Sydney 200

Compact Street Directory

18th Edition

- cafés
- restaurants
- pubs
- shops
- accommodation
- transport

Australian Owned Family Company

We've Got Australia Covered

23 24 25 26 27 28 29 30 31 32 33 34 35 36

51 52 53 54 55 56 57 58 59 60 61 62 63 64 65 66

81 82 83 84 85 86 87 88 89 90 91 92 93 94 95 96

111 112 113 114 115 116 117 118 119 120 121 122 123 124 125 126

141 142 143 144 145 146 147 148 149 150 151 152 153 154 155 156

171 172 173 174 175 176 177 178 179 180 181 182 183 184 185 186

201 202 203 204 205 206 207 208 209 210 211 212 213 214 215 216

231 232 233 234 235 236 237 238 239 240 241 242 243 244 245 246

261 262 263 264 265 266 267 268 269 270 271 272 273 274 275 276

291 292 293 294 295 296 297 298 299 300 301 302 303 304 305 306

321 322 323 324 325 326 327 328 329 330 331 332 333 334 335 336

349 350 351 352 353 354 355 356 357 358 359 360 361 362 363 364 365 366

379 380 381 382 383 384 385 386 387 388 389 390 391 392 393 394 395 396

409 410 411 412 413 414 415 416 417 418 419 420 421 422 423 424 425 426

439 440 441 442 443 444 445 446 447 448 449 450 451 452 453 454 455 456

469 470 471 472 473 474 475 476 477 478 479 480 481 482 483 484 485 486

499 500 501 502 503 504 505 506 507 508 509 510 511 512 513 514 515 516

529 530 531 532 533 534 535 536 537 538 539 540 541 542 543 544 545 546

PICTON MAPS 561 - 566
BARGO MAP 567

APPIN MAP 568

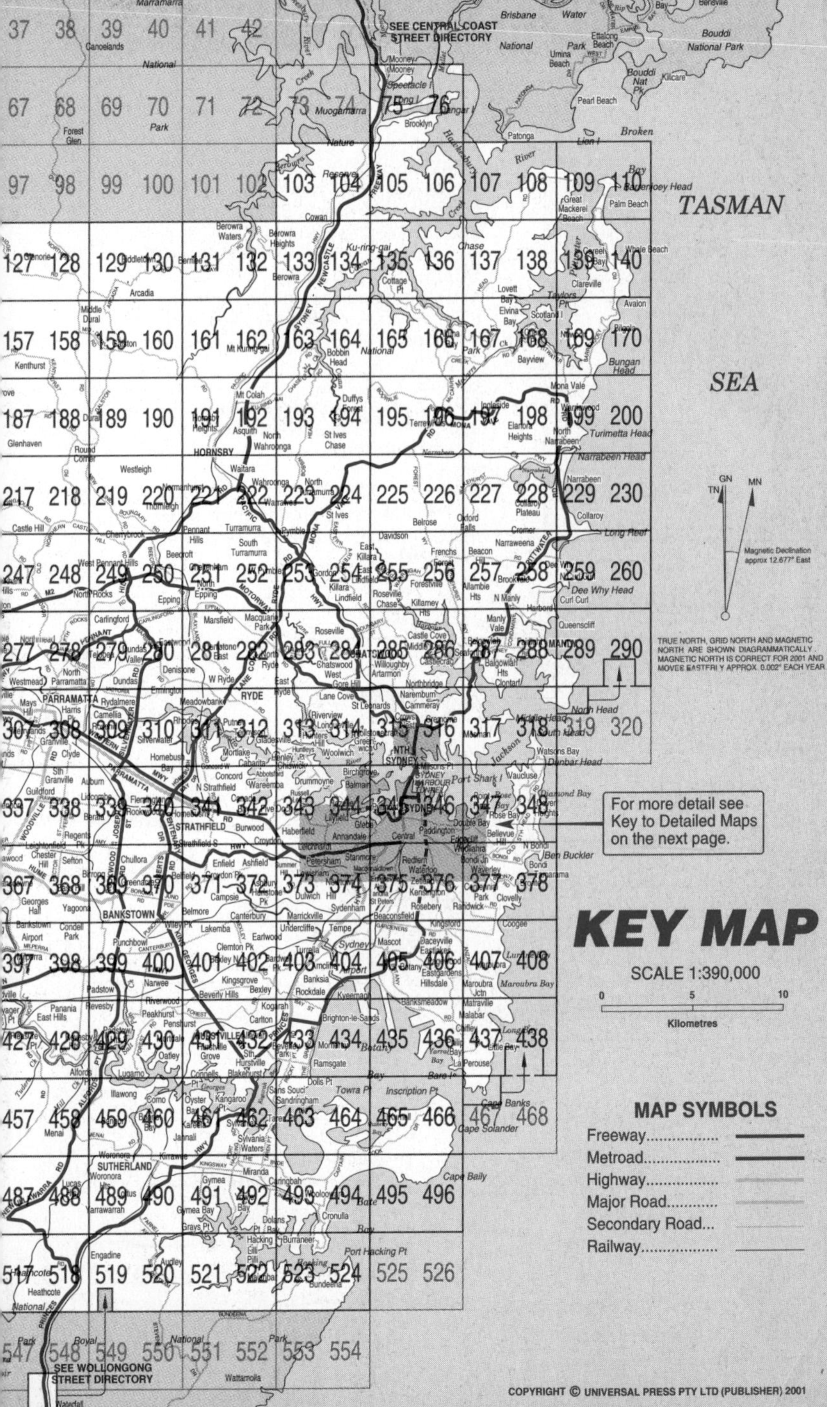
KEY MAP
SCALE 1:390,000
0
5
10
Kilometres
MAP SYMBOLS
Freeway
Metroad
Highway
Major Road
Secondary Road
Railway
For more detail see Key to Detailed Maps on the next page.
TRUE NORTH, GRID NORTH AND MAGNETIC NORTH ARE SHOWN DIAGRAMMATICALLY. MAGNETIC NORTH IS CORRECT FOR 2001 AND MOVES EASTERLY APPROX. 0.002° EACH YEAR
TN
GN
MN
Magnetic Declination approx 12.677° East
SEE CENTRAL COAST STREET DIRECTORY
SEE WOLLONGONG STREET DIRECTORY
TASMAN
SEA
Brisbane Water National Park
Bouddi National Park
Ku-ring-gai Chase National Park
HORNSBY
PARRAMATTA
RYDE
STRATHFIELD
BANKSTOWN
SUTHERLAND
NTH SYDNEY
SYDNEY
Botany Bay
Port Hacking
North Head
Long Reef
Cape Solander
Cape Baily
Waterfall
COPYRIGHT © UNIVERSAL PRESS PTY LTD (PUBLISHER) 2001

KEY & SCALES TO DETAILED MAPS

City Area

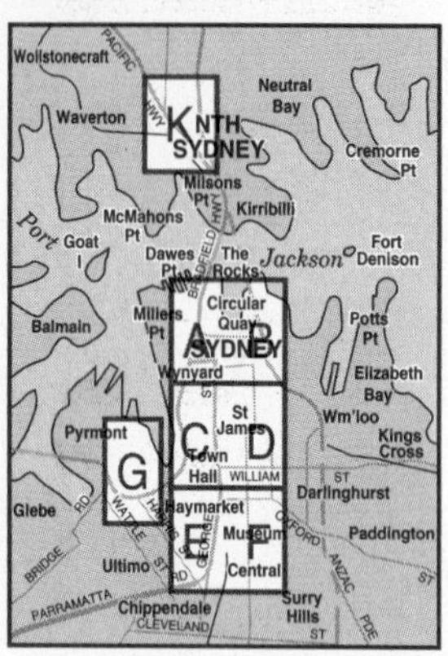

SCALE 1 : 6 250
MAPS A to G and K are City Area Maps and each map covers 625m east-west and 1 km north-south.

SCALE 1 : 7 500
MAP H is a detailed Darling Harbour map and covers 750m east-west and 1.2km north-south.

SCALE 1 : 20 800
MAP J is a detailed Parking map and covers 1.4km east-west and 3.4km north-south.

SCALE 1 : 20 340
MAP L & M are detailed Homebush Bay maps and cover 3.2km east-west and 4km north-south.

Inner Suburb Area

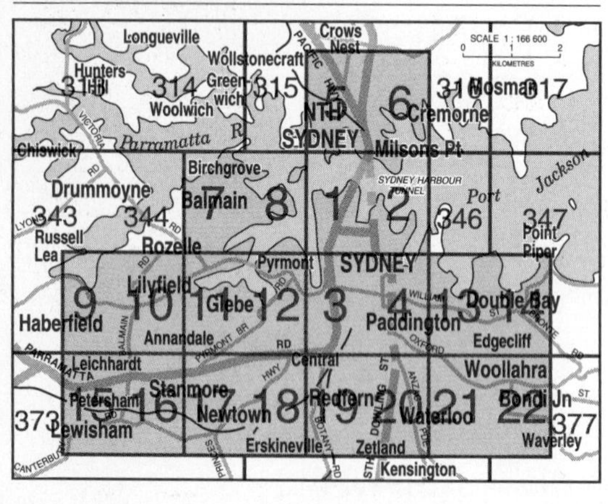

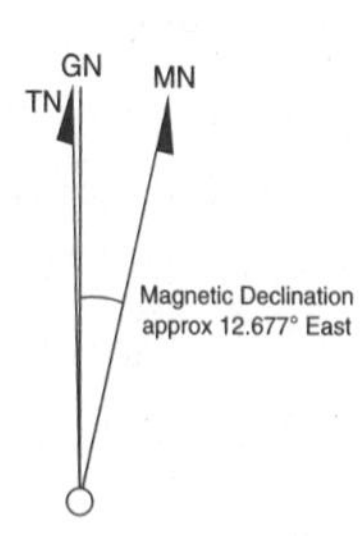

TRUE NORTH, GRID NORTH AND MAGNETIC NORTH ARE SHOWN DIAGRAMMATICALLY. MAGNETIC NORTH IS CORRECT FOR 2001 AND MOVES EASTERLY APPROX 0.002° EACH YEAR.

Map Scales

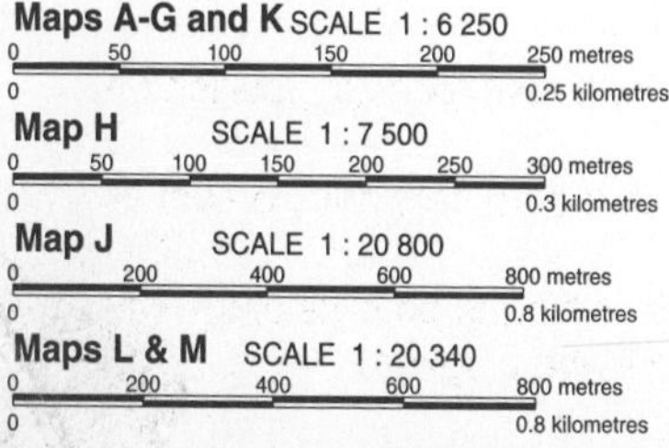

Maps 1-22 SCALE 1 : 12 500
0 100 200 300 400 500 metres
0 0.5 kilometres

Maps 53-566 SCALE 1 : 25 000
0 200 400 600 800 1 000 metres
0 1 kilometres

Maps 567-568 SCALE 1 : 27 500
0 200 400 600 800 1 000 metres
0 1 kilometres

MAP SYMBOLS

Freeway or Motorway	WARRINGAH FREEWAY
Highway or Main Traffic Route	PRINCES HIGHWAY
Trafficable Road	JONES AV
Un-trafficable / Proposed Road	THOMAS ST
Traffic Light, Level Crossing & Roundabout	
Road and Railway Bridges	
One-way Traffic Route	
National and State Route Numbers	1 33
Metroad and Tourist Route Numbers	5 14
Proposed Freeway	Proposed Freeway
Direction of Sydney City Centre	CITY
Distance by Road from GPO	22
Railway Line, Station (distance from Central)	Dulwich Hill 8
Suburb Name	EASTWOOD
Locality Name	Audley
Walking Tracks, Horse Tracks and Cycleways	
Park, Reserve or Golf Course	
School or Hospital	
Caravan Park, Cemetery, Shopping Centre,etc	
Mall, Plaza	

Car Park	P	Place of Worship	
Council Office	Cncl Off	Point of Interest	Museum
Fire Station	Fire Station	Police Station	★
Hospital	✚	Post Office	
Library		Rural Fire Service	RFS
Picnic Area		Shopping Centre	

STREET MAPS overlap on each page to help in re-locating position on an adjoining page.
ADJOINING MAP NUMBERS are shown in the borders and corners of the street maps.
REFERENCE NUMBERS AND LETTERS within the borders of the street maps are the reference co-ordinates given in the indexes.

the rocks

citysideguide

Sydney is Australia's most vibrant city. The *Cityside Guide* covers Sydney's CBD and inner city areas and includes sightseeing and shopping suggestions; restaurant and cafe recommendations; listings of Sydney's best museums, galleries, theatres, cinemas, pubs, bars, nightclubs and backpacker and youth hostels; and comprehensive public transport information.

cityside guide

around the harbour

Sydney Harbour and its surroundings makes the City of Sydney spectacular. Sydneysiders are fortunate to have this stunning all-year-round playground at their disposal. Here you can sail from Rushcutters Bay, windsurf at Balmoral Beach, swim in harbourside pools and beaches, picnic at waterfront parks or sightsee from a ferry. Circular Quay, Sydney's ferry terminal, is the departure point for scenic cruises and ferry rides around picturesque Sydney Harbour and between harbourside suburbs.
For ferry timetables visit the Sydney Ferries Information Office (9207 3166) opposite Wharf 4 or call the Public Transport Info Line (131 500). Contact Australian Travel Specialists (9247 5151) at Wharf 6 for commercial cruises and tall ship sailing.

• **Circular Quay (Map B, Ref D6; Map 1, Ref J11)**, at the northern edge of the **Central Business District (CBD)**, is a pulsating, public waterfront space. Enjoy the harbour activity, watch buskers perform or have coffee at Rossini's (9247 8026), before catching a ferry to one of Sydney's many harbourside attractions.

• **Sydney Opera House (Map B, Ref J1)** (9250 7111), at **Bennelong Point**, took fourteen years to complete and is widely regarded as one of the architectural wonders of the world. This living sculpture of white sails or shells, is Sydney's most popular attraction and busiest performing arts venue, containing a concert hall, theatres, restaurants, cafes and extensive exterior public walkways.

• **Sydney Harbour Bridge (Map 1, Ref J5)**, the world's widest long span bridge, was completed in 1932 and links the city to Sydney's north side. The south east **Pylon Lookout** (9247 3408) houses an exhibition illustrating the impressive construction of 'The Coathanger'. To view the Harbour from the top of the Bridge's arch, contact **Bridge Climb** (9252 0077).

• **The Rocks (Map B, Ref A3)** (The Rocks Heritage and Information Centre, George St, 9255 1788) provides visitors with a taste of Sydney's colonial past. The sandstone **Cadman's Cottage** (110 George St, 9247 8861) is the oldest surviving building. **Campbell's Storehouses** (7-27 Circular Quay West), former bond stores completed in 1890, now contain galleries and waterfront restaurants. Historic pubs such as the cosy **Lord Nelson Brewery Hotel** (cnr Kent and Argyle Sts, 9251 4044), built in 1842, are perfect for a brewed-on-the-premises ale after a day's sightseeing. Book for the popular night sky viewings at the astronomy museum, **Sydney Observatory** (Watson Rd, Observatory Hill, 9217 0485).

• **Fort Denison (Map 2, Ref K6)** (9247 5033) was constructed to defend Sydney during the 1850s on **Pinchgut Island**, so-named because of the limited rations left for convicts incarcerated there. Book a tour to explore the island's barracks, tower and gun battery or plan a picnic to watch holiday fireworks displays.

• **Taronga Zoological Park (Map 316, Ref K14)** (Bradley's Head Rd, Mosman, 9969 2777), with its magnificent harbour views, is a conservation leader. Once voted the world's best zoo, it utilises moats where possible, instead of bars and fences and its enclosures resemble animals' natural environments. Highlights include the nocturnal exhibit, native Australian animals, the Koala House and the Walk-through Rainforest.

• The holiday atmosphere at **Manly (Map 288, Ref H9)** (Manly Visitor Information Centre, Ocean Beach, North Steyne, (9977 1088) is due to its prime location, sandwiched between the harbour and open sea. Take a JetCat or ferry to visit **Oceanworld** (West Esplanade, 9949 2644), an aquarium with three daily live shows of Dangerous Australian Creatures, sharks and the colourful coral and marine-life of the Great Barrier Reef. Enjoy free entertainment, shops and cafes at **Manly Wharf**, stroll along downtown Manly's **Corso** or through the pretty backstreets to the surf beach and promenade. Explore **Fairy Bower** and secluded **Shelly Beach**, or visit the historic **Quarantine Station** (9247 5033) at **North Head**.

• **Watsons Bay (Map 318, Ref E13)** offers panoramic harbour and city views from **Wharf Beach**, a perfect place to enjoy a swim and dine on fresh seafood as the sun goes down. Stroll around the charming, village-like suburb or swim at nearby **Camp Cove**. Explore **South Head**, the harbour's southern entrance, and climb **The Gap's** dramatic cliffs with views of the crashing waves below.

• **Darling Harbour (Map H)** (9286 0111) can be reached by foot, **monorail** (8584 5288) or **light rail** (8584 5288), but it's more fun to take the ferry trip, going beneath the vast **Sydney Harbour Bridge** via **Balmain** to Aquarium Pier, home to **Sydney Aquarium** (9262 2300). There you can see the platypus, seals and penguins and walk through perspex tunnels while sharks, fish, rays and eels swim around you. Wander across **Pyrmont Bridge**, the world's oldest electrically-operated swingspan bridge, to the shops and eateries at the **Harbourside Festival Marketplace**. Visit the adjacent **National Maritime Museum** or the interactive indoor theme park, **Sega World** (9273 9273). Take a relaxing stroll amid the waterfalls, bridges and Cantonese pavilions of the tranquil **Chinese Gardens**, before catching a film on the world's largest screen at the **IMAX Theatre** (9281 3300). **Chinatown**, **Powerhouse Museum**, **Sydney Fish Markets** and **Sydney Star City Casino** are close by.

• **Milsons Point (Map 1, Ref K1)** is a great walking destination. Alight at **Milsons Point Wharf**, at the historic fun fair, and walk across **Bradfield Park** to admire the massive **Sydney Harbour Bridge** above you. Enjoy the harbour views in between laps at the **North Sydney Olympic Pool** (Alfred St, Milsons Point, 9955 2309), then wander along Blues Point Road for a snack at a cafe before walking to nearby **McMahons Point** for a return ferry to Circular Quay.

• **Cockle Bay Wharf (Map H)** (9269 9800) at **Darling Park**, on the city side of **Darling Harbour**, is a newly redeveloped harbourside venue. Once the site of industrial docklands, it has now become a well utilised public area boasting an array of eateries, take away outlets, a Museum of Contemporary Art store, pub and nightclub. Restaurants such as **Ampersand** (Level 2, Cockle Bay Wharf, 9264 6666) and **Chinta Ria...The Temple of Love** (Level 2, The Roof Terrace, Cockle Bay Wharf, 9264 3211) are exciting additions to Sydney's eating scene; while nightclub **Home** has taken its place in the city's clubbing scene. Rub shoulders with music and film industry types, city workers and inner city groovers at **Pontoon Bar** (Shop 112, Cockle Bay Wharf, 9267 7099).

city sights

• **AMP Tower (Map D, Ref A7)** (Centrepoint, 100 Market St, 9229 7430) is the tallest public building in the southern hemisphere. Its 360-degree views provide the best vantage point from which to familiarise yourself with Sydney. An observation level, coffee shop and two revolving restaurants offer magnificent views of the CBD, Blue Mountains to the west, Botany Bay to the south, Pittwater to the north and from across the harbour out to sea.

• **Hyde Park (Map D, Ref E10)**, on the eastern border of the CBD, is the perfect place to take a picnic lunch. Do as the office workers do and watch the chess players, or bask in the sun on the grass by the **Archibald Fountain** or sunken **Sandringham Garden**. Stroll along the tree-covered walkways to the pretty poplar-lined **Pool of Remembrance** to admire the Art Deco **Anzac Memorial**, where a photographic and military exhibition can be viewed.

• **St Mary's Cathedral (Map D, Ref H9)** (Cathedral & College Sts, 9220 0400), a magnificent Gothic Revival-style cathedral, opened in 1882; the twin southern spires proposed by the original architect have recently been built. Choral Eucharist at 10.30am. Join a guided tour, (daily, at noon), on religious significance and architecture, and see the beautiful marble terrazzo floor in the Cathedral Crypt. Visit the historical exhibition: 'The First Australian Catholics, From Convict Ships to the Great Fire', (4 Sept 2000 to 3 Sept 2001).

• **Macquarie Street (Maps B & D)** extends from **Hyde Park** to **Bennelong Point** and contains many elegant examples of Georgian architecture worth visiting. **Hyde Park Barracks** (9223 8922), originally designed to house convicts, is now a museum featuring changing exhibitions on Australia's history and culture; it has cafe/restaurant. **Sydney Mint Museum** (9217 0311) contains exhibitions on gold and silver. For good luck, rub the snout of the brass boar **Il Porcellino** at the front of grand **Sydney Hospital**; then admire the Art Deco fountain in the inner courtyard. **Parliament House** (9230 2111), the seat of the New South Wales Government, has illuminating displays on the building's development and the State's legislative history. The majestic **State Library** (9273 1414) warrants a visit just for the Mitchell Library's reading room with its impressive skylight; free tours Tues 11-12am, Thurs 2-3pm.

• **The Domain (Map D, Ref K6)**, the grassy parkland behind Macquarie Street, is a public rallying point, site of summer concerts and favourite exercise and lunch spot for city workers. From its eastern edge near the **Art Gallery of NSW** you can view historic **Woolloomooloo Finger Wharf, Garden Island** and **Potts Point**. The harbourside **Andrew 'Boy' Charlton Pool** is on the way to **Mrs Macquarie's Chair**, an ideal place to sit and take in the harbourside activity.

• **Royal Botanic Gardens (Map 2, Ref D15)** (9231 8111) extends over 30 lush hectares from **Mrs Macquarie's Chair** around **Farm Cove** to **Bennelong Point**. Explore Australia's first farm, Palm Grove; Sydney Tropical Centre; the National Herbarium of New South Wales and the Herb Garden; or relax in the Rose Garden's rotunda, the site of many weddings. Situated on the Macquarie Street side of the gardens, **Government House** (9931 5222), formerly the official residence of the Governor, houses collections of 19th- and early 20th-century furnishings.

• **Martin Place (Map C, Ref K2)**, a plaza between George and Macquarie Streets, contains the 1929 Art Deco **Cenotaph** where annual Anzac Day war remembrance services are held; the Renaissance-style **General Post Office**, recently refurbished, and other grand buildings such as the Commonwealth Bank. Daily lunch time concerts are held in the amphitheatre.

• **Pitt Street Mall (Map C, Ref K6)**, between King and Market Streets, is Sydney's shopping heart. Here you will find the ornate **Strand Arcade** (9232 4199), a lovingly restored Victorian-era shopping centre that is a window shopper's delight.

• **State Theatre (Map C, Ref J9)** (1902 262 588), nearby on Market Street, is a salubrious 1929 movie palace in the Cinema Baroque style, containing a magnificent Wurlitzer organ and a 20 000 piece chandelier. It is a premier venue for concerts, theatre and special events and is home to the annual Sydney Film Festival.

• **Queen Victoria Building (Map C, Ref H10)** (George St, York, Market and Park Sts, 9264 1864), is a majestic Romanesque shopping arcade. Built in 1898, it was originally a fresh produce market. The restoration retained many original features, including the giant domes and roof statues, transforming it into an up-market retail complex. An underground promenade connects Town Hall railway station to Sydney Central Plaza and Grace Bros Department Store.

• **Sydney Town Hall (Map C, Ref G13)** (483 George St, 9265 9333), is an excellent example of high Victorian architecture. As Sydney's civic centre, it is a venue for concerts, balls, dances and public meetings and continues the tradition of being Sydney's favourite city meeting place.

Sydney city boasts a wide variety of attractions to interest both locals and tourists alike. From the charming sandstone architecture of The Rocks, to the majestic grandeur of the Queen Victoria Building; from the city's lively shopping malls to the peaceful Royal Botanic Gardens; from bustling Martin Place to elegant Macquarie Street, there are numerous sights worth seeing. Take a walking tour of the many outdoor monuments, statues and fountains around the city by following Sydney City Council's map (1300 651 301) of either the Sydney Open Museum or the Sydney Sculpture Walk. The NSW Visitor Info Line (132 077) and Sydney Visitors Centre (Martin Place, between Castlereagh & Elizabeth Sts, 9235 2424) can also suggest places of interest.

There are fantastic views of Sydney Harbour from the Star City casino near Darling Harbour in Pyrmont, where there are 5 restaurants, cafes, the Lyric Theatre and various shops. Star City can be accessed via foot, car, bus, monorail or light rail.

Sydney's major sights can be seen on foot, or you can ride a train, bus or monorail (8584 5288) around the CBD. The Sydney Explorer bus stops at 26 prime attractions. Phone the Public Transport Infoline (131 500) for details.

cityside guide

shopping & markets

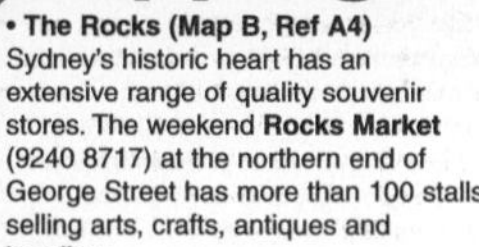

Sydney offers world-class shopping. Vibrant retail streets, elegant arcades, modern malls, large department stores and colourful markets in the CBD and city fringe offer an impressive range of high quality, locally made and imported goods. From indigenous art and handmade crafts at The Rocks to funky clothes and innovative jewellery on Oxford Street, there are temptations for all tastes and budgets. Bargains can be found at weekend markets spanning from Paddington and Bondi to Balmain and Glebe. Factory and designer seconds stores in Surry Hills and Redfern sell remarkably reduced items from labels such as Marcs and Diesel. Most shops open from 9.00 am – 5.30 pm weekdays, until 9.00 pm Thursday nights and 9.00 am – 4.00 pm Saturdays. Many stores are also open on Sundays in tourist areas such as Darling Harbour, Kings Cross, Bondi and in parts of the city such as Pitt St Mall and the Queen Victoria Building.

• The Rocks (Map B, Ref A4)
Sydney's historic heart has an extensive range of quality souvenir stores. The weekend **Rocks Market** (9240 8717) at the northern end of George Street has more than 100 stalls selling arts, crafts, antiques and jewellery.
Aboriginal and Tribal Art Centre
117 George St, The Rocks, 9241 5998
Indigenous paintings and artifacts.
Australian Craftworks
127 George St, The Rocks, 9247 7156
Ceramics, textiles and pottery.

• Pitt Street Mall & George Street (Map C, Ref K6)
A wide variety of specialty stores can be found on George Street and in the shopping centres on the mall, such as **Skygarden**, **Strand Arcade**, **Mid City Centre**, **Centrepoint** and **Sydney Central Plaza**.
Australian Geographic Shop
Shop 34, Centrepoint, 9231 5055
Environmentally friendly products.
Gowings
Cnr George & Market Sts, 9264 6321
Basic menswear, footwear, travel goods and cheep haircuts.
Dinosaur Designs
Shop 77, Strand Arcade, 9223 2953
Fun and funky homewares and jewellery made from jewel-coloured resin.

• Castlereagh Street, CBD (Map D, Ref B6)
Exclusive international couture and Australian designer labels can be found at the **MLC Centre** and the Castlereagh Street stores of **Chanel**, **Louis Vuitton** and **Hermes**. **Cartier** and **Tiffany & Co** are at **Chifley Plaza** and **Emporio Armani** is in **Martin Place**.
Chanel Boutique
70 Castlereagh St, 9233 4800
Fabulous French garments.
David Jones Department Store
Castlereagh & Elizabeth Sts, 9266 5544
Fashion, fragrances, furnishings and **Food Hall**.

• Queen Victoria Building (QVB) (Map C, Ref H10)
This majestic shopping centre contains more than 200 stores selling quality souvenirs, homeware, knitwear, lingerie, cosmetics, shoes, jewellery and fashion, including chain stores **Country Road**, **Esprit**, **Lush** and **Gap**.
ABC Shop
Shop 48, first floor, QVB, 9333 1635
TV-related books, videos, CDs and souvenirs.
Red Earth
Shop M12, lower floor, QVB, 9264 4019
Natural beauty products.

• Darling Harbour (Map H)
The **Harbourside Festival Marketplace** is home to over 200 stores offering souvenirs, fashion, bush and beach wear, CDs, books and crafts. There is also a wide choice of eateries.
Redline Sports
Shop 223, 9281 9180
Motor racing merchandise.
Surf Dive 'N' Ski
Shop 205-207, 9281 4040
Everything for the watersports lover.

• Chinatown (Map E, Ref D4)
This cosmopolitan part of town has everything from traditional herbalists to hip designer labels plus 92 specialist shops at **Market City** (Hay & Quay Sts). Go to bustling **Paddy's Markets** (Hay & Quay Sts, weekends) for fresh produce, plants, pets, toys and clothes.
Accessories Shop
Sussex Centre, Sussex St, 9281 5595
Versace, Gaultier, Dolce & Gabbana.
Chinatown Centre Food Hall
25 Dixon St, 9281 7568
Popular, varied and exotic types of food.

• Oxford Street, Darlinghurst (Map F, Ref G3)
Leather, gymwear, fashion, music, books and homeware are all to be found on the lower end of this popular street.
Fish
33 Oxford St, Darlinghurst, 9267 5142
Dance and alternative music.
Home
153 Oxford St, Darlinghurst, 9332 4840
Stylish essentials for city living.

• Crown Street, Darlinghurst (Map F, Ref K9)
Scattered along Crown Street are shops selling inner-city fashion and accessories, from retro groove to basic black, interspersed with interesting and varied bric-a-brac and interior design stores.
Route 66
257 Crown St, Darlinghurst, 9331 6686
Classic jeans, jackets and cowboy garb.

• Oxford Street, Paddington (Map 4, Ref H15)
Sydney's innovative young designer fashion labels can be found at the upper end of Oxford Street, interspersed with interesting bookshops, gift and homeware stores. On Saturday check out **Paddington Bazaar** (9331 2646), the coolest markets in town.
Ariel Booksellers
42 Oxford St, Paddington, 9332 4581
Quality books: fiction, film, art and design; great novelty cards and slick gift-wrapping.
Mambo
17 Oxford St, Paddington, 9331 8034
Wild and colourful beach and street wear.

culture & entertainment

MUSEUMS

• Australian Museum (Map D, Ref G14)
6 College St, Sydney, 9320 6000
Natural history museum of Australia and the Pacific.

• The Museum of Sydney (Map B, Ref E11)
Cnr Phillip and Bridge Sts, Sydney, 9251 5988
State-of-the-art museum imaginatively brings Sydney's past to life on the site of the first government house.

• Powerhouse Museum (Map 3, Ref B11)
500 Harris St, Ultimo, 9217 0111
Interactive museum featuring the extraordinary and the everyday.

• National Maritime Museum (Map 3, Ref A3)
Darling Harbour, 9298 3777
Exhibits our connection to the coast and sea.

GALLERIES

• Art Gallery of New South Wales (Map 4, Ref D2)
Art Gallery Rd, The Domain, 9225 1744 (Recorded info: 9225 1790)
Australia's foremost collection of Australian, Asian and European art.

• Museum of Contemporary Art (Map B, Ref A5)
Circular Quay West, The Rocks, 9252 4033
Adventurous collection of modern art, Aboriginal paintings and video art.

• State Library of NSW (Map B, Ref G16)
Macquarie St, Sydney, 9273 1414
Exhibitions of art, photography, drawings and unusual treasures.

• Artspace/The Gunnery (Map 4, Ref G3)
43-51 Cowper Wharf Road, Woolloomooloo, 9368 1899
Installations and performances.

• Australian Centre for Photography (Map 21, Ref B1)
257 Oxford St, Paddington, 9332 1455
Contemporary photography, courses and public photographic facilities.

• Brett Whiteley Studio (Map 20, Ref C4)
2 Raper St, Surry Hills, 9225 1881
The artist's works and memorabilia, displayed in his former home.

• Byron Mapp Gallery (Map 4, Ref K16)
178 Oxford St, Paddington, 9331 2926
Gallery-bookstore-cafe, featuring local and international photography.

• Aboriginal Art Centres
117 George St, The Rocks, 9247 9625
7 Walker Lane, Paddington, 9360 6839
Upper Concourse, Opera House, Bennelong Point, 9247 4344
Australian indigenous art and craft.

MUSIC AND PERFORMING ARTS

• Sydney Opera House (Map B, Ref J1)
Bennelong Point, 9250 7777
Showcases performances by Opera Australia, Australian Ballet, Sydney Theatre Company, Sydney Dance Company and Sydney Symphony Orchestra.

• The Performance Space (Map 19, Ref D5)
199 Cleveland Street, Redfern, 9319 5091
Experimental dance, movement, mime and performance arts.

• The Wharf Theatre (Map 1, Ref F7)
Pier 4, Hickson Rd, Millers Point, 9250 1700
Exciting theatre, dramatic water views and the Wharf Restaurant (9250 1761).

• State Theatre (Map C, Ref J8)
49 Market St, Sydney, 9373 6655 (Ticket Master 1902 262 588)
An opulence theatre, staging musicals, concerts and, mid year, the Sydney Film Festival.

• Capitol Theatre (Map E, Ref H7)
13-17 Campbell St, Haymarket, 9320 5000
Lavishly restored 1920s theatre, with a starry-sky ceiling.

• Seymour Theatre Centre (Map 18, Ref G4)
Cnr Cleveland St & City Rd, Chippendale, 9364 9400 (Box Office 9351 7940)
A mix of exciting musical performances and theatre.

• Belvoir Street Theatre (Map 19, Ref G4)
25 Belvoir St, Surry Hills, 9699 3444
Experimental and leading-edge productions.

• The Stables Theatre (Map 4, Ref H10)
10 Nimrod St, Kings Cross, 9361 3817
A venue for showing new Australian works.

CINEMAS

• Hoyts (Map C, Ref G16)
505 George St, Sydney, 9273 7373
Multiplex with blockbuster movies.

• Greater Union (Map C, Ref G16)
525 George St, Sydney, 9267 8666
Mostly mainstream movies.

• Village/Hoyts (Map C, Ref G16)
505 George St, Sydney, 9273 7373
Multiplex with blockbuster movies.

• Palace Academy Twin (Map 4, Ref F14)
3a Oxford St, Paddington, 9361 4453
Quality international arthouse.

• Verona Cinema (Map 4, Ref G15)
17 Oxford St, Paddington, 9360 6099 (Info Line: 9360 6296)
Small theatres, screening an eclectic range of films.

• Chauvel Cinema (Map 21, Ref A1)
149 Oxford St, Paddington, 9361 5398
Australian cinema, independent international and movie classics

• Dendy Cinemas
MLC Centre **(Map D, Ref A2)**, 19 Martin Place, Sydney, 9233 8166
East Circular Quay **(Map B, Ref G6)**, Sydney, 9247 3800
261 King St, Newtown **(Map 17, Ref G11)**, 9550 5699
Independent Australian and international films

Sydney's diverse and exciting cultural scene is reflected in the remarkable range of galleries, museums, theatres and cinemas; and the orchestras, classical and modern dance, opera and theatre companies which make Sydney their home. *Sydney Morning Herald's Friday Metro* supplement contains a comprehensive weekly listing of entertainment, cultural activities, exhibitions and events, or check out the *Sydney Morning Herald's* Citysearch website (citysearch.com.au) for the comprehensive low-down on what to do, where in Sydney. Free weekly papers *Beat, Drum Media, 3D World* and *On the Street* specialise in live music, dance clubs and the arts, while *What's On In Sydney* is an invaluable guide for tourists.
Purchase tickets to concerts, events and exhibitions from either the venues, Ticketek (9266 4800) and Ticket Master (9320 9000), or buy cheap tickets from HalfTix (9286 3310) in 201 Sussex St (Cnr Market & Sussex Sts) after 9 am each day for same day performances or exhibitions.

cityside guide

restaurants & cafes

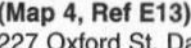

Sydney's exciting eating scene offers an overwhelming choice of ethnically diverse restaurants and cafes, taking advantage of the fabulous fresh local produce. Sydney's top-end restaurants provide sublime dining experiences and often require reservations to be made weeks in advance. Your culinary memories will make them well worth both the trouble and expense.
A vast range of economical eateries abound across the city — from Asian in Chinatown, Spanish in Liverpool Street, Italian in East Sydney and everything from Mediterranean to Morrocan in Darlinghurst and Potts Point.

Prices	(GST Incl.)
$	under $10
$$	$10 - $20
$$$	$20 - $30
$$$$	$30 - $40
$$$$$	$40 and over

Prices are per person, excluding drinks, corkage and tips, and based on two courses.

RESTAURANTS

• **Angkor Wat Cambodian Restaurant $$ (Map 4, Ref E13)**
227 Oxford St, Darlinghurst, 9360 5500
Fresh and fragrant flavours in a warm and exotic environment.

• **Capitan Torres $$ (Map E, Ref F2)**
73 Liverpool St, Sydney, 9264 5574
Family-run rustic bar; Spanish sangria makes an excellent companion to 20 plus types of tapas.

• **Chinta Ria...The Temple of Love $$ (Map C, Ref 35)**
Level 2, The Roof Terrace, Cockle Bay Wharf, Darling Park, 9264 3211
Malaysian inspired cuisine.

• **Darley Street Thai $$$$$ (Map 4, Ref J8)**
30 Bayswater Rd, Kings Cross, 9358 6530
Experience colour and spice in both the decor and creative Thai cuisine.

• **Dhaba Indian Street Eatery $$ (Map 20, Ref B7)**
466 Cleveland St, Surry Hills, 9319 6260
Inexpensive and cheerful north and south Indian food with a tasty range of tandoor breads.

• **Edna's Table $$$$ (Map C, Ref F9)**
204 Clarence St, Sydney, 9267 3933
Showcases Australian bush foods.

• **Eleni's $$$ (Map 4, Ref E9)**
185a Bourke St, East Sydney, 9331 5306
Intimate, Aegean-inspired setting; innovative and modern Greek flavours; very popular, so book to beat regulars; BYO.

• **Fez $$ (Map 4, Ref H11)**
247 Victoria St, Darlinghurst, 9360 9581
Contemporary Middle Eastern; breakfasts and mezze plates recommended; bright, breezy Morrocan-style decor.

• **Forty One $$$$$ (Map B, Ref D16)**
Level 41, Chifley Tower, Chifley Square, Sydney, 9221 2500
Modern Australian cuisine, with magnificent views of Sydney.

• **Fu Manchu $$ (Map 4, Ref H11)**
249 Victoria St, Darlinghurst, 9360 9581
Asian noodle bar, with fun atmosphere and funky decor.

• **Kam Fook Restaurant $$$$ (Map E, Ref D7)**
Level 3, Market City, 9 Hay St, Haymarket, 9211 8988
Sydney's largest Chinese restaurant, with 100 styles of dim sim.

• **Macleay Street Bistro $$$ (Map 4, Ref K3)**
73a Macleay St, Potts Point, 9358 4891
Popular for top quality steak and mash, BYO.

• **Mezzaluna $$$$$ (Map 4, Ref J5)**
123 Victoria St, Potts Point, 9357 1988
Excellent, contemporary Italian cuisine, with spectacular city views from the terrace.

• **Odeon $$$ (Map 4, Ref K4)**
32 Orwell St, Potts Point 9331 0172
Popular, with modern decor and an appealing menu.

• **Paramount $$$$$ (Map 4, Ref K3)**
73 Macleay St, Potts Point, 9358 1652
Stylish, contemporary Australian cuisine.

• **The Pig and The Olive Pizzeria $$ (Map 4, Ref K3)**
71A Macleay St, Potts Point, 9357 3745
Popular eatery, with gourmet pizzas.

• **Rockpool $$$$$ (Map A, Ref K5)**
107 George St, The Rocks, 9252 1888
Freshest seafood, innovative cuisine, East meets West.

• **Wang Shim Re $$ (Map 4, Ref K6)**
36 Llankelly Pl, Kings Cross, 9356 2224
Great value Korean banquet of spicy barbecued seafood and meats.

• **Tetsuya's $$$$$ (Map 344, Ref E7)**
729 Darling St, Rozelle, 9555 1017
Top Sydney restaurant, with a sensational Japanese-French cuisine.

• **A Touch of Thai $$ (Map 4, Ref H8)**
230 William St, Kings Cross, 9326 9343
Delicious Thai curries, daily specials.

• **Yipiyiyo $$$ (Map 4, Ref C13)**
290 Crown St, Darlinghurst, 9332 3114
Tasty Sante Fe style cuisine.

CAFES & FAST EATS

BBQ King $$ (Map E, Ref F4)
18 Goulburn St, Chinatown, 9267 2586
Traditional Chinese barbecued meats; where the chefs go for a late night bite.

• **Bangkok and Penang Curry Laksa House $ (Map E, Ref D2)**
Harbour Plaza Food Court, Dixon St Mall
The best authentic Malaysian curry laksa in Sydney.

• **Cafe Hernandez $$ (Map 4, Ref J8)**
60 Kings Cross Rd, Rushcutters Bay, 9331 2343
Strong Spanish coffee, open late.

• **Hard Rock Cafe $$ (Map 4, Ref D8)**
121-129 Crown St, Darlinghurst, 9331 1116
American style, cafe-restaurant.

• **Harry's Cafe de Wheels $ (Map 4, Ref G3)**
Cowper Wharf Rd, Woolloomooloo
Stand-up eating of Sydney's best pies and peas at this Sydney icon.

• **Ippon Sushi $$ (Map E, Ref E6)**
404 Sussex St, Chinatown, 9212 7669
Choose fresh, cheap Japanese sushi from the conveyor belt.

• **Le Petit Creme $$ (Map 4, Ref G10)**
118 Darlinghurst Rd, Darlinghurst, 9361 4738
Arrive early for the Eggs Benedict weekend special and le bowl of coffee.

• **MCA Cafe $$ (Map B, Ref B6)**
MCA, Circular Quay West, 9241 4253
Stylish contemporary Australian food, with spectacular harbour views.

• **Planet Hollywood $$ (Map E, Ref H1)**
Level 2, 600 George St, Sydney, 9267 7827
Great food, great service guaranteed.

• **QVB Jet $ (Map C, Ref H11)**
Shop G55, Queen Victoria Building, York St, Town Hall end, 9283 5004
Sip strong lattes in outdoor European style seating.

• **Spring $ (Map 4, Ref K2)**
Challis Ave, Potts Point, 9331 0190
Tiny cafe with sunny sidewalk and coffee with a kick.

• **Starbuck's Coffee $ (Map D, Ref C12)**
Cnr Park & Elizabeth Sts, Sydney, 9268 0184 Leading world retailer of specialty coffee.

• **The Vinyl Lounge $$ (Map 13, Ref C5)**
1/17 Elizabeth Bay Rd, Elizabeth Bay, 9326 9224 Very French, the chef ensures all baguettes are the same size.

• **Wedge Cafe $ (Map 13, Ref B5)**
70 Elizabeth Bay Rd, Elizabeth Bay, 9326 9015 Great coffee, food and service.

bars, clubs & pubs

CITY DRINKING

• 'The Bar' Sir Stamford (Map B, Ref G8)
93 Macquarie St, Sydney, 9252 4600
Elegant decor, located at Circular Quay.

• Brooklyn Hotel (Map A, Ref J11)
Cnr George & Grosvenor Sts, Sydney, 9247 6744
Attracts business people; interesting view of the street.

• 'Hotel' CBD (Map C, Ref G4)
Cnr King and York St, Sydney, 9299 1700
Good atmosphere, one of the best bars in the city centre.

• Customs House Bar (Map B, Ref B11)
Sydney Renaissance Hotel, Macquarie Place, Sydney, 9259 7000
Attracts many city workers who unwind with a drink under the trees.

• Dendy Bar (Map C, Ref K2)
19 Martin Place, Sydney, 9233 8166
At Dendy Cinema, perfect for a post-film drink and discussion.

• Horizon's Bar (Map A, Ref G7)
Level 36, ANA Hotel, 176 Cumberland St, The Rocks, 9250 6000
Sip a cocktail and savour the view.

• Sydney Cove Oyster Bar (Map B, Ref G3)
1 Circular Quay East, 9247 2937
Waterside, outdoor eating with a wide choice of oysters, Australian beers and sparkling wines.

PADDINGTON & DARLINGHURST BARS

• Burdekin Hotel (Map 4, Ref E3)
2 Oxford St, Darlinghurst, 9331 3066
Join the Dugout Bar's cigar set or boogie at the main bar.

• Elephant Bar (Map 13, Ref C14)
The Royal Hotel, Five Ways, Paddington, 9331 2604
Sip on a drink and enjoy the sunset views over eastern Sydney.

• Fringe Bar (Map 4, Ref H15)
106 Oxford St, Paddington, 9360 3554
A big, popular bar, with pool tables and booths.

• Gilligan's (Map 4, Ref D12)
Above Oxford Hotel, Taylor Square, Darlinghurst, 9331 3467
Open from 5pm, with the wildest cocktails in Sydney.

• Grand Pacific Blue Room (Map 4, Ref F14)
Cnr Oxford and South Dowling Sts, Darlinghurst, 9331 7108
Cocktails and classics.

• 'International' Bar (Map 4, Ref H10)
Top of the Town Hotel, Level 14, 227 Victoria St, Darlinghurst, 9361 0911
View the spectacular city skyline while lounging in the comfortable booths.

• 'Judgement' Bar (Map 4, Ref D13)
Courthouse Hotel (upstairs), Taylor Square, Darlinghurst, 9360 4831
Interesting decor.

• Lizard Lounge (Map F, Ref H4)
Exchange Hotel (upstairs), 34 Oxford St, Darlinghurst, 93311936
Meet all types while enjoying the complementary happy hour snacks.

• L'otel (Map 4, Ref G10)
114 Darlinghurst Rd, Darlinghurst, 9360 6868 A hip crowd squeezes into this small, fun bar.

INNER CITY PUBS

• Clock Hotel (Map 20, Ref C2)
470 Crown St, Surry Hills, 9331 5333
This revamped pub now attracts an eclectic, young, inner city crowd.

• Cricketer's Arms Hotel (Map 20, Ref E1)
106 Fitzroy St, Surry Hills, 9331 3301
Funky music and cool beer garden.

• Hopetoun Hotel (Map 20, Ref D1)
Cnr Bourke & Fitzroy Sts, Surry Hills, 9361 5257 A small underground bar with live music every night.

• Lord Nelson Brewery Hotel (Map A, Ref C2)
cnr Kent and Argyle Sts, 9251 4044
This cosy, sandstone historic pub brews their own ales, over 150 years old.

• O Bar, Clarendon Hotel (Map 19, Ref K3)
156 Devonshire St, Surry Hills, 9319 6881
Stylish drinking and dining.

• Paddington Inn (Map 21, Ref D2)
338 Oxford St, Paddington, 9380 5277
A fun, local pub, popular after Saturday's markets.

• Palace Hotel (Map 4, Ref E16)
122 Flinders St, Darlinghurst, 9361 5170
Several levels, pool tables and great quality pub food.

• The Spirit of Sydney Hotel (Map F, Ref K10)
320 Crown St, Surry Hills, 9331 1186
Pleasant setting, refurbished cocktail bar upstairs.

NIGHTCLUBS

• Tantra Bar (Map 4, Ref D12)
169 Oxford St, Darlinghurst, 9331 7729
Popular with toned body and pierced navel set.

• Goodbar (Map 4, Ref F14)
11 Oxford St, Paddington, 9360 6759
Two bars, with dance music, live bands and percussion.

• Q Bar (Map F, Ref H4)
44 Oxford St, Darlinghurst, 9360 1375
Pool tables, pinball, three bars and two funky dance spaces.

• Retro (Map C, Ref C2)
Bristol Arms Hotel, 81 Sussex St, Sydney, 9262 5491
Five levels of disco, indie, britpop, techno and '70s, '80s and '90s pop.

• Soho (Map 4, Ref H6)
171 Victoria St, Kings Cross, 9358 4221
Play pool, chat or dance to disco hits.

Like most great cities of the world, Sydney has a wide range of bars, pubs and nightclubs to suit all types and tastes. There are after work bars offering cheap drinks during 'happy hour'; sophisticated bars in international hotels; upmarket pubs providing complementary snacks; fun cocktail bars; noisy pubs with live music; restaurant bars where you drink and eat; large nightclubs offering pinball, pool and dancing; and dingy late-nighters where you go when there's nowhere else to go. Opening and closing hours vary, although night-clubbing in Sydney begins late, around 10 pm or 11 pm, with many clubs staying open until sunrise.

city fringe

The fringes of Sydney's CBD house an array of interesting suburbs well worth exploring for their own distinct characters, whether it be the ethnic diversity of Newtown, the Italianness of Leichhardt, the bohemian nature of Surry Hills, the refined atmosphere of Woollahra or the leisurely mood of Bronte. Many a day can be easily filled in any one area, visiting heritage sites, shopping at weekend markets, dining in local cafes or restaurants, lazing in community parks or just wandering the streets taking in the unique architecture and atmosphere.
Many suburbs, such as Glebe and Paddington, are within walking distance from the city centre. Other areas like Bondi Beach and Newtown can readily be reached by bus or train. Call the Public Transport Infoline (131 500) for details.

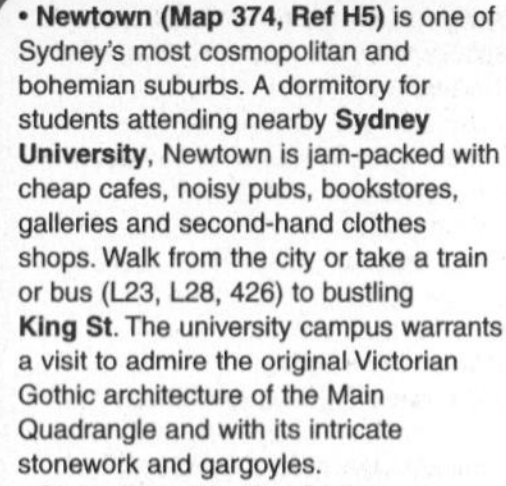

• **Newtown (Map 374, Ref H5)** is one of Sydney's most cosmopolitan and bohemian suburbs. A dormitory for students attending nearby **Sydney University**, Newtown is jam-packed with cheap cafes, noisy pubs, bookstores, galleries and second-hand clothes shops. Walk from the city or take a train or bus (L23, L28, 426) to bustling **King St**. The university campus warrants a visit to admire the original Victorian Gothic architecture of the Main Quadrangle and with its intricate stonework and gargoyles.

• **Glebe (Map 345, Ref C15)** is home to Sydney's cafe society. **Glebe Point Rd** is lined with many cafes and eateries. The colourful **Badde Manors** cafe (37 Glebe Point Rd, 9660 3797) is a Glebe icon, while **Russel's Natural Food Market** (55 Glebe Point Rd, 9660 8144), as the name suggests, is a megastore for organic and macrobiotic food supplies. Bookstores are also a Glebe feature, drawing literary types to explore everything from pulp crime and collector comics to feminist writings and new age tracts. **Gleebooks** (49 Glebe Point Rd, 9660 2333) has an eclectic range, while their secondhand store a few blocks up (191 Glebe Point Rd, 9552 2526) specialises in children's books and offers many bargains. Wander the side streets, which have rows of workers cottages and historic stately mansions. Bargain-hunt for bric-a-brac or secondhand clothes on Saturdays at **Glebe Markets** (Glebe Public school, Glebe Point Rd); or head to the end of Glebe Point Rd to **Jubilee Park**, for stunning city views and the striking outline of **Glebe Island Bridge**. Catch a bus from the city (431, 433).

• **Balmain (Map 344, Ref J5)** should be visited on Saturday to explore the treasure trove of **Balmain Markets** at St Andrews churchyard, opposite **Gladstone Park**. Take a bus (441) from Town Hall, or ferry from Circular Quay to **Darling St Wharf**, and walk up to Balmain Village through the historic narrow streets with their quaint sandstone cottages and Victorian terraces. Browse in the bookstores and gift shops, lunch in a cafe or pub or buy picnic food from a delicatessen or patisserie to take to one of Balmain's many waterfront parks. **Birchgrove Park**, **Mort Bay Park** and **Illoura Reserve** all have city skyline or Darling Harbour views.

• **Leichhardt (Map 343, Ref J14)** is Sydney's Little Italy. Scores of Italian restaurants, late-night cafes, delis, bakeries and shops line **Norton and Marion Sts**, giving the suburb its distinct Italian flavour. Take a bus (461, 480, 483) to Norton St and embark on a culinary tour of the area. Enjoy traditional homestyle Italian cuisine or contemporary variations in one of the many cafes or restaurants such as **Portofino** (166 Norton St, 9550 0782), but save room for Sydney's best gelato at **Bar Italia** (169–171 Norton St, 9560 9981).

• **Woollahra (Map 347, Ref A15)** is Sydney's premier antiques centre. Catch the bus (380, 382, 389) along **Oxford St** and alight at **Queen St**, the heart of this exclusive suburb. Hours can be spent in the fine antiques and interior design stores, galleries and shops. Explore the back streets, which have grand homes and terrace houses, or walk to nearby **Centennial Park** (9331 5056) where you can laze by the lake, feed the ducks or join a nature walk. If you're feeling more energetic, you can hire a bicycle, rollerblades or a horse.

• **Double Bay (Map 347, Ref D15)** is home to Sydney's society set. Take the train to **Edgecliff** or bus (324, 325) to this prestigious harbourside suburb and take in its village-like atmosphere. Browse in the exclusive designer boutiques or dine at a sophisticated restaurant or coffee shop. Walk up to hilly **Darling Point** and admire **Lindesay** (9363 2401), an impressive house built in 1834 that opens for exhibitions and special events. Alternatively, explore ritzy **Vaucluse** to the east where you can visit the Gothic mansion and museum **Vaucluse House** (9388 7922) and enjoy their famous Devonshire teas.

• **Bondi Beach (Map 378, Ref E4)** is synonymous with surf, sand and sun. It's now as popular for its buzzy **Campbell Pde** cafe scene and **Sunday Bondi Markets**. Take a bus (380, 382, 389) or the Bondi and Bay Explorer (Transport Info Line 131 500), which stops around Sydney Harbour and its shores, continuing on to Bondi Beach. There is much to do along the lively promenade: rollerblade, skateboard, jog, walk the dog, eat fresh seafood on the beach, attend a play, film, dance, band or festival at **Bondi Pavilion**. To take an invigorating walk to see breathtaking ocean views, head south from Notts Ave past Bondi Icebergs' clubhouse and along the rocky headland path to tiny **Tamarama** and **Bronte** beaches.

• **Bronte (Map 378, Ref B8)** is a small, protected white sandy beach that is favoured by families that flock to its pretty wooded park and barbecue area on weekends. Bronte can be reached by bus (378) from the city or by foot from Bondi Beach around the popular cliff edge trail, with its spectacular open ocean views. Be sure to take food for the BBQ as the fish and chips queue is always long. Perhaps try one of the excellent cafes across the road such as **Sejuiced** (9389 9538), which offers fresh fruit juices.

BACKPACKER & YOUTH HOSTELS

AA Tremayne Backpackers (Map 6, Ref C15)
89 Carabella St, Kirrabilli, 9955 4144

YHA New South Wales (Map C, Ref E9)
422 Kent St, Sydney, 9261 1111

Backpackers Accommodation (Map 12, Ref B12)
256-258 Glebe Point Rd, Glebe, 9660 8133

Backpackers Accommodation (Map E, Ref J6)
412 Pitt St, Sydney, 9571 9049

CB Hotel - Backpackers Accommodation (Map E, Ref J6)
417 Pitt St, Sydney, 9211 5115

Backpackers Connection (Map 13, Ref A7)
2 Roslyn St, Elizabeth Bay, 9358 4844

Bee-Hive Hostel (Map 18, Ref K4)
103 Cleveland St, Sydney, 9699 5315

Bell City - Country Stays (Map 18, Ref H2)
42 City Rd, Chippendale, 9211 5197

Crown Budget Inn (Map 4, Ref C10)
199-203 Crown St, Darlinghurst, 9360 9744

Dury House (Map 4, Ref J7)
34B Darlinghurst Rd, Kings Cross, 9368 0188

Excelsior Hotel (Map 3, Ref K16)
64 Foveaux St, Surry Hills, 9211 4945

Fact Free Youth Service (Map 19, Ref G13)
703 Elizabeth St, Waterloo, 9319 2708

Funk House – Backpacker (Map 4, Ref K6)
23 Darlinghurst Rd, Kings Cross, 9358 6455

George Street Private Hotel (Map E, Ref G7)
700A George St, Sydney, 9211 1800

Glebe Point YHA (Map 12, Ref B12)
262 Glebe Point Rd, Glebe, 9692 8418

Globe Backpackers Hostel (Map 4, Ref J7)
40 Darlinghurst Rd, Kings Cross, 9326 9675

Harbour City Hotel (Map 4, Ref D5)
50 Sir John Young Cres, Woolloomooloo, 9380 2922

Jolly Swagman Backpackers (Map 4, Ref K5)
27 Orwell St, Potts Point, 9358 6400

Gracelands Budget Accommodation (Map 20, Ref D7)
461 Cleveland St, Surry Hills, 9699 1399

Kangaroo Bak-Pak (Map 20, Ref D7)
665 South Dowling St, Surry Hills, 9319 5915

Kings Cross Holiday Apartments (Map 4, Ref F8)
169 William St (Forbes Square), Kings Cross, 9361 0637

Nomads Captain Cook Hotel (Map 20, Ref F2)
162 Flinders St, Darlinghurst, 9331 6487

Nomads City Central Backpackers (Map E, Ref F9)
752 George St, Sydney, 9212 4833

Nomads Downtown City Backpackers (Map E, Ref G5)
611 George St, Sydney, 9211 8801

Nomads Forest Lodge (Map 12, Ref A16)
117 Arundel St, Glebe, 9660 1872

Original Backpackers Lodge (Map E, Ref J6)
162 Victoria St, Potts Point, 9356 3232

Pink House Travellers Hostel (Map 13, Ref A7)
6 Barncleuth Square, Kings Cross, 9358 1689

Plane Tree Lodge (Map E, Ref J6)
174 Victoria St, Potts Point, 9356 4551

Potts Point House (Map E, Ref J5)
154 Victoria St, Potts Point, 9368 0733

Redback Steve Sydney Backpackers (Map F, Ref B7)
198 Elizabeth St, Surry Hills, 9211 4200

Royal Nomads (Map 18, Ref F8)
370 Abercrombie St, Darlington, 9698 8557

Sydney Central Backpackers (Map 4, Ref J5)
16 Orwell St, Potts Point, 9358 6600

Sydney Central YHA (Map E, Ref G11)
Cnr Pitt St & Rawson Pl, Sydney, 9281 9111

Sydney City Centre (Map D, Ref D1)
7 Elizabeth St, Sydney, 9221 7528

Tokyo Joe's Budget Accommodation (Map 4, Ref E7)
132 Bourke St, Woolloomooloo, 9331 0822

Travellers Rest (Map 4, Ref J5)
156 Victoria St, Kings Cross, 9358 4606

The Virgin Backpackers (Map 4, Ref J5)
144 Victoria St, Kings Cross, 9357 4733

Wattle House Travellers Accommodation (Map 11, Ref K12)
44 Hereford St, Glebe, 9552 4997

There are many reasonably priced places for travellers on a limited budget to stay in Sydney. All types of people stay in youth and backpacker hostels, groups of young people, older people, singles or families. Some hostels attract younger and exuberant people while others have a quieter atmosphere. It is always a good idea to ring ahead so that you end up staying in the place most suitable for your needs.
Listed are backpacker and youth hostels within the city, from Kings Cross to Glebe. However, there are many other hostels in the surrounding suburbs, especially in Manly and Bondi. Both of these suburbs have very popular and beautiful beaches and are only around 20 minutes travel by public transport to the CBD, making them an attractive place to stay. For contact details, check listings in Sydney's Yellow Pages telephone directory.

public transport

Sydney's extensive public transport system is both convenient and clean. As many of Sydney's sights are within easy walking distance, sightseeing is generally best done on foot. Driving into the city is not recommended; the network of buses, trains, ferries, light rail and taxis will assist you reach any destination. Ferries offer a scenic route between the city and harbourside suburbs — and they are even worth taking just for the ride. The Manly ferry is a must do for visitors, but other round-the-harbour trips such as the run to Watsons Bay are well worth the trip. You can stop off for fresh fish and chips and a spectacular view, as a reward for your efforts. Inner city areas can readily be reached by bus or train, as can Sydney's vast suburban sprawl.

• Getting to and around Sydney
For information on how to travel in Sydney by bus, train or ferry contact the Public Transport Info Line between 6am to 10pm daily (131 500). They provide details of routes, fares and timetables. Composite tickets are offered, which combine travel by bus, train and ferry at a cheaper price. These tickets can be purchased from State Transit Information Kiosks, Ticket Kiosks, newsagents, train stations and newspaper stands. Metro Light Rail (85845288) and Metro Monorail (85845288) can be contacted for details of their services.
To get to and from **Sydney's Airport (Map 404)** Domestic and International Flight Terminals, taxis, buses and trains are the primary options. The airport is 9 kilometres from the city centre, and although there are many taxis, the queues during peak hour can be long. State Transit offers four buses: Airport Express 350 to Kings Cross, Airport Express 300 to Circular Quay, metro route bus 100 from Dee Why via the city and metro route bus 400, which travels from Bondi Junction to Burwood via the airport. There are also bus services to a number of city hotels offered by Kingsford Smith Sydney Airporter (9667 0663). The Airport Shuttle (9317 3311) takes passengers between the airport and Darling Harbour and city hotels.
Homebush Bay (Map M), the home of the Sydney 2000 Olympic and Paralympic Games, is situated 16 kilometres from the city centre. To get there on weekdays, catch a Cityrail train to Strathfield or Lidcombe and connect with a Sydney Bus service to Homebush Bay. On weekends, rail services operate directly from Central Station to Olympic Park Station within close walking distance to the venues at Homebush Bay.

• Train Travel
Cityrail, www.cityrail.nsw.gov.au; Public Transport Info Line: 131 500. The Cityrail network offers convenient and regular train services, between 4:30am and midnight daily. Central Station in the city is the main urban and country terminus. To move around the city quickly, use the underground City Circle loop, which links all the stops in the CBD. Sydney's wider rail network has 6 major lines, extending to the Blue Mountains in the west, Berowra in the north, Bondi Junction in the east and Waterfall in Sydney's south. For a full listing of the suburban lines, please refer to the Cityrail Suburban Network map on the back cover of this directory. In the evening, be sure to stand in the designated 'Nightsafe' area and travel in carriages marked with a blue light, as they are near the train guard. After midnight, Cityrail provides the Nightride bus service, which replaces the train service — a handy tip is to arrange for a taxi to meet you once you reach your destination. Please refer to the map of the Nightride Bus network on the inside back cover of this directory. Most tickets are either single or return, however weekly and monthly tickets are offered at a cheaper rate, contact the Public Transport Info Line (131 500) for details.
• The Rail Link to Sydney Airport (131 500), Mascot, is a fast rail from Central Train Station to the Domestic and International Air Terminals.
It operates every 7 minutes and a one-way journey takes 10 minutes. Luggage space is available. Lifts operate at Central. The price is $10 one-way per person or $15 return per person.

• The Bus System
State Transit Authority, www.sydneybuses.nsw.gov.au; Public Transport Info Line: 131 500. **Sydney Buses** provide a reliable service that links up effectively with the train and ferry systems. The major city bus terminals are at Circular Quay, Wynyard, the western side of the Queen Victoria Building and Central Station. The route number and destination are displayed on the front, left side and back of all buses. Single journey tickets are purchased on the bus, but Travelten tickets, which allow you to make 10 bus trips, are more economical if you use buses frequently. Express buses are marked with an 'X' at the front, while Limited stop buses are marked with an 'L' in front of the route number. Additional buses are provided for special and sporting events. Contact State Transit Authority for details (9941 6814).
A number of **private bus companies** operate to and between Sydney's outlying suburbs, such as Westbus (9890 0000 or 131 500); Shorelink (9457 8888) for the Sydney's northern suburbs; Harris Park Buses (9689 1066) for Sydney's western suburbs; Hopkins (9632 3344) for Sydney's western suburbs: and Forest Coast Lines (9450 2277) for the north shore suburbs.

• Ferry Travel
Sydney Ferries Information Office is opposite Wharf 4, Circular Quay, 9207 3166, Public Transport Info Line, 131 500. **Ferries** have taken passengers on scenic journeys across Sydney Harbour for more than a century. Circular Quay is the city departure point for ferries, which operate daily, travelling to the eastern suburbs, North Shore and up the Parramatta River to Parramatta. Many ferry stops are also key tourist destinations, such as Darling Harbour, Manly, Watsons Bay, Balmain and Taronga Park Zoo. The ferries are conveniently linked to the train and bus

networks at Circular Quay. State Transit also offers a number of reasonably priced sightseeing cruises. Private harbour tour operators are Hegarty's Ferries (9206 1167), which offers a Circular Quay and Inner Harbour Loop tour, and Matilda Cruises – Rocket Ferry Services (9264 7377), running between Darling Harbour, the Star City Casino and Circular Quay. A map of the Sydney Ferry Network is included in this directory opposite the back inside cover of this directory.

• Light Rail & Monorail

Metro Light Rail, 8584 5288, operates 24 hours daily, Metro Light Rail runs trams every 8 to 15 minutes. Services run between Central and Wentworth Park, going to Capitol Square, Haymarket, Sydney Convention and Exhibition Centre, Pyrmont Bay, Star City, Sydney Fish Market, Glebe, Jubilee Park, Rozelle Bay and Lilyfield, 6 am – midnight. Tickets can be purchased on the tram.

Metro Monorail, 8584 5288

The Monorail runs from: Sundays 8am – 10pm, Monday to Wednesday 7 am – 10 pm, Thursday to Saturday 7 am – midnight, every 3 to 5 minutes. It connects key sightseeing spots such as the Powerhouse Museum, City Centre, Darling Park, as well as Harbourside stop - attractions including Star City and the National Maritime Museum. Purchase your ticket at the Monorail station. The Monorail Day Pass for $7 provides unlimited rides for an entire day.

• Travelling by Taxi

Efficiently organised, flexible and readily available, Sydney's taxi operators provide a fast service. To catch a cab, you can either hail one on the street – vacant cabs have an illuminated orange light on their roof; wait at a taxi rank in the queue; or telephone a company and order a cab to collect you from your location. Phone numbers for Sydney's many taxi companies are available by contacting Telstra (1223). The flagfall is currently $2.35 once the meter has started. There is a cost of $1.32 per kilometre, which has a 20% surcharge between 10 pm – 6 am. A $1.10 surcharge is charged if you book by telephone. Passengers pay for all bridge and road tolls, including some return tolls.

• Disabled Access

For information to assist people with a disability to readily travel around Sydney, contact NICAN (1800 806 769), IDEAS (1800 029 904) or Australian Quadriplegics Association's 'Ask AQA' help-line (1800 819 775). A number of taxis are specifically designed to enable passengers with wheelchairs to travel comfortably; they can be booked by phoning any of the major taxi companies.

• Purchasing Tickets

Sydney's public transport network offers a range of tickets including singles, returns, all-day, weekly and long term tickets. Some tickets allow you to catch a bus, train or ferry using the same ticket. In terms of train travel, for people who only travel occasionally, single or return tickets are usually the best option, and during the day off-peak tickets are available at a discounted price. For frequent travellers, Cityrail offers a 7 day rail pass; flexipasses offer substantial discounts and can be purchased for between 4 weeks and 1 year periods. For travelling by bus, single tickets can be purchased on the bus from the driver; while for frequent travellers there are Travelten tickets, which allow 10 journeys within the bus route sections covered by the ticket; a good option for sightseeing is the Bus Tripper ticket, a 1 day ticket which allows unlimited travel in the Sydney bus network, and is also valid on the Sydney and Bondi & Bay Explorers. For occasional ferry travellers, single and return tickets can be purchased from ticket booths at ferry terminals; for more regular travellers the FerryTen ticket allows for 10 rides on Sydney Ferry services. Sydney Light Rail offers weekly tickets and day passes, which provide unlimited travel on the day of purchase; or single and return tickets. Sydney Monorail offers a standard fare, all-day pass, family pass and free tickets for children under 5 years of age. There are also a number of tickets that combine train, bus and ferry travel. The CityHopper provides unlimited train and bus travels within a limited area covering the CBD and some of the inner city. DayRover tickets provide unlimited all-day travel in Cityrail suburban trains, Sydney Buses and Sydney Ferries. DayPasses allow unlimited travel on Sydney Buses and Sydney Ferries for one day. TravelPasses are available for periods of a week, a quarter or a year, and are colour-coded depending on the boundaries they are valid to travel in, allowing unlimited train, bus and ferry travel within the specified boundaries during the time period of the ticket. The SydneyPass is a good option for visitors wishing to explore Sydney over a few days; it provides for unlimited travel for either 3, 5 or 7 day periods and can be used on trains, buses and ferries within a specified boundary. For more detailed information on any of these ticketing options contact the Public Transport Info Line (131 500).

Special Events Arrangements

Sydney's range of special attractions and events can be enjoyed with the assistance of Sydney's extensive public transport system. Major sporting and entertainment events are accompanied by special transport arrangements for all major venues. The Moore Park precinct — including Sydney Cricket Ground (SCG), Sydney Football Stadium (SFS) and the Fox Studios Complex — all have State Transit shuttle buses arranged for special events held at their major venues, leaving from Chalmers St, near Central train station. A new bus station has been constructed opposite the SCG at Moore Park, to provide speedy access to all major events held at this location. Additional bus and train services are provided for New Year's Eve celebrations to and from the CBD. Late night bus services are available from midnight from the Town Hall station Nightride Bus stops. Cityrail and Sydney Buses also provide additional services for the Australia Day public holiday.

SUBURBS and LOCALITIES

Listed below are the suburbs and localities included in this directory, together with their postcodes and map references.

Suburbs and localities are differentiated in the index as follows:

Abbotsbury — Suburb
Anzac Village — Locality shown on the maps
Avalon Heights — Local name
Map reference indicates approximate location

Note: Streets are indexed to suburbs only, not localities.

Name	Postcode	Map	Ref
Abbotsbury	2176	333	B9
Abbotsford	2046	342	H2
Abbotsford Point	2046	312	H16
Acacia Gardens	2763	214	K14
Agnes Banks	2753	117	C10
Airds	2560	512	B11
Akuna Bay	2084	166	G5
Alexandria	2015	375	D10
Alfords Point	2234	459	B1
Allambie	2100	257	G15
Allambie Heights	2100	257	E12
Allawah	2218	432	F8
Ambarvale	2560	511	A13
Annandale	2038	344	F15
Annangrove	2156	186	C4
Anzac Village	2173	396	A13
Appin	2560	568	E6
Arcadia	2159	130	C9
Arncliffe	2205	403	E7
Arndell Park	2148	273	G9
Artarmon	2064	284	J15
Ashbury	2193	372	E9
Ashcroft	2168	394	F1
Ashfield	2131	372	G4
Asquith	2077	192	B12
Auburn	2144	339	C4
Auburn North	2144	309	F15
Auburn South	2144	339	D7
Auburn West	2144	338	J7
Audley	2232	520	C7
Austral	2171	391	E7
Avalon	2107	169	H1
Avalon Beach	2107	170	D2
Avalon Heights	2107	169	H1
Avalon North	2107	139	K13
Badgerys Creek	2171	358	E7
Bald Face	2221	462	H3
Balgowlah	2093	287	G10
Balgowlah Heights	2093	287	J13
Balls Head	2060	315	J16
Balmain	2041	344	J5
Balmain East	2041	345	E4
Balmoral	2088	317	C4
Balmoral Beach	2088	317	F6
Balmoral Heights	2088	317	C5
Bangor	2234	459	G12
Banksia	2216	403	G13
Banksmeadow	2019	436	B2
Bankstown	2200	369	F13
Bankstown Airport	2200	367	G16
Bankstown South	2200	399	H7
Bankstown West	2200	368	K16
Bantry Bay	2087	286	K3
Barden Ridge	2234	488	E1
Bardwell Park	2207	402	J8
Bardwell Valley	2205	403	B8
Bargo	2574	567	H7
Bass Hill	2197	368	B7
Baulkham Hills	2153	247	C11
Bayview	2104	168	G13
Beacon Hill	2100	257	H2
Beaconsfield	2015	375	F12
Beauty Point	2088	287	A16
Beecroft	2119	250	C5
Belfield	2191	371	C11
Belimbla Park	2570	501	F9
Bella Vista	2153	246	B3
Bellevue Hill	2023	347	E14
Belmore	2192	371	E15
Belrose	2085	226	D9
Ben Buckler	2026	378	J3
Berala	2141	339	E14
Berkshire Park	2765	180	B6
Berowra	2081	133	C12
Berowra Heights	2082	133	E6
Berowra Waters	2082	132	E4
Berrilee	2159	131	J9
Berrys Bay	2060	315	E15
Beverley Park	2217	433	B12
Beverly Hills	2209	401	D12
Beverly Hills North	2209	401	B10
Bexley	2207	402	E15
Bexley North	2207	402	D12
Bexley South	2207	432	H2
Bexley West	2207	402	E14
Bickley Vale	2570	505	H10
Bidwill	2770	211	F14
Bilgola	2107	169	J4
Bilgola Plateau	2107	169	F4
Birchgrove	2041	344	H1
Birkenhead Point	2047	344	C3
Birrong	2143	369	A6
Blackett	2770	241	C2
Blacktown	2148	244	G11
Blacktown North	2148	244	J11
Blacktown South	2148	274	F4
Blacktown West	2148	244	B16
Blackwattle Bay	2009	345	A11
Blair Athol	2560	511	B1
Blairmount	2559	481	A13
Blakehurst	2221	432	C14
Blaxcell	2142	338	E6
Blaxland	2774	233	H5
Blaxlands Ridge	2758	56	B2
Bligh Park	2756	150	E6
Blue Mountains National Park		264	D11
Blues Point	2060	345	H1
Bobbin Head	2074	163	H12
Bondi	2026	377	J3
Bondi Beach	2026	378	E4
Bondi Junction	2022	377	C4
Bondi South	2026	378	C5
Bonnet Bay	2226	460	C12
Bonnie Vale	2230	523	D9
Bonnyrigg	2177	363	J8
Bonnyrigg Heights	2177	363	D5
Boronia Park	2111	313	C5
Bossley Park	2176	333	G6
Botany	2019	405	H14
Bow Bowing	2566	452	F13
Bowen Mountain	2753	84	B9
Box Hill	2765	154	B8
Bradbury	2560	511	E12
Bradleys Head	2088	347	D2
Breakfast Point	2137	312	C13
Brickfield Hill	2000	345	H13
Brighton-Le-Sands	2216	434	B1
Bringelly	2171	387	J10
Broadway	2007	3	B16
Bronte	2024	377	J8
Brooklyn	2083	76	B11
Brookvale	2100	258	C10
Brownlow Hill	2570	475	E6
Brush Farm	2122	280	G9
Bundeena	2230	523	G11
Bungan Beach	2106	169	J16
Burraneer	2230	493	E16
Burwood	2134	342	A12
Burwood Heights	2136	372	A4
Busby	2168	363	H14
Cabarita	2137	342	E2
Cabarita Junction	2137	342	B3
Cabramatta	2166	365	G5
Cabramatta Heights	2166	365	B8
Cabramatta West	2166	365	A5
Cabravale	2166	365	K5
Cambridge Gardens	2747	237	H2
Cambridge Park	2747	237	G8
Camden	2570	477	C13
Camden South	2570	507	E14
Camellia	2142	309	B4
Cammeray	2062	316	A6
Campbelltown	2560	511	D3
Campbelltown North	2560	511	J4
Camperdown	2050	374	H3
Campsie	2194	372	C13
Campsie South	2194	372	A16
Canada Bay	2046	342	E8
Canley Heights	2166	365	E1
Canley Vale	2166	366	C4
Canterbury	2193	372	F12
Caravan Head	2225	461	F4
Careel Bay	2107	140	B11
Caringbah	2229	492	H9
Caringbah South	2229	492	J12
Carlingford	2118	279	G3
Carlingford Heights	2118	279	C5
Carlingford North	2118	250	C13
Carlton	2218	432	G5
Carnes Hill	2171	392	D9
Carramar	2163	366	J2
Carss Park	2221	432	G14
Cartwright	2168	394	C5
Castle Cove	2069	285	J2
Castlecrag	2068	286	D10
Castle Hill	2154	217	H11
Castlereagh	2749	176	C7
Casula	2170	394	J14
Catherine Field	2171	449	J8
Cattai	2756	94	E4

Name	Postcode	Map	Ref
Cawdor	2570	506	G9
Cecil Hills	2171	362	H4
Cecil Park	2171	332	C13
Centennial Park	2021	376	J5
Central	2000	345	J16
Charing Cross	2024	377	F7
Chatham Village	2170	425	A1
Chatswood	2057	284	J6
Chatswood West	2057	283	J10
Chatsworth	2759	269	K8
Cheltenham	2119	251	A8
Cherrybrook	2126	219	G6
Chester Hill	2162	368	D3
Chester Hill North	2162	338	B13
Chifley	2036	437	B8
Chinatown	2000	3	E11
Chippendale	2008	375	E1
Chipping Norton	2170	396	J2
Chiswick	2046	343	E2
Chowder Bay	2088	317	F13
Chullora	2190	370	C3
Church Hill	2000	345	H7
Church Point	2105	168	G6
Circular Quay	2000	345	K6
Claremont Meadows	2747	268	K3
Clarendon	2756	120	C11
Clareville	2107	169	E2
Claymore	2559	481	D10
Clemton Park	2206	402	C5
Clifton Gardens	2088	317	F14
Clontarf	2093	287	E13
Clovelly	2031	377	H11
Clovelly West	2031	377	F12
Clyburn	2144	309	A15
Clyde	2142	308	H12
Coasters Retreat	2108	139	A4
Cobbitty	2570	446	B10
Cockatoo Island	2000	314	F16
Cogra Bay	2083	76	D1
Colebee	2761	212	H12
Collaroy	2097	229	D12
Collaroy Beach	2097	229	B10
Collaroy Plateau	2097	228	H10
Colyton	2760	270	D3
Comleroy	2758	56	B6
Como	2226	460	G6
Como West	2226	460	F6
Concord	2137	341	J3
Concord East	2137	342	B5
Concord North	2138	311	E14
Concord South	2137	342	K9
Concord West	2138	341	E3
Condell Park	2200	398	E4
Connells Point	2221	431	G14
Coogee	2034	377	E14
Coogee North	2034	377	J14
Cornwallis	2756	90	J15
Cottage Point	2084	135	F8
Couridjah	2571	564	J15
Cowan	2081	104	B14
Cranebrook	2749	207	D10
Cremorne	2090	316	E10
Cremorne Junction	2090	316	F6
Cremorne Point	2090	316	F14
Cromer	2099	228	A14
Cromer Heights	2099	227	G13
Cronulla	2230	493	H13
Cronulla South	2230	523	K1
Crows Nest	2065	315	F5
Croydon	2132	342	E12
Croydon North	2132	342	H12
Croydon Park	2133	372	C7
Curl Curl	2096	258	K13
Currans Hill	2567	479	K12
Currawong Beach	2108	109	B16
Daceyville	2032	406	F4
Dangar Island	2083	76	G5
Darling Harbour	2000	345	F12
Darlinghurst	2010	346	C13
Darling Point	2027	346	J10
Darlington	2008	375	D4
Davidson	2085	255	E3
Dawes Point	2000	345	H3
Dean Park	2761	242	J1
Dee Why	2099	258	G6
Dee Why Beach	2099	259	B6
Dee Why North	2099	83	J14
Dee Why West	2099	83	D9
Denham Court	2565	422	D11
Denistone	2114	281	E12
Denistone East	2122	281	J11
Denistone West	2114	281	A13
Dharruk	2770	241	B6
Diamond Bay	2030	348	H5
Dobroyd Head	2093	288	C16
Dobroyd Point	2045	343	G11
Dolans Bay	2229	492	K16
Dolls Point	2219	463	G1
Doonside	2767	243	B11
Double Bay	2028	347	D15
Dover Heights	2030	348	H11
Drummoyne	2047	343	H4
Duffys Forest	2084	195	C4
Dulwich Hill	2203	373	E8
Dundas	2117	279	G14
Dundas Valley	2117	280	B8
Dundas West	2117	279	A11
Dunheved	2760	239	F5
Dural	2158	189	D10
Eagle Vale	2558	481	G7
Earlwood	2206	402	G4
Earlwood West	2206	372	G16
Eastern Creek	2766	273	A11
Eastgardens	2036	406	F9
East Hills	2213	427	J2
East Killara	2071	254	H8
East Kurrajong	2758	56	K3
Eastlakes	2018	406	C6
East Lindfield	2070	254	K14
East Roseville	2069	285	C2
East Ryde	2113	283	C15
East Sydney	2010	4	C8
Eastwood	2122	281	E7
Ebenezer	2756	63	E10
Edensor Park	2176	363	G1
Edgecliff	2027	346	K15
Edmondson Park	2171	423	D4
Elanora Heights	2101	198	B14
Elderslie	2570	507	E4
Elizabeth Bay	2011	346	G9
Ellis Lane	2570	476	E6
Elvina Bay	2105	168	E3
Emerton	2770	240	K5
Emu Heights	2750	235	B1
Emu Plains	2750	235	G6
Enfield	2136	371	H5
Enfield South	2133	371	F6
Engadine	2233	518	G5
Engineer Barracks	2170	425	C2
Enmore	2042	374	F8
Epping	2121	251	D14
Epping West	2121	250	F15
Ermington	2115	310	F5
Erskine Park	2759	270	J16
Erskineville	2043	375	A9
Erskineville South	2043	374	K9
Eschol Park	2558	481	A3
Eveleigh	2015	375	D5
Fairfield	2165	336	G9
Fairfield East	2165	337	C12
Fairfield Heights	2165	336	B10
Fairfield West	2165	335	D10
Fairlight	2094	288	C6
Fairy Bower	2095	288	K11
Faulconbridge	2776	171	B14
Fiddletown	2159	129	G3
Five Dock	2046	343	B9
Flemington	2140	340	F9
Forest Lodge	2037	344	J15
Forestville	2087	255	F9
Forty Baskets Beach	2093	288	B12
Fox Valley	2076	221	G16
Freemans Reach	2756	90	D6
Frenchs Forest	2086	256	J1
Frenchs Forest East	2086	257	B5
Fullers Bridge	2067	283	K8
Gallows Hill	2000	345	J6
Galston	2159	159	E7
Garden Island	2000	346	G4
Georges Hall	2198	367	H13
Georges Heights	2088	317	J9
Gilead	2560	539	H7
Girraween	2145	276	B12
Gladesville	2111	312	J7
Glebe	2037	345	C15
Glebe Island	2039	344	K9
Glebe Point	2037	11	H6
Glen Alpine	2560	510	D12
Glenbrook	2773	234	D13
Glendenning	2761	242	F6
Glenfield	2167	424	D6
Glenhaven	2156	217	J2
Glenmore	2570	503	G5
Glenmore Park	2745	266	H9
Glenorie	2157	128	A5
Glenwood	2768	215	C16
Glossodia	2756	59	G7
Goat Island	2000	345	E2
Golden Grove	2008	18	E8
Goodyears	2142	309	D5
Gordon	2072	253	F8
Gore Hill	2065	315	B5
Grantham Heights	2147	275	E8
Granville	2142	308	F13
Granville North	2142	308	J8
Grasmere	2570	476	A12
Grays Point	2232	491	C14
Great Mackerel Beach	2108	109	C14
Greenacre	2190	370	G10
Greendale	2745	385	H7
Greenfield Park	2176	334	B15
Green Valley	2168	363	B11
Greenwich	2065	315	B7
Greenwich Point	2065	314	H14
Greystanes	2145	306	A7
Gronos Point	2756	93	E5
Grose Vale	2753	85	F12
Grose Wold	2753	116	B7
Guildford	2161	337	J6
Guildford East	2161	338	D7
Guildford Heights	2161	337	H5
Guildford North	2160	338	A2
Guildford West	2161	336	H4
Gundamaian	2232	521	J1
Gunnamatta Bay	2230	493	G14
Gymea	2227	491	F5
Gymea Bay	2227	491	G9
Haberfield	2045	343	D13
Hammondville	2170	396	J14
Harbord	2096	288	D1
Harbord West	2096	258	E14
Hardies	2142	309	A5
Harrington Park	2567	478	J3
Harris Park	2150	308	G5
Hassall Grove	2761	212	A15
Hawkesbury Heights	2777	174	F2
Hawkesbury River		76	C11
Haymarket	2000	345	J14
Heathcote	2233	518	E12
Hebersham	2770	241	E3
Heckenberg	2168	364	B14
Henley	2111	313	A14
Hewitt	2759	270	H12
Hillsdale	2036	406	G15
Hillside	2157	127	B3
Hilltop		307	A8
Hinchinbrook	2168	363	C16
HMAS Penguin	2091	317	G7
Hobartville	2753	118	D7
Holroyd	2160	307	K11
Holsworthy	2173	426	D5
Holsworthy Barracks	2173	426	E9
Homebush	2140	341	B4
Homebush Bay	2127	340	J2
Homebush West	2140	340	H10
Hookhams Corner	2077	191	F11
Horningsea Park	2171	392	D12
Hornsby	2077	221	E3
Hornsby Heights	2077	191	E5
Horsley Park	2164	302	E12
Hoxton Park	2171	392	F9
Hunters Hill	2110	313	G10
Huntingwood	2148	273	E13
Huntleys Point	2111	313	E14
Hurlstone Park	2193	373	A12
Hurstville	2220	432	B4
Hurstville Grove	2220	431	H11
Illawong	2234	459	E6
Ingleburn	2565	453	E9

Name	Postcode	Map	Ref
Ingleburn Military Camp	2174	423	C10
Ingleburn Village	2174	423	C8
Ingleside	2101	197	G5
Jamisontown	2750	265	J1
Jannali	2226	460	H11
Jannali West	2226	460	F13
Kangaroo Point	2224	461	J5
Kareela	2232	461	D10
Kearns	2558	451	B15
Kellyville	2155	216	D6
Kemps Creek	2171	360	C8
Kensington	2033	376	B13
Kenthurst	2156	187	E5
Kentlyn	2560	513	E5
Killara	2071	254	C11
Killarney Heights	2087	255	J15
Kings Cross	2011	4	J8
Kingsford	2032	406	J5
Kingsgrove	2208	401	H9
Kings Langley	2147	245	F6
Kings Park	2148	244	G4
Kingsway	2208	401	G15
Kingswood	2747	237	F14
Kirkham	2570	477	H8
Kirrawee	2232	491	A3
Kirribilli	2061	316	C16
Kissing Point	2074	252	B9
Kogarah	2217	433	E4
Kogarah Bay	2217	432	K14
Kogarah South	2217	433	C8
Kogarah West	2207	432	K15
Ku-Ring-Gai Chase National Park		163	G1
Kurmond	2757	86	F5
Kurnell	2231	465	K8
Kurraba Point	2089	316	E16
Kurrajong	2758	85	G3
Kurrajong Heights	2758	53	G5
Kurrajong Hills	2758	54	F14
Kyeemagh	2216	404	A13
Kyle Bay	2221	431	K15
Lakemba	2195	401	C2
Lake Parramatta	2151	278	E7
Lakesland	2572	561	A7
Lalor Park	2147	245	F13
Lane Cove	2066	314	B2
Lane Cove North	2066	284	A14
Lane Cove West	2066	283	G15
Lansdowne	2163	367	C6
Lansvale	2166	366	H7
La Perouse	2036	436	H15
Lapstone	2773	264	G2
Lavender Bay	2060	315	J14
Leichhardt	2040	343	J14
Leightonfield	2163	367	G1
Leonay	2750	235	A14
Leppington	2171	421	D7
Lethbridge Park	2770	240	F2
Leumeah	2560	482	D15
Lewisham	2049	373	F6
Liberty Grove	2138	311	C13
Lidcombe	2141	339	F9
Lilli Pilli	2229	522	E2
Lilyfield	2040	344	D11
Lindfield	2070	284	B2
Linley Point	2066	313	H7
Linns Hill	2570	443	F1
Little Bay	2036	437	E12
Liverpool	2170	395	C6
Liverpool North	2170	365	A16
Liverpool South	2170	395	B8
Liverpool West	2170	394	H5
Llandilo	2747	208	D4
Loftus	2232	489	J9
Loftus Heights	2232	489	K11
Londonderry	2753	148	C12
Long Bay	2036	437	G4
Long Point	2564	454	E10
Long Reef	2097	259	D2
Longueville	2066	314	E9
Loquat Valley	2104	168	K12
Lovett Bay	2105	168	C2
Lowlands	2753	88	E11
Lucas Heights	2234	487	G8
Luddenham	2745	356	E1
Lugarno	2210	429	H11
Lugarno North	2210	430	A10
Lurline Bay	2035	407	J8
Lurnea	2170	394	F10
McCallums Hill	2195	401	D8
Macdonaldtown	2042	17	K11
McGraths Hill	2756	121	H10
McMahons Point	2060	315	F15
Macquarie Fields	2564	424	H15
Macquarie Links	2565	423	D14
Macquarie Park	2113	282	H3
Macquarie University	2109	252	B16
Maianbar	2230	523	C7
Malabar	2036	437	E7
Malabar Heights	2036	437	F8
Manahan	2200	399	B4
Manly	2095	288	J8
Manly East	2095	288	J11
Manly Vale	2093	287	J2
Manly West	2093	287	J2
Maraylya	2765	124	H5
Marayong	2148	243	J4
Marayong Heights	2148	244	B4
Marayong South	2148	244	C11
Maroota South	2756	64	E3
Maroubra	2035	407	D11
Maroubra Junction	2035	407	D9
Maroubra South	2035	407	D15
Marrickville	2204	373	J13
Marrickville South	2204	373	J16
Marrickville West	2204	373	E14
Marsden Park	2765	181	H12
Marsfield	2122	281	H2
Martin Place	2000	345	K9
Mascot	2020	405	C4
Matraville	2036	436	H6
Mays Hill	2145	307	H5
Meadowbank	2114	311	C3
Melrose Park	2114	310	J1
Melville	2759	269	J12
Menai	2234	458	G5
Menangle	2568	538	J14
Menangle Park	2563	538	H7
Merrylands	2160	307	F11
Merrylands West	2160	306	J12
Middle Cove	2068	286	C9
Middle Dural	2158	158	F7
Middle Harbour	2088	317	F1
Middle Head	2088	318	B7
Miller	2168	393	H4
Millers Point	2000	345	F5
Mill Hill	2022	377	B4
Milperra	2214	397	E8
Milperra Bridge	2170	397	E6
Milsons Point	2061	315	K16
Minchinbury	2770	271	D8
Minto	2566	482	D3
Minto Heights	2566	483	H5
Miranda	2228	492	B6
Miranda North	2228	492	E2
Mobbs Hill	2118	280	B3
Model Farms	2153	247	H16
Mona Vale	2103	199	D5
Monterey	2217	433	H7
Mooney Mooney	2083	75	F1
Moorebank	2170	395	F10
Moorebank Village	2170	395	F12
Moore Park	2021	376	C6
Morning Bay	2108	138	G15
Mortdale	2223	431	B5
Mortlake	2137	312	A12
Mosman	2088	316	K10
Mount Annan	2567	479	D12
Mt Colah	2079	192	B2
Mount Druitt	2770	241	F13
Mt Hunter	2570	504	H9
Mt Kuring-Gai	2080	162	K10
Mt Lewis	2190	370	C15
Mt Pritchard	2170	364	G10
Mt Riverview	2774	234	G3
Mt Vernon	2759	331	B11
Mowbray Park	2571	561	E6
Mulgoa	2745	295	F11
Mulgrave	2756	151	H3
Museum	2000	345	K13
Narellan	2567	478	H11
Narellan Vale	2567	478	K11
Naremburn	2065	315	E2
Narrabeen	2101	229	C6
Narrabeen Peninsula	2101	229	E1
Narraweena	2099	258	C3
Narwee	2209	400	H11
Nelson	2765	154	J9
Neutral Bay	2089	316	B10
Neutral Bay Junction	2089	316	D9
Newington	2127	310	C13
Newport	2106	169	F10
Newport Beach	2106	170	A9
Newtown	2042	374	H5
Newtown South	2042	374	G8
Normanhurst	2076	221	G11
Normanhurst West	2120	221	D9
North Balgowlah	2093	287	E5
North Bankstown	2199	369	F11
North Bondi	2026	348	E14
Northbridge	2063	286	B15
North Cremorne	2090	316	E6
North Cronulla	2230	494	D8
North Curl Curl	2099	258	J11
North Engadine	2233	488	G10
North Epping	2121	251	F11
North Head	2095	290	E16
North Manly	2100	258	B14
Northmead	2152	277	J6
North Narrabeen	2101	228	H2
North Parramatta	2151	278	F7
North Richmond	2754	87	F11
North Rocks	2151	249	A13
North Ryde	2113	282	F10
North St Ives	2075	224	E6
North Steyne	2095	288	J8
North St Marys	2760	240	B7
North Strathfield	2137	341	E7
North Sydney	2060	315	J11
North Turramurra	2074	223	G4
North Wahroonga	2076	222	H1
North Willoughby	2068	285	G8
Northwood	2066	314	G8
Oakdale	2570	500	C10
Oakhurst	2761	242	B3
Oakville	2765	153	E5
Oatlands	2117	279	C11
Oatley	2223	431	B13
Oatley West	2223	430	G11
Old Guildford	2161	337	F10
Old Toongabbie	2146	277	E6
Olympic Park	2140	340	H1
Orange Grove	2040	344	B11
Orangeville	2570	443	E13
Oran Park	2570	448	H8
Orchard Hills	2748	267	J9
Osborne Park	2066	314	G4
Oxford Falls	2100	227	C14
Oxley Park	2760	270	F1
Oyster Bay	2225	461	E4
Paddington	2021	346	F16
Padstow	2211	399	E14
Padstow Heights	2211	429	C8
Padstow North	2211	399	C11
Pagewood	2035	406	E7
Palm Beach	2108	139	K2
Panania	2213	428	C3
Parklea	2768	215	B13
Parramatta	2150	308	E2

Name	Postcode	Map	Ref
Parramatta East	2150	278	K16
Peakhurst	2210	430	G4
Peakhurst Heights	2210	430	D7
Peakhurst South	2210	430	C9
Peakhurst West	2210	430	A9
Pearces Corner	2076	222	B7
Pendle Hill	2145	276	F12
Pennant Hills	2120	220	F13
Penrith	2750	236	F13
Penshurst	2222	431	E3
Petersham	2049	373	J4
Phillip Bay	2036	436	J9
Picnic Point	2213	428	E9
Picton	2571	563	J6
Pitt Town	2756	92	H12
Pitt Town Bottoms	2756	92	B11
Pleasure Point	2171	427	F7
Plumpton	2761	242	A6
Point Piper	2027	347	D8
Port Botany	2036	436	C7
Port Hacking	2229	522	J3
Potts Hill	2143	369	C4
Potts Point	2011	346	E10
Prairiewood	2176	334	G9
Prestons	2170	393	E11
Prospect	2148	275	C14
Punchbowl	2196	400	C1
Punchbowl South	2196	400	B7
Putney	2112	312	B7
Pymble	2073	253	B3
Pyrmont	2009	345	E9
Quakers Hill	2763	214	B10
Queenscliff	2096	288	F2
Queens Park	2022	377	C5
Raby	2566	451	E14
Ramsgate	2217	433	E13
Ramsgate Beach	2217	433	G11
Randwick	2031	377	C12
Randwick South	2031	407	B2
Redfern	2016	375	H4
Regents Park	2143	369	C1
Regentville	2745	265	E3
Revesby	2212	398	G11
Revesby Heights	2212	428	K6
Revesby North	2212	398	J12
Rhodes	2138	311	D10
Richmond	2753	118	C4
Richmond East	2753	119	B5
Riverstone	2765	182	G7
Riverview	2066	313	K6
Riverwood	2210	400	C11
Rockdale	2216	403	F14
Rodd Point	2046	343	F8
Rogans Hill	2154	218	G14
Rookwood	2141	340	D10
Rooty Hill	2766	272	E2
Rose Bay	2029	348	A8
Rose Bay North	2030	348	H8
Rosebery	2018	375	H14
Rosehill	2142	308	J7
Roselands	2196	400	G8
Roselea	2118	250	A12
Rosemeadow	2560	540	F5
Roseville	2069	284	J3
Roseville Chase	2069	285	F1
Rossmore	2171	389	G8
Round Corner	2158	188	F14
Rouse Hill	2155	184	E9
Royal National Park	2232	520	F6
Rozelle	2039	344	E7
Ruse	2560	512	E4
Rushcutters Bay	2011	346	G12
Russell Lea	2046	343	D4
Rydalmere	2116	309	E2
Ryde	2112	312	C2
Sadleir	2168	394	B2
St Andrews	2566	481	J4
St Clair	2759	270	C11
St Helens Park	2560	541	D5
St Ives	2075	224	F12
St Ives Chase	2075	223	H3
St James	2000	345	K10
St Johns Park	2176	364	F1
St Leonards	2065	315	C4
St Marys	2760	239	E9
St Peters	2044	374	H15
Sandown	2192	309	E5
Sandringham	2219	463	E4
Sandy Point	2171	428	B10
Sans Souci	2219	433	E15
Scheyville	2756	123	G5
Schofields	2762	183	F14
Scotland Island	2105	168	G1
Scotts Hill	2570	443	K5
Seaforth	2092	287	B9
Sefton	2162	368	F4
Seven Hills	2147	275	G5
Seven Hills North	2147	246	D11
Seven Hills West	2147	245	C16
Shalvey	2770	210	K15
Shanes Park	2760	209	G7
Sherwood Grange	2160	306	G13
Silverdale	2752	354	D10
Silverwater	2128	309	G13
Smeaton Grange	2567	479	F8
Smithfield	2164	335	H3
Smithfield West	2164	335	D3
Sorlie	2086	256	B3
South Coogee	2034	407	K5
South Curl Curl	2096	258	K15
South Engadine	2233	518	H7
South Granville	2142	338	F4
South Hurstville	2221	432	B9
South Penrith	2750	266	G3
South Steyne	2095	288	H10
South Turramurra	2074	251	J7
South Wentworthville	2145	307	B5
South Windsor	2756	120	J15
Spectacle Island	2000	344	C1
Spit Junction	2088	317	A4
Spring Farm	2570	507	H8
Springwood	2777	201	F2
Stanhope Gardens	2768	215	E7
Stanmore	2048	374	D6
Strathfield	2135	341	E13
Strathfield South	2136	371	B6
Strawberry Hills	2010	19	K3
Summer Hill	2130	373	B4
Surry Hills	2010	346	A15
Sutherland	2232	490	C2
Sydenham	2044	374	E15
Sydney	2000	345	G8
Sydney (GPO)	2001	345	J9
Sylvania	2224	461	J10
Sylvania Heights	2224	461	F11
Sylvania Waters	2224	462	E11
Tahmoor	2573	566	E12
Tamarama	2026	378	E7
Tarban	2111	313	D12
Taren Point	2229	462	K12
Taronga Zoological Park	2088	317	A14
Taverners Hill	2040	373	H4
Taylors Point	2107	169	C2
Telopea	2117	279	F9
Tempe	2044	404	D2
Tennyson	2754	57	J9
Tennyson	2111	312	E10
Terrey Hills	2084	196	B7
The Basin	2108	138	G3
The Cross Roads	2170	424	B3
The Oaks	2570	502	G11
Theresa Park	2570	444	H5
The Rocks	2000	345	K4
The Slopes	2754	56	H7
The Spit	2088	287	C13
The Trongate	2142	338	F2
Thirlmere	2572	565	E4
Thompsons Corner	2125	249	J5
Thornleigh	2120	220	J13
Tom Uglys Point	2221	462	F5
Toongabbie	2146	276	E8
Toongabbie West	2146	276	G7
Town Hall	2000	3	H6
Towra Point	2231	464	D4
Tregear	2770	240	D6
Turramurra	2074	222	G15
Turrella	2205	403	E4
Ultimo	2007	345	E14
Undercliffe	2206	403	F3
University of NSW	2052	376	G14
University of Sydney	2006	375	B1
Valley Heights	2777	202	H6
Varroville	2566	451	H5
Vaucluse	2030	348	C4
Vaucluse Heights	2030	348	D6
Villawood	2163	367	G3
Villawood East	2163	367	G4
Vineyard	2765	152	H11
Voyager Point	2171	427	E3
Wahroonga	2076	222	G6
Wahroonga South	2076	221	H16
Waitara	2077	221	J2
Waitara East	2077	222	B3
Wakehurst	2085	226	B16
Wakeley	2176	334	K13
Wallacia	2745	324	J15
Wallgrove	2164	272	G11
Wareemba	2046	343	A5
Warragamba	2752	353	E6
Warrawee	2074	222	G10
Warriewood	2102	199	A10
Warrimoo	2774	203	F13
Warumbul	2229	521	K7
Warwick Farm	2170	365	K12
Waterfall	2233	519	C14
Waterloo	2017	375	G7
Watsons Bay	2030	318	G11
Wattle Grove	2173	396	A15
Waverley	2024	377	G7
Waverley South	2024	377	H10
Waverton	2060	315	E13
Wedderburn	2560	540	C12
Wentworthville	2145	277	B14
Werombi	2570	443	F7
Werrington	2747	239	C12
Werrington County	2747	238	K7
Werrington Downs	2747	238	B4
West Gordon	2072	253	C10
West Hoxton	2171	392	B4
Westleigh	2120	220	F4
West Lindfield	2070	283	G2
Westmead	2145	307	E1
West Pennant Hills	2125	249	D4
West Pymble	2073	252	J11
West Ryde	2114	281	G14
Wetherill Park	2164	334	D2
Whalan	2770	241	B11
Whale Beach	2107	140	D6
Wheeler Heights	2097	228	F9
White Bay	2039	344	K7
Wilberforce	2756	92	B4
Wiley Park	2195	400	G1
Willmot	2770	210	D12
Willoughby	2068	285	H11
Windsor	2756	121	C11
Windsor Downs	2756	180	J2
Wingala	2099	258	H11
Winmalee	2777	173	F10
Winston Hills	2153	277	C2
Wollstonecraft	2065	315	D9
Wondabyne	2250	76	H1
Woodbine	2560	481	H13
Woodcroft	2767	243	G8
Woodpark	2164	306	G14
Woollahra	2025	377	B1
Woollahra Point	2028	347	G7
Woolloomooloo	2011	346	D11
Woolooware	2230	493	E11
Woolwich	2110	314	F13
Woronora	2232	460	A15
Woronora Heights	2233	489	F4
Wynyard	2000	1	E16
Yagoona	2199	369	C11
Yanderra	2574	567	C13
Yarra Junction	2036	436	K12
Yarramundi	2753	145	H7
Yarrawarrah	2233	489	F12
Yellow Rock	2777	204	D4
Yennora	2161	337	D10
Yowie Bay	2228	492	A12
Yowie Point	2228	492	A15
Zetland	2017	375	K11

STREET INDEX

ABBREVIATIONS USED IN THE STREET INDEX

ABBREVIATIONS FOR DESIGNATIONS

Alley	al	Cross	cs	Junction	jnc	Return	rtn
Approach	app	Crossing	csg	Key	key	Ridge	rdg
Arcade	arc	Curve	cve	Lane	la	Rise	ri
Avenue	av	Dale	dle	Link	lk	Road	rd
Bend	bnd	Down/s	dn	Loop	lp	Roadway	rdy
Boulevard	bvd	Drive	dr	Mall	ml	Route	rte
Bowl	bl	Driveway	dwy	Mead	md	Row	row
Brace	br	East	e	Meander	mdr	Serviceway	swy
Brae	br	Edge	edg	Mews	mw	South	s
Break	brk	Elbow	elb	Motorway	mwy	Square	sq
Brook	brk	End	end	Nook	nk	Strand	sd
Broadway	bwy	Entrance	ent	North	n	Street	st
Brow	brw	Esplanade	esp	Outlook	out	Tarn	tn
Bypass	bps	Expressway	exp	Parade	pde	Terrace	tce
Centre	ctr	Fairway	fy	Park	pk	Tollway	twy
Chase	ch	Freeway	fwy	Parkway	pky	Top	top
Circle	cir	Frontage	fr	Pass	ps	Tor	tor
Circuit	cct	Garden/s	gdn	Pathway	pwy	Track	tr
Circus	crc	Gate/s	gte	Place	pl	Trail	trl
Close	cl	Gateway	gwy	Plaza	plz	Turn	trn
Common	cmn	Glade	gld	Pocket	pkt	Underpass	ups
Concourse	cnc	Glen	gln	Point/Port	pt	Vale	va
Copse	cps	Grange	gra	Promenade	prm	View	vw
Corner	cnr	Green	grn	Quadrant	qd	Vista	vst
Corso	cso	Grove	gr	Quay/s	qy	Walk	wk
Court	ct	Grovet	gr	Ramble	ra	Walkway	wky
Courtyard	cyd	Haven	hvn	Reach	rch	Way	wy
Cove	cov	Heights	hts	Reserve	res	West	w
Crescent	cr	Highway	hwy	Rest	rst	Wynd	wyn
Crest	cst	Hill	hill	Retreat	rt		

ABBREVIATIONS FOR SUBURB NAMES

Where it has been necessary to abbreviate the suburb names in the street index the following conventions have been used. If any difficulty is experienced with the suburban manes refer to the SUBURBS and LOCALITIES index.

Airport	Aprt	Forest	Frst	Lookout	Lkt	Reserve	Res
Basin	Bsn	Garden/s	Gdn	Lower	Lr	Ridge	Rdg
Bay	B	Grove	Gr	Meadows/s.	Mdw	River	R
Beach	Bch	Gully	Gly	Mount	Mt	Rocks	Rks
Bridge	Br	Harbor/our	Hbr	Mountain/s	Mtn	Saint	St
Central	Ctrl	Head/s	Hd	North	N	South	S
Chase	Ch	Headland	Hd	Paradise	Pdse	Terminal	Term
Corner	Cnr	Heights	Ht	Park	Pk	University	Uni
Creek	Ck	Hill/s	Hl	Plain/s	Pl	Upper	Up
Crossing	Csg	Island	I	Plateau	Plat	Valley	Vy
Down/s	Dn	Junction	Jctn	Pocket	Pkt	Vale	Va
East	E	Lagoon	Lgn	Point/Port.	Pt	Village	Vill
Field/s	Fd	Lakes	L	Range	Rge	Waters	Wtr
Flat	Fl	Lodge	Ldg	Reach	Rch	West	W

NON-STANDARD ABBREVIATIONS FOR SUBURB NAMES

Banksmeadow	Bnksmeadw	**Harrington Park**	Harringtn Pk	**North Wahroonga**	N Wahrnga
Bankstown Airport	Bnkstn Aprt	**Hawkesbury Heights**	Hawkesbry Ht	**North Willoughby**	N Willghby
Brighton-Le-Sands	Btn-Le-Sds	**Hinchinbrook**	Hinchinbrk	**Old Guildford**	Old Guildfrd
Cabramatta West	Cabramtta W	**Homebush West**	Homebsh W	**Old Toongabbie**	Old Tngabbie
Cambridge Gardens	Cmbrdg Gdn	**Horningsea Park**	Horngsea Pk	**Pitt Town Bottoms**	Pitt Twn Bttms
Cambridge Park	Cambrdg Pk	**Huntingwood**	Huntingwd	**Rosemeadow**	Rsemeadow
Campbelltown	Campbelltwn	**Kings Langley**	Kings Lngly	**Royal National Park**	Royal N P
Camperdown	Camperdwn	**Ku-ring-gai Chase National Park**	Krngai Ch N P	**Rushcutters Bay**	Rcuttrs Bay
Centennial Park	Centnnial Pk	**Lethbridge Park**	Lethbrdg Pk	**Smeaton Grange**	Smeaton Gra
Chatswood West	Chatswd W	**Macquarie Fields**	Mcquarie Fd	**South Wentworthville**	S Wntwthvle
Chipping Norton	Chipping Ntn	**Macquarie Links**	Mcquarie Lk	**Stanhope Gardens**	Stanhpe Gdn
Claremont Meadows	Clarmnt Ms	**Macquarie Park**	Mcquarie Pk	**Warwick Farm**	Warwck Frm
Edmondson Park	Edmndsn Pk	**Meadowbank**	Meadowbnk	**Wentworthville**	Wentwthvle
Faulconbridge	Faulconbdg	**Merrylands West**	Merrylnds W	**Werrington County**	Wrrngtn Cty
Freemans Reach	Freemns Rch	**Mooney Mooney**	Mooney	**Werrington Downs**	Wrrngtn Dns
Great Mackerel Beach	Gt Mckrl Bch	**Mount Ku-ring-gai**	Mt Krngai	**West Pennant Hills**	W Pnnant Hl
Greenfield Park	Greenfld Pk	**North Turramurra**	N Turramrra	**Wollstonecraft**	Wollstncraft
Hammondville	Hamondvle			**Woolloomooloo**	Woolmloo

SPECIAL NOTE

The LANES shown in *italics* in the street index are not chartered on the street maps.
For reasons of clarity it is not practical to show them.

A

AARON
pl. Carlingford 249 J16
pl. Plumpton 242 A11
pl. Wahroonga 222 A8
pl. Warragamba 353 H12
ABADAL
pl. Ingleburn 453 H8
ABAROO
st. Ryde 282 E16
ABBE RECEVEUR
pl. Little Bay 437 A12
ABBERTON
st. Jamisontown 266 C4
ABBEVILLE
cl. Prestons 392 K12
ABBEY
av. Greenacre 370 F11
la. Parramatta 278 F15
la. Wrrngtn Dns, off Abbey Row 238 D5
pl. Cherrybrook 219 E14
rd. Kemps Ck 330 G7
row. Wrrngtn Dns 238 D5
st. Hunters Hill 313 A7
st. Randwick 377 A12
wy. Glenhaven 218 B5
ABBOTFORD
la. Kensington 376 E9
st. Kensington 376 F9
ABBOTSBURY
dr. Horsley Pk 332 B5
ABBOTSFORD
pde. Abbotsford 342 H1
rd. Homebush 341 B10
rd. Picton 563 C1
ABBOTSFORD COVE
dr. Abbotsford 342 K2
ABBOTT
av. Sefton 338 F15
cl. Edensor Pk 333 H14
la. Cammeray, off Abbott St 315 J4
pl. Glenorie 128 D10
pl. Ingleburn 452 J10
rd. Artarmon 284 K16
rd. Heathcote 518 D9
rd. N Curl Curl 258 E10
rd. Seven Hills 246 A14
st. Balgowlah Ht 287 G14
st. Cammeray 315 J4
st. Coogee 377 E14
st. Merrylands 308 D16
ABBOTTS
la. Mt Hunter 504 J1
rd. Kemps Ck 330 E7
ABDALE
cr. Glenwood 215 H13
ABEBE BIKILA
st. Newington M A14
st. Newington 310 B14
A'BECKETT
av. Ashfield 372 H4
st. Granville 308 G9
st. Granville 308 J9
ABEL
la. Petersham 15 H10
pl. Cronulla 493 K11
st. Canley Ht 335 C16
st. Greenacre 370 F15
st. Jamisontown 236 D15
ABELIA
cl. Cherrybrook 219 K5
st. Tahmoor 566 A11
wy. Blacktown 274 F12
ABER
gr. Mount Druitt 271 C2
ABERCORN
st. Bexley 402 G13
ABERCROMBIE
av. Seven Hills 275 E10
la. Sydney A K12
st. Cabramtta W 365 B8
st. Chippendale 19 A1
st. Darlington 18 E8
st. Leumeah 482 C16
st. Redfern 19 A5
ABERDARE
pl. Cartwright 394 E4
ABERDEEN
cct. Glenmore Pk 266 H8
pl. Stanhpe Gdn 215 F9
rd. Busby 363 K16
rd. St Andrews 452 B13
rd. Winston Hills 277 E3
st. Bossley Park 334 B12
st. Cambrdg Pk 237 K8
ABERFELDY
cr. St Andrews 482 A1
ABERFOYLE
pl. Grasmere 475 K15
rd. Wedderburn 540 C9
rd. Wedderburn 541 J16
ABERGELDIE
st. Dulwich Hill 373 B8
ABERMAIN
pl. Cartwright 394 D4
ABERNETHY
st. Seaforth 286 K9
ABICHT
cl. Kemps Ck 360 G10
ABIGAIL
la. Newtown 17 E11
st. Hunters Hill 313 D8
st. Seven Hills 275 J4
ABINGDON
rd. Roseville 284 B5
st. Chipping Ntn 366 F16
st. N Balgowlah 287 G5
ABINGTON
cr. Glen Alpine 510 A14
ABONYI
pl. Glenwood 215 J16
ABOUD
av. Kingsford 406 C2
ABOUKIR
st. Dover Ht 348 G12
st. Rockdale 403 F16
ABRAHAM
cl. Menai 458 H11
st. Rooty Hill 241 J12
ABRAHAMS
wy. Claymore 481 E10
ABUKLEA
rd. Eastwood 281 G3
rd. Epping 281 D2
rd. Marsfield 281 G3
ACACIA
av. Glenmore Pk 265 G8
av. Greenacre 370 D15
av. Oakdale 500 B13
av. Prestons 394 A15
av. Punchbowl 400 D2
av. Ruse 512 F7
av. Ryde 312 D6
av. St Marys 239 G14
cl. Turramurra 252 D3
ct. Narellan Vale 478 K11
ct. Oatlands 279 B8
gr. Stanhpe Gdn 215 E10
la. Belmore 371 F16
la. Eastwood 281 H8
la. Roseville 284 K5
pl. Greystanes 305 E11
rd. Berowra 133 D15
rd. Kirrawee 490 H6
rd. Seaforth 286 K6
rd. Sutherland 490 H6
rd.n, Kirrawee 490 H4
rd.n, Sutherland 490 H4
st. Belmore 371 F16
st. Cabramatta 365 H8
st. Collaroy Plat 228 H10
st. Eastwood 281 H8
st. Oatley 431 A10
st. Rooty Hill 272 D4
st. Rydalmere 279 J16
tce. Bidwill 211 F14
ACCLAIM
la. Luddenham 356 F12
ACE
av. Fairfield 336 F9
ACER
ct. Cherrybrook 219 H8
gln. Castle Hill 218 F16
ACHIEVEMENT
av. Glenbrook 264 D3
ACHILLES
rd. Engadine 488 E14
ACHILPA
cl. Bangor 459 H15
ACKLING
st. Baulkham Hl 247 H8
ACLAND
st. Guildford 337 D5
ACOLA
ct. Wattle Grove 396 B15
ACORN
cl. Mt Colah 162 E13
gr. Elderslie 507 F2
st. Emu Plains 235 A11
ACRES
la. Ingleburn 453 F8
pl. Bligh Park 150 H7
rd. Kellyville 216 D5
ACRI
st. Prestons 393 E15
ACRON
rd. St Ives 224 G11
ACROPOLIS
av. Rooty Hill 271 H3
ACTINOTUS
av. Caringbah 492 J12
ACTION
st. Greenacre 370 A9
ACTIVE
pl. Kellyville 185 K14
ACTON
st. Croydon 342 E13
st. Hurlstone Pk 372 J13
st. Sutherland 490 F1
ACUBA
gr. Quakers Hill 214 C11
ADA
av. Brookvale 258 D12
av. Strathfield 341 A16
av. Wahroonga 222 C11
av.s, Wahroonga 222 C13
la. Erskineville 18 C14
la. Randwick 377 B14
pl. Carlingford 249 J15
pl. Doonside 243 D8
pl. Pyrmont 12 H6
pl. Ultimo 12 J9
st. Bexley 402 C16
st. Canley Vale 366 E3
st. Concord 341 H9
st. Cremorne 316 F7
st. Erskineville 18 C14
st. Harris Park 308 E5
st. Kingsgrove 401 G6
st. North Ryde 282 D9
st. Oatley 431 D11
st. Padstow 429 F3
st. Randwick 377 C15
ADAH
st. Guildford 338 D4
ADAIR
pl. East Killara 254 H8
ADALUMA
av. Bangor 459 F15
ADAM
cl. Berowra 133 H10
cl. S Windsor 150 J3
pl. Glenhaven 217 H2
pl. Lalor Park 245 E10
pl. Mcquarie Fd 424 A14
st. Campsie 372 C10
st. Fairfield 336 E9
st. Guildford 338 C3
st. Ryde 282 C15
ADAMINABY
st. Heckenberg 364 B12
ADAMS
av. Malabar 437 F7
av. Turramurra 223 E11
cr. St Marys 269 K3
la. Baulkham Hl 247 D11
la. Bondi Jctn 22 K9
la. Concord 342 B1
rd. Luddenham 356 J3
st. Curl Curl 258 J13
st. Frenchs Frst 256 C3
ADAMSON
av. Dundas Vy 280 B11
av. Thornleigh 221 B8
st. Glenfield 424 H12
ADARE
pl. Killarney Ht 255 K15
pl. Tregear 240 E7
ADCOCH
pl. Bidwill 211 B16
ADDER
st. Beecroft 250 G4
ADDERLEY
st.e, Lidcombe 309 J16
st.w, Auburn 309 D13
ADDERSTONE
av. N Sydney 6 C11
ADDERTON
rd. Carlingford 279 H6
rd. Dundas 279 H6
rd. Telopea 279 H6
ADDINGTON
av. Ryde 311 J2
ADDISCOMBE
rd. Manly Vale 288 C4
ADDISON
av. Concord 341 K7
av. Little Bay 437 G14
av. Roseville 285 A3
gr. Bidwill 211 C16
rd. Ingleside 197 F7
rd. Manly 288 G14
rd. Marrickville 15 J14
rd. Petersham 15 J14
st. Balmain 7 C7
st. Kensington 376 D12
st. Thirlmere 562 E8
st. Wetherill Pk 334 E6
wy. West Hoxton 392 A13
ADDLESTONE
rd. Merrylands 307 G14
ADDY
la. N Strathfield 341 F7
ADELAIDE
av. Campbelltwn 512 B5
av. E Lindfield 254 K14
gr. Bella Vista 246 G2
la. Oxley Park, off Adelaide St 270 G2
pde. Woollahra 22 K3
pl. Cecil Hills 362 J4
pl. Surry Hills 19 K3
pl. Sylvania 461 K8
rd. Padstow 429 F3
st. Balgowlah Ht 287 G14
st. Belmore 371 F14
st. Bondi Jctn 22 K3
st. Meadowbnk 311 B2
st. Oxley Park 269 K1
st. Rooty Hill 242 A14
st. St Marys 269 K1
st. Surry Hills 19 K2
st. West Ryde 281 B16
st. Woollahra 22 K3
ADELINE
st. Bass Hill 367 K7
st. Rydalmere 279 D15
ADELLA
av. Blacktown 243 K15
ADELONG
cl. Emu Plains 234 K7
cl. Wakeley 334 H13
pl. Camden S 507 B13
pl. Wahroonga 222 C13
st. Sutherland 490 D3
ADELPHI
cr. Doonside 243 D8
rd. Marsfield 282 C5
st. Rouse Hill 184 J7
st. Rouse Hill 184 K9
ADEN
st. Quakers Hill 214 E13
st. Seaforth 287 B10
ADEPT
la. Bankstown 399 F6
ADHARA
st. Erskine Park 301 A1
ADINA
av. Phillip Bay 436 K12
cl. Fairfield W 335 F12
pl. Beverly Hills 401 C12
pl. Bradbury 511 D15
rd. Curl Curl 258 K13
st. Miranda 491 K5
st. Seven Hills 245 K14
st. Telopea 279 G7
wy. La Perouse 436 K13
ADLER
pde. Greystanes 306 G7
pde. Greystanes 306 G9
ADMIRALTY
wy. Minto 482 H7
ADNA
st. Plumpton 242 C6
ADNUM
la. Bankstown, off Fetherstone St 369 E16
ADOLPHUS
cl. Hinchinbrk 363 B14
st. Balmain 8 B10
st. Canley Ht 365 G4
st. Naremburn 315 G2
ADOR
av. Rockdale 403 G16
ADRIAN
av. Lurnea 394 D8
ct. Carlingford 279 D4
pl. Balgowlah Ht 287 H14
pl. Greystanes 306 F6
st. Glenwood 215 J14
st. Mcquarie Fd 424 A14
ADRIENNE
st. Glendenning 242 F5
ADVANCE
st. Schofields 183 C16
ADY
st. Hunters Hill 313 J11
AEOLIA
la. Randwick, off Aeolia St 377 B16
st. Randwick 377 B16
AEOLUS
av. Ryde 282 A13
AERO
rd. Ingleburn 453 C2
st. Btn-le-Sds 433 H1
AERODROME
rd. Cobbitty 476 K10
AFTERNOON
ct. St Clair 270 C14
AFTON
pl. Quakers Hill 214 E12
AGAR
st. Marrickville 16 E16
AGATE
pl. Eagle Vale 481 D8
AGATHA
pl. Oakhurst 241 K4
AGINCOURT
pl. Glenwood 245 H2
rd. Marsfield 281 J2
AGIUS
st. Winston Hills 277 C1
AGNES
st. Strathfield 341 E16
AGNEW
cl. Bossley Park 334 C11
AGONIS
cl. Banksia 403 G12
AGRA
pl. Riverstone 183 A4
AGRAFE
pl. Minchinbury 272 A10
AGRIPPA
st. Rsemeadow 540 G2
AHEARN
av. S Coogee 407 H4
AHMET
ct. Oakhurst 242 D2
AIKEN
rd. W Pnnant Hl 249 A7
AILSA
av. Blacktown 275 B3
cl. E Lindfield 255 B10
pl. Riverstone 182 K5
wy. Canley Vale 366 G6
AIMEE
st. Quakers Hill 214 C9
AINSBURY
rd. St Marys 269 F6
AINSLEE
ct. Cranebrook 206 J9
AINSLEY
av. Glendenning 242 E2
AINSLIE
cl. St Ives Ch 224 A6
pde. Carlingford 249 H14
pl. Condell Park 398 G2
pl. Ruse 512 G4
st. Fairfield W 335 F8
st. Kingsford 407 A4
AINSWORTH
cr. Wetherill Pk 334 H3
st. Leichhardt 10 D11
st. Lilyfield 10 D11
AINTREE
cl. Casula 424 E1
AIRD
st. Parramatta 308 B4
AIRDS
rd. Minto 482 C7
AIRDSLEY
la. Bradbury 511 D13
AIREDALE
av. Earlwood 402 F6
AIRLIE
cr. Cecil Hills 362 G3
pl. Oatlands 278 J10

AIRPORT
av. Bnkstn Aprt 367 K16
dr. Mascot 404 D4
AIRSTRIP
rd. Pitt Town 93 B15
AITAPE
cr. Whalan 240 H10
pl. Holsworthy 426 C3
AITCHANDAR
rd. Ryde 312 E1
AITKEN
av. Queenscliff 288 F3
AJAX
pl. Blacktown 245 D8
pl. Engadine 488 J14
AJUGA
ct. Voyager Pt 427 D5
AKMA
cl. Bonnyrigg 363 K9
AKOONAH
cl. Westleigh 220 F2
pl. Peakhurst 430 C9
AKORA
av. Baulkham Hl 247 C5
cl. Chipping Ntn 396 F6
st. Frenchs Frst 256 F6
AKRON
pl. Toongabbie 275 F14
AKUNA
av. Bangor 459 G14
av. Bangor 459 G15
av. Bradbury 511 F15
av. Bradbury 511 G14
la. Mona Vale 199 C4
ALABAMA
av. Bexley 432 F3
ALABASTER
pl. Eagle Vale 481 D8
ALADORE
av. Cabramatta 365 F8
ALAINE
pl. Cecil Park 332 D10
ALAM
pl. Campbelltwn 511 K3
st. Blacktown 244 B12
st. Colyton 270 B6
ALAMAR
cr. Quakers Hill 214 F16
ALAMEDA
wy. Warriewood 198 K6
ALAMEIN
av. Carlingford 250 A14
av. Liverpool 394 K3
av. Mt Annan 479 A10
av. Narellan Vale 479 A10
av. Narraweena 258 C4
rd. Bossley Park 334 A5
rd. Revesby Ht 428 J6
st. Engadine 489 A10
ALA MOANA
rd. E Kurrajong 57 B2
ALAN
av. Hornsby 191 E10
av. Ryde 281 K11
av. Seaforth 287 A11
rd. Berowra Ht 133 B8
st. Box Hill 154 B16
st. Cammeray 316 C4
st. Fairfield 336 G12
st. Mount Druitt 271 B4
st. Rydalmere 309 B2
st. Yagoona 368 J11
ALANA
dr. W Pnnant Hl 248 J6
pl. St Ives Ch 224 A3
ALANAS
av. Oatlands 278 K11
ALAN BOND
pl. Marsfield 282 B3
ALASKA
la. Parramatta, off Thomas St 308 E1
ALBAN
st. Lidcombe 339 J1
ALBANY
cl. Wakeley 334 H15
cr. East Killara 254 K5
la. Colyton 270 G8
la. Crows Nest 315 E5
la. St Leonards 315 E5
la. Stanmore 16 G6
pl. Kareela 461 D14
pl. Kearns 451 C16
rd. Petersham 16 B8
rd. Stanmore 16 B8
st. Busby 363 H15
st. Crows Nest 315 E6
st. Ermington 280 D12
st. St Leonards 315 E6
ALBATROSS
av. Hinchinbrk 393 C2
cct. Woronora Ht 489 D5
ALBEMARLE
av. Rose Bay 348 B11
la. Rose Bay, off Albemarle Av 348 C11
pl. Cecil Hills 362 F1
st. Dundas 279 G14
st. Narrabeen 229 B3
ALBERMARLE
st. Marrickville 373 F13
st. Newtown 17 C11
ALBERT
av. Chatswood 284 H11
av. Sylvania 461 G13
av. Thirlmere 562 B16
cr. Burwood 342 B14
cr. Croydon 342 B14
dr. Killara 283 D2
la. Bronte 377 K9
la. Forest Lodge 11 F14
la. Hornsby 191 H16
la. Hornsby 221 H1
la. Chatswood, off Albert Av 284 H10
la. Earlwood, off Banks Rd 403 B4
pde. Ashfield 342 H16
pde. Rooty Hill 272 E4
pl. Bligh Park 150 E6
pl. Leumeah 482 G12
rd. Auburn 339 A11
rd. Avalon 140 D11
rd. Beecroft 250 C4
rd. Croydon Pk 372 C8
rd. Strathfield 341 A13
sq. Paddington 21 C1
st. Banksia 403 F12
st. Belfield 371 F13
st. Belmore 371 F13
st. Berala 339 D9
st. Bexley 432 E1
st. Botany 405 J12
st. Bronte 377 K9
st. Cabramatta 366 A10
st. Campsie 371 F13
st. Drummoyne 343 K2
st. Edgecliff 14 A13
st. Erskineville 17 J13
st. Forest Lodge 11 E13
st. Gladesville 312 J6
st. Granville 308 F9
st. Greenwich 314 K13
st. Guildford W 306 J16
st. Harbord 288 G1
st. Hornsby 191 J16
st. Hurstville 431 K9
st. Ingleburn 453 A8
st. Leichhardt 15 E5
st. Lurnea 394 E9
st. McGraths Hl 122 A10
st. Mount Druitt 270 J2
st. Narrabeen 229 A4
st. Newtown 17 B10
st. N Parramatta 278 C14
st. Paddington 21 D1
st. Petersham 15 K14
st. Randwick 377 B13
st. Redfern 19 D9
st. Revesby 398 H14
st. Riverstone 153 A13
st. Rozelle 10 J4
st. St Peters 374 J13
st. Sydney B F8
st. Sydney 2 A12
st. Warrimoo 203 B14
st. Werrington 239 A11
st.e, N Parramatta 278 H15
st.s, Hornsby 221 H2
ALBERTA
av. Cowan 104 B13
st. Jannali 460 G12
st. Sydney F D5
ALBERTO
st. Lilyfield 10 F2
ALBI
pl. Randwick 377 C14
ALBILLO
pl. Eschol Park 481 D3
ALBION
av. Merrylands 307 J13
av. Paddington 4 F16
av. Pymble 252 K1
cl. Bossley Park 333 E9
la. Annandale 16 E4
la. Mosman 317 B6
la. St Peters 374 F14
la. Waverley 377 G9
pl. Baulkham Hl 246 J2
pl. Engadine 489 A8
pl. Sydney E G1
st. Annandale 16 E3
st. Clovelly 377 F10
st. Concord 342 B2
st. Dundas 279 F13
st. Harris Park 308 E6
st. Leichhardt 16 E3
st. Marrickville 373 J13
st. Pennant Hills 220 J16
st. Randwick 377 F10
st. Roselands 401 A7
st. Rozelle 344 D8
st. Surry Hills F B12
st. Surry Hills 3 J14
st. Waverley 377 F10
wy. Surry Hills F C13
ALBUERA
rd. Epping 281 C3
ALBURY
av. Campbelltwn 512 C5
ct. Harringtn Pk 478 G7
st. Yagoona 368 J9
ALBYN
rd. Strathfield 341 C15
st. Bexley 402 K14
ALCHIN
st. Dharruk 241 B7
ALCOCK
av. Casula 424 D3
av. Casula 424 F4
ALCOOMIE
st. Villawood 367 D3
ALDAN
pl. St Clair 269 J14
ALDEBARAN
st. Cranebrook 207 F6
ALDEN
gr. Oakhurst 241 K1
ALDER
av. Lane Cove W 283 H15
dr. St Ives 224 E5
gr. Menai 458 K14
st. Clontarf 287 H15
ALDERNEY
rd. Merrylands 307 A10
st. Minto 482 G7
ALDERSON
av. Liverpool 394 H9
av. North Rocks 248 F11
ALDERTON
av. Springwood 201 H1
ALDGATE
st. Prospect 275 B12
st. Sutherland 490 G5
ALDINGA
pl. Bradbury 541 D1
pl. Clarmnt Ms 268 H2
pl. Forestville 255 H10
ALDINGTON
rd. Kemps Ck 300 G13
ALDOUS
cl. Hornsby Ht 161 J8
ALE
st. Ingleburn 454 A10
ALEPPO
st. Quakers Hill 214 F13
ALERT
pl. Yagoona 368 E15
ALETA
cl. Wahroonga 251 G2
wy. Seven Hills 275 K6
ALEX
av. Schofields 213 H5
pl. Baulkham Hl 217 A16
pl. Bligh Park 150 H9
rd. Yowie Bay 492 B13
ALEXANDER
av. Mosman 317 D10
av. N Willghby 285 F9
av. Taren Point 462 J14
cr. Mcquarie Fd 423 J16
la. Surry Hills 20 C2
la. Crows Nest, off Pacific Hwy 315 G7
pde. Blacktown 273 J8
pde. Carlingford 250 B15
pde. Roseville 284 F6
rd. Avalon 140 E11
st. Alexandria 18 G13
st. Auburn 339 A14
st. Balmain 8 B7
st. Bligh Park 150 B6
st. Collaroy 229 A12
st. Coogee 407 G2
st. Crows Nest 315 G7
st. Dundas Vy 280 A7
st. Eveleigh 18 G12
st. Manly 288 F6
st. Paddington 21 B2
st. Penshurst 431 G8
st. Smithfield 335 H7
st. Surry Hills 20 C2
st. Sylvania 461 K11
st. Tamarama 378 C6
st. Yagoona 368 K9
ALEXANDRA
av. Croydon 342 E12
av. Westmead 277 E16
cct. St Clair 269 J8
cr. Bayview 169 A13
cr. Glenbrook 264 E1
la. Glebe 11 G8
la. St Clair, off Alexandra Cct 269 J8
pde. Rockdale 403 C16
pl. Carlingford 249 E14
pl. Glendenning 242 H5
rd. Glebe 11 G8
st. Ashfield 342 H14
st. Blacktown 274 E14
st. Concord 341 H9
st. Drummoyne 343 K2
st. Hunters Hill 313 J11
st. Turrella 403 E6
ALEXANDRIA
av. Eastwood 281 E6
la. Surry Hills 20 C6
pde. S Coogee 407 J5
pde. Wahroonga 221 J3
pde. Waitara 221 J3
pl. Busby 363 J16
ALEXANDRINA
ct. Wattle Grove 396 B14
ALEXIS
pl. Rsemeadow 540 H3
ALEX POPOV
av. Newington L K14
av. Newington 310 B13
ALFA
pl. Ingleburn 453 F13
ALFORD
st. Quakers Hill 243 D4
ALFORDS POINT
rd. Alfords Point 429 C15
rd. Illawong 459 B5
rd. Menai 458 G10
rd. Padstow Ht 429 C15
ALFRED
av. Woolooware 493 J8
la. Rozelle 10 K3
la. Mascot, off Wentworth Av 405 F6
pl. Quakers Hill 213 K8
pl. S Turramrra 252 A8
rd. Brookvale 258 B9
rd. Chipping Ntn 396 E4
rd. Forest Lodge 11 F14
rd. Narraweena 258 B9
st. Annandale 10 G15
st. Bronte 377 K7
st. Campsie 402 A3
st. Cromer 228 D16
st. Croydon 342 F11
st. Granville 308 G10
st. Harris Park 308 H8
st. Hurstville 432 C6
st. Leichhardt 10 C11
st. Lewisham 15 B8
st. Lilyfield 10 C11
st. Marrickville 373 E15
st. Mascot 405 F6
st. Merrylands 307 H10
st. Narraweena 258 C6
st. Parramatta 308 H8
st. Ramsgate Bch 433 G13
st. Rhodes 311 C12
st. Rhodes 311 D11
st. Rosehill 308 H8
st. Rozelle 11 A2
st. St Peters 374 F14
st. Sans Souci 433 G16
st. Sydney B A7
st. Sydney 1 H12
st. Westmead 277 H16
st. Woolwich 314 D14
st.n, Neutral Bay 5 K9
st.n, N Sydney 5 K9
st.s, Milsons Pt K K16
st.s, Milsons Pt 5 J13
ALFREDA
st. Coogee 377 G16
ALGERNON
st. Oatley 461 B1
ALGIE
cr. Kingswood 238 B14
ALGONA
st. Bilgola 169 F7
ALIBERTI
dr. Blacktown 273 J7
ALICANTE
st. Minchinbury 271 G9
ALICE
av. Newtown 374 G9
av. Russell Lea 343 D6
cl. Collaroy Plat 228 C9
ct. Cherrybrook 219 D9
la. Newtown 374 H9
la. Randwick, off Pine St 377 F9
pl. Cecil Hills 362 J7
st. Auburn 339 C4
st. Caringbah 492 G15
st. Harris Park 308 F6
st. Jannali 460 G13
st. Mcquarie Fd 424 B16
st. Newtown 374 G10
st. Padstow 399 D15
st. Rooty Hill 241 K14
st. Rosehill 308 F6
st. Rozelle 10 J4
st. Sans Souci 433 B14
st. Seven Hills 275 G3
st. Turramurra 222 K8
st. Wiley Park 400 J2
st.n, Wiley Park 400 H2
ALICE HANCOX
cl. Castle Hill, off Vittoria Smith Av 218 H13
ALICIA
la. Roselands 401 C4
pl. Kenthurst 155 J5
rd. Mt Krng-gai 162 J12
ALICK
st. Cabramatta 365 E10
ALINDA
cl. Middle Dural 157 K1
ALINGA
pl. Doonside 243 E16
st. Cabramtta W 365 C8
ALINJARRA
rd. Tennyson 58 B5
ALINTA
cl. Thornleigh 221 C13
ALISON
la. Coogee 377 G14
rd. Coogee 377 E14
rd. Cromer 228 H15
rd. Kensington 376 E8
rd. Randwick 376 E8
st. Ashbury 372 D7
st. Croydon Pk 372 D7
st. Eastwood 281 J7
st. Roseville 284 C7
st. Russell Lea 343 E7
st. Seven Hills 245 D16
ALKARINGA
rd. Miranda 491 H8
ALKIRA
cct. Narraweena 257 J3
pl. Caringbah 493 C16
rd. Carlingford 249 F14
rd. St Ives 224 B15
ALKOO
av. Little Bay 437 B10
ALKOOMIE
av. Forestville 255 J9
av. S Penrith 266 H2
pl. Pymble 252 K8
st. Beverly Hills 401 B10
ALLAMBEE
cr. Beverly Hills 401 B11

ALLAMBI
st. Colyton 270 G6
ALLAMBIE
av. Caringbah 492 G15
av. E Lindfield 255 A13
av. Northmead 277 G7
rd. Allambie Ht 257 B9
rd. Castle Cove 285 K5
rd. Edensor Pk 333 F14
rd. Frenchs Frst 257 A7
ALLAN
av. Belmore 371 C14
av. Clovelly 377 K12
av. Ryde 311 J1
av. Turramurra 222 G14
la. Mowbray Pk 561 J7
la. Roseville Ch 285 D1
rd. Mulgoa 325 B1
st. Bexley 402 F13
st. Kangaroo Pt 461 J4
st. Lidcombe 339 F11
st. Roseville Ch 285 D1
ALLANDALE
dr. Baulkham Hl 246 H5
ALLANS
av. Petersham 15 E13
ALLARA
av. N Turramrra 223 F6
pl. Castle Hill 218 K6
ALLARD
av. Roseville Ch 285 G1
pl. Hassall Gr 211 K16
pl. Ingleburn 453 G10
st. Penrith 237 D2
ALLARS
st. Denistone W 280 J12
ALLAWAH
av. Carss Park 432 G15
av. Elanora Ht 198 E16
av. Sefton 368 E5
cl. Bangor 459 J15
cl. Mt Colah 162 B15
ct. Erskine Park 300 D2
la. *Carss Park, off Allawah Av 432 F14*
pl. Greenwich 315 A7
rd. Pymble 253 A3
st. Blacktown 274 D2
ALLAY
st. Blacktown 243 K10
ALLDER
st. Yagoona 369 A8
ALLEGRA
av. Belmore 401 E4
la. *Belmore, off Allegra Av 401 E3*
ALLEN
av. Alexandria 18 E14
av. Bilgola 170 B5
av. Ingleburn 422 H12
la. Alexandria 18 H13
la. Glebe 11 H8
pl. Menai 458 H14
pl. Minto 452 J16
pl. Penrith 236 J10
pl. Wetherill Pk 334 D2
rd. Blacktown 245 A9
st. Arncliffe 403 H7
st. Blaxland 233 K7
st. Canterbury 372 C15
st. Glebe 11 H8
st. Harris Park 308 E7
st. Homebush 341 D7
st. Leichhardt 9 D13
st. N Strathfield 341 D7
st. Pyrmont 12 J7
st. S Hurstville 432 B10
st. S Wntwthvle 307 A5
st. Waterloo 19 D16
wy. Dural 188 H13
ALLENA
cl. Georges Hall 367 K11
ALLENBY
cr. Strathfield 341 B14
la. Clontarf 287 F15
rd. Rossmore 389 F16
st. Canley Ht 365 D2
st. Clontarf 287 F14
st. Doonside 273 F1
ALLENBY PARK
pde. Allambie Ht 257 G11
ALLENDALE
st. Marayong 244 C6
ALLENGROVE
cr. North Ryde 282 H7
ALLENS
pde. Bondi Jctn 22 J9
ALLERTON
rd. Beecroft 250 D9
ALLEYNE
av. N Narrabeen 198 J16
st. Chatswood 285 E6
ALLIANCE
av. Revesby 398 E11
ALLIBONE
st. Ashbury 372 H6
ALLIEDALE
cl. Hornsby 221 G5
ALLIES
rd. Barden Rdg 488 G5
ALLIGATOR
pl. Kearns 451 B16
ALLINGHAM
st. Condell Park 398 B1
ALLINGTON
cr. Elanora Ht 198 E13
ALLIOTT
st. Bradbury 511 H11
ALLIRA
pl. Hassall Gr 211 K13
ALLISON
av. Condell Park 398 E1
av. Lane Cove 314 G2
cr. Menai 458 H12
dr. Glenmore Pk 265 J7
pde. Croydon 372 D2
rd. Cronulla 493 J15
rd. Guildford 337 D6
ALLISTER
st. Cremorne 316 F9
ALLMAN
av. Summer Hill 373 B4
st. Campbelltwn 511 E6
ALLOWRIE
rd. Villawood 367 B3
ALLPORT
wy. *Claymore, off Colquhoun Wy 481 C11*
ALL SAINTS
cl. Cherrybrook 219 F14
ALLSOPP
av. Baulkham Hl 248 C8
dr. Cmbrdg Gdn 237 G3
ALLUM
pl. Glebe 12 C11
st. Bankstown 369 B16
st. Haberfield 343 A13
st. Yagoona 369 B16
ALLUNGA
cl. Mona Vale 169 E16
ALLWOOD
cr. Lugarno 429 H12
ALLWORTH
dr. Davidson 255 C2
ALMA
av. Campsie 371 G13
av. Enmore 16 H15
cr. Emu Heights 205 B16
pl. Rooty Hill 242 A16
pl. Thirlmere 565 D2
rd. Leppington 419 J9
rd. Mcquarie Pk 282 G1
rd. Maroubra 407 B9
rd. Padstow 429 B4
st. Ashfield 372 G5
st. Clontarf 287 G15
st. Granville 308 A7
st. Hurstville 431 K7
st. Paddington 13 D12
st. Parramatta 308 A7
st. Pymble 253 D2
st. Rydalmere 309 J2
st. Vineyard 151 K9
ALMADA
st. Engadine 489 C9
ALMANDINE
pl. Eagle Vale 481 G5
ALMERIA
av. Baulkham Hl 246 H13
ALMETA
st. Schofields 213 J6
ALMONA
st. Glenwood 215 H11
ALMOND
st. Wentwthvle 277 A8
ALMORA
la. *Mosman, off Upper Almora St 317 C6*
ALOE
st. Quakers Hill 243 F3
AL OERTER
av. Newington M C15
av. *Newington, off Kieren Perkins Av 310 A15*
ALOHA
st. Mascot 405 D3
ALONSO
cl. Rsemeadow 540 J6
ALPEN
la. Mount Druitt 241 B16
ALPHA
av. Roselands 400 K8
rd. Camden 507 B1
rd. Greystanes 305 E11
rd. Lane Cove 314 E4
rd. Northbridge 285 G15
rd. Willoughby 285 G15
st. Blacktown 244 F16
st. Chester Hill 337 H10
ALPHILL
av. Cabramatta 366 C6
ALPHIN
st. Lidcombe 339 H11
ALPHONSUS
wy. Auburn 338 K2
ALPIN
gr. Oakhurst 242 A4
ALPINE
cct. St Clair 269 G9
la. *St Clair, off Alpine Cct 269 F9*
pl. Engadine 488 C12
pl. Mcquarie Fd 454 D3
wy. Glenwood 245 G1
ALPITA
st. Kareela 461 C14
ALROY
cr. Hassall Gr 212 B16
ALSACE
av. Bardwell Vy 402 K10
la. Peakhurst 430 C13
ALSON
st. Mount Druitt 271 D2
ALSOP
pl. Bligh Park 150 C7
ALSTON
dr. Berowra Ht 132 J3
st. Bexley North 402 C13
st. Glenmore Pk 266 E8
st. Kingsgrove 402 C13
wy. Roseville 284 E5
ALT
cl. West Hoxton 392 B12
cr. Davidson 225 C16
la. Queens Park 22 F12
pl. Doonside 273 E3
st. Ashfield 342 H16
st. Haberfield 343 C13
st. Queens Park 22 E12
st. Smithfield 336 C6
ALTAIR
pl. Hinchinbrk 393 D5
pl. Jamisontown 266 E2
ALTHORPE
dr. Green Valley 362 K8
ALTO
av. Seaforth 287 A4
pl. Artarmon 314 G1
st. S Wntwthvle 307 B6
ALTON
av. Concord 341 G7
la. Newtown 17 F12
st. Merrylands 307 J15
st. Woollahra 22 A2
ALTONA
av. Forestville 256 A7
pl. Blacktown 274 C3
pl. Greenacre 370 B11
pl. North Rocks 248 J16
st. Abbotsford 342 J1
st. Hornsby Ht 161 H16
ALUA
cl. North Manly 258 A13
ALVA
pl. Riverstone 183 C9
ALVERNA
st. Rooty Hill 272 D7
ALVERSTONE
st. Riverwood 400 B11
ALVIS
pl. Ingleburn 453 J10
pl. Plumpton 241 G10
ALVISTON
st. Strathfield 341 E14
ALVONA
av. St Ives 254 A1
ALWYN
av. Wallacia 324 J12
cr. Glenwood 215 H13
ALYAN
pl. St Helens Pk 541 A7
ALYSSE
cl. Baulkham Hl 247 C1
AMADIO
pl. Mt Pritchard 364 J9
AMALFI
pl. Longueville 314 C10
st. Lurnea 394 G11
AMANDA
cl. Berowra Ht 133 A6
cl. Dean Park 213 A16
pl. Annangrove 155 D4
pl. Ingleburn 453 D12
AMARAL
st. Narraweena 258 B5
AMARANTHUS
pl. Mcquarie Fd 454 B5
AMARINA
av. Bass Hill 367 K5
av. Greenacre 370 G9
AMARNA
pde. Roseville 284 K1
AMAROO
av. Blaxland 234 E7
av. Castle Cove 285 J4
av. Elanora Ht 198 B16
av. Georges Hall 367 F12
av. Mt Colah 191 K2
av. Strathfield 371 B4
av. Wahroonga 222 C11
cr. Mosman 317 E9
cr. Mosman 317 F9
st. Bonnyrigg 364 B9
st. Kingswood 237 K12
st. Sylvania 461 G15
AMAROO PARK
dr. Annangrove 155 D11
AMARYLLIS
wy. Bidwill 211 D13
AMAX
av. Girraween 275 H15
AMAZON
la. *St Clair, off Amazon Pl 269 K16*
pl. Kearns 481 D1
pl. St Clair 269 J16
rd. Seven Hills 275 E9
AMBER
cl. Bossley Park 334 A7
cl. Thornleigh 220 K12
la. Woolooware 493 F7
pl. Bass Hill 367 F8
pl. Eagle Vale 481 A7
AMBERDALE
av. Picnic Point 428 D9
AMBERLEA
ct. Castle Hill 218 J6
st. Glenwood 245 G3
AMBERWOOD
pl. Castle Hill 218 H16
pl. Menai 458 H13
wy. Castle Hill 218 G15
AMBLECOTE
pl. Tahmoor 565 J8
AMBLER
cl. Emu Heights 235 C5
pl. Narellan Vale 478 K16
AMBLESIDE
dr. Castle Hill 247 K5
st. Collaroy Plat 228 D12
AMBON
av. Holsworthy 426 F8
cl. Bossley Park 334 A5
rd. Holsworthy 396 C15
AMBROSE
la. *Condell Park, off Ambrose St 398 H4*
st. Condell Park 398 H4
st. Glendenning 242 H5
st. Hunters Hill 313 K11
AMBROSIA
st. Mcquarie Fd 454 D6
AMBRYM
av. Frenchs Frst 255 J2
AMBULANCE
av. Haymarket E E14
av. Haymarket 3 E15
AMBYNE
st. Woolooware 493 E8
AMEDE
pl. Illawong 459 K3
AMELIA
cl. Cecil Hills 362 F5
cr. Canley Ht 335 B14
gr. Pitt Town 92 H11
pl. N Narrabeen 198 G14
st. North Ryde 282 G8
st. Waterloo 20 B16
wy. Bidwill 211 H13
AMELIA GODBEE
av. Glenhaven 218 B1
AMERICAN
ml. Rooty Hill 272 F5
AMESBURY
av. St Ives 224 B16
av. Sefton 368 F1
AMETHYST
pl. Eagle Vale 481 C7
AMHERST
st. Cammeray 315 J5
st. Guildford 337 E2
AMIENS
av. Engadine 488 F16
av. Milperra 397 E11
av. Mosman 317 A3
cl. Bossley Park 334 A6
rd. Clontarf 287 F14
rd. Moorebank 395 D12
st. Gladesville 312 G12
wy. Matraville 407 B15
AMILCAR
st. Ingleburn 453 G12
AMINTA
cr. Hassall Gr 211 K14
AMINYA
cr. Bradbury 541 D1
pl. Baulkham Hl 248 B10
pl. Riverview 313 K5
pl. St Ives 224 B14
AMITAF
av. Caringbah 492 E10
AMOR
st. Asquith 191 H9
st. Hornsby 191 H9
AMOS
la. Elizabeth Bay 13 A6
pl. Marayong 244 C6
pl. Sylvania 461 K12
pl. Westmead 307 J3
rd. West Hoxton 391 J7
st. Parramatta 307 F4
st. Westmead 307 F4
AMOUR
av. Maroubra 407 F9
st. Milperra 398 A8
st. Revesby 398 A8
AMOURIN
st. North Manly 258 C13
AMPHITHEATRE
cct. Baulkham Hl 246 G9
AMRON
pl. Acacia Gdn 214 H16
AMSTERDAM
st. Oakhurst 242 C3
AMUNDSEN
st. Leumeah 482 H13
st. Tregear 240 F7
AMUR
pl. Kearns 451 B15
AMY
cl. Glendenning 242 E2
la. Campsie 372 A13
la. *Erskineville, off Macdonald St 374 K9*
pl. Hornsby Ht 161 J11
pl. Narellan Vale 478 H15
rd. Riverwood 429 J1
st. Blakehurst 432 A15
st. Campsie 371 J14
st. Erskineville 374 K10
st. Marrickville 374 A9
st. Regents Pk 369 B1
st. Turrella 403 D5
AMY HAWKINS
cct. Kellyville 217 B1
ANAKAI
dr. Jamisontown 236 A16

ANANA
rd. Elanora Ht 198 F15
rd. N Narrabeen 198 F15
ANASTASIO
rd. Liverpool 364 J15
ANATOL
pl. Pymble 253 G4
ANCHORAGE
la. St Clair, off Anchorage St 270 J13
st. St Clair 270 J13
ANCILIA
cl. Quakers Hill 213 F7
ANCONA
av. Toongabbie 276 D7
rd. Turramurra 223 A7
ANCRUM
st. N Sydney 5 B9
ANCURA
ct. Wattle Grove 396 B16
ANDAMAN
st. Kings Park 244 F2
ANDAMOOKA
pl. Cartwright 394 B4
ANDERSON
av. Blackett 241 A3
av. Dundas 279 B15
av. Liverpool 394 J3
av. Mt Pritchard 364 E10
av. Panania 398 B16
av. Richmond 118 D9
av. Ryde 311 J2
av. S Turramrra 252 A9
cl. Appin 568 F7
la. Belmore 401 G2
la. Penrith 237 B11
la. Ryde 311 H2
la. Concord, off Archer St 342 A2
la. Sefton, off Torrington Av 368 G3
pl. Cottage Pt 135 F9
pl. S Windsor 120 H15
rd. Badgerys Ck 359 B6
rd. Concord 342 A2
rd. Kings Lngly 246 C10
rd. Mortdale 430 G6
rd. Northmead 278 A4
rd. Smeaton Gra 479 C5
st. Alexandria 18 J14
st. Bnksmeadw 406 A12
st. Belmore 401 G1
st. Bexley 432 F4
st. Chatswood 284 J8
st. Double Bay 14 D11
st. Kingsford 406 H3
st. Neutral Bay 6 F6
st. Panania 428 B2
st. Parramatta 308 D6
st. St Helens Pk 541 B6
st. Westmead 307 G4
ANDERTON
st. Marrickville 373 H11
ANDORA
pl. Glen Alpine 510 G11
ANDORRA
cl. Glendenning 242 J4
ANDOVE
st. Belrose 226 B14
ANDOVER
cr. Hebersham 241 F6
la. Allawah 432 G8
st. Carlton 432 G7
ANDRE
pl. Blacktown 274 E10
ANDREA
cl. Bonnyrigg 364 F5
ANDREAS
st. Petersham 15 F6
ANDREW
av. Canley Ht 365 C1
av. West Pymble 253 A12
cl. Mt Colah 192 C5
la. Melrose Pk 310 J2
pl. Birrong 368 K4
pl. Earlwood 403 F4
pl. Girraween 276 D12
pl. North Rocks 248 G15
rd. Kellyville 186 D7
st. Belrose 225 D15
st. Bronte 378 A8
st. Brooklyn 75 K11
st. Clovelly 377 K12
st. Melrose Pk 310 J3
st. Richmond 119 D4
st. West Ryde 310 J3
ANDREW CHARLTON
av. Newington M B15
av. Newington, off Kip Keino Av 309 K15
ANDREW LLOYD
dr. Doonside 273 E5
ANDREW NASH
la. Parramatta, off George St 308 D2
ANDREWS
av. Ashbury 372 G9
av. Bondi 378 B5
av. Toongabbie 276 F10
cct. Horngsea Pk 392 F12
la. N Sydney K A3
la. N Sydney 5 E6
pl. St Helens Pk 541 A8
pl. Yellow Rock 173 G14
rd. Cranebrook 237 B1
ANDREW THOMPSON
dr. McGraths Hl 121 J12
pl. Colyton 270 H9
ANDREW TOWN
pl. Richmond 118 C5
ANDRO
pl. Werrington 238 G10
ANDROMEDA
cr. Engadine 488 D11
dr. Cranebrook 207 F5
ANDY
st. Guildford W 336 J3
ANDYS
ct. St Clair 269 G11
ANEBO
st. Liverpool 394 K4
ANELLA
av. Castle Hill 217 C12
ANEMBO
av. Georges Hall 367 J11
cr. Killara 283 F1
pl. Eastwood 281 F2
rd. Berowra 133 D15
rd. Duffys Frst 194 J7
st. Bradbury 511 G15
ANEMONE
pl. Kirrawee 461 A14
ANEURA
ct. Wattle Grove 396 C15
ANGARA
cct. Glenwood 245 J2
cl. Kearns 451 C16
ANGAS
cl. Barden Rdg 488 J3
st. Meadowbnk 311 F4
st. Wrrngtn Cty 238 H7
ANGEL
cl. Cherrybrook 219 F15
ct. Glenwood 245 D2
la. Newtown 17 H13
pl. Cherrybrook 219 F15
pl. Forestville 256 B8
pl. Sydney C J1
pl. Sydney 3 G1
rd. Strathfield 341 G16
st. Newtown 17 G16
st. Wrrngtn Cty 238 G6
ANGELA
st. Cecil Hills 362 F4
ANGELINA
cr. Cabramatta 365 E10
ct. Green Valley 362 K9
ANGELINI
av. Rozelle 10 H1
ANGELO
av. Liverpool 394 H10
st. Burwood 371 J2
st. N Sydney K B1
st. N Sydney 5 E5
st. Woolwich 314 G12
ANGLE
rd. Grays Point 491 A14
rd. Leumeah 482 B14
rd.s, Leumeah 512 C1
st. Balgowlah 287 J8
ANGLEDOOL
av. Hinchinbrk 392 H3
ANGLESEA
st. Bondi 377 H4
ANGLE VALE
rd. Edensor Pk 363 D1
ANGLO
la. Greenwich 315 B7
rd. Campsie 371 J14
rd. Greenwich 315 B7
sq. Carlton 432 J8
st. Chatswd W 284 F9
ANGOPHORA
av. Kingswood 267 G2
cct. Mt Annan 509 F3
cr. Forestville 255 E8
ct. Voyager Pt 427 B5
gr. Greenacre 370 F5
pl. Alfords Point 459 B3
pl. Castle Hill 248 E3
pl. Pennant Hills 250 J4
pl. Valley Ht 202 G9
ANGORRA
rd. Terrey Hills 196 C6
ANGOURIE
ct. Dural 219 B3
pl. Bow Bowing 452 C14
ANGUS
av. Auburn 339 B9
av. Epping 280 E1
av. Lane Cove 314 G2
av. Peakhurst 430 G3
av. Rooty Hill 271 H6
cr. Yagoona 368 H10
pl. Busby 363 K16
pl. St Andrews 482 A3
rd. Kenthurst 188 D8
rd. Schofields 212 H4
rd. Smeaton Gra 479 F5
st. Earlwood 402 D6
ANICH
pl. Prestons 423 A1
ANIMBO
st. Miranda 491 K6
ANISEED
st. Prestons 393 H14
ANITA
st. Glenwood 215 E12
ANITRA
av. Kareela 461 D12
pl. Shalvey 210 H15
ANJOU
cct. Cecil Hills 362 C4
ANJUDY
cl. Casula 394 F16
ANKA
av. Old Tngabbie 276 J10
ANKALI
pl. North Manly 258 A14
ANN
cr. Mt Pritchard 364 H13
pl. Bligh Park 150 F8
pl. Cecil Hills 363 A3
pl. Narellan Vale 508 J2
st. Arncliffe 403 H7
st. Balmain 8 A10
st. Bondi Jctn 22 J8
st. Earlwood 372 G16
st. Enfield 371 H4
st. Fairfield Ht 335 J10
st. Faulconbdg 172 B5
st. Frenchs Frst 256 D6
st. Lidcombe 339 H7
st. Longueville 314 D8
st. Marrickville 373 J13
st. N Willghby 285 G10
st. Surry Hills F E12
st. Surry Hills 3 K14
st. Willoughby 285 G10
ANNABELLA
rd. Camden 506 K5
ANNABELLE
cr. Kellyville 216 F5
pl. Mt Colah 162 E16
pl. Pymble 253 A9
ANNAM
rd. Bayview 168 J15
ANNAN
pl. Baulkham Hl 246 G11
ANNANDALE
st. Annandale 16 G4
st. Darling Point 13 H6
ANNANGROVE
rd. Annangrove 187 B7
rd. Kenthurst 187 B7
rd. Rouse Hill 184 H5
ANNE
av. Seven Hills 245 A16
cr. Blaxland 234 C5
pl. Cherrybrook 219 K4
pl. Wahroonga 223 B5
pl. Wilberforce 92 C2
st. Blacktown 274 C4
st. Oatlands 278 K11
st. Revesby 399 A12
st. St Marys 239 F8
wy. Mcquarie Fd 424 F15
ANNELIESE
pl. Castle Hill 218 C10
ANNE MARIE
cl. St Ives 223 K16
pl. Belfield 371 F10
pl. Carlingford 249 E14
ANNESLEY
st. Leichhardt 10 C12
ANNETT
st. Emu Plains 235 F12
ANNETTE
av. Ingleburn 453 B6
av. Kogarah 433 E5
pl. Baulkham Hl 248 C7
pl. Belrose 226 B16
pl. Richmond 118 G7
st. Cabramtta W 365 B6
st. Oatley 431 C16
ANNE WILLIAM
dr. W Pnnant Hl 249 F7
ANNIE
la. West Ryde 281 B16
st. Hurstville 401 J16
ANNIE SPENCE
cl. Emu Heights 235 B3
ANNIVERSARY
st. Botany 405 H16
ANNUAL
la. St Clair 270 C14
ANSCHAU
cr. Windsor 121 D8
ANSELM
st. Strathfield S 371 A4
ANSON
pl. Castle Hill 247 F1
ANTARES
av. Hinchinbrk 393 D4
pl. Cranebrook 207 F5
ANTHEA
pl. Dean Park 212 K16
ANTHONY
av. Mt Riverview 234 C1
av. Padstow 429 C3
cl. Beacon Hill 257 H5
cl. St Ives 254 A1
cr. Kingswood 238 A14
dr. Rsemeadow 540 G3
la. Matraville 406 J15
la. West Ryde, off Anthony Rd 281 D15
rd. Bargo 567 J1
rd. Castle Hill 217 J15
rd. Catherine Fd 419 F7
rd. Denistone 281 C12
rd. Leppington 419 F7
rd. West Ryde 281 D12
st. Blacktown 245 A7
st. Carlingford 250 B16
st. Chatswood 285 A10
st. Croydon 342 F16
st. Epping 250 B16
st. Fairfield 336 E7
st. Matraville 406 K15
st. Yagoona 369 D8
ANTILL
cl. Camden S 507 A10
cr. Baulkham Hl 247 H5
pl. Blackett 241 C2
pl. Mt Pritchard 364 J9
rd. Mt Pritchard 364 H9
st. Blaxland 234 A7
st. Picton 563 E11
st. Thirlmere 565 B5
st. Yennora 337 D9
wy. Airds 511 J16
ANTIQUE
cr. Woodcroft 243 F7
ANTOINE
st. Rydalmere 309 G3
ANTOINETTE
av. Narellan Vale 508 E1
cl. Warrawee 222 E13
ANTON
pl. Bonnyrigg 363 J9
rd. Luddenham 357 F1
ANTONIA
cr. Cranebrook 207 B13
ANTONIETTA
st. Cabramatta 365 E11
ANTONIO
cl. Rsemeadow 540 K4
st. St Johns Pk 364 G2
ANTRIM
st. Hebersham 241 F3
ANTWERP
st. Auburn 338 K10
st. Bankstown 399 A6
ANULLA
pl. Wahroonga 222 A7
ANVIL
pl. Jamisontown 236 B15
rd. Seven Hills 276 E3
ANZAC
av. Cammeray 315 K7
av. Collaroy 229 A15
av. Collaroy Plat 228 J14
av. Denistone 281 F14
av. Engadine 518 J1
av. Fairfield 336 F13
av. Ryde 281 F14
av. Smeaton Gra 479 C9
av. West Ryde 281 F14
la. Campbelltwn 511 E4
la. West Ryde, off Wattle St 281 E15
mw. Holsworthy 396 B14
pde. Chifley 437 C5
pde. Kensington 376 E9
pde. Kingsford 406 F1
pde. La Perouse 436 J14
pde. La Perouse 436 K14
pde. Little Bay 437 A11
pde. Malabar 437 C5
pde. Maroubra 407 A6
pde. Matraville 407 B15
pde. Moore Park 20 G4
pde. Phillip Bay 436 K13
rd. Bangor 459 B13
rd. Holsworthy 396 B14
rd. Moorebank 395 F13
rd. Wattle Grove 395 F13
sq. Campsie 371 K13
st. Canterbury 372 E16
st. Chullora 369 H10
st. Greenacre 369 H10
st. Miranda 492 D6
st. N St Marys 239 K10
ANZIO
av. Allambie Ht 257 C9
AOMA
st. Scotland I 168 H3
APACHE
gr. Stanhpe Gdn 215 C11
rd. Bossley Park 333 K10
APANIE
pl. Westleigh 220 E8
APAP
av. Castle Hill 217 C6
APARA
st. Forestville 255 F10
APERTA
pl. Beacon Hill 257 K7
APEX
av. Picnic Point 428 F7
st. Blacktown 274 D7
st. Liverpool 365 B15
st. Naremburn 315 F1
APIA
pl. Lethbrdg Pk 240 F2
st. Guildford 337 E5
APLIN
cl. St Ives Ch 223 J6
rd. Bonnyrigg Ht 363 E8
APOLLO
av. Baulkham Hl 246 K14
av. West Pymble 252 G12
cl. St Clair 269 F11
pl. Eastwood 280 E7
pl. Lane Cove W 283 F15
pl. Port Hacking 522 K3
st. Greenfld Pk 334 C13
st. Warriewood 198 H5
APPALOOSA
cct. Blairmount 481 A14
APPIAN
cct. Baulkham Hl 246 G10
wy. Burwood 371 K2
APPIN
pl. Engadine 489 D10
pl. St Marys 239 F4
rd. Ambarvale 511 B15
rd. Appin 568 G9
rd. Bradbury 511 B15
rd. Campbelltwn 511 B15
rd. Gilead 540 H15
rd. Rsemeadow 540 H15

rd. St Helens Pk...540 H15
APPLAUSE
st. Riverwood......400 C10
APPLE
pl. Mcquarie Fd....454 A4
st. Wentwthvle.....277 B8
APPLEBEE
st. St Peters.........374 J12
APPLEBOX
av. Glenwood.......215 H16
APPLEBY
ct. Agnes Banks...117 E16
pl. Plumpton.......242 B8
APPLECROSS
av. Castle Hill.......218 A7
APPLEGUM
pl. Mt Riverview...234 E3
pl. Prestons.........393 K14
APPLETON
av. Lurnea...........394 D11
APPLETREE
dr. Cherrybrook...219 J7
gr. Oakhurst.........211 H16
pl. Menai.............458 H13
APPS
av. N Turramrra....223 D8
pl. Narellan Vale...508 K1
APSLEY
av. Kingsford.........406 H4
ct. Cranebrook.....206 J9
la. Kingsford.........406 H4
pl. Campbelltwn...511 J8
pl. Taren Point.....462 G13
st. Guildford.........337 E1
st. Penshurst.......431 F5
AQUA
pl. Marayong.......244 B5
AQUAMARINE
dr. Eagle Vale.......481 E8
AQUARIUS
cr. Erskine Park...300 K1
la. Erskine Park, off Aquarius Cr.....300 K1
AQUATIC
dr. Frenchs Frst....257 A7
AQUILA
la. Erskine Park, off Pegasus St......301 A2
pl. Erskine Park...301 A2
AQUILINA
dr. Plumpton.......242 D11
ARA
cr. Narraweena....258 A1
pl. Hinchinbrk......393 E3
ARAB
rd. Padstow.........399 C15
ARABANOO
st. Seaforth..........287 C7
ARABELLA
pl. Bella Vista.......246 G5
st. Longueville.....314 D9
st. Northwood.....314 D9
ARAFURA
av. Cranebrook.....207 C10
ARAGON
st. Cecil Hills........362 D4
ARAKOON
av. Penrith...........237 D7
ARALUEN
av. Moorebank.....396 G6
av. St Marys.........239 G14
pl. Bayview..........168 F11
pl. Camden S.......507 D12
pl. Glenhaven......217 H2
pl. Sutherland......460 H15
rd. Lansvale.........366 C10
st. Kingsford.........407 A4
ARAMON
cl. Edensor Pk.....363 E2
ARANA
cl. Bangor...........459 J15
cl. Banksia..........403 G12
cl. Georges Hall...368 A15
pl. Cabramtta W..365 C7
st. Manly Vale......287 G3
ARANDA
dr. Davidson........255 E2
dr. Frenchs Frst....255 E2
ARANDA PATH
Winmalee.......173 B10
ARARAT
cl. Bossley Park...333 E9
ARBOR
gln. Castle Hill.......217 E2
ARBOUR
gr. Quakers Hill....213 G9
ARBROATH
pl. St Andrews.....482 A3
ARBUTUS
st. Canley Ht........365 E3
st. Canley Vale.....365 E3
st. Mosman.........317 C6
ARCADIA
av. Drummoyne....344 B3
av. Gymea Bay.....491 C11
av. Woolooware...493 F7
cr. Berowra..........133 C11
la. Coogee...........377 H14
la. Glebe................11 G10
la. Colyton, off Arcadia Pl........270 B8
pl. Colyton...........270 B8
rd. Arcadia...........129 E16
rd. Chester Hill.....368 D1
rd. Galston...........159 D2
rd. Glebe................11 G10
st. Coogee...........377 G14
st. Merrylnds W...307 A12
st. Penshurst.......431 C1
ARCADIAN
cct. Carlingford......279 B4
ARCHBALD
av. Btn-le-Sds.......403 K15
ARCHBOLD
av. Rouse Hill.......185 D1
rd. Eastern Ck......271 E12
rd. E Lindfield........254 H15
rd. Lindfield..........254 H15
rd. Minchinbury...271 E12
rd. Roseville.........284 J1
ARCHDALE
wky. Wahroonga.....222 D7
ARCHDALL
gr. Bella Vista.......246 F4
ARCHER
cl. Bossley Park...333 K8
cr. Bankstown......399 D6
ct. St Clair............270 E11
la. Windsor Dn....180 H1
pl. Maroubra........407 C8
pl. Minto.............483 A3
row. Menai...........458 K15
st. Blacktown.......274 B6
st. Burwood.........342 B12
st. Chatswood......284 J6
st. Concord..........341 K2
st. Mosman.........317 A8
st. Mount Druitt...271 B4
st. Roseville.........284 J6
wy. West Hoxton...392 D10
ARCHIBALD
cr. Rsemeadow....540 G8
st. Belmore..........401 H5
st. Granville.........308 G14
st. Padstow.........399 B13
ARCHITECTS
pl. St Clair...........270 B10
ARCTURUS
cl. Cranebrook.....207 F6
ARDATH
av. Panania..........428 B5
ARDEN
la. Clovelly, off Arden St..........377 H12
pl. Frenchs Frst....256 G3
rd. Pymble...........253 A2
st. Clovelly...........377 H12
st. Coogee...........377 H16
st. S Coogee........407 G3
st. Waverley.........377 H12
ARDGRYFFE
st. Burwood Ht....372 A4
ARDILL
la. Warrimoo.......203 B15
ARDING
st. Lane Cove W...284 B15
ARDISIA
pl. Loftus............489 K12
ARDITTOS
la. Strathfield.......341 E12
ARDNO
st. Busby.............363 G14
ARDRISHAIG
pl. Glenhaven.......218 F6
ARDROSSAN
cr. St Andrews.....451 K14
rd. Engadine.........488 J11
ARDSLEY
av. Frenchs Frst....256 D3
ARDUA
pl. Engadine.........488 D15
ARELEY
ct. Jamisontown..266 E5
ARGO
pl. Miranda..........461 J16
wy. Airds..............512 C11
ARGONNE
st. N Strathfield....341 C3
ARGOWAN
rd. Schofields.......183 B16
ARGUIMBAU
st. Annandale........10 J13
ARGUS
la. Parramatta......308 F3
ARGYLE
av. Ryde..............312 B2
cr. S Coogee........407 E6
la. Millers Point.......A B3
pl. Bonnyrigg Ht...363 B6
pl. Emu Plains......235 B9
pl. Kareela............461 B14
pl. Mcquarie Fd....423 J16
pl. Millers Point.......A C2
pl. Millers Point.......1 D9
pl. W Pnnant Hl....249 A6
st. Arncliffe..........403 H7
st. Auburn............309 D15
st. Bilgola.............169 F8
st. Camden...........477 B15
st. Carlton............432 J6
st. Dawes Point.......A D2
st. Dawes Point.......1 E9
st. Millers Point.......A D2
st. Millers Point.......1 E9
st. Parramatta......308 B4
st. Penshurst.......431 B2
st. Picton.............563 D13
st. Picton.............563 E11
st. Riverstone.......182 F13
st. S Windsor........120 J12
st. The Rocks..........A J3
st. The Rocks..........1 G10
ARGYLE REACH
rd. Freemns Rch....91 E12
rd. Wilberforce......91 G8
ARGYLE STAIRS
The Rocks..........A J3
ARGYLL
pl. Cheltenham.....250 J6
rd. Winmalee........173 C12
rd. Winmalee........173 D12
ARIANA
pl. Acacia Gdn......214 J16
ARIANNA
av. Normanhurst...221 J11
ARIEL
cr. Cranebrook.....207 C16
pl. Rsemeadow....540 K6
ARIELLA
pl. Edensor Pk.....333 E14
ARIES
pl. Erskine Park....270 G15
ARIETTA
cct. Harringtn Pk....478 F7
ARIKA
cl. Bangor............459 G15
ARILLA
av. Riverwood......400 F11
pl. Bangor............459 J15
rd. Pymble...........253 A3
ARINA
rd. Bargo.............567 K12
ARINYA
st. Kingsgrove......401 K7
ARISAIG
pl. St Andrews.....451 K16
ARISTOTLE
la. Winmalee........173 J8
ARIZONA
pl. North Rocks....278 H2
pl. Riverwood......400 A12
pl. Stanhpe Gdn...215 C11
ARJEZ
pl. Marayong........244 B5
ARK
pl. Riverstone.......183 A4
ARKANA
pl. Engadine........489 A8
st. Telopea...........279 D7
ARKANSAS
pl. Kearns............451 C16
ARKELL
dr. Bligh Park.......150 H5
ARKENA
av. Epping...........250 C14
ARKLAND
st. Cammeray......316 B4
ARKLEY
st. Bankstown.....399 F6
ARLENE
pl. Plumpton.......241 G10
ARLEWIS
st. Chester Hill.....338 B14
ARLEY
pl. North Rocks...248 K13
ARLINGTON
av. Castle Hill.......217 G10
av. Riverstone......183 G9
dr. Fairlight.........288 C10
st. Dulwich Hill....373 B8
st. Five Dock.......342 J12
st. Rockdale........403 B13
ARMATA
ct. Wattle Grove..426 B1
ARMEN
wy. Hornsby Ht.....161 G16
ARMENTIERES
av. Milperra.........397 G11
wy. Matraville.......407 B15
ARMIDALE
av. Hoxton Park...392 G6
pl. Engadine........488 G12
ARMINE
wy. Kellyville.........185 J14
ARMITAGE
dr. Glendenning...242 E3
dr. Glendenning...242 F2
la. Mosman, off Rosherville Rd..317 D2
ARMITREE
st. Kingsgrove.....401 E7
st. Kingsgrove.....401 F8
ARMOUR
av. Camden S......507 B14
ARMSTEIN
cr. Werrington.....238 F11
la. Werrington, off Armstein Cr....238 G11
ARMSTRONG
ct. Bnkstn Aprt....367 J16
la. Lidcombe.......339 H10
pl. Castle Hill.......218 C10
pl. Dean Park......242 H1
st. Ashcroft.........394 D1
st. Ashfield..........372 J7
st. Cammeray......315 H4
st. Raby..............451 D12
st. Seaforth.........286 K4
st. Willoughby.....285 E15
st.e, Willoughby.....285 F16
ARMYTAGE
pl. Glen Alpine.....510 E13
ARNCLIFFE
rd. Earlwood........403 C4
st. Arncliffe.........403 H7
ARNDELL
st. Camden S......507 B10
st. Windsor.........121 E7
wy. Minto............482 H6
ARNDILL
av. Baulkham Hl...247 E3
ARNETT
st. Pendle Hill......306 F2
ARNHEM
pl. Leumeah........482 F9
pl. Willmot..........210 C12
rd. Allambie Ht.....257 B8
ARNO
tce. Glenwood.......245 K4
ARNOLD
av. Camden S......507 C16
av. Green Valley...363 A11
av. Kellyville.........215 J8
av. St Marys........270 A4
av. Yagoona.........369 C10
la. Darlinghurst.......F K8
la. Panania..........428 D2
pl. Darlinghurst.......F J6
pl. Glenwood.......215 K16
pl. Menai............458 H11
st. Killara.............254 B12
st. Leumeah........512 C2
st. N Richmond.....87 C14
st. Peakhurst.......430 B3
st. Queens Park.....22 H13
st. Ryde..............312 D5
st. Wetherill Pk....334 E6
ARNOLD JANSSEN
dr. Kellyville.........185 K16
dr. Kellyville.........215 K1
ARNOTT
cr. Warriewood....199 D11
pl. Wetherill Pk....304 E13
rd. Marayong.......244 A4
ARNOTTS
pl. Huntingwd......273 E12
AROA
pl. Glenfield.........424 D13
ARONIA
av. St Ives............224 G9
AROONA
rd. Oxford Falls....227 A13
ARRABRI
pl. Warriewood....199 B8
ARRAGONG
st. Bangor...........459 J15
ARRAN
pl. St Andrews.....481 J3
ARRAS
pde. Ryde..............312 C3
ARRAWATTA
cl. Edensor Pk.....333 D14
ARRIONGA
pl. Hornsby.........191 D12
ARRIVAL
ct. Mascot...........404 D6
ARROW
la. Old Tngabbie..277 F10
pl. Raby..............481 F1
ARROWFIELD
av. Burwood........371 H1
dr. Wattle Grove...396 A16
ARROWHEAD
rd. Greenfld Pk.....333 K12
ARROWSMITH
st. Glenwood.......215 E15
ARRUNGA
av. Roseville.........284 G1
rd. Arcadia..........129 C15
st. Dundas..........279 F14
ARTARMON
rd. Artarmon........285 A14
rd. Willoughby.....285 D16
ARTEGALL
st. Bankstown......399 A8
ART GALLERY
rd. Campbelltwn...511 C7
rd. Sydney...............D J6
rd. Sydney...............4 C3
ARTHUR
av. Blacktown.......244 A11
av. Cronulla..........494 A15
la. Fairlight...........288 D7
la. Lavender Bay......K H14
la. Lavender Bay......5 H12
la. Randwick.......377 A14
la. Surry Hills........20 C3
pl. Bonnet Bay.....460 B7
st. Ashfield..........372 G4
st. Auburn...........338 J5
st. Balmain.............7 C8
st. Bankstown......399 B7
st. Baulkham Hl...247 H12
st. Bellevue Hill......14 H14
st. Bexley............402 H13
st. Bonnet Bay......460 C7
st. Burwood Ht....372 B4
st. Cabramatta.....365 J7
st. Carlton...........432 H9
st. Chipping Ntn..397 A4
st. Concord.........341 H5
st. Croydon.........372 B4
st. Croydon Pk.....372 B4
st. Dee Why.........258 F4
st. Dover Ht.........348 F14
st. Edgecliff............13 J12
st. Fairlight..........288 E7
st. Five Dock........343 D8
st. Forest Lodge....11 F13
st. Forestville.......255 D8
st. Granville.........308 H10
st. Granville.........308 H8
st. Hornsby.........191 J13
st. Killara............254 A8
st. Lavender Bay.....K H15
st. Lavender Bay.....5 H11
st. Leichhardt........10 A14
st. McMahons Pt....K H14
st. Marrickville.....373 H13
st. Marsden Pk....182 B14

st. Mascot 405 H4
st. Merrylnds W 307 A12
st. Parramatta 308 J6
st. Punchbowl 400 C4
st. Randwick 376 K14
st. Redfern 19 J6
st. Rodd Point 343 D8
st. Rookwood 340 E10
st. Rosehill 308 J6
st. Rosehill 308 H8
st. Ryde 282 C12
st. Strathfield 340 J11
st. Surry Hills 20 B2
st. Surry Hills 20 C3
st. Warrimoo 203 B14
st.n, N Sydney K H10
st.n, N Sydney 5 H9
ARTHUR PHILLIP
dr. N Richmond 86 K13
ARTHURS
cir. Mt Colah 162 D9
ARTHURSLEIGH
st. Burwood 342 B11
ARTHUR TAYLOR
av. Matraville 436 G9
ARTIE
st. Carramar 366 G1
ARTILLERY
cr. Holsworthy 426 F3
cr. Seven Hills 245 H16
dr. Manly 289 B13
rd. Holsworthy 425 D11
ARTISAN
rd. Seven Hills 276 F2
ARTLETT
st. Edgecliff 13 F11
ARTORNISH
pl. Rooty Hill, off Barker St 272 C1
ARU
pl. Kings Park 244 J2
ARUM
pl. Mcquarie Fd 454 D6
wy. Cherrybrook 219 G14
ARUMA
av. Kellyville 216 H8
cl. Chipping Ntn 396 D5
pl. Dharruk 241 C9
ARUNDEL
st. Engadine 489 A11
st. Forest Lodge 11 K16
st. Glebe 18 C1
st. Longueville 314 D9
st. West Pymble 252 G10
wy. Cherrybrook 219 C14
ARUNDELL
st. Dharruk 241 A7
ARUNDEL PARK
dr. St Clair 270 F14
ARUNDLE
rd. Bass Hill 367 J8
rd. Horsley Pk 302 D14
ARUNTA
av. Green Valley 363 G11
cl. Bangor 459 F15
cr. Leumeah 482 G11
ARWON
av. Casula 394 E16
ASAPH
cl. Hornsby Ht 161 E15
ASCHE
st. Doonside 243 B9
ASCOT
av. Wahroonga 222 C2
dr. Chipping Ntn 366 F15
dr. Chipping Ntn 366 G13
pl. Miranda 492 B3
pl. S Penrith 266 H1
pl. Wilberforce 92 A2
rd. Kenthurst 157 H9
st. Bexley 402 H13
st. Canley Ht 365 E4
st. Kensington 376 F11
st. Randwick 376 F11
ASEKI
av. Glenfield 424 C14
ASH
av. Caringbah 492 F13
cl. Bossley Park 333 H11
la. Haberfield 343 A13
pl. Bradbury 511 D9
pl. Lugarno 429 H16
pl. Narellan Vale 478 J14
pl. S Coogee 407 E6
rd. Prestons 393 G13
rd. Prestons 393 J8
st. Blacktown 243 K15
st. Cherrybrook 219 G12
st. Georges Hall 367 F11
st. Greystanes 306 E4
st. N St Marys 239 K10
st. Sydney C J1
st. Sydney 3 G1
ASHBURN
la. Gladesville 312 H11
pl. Gladesville 312 G12
ASHBURNER
st. Manly 288 H11
ASHBURTON
av. S Turramrra 252 B10
ct. Kellyville 186 H16
ASHBY
av. Yagoona 369 C10
cl. Bargo 567 A3
la. Randwick 377 D9
st. Guildford 338 A7
st. Kingsgrove 401 G13
st. Prospect 274 F12
ASHCOTT
st. Kings Lngly 245 D7
ASHCROFT
av. Casula 394 K14
st. Ermington 280 B13
st. Georges Hall 367 E14
ASHDOWN
pl. Frenchs Frst 256 F3
ASHER
pl. Campbelltwn 511 E6
st. Coogee 407 G2
ASHERS
la. Artarmon 314 J2
ASHFIELD
pl. Glen Alpine 540 C2
ASHFORD
av. Castle Hill 217 F13
av. Milperra 397 J11
cl. Hinchinbrk 392 H5
gr. St Clair 270 G14
la. St Clair, off Ashford Gr 270 G14
rd. Cherrybrook 219 C14
rd. Vineyard 152 F12
st. Ashfield 372 J8
ASHFORDBY
st. Chipping Ntn 396 F1
ASHGATE
av. Vaucluse 348 C6
ASHGROVE
cr. Blacktown 274 F9
st. St Johns Pk 364 E1
ASHLAR
st. St Ives 224 D6
ASHLEIGH MADISON
wy. Mt Colah 191 K4
ASHLEY
av. W Pnnant Hl 249 G8
cl. St Johns Pk 364 E1
gr. Gordon 253 H5
la. Hornsby 221 F1
la. Westmead 277 G16
pde. Fairlight 288 B10
st. Chatswood 284 J7
st. Hornsby 221 E1
st. Roseville 285 A6
st. Tamarama 378 A7
ASHMEAD
av. Castle Hill 217 H9
av. Revesby 428 H2
rd. Minto 483 B1
rd. Minto 483 C1
ASHMONT
pl. Prestons 393 B15
ASHMORE
av. Pymble 252 J2
st. Erskineville 375 A8
ASHTON
av. Chester Hill 338 A15
av. Earlwood 372 J16
av. Ermington 310 B3
av. Forestville 255 K9
av. Seaforth 287 A12
cl. Eagle Vale 480 K9
la. Paddington 21 E1
pl. Doonside 273 F2
pl. Mt Pritchard 364 J12
st. Queens Park 22 C11
st. Rockdale 433 D2
ASHTONS
rd. Grose Wold 116 A9
ASHUR
cr. Greenfld Pk 334 A15
ASHWELL
rd. Blacktown 274 F2
ASHWICK
cct. St Clair 270 G10
ASHWOOD
cl. Menai 458 H14
rd. Kenthurst 187 C3
ASHWORTH
av. Belrose 225 E14
ASPEN
cl. Prestons 393 J13
st. Bossley Park 333 H9
st. S Penrith 267 D5
ASPINALL
av. Minchinbury 272 B8
pl. Mulgrave 121 H16
pl. Woolwich 314 G11
ASPLIN
pl. Kurrajong Hl 55 F7
ASQUITH
av. Rosebery 375 J16
av. Winston Hills 247 J15
st. Oatley 431 E12
st. Silverwater 309 E12
ASSETS
st. Campsie 371 K12
ASSISI
pl. Rooty Hill 272 D7
ASSUNTA
st. Rooty Hill 272 D7
ASTELIA
st. Mcquarie Fd 454 C4
ASTER
av. Asquith 191 K9
av. Miranda 492 D2
av. Punchbowl 399 G4
cl. Glenmore Pk 265 F10
pl. Quakers Hill 243 F3
st. Eastwood 281 D7
st. Greystanes 305 J12
ASTLEY
av. Padstow 429 E1
pl. Edensor Pk 363 G4
wy. Casula 424 G4
ASTOLAT
st. Randwick 377 C11
ASTON
av. Lucas Ht 487 F12
av. S Penrith 267 B1
cl. Hoxton Park 392 K6
gdn. Bellevue Hill 347 F11
la. S Penrith, off Aston Av 267 B1
pl. Bellevue Hill 347 F11
pl. Leumeah 482 B14
rd. Kenthurst 187 E8
st. Hunters Hill 313 A7
ASTOR
st. Moorebank 396 E7
ASTORIA
cct. Maroubra 407 B12
ASTORIA PARK
rd. Baulkham Hl 246 F10
ASTRAL
dr. Doonside 243 G15
ASTRID
av. Baulkham Hl 247 E7
cl. Cabramatta 365 E11
ASTROLABE
rd. Daceyville 406 E3
ASTRON
cr. Bexley North 402 D9
ASTWIN
st. Croydon 342 G14
ASTWOOD
st. Colyton 270 D8
ATAMI
pl. Picnic Point 428 A7
ATCHISON
la. Crows Nest 315 E5
la. St Leonards 315 E5
rd. Mcquarie Fd 453 K1
st. Crows Nest 315 E5
st. St Leonards 315 E5
st. St Marys 269 F5
ATHABASKA
av. Seven Hills 275 H8
ATHEL
st. Georges Hall 367 F11
st. N St Marys 240 C13
ATHELLA
pl. Dural 219 C7
ATHELSTANE
av. Arncliffe 403 D9
ATHEL TREE
cr. Bradbury 511 F14
ATHENA
av. St Ives 224 G7
ct. St Clair 269 G11
ATHENE
pl. Collaroy Plat 228 K13
ATHENS
av. Hassall Gr 212 A16
ATHERDEN
st. The Rocks A K1
ATHERTON
cr. Auburn 339 B12
rd. Engadine 489 A10
st. Fairfield W 335 E10
ATHLONE
cr. Killarney Ht 256 D15
st. Blacktown 273 K1
st. Cecil Hills 362 H9
ATHOL
pl. Carlingford 279 C3
st. Frenchs Frst 255 J1
st. Leichhardt 9 D12
st. S Coogee 407 G4
ATHOL WHARF
rd. Mosman 317 A15
ATKA
st. Tregear 240 C6
ATKINS
av. Carramar 336 H16
av. Russell Lea 343 E4
cr. Richmond 118 D8
ct. Baulkham Hl 247 E2
pl. Barden Rdg 488 F3
rd. Ermington 280 E16
rd. Ermington 310 E1
ATKINSON
av. Padstow 399 B10
cl. Glenmore Pk 265 J6
rd. Taren Point 463 A15
st. Arncliffe 403 B11
st. Liverpool 395 A7
ATLANTA
pl. Casula 395 A12
ATLANTIC
pl. Kellyville 185 K14
ATLAS
pl. Winston Hills 277 C1
wy. Kellyville 185 J14
wy. Narellan Vale 508 J2
ATNATU
wy. Doonside 243 F16
ATOLL
pl. Quakers Hill 213 F14
ATTAR
st. Guildford 337 K4
ATTARD
av. Marayong 244 D7
ATTILIO
pl. Edensor Pk 363 H4
ATTLEE
pl. Winston Hills 277 J2
ATTOW
st. Winston Hills 277 C3
ATTUNGA
av. Earlwood 402 F6
av. Moorebank 396 F11
av. W Pnnant Hl 249 J1
pl. Bradbury 511 F15
pwy. Moorebank, off Attunga Av 396 F10
rd. Blaxland 233 E4
rd. Miranda 492 A7
rd. Newport 169 K7
rd. Roseville Ch 255 D14
rd. Yowie Bay 492 A13
st. Baulkham Hl 247 C5
st. Seven Hills 275 E4
st. Woollahra 22 F2
AUBER
gln. St Clair 300 C2
la. St Clair, off Auber Gln 300 C2
AUBERT
st. Narellan 478 G13
AUBIN
st. Neutral Bay 6 D8
AUBREEN
st. Collaroy Plat 228 J12
AUBREY
cl. Castle Hill 248 E2
pl. Berowra 133 H9
rd. Northbridge 286 F16
st. Ingleburn 453 E7
st. S Granville 338 F3
st. Stanmore 16 C11
AUBURN
rd. Auburn 339 C11
rd. Auburn 339 D7
rd. Berala 339 C11
rd. Birrong 368 K6
rd. Regents Pk 369 A5
rd. Yagoona 368 K11
st. Hunters Hill 313 A8
st. Parramatta 307 H7
st. Sutherland 490 G4
st.s, Sutherland 490 G6
AUCKLAND
st. Bonnyrigg Ht 363 C6
st. Engadine 518 H6
AUDINE
av. Epping 280 E3
AUDLEY
la. Petersham 15 H11
rd. Royal N P 520 E2
st. Petersham 15 H11
AUDREY
pde. Condell Park 398 J5
pl. Quakers Hill 213 G8
st. Balgowlah 287 F9
st. Thirlmere 565 D2
AUGUSTA
ct. Rouse Hill 185 B9
la. Allawah 432 F9
la. Manly 288 F8
la. St Clair, off Augusta Pl 270 J11
pl. St Clair 270 J11
rd. Fairlight 288 E7
rd. Manly 288 E7
st. Allawah 432 G9
st. Bankstown 399 A4
st. Blacktown 274 F14
st. Casula 395 A13
st. Concord 341 K1
st. Condell Park 398 H4
st. Five Dock 343 C10
st. Punchbowl 400 C9
st. Strathfield 371 A2
AUGUSTINE
st. Hunters Hill 313 B9
AUGUSTUS
la. Enmore 17 A12
st. Enmore 17 A12
wy. Ambarvale 510 K15
AUKANE
st. Green Valley 362 K11
AULD
av. Eastwood 280 J7
av. Milperra 397 B7
pl. Eagle Vale 481 B9
pl. Schofields 183 E15
AULT
pl. Illawong 459 K6
AULUBA
rd. S Turramrra 252 B6
AUMUNA
rd. Terrey Hills 195 K9
AURELIA
st. Toongabbie 276 B8
AURORA
dr. Tregear 240 E7
dr. Whalan 240 F8
pl. Eveleigh 18 E12
AUSTEN
cl. Wetherill Pk 334 G6
pl. Kellyville 215 F3
AUSTIN
av. Beverly Hills 430 K1
av. Campbelltwn 511 H9
av. Croydon 372 B3
av. Homebsh W 340 H7
av. N Curl Curl 259 A10
bvd. Picnic Point 428 E7
cr. Belfield 371 E11
cr. Lane Cove 314 D2
cr. Wentwthvle 277 D9
la. Surry Hills 20 C4
pl. Orchard Hills 268 D8
st. Fairlight 288 B8
st. Illawong 459 H6
st. Lane Cove 314 D3
AUSTIN WOODBURY
pl. Toongabbie 276 H6
AUSTRAL
av. Beecroft 250 C8
av. Lindfield 284 B5

av. North Manly....258 B15
av. Westmead......307 E1
pde. Fairfield.........336 D15
pl. St Helens Pk...541 A6
st. Kogarah..........433 D8
st. Malabar..........437 D4
st. Mount Druitt...241 C13
st. Penshurst.......431 D5
AUSTRALIA
av. Homebush B ... 340 J1
av. Matraville........436 F3
av. Newington.........M G4
av. Newington.........M A6
la. Camperdwn......17 D6
la. Camperdwn......17 D8
la. Woollahra.........22 H4
rd. Barden Rdg....488 G2
st. Bass Hill.........368 D10
st. Camperdwn......17 C4
st. Croydon.........342 H13
st. Hurstville........432 A9
st. Merrylands.....308 A13
st. Newtown.........17 E8
st. St Marys.........269 K1
AUSTRALIS
av. Wattle Grove...396 B16
cl. Cranebrook.....207 H6
AUSTRALORP
av. Seven Hills......275 E5
AUTUMN
gr. Glendenning...242 H4
pl. Guildford........337 C2
AUTUMN LEAF
gr. Cherrybrook...219 J15
pde. St Clair..........270 C13
AVALON
av. Lane Cove W...283 H16
cl. Bossley Park...333 F9
pde. Avalon...........169 K1
pl. Woodbine.......481 J9
st. Birrong..........369 A5
st. Turramurra.....223 D12
AVELINE
pl. Hassall Gr.......211 K13
AVELING
st. Blakehurst......432 C16
AVENAL
st. Arncliffe..........403 G10
st. Guildford........337 D2
AVENEL
rd. Gymea Bay.....491 C8
st. Canley Vale.....365 J1
AVENUE
la. Glebe...........11 H8
rd. Glebe...........11 H8
rd. Hunters Hill....313 E10
rd. Mosman........316 H10
AVENUE OF AFRICA
Newington.........L G12
Newington......310 C10
AVENUE OF ASIA
Newington.........L G12
Newington......310 C11
AVENUE OF EUROPE
Newington.........L H13
Newington......310 B11
AVENUE OF OCEANIA
Homebush B....310 C11
Newington.........L J11
Newington......310 C11
AVENUE OF THE AMERICAS
Newington.........L G13
AVERIL
pl. Lindfield.........284 C2
AVERILL
st. Rhodes...........311 E7
AVERY
av. Kirrawee.........491 B4
st. Normanhurst..221 E7
wy. Narellan Vale...508 K1
AVIA
cl. Raby...........451 B13
AVIAN
cr. Lane Cove W..283 G12
AVIATION
pl. Bnkstn Aprt....397 J1
AVISFORD
st. Fairfield..........336 B14
AVOCA
av. Belfield...........371 E9
av. Emu Plains.....236 B7
cl. West Hoxton...392 E6
la. Randwick.......407 B1
la. Bondi, off Avoca St..........378 A5
la. Canley Ht, off Birchgrove Av...364 K3
pl. Woodbine.......481 K10
rd. Canley Ht........365 A3
rd. Grose Wold.....115 F7
rd. Silverdale........383 A11
rd. Silverdale........413 A1
rd. Turramurra.....222 H16
rd. Wakeley..........335 A16
st. Bondi.............377 K5
st. Glenbrook........264 C1
st. Kingsford........407 A5
st. Randwick........377 B16
st. Yagoona.........369 D10
AVOCET
pl. Hinchinbrk......393 C2
AVON
cl. Asquith...........192 D10
cl. Pymble...........252 K4
grn. W Pnnant Hl...249 C5
la. Glebe..............12 A9
la. St Clair, off Avon Pl...........269 J13
pl. Kirrawee.........491 A10
pl. Leumeah.........482 D12
pl. St Clair...........269 J13
pl. Toongabbie.....276 G7
pl. Windsor Dn....151 B12
rd. Bringelly.........387 F5
rd. Dee Why.........258 J6
rd. North Ryde......282 H9
rd. Pymble...........253 B2
st. Bankstown......369 D12
st. Cammeray......316 B5
st. Canley Ht........365 A3
st. Glebe..............12 A9
AVONA
av. Glebe..............11 K8
cr. Seaforth..........287 C11
AVONDALE
pl. Cartwright.......394 E4
pl. West Pymble..252 H7
rd. Pitt Town..........93 H16
rd. Scheyville.......123 D1
AVON DAM
rd. Bargo.............567 G8
AVONLEA
cr. Bass Hill.........368 C8
dr. Carlingford......250 C13
st. Canley Ht........335 E15
AVONLEIGH
ct. Glenwood.......245 G2
wy. W Pnnant Hl...249 C3
AVRIL
ct. Kellyville.........216 G3
AVRO
pl. Raby..............451 G15
rd. Lane Cove W...283 G12
st. Bnkstn Aprt....367 H16
st. Mascot...........404 K4
AWABA
la. Mosman, off Killarney St......317 B4
pl. Warriewood....199 C9
st. Mosman.........316 H3
st. Mosman.........317 A4
AWATEA
pl. Engadine.........518 F5
pl. Lethbrdg Pk....240 E2
rd. St Ives Ch.......223 K2
AXAM
wy. Narellan Vale...509 A1
AXFORD
pl. Fairfield W......335 A9
AXINITE
pl. Eagle Vale.......481 G9
AXON
pl. Bonnyrigg.......364 B6
AYCLIFFE
av. Hebersham.....241 F8
AYLES
rd. Winston Hills..246 G16
AYLESBURY
cr. Chipping Ntn...396 G2
st. Botany...........405 H12
st. Newtown..........17 K7
AYLETT
st. N St Marys......239 J8
AYLSHAM
cl. Chipping Ntn...366 G13
AYLWARD
av. Quakers Hill....214 B10
AYR
pl. Riverstone.......183 C8
st. Ashbury..........372 E8
st. Banksia..........403 J13
AYRES
cr. Georges Hall...367 J15
cr. Leumeah.........482 G10
gr. Mount Druitt...241 F15
rd. St Ives............224 D7
rd.w, St Ives............224 B7
AYRSHIRE
st. Bossley Park...334 B11
st. Busby............363 K16
wy. Narellan Vale...508 J2
AYRTON
st. Blacktown.......273 J7
AYSHFORD
st. Casula............424 B3
AZALEA
ct. Glenmore Pk...265 G8
gdn. Wahroonga.....223 C6
gr. Castle Hill.......217 F16
gr. Pennant Hills....250 G2
pl. Loftus............489 K9
pl. Mcquarie Fd....453 K6
pl. Panania..........428 E5
st. Blacktown.......274 E12
st. Greystanes......305 H11
AZILE
ct. Carlingford......279 F6
AZTEC
cl. Greenfld Pk.....333 K14
AZZOPARDI
av. Glendenning....242 E5

B

BAANYA
pl. Cranebrook.....207 D15
BAARTZ
tce. Glenwood.......215 H16
BABBAGE
rd. Roseville.........285 D3
rd. Roseville Ch....255 E16
BABBIN
av. Caringbah.......492 F9
BACH
av. Emerton..........240 H6
cl. Cranebrook.....207 D15
pl. Bonnyrigg Ht...363 D7
pl. Engadine.........518 E5
BACHELL
av. Lidcombe..........M K12
av. Lidcombe........340 C6
BACK
cl. Kearns...........451 C16
BACKS
pl. Narellan Vale...478 H15
BADAJOZ
rd. North Ryde.....282 G15
rd. Ryde..............282 G15
BADANA
pl. Cromer...........228 D15
BADARENE
pl. E Lindfield.......255 A11
BADCOE
rd. Cromer...........227 K13
BADDELEY
st. Padstow..........399 B16
BADEN
av. Bass Hill.........368 A6
pl. Blaxland.........233 D3
rd. Neutral Bay........6 J14
st. Coogee...........377 H15
st. Greystanes......306 E10
BADENOCH
av. Glenhaven.......218 B6
BADEN POWELL
av. Kingswood.....237 G15
pl. Lakemba.........401 C4
pl. North Rocks....249 A13
pl. Winston Hills...277 F6
st. Brooklyn..........75 K11
BADGALLY
rd. Blairmount......480 K11
rd. Campbelltwn...511 E1
rd. Claymore........480 K11
rd. Eagle Vale.......480 K11
rd. The Oaks.........502 D13
rd. Woodbine.......481 C15
BADGER
av. Sefton............368 F5
pl. Green Valley....363 A8
BADGERY
av. Homebush......340 J11
wy. Bonnyrigg......364 C4
BADGERYS CREEK
rd. Badgerys Ck...328 G16
rd. Bringelly.........388 B7
BADHAM
av. Mosman.........316 H12
st. Merrylands.....308 C16
st. Woolmloo, off Crown St.........4 D6
BADMINTON
rd. Croydon.........372 B3
BADTO
av. Gymea............491 C4
BAECKEA
pl. Oxford Falls....226 H15
BAGALA
av. Glenwood.......215 H16
BAGDAD
st. Regents Pk.....369 B2
BAGGOT
pl. Baulkham Hl...247 C2
BAGLIN
st. Bronte...........377 H10
BAGO
st. Pendle Hill......276 G12
BAGUETTE
cl. Casula...........394 G16
BAHRI
pl. Glenwood.......245 K4
BAIL
wy. Glenwood.......215 F13
BAILEY
av. Lane Cove W..284 A12
av. West Hoxton..391 G8
cr. N Epping........251 E8
pde. Peakhurst.......430 F1
pl. Blacktown......243 K9
st. Newtown..........17 E13
st. Westmead......307 G1
BAILEYANA
ct. Wattle Grove..426 B1
BAILEYS
la. Kurrajong Hl.....54 J16
BAILLEY
st. Leumeah........512 D1
BAIN
gr. Quakers Hill....214 E15
pl. Barden Rdg....488 H2
pl. Dundas Vy.......280 C9
st. Glenbrook......264 A2
BAINBRIDGE
av. Chipping Ntn..396 B5
av. Ingleburn.......453 A12
cr. Rooty Hill.......271 H4
BAINES
cl. Mulgoa...........324 C5
BAINTON
pl. Doonside........243 E16
rd. Mt Pritchard....364 K9
BAIRD
av. Matraville.......406 H16
av. Ryde.............312 E2
ct. W Pnnant Hl...249 F7
la. Sefton...........368 E6
la. Matraville, off Baird Av.........406 H16
st. Bass Hill.........368 E8
st. Sefton...........368 E8
BAKEHOUSE
pl. The Rocks..........A K5
BAKER
cl. Bossley Park..333 H11
cr. Baulkham Hl...248 A9
la. Bundeena.......524 B10
pl. Lindfield.........284 A1
pl. Minto............453 D15
pl. Penshurst.......431 E2
st. Bnksmeadw....406 B12
st. Blacktown......245 A15
st. Bundeena.......524 A9
st. Carlingford.....279 F5
st. Enfield...........371 J4
st. Galston..........159 E9
st. Kensington......376 B11
st. Merrylands.....307 J16
st. Oatley...........430 H13
st. Springwood....202 D10
st. Windsor.........121 D7
BAKERI
ct. Voyager Pt.....427 B4
BAKERS
la. Forest Lodge....17 J1
la. Kemps Ck.......300 B12
la. Strathfield, off Cooper St........341 F10
la. Earlwood, off Homer St........403 A3
la. St Peters, off Mary St...........374 G14
rd. Church Point..168 G9
BALA
pl. Marayong.......243 K6
BALACLAVA
la. Alexandria........19 A16
rd. Berowra..........133 E10
rd. Eastwood.......281 D6
rd. Emu Heights...235 A2
rd. Mcquarie Pk...281 J3
rd. Marsfield........281 J3
BALAKA
dr. Carlingford.....249 C16
BALALA
ct. Wattle Grove...396 A16
BALANADA
av. Chipping Ntn..396 G6
BALANAMING
la. Petersham........15 G11
BALANDRA
pl. Kareela...........461 E10
BALARANG
pl. Bangor...........459 D10
BALBEEK
av. Blacktown.......243 K11
BALBOA
pl. Willmot...........210 C13
st. Kurnell............465 G8
BALDER
st. Doonside........243 F15
BALDI
av. Panania..........398 C14
BALDINI
pl. Hinchinbrk......393 A3
BALDO
st. Edensor Pk.....333 H12
BALDRY
st. Chatswood.....285 A8
BALDWIN
av. Asquith..........192 B10
av. Glenfield.........424 E10
av. Winston Hills..247 H16
st. Erskineville.......17 K13
st. Gordon...........253 K5
st. Padstow.........429 B1
wy. Currans Hill....479 F12
BALEMO
pl. Bangor...........459 B12
BALFOUR
av. Caringbah.......492 G3
dr. Kellyville.........186 B15
la. Bellevue Hill....347 H14
la. Kensington......376 D10
la. Lindfield..........254 C16
la. Wollstncraft.....315 D8
rd. Bellevue Hill....347 H11
rd. Kensington......376 D12
rd. Narwee...........400 J15
rd. Rose Bay........347 H11
st. Allawah...........432 G8
st. Chippendale......19 B4
st. Dulwich Hill....373 D13
st. Greenwich......314 J6
st. Lindfield..........254 C16
st. Northmead.....277 K12
st. Wollstncraft....315 D8
BALGA
cl. Berowra Ht.....132 H10
BALGANG
av. Kirrawee.........491 B4
BALGOWLAH
rd. Balgowlah.......287 H6
rd. Fairlight..........288 A7
rd. Manly.............288 D6
BALI
dr. Quakers Hill....213 H9
BALIGA
av. Caringbah.......492 E10
BALIMBA
pl. Whalan..........240 K9
BALIMO
pl. Glenfield.........424 G11
BALIN
pl. Blacktown.......274 K7
BALINTORE
dr. Castle Hill.......218 C7
dr. Castle Hill.......218 D8
BALKE
st. Minto.............452 J13

BALL
av. Eastwood....... 281 C6
la. *Colyton, off Ball St............ 270 C3*
pl. Willmot.......... 210 D13
st. Colyton........... 270 C3
BALLAH
ct. S Penrith........ 266 H6
la. *S Penrith, off Ballah Ct......... 266 H6*
BALLA MACHREE
wy. Gymea Bay..... 491 E9
BALLANDA
av. Lugarno......... 430 B15
pl. Bangor........... 459 D12
pl. Dural............. 158 E13
st. Frenchs Frst... 256 D8
BALLANDELLA
rd. Pendle Hill...... 276 E12
rd. Toongabbie.... 276 E12
BALLANTRAE
dr. St Andrews..... 451 K15
BALLANTYNE
rd. Mortdale......... 430 G9
st. Mosman......... 316 K9
BALLAR
av. Gymea Bay..... 491 H9
BALLARAT
av. St Clair........... 270 B10
pl. Cartwright....... 394 B5
pl. St Johns Pk.... 364 H1
BALLARD
pl. Doonside........ 273 E3
BALLAST POINT
rd. Birchgrove.......... 7 J3
BALLATER
wy. Kellyville......... 217 B2
BALLENY
pl. Tregear........... 240 F5
BALLERDO PATH
Winmalee....... 173 C9
BALLINA
av. Killarney Ht..... 286 B1
cl. Hoxton Park... 392 K7
pl. Bangor........... 459 B11
pl. Bossley Park.. 333 F10
st. Georges Hall... 367 J13
st. Greystanes..... 305 H4
BALLS HEAD
dr. Waverton....... 315 D15
rd. Waverton....... 315 D14
BALLYBUNNION
tce. Glenmore Pk.. 266 F8
BALLYLEANEY
pl. Erskine Park... 300 F2
BALLYMENA
st. Hebersham..... 241 F4
wy. Kellyville......... 217 C2
BALLYSHANNON
rd. Killarney Ht..... 255 J13
BALMAIN
pl. Doonside........ 273 E2
rd. Leichhardt........ 10 B14
rd. Leichhardt........ 16 B1
rd. Lilyfield............ 10 B6
rd. Lilyfield............ 10 C5
rd. McGraths Hl... 121 K13
st. Cartwright...... 394 D5
wy. Minto............ 483 A2
BALMARINGA
av. S Turramrra.... 252 B5
BALMORAL
av. Croydon Pk.... 371 K9
av. Mosman......... 317 C7
cct. Cecil Hills....... 362 F4
cr. Georges Hall... 367 H14
dr. Cambrdg Pk.... 237 J9
pl. Carlingford..... 279 C5
rd. Ingleburn....... 453 K15
rd. Kellyville......... 215 J12
rd. Mortdale......... 430 G8
rd. Northmead..... 277 H11
st. Blacktown...... 274 E2
st. Hornsby......... 192 A16
st. Waitara........... 222 A4
BALOG
st. St Marys......... 270 A7
BALOOK
cr. Bradbury........ 511 B16
BALOWRIE
st. Yowie Bay...... 492 C11
BALSON
cl. Abbotsbury.... 333 A15
BALTHASAR
cl. Rsemeadow.... 540 H4
BALTIC
la. Newtown.......... 17 D11
st. Fairlight.......... 288 D7
st. Newtown.......... 17 C11
BALTIMORE
rd. Mortdale......... 430 H9
st. Belfield........... 371 E11
BALYATA
av. Caringbah....... 493 B12
BAMBARA
av. Bradbury........ 541 D1
cr. Beecroft.......... 250 C11
pl. Baulkham Hl... 248 C10
rd. Frenchs Frst.... 256 B1
st. Dharruk.......... 241 C9
BAMBI
cl. Cranebrook..... 207 B10
st. Ryde.............. 282 D15
BAMBIL
pl. Blaxland......... 234 E8
rd. Berowra......... 133 D16
st. Georges Hall... 367 G13
st. Greystanes..... 305 J10
BAMBOO
av. Earlwood........ 403 H3
wy. Stanhpe Gdn... 215 D9
BAMBRA
av. Roselands...... 400 J6
BAMBRIDGE
la. *Riverstone, off Pitt St............. 182 J8*
st. Chester Hill..... 368 B5
BAMENT
pl. Minchinbury... 271 F8
BAMFIELD
av. Yagoona......... 368 F12
BAMFORD
pl. Lalor Park....... 245 G10
BAMPI
pl. Castle Cove..... 286 D5
BAMPTON
av. Illawong......... 459 A7
BANACA
st. S Turramrra.... 252 D6
BANARO
av. Whalan........... 240 K10
BANBAL
rd. Engadine........ 488 H14
BANBURY
cr. Chipping Ntn.. 396 E3
BANCKS
av. Thornleigh...... 221 B10
BANCROFT
av. Roseville........ 284 H4
av. W Pnnant Hl... 220 B15
la. *Roseville, off Bancroft Av..... 284 H4*
rd. Abbotsbury..... 333 B15
st. Oakhurst......... 241 H1
BANDA
pl. Fairfield W...... 335 F9
BANDAIN
av. Kareela.......... 461 C14
BANDALONG
av. West Pymble.. 253 B13
cr. Bangor........... 459 D11
BANDERRA
rd. S Penrith........ 237 B15
BANDO
rd. Cronulla......... 494 A9
rd. Girraween....... 276 C12
BANDON
rd. Vineyard......... 152 F10
BANFF
pl. Winston Hills.. 277 E3
BANGALAY
pl. Leonay........... 234 K14
pl. Mcquarie Fd.... 454 G3
st. Georges Hall... 367 G11
BANGALEE
pl. Bangor........... 459 D11
BANGALLA
av. Bradbury........ 511 F15
av. Chipping Ntn.. 396 F4
pl. Forestville....... 255 H11
rd. Concord W..... 311 D15
rd. Rose Bay........ 348 E12
st. Turramurra..... 222 G9
st. Warrawee....... 222 G9
BANGALLEY
wy. *Avalon, off Barrenjoey Rd. 140 D13*
BANGALOW
av. Beecroft.......... 250 C5
av. Chipping Ntn... 396 G4
av. Mona Vale....... 199 D1
pl. Baulkham Hl... 247 A7
pl. Stanhpe Gdn... 215 B10
BANGAR
cl. Killarney Ht..... 256 A16
BANGAROO
st. Bangor........... 459 D12
st. N Balgowlah.... 287 D6
BANGOR
rd. Glenorie.......... 128 E16
st. Auburn........... 338 J1
st. Guildford........ 337 D4
BANGU
pl. Glenmore Pk... 266 B11
BANJO
cr. Emu Plains...... 235 A8
ct. Castle Hill........ 217 D9
pl. Springwood..... 202 J1
st. Heathcote....... 518 C15
BANJO PATERSON
cl. Glenmore Pk... 265 K5
pl. Padstow Ht..... 429 D7
BANK
la. Kogarah.......... 433 C4
la. McMahons Pt..... 5 B10
la. N Sydney............ 5 B10
st. Lidcombe........ 339 G10
st. McMahons Pt..... 5 B10
st. Meadowbnk.... 311 E4
st. N Sydney............ 5 B10
st. Pyrmont........... 12 C3
st. West Ryde...... 311 E4
BANKS
av. Berrilee........... 131 D9
av. Daceyville....... 406 F8
av. Eastgardens.... 406 E11
av. N Turramrra.... 223 E3
av. Pagewood....... 406 E11
dr. St Clair........... 269 G9
la. Earlwood.......... 403 A4
pl. Camden S....... 507 A11
rd. Busby............ 363 F16
rd. Castle Hill........ 218 E9
rd. Earlwood......... 403 A4
rd. Miller............. 393 E5
st. Ashfield.......... 342 G16
st. Campbelltwn... 511 K6
st. Maroubra........ 407 J9
st. Mays Hill......... 307 H6
st. Monterey........ 433 H6
st. Padstow......... 399 E15
st. Parramatta...... 307 H6
BANKSHILL
cr. Carlingford...... 280 B5
BANKSIA
av. Banksia.......... 403 E12
av. Engadine......... 488 G16
cl. Kings Lngly..... 245 J10
cr. Fairfield E....... 336 J12
dr. Valley Ht......... 202 E5
pl. Arcadia........... 129 G7
pl. Canada Bay..... 342 E8
pl. Greystanes...... 305 F11
pl. Ingleburn........ 453 D8
pl. Kenthurst........ 156 J15
pl. Lugarno.......... 429 H14
pl. Oakdale........... 500 C13
pl. Wattle Grove... 396 B16
rd. Bellevue Hill.... 377 J1
rd. Caringbah....... 492 J6
rd. Caringbah....... 493 A7
rd. Greenacre....... 369 H11
rd. Mt Annan........ 509 D3
st. Botany............ 405 F11
st. Couridjah........ 564 F16
st. Dee Why......... 259 A8
st. Eastwood........ 281 H8
st. Normanhurst.. 221 D12
st. N St Marys...... 240 A10
st. Pagewood....... 405 K10
st. S Granville...... 338 G2
st. Stanhpe Gdn... 215 D10
BANKSIDE
av. Earlwood........ 403 F2
BANN
wy. *Wentwthvle, off Portadown Rd.. 277 D11*
BANNER
rd. Kingsgrove..... 402 A13
BANNERMAN
cr. Rosebery........ 375 K16
rd. Glenhaven....... 187 B12
rd. Kenthurst........ 187 B12
st. Cremorne........... 6 J6
st. Ermington....... 310 D2
st. Mortdale......... 430 G9
BANNISTER
pl. Mt Pritchard.... 364 F12
wy. Wrrngtn Cty.... 238 F4
BANNOCKBURN
av. St Andrews..... 481 J2
la. N Turramrra.... 223 D8
rd. Pymble........... 223 C11
rd. Turramurra..... 223 C11
BANOOL
av. St Ives........... 223 H9
av. S Penrith........ 266 H1
la. *S Penrith, off Banool Av........ 266 H1*
st. Chester Hill..... 338 A16
st. Kareela........... 461 C12
BANQUO
pl. Rsemeadow.... 540 D3
BANTRY BAY
rd. Frenchs Frst.... 256 G10
BANYEENA
pl. Belrose........... 226 C15
BANYULA
pl. Killara............. 253 E15
pl. Mt Colah......... 162 F11
BANYULE
ct. Wattle Grove... 425 K1
BANZ
pl. Glenfield.......... 424 G9
BAPAUME
pde. Matraville........ 407 A16
pl. Milperra.......... 397 H10
rd. Moorebank...... 395 D12
rd. Mosman......... 317 A3
BAPTIST
la. Redfern............ 19 K11
st. Redfern............ 20 A10
BARA
pl. Quakers Hill.... 243 H1
BARABA
cl. Glenmore Pk... 266 D8
BARADINE
pl. Yarrawarrah.... 489 F14
wy. Hoxton Park.... 392 H8
BARAGOOLA
av. Phillip Bay....... 436 J10
st. Fairfield W....... 335 E14
BARALGA
cr. Riverwood...... 400 F11
BARAMBAH
la. Roseville......... 285 C5
rd. Roseville......... 285 C4
BARANA
pde. Roseville Ch.... 255 F16
pl. Kareela........... 461 B12
BARANBALI
av. Seaforth.......... 287 B6
st. Beverly Hills.... 401 E11
st. Doonside........ 243 C14
BARANGAROO
rd. Toongabbie..... 276 D7
BARARA
pl. Fairfield W....... 335 F15
BARASI
pl. Kenthurst........ 157 J6
BARB
pl. Blairmount...... 480 K14
BARBARA
bvd. Seven Hills...... 245 C16
cr. Merrylands...... 307 E14
ct. Mona Vale....... 198 K4
pl. Lugarno.......... 429 K15
st. Fairfield........... 336 E12
BARBARO
la. Horsley Pk...... 332 A2
BARBER
av. Eastlakes........ 405 K3
av. Kingswood...... 237 C12
av. Penrith............ 237 C12
la. Panania........... 398 C16
pl. Glenwood........ 215 D15
BARBERS
rd. Chester Hill..... 337 H10
rd. Guildford......... 337 H10
BARBOUR
rd. Thirlmere........ 565 A5
BARCELONA
dr. Prestons......... 393 K15
BARCHAM
ct. W Pnnant Hl.... 249 A9
BARCLAY
cl. Pymble........... 252 K4
rd. North Rocks.... 249 A14
st. Marrickville..... 374 C14
st. Quakers Hill.... 213 F15
st. Waverley........ 377 H10
BARCOM
av. Darlinghurst....... 4 J12
av. Darlinghurst....... 4 G13
av. Paddington......... 4 G13
st. Merrylnds W.. 307 B14
BARCOO
av. Leumeah........ 482 B15
cl. Erskine Park.... 270 G15
la. *St Clair, off Barcoo Cl........ 270 G15*
pl. St Ives........... 254 D4
st. Peakhurst....... 430 D8
st. Roseville........ 285 C4
BARCOO ISLAND
Sylvania Wtr... 462 F12
BARCOOLA
pl. Bayview.......... 168 C11
BARCOTE
pl. Castle Hill....... 219 A8
BARD
ct. St Clair........... 270 C16
BARDEN
la. Randwick....... 377 A11
rd. Barden Rdg.... 458 G16
st. Arncliffe......... 403 F8
st. Northmead..... 277 J12
st. Tempe............ 404 C3
BARDIA
ct. Mt Annan....... 479 C11
pde. Holsworthy..... 396 D16
pl. Bossley Park.. 334 B5
pl. E Lindfield...... 254 K10
rd. Carlingford..... 249 K13
BARDO
rd. Newport......... 169 E11
st. Glenmore Pk.. 266 D7
BARDOLPH
av. Rsemeadow... 540 G8
BARDON
cl. St Johns Pk..... 334 F16
BARDOO
av. N Balgowlah... 287 C4
BARDSLEY
cct. Rouse Hill....... 184 J6
gdn. N Sydney........ 315 J7
BARDWELL
cr. Earlwood........ 402 G5
la. *Mosman, off Holt Av............ 316 J9*
rd. Bardwell Pk.... 402 J7
rd. Bardwell Vy.... 403 A7
rd. Mosman......... 316 J8
wky. *Bardwell Pk, off Crewe St......... 402 J6*
BARE
av. Lurnea........... 394 D7
st. Bnksmeadw.... 346 C1
BAREE
pl. Warriewood.... 199 B8
BAREENA
av. Wahroonga.... 222 D4
dr. Balgowlah Ht.. 287 H14
pl. Hamondvle..... 396 E14
pl. Marsfield......... 251 J14
rd. Avalon........... 140 E13
st. Cabramatta..... 366 B5
st. Canley Vale..... 366 B5
st. Lilli Pilli.......... 522 E4
st. Strathfield....... 340 K16
wk. Wahroonga.... 222 E5
BARELLAN
av. Carlingford..... 280 C2
av. Turramurra..... 252 F1
st. Merrylands..... 306 J10
BARFF
rd. Camperdwn...... 18 E2
rd. Ingleburn....... 453 A10
BARFIL
cr. S Wntwthvle... 306 J4
BARGAROO
av. Glenmore Pk.. 266 H15
BARGO
pl. Prestons......... 392 K16
rd. Bargo............. 567 F7
st. Maianbar........ 523 B7
BARGO RIVER
rd. Couridjah....... 564 E16
rd. Couridjah....... 565 A16

rd. Couridjah 565 E16
rd. Tahmoor 565 E16
BARHAM
st. Heckenberg 364 A12
st. Maianbar 523 B7
st. Parramatta 278 J15
BARILLA
pl. Bonnyrigg Ht 362 K6
st. Bonnyrigg Ht 363 A5
BARINA
cr. Emu Plains 234 K8
pl. Blaxland 234 D5
rd. Riverview 314 C5
BARINA DOWNS
rd. Baulkham Hl 246 G1
rd. Bella Vista 246 G1
BARINGA
av. Seaforth 287 B6
cl. Belrose 225 K11
cl. Green Valley 363 H11
rd. Earlwood 402 D4
rd. Engadine 488 H16
rd. Mortdale 430 G9
rd. Northbridge 285 J16
st. Berowra Ht 133 B10
st. Blaxland 233 F5
st. North Ryde 282 E8
BARISTON
av. Cremorne 316 G5
BARITE
pl. Eagle Vale 481 F6
BARJADDA
av. Sylvania 462 B11
BARK
pl. Kings Lngly 245 E8
BARKALA
pl. Westleigh 220 G4
BARKDUK
av. Miranda 491 J5
BARKER
av. Silverwater 309 J15
cl. Camden S 506 K10
dr. Castle Hill 218 J13
la. Lewisham 15 C8
la. Kingsford, off Houston Rd 376 F16
pl. Leumeah 482 D16
rd. Strathfield 341 A14
st. Bossley Park 334 C11
st. Cambrdg Pk 237 F7
st. Kensington 376 E16
st. Kingsford 376 E16
st. Lewisham 15 B8
st. Randwick 376 E16
st. Rooty Hill 272 D2
st. St Marys 269 E5
BARKERS LODGE
rd. Mowbray Pk 562 E1
rd. Oakdale 500 C16
rd. Picton 563 A2
BARKL
av. Padstow 429 C1
BARKLEY
cl. Cherrybrook 219 C14
st. Carramar 366 J1
BARKLY
cl. Bonnyrigg Ht 363 G5
dr. Windsor Dn 180 G1
BARLEY
gln. Wrrngtn Dns 238 B5
BARLOW
cr. Canley Ht 364 K3
pl. Georges Hall 367 J12
pl. Horngsea Pk 392 C15
st. Cambrdg Pk 237 J6
st. Haymarket E F10
st. Haymarket 3 F13
BARNABY
pl. Ambarvale 510 K15
BARNARD
cr. Oakhurst 241 H4
pl. St Helens Pk 541 A8
BARNARDO
cl. Wahroonga 221 K10
BARNARDS
av. Hurstville 401 J16
BARNCLEUTH
la. Potts Point 4 K6
sq. Elizabeth Bay 13 A6
sq. Potts Point 13 A6
BARNES
av. Earlwood 372 F16
cr. Menai 458 D10
la. Blacktown 274 D6
pl. Rouse Hill 184 K7
rd. Frenchs Frst 257 B3
rd. Llandilo 179 G15
st. Girraween 276 B10
st. Lidcombe 339 J11
st. Minto 453 C16
BARNET
av. Rookwood 340 A12
pl. Doonside 273 H2
st. Glenbrook 234 C15
BARNETT
la. Bondi Jctn 377 H2
la. Darlinghurst 4 D8
la. S Penrith, off Barnett St 266 F3
pl. Cabramtta W 365 C6
st. Ashcroft 394 F2
st. S Penrith 266 F3
BARNETTS
rd. Berowra Ht 133 A10
rd. Winston Hills 277 C4
BARNEY
pl. Davidson 225 C15
st. Drummoyne 343 F5
st. N Parramatta 278 B11
BARNFIELD
pl. Dean Park 212 K16
BARNIER
dr. Quakers Hill 214 B8
BARNSBURY
gr. Bardwell Pk 402 H8
gr. Bexley North 402 F10
gr. Dulwich Hill 373 F10
BARNSLEY
pl. Menai 458 J14
BARNSTAPLE
la. Five Dock 343 A8
rd. Five Dock 343 A9
rd. Rodd Point 343 A9
rd. Russell Lea 343 A9
BARNWELL
pl. Cecil Hills 362 G3
BARODA
la. Elizabeth Bay 13 A5
st. Elizabeth Bay 13 A5
BAROMBAH
rd. Epping 250 J12
BARON
cl. Kings Lngly 245 D6
BARONBALI
st. Dundas 279 H13
BARONESA
la. S Penrith, off Baronesa Rd 237 C16
rd. S Penrith 237 B16
BARONGA
av. Queens Park 22 E14
BARONS
av. Carlingford 279 D5
cr. Hunters Hill 313 D4
BARONTA
st. Blacktown 275 A2
BAROO
st. Thirlmere 565 C5
BAROOGA
av. Bradbury 511 F16
BAROOK
pl. Mt Pritchard 364 D9
BAROONA
pl. Seven Hills 246 B13
rd. Northbridge 315 J1
st. Church Point 168 F8
st. Dangar I 76 J7
BAROSSA
cl. St Clair 270 D12
ct. Baulkham Hl 246 H4
dr. Minchinbury 271 J9
pl. Edensor Pk 333 D16
pl. Mona Vale 199 B5
BARR
st. Balmain 7 C9
st. Camperdwn 17 G1
st. Colyton 270 F8
st. Mortdale 430 J8
st. North Ryde 282 H7
BARRABA
pl. Bella Vista 246 F8
BARRABOOKA
st. Clontarf 287 H16
BARRA-BRUI
cr. St Ives 254 C3
BARRACE
rd. Mosman, off Middle Head Rd 317 F10
BARRACK
cct. Mcquarie Lk 423 E14
la. Parramatta 308 D3
la. Sydney C G2
st. Sydney C F2
st. Sydney 3 G1
BARRACKS
st. Emu Plains 235 C10
BARRACLOUGH
wy. Bonnyrigg 364 B4
BARRACLUFF
av. Bondi Beach 378 A2
BARRAGIL
mw. Mt Annan 479 H16
BARRAKEE
pl. Westleigh 220 G3
BARRALLIER
wy. St Clair 270 E11
BARRARAN
st. Gymea Bay 491 E11
BARRATT
av. Camden S 507 B13
st. Hurstville 432 A5
wy. Minto 482 K1
BARRATTA
pl. Bangor 459 C11
BARRAWARN
pl. Castle Hill 218 B12
BARRAWINGA
st. Telopea 279 G8
BARRE
st. Hurlstone Pk 373 A11
BARREMMA
rd. Lakemba 371 B14
BARREN
cl. Green Valley 363 A12
BARRENJOEY
cl. Woodbine 481 H11
rd. Avalon 140 C10
rd. Bilgola 170 A5
rd. Mona Vale 199 E4
rd. Newport 169 H16
rd. Palm Beach 139 H2
BARRETT
av. Thornleigh 220 J11
pl. Cranebrook 207 F8
pl. Randwick 377 E10
st. Guildford 337 G3
BARRIE
pl. Davidson 255 D1
pl. Leumeah 512 C3
st. East Killara 255 A8
BARRIER
cl. Casula 424 C1
pl. Illawong 459 H3
st. Homebush B M A6
BARRIGON
gr. Menai 458 J14
BARRINGTON
ct. Holsworthy 426 E5
dr. Dural 219 C4
pl. Carlingford 279 E2
rd. Silverdale 384 A4
st. Bossley Park 334 C9
st. Ruse 512 F5
BARRON
pl. Bossley Park 333 G5
BARRON FIELD
dr. Glenmore Pk 265 H5
BARROW
cl. Green Valley 363 B12
pl. Silverdale 353 H16
st. Revesby 399 A15
BARRY
av. Catherine Fd 419 C2
av. Mortdale 430 G6
av. Rossmore 419 C2
cr. Padstow Ht 429 G7
la. Neutral Bay 6 G3
pl. Bidwill 211 C16
pl. Cherrybrook 219 F16
pl. Wentwthvle 307 C3
rd. Chipping Ntn 366 J16
rd. Kellyville 185 J7
rd. Menai 458 G13
st. Cambrdg Pk 237 G9
st. Clovelly 377 G12
st. Neutral Bay 6 F4
BARRY COE
pl. Cranebrook 207 G10
BARSBY
av. Allawah 432 F7
BARSDEN
st. Camden 506 K1
BARSEDEN
st. Bonnyrigg 364 D4
BARTIL
cl. Epping 251 E14
BARTLETT
la. Paddington 20 G1
st. Ermington 280 B14
st. S Wntwthvle 307 B7
st. Summer Hill 373 C6
BARTLEY
la. Chippendale 19 B3
st. Cabramatta 365 H5
st. Canley Vale 365 H5
st. Chippendale 19 B4
BARTOK
gr. St Clair 300 B1
pl. Bonnyrigg Ht 363 D5
BARTON
av. Haberfield 343 E14
av. Hurlstone Pk 373 A11
av. W Pnnant Hl 249 A8
cr. N Wahrnga 222 G1
rd. Artarmon 285 A16
st. Concord 342 A1
st. Ermington 310 E1
st. Kogarah 433 D8
st. Marsden Pk 181 K13
st. Monterey 433 D8
st. N Parramatta 278 K14
st. Smithfield 336 A8
st. Strathfield S 371 C5
BARUDA
pl. Erskine Park 270 F16
BARUNGA
st. Concord W 311 F15
BARWELL
av. Castle Hill 218 B15
BARWING
pl. Woronora Ht 489 F4
BARWON
av. Homebush B M A6
av. S Turramrra 251 K5
cr. Matraville 436 K2
ct. Wattle Grove 395 J12
pl. Campbelltwn 512 A7
pl. Sylvania Wtr 462 E10
rd. Lane Cove W 313 J1
rd. Mortdale 430 H9
st. Greystanes 306 C5
BARWON PARK
rd. Alexandria 374 J12
rd. St Peters 374 J12
BARWOOD
cl. Westleigh 220 G2
BASIL
rd. Bexley 432 C1
st. Riverwood 399 J16
BASILDON
pl. Hebersham 241 F6
rd. Canley Ht 365 B4
BASILISK
pl. Whalan 240 J9
BASINGSTOKE
pl. Hebersham 241 F5
BASS
av. East Hills 427 G3
cl. Hinchinbrk 363 B16
dr. Baulkham Hl 247 B11
pl. Camden S 506 J13
pl. Mt Colah 162 C11
pl. Ruse 512 F3
pl. St Ives 224 A8
pl. Willmot 210 B12
rd. Earlwood 403 B1
rd. Ingleburn 423 A10
rd. Lansvale 367 B10
st. Colyton 270 E8
st. Ermington 280 C15
st. Kingsford 406 K4
st. Port Hacking 522 J2
st. Putney 312 D7
BASSELL
la. Seven Hills 245 G16
BASSETT
pl. Castle Hill 218 J11
pl. Menai 458 H13
st. Hurstville 431 E1
st. Mona Vale 199 D1
BASSIA
pl. Alfords Point 428 K13
BASTABLE
st. Croydon 372 F1
BASTILLE
cl. Padstow Ht 429 H7
BATAAN
cl. Illawong 459 J4
pl. Kings Park 244 K3
pl. Lethbrdg Pk 210 K16
BATAVIA
pl. Baulkham Hl 246 G6
pl. Illawong 459 F5
pl. Willmot 210 E14
BATCHELOR
av. Panania 398 A16
cl. Menai 458 H15
BATE
av. Allambie Ht 257 G16
BATE BAY
rd. Cronulla 494 B6
BATEHAVEN
cl. Prestons 392 K13
BATEMAN
cr. Bass Hill 367 F8
pl. Bligh Park 150 C6
BATEMANS
rd. Gladesville 312 K11
BATES
av. Blaxland 233 F9
av. Paddington 13 B13
av. S Wntwthvle 306 H7
cl. Elderslie 507 J4
dr. Kareela 461 B11
dr. Kareela 461 C14
dr. Kirrawee 461 D14
pl. Doonside 273 H1
pl. Edensor Pk 333 J14
st. Birchgrove 7 J3
st. Homebush 340 K9
st. Strathfield 340 K9
wy. Ambarvale 540 K1
BATH
la. Avalon 170 C2
rd. Kareela 461 B14
rd. Kirrawee 491 B3
rd.s, Kirrawee 491 A6
st. Monterey 433 H7
BATHO
st. Harbord 258 J15
BATHURST
la. Woollahra 22 H3
st. Berala 339 E13
st. Greystanes 305 J3
st. Gymea 461 G16
st. Leumeah 512 C3
st. Liverpool 395 C4
st. Liverpool 395 D1
st. Pitt Town 92 H15
st. Sydney C D14
st. Sydney 3 E7
st. Wakeley 334 H13
st. Warwck Frm 365 D16
st. Woollahra 22 H3
BATLOW
pl. Bossley Park 333 E13
st. Heckenberg 364 A13
BATMAN
cr. Springwood 202 C11
la. Surry Hills F E11
pl. St Johns Pk 364 G1
rd. Ingleburn 422 J14
wk. Parramatta, off Macquarie St 308 D3
BATT
st. Jamisontown 266 D1
st. Penrith 266 D1
st. Sefton 368 E5
BATTEN
av. Melrose Pk 310 J1
cct. S Windsor 150 F1
cr. Ermington 280 A15
pl. Doonside 273 H1
BATTENBERG
cl. Cecil Hills 362 D5
BATTERSEA
st. Abbotsford 312 H16
BATTERY
rd. Mosman 317 K6
st. Clovelly 377 J13
BATTLE
bvd. Seaforth 287 B11
BATTLEMENT
cr. Castle Hill 217 F3
BATTUNGA
pl. Engadine 489 D10

BATTY
st. Rozelle 7 F14
BATTYE
av. Beverley Pk 433 B8
BAUDIN
cl. Illawong 459 C4
cr. Fairfield W 335 D11
pl. Willmot 210 A11
BAUER
ct. Mt Annan 509 G3
rd. Cabramatta W 365 B9
BAULKHAM HILLS
rd. Baulkham Hl 247 A12
BAUMANS
rd. Peakhurst 430 G1
rd. Riverwood 400 F15
BAUXITE
pl. Eagle Vale 481 D8
BAVIN
av. Ryde 282 B16
BAX
gln. St Clair 300 B2
BAXTER
av. Kogarah 433 D3
av. Springwood 202 C1
cr. Glendenning 242 H6
dr. Old Tngabbie 277 A5
la. Kogarah 433 D3
la. Picton 563 H5
rd. Bass Hill 367 F6
rd. Mascot 405 B5
st. S Penrith 237 A15
BAY
la. Cronulla 523 H1
la. Ultimo 12 H14
pde. Malabar 437 F4
pl. Quakers Hill 243 K1
rd. Arcadia 130 F9
rd. Berowra Wtr 132 A6
rd. Berrilee 132 A6
rd. N Sydney K A1
rd. N Sydney 5 A6
rd. Oatley 430 G11
rd. Russell Lea 343 D3
rd. Taren Point 462 J15
rd. Waverton 5 A6
st. Birchgrove 7 H4
st. Birchgrove 7 H5
st. Botany 405 F11
st. Btn-le-Sds 433 G1
st. Coogee 407 F2
st. Croydon 342 F12
st. Double Bay 14 C10
st. Glebe 12 H13
st. Greenwich 314 J10
st. Mosman 316 K3
st. North Bondi 378 G3
st. Pagewood 405 J10
st. Rockdale 403 D15
st. Ryde 312 D3
st. Tempe 404 A3
st. Ultimo 12 H13
vst. Lilli Pilli 522 G1
BAYAN
pl. Bargo 567 E13
BAYARD
la. Concord, off Bayard St 312 A15
st. Concord 312 A15
st. Mortlake 312 A15
BAYBERRY
wy. Castle Hill 218 G16
BAYDON
st. Castle Hill 219 A8
BAYFIELD
rd. Arcadia 159 H2
rd. Galston 159 H2
rd. Galston 159 H7
rd. Greystanes 306 B11
BAYHAVEN
pl. Gymea Bay 491 H12
BAYLDON
pl. Glenmore Pk 266 A6
BAYLEY
rd. S Penrith 267 A6
st. Marrickville 373 E13
BAYLIS
pl. N Richmond 86 K13
BAYLY
ct. Richmond 118 H7
st. Minchinbury 272 G9
BAYNES
st. Mount Druitt 271 A2
BAYNTON
pl. St Helens Pk 541 A6
BAYSIDE
dr. Lugarno 430 B14
pl. Caringbah 492 E10
st. Lilyfield 9 G6
BAYSWATER
av. Hurstville Gr 431 G11
rd. Darlinghurst 13 B9
rd. Lindfield 284 D4
rd. Potts Point 4 J8
rd. Rcutters Bay 13 B9
st. Drummoyne 343 H1
st. St Johns Pk 364 C3
BAYTON
st. Oxley Park 270 D2
BAY VIEW
st. Lavender Bay 5 F14
BAYVIEW
av. Earlwood 403 C2
av. Mosman 317 D8
cr. Annandale 11 B6
cr. Henley 313 C14
la. Annandale 11 B6
la. Earlwood, off Bayview St 403 E2
pl. Bayview 169 B14
pl. Frenchs Frst 256 J5
rd. Canada Bay 342 E10
rd. Peakhurst 430 D11
rd. Woolooware 493 D13
st. Arncliffe 403 D10
st. Bexley 402 J11
st. Bronte 378 A8
st. Concord 342 B3
st. Glebe 12 C10
st. Kogarah Bay 432 K12
st. Mt Krng-gai 163 B10
st. Northwood 314 G7
st. Pyrmont 8 G15
st. Scotland I 168 H4
st. Tennyson 312 D9
BAYVIEW HILL
la. Rose Bay 348 A7
rd. Rose Bay 348 B7
BAYVILLE
st. Balmain 344 E5
BAYWATER
dr. Homebush B L D4
dr. Homebush B 310 J8
BAZENTIN
st. Belfield 371 B11
BEACH
av. Vaucluse 318 G16
la. Coogee 377 H14
la. Emu Plains, off Beach St 235 F13
la. Mosman, off Military Rd 317 B6
rd. Bondi Beach 378 C1
rd. Collaroy 229 D14
rd. Dulwich Hill 373 E10
rd. Newport 169 H15
rd. North Bondi 348 B16
rd. Palm Beach 109 K14
st. Blakehurst 462 F1
st. Bundeena 524 A9
st. Clovelly 377 H15
st. Coogee 377 H15
st. Coogee 407 H2
st. Cronulla 524 A2
st. Curl Curl 258 J15
st. Double Bay 14 D7
st. Emu Plains 235 F13
st. Kogarah 433 D2
st. Tennyson 312 D10
BEACHCOMBER
av. Bundeena 524 A11
pl. Chipping Ntn 366 K15
BEACH PARK
av. Cronulla 493 K13
BEACHVIEW
pl. Brookvale 257 H10
BEACON
av. Beacon Hill 257 J8
av. Glenhaven 217 J3
av. Ryde 311 K5
BEACON HILL
rd. Beacon Hill 257 J7
rd. Brookvale 257 J7
BEACONIA
cl. Mona Vale 169 D16
BEACONSFIELD
av. Concord 342 A6
av. Kingsgrove 402 B7
la. Concord, off Beaconsfield Av 342 A6
la. Alexandria, off Beaconsfield St 375 F14
la. Beaconsfield, off Beaconsfield St 375 G13
pde. Lindfield 284 C1
rd. Chatswd W 284 A11
rd. Chatswd W 284 C12
rd. Lane Cove W 284 A11
rd. Lane Cove W 284 C12
rd. Mortdale 430 H9
rd. Mosman 317 E9
rd. Rooty Hill 272 C5
rd. Rooty Hill 272 C7
st. Alexandria 375 F13
st. Beaconsfield 375 F13
st. Bexley 403 A16
st. Milperra 398 B12
st. Newport 169 F13
st. Revesby 398 B12
st. Silverwater 309 F13
BEACONVIEW
st. Balgowlah Ht 287 K14
BEACROFT
pl. Cranebrook 207 D13
BEAGLE
pl. Willmot 210 B12
BEAHAN
pl. Cherrybrook 219 K13
BEAL
pl. Glenmore Pk 266 A6
BEALE
cr. Fairfield W 335 C13
cr. Peakhurst 430 E6
st. Georges Hall 367 D15
st. Liverpool 395 B4
BEAMES
av. Mount Druitt 241 C16
av. Rooty Hill 272 B1
st. Lilyfield 10 C9
BEAMISH
la. Campsie 372 A13
rd. Northmead 277 J11
st. Campsie 372 A11
st. Padstow 399 D12
BEAN
pl. Bonnyrigg 364 C6
BEARD
pl. Glenorie 128 C14
BEARING
rd. Seven Hills 276 E1
BEASLEY
pl. S Windsor 150 K2
BEATHAM
pl. Milperra 397 G10
BEATRICE
cl. Berowra Ht 133 A7
st. Ashfield 372 F2
st. Auburn 339 C4
st. Balgowlah Ht 287 F14
st. Bass Hill 367 K7
st. Cecil Hills 362 K3
st. Clontarf 287 F14
st. Hurstville 431 H1
st. Lane Cove W 313 G2
st. Lidcombe 339 G12
st. North Ryde 282 H8
st. Rooty Hill 242 A13
BEATSON
la. Kingswood 237 D16
BEATTIE
av. Denistone E 281 J12
la. Surry Hills 19 H1
st. Balmain 7 F10
st. Rozelle 7 A12
BEATTY
la. Maroubra 407 C11
pde. Georges Hall 367 D13
st. Balgowlah Ht 288 A12
st. Maroubra 407 C11
st. Mortdale 430 H8
st. St Marys 270 A6
BEAU
ct. Quakers Hill 213 H7
BEAUCHAMP
av. Chatswood 284 K7
la. Surry Hills F D11
rd. Bnksmeadw 436 D2
rd. Hillsdale 406 F16
rd. Maroubra 407 C14
rd. Matraville 406 F16
st. Marrickville 373 E14
st. Wiley Park 400 G4
BEAUFIGHTER
st. Raby 451 F16
BEAUFORD
av. Caringbah 492 E15
BEAUFORT
pl. Chullora 370 C4
rd. Blacktown 275 B7
st. Croydon Pk 372 B6
st. Guildford 337 E3
st. Northmead 277 J11
BEAUMARIS
av. Castle Hill 217 B9
cr. Mortdale 430 G10
dr. Menai 458 H9
st. Enfield 371 G3
BEAUMETZ
wy. Matraville 407 A16
BEAUMOND
av. Maroubra 407 J10
BEAUMONT
av. Denistone 281 A12
av. Glenwood 215 H13
av. N Richmond 87 F13
cr. Bayview 169 A15
dr. Kellyville 185 J14
pl. Castle Hill 248 A3
rd. Killara 253 E15
rd. Mt Krng-gai 162 G3
st. Auburn 338 K8
st. Campsie 371 J16
st. Kingsgrove 402 B9
st. Rose Bay 348 D12
st. Smithfield 335 B5
st. Waterloo 19 G12
BEAUMOUNT
st. Chippendale 18 J4
BEAUTY
dr. Whale Beach 140 C9
BEAUTY POINT
cr. Leonay 264 K2
rd. Mosman 287 A15
BEAVORS
st. Prairiewood 334 J9
BEAZLEY
pl. Baulkham Hl 246 K14
st. Ryde 312 E3
BEBE
av. Revesby 428 J2
la. Revesby 428 J2
BECHARRY
rd. Blacktown 243 K11
BECK
rd. Old Tngabbie 276 K10
st. N Epping 251 J10
BECKE
ct. Glenmore Pk 265 K9
BECKENHAM
st. Canley Vale 366 F4
BECKET
ct. S Penrith 266 K4
BECKHAUS
st. St Johns Pk 364 J2
BECKMAN
pde. Frenchs Frst 255 G1
pl. Tennyson 58 B9
BECKTON
pl. Lilli Pilli 522 F2
BECKY
av. North Rocks 279 A1
BECQUEREL
pl. Lucas Ht 487 F13
BEDDEK
st. McGraths Hl 121 H11
BEDDINGTON
ct. Wattle Grove 426 C5
BEDE
st. Lidcombe 339 H9
st. Strathfield S 371 A4
BEDERVALE
ct. Wattle Grove 426 A1
BEDFORD
av. N Turramrra 223 F8
cr. Collaroy 229 B16
cr. Dulwich Hill 373 E13
la. Newtown 17 B10
pl. Rockdale 403 H15
pl. S Coogee 407 H6
pl. Sylvania 462 A11
rd. Blacktown 244 K11
rd. Homebsh W 340 K6
rd. N Epping 251 H11
st. Earlwood 402 G2
st. Emu Plains 234 K11
st. Newtown 17 B11
st. N Willghby 285 F8
st. Surry Hills 19 G3
BEDIVERE
st. Blacktown 274 K7
BEDLEY
pl. Cranebrook 207 E14
BEDNAL
rd. Springwood 201 G2
BEDWIN
rd. Marrickville 374 G12
rd. St Peters 374 G12
BEECH
pl. Lugarno 429 J14
pl. Mcquarie Fd 454 G1
rd. Casula 423 J3
rd. Prestons 393 J16
rd. Prestons 393 J15
st. Quakers Hill 243 F5
BEECHCRAFT
av. Raby 451 F15
BEECHWOOD
av. Greystanes 306 F11
pde. Cherrybrook 219 G8
pl. Bass Hill 367 J8
BEECHWORTH
pl. Mt Colah 162 F14
rd. Pymble 253 A2
BEECROFT
rd. Beecroft 250 D3
rd. Cheltenham 251 A12
rd. Epping 251 A12
rd. Pennant Hills 250 D3
rd. Wilberforce 62 A14
BEE FARM
rd. Springwood 201 G9
BEEF CATTLE
rd. Richmond 118 J13
rd. Richmond 119 A14
BEEHAG
av. Arncliffe 403 E11
st. Kyeemagh 404 B13
BEELAR
st. Canley Ht 365 B1
BEELONG
st. Dharruk 241 A6
BEEMERA
st. Fairfield Ht 335 H10
BEEMRA
st. Auburn 309 C15
BEERSHEBA
pde. Holsworthy 426 D11
BEESON
st. Leichhardt 15 B4
BEETHOVEN
pl. Cranebrook 207 H9
st. Engadine 518 D5
st. Seven Hills 246 D12
BEGA
av. Little Bay 437 B11
cl. Prestons 393 A13
pl. Bossley Park 333 G9
pl. Georges Hall 367 J11
rd. Jannali 460 H10
rd. Northbridge 286 B15
st. Marayong 243 J7
st. Pendle Hill 276 C16
st. St Marys 269 K5
BEGG
la. Paddington 13 B15
BEGGS
rd. Eastern Ck 272 G6
st. Roselands 400 K10
BEGONIA
av. Cabramatta 365 G11
ct. Glenmore Pk 265 H8
pl. Mcquarie Fd 454 A7
pl. Woolooware 493 D9
rd. Normanhurst 221 D13
st. Pagewood 405 K10
BEGOVICH
cr. Abbotsbury 333 A15
BEIHLER
la. Ryde 282 A14
BELAH
av. Vaucluse 348 H1
gdn. Vaucluse 318 H16
pl. Mcquarie Fd 424 E16
BEL-AIR
rd. Penrith 237 B7
BELAIR
av. Caringbah 493 B10
cl. Hornsby 191 K15
pl. Bayview 169 A15
pl. Mt Krng-gai 163 B10

pl. Prairiewood....334 F7
st. Bow Bowing....452 D14
st. Punchbowl.....400 A7
BELAR
av. Villawood........367 C4
av. Villawood........367 E5
rd. Camden..........507 A8
st. St Marys.........239 G14
BELARADA
cl. Bangor...........459 B11
BELBOWRIE
cl. Bangor...........459 C10
cl. Galston...........159 G13
gln. St Clair...........270 B16
BELCOTE
rd. Longueville.....314 C10
BELEMBA
av. Roselands......401 B5
BELFAST
pl. Killarney Ht.....286 B1
BELFIELD
la. Belfield...........371 D9
rd. Bossley Park...333 F13
rd. Edensor Pk.....333 G13
BELFORD
pl. Greenacre.......369 K10
st. Ingleburn........453 A9
BELGENNY
av. Camden..........507 B6
BELGIAN
st. Westmead......307 J3
BELGICA
st. Tregear...........240 D5
BELGIUM
av. Roseville.........284 G2
st. Auburn...........338 J10
st. Lidcombe.......340 B5
st. Riverwood......400 B11
BELGRAVE
esp. Sylvania..........462 E8
esp. Sylvania Wtr...462 C11
la. Bronte............377 J7
la. Cremorne, off Ben Boyd La....316 D8
la. Neutral Bay, off Ben Boyd La....316 D8
st. Bronte............377 J6
st. Burwood.........341 H16
st. Cremorne.......316 D8
st. Kogarah..........433 B5
st. Manly.............288 G10
st. Petersham........15 J13
BELIMLA
st. Auburn...........309 C16
BELINDA
cr. Glenwood.......245 E2
cr. N Epping........251 B9
ct. Castle Hill.......217 C10
pl. Mays Hill.........307 F6
pl. Newport..........169 G9
rd. Alfords Point...459 C2
st. Bass Hill.........367 H8
BELL
av. Beverly Hills....400 H16
av. Kogarah Bay...432 J12
av. Lindfield.........283 H2
av. Richmond.......118 B8
av. West Ryde......280 G13
cr. Fairfield..........336 H11
cr. Leumeah.........512 E1
la. Glebe.................11 J10
la. Randwick.......377 A13
pl. Burraneer.......523 E3
pl. Moorebank.....396 E10
pl. Mt Pritchard...364 J11
rd. Londonderry...148 F9
st. Concord.........341 H8
st. Glebe................11 H11
st. Gordon..........254 B7
st. Hornsby.........191 J11
st. Maroubra.......407 E9
st. Panania.........428 D4
st. Riverwood......400 A10
st. S Windsor.......120 J12
st. Thirlmere........565 A5
st. Toongabbie....276 H5
st. Vaucluse.........318 G16
BELLA
pl. Barden Rdg....488 H1
st. Randwick........377 E9
BELLAMBI
pl. Cartwright.......394 E4
st. Northbridge....285 K15
BELLAMY
av. Eastwood.......281 F4
la. Eastwood, off Bellamy Av......281 F4
st. Pennant Hills...220 D16
BELLAMY FARM
rd. W Pnnant Hl...249 E7
BELLARA
av. N Narrabeen....198 G15
BELLATA
ct. Glenbrook.......264 D2
pl. Hinchinbrk......392 J4
BELLATRIX
la. Cranebrook, off Bellatrix St......207 D5
st. Cranebrook......207 E5
BELLA VISTA
dr. Bella Vista.......246 E3
st. Heathcote.......518 D11
BELLBIRD
av. Kurrajong Ht.....54 B14
cl. Canada Bay.....342 E8
cr. Blaxland..........234 B7
cr. Bowen Mtn.......83 K9
cr. Forestville.......255 K12
ct. Quakers Hill....213 J10
dr. W Pnnant Hl...249 D7
pl. Cartwright.......394 D4
pl. Kareela...........461 C13
rd. Wedderburn....540 A11
st. Canterbury......402 D2
BELLBROOK
av. Emu Plains.....235 G9
av. Hornsby..........191 J16
BELLE ANGELA
dr. Theresa Park...444 H8
BELLEDALE
cl. St Clair............270 E14
BELLENDEN
pl. Dural..............219 B2
BELLEREEVE
av. Mt Riverview...234 B4
BELLEREVE
pl. Leonay............234 J13
BELLETTE
cl. Abbotsbury.....333 A13
BELLEVALE
ct. Stanhpe Gdn...215 G9
BELLEVARDE
pde. Mona Vale.......199 F1
BELLEVERDE
av. Strathfield.......371 B4
BELLEVISTA
st. Blacktown.......274 B3
BELLEVUE
av. Avalon............170 A3
av. Denistone.......281 A11
av. Georges Hall...367 K13
av. Greenwich......315 A6
av. Lakemba.........400 K1
av. Paddington.......13 A16
av. West Ryde......281 B14
cl. Rossmore........389 G5
ct. Arncliffe..........403 H10
dr. Carlingford......249 D14
gdn. Bellevue Hill, off Kendall St.........377 G2
la. Arncliffe..........403 H11
la. Glebe................12 E10
la. Hurstville........432 C7
la. Surry Hills..........F E15
la. West Ryde, off Dickson Av.......281 C15
pde. Allawah.........432 C7
pde. Caringbah......493 A6
pde. Carlton...........432 E9
pde. Hurstville........432 C7
pde. N Curl Curl......258 J9
pl. N Curl Curl.......258 K9
rd. Bellevue Hill......14 F10
rd. Regentville......235 E16
st. Arncliffe..........403 H11
st. Blacktown.......274 B4
st. Cammeray.......315 K5
st. Chatswd W......284 B10
st. Fairlight...........288 C9
st. Glebe................12 E10
st. Kogarah..........433 A6
st. Maroubra........407 H10
st. N Parramatta...278 D12
st. Riverstone.......183 C6
st. St Peters.........374 E16
st. Surry Hills..........F E16
st. Surry Hills...........3 K16
st. Tempe............404 E1
st. Thornleigh......221 A14
BELLEVUE PARK
rd. Bellevue Hill....377 H1
BELLFIELD
av. Rossmore.......389 D11
BELLINGARA
rd. Miranda..........461 K16
rd. Sylvania..........462 B13
BELLINGEN
wy. Hoxton Park....392 H8
BELLINGER
cl. Narellan Vale...478 G15
pl. Sylvania Wtr....462 F15
rd. Ruse..............512 C8
BELLINGHAM
av. Glendenning....242 F3
st. Narellan..........478 D8
BELLINI
la. St Clair, off Bellini Pl..........300 A2
pl. St Clair............300 B2
BELLOC
cl. Wetherill Pk.....334 E5
pl. Winston Hills...247 G16
BELLOMBI
st. Campsie..........372 D12
BELLONA
av. Homebush......341 A5
av. Regents Pk.....368 H1
st. Winston Hills...277 A2
BELLOTTI
av. Winston Hills...277 F1
BELLS
av. Cammeray.......316 A6
la. Kurmond...........86 F2
la. Strathfield, off Morwick St.......341 G13
rd. Grose Vale.......85 B13
rd. Oatlands..........279 C13
rd. Schofields.......212 E4
BELLS LINE OF
rd. Kurmond..........56 A16
rd. Kurrajong..........55 B15
rd. Kurrajong Ht....54 A4
rd. Kurrajong Hl.....54 D12
rd. N Richmond.......87 C10
BELLTREE
cr. Castle Hill........218 K5
BELLTREES
cl. Glen Alpine......510 C11
BELLWOOD
cl. Werrington......239 B11
pl. Castle Hill........219 B9
BELMONT
av. Penshurst.......431 H6
av. Sans Souci......433 F16
av. Wollstncraft....315 D9
la. Alexandria........18 G16
la. Mosman.........317 A8
la. Wollstncraft, off Shirley Rd........315 D9
pde. Mt Colah.........192 B5
rd. Glenfield.........424 D10
rd. Mosman.........316 H7
st. Alexandria........18 G16
st. Merrylands......307 E16
st. Sutherland......490 F4
st.s, Sutherland......490 F6
BELMORE
av. Belmore..........371 D15
av. Mount Druitt...241 B15
la. Cromer...........227 J13
la. Enmore...........17 B13
la. Ryde...............311 K2
la. Surry Hills..........F B14
la. Sydenham........374 D16
la. Surry Hills, off Belmore St........3 K16
pl. Paddington........13 C16
rd. Bringelly..........418 C1
rd. Eastern Ck.......272 H8
rd. Peakhurst........430 A7
rd. Punchbowl......400 B14
rd. Randwick........377 A13
rd. Riverwood......400 B14
rd. Riverwood......400 B16
st. Arncliffe..........403 G8
st. Burwood.........341 K15
st. Enmore...........17 B13
st. N Parramatta...278 E13
st. Penrith............236 J9
st. Rozelle...........344 E8
st. Ryde...............311 H4
st. Surry Hills..........F D15
st. Surry Hills..........3 K16
st. Tempe............374 D16
st. Villawood.......337 B16
st.e, Oatlands........279 A12
wk. Arncliffe, off Station St........403 G7
BELROSE
ct. Bankstown.....368 H15
pl. Prospect.........275 D12
BELTANA
av. Bonnyrigg.......363 K8
av. Terrey Hills.....196 F6
cl. Bangor...........459 B12
ct. Wattle Grove..425 K2
pl. Glen Alpine.....510 D16
pl. Leonay............234 K13
pl. Wahroonga.....251 G1
st. Denistone.......281 H13
BELUS
wy. Doonside........243 E15
BELVEDERE
arc. Cabramatta, off John St..........365 H7
av. Castle Hill.......217 H12
st. Mt Pritchard...364 B11
BELVOIR
rd. Moorebank.....425 B4
st. Surry Hills........19 G4
BEMBRIDGE
st. Carlton...........432 H7
BEN
pl. Kellyville.........185 J13
pl. Kings Lngly.....245 K6
st. Marsden Pk....182 A12
BENAARA
gdn. Castle Hill.......218 A16
BENA BENA
pl. Holsworthy.....426 C2
BENALLA
av. Ashfield..........372 G1
av. Kellyville.........216 G7
cr. Marayong.......243 K4
BENALONG
st. St Marys........239 F14
BENARES
cr. Acacia Gdn.....214 G16
BENAROON
av. St Ives...........223 J10
rd. Belmore.........371 A12
rd. Lakemba........371 A12
BENAUD
cl. Menai.............458 F9
ct. St Clair...........269 K16
la. St Clair, off Benaud Ct.........269 K16
pl. Telopea..........279 H10
st. Blacktown.......274 F4
st. Greystanes.....306 A9
BENBOW
cl. Stanhpe Gdn..215 B10
BEN BOYD
la. Cremorne.......316 C8
la. Neutral Bay.....316 C8
rd. Cremorne.......316 C10
rd. Neutral Bay.........6 E4
BEN BULLEN
rd. Glenorie.........128 K1
BENBURY
st. Quakers Hill....214 B8
BENCOOLEN
av. Denistone.......281 C14
av. West Ryde......281 C14
BENCUBBIN
st. Sadleir............394 A1
BENDA
st. Belmore.........371 C14
BENDIGO
cl. Wakeley.........334 H13
pl. Cartwright......394 A5
BENDTREE
wy. Castle Hill.......248 G4
BEN EDEN
st. Bondi Jctn......377 G3
BENEDICT
cl. Cecil Hills.......362 D5
ct. Holroyd..........308 A10
BENEDICTINE
pl. Cherrybrook...219 E14
BENELONG
av. Smithfield.......335 D7
cr. Bellevue Hill....347 J16
la. Cremorne, off Grasmere Rd...316 D7
rd. Cremorne.......316 E6
st. Seaforth.........287 C7
BENFIELD
pde. Panania..........398 C14
BENGHAZI
rd. Carlingford.....249 K13
st. Bossley Park...334 A6
BENHAM
rd. Minto.............452 K16
st. Dulwich Hill....373 D6
BENINE
dr. Cambrdg Pk...238 C8
BENJAMIN
la. Glenbrook.......233 J14
pl. Currans Hill....479 K14
rd. Mt Pritchard...364 H9
st. Bexley North...402 G9
st. Greystanes.....306 F8
BENJI
pl. Dean Park.......242 J2
BEN LOMOND
rd. Minto.............482 C2
rd. Minto Ht.........483 A6
st. Bossley Park...333 D11
BENNABRA
pl. Frenchs Frst....255 J3
BENNALONG
st. Granville.........308 A13
st. Merrylands.....308 A13
BENNELONG
pl. E Kurrajong......60 H2
pl. Narellan..........478 E15
rd. Homebush B.......L G5
rd. Homebush B......M C4
rd. Homebush B...340 K1
st. Ruse..............512 H5
BENNET
pl. Maroubra.......407 D15
BENNETT
av. Carramar........366 K4
av. Darling Point....13 J3
av. Five Dock.......343 B8
av. Roselands......401 B7
av. Strathfield S....371 E5
gr. Bidwill............211 C15
la. Kurrajong Ht.....54 A7
la. Mortlake.........312 A15
la. Riverwood......400 A15
pl. Castle Hill.......218 F11
pl. Surry Hills........20 D2
rd. Colyton...........270 C9
rd. Londonderry...149 F10
rd. Riverwood......400 A15
rd. St Clair...........270 D11
rd. S Granville......338 G4
st. Bass Hill.........367 K4
st. Bondi.............377 J5
st. Burwood........342 C11
st. Chester Hill.....367 K4
st. Cremorne...........6 H4
st. Curl Curl.........258 F13
st. Dee Why.........258 F4
st. Glenbrook.......233 H16
st. Kingsgrove.....402 B13
st. Minto.............482 K10
st. Mortlake.........312 A14
st. Neutral Bay.........6 H4
st. Newtown..........18 C9
st. Surry Hills........20 D2
st. Wentwthvle.....307 A2
st. West Ryde......281 A15
BENNETTS
rd.e, Dundas..........280 B13
rd.w, Dundas..........279 H14
BENNETTS GROVE
av. Paddington.......13 C16
BEN NEVIS
rd. Cranebrook.....207 D14
BENNING
av. S Turramrra....252 A9
BENNISON
rd. Hinchinbrk......392 K1
BENNY
la. Yagoona.........369 B13
pl. St Helens Pk...541 B8
BENOWIE
cl. Berowra Ht.....132 J5
BENOWRA
pl. Belrose...........225 E15
BENSBACH
rd. Glenfield.........424 D13
BENSLEY
rd. Ingleburn........453 F16
rd. Mcquarie Fd...453 K10
rd. Minto.............453 F16

BENSON
cl. Wahroonga....222 C5
la. West Ryde......281 J13
rd. Ingleburn.......452 J3
st. Carramar........366 H1
st. S Wntwthvle...307 D5
st. West Ryde......281 J13
BENSONS
la. Lowlands.......118 J4
BENT
la. Greenwich......314 K9
la. Neutral Bay.........6 C1
pl. Ruse..............512 G1
st. Carlton...........432 J5
st. Chester Hill.....338 B16
st. Chipping Ntn..366 F14
st. Concord.........342 A4
st. Greenwich......314 K9
st. Lindfield.........254 C16
st. Moore Park......21 A9
st. Neutral Bay.........6 B3
st. Paddington.......21 C4
st. Petersham........16 B10
st. St Marys.........239 F8
st. Sydney..............B C12
st. Sydney..............1 J14
st. Villawood.......367 B4
BENTINCK
dr. Green Valley...363 B10
BENTLEY
av. Forestville.......256 B8
av. Kellyville.........185 E9
gr. Menai............458 J15
la. Pendle Hill......276 E14
rd. Colyton...........270 E6
st. Balgowlah......287 K9
st. Rooty Hill.......271 H2
st. Wetherill Pk....333 J2
BENTON
av. Artarmon........284 J15
BENTS BASIN
rd. Silverdale.......354 F10
rd. Warragamba..324 G14
BENVENUE
st. Kingsford.......407 A6
BENWERRIN
av. Baulkham Hl...247 B5
av. Carss Park......432 F14
cl. East Killara.....254 H5
cr. Grasmere........505 H4
la. Carss Park......432 F13
BERALA
st. Berala.............339 E12
BERALLIER
dr. Camden S......507 A12
BEREN
la. Cranebrook....207 D14
pl. Cranebrook....207 D15
BERENBEL
pl. Westleigh.......220 E9
BERENICE
st. Roselands......401 A9
BERENICES
wy. Chatswd W.....284 F10
BERES
rd. Greendale.......384 K8
BERESFORD
av. Bankstown.....369 G11
av. Baulkham Hl...248 A8
av. Beverly Hills...401 D15
av. Chatswd W.....284 F12
av. Croydon Pk.....372 C5
av. Greenacre.......369 G10
cr. Bellevue Hill....347 G12
pde. Kingsgrove.....402 B7
rd. Bellevue Hill....347 G11
rd. Caringbah.......492 G3
rd. Greystanes.....305 K5
rd. Rose Bay........347 G11
rd. Strathfield.......341 B12
rd. Strathfield.......341 D11
rd. Thornleigh......221 C6
st. Mascot...........405 E7
st. St Marys.........270 A5
BERG
st. Blacktown......274 J8
BERGALIA
cl. Prestons.........393 A12
BERGER
rd. S Windsor......150 J3
BERGIN
pl. Minchinbury...271 J10
st. Denistone W...280 J11
BERGONIA
st. Mona Vale......198 K3

BERILDA
av. Warrawee.......222 D14
BERITH
rd. Greystanes.....306 F4
st. Auburn...........339 B8
st. Collaroy Plat...228 F11
st. Kingsgrove.....402 B10
BERKELEY
cl. Berowra Ht.....133 A10
st. Peakhurst.......430 C8
st. S Wntwthvle...307 B6
st. Yanderra.........567 B16
BERKLEY
rd. Padstow Ht.....429 G9
wy. Rsemeadow....540 J2
BERKSHIRE
rd. Riverstone......182 G10
BERLIET
pl. Ingleburn........453 K7
BERMILL
st. Rockdale........433 G2
BERMUDA
pl. Burraneer.......493 F13
pl. Kings Park......244 F3
rd. Tahmoor.........566 G10
BERNA
la. Canterbury......372 F15
st. Canterbury......372 F14
BERNACCI
st. Tregear...........240 C4
BERNADETTE
pl. Baulkham Hl...247 B3
pl. Fairfield..........336 E6
BERNADOTTE
st. Riverwood......400 E15
BERNARD
av. Bardwell Pk....402 G8
av. Gladesville......312 H13
la. Crows Nest, off Emmett St.......315 H8
pl. Castle Hill.......248 C4
pl. Cherrybrook...219 D13
pl. Mount Druitt...271 A4
rd. Padstow Ht.....429 F9
st. Lidcombe.......339 H10
st. Westmead......307 F5
BERNARDO
st. Rsemeadow....540 J8
BERNARRA
pl. Cranebrook.....207 D15
BERNE
st. St Peters.........374 G15
BERNERA
rd. Prestons.........393 C15
BERNICE
st. Seven Hills......246 B11
BERNIE
av. Forestville.......255 K12
st. Bundeena.......524 A10
st. Greystanes.....306 E11
BERNIER
st. Minchinbury...272 B8
wy. Green Valley...363 A9
BERNOTH
pl. Edensor Pk.....363 D3
BERONGA
av. Hurstville........402 B16
st. N Strathfield...341 E5
BEROWRA
pde. Berowra.........133 G13
rd. Mt Colah.........192 C5
BEROWRA WATERS
rd. Berowra..........133 A9
rd. Berowra Ht.....133 A9
rd. Berowra Wtr...132 H4
BERRARA
cl. Prestons.........393 C13
BERRICO
pl. Bangor...........459 C10
pl. Bargo.............567 D7
BERRIDALE
av. S Penrith........266 F5
la. S Penrith, off Berridale Av....266 F5
pl. Heckenberg....364 A12
BERRIGAN
cl. St Clair...........270 B16
cr. Mcquarie Fd....454 D1
pl. Bossley Park...333 F9
st. Northmead.....277 K3
BERRIL
pl. Glenmore Pk...266 D10
BERRILLE
rd. Narwee..........400 K14

BERRILLEE
la. Turramurra.....223 B14
st. Turramurra.....223 B13
BERRIMA
av. Padstow.........429 F5
pl. Doonside........243 C11
st. Heathcote.......518 E9
BERRIMILLA
wy. Kellyville.........185 J15
BERRINDA
pl. Frenchs Frst....255 K3
BERRING
av. Roselands.......400 K8
BERRIPA
cl. North Ryde.....282 G14
BERRY
av. Fairlight..........288 D9
av. Naremburn.....315 D3
av. N Narrabeen....199 B14
cl. Grasmere........475 J15
gr. Menai.............459 A12
la. St Leonards.....315 C7
pl. Wrrngtn Cty....238 F9
rd. St Leonards....315 C7
st. Cronulla..........494 B6
st. Granville.........308 H12
st. Mount Druitt...271 B2
st. N Sydney...........K C3
st. N Sydney...........K A4
st. N Sydney............5 D6
st. Prairiewood....334 K8
st. Prestons.........392 H14
st. Regents Pk.....369 C2
st. Rosebery........405 H2
BERRYMAN
st. North Ryde.....282 K10
BERRY PARK
wy. Mt Colah.........192 D5
BERT
la. N Parramatta...278 G14
BERTANA
cr. Warriewood....199 A6
BERTHA
rd. Cremorne............6 J5
st. Fairfield...........336 G13
st. Merrylands.....307 J16
BERTRAM
cr. Beverley Pk.....433 B8
la. Mortlake.........312 A15
pl. Narellan Vale...479 B11
st. Chatswood......285 A9
st. Concord..........312 A15
st. Eastwood.........281 C5
st. Mortlake.........312 A15
st. Yagoona.........368 E13
BERTRAND
cl. Marsfield........282 B4
rd. N Turramrra....223 F1
BERWICK
la. Darlinghurst........4 D10
pl. Menai.............458 J5
pwy. Winston Hills..277 F4
st. Coogee...........407 F1
st. Guildford........337 D4
BERWIN
pl. Baulkham Hl...247 E8
BERYL
av. Mt Colah.........162 C12
cl. Claymore.........481 G9
pl. Greenacre.......370 D7
pl. Rooty Hill........242 A13
st. Westmead......307 H2
BESANT
pl. Rooty Hill........272 A5
BESBOROUGH
av. Bexley............402 G15
BESFORD
wy. Minto.............482 K5
BESLEY
st. Cambrdg Pk....237 K7
BESSBROOK
wy. Wentwthvle, off Tanderagee St..277 D10
BESSEMER
st. Blacktown.......244 G10
BEST
cr. Kirrawee.........490 H5
pl. Prairiewood....335 A8
rd. Middle Dural...158 C5
rd. Seven Hills......275 H2
st. Lane Cove.......313 J2
st. Woolmloo...........4 G5
BESTIC
st. Kyeemagh.......404 A14

st. Rockdale.........403 E13
BESWICK
av. North Ryde.....282 E6
BESZANT
st. Merrylands......308 B15
BETA
pl. Engadine.........518 D3
pl. Quakers Hill....214 D13
rd. Lane Cove.......314 E4
BETH
wy. Glenwood.......215 H12
BETHAM
pl. Kirrawee..........490 J8
BETHANY
ct. Baulkham Hl....216 K16
BETHEL
cl. Rooty Hill........271 K6
la. Paddington........4 J15
st. Toongabbie.....276 F7
BETHEL STEPS
The Rocks..........B B1
BETOLA
st. Ryde..............282 C13
BETSEY
wy. Ambarvale.......510 K16
BETTINA
ct. Greenacre.......370 E16
pl. Dural...............188 G12
st. Merrylnds W...307 A15
BETTINGTON
rd. Carlingford......279 A5
rd. Oatlands..........279 B13
rd. Telopea...........279 B5
st. Millers Point.......A A1
st. Millers Point.......1 C9
BETTONG
cr. Bossley Park...333 F7
pl. St Helens Pk....541 H1
BETTOWYND
rd. Pymble...........223 C15
BETTS
av. Blakehurst.......432 F12
av. Five Dock.......343 C8
pl. W Pnnant Hl....249 E10
rd. Merrylnds W...306 F15
rd. Smithfield.......306 F15
rd. Woodpark.......306 F15
st. Parramatta......278 F16
st. West Ryde......281 D14
BETTY
av. Winston Hills...277 F5
pl. Thirlmere........562 D16
pl. Thirlmere........565 D1
st. Blacktown.......274 G8
st. Roseville..........285 B4
BETTY CUTHBERT
av. Ermington.......310 B2
BETTY HENDRY
pde. North Ryde.....282 J9
BETULA
pl. Loftus............489 J11
BEULAH
pl. Engadine.........518 E3
st. Kingsford.........406 J5
st. Kirribilli..............2 D3
BEVAN
pl. Carlingford......279 J1
st. Northmead......277 J11
BEVANS
rd. Galston...........160 B8
BEVERLEY
cr. Chester Hill.....337 H10
cr. Marsfield.........282 B7
cr. Penshurst.......431 H6
cr. Roselands.......401 B9
la. Darling Point....13 K1
pl. Cherrybrook....219 E6
pl. Curl Curl.........258 J14
pl. Wrrngtn Cty....238 D8
rd. Campbelltwn...511 H2
BEVERLY
pl. Beverly Hills....401 A16
pl. Plumpton........242 C11
BEVIN
av. Five Dock.......342 G9
BEXLEY
rd. Bexley............402 H12
rd. Bexley North...402 E10
rd. Campsie..........402 B1
rd. Earlwood.........402 C5
rd. Kingsgrove......402 C5
st. Mt Pritchard....364 C11
BEYER
pl. Currans Hill.....479 H11

BIAMI
cl. Bangor...........459 C12
BIANCA
pl. Acacia Gdn.....244 J1
pl. Rsemeadow...540 H5
BIARA
av. Campsie.........402 B3
cl. Marsfield.........282 B3
pl. Turramurra.....223 C8
st. Bargo.............567 C5
st. Chester Hill.....338 A15
BIARGAR
av. Miranda..........491 J5
BIBBALONG
la. Blacktown......273 H3
BIBBENLUKE
av. Duffys Frst......194 G7
BIBBY
st. Carlton...........432 G11
st. Chiswick.........343 C2
BIBBYS
pl. Bonnyrigg......364 B3
rd. St Johns Pk....364 B2
BIBURY
cl. Chipping Ntn..396 D4
BICANE
cl. Edensor Pk.....363 D2
BICHEND
cl. West Hoxton..392 C6
BICKELL
rd. Mosman.........317 A2
BICKERTON
av. Green Valley...362 K13
BICKLEIGH
st. Abbotsford.....342 K4
st. Wareemba......342 K4
BICKLEY
rd. S Penrith........267 A7
BIDDY
pl. Ambarvale......510 G14
BIDGEE
rd. Ryde..............282 E16
BIDURA
cl. Glen Alpine.....510 F10
BIDURGAL
av. Kirrawee.........491 C4
BIDWILL
sq. Bidwill............211 E16
BIFFINS
la. Cawdor..........505 D16
la. Mt Hunter.......505 D16
BIGGE
st. Liverpool........395 E4
st. Warwck Frm....365 F16
wy. Minto.............482 K6
BIG HILL
rd. The Oaks........503 B2
BIGLAND
av. Denistone.......281 B13
av. West Ryde.......281 B13
BIGNELL
la. Annandale........17 D3
st. Illawong.........460 F1
BIJA
dr. Glenmore Pk..266 B9
BIJIJI
st. Pendle Hill......276 G12
BIJOU
la. Haymarket.........E C13
BILAMBEE
av. Bilgola............169 G4
la. Bilgola............169 H4
BILBERRY
av. Bilgola............169 H4
BILBETTE
pl. Frenchs Frst...257 B3
BILBOA
pl. Edensor Pk.....363 C1
BILBY
pl. Quakers Hill....214 E12
BILDERA
pl. Grays Point.....491 E15
BILGA
av. Bilgola............169 H4
cr. Malabar..........437 D8
st. Kirrawee.........490 K6
BILGOLA
av. Bilgola............170 A5
st. Campbelltwn..511 J6
tce. Bilgola............170 A5
BILKURRA
av. Bilgola............169 H4

BILLA
rd. Bangor 459 C12
BILLABONG
av. Turramurra 223 A10
gln. Wrrngtn Dns 238 E4
pl. Rouse Hill 185 D7
st. Pendle Hill 276 E14
BILLAGAL
pl. Blaxland 234 A6
BILLARA
av. Gymea Bay 491 D8
BILLARGA
rd. Westleigh 220 F5
BILLARONG
av. Dee Why 258 J2
BILL BARNACLE
av. Faulconbdg 171 G12
BILLEROY
av. Baulkham Hl 246 J7
BILLETT
st. Silverdale 353 J13
BILLIKIN
wy. Ambarvale 511 A16
BILLING
la. Greenacre, off Glover St 370 F3
BILLINGTON
pl. Emu Plains 236 A7
BILL NORTHAM
av. Newington L F16
av. Newington, off Mark Spitz Av 309 K14
BILLONG
av. Vaucluse 348 E5
st. Neutral Bay 6 H9
BILL ROYCROFT
av. Newington M C16
av. Newington 309 K15
BILLYARD
av. Elizabeth Bay 13 A3
av. Wahroonga 222 F7
gr. Turramurra 222 K7
la. Wahroonga, off Illoura Av 222 E7
pl. Carlingford 279 F4
wk. Wahroonga, off Cleveland St 222 E7
BILMARK
pl. Btn-le-Sds 403 K14
BILOELA
pl. Gymea Bay 491 H10
st. Villawood 367 E3
st. Villawood 367 F3
BILOOLO
rd. Green Valley 363 J10
BILPIN
cl. Bangor 459 C12
pl. Bossley Park 333 D10
st. Greystanes 305 F9
BILSTON
st. Berowra 133 E9
BILWARA
av. Bilgola 169 G4
cr. S Penrith 266 J7
BILYANA
pl. Rouse Hill 129 C5
BIMAN
pl. Whalan 240 K10
BIMBADEEN
av. Bradbury 511 F16
av. Lugarno 430 A13
av. Miranda 492 D4
cr. Frenchs Frst 256 J5
st. Epping 280 G5
BIMBAI
cl. Bangor 459 D12
BIMBI
pl. Bonnyrigg 363 J9
BIMBIL
av. Mt Colah 192 A4
pl. Castle Hill 218 A12
pl. Killara 283 E3
st. Blacktown 244 A14
BIMBIMBIE
pl. Bayview 168 K15
BIMBIRI
st. Horngsea Pk 392 D15
BIMBURRA
av. St Ives 223 H9
BINALONG
av. Allambie Ht 257 F14
av. Caringbah 492 F6
av. Georges Hall 367 H11
rd. Belimbla Pk 501 D14
rd. Kenthurst 156 H7
rd. Mt Colah 162 B16
rd. Old Tngabbie 276 H14
rd. Pendle Hill 276 H14
rd. Toongabbie 276 H14
rd. Wentwthvle 276 H14
rd. Yellow Rock 174 K14
st. West Pymble 252 J10
BINARA
cl. Hamondvle 396 G14
BINAVILLE
av. Burraneer 523 E2
BINBA
pl. Brookvale 258 C8
BINBURRA
av. Avalon 140 D13
BINDA
cr. Little Bay 437 B10
pl. Baulkham Hl 246 K9
rd. Yowie Bay 492 A11
st. Merrylnds W 307 B12
BINDAREE
pl. Kellyville 216 F2
st. Hebersham 241 F9
st. Lansvale 367 B10
BINDEA
st. Como 460 F8
st. Jannali 460 F8
st. Mt Pritchard 364 C10
BINDEE
cl. Glenmore Pk 266 A7
BINDER
st. Hurstville 431 H1
BINDI
pl. Beacon Hill 257 F5
BINDON
pl. Kellyville 216 F2
BINDOOK
cr. Terrey Hills 196 D7
BINDOWAN
pl. Erskine Park 300 D2
BINET
wy. Glenhaven 218 D5
BINGARA
cr. Bella Vista 246 E7
dr. Sandy Point 427 K10
rd. Beecroft 250 C11
rd. Mcquarie Fd 453 J2
st. West Pymble 253 A13
BINGARRA
pl. Bargo 567 D7
BINGHAM
pl. Edensor Pk 333 J15
BINHAM
pl. Chipping Ntn 366 G13
BINNA BURRA
st. Villawood 367 D2
BINNARI
rd. Hornsby Ht 191 G5
BINNAWAY
av. Hoxton Park 392 G8
BINNEY
rd. Kings Park 244 F4
st. Caringbah 492 H15
BINNING
la. Erskineville 18 B16
st. Erskineville 18 C16
BINNIT
pl. Glenmore Pk 266 B12
BINNOWEE
av. St Ives 223 K9
pl. Bayview 169 A15
BINOMEA
pl. Pennant Hills 250 G2
BINYA
cl. Hornsby Ht 162 A7
pl. Como 460 H6
st. Blaxland 234 E6
st. Pendle Hill 276 G12
BINYON
cl. Wetherill Pk 334 H4
BIRALEE
cr. Beacon Hill 257 K6
BIRCH
av. Casula 394 G14
gr. Baulkham Hl 248 B12
pl. Bidwill 211 D14
pl. Kirrawee 490 K1
pl. Mcquarie Fd 424 F16
st. Bnkstn Aprt 368 B16
st. Condell Park 368 B16
st. East Ryde 283 A14
st. N St Marys 240 A11
BIRCHGROVE
av. Canley Ht 364 K3
rd. Balmain 7 D6
rd. Birchgrove 7 D6
BIRD
av. Guildford 337 K4
av. Lurnea 394 G9
la. St Clair, off Banks Dr 269 H11
pl. St Clair 269 H11
pl. St Helens Pk 541 C3
pl. West Hoxton 392 A10
st. Ryde 282 H16
BIRDS
la. Bondi Jctn 22 J9
la. Maraylya 125 A14
BIRDSALL
av. Condell Park 398 H4
BIRDSVILLE
cr. Leumeah 482 G10
BIRDWOOD
av. Belfield 371 F9
av. Cabramtta W 364 G7
av. Collaroy 229 C13
av. Daceyville 406 G6
av. Doonside 243 E16
av. East Killara 254 D8
av. Holsworthy 396 A13
av. Killara 254 D8
av. Lane Cove 314 D1
av. Pagewood 406 G6
av. Winmalee 172 H13
cl. Narrabeen 228 G7
la. Lane Cove 314 D1
la. Georges Hall, off Georges Cr 367 F14
rd. Bnkstn Aprt 367 G14
rd. Georges Hall 367 G14
st. Denistone E 281 J11
st. Sylvania 461 J8
BIRGITTE
cr. Cecil Hills 362 G7
BIRINTA
st. Narraweena 258 A2
BIRK
pl. Bligh Park 150 G6
BIRKDALE
cct. Glenmore Pk 266 F10
cr. Liverpool 395 C9
BIRKLEY
la. Fairlight 288 E8
la. Manly 288 E8
rd. Manly 288 E8
BIRMINGHAM
av. Villawood 337 G16
rd. S Penrith 266 F4
st. Alexandria 375 E16
st. Merrylands 307 H10
BIRNAM
av. Blacktown 243 J15
gr. Strathfield 341 C16
BIRNIE
av. Homebush B M H10
av. Homebush B 340 E4
av. Lidcombe M K11
av. Lidcombe 340 C6
BIROK
av. Engadine 518 K1
BIRRAMAL
rd. Duffys Frst 194 H7
BIRR CROSS
rd. Moorebank 425 C4
BIRRELL
la. Queens Park 22 D11
st. Bondi 377 H6
st. Bondi Jctn 22 D9
st. Tamarama 377 H6
st. Waverley 377 H6
BIRRELLEA
av. Earlwood 402 E5
BIRRIGA
av. Chester Hill 368 B2
rd. Bellevue Hill 377 J1
rd. Croydon 342 G13
BIRRIMA
st. N Balgowlah 287 H5
BIRRIWA
av. Belfield 371 B8
pl. Baulkham Hl 246 H6
pl. Northwood 314 G8
st. Greystanes 305 G9
BIRRONG
av. Belrose 225 H15
av. Birrong 368 K6
BIRRU
pl. Belrose 225 K14
BIRTLES
av. Pendle Hill 276 G11
BIRTLEY
pl. Elizabeth Bay 13 A6
BIRUBI
av. Gymea 491 E1
av. Pymble 223 C14
cr. Bilgola 169 E8
BIRUNNA
av. Gymea 491 G1
BISCAYNE
av. S Wntwthvle 306 K9
BISCOE
pl. Tregear 240 F8
BISDEE
pl. Engadine 489 C13
BISHOP
av. W Pnnant Hl 249 K2
av. Matraville, off Cemetery Av 436 G8
cl. Green Valley 363 B12
cl. S Windsor 150 F2
cr. Bonnyrigg 364 E5
rd. Menai 458 G15
st. Cabarita 342 D1
st. Newport 169 G11
st. Petersham 15 F15
st. Revesby 399 A11
st. St Peters 374 J14
BISHOPGATE
av. Castle Hill 217 G4
la. Camperdwn 17 D9
st. Camperdwn 17 D9
st. Newtown 17 D9
BISHOPS
av. Randwick 377 F12
BISHOPSCOURT
pl. Glen Alpine 510 B12
BISMARCK
st. McGraths Hl 122 B14
BISMARK
rd. Northmead 278 D5
BISMIRE
st. Panania 398 A15
BITTERN
cl. Erskine Park 270 H14
cl. Hinchinbrk 393 D2
gr. Glenwood 215 F14
BIWA
cl. St Clair 269 G15
la. St Clair, off Rotarua Rd 269 F16
BIX
rd. Dee Why 258 F3
BIZET
pl. Bonnyrigg Ht 363 D7
BLACK
cl. Illawong 459 F5
st. Marrickville 374 E10
st. Vaucluse 348 D6
BLACKALL
st. Revesby 399 B14
BLACK ASH
pl. Hornsby Ht 162 A5
BLACKBIRD
gln. Erskine Park 271 A14
la. St Clair, off Blackbird Gln 271 A14
BLACKBURN
av. North Rocks 249 A16
av. West Hoxton 392 A10
pl. Gymea Bay 491 D7
rd. Wedderburn 540 A16
st. St Ives 224 F7
st. Surry Hills F B9
BLACKBUTT
av. Bradbury 511 F11
av. Lugarno 429 J11
av. Pennant Hills 250 K4
cir. Mt Riverview 204 E15
cr. Greystanes 306 E12
pl. Engadine 488 H16
pl. Leonay 235 A16
pl. The Oaks 502 E12
st. Bossley Park 333 G9
BLACKBUTTS
rd. Frenchs Frst 255 F2
BLACKET
pl. West Hoxton 392 B10
st. Heathcote 518 H10
BLACKETT
dr. Castle Hill 247 F3
pl. Cabramtta W 365 B4
st. Kings Park 244 D2
BLACKFORD
cr. S Penrith 266 G4
st. Fairfield E 337 D14
BLACKFRIAR
pl. Wetherill Pk 335 A1
BLACKFRIARS
la. Chippendale 19 A2
pl. Chippendale 19 A1
st. Chippendale 19 A1
BLACK LION
pl. Kensington 376 C9
BLACKMAN
cr. Horngsea Pk 392 G15
cr. S Windsor 120 K16
ct. Wrrngtn Cty 238 E5
la. Bass Hill 368 E10
la. Yagoona 368 E10
BLACKMORE
la. Redfern 19 K11
pl. Wetherill Pk 334 F6
rd. Smeaton Gra 479 B8
BLACKS
rd. Arcadia 159 D2
rd. W Pnnant Hl 248 H7
BLACKSHAW
av. Mortdale 430 H7
BLACKSMITH
cl. Stanhpe Gdn 215 F9
st. Greenfld Pk 334 D13
BLACKSTONE
st. Wetherill Pk 305 C16
BLACK SWAN
pl. Yarramundi 145 E6
BLACKTHORN
cct. Menai 458 K12
BLACKTOWN
rd. Blacktown 275 A2
rd. Freemns Rch 90 G3
rd. Londonderry 149 F1
rd. Prospect 275 C11
rd. Richmond 118 K8
rd. S Windsor 149 F1
BLACKWALL POINT
rd. Abbotsford 342 K2
rd. Chiswick 343 A2
BLACK WATTLE
gr. Narellan Vale 479 A14
pl. Sydney 3 D6
st. Peakhurst 430 E4
BLACKWATTLE
la. Ultimo 12 J14
pl. Alfords Point 459 A1
pl. Cherrybrook 219 J8
pl. Sydney C B12
BLACKWELL
av. St Clair 270 A16
BLACKWOOD
av. Ashfield 372 F5
av. Casula 394 J15
av. Clovelly 378 A12
av. Dulwich Hill 373 E11
av. Minto 452 J15
av. Mt Krng-gai 162 J14
cl. Beecroft 250 D3
cl. Bossley Park 333 E9
cr. Mcquarie Fd 454 E1
la. Dulwich Hill, off Blackwood Av 373 E11
pl. Oatlands 278 G10
rd. Merrylands 307 C9
rd. N Curl Curl 258 K10
rd. Vineyard 152 D7
st. Belfield 371 D10
st. Miranda 491 K7
BLADES
pl. Mt Annan 479 F15
BLAIKIE
rd. Jamisontown 235 J15
BLAIN
st. Toongabbie 276 F9
BLAIR
av. Croydon 342 E13
av. East Hills 427 J4
av. St Marys 239 H15
la. St Marys, off Blair Av 239 H15
pl. Cabramatta 366 A10
pl. Minto 453 C16
pl. St Ives 253 K2
st. Bondi Beach 378 C1
st. Gladesville 312 H10
st. North Bondi 378 C1

BLAIR ATHOL
dr. Blair Athol 511 A3
BLAIRGOWIE
pl. Oatlands 278 J11
BLAIRGOWRIE
cct. St Andrews 452 B16
la. Dulwich Hill, off Windsor Rd 373 D6
st. Dulwich Hill 373 D6
BLAKE
av. Blakehurst 462 F3
av. Hunters Hill 314 B13
cl. Wetherill Pk 334 J6
pl. Eagle Vale 481 B9
rd. Mt Annan 479 D15
st. Balmain 8 C10
st. Dover Ht 348 D10
st. Kogarah 433 A6
st. Quakers Hill 213 K8
st. Rose Bay 348 D10
BLAKEFORD
av. Ermington 280 E15
BLAKESLEY
rd. Allawah 432 F10
rd. Carlton 432 F10
rd. S Hurstville 432 C11
st. Chatswood 285 A8
BLAMEY
av. Caringbah 492 G15
pl. Doonside 273 F1
pl. Revesby 398 J16
pl. St Ives 224 F16
rd. Holsworthy 396 A13
st. Allambie Ht 257 H16
st. Colyton 270 B5
st. North Ryde 282 J11
st. Revesby 398 H16
wy. Cherrybrook, off Tennyson Cl 219 E10
BLAMIRE
la. Marrickville 373 J14
BLANC
av. East Hills 428 A4
BLANCHE
av. Padstow 429 E2
st. Belfield 371 B9
st. Minto 482 F2
st. Oatley 431 E11
BLAND
rd. Oakville 124 E7
rd. Springwood 202 A2
st. Ashfield 372 J2
st. Bradbury 511 E8
st. Carramar 336 H16
st. Haberfield 343 A15
st. Woolmloo 4 F3
BLANDFORD
av. Bronte 377 H7
st. Collaroy Plat 228 J12
BLANE
st. Granville 308 C10
BLANTYRE
cl. Thornleigh 221 C12
BLARNEY
av. Killarney Ht 286 B1
BLATTMAN
av. Oakdale 500 C12
cl. Blacktown 273 H5
st. Colyton 270 C7
BLAXCELL
pl. Harringtn Pk 478 F6
st. Granville 308 F16
st. Guildford 338 D9
st. S Granville 338 E3
BLAXLAND
av. Luddenham 356 H2
av. Newington L G10
av. Newington L H11
av. Newington 310 D11
av. Newington 310 D12
av. Penrith 237 B9
dr. Illawong 459 E6
la. Penrith, off Blaxland Av 237 B9
la. Ryde, off Devlin St 311 K1
pl. Glenhaven 218 B3
pl. Milperra 397 J7
rd. Bellevue Hill 347 J16
rd. Camden S 506 K12
rd. Campbelltwn 511 B4
rd. Denistone 281 F10
rd. Denistone E 281 F10
rd. Eastwood 281 F10
rd. Epping 281 C1
rd. Ingleburn 423 A9
rd. Killara 253 D15
rd. Orchard Hills 298 C10
rd. Rhodes 311 D9
rd. Ryde 312 A2
st. Frenchs Frst 256 E2
st. Hunters Hill 313 B6
st. Lalor Park 245 D13
st. Matraville 437 A2
st. Silverwater L D16
st. Silverwater 309 K8
st. Yennora 337 B10
BLAXLANDS CORNER
Lane Cove 314 F5
BLEND
pl. Woodcroft 243 G7
BLENHEIM
av. Rooty Hill 241 J13
la. Queens Park 22 J13
pl. Glenfield 424 F9
pl. St Clair 270 F14
rd. Carlingford 279 F5
rd. Lindfield 254 D14
rd. North Ryde 283 A11
rd. Schofields 182 H15
st. Croydon Pk 371 F7
st. Queens Park 22 K11
st. Randwick 376 K14
BLENMAN
av. Punchbowl 400 A7
BLETCHLEY
pl. Hebersham 241 F5
BLICK
pde. Canterbury 372 H13
BLIGH
av. Camden S 506 J10
av. Lurnea 394 B12
cl. Georges Hall 368 C15
cr. Seaforth 286 J9
ct. St Clair 270 A11
la. Eastwood 281 F5
pl. Kellyville 215 G4
pl. Randwick 377 D11
st. Burwood Ht 371 K3
st. Chifley 437 C3
st. East Killara 254 F7
st. Eastwood 281 F5
st. Guildford 338 C8
st. Kirrawee 490 J7
st. Kirribilli 6 A15
st. Milsons Pt 6 A15
st. Northbridge 286 A16
st. Riverstone 183 C11
st. Silverwater 309 H14
st. Sydney B C15
st. Sydney 1 J16
st. Villawood 337 B15
BLIGHS
rd. Cromer 227 J12
BLIND
rd. Nelson 155 A8
BLOMFIELD
rd. Denham Ct 422 G15
BLOODWOOD
pl. Bradbury 511 E9
rd. Fiddletown 130 A3
rd. Ingleside 197 F3
BLOOMFIELD
la. Surry Hills 4 D14
st. S Coogee 407 H5
st. Surry Hills 4 D14
BLOOMSBURY
av. Pymble 253 E4
BLOXSOME
la. Mosman 316 G9
BLUCHER
st. Sans Souci 463 C6
BLUE
pl. Wetherill Pk 334 D5
st. N Sydney K C11
st. N Sydney 5 F10
BLUE ANCHOR
la. Sydney A K8
BLUE BELL
pl. Heathcote 518 E9
rd. Heathcote 518 E9
BLUEBELL
cl. Glenmore Pk 265 H8
BLUEBERRY
ct. Narellan Vale 478 H14
dr. Colyton 270 H6
pl. Alfords Point 459 C1
BLUEBIRD
rd. Cranebrook 207 B11
BLUEBUSH
cl. Bossley Park 333 J9
BLUE CRANE
cl. W Pnnant Hl 248 F8
BLUE CREST
pl. Kingswood 267 H3
BLUEFISH
dr. Manly 289 A13
BLUE GUM
av. Chatswd W 284 F8
av. Gymea Bay 491 E8
av. Ingleburn 453 F5
av. Roseville 284 F8
cr. Blaxland 234 C9
cr. Stanhpe Gdn 215 B11
dr. East Ryde 283 A15
rd. Annangrove 156 A14
rd. Kenthurst 156 A14
rd. Wentwthvle 277 A9
BLUEGUM
av. Prestons 394 C14
av. S Penrith 267 B1
cr. Frenchs Frst 256 F4
cr. Picnic Point 428 H7
gr. Glenwood 245 H2
pl. Roseville 284 C6
st. Normanhurst 221 E13
wy. Menai 458 J10
BLUE GUMS
wy. Castle Hill 218 J13
BLUE HILLS
cr. Blacktown 244 B16
dr. Glenmore Pk 266 E13
BLUE JAY
ct. W Pnnant Hl 249 D7
BLUE RIDGE
cr. Berowra Ht 132 K5
ct. Glenhaven 218 E2
BLUES POINT
rd. McMahons Pt K A15
rd. McMahons Pt 5 D16
rd. N Sydney K A16
rd. N Sydney 5 D16
BLUETT
av. East Ryde 282 J15
cr. Doonside 243 C6
st. Marayong 244 D7
BLUE WREN
pl. Oakdale 500 F11
BLUEWREN
cl. Glenmore Pk 265 K12
BLUFF
st. Green Valley 363 B11
BLUNDELL
cr. Kellyville 216 D2
st. Marsfield 282 A5
BLUNT
pl. Rsemeadow 540 G7
BLYTHE
av. Glenwood 215 H12
BLYTHESWOOD
av. Turramurra 222 D14
av. Warrawee 222 D14
BOAB
pl. Casula 423 K1
BOADA
pl. Winston Hills 277 G2
BOAKE
cl. Glenmore Pk 265 K7
BOALA
pl. Engadine 489 C9
BOAMBILLEE
av. Vaucluse 348 D2
BOANBONG
rd. Palm Beach 140 A4
BOARD
st. Lidcombe 339 H7
st. N Parramatta 278 B11
BOARDMAN
st. Dundas Vy 280 D10
st. Yagoona 369 F7
BOATWRIGHT
av. Lugarno 430 A8
BOB
rd. Moorebank 425 A5
BOBADAH
st. Kingsgrove 402 A8
BOBART
st. Parramatta 308 A5
BOBBIN
pl. Bangor 459 C13
BOBBIN HEAD
rd. Krngai Ch NP 163 J16
rd. N Turramrra 223 E7
rd. Pymble 223 E7
rd. Turramurra 223 E7
BOBBY PEARCE
av. Newington L K12
av. Newington 310 C13
BOBIN
rd. Sadleir 364 B16
BOBS
pl. Matraville 406 K16
BOBS RANGE
rd. Orangeville 443 J16
BOBUCK
pl. St Helens Pk 541 H2
BOCKING
av. Bradbury 511 E7
BOCKS
rd. Oakville 152 K7
BODALLA
cr. Bangor 459 B12
ct. Wattle Grove 426 B3
st. Fairfield Ht 335 H8
BODE
pl. Barden Rdg 458 G16
BODEN
av. Strathfield 340 J15
pl. Castle Hill 217 D9
rd. Seven Hills 276 F1
BOEING
cr. Raby 451 G13
pl. Btn-le-Sds 433 J1
pl. St Clair 270 D16
rd. Mascot 404 J4
BOFFIN
pl. Ambarvale 510 F16
BOGALARA
rd. Old Tngabbie 276 J11
BOGAN
av. Baulkham Hl 247 G4
av. Sylvania Wtr 462 E10
pl. Ruse 512 E7
pl. Seven Hills 275 F10
pl. Wahroonga 222 A15
st. Greystanes 306 A4
st. Summer Hill 373 E3
BOGIE
la. Allawah 432 C7
la. Hurstville 432 C7
BOGONG
pl. Prairiewood 334 F7
BOGOTA
av. Neutral Bay 6 J7
BOHAN
wy. Minto 482 H6
BOHEMIA
st. Malabar 437 F6
BOHR
cr. Lucas Ht 487 H11
BOILER
cl. Blacktown 274 C14
BOKANA
pl. North Rocks 248 J16
BOKHARA
cr. Greystanes 306 C5
BOLAND
av. Springwood 201 J2
la. Marrickville 373 K10
la. Springwood 201 K2
BOLARO
av. Greystanes 305 G10
av. Gymea 491 F2
BOLD
st. Burwood 371 J1
st. Cabramtta W 364 J7
st. Granville 308 F10
BOLDERO
cr. Glenmore Pk 266 H13
BOLDREWOOD
av. Casula 424 F2
pl. Cherrybrook 219 C8
rd. Blackett 241 B3
BOLGER
st. Campbelltwn 510 K7
BOLINDA
st. Busby 363 G12
BOLINGBROKE
pde. Fairlight 288 B10
BOLIVIA
st. Cabramatta 365 G8
BOLLARD
pl. Picton 563 C13
BOLTA
pl. Cromer 258 A1
BOLTON
av. Mt Colah 192 C5
av. Mt Pritchard 364 F9
pl. Pymble 253 J2
st. Guildford 337 G7
st. Prospect 275 D12
st. St Peters 374 E14
st. Sydenham 374 E14
BOLTONS
st. Horngsea Pk 392 D15
BOLWARRA
av. West Pymble 253 C14
cr. Castle Hill 248 G2
rd. N Narrabeen 198 G13
BOMADERRY
dr. Prestons 393 D16
BOMBALA
cr. Quakers Hill 243 K3
st. Pendle Hill 276 C16
BOMBARDIERE
pl. Baulkham Hl 248 B7
BOMBAY
st. Lidcombe 339 K6
BOMBELL
av. Engadine 518 F3
BOMBO
cl. Prestons 393 A16
pl. Bangor 459 C13
BOMBORA
av. Bundeena 524 B11
BON
st. Chipping Ntn 396 C5
BONA
cr. Morning Bay 138 E13
BON ACCORD
av. Bondi Jctn 377 G3
la. Bondi Jctn, off Bon Accord Av 377 G2
BONALBO
st. Kingsgrove 402 B9
BONANZA
la. Sans Souci 433 C16
pde. Sans Souci 433 C16
BONAPARTE
st. Riverwood 400 D14
BONAR
st. Arncliffe 403 G7
st. Telopea 279 F8
BONA VISTA
av. Maroubra 407 H10
BOND
av. Toongabbie 276 F7
cr. Wetherill Pk 333 G4
la. Mosman, off Bond St 316 J4
pl. Ellis Lane 476 D6
pl. Illawong 459 F7
st. Hurstville 431 K4
st. Maroubra 407 H10
st. Mosman 316 K5
st. North Ryde 282 D11
st. Sydney A J13
st. Sydney 1 G15
BONDELL
av. Gymea 491 G2
BONDI
pl. Woodbine 481 F13
rd. Bondi 377 F3
rd. Bondi Jctn 377 F3
st. Bundeena 523 J11
BONDS
rd. Peakhurst 430 E1
rd. Punchbowl 400 E7
rd. Riverwood 400 E13
rd. Riverwood 400 E16
rd. Roselands 400 E7
rd. Thirlmere 564 A3
st. Austral 390 F8
BONEDA
cl. Annangrove 155 K16
BONGALONG
st. Naremburn 315 E3
BONHAM
st. Canley Vale 366 E2
BON MART
Winston Hills 277 G2
BONNEFIN
pl. Castle Hill 218 E16
rd. Hunters Hill 313 D8
BONNER
av. Manly 288 H5
rd. Agnes Banks 117 D13
BONNET
av. Como 460 D6
BONNEY
cl. St Ives Ch 224 A6

pl. Doonside 273 E4
pl. St Helens Pk 541 C5
st. Sans Souci 433 A16
BONNIE DOON
pl. Burraneer 523 E3
BONNIE FIELD
cl. Catherine Fd 449 D3
BONNIE VIEW
st. Gymea 491 D6
BONNIEVIEW
st. Woolooware 493 D12
BONNYRIGG
av. Bonnyrigg 363 K5
BONTON
rd. Springwood 202 C7
BONTOU
rd. Pymble 223 K16
rd. St Ives 223 K16
BONUS
st. North Bondi 348 C15
BONZER
pl. Glendenning 242 E5
BOOBOOK
pl. Ingleburn 453 F10
BOOKER
rd. Hawksbry Ht 174 G3
BOOKS
cr. McGraths Hl 121 K12
st. Dean Park 212 H15
BOOLA
av. Yennora 337 B8
pl. Cromer 228 E13
pl. Westleigh 220 G9
BOOLARONG
av. Chipping Ntn 396 G5
rd. Pymble 223 F14
BOOLEROO
pl. Westleigh 220 G6
BOOLIGAL
rd. Terrey Hills 195 H3
BOOMERANG
av. Earlwood 402 G5
av. Lilli Pilli 522 G1
cr. Raby 451 E12
dr. Glossodia 59 G4
pl. Cmbrdg Gdn 237 F4
pl. Seven Hills 275 H2
rd. Collaroy Plat 228 H13
rd. Edensor Pk 363 H3
rd. Springwood 201 G3
st. Granville 308 B11
st. Haberfield 343 E12
st. Maroubra 407 G9
st. Turramurra 223 A12
BOOMI
pl. Woronora 459 K16
BOON
rd. Londonderry 148 F16
BOONA
rd. Terrey Hills 195 H7
BOONAH
av. Eastgardens 406 F12
la. Eastgardens 406 G12
st. Wentwthvle 276 K11
BOONAL
st. Baulkham Hl 247 A6
BOONARA
av. Bondi 378 A5
la. Bondi, off Boonara Av 378 A5
BOONDAH
pl. Kareela 461 B12
pl. Warrawee 222 H10
rd. Warriewood 199 A11
BOONGARY
st. St Helens Pk 541 J1
BOONGIL
st. West Pymble 252 J8
BOONOKE
cr. Miller 393 H2
pl. Airds 512 C12
wy. Airds 512 C13
BOORABA
av. Lindfield 283 H6
BOORAGUL
st. Beverly Hills 401 B10
BOORALEE
st. Botany 405 C12
BOORALIE
rd. Duffys Frst 195 A2
rd. Terrey Hills 196 A5
BOORALLA
rd. Edensor Pk 333 K16
BOORARA
av. Oatley 430 K16
av. Oatley 431 A15
BOOREA
av. Lakemba 371 A14
st. Blaxland 233 H6
st. Lidcombe 339 G3
BOOREE
ct. Wattle Grove 426 A2
BOOREEA
st. Blacktown 274 E2
BOORIMA
pl. Cronulla 494 A14
BOORROO
st. Kangaroo Pt 461 J4
BOOTES
av. Hinchinbrk 393 E4
BOOTH
la. Annandale 11 B14
pl. Cherrybrook 219 K10
pl. Minchinbury 271 F9
st. Annandale 11 A14
st. Arncliffe 403 H6
st. Balmain 7 H11
st. Camperdwn 17 D1
st. Marsfield 282 C4
st. Westmead 307 H4
BOOTIE
pl. Kings Lngly 246 D10
BOOTLE
pl. Cranebrook 207 G12
BOOTLES
la. Pitt Town 92 H12
BOOTS
la. Ingleburn 453 D5
BOOYONG
av. Caringbah 492 J4
av. Lugarno 430 A13
st. Cabramatta 365 H10
BORA
pl. Toongabbie 276 H10
pl. Wilberforce 92 C1
BORAMBIL
pl. Longueville 314 E6
pl. Oyster Bay 461 D4
st. Warrawee 222 F10
BORDEAUX
pl. Orchard Hills 268 H14
BORDER
cl. Elderslie 507 K1
cl. Hinchinbrk 363 A14
la. Mosman 317 D4
rd. Horsley Pk 332 H8
BORDLEY
pl. Oakhurst 242 B5
BOREC
rd. Penrith 236 F3
BOREE
pl. Bangor 459 C12
pl. Mcquarie Fd 454 F4
pl. Wrrngtn Dns 238 B3
pl. Westleigh 220 E7
rd. Forestville 255 D8
st. Marsfield 282 A4
BORELLA
rd. Milperra 397 D9
BORG
pl. Prairiewood 334 E12
BORGAH
st. Carss Park 432 F14
BORGNIS
st. Belrose 225 E16
st. Davidson 225 E16
BORLAISE
st. Willoughby 285 E14
BORNEO
ct. Bossley Park 334 B5
BORO
pl. Prestons 393 B13
BORODIN
cl. Cranebrook 207 F9
BORODINO
pl. Narellan Vale 479 A16
BOROJEVIC
st. Bonnyrigg Ht 363 A5
BOROMI
wy. Cromer 227 K11
BORONGA
av. West Pymble 252 H13
cl. Bangor 459 B11
pl. Berowra Ht 133 B10
BORONIA
av. Beecroft 250 F9
av. Burwood 342 C13
av. Cheltenham 250 F9
av. Croydon 372 C3
av. Engadine 518 H2
av. Epping 280 G1
av. Hunters Hill 313 C7
av. Mt Annan 509 C3
av. Russell Lea 343 D5
av. Turramurra 252 E1
cr. Stanhpe Gdn 215 E10
cr. Winmalee 173 K6
dr. Voyager Pt 427 B5
gr. Heathcote 518 H12
la. Denistone E 281 G9
la. Redfern 20 B8
la. Seaforth 286 K7
la. Mosman, off Brady St 317 A5
pde. Lugarno 430 B15
pde.w, Lugarno 430 A14
pl. Cheltenham 250 J11
rd. Bellevue Hill 347 J14
rd. Bossley Park 333 F10
rd. Glenorie 127 G8
rd. Greenacre 369 J11
rd. Ingleside 198 A4
rd. Kentlyn 483 F12
rd. N St Marys 239 J7
rd. N St Marys 240 B9
st. Belfield 371 B11
st. Concord W 311 E14
st. Cronulla 523 K2
st. Dee Why 259 A7
st. Ermington 310 D4
st. Kensington 376 E11
st. Kyle Bay 431 J15
st. Lalor Park 245 B11
st. N Balgowlah 287 F6
st. Redfern 19 K8
st. S Granville 338 G2
st. S Wntwthvle 306 K5
st. Wollstncraft 315 D8
BORRODALE
rd. Kingsford 406 D2
BORROWDALE
cl. Lurnea 394 C12
cl. Narellan 478 E14
pl. Beacon Hill 257 F4
pl. Bligh Park 150 C5
wy. Cranebrook 207 D11
wy. Kellyville 185 K14
BORTFIELD
dr. Chiswick 343 D1
BORTHWICK
st. Minto 482 G7
BORU
pl. Killarney Ht 286 D2
BOSAVI
st. Glenfield 424 G14
BOSCI
rd. Ingleburn 452 K5
BOSCO
pl. Schofields 213 J6
BOSCOBEL
rd. Londonderry 177 G4
BOSLEY
av. Liverpool 364 K15
BOSNJAK
av. Edensor Pk 333 G15
BOSSLEY
rd. Bossley Park 333 F7
tce. Woolmloo 4 E5
BOSTOCK
st. Richmond 120 A5
BOSTON
cl. Hinchinbrk 392 K1
pl. St Clair 270 G13
pl. Toongabbie 275 F14
rd. Kellyville 216 A11
BOSWORTH
st. Richmond 118 F5
BOTANIC
rd. Mosman 317 D8
BOTANY
bvd. Kings Lngly 246 A10
bvd. Seven Hills 246 A10
cir. Matraville 436 G8
la. Alexandria 19 B13
la. Kingsford 406 J1
la. Mascot 405 E6
la. St Clair, off Bennett Rd 270 C12
pl. Bondi Jctn 377 F5
pl. Ruse 512 G8
pl. Yagoona 368 H11
rd. Alexandria 19 B12
rd. Bnksmeadw 435 J1
rd. Bnksmeadw 436 C3
rd. Beaconsfield 375 F16
rd. Botany 405 E9
rd. Mascot 405 E5
rd. Matraville 436 C3
rd. Port Botany 436 C3
rd. Rosebery 405 E5
rd. Waterloo 19 B12
rd. Zetland 375 F16
st. Allawah 432 E4
st. Bondi Jctn 377 F5
st. Kensington 376 K16
st. Kingsford 406 H5
st. Randwick 406 J3
BO TREE
pl. Prestons 393 J15
BOTTLE BRUSH
dr. Faulconbdg 171 D12
pl. Colyton 270 H6
rd. Westleigh 220 H8
BOTTLEBRUSH
av. Bradbury 511 F10
av. Lugarno 430 A9
cl. Picton 561 C4
dr. Cranebrook 237 E1
gr. Acacia Gdn 214 J15
la. Cranebrook, off Greygums Rd 207 E16
pl. Alfords Point 429 B15
BOTTLE FOREST
rd. Heathcote 518 J11
BOTTLES
rd. Plumpton 241 K7
BOUCHET
cr. Minchinbury 271 K8
BOUDDI
st. Bow Bowing 452 C15
BOUGAINVILLE
av. Bossley Park 333 K6
ct. Maroubra 407 C14
rd. Blackett 241 A1
rd. Glenfield 424 E12
rd. Lethbrdg Pk 240 G2
BOUGHTON
st. Richmond 118 J7
BOULT
cl. Bligh Park 150 D5
BOULTON
av. Baulkham Hl 247 E4
st. Putney 311 K6
BOUNDARY
la. Cabramatta 365 J8
la. Cabramatta 365 K8
la. Darlington 18 E8
la. Paddington 4 J12
la. Paddington 4 K12
rd. Box Hill 153 D13
rd. Carlingford 279 J3
rd. Cherrybrook 219 G13
rd. Chester Hill 338 E13
rd. Cranebrook 206 K8
rd. Faulconbdg 201 D1
rd. Glossodia 60 C8
rd. Heathcote 518 D14
rd. Liverpool 394 G9
rd. Lurnea 394 G9
rd. Maraylya 124 A15
rd. Mortdale 430 G3
rd. N Epping 251 E8
rd. Northmead 277 K11
rd. Oakville 153 D13
rd. Oatley 431 A8
rd. Peakhurst 430 G3
rd. Pennant Hills 250 E1
rd. Pennant Hills 250 F1
rd. Schofields 183 G11
rd. Sefton 338 E13
rd. Springwood 201 D1
rd. Vineyard 153 D13
rd. Wahroonga 222 F2
st. Alexandria 19 A10
st. Berowra 133 E12
st. Castle Cove 285 E3
st. Clovelly 377 J11
st. Clovelly 378 A12
st. Croydon 342 D15
st. Darlinghurst 4 H13
st. Darlington 18 H5
st. Granville 308 A8
st. Paddington 4 H13
st. Parramatta 308 A8
st. Redfern 18 K10
st. Roseville 284 J5
st. Roseville Ch 285 E3
st. Thirlmere 564 J10
st. Thirlmere 565 A10
st. Warriewood 198 E6
BOUNTY
av. Castle Hill 217 H10
av. Kirrawee 491 A9
cr. Bligh Park 150 H9
pl. Old Tngabbie 277 C7
BOURKE
la. Paddington 4 K16
la. Queens Park 22 H12
la. Redfern 20 B11
la. Pymble, off Bannockburn Rd 223 C13
pl. Abbotsford 343 A4
pl. Blairmount 480 K13
pl. Botany 405 F11
pl. Camden S 506 K12
rd. Alexandria 375 B15
rd. Mascot 405 B2
rd. Mascot 405 B3
rd. Pendle Hill 276 G13
st. Blaxland 233 D5
st. Darlinghurst 4 E12
st. Liverpool 395 C5
st. N Parramatta 278 B10
st. Pymble 223 C13
st. Queens Park 22 H13
st. Redfern 20 B11
st. Richmond 118 J8
st. Riverstone 182 H5
st. Smithfield 335 E7
st. Surry Hills 4 D16
st. Waterloo 375 H9
st. Woolmloo 4 E7
st. Zetland 375 H9
BOURMAC
av. Northbridge 286 F15
BOURNE
st. Marrickville 374 E11
st. Wentwthvle 277 A15
BOURNEMOUTH
ct. Bundeena 524 A11
BOUSSOLE
rd. Daceyville 406 E3
BOUVARDIA
st. Asquith 191 K10
st. Caringbah 492 H16
st. Punchbowl 400 D1
st. Russell Lea 343 C4
BOVIS
pl. Rooty Hill 272 C6
BOW
la. Kingsford 406 H2
pl. Glen Alpine 510 B14
BOWAGA
av. Blaxland 234 E7
BOWATER
cl. N Wahrnga 222 K1
BOW BOWING
cr. Bradbury 511 H12
BOWDEN
bvd. Yagoona 369 C9
cl. Green Valley 363 B11
cr. Connells Pt 461 G1
la. Woollahra 22 A5
pl. Belfield 371 E12
st. Alexandria 375 E9
st. Cabramatta 365 D11
st. Guildford 337 A1
st. Harris Park 308 F8
st. Meadowbnk 311 E5
st. Merrylnds W 307 B16
st. N Parramatta 278 J15
st. Ryde 311 G2
st. Woollahra 21 K5
BOWEN
av. S Turramrra 252 A10
cl. Cherrybrook 219 C10
pl. Maroubra 407 D16
pl. Seven Hills 275 D6
st. Chatswd W 284 H13
BOWENIA
ct. Stanhpe Gdn 215 E10
BOWEN MOUNTAIN
rd. Bowen Mtn 84 A12
rd. Grose Vale 84 D11
BOWER
la. Manly 288 K11
st. Bankstown 369 B14
st. Manly 288 K11
st. Plumpton 242 B10
st. Roselands 401 D6

BOWER BIRD
ct. Kenthurst....... 158 A15
BOWER-BIRD
st. Hinchinbrk...... 393 B4
BOWERBIRD
av. Ingleburn....... 453 F9
cr. St Clair.......... 269 J10
BOWERMAN
pl. Cherrybrook... 219 F15
BOWERS
pl. Leumeah........ 482 K11
BOWES
av. Edgecliff.......... 13 H13
av. Killara............ 253 F15
av. S Penrith........ 266 H2
cl. Cecil Hills....... 362 J9
pl. Doonside........ 273 E2
BOWIE
pl. Wetherill Pk.... 334 D5
BOWLER
av. Fairfield.......... 336 D9
BOWLERS
av. Bexley........... 403 A14
BOWLING GREEN
la. Avalon........... 170 A1
BOWMAN
av. Camden S...... 507 B13
av. Castle Hill....... 247 J4
av. Frenchs Frst... 256 D2
rd. Londonderry.. 148 G13
st. Drummoyne.... 343 G4
st. Mortdale........ 430 H8
st. Pyrmont.......... 12 C2
st. Richmond...... 119 B5
wy. Minto............ 482 K1
BOWMANS
rd. Kings Park...... 244 E5
BOWMER
st. Banksia.......... 403 D12
BOWNESS
ct. Kellyville......... 186 K15
st. Collaroy Plat... 228 D9
BOWNS
rd. Kogarah......... 433 A6
BOWOOD
av. Bexley........... 402 H14
la. St Marys, off
Bowood Pl...... 270 A6
pl. St Marys......... 270 A6
rd. Mt Vernon...... 331 B7
BOWRA
cl. Bangor........... 459 C12
BOWRAL
cl. Hornsby Ht..... 161 J7
la. Kensington..... 376 F11
rd. Blacktown...... 274 F2
st. Greystanes..... 305 H4
st. Kensington..... 376 E11
st. North Rocks.... 279 A2
BOWREY
pl. Shalvey.......... 211 C12
BOWTELL
av. St Johns Pk.... 364 J2
BOX
av. Wilberforce....... 62 G12
la. Jannali........... 460 H12
pl. Mcquarie Fd... 454 H3
rd. Box Hill.......... 184 E1
rd. Caringbah........ 462 G15
rd. Casula........... 424 B2
rd. Jannali........... 460 H12
rd. Kareela........... 461 B13
rd. Prestons......... 394 B16
rd. Rouse Hill....... 184 E1
rd. Sylvania......... 461 J14
rd. Sylvania Wtr... 462 G15
rd. Wakeley......... 334 F13
BOXER
pl. Rooty Hill....... 272 D5
BOXLEY
cr. Bankstown..... 399 G6
BOXSELL
cl. Menai............ 458 K11
BOXWOOD
pl. Cherrybrook... 219 E10
BOYCE
av. Strathfield....... 341 A11
la. Glebe................ 11 H12
la. Maroubra........ 407 E10
pl. Ruse.............. 512 H7
rd. Maroubra....... 406 H8
rd. Maroubra....... 407 A9
st. Glebe................ 11 H12
st. Ryde.............. 282 E14

wy. Clarmnt Ms..... 268 G3
BOYD
av. Lugarno.......... 429 K10
av. W Pnnant Hl... 249 K3
ct. Harringtn Pk... 478 E7
la. Gladesville...... 313 A3
la. Glenbrook....... 234 A14
la. Neutral Bay......... 6 D8
la. Berala, off
Sixth Av.......... 339 D16
pl. Barden Rdg.... 458 G16
pl. Wrrngtn Cty.... 238 E5
st. Austral........... 390 E11
st. Blacktown....... 244 K16
st. Cabramtta W.. 364 K7
st. Claymore........ 481 C8
st. Eagle Vale....... 481 C8
st. Turramurra..... 222 H14
BOYER
pl. Minto............. 453 A16
rd. Beacon Hill..... 257 E4
BOYLE
la. Sutherland...... 490 E3
pl. Shalvey........... 211 B15
st. Balgowlah....... 287 K9
st. Cremorne....... 316 F11
st. Croydon Pk..... 372 A6
st. Ermington...... 310 D4
st. Mosman......... 316 F11
st. Sutherland...... 490 E3
BOYLES
la. Valley Ht......... 203 E7
BOYLSON
pl. Cromer........... 227 H13
BOYNE
av. Pendle Hill...... 306 E1
pl. Baulkham Hl... 246 J4
pl. Killarney Ht..... 256 B15
pl. Wahroonga..... 222 B14
BOYNTON
st. Blaxland......... 233 D6
BOYS
av. Blacktown....... 244 H15
BOYTHORN
av. Ambarvale...... 510 J14
BOZ
pl. Ambarvale...... 511 A14
BRABHAM
dr. Eastern Ck...... 273 C13
BRABYN
st. Denistone E.... 281 F9
st. Fairfield W...... 335 C8
st. N Parramatta.. 278 H15
st. Parramatta...... 278 H15
st. Windsor......... 120 K11
BRACHER
st. East Hills........ 427 J2
BRACK
cl. Abbotsbury..... 333 C12
BRACKEN
cl. Berowra.......... 163 C1
cl. Engadine........ 488 K15
BRACKEN FELL
cl. Castle Hill....... 217 G10
BRACKNELL
av. Hebersham...... 241 F5
rd. Canley Ht....... 365 A3
BRAD
pl. Kings Lngly..... 245 F8
BRADBURY
av. Bradbury........ 511 E6
av. Campbelltwn... 511 E6
st. Tahmoor......... 565 K10
BRADDOCK
pl. Winston Hills.. 247 K15
BRADDON
la. Oxley Park, off
Braddon St...... 240 F16
pl. Edensor Pk..... 363 G3
st. Blacktown...... 273 K4
st. Concord......... 312 A16
st. Oxley Park...... 240 D15
BRADEY
av. Hamondvle..... 396 E15
BRADFIELD
cr. Bonnyrigg....... 364 A5
hwy. Dawes Point....... A G4
hwy. Dawes Point....... 1 G8
hwy. Millers Point....... A G4
hwy. Millers Point....... 1 G8
hwy. Milsons Pt.......... 5 K13
pl. Doonside........ 273 G4
rd. Lindfield......... 283 F4
st. Leumeah........ 482 D16

BRADFORD
la. Balmain.............. 7 J11
st. Alexandria....... 375 E16
st. Balmain.............. 7 J11
st. Pymble........... 223 E14
BRADLEY
av. Bellevue Hill.... 347 H16
av. Berala............ 339 D15
cr. Wiley Park...... 400 H5
ct. W Pnnant Hl.... 248 J7
dr. Carlingford...... 249 J15
la. Elizabeth Bay..... 13 B6
la. Randwick, off
Bradley St........ 376 K13
pl. Illawong.......... 460 A4
pl. Liberty Gr....... 311 C13
pl. Ruse.............. 512 H4
rd. N Richmond...... 87 B13
rd. S Windsor....... 150 E2
st. Drummoyne.... 343 F3
st. Ingleburn........ 453 C10
st. Mulgoa........... 296 G1
st. Randwick......... 376 K13
BRADLEYS HEAD
rd. Mosman......... 317 B9
BRADLY
av. Milsons Pt.......... 6 B12
BRADMAN
av. St Clair........... 270 A15
rd. Menai............ 458 E9
rd. Shalvey........... 211 A15
st. Greystanes...... 305 J9
st. Greystanes...... 306 B9
st. Merrylands..... 308 B15
st. Narwee........... 400 K15
BRADSHAW
av. Moorebank..... 395 G9
pl. Prairiewood.... 334 J8
BRADY
pl. Glenmore Pk... 266 A5
pl. Kellyville......... 216 G5
pl. Prairiewood.... 334 D10
st. Croydon.......... 342 C16
st. Merrylands..... 308 B12
st. Mosman......... 317 A5
wy. Bonnyrigg....... 364 D5
BRADYN
pl. Glenmore Pk... 265 F7
BRAE
st. Bronte............ 377 H9
st. Prospect......... 274 H13
BRAEFIELD
pl. Castle Hill........ 218 B7
BRAEKELL
pl. Kellyville......... 186 J15
BRAEMAR
av. Auburn........... 309 E15
av. Kellyville......... 217 B3
av. St Andrews..... 451 K15
dr. S Penrith......... 267 A2
pl. Roseville......... 255 A16
st. Smithfield....... 336 B5
BRAEMORE
ct. Castle Hill........ 218 K6
BRAESIDE
av. Penshurst....... 431 G7
av. Smithfield....... 335 G5
cr. Earlwood........ 402 D7
cr. Glen Alpine..... 510 E14
pl. Engadine......... 488 J12
rd. Greystanes...... 306 E6
st. Wahroonga..... 222 F5
BRAESMERE
rd. Panania.......... 427 K1
BRAHMA
cl. Bossley Park... 334 A12
rd. N Richmond...... 87 K6
BRAHMS
st. Seven Hills...... 246 D13
wy. Clarmnt Ms..... 268 F3
BRAIDWOOD
av. N Epping......... 251 E8
dr. Prestons......... 392 J16
dr. Prestons......... 392 J15
dr. Prestons......... 393 A16
dr. Prestons......... 422 K1
st. Strathfield S.... 370 H3
BRAIKFIELD
av. Kemps Ck....... 359 J7
BRAIN
av. Lurnea........... 394 D11
BRALLAS
av. St Ives Ch....... 223 J6
BRALLOS
av. Holsworthy..... 396 D15

BRAMBLE
pl. Mcquarie Fd.... 454 E5
pl. Whalan........... 240 J9
BRAMHALL
av. Punchbowl...... 399 J7
BRAMLEY
av. Newport.......... 169 J11
st. Fairfield W....... 335 B8
BRAMPTON
cl. Hinchinbrk...... 363 B16
dr. Kellyville.......... 185 J13
dr. Kellyville.......... 186 A14
dr. Kellyville.......... 216 A1
pl. Greystanes...... 305 J1
BRAMSTON
av. Earlwood......... 402 F2
BRAMWELL
pl. Illawong.......... 460 A3
BRANCOURT
av. Bankstown...... 369 C13
av. Bankstown...... 369 C16
av. Yagoona......... 369 C13
BRAND
st. Artarmon........ 284 K14
st. Croydon.......... 342 D15
st. Dundas Vy...... 279 J6
BRANDE
st. Belmore.......... 371 C15
BRANDERS
la. N Richmond..... 87 C6
BRANDLING
la. Alexandria........ 18 F13
st. Alexandria........ 18 F13
BRANDON
av. Bankstown...... 399 C1
la. Bankstown, off
Brandon Av..... 399 D2
pl. St Ives............ 224 F7
st. Clovelly.......... 377 H11
BRANDOWN
av. Austral........... 361 G15
BRANDS
la. Warriewood.... 198 K8
BRANKSOME
wy. Glenmore Pk... 266 F15
BRANSBY
pl. Mt Annan........ 479 G13
BRANSFIELD
st. Tregear.......... 240 F6
BRANSGROVE
rd. Panania.......... 397 J13
rd. Revesby.......... 398 A13
st. Wentwthvle..... 307 B3
BRANTWOOD
st. Sans Souci...... 463 B5
BRASSIE
st. North Bondi.... 348 C16
BRATSELL
st. Moorebank...... 396 C11
BRAUNBECK
st. Bankstown...... 369 B15
BRAY
av. Earlwood......... 402 G6
ct. North Rocks.... 249 B16
gr. Menai............. 458 K15
la. Neutral Bay........ 6 A8
la. N Sydney........... 6 A8
la. Erskineville, off
Bray St.............. 374 J10
pl. Ambarvale....... 510 F15
st. Drummoyne.... 343 G3
st. Dundas........... 280 A12
st. Erskineville...... 374 K10
st. Fairfield........... 336 E7
st. Mosman......... 316 H4
st. N Sydney........... 5 K8
BRAYE
pl. Padstow Ht..... 429 F7
BRAYS
rd. Breakfast Pt..... 341 K1
rd. Concord.......... 341 K1
BRAYTON
cl. Prestons......... 392 H15
BRAZIER
st. Guildford......... 338 B7
BREAKFAST
rd. Marayong........ 243 K7
BREAKWELL
la. Mortdale......... 431 A4
st. Mortdale......... 430 K5
BREAM
st. Como............. 460 E6
st. Coogee........... 377 E15

BREASLEY
av. Yagoona......... 368 J12
pl. Yagoona......... 369 A11
BRECHIN
cl. Emu Plains..... 235 E14
rd. St Andrews..... 451 K15
BRECON
ct. Castle Hill....... 218 C11
BREDBO
st. Prestons......... 393 B13
BREDON
av. W Pnnant Hl... 218 K16
pl. Jamisontown.. 266 C4
BREELLEN
cl. Tahmoor........ 565 F12
BREEZA
pl. Bangor........... 459 B13
BREILLAT
la. Annandale........ 11 A8
st. Annandale........ 11 A8
BRELL
pl. Kingswood..... 237 F9
BRELOGAIL
st. Northmead..... 277 J11
BREMER
pl. Hinchinbrk..... 392 K1
BREN
cl. St Clair........... 269 K12
BRENAN
st. Fairfield.......... 335 J6
st. Lilyfield............ 10 G8
st. Smithfield....... 335 J6
BRENDA
av. Lidcombe....... 340 B7
ct. North Rocks... 248 J15
rd. Kemps Ck....... 360 B11
st. Ingleburn....... 453 A9
wy. Epping........... 251 C15
BRENDAN
pl. Quakers Hill.... 213 K9
BRENDON
pl. Carlingford..... 279 J1
st. North Ryde..... 282 C9
BRENNAN
cl. Asquith.......... 192 A14
la. Newtown.......... 17 G12
pl. Blackett.......... 241 B1
pl. Minto............ 482 J1
st. Alexandria........ 19 A15
st. Yagoona......... 368 F10
BRENNANS
la. Russell Lea..... 343 D4
rd. Arncliffe.......... 403 J10
BRENNANS DAM
rd. Vineyard......... 152 C3
BRENT
st. Rozelle............... 7 B15
st. Russell Lea..... 343 E6
BRENTFORD
rd. Wahroonga.... 222 B6
BRENTIN
pl. Hebersham..... 241 E10
BRENTWOOD
av. Richmond...... 118 G7
av. Turramurra..... 222 G11
av. Warrawee....... 222 G11
gr. Wrrngtn Dns.. 237 J4
pl. Frenchs Frst... 257 A2
st. Fairfield W...... 335 B8
wy. Castle Hill...... 248 H3
BRERETON
av. Marrickville..... 373 J9
la. Marrickville, off
Brereton Av..... 373 K10
st. Gladesville...... 312 G7
BRETON
pl. Emu Heights... 235 B2
BRETT
av. Balmain East...... 8 G7
av. Hornsby Ht..... 191 E2
av. Wentwthvle.... 277 A10
pl. Ingleburn....... 453 E11
pl. W Pnnant Hl... 249 H4
st. Kings Lngly..... 245 G9
st. Revesby......... 428 H1
st. Tennyson....... 312 E10
BREUC
pl. Box Hill.......... 154 E13
BREUST
pl. Punchbowl..... 400 C3
BREWER
av. Liberty Gr....... 311 B10
cr. S Wntwthvle... 307 D5
pl. Lugarno......... 430 A12

st. Concord 342 A4
st. Marsden Pk 182 A10
BREWERS
la. Freemns Rch 91 B2
BREWON
cl. Bossley Park 333 F9
BREWONGLE
av. Penrith 237 E4
BREWSTER
pl. Leumeah 482 F12
BREYLEY
st. Cambrdg Pk 237 J8
BRIAL
pl. Minto 482 H8
BRIALY
pl. Picton 561 D4
BRIAN
st. Merrylnds W 306 H12
st. Ryde 282 A9
BRIAR
la. St Peters, off Henry St 374 F14
pl. Georges Hall 367 H11
rd. Airds 511 J13
rd. Bradbury 511 J13
st. St Ives 224 D11
BRIARWOOD
av. Glenmore Pk 266 H13
BRIBIE
cl. Green Valley 363 A12
BRICE
cl. Illawong 459 K5
wy. St Helens Pk 540 K7
BRICKENDON
ct. Wattle Grove 395 K16
BRICKETWOOD
dr. Woodcroft 243 G7
BRICKFIELD
pl. Blacktown 275 A4
rd. Windsor 121 B13
st. N Parramatta 278 E16
st. Parramatta 278 E16
st. Ruse 512 H3
BRIDDON
cl. Pennant Hills 220 D14
BRIDGE
la. Drummoyne 313 G15
la. Glebe 12 D10
la. Sydney A J12
la. Belmore, off Gladstone St 371 D16
rd. Belmore 371 D16
rd. Blaxland 233 C5
rd. Forest Lodge 11 H15
rd. Glebe 12 C11
rd. Homebush 341 A10
rd. Hornsby 191 G14
rd. Hornsby 191 H14
rd. Manly 288 H4
rd. Marsfield 282 A8
rd. North Ryde 282 A8
rd. Parramatta 277 K13
rd. Queenscliff 288 H3
rd. Ryde 282 A8
rd. Stanmore 17 A6
rd. Ultimo 12 D9
rd. Westmead 307 D3
st. Balmain 344 E4
st. Bexley 402 C16
st. Brooklyn 76 C11
st. Cabramatta 365 K8
st. Epping 251 A16
st. Erskineville 18 A16
st. Erskineville 18 B14
st. Granville 308 F10
st. Hurstville 431 F5
st. Lane Cove 314 A3
st. Lidcombe 339 H8
st. Padstow 399 G15
st. Parramatta 279 A16
st. Penshurst 431 F5
st. Picton 563 A14
st. Picton 565 D1
st. Pymble 253 E5
st. Rydalmere 309 C1
st. Schofields 183 B14
st. Sydney A K11
st. Sydney 1 H14
st. Tempe 374 C15
st. Thirlmere 565 D1
st. Werrington 239 C16
st. Windsor 121 D7
st. Artarmon, off Cameron Av 284 K15
st.w, Lidcombe, off Samuel St 339 G8
BRIDGE END
Wollstncraft 315 D10
BRIDGE QUARRY
pl. Glenbrook 234 D11
BRIDGES
av. Croydon 342 F13
av. Holsworthy 396 B13
rd. Moorebank 395 H5
st. Kurnell 465 H9
st. Maroubra 407 F13
BRIDGE STAIRS
. The Rocks A G3
BRIDGET
pl. Kellyville 215 G5
BRIDGE VIEW
st. Blacktown 274 F8
BRIDGEVIEW
av. Cammeray 315 J4
cr. Forestville 255 F11
cr. Mt Riverview 204 G16
cr. Thornleigh 221 B13
rd. Beverly Hills 430 J2
rd. Engadine 489 D14
BRIDLE
av. Currans Hill 479 K9
av. Oakdale 500 G11
BRIDPORT
cl. West Hoxton 392 D7
BRIENS
rd. Northmead 277 G11
rd. Wentwthvle 277 D13
BRIER
cr. Quakers Hill 243 G4
pl. Mt Pritchard 364 E9
BRIERLEY
cr. Plumpton 241 H11
pl. Eagle Vale 480 K9
BRIERLY
st. Mosman 316 G9
BRIERWOOD
pl. Frenchs Frst 255 J1
BRIERY
pl. Cranebrook 207 E12
BRIGADOON
av. Glenmore Pk 266 F12
ct. Epping 281 C3
BRIGALOW
av. Camden S 507 B11
av. Casula 394 E14
pl. Engadine 489 F9
pl. Westleigh 220 E9
st. Cabramatta 365 G9
BRIGANTINE
st. Chipping Ntn 366 K15
BRIGG
rd. Epping 281 C2
BRIGGS
pl. Doonside 273 F4
pl. St Helens Pk 541 A11
st. Camperdwn 17 F4
BRIGHT
cl. Edensor Pk 333 J14
st. Guildford 338 A5
st. Marrickville 16 B15
st. Ryde 312 E3
BRIGHTMAN
cr. Bidwill 241 G1
BRIGHTMORE
la. Cremorne, off Illiliwa St 316 E7
st. Cremorne 316 E6
BRIGHTON
av. Btn-le-Sds 433 K5
av. Campsie 372 A10
av. Croydon Pk 372 B8
av. Panania 398 C16
bvd. Bondi Beach 378 E1
bvd. North Bondi 378 E1
la. Croydon Pk 372 C5
la. Petersham 15 K9
la. Riverstone 183 B11
pde. Btn-le-Sds 433 K1
rd. Coogee 377 E15
rd. Peakhurst 400 F16
st. Balgowlah 287 G7
st. Botany 405 K13
st. Bundeena 523 K11
st. Croydon 372 C3
st. Croydon Pk 372 C5
st. Curl Curl 258 E13
st. Greystanes 305 K8
st. Harbord 258 E13
st. Kogarah Bay 432 J11
st. Petersham 15 F9
st. Riverstone 183 A12
BRIGID
pl. Quakers Hill 214 F15
BRINAWA
st. Mona Vale 199 A5
BRINDABELLA
dr. Horngsea Pk 392 F16
la. Narellan 478 B10
pl. W Pnnant Hl 248 J5
st. Ruse 512 H7
BRINDISI
pl. Avalon 139 H14
BRINGELLY
av. Pendle Hill 276 G14
la. Kingswood, off Bringelly Rd 237 H13
pl. Bonnyrigg Ht 363 B5
rd. Austral 391 A16
rd. Bringelly 388 E13
rd. Horngsea Pk 392 A16
rd. Kingswood 237 G16
rd. Leppington 421 A1
rd. Rossmore 389 B14
rd. West Hoxton 421 H1
BRIONY
pl. Mona Vale 198 K3
BRISBANE
av. E Lindfield 254 J14
av. Lurnea 394 D13
av. Mt Krng-gai 162 J13
av. Rodd Point 9 B1
la. Waterloo 19 G13
pl. Cromer 227 J13
rd. Campbelltwn 512 B6
rd. Castle Hill 218 E14
rd. Riverstone 182 H1
rd. St Johns Pk 334 D16
rd. Vineyard 152 G14
st. Bondi Jctn 22 H9
st. Chifley 437 A5
st. Fairlight 288 C8
st. Harris Park 308 F7
st. Illawong 459 H4
st. Oxley Park 240 E16
st. St Marys 239 K15
st. Surry Hills F E7
st. Surry Hills 3 K12
BRISCOE
cr. Kings Lngly 245 C5
BRISSENDEN
av. Collaroy 229 C13
BRISTOL
av. Pymble 253 J1
av. Raby 451 G15
av. Wahroonga 221 J11
cct. Blacktown 274 B7
la. N Narrabeen 228 J2
rd. Hurstville 432 A3
st. Merrylnds W 306 K15
st. N Parramatta 278 C9
BRISTOW
la. Peakhurst 430 F2
BRITANNIA
av. Burwood 341 K11
av. Merrylands 307 K13
la. Woollahra 21 J3
rd. Castle Hill 217 J12
st. Pennant Hills 250 J2
BRITTAIN
cr. Hillsdale 406 G14
BRITTANIA
pl. Bligh Park 150 E7
BRITTANY
pl. Peakhurst 430 C13
BRITTEN
cl. Cranebrook 207 H9
pl. Bossley Park 333 J12
BRITTON
cl. Elderslie 507 G2
st. Smithfield 336 B1
BRIXHAM
pl. Chipping Ntn 366 G16
BRIXTON
rd. Berala 339 E13
rd. Lidcombe 339 E13
BROAD
st. Bass Hill 368 D7
st. Cabramatta 365 D8
st. Croydon Pk 371 K8
st. Prospect 275 B11
BROAD ARROW
rd. Beverly Hills 401 A13
rd. Narwee 400 K14
rd. Riverwood 400 D15
BROADBENT
st. Kingsford 406 K5
BROADFORD
st. Bexley 402 J11
st. St Andrews 452 A12
BROADHURST
pl. Baulkham Hl 246 K12
rd. Ingleburn 453 A7
BROADLEAF
cr. Kellyville 215 K1
BROADLEYS
la. Marrickville, off Malakoff St 373 K12
BROADMEADOWS
st. St Johns Pk 364 F3
BROADOAK
pl. Castle Hill 218 J7
BROADSIDE
st. Balmain East 8 D9
BROADSWORD
pl. Castle Hill 217 G5
BROADWAY
Chippendale 18 G1
Punchbowl 400 E5
Ultimo 3 C16
BROCAS
pl. Quakers Hill 214 E13
BROCK
av. St Marys 239 H16
la. St Marys, off Brock Av 239 H16
st. Mount Druitt 271 F3
BROCKAMIN
dr. S Penrith 267 C5
BROCKLEHURST
la. Kingsgrove 402 A11
BROCKLEY
st. Lilyfield 10 H3
st. Rozelle 10 H3
BROCKMAN
av. Revesby Ht 429 A7
st. Wakeley 334 J12
BROCKS
la. Newtown 18 A9
BROCKWELL
pl. Blakehurst 432 F16
BRODERICK
st. Balmain 344 E4
st. Camperdwn 17 F3
BRODIE
av. Little Bay 437 G13
cir. Baulkham Hl 248 A11
st. Baulkham Hl 248 A10
st. Paddington 4 K16
st. Rydalmere 309 B2
st. Yagoona 368 G9
BROE
av. Arncliffe 403 F7
av. East Hills 427 H5
BROGO
pl. Prestons 393 C13
BROKENWOOD
pl. Baulkham Hl 246 J2
pl. Cherrybrook 219 E12
BROLEN
wy. Cecil Park 331 J12
BROLGA
cr. Green Valley 363 F14
gln. St Clair 270 E12
pl. Belrose 225 F14
pl. Gymea Bay 491 G9
pl. Ingleburn 453 D8
wy. W Pnnant Hl 249 E7
BROMBOROUGH
rd. Roseville 284 E5
BROMFIELD
av. Prospect 275 C11
av. Toongabbie 276 E9
BROMLEY
av. Greenacre 370 B13
av. Pymble 253 G3
av. Cremorne, off Kareela Rd 316 G12
rd. Emu Heights 235 A6
st. Canley Vale 366 G5
wy. Glenhaven 218 D5
BROMPTON
rd. Kensington 376 C10
st. Marrickville 374 D10
BROMUS
pl. Mcquarie Fd 454 G5
BROMWICH
pl. Menai 458 H7
st. Greystanes 306 A10
BRON
cl. W Pnnant Hl 248 H5
BRONHILL
av. East Ryde 283 B16
BRONSDON
st. Smithfield 335 B4
BRONSGROVE
cl. S Penrith 267 B7
BRONTE
av. Glenwood 215 H14
cl. West Hoxton 392 E6
cl. Wetherill Pk 334 H6
pl. Winston Hills 277 F2
pl. Woodbine 481 D14
rd. Bondi Jctn 22 J7
rd. Bondi Jctn 22 J9
rd. Bronte 377 J8
rd. Waverley 377 E6
wy. Glenmore Pk 266 G12
BRONTE MARINE
dr. Bronte 378 B8
BRONTI
st. Mascot 405 E7
BRONZEWING
st. Ingleburn 453 F6
st. Tahmoor 565 C11
st. Tahmoor 565 J13
st. Thirlmere 565 B9
BROOK
la. Fairfield Ht 335 K9
la. Crows Nest, off Brook St 315 G5
rd. Currans Hill 479 G6
rd. Glenbrook 264 C4
rd. Seaforth 287 D8
st. Coogee 377 G16
st. Crows Nest 315 G5
st. Marayong 243 G5
st. Naremburn 315 G4
BROOKDALE
tce. Glenbrook 234 D16
BROOKE
av. Castle Hill 217 C10
pl. Silverdale 353 K13
st. Bass Hill 367 G8
st. Engadine 489 A16
BROOKER
av. Beacon Hill 257 E4
av. Oatlands 279 A13
st. Colyton 270 C3
BROOKES
la. Newtown 17 E9
st. Hunters Hill 314 B12
st. Thornleigh 221 D7
BROOKFIELD
av. Wrrngtn Dns 238 B5
pl. St Ives 223 H8
rd. Minto 482 H4
BROOKHOLLOW
av. Baulkham Hl 216 H15
BROOKLANDS
rd. Glenbrook 264 D2
BROOKLYN
la. Double Bay 14 B10
la. Tempe, off Brooklyn St 404 C2
rd. Brooklyn 75 C11
st. Burwood 342 B15
st. Strathfield S 371 B5
st. Tempe 404 B1
BROOKPINE
pl. W Pnnant Hl 248 K3
BROOKS
la. Agnes Banks 146 K1
rd. Denham Ct 452 G1
rd. Ingleburn 452 G1
st. Guildford 337 D6
st. Linley Point 313 H7
st. Mcquarie Fd 454 B3
BROOKSBANK
rd. Gilead 539 F11
BROOKS BEND
Mt Annan 479 B16
BROOKS POINT
rd. Appin 568 A12
BROOKVALE
av. Brookvale 257 K10
BROOKVIEW
st. Currans Hill 479 J10
BROOM
pl. Loftus 489 J10
pl. St Andrews 452 A14

BROOMAN
st. Prestons 422 K1
BROOME
av. Centnnial Pk 22 B6
pl. Bligh Park 150 C5
st. Maroubra 407 D15
BROOMFIELD
st. Cabramatta 365 J10
st. Canley Vale 365 K6
BROOS
rd. Oakville 152 F3
BROTCHIE
av. Matraville 436 G8
BROTHERS
av. Cammeray 316 C3
av. Northbridge 316 C3
pl. Narellan Vale 479 A16
st. Dundas Vy 280 A11
BROTHERSON
av. Matraville 436 G4
BROTHERTON
st. S Wntwthvle 307 B7
BROUGHAM
la. Glebe 12 C11
la. Potts Point 4 G7
la. Woolmloo 4 G7
la. Emu Plains, off Brougham St 235 B12
pl. Raby 451 E12
st. Emu Plains 235 B12
st. Potts Point 4 H7
st. Woolmloo 4 H7
BROUGHTON
av. Castle Hill 218 J14
cr. Appin 568 G9
ct. Kellyville 217 A3
la. Drummoyne 343 H4
la. Glebe 12 E13
pl. Barden Rdg 488 F3
pl. Davidson 225 B16
rd. Artarmon 284 H16
rd. Strathfield 341 B11
st. Ashfield 342 H15
st. Camden 507 A3
st. Campbelltwn 511 G3
st. Canterbury 372 F12
st. Concord 341 K10
st. Drummoyne 343 H5
st. Glebe 12 D11
st. Hinchinbrk 362 K16
st. Kirribilli 6 A13
st. Milsons Pt 6 A13
st. Mortdale 431 A7
st. Old Guildfrd 337 E9
st. Paddington 13 D15
st. Parramatta 308 H2
st. Sans Souci 463 A1
st. Woolmloo 4 D6
BROULA
av. Baulkham Hl 246 H8
cl. Caringbah 492 F6
rd. Wahroonga 223 C4
BROULEE
pl. Carlingford 280 C5
pl. Engadine 518 G1
BROWALLIA
cr. Loftus 489 K10
BROWLEE
pl. Mt Pritchard 364 K10
BROWN
av. Botany 405 J11
cl. Menai 458 G15
la. Newtown 17 J11
la. Paddington 4 K13
pl. Mt Annan 509 G3
pl. Shalvey 211 B14
rd. Bonnyrigg 363 K8
rd. Bonnyrigg Ht 363 G6
rd. Maroubra 407 F15
st. Alexandria 18 G15
st. Ashfield 372 H2
st. Bronte 377 H8
st. Camperdwn 17 J7
st. Chatswood 284 H10
st. Chester Hill 337 H12
st. Forestville 255 K7
st. Lewisham 15 A9
st. Lewisham 15 B7
st. Newtown 17 H7
st. Newtown 17 J10
st. N Parramatta 278 D10
st. Paddington 4 K14
st. Penrith 236 G13
st. Riverstone 182 D11
st. St Peters 374 G13
st. Smithfield 335 C6
BROWNE
pde. Warwck Frm 365 F16
pl. Baulkham Hl 247 D1
st. Campbelltwn 511 F3
BROWNING
av. Campbelltwn 512 B3
av. Lakemba 401 A1
cl. Mount Druitt 241 F11
cl. Wetherill Pk 334 H6
la. Hurlstone Pk 372 K11
pl. Lalor Park 245 J13
rd. N Turramrra 223 F7
st. Campsie 372 A11
st. East Hills 427 K5
BROWNLOW
ct. Wattle Grove 425 K1
pl. Ambarvale 510 G13
BROWNLOW HILL LOOP
rd. Brownlow Hl 475 C8
BROWNS
av. Austral 391 E14
av. Austral 421 E1
av. Enmore 16 F14
la. N Sydney K A2
la. N Sydney 5 E5
la. Hunters Hill, off Ady St 313 K10
rd. Blaxland 233 G6
rd. Blaxlands Rdg 56 C1
rd. Gordon 253 F10
rd. The Oaks 502 G8
rd. Wahroonga 221 E15
rd. Wilberforce 62 A11
BROWSE
pl. Green Valley 363 A9
BROXBOURNE
st. Westmead 307 G4
BRUBRI
st. Busby 363 H13
BRUCE
av. Belfield 371 E12
av. Caringbah 492 E15
av. Clovelly 378 A13
av. Killara 253 J10
av. Manly 288 G13
av. Panania 428 E4
la. Kingsford 406 F2
la. Newtown 17 K11
la. N Curl Curl 259 B10
la.e, Stanmore 16 D9
la.w, Stanmore 16 C9
pl. Kellyville 185 K5
rd. Glenbrook 264 A5
rd. Vineyard 152 D7
st. Ashfield 373 A2
st. Bexley 432 H3
st. Blacktown 244 K15
st. Btn-le-Sds 433 K1
st. Crows Nest 315 F8
st. Kingsford 406 F2
st. Kogarah Bay 432 H13
st. Lansvale 366 F9
st. Marrickville 373 E16
st. Merrylnds W 306 G13
st. Mona Vale 199 D10
st. Rozelle 7 A12
st. Ryde 282 D13
st. Springwood 202 C10
st. Stanmore 16 C9
st. Waterloo 20 B15
st. Wollstncraft 315 F8
BRUCE BENNETTS
pl. Maroubra 406 K9
BRUCEDALE
av. Epping 281 D1
dr. Baulkham Hl 247 F4
BRUCE NEALE
dr. Penrith 236 D7
BRUCHHAUSER
cr. Elderslie 507 H1
BRUCKNER
pl. Clarmnt Ms 268 G2
BRUDENELL
av. Leumeah 481 K16
BRUMBY
cr. Emu Heights 235 C5
la. Emu Heights, off Brumby Cr 235 B5
st. Surry Hills 19 H3
BRUNDAH
rd. Tahmoor 565 D6
rd. Tahmoor 565 G5
rd. Thirlmere 565 D6
BRUNDY
cl. W Pnnant Hl 249 C8
BRUNE
st. Doonside 243 C5
BRUNEI
cr. Holsworthy 426 D4
BRUNEL
cl. Cherrybrook 219 K7
BRUNETTE
dr. Castle Hill 248 B5
BRUNKER
rd. Chullora 369 G8
rd. Greenacre 369 G8
rd. Potts Hill 369 A7
rd. Yagoona 369 A7
BRUNSWICK
av. Liberty Gr 311 B10
av. Strathfield 341 E14
cl. Colyton 270 F9
cr. St Johns Pk 334 D16
pde. Ashfield 372 F4
st. Granville 308 C14
st. Merrylands 308 B14
st. Waterloo 19 H13
BRUNSWICK HEADS
cr. Hoxton Park 392 J6
BRUNTON
pl. Marsfield 251 J13
st. Panania 428 D4
BRUSH
cl. Green Valley 363 B10
rd. Eastwood 280 G8
rd. West Ryde 280 H12
wy. Airds 512 F10
BRUSHBOX
pl. Bradbury 511 E10
pl. Cherrybrook 219 J8
BRUSHFORD
av. Castle Hill 248 C5
BRUSHWOOD
dr. Alfords Point 459 B2
dr. Rouse Hill 185 B7
pl. Hornsby 221 B2
BRUSSELS
cr. Rooty Hill 271 J2
st. Mascot 405 G6
st. N Strathfield 341 C4
st. S Granville 338 G3
BRUTON
wy. Canley Vale 366 F5
BRUTUS
wy. Rsemeadow 540 J3
BRUXNER
pl. Doonside 273 G4
BRUZZANO
pl. Cromer 258 G1
BRYAN
av. Normanhurst 221 E9
BRYANT
la. Rockdale 403 E14
pl. Fairfield W 335 D9
st. Narwee 400 K14
st. Padstow 399 C11
st. Rockdale 403 E14
wy. Claymore 481 C12
BRYCE
av. St Ives 254 E1
BRYSON
la. Toongabbie 276 G8
st. Chatswood 284 H13
st. Toongabbie 276 G8
BUANGI
pl. Gymea Bay 491 E11
BUCHAN
av. Edmndsn Pk 422 H5
pl. Kings Lngly 245 G6
pl. Wetherill Pk 334 F6
BUCHANAN
av. Bonnet Bay 460 B10
la. Windsor Dn 180 K4
st. Balmain 7 G14
st. Carlton 432 K6
BUCKARA
cl. Erskine Park 300 D2
BUCKERIDGE
pl. Kellyville 216 G5
BUCKETT
pl. Kurrajong 85 C2
BUCKHURST
av. Point Piper 14 J4
BUCKINBAH
pl. Lilli Pilli 522 F2
BUCKINGHAM
av. Normanhurst 221 F9
cr. Chipping Ntn 366 H15
la. Killara 253 J13
rd. Baulkham Hl 247 D5
rd. Killara 253 J14
st. Canley Ht 365 G2
st. Canley Vale 365 G2
st. Pitt Town 92 H14
st. Surry Hills 19 G4
BUCKLAND
av. Carlingford 279 H1
la. Alexandria 18 J14
la. Newtown 17 J10
rd. Casula 394 K15
rd. Casula 395 A13
rd. St Clair 269 J8
rd. Springwood 202 C1
st. Alexandria 19 A13
st. Chippendale 18 K3
st. Greenacre 370 E8
BUCKLE
av. Engadine 488 D15
BUCKLEY
av. Revesby 398 K15
cl. Fairfield W 335 A9
la. Marrickville 374 D14
st. Marrickville 374 C14
BUCKLEYS
rd. Winston Hills 276 H2
BUCKNELL
la. Newtown 17 K9
st. Newtown 17 K9
BUCKRA
st. Turramurra 223 D11
BUCKRIDGE
st. Pitt Town 92 J16
BUCKWALL
av. Greenacre 370 B14
BUCKWELL
dr. Hassall Gr 211 K15
BUDAPEST
st. Rooty Hill 271 J4
BUDBURY
st. Harringtn Pk 478 F6
BUDD
av. Little Bay 437 B12
st. Drummoyne 343 F4
BUDDS
la. Stanmore 16 B8
BUDERIM
av. Kareela 461 B12
BUDGE
cl. Glenmore Pk 265 F7
la. Glenmore Pk, off Budge Cl 265 G7
BUDGEREE
rd. Toongabbie 276 D9
BUDGERIGAR
st. Green Valley 363 F11
BUDINS
rd. Kenthurst 187 D6
BUDYAN
rd. Grays Point 491 B15
BUENA VISTA
av. Denistone 281 B11
av. Mona Vale 198 J5
av. Mosman 317 C13
rd. Winmalee 173 A14
wy. St Ives 224 F6
BUFFALO
pl. Toongabbie 275 G13
rd. Gladesville 312 G3
rd. Ryde 282 B15
wy. Airds 511 J16
wy. Kellyville 186 A15
BUGATTI
dr. Ingleburn 453 H9
BUGDEN
av. Milperra 397 E11
pl. Campbelltwn 511 A7
BUGONG
st. Prestons 392 H13
BUICK
pl. Ingleburn 453 G10
rd. Cromer 258 E1
BUIN
pl. Glenfield 424 C13
BUIST
st. Bass Hill 368 B8
st. Sefton 368 D8
st. Yagoona 368 D8
BUJAN
st. Glenmore Pk 266 C12
BUJARA
pl. Bangor 459 D12
BUJWA BAY
rd. Cowan 104 B12
BUKA
pl. Glenfield 424 G9
BUKARI
wy. Glenmore Pk 266 D8
BULA
av. Campsie 401 K3
BULAH
cl. Berowra Ht 132 J10
wy. Seven Hills 275 K6
BULARA
st. Duffys Frst 165 A15
BULBA
rd. Engadine 489 F9
BULBERRY
pl. Engadine 489 F9
BULBI
av. Winmalee 173 A10
pl. Glenmore Pk 266 B12
BULBINE
st. Engadine 518 E2
BULBUL
av. Green Valley 363 F13
BULGA
cl. Hornsby Ht 161 J12
pl. Hoxton Park 392 H7
rd. Dover Ht 348 G8
BULGALLA
pl. Caringbah 492 H12
BULIMBA
av. Kareela 461 B12
BULKARA
rd. Bellevue Hill 14 H9
BULKIRA
rd. Epping 281 C3
BULL
pl. Harringtn Pk 478 D1
st. Warwck Frm 365 J16
BULLARA
cr. Narraweena 258 A3
BULLAWAI
pl. Beecroft 250 E10
BULLDOG
rd. Moorebank 425 A3
BULLECOURT
av. Engadine 518 F1
av. Milperra 397 G9
av.n, Mosman 317 A1
av.s, Mosman 317 A3
la. Ultimo 3 A10
wy. Matraville 407 B15
BULLER
la. Lane Cove 314 F1
rd. Artarmon 284 J15
st. Bellevue Hill 377 H1
st. Jannali 460 H13
st. N Parramatta 278 F16
st. Parramatta 278 F16
st. S Turramrra 252 C6
BULLETIN
pl. Sydney B B9
BULLI
cl. Prestons 392 J14
rd. Old Tngabbie 276 F9
rd. Toongabbie 276 F8
rd. Wentwthvle 277 A9
st. Badgerys Ck 358 G8
BULLI APPIN
rd. Appin 568 H13
BULLIVANT
la. N Sydney K F3
BULLOCK
av. Chester Hill 337 J12
BULLS
av.w, Burraneer 523 E1
rd. Burraneer 523 E1
rd. Wakeley 334 H15
BULMANN
av. Horngsea Pk 392 F16
BULOLO
dr. Whalan 240 J10
pl. Glenfield 424 G9
BULU
dr. Glenmore Pk 265 K10
BULUMIN
st. Como 460 G5
BULWARA
rd. Pyrmont 12 G4
rd. Pyrmont 12 H6
rd. Ultimo 3 A12
BULWARRA
av. Sefton 368 E5
pl. Berowra Ht 133 D8

st. Caringbah 492 H9
BUMBERA
st. Prestons 392 H15
BUMBORAH POINT
rd. Matraville 436 F7
rd. Port Botany 436 F7
BUNA
cl. Glenmore Pk 266 D12
cl. Mt Annan 479 C12
cl. N Turramrra 223 D1
ct. Ryde 282 E14
pl. Allambie Ht 257 D10
pl. Glenfield 424 H12
rd. Holsworthy 426 G9
st. Holsworthy 426 D3
BUNARBA
rd. Gymea Bay 491 F8
BUNBIE
la. West Ryde 311 F1
BUNBINLA
av. Mt Riverview 234 D1
BUNBURY
av. Sutherland 460 C14
rd. Mcquarie Fd 453 J2
BUNCE
pl. Wrrngtn Cty 238 G5
rd. Liverpool 394 H2
BUNDA
pl. Glenmore Pk 266 D11
BUNDABAH
av. St Ives 224 B9
BUNDAH
st. Winmalee 173 A10
BUNDALEER
st. Belrose 225 K4
BUNDANOON
pl. Hornsby Ht 191 H5
rd. Engadine 489 A6
rd. Prestons 392 K16
rd. Woronora Ht 489 A6
BUNDARA
cl. Mona Vale 169 E16
st. Beverly Hills 401 E13
wy. Baulkham Hl 246 E11
BUNDARRA
av.n, Wahroonga 222 C5
av.s, Wahroonga 222 B7
ct. Wattle Grove 395 K12
rd. Bellevue Hill 347 H15
rd. Campbelltwn 511 K6
rd. Regentville 235 E16
st. Lansvale 366 G8
st. Waterfall 519 D13
BUNDEENA
dr. Bundeena 523 H9
dr. Royal N P 523 B14
rd. Woodbine 481 F12
BUNDELL
st. Harringtn Pk 478 E2
BUNDELUK
cr. Glenmore Pk 266 C12
BUNDEMAR
st. Miller 393 H2
wy. Airds 512 E10
BUNDILLA
av. Winston Hills 277 F6
pl. Dee Why 258 E4
BUNDOCK
la. Randwick 407 B3
la. S Coogee 407 B3
st. Kingsford 407 B3
st. Randwick 407 B3
st. S Coogee 407 B3
BUNDOON
la. Manly 288 F7
BUNDY
cl. Mcquarie Fd 454 H5
BUNGAL
st. Engadine 488 G14
BUNGALOE
av. Balgowlah 287 H12
av. Balgowlah Ht 287 H12
BUNGALOW
av. Pymble 253 C1
cr. Bankstown 369 D16
pde. Wrrngtn Dns 238 B6
rd. Peakhurst 400 E16
rd. Plumpton 241 J10
rd. Roselands 401 A9
BUNGAN
la. Mona Vale 199 C4
pl. Woodbine 481 K8
st. Mona Vale 199 B4
BUNGAN HEAD
rd. Newport 169 H13
BUNGAREE
la. Mosman, off Beaconsfield Rd 317 E8
pl. Miller 393 H3
rd. Pendle Hill 276 F13
rd. Toongabbie 276 F13
rd. Yellow Rock 174 J14
BUNGARN
pl. Caringbah 493 A12
BUNGARRA
cr. Chipping Ntn 396 G4
BUNGARRIBEE
rd. Blacktown 274 B2
rd. Doonside 273 F2
BUNGAY
st. Leichhardt 10 F14
BUNGENDORE
st. Ingleside 197 E5
BUNGONIA
ct. Wattle Grove 395 J12
rd. Leumeah 482 D14
st. Prestons 392 H15
BUNGOONA
av. Elanora Ht 198 A16
BUNGOWEN
av. Thornleigh 221 A7
BUNGULLA
st. Sadleir 364 A16
BUNKER
pde. Bonnyrigg 364 C5
st. Minchinbury 271 H9
st. Minto 452 H14
BUNN
la. Pyrmont 12 J5
st. Pyrmont 12 J5
BUNNAL
av. Winmalee 173 B11
BUNNERONG
rd. Chifley 436 K6
rd. Daceyville 406 G4
rd. Eastgardens 406 G12
rd. Hillsdale 406 G12
rd. Kingsford 406 G4
rd. Maroubra 406 G12
rd. Matraville 436 H1
rd. Pagewood 406 G4
rd. Pagewood 406 G8
BUNNING
pl. Doonside 273 G2
BUNROY
cr. Horngsea Pk 392 F15
BUNSEN
av. Emerton 240 J4
BUNT
av. Greenacre 370 B10
BUNTING
st. Emerton 241 A6
BUNYA
cl. Baulkham Hl 246 K2
cr. Bowen Mtn 83 K10
pde. S Coogee 407 J6
pl. Glenmore Pk 265 H11
pl. Mcquarie Fd 454 G4
pl. Spring Farm 508 E1
pl. Wakeley 334 H12
rd. Bidwill 241 F1
wy. Horngsea Pk 392 F14
BUNYALA
la. Carss Park 432 F15
st. Blakehurst 432 E15
st. Carss Park 432 E14
BUNYAN
pl. Bangor 459 B12
rd. Glenbrook 234 A12
rd. Leonay 235 C14
st. Wetherill Pk 334 E6
BUNYANA
av. Wahroonga 223 B5
BUNYARRA
dr. Emu Plains 235 A9
BUNYIP BLUE GUM
rd. Faulconbdg 171 F12
BUNYULA
rd. Bellevue Hill 347 J15
BURAN
cl. Mount Druitt 241 E15
BURANDA
cr. St Johns Pk 334 C16
BURBANG
cr. Rydalmere 309 G2
BURBANK
av. East Hills 427 J6
av. Picnic Point 427 K7
BURBONG
st. Kingsford 406 K4
BURCH
la. Mascot, off Hughes Av 405 E2
BURCHMORE
rd. Manly Vale 288 B4
BURDEKIN
cr. St Ives 254 D4
ct. Wattle Grove 396 A13
la. Surry Hills 20 E4
pl. Engadine 488 J9
rd. Quakers Hill 213 F6
rd. Wilberforce 92 H1
BURDETT
cr. Blacktown 244 A16
st. Canley Ht 365 H4
st. Hornsby 221 H1
st. Wahroonga 222 A1
BURFITT
pde. Glenbrook 263 K1
rd. Riverstone 182 F15
st. Leichhardt 9 D14
BURFORD
st. Colyton 270 F6
st. Merrylands 307 F14
st. Minto 452 J13
BURGAN
cl. Menai 458 H13
BURGE
st. Vaucluse 348 F5
BURGESS
rd. Freemns Rch 90 D5
rd. Freemns Rch 90 F4
rd. S Penrith 267 C2
st. Beverley Pk 433 C10
st. Richmond 118 J5
BURGOYNE
la. Gordon 253 H6
la. Mt Lewis, off Frank St 369 K16
st. Gordon 253 H6
BURGUNDY
cl. Cecil Hills 362 E1
ct. Eschol Park 481 C5
pl. Minchinbury 271 K9
BURILLA
av. N Curl Curl 258 F10
BURING
av. Leonay 235 B16
cr. Minchinbury 271 H9
BURKE
av. Berala 339 D12
av. Wrrngtn Cty 238 H8
cr. Oatley 430 H13
pl. Mt Colah 162 B11
pl. St Johns Pk 364 H1
rd. Cronulla 493 K9
rd. Ingleburn 422 K9
rd. Lalor Park 245 F13
sq. Lansdowne 367 C5
st. Appin 568 H12
st. Blacktown 274 B6
st. Chifley 437 A4
st. Como 460 F7
st. Concord W 341 E1
st. Newport 169 K7
st. Oatley 430 H13
st. Ruse 512 F3
st. Ryde 282 F15
st. Telopea 279 G11
BURLEIGH
av. Caringbah 493 A4
st. Burwood 342 A14
st. Lindfield 284 E3
BURLEY
cl. Illawong 459 K3
rd. Horsley Pk 302 D11
rd. Padstow 429 E1
st. Lane Cove W 284 F16
BURLEY GRIFFIN
cl. St Clair 270 B11
BURLINGTON
av. Earlwood 372 G16
la. Crows Nest 315 G7
rd. Homebush 341 B9
st. Crows Nest 315 G7
st. Monterey 433 G8
st. Northmead 277 K11
BURLISON
st. Warwck Frm 365 G13
BURMAH
rd. Denistone 281 B12
BURNE
av. Dee Why 258 F6
BURNELL
pl. Darlinghurst 4 C9
st. Drummoyne 343 F7
st. Russell Lea 343 F7
BURNETT
av. Mt Annan 509 H1
pl. Sylvania Wtr 462 C12
st. Hurlstone Pk 373 A14
st. Mays Hill 307 H6
st. Merrylands 307 C11
st. Parramatta 307 H6
st. Redfern 19 F7
wk. Denistone 281 C12
BURNHAM
av. Glenwood 215 D14
pl. N Parramatta 278 C9
st. Belfield 371 E12
BURNIE
la. Clovelly, off Winchester Rd 377 J11
st. Blacktown 275 B2
st. Clovelly 377 J12
BURNLEIGH
cr. Cmbrdg Gdn 237 J1
BURNLEY
av. N Turramrra 223 G7
BURNS
av. Mcquarie Fd 454 A3
cl. Rooty Hill 271 K6
cr. Chiswick 343 C2
la. Caringbah 492 H7
la. Petersham 15 K8
la. Picnic Point 428 F8
pl. Springwood 201 K12
rd. Campbelltwn 512 A2
rd. Heathcote 518 C16
rd. Kellyville 215 H9
rd. Leumeah 512 A2
rd. Picnic Point 428 D8
rd. St Ives 223 A6
rd. Springwood 202 A11
rd. Thirlmere 561 J12
rd. Turramurra 223 A6
rd. Wahroonga 222 D5
rd. Wakeley 334 H16
rd. Winston Hills 276 H1
rd.n, Beecroft 250 B6
rd.s, Beecroft 250 B7
st. Campsie 372 B10
st. Croydon 342 H12
st. Marsfield 282 C7
st. Petersham 15 K8
BURNS BAY
rd. Lane Cove 313 F8
rd. Lane Cove 313 J2
rd. Lane Cove W 313 F8
rd. Linley Point 313 F8
BURNSIDE
gr. Windsor Dn 180 K3
st. N Parramatta 278 F11
BURNT
st. Seaforth 286 K3
BURNT BRIDGE CREEK DEVIATION
Balgowlah 287 E8
Manly Vale 287 E8
N Balgowlah 287 E8
Seaforth 287 E8
BURR
cl. Bossley Park 334 C10
BURRA
cl. Glenmore Pk 266 B9
cl. Mt Colah 162 D16
pl. Greystanes 305 F10
rd. Artarmon 285 A15
st. Busby 363 H14
st. Pendle Hill 276 G12
BURRABIRRA
av. Vaucluse 348 D3
BURRABOGEE
rd. Old Tngabbie 276 E11
rd. Pendle Hill 276 E11
rd. Toongabbie 276 E11
BURRADDAR
av. Engadine 488 G14
BURRADOO
cl. North Rocks 279 A2
rd. Beverly Hills 401 A11
rd. Lansvale 366 D9
st. Caringbah 492 G12
st. Padstow 429 G3
BURRAGA
av. Terrey Hills 196 C5
pl. Glenmore Pk 266 B8
pl. Lindfield 284 A2
BURRAGATE
st. Prestons 393 C15
BURRAGORANG
av. Woodcroft 243 F11
rd. Belimbla Pk 501 B10
rd. Bickley Vale 505 B7
rd. Brownlow Hl 505 B7
rd. Glenmore 503 C4
rd. Grasmere 505 J7
rd. Mt Hunter 505 B7
rd. Oakdale 500 B13
rd. Ruse 512 F8
rd. The Oaks 502 J9
st. Oakdale 500 G11
st. The Oaks 502 E11
BURRAHPORE
la. Woolmloo 4 F7
BURRALOO
st. Frenchs Frst 256 G1
BURRALOW
rd. Kurrajong Ht 53 H13
BURRAMY
cl. Bossley Park 333 G7
BURRAN
av. Mosman 317 E3
BURRANDONG
cr. Baulkham Hl 246 J10
BURRANEER
av. St Ives 254 D3
cl. Allawah 432 C8
cr. Greenacre 369 K11
st. Leumeah 482 C15
BURRANEER BAY
rd. Caringbah 492 E10
rd. Cronulla 493 A11
rd. Woolooware 493 A11
BURRAWAL
pl. Cromer 227 K11
BURRAWALLA
rd. Caringbah 493 B6
BURRAWANG
dr. Nelson 155 D8
pl. Alfords Point 429 A13
st. Cherrybrook 219 K5
BURRAWONG
av. Mosman 317 D13
cr. Elderslie 477 F16
rd. Avalon 140 D11
BURRELL
cr. Baulkham Hl 247 E11
pde. Blacktown 273 H4
rd. Kenthurst 156 C9
st. Beverly Hills 401 F14
BURREN
st. Erskineville 18 A11
st. Eveleigh 18 A11
st. Newtown 18 A11
BURRENDONG
pl. Avalon 139 K15
rd. Leumeah 482 D12
BURRIA
pl. Winmalee 173 B10
BURRILL
pl. Leumeah 482 F14
BURRIMUL
st. Kingsgrove 401 F6
BURRINGBAR
st. N Balgowlah 287 C5
BURRINJUCK
dr. Woodcroft 243 G10
pl. Miranda 491 H7
st. Leumeah 482 E13
BURROGY
la. Mosman, off Cardinal St 316 J5
BURROWAY
rd. Homebush 311 A6
rd. Homebush B L B2
st. Neutral Bay 6 H5
BURROWES
gr. Dean Park 212 F16
BURROWS
av. Chester Hill 338 B13
av. Sydenham 374 D14
la. Minto, off Erica La 482 F2
rd. Alexandria 375 A15
rd. St Peters 375 A15
rd.s, St Peters 374 H16
st. Arncliffe 403 H8

BURRSWOOD
cl. Belrose 225 K12
BURRUNDULLA
cr. Airds 511 K14
BURSARIA
cr. Glenmore Pk 265 F10
rd. Mt Annan 509 D4
BURSILL
st. Guildford 337 H3
BURT
st. Rozelle 10 K3
BURTENSHAW
st. Panania 398 D14
BURTON
av. Chester Hill 338 D15
av. Moorebank 396 D11
av. Northmead 278 B2
la. Glebe 12 C9
la. Milsons Pt, off Alfred St 5 K15
la. Randwick, off Prince St 376 K11
st. Balgowlah 287 K9
st. Concord 341 K10
st. Darlinghurst 4 D11
st. Glebe 12 B10
st. Linley Point 313 G7
st. Milsons Pt 5 K15
st. Mosman 316 J2
st. Randwick 376 K11
st. Werrington 238 E8
st. Wrrngtn Cty 238 E8
BURU
pl. Kings Park 244 J2
BURUNDA
st. Como 460 E6
BURUWAN
la. Annandale 11 B6
BURWOOD
pl. St Johns Pk 364 G4
rd. Belfield 371 D10
rd. Belmore 371 D13
rd. Burwood 341 K15
rd. Burwood Ht 371 J8
rd. Concord 342 B8
rd. Croydon Pk 371 J8
rd. Enfield 371 J8
BURY
rd. Guildford 337 J4
BUSACO
rd. Marsfield 252 C12
BUSBY
av. Edensor Pk 363 E1
la. Woolmloo D K13
la. Woolmloo 4 C6
la. Bronte, off Busby Pde 377 K10
pde. Bronte 377 J11
pl. Frenchs Frst 255 H4
rd. Busby 393 J1
BUSH
pl. Glenbrook 264 B4
rd. Kenthurst 125 E4
tr. Belrose 226 D6
BUSHELLS
la. Freemns Rch 90 G12
pl. Wetherill Pk 304 B16
BUSHEY
pl. Dee Why 258 J8
BUSHLAND
av. Forestville 255 K10
cr. Carlingford 249 F16
dr. Padstow Ht 429 D8
pl. Erskine Park 270 F16
pl. Kenthurst 188 D4
BUSHLANDS
av. Gordon 253 F10
av. Hornsby Ht 191 G8
pl. Hornsby Ht 191 F8
BUSHLARK
pl. Clarmnt Ms 268 J4
BUSHLEY
pl. Jamisontown 266 C2
BUSHRANGERS
hill, Newport 169 H13
BUSHVIEW
dr. Kellyville 186 K15
BUSHY
gln. Glenhaven 217 K5
BUTCHERBIRD
pl. Glenmore Pk 265 K12
BUTE
pl. St Andrews 481 K5

BUTIA
wy. Stanhpe Gdn 215 E10
BUTLER
av. Bossley Park 334 B7
av. Campsie 371 J13
cl. Menai 459 A10
cr. Bnkstn Aprt 397 K1
cr. S Penrith 237 B15
la. Hurstville 432 A6
la. S Penrith, off Butler Cr 237 C15
pl. Lalor Park 245 G14
rd. Hurstville 432 A6
wy. S Windsor 150 F1
BUTLERS
cl. West Hoxton 392 D7
BUTLIN
av. Darlington 18 E5
BUTT
st. Surry Hills 19 H3
BUTTERCUP
pl. Mt Annan 509 E4
st. Mcquarie Fd 454 C5
BUTTERFIELD
pl. Mt Annan 509 C1
st. Blacktown 244 G11
st. Thornleigh 221 C13
BUTTSWORTH
la. Wilberforce 91 K7
BUVELOT
wy. Claymore 481 D13
BUXTON
pl. N Turramrra 223 G7
pl. Prestons 392 J14
BUYU
rd. Glenmore Pk 266 D10
BUYUMA
pl. Avalon 139 J14
st. Carlingford 280 D7
BY
st. N Parramatta 278 C11
BYAMEE
st. East Killara 254 J6
BYANBI
pl. Castle Hill 248 C6
BYDOWN
st. Neutral Bay 6 F3
BYER
st. Enfield 371 G3
BYFIELD
st. Mcquarie Pk 282 F3
BYGRAVE
st. Ryde 282 H15
BYKOOL
av. Kingsgrove 401 E8
BYLONG
pl. Ruse 512 F8
BYLOSS
st. Chester Hill 338 A13
BYNA
st. Malabar 437 E8
BYNG
la. Maroubra 407 B10
st. Maroubra 407 B11
BYNYA
rd. Palm Beach 140 B3
BYORA
cr. Northbridge 286 E14
BYRD
av. Kingsford 406 J4
pl. Tregear 240 E5
st. Canley Ht 365 C3
BYRNE
av. Drummoyne 343 D3
av. Russell Lea 343 D3
av. S Coogee 407 F7
bvd. Marayong 243 K8
cr. Maroubra 407 F14
pl. Camden 506 K8
pl. Prairiewood 334 J8
st. Ashcroft 364 E16
st. Auburn 309 B15
st. Lapstone 264 G5
st. Wentwthvle 277 C16
wy. Bradbury 511 J12
wy. Glenmore Pk 265 E11
BYRNES
av. Neutral Bay 316 B8
st. Bexley 432 H4
st. Botany 405 E11
st. Marrickville 373 K14
st. N Parramatta 278 C9
st. Rozelle 344 C7
st. S Granville 338 G2

BYRON
av. Campbelltwn 512 A3
av. Ryde 282 D12
av. St Ives 224 B14
av. Wallacia 324 J13
la. Mount Druitt 241 C13
pl. Illawong 459 E5
pl. Northmead 278 B5
rd. Guildford 337 C7
rd. Leppington 421 B9
rd. Tahmoor 565 D14
rd. Tahmoor 565 E14
rd. Yennora 337 C7
st. Campsie 372 A9
st. Coogee 377 E16
st. Croydon 342 G12
st. Peakhurst 430 C7
BYRON BAY
cl. Hoxton Park 392 H6
BY THE SEA
rd. Mona Vale 199 E3
BYWONG
pl. Bonnyrigg 364 A10
pl. Sylvania 461 G14

C

CABARITA
pl. Caringbah 492 E9
rd. Avalon 139 H9
rd. Cabarita 342 D2
rd. Concord 342 B3
CABBAGE TREE
rd. Bayview 169 A16
rd. Grose Vale 85 A16
rd. Grose Vale 115 A3
rd. Grose Vale 115 A4
rd. Ingleside 168 C16
CABBAN
st. Mosman 317 A11
CABER
cl. Dural 219 B8
CABERNET
av. Eschol Park 481 C2
cct. Orchard Hills 268 F15
CABLE
pl. Eastern Ck 272 G7
st. Wollstncraft 315 C11
CABLES
pl. Waverley 377 F8
CABRAMATTA
av. Miller 393 F5
rd. Cremorne 316 H8
rd. Mosman 316 H8
rd. Woolooware 493 E11
rd.e, Cabramatta 366 A7
rd.w, Bonnyrigg 364 D7
rd.w, Cabramatta 365 B9
rd.w, Cabramtta W 364 D7
rd.w, Mt Pritchard 364 D7
CABRAMURRA
st. Heckenberg 364 A14
CACIA
av. Seven Hills 245 J14
CADAC
pl. Schofields 213 K6
CADBURY
st. Quakers Hill 213 G14
CADDENS
rd. Clarmnt Ms 268 D4
rd. Kingswood 267 F3
CADDIES
pl. Glenwood 215 B14
CADDO
cl. Greenfld Pk 333 K14
CADELL
gln. St Clair 270 D10
la. St Clair, off Cadell Gln 270 C10
CADENCE
pl. Kareela 461 D12
CADIA
st. Kogarah 433 B2
CADIGAL
av. Pyrmont 12 E1
CADILLAC
pl. Ingleburn 453 H9
CADMAN
cr. Castle Hill 217 H14
pl. Woodcroft 243 F6
CADOGAN
la. Marrickville 374 D12
rd. Mcquarie Fd 454 C4
st. Marrickville 374 D12

CADOW
st. Frenchs Frst 256 E1
st. Pymble 253 B9
CADWELLS
rd. Kenthurst 126 H15
rd. Kenthurst 156 H1
CAERLEON
cr. Randwick 377 D11
CAERNARVON
cl. Kirkham 477 C9
CAESAR
cl. Prairiewood 334 D12
la. St Clair, off Caesar Wy 270 C16
wy. St Clair 270 C16
CAHILL
exp. Sydney A K7
exp. Sydney 1 H12
exp. The Rocks A K7
exp. The Rocks 1 H12
la. Annandale 17 B3
la. Greenacre 370 B6
pl. Marrickville 373 F16
st. Annandale 17 B3
st. Beverly Hills 401 D14
st. Smithfield 335 F6
CAHIR
la. Marrickville 373 K12
CAHORS
rd. Padstow 399 C14
CAIN
pl. Plumpton 242 B10
CAINES
cr. St Marys 269 J7
la. St Marys, off Caines Cr 269 J7
CAINS
pl. Waterloo 19 E12
CAIRA
pl. Quakers Hill 244 A1
CAIRD
cl. Edensor Pk 363 C2
pl. Seven Hills 245 K15
st. Wentwthvle 277 C9
CAIRDS
av. Bankstown 369 D15
CAIRNES
la. Glenorie 128 D2
rd. Glenorie 128 D4
CAIRNGORM
av. Glenhaven 218 A6
CAIRNS
av. Rodd Point 343 D8
pl. Wakeley 334 H15
st. Riverwood 400 B16
CAIRO
av. Padstow 399 B15
av. Revesby 399 B15
st. Cammeray 316 A4
st. Rockdale 403 E16
st. S Coogee 407 H4
CAITHNESS
cr. Winston Hills 277 D2
st. Killara 253 K13
CALABASH
rd. Arcadia 130 F7
CALABRESE
st. Blairmount 481 A15
CALABRIA
pl. Erskine Park 300 F2
st. Prestons 393 E13
CALABRO
av. Liverpool 394 H7
av. Lurnea 394 H7
CALABY
st. Toongabbie 276 H8
CALADENIA
cl. Elanora Ht 197 H13
st. Rooty Hill 272 C3
CALAIS
pl. Erskine Park 270 H15
CALALA
st. Mount Druitt 241 C13
CALANDRA
av. Quakers Hill 214 A7
CALARIA
cl. Edensor Pk 363 D1
CALBINA
rd. Earlwood 402 C3
rd. Northbridge 315 J1
CALCA
cr. Forestville 255 K14
CALCITE
pl. Eagle Vale 481 C8

CALDARRA
av. Engadine 518 J2
pl. Westleigh 220 G2
CALDER
cl. Rydalmere 279 H15
la. Darlington 18 H5
pl. St Ives 224 B6
rd. Darlington 18 H6
rd. Rydalmere 279 D14
st. N Curl Curl 258 F10
CALDERON
la. Padstow 429 C3
CALDERWOOD
rd. Galston 160 D13
CALDWELL
la. Bexley North 402 D10
pde. Yagoona 369 B11
pl. Blacktown 274 J3
pl. Edensor Pk 333 G13
st. Darlinghurst 4 J10
st. S Windsor 150 J3
CALDY
pl. Glenhaven 217 K4
CALEDONIA
cr. Peakhurst 430 B5
la. Paddington 21 G2
st. Paddington 21 G2
CALEDONIAN
av. Winston Hills 277 D3
rd. Rose Bay 348 B9
st. Bexley 403 A15
CALEEN
st. Glenwood 245 F1
CALEY
cr. Lapstone 264 H4
dr. Mt Annan 509 D9
pl. Barden Rdg 488 G1
pl. Horngsea Pk 392 F15
rd. Bradbury 511 G13
st. Chifley 437 A4
CALEYI
wy. Belrose 226 B10
CALGA
av. Bronte 378 B10
av. Malabar 437 E8
av. Normanhurst 221 D12
pl. Bronte 378 B10
pl. Old Tngabbie 276 K8
pl. Sylvania 461 G14
st. Roseville Ch 285 F2
CALGAROO
cr. Kingswood 237 H16
CALIBAN
pl. Rsemeadow 540 K6
CALIDA
cr. Hassall Gr 212 A15
CALIDORE
st. Bankstown 399 A7
CALLA
gr. Pendle Hill 276 G13
CALLABONNA
pl. Woodcroft 243 F12
CALLAGHAN
la. Ryde, off Badajoz Rd 282 G15
st. Ryde 282 H15
CALLAGHER
st. Mount Druitt 271 D1
CALLAN
st. Rozelle 344 C7
wy. Wentwthvle 277 D10
CALLICOMA
rd. Seaforth 286 K7
CALLIOPE
la. Mosman, off Calliope St 316 G10
pl. Busby 363 J13
rd. Miranda 492 C7
st. Guildford 337 D4
st. Mosman 316 G10
CALLISTEMON
cl. Alfords Point 429 C15
cl. Baulkham Hl 247 C15
cl. N Epping 251 C11
gr. Greenacre 370 F6
st. Mt Annan 509 C2
CALLISTO
dr. Cranebrook 207 D11
CALLOW
la. Kingswood 237 J15
pl. Woodcroft 243 E10
CALMAR
cl. Glen Alpine 510 C14

CALMSLEY
pl. Horsley Pk...332 C5
CALOOL
cr. Belrose...225 H12
rd. Beecroft...250 D12
st. Lidcombe...339 J4
CALOOLA
av. Penrith...237 E6
cr. Beverly Hills...401 E11
cr. Penshurst...431 H7
pl. Baulkham Hl...246 J10
rd. Wentwthvle...277 A11
st. Condell Park...398 E1
CALPAC
pl. Old Tngabbie...276 H11
CALPURNIA
wy. Rsemeadow...540 H2
CALVADOS
st. Glenfield...424 E13
CALVER
av. Mt Riverview...204 C16
CALVERT
av. Killara...253 G12
la. Marrickville, off Fernbank St...374 A13
pde. Newport...169 K11
st. Marrickville...373 K13
CALVERTS
rd. Orchard Hills...268 D13
CALYPSO
av. Mosman...316 K10
pl. Miranda...491 K10
rd. Cranebrook...207 C15
CALYPTA
gr. Quakers Hill...214 F11
CAM
la. North Ryde...282 J8
st. Cambrdg Pk...237 G9
st. North Ryde...282 J7
st. Wahroonga...222 A6
CAMBAGE
ct. Frenchs Frst...255 E4
CAMBALAN
st. Bargo...567 D1
CAMBERWELL
rd. Vineyard...152 F12
CAMBEWARRA
av. Castle Hill...248 B3
cr. Berowra Ht...132 K7
rd. Fairfield W...335 E10
st. Ruse...512 G7
CAMBOURNE
av. St Ives...224 H7
CAMBRAI
av. Engadine...518 H1
pl. Milperra...397 D12
CAMBRIAN
av. Voyager Pt...427 E4
CAMBRIDGE
av. Bankstown...399 A2
av. Glenfield...424 G8
av. Moorebank...425 A9
av. Narraweena...258 D2
av. North Rocks...278 H2
av. Vaucluse...348 F1
av. Windsor...120 J11
la. Chatswood...284 J9
la. Enmore...17 A13
la. Paddington...13 E13
la. Cambrdg Pk, off Cambridge St...237 F9
pl. Narellan...478 G11
rd. Artarmon...284 K13
rd. Drummoyne...313 H15
st. Berala...339 D10
st. Blacktown...244 K11
st. Cambrdg Pk...237 G9
st. Cammeray...315 J4
st. Canley Ht...365 D3
st. Enmore...17 A13
st. Epping...251 B15
st. Fairfield W...335 D16
st. Fairfield W...335 E13
st. Gladesville...312 J7
st. Harris Park...308 E7
st. Ingleburn...453 E5
st. Lidcombe...339 D10
st. Merrylands...307 F13
st. Mount Druitt...241 C11
st. N Willghby...285 F8
st. Paddington...13 E13
st. Penshurst...431 D1
st. Rozelle...344 D8
st. S Turramrra...252 B8
st. Stanmore...16 F10
st. The Rocks...A J4
st. Valley Ht...202 H10
CAMDEN
bps. Camden...507 A9
bps. Camden S...507 A9
bps. Elderslie...507 J4
bps. Narellan...478 F16
bps. Narellan Vale...478 F16
bps. Spring Farm...507 J4
gdn. N Turramrra...223 F2
la. Newtown...17 F16
la. Pyrmont...12 J7
rd. Campbelltwn...511 C6
st. Enmore...374 G9
st. Fairfield Ht...335 K10
st. Newtown...17 F16
st. Penrith...236 G1
st. Sylvania...462 B13
wy. Bidwill...211 F16
CAMDEN VALLEY
wy. Casula...423 G3
wy. Catherine Fd...449 E15
wy. Currans Hill...479 A6
wy. Edmndsn Pk...422 F1
wy. Elderslie...477 F15
wy. Harringtn Pk...478 D10
wy. Horngsea Pk...392 C16
wy. Kirkham...477 F15
wy. Leppington...421 H5
wy. Narellan...478 D10
wy. Oran Park...449 E15
wy. Prestons...392 C16
wy. Prestons...423 B2
wy. Smeaton Gra...479 A6
CAMDEN VIEW
dr. Narellan...478 C10
CAMELLIA
av. Glenmore Pk...265 F10
ct. Cherrybrook...219 G7
gr. Gymea Bay...491 C8
pl. Lalor Park...245 B10
st. Greystanes...306 A12
CAMELOT
cl. Kirkham...477 E8
cl. Mt Colah...162 G14
ct. Carlingford...279 A4
dr. Cranebrook...207 A12
pl. St Ives...254 A2
CAMEO
cr. St Clair...269 H13
pl. Eagle Vale...481 B7
CAMERA
st. Manly...288 F9
CAMERON
av. Artarmon...285 A15
av. Bass Hill...368 D13
av. Baulkham Hl...247 G5
av. Earlwood...402 H3
av. Manly...288 G4
av. W Pnnant Hl...249 G1
cr. Ryde...282 D16
ct. Merrylnds W...306 J14
pl. Alfords Point...429 C13
pl. Parramatta...278 J15
pl. St Helens Pk...541 B8
rd. Pymble...253 J3
st. Balmain...7 G4
st. Banksia...403 F13
st. Bexley...432 H4
st. Birchgrove...7 G4
st. Doonside...243 B11
st. Edgecliff...13 H12
st. Jamisontown...266 B2
st. Lidcombe...339 F9
st. Richmond...118 G8
st. Rockdale...403 F16
st. Strathfield...371 E2
CAMILLA
wy. Ambarvale...510 K15
CAMILLE
pl. Glenhaven...187 K15
st. Sans Souci...433 C16
CAMILLERI
av. Quakers Hill...213 G7
CAMILLO
st. Pendle Hill...306 D1
st. Seven Hills...245 G14
CAMIRA
cl. Belrose...225 J14
pl. Bonnyrigg...363 J9
st. Maroubra...407 E12
st. St Marys...239 G13
st. Villawood...367 G5
st. West Pymble...252 K14
CAMIRI
st. Hornsby Ht...191 G1
CAMMARAY
rd. Castle Cove...286 D6
CAMMARLIE
st. Panania...427 J1
CAMMERAY
av. Cammeray...315 K6
rd. Cammeray...316 B5
CAMORTA
cl. Kings Park...244 H3
CAMP
la. Bondi Jctn...22 E5
st. Watsons Bay...318 E13
CAMPASPE
av. Wiley Park...400 G4
CAMPBELL
av. Cromer...228 H16
av. Dee Why...258 H1
av. Lane Cove...314 G5
av. Lilyfield...9 J5
av. Normanhurst...221 E10
av. Paddington...4 J13
cl. Minto...482 K9
cr. Glenorie...128 G1
dr. Wahroonga...222 A14
la. Glebe...12 C14
la. Narellan...478 E9
la. Newtown...17 D11
la. St Peters...374 K14
la. Clovelly, off Park La...378 A12
pde. Bondi Beach...378 D3
pde. Manly Vale...287 H2
pl. Merrylands...307 H16
rd. Alexandria...374 K14
rd. Kenthurst...156 F15
rd. St Peters...374 K14
st. Abbotsford...342 K4
st. Artarmon...314 K3
st. Auburn...309 C15
st. Balmain...7 K9
st. Berala...339 C13
st. Bexley...432 H1
st. Blacktown...244 H16
st. Clovelly...378 A12
st. Darlinghurst...4 A13
st. Eastwood...280 J10
st. Fairfield E...336 K14
st. Glebe...12 D13
st. Gymea...461 G16
st. Haymarket...E G7
st. Haymarket...3 G12
st. Hunters Hill...313 K10
st. Liverpool...395 B1
st. Liverpool...395 C1
st. Luddenham...356 G3
st. Narellan...478 E8
st. Newtown...17 J8
st. Northmead...277 K8
st. N Richmond...87 B13
st. Parramatta...308 B5
st. Picton...563 G8
st. Punchbowl...400 C5
st. Ramsgate...433 D15
st. Riverstone...183 B5
st. St Peters...374 H12
st. Sans Souci...433 D15
st. S Windsor...120 H13
st. Surry Hills...F B8
st. Surry Hills...4 A13
st. Thirlmere...564 K5
st. Villawood...336 K14
st. Waverley...377 G7
CAMPBELLFIELD
av. Bradbury...511 D13
CAMPBELL HILL
rd. Chester Hill...338 B15
rd. Guildford...338 B15
CAMPBELLS
rd. Cobbitty...415 B7
CAMPBELLTOWN
rd. Bow Bowing...452 C14
rd. Campbelltwn...511 J2
rd. Denham Ct...422 F15
rd. Glenfield...423 J6
rd. Ingleburn...452 C14
rd. Leumeah...481 J15
rd. Minto...482 A3
rd. St Andrews...452 C14
CAMPFIRE
ct. Wrrngtn Dns...238 E4
CAMPHORLAUREL
ct. Doonside...243 G16
CAMPI
ct. Prestons...422 K1
CAMPION
st. Wetherill Pk...334 K4
CAMPSIE
la. Canterbury, off Wonga St...372 D12
st. Campsie...371 G14
st. Campsie...371 H13
CAMPTON
av. Cambrdg Pk...238 A10
ct. Carlingford...250 C13
CAMPUS
dr. Richmond...119 A11
CANADA
cl. Minto...482 G5
CANADIAN
pl. Kearns...450 J16
CANAL
rd. Greystanes...306 E12
rd. Greystanes...306 E13
rd. Leichhardt...9 D9
rd. Lilyfield...9 E7
rd. St Peters...374 G15
CANARA
av. Phillip Bay...436 J11
pl. Frenchs Frst...255 F2
pl. Palm Beach...139 J2
pl. Smithfield...335 E4
CANARY
cl. St Clair...269 H10
CANARYS
rd. Roselands...400 K7
CANBERRA
av. Casula...394 J15
av. Richmond...119 K4
av. St Leonards...315 D7
av. Turramurra...223 C10
cr. Campbelltwn...512 B6
cr. E Lindfield...255 B15
la. Randwick...407 B2
pwy. Casula, off Canberra Av...394 K15
rd. Sylvania...462 C9
st. Epping...251 A13
st. Hurlstone Pk...372 H13
st. Lane Cove W...284 B15
st. Oxley Park...240 A16
st. Randwick...407 C3
st. St Johns Pk...364 F1
st. St Marys...240 A16
CANDICE
cr. Stanhpe Gdn...215 B10
CANDLEBARK
cct. Glenmore Pk...265 H11
CANDLEBUSH
cr. Castle Hill...248 F5
CANDLEWOOD
st. Bossley Park...333 G9
CANDOWIE
cr. Baulkham Hl...248 C8
CANEA
cr. Allambie Ht...257 D10
CANHAM
cl. Castle Hill...247 H1
CANIDIUS
st. Rsemeadow...540 E3
CANISIUS
cl. Pymble...223 F15
CANLEY VALE
rd. Canley Ht...365 A2
rd. Canley Vale...365 J3
rd. St Johns Pk...334 F15
rd. Wakeley...334 F15
rd. Wetherill Pk...334 C3
CANN
st. Bass Hill...368 B6
st. Bass Hill...368 B9
st. Guildford...337 D7
CANNA
pl. Quakers Hill...243 E3
pl. St Andrews...482 A1
CANNAN
cl. Cherrybrook...219 C11
CANNERY
rd. Plumpton...241 K7
CANNES
dr. Avalon...139 J13
CANNING
pl. Pitt Town...93 F8
CANNON
la. Stanmore...16 E5
st. Prospect...275 B11
st. Stanmore...16 E5
CANNONS
pde. Forestville...255 K11
CANOBOLAS
pl. Yarrawarrah...489 D13
st. Fairfield W...335 E11
CANONBURY
gr. Bexley North...402 E12
gr. Bexley North...402 G10
gr. Dulwich Hill...373 E12
CANOON
rd. S Turramrra...251 K5
CANOONA
av. Windsor Dn...150 E14
CANOPUS
cl. Engadine...488 D13
cl. Erskine Park...300 H1
CANOWIE
pl. Busby...363 G14
CANROBERT
st. Mosman...316 K9
CANSDALE
pl. Castle Hill...217 J7
st. Blacktown...273 H4
CANTELLO
av. Hamondvle...396 H15
CANTERBURY
rd. Bankstown...399 A9
rd. Belmore...401 B4
rd. Campsie...372 B16
rd. Canterbury...372 G13
rd. Glenfield...424 E14
rd. Hurlstone Pk...372 G13
rd. Lakemba...401 B4
rd. Punchbowl...399 A9
rd. Revesby...399 A9
rd. Roselands...400 H6
rd. St Johns Pk...364 H3
rd. Wiley Park...400 H6
CANTERTON
st. Hurlstone Pk...372 J12
CANTON
st. Canterbury...372 E15
st. Kings Park...244 E2
CANTOR
cr. Croydon...342 F15
la. Croydon, off Cantor St...342 F15
st. Croydon...342 F15
CANTRELL
st. Bankstown...368 G15
st. Yagoona...368 G15
CANTRILL
av. Maroubra...407 E8
CANTWELL
st. Glenwood...215 C14
CANUNGRA
pl. Elanora Ht...198 C15
CANVA
st. Canley Vale...366 D5
CANYON
dr. Stanhpe Gdn...215 B12
pl. Engadine...488 C13
rd. Baulkham Hl...248 A13
CAPE
pl. Cherrybrook...219 J6
CAPE BARRON
av. Green Valley...363 A14
CAPELLA
pl. Normanhurst...221 E12
rd. Hinchinbrk...393 E3
st. Erskine Park...270 H16
CAPER
pl. Quakers Hill...243 E3
CAPERTEE
st. Ruse...512 F7
CAPE SOLANDER
dr. Kurnell...466 F5
CAPITAL
pl. Sylvania...462 D9
CAPITOL HILL
dr. Mt Vernon...331 A8
CAPPARIS
cct. Bidwill...211 D13
CAPPER
st. Lindfield...254 G16
CAPRERA
rd. Northmead...278 A6
CAPRI
cl. Avalon...139 J12
cl. Heathcote...518 E7
pl. Erskine Park...300 E1
CAPRICORN
av. Cranebrook...207 F15
rd. Kings Lngly...245 D7

CAPTAIN COOK
dr. Caringbah ... 492 H2
dr. Cronulla ... 493 E6
dr. Kurnell ... 465 A15
dr. Willmot ... 210 B11
dr. Woolooware ... 493 E6
CAPTAIN HUNTER
rd. Bayview ... 168 E8
CAPTAIN JACKA
cr. Daceyville ... 406 F3
CAPTAIN PIPERS
rd. Vaucluse ... 348 D5
CAPTAINS
rd. Penrith ... 236 A10
CAPTAIN STROM
pl. Dundas Vy ... 279 J6
CAPUA
pl. Avalon ... 139 J14
CAPULET
pl. Rsemeadow ... 540 H4
CARA
ct. S Penrith ... 266 K7
CARABEELY
pl. Harringtn Pk ... 478 F5
CARABEEN
st. Cabramatta ... 365 G9
CARABELLA
rd. Caringbah ... 493 A5
st. Kirribilli ... 6 B14
st. Milsons Pt ... 6 B14
CARAHERS
la. The Rocks ... A H6
CARAMAR
st. Dharruk ... 241 B8
CARANDINI
st. St Helens Pk ... 541 B7
CARANYA
pl. Cabramtta W ... 365 C6
CARATEL
cr. Marayong ... 243 J5
CARAVAN HEAD
rd. Oyster Bay ... 461 A6
CARAWA
rd. Cromer ... 228 B16
CARAWATHA
st. Beecroft ... 250 E11
st. Villawood ... 367 C4
CARBASSE
cr. St Helens Pk ... 540 K10
CARBEEN
av. St Ives ... 223 J10
rd. Westleigh ... 220 D8
CARBERRY
ct. Kellyville ... 217 A1
la. Campbelltwn ... 511 E5
CARBETHON
cr. Beverly Hills ... 401 D9
CARBINE
cl. Casula ... 424 E1
CARBONI
st. Liverpool ... 395 A2
CARBOONA
av. Earlwood ... 403 G3
CARCLEW
pl. Glen Alpine ... 510 D11
CARCOAR
cl. Erskine Park ... 300 C3
CARCOOLA
av. Chipping Ntn ... 396 H4
cr. Normanhurst ... 221 F7
rd. Cromer ... 228 B15
rd. St Ives ... 224 D12
st. Campbelltwn ... 511 K7
st. Canley Vale ... 366 B4
st. Castle Hill ... 218 C11
CARDEN
av. Wahroonga ... 222 A5
CARDEW
wy. Bradbury ... 511 J11
CARDIFF
st. Blacktown ... 244 K14
st. Engadine ... 489 C15
wy. Castle Hill ... 248 A3
CARDIGAN
la. Camperdwn ... 17 A9
la. Camperdwn ... 17 B6
pl. Camperdwn ... 17 B4
rd. Greenacre ... 370 A7
rd. Roseville Ch ... 255 E14
st. Auburn ... 339 A1
st. Camperdwn ... 17 A6
st. Glebe ... 12 D10
st. Guildford ... 337 E3
st. Stanmore ... 17 A9
CARDILLO
st. Wentwthvle ... 277 E13
CARDINAL
av. Beecroft ... 250 A5
av. W Pnnant Hl ... 249 K2
st. Mosman ... 316 J6
CARDINAL CLANCY
av. Glendenning ... 242 G5
CARDWELL
st. Balmain ... 7 E6
st. Canley Vale ... 365 K1
CAREDEN
av. Beacon Hill ... 257 J4
CAREEBONG
rd. Frenchs Frst ... 256 E7
CAREEL BAY
cr. Avalon ... 139 J11
CAREEL HEAD
rd. Avalon ... 140 D11
CAREFREE
rd. N Narrabeen ... 228 G2
CAREW
la. Marrickville ... 373 K11
st. Dee Why ... 258 H8
st. Mount Druitt ... 241 G11
st. Padstow ... 429 B5
CAREX
cl. Glenmore Pk ... 265 H13
CAREY
la. Glenbrook ... 234 A13
la. Randwick, off Carey St ... 377 F11
st. Bass Hill ... 367 K10
st. Liverpool ... 395 C6
st. Manly ... 288 H14
st. Randwick ... 377 F11
CARGELLIGO
pl. Woodcroft ... 243 H11
CARHULLEN
st. Merrylands ... 308 A12
CARIBBEAN
pl. Mt Colah ... 162 E13
CARIBOU
cl. St Clair ... 270 D16
pl. Raby ... 451 G14
CARIEVILLE
la. Balmain ... 7 A6
st. Balmain ... 7 A7
CARILLA
st. Burwood ... 341 J13
CARILLON
av. Camperdwn ... 17 H7
av. Newtown ... 17 H7
CARINA
av. Hinchinbrk ... 393 D3
la. Oyster Bay, off Drummond Rd. 461 B7
pl. Castle Hill ... 218 J9
pl. Cranebrook ... 207 F7
pl. St Johns Pk ... 364 C1
rd. Oyster Bay ... 461 C6
rd. Turramurra ... 252 E5
CARINDA
dr. Glenhaven ... 187 G16
dr. S Penrith ... 266 K2
la. S Penrith, off Carinda Dr ... 266 K2
st. Ingleburn ... 453 A9
CARINGAL
pl. St Ives ... 223 G10
st. Chipping Ntn ... 396 G4
CARINGBAH
rd. Caringbah ... 492 F9
rd. Woolooware ... 493 A9
CARINGTON
st. Riverstone ... 182 E15
CARINYA
av. Beverly Hills ... 431 A1
av. Btn-le-Sds ... 403 K15
av. Mascot ... 405 D2
av. St Marys ... 239 G16
cl. Allambie Ht ... 257 G16
pl. Carss Park ... 432 G13
pl. Kirrawee ... 490 J1
pl. Moorebank ... 396 F7
rd. Girraween ... 276 C10
rd. Mt Colah ... 191 K4
rd. Picnic Point ... 428 B12
rd. Pymble ... 223 G14
st. Blacktown ... 244 E16
CARINYAH
cr. Castle Hill ... 218 A11
CARIOCA
ct. W Pnnant Hl ... 249 B1
wy. W Pnnant Hl ... 249 B1
CARISBROOK
st. Linley Point ... 313 H7
CARISSA
av. St Ives ... 224 F8
pl. Alfords Point ... 458 K3
CARL
ct. Eastern Ck ... 273 K15
pl. Kings Lngly ... 246 B11
CARLEEN
cl. Werrington ... 238 E10
CARLENE
av. Padstow ... 429 G5
CARLINGFORD
rd. Carlingford ... 280 A2
rd. Epping ... 251 A15
st. Regents Pk ... 369 A2
st. Sefton ... 368 G2
CARLISLE
av. Bidwill ... 211 E16
av. Blackett ... 241 D8
av. Colyton ... 270 K7
av. Dharruk ... 241 D8
av. Hebersham ... 241 D8
av. Minchinbury ... 271 B6
av. Mount Druitt ... 241 C16
cl. Hinchinbrk ... 393 B1
cl. Mcquarie Pk ... 252 J16
cr. Beecroft ... 249 K6
cr. Kellyville ... 186 J16
rd. Bargo ... 567 B14
rd. Yanderra ... 567 B14
st. Ashfield ... 372 G4
st. Collaroy Plat ... 228 E11
st. Ingleburn ... 453 B7
st. Leichhardt ... 9 G15
st. Rose Bay ... 348 C10
st. Tamarama ... 378 B6
CARL LEWIS
wy. Newington ... L K12
wy. Newington ... 310 C13
CARLON
st. Harringtn Pk ... 478 G6
CARLOS
rd. Artarmon ... 285 A14
CARLOTTA
av. Gordon ... 253 G6
la. Greenwich, off Ffrench St ... 314 K9
rd. Double Bay ... 14 F11
st. Artarmon ... 314 K3
st. Greenwich ... 315 A9
CARLOW
cr. Killarney Ht ... 256 C15
st. N Sydney ... 5 F1
CARLOWRIE
cr. East Hills ... 428 A4
CARLTON
arc. Sydney ... 3 J2
cr. Carss Park ... 432 H14
cr. Kogarah Bay ... 432 H14
cr. Summer Hill ... 373 B3
dr. Liberty Gr ... 311 C15
la. Kensington ... 376 F10
pde. Allawah ... 432 F7
pde. Carlton ... 432 F7
pde. Punchbowl ... 399 J8
rd. Cecil Hills ... 362 E7
rd. North Rocks ... 248 H12
rd. Thirlmere ... 562 A16
rd. Thirlmere ... 565 A2
st. Arncliffe ... 403 B11
st. Chippendale ... 19 B2
st. Granville ... 308 E11
st. Harbord ... 258 H16
st. Kensington ... 376 F10
st. Manly ... 288 G7
st. Riverstone ... 182 J9
st. Waverley ... 377 H10
wy. Minto ... 482 K2
CARLY
pl. Quakers Hill ... 214 C13
CARLYLE
cr. Cmbrdg Gdn ... 237 G4
la. Wollstncraft ... 315 D8
la. Cmbrdg Gdn, off Carlyle Cr ... 237 G4
rd. E Lindfield ... 255 B14
st. Bossley Park ... 334 C8
st. Enfield ... 371 H3
st. Wollstncraft ... 315 E8
CARMAN
st. Schofields ... 183 C15
CARMARTHEN
st. Menai ... 458 J9
CARMEL
cl. Baulkham Hl ... 247 C1
pl. Winston Hills ... 276 H1
st. Glenbrook ... 233 K14
CARMELITA
cct. Rouse Hill ... 185 B6
CARMEN
cr. Cherrybrook ... 219 J3
dr. Carlingford ... 249 E11
pl. Caringbah ... 493 A14
pl. Freemns Rch ... 90 A4
st. Bankstown ... 369 C14
st. Guildford W ... 336 J2
st. Marsfield ... 282 B7
st. St Ives ... 224 E13
CARMICHAEL
dr. West Hoxton ... 392 B5
dr. West Hoxton ... 392 F6
CARMINYA
st. Kensington ... 376 B10
CARNARVON
av. Glenhaven ... 218 C5
dr. Frenchs Frst ... 256 G2
rd. Bow Bowing ... 452 E14
rd. Riverstone ... 182 E11
rd. Roseville ... 254 K16
rd. Schofields ... 212 H1
st. Carlton ... 432 H7
st. Silverwater ... M A16
st. Silverwater ... 309 E12
st. Yarrawarrah ... 489 G13
st. Wakeley, off Bulls Rd ... 334 K11
CARNATION
av. Bankstown ... 399 H1
av. Casula ... 394 G12
av. Clarmnt Ms ... 238 H16
av. Old Guildfrd ... 337 F8
st. Greystanes ... 306 A11
CARNAVON
cr. Georges Hall ... 367 J13
CARNE
cl. Austral ... 391 D8
pl. Oxley Park ... 240 D15
wy. Bidwill ... 211 H14
CARNEGIE
cct. Chifley ... 436 K5
pl. Blacktown ... 244 F9
pl. Castle Hill ... 247 J1
rd. Chester Hill ... 368 C3
st. Auburn ... 338 K6
CARNEY
la. Mosman, off Avenue Rd ... 317 B8
st. Casula ... 394 C16
CARNIVAL
wy. Kellyville ... 186 C16
CARNOUSTIE
pl. Glenmore Pk ... 266 F11
CAROB
pl. Cherrybrook ... 219 E7
CAROL
av. Jannali ... 460 F14
cr. Roselands ... 400 F8
CAROLE
av. Baulkham Hl ... 247 K10
st. Seven Hills ... 246 B11
CAROLES
rd. Orangeville ... 443 C14
CAROLINE
cr. Georges Hall ... 367 F10
la. Balmain ... 8 B8
la. Redfern ... 18 K6
st. Balmain ... 8 B8
st. Earlwood ... 372 G16
st. Guildford ... 338 C6
st. Kingsgrove ... 402 A10
st. Oyster Bay ... 461 A6
st. Redfern ... 18 K6
st. Westmead ... 277 H15
wy. Minto ... 482 J2
CAROLINE CHISHOLM
dr. Camden S ... 507 B10
dr. Winston Hills ... 277 A1
la. Lane Cove ... 313 H4
CAROLYN
av. Beacon Hill ... 257 J5
av. Carlingford ... 249 G12
ch. Orchard Hills ... 267 B13
cl. Castle Hill ... 217 J9
st. Greystanes ... 306 F4
st. Silverwater ... 309 J10
CAROMA
av. Kyeemagh ... 404 B14
CARONIA
av.e, Cronulla ... 493 J11
av.w, Cronulla ... 493 F10
av.w, Woolooware ... 493 F10
CAROONA
wy. Glenwood ... 215 F16
CAROTANA
st. Padstow ... 399 A13
CAROUSEL
cl. Cromer ... 258 G2
CARPENTER
av. Rookwood ... 340 B12
cr. Warriewood ... 199 D11
la. Ashcroft, off Sutton Rd ... 364 E16
pl. Minchinbury ... 271 G7
st. Colyton ... 269 J3
st. St Marys ... 269 J3
CARR
la. Coogee ... 407 E1
pl. Bradbury ... 511 J11
rd. Bringelly ... 387 F8
st. Chatswd W ... 284 E11
st. Coogee ... 407 E1
st. Waverton ... 5 A6
CARRABAI
pl. Baulkham Hl ... 248 A11
CARRAMAR
av. Carramar ... 366 H2
av. North Ryde ... 283 B13
cr. Miranda ... 492 E5
cr. Winmalee ... 173 F12
gr. Terrey Hills ... 196 D6
pl. Peakhurst ... 430 C9
rd. Lindfield ... 283 F4
st. Berowra ... 133 F11
CARRAMARR
rd. Castle Hill ... 218 B13
CARRANYA
rd. Riverview ... 314 B6
CARRARA
pl. Plumpton ... 241 H11
rd. Vaucluse ... 348 B4
CARRBRIDGE
dr. Castle Hill ... 218 C7
CARRE
av. Canley Ht ... 335 E16
CARRICK
cl. West Hoxton ... 392 D7
CARRINGTON
av. Bellevue Hill ... 347 F13
av. Caringbah ... 492 F4
av. Cromer ... 228 B13
av. Hurstville ... 431 G1
av. Mortdale ... 431 D8
av. Mosman ... 316 K2
av. Strathfield ... 341 F13
cct. Leumeah ... 482 D16
dr. Centnnial Pk ... 21 G6
la. Coogee ... 377 E14
la. Petersham ... 15 J9
la. Bellevue Hill, off Carrington Av ... 347 F13
la. N Strathfield, off Carrington St ... 341 F8
pde. Curl Curl ... 258 K16
pde. Harbord ... 258 K16
rd. Bringelly ... 418 H2
rd. Castle Hill ... 217 D13
rd. Coogee ... 377 D15
rd. Guildford ... 337 D6
rd. Hornsby ... 191 F11
rd. Londonderry ... 148 C10
rd. Marrickville ... 373 K16
rd. Randwick ... 377 D15
rd. Wahroonga ... 222 E2
rd. Waverley ... 377 F10
sq. Campsie ... 371 J13
st. Auburn ... 339 A3
st. Balmain ... 7 C11
st. Bexley ... 402 H16
st. Campsie ... 371 J13
st. Granville ... 308 E13
st. Lewisham ... 15 C7
st. Lilyfield ... 10 D4
st. N Strathfield ... 341 F8
st. Parramatta ... 307 K7
st. Penshurst ... 431 G5
st. Revesby ... 398 C10
st. St Marys ... 269 J6
st. Seven Hills ... 275 K4
st. Summer Hill ... 373 D6
st. Sydney ... A G16
st. Sydney ... 1 F16
st. Wahroonga ... 222 D2

CARRISBROOK
av. Bexley North...402 F10
av. Punchbowl...400 A1
CARROL
ct. Menai...458 J14
CARROLL
cr. Plumpton...242 B11
la. Woollahra...22 K5
la. Mosman, off Ourimbah Rd..317 A5
pl. Westleigh...220 E8
st. Beverley Pk...433 C10
st. Lidcombe...339 G10
st. Warwck Frm...365 E13
st. Wetherill Pk...334 F5
CARROWBROOK
av. Glenwood...245 F1
CARRS
rd. Galston...159 F4
rd. Wilberforce...61 G5
CARRUTHERS
dr. Dolls Point...463 H2
dr. Horngsea Pk...392 F16
dr. Sans Souci...433 H16
st. Penshurst...431 C4
CARSHALTON
st. Croydon...372 E5
st. Croydon Pk...372 E5
CARSON
cr. Bexley North...402 C10
st. Dundas Vy...280 E10
st. Panania...398 E15
st. Pymble...253 E1
CARSONS
la. St Marys...239 G16
CARSTAIRS
pl. St Andrews...482 B2
CARSTONE
wy. Ambarvale...510 K16
CARTELA
cr. Smithfield...335 E4
CARTER
cr. Gymea Bay...491 E9
cr. Padstow Ht...429 E8
la. Marrickville...373 F14
la. Randwick, off Castle La...377 B10
pl. Claymore...481 B10
rd. Brookvale...258 D10
rd. Menai...458 H13
st. Belfield...371 D12
st. Bronte...377 H8
st. Cammeray...316 A5
st. Gordon...254 A7
st. Greystanes...305 H9
st. Homebush B...340 C2
st. Newington...M F13
st. Randwick...377 B9
st. Seven Hills...276 A4
CARTERET
av. Willmot...210 D13
CARTERS
rd. Dural...189 E3
rd. Grose Vale...84 G11
CARTHONA
av. Darling Point...14 A1
CARTIER
cr. Green Valley...363 B9
st. Bonnyrigg...363 H8
CARTLEDGE
av. Miranda...491 J6
CARTMORE
la. Surry Hills...20 B6
CARTREF
la. Mosman, off Rangers Av...316 G9
CARTWRIGHT
av. Busby...393 H1
av. Cartwright...393 H1
av. Homebush...341 B6
av. Merrylands...307 B11
av. Miller...393 H1
av. Sadleir...393 H1
cl. Glenmore Pk...265 F7
cr. Lalor Park...245 G11
st. Bonnyrigg Ht...363 G6
st. S Windsor...150 H2
CARVER
cr. Baulkham Hl...247 G6
pl. Dundas Vy...280 C8
CARVERS
rd. Oyster Bay...461 A8
CARVOSSA
pl. Bligh Park...150 J6

CARWAR
av. Carss Park...432 G13
la. Carss Park...432 G12
CARY
gr. Minto...482 C2
la. Bondi Jctn...22 K8
st. Baulkham Hl...248 B9
st. Drummoyne...344 B4
st. Emu Plains...235 E11
st. Leichhardt...15 G2
st. Marrickville...373 H16
wy. Villawood...337 A16
CARYSFIELD
rd. Bass Hill...368 C12
rd. Georges Hall...368 C12
CARYSFORT
st. Hurstville...432 A8
CASABLANCA
av. Kellyville...186 B16
CASANDA
av. Smithfield...335 C4
CASBEN
cl. Carlingford...250 D12
CASBY
pl. Ambarvale...510 G13
CASCADE
la. Paddington...13 E13
rd. Cranebrook...207 A12
st. Paddington...13 E16
st. Seven Hills...275 C10
CASCADES
cl. West Hoxton...392 D5
CASERTA
pl. Allambie Ht...257 D8
CASEY
pl. Blackett...241 D3
CASH
pl. Prairiewood...334 E11
CASHEL
cr. Killarney Ht...255 H12
CASHMAN
dr. Kurrajong...55 E11
pl. Edensor Pk...333 J14
rd. Btn-le-Sds...404 A15
st. Rozelle...10 K4
CASHMANS
la. Five Dock, off Ramsay Rd...342 K10
CASHMERE
av. Rouse Hill...185 E2
dr. Elderslie...507 J1
CASINO
pl. Hoxton Park...393 B7
rd. Greystanes...305 G3
st. Bossley Park...333 D13
st. Eastlakes...406 A4
st. Glenwood...245 G1
CASPIAN
pl. Woronora Ht...489 F5
CASS
ct. Currans Hill...479 J14
pl. Cranebrook...207 E13
CASSAM
pl. Valley Ht...202 D4
CASSANDRA
av. St Ives...224 D14
cr. Heathcote...518 F9
pl. Carlingford...279 K2
CASSAR
cr. Cranebrook...207 G6
CASSIA
cl. Bossley Park...333 E8
cl. St Clair...269 H9
gr. Beecroft...250 F3
la. Dee Why...258 K9
pl. Bass Hill...368 A10
pl. Eastwood...281 C5
pl. Loftus...489 J11
pl. Mcquarie Fd...454 E1
st. Dee Why...258 K9
CASSIDY
st. Denham Ct...422 C4
CASSILIS
st. Monterey...433 G8
CASSINA
pl. Baulkham Hl...246 G9
CASSINIA
ct. Wattle Grove...426 A2
pl. Mt Annan...509 F4
CASSINO
cl. Allambie Ht...257 D9
CASSINS
av. N Sydney...5 F1
la. N Sydney...5 F1

CASSIUS
wy. Rsemeadow...540 H3
CASSOLA
pl. Penrith...236 E2
CASTELNAU
st. Caringbah...492 G11
CASTLE
cct. Seaforth...286 K6
cct. Westleigh...220 F8
cr. Belrose...225 J14
la. Randwick, off Carter St...377 B9
pl. Castle Hill...218 B14
pl. Padstow Ht...429 H5
pl. Sylvania...461 J14
rd. Orchard Hills...267 E5
rd. Richmond...118 G11
st. Blacktown...274 C5
st. Blakehurst...462 C4
st. Castle Hill...218 A13
st. Castlereagh...176 A5
st. N Parramatta...278 C11
st. Randwick...377 B9
CASTLE CIRCUIT
cl. Seaforth...286 J5
CASTLECOVE
dr. Castle Cove...285 F4
CASTLEFERN
ct. Kellyville...186 K15
CASTLEFIELD
la. Bondi, off Castlefield St...378 A4
st. Bondi...378 A4
CASTLE HILL
rd. Castle Hill...218 H14
rd. Cherrybrook...249 D1
rd. W Pnnant Hl...249 D1
CASTLE HOWARD
rd. Beecroft...250 F9
rd. Cheltenham...250 F9
CASTLE LEA
ct. Castle Hill...219 A12
CASTLEREAGH
cr. Sylvania Wtr...462 D11
la. Redfern...19 G7
la. Penrith, off Castlereagh Rd..236 F7
rd. Agnes Banks...117 A14
rd. Castlereagh...205 G11
rd. Penrith...236 F7
rd. Richmond...117 H8
rd. Wilberforce...91 K1
st. Bossley Park...333 F5
st. Concord...341 H6
st. Haymarket...F B7
st. Haymarket...F A8
st. Haymarket...3 H11
st. Liverpool...395 C4
st. Penrith...236 H13
st. Riverstone...182 K8
st. Sydney...D A16
st. Sydney...3 H11
st. Tahmoor...565 H12
st. Tahmoor...565 J10
CASTLE ROCK
cr. Clontarf...287 G15
ct. Wattle Grove...395 K14
CASTLEROCK
av. Glenmore Pk...266 H8
CASTLESTEAD
st. Concord W...311 D14
CASTLEWOOD
av. Woolooware...493 E10
dr. Castle Hill...248 H1
CASTRA
pl. Double Bay...14 F7
CASUARINA
av. Glenorie...128 C5
cct. Kingswood...267 H2
cl. The Oaks...502 E14
ct. Wattle Grove...396 C16
dr. Cherrybrook...219 G13
pl. Mcquarie Fd...454 B5
rd. Alfords Point...429 C14
rd. Gymea Bay...491 F12
CASULA
pl. Forestville...255 H9
rd. Casula...394 H15
CASURINA
pl. Narellan Vale...478 J14
CAT
pl. Seven Hills...275 B5
CATALINA
cr. Avalon...140 D14
pl. Kellyville...186 F16
pl. Raby...481 H1
st. Mascot...404 K4
st. N St Marys...239 J10
CATALPA
av. Avalon...139 J15
av. Blaxland...233 G6
cr. Turramurra...222 H16
gr. Menai...458 K13
wy. Blacktown...274 E12
CATANIA
pl. Quakers Hill...214 D9
CATARACT
pl. Leumeah...482 E13
rd. Appin...568 E14
rd. Box Hill...154 A1
CATCHMENT
cl. Mulgoa...323 E4
CATCHPOLE
av. Richmond...118 D6
st. St Helens Pk...541 C3
CATERSON
dr. Castle Hill...217 E9
CATES
pl. St Ives...224 D8
CATHAN
st. Quakers Hill...214 E11
CATHCART
st. Fairfield...336 A16
CATHEDRAL
st. Sydney...D J10
st. Sydney...4 B5
st. Woolmloo...4 B5
st. Woolmloo...4 E6
CATHERINE
av. Lurnea...394 D10
cr. Blaxland...234 C7
cr. Rooty Hill...272 C2
la. Belmore...401 H1
st. Glebe...12 B16
st. Kurrajong...85 F3
st. Leichhardt...16 D3
st. Lilyfield...10 F8
st. Punchbowl...370 B16
st. Rockdale...433 C1
st. Rozelle...10 J2
st. St Ives...224 D13
st. Werrington...238 H9
st. Windsor...121 B9
CATHERINE FIELD
rd. Catherine Fd...449 D1
CATHY
st. Blaxland...233 J11
wy. Seven Hills...275 K5
CATKIN
wy. Mcquarie Fd...454 G4
CATLETT
av. North Rocks...248 K16
CATO
cl. Edensor Pk...363 F3
pl. Blackett...241 D3
pl. Illawong...459 D5
wy. Casula...424 F3
CATON
pl. Quakers Hill...213 H16
CATRIONA
cl. Berowra Ht...133 A6
CATTAI
ct. Holsworthy...426 E5
pl. Kenthurst...188 D6
rd. Cattai...94 C4
rd. Pitt Town...93 A13
CATTAI CREEK
dr. Kellyville...187 A16
dr. Kellyville...216 K1
dr. Kellyville...217 C1
CATTAI RIDGE
rd. Glenorie...128 D12
rd. Maraylya...95 B13
CATTON
pl. Menai...458 J14
CAULFIELD
cr. St Johns Pk...364 E2
CAVALLARO
ct. Mount Druitt...241 D11
CAVALLI
wy. Clarmnt Ms...268 F4
CAVAN
pl. Airds...512 B13
rd. Killarney Ht...255 K13
CAVE
av. North Ryde...282 C9
cl. Green Valley...363 B11
rd. Strathfield...370 J2

CAVELL
av. Rhodes...311 E7
CAVENDISH
av. Blacktown...275 A7
la. Stanmore...16 F12
st. Concord W...341 D1
st. Enmore...16 E11
st. Pennant Hills..220 K16
st. Stanmore...16 E11
CAVERSHAM
ct. Cherrybrook...219 F9
CAVES
la. Dulwich Hill...373 E9
CAVEY
st. Marrickville...373 K14
CAVILL
av. Ashfield...372 G2
st. Harbord...288 F2
st. Hebersham...241 F10
st. Queenscliff...288 F2
CAWARRA
pl. Fairfield...336 F7
pl. Gordon...253 E9
rd. Caringbah...492 J6
st. Eastern Ck...272 F7
CAWARRAH
rd. Middle Cove...285 J8
CAWDOR
pl. Acacia Gdn...214 H16
pl. Rsemeadow...540 D3
rd. Camden...506 H4
rd. Cawdor...506 C16
rd. Cawdor...537 A10
CAWDOR FARMS
rd. Grasmere...475 H16
CAWTHORNE
st. Hornsby Ht...191 G7
CAYLEY
av. Punchbowl...400 B6
pl. Cabramtta W..364 F6
CECIL
av. Castle Hill...217 K14
av. Pennant Hills..250 J1
la. Paddington...13 G14
pl. Greenfld Pk...334 C16
pl. Cecil Park...331 G8
rd. Hornsby...192 C14
rd. Newport...169 G16
rd. Rose Bay...348 D8
st. Ashfield...373 A1
st. Caringbah...492 K16
st. Denistone E...281 H10
st. Dolans Bay...492 K16
st. Fairlight...288 E8
st. Gordon...253 G11
st. Guildford...337 G2
st. Hurstville Gr...431 H9
st. Merrylands...307 G16
st. Monterey...433 H6
st. Paddington...13 G14
st. Scotland I...168 H4
st. Wareemba...342 K6
CECIL HEALY
av. Newington...L F16
av. Newington...310 A16
CECILIA
st. Belmore...371 E13
st. Marrickville...373 K11
st. Toongabbie...276 B7
CECIL MUNRO
av. Cronulla, off Ozone St...494 A12
CECILY
st. Belfield...371 B10
st. Lilyfield...10 G2
CEDAR
av. Bradbury...511 E14
cl. Bossley Park...333 H9
cr. N St Marys...240 A11
gr. Castle Hill...217 D10
gr. Frenchs Frst...256 F2
la. N St Marys, off Cedar Cr...240 A12
pl. Blacktown...274 B7
pl. Ermington...280 D13
pl. Kirrawee...490 K5
pl. S Coogee...407 E6
pl. The Oaks...502 F13
rd. Casula...423 K3
rd. Prestons...394 A15
st. Greystanes...306 E4
st. Lugarno...429 G16
st. Normanhurst..221 D12
CEDAR CREEK
rd. Thirlmere...561 H11

rd. Thirlmere 561 H12
CEDAR WATTLE
pl. Narellan Vale 478 K14
CEDARWOOD
cl. Greystanes 306 F12
dr. Cherrybrook 219 H15
gr. Dean Park 212 F16
pl. Carlingford 249 D15
CEDRIC
la. Mosman, off Mulbring St 317 D9
st. Mcquarie Fd 423 K15
CELEBES
st. Kings Park 244 K2
CELEBRATION
rd. Sadleir 364 B16
CELESTE
av. Castle Hill 217 C7
ct. Rooty Hill 272 A5
CELESTIAL
pl. Cranebrook 207 G5
CELIA
pl. Kings Lngly 245 G8
rd. Kellyville 185 F1
st. Granville 308 F15
CELOSIA
pl. Loftus 489 H13
CELTIS
pl. Mcquarie Fd 454 F2
CEMETERY
av. Matraville 436 G8
rd. Riverstone 182 E10
CENTAUR
st. Padstow 429 A2
st. Revesby 429 A5
st. Revesby Ht 429 A5
CENTAURI
cct. Cranebrook 207 E5
CENTAURUS
dr. Hinchinbrk 393 D4
CENTENARY
av. Hunters Hill 313 D11
av. Matraville 436 J8
av. Moorebank 395 K11
dr. Homebsh W 340 F12
dr. Mosman 316 H11
dr. Strathfield 340 F12
rd. Merrylands 306 K5
rd. S Wntwthvle 307 A5
CENTENNIAL
av. Chatswd W 284 E11
av. Lane Cove 284 B16
av. Lane Cove W 313 J1
av. Randwick 377 C9
ct. Mt Vernon 331 E3
la. Centnnial Pk 21 C10
la. Ellis Lane 476 C13
sq. Centnnial Pk 21 G4
sq. Paddington 21 G4
st. Marrickville 373 K10
CENTENNIAL PARK
ct. Wattle Grove 426 A3
CENTRAL
av. Chipping Ntn 366 F16
av. Chipping Ntn 366 H15
av. Como 460 F4
av. Eastwood 280 K5
av. Eveleigh 18 H11
av. Lane Cove 314 E2
av. Lilyfield 10 C2
av. Manly 288 H9
av. Marrickville 373 K13
av. Mosman 317 A1
av. Thornleigh 221 A13
av. Westmead 277 H16
la. Chipping Ntn 366 G14
la. Marrickville, off Victoria Rd 374 B13
pl. Baulkham Hl 247 H11
rd. Avalon 139 J15
rd. Beverly Hills 430 J1
rd. Miranda 492 A3
st. Belfield 371 D10
st. Naremburn 315 F2
st. Sydney E H1
st. Sydney 3 G9
CENTRAL PARK
dr. Bow Bowing 452 D15
CENTRE
av. Roselands 400 J7
cr. Blaxland 234 C6
la. Kingsford, off Kennedy St 406 J1
pl. Wetherill Pk 334 E1
rd. Mascot 404 C6
st. Blakehurst 462 D1
st. Leichhardt 16 D2
st. Penshurst 431 E6
st. Redfern 19 H6
CENTURY
cct. Baulkham Hl 216 G15
CEPHEUS
la. Erskine Park, off Cepheus Pl 300 F1
pl. Erskine Park 300 F1
CERAMIC
la. Manly 288 G5
wy. Woodcroft 243 E9
CEREMONIAL
dr. Richmond 118 J10
dr. Richmond 119 A10
CERES
pl. Rsemeadow 540 K5
st. Penrith 237 D2
CESSNA
pl. Raby 481 G2
CESTRUM
av. Mcquarie Fd 454 F5
CETUS
pl. Erskine Park 301 B3
CEVU
av. Willoughby 285 G13
CHABLIS
pl. Eschol Park 481 B6
pl. Minchinbury 272 B9
pl. Orchard Hills 268 F15
CHAD
pl. St Clair 299 J3
CHADD
st. Galston 160 F5
CHADDERTON
st. Cabramatta 366 E6
st. Canley Vale 366 E6
CHADLEY
ct. Cherrybrook 219 H13
pl. West Hoxton 392 A10
CHADWICK
av. Marrickville 373 D15
av. Regents Pk 339 D16
cr. Fairfield W 335 B13
st. Lucas Ht 487 J11
st. Putney 312 A9
CHADWORTH
pl. Castle Hill 248 B6
CHAFFEY
pl. Bonnyrigg Ht 363 E7
CHAINMAIL
cr. Castle Hill 217 E3
CHAIN-O-PONDS
cct. Mt Annan 479 A16
rd. Mulgoa 295 F9
CHAKOLA
av. Hornsby Ht 191 G4
pl. Kirrawee 461 D16
CHALCEDONY
st. Eagle Vale 481 G7
CHALDER
av. Marrickville 374 D11
la. Marrickville, off Chalder St 374 C10
st. Marrickville 374 C11
st. Newtown 17 H8
CHALET
pl. Minchinbury 272 A8
rd. Kellyville 216 E5
CHALEYER
st. N Willghby 285 F7
st. Rose Bay 348 C13
CHALFORD
av. Canterbury 402 E1
CHALIS
la. Randwick, off Castle St 377 B9
CHALLENGER
dr. Belrose 225 H6
la. Cranebrook, off Pensax Rd 207 G14
pl. Birchgrove 7 K4
st. Voyager Pt 427 D4
wy. Cranebrook 207 G14
CHALLIS
av. Dulwich Hill 373 F12
av. Potts Point 4 J2
av. Turramurra 222 K10
st. Randwick 377 B9
CHALLONER
av. Chipping Ntn 396 E4
CHALMER
cl. St Johns Pk 364 E1
CHALMERS
av. Beacon Hill 257 H7
av. Emu Plains 235 J10
cr. Mascot 405 A3
cr. Old Tngabbie 276 J11
la. Surry Hills 19 G3
rd. Strathfield 341 B16
st. Belmore 401 C3
st. Haymarket 19 G4
st. Lakemba 401 C3
st. Redfern 19 F10
st. Surry Hills 19 G4
CHAMBERLAIN
av. Caringbah 492 G4
av. Rose Bay 348 C8
dr. Smithfield 335 B6
rd. Bexley 402 H12
rd. Guildford 337 J7
rd. Padstow 429 D5
rd. Padstow Ht 429 D6
st. Campbelltwn 511 H2
st. Narwee 400 J14
CHAMBERS
av. Bondi Beach 378 B3
ct. Epping 251 B16
st. Wrrngtn Cty 238 F9
CHAMELEON
dr. Erskine Park 300 D3
la. Erskine Park, off Chameleon Dr 300 F1
CHAMPION
rd. Glenorie 128 G13
rd. Tennyson 312 E11
st. Glenfield 424 H10
CHAMPNESS
cr. St Marys 239 J15
la. St Marys, off Champness Cr 239 K15
CHANCERY
st. Canley Vale 366 E5
CHANDLER
av. Chippendale 18 H1
av. Cowan 104 C14
av. Chippendale, off City Rd 18 H2
st. Rockdale 433 D2
st. Rooty Hill 271 J6
CHANDOS
la. Crows Nest, off Alexander St 315 F5
rd. Bargo 567 C15
rd. Horsley Pk 303 A12
rd. Yanderra 567 C15
st. Ashfield 343 A16
st. Canley Vale 365 J2
st. Crows Nest 315 E5
st. Haberfield 343 B16
st. Manly Vale 287 J5
st. Naremburn 315 E5
st. St Leonards 315 E5
CHANEL
st. Toongabbie 276 G4
CHANG
pl. Kearns 481 B1
CHANNEL
pl. Mt Annan 479 G15
st. Dulwich Hill 373 D7
CHANNEY
cl. Bossley Park 333 H7
CHANSA
pl. Blacktown 273 K5
CHANT
av. Pagewood 406 G7
CHANTER
rd. Thirlmere 564 G9
CHAPALA
cl. St Ives 224 E8
CHAPEL
cct. Prospect 274 J13
cl. Cherrybrook 219 E14
la. Alexandria 18 K10
la. Alexandria 19 A10
la. Baulkham Hl 246 G8
la. Baulkham Hl 247 B4
la. Belmore 401 F3
la. Marrickville 374 B10
la. Rockdale 403 D16
la. St Marys, off Champness Cr 239 J15
la. Crows Nest, off Holterman St 315 F6
rd. Bankstown 369 E16
rd. Vaucluse 348 D2
rd.s, Bankstown 399 C7
st. Belmore 401 D2
st. Darlinghurst 4 D9
st. Kingsgrove 401 D2
st. Kogarah 433 C6
st. Lakemba 401 D2
st. Lilyfield 9 H4
st. Marrickville 374 C10
st. Randwick 377 C11
st. Richmond 118 E3
st. Rockdale 403 E16
st. Roselands 401 D2
st. St Marys 239 H16
CHAPERON
cr. Minto 453 B15
CHAPLAIN
pl. Bligh Park 150 J7
CHAPLIN
cr. Quakers Hill 243 H1
dr. Lane Cove 283 F16
CHAPMAN
av. Beecroft 250 B5
av. Castle Hill 217 H13
av. Chatswood 284 J11
av. Maroubra 407 G11
av. Penrith 236 H13
cct. Currans Hill 479 H9
la. Annandale 10 J15
la. Surry Hills 20 E3
la. Lindfield, off Tyron Rd 254 D16
pde. Faulconbdg 171 D13
pl. Wakeley 334 G14
rd. Annandale 11 D6
rd. Vineyard 152 H9
st. Gladesville 312 E7
st. Green Valley 363 B13
st. Gymea 491 E3
st. Gymea 491 E6
st. Strathfield 341 F10
st. Summer Hill 373 E4
st. Surry Hills 20 E3
st. Tahmoor 565 H10
st. Werrington 238 K12
st. West Hoxton 392 C10
CHAPPEL
av. Green Valley 363 A9
ct. Mt Annan 479 C12
CHARADE
st. Riverwood 400 C10
CHARD
rd. Brookvale 258 B10
CHARDONNAY
av. Eschol Park 481 A4
rd. St Clair 270 G11
CHARKER
cl. Harringtn Pk 478 C3
CHARKERS
st. S Penrith 266 H6
CHARLBURY
st. Chipping Ntn 396 F2
CHARLECOT
st. Dulwich Hill 373 G10
CHARLEMONT
wy. Wentwthvle 277 E11
CHARLEROI
rd. Belrose 226 A9
CHARLES
ct. North Rocks 278 F3
la. Burwood 342 B15
la. Forest Lodge 11 G15
la. Mosman, off Muston St 317 C9
pl. Cherrybrook 219 H5
pl. Jannali 460 H11
pl. Mt Annan 509 F2
st. Arncliffe 403 H9
st. Balmain 8 C10
st. Baulkham Hl 247 G13
st. Blacktown 245 A8
st. Burwood 342 C15
st. Canterbury 372 E13
st. Carlingford 279 G6
st. Castlecrag 286 A11
st. Eastlakes 405 J6
st. Enmore 17 A12
st. Erskineville 18 A13
st. Fairlight 288 D8
st. Five Dock 343 A7
st. Forest Lodge 11 G15
st. Granville 308 F15
st. Guildford W 336 H3
st. Harbord 288 H2
st. Killara 283 E2
st. Leichhardt 9 G10
st. Lilyfield 9 G7
st. Lindfield 283 E2
st. Liverpool 395 B8
st. McGraths Hl 121 J11
st. Marrickville 374 B9
st. Marsden Pk 182 A12
st. N Richmond 87 D13
st. N Sydney K B5
st. N Sydney 5 E7
st. Oatlands 279 A10
st. Oatley 431 B15
st. Parramatta 308 E4
st. Petersham 16 C5
st. Putney 311 K8
st. Redfern 20 C8
st. Riverwood 400 E16
st. Ryde 312 B5
st. St Marys 239 E5
st. Smithfield 335 B6
st. Springwood 201 F3
st. Woolmloo 4 F5
CHARLES BABBAGE
av. Currans Hill 479 G12
CHARLESCOTTE
av. Punchbowl 400 D7
CHARLES HACKETT
dr. St Marys 239 F16
CHARLES HAYMAN
la. Collaroy 229 B14
CHARLES STURT
dr. Wrrngtn Cty 238 F9
CHARLES TODD
cr. Wrrngtn Cty 238 E7
la. Wrrngtn Cty, off Charles Todd Cr 238 E7
CHARLESTON
av. Earlwood 402 E6
CHARLESWORTH
cl. Catherine Fd 449 G8
CHARLIE YANKOS
st. Glenwood 215 K16
CHARLISH
la. Lane Cove 313 K1
CHARLOTTE
av. Marrickville 373 K15
cl. Lurnea 394 B12
cr. Canley Vale 366 F4
gr. Bella Vista 246 G3
la. Darlinghurst F G2
la. Pennant Hills 250 J1
pl. Beacon Hill 257 F2
pl. Bligh Park 150 D4
pl. Illawong 459 G3
rd. Pennant Hills 250 J1
rd. Port Botany 436 B9
rd. Rooty Hill 271 J3
st. Ashfield 372 J1
st. Campsie 401 K1
st. Dundas Vy 280 B7
st. Lilyfield 10 C10
st. Marsden Pk 181 J12
st. Merrylands 307 C16
st. Rozelle 10 K1
wy. Minto 482 H7
CHARLTON
av. Chipping Ntn 366 E15
av. Turramurra 223 E12
dr. Castle Hill 219 A13
la. Brookvale 258 B11
pl. Menai 458 E13
pl. St Clair 270 C9
pwy. Chipping Ntn, off Charlton Av 366 E14
rd. Lalor Park 245 E10
st. Abbotsford 342 J2
st. Yagoona 369 C9
wy. Glebe 11 K8
CHARLTONS CREEK
rd. Berrilee 131 D11
CHARM
pl. Peakhurst 429 K6
CHARMAINE
av. Greenacre 370 C7
CHARMAN
av. Maroubra 406 H7
CHARMER
cr. Minchinbury 271 G8
CHARMIAN
pl. Rsemeadow 540 H3
CHARNWOOD
ct. Glen Alpine 510 E9
CHARTER
st. Sadleir 394 B2
CHASE
av. Roseville Ch 255 E14
dr. Acacia Gdn 214 J16

CHASELING
av. Springwood 201 G1
pl. The Oaks 502 E10
st. Greenacre 370 D13
CHASSELAS
av. Eschol Park 481 A4
CHATEAU
cl. Kellyville 185 E7
cr. St Clair 270 B9
tce. Quakers Hill 213 G9
CHATFIELD
av. Belfield 371 C8
st. Ryde 312 D1
CHATHAM
av. Moorebank 425 A3
cl. Belrose 226 A13
ct. Cherrybrook, off Glamorgan Wy. 219 E9
pl. Abbotsford 342 K2
pl. N Turramrra 223 E6
rd. Denistone 281 B12
rd. Eastwood 281 B11
rd. West Ryde 281 B12
st. Botany 405 G12
st. Canley Ht 365 G4
st. Pitt Town 92 H15
st. Randwick 377 D15
CHATRES
st. St Clair 270 F11
CHATSWOOD
av. Chatswood 285 B8
CHATSWORTH
rd. St Clair 270 D10
st. Fairfield 336 B14
CHAUCER
cr. Leumeah 512 B2
pl. Winmalee 173 J9
rd. Riverstone 182 C10
st. Wetherill Pk 334 G6
CHAUSSON
pl. Cranebrook 207 G8
CHAUVEL
av. Holsworthy 396 B13
av. Milperra 397 E12
cl. Wahroonga 223 B5
st. North Ryde 282 J11
CHAVIN
pl. Greenfld Pk 333 K13
CHEAL
la. Neutral Bay 6 F1
CHEATLE
st. East Hills 427 H2
CHECKLEY
ct. Ermington 280 B15
st. Abbotsford 342 H1
CHEDDAR
st. Blakehurst 432 D12
CHEDLEY
pl. Marayong 244 D8
CHEERS
st. West Ryde 280 J13
CHEERYBLE
pl. Ambarvale 510 K14
CHEESMANS
rd. Maroota S 64 J4
CHEGWYN
av. Matraville 436 H8
la. Botany, off Chegwyn St 405 E12
st. Botany 405 E11
CHELLASTON
st. Camden 507 B3
CHELMSFORD
av. Artarmon 285 D16
av. Artarmon 315 C1
av. Bankstown 399 B2
av. Belmore 401 H2
av. Botany 405 F15
av. Cronulla 523 K3
av. Croydon 372 C1
av. E Lindfield 254 G16
av. Epping 280 H3
av. Haberfield 343 D12
av. Lindfield 284 E2
av. Maroubra 407 C15
av. Naremburn 315 C1
av. Willoughby 285 D16
rd. Asquith 192 D10
rd. S Wntwthvle 306 J5
st. Camperdwn 17 D10
st. Newtown 17 D10
CHELSEA
av. Baulkham Hl 247 H8
dr. Canley Ht 335 C16
pl. Colyton 270 E6
pl. Glenfield 424 C11
rd. W Pnnant Hl 219 K16
st. Merrylands 307 B10
st. Redfern 20 C8
tce. Glenwood 215 H14
CHELSEA GARDEN
ct. Wattle Grove 426 B5
CHELTENHAM
av. Cambrdg Pk 237 K8
cl. Castle Hill 218 E12
rd. Burwood 342 C14
rd. Cheltenham 250 H10
rd. Croydon 342 C14
st. Chipping Ntn 366 F15
st. Rozelle 10 J3
CHEPSTOW
st. Randwick 377 B10
CHERANA
cr. Forestville 255 E9
pl. Kareela 461 E12
CHERIE
pl. Bass Hill 367 F7
CHERITON
av. Castle Hill 218 A15
CHEROKEE
av. Greenfld Pk 333 K14
pl. Raby 451 H16
CHERRY
av. Carlingford 249 E16
ct. Marsfield 282 A4
pl. Castle Cove 286 D7
pl. Mcquarie Fd 454 C5
pl. Prestons 393 H14
st. Marsden Pk 182 A13
st. Mt Pritchard 364 E9
st. Warrawee 222 G13
CHERRYBROOK
ch. Londonderry 178 C1
rd. Lansvale 366 C10
rd. W Pnnant Hl 219 J15
CHERRYWOOD
av. Mt Riverview 234 D3
av. Wahroonga 223 B4
cl. Cranebrook 207 E7
gr. Menai 458 K13
CHERTSEY
av. Bankstown 399 B3
CHERYL
cr. Newport 169 E9
pl. Castle Hill 217 C10
pl. Plumpton 242 D11
CHERYLE
av. Chester Hill 337 J10
CHESHAM
pde. Glenfield 424 E9
pl. Chipping Ntn 366 G14
pl. Plumpton 241 H8
st. St Marys 239 J14
CHESNUT
cr. Prestons 393 K15
CHESSELL
la. Ashfield, off Brown St 372 H2
CHESTER
av. Baulkham Hl 247 B13
av. Cambrdg Pk 237 H10
av. Maroubra 407 C12
la. Woollahra 22 E4
la. Zetland, off Joynton Av 375 H12
pl. Ermington 280 D14
pl. Narraweena 258 C2
rd. Ingleburn 453 B7
rd. Turramurra 223 D9
st. Annandale 17 B1
st. Annandale 17 C1
st. Blacktown 244 B15
st. Epping 251 B14
st. Merrylands 307 F8
st. Mount Druitt 241 C14
st. Petersham 15 H12
st. Schofields 183 E12
st. Sylvania 461 J13
st. Woollahra 22 E3
CHESTERFIELD
la. Bronte 377 J10
pde. Bronte 377 J10
rd. Epping 280 J3
rd. S Penrith 266 K3
CHESTER HILL
rd. Bass Hill 368 A8
rd. Chester Hill 368 B4
CHESTERMAN
cr. Davidson 255 B1
CHESTERTON
ct. Cmbrdg Gdn 237 H5
CHESTNUT
av. Telopea 279 G12
cr. Bidwill 211 D13
dr. Banksia 403 F12
dr. Glossodia 59 C6
rd. Auburn 339 A6
rd. Mt Colah 162 E13
st. Loftus 489 J12
CHETWYN
pl. Wentwthvle 277 C12
CHETWYND
rd. Guildford 337 D3
rd. Merrylands 307 E16
CHEVALIER
cr. Hunters Hill 314 A14
wy. Claymore 481 B12
CHEVIOT
dr. Cobbitty 416 F6
pl. Airds 512 A12
st. Ashbury 372 D8
st. Mount Druitt 241 C13
CHEVROLET
pl. Ingleburn 453 K7
CHEYENNE
rd. Greenfld Pk 333 K14
CHEYNE
rd. Terrey Hills 196 F5
wk. Castlecrag 286 F12
wk. W Pnnant Hl 219 J16
CHIANTI
ct. Glenwood 246 A3
CHICAGO
av. Blacktown 244 G12
av. Maroubra 407 C14
CHICHESTER
st. Maroubra 406 K10
CHICK
st. Roselands 400 H10
CHICKASAW
cr. Greenfld Pk 334 A16
CHIENTI
pl. Prestons 393 H15
CHIFLEY
av. Sefton 338 F16
cl. N Wahrnga 192 G16
pl. Bligh Park 150 G8
sq. Sydney B D16
sq. Sydney 1 K16
st. Smithfield 335 C2
st. Wetherill Pk 335 C2
wy. Penrith 237 B7
CHILAW
av. St Marys 269 G6
CHILCOTT
rd. Berrilee 131 D8
CHILDERS
st. Bonnyrigg Ht 363 F6
CHILDREY
pl. Castle Hill 219 A9
CHILDS
pl. Mt Annan 479 G15
pwy. Chipping Ntn, off Childs Rd 396 G1
rd. Chipping Ntn 396 F2
st. East Hills 427 J1
st. Lidcombe 339 H7
st. Panania 427 J1
CHILE
pl. Seven Hills 275 H4
CHILTERN
cr. Castle Hill 217 H10
rd. Guildford 337 H8
rd. Ingleside 197 J4
rd. Willoughby 285 F14
CHILTON
av. Oakhurst 242 D3
pde. Warrawee 222 G8
CHILVERS
la. Maroota S 65 K5
rd. Thornleigh 221 A10
CHILWORTH
cl. Beecroft 250 D7
CHINDOO
cl. Kingswood 267 F3
la. Kingswood, off Chindoo Cl 267 F3
CHIOS
pl. Rooty Hill 272 A3
CHIPALEE
ct. Erskine Park 300 E2
CHIPILLY
av. Engadine 518 G1
CHIPMAN
st. Eastlakes 405 J5
CHIPP
ct. Bella Vista 246 E3
CHIPPEN
la. Chippendale 19 C4
st. Chippendale 19 B4
CHIPPENHAM
pl. Chipping Ntn 366 G13
st. Chipping Ntn 366 G14
CHIPPING
pl. S Penrith 266 F4
CHIRCAN
st. Old Tngabbie 277 A6
CHISHOLM
av. Avalon 139 H15
av. Belmore 401 J4
av. Wrrngtn Cty 238 F9
cr. Blaxland 233 E9
cr. Bradbury 511 E9
pl. Windsor 121 D16
rd. Auburn 338 J6
rd. Catherine Fd 449 F3
rd. Sefton 368 H1
st. Belfield 371 B8
st. Darlinghurst 4 E14
st. Greenwich 315 A10
st. North Ryde 282 J8
st. Quakers Hill 213 H14
st. Smithfield 336 C5
st. S Turramrra 252 A5
CHISOLM
rd. Kurnell 465 J12
CHISWICK
la. Woollahra 22 B1
pl. Cherrybrook 219 C10
rd. Auburn 338 K7
rd. Greenacre 369 K10
rd. S Granville 338 E6
st. Chiswick 343 D1
st. Strathfield S 371 E7
CHITTICK
la. Cobbitty 446 J13
CHIVE
pl. Quakers Hill 243 G4
CHIVERS
av. Lugarno 429 K10
pl. Tahmoor 566 D8
CHOMA
wy. Leppington 420 A10
CHOPIN
cl. Bonnyrigg Ht 363 E5
cr. Clarmnt Ms 268 G3
st. Seven Hills 246 D13
CHORLEY
av. Cheltenham 250 K7
CHOWDER BAY
rd. Mosman 317 G11
CHOWNE
pl. N Willghby 285 G6
pl. Yennora 336 K11
st. Pyrmont 8 D16
st. Pyrmont 12 D1
CHRIS
pl. Dean Park 212 J16
st. Lansvale 367 B10
st. Windsor 121 K6
CHRISALEX
pl. St Clair 269 J8
CHRISAN
cl. Werrington 238 K10
CHRIS BANG
cr. Vaucluse 348 F6
CHRISTABEL
pl. Cecil Hills 362 F3
CHRISTEL
av. Carlingford 249 D13
CHRISTENSEN
cr. Oatley 430 D14
CHRISTIAN
rd. Punchbowl 400 D8
CHRISTIE
la. Glebe 12 G13
la. Surry Hills 20 A5
la. St Leonards, off Christie St 315 D6
rd. Mcquarie Pk 252 E15
st. Liverpool 395 A8
st. Minto 452 H16
st. Prairiewood 334 E10
st. St Leonards 315 D5
st. St Marys 239 C8
st. S Penrith 236 J15
st. Werrington 239 C8
st. Windsor 121 B9
st. Wollstncraft 315 D5
CHRISTIES
la. Zetland, off Merton St 375 H10
CHRISTINA
pl. Kareela 461 E12
rd. Villawood 337 E16
st. Longueville 314 E7
st. Rydalmere 309 H1
CHRISTINE
av. Ryde 282 C10
cr. Lalor Park 245 H12
ct. Kellyville 217 C3
st. Northmead 277 F10
st. S Penrith 267 C3
CHRISTMAS
pl. Green Valley 363 B10
CHRISTOPHER
av. Camden 507 B6
av. Georges Hall 367 F9
pl. Beacon Hill 257 E3
pl. N Richmond 87 B16
pl. Woolooware 493 E13
st. Baulkham Hl 247 H7
CHRYSANTHEMUM
av. Lurnea 394 F12
CHUBB
pl. Rooty Hill 241 K14
CHUDLEIGH
st. Rydalmere 279 F15
CHULLORA
cr. Engadine 488 D14
CHUNOOMA
rd. N Wahrnga 222 G1
CHURCH
av. Mascot 405 A1
av. Westmead 307 E2
la. Allawah 432 D8
la. Cranebrook 206 G1
la. Glebe 11 K10
la. N Sydney 5 E3
la. Pitt Town 92 G14
la. Randwick 377 A11
la. Ryde 311 K2
la. Surry Hills 4 D14
pl. Paddington 21 F4
rd. Denham Ct 422 E15
rd. Moorebank 395 F9
rd. Mulgoa 325 D2
rd. Wilberforce 92 B1
rd. Yagoona 369 A11
st. Appin 568 G12
st. Appin 568 J13
st. Ashfield 342 H14
st. Balmain 7 G8
st. Birchgrove 7 G8
st. Blakehurst 462 E2
st. Burwood 342 A16
st. Cabramatta 365 J10
st. Camperdwn 17 F4
st. Canterbury 372 H13
st. Castle Hill 248 B1
st. Castlereagh 176 G16
st. Chatswood 285 C9
st. Cranebrook 176 G16
st. Croydon 342 F13
st. Drummoyne 343 K3
st. Eastern Ck 272 G5
st. Elderslie 507 F1
st. Granville 308 C6
st. Greenwich 314 J12
st. Harris Park 308 C6
st. Hunters Hill 313 F11
st. Hurlstone Pk 372 H13
st. Lidcombe 339 H8
st. Lidcombe 340 B8
st. Lilyfield 9 G5
st. Mcquarie Fd 453 J2
st. Marrickville 373 H14
st. Mt Krng-gai 163 A12
st. Newtown 17 G7
st. N Parramatta 278 B10
st. N Sydney 5 E3
st. N Willghby 285 C9
st. Old Guildfrd 337 G10
st. Paddington 4 F16
st. Parramatta 308 C1
st. Parramatta 308 C4
st. Peakhurst 430 B3
st. Petersham 16 A11
st. Pitt Town 92 G15
st. Pymble 253 E2
st. Randwick 376 K12
st. Riverstone 182 J6

st. Rossmore 389 F14
st. Ryde 311 H5
st. Ryde 311 K3
st. St Peters 374 H13
st. S Windsor 120 G14
st. Waverley 377 F6
st. W Pnnant Hl 249 J4
st. Windsor 120 G14
st. Woolooware 493 E10
st. Parramatta, off George St 308 C3
CHURCH HILL
la. Gordon 253 H8
CHURCHILL
av. Kirrawee 491 A5
av. Riverwood 400 F14
av. Strathfield 341 E12
av. Wahroonga 222 C4
cr. Allambie Ht 257 D12
cr. Cammeray 316 D5
cr. Concord 341 H5
ct. Narellan Vale 479 A11
dr. Northmead 277 H2
dr. Winston Hills 277 H2
pl. Springwood 201 D2
rd. East Killara 254 E8
rd. Padstow Ht 429 F8
rd. Rose Bay 348 C8
st. Bardwell Pk 402 G9
st. Fairfield 336 A12
st. Fairfield Ht 336 A12
st. Guildford 338 D7
st. Silverwater 309 H13
st. Springwood 201 D1
CHURCH STREET
ml. Parramatta, off Church St 308 C3
CHUSAN
pl. Plumpton 242 C5
CHUTER
av. Monterey 433 G9
av. Ramsgate Bch 433 F13
av. Sans Souci 433 F16
st. McMahons Pt 5 C11
CICADA GLEN
rd. Ingleside 197 K1
CICERO
wy. Rsemeadow 540 H2
CIGOLINI
pl. Kellyville 216 G3
CILENTO
cr. East Ryde 282 K16
CINDY
pl. Colyton 270 E3
CINI
pl. Quakers Hill 213 G13
CINNABAR
st. Eagle Vale 481 G4
CIPOLIN
cl. Eagle Vale 481 G8
CIRCULAR
qy. Sydney B D7
qy. Sydney 1 J12
CIRCULAR QUAY
e. Sydney B F7
e. Sydney 2 A12
w. The Rocks B B3
w. The Rocks 1 J9
CIRELLA
cl. North Manly 258 A13
CIRRUS
pl. Bnkstn Aprt 397 J1
CISTICOLA
st. Hinchinbrk 363 E16
CITADEL
cr. Castle Hill 217 H4
pl. Glenwood 246 C6
CITRINE
cl. Bossley Park 333 K7
CITRINUS
pl. Narellan Vale 478 J13
CITROEN
pl. Ingleburn 453 G11
CITRON
pl. Oakhurst 241 J1
CITRUS
av. Hornsby 191 H12
gr. Carlingford 279 F2
CITY
rd. Camperdwn 18 D6
rd. Chippendale 18 D6
rd. Darlington 18 D6
rd. Newtown 18 D6
CITY VIEW
rd. Pennant Hills 250 F1
CITY WEST LINK
rd. Lilyfield 9 E7
rd. Lilyfield 10 F8
rd. Lilyfield 343 H12
rd. Rozelle 10 F8
CIVIC
arc. Chatswood, off Victoria Av 284 K9
av. Kogarah 433 F7
av. Pendle Hill 276 E13
dr. Bankstown 369 F15
dr. Dee Why 258 G5
la. Frenchs Frst 256 A3
la. Blacktown, off Campbell St 244 G16
la. Mosman, off Clifford St 317 A6
pl. Parramatta 308 C4
rd. Auburn 339 D3
CLACK
rd. Chester Hill 337 H11
CLACKMANNAN
rd. Winston Hills 277 E4
CLADDEN
cl. Pennant Hills 250 J2
CLAFTON
av. Northbridge 286 A15
CLAIR
cr. Padstow Ht 429 C7
CLAIRE
pl. Baulkham Hl 247 D2
st. Naremburn 315 F1
CLAIRVAUX
rd. Vaucluse 348 C6
CLANALPINE
st. Eastwood 281 A9
st. Mosman 317 A11
CLANCY
la. Seven Hills 275 G2
st. Padstow Ht 429 E6
st. Padstow Ht 429 G6
st. Smithfield 335 K6
CLANVILLE
rd. Roseville 284 F3
CLANWILLIAM
st. Chatswood 285 C10
st. Eastwood 280 J11
st. N Willghby 285 C10
CLAPHAM
rd. Regents Pk 368 G1
rd. Sefton 368 G1
CLAPTON
pl. Darlinghurst 4 F9
CLARA
st. Erskineville 18 C13
st. Newtown 374 G9
st. Randwick 377 A14
CLARE
cr. Oakville 122 E13
cr. Russell Lea 343 C6
pl. Killarney Ht 286 C1
st. Blacktown 274 E11
st. Cabramtta W 364 G5
st. Gladesville 312 G12
st. Glebe 11 K13
st. Rozelle 7 B12
st. Surry Hills 4 E15
st. Sylvania 462 D7
CLAREMONT
av. Canley Ht 335 E16
av. Greenacre 369 G9
cct. Glen Alpine 510 D16
cr. Hinchinbrk 363 B14
cr. Windsor 120 J9
ct. Wattle Grove 425 K4
dr. Bargo 567 B2
grn. W Pnnant Hl 249 C4
pl. S Penrith 266 F4
rd. Burwood Ht 372 A3
st. Balmain 7 A9
st. Campsie 371 J15
st. Merrylands 307 J15
st. Penshurst 431 F9
st. Richmond 119 A6
CLAREMOUNT
pl. Cherrybrook 219 D12
CLARENCE
av. Dee Why 258 J5
av. Homebush B M A6
av. Killara 254 C13
cr. Sylvania Wtr 462 D11
la. Sydney A D13
la. St Clair, off Clarence Rd 300 B1
pl. Double Bay 14 G14
rd. Cattai 94 G2
rd. Rockdale 403 A12
rd. St Clair 300 B1
st. Balgowlah 287 J11
st. Belfield 371 E10
st. Blacktown 243 J13
st. Burwood 342 A15
st. Canley Ht 335 F16
st. Condell Park 399 A4
st. Glenbrook 234 A14
st. Lidcombe 339 G7
st. Mcquarie Fd 423 J16
st. Matraville 436 K2
st. Merrylands 307 E11
st. North Ryde 283 B11
st. Penshurst 431 E3
st. Smithfield 335 H2
st. Strathfield 341 F9
st. Sydney C E2
st. Sydney 3 E1
st. Wentwthvle 277 C12
CLARENDON
ct. Wattle Grove 425 J3
dr. Stanhpe Gdn 215 G9
la. Stanmore 16 G7
la.w, Stanmore 16 F7
pl. Airds 511 K15
pl. Burwood 341 K14
rd. Riverwood 429 K2
rd. Stanmore 16 E7
st. Artarmon 314 J2
st. Richmond 119 D4
st. Vaucluse 348 E6
st. Waterloo 19 H11
CLARET
pl. Eschol Park 481 E3
st. Bossley Park 333 H9
CLARET ASH
gr. Menai 458 K14
CLAREVALE
st. Edensor Pk 333 D16
CLAREVILLE
av. Sandringham 463 D5
av. Sans Souci 463 E1
cl. Belfield 371 D8
cl. Woodbine 481 H11
CLARGO
st. Dulwich Hill 373 B10
CLARIBEL
st. Bankstown 399 A8
CLARICE
cr. Campbelltwn 511 J5
CLARIDGE
cl. Cherrybrook 219 D15
CLARINDA
st. Hornsby 191 E10
CLARISSA
pl. Ambarvale 511 B13
pl. Castle Hill 248 C6
CLARK
pl. Minto 482 J8
rd. Londonderry 149 B5
rd. Milsons Pt 6 A12
rd. Neutral Bay 6 B8
rd. N Sydney 6 A12
CLARKE
av. Richmond 118 C8
cl. Hinchinbrk 393 A1
cl. Prairiewood 334 J7
dr. Castle Hill 218 H13
la. Bass Hill 368 D11
la. Earlwood 402 H4
la. Panania 428 F2
la. Crows Nest, off Oxley St 315 E6
la. St Leonards, off Oxley St 315 E6
pl. Castle Hill 218 E12
pl. Killara 254 F11
pl. Menai 458 E12
pl. Mt Annan 479 G16
pl. Punchbowl, off Turner St 400 C4
rd. Hornsby 221 E5
rd. Pennant Hills 250 J4
rd. Waitara 221 H5
rd. Woolwich 314 E13
st. Annandale 16 F3
st. Bass Hill 368 D13
st. Berala 339 B12
st. Chatswd W 284 E9
st. Crows Nest 315 F6
st. Earlwood 402 H4
st. Granville 308 C12
st. Guildford 337 C7
st. Narrabeen 229 A8
st. Riverstone 183 F5
st. Rydalmere 279 G16
st. Sydney F C4
st. Sydney 3 J10
st. Vaucluse 348 G4
st. West Ryde 281 H15
st.n, Peakhurst 429 K3
st.s, Peakhurst 429 K5
st.w, Narrabeen 228 J8
wy. Kenthurst 126 A16
CLARKES
rd. Ramsgate 433 D12
CLAROS
cl. Hornsby Ht 161 H13
CLASSEN
st. Sylvania 462 A13
CLASSERS
pl. Currans Hill 480 A10
CLAUDARE
st. Collaroy Plat 228 H12
CLAUDE
av. Cremorne 6 K6
st. Chatswood 284 K10
CLAUDE JAMES
cr. Regents Pk 369 E1
CLAUDIA
rd. Toongabbie 275 G11
CLAUDIUS
pl. Rsemeadow 540 D2
CLAVERDON
av. Picnic Point 428 G9
CLAVERING
rd. Seaforth 286 J7
CLAXTON
cct. Rouse Hill 184 J8
CLAY
pl. Eagle Vale 481 E7
st. Balmain 7 D12
CLAYPOLE
st. Ambarvale 540 E1
CLAYTON
la. Camperdwn 17 D7
pl. Girraween 276 A16
pl. W Pnnant Hl 249 A8
st. Balmain 7 J8
st. Blacktown 244 A12
st. Peakhurst 430 B2
st. Prairiewood 335 A9
st. Ryde 312 D2
wy. Clarmnt Ms 268 F4
CLEAL
st. Ermington 280 C15
CLEARVIEW
pl. Brookvale 257 H10
CLEARY
av. Belmore 371 D15
av. Forestville 256 B7
cl. Edensor Pk 363 F2
la. St Clair, off Cleary Pl 270 B12
la. Belmore, off Dean Av 371 E15
pl. Blackett 241 D2
pl. Casula 424 D4
pl. St Clair 270 A12
CLEAVER
pl. Ambarvale 510 K15
CLEEVE
cl. Mount Druitt 241 E16
pl. Cmbrdg Gdn 237 F3
CLEG
st. Artarmon 315 B2
CLEGG
pl. Glenhaven 217 K4
pl. Prairiewood 334 J9
CLELAND
rd. Artarmon 285 B16
st. Mascot 405 H5
CLEM
pl. Shalvey 211 B14
CLEMATIS
cl. Cherrybrook 220 A7
pl. Mcquarie Fd 454 D2
pl. Mt Annan 509 E4
CLEMENT
cl. Pennant Hills 250 G3
la. Rcuttrs Bay 13 B8
pl. Ingleburn 453 H8
pl, Rcuttrs Bay 13 C8
st. Guildford 337 D6
st. Rooty Hill 242 B16
st. Rcuttrs Bay 13 B8
st. Strathfield S 371 E6
CLEMENTINA
cct. Cecil Hills 362 D4
CLEMENTS
av. Bankstown 399 E7
pde. Kirrawee 491 B4
st. Drummoyne 343 F6
st. Russell Lea 343 F6
CLEMENTSON
dr. Rossmore 359 G16
CLEMSON
st. Kingswood 237 F15
CLEMTON
av. Earlwood 402 C5
pl. Earlwood, off Clemton Av 402 D5
CLENNAM
av. Ambarvale 510 G12
CLENT
st. Jamisontown 266 C5
CLEONE
st. Guildford 338 A4
CLEOPATRA
dr. Rsemeadow 540 E2
CLERGY
rd. Wilberforce 91 K1
CLERKE
pl. Kings Lngly 246 C11
CLERKENWELL
st. Ambarvale 510 G15
CLERMISTON
av. Roseville 285 A4
CLERMONT
av. Concord 341 F5
av. N Strathfield 341 F5
av. Ryde 282 A12
la. Concord, off Wellbank St 341 F5
la. N Strathfield, off Wellbank St 341 F5
CLEVEDON
rd. Hurstville 431 K2
st. Botany 405 H13
CLEVELAND
av. Cromer 228 A14
av. Surry Hills 20 A6
la. Chippendale 18 H3
pl. Bonnet Bay 460 B9
rd. Riverstone 182 C10
st. Chippendale 18 H4
st. Darlington 18 H4
st. Ermington 280 E11
st. Moore Park 20 D7
st. Redfern 19 J6
st. Strathfield S 370 K6
st. Surry Hills 19 J6
st. Wahroonga 222 E7
CLEVELEY
av. Kings Lngly 245 A5
CLEY
pl. Prospect 274 K11
CLIFF
av. Northbridge 315 K2
av. N Wahrnga 222 J2
av. Peakhurst 430 B12
av. Winston Hills 277 F6
pl. Cranebrook 207 B11
rd. Collaroy 229 C14
rd. Epping 250 H15
rd. Freemns Rch 89 F6
rd. Northwood 314 H8
st. Manly 288 J11
st. Milsons Pt K J16
st. Milsons Pt 5 J13
st. Picton 563 F2
st. Watsons Bay 318 F12
tce. Forest Lodge 11 F13
CLIFFBROOK
cr. Leonay 235 A16
pde. Clovelly 377 K14
CLIFFE
st. Picton 563 F2
st. Regents Pk 369 G2
CLIFF HAVEN
pl. Miranda 491 K9
CLIFFORD
av. Canley Vale 365 K4
av. Fairlight 288 C10
av. Thornleigh 221 C15
cr. Ingleburn 453 D12
la. Canley Vale, off Clifford Av 366 A4

rd. Miranda 492 A7
st. Coogee 407 F2
st. Gordon 254 B7
st. Mosman 317 B6
st. Panania 428 B5
st. Rockdale 403 B14
CLIFF POINT
pl. Frenchs Frst 257 A2
CLIFFVIEW
rd. Berowra Ht 133 D5
CLIFT
cl. Edensor Pk 363 G2
CLIFTON
av. Burwood 342 B16
av. Glenbrook 264 C1
av. Kemps Ck 360 D1
la. Bronte, off Busby Pde 377 K11
pl. Cartwright 394 C5
pl. Cherrybrook 219 B14
rd. Clovelly 377 J12
rd. Marsden Pk 182 A16
rd. Riverstone 182 A15
res. Surry Hills F K13
res. Surry Hills 4 C15
st. Balmain East 8 F7
st. Blacktown 244 J15
st. Mosman 317 D12
st. Oatley 461 C1
st. Waverton 5 A8
st. West Ryde 280 J14
CLIMUS
st. Hassall Gr 212 B15
CLINGAN
av. Lurnea 394 D9
CLINIC
cct Narrabeen, off Snake Gulley Cl. 228 E8
CLINKER
gr. Woodcroft 243 F6
CLINTON
cl. Berowra Ht 132 J9
dr. Narellan 478 J11
st. Quakers Hill 214 B8
CLIO
la. Maroubra 407 C10
st. Sutherland 490 F1
st. Wiley Park 400 K4
CLIPPER
cl. Chipping Ntn 366 K15
CLIPSHAM
la. Gordon, off St Johns Av 253 H8
CLISBY
wy. Matraville 437 C1
CLISDELL
av. Canterbury 402 D1
st. Surry Hills 19 J4
CLISSOLD
la. Campsie 372 A12
pde. Campsie 372 A12
rd. Wahroonga 223 C6
st. Ashfield 372 J6
st. Cambrdg Pk 238 A7
CLIVE
cr. Bayview 168 H12
rd. Eastwood 281 A7
rd. Riverstone 182 F8
st. Fairfield 336 F15
st. Revesby 428 H5
st. Roseville 285 D3
st. Roseville Ch 285 D3
CLIVEDEN
ct. Wattle Grove 426 B3
CLONCURRY
pl. Wakeley 334 G14
CLONTARF
cl. Woodbine 481 J10
st. Seaforth 287 A5
st. Seaforth 287 A7
CLOPTON
dr. Killara 254 C8
CLORINDA
st. Rooty Hill 272 C5
CLOSE
pl. Hebersham 241 F1
st. Canterbury 372 G14
st. S Coogee 407 J6
st. Thirlmere 564 J4
st. Thirlmere 565 A5
CLOTHIER
rd. Menai 459 A11
CLOUGH
av. Illawong 459 K2
CLOUTA
pl. Emu Plains 234 J9
CLOVE
la. Randwick, off Darley La 377 B9
CLOVELLY
cct. Kellyville 215 F4
pl. Woodbine 481 F14
rd. Clovelly 377 F12
rd. Coogee 377 F12
rd. Hornsby 221 D3
rd. Randwick 377 B9
st. Clovelly 377 K13
st. Watsons Bay 318 G14
CLOVER
cl. Carlingford 279 J5
pl. Mcquarie Fd 454 E6
CLOVERDALE
cct. Glenmore Pk 266 F14
CLOVERTOP
pl. Wrrngtn Dns 238 B5
CLOWER
av. Rouse Hill 185 A8
CLUB
la. Ermington, off River Rd 310 B3
CLUBB
cr. Miranda 492 B3
st. Rozelle 344 C7
CLUCAS
rd. Dharruk 241 C10
rd. Regents Pk 369 E1
CLUDEN
cl. Toongabbie 276 H6
CLUMP
pl. Green Valley 362 K10
CLUNE
cl. Casula 424 E4
pl. Blackett 241 D2
CLUNES
la. Canterbury 372 D14
CLUNIES
pl. Bonnyrigg Ht 363 F7
CLUNIES ROSS
st. Greystanes 275 E16
st. Prospect 275 E16
CLUSTER
pl. Cranebrook 207 F11
CLWYDON
cl. Belrose 226 B12
pl. Wahroonga 222 E6
CLYBURN
av. Jamisontown 266 B3
CLYDE
av. Cronulla 493 K15
av. Moorebank 396 E13
av. St Clair 269 H14
la. Kurrajong Ht 54 C14
pl. Campbelltwn 511 K9
pl. Mt Hunter 504 K7
pl. Wahroonga 222 A14
rd. Dee Why 258 K6
st. Croydon Pk 372 A7
st. Granville 308 G16
st. Guildford 337 E4
st. North Bondi 348 D14
st. Randwick 377 C14
st. Rydalmere 309 D2
st. Silverwater L C16
st. Silverwater 309 K8
st. S Granville 338 F8
st. Vineyard 152 F14
CLYDEBANK
cr. Glen Alpine 510 A13
CLYDESDALE
dr. Blairmount 480 K14
la. Richmond 118 G13
pl. Pymble 253 B2
CLYFFORD
pl. Panania 428 E6
COACH HOUSE
pl. Kurrajong Ht 53 K3
rd. Kurrajong Ht 53 K3
COACHLINE
pl. Belrose 226 A11
COACHMAN
cr. Kellyville 215 C2
COACHWOOD
cl. Rouse Hill 185 B7
cr. Alfords Point 459 A2
cr. Bradbury 511 F12
cr. Picton 563 E13
COAL
st. Silverwater 309 J10
COALLEE
pl. S Penrith 267 A3
COAST
av. Cronulla 494 A16
COAST HOSPITAL
rd. Little Bay 437 G14
COASTVIEW
pl. Harbord 258 K16
COATES
pl. Wetherill Pk 303 J15
st. Mount Druitt 271 D4
wy. Claymore 481 A11
COATES PARK
rd. Cobbitty 416 B14
COBAC
av. Eastwood 280 J5
COBAH
rd. Arcadia 129 E12
rd. Arcadia 129 J7
rd. Fiddletown 129 J7
COBAIN
pl. Acacia Gdn 214 G15
COBAR
cl. Wakeley 334 H13
pl. Cartwright 394 A4
pl. Erskine Park 270 K16
st. Dulwich Hill 373 A9
st. Greystanes 305 H3
st. Willoughby 285 C14
wy. Mcquarie Pk 282 E4
COBARGO
rd. Gymea Bay 491 C10
COBB
av. Jamisontown 266 C1
la. Blacktown, off Campbell St 244 H16
pl. Ambarvale 511 B14
st. Frenchs Frst 256 E4
COBBADAH
av. Pennant Hills 250 J4
pl. Harbord 258 D15
COBBETT
st. Wetherill Pk 334 D4
st. Wetherill Pk 334 F3
COBBITTEE
la. Mosman, off Cobbittee St 317 G9
st. Mosman 317 G9
COBBITTY
av. Croydon Pk 371 K6
rd. Brownlow Hl 475 H2
rd. Cobbitty 447 C14
rd. Harringtn Pk 447 J13
rd. Harringtn Pk 448 D13
rd. Oran Park 448 D13
COBBITY
av. Wrrngtn Dns 237 K3
st. Seven Hills 246 C14
COBBLER
cr. Minchinbury 271 F9
COBBLERS
cl. Kellyville 186 H16
COBBLERS BEACH
rd. Mosman 317 J6
COBBLESTONE
ct. Glenhaven 218 B4
gr. Woodcroft 243 F9
pl. Wrrngtn Dns 238 C5
COBBY
pl. Bidwill 211 C14
COBCROFT
rd. Wilberforce 61 K13
COBDEN
av. Lane Cove 314 G2
la. Enfield 371 H2
la. Belmore, off Rydge St 401 G1
st. Belmore 401 H1
st. Enfield 371 H3
COBHAM
av. Melrose Pk 280 H15
la. Melrose Pk 280 H15
st. Horsley Pk 332 D2
st. Ingleburn 453 B6
st. Kings Park 244 E5
st. Maroubra 406 G10
st. Yanderra 567 B16
COBOURG
pl. Bow Bowing 452 D13
COBRA
pl. Raby 451 B14
st. Cranebrook 207 B9
COBRAN
rd. Cheltenham 251 B9
COBURG
pl. St Johns Pk 364 G1
rd. Wilberforce 61 K15
rd. Wilberforce 92 C1
COCHRAN
pl. Abbotsbury 333 B14
COCHRANE
st. Minto 482 J10
COCKATIEL
cct. Green Valley 363 F10
COCKATOO
cl. Hinchinbrk 363 A14
la. St Clair, off Cockatoo Rd 270 J14
rd. Erskine Park 270 J14
COCKBURN
cr. Fairfield E 336 J12
COCKLE
pl. N Turramrra 193 D15
COCKROFT
pl. Lucas Ht 487 J11
COCKTHORPE
rd. Auburn 339 F7
COCO
dr. Glenmore Pk 266 A7
COCOS
av. Eastwood 281 A4
cl. Green Valley 363 C10
pl. Quakers Hill 213 F13
COCUPARA
av. Lindfield 283 K3
CODLIN
st. Ambarvale 510 J12
CODRINGTON
st. Darlington 18 F7
st. Fairfield 336 B15
CODY
pl. Oakhurst 242 A4
COE
pl. Riverstone 183 C8
COEN
cl. Bossley Park 333 F11
COFFEY
st. Ermington 310 B4
wy. Claymore, off Colquhoun Wy 481 C11
COFFS HARBOUR
av. Hoxton Park 392 K9
COFTON
ct. Wrrngtn Cty 238 F6
COGAN
pl. Lane Cove 314 H5
COGGINS
pl. Mascot 404 K2
COGHILL
st. Narellan 478 E10
COGHLAN
cr. Doonside 243 A14
COHEN
av. Rookwood 339 K11
st. Fairlight 288 C8
st. Merrylands 308 C15
COILA
pl. Woodpark 306 G14
st. Turramurra 223 A10
COLAC
pl. Marayong 243 J7
COLAH
rd. Mt Colah 192 C4
COLANE
st. Concord W 311 E15
COLBARRA
pl. W Pnnant Hl 249 B6
COLBECK
st. Tregear 240 E5
COLBOURNE
av. Glebe 12 D12
COLBRAN
av. Kenthurst 187 A9
COLDEN
st. Picton 563 G4
COLDENHAM
dr. Picton 561 F3
wy. Airds 512 A13
COLDSTREAM
st. S Coogee 407 G5
COLE
av. Baulkham Hl 246 F12
cr. Liberty Gr 311 B10
la. Bankstown 369 D16
la. Hurstville 432 B7
pl. St Marys 269 E2
st. Brooklyn 75 G12
st. S Hurstville 432 B8
COLEBEE
cr. Hassall Gr 212 A13
pl. Narellan 478 E15
COLEBORNE
av. Mortdale 431 C8
COLECHIN
st. Yagoona 368 G13
COLEMAN
av. Bankstown 369 C15
av. Carlingford 279 J5
av. Homebush 341 A6
av. Regents Pk 369 D1
pl. Blacktown 244 F9
rd. Minto Ht 483 D9
rd. Wedderburn 540 B10
st. Mascot 405 A5
st. Merrylands 307 D7
st. S Wntwthvle 307 D7
COLENSO
cr. Daceyville 406 F3
COLERAINE
av. Killarney Ht 256 B15
st. Fairfield 336 B14
COLERIDGE
rd. Wetherill Pk 334 H5
st. Leichhardt 10 D15
st. Pymble 223 D16
st. Riverwood 399 K14
COLES
pde. Newport 169 J9
rd. Harbord 258 D15
st. Concord 341 J9
COLETTE
pl. East Killara 254 G8
COLEVILE
pl. Rsemeadow 540 H8
COLEY
pl. Bligh Park 150 H8
COLGATE
av. Balmain 8 B9
COLIN
av. Riverwood 400 A16
pl. Carlingford 249 G13
pl. Westleigh 220 H4
st. Cammeray 316 A4
st. Lakemba 370 H15
COLINDIA
av. Neutral Bay 6 C7
COLING
pl. Quakers Hill 214 D13
COLL
pl. St Andrews 482 A3
COLLARENEBRI
rd. Hinchinbrk 392 H4
COLLAROY
av. Peakhurst 430 G1
rd. Woodbine 481 K10
st. Collaroy 229 A12
COLLEEN
av. Picnic Point 428 B6
cl. Cherrybrook 219 K5
COLLEGE
cr. Hornsby 221 G4
cr. St Ives 224 C12
dr. Richmond 118 G10
la. Darlinghurst F G1
la. Petersham 16 C13
la. Rose Bay 347 G12
la. Bellevue Hill, off Cranbrook Rd 347 F12
rd. Campbelltwn 511 J9
rd.n, Lane Cove 314 A3
rd.s, Riverview 313 K5
st. Balmain 7 G8
st. Cambrdg Pk 237 H10
st. Croydon 342 E16
st. Darlinghurst D G16
st. Darlinghurst 4 A8
st. Drummoyne 343 J3
st. Gladesville 312 G5
st. Liverpool 395 F3
st. Manly 288 K12
st. Newtown 17 E15
st. Richmond 118 H8
st. Sydney D G16
st. Sydney 4 A8
COLLEN
pl. Cranebrook 207 D13
COLLESS
st. Penrith 237 B14
COLLETT
cr. Kings Lngly 246 C9
pde. N Parramatta 278 K15

COLLEY
pl. Hebersham 241 G3
COLLICOTT
pl. Barden Rdg 488 G2
COLLIE
ct. Wattle Grove 395 H12
pl. Bonnyrigg 364 A8
COLLIER
av. Beverly Hills 401 A14
cl. St Helens Pk 541 B2
pl. Maroubra 407 D12
COLLIMORE
av. Liverpool 395 B2
COLLING
av. Wrrngtn Cty 238 F4
COLLINGS
st. Wahroonga 222 C2
COLLINGWOOD
av. Cabarita 342 D2
av. Earlwood 402 K3
st. Bronte 378 A10
st. Drummoyne 343 J1
st. Manly 288 F6
st. Woolwich 314 E13
COLLINS
av. Lurnea 394 D10
av. Rose Bay 348 A10
cl. Edensor Pk 363 F4
cr. Lapstone 264 G5
cr. Yagoona 368 F15
ct. Rouse Hill 184 K8
gr. Mt Annan 479 H15
la. Annandale 10 H15
la. Surry Hills 20 B3
la. Beaconsfield, off Collins St 375 F13
pl. Engadine 488 G16
prm. Ingleburn 453 C13
prm. Minto 453 C13
rd. St Ives 223 K11
rd. St Ives Ch 223 K6
st. Alexandria 375 E12
st. Annandale 17 A1
st. Beaconsfield 375 E12
st. Belmore 401 D1
st. N Narrabeen 199 C14
st. North Ryde 282 J9
st. Pagewood 406 A11
st. Pendle Hill 276 E16
st. Rozelle 7 C14
st. St Marys 269 G5
st. Seven Hills 245 F16
st. Surry Hills 20 B2
st. Tempe 404 B1
COLLINS BEACH
rd. Manly 288 K15
COLLINSVILLE
pl. Miller 393 F4
COLLIS
pl. Minto 452 K15
COLLITH
av. S Windsor 150 F4
COLLITT
cr. Cranebrook 207 F13
la. Cranebrook, off Sherringham La 207 F13
COLLY
pl. Busby 363 G15
COLO
ct. Wattle Grove 395 K13
la. Blacktown 274 H1
pl. Campbelltwn 512 A7
pl. Greystanes 306 A3
st. Couridjah 564 F16
COLONEL BRAUND
cr. Daceyville 406 G3
COLONEL PYE
dr. Cobbitty 416 C5
COLONEL WOODS
dr. Narrabeen 228 G8
COLONG
cl. Hoxton Park 392 J6
cr. Leumeah 482 D14
COLONIAL
dr. Bligh Park 150 B5
pl. Casula 395 A12
st. Campbelltwn 511 H7
COLOOLI
lp. Narrabeen, off Stack St 228 G8
rd. Narrabeen 228 G7
COLORADO
dr. St Clair 270 G13
st. Kearns 450 J16
COLOSSEUM
cr. Baulkham Hl 246 F9
COLQUHOUN
st. Rosehill 309 C8
wy. Claymore 481 C11
COLSON
cr. Monterey 433 G6
cr. Wrrngtn Cty 238 F5
COLSTON
st. Ryde 281 K16
COLT
pl. Cranebrook 237 F1
COLUMBA
la. St Clair, off Columba Pl 270 G16
pl. Erskine Park 300 G1
COLUMBIA
ct. Baulkham Hl 216 K14
la. Homebush 341 E9
rd. Seven Hills 275 C10
st. Kearns 450 J16
wy. Baulkham Hl 216 J14
COLUMBINE
av. Bankstown 399 H4
av. Punchbowl 399 H4
cl. Loftus 489 J7
COLUMBUS
av. St Clair 270 H11
COLVILLE
pl. Bonnyrigg Ht 363 C7
rd. Yellow Rock 204 H1
st. Kings Lngly 246 A7
COLVIN
av. Carlton 432 H10
av. Kingsgrove 401 K11
cr. Denistone E 281 H9
pl. Frenchs Frst 256 A1
COLWELL
cr. Chatswd W 284 C12
st. Kingsgrove 401 F13
COLYTON
rd. Minchinbury 271 E6
COMANCHE
rd. Bossley Park 333 K12
COMBARA
av. Caringbah 492 K9
av. Castle Hill 247 F1
COMBE
pl. West Pymble 252 F12
COMBER
cr. Pendle Hill 276 F13
st. Paddington 4 H14
COMBERFORD
cl. Prairiewood 334 D10
COMBET
pl. Minchinbury 271 H9
COMBINGS
pl. Currans Hill 480 A10
COMBLES
pde. Matraville 407 A16
COMBOYNE
av. Hoxton Park 392 H9
pl. St Clair 270 B16
COMER
st. Burwood 341 K12
COMEROY
cr. Frenchs Frst 256 F1
COMET
cct. Kellyville 185 K13
gln. St Clair 270 E15
pl. Raby 481 G3
pl. Springwood 172 G15
st. Ashfield 342 J16
COMETROWE
st. Drummoyne 343 G2
COMIN
pl. Abbotsbury 333 C10
COMLEROY
rd. Blaxlands Rdg 56 D4
rd. Comleroy 56 A12
rd. Kurrajong 55 J14
COMMERCE
la. Glenbrook 264 A1
la. Glossodia 59 F9
la. Balgowlah Ht, off Dobroyd Rd 287 J14
COMMERCIAL
dr. Regents Pk 338 K16
la. Merrylands, off Bertha St 308 A16
rd. Kellyville 185 B11
rd. Kingsgrove 401 J10
rd. Lalor Park 245 E12
rd. Lilyfield 9 H6
rd. Rouse Hill 185 B11
rd. Vineyard 152 E3
COMMISSIONERS
rd. Denistone 281 G13
COMMODORE
cr. McMahons Pt 5 A10
st. McMahons Pt 5 B10
st. Newtown 374 H10
COMMONS
st. Hurlstone Pk 373 A13
COMMONWEALTH
av. Mosman 317 G11
cr. N St Marys 239 H8
la. Surry Hills F D14
pde. Manly 288 E10
rd. Lindfield 254 A15
st. Surry Hills F C15
st. Surry Hills 3 J15
st. Sydney F D9
st. Sydney 3 K12
COMMUNITY
pl. Greenacre 370 C12
COMO
cl. St Clair 269 G14
ct. Wattle Grove 395 K14
la. Cremorne 316 C7
la. St Clair, off Como Cl 269 G14
pde. Como 460 H5
pde. Como 460 H6
pl. St Johns Pk 364 H3
rd. Greenacre 370 D5
rd. Oyster Bay 461 C7
st. Blakehurst 462 C2
st. Merrylnds W 307 C13
COMPER
st. Bnkstn Aprt 397 K1
COMPTON
av. Lurnea 394 E9
grn. W Pnnant Hl 249 C6
st. Bass Hill 368 B6
CONCETTINA
dr. Prestons 392 H14
CONCISE
st. Balgowlah Ht 287 K13
CONCORD
av. Concord W 311 C16
la. Erskineville, off Concord St 374 K10
la. N Strathfield, off Nelson Rd 341 F7
pl. Gladesville 312 J8
pl. St Johns Pk 364 H4
rd. Concord 341 E1
rd. Concord W 341 E1
rd. N Strathfield 341 E1
rd. Rhodes 311 D9
st. Erskineville 374 K10
CONCORDE
pl. Raby 451 H16
pl. St Clair 270 F14
CONDAMINE
st. Allambie Ht 257 K14
st. Balgowlah 287 K8
st. Campbelltwn 511 G6
st. Manly Vale 287 K4
st. North Manly 257 K14
st.s, Balgowlah 287 J12
st.s, Balgowlah Ht 287 J12
CONDELLO
cr. Edensor Pk 333 H14
CONDER
av. Mt Pritchard 364 J12
st. Burwood 341 J16
wy. Claymore 481 B12
CONDON
av. Panania 428 F3
st. Caringbah 492 H9
CONDOR
cr. Blakehurst 432 A13
pl. Abbotsbury 333 B12
pl. Glenmore Pk 266 A13
st. Quakers Hill 214 F13
CONDOVER
st. N Balgowlah 287 G5
CONEILL
pl. Forest Lodge 11 E12
CONEY
rd. Earlwood 402 J3
CONFERTA
ct. Wattle Grove 396 B16
CONGEWOI
la. Mosman 316 H4
rd. Mosman 316 J4
CONGHAM
rd. West Pymble 252 H12
CONGO
pl. Kearns 451 A14
CONGRESSIONAL
dr. Liverpool 395 B9
CONIE
av. Baulkham Hl 247 G12
CONIFER
cl. Stanhpe Gdn 215 D11
ct. Greystanes 306 F10
pl. Engadine 518 F3
CONISTON
pl. Castle Hill 247 K5
st. Collaroy Plat 228 D11
CONJOLA
cr. Leumeah 482 F15
pl. Gymea Bay 491 C10
pl. Hamondvle 396 F14
pl. Woodcroft 243 F11
CONLAN
st. Bligh Park 150 K7
CONNAUGHT
st. Brookvale 258 B8
st. Narraweena 258 B8
CONNECTICUT
av. Five Dock 343 B11
CONNELL
cl. Baulkham Hl 246 K4
rd. Oyster Bay 461 F6
CONNELLAN
cr. Picton 563 E9
CONNELLS POINT
rd. Connells Pt 431 K14
rd. S Hurstville 431 K14
CONNELLY
st. Penshurst 431 F5
CONNELS
rd. Cronulla 493 G11
rd. Woolooware 493 G11
CONNEMARA
av. Killarney Ht 286 C2
CONNEMARRA
st. Bexley 432 J2
CONNER
cl. Liberty Gr 311 B10
CONNOLLY
av. Padstow Ht 429 D6
la. Beaconsfield, off Reserve St 375 F12
CONNOR
pl. Illawong 459 D7
pl. Rouse Hill 185 C7
pl. Tahmoor 565 J9
CONRAD
rd. Kellyville 215 A6
st. North Ryde 283 B13
st. Richmond 118 J7
st. Wetherill Pk 334 D6
CONROY
la. Revesby 398 H15
rd. Wattle Grove 426 B3
CONSERVATORIUM
rd. Sydney B H10
rd. Sydney 2 B13
CONSETT
av. Bondi Beach 378 C3
st. Concord W 341 D2
st. Dulwich Hill 373 D10
CONSOLO
av. Glenwood 215 G10
CONSTANCE
av. Oxley Park 240 E15
cl. Epping 251 C12
st. Guildford 338 A3
st. Revesby 398 K13
CONSTELLATION
rd. Mascot 404 K4
CONSTITUTION
ct. Carlingford 279 D4
la. Dulwich Hill, off Union St 373 C8
rd. Dulwich Hill 373 C8
rd. Meadowbnk 311 E3
rd. Ryde 311 E3
rd. Wentwthvle 277 B9
rd.w, Meadowbnk 311 B2
CONSUL
rd. Brookvale 258 A9
rd.n, Narraweena 258 A7
CONTAPLAS
st. Arndell Park 273 F7
CONTINUA
ct. Wattle Grove 396 C15
CONVAIR
pl. Raby 451 E12
CONVENT
la. Marrickville 373 K12
la. Woollahra 22 K5
CONVICT
pl. Castle Hill 218 F13
CONWAY
av. Cambrdg Pk 237 H10
av. Concord W 341 C3
av. N Strathfield 341 C3
av. Randwick 377 F11
av. Rose Bay 348 C9
av. St Ives 224 K2
ct. Baulkham Hl 247 A3
pl. Kings Lngly 245 F6
pl. Oatlands 279 C13
pl. St Peters 374 G13
rd. Bankstown 369 F14
st. Menai 458 K9
COOBA
pl. Mcquarie Fd 454 E2
st. Lidcombe 339 J6
COODE
pl. Bonnyrigg 364 B5
COOEEYANA
pde. Mt Lewis 370 B15
COOGAN
pl. Campbelltwn 511 E4
pl. Dean Park 212 H16
COOGARAH
st. Blakehurst 462 D2
COOGEE
pl. Woodbine 481 D15
st. Randwick 377 C14
COOGEE BAY
rd. Coogee 377 C15
rd. Randwick 377 C15
COOGHANS
la. Five Dock, off Lyons Rd W 342 K8
COOINDA
cl. Marsfield 281 J1
pl. Baulkham Hl 248 B7
pl. Bilgola 169 F5
pl. Doonside 243 A14
pl. Northmead 278 A2
st. Colyton 270 G6
st. Engadine 489 D14
st. Seven Hills 246 A14
COOK
av. Canada Bay 342 D8
av. Canley Vale 366 G3
av. Daceyville 406 F4
cr. East Hills 427 F5
la. Bondi Jctn 22 K6
la. St Clair, off Cook Pde 269 J14
la. Mortdale, off Cook St 431 C7
la. St Marys, off Cook St 269 H3
la. Zetland, off Joynton Av 375 J10
pde. St Clair 269 J16
pl. Lalor Park 245 C13
rd. Centnnial Pk 21 C11
rd. Killara 253 K15
rd. Marrickville 374 D10
rd. Moore Park 21 C11
rd. Oakhurst 241 J1
rd. Oyster Bay 461 D4
rd. Ruse 512 G2
st. Baulkham Hl 247 K13
st. Caringbah 492 J14
st. Croydon Pk 371 K7
st. Forestville 256 B10
st. Glebe 11 J8
st. Kurnell 466 B10
st. Lewisham 15 B7
st. Lidcombe 339 G9
st. Mortdale 431 C7
st. North Ryde 282 C8
st. Randwick 377 A12
st. Rozelle 10 H1
st. St Marys 269 H3
st. Sutherland 490 F4
st. Telopea 279 J9
st. Tempe 404 A3
st. Turrella 403 D6
st. Woolooware 493 H7
tce. Mona Vale 199 D9
COOKE
wy. Epping 250 G14

COOKNEY
pl. West Hoxton...392 C10
COOKS
av. Canterbury......372 D15
la. Canterbury, off Cooks Av........372 D15
COOKSEY
av. Harbord..........258 H14
COOKSON
pl. Glenwood.......215 C13
COOKS RIVER
av. Mascot...........404 C7
COOLABAH
av. Greenwich......315 A8
av. Turramurra......223 C11
cl. Thornleigh......221 B7
cr. Forestville.......256 C9
cr. Glenmore Pk...266 F12
la. Greenwich......315 A8
pl. Blacktown.......273 K6
pl. Caringbah.......492 J3
pl. Mcquarie Fd....454 G1
pl. Turramurra.....223 C11
rd. Valley Ht.........202 F9
st. Beverly Hills....401 C9
COOLAH
av. Campbelltwn...511 K7
pl. Lansvale.........366 G8
wy. Hoxton Park....392 G8
COOLALIE
av. Camden S.......507 B11
pl. Allambie Ht....257 F16
pl. Kenthurst........157 B9
st. Villawood........367 E4
COOLAMON
cl. Arcadia...........130 J9
rd. Agnes Banks...146 A3
COOLANGATTA
av. Burraneer.......493 E15
av. Elanora Ht.......198 D16
COOLARN
st. Chipping Ntn ..396 H4
COOLAROO
cr. Lurnea............394 G7
rd. Lane Cove W ..284 C13
COOLATAI
cr. Bossley Park...333 G12
COOLAWIN
rd. Avalon............169 K2
rd. Northbridge....286 F16
COOLEEN
la. Blakehurst......432 B13
st. Blakehurst......432 C13
COOLEENA
rd. Elanora Ht.......198 F13
COOLGARDIE
pl. Sutherland......460 D14
COOLGUN
la. Eastwood 281 A8
COOLIBAH
la. S Penrith, off Coolibah Pl.....266 H6
pl. S Penrith........266 G6
st. Castle Hill.......218 B11
st. Merrylnds W...306 K12
COOLIBAR
st. Canley Ht........365 A1
COOLIDGE
cr. Bonnet Bay.....460 A8
COOLINGA
st. Mcquarie Pk...282 H5
COOLOCK
cr. Baulkham Hl...247 C2
COOLONG
cr. St Clair...........269 H8
rd. Vaucluse.........348 B1
st. Castle Hill.......217 G16
COOLOONGATTA
rd. Beverly Hills....401 B10
COOLOWIE
rd. Terrey Hills.....195 K9
COOLUM
pl. Yowie Bay.......492 C10
COOMA
ct. Wattle Grove...396 B16
rd. Greystanes.....305 G3
st. Carramar........366 H1
st. Dharruk..........241 C8
COOMALIE
av. Castle Hill.......248 F2
COOMASSIE
av. Faulconbdg.....201 C1
COOMBAH
pl. Engadine........518 G7

COOMBES
dr. Penrith............237 A6
COONABARABRAN
cr. Hoxton Park....392 J7
pl. Caringbah.......493 C14
COONAH
pde. Riverview........313 H6
COONAMBLE
st. Hoxton Park....392 G7
COONANBARRA
rd. N Wahrnga.....222 E3
rd. Wahroonga.....222 D7
COONANGA
rd. Avalon............140 E15
COONARA
av. W Pnnant Hl...249 A4
COONARDOO
cl. Canada Bay.....342 F9
pl. Castle Hill........218 A12
COONAWARRA
dr. St Clair............270 E13
rd. Terrey Hills.....195 H8
st. Edensor Pk.....333 D16
COONEY
rd. Artarmon........285 B15
st. North Ryde.....282 G9
COONGRA
st. Busby.............363 G12
COONONG
rd. Concord W.....311 D15
rd. Gymea Bay.....491 D12
st. Busby.............363 H15
wy. Airds...............512 E10
COOPER
av. Moorebank.....395 F8
cl. Beacon Hill.....257 K5
cr. Smithfield.......336 C5
cr. Wahroonga.....222 B15
ct. Castle Hill........218 C10
la. Maroubra........407 C11
la. Paddington.......13 A14
la. Surry Hills.........19 K1
la. Cremorne, off Belgrave St......316 D8
la. Neutral Bay, off Belgrave St......316 D8
la. Yagoona, off Cooper Rd.......369 B12
la. Penrith, off Cooper St........237 E3
la. Strathfield, off Cooper St........341 G11
pl. Currans Hill.....479 H9
rd. Birrong...........369 B7
rd. Yagoona...........369 B10
st. Balmain..............8 C9
st. Blacktown.......274 D3
st. Double Bay.......14 A9
st. Engadine.........518 H5
st. Kingsford........407 C7
st. Maroubra........407 C9
st. Marsfield........282 A5
st. Paddington.......13 A13
st. Penrith............237 E3
st. Penrith............237 C3
st. Redfern.............19 H7
st. Smithfield.......305 H15
st. Strathfield.......341 G11
st. Surry Hills.........19 J1
st. Waterloo...........19 C12
COOPERNOOK
av. E Lindfield.......255 B11
av. Gymea Bay.....491 G13
COOPER PARK
rd. Bellevue Hill....347 F16
COOPWORTH
rd. Elderslie..........507 K2
COORA
av. Belrose...........225 J15
pl. Connells Pt......431 G15
rd. Westleigh........220 G3
rd. Yowie Bay.......492 B12
st. Sans Souci.....433 F16
COORABAN
rd. Milperra..........398 B6
COORABIN
pl. Riverwood.......400 C12
rd. Northbridge....286 C14
COORADILLA
pl. Bradbury.........541 E1
COORI
pl. Bonnyrigg.......364 A9
COORIENGAH HEIGHTS
rd. Engadine.........488 F13

COORILLA
av. Croydon Pk.....372 D9
COOROY
cr. Yellow Rock....204 K1
COORUMBENE
ct. Bella Vista.......246 H1
COOT
pl. Erskine Park....270 K14
pl. Hinchinbrk......363 E16
COOTAMUNDRA
dr. Allambie Ht.....257 E13
rd. Hornsby Ht.....161 J7
COOTHA
cl. Bossley Park...334 C5
COOWARRA
dr. St Clair...........270 B16
la. St Clair, off Coowarra Dr....300 B1
COOYAL
pl. Glenwood.......215 F16
COOYONG
cr. Toongabbie.....276 D7
rd. Terrey Hills......196 A8
COPAIN
pl. S Penrith.........266 H4
COPE
pl. Bass Hill..........368 C12
st. Lane Cove........313 G4
st. Lane Cove W...313 G4
st. Redfern............19 B10
st. Waterloo..........19 C12
COPELAND
av. Newtown..........18 A12
la. Alexandria........18 E15
rd. Beecroft..........249 K8
rd. Emerton..........240 G2
rd. Engadine.........518 G6
rd. Heathcote........518 G9
rd. Lethbrdg Pk....240 G2
rd. Wilberforce......61 K16
rd.e, Beecroft.........250 F6
st. Alexandria.........18 E15
st. Erskineville.......18 E15
st. Liverpool.........395 C3
st. Penrith............237 D10
st. Richmond.......119 A5
COPPABELLA
cr. Bradbury........511 G15
rd. Middle Dural...158 J9
COPPERFIELD
dr. Ambarvale.......510 K16
dr. Rsemeadow....540 J5
COPPERLEAF
pl. Castle Hill........248 H3
pl. Cherrybrook.....219 H7
wy. Castle Hill........248 G4
COPPIN
pl. Doonside........243 C5
pl. Shalvey...........211 B13
COPPINS
cl. St Ives.............254 B1
pl. Castle Hill........248 A5
COPPLESTONE
pl. Castle Hill........218 J7
COPPSLEIGH
cl. Westleigh........220 G6
COQUET
wy. Green Valley....363 A11
CORAKI
av. Campbelltwn...512 A6
cl. Bonnyrigg.......363 K8
pl. Westleigh........220 D8
rd. Bass Hill..........367 K5
CORAL
av. Kentlyn...........513 A3
av. Padstow.........399 B16
cl. Avalon.............140 E10
cr. Kellyville..........216 G6
ct. Cherrybrook....220 A7
la. Cambrdg Pk, off Coral Pl.........238 C7
pl. Cambrdg Pk.....238 C7
pl. Canley Vale.....366 C2
pl. N Richmond.....87 B15
pl. Quakers Hill....213 F14
rd. Woolooware....493 C11
st. Balgowlah.......287 E9
st. Marsfield.........281 J1
CORALGUM
pl. Blacktown.......275 A4
CORAL HEATH
av. Westleigh........220 G8
CORALIE
st. Wareemba......343 A4

CORAL PEA
ct. Colyton..........270 H6
CORAL TREE
dr. Carlingford.....249 G11
dr. Carlingford.....249 H11
CORAMANDEL
av. Winmalee.......173 J7
CORAMBA
st. N Balgowlah...287 C5
CORANG
rd. Westleigh.......220 G6
st. Ruse..............512 C8
CORANTO
st. Wareemba......343 A5
CORBEN
av. Moorebank.....396 C11
st. Surry Hills.........F F16
st. Surry Hills..........4 A16
CORBETT
pl. Barden Rdg....488 G5
st. Bankstown.....369 F12
CORBIN
av. Quakers Hill....214 E8
av. S Penrith........266 K5
st. Ingleburn.......453 E13
CORBY
av. Concord.........342 C7
pl. Chipping Ntn ..366 G16
CORCORAN
st. Riverstone......182 D13
CORD
pl. Ingleburn........453 K8
CORDEAUX
cr. Sylvania Wtr...462 E14
st. Campbelltwn ..511 F4
st. Leppington.....420 B6
CORDELIA
cr. Green Valley...363 B11
cr. Rooty Hill........271 J3
st. Rsemeadow...540 J6
CORDEN
av. Five Dock.......342 H8
CORDNERS
la. Cornwallis........90 K15
COREA
st. Miranda..........461 K14
st. Sylvania.........461 K12
COREE
pl. St Ives............224 B15
rd. Artarmon........284 K13
COREEN
av. Cecil Park.......331 F10
av. Loftus............489 K6
av. Peakhurst.......430 H3
av. Penrith...........237 A7
av. Terrey Hills.....196 D4
cl. Berowra Ht.....132 K3
pl. Banksia..........403 H12
pl. Blaxland.........234 E9
CORELLA
cr. Glenmore Pk..266 C13
ct. W Pnnant Hl...249 D6
rd. Green Valley...363 F10
rd. Kirrawee.........491 B6
rd. Lalor Park.......245 J11
st. Harbord..........258 H14
CORELLI
cr. Clarmnt Ms....268 G4
CORE PARK
rd. Warragamba..353 E3
CORFIELD
rd. Prestons.........422 K1
CORFU
st. Woolmloo..........4 F7
CORIN
wy. Bonnyrigg......364 A5
CORINDA
st. St Johns Pk....364 D1
CORINDI
cl. Hoxton Park...392 J8
CORINGLE
cl. Woodcroft......243 F11
CORINNE
st. Acacia Gdn.....214 G15
CORINTH
rd. Heathcote.......518 E7
CORIO
dr. St Clair...........299 K2
la. St Clair, off Corio Dr..........299 K2
rd. Prairiewood....334 J8
CORISH
cir. Bnksmeadw....406 E12
cir. Eastgardens...406 E12

CORK
pl. Bidwill............211 D16
CORKERY
cr. Allambie Ht.....257 G13
CORLETTE
wy. Bonnyrigg.......364 B3
CORLISS
st. Regents Pk.....369 A2
CORMACK
pl. Glendenning...242 E3
rd. Beacon Hill.....257 J4
st. Balgowlah.......287 K7
CORMISTON
av. Concord.........341 K5
CORMO
cl. Elderslie.........507 J3
CORMORANT
av. Hinchinbrk......393 E1
cr. Glenmore Pk...265 J13
st. Grays Point.....491 D15
CORNDEW
cr. Wrrngtn Dns...238 A5
la. Wrrngtn Dns, off Corndew Cr.....238 A5
CORNELIA
rd. Middle Dural...158 C5
rd. Toongabbie....276 A7
st. Wiley Park......400 F1
CORNELIAN
av. Eagle Vale.......481 G5
CORNELIUS
la. Regentville, off Cornelius Pl....265 J4
pl. Regentville......265 H4
CORNELL
st. Blacktown.......275 C2
st. Leonay...........235 C15
CORNHILL
pl. Cherrybrook...219 F8
CORNICHE
rd. Church Point..168 G10
CORNISH
av. Beacon Hill.....257 H6
CORNOCK
av. Toongabbie....276 G10
CORNUTA
cl. Narellan Vale..478 K15
CORNWALL
av. Turramurra.....222 F16
pl. Bella Vista.......246 H4
rd. Auburn...........339 A11
rd. Ingleburn........453 A6
st. Agnes Banks...117 E15
st. N Epping........251 H11
CORNWALLIS
la. Redfern............19 A9
rd. Cornwallis.......120 J7
st. Eveleigh...........18 K9
st. Redfern............19 A9
CORNWELL
av. Richmond.......118 C8
rd. Allambie Ht.....287 J1
CORNWELLS
la. Lowlands..........88 H14
COROMANDEL
cl. Baulkham Hl...246 H5
rd. Ebenezer..........63 G7
wy. Minto.............482 H6
CORONA
av. Roseville.........284 G6
rd. Fairfield W......335 C13
CORONATA
wy. Mcquarie Fd...424 D16
CORONATION
av. Cronulla..........493 K16
av. Eastwood.......280 K10
av. Five Dock.......343 A10
av. Kings Park.......244 F6
av. Mosman.........317 E8
av. Peakhurst.......430 D5
av. Petersham........15 K15
dr. Green Valley...363 A9
gr. Cmbrdg Gdn...237 H5
la. Cmbrdg Gdn, off Coronation Gr..237 H5
pde. Enfield..........371 F7
pde. Strathfield S...371 F7
rd. Baulkham Hl...247 E10
st. Mona Vale......199 D8
st. Hornsby, off Jersey St.........191 G16
CORONET
ct. North Rocks...278 J4

CORONGA
cr. Killara 253 F15
CORR
la. Werrington 238 J12
CORREA
ct. Voyager Pt 427 D6
pl. Mcquarie Fd 454 F6
CORREY
pl. Carlingford 279 K2
CORREYS
av. Concord 341 F4
av. N Strathfield 341 F4
CORRIE
rd. North Manly 258 B15
CORRIEDALE
cl. Elderslie 507 J1
st. Miller 393 G2
st. Wakeley 364 K1
CORRIN
ct. Wattle Grove 396 B14
CORRY
ct. N Parramatta 278 H13
st. Bonnyrigg 363 J7
CORRYONG
st. Fairfield W 335 C8
CORRYTON
ct. Wattle Grove 425 H4
pl. Glen Alpine 510 C15
CORSAIR
cr. Cranebrook 207 A10
st. Raby 481 G1
CORUNDUM
cl. Eagle Vale 481 G4
CORUNNA
av. Leumeah 482 G16
av. North Rocks 279 A2
la. Stanmore 16 E5
rd. Eastwood 281 E4
rd. Petersham 16 B6
rd. Stanmore 16 B6
CORVUS
cl. Glenmore Pk 265 H13
rd. Hinchinbrk 393 E5
CORY
av. Padstow 399 C15
pl. Prospect 274 J11
CORYMBIA
cct. Oxford Falls 226 G15
CORYULE
pl. Warriewood 199 B7
COSFORD
cl. Chipping Ntn 396 E1
COSGROVE
cr. Kingswood 238 A14
rd. Belfield 371 A9
rd. Strathfield S 370 J5
COSIMO
st. Ryde 282 A11
st. Toongabbie 276 H7
COSMOS
pl. Mcquarie Fd 454 E7
COSSINGTON
wy. Claymore 481 D13
COSTAIN
pl. Seven Hills 275 D6
COSTATA
ct. Voyager Pt 427 C5
pl. Mcquarie Fd 454 G2
COSTELLO
pl. Seven Hills 246 D14
COSTENS POINT
rd. Royal N P 522 E11
COSTER
st. Frenchs Frst 257 A4
COTENTIN
rd. Belrose 225 K9
COTSWOLD
av. Castle Hill 217 H10
cl. Belrose 226 B12
rd. Dural 189 E8
rd. Horsley Pk 332 K8
rd. Strathfield 371 D2
st. Westmead 307 G3
COTTAGE
st. Werrington 238 D11
wy. Lilyfield 10 B4
COTTAGE POINT
rd. Cottage Pt 135 E13
rd. Krngai Ch NP 165 F1
COTTAM
av. Bankstown 399 E7
COTTEE
dr. Epping 280 D4
COTTENHAM
av. Kensington 376 D16
av. Kingsford 406 D2
COTTER
la. Glebe 11 H7
pl. Greystanes 306 A4
pl. Leumeah 482 D13
pl. Quakers Hill 214 C14
COTTERILL
st. Plumpton 241 H7
COTTERS
la. Revesby Ht, off Sandakan Rd 428 K6
COTTON
gr. Stanhpe Gdn 215 C10
st. N Epping 251 J10
COTTONWOOD
cr. Mcquarie Fd 454 G2
cr. Mcquarie Pk 282 E3
gr. Menai 459 A14
pl. Castle Hill 248 H2
wy. Hornsby Ht 161 G16
COTTRELL
pl. Baulkham Hl 247 F5
pl. Fairfield W 334 K9
pl. Fairfield W 335 A9
COTULA
pl. Glenmore Pk 265 H12
pl. Mcquarie Fd 454 F4
pl. Mt Annan 509 E4
COUCAL
av. Hinchinbrk 393 E1
pl. Ingleburn 453 F9
COUGAR
pl. Raby 451 E13
COUGHLAN
rd. Blaxland 233 D12
COULL
st. Picton 563 F5
st. Picton 563 F6
COULMAN
st. Kings Park 244 E2
COULON
st. Rozelle 7 A15
COULSON
st. Erskineville 375 A10
COULTER
st. Gladesville 312 H9
COULTON
la. Surry Hills 20 D4
st. Bondi 377 K5
COUNCIL
la. Fairfield, off Smart St 336 F12
pl. Sydney C F7
st. Bondi Jctn 377 G5
st. Marrickville 374 B10
st. N Willghby 285 E10
st. St Peters 374 H11
COUNTESS
st. Mosman 316 J5
COUNTY
av. Paddington 13 A16
dr. Cherrybrook 219 A14
COUPS
pl. Wahroonga 222 C13
COURALLIE
av. Homebsh W 340 G7
av. Pymble 253 A6
rd. Northbridge 286 D14
COURANGA
st. Lilli Pilli 522 G1
COURLAND
st. Five Dock 342 H11
st. Randwick 377 D15
COURT
av. Kingsford 406 E2
pl. Menai 458 G6
rd. Double Bay 14 D11
rd. Fairfield 336 F11
st. Windsor 121 E7
COURTENAY
av. Rookwood 340 C15
rd. Rose Bay 348 D9
COURTLAND
av. Tahmoor 566 A12
COURTLEY
rd. Beacon Hill 257 D6
COURTNEY
rd. Padstow 429 C5
COURTYARD
pl. Castle Hill 217 F4
COUSINS
rd. Beacon Hill 257 H5
COUTTS
cr. Collaroy 259 A1
COVE
av. Manly 288 G13
cct. Castle Cove 285 H4
cl. St Clair 269 J11
la. St Clair, off Netherton Av 269 J11
st. Birchgrove 7 F3
st. Haberfield 342 K13
st. Hunters Hill 313 E4
st. S Turramrra 251 K7
st. Watsons Bay 318 E12
COVELEE
cct. Middle Cove 285 J9
COVENEY
st. Bexley North 402 D11
COVENTRY
cr. N Epping 251 G12
pl. Mount Druitt 240 H14
pl. West Pymble 252 G8
rd. Cabramatta 365 E7
rd. Strathfield 341 B12
COVENY
st. Doonside 243 A11
st. Warragamba 353 G13
COVER
st. Auburn 339 A2
st. Birchgrove 7 H3
COVERDALE
st. Carlingford 250 C13
COW
la. Darlinghurst 4 J11
la. Hurstville 432 B7
COWAL
wy. Woodcroft 243 J9
COWAN
cl. Seven Hills 246 C12
dr. Cottage Pt 135 E10
pl. Glenmore Pk 266 A8
pl. Prairiewood 334 K9
pl. St Helens Pk 540 K10
rd. Mt Colah 192 B4
rd. Mt Colah 192 C4
rd. St Ives 223 J12
st. Brooklyn 75 J11
st. Oyster Bay 461 C6
COWARD
st. Mascot 404 J2
st. Mascot 405 B2
st. Rosebery 405 E3
COWDERY
la. Strathfield 341 H11
st. Glenbrook 233 K16
wy. Currans Hill 479 J12
COWDREY
wy. Bonnyrigg 364 B4
COWDROY
av. Cammeray 316 C4
COWE
cl. Bonnyrigg Ht 363 G5
COWELL
st. Gladesville 312 J10
st. Ryde 312 A3
COWELLS
la. Ermington 280 E13
COWL
st. Greenacre 370 E8
COWLAND
av. East Hills 427 H4
COWLES
rd. Mosman 316 K8
COWLEY
cr. Prospect 274 J10
cr. Prospect 274 G11
COWPASTURE
pl. Wetherill Pk 333 F3
rd. Abbotsbury 333 D15
rd. Bonnyrigg Ht 363 A5
rd. Bossley Park 333 D15
rd. Cecil Hills 362 J9
rd. Cecil Park 362 J11
rd. Edensor Pk 363 A5
rd. Green Valley 362 J9
rd. Hinchinbrk 392 G4
rd. Horngsea Pk 392 C13
rd. Horsley Pk 333 G2
rd. Hoxton Park 392 C13
rd. Leppington 421 F5
rd. West Hoxton 392 C13
rd. Wetherill Pk 333 G2
COWPE
la. Eastern Ck 272 J11
COWPER
av. Pagewood 406 C8
cir. Quakers Hill 213 G14
ct. Milperra 397 F10
dr. Camden S 506 K11
la. Glebe 12 F13
la. Milperra 397 E11
pl. Barden Rdg 488 G3
pl. Connells Pt 431 H15
pl. Turramurra 222 H13
pl. Wetherill Pk 334 K6
st. Campsie 372 B10
st. Glebe 12 F15
st. Granville 308 F10
st. Leumeah 512 B1
st. Longueville 314 D8
st. Marrickville 16 G16
st. Marrickville 374 D9
st. Parramatta 308 D5
st. Picton 563 E10
st. Picton 563 F10
st. Randwick 376 K11
COWPER WHARF
rdy. Potts Point 4 F2
rdy. Woolmloo 4 F2
COWRA
cl. Bonnyrigg Ht 363 B7
pl. Cronulla 523 J4
pl. Leumeah 512 D3
st. Greystanes 305 H1
COWRANG
av. Terrey Hills 196 D5
COX
av. Bondi Beach 378 B2
av. Kingswood 237 C11
av. Penrith 237 C11
cr. Dundas Vy 279 K7
cr. Richmond 118 E7
la. Toongabbie 276 C8
pl. Gymea 461 G16
pl. Ingleburn 453 C12
pl. Mortdale 431 B6
pl. Mt Pritchard 364 B11
pl. West Hoxton 392 B10
st. Coogee 407 F3
st. Elderslie 507 G1
st. Glenbrook 263 J2
st. S Windsor 120 D16
st. Windsor 120 H12
COXS
av. Liverpool 395 A8
la. Lane Cove 314 C1
rd. East Ryde 283 A13
rd. North Ryde 282 F9
CRABB
pl. Cabramatta 365 E11
CRABBES
av. N Willghby 285 E9
CRACKENBACK
ct. Glenhaven 218 A5
CRADDOCK
st. Wentwthvle 306 G1
CRAG
cr. Bowen Mtn 83 K7
CRAGG
st. Condell Park 398 H3
CRAGSIDE
pl. Glenhaven 218 A5
CRAIG
av. Baulkham Hl 247 H14
av. Leumeah 512 B1
av. Manly 288 H13
av. Moorebank 396 D9
av. Oxley Park 270 F2
av. Vaucluse 348 F6
pl. Davidson 255 E2
st. Blacktown 274 C5
st. Punchbowl 399 J9
st. St Ives Ch 224 B2
st. Smithfield 335 D7
st. Woolooware 493 E12
CRAIGAVON
wy. Wentwthvle 277 E10
CRAIGEND
st. Darlinghurst 13 A9
st. Darlinghurst 13 B9
CRAIGHOLM
st. Sylvania 461 J12
CRAIGIE
av. Padstow 429 D3
CRAIGLANDS
av. Gordon 253 D9
CRAIGLEA
gdn. Carlingford 250 D13
st. Blacktown 274 J3
st. Guildford 337 E6
CRAIGMORE
dr. Kellyville 216 K1
CRAIGSLEA
pl. Canley Ht 335 C16
CRAIGTON
pl. Glenhaven 218 E6
CRAIK
av. Austral 391 E2
CRAIN
ct. Harringtn Pk 478 C2
CRAKANTHORP
la. Picton 563 F5
CRAMER
cr. Chatswd W 284 C13
cr. Lane Cove W 284 C13
pl. Glenwood 215 J14
CRAMMOND
av. Bundeena 523 G8
bvd. Caringbah 492 J2
pl. Minto 453 A14
CRAMPTON
dr. Springwood 172 E12
CRANA
av. E Lindfield 255 A13
av. S Coogee 407 J5
pl. Forestville 255 J8
rd. Brownlow Hl 475 K9
st. St Marys 239 G16
CRANBERRY
st. Loftus 490 A9
st. Mcquarie Fd 454 D6
CRANBOURNE
st. Riverstone 183 D11
CRANBROOK
av. Cremorne 316 F9
av. Roseville 284 J1
cl. West Hoxton 392 D9
la. Bellevue Hill 347 F11
la. Cronulla 493 H12
la. Cremorne, off Cranbrook Av 316 F8
pl. Illawong 460 E1
rd. Bellevue Hill 347 F13
st. Botany 405 F13
CRANDON
rd. Epping 251 D16
CRANE
av. Green Valley 363 E14
av. Haberfield 343 D12
la. Concord 342 B8
pl. Bellevue Hill 14 G8
pl. Cranebrook 207 A5
pl. Double Bay 14 G8
pl. Wetherill Pk 335 A5
rd. Castle Hill 218 D15
st. Concord 342 A7
st. Homebush 341 B8
st. Springwood 201 E4
CRANEBROOK
rd. Castlereagh 206 H15
rd. Cranebrook 206 H15
CRANE LODGE
pl. Palm Beach 140 B9
CRANFIELD
pl. Camden S 506 K14
CRANFORD
av. St Ives 223 K9
CRANNEY
pl. Lalor Park 245 F14
CRANSTONS
rd. Middle Dural 158 D3
CRATER
rd. N Balgowlah 287 G4
CRAVEN
pl. Mt Annan 509 H1
CRAWFORD
av. Shalvey 210 J13
la. Tahmoor 565 K12
la. Emu Plains, off Crawford St 235 B9
pl. Beacon Hill 257 H8
pl. Dundas Vy 280 A6
pl. Marrickville 373 G12
pl. Surry Hills F F13
rd. Btn-le-Sds 433 H4
rd. Doonside 243 A12
rd. Mt Krng-gai 162 J10
st. Berala 339 D12
st. Blakehurst 432 B13
st. Emu Plains 235 B9
st. Old Guildfrd 337 G9
swy. Liverpool 395 E4

CRAWLEY
av. Hebersham 241 G8
st. Merrylands 307 J9
CRAYFORD
cr. Mt Pritchard 364 C11
CREBRA
wy. Mt Annan 509 E3
CREDA
pl. Baulkham Hl 248 D10
CREE
cr. Greenfld Pk 333 K16
CREEK
rd. St Marys 239 F15
st. Balmain 7 F11
st. Colyton 270 J7
st. Forest Lodge 11 E15
st. Riverstone 182 H9
CREEK RIDGE
rd. Freemns Rch 90 E1
rd. Glossodia 60 C11
rd. Glossodia 61 A6
CREEKWOOD
dr. Voyager Pt 427 B5
CREER
pl. Narraweena 257 K4
st. Randwick 407 C2
CREEWOOD
la. Concord, off Creewood St 341 G7
st. Concord 341 G7
CREGO
rd. Glenhaven 218 D4
CREIGAN
rd. Bradbury 511 J13
CREMA
pl. Edensor Pk 333 J15
CREMONA
pl. Oakhurst 242 D1
rd. Como 460 H5
CREMORNE
la. Cremorne Pt 316 F13
rd. Cremorne Pt 316 F13
CREOLE
st. Berowra 133 C11
CRESCENT
av. Manly 288 F7
av. Ryde 312 C1
cl. Warrawee 222 E8
la. Newtown 17 E13
pl. Milsons Pt 6 A14
rd. Caringbah 492 E14
rd. Mona Vale 169 F16
rd. Newport 169 F14
st. Fairlight 288 E8
st. Granville 308 B10
st. Haberfield 9 A6
st. Hunters Hill 314 A12
st. Redfern 20 B12
st. Rozelle 11 C1
st. Waterloo 20 B12
CRESS
pl. Mcquarie Fd 454 F6
pl. Quakers Hill 243 E4
CRESSBROOK
dr. Wattle Grove 425 J3
CRESSFIELD
av. Carlingford 279 F4
CRESSY
av. Kellyville 215 H3
rd. East Ryde 282 J15
rd. Mt Vernon 331 A14
rd. North Ryde 282 J15
rd. North Ryde 283 A13
rd. Ryde 312 E4
rd. Ryde 312 H1
st. Canterbury 372 D16
st. Rosebery 375 H13
CREST
pl. Engadine 488 C15
pl. Jamisontown 266 C4
rd. Warragamba 353 B4
CRESTA
cl. St Ives 224 A13
CRESTANI
pl. Edensor Pk 333 J16
CRESTBROOK
st. Seven Hills 245 C15
CRESTREEF
dr. Acacia Gdn 214 G15
CRESTVIEW
av. Kellyville 216 G1
dr. Glenwood 246 B5
pl. Cherrybrook 219 D13
pl. Cranebrook 207 A12
CRESTWOOD
av. Thornleigh 221 B5
dr. Baulkham Hl 246 J3
wk. Baulkham Hl 247 B7
CRESWELL
st. Revesby 398 E14
CRESWICK
pl. Dharruk 241 D8
CRETE
pl. E Lindfield 254 K11
pl. Lugarno 429 K8
st. Narraweena 258 D6
CRETNEY
pl. Peakhurst 430 D7
CREWE
pl. Rosebery 375 J14
st. Bardwell Pk 402 J7
CREWS
rd. Seven Hills 246 B11
CRICK
av. Elizabeth Bay 13 A4
st. Chatswood 285 B7
CRICKETERS ARMS
rd. Prospect 274 F16
CRIEFF
st. Ashbury 372 D9
CRIMEA
rd. Marsfield 251 H14
st. Parramatta 307 H7
CRIMSON
la. Ashbury 372 H6
st. Ashbury 372 H6
CRINAN
ct. Castle Hill 218 D7
la. Hurlstone Pk 372 K11
st. Hurlstone Pk 372 K11
CRINUM
pl. Mcquarie Fd 454 F5
CRIPPLE
rd. Blaxland 233 G4
CRIPPS
av. Kingsgrove 401 G6
CRISPIN
pl. Quakers Hill 214 B12
CRISPSPARKLE
dr. Ambarvale 540 F1
CRITCHETT
rd. Chatswd W 284 G12
CRITERION
cr. Doonside 243 C6
CROATIA
av. Edmndsn Pk 423 B4
pl. Quakers Hill 214 A10
CROCKET
wy. Minto 482 K5
CROCODILE
dr. Green Valley 363 B9
CROCUS
pl. Quakers Hill 243 F3
CROFT
av. Merrylands 307 B11
pl. Bradbury 511 J13
pl. Glenwood 246 B5
CROFTS
av. Hurstville 432 A5
la. Rockdale 403 D15
CROISSY
av. Hunters Hill 313 J12
CROKER
cr. Colyton 270 D5
la. Colyton, off Croker Cr 270 D5
pl. Green Valley 362 J12
pl. Guildford W 336 J1
CROMARTY
cr. Winston Hills 277 C3
pl. St Andrews 481 K5
CROMDALE
st. Mortdale 430 J8
CROMER
pl. St Johns Pk 364 E2
rd. Cromer 227 J11
CROMERTY
pl. Glenhaven 218 D5
CROMER VALLEY
rd. Belrose 227 B7
rd. Cromer 227 B7
rd. Oxford Falls 227 B7
CROMMELIN
cr. St Helens Pk 541 A6
CROMPTON
pl. W Pnnant Hl 249 B3
CROMWELL
pl. Malabar 437 D2
st. Croydon 372 E5
st. Croydon Pk 372 E5
st. Leichhardt 9 H14
CRONDALL
st. Bonnyrigg Ht 363 A7
CRONIN
av. Penshurst 431 H7
pl. Bonnyrigg 364 D4
st. Penrith 237 B14
CRONULLA
cr. Woodbine 481 D15
la. Allawah 432 E4
st. Allawah 432 E5
st. Cronulla 493 K13
CROOKED
la. N Richmond 87 D10
CROOKS
la. Newtown 17 H10
CROOKSTON
dr. Camden S 507 A13
CROOKWELL
av. Miranda 491 J7
CROOT
st. Hurstville 401 H15
CROPLEY
dr. Baulkham Hl 247 C13
la. Rhodes, off Cropley St 311 F8
st. Rhodes 311 E8
CROQUET
la. Mosman 317 D10
CROSBY
av. Hurstville 432 D3
cr. Fairfield 336 E7
st. Denistone W 280 K12
st. Greystanes 306 E3
st. Greystanes 306 F3
CROSIO
pl. Bonnyrigg 364 F6
CROSS
la. Double Bay 14 E9
la. Enmore 17 A15
la. Kogarah 433 D4
la. Mortdale 431 C7
la. Woolmloo 4 F6
pl. Bligh Park 150 K7
pl. Mt Annan 479 G16
rd. Longueville 314 B9
rd. Orchard Hills 267 C11
rd. Regentville 235 E16
rd. Woolooware 493 F13
st. Balgowlah 287 J6
st. Bankstown 399 G2
st. Baulkham Hl 248 B9
st. Bronte 378 A7
st. Brookvale 257 J11
st. Campsie 402 B1
st. Concord 341 G6
st. Croydon 342 D14
st. Doonside 243 A13
st. Double Bay 14 B8
st. Five Dock 342 J10
st. Forest Lodge 11 G15
st. Glebe 11 G15
st. Glenbrook 264 A1
st. Guildford 337 F6
st. Hurstville 432 A5
st. Kemps Ck 360 B3
st. Kogarah 433 E4
st. Kyle Bay 431 J16
st. Lidcombe 339 K6
st. Merrylands 307 A9
st. Miranda 492 D7
st. Mortdale 431 C6
st. Mosman 317 C11
st. Pymble 253 B7
st. Pyrmont 12 F1
st. Rozelle 7 A14
st. Ryde 312 E6
st. Strathfield 371 D4
st. Tahmoor 566 D11
st. Warrimoo 203 F11
CROSSING
la. Concord, off Ada St 341 G9
CROSSLAND
st. Merrylands 338 C1
CROSSLANDS
rd. Galston 160 B10
CROSSLEY
av. McGraths Hl 122 A13
st. Ingleburn 453 F13
CROSTON
rd. Engadine 489 E8
CROSWELL
pl. N Parramatta 278 E10
CROTON
pl. Mcquarie Fd 454 C4
CROTOYE
pl. Marsfield 281 K6
CROW
pl. Bossley Park 333 K11
CROWBILL
pl. Erskine Park 270 J13
CROWEA
pl. Oxford Falls 226 H15
CROWGEY
st. Rydalmere 279 C16
CROWLE
rd. S Penrith 267 A4
CROWLEY
cr. Melrose Pk 310 K4
rd. Berowra 133 D13
CROWLEYS
la. Agnes Banks 117 C8
CROWN
cl. Henley 313 B13
la. Darlinghurst 4 C8
mw. Bella Vista 246 E4
pl. Tahmoor 565 F7
rd. Pymble 223 C13
rd. Queenscliff 288 F2
st. Darlinghurst F K9
st. Darlinghurst 4 C12
st. Epping 250 J16
st. Fairfield E 337 A11
st. Glebe 12 G14
st. Granville 307 K8
st. Harris Park 308 F7
st. Henley 313 B14
st. Riverstone 182 H4
st. St Peters 374 J13
st. Surry Hills F J16
st. Surry Hills F K9
st. Surry Hills 4 B16
st. Surry Hills 20 B5
st. Woolmloo 4 C12
tce. Bella Vista 246 E4
CROWS NEST
rd. Waverton 5 A5
rd. Wollstncraft 5 A5
CROWTHER
av. Greenwich 314 J5
CROXON
cr. Lalor Park 245 G11
CROYDON
av. Croydon 372 D5
av. Croydon Pk 372 C9
la. Petersham 15 K7
la. Cronulla, off Cronulla St 493 K13
la. Lakemba, off Croydon St N 400 K1
rd. Bexley 402 A15
rd. Croydon 342 F16
rd. Hurstville 402 A15
st. Cronulla 493 K12
st. Lakemba 401 A2
st. Petersham 15 J7
st.n, Lakemba 400 K1
CROZET
st. Kings Park 244 F3
CROZIER
rd. Belrose 225 K5
st. Eagle Vale 481 B9
CRUCIE
av. Bass Hill 367 G6
CRUCIS
la. Erskine Park, off Crucis Pl 300 J3
pl. Erskine Park 300 J2
CRUDGE
rd. Marayong 244 A7
CRUIKSHANK
av. Elderslie 507 G1
st. Stanmore 17 A5
CRUMMOCK
st. Collaroy Plat 228 D12
CRUMP
st. Mortdale 431 A6
CRUSADE
av. Padstow 399 C16
pl. Woolooware 493 C10
CRUSADER
rd. Galston 160 E13
CRUX
la. Mosman 316 J11
st. Mosman 316 J10
CRYSTAL
la.w, Petersham 16 A9
pl. Doonside 243 E8
st. Greystanes 306 A2
st. Newport 169 D10
st. Petersham 16 A9
st. Rozelle 344 D7
st. Sylvania 461 H12
wy. Mt Annan 479 C15
CUBBY
cl. Castle Hill 217 B10
CUBITT
cr. Quakers Hill 214 D12
dr. Denham Ct 422 C7
CUDAL
cl. Terrey Hills 196 E5
pl. Carlingford 249 D13
pl. Kirrawee 490 J6
CUDDLEPIE
pl. Faulconbdg 171 D15
CUDGEE
cl. Baulkham Hl 246 H9
la. Penrith, off Cudgee Rd 237 E4
pl. Dharruk 241 D9
pl. Greystanes 305 K10
rd. Gymea Bay 491 G8
rd. Penrith 237 E4
st. Turramurra 223 A9
CUDGEGONG
rd. Rouse Hill 184 C8
rd. Ruse 512 B8
CULBARA
pl. Allambie Ht 257 G15
CULBURRA
rd. Miranda 492 B1
st. Prestons 393 C14
CULDEES
rd. Burwood Ht 372 A3
CULGOA
av. Eastwood 281 J5
ct. Wattle Grove 395 K13
pl. Sylvania Wtr 462 E9
st. Chatswd W 284 B9
CULL
rd. Harringtn Pk 478 E2
CULLAMINE
rd. Duffys Frst 164 H16
CULLEN
av. Mosman 317 C9
av. Richmond 119 K3
la. Maianbar 523 A8
pl. Dharruk 241 B8
pl. Minto 482 J9
pl. Smithfield 306 C15
st. Forestville 255 E9
st. Lane Cove W 313 H2
st. Maianbar 523 A8
CULLENS
av. Liverpool 394 J9
la. Hunters Hill 313 H10
pl. Liverpool 394 J10
rd. Punchbowl 400 A7
CULLENYA
cl. Berowra 133 A16
CULLIS
pl. Woodpark 306 H14
CULLODEN
rd. Mcquarie Pk 252 A16
rd. Marsfield 281 H2
CULLUM
st. Bossley Park 333 H11
CULMARA
pl. Engadine 489 B10
CULMONE
cl. Edensor Pk 363 F4
CULTOWA
rd. Pymble 253 B7
CULVER
st. Monterey 433 F10
st. S Wntwthvle 307 A7
CULVERSTON
av. Denham Ct 422 C5
rd. Minto 482 C8
CULWORTH
av. Killara 254 A12
CULWULLA
st. S Hurstville 432 B9
CULYA
st. Marayong 243 H6
CUMBEE
la. Caringbah 493 B16
CUMBERLAND
av. Castle Hill 217 J10

av. Collaroy.......... 259 A1
av. Dee Why 258 K2
av. Georges Hall... 368 C15
av. Lane Cove W.. 283 G13
hwy. Beecroft.......... 249 J14
hwy. Cabramatta..... 365 B11
hwy. Cabramtta W .. 365 D7
hwy. Canley Ht........ 365 D7
hwy. Carlingford 279 F6
hwy. Fairfield W...... 335 D15
hwy. Greystanes 306 H7
hwy. Liverpool........ 365 B11
hwy. Merrylnds W .. 306 F14
hwy. Normanhurst.. 221 E10
hwy. Northmead 277 C11
hwy. N Parramatta .. 278 H10
hwy. Oatlands......... 278 H10
hwy. Pennant Hills .. 250 A3
hwy. Smithfield........ 335 H7
hwy. S Wntwthvle.... 306 H7
hwy. Thornleigh...... 221 E10
hwy. Wahroonga 221 E10
hwy. Warwck Frm... 365 B11
hwy. Wentwthvle.... 277 C11
hwy. W Pnnant Hl... 249 J14
hwy. Woodpark...... 306 F14
pl. Colyton........... 270 F8
pl. The Rocks ....A J5
rd. Auburn........... 339 A4
rd. Greystanes 306 C6
rd. Ingleburn 453 B13
rd. Minto 453 B12
sq. Newington, off Monterey St.... 310 D11
st. Blacktown 274 H6
st. Cabramatta....... 366 A8
st. Carlton 432 G6
st. Epping............. 280 D3
st. Homebush B ..... M A6
st. The Rocks ....A F9
st. The Rocks 1 F13

CUMBERNAULD
cr. Dharruk.......... 241 C6

CUMBORA
cct. Berowra 133 B13

CUMBRAE
cl. Erskine Park ... 300 F2
pl. Oatlands.......... 278 H10

CUMBRIAN
cl. Northmead 278 C5

CUMMING
av. Concord 341 F3
av. Concord W...... 341 F3
cr. Quakers Hill.... 213 H14

CUMMINGS
cr. Lansvale.......... 366 H8

CUMMINS
rd. Menangle Pk .. 539 B6

CUNLIFFE
rd. East Killara 254 G7

CUNNEEN
st. Mulgrave......... 121 H15

CUNNINGHAM
cl. St Clair 270 D10
cr. Blacktown 245 B12
cr. Ingleburn 423 B11
dr. Mt Annan 509 J5
pl. Camden S 506 K11
pl. S Windsor 150 H1
pwy. Moorebank, off Cunningham St... 395 J8
rd. Ingleburn 423 A9
st. Haymarket.......... E H6
st. Matraville 437 B2
st. Moorebank..... 395 J9
st. N Sydney........... 5 F2
st. Telopea 279 G11

CUNNINGHAME
st. Fairfield 336 D10

CUPANIA
cr. Bidwill............ 211 E13

CUPAR
pl. St Andrews..... 451 K16

CUPITTS
la. Richmond 120 B3

CURAC
pl. Casula............ 424 C3

CURAGUL
rd. N Turramrra ... 193 E14

CURBAN
st. Balgowlah Ht.. 287 J13

CURIE
av. Little Bay 437 G13
av. Lucas Ht......... 487 H12

CURL CURL
pde. Curl Curl......... 258 H13
pl. Woodbine........ 481 J9

CURLEW
av. Newington .... L H10
av. Newington 310 E11
cl. Woronora Ht... 489 B3
st. Glenwood 215 E14

CURLEW CAMP
rd. Mosman 316 J12

CURLEWIS
st. Ashcroft.......... 364 F15
st. Bondi Beach ... 378 B1

CURRA
cl. Frenchs Frst.... 255 K2
pl. Greystanes 305 K10

CURRAGHBEENA
rd. Mosman 316 J13

CURRAGUNDI
av. Belrose........... 226 B10

CURRAH
rd. Como 460 G5

CURRAN
av. Mcquarie Fd.... 453 J2
rd. Marayong 244 A8
st. Prairiewood 335 A7

CURRANA
st. Beverly Hills.... 401 C9

CURRANS HILL
dr. Currans Hill 479 G11

CURRAWANG
pl. Como 460 H6
st. Cammeray 316 B4
st. Carss Park 432 F13
st. Concord W 311 E13

CURRAWEELA
st. Forestville 255 K7

CURRAWONG
av. Lane Cove W .. 313 H1
av. Normanhurst .. 221 F12
av. Palm Beach ... 140 B9
av. Valley Ht......... 202 E5
cr. Bowen Mtn 84 A8
cr. Leonay 234 K13
pl. Blaxland 234 E5
rd. Berowra Ht 132 J8
rd. Glenorie.......... 127 K9
st. Glenwood 215 C16
st. Green Valley ... 363 E9
st. Ingleburn 453 G7

CURRENCY
rd. Freemns Rch 60 J10

CURRENT
st. Padstow 429 H2

CURREY
pl. Fairfield W 335 A11

CURRIE
av. Annangrove 186 E4
rd. Forestville 256 C9
rd. Oakville........... 122 H12

CURRINGA
rd. Villawood........ 367 A3

CURRONG
cct. Terrey Hills 196 D8
pl. S Turramrra 252 B9
st. S Wntwthvle ... 306 J7

CURRY
la. Artarmon 314 K2
pl. Seven Hills...... 275 G8
st. Eastern Ck 272 G2
st. Rooty Hill 272 G2

CURT
pl. Quakers Hill 214 A10
st. Ashfield 343 A16

CURTALE
ct. Green Valley ... 363 C10

CURTIN
av. Abbotsford 343 A4
av. N Wahrnga 192 E15
cr. Maroubra 407 E14
gr. Penrith 237 C6
la. Canterbury...... 372 F15
pl. Concord 341 H5
pl. Condell Park ... 398 G1
pl. Sydney ....A J14
pl. Sydney 1 G15
pl. Westmead 307 E3
st. Cabramatta 366 A5
st. Canley Vale 366 A5

CURTIS
av. Taren Point..... 462 G13
cl. Cherrybrook 249 E1
cr. Moorebank 396 D9
ct. Carlingford 279 F7
la. Catherine Fd.... 449 D6
pl. Kings Park...... 244 F2
rd. Balmain 7 F6
rd. Chester Hill 338 A14
rd. Kellyville 186 A13
rd. Mulgrave 121 H15
st. Banksia........... 403 D12
st. Caringbah 492 G7
st. Ryde............... 312 E6

CURTISS
pl. Raby.............. 481 E1

CURVERS
dr. Mt Riverview... 234 C1

CURZON
rd. Padstow Ht 429 B5
st. Ryde............... 282 A16
wy. Ambarvale 511 A16

CUSACK
av. Casula............ 424 G3
cl. St Helens Pk ... 541 C3
pl. Blackett.......... 241 D3
rd. Oakville.......... 124 C8
st. Denistone W ... 280 J12
st. Merrylnds W ... 307 A16

CUSAK
cl. Edensor Pk 333 H16

CUSCUS
pl. St Helens Pk ... 541 H2

CUSHER
wy. Wentwthvle, off Portadown Rd .. 277 D11

CUSTOM HOUSE
la. Sydney .... B D9

CUSTOMS OFFICERS STAIRS
The Rocks........... 1 J8

CUTBUSH
av. Belfield............ 371 C9

CUTCLIFFE
av. Regents Pk 369 F2

CUTHBERT
av. Kellyville 215 H5
cr. Edensor Pk 363 D2
cr. Revesby......... 428 H2
pl. Menai 458 F12
st. Queens Park 22 E11

CUTHEL
pl. Campbelltwn ... 511 K2
st. Badgerys Ck.... 359 C4

CUT HILL
rd. Cobbitty.......... 446 D9

CUTHILL
st. Randwick........ 377 B15

CUTLER
av. St Marys 270 A1
cct. Narrabeen....... 228 F6
cl. Westleigh........ 220 H8
la. St Marys, off Cutler Av......... 270 A2
pde. North Ryde 282 K11
pl. Cromer 227 K11
rd. Clontarf........... 287 G15
rd. Engadine......... 518 E4
rd. Lansvale 366 E8
st. Bondi.............. 378 B4

CUTLER FOOTWAY
Paddington 4 J13

CUTLER HALL
wy. Narrabeen, off Cutler Cct 228 F7

CUVEE
pl. Minchinbury ... 271 K10

CUZCO
st. S Coogee 407 H6

CYCAS
pl. Stanhpe Gdn... 215 D10

CYCLAMEN
pl. Mcquarie Fd.... 454 E5

CYGNET
av. Green Valley.... 363 D14
pl. Illawong.......... 459 C5
pl. Willmot........... 210 F12

CYGNUS
cl. Doonside 243 E13
pl. Cranebrook..... 207 G7

CYNTHEA
rd. Palm Beach..... 140 A4

CYNTHIA
av. Castle Hill........ 248 A5
st. Pymble 252 K7
wk. Pymble 252 K7

CYPERUS
pl. Glenmore Pk... 265 H14

CYPRESS
cl. Alfords Point... 458 K3
ct. Baulkham Hl.... 248 B11
dr. Lugarno 429 K8
la. Blacktown, off Kildare Rd 243 K15
pl. Liverpool......... 395 B9
rd. N St Marys...... 240 C12
st. Normanhurst... 221 D13

CYPRIAN
st. Mosman 317 C1

CYPRUS
st. Mcquarie Fd 453 K4

CYRIL
pl. Baulkham Hl.... 247 E11
st. Greystanes...... 306 G4

CYRUS
av. Wahroonga 222 A12

D

DABAGE
pl. Kurrajong Ht 54 A5

DACEY
av. Moore Park 20 D15
pl. Doonside 273 F3

DACRE
la. Malabar........... 437 E3
st. Malabar........... 437 E3

DADLEY
st. Alexandria 18 H13

DADSWELL
pl. Mt Pritchard 364 K11

DAFFODIL
pl. Glenmore Pk ... 265 G7
st. Eastwood 281 D7
st. Greystanes...... 306 C12
st. Marayong........ 244 B6

DAGMAR
cr. Blacktown 274 C3

DAHLIA
pl. Clarmnt Ms 238 H16
pl. Prestons 393 J14
st. Greystanes...... 305 G11
st. Quakers Hill 243 E2

DAIHATSU
dr. Riverwood, off Applause St..... 400 C10

DAIMLER
pl. Ingleburn 453 H12

DAINES
pde. Beacon Hill...... 257 F6

DAINTON
av. St Ives............ 224 D11

DAINTREE
dr. Wattle Grove ... 426 A4
gln. St Clair 270 D11
la. St Clair, off Daintree Gln 270 D11
pl. Dural.............. 219 A3
pl. Kellyville.......... 216 G2
wy. Menai............. 458 H10

DAINTREY
cr. Randwick 377 C16
st. Fairlight........... 288 D8

DAIRY
ct. Glenwood 215 E13
rd. Belimbla Pk..... 501 D8

DAISY
av. Penshurst 431 G6
la. Bargo.............. 567 A5
pl. Clarmnt Ms 238 H16
pl. Lalor Park 245 C11
pl. Mcquarie Fd 454 D5
st. Chatswood 284 J8
st. Croydon Pk..... 372 A5
st. Dee Why 259 A8
st. Greystanes...... 305 H7
st. N Balgowlah.... 287 F6
st. Revesby.......... 398 F10
st. Roselands 400 F8

DAKARA
cl. Pymble 252 J4
dr. Frenchs Frst 256 A2
pl. Frenchs Frst 256 B2

DAKING
st. N Parramatta ... 278 B10

DAKOTA
ct. Stanhpe Gdn ... 215 C12
dr. Bossley Park ... 333 K11
pl. Raby 451 B13
pl. St Clair 269 F13

DALBERTIS
st. Abbotsbury 333 A13

DALBY
pl. Chipping Ntn .. 366 H16
pl. Eastlakes........ 405 K2

DALCASSIA
st. Hurstville........ 431 K4

DALE
av. Chippendale 19 B4
av. Liverpool........ 394 F5
cl. Thornleigh...... 220 H12
cr. Narwee........... 400 G15
gr. Hebersham..... 241 F10
la. Mcquarie Fd ... 453 K2
pde. Bankstown 399 D1
pl. Cranebrook 237 D1
pl. North Rocks ... 248 J12
pl. Winston Hills .. 277 H3
st. Brookvale 258 A11
st. Fairfield 336 F13
st. Seven Hills 245 D15

DALES
cl. Blairmount 481 A14
rd. Silverdale 353 K12

DALEY
cl. Belimbla Pk 501 G16
pl. Fairfield W 335 B12
rd. Yagoona......... 369 B10
st. Pendle Hill...... 276 D16

DALEY THOMPSON
st. Newington......... M B16
st. Newington...... 309 K15

DALGETY
rd. Millers Point....... A A1
rd. Millers Point....... 1 C8
tce. Millers Point....... 1 C8

DALHOUSIE
st. Haberfield....... 343 C16

DALKEITH
la. Sans Souci 433 C13
pl. St Helens Pk... 511 J16
rd. Cherrybrook ... 219 B14
st. Busby............. 363 G16
st. Northbridge.... 285 K15
st. Ramsgate....... 433 C13
st. Sans Souci 433 C13

DALLAS
av. S Penrith 266 K4
pl. St Ives............ 224 G9
pl. Toongabbie 275 H11

DALLEY
av. Pagewood 406 B9
av. Vaucluse 348 C6
la. Redfern 20 B8
la. Pagewood, off Holloway St 406 B10
la. Bondi Jctn, off Waverley Cr 377 F3
rd. Heathcote....... 518 G9
st. Harris Park 308 E8
st. Jamisontown.. 265 J2
st. Kogarah 432 K4
st. Lidcombe 340 B7
st. Queenscliff 288 E2
st. Sydney ....A K11
st. Sydney 1 H13
st. Bondi Jctn, off Waverley St 377 G4

DALLEYS
rd. Naremburn..... 315 D3
rd. St Leonards.... 315 D3

DALLWOOD
av. Epping 250 E16

DALMAN
pl. Baulkham Hl... 246 H6
pl. Sylvania 462 B10

DALMAR
pl. Carlingford 280 D5
st. Croydon 342 G12

DALMATIA
av. Edmndsn Pk... 423 A4
st. Carramar 336 J15

DALMENY
av. Rosebery........ 375 K14
av. Rosebery........ 405 J1
av. Russell Lea..... 343 D7
dr. Prestons......... 393 E14
dr. Prestons......... 393 D16
rd. Northbridge.... 286 E15

DALPRA
cr. Bossley Park .. 333 E12

DALPURA
pl. Bangor........... 459 A15
st. Cromer........... 228 D14

DALRAY
st. Lalor Park....... 245 E9

DALRYMPLE
av. Chatswd W.....284 D14
av. Chatswd W.....284 F13
av. Lane Cove W..284 D14
cr. Pymble...........223 J16
pl. Barden Rdg....488 G2
DALSTRAITH
pl. Glen Alpine.....510 D14
DALTON
av. Condell Park...398 E1
av. Eastwood.......281 E9
av. Homebush......341 A7
av. Lucas Ht.........487 K12
cl. Rouse Hill.......185 D4
la. Mosman, off Awaba St.........317 A4
pl. Fairfield W......335 A11
pl. Prestons.........393 C13
rd. Mosman.........317 A4
rd. St Ives Ch.......223 K4
st. Colyton...........270 G5
DALWOOD
av. Seaforth..........287 A8
pl. Carlingford.....249 E13
pl. Eschol Park....481 F3
pl. Mt Annan........509 J1
DALY
av. Concord.........341 H9
av. N Wahrnga.....222 K2
ct. Wrrngtn Cty....238 F7
la. Wrrngtn Cty, off Daly Ct............238 F7
rd. Faulconbdg.....171 C10
st. Bilgola............169 G6
DALZIEL
av. Panania..........428 C3
st. Engadine........489 D13
st. Fairfield W......335 A12
DAMEELI
av. Kirrawee.........491 A4
DAME MARY GILMORE
rd. Oatley.............430 G11
DAMIEN
av. Greystanes.....306 G5
av. S Penrith........266 K5
DAMON
av. Epping............250 E15
cl. Glendenning...242 H4
DAMOUR
av. E Lindfield......254 J12
st. Holsworthy.....396 D16
DAMPIER
av. Wrrngtn Cty....238 F5
cr. Fairfield W......335 C9
pl. Leumeah.........482 F11
pl. Prestons.........393 H7
pl. Whalan...........240 J9
st. Chifley............437 A5
st. Kurnell............465 J9
DAMSEL
ct. Castle Hill.......217 G4
DAN
av. Blacktown.......244 B13
av. Maroubra.......407 F14
cr. Castle Hill.......218 F15
cr. Colyton...........270 B5
cr. Lansvale.........366 E9
st. Campbelltwn...511 J3
st. Marsfield.........282 A7
st. Merrylands.....307 C10
DANA
cl. Castle Hill.......247 F2
pde. Regents Pk.....369 A3
DANALAM
st. Liverpool........394 K8
DANBURITE
pl. Eagle Vale.......481 H4
DANBURY
cl. Marsfield........282 A6
DANBY
st. Prospect.........275 A11
DANDAR
pl. Bradbury........511 C15
DANDARBONG
av. Bangor...........459 B14
av. Carlingford.....280 D7
DANDENONG
cl. Bossley Park...334 B6
cr. Ruse...............512 H6
rd. Terrey Hills.....196 E6
DANELLA
st. The Oaks........502 F9
DANGAR
cl. Hinchinbrk......363 B13
pl. Chippendale......19 A3
pl. Davidson........255 C2
rd. Brooklyn...........76 D11
st. Chippendale......19 A4
st. Lindfield..........254 F14
st. Randwick..........377 A10
wy. Airds...............512 A14
DANGIN
cl. Bonnyrigg.......364 C9
DANIEL
av. Baulkham Hl...246 J12
cl. Cherrybrook....220 A6
la. St Clair, off Daniel Pde.......269 J9
pde. St Clair...........269 J9
pl. Green Valley....362 K10
st. Botany............405 G10
st. Granville.........308 C11
st. Greystanes......306 D8
st. Leichhardt..........9 C15
st. Wetherill Pk....334 E3
DANIELA
pl. Blacktown.......273 G5
DANIELS
rd. Bidwill.............211 H16
rd. Bidwill.............241 G3
rd. Hassall Gr.......211 H16
rd. Hebersham......241 G3
rd. Oakhurst..........241 G3
st. Chippendale......18 J2
DANIEL WILLIAMS
pl. Glenbrook.......234 D11
DANKS
st. Waterloo...........19 J12
DANNY
rd. Lalor Park.......245 D11
st. Werrington.....238 H11
DANS
av. Coogee...........377 G12
DANTIC
pl. Cherrybrook....219 B12
DANUBE
cr. Kearns............451 A14
pl. St Clair............270 B8
DAPHINE
la. Kingswood, off Daphine Cl.......238 A14
DAPHNE
av. Bankstown......399 G3
av. Castle Hill........247 J4
cl. Cherrybrook....220 A6
cl. Kingswood......238 A14
la. Botany............405 E10
pl. Blacktown.......244 K10
pl. Mcquarie Fd....454 F7
st. Botany............405 E10
st. Caringbah.......492 H16
st. Merrylands.....307 C10
st. West Ryde......280 H13
DAPLYN
wy. Claymore........481 A12
DAPTO
cl. Prestons.........393 A14
pl. Bangor............459 A14
DARA
cr. Glenmore Pk...266 C7
D'ARAM
st. Hunters Hill.....313 H10
DARANGAN
cl. Waterfall.........519 D11
DARAYA
rd. Marayong.......244 A8
st. Colyton...........270 B6
DARCEY
rd. Castle Hill........248 E4
st. Prestons.........393 B10
D'ARCY
av. Lidcombe.......339 H11
wy. Minto..............482 K1
wy. Minto..............483 A1
DARCY
av. Appin.............568 F9
pl. E Kurrajong.......56 G4
rd. Wentwthvle.....276 H13
rd. Wentwthvle.....277 A14
rd. Westmead.......277 A14
st. Casula.............423 H2
st. Granville.........308 K11
st. Marsfield.........282 A5
st. Parramatta......308 C4
D'ARCY IRVINE
dr. Castle Hill........218 K12
DARDANELLES
rd. Chatswd W.....284 F11
st. Mortdale.........431 D8
DARE
st. Glenwood.......215 C13
DAREEN
st. Beacon Hill.....257 B5
st. Frenchs Frst....257 B5
DARGAN
st. Naremburn......315 E2
st. S Windsor.......150 K1
st. Yagoona.........368 F14
DARGHAN
la. Glebe...............12 E10
st. Glebe...............12 E10
DARGIE
pl. Eagle Vale.......481 A9
st. Mt Pritchard....364 J10
DARICE
pl. Plumpton.........242 D12
DARIUS
av. N Narrabeen....199 B15
DARK
cl. Edensor Pk.....363 F3
DARKON
pl. Oakhurst.........241 H2
DARLEY
la. Newtown.........374 J10
la. Randwick..........22 D16
pl. Darlinghurst.......4 F11
rd. Bardwell Pk.....402 J7
rd. Centnnial Pk.....22 B16
rd. Leichhardt..........9 C13
rd. Manly.............288 H10
rd. Randwick........376 H10
st. Darlinghurst.......4 F11
st. Forestville.......255 K13
st. Killarney Ht.....255 K13
st. Marrickville.....373 F11
st. Mona Vale.......199 C2
st. Neutral Bay........5 K6
st. Newtown.........374 H11
st. Sans Souci......433 B15
st. Thirlmere........562 D16
st. Thirlmere........565 D1
st.e, Mona Vale......199 E4
st.w, Mona Vale......199 B1
DARLING
av. Kentlyn...........512 J7
av. Lurnea............394 D13
av. Ruse...............512 H1
av. Ruse...............512 J7
dr. Haymarket..........E A8
dr. Haymarket...........3 A9
dr. Sydney...............3 A4
la. Glebe...............12 D10
la. Kensington, off Darling St........376 E12
pl. Sylvania Wtr....462 E10
st. Abbotsbury.....333 A13
st. Balmain.............7 F8
st. Balmain East......8 C9
st. Bronte.............378 A7
st. Chatswood......284 K5
st. Glebe...............12 D10
st. Greystanes......306 A5
st. Homebush B.....M B6
st. Kensington......376 E12
st. Penrith............237 A14
st. Roseville.........284 K5
st. Rozelle............344 D8
st. St Ives............224 F9
DARLINGHURST
rd. Darlinghurst.......4 F13
rd. Potts Point.........4 J7
DARLING ISLAND
rd. Pyrmont.............8 H16
DARLING POINT
rd. Darling Point....13 H9
DARLINGTON
dr. Cherrybrook....219 C11
la. Darlington........18 D7
rd. Darlington........18 D7
rd. Newtown..........18 D7
DARLY
pl. Dharruk...........241 C8
st. Miranda..........492 C6
DARMENIA
av. Greystanes......306 E11
DARMOUR
av. Allambie Ht.....257 C10
DARNAY
pl. Ambarvale.......540 E1
DARNLEY
st. Gordon...........253 K4
DAROOK PARK
rd. Cronulla..........523 H1
DARRA
pl. St Johns Pk....364 D1
DARRAGH
la. Haberfield..........9 A15
DARRAMBAL
av. Baulkham Hl...248 C10
DARRELL
pl. Oakhurst.......241 K4
DARREN
ct. Glenwood.......215 K16
DARRI
av. N Wahrnga.....222 F3
av. S Penrith........266 F2
DARRYL
pl. Gymea Bay.....491 F8
DART
rd. Bringelly.........388 A9
DARTBROOK
rd. Auburn..........339 F2
DARTFORD
rd. Thornleigh......221 D6
st. Mt Pritchard...364 B11
DARTLE
wy. Ambarvale......511 A15
DARTMOOR
cct. Emu Heights...235 A5
la. Emu Heights, off Dartmoor Cct..235 B6
DART THRU
la. Croydon Pk....372 B6
DARU
pl. Glenfield.........424 F10
wy. Whalan...........241 B10
DARVALL
rd. Denistone W...280 J12
rd. Eastwood........280 G8
rd. West Ryde......280 J12
st. Balmain.............7 J11
st. Centnnial Pk.....21 D9
st. St Leonards.....315 E4
DARVELL
st. Bonnyrigg Ht..363 G5
DARVILL
rd. Orchard Hills..268 B13
DARWIN
av. Little Bay........437 G14
cl. Wakeley.........334 K13
dr. Lapstone........264 H2
pl. Barden Rdg....458 G16
rd. Campbelltwn..512 B6
st. Carlingford.....280 A1
st. West Ryde......281 A16
DARYL
st. Merrylnds W..306 H12
wy. Claymore.......481 D12
DASEA
st. Chullora.........369 G5
DASHMERE
st. Bossley Park..333 K9
DASSAULT
cl. Raby.............451 F12
DATCHETT
st. Balmain.............8 F9
st. Balmain East......8 F9
DATE
pl. Glenwood.......215 J16
DAUNT
av. Matraville.......406 J16
DAVENEY
wy. W Pnnant Hl...248 K2
DAVENPORT
dr. Wallacia.........324 K15
DAVESTA
rd. Springwood...172 C16
DAVEY
ct. Emu Heights...235 A6
rd. Dural.............188 G7
st. Jannali...........460 K12
st. Lidcombe.......339 K9
DAVID
av. Caringbah.......492 H14
av. Casula...........394 G13
av. North Ryde......282 F6
cl. St Ives Ch.......224 A5
la. Blacktown......244 G16
la. Forest Lodge....11 J16
la. Crows Nest, off Emmett St.......315 G8
pl. Mt Annan.......479 H15
pl. Peakhurst.......430 A3
pl. Seaforth.........286 J12
rd. Barden Rdg....488 G3
rd. Castle Hill......219 A14
rd. Cherrybrook...219 A14
rd. Collaroy Plat...228 J14
rd. Emu Plains.....235 F7
rd. Springwood....202 A4
rd.e, Springwood....202 B5
st. Concord.........342 A8
st. Crows Nest.....315 G8
st. Croydon.........372 C2
st. Dundas Vy......280 A9
st. Earlwood........403 D3
st. Forest Lodge....11 H16
st. Glenbrook.......234 A14
st. Greenacre.......370 E7
st. Marrickville.....373 H12
st. Mascot...........405 H4
st. Mosman.........317 D12
st. Mt Pritchard...364 G10
st. S Wntwthvle...306 J9
st. Wilberforce.......91 K4
DAVIDSON
av. Concord.........341 F5
av. Forestville.......255 H9
av. North Rocks....278 J3
av. N Strathfield....341 F5
av. Warrawee.......222 H9
cl. St Clair..........270 A14
cr. Maroubra.......407 C15
la. Concord.........341 G4
la. Lakemba.........401 A2
la. St Clair, off Davidson Cl.....269 K14
pde. Cremorne.......316 G5
pl. Airds.............512 D11
rd. Guildford........338 C10
rd. Menai............458 G8
st. Balmain.............7 F11
st. Greenacre.......370 G2
DAVID THEILE
av. Newington.........M C16
av. Newington......309 K15
DAVIES
av. Springwood....201 C7
av. Vaucluse.........348 G1
ct. Baulkham Hl...247 G14
la. Surry Hills........20 C4
rd. Padstow.........399 F13
rd. Seven Hills.....275 D4
st. Chatswd W.....284 E9
st. Leichhardt.........15 C2
st. Marsden Pk....182 A11
st. Merrylands.....307 D15
st. Mount Druitt....240 H16
st. Newington.........L H11
st. Newington......310 D11
st. N Parramatta..278 C9
st. Surry Hills........20 B4
wy. Claymore........481 B12
DAVIESIA
pl. Glenmore Pk...265 H14
DAVINA
cr. Cecil Hills.......362 J5
DAVIS
av. Baulkham Hl...248 A7
av. Epping...........281 D4
la. Bankstown......369 F11
la. Pitt Twn Bttms..122 B3
la. Woollahra.........22 H5
la. Yagoona.........369 F11
pl. Bligh Park......150 D5
pl. Glenhaven......217 J1
pl. Menai............458 K10
pl. Rooty Hill.......272 C3
pl. Thirlmere........565 B1
rd. Marayong.......244 C10
rd. Wetherill Pk....304 E13
st. Dulwich Hill....373 D7
st. Richmond.......120 A5
swy. Liverpool, off Northumberland St.....................395 D3
DAVISON
la. Picton............563 F3
st. Cromer...........228 D16
st. Merrylands.....307 E7
DAVOREN
la. Surry Hills........20 C2
DAVY
pl. St Helens Pk...541 A10
st. Warwck Frm...365 E15
DAVY ROBINSON
dr. Chipping Ntn..397 A6
DAWES
av. Castle Hill.......217 G13
av. Regents Pk.....369 E3
cr. Eastwood........281 G8
pl. Barden Rdg....488 F3

pl. Bligh Park ... 150 J8
pl. Cherrybrook ... 219 G12
pl. Lapstone ... 264 J3
pl. Ruse ... 512 H4
rd. Belrose ... 226 C14
st. Little Bay ... 437 B12
st. Mt Pritchard ... 364 C9
st. Wentwthvle ... 306 G2
DAWKINS
pl. Ambarvale ... 510 J12
DAWN
av. Chester Hill ... 368 D6
av. Mt Pritchard ... 364 D12
cl. Lurnea ... 394 C6
cr. Mt Riverview ... 234 C1
cr. Regents Pk ... 339 B15
dr. Seven Hills ... 245 B16
st. Greystanes ... 305 G7
st. Peakhurst ... 430 C6
DAWN FRASER
av. Homebush B ... M F9
av. Homebush B ... 340 E2
DAWSON
av. Camden S ... 506 K15
av. Earlwood ... 402 G3
av. Thornleigh ... 221 C14
la. Bass Hill ... 368 D10
la. Woollahra ... 22 H5
ml. Mount Druitt ... 241 E16
pl. Bass Hill ... 367 H7
pl. Menai ... 458 K11
pl. Ruse ... 512 E5
pl. Turramurra ... 252 D3
rd. Mt Hunter ... 505 B8
st. Croydon ... 342 F12
st. Epping ... 250 F12
st. Fairfield Ht ... 335 G12
st. Naremburn ... 315 J2
st. Rookwood ... 340 C12
st. Surry Hills ... 19 H3
DAX
pl. Prospect ... 274 H10
DAY
av. Kensington ... 376 C15
av. Richmond ... 118 E9
la. Kensington ... 376 E16
la. Kingsford ... 406 E2
pl. Minto ... 482 K9
pl. Prospect ... 274 J10
rd. Cheltenham ... 251 A8
st. Ashcroft ... 394 E1
st. Avalon ... 140 A14
st. Chatswood ... 284 H9
st. Colyton ... 270 C4
st. Drummoyne ... 344 A3
st. Lansvale ... 366 J7
st. Leichhardt ... 15 G1
st. Marrickville ... 373 G16
st. Sydney ... C C13
st. Sydney ... E D1
st. Windsor ... 121 B10
st.n, Silverwater ... 310 A14
st.s, Lidcombe ... 339 J1
DAYDREAM
av. Hinchinbrk ... 393 A1
st. Warriewood ... 198 G4
DAYMAN
pl. Marsfield ... 251 J15
DAYMAR
pl. Avalon ... 139 J12
pl. Castle Cove ... 286 B5
DAYRELL
av. Mosman ... 317 G9
DAYS
av. Hurstville ... 431 K9
DEADMAN
rd. Moorebank ... 395 J8
DEAKIN
av. Glenwood ... 215 H13
av. Haberfield ... 343 D15
av. Penrith ... 237 C7
cl. Springwood ... 202 E11
pl. Bonnyrigg ... 364 C3
pl. East Killara ... 254 H6
pl. Kirrawee ... 490 J5
pl. W Pnnant Hl ... 249 A8
st. Concord ... 311 K15
st. Ermington ... 280 E16
st. Forestville ... 256 A7
st. Silverwater ... 309 E13
st. West Ryde ... 311 A1
DEAL
cl. Green Valley ... 363 B10
DEAN
av. Belmore ... 371 E15
cl. Oakdale ... 500 D11
cr. Ermington ... 280 G15
ct. Baulkham Hl ... 247 B14
la. Crows Nest, off Willoughby La ... 315 F7
pl. Penrith ... 236 K5
st. Caringbah ... 492 F14
st. Granville ... 308 E11
st. Greystanes ... 306 E7
st. Strathfield S ... 371 B6
st. W Pnnant Hl ... 249 K2
DEANE
pl. Bligh Park ... 150 G7
st. Burwood ... 342 A14
st. Glenbrook ... 263 J1
DEANS
rd. Airds ... 512 B11
DEBBIE
cct. Mount Druitt ... 241 H12
DEBBY
wy. Toongabbie ... 276 A6
DEBENHAM
av. Leumeah ... 482 H12
DEBORAH
av. Lidcombe ... 340 A7
cl. Fairfield ... 336 E6
cl. Mt Colah ... 192 A4
cr. Cambrdg Pk ... 237 J7
pl. Eastwood ... 281 F4
pl. Punchbowl ... 400 E7
pl. Riverstone ... 183 B7
rd. Annangrove ... 186 D3
st. Greystanes ... 305 H6
DEBRINCAT
av. N St Marys ... 239 K11
av. Tregear ... 240 D9
av. Whalan ... 240 D9
DE BURGH
rd. Killara ... 253 E15
DEBUSSY
pl. Cranebrook ... 207 J9
DE CASTELLA
dr. Blacktown ... 273 G6
DECCAN
wy. Bidwill ... 211 G13
DE CHAIR
av. Springwood ... 202 B5
rd. Narraweena ... 258 C7
DECKER
pl. Huntingwd ... 273 J12
DEE
pl. Prospect ... 274 K13
DEEBAN
wk. Cronulla ... 493 J12
DEEBLE
st. Tennyson ... 312 E11
DEED
pl. Northmead ... 277 H7
DEEPFIELDS
rd. Catherine Fd ... 449 H2
DEEP POOL
wy. Mt Annan ... 479 D14
DEEPWATER
rd. Castle Cove ... 285 F4
DEERWOOD
av. Liverpool ... 395 B10
DEESIDE
av. Baulkham Hl ... 246 K12
cl. S Penrith ... 266 K2
la. S Penrith, off Deeside Cl ... 266 K2
DEE WHY
la. N Curl Curl, off Headland Rd ... 259 C9
pde. Dee Why ... 258 J5
pl. Woodbine ... 481 H9
DEFARGE
wy. Ambarvale ... 541 A1
DEFOE
la. Wiley Park ... 400 F2
pl. Wetherill Pk ... 334 G5
pl. Winston Hills ... 247 F16
st. Wiley Park ... 400 F2
DEFRIES
pl. Doonside ... 273 F4
DEHAVILLAND
cr. Raby ... 451 H15
DEHLSEN
av. W Pnnant Hl ... 249 H6
DEIRDRE
dr. Riverstone ... 183 C7
DELA
cl. Dee Why ... 258 E5
cl. St Ives Ch ... 224 A5
DELAGE
pl. Ingleburn ... 453 K7
DELAGOA
pl. Caringbah ... 492 K7
DELAIGH
av. Baulkham Hl ... 247 C7
av. N Curl Curl ... 258 H10
DELAMERE
st. Canley Vale ... 335 J16
DELANEY
av. Silverdale ... 353 J15
dr. Baulkham Hl ... 247 B1
dr. Doonside ... 243 C5
la. Revesby Ht ... 428 J5
DE LANGE
pl. Oakhurst ... 242 C1
DELANGE
rd. Putney ... 312 A8
DELARUE
st. Richmond ... 119 K5
DE LA SALLE
pl. Castle Hill ... 218 K10
DELAUNAY
st. Ingleburn ... 453 F13
DE LAURET
av. Newport ... 169 E7
DELAVOR
pl. Glenhaven ... 217 J3
DELAWARE
av. St Ives ... 224 C8
rd. Ermington ... 280 C13
rd. Horsley Pk ... 301 K16
st. Epping ... 250 H15
DELECTA
av. Clareville ... 169 F1
av. Mosman ... 286 K15
DELEWARE
rd. Riverstone ... 182 E9
DELFIN
dr. Wattle Grove ... 395 H13
DELGARNO
rd. Bonnyrigg Ht ... 363 E8
DELGAUN
pl. Baulkham Hl ... 246 J11
DELHI
rd. Chatswd W ... 283 B9
rd. Mcquarie Pk ... 283 B9
rd. North Ryde ... 283 B9
st. Lidcombe ... 340 A6
DELIA
av. Revesby ... 398 J15
pde. Engadine ... 518 F4
DELIVERY
dr. Randwick, off Hospital Rd ... 377 A15
DELL
pl. Georges Hall ... 367 H9
st. Belrose ... 225 K5
st. Blacktown ... 274 A3
st. Woodpark ... 306 G16
DELLA
pl. Glendenning ... 242 G3
DELLER
av. Cabramtta W ... 365 A8
pl. Blakehurst ... 432 D13
DELLIT
pl. Doonside ... 273 G3
DELLS
la. Lowlands ... 88 H11
DELLVIEW
la. Tamarama, off Silva St ... 378 B6
st. Glenbrook ... 264 B2
st. Tamarama ... 378 C6
DELLWOOD
av. Earlwood ... 372 J16
st. Bankstown ... 399 D4
st. Chatswd W ... 284 E12
st. S Granville ... 338 E4
DELMAR
pde. Dee Why ... 258 G7
pde. Gladesville ... 312 F12
DELOITTE
av. Birchgrove ... 7 H1
DELORAINE
cl. Hinchinbrk ... 363 A16
dr. Leonay ... 234 J14
DELPHINIUM
pl. Kellyville ... 216 D3
wy. Kellyville, off Delphinium Pl ... 216 D3
DELRAY
av. Wahroonga ... 223 B4
DELTA
cl. Raby ... 451 D11
pl. Blacktown ... 245 D8
pl. Lane Cove ... 314 F5
pl. Sutherland ... 490 B1
rd. Lane Cove ... 314 F4
row. Wrrngtn Dns ... 238 E4
DELVES
st. Mortdale ... 430 J5
DELWOOD
cl. Mona Vale ... 199 E1
DEMAINE
av. Bexley North ... 402 D9
DE MESTRE
pl. Sydney ... A J15
DEMETRIUS
rd. Rsemeadow ... 540 D3
DE MEYRICK
av. Casula ... 394 E12
av. Lurnea ... 394 E12
DE MILHAU
rd. Hunters Hill ... 313 D11
DEMPSEY
pl. Drummoyne ... 343 H2
st. Emu Heights ... 235 A5
st. North Ryde ... 282 E11
DEMPSTER
cr. Regents Pk ... 339 B16
DENAWEN
av. Castle Cove ... 285 K5
DENBERN
st. Bossley Park ... 334 A8
st. Dean Park ... 242 H2
DENBIGH
pl. Harringtn Pk ... 478 E5
pl. Menai ... 458 H9
DENBY
st. Marrickville ... 374 D9
DENDROBIUM
cr. Elanora Ht ... 197 J15
DENEB
pl. Hinchinbrk ... 393 D5
DENFIELD
cct. St Helens Pk ... 541 A5
la. Tahmoor ... 565 J13
DENGATE
av. Ashfield ... 372 J2
st. Epping ... 250 F16
DENHAM
la. Surry Hills ... 4 D14
la. Bondi, off Edward St ... 378 B4
pl. Dundas ... 279 E13
rd. Kenthurst ... 187 K9
st. Bondi ... 378 B5
st. Bondi Beach ... 378 B5
st. Rhodes ... 311 E8
st. Surry Hills ... 4 C14
DENHAM COURT
rd. Denham Ct ... 422 A13
DENIEHY
st. Granville ... 309 A11
DENING
cl. Chipping Ntn ... 366 E16
st. Drummoyne ... 343 F2
DENINTEND
pl. S Penrith ... 266 F3
DENISE
av. Glenbrook ... 263 J2
cr. Peakhurst ... 430 C4
pl. Hornsby ... 221 E6
DENISON
av. Lurnea ... 394 E13
la. Camperdwn ... 17 D8
la. Newtown ... 17 D8
pl. Appin ... 568 F8
pl. Cromer ... 227 H13
pl. Windsor Dn ... 180 K3
rd. Dulwich Hill ... 373 D9
rd. Lewisham ... 15 A13
st. Arncliffe ... 403 E6
st. Bnksmeadw ... 406 E13
st. Bondi Jctn ... 22 E11
st. Camperdwn ... 17 C4
st. Carramar ... 366 K3
st. Concord ... 342 B2
st. Eastgardens ... 406 E13
st. Granville ... 308 A7
st. Hillsdale ... 406 E13
st. Hornsby ... 191 J14
st. Manly ... 288 H8
st. Newtown ... 17 D8
st. N Sydney ... K F7
st. N Sydney ... 5 G7
st. Parramatta ... 308 A7
st. Penshurst ... 431 H7
st. Queens Park ... 22 E11
st. Rozelle ... 10 H1
st. Ruse ... 512 H3
st. Villawood ... 367 A3
DENISTONE
rd. Denistone ... 281 D9
rd. Eastwood ... 281 D9
rd. N Parramatta ... 278 G8
DENIS WINSTON
dr. Doonside ... 273 F2
DENLEY
la. St Ives ... 223 K12
DENMAN
av. Caringbah ... 492 J7
av. Haberfield ... 343 B14
av. Wiley Park ... 400 H4
av. Woolooware ... 493 D8
ct. Glenwood ... 245 G1
la. Glebe ... 12 E12
pde. Normanhurst ... 221 F9
rd. Georges Hall ... 367 F11
st. Eastwood ... 280 H10
st. Hurstville ... 431 J8
st. Turramurra ... 222 F14
DENMARK
rd. Riverstone ... 182 H10
st. Merrylands ... 307 G15
DENMEAD
st. Thirlmere ... 565 C10
DENNING
st. Petersham ... 16 B13
st. S Coogee ... 407 H4
DENNIS
av. Wahroonga ... 222 B12
av. West Hoxton ... 362 B15
pl. Beverly Hills ... 401 B15
st. Campbelltwn ... 512 A5
st. Colyton ... 270 J9
st. Ermington ... 310 A1
st. Greystanes ... 306 E7
st. Lakemba ... 371 B16
st. Lakemba ... 401 B1
st. Lalor Park ... 245 E12
st. Thirlmere ... 565 C7
DENNISON
cl. Rouse Hill ... 129 D6
DENNISTOUN
av. Guildford ... 337 A5
av. Guildford W ... 336 H5
av. Yennora ... 336 H5
DENNY
rd. Picnic Point ... 428 B7
DENT
cl. Hinchinbrk ... 363 B14
pl. Shalvey ... 210 K14
st. Bnksmeadw ... 435 J1
st. Epping ... 250 C16
st. Jamisontown ... 236 E14
DENTON
gr. Quakers Hill ... 214 A9
la. Cabramatta, off Arthur St ... 365 J7
pl. Wallacia ... 324 K15
DENTS
pl. Gymea Bay ... 491 C9
DENVER
pl. Toongabbie ... 275 H12
rd. St Clair ... 270 G11
DENYA
cl. Glenmore Pk ... 266 E8
DENZIL
av. St Clair ... 270 A9
la. St Clair, off Denzil Av ... 269 K10
DEODAR
wy. Blacktown ... 274 E12
DEODARA
gdn. N Turramrra ... 223 D2
DEPARTURE
plz. Mascot ... 404 D6
DEPOT
la. Marrickville, off Malakoff St ... 373 K12
pl. Bankstown ... 369 D16
rd. Mortdale ... 430 F7
st. Rooty Hill ... 272 D1
DEPTFORD
av. Kings Lngly ... 245 G5
DERBY
cr. Chipping Ntn ... 396 H1
la. Camperdwn ... 17 D6
la. Surry Hills ... F J14

pl. Camperdwn......17 C5
pl. Glebe......12 F16
pl. Glossodia......59 B9
pl. Yarrawarrah......489 E13
pwy. *Chipping Ntn, off Derby Cr......366 H16*
pwy. *Chipping Ntn, off Derby Cr......396 H1*
rd. Hornsby......222 C1
st. Blacktown......244 C15
st. Camperdwn......17 C6
st. Canley Ht......365 D4
st. Epping......251 B12
st. Kingswood......237 E13
st. Kogarah......433 B5
st. Merrylands......308 B16
st. Minto......452 H16
st. Minto Ht......483 F1
st. Penrith......237 A12
st. Rooty Hill......242 C15
st. St Ives......224 C15
st. Silverwater......309 F11
st. Vaucluse......318 G16
DERBYSHIRE
av. Toongabbie......276 F9
rd. Leichhardt......10 A10
rd. Lilyfield......10 A8
DEREK
pl. Hassall Gr......212 C15
DERMONT
st. Hassall Gr......211 J14
DERNA
av. Holsworthy......426 E8
cr. Allambie Ht......257 F11
rd. Holsworthy......396 C16
DERNANCOURT
av. Engadine......518 J1
pde. Milperra......397 H11
DEROWIE
av. Homebush......341 A7
DERRIA
st. Canley Ht......365 D3
DERRIBONG
cr. Bangor......459 C13
pl. Thornleigh......221 B6
st. Villawood......367 D4
DERRIG
rd. Tennyson......58 B11
DERRILIN
cl. Bangor......459 B14
DERRING
la. Kurrajong......55 C12
DERRIWONG
la. Dural......189 B11
rd. Dural......188 G8
rd. Dural......189 A13
DERRY
wy. Bonnyrigg......364 B3
DERWENT
av. N Wahrnga......222 K2
ct. Wattle Grove......395 H12
la. Glebe......12 C14
pde. Blacktown......274 A4
pl. Bligh Park......150 G7
pl. Bossley Park......333 F5
pl. Castle Hill......247 K5
pl. Kearns......481 C1
pl. St Clair......300 C1
rd. Bringelly......387 K5
st. Collaroy Plat......228 D11
st. Glebe......12 C14
st. Mount Druitt......241 C12
st. S Hurstville......432 B10
DE SAXE
cl. Thornleigh......220 G11
DESBOROUGH
rd. Colyton......269 J5
rd. St Marys......269 J5
DESDEMONA
st. Rsemeadow......540 F6
DESLEY
cr. Prospect......274 H13
DESLIE
av. Werrington......238 F11
DESMOND
st. Eastwood......281 H3
st. Ingleburn......453 C10
st. Merrylands......307 B13
st. Merrylnds W......307 B13
DESOUTTER
av. Bnkstn Aprt......367 J16
DESPOINTES
st. Marrickville......373 K12
DETTMANN
av. Longueville......314 C8
DETZNER
pl. Whalan......240 K9
DEVANEY
av. Glenmore Pk......265 J8
st. Blackett......241 D2
DEVENISH
st. Greenfld Pk......334 B12
DEVERE
av. Belrose......226 A13
DEVERON
pl. St Andrews......481 K1
DE VILLIERS
av. Chatswd W......284 E11
DE VILNITS
pde. Penrith......236 F10
DEVILS
cr. Bowen Mtn......83 J7
DEVINE
st. Erskineville......374 K10
DEVITT
cr. The Oaks......502 F14
pl. Hillsdale......406 H15
st. Blacktown......244 J16
st. Narrabeen......229 A7
DEVLIN
pl. Menai......458 J6
pl. Quakers Hill......214 B12
rd. Castlereagh......145 H14
rd. Londonderry......177 A1
rd. N Epping......251 C10
st. Ashcroft......364 F15
st. Ryde......311 K2
wy. Bonnyrigg......364 C6
DEVON
cl. Bossley Park......334 B12
pl. Busby......363 K15
pl. Collaroy......229 A15
pl. Galston......159 E10
pl. Narellan Vale......508 J2
pl. North Rocks......278 J2
rd. Bardwell Pk......402 J7
rd. Cambrdg Pk......237 K9
rd. Ingleburn......452 K6
st. N Epping......251 E11
st. Rooty Hill......272 D3
st. Rosehill......309 C8
st. Wahroonga......223 C4
DEVONPORT
st. Wakeley......334 G16
DEVONSHIRE
rd. Kemps Ck......360 C16
rd. Rossmore......390 B7
st. Chatswood......284 K11
st. Crows Nest......315 G6
st. Croydon......372 B2
st. Surry Hills......19 H2
DEWAR
pl. Riverstone......183 C8
pl. St Andrews......451 J14
st. Campsie......371 K13
DEWBERRY
cl. Menai......458 J13
wy. Castle Hill......248 H3
DEWDNEY
rd. Emu Plains......235 H11
DEWDROP
pl. Wrrngtn Dns......238 C4
DEWEY
ct. Maroubra......407 E14
pl. St Helens Pk......540 K11
DEWHURST
av. Castle Hill......218 B10
DE WITT
la. Bankstown......399 D4
pl. Fairfield W......335 C10
pl. Willmot......210 E13
st. Bankstown......399 D5
DEWRANG
av. Bradbury......511 D15
av. Elanora Ht......198 E16
st. Carss Park......432 F13
st. Lidcombe......339 J4
DEWSBURY
st. Botany......405 E14
swy. Liverpool......395 E3
DEXTER
la. Rockdale......403 B15
pl. Plumpton......242 C10
st. St Helens Pk......541 A6
DHARUG
cl. Mulgoa......324 A5
DIAMANTINA
av. Windsor Dn......151 A16
cl. St Clair......270 G12
DIAMOND
av. Glenwood......215 E14
av. Granville......308 F12
cr. Bonnyrigg......363 G8
pl. Eagle Vale......481 C7
DIAMOND BAY
rd. Vaucluse......348 E6
DIAMOND HILL
dr. Kurrajong Hl......55 C8
DIAMONTINA
av. Kearns......451 C16
DIANA
av. Kellyville......216 D3
av. Roselands......400 J7
av. West Pymble......252 G12
ct. Cecil Hills......363 A4
pl. S Penrith......267 B7
st. Pendle Hill......306 E2
DIANE
cl. Greenacre......370 C6
dr. Lalor Park......245 H12
st. Marsfield......281 K4
DIANELLA
pl. Kingswood......267 H2
pl. Mt Annan......509 E4
st. Caringbah......492 J5
DIANNE
pl. Berowra Ht......132 J9
pl. Hawksbry Ht......174 J4
DIANTHUS
pl. Jannali......460 J10
DIBBLE
av. Marrickville......373 D14
DIBBLER
pl. St Helens Pk......541 G2
DIBBS
la. Alexandria......18 F15
st. Alexandria......18 F15
st. Canterbury......372 E14
st. Centnnial Pk......20 K14
DICK
st. Balmain......7 G11
st. Chippendale......19 A2
st. Harbord......258 K16
st. Henley......313 B14
st. Randwick......377 E12
DICKENS
dr. Centnnial Pk......21 F11
rd. Ambarvale......511 A14
rd. Wetherill Pk......334 H6
st. Winston Hills......247 F16
DICKENSON
st. Panania......398 D14
DICKIN
av. Sandringham......463 D2
DICKINSON
av. Croydon......372 D2
DICKSON
av. Artarmon......314 J3
av. W Pnnant Hl......249 D10
av. West Ryde......281 B14
la. Bronte......377 J6
la. West Ryde......281 C15
la. *Newtown, off King La......374 J10*
rd. Denham Ct......422 F16
rd. Leppington......420 G6
st. Bronte......377 J7
st. Haberfield......343 D15
st. Newtown......374 H10
st. Strathfield......341 A12
DIEFFENBACH
tce. Bidwill......211 E16
DIETZ
la. Oakdale......500 F4
DIFFEY
la. Yagoona......368 H11
st. Yagoona......368 H11
DIGBY
pl. Chipping Ntn......366 G16
DIGGER
cr. Gt Mckrl Bch......109 A13
DIGGERS
av. Gladesville......312 J4
la. *Canley Vale, off Freeman Av......366 A3*
DIGGINS
st. Kellyville......186 A14
DIGHT
st. Richmond......119 B4
st. Windsor......121 B10
DILGA
cl. Bangor......459 C14
cr. Erskine Park......270 G15
st. Kings Lngly......245 G7
DILKARA
ct. Menai......459 A16
DILKE
rd. Padstow......429 F6
rd. Padstow Ht......429 F8
DILKERA
cl. Hornsby......191 C13
rd. Glenorie......127 K4
DILLON
cl. Barden Rdg......488 H2
la. Paddington......13 A12
pl. Oakhurst......242 C2
st. Paddington......4 K12
st. Ramsgate......433 D13
DILLWYNIA
dr. Glenmore Pk......265 H13
DILLWYNNIA
gr. Heathcote......518 H12
DILSTON
cl. West Hoxton......392 E6
DI MASCIO
pl. Oakhurst......211 H16
DIMBY
pl. Busby......363 G15
DIMENT
wy. Hurstville......432 A6
DINA BETH
av. Blacktown......273 J1
DIND
st. Milsons Pt......5 J16
DINDIMA
pl. Bangor......459 B14
pl. Belrose......226 B14
DINE
la. Randwick......407 B1
pl. Camden S......506 K13
st. Randwick......377 B16
DINGLE
st. Riverstone......183 A5
DINJERRA
cl. Bangor......459 A15
cr. Oatley......461 A1
DINMORE
pl. Castle Hill......219 A9
DINO
cl. Rooty Hill......271 J3
DINORA
st. Belmore......371 C14
DINTON
st. Prospect......274 K10
D'INZEO
pl. Hinchinbrk......393 A4
DION
pl. Plumpton......241 H8
DIONE
ct. St Clair......269 G11
DIOSMA
pl. Engadine......488 E14
DIPROSE
st. Fairfield......336 J15
DIRE STRAITS
wy. Berala......339 C15
DIRK
cl. Green Valley......363 B10
DISALVO
cl. Cabramtta W......365 C5
DISCOVERY
av. Willmot......210 C12
pl. Oyster Bay......461 D3
DISPENSARY
la. Campsie......371 K12
DISRAELI
rd. Winston Hills......277 J1
DISTILLERS
pl. Huntingwd......273 G12
DIVE
st. Matraville......406 J15
DIVISION
la. *Coogee, off Brook St......377 G13*
st. Coogee......377 G13
DIXMUDE
st. S Granville......338 G5
DIXON
av. Frenchs Frst......257 B3
cl. Illawong......459 H4
la. *Revesby, off Blamey Pl......398 J16*
rd. Blaxland......234 B4
st. Abbotsbury......333 C15
st. Haymarket......E D3
st. Haymarket......3 E10
st. Mount Druitt......271 E5
st. Parramatta......308 B7
st. Sydney......E D3
st. Sydney......3 E10
DIXSON
av. Dulwich Hill......373 B8
DOAK
av. Llandilo......178 D13
DOBBIE
pl. Glenorie......128 C5
DOBELL
cct. St Clair......270 B13
la. *St Clair, off Dobell Cct......270 B13*
pl. Kenthurst......158 A9
pl. St Ives......224 C9
rd. Claymore......481 C13
rd. Eagle Vale......480 K10
rd. Engadine......489 A15
st. Mt Pritchard......364 J11
DOBROYD
av. Camden......507 A9
la. Haberfield......9 B5
pde. Haberfield......342 K12
pde. Haberfield......343 G11
pde. Haberfield......343 D11
pde. Haberfield......343 C12
pde. Haberfield......343 B12
rd. Balgowlah Ht......287 J14
DOBROYD SCENIC
dr. Balgowlah Ht......287 K15
DOBSON
cl. Edensor Pk......363 F3
cr. Baulkham Hl......247 H10
cr. Dundas Vy......280 D10
cr. Ryde......282 C14
pl. Emu Heights......234 K6
st. Thornleigh......220 H10
DOBSON DORKING
pl. Faulconbdg......171 K12
DOBU
pl. Glenfield......424 G10
DOCHARTY
rd. Bradbury......511 J11
DOCK
rd. Birchgrove......7 J4
DOCKER
la. Chippendale......18 K2
DOCOS
cr. Bexley......432 D2
DOCTOR LAWSON
pl. Rooty Hill......272 F5
DODD
pl. Cranebrook......207 G12
DODDS
st. Naremburn......315 F3
DODFORD
rd. Llandilo......178 E14
DODS
pl. Doonside......273 F2
DODSON
av. Cronulla......493 H12
cr. Winston Hills......277 G4
DOHENY
cl. Baulkham Hl......247 B1
DOHERTY
av. Glenhaven......218 C2
st. Quakers Hill......214 F12
DOIG
av. Denistone E......281 H10
st. Wentwthvle......277 D10
DOLAN
la. Woollahra......22 F4
st. Ryde......312 E3
DOLANS
rd.s, Woolooware......493 D12
DOLGE
pl. Ambarvale......510 H15
DOLLIN
st. Colyton......270 C7
DOLOMITE
pl. Eagle Vale......481 E5
rd. Cranebrook......207 D14
DOLPHIN
cl. Clarmnt Ms......238 J16
cl. Green Valley......363 A12
cr. Avalon......140 D10
la. Coogee......377 E15
st. Coogee......377 E15
st. Randwick......377 C15
DOMAIN
ct. Bella Vista......246 J4

DOMBEY
pl. Ambarvale...... 510 J13
DOMINIC
st. Woolooware... 493 C12
DOMINION
cr. Mosman......... 317 F10
DOMINISH
cr. Camden S 506 K15
DON
cl. St Clair 269 K16
pl. Kearns............ 451 B15
st. Kurrajong Ht..... 53 K7
st. Newtown.......... 17 D14
DONAHUE
cl. Prairiewood.... 334 E9
DONALBAIN
cct. Rsemeadow ... 540 C4
DONALD
av. Epping............ 281 E3
pl. Bondi Jctn........ 22 J10
st. Carlingford 279 J2
st. Hurstville....... 431 H1
st. North Ryde..... 283 A10
st. Old Guildfrd.... 337 E11
st. Picnic Point.... 428 B7
st. Yennora 337 E11
DONALDSON
st. Bradbury 511 G10
st. Pagewood 406 D8
DONATO
st. Smithfield....... 336 A5
DONCASTER
av. Casula 394 G16
av. Cawdor 506 D16
av. Kensington...... 376 E15
av. Kingsford 406 E2
av. Narellan.......... 478 H10
av. West Pymble .. 252 G9
DONE
st. Arncliffe.......... 403 G7
DONEGAL
av. Smithfield....... 335 E2
pl. Rouse Hill....... 185 D8
rd. Killarney Ht..... 286 B2
DONELLY
pl. Frenchs Frst ... 255 G1
DONGOLA
cct. Schofields 213 J5
DONINGTON
av. Georges Hall... 368 C14
DON JUAN
av. Randwick 377 B15
DONLEA
wy. Mt Colah 162 E15
DON MILLS
av. Hebersham..... 241 F4
DONNA
pl. Acacia Gdn..... 214 G14
pl. Miranda.......... 491 J1
DONNAN
st. Bexley 402 G15
DONNELLAN
cct. Clovelly 377 K13
pl. Blacktown, off Campbell St.... 244 H16
pl. Blacktown, off Campbell St.... 274 H1
DONNELLY
cl. Liberty Gr 311 B10
st. Balmain 7 J12
st. Crows Nest..... 315 F4
st. Guildford 337 B2
st. Naremburn..... 315 F4
st. Putney............ 312 C7
DONOHOES
av. Mulgoa........... 323 K3
DONOHUE
st. Kings Park...... 244 D1
DONOVAN
av. Maroubra 406 G12
pl. Bonnyrigg 364 D5
st. Eastwood 281 J8
st. Revesby Ht..... 428 K6
DONS
rd. Dural.............. 189 E15
DOODSON
av. Lidcombe....... 339 J7
DOODY
st. Alexandria 375 D14
st. Gladesville...... 312 G11
DOOHAT
av. N Sydney...........K A2
av. N Sydney............ 5 E5
la. N Sydney...........K A3
DOOLAN
la. Balmain 7 A8
st. Dean Park....... 212 F16
DOOLEY
av. Bass Hill 368 C13
DOOMBEN
av. Eastwood 281 B6
cl. Casula 394 D15
DOON
dr. Sans Souci 462 K5
pl. St Andrews..... 482 A1
st. Marayong....... 243 G6
DOONKUNA
st. Beverly Hills.... 401 D8
DOONMORE
st. Penrith 237 A14
DOONSIDE
cr. Blacktown....... 243 J13
cr. Blacktown....... 244 B14
cr. Doonside........ 243 C13
cr. Woodcroft 243 C13
rd. Arndell Park.... 273 D9
rd. Doonside........ 243 C15
DORA
cr. Dundas........... 279 G14
st. Blacktown....... 274 E6
st. Hurstville........ 431 G1
st. Marsfield 282 C4
DORADILLO
pl. Eschol Park 481 B4
DORADO
pl. Hinchinbrk...... 393 D3
st. Erskine Park ... 270 F16
DORAHY
st. Dundas........... 279 K12
DORAL
pl. Liverpool 395 A10
DORAN
av. Lurnea........... 394 E7
dr. Castle Hill 217 F12
st. Kingsford........ 406 E2
DORCAS
pl. Rsemeadow.... 540 J10
DORE
pl. Mt Annan........ 479 H15
DOREEN
cr. Baulkham Hl ... 247 C10
DORHAUER
la. Woollahra......... 21 K4
pl. Woollahra......... 21 J4
DORIS
av. Earlwood 402 G3
av. Miranda.......... 461 J16
la. N Sydney............ 6 A9
pl. Emerton 240 K5
st. Greystanes 305 G5
st. N Sydney............ 6 A9
st. Picnic Point 428 B8
st. Ashfield, off Heighway Av ... 372 G2
DORKING
rd. Cabarita.......... 342 E1
DORLTON
st. Kings Lngly 245 E7
DORMAN
cr. Lindfield 283 H2
DORMER
cl. Elderslie.......... 507 K2
gr. Quakers Hill 214 D14
DORMITORY HILL
rd. Scheyville 124 A6
DORNOCH
ct. Castle Hill 218 E7
st. Winston Hills .. 277 D3
DOROTHY
cr. Colyton........... 270 E5
ct. Baulkham Hl ... 247 D3
st. Cromer 228 C15
st. Freemns Rch 90 D2
st. Hebersham 241 F10
st. Merrylands 307 C7
st. Mt Pritchard ... 364 G11
st. Rydalmere 309 J3
st. Ryde.............. 282 A10
st. Sefton............ 338 E13
st. Wentwthvle..... 276 J13
DORRE
pl. Green Valley ... 363 B10
DORRIE
pl. Quakers Hill 214 C13
DORRIGO
av. Hoxton Park.... 392 K6
av. N Balgowlah ... 287 B4
cl. Bangor 459 C14
cr. Bow Bowing ... 452 D15
la. Sans Souci 463 A5
DORRINGTON
cr. S Windsor....... 151 B8
pl. Glenmore Pk... 266 A5
DORRIT
wy. Ambarvale 511 B15
DORRITT
st. Lane Cove....... 314 E3
DORSET
av. Northmead...... 278 C4
cl. Belrose 225 K11
cl. Elderslie.......... 507 K1
cl. Wakeley.......... 364 J1
dr. St Ives 223 K16
dr. St Ives 224 A14
pl. Miller 393 H3
rd. Heathcote 518 D10
rd. Northbridge 316 F1
st. Blacktown....... 274 G6
st. Cambrdg Pk.... 237 J8
st. Epping............ 251 D13
DOT
la. Leichhardt 16 A4
st. Marrickville 373 G12
DOTTEREL
pl. Ingleburn........ 453 H6
pl. Woronora Ht... 489 E5
st. Hinchinbrk...... 393 D1
DOUGAN
st. Ashfield 372 F6
DOUGHERTY
la. N Willghby...... 285 D10
st. Rosebery 405 H3
DOUGLAS
av. Chatswood...... 285 D6
av. N Epping......... 251 F8
av. Wahroonga..... 222 D3
cl. Green Valley.... 363 C11
la. Randwick........ 377 F11
la. Stanmore.......... 16 D9
pde. Dover Ht 348 G14
pl. Miranda 461 J16
rd. Blacktown 273 E4
rd. Doonside 273 E4
rd. Kurrajong Ht 54 B8
rd. Quakers Hill 213 G13
st. Bardwell Vy..... 402 J9
st. Clovelly........... 377 F10
st. Earlwood 402 D7
st. Fairfield........... 336 F9
st. Faulconbdg..... 171 C15
st. Merrylands 307 A9
st. N Richmond 87 E10
st. Panania........... 428 D5
st. Putney 311 K8
st. Randwick........ 377 F10
st. Redfern............. 19 E10
st. Richmond 118 D6
st. St Ives 224 B10
st. Springwood 201 D1
st. Stanmore.......... 16 B9
st. Waterloo........... 19 E10
DOUGLAS FARM
rd. Kurrajong Hl 54 J7
DOUGLAS HAIG
st. Oatley 430 H12
DOUGLAS McMASTER
pl. Llandilo.......... 209 G2
DOUGLASS
av. Carlingford...... 249 J15
la. Sydney ....E F2
pl. Cromer 228 A16
st. Sydney ....E E2
DOULTON
av. Beacon Hill...... 257 G8
dr. Cherrybrook.... 219 C13
DOUNE
ct. Castle Hill........ 218 E7
DOURO
pl. Airds............... 511 K15
st. Marayong 243 J7
DOUST
pl. Grasmere........ 475 J16
pl. Shalvey........... 211 C13
st. Bass Hill 368 C7
st. Chester Hill 368 C7
DOVE
cl. Woronora Ht... 489 E2
la. Randwick........ 377 F10
pl. Hinchinbrk...... 363 C16
pl. Ingleburn........ 453 H7
pl. St Clair............ 269 H11
st. Revesby.......... 399 A12
DOVECOTE
gln. Wrrngtn Dns ... 237 K4
DOVELEY
rd. Como.............. 460 E6
DOVER
ct. Castle Hill........ 219 A11
la. Rose Bay, off Dover Rd......... 348 C11
pl. Engadine......... 489 C16
pl. West Hoxton ... 392 C8
rd. Dover Ht 348 D11
rd. Rose Bay......... 348 B10
st. Botany 405 F12
st. Marsfield 281 K4
st. Summer Hill 373 E4
DOW
pl. Marayong........ 244 A4
DOWD
la. East Ryde 282 K16
DOWDING
cl. Cecil Hills 362 J8
st. Panania........... 398 B14
DOWE
pl. Bligh Park 150 D6
DOWEL
st. Chatswood...... 285 A6
DOWLAND
st. Bonnyrigg Ht... 363 D7
DOWLE
pl. Camden S 507 B16
DOWLES
la. Bickley Vale..... 505 J12
DOWLING
la. Kensington, off Ingram St 376 A12
pl. S Windsor....... 120 K15
st. Arncliffe 403 D7
st. Bardwell Vy..... 403 D7
st. Kensington...... 376 A12
st. Leumeah......... 482 D15
st. Queenscliff 288 F2
st. Woolmloo 4 G7
st. Zetland............ 376 A12
DOWNES
cl. Illawong 459 K4
cr. Currans Hill 479 G10
st. Belfield 371 D9
st. Colyton 270 D7
st. N Epping 251 J9
DOWNEY
la. Fairfield, off Harris St 336 E12
st. Bexley 402 F16
DOWNING
av. Cmbrdg Gdn ... 237 G1
av. Regents Pk...... 369 E1
pl. Gladesville....... 313 A11
st. Epping 250 F14
st. Picton 563 G2
DOWNPATRICK
rd. Killarney Ht 255 K15
DOWNSHIRE
pde. Chester Hill 368 C4
pl. Dawes Point....... 1 F8
st. Dawes Point....... 1 F8
DOWRENA
pl. Berowra 133 D10
DOWSETT
rd. Kingsgrove...... 402 A12
DOYLE
cl. Wetherill Pk..... 334 D4
pl. Baulkham Hl.... 246 J15
pl. Gordon 253 D12
pl. Marayong........ 244 C3
rd. Padstow.......... 429 D1
rd. Revesby.......... 399 A13
DRACIC
st. S Wntwthvle.... 306 J9
DRAGO
rd. Hinchinbrk...... 393 D4
DRAKE
av. Caringbah 492 K4
la. Jamisontown, off Drake St 266 D5
pl. Blacktown 275 A7
pl. Shalvey........... 211 B13
st. Artarmon 284 J14
st. Concord.......... 342 A1
st. Jamisontown .. 266 D5
st. Panania........... 398 D16
DRAKES
la. Ashfield........... 372 J3
DRANSFIELD
av. Mascot............ 405 F7
rd. Edensor Pk..... 363 F4
DRAPER
av. Roselands 400 F7
st. Glenwood....... 215 D14
DRAVA
pl. Kearns........... 451 B16
DRAVET
st. Padstow......... 399 B11
DRAWBRIDGE
pl. Castle Hill....... 217 E4
DRAYTON
av. Castle Hill....... 248 A5
pl. Edensor Pk..... 333 F14
DREADNOUGHT
rd. Oxford Falls.... 227 A16
st. Roselands 401 B5
DREAM HOUSE
la. Mosman, off Spit Rd 287 B16
DREDGE
av. Moorebank..... 396 D7
pwy. Moorebank, off Dredge Av....... 396 E7
DREMEDAY
st. Northmead 248 B15
DRESDEN
av. Beacon Hill..... 257 F7
av. Castle Hill....... 247 F1
DRESS CIRCLE
rd. Avalon............ 170 A4
DREW
pl. Belrose........... 256 A1
st. Greenacre....... 370 G11
st. Westmead 307 H3
DRIFT
rd. Richmond 117 H7
DRISCOLL
av. Rooty Hill 272 B5
pl. Barden Rdg.... 488 F4
st. Abbotsbury 333 B15
DRIVER
av. Moore Park 20 H3
av. Wallacia 324 K13
pl. Bonnyrigg 364 C4
st. Denistone W... 280 K13
DROMANA
rd. Marsden Pk.... 181 K14
DRONE
st. Greenacre....... 370 H10
DROOD
pl. Ambarvale...... 510 J14
DROVER
rd. Bnkstn Aprt.... 367 H16
DROVERS
wy. Lindfield......... 284 C2
DRUERY
la. Hurstville........ 431 K8
DRUITT
la. Camden.......... 506 H8
la. Camden S 506 H8
la. Cawdor 506 H8
la. Sydney ....C E13
pl. Sydney ....C E11
pl. Wrrngtn Cty ... 238 E9
st. Mount Druitt... 241 C11
st. Sydney ....C E12
st. Sydney 3 E6
DRUMALBYN
rd. Bellevue Hill... 347 G13
st. Ingleburn 453 C9
DRUMARD
av. Leumeah........ 482 C14
DRUMCLIFF
av. Killarney Ht..... 255 K15
DRUMMOND
la. Belmore 401 F2
la. Warwck Frm.... 365 G16
rd. Kurrajong......... 85 E3
rd. Oyster Bay....... 461 A7
st. Belmore 401 F1
st. S Windsor 120 G15
st. Warwck Frm... 365 G16
DRUMMOYNE
av. Drummoyne ... 313 G15
cr. St Johns Pk.... 364 G4
DRURY
la. Mosman, off Gordon St....... 317 D8
pl. Hebersham..... 241 G1
DRYAD
pl. Leonay........... 264 J2
DRYBERRY
av. St Clair........... 269 G16

DRY DEN
pl. Wetherill Pk....334 J6
DRYDEN
av. Carlingford.....249 E13
av. Oakhurst.........242 A5
rd. N Turramrra.....223 E7
st. Campsie.........372 B11
DRY LAKES
rd. Thirlmere........564 A4
DRYNAN
st. Summer Hill...373 B5
DRYSDALE
av. Picnic Point....428 E8
cr. Plumpton.......242 C7
pl. Casula............424 F2
pl. Kareela...........461 D13
rd. Elderslie..........507 J2
rd. Mt Pritchard...364 J11
st. Claymore.......481 A10
st. Eagle Vale.......481 A9
DUARDO
st. Edensor Pk.....333 H15
DUBARDA
st. Engadine........488 F16
DUBBO
pl. Bangor...........459 C14
st. Quakers Hill....244 A2
DUBLIN
av. Killarney Ht.....256 C16
st. Glendenning...242 J3
st. Smithfield.......335 D6
DUCHESS
av. Rodd Point.....343 E8
wy. Minto.............482 J7
DUCK
pl. Hinchinbrk......393 D1
st. Auburn...........309 B13
DUCKER
av. Richmond.......118 E9
DUCKMALLOIS
av. Blacktown.......274 G5
DUCROS
st. Petersham........15 F13
DUDLEY
av. Bankstown......399 C4
av. Blacktown.......244 B15
av. Caringbah.......492 J11
av. Roseville.........284 J2
la. Woollahra.........22 G5
pl. Tahmoor..........565 F12
rd. Guildford........338 D10
rd. Rose Bay........348 D8
st. Asquith...........192 B9
st. Auburn...........339 B3
st. Balgowlah.......287 F8
st. Berala............339 D10
st. Bondi.............378 C5
st. Coogee...........407 D1
st. Haberfield.......343 E13
st. Hurstville........431 F1
st. Kirrawee.........491 C1
st. Lidcombe........339 D10
st. Marrickville.....373 E13
st. Mount Druitt...241 C14
st. Paddington.......21 E1
st. Pagewood......405 K10
st. Penshurst.......431 H7
st. Punchbowl.....400 D3
st. Punchbowl.....400 E4
st. Randwick.......377 D16
st. Rydalmere......279 C16
DUER
pl. Cherrybrook...219 J11
DU FAUR
st. N Turramrra....193 F12
DUFEK
pl. Tregear...........240 B5
DUFF
pl. Castle Hill.......218 B9
rd. Cecil Park.......331 E13
st. Arncliffe..........403 D7
st. Burwood..........341 K16
st. Turramurra......222 F15
DUFFY
av. Grose Vale........85 D15
av. Kingsgrove.....401 K6
av. Thornleigh.......221 A10
av. Westleigh........220 E9
st. Merrylnds W...306 J14
DUGALD
rd. Mosman.........317 D8
st. Riverstone......183 D8
DUGGAN
cr. Connells Pt.....431 J13
pl. Lalor Park.......245 E14

DUGUID
st. Mascot...........405 A5
DUIGNAN
cl. Epping............281 D3
DUKE
av. Concord..........342 D5
av. Rodd Point.....343 E8
cl. Green Valley....362 K11
pl. Balmain East.......8 E8
rd. Wilberforce.......92 A1
st. Balmain East.......8 E7
st. Btn-le-Sds........433 K3
st. Campsie.........372 B13
st. Canley Ht.......365 G1
st. East Hills.........427 K4
st. Forestville.......255 F10
st. Granville.........308 E9
st. Kensington.....376 D11
st. Merrylands.....307 A9
st. Rooty Hill.......241 H13
st. Strathfield.......341 E11
DUKE OF EDINBURGH
pde. Clontarf...........287 F15
DUKES
pl. Emu Plains.....235 C11
DUKIC
st. Bonnyrigg Ht..363 A7
DULCIE
st. Seven Hills......245 B16
DULIN
cl. Bangor............459 B15
DULWA
rd. Menai.............459 A4
DULWICH
rd. Chatswd W.....284 F7
rd. Roseville.........284 F7
rd. Vineyard.........152 F11
st. Dulwich Hill....373 E9
DUMARESQ
rd. Rose Bay........348 B8
st. Campbelltwn...511 E5
st. Gordon...........253 F8
DUMAS
pl. Winston Hills..247 E16
DU MAURIER
pl. Wetherill Pk....335 A6
DUMBARTON
pl. Engadine.........489 A8
st. McMahons Pt.....5 B12
DUMBLE
st. Seven Hills......275 D3
DUMFRIES
rd. St Andrews.....451 K16
st. Winston Hills..277 E5
DUMIC
pl. Cromer...........228 E15
DUMPU
st. Holsworthy.....426 G7
DUNALLEY
st. West Hoxton...392 D5
DUNARA
gdn. Point Piper........14 K2
DUNBAR
av. Regents Pk.....369 C2
av. Wrrngtn Cty....238 E8
cl. Normanhurst..221 F11
pl. Illawong..........459 D1
pl. Kellyville.........217 A2
pl. Mt Annan........479 E16
st. Ryde..............281 K16
st. St Andrews.....452 A13
st. Silverdale........353 H16
st. Watsons Bay...318 G15
DUNBARS
rd. Werombi.........443 D6
DUNBIER
av. Lurnea............394 F7
DUNBIL
ct. Bangor............459 B15
DUNBLANE
st. Camperdwn......17 F4
DUNCAN
cl. Glenmore Pk...265 F9
cr. Collaroy Plat...228 K13
la. Maroubra........407 E11
pl. Epping............280 J1
st. Arncliffe..........403 J8
st. Balmain.............8 A9
st. Drummoyne....343 J5
st. Maroubra........407 E11
st. Minto Ht.........483 J2
st. Punchbowl......400 D5
st. Richmond.......120 B5

DUNCANS
rd. Greendale.......355 A14
DUNCANSBY
cr. St Andrews.....452 B15
DUNCRAIG
dr. Kellyville..........186 K15
DUNDAS
pl. Wakeley..........334 G13
st. Coogee...........407 H3
DUNDEE
pl. St Andrews.....481 J3
st. Cambrdg Pk....237 H9
st. Engadine.........488 J10
st. Sadleir...........364 C16
DUNDILLA
rd. Frenchs Frst....256 D2
DUNDRA
cl. Bangor............459 B14
DUNEBA
av. Kirrawee..........491 A8
av. West Pymble...253 B12
dr. Westleigh........220 E9
pl. Frenchs Frst....255 K2
DUNGARA
cr. Glenmore Pk...266 C11
cr. Stanhpe Gdn...215 D8
pl. Winmalee........173 A10
DUNGARTH
la. Emu Heights, off
Dungarth Pl.....234 K6
pl. Emu Heights...234 K6
DUNGATE
la. Sydney...............F A2
DUNGOG
pl. Bangor............459 C13
DUNGOWAN
la. Manly, off
Ashburner St...288 H10
DUNHEVED
cct. St Marys.........239 F6
rd. Cmbrdg Gdn...237 G5
rd. Cambrdg Pk....238 A6
rd. Wrrngtn Cty....238 G7
rd. Wrrngtn Dns...238 A6
DUNK
cl. Green Valley....363 A13
pl. Kings Lngly.....245 E6
DUNKELD
av. Baulkham Hl....246 J10
av. Hurlstone Pk...372 J12
cl. Burraneer........493 E15
la. Hurlstone Pk...372 J12
pl. Dural..............219 G4
pl. St Andrews.....452 C12
DUNKIRK
av. Kingsgrove......402 B5
DUNKLEY
ct. Rooty Hill........272 C5
pl. Werrington.......238 K10
st. Smithfield.......335 B7
DUNLEA
rd. Engadine.........518 F3
DUNLEAVY
st. Prairiewood.....334 D11
DUNLEY
pl. Castle Hill.......219 A8
DUNLOP
la. Roselands.......400 H6
pl. Picton............563 E10
st. Epping............280 E3
st. N Parramatta...278 B12
st. Roselands.......400 J6
st. Strathfield S....371 B6
wy. Minto.............482 J8
DUNMORE
av. Carlingford......279 F5
cr. Casula............394 K15
pl. Barden Rdg.....488 H4
pl. Wrrngtn Cty....238 F4
rd. Epping............250 K12
rd. West Ryde......281 C16
st. Croydon Pk.....372 B7
st. Pendle Hill.......276 E15
st. Wentwthvle.....277 A16
st.n, Bexley............402 K15
st.s, Bexley............433 A1
DUNN
pl. Cranebrook.....207 E13
pl. Prairiewood.....334 E10
rd. Smeaton Gra...479 D5
DUNNA
la. Glenmore Pk, off
Dunna Pl.........266 C11
pl. Glenmore Pk...266 C11

DUNNING
av. Rosebery........375 G16
av. Zetland...........375 G16
DUNNS
la. Burwood.......341 K13
rd. Maraylya........124 E3
DUNOIS
st. Longueville.....314 D8
DUNOON
av. West Pymble..253 B12
pl. Bangor...........459 B13
st. Berowra Ht.....132 J11
DUNRAVEN
wy. Cherrybrook...219 B14
DUNROSSIL
av. Carlingford.....250 A16
av. Casula...........394 J12
av. Fairfield E.......336 J12
DUNSHEA
pl. Guildford........337 B3
st. Denistone W...280 K12
DUNSMORE
st. Rooty Hill.......272 E2
DUNSTABLE
rd. Blacktown......244 K10
DUNSTAFFENAGE
st. Hurlstone Pk..372 K12
DUNSTAFFNAGE
pl. Erskine Park...300 F3
DUNSTAN
av. Milperra.........397 D10
pl. Bligh Park.......150 K6
pl. Engadine.........518 E4
st. Croydon Pk....372 D9
st. Fairfield W......334 J10
DUNTROON
av. Epping...........250 F16
av. Roseville........285 B3
av. Roseville Ch...285 D2
av. St Leonards....315 D7
la. Hurlstone Pk, off
Duntroon St....373 B10
st. Hurlstone Pk..373 A13
st. Hurlstone Pk..373 B11
DUNWELL
av. Loftus...........490 B9
DUPAS
st. Smithfield.......305 K14
DURABA
pl. Caringbah.......492 J6
pl. S Penrith........266 J7
DURACK
cl. Edensor Pk.....363 E4
pl. Casula...........424 F2
pl. St Helens Pk...541 A7
pl. St Ives...........224 F8
DURAL
cr. Engadine........489 E8
la. Hornsby.........221 F1
pl. Dharruk..........241 D10
rd. Maraylya..........94 F15
st. Dural.............158 B16
st. Hornsby.........221 E1
st. Kenthurst.......188 B1
DURALI
av. Winmalee.......173 A9
rd. Glenmore Pk..266 D12
DURANT
la. Yagoona.........369 A11
pl. Cherrybrook...219 F16
DURBAN
wy. Minto.............482 K2
DURBAR
av. Kirrawee.........491 B3
DURDANS
av. Rosebery........375 F16
DURDEN
pl. Ambarvale......540 E1
DURHAM
av. St Ives, off
Denley La........223 K12
cl. Bonnyrigg Ht..363 C4
cl. Dural.............188 G1
cl. Mcquarie Pk...252 J16
gr. Windsor Dn....151 B16
la. Springwood...201 F3
la. Stanmore.........16 J9
la. Dulwich Hill, off
Durham St.......373 E10
pl. Sylvania.........461 J13
rd. Schofields......212 H5
st. Allawah.........432 D6
st. Carlton..........432 D6
st. Concord.........342 E6

st. Dulwich Hill....373 E10
st. Hunters Hill....313 F11
st. Hurstville........432 D6
st. Minto.............452 G16
st. Mount Druitt...271 A1
st. N Epping........251 C9
st. Oxley Park......240 G16
st. Rosehill..........309 E8
st. Stanmore.........16 J9
DURI
cl. Bangor...........459 B13
pl. Bonnyrigg.......364 A9
st. Malabar..........437 F8
DURKIN
pl. Peakhurst.......430 G3
DURNESS
pl. St Andrews.....452 A13
DURRAS
cl. Woodcroft......243 F11
pl. Leumeah........482 F15
st. Prestons.........422 K1
DURROW
av. Killarney Ht....256 C16
DURSLEY
rd. Yennora..........336 G6
DURUMBIL
rd. Duffys Frst......195 F3
D'URVILLE
av. Tregear...........240 F6
DURWARD
st. Dean Park.......212 G16
DUTBA
la. Glenmore Pk, off
Dutba Pl.........266 B10
pl. Glenmore Pk...266 B10
DUTCH
la. St Clair, off
Dutch Pl..........269 F11
pl. Oakhurst.........242 C3
pl. St Clair...........269 G11
DUTERREAU
wy. Claymore........481 E11
DUTRUC
st. Randwick.......377 C13
DUTTON
la. Cabramatta.....365 J7
pl. Glenmore Pk...266 A7
st. Bankstown......369 A14
st. Yagoona.........369 A14
DUVAL
st. Hebersham.....241 G2
DUXFORD
la. Paddington, off
Broughton St....13 D15
st. Paddington.......13 C15
DWIGHT
st. Greystanes.....306 D7
DWYER
av. Blakehurst......432 E12
av. Little Bay........437 A12
cl. Fairfield W......335 A13
cr. Seven Hills.....245 D15
la. Blakehurst......432 F12
la. Woollahra.........21 J4
pl. St Helens Pk...541 A7
pl. S Penrith........236 K16
rd. Bringelly.........387 A6
rd. Leppington.....450 C1
st. Chippendale........E A16
st. Chippendale........3 C16
st. Gymea............491 G2
st. Ryde...............282 G15
DYCE
pl. St Andrews.....481 K1
DYGAL
st. Mona Vale......199 B3
DYINDA
pl. Miranda..........492 A1
DYLAN
pl. W Pnnant Hl...248 H7
DYMOND
rd. Bargo.............567 F5
DYMPNA
st. Cromer...........228 F13
DYSON
la. Woollahra.........22 J4
pl. Fairfield W......335 B12
pl. Glenmore Pk...265 K8
st. Putney............312 A9
wy. Blackett.........241 B2
wy. Claymore........481 B12

E

EACHAM
st. Fairfield W 335 G8
EAGAR
la. Sydney E E3
st. Sydney E F3
EAGLE
pl. St Johns Pk 334 C16
rd. Theresa Park 414 D12
st. Ryde 311 K3
st. Wallacia 324 J13
EAGLE CREEK
rd. Werombi 443 D6
EAGLEHAWK
pl. W Pnnant Hl 248 E8
st. Heckenberg 363 K14
EAGLEMONT
cr. Campbelltwn 511 H4
EAGLE VALE
dr. Eagle Vale 481 B6
dr. Eschol Park 481 B6
EAGLEVIEW
rd. Ingleburn 453 C16
rd. Minto 483 A4
EALING
pl. Quakers Hill 214 D9
EALT
st. Riverstone 181 K8
EAMES
av. Baulkham Hl 247 C10
EARL
la. Randwick, off Stephen St 377 B9
pl. Cecil Hills 362 K5
pl. Potts Point 4 J6
st. Beacon Hill 257 E6
st. Canley Ht 365 G2
st. Canley Vale 365 G2
st. Hunters Hill 313 B6
st. Merrylands 338 B1
st. Mosman 316 J5
st. Mount Druitt 241 E13
st. Potts Point 4 J6
st. Randwick 377 B9
st. Roseville 285 A2
st. Wilberforce 91 J5
EARLE
av. Ashfield 342 K14
st. Arncliffe 403 C10
st. Cremorne 316 C6
st. Doonside 243 B12
st. Harringtn Pk 478 F8
st. Narellan 478 F8
wy. Claymore 481 B11
EARLS
av. Riverwood 400 E12
ct. Cherrybrook 219 E12
ct. Roseville Ch 255 F15
EARLWOOD
av. Earlwood 402 J3
cr. Bardwell Pk 402 H8
EARLY
st. Parramatta 308 B6
EARN
pl. St Andrews 482 A2
EARNGLEY
la. Edgecliff 13 F10
EARNSHAW
st. Gladesville 312 K9
EAST
av. Cammeray 316 B3
cr. Hurstville Gr 431 H11
dr. Bexley North 402 C9
esp. Manly 288 G11
la. Randwick 407 B2
la. St Marys 239 H16
pde. Campsie 372 D12
pde. Canley Vale 366 C2
pde. Couridjah 564 D16
pde. Denistone 281 B8
pde. Eastwood 281 B8
pde. Fairfield 336 D16
pde. Sutherland 490 D4
rd. Riverstone 182 F9
st. Bardwell Vy 403 B8
st. Blakehurst 462 D2
st. Couridjah 564 H16
st. Five Dock 342 K9
st. Granville 308 G11
st. Greenwich 314 K13
st. Kurrajong Ht 54 D8
st. Lidcombe 339 J12
st. Marrickville 16 D16
st. Parramatta 279 B16
st. Redfern 19 E9
tce. Bankstown 399 G1
EAST BANK
st. Collaroy 229 B13
EASTBANK
av. Lansvale 366 E9
EASTBOURNE
av. Avalon 140 C15
av. Clovelly 378 A13
av. Wahroonga 222 A9
rd. Darling Point 13 K6
rd. Homebsh W 340 F10
wy. Bella Vista 246 E5
EASTCOTE
rd. N Epping 251 G10
EAST CRESCENT
st. McMahons Pt 5 E16
EASTER
st. Leichhardt 15 E5
EASTERBROOK
pl. S Penrith 266 J5
EASTERN
av. Camperdwn 18 E3
av. Dover Ht 348 F8
av. Kensington 376 D16
av. Kingsford 376 D16
av. Panania 428 G3
av. Revesby 428 G3
cct. Parramatta 278 A12
rd. Doonside 243 A15
rd. Matraville 406 K16
rd. Quakers Hill 213 G13
rd. Rooty Hill 272 F3
rd. Turramurra 222 J13
rd. Wahroonga 222 K5
EASTERN ARTERIAL
rd. East Killara 254 E10
rd. E Lindfield 254 E10
rd. Gordon 254 D7
rd. Killara 254 E10
rd. Lindfield 254 E10
rd. St Ives 254 C2
EASTERN DISTRIBUTOR
Darlinghurst 346 C13
Moore Park 20 D13
Moore Park 376 B7
Redfern 376 B7
Surry Hills 376 B7
EASTERN VALLEY
wy. Castle Cove 285 E4
wy. Castlecrag 285 J15
wy. Chatswood 285 E4
wy. Middle Cove 285 E4
wy. Northbridge 285 J15
wy. N Willghby 285 E4
wy. Roseville 285 E4
wy. Willoughby 285 J15
EASTGATE
av. East Killara 254 G9
EAST KURRAJONG
rd. Comleroy 56 F5
rd. E Kurrajong 56 F5
EASTLEA
av. Springwood 171 F16
gdn. Springwood 171 F16
EASTLEWOOD
st. Narellan 478 H10
EAST MARKET
st. Richmond 118 G8
EASTMORE
pl. Maroubra 406 H7
EASTON
av. Sylvania 461 K9
rd. Berowra Ht 133 A11
st. Rozelle 10 J3
EASTVIEW
av. North Ryde 282 D8
dr. Orangeville 473 B1
rd. Church Point 168 F7
st. Greenwich 315 C8
EAST WILCHARD
rd. Castlereagh 176 D12
rd. Cranebrook 176 H15
EASTWOOD
av. Eastwood 281 A4
av. Epping 280 J4
rd. Leppington 420 A9
EASY
st. Randwick 377 A16
st. Randwick 407 A1
EATHER
av. North Rocks 248 F12
rd. Ingleburn 422 H13
EATON
av. Normanhurst 221 G8
pl. Chiswick 343 D1
rd. Luddenham 356 K4
rd. W Pnnant Hl 249 C10
rd. W Pnnant Hl 249 G9
sq. Allambie Ht 257 B8
st. Agnes Banks 117 D12
st. Balmain 7 K10
st. Neutral Bay 6 A5
st. Rooty Hill 271 K5
st. Willoughby 285 F12
EBAL
pl. Seven Hills 275 D11
EBB
st. Quakers Hill 214 C11
EBB TIDE
st. Chipping Ntn 366 J15
EBDEN
st. Quakers Hill 214 A9
EBENEZER WHARF
rd. Ebenezer 63 A10
EBER
pl. Minchinbury 271 G10
EBLEY
st. Bondi Jctn 22 F8
EBON
la. Erskineville 17 J16
EBONY
av. Carlingford 249 C15
av. North Rocks 249 C15
cl. Casula 394 F14
cr. Quakers Hill 243 D2
pl. Mcquarie Fd 454 H3
pwy. Casula, off Ebony Cl 394 F14
row. Menai 458 K14
EBOR
pl. Hoxton Park 392 H6
rd. Palm Beach 140 A4
EBRO
pl. Kearns 481 A2
st. Seven Hills 275 F9
EBSWORTH
rd. Rose Bay 348 D9
ECCLES
av. Ashfield 372 G1
pl. Prairiewood 334 F7
st. Ermington 280 B16
ECHIDNA
pl. Blaxland 233 D12
ECHO
cl. Penrith 237 C2
pl. Winston Hills 277 A1
st. Cammeray 316 A5
st. Roseville 285 C1
ECHUCA
cl. Bonnyrigg 363 K10
ECHUNGA
rd. Duffys Frst 195 F3
ECOLE
av. Winmalee 173 F5
la. Carlton 432 K8
st. Carlton 432 K8
ECONO
pl. Warragamba 353 J8
EDDIE
av. Panania 428 B3
rd. Minchinbury 271 B6
EDDY
av. Haymarket E H12
av. Haymarket 3 G14
rd. Chatswd W 284 E12
st. Merrylnds W 306 G12
st. Thornleigh 220 J12
EDDYSTONE
rd. Bexley 402 G13
rd. Bexley 402 J12
EDEL
pl. Fairfield W 335 C9
EDELWEISS
pl. Lugarno 430 A14
EDEN
av. Croydon Pk 371 J7
av. Punchbowl 400 B8
av. S Turramrra 252 C9
dr. Asquith 192 D9
gln. St Clair 269 J14
la. N Sydney 5 D2
la. S Turramrra 252 D10
pl. Bossley Park 333 F10
pl. Caringbah 492 E14
pl. Prestons 392 J16
pl. Winston Hills 247 H16
st. Arncliffe 403 G9
st. Chatswood 285 D7
st. Marayong 244 B8
st. N Sydney 5 E1
st. Ryde 282 D11
EDENBOROUGH
rd. Lindfield 284 B4
EDENHOLME
rd. Russell Lea 343 C4
rd. Wareemba 343 A4
st. West Pymble 252 F11
EDENLEE
st. Epping 280 H3
EDEN PARK
dr. Mcquarie Pk 282 K5
EDENSOR
rd. Bonnyrigg 364 E4
rd. Cabramtta W 364 E4
rd. Edensor Pk 333 D16
rd. Greenfld Pk 363 K1
rd. St Johns Pk 364 E4
st. Epping 251 A13
EDGAR
cr. Belfield 371 E10
la. Tempe, off Edgar St 404 A1
pl. Kings Lngly 245 H7
st. Auburn 339 A5
st. Bankstown 368 H15
st. Baulkham Hl 247 G13
st. Chatswd W 284 F10
st. Condell Park 398 G6
st. Condell Park 398 G8
st. Eastwood 281 D7
st. Harbord 288 K1
st. Kingsford 407 C7
st. Mcquarie Fd 424 A16
st. Revesby 398 G8
st. St Marys 269 G3
st. Strathfield 340 J13
st. Tempe 404 A1
st. Yagoona 368 H15
EDGAR BUGGY
st. Merrylands 337 H1
EDGBASTON
rd. Beverly Hills 401 A16
EDGE
st. Lakemba 400 J4
st. Wiley Park 400 J4
EDGECLIFF
pl. Engadine 488 D16
pl. Peakhurst 430 B11
rd. Edgecliff 14 B12
rd. Glenhaven 187 H13
rd. Woollahra 22 C1
rd. Woolwich 314 E14
sq. Edgecliff 13 K12
EDGECLIFFE
av. S Coogee 407 H7
bvd. Collaroy Plat 228 H9
esp. Seaforth 287 A11
EDGECOMBE
av. Moorebank 396 B7
av. Wahroonga 221 K12
rd. St Ives 224 B6
EDGECUMBE
av. Coogee 407 F2
EDGEHILL
av. Botany 405 F15
st. Carlton 432 J5
EDGELY
st. Surry Hills 20 C5
EDGEWARE
la. Enmore 17 A15
rd. Enmore 17 A15
rd. Newtown 374 G10
rd. Prospect 275 B12
EDGEWATER
dr. Bella Vista 216 A15
pde. Parramatta 308 D1
EDGEWOOD
pl. St Ives 224 A16
EDGEWORTH
pl. Cartwright 394 A6
EDGEWORTH DAVID
av. Hornsby 221 H2
av. Wahroonga 222 B3
av. Waitara 221 H2
EDINA
av. Waverley 377 F6
EDINBURGH
av. Carlingford 279 D4
cct. Cecil Hills 362 J4
cl. Woolooware 493 G7
cr. St Andrews 452 A13
cr. Woolooware 493 F7
dr. Revesby 428 J5
dr. Revesby Ht 428 J5
pl. Winston Hills 277 F4
rd. Castlecrag 285 H12
rd. Forestville 255 G9
rd. Marrickville 374 E10
rd. Willoughby 285 H12
st. Tahmoor 566 A16
EDISON
la. Belmore 371 G16
pde. Winston Hills 277 B5
pl. Leumeah 482 E16
st. Belmore 371 G16
EDITH
av. Concord 342 C6
av. Liverpool 364 K16
av. Mcquarie Fd 454 A2
la. Leichhardt 15 F2
la. St Peters, off Edith St 374 H14
pl. Northmead 278 C5
pwy. Liverpool, off Edith Av 364 J15
st. Bardwell Pk 403 B6
st. Castlecrag 286 A12
st. Girraween 276 C13
st. Hurstville 401 J16
st. Kingswood 237 J16
st. Lansdowne 367 B5
st. Leichhardt 15 F1
st. Lidcombe 339 K4
st. Marsfield 282 B8
st. Mount Druitt 271 B2
st. St Peters 374 G13
EDMONDSON
av. Austral 391 C7
av. St Marys 270 A1
cr. Carramar 366 K4
dr. Narrabeen 228 G8
st. North Ryde 282 K9
EDMUND
pl. Cecil Hills 362 E2
pl. Rsemeadow 540 J7
st. Beverly Hills 401 E16
st. Chatswood 284 K7
st. Lindfield 283 F3
st. Queens Park 377 F8
st. Riverstone 153 A13
st. Riverstone 183 C1
EDMUND BLACKET
cl. St Clair 270 C11
EDMUND HOCK
av. Avalon 170 B2
EDMUNDS
st. Carramar 366 J2
EDMUNDSON
cl. Thornleigh 220 H11
EDNA
av. Merrylnds W 307 B14
av. Mt Pritchard 364 F12
av. Penshurst 431 G6
av. Springwood 202 A11
av. Toongabbie 276 C4
la. Kingswood, off Edna St 237 J15
pl. Dee Why 258 G3
pl. Ermington 280 C13
pl. Ingleburn 453 C10
pl. Kings Lngly 245 K6
st. Bass Hill 368 D11
st. Kingswood 237 J15
st. Lilyfield 10 G11
st. N Willghby 285 H10
st. Sans Souci 463 C4
st. Warrimoo 203 E13
st. Wiley Park 400 F1
EDROM
cl. Prestons 393 B16
cl. Prestons 423 B1
EDSEL
pl. Hassall Gr 211 J14
EDUCATION
la. Cremorne, off Murdoch St 316 F9
EDWARD
av. Kensington 376 E16
av. Kingsford 406 E1
av. Miranda 492 E1
av. Mulgoa 265 C3
cl. Werrington 238 K10
la. Bondi 378 A3
la. Darlington 18 K6
la. Dulwich Hill 373 E6
la. Glebe 11 G7

la. Pyrmont 12 J5
la. Concord, off Edward St 341 G9
pl. Canley Ht 335 B16
rd. Marayong 244 A7
st. Balmain East 8 J10
st. Bankstown 399 B6
st. Baulkham Hl 247 J5
st. Bexley North 402 B11
st. Bondi 377 K3
st. Bondi Beach 377 K3
st. Botany 405 F11
st. Camden 477 B14
st. Carlton 432 H9
st. Concord 341 G9
st. Cranebrook 207 B9
st. Darlington 18 K5
st. Glebe 11 H7
st. Gordon 253 K7
st. Guildford W 336 H2
st. Kingsgrove 402 B11
st. Kingswood 237 J16
st. Kurrajong Ht 54 B7
st. Lilyfield 10 C7
st. Lurnea 394 G11
st. Mcquarie Fd 423 K14
st. Marrickville 374 B11
st. Narraweena 258 A6
st. Northmead 277 F10
st. N Sydney 5 D5
st. Oatley 431 D10
st. Pyrmont 12 J4
st. Riverstone 182 G2
st. Ryde 312 A2
st. Strathfield S 371 D6
st. Summer Hill 373 E5
st. Sylvania 461 F12
st. The Oaks 502 F13
st. Turrella 403 F6
st. Waverton 5 D5
st. Willoughby 285 E15
st. Woollahra 22 H2
EDWARD BENNETT
dr. Cherrybrook 249 E1
EDWARD HOWE
pl. Narellan Vale 509 A1
EDWARDS
av. Beecroft 250 A10
la. Killara 254 C10
pl. Penrith 236 K10
rd. Barden Rdg 488 G8
rd. Box Hill 154 J15
rd. Lakemba 370 H14
rd. Lowlands 88 F8
rd. Middle Dural 158 J4
rd. Nelson 155 A15
rd. Rouse Hill 155 A15
rd. Wahroonga 221 H7
EDWARDS BAY
rd. Mosman 317 D4
EDWIN
av. Avalon 140 A14
la. Cammeray, off Edwin St 315 J6
pl. Glenwood 245 H3
pl. Liverpool 394 J8
st. Cammeray 315 J6
st. Colyton 270 G5
st. Drummoyne 343 J3
st. Fairlight 288 D8
st. Greenwich 315 A10
st. Mortlake 312 A14
st. Oatlands 279 A13
st. Regents Pk 369 B2
st. Tempe 404 A2
st.n, Croydon 342 F16
st.s, Croydon 372 E2
EDWINA
pl. Plumpton 241 J10
EDWIN FLACK
av. Homebush B M C10
av. Homebush B 340 D1
EDWIN WARD
pl. Mona Vale 169 E16
EERAWY
rd. Allambie Ht 257 H15
EFFINGHAM
st. Mosman 317 C10
EGAN
la. Newtown 17 D14
pl. Beacon Hill 257 H4
pl. Woolmloo 4 E7
st. Bankstown 399 C1
st. Newtown 17 J8
EGANS
rd. Oakdale 500 E11
EGERTON
st. Silverwater 309 J11
EGGLETON
st. Blacktown 245 B6
st. Campbelltwn 510 J7
EGLINGTON
st. Lidcombe 339 H12
EGLINTON
la. Glebe 11 G7
rd. Glebe 11 G7
EGRET
cl. Bella Vista 246 F1
pl. Clarmnt Ms 268 H5
pl. Hinchinbrk 363 D16
pl. Ingleburn 453 H7
pl. Quakers Hill 214 E11
pl. Woronora Ht 489 E5
pl. Yarramundi 145 D4
wy. Mt Annan 509 B1
EGYPT
st. Holsworthy 426 E10
EIGER
pl. Cranebrook 207 F14
st. Seven Hills 275 C9
EIGHTEENTH
av. Austral 361 G15
st. Warragamba 353 E5
EIGHTH
av. Austral 391 A11
av. Campsie 371 H12
av. Jannali 461 A12
av. Llandilo 208 C6
av. Loftus 489 J7
av. Seven Hills 275 J4
av. Shanes Park 209 A8
EILDON
ct. Wattle Grove 396 B15
st. Wentwthvle 277 A10
EILEEN
av. Beverly Hills 401 A12
la. Campsie 372 B14
st. N Balgowlah 287 C6
st. Picnic Point 428 C8
st. Ryde 282 C14
EINSTEIN
av. Lucas Ht 487 G13
st. Winston Hills 277 C5
EISENHOWER
pl. Bonnet Bay 460 A9
ELABANA
cr. Castle Hill 219 B9
EL ADEM
rd. Holsworthy 426 D8
ELAINE
av. Avalon 140 C15
ct. Werrington 238 J11
pl. Hornsby 192 D16
pl. Middle Dural 128 C16
st. Regents Pk 368 K2
ELAMANG
av. Kirribilli 6 C14
ELANORA
av. Blacktown 274 E3
cl. Baulkham Hl 247 F14
pl. Cecil Hills 362 D4
rd. Elanora Ht 198 D14
st. Rose Bay 347 J11
ELAROO
av. La Perouse 436 J12
av. Phillip Bay 436 J12
ELATA
ct. Wattle Grove 396 B16
pl. Kingswood 267 J2
wy. Bidwill 211 E13
ELAYNE
pl. Guildford 338 B8
ELBA
wy. Glenwood 246 A3
ELBE
pl. Kearns 451 A15
st. Seven Hills 275 H8
ELBERTA
av. Castle Hill 247 G2
ELBON
av. Epping 280 D1
ELBRUS
st. Seven Hills 275 C9
ELCAR
pl. Chullora 369 J5
ELCEDO
la. Greenwich 315 A6
ELCHO
cl. Green Valley 362 K13
ELDER
av. Baulkham Hl 247 D5
la. Wrrngtn Cty, off Elder Pl 238 G4
pl. Alfords Point 459 B1
pl. Mcquarie Fd 454 G2
pl. Wrrngtn Cty 238 G4
rd. Dundas 279 F14
wy. Mt Annan 509 F1
ELDERBERRY
pl. Cherrybrook 219 K13
ELDERSHAW
rd. Edensor Pk 333 G16
ELDERSLIE
ct. Wattle Grove 425 K2
ELDON
av. Georges Hall 368 B15
grn. W Pnnant Hl 249 D5
la. Beecroft 250 B7
st. Pitt Town 92 H15
st. Riverwood 400 B16
ELDRED
st. Warragamba 353 G13
ELDRIDGE
rd. Bankstown 399 A7
rd. Condell Park 398 F6
rd. Greystanes 306 C11
st. Cherrybrook 219 K5
ELEANOR
av. Belmore 401 F5
cr. Rooty Hill 241 K15
st. Rosehill 308 G8
ELEBANA
st. Colyton 270 G6
ELECTRA
pl. Raby 451 G13
st. Heathcote 518 F9
ELEGANS
av. St Ives 224 E15
ELEHAM
rd. Lindfield 254 C15
ELENA
la. Belmore 401 H1
ELEVATED
rd. The Rocks B B2
rd. The Rocks 1 J9
ELEVATION
av. Balgowlah Ht 287 K14
ELEVENTH
av. Austral 391 B7
st. Mascot 405 B7
st. Warragamba 353 F5
ELEY HAWKINS
dr. Warrimoo, off Great Western Hwy 203 B12
ELFORD
cr. Merrylnds W 306 J12
ELFRED
st. Paddington 4 K15
ELFRIDA
st. Mosman 317 A11
ELFRIEDA
st. Old Tngabbie 277 B6
ELGA
pl. Cherrybrook 219 F16
ELGAR
cl. Bonnyrigg Ht 363 E6
pl. Narellan Vale 478 G15
pl. Seven Hills 246 E11
ELGATA
cl. Avalon 139 J12
cr. Bradbury 511 E16
ELGATTA
pl. Epping 250 F13
ELGER
st. Glebe 12 G13
ELGIN
av. St Andrews 451 K15
pl. Winston Hills 277 E3
st. Gordon 253 K4
st. Schofields 183 B16
st. Woolwich 314 E13
wy. Kellyville 217 B2
ELIAS
wy. Kellyville 186 A14
ELIM
pl. Chippendale 18 H1
ELIMATTA
rd. Mona Vale 199 A6
st. Lidcombe 339 J3
ELIZA
av. Liberty Gr 311 B10
pl. Glenmore Pk 265 F9
st. Fairfield Ht 335 J13
st. Newtown 17 F11
wy. Leumeah 482 C13
ELIZABETH
av. Ashfield 372 K3
av. Ashfield 373 A3
av. Dulwich Hill 373 A9
av. Kurmond 86 E1
av. Mascot 405 D5
cl. Appin 568 F10
cr. Kingswood 237 F16
cr. Northmead 278 A4
cr. Yagoona 368 H12
dr. Abbotsbury 363 D3
dr. Ashcroft 364 C8
dr. Badgerys Ck 328 B14
dr. Bonnyrigg 364 C8
dr. Bonnyrigg Ht 363 D3
dr. Cecil Hills 362 F1
dr. Cecil Park 361 B1
dr. Edensor Pk 363 D3
dr. Kemps Ck 361 B1
dr. Liverpool 395 A1
dr. Luddenham 327 B11
dr. Mt Pritchard 364 C8
la. Campsie 372 B15
la. Redfern 19 G7
la. Seven Hills 275 F4
la. Randwick, off Elizabeth St 377 A13
la. Parramatta, off Thomas St 308 E1
pde. Lane Cove W 284 B15
pl. Brookvale 258 A10
pl. Cronulla 494 B14
pl. Darling Point 13 K7
pl. Galston 159 H9
pl. Paddington 21 E2
plz. N Sydney K E8
rd. Mt Riverview 234 C1
st. Allawah 432 F7
st. Artarmon 284 J13
st. Ashfield 372 F1
st. Avalon 139 K12
st. Berala 339 C13
st. Berowra Ht 133 A6
st. Burwood 342 A15
st. Camden 477 B14
st. Campsie 401 J2
st. Croydon 342 F16
st. Five Dock 342 H8
st. Granville 308 C13
st. Guildford 337 F2
st. Haymarket F A15
st. Haymarket 3 H16
st. Hurstville 431 K3
st. Kingsgrove 402 B13
st. Liverpool 395 E2
st. Newtown 18 A8
st. N Richmond 87 C12
st. Paddington 21 D3
st. Paddington 21 E2
st. Parramatta 308 E1
st. Picton 563 F3
st. Randwick 377 A13
st. Redfern 19 G15
st. Riverstone 182 K9
st. Rooty Hill 242 A15
st. Rozelle 10 K2
st. Ryde 282 E13
st. Surry Hills F A15
st. Surry Hills 19 H7
st. Sydney D C16
st. Sydney 3 J6
st. Wahroonga 221 J13
st. Waterloo 19 G15
st. Wetherill Pk 334 E3
st. Windsor 121 A8
st. Zetland 375 J9
wy. Airds 512 B11
ELIZABETHAN
pl. St Ives Ch 224 A6
ELIZABETH BAY
cr. Elizabeth Bay 13 D5
rd. Elizabeth Bay 13 B6
rd. Elizabeth Bay 13 C5
rd. Rcuttrs Bay 13 C5
ELIZABETH HAKE
cl. Castle Hill, off Vittoria Smith Av 218 J13
ELIZABETH HENRIETTA
cct. Mcquarie Lk 423 F14
ELIZABETH MACARTHUR
av. Camden S 507 B12
dr. Bella Vista 246 C2
ELK
pl. Cranebrook 237 D1
pl. Seven Hills 275 C9
st. Marsfield 281 G1
ELKE
cr. Chester Hill 368 C6
wy. Toongabbie 276 A5
ELKHORN
pl. Alfords Point 429 A14
ELLA
st. Artarmon 315 C3
st. Rydalmere 309 K5
st. St Leonards 315 C3
ELLALONG
pl. Doonside 243 E10
pl. Cremorne, off Ellalong Rd 316 F5
rd. Cremorne 316 F5
rd. N Turramrra 223 F8
ELLAM
dr. Seven Hills 275 D7
ELLAMATTA
av. Mosman 317 C10
ELLEN
pl. Ingleburn 453 D10
st. Curl Curl 258 J15
st. Panania 428 E3
st. Randwick 407 D2
st. Randwick 407 D3
st. Rozelle 7 A16
st. Ryde 281 K9
ELLENDALE
rd. Kenthurst 157 G14
ELLENGOWAN
cr. Whalan 240 J9
ELLEN SUBWAY
Mortdale 431 C8
ELLERMAN
av. Kenthurst 188 D4
ELLERSLIE
dr. W Pnnant Hl 249 A6
rd. Bexley 402 F12
rd. Bexley North 402 F12
ELLERSTON
ct. Wattle Grove 396 A16
ELLERY
cl. St Ives Ch 224 B1
pde. Seaforth 287 A9
pl. Caringbah 493 A15
st. Bossley Park 334 B8
ELLESMERE
av. Hunters Hill 313 J11
av. Schofields 183 A15
ct. Wattle Grove 395 K14
rd. Gymea Bay 491 G12
st. Panania 398 D13
ELLIM
pl. Cranebrook 207 D8
ELLIMATTA
st. Rydalmere 279 J16
wy. Cherrybrook, off Tennyson Cl 219 D10
ELLIOT
pl. Hillsdale 406 G14
st. Beacon Hill 257 H8
ELLIOTDALE
cl. Elderslie 507 K3
ELLIOTT
av. East Ryde 282 K15
av. Erskineville 18 C16
pl. Baulkham Hl 246 J3
pl. Cherrybrook 219 J10
pl. St Helens Pk 541 A9
rd. Menai 458 F12
st. Balmain 344 E4
st. Belfield 371 D7
st. Kings Park 244 D4
st. Kingswood 237 E16
st. Lalor Park 245 C9
st. North Bondi 348 C14
st. N Strathfield 341 D7
st. N Sydney 5 H3
st. Picnic Point 428 A7
ELLIS
av. Alexandria 375 D16
av. Ingleburn 453 E7
cr. Miller 363 G16
la. Ellis Lane 476 B11
pde. Yennora 337 A10
pl. Kings Lngly 245 K6
rd. Beacon Hill 257 E5

st. Botany 405 J10
st. Chatswood 284 H11
st. Concord 342 A3
st. Condell Park 398 F5
st. Merrylands 307 C9
st. Oatlands 279 A9
st. St Marys 269 E2
st. Sylvania 462 E8
ELLIS BENT
rd. Greendale 385 A9
ELLISON
la. Greenwich 314 K10
pl. Emu Plains 235 G9
pl. Pymble 253 C7
rd. Castlereagh 176 D13
rd. Springwood 172 G14
ELLISTON
pl. Barden Rdg 488 G5
st. Chester Hill 338 C14
ELLSMORE
av. Killara 253 K15
ELLSWORTH
dr. Tregear 240 B4
st. Leumeah 482 K11
ELM
av. Belrose 225 H11
ct. Cherrybrook 219 G13
pl. Narellan Vale 479 A12
pl. North Rocks 278 E2
pl. Rydalmere 309 H1
pl. Wentwthvle 277 A8
pl. Woolooware 493 C11
rd. Auburn 339 A7
st. Burwood Ht 371 K3
st. Greystanes 306 F9
st. Lugarno 429 H16
st. N St Marys 239 H11
st. Schofields 184 A12
st. Villawood 367 A2
ELMBRIDGE
rd. Jamisontown 266 C2
ELMSLEA
pl. Airds 512 C10
ELONERA
st. Rydalmere 309 G2
ELOORA
st. Lane Cove W 313 H2
ELOUERA
cr. Moorebank 396 G7
cr. Woodbine 481 D14
ct. Clarmnt Ms 268 H1
la. Blacktown 275 B2
rd. Avalon 169 K1
rd. Cronulla 494 A10
rd. Westleigh 220 E8
st. Beverly Hills 401 C11
ELOURA
pl. Bonnyrigg 364 A7
st. Dharruk 241 B7
ELPHICK
av. Mascot 405 D2
ELPHIN
st. Tahmoor 565 H9
ELPHINSTONE
pl. Davidson 225 B16
rd. S Coogee 407 F4
st. Cabarita 342 D1
ELRINGTON
pl. Cartwright 394 C5
ELSE
pl. Springwood 201 K2
ELSEY
pl. Leumeah 482 G11
ELSHAM
rd. Auburn 339 E7
ELSIE
st. Burwood 341 K13
st. Earlwood 372 G16
st. Scotland I 168 J4
ELSINORE
st. Merrylands 307 G15
ELSMERE
st. Kensington 376 F10
ELSMORE
pl. Carlingford 280 C3
ELSOM
st. Kings Lngly 244 K5
ELSTON
av. Denistone 281 E11
av. Narwee 400 G14
la. Narwee, off Elston Av 400 G13
ELSWICK
la. Leichhardt 15 F4
st. Leichhardt 15 G1
st. Petersham 15 K5
st.n, Leichhardt 9 F10
ELTHAM
pl. Cecil Hills 362 D6
pl. Heathcote 519 A11
st. Beacon Hill 257 K4
st. Blacktown 275 A9
st. Dulwich Hill 15 A13
st. Dulwich Hill 373 E7
st. Gladesville 312 H6
st. Lewisham 15 A13
st. Lewisham 373 E7
ELTON
pl. Plumpton 241 H7
ELTONS
rd. Silverdale 383 D6
ELVA
av. Killara 253 K10
st. Cabramtta W 365 B6
st. Strathfield 341 F11
st. Toongabbie 276 G8
ELVINA
av. Avalon 140 A15
av. Newport 169 D7
st. Dover Ht 348 E8
st. Greystanes 305 J6
ELVY
pl. Newtown 18 D8
st. Bargo 567 A2
ELWIN
st. Peakhurst 429 J3
st. Strathfield 341 C14
ELWOOD
cr. Quakers Hill 213 E15
pl. St Johns Pk 364 H2
ELWYN
cl. Mona Vale 199 A4
ELY
pl. Marayong 243 J6
st. Revesby 398 G13
ELYARD
cr. West Hoxton 392 A12
st. Narellan 478 F11
EMANUEL
la. Rosebery, off Queen St 375 G13
EMERALD
dr. Eagle Vale 481 B7
pl. Cartwright 393 J5
pl. Emu Plains 235 E13
pl. Grays Point 491 C15
rd. Seven Hills 275 C7
st. Emu Plains 235 D13
st. Narrabeen 229 B1
st. W Pnnant Hl 248 J6
EMERSON
pl. Menai 458 H7
st. Leumeah 512 B2
st. Shalvey 211 A13
st. Wetherill Pk 334 J5
EMERSTAN
dr. Castle Cove 286 E6
EMERT
pde. Emerton 240 H7
st. Greystanes 306 H4
st. S Wntwthvle 306 H4
st. Wentwthvle 306 J1
EMERY
av. Yagoona 369 E10
st. Rooty Hill 271 K3
EMEX
pl. Mcquarie Fd 454 D4
EMILIA
cl. Rsemeadow 540 G6
pl. Prestons 393 F13
EMILY
av. Emu Plains 235 H10
pl. Cherrybrook 219 G16
st. Breakfast Pt 312 B16
st. Hurstville 401 J15
st. Leichhardt 16 D2
st. Mortlake 312 B16
st. Mount Druitt 271 C4
st. Rozelle 10 J2
EMIL ZATOPEK
av. Newington L F16
av. Newington, off Newington Dr 310 B13
EMLYN
pl. Kellyville 186 B16
EMMA
cl. Bonnyrigg 364 C5
cr. Wentwthvle 277 B9
gr. Glenwood 215 D13
pde. Winmalee 172 K13
pl. Ambarvale 510 G14
pl. Berowra 133 G9
st. Lakemba 370 J16
st. Leichhardt 10 F15
st. Mona Vale 198 J4
EMMALINE
st. Ramsgate Bch 433 G11
EMMANUEL
tce. Glenwood 215 J12
EMMAUS
rd. Ingleside 197 E3
EMMERICK
st. Lilyfield 9 K6
EMMETT
cl. Picton 563 H4
la. Crows Nest 315 G8
pl. Killarney Ht 256 C16
st. Crows Nest 315 G8
st. Tahmoor 565 J12
EMMETTS FARM
rd. Rossmore 389 F5
EMPEROR
pl. Forestville 256 C8
pl. Kenthurst 157 E14
EMPIRE
av. Blakehurst 432 C16
av. Concord 342 B5
ct. Carlingford 279 D4
la. Sydney A K15
la. Marrickville, off Victoria Rd 374 F10
pl. Illawong 459 E4
st. Haberfield 343 C14
EMPRESS
cct. Rouse Hill 185 E3
la. Hurstville 432 A7
st. Hurstville 432 B7
EMPYREAN
gr. Doonside 243 F15
EMU
av. Hinchinbrk 363 C16
cl. Bossley Park 334 C10
la. Canterbury 372 D14
pl. Hornsby Ht 161 J8
rd. Glenbrook 264 D5
st. Canterbury 372 D14
st. Collaroy Plat 228 H13
st. Strathfield 371 G1
st. West Ryde 280 G11
EMU PLAINS
rd. Mt Riverview 204 F15
ENDEAVOUR
av. La Perouse 436 J14
av. St Clair 270 A12
cl. Castle Hill 217 J9
dr. Beacon Hill 257 G4
dr. Narrabeen 228 F8
dr. Winmalee 173 H7
la. Sans Souci 463 A3
la. St Clair, off Endeavour Av 270 A12
pl. Riverwood 400 E14
rd. Caringbah 493 B3
rd. Daceyville 406 F3
rd. Georges Hall 367 D15
st. Chatswood 284 J9
st. Ruse 512 G3
st. Sans Souci 463 A2
st. Seven Hills 275 D2
st. Sylvania 462 D9
st. Wahroonga 223 A5
st. West Ryde 281 C15
ENDERBY
cl. Hinchinbrk 362 K14
pl. Barden Rdg 458 J16
st. Tregear 240 F8
ENDGATE
gln. Wrrngtn Dns 237 K3
ENFIELD
av. N Richmond 87 C15
cl. St Johns Pk 364 H4
st. Jamisontown 266 C5
st. Marrickville 373 H10
ENGADINE
av. Engadine 518 G4
pl. Engadine 518 J3
ENGEL
av. Marsfield 281 H3
ENGESTA
av. Camden 506 K7
ENGLAND
av. Marrickville 16 E16
rd. Ingleburn 422 J14
st. Btn-le-Sds 433 H2
wk. Lalor Park 245 D11
ENGLART
pl. Baulkham Hl 247 F7
ENGLEWOOD
wy. Glenmore Pk 266 E10
ENGLISH
av. Camden S 507 B15
av. Castle Hill 248 A4
la. Kogarah 433 B7
st. Camperdwn 17 G6
st. Carlton 432 K6
st. Glenfield 424 E10
st. Kogarah 433 A7
st. Revesby 398 K14
st. Woolooware 493 D10
ENGLORIE PARK
dr. Ambarvale 510 F16
dr. Campbelltwn 510 H10
dr. Campbelltwn 510 F16
dr. Glen Alpine 510 F16
dr. Rsemeadow 540 C2
ENID
av. Granville 308 F12
av. Roselands 401 B8
pl. Ingleburn 453 E10
st. Denistone 281 G12
st. Greystanes 305 J8
ENMORE
la. Enmore 17 A14
rd. Enmore 17 A14
rd. Marrickville 16 K16
rd. Marrickville 374 E10
rd. Newtown 17 A14
ENNERDALE
cr. Collaroy Plat 228 E9
ENNIS
av. Killarney Ht 286 B1
la. Balmain 7 E12
pl. Lalor Park 245 F13
rd. Milsons Pt 5 K12
st. Balmain 7 E11
ENOCH
pl. Winston Hills 277 B4
ENOGGERA
rd. Beverly Hills 401 A10
ENRIGHT
st. East Hills 427 H2
ENSIGN
pl. Castle Hill 218 A11
ENTERPRISE
av. Padstow 399 E12
dr. Glendenning 242 F6
pl. Wetherill Pk 333 K4
rd. Cranebrook 207 A9
ENTRANCE
rd. Parramatta 278 B13
EOS
pl. Schofields 213 B1
EPACRIS
av. Caringbah 492 J13
av. Forestville 256 A8
EPHRAIM HOWE
pl. Narellan Vale 508 K2
EPIC
pl. Villawood 337 J15
EPIDOTE
cl. Eagle Vale 481 F9
EPO
pl. Glenfield 424 F9
EPPING
av. Eastwood 280 J5
av. Epping 280 K4
cl. Cambrdg Pk 237 J10
dr. Frenchs Frst 256 F3
rd. Double Bay 14 E12
rd. Epping 251 C16
rd. Lane Cove W 283 H14
rd. Mcquarie Pk 282 D4
rd. Marsfield 251 C16
rd. North Ryde 282 D4
EPPING FOREST
dr. Eschol Park 481 A1
dr. Kearns 481 A1
EPPLESTON
pl. West Pymble 252 J10
wk. West Pymble, off Eppleston Pl 252 J11
EPSOM
pwy. Chipping Ntn, off Epsom Rd 396 E2
rd. Chipping Ntn 396 B6
rd. Rosebery 375 H12
rd. Zetland 375 H12
EPWORTH
pl. N Narrabeen 198 F11
EQUESTRIAN
dr. Picton 563 B1
st. Glenwood 245 J3
EQUITY
la. Erskineville 18 B14
pl. Canley Vale 365 J4
ERANG
av. Kirrawee 491 A6
st. Carss Park 432 G13
ERAWAR
cl. Westleigh 190 J16
ERBY
pl. Parramatta 308 C2
ERCILDOUNE
av. Beverley Pk 433 C9
av. Kogarah 433 C9
EREBUS
cr. Tregear 240 F8
ERIC
av. Bass Hill 368 C13
av. Merrylands 307 D16
cl. Emu Plains 234 K7
cr. Lidcombe 340 A8
la. Mosman, off Earl St 316 J5
rd. Artarmon 284 H15
st. Bundeena 524 B12
st. Eastwood 280 G9
st. Harbord 258 G16
st. Lilyfield 10 B7
st. Wahroonga 223 B6
ERICA
cl. Westleigh 220 E8
cr. Georges Hall 367 H15
la. Minto 482 F2
pl. Minto 482 F2
pl. Rooty Hill 272 C4
st. Kurmond 86 E1
ERIC COOPER
dr. Castle Hill 217 B8
ERIC FELTON
st. Castle Hill, off Old Castle Hill Rd 218 C13
ERIE
la. Petersham 16 B8
pl. St Clair 269 H16
pl. Seven Hills 275 E6
st. S Granville 338 G8
ERIN
pl. Casula 423 H3
ERINA
av. Five Dock 343 B8
cl. Bossley Park 333 H8
pl. S Windsor 150 D2
st. Eastwood 281 F4
ERINLEIGH
ct. Kellyville 216 D1
ERITH
st. Blacktown 275 A9
st. Botany 405 D12
st. Mosman 316 H6
ERLESTOKE
pl. Castle Hill 219 A10
ERMINGTON
la. Ermington 310 C2
st. Botany 405 J14
ERNA
av. Lansvale 366 K8
pl. Quakers Hill 214 D12
ERNEST
av. Chipping Ntn 366 H15
la. Crows Nest 315 H6
pl. Crows Nest 315 F6
st. Balgowlah Ht 287 G13
st. Cammeray 315 H7
st. Cremorne 315 H7
st. Crows Nest 315 H7
st. Glenwood 215 D13
st. Guildford 337 E6
st. Hunters Hill 313 J10
st. Lakemba 401 A4
st. Lugarno 430 A9
st. Neutral Bay 315 H7
st. Sefton 368 H3
st.n, Lakemba 400 J1
ERNST
pl. Edensor Pk 333 H12
ERNSTINE HILL
cl. Glenmore Pk 265 K7
EROLA
cir. Lindfield 283 K3

EROS
pl. Rsemeadow....540 F2
pl. Winston Hills..277 F3
ERRICA
st. Greenfld Pk.....334 C13
ERRIGAL
pl. Killarney Ht.....286 D1
ERRINGHI
pl. McGraths Hl...122 A13
ERROL
pl. Quakers Hill....214 F13
ERROL FLYNN
bvd. Moore Park.......21 A9
ERSKINE
rd. Caringbah.......462 H16
st. Chatswood.....284 K11
st. Riverwood......400 C16
st. Sydney..............C D1
st. Sydney...............3 E1
wy. Minto.............483 A1
ERSKINE PARK
rd. Erskine Park...299 K5
rd. St Clair...........270 E16
ERSKINEVILLE
la. Erskineville.......18 A15
la. Newtown..........17 J13
rd. Erskineville.......17 H12
rd. Newtown..........17 H12
ERVINE
st. Winston Hills..277 E1
ERYNE
pl. Dural..............219 B7
ESCHOL PARK
dr. Eschol Park....481 C3
dr. Kearns............481 C3
ESDAILE
pl. Arncliffe..........403 E9
ESHELBY
st. Green Valley...363 C11
ESHER
la. Burwood, off
Burwood Rd....342 A10
mw. Wattle Grove...425 K4
st. Burwood.........342 A11
ESK
av. Green Valley...362 J11
la. Marrickville, off
Grove St..........373 J15
st. Marrickville.....373 J15
st. N Wahrnga.....223 B1
ESKDALE
cl. Narellan Vale...508 F2
st. Minchinbury....272 C8
ESME
av. Chester Hill.....338 C15
ESMOND
pl. Wakeley..........334 G13
ESPALIER
pl. Minchinbury...272 B10
ESPERANCE
cr. Wakeley..........334 K11
pl. Yarrawarrah....489 H13
ESPLANADE
. Elizabeth Bay....13 C4
. Mona Vale......169 D14
ESPLIN
av. Strathfield.......341 H15
ESSENDON
st. St Johns Pk....364 F3
ESSEX
av. Castle Hill.......217 K11
st. Blacktown.......244 B13
st. Epping............281 D1
st. Guildford..........337 C4
st. Killara.............253 G11
st. Marrickville.......16 A16
st. Minto.............452 E16
st. The Rocks..........A G8
st. The Rocks..........1 F12
ESSEY
pl. Merrylands.....307 E8
ESSILIA
st. Collaroy Plat...228 H12
ESSINGTON
cr. Sylvania..........461 K13
st. Wentwthvle.....307 B3
ESSON
pl. Glenmore Pk...265 J6
ESTELLA
pl. Ambarvale......510 H15
ESTELLE
pl. Frenchs Frst....256 A3
ESTHER
la. Surry Hills........20 B4
la. Mosman, off
Esther Rd........317 D6
rd. Mosman.........317 D6
st. Greystanes......305 K8
st. Surry Hills.........20 C4
st. Winston Hills..277 A4
ESTONIAN
rd. Thirlmere........561 A16
rd. Thirlmere........564 A1
ESTRAMINA
wy. Minto.............482 J7
ETA
st. Blacktown.......274 C4
ETCHELL
la. Cranebrook, off
Etchell Pl.........207 A10
pl. Cranebrook.....207 A10
ETELA
st. Belmore..........371 E15
ETHAM
av. Darling Point.....13 K4
ETHEL
av. Brookvale........258 D12
la. Allawah...........432 E5
la. Eastwood........281 C7
st. Balgowlah.......287 E10
st. Burwood.........342 A16
st. Carlton............432 E4
st. Condell Park...398 E6
st. Eastwood........281 C7
st. Erskineville.......18 C14
st. Hornsby..........191 F9
st. Merrylands.....307 K16
st. Randwick.........407 C2
st. Seaforth..........287 E10
st. Vaucluse.........348 F7
ETHELL
rd. Kirrawee.........461 C15
ETHERDEN
rd. Bligh Park.......150 J6
ETHIE
rd. Beacon Hill......257 D8
ETHNE
av. Randwick........377 C10
ETIVAL
st. Palm Beach.....140 B10
ETNA
cl. Cranebrook.....207 E14
pl. Bossley Park...334 B10
ETON
ct. Cambrdg Pk....238 A8
la. Camperdwn......17 D7
la. Sutherland......490 E4
rd. Cambrdg Pk....237 F6
rd. Lindfield..........284 B5
st. Bexley............402 H14
st. Camperdwn......17 D7
st. Fairfield...........336 D7
st. Smithfield........335 K5
st.n, Sutherland......490 E5
st.s, Sutherland......490 E6
ETONVILLE
pde. Croydon..........342 G16
ETRUSCAN
ct. Glenwood.......245 K4
ETTALONG
pl. Woodbine........481 K11
rd. Greystanes.......306 D4
st. Auburn...........339 A8
st. Collaroy Plat...228 F11
ETTLESDALE
rd. Spring Farm....507 H6
ETTRICK
st. Ashbury..........372 F8
EUCALYPT
rd. Springwood....202 B2
EUCALYPTUS
cl. St Ives............253 K1
ct. Baulkham Hl...247 E14
ct. Stanhpe Gdn...215 B11
dr. Cranebrook.....237 E1
dr. Mcquarie Fd....424 E16
dr. Westleigh........220 F8
st. Alfords Point...459 B3
st. Peakhurst.......430 E4
st. St Ives............254 A1
st. Wentwthvle......277 A9
EUCHORA
la. Springwood....202 B1
EUCLA
cr. Malabar..........437 F8
pl. Sutherland......460 C14
EUCLASE
pl. Eagle Vale.......481 F8
EUCLID
st. Winston Hills...277 D5
EUCRA
st. Schofields.......213 K6
EUCUMBENE
cr. Heckenberg.....363 K12
dr. Woodcroft.......243 H8
la. St Clair, off
Eucumbene Pl..269 J16
pl. St Clair............269 J16
EUDON
st. Doonside........243 C4
EUGENES
gln. Kellyville..........185 J14
EUGENIA
st. Loftus.............489 K9
wy. Bidwill.............211 G13
EULABAH
av. Earlwood.........402 C5
EULALIA
st. West Ryde......280 H14
EULALIE
av. Randwick........377 C12
EULBERTIE
av. Warrawee........222 F12
EULDA
st. Belmore..........371 B14
EULO
pde. Ryde..............282 A13
EUMINA
st. Beverly Hills....401 D10
EUMUNG
ct. Wattle Grove...426 A2
EUNGAI
pl. N Narrabeen....198 F15
EUPHRATES
pl. Kearns............451 B14
EURABALONG
rd. Burraneer........523 E4
EURABBA
rd. Duffys Frst......195 A1
EURABBIE
gln. St Clair...........270 A15
pl. Mcquarie Fd....454 E4
st. Cabramatta.....365 H10
EURALLA
st. Westmead.......307 F3
EUREKA
cr. Sadleir............394 C3
gr. Glenwood.......215 C15
EURELLA
av. N Balgowlah....287 D4
st. Burwood.........342 B13
EURIMBLA
av. Randwick........376 K15
EUROA
pl. Engadine.........489 D9
EUROBIN
av. Manly.............288 F4
EUROKA
la. N Sydney...........5 B8
rd. Glenbrook.......264 A1
rd. Mulgoa..........294 D14
rd. Westleigh........220 F9
st. Ingleburn........453 B10
st. Northbridge.....286 A15
st. N Sydney...........5 B8
st. Waverton...........5 B8
EURONG
st. Wahroonga.....251 G1
EURYALUS
st. Mosman.........286 K16
EUSTACE
pde. Killara............253 D16
st. Fairfield...........335 K13
st. Fairfield Ht.........335 K13
st. Manly..............288 F9
EUSTON
la. Alexandria.......375 C11
rd. Alexandria.......375 C11
rd. Auburn............338 J3
rd. Hurlstone Pk....372 K12
st. Rydalmere.....309 D2
EUTHELLA
av. Hunters Hill.....313 E11
EVA
av. Green Valley....362 K11
la. Northwood......314 H9
pl. Glenfield.........424 H13
pl. Northmead......277 H8
st. Condell Park....398 H5
st. Greystanes......305 K6
st. Northwood......314 H8
st. Roselands.......400 F9
EVALINE
st. Campsie.........371 J15
st. Canterbury.....372 A14
EVAN
la. Waterloo..........19 J12
pl. Kings Lngly....245 A5
st. Gladesville.....312 H8
st. Penrith...........237 A13
st. S Penrith........266 J3
st. S Penrith........266 J4
EVANDA
st. Berowra.........133 F10
EVANDALE
ct. Wattle Grove..425 J5
EVANS
av. Eastlakes........405 J2
av. Eastlakes........406 A2
av. Moorebank......396 C7
cr. Richmond......119 C3
la. Eastlakes.........405 K2
la. Redfern...........19 A5
la. St Leonards....315 D4
la. Mosman, off
Muston St.......317 C6
pde. Lapstone........264 G4
pl. Mt Pritchard....364 K9
rd. Carlingford.....280 A7
rd. Dundas Vy......280 A7
rd. Glenhaven......217 K2
rd. Hornsby Ht......191 G4
rd. Rooty Hill.......272 D6
rd. Rcuttrs Bay......13 C6
rd. Telopea..........279 H10
rd. Wilberforce......61 K12
st. Balmain.............7 B13
st. Bronte............377 J9
st. Como.............460 H8
st. Fairfield Ht.......335 H11
st. Harbord..........258 H16
st. Newington..........L G11
st. Newington.....310 D11
st. Peakhurst.......429 K5
st. Randwick........377 A9
st. Rozelle.............7 A16
st. Sans Souci.......463 B2
st. West Pymble..252 F7
wy. Minto.............482 J5
EVE
ct. Cabramatta.....365 G11
pl. Berowra Ht.....133 F8
pl. Winston Hills..276 H2
st. Arncliffe..........403 J9
st. Banksia..........403 J13
st. Erskineville.....375 A10
st. Guildford.........338 C5
st. Strathfield.......371 D4
EVELEIGH
st. Redfern............19 A6
EVELYN
av. Concord..........342 C7
av. Turramurra.......223 B11
cl. Wetherill Pk.....334 F4
cr. Berowra Ht.....133 C6
pl. Belrose...........226 B16
pl. Glendenning...242 F4
st. Baulkham Hl...247 G13
st. Greenwich.......314 K10
st. Mcquarie Fd...454 B6
st. S Coogee.........407 G4
st. Sylvania.........462 C10
st. Sylvania Wtr...462 C10
st.n, Sylvania.........462 E9
EVENING
row. St Clair..........270 C13
EVENSTAR
pl. St Clair...........270 D14
EVERARD
st. Hunters Hill....313 A7
EVEREST
st. Seven Hills.....275 B9
EVERETT
pl. Annangrove....155 D6
st. Maroubra.......406 K8
wy. Wahroonga....222 C7
EVERGOLD
pl. Eagle Vale.......481 B8
EVERGREEN
av. Bradbury........511 D11
wy. Kellyville.........185 E6
EVERITT
cr. Minchinbury...272 C10
pl. Strathfield S...371 E6
EVERLEY
rd. Auburn...........338 H12
rd. Sefton............338 F11
EVERS
cl. Edensor Pk.....363 F3
EVERTON
rd. Belrose...........226 A15
rd. Faulconbdg.....171 A16
rd. Strathfield.......341 G11
st. Pymble...........253 D3
EVERVIEW
av. Mosman.........316 K4
EVESHAM
ct. Baulkham Hl...216 H16
pl. Chipping Ntn..366 G13
EVESSON
la. Woollahra.........22 K4
EVOE
pl. Doonside........243 A10
EWAN
st. Mascot...........405 A5
EWART
la. Dulwich Hill....373 D13
st. Dulwich Hill....373 C12
wy. Claymore, off
Colquhoun Wy.. 481 C11
EWELL
la. Bondi.............377 J6
st. Balmain..............7 B12
st. Bondi.............377 J5
EWEN
st. Roselands......400 H6
EWENTON
la. Balmain..............8 C11
st. Balmain..............8 C11
EWING
av. Little Bay........437 G14
pl. Bligh Park.......150 K7
EWOS
pde. Cronulla..........493 K16
EXBURY
ct. Wattle Grove...426 B5
EXCALIBUR
av. Castle Hill.......217 G5
cl. Mt Colah.........162 E11
EXCELLER
av. Bankstown......399 F7
EXCELSIOR
av. Belfield...........371 C7
av. Castle Hill.......247 F2
av. Castle Hill.......248 A4
pde. Marrickville.....373 H16
rd. Cronulla..........493 H12
rd. Mt Colah.........162 E11
st. Concord..........342 B7
st. Guildford.........338 B4
st. Guildford.........338 B7
st. Leichhardt........15 H3
st. Merrylands.....308 C16
wy. Castle Hill.......247 F2
EXCHANGE
rd. Smeaton Gra..479 A9
EXELL
st. Bnksmeadw....436 A2
EXETER
gr. Kings Lngly....245 G4
pl. Bidwill............241 E1
pl. North Rocks...278 J2
rd. Homebsh W...340 G9
rd. Kemps Ck.......360 B6
rd. Wahroonga.....222 A11
st. Camden..........477 A14
EXFORD
ct. Wattle Grove...425 J2
EXHIBITION
pde. Mt Pritchard...364 F13
pl. Haymarket..........E A3
pl. Haymarket..........3 C9
EXILE
la. Concord.........342 E5
EXLEY
pl. S Penrith........266 K6
rd. Wedderburn...540 A15
EXMOOR
pl. Blairmount......481 B14
EXMOUTH
pl. Yarrawarrah....489 G13
EXPERIMENT
st. Pyrmont...........12 J5
EXPLORER
st. Eveleigh...........18 D12
EXPLORERS
rd. Glenbrook.......264 C1
rd. Glenbrook.......264 C3
rd. Lapstone........264 C3
wy. St Clair..........270 D11

EXTON
wy. Rsemeadow ... 540 J2
EYLES
av. Epping ... 250 C16
st. Telopea ... 279 H10
EYNHAM
rd. Milperra ... 397 F11
EYRE
av. Ingleburn ... 423 B10
pl. Camden S ... 507 B10
pl. Kirrawee ... 460 J16
pl. Mt Colah ... 162 C11
st. Chifley ... 437 A6
st. Lalor Park ... 245 B14
st. Smithfield ... 335 D1
st. Wrrngtn Cty ... 238 G8
EZZY
la. Chester Hill ... 337 F13

F

F3
Asquith ... 192 D16
Berowra ... 163 A9
Brooklyn ... 75 A13
Cowan ... 104 E13
Krngai Ch NP ... 192 D16
Mooney ... 75 A13
Mt Colah ... 162 F16
Mt Krng-gai ... 163 A9
N Wahrnga ... 222 B6
Wahroonga ... 222 B6
F6
Waterfall ... 519 D16
FABIAN
pl. Mona Vale ... 199 A5
pl. Rsemeadow ... 540 G6
FABOS
pl. Croydon Pk ... 372 D6
pl. Smithfield ... 335 J7
FABRY
st. Botany ... 405 G13
FACER
ct. Castle Hill ... 217 F15
FACEY
cr. Lurnea ... 394 B8
FACTORY
ct. Padstow ... 399 G12
rd. Regentville ... 265 E1
st. Granville ... 308 H15
st. Haymarket ... E C5
st. N Parramatta ... 278 C13
FADDEN
pl. N Wahrnga ... 192 F14
rd. Springwood ... 202 D12
FAGAN
pl. Bonnyrigg ... 363 J10
FAGANS
rd. Arcadia ... 129 G11
FAHEY
la. Marrickville, off Philpott St ... 374 D9
FAHY
pl. Loftus ... 490 B6
FAIR
rd. Glenorie ... 96 E4
FAIRBAIRN
av. Clontarf ... 287 E12
av. East Killara ... 254 F8
FAIRBURN
av. W Pnnant Hl ... 249 J3
cr. Minchinbury ... 272 C8
rd. Wedderburn ... 540 E13
FAIREY
rd. S Windsor ... 121 B16
rd. Windsor ... 121 A12
FAIRFAX
rd. Bellevue Hill ... 14 G9
rd. Mosman ... 317 C2
FAIRFIELD
av. Windsor ... 120 J10
pl. Jamisontown ... 266 B1
rd. Guildford W ... 336 H2
rd. Woodpark ... 306 H16
rd. Yennora ... 336 F7
st. Fairfield ... 336 G12
st. Fairfield E ... 336 J11
st. Old Guildfrd ... 337 A11
st. Yennora ... 337 A11
FAIRFORD
rd. Padstow ... 399 F11
FAIRFOWL
la. Dulwich Hill, off Fairfowl St ... 373 F10
st. Dulwich Hill ... 373 F10

FAIRGREEN
pl. Castle Hill ... 217 J7
FAIRHOLM
st. Strathfield ... 371 D1
FAIRLAND
av. Greenacre ... 370 C10
FAIRLAWN
av. Turramurra ... 223 B11
cl. Lansvale ... 366 D10
FAIRLIGHT
av. East Killara ... 254 F10
av. Fairfield ... 336 E14
cr. Fairlight ... 288 B10
pl. Woodbine ... 481 J9
rd. Mulgoa ... 295 A16
st. Fairlight ... 288 B9
st. Five Dock ... 342 K11
st. Lilyfield ... 9 G8
st. Manly ... 288 C9
FAIRMONT
av. Baulkham Hl ... 216 J16
FAIRMOUNT
cct. Glenwood ... 246 A5
st. Dulwich Hill ... 373 D6
st. Lakemba ... 370 H15
st. Merrylands ... 307 A8
FAIRPORT
st. N Curl Curl ... 258 G10
FAIRS
av. Woolooware ... 493 E10
FAIRVIEW
av. Engadine ... 518 D4
av. Roselands ... 400 H6
av. St Ives Ch ... 223 K4
pl. Mt Krng-gai ... 162 J10
rd. Cabramatta ... 366 C7
rd. Canley Vale ... 366 C7
st. Arncliffe ... 403 B10
st. Concord ... 341 J6
st. Guildford ... 337 B2
FAIRWATER
dr. Harringtn Pk ... 478 D5
FAIRWAY
av. Kogarah ... 433 E6
av. Mortdale ... 430 G8
av. Pymble ... 223 H14
av. Springwood ... 172 D13
cl. Manly Vale ... 288 C5
dr. Kellyville ... 216 E10
pl. Narellan ... 478 C9
FAIRWAYS
av. Leonay ... 235 B15
cr. Springwood ... 172 B13
FAIRWEATHER
pl. Eagle Vale ... 481 E9
st. Bellevue Hill ... 347 F15
FAIRY BOWER
rd. Manly ... 288 J12
FAIRY DELL
cl. Westleigh ... 220 G9
FAIRYLAND
av. Chatswd W ... 283 J10
FAIRYWREN
cl. Glenmore Pk ... 265 J12
FAITH
ct. Georges Hall ... 367 G10
FAITHFULL
pl. Airds ... 512 D10
st. Elderslie ... 477 G16
st. Richmond ... 119 B4
wy. Airds ... 512 D10
FALCON
cct. Green Valley ... 363 D12
cl. Greenfld Pk ... 334 C12
cr. Clarmnt Ms ... 268 J4
la. Clarmnt Ms, off Falcon Cr ... 268 J4
la. Crows Nest, off Sophia St ... 315 G7
pl. Ingleburn ... 453 G6
st. Crows Nest ... 315 G7
st. Neutral Bay ... 315 G7
st. Newington ... L F16
st. Newington ... 310 C11
st. N Sydney ... 315 G7
wy. Glenwood ... 215 F14
FALCONER
st. West Ryde ... 281 G16
FALKINER
wy. Airds ... 512 C12
FALKIRK
dr. Kellyville ... 217 B2
pl. Dharruk ... 241 D6
pl. St Andrews ... 481 J1

FALKLAND
cl. Winmalee ... 173 B12
pl. St Andrews ... 481 K2
FALKLANDS
av. Bossley Park ... 334 A8
FALL
st. Cammeray ... 316 C5
st. Cremorne ... 316 C5
st. Revesby ... 398 K13
FALLEN LEAF
ct. W Pnnant Hl ... 248 J3
FALLON
dr. Dural ... 219 D5
st. Quakers Hill ... 214 E16
st. Rydalmere ... 310 A5
FALLONS
rd. Orangeville ... 443 G12
FALLOWFIELD
ct. Wrrngtn Dns ... 237 K5
la. Wrrngtn Dns, off Fallowfield Ct ... 237 K5
FALLOWS
wy. Cherrybrook ... 219 E15
FALLS
st. Leichhardt ... 9 E10
FALMAR
pl. Woronora Ht ... 489 D3
FALMER
st. Abbotsbury ... 333 A14
FALMOUTH
rd. Quakers Hill ... 243 G5
FALSTAFF
pl. Rsemeadow ... 540 G7
FAN
wy. Stanhpe Gdn ... 215 D10
FANE
pl. Doonside ... 243 B8
FANNICH
pl. St Andrews ... 452 B14
FANNIN
pl. Kings Lngly ... 245 A2
FANNING
st. Tempe ... 404 C3
FANNY
pl. Surry Hills ... 20 D2
FANTAIL
cr. Erskine Park ... 270 K15
la. St Clair, off Fantail Cr ... 271 A15
pl. Green Valley ... 363 D10
pl. Ingleburn ... 453 G10
FANTOME
st. Voyager Pt ... 427 D4
FARADAY
av. Rose Bay ... 348 B12
la. Meadowbnk ... 311 E3
rd. Leumeah ... 482 E16
rd. Padstow ... 429 D2
FARAH
pl. Yagoona ... 368 H11
FARHALL
pl. Glenhaven ... 218 A4
FARIOLA
st. Silverwater ... 309 J11
FARLEIGH
st. Ashfield ... 372 J6
FARLEY
pl. Londonderry ... 148 C10
rd. Cecil Park ... 332 G9
FARLOW
pl. Kingswood ... 237 E9
FARM
rd. Kenthurst ... 155 J3
rd. Mulgoa ... 295 E14
rd. Riverstone ... 181 K7
rd. Springwood ... 202 B9
st. Gladesville ... 312 G6
FARMAN
pl. Raby ... 451 C12
FARMER
cl. Glenwood ... 215 F12
pl. St Clair ... 270 A10
rd. Clontarf ... 287 E11
FARMHOUSE
pl. Mt Annan ... 479 K11
FARMING
av. Lowlands ... 88 J14
FARMINGDALE
dr. Blacktown ... 274 D10
FARMRIDGE
wy. Glenhaven ... 218 C3
FARMVIEW
dr. Cranebrook ... 207 C15

FARNBOROUGH
ct. Wattle Grove ... 426 B4
rd. Dural ... 189 H4
FARNELL
av. Carlingford ... 249 E15
av. Royal N P ... 490 B14
rd. Yagoona ... 369 A10
st. Curl Curl ... 258 K13
st. Granville ... 308 B15
st. Hunters Hill ... 313 C6
st. Merrylands ... 308 B15
st. West Ryde ... 280 F12
st. Surry Hills, off Sandwell St ... 20 D1
FARNHAM
av. Randwick ... 377 D14
av. Roselands ... 400 F7
rd. Quakers Hill ... 214 F13
FARNINGHAM
st. Mt Pritchard ... 364 B11
FARNSWORTH
av. Campbelltwn ... 511 G9
av. Warragamba ... 353 E9
FARNWORTH
la. Point Piper, off Wyuna Rd ... 347 F8
FARR
st. Banksia ... 403 F16
st. Marrickville ... 374 B11
st. Rockdale ... 403 F16
FARRAN
la. Woollahra ... 22 E4
st. Lane Cove W ... 283 K13
FARRANT
pl. Carlingford ... 249 H15
FARRAR
av. Krngai Ch NP ... 163 J15
av. Rookwood ... 340 A12
pl. Bonnyrigg Ht ... 363 F7
pl. Jamisontown ... 266 B3
pl. Lalor Park ... 245 B12
st. Arncliffe ... 403 D9
st. Balgowlah Ht ... 287 J12
FARRELL
av. Darlinghurst ... 4 G8
pl. Fairfield W ... 334 K10
rd. Bass Hill ... 367 F7
rd. Kingsgrove ... 402 A13
st. Hebersham ... 241 F4
FARRELLS
la. Castlereagh ... 206 G8
la. Cranebrook ... 206 G8
FARRELLYS
av. Tamarama ... 378 A5
FARRENDON
pl. Mt Annan ... 509 E1
FARRER
av. W Pnnant Hl ... 248 K9
pl. Frenchs Frst ... 255 H5
pl. Oyster Bay ... 461 C5
pl. Sydney ... B D12
FARRIER
pl. Castle Hill ... 217 F5
FARRINGTON
pde. North Ryde ... 282 H10
st. Minchinbury ... 272 C10
FARROW
la. Tempe ... 404 B2
rd. Campbelltwn ... 511 E3
FARTHING
pl. Maroubra ... 407 D15
FARVIEW
rd. Bilgola ... 169 H6
FASSIFERN
pl. Cartwright ... 394 B4
FAUCETT
la. Woolmloo ... 4 D6
FAULDS
rd. Guildford W ... 337 A4
FAULKLAND
cr. Kings Park ... 244 F3
FAULKNER
st. Old Tngabbie ... 277 B7
FAUNA
pl. Kirrawee ... 490 J4
rd. Erskine Park ... 270 E16
st. Earlwood ... 402 J5
FAUNCE
st. Burwood Ht ... 371 K4
FAUST
gln. St Clair ... 270 D15
FAUX
st. Wiley Park ... 400 F4

FAVA
pl. Rooty Hill ... 271 K3
FAVELL
av. Rouse Hill ... 184 J8
st. Toongabbie ... 276 G9
FAVERSHAM
cr. Chipping Ntn ... 366 G15
la. Marrickville, off Hans Pl ... 374 C12
st. Marrickville ... 374 C12
FAWCETT
st. Balmain ... 7 K10
st. Glenfield ... 424 C12
st. Ryde ... 282 A11
FAWKENER
pl. Wrrngtn Cty ... 238 G6
FAWKNER
pl. Barden Rdg ... 488 H5
FAY
pl. Marsfield ... 281 K6
st. N Curl Curl ... 258 F10
FAYE
av. Blakehurst ... 432 D13
av. Earlwood ... 372 H16
st. Seven Hills ... 245 B16
FEARN
st. Toongabbie ... 276 H8
FEATHER
la. St Clair, off Feather St ... 269 G14
st. St Clair ... 269 G14
FEATHERWOOD
av. Cherrybrook ... 219 J5
wy. Castle Hill ... 248 F5
FEATON
pl. Mortdale ... 430 H8
FEDERAL
av. Ashfield ... 373 A3
pde. Brookvale ... 258 B8
pde.w, Brookvale ... 258 A8
rd. Glebe ... 11 G6
rd. Seven Hills ... 275 D2
rd. West Ryde ... 311 C2
FEDERATION
pl. Frenchs Frst ... 256 G1
pl. Sadleir ... 394 C2
rd. Newtown ... 17 F9
FEDOTOW
pl. Rooty Hill ... 271 H3
FEHON
rd. Chatswd W ... 284 H12
FEILBERG
pl. Abbotsford ... 343 B3
FELD
av. Elderslie ... 507 F3
FELDSPAR
rd. Eagle Vale ... 481 F5
FELICIA
pl. Blacktown ... 244 K10
FELL
pl. Schofields ... 212 H1
FELLOWS
rd. Bonnyrigg Ht ... 363 G5
FELS
av. Springwood ... 202 B5
FELTON
av. Lane Cove W ... 284 B14
rd. Carlingford ... 279 B5
rd. Carlingford ... 279 F4
st. Horsley Pk ... 302 F16
st. Telopea ... 279 D7
FELUGA
pl. Acacia Gdn ... 214 G15
FENCHURCH
st. Prospect ... 275 C12
FENDER
pl. Chifley ... 437 B5
FENECH
pl. Quakers Hill ... 213 H7
FENNELL
st. Parramatta ... 278 B15
FENTON
av. Caringbah ... 493 B4
av. Maroubra ... 407 G12
cr. Minto ... 483 A2
st. Panania ... 427 K1
FENWICK
av. Roselands ... 400 J7
cl. Kellyville ... 217 A2
pl. Westmead ... 307 F2
st. Bankstown ... 368 J15
st. Yagoona ... 368 J15
FEODORE
dr. Cecil Hills ... 362 E5

FERAMIN
av. Whalan..........240 J8
FERDINAND
pl. Rsemeadow....540 K5
st. Birchgrove..........7 F3
st. Hunters Hill....313 H10
FERGERSON
av. Fairfield..........336 E9
FERGUSON
av. Castle Hill.......248 C6
av. Thornleigh......221 C15
av. Wiley Park......400 H4
cl. Menai............458 F12
cr. Ingleburn.........423 B13
la. Chatswood.......284 J9
la. Grasmere..........506 E1
la. Chatswood, off Archer St.........284 K9
rd. Springwood....201 G4
st. Forestville.......255 F7
st. Forestville.......255 K8
st. Maroubra.......407 A10
FERGUSSON
st. Glenfield.........424 G8
FERMI
st. Lucas Ht.........487 G12
FERMO
rd. Engadine........489 C9
FERMOY
av. Bayview..........169 A13
rd. Marsden Pk....182 C14
FERN
av. Bradbury........511 C11
av. Wahroonga.....222 B4
cct.e, Menai............458 K14
cct.w, Menai............458 J14
pl. Blacktown.......244 K9
pl. Leonay...........234 J15
pl. Woollahra........377 F3
rd. Hunters Hill....314 A14
st. Clovelly...........377 F10
st. Pymble............253 F4
st. Randwick.......377 G12
FERNBANK
la. Marrickville, off Fernbank St.....374 A13
pl. Cherrybrook...219 B13
st. Marrickville.....374 A13
FERNBROOK
pl. Castle Hill.......218 K6
FERNCLIFFE
rd. Glenhaven......218 A3
FERNCOURT
av. Chatswood.....285 A5
av. Roseville.........285 A5
FERN CREEK
rd. Warriewood....198 G8
FERNCREEK
ct. Kellyville........186 K14
FERNDALE
av. Blaxland.........233 K8
av. Carlingford.....279 C3
cl. Wentwthvle.....277 D10
la. Newtown, off Camden St......374 H9
rd. Badgerys Ck...357 K3
rd. Beecroft..........250 E9
rd. Normanhurst..221 H12
rd. Revesby.........428 G4
st. Chatswd W.....284 D12
st. Ingleburn........454 A10
st. Newtown..........17 D16
FERNDELL
st. Sefton.............338 E12
st. S Granville......338 E12
FERNGREEN
wy. Castle Hill.......248 J2
FERNGROVE
pl. Chester Hill.....338 D12
rd. Canley Ht........335 D16
FERNHILL
av. Epping............250 J13
pl. Glen Alpine.....510 F10
pl. Grays Point.....491 D14
pl. Wrrngtn Dns...237 J5
st. Hurlstone Pk...373 A11
FERNHURST
av. Cremorne......316 G4
FERNLEA
pl. Canley Ht........335 D16
FERNLEAF
cr. Kellyville.........185 K16
ct. Wattle Grove...396 B16

FERNLEIGH
av. Rose Bay........348 C9
cl. Cherrybrook....219 D15
cl. Ryde...............312 B4
gdn. Rose Bay........348 C9
pl. Glen Alpine......510 B16
rd. Caringbah.......493 B15
FERNS
la. Five Dock, off Lyons Rd W....342 K8
FERN TREE
cl. Hornsby..........191 F13
FERNTREE
cl. Glenmore Pk...265 H11
rd. Engadine.........488 E16
FERNVALE
av. West Ryde......281 C14
FERNVIEW
pl. Cranebrook.....207 B11
pl. Glenwood.......246 A5
FEROX
ct. S Penrith.........266 G3
FEROZA
st. Riverwood......400 C10
FERRABETTA
av. Eastwood........281 J7
FERRARI
pl. Ingleburn........453 J7
FERRARO
cl. Edensor Pk.....363 E2
cr. West Hoxton...391 K13
FERRERS
rd. Eastern Ck......273 A16
rd. Horsley Pk......303 D16
FERRIER
cr. Minchinbury...271 F6
dr. Menai.............458 H5
pde. Campsie.........402 B3
rd. Birrong...........368 G7
rd. Sefton.............368 G7
rd. Yagoona.........368 G7
st. Rockdale.........403 B14
FERRINGTON
cr. Liverpool........394 H4
FERRIS
st. Annandale.........16 F3
st. Ermington.......310 E2
st. N Parramatta...278 B11
FERRY
av. Beverley Pk.....433 A11
la. Drummoyne....343 K2
la. Glebe...............12 A9
rd. Glebe...............12 A10
rd. Lansvale.........366 K9
st. Hunters Hill.....313 J12
st. Kogarah..........433 A5
FESQ
pwy. Winmalee........172 K14
FESTIVAL
st. Sadleir............394 C1
FETHERSTONE
st. Bankstown......369 E16
FEWINGS
st. Clovelly...........377 H12
FEWTRELL
av. Revesby Ht.....428 K8
FFRENCH
st. Greenwich......314 K8
FIASCHI
pl. S Windsor.......150 E3
FIAT
pl. Ingleburn........453 K7
FICUS
pl. Mcquarie Fd....454 B4
pl. Narellan Vale...478 J13
FIDDENS WHARF
rd. Killara.............253 G16
FIDDICK
pl. Menai.............458 G14
FIDDLEWOOD
gr. Menai.............458 J15
FIELD
av. Rookwood.......340 D13
cl. Moorebank......395 J7
la. Mosman, off Clifford St.........317 B6
pl. Blackett...........241 A1
pl. Cranebrook.....207 G10
pl. Currans Hill.....479 K11
pl. Illawong..........459 H5
pl. Telopea...........279 G9
pl. Wahroonga......222 E11
FIELDERS
st. Seven Hills.....245 F16

FIELDING
cl. Wetherill Pk.....334 J6
st. Collaroy..........229 B12
FIELD OF MARS
av. S Turramrra.....251 K5
FIELDS
rd. Ingleburn........453 J6
rd. Mcquarie Fd....453 J6
FIFE
cr. Blacktown.......275 A10
pl. Cecil Hills........362 H9
FIFTEENTH
av. Austral...........391 A2
av. Kemps Ck.......390 A1
av. Rossmore........390 D1
av. West Hoxton....392 A4
st. Warragamba...353 E7
FIFTH
av. Austral...........391 A15
av. Berala............339 D14
av. Blacktown.......244 H13
av. Campsie.........371 J10
av. Canley Vale.....366 C3
av. Condell Park....398 E5
av. Cremorne........316 G5
av. Denistone.......281 D10
av. Jannali............460 K10
av. Llandilo...........207 K1
av. Loftus.............489 K7
av. Mcquarie Fd....454 F5
av. Seven Hills......275 J3
rd. Berkshire Pk....179 H5
st. Ashbury..........372 G8
st. Granville.........308 F14
st. Mascot............404 K6
st. Warragamba....353 G7
FIG
la. Ultimo...............12 J9
la. Pymble, off Peace Av.........253 H1
pl. Eastwood........281 D7
pl. Mt Pritchard....364 D8
st. Pyrmont............12 H9
tce. Glenwood.......215 C14
FIG TREE
av. Abbotsford......342 K2
av. Telopea..........279 H9
la. N Sydney...........5 H1
la. Woollahra, off Fletcher St.......377 F2
st. Lane Cove.......313 K2
FIGTREE
av. Randwick........377 D9
cr. Glen Alpine......510 C14
dr. Homebush B.....M F6
dr. Homebush B....340 H2
rd. Hunters Hill.....313 E9
FIJI
av. Lethbrdg Pk....240 E3
FILEY
st. Blacktown.......274 G9
FILLMORE
rd. Bonnet Bay......460 C10
FINCH
av. Concord..........342 C7
av. East Ryde.......282 K16
av. Rydalmere......309 J1
ct. Revesby..........398 B10
pl. Davidson.........225 C15
pl. Greystanes......306 C3
pl. Hinchinbrk.......393 E1
pl. Ingleburn.........453 F10
pl. Lugarno..........429 H13
pl. St Clair............269 G12
pl. Woronora Ht....489 F2
FINCHLEY
pl. Glenhaven.......218 C2
pl. Turramurra......223 B7
FINDLAY
av. Roseville.........284 F7
la. Dulwich Hill.....373 E9
FINDLEY
rd. Bringelly.........387 A11
FINEGAN
la. Yagoona, off Brodie St.........368 G9
FINGAL
av. Glenhaven.......217 H1
FINGLETON
cl. Rouse Hill.......184 K6
cl. Rouse Hill.......185 A6
FINIAN
av. Killarney Ht.....255 J14
FINISTERRE
av. Whalan...........240 G8

FINLAY
av. Beecroft.........250 C10
av. Mt Pritchard....364 F14
rd. Turramurra.....222 D15
rd. Warrawee.......222 D15
st. Blacktown......274 J6
FINLAYS
av. Earlwood........403 B4
la. Earlwood, off Finlays Av.......403 B4
FINLAYSON
st. Lane Cove......314 B1
st. S Wntwthvle...307 A5
FINLEY
pl. Glenhaven......187 K14
FINN
cl. Cranebrook....206 K10
pl. Marayong.......244 C7
FINNAN
pl. Bligh Park.......150 G9
FINNEY
la. Hurstville........432 A7
st. Hurstville........432 B7
st. Old Tngabbie..276 J10
FINNIE
av. Matraville.......436 H8
FINNS
la. Merrylands, off Merrylands Rd...307 H13
rd. Menangle.......537 C14
FINSCHHAFEN
st. Holsworthy.....426 D4
FINTRY
ct. Kellyville.........217 A1
FINUCANE
cr. Matraville.......437 B1
FIONA
av. Castle Hill.......247 G1
av. Wahroonga....223 C4
cl. Padstow Ht.....429 C5
pl. Ingleburn.......453 D11
rd. Beecroft.........250 C8
st. Belrose...........226 A10
st. Mt Pritchard...364 C10
st. Woodpark......306 H16
wy. Toongabbie....276 A5
FIR
pl. Lugarno.........429 J16
FIREBALL
av. Cranebrook....207 B10
la. Cranebrook, off Fireball Av.......207 B9
FIRENZE
st. Glenwood.......245 K4
FIRESTONE
cr. Glenmore Pk..266 E11
FIRETAIL
gr. Plumpton.......242 B8
FIRE TRAIL
rd. Castlereagh....176 H8
rd. Londonderry..147 A14
rd. Londonderry..176 J5
FIRMSTONE
gdn. Arncliffe..........403 J10
FIRST
av. Allawah..........432 C8
av. Belfield...........371 G10
av. Berala............339 F15
av. Blacktown.......244 H15
av. Campsie.........371 G10
av. Canley Vale.....366 A4
av. Eastwood........281 C8
av. Epping...........280 G3
av. Five Dock.......343 A10
av. Gymea Bay.....491 C10
av. Hoxton Park...393 A6
av. Hurstville........432 C8
av. Jannali...........460 J11
av. Lane Cove......314 G3
av. Lindfield.........254 E12
av. Loftus............490 B5
av. Mcquarie Fd...424 A16
av. Maroubra.......407 G9
av. Narrabeen......228 G9
av. North Ryde.....282 H12
av. N Willghby.....285 G10
av. Rodd Point.....343 D9
av. Seven Hills.....275 H2
av. Toongabbie....276 F8
av. Willoughby.....285 G10
la. Kingswood, off First St.........237 H16
rd. Berkshire Pk...180 D1
st. Ashbury.........372 G9
st. Granville........308 H13

st. Kingswood.....237 H16
st. Parramatta.....279 A15
st. Warragamba...353 G7
wk. Chester Hill.....337 J13
FIRST FARM
dr. Castle Hill.......218 E11
FIRST FLEET
av. W Pnnant Hl...249 B2
FIRST ORCHARD
av. Bella Vista.......246 E7
FIRTH
av. Green Valley...363 G11
av. Strathfield........341 A16
st. Arncliffe..........403 G9
st. Waverley........377 H10
FIR TREE
av. West Ryde......280 H14
FISCHER
la. Kingsford.......406 K5
st. Kingsford.......406 K5
FISHBOURNE
rd. Allambie Ht.....257 J15
FISHBURN
cl. Lurnea............394 C12
cr. Castle Hill.......217 G13
pl. Beacon Hill.....257 G3
pl. Bligh Park.......150 C5
pl. Narellan.........478 F14
rd. Galston..........160 C10
rd. Port Botany....436 A11
FISHER
av. N Wahrnga.....192 F15
av. Pennant Hills..250 F1
av. Ryde..............282 F12
av. S Penrith........237 B15
av. Vaucluse.........348 B4
cr. Pendle Hill......276 D15
la. Narwee...........400 H14
pl. Campbelltwn...511 H8
pl. Narwee...........400 J14
rd. Camperdwn......18 D3
rd. Dee Why.........258 G6
rd. Lalor Park.......245 G10
rd. Maraylya...........94 G12
rd.n, Cromer..........258 F1
st. Balgowlah Ht..288 A14
st. Cabramatta.....365 K6
st. Petersham........15 J11
st. Silverwater.....309 F12
st. Yagoona.........368 K8
FISHERMANS
rd. Malabar..........437 F3
FISHERS
res. Petersham........15 J8
FISK
cl. Bonnyrigg Ht..363 E7
FITCH
av. Penrith...........236 B10
FITTON
pl. St Helens Pk...540 K8
st. Doonside........243 B8
FITZELL
pl. Brookvale.......257 J10
FITZGERALD
av. Beverley Pk.....433 C9
av. Edensor Pk.....363 J2
av. Hamondvle.....396 G14
av. Kogarah.........433 C9
av. Maroubra.......406 H12
cr. Blackett..........241 D1
cr. Strathfield.......370 K3
la. Maroubra.......407 F13
la. Queens Park.....22 H11
pl. Glenmore Pk...265 K6
rd. Ermington......280 F14
st. Newtown..........17 G7
st. Queens Park.....22 H11
st. Windsor..........121 C8
wy. Bella Vista.......246 H4
FITZGIBBON
la. Rsemeadow....540 K4
FITZPATRICK
av. Scotland I.......168 G3
av.e, Frenchs Frst...256 E6
av.w, Frenchs Frst...256 C6
cr. Casula...........394 G13
la. Bankstown, off Stanley St.......399 F2
pl. Bligh Park.......150 H9
rd. Mt Annan........479 F14
st. Marsfield.........282 B6
st. Menangle Pk...539 B2
st. Revesby.........398 D10
FITZROY
av. Balmain.............7 C6

av. Pymble 223 D13
cl. Hinchinbrk 363 A15
cl. St Johns Pk 364 G2
cr. Leumeah 481 K16
la. Newtown 17 C11
la. Newtown 18 A8
la. Pymble 223 D13
la. Surry Hills 20 E1
la. Windsor Dn 180 G2
la. Emu Plains, off Fitzroy St 235 H10
pl. Kellyville 215 F4
pl. Surry Hills F K16
pl. Sylvania Wtr 462 C14
rd. Cromer 227 K14
st. Abbotsford 312 J16
st. Burwood 342 B16
st. Campsie 371 J16
st. Croydon 372 C1
st. Emu Plains 235 G9
st. Killara 253 G12
st. Kirribilli 5 K16
st. Marrickville 374 C12
st. Milsons Pt 5 K16
st. Newtown 18 B9
st. Surry Hills F G15
st. Surry Hills 4 A16
st. Surry Hills 20 D1
wy. Bidwill 211 E16

FITZSIMMONS
av. Lane Cove W 283 G13

FITZSIMONS
la. Gordon 253 E6

FITZWATER
wy. Rsemeadow 540 J3

FITZWILLIAM
rd. Old Tngabbie 276 F6
rd. Toongabbie 276 F6
rd. Vaucluse 348 D1
st. Parramatta 308 C4

FIVEASH
st. St Helens Pk 540 K7

FIVE WAYS
Killara 254 C12
Paddington 13 B14

FIZELL
pl. Minchinbury 271 F7

FLACK
av. Hillsdale 406 G16
cl. Edensor Pk 363 D3

FLAGSTAFF
st. Engadine 489 C8
st. Gladesville 312 J9
st. Stanhpe Gdn 215 C12

FLAHERTY
bvd. S Granville 338 G4

FLAME
cr. Mcquarie Fd 454 E3
pl. Blacktown 274 C7

FLAME TREE
pl. Cherrybrook 219 H14

FLAMINGO
ct. Bella Vista 246 H2
gr. Plumpton 242 A10
pl. Pendle Hill 276 B16

FLANAGAN
av. Moorebank 396 C7

FLANDERS
av. Matraville 437 A1
av. Milperra 397 G12
av. Mt Krng-gai 162 J14

FLAT
cl. Green Valley 363 C8
st. Leichhardt 9 E10

FLAT ROCK
dr. Naremburn 315 G1
dr. Northbridge 315 G1
rd. Gymea Bay 491 G12
rd. Kingsgrove 402 C8

FLAUMONT
av. Riverview 314 B6

FLAVEL
st. S Penrith 267 D6

FLAVELLE
st. Concord 341 H4

FLAX
pl. Mcquarie Fd 454 F6
pl. Quakers Hill 213 K10

FLEECE
cl. St Clair 270 F12

FLEET
av. Earlwood 402 E4
la. Chatswood, off Albert Av 284 H10
la. Mosman, off Orlando Av 316 G11
pl. Beacon Hill 257 G3
pl. Bligh Park 150 G6
st. Carlton 432 F5
st. N Parramatta 278 B14
st. Parramatta 278 B14
st. Summer Hill 373 D4

FLEET STEPS
Sydney 2 G12

FLEETWOOD
st. Shalvey 211 A15

FLEMING
st. Beverly Hills 401 F14
st. Carlingford 250 A16
st. Little Bay 437 G15
st. Northwood 314 G7
st. St Marys 269 K2

FLEMINGS
la. Darlinghurst 4 E16

FLEMINGTON
cl. Casula 394 E16
rd. Homebsh W 340 J6
st. St Johns Pk 364 G4

FLEMMING
cl. Merrylnds W 306 K12
gr. Doonside 273 E5

FLERS
av. Earlwood 402 J1
st. Allambie Ht 257 D11
wy. Matraville 407 B16

FLETCHER
av. Blakehurst 462 C4
av. Miranda 492 A6
cl. Elderslie 507 J4
cl. Old Tngabbie 277 E10
la. Woollahra, off Fletcher St 377 F2
pl. Davidson 225 C15
rd. Heathcote 518 B15
st. Auburn 338 K3
st. Bondi 378 B5
st. Burwood 341 H13
st. Campsie 371 K16
st. Glenbrook 233 H15
st. Marrickville 373 J13
st. Minto 452 K16
st. Northmead 277 K6
st. Revesby 398 F11
st. S Penrith 267 B3
st. Tamarama 378 B5
st. Vineyard 153 B9
st. Woollahra 22 J3

FLEUR
cl. W Pnnant Hl 249 H4

FLEURBAIX
av. Milperra 397 G10
av. Milperra 397 F14
av. Panania 397 F14

FLEURS
rd. Mt Vernon 331 A13
st. Minchinbury 272 B9

FLIDE
st. Caringbah 492 G6

FLINDERS
av. Baulkham Hl 247 B11
av. Camden S 506 K12
av. Orchard Hills 269 A9
av. St Ives 224 D11
cr. Ermington 280 D16
cr. Hinchinbrk 363 A15
cr. Ingleburn 423 B10
pl. Davidson 225 B14
pl. Mt Colah 162 C13
pl. N Richmond 87 E15
rd. Earlwood 373 B16
rd. Georges Hall 367 F12
rd. North Ryde 282 C9
rd. Woolooware 493 G8
st. Darlinghurst 4 E14
st. Ermington 280 D15
st. Fairfield W 335 E11
st. Matraville 437 A2
st. Moore Park 20 F1
st. Mount Druitt 240 J16
st. Paddington 20 F1
st. Ruse 512 E3
st. Surry Hills 4 E14

FLINT
av. Penrith 236 H14
pl. Illawong 460 A4
pl. Kellyville 216 D5
st. Eastgardens 406 G13
st. Hillsdale 406 G13
st. Ingleburn 453 E5
st. Kings Lngly 245 A2

FLINTLOCK
dr. St Clair 269 K12
la. St Clair, off Banks Dr 269 J12

FLITCROFT
pl. Glenmore Pk 265 G6

FLITTON VALLEY
cl. Frenchs Frst 256 A2

FLOOD
av. Revesby 398 J15
la. Bondi Jctn, off Bondi Rd 377 H4
st. Bondi 377 H4
st. Clovelly 377 J13
st. Leichhardt 15 E5

FLOODS
pl. Surry Hills 4 D16

FLORA
av. Mt Colah 192 C1
av. S Penrith 266 G2
cl. Merrylnds W 306 J14
ct. Baulkham Hl 217 A16
ct. Baulkham Hl 247 A1
st. Arncliffe 403 J7
st. Erskineville 374 K10
st. Kirrawee 491 A4
st. Mascot 405 E4
st. Narwee 400 G15
st. Oyster Bay 461 A6
st. Plumpton 242 C6
st. Roselands 401 C5
st. Sutherland 490 F3

FLORABELLA
st. Warrimoo 203 B16

FLOREAT
pl. Seven Hills 275 E5

FLORENCE
av. Collaroy 229 D14
av. Denistone 281 E11
av. Eastlakes 406 A4
av. Kurrajong 85 C1
av. Minto Ht 483 J6
cl. Bargo 567 C2
ct. N Balgowlah 287 E6
la. Cremorne, off Murdoch St 316 F10
pl. Epping 250 E13
st. Cremorne 316 F10
st. Glendenning 242 D3
st. Hornsby 221 J1
st. Hurlstone Pk 372 J11
st. Mt Pritchard 364 H14
st. Oakhurst 242 D3
st. Prospect 274 G16
st. Ramsgate Bch 433 G12
st. St Peters 374 G13
st. S Wntwthvle 306 K4
st. Strathfield 341 C14
tce. Scotland I 168 J2

FLOREY
av. Pymble 223 E15
cr. Mt Pritchard 364 H11
cr. Springwood 202 E11
pl. Abbotsford 343 A3
pl. Barden Rdg 488 H6

FLORIAN
gr. Oakhurst 242 A2

FLORIBUNDA
av. Glenmore Pk 265 H7
rd. Kemps Ck 360 E8

FLORIDA
av. Ermington 280 E11
cr. Riverwood 400 A14
pl. Seven Hills 275 D5
rd. Palm Beach 139 K1
st. Sylvania 462 C8

FLORRIE
st. Granville 308 C12

FLOSS
st. Hurlstone Pk 372 J12
st. Hurlstone Pk 373 B12

FLOWER
la. Maroubra 407 D11
st. Maroubra 407 D10

FLOWERDALE
rd. Liverpool 394 J4

FLOYD
pl. Mt Pritchard 364 H10

FLOYDS
rd. Maroota S 66 A2

FLUORITE
pl. Eagle Vale 481 D6

FLUSHCOMBE
rd. Blacktown 274 G7

FLYNN
cr. Leumeah 482 F11
pl. Bonnyrigg Ht 363 F7

FOAL
wy. Glenwood 245 J3

FOAM
st. Harbord 258 H15

FOAMCREST
av. Newport 169 J10

FOCH
av. Gymea 491 C2

FOGG
pl. Yellow Rock 204 A5

FOGGITS
wk. Hunters Hill 313 B11

FOLEY
la. Georges Hall 367 J13
pl. Castle Hill 218 K10
st. Darlinghurst F K5
st. Darlinghurst 4 C11
st. Georges Hall 367 J14
st. Mona Vale 198 J5

FOLINI
av. Northmead 278 A2

FOLKARD
st. North Ryde 282 G8

FOLKESTONE
pde. Botany 405 E14
pl. Dural 219 B5

FOLLY
rd. Silverdale 354 E11

FONDA
pl. Glendenning 242 F3

FONTAINE
st. Chatswood 285 B6

FONTAINEBLEAU
st. Sans Souci 463 A5

FONTANA
cl. St Clair 300 C2

FONTENOY
rd. Mcquarie Pk 282 J1

FONTHILL
pl. Airds 512 C10

FONTI
st. Eastwood 281 G6

FOORD
av. Hurlstone Pk 372 K14

FOOTMAN
cr. Kellyville 215 C2

FOOTS
pl. Maroubra 407 G8

FOOTSCRAY
st. St Johns Pk 364 E3

FORAY
st. Guildford W 336 F5
st. Yennora 336 F5

FORBES
av. Belmore 401 H2
cl. Abbotsbury 333 C16
cr. Engadine 488 F13
la. Newtown 18 D8
la. Turramurra 222 H14
la. Warwck Frm 365 G16
pl. Allambie Ht 257 F13
pl. Leumeah 481 J16
pl. Newtown 18 C8
rd. Marayong 244 D7
st. Croydon Pk 372 D7
st. Darlinghurst 4 E12
st. Emu Plains 235 A11
st. Hornsby 221 F2
st. Liverpool 395 G1
st. Newtown 18 C8
st. Paddington 13 J16
st. Warwck Frm 365 G16
st. Windsor 121 B11
st. Woolmloo 4 F5
st. Woolmloo 4 F7
wy. Mcquarie Lk 423 G14

FORCETT
cl. West Hoxton 392 E8

FORD
la. Burwood, off Railway Pde 342 A14
pl. Erskine Park 270 G15
pl. Ingleburn 453 K7
rd. Maroubra 407 F14
st. Balmain 7 H9
st. Greenacre 370 G7
st. Greenwich 314 J10
st. Huntingwd 273 G13
st. North Ryde 282 D8
st. Old Tngabbie 276 H10

FORDE
pl. Currans Hill 479 J11
pl. N Wahrnga 192 F15

FORE
st. Canterbury 372 E14

FOREMAN
la. Tempe 404 C1
pl. Barden Rdg 488 J1
st. Glenfield 424 E8
st. Tempe 404 C1

FORESHORE
rd. Bnksmeadw 435 H1
rd. Botany 405 C13

FOREST
cl. Cherrybrook 219 A14
cr. Kellyville 185 K16
gln. Cherrybrook 219 E9
gr. Epping 281 C1
gr. Lansvale 366 D9
pl. Galston 159 F10
rd. Arncliffe 403 A11
rd. Baulkham Hl 248 A13
rd. Bexley 402 G16
rd. Double Bay 14 E12
rd. Gymea 491 D7
rd. Gymea Bay 491 D7
rd. Heathcote 518 K10
rd. Hurstville 431 K5
rd. Hurstville 432 C6
rd. Kirrawee 490 E5
rd. Kirrawee 490 H6
rd. Lugarno 429 K12
rd. Miranda 491 J8
rd. Mortdale 431 A3
rd. Peakhurst 430 E3
rd. Penshurst 431 F4
rd. Sutherland 490 E5
rd. Warriewood 198 F6
st. Forest Lodge 11 K16
st. Glebe 11 K16
wy. Belrose 226 A2
wy. Frenchs Frst 256 C1
wy. Terrey Hills 195 K16
wy. Wrrngtn Cty 238 F5

FORESTER
cr. Cherrybrook 219 H4
pl. Bossley Park 333 E10

FOREST GLEN
cr. Belrose 226 B15
dr. Cranebrook 207 B8
wy. Menai 458 H14

FORESTGROVE
dr. Menai 458 K13

FOREST GUM
pl. Greystanes 306 C3

FOREST HILL
rd. Werombi 413 H13

FOREST KNOLL
Castle Hill 218 J16
av. Bondi Beach 378 B3

FORESTVILLE
av. Forestville 255 J10

FORESTWOOD
cr. W Pnnant Hl 249 G4

FORGE
pl. Narellan 478 C8
st. Blacktown 244 H9

FORK
la. Kurmond 86 D4

FORMAN
av. Glenwood 215 E15

FORMER HUME
hwy. Camden 507 A15
hwy. Camden S 507 A15

FORMOSA
st. Drummoyne 343 J3
st. Sylvania 461 K12
st. Sylvania 462 A9

FORNASIER
la. Canley Vale, off Canley Vale Rd 366 A3

FORREST
av. Earlwood 402 E7
av. N Wahrnga 222 F1
cr. Camden 507 B2
rd. East Hills 427 G3
rd. Lalor Park 245 C13
rd. Ryde 312 E1
st. Chifley 437 A6
st. Ermington 280 E16
st. Haberfield 343 E14

FORRESTER
pl. Maraylya 94 K13
rd. Lethbrdg Pk 240 A4
rd. N St Marys 240 A4

rd. St Marys 239 H12
rd. Tregear 240 A4
st. Kingsgrove 401 J9
FORRESTERS
cl. Woodbine 481 H11
FORRESTWOOD
pl. Prospect 274 H12
FORSHAW
av. Chester Hill 338 D16
av. Peakhurst 430 H2
FORSTER
la. West Ryde 281 F14
pl. Dundas Vy 280 D9
pl. Penrith 237 B7
st. Blakehurst 432 E13
st. Concord 341 K10
st. Mascot 405 D3
st. West Ryde 281 F14
FORSYTH
cl. Wetherill Pk 334 A3
la. Glebe 12 B8
pl. Oatlands 279 A14
st. Belmore 401 G6
st. Glebe 11 K9
st. Killara 253 K9
st. Kingsford 406 G1
st. Kingsgrove 401 G6
st. N Willghby 285 D10
st. West Ryde 311 G1
FORT
pl. Quakers Hill 214 E16
st. Petersham 15 H6
FORTESCUE
st. Bexley North 402 D10
st. Chiswick 343 C1
FORTH
st. Woollahra 22 B2
FORTHORN
pl. N St Marys 239 K12
FORTINBRAS
cl. Rsemeadow 540 J8
FORTRIL
av. Bankstown 399 F7
FORTUNATO
gr. Prestons 392 K14
st. Prestons 392 J14
FORTUNE
gr. Kellyville 186 G16
FORUM
cr. Baulkham Hl 246 G11
dr. Heathcote 518 E7
FORWOOD
av. Turramurra 252 D4
FOSS
st. Blacktown 274 K9
st. Forest Lodge 11 G16
st. Glebe 11 G16
st. Hunters Hill 313 J11
FOSTER
av. Bellevue Hill 347 G15
cl. West Hoxton 391 K4
la. Leichhardt 15 D2
la. Surry Hills F B10
pl. Quakers Hill 213 K16
st. Leichhardt 15 C1
st. Surry Hills F B9
st. Surry Hills 3 J13
st. Valley Ht 202 F6
FOSTERS
la. Bickley Vale 505 E11
la. Mt Hunter 505 E11
FOTEA
cl. Edensor Pk 333 F15
FOTHERINGHAM
la. Marrickville, off Cowper St 374 E9
st. Enmore 16 J16
FOUCART
st. Rozelle 10 H2
FOUNDRY
rd. Seven Hills 246 E15
FOUNTAIN
av. Croydon Pk 371 G8
st. Alexandria 18 H15
FOURTEENTH
av. Austral 390 H3
st. Warragamba 353 F7
FOURTH
av. Austral 390 K16
av. Berala 339 D15
av. Blacktown 244 G13
av. Campsie 371 J10
av. Canley Vale 366 C3
av. Condell Park 398 D5
av. Eastwood 281 D9
av. Jannali 460 K10
av. Lane Cove 314 G4
av. Lindfield 254 F13
av. Llandilo 177 K14
av. Llandilo 178 C16
av. Loftus 489 K6
av. Mcquarie Fd 454 C3
av. N Willghby 285 H9
av. Seven Hills 275 J3
av. Willoughby 285 H9
rd. Berkshire Pk 179 K4
st. Ashbury 372 G8
st. Granville 308 G14
st. Mascot 404 K6
st. Parramatta 279 A16
st. Warragamba 353 F7
FOVEAUX
av. Lurnea 394 D13
cct. Harringtn Pk 478 C2
pl. Airds 511 K15
pl. Barden Rdg 488 G3
pl. Cromer 227 H12
st. Surry Hills F A15
st. Surry Hills 20 A1
tce. Bella Vista 246 G3
wy. Mcquarie Lk 423 F13
FOWKES
wy. West Hoxton 392 B13
FOWLER
av. Bexley North 402 F10
cr. Maroubra 407 G8
cr. S Coogee 407 G8
la. Camperdwn 17 E6
rd. Guildford 337 A4
rd. Guildford W 337 A4
rd. Illawong 459 D4
rd. Merrylands 307 B16
rd. Merrylnds W 307 B16
st. Camperdwn 17 E6
st. Leichhardt 10 C15
st. Seven Hills 275 D5
st.n, Woolooware 493 G9
st.s, Woolooware 493 G9
FOX
av. Erskineville 18 E16
cr. Padstow 429 B1
pl. Penrith 237 D3
rd. East Ryde 282 K14
st. Granville 308 A10
st. Lane Cove 314 B3
st. Malabar 437 F4
st. Narellan 478 E9
st. Riverview 314 B3
wy. Claymore 481 D11
FOXALL
rd. Kellyville 186 D8
st. Elanora Ht 198 D11
FOXGLOVE
rd. Mt Colah 162 F13
FOX GROVE
av. Casula 423 J2
FOX HILLS
cr. Prospect 275 E14
FOXLOW
pl. Airds 512 D11
st. Canley Ht 335 B15
FOXS
la. Ashfield, off Brown St 372 H3
FOXTON
st. Quakers Hill 214 D11
FOX VALLEY
rd. Denham Ct 421 J9
rd. Wahroonga 221 H16
rd. Wahroonga 222 B12
FOXWOOD
av. Quakers Hill 213 H11
cl. Silverdale 383 J3
wy. Cherrybrook 219 D13
FOY
la. Sydney F B6
st. Balmain 7 F12
FOYLE
av. Birrong 369 A6
FRAGAR
rd. S Penrith 267 B6
FRAM
pl. Tregear 240 G7
FRAMPTON
av. Marrickville 374 B13
av. St Clair 270 F15
la. Marrickville 374 B13
st. Lidcombe 339 J3
FRANCE
st. Canterbury 372 F16
FRANCES
av. Strathfield S 371 D5
la. Randwick, off Frances St 377 A12
pl. Miranda 492 E2
rd. Putney 312 B7
st. Lidcombe 339 K5
st. Lindfield 284 B2
st. Merrylands 307 C8
st. Narellan 478 H10
st. Northmead 277 J9
st. Randwick 376 K12
st. S Wntwthvle 307 C8
FRANCESCO
cr. Bella Vista 246 D8
FRANCINE
st. Seven Hills 245 H14
FRANCIS
av. Btn-le-Sds 403 J16
av. Emu Plains 235 J9
la. Darlinghurst F H1
la. Emu Plains, off Francis Av 235 J9
la. Manly, off Raglan St 288 H8
pl. Currans Hill 479 K13
rd. Artarmon 284 J15
rd. Faulconbdg 171 C11
rd. Rooty Hill 272 A2
st. Artarmon 315 C1
st. Bondi 377 K2
st. Bondi Beach 378 B3
st. Bringelly 387 C8
st. Cambrdg Pk 238 D9
st. Campsie 372 B14
st. Carlton 432 H9
st. Castle Hill 248 B1
st. Colyton 270 G4
st. Darlinghurst F G1
st. Darlinghurst 4 A9
st. Dee Why 258 F6
st. Earlwood 402 E3
st. Enmore 17 A15
st. Epping 280 H2
st. Fairfield 336 C15
st. Fairlight 288 E8
st. Glebe 12 F16
st. Homebush 340 K11
st. Hunters Hill 314 A13
st. Leichhardt 9 H10
st. Leichhardt 9 H12
st. Lilyfield 9 H7
st. Longueville 314 D8
st. Manly 288 E8
st. Marrickville 373 H13
st. Mascot 405 H5
st. Minto 452 J14
st. Mount Druitt 240 J16
st. Naremburn 315 C1
st. Naremburn 315 C3
st. Richmond 118 E2
st. Strathfield 340 K11
FRANCISCO
cr. Rsemeadow 540 J9
FRANCIS GREENWAY
av. St Clair 270 A9
dr. Cherrybrook 219 G12
FRANCIS MARTIN
dr. Randwick, off Hospital Rd 377 A16
FRANCIS OAKES
wy. W Pnnant Hl 249 E9
FRANGIPANE
av. Liverpool 394 J6
FRANGIPANI
ct. Erskine Park 300 E3
pl. Caringbah 492 E13
FRANK
st. Gladesville 312 F5
st. Guildford 337 A1
st. Guildford 337 B2
st. Mount Druitt 271 C4
st. Mt Lewis 369 K16
st. Wetherill Pk 304 F15
FRANK BEAMES
la. Harris Park 308 F6
FRANK BEAUREPAIRE
av. Newington M D15
av. Newington 310 A16
FRANKI
av. Woolwich 314 E13
la. Prospect 275 D15
FRANKIE
la. Concord 342 A10
FRANKISH
pl. W Pnnant Hl 248 G7
FRANKLIN
cr. Blackett 241 A1
pl. Bossley Park 333 E10
pl. Carlingford 249 K15
pl. Colyton 270 G7
rd. Cherrybrook 219 D16
rd. Chipping Ntn 396 B6
rd. Woolooware 493 H10
st. Chifley 437 B3
st. Leumeah 482 D15
st. Malabar 437 D3
st. Matraville 436 J2
st. Mays Hill 307 J7
st. Parramatta 307 J7
FRANKLYN
st. Concord 341 H9
st. Glebe 12 F15
FRANK OLIVERI
dr. Chipping Ntn 366 J15
FRANKSON
pl. Mona Vale 199 E2
FRANKUM
dr. Orangeville 473 C1
FRANLEE
rd. Dural 188 G14
FRASCATTI
la. Mosman 317 E9
FRASER
av. Eastgardens 406 F12
av. Kellyville 215 J5
pl. Mt Annan 509 G3
pl. Shalvey 210 K13
rd. Canley Vale 366 D4
rd. Cowan 104 B14
rd. Normanhurst 221 G9
rd. Springwood 172 B16
st. Auburn 338 K10
st. Homebush 340 J11
st. Homebsh W 340 J11
st. Lane Cove W 283 K15
st. Mcquarie Fd 424 A14
st. Randwick 377 D10
st. Rockdale 433 G2
st. Strathfield 340 J12
st. Wentwthvle 277 A9
st. Westmead 307 F5
FRATERS
av. Sans Souci 463 A6
FRAZER
av. Lurnea 394 E12
pl. Birrong 368 J7
st. Collaroy 229 B11
st. Dulwich Hill 15 C16
st. Lakemba 371 A13
st. Lilyfield 9 G5
st. Marrickville 15 C16
st. Tahmoor 565 G12
FRAZIER
cl. Liberty Gr 311 B10
FREAME
st. Wentwthvle 276 K16
FRED
la. Lilyfield 10 G1
la. Rozelle 10 G1
st. Lewisham 373 E6
st. Lilyfield 10 G2
FREDA
pl. Hamondvle 396 C13
st. Panania 428 A6
FRED ALLEN
pl. Rooty Hill 272 B2
FREDBEN
av. Cammeray 315 J5
la. Cammeray, off Fredben Av 315 J5
FREDBERT
st. Lilyfield 10 A5
FREDDIE LANE
av. Newington L G16
av. Newington 310 A15
FREDE
la. Marrickville 373 J15
FREDERICK
av. Beverly Hills 401 C14
av. S Granville 338 E3
la. Oatley 431 C12
la. Rockdale 403 C15
pl. Kurrajong Ht 53 K7
rd. Cecil Hills 362 G8
rd. Taren Point 462 J10
st. Artarmon 315 B3
st. Ashfield 372 F2
st. Bankstown 369 G12
st. Blacktown 245 A8
st. Campsie 372 B12
st. Canterbury 372 G11
st. Concord 342 B2
st. Fairfield 336 C14
st. Hornsby 221 D2
st. Killara 283 E1
st. Lalor Park 245 E9
st. Lidcombe 339 K8
st. Miranda 492 E6
st. North Bondi 348 F16
st. Oatley 431 C12
st. Pendle Hill 306 E2
st. Petersham 16 A11
st. Randwick 407 D2
st. Rockdale 403 A13
st. Ryde 312 C5
st. St Leonards 315 B3
st. St Peters 374 E14
st. Sydenham 374 E14
FREDRIKA
pl. Carlingford 249 E13
FREEBODY
cl. S Windsor 150 K1
FREEDOM
plz. Cabramatta, off Arthur St 365 J7
FREEMAN
av. Canley Vale 365 K2
av. Castle Hill 247 J2
av. Oatley 430 H14
cct. Ingleburn 452 J10
pl. Carlingford 280 E4
pl. Chester Hill 338 E16
pl. Concord 342 B5
rd. Agnes Banks 117 D11
rd. Chatswd W 284 G11
rd. Heathcote 518 D11
st. Colyton 270 C5
st. Lalor Park 245 F12
st. Warwck Frm 365 H14
FREEMANS
la. Glenorie 128 J16
FREEMANS REACH
rd. Freemns Rch 121 C3
FREEMANTLE
pl. Wakeley 334 H15
FREEMASONS ARMS
la. Parramatta, off George St 308 C2
FREESIA
pl. Glenmore Pk 265 H7
FREESTONE
av. Carlingford 249 C15
FREITAS
la. Lidcombe, off Olympic Dr 339 G9
FREMANTLE
pl. Yarrawarrah 489 G13
FREMLIN
st. Botany 405 J16
FREMONT
av. Ermington 280 C13
st. Concord W 311 E12
FRENCH
av. Bankstown 369 E14
av. Toongabbie 276 C5
la. Kogarah 433 D3
la. Maroubra 407 E10
pl. Currans Hill 479 K14
pl. Hinchinbrk 362 K16
st. Artarmon 284 H16
st. Kingswood 238 C13
st. Kogarah 433 D3
st. McMahons Pt 5 D14
st. Maroubra 407 E11
FRENCHMANS
rd. Randwick 377 C11
FRENCHS
la. Summer Hill 15 A6
pl. Belrose 225 E14
rd. Willoughby 285 F14
FRENCHS FOREST
rd. Seaforth 287 B7
rd.e, Frenchs Frst 256 J5
rd.w, Frenchs Frst 256 F4
FRENSHAM
pl. Dural 188 G13
FRERE
pl. Cherrybrook 220 B13
FRERES
rd. Kentlyn 483 G14

FRESHWATER
cl. Woodbine 481 H10
FREYA
cr. Shalvey 210 H13
st. Kareela 461 D12
FREYCINET
cl. Dural 219 B3
FRIAR
pl. Ingleburn 453 H7
FRIARBIRD
cr. Glenmore Pk 265 H12
FRICOURT
av. Earlwood 402 J2
FRIEDLANDER
pl. St Leonards, off Nicholson St 315 E6
FRIEDMANN
pl. S Penrith 267 A5
FRIEND
av. Five Dock 342 G8
pl. Blacktown 274 D10
st. Merrylands 307 C6
wy. Mt Pritchard 364 J11
FRIENDSHIP
av. Kellyville 216 C2
pl. Beacon Hill 257 H4
pl. Bligh Park 150 C5
pl. Illawong 459 G7
rd. Port Botany 436 B10
st. Dundas Vy 280 B6
wy. Minto 482 J7
FRIESIAN
st. Busby 363 K16
FRIGATE-BIRD
av. Hinchinbrk 393 B3
FRIPP
cr. Beverly Hills 401 A15
la. Springwood 171 F16
st. Arncliffe 403 C9
FRITH
av. Normanhurst 221 J8
st. Doonside 243 D6
FROBISHER
av. Caringbah 492 K4
FROGGATT
cr. Croydon 342 E15
FROGMORE
la. Mascot 405 F6
rd. Orchard Hills 267 D7
st. Mascot 405 F6
FROME
pl. Castle Hill 217 H10
st. Fairfield W 335 G9
FROMELLES
av. Milperra 397 G10
av. Seaforth 287 A6
wy. Matraville 407 A15
FRONTIGNAN
st. Eschol Park 481 A5
FROST
av. Matraville 436 H8
av. Narellan 478 G14
cl. St Clair 299 K2
ct. Wetherill Pk 334 H6
la. Chester Hill 368 C1
rd. Campbelltwn 511 C1
st. Earlwood 402 D7
FRUTICOSA
wy. Mcquarie Fd 454 G3
FRY
pl. Quakers Hill 213 G15
st. Chatswood 285 C11
FRYAR
row. Tarban 313 B12
FRYER
av. Wentwthvle 276 K14
st. Mt Annan 479 D16
FUCHSIA
cr. Mcquarie Fd 454 A3
cr. Quakers Hill 243 E3
ct. Baulkham Hl 247 F14
pl. Bossley Park 333 F8
FUGGLES
rd. Kenthurst 156 K9
rd. Kenthurst 157 A10
FULBOURNE
av. Pennant Hills 220 H14
FULHAM
st. Busby 363 J12
st. Newtown 17 D16
FULLAGAR
rd. Wentwthvle 307 A3
FULLAM
rd. Blacktown 274 G6
FULLARTON
st. Telopea 279 J8
FULLER
av. Earlwood 402 F1
av. Hornsby 221 G3
pl. St Clair 270 H10
st. Badgerys Ck 358 F8
st. Chester Hill 337 H11
st. Collaroy Plat 228 G11
st. Mount Druitt 271 D2
st. Narrabeen 228 G11
st. Seven Hills 275 K5
FULLERS
rd. Chatswd W 284 A9
rd. Chatswd W 284 D10
rd. Glenhaven 218 C3
FULLERTON
cct. St Helens Pk 541 D4
cr. Bligh Park 150 C6
cr. Riverwood 400 F14
pl. Glenmore Pk 265 K7
st. Woollahra 14 B16
st. Woollahra 22 B1
FULLFORD
st. Dundas Vy 280 B10
FULLWOOD
pl. Claymore 481 F11
FULTON
av. Wentwthvle 277 B12
la. Penrith 237 A11
pl. Kellyville 186 E9
pl. N Richmond 86 K14
rd. Marsden Pk 211 H6
st. Penrith 237 A11
FUNDA
cr. Lalor Park 245 F14
pl. Brookvale 257 K10
FUR
pl. Rooty Hill 241 K12
FURBER
la. Centnnial Pk 21 D7
la. Moore Park 21 D7
pl. Davidson 225 B14
rd. Centnnial Pk 21 D6
FURCI
av. Edensor Pk 333 H15
FURLONG
av. Casula 424 C1
pwy. Casula, off Furlong Av 394 C16
FURNER
av. Camden S 506 K14
FURSORB
st. Marayong 244 B7
FURY
st. Kingswood 237 H15
FUTUNA
st. Hunters Hill 314 A12
FUTURA
pl. Toongabbie 276 F5
FYALL
av. Wentwthvle 276 J14
st. Ermington 280 B13
FYFE
pl. Glenfield 424 F13
pl. N Sydney 5 F3
rd. Kellyville 214 J6
FYNE
cl. St Andrews 451 K12
FYSH
pl. Bidwill 211 C16

G

GABEE
pl. Malabar 437 E8
GABO
cr. Sadleir 364 A16
ct. Baulkham Hl 247 D1
pl. Gymea 491 F2
GABRIELLA
av. Cecil Hills 362 G7
GABRIELLE
av. Baulkham Hl 247 B8
cl. Mt Colah 162 F14
GABRIELS
la. St Marys 239 F16
GADARA
dr. S Penrith 266 F6
GADDS
la. Kurmond 57 C14
GADSHILL
pl. Rsemeadow 540 C3
GAERLOCH
av. Tamarama 378 C7
GAGA
rd. Illawong 459 F4
GAGGIN
st. Parramatta 278 H16
GAGOOR
cl. Clarmnt Ms 268 H2
la. Clarmnt Ms, off Gagoor Cl 268 H2
GAHNIA
wy. Winmalee 172 H13
GAIETY
pl. Doonside 243 B8
GAIL
pl. Bankstown 369 B16
GAILES
st. Sutherland 460 G16
GAINFORD
av. Matraville 407 A14
GAINSFORD
dr. Kellyville 215 H5
GAIWOOD
pl. Castle Hill 248 H1
GAL
cr. Moorebank 396 B9
GALA
av. Croydon 372 C4
GALAH
cl. St Clair 269 J10
GALAHAD
cl. Mt Colah 162 E11
cr. Castle Hill 217 G7
GALASHIELS
av. St Andrews 481 J2
GALATEA
st. Plumpton 241 G8
GALAXY
pl. Raby 451 H14
rd. Luddenham 326 D8
GALBA
cl. Prestons 392 K16
GALE
pl. Oakhurst 211 J16
rd. Maroubra 406 H8
st. Concord 342 B1
st. Ryde 311 G4
st. Woolwich 314 E13
GALEA
dr. Glenwood 245 D2
GALEN
st. Hornsby 221 F3
GALENA
pl. Eagle Vale 481 G4
GALGA
st. Sutherland 460 D16
GALILEE
cl. Bossley Park 333 K8
GALLAGHER
st. St Helens Pk 541 B9
GALLARD
st. Denistone E 281 H10
GALLEON
cl. Chipping Ntn 366 J15
GALLIMORE
av. Balmain East 8 G7
GALLIPOLI
cl. Narrabeen, off Endeavour Dr 228 F8
la. Concord, off Gallipoli St 342 A5
st. Bankstown 398 K7
st. Bossley Park 333 J6
st. Concord 342 A5
st. Condell Park 398 K7
st. Hurstville 432 A8
st. Lidcombe M K12
st. Lidcombe 340 C5
st. St Marys 269 F6
GALLOP
gr. Lalor Park 245 G11
st. Warwck Frm 365 G14
GALLOWAY
cr. St Andrews 482 A1
st. Bossley Park 334 C12
st. Busby 393 K1
st. N Parramatta 278 C13
GALLUS
pl. Rsemeadow 540 E2
GALSTON
rd. Dural 189 B6
rd. Galston 159 G11
rd. Hornsby 191 E1
rd. Hornsby Ht 191 E1
GALTON
st. Smithfield 335 C2
st. Wetherill Pk 335 C2
GALVIN
rd. Llandilo 179 C14
st. Elderslie 507 G1
st. Maroubra 407 C10
GALWAY
av. Killarney Ht 286 B1
ct. St Clair 269 K10
pl. Smithfield 335 F2
GAMA
rd. Cranebrook 207 E10
GAMACK
ct. Rouse Hill 185 A8
GAMAY
pl. Minchinbury 272 B7
GAMBIA
pl. Cranebrook 207 E10
st. Kearns 481 C1
GAMBIER
av. Sandy Point 427 K10
st. Bossley Park 334 B9
GAMBOOLA
wy. Airds 512 B14
GAME
st. Bonnyrigg 363 K7
GAMENYA
av. S Penrith 267 A1
pl. Engadine 489 F8
GAMMA
rd. Lane Cove 314 F3
GAMMELL
st. Rydalmere 309 K3
GAMMIE
av. Matraville 436 G8
GAMUT
rd. Engadine 489 F8
GANDELL
cr. S Penrith 266 G5
la. S Penrith, off Gandell Cr 266 G5
GANDER
pl. Hinchinbrk 363 E15
GANDY
la. Greenacre 370 G2
GANGES
wy. Kellyville 185 K14
GANGURLIN
st. Heckenberg 364 B13
GANMAIN
cr. Milperra 397 F11
rd. Pymble 223 F15
GANNET
pl. Acacia Gdn 214 J16
pl. Hinchinbrk 393 C2
pl. Woronora Ht 489 C5
st. Gladesville 313 A5
st. Raby 481 G3
GANNON
av. Dolls Point 463 G1
cl. Bradbury 511 J10
la. Tempe 404 B3
st. Kurnell 466 C7
st. Tempe 404 A2
GANNONS
av. Hurstville 432 B1
rd. Caringbah 493 C7
rd.s, Caringbah 493 B15
GANORA
st. Gladesville 313 A4
GAP
rd. Watsons Bay 318 G14
GARAH
cl. Westleigh 220 E7
GARBALA
rd. Gymea 491 F1
GARBETT
pl. Doonside 273 E4
GARBUTT
pl. Oakdale 500 E11
GARDA
st. Seven Hills 275 H7
GARDEN
cl. Hinchinbrk 362 K15
ct. W Pnnant Hl 248 J9
gr. Beverly Hills 400 K16
la. Belmore 401 F3
la. Maroubra 407 B10
la. Eastlakes, off Maloney La 405 J4
pl. Bonnyrigg 364 E6
pl. Picnic Point 428 D7
sq. Faulconbdg 201 C1
sq. Gordon 253 J6
st. Alexandria 18 K11
st. Belmore 401 F4
st. Blacktown 245 B8
st. Eastlakes 405 J4
st. Eveleigh 18 K11
st. Kingsford 407 B10
st. Kogarah 433 A7
st. Maroubra 407 B10
st. Marrickville 374 E13
st. Mt Pritchard 364 J13
st. N Narrabeen 198 J13
st. Telopea 279 F9
st. Warriewood 198 H10
wy. Lilyfield 10 B4
GARDENER
av. Ryde 282 D16
GARDENERS
la. Kingsford 406 F2
la. West Ryde 281 A15
rd. Alexandria 375 B16
rd. Daceyville 406 B2
rd. Eastlakes 406 B2
rd. Kensington 406 B2
rd. Kingsford 406 B2
rd. Mascot 375 B16
rd. Rosebery 405 C1
GARDEN HILL
rd. Mulgoa 325 K2
GARDENIA
av. Bankstown 399 H2
av. Emu Plains 235 F9
av. Lane Cove W 313 K1
gr. Lalor Park 245 D11
pde. Greystanes 305 K12
pl. Castle Hill 248 H2
pl. Mcquarie Fd 454 E5
st. Asquith 191 K9
st. Cronulla 524 A2
GARDENSET
gr. Blacktown 274 D10
GARDENVALE
rd. Oatlands 279 C12
GARDERE
av. Curl Curl 258 H14
av. Harbord 258 H14
st. Caringbah 492 G6
GARDINER
av. Banksia 403 C12
cr. Fairfield W 335 E11
rd. Badgerys Ck 358 H2
rd. Galston 159 G10
st. Bondi Jctn 22 H9
st. Minto 482 K4
GARDINIA
st. Narwee 400 G15
GARDNER
st. Rooty Hill 272 A6
GARDYNE
st. Bronte 377 J8
GAREMA
cct. Kingsgrove 401 G8
GAREMYN
rd. Middle Dural 158 D3
GARETH
cl. Mt Colah 162 F11
st. Blacktown 274 H8
GARFIELD
av. Bonnet Bay 460 C9
la. Carlton, off Shaftsbury St 432 H7
rd. Horsley Pk 331 G5
rd.e, Riverstone 182 J8
rd.w, Marsden Pk 181 J16
rd.w, Riverstone 182 D12
st. Carlton 432 H7
st. Five Dock 342 H10
st. McGraths Hl 122 B12
st. Oakville 122 B12
st. Wentwthvle 306 J3
st. Wentwthvle 306 K2
GARGERY
st. Ambarvale 510 F14
GARIE
cl. Woodbine 481 F12
pl. Frenchs Frst 256 J4
pl. S Coogee 407 H5
GARIGAL
pl. Mona Vale 199 B2
rd. Belrose 225 K1
GARING
st. Richmond 120 B6
GARLAND
av. Epping 280 K2
cr. Bonnyrigg Ht 363 B3
rd. Naremburn 315 F1
wy. Ambarvale 511 A15

GARLICKS RANGE
rd. Orangeville.....473 A10
GARLING
pl. Barden Rdg.....488 G5
pl. Currans Hill.....479 J10
rd. Kings Park......244 H5
st. Lane Cove W..283 K16
wy. Claymore........481 C10
GARMENT
st. Fairfield W......335 B8
st. Prairiewood....335 B8
GARNER
av. Frenchs Frst....256 G7
st. St Marys.........269 G2
GARNERS
av. Marrickville.....374 A12
la. Marrickville.....374 A12
GARNET
av. Lilyfield............10 E7
cr. Killara.............254 D12
la. Dulwich Hill....373 C11
pl. Cartwright.......393 K5
pl. Kellyville.........185 E9
rd. Gymea.............461 G15
rd. Kareela............461 B14
rd. Kirrawee..........461 B14
rd. Miranda...........461 G15
st. Bossley Park...334 B9
st. Dulwich Hill....373 B11
st. Eagle Vale.......481 F6
st. Hurlstone Pk...373 B11
st. Killara.............254 D12
st. Rockdale.........433 F1
st. S Coogee.........407 H4
GARNETT
st. Guildford.........338 C4
st. Merrylands......338 C4
GARNSEY
av. Panania...........428 F5
GARONNE
st. Kearns............451 D16
st. Seven Hills......275 G7
GARRALLAN
pl. Airds.............512 C10
GARRAN
la. Glebe...............12 A7
st. Fairfield W......335 F11
GARRARD
la. Balmain East........8 D9
st. Granville.........308 D13
GARRAWEEN
av. N Balgowlah...287 C4
GARREFFA
cl. Edensor Pk.....333 J13
GARRETT
av. Glenhaven......218 D3
av. S Turramrra....252 B8
av. Terrey Hills.....196 F5
pl. Shalvey...........211 A15
rd. Beecroft..........250 F5
st. Kingsford........407 B8
st. Maroubra........407 B8
wy. Glenwood.......246 B5
GARRICK
av. Hunters Hill....313 K12
la. St Clair, off St Clair Av.......269 H8
pl. Doonside........243 B7
rd. St Clair...........269 G8
rd. St Ives............224 B10
GARRISON
rd. Bossley Park...333 H8
wy. Glenwood.......246 B5
GARRONG
rd. Lakemba.........371 A15
GARRY
ct. Georges Hall...367 K15
GARSWOOD
rd. Glenmore Pk...266 F9
GARTFERN
av. Five Dock........343 A6
GARTHONS
la. Hurstville........431 J5
GARTHOWEN
av. Lane Cove.......313 K2
cr. Castle Hill.......218 E13
GARTMORE
av. Bankstown......399 F5
GARTUNG
rd. Galston...........159 C4
GARTY
la. Greenacre.......370 G2
GARVAN
rd. Heathcote.......518 C15

GARY
gr. Marayong........244 D6
st. Castle Hill........248 B3
st. Merrylnds W...306 J13
GAS
la. Millers Point......A C9
la. N Sydney...........K D10
GASCOGNE
st. Prestons.........393 H15
GASCOIGNE
rd. Birrong...........368 H7
rd. Yagoona..........368 H8
st. Penrith............237 D9
GASCOYNE
pl. Illawong..........460 B3
GASMATA
cr. Whalan...........240 H10
GASPARD
pl. Ambarvale.......510 H13
GAS WORKS
rd. Wollstncraft....315 D11
GATACRE
av. Lane Cove.......314 F1
GATE
rd. Blacktown.......244 G9
GATEHOUSE
cct. Wrrngtn Dns...238 A3
GATENBY
pl. Barden Rdg.....458 H16
GATES
rd. Luddenham....326 F1
GATHREY
cr. Kings Lngly.....245 D5
GATLEY
ct. Wattle Grove...426 A5
GATTO
pl. West Hoxton...392 C7
GAUSS
pl. Tregear...........240 E5
GAUTHORPE
st. Rhodes...........311 D8
GAVIN
pl. Cherrybrook....219 J9
pl. Kings Lngly.....245 K6
GAWAIN
ct. Glenhaven.......217 J5
GAWLER
pl. Bossley Park...333 E10
pl. N Turramrra....223 D1
GAY
st. Castle Hill........218 D12
st. Lane Cove W...284 D15
GAYLINE
dr. Narellan Vale...479 B13
GAYMARK
la. Penrith............236 J10
GAZA
av. Hunters Hill.....313 E5
la. West Ryde, off Gaza Rd..........281 D15
rd. Naremburn......315 F1
rd. West Ryde.......281 D16
st. Holsworthy......426 D10
GAZALA
rd. Holsworthy......426 E7
GAZANIA
rd. Faulconbdg.....171 E14
GAZELLE
ct. Glenwood........215 K16
pl. Werrington......238 E11
st. Glenfield.........424 F9
GAZI
cl. Bossley Park...334 A6
GAZZARD
st. Birrong...........368 K6
GEAKES
rd. Freemns Rch....61 A14
rd. Glossodia..........61 A8
rd. Wilberforce.......61 A8
GEARS
av. Drummoyne....343 F4
GEDDES
pl. Cabramtta W...365 C8
st. Balgowlah Ht..288 A13
st. Botany............405 J16
GEE
wy. Minto.............482 K2
GEEBUNG
cl. Arcadia...........129 J10
ct. Voyager Pt......427 C4
GEEHI
pl. Heckenberg....364 A14
GEELANS
rd. Arcadia...........130 A14

GEELONG
cr. St Johns Pk....364 E3
rd. Cromer...........228 D16
rd. Engadine.........489 C9
GEER
av. Sans Souci......463 B2
GEES
av. Strathfield.......371 E5
GEEVES
av. Rockdale.........403 D15
la. Pennant Hills...220 G16
la. Pennant Hills...250 G1
GEEWAN
av. Kellyville..........216 F2
pl. Clarmnt Ms.....268 H2
GEHRIG
la. Annandale........17 C2
GELDING
st. Dulwich Hill.....373 C7
GELLING
av. Strathfield.......341 C16
GEM
pl. Greystanes......306 C2
GEMALLA
st. Bonnyrigg.......363 K9
GEMALONG
pl. Glenmore Pk...266 G15
GEMAS
pl. St Ives Ch........223 J6
st. Holsworthy.....426 D1
GEMEREN
gr. W Pnnant Hl....248 K7
GEMINI
cl. S Penrith.........267 B6
GEMOORE
st. Smithfield........335 B7
GEMSTONE
wy. Oakhurst, off Dillon Pl...........242 C2
GENDERS
av. Burwood.........371 H1
la. Burwood, off Genders Av......371 H1
GENERAL BRIDGES
cr. Daceyville........406 G3
GENERAL HOLMES
dr. Botany............405 D7
dr. Btn-le-Sds.......404 B16
dr. Kyeemagh.......404 B16
dr. Mascot............404 B16
GENEVA
cr. Seven Hills......275 H7
pl. Engadine.........489 B9
rd. Cranebrook.....207 G5
st. Berowra..........133 E16
GENISTA
st. Loftus.............490 A10
GENNER
st. Denistone W...281 A12
GENOA
st. Como.............460 J6
GENTIAN
av. Mcquarie Fd....454 G5
pl. Lugarno..........430 A14
GENTLE
cl. Casula............424 B3
st. Lane Cove.......314 A1
st.w, Lane Cove W...314 A1
GENTY
st. Campbelltwn...511 H4
GEOFFREY
cr. Loftus.............490 A11
st. S Turramrra....252 C7
st. Wentwthvle.....277 A10
GEORGANN
st. Turramurra.....223 A8
GEORGE
la. Paddington......21 D4
la. Eastlakes, off George St........405 J4
pde. Baulkham Hl...247 G14
pl. Artarmon........284 H16
rd. Leppington......420 C15
rd. Wilberforce......91 K3
st. Appin.............568 J13
st. Appin.............568 J14
st. Avalon............139 K11
st. Balmain.............7 C13
st. Bankstown......369 D11
st. Bardwell Vy.....402 J10
st. Bexley............402 J10
st. Blacktown.......244 H15
st. Box Hill...........154 D9
st. Brooklyn..........76 D12

st. Burwood........341 J13
st. Burwood Ht....371 K4
st. Campbelltwn..511 G8
st. Canley Ht.......365 G1
st. Concord W.....341 C1
st. Dover Ht........348 E8
st. Eastlakes.......405 J4
st. Epping...........280 G1
st. Erskineville.......18 A16
st. Gladesville......312 G10
st. Granville.........308 H11
st. Greenwich......314 J13
st. Guildford........337 C3
st. Haymarket.........E E12
st. Haymarket.........E F6
st. Haymarket.........3 D16
st. Hornsby.........221 G1
st. Hunters Hill....313 D11
st. Kingswood.....238 B13
st. Leichhardt........15 D5
st. Lidcombe.......339 G9
st. Liverpool........395 E4
st. Manly.............288 E9
st. Marrickville.....373 H10
st. Miranda..........492 B7
st. Mortdale.........431 B9
st. Mount Druitt...271 F5
st. N Strathfield...341 D4
st. Paddington.......21 F3
st. Parramatta.....308 C2
st. Pennant Hills..250 J1
st. Penshurst.......431 C3
st. Randwick.......377 C13
st. Redfern...........19 C9
st. Riverstone......182 H4
st. Rockdale........403 E15
st. St Marys.........269 D2
st. Schofields......182 H15
st. Seven Hills.....275 G3
st. S Hurstville.....432 C8
st. S Windsor......120 E16
st. Springwood....202 A2
st. Sydenham......374 E14
st. Sydney.............C H16
st. Sydney.............1 G16
st. Sydney.............3 G6
st. Tahmoor........565 J12
st. Tahmoor........565 K10
st. The Rocks.........A J10
st. The Rocks.........1 H8
st. Ultimo..............E C15
st. Ultimo..............3 D16
st. Warwck Frm....365 E16
st. Waterloo..........19 D12
st. Waterloo..........19 E16
st. Windsor.........120 H13
st. Windsor.........121 B9
st. Yagoona........369 D11
GEORGE BRANSBY
av. Harringtn Pk...478 C2
GEORGE CALEY
pl. Mt Annan.......509 H2
GEORGE HUNTER
dr. Narellan.........478 H8
GEORGE MOBBS
dr. Castle Hill.......248 B5
GEORGE MUIR
cl. Baulkham Hl...248 D10
GEORGE PING
dr. Thirlmere.......564 J6
GEORGES
av. Berala............339 G12
av. Lidcombe........339 G12
cr. Georges Hall...367 F13
cr. Roselands......400 K9
pde. Glenfield.......424 K12
rd. Vaucluse........348 G2
swy. Liverpool......395 D4
GEORGES RIVER
cr. Oyster Bay......461 C4
rd. Airds.............512 A9
rd. Campbelltwn..512 A9
rd. Croydon Pk....371 G7
rd. Jannali...........460 J12
rd. Kentlyn..........513 A7
rd. Lansvale.........366 G8
rd. Oyster Bay......461 A10
rd. Ruse.............512 A9
GEORGIA
tce. Kellyville.........187 A16
GEORGIA LEE
pl. Clareville........169 E2
GEORGIAN
av. Carlingford.....249 G15

GEORGIANA
cr. Ambarvale......511 B11
GEORGINA
av. Elanora Ht.....198 F15
cl. Wahroonga.....221 K14
la. Newtown..........18 B9
rd. Mt Vernon......331 D12
st. Bass Hill.........368 D14
st. Bonnyrigg Ht..363 B7
st. Newtown..........18 A9
GERALD
av. Roseville.........284 H2
cr. Doonside........243 E5
rd. Illawong.........459 A6
st. Cecil Hills.......362 J7
st. Greystanes.....306 F6
st. Marrickville.....374 B14
GERALDINE
av. Baulkham Hl...247 D8
GERALDTON
pl. Yarrawarrah....489 F12
GERANIUM
av. Mcquarie Fd...454 F6
cl. Glenmore Pk...265 G13
GERARD
av. Condell Park...368 F16
la. Cremorne.......316 E7
la. Gladesville, off Gerard St........312 H8
st. Alexandria........18 K12
st. Cremorne.......316 F7
st. Gladesville......312 H8
GERBULIN
st. Glendenning...242 F3
GERLEE
pl. Quakers Hill....214 F9
GERMAINE
av. Mt Riverview..234 B3
GERONIMO
cl. Greenfld Pk.....334 A14
GERRALE
st. Cronulla..........493 K13
GERRING
st. Colyton...........270 B6
GERRISH
st. Gladesville......312 K7
GERROA
av. Bayview..........169 B14
pl. Prestons.........393 A14
GERSHAM
gr. Oakhurst.........242 A4
GERSHWIN
cr. Clarmnt Ms.....268 G3
GERTRUDE
av. Newport.........169 J13
rd. Ingleburn........453 D12
st. Arncliffe.........403 K6
st. Balgowlah Ht..287 G12
st. Beacon Hill.....257 E7
GETYUNGA
rd. Oyster Bay......461 C4
GEUM
pl. Mcquarie Fd...454 F6
GHURKA
st. Sadleir............394 B2
GIBB
av. Casula............394 J11
cl. N Parramatta..278 G12
pl. Springwood....201 D1
st. North Ryde.....282 E8
GIBBENS
la. Camperdwn......17 E6
st. Camperdwn......17 E6
GIBBER
pl. Annangrove....186 H4
GIBBES
la. Newtown..........17 H14
st. Banksia...........403 F16
st. Chatswood......285 E5
st. Jamisontown..265 J2
st. Newtown..........17 G14
st. Regentville......265 G4
st. Rockdale........403 F16
GIBBINS
cl. Hornsby.........191 G9
GIBBON
rd. Baulkham Hl...246 G15
rd. Winston Hills..246 G15
GIBBONS
la. Arncliffe.........403 B10
pl. Marayong........244 C8
st. Auburn...........339 D1
st. Eveleigh...........19 A9
st. Oatlands.........279 D6

st. Redfern 19 A9
st. Telopea 279 D6
wy. Claymore 481 C12
GIBBS
la. Manly Vale 287 H2
la. Newtown 17 D10
st. Auburn 338 K5
st. Croydon 342 E15
st. Manly Vale 287 H3
st. Miranda 492 A5
GIBLETT
av. Thornleigh 220 H11
GIBRAN
pl. St Ives 224 E16
GIBSON
av. Casula 394 J12
av. Chatswood 284 J7
av. Padstow 399 C9
av. Werrington 238 K11
la. Horsley Pk 302 E16
pl. Blacktown 274 C5
pl. Chifley 437 B6
pwy. Casula, off Gibson Av 394 K12
rd. Denham Ct 452 G3
rd. Mosman 317 C8
st. Bronte 377 H8
st. Pagewood 405 K10
st. Richmond 118 G7
st. Warragamba 353 G14
st. Waterloo 19 F13
st. Waverley 377 H8
st. Yarrawarrah 489 F11
GIDDINGS
av. Cronulla 493 K14
GIDEON
st. Winston Hills 276 H2
GIDGEE
st. Cabramatta 365 G9
GIDJI
rd. Miranda 491 K5
GIDLEY
cr. Claymore 481 A11
st. St Marys 239 H16
GIDYA
st. Frenchs Frst 256 F4
GIFFARD
st. Silverwater 309 J10
GIFFNOCK
av. Mcquarie Pk 282 G4
GILAI
pl. Allambie Ht 257 G15
GILBA
rd. Girraween 275 J11
rd. Pendle Hill 276 A12
GILBERT
cr. Kings Lngly 245 A5
pl. Frenchs Frst 256 G8
rd. Castle Hill 217 F10
rd. Glenhaven 217 J6
st. Cabramatta 365 D7
st. Colyton 270 B7
st. Dover Ht 348 E11
st. Manly 288 G10
st. N Parramatta 278 D11
st. Sylvania 462 A12
wy. Minto 482 K1
GILBULLA
av. Camden 507 A3
GILCHRIST
dr. Campbelltwn 510 K9
pl. Balmain East 8 E8
GILDA
av. S Penrith 266 F2
av. Wahroonga 222 D10
st. North Ryde 283 C11
wy. Toongabbie 276 B5
GILDEA
av. Five Dock 343 A7
GILDERTHORPE
av. Randwick 377 D10
GILES
cl. Glenmore Pk 265 K6
cr. Ruse 512 F3
pl. Bligh Park 150 J7
pl. Cabramatta 365 E10
pl. Plumpton 241 G9
st. Chifley 437 A6
st. Yarrawarrah 489 F11
GILGANDRA
av. Thornleigh 221 A8
rd. North Bondi 348 C15
st. West Hoxton 392 G7
GILHAM
st. Castle Hill 218 B11
st. Chatswood 284 J13
GILI
pl. Glenmore Pk 266 A7
GILJA
gln. Kingswood 267 J2
GILL
av. Liverpool 394 K9
la. Strathfield S 370 J3
pl. Ruse 512 G1
pl. Schofields 183 D15
GILLEN
cl. Bonnyrigg Ht 363 F7
ct. Wrrngtn Cty 238 H4
GILLES
cr. Beacon Hill 257 J5
GILLESPIE
av. Alexandria 375 E16
pl. Windsor 121 A10
st. Liverpool 395 B6
GILLHAM
av. Caringbah 492 G14
GILLIAN
cr. Hassall Gr 211 H15
pde. West Pymble 252 J13
pl. Punchbowl 399 J3
GILLIANA
pl. Frenchs Frst 255 H3
GILLIAN ROLTON
av. Newington L G16
av. Newington, off Jon Henricks Av 309 K15
GILLIES
av. Haberfield 343 C15
la. Lakemba 401 B1
st. Annandale 10 J12
st. Lakemba 401 B2
st. Wollstncraft 5 A1
GILLIGANS
rd. Dural 189 F2
GILLIVER
av. Vaucluse 348 C5
cr. Greenacre 370 C8
GILLIVERS
pl. Lidcombe 339 K7
GILLOOLY
av. Matraville 436 K9
GILLOTT
wy. St Ives 224 B12
GILLWINGA
av. Caringbah 492 F12
GILMORE
av. Collaroy Plat 228 G13
av. Kirrawee 490 J2
av. Leumeah 512 C2
cl. Glenmore Pk 265 K7
rd. Casula 424 F5
rd. Lalor Park 245 E10
st. Cabramatta 365 J5
GILMOUR
cl. Glenhaven 218 C1
la. Colyton, off Gilmour St 270 H8
pl. Penshurst 431 D2
st. Colyton 270 H8
GILPIN
la. Camperdwn 17 B9
pl. Plumpton 242 D10
st. Camperdwn 17 B9
st. Newtown 17 B9
GILROY
la. Turramurra, off Gilroy Rd 222 J14
rd. Turramurra 222 J13
GILWINGA
dr. Bayview 168 C12
GIMLET
cl. Kingswood 237 H16
cl. Kingswood 267 H1
pl. Mcquarie Fd 454 E3
GINAHGULLA
rd. Bellevue Hill 14 J7
GINAHGULLAH
av. Grose Vale 85 H9
GINDURRA
av. Castle Hill 217 C8
cl. Hamondvle 396 G14
GIOVANNA
ct. Castle Hill 217 C7
GIPPS
av. Little Bay 437 A12
cl. Turramurra 252 B3
pl. Cromer 227 G12
rd. Greystanes 305 D11
rd. Smithfield 305 D13
st. Arncliffe 403 C8
st. Bardwell Vy 403 C8
st. Birchgrove 7 F6
st. Bradbury 511 G14
st. Bronte 377 H8
st. Clarmnt Ms 239 A16
st. Clarmnt Ms 268 J4
st. Concord 341 H8
st. Drummoyne 343 F4
st. Paddington 4 J15
st. Pyrmont 12 H5
st. Smithfield 335 C7
st. Werrington 239 A15
GIPSY
st. Bnkstn Aprt 397 K1
GIRA
pl. Dharruk 241 D8
GIRARD
st. Harbord 288 D2
GIRD
pl. Marayong 243 K6
GIRILANG
av. Vaucluse 348 E6
GIRRA
av. S Penrith 266 J1
rd. Blacktown 243 H16
st. Fairfield W 335 G10
GIRRALONG
av. Baulkham Hl 248 A7
GIRRAWEEN
av. Como 460 F6
av. Lane Cove W 284 A14
rd. Girraween 275 K16
st. Kingsgrove 402 A9
GIRRILANG
rd. Cronulla 494 A8
GIRROMA
st. Carss Park 432 G13
GISSING
st. Wetherill Pk 334 F4
GIUFFRE
pl. W Pnnant Hl 249 H7
GLADE
pl. Engadine 488 K15
pl. W Pnnant Hl 249 C2
st. Balgowlah Ht 287 J13
GLADES
av. Gladesville 312 G10
GLADESVILLE
rd. Hunters Hill 313 B10
GLADIATOR
st. Raby 451 D13
GLADSTONE
av. Hunters Hill 314 C13
av. Mosman 317 B8
av. Ryde 312 A4
av. Warrawee 222 H11
la. Marrickville 374 A13
la. Newtown 17 C13
la. Kogarah, off Gladstone St 433 C3
pde. Lindfield 284 C3
pde. Riverstone 183 A10
pl. West Hoxton 392 D8
rd. Castle Hill 217 B15
st. Balmain 7 K10
st. Belmore 401 D1
st. Bexley 402 J16
st. Burwood 341 J12
st. Cabramatta 365 F7
st. Canley Ht 365 F4
st. Concord 342 B7
st. Enmore 17 A11
st. Kogarah 433 C3
st. Lilyfield 10 H10
st. Marrickville 374 A13
st. Merrylands 307 J12
st. Newport 169 E12
st. Newtown 17 A11
st. N Parramatta 278 E13
st. Stanmore 17 A11
st. Surry Hills 19 J2
st. Vaucluse 318 F16
GLADSWOOD
av. S Penrith 267 B2
gdn. Double Bay 14 F6
GLADYS
av. Frenchs Frst 256 G4
av. Wahroonga 223 A4
cr. Seven Hills 245 C16
st. Kingswood 237 D16
st. Rydalmere 309 J3
GLAISHER
pde. Cronulla 523 K4
GLAMIS
st. Kingsgrove 401 F8
GLAMORGAN
st. Blacktown 274 H7
wy. Cherrybrook 219 F9
GLANARA
ct. Wattle Grove 426 A1
GLANCE
rd. The Slopes 56 K11
GLANDORE
st. Woolooware 493 G6
GLANFIELD
st. Maroubra 406 H9
GLANMIRE
rd. Baulkham Hl 247 A9
GLANVILLE
av. Pagewood 406 G6
GLASGOW
av. Bondi Beach 378 D1
st. Holsworthy 396 B14
st. St Andrews 452 B14
st. Winston Hills 277 D4
GLASSOP
la. Yagoona 368 F13
st. Balmain 7 A8
st. Bankstown 368 J13
st. Caringbah 492 K6
st. Yagoona 368 F13
GLEAM
pl. Cranebrook 206 H8
GLEBE
cl. Appin 568 G14
la. Glebe 12 D13
pl. Penrith 237 D9
pl. St Johns Pk 364 F5
rd. Pitt Town 122 K1
st. Edgecliff 13 J13
st. Glebe 12 D13
st. Parramatta 307 K6
st. Randwick 377 E12
GLEBE POINT
rd. Glebe 12 C14
GLEDITSIA
cl. Narellan Vale 479 A11
GLEDSWOOD
pl. Glen Alpine 510 G12
GLEESON
av. Baulkham Hl 247 E10
av. Condell Park 398 K6
av. Sydenham 374 D14
pl. Abbotsbury 333 C12
GLEN
av. Randwick 377 D13
la. Bondi 378 B5
la. Glebe 11 G11
la. Glenbrook 264 A1
la. Randwick 377 E12
pl. Currans Hill 479 K11
pl. Pendle Hill 276 C16
rd. Castle Hill 218 H14
rd. Emu Heights 234 K6
rd. Oatley 430 J10
rd. Roseville 284 D6
st. Belrose 225 J16
st. Blaxland 233 D5
st. Bondi 378 B5
st. Eastwood 281 A8
st. Galston 159 F9
st. Glenbrook 264 A1
st. Granville 308 E13
st. Harbord 258 G16
st. Marrickville 373 F15
st. Milsons Pt 5 J15
st. Mosman 316 K3
st. Paddington 13 B13
GLENAEON
av. Belrose 226 B8
GLEN ALLAN
rd. Rossmore 390 A15
GLEN ALPINE
dr. Glen Alpine 510 E10
GLENALVON
pl. West Hoxton 392 B11
GLENANNE
pl. Tahmoor 565 F7
GLENARM
cr. Killarney Ht 256 B15
GLENARVON
st. Strathfield 371 A1
GLEN AVON
av. Narwee 400 H15
GLENAVON
pl. Glen Alpine 510 E13
GLENAVY
st. Wentwthvle 276 K15
GLEN-AYR
av. Yowie Bay 492 C10
GLENAYR
av. Bondi Beach 378 C2
av. Denistone W 280 K13
av. North Bondi 348 D16
av. West Ryde 280 K13
gr. W Pnnant Hl 249 B1
la. Bondi Beach, off Blair St 378 C1
GLENBAWN
pl. Leumeah 482 D13
pl. Woodcroft 243 J11
GLENBROOK
cr. Georges Hall 367 J10
pl. The Oaks 502 E13
rd. Blaxland 233 J14
rd. Glenbrook 233 J14
st. Jamisontown 266 B2
GLENCARRON
av. Mosman 317 C4
GLENCOE
av. Chatswd W 284 F8
av. Oatlands 278 H10
av. Wrrngtn Cty 238 D9
cl. Berowra 133 G10
rd. Woollahra 22 E1
st. Sutherland 490 G4
st.s, Sutherland 490 F6
GLENCORSE
av. Milperra 397 G12
GLENCROFT
rd. Roseville 284 J4
GLENDA
pl. Mt Krng-gai 162 J11
pl. North Rocks 248 J13
pl. Plumpton 241 J8
GLENDALE
av. Mt Pritchard 364 H14
av. Narwee 400 J13
av. Padstow 429 D3
dr. Lilyfield 10 C5
gr. W Pnnant Hl 249 A3
pl. Jannali 460 J13
rd. Cowan 133 K2
rd. Turramurra 223 A8
GLEN DAVIS
av. Bossley Park 333 E11
GLENDENNING
rd. Glendenning 242 F11
GLENDEVIE
st. West Hoxton 392 D6
GLENDIVER
rd. Glenmore 503 A12
rd. The Oaks 502 F12
GLENDON
rd. Double Bay 14 F12
GLENDOWER
av. Eastwood 281 H5
st. Gilead 540 F7
st. Rsemeadow 540 F7
GLENEAGLES
av. Killara 253 F15
cr. Hornsby 192 D15
pl. St Andrews 481 K4
wy. Glenmore Pk 266 E9
GLENELG
ct. Wattle Grove 395 H13
pl. Beecroft 250 G7
pl. St Ives Ch 223 K3
st. Sutherland 460 F16
GLEN ELGIN
cr. Edensor Pk 333 D15
GLENELGIN
rd. Winmalee 173 D12
GLENELL
st. Blaxland 233 J10
GLENELLA
av. Beverly Hills 400 J16
wy. Minto 482 G9
GLENESS
pl. Glenorie 127 J13
GLENFARNE
st. Bexley 432 G2
GLENFERN
cl. W Pnnant Hl 248 G8
cr. Bossley Park 334 A9
pl. Gymea Bay 491 E8
rd. Epping 250 J16

GLENFERRIE
av. Cremorne, off Iredale Av 316 F11
GLENFIELD
dr. Currans Hill 479 K13
rd. Casula 424 A5
rd. Glenfield 424 A5
rd. Glenfield 424 E7
GLENGARIFF
av. Killarney Ht 256 A16
GLENGARRIE
rd. Marsden Pk 211 D5
GLENGARRY
av. N Turramrra 223 E2
dr. Glenmore Pk 266 G12
dr. Glenmore Pk 266 G14
la. Carlingford 280 A2
la. Mosman, off Effingham St 317 C10
GLENGYLE
ct. Wattle Grove 425 K2
GLENHARE
la. Glenbrook, off Moore St 233 K15
GLENHAVEN
pl. Oyster Bay 461 C5
rd. Glenhaven 218 C1
rd. Kellyville 186 J15
GLEN HELEN
gr. Dural 219 B3
GLENHOPE
rd. W Pnnant Hl 249 B3
GLENIDOL
rd. Oakville 152 H4
GLEN INNES
rd. Hinchinbrk 392 H6
rd. Hoxton Park 392 H6
GLENISIA
av. Georges Hall 367 J11
GLENLEA
st. Canley Ht 335 D15
GLENLEE
cl. Mt Krng-gai 162 K13
ct. Narellan Vale 508 F2
rd. Gllead 509 E14
rd. Glen Alpine 509 E14
rd. Menangle Pk 509 E14
rd. Spring Farm 508 E7
GLENLEIGH
av. Mulgoa 324 C6
GLEN LOGAN
rd. Bossley Park 333 E10
GLEN MARGARET
av. Lurnea 394 E12
GLENMORE
la. S Penrith, off Glenmore Pl 266 F4
pky. Glenmore Pk 265 H9
pky. Glenmore Pk 265 G5
pl. S Penrith 266 F3
rd. Edgecliff 13 F12
rd. Paddington 4 J15
rd. Paddington 13 F12
st. Naremburn 315 F3
GLENN
av. Northmead 277 H9
pl. N Richmond 87 C13
pl. Yagoona 368 K8
st. Dean Park 242 G1
GLENNIE
st. Colyton 270 D8
GLENOAK
wy. Cherrybrook 219 C9
GLENORA
rd. Yarrawarrah 489 E14
GLENORE
rd. Canterbury 402 D1
GLEN ORMOND
av. Abbotsford 342 J3
GLEN OSMOND
cr. Bossley Park 333 E10
GLENRIDGE
av. W Pnnant Hl 249 B2
GLENROCK
av. Edgecliff 13 J11
av. Wahroonga 223 C5
ct. Wattle Grove 426 A1
pl. Glen Alpine 510 E13
GLENROE
av. W Pnnant Hl 249 B3
GLENROSE
pl. Belrose 225 H16
GLENROTHES
pl. Dharruk 241 D7
GLENROWAN
av. Kellyville 216 G6
dr. Harringtn Pk 478 C2
wy. St Clair 270 D12
GLENROY
av. Middle Cove 285 J7
cr. St Johns Pk 364 F1
pl. Glenwood 245 H3
pl. Middle Dural 158 C9
GLENSHEE
pl. Glenhaven 218 E6
pl. St Andrews 481 J6
GLENSIDE
st. Balgowlah Ht 287 K13
GLENTON
st. Abbotsbury 333 B13
GLENTREES
av. Forestville 256 A12
pl. Cherrybrook 219 H10
GLENUGIE
st. Maroubra 407 E12
GLENVALE
cl. W Pnnant Hl 249 H6
GLENVIEW
av. Earlwood 402 F4
av. Revesby 398 F15
cr. Hunters Hill 314 A13
gr. Glendenning 242 H4
la. Paddington 4 K12
la. Earlwood, off Glenview Av 402 F4
la. St Marys, off Glenview St 269 K4
pl. Engadine 488 J14
rd. Hunters Hill 314 B13
rd. Mt Krng-gai 162 J11
st. Gordon 253 K5
st. Greenwich 315 A9
st. Kogarah Bay 432 K12
st. Paddington 4 K12
st. St Marys 269 J5
GLENWALL
st. Kingsgrove 401 G14
GLENWARI
st. Sadleir 394 A1
GLENWOOD
av. Coogee 377 F16
st. Beecroft 250 A10
wy. Castle Hill 218 G16
GLENWOOD PARK
dr. Glenwood 215 D16
GLENWORTH
pl. Theresa Park 445 B4
GLOBE
st. The Rocks A J6
GLORIA
cl. Mt Colah 162 F12
pl. S Penrith 267 C5
st. Merrylnds W 306 J13
GLORY
wy. Kellyville 185 J13
GLOSSOP
st. N St Marys 239 J11
GLOUCESTER
av. Burwood 341 K13
av. Merrylands 307 D16
av. N Parramatta 278 E10
av. Padstow 429 D1
av. West Pymble 252 G13
pl. Kensington 376 C11
rd. Beverly Hills 401 E14
rd. Epping 251 F13
rd. Hoxton Park 392 H10
rd. Hurstville 431 F1
st. Bexley 432 E2
st. Bonnyrigg Ht 363 A5
st. Concord 341 K1
st. Mcquarie Fd 423 K15
st. N Balgowlah 287 C4
st. Rockdale 403 C14
st. The Rocks A G10
st. The Rocks A H6
st. The Rocks 1 G11
st. The Rocks 1 F13
wk. The Rocks A J2
GLOVER
av. Quakers Hill 214 E9
la. Mosman, off Glover St 316 H8
pl. West Hoxton 392 C11
st. Greenacre 370 F3
st. Lilyfield 9 J2
st. Mosman 316 H7
st. N Willghby 285 F9
GLYN
av. Picnic Point 428 H8
st. Wiley Park 400 F2
GLYNN
cl. Cranebrook 207 B14
GNARBO
av. Carss Park 432 F15
la. Carss Park, off Allawah Av 432 F15
GOBURRA
pl. Engadine 518 D4
GODALLA
rd. Freemns Rch 60 D12
GODDARD
cr. Quakers Hill 214 C10
st. Erskineville 375 A10
st. Newtown 17 E14
st. Turrella 403 F5
GODERICH
la. Potts Point 4 J8
GODFREY
av. Turramurra 222 H16
av. West Hoxton 391 K4
rd. Artarmon 285 C13
st. Banksia 403 D11
st. Hurstville Gr 431 F9
st. Penshurst 431 F9
GODWIN
st. Bexley 402 J13
GODWIT
cl. Hinchinbrk 363 E15
GOGOL
pl. Wetherill Pk 335 A4
GOLD
st. Blakehurst 462 C3
GOLDEN
gr. Beacon Hill 257 G2
gr. Bligh Park 150 D4
gr. Cherrybrook 219 D14
gr. Freemns Rch 89 K3
gr. Stanhpe Gdn 215 A10
gr. Westleigh 220 F7
GOLDEN GROVE
av. Kellyville 216 E1
st. Darlington 18 D8
st. Newtown 18 D8
GOLDEN STAVE
wy. Berala 339 C14
GOLDEN VALLEY
dr. Glossodia 59 C8
GOLDERS GREEN
wy. Glenhaven 218 D5
GOLDFINCH
pl. Bella Vista 246 F1
pl. Grays Point 491 F14
st. Moorebank 396 C10
GOLDIE
av. Bondi Jctn 377 G5
pl. Colyton 270 G4
GOLDING
dr. Glendenning 242 G4
GOLDMAN
la. Double Bay 14 C10
la. Double Bay, off Knox St 14 D9
GOLDMARK
cr. Cranebrook 207 G10
cr. Cranebrook 207 G9
la. Cranebrook, off Goldmark Cr 207 J9
GOLDSBOROUGH
la. Yennora 337 C11
GOLDSMITH
av. Campbelltwn 510 H6
av. Killarney Ht 286 D1
av. Winston Hills 277 G1
cl. Wetherill Pk 334 J6
GOLF
av. Mona Vale 199 E4
pde. Manly 288 F5
GOLF COURSE
dr. Glen Alpine 510 E12
GOLFERS
la. Roseville 255 A16
pde. Pymble 253 A6
GOLF LINKS
rd. Killara 253 G14
GOLFVIEW
dr. Wallacia 324 K13
GOLIATH
av. Winston Hills 276 H3
GOLLAN
av. Oatlands 278 J9
GOLSPIE
cl. Prestons 392 H15
GONA
gr. Narraweena 258 C6
pl. Glenfield 424 G12
st. Holsworthy 426 E2
GONDOLA
rd. N Narrabeen 228 H1
GOOBARAH
rd. Burraneer 523 D2
GOOD
st. Granville 308 F10
st. Harris Park 308 G8
st. Parramatta 307 J4
st. Rosehill 308 G8
st. Westmead 307 H2
GOODACRE
av. Fairfield W 335 B14
av. Miranda 492 C1
av. Winston Hills 277 G3
GOODALL
st. Pendle Hill 276 F14
GOODCHAP
rd. Chatswd W 284 G12
st. Surry Hills F G10
st. Surry Hills 4 A13
GOODE
pl. Currans Hill 479 H9
GOODEN
dr. Baulkham Hl 247 A12
GOODENIA
ct. Voyager Pt 427 D5
rd. Mt Annan 509 C3
GOODENOUGH
st. Glenfield 424 H8
GOODHALL
av. Baulkham Hl 246 J15
GOODHOPE
la. Paddington 13 C14
st. Paddington 13 C14
GOODIA
wy. Bidwill 211 G13
GOODIER
pl. Kenthurst 156 J11
GOODIN
rd. Winston Hills 247 K15
GOODLANDS
av. Thornleigh 220 J12
GOODLET
cl. Lane Cove W, off Walkers Dr 283 F12
la. Surry Hills 19 J5
st. Ashbury 372 E7
st. Merrylands 307 F11
st. Surry Hills 19 J5
st. Thirlmere 565 A3
GOODMAN
pl. Cherrybrook 219 J6
wy. Bonnyrigg 364 B4
GOODMANS
tce. Surry Hills 19 J2
GOODOOGA
cl. Hinchinbrk 392 G4
GOODRICH
av. Kingsford 376 C15
rd. Cecil Park 331 K11
GOODS
rd. Oakville 152 H2
GOODSELL
st. Minto 482 K9
st. St Peters 374 J11
GOODSIR
cl. Rossmore 389 J6
st. Rozelle 7 C13
GOODSTATE
pl. Chester Hill 368 A2
GOODWIN
av. Ashfield 372 J8
av. Mt Lewis 370 B15
cr. Minto 482 H5
rd. Newport 169 G9
st. Denistone 281 G13
st. Narrabeen 229 A7
st. West Ryde 281 G13
st. Woolooware 493 G8
GOODWOOD
st. Kensington 376 F10
GOODWYN
rd. Berowra 133 D14
GOOLAGONG
av. Toongabbie 276 F5
ct. Milperra 397 F11
pl. La Perouse 436 J13
pl. Menai 458 H6
GOOLD
st. Chippendale 19 D1
GOOLGUNG
av. Baulkham Hl 248 A10
GOOLMA
pl. Hornsby 192 D13
GOOLWA
cr. Cranebrook 207 F9
GOOMERAH
cr. Darling Point 13 J4
GOONAROI
st. Villawood 367 J5
GOONDA
av. La Perouse 436 K12
GOONDAH
rd. Engadine 489 C10
st. Villawood 367 E4
GOONDARI
rd. Allambie Ht 257 G14
GOONGOORA
cl. Jamisontown 266 A4
GOORA
st. Little Bay 437 B11
GOORARI
av. Bella Vista 246 F6
GOORAWAHL
av. La Perouse 436 J14
GOORAWAY
dr. Castle Hill 217 J7
pl. Berowra Ht 132 K5
GOOREEN
st. Lidcombe 339 K3
GOORGOOL
rd. Bangor 459 H14
GOORIWA
pl. Engadine 488 E13
GOOROA
st. Carss Park 432 G13
GOOSE
cl. Hinchinbrk 363 D15
GOOSEBERRY
la. Mosman 317 G8
pl. Glenwood 215 E14
GORADA
av. Kirrawee 491 C6
GORDON
av. Castle Hill 218 B11
av. Chatswood 284 H12
av. Coogee 377 J14
av. Ingleburn 453 F3
av. S Granville 338 F5
cr. Denistone 281 D11
cr. Lane Cove W 284 B14
cr. Stanmore 16 B10
la. Paddington 21 D3
la. Petersham 15 G11
pl. Bronte 377 J10
pl. Narellan Vale 478 G16
pl. Windsor Dn 180 K4
rd. Auburn 339 A8
rd. Schofields 183 J14
sq. Marrickville 16 B16
st. Annandale 17 C2
st. Bankstown 369 D15
st. Blacktown 244 J15
st. Btn-le-Sds 433 K1
st. Burwood 341 J13
st. Campsie 372 C10
st. Caringbah 492 J6
st. Carramar 336 J15
st. Clontarf 287 F13
st. Eastwood 281 D6
st. Fairfield 336 J15
st. Hurstville 431 K4
st. Manly Vale 287 K2
st. Marrickville 374 D9
st. Mosman 317 D9
st. Paddington 21 C3
st. Penrith 236 G1
st. Petersham 15 F11
st. Randwick 377 B11
st. Rosebery 405 H3
st. Rozelle 11 B2
st. Rydalmere 310 A2
st. St Marys 269 K2
st. Thirlmere 565 B1
GORDONIA
gr. Baulkham Hl 247 E16
GORDON McKINNON
la. Harris Park 308 E6
GORDON PARKER
st. Revesby 398 E10

GORDONS
la. Concord, off Finch Av 342 B8
GORE
av. Kirrawee 490 J8
cr. Bella Vista 246 G5
la. Kirrawee 490 H8
pl. Willmot 210 D12
st. Arncliffe 403 E10
st. Greenwich 315 A8
st. Harbord 288 H2
st. Parramatta 278 H16
GORE HILL
fwy. Artarmon 315 A1
fwy. Lane Cove 314 J1
fwy. Naremburn 315 A1
GORINSKI
rd. Toongabbie 276 G4
GORMAN
av. Panania 428 E4
pl. Cranebrook 207 D10
st. Marrickville 374 B11
st. Willoughby 285 E15
GORMLEY
st. Freemns Rch 89 F6
st. Lidcombe 339 J11
GORNALL
av. Earlwood 372 G15
GOROKA
pl. Beacon Hill 257 E8
st. Glenfield 424 F10
st. Whalan 240 H10
GORRICKS
la. Freemns Rch 90 G5
GORSE
cl. Loftus 489 K10
st. Prospect 274 G10
GORT
rd. Engadine 488 K12
GORTON
cl. Penrith 237 B7
GOSBELL
la. Paddington 13 B11
st. Paddington 13 A11
GOSBY
av. Miranda 491 J5
GOSHA
cl. Rooty Hill 271 H6
GOSHAWK
cr. Woronora Ht 489 D2
pl. Green Valley 363 C12
GOSLING
av. Green Valley 363 C14
st. Emu Heights 234 J6
st. Greenacre 370 E14
GOSPER
st. Windsor 120 J10
GOSPORT
st. Cronulla 493 J10
GOSSAMER
pl. Mcquarie Fd 454 E4
GOSSE
ct. St Clair 270 D10
la. St Clair, off Gosse Ct 270 D10
pl. Bonnyrigg Ht 363 F8
GOSSELL
gr. Carlingford 249 C13
GOTHER
av. Greenwich 314 K13
GOTTENHAM
la. Glebe 12 C12
st. Glebe 12 C11
GOTTWALD
pl. W Pnnant Hl 249 H6
GOUDA
cl. Abbotsbury 333 B14
GOUGH
av. Chester Hill 337 K12
dr. Castle Hill 218 K13
st. Emu Plains 235 C12
st. Granville 307 K10
GOULBURN
la. Surry Hills F E7
st. Darlinghurst F C5
st. Haymarket E D4
st. Haymarket 3 E10
st. Kings Park 244 E6
st. Liverpool 395 F2
st. Ruse 512 C9
st. St Ives 223 K15
st. Surry Hills F C5
st. Surry Hills 3 J11
st. Sydney E D4
st. Sydney 3 E10
st. Warwck Frm 365 F16
swy. Liverpool 395 F1
GOULBURN PENINSULA
Sylvania Wtr 462 D14
GOULD
av. Kellyville 215 J5
av. Lewisham 15 C15
av. Narraweena 258 D1
av. St Ives Ch 224 A1
la. Lewisham 15 C13
pl. Menai 458 E15
pl. Parramatta 308 J1
rd. Claymore 481 E10
rd. Eagle Vale 481 E10
st. Bankstown 368 H14
st. Bondi Beach 378 D3
st. Campsie 372 C13
st. Canterbury 372 C13
st. Strathfield S 370 J4
st.n, North Bondi 348 E16
GOULDING
rd. Ryde 282 D13
GOULDSBURY
st. Mosman 317 A7
GOURLAY
av. Balgowlah 287 K11
GOVE
av. Green Valley 363 J11
GOVER
st. Peakhurst 430 C2
GOVERNMENT
rd. Bargo 567 J2
rd. Beacon Hill 257 E7
rd. Berkshire Pk 179 H13
rd. Brooklyn 76 B11
rd. Cromer 227 K13
rd. Hinchinbrk 392 G4
rd. Hornsby 221 G2
rd. Mona Vale 198 K2
rd. Mosman 287 A16
GOVERNMENT HOUSE
dr. Emu Plains 235 D9
GOVERNOR MACQUARIE
dr. Chipping Ntn 396 H1
dr. Warwck Frm 365 K15
GOVERNOR PHILLIP
pl. W Pnnant Hl 248 H8
GOVERNORS
dr. Concord 342 F6
dr. Lapstone 264 H3
rd. Mosman 317 K6
wy. Mcquarie Lk 423 E15
wy. Oatlands 278 K8
wy. Oatlands 279 A7
GOVETT
la. Randwick, off Govett St 376 K10
pl. Davidson 225 A15
st. Mt Pritchard 364 C10
st. Randwick 376 K9
GOW
av. Port Hacking 522 K3
la. Cornwallis 120 G1
st. Abbotsford 342 J2
st. Balmain 7 C5
st. Padstow 399 C9
GOWAN
ct. Carlingford 279 B5
pl. Denham Ct 452 G4
GOWAN BRAE
av. Oatlands 278 K10
GOWER
cl. Wetherill Pk 334 J5
st. Ashfield 373 C2
st. Hurlstone Pk 372 K12
st. Summer Hill 373 C2
GOWLLAND
pde. Panania 398 D13
GOWRIE
av. Bondi Jctn 377 G3
av. Punchbowl 399 K5
cl. St Ives 224 F6
cr. Westmead 307 E2
dr. Castle Hill 218 K13
la. Newtown 17 H15
pl. Cabramatta 365 C11
pl. Cromer 227 H13
st. Bondi Jctn 22 D6
st. Cronulla 523 K4
st. Newtown 17 H16
st. Ryde 312 A3
GOYA
pl. Old Tngabbie 276 K6
GOYEN
av. Bexley 403 A15
pl. Padstow 429 E5
GOZO
rd. Greystanes 305 H8
GRACE
av. Beecroft 249 K5
av. Cabramatta 365 F9
av. Condell Park 398 D1
av. Forestville 256 C7
av. Frenchs Frst 256 C3
av. Lakemba 401 C3
av. Lidcombe 340 A2
av. Riverstone 183 A4
cr. Merrylands 307 E15
st. Carlingford 279 F7
st. Kingswood 237 F16
st. Lane Cove 314 A2
st. Liverpool 394 H3
st. Telopea 279 F7
GRACE CAMPBELL
cr. Hillsdale 406 F15
GRACELANDS
dr. Quakers Hill 213 H7
GRACEMAR
av. Panania 428 A5
GRACEMERE
ct. Wattle Grove 425 K1
pl. Glen Alpine 510 F11
st. Concord W 341 E5
GRACILIS
wy. Bidwill 211 D16
GRADY
gdn. Smithfield 335 D4
st. Quakers Hill 214 B13
GRAEME
pl. Freemns Rch 90 E2
GRAF
av. Potts Hill 369 E8
av. West Ryde 281 D15
av. Yagoona 369 E8
GRAFTON
av. Naremburn 315 H3
cr. Dee Why 258 H3
la. Balmain 8 D11
la. Chippendale 18 J1
la. Bondi Jctn, off Adelaide St 377 F3
pl. Jamisontown 266 C2
st. Balmain 8 C11
st. Blacktown 274 J1
st. Bondi Jctn 22 E5
st. Cammeray 316 C6
st. Chippendale 18 J1
st. Cremorne 316 C6
st. Eastlakes 406 A4
st. Greystanes 305 H4
st. Sutherland 490 E6
GRAHAM
av. Casula 394 D11
av. Eastwood 281 F6
av. Harbord 258 H16
av. Lurnea 394 D11
av. Marrickville 373 J11
av. Miranda 461 J16
av. Pymble 253 D1
av. Rookwood 340 E10
av. Wentwthvle 276 J14
cl. Berowra Ht 133 F8
cl. Cranebrook 207 A13
cr. Baulkham Hl 247 J13
pl. Earlwood 402 F6
pl. Picnic Point 428 H7
rd. Leppington 419 J6
rd. Narwee 400 G12
rd. Rossmore 419 J6
st. Auburn 339 C11
st. Berala 339 C11
st. Bundeena 524 A10
st. Doonside 243 B12
st. Greystanes 306 D5
st. Lane Cove 314 B1
st. Rozelle 11 C1
st. Silverdale 353 H14
GRAHAME
av. Glenfield 424 F8
st. Blaxland 233 H11
GRAHAM HILL
rd. Narellan 478 D8
GRAINGER
av. Ashfield 372 J2
av. Mt Pritchard 364 H9
av. N Curl Curl 258 J10
pl. N Richmond 86 K14
st. Marsden Pk 181 K13
GRANARY
ct. Wrrngtn Dns 238 B4
la. Wrrngtn Dns, off Granary Ct 238 B4
GRAND
av. Camellia 309 B5
av. Rosehill 309 B5
av. Westmead 307 E1
av. West Ryde 311 B2
av.n, Camellia 308 K4
dr. Centnnial Pk 21 D11
pde. Glossodia 59 D7
pde. Homebush B M C8
GRAND FLANEUR
av. Richmond 118 B5
GRAND HAVEN
rd. E Kurrajong 57 D1
GRANDIS
pl. Kingswood 267 J2
GRANDOAKS
pl. Castle Hill 218 H16
wy. Castle Hill 218 H16
GRAND VIEW
ct. Bella Vista 246 D8
dr. Mt Riverview 204 G14
GRANDVIEW
av. Seven Hills 275 F10
cr. Lugarno 429 K10
dr. Bilgola 169 G7
dr. Campbelltwn 511 F9
dr. Newport 169 G7
gr. Seaforth 287 B9
la. Bowen Mtn 84 C12
la. Pymble 253 D3
pde. Caringbah 493 C13
pde. Epping 250 H16
pde. Mona Vale 199 G1
st. Naremburn 315 D1
st. Parramatta 278 J16
st. Pymble 253 D3
st. S Penrith 266 J2
GRANGE
av. Marsden Pk 211 J3
av. Schofields 183 A16
cr. Cmbrdg Gdn 237 G3
la. Cmbrdg Gdn, off Grange Cr 237 G4
rd. Glenhaven 218 B2
rd. Minto 482 A11
GRANGEWOOD
pl. W Pnnant Hl 248 G6
GRANITE
pl. Eagle Vale 481 E7
pl. Hinchinbrk 362 K15
GRANT
av. Cabramatta 365 C9
cl. Epping 250 G15
cl. Kemps Ck 360 G10
cr. Merrylands 306 J10
gld. Bella Vista 246 G2
pl. Bonnet Bay 460 C9
pl. St Ives 224 A16
st. Blacktown 243 J10
wy. Minto 482 K7
GRANTHAM
cr. Dangar I 76 H7
la. Potts Point 4 J1
pl. Chipping Ntn 366 F13
rd. Seven Hills 275 F4
st. Burwood 341 J11
st. Carlton 432 J5
st. Potts Point 4 K1
st. Riverstone 153 B14
GRANTOWN
ct. Castle Hill 218 D7
GRANVILLE
st. Fairfield 336 C7
st. Fairfield Ht 336 B9
GRAPHITE
pl. Eagle Vale 481 E6
GRASMERE
av. Northmead 278 C5
cr. Collaroy Plat 228 E10
la. Cremorne 316 C7
rd. Cremorne 316 C6
GRASSMERE
av. S Penrith 266 F2
gr. Grasmere 475 K16
rd. Killara 254 A16
st. Guildford 337 K5
GRASSY
cl. Hinchinbrk 363 A14
GRATTAN
cr. Frenchs Frst 256 F10
GRAWIN
cl. Hinchinbrk 392 H4
GRAY
av. Kogarah 433 C7
cr. Eastlakes 405 K2
cr. Yagoona 368 J10
la. Kogarah 433 C7
la. Sutherland, off President Av 490 D4
pl. Bradbury 511 G11
pl. Kings Lngly 246 A9
pl. Wetherill Pk 335 A3
st. Annandale 10 K9
st. Bondi Jctn 22 J8
st. Granville 308 G9
st. Henley 313 B14
st. Kogarah 433 B5
st. Kogarah 433 C7
st. Mt Colah 192 D4
st. Randwick 377 C15
st. Sutherland 490 E4
GRAYLIND
av. W Pnnant Hl 249 G1
cl. Collaroy 229 A11
pl. Vaucluse 348 C5
GRAYLING
rd. West Pymble 252 K9
GRAYS
la. Cranebrook 207 C8
la. Waterloo 19 C11
GRAYS FOLLY
pl. Theresa Park 444 G7
GRAYSON
rd. N Epping 251 D10
st. Glendenning 242 G3
GRAY SPENCE
cr. W Pnnant Hl 249 B8
GRAYS POINT
rd. Grays Point 491 A14
GRAZIER
cr. Wrrngtn Dns 238 D6
pl. Minchinbury 271 F9
GREAT BUCKINGHAM
st. Redfern 19 G7
GREAT NORTH
rd. Abbotsford 342 J2
rd. Five Dock 342 J11
rd. Wareemba 343 A7
GREATREX
av. Regents Pk 369 D1
GREAT SOUTHERN
rd. Bargo 567 E1
GREAT THORNE
st. Edgecliff 13 J13
GREAT WESTERN
hwy. Annandale 16 D4
hwy. Arndell Park 273 A9
hwy. Ashfield 342 G11
hwy. Auburn 309 E14
hwy. Blacktown 274 A12
hwy. Blaxland 233 D4
hwy. Burwood 342 G11
hwy. Camperdwn 17 H2
hwy. Canada Bay 342 G11
hwy. Colyton 270 A2
hwy. Concord 342 G11
hwy. Croydon 342 G11
hwy. Doonside 273 A9
hwy. Eastern Ck 273 A9
hwy. Emu Plains 234 J10
hwy. Faulconbdg 201 C1
hwy. Five Dock 342 G11
hwy. Forest Lodge 17 H2
hwy. Girraween 275 B14
hwy. Glebe 17 H2
hwy. Glenbrook 233 D4
hwy. Granville 308 D9
hwy. Greystanes 305 J1
hwy. Haberfield 373 D2
hwy. Homebush 342 G11
hwy. Homebsh W 340 A2
hwy. Huntingwd 273 A9
hwy. Kingswood 237 E12
hwy. Lapstone 264 F1
hwy. Leichhardt 15 E6
hwy. Lewisham 15 E6
hwy. Lidcombe 340 A2
hwy. Mays Hill 307 A4
hwy. Minchinbury 271 B4
hwy. Mount Druitt 271 B4
hwy. Oxley Park 270 A2
hwy. Parramatta 307 A4
hwy. Pendle Hill 305 J1
hwy. Penrith 236 G10
hwy. Petersham 15 E6

hwy. Prospect.........275 B14
hwy. Rooty Hill.......272 B7
hwy. St Marys.........269 C1
hwy. S Wntwthvle...307 A4
hwy. Springwood....201 C1
hwy. Stanmore..........16 D4
hwy. Summer Hill....373 D2
hwy. Valley Ht.........202 D4
hwy. Warrimoo........203 A13
hwy. Wentwthvle.....307 A4
hwy. Werrington.....238 D14
hwy. Westmead.......307 A4
GREBE
pl. Hinchinbrk......393 E1
st. Erskine Park..270 F16
st. Ingleburn........453 G8
GRECH
st. Glenwood.......245 F2
GRECIA
la. Mosman.........317 C1
GRECO
pl. Rsemeadow....540 D4
GREEK
st. Glebe................12 G15
GREEN
av. Smithfield.......335 K6
la. Bradbury........511 E13
la. Kogarah..........433 D4
pde. Valley Ht.........202 G7
pl. Oyster Bay......461 B5
pl. Peakhurst.......430 B6
rd. Kellyville.........216 K1
sq. Alexandria, off Botany Rd.......375 G10
st. Bnksmeadw...406 B11
st. Blacktown.......274 J8
st. Brookvale........257 K11
st. Cremorne Pt...316 G13
st. Glenbrook.......234 B16
st. Kogarah..........433 D4
st. Maroubra........407 B9
st. Pleasure Pt.....427 H7
st. Revesby.........398 B10
st. Tempe............404 A3
st. Wallacia..........324 K13
st. Woolooware...493 H10
GREENACRE
dr. Tahmoor.........566 C13
rd. Bankstown......369 H13
rd. Connells Pt.....431 K13
rd. Greenacre.......369 J13
rd. S Hurstville.....431 K13
GREENAWAY
av. Camden S.......507 B9
GREENBANK
dr. Glenhaven......217 J4
dr. Wrrngtn Dns...238 D5
st. Hurstville.......431 K7
st. Marrickville.....373 H14
GREENDALE
av. Frenchs Frst....256 D2
av. Pymble...........223 F14
cr. Chester Hill.....338 C15
rd. Bringelly.........387 A13
rd. Greendale.......355 B13
rd. Wallacia..........324 J13
st. Greenwich.......315 B8
GREENE
av. Ryde..............282 C16
GREENFIELD
av. Middle Cove....285 J7
pde. Bankstown......399 E1
pl. Forestville.......256 C9
pl. Maraylya...........94 A11
rd. Greenfld Pk.....334 B13
rd. Prairiewood....334 B13
st. Bnksmeadw....435 K1
GREENFIELDS
pl. Theresa Park..445 A3
GREENFINCH
st. Green Valley...363 F12
GREENGATE
la. Killara.............253 J10
rd. Airds..............511 J16
rd. Killara.............253 J11
rd. St Helens Pk...511 J16
GREENHALG
rd. Cranebrook.....207 D14
GREENHALGH
la. Padstow.........429 E1
GREENHAVEN
dr. Emu Heights...234 K4
dr. Pennant Hills..250 G3
pl. Silverdale........354 A14
rd. Grays Point.....491 A13
GREENHILL
av. Normanhurst..221 D12
cl. Castle Hill......218 B10
cr. St Ives Ch.......223 J4
dr. Glenwood.......245 K3
GREEN HILLS
dr. Silverdale........383 J2
GREENHILLS
av. Moorebank.....395 G13
av. Moorebank.....395 H10
av. S Penrith.........236 H16
rd. Holsworthy.....425 F10
st. Croydon..........372 D5
st. Croydon Pk.....372 D5
GREENKNOWE
av. Elizabeth Bay.....13 A5
GREENLANDS
av. Peakhurst.......430 G1
rd. Lane Cove W...284 C14
GREENLEAF
st. Wentwthvle.....277 A7
GREENLEE
st. Berala............339 C15
GREENLEES
av. Concord..........342 B5
GREENMEADOWS
cr. Toongabbie.....276 E6
GREENMOUNT
wy. Mt Colah.........192 D5
GREENOAKS
av. Bradbury.........511 D13
av. Cherrybrook....219 H15
av. Darling Point.....13 J7
GREEN POINT
rd. Oyster Bay......461 A7
GREENS
av. Oatlands.........279 B12
dr. Cammeray......316 B5
rd. Paddington.........4 G16
rd. Warrimoo.......202 K13
GREENSBOROUGH
av. Rouse Hill.......185 B8
GREENSLOPE
st. S Wntwthvle...306 H5
GREENSTEAD
la. Randwick.......377 B13
GREENTREE
pl. Wilberforce.......92 A1
GREENVALE
gr. Hornsby..........221 F6
pl. Castle Hill.......248 D5
st. Fairfield W......335 D12
GREEN VALLEY
rd. Busby............363 A10
rd. Green Valley....363 A10
GREENVALLEY
av. St Ives...........224 D4
GREENVIEW
pde. Berowra.........163 D2
GREENWAY
av. Shalvey...........211 A14
cr. Windsor..........120 K8
dr. Milsons Pt..........5 K12
dr. Pymble...........252 J7
dr. S Penrith.........267 A1
dr. West Hoxton...392 A10
dr. West Pymble..252 J7
la. Springwood....202 A3
la. The Rocks..........A K3
pde. Revesby..........398 F11
pl. Horsley Pk......331 G1
st. Gymea............491 G1
st. Ruse..............512 G1
GREENWELL
rd. Prestons.........392 K15
GREENWICH
cl. St Johns Pk....364 F5
pl. Kellyville.........216 D2
rd. Greenwich......315 A6
GREENWOOD
av. Bankstown......399 C1
av. Narraweena.....258 B3
av. S Coogee........407 G4
cl. Hamondvle.....396 H15
gr. Blacktown.......244 D15
la. Enfield............371 H2
pl. Harbord..........258 H16
pl. St Helens Pk...541 C2
rd. Kellyville........216 F3
GREER
st. Bonnyrigg Ht..363 E8
st. Merrylands.....307 D13
GREG
pl. Dean Park.......212 J16
GREGGS
rd. Kurrajong.........85 C5
GREGORACE
pl. Bonnyrigg.......363 J6
GREGORY
av. Baulkham Hl....247 A11
av. Croydon..........342 G15
av. N Epping.........251 E12
av. Oxley Park.......270 F3
cr. Beverly Hills....401 A15
la. Earlwood.........402 K4
pl. Harris Park......308 H5
rd. Leppington......419 E6
st. Ermington.......310 F5
st. Fairfield W.......335 B13
st. Glendenning....242 E2
st. Granville..........308 E16
st. Greystanes......306 E3
st. Maroubra.......407 H6
st. N Richmond.....87 B14
st. Rsemeadow....540 H4
st. Roseville.........284 J2
st. Ryde..............312 D7
st. S Coogee........407 H6
st. Strathfield S....371 A5
st. Yagoona.........368 E12
tce. Lapstone.........264 H4
GREGSON
pl. Quakers Hill....214 E8
GREG TAYLOR
av. Matraville........436 K8
GREIG
pl. Engadine.........518 D4
pl. Seven Hills......246 E13
GRENACHE
pl. Eschol Park.....481 A5
GRENADA
st. Fairfield W.......335 B11
GRENFELL
av. N Narrabeen....228 J2
st. Blakehurst.......432 C15
GRENVILLE
av. Cabarita..........342 E1
av. Caringbah.......493 A4
st. Pitt Town..........92 G14
GRESHAM
av. W Pnnant Hl....249 G8
st. Cowan............104 B13
st. Sydney................B B12
st. Sydney................1 J14
GRETA
pl. Cartwright.......394 D4
pl. Hebersham......241 G3
GRETCHEN
av. Earlwood.........402 E5
GRETEL
st. Greenfld Pk.....334 D15
GRETNA
cl. West Hoxton....392 E6
pl. St Andrews.....482 A2
GRETTA
pl. Kellyville..........186 J16
GREVILLE
st. Chatswd W.....284 C13
st. Chatswd W.....284 D9
st. Clovelly...........377 G11
st. Randwick.........377 G11
GREVILLEA
av. St Ives............224 D14
cl. Bossley Park...333 E8
cr. Greystanes.......305 E11
cr. Hornsby Ht......191 G5
cr. Mcquarie Fd....454 G4
cr. Prestons.........394 A14
cr. Stanhpe Gdn...215 D11
dr. St Clair............270 A15
gr. Baulkham Hl....247 D16
gr. Heathcote........518 J11
gr. Narellan Vale...478 K14
la. St Clair, off Grevillea Dr......270 A15
pl. Kenthurst.........156 K15
pl. S Coogee........407 E6
pwy. Valley Ht.........202 E5
rd. Chester Hill.....368 C1
st. Collaroy Plat....228 H11
GREX
av. Minchinbury....271 D7
GREY
st. Carlton............432 F4
st. Emu Plains......235 A11
st. Glenbrook.......264 C2
st. Silverwater......309 J14
GREYCAIRN
pl. Woollahra........22 E3
GREYCLIFFE
av. Pennant Hills..220 F16
av. Vaucluse.........348 B2
st. Queenscliff......288 G4
GREY GUM
rd. Mt Colah........191 K2
GREYGUM
av. Rouse Hill......184 K7
pl. Gymea Bay.....491 F11
GREYGUMS
rd. Cranebrook....207 B13
GREYSTANES
rd. Greystanes.....305 G8
GREYSTOKE
st. Collaroy Plat...228 D9
GREYSTONES
rd. Killarney Ht....255 K14
GREYWOOD
st. Cherrybrook...219 C11
GRIBBENMOUNT
rd. Galston..........159 H8
GRIBBLE
pl. Blacktown......244 E15
GRIDE
pl. Ambarvale......511 B14
GRIEVE
cr. Milperra.........397 E11
GRIFFIN
av. Bexley...........432 J3
pde. Illawong.........459 K3
pl. Doonside.........273 F3
pl. Kenthurst.......157 K5
rd. Dee Why........259 A12
rd. N Curl Curl.....259 A12
st. Manly.............288 E9
st. Surry Hills........20 B1
GRIFFINS
rd. Tennyson.........58 A5
GRIFFITH
av. North Bondi....348 C16
av. Roseville Ch...285 F2
cl. Galston..........159 G10
GRIFFITHS
av. Bankstown.....399 H1
av. Camden S.....507 B16
av. McGraths Hl...121 K12
av. Punchbowl.....399 H1
av. West Ryde......311 G1
la. West Ryde......281 G16
pl. Eagle Vale.......480 K11
st. Ashfield.........372 J10
st. Balgowlah......287 J7
st. Blacktown......274 K1
st. Ermington......310 C2
st. Fairlight.........288 A7
st. Hurlstone Pk..372 J10
st. N St Marys.....239 J9
st. Oatley............431 A9
st. Sans Souci.....463 B2
st. Tempe............404 A2
st. Wentwthvle....307 B3
st. Woolmloo..........4 F4
GRIGG
av. N Epping........251 D11
cl. Ellis Lane........476 C11
st. Oatley............431 D10
GRIGOR
pl. Allambie Ht.....257 D12
GRIMES
la. Carlingford.....280 D5
la. Epping...........280 D5
pl. Bonnyrigg......364 B8
pl. Davidson........225 B15
GRIMLEY
cl. Penrith...........237 F2
la. Penrith, off Grimley Cr......237 F2
GRIMMET
av. Rouse Hill......184 K7
GRIMMETT
ct. St Clair..........269 K16
la. St Clair, off Grimmett Ct....269 K16
st. Greystanes....305 H8
GRIMSON
cr. Liverpool........365 B16
la. Liverpool, off Grimson Cr.....365 B16
GRIMWIG
cr. Ambarvale......510 H12
GRIMWOOD
st. Granville.........308 B11
GROGAN
st. Croydon.........342 E11
GRONO
pl. McGraths Hl...121 K13
GRONO FARM
rd. Wilberforce.......62 H15
GROOTE
av. Hinchinbrk......363 A15
GROSE
av. Lurnea............394 B13
av. N St Marys......239 J8
la. Bowen Mtn.......84 E15
la. Grose Vale........84 E15
pl. Camden S.......507 B9
pl. Ruse..............512 G8
pl. Seven Hills.....275 F10
rd. Faulconbdg.....171 B16
st. Camperdwn......17 G5
st. Glebe................12 G16
st. Little Bay........437 A13
st. Parramatta......278 C15
st. Richmond.......118 G6
GROSE RIVER
rd. Grose Wold....116 E8
GROSE VALE
rd. Grose Vale........84 J9
rd. Kurrajong.........85 A6
rd. N Richmond.....87 A16
GROSE VALE COMMUNITY CENTRE
rd. Grose Vale........85 A15
GROSE VALLEY
ct. Faulconbdg.....171 D11
GROSE WOLD
rd. Grose Vale........85 C15
rd. Grose Wold....115 H5
GROSVENOR
cr. Cronulla..........493 G13
cr. Summer Hill...373 C3
la. Cremorne...........6 H1
la. Neutral Bay.........6 H1
la. Lindfield, off Grosvenor Rd.284 D3
pl. Brookvale.......258 B12
pl. W Pnnant Hl...249 D2
rd. Lindfield.........283 J5
rd. S Hurstville.....432 C11
st. Bondi Jctn........22 J5
st. Cremorne.......316 D8
st. Croydon.........342 D16
st. Kensington.....376 D13
st. Neutral Bay.....316 C8
st. N Wahrnga.....192 F16
st. Sydney...............A G11
st. Sydney................1 F14
st. Wahroonga.....222 F5
st. Woollahra.........22 J5
GROSVERNOR
la. Bondi Jctn........22 H6
GROUNDSEL
av. Mcquarie Fd...454 E5
GROUT
pl. Menai............458 E11
pl. Rouse Hill.......184 K5
GROVE
av. Hurstville Gr...431 E7
av. Narwee...........400 G11
av. Penshurst.......431 E7
la. Eastwood.......281 G7
la. Lilyfield............10 F5
pl. Prospect.........275 A10
st. Birchgrove..........7 G4
st. Bondi.............377 K5
st. Casula...........394 H11
st. Dulwich Hill....373 D9
st. Earlwood........402 H2
st. Eastwood.......281 G8
st. Guildford........337 F3
st. Lilyfield............10 E5
st. Marrickville.....373 J15
st. St Peters........374 F14
GROVER
av. Cromer..........227 K15
cr. Mulgoa...........296 D11
st. Lapstone........264 G4
GROVES
av. Mulgrave........151 H2
rd. Minto Ht.........483 G2
GROVEWOOD
pl. Castle Hill.......218 J6
GRUMMAN
la. St Clair, off Grumman Pl...270 E15
pl. Raby..............451 D15
pl. St Clair..........270 E15
GRUNER
pl. Mt Pritchard...364 J11

wy. Claymore........ 481 D11
GUAM
pl. Kings Park...... 244 F2
GUARDIAN
av. Kellyville......... 185 H11
cr. Bligh Park....... 150 E8
pde. Beacon Hill..... 257 F3
GUELPH
st. Regents Pk..... 368 J2
GUERIE
st. Marayong....... 244 C3
GUERIN
la. Bass Hill......... 367 K4
st. Doonside........ 243 C6
GUERNSEY
av. Minto............. 452 K16
st. Busby.............. 363 J16
st. Guildford......... 337 D7
wy. Stanhpe Gdn .. 215 F10
GUESS
av. Arncliffe.......... 403 H5
GUEUDECOURT
av. Earlwood........ 402 J1
GUIHEN
st. Annandale........ 17 C1
GUILD
st. Old Tngabbie.. 277 E8
GUILDFORD
la. Cambrdg Pk, off Guildford Rd... 237 J10
pl. Leumeah........ 482 C16
rd. Cambrdg Pk ... 237 J11
rd. Guildford......... 337 G5
rd.w, Guildford........ 337 A3
rd.w, Guildford W..... 337 A3
GUILFOYLE
av. Double Bay....... 14 B8
st. Berala............. 339 C12
GUINEA
st. Kogarah......... 433 A4
GUINEVIERE
ct. Castle Hill....... 217 G4
GUIREN
pl. Toongabbie.... 276 G6
GUISE
av. Casula............ 394 C15
pwy. Casula, off Guise Av......... 394 D16
rd. Bradbury........ 511 F10
GULIA
st. Mona Vale...... 198 G1
GULL
pl. Erskine Park... 270 H14
pl. Hinchinbrk...... 363 E16
pl. Lugarno......... 429 H12
pl. Prospect......... 274 J11
st. Little Bay........ 437 G15
GULLALIE
cir. Blaxland......... 233 K6
GULLIVER
st. Brookvale....... 258 A9
GULLY
rd. Valley Ht......... 202 G3
GULLY GULLY
rd. Mooney............ 75 D2
GUM
st. Greystanes..... 306 E4
st. Riverstone...... 182 K3
GUMBLETON
pl. Narellan Vale .. 508 H1
GUM BLOSSOM
dr. Westleigh....... 220 H9
GUMBOOYA
st. Allambie Ht..... 257 H14
GUMBUYA
av. Baulkham Hl... 246 H7
GUMDALE
av. St Johns Pk.... 364 C1
GUM GROVE
pl. W Pnnant Hl... 249 H9
GUM LEAF
cl. Hornsby Ht..... 162 A9
GUMLEAF
pl. W Pnnant Hl... 249 G3
row. Wrrngtn Dns .. 238 D6
GUMNUT
cl. Blaxland......... 233 F4
cl. Kellyville......... 186 C15
pl. Cherrybrook... 219 F12
pl. Mcquarie Fd ... 454 E1
rd. Cherrybrook... 219 F11
GUMNUT BABY
wk. Faulconbdg 171 D14
GUMTREE
la. Double Bay....... 14 C10
wy. Smithfield....... 335 G7
GUNARA
tce. Glenmore Pk... 265 K10
GUNBALANYA
av. Beecroft.......... 250 C4
GUNBOWER
rd. Bowen Mtn....... 84 B10
GUNDAGAI
cr. Wakeley.......... 334 F14
GUNDAH
rd. Mt Krng-gai.... 162 J5
GUNDAIN
la. Kirrawee, off Gundain Rd..... 461 D16
rd. Kirrawee........ 461 D16
GUNDAMAIAN ROAD SERVICE
trl. Royal N P....... 521 H4
GUNDAROO
st. Villawood........ 367 E4
GUNDARY
cl. Prestons......... 422 J1
GUNDAWARRA
pl. Kenthurst........ 157 G9
st. Lilli Pilli........... 522 G1
GUNDIBRI
st. Busby............. 363 H14
GUNDIMAINE
av. Neutral Bay......... 6 J9
GUNDOWRINGA
pl. Airds............. 512 A10
GUNDY
pl. Westleigh....... 220 F10
GUNELL
pl. Cranebrook..... 207 F13
GUNGAH BAY
rd. Oatley............. 430 J12
GUNGARLIN
dr. Horngsea Pk... 392 F14
GUNGAROO
pl. Beverly Hills.... 401 B10
GUNGARTEN
cl. Kellyville......... 216 C1
GUNGURRU
st. Kingswood..... 267 H2
GUNJULLA
pl. Avalon............ 139 J16
GUNN
pl. St Helens Pk... 540 K9
rd. Lalor Park....... 245 F10
GUNNAMATTA
rd. Cronulla.......... 493 G13
rd. Woolooware... 493 G13
GUNNEDAH
rd. Hoxton Park.... 392 H7
GUNNERS
mw. Holsworthy..... 426 F4
GUNNING
cl. Prestons......... 393 D16
GUNSYND
av. Casula............ 394 G15
GUNTAWONG
rd. Rouse Hill....... 183 K9
GUNYA
pl. Hebersham..... 241 E10
st. Regents Pk..... 369 A2
GUNYAH
cr. Roselands...... 401 D6
pl. Avalon............ 140 A13
pl. Glen Alpine...... 510 D13
st. Cronulla.......... 523 J2
st. Marsfield........ 281 G2
st. Northbridge.... 286 A16
GUNYAH PATH
. Winmalee....... 173 A9
GURA
pl. Glenmore Pk... 266 C6
GURGAR
pl. Harringtn Pk... 478 G2
GURIN
av. Killara............ 253 E14
GURLEY
pl. Bonnyrigg....... 363 J10
GURNER
av. Austral........... 361 A15
av. Kemps Ck....... 360 E13
la. Paddington....... 13 D14
pl. Kellyville......... 216 G5
st. Paddington....... 13 D14
GURNEY
cr. Fairfield W...... 335 A12
cr. Seaforth.......... 286 J8
rd. Chester Hill..... 337 G12
GURRAWILLIE
st. Villawood........ 367 J3
GURRIER
av. Miranda.......... 492 C4
GURRIGAL
st. Mosman......... 316 K6
GUTHEGA
cl. Woodcroft...... 243 H9
cr. Heckenberg.... 364 A12
pl. Bossley Park... 334 C8
GUTHRIE
av. Cremorne............ 6 J6
GUY
pl. Emu Heights... 205 A15
pl. Rooty Hill........ 271 K5
GUYONG
st. Lindfield.......... 283 H6
GUYRA
cl. Bossley Park... 333 F11
rd. Hinchinbrk...... 392 G5
GUYS
pl. St Johns Pk.... 364 G1
GWANDALAN
cr. Berowra.......... 133 A16
pl. Emu Plains..... 235 E12
rd. Edensor Pk..... 363 F2
rd. Padstow......... 399 C12
st. Emu Plains..... 235 E11
GWAWLEY
pde. Miranda.......... 462 E16
GWEA
av. Daceyville....... 406 F4
GWEN
cr. Warrimoo....... 203 C11
pl. Padstow Ht..... 429 B6
pl. W Pnnant Hl... 249 E10
GWENDALE
cr. Eastwood........ 281 D5
GWYDIR
av. Matraville........ 436 K1
av. N Turramrra.... 193 D14
av. Quakers Hill.... 213 K7
pl. Campbelltwn... 512 A8
st. Engadine......... 488 E12
st. Greystanes...... 306 A4
st. Homebush B...... M B6
wy. Glenhaven....... 218 D6
GWYN
cl. St Ives............ 224 G10
st. Doonside........ 243 D9
GWYNELLEN
pl. Cherrybrook.... 219 D8
GWYNN
cl. Emu Plains..... 235 A10
GWYNNE
st. Ashcroft.......... 364 D16
GWYNN HUGHES
rd. Bargo............. 567 A6
GYMEA
pl. Jamisontown.. 266 D5
GYMEA BAY
rd. Gymea........... 491 E3
rd.s, Gymea........... 491 D8
rd.s, Gymea Bay..... 491 E9
GYMKHANA
pl. Glenwood....... 245 J3
GYMNASIUM
rd. Mcquarie Pk.... 252 B15
GYMPIE
pl. Wakeley.......... 334 H13
GYPSUM
pl. Eagle Vale....... 481 H6
GYRA
pl. Dharruk.......... 241 B6

H

HABERFIELD
rd. Haberfield....... 373 D1
HACKETT
pl. North Rocks.... 248 F15
st. Ultimo................. 3 A11
HACKING
av. Wrrngtn Cty.... 238 F6
dr. Narellan Vale... 478 F16
HACKNEY
st. Greystanes...... 306 B4
HADDENHAM
st. Chipping Ntn... 366 H15
HADDIN
cl. Turramurra..... 222 H13
pl. Kirkham.......... 477 C8
HADDON
cl. Bonnyrigg Ht... 363 H5
cr. Revesby.......... 398 K14
pl. Picton............. 563 F12
HADDON RIG
pl. Airds.............. 512 D12
pl. Miller............. 393 G2
HADLEIGH
av. Collaroy.......... 259 B1
HADLEY
pl. Jamisontown.. 266 D5
HADLOW
cl. Kellyville.......... 185 K15
HADRIAN
av. Blacktown....... 275 A8
HAERSE
av. Chipping Ntn... 396 B5
HAFEY
rd. Kenthurst........ 157 J6
HAFLINGER
cl. Emu Heights... 235 C3
HAGEN
pl. Glenfield.......... 424 G13
pl. Whalan........... 241 A8
HAGUE
gr. Oakhurst......... 242 C2
HAHN
st. Lucas Ht......... 487 H12
HAIG
av. Daceyville........ 406 F4
av. Denistone E..... 281 J11
av. Georges Hall... 367 D15
av. Summer Hill..... 15 A7
la. Maroubra........ 407 B10
la. Woolmloo.......... 4 C6
st. Bexley............ 432 D1
st. Chatswood...... 285 D7
st. Maroubra........ 407 B10
st. Mt Pritchard.... 364 G8
st. Roseville......... 285 C1
st. Wentwthvle..... 307 C2
HAIGH
av. Belrose........... 225 H15
av. Roselands....... 400 J7
pl. Castle Hill........ 218 F15
HAINES
av. Carlingford...... 249 C13
gr. Mt Annan........ 509 H1
pl. Menangle........ 538 G16
HAINING
st. Cambrdg Pk.... 237 K7
HAINSWORTH
st. Westmead....... 277 J13
HAIR
cl. Greenfld Pk..... 334 C12
HAITE
cl. West Pymble... 252 F9
HAKEA
av. Belrose........... 225 F16
av. Frenchs Frst.... 255 F1
cl. Casula............ 394 F13
cr. Galston........... 159 D10
ct. St Clair........... 269 G8
pl. Baulkham Hl.... 247 C15
pl. Epping............ 280 E4
pl. Mcquarie Fd.... 454 G4
st. Engadine......... 489 C13
st. Mt Annan........ 509 F3
st. Stanhpe Gdn... 215 C10
HALCROWS
rd. Glenorie........... 95 F1
HALCYON
av. Padstow.......... 399 D12
av. Wahroonga..... 222 H8
av. Winmalee........ 172 K11
ct. Harringtn Pk.... 478 G5
st. Gladesville....... 312 K6
HALDANE
cr. Lane Cove...... 314 G2
la. Lane Cove....... 314 G2
st. Asquith........... 192 A10
HALDIS
pl. Plumpton........ 241 H7
HALDON
la. Lakemba......... 401 B4
st. Lakemba......... 401 A1
st.n, Lakemba......... 401 A1
HALE
cr. S Windsor....... 150 K2
pl. Fairfield Ht..... 336 B11
rd. Mosman......... 316 H6
st. Botany........... 405 C12
HALELUKA
cr. Plumpton........ 242 D10
HALES
pl. Blackett.......... 241 A4
HALESMITH
rd. Mona Vale...... 169 D14
HAL HAMMOND
pl. Belrose........... 226 B13
HALIFAX
av. Roselands...... 400 G10
ct. St Clair........... 270 E15
la. St Clair, off Halifax Ct........ 270 E16
st. Raby............... 451 D15
HALINDA
st. Whalan........... 240 K7
HALL
av. Collaroy Plat... 228 G12
av. Thornleigh...... 221 A11
cr. Padstow......... 429 F5
cr. Padstow Ht..... 429 F5
dr. Menai............. 458 E15
pl. Eagle Vale...... 481 A10
pl. Fairfield W...... 334 K10
pl. Guildford W.... 336 K1
pl. Minto.............. 452 J13
rd. Hornsby......... 221 E4
st. Auburn........... 339 E1
st. Belmore......... 371 G14
st. Bondi Beach... 378 A1
st. Chifley............ 437 B8
st. Pitt Town.......... 92 H8
st. St Marys........ 269 E5
st. S Turramrra... 252 A6
st. West Ryde...... 281 B14
HALLAM
av. Lane Cove W.. 283 H16
wy. Cherrybrook, off Tennyson Cl.... 219 D9
HALLEN
pl. West Hoxton .. 392 B13
rd. Cherrybrook... 219 J12
HALLEY
av. Bexley............ 402 G15
st. Five Dock....... 343 A6
HALLORAN
av. Davidson........ 225 C16
st. Lilyfield............ 10 F6
HALLS
la. Woollahra......... 21 H3
rd. Arcadia........... 159 B2
rd. Galston........... 159 B2
rd. Maroota S........ 64 J2
HALLSTROM
cl. Northbridge.... 286 G16
pl. Mona Vale...... 199 C2
pl. Wetherill Pk.... 333 J2
HALMAHERA
cr. Lethbrdg Pk... 240 J1
HALSALL
st. Granville......... 308 D10
HALSLEY
st. Hassall Gr....... 211 K15
HALSTEAD
st. S Hurstville..... 431 K10
HAM
st. S Windsor...... 120 F15
st. S Windsor...... 120 H16
HAMBIDGE
pl. Bow Bowing... 452 D14
HAMBLEDON
av. Baulkham Hl... 247 E3
av. Castle Hill...... 247 E3
rd. Quakers Hill.... 213 J12
rd. Schofields...... 214 A5
wy. West Hoxton .. 392 B12
HAMBLY
st. Botany........... 405 J12
st. Fairfield W...... 335 D13
HAMBRIDGE
rd. Bargo............. 567 B4
rd. Bargo............. 567 D3
HAMBRO
av. Glenwood....... 215 E13
HAMEL
cl. Milperra......... 397 H11
cr. Earlwood........ 402 K1
rd. Matraville....... 407 A16
rd. Mt Pritchard.... 364 B10
HAMELIN
pl. Illawong......... 459 D6
HAMER
st. Epping........... 250 E13
st. Kogarah Bay... 432 H12
HAMERSLEY
pl. Bow Bowing... 452 C14

st. Fairfield W ... 335 F10
HAMILTON
av. Earlwood ... 402 H3
av. Holsworthy ... 396 B13
av. Naremburn ... 315 H4
av. Matraville, off Cemetery Av ... 436 H8
cr. Ryde ... 311 G5
cr.w, Ryde ... 311 G4
dr. Centnnial Pk ... 21 G8
la. Naremburn ... 315 H4
pde. Pymble ... 253 B8
pl. Narellan ... 478 G12
rd. Fairfield ... 335 H13
rd. Fairfield Ht ... 335 H13
rd. Fairfield W ... 335 A11
rd. Kentlyn ... 513 C4
st. Allawah ... 432 G7
st. Arncliffe ... 403 A10
st. Coogee ... 377 G14
st. Granville ... 308 J10
st. Lidcombe ... 339 G9
st. N Strathfield ... 341 D6
st. Riverstone ... 183 A4
st. Riverview ... 314 A4
st. Rose Bay ... 348 C10
st. S Wntwthvle ... 307 B5
st. Sydney ... A K14
st. Vineyard ... 152 F12
st. Rozelle, off Merton St ... 344 E7
st.e, N Strathfield ... 341 D6
wy. Kellyville ... 185 J14
HAMISH
ct. Kellyville ... 186 B16
HAMLET
cl. St Clair ... 300 C1
cr. Rsemeadow ... 540 J7
la. Mosman, off Raglan St ... 317 B9
HAMLEY
rd. Mt Krng-gai ... 162 K6
HAMMAL
wy. Minto ... 482 J5
HAMMENT
pl. Glenbrook, off Great Western Hwy ... 234 B16
HAMMERLI
wy. Shalvey ... 210 J12
HAMMERS
rd. Northmead ... 277 H8
rd. Old Tngabbie ... 277 E8
HAMMERSLEY
rd. Grays Point ... 491 A13
HAMMERSMITH
rd. Homebsh W ... 340 H6
HAMMON
av. Doonside ... 243 G16
HAMMOND
av. Croydon ... 342 G12
av. Normanhurst ... 221 F8
ct. Baulkham Hl ... 247 C14
pl. Campbelltwn ... 511 F8
pl. Mascot ... 405 C9
pl. Narwee ... 400 H10
HAMPDEN
av. Cremorne ... 6 K1
av. Darling Point ... 13 J3
av. Marrickville ... 373 G16
av. Wahroonga ... 223 B6
pl. Raby ... 451 H13
rd. Abbotsford ... 343 A4
rd. Artarmon ... 284 J14
rd. Lakemba ... 370 J14
rd. Pennant Hills ... 250 H2
rd. Russell Lea ... 343 A4
rd. S Wntwthvle ... 306 J5
rd. Wareemba ... 343 A4
st. Ashfield ... 372 F4
st. Belrose ... 226 B12
st. Beverly Hills ... 401 C15
st. Hurlstone Pk ... 373 B12
st. Mosman ... 317 B3
st. North Rocks ... 278 H1
st. N Sydney ... K J2
st. N Sydney ... 5 J5
st. Paddington ... 13 F13
HAMPSHIRE
av. W Pnnant Hl ... 249 C2
av. West Pymble ... 252 K15
ct. Cherrybrook, off Glamorgan Wy ... 219 E9
la. Camperdwn ... 17 E4
pl. Seven Hills ... 275 F5
pl. Wakeley ... 334 J15
st. Camperdwn ... 17 E3
st. Cronulla ... 493 J16
HAMPSON
av. Maroubra ... 407 E8
HAMPSTEAD
rd. Auburn ... 309 C15
rd. Dulwich Hill ... 373 C7
rd. Homebsh W ... 340 H10
HAMPTON
cl. Castle Hill ... 248 A3
cr. Prospect ... 274 J14
ct. Wattle Grove ... 426 C3
rd. Sylvania Wtr ... 462 C13
st. Balmain ... 7 C7
st. Canley Vale ... 366 A1
st. Croydon Pk ... 372 A8
st. Fairfield ... 336 B16
st. Fairfield ... 336 C15
st. Hurstville Gr ... 431 G10
HAMPTON COURT
rd. Carlton ... 432 H8
HAMRUN
cct. Rooty Hill ... 271 K5
HANBURY
cl. S Penrith ... 267 D5
st. Greystanes ... 306 F7
HANCEY
av. North Rocks ... 248 E14
HANCKEL
rd. Oakville ... 153 E1
HANCOCK
dr. Cherrybrook ... 219 D7
pl. Edensor Pk ... 333 K16
st. Bexley ... 402 D15
st. Rozelle, off Belmore St ... 344 E8
HANCOTT
st. Ryde ... 282 B13
HAND
av. Penrith ... 236 K13
HANDCOCK
la. Greenwich, off Greenwich Rd ... 315 A9
HANDEL
av. Emerton ... 240 J6
st. Bonnyrigg Ht ... 363 D7
HANDLE
st. Bass Hill ... 367 K10
HANDLEY
av. Bexley North ... 402 F11
av. Thornleigh ... 221 B15
av. Turramurra ... 223 C10
pl. Raby ... 451 G13
st. Auburn ... 338 J5
st. Marrickville ... 374 C9
HANDOUB
pde. Dee Why ... 259 C9
pde. N Curl Curl ... 259 C9
HANDS
la. Surry Hills ... F C10
HANGER
pl. Narellan ... 478 G13
HANIGAN
st. Penshurst ... 431 E6
HANKINS
ct. Greenacre ... 370 E6
HANKS
st. Ashbury ... 372 J9
st. Ashfield ... 372 J9
HANLAN
st. Cranebrook ... 207 A9
HANLON
cl. Minto ... 453 A14
HANLY
st. Lansdowne ... 367 A7
HANNA
av. Lurnea ... 394 F12
pl. Oakhurst ... 241 J3
st. Botany ... 405 H16
HANNABUS
pl. Mulgrave ... 151 J1
HANNAFORD
st. Campbelltwn ... 511 H8
HANNAH
av. Kellyville ... 217 C1
pl. Mt Annan ... 479 D16
st. Beecroft ... 249 K6
st. Westmead ... 307 G4
HANNAH BELLAMY
pl. W Pnnant Hl ... 249 E5
HANNAM
pl. Campbelltwn ... 510 J10
st. Bardwell Vy ... 403 C6
st. Darlinghurst ... 4 E15
st. Turrella ... 403 C6
HANNAN
st. Maroubra ... 406 J9
HANNANS
rd. Narwee ... 400 C13
rd. Riverwood ... 400 C13
HANNON
st. Botany ... 405 G14
HANNONS
av. Peakhurst ... 430 E4
HANOVER
av. N Epping ... 251 G8
st. Cecil Hills ... 362 D6
st. Rozelle ... 7 B14
st. Wilberforce ... 91 J2
HANS
pl. Casula ... 424 H1
pl. Marrickville ... 374 C12
HANSARD
st. Zetland ... 375 H12
HANSEN
av. Earlwood ... 402 F2
av. Galston ... 159 D9
HANSENS
rd. Minto Ht ... 482 J13
HANSFORD
pde. Bilgola ... 169 E4
HANSLOW
st. Surry Hills ... F K16
HANSON
st. Fairfield ... 337 A13
st. Fairfield E ... 337 A13
HANWELL
swy. Liverpool ... 395 E3
HANWOOD
pl. Edensor Pk ... 363 C1
HAPP
st. Auburn ... 339 B3
HARAH
cl. Bonnyrigg ... 363 K9
HARAN
st. Mascot ... 405 C2
HARBER
st. Alexandria ... 375 A14
st. St Peters ... 374 K14
HARBORD
rd. Brookvale ... 258 E12
rd. Dee Why ... 258 E12
rd. Harbord ... 258 E14
rd. N Curl Curl ... 258 E12
rd. North Manly ... 258 E14
rd. Woodbine ... 481 J11
st. Granville ... 308 K11
HARBOUR
la. Middle Cove ... 285 K8
st. Clontarf ... 287 G16
st. Cronulla ... 523 K3
st. Haymarket ... E C2
st. Haymarket ... 3 D8
st. Mosman ... 316 K7
st. Sydney ... E C2
st. Sydney ... 3 D8
HARBOURNE
la. Kingsford, off Harbourne Rd ... 376 G16
rd. Kingsford ... 406 G1
HARBOUR VIEW
cr. Lavendaer Bay ... K H16
cr. Lavender Bay ... 5 H12
st. Clontarf ... 287 F11
HARBOURVIEW
cr. Abbotsford ... 343 A2
la. Woollahra ... 22 H4
HARCOURT
av. Campsie ... 371 H13
av. East Hills ... 427 J4
cl. Castle Hill ... 218 K7
gr. Glenwood ... 245 G3
pde. Rosebery ... 375 G16
pl. Eagle Vale ... 481 A8
st. East Killara ... 254 E7
HARCUS
st. Merrylands ... 307 D13
HARDEN
av. Northbridge ... 285 J15
cr. Georges Hall ... 367 H12
rd. Artarmon ... 285 B15
st. Canley Ht ... 335 A16
HARDIE
av. Summer Hill ... 373 C4
la. Mascot ... 405 E6
st. Darlinghurst ... 4 G11
st. Mascot ... 405 E6
st. Neutral Bay ... 6 D2
HARDIMAN
av. Randwick ... 377 C16
HARDING
la. Bexley ... 402 H12
pl. Bonnet Bay ... 460 B9
pl. Minto ... 482 G5
HARDWICKE
st. Riverwood ... 430 C1
st. The Oaks ... 502 G14
HARDY
av. Riverwood ... 400 C13
la. Riverwood ... 400 B13
pl. Casula ... 424 F4
st. Ashbury ... 372 H10
st. Ashfield ... 372 H10
st. Blackett ... 241 A3
st. Dover Ht ... 348 E14
st. Eschol Park ... 481 B6
st. Fairfield ... 336 C11
st. Hurlstone Pk ... 372 H10
st. North Bondi ... 348 E14
HARE
st. Glenbrook ... 233 K15
HAREDALE
st. Ambarvale ... 540 D2
HAREFIELD
cl. N Epping ... 251 H10
HAREWOOD
pl. Cecil Hills ... 362 J8
pl. Warriewood ... 199 D11
HARFORD
av. East Hills ... 427 K3
st. Jamisontown ... 236 E15
st. North Ryde ... 282 K13
HARGRAVE
la. Darlinghurst ... F J2
la. Darlinghurst ... F H2
la. Paddington ... 13 F14
rd. Auburn ... 339 D7
rd. Lalor Park ... 245 B12
st. Darlinghurst ... F H2
st. Darlinghurst ... 4 B9
st. Kingswood ... 237 F13
st. Leumeah ... 512 D1
st. Paddington ... 13 F15
HARGRAVES
av. Punchbowl ... 400 E8
pl. Maroubra ... 407 D15
pl. Wetherill Pk ... 304 D16
st. Allambie Ht ... 257 J15
HARGREAVES
st. Condell Park ... 398 D2
HARKEITH
st. Mona Vale ... 199 D3
HARKNESS
av. Glenorie ... 128 C5
rd. Oakville ... 153 D9
st. Woollahra ... 22 G4
HARLAND
st. Ashfield ... 372 K8
st. Fairlight ... 288 B7
HARLECH
cl. Menai ... 458 K8
ct. Castle Hill ... 218 K11
HARLEY
cr. Condell Park ... 398 B3
cr. Eastwood ... 280 K4
pl. Kellyville ... 216 D4
rd. Avalon ... 140 E16
st. Alexandria ... 375 D9
st. Sylvania ... 461 H11
st. Yanderra ... 567 B16
HARLOW
av. Hebersham ... 241 F8
HARLOWE
pl. Bronte ... 378 A7
HARMAN
st. Ingleburn ... 453 A11
HARMER
st. Woolmloo ... 4 F5
HARMONY
st. Ashbury ... 372 D9
HARMSTON
av. Frenchs Frst ... 257 A5
HARNESS
pl. Wrrngtn Dns ... 238 A4
HARNETT
av. Marrickville ... 373 G14
av. Mosman ... 316 H11
pl. Chatswd W ... 284 C11
st. N Sydney ... K G2
st. N Sydney ... 5 H5
st. Woolmloo ... 4 H3
HARNEY
st. Marrickville ... 373 G11
HARNLEIGH
av. Woolooware ... 493 D8
av.s, Woolooware ... 493 D9
HAROLD
av. Pennant Hills ... 250 J1
av. Richmond ... 118 E8
av. Scotland I ... 168 J5
pl. Dee Why ... 258 F2
st. Blacktown ... 244 K14
st. Campsie ... 372 A13
st. Fairfield ... 336 C14
st. Guildford ... 337 J2
st. Ingleburn ... 453 H8
st. Mcquarie Fd ... 424 D16
st. Matraville ... 436 G2
st. Mt Lewis ... 369 K15
st. Newtown ... 17 H15
st. Parramatta ... 278 C14
HARP
st. Belmore ... 401 G4
st. Campsie ... 401 G4
HARPER
cl. Mt Annan ... 479 J15
cl. Tahmoor ... 565 K13
pl. Frenchs Frst ... 255 F4
pl. Kellyville ... 216 F4
st. Merrylands ... 307 J15
st. N Epping ... 251 F11
wy. Ingleburn ... 453 A10
wy. Menai, off Forest Glen Wy ... 458 J14
HARPUR
cl. Glenmore Pk ... 265 J6
cr. S Windsor ... 150 E2
pl. Casula ... 424 E4
pl. Lalor Park ... 245 E11
st. Fairfield W ... 335 B13
HARRABROOK
av. Five Dock ... 342 K12
HARRADANCE
pl. Liverpool ... 394 J9
HARRADEN
dr. West Hoxton ... 391 K12
HARRADINE
cr. Bligh Park ... 150 E5
HARRICKS
pl. Bonnyrigg ... 364 B5
HARRIER
av. Green Valley ... 363 C12
av. Raby ... 481 F2
pl. Clarmnt Ms ... 268 J5
pl. Woronora Ht ... 489 E2
HARRIES
wky. Revesby ... 428 H2
HARRIET
av. Castle Hill ... 247 G1
pl. Currans Hill ... 480 A12
st. Marrickville ... 374 A15
HARRIETT
cl. Glenmore Pk ... 265 F11
la. Glenmore Pk, off Harriett Cl ... 265 F10
HARRIETTE
la. Neutral Bay ... 6 H8
st. Neutral Bay ... 6 F7
HARRINGTON
av. Warrawee ... 222 H10
la. Enmore ... 16 G14
la. The Rocks, off Globe St ... 1 H11
pky. Harringtn Pk ... 478 F3
st. Cabramtta W ... 364 J7
st. Elderslie ... 477 F16
st. Enmore ... 16 G13
st. The Rocks ... A H10
st. The Rocks ... A J6
st. The Rocks ... 1 G13
HARRIOTT
la. Waverton ... 5 A6
st. Waverton ... 5 A5
HARRIS
ct. Five Dock ... 342 G10
la. Fairfield, off Hamilton Rd ... 336 E13
la. Jamisontown, off Harris St ... 236 C15
pl. Baulkham Hl ... 247 F5
pl. West Hoxton ... 392 C11
rd. Dural ... 189 D15
rd. Five Dock ... 342 G11
rd. Normanhurst ... 221 E9
rd. Wentwthvle ... 277 D11
st. Balmain ... 7 A11

st. Condell Park...398 G7
st. Fairfield...336 C13
st. Guildford...337 C3
st. Harris Park...308 F7
st. Ingleburn...453 E7
st. Jamisontown..236 B15
st. Merrylands...307 C16
st. N St Marys...239 H13
st. Paddington...13 H15
st. Parramatta...308 F7
st. Pyrmont...12 F1
st. Rosebery...405 G3
st. Sans Souci...462 J5
st. Thirlmere...562 D7
st. Ultimo...E A13
st. Ultimo...3 A10
st. Warriewood...198 J5
st. Willoughby...285 F14
st. Windsor...121 C14
st. Woolooware...493 F12
HARRISON
av. Bonnet Bay...460 B10
av. Concord W...311 D12
av. Eastwood...280 H8
av. Maroubra...407 G8
la. Cremorne...6 K3
rd. Kentlyn...513 C8
st. Ashcroft...394 E2
st. Cremorne...6 H3
st. Greenwich...314 J13
st. Marrickville...373 H11
st. Old Tngabbie..277 F9
st. Revesby...398 F15
HARRISONS
la. Glenorie...128 F5
HARROD
st. Prospect...275 A12
HARROW
av. Lansvale...366 D9
la. Stanmore...16 J10
rd. Auburn...339 B11
rd. Auburn...339 C7
rd. Berala...339 B11
rd. Bexley...403 A14
rd. Cambrdg Pk...238 B9
rd. Glenfield...424 G13
rd. Kogarah...433 C1
rd. Stanmore...16 H10
rd.n, Glenfield...424 G9
rd.s, Glenfield...424 D13
st. Marayong...243 H6
st. Sylvania...462 C7
HARROWER
pl. Glenmore Pk..265 K6
HARRY
av. Lidcombe...339 K5
pl. Bella Vista...246 D7
st. Eastlakes...405 J5
HARRY KNOX
pl. Harbord...258 F13
HARRY LAWLER
rd. Cranebrook...207 C15
HARSLETT
cr. Beverley Pk...433 A10
HARST
pl. Belrose...226 A10
HARSTON
av. Mosman...316 K3
HART
dr. Wentwthvle...277 A15
pl. Kellyville...216 G8
pl. St Clair...270 C9
rd. S Windsor...150 G2
st. Balmain East...8 C9
st. Dundas Vy...280 A8
st. Lane Cove W...283 K13
st. Redfern...19 B5
st. Smithfield...335 E3
st. Surry Hills...19 J2
st. Tempe...404 B3
st. Warwck Frm...365 H16
HARTAM
st. Kings Lngly...245 F5
HARTFORD
av. Glen Alpine...510 D15
HARTHOUSE
rd. Ambarvale...510 G16
HARTIGAN
av. Emu Plains...235 F9
wy. Bradbury...511 J12
HARTILL-LAW
av. Earlwood...402 J5
HARTINGTON
st. Granville...308 E13
st. Rooty Hill...242 C14
HARTLAND
st. Northmead...277 K5
HARTLEY
cl. Bligh Park...150 K7
cl. N Turramrra...223 E1
pl. Ruse...512 F8
pl. Wrrngtn Cty...238 H8
rd. Currans Hill...479 F12
rd. Seven Hills...275 G1
rd. Smeaton Gra..479 B7
st. Rozelle...7 B16
HARTNETT
pl. Doonside...273 E1
HARTOG
av. Fairfield W...335 D11
av. Willmot...210 C12
dr. Wrrngtn Cty...238 H4
la. Wrrngtn Cty, off Henry Lawson Av...238 H5
pl. Illawong...459 F5
HARTREE
pl. Cherrybrook...220 A10
HARTZELL
pl. Bnkstn Aprt...367 K16
HARVARD
cct. Rouse Hill...185 D4
la. Sutherland...490 D1
st. Gladesville...312 J8
HARVEST
dr. Wrrngtn Cty...238 D4
dr. Wrrngtn Dns...238 D4
HARVEY
av. Moorebank...396 E7
av. Padstow...429 D5
cct. St Clair...270 B13
la. St Clair, off Harvey Cct...270 B13
pl. Cherrybrook...219 G16
pl. Menai...458 E10
pl. Toongabbie...276 B9
pwy. Moorebank, off Harvey Av...396 D7
rd. Ingleside...197 C6
rd. Kings Park...244 C2
st. Little Bay...437 G15
st. Mcquarie Fd...424 B16
st. Parramatta...308 G2
st. Pyrmont...12 F1
st.e, Seaforth...287 A9
st.w, Seaforth...287 A9
HARWOOD
av. Chatswood...285 D7
av. Mt Krng-gai...163 B11
cct. Glenmore Pk...265 J4
la. Pyrmont...12 K4
pl. St Helens Pk...541 A10
st. Pyrmont...12 J4
st. Seven Hills...275 J6
HASCOMBE
la. St Clair, off Hascombe Wy..270 F13
wy. St Clair...270 F13
HASLEM
dr. Rookwood...340 A14
HASLEWOOD
pl. Hinchinbrk...363 B16
HASLUCK
pl. Glenmore Pk...265 J6
rd. Bonnyrigg...363 H7
HASSALL
st. Camellia...308 H4
st. Elderslie...477 G14
st. Harris Park...308 H4
st. Harris Park...308 E4
st. Parramatta...308 E4
st. Smithfield...335 C3
st. Westmead...307 G2
st. Wetherill Pk...335 C3
HASSELBURGH
rd. Tregear...240 F8
HASSELL
st. St Ives...224 D6
HASSELT
rd. Shanes Park...209 F4
HASSETT
cl. Menai...458 G9
la. St Clair, off Hassett Pl...269 K16
pl. Rouse Hill...184 J8
pl. St Clair...269 K16
HASTINGS
av. Chifley...437 A7
cr. Greystanes...306 A3
la. Surry Hills...20 B6
la. Marrickville, off Livingstone Rd..373 J11
pde. Bondi Beach...378 E1
pde. North Bondi...378 E1
pl. Campbelltwn...511 K9
pl. Sylvania Wtr...462 D10
rd. Beverley Pk...433 C12
rd. Castle Hill...218 H7
rd. Glenhaven...218 H7
rd. Warrawee...222 G10
st. Botany...405 F12
st. Lidcombe...339 K2
st. Marrickville...373 J11
HATCHINSON
cr. Jamisontown..265 K2
HATFIELD
pl. Hebersham...241 F6
rd. Canley Ht...365 C4
st. Blakehurst...462 C1
st. Lane Cove W...283 K13
st. Mascot...405 D5
HATHAWAY
rd. Lalor Park...245 G10
HATHERN
st. Leichhardt...15 B5
HATHERTON
rd. Lethbrdg Pk...240 C3
rd. Tregear...240 C3
HATHOR
st. Doonside...243 F15
HATTAH
wy. Bow Bowing...452 E12
HATTERSLEY
st. Arncliffe...403 E11
st. Banksia...403 E12
HATTON
la. Ryde, off Gladstone Av...312 A3
pl. Barden Rdg...488 H3
st. Ryde...312 B3
HAUGHTON
ct. Wattle Grove...426 B4
st. Carramar...336 H16
st. Linley Point...313 G8
HAULTAIN
st. Minto...452 K13
HAVANNAH
pl. Illawong...459 E5
HAVARD
pl. Ashcroft...394 E1
HAVELOCK
av. Coogee...407 F1
av. Engadine...488 D14
st. McGraths Hl...122 B12
st. S Turramrra...252 C5
HAVEN
ct. Cherrybrook...219 B12
pl. Kenthurst...188 C13
st. Merrylands...307 B10
st. Plumpton...242 A10
HAVENDALE
av. Penshurst...431 H6
HAVEN VALLEY
wy. Lansvale...366 C10
HAVENWOOD
pl. Blacktown...274 A8
HAVERHILL
av. Hebersham...241 E8
HAVILAH
av. Wahroonga...221 K10
ct. Wattle Grove...426 A1
la. Lindfield...254 D15
pl. Carlingford...279 J1
rd. Lindfield...254 D15
st. Chatswood...285 A8
HAVISHAM
wy. Ambarvale...511 A15
HAWAII
av. Lethbrdg Pk...240 F2
HAWDON
av. Wrrngtn Cty...238 E8
cl. Elderslie...507 H3
HAWEA
pl. Belrose...226 A16
HAWICK
ct. Kellyville...187 A16
HAWK
cl. Green Valley...363 D12
pl. Erskine Park...270 E16
st. Penshurst...431 B3
HAWKE
la. Kings Lngly...245 K9
pl. Kings Lngly...245 J9
HAWKEN
st. Newtown...374 G10
HAWKER
pl. Raby...451 D16
pl. West Hoxton...392 C12
st. Kings Park...244 C2
HAWKESBURY
av. Dee Why...258 J4
cr. Brooklyn...75 G12
esp. Sylvania Wtr...462 F13
rd. Hawksbry Ht...175 A4
rd. Springwood...202 B2
rd. Westmead...307 E4
rd. Winmalee...173 H7
st. Fairfield W...335 C14
st. Homebush B...M A7
st. Pitt Town...92 H9
HAWKESWORTH
pde. Kings Lngly...245 A5
pl. Cherrybrook...219 K7
HAWKEY
cr. Camden...507 B5
HAWKHURST
st. Marrickville...373 J10
HAWKINS
av. Luddenham...356 H1
pde. Blaxland...233 E10
pl. Wilberforce...92 A3
rd. Tahmoor...565 J16
st. Artarmon...284 J14
st. Blacktown...275 A6
HAWKRIDGE
pl. Dural...219 B5
HAWKSLEY
st. Waterloo, off Bourke St...375 J9
HAWKSVIEW
st. Guildford...337 C1
st. Merrylands...307 C16
HAWLEY
ct. St Ives...224 C8
HAWTHORN
pl. Cherrybrook...219 K6
rd. Penrith...237 C8
st. Loftus...489 H11
st. St Johns Pk...364 G2
HAWTHORNE
av. Chatswd W...284 B10
av. Rookwood...340 C14
pde. Haberfield...15 A2
pl. Mcquarie Fd...454 F2
rd. Bargo...567 F3
rd. Bargo...567 F7
st. Leichhardt...15 C1
st. Ramsgate Bch.433 F12
HAY
av. Caringbah...492 J7
cl. St Clair...269 J14
la. Caringbah, off Hay Av...492 J7
la. Randwick, off Hay St...376 K16
pl. Quakers Hill...244 A4
pl. Wakeley...334 K12
st. Ashbury...372 D9
st. Collaroy...229 C14
st. Croydon Pk...372 D7
st. Haymarket...E D7
st. Haymarket...E J8
st. Haymarket...3 E12
st. Leichhardt...16 B4
st. Liverpool...395 C6
st. Randwick...376 K16
st. Vaucluse...348 D7
st. West Ryde...281 A15
HAYBERRY
la. Crows Nest, off Bernard La...315 H8
st. Crows Nest...315 G8
HAYBURN
av. Rockdale...403 D16
HAYDEN
la. Darlinghurst...4 G10
pl. Botany...405 G16
pl. Darlinghurst...4 G11
pl. Engadine...518 E5
HAYDN
pl. Bonnyrigg Ht...363 E6
st. Seven Hills...246 E13
HAYDOCK
la. Revesby...398 J15
HAYES
av. Kellyville...216 K3
av. Northmead...277 H9
av. S Wntwthvle...307 D5
ct. Harringtn Pk...478 F7
pl. Bonnet Bay...460 C10
pl. Minto...452 K13
rd. Rosebery...375 G15
rd. Seven Hills...275 C4
rd. Wilberforce...61 A4
st. Balgowlah...287 K5
st. Lidcombe...339 G12
st. Neutral Bay...6 E10
HAYLE
st. St Ives...224 H8
HAYLEN
pl. Blackett...241 B2
pl. Edensor Pk...363 G1
HAYLEY
gr. Blacktown...273 G6
pl. Cherrybrook...219 H5
HAYMAN
av. Hinchinbrk...393 A1
st. N Richmond...87 C14
HAYMET
st. Blaxland...233 H11
st. Kirrawee...490 J6
HAYNES
av. Seven Hills...245 C15
st. Penrith...237 B10
HAYTER
pde. Camden S...506 J15
HAYWARD
st. Kingsford...406 H4
HAYWOOD
cl. Wetherill Pk...335 A3
pl. Greystanes...305 J1
st. Epping...250 D16
HAZEL
av. Lurnea...394 C10
cl. Cranebrook...207 B13
pl. Burraneer...493 F15
pl. Ingleburn...453 E11
st. Bass Hill...367 E10
st. Georges Hall...367 E10
st. Girraween...276 A16
st. Lansdowne...367 E10
HAZELBANK
pl. N Sydney...5 E2
rd. N Sydney...5 A3
rd. Wollstncraft...5 A3
HAZELDEAN
av. Hebersham...241 F10
pl. Kenthurst...157 D2
wy. Airds...512 F10
HAZELGLEN
av. Panania...398 C15
HAZELMEAD
rd. Asquith...192 B9
HAZLEWOOD
pl. Epping...250 J15
HEADLAND
rd. Castle Cove...285 H4
rd. N Curl Curl...258 F9
HEALD
rd. Ingleburn...452 K7
HEALEY
cct. Huntingwd...273 F13
wy. Killarney Ht...255 G15
HEANEY
cl. Mt Colah...162 E14
HEAPEY
st. Blacktown...274 F9
HEARD
av. Tregear...240 G7
st. Denistone E...281 H10
HEARN
st. Leichhardt...16 D3
HEARNE
cl. Eastlakes...405 K2
st. Bligh Park...150 H5
st. Mortdale...430 H5
HEARNSHAW
st. North Ryde...282 K9
HEART
pl. Blacktown...244 C15
HEATH
cl. East Killara...254 G6
la. Heathcote...518 G12
la. Hunters Hill...313 F11
la. Ryde...281 K12
pl. Heathcote...518 K10
rd. Blakehurst...432 D13
rd. Kellyville...186 D7
rd. Leppington...420 E6
st. Asquith...191 K12
st. Auburn...338 K6
st. Bankstown...369 F13

st. Bexley North 402 E12
st. Concord 311 K16
st. Five Dock 343 C9
st. Granville 338 G1
st. Kingswood 238 B12
st. Merrylands 307 G8
st. Mona Vale 199 F3
st. Prospect 274 G10
st. Punchbowl 400 A6
st. Randwick 377 C15
st. Ryde 281 K12
st. Turrella 403 C6

HEATHCLIFF
cr. Balgowlah Ht 287 K14

HEATHCOTE
rd. Engadine 518 C1
rd. Hamondvle 426 F1
rd. Heathcote 518 C1
rd. Holsworthy 427 H11
rd. Lucas Ht 487 A12
rd. Moorebank 395 H7
rd. Pleasure Pt 427 B6
rd. Sandy Point 427 H11
rd. Voyager Pt 427 B6
st. Picton 563 F9
st. Rockdale 403 B13

HEATHER
cl. Baulkham Hl 247 E6
pl. Acacia Gdn 214 G15
pl. Hornsby Ht 161 G11
pl. Wilberforce 92 A2
rd. Winmalee 173 E8
st. Caringbah 492 J15
st. Collaroy Plat 228 E12
st. Girraween 276 A16
st. Leonay 234 J15
st. Loftus 489 J10
st. Yagoona 368 E13

HEATHERBRAE
pl. Castle Hill 218 E12

HEATHERFIELD
cl. Catherine Fd 449 E1

HEATHER GLEN
rd. Yellow Rock 173 F15

HEATHERWOOD
cl. Winmalee 173 B12

HEATHFIELD
pl. Airds 512 A11

HEATLEY
cl. Abbotsbury 333 D14

HEATON
av. Clontarf 287 E11

HEAVEY
st. Werrington 238 F10

HEBBLEWHITE
pl. Bonnyrigg 364 A6

HEBBURN
pl. Cartwright 394 D4

HEBE
pl. Kellyville 186 J15
st. Greenacre 370 J12

HEBER
pl. Prospect 274 K13
st. Hurstville 431 H1

HEBRIDES
pl. St Andrews 482 A4

HECKENBERG
av. Busby 393 K2
av. Heckenberg 364 A16
av. Sadleir 364 A16
rd. Glenorie 128 K1

HECTOR
rd. Willoughby 285 D14
st. Bass Hill 368 C10
st. Chester Hill 368 D6
st. Greystanes 306 E6
st. Illawong 459 K6
st. Sefton 338 E16

HEDDA
st. Oakhurst 241 K4

HEDGER
av. Ashfield 342 G15

HEDGES
av. Strathfield 370 J2
st. Fairfield 336 F8

HEDLEY
st. Greystanes 306 E9
st. Marayong 244 C10
st. Riverwood 430 B1

HEDLUND
st. Revesby 428 J1

HEELEY
la. Paddington 13 B16
st. Paddington 13 B16

HEFFERMAN
la. Cranebrook, off Hefferman Rd 207 E13
rd. Cranebrook 207 D13

HEFFERNAN
cr. Richmond 119 K4

HEFFRON
rd. Eastgardens 406 D8
rd. Lalor Park 245 F9
rd. Pagewood 406 D8

HEGARTY
la. Bondi Jctn 22 F5
st. Glebe 11 J13

HEGEL
av. Emerton 240 K7

HEGERTY
st. Rockdale 403 C16

HEGGIE
la. Punchbowl 400 D4

HEIDELBERG
av. Newington M A13
av. Newington 310 B14

HEIDI
pl. W Pnnant Hl 249 B9

HEIGHTS
cr. Middle Cove 285 J8
pl. Hornsby Ht 161 F14

HEIGHWAY
av. Ashfield 372 E1
av. Croydon 372 E1

HEINDRICH
av. Padstow 399 D15

HEINE
av. Emerton 240 J7

HEINZE
av. Mt Pritchard 364 H8

HELDER
st. Ingleburn 454 A10

HELEN
ct. Castle Hill 248 B2
pl. Rooty Hill 241 K15
st. Epping 280 C1
st. Lane Cove W 284 F16
st. Sefton 368 F3
st. Sefton 368 G1
st. Smithfield 335 B3
st. Westmead 277 J15
st.n, Sefton 338 G16

HELENA
av. Emerton 240 H7
rd. Cecil Hills 362 H6
rd. Minto Ht 483 J5
st. Auburn 339 C5
st. Guildford W 336 J1
st. Kirrawee 490 H7
st. Lilyfield 10 C6
st. Randwick 407 B2

HELGA
av. Padstow 429 E4
pl. Hassall Gr 212 A13

HELICIA
rd. Mcquarie Fd 454 G7

HELIODOR
pl. Eagle Vale 481 G8

HELIOS
cr. Doonside 243 E14

HELIOTROPE
cr. Blacktown 274 E12

HELLES
av. Moorebank 395 D10

HELMAN
pl. Ingleburn 452 J11

HELM COTTAGE
st. Blair Athol 511 A3

HELP
st. Chatswood 284 H9

HELVETIA
av. Berowra 163 D2
la. Earlwood 402 J3

HELY
ct. Wrrngtn Cty 238 F5

HEMERS
rd. Dural 189 H15

HEMINGWAY
cr. Fairfield 336 D6

HEMMINGS
st. Penrith 237 B9

HEMPHILL
av. Mt Pritchard 364 F10

HEMSBY
st. Doonside 243 E5

HEMSWORTH
av. Northmead 277 H9

HENDERSON
av. Panania 428 B4
cr. Jamisontown 266 D3
la. Alexandria 18 E13
rd. Alexandria 18 E13
rd. Bexley 402 F14
rd. Eveleigh 18 E13
rd. Ingleburn 453 D1
rd. Mcquarie Fd 453 H4
st. Bondi 377 K4
st. Denistone E 281 F9
st. Merrylands 307 J9
st. Turrella 403 D5

HENDLE
cl. Baulkham Hl 246 J5

HENDON
grn. W Pnnant Hl 249 C4

HENDRA
cl. St Johns Pk 364 E1
st. Warwck Frm 395 K1

HENDREN
pl. Colyton 270 G6

HENDRENS
rd. Ebenezer 63 F10

HENDY
av. Collaroy 229 A14
av. Coogee 407 D3
av. Panania 428 F1
av. S Coogee 407 D3

HENLEY
cl. Belrose 225 K13
cl. Castle Hill 248 F3
cl. Hornsby Ht 191 F9
gr. St Clair 270 G10
rd. Homebsh W 340 G10
st. Drummoyne 343 H5
st. Lane Cove W 283 J16
st. Rosebery 405 F2

HENLEY MARINE
dr. Drummoyne 343 J6
dr. Five Dock 343 B12
dr. Rodd Point 343 E9
dr. Russell Lea 343 E9

HENNESSY
st. Croydon 342 E16

HENNESY
cr. Shalvey 211 A13

HENNING
av. Kingsford 407 D7
av. Maroubra 407 D7
av. S Coogee 407 D7

HENNINGS
la. Newtown 17 K11

HENRICKS
av. Drummoyne 313 G16
pl. Beacon Hill 257 J8

HENRIETTA
cl. Cecil Hills 362 D3
dr. Narellan Vale 508 F2
la. Double Bay 14 B10
la. Manly, off Raglan St 288 H9
st. Chippendale 19 B3
st. Double Bay 14 B10
st. Waverley 377 G8

HENRY
av. Sylvania 461 H13
av. Ultimo 12 J9
la. Lewisham 15 B10
la. St Leonards 315 E5
la. Sydenham, off Reilly La 374 E15
la.n, Lewisham 15 B10
pl. Narellan Vale 508 K2
pl. Plumpton 241 G10
rd. Riverwood 399 J15
rd. Vineyard 152 B2
st. Ashfield 342 J13
st. Balmain 7 C13
st. Baulkham Hl 247 K8
st. Carlton 432 J5
st. Cecil Hills 362 H7
st. Dee Why 259 A9
st. Five Dock 342 H9
st. Gordon 253 J8
st. Guildford 337 H7
st. Leichhardt 9 K9
st. Lewisham 15 B10
st. Lidcombe 339 J10
st. Lilyfield 9 K8
st. Old Guildfrd 337 E7
st. Parramatta 308 F1
st. Penrith 237 A10
st. Picton 563 C15
st. Punchbowl 370 C16
st. Queens Park 22 K15
st. Randwick 407 D2
st. Ryde 312 C5
st. St Peters 374 E15
st. Strathfield 371 G1
st. Sydenham 374 E15
st. Tempe 374 D16
st. Turrella 403 E5

HENRY COX
dr. Mulgoa 324 C1

HENRY KENDALL
av. Padstow Ht 429 C6
cl. Heathcote 518 C15
cr. Mascot 405 D2

HENRY LAWSON
av. Abbotsford 342 J3
av. McMahons Pt 5 E16
av. Wrrngtn Cty 238 E6
dr. Bnkstn Aprt 397 C1
dr. East Hills 427 F5
dr. Georges Hall 367 C16
dr. Lansdowne 367 B6
dr. Milperra 397 C1
dr. Padstow 429 F6
dr. Padstow Ht 429 A9
dr. Panania 428 B9
dr. Peakhurst 430 A3
dr. Picnic Point 428 B9
dr. Revesby Ht 429 A9
rd. Peakhurst 430 D4

HENSHAW
cl. Bonnyrigg 364 F6

HENSON
la. Ultimo 12 K12
st. Btn-le-Sds 403 K16
st. Marrickville 373 F15
st. Merrylands 307 D12
st. Summer Hill 373 B7
st. Toongabbie 276 H8

HENSTOCK
rd. Arcadia 129 C12

HENTIC
ct. Wrrngtn Cty 238 H5

HENTY
pl. Bonnyrigg 363 H7
pl. Quakers Hill 214 B9
rd. Ingleburn 422 K13
st. Yagoona 368 G9

HENVILLE
pl. Bass Hill 367 G7

HENZE
cr. Clarmnt Ms 268 G4

HEPBURN
av. Carlingford 280 C2
av. Gladesville 312 H8
rd. North Rocks 248 H12

HERA
pl. St Clair 269 G11
pl. Winston Hills 277 D1

HERAKLES
pl. Doonside 243 F16

HERALD
pl. Kellyville 185 K14
sq. Sydney A K8

HERB ELLIOTT
av. Homebush B M E7
av. Homebush B 340 G1

HERBER
pl. Wahroonga 222 C11

HERBERT
av. Newport 169 C7
av. Wahroonga 222 B2
la. Newtown 17 J12
la. West Ryde, off Herbert St 281 F16
pl. Narellan 478 G15
pl. Smithfield 336 C2
rd. Edgecliff, off New McLean St 13 J12
st. Artarmon 315 B2
st. Bankstown 399 C7
st. Cambrdg Pk 238 A10
st. Dulwich Hill 373 F9
st. Kemps Ck 359 K11
st. Malabar 437 D4
st. Manly 288 E6
st. Marsden Pk 182 A12
st. Merrylands 308 B13
st. Mortlake 312 B16
st. Newtown 17 J12
st. Oatley 431 C16
st. Pyrmont 8 F15
st. Regentville 265 F4
st. Rockdale 403 A12
st. St Leonards 315 B2
st. Summer Hill 373 B6
st. West Ryde 281 F15

HERBERTO
la. Glebe 11 K10

HERBERTON
av. Hunters Hill 313 F11

HERBORN
pl. Minto 452 K14

HERCULES
av. Padstow 429 C2
cl. Cranebrook 207 E6
cl. Raby 451 H14
la. Dulwich Hill 373 D11
pl. Bligh Park 150 E7
rd. Btn-le-Sds 433 K4
st. Ashfield 372 J3
st. Chatswood 285 B9
st. Dulwich Hill 373 D11
st. Fairfield E 337 A15
st. Surry Hills 19 J1
st. Villawood 337 A15

HEREFORD
pl. Minto Ht 482 J13
pl. S Wntwthvle 306 H6
pl. West Pymble 252 H14
st. Busby 393 J1
st. Forest Lodge 11 F15
st. Glebe 11 J13
st. Richmond 118 E6

HEREWARD
hwy. Blacktown 274 H3
st. Maroubra 407 G11

HERFORD
st. Botany 405 J16

HERING
av. Emerton 240 K6

HERITAGE
ct. Castle Hill 248 E4
ct. Dural 219 B6
dr. Illawong 459 E4
pl. Glenwood 245 F3
wy. Glen Alpine 510 C13

HERLEY
av. Rossmore 390 E4

HERMAN
cr. Hornsby Ht 161 F15

HERMES
pl. Emu Plains 235 F8

HERMIES
av. Milperra 397 G11

HERMINGTON
st. Epping 280 E1

HERMIT
av. Vaucluse 348 B6

HERMITAGE
av. Kellyville 185 F9
cr. Cartwright 394 C4
ct. Orchard Hills 268 E5
la. West Ryde, off Hermitage Rd 281 F16
pl. Eschol Park 481 A4
pl. Minchinbury 271 K9
rd. Kurrajong Hl 54 H12
rd. West Ryde 281 F16

HERMOSA
ct. Castle Hill 217 D9

HERMOYNE
st. West Ryde 280 G13

HERON
av. Georges Hall 367 K13
cr. St Clair 270 B14
cr. Yarramundi 145 C4
ct. Castle Hill 218 D8
pl. Dee Why 258 H2
pl. Grays Point 491 F14
pl. Hinchinbrk 393 C1
pl. Ingleburn 453 F7

HERRICK
cl. West Hoxton 392 E5
st. Blacktown 275 A8
st. Wetherill Pk 334 D4

HERRING
rd. Mcquarie Pk 282 D3
rd. Marsfield 282 A6

HERRON
wk. Mosman, off Raglan St 316 H14

HERSEY
st. Blaxland 233 H11

HERSHON
st. St Marys 269 K6

HERSTON
rd. St Johns Pk 364 C2

HERTZ
pl. Emerton ... 240 J4
HERVEY
st. Georges Hall... 367 E13
HESELTINE
pl. Rooty Hill ... 272 B4
HESPERUS
st. Pymble... 252 K7
HESSEL
pl. Emu Heights... 234 J7
HESSION
rd. Nelson... 155 A14
rd. Oakville ... 124 A12
HESTEN
la. Rockdale, off Gloucester St.. 403 C14
la. Rockdale, off Walz St... 403 C15
HESTER
st. Castlereagh ... 146 D15
wy. Kellyville... 186 A15
HESWELL
av. Morning Bay... 138 G14
HEVINGTON
rd. Auburn... 339 E7
HEVRELL
ct. Glenwood... 215 D14
HEWETT
la. Penrith, off Warwick St... 236 J13
HEWIN
cl. Liberty Gr... 311 B10
HEWISON
av. Green Valley... 363 C11
wy. Minto ... 482 H8
HEWIT
av. Glebe... 12 A14
HEWITT
av. Greystanes... 306 F11
av. Wahroonga ... 221 K11
pl. Minto ... 482 J9
st. Colyton... 270 G9
st. Greenacre... 370 F9
HEWLETT
st. Bronte ... 377 K7
st. Granville... 308 C11
HEWS
ct. Belrose... 226 C13
pde. Belrose... 226 A13
HEXHAM
pl. Wetherill Pk... 304 A15
HEXTOL
st. Croydon Pk ... 371 H9
HEYDE
av. Strathfield... 341 B13
HEYDON
av. Warrawee... 222 F11
st. Enfield... 371 J3
st. Mosman... 317 A5
HEYSEN
av. Ermington ... 310 B5
cl. Pymble... 253 F1
pl. Casula... 424 H2
st. Abbotsbury ... 333 B11
HEYSON
wy. Claymore... 481 F11
HEYWARD
cl. Jamisontown.. 266 C2
HEYWOOD
cl. Hinchinbrk... 362 K16
ct. Bella Vista ... 246 H3
HEZLET
st. Chiswick... 343 E1
HEZLETT
rd. Kellyville... 186 C11
HIBBERTIA
pl. Westleigh ... 220 G8
HIBBERTS
la. Freemns Rch... 90 D3
HIBBLE
st. West Ryde... 311 A2
HIBERNIA
pl. Harringtn Pk... 478 G5
HIBERTIA
pl. Mt Annan ... 509 E2
HIBISCUS
av. Carlingford... 249 C16
cl. Alfords Point .. 429 B13
cr. Mcquarie Fd ... 454 D2
ct. St Clair ... 270 B15
pl. Cherrybrook ... 219 F11
st. Greystanes... 305 G11
HICKETTS
av. Glebe... 11 K7
HICKEY
cl. Abbotsbury... 333 C11
la. Darlinghurst ... 13 A9
pl. Mt Annan... 479 F15
HICKEYS
rd. Penrith ... 237 A5
HICKLER
gr. Bidwill ... 211 C14
HICKORY
cl. Alfords Point... 459 C2
mw. Wattle Grove... 396 C16
pl. Dural ... 219 B6
pl. Mcquarie Fd... 424 G16
pl. St Clair ... 270 G11
st. Greystanes ... 306 D4
HICKS
av. Mascot ... 405 G6
av. S Turramrra ... 252 A4
pl. Kings Lngly ... 245 J8
HICKSON
rd. Dawes Point ... 1 D8
rd. Millers Point ...A B4
rd. Millers Point ... 1 D10
rd. Millers Point ... 1 D8
rd. Sydney ...A B4
rd. Sydney ... 1 D10
rd. The Rocks ...B A1
rd. The Rocks ... 1 H8
st. Botany... 405 E10
HICKSON STEPS
Dawes Point ... 1 G6
HIDES
st. Glenfield ... 424 H11
HIGGERSON
av. Engadine ... 518 F5
HIGGINBOTHAM
rd. Gladesville ... 312 G3
rd. Ryde... 312 G3
HIGGINS
la. Penrith ... 236 K11
pl. Westleigh ... 220 J2
st. Condell Park ... 398 D1
st. Penrith ... 237 A11
HIGGS
la. Turramurra, off William St ... 222 H14
pl. Cranebrook... 207 C10
st. Coogee ... 407 D2
st. Randwick ... 407 D2
HIGH
la. Millers Point ...A B3
la. Moorebank... 395 G7
la. Waverley, off High St... 377 G8
st. Balmain ...7 A10
st. Bankstown... 399 B5
st. Berowra... 133 E11
st. Cabramtta W .. 365 A8
st. Campbelltwn... 511 F8
st. Canterbury... 372 E16
st. Caringbah... 492 G8
st. Carlton ... 432 F4
st. Chatswood ... 285 D6
st. Concord ... 341 J5
st. Dee Why... 258 E4
st. Edgecliff ... 13 K13
st. Epping... 281 B1
st. Gladesville ... 313 A3
st. Glenbrook... 234 B13
st. Granville ... 308 D7
st. Gymea... 491 D6
st. Harris Park ... 308 D7
st. Hornsby ... 221 G1
st. Hunters Hill ... 313 C5
st. Kensington ... 376 F14
st. Kogarah... 433 A7
st. McGraths Hl ... 121 J11
st. Manly ... 288 J12
st. Marrickville... 373 K15
st. Mascot ... 405 B5
st. Millers Point ...A B3
st. Millers Point ... 1 D10
st. Milsons Pt... 6 A11
st. Mt Krng-gai ... 163 B11
st. N Sydney ... 6 A11
st. N Willghby... 285 F10
st. Penrith ... 236 D7
st. Penrith ... 236 H10
st. Penrith ... 237 A11
st. Randwick ... 377 A15
st. Strathfield ... 371 B3
st. Waverley ... 377 G8
st. Willoughby ... 285 F10
st. Willoughby ... 285 G15
st. Woolooware ... 493 H8
HIGHBRIDGE
rd. Killara ... 253 F13
HIGHBROOK
pl. Castle Hill... 218 K7
HIGHBURY
st. Croydon... 372 E2
HIGHCLAIRE
pl. Glenwood ... 245 H3
HIGHCLERE
av. Banksia... 403 H13
av. Burwood... 371 H1
av. Punchbowl... 370 D16
cr. North Rocks... 279 A2
pl. Castle Hill... 218 H8
HIGHCLIFF
la. Earlwood ... 403 E3
rd. Earlwood ... 403 E3
HIGHERDALE
av. Miranda ... 492 C4
HIGHETT
pl. Glenhaven... 218 A2
HIGHFIELD
cr. Strathfield ... 371 E4
la. Lindfield... 254 A16
pl. Kellyville ... 186 B15
rd. Guildford ... 338 D9
rd. Lindfield... 283 H1
rd. Quakers Hill ... 214 A14
HIGHGATE
cct. Kellyville ... 185 E6
pl. Cherrybrook... 219 D13
pl. Glenwood ... 246 B4
rd. Lindfield... 254 D15
st. Auburn ... 309 B14
st. Bexley... 402 F13
st. Strathfield ... 371 D1
HIGHGROVE
ct. Cecil Hills... 362 G3
HIGH HOLBORN
st. Surry Hills... 20 A6
HIGHLAND
av. Bankstown... 369 A15
av. Roselands... 400 F7
av. Toongabbie... 276 C5
av. Yagoona ... 369 A15
cr. Earlwood ... 403 C3
rd. Peakhurst ... 430 G1
rdg. Middle Cove... 285 K8
st. Guildford ... 337 K2
HIGHLANDS
av. Gordon ... 253 G5
av. Rouse Hill ... 185 E3
av. Wahroonga ... 222 B4
cr. Blacktown ... 274 B2
HIGHPOINT
dr. Blacktown ... 274 B8
pl. Como... 460 E5
HIGHS
rd. W Pnnant Hl ... 219 A15
HIGH SCHOOL
dr. Winmalee... 173 H7
HIGHVIEW
av. Faulconbdg... 171 E14
av. Greenacre ... 369 J13
av. Manly Vale... 287 K4
av. Neutral Bay ... 6 D4
av. Penrith... 237 B6
av. Queenscliff... 288 G2
cl. N Epping... 251 C10
cr. Oyster Bay ... 461 B6
la. Neutral Bay ... 6 D4
st. Blacktown ... 274 C7
HIGHWORTH
av. Bexley... 402 H14
HILAND
cr. Smithfield ... 336 A6
HILAR
av. Carlingford... 279 E4
HILARY
cr. Dundas... 279 K13
st. Winston Hills .. 276 G1
HILDA
av. Casula... 394 H12
av. Scotland I ... 168 G4
rd. Baulkham Hl ... 247 A11
st. Bass Hill ... 367 K6
st. Blaxland... 234 B5
st. Prospect... 274 K12
HILDEGARD
pl. Baulkham Hl ... 247 B2
HILDER
rd. Balgowlah Ht .. 287 H12
rd. Ermington... 310 B4
st. Elderslie... 477 J14
wy. Claymore ... 481 D12
HILDERLEIGH
cl. Faulconbdg ... 171 B13
HILES
la. Alexandria ... 19 B16
st. Alexandria ... 19 B16
HILL
av. Richmond ... 118 C9
la. Campsie... 372 B14
la. Carlton ... 432 K5
rd. Birrong ... 368 J6
rd. Homebush B ... L E5
rd. Homebush B ... 340 B2
rd. Lidcombe... 340 B2
rd. Lurnea ... 394 C10
rd. Newington ... L K10
rd. Newington ... L H8
rd. Newington ... M E13
rd. W Pnnant Hl... 249 B5
st. Arncliffe ... 403 D7
st. Balgowlah ... 288 A9
st. Baulkham Hl... 247 J9
st. Berowra ... 133 E13
st. Cabramatta ... 365 H7
st. Camden ... 477 B16
st. Campsie... 372 A14
st. Carlton ... 432 J5
st. Coogee ... 377 G15
st. Dulwich Hill... 373 D8
st. Fairlight... 288 A9
st. Five Dock ... 342 K6
st. Glenbrook ... 234 B15
st. Hurstville... 432 C6
st. Leichhardt... 10 B13
st. Marrickville ... 373 F15
st. N Sydney ... K F9
st. N Sydney ... 5 G9
st. Picton ... 563 D11
st. Queenscliff ... 288 G2
st. Roseville ... 284 G4
st. Strathfield S ... 371 E5
st. Surry Hills ... 4 D15
st. Wareemba ... 342 K6
st. Warriewood ... 199 C9
st. Wentwthvle ... 277 A15
st. Woolooware... 493 F11
HILLARD
st. Wiley Park... 370 G16
HILLARY
cl. Eastlakes... 406 A3
pde. Matraville ... 437 C2
st. Greystanes ... 306 D9
st. West Pymble ... 252 F11
HILLAS
av. Kellyville... 216 G4
HILLBAR
la. Glenbrook ... 234 B15
HILL CLIMB
dr. Annangrove ... 155 H11
HILLCOT
st. Hurlstone Pk ... 372 J10
HILLCREST
av. Ashfield... 372 J7
av. Bardwell Vy ... 402 H10
av. Epping ... 250 H14
av. Gladesville ... 312 K11
av. Greenacre ... 369 K14
av. Hurstville... 431 H8
av. Hurstville Gr ... 431 E10
av. Mona Vale ... 199 H1
av. Moorebank ... 396 C11
av. Mt Lewis ... 369 J16
av. Oatley ... 431 E10
av. Penrith... 237 B6
av. Penshurst ... 431 E10
av. Strathfield S ... 371 E6
av. Villawood ... 367 B3
av. Winston Hills... 277 D2
dr. St Ives... 224 D8
la. Tempe ... 374 B16
la. Emu Heights, off Hillcrest Rd... 235 A2
pl. North Manly ... 288 C1
rd. Berowra ... 133 D10
rd. Emu Heights ... 235 A2
rd. Pennant Hills... 220 G16
rd. Quakers Hill ... 214 A15
rd. Wedderburn ... 541 F15
rd. Yarramundi ... 145 A8
st. Homebush ... 341 B7
st. Punchbowl ... 400 D5
st. Tempe ... 374 C16
st. Wahroonga ... 222 J6
st. Wiley Park ... 400 D5
HILLCROSS
st. Lugarno ... 429 K14
HILL END
rd. Doonside... 243 C13
HILLEND
pl. Wakeley ... 334 G14
HILLGATE
av. Castle Hill ... 219 B11
HILLIARD
dr. Castle Hill ... 218 J12
HILLIER
rd. Liverpool ... 395 A3
st. Concord W ... 341 E4
st. Edensor Pk... 363 C2
st. Merrylands ... 307 E9
HILLIGER
rd. S Penrith ... 267 C2
HILLINA
wy. Mcquarie Fd ... 454 H4
HILLMAN
av. Rydalmere ... 309 J1
HILLMONT
av. Thornleigh... 221 B13
HILLOAK
ct. Castle Hill ... 218 K6
wy. Menai ... 458 H13
HILLPINE
av. Kogarah ... 433 C9
pl. Terrey Hills ... 196 D4
HILLS
av. Epping ... 250 E16
st. Bnksmeadw ... 435 K1
HILLSBOROUGH
ct. Cherrybrook ... 219 D12
wy. Baulkham Hl ... 216 K16
HILLSIDE
av. Belmore ... 401 K4
av. St Ives Ch ... 224 A5
av. Vaucluse ... 348 C7
cct. Cranebrook ... 207 D8
cr. Epping ... 281 A3
cr. Glenbrook ... 234 E16
dr. Harringtn Pk ... 478 C3
la. Blacktown ... 275 B2
la. Carlingford ... 249 G11
pde. Mt Colah ... 162 B16
pl. Glen Alpine ... 510 G10
pl. W Pnnant Hl ... 249 J9
rd. Blacktown ... 274 B4
rd. Newport ... 169 J7
st. Chatswd W ... 284 F8
st. Roseville ... 284 F8
HILLSLOPE
rd. Newport ... 169 H7
HILLTOP
av. Blacktown ... 274 A3
av. Currans Hill ... 480 A9
av. Marrickville... 403 E1
av. Mt Pritchard ... 364 F13
av. Padstow Ht... 429 G7
cr. Campbelltwn ... 511 F9
cr. Fairlight ... 288 A9
cr. Fairlight ... 288 C9
ct. Castle Hill ... 217 B10
rd. Avalon ... 139 G16
rd. Merrylands ... 307 C8
rd. Penrith ... 237 C6
rd. Tennyson ... 57 G12
st. Kingsgrove ... 402 A5
HILLVIEW
av. Bankstown ... 369 J15
av. S Penrith ... 266 J1
la. Eastwood ... 281 A8
la. Sans Souci ... 433 C14
pde. Lurnea... 394 B11
pl. Glendenning ... 242 H5
pl. Narellan... 478 H13
rd. Eastwood ... 281 A7
rd. Kellyville ... 185 F5
st. Auburn ... 339 A10
st. Hornsby Ht ... 161 H12
st. Narellan... 478 H13
st. Roselands ... 401 D4
st. Sans Souci ... 433 B14
HILLY
st. Mortlake... 312 A13
HILMA
st. Collaroy Plat ... 228 K14
HILMER
st. Frenchs Frst ... 256 G6
HILSDEN
st. Rooty Hill ... 272 B5
HILTON
av. Roselands ... 400 J9

av. Sydenham 374 E16
cl. Rouse Hill 185 F4
cr. Casula 424 G1
pl. Kenthurst 157 G8
rd. Cmbrdg Gdn ... 237 H4
rd. Springwood ... 202 C6
st. Greystanes ... 306 E9
HILTON PARK
rd. Tahmoor 565 H6
rd. Tahmoor 565 J7
HILTS
rd. Strathfield 341 F10
HILVERSUM
cr. Belrose 226 B4
HILWA
st. Villawood 367 C2
HIMALAYA
cr. Seven Hills 275 B8
HINCHEN
st. Guildford 338 A6
HINCHINBROOK
dr. Hinchinbrk 363 A15
HINCKS
st. Kingsford 406 J4
HIND
pl. Chipping Ntn .. 396 C4
HINDEMITH
av. Emerton 240 J6
HINDER
cl. Abbotsbury 333 B11
HINDLE
tce. Bella Vista 246 F4
HINDMARSH
rd. Liverpool 365 A15
st. Cranebrook 207 D8
HINDSON
pl. Belrose 226 B15
HINEMOA
av. Normanhurst .. 221 J11
st. Panania 428 C5
HINES
pl. Mt Annan 509 E1
HINGERTY
pl. S Penrith 266 K6
HINKLER
av. Caringbah 492 G5
av. Condell Park ... 398 C2
av. Ryde 281 J16
av. S Turramrra 251 K6
av. Warwck Frm ... 365 E15
cr. Lane Cove W .. 283 G12
ct. Drummoyne ... 343 G1
pl. Doonside 273 F4
pwy. Warwck Frm, off Hinkler Av 365 F15
st. Btn-le-Sds 433 H1
st. Ermington 280 A15
st. Greenwich 314 J6
st. Maroubra 406 G11
st. Smithfield 335 E2
HINTON
cl. St Johns Pk ... 364 J2
gln. N St Marys 239 J8
la. N St Marys, off Hinton Gl 239 J8
pl. Chipping Ntn .. 366 E14
HINXMAN
rd. Castlereagh 176 B4
HIPWOOD
st. Milsons Pt 6 B12
st. N Sydney 6 B12
HIRST
pl. Fairfield W 335 A12
st. Arncliffe 403 C8
st. Bardwell Vy 403 C8
HISHION
pl. Georges Hall ... 367 K14
HISPANO
pl. Ingleburn 453 J8
HITTER
av. Bass Hill 368 B7
av. Casula 394 K11
av. Mt Pritchard ... 364 H13
HIXSON
st. Bankstown 399 D5
HOAD
pl. Greystanes 306 B11
pl. Menai 458 F7
pl. Shalvey 211 A13
HOADLEY
pl. Arndell Park ... 273 H10
HOBART
av. Campbelltwn ... 512 B5
av. E Lindfield 254 K15

pl. Illawong 459 G5
pl. Wakeley 334 H15
st. Oxley Park 240 A14
st. Richmond 119 C4
st. Riverstone 153 B16
st. Riverstone 182 H3
st. St Marys 240 A14
HOBBITS
gln. Wrrngtn Dns ... 237 J4
HOBBS
st. Bligh Park 150 J6
st. Kingsgrove 401 H11
st. Lewisham 15 C10
HOBBY
cl. S Penrith 266 G5
la. S Penrith, off Hobby Cl 266 G5
HOBLER
av. West Hoxton ... 392 B10
HOBSON
pl. Plumpton 242 C10
HOCKING
av. Earlwood 403 A4
la. Earlwood, off Hocking Av 403 A4
pl. Erskine Park ... 300 K1
HOCKLEY
rd. Eastwood 280 F6
HODDLE
av. Bradbury 511 E9
av. Campbelltwn ... 511 E9
cr. Davidson 255 E2
pl. West Hoxton ... 392 A11
st. Paddington 13 C13
HODGE
st. Hurstville 431 J1
HODGES
pl. Currans Hill 479 G11
st. Kings Lngly 245 A3
HODGKINSON
cr. Panania 428 E1
HODGSON
av. Cremorne 316 F12
av. Cremorne Pt ... 316 F12
cl. Wedderburn ... 540 C10
cr. Baulkham Hl ... 247 D13
rd. Glenbrook 264 C4
st. Randwick 377 B11
HODKIN
pl. Ingleburn 453 A11
HOFF
st. Mt Pritchard ... 364 K11
HOFFMAN
la. Newtown 17 E12
pl. Oakhurst 242 C4
HOFFMANN
pwy. Springwood ... 201 D1
HOFFMANS
la. Balmain 7 J9
HOGAN
av. Bass Hill 367 F7
av. Green Valley ... 362 K8
av. Sydenham 374 E14
la. Panania 428 D2
pl. Kingswood 267 E2
pl. Mt Annan 479 E15
pl. Quakers Hill 214 C12
st. Balgowlah Ht .. 287 K12
HOGANS
dr. Bargo 567 B3
dr. Bargo 567 D1
HOGARTH
av. Dee Why 258 F5
HOGBEN
st. Kogarah 433 C5
HOGUE
pl. Mt Annan 509 D1
HOLBEACH
av. Tempe 404 B4
HOLBECHE
rd. Arndell Park ... 273 E8
HOLBORN
av. Dee Why 258 G3
st. Ambarvale 510 G12
HOLBOROW
st. Croydon 372 D5
st. Croydon Pk 372 D5
HOLBORROW
av. Richmond 118 B7
HOLBROOK
av. Kirribilli 2 F1
ct. Stanhpe Gdn ... 215 D12
st. Bossley Park ... 333 G10

HOLBURN
cr. Kings Lngly 245 G8
HOLCROFT
pl. Cherrybrook ... 219 K7
HOLDEN
av. Epping 250 G13
st. Ashbury 372 H10
st. Ashfield 372 J6
st. Canterbury 372 H10
st. Chester Hill 337 K11
st. Maroubra 406 H11
st. Northwood 314 G7
st. Redfern 19 B6
st. Toongabbie 276 G8
HOLDIN
st. Bonnyrigg 364 A7
HOLDSWORTH
av. Rcuttrs Bay 13 C6
av. St Leonards 315 C7
dr. Mt Annan 479 A12
dr. Narellan Vale ... 479 A12
la. Newtown 18 C10
la. Paddington 4 G14
rd. Neutral Bay 6 C6
st. Merrylands 307 C14
st. Neutral Bay 6 B6
st. Newtown 18 C10
st. Woollahra 21 K1
HOLFORD
cr. Gordon 253 D8
rd. Cabramtta W ... 365 B6
HOLKER
st. Homebush B ... 309 K9
st. Silverwater ...... L E16
st. Silverwater 309 K9
HOLKER BUSWAY
Homebush B ...... L J7
Homebush B ... 310 F12
HOLKHAM
av. Randwick 376 K11
HOLLAND
av. Rockdale 403 B12
cr. Casula 394 J14
cr. Frenchs Frst ... 256 E5
ct. Glenmore Pk ... 266 F15
pl. Lakemba 370 J14
pl. Telopea 279 J11
rd. Bellevue Hill 14 J16
rd. Glenhaven 187 H13
st. Birrong 369 B5
st. Chatswood 285 B11
st. Cronulla 493 H12
st. N Epping 251 E10
st. St Peters 374 K14
st. Springwood 202 A2
HOLLANDS
av. Marrickville 373 G12
HOLLEY
la. Beverly Hills 430 J3
rd. Beverly Hills 430 J2
HOLLIDAY
av. Berowra 133 C11
av. Berowra Ht 133 C11
la. Auburn 339 E2
HOLLIER
pl. Baulkham Hl ... 247 D10
rd. Picton 561 C4
st. Cambrdg Pk ... 238 A6
HOLLINGS
cr. Heathcote 518 G9
pl. Plumpton 241 G9
HOLLINGSHED
la. Mascot, off Johnson St 405 E6
st. Mascot 405 E6
HOLLINSWORTH
rd. Marsden Pk 211 J11
HOLLIS
av. Denistone E 281 E8
la. Newtown 18 B9
st. Wentwthvle 277 B9
st. Wentwthvle 277 C9
HOLLISTER
pl. Carlingford 249 G14
HOLLOWAY
la. Pagewood, off Holloway St 406 B10
pl. Curl Curl 258 F12
st. Pagewood 405 K10
HOLLOWFORTH
av. Neutral Bay 6 H10
HOLLOWS
pl. Bonnyrigg 363 H8

HOLLY
av. Chipping Ntn .. 396 D5
av. Ryde 312 G3
rd. Cherrybrook ... 219 H12
st. Caringbah 493 A11
st. Castle Cove 285 F3
HOLLYDALE
pl. Prospect 275 B10
HOLLYDENE
cr. Edensor Pk 333 D16
HOLLYLEA
rd. Leumeah 481 K13
HOLLYWOOD
av. Bondi Jctn 22 K8
cr. Willoughby 285 F11
dr. Lansvale 366 G8
rd. Newport 169 J12
st. Merrylands 307 A8
st. Monterey 433 G10
st. S Wntwthvle ... 307 A8
HOLMAN
pl. St Helens Pk ... 541 B3
st. Canley Ht 335 A16
HOLMEGATE
cr. Cranebrook 207 G11
HOLMES
av. Ashbury 372 E8
av. Clontarf 287 E14
av. Oatlands 279 D12
av. Sefton 338 F15
cr. Richmond 119 K5
rd. Minto 482 C2
st. Colyton 270 D6
st. Kingsford 407 A6
st. Lalor Park 245 G13
st. Turramurra 222 F15
HOLMESDALE
st. Marrickville 374 A10
HOLMLEA
pl. Engadine 488 F11
HOLMWOOD
av. Strathfield S ... 371 C5
la. Newtown, off King La 374 J10
st. Newtown 374 H9
HOLROYD
rd. Merrylands 307 B11
HOLST
cl. Bonnyrigg Ht .. 363 E7
HOLSTEIN
cl. Emu Heights ... 235 B3
HOLSTON
st. Casula 395 A12
HOLT
av. Cremorne 316 G8
av. Mosman 316 G8
av. N Wahrnga 192 G16
cr. Marrickville 403 H1
ct. Penrith 237 C6
pl. Dundas Vy 280 B11
rd. Sylvania 461 J11
rd. Sylvania 462 A11
rd. Taren Point 462 G12
st. Ashcroft 364 F16
st. Doonside 243 C8
st. Double Bay 13 K10
st. McMahons Pt 5 D11
st. Newtown 17 E15
st. Newtown 17 F15
st. North Ryde 282 F6
st. Stanmore 16 E11
st. Surry Hills ...... F B16
st. Surry Hills 19 J1
HOLTERMAN
pl. Cartwright 393 J6
HOLTERMANN
st. Crows Nest 315 G6
HOLTS POINT
pl. Sylvania Wtr ... 462 F10
HOLWAY
st. Eastwood 280 H7
HOLWOOD
av. Ashfield 372 K8
HOLYWOOD
wy. Glenmore Pk .. 266 H8
HOMANN
av. Leumeah 512 A1
HOMEBUSH
rd. Homebush 341 D13
rd. Strathfield 341 D16
rd. Strathfield S ... 371 C5
st. St Johns Pk 364 H4
HOMEBUSH BAY
dr. Concord W 311 C16

dr. Homebush 341 A3
dr. Homebush B ... 340 J5
dr. Newington ...... M J4
dr. Rhodes 311 C16
HOMEDALE
av. Bexley North ... 402 E12
av. Concord 341 G6
cr. Connells Pt 431 J12
rd. Bankstown 399 G7
st. Springwood 201 H4
HOMELANDS
av. Carlingford 279 G7
HOMELEA
av. Panania 397 K15
HOMEPRIDE
av. Warwck Frm ... 365 D14
HOMER
la. Earlwood 402 J3
pl. Caringbah 493 B16
pl. Wetherill Pk ... 335 A5
st. Earlwood 402 H4
st. Kingsgrove 401 K7
st. Winston Hills .. 277 E1
HOMESTEAD
av. Chipping Ntn .. 366 G12
av. Collaroy 229 B13
cct. Glenfield 423 G14
ct. Bella Vista 246 G2
rd. Bonnyrigg Ht .. 363 H5
rd. Orchard Hills .. 267 B9
HOMEWOOD
av. Hornsby 221 E6
HONDA
rd. Neutral Bay 6 J7
HONEMAN
cl. Huntingwd 274 B12
HONEYCUP
cl. Westleigh 220 G8
HONEYEATER
cr. Blaxland 233 E11
la. St Clair, off Honeyeater Pl .. 270 K13
pl. Erskine Park ... 270 K13
pl. Hinchinbrk 363 E15
pl. Ingleburn 453 F9
pl. Woronora Ht ... 489 F2
tce. Glenwood 215 F14
HONEYSUCKLE
av. Glenmore Pk ... 265 G9
pl. Kellyville 216 E1
pl. Leonay 234 K14
st. Jannali 460 J9
HONEYTREE
pl. Baulkham Hl ... 246 J3
HONITON
av.e, Carlingford 279 K6
av.w, Carlingford 279 J6
HONOR
st. Ermington 310 D4
HONOUR
av. Fairfield 336 G14
HOOD
av. Earlwood 402 E4
av. Rodd Point 9 A1
cl. Wetherill Pk 334 H6
la. Old Tngabbie .. 277 F8
st. Miranda 491 K7
st. Old Tngabbie .. 277 F8
st. Yagoona 368 E10
HOOK
cl. Hinchinbrk 363 A16
pl. Wakeley 334 H12
HOOP
pl. Spring Farm ... 508 E1
HOOPER
la. Randwick 377 E10
st. Clovelly 377 E9
st. Randwick 377 E9
HOOVER
pl. Bonnet Bay 460 E11
pl. Cromer 228 D14
HOP-BUSH
pl. Mt Annan 509 F3
HOPE
av. North Manly ... 258 A15
cr. Bossley Park ... 334 C6
pl. McGraths Hl ... 122 A12
st. Blaxland 233 F7
st. Ermington 310 F3
st. Harringtn Pk ... 478 F6
st. Penrith 237 B12
st. Pymble 253 E1
st. Regents Pk 369 B3
st. Rosehill 308 J6

st. Seaforth 287 E9
st. Seven Hills 245 F15
st. Strathfield S 371 A8
st. Warwck Frm 365 K16
HOPE FARM
rd. Cattai 63 K12
HOPETOUN
av. Chatswood 284 J12
av. Denistone E 281 F10
av. Mosman 317 D2
av. Vaucluse 348 E4
av. Watsons Bay 318 F16
la. Camperdwn 17 E7
la. Paddington 13 E16
mw. Vaucluse 348 D3
st. Camperdwn 17 E7
st. Hurlstone Pk 373 A13
st. Paddington 13 E16
st. Petersham 16 B10
HOPEWELL
la. Paddington 4 H15
st. Paddington 4 H15
HOPKINS
pl. Austral 391 C8
pl. Forestville 255 G9
pl. N Turramrra 193 E14
st. Wentwthvle 277 C12
st. Wetherill Pk 334 G4
HOPMAN
av. Menai 458 G7
cr. Shalvey 210 J14
st. Greystanes 306 A10
HOPPING
rd. Ingleburn 453 A11
HOPPYS
la. Kingsgrove 401 H11
HOPSON
av. Camden S 507 C13
HORACE
st. St Ives 254 B1
st. Waverton 315 D12
HORAN
rd. Glenorie 126 H3
HORANS
la. Grose Vale 84 F6
HORATIO
pl. Plumpton 241 H9
st. Rsemeadow 540 J6
HORBLING
av. Georges Hall 368 C15
HORBURY
la. Newtown 17 D12
st. Sans Souci 433 E16
HORDERN
av. Petersham 16 A7
av. Putney 311 K7
la. Mosman 317 B5
pde. Croydon 372 F1
pl. Camperdwn 17 B5
pl. Mosman 317 A5
st. Newtown 17 H8
HORDERNS
la. Bundeena 523 H9
pl. Potts Point 4 H4
HORIZON
pl. Cranebrook 206 J8
HORLER
av. Vaucluse 348 E2
HORN
cl. Abbotsbury 333 B14
HORNBY
av. Sutherland 460 E15
HORNE
pl. Bargo 567 A4
pl. Blackett 241 B2
HORNER
av. Mascot 405 G5
HORNET
pl. Raby 451 H16
st. Greenfld Pk 334 B15
HORNING
pde. Manly Vale 287 J4
st. Kurnell 465 H10
HORNINGSEA PARK
dr. Horngsea Pk 392 E14
dr. Horngsea Pk 392 F16
HORNS
av. Gymea Bay 491 D12
HORNSBY
st. Hornsby 221 H3
HORNSEY
cl. Bonnyrigg Ht 363 B6
rd. Homebsh W 340 G10
st. Burwood 341 J14

st. Rozelle 11 B2
HORNSEYWOOD
av. Penrith 236 K14
HORSELL
av. Arncliffe 403 D8
HORSESHOE
cct. St Clair 299 H2
HORSFALL
st. Ermington 280 B16
HORSHAM
pl. Chipping Ntn 366 H15
HORSLEY
av. N Willghby 285 E10
rd. Horsley Pk 302 E16
rd. Milperra 398 A11
rd. Panania 398 A11
rd. Panania 398 A15
rd. Revesby 398 A15
HORSNELL
la. Mosman, off Civic La 317 A6
HORST
pl. Mona Vale 199 A2
HORTICULTURE
dr. Richmond 118 F11
HORTON
la. Bass Hill 368 D13
la. Yagoona 368 D13
st. Bass Hill 368 E13
st. Marrickville 374 A9
st. Mt Pritchard 364 A11
st. Yagoona 368 E13
HORWOOD
av. Baulkham Hl 247 J14
av. Killara 283 D2
pl. Kings Lngly 245 B3
pl. Parramatta 308 C3
HOSIER
pl. Bligh Park 150 C6
HOSKING
av. West Hoxton 392 C8
cr. Glenfield 424 D10
pl. Sydney D B1
st. Balmain East 8 G10
st. Cranebrook 207 C11
wy. Bonnyrigg 364 C5
HOSKINS
av. Bankstown 399 D6
HOSPITAL
la. Marrickville, off Stanley St 373 J11
la. Crows Nest, off Willoughby La 315 F6
rd. Concord W 311 E13
rd. Randwick 377 A15
rd. Sydney D H5
HOTHAM
pde. Artarmon 314 H2
rd. Gymea 491 C5
rd. Kirrawee 461 D16
st. Chatswd W 284 H7
HOTSON
av. Matraville 436 J8
HOTSPUR
cl. Rsemeadow 540 H8
HOUGH
st. Bondi Jctn 22 D9
st. Colyton 270 J9
HOUGHTON
cl. Quakers Hill 213 D14
HOUISON
pl. Parramatta, off Horwood Pl 308 C3
st. Westmead 307 G2
HOURGLASS
gln. St Clair 270 D14
HOURIGAN
la. Potts Point 4 H6
HOUSMAN
av. Kellyville 215 J5
st. Wetherill Pk 334 E6
HOUSTON
la. Kensington 376 F16
la. Kingsford 406 F1
pl. Mt Pritchard 364 E8
rd. Kensington 376 F16
rd. Kingsford 406 F1
rd. Yagoona 369 A8
st. Gymea 491 G5
HOUTMAN
av. Willmot 210 D12
HOVEA
ct. Voyager Pt 427 C5
pl. Glenmore Pk 265 J9

pl. Kirrawee 491 A10
pl. Mcquarie Fd 454 D4
pl. Mt Annan 509 E3
HOVELL
rd. Ingleburn 422 J14
rd. Smithfield 305 F13
st. Narellan 478 F12
HOVEY
av. St Ives 254 D1
HOWARD
av. Dee Why 258 H6
av. Northmead 277 K10
cl. Green Valley 363 A8
la. Lindfield 254 G16
la. Randwick, off Howard St 407 B1
pl. Castle Hill 248 D4
pl. Hebersham 241 F7
pl. Hunters Hill 313 E11
pl. N Epping 251 G11
pl. Randwick 407 D1
rd. Minto Ht 483 K6
rd. Padstow 399 C16
st. Canterbury 372 D15
st. Greystanes 306 E5
st. Lansvale 366 K11
st. Lindfield 254 G16
st. Randwick 407 B1
st. Strathfield 340 J13
st. Telopea 279 J7
st. Ultimo 12 K16
HOWARTH
rd. Lane Cove W 284 G16
HOWE
av. Horngsea Pk 392 F16
pl. Canley Ht 365 A4
pl. Kings Lngly 245 H6
st. Campbelltwn 511 F4
st. Malabar 437 F5
st. Westmead 307 G4
HOWELL
av. Lane Cove 313 K3
av. Matraville 406 K16
cl. Newport 169 J8
cr. S Windsor 150 J1
pl. Lane Cove 314 A2
rd. Londonderry 149 B13
HOWES
cl. Westleigh 220 J1
rd. E Kurrajong 57 F3
st. Richmond 118 F6
HOWIE
av. Woolooware 493 J10
HOWITT
pl. Bonnyrigg 364 B8
HOWLETT
cl. Chipping Ntn 396 D4
HOWLEY
st. Five Dock 343 C9
HOWSE
cr. Cromer 227 J14
HOWSON
av. Turramurra 252 A2
HOXTON PARK
rd. Cartwright 393 G6
rd. Hinchinbrk 393 A6
rd. Hoxton Park 393 A6
rd. Liverpool 395 A6
rd. Lurnea 394 F5
HOYA
pl. Cherrybrook 220 A7
HOYLE
av. Castle Hill 217 D14
dr. Dean Park 242 G1
pl. Greenfld Pk 334 A14
pl. S Penrith 267 A6
HOYS
rd. Lansvale 366 E9
HUBER
av. Cabramatta 365 G6
HUBERT
st. Condell Park 398 H6
st. Fairfield 335 K14
st. Harbord 258 E14
st. Leichhardt 9 G10
st. Lilyfield 9 G7
HUCKSTEPP
swy. Liverpool 395 D4
swy. Liverpool, off Northumberland St 395 D3
HUDDART
av. Normanhurst 221 F10
la. Randwick 376 K9

HUDDLESTON
st. Colyton 270 G7
HUDSON
av. Castle Hill 217 A14
av. Willoughby 285 F13
cl. S Turramrra 252 D5
pde. Avalon 139 G16
pde. Birrong 369 A6
pde. Clareville 169 D2
pl. Ingleburn 453 J8
pl. Mulgrave 151 H1
rd. Frenchs Frst 257 B6
st. Annandale 10 J10
st. Homebush 341 A8
st. Hurstville 432 A3
st. Lewisham 15 A10
st. Redfern 19 A5
st. Seven Hills 275 J6
st. S Granville 338 F1
st. Tempe 374 C16
st. Wentwthvle 307 C2
wy. Currans Hill 479 G11
HUEN
pl. Tahmoor 565 G9
HUETT
pl. Berowra 133 G10
HUGH
av. Dulwich Hill 373 A9
av. Peakhurst 430 E2
pl. Greystanes 306 E9
pl. Kings Lngly 245 F8
st. Ashfield 372 H4
st. Belmore 371 A12
HUGHES
av. Castle Hill 217 G14
av. Ermington 310 F1
av. Maroubra 407 D16
av. Mascot 405 D2
av. Penrith 237 C7
av. Richmond 118 B7
la. Potts Point 4 J5
pl. Chester Hill 368 A2
pl. E Lindfield 255 A12
pl. Potts Point 4 J5
rd. Glenorie 129 B2
st. Cabramatta 365 E6
st. Earlwood 402 H6
st. Kings Lngly 246 B10
st. Leumeah 481 J15
st. Londonderry 148 B9
st. Petersham 16 C5
st. Potts Point 4 J5
st. West Ryde 311 D1
st. Woolooware 493 E9
HUGHES STEPS
Mosman 286 K15
Mosman 287 A15
HUGO
pl. Quakers Hill 214 F13
st. Redfern 19 A6
HUIE
st. Cabramatta 365 E10
HULL
av. Lurnea 394 E9
pl. Moorebank 395 H4
pl. Seven Hills 275 C5
rd. Beecroft 250 B1
rd. W Pnnant Hl 220 A15
HULLICK
la. East Hills 427 G5
HULLS
rd. Leppington 450 E1
HUMBER
pl. Ingleburn 453 J8
HUMBERSTONE
av. Gymea 491 G1
HUME
av. Castle Hill 218 A16
av. Ermington 280 B16
av. St Ives 224 E10
cr. Wrrngtn Cty 238 G7
dr. West Hoxton 392 A12
hwy. Ashfield 372 E2
hwy. Bankstown 369 C12
hwy. Bargo 567 G16
hwy. Bass Hill 368 B9
hwy. Blairmount 481 B14
hwy. Burwood Ht 371 C5
hwy. Cabramatta 366 B10
hwy. Campbelltwn 481 B15
hwy. Canley Vale 366 B10
hwy. Carramar 366 B10
hwy. Casula 424 B3
hwy. Claymore 481 B15
hwy. Croydon 372 E2

hwy. Denham Ct 422 K16
hwy. Eagle Vale 481 B15
hwy. Enfield 371 D5
hwy. Gilead 509 H16
hwy. Glen Alpine 510 A8
hwy. Glenfield 423 B15
hwy. Greenacre 369 C12
hwy. Greenacre 370 B6
hwy. Ingleburn 423 B15
hwy. Lansdowne 367 D5
hwy. Lansvale 366 B10
hwy. Liverpool 395 A9
hwy. Menangle 539 B16
hwy. Menangle Pk 509 H16
hwy. Mt Annan 510 A8
hwy. Raby 481 B15
hwy. St Andrews 481 B15
hwy. Strathfield S 371 D5
hwy. Summer Hill 373 A3
hwy. Varroville 451 J15
hwy. Villawood 367 E5
hwy. Warwck Frm 365 F16
hwy. Woodbine 481 B15
hwy. Yagoona 369 C12
hwy. Yanderra 567 G16
la. Crows Nest 315 F6
pl. Frenchs Frst 256 C1
pl. Mt Colah 162 D12
rd. Cronulla 493 K7
rd. Ingleburn 422 J14
rd. Lapstone 264 H3
rd. Smithfield 305 F13
st. Campbelltwn 511 J7
st. Chifley 437 B3
st. Crows Nest 315 F6
st. Homebush B M B6
st. Narellan 478 F11
st. Wollstncraft 315 E7
HUMPHREY
pl. Milsons Pt 6 A15
st. Lidcombe 339 F10
st. Rosebery 405 H3
HUMPHREYS
av. Casula 394 H12
wy. Claymore 481 E12
HUMPHRIES
la. Hurstville, off Crofts Av 432 A6
la. Blacktown, off Sunnyholt Rd 244 H15
rd. Bonnyrigg 364 E6
rd. Mt Pritchard 364 D9
rd. St Johns Pk 364 H3
rd. Wakeley 335 A15
HUNGERFORD
dr. Glenwood 245 F1
HUNT
av. Dural 189 E10
la. Lakemba 401 D3
pl. Wrrngtn Cty 238 G8
st. Croydon 342 G15
st. Enfield 371 J4
st. Glenbrook 263 K1
st. Guildford W 336 H4
st. N Parramatta 278 B10
st. Schofields 183 C15
st. Surry Hills F D7
st. Surry Hills 3 K12
HUNTER
av. Lurnea 394 B13
av. Matraville 436 J2
av. St Ives 254 C1
cr. N Sydney K B12
cr. N Sydney 5 E10
la. Greenacre 370 E6
la. Hornsby 191 H16
la. Hornsby 221 H1
la. Penshurst 431 D6
la. Woolwich, off Gale St 314 F13
la. Mosman, off Hunter Rd 317 D5
pl. Castle Hill 218 C10
rd. Mosman 317 D6
st. Abbotsford 342 H1
st. Auburn 309 E15
st. Blacktown 273 H5
st. Camden S 507 B9
st. Campbelltwn 511 K9
st. Condell Park 398 J4
st. Dover Ht 348 G9
st. Emu Plains 235 G12
st. Fairfield 336 C12
st. Heathcote 518 G10
st. Homebush B M B6
st. Hornsby 221 H1

rd. Emu Heights...235 A1
st. Granville.........308 B7
st. Mosman.........316 J3
st. Parramatta.....308 B7

INLET
rd. Brooklyn..........76 A10

INMAN
rd. Cromer..........228 G15
st. Maroubra.......407 J9

INNES
av. Hornsby.........221 F4
cr. Mount Druitt...241 A16
pl. Werrington.....238 G11
rd. Greenwich......314 J5
rd. Manly Vale.....288 A3
st. Campbelltwn..511 H5
st. Five Dock.......342 K8
st. Thirlmere.......562 F16
st. Thirlmere.......565 F1

INNESDALE
rd. Arncliffe.........403 K7

INNIS
pl. Kurrajong Hl.....55 E5

INNISFAIL
rd. Wakeley.........334 J13

INSIGNIA
st. Sadleir...........394 B1

INSPIRATION
pl. Berrilee..........131 E13

INSTITUTE
dr. Little Bay.......437 G15
rd. Westmead.......277 F14

INTER-TERMINAL ACCESS
rd. Bnksmeadw....436 C4
rd. Port Botany....436 C4

INTREPID
pl. Greenfld Pk....334 E14

INVERALLAN
av. West Pymble..253 A9

INVERARY
dr. Kurmond..........86 J3
st. Concord.........341 H8

INVERELL
av. Hinchinbrk......392 H4

INVERGOWRIE
av. Glen Alpine.....510 D15
cl. W Pnnant Hl...249 A3

INVERNESS
av. Frenchs Frst...257 A5
av. Penshurst.......431 C2
cct. Cecil Hills.......362 E5
cr. Glenhaven......218 C5
pl. Kareela..........461 B14
pl. St Andrews......452 A16
rd. Riverstone......183 C8
rd. S Penrith........266 K2
st. Bronte...........377 J10

INVESTIGATOR
av. Yagoona.........368 E15

INWOOD
cl. Castle Hill.......218 K13

IOLANTHE
st. Campbelltwn..511 G2

IONA
av. North Rocks...278 G2
av. West Pymble..252 K9
ct. Mona Vale......169 D15
ct. Yennora.........337 A8
la. Paddington.........4 G15
pl. Bass Hill.........368 A10
pl. St Andrews......452 A16
st. Blacktown......273 K1

IOWA
cl. St Clair..........269 G13

IPEL
cl. St Clair..........269 G16

IPOH
st. Holsworthy.....426 F11

IPSWICH
av. Glenwood.......215 G12

IRAGA
av. Peakhurst.......430 H2
pl. Forestville.......256 C7

IRAKING
av. Moorebank.....396 A7

IRALBA
av. Emu Plains.....235 A9

IRAMIR
pl. Warriewood....198 K6

IRAS
pl. Rsemeadow...540 E2

IRBY
pl. Quakers Hill....243 K2

IREDALE
av. Cremorne.......316 F11
la. Cremorne, off Hodgson Av....316 F12
st. Newtown........374 J9

IRELAND
st. Burwood.........371 J1
st. St Clair..........269 H10

IRELANDS
rd. Blacktown.......243 J13

IRENE
cr. Eastwood........281 H4
cr. Hurstville........401 K15
la. Panania..........428 A6
pl. Ingleburn........453 E11
st. Kogarah..........433 D9
st. Panania..........428 A6
st. S Penrith.........267 C3
st. Wareemba......342 K5

IRETON
st. Malabar..........437 D4

IRIS
av. Riverwood......399 K10
ct. Glenmore Pk...265 G7
pl. Blacktown.......245 C8
st. Beacon Hill.....257 A4
st. Frenchs Frst....257 A4
st. Guildford W....336 G2
st. North Ryde.....282 D8
st. Paddington.......20 G1
st. Sefton............368 G4

IRMA
pl. Oakhurst.........241 H4

IRON
st. N Parramatta..278 C10

IRON BARK
gr. Bella Vista.......246 H3
wy. Colyton...........270 H6

IRONBARK
av. Camden..........507 A8
av. Casula............394 E14
cl. Alfords Point...429 C16
cr. Blacktown.......273 K7
cr. Mcquarie Fd....454 F1
dr. Cranebrook.....207 F16
dr. Wilberforce.......62 G13
gr. Greenacre.......370 G5
pl. Westleigh.......220 F7
rd. Bargo............567 F3

IRONMONGER
av. Rouse Hill, off Grimmet Av.....184 K7

IRONSIDE
av. St Helens Pk...541 C2
st. St Johns Pk....364 D1

IRRABELLA
pl. Erskine Park...300 D2

IRRARA
st. Croydon.........342 E14

IRRAWONG
rd. N Narrabeen...198 F11

IRRIBIN
st. Marayong.......243 H6

IRRIGATION
rd. Merrylands.....306 J9
rd. S Wntwthvle...306 J9

IRRUBEL
rd. Caringbah.......493 B6
rd. Newport.........169 E10

IRRUKA
pl. Cranebrook.....207 H11

IRVINE
cr. Ryde..............312 D3
pl. Bella Vista.......246 B1
pl. Ruse..............512 H6
st. Bankstown......399 B6
st. Elderslie.........477 K16
st. Kingsford........406 J6

IRVING
st. Parramatta......308 K1
wy. Doonside........273 E3

IRWIN
cr. Bexley North...402 F9
ct. Narellan Vale...478 K16
pl. Wentwthvle.....307 B3
st. N Parramatta..278 C10
st. Werrington.....238 J9

IRWINE
rd. Caringbah.......493 B16

ISA
cl. Bossley Park...334 B10
pl. Cartwright.......393 K5

ISAAC
pl. Quakers Hill....213 J8
pl. Ruse..............512 D4
st. Peakhurst.......430 B6

ISAAC SMITH
pde. Kings Lngly.....245 B4
rd. Castlereagh.....176 B7
st. Daceyville.......406 E3

ISABEL
av. Vaucluse.........348 E6
cl. Cherrybrook....219 D8
st. Belmore..........371 F15
st. Cecil Hills........362 E1
st. Ryde..............282 B16

ISABELLA
cl. Bella Vista.......246 G2
la. Queens Park.....22 J12
st. Balmain.............7 C9
st. Camperdwn......17 E2
st. N Parramatta...278 E14
st. Queens Park.....22 J11
st. Revesby..........398 K16
st. Werrington.....238 H10

ISABELLE
st. Seven Hills......275 J6

ISAR
st. Seven Hills......275 G8

ISCA
pl. Glenmore Pk...266 G12

ISCHIA
st. Cronulla..........524 A4

ISIS
la. Kingsford........406 J4
pl. Quakers Hill....243 G5
st. Fairfield W......335 D8
st. Wahroonga......222 B7

ISLA
pl. Belrose...........225 K11

ISLAND
pl. Kurrajong Ht.....54 B6

ISLAY
st. Winston Hills..277 B3

ISLER
st. Gladesville......313 A11

ISLES
pl. Plumpton.........241 H11

ISLINGTON
cr. Greenacre.......369 J10
st. Cranebrook.....207 C10

ISMAY
av. Homebush......341 C6

ISMONA
av. Newport..........169 J8

ISOBEL
cl. Mona Vale.......199 A3

ISOBELL
av. W Pnnant Hl...249 D8

ITHACA
cl. St Johns Pk....334 E16
rd. Elizabeth Bay.....13 C4
st. Emu Plains.....235 C9

ITHIER
la. Quakers Hill....213 H13

IVAN
cl. Illawong..........460 F1
st. Greystanes......306 C6
st. Minchinbury...271 G7

IVANHOE
pl. Mcquarie Pk....282 D4
pl. Oatlands.........278 H11
rd. Croydon..........342 F14
st. Ingleburn........453 B10
st. Marrickville.....373 J15
st. St Johns Pk....364 H1

IVERS
pl. Minto.............483 A2

IVERYS
la. Newtown..........18 C10

IVES
av. Liverpool........394 H9
ct. St Clair...........300 C2
la. Crows Nest, off Willoughby La..315 F5

IVEY
st. Lindfield..........284 A3

IVOR
st. Lidcombe........340 A4

IVORY
la. Leichhardt........15 F2
pl. Jamisontown..266 B4
pl. Richmond.......117 J6

IVY
av. McGraths Hl....122 A10
la. Darlington.........18 J5
la. Randwick, off Ivy St.............407 C1
pl. Cherrybrook....219 H11
pl. Kenthurst........187 J1
rd. Mosman.........317 D13
st. Botany............405 F10
st. Canterbury......372 E15
st. Chatswd W.....284 F13
st. Darlington........18 H5
st. Greenacre.......370 E7
st. Liverpool.........395 B7
st. Randwick........407 C1
st. Ryde..............282 F15
st. Toongabbie.....276 B5
st. Wollstncraft....315 E10

IWAN
pl. Kellyville..........216 B1

IWUNDA
rd. Guildford.........338 D9
rd. Lalor Park.......245 E12

IXION
la. Cammeray, off Amherst St......315 K5
st. Winston Hills...277 C1

J

JABEZ
st. Marrickville.....374 C9

JABIRU
cl. Mona Vale.......169 E16
pl. Blacktown.......274 B9
pl. Ingleburn........453 F10
pl. Woronora Ht...489 F2
st. Green Valley...363 D14

JACANA
cl. Wahroonga.....223 C3
gr. Heathcote........519 A10
pl. Ingleburn........453 F6
pl. W Pnnant Hl....248 F8
wy. Glenmore Pk...265 K13
wy. Plumpton, off Sanctuary Park Dr...................242 A9

JACARANDA
av. Baulkham Hl....247 K10
av. Blaxland..........233 G5
av. Bradbury.........511 E13
av. Lugarno..........430 B14
cr. Casula............394 F13
dr. Cabarita..........342 E3
dr. Georges Hall...367 F11
dr. Parramatta......278 A12
pl. Beecroft..........250 F3
pl. Doonside.........243 G16
pl. Manly Vale......287 J5
pl. S Coogee........407 F5
rd. Caringbah.......492 K10
st. Cabarita..........342 E3

JACEVA
pl. Cattai...............94 D4

JACINTA
av. Beecroft..........250 D4
pl. Picton.............561 F4

JACKA
st. St Marys.........270 A2

JACKAMAN
st. Bondi.............377 K6

JACKARANDA
rd. N St Marys......240 A9

JACKIE JOYNER
av. Newington.........L G16
av. Newington......309 K15

JACK McLURE
pl. Northbridge.....285 K14

JACK O'SULLIVAN
rd. Moorebank......396 B7

JACK RUSSELL
rd. Berrilee..........131 H10

JACKS
ct. Currans Hill.....479 G13

JACKSON
av. Miranda..........492 B5
cl. Menai.............458 F13
cr. Chester Hill.....338 D16
cr. Denistone E....281 G10
cr. Pennant Hills...220 F12
pl. Cabramtta W...365 B8
pl. Earlwood.........403 E4
pl. Kellyville.........215 K5
rd. Lalor Park.......245 C10
rd. Luddenham.....357 F2
st. Balgowlah.......287 J9
st. Ermington.......310 B3
st. Marsden Pk.....182 A14

JACKSONS
rd. Warriewood....199 A13

JACLYN
st. Ingleburn.......453 C9

JACOB KING
pl. Emu Plains.....235 G9

JACOBS
av. Asquith..........192 B11
cl. Menai.............458 G15
cl. N Epping.........251 F9
pl. Bligh Park.......150 D6
st. Bankstown.....369 F15

JACOBSON
av. Kyeemagh......404 B14

JACQUELENE
cl. Bayview..........168 E8

JACQUELINE
cr. Greenacre.......370 C10
pl. Kurmond..........86 E1
pl. Moorebank.....396 F13

JACQUELINE PEREIRA
st. Newington.........L G16
st. Newington, off Newington Dr. 310 A15

JACQUES
av. Peakhurst.......430 B2
la. Balmain..............7 D8
pl. Minchinbury...271 H7
st. Balmain..............7 D8
st. Chatswood.....285 C9
st. Kingsford.......406 H3

JACQUIE
st. Cabramatta.....365 E9

JACQUINOT
ct. Moorebank.....425 B4
pl. Glenfield.........424 E12
rd. Moorebank.....425 B4

JADCHALM
st. W Pnnant Hl...249 J3

JADE
ct. Georges Hall...367 J11
pl. Eagle Vale......481 C8
pl. St Clair..........269 J13
pl. Seven Hills.....275 C7
pl. W Pnnant Hl...249 H5

JAEGER
pl. Woronora Ht..489 B4

JAF
pl. Blairmount.....481 B14

JAFFA
rd. Dural.............188 J13
st. Fairfield W......335 F13

JAGELMAN
rd. Badgerys Ck...358 D9

JAGGERS
pl. Ambarvale......511 A11

JAGO
pl. Toongabbie....276 G5
st. Greenwich......314 K11

JAGUNGAL
pl. Heckenberg....364 C14

JAKARI
cr. Whalan..........240 H12

JAMAICA PARK
rd. Ellis Lane........476 B8

JAMBEROO
av. Baulkham Hl...246 K8
av. Terrey Hills.....196 D6
la. Double Bay.......14 E9
pl. Bangor...........459 J12

JAMES
av. Lurnea...........394 C11
cl. Menai.............459 A12
la. Balmain East......8 H8
la. Paddington.......13 D13
la. Sydney...............C D15
la. Waitara..........221 H3
la. Woollahra.........21 H4
pl. Castle Hill........217 G15
pl. Darlinghurst.......4 D12
pl. Hillsdale.........406 G14
pl. N Sydney............5 F3
rd. Brooklyn..........76 A11
st. Allambie Ht.....257 K16
st. Balmain.............7 F11
st. Baulkham Hl...247 J11
st. Blakehurst......432 D16
st. Bondi Jctn......377 F5
st. Canterbury.....372 F11
st. Carlingford.....279 H4
st. Chatswd W....284 G10
st. Enmore.........374 G9
st. Fairfield E.......337 A12
st. Five Dock.......342 H8
st. Glossodia.........59 F10
st. Guildford W....336 H4

st. Hornsby 221 H3
st. Hunters Hill 313 D9
st. Ingleburn 453 E4
st. Leichhardt 9 J9
st. Lidcombe 339 J9
st. Lilyfield 9 J8
st. Manly 288 E9
st. Melrose Pk 311 A3
st. Mosman 317 B1
st. Northwood 314 G8
st. Petersham 15 K12
st. Punchbowl 399 H7
st. Redfern 19 D5
st. Redfern 19 G5
st. Riverstone 183 A10
st. Seven Hills 275 C4
st. S Windsor 120 G14
st. Strathfield S 371 C6
st. Summer Hill 373 B7
st. Sydney C D16
st. Wallacia 325 D16
st. Waterloo 19 D16
st. Woollahra 21 H4
wy. Mt Annan 479 D16
JAMES BAILEY
dr. Harringtn Pk 478 D1
JAMES BARNETT
gln. St Clair 270 B11
la. St Clair, off James Barnett Gln 270 B11
JAMES BELLAMY
pl. W Pnnant Hl 249 E6
JAMES COOK
dr. Castle Hill 218 H13
dr. Kings Lngly 245 A3
JAMES COOK ISLAND
Sylvania Wtr 462 D12
JAMES CRAIG
rd. Rozelle 11 D4
JAMES FLYNN
av. Harringtn Pk 478 G7
JAMES HENTY
dr. Dural 219 A6
JAMES KING
la. Mosman, off Union St 317 C11
JAMES MEEHAN
st. Windsor 121 B14
wy. Mcquarie Lk 423 E14
JAMES MILEHAM
dr. Kellyville 186 H16
dr. Kellyville 216 F1
JAMESON
la. Sans Souci 463 A2
JAMES RANDALL
pl. Glenbrook 234 C12
JAMES RUSE
cl. Windsor 121 A8
dr. Camellia 308 K4
dr. Granville 308 J11
dr. N Parramatta 278 C9
dr. Oatlands 278 C9
dr. Oatlands 279 A16
dr. Parramatta 308 K4
dr. Rosehill 308 J11
JAMES WHEELER
pl. Collaroy Plat 228 C9
JAMIESON
av. Baulkham Hl 247 G6
av. Fairlight 288 C7
av. N Curl Curl 258 J10
cl. Horsley Pk 332 C1
la. Fairfield E 337 A14
la. Greenacre 370 E13
pde. Collaroy 229 B15
sq. Forestville 256 A9
st. Emu Plains 235 A10
st. Granville 308 E11
st. Newington L F11
st. Revesby 428 K1
st. Silverwater 310 D10
wy. Thornleigh 220 K10
JAMISON
pl. Barden Rdg 488 H1
rd. Jamisontown 235 J13
rd. Kingswood 237 D15
rd. S Penrith 237 A14
st. Blaxland 234 A5
st. Luddenham 356 H2
st. Ruse 512 F8
st. Sydney A E13
st. Sydney 1 F15
JAN
av. Lurnea 394 C9
pl. Greystanes 305 J7
pl. Quakers Hill 213 K8
st. Picton 561 E3
JANACEK
pl. Bonnyrigg Ht 363 D4
JANALI
av. Bonnyrigg 364 A10
JANAMBA
av. Kellyville 216 F4
JANDIGA
pl. Winmalee 173 A11
JANE
ct. Narellan Vale 508 H2
ct. Narellan Vale 508 J2
pl. Cecil Hills 363 B3
pl. Dural 188 H7
pl. Heathcote 518 H9
st. Balmain 7 K10
st. Blacktown 274 K1
st. Penrith 236 F8
st. Randwick 406 K1
st. Smithfield 335 B5
JANELL
cr. Carlingford 279 K4
JANET
av. Thornleigh 220 J13
st. Bass Hill 368 A11
st. Drummoyne 343 F5
st. Merrylands 307 C7
st. Mount Druitt 271 D5
st. Russell Lea 343 F5
JANET EVANS
av. Newington M C15
av. Newington 309 K16
JANETTE
pl. Oakdale 500 E12
JANICE
av. Padstow 429 G5
av. Smithfield 335 H5
dr. Tahmoor 566 A11
pl. Cherrybrook 219 C12
pl. Narraweena 258 C3
st. Seven Hills 245 B16
JANITA
cr. Mt Colah 162 D14
pl. Bossley Park 333 H11
JANNALI
av. Jannali 460 F16
av. Sutherland 490 F1
cr. Jannali 460 K10
JANNARN
gr. Seven Hills 246 A13
JANPIETER
rd. Box Hill 154 G3
rd. Maraylya 125 A14
JANSZ
pl. Fairfield W 335 C11
JAPONICA
pl. Loftus 490 A9
rd. Epping 250 E13
JAPURA
pl. Kearns 450 K15
JAQUES
av. Bondi Beach 378 C3
JAQUETTA
cl. Cecil Hills 362 E2
JARANDA
st. Berowra 133 F10
JARDIN
wy. Mount Druitt 241 E11
JARDINE
dr. Edmndsn Pk 422 G3
JARI
cl. St Clair 269 F15
JARLEY
pl. Ambarvale 510 G15
JARNDYCE
av. Ambarvale 511 A13
JAROCIN
av. Glebe 11 K14
JARRA
cr. Glenmore Pk 266 A9
JARRAH
av. Bradbury 511 F13
av. Prestons 394 C15
cl. Alfords Point 459 C1
pl. Bossley Park 333 F8
pl. Castle Hill 248 F1
pl. Doonside 243 G16
pl. Faulconbdg 171 E13
pl. Frenchs Frst 255 G1
JARRETT
la. Leichhardt, off Jarrett St 373 J3
st. Campsie 402 A3
st. Leichhardt 15 H4
JARVIE
av. Petersham 15 E15
la. Marrickville, off Northcote St 373 K11
JARVIS
pl. Hebersham 241 G3
st. Thirlmere 565 B6
JARVISFIELD
rd. Picton 561 D4
rd. Picton 563 K1
JASMINE
av. Padstow Ht 429 D7
av. Quakers Hill 243 E2
cl. Arcadia 130 H3
cl. Glenmore Pk 265 G9
cr. Cabramatta 365 G10
ct. Cherrybrook 219 K12
pl. Castle Hill 248 G1
pl. Greystanes 305 G11
pl. Sylvania 462 B13
rd. Normanhurst 221 J9
st. Botany 405 G10
tce. Bidwill 211 E15
wy. Castle Hill 248 G1
JASNAR
st. Greenfld Pk 334 C15
JASON
av. S Penrith 266 J6
la. S Penrith, off Jason Av 266 J5
pl. North Rocks 248 J16
st. Greystanes 306 C6
st. Miranda 461 J16
JASPER
ct. Prestons 392 H14
pl. Ambarvale 540 F2
rd. Baulkham Hl 247 A8
rd. Baulkham Hl 247 D9
st. Greystanes 306 D9
st. Seaforth 286 K9
JAUNCEY
pl. Hillsdale 406 H14
JAVA
pl. Kellyville 185 J13
pl. Quakers Hill 214 B11
JAVELIN
la. St Clair, off Javelin Row 270 F15
pl. Raby 451 G15
row. St Clair 270 F15
JAY
av. Belfield 371 D10
pl. Oxley Park 240 F16
pl. Rooty Hill 271 K4
st. Lidcombe 339 F10
JAYELEM
cr. Padstow 399 G14
JAYNE
st. West Ryde 280 G11
JEAN
av. Miranda 461 J16
st. Greenacre 370 F3
st. Kingswood 237 D15
st. North Rocks 278 B8
st. Rydalmere 309 H4
st. Seven Hills 245 D16
st. Villawood 337 A16
JEANETTE
av. Mona Vale 198 H3
st. East Ryde 283 B15
st. Padstow 399 E15
st. Regentville 265 J4
st. Seven Hills 245 E16
JEANNERET
av. Hunters Hill 314 A13
JED
pl. Marayong 244 A8
JEDDA
pl. Mona Vale 199 E1
rd. Lurnea 394 B9
rd. Prestons 393 E8
JEENGA
pl. Sylvania 461 G15
JEFFERIES
pl. Prairiewood 334 J8
JEFFERSON
av. St Ives 224 C7
cr. Bonnet Bay 460 D11
gr. Kenthurst 157 C14
JEFFERY
av. N Parramatta 278 D10
JEFFREY
av. Greystanes 306 D6
av. St Clair 299 K2
st. Canterbury 372 G13
st. Kirribilli 6 B16
st. Kurnell 466 E8
JELENA
pl. Bossley Park 333 G12
JELLICOE
av. Kingsford 407 A4
st. Balgowlah Ht 288 A14
st. Caringbah 492 G11
st. Concord 342 A5
st. Condell Park 398 J7
st. Hurstville Gr 431 G10
st. Lidcombe M J13
st. Lidcombe 340 B5
JELLIE
pl. Oakhurst 242 C4
JELLINGAL
rd. Engadine 489 B12
JEM
pl. Blacktown 275 A9
JENDI
av. Bayview 168 J12
JENKINS
av. Penrith 237 D10
la. Crows Nest, off Brook St 315 G5
la. S Wntwthvle, off Hereford Pl 306 H6
rd. Carlingford 279 H4
st. Berala 339 B14
st. Cammeray 315 H5
st. Chatswd W 284 G10
st. Collaroy 229 A11
st. Dundas 280 B13
st. Millers Point A C10
st. Mona Vale 199 C7
st. Regents Pk 339 B14
JENKYN
pl. Bligh Park 150 E5
JENNA
cl. Allambie Ht 287 G1
cl. Rooty Hill 271 K2
JENNER
rd. Dural 219 B7
st. Baulkham Hl 247 J10
st. Little Bay 437 G14
st. Seaforth 287 A9
wy. Minto 482 H7
JENNIE
pl. Carlingford 249 C14
JENNIFER
av. Allambie Ht 257 F14
av. Blacktown 273 K2
pl. Baulkham Hl 247 A14
pl. Cherrybrook 219 K4
pl. Smithfield 335 G8
st. Little Bay 437 B13
st. Ryde 282 A13
JENNINGS
av. Bass Hill 367 G7
rd. Faulconbdg 171 D6
rd. Heathcote 518 D14
st. Alexandria 18 F14
st. Matraville 406 G16
JENNY
pl. Oakville 122 E12
pl. Rooty Hill 272 C2
JENOLA
la. Woolooware 493 C9
JENOLAN
cl. Hornsby Ht 161 J9
ct. Wattle Grove 395 H13
st. Leumeah 482 D14
JENSEN
av. Vaucluse 348 G4
pl. Engadine 518 F4
pl. S Coogee 407 H7
st. Colyton 270 H8
st. Condell Park 398 E2
st. Fairfield W 335 A11
JEREMY
wy. Cecil Hills 362 H9
JERILDERIE
av. Kellyville 216 G7
JEROME
av. Winston Hills 247 E16
JERRARA
st. Engadine 488 J13
JERRAWA
pl. Glenhaven 187 J14
JERSEY
av. Mortdale 431 B4
gln. St Clair 270 A13
la. Hornsby, off Coronation St 191 G16
la. S Wntwthvle 306 H6
la. Five Dock, off Barnstaple Rd 343 A8
pde. Minto 482 H9
pl. Cromer 227 H14
rd. Artarmon 284 J16
rd. Blackett 241 A5
rd. Bringelly 388 K14
rd. Dharruk 241 A5
rd. Emerton 240 J4
rd. Greystanes 306 H9
rd. Hebersham 241 A5
rd. Maroubra 406 J15
rd. Matraville 406 J15
rd. Merrylands 306 H10
rd. Oakhurst 241 H5
rd. Plumpton 241 H5
rd. Schofields 212 J7
rd. S Wntwthvle 306 H9
rd. Strathfield 341 G15
rd. Woollahra 21 G3
st. Busby 393 J1
st. Hornsby 191 G15
st. Marrickville 373 H13
st. Mt Colah 192 A5
st. Richmond 119 A5
st. Turramurra 222 J15
st.n, Asquith 191 H13
st.n, Hornsby 191 H13
JERSEYWOLD
av. Springwood 201 H3
JERVIS
dr. Illawong 459 A7
st. Ermington 310 F2
st. Fairfield 336 F8
st. Prestons 392 K16
JERVOIS
av. Centnnial Pk 21 E9
JESMOND
av. Dulwich Hill 373 B10
av. Vaucluse 318 G16
cr. Beecroft 250 A4
st. Surry Hills F K14
st. Surry Hills 4 C15
JESSE OWENS
av. Newington M D15
av. Newington 309 K16
JESSICA
gdn. St Ives 224 G5
pl. Mt Colah 162 D15
pl. Plumpton 241 J7
pl. Rsemeadow 540 K4
JESSIE
st. Smithfield 335 G8
st. Westmead 277 J14
JESSON
la. Surry Hills 20 B4
st. Surry Hills 20 B3
JESSOP
pl. Westmead 307 E3
JESSUP
pl. Glenmore Pk 265 E9
JET
pl. Eagle Vale 481 E9
JETTY
rd. Putney 312 C9
JEWELL
cl. Hamondvle 426 G1
JEWELSFORD
rd. Wentwthvle 306 G2
JIBBON
pl. Woodbine 481 G12
st. Cronulla 524 A3
JILL
st. Marayong 244 A9
JILLAK
cl. Glenmore Pk 266 A11
JILLIAN
pl. Mcquarie Fd 424 F15
JILLIBY
pl. Belrose 225 K15
JILLONG
st. Rydalmere 279 J14
JIMADA
av. Frenchs Frst 257 A4
JIMBI
pl. Glenmore Pk 266 B8
JIMBOUR
ct. Wattle Grove 425 J4

JIMBUCK
cl. Glenmore Pk .. 266 B11
JIM RING
la. Birrong, off Rodd St 369 A5
JIM SIMPSON
la. Blacktown, off Main St.......... 244 G15
JINATONG
st. Miranda.......... 491 J2
JINCHILLA
rd. Terrey Hills..... 196 C6
JINDABYNE
av. Baulkham Hl... 248 A8
cct. Woodcroft...... 243 G12
cr. Peakhurst....... 430 C9
st. Bossley Park .. 333 E11
st. Frenchs Frst ... 256 E1
st. Heckenberg 363 K13
JINDALEE
pl. East Killara 254 J6
pl. Riverwood...... 400 D11
JINDALLA
cr. Hebersham..... 241 D9
JINGARA
pl. Sylvania 461 G14
JINIWIN
pl. Ambarvale...... 510 K11
JINKINS
pl. Ambarvale...... 510 H14
JINNA
rd. Peakhurst....... 430 D10
JIPP
st. Penrith........... 237 A14
JIRANG
pl. Glenmore Pk .. 266 A8
JIRI
pl. Engadine 518 G4
JIRRAMBA
ct. Glenmore Pk .. 266 B7
JIRRANG
cl. Mount Druitt... 241 E16
JOADJA
cr. Glendenning... 242 G5
rd. Prestons......... 393 F8
JOALAH
av. Blaxland 234 E9
cl. St Ives........... 224 D16
cr. Berowra Ht..... 133 B10
rd. Duffys Frst...... 194 H3
JOAN
la. Belmore 401 G3
pl. Baulkham Hl... 247 K9
pl. Currans Hill 479 K13
pl. Greystanes 305 J6
pl. Mount Druitt... 271 A3
st. Chester Hill..... 368 C5
st. Hurstville........ 431 H1
JOANIE
pl. Glendenning... 242 F2
JOANNA
st. S Penrith........ 266 K5
JOANNE
cl. Cherrybrook ... 219 E6
ct. Sefton 368 H3
pl. Bilgola........... 169 E7
JOB
st. Harbord.......... 258 C14
JOCARM
av. Condell Park... 398 F1
JOCELYN
av. Marrickville..... 373 F11
bvd. Quakers Hill.... 213 J7
la. N Curl Curl, off Jocelyn St....... 258 F9
st. Chester Hill..... 368 B4
st. N Curl Curl 258 G9
JOCKBET
st. Agnes Banks .. 147 F2
st. Londonderry .. 147 F2
JOCKEY
cl. Casula........... 394 F16
JODIE
pl. Quakers Hill.... 244 A2
JODY
pl. St Clair 299 K2
JOEL
pl. Kings Lngly.... 246 C10
JOFFRE
cr. Daceyville...... 406 G4
st. Gymea Bay..... 491 D7
st. S Hurstville..... 432 B10
JOHANNA
pl. Schofields...... 213 H5

JOHN
av. Mcquarie Fd.... 454 A3
la. Glebe............... 11 K14
la. Randwick, off John St........... 376 J10
pl. Cecil Hills........ 362 E2
rd. Cherrybrook ... 219 C13
st. Ashfield.......... 342 G15
st. Avalon........... 140 C12
st. Bardwell Vy 403 B7
st. Baulkham Hl ... 247 H13
st. Beecroft.......... 250 B10
st. Bexley............. 402 F15
st. Blacktown....... 274 C5
st. Burwood......... 341 K13
st. Cabramatta..... 365 D6
st. Cabramtta W .. 365 A6
st. Camden.......... 477 A14
st. Canterbury...... 372 F12
st. Concord 341 J8
st. Cronulla......... 523 K2
st. Croydon 342 G15
st. Ermington .... L A15
st. Erskineville 18 A13
st. Glebe.............. 11 K13
st. Granville.......... 308 B13
st. Hunters Hill 313 B9
st. Hurstville 431 J2
st. Kogarah Bay ... 432 J11
st. Leichhardt 10 F15
st. Lidcombe 339 J4
st. McMahons Pt 5 B11
st. Marsden Pk 181 K11
st. Mascot 405 B2
st. Merrylands 308 B13
st. Newtown 374 H11
st. Petersham 16 A14
st. Punchbowl 399 H7
st. Pyrmont 12 E2
st. Queens Park ... 377 E8
st. Randwick 376 J10
st. Rooty Hill 271 J5
st. Rydalmere 309 H3
st. St Marys 269 E3
st. Schofields 182 H14
st. Strathfield S.... 371 A5
st. Tempe............ 374 C16
st. The Oaks 502 F12
st. Waterloo........... 19 C14
st. West Ryde 280 G11
st. Woollahra 21 J5
JOHN ALBERT
cl. Kellyville 216 H7
JOHN BATMAN
av. Wrrngtn Cty.... 238 G5
JOHN BOY
pl. Blacktown....... 273 J7
JOHN DAVEY
av. Cronulla.......... 494 B7
JOHN DEVITT
av. Newington .... M B13
av. Newington 310 B15
JOHN DWYER
rd. Lalor Park....... 245 F12
JOHN DYKES
av. Vaucluse......... 348 G1
JOHN FORREST
av. Sutherland...... 460 C14
JOHN HINES
av. Minchinbury ... 270 K5
av. Minchinbury ... 271 A5
JOHN HUGHES
pl. Wahroonga..... 222 B6
JOHN HUNTER
gr. Mt Annan........ 479 H16
JOHN IAN WING
pde. Homebush B... 310 A15
pde. Newington .... M C14
pde. Newington 310 A15
JOHN KIDD
dr. Blair Athol 511 C2
JOHN KONRADS
av. Newington .... M B13
av. Newington 310 A15
JOHN MARSHALL
av. Newington .... L G16
av. Newington 310 A16
JOHN McLENNON
cct. Harringtn Pk... 478 D2
JOHN MILLER
st. Ryde............. 282 H16
JOHN NORTHCOTT
pl. Surry Hills 19 K4
JOHN OXLEY
av. Werrington 238 G7
av. Wrrngtn Cty.... 238 G7
dr. Davidson 255 E4
dr. Frenchs Frst.... 255 E4
JOHN RADLEY
av. Dural 219 B8
JOHNS
av. Normanhurst .. 221 G7
JOHN SAVAGE
cr. W Pnnant Hl ... 219 J16
JOHNSON
av. Camden S....... 506 K10
av. Dulwich Hill 373 A9
av. Kenthurst........ 156 A7
av. Melrose Pk...... 280 J16
av. Seven Hills...... 245 K14
cl. Bonnet Bay 460 A9
la. Mascot 405 E6
pl. Ruse.............. 512 H4
pl. Springwood 172 G16
rd. Campbelltwn... 481 B16
rd. Galston 159 D10
st. Alexandria........ 375 G11
st. Beaconsfield ... 375 G11
st. Chatswood...... 285 A11
st. Harbord 258 E15
st. Hunters Hill..... 313 B10
st. Lindfield.......... 283 F3
st. Mascot 405 E6
JOHNSTON
av. Cammeray 316 D4
av. Kirrawee 490 K7
av. Kogarah Bay ... 432 H12
av. Lurnea 394 C13
cr. Lane Cove W... 283 K15
la. Annandale......... 11 A16
la. Lane Cove W... 313 H3
la. Marrickville 373 J16
pde. Maroubra........ 407 D7
pde. Maroubra........ 407 E7
pde. S Coogee 407 E7
rd. Bargo............. 567 G8
rd. Bass Hill 367 F7
rd. Eastwood......... 280 F6
st. Annandale......... 16 H3
st. Balmain East....... 8 G9
st. Earlwood 402 E8
st. Pitt Town 92 H9
st. Windsor.......... 121 C8
JOHNSTONE
st. Guildford W 336 K5
st. Peakhurst 429 K4
JOHN SULMAN
la. St Clair, off John Sulman Pl. 270 B11
pl. St Clair............ 270 B11
JOHN TEBBUT
pl. Richmond....... 118 E4
JOHN TIPPING
gr. Penrith............ 236 F10
JOHN WALL
la. Yagoona 369 E11
JOHN WARREN
av. Glenwood 215 J16
JOHORE
pl. E Lindfield....... 254 J12
rd. Holsworthy 426 F10
JOINER
pl. Bonnyrigg....... 364 D6
JOKIC
st. Bonnyrigg Ht .. 362 K7
JOLLY
st. Castlereagh..... 176 E8
JOLY
pde. Hunters Hill..... 313 C11
JONATHAN
pl. Miranda 491 J1
st. Greystanes...... 306 C7
JONATHON
pl. Cherrybrook 219 J7
pl. Frenchs Frst 256 B4
JONES
av. Kingsgrove 402 C8
av. Monterey 433 H9
ct. Currans Hill..... 479 G13
la. Pyrmont 12 H8
la. Redfern............ 19 D8
la. Rosebery, off Hayes Rd 375 G15
la. Kingswood, off Jones St.......... 237 H16
pl. Mt Pritchard 364 D11
rd. Castlereagh..... 175 G6
rd. Eastwood........ 280 G6
rd. Kenthurst........ 187 G1
st. Beacon Hill...... 257 C5
st. Blacktown 274 J5
st. Concord.......... 342 A6
st. Croydon.......... 342 G14
st. Engadine......... 518 F1
st. Kingswood...... 237 H16
st. Pyrmont........... 12 E2
st. Pyrmont........... 12 H9
st. Ryde 282 D15
st. Ultimo............. 12 K12
st. Wentwthvle..... 306 F2
JONES BAY
rd. Pyrmont........... 12 H1
JON HENRICKS
av. Newington .... M B16
av. Newington 309 K15
JONQUIL
pl. Alfords Point ... 459 A3
pl. Glenmore Pk ... 265 G10
JOPLING
cr. Lalor Park 245 B11
st. North Ryde 283 A12
JORDAN
av. Beverly Hills 401 A12
av. Glossodia......... 59 K11
cl. Mt Colah 162 E16
la. Valley Ht 202 H10
pl. Kearns 451 A15
rd. Moorebank....... 425 B1
rd. Wahroonga 221 K16
st. Fairfield W....... 335 C9
st. Gladesville....... 312 H9
st. Rosehill.......... 308 H8
st. Seven Hills 245 F15
st. Wentwthvle 307 C1
JORDANA
pl. Castle Hill 248 E4
JORDANS
la. Matraville 436 J4
JORDON
st. Cambrdg Pk.... 238 A7
JORGENSEN
av. St Clair 270 D10
JORJA
pl. Kellyville.......... 216 D1
JOSEPH
cl. Liberty Gr........ 311 B10
cr. Sefton 368 F6
la. Yagoona 369 E10
rd. Leppington 420 B9
st. Ashfield........... 372 J5
st. Avalon............ 140 A13
st. Berala 339 G16
st. Blacktown 274 E6
st. Blakehurst 432 C15
st. Cabramatta 365 C8
st. Cabramtta W ... 365 C8
st. Chipping Ntn ... 396 C5
st. Kingswood...... 237 H11
st. Lane Cove 314 G3
st. Lidcombe 339 G16
st. Lidcombe........ 339 H10
st. Lilyfield 10 D6
st. Regents Pk...... 369 G2
st. Richmond 118 K7
st. Rozelle 7 B16
st. Rydalmere 279 E15
JOSEPH BANKS
ct. Mt Annan 509 G4
dr. Kings Lngly..... 245 H7
JOSEPHINE
cr. Cherrybrook.... 219 J4
cr. Georges Hall ... 367 F10
cr. Moorebank...... 396 C11
st. Merrylnds W ... 306 H13
st. Riverwood 400 C14
wy. Glendenning, off Tony Pl............ 242 F1
JOSEPHSON
st. Paddington 20 F2
JOSHUA
rd. Freemns Rch.... 61 A11
wy. Cranebrook 207 E13
wy. Dean Park, off Medea Pl 212 F15
JOSHUA MOORE
dr. Horngsea Pk ... 392 C14
JOSQUIN
wy. Clarmnt Ms 268 F4
JOSSELYN
pl. Concord.......... 342 B3
JOUBERT
st.n, Hunters Hill..... 313 F9
st.s, Hunters Hill..... 313 E11
JOWARRA
pl. Bow Bowing.... 452 E13
wy. Merrylnds W .. 306 K11
JOWETT
pl. Ingleburn 453 J8
JOWYN
pl. Kirrawee......... 491 C3
JOY
av. Earlwood........ 402 J4
la. Earlwood, off Joy Av 402 J4
pl. Maroubra 407 C15
st. Gladesville...... 313 A4
st. Mt Pritchard ... 364 G10
JOYCE
av. Picnic Point.... 428 D8
dr. Mascot........... 405 B6
pl. Dural 219 C7
st. Fairfield 336 A13
st. Glenwood....... 245 D2
st. Pendle Hill...... 276 E14
st. Punchbowl 399 J9
JOYCELYN
cl. Hornsby Ht..... 161 J12
JOYLYN
rd. Annangrove.... 155 E12
JOYNER
st. Westmead 307 J4
JOYNT
av. Milperra 397 F10
JOYNTON
av. Zetland 375 J11
JUBA
cl. St Clair 269 J16
JUBILEE
av. Beverley Pk 433 A8
av. Carlton 432 J7
av. Pymble........... 252 K1
av. Warriewood.... 198 F5
la. Parramatta 308 D6
la. Lewisham, off Jubilee St.......... 15 B10
pl. Balmain.............. 8 D10
pl. Balmain East 8 D10
st. Lewisham......... 15 B9
st. Wahroonga 222 C2
JUDD
av. Hamondvle..... 396 H16
la. Oatley............ 431 D10
st. Banksia 403 C12
st. Berkshire Pk ... 179 H11
st. Cronulla 493 K9
st. Mortdale......... 431 D9
st. Oatley............ 431 D10
st. Penshurst....... 431 D9
JUDE
av. Kogarah Bay... 432 H11
JUDGE
la. Woolmloo 4 F7
la. Randwick, off Coogee Bay Rd.. 377 C15
pl. Woolmloo 4 G6
pl. Randwick, off Judge St.......... 377 C15
st. Randwick 377 C15
st. Woolmloo 4 G7
JUDGES
la. Waverley, off Bronte Rd 377 F8
JUDITH
av. Cabramatta..... 365 C10
av. Mt Colah 192 B3
av. Mt Riverview .. 234 D2
av. Seven Hills 275 D5
cl. Werrington 238 J11
pl. Cromer........... 228 C15
st. Baulkham Hl... 247 K11
st. Berala 339 B13
st. Chester Hill..... 368 D2
st. Pendle Hill...... 306 C1
st. Seaforth 286 K2
JUDITH ANDERSON
dr. Doonside........ 243 B9
JUDSON
rd. Thornleigh...... 221 C8
JUGIONG
st. West Pymble.. 252 G10
JUKES
cl. Barden Rdg 488 H6
JULAR
pl. Jamisontown.. 266 D6
JULIA
cl. Cherrybrook ... 220 A13
cl. West Hoxton .. 391 K4
gr. Castle Hill 217 C7
st. Ashfield.......... 342 K16

JULIAN
pl. Arcadia 130 A16
pl. Sefton 368 F5
st. Mosman 316 H3
st. Willoughby 285 E14
wy. Claymore 481 E11
JULIANA
cr. Baulkham Hl 246 H5
pl. Bligh Park 150 E8
wy. Cherrybrook 219 A14
JULIANNE
pl. Canley Ht 365 C4
JULIE
av. Campsie 402 A4
cr. St Clair 269 H8
ct. Kellyville 186 B16
st. Blacktown 274 E7
st. Marsfield 282 B8
JULIET
cl. Rsemeadow 540 H4
JULIETT
la. Marrickville 16 K16
la. Marrickville 374 E8
st. Enmore 16 K16
st. Marrickville 16 K16
st. Marrickville 374 F8
JULIETTE
av. Punchbowl 370 B16
JULIUS
av. North Ryde 283 C10
rd. Rsemeadow 540 J2
st. Fairfield W 335 C13
JULL
pl. St Helens Pk 541 A9
JUMAL
pl. Smithfield 306 D15
JUMBUNNA
pl. Terrey Hills 196 C7
JUNCTION
la. N Sydney K H11
la. Wahroonga 223 A4
la. Woolmloo 4 E5
rd. Baulkham Hl 247 C16
rd. Beverly Hills 400 H16
rd. Heathcote 518 G10
rd. Leumeah 482 G16
rd. Moorebank 396 A10
rd. Peakhurst 430 H1
rd. Riverstone 153 E16
rd. Ruse 512 E8
rd. Schofields 183 E14
rd. Summer Hill 373 B6
rd. Wahroonga 222 E3
rd. Winston Hills 247 C16
st. Auburn 309 C13
st. Cabramatta 365 K9
st. Forest Lodge 11 H16
st. Gladesville 312 J10
st. Granville 308 D8
st. Marrickville 373 K15
st. Miranda 492 D3
st. Mortdale 431 B4
st. Old Guildfrd 337 D8
st. Ryde 311 H4
st. Silverwater 309 C13
st. Strathfield S 371 B5
st. Woollahra 22 J5
st. Woolmloo 4 F5
st. Yennora 337 D8
JUNE
pl. Glenhaven 218 B1
pl. Gymea Bay 491 C9
st. Bankstown 399 C4
st. Blacktown 274 H8
st. Seven Hills 245 C15
JUNEE
cl. Bossley Park 333 G9
cr. Kingsgrove 402 B6
ct. Minto 482 F9
st. Marayong 243 K8
JUNIA
av. Toongabbie 276 B8
JUNIOR
st. Leichhardt 15 H3
JUNIPER
pl. Baulkham Hl 248 B11
pl. Prestons 393 K15
pl. Sylvania 462 A9
wy. Blacktown 274 E12
wy. Mcquarie Fd 454 H4
JUNO
pde. Greenacre 370 E11
JUPITER
ct. Cranebrook 207 F15
la. Cranebrook, off Pensax Rd 207 F14
rd. Kellyville 216 C2
rd. Kellyville 216 C3
st. Gladesville 312 K9
st. Lansvale 366 J8
st. Winston Hills 277 C1
JUPP
pl. Eastwood 281 E4
JURA
cl. Cranebrook 207 E15
cr. Winmalee 173 E12
pl. St Andrews 481 J1
pl. Seven Hills 275 C8
JURDS
la. Ryde 281 K9
JURY
wy. Minto 482 J7
JUSTIN
pl. Quakers Hill 214 F12
st. Lilyfield 10 F4
st. Smithfield 335 J5
JUSTINE
av. Baulkham Hl 247 C8
cl. Bargo 567 B4
JUSTUS
st. North Bondi 348 C15
JUVENIS
av. Oyster Bay 461 C3

K

KABAN
st. Doonside 243 D14
KABARLI
rd. Lalor Park 245 E13
KABLE
rd. Bradbury 511 G13
st. Windsor 121 C7
KABUL
cl. St Clair 269 K16
la. St Clair, off Kabul Cl 269 K16
KADER
st. Bargo 567 A5
st. Bargo 567 D6
KADIERA
cl. Wallacia 325 A15
KADIGAL
pl. Beacon Hill 257 D6
KADINA
pl. Quakers Hill 214 B16
KAFFIR
cl. Cherrybrook 219 E7
KAGA
pl. Marsfield 281 K5
KAGA PATH
Blaxland 233 G13
KAHIBAH
rd. Mosman 317 F10
rd. Mosman 317 F9
KAIN
av. Matraville 437 C1
pl. Bonnyrigg 364 C6
KAIRAWA
st. S Hurstville 432 C10
KALA
cct. St Clair 269 H14
la. St Clair, off Kala Cct 269 H14
KALAMBO
pl. St Clair 270 H11
KALANA
cl. Moorebank 396 H7
KALANG
av. Killara 254 C9
av. St Marys 239 F15
la. Yowie Bay 492 C10
rd. Edensor Pk 333 D16
rd. Edensor Pk 363 D2
rd. Elanora Ht 198 D14
rd. Greystanes 306 B6
rd. Kenthurst 187 F6
rd. Mt Colah 191 K5
rd. Seven Hills 275 G4
KALAUI
st. N Balgowlah 287 E4
KALBARRI
cr. Bow Bowing 452 C13
KALESKI
st. Moorebank 395 G9
KALGAL
st. Frenchs Frst 255 J1
KALGOORLIE
pl. Cartwright 393 K5
pl. Sutherland 460 D14
st. Leichhardt 9 F13
st. Willoughby 285 D13
KALIANNA
cr. Beacon Hill 257 H8
KALIMNA
dr. Baulkham Hl 247 A7
st. Moorebank 396 F7
KALINDI
pl. St Clair 270 H11
la. St Clair, off Kalindi Pl 270 H11
KALINYA
st. Newport 169 E12
KALKADA
av. Gymea Bay 491 E11
KALLANG
pde. Wahroonga 221 J16
KALLAROO
rd. Riverview 314 C7
rd. Terrey Hills 195 K7
st. Mosman 316 K11
KALLAWATTA
gr. McGraths Hl 122 B10
KALLISTA
av. St Ives 254 E1
KALMIA
pl. Miranda 491 K5
KALOE
pl. Marayong 244 B3
KALOONA
pl. Kirrawee 460 J16
KALORA
av. Dee Why 258 J1
av. Fairfield W 335 G14
KALUA
pl. Glenmore Pk 266 B6
KALUGA
st. Busby 363 H13
KALUMNA
cl. Cherrybrook 219 F12
KALUNA
av. Smithfield 336 B5
st. Putney 312 A8
KALUNGA
la. Rooty Hill 242 D16
la. Rooty Hill 272 C1
KALYAN
av. Bradbury 511 F16
KAMAROOKA
cr. W Pnnant Hl 249 G5
KAMBAH
pl. W Pnnant Hl 249 A8
KAMBALA
cr. Fairfield W 335 F14
pl. Bellevue Hill 347 F15
rd. Bellevue Hill 14 J9
KAMBALDA
pl. Yarrawarrah 489 E13
KAMBER
rd. Terrey Hills 196 C12
KAMBORA
av. Davidson 255 D1
av. Frenchs Frst 255 D1
KAMERUKA
rd. Northbridge 285 K14
KAMILAROI
rd. Bayview 169 A14
KAMILAROY
rd. West Pymble 253 A12
KAMIRA
av. Villawood 367 C1
ct. Villawood 367 C1
rd. Lilli Pilli 522 F3
KAMIRI
st. Seaforth 287 B5
KAN
cl. St Clair 269 H15
KANA
cl. Cranebrook 207 E6
KANADAH
av. Baulkham Hl 246 J8
KANANDAH
rd. Engadine 488 C13
KANANGRA
av. Baulkham Hl 247 B4
cr. Balgowlah 287 E11
cr. Cherrybrook 219 J7
cr. Clontarf 287 E11
cr. Elderslie 477 H16
cr. Ruse 512 F5
ct. Wattle Grove 426 B4
rd. Terrey Hills 196 F7
KANANGUR
av. Gymea 491 H1
KANANOOK
av. Bayview 168 H10
KANDARA
cl. Middle Dural 157 H1
KANDOS
st. Glenwood 245 F1
KANDRA
rd. Beacon Hill 257 H8
KANDY
av. Epping 251 A12
KANE
pl. Casula 424 D3
pl. Glendenning 242 E4
st. Guildford 337 F4
KANERUKA
pl. Baulkham Hl 246 K8
KANGAROO
cl. Green Valley 363 A12
la. Manly, off Carlton St 288 G7
pl. Emu Plains 235 A11
rd. Collaroy Plat 228 J13
rd. Tahmoor 565 B13
st. Manly 288 F7
KANGAROO POINT
rd. Kangaroo Pt 461 J7
KANILI
av. Baulkham Hl 247 B15
KANIMBLA
cr. Bilgola 169 H7
st. Ruse 512 F8
KANINA
pl. Cranebrook 207 B13
KANINI
cl. Cromer 227 K16
KANNAN
pl. Kirrawee 461 D15
KANNING
av. Gymea Bay 491 E8
KANO
cl. Bonnyrigg 364 C8
KANOONA
av. Homebush 341 A7
av. St Ives 223 J11
st. Caringbah 492 F8
KANOWAR
av. East Killara 254 J6
KANSAS
pl. Toongabbie 275 H12
KANUKA
st. Bossley Park 333 F8
KANYA
st. Frenchs Frst 256 F8
KAPALA
av. Bradbury 511 E16
KAPITI
st. St Ives Ch 223 J2
KAPOVIC
st. Edensor Pk 363 F1
KAPUNDA
pl. Belrose 226 A14
KAPUTAR
ct. Holsworthy 426 C5
pl. Prairiewood 334 F7
KAPYONG
st. Belrose 226 A15
KARA
cr. Bayview 168 K13
la. Peakhurst 430 B10
la. Randwick, off Howard St 407 B1
st. Lane Cove W 284 E16
st. Randwick 407 B1
st. Sefton 368 E3
KARABAH
pl. Frenchs Frst 257 C4
tce. Warrimoo 203 C15
KARABAR
st. Fairfield Ht 335 H9
KARABI
cl. Glenmore Pk 266 C10
KARABIL
cr. Baulkham Hl 248 C8
KARA KAROOK
st. Maianbar 523 B8
KARALEE
cl. Marsfield 281 K1
rd. Galston 160 J7
KARALTA
cr. Belrose 225 G14
KARAMARRA
rd. Engadine 488 H13
KARANA
pl. Chatswd W 284 C10
KARANGI
pl. Illawong 460 B4
rd. Whalan 241 A9
KARANI
av. Guildford W 336 G3
KARDA
pl. Gymea 491 F1
KARDELLA
av. Killara 254 D11
cr. Narwee 400 K13
ct. Condell Park 368 H16
la. Killara 254 E11
KARDINIA
rd. Mosman 317 D13
KAREELA
av. Penrith 237 E6
cr. Greenacre 370 B13
la. Cremorne Pt 316 F12
la. Penrith, off Kareela Av 237 E5
rd. Baulkham Hl 247 F7
rd. Chatswd W 284 E8
rd. Cremorne Pt 316 F12
rd. Cremorne, off Hodgson Av 316 F12
st. Doonside 243 B15
KAREELAH
rd. Hunters Hill 313 G12
KAREEMA
st. Balgowlah 287 F10
KAREENA
rd.n, Miranda 492 E5
rd.s, Miranda 492 E7
KARELLA
av. Villawood 367 B2
KAREN
av. Picnic Point 428 D8
ct. Baulkham Hl 247 A10
ct. Cranebrook 206 J8
pl. Faulconbdg 171 D15
pl. Ingleburn 453 D12
pl. Mount Druitt 270 K1
pl. Silverdale 354 B11
rd. Rossmore 419 E3
rd. St Ives 224 F9
KAREN MORAS
dr. Ryde 312 E5
KARIBOO
cl. Mona Vale 199 E1
KARILLA
av. Lane Cove W 284 C15
KARIMBLA
rd. Miranda 491 J4
KARINA
cr. Belrose 226 D15
KARINGAL
av. Carlingford 279 E3
cr. Frenchs Frst 256 E6
ct. Marsfield 281 K1
pl. Greenacre 370 B14
rd. Riverview 314 C7
st. Kingsgrove 401 J9
st. Seaforth 287 B7
KARINI
cl. Green Valley 363 H11
KARINYA
pl. Kellyville 216 C2
pl. Wahroonga 221 H6
KARIOLA
st. Lane Cove W 284 C15
KARIUS
st. Glenfield 424 H9
KARIWARA
st. Dundas 279 G13
KARLOO
cl. Moorebank 396 H6
pde. Newport 169 H15
st. Turramurra 223 B10
KARLOON
rd. W Pnnant Hl 249 H9
KARNAK
st. Denistone E 281 F9
KARNE
st. Narwee 400 G13
st. Riverwood 400 G13
st. Roselands 400 G13
KARNU
pl. Kareela 461 D14
KARONGA
cl. Epping 250 D15
KAROO
av. E Lindfield 255 A13

cr. Hornsby Ht..... 161 F15
pl. Malabar.......... 437 D8

KAROOL
av. Earlwood........ 372 H16

KAROOLA
cr. Caringbah....... 492 F4
st. Brooklyn........... 76 D11
st. Busby............. 363 J14
st. Narraweena.... 258 C2

KAROOM
av. St Ives............ 223 H9

KAROON
av. Canley Ht........ 335 B15

KARRABA
st. Sefton............ 368 G6

KARRABAH
rd. Auburn........... 309 C16

KARRABEE
av. Tarban............ 313 B12
st. Dee Why........ 258 E7

KARRABUL
pl. Bossley Park .. 333 F6
rd. Airds.............. 511 H16
rd. St Helens Pk.... 541 G3

KARRANGA
av. Killara............ 254 B11

KARREE
pl. Heathcote....... 518 E10

KARRI
pl. Alfords Point .. 429 A14
pl. Bradbury........ 511 E10

KARRIL
av. Beecroft.......... 249 K12

KARRONG
st. Clarmnt Ms.... 268 G2

KARUAH
pl. Engadine........ 488 K8
rd. Penrith........... 237 C5
rd. Turramurra..... 222 J11
st. Campbelltwn .. 511 K7
st. Doonside........ 243 B7
st. Greenacre....... 370 E11
st. Greystanes..... 306 C7
st. Strathfield....... 340 H13

KARUK
st. Glenmore Pk .. 266 E11

KARWARRA
pl. Peakhurst....... 430 C9

KASCH
cl. Tahmoor........ 565 D12

KASHMIR
av. Quakers Hill.... 214 D7

KASIE
la. St Clair, off
Kasie Pl.......... 299 J3
pl. St Clair.......... 299 K3

KASTELAN
st. Blacktown...... 273 J3

KATANDRA
cl. Avalon........... 139 J16

KATANNA
rd. Wedderburn... 540 D14

KATAVICH
cr. Bonnyrigg Ht .. 363 C4

KATE
pl. Cherrybrook... 219 J4
pl. Quakers Hill.... 213 K7
st. Turramurra..... 252 E2

KATELLA
pl. Airds............. 512 B14

KATER
pl. Croydon Pk.... 372 A5

KATH
pl. Kings Lngly.... 245 C4

KATHERIN
rd. Baulkham Hl... 247 E11

KATHERINE
cl. Cranebrook.... 207 D4
cl. Galston........... 160 F11
pl. Castle Hill....... 248 C1
st. Cecil Hills....... 362 J3
st. Leumeah........ 482 F12
st. Chatswood, off
Victoria Av...... 284 H10

KATHLEEN
av. Castle Hill....... 217 F11
av. Lurnea........... 394 D10
la. Emu Plains, off
Kathleen St...... 235 B9
pde. Picnic Point.... 428 D7
pl. Thirlmere........ 565 C6
st. Emu Plains..... 235 A9
st. North Ryde..... 282 H8
st. Wiley Park...... 400 J2

KATHRYN
pl. Gymea Bay..... 491 F8
pl. Lalor Park....... 245 C13

KATHY
cl. Pymble........... 223 B14
wy. Dean Park....... 212 F15

KATHY WATT
av. Newington.......... L G16
av. Newington....... 310 B12

KATIA
st. N Parramatta .. 278 F12

KATINA
st. Turramurra..... 223 A11

KATINKA
st. Bonnyrigg....... 364 D7

KATNOOK
pl. W Pnnant Hl... 249 A2

KATOA
cl. N Narrabeen... 198 J13
pl. Marsfield........ 282 A3

KATRINA
av. Mona Vale...... 198 J2
cl. Richmond....... 118 E7
cr. Cabramtta W .. 364 H6
ct. Normanhurst .. 221 J11
pl. Baulkham Hl... 247 G13
pl. Ermington...... 280 D14
pl. Roselands...... 401 E4
rd. Bringelly......... 418 J3
st. Seven Hills...... 245 K12

KATTA
cl. Hornsby......... 191 J7

KAUAI
pl. Kings Park...... 244 H3

KAURI
av. Berowra.......... 163 D1
pl. Blaxland......... 234 B8
st. Blacktown....... 244 A15
st. Cabramatta..... 365 G10

KAVENAGH
cl. Prairiewood.... 335 A8

KAVIENG
av. Whalan.......... 241 A8

KAWANA
cl. Epping............ 250 H13
ct. Bella Vista....... 246 D7
pl. Bangor........... 459 J14
pl. Erskine Park.... 270 G16
st. Bass Hill......... 367 K6
st. Frenchs Frst.... 255 G3

KAY
cl. Cherrybrook... 220 A11
cl. Jamisontown... 266 B2
cl. Mona Vale...... 198 H3
la. Jamisontown, off
Kay Cl............ 266 B2
st. Blacktown....... 274 H7
st. Carlingford..... 280 C4
st. Granville........ 308 K10
st. Old Guildfrd.... 337 F7

KAYLEY
pl. Glenhaven...... 218 D3

KAYLYN
pl. Mount Druitt... 241 G12

KAYS
av.e, Marrickville..... 373 F13
av.w, Dulwich Hill.... 373 E12

KAZANIS
ct. Werrington..... 239 A12

KEA
cl. Acacia Gdn..... 214 G15

KEADY
wy. Wentwthvle..... 277 E11

KEARNEY
ct. Baulkham Hl... 247 A2
pl. Bonnyrigg....... 363 J8
rd. Maroota S......... 66 E1

KEARNS
av. Kearns........... 451 C16
la. Yagoona.......... 369 D11
pl. Horngsea Pk... 392 C14

KEARY
st. Willoughby...... 285 F12

KEATES
av. Padstow Ht..... 429 E6

KEATING
pl. Denham Ct..... 422 G16
st. Lidcombe........ 339 J7
st. Maroubra....... 407 C7
wy. Narellan Vale... 508 G1

KEATO
av. Hamondvle..... 396 F16

KEATS
av. Riverwood...... 400 C13

av. Rockdale......... 403 C16
av. Ryde.............. 282 D12
cl. Wetherill Pk.... 334 H5
pl. Heathcote....... 518 C16
pl. Ingleburn........ 453 C12
pl. Winston Hills .. 277 G1
rd. N Turramrra.... 223 E7
st. Carlingford...... 250 B16

KEDA
cct. N Richmond..... 87 D16

KEDDIE
pl. Riverstone...... 183 C9

KEDRON
av. Beecroft.......... 250 C8
pl. St Johns Pk.... 334 E15
rd. Ingleside......... 197 A8
st. Glenbrook....... 233 K13

KEDUMBA
cr. N Turramrra.... 223 F2

KEECH
rd. Castlereagh..... 176 E12

KEEDEN
pl. Bonnyrigg....... 364 A7

KEEGAN
av. Glebe................ 12 B11
pl. Forestville....... 256 A12
rd. Bass Hill......... 367 G8

KEELE
st. Como............. 460 E5
st. N Sydney........ 315 H8
st. Vaucluse......... 318 F15

KEELENDI
rd. W Pnnant Hl... 250 A1

KEELER
st. Carlingford...... 280 A2

KEELO
st. Quakers Hill.... 243 D4

KEENAN
la. Chester Hill..... 368 C2
st. Mona Vale....... 199 B3

KEENE
st. Baulkham Hl... 247 F10

KEERA
st. Quakers Hill.... 243 F5

KEESING
cr. Blackett........... 241 D4
st. Edensor Pk..... 363 G3

KEEVIN
st. Roselands....... 401 A7

KEEYUGA
rd. Huntleys Pt..... 313 F13

KEGWORTH
st. Leichhardt........ 15 B3

KEIGHRAN
pl. Cherrybrook.... 219 E6
pl. Minto............. 482 H8

KEILEY
st. Marsfield........ 281 K5

KEIR
av. Hurlstone Pk... 372 K14

KEIRA
av. Greenacre....... 370 F4
cl. Terrey Hills..... 196 D5
pl. Beecroft.......... 249 K12
pl. Ruse.............. 512 F4

KEIRAN
la. Bondi Jctn........ 22 F9
st. Bondi Jctn........ 22 F9

KEIRLE
rd. Kellyville......... 215 A4
st. North Manly.... 258 B14

KEITH
ct. Cherrybrook.... 219 F6
la. Dulwich Hill..... 373 D12
pl. Baulkham Hl... 247 E11
st. Clovelly........... 377 K12
st. Dulwich Hill..... 373 D12
st. Earlwood......... 373 A16
st. Lindfield.......... 284 G1
st. Peakhurst........ 430 E1
st. S Penrith......... 266 J2
wy. Mosman......... 317 A12

KEITH SMITH
av. Mascot........... 404 J6

KELBRAE
cl. Castle Hill........ 247 J1

KELBURN
pl. Airds.............. 512 B13
rd. Roseville......... 284 F2

KELD
pl. Blacktown....... 244 D15

KELDIE
st. Forestville....... 255 K6

KELHAM
st. Glendenning.... 242 G7

KELLAWAY
pl. Wetherill Pk..... 304 G15
st. Doonside........ 243 B7
st. East Ryde........ 282 J16

KELLER
pl. Casula............ 395 A12

KELLERMAN
dr. St Helens Pk.... 540 K9

KELLETT
pl. Rcuttrs Bay........ 4 K7
st. Potts Point......... 4 J7
wy. Potts Point......... 4 K7

KELLICAR
rd. Campbelltwn... 510 H8

KELLICK
st. Waterloo.......... 19 F13

KELLOGG
rd. Rooty Hill........ 242 F13

KELLOWAY
av. Camden.......... 507 A7

KELLS
la. Darlinghurst....... 4 D11
rd. Ryde.............. 312 D1

KELLY
cl. Baulkham Hl.... 247 A2
cl. Mount Druitt... 241 E15
la. Brooklyn.......... 75 F12
la. Matraville........ 436 G2
la. Padstow, off
Watson Rd...... 399 D14
pl. Mt Pritchard.... 364 H14
rd. Ingleburn........ 422 G10
st. Austral............ 390 F15
st. Henley............ 313 B14
st. Matraville........ 436 G1
st. Punchbowl...... 400 B3
st. Sylvania.......... 461 K13
st. Ultimo.............. 12 H14

KELLYS
esp. Northwood...... 314 F7
la. Maroota S........ 66 C5

KELMSCOTT
la. St Clair, off
Kelmscott Wy.. 270 G14
wy. St Clair........... 270 F14

KELPA
pl. Allambie Ht, off
Roosevelt Av... 257 D12

KELRAY
pl. Asquith........... 192 A13

KELSALL
pl. Barden Rdg..... 488 G5
st. Doonside........ 273 E4

KELSEY
st. Arncliffe.......... 403 F7

KELSO
cl. Bonnyrigg Ht... 363 C6
cr. Moorebank....... 395 K7
la. Blacktown....... 274 H1
la. Randwick......... 377 A12
pl. St Andrews..... 452 A15
st. Burwood Ht..... 372 A3
st. Engadine......... 489 A8

KELTON
pl. Engadine......... 488 K8

KELVEDON
la. Marsden Pk..... 182 B11

KELVIN
ct. Oatlands.......... 279 A10
gr. Winston Hills... 277 F6
pde. Picnic Point..... 428 B7
pl. Busby............. 363 H16
rd. St Ives............ 224 D16
st. Ashbury.......... 372 F8

KELVIN PARK
dr. Bringelly.......... 388 G12

KEMBLA
av. Chester Hill..... 368 D1
cr. Ruse............... 512 F4
st. Arncliffe.......... 403 D8
st. Croydon Pk..... 371 F7
st. Dharruk........... 241 C8
st. Wakeley.......... 334 H14

KEMBLE
la. Mosman......... 317 A8
pl. Bilgola............ 169 F8

KEMERTON
la. St Clair, off
Kemerton St.... 269 J11
st. St Clair........... 269 J10

KEMIRA
pl. Cartwright....... 394 D5

KEMMEL
cl. Bossley Park .. 334 B10

KEMMIS
st. Randwick....... 377 D11

KEMP
av. Kirrawee......... 490 K8
av. Matraville....... 436 J2
pl. Bonnyrigg....... 364 D5
pl. Glenorie......... 126 E4
pl. Minto............. 482 G9
pl. Tregear.......... 240 E7
st. Granville......... 308 G10
st. Mortdale......... 431 A6
st. Tennyson....... 312 E9

KEMPBRIDGE
av. Seaforth......... 287 E9

KEMPE
pde. Kings Lngly.... 246 B10

KEMPSEY
cl. Dee Why........ 258 H3
la. Jamisontown, off
Kempsey St.... 266 D5
pl. Bossley Park .. 333 D13
st. Blacktown...... 274 J2
st. Jamisontown.. 266 D5
wy. Hoxton Park... 392 G9

KEMPT
st. Bonnyrigg...... 363 K6

KENARF
cl. Kingswood..... 238 A14

KENBURN
av. Cherrybrook... 219 G10

KENDAL
cr. Collaroy Plat... 228 E11

KENDALL
dr. Casula........... 424 C3
dr. Casula........... 424 F2
la. Surry Hills........ 20 D3
la. The Rocks.......... A K3
pl. Kareela........... 461 C13
pl. Kellyville......... 186 G12
rd. Castle Cove..... 285 F3
st. Cabarita.......... 342 D1
st. Campbelltwn.. 512 A4
st. Ermington...... 310 B2
st. Fairfield W...... 335 B13
st. Granville......... 308 J11
st. Harris Park..... 308 E5
st. Mortdale......... 430 J7
st. Penrith........... 237 C11
st. Pymble........... 253 A9
st. Riverstone...... 182 E14
st. Rydalmere....... 310 B2
st. Sans Souci..... 463 A3
st. Surry Hills........ 20 D3
st. Thirlmere....... 562 D11
st. West Pymble.. 252 J10
st. Woollahra....... 377 G2

KENDEE
st. Sadleir........... 364 C15

KENEALLY
cr. Edensor Pk..... 333 G16
wy. Casula........... 424 G3

KENELDA
av. Guildford........ 338 A2

KENGE
pl. Ambarvale...... 510 G15

KEN HALL
pl. Agnes Banks.. 117 C12

KENIBEA
pl. Dee Why........ 258 H1

KENILWORTH
cr. Cranebrook..... 207 A6
la. Bondi Jctn, off
Flood La......... 377 H3
rd. Dundas Vy...... 280 B6
rd. Lindfield......... 254 C14
st. Bondi Jctn...... 377 G3
st. Croydon......... 342 F15
st. Miller.............. 393 F2

KENJI
pl. Blacktown...... 273 J7

KENLEY
rd. Normanhurst.. 221 E9

KENMARE
rd. Londonderry .. 148 B11

KENNA
pl. Cromer........... 227 K12
pl. Gymea........... 491 C6

KENNEDIA
pl. Mt Annan....... 509 C2

KENNEDY
av. Belmore......... 371 C14
cr. Bonnet Bay..... 460 D8

dr. S Penrith 236 J15
gr. Appin 568 G9
la. Gladesville 313 A3
la. Kingsford 376 J16
pde. Lalor Park 245 G14
pl. Bayview 168 D8
pl. St Ives 224 G16
st. Appin 568 G12
st. Appin 568 G9
st. Gladesville 313 A3
st. Guildford 338 C8
st. Kingsford 376 J16
st. Liverpool 394 H3
st. Panania 428 F6
st. Picnic Point 428 F8
st. Revesby 428 F6
st. Ruse 512 F2
st. Woolmloo 4 D7
wy. Bonnyrigg 364 D6

KENNELLY
st. Colyton 270 F8

KENNETH
av. Baulkham Hl 247 F11
av. Kirrawee 490 J2
av. Panania 428 E1
cr. Dean Park 242 H2
la. Kingsford, off Kennedy St 376 J16
pl. Dural 219 D5
rd. Balgowlah 288 A5
rd. Fairlight 288 A5
rd. Manly 288 A5
rd. Manly Vale 287 J4
rd. Manly Vale 288 A5
st. Longueville 314 D9
st. Mcquarie Fd 424 A16
st. Ryde 312 D4
st. Tamarama 378 C6

KENNETH SLESSOR
dr. Glenmore Pk 265 J6

KENNETT
pl. Glenfield 424 D10

KENNIFF
st. Rozelle 10 K1

KENNINGTON
av. Quakers Hill 214 C12

KENNINGTON OVAL
Auburn 339 A12

KENNY
av. Casula 394 G13
av. Chifley 437 B8
av. St Marys 240 A14
cl. St Helens Pk 541 C3
la. Marayong 244 D6
pl. Dundas Vy 279 H5
pl. Fairfield W 334 K10
rd. Pagewood 406 F9

KENNY HILL
rd. Currans Hill 510 C1

KENOMA
pl. Arndell Park 273 H9

KENS
rd. Frenchs Frst 255 H2
rd. Yarramundi 145 B1

KENSINGTON
cl. Cecil Hills 362 D7
dr. Harringtn Pk 478 C1
la. Harringtn Pk 478 C2
la. Waterloo 19 G14
la. Kogarah, off Kensington St 433 B5
mw. Waterloo 19 H14
rd. Kensington 376 D13
rd. Summer Hill 373 D2
st. Chippendale 19 C1
st. Kogarah 433 B5
st. Punchbowl 400 B9
st. Waterloo 19 H14

KENSINGTON PARK
rd. Schofields 183 B13

KENT
av. Croydon Pk 371 K6
av. Roselands 400 J7
la. Newtown 17 D11
la. Newtown 17 E16
la. Turramurra 223 E10
pl. Beverly Hills 430 J1
pl. Bossley Park 333 H11
pl. Colyton 270 E4
pl. Heathcote 518 D11
rd. Clarmnt Ms 268 J9
rd. Marsfield 282 B6
rd. Mascot 404 K3
rd. Mascot 405 A1
rd. Narellan Vale 478 H16
rd. North Ryde 282 B6
rd. Orchard Hills 268 J9
rd. Rose Bay 347 K11
rd. Tahmoor 566 F7
rd. Turramurra 223 E9
st. Baulkham Hl 247 C7
st. Belmore 401 E1
st. Blacktown 244 D13
st. Collaroy 229 A14
st. Epping 250 H12
st. Glenbrook 234 B14
st. Hamondvle 396 G14
st. Millers Point A C1
st. Millers Point 1 D10
st. Minto 482 G3
st. Newtown 17 D16
st. Regents Pk 339 B16
st. Rockdale 403 E14
st. Sydney C D2
st. Sydney 3 E2
st. Waverley 377 H10
st. Winmalee 172 H14

KENTHURST
pl. Chester Hill 368 B5
rd. Dural 188 E11
rd. Kenthurst 188 B1
rd. Kenthurst 188 E11
rd. St Ives 224 A10

KENTIA
ct. Stanhpe Gdn 215 C9
pde. Cherrybrook 219 F7
pl. Alfords Point 429 B13

KENTUCKY
dr. Glossodia 58 K8
rd. Riverwood 400 A12

KENTVILLE
av. Annandale 11 B7
la. Annandale 11 B7

KENTWELL
av. Castle Hill 218 A14
av. Concord 341 H7
av. Thornleigh 220 J10
dr. S Windsor 151 A7
rd. Allambie Ht 257 G16
rd. North Manly 258 A16
st. Baulkham Hl 247 E12

KENTWOOD
pl. Narellan 478 G11

KENWARD
av. Chester Hill 338 A14

KENWICK
la. Beecroft 250 D7

KENWOOD
rd. Wedderburn 540 B11

KENWORTHY
st. Rydalmere 279 E14

KENWYN
cl. St Ives 224 J8
st. Bonnyrigg Ht 362 K7
st. Hurstville 432 D4

KENYON
cr. Doonside 243 D6
la. Fairfield 336 E12
rd. Bexley 432 D2
st. Fairfield 336 D12

KENYONS
rd. Merrylnds W 307 A13

KEON
pl. Quakers Hill 214 F11

KEPOS
la. Redfern 20 A11
st. Redfern 20 A11

KEPPEL
av. Concord 341 H8
av. Riverwood 400 A16
cct. Hinchinbrk 362 K14
rd. Ryde 282 E12
st. Kings Lngly 245 E6

KERELA
av. Wahroonga 221 H16

KEREMA
pl. Glenfield 424 C13

KERILEE
ct. Bella Vista 246 H1

KERIN
av. Five Dock 342 K7

KERLE
cr. Castle Hill 218 J14

KERR
av. Bundeena 523 G8
cl. Narraweena 258 D3
cr. Pagewood 406 G7
pde. Auburn 339 E3
rd. Ingleburn 453 D3
st. Appin 568 F10
st. Hornsby 191 E11

KERRABEE
ct. Engadine 488 K10

KERRAN
cl. Cambrdg Pk 238 A11
la. Cambrdg Pk, off Kerran Cl 238 A11

KERRAWAH
av. St Ives 223 K7

KERRIBEE
pl. Carlingford 249 H10

KERRIDGE
pl. Forest Lodge 18 A1

KERRIE
av. Regents Pk 369 A3
cr. Panania 397 K16
cr. Peakhurst 430 B4
pl. Hornsby 191 J9
rd. Oatlands 278 J12
st. Woodpark 306 H16

KERRINEA
rd. Sefton 368 F3

KERRS
rd. Berala 339 F10
rd. Castle Hill 247 J1
rd. Lidcombe 339 F10
rd. Mt Vernon 330 G12

KERRUISH
av. Homebsh W 340 G8

KERRY
av. Epping 250 F11
av. Springwood 202 A5
cl. Beacon Hill 257 H5
cr. Roselands 401 C8
pl. Oakdale 500 D13
rd. Blacktown 243 J16
rd. Schofields 212 K4

KERSLAKE
av. Regents Pk 369 C3
gr. Menai 458 H15

KERSTIN
st. Quakers Hill 213 H9

KERULORI
cl. Hornsby Ht 161 H12

KERWICK
ct. Baulkham Hl 247 B3

KERWIN
cir. Hebersham 241 F1

KERYN
pl. Cabramatta 365 E10

KESAWAI
pl. Holsworthy 426 D2

KESSELL
av. Homebsh W 340 H10

KESTER
cr. Oakhurst 241 K3

KESTON
av. Mosman 317 A8
la. Mosman, off Keston Av 317 A8

KESTREL
av. Hinchinbrk 393 B3
cr. Erskine Park 270 K13
la. St Clair, off Kestrel Cr 270 K13
pl. Bnkstn Aprt 397 J1
pl. Ingleburn 453 G5
pl. Woronora Ht 489 C5
wy. Yarramundi 145 C6

KESWICK
av. Castle Hill 247 K5
st. Dee Why 259 A8
st. Georges Hall 367 H14

KETHEL
rd. Cheltenham 250 J7

KETTLE
la. Ultimo 12 H15
st. Redfern 19 H9

KEVIN
av. Avalon 140 A14
av. Scotland I 168 J3
pl. Thirlmere 565 A2
st. Wentwthvle 277 D10

KEVIN COOMBS
av. Homebush B M B9
av. Homebush B 310 E14

KEW
cl. Belrose 225 K13
pl. Dharruk 241 B7
pl. St Johns Pk 364 G3
wy. Airds 511 H16

KEW GARDENS
ct. Wattle Grove 426 A3

KEWIN
av. Mt Pritchard 364 D8

KEWOL
pl. Port Hacking 522 J2

KEY
ct. Baulkham Hl 246 J12

KEYNE
st. Prospect 275 A12

KEYPORT
cr. Glendenning 242 G4

KEYS
cl. Westleigh 220 J1
pde. Milperra 397 B9
pl. Liverpool 394 K4

KEYSOR
pl. Milperra 397 G9
rd. Pagewood 406 G7

KEYWORTH
dr. Blacktown 275 A7

KHANCOBAN
st. Heckenberg 363 K13

KHARTOUM
av. Gordon 253 J7
la. Gordon 253 J8
rd. Mcquarie Pk 282 G3

KIA
pl. Ambarvale 511 B13

KIAH
cl. Bayview 168 J16
cl. Hornsby Ht 191 G4
pl. Baulkham Hl 247 A5
pl. Bonnyrigg 364 B9
pl. Greystanes 306 B7
pl. Miranda 491 H5

KIAKA
cr. Jamisontown 266 D6

KIALBA
rd. Campbelltwn 481 H16

KIAMA
cl. Terrey Hills 196 E6
pl. Emu Plains 234 K9
st. Greystanes 305 J2
st. Miranda 462 B15
st. Padstow 429 F3
st. Prestons 392 K14

KIAMALA
cr. Killara 254 C14

KIANDRA
cl. Terrey Hills 196 E5
pl. Heckenberg 364 A15
pl. Wakeley 334 F14

KIANGA
cl. Prestons 422 J1

KIAORA
la. Double Bay 14 D10
rd. Double Bay 14 E10

KIARA
cl. Bangor 459 H14
cl. N Sydney 6 C11
st. Marayong 244 C2

KIARELLAS
dr. Lane Cove W, off Whitfield Av 283 F12

KIATA
cr. Doonside 243 H14

KIBAH
st. Busby 363 J13

KIBBLE
pl. Narellan 478 C8

KIBER
dr. Glenmore Pk 266 E11
dr. Glenmore Pk 266 C12

KIBO
rd. Regents Pk 339 C16

KIDD
cl. Bidwill 211 G16
ct. Currans Hill 479 H13
pl. Minto 453 B14
st. Richmond 119 K5

KIDMAN
la. Paddington 4 H15
st. Blaxland 233 H13
st. Coogee 377 F16

KIDMANS
tce. Woolmloo, off Junction La 4 E5

KIDNER
cl. Castle Hill 218 J13

KIERANS
pl. Duffys Frst 194 G7

KIEREN
dr. Blacktown 273 G5

KIEREN PERKINS
av. Newington M A15
av. Newington 310 A14

KIEV
st. Merrylands 307 C11

KIEWA
cl. Bayview 168 J16
pl. Kirrawee 460 K15
rd. St Marys 239 H3

KIEWARRA
st. Kingsgrove 401 F7

KIHILLA
rd. Auburn 309 C16
st. Fairfield Ht 335 H9

KIKORI
cr. Whalan 241 A9
pl. Glenfield 424 F10

KILBORN
pl. Menai 458 G12

KILBRIDE
av. Dharruk 241 C5
st. Hurlstone Pk 372 H13

KILBURN
cl. Beacon Hill 257 K9

KILBY
pl. Illawong 459 J6

KILCARN
pl. Wakeley 334 G14

KILDARE
gr. Killarney Ht 286 D2
la. Coogee, off Beach St 377 J14
rd. Blacktown 244 B16
rd. Doonside 243 D14

KILGOUR
ct. Glen Alpine 510 F9

KILIAN
st. Winston Hills 246 J16

KILKEE
av. Kingsgrove 402 B6

KILKENNY
av. Killarney Ht 256 B14
av. Smithfield 335 E2
rd. S Penrith 266 K2

KILLALA
av. Killarney Ht 255 J13

KILLALOE
av. Pennant Hills 250 C1

KILLANOOLA
st. Villawood 367 G4

KILLARA
av. Killara 254 A14
av. Kingsgrove 402 B6
av. Panania 398 A15
av. Riverwood 400 A14
cr. Winmalee 173 F4
pl. Dharruk 241 C7

KILLARNEY
av. Blacktown 274 A1
av. Glenmore Pk 266 H8
cl. Castle Hill 248 E2
ct. McGraths Hl 121 J11
dr. Killarney Ht 256 A15
la. Mosman, off Killarney St 317 B4
st. Mosman 317 A3

KILLAWARRA
pl. Wahroonga 222 E2
rd. Duffys Frst 195 A6

KILLEATON
st. St Ives 223 H10

KILLEEN
st. Auburn 338 H8
st. Balmain 8 D9
st. Balmain East 8 D9
st. Wentwthvle 307 B2

KILLINGER
av. Liverpool 394 J1

KILLOOLA
st. Concord W 311 D13

KILLURAN
av. Emu Heights 234 K5

KILLYLEA
wy. Wentwthvle 277 E11

KILMARNOCK
rd. Engadine 488 J10

KILMINSTER
la. Woollahra 22 B2

KILMOREY
st. Busby 363 G15

KILMORY
pl. Mt Krng-gai 162 K14

KILN
pl. Woodcroft 243 F9

KILNER
la. Camperdwn 17 B4

KILPA
pl. St Ives 254 A3
KIM
av. Regents Pk 369 A3
cl. Cabramatta 365 E11
cl. Thirlmere 564 J4
pl. Ingleburn 453 E12
pl. Quakers Hill 214 E16
pl. Toongabbie 276 G9
st. Gladesville 312 K3
KIMBA
cl. Westleigh 220 G6
KIMBAR
pl. Yarrawarrah 489 E14
KIMBARRA
av. Baulkham Hl 248 A8
av. Camden 507 A4
cl. Berowra Ht 133 D6
rd. Pymble 252 K2
KIMBER
la. Forest Lodge 11 H16
la. Haymarket E D5
KIMBERLEY
av. Lane Cove 314 F1
cr. Fairfield W 335 F9
ct. Bella Vista 246 E8
gr. Rosebery 375 K14
la. Hurstville 431 K3
la. Windsor Dn 181 A1
pl. Gymea Bay 491 J9
rd. Carlingford 250 B13
rd. Hurstville 432 A2
st. East Killara 254 H5
st. Guildford 338 B2
st. Leumeah 482 E10
st. Merrylands 338 B2
st. Rooty Hill 241 K15
st. Vaucluse 348 F7
KIMBRIKI
rd. Ingleside 196 H11
KIMO
pl. Marayong 244 B3
st. N Balgowlah 287 F5
st. Roseville 284 B5
KIMPTON
st. Banksia 403 C12
KIMS
av. Lugarno 429 K16
KINALDY
cr. Kellyville 186 K16
KINARRA
av. Kellyville 216 F4
KINCHEGA
cr. Glenwood 215 E15
ct. Holsworthy 426 C5
ct. Wattle Grove 426 C5
pl. Bow Bowing 452 D14
KINCRAIG
ct. Castle Hill 218 D7
KINCUMBER
pl. Engadine 489 B10
rd. Bonnyrigg 363 J9
KINDEE
av. Bonnyrigg 363 K9
KINDELAN
rd. Winston Hills 246 H16
KINDER
st. Lalor Park 245 F10
KINDILAN
pl. Miranda 492 E5
KINDILEN
cl. Rouse Hill 185 D6
KING
av. Balgowlah 287 K9
la. Balmain 7 D7
la. Moorebank 395 G8
la. Newtown 374 J9
la. Randwick 377 A11
la. Waverton 5 A4
la. Wollstncraft 5 A4
la. Penrith, off King St 237 C9
la. Rockdale, off King St 403 D15
la. Marrickville, off Renwick St 373 J16
la. Mascot, off Sutherland St 405 F5
pl. Kings Lngly 245 C3
rd. Camden S 506 K11
rd. Fairfield W 335 A13
rd. Hornsby 192 A15
rd. Hornsby 192 C15
rd. Ingleside 197 J7
rd. Prairiewood 335 A8
rd. Wahroonga 222 D1
rd. Wilberforce 91 K4
sq. Bidwill 211 G15
st. Alexandria 374 H8
st. Appin 568 G11
st. Ashbury 372 F9
st. Ashfield 372 G4
st. Auburn 309 D14
st. Balmain 7 D7
st. Berowra 133 E12
st. Bondi 377 J5
st. Campbelltwn 511 G3
st. Canterbury 372 F10
st. Concord W 311 C16
st. Croydon 342 D15
st. Dundas Vy 280 C9
st. Eastlakes 405 J5
st. Enfield 371 F4
st. Glenbrook 233 J14
st. Guildford W 336 H1
st. Heathcote 518 F10
st. Hunters Hill 313 E11
st. Kogarah 433 A4
st. Maianbar 522 K9
st. Manly Vale 287 G3
st. Marrickville 374 B10
st. Mascot 405 A4
st. Mt Krng-gai 163 A13
st. Naremburn 315 G2
st. Narrabeen 229 A5
st. Newport 169 F10
st. Newtown 17 G12
st. Newtown 374 H8
st. Parramatta 307 K5
st. Penrith 237 C10
st. Randwick 376 J10
st. Riverstone 182 H6
st. Rockdale 403 D15
st. Rossmore 390 C15
st. St Marys 269 H1
st. St Peters 374 H8
st. S Hurstville 432 C10
st. Sydney C D4
st. Sydney 3 E2
st. Tahmoor 565 G11
st. Turramurra 222 H12
st. Waverton 315 D11
st. Wilberforce 91 J4
st. Wollstncraft 5 A4
st. Wollstncraft 315 D11
KINGARTH
st. Busby 363 G13
KINGDOM
pl. Kellyville 215 H4
KINGDON
pde. Long Point 454 E13
KING EDWARD
av. Bayview 169 B13
st. Croydon 342 D11
st. Pymble 253 E3
st. Rockdale 403 B15
st. Roseville 285 B5
KINGFISHER
av. Bossley Park 333 F7
av. Hinchinbrk 363 C15
cr. Grays Point 491 F14
dr. Duffys Frst 195 C1
pl. Glendenning 242 H5
pl. W Pnnant Hl 249 D6
st. Ingleburn 453 H8
wy. St Clair 270 F13
KING GEORGE
st. Lavender Bay 5 E13
st. McMahons Pt 5 E13
KING GEORGES
rd. Beverly Hills 401 A10
rd. Blakehurst 432 A9
rd. Hurstville 431 F3
rd. Penshurst 431 F3
rd. Roselands 400 K7
rd. S Hurstville 432 A9
rd. Wiley Park 400 G1
KINGHORNE
rd. Bonnyrigg Ht 363 H6
KING MAX
st. Mosman 317 C10
KINGMORE
la. Glenbrook 233 K15
KINGS
av. Roseville 284 F6
la. Btn-le-Sds 433 K4
la. Darlinghurst F K4
la. Darlinghurst 4 C10
pl. Beverly Hills 401 F15
pl. Carlingford 279 B6
pl. Kingsgrove 401 F15
rd. Btn-le-Sds 433 H3
rd. Castle Hill 217 C8
rd. Denistone E 281 G10
rd. Five Dock 342 G10
rd. Ingleburn 453 G4
rd. Vaucluse 348 G3
KINGS BAY
av. Five Dock 342 G9
KINGSBURY
la. Kingswood, off Kingsbury Pl 238 C12
pl. Jannali 460 K13
pl. Kingswood 238 C13
st. Croydon Pk 371 G6
KINGSCLARE
st. Leumeah 481 K15
st. Leumeah 482 B16
KINGSCLEAR
la. Alexandria 18 G13
rd. Alexandria 18 G13
KINGSCOTE
pl. Kingswood 267 H3
KINGSCOTT
pl. Castle Hill 218 J8
KINGS CROSS
rd. Darlinghurst 4 H8
rd. Potts Point 4 H8
rd. Rcuttrs Bay 13 A9
KINGSDALE
rd. Prestons 392 K16
KINGSFIELD
av. Glenmore Pk 266 F14
KINGSFORD
av. Eastwood 281 J6
av. Five Dock 343 A11
av. S Turramrra 251 K7
st. Blacktown 245 C7
st. Ermington 280 A14
st. Maroubra 406 G10
st. Smithfield 335 F3
KINGSGROVE
av. Bexley North 402 A9
av. Kingsgrove 402 A9
rd. Belmore 401 H3
rd. Kingsgrove 401 K9
KINGSHILL
rd. Mulgoa 295 F13
KINGSLAND
rd. Berala 339 C16
rd. Regents Pk 369 C2
rd. Strathfield 371 E1
rd.n, Bexley North 402 F9
rd.s, Bexley 402 H12
KINGSLANGLEY
rd. Greenwich 314 J6
KINGSLEA
pl. Canley Ht 335 E15
KINGSLEY
cl. S Windsor 120 H15
cl. Wahroonga 222 A9
gr. Kingswood 238 B12
la. Kingswood, off Kingsley Gr 238 C12
st. Blackett 241 B4
KINGS LYNN
ct. W Pnnant Hl 249 G5
KINGSMERE
dr. Glenwood 245 H3
KINGS PARK
cct. Five Dock 342 G9
rd. Five Dock 342 G9
KINGSTON
av. Concord 312 A15
av. Panania 428 F3
cl. W Pnnant Hl 249 A8
la. Camperdwn 17 B10
la. Newtown 17 B10
pl. Abbotsbury 363 C1
pl. Airds 511 J14
rd. Camperdwn 17 A9
rd. Mt Annan 479 G14
rd. Newtown 17 A10
st. Botany 405 E13
st. Haberfield 343 D15
KINGSVIEW
wy. Glenwood, off Citadel Pl 246 C7
KINGSWAY
Beverly Hills 401 G14
Caringbah 492 H5
Cronulla 493 J11
Dee Why 258 H4
Gymea 491 D3
Kingsgrove 401 G14
Miranda 492 C4
Woolooware 493 E9
KINGSWOOD
rd. Engadine 489 A12
rd. Orchard Hills 267 H12
KINGTON
la. Cranebrook, off Pendock Rd 207 F14
pl. Cranebrook 207 F14
st. Minchinbury 272 E8
KINGUSSIE
av. Castle Hill 218 B7
KING WILLIAM
st. Greenwich 314 K9
KINKA
rd. Duffys Frst 195 C7
rd. Terrey Hills 195 C7
KINKUNA
st. Busby 363 G13
KINLEY
pl. Baulkham Hl 247 H10
KINMONT
rd. S Penrith 267 C6
KINNANE
cr. Acacia Gdn 214 H14
KINNARD
wy. Kellyville 217 A1
KINNEAR
st. Harringtn Pk 478 D2
st. Harringtn Pk 478 F2
KINROSS
ct. Wattle Grove 426 A5
pl. Engadine 518 F4
pl. Revesby 428 G5
pl. St Andrews 452 A15
st. Riverstone 183 C9
KINROSS PATH
Winmalee 173 E12
KINSDALE
cl. Killarney Ht 255 H12
KINSEL
av. Kingsgrove 401 H14
gr. Bexley 402 J15
KINSELA
st. Illawong 460 B4
KINSELLA
ct. Kellyville 186 K16
KINSON
cr. Denistone 281 C11
KINTORE
st. Dulwich Hill 373 D10
st. Wahroonga 222 G4
KINTYRE
pl. St Andrews 481 K4
st. Cecil Hills 362 D3
KIOGLE
st. Wahroonga 221 H16
KIOLA
pl. Castle Hill 218 A11
rd. Northbridge 285 K15
st. Smithfield 336 A4
KIOLOA
wy. Merrylnds W 306 J11
KIORA
av. Mosman 317 C2
cr. Yennora 337 A9
ct. Prestons 392 H13
la. Miranda 492 A4
rd.n, Miranda 492 A4
rd.s, Miranda 491 K9
rd.s, Yowie Bay 491 K9
st. Canley Ht 365 E3
st. Canley Vale 365 E3
st. Panania 398 C16
KIOWA
pl. Bossley Park 333 K10
KIPARA
cr. Warragamba 353 G3
KIPARRA
cr. S Penrith 266 G6
st. Engadine 488 F12
st. Pymble 253 C9
KIP KEINO
av. Newington L G16
av. Newington 309 K15
KIPLING
dr. Colyton 270 J8
rd. Wetherill Pk 334 J6
KIPPARA
pl. Bradbury 511 E14
rd. Dover Ht 348 E14
KIPPAX
la. St Clair, off Kippax Pl 269 K15
pl. Menai 458 F8
pl. St Clair 269 K15
pl. Shalvey 211 A15
st. Greystanes 305 J9
st. Surry Hills F A16
st. Surry Hills 3 H16
KIPPIST
av. Minchinbury 271 B6
KIRA
av. Northmead 248 B16
KIRAWA
cl. Turramurra 222 G13
KIRBY
pl. St Ives 224 F7
st. Dundas 279 H12
st. Rydalmere 309 K3
KIRIWINA
pl. Glenfield 424 F9
KIRK
av. Guildford 338 D7
cr. Kirrawee 491 A7
pl. Carlingford 249 J16
st. Chatswood 284 J9
st. Ultimo 12 K10
KIRKBRIDE
wy. Lilyfield 10 E1
KIRKBY
pl. Miranda 492 B5
KIRKCALDY
ct. Kellyville 217 B1
KIRKETON
rd. Darlinghurst 4 G9
KIRKHAM
la. Elderslie 477 E6
la. Kirkham 477 E6
mw. Wattle Grove 425 J5
rd. Auburn 338 J12
st. Beecroft 250 F8
st. Narellan 478 E9
KIRKMAN
la. Chester Hill 337 K12
rd. Blacktown 274 D2
KIRKOSWALD
av. Mosman 317 D3
KIRK PATRICK
la. Petersham 15 J7
KIRKPATRICK
av. West Hoxton 391 J5
st. N Turramrra 193 F13
wy. Berowra Wtr 132 F2
KIRKSTONE
rd. Collaroy Plat 228 D12
KIRKTON
pl. Edensor Pk 333 F16
KIRKWOOD
av. N Epping 251 C10
ct. Castle Hill 248 J2
rd. Cronulla 494 B7
st. Seaforth 286 K2
KIRRA
pl. Wilberforce 91 K1
rd. Allambie Ht 257 F12
KIRRANG
av. Villawood 367 B2
st. Beverly Hills 401 C11
st. Cromer 227 K16
st. Wareemba 343 A6
KIRRAWEE
av. Kirrawee 490 K6
KIRRIBILLI
av. Kirribilli 2 B1
KIRRIFORD
wy. Carlingford 249 J10
KIRRILY
pl. Bass Hill 367 F7
wy. Castle Hill 248 G3
KIRSTY
cr. Hassall Gr 212 B14
KISDON
cr. Prospect 274 J12
KISSING POINT
rd. Dundas 279 A14
rd. Dundas 280 A12
rd. Dundas Vy 279 A14
rd. Ermington 280 C12
rd. N Parramatta 279 A14
rd. Oatlands 279 A14
rd. S Turramrra 252 B9
rd. Turramurra 222 G16
KISTA DAN
av. Tregear 240 D5
KIT
pl. Rooty Hill 272 B5

rd. Kurrajong 85 E1
rd. Lurnea 394 E14
rd. N St Marys 240 A13
rd. Prestons 393 G13
rd. Richmond 117 K1
st. Cabramatta 365 G8
st. Cheltenham 251 A5
st. Pennant Hills 250 K4
st. Sutherland 460 E16
KURRAMATTA
pl. Cronulla 493 G12
KURRARA
st. Lansvale 366 F8
KURRAWA
av. Coogee 407 H1
KURRAWONG
la. Mosman, off Warringah La 317 C3
KURREWA
pl. Kareela 461 C10
KURRI
st. Lane Cove W 284 D15
st. Loftus 489 K11
KURU
st. N Narrabeen 198 J14
KURUK
pl. Turramurra 252 E5
KURWIN
st. Engadine 488 H10
KUTA
pl. Quakers Hill 213 H9
KUTMUT
st. Glenmore Pk 266 D9
KUTTABUL
pl. Elanora Ht 198 F12
KUYORA
pl. N Narrabeen 198 G12
KWANI
pl. Narraweena 258 B2
KYALITE
st. Glenwood 245 F1
KYANITE
pl. Eagle Vale 481 G5
KYARRA
tce. Glenmore Pk 266 H12
KYD
pl. Wetherill Pk 334 G3
KYDRA
cl. Prestons 393 B16
cl. Prestons 423 B1
KYEEMA
pde. Belrose 225 H15
pl. Bow Bowing 452 C16
pl. Doonside 243 H16
st. Picton 561 D2
KYEEMAGH
av. Mascot 404 E12
KYLE
av. Glenhaven 218 D2
pde. Connells Pt 431 J14
pde. Kyle Bay 431 J15
st. Arncliffe 403 H8
KYLEANNE
pl. Dean Park 242 H1
KYLIE
av. Killara 254 B9
cr. W Pnnant Hl 249 B11
pde. Punchbowl 399 K9
pl. Camden S 507 B13
pl. Frenchs Frst 256 F8
pl. Ingleburn 453 D10
wy. Casula 424 F2
KYLIE TENNANT
cl. Glenmore Pk 265 J7
KYMEA
pl. Hebersham 241 E9
KYNASTON
av. Randwick 376 K12
KYNGDON
st. Cammeray 315 H4
KYOGLE
pl. Frenchs Frst 256 F8
pl. Grays Point 491 B14
pl. Hoxton Park 393 A6
rd. Bass Hill 367 K5
rd. Northbridge 285 K14
st. Eastlakes 405 K5
st. Maroubra 407 E12
KYONG
st. Lane Cove W 284 C16
KYRA
pl. Rooty Hill 241 J14
KYRE
cr. Emu Plains 234 K8
KYWONG
av. Castle Hill 218 B11
av. Pymble 253 F2
rd. Berowra 133 B16
rd. Elanora Ht 198 D13
st. Telopea 279 F7

L

LA BOHEME
av. Caringbah 492 D11
LABRADOR
st. Rooty Hill 272 C5
LABUAN
rd. Wattle Grove 396 B15
LACEBARK
wy. Castle Hill 248 G2
LACEY
pl. Blacktown 275 A3
st. Kogarah Bay 432 J11
st. Surry Hills 20 A2
LACHAL
av. Kogarah 433 D6
LACHLAN
av. Harringtn Pk 478 D6
av. Mcquarie Pk 282 E3
av. Sylvania Wtr 462 F10
av. West Pymble 252 H9
dr. Winston Hills 277 A2
gr. Carlingford 279 J7
pl. Berowra 133 B15
pl. Campbelltwn 511 G9
pl. Silverdale 354 B10
st. Bossley Park 333 G6
st. Liverpool 365 D16
st. Liverpool 365 F16
st. Revesby 399 A9
st. St Marys 269 C1
st. Warwck Frm 365 D16
st. Warwck Frm 365 F16
st. Waterloo 20 A14
LACK
pl. Werrington 238 F10
LACKENWOOD
cr. Galston 159 E9
LACKEY
pl. Currans Hill 479 J11
st. Fairfield 336 D14
st. Merrylands 338 B1
st. N Parramatta 278 D9
st. St Peters 374 H12
st. S Granville 338 E1
st. Summer Hill 373 C4
LACKS
pl. Blair Athol 511 A3
LACOCKE
wy. Airds 511 J15
LACROZIA
la. Darlinghurst 4 H13
LACY
pl. Mt Annan 479 H16
LADBROKE
st. Milperra 398 A8
LADBURY
av. Penrith 236 B10
LADY
ct. Stanhpe Gdn 215 D9
st. Mt Colah 191 K5
LADY ANN
wy. Narellan Vale 478 H15
LADY CARRINGTON
dr. Royal N P 520 D8
LADY CUTLER
av. Bankstown 369 G15
LADY DAVIDSON
cct. Forestville 255 K6
LADY GAME
dr. Chatswd W 283 J6
dr. Killara 253 B15
dr. Lindfield 283 G1
dr. West Pymble 253 B15
LADY JAMISON
dr. Glenmore Pk 265 F8
LADY PENRHYN
cl. Lurnea 394 B12
dr. Beacon Hill 257 G2
pl. Bligh Park 150 C4
LADY WOODWARD
pl. Miller 393 J3
LAE
pl. Allambie Ht 257 C8
pl. Glenfield 424 H10
pl. Narellan Vale 478 K10
pl. Narellan Vale 479 A10
pl. Whalan 240 K8
rd. Holsworthy 426 C3
LAGANA
pl. Wetherill Pk 334 A4
LAGGAN
av. Balmain 344 E4
LAGO
pl. St Clair 269 G15
LAGONDA
av. Killara 254 A9
dr. Ingleburn 453 H12
LAGOON
dr. Blaxland 233 H13
dr. Glenbrook 233 H13
st. Narrabeen 229 A4
LAGOON FLATS
pl. Cawdor 506 D16
LAGOON VIEW
rd. Cromer 258 D1
LAGUNA
dr. Glenmore Pk 266 E10
pl. Glen Alpine 510 A14
rd. Bilgola 169 J5
rd. Northbridge 286 F16
st. Caringbah 492 F8
st. Vaucluse 348 E5
LAING
av. Killara 254 A9
LAITOKI
rd. Terrey Hills 196 B7
LAKE
st. Collaroy Plat 228 D11
st. N Parramatta 278 F10
wy. Narellan 478 B9
LAKELAND
cct. Harringtn Pk 478 E3
rd. Cattai 94 A6
LAKEMBA
st. Belmore 371 C15
st. Lakemba 371 A16
st. Wiley Park 400 G2
LAKE PARK
rd. N Narrabeen 199 B15
LAKER
st. Blacktown 274 H6
LAKES
st. Penrith 206 G16
st. Thirlmere 564 E3
LAKESIDE
av. Monterey 433 F9
cr. North Manly 288 D3
rd. Eastwood 281 A6
rd. Narrabeen 228 K7
st. Currans Hill 479 J9
LAKESLAND
rd. Lakesland 561 A6
LAKEVIEW
cl. Baulkham Hl 216 J16
ct. Harringtn Pk 478 E4
pde. Warriewood 199 C10
pl. Glen Alpine 540 D1
LAKEWOOD
cr. Casula 395 B11
dr. Woodcroft 243 F10
LALANDA
cl. Cranebrook 207 F5
LALCHERE
st. Curl Curl 258 K12
LALICH
av. Bonnyrigg 364 A9
LALOKI
st. Seven Hills 275 H7
LALOR
cr. Engadine 488 K12
dr. Springwood 202 D11
rd. Quakers Hill 213 K13
st. Cabramatta 365 E11
st. Glenfield 424 F9
LALS
pde. Villawood 337 A16
LA MASCOTTE
av. Concord 342 C6
LAMATTINA
pl. Green Valley 362 J8
LAMB
av. Campsie 371 H10
cl. Wetherill Pk 334 F6
cr. Merrylands 337 K1
pl. Elderslie 507 H1
st. Bellevue Hill 347 F15
st. Glendenning 242 F5
st. Lilyfield 10 F4
st. Marsden Pk 182 A11
st. Oakhurst 242 C5
st. Plumpton 242 C5
LAMBE
pl. Cherrybrook 219 H13
st. West Hoxton 392 A13
LAMBERT
av. Ermington 310 B3
av. Plumpton 242 C8
cr. Baulkham Hl 246 K16
pl. Leumeah 482 C16
pl. Mt Pritchard 364 H11
rd. Bardwell Pk 402 K7
st. Cammeray 316 C5
st. Camperdwn 17 E2
st. Cremorne 316 C5
st. Erskineville 18 A15
st. West Ryde 280 G12
st. Yagoona 369 E8
LAMBETH
pl. Illawong 459 G6
rd. Schofields 183 C13
st. Panania 428 B4
st. Picnic Point 428 B8
LAMBIE
pl. Ruse 512 G8
LAMBS
rd. Artarmon 315 C1
LAMER
pl. West Hoxton 391 K12
LAMERTON
st. Oakhurst 242 A3
LAMETTE
st. Chatswood 285 B7
LAMINGTON
pl. Bow Bowing 452 C13
LAMMING
pl. St Marys 269 K7
LAMOND
dr. Turramurra 222 G13
LAMONERIE
st. Toongabbie 276 E10
LAMONT
pl. Cartwright 393 K5
pl. S Windsor 150 E2
st. Parramatta 308 D1
st. Wollstncraft 315 E7
LAMORNA
av. Beecroft 249 K10
LAMROCK
av. Bondi Beach 378 A2
av. Glossodia 60 G4
av. Russell Lea 343 D7
pl. Bondi Beach, off Lamrock Av 378 C4
st. Emu Plains 236 A7
LAMSON
pl. Greenacre 370 C6
LANA
cl. Kings Park 244 G2
LANAI
pl. Beacon Hill 257 H5
LANARK
av. Earlwood 402 H3
ct. Castle Hill 218 D8
pl. St Andrews 451 J16
LANCASHIRE
pl. Gymea 491 F3
LANCASTER
av. Beecroft 250 A3
av. Cecil Hills 362 F2
av. Melrose Pk 310 J2
av. Punchbowl 399 H6
av. St Ives 224 C14
cr. Collaroy 259 B1
cr. Kingsford 406 H5
dr. Marsfield 281 K2
la. Seaforth 286 K10
rd. Dover Ht 348 E9
st. Blacktown 274 A2
st. Ingleburn 453 A5
wy. W Pnnant Hl 248 J4
LANCASTRIAN
rd. Mascot 404 J4
LANCE
av. Blakehurst 432 E14
cr. Greystanes 306 E8
la. Millers Point A B5
LANCELEY
av. Carlingford 249 G15
pl. Abbotsbury 333 C11
pl. Artarmon 315 A3
LANCELOT
ct. Castle Hill 217 F5
st. Allawah 432 F7
st. Bankstown 399 A3
st. Blacktown 274 G8
st. Concord 341 K2
st. Condell Park 398 H3
st. Five Dock 342 H9
st. Mt Colah 162 F13
st. Punchbowl 400 A5
LANCEWOOD
rd. Dural 188 F6
LANCIA
dr. Ingleburn 453 E12
LANDAIS
la. Emu Heights, off Landais Pl 235 B3
pl. Emu Heights 235 B4
LANDENBURG
pl. Greenwich 314 K11
LANDER
av. Blacktown 244 F13
la. Darlington 18 H6
st. Darlington 18 G7
st. Leumeah 481 K16
LANDERS
rd. Lane Cove W 284 C16
st. Werrington 239 A12
LANDON
st. Fairfield E 336 K14
LANDOR
rd. Barden Rdg 488 J1
LANDRA
av. Mt Colah 192 D1
LANDS
la. Newtown 17 C9
LANDSCAPE
av. Forestville 256 C10
st. Baulkham Hl 247 F9
LANDSDOWNE
cl. Hornsby Ht 161 K8
rd. Lansdowne 367 D6
rd. Orchard Hills 268 F9
LANDY
av. Penrith 237 C3
cl. Edensor Pk 363 E3
cl. Menai 458 E13
pl. Beacon Hill 257 J8
pl. Kellyville 215 G6
rd. Lalor Park 245 D10
st. Matraville 437 C2
LANE
gr. Schofields 213 C1
pl. Minto 453 A15
st. Wentwthvle 307 A3
LANE COVE
rd. Ingleside 197 K5
rd. Mcquarie Pk 282 E9
rd. North Ryde 282 E9
rd. Ryde 282 A16
LANFORD
av. Killarney Ht 255 H12
LANG
av. Pagewood 406 B9
cr. Blackett 241 A2
pl. Glenmore Pk 265 K8
rd. Casula 394 J14
rd. Centnnial Pk 21 D11
rd. Earlwood 373 B14
rd. Kenthurst 155 K4
rd. Moore Park 20 J10
rd. S Windsor 150 G2
st. Croydon 342 F13
st. Mosman 316 J5
st. Padstow 429 B5
st. Smithfield 336 B7
st. Sydney A G12
st. Sydney 1 F14
LANGDALE
av. Revesby 399 A13
pl. Collaroy Plat 228 E10
LANGDON
av. Campbelltwn 511 G2
rd. Baulkham Hl 246 J16
rd. Winston Hills 276 J1
LANGER
av. Caringbah 492 J16
av. Dolans Bay 492 J16
st. Banksia 403 E13
LANGFORD
rd. Dural 188 G4
LANGFORD SMITH
cl. Kellyville 216 K2
LANGHAM
pl. Belrose 225 E15
LANGHOLM
ct. Kellyville 217 B3
LANGLAND
st. Wetherill Pk 334 F6

LANGLANDS
rd. Annangrove 155 J16
LANGLEE
av. Waverley 377 H6
la. Bronte, off Brown St 377 H7
LANGLEY
av. Cremorne 316 G7
av. Glenmore Pk 265 J8
la. Glenmore Pk, off Langley Av 265 J8
pl. Blackett 241 D2
pl. Richmond 117 J7
st. Darlinghurst 4 D11
wy. Rsemeadow 540 J2
LANGMEAD
rd. Silverdale 354 C12
LANGSHAW
pl. Connells Pt 431 J13
LANGSTON
pl. Epping 251 B16
LANGSWORTH
wy. Five Dock 342 K11
LANGTRY
av. Auburn 339 B4
LANHAMS
rd. Wedderburn 541 F15
rd. Winston Hills 277 B2
LANSBURY
st. Edensor Pk 363 F3
LANSDOWNE
cr. Oatley 430 J14
la. Surry Hills 20 A4
pde. Oatley 430 H14
rd. Brownlow Hl 475 E10
rd. Canley Vale 366 C4
st. Arncliffe 403 A10
st. Concord 342 A9
st. Eastwood 281 D6
st. Greenwich 314 K6
st. Merrylands 337 J1
st. Parramatta 307 H6
st. Parramatta 308 B6
st. Penshurst 431 E7
st. Surry Hills 20 A5
LANTANA
av. Collaroy Plat 228 F9
dr. Faulconbdg 171 E13
rd. Engadine 488 H14
st. Mcquarie Fd 454 D4
LANYON
ct. Wattle Grove 426 A2
pl. Newport 169 D10
LA PEROUSE
st. Fairlight 288 B8
LAPIS
cr. Bardwell Vy 403 A9
LAPISH
av. Ashfield 372 G3
LAPSTONE
cr. Blaxland 233 G12
pl. Leonay 265 A3
LAPWING
wy. Plumpton, off Sanctuary Park Dr 242 A10
LARA
cl. Illawong 459 H4
pl. Frenchs Frst 256 E1
LARAPINTA
cr. St Helens Pk 541 H1
cr. St Helens Pk 541 H3
pl. Glenhaven 187 D14
LARBERT
av. Wahroonga 222 J8
pl. Prestons 392 J13
LARCHMONT
av. East Killara 254 F9
pl. W Pnnant Hl 249 H9
LARCOMBE
st. Regents Pk 369 D1
LARIEN
cr. Birrong 369 A7
cr. Yagoona 369 A7
LARISA LATYNINA
wk. Newington L H12
LARISSA
av. W Pnnant Hl 249 G3
rd. Allambie Ht 257 C9
LARK
pl. Green Valley 363 E11
pl. Greystanes 306 C3
pl. Ingleburn 453 H8
pl. Wallacia 324 K13
st. Belmore 371 G15
LARKARD
st. North Ryde 282 H7
LARKEN
av. Baulkham Hl 247 A14
LARKHALL
av. Earlwood 402 H3
la. Earlwood, off Larkhall Av 402 H3
LARKHILL
av. Riverwood 400 D16
LARKIN
la. Roseville 284 G5
pl. Camden 477 B15
st. Camperdwn 17 H1
st. Riverwood 400 E11
st. Roseville 284 G5
st. Tahmoor 565 J12
st. Waverton 315 E13
LARKSPUR
pl. Heathcote 518 E9
LARKVIEW
av. Chester Hill 337 K14
LARMER
pl. Narraweena 258 D2
LARNACH
pl. Elderslie 477 G15
LARNE
pl. Killarney Ht 255 K14
LARNOCK
av. Pymble 253 J2
LARNOOK
cl. Oatlands 279 B14
LAROOL
av. Lindfield 284 B4
av. Oatley 431 B13
cr. Castle Hill 218 B13
cr. Thornleigh 221 A8
pl. Engadine 489 A12
rd. Terrey Hills 196 A9
LAROSE
av. Matraville 437 A2
LAROW
pl. Bonnyrigg 364 A10
LARRA
cr. North Rocks 248 F12
ct. Wattle Grove 425 J2
pl. Dundas Vy 279 J8
pl. Glen Alpine 510 C16
st. Yennora 337 B9
LARRY
pl. Annangrove 155 F2
LASA
st. Cabramatta 366 C8
LASBURN
cr. Carlingford 279 G2
LASCELLES
av. Greenacre 370 E14
la. Greenacre 370 E14
rd.n, Narraweena 258 A4
rd.s, Narraweena 258 A6
st. Cecil Hills 362 G8
LASSETER
av. Chifley 437 A7
LASSETTER
pl. Ruse 512 F2
LASSWADE
st. Ashbury 372 E8
LATAN
wy. Stanhpe Gdn 215 B10
LATHAM
pl. Canley Vale 366 D6
tce. Newington L H12
tce. Newington 310 C11
LATIMER
rd. Bellevue Hill 347 J14
LATINA
cct. Prestons 393 F13
LATONA
av. Vineyard 152 E6
la. Pymble 252 K7
st. Pymble 252 K8
st. Winston Hills 277 B1
LA TROBE
cl. Barden Rdg 488 H1
LATTY
st. Fairfield 336 F15
LATVIA
av. Greenacre 370 D8
LAUDER
st. Doonside 243 E6
LAUDERDALE
av. Fairlight 288 A9
st. West Hoxton 392 F7
LAUMA
av. Greenacre 370 A9
LAUNCELOT
av. Croydon Pk 371 J7
LAUNDESS
av. Panania 398 B14
LAURA
cl. Bargo 567 C5
pl. St Clair 270 J12
st. Gladesville 313 B3
st. Merrylands 307 E7
st. Mount Druitt 241 C10
st. Newtown 374 G10
st. Seaforth 287 A12
LAURANTUS
swy. Liverpool 395 D3
LAUREL
av. Turramurra 222 H12
ch. Forestville 255 G10
cl. Hornsby 191 H10
cr. Revesby 399 A11
gr. Menai 458 K13
pl. Lalor Park 245 B10
pl. Liverpool 394 J9
pl. Mcquarie Fd 454 G1
rd.e, Ingleside 198 C6
rd.w, Ingleside 198 B4
st. Carramar 366 J3
st. N Willghby 285 D11
st. Willoughby 285 D11
LAUREN
av. Castle Hill 248 C2
pl. Cherrybrook 220 A3
pl. Plumpton 241 G9
LAURENCE
av. Bundeena 523 H9
av. Turramurra 222 K10
rd. Londonderry 149 C13
st. Greystanes 306 D7
st. Manly 288 D10
st. Pennant Hills 220 D14
st. Richmond 118 D9
st. Sans Souci 433 D15
LAURIE
rd. Dural 189 J8
rd. Manly Vale 288 B5
LAURIETON
rd. Hoxton Park 392 H10
LAURINA
av. Earlwood 372 H16
av. Engadine 489 B16
LAURISTON
pl. Glen Alpine 510 F10
pl. St Clair 270 G14
LAVARACK
st. Ryde 282 C12
LAVENDER
av. Bexley 402 D16
av. Punchbowl 399 H4
cl. Casula 423 J2
cl. Glenmore Pk 265 H9
cr. Lavender Bay K C15
cr. Lavender Bay 5 F12
pl. Alfords Point 459 A1
pl. Blacktown 245 B9
pl. Fairfield W 335 B10
pl. St Helens Pk 541 A8
st. Five Dock 342 H11
st. Lavender Bay K C14
st. Lavender Bay 5 F11
st. McMahons Pt K C14
st. McMahons Pt 5 F11
st. Milsons Pt K C14
st. Milsons Pt 5 F11
st. Narellan 478 F13
st. N Sydney K C14
LAVER
av. Menai 458 G7
pl. Greystanes 305 K11
st. Shalvey 210 K13
LAVERACK
cr. S Granville 338 G4
LAVIN
cr. Wrrngtn Cty 238 E7
LAVINGTON
av. Chipping Ntn 366 E15
pwy. Chipping Ntn, off Lavington Pwy 366 E14
st. Yagoona 368 J8
LAVINIA
pl. Ambarvale 511 B13
st. Merrylands 338 C2
st. Riverstone 183 B10
st. Seven Hills 275 H9
st. S Granville 338 C2
LA'VISTA
gr. Castle Hill 217 C6
LAVONI
st. Mosman 317 D5
LAW
cr. Tregear 240 C3
st. North Rocks 279 A3
LAWFORD
st. Fairfield W 335 F11
st. Greenacre 370 F4
LAWLER
st. Panania 428 B6
LAWLEY
cr. Pymble 252 J3
st. Bossley Park 334 C7
LAWN
av. Bradbury 511 D9
av. Campsie 402 B3
av. Lane Cove W 313 K1
LAWNDALE
av. North Rocks 249 A15
LAWRENCE
cr. Lucas Ht 487 H12
la. Alexandria 18 H16
rd. Kenthurst 157 D3
st. Alexandria 18 H16
st. Chatswood 285 C8
st. Fairfield 336 D7
st. Harbord 288 F1
st. Peakhurst 430 C2
st. Seven Hills 275 G8
st. West Ryde 280 G11
LAWRENCE HARGRAVE
rd. Warwck Frm 365 E14
LAWRY
pl. Shalvey 211 B14
st. Greystanes 306 A9
LAWS
la. Strathfield S 371 C6
LAWSON
av. Camden S 506 K13
av. Marrickville 15 F16
la. Bondi Jctn 22 E9
la. Naremburn 315 E4
la. Paddington 13 D12
pde. St Ives 224 D12
pl. Barden Rdg 488 G1
pl. Castle Hill 218 A9
pl. Cherrybrook 220 B12
pl. Manly 288 F8
rd. Badgerys Ck 329 C16
rd. Ingleburn 423 A9
rd. Springwood 202 C2
sq. Redfern 19 B7
st. Balmain 7 B9
st. Bondi Jctn 22 F9
st. Campbelltwn 512 A5
st. Eastwood 280 F9
st. Emu Plains 235 F10
st. Ermington 310 B2
st. Eveleigh 19 A7
st. Fairfield 336 E14
st. Lalor Park 245 B11
st. Matraville 437 B1
st. Paddington 13 B12
st. Panania 398 A13
st. Penrith 236 K10
st. Redfern 19 A7
st. Sans Souci 463 A4
LAWTON
pl. Oakhurst 242 A4
LAYBUTT
rd. Lalor Park 245 F10
LAYCOCK
av. Cronulla 493 K13
pl. Bonnyrigg 364 C6
rd. Hurstville Gr 431 F6
rd. Penshurst 431 F6
st. Bexley North 402 C11
st. Cranebrook 207 A13
st. Mascot 405 B2
st. Neutral Bay 6 D1
LAYDEN
av. Engadine 518 H4
LAYTON
av. Blaxland 233 H7
ct. Harrington Pk 478 F1
st. Camperdwn 17 E2
st. Wentwthvle 276 H16
wy. Kellyville 185 K15
LEA
av. N Willghby 285 D11
av. Russell Lea 343 B7
rd. Bringelly 388 B9
st. Croydon 372 C1
st. Quakers Hill 244 A3
LEABONS
la. Seven Hills 275 B4
LEACH
rd. Guildford W 336 H4
LEACOCKS
la. Casula 424 F4
LEADENHAM
pl. Chipping Ntn 366 H16
LEADER
st. Padstow 429 B3
LEAGAY
cr. Frenchs Frst 257 B4
LEAH
av. Picnic Point 428 E6
cl. Smithfield 335 F8
LEAL
ct. Pymble 253 J3
LEAMINGTON
av. Newtown 18 B11
la. Newtown 18 B11
rd. Dundas 279 F12
LEANE
pl. Cranebrook 207 G10
LEANNE
pl. Quakers Hill 214 B15
LEAR
cl. St Clair 270 D15
pl. Rsemeadow 540 J7
LEARMONTH
av. Balgowlah 287 K8
st. Haberfield 9 A7
st. Rooty Hill 272 D3
LEAT
pl. Blacktown 244 D15
LEATHERWOOD
ct. Baulkham Hl 247 C16
LEAVESDEN
pl. Sylvania 461 K7
LEAWARRA
st. Engadine 488 G11
LEAWILL
pl. Gladesville 312 J4
LEDBURY
pl. Chipping Ntn 396 H2
LEDGER
cl. Casula 394 G15
pwy. Casula, off Ledger Cl 394 G15
rd. Merrylands 307 J8
LEE
av. Beverly Hills 401 D14
av. Ryde 311 K1
cl. Edensor Pk 333 H13
la. Sydenham, off Yelverton St 374 F15
pl. Illawong 458 K7
pl. Killarney Ht 256 D15
pl. St Ives Ch 224 B1
rd. Beacon Hill 257 H6
rd. Cherrybrook 220 B15
rd. Winmalee 173 C11
st. Chippendale E C16
st. Chippendale 3 D16
st. Condell Park 398 F3
st. Emu Plains 235 J6
st. Haymarket E C16
st. Haymarket 3 D16
st. Randwick 407 C1
st. Seven Hills 245 G14
LEE AND CLARK
rd. Kemps Ck 360 B15
LEEDER
av. Penshurst 431 G6
LEEDHAM
pl. Riverwood 400 A10
LEEDS
pl. Turramurra 222 F16
st. Merrylands 307 F10
st. Rhodes 311 E7
LEE HOLM
rd. St Marys 239 E7
LEEMING
st. Mt Krng-gai 163 A12
LEEMON
st. Condell Park 398 E3
LEES
av. Croydon Pk 371 G8
cr. Blacktown 274 J5
ct. Sydney D A4
pl. Kellyville 186 A15
rd. Kingsgrove 401 D8
LEESWOOD
ct. Wattle Grove 425 K4

LEETON
av. Coogee 377 F14
cr. Panania 398 E16
st. Merrylands 306 J10
LEGANA
st. West Hoxton 392 F6
LEGGE
st. Roselands 401 D4
LEGGO
st. Badgerys Ck 358 F6
LE HANE
plz. Caringbah 492 K14
LEHMANN
av. Glenmore Pk 265 K4
av. Liverpool 394 H1
LEHN
rd. East Hills 427 H4
LEICESTER
av. Strathfield 341 F10
pl. Miller 393 G3
sq. Blacktown 274 A3
st. Bexley 432 E1
st. Chester Hill 368 C1
st. Epping 250 E14
st. Leumeah 482 E11
st. Marrickville 374 E10
st. Narellan 478 H11
st. Wakeley 364 J1
wy. St Clair 270 F13
LEICHHARDT
av. Fairfield W 335 C9
av. Glebe 11 J7
av. Wrrngtn Cty 238 G4
cr. Sylvania 462 A12
la. Waverley, off Leichhardt St 377 G9
rd. Ingleburn 422 J14
st. Bronte 377 H9
st. Chifley 436 K6
st. Darlinghurst 4 H12
st. Glebe 11 J7
st. Horngsea Pk 392 D14
st. Lalor Park 245 D14
st. Leichhardt 10 B16
st. Ruse 512 E4
st. Waverley 377 H9
LEIGH
av. Concord 341 J8
av. Roselands 400 G10
cr. Claymore 481 D9
pl. Ashcroft 364 E15
pl. Kings Lngly 246 B9
pl. Riverwood 400 F10
pl. S Windsor 150 J2
pl. W Pnnant Hl 249 D9
st. Merrylands 307 C16
LEIGHDON
st. Bass Hill 368 D14
LEIGHTON
pl. Hornsby 192 B14
st. Rooty Hill 272 E4
LEIHA
pl. Tahmoor 565 H8
LEILA
st. Berala 339 G13
LEILANI
cl. Casula 394 F15
LEINSTER
av. Killarney Ht 256 D16
st. Paddington 21 B3
LEIST
wy. Claymore, off Duterreau Wy 481 E11
LEISURE
cl. Mcquarie Pk 282 J1
LEITCH
av. Londonderry 149 A14
LEITH
pl. St Andrews 482 A2
rd. Pennant Hills 220 E16
st. Ashbury 372 D7
st. Croydon Pk 372 D7
LEITZ
st. Liverpool 395 A1
LELAND
st. Penrith 236 F1
LELIA
av. Freemns Rch 90 D2
LE MAIRE
av. Lethbrdg Pk 240 D3
LEMAIRES
la. Glenbrook 233 G15
LE MERTON
pl. Rooty Hill 271 J2
LEMKO
pl. Penrith 236 G3
LEMM
st. Birchgrove 8 A4
LEMNOS
av. Milperra 397 D12
st. N Strathfield 341 D7
LEMON
cl. Prairiewood 334 H7
gr. Glenwood 215 E13
LEMONGRASS
pl. Cherrybrook 219 E10
LEMON GROVE
rd. Penrith 237 A9
LEMONGROVE
av. Carlingford 249 F16
LEMONGUM
pl. Alfords Point 459 C2
pl. Quakers Hill 214 A7
LEMON TREE
cl. Frenchs Frst 256 H1
LEMONWOOD
pl. Castle Hill 248 F4
LEN
cl. Plumpton 242 A11
LENA
av. Allambie Ht 257 C9
pl. Kearns 451 B16
pl. Merrylands 307 E9
pl. Tregear 240 D4
st. Granville 308 D12
st. Mt Pritchard 364 E8
st. Sandringham 463 E5
LENNA
pl. Jannali 460 H14
LENNARTZ
st. Croydon Pk 371 G7
LENNOX
pl. Barden Rdg 488 G1
pl. St Andrews 481 K1
pl. West Hoxton 392 A12
pl. Wetherill Pk 305 C16
st. Banksia 403 G14
st. Bellevue Hill 347 G16
st. Colyton 270 F6
st. Glenbrook 233 J16
st. Gordon 253 K5
st. Mosman 317 A12
st. Newtown 17 E11
st. Normanhurst 221 D8
st. Northmead 277 K5
st. Old Tngabbie 276 H11
st. Parramatta 308 B6
st. Richmond 118 H6
st. Rockdale 403 G14
LENNOX BRIDGE
Glenbrook 234 E11
LENORDS
la. Kurrajong 85 F1
LENORE
la. Erskine Park 300 C4
pl. Lidcombe 340 B6
st. Russell Lea 343 E6
LENTARA
ct. Georges Hall 367 F13
rd. Bayview 168 G12
LENTHALL
st. Kensington 376 B13
LENTHEN
la. Botany 405 H15
LENTON
av. Fairfield W 335 C12
cr. Oakhurst 241 K4
pde. Waterloo 19 F12
pl. North Rocks 248 E16
LEO
av. Lurnea 394 C9
cr. Greystanes 306 D6
pl. Erskine Park 300 G2
pl. Hebersham 241 E8
pl. Telopea 279 F7
rd. Pennant Hills 220 D16
st. Hunters Hill 313 A7
st. Mt Pritchard 364 E8
LEOFRENE
av. Marrickville 373 K14
LEON
av. Georges Hall 367 G10
av. Roselands 400 G8
pl. Ingleburn 453 J9
st. Wilberforce 91 K5
LEONARD
av. Greystanes 306 G6
av. Kingsford 406 D2
cr. Earlwood 403 B1
la. Colyton, off Leonard Pl 270 D6
pl. Bonnyrigg 363 K8
pl. Colyton 270 D5
pl. Marsfield 282 B5
st. Bankstown 399 F3
st. Blacktown 244 A12
st. Colyton 270 C5
st. Hornsby 221 H3
st. Thirlmere 565 A7
st. Waitara 221 H3
LEONARDS
wy. Kellyville 185 K16
LEONAY
pde. Leonay 235 A16
st. Sutherland 460 C16
LEONE
av. Baulkham Hl 247 B1
LEONELLO
pl. Edensor Pk 333 H14
LEONG
pl. Baulkham Hl 247 E8
LEONIE
cr. Berala 339 B14
pl. Hassall Gr 212 B15
LEONORA
av. Kingsford 406 J6
av. St Ives 224 C7
cl. Hornsby Ht 161 K12
st. Earlwood 402 F5
LEONTES
cl. Rsemeadow 540 J8
LEOPARDWOOD
pl. Mcquarie Fd 454 F1
LEOPOLD
pl. Cecil Hills 362 G5
st. Ashbury 372 E7
st. Croydon Pk 372 E7
st. Merrylands 307 J9
st. Rooty Hill 241 J14
LERIDA
av. Camden 507 B3
LERWICK
pl. St Andrews 452 A14
LES BURNETT
la. Harris Park 308 E7
LESLEY
av. Carlingford 279 D2
av. Revesby 428 H2
cl. Elanora Ht 198 F13
cr. Mortdale 430 K4
LESLIE
ct. Wrrngtn Cty 238 F6
la. Wrrngtn Cty, off Leslie Ct 238 F6
rd. Bexley 432 C1
rd. Glenbrook 234 C16
st. Bass Hill 368 B11
st. Blacktown 274 A5
st. North Ryde 282 D6
st. Roselands 401 C6
st. Tempe 374 C16
st. Winmalee 173 F6
wk. Narrabeen 228 G8
LESNIE
av. Matraville 436 K8
LES SHORE
pl. Castle Hill 218 C13
LESSING
st. Emerton 240 H7
st. Hornsby 191 K13
LESTER
pl. Abbotsford 342 K3
rd. Greystanes 306 D8
rd. Revesby 399 A13
st. Lurnea 394 F6
LESWELL
la. Woollahra 22 E4
st. Bondi Jctn 22 E5
LETHBRIDGE
av. Werrington 238 J11
st. Penrith 237 A12
st. St Marys 239 J15
LETI
pl. Marayong 244 B4
LETITIA
st. Oatley 431 B15
st. Oatley 431 C12
LETTER BOX
la. Illawong 460 C2
LEUMEAH
av. Baulkham Hl 246 J6
cl. W Pnnant Hl 220 A16
rd. Leumeah 482 D13
st. Cronulla 493 H16
LEUNA
av. Wahroonga 251 H3
LEURA
cl. Bossley Park 333 E13
pl. Prospect 275 C11
rd. Auburn 338 K8
rd. Double Bay 14 E10
LEVEL CROSSING
rd. Vineyard 151 J9
LEVEN
pl. Northmead 278 C5
pl. St Andrews 481 K1
LEVENDALE
st. West Hoxton 392 D7
LEVER
st. Rosebery 405 F2
LEVERTON
cl. St Ives 224 E14
LE VESINET
dr. Hunters Hill 314 A14
LEVETT
av. Beverly Hills 401 A14
LEVEY
st. Arncliffe 403 K7
st. Chippendale 19 A3
LEVICK
rd. Greystanes 306 F9
st. Cremorne 316 F6
LEVUKA
st. Cabramatta 366 A8
LEVY
av. Matraville 436 H8
cl. Hamondvle 426 G1
st. Glenbrook 233 J14
st. Pendle Hill 306 F1
st. Putney 312 B7
LEWERS
cl. Abbotsbury 333 A14
LEWIN
cr. Bradbury 511 H13
cr. Chipping Ntn 396 E5
st. Blaxland 234 A5
st. Springwood 201 E2
LEWINS
la. Earlwood, off Clarke St 402 H4
st. Earlwood 402 H3
LEWIS
ct. Castle Hill 248 C4
la. N Strathfield 341 F6
la. Tahmoor 565 K12
la. Cmbrdg Gdn, off Lewis Rd 237 G5
pl. Bonnyrigg Ht 363 C5
pl. Panania 428 D4
rd. Cmbrdg Gdn 237 F5
rd. Liverpool 395 A1
st. Appin 568 E10
st. Avalon 140 C13
st. Balgowlah Ht 287 G13
st. Bexley 402 G16
st. Bradbury 511 E8
st. Cronulla 493 K14
st. Dee Why 258 E5
st. Epping 280 G1
st. Lapstone 264 G5
st. Merrylands 307 B7
st. Regents Pk 369 E3
st. Schofields 183 C15
st. S Wntwthvle 307 B7
st. Warragamba 353 G12
LEWISHAM
st. Dulwich Hill 373 E9
LEXCEN
pl. Marsfield 282 B4
LEXIA
cl. Mona Vale 199 A5
LEXINGTON
av. Eastwood 280 F6
av. St Clair 270 H13
dr. Bella Vista 216 A15
dr. Bella Vista 246 B1
la. St Clair, off Lexington Av 270 H14
pl. Maroubra 407 D13
LEYLAND
pl. Ingleburn 453 G11
LEYLANDS
pde. Belmore 401 D2
pde. Lakemba 401 D2
LEYS
av. Lilyfield 10 E11
LEYSDOWN
av. North Rocks 249 B15
LEYTE
av. Lethbrdg Pk 240 D2
LIANE TOOTH
av. Newington L H16
av. Newington, off Kieren Perkins Av 310 A14
LIBBY COSMALA
cl. Newington L H16
LIBBY KOSMALA
cl. Newington 310 C12
LIBERA
av. Padstow 399 D13
LIBERATOR
st. Raby 451 C15
wy. St Clair 270 E14
LIBERATOR GENERAL SAN MARTIN
dr. Krngai Ch NP 167 A9
LIBERTY
rd. Huntingwd 273 D11
st. Belmore 401 G3
st. Enmore 16 K13
st. Enmore 17 A12
wy. Kellyville 185 F6
wy. Old Tngabbie 277 C6
LIBRA
pl. Erskine Park 300 K2
LIBYA
cr. Allambie Ht 257 F11
pl. Marsfield 252 B13
LICHEN
pl. Westmead 307 J3
LIDBURY
st. Berala 339 B12
LIDCO
st. Arndell Park 273 F9
LIDDLE
st. N St Marys 239 J8
LIDELL
pl. Bonnyrigg Ht 363 B7
LIDO
av. N Narrabeen 228 J1
LIDWINA
pl. Cromer 228 A16
LIEGE
st. Russell Lea 343 E5
LIEUTENANT BOWEN
dr. Bowen Mtn 83 K13
rd. Bowen Mtn 83 K10
LIFFEY
pl. Woronora 460 B15
LIGAR
st. Fairfield Ht 335 H11
LIGATO
pl. Liverpool 364 J16
LIGHT BODY
wy. Narellan Vale 508 G1
LIGHTCLIFF
av. Lindfield 254 F15
LIGHT HORSE
pde. Holsworthy 426 E4
LIGHTNING
st. Raby 481 G3
LIGHTNING RIDGE
rd. Hinchinbrk 392 H3
LIGHTWOOD
st. Ambarvale 510 G15
wy. Kellyville 185 K16
LIGNITE
pl. Eagle Vale 481 E9
LIGUORI
wy. Pennant Hills 250 H2
LIGURIA
st. Maroubra 407 H7
st. S Coogee 407 H7
LIHON
st. Lane Cove W 313 G3
LILAC
pl. Eastwood 281 G7
pl. Jamisontown 266 B4
pl. Quakers Hill 213 K10
st. Loftus 490 A12
st. Punchbowl 400 D1
LILIAN
la. Campsie 371 H14
st. Campbelltwn 511 H5
st. Campsie 371 J13
LILIAN FOWLER
pl. Marrickville 374 D12

LILLA
pl. Quakers Hill....214 D12
rd. Pennant Hills..250 E2
LILLAS
pl. Minto.............482 J1
LILLE
pl. Milperra.........397 H11
LILLEY
st. St Clair...........269 G14
LILLIAN
cr. Revesby.........398 H14
rd. Annangrove....155 C1
rd. Riverwood......399 J15
st. Berala............339 F13
LILLIE
st. N Curl Curl......258 H11
LILLIHINA
av. Cromer...........258 B1
LILLI PILLI
av. Beverley Pk.....433 B8
cl. Peakhurst.......430 E4
st. Epping...........250 G15
LILLI PILLI POINT
rd. Lilli Pilli..........522 E4
LILLIS
st. Cammeray......315 K7
LILLY PILLY
ct. Kellyville, off Lilly Pilly Pl.....185 J14
pl. Kellyville.........185 J14
LILLYVICKS
cr. Ambarvale......510 J13
LILY
av. Riverwood......399 K10
ct. Glenmore Pk....265 H9
ct. Narellan Vale...479 A15
la. Allawah..........432 D5
pl. Lalor Park.......245 H13
st. Auburn...........339 B4
st. Burwood Ht....371 K4
st. Croydon Pk.....371 K4
st. Hurstville........432 D5
st. North Ryde......282 D8
st. Wetherill Pk....334 G6
LILYDALE
av. Peakhurst.......430 E5
st. Marrickville.....373 J11
LILYFIELD
cl. Catherine Fd...449 F2
rd. Lilyfield..............9 F6
rd. Rozelle............11 A3
LIMA
cl. Clarmnt Ms.....268 J1
la. Clarmnt Ms, off Lima Cl..........268 J2
pl. Erskine Park...270 H15
st. Greenacre.......370 G14
LIME
gr. Carlingford.....279 F1
st. Cabramtta W..364 J7
st. Quakers Hill....243 E3
LIME KILN
rd. Lugarno..........430 A15
LIMONITE
pl. Eagle Vale.......481 D7
LIMPOPO
cr. Seven Hills......275 F9
LINARA
cct. Glenmore Pk...265 J11
LINCLUDEN
pl. Airds..............512 C10
pl. Oatlands.........278 J10
LINCOLN
av. Castlecrag.......285 K10
av. Collaroy..........229 A16
av. Riverstone......183 C10
cl. Asquith...........191 K7
cr. Bonnet Bay.....460 F9
cr. Sydney..............4 F1
cr. Woolmloo..........4 F1
dr. Cambrdg Pk....237 J9
la. Stanmore.........16 K9
la. Cambrdg Pk, off Lincoln Dr.......238 A9
pl. Castle Hill.......218 B16
pl. Edgecliff..........14 A13
rd. Cecil Park.......331 H7
rd. Georges Hall...368 C15
rd. Horsley Pk......331 K6
rd. St Ives...........224 A10
st. Belfield...........371 G12
st. Campsie..........371 G13
st. Dulwich Hill....373 G10
st. Eastwood.......281 G3
st. Lane Cove W...313 F1
st. Miller..............393 F4
st. Minto..............482 E2
st. Stanmore.........16 J9
tce. Marsden Pk....182 B14
LIND
av. Oatlands.........279 A9
LINDA
av. Bass Hill.........367 E6
av. Oatley.............430 K8
pl. Merrylands.....308 A15
st. Belfield...........371 C10
st. Fairfield Ht.....335 G12
st. Hornsby..........191 H16
st. Seven Hills......246 A13
LINDE
rd. Glendenning...242 H4
LINDEL
pl. Lindfield..........284 B1
LINDEMAN
cr. Green Valley....363 A13
LINDEN
av. Belrose...........225 K5
av. Punchbowl......400 A5
av. Pymble...........252 K2
av. Woollahra.........22 F1
cl. Pymble...........253 A3
cr. Cranebrook.....207 D7
cr. Lugarno..........429 J12
dr. Freemns Rch....89 H4
gr. Ermington.......310 F1
la. Surry Hills...........4 D14
pl. Seven Hills.....245 H14
st. Mascot...........405 G4
st. Mount Druitt...241 B15
st. Sutherland......460 D15
st. Sutherland......490 D4
st. Toongabbie.....276 C8
wy. Castlecrag.......286 F11
LINDESAY
st. Campbelltwn...511 E6
st. Leumeah.........511 K3
LINDFIELD
av. Concord..........342 C6
av. Killara............254 C14
av. Lindfield..........254 C14
av. Winmalee.........173 E4
pl. Dean Park.......212 F16
LINDISFARNE
cr. Carlingford......279 G1
LINDLEY
av. Mcquarie Fd...424 B15
av. Narrabeen.......228 J8
sq. Bidwill............211 E15
LINDRIDGE
pl. Colyton...........270 A7
st. S Penrith.........267 A7
LINDSAY
av. Darling Point.....14 A1
av. Ermington.......310 B5
av. Smithfield.......335 E5
av. Summer Hill....373 B5
cl. Pymble...........223 E15
cr. S Penrith.........267 A5
la. Darlinghurst........4 K11
la. Mosman..........316 H8
pl. Doonside........243 D11
pl. Glossodia..........59 C6
pl. Mt Pritchard....364 J11
pl. Richmond.......118 B5
rd. Faulconbdg......171 J11
st. Baulkham Hl...247 F11
st. Burwood..........371 H2
st. Campsie.........372 C10
st. Caringbah.......492 F12
st. Neutral Bay.........6 D3
st. Panania...........398 C14
st. Phillip Bay.......436 K11
st. Rockdale..........433 F2
st. Wentwthvle......277 A14
LINDSAY GORDON
pl. Heathcote.......518 D15
LINDSELL
pl. Tahmoor.........565 G12
LINDSEY
pl. Elderslie..........507 J1
LINDUM
pl. St Johns Pk....334 F16
rd. Kurnell...........465 B16
LINDWALL
cl. Menai.............458 F9
ct. St Clair..........269 K15
la. St Clair, off Lindwall Ct......269 K15
pl. Rouse Hill.......184 K7
pl. Shalvey...........211 A15
LINEATA
pl. Glenmore Pk...265 H13
LINEY
av. Campsie..........401 K4
LINFORD
pl. Kellyville..........216 A2
LINGARD
st. Randwick........377 B13
LINGAYEN
av. Lethbrdg Pk....240 E2
LINGELLEN
st. Berowra Ht......133 A7
LINIFOLIA
mw. Wattle Grove...396 B16
LINIGEN
pl. St Ives............224 G6
LINK
rd. Bnkstn Aprt.....367 F15
rd. Hornsby..........191 G9
rd. Mascot............404 D5
rd. Mt Annan........479 E14
rd. St Ives...........224 B11
rd. Zetland...........376 A12
st. Manly Vale......287 J4
LINKMEAD
av. Clontarf...........287 E11
LINKS
av. Cabramatta.....365 C10
av. Concord..........341 G4
av. Cronulla..........494 B7
av. Milperra..........397 C10
av. Roseville.........285 C1
la. Concord..........341 G4
rd. St Marys.........239 E2
st. Glenmore Pk...266 J8
wy. Narellan.........478 B10
LINKSLEY
av. Glenhaven.......217 J5
LINKSVIEW
av. Leonay...........235 B15
pl. Comleroy.........56 B8
rd. Springwood....172 C12
LINLEE
st. Girraween.......276 B15
LINLEY
cl. Carlingford......279 B4
la. Linley Point, off Burns Bay Rd..313 G6
pl. Cecil Hills.......362 G9
pl. Linley Point.....313 G8
wy. Ryde.............312 A4
LINNE
pl. Hinchinbrk......392 K1
LINNET
pl. Quakers Hill....214 D12
st. Winmalee........173 J6
LINSLEY
st. Gladesville.......312 H10
LINTHORN
av. Croydon Pk.....371 G8
LINTHORNE
st. Guildford........338 A3
LINTHORPE
la. Newtown..........17 H12
st. Newtown..........17 J12
LINTINA
av. Tahmoor.........565 K13
LINTON
av. Revesby.........398 J14
av. West Ryde......281 G16
la. West Ryde......281 G16
st. Baulkham Hl....248 B13
LINUM
pl. Mt Annan........509 F3
st. Mcquarie Fd....454 E6
LINWOOD
av. Bexley............403 A14
st. Guildford W....336 J4
LION
la. Randwick, off Oberon St.......407 B2
st. Croydon..........372 E3
st. Randwick.........407 B2
LIONEL
av. North Ryde.....283 A12
st. Georges Hall...367 D14
st. Ingleburn........453 D7
LIONS
av. Lurnea...........394 E7
LIPARI
pl. Acacia Gdn.....214 H15
LIPSIA
pl. Carlingford......279 E2
LIPSOM
av. Bondi Jctn, off James St........377 G5
LIQUIDAMBER
dr. Narellan Vale..478 K12
LISA
cl. Narellan..........478 H12
cl. Westleigh.......220 E7
cr. Castle Hill.......217 G10
pl. Bilgola............169 F3
pl. Leonay...........234 K14
st. Quakers Hill....214 C16
LISA VALLEY
cl. Wahroonga....221 F15
LISBON
ct. Castle Hill.......247 H3
rd. Kenthurst........157 H14
st. Fairfield E.......337 B12
st. Mount Druitt...241 C12
st. Sylvania.........461 J10
LISGAR
av. Baulkham Hl...247 C6
la. Hornsby.........221 D1
rd. Hornsby.........221 D1
st. Merrylands.....338 C1
st. S Granville......338 C1
LISLE
ct. W Pnnant Hl...249 G9
st. Narrabeen......229 B1
LISMORE
av. Dee Why........258 H3
cl. Bossley Park..333 D13
st. Blacktown......274 J2
st. Eastlakes........406 A4
st. Hoxton Park....392 K7
st. Pendle Hill......276 D13
LISSON
pl. Minto............452 K14
LISTER
av. Cabramtta W..365 B7
av. Ermington......310 A3
av. Little Bay........437 G14
av. Rockdale........403 D16
av. Seaforth.........287 A5
pl. Rooty Hill.......241 J14
st. N Wahrnga.....222 H2
st. Winston Hills..277 E5
LISZT
pl. Cranebrook....207 G8
LITCHFIELD
pl. St Helens Pk...541 D4
LITERATURE
pl. Blackett..........241 C2
LITHGOW
av. Yagoona.........369 E9
st. Campbelltwn..511 F5
st. Russell Lea.....343 E6
st. St Leonards.....315 D6
st. Wollstncraft....315 D6
LITORIA
pl. Glenmore Pk..265 H13
LITTIMER
wy. Ambarvale......510 K16
LITTLE
la. Lane Cove......314 E2
pl. Whale Beach..140 C9
rd. Bankstown......369 A16
rd. Yagoona.........369 A16
st. Austral...........390 F11
st. Balmain...............7 F10
st. Cambrdg Pk...238 B7
st. Camden..........506 K3
st. Dee Why........258 E6
st. Dulwich Hill.....373 E7
st. Granville.........308 C11
st. Lane Cove......314 E2
st. Marayong.......244 A9
st. Maroubra.......407 F11
st. Mosman.........317 C5
st. Parramatta.....308 E4
st. Smithfield.......335 K3
st. Yellow Rock...174 H16
LITTLE ADA
st. Canley Vale.....366 E4
LITTLE ALBION
st. Surry Hills.........F E13
LITTLE ALFRED
st. N Sydney............5 K10
LITTLE ARTHUR
st. Balmain..............7 C8
LITTLE BAY
rd. Chifley...........437 A9
rd. Little Bay........437 A9
LITTLE BEATTIE
st. Balmain...............7 D10
LITTLE BLOOMFIELD
st. Surry Hills..........4 C14
LITTLE BOURKE
st. Surry Hills..........4 D14
LITTLEBOY
st. Kings Lngly....245 A5
LITTLE BRIGHTON
st. Petersham........15 G9
LITTLE BUCKINGHAM
st. Surry Hills........19 H4
LITTLE BURTON
st. Darlinghurst.......F K5
LITTLE BYRNE
st. Camden..........506 K3
LITTLE CHAPEL
st. St Marys.........239 H15
LITTLE CHURCH
st. Ryde..............311 K3
st. Windsor.........121 B9
LITTLE CLEVELAND
st. Redfern............20 C7
LITTLE COLLINS
st. Surry Hills........20 A2
LITTLE COMBER
st. Paddington.........4 G14
LITTLE COMMODORE
st. Newtown, off Pearl St..........374 H10
LITTLE CORMISTON
av. Concord..........341 K5
LITTLE DARLING
st. Balmain...............7 E8
LITTLE DOWLING
st. Paddington.........4 F16
LITTLE EDWARD
st. Balmain East.......8 H10
st. Pyrmont...........12 J4
LITTLE EVELEIGH
st. Eveleigh............18 K7
st. Eveleigh............19 A7
st. Redfern............19 A7
LITTLEFIELDS
rd. Luddenham....325 J1
rd. Mulgoa..........295 D16
LITTLE FOREST
rd. Lucas Ht.........487 D9
LITTLE HAY
st. Haymarket..........E D6
st. Haymarket..........3 E11
LITTLE HUNTER
st. Sydney...............A J14
LITTLE JANE
st. Penrith...........236 H9
LITTLE LLEWELLYN
st. Balmain...............7 E9
LITTLE MONTAGUE
st. Balmain...............7 E10
LITTLE MORT
st. Randwick.......376 K10
LITTLE MOUNT
st. Pyrmont...........12 G4
LITTLE NAPIER
st. Paddington.........4 F15
LITTLE NICHOLSON
st. Balmain East.......8 F9
LITTLE NORTON
la. Surry Hills..........F H16
st. Surry Hills..........F H16
st. Surry Hills..........4 B16
LITTLE OXFORD
st. Darlinghurst.......4 C12
LITTLE PIER
st. Haymarket..........E A4
LITTLE QUEEN
st. Chippendale......19 A3
st. Newtown..........18 B7
LITTLE QUEENS
la. Vaucluse.........348 B5
LITTLE REGENT
st. Chippendale........E B16
st. Chippendale........3 D16
LITTLE RILEY
st. Surry Hills..........F G13
st. Surry Hills..........F G16
st. Surry Hills..........4 A14
st. Surry Hills........20 A3
LITTLE SELWYN
st. Paddington.........4 F16
LITTLE SMITH
st. Surry Hills..........F F11

LITTLE SPRING
st. N Sydney K F6
st. N Sydney 5 G7
LITTLE STEPHEN
st. Balmain 7 H10
LITTLE STEWART
st. Paddington 21 B2
LITTLE SURREY
st. Darlinghurst 4 H10
LITTLE TARONGA
wy. Faulconbdg 171 B13
LITTLE THEODORE
st. Balmain 7 D9
LITTLETON
st. Riverwood 400 C15
LITTLE TURRIELL BAY
rd. Lilli Pilli 522 H2
rd. Port Hacking 522 H2
LITTLE WALKER
st. N Sydney K H10
st. N Sydney 5 H9
LITTLE WEST
st. Darlinghurst 4 J10
LITTLE WILLANDRA
rd. Cromer 228 A16
LITTLE WONGA
rd. Cremorne 316 F5
LITTLE WYNDHAM
st. Alexandria 19 A11
LITTLE YOUNG
st. Cremorne 316 E5
st. Redfern 19 J7
LITTON
st. Emu Heights 235 A4
LIVERPOOL
la. Darlinghurst F K3
la. Darlinghurst 4 C10
rd. Ashfield 372 C2
rd. Burwood Ht 372 C2
rd. Cabramatta 366 E8
rd. Canley Vale 366 E8
rd. Croydon 372 C2
rd. Enfield 371 A3
rd. Strathfield 371 A4
rd. Strathfield S 371 A3
rd. Summer Hill 373 B3
st. Bundeena 523 H10
st. Cabramatta 365 K10
st. Darlinghurst F C3
st. Darlinghurst 4 C10
st. Dover Ht 348 C12
st. Ingleburn 453 A6
st. Liverpool 394 G10
st. Lurnea 394 G10
st. Paddington 4 J13
st. Pitt Town 92 H14
st. Rose Bay 348 C12
st. Sydney E D1
st. Sydney 3 F9
LIVINGSTON
av. Dharruk 241 C6
LIVINGSTONE
av. Baulkham Hl 247 J14
av. Botany 405 G15
av. Ingleburn 453 C12
av. Pymble 253 A8
ct. Shanes Park 179 K16
la. Botany, off Livingstone Av 405 G15
la. Burwood, off Livingstone St 341 K15
pl. Mt Colah 162 D12
pl. Newport 169 G12
rd. Lidcombe 339 F8
rd. Marrickville 15 H16
rd. Marrickville 373 G13
rd. Petersham 15 H16
st. Burwood 341 K15
wy. Thornleigh 220 K10
LIVISTONA
la. Palm Beach 139 K1
LIVORNO
gr. Glenwood 246 A4
LIZ
pl. Ashfield 372 G2
LIZARD
cl. Green Valley 363 A12
LIZZIE WEBBER
pl. Birchgrove 7 K4
LLANBERIS
dr. Menai 459 A8
LLANDAFF
st. Bondi Jctn 377 F4
LLANDILO
av. Strathfield 341 E16
rd. Berkshire Pk 179 H5
rd. Llandilo 179 A16
LLANFOYST
st. Randwick 377 B14
LLANGOLLAN
av. Enfield 371 J5
LLANKELLY
pl. Potts Point 4 K6
LLEWELLYN
av. Villawood 367 E1
la. Marrickville 374 F9
la. Lindfield, off Llewellyn St 284 E2
st. Balmain 7 D9
st. Lindfield 284 D2
st. Marrickville 374 F9
st. Oatley 431 A15
st. Rhodes 311 E8
LLOYD
av. Cremorne 316 F4
av. Hunters Hill 313 K11
av. Yagoona 369 E9
pl. Casula 424 C4
st. Bexley 402 H11
st. Blacktown 273 J3
st. Greystanes 306 D6
st. Oatley 430 G12
st. Sans Souci 433 B13
LLOYD GEORGE
av. Concord 341 H9
av. Winston Hills 247 J16
LLOYD REES
dr. Lane Cove W 313 F1
LLOYDS
av. Carlingford 279 J4
wy. Bargo 567 A4
LOADER
av. Beverly Hills 401 A16
LOBB
cr. Beverley Pk 433 A9
LOBELIA
cr. Quakers Hill 243 F4
pl. Gymea 491 C6
st. Chatswd W 283 J11
st. Mcquarie Fd 454 B6
LOBLAY
cr. Bilgola 169 F4
LOCH
av. Centnnial Pk 21 J12
av. Penshurst 431 C2
la. Campsie 371 J14
st. Campsie 371 H13
st. Harbord 258 J15
LOCHALSH
st. St Andrews 451 K12
LOCH AWE
cr. Carlingford 250 A15
LOCHEE
av. Minto 452 G16
LOCH ETIVE
pl. Narraweena 258 A4
LOCHIEL
pl. Georges Hall 367 H14
rd. Engadine 488 H12
LOCHINVAR
pde. Carlingford 249 H14
rd. Revesby 428 G4
st. Winmalee 173 C12
LOCHINVER
pl. St Andrews 452 B15
LOCH LOMOND
cr. Burraneer 523 D4
LOCH MAREE
av. Thornleigh 221 B12
cr. Connells Pt 431 H16
pde. Concord W 311 E11
pl. Vaucluse 348 C2
st. Kingsford 407 B8
st. Maroubra 407 B8
LOCH NESS
pl. Hornsby 221 A1
LOCHNESS
pl. Engadine 488 J12
LOCHVILLE
st. Wahroonga 222 E4
st. Wahroonga 222 C4
LOCK
av. Padstow 399 F16
la. Forest Lodge 11 H16
rd. Wilberforce 61 C16
st. Blacktown 274 J7
st. Girraween 276 B15
st. Ryde 282 J15
LOCKE
st. Wetherill Pk 334 F4
LOCKER
av. Lurnea 394 C9
LOCKERBIE
rd. Thornleigh 221 C8
LOCKHART
av. Castle Hill 217 K10
av. Balmain, off Elliott St 344 E4
ct. Harringtn Pk 478 E4
pl. Belrose 226 A9
LOCKHEED
cct. St Clair 270 E16
st. Raby 481 G3
LOCKINVAR
pl. Hornsby 191 C16
LOCKLEY
pde. Roseville Ch 285 G1
LOCKSLEY
av. Merrylands 307 J14
cl. Wahroonga 221 K11
rd. Bexley 432 D2
st. Killara 254 B12
st. Woolooware 493 H7
LOCKUNDY
la. Hurstville 431 G1
LOCKWOOD
av. Frenchs Frst 255 H1
av. Greenacre 370 C5
gr. Bidwill 211 B16
st. Asquith 191 K12
st. Merrylands 307 F11
LOCKYER
av. Wrrngtn Cty 238 F6
cl. Dural 219 A3
LOCOMOTIVE
st. Eveleigh 18 G11
LODDON
cl. Bossley Park 333 G5
cr. Campbelltwn 511 J8
LODER
cr. S Windsor 150 F2
la. Punchbowl 400 A4
pl. Glen Alpine 510 B15
LODESTONE
pl. Eagle Vale 481 H6
LODGE
av. Old Tngabbie 277 C7
la. Harbord 258 J16
la. Mosman, off Rangers Av 316 G9
pl. Chester Hill 368 A4
pl. Wetherill Pk 335 A5
rd. Cremorne 316 G3
st. Balgowlah 287 J6
st. Forest Lodge 12 A15
st. Glebe 12 A15
st. Hornsby 191 J10
LODGES
rd. Elderslie 478 A16
rd. Narellan 478 D15
LODI
cl. West Hoxton 392 D5
LODORE
pl. Northmead 278 B6
LOFBERG
rd. West Pymble 253 A10
LOFTS
av. Roselands 401 D5
LOFTUS
av. Loftus 489 J13
av. Sutherland 490 B8
cr. Homebush 341 A8
la. Homebush 341 B8
la. Sydney B D10
rd. Bringelly 388 C14
rd. Darling Point 13 G7
rd. Pennant Hills 250 C1
rd. Yennora 337 A8
st. Ashfield 373 A1
st. Bundeena 524 A9
st. Campsie 371 H13
st. Campsie 371 H14
st. Concord 342 B10
st. Dulwich Hill 373 E10
st. Fairfield E 337 A14
st. Glenfield 424 H13
st. Leichhardt 9 B15
st. Marsden Pk 181 J13
st. Merrylands 308 A13
st. Narrabeen 229 B2
st. Regentville 265 F4
st. Riverstone 182 H2
st. Sydney B C11
st. Sydney 1 J13
st. Turrella 403 E5
LOFTY
cr. Bossley Park 334 B9
pl. Cranebrook 207 F9
pl. Ruse 512 F6
LOGAN
av. Haberfield 373 D1
st. Loftus 490 A11
LOGANS
pl. Quakers Hill 214 D8
LOGIE
rd. Kenthurst 186 K11
LOIRE
pl. Kearns 451 A14
LOIS
ct. Jamisontown 266 B2
la. Minto 452 F16
la. Pennant Hills 220 C15
pl. Merrylands 307 E11
st. Northmead 278 A1
LOLA
pl. Miranda 461 K16
rd. Dover Ht 348 G14
LOLITA
av. Forestville 255 E9
LOLOMA
pl. Rooty Hill 241 K13
st. Cabramatta 366 B8
LOMANDRA
cct. Castle Hill 217 D6
cr. Mt Annan 509 C2
pl. Alfords Point 429 A15
pl. S Coogee 407 E5
LOMANI
st. Busby 363 G16
LOMATIA
la. Springwood 201 K1
LOMAX
st. Epping 280 E4
LOMBARD
la. Glebe 12 A11
pl. Bella Vista 246 H2
pl. Prospect 275 C12
st. Balgowlah 287 H7
st. Fairfield 335 G13
st. Fairfield W 335 G13
st. Glebe 12 B11
st. Northmead 277 J7
LOMOND
cr. Winston Hills 277 C4
ct. Wattle Grove 395 K15
pl. Castle Hill 218 E7
st. Guildford W 336 J5
st. Wakeley 334 J12
LONACH
cl. Baulkham Hl 247 A2
LONARD
av. Wiley Park 400 J4
LONDON
ct. Cecil Hills 362 D7
la. Campsie, off London St 371 K12
pl. Grose Wold 116 B6
rd. Berala 339 E12
rd. Lidcombe 339 E12
st. Blacktown 243 K13
st. Campsie 371 K12
st. Enmore 17 A12
LONDONDERRY
dr. Killarney Ht 256 B14
rd. Londonderry 177 K12
rd. Richmond 118 E10
LONE PINE
av. Chatswd W 284 F12
av. Milperra 397 D11
pde. Matraville 407 B16
pl. N Balgowlah 287 B4
LONG
av. East Ryde 283 A14
cl. Green Valley 363 B10
cl. Menai 458 G6
st. Richmond 118 C6
st. Smithfield 305 E14
st. Strathfield 371 D3
LONG ANGLE
rd. Yellow Rock 173 F16
LONGBOW
cl. Old Tngabbie 277 E9
LONGDON
cl. S Penrith 267 D5
la. S Penrith, off Longdon Cl 267 C5
LONGDOWN
st. Newtown 17 J8
LONGFELLOW
st. Wetherill Pk 335 A6
LONGFIELD
st. Cabramatta 366 A6
LONGFORD
st. Roseville 284 C6
LONG HAI
rd. Moorebank 395 C16
LONGHURST
rd. Minto 453 A14
rd. Minto 482 J4
LONGLEAT
la. Kurmond 86 A2
rd. Kurmond 56 D16
LONGLEY
pl. Castle Hill 217 D6
wy. S Windsor 150 F2
LONGLEYS
rd. Badgerys Ck 358 B4
rd. Luddenham 357 G4
LONGPORT
st. Lewisham 15 A9
LONGREACH
pl. Bella Vista 246 G1
LONG REEF
cr. Woodbine 481 H9
LONGS
la. The Rocks A H6
LONGSTAFF
av. Chipping Ntn 396 C5
la. Chipping Ntn 396 E5
wy. Claymore 481 E11
LONG TAN
pl. Scheyville 123 D8
LONGUEVILLE
rd. Lane Cove 314 E1
LONGVIEW
rd. Mulgoa 295 J14
st. Balmain 344 E5
st. Eastwood 281 H5
st. Five Dock 342 J11
LONGWORTH
av. Eastlakes 405 K3
av. Point Piper 347 F8
cr. Castle Hill 219 A10
la. Point Piper, off Longworth Av 347 F8
LONICERA
pl. Cherrybrook 219 K14
LONSDALE
av. Berowra Ht 133 B6
av. Pymble 252 K4
pl. W Pnnant Hl 249 H5
st. Lilyfield 10 E9
st. St Marys 269 G4
LOOKES
av. Balmain East 8 G8
LOOKOUT
av. Blaxland 234 C8
av. Dee Why 259 B9
dr. Mt Pritchard 364 F14
LOOMBAH
av. E Lindfield 254 J13
av. S Penrith 266 G1
rd. Dover Ht 348 F14
st. Bilgola 169 E6
LOOP
rd. Mt Annan 479 E14
LOORANA
rd. Leumeah 482 B15
st. Roseville Ch 285 E2
LOPEZ
la. Bankstown 399 F1
LOQUAT VALLEY
rd. Bayview 168 J13
LORAINE
av. Caringbah 492 G14
LORANDO
av. Sefton 338 F16
LORANTHUS
cr. Bidwill 211 F13
LORD
av. Dundas Vy 279 K9
pl. Barden Rdg 488 F3
rd. Orchard Hills 267 D9
st. Belrose 226 D15
st. Botany 405 E9
st. Cabramtta W 364 K7
st. Haberfield 373 E2
st. Mt Colah 192 C6
st. Narellan 478 F11
st. Newtown 374 H11

st. N Sydney 5 D8
st. Rockdale 403 E15
st. Roseville 284 H4
wy. Glenwood 215 J16
LORD CASTLEREAGH
cct. Mcquarie Lk 423 E14
LORD ELDON
dr. Harringtn Pk 478 D2
LORD HOWE
dr. Green Valley 363 A11
dr. Green Valley 363 A11
dr. Hinchinbrk 363 A13
dr.n, Green Valley 363 A8
st. Dover Ht 348 F13
LORDS
av. Asquith 192 A9
rd. Leichhardt 15 B3
LORENZO
cr. Rsemeadow 540 K4
LORETTA
av. Como 460 H5
pl. Belrose 225 K14
pl. Glendenning 242 J3
LORIKEET
av. Ingleburn 453 F10
cr. Green Valley 363 D9
pl. St Clair 270 G13
wy. W Pnnant Hl 249 D7
LORING
pl. Quakers Hill 214 B11
LORKING
st. Canterbury 372 E16
LORNA
av. Blakehurst 432 C15
av. North Ryde 282 H7
la. Stanmore 16 C8
LORNE
av. Kensington 376 E13
av. Killara 253 K12
av. S Penrith 266 H2
pl. Bossley Park 333 D11
st. Girraween 276 A15
st. Prospect 274 K10
st. Summer Hill 373 C5
LOROY
cr. Frenchs Frst 255 G1
LORRAINE
av. Arncliffe 403 A10
av. Bardwell Vy 403 A10
av. Padstow Ht 429 H7
pl. Merrylnds W 307 B15
pl. Oatlands 278 J12
st. N Strathfield 341 C5
st. Peakhurst 430 E6
st. Seven Hills 245 J15
LORRINA
cl. W Pnnant Hl 249 K1
LOSCOE
st. Fairfield 336 E8
LOSTOCK
pl. Leumeah 482 E13
LOT
la. Hunters Hill 313 H10
LOTHIAN
st. Winston Hills 277 F4
LOTOS
la. Petersham 15 G8
st. Petersham 15 G8
LOTUS
cl. Baulkham Hl 246 J4
pl. Mcquarie Fd 454 D6
LOUDEN
av. Illawong 460 C3
st. Canada Bay 342 D10
LOUDON
av. Haberfield 343 D12
LOUGH
av. Guildford 337 K7
la. Guildford 337 K7
LOUGHLIN
st. Rozelle 7 C16
LOUIE
la. Revesby, off Louie St 399 C11
st. Padstow 399 B11
LOUIS
st. Granville 308 B14
st. Merrylands 308 B14
st. Redfern 19 A6
tce. Hurstville 431 K1
LOUISA
rd. Birchgrove 7 F3
st. Auburn 339 E5
st. Earlwood 402 G2
st. Oatley 431 E11
st. Summer Hill 373 B4
LOUISE
av. Baulkham Hl 247 B9
av. Chatswd W 284 A9
av. Ingleburn 453 C4
pl. Bonnyrigg 364 B5
pl. Cecil Hills 362 J4
st. Dean Park 242 H1
st. Jannali 460 G13
wy. Cherrybrook 219 C15
LOUISE SAUVAGE
pwy. Newington L H16
pwy. Newington, off Michael Jordan Av 310 B15
LOUISIANA
pl. Riverwood 400 B13
LOURDES
av. Lindfield 254 E13
LOUTH
pl. Hoxton Park 392 F7
LOVAT
av. Earlwood 372 K16
st. West Pymble 252 H11
LOVE
av. Emu Plains 235 H11
la. Guildford 337 G5
pl. Picton 563 G1
st. Blacktown 244 A10
LOVEGROVE
dr. Quakers Hill 213 H14
LOVELL
rd. Denistone E 281 E8
rd. Eastwood 281 E8
LOVERIDGE
st. Alexandria 19 A16
LOVERING
pl. Newport 169 K12
LOVES
av. Oyster Bay 461 B9
LOVETT
st. Manly Vale 288 A3
st. Thornleigh 220 J13
LOVILLE
av. Peakhurst 430 D10
av. Seven Hills 245 C15
LOVONI
st. Cabramatta 366 B10
LOW
st. Hurstville 401 H16
st. Mt Krng-gai 163 A12
st. Smithfield 336 A4
LOWAN
pl. Kellyville 216 J1
pl. Woronora Ht 489 D5
LOWANA
av. Kirrawee 491 B5
av. Merrylands 307 E10
av. Roseville 284 G2
cr. Seven Hills 246 C12
pl. Beverly Hills 401 B13
st. Villawood 367 G5
LOWANNA
av. Baulkham Hl 247 B4
dr. S Penrith 266 G7
pl. Hornsby 221 C1
st. Belrose 225 K16
st. Scotland I 168 J4
LOWE
cr. Elderslie 477 H15
rd. Bexley North 402 F9
rd. Hornsby 192 B16
st. Clovelly 378 A14
st. Merrylands 307 K15
LOWER ALMORA
st. Mosman 317 D6
LOWER AVON
st. Glebe 12 B10
LOWER BEACH
st. Balgowlah 287 H10
LOWER BLIGH
st. Northbridge 286 A14
LOWER BOYLE
st. Mosman 316 G11
LOWER CAMPBELL
st. Surry Hills F J8
LOWER CLIFF
av. Northbridge 316 A2
LOWER FORT
st. Dawes Point A F2
st. Dawes Point 1 F9
st. Millers Point A F2
st. Millers Point 1 F9
LOWER MOUNT
st. Wentwthvle 277 A13
LOWER PLATEAU
rd. Bilgola 169 E5
LOWER PUNCH
st. Mosman 317 C5
LOWER SERPENTINE
rd. Greenwich 314 J14
LOWER SPOFFORTH
wk. Cremorne, off Lower Boyle St 316 F11
LOWER ST GEORGES
cr. Drummoyne 313 K16
LOWER WASHINGTON
dr. Bonnet Bay 460 B8
dr. Bonnet Bay 460 E10
LOWER WILSONS
rd. Bardwell Vy 403 A8
LOWER WYCOMBE
rd. Neutral Bay 6 F10
LOWERY
cl. Emu Plains 234 K10
LOWES
dr. Cobbitty 416 H6
LOWING
cl. Forestville 255 K8
LOWRY
av. West Hoxton 391 G7
cr. St Ives 253 K2
pl. Prairiewood 334 K9
pl. Woronora Ht 489 B5
rd. Lalor Park 245 J10
st. Mt Lewis 370 A16
LOWTHER PARK
av. Warrawee 222 G12
LOXTON
pl. Bossley Park 333 E11
pl. Forestville 256 B6
LOXWOOD
av. Cambrdg Pk 238 C8
LOY
pl. Quakers Hill 243 K3
LOYALTY
rd. North Rocks 278 F2
sq. Balmain 7 H9
LOZANO
pl. Bossley Park 333 K10
LUCAN
pl. Minchinbury 271 K8
LUCAS
av. Malabar 437 F6
av. Moorebank 396 E8
av. Russell Lea 343 C5
cct. Kellyville 215 G4
la. Camperdwn 17 F5
rd. Burwood 342 C14
rd. East Hills 427 K5
rd. Lalor Park 245 F15
rd. Seven Hills 245 F15
st. Camperdwn 17 G5
st. Cronulla 524 A2
st. Emu Plains 235 C12
st. Guildford 337 B3
wy. Ingleburn 453 A10
LUCASVILLE
rd. Glenbrook 234 B16
LUCE
pl. St Andrews 481 K6
LUCENA
cr. Lethbrdg Pk 240 D2
LUCERNE
av. S Wntwthvle 306 K9
st. Belmore 371 B13
LUCIA
av. Baulkham Hl 247 E9
av. St Ives 224 F11
LUCIDUS
pl. Glenmore Pk 265 H14
LUCILLE
cr. Casula 394 H12
LUCINDA
av. Bass Hill 367 E7
av. Georges Hall 367 E7
av. Springwood 201 F1
av. Wahroonga 222 A11
av.s, Wahroonga 222 A13
gr. Winston Hills 277 A2
rd. Greystanes 306 G8
rd. Marsfield 282 A7
LUCIUS
pl. Rsemeadow 540 C3
st. Bondi Beach 378 B4
LUCKNOW
st. Willoughby 285 D15
LUCRETIA
av. Longueville 314 E9
rd. Seven Hills 275 E7
rd. Toongabbie 275 H10
LUCULIA
av. Baulkham Hl 247 D14
LUCY
av. Lansvale 366 K8
cl. Hornsby 191 J10
ct. Ashfield 342 H14
st. Ashfield 342 H14
st. Kingswood 237 D16
st. Merrylnds W 306 J13
LUDDENHAM
rd. Luddenham 327 H12
rd. Orchard Hills 299 C5
rd. St Clair 269 E16
LUDGATE
st. Concord 341 J5
st. Fairfield 336 D5
st. Roselands 401 A5
LUDLOW
rd. Castle Hill 218 D16
LUDMILA
cl. Carlingford 279 F3
LUDOVIC
cl. Beecroft 250 D4
LUDWIG
sq. Bidwill 211 G14
LUE
pl. Airds 512 B10
LUFF
pl. Ingleburn 453 A11
st. Botany 405 G14
LUGANO
av. Burraneer 523 E2
av. Springwood 201 F3
ct. Springwood 201 F2
LUGAR
st. Bronte 377 H9
LUGAR BRAE
av. Bronte 377 H9
LUGARD
st. Penrith 236 G2
LUGARNO
av. Leumeah 482 C15
pde. Lugarno 429 J15
pl. The Oaks 502 A12
LUKAS
av. Kenthurst 158 B16
LUKE
av. Burwood 342 C11
pl. Rooty Hill 272 B1
rd. Londonderry 178 C7
st. Hunters Hill 313 D10
LUKER
st. Elderslie 507 F2
LUKES
la. Baulkham Hl 247 D5
LUKIS
av. Richmond 119 B6
st. Richmond 119 K5
LULAND
st. Botany 405 D12
LUMEA
pl. Dharruk 241 C9
LUMEAH
av. Elanora Ht 198 D16
av. Punchbowl 400 D8
rd. Lindfield 284 C3
st. Merrylands 308 A15
LUMLEY
st. Granville 308 E12
LUMSDAINE
av. East Ryde 313 B1
dr. Harbord 288 K2
st. Picton 563 F6
LUMSDEN
st. Cammeray 316 A5
LUNA
st. Milsons Pt 5 K11
LUNAR
av. Heathcote 518 E14
LUND
st. Denistone 281 G13
LUNDY
av. Kingsgrove 402 B7
LUNN
ct. Cabramatta 365 H10
LUONGO
cl. Prestons 393 B13
LUPIN
av. Riverwood 399 K10
av. Villawood 337 B16
pl. Greystanes 306 A11
LUPTON
pl. Horngsea Pk 392 F14
pwy. Warrimoo 203 C15
LURGAN
st. Wentwthvle 277 D10
LURLINE
st. Maroubra 407 J9
LURNEA
av. Georges Hall 367 G13
cr. Forestville 255 H9
LURR
pl. Bonnyrigg 364 A7
LUSKIN
pl. Bossley Park 333 K9
LUSS
ct. Glenhaven 218 E7
LUSTY
pl. Moorebank 396 F6
st. Arncliffe 403 J5
st. Arncliffe 403 H5
LUTANA
pl. Baulkham Hl 248 B8
LUTANDA
cl. Pennant Hills 220 C15
LUTHER
rd. Winmalee 172 K12
LUTON
pl. Colyton 270 E5
pl. St Ives 224 A9
rd. Blacktown 244 K10
LUTTRELL
st. Glenmore Pk 265 J10
st. Glenmore Pk 265 K7
st. Richmond 118 D10
wy. Minto 482 K5
LUXFORD
rd. Bidwill 211 A14
rd. Emerton 240 G6
rd. Hassall Gr 241 K1
rd. Lethbrdg Pk 240 F2
rd. Londonderry 148 K5
rd. Mount Druitt 241 E14
rd. Oakhurst 241 K1
rd. Shalvey 211 A14
rd. Tregear 240 G6
rd. Whalan 240 G6
LUXOR
pde. Roseville 284 K1
LUYTEN
cl. Cranebrook 207 E6
LUZON
av. Lethbrdg Pk 240 D2
LYALL
av. Dean Park 212 K16
st. Leichhardt 9 D12
LYCETT
av. Kellyville 215 F3
LYDBROOK
st. Wentwthvle 277 D15
LYDHAM
av. Rockdale 403 A12
pl. Castle Hill 219 A10
LYDIA
pl. Hassall Gr 211 J14
LYELL
pl. Bow Bowing 452 C15
pl. Cartwright 394 A5
st. Bossley Park 334 C7
LYGON
pl. Castle Hill 217 J11
wy. Cranebrook 207 G13
LYLA
st. Narwee 400 G14
LYLE
av, Lindfield 283 K5
st. Girraween 276 A15
st. Hurstville 401 H15
st. Ryde 281 K9
LYLY
rd. Allambie Ht 257 H13
LYMERSTON
st. Tempe 404 C1
LYMINGE
rd. Croydon Pk 371 K8
LYMINGTON
st. Bexley 402 H16
LYMM
st. Belrose 225 J13
LYMOORE
av. Thornleigh 221 C9
LYN
cct. Jamisontown 266 B2

la. Jamisontown, off Lyn Cct 266 C3
pde. Prestons 394 A8
pl. Wentwthvle 277 C9

LYNBARA
av. St Ives 254 A1

LYNBRAE
av. Beecroft 250 C10

LYNCH
av. Caringbah 492 G13
av. Enmore 374 F9
av. Queens Park 22 D12
cl. Carlingford 279 G3
la. Marrickville 374 F9
rd. Faulconbdg 171 D10
rd. Glenbrook 264 B2

LYNDEL
cl. Quakers Hill 213 J9
pl. Castle Hill 218 D15

LYNDELLE
pl. Carlingford 250 C14

LYNDEN
av. Carlingford 249 H14

LYNDHURST
cr. Hunters Hill 313 H11
ct. Wattle Grove 425 J5
ct. W Pnnant Hl 249 C2
pl. Glen Alpine 510 C13
st. Gladesville 312 H4
st. Glebe 12 D11
st. Riverstone 182 D12
wy. Belrose 226 C10
wy. Cherrybrook, off Purchase Rd 219 D10

LYNDIA
st. Ingleburn 453 C10

LYNDLEY
st. Busby 363 G15

LYNDON
st. Fairfield 336 E15
wy. Beecroft 250 A4

LYNE
la. Alexandria 18 G13
rd. Cheltenham 250 K11
st. Alexandria 18 G13

LYNEHAM
pl. W Pnnant Hl 249 A8

LYNESTA
av. Bexley North 402 D10
av. Fairfield W 335 B12

LYNETTE
av. Carlingford 249 H13
cl. Hornsby Ht 191 H1
cr. S Wntwthvle 307 E5
pl. Belrose 226 A13

LYNNE
pl. Hornsby 221 F6

LYNN RIDGE
av. Gordon 253 E10

LYNROB
pl. Thornleigh 220 G11

LYNSTOCK
av. Castle Hill 218 D12

LYNTON
grn. W Pnnant Hl 249 D5

LYNVALE
cl. Lane Cove W 284 G14

LYNWEN
cr. Banksia 403 H12

LYNWOOD
av. Cromer 258 E2
av. Dee Why 258 E2
av. Doonside 243 J14
av. Killara 254 A11
av. Narraweena 258 E2
cl. Pennant Hills 220 F14
la. Blakehurst 432 C13
pl. Castle Hill 217 J9
rd. St Helens Pk 541 H3
st. Blakehurst 432 C14

LYNX
pl. Cranebrook 207 G5
pl. Quakers Hill 214 C9

LYON
av. Punchbowl 399 K7
av. S Turramrra 252 A5
cl. Killara 253 J12
pl. Cecil Hills 362 G3
st. Mascot 405 F4

LYONPARK
rd. Mcquarie Pk 282 F4

LYONS
av. Cabramatta 365 D10
la. Sydney F E4
pl. Cherrybrook 219 D9
pl. Drummoyne 343 K1
pl. St Clair 270 B10
rd. Camperdwn 17 F1
rd. Drummoyne 343 E5
rd. Five Dock 343 A8
rd. Russell Lea 343 E5
rd.w. Canada Bay 342 E7
rd.w. Five Dock 342 G8
st. Dover Ht 348 E12
st. Strathfield 341 G13
wy. Minto 482 K2
wy. Minto 483 A2

LYPTUS
wy. Plumpton 241 G9

LYRA
la. Seven Hills 246 C14
pl. Hinchinbrk 393 D4

LYREBIRD
cr. Green Valley 363 D10
cr. St Clair 269 H11
ct. Kenthurst 158 A16
la. St Clair, off Banks Dr 269 H12
pl. Ingleburn 453 F9
pl. St Ives Ch 223 K1

LYSAGHT
rd. Wedderburn 540 B16

LYSANDER
av. Rsemeadow 540 H9

LYTE
pl. Prospect 275 A12

LYTHAM
ct. Glenmore Pk 266 G8

LYTON
st. Blacktown 244 B14

LYTTON
la. Riverstone 182 D8
pl. Campbelltwn 511 K2
rd. Riverstone 182 F9
st. Cammeray 315 K7
st. Wentwthvle 307 B3

M

M2
mwy. Baulkham Hl 246 J15
mwy. Beecroft 250 A9
mwy. Carlingford 249 A13
mwy. Cheltenham 251 F12
mwy. Epping 250 A10
mwy. Mcquarie Pk 283 A5
mwy. Marsfield 251 F12
mwy. N Epping 251 F12
mwy. North Rocks 248 B14
mwy. North Ryde 283 A5

M4
Auburn 309 C12
Blacktown 273 C14
Clarmnt Ms 269 B7
Eastern Ck 272 C11
Emu Plains 235 A12
Glenbrook 234 H15
Granville 308 C8
Greystanes 306 E3
Harris Park 308 C8
Homebush 341 A7
Homebush B 340 A1
Homebsh W 340 A1
Huntingwd 273 C14
Jamisontown 265 G1
Lapstone 234 H15
Leonay 234 H15
Lidcombe 340 A1
Mays Hill 307 B4
Merrylands 307 B4
Minchinbury 271 C10
N Strathfield 341 A7
Orchard Hills 267 D8
Parramatta 308 C8
Prospect 275 B16
St Clair 270 A8
Silverwater 309 C12
S Penrith 266 D6
S Wntwthvle 307 B4

M5
Beverly Hills 400 A11
Casula 423 G5
Hamondvle 396 C12
Liverpool 393 K16
Lurnea 393 K16
Milperra 397 B14
Moorebank 396 C12
Narwee 400 A11
Padstow 399 B11
Panania 398 B12
Prestons 423 G5
Revesby 398 B12
Riverwood 400 A11

MAAS
st. Cromer 258 C1

MABEL
st. Hurstville 431 K7
st. Kingsgrove 402 B12
st. Willoughby 285 D12

McADAM
pl. Lalor Park 245 H11

McALEER
st. Leichhardt 15 D6

McALISTER
av. Cronulla 494 A13
av. Engadine 518 G3
la. Chippendale 19 A3
rd. Galston 160 D4

McANALLY
la. Randwick, off Carrington Rd 377 D16

McANDREW
cl. Lurnea 394 F12

McARDLE
st. Ermington 280 B14

MACARTHUR
av. Crows Nest 315 J7
av. Pagewood 406 C8
av. Revesby 398 J16
av. Strathfield 371 C3
cr. Westmead 307 E3
dr. Holsworthy 426 F7
dr. St Clair 270 A10
pde. Dulwich Hill 373 E11
pl. Ruse 512 G1
rd. Elderslie 477 F16
rd. Kellyville 217 D5
rd. Spring Farm 507 G5
st. Ermington 310 E1
st. Homebush B M B6
st. N Parramatta 278 G12
st. Parramatta 308 F3
st. St Ives 254 D1
st. Sylvania 462 A14
st. Ultimo 12 J13
st. Villawood 337 C15
wy. Bidwill 211 F15

McARTHUR
st. Guildford 337 J2

MACARTNEY
av. Chatswd W 284 E9
cr. Hebersham 241 E1
st. Ermington 310 D3
st. Miranda 461 K16

MACAULAY
la. Stanmore 16 G5
la.w. Stanmore 16 F5
rd. Stanmore 16 F6
st. Wetherill Pk 334 E4

MACAULEY
av. Bankstown 399 D3
st. Leichhardt 9 G14

McAULEY
cl. Heathcote 518 C15
cr. Emu Plains 235 F8
pl. Waitara 221 K5

McAULIFFE
pl. Silverdale 353 J13

MACBETH
gr. St Clair 270 C16
wy. Rsemeadow 540 K2

McBRIAN
pl. Wakeley 334 F15

McBRIDE
av. Hunters Hill 313 J10

McBRIEN
pl. Frenchs Frst 255 E4

McBURNEY
av. Mascot 405 E8
la. Kirribilli 6 D16
la. Mascot 405 E7
rd. Cabramatta 365 E5
st. Naremburn 315 H3

McCABE
cl. Prairiewood 334 K9
cl. St Clair 269 K16
la. St Clair, off McCabe Cl 269 K16
pl. Chatswood 285 F6
pl. Menai 458 F9
pl. Rouse Hill 184 K7
st. Greystanes 305 H9

McCAHONS
av. Georges Hall 367 K11

McCALL
av. Camden S 507 B14
av. Croydon Pk 371 J7

McCALLUM
av. East Ryde 313 C2
st. Roselands 401 D6

McCALLUMS
av. Berrilee 131 E9

McCANN
pl. Hassall Gr 212 B14
rd. Leppington 420 C2
rd. Rossmore 419 G1
rd. Rossmore 420 C2
rd. Yellow Rock 204 J5
wy. Minto 482 K1

McCARRS CREEK
rd. Church Point 168 C10
rd. Krngai Ch NP 166 G14
rd. Terrey Hills 196 F7

McCARTHY
la. Annandale 17 A3
la. Concord 341 J4
la. Woolmloo D K13
pl. Woolmloo 4 C7
st. Fairfield W 334 K10
st. Richmond 119 K5

McCARTHYS
la. Castlereagh 206 D11

McCARTNEY
cr. St Clair 270 A16
la. St Clair, off McCartney Cr 270 A16
pwy. Warwck Frm, off McCartney St 365 E14
st. Warwck Frm 365 E14

McCAULEY
cr. Glenbrook 234 F16
la. Alexandria 19 B16
st. Alexandria 19 A16
st. Matraville 436 E3

McCLEAN
st. Blacktown 243 J12
st. Georges Hall 367 K11

McCLEER
st. Rozelle 344 D7

McCLELLAND
st. Chester Hill 368 A5
st. N Willghby 285 G9

McCLYMONTS
rd. Kenthurst 125 C12
rd. Maraylya 125 C12

McCONVILLE
la. Beaconsfield, off Connolly La 375 G11

McCORMACK
pl. Denham Ct 452 F5
st. Arndell Park 273 E9

McCOURT
st. Wiley Park 370 H16

McCOWEN
rd. Ingleside 197 D3

McCOY
la. Btn-le-Sds 433 J2
st. Toongabbie 276 A5
st. Toongabbie 276 B4

McCRAE
dr. Camden S 506 K12
pl. Blackett 241 C3

McCREA
cl. Edensor Pk 363 G4

McCREADY
pl. Berowra 133 H11

McCREDIE
dr. Horngsea Pk 392 F13
rd. Guildford W 336 H3
rd. Smithfield 336 E3

McCROSSIN
av. Birrong 368 J7

McCUBBENS
la. Sutherland, off Old Princes Hwy 490 E3

McCUBBIN
pl. Casula 424 E2
pl. Mt Pritchard 364 J12
pl. Plumpton 242 C7
wy. Claymore 481 F10

McCULLOCH
rd. Blacktown 243 J13
st. Riverstone 183 C6
st. Russell Lea 343 E7

McCUSKER
cr. Cherrybrook 219 D11

MACDONALD
av. Lalor Park 245 G11
av. Lurnea 394 E7
cr. Bexley North 402 E11
la. Paddington 4 K13
rd. Ingleburn 423 A14
st. Erskineville 375 A9
st. Lakemba 370 J15
st. Paddington 4 K13
st. Ramsgate 433 D14
st. Sans Souci 433 D14
st. Vaucluse 348 G5

McDONALD
av. Auburn 339 B10
av. Winston Hills 277 J1
cr. Strathfield 341 G16
la. Bankstown 399 E2
la. N Sydney K F11
la. Potts Point 4 K2
pl. McGraths Hl 122 A14
pl. Rooty Hill 241 K12
st. Balmain 7 J9
st. Berala 339 E12
st. Cronulla 494 A11
st. Harbord 258 D16
st. Illawong 459 K4
st. Leichhardt 16 A1
st. Mortlake 312 A15
st. North Rocks 249 B16
st. Potts Point 4 K2
wy. Greenacre 370 G5

MACDONNELL
av. Fairfield W 335 F11

McDONNELL
st. Raby 451 C12

McDOUGALL
av. Baulkham Hl 247 F4
la. Castle Hill 218 C15
st. Kensington 376 B11
st. Milsons Pt 6 A12

MACDUFF
wy. Rsemeadow 540 K2

MACEDON
pl. Warriewood 199 C10
st. Bossley Park 334 B10

McELHONE
pl. Surry Hills 20 E2
st. Woolmloo 4 H4
st. Woolmloo 4 G7

McELIVER
wy. Minto 482 J5

McENCROE
st. Strathfield S 371 A4

MACERI
pl. Edensor Pk 333 J15

McEVOY
cl. Hamondvle 396 F14
rd. Padstow 399 F14
st. Alexandria 19 A16
st. Waterloo 19 A16

McEWAN
av. Winston Hills 277 G3
cct. Mt Annan 479 F15

McFADYEN
st. Botany 405 E13

McFALL
pl. Rooty Hill 271 K3
st. Botany 405 D12

MACFARLANE
pde. Sylvania 461 H13
st. Davidson 225 A16

McFARLANE
dr. Minchinbury 271 F8
st. Merrylands 307 G12

McGANN
pl. Cranebrook 207 E14

McGARVIE
st. Paddington 21 F2

McGEE
pl. Baulkham Hl 248 C10
pl. Fairfield W 334 K10

McGETTIGAN
la. Panania 398 E15

McGILL
pl. Menai 458 E14
st. Lewisham 15 A10

McGILVRAY
pl. Rouse Hill 184 K6

McGIRR
pde. Warwck Frm 365 F15
pl. Abbotsford 343 A3
st. Padstow 399 B16

McGOVERN
cr. Merrylnds W 307 A13

McGOVETT
pl. Menai 458 K12
McGOWAN
av. Marrickville 403 H1
st. Putney 312 C10
McGOWEN
av. Malabar 437 E5
cr. Liverpool 395 C8
McGRATH
av. Earlwood 402 F1
av. Five Dock 342 K8
pl. Currans Hill 479 H12
rd. McGraths Hl 121 K14
McGRATHS
la. Kensington 376 F11
MACGREGOR
st. Croydon 342 E14
McGREGOR
st. Kingsgrove 401 H13
st. North Ryde 282 G6
McGUIRK
wy. Rouse Hill 185 A8
McHALE
la. Sefton 338 E15
wy. Nelson 154 J13
McHATTON
pl. Hassall Gr 211 J15
st. N Sydney 5 C4
st. Waverton 5 C4
McHENRY
rd. Cranebrook 207 C14
McILVENIE
st. Canley Ht 365 C3
McILWAINS
st. Ashcroft 364 E15
McILWRAITH
st. Wetherill Pk 334 A3
MACINA
pl. St Clair 269 H13
McINNES
pl. Ingleburn 453 B11
MACINTOSH
st. Mascot 405 D4
st. Melrose Pk 310 K3
McINTOSH
av. Padstow Ht 429 G6
la. Neutral Bay 6 B1
la. Newtown 17 E12
rd. Beacon Hill 257 J4
rd. Dee Why 258 E5
rd. Narraweena 257 J4
st. Chatswood 284 H9
st. Fairfield 336 G15
st. Gordon 253 K8
st. Kings Park 244 D2
st. The Oaks 502 D12
MACINTYRE
cr. Ruse 512 C8
cr. Sylvania Wtr 462 D13
McINTYRE
av. Btn-le-Sds 403 K15
av. St Clair 269 G16
la. Gordon 253 G7
la. St Clair, off McIntyre Av 269 G16
pl. Castle Hill 217 K7
st. Gordon 253 F7
st. Oatley 430 J12
McIVER
av. West Hoxton 362 B16
pl. Maroubra 407 D14
MACK
st. Wentwthvle 306 H2
MACKANESS
cl. Five Dock 342 G8
MACKAY
pl. Leumeah 482 H12
rd. S Granville 338 G4
st. Ashfield 342 G16
st. Caringbah 492 J7
st. Emu Plains 235 C11
wy. Rouse Hill 184 J6
McKAY
av. Moorebank 396 D7
dr. Silverdale 353 H15
pl. Minchinbury 271 K7
rd. Hornsby Ht 161 E15
rd. Palm Beach 139 K4
st. Dundas Vy 280 B9
st. Toongabbie 276 G5
McKEARNS
pl. Arncliffe 403 H9
McKECHNIE
st. Epping 250 C16
McKEE
rd. Theresa Park 444 D7
st. Ultimo 12 K13
McKELL
av. Casula 394 K12
cl. Bonnyrigg 363 K6
st. Birchgrove 7 J6
MACKELLAR
cir. Springwood 202 H1
pl. Campbelltwn 512 B4
rd. Hebersham 241 E2
st. Casula 424 G3
st. Emu Plains 235 K7
McKELLAR
cr. S Windsor 150 H2
MACKEN
cl. Edensor Pk 363 E3
cr. Oatley 430 J13
st. Liverpool 365 B16
st. Oatley 430 J13
McKENDRICK
pl. Warrimoo 202 J13
McKENNY
wy. Narellan Vale 508 H1
McKENSIE
pl. McGraths Hl 121 K12
MACKENZIE
av. Glenmore Pk 265 G6
bvd. Seven Hills 275 F8
pl. Kearns 481 B2
st. Bondi Jctn 22 H9
st. Canley Vale 366 B4
st. Concord W 341 E2
st. Homebush 341 A11
st. Lavender Bay K D13
st. Lavender Bay 5 F11
st. Leichhardt 10 C14
st. Lilyfield 10 C14
st. Lindfield 254 E14
st. Revesby 399 A13
st. Rozelle 7 B16
st. Strathfield 341 A11
McKENZIE
av. Chifley 437 C10
cr. Wilberforce 62 C16
la. Earlwood 402 G3
pl. Menai 458 E9
st. Campsie 371 J16
wk. Cambrdg Pk, off Cambridge St 237 J9
McKEON
st. Maroubra 407 G11
McKEOWN
st. Prairiewood 334 H7
McKERN
st. Campsie 371 J16
st. Wentwthvle 307 A1
McKEVITTE
av. East Hills 427 J2
MACKEY
st. Surry Hills F F11
st. Surry Hills F H12
MACKEYS
st. Horngsea Pk 392 E14
McKIBBIN
st. Canley Ht 365 A2
MACKIE
la. Mosman 316 H5
MACKILLOP
cr. St Helens Pk 540 K10
dr. Baulkham Hl 247 A3
pl. Erskine Park 270 E16
McKILLOP
pl. Dundas Vy 279 J7
rd. Beacon Hill 257 K6
MACKIN
cl. Barden Rdg 488 F7
McKINLEY
av. Bonnet Bay 460 C11
pl. Cherrybrook 219 J9
MACKINNON
av. Padstow 399 B12
st. St Helens Pk 541 A9
McKINNON
av. Five Dock 343 A7
McKINNONS
rd. Wilberforce 61 C11
MACKLIN
st. Pendle Hill 276 D15
MACKS
gln. Kellyville 185 K16
MACKSVILLE
st. Hoxton Park 392 K8
McKYE
st. Waverton 315 E11
McLACHLAN
av. Artarmon 314 J1
av. Darlinghurst 13 B11
av. Rcutters Bay 13 B10
wy. Darlinghurst 13 A11
McLAREN
gr. St Clair 270 E13
pl. Ingleburn 453 J7
st. Blackett 241 B4
st. Carramar 366 K1
st. N Sydney K G1
st. N Sydney 5 E4
McLAUGHLAN
pl. Paddington 4 K15
McLAUGHLINE
cct. Bradbury 511 J9
MACLAURIN
av. East Hills 427 G4
pde. Roseville 284 G5
st. Penshurst 431 H8
MACLEAN
st. Woolmloo 4 G3
McLEAN
av. Chatswd W 284 E9
cr. Mosman 317 C1
rd. Campbelltwn 511 K4
st. Auburn 339 A3
st. Emu Plains 235 E12
st. Ingleside 198 A8
st. Liverpool 394 H1
MACLEAY
av. Wahroonga 223 C4
cr. St Marys 269 J5
ct. Harringtn Pk 478 F6
pl. Earlwood 402 F3
pl. Sylvania Wtr 462 C11
st. Bradbury 511 F13
st. Elizabeth Bay 4 K6
st. Greystanes 306 A3
st. North Bondi 348 E14
st. Potts Point 4 K6
st. Ryde 282 E13
st. S Coogee 407 G6
McLENNAN
av. Randwick 377 C11
MACLEOD
rd. Grose Wold 115 D9
McLEOD
av. Lindfield 284 H1
av. Roseville 284 H1
rd. Middle Dural 158 C1
st. Hurstville 432 B3
st. Mosman 316 H13
MAC MAHON
pl. Menai 458 H11
MACMAHON
st. Hurstville 432 A5
st. N Willghby 285 E8
McMAHON
av. Liverpool 365 A15
cl. Penrith 237 D7
gr. Glenwood 215 C14
rd. Yagoona 368 J11
McMAHONS
rd. Lane Cove 314 F6
rd. Longueville 314 F6
rd. Wilberforce 62 B1
McMAHONS PARK
rd. Kurrajong 85 C1
McMANUS
pl. Lugarno 430 A14
st. McMahons Pt 5 D15
MACMILLAN
st. Seaforth 287 A8
McMILLAN
av. Sandringham 463 E2
av. Winston Hills 277 K1
rd. Artarmon 284 K16
st. Heckenberg 364 B12
st. Yagoona 369 D9
McMINN
pl. Narellan Vale 478 G16
McMULLEN
av. Carlingford 250 A13
av. Castle Hill 218 D14
McMURDO
av. Tregear 240 F6
McNAIR
av. Kingsford 406 K3
MACNAMARA
av. Concord 341 H6
pl. Appin 568 F14
McNAMARA
av. Richmond 120 A6
rd. Cromer 227 J13
McNAMEE
pl. Kellyville 217 D1
McNAUGHTON
st. Jamisontown 236 B15
McPHEE
pl. Bligh Park 150 B5
st. Chester Hill 338 D15
MACPHERSON
rd. Londonderry 149 A8
st. Bronte 377 J10
st. Cremorne 316 G5
st. Hurstville 401 H15
st. Mosman 316 G5
st. Warriewood 198 G7
st. Waverley 377 G9
McPHERSON
av. Punchbowl 399 K5
la. Carlton 432 G9
la. Zetland, off Joynton Av 375 J9
la. Meadowbnk, off McPherson St. 311 F2
pl. Illawong 459 J3
pl. Ruse 512 H6
rd. Smeaton Gra 479 F11
st. Bnksmeadw 435 K1
st. Bnksmeadw 436 D1
st. Carlton 432 G8
st. Revesby 398 K15
st. Wakeley 334 H12
st. West Ryde 311 F2
McQUADE
av. S Windsor 120 G12
MACQUARIE
av. Camden 507 A5
av. Campbelltwn 511 J6
av. Kellyville 215 G4
av. Leumeah 512 C3
av. Penrith 237 A9
cct. Holsworthy 426 C9
dr. Cherrybrook 219 H9
la. Parramatta 308 D3
pl. Denistone E 281 J10
pl. Glossodia 59 F8
pl. Mortdale 431 B8
pl. Sydney B B11
pl. Tahmoor 565 F10
rd. Appin 568 B7
rd. Appin 568 D10
rd. Auburn 339 D1
rd. Earlwood 403 B2
rd. Greystanes 305 G11
rd. Ingleburn 453 E4
rd. Mcquarie Fd 453 D4
rd. Pymble 253 H2
rd. Rouse Hill 184 C11
rd. Springwood 201 D3
rd. Vaucluse 348 G2
rd. Wilberforce 91 K2
st. Annandale 16 D4
st. Chatswood 285 A5
st. Chifley 437 A6
st. Cromer 227 H12
st. Fairfield 336 A12
st. Greenacre 370 D13
st. Gymea 461 H16
st. Homebush B M B6
st. Leichhardt 16 D4
st. Liverpool 395 C6
st. Liverpool 395 E1
st. Parramatta 308 A3
st. Rosebery 405 J2
st. Roseville 285 A5
st. S Windsor 120 G15
st. Sydney D F5
st. Sydney 4 A3
st. Warwck Frm 365 E16
st. Windsor 121 A11
tce. Balmain 7 E6
MACQUARIE GROVE
rd. Camden 477 A11
rd. Cobbitty 447 F15
rd. Harringtn Pk 447 F15
rd. Kirkham 477 A9
MACQUARIE LINKS
dr. Glenfield 423 G12
dr. Mcquarie Lk 423 D16
MACQUEEN
pl. Mt Riverview 234 D4
McRAE
pl. N Turramrra 223 D7
rd. Sans Souci 433 G16
st. Petersham 15 H15
McRAES
av. Penshurst 431 E7
McROBERTS
st. N Parramatta 278 G10
McTAGGART
rd. N Turramrra 193 E12
MACTIER
av. Milperra 397 F12
st. Narrabeen 228 H7
st. Narrabeen 229 A8
MACULATA
cr. Mcquarie Fd 454 D2
pl. Kingswood 267 J1
McVEY
pl. Rooty Hill 241 K12
McVICARS
la. Lidcombe 339 H10
McVICKER
st. Moorebank 396 D10
MADAGASCAR
dr. Kings Park 244 F2
MADANG
av. Whalan 240 J12
pl. Glenfield 424 G14
rd. Belrose 226 B3
st. Holsworthy 426 D4
wy. Matraville 407 C16
MADDECKS
av. Moorebank 396 C8
MADDEN
la. Blacktown 245 D8
MADDENS
rd. N Richmond 87 D6
MADDISON
la. Redfern 20 C9
st. Redfern 20 C10
MADDOCK
st. Dulwich Hill 373 C7
MADDOX
st. Alexandria 375 C10
MADDY
wy. Stanhpe Gdn 215 C9
MADEIRA
av. Kings Lngly 245 D7
pl. Surry Hills 19 J2
st. Sylvania 462 B7
wy. Minto 482 K2
MADELEINE
ct. Mt Colah 162 F14
pl. Kingsford 407 C4
MADELINE
av. Northmead 278 A5
st. Belfield 371 B8
st. Fairfield 335 G14
st. Fairfield W 335 G14
st. Hunters Hill 313 H10
st. Strathfield S 371 A7
MADIGAN
dr. Wrrngtn Cty 238 F6
gr. Thirlmere 565 C4
MADISON
cct. St Clair 269 F13
la. St Clair, off Madison Cct 269 G12
pl. Bonnet Bay 460 D11
pl. Kellyville 216 C2
pl. Schofields 213 H5
MADOLINE
pl. Springwood 201 J2
MADONNA
st. Winston Hills 246 G15
MADRERS
av. Kogarah 433 D9
MADRID
pl. Glendenning 242 G3
MADSON
pl. Bonnyrigg 364 B6
MAE
cr. Panania 398 B13
MAEVE
av. Kellyville 216 J3
MAFEKING
av. Lane Cove 314 F1
MAGARRA
pl. Seaforth 287 D10
MAGDALA
rd. North Ryde 283 B12
MAGDALENE
st. St Marys 269 J1
MAGDELLA
st. Birrong 369 A5
MAGEE
la. Glenfield 424 D10

pl. Killarney Ht..... 256 D15
st. Ashcroft......... 364 F16
MAGELLAN
av. Lethbrdg Pk ... 240 G5
st. Fairfield W...... 335 D9
MAGENTA
la. Paddington......... 4 F15
MAGGA DAN
av. Tregear.......... 240 C5
MAGGIOTTO
pl. Mt Pritchard ... 364 K10
MAGIC
gr. Mosman......... 317 A11
MAGIC PUDDING
pl. Faulconbdg 171 F11
MAGILL
st. Randwick 376 K16
MAGNA
wy. Oakhurst, off
Alpin Gr.......... 242 A4
MAGNETIC
av. Hinchinbrk...... 393 A1
MAGNEY
av. Regents Pk..... 369 A3
la. Woollahra....... 377 F2
pl. Bella Vista 246 F4
st. Woollahra......... 22 G4
MAGNOLIA
av. Baulkham Hl ... 247 F14
av. Epping........... 250 E12
cl. Casula 423 K2
cl. Frenchs Frst ... 256 H1
dr. Picton 561 B3
pl. Mcquarie Fd ... 453 K6
st. Greystanes 306 C13
st. Kirrawee......... 460 J15
st. N St Marys 240 B9
MAGNUM
pl. Minto 482 E9
MAGOWAR
rd. Girraween....... 275 J13
rd. Pendle Hill...... 276 A14
MAGPIE
ct. Glenwood....... 215 E14
pl. Glenmore Pk .. 265 J12
pl. Ingleburn 453 H5
rd. Green Valley ... 363 D8
MAGRA
pl. Kings Lngly 245 C5
MAGRATH
pl. Emu Plains 235 E8
MAGREE
cr. Chipping Ntn .. 396 E5
MAGUIRES
rd. Maraylya 124 E10
MAGYAR
pl. Oakhurst 242 D2
MAHAN
wy. Minto 483 A1
MAHBUHAY
gr. Mount Druitt ... 241 D12
MAHER
cl. Beecroft.......... 249 K11
la. Hurstville, off
Maher St......... 432 A7
st. Hurstville......... 431 J8
MAHNKEN
av. Revesby 399 A13
MAHOGANY
cl. Alfords Point .. 429 C14
cl. Cranebrook 237 F1
cl. Glenwood....... 215 J16
ct. Castle Hill 218 K7
pl. Mcquarie Fd ... 454 E2
st. Prestons......... 393 H14
wy. Greenacre....... 370 F5
MAHON
ct. Ingleburn 453 A12
st. West Ryde...... 281 H14
MAHONEY
la. Edgecliff........... 13 E9
MAHONGA
st. Tahmoor 565 K10
MAHONS CREEK
rd. Yarramundi 145 A3
MAHONY
rd. Riverstone...... 182 K5
rd. Wentwthvle 277 B11
MAHRATTA
av. Wahroonga 222 B11
MAI
pl. Hebersham..... 241 D10
MAIANBAR
rd. Royal N P 522 B15
MAIDA
rd. Epping............ 281 C2
st. Five Dock........ 342 G8
st. Lilyfield............ 10 E4
MAIDEN
la. Surry Hills 4 D14
st. Greenacre 370 E11
MAIDOS
pl. Quakers Hill 214 D11
MAIDSTONE
pl. Glenmore Pk... 266 E12
st. Picton............. 563 F11
MAILEY
cct. Rouse Hill....... 184 J5
pl. Shalvey........... 211 B15
MAIN
la. Merrylands 307 H12
st. Blacktown....... 244 H16
st. Earlwood 402 D4
st. Horngsea Pk... 392 E11
st. Mt Annan........ 479 D13
MAINERD
av. Bexley North ... 402 F11
MAINO
cl. Green Valley ... 363 H11
MAINSBRIDGE
av. Liverpool 394 H4
MAIN SOUTHERN
rd. Camden.......... 506 E10
rd. Cawdor........... 506 E10
MAINTENANCE
la. Richmond....... 118 F13
MAISMONDE
pl. Carlingford 280 E6
MAITLAND
av. Kingsford........ 406 C2
pl. Baulkham Hl... 216 H14
pl. Kirrawee......... 491 B7
st. Davidson 255 D3
st. Killara............ 253 H12
wy. Airds 511 H15
MAJESTIC
dr. Stanhpe Gdn... 215 D10
MAJOR
rd. Merrylands 307 E11
st. Coogee........... 377 J15
st. Mosman.......... 317 A12
st. Punchbowl 400 C8
MAJOR CLEWS
pl. Horngsea Pk... 392 E16
MAJORS
la. Concord, off
Brewer St........ 341 K4
MAJORS BAY
rd. Concord 341 J1
MAJURA
cl. St Ives Ch....... 194 B16
MAKIM
st. N Curl Curl...... 258 F9
MAKINSON
st. Gladesville 312 K9
MALA
cr. Blacktown....... 244 B12
st. Smithfield 335 B3
MALABAR
rd. Dural 188 E15
rd. Maroubra 407 C16
rd. S Coogee........ 407 F4
st. Canley Vale..... 366 B1
st. Fairfield 335 K15
MALABINE
la. S Penrith, off
Malabine Pl...... 266 H7
pl. S Penrith 266 H7
MALACHITE
rd. Eagle Vale....... 481 A8
MALACOOTA
rd. Northbridge 286 B16
MALAHIDE
rd. Pennant Hills .. 220 E16
MALAKOFF
st. Marrickville..... 373 K12
MALAKUA
st. Whalan........... 240 K11
MALANDA
pl. St Marys......... 269 C4
MALAWA
pl. Bradbury 511 C15
MALBARA
cr. Frenchs Frst.... 255 K2
MALBEC
pl. Eschol Park 481 C3
MALCOLM
av. Mt Pritchard ... 364 F9
av. Werrington 238 H10
la. Erskineville 18 B16
st. Blacktown....... 274 J5
st. Erskineville 18 B16
st. Mascot 405 H4
st. Narrabeen....... 229 C1
wy. Rsemeadow.... 540 K2
MALDON
st. S Penrith......... 266 F5
MALEY
gr. Glenwood 215 K15
st. Guildford 337 C5
MALGA
av. Roseville Ch.... 255 E16
MALIBU
st. Bundeena 524 B11
MALING
av. Ermington....... 310 C3
MALINYA
cr. Moorebank 396 F11
rd. Allambie Ht..... 257 H14
MALLACOOTA
cl. Prestons 393 B16
cl. Prestons 423 A1
pl. Woodcroft 243 F10
st. Wakeley.......... 334 H12
MALLAM
rd. Picton 561 C3
MALLARD
dr. Oatley 430 E12
st. Woronora Ht.... 489 B3
MALLAWA
rd. Duffys Frst...... 194 J1
MALLEE
ct. Holsworthy 426 D5
pl. Mcquarie Fd.... 454 E2
st. Cabramatta 365 J9
st. N St Marys...... 240 B12
st. Quakers Hill 243 J1
MALLENY
st. Ashbury.......... 372 E9
MALLET
cl. Kingswood...... 267 H1
MALLETT
la. Camperdwn 17 F6
st. Annandale......... 17 D2
st. Camperdwn 17 D2
MALLEY
av. Earlwood 402 D5
MALLORY
st. Dean Park....... 242 J1
MALLOW
pl. Cabramtta W... 365 B4
MALO
rd. Whale Beach ... 140 C8
MALONE
cr. Dean Park....... 242 K1
MALONEY
la. Eastlakes 405 J4
st. Blacktown....... 273 K3
st. Mascot 405 J5
st. Mascot 405 H6
st. Rosebery 405 J5
MALONGA
av. Kellyville 216 G3
MALORY
av. West Pymble .. 252 H9
cl. Wetherill Pk 334 E4
MALOUF
pl. Blacktown....... 243 J9
st. Canley Ht........ 365 B3
st. Colyton........... 270 B4
st. Guildford W 336 H2
MALSBURY
rd. Hornsby.......... 221 G8
rd. Normanhurst .. 221 G8
MALTA
pl. Rooty Hill........ 271 H3
st. Fairfield E........ 337 B14
st. N Strathfield.... 341 D6
MALTON
grn. W Pnnant Hl .. 249 D5
rd. Beecroft.......... 250 G5
rd. Cheltenham..... 251 A7
rd. N Epping......... 251 E9
MALUA
st. Dolls Point 463 G1
MALUKA
pl. Kingsgrove 401 H14
MALVERN
av. Baulkham Hl ... 247 A13
av. Chatswood...... 284 K8
av. Croydon.......... 372 D1
av. Manly 288 G6
av. Merrylands...... 307 J14
av. Roseville 285 C3
av. Roseville Ch 285 D3
cl. St Johns Pk..... 364 F3
cr. Strathfield 341 F16
rd. Glenwood 215 B16
rd. Miranda 492 D4
st. Panania........... 428 C5
MALVINA
st. Ryde 312 E1
MALVOLIO
st. Rsemeadow 540 F5
MAMBLE
pl. S Penrith 267 B7
MAME
pl. Kearns 451 A15
MAMIE
av. Seven Hills 245 B16
MAMMONE
cl. Edensor Pk 333 J14
MAMRE
cr. Airds 512 A14
la. St Clair, off
Mamre Rd 269 F10
rd. Kemps Ck 330 A2
rd. St Clair 269 F14
rd. St Marys 269 G6
MANAHAN
st. Condell Park.... 398 D2
MANAM
pl. Glenfield......... 424 J9
MANAR
pl. Prestons 392 J16
MANARA
pl. Seven Hills 275 F5
MANCHESTER
rd. Auburn........... 338 K1
rd. Gymea 491 F4
rd. Gymea 491 F6
st. Dulwich Hill..... 373 C7
st. Merrylands...... 307 G10
wy. Currans Hill..... 479 G11
MANDA
pl. Rooty Hill 272 A6
MANDALONG
tce. Glenmore Pk ... 266 F12
MANDARIN
st. Fairfield E 337 C15
st. Villawood 337 C15
wy. Glenwood 215 F11
MANDEMAR
av. Homebsh W 340 F7
MANDIBLE
st. Alexandria....... 375 F10
MANDINA
pl. Bringelly.......... 389 A5
MANDOLONG
la. Mosman 317 D6
rd. Mosman 317 B6
st. Bonnyrigg Ht... 363 A6
MANDOO
dr. Doonside 243 E15
MANDOON
rd. Girraween 275 J14
MANDUR
pl. Caringbah 492 H12
MANEROO
rd. Allambie Ht 257 F13
MANETTE
pl. Ambarvale....... 510 J11
MANEY
st. Rozelle 11 B1
MANGALOO
st. Berowra Ht...... 133 A8
MANGARIVA
av. Emerton.......... 240 G6
av. Lethbrdg Pk 240 G6
MANGIRI
rd. Beecroft.......... 250 C3
MANGROVE
la. Taren Point 463 A14
rd. Brooklyn 75 E12
MANIFOLD
rd. Blackett.......... 241 C1
MANILA
rd. Lethbrdg Pk 240 G5
MANILDRA
av. Carlingford...... 279 D2
st. Earlwood......... 402 F6
st. Prestons 393 E15
MANILLA
pl. Woronora 459 K16
rd. Hoxton Park.... 392 H6
MANINS
av. Kingsgrove..... 401 K7
MANION
av. Rose Bay........ 347 J12
MANLY
la. Fairlight, off
Birkley Rd....... 288 E8
la. Manly, off
Birkley Rd....... 288 E8
pl. Kings Lngly 245 D5
pl. Woodbine 481 H9
rd. Balgowlah 287 C11
rd. Clontarf 287 C11
rd. Mulgoa........... 293 J11
rd. Seaforth 287 C11
MANN
pl. St Helens Pk... 541 A6
st. Chatswood 285 E6
st. Glenbrook 233 K16
MANNA
ct. Mt Riverview .. 204 E15
pl. Bossley Park .. 333 G9
pl. Kingswood 237 H16
wy. Silverdale 353 K16
MANNA GUM
rd. Narellan Vale .. 479 A14
MANNERIM
pl. Castle Cove 286 B6
MANNIKIN
dr. Woronora Ht .. 489 B4
pl. Mount Druitt... 241 E12
MANNING
av. Strathfield S ... 371 D5
cl. McGraths Hl ... 121 K12
pde. Dundas Vy...... 279 K10
pl. Currans Hill 479 F12
pl. Seven Hills 275 F10
rd. Camperdwn..... 18 B2
rd. Double Bay....... 14 C11
rd. Gladesville...... 313 A12
rd. Hunters Hill 313 A12
rd. Killara............ 253 D16
rd. North Ryde..... 282 H11
rd. Woollahra......... 22 F1
st. Campbelltwn .. 511 K9
st. Homebush B ..... M C6
st. Kingswood 237 J16
st. N Balgowlah ... 287 B3
st. Oyster Bay....... 461 A7
st. Potts Point 4 K4
st. Prospect......... 274 F16
st. Queens Park..... 22 G13
st. Rozelle 344 C7
st. Warwck Frm ... 365 J16
MANNIX
ct. Harringtn Pk... 478 D1
pde. Warwck Frm ... 365 G15
pl. Quakers Hill.... 214 B9
st. Bonnyrigg Ht.. 363 F8
st. Warwck Frm ... 365 G15
MANNOW
av. West Hoxton .. 392 B6
MANNS
av. Greenwich 314 K12
av. Neutral Bay......... 6 E9
pl. Greenwich, off
O'Connell St.... 314 K14
rd. Wilberforce 93 F5
MANOOKA
cr. Bradbury 511 C15
pl. Kareela 461 D14
pl. Warriewood.... 199 A7
rd. Currans Hill 480 A9
MANOR
gln. Wrrngtn Dns .. 238 D5
pl. Baulkham Hl... 247 F7
rd. Hornsby 191 C13
rd. Ingleside 197 J5
MANOR HILL
rd. Miranda.......... 461 J14
MANORHOUSE
bvd. Quakers Hill.... 213 F9
MANSFIELD
av. Caringbah....... 492 K8
la. Glebe 11 J10
rd. Galston 159 J4
st. Girraween....... 276 B16
st. Glebe 11 J10
st. Rozelle 7 B15
st. Wetherill Pk 334 J5
MANSION
ct. Quakers Hill.... 213 G9
la. Potts Point 4 K7
rd. Bellevue Hill.... 347 F14
st. Marrickville..... 403 H1

MANSION POINT
rd. Grays Point 491 E16
MANSON
pl. Clovelly 377 G11
rd. Strathfield 341 G10
st. S Wntwthvle 307 C5
st. Telopea 279 G11
MANTAKA
st. Blacktown 275 A2
MANTALINI
st. Ambarvale 510 H14
MANTILLUS
gr. Baulkham Hl 246 H4
MANTON
av. Newington L H10
av. Newington 310 D11
MANTURA
ct. Winston Hills 276 H1
MANUELA
pl. Curl Curl 258 E12
MANUKA
av. Baulkham Hl 247 D15
cir. Cherrybrook 219 G11
cr. Bass Hill 368 A10
st. Wentwthvle 277 C12
MANUS
pl. Glenfield 424 G9
MANWARING
av. Maroubra 407 D16
MAPITI
pl. Acacia Gdn 214 G16
MAPLE
av. Pennant Hills 220 F15
cl. Canada Bay 342 F9
cr. Ermington 280 D13
ct. Greenacre 370 B14
gr. Narellan 478 C10
la. N St Marys, off Maple Rd 240 B11
pl. Belrose 225 J14
pl. Mcquarie Fd 424 E16
pl. Wentwthvle 277 A9
rd. Casula 423 J2
rd. N St Marys 239 J8
st. Bowen Mtn 83 K7
st. Cabramatta 365 G8
st. Caringbah 492 J15
st. Dural 188 H12
st. Greystanes 306 E4
st. Lugarno 429 H15
MAPLELEAF
dr. Padstow 429 G2
MAPLES
av. Killara 254 A11
MARA
cl. Bonnyrigg 363 J10
cr. Mooney 75 E1
MARAGA
pl. Doonside 243 F16
MARAKET
av. Blaxland 234 D9
MARALINGA
av. Elanora Ht 198 B16
pl. W Pnnant Hl 249 G6
MARAMBA
cl. Kingsgrove 401 F7
MARAMPO
st. Marayong 243 H5
MARANA
rd. Earlwood 402 C3
rd. Northbridge 315 K1
st. Blacktown 274 F5
MARANATHA
cl. W Pnnant Hl 248 G7
st. Rooty Hill 271 K6
MARANIE
av. St Marys 269 K5
MARANOA
pl. Wahroonga 223 C4
st. Auburn 338 J11
MARANTA
st. Hornsby 191 F11
MARANUI
av. Dee Why 258 F4
MARATHON
av. Darling Point 13 K7
av. Newington L K13
av. Newington 310 B13
la. Darling Point 13 K7
mw. Double Bay 14 B7
rd. Darling Point 13 K6
MARAU
pl. Yellow Rock 204 G1
MARBLE
cl. Bossley Park 334 A8
MARCEAU
dr. Concord 342 D6
MARCEL
av. Coogee 377 F12
av. Randwick 377 F12
cr. Blacktown 274 K2
pl. Baulkham Hl 247 K7
MARCELLA
st. Bankstown 399 G4
st. Bankstown 399 G5
st. Kingsgrove 401 K5
st. N Epping 251 D9
MARCELLUS
pl. Rsemeadow 540 H6
MARCH
pl. Earlwood 403 B5
st. Bellevue Hill 347 F15
st. Richmond 118 F4
MARCHMONT
pl. Airds 512 B10
MARCIA
la. Hurlstone Pk, off Duntroon St 373 A12
st. Hurlstone Pk 373 A12
st. Toongabbie 276 A6
MARCIANO
cl. Edensor Pk 363 G4
MARCO
av. Panania 397 J16
av. Revesby 398 D16
MARCOALA
pl. St Ives 224 D10
MARCONI
pl. Little Bay 437 B13
rd. Bossley Park 333 H10
rd. Bossley Park 333 H7
st. Winston Hills 277 C5
MARCUS
pl. Frenchs Frst 255 K3
st. Asquith 191 K7
st. Kings Park 244 E3
MARCUS CLARK
wy. Hornsby 191 E12
MARCUS CLARKE
cr. Glenmore Pk 265 J8
MARDEN
st. Artarmon 314 H1
st. Georges Hall 367 G12
MARDI
ct. Kellyville 217 D2
st. Girraween 276 A14
MARE
ct. Harringtn Pk 478 F1
MAREE
av. Cabramtta W 365 C4
pl. Blacktown 243 K9
pl. Condell Park 398 F1
MARELLA
av. Kellyville 216 H2
MARETIMO
st. Balgowlah 287 F10
MARGA
rd. Gymea Bay 491 H9
MARGARET
av. Hornsby Ht 191 E2
cr. Lugarno 429 K16
ct. Shalvey 210 K13
la. Newtown 17 D16
la. Stanmore 16 D5
la. Sydney A G13
pl. Lane Cove W 283 G13
pl. Paddington 4 K16
st. Abbotsford 343 C3
st. Ashfield 342 H16
st. Beacon Hill 257 E7
st. Belfield 371 E9
st. Dulwich Hill 373 E11
st. Fairfield 335 G14
st. Fairfield W 335 G14
st. Fairlight 288 D10
st. Granville 308 D10
st. Greenacre 370 G3
st. Kingsgrove 401 J12
st. Kogarah 433 D9
st. Mays Hill 307 G7
st. Minto 482 G2
st. Newtown 17 D16
st. Northmead 278 A4
st. N Sydney 6 A10
st. Petersham 16 B5
st. Picton 563 G3
st. Redfern 19 A9
st. Riverstone 183 G8
st. Roseville 285 B3
st. Rozelle 344 D6
st. Russell Lea 343 C3
st. Ryde 312 E5
st. St Marys 269 G5
st. Seven Hills 275 F4
st. Stanmore 16 B5
st. Strathfield 341 F13
st. Sydney A F14
st. Sydney 1 F15
st. Woolwich 314 D13
tce. Silverdale 354 B16
wy. Cecil Hills 362 H4
MARGARETA
cl. Guildford 337 D3
MARGATE
st. Botany 405 G14
st. Ramsgate 433 D12
st. Sans Souci 433 E14
MARGO
pl. Schofields 213 J5
MARGOT
pl. Castle Hill 217 H16
MARGUERETTE
st. Ermington 310 D3
MARGUERITE
av. Mt Riverview 234 D2
cr. W Pnnant Hl 220 A15
MARI
cl. Glenmore Pk 266 D9
MARIA
la. Newtown, off Darley St 374 J10
pl. Blacktown 274 E5
pl. Oakdale 500 D12
st. Petersham 15 G13
st. Strathfield S 371 D7
MARIALA
ct. Holsworthy 426 D5
MARIA LOCK
gr. Oakhurst 242 D4
MARIAM
cl. Cherrybrook 219 B15
MARIAN
ct. Baulkham Hl 247 B1
la. Enmore 17 B14
st. Enmore 17 B14
st. Eveleigh 19 A8
st. Guildford 337 H4
st. Killara 254 A13
st. Redfern 19 A8
st. S Coogee 407 F3
MARIANA
cl. St Ives 224 D14
cr. Lethbrdg Pk 240 G3
MARIANI
cl. Bossley Park 333 G11
MARIE
av. Glenwood 245 F3
cl. Bligh Park 150 H6
cr. Mona Vale 198 J3
la. Belmore 371 E16
st. Belmore 401 D1
st. Castle Hill 247 J2
st. Lurnea 394 E10
st. Wentwthvle 277 A10
MARIEANNE
pl. Minchinbury 271 D7
MARIEBA
rd. Kenthurst 157 A6
MARIE DODD
cr. Blakehurst 462 D3
MARIE PITT
pl. Glenmore Pk 265 H5
MARIGOLD
av. Marayong 244 B7
cl. Glenmore Pk 265 G10
la. Glenmore Pk, off Marigold Cl 265 F10
pl. Revesby 398 B11
st. Revesby 398 B11
MARIKO
pl. Blacktown 273 J7
MARILLIAN
av. Waitara 221 H5
MARILYN
st. North Ryde 282 G8
MARIN
pl. Glendenning 242 F5
pl. Merrylands 307 C11
pl. Prestons 393 A16
MARINA
cl. Bossley Park 333 K9
cl. Mt Krng-gai 162 K6
cr. Cecil Hills 362 K3
cr. Greenacre 369 H12
cr. Gymea Bay 491 E13
pl. Belrose 225 J15
rd. Baulkham Hl 246 J12
st. Kingsgrove 401 J12
MARINE
cr. Hornsby Ht 191 D8
dr. Oatley 430 G15
esp. Cronulla 494 C7
pde. Avalon 140 E16
pde. Double Bay 14 B6
pde. Homebush B L F4
pde. Homebush B 310 K9
pde. Manly 288 K10
pde. Maroubra 407 G12
pde. Watsons Bay 318 F15
rd. Avalon 140 F14
MARINEA
st. Arncliffe 403 F11
MARINELLA
st. Manly Vale 287 H5
MARINER
cr. Abbotsbury 333 C15
rd. Illawong 459 C3
MARINNA
rd. Elanora Ht 198 E14
MARION
cr. Lapstone 264 H5
st. Auburn 339 E5
st. Bankstown 369 A16
st. Bnkstn Aprt 367 H15
st. Blacktown 274 H2
st. Cecil Hills 362 G5
st. Condell Park 368 C16
st. Georges Hall 367 H15
st. Gymea 491 G3
st. Haberfield 373 E1
st. Harris Park 308 E6
st. Leichhardt 15 G1
st. Parramatta 308 D6
st. Seven Hills 245 D16
st. Strathfield 340 J14
st. Thirlmere 565 D3
MARIPOSA
rd. Bilgola 169 H6
MARIST
pl. Parramatta 278 C16
MARJORIE
cr. Maroubra 406 H7
st. Roseville 284 G1
st. Sefton 368 H1
MARJORIE JACKSON
pky. Homebush B L K6
pky. Homebush B 310 H13
MARJORY
pl. Baulkham Hl 248 A10
MARJORY THOMAS
pl. Balgowlah 288 A7
MARK
la. Roselands 401 C7
la. Sydney C D5
pl. Bilgola 169 F4
pl. Cherrybrook 219 F8
pl. Penrith 236 E3
rd. Nelson 154 H9
rd. Rossmore 419 K4
st. Canley Ht 365 A2
st. Dundas Vy 280 D10
st. Hunters Hill 313 B9
st. Lidcombe 339 J9
st. Merrylands 306 K10
st. Mount Druitt 271 C3
st. St Marys 270 A5
MARKELL
pl. Liverpool 394 J5
MARKET
la. Manly 288 G10
la. Merrylands, off Baker St 307 J16
row. Sydney C G10
st. Appin 568 G10
st. Clarmnt Ms 269 B1
st. Condell Park 398 K4
st. Drummoyne 343 H6
st. Moorebank 395 G9
st. Naremburn 315 G2
st. Parramatta 308 C1
st. Randwick 377 C10
st. Randwick 377 D9
st. Riverstone 182 J7
st. Rockdale 403 D15
st. Smithfield 335 G5
st. Sydney C D8
st. Sydney 3 E4
st. Tahmoor 565 G12
st. West Ryde 281 D15
st.e, Naremburn 315 H2
MARKETOWN
la. Riverstone, off Garfield Rd E 182 J8
MARKET PLACE
st. Horngsea Pk 392 E11
MARKEY
st. Guildford 338 D5
MARKHAM
av. Ashfield 372 H2
av. Penrith 237 D11
cl. Mosman 317 E10
ct. Acacia Gdn 214 H16
pl. Ashfield 372 H2
st. Holsworthy 426 C4
MARKOVINA
st. Edensor Pk 333 F16
MARKS
av. Seven Hills 245 H14
la. Bass Hill 368 A5
la. Chester Hill 368 A5
la. Tamarama 378 D6
st. Bass Hill 368 A5
st. Chester Hill 368 A5
st. Chester Hill 368 B5
st. Naremburn 315 H3
MARK SPITZ
av. Newington M C16
av. Newington 309 K15
MARKWELL
pl. Agnes Banks 117 E11
MARL
pl. Eagle Vale 481 F7
MARLBOROUGH
av. Harbord 258 C15
la. Glebe 12 B11
pl. St Ives 223 J7
rd. Homebsh W 340 G8
rd. Willoughby 285 G15
st. Drummoyne 343 H1
st. Fairfield Ht 336 B9
st. Glebe 12 B12
st. Leichhardt 9 G16
st. Smithfield 336 B9
st. Surry Hills 20 A5
MARLE
av. The Oaks 502 F9
MARLEE
rd. Engadine 489 E9
st. Hornsby 191 H8
st. N Balgowlah 287 G5
MARLENE
cr. Greenacre 370 F1
pl. Belmore 401 F6
st. Freemns Rch 90 A3
MARLEY
cr. Bonnyrigg Ht 363 B3
st. Ambarvale 511 A14
MARLIS
av. Revesby 398 E11
MARLO
rd. Cronulla 494 A9
MARLOCK
pl. Alfords Point 429 C13
pl. Mcquarie Fd 454 D4
st. Kingswood 267 H1
MARLOO
pl. St Helens Pk 541 H3
MARLOW
av. Denistone 281 F13
la. Denistone 281 F12
pl. Campbelltwn 511 H9
rd. Artarmon 285 C13
MARLOWE
st. Campsie 372 A15
st. Wetherill Pk 334 K4
MARMADUKE
st. Burwood 342 A14
MARMION
la. Abbotsford 312 K16
la. Camperdwn 17 B8
rd. Abbotsford 312 K16
st. Birrong 369 B5
st. Camperdwn 17 B8
wy. Kellyville 185 J14
MARMORA
st. Harbord 258 G16
MARNE
la. St Clair, off Marne Pl 269 G16
pl. St Clair 269 G15

st. Vaucluse........348 G5
MARNIE
gr. Kings Lngly....245 K8
MARNOO
pl. Belrose..........226 C15
MARNPAR
rd. Seven Hills.....246 A13
MAROA
cr. Allambie Ht.....287 G1
MARONG
st. Panania..........398 D16
MARONI
pl. St Clair..........269 F14
MAROOBA
pl. Engadine........488 G11
rd. Northbridge....285 K15
MAROOK
st. Carlingford.....280 E6
MAROOPNA
rd. Yowie Bay......492 A10
MAROUBRA
cr. Woodbine.......481 F13
la. Maroubra.......407 B10
rd. Maroubra.......406 H9
rd. Maroubra.......407 G10
MARPLE
av. Villawood.......367 F1
MARQUESA
cr. Lethbrdg Pk...240 F3
MARQUET
st. Rhodes..........311 C9
MARRA
pl. Sylvania.........462 E8
MARRAKESH
pl. Arcadia...........129 B12
MARRICKVILLE
av. Marrickville.....373 G12
la. Marrickville.....374 A13
rd. Dulwich Hill....373 F10
rd. Marrickville.....373 F10
MARRIOTT
gr. Castle Hill.......217 D10
rd. Bonnyrigg......363 F9
rd. Bonnyrigg Ht..363 F9
st. Redfern............19 K11
st. Redfern............20 A7
MARRON
pl. Beecroft..........250 A12
MARROO
st. Bronte............377 J11
MARS
la. Gladesville......313 A3
rd. Lansvale.........366 H8
rd. Lane Cove W..283 E16
st. Epping............280 D2
st. Gladesville......312 K10
st. Padstow.........429 B3
st. Revesby.........428 J3
MARSALA
st. Mosman.........287 A15
MARSANNE
pl. Eschol Park....481 C2
MARSDEN
av. Elderslie.........507 H1
av. Kellyville.........215 G4
cl. Bossley Park..334 D11
cr. Bligh Park.......150 E5
cr. Peakhurst.......430 E1
la. Riverstone......182 C9
rd. Barden Rdg....458 G16
rd. Carlingford.....280 B4
rd. Dundas Vy......280 B4
rd. Liverpool.......395 A1
rd. Riverstone......182 E9
rd. St Marys.........270 A7
rd. West Ryde......280 F11
st. Camperdwn......17 F3
st. Granville.........308 B7
st. Lidcombe.........339 J9
st. Parramatta.....308 B5
st. Ruse.............512 G2
MARSH
av. Woolooware....493 J8
pde. Casula...........394 K14
pl. Cranebrook....207 D10
pl. Lane Cove......314 G3
pl. The Oaks.......502 F14
rd. Warragamba..353 F15
st. Arncliffe..........403 J8
st. Condell Park...398 F2
st. Granville.........308 H11
st. Wakeley.........364 K1
MARSHALL
av. Bargo............567 F10
av. Moorebank.....396 E12
av. St Leonards....315 C6
av. Warrawee.......222 D13
cl. Hornsby Ht.....161 J10
cr. Beacon Hill.....257 H9
la. Panania..........398 B16
la. Petersham........16 C13
la. St Leonards, off
Berry Rd.........315 C6
rd. Dundas Vy......279 H9
rd. Kirrawee.........461 C16
rd. Mt Riverview...234 B4
rd. Telopea...........279 H9
st. Balmain...............7 K8
st. Bankstown......399 E6
st. Bnkstn Aprt....368 B16
st. Kogarah..........433 D7
st. Manly.............288 H13
st. Paddington.........4 F14
st. Petersham........16 B13
st. Surry Hills........20 D2
MARTEN
cl. Prestons.........392 J16
cl. Prestons.........422 J1
MARTENS
cct. Kellyville.........215 G3
la. Mosman, off
Raglan St........317 C9
la. Cremorne, off
Waters La.......316 D8
la. Neutral Bay, off
Waters La.......316 D8
pl. Abbotsbury.....333 B11
wy. Claymore........481 B10
MARTHA
av. Northmead.....277 K6
cr. Cranebrook.....207 D11
la. Cranebrook, off
Martha Cr........207 D10
st. Granville.........308 K11
st. Hunters Hill....313 K11
st. Yagoona.........369 A10
wy. Ambarvale......510 K15
MARTI
pl. Hebersham.....241 E10
MARTIN
av. Arncliffe..........403 G6
av. Pagewood......406 C8
bvd. Plumpton.......241 K11
cr. Milperra..........397 C10
cr. Woodpark.......306 H14
gr. Colyton...........270 G9
la. Roseville.........284 H3
pl. Dural..............188 G12
pl. Dural..............188 H13
pl. Mortdale.........431 A8
pl. Mt Annan........479 H14
pl. Sydney..............C K2
pl. Sydney..............3 G1
rd. Badgerys Ck...329 D16
rd. Centnnial Pk....21 A14
rd. Galston...........159 H9
rd. Moore Park.......20 J14
rd. Oakville...........124 E6
st. Blakehurst......432 A14
st. Emu Plains....235 C10
st. Haberfield......343 B12
st. Harbord..........288 D1
st. Heathcote.......518 F11
st. Hunters Hill....313 E9
st. Lidcombe.......340 A8
st. Mulgoa...........265 D4
st. Paddington.......21 B3
st. Regentville.....265 D4
st. Roselands......400 F9
st. Ryde..............282 D14
st. St Leonards....315 F4
MARTINA
st. Plumpton.......241 J11
MARTINDALE
av. Baulkham Hl...247 F5
ct. Wattle Grove...395 K16
MARTINE
av. Camden S.......507 B11
MARTIN LUTHER
la. Allambie Ht.....257 A10
pl. Allambie Ht.....257 B10
MARTINO
cl. Prestons.........422 H1
MARTINS
av. Bondi.............377 J2
la. Carlingford.....279 G6
la. Freemns Rch....90 J2
MARTLEY
la. Cranebrook, off
Martley Wy......207 F14
wy. Cranebrook.....207 F14
MARTON
cr. Kings Lngly.....245 G8
MARULAN
wy. Prestons.........392 H15
MARUM
st. Ashcroft..........364 F14
MARVELL
rd. Wetherill Pk....334 E6
MARVILLE
av. Kingsford........406 H6
MARWOOD
dr. Beecroft..........250 C10
MARX
av. Beverley Pk.....433 B9
pl. Quakers Hill....243 K1
MARY
av. Cranebrook.....206 H8
cr. Liverpool........394 H9
la. Bundeena.......523 K10
la. Surry Hills..........F C14
pde. Rydalmere.......309 C1
pl. Bligh Park.......150 F7
pl. Paddington.........4 J15
pl. Surry Hills...........4 D15
st. Auburn...........339 A3
st. Beacon Hill......257 E6
st. Beecroft..........250 E7
st. Blacktown........244 A11
st. Bundeena.......524 A9
st. Burwood.........342 A14
st. Drummoyne....343 F5
st. Ermington.......310 H3
st. Glebe...............11 H6
st. Granville........308 E11
st. Hunters Hill....313 C10
st. Jannali...........460 G12
st. Lidcombe.......339 J8
st. Lilyfield...............9 H4
st. Lilyfield...............9 J7
st. Longueville.....314 C9
st. Mcquarie Fd....424 E15
st. Merrylands.....337 E1
st. Newtown..........17 G11
st. Northmead......278 A3
st. N Parramatta...278 D11
st. Regents Pk.....368 J2
st. Rhodes..........311 D10
st. Riverwood......399 K14
st. Rooty Hill........241 K15
st. Rozelle.............10 J4
st. St Peters.........374 F14
st. Schofields.......182 H14
st. Surry Hills..........F B14
st. Surry Hills...........3 J15
st. The Oaks........502 E11
st. Turrella...........403 D6
st. Wetherill Pk....334 J6
st. Wiley Park......400 J4
MARY ANN
st. Ultimo..............12 K14
MARY ANNE
cl. Mt Annan........509 F2
MARY BROWN
pl. Blair Athol.......511 B2
MARYFIELDS
dr. Blair Athol.......510 J2
MARY GILMORE
pl. Heathcote.......518 C15
MARY-HELEN
ct. Baulkham Hl...247 A1
MARY HOWE
pl. Narellan Vale...508 J2
MARY IRENE
pl. Castle Hill........248 F2
MARYL
av. Roselands.......401 B8
MARY MARGARET
la. Mosman.........317 D13
MARY ROSE
st. Green Valley....362 K9
MARYVALE
av. Liverpool.........394 G4
MARY WALL
cr. Berowra..........133 G9
MARY WOLLSTONECRAFT
la. Milsons Pt..........5 K16
MASCOT
dr. Eastlakes........405 J3
MASEFIELD
pl. Woolooware...493 C12
MASER
st. Cranebrook.....207 F10
MASERATI
dr. Ingleburn........453 G11
MASHMAN
av. Kingsgrove......401 K11
av. Wentwthvle.....306 J1
MASIKU
pl. Glendenning....242 E4
MASLIN
cr. Quakers Hill....214 A11
MASON
av. Cheltenham.....250 H9
av. Richmond.......118 D6
la. Bondi, off
Jackaman St....377 K6
pl. Barden Rdg.....488 F7
pl. Bonnyrigg.......364 D6
rd. Box Hill..........154 C13
st. Camperdwn.....17 E2
st. Denistone E.....281 G10
st. Maroubra........406 H8
st. Merrylands......307 D13
st. Mount Druitt....240 H16
st. Parramatta......278 H16
st. Thirlmere........564 J4
st. Thirlmere........565 A4
MASONS
dr. N Parramatta...278 H8
la. N Parramatta...278 H7
MASSA
la. Clarmnt Ms, off
Massa Pl..........268 J3
pl. Clarmnt Ms.....268 J3
MASSEY
la. Gladesville.......312 J9
pl. St Ives Ch.......223 K6
st. Cammeray.......315 H4
st. Carlton............432 G11
st. Gladesville.......312 J9
wy. Glenmore Pk...265 H5
MASSIE
st. Ermington.......310 F3
MASTERFIELD
st. Rossmore.......389 C16
MASTERS
pl. Girraween.......276 B14
pl. Penrith............236 J10
MATAHIL
cl. Harringtn Pk....478 H7
MATARO
cl. Edensor Pk.....333 C16
pl. Eschol Park.....481 E3
MATHERS
pl. Menai.............458 G15
MATHESON
av. Chatswood......285 C11
av. Mt Pritchard....364 F11
av. N Richmond.....87 D15
gr. Hassall Gr.......211 J15
MATHEW
la. Belmore..........371 A12
pl. West Hoxton...392 D10
MATHEWS
pl. Menai.............458 F12
st. Davidson.........225 A15
MATHEWSON
st. Eastgardens....406 G13
MATHIESON
st. Annandale........17 B3
MATHINNA
cct. West Hoxton...392 D6
MATHIS
pl. Ingleburn........453 J6
MATIKA
pl. Lethbrdg Pk....210 G15
MATILDA
gr. Kellyville.........185 K15
st. Rozelle.............10 G1
wy. Glenwood.......245 K5
MATINGARA
wy. Wallacia..........354 K2
MATONG
pl. Gymea Bay......491 G10
st. Gordon..........254 A7
MATORA
la. Cremorne........316 D5
MATRA
pl. Raby...............451 H13
MATRUM
st. Holsworthy.....426 E6
MATSON
cr. Miranda..........492 C7
MATTERSON
la. Redfern............20 B7
MATTHES
st. Yennora.........337 B11
MATTHEW
av. Heckenberg....363 K13
cl. Galston..........160 J10
cl. Mt Annan.......509 D1
cl. St Ives...........224 F10
cr. Blacktown......274 D4
la. Crows Nest, off
Atchison St.....315 H5
pde. Blaxland.........233 J9
pl. Bella Vista......246 F2
pl. Richmond.......119 C3
rd. Lidcombe........339 F10
st. Beverley Pk....433 A12
st. Crows Nest.....315 G5
st. Hunters Hill....313 D10
st. Merrylands......307 C15
wy. W Pnnant Hl...219 A16
MATTHEW FLINDERS
pl. Burraneer.......523 D3
MATTHEWS
av. East Hills........427 K4
av. Lane Cove.......313 K2
la. Picton............563 H10
sq. Ingleburn.......453 E8
st. Carramar.......336 J16
st. Emu Heights...235 A5
st. Greenacre.......370 G11
st. Punchbowl.....400 D4
MATTS
av. Panania..........398 C14
la. Revesby.........398 H15
MAUBEUGE
st. S Granville......338 G6
MAUD
cl. Cecil Hills.......362 G7
la. Marrickville......374 B14
st. Blacktown......274 H8
st. Fairfield Ht.....335 G12
st. Fairfield W......335 G14
st. Granville.........308 E12
st. Lidcombe.......339 K6
st. Randwick........376 K16
MAUDE
st. Regents Pk.....369 B3
MAUGHAM
cr. Wetherill Pk....334 G3
MAUGHAN
st. Lalor Park.......245 E13
MAUNDER
av. Girraween.......276 B14
av. St Ives...........224 C8
pl. Warragamba..353 E8
st. Regents Pk.....369 D2
MAUREEN
pl. Blacktown......274 B3
MAURICE
la. St Clair, off
Maurice St......270 A9
st. Marsden Pk....182 B14
st. St Clair...........270 A9
MAURITIUS
av. Georges Hall...368 C15
MAVICK
cr. Leumeah........511 K1
MAVIS
av. Peakhurst.......430 H4
st. Greystanes.....305 G7
st. North Ryde.....282 D9
st. Revesby.........398 J9
st. Rooty Hill.......272 D1
MAVOR
cr. Frenchs Frst...256 C8
MAWARRA
av. Miranda..........491 J5
cl. Forestville.......255 G8
cr. Kellyville.........216 E3
cr. Marsfield........251 H15
MAWBANNA
pl. West Hoxton..392 E5
MAWSON
av. Beecroft.........250 D10
cr. Ermington.......310 C1
ct. Wrrngtn Cty...238 F8
dr. Cartwright......393 J5
la. Chifley, off
Mawson Pde...437 B7
pde. Chifley...........437 B7
pl. Pitt Town.........92 J15
rd. Tregear..........240 C5
st. Bardwell Vy....403 C7
st. Leumeah.......482 J10

st. Punchbowl 399 J4
st. St Ives 224 C7
MAX
st. Kurrajong Ht 54 A7
MAX ALLEN
dr. Lindfield 283 G8
MAXIM
la. West Ryde, off Maxim St 281 D16
pl. St Marys 239 G10
st. West Ryde 281 D16
MAXINE
rd. Greystanes 306 G9
MAXWELL
av. Maroubra 407 G11
av. Milperra 397 E14
cl. Illawong 459 D1
la. Glebe 11 G10
la. Pagewood, off Maxwell Rd 406 G9
pde. Frenchs Frst 256 C9
pl. Blaxland 233 F6
pl. Narellan 478 J8
pl. W Pnnant Hl 249 C9
rd. Glebe 11 F9
rd. Pagewood 406 G9
st. Blacktown 274 D3
st. Mcquarie Fd 424 A14
st. Mona Vale 198 J3
st. S Penrith 266 F2
st. S Turramrra 252 C8
MAXWELLS
av. Ashcroft 364 F16
av. Sadleir 394 B3
MAXWELTON
pl. Narraweena 258 C5
MAY
av. Rossmore 389 C12
la. Eastwood 281 C7
la. Neutral Bay 6 G1
la. St Peters 374 J11
la. Dulwich Hill, off Union St 373 C10
pl. Illawong 459 H6
pl. St Andrews 482 A3
rd. Dee Why 258 D7
rd. Narraweena 258 D7
st. Bardwell Pk 403 A7
st. Dulwich Hill 373 B10
st. Eastwood 281 B7
st. Fairfield 336 J14
st. Glenbrook 234 D16
st. Hornsby 191 J16
st. Lilyfield 10 C5
st. Merrylands 308 D15
st. St Peters 374 H12
st. Turramurra 252 D2
st. Wentwthvle 277 A10
wk. Lalor Park 245 H11
MAYA
cl. Bossley Park 333 K12
MAYBERRY
cr. Liverpool 395 A2
MAYBROOK
av. Cromer 227 G13
MAYBUSH
ct. Schofields 213 H5
pl. Cherrybrook 219 J14
wy. Castle Hill 248 F1
MAYCOCK
st. Denistone E 281 H10
MAYDA
pl. Kellyville 186 A15
MAYES
st. Annandale 16 G1
MAYFAIR
av. Kellyville 185 E8
cr. Beverly Hills 401 A13
pl. E Lindfield 255 D12
rd. Mulgoa 295 A7
st. Auburn 338 K14
MAY FARM
rd. Brownlow Hl 475 F16
rd. Brownlow Hl 505 D3
rd. Mt Hunter 505 D4
MAYFIELD
av. Pymble 253 A2
av. Woolwich 314 F13
st. Wentwthvle 277 C13
MAYGAR
cl. Milperra 397 D13
MAY GIBBS
pl. Frenchs Frst 256 G3
wy. Frenchs Frst 256 H3

MAYLIE
cl. Ambarvale 510 H13
MAYMAN
row. Menai 458 J12
MAYNE
la. Abbotsford 342 J3
st. Wilberforce 91 K3
MAYO
pl. Killarney Ht 256 D16
rd. Llandilo 179 B16
st. Little Bay 437 G14
MAYOR
st. Kogarah Bay 432 H13
MAYTONE
av. Killara 254 C8
MAYVIC
st. Greenacre 370 G7
MAZARI
gr. Stanhpe Gdn 215 A10
MAZARIN
st. Riverwood 400 D14
MAZE
av. Ryde 312 C2
cr. Darlington 18 E5
la. Chippendale 18 H3
MAZEPA
av. S Penrith 267 D1
pl. Lidcombe 340 B7
MEACHER
st. Mount Druitt 241 D12
MEAD
dr. Chipping Ntn 366 J14
pl. Chipping Ntn 366 K14
st. Banksia 403 F13
MEADE
st. Allawah 432 E9
MEADOW
cl. Beecroft 250 F10
cr. Meadowbnk 311 D4
la. Wollstncraft, off Rocklands Rd 315 E10
pl. Kellyville 216 E1
pl. Miranda 461 J15
rd. Schofields 212 G8
st. Concord 341 J7
MEADOWBANK
la. West Ryde 311 A1
MEADOWLAND
rd. Peakhurst 400 F16
MEADOWS
rd. Cabramtta W 364 F8
rd. Mt Pritchard 364 D12
rd. N Richmond 58 E15
st. Merrylands 308 B15
wy. Minto 482 J4
MEADOWVIEW
wy. Wrrngtn Dns 237 J5
MEADWAY
cl. Pymble 253 J4
MEAGER
av. Padstow 399 G16
MEAGHER
av. Maroubra 407 E14
st. Chippendale 19 B3
MEAKEM
st. Hurstville 431 J5
MEAKIN
cr. Chester Hill 338 D16
st. Merrylands 307 F15
MEALIA
la. Edgecliff 13 F11
MEANDER
cl. West Hoxton 392 D6
MEARES
rd. McGraths Hl 121 K13
MEARS
av. Randwick 377 B15
MEATH
pl. Blacktown 243 J15
pl. Killarney Ht 256 E16
MEATWORKS
av. Oxford Falls 227 B14
MECHANIC
st. Newtown 17 H10
MECKIFF
av. North Rocks 278 J3
cl. Menai 458 E9
MEDCALFE
pl. Edensor Pk 363 E3
MEDEA
pl. Dean Park 212 F15
MEDHURST
rd. Gilead 539 F10

MEDIATI
av. Kellyville 216 G7
MEDICH
pl. Bringelly 388 E10
MEDICI
pl. Glenwood 246 A4
MEDIKA
pl. Kirrawee 461 D15
MEDLEY
av. Liverpool 365 A14
MEDLOW
dr. Quakers Hill 243 H1
MEDORA
la. Cabarita 312 E15
st. Cabarita 312 D16
MEDUSA
st. Mosman 287 A16
MEDWAY
rd. Bringelly 387 K11
rd. Bringelly 388 A12
st. Bexley 402 H14
MEDWIN
pl. Quakers Hill 214 C11
MEEGAN
pl. Colyton 270 F8
MEEHAM
st. West Hoxton 392 A12
MEEHAN
av. Hamondvle 396 D13
av. Wrrngtn Cty 238 J5
la. Georges Hall 367 H9
la. Matraville 437 D3
la. Wrrngtn Cty, off Meehan Av 238 H5
pl. Baulkham Hl 247 F3
pl. Campbelltwn 511 E8
pl. Harringtn Pk 478 E5
pl. Kirrawee 490 H7
rd. Cromer 228 C15
st. Granville 308 A8
st. Matraville 437 C1
tce. Harringtn Pk 478 F5
MEEKATHARRA
pl. Yarrawarrah 489 H12
MEEKS
cr. Faulconbdg 171 A15
la. Kingsford 406 G1
la. Marrickville, off Meeks Rd 374 A14
rd. Marrickville 374 A14
st. Kingsford 406 G1
MEELA
st. Blacktown 273 K3
MEGALONG
av. N Willghby 285 H8
cr. Campbelltwn 512 A7
MEGAN
av. Bankstown 399 F4
av. Smithfield 335 F2
rd. Galston 160 F10
st. Telopea 279 D6
MEIG
pl. Marayong 244 D9
MEITNER
pl. Lucas Ht 487 J12
MEKEO
pl. Glenfield 424 G13
MEKONG
pl. Kearns 481 B1
MELALEUCA
cl. Castle Hill 248 G4
cr. Carlingford 280 E8
dr. Mcquarie Fd 454 F3
dr. St Ives 224 D15
gr. Greenacre 370 F6
la. Mosman, off Mandolong Rd 317 B6
la. Kingswood, off Melaleuca Pl 267 F2
pl. Alfords Point 429 B15
pl. Kingswood 267 G2
pl. Prestons 393 J16
rd. Narellan Vale 478 H14
st. Newport 169 K13
st. Stanhpe Gdn 215 D10
MELANESIA
av. Lethbrdg Pk 240 G3
MELANIE
pl. Bella Vista 246 F6
st. Bankstown 369 C13
st. Hassall Gr 211 K15
st. Yagoona 369 C13
MELBA
av. Chifley 437 B7

dr. East Ryde 282 K15
pl. Casula 424 G1
pl. St Helens Pk 541 D3
rd. Lalor Park 245 C10
MELBOURNE
av. Mona Vale 199 D9
rd. E Lindfield 254 K13
rd. Riverstone 182 G1
rd. St Johns Pk 364 D3
rd. Winston Hills 247 J16
st. Concord 341 J9
st. Fairlight 288 B8
st. Oxley Park 270 G1
MELDON
pl. Stanhpe Gdn 215 G9
MELDRUM
av. Miranda 492 C1
av. Mt Pritchard 364 J11
st. Ryde 282 G15
wy. Claymore 481 D12
MELFORD
st. Hurlstone Pk 372 J13
MELHAM
av. Panania 398 D14
MELIA
ct. Castle Hill 218 J14
pl. Mcquarie Fd 424 F16
MELINDA
cl. Kellyville 185 J15
MELINGA
pl. Revesby 428 G4
MELINZ
pl. Quakers Hill 214 F12
MELISSA
pl. Cherrybrook 219 F7
pl. Kings Park 244 G6
pl. W Pnnant Hl 248 K7
st. Auburn 338 G14
MELITA
rd. Cambrdg Pk 237 H8
MELKARTH
pl. Doonside 243 E16
MELKIN
end, Gordon 253 J6
MELLA
pl. West Hoxton 392 C5
MELLFELL
rd. Cranebrook 207 F10
MELLICK
st. Fairfield W 335 F13
MELLIODORA
wy. Mcquarie Fd 454 F3
MELLOR
pl. Bonnyrigg Ht 363 A7
pl. Hebersham 241 F9
st. West Ryde 311 F1
MELNOTTE
av. Roseville 284 J5
MELODY
la. Collaroy 229 A15
la. Coogee 377 E15
st. Coogee 377 E16
st. Toongabbie 276 B5
MELROSE
av. Lakemba 400 K3
av. Quakers Hill 243 G2
av. Sylvania 461 K9
av. Wiley Park 400 K3
la. Woollahra 21 F4
pde. Clovelly 377 K13
pl. Bossley Park 333 E12
rd. Abbotsford 343 A2
rd. Chiswick 343 A2
st. Brooklyn 75 F11
st. Chester Hill 338 C16
st. Croydon Pk 372 A7
st. Epping 280 J2
st. Homebush 341 D11
st. Lane Cove W 284 A12
st. Mosman 316 J6
MELTON
rd. Glenorie 127 H9
st.n, Silverwater 309 G14
st.s, Auburn 309 G15
MELUCA
cr. Hornsby Ht 191 D1
MELVILLE
av. Cabramatta 366 A6
av. Strathfield 340 H15
cl. Berowra 133 C16
cl. Hinchinbrk 393 A1
la. Newtown 17 E12
pl. Barden Rdg 488 F2
rd. Rooty Hill 272 A4

rd. St Clair 269 J12
st. Ashbury 372 F8
st. Parramatta 308 H1
st. Ryde 281 J15
st. West Ryde 281 H15
MELVIN
st.n, Beverly Hills 401 A14
st.s, Beverly Hills 401 B15
MELWOOD
av. Forestville 255 J12
av. Killarney Ht 255 K14
MEMA
pl. Quakers Hill 243 H3
MEMBREY
st. Granville 308 F16
MEMMANG
pl. Kirrawee 461 D15
MEMORIAL
av. Ingleburn 453 B4
av. Kellyville 216 E8
av. Liverpool 395 A4
av. Merrylands 307 H14
av. Penrith 236 D8
av. Rookwood 340 C15
av. St Ives 224 A11
dr. Granville 308 G12
dr. Padstow 399 E15
dr. Richmond 120 A6
MEMPHIS
cr. Toongabbie 275 H11
st. Minto 452 G13
st. Minto 452 J13
st. Mount Druitt 241 A16
MEMTEC
pky. S Windsor 121 A15
MENA
av. Lansvale 367 A8
st. Belfield 371 C11
st. N Strathfield 341 C4
wy. Bidwill 211 F13
MENAI
rd. Bangor 459 A13
rd. Bangor 459 H13
rd. Menai 458 H12
rd. Woronora 459 K14
MENANGLE
rd. Camden 507 A3
rd. Campbelltwn 511 A6
rd. Gilead 509 K16
rd. Glen Alpine 510 C10
rd. Menangle 538 H16
rd. Menangle Pk 538 J11
st. Picton 563 G4
st.w, Picton 563 F3
MENDANA
st. Lethbrdg Pk 240 F4
MENDELEEF
av. Lucas Ht 487 F12
MENDELSSOHN
av. Emerton 240 H5
MENDI
pl. Glenfield 424 B13
pl. Whalan 240 H12
MENDOS
pl. Engadine 489 F7
MENIN
pl. Milperra 397 G12
rd. Matraville 407 A16
rd. Oakville 153 B7
MENINDEE
av. Leumeah 482 F13
wy. Woodcroft 243 H10
MENSA
pl. Castle Hill 218 K9
pl. Jamisontown 266 D6
MENTHA
pl. Mcquarie Fd 454 B4
MENTMORE
av. Rosebery 375 G16
MENTONE
av. Cronulla 494 A13
MENUS
pl. Rsemeadow 540 H2
MENZIES
arc. Sydney 1 G16
cct. St Clair 270 A12
la. Marsfield 281 G2
la. St Clair, off Menzies Cct 270 A13
pl. Edensor Pk 333 H13
rd. Marsfield 281 G1
MEPUNGA
st. Concord W 341 F2

MERA
st. Guildford 337 C4
MERAUKE
st. Whalan 240 J11
MERCATOR
cr. Willmot 210 E14
MERCEDES
pl. Kareela 461 D11
rd. Ingleburn 453 H13
MERCER
cr. Beverly Hills 400 K16
st. Castle Hill 218 D15
st. Castle Hill 218 E15
MERCHANT
st. Mascot 405 E7
st. Stanmore 16 G12
MERCURY
pl. Kings Lngly 246 B8
st. Beverly Hills 400 J14
st. Narwee 400 J14
MERCUTIO
pl. Gilead 540 F8
MERCY
av. Chester Hill 337 K12
MERDLE
pl. Ambarvale 540 F1
MEREDITH
av. Hornsby Ht 191 D8
av. Kellyville 216 G5
cl. Fairfield 336 E6
cr. St Helens Pk 541 B8
pl. Frenchs Frst 256 F7
rch. Westleigh 220 H7
st. Bankstown 369 D15
st. Blaxland 233 E9
st. Epping 280 F4
st. Homebush 341 B11
st. Strathfield 341 B11
wy. Cecil Hills 362 E1
MEREIL
st. Campbelltwn 511 K3
MERELYN
rd. Belrose 226 B16
MERELYNNE
av. W Pnnant Hl 248 K8
MEREVALE
pl. Oakhurst 241 J4
MERIDIAN
pl. Bella Vista 216 A16
pl. Doonside 243 H16
st. Eastlakes 405 J6
MERIEL
st. Sans Souci 463 A5
MERINDA
av. Baulkham Hl 248 B8
av. Epping 250 F11
pl. Bonnyrigg 364 B8
st. Lane Cove W 283 J14
st. St Marys 239 F14
MERINDAH
rd. Baulkham Hl 247 A7
wy. Kurrajong 55 J10
MERINO
cct. St Clair 270 D12
cr. Airds 511 H15
dr. Elderslie 507 H1
pl. Sylvania 462 B13
st. Miller 393 G2
MERION
ct. Glenmore Pk 266 G9
MERITON
st. Gladesville 312 G12
MERLE
st. Bass Hill 368 D7
st. N Epping 251 C8
st. Sefton 338 F13
MERLEN
cr. Yagoona 369 B9
MERLENE OTTEY
av. Newington L H16
av. Newington 310 A14
MERLEY
rd. Strathfield 341 A13
MERLIN
cl. Mt Colah 162 D8
ct. Castle Hill 217 H4
pl. Emu Heights 235 C3
st. Blacktown 274 G8
st. Neutral Bay 6 B1
st. Neutral Bay 316 A8
st. Roseville 284 K1
st. The Oaks 502 F13
st. The Oaks 502 G10
MERLOT
pl. Edensor Pk 333 C16
MERMAID
av. Maroubra 407 H8
MERNAGH
st. Ashcroft 364 E15
MEROO
cl. Wakeley 334 J13
st. Auburn 338 J11
st. Blacktown 244 D16
MERRANG
ct. Wattle Grove 425 J6
MERREDIN
cl. Yarrawarrah 489 F13
MERRENBURN
av. Naremburn 315 G3
MERRETT
cr. Greenacre 370 C9
MERRI
av. Peakhurst 430 D9
pl. St Johns Pk 364 F2
MERRIC
ct. Oakhurst 242 A4
MERRICK
av. Lakemba 371 A14
pl. N Richmond 87 A12
wy. Glenhaven 217 K6
MERRIDONG
rd. Elanora Ht 198 F13
MERRILEE
cr. Frenchs Frst 255 K3
MERRILONG
av. Mt Krng-gai 163 B10
st. Castle Hill 247 G3
MERRIMAN
cl. Elderslie 507 H2
pl. Airds 512 B11
st. Kyle Bay 432 A15
st. Millers Point A A1
st. Millers Point 1 C9
MERRIN
cl. St Helens Pk 541 E2
MERRINA
st. Hebersham 241 E9
MERRINDAL
cl. Cranebrook 207 E7
MERRINGTON
pl. Woolwich 314 F14
MERRIS
pl. Milperra 397 H10
st. Kingsgrove 401 H6
MERRIT
pl. Mcquarie Fd 454 G4
MERRIVALE
la. Turramurra 223 F12
rd. Pymble 223 D16
rd. St Ives 223 D16
MERRIVILLE
rd. Kellyville 215 B2
MERRIWA
av. Hoxton Park 392 G7
pl. Cherrybrook 219 D10
pl. Yarrawarrah 489 E14
st. Gordon 253 E7
MERROO
rd. Kurrajong 55 D9
MERRYL
av. Old Tngabbie 276 J8
MERRYLANDS
rd. Greystanes 306 F10
rd. Merrylands 307 B11
rd. Merrylnds W 307 B11
MERRYN
cl. Cobbitty 448 A13
cl. Harringtn Pk 448 A13
MERRYVALE
rd. Minto 482 C2
MERRYVILLE
ct. Wattle Grove 425 K2
MERRYWEATHER
cl. Minto 483 A2
MERSEY
cl. Bossley Park 333 F5
rd. Bringelly 387 G3
st. Woronora 460 A16
MERTON
av. Cmbrdg Gdn 237 G2
la. Stanmore 16 C11
st. Dean Park 242 G1
st. Kogarah Bay 432 K11
st. Petersham 16 C10
st. Rozelle 7 A13
st. Stanmore 16 C10
st. Zetland 375 J10
st.n, Sutherland 490 E4
st.s, Sutherland 490 E6
MERTZ
pl. Leumeah 482 J11
MERU
pl. St Clair 269 F12
MERVILLE
st. Concord W 311 E12
MERYLA
st. Burwood 342 A12
MERYLL
av. Baulkham Hl 247 F10
MESA
wy. Stanhpe Gdn 215 C11
MESSINA
cr. Bonnyrigg Ht 362 K7
MESSINES
av. Milperra 397 H11
pl. Matraville 407 B16
MESSITER
st. Campsie 372 C16
META
st. Caringbah 492 K2
st. Croydon 342 E16
st. Ryde 282 H14
METCALF
av. Carlingford 249 G16
METCALFE
av. Moorebank 396 D9
la. Lidcombe 339 F8
st. Cammeray 315 J6
st. Maroubra 407 C8
METELLA
cr. Belfield 371 G13
rd. Toongabbie 275 E14
METEOR
pl. Raby 451 D16
METEREN
cl. Milperra 397 E13
METHIL
pl. St Andrews 452 A12
METHUEN
av. Mosman 317 F10
pde. Riverwood 400 E12
METHVEN
st. Mount Druitt 241 D13
METROPOLITAN
rd. Enmore 17 B14
METTERS
pl. Wetherill Pk 334 B2
METZ
pl. Plumpton 241 G7
METZLER
pl. Gordon 253 G5
MEURANTS
la. Glenwood 245 B1
la. Ramsgate 433 D12
MEWS
la. Marrickville 373 G15
MEWTON
rd. Maraylya 94 J15
MEY
cl. Cecil Hills 362 G4
MEYERS
av. Hunters Hill 313 F6
la. Sefton 368 F1
MEYMOTT
st. Coogee 407 D1
st. Randwick 407 D1
MEZEN
pl. St Clair 299 J1
MIA
pl. Clareville 169 F2
pl. Marayong 244 C3
MIAMBA
av. Carlingford 279 D1
MIAMI
cl. Greenfld Pk 333 K13
pl. Cranebrook 207 H11
pl. Frenchs Frst 256 G7
st. Glenwood 215 H12
MIA MIA
st. Girraween 276 D12
MIANGA
av. Engadine 518 J2
MIAX
pl. Dharruk 241 B8
MICA
pl. Eagle Vale 481 A8
MICAWBER
st. Ambarvale 511 A14
MICHAEL
av. Belfield 371 F12
av. Luddenham 356 H2
cl. Cranebrook 207 B14
pl. Ingleburn 453 C10
st. N Richmond 87 B14
st. North Ryde 282 D7
MICHAEL JORDAN
av. Newington L H16
av. Newington 310 B15
MICHAELS
cr. Punchbowl 399 H5
MICHAEL WENDEN
av. Newington L H16
av. Newington, off Newington Dr 310 C13
MICHELAGO
cct. Prestons 393 B13
MICHELE
av. Cambrdg Pk 237 H7
ct. Regents Pk 339 B16
la. Kingsgrove, off Bykool Av 401 E8
pl. Camden S 507 C11
pl. Turramurra 222 K7
rd. Cromer 228 H16
MICHELL
rd. Thirlmere 564 E6
MICHELLE
dr. Wentwthvle 277 C10
pl. Blaxland 234 F8
pl. Dural 188 G13
pl. Marayong 244 A6
MICHIGAN
av. Asquith 192 B11
rd. Riverwood 399 K12
rd. Seven Hills 275 E6
MIDDLE
la. Kingsford 406 G1
rd. Oxford Falls 227 A12
st. Kingsford 406 G1
st. McMahons Pt 5 E16
st. Marrickville 16 C15
st. Randwick 406 G1
MIDDLE HARBOUR
pl. Belrose 225 F14
rd. E Lindfield 254 F16
rd. Lindfield 284 E1
MIDDLE HEAD
rd. Mosman 317 C9
MIDDLEHOPE
st. Bonnyrigg Ht 363 A6
MIDDLEMISS
st. Lavender Bay K G13
st. Lavender Bay 5 H11
st. Mascot 405 F4
st. Rosebery 405 F4
MIDDLETON
av. Castle Hill 217 G13
av. Cranebrook 207 E9
av. Richmond 119 J4
av. Richmond 119 J6
cr. Bidwill 211 B15
pl. Picton 561 C4
rd. Chester Hill 337 G12
rd. Cromer 228 E14
rd. Leumeah 512 B2
st. Petersham 16 C13
MID-DURAL
rd. Galston 159 A7
rd. Middle Dural 158 J7
MIDELTON
av. Bexley North 402 F10
av. North Bondi 348 E15
MIDIN
cl. Glenmore Pk 266 C9
pl. Mount Druitt 241 F15
MIDLOTHIAN
av. Beverly Hills 401 A12
rd. St Andrews 452 A12
MIDSON
rd. Eastwood 280 H1
rd. Epping 280 H1
rd. Oakville 123 K13
MIDWAY
dr. Maroubra 407 C13
pl. Lethbrdg Pk 240 F3
MIDWINTER
row. St Clair 270 D14
MIFSUD
cr. Oakhurst 241 H3
st. Girraween 276 A10
MIGGS
pl. Ambarvale 511 A10
MIKADO
wy. Doonside 243 F16
MIKARIE
pl. Kirrawee 461 D15
MIKKELSEN
av. Tregear 240 F7
MILA
pl. Marayong 243 J6
MILAK
pl. Whalan 240 H12
MILAN
st. Prestons 393 F16
MILANO
pl. Edensor Pk 363 F1
MILBA
rd. Caringbah 493 C6
MILBURN
pl. St Ives Ch 194 B16
rd. Gymea 491 E2
st. Quakers Hill 214 C12
MILDARA
pl. Edensor Pk 333 D15
pl. W Pnnant Hl 249 A2
MILDRED
av. Hornsby 191 H13
av. Manly Vale 287 H4
st. Warrawee 222 D14
st. Wentwthvle 306 J1
MILDRED DIDRIKSEN
av. Newington L H16
av. Newington, off Jon Henricks Av 309 K15
MILDURA
pl. Prestons 393 E14
st. Killara 253 G14
MILE END
rd. Rouse Hill 184 K8
rd. Rouse Hill 185 B6
MILEHAM
av. Baulkham Hl 247 H5
av. Castle Hill 247 H5
st. S Windsor 120 G16
st. Windsor 121 A11
wy. Minto 482 H6
MILES
st. Bnkstn Aprt 367 K16
st. Brookvale 258 D12
st. Chester Hill 338 C16
st. Mascot 405 D1
st. Surry Hills 20 B4
MILES FRANKLIN
cl. Glenmore Pk 265 K6
MILFORD
av. Panania 428 A5
dr. Rouse Hill 185 C7
gr. Cherrybrook 219 A13
pl. Turramurra 252 F5
rd. Ellis Lane 476 A9
rd. Londonderry 148 F10
rd. Miranda 492 D3
rd. Peakhurst 400 F16
st. Randwick 377 B14
wy. Wentwthvle 277 E11
MILGA
rd. Avalon 140 E13
MILGATE
la. Campbelltwn 511 E4
MILGUY
av. Castle Hill 247 F1
MILHAM
av. Eastwood 281 F5
cr. Forestville 255 D8
st. St Marys 269 J4
MILI
pl. Kings Park 244 J2
MILITARY
dr. Lilyfield 10 A1
la. Cremorne 6 H2
rd. Cremorne 316 C9
rd. Dover Ht 348 F8
rd. Guildford 337 G4
rd. Matraville 436 G8
rd. Merrylands 307 J16
rd. Mosman 316 H6
rd. Neutral Bay 6 F1
rd. North Bondi 378 G1
rd. Vaucluse 348 F7
rd. Watsons Bay 318 G14
MILK
av. Vaucluse 348 E2
MILL
dr. North Rocks 248 F12
la. Hurlstone Pk 373 A12
la. The Rocks B A2
pl. St Clair 270 E10

rd. Campbelltwn...481 H14
rd. Kurrajong...55 F12
rd. Kurrajong Hl...54 J12
rd. Liverpool...395 C6
st. Bnksmeadw...406 D12
st. Carlton...432 G4
st. Currans Hill...479 J10
st. Hurlstone Pk...373 A12
st. Riverstone...182 J6
MILLAR
cr. Dural...188 H12
st. Drummoyne...343 G5
MILLARD
cr. Plumpton...241 G9
MILLBROOK
pl. Cherrybrook...219 E12
MILLEN
st. Kingswood...238 A13
MILLENNIUM
ct. Matraville...436 J7
ct. Silverwater...309 G11
MILLER
av. Ashfield...372 G3
av. Bexley North...402 F11
av. Dundas Vy...280 E10
av. Hornsby...191 H14
la. Cammeray...315 K5
la. Petersham...15 F16
la. Pyrmont...12 G4
pl. Menai...458 F10
pl. Mt Pritchard...364 J10
pl. Tahmoor...565 G9
rd. Bass Hill...367 J6
rd. Chester Hill...337 J11
rd. Chester Hill...367 J6
rd. Glenorie...126 D3
rd. Miller...393 G4
rd. Villawood...367 J6
st. Bondi...378 A4
st. Cammeray...315 J6
st. Crows Nest...315 J6
st. Haberfield...343 C13
st. Kingsgrove...402 B5
st. Kingsgrove...402 C6
st. Lavender Bay...K C14
st. Lavender Bay...5 F11
st. McMahons Pt...K C14
st. McMahons Pt...5 F11
st. Merrylands...307 H13
st. Mount Druitt...271 C3
st. N Sydney...K D10
st. N Sydney...K C14
st. N Sydney...K D6
st. N Sydney...5 F11
st. N Sydney...5 F7
st. Petersham...15 G15
st. Pyrmont...12 F4
st. S Granville...338 E7
st. S Penrith...236 H15
wy. Claymore...481 D11
MILLERS
rd. Cattai...94 B7
wy. W Pnnant Hl...248 H7
MILLET
row. Wrrngtn Dns...238 E5
MILLETT
rd. Mosman...316 J10
st. Hurstville...431 F1
MILLEWA
av. Wahroonga...222 C6
av. Warrawee...222 C6
la. Wahroonga, off Millewa Av...222 D6
MILL HILL
rd. Bondi Jctn...22 D8
MILLICENT
st. Greystanes...305 J1
MILLIE
st. Guildford...337 E6
MILLIGAN
la. Cranebrook, off Milligan Rd...207 C13
rd. Cranebrook...207 C13
MILLING
st. Hunters Hill...313 A8
MILL POND
rd. Botany...405 D8
MILLS
av. Asquith...191 K7
av. North Rocks...249 A16
cr. Burwood...342 C12
la. Chatswood...284 K9
la. Winmalee...173 J7
pl. Beacon Hill...257 D7
rd. Glenhaven...187 F16
rd. Londonderry...148 G15
st. Croydon...372 D3
st. Lidcombe...339 J7
st. Merrylands...307 A10
MILLSTREAM
gr. Dural...219 A3
rd. Wrrngtn Dns...237 K5
MILLWOOD
av. Chatswd W...284 A8
av. Narellan...478 C9
MIL MIL
st. McMahons Pt...5 D14
MILNE
av. Kingswood...237 G15
av. Matraville...406 H16
cl. Wetherill Pk...335 A7
la. Tempe, off Lymerston St...404 D1
la. Merrylands, off Terminal Pl...307 J13
pl. Narellan Vale...478 K10
st. Ryde...282 G16
st. Tahmoor...565 F12
MILNER
av. Hornsby...221 C4
av. Kirrawee...490 H6
cr. Wollstncraft...315 C9
la. Mosman, off Milner St...317 A10
rd. Artarmon...284 J16
rd. Guildford...337 H7
rd. Peakhurst...400 F16
st. Mosman...317 A9
MILPARINKA
av. Glenwood...245 F1
cl. Hoxton Park...392 F7
MILPERA
pl. Cromer...228 B16
MILPERRA
rd. Bnkstn Aprt...397 G6
rd. Milperra...397 G6
rd. Revesby...397 G6
MILRAY
av. Wollstncraft...315 B11
st. Lindfield...254 D15
MILROY
av. Kensington...376 B10
st. North Ryde...282 E8
MILSON
pde. Normanhurst...221 D9
pde. Thornleigh...221 D9
rd. Cremorne Pt...316 F13
rd. Doonside...243 E12
rd. Woodcroft...243 E12
MILSOP
pl. Mortdale...431 B4
st. Bexley...432 H4
MILSTED
rd. Terrey Hills...196 E5
MILTON
av. Eastwood...280 G7
av. Mosman...317 B11
av. Woollahra...22 F2
cl. Wetherill Pk...334 K5
cr. Leumeah...512 B2
cr. Prestons...392 H13
la. Burwood, off Neich Pde...342 A11
la. Ashfield, off Norton St...372 F3
pl. Frenchs Frst...256 D8
pl. Greystanes...306 C11
rd. N Turramrra...223 F3
rd. Riverstone...182 D10
st. Ashbury...372 F5
st. Ashfield...372 F4
st. Ashfield...372 F5
st. Bankstown...369 G14
st. Burwood...342 A11
st. Carlingford...280 A1
st. Chatswood...285 B7
st. Colyton...270 H7
st. Granville...308 C10
st. Leichhardt...10 D14
st. Lidcombe...339 F7
st. Riverstone...182 F13
st. Rydalmere...309 J4
st. Thirlmere...562 C15
st.n, Ashfield...372 F2
wy. Shalvey...210 J14
MILVAY
pl. Ambarvale...511 B15
MIMA
st. Sefton...368 G2
MI MI
st. Oatley...431 A12
MIMIKA
av. Whalan...240 J12
MIMOS
st. Denistone W...281 A13
MIMOSA
av. Toongabbie...276 C5
cl. St Clair...270 B15
gr. Glenwood...245 G2
rd. Bossley Park...334 A10
rd. Greenacre...369 J12
rd. Greenfld Pk...334 A12
rd. Turramurra...252 E3
st. Bargo...567 D5
st. Bexley...402 E14
st. Frenchs Frst...255 F3
st. Granville...308 G16
st. Heathcote...519 A10
st. Oatley...431 A14
st. S Hurstville...432 A11
st. Westmead...307 H3
MIMULUS
la. Regents Pk...369 B2
pl. Caringbah...492 E13
pl. Mcquarie Fd...454 G4
MINA
rd. Menai...458 H10
MINAGO
pl. Castle Hill...218 A7
MINAHAN
pl. Plumpton...241 G9
MINA ROSA
st. Enfield...371 G4
MINARTO
la. N Narrabeen...228 K2
MINCHIN
av. Richmond...118 D9
dr. Minchinbury...271 J7
MINCHINBURY
st. Eastern Ck...272 D7
tce. Eschol Park...481 A6
MINDA
pl. Whalan...240 H11
MINDANAO
av. Lethbrdg Pk...240 F3
MINDAR
st. Como...460 H7
MINDARIBBA
av. Rouse Hill...185 D7
MINDARIE
st. Lane Cove W...283 J14
MINDONA
wy. Woodcroft...243 J11
MINDORO
pl. Lethbrdg Pk...240 G5
MINELL
ct. Harringtn Pk...478 E1
MINER
gln. Erskine Park...271 A11
pl. Ingleburn...453 F7
MINERAL SPRINGS
rd. Picton...563 G11
MINERVA
cr. Kellyville...186 A14
pl. Prestons...392 K13
rd. Wedderburn...540 B11
st. Kirrawee...490 H5
MINGA
st. Ryde...282 F15
MINIMBAH
rd. Northbridge...286 D14
MINJ
pl. Glenfield...424 J9
MINKARA
rd. Bayview...168 E15
MINMAI
rd. Chester Hill...337 F13
rd. Mona Vale...198 G2
MINNA
cl. Belrose...225 H1
st. Burwood...371 H1
MINNAMORRA
av. Earlwood...403 A5
MINNAMURRA
av. Miranda...492 F3
av. Pymble...253 C8
cct. Prestons...393 B16
cct. Prestons...423 A1
gr. Dural...219 A3
pl. Pymble...253 C9
rd. Northbridge...286 D15
MINNEAPOLIS
cr. Maroubra...407 C13
MINNEK
cl. Glenmore Pk...266 C11
MINNESOTA
av. Five Dock...343 B11
av. Riverwood...400 A13
MINNIE
st. Belmore...371 A12
MINNS
rd. Gordon...253 J6
MINOGUE
cr. Forest Lodge...11 E13
cr. Forest Lodge...11 E14
MINORCA
wy. Minto...482 H7
MINSTREL
pl. Rouse Hill...185 C6
MINT
cl. St Clair...269 G11
la. St Clair, off Mint Cl...269 G11
pl. Quakers Hill...243 F4
MINTARO
av. Strathfield...371 C2
MINTER
st. Canterbury...372 G13
MINTO
av. Haberfield...343 E12
cl. Bonnyrigg Ht...363 C4
pl. Erskine Park...270 J15
rd. Minto...453 A14
st. Hebersham...241 D9
MINTOFF
pl. Dean Park, off Raupach St...212 F16
MINTON
av. Dolls Point...463 E1
MINUET
ct. Glenwood...245 C1
MINYA
av. Kingsford...406 D2
MIOWERA
av. Carss Park...432 E15
rd. Chester Hill...337 F14
rd. Northbridge...286 F15
rd. N Turramrra...223 G6
MIRAGE
av. Raby...481 E1
MIRAMBENA
cl. Cherrybrook...220 A13
MIRAMONT
av. Riverview...314 A6
MIRANDA
cl. Cherrybrook...219 J3
pl. Rsemeadow...540 K6
rd. Miranda...492 C2
rd. Miranda...492 C5
st. S Penrith...267 C5
MIRANG
pl. Engadine...488 J9
MIRBELIA
ct. Voyager Pt...427 C5
pde. Elanora Ht...197 J12
pde. Ingleside...197 J12
pl. Caringbah...493 B6
MIRCA
pl. Appin...568 C7
MIRETTA
pl. Castle Hill...247 J3
MIRI
cr. Holsworthy...426 D2
ct. St Ives...223 K16
MIRIAM
cl. Smithfield...336 B7
ct. Baulkham Hl...247 C2
rd. Denistone...281 D12
rd. West Ryde...281 D12
st. Bass Hill...368 C10
MIRIMAR
av. Bronte...378 B7
MIROOL
st. Denistone W...280 K13
st. West Ryde...280 K13
MIRRA
pl. Cromer...228 D14
MIRRABOOK
pl. Heathcote...518 F10
MIRRABOOKA
av. Strathfield...341 B11
cr. Little Bay...437 A11
ct. Emu Heights...234 K5
st. Bilgola...169 E5
MIRRADONG
pl. Kirribilli...2 E3
MIRRAL
rd. Caringbah...492 G15
rd. Lilli Pilli...522 G1
MIRRI
pl. Glenmore Pk...266 B10
MIRROOL
st. N Narrabeen...198 G16
st. N Narrabeen...228 G2
st. N Wahrnga...192 E15
MISIMA
pl. Glenfield...424 J10
MISSENDEN
rd. Camperdwn...17 G3
rd. Newtown...17 J6
MISSISSIPPI
cr. Kearns...451 A15
rd. Seven Hills...275 D9
MISSOURI
pl. Riverwood...400 A13
st. Kearns...451 A14
MISTLETOE
av. Clarmnt Ms...238 J16
av. Mcquarie Fd...454 B6
st. Loftus...489 K11
MISTRAL
av. Mosman...316 K11
pl. Shalvey...210 J13
st. Greenfld Pk...334 C13
MISTY
gln. Wrrngtn Dns...238 B4
MITALA
st. Newport...169 D10
MITCHAM
rd. Bankstown...369 B15
st. Punchbowl...400 A7
MITCHELL
av. Jannali...460 F12
cl. Tahmoor...565 K13
cr. Turramurra...222 C16
cr. Warrawee...222 C16
dr. Glossodia...59 G9
dr. West Hoxton...392 B12
la. Alexandria...18 G15
la. Mosman, off Mitchell Rd...317 B3
la.e, Glebe...12 F13
la.w, Glebe...12 E13
pl. Kenthurst...188 E7
rd. Alexandria...18 G16
rd. Alexandria...375 B10
rd. Brookvale...258 C12
rd. Cronulla...494 A10
rd. Darling Point...13 K4
rd. Dural...190 A9
rd. Erskineville...375 B10
rd. Moorebank...395 J9
rd. Mosman...317 B3
rd. Palm Beach...140 A3
rd. Pitt Town...93 B11
rd. Rose Bay...348 D8
rd. Strathfield...340 G12
st. Arncliffe...403 E8
st. Bondi Beach...378 D1
st. Camden...477 A15
st. Campbelltwn...511 J7
st. Carramar...336 H16
st. Centnnial Pk...21 E7
st. Chifley...437 A3
st. Condell Park...398 F3
st. Croydon Pk...371 G5
st. Enfield...371 G5
st. Ermington...280 D16
st. Five Dock...343 B7
st. Glebe...12 D16
st. Greenwich...314 J13
st. Lalor Park...245 C13
st. McMahons Pt...5 C13
st. Marrickville...374 C11
st. Naremburn...315 E5
st. North Bondi...378 D1
st. Putney...312 B8
st. St Leonards...315 E5
st. St Marys...269 H3
st. S Penrith...236 H14
st. Villawood...337 A16
wy. Eveleigh...18 K10
MITCHELL PARK
rd. Cattai...94 F3
MITCHELLS
ps. Blaxland...233 K9
ps. Glenbrook...234 F10
MITTABAH
rd. Asquith...191 J8
rd. Hornsby...191 J8

MITTIAMO
st. Canley Ht........ 365 B1
MITUMBA
rd. Seven Hills..... 275 C10
MIVO
st. Holsworthy..... 426 D1
MIYAL
pl. Engadine........ 518 H2
MOALA
st. Concord W..... 311 E15
MOANI
av. Gymea........... 491 D4
MOATE
av. Btn-le-Sds...... 433 K2
MOBBS
la. Carlingford..... 280 E6
la. Epping........... 280 E6
MOCATTA
av. Pymble........... 253 E3
MODEL FARMS
rd. Northmead..... 277 H1
rd. Winston Hills.. 247 H16
MODERN
av. Canterbury..... 402 E1
MOFFAT
pl. Minto............ 482 H9
MOFFATT
dr. Lalor Park....... 245 H10
wy. Kellyville......... 185 J14
MOFFATTS
dr. Dundas Vy...... 279 J10
MOFFITT
cr. Edensor Pk..... 333 G15
MOFFITTS
la. Ellis Lane........ 476 C6
MOGILA
st. Seven Hills..... 275 E4
MOGO
ct. Prestons......... 392 J13
pl. Glenmore Pk.. 266 B11
MOHAVE
pl. Bossley Park.. 334 A12
MOHAWK
cr. Greenfld Pk.... 334 A16
pl. Erskine Park... 271 A16
MOIR
av. Northmead..... 277 J6
pl. Bidwill............ 211 B16
st. Smithfield....... 335 E3
MOIRA
av. Denistone W... 281 A14
av. West Ryde...... 281 A14
cr. Coogee........... 377 F13
cr. Randwick....... 377 F13
cr. St Marys......... 269 J4
la. St Marys, off Moira Cr......... 269 K3
pl. Frenchs Frst... 256 F10
st. Sutherland...... 460 H16
MOJO
pl. Greenfld Pk.... 333 K13
MOKARI
st. N Richmond..... 87 C14
MOKERA
av. Kirrawee......... 461 A15
MOLES
rd. Wilberforce....... 61 B1
MOLESWORTH
la. Longueville..... 314 E7
MOLISE
av. Kellyville......... 186 H16
MOLLE
pl. Narellan Vale.. 478 G16
MOLLER
av. Birrong........... 369 A6
MOLLISON
cr. Ermington...... 280 A16
MOLLOY
av. S Coogee........ 407 G7
ct. Mortdale......... 430 F6
pl. Minchinbury.... 272 C9
MOLLS
la. Mowbray Pk... 561 J8
MOLLUSO
cl. Wakeley......... 334 G15
MOLLYMOOK
st. Prestons......... 393 B13
MOLONG
rd. Gymea Bay..... 491 E12
st. N Curl Curl..... 259 B11
st. Quakers Hill.... 243 K1
wy. Bidwill............ 211 E13
MOLONGLO
rd. Seven Hills..... 275 E10

MOLYNEAUX
av. Kings Lngly.... 245 J7
MOMBRI
st. Merrylands..... 307 K12
MONA
la. Darling Point.... 13 F8
rd. Darling Point.... 13 G9
rd. Menai............. 458 K11
rd. Riverwood...... 400 E15
st. Allawah.......... 432 E7
st. Auburn........... 339 A2
st. Bankstown...... 399 E1
st. Mona Vale...... 199 C1
st. S Granville...... 338 G1
st. Wahroonga..... 222 J7
MONACO
av. Kellyville......... 185 F8
pl. Prestons......... 393 C15
pl. Quakers Hill.... 214 E13
MONAGHAN
st. Minto............. 482 H2
MONAHAN
av. Banksia.......... 403 E13
MONARCH
cct. Glenmore Pk... 266 B13
cl. Rouse Hill....... 185 E5
pl. Quakers Hill.... 213 K8
MONARO
av. Kingsgrove..... 401 H12
cl. Bossley Park... 333 K9
pl. Beacon Hill..... 258 A5
pl. Emu Plains..... 234 K7
pl. Heckenberg.... 364 A15
st. Homebush B......M C6
st. Seven Hills...... 246 C13
MONASH
av. East Hills........ 427 H4
av. East Killara...... 254 G10
av. Gt Mckrl Bch... 109 A13
av. Holsworthy..... 396 B13
cr. Clontarf.......... 287 E14
gdn. Pagewood....... 406 F7
pde. Croydon........ 342 E12
pde. Dee Why......... 259 B9
pl. Bonnyrigg....... 364 A6
rd. Blacktown....... 273 J1
rd. Doonside........ 273 G1
rd. Gladesville...... 312 H5
rd. Menai............. 458 J6
st. Wentwthvle..... 306 J3
MONASTERY
pl. Cherrybrook.... 219 F15
MONA VALE
pl. Woodbine....... 481 J10
rd. Ingleside........ 197 B9
rd. Krngai Ch NP.. 224 F4
rd. Mona Vale...... 198 G3
rd. Pymble........... 253 F4
rd. St Ives........... 224 C10
rd. Terrey Hills..... 195 H16
rd. Warriewood.... 198 B6
MONCKTON
pl. Glenfield........ 424 H11
MONCRIEFF
cl. St Helens Pk... 541 C3
dr. East Ryde....... 282 K15
pl. Milperra.......... 397 E10
rd. Lalor Park....... 245 C9
MONCUR
av. Belmore.......... 401 H4
la. Woollahra......... 21 J3
st. Marrickville..... 373 G14
st. Woollahra......... 21 J3
MONDIAL
pl. West Ryde...... 281 H13
MONDOVI
cl. Prestons......... 393 H16
MONDS
la. Picton............ 561 A4
la. Picton............ 563 E1
MONFARVILLE
st. St Marys......... 269 H5
MONFORD
pl. Cremorne....... 316 E8
MONGA
pl. Prestons......... 392 J15
MONGON
pl. St Helens Pk... 541 H3
MONI
wy. Doonside........ 243 F15
MONICA
av. Hassall Gr....... 211 K16
cl. Lurnea............ 394 D6
pl. Jamisontown... 265 K3

pl. Tahmoor......... 565 H8
MONIE
av. East Hills......... 427 G4
MONIER
sq. Villawood........ 367 G1
MONITOR
rd. Merrylands..... 307 F12
MONK
av. Arncliffe.......... 403 G6
MONKEY
rd. The Oaks........ 502 B7
MONKS
la. Alexandria......... 18 D13
la. Erskineville....... 18 D13
la. Mt Hunter....... 504 H5
MONMOUTH
av. East Killara...... 254 F9
st. Randwick........ 377 B10
MONOMEETH
pl. Miranda.......... 462 A16
st. Bexley............ 402 J15
MONRO
av. Kirrawee......... 491 A2
MONROE
st. Blacktown....... 274 H4
st. Ermington....... 280 E12
MONS
av. Maroubra........ 407 C10
av. West Ryde...... 311 C1
rd. N Balgowlah.... 287 B4
rd. Wentwthvle..... 277 E13
rd. Westmead...... 277 E13
st. Canterbury...... 372 D16
st. Condell Park.... 398 J9
st. Lidcombe..........M K13
st. Lidcombe........ 340 B5
st. Revesby.......... 398 J9
st. Russell Lea...... 343 D5
st. S Granville...... 338 G3
st. Vaucluse......... 348 G5
MONSERRA
rd. Allambie Ht..... 257 F13
MONT
pl. St Clair........... 269 G9
MONTAGUE
cl. Green Valley.... 363 A13
pl. Rsemeadow.... 540 G4
rd. Cremorne........ 316 G5
st. Balmain............. 7 E9
st. Fairfield Ht...... 335 H9
st. Greystanes...... 306 C7
st. Illawong.......... 459 C6
st. North Manly.... 258 A14
MONTAH
av. Killara............ 254 C9
MONTANA
av. North Rocks.... 278 G2
cr. Riverwood...... 399 K12
wy. Mcquarie Fd.... 454 H4
MONTAUBAN
av. Seaforth......... 287 A7
MONT CLAIR
la. Darlinghurst........ 4 F11
MONTE BELLO
cl. Green Valley.... 362 K14
MONTECLAIR
av. Liverpool........ 395 A10
MONTEITH
la. Turramurra..... 222 D15
la. Warrawee....... 222 D15
pl. Baulkham Hl.... 247 D6
st. Turramurra..... 222 D15
st. Warrawee....... 222 D15
MONTELIMAR
pl. Wallacia.......... 325 A13
MONTELLA
pl. Prestons......... 393 F14
MONTERAY
tce. Glenmore Pk... 266 F14
MONTEREY
pde. Ermington....... 280 E11
pl. Cherrybrook.... 219 D11
rd. Bilgola............ 169 H6
st. Monterey......... 433 F9
st. Newington..........L J16
st. Newington....... 310 D12
st. St Ives............ 224 D6
st. S Wntwthvle... 307 A7
MONTERRA
av. Peakhurst....... 430 D8
MONTGOMERY
av. Revesby.......... 398 K16
av. S Granville...... 338 E6
rd. Bonnyrigg....... 363 J9

rd. Carlingford...... 250 B15
st. Kogarah.......... 433 C4
st. Miranda.......... 492 C3
st. Narellan Vale... 479 B10
MONTI
pl. N Richmond..... 87 C13
MONTORE
rd. Minto............. 482 C4
MONTPELIER
dr. The Oaks......... 502 D16
st. Neutral Bay........ 6 B5
MONTREAL
av. Killara............ 283 E1
MONTROSE
av. Fairfield E........ 337 B14
av. Merrylands...... 307 K14
pl. St Andrews..... 451 K12
rd. Abbotsford..... 342 K1
rd. Winmalee........ 173 B12
st. Quakers Hill.... 213 K14
st. Turramurra..... 222 E16
MONTVIEW
pde. Hornsby Ht..... 191 E1
wy. Glenwood, off Crestview Dr.... 246 B6
MOOCULTA
st. Russell Lea..... 343 B6
MOODIE
la. Cammeray...... 316 A8
st. Cammeray...... 315 K8
st. Rozelle............ 344 D8
MOODY
st. Rooty Hill........ 272 C4
MOOKARA
pl. Port Hacking... 522 H1
MOOKI
st. Miranda.......... 492 C6
MOOLA
pde. Chatswd W..... 284 D13
pde. Lane Cove W... 284 D13
MOOLAH
rd. Terrey Hills...... 196 C6
MOOLANA
pde. S Penrith......... 266 G7
rd. Bnksmeadw.... 405 K15
MOOLANDA
av. W Pnnant Hl.... 249 C10
MOOMBARA
av. Peakhurst........ 430 H3
cr. Port Hacking... 522 J3
MOOMIN
pl. Busby............. 363 J15
st. Lalor Park....... 245 H10
MOONA
av. Baulkham Hl.... 246 K7
av. Matraville........ 436 H4
pde. Wahroonga..... 221 H16
rd. Kirrawee.......... 460 J15
st. Hornsby.......... 191 H8
MOONAH
cl. St Ives Ch....... 194 B15
cl. West Hoxton... 392 E6
gr. St Clair............ 270 B15
pl. Mcquarie Fd.... 454 D4
rd. Alfords Point... 429 A13
MOONARIE
pl. Cromer........... 228 A15
MOONBEAM
cl. St Clair........... 270 D13
MOONBI
cl. Greenfld Pk..... 334 C15
cr. Frenchs Frst.... 256 E2
pl. Kareela............ 461 E10
rd. Penrith............ 237 D3
MOONBIE
st. Summer Hill.... 373 C6
MOONBRIA
pl. Airds.............. 512 C12
st. Naremburn...... 315 E3
MOONDANI
la. Beverly Hills, off Moondani Rd... 401 A10
rd. Beverly Hills.... 401 A10
MOONDO
st. Greenacre....... 370 F11
MOONEY
av. Blakehurst...... 432 A14
av. Earlwood......... 402 F2
pl. Ruse.............. 512 C8
st. Lane Cove W... 284 A12
st. Strathfield S.... 371 B5
MOONLIGHT
rd. Prairiewood..... 334 E10

MOON POINT
rd. Illawong......... 459 D4
MOONS
av. Lugarno......... 429 F14
MOONSHINE
av. Cabramtta W.. 364 G6
MOONSTONE
pl. Eagle Vale....... 481 E6
MOONYEAN
pl. Cromer........... 228 C16
MOORA
st. Chester Hill..... 338 A15
MOORAL
av. Punchbowl..... 400 A9
MOORAMBA
av. Riverview....... 314 A5
rd. Dee Why........ 258 F7
MOORAMIE
av. Kensington..... 376 E15
MOORANYAH
cl. Woodcroft...... 243 H12
MOORE
av. Lindfield......... 283 F1
cr. Faulconbdg.... 171 D14
cr. Faulconbdg.... 171 C15
la. Campsie......... 372 B10
la. East Hills........ 427 J4
la. Harbord.......... 288 G1
la. Leichhardt........ 10 F12
la. Rozelle.............. 7 D16
pl. Bligh Park...... 150 E5
pl. Currans Hill.... 479 J12
pl. Doonside........ 243 D5
rd. Harbord.......... 288 G1
rd. Oakdale.......... 500 D11
rd. Springwood.... 202 B1
st. Bnksmeadw.... 406 C11
st. Bardwell Pk.... 402 J8
st. Bexley............ 402 A16
st. Blaxland......... 234 B6
st. Bondi............ 377 K4
st. Cabarita.......... 342 D1
st. Campbelltwn.. 511 F5
st. Campsie......... 372 B10
st. Canley Vale..... 366 F4
st. Clontarf.......... 287 G15
st. Coogee........... 377 J14
st. Drummoyne... 343 F3
st. Glenbrook....... 233 J15
st. Hurstville........ 402 A16
st. Lane Cove W.. 283 H15
st. Lansdowne..... 367 B4
st. Leichhardt........ 10 C12
st. Liverpool........ 395 A3
st. Roseville......... 285 B2
st. Rozelle.............. 7 C14
st. St Clair........... 269 K11
st. Strathfield....... 341 J10
st. Sutherland...... 490 D3
st. Vaucluse........ 318 G15
st.w, Leichhardt........ 10 A11
MOOREBANK
av. Moorebank..... 395 E10
MOORECOURT
av. Springwood... 201 G3
MOOREFIELD
av. Hunters Hill.... 313 G11
av. Kogarah......... 433 E6
la. Kogarah......... 433 C4
MOOREFIELDS
la. Beverly Hills, off Moorefields Rd.. 401 A10
rd. Beverly Hills.. 401 B9
rd. Kingsgrove..... 401 B9
rd. Roselands...... 401 B9
MOOREHEAD
av. Silverdale...... 353 H15
MOOREHOUSE
cr. Edensor Pk..... 363 H1
MOORE-OXLEY
st. Bradbury........ 511 D6
st. Campbelltwn.. 511 D6
MOORE PARK
rd. Moore Park...... 20 G2
rd. Paddington....... 20 G2
MOORES
la. Alexandria........ 19 B15
rd. Glenorie......... 128 J3
wy. Glenmore....... 503 E4
wy. The Oaks....... 503 E4
MOORESFIELD
la. Ellis Lane....... 476 D9
MOORES STEPS
Sydney...............B G5

MOORFOOT
rd. St Andrews 451 J15
MOORGATE
la. Chippendale 18 J1
st. Chippendale 18 K1
st. Toongabbie 276 H7
MOORHEN
st. Ingleburn 453 G5
MOORHOUSE
av. St Ives 254 D4
MOORILLA
av. Carlingford 249 G11
st. Dee Why 258 E8
MOORINA
av. Matraville 436 H4
cl. Greenfld Pk 334 D14
rd. Pymble 223 G14
MOORLAND
rd. Tahmoor 566 B10
rd. Tahmoor 566 C9
MOORLANDS
rd. Ingleburn 452 J8
MORAGO
wy. Airds 512 E10
MORAN
cl. Bonnyrigg Ht 363 E8
pl. Currans Hill 479 J13
st. Mosman 316 K12
wy. Minto 482 H8
MORANDOO
rd. Elanora Ht 198 F14
MORANT
st. Edensor Pk 363 H2
MORAR
pl. St Andrews 452 C12
MORAY
pl. Sylvania 461 G10
st. Richmond 118 J8
st. Winmalee 173 F13
MORDEN
st. Cammeray 315 K6
MOREE
av. Westmead 307 E1
pl. Bossley Park 333 E10
st. Gordon 253 F8
MOREHEAD
av. Mount Druitt 241 G11
st. Redfern 19 H14
st. Waterloo 19 H14
MORELLA
av. Sefton 368 E6
pl. Castle Cove 286 C6
rd. Mosman 317 D12
rd. Whale Beach 140 B6
MOREN
st. Blacktown 274 F7
MORESBY
av. Glenfield 424 C13
cr. Whalan 240 H12
pl. Allambie Ht 257 E11
MORESTONE
pl. Windsor Dn 180 K1
MORETON
av. Kingsgrove 401 J12
cl. Hinchinbrk 363 B15
rd. Illawong 459 C5
rd. Minto Ht 483 G6
st. Concord 342 B9
st. Lakemba 401 C1
MORETON BAY
av. Spring Farm 508 E1
sq. Bidwill 241 F1
MORETON PARK
rd. Menangle 538 K16
MOREY
pl. Kings Lngly 245 C3
MORGAN
av. Matraville 436 G8
cl. Prairiewood 334 E12
la. Bankstown, off West Tce 399 F1
pl. Bligh Park 150 H8
pl. Glendenning 242 J4
pl. Strathfield 370 K2
rd. Belrose 226 B8
rd. Mt Annan 479 D15
st. Beverly Hills 401 C14
st. Botany 405 J11
st. Earlwood 402 G5
st. Ingleburn 453 E13
st. Kingsgrove 401 G12
st. Merrylands 307 F7
st. Miller 393 G4
st. Petersham 15 E14
st. Thornleigh 220 G12
MORIAC
st. Warriewood 198 K6
MORIAL
la. Pymble, off Peace Av 253 H1
MORIARTY
rd. Chatswd W 284 H13
MORIL
av. Mt Riverview 204 E16
MORINDA
st. Mt Annan 509 C3
MORISON
dr. Lurnea 394 B11
la. Panania 428 B6
MORLEY
av. Hamondvle 396 G15
av. Kingswood 237 K12
av. Rosebery 375 G14
ct. Baulkham Hl 246 H4
la. Kingswood, off Kingsley Gr 238 B12
st. Sutherland 490 E5
MORNA
pl. Kareela 461 E11
pl. Quakers Hill 214 D11
pl. Turramurra 252 F5
st. Greenfld Pk 334 E13
MORNINGBIRD
cl. St Clair 270 D13
la. St Clair, off Morningbird Cl. 270 D13
MORNINGTON
av. Castle Hill 247 H1
pl. Hinchinbrk 393 B2
MORO
av. Padstow 399 D13
MOROBE
st. Whalan 240 H12
MORONA
av. Wahroonga 251 G2
MORONEY
av. Castle Hill 217 B7
cl. Blacktown 273 G5
MOROTAI
av. Riverwood 400 A15
cr. Castlecrag 285 K13
rd. Revesby Ht 428 J6
st. Whalan 240 J11
MORPHETT
st. Kingswood 238 B14
MORREL
pl. Kingswood 267 H1
MORRELL
cr. Quakers Hill 213 H8
st. Woollahra 21 K2
MORRICE
st. Lane Cove 314 C4
MORRIS
av. Croydon Pk 372 C8
av. Kingsgrove 401 J13
av. Thornleigh 220 H11
av. Wahroonga 223 A3
cl. Menai 458 D10
la. Burwood 341 J16
la. St Marys, off Morris St 270 A3
pl. Ingleburn 453 G11
pl. Maroubra 407 D13
st. Dundas Vy 280 E8
st. Merrylands 307 D14
st. Regents Pk 369 A3
st. St Marys 269 J2
st. Seven Hills 245 H15
st. Smithfield 335 K6
st. Summer Hill 373 C5
MORRISEY
wy. Rouse Hill 185 E2
MORRISON
av. Chester Hill 368 D4
av. Engadine 488 J16
pl. Pennant Hills 220 C13
rd. Gladesville 312 E8
rd. Putney 312 A6
rd. Ryde 311 J3
rd. Tennyson 312 E8
st. Glenmore Pk 265 J9
MORRISSEY
rd. Erskineville 17 K16
MORSE
pl. Blaxland 233 G6
st. Villawood 337 A16
MORSHEAD
av. Carlingford 250 B13
cr. S Granville 338 G4
dr. Connells Pt 431 G13
dr. Hurstville Gr 431 F13
dr. Hurstville Gr 431 G13
dr. S Hurstville 431 J13
rd. Narellan Vale 479 B12
st. Colyton 270 C5
st. North Ryde 282 K8
MORT
cl. Barden Rdg 488 G3
la. Randwick 377 A10
la. Surry Hills 20 D6
pl. Glenmore Pk 265 E10
st. Balmain 7 H8
st. Blacktown 245 A14
st. Granville 308 D9
st. Randwick 376 K9
st. Surry Hills 20 C6
MORTAIN
av. Allambie Ht 257 C9
MORTIMER
cl. Cecil Hills 362 F2
la. Emu Plains, off Mortimer St 235 H9
st. Emu Plains 235 G9
st. Minto 482 K2
st. Yanderra 567 B16
MORTIMER LEWIS
dr. Tarban 313 C13
la. St Clair, off Mortimer Lewis Cr 270 B11
gr. St Clair 270 B11
MORTLAKE
la. Concord, off Archer St 342 B2
st. Concord 342 B1
MORTLEY
av. Haberfield 343 E11
MORTON
av. Carlingford 249 D12
av. Dulwich Hill 15 B15
cl. Wakeley 334 H12
ct. Wattle Grove 426 B3
la. Woollahra 21 K4
la. Wollstncraft, off Sinclair St 315 F8
rd. Lalor Park 245 E13
st. Lilyfield 9 G4
st. N Richmond 87 B12
st. Parramatta 308 H2
st. Wollstncraft 5 A1
tce. Harringtn Pk 478 E5
MORTS
rd. Mortdale 431 A5
MORUBEN
rd. Mosman 317 B5
MORUYA
av. Sylvania Wtr 462 G12
cl. Prestons 392 K15
cr. Greystanes 305 H5
MORVAN
st. Denistone W 281 A13
st. West Ryde 281 A13
MORVEN
ct. Castle Hill 218 C7
st. Old Guildfrd 337 F9
MORVEN GARDENS
la. Greenwich 314 K5
MORWICK
st. Strathfield 341 G13
MOSELEY
st. Carlingford 279 H2
MOSELLE
pl. Eschol Park 481 C5
MOSELY
av. S Penrith 266 F3
st. Strathfield 341 G11
MOSES
st. Windsor 120 K9
MOSMAN
pl. Barden Rdg 488 H6
sq. Mosman, off Military Rd 317 A6
st. Mosman 316 H12
MOSS
gln. Cranebrook 207 B12
la. Mosman 287 A16
pl. Galston 159 E8
pl. St Helens Pk 540 K10
pl. Westmead 307 J3
st. Chester Hill 337 K11
st. Northmead 277 H7
st. Sans Souci 463 B5
st. West Ryde 281 A16
MOSSBERRY
st. Blair Athol 511 A3
MOSSGIEL
st. Fairlight 288 E7
MOSSGLEN
st. Minto 482 J3
MOTH
cl. Cranebrook 207 B10
pl. Raby 481 G1
MOTORKHANA
rd. Leppington 451 A1
MOTTLE
gr. Woodcroft 243 F7
MOTU
pl. Glenfield 424 F13
MOULAMEIN
tce. Glenwood 215 E15
MOULTON
av. Newington L H11
av. Newington 310 D11
MOUNT
av. Roselands 400 G6
cl. Cranebrook 207 B12
la. Coogee, off Dolphin St 377 F15
st. Arncliffe 403 D10
st. Bonnyrigg Ht 363 B4
st. Coogee 377 F14
st. Coogee 377 F16
st. Georges Hall 368 B13
st. Glenbrook 234 E16
st. Hunters Hill 313 G11
st. Hurlstone Pk 372 J10
st. Mt Colah 192 A5
st. Mount Druitt 241 F16
st. N Sydney K A7
st. N Sydney K F8
st. N Sydney 5 E8
st. N Sydney 5 G8
st. Pyrmont 12 F2
st. Redfern 20 D8
st. Strathfield 371 F2
st. Wentwthvle 277 A11
st. West Ryde 281 J14
MT ADELAIDE
st. Darling Point 13 K6
MOUNTAIN
av. Yarramundi 115 F15
cr. Mt Pritchard 364 G10
la. Ultimo 12 J14
st. Engadine 488 D13
st. Epping 250 F14
st. Ultimo 12 J15
MOUNTAIN VIEW
av. Glen Alpine 510 E15
cl. Kurrajong Hl 55 E5
cl. Vineyard 152 F4
cr. W Pnnant Hl 249 F8
pl. Narellan 478 B9
rd. Berowra 133 C16
MOUNTAINVIEW
cr. Penrith 237 A9
MT ANNAN
dr. Mt Annan 479 J16
dr. Mt Annan 509 C2
dr. Mt Annan 509 E5
MT AUBURN
rd. Auburn 339 C10
rd. Berala 339 C10
MOUNTBATTEN
st. Oatley 431 E10
MT CARMEL
pl. Engadine 488 E12
MT DRUITT
pl. Mount Druitt 241 B16
rd. Mount Druitt 271 A3
MOUNTFORD
av. Greystanes 305 K1
av. Guildford 337 H4
MOUNTFORT
st. Lalor Park 245 B13
MT HUON
cct. Glen Alpine 510 F9
MT IDA
st. Gordon 254 B5
MT LEWIS
av. Mt Lewis 370 B16
av. Punchbowl 370 B16
MT MORRIS
la. Woolwich, off Mt Morris St 314 G12
st. Woolwich 314 H12
MT PLEASANT
av. Burwood 341 J12
av. Frenchs Frst 256 B2
av. Mona Vale 199 E2
av. Normanhurst 221 G13
MOUNTSIDE
av. Mt Colah 192 D3
MT SION
pl. Glenbrook 234 A11
MOUNT STREET
wk. Pyrmont 8 E16
wk. Pyrmont 12 E1
MT SUGARLOAF
dr. Glen Alpine 510 B15
dr. Glen Alpine 540 B1
MT VERNON
la. Glebe 12 B15
pde. Blakehurst 462 D1
rd. Mt Vernon 331 A16
st. Glebe 12 A15
MOUNTVIEW
av. Beverly Hills 400 H14
av. Chester Hill 337 K11
av. Doonside 243 D14
av. Narwee 400 H14
pl. Bilgola 169 E8
MT WILLIAM
st. Gordon 253 G6
MOURNE
cl. Killarney Ht 256 A16
MOUTRIE
pl. Castle Hill 218 E13
MOVERLY
rd. Kingsford 407 B7
rd. Maroubra 407 B7
rd. S Coogee 407 F7
MOWATT
st. Narellan 478 G13
MOWBRAY
cl. Castle Hill 218 J6
rd. Artarmon 284 J13
rd. Chatswood 284 J13
rd. Willoughby 285 F13
rd.w, Chatswd W 284 D14
rd.w, Lane Cove W 283 F12
st. Prestons 393 A13
st. Sylvania 462 D8
wy. Rsemeadow 540 J3
MOWBRAY PARK
rd. Mowbray Pk 561 B7
MOWER
pl. S Windsor 150 J1
MOWLA
av. Jamisontown 266 A3
MOWLE
st. Westmead 307 G2
MOXHAM
la. Cranebrook, off Moxham St 207 D9
st. Cranebrook 207 D9
st. N Parramatta 278 C10
MOXHAMS
rd. Northmead 277 H6
rd. Winston Hills 277 G5
MOXON
rd. Punchbowl 399 H7
MOYA
cr. Kingsgrove 401 K11
MOYARTA
st. Hurstville 431 H2
MOYES
st. Marrickville 373 H14
MOYRAN
pde. Grays Point 491 A16
MOZART
pl. Bonnyrigg Ht 363 E7
pl. Cranebrook 207 G8
st. Seven Hills 246 D13
MRS MACQUARIE
dr. Frenchs Frst 256 H2
MRS MACQUARIES
rd. Sydney 2 F15
MUBO
cr. Holsworthy 426 C3
MUCCILLO
st. Quakers Hill 214 F14
MUDGEE
pl. St Clair 270 E14
MUDIE
pl. Blackett 241 C4
MUDIES
rd. St Ives 223 H8
MUELLER
pl. Tregear 240 F5

wy. Mt Annan 509 G3
MUHAMMED ALI
pde. Newington.......... L J16
pde. Newington, off Newington Dr .. 310 B13
MUIR
pl. St Andrews..... 452 A13
pl. Wetherill Pk..... 304 F13
rd. Chullora 369 G5
rd. Yagoona......... 369 G5
MUIRBANK
av. Hunters Hill 313 J12
MUIRFIELD
cr. Glenmore Pk .. 266 F8
MUJAR
pl. Winmalee....... 173 C9
MULAWA
pl. Frenchs Frst ... 255 H2
MULBERRY
st. Loftus 489 J10
MULBRING
st. Mosman......... 317 D9
MULGA
pl. Kirrawee......... 460 K14
pl. Mcquarie Fd ... 454 D1
rd. Oatley............ 431 A12
st. N St Marys 240 C11
st. Punchbowl..... 399 K4
MULGARA
pl. Bossley Park .. 333 F7
pl. St Helens Pk... 511 H16
MULGI
st. Blacktown 274 G8
MULGOA
rd. Glenmore Pk .. 265 F4
rd. Jamisontown.. 236 C15
rd. Mulgoa........... 265 B9
rd. Mulgoa........... 295 C6
rd. Penrith 236 C15
rd. Regentville 265 F4
rd. Wallacia 324 J12
MULGOWRIE
cr. Balgowlah Ht.. 287 J15
MULGRAVE
rd. Mulgrave........ 121 G16
MULGRAY
av. Baulkham Hl... 247 E10
av. Maroubra 407 E10
MULHERON
av. Baulkham Hl... 247 A12
MULHOLLANDS
rd. Mowbray Pk... 561 D7
rd. Mowbray Pk... 562 A7
rd. Thirlmere....... 561 D7
rd. Thirlmere....... 562 A7
MULL
pl. St Andrews..... 481 J2
MULLA
rd. Yagoona......... 369 C13
MULLANE
av. Baulkham Hl... 247 B12
MULLENDERREE
st. Prestons......... 392 H16
st. Prestons......... 422 J1
MULLENS
rd. N Richmond 87 A1
st. Balmain 7 E12
st. Rozelle 7 D14
MULLET
pl. Warriewood.... 199 C10
MULLEY
pl. Belrose........... 225 H12
MULLIGAN
cl. St Clair 270 D10
la. St Clair, off Mulligan Cl 270 C10
st. Bossley Park .. 334 B9
MULLINS
st. Sydney............... C G10
MULLION
cl. Hornsby Ht..... 191 H4
MULLOO
la. Cranebrook, off Mulloo Pl......... 207 J10
pl. Cranebrook 207 J10
MULLUMBIMBY
av. Hoxton Park ... 392 H6
MULQUEENEY
la. Newtown.......... 17 E12
MULVIHILL
st. West Ryde...... 311 F1
MULWARREE
av. Randwick 376 K11
MULYAN
av. Carlingford 280 D6
st. Como 460 G8
MUMFORD
rd. Cabramtta W .. 365 B9
MUNCASTER
pl. Cranebrook..... 207 F12
MUNDAKAL
av. Kirrawee 490 J6
MUNDAMATTA
st. Villawood........ 367 H6
MUNDARA
pl. Narraweena 258 C5
MUNDARDA
pl. St Helens Pk... 541 G3
MUNDARRAH
st. Clovelly........... 377 J13
MUNDAY
pl. Currans Hill 479 H13
st. Warwck Frm ... 365 J15
MUNDERAH
st. Wahroonga..... 222 D9
MUNDIN
st. Doonside........ 243 C9
MUNDON
pl. W Pnnant Hl ... 249 G10
MUNDOWI
rd. Mt Krng-gai 162 G6
MUNDOWIE
pl. Clarmnt Ms..... 268 J2
MUNDOWY
pl. Bradbury 511 C16
MUNDURRA
pl. Kellyville 216 E2
MUNDY
st. Emu Plains 235 D9
MUNEELA
pl. Yowie Bay....... 492 C11
MUNGADAL
wy. Airds 512 E10
MUNGARRA
av. St Ives 223 H10
pl. W Pnnant Hl ... 248 J7
MUNGERIE
rd. Kellyville 185 G12
MUNMORA
pl. Oxley Park 240 E15
MUNMORAH
cct. Woodcroft 243 J9
st. Leumeah 482 F15
MUNMURRA
rd. Riverwood 400 E15
MUNN
pl. Toongabbie 276 H7
MUNNI
st. Newtown 17 H16
st. Woolooware ... 493 D11
MUNNUMBA
av. Belrose........... 226 B13
MUNOORA
st. Seaforth.......... 287 A9
MUNRO
st. Baulkham Hl ... 248 A6
st. Canley Vale..... 366 E5
st. Eastwood 281 E4
st. Greystanes 305 D11
st. Lane Cove W .. 284 A16
st. McMahons Pt 5 B13
st. Sefton............ 338 F15
MUNROE
pl. Hamondvle..... 396 E15
MUNROS
la. Glenorie.......... 128 G8
MUNYANG
st. Heckenberg 364 A13
MURA
la. Baulkham Hl ... 247 B6
MURABAN
pl. Belrose........... 226 B12
rd. Dural 189 K4
MURCH
pl. Eagle Vale....... 481 A11
MURCHISON
st. St Ives 224 B8
st. Sylvania......... 461 K12
MURDOCH
cr. Connells Pt 431 G16
ct. Harringtn Pk ... 478 D5
rd. Orangeville 443 F12
st. Blackett 241 C1
st. Cremorne 316 F9
st. Ermington 310 D2
st. Rozelle 7 C14
st. Turramurra 223 D10
MURDOCK
cr. Lugarno.......... 429 J10
la. Guildford 337 F3
st. Cronulla.......... 494 C7
st. Guildford 337 F3
MURIEL
av. Epping 281 E2
av. Rydalmere 309 C2
la. Hornsby.......... 191 J16
la. Hornsby.......... 221 J2
st. Faulconbdg 171 C13
st. Hornsby.......... 221 J2
MURNDAL
ct. Wattle Grove ... 425 H4
MURONGA
pl. Kirrawee 461 D16
MURPHY
av. Liverpool 394 K5
pl. Blackett.......... 241 B3
st. Blaxland.......... 233 H12
st. Merrylnds W ... 307 A15
st. Revesby.......... 398 K16
wy. Minto 482 K1
wy. Minto 483 A1
MURPHYS
la. Croydon, off Young St......... 342 E14
MURRABIN
av. Matraville........ 436 G3
MURRALAH
pl. Lane Cove....... 313 J3
MURRALIN
la. Sylvania.......... 462 B8
MURRALONG
av. Five Dock........ 342 K11
rd. Mt Colah 162 A15
MURRAMI
av. Caringbah 493 B5
MURRANDAH
av. Camden 507 A4
MURRAY
av. Springwood 201 F1
ct. Wattle Grove ... 395 J12
la. Lane Cove W... 284 E15
la. Marrickville 373 E13
pl. Blacktown 274 H5
rd. Beecroft.......... 250 G9
rd. Harbord 288 H1
rd. Pagewood........ 406 G8
st. Bronte............ 377 J8
st. Camden 477 A16
st. Campbelltwn ... 511 K8
st. Croydon.......... 372 C1
st. Greenacre 370 E3
st. Lane Cove W... 284 E15
st. Lidcombe 339 F11
st. Maroubra........ 407 B14
st. Marrickville 374 F11
st. Merrylands 307 G9
st. Northmead....... 277 K7
st. N Parramatta... 278 J14
st. Pyrmont 12 K6
st. Russell Lea 343 D5
st. St Marys 269 K6
st. Smithfield 335 K8
st. Sydney 12 K6
st. Waterloo........... 20 B15
st. West Ryde 281 A14
MURRAY FARM
rd. Beecroft.......... 249 K11
rd. Carlingford...... 249 E12
MURRAY ISLAND
Sylvania Wtr ... 462 E11
MURRAY JONES
dr. Bnkstn Aprt..... 397 J6
MURRAY PARK
rd. Kenthurst........ 187 A2
MURRAY ROSE
av. Homebush B...... M D7
av. Homebush B... 340 G1
MURRAYS
rd. Tennyson.......... 57 J7
MURRELL
pl. Dural 219 A5
st. Ashfield 372 K3
MURRILLS
cr. Winston Hills .. 247 K15
MURRIVERIE
rd. North Bondi 348 C15
MURRONG
pl. La Perouse 436 J12
MURROOBAH
rd. Wallacia.......... 324 K14
MURRUA
rd. N Turramrra 193 E13
MURRUMBA
pl. Castle Hill........ 217 K8
pl. East Killara 254 K6
MURRUMBIDGEE
av. Sylvania Wtr 462 F13
st. Bossley Park ... 333 H6
st. Heckenberg...... 364 A15
MURRUMBURRAH
st. Wakeley 334 H14
MURTHA
st. Arndell Park 273 J10
MURU
av. Winmalee........ 173 A11
dr. Glenmore Pk ... 266 B11
la. Glenmore Pk, off Muru Dr 266 C11
MURUBA
av. Carlingford 279 E3
MURULLA
pl. Airds 511 J15
MURWILLUMBAH
av. Hoxton Park 393 A6
MUSCAT
gr. Glenwood 215 D14
pl. Eschol Park 481 C2
pl. Orchard Hills ... 268 D9
rd. Warwck Frm.... 365 K13
MUSCATEL
wy. Orchard Hills ... 268 F12
MUSCHARRY
rd. Londonderry ... 148 C10
MUSCIO
st. Colyton 270 C4
MUSCIOS
rd. Glenorie 128 J12
MUSGRAVE
av. Centnnial Pk..... 22 B16
av. Queens Park..... 22 B16
cr. Fairfield W........ 335 E9
pl. Ruse............... 512 F6
st. Mosman 316 H13
st. Turramurra 223 E12
MUSGROVE
cr. Doonside 243 E8
MUSSELBURGH
cl. Glenmore Pk ... 266 E10
MUSSON
la. Richmond 118 G4
MUSTANG
av. St Clair 270 F11
dr. Raby 451 D16
MUSTON
la. Sutherland, off Flora St.......... 490 E3
pl. Glenhaven........ 187 K16
st. Mosman 317 C7
MUSWELLBROOK
rd. Hoxton Park 392 G9
st. Glenwood 245 G1
MUTCH
av. Kyeemagh 404 A14
MUTTAMA
av. Kirrawee.......... 491 B6
rd. Artarmon 284 K13
st. Wahroonga 251 J1
MUTUAL
dr. Old Tngabbie... 277 C7
rd. Mortdale 431 A5
MYAHGAH
mw. Mosman, off Vista St........... 317 A6
rd. Mosman 317 A7
MYALL
av. Vaucluse 348 H1
av. Wahroonga 222 E11
cr. Strathfield 340 H12
pl. Leumeah 482 F14
rd. Casula............ 424 C1
rd. Mt Colah 192 D5
st. Auburn............ 338 K11
st. Belmore 371 F16
st. Cabramatta 365 H8
st. Concord W....... 311 F16
st. Doonside 243 D15
st. Merrylands 307 E16
st. Oatley 430 K13
st. Punchbowl 400 A3
MYALLIE
av. Baulkham Hl.... 247 C16
MYALORA
st. Russell Lea 343 C6
MYAMBA
rd. Collaroy.......... 229 A16
MYCUMBENE
av. E Lindfield 255 A15
MYDDLETON
av. Fairfield 336 C8
MYDELL
st. Kingsgrove 401 F9
MYEE
av. Strathfield....... 340 J15
cr. Baulkham Hl... 246 F11
cr. Lane Cove W .. 313 F3
rd. Mcquarie Fd ... 453 H2
st. Lakemba 401 A3
st. Merrylands 307 H15
MYERLA
cr. Connells Pt..... 431 H16
MYERS
st. Roselands 401 D5
st. Sans Souci 463 A1
MYLER
st. Five Dock 342 G9
MYLES
pl. Minto 452 K15
MYNAH
cl. St Clair 270 E12
MYOLA
rd. Newport 169 J12
MYOORA
rd. Terrey Hills 195 J14
st. Pymble........... 253 A2
st. Seven Hills 245 K13
MYORA
cl. Green Valley ... 363 H10
MYPOLONGA
av. Gymea Bay 491 H10
MYRA
av. Ryde 282 B15
la. Dulwich Hill.... 373 C11
pl. Ingleburn 453 C10
pl. Oatley........... 431 B15
rd. Dulwich Hill.... 373 C11
st. Frenchs Frst ... 257 B4
st. Plumpton 242 C7
st. Wahroonga 222 A4
MYRNA
rd. Strathfield....... 341 A15
MYRTLE
ct. Voyager Pt 427 C4
gr. Bella Vista 246 G6
la. Chippendale 18 H2
la. Stanmore 16 G8
la.w, Stanmore 16 E7
pl. St Ives........... 224 B10
rd. Bankstown 369 G14
rd. Clarmnt Ms 268 J3
rd. Greenfld Pk 334 E13
rd. Prairiewood.... 334 E13
st. Botany........... 405 H9
st. Chippendale 18 H2
st. Chippendale 19 A3
st. Crows Nest......... 5 D1
st. Granville......... 308 G16
st. Kensington..... 376 B12
st. Leichhardt 15 E3
st. Loftus 489 J13
st. Marrickville..... 374 A15
st. Minto Ht......... 483 F7
st. Normanhurst.. 221 E13
st. N Balgowlah ... 287 F6
st. N Sydney............ 5 D1
st. Oatley............ 430 K12
st. Oatley............ 431 A13
st. Pagewood 405 H9
st. Prestons......... 393 K14
st. Prospect......... 274 G11
st. Rydalmere 309 G1
st. Stanmore 16 E8
MYRTLE CREEK
av. Tahmoor 566 B8
MYRTUS
cr. Bidwill............ 211 F13
MYSON
dr. Cherrybrook ... 219 E13
MYUNA
cl. Westleigh 220 E7
cr. Seven Hills 275 C7
pl. Camden S 507 C10
pl. Port Hacking .. 522 H2
rd. Dover Ht......... 348 F10

N

NAALONG
pl. Cranebrook 207 H11
NABIAC
av. Belrose 225 H12
av. Gymea Bay 491 G8
pl. Westleigh 220 G10
NABILLA
rd. Palm Beach 139 G2
NADA
st. Old Tngabbie 276 K7
NADENE
pl. Pymble 253 C7
NADIA
pl. Guildford 338 B7
NADIA COMANECI
av. Newington L J16
av. Newington, off Newington Dr 310 B12
NADIE
pl. Kings Lngly 245 K7
NADINE
cl. Cherrybrook 219 J4
NADZAB
rd. Holsworthy 426 F9
NAGLE
av. Springwood 172 E12
cl. Menai 458 H6
pl. N Turramrra 193 F12
st. Liverpool 395 C7
st. Maroubra 406 K11
wy. Quakers Hill 214 B12
NAILON
pl. Mona Vale 199 C1
NAIRANA
dr. Marayong 244 B4
NAIRN
st. Kingsgrove 402 B9
NAIROBI
pl. Toongabbie 275 E13
NALAURA
cl. Beecroft 250 B6
NALLADA
pl. Beecroft 250 B12
rd. Alfords Point 429 C14
NALONG
st. St Clair 270 F10
NALYA
av. Baulkham Hl 246 K7
la. Berowra Ht 132 J5
rd. Berowra Ht 132 J6
rd. Narraweena 258 B1
NAMAN
cl. Bossley Park 334 B5
NAMARA
pl. Engadine 518 G6
NAMATJIRA
av. Londonderry 148 C9
cl. Eagle Vale 481 A10
pl. Chifley 437 B9
pwy. Winmalee 172 K10
NAMBA
rd. Duffys Frst 194 H4
NAMBOUR
pl. Engadine 489 E9
NAMBUCCA
pl. Clarmnt Ms 268 K1
pl. Padstow Ht 429 G8
rd. Terrey Hills 196 C5
st. Ruse 512 E6
st. Turramurra 223 C8
NAMBUCCA HEADS
cr. Hoxton Park 392 H9
NAMBUNG
pl. Bow Bowing 452 D13
NAME
la. Dulwich Hill 373 E7
NAMOI
ct. Wattle Grove 395 H13
la. Georges Hall, off Surrey Av 368 B16
pl. E Lindfield 255 B14
pl. Ruse 512 B9
pl. Sylvania Wtr 462 D10
pl. Toongabbie 275 F10
rd. Matraville 436 K1
rd. Northbridge 316 B1
st. Greystanes 305 K4
st. N Epping 251 E10
NAMONA
st. N Narrabeen 199 A14
NAMUR
st. S Granville 338 G5

NANBAREE
rd. Ryde 282 E16
NANCARROW
av. Ryde 311 F4
la. Ryde 311 F4
NANCE
av. Cabramatta 365 D9
la. Croydon Pk 372 B6
NANCY
pl. Ambarvale 510 F15
pl. Galston 159 H8
st. North Bondi 348 D15
st. Pendle Hill 306 C1
st. St Marys 269 J3
NANCYE
st. Randwick 377 C16
NANDEWAR
pl. Airds 512 A10
NANDI
av. Frenchs Frst 256 J4
NANDINA
tce. Avalon 139 K15
NANETTE
pl. Castle Hill 217 H11
NANGANA
rd. Bayview 168 J14
NANGAR
pl. Emu Plains 235 A8
st. Fairfield W 335 E12
NANNA GLEN
rd. Hoxton Park 392 J9
NANOWIE
av. Wahroonga 221 J12
st. Narwee 400 H13
NANT
st. Bnksmeadw 436 C1
NAOI
pl. Glenmore Pk 266 A11
NAOLI
la. St Clair, off Naoli Pl 269 G14
pl. St Clair 269 G13
NAOMI
ct. Cherrybrook 219 K4
st.n, Winston Hills 248 A16
st.s, Northmead 278 A1
NAPIER
av. Emu Plains 235 K8
av. Lurnea 394 C13
cr. North Ryde 282 G7
la. Emu Plains, off Napier St 235 K8
pl. Bossley Park 334 C8
pl. Ingleburn 453 F13
st. Canterbury 372 E16
st. Dover Ht 348 F11
st. Drummoyne 343 K1
st. Engadine 518 G6
st. Lindfield 284 B3
st. Malabar 437 E6
st. Mays Hill 307 J5
st. N Strathfield 341 F7
st. N Sydney K B4
st. N Sydney 5 E6
st. Paddington 4 F15
st. Parramatta 307 J5
st. Petersham 15 G15
st. Rooty Hill 242 C14
NAPOLEON
rd. Greenacre 370 D15
st. Mascot 405 F4
st. Riverwood 400 D14
st. Rosebery 405 F4
st. Rozelle 7 A14
st. Sans Souci 463 C5
st. Sydney A C13
st. Sydney 1 D15
NAPOLI
rd. Minto Ht 484 B7
st. Padstow 399 A9
st. Revesby 399 A9
NAPPER
av. Riverwood 400 C16
st. S Coogee 407 H5
NAPULYA
st. Duffys Frst 165 A14
NAPUNYAH
wy. St Clair 270 A16
NARA
pl. St Ives 224 D7
NARABANG
wy. Belrose 225 H1
NARAMBI
cl. Berowra Ht 132 J10

NARANGA
av. Engadine 518 G5
NARANGANAH
av. Gymea Bay 491 F12
NARANGHI
av. Telopea 279 E9
st. Busby 363 G13
NARANI
cr. Earlwood 402 D2
cr. Northbridge 286 C16
NARCISSUS
av. Quakers Hill 243 D3
NARDANGO
rd. Bradbury 511 C16
NARDOO
rd. Willoughby 285 D13
st. Ingleburn 453 B7
st. Ingleburn 453 C6
wy. Mt Annan 479 C14
NARDU
la. S Penrith, off Nardu Pl 266 H7
pl. S Penrith 266 H7
NAREE
rd. Frenchs Frst 256 D4
NAREEN
pde. N Narrabeen 228 K1
NARELLAN
cr. Bonnyrigg Ht 363 C7
rd. Blairmount 510 C1
rd. Campbelltwn 510 C1
rd. Currans Hill 479 B10
rd. Mt Annan 479 B10
rd. Narellan 478 J9
rd. Narellan Vale 478 J9
rd. Smeaton Gra 479 B10
NARELLE
av. Castle Hill 248 C2
av. Pymble 253 G4
av.e, Castle Hill 248 C3
cr. Greenacre 370 C8
pl. Silverdale 354 A11
st. Mount Druitt 271 A3
st. North Bondi 348 D14
st. N Epping 251 D10
NARENA
cl. Beecroft 250 F3
NARETHA
la. Green Valley 363 F10
NARGONG
rd. Allambie Ht 257 G13
NARIEL
pl. Peakhurst 430 D9
st. St Marys 239 G13
NARLA
rd. Bayview 168 F12
NAROO
rd. Terrey Hills 196 G5
NAROOMA
av. S Penrith 266 F6
cl. Panania 428 G3
dr. Prestons 393 C16
pl. Gymea Bay 491 C9
rd. Northbridge 286 C15
NARRABEEN
rd. Leumeah 482 F12
st. Narrabeen 229 A5
NARRABEEN PARK
pde. Mona Vale 199 D9
pde. N Narrabeen 199 D14
pde. Warriewood 199 D14
NARRABRI
st. Quakers Hill 243 K3
NARRABURRA
cl. Mt Colah 191 K6
NARRAGA
pl. Gymea Bay 491 D8
NARRAMORE
st. Kingsgrove 402 A14
NARRAN
ct. Woodcroft 243 H10
pl. Glenmore Pk 266 C6
NARROMINE
pl. Bonnyrigg Ht 363 C5
wy. Mcquarie Pk 282 E4
NARROW
la. Paddington, off Broughton St 13 D15
NARROY
rd. N Narrabeen 228 J1
NARRUN
cr. Dundas 279 F11
NARRYNA
pl. Glen Alpine 510 B16

NARTEE
pl. Wilberforce 92 B1
NARVA
pl. Seven Hills 275 G6
NARWEE
av. Narwee 400 H14
NASH
la. Carramar 366 H3
pl. Blacktown 244 B12
pl. Currans Hill 479 G13
pl. North Ryde 283 B12
st. S Penrith 267 A4
NASHS
la. Concord 312 A15
NASSAU
cl. Bossley Park 333 K6
NATAL
pl. Seven Hills 275 H4
NATALIE
cl. Casula 423 K3
cl. Hornsby Ht 191 G3
cr. Fairfield W 335 E12
ct. Glenhaven 218 D2
pl. Oakhurst 242 D2
NATASHA
pl. Picton 561 G3
NATCHEZ
cr. Greenfld Pk 333 K15
NATHAN
cr. Dean Park 212 H15
la. Willoughby 285 F15
la. Mosman, off Harbour St 316 K6
la. Mosman, off Vista St 316 K6
pl. Engadine 518 E3
st. Coogee 377 E15
st. Mulgoa 296 F1
NATHANIEL
pde. Kings Lngly 245 E7
NATIONAL
av. Loftus 490 A12
la. Rozelle 7 A14
st. Cabramatta 365 K10
st. Leichhardt 15 F4
st. Rozelle 7 A14
st. Warwck Frm 365 J16
NATIONAL PARK
rd. Holsworthy 426 H6
NATTAI
cl. Thornleigh 221 B6
pl. Banksia 403 H12
st. Couridjah 564 G13
st. Couridjah 565 A14
st. Loftus 490 B10
st. Ruse 512 B9
st. Seven Hills 246 C13
NATUNA
pl. Lethbrdg Pk 240 K1
st. N Narrabeen 198 J13
NAUGHTON
av. Lansdowne 367 D7
st. Greenacre 370 G7
NAURU
cr. Lethbrdg Pk 240 J1
NAVAHO
st. Bossley Park 334 A10
NAVAJO
cl. Stanhpe Gdn 215 D11
NAVINS
la. Zetland, off Elizabeth St 375 H10
NAYLA
cl. Bardwell Vy 403 C7
NAYLOR
pl. Ingleburn 453 A11
NEA
cl. Glenmore Pk 266 C8
st. Chatswood 284 J12
NEAGLE
la. Colyton, off Neagle St 270 E7
st. Colyton 270 E7
NEAL
pl. Appin 568 G13
pl. Minto 482 H8
NEALE
av. Cherrybrook 219 E15
av. Forestville 256 A11
st. Belmore 371 C13
st. St Marys 269 E1
wy. Berrilee 131 E12
NEALES
la. Penrith 237 A10

NEBO
pl. Cartwright 394 C5
NEBULA
gln. N St Marys 239 K7
NECROPOLIS
cct. Rookwood 340 A11
dr. Rookwood 339 K10
dr. Rookwood 340 B11
NEEDLEBRUSH
cl. Alfords Point 459 B1
NEEDLEWOOD
cl. Rouse Hill 185 A7
gr. Padstow Ht 429 D8
NEENAN
pl. Erskine Park 270 H16
NEERIM
cl. Berowra 133 E9
rd. Castle Cove 285 J3
NEERINI
av. Smithfield 336 A8
NEETA
av. Cambrdg Pk 238 C8
NEEWORRA
rd. Northbridge 286 D15
NEICH
pde. Burwood 342 A11
rd. Glenorie 126 J1
rd. Maraylya 124 G1
NEICHS
la. Concord 342 B10
NEIL
pl. Canley Ht 365 D1
st. Bundeena 524 B8
st. Epping 280 F2
st. Holroyd 307 H11
st. Hornsby 221 E6
st. Merrylands 307 H11
st. North Ryde 283 A12
NEILD
av. Darlinghurst 13 B12
av. Paddington 13 B12
NEILSON
av. Peakhurst 430 G2
cl. Glenmore Pk 265 J6
cr. Bligh Park 150 G8
st. Granville 308 G16
wy. Blackett 241 B2
NEIRBO
av. Hurstville 431 J6
NEIWAND
av. Kellyville 215 H6
NELL
pl. Ambarvale 511 A14
NELLA
st. Padstow 429 F4
NELLA DAN
av. Tregear 240 C5
NELLELLA
st. Blakehurst 432 B14
NELLIE
st. Lalor Park 245 D9
NELLIE STEWART
dr. Doonside 243 D5
NELLIGEN
cl. Prestons 393 C14
NELLO
pl. Wetherill Pk 334 C4
NELSON
av. Belmore 401 G3
av. Bronte 378 A9
av. Padstow 399 C9
la. Annandale 11 C14
la. Waterloo 19 E11
la. Woollahra 22 C3
pde. Hunters Hill 314 C14
pl. Petersham 15 G11
rd. Box Hill 184 D2
rd. Cattai 94 G3
rd. Earlwood 403 B2
rd. Ingleburn 423 A12
rd. Killara 254 D13
rd. Lindfield 254 E15
rd. Nelson 154 F16
rd. N Strathfield 341 F7
rd. Yennora 337 A9
st. Annandale 17 A3
st. Bondi Jctn 22 D5
st. Chatswood 284 H13
st. Dulwich Hill 373 E7
st. Engadine 488 J14
st. Fairfield 336 C11
st. Fairfield Ht 336 A11
st. Gladesville 312 H4
st. Gordon 253 K7

NIGHTMIST
gr. St Clair 270 D15
la. St Clair, off Nightmist Gr.... 270 E15
NILAND
cr. Blackett 241 B2
pl. Edensor Pk.....363 J3
wy. Casula 424 G2
NILE
av. Seven Hills......275 F7
cl. Marsfield 251 K13
pl. Kearns............481 A1
pl. St Clair 270 B9
st. Fairfield Ht......335 H10
NILLERA
av. Terrey Hills.....196 C6
NILSON
av. Hillsdale..........406 F15
NILSSON
la. Botany............405 F11
NIMBEY
av. Narraweena 258 B6
NIMBIN
av. Hoxton Park....393 B7
pl. Yarrawarrah....489 E14
st. N Balgowlah ...287 C4
NIMBRIN
st. Turramurra.....252 D4
NIMOOLA
rd. Engadine........489 D9
NIMROD
pl. Tregear...........240 E4
st. Darlinghurst 4 H10
NINA
pl. Kurrajong Ht.....53 K7
pl. Oakhurst..........241 H1
st. Revesby 398 K12
NINDI
cr. Glenmore Pk...266 C6
NINETEENTH
av. Hoxton Park....392 G7
st. Warragamba...353 E9
NINEVEH
cr. Greenfld Pk.....334 A15
NINNIS
st. Leumeah 482 H11
NINTH
av. Austral............391 A10
av. Belfield...........371 H13
av. Campsie 371 H13
av. Cranebrook.....208 F9
av. Jannali............461 A12
av. Llandilo 207 K8
av.n, Loftus............490 A8
av.s, Loftus...........489 H11
rd. Berkshire Pk...180 C10
st. Mascot 405 A7
st. Warragamba...353 F5
NIOBE
la. Turramurra.....252 E1
NIOKA
pl. Bankstown......369 H13
pl. Caringbah.......492 F6
pl. St Ives Ch.......223 K4
rd. Narrabeen.......228 H7
rd. Penrith 237 C3
st. Gladesville......312 F8
NIPIGON
rd. Seven Hills......275 G6
NIRIMBA
av. Narwee...........400 G13
av. N Epping 251 E9
cr. Heathcote........518 J9
dr. Quakers Hill....213 H12
dr. Schofields 213 H12
NIRRANDA
st. Concord W.....341 F1
NIRVANA
st. Pendle Hill......276 E12
NITH
pl. St Andrews.....451 J14
NITHDALE
st. Pymble...........223 D15
NITHSDALE
la. Sydney ....F B5
la. Sydney ....F D4
st. Sydney ....F C5
st. Sydney 3 J11
NIX
av. Malabar 437 F7
NIXON
av. Ashfield 372 H2
la. Strathfield.......341 J11
pl. Bonnet Bay.....460 B8
pl. Cherrybrook....219 G6
rd. Thirlmere 562 B14
st. Emu Plains 235 E9
st. Glenwood 215 J14
NOAKES
pde. Lalor Park.......245 F13
NOBBS
la. Surry Hills.........20 D5
rd. Yagoona 369 A9
st. S Granville 338 F2
st. Surry Hills.........20 D4
NOBEL
pl. Castle Hill........217 K13
pl. Winston Hills ..277 D5
NOBLE
av. Greenacre 370 B10
av. Mt Lewis.........370 A16
av. Punchbowl......370 A16
av. Strathfield 371 C4
cl. Kings Lngly......245 D7
cl. Menai 458 G8
la. St Clair, off Noble Pl...........269 K15
pl. St Clair............269 K15
pl. Telopea...........279 F9
st. Allawah...........432 D7
st. Canley Vale 366 F2
st. Concord...........342 A2
st. Five Dock.........343 C8
st. Hornsby...........221 E4
st. Mosman 316 K8
st. Old Tngabbie ..277 C8
st. Rodd Point 343 C8
wy. Rouse Hill.......184 J7
NOCK
la. Mosman, off Avenue Rd.......317 A9
NOCKOLDS
av. Punchbowl......370 A16
NODDY
pl. Hinchinbrk......363 F16
NOEL
st. Georges Hall ...367 H14
st. Marayong 244 D11
NOELA
pl. Oxley Park 270 D2
NOELENE
st. Fairfield W 335 G11
NOELINE
av. Mcquarie Fd....454 B2
st. Hurstville 401 G16
NOFFS
pl. Bonnyrigg Ht ..363 F6
NOLA
la. Roseville, off Nola Rd...........284 G6
pl. Baulkham Hl ...247 D1
rd. Roseville.........284 G5
st. Marsfield 282 C4
NOLAN
av. Clovelly...........377 G11
av. Engadine.........518 K1
cr. Naremburn 315 D2
cr. Westmead 307 F2
pl. Balgowlah Ht ..287 J14
pl. Mt Pritchard.....364 K10
pl. Seven Hills......245 K14
st. Casula.............424 E4
NOLLAN
pl. Kenthurst........156 K8
NOLLANDS
rd. Fiddletown 129 J4
NOLLER
pde. Parramatta......308 G4
NOMAD
gr. St Clair............270 E15
pl. Raby...............481 H2
NOOAL
st. Newport..........169 E10
NOOK
av. Neutral Bay 6 A5
la. Neutral Bay 6 A5
la. West Ryde 281 F16
pl. Leonay............235 A16
NOOLA
av. Kellyville 216 J8
NOOLINGA
rd. Bayview 168 J10
NOONAN
rd. Ingleburn 453 B1
NOONBINNA
cl. Northbridge 286 A14
cr. Northbridge 286 B14
NOONGAH
pl. Canada Bay 342 E8
st. Bargo.............567 C7
NOORA
av. Little Bay.........437 A10
pl. Marayong........244 C2
st. Lidcombe........339 H5
NOORAL
st. Bargo..............567 E8
NOORONG
av. Frenchs Frst....256 G1
cl. Baulkham Hl....247 C5
NORA
ct. Rouse Hill 184 K9
ct. Rouse Hill 185 A9
NORBAR
la. Kingsford 376 J16
NORE
pl. Minto 482 K4
NOREE
pl. Wrrngtn Dns ...238 A3
NORFOLK
av. Beverly Hills 401 D15
av. Collaroy 229 A16
av. Fairfield W.......335 B10
la. Paddington 13 E15
la. Matraville, off Franklin St.........436 J2
pde. Matraville 436 J2
pl. Carlingford......279 B3
pl. Miranda 492 D6
pl. N Richmond..... 87 H13
rd. Cambrdg Pk....237 H10
rd. Epping 251 D14
rd. Greenacre 370 E6
rd. Longueville 314 B9
rd. N Epping.........251 D10
st. Blacktown 244 C13
st. Ingleburn 453 C6
st. Killara 253 G11
st. Liverpool.........395 C5
st. Mount Druitt ...240 K16
st. Newtown.......... 17 G14
st. Paddington 13 E15
swy. Liverpool.........395 C5
wy. North Ryde 282 J13
NORIKA
pl. Toongabbie.....276 E10
NORMA
av. Belmore 401 F5
av. Eastwood 281 G7
cl. Bargo.............567 A2
cr. Cheltenham.....250 K7
pl. Merrylands......307 E15
rd. Palm Beach.....140 C4
NORMAC
rd. Girraween 276 A11
st. Roseville Ch ...285 G1
NORMAN
av. Auburn............339 A12
av. Dolls Point 463 F1
av. Hamondvle......396 F15
av. Thornleigh 221 A4
cr. Claymore 481 C12
pl. Bligh Park 150 K7
st. Allawah 432 F9
st. Berala 339 D10
st. Concord..........341 H1
st. Condell Park....398 H2
st. Darlinghurst.........F J4
st. Darlinghurst 4 B10
st. Five Dock 343 C10
st. Merrylands......307 B8
st. Peakhurst.........430 F5
st. Prospect 274 G13
st. Punchbowl......400 B6
st. Rozelle............344 E6
swy. Hamondvle......396 F15
NORMANBY
rd. Auburn............339 B1
st. Fairfield E 337 A14
st. Villawood 337 A14
NORMANDY
rd. Allambie Ht 257 C10
tce. Leumeah.........482 F11
NORMANHURST
rd. Normanhurst...221 G10
st. Elvina Bay 168 C4
NORMAN LINDSAY
cr. Faulconbdg 171 H11
NORMANS
rd. Silverdale 354 C15
NORMIC
av. Blaxland 234 A8
la. Blaxland 234 A8
NORMURRA
av. N Turramrra ... 223 F5
NORN
cl. Greenfld Pk 334 D14
NORRIE
pl. Oakhurst 242 A2
st. Yennora 337 A8
NORRIS
pl. Narellan Vale .. 478 K16
wy. Wentwthvle, off Portadown Rd. 277 D11
NORSEMAN
cl. Green Valley ... 363 J11
pl. Yarrawarrah ... 489 F13
NORTH
av. Cammeray...... 315 K3
av. Leichhardt........ 16 E1
av. Rossmore 389 J14
av. Westmead...... 277 E15
cir. Blaxland 233 H6
cr. Lilyfield 10 E1
pde. Auburn............ 339 E3
pde. Campsie.......... 372 A12
pde. Guildford......... 337 G7
pde. Hunters Hill 313 H10
pde. Mount Druitt... 241 C16
pde. Rooty Hill 272 A1
rd. Denistone E.... 281 K10
rd. Eastwood 281 G5
rd. N Curl Curl 258 K10
rd. Ryde 281 K11
st. Auburn 339 A6
st. Balmain.............. 7 E7
st. Fairfield 336 E15
st. Gymea............. 491 E4
st. Leichhardt........... 9 G11
st. Marrickville....... 16 C14
st. Mt Colah 162 B16
st. Penrith 237 A9
st. Schofields 182 H15
st. Thirlmere 565 A1
st. Thirlmere 565 B2
st. Windsor 121 F7
tce. Bankstown 369 F16
NORTHAM
av. Bankstown 399 A8
dr. North Rocks ... 279 A3
st. Belrose........... 225 K15
NORTHAMPTON DALE
rd. Appin 568 B14
NORTH ARM
rd. Middle Cove ... 285 K7
NORTH AVALON
rd. Avalon............ 140 D14
NORTHBROOK
pl. Illawong 459 D5
st. Bexley 432 H1
NORTHBURY
ct. Glen Alpine..... 510 C11
NORTHCLIFF
st. Milsons Pt.......... 5 J16
NORTHCLIFFE
av. Narraweena.... 258 A7
NORTHCOTE
av. Caringbah....... 492 J12
av. Fairlight.......... 288 A9
av. Killara............ 254 A10
la. Glebe 11 G6
rd. Glebe 11 G6
rd. Greenacre........ 370 A8
rd. Hornsby 192 A16
rd. Lindfield 254 E14
st. Auburn 339 A2
st. Canterbury 372 C16
st. Earlwood 402 C2
st. Haberfield....... 343 A13
st. Marrickville..... 373 K11
st. Mortlake......... 312 A14
st. Naremburn..... 315 D4
st. Rose Bay........ 348 E9
st. St Leonards.... 315 D4
st. Sans Souci 433 B15
NORTHCOTT
av. Kingsgrove..... 401 J11
la. Parramatta 278 B15
rd. Blacktown 245 C10
rd. Cromer.......... 227 G12
rd. Lalor Park...... 245 C10
st. North Ryde..... 282 D10
st. S Wntwthvle ... 306 J8
wy. Cherrybrook, off Tennyson Cl.... 219 E10
NORTH COURT
rd. Russell Lea..... 343 D5
NORTH EAST
cr. Lilli Pilli.......... 522 G3
NORTHEND
av. S Penrith 266 G3
NORTHERN RIVERS
av. Homebush B.......M B9
NORTH FORT
rd. Manly 290 B13
NORTH HARBOUR
st. Balgowlah....... 287 J11
NORTH HEAD SCENIC
dr. Manly 289 A16
NORTHLAND
rd. Bellevue Hill..... 14 H16
NORTH LIVERPOOL
rd. Bonnyrigg 363 K11
rd. Bonnyrigg Ht .. 363 A8
rd. Green Valley ... 363 A8
rd. Heckenberg 363 K11
rd. Mt Pritchard ... 363 K11
NORTHMEAD
av. Northmead 277 J9
NORTH ROCKS
rd. Carlingford 249 H13
rd. N Parramatta .. 278 B8
rd. North Rocks ... 249 A16
rd. North Rocks ... 278 C8
NORTHROP
st. Raby............... 451 C13
NORTH STEYNE
Manly 288 H5
rd. Woodbine....... 481 D15
NORTHUMBERLAND
av. Mt Colah......... 192 C1
av. Stanmore 16 H5
la. Clovelly, off Warner Av....... 378 B12
la.e, Stanmore 16 J5
la.w, Stanmore 16 H5
rd. Auburn 309 E16
st. Blacktown....... 274 H6
st. Bonnyrigg Ht .. 363 A7
st. Clovelly.......... 378 B12
st. Liverpool 395 D4
st. Woolwich 314 D12
swy. Liverpool 395 D4
NORTH VANDERVILLE
st. The Oaks 502 F9
NORTHVIEW
pl. Mt Colah......... 192 A3
rd. Palm Beach 109 K15
NORTH WEST ARM
rd. Grays Point..... 491 B11
rd. Gymea............ 491 B9
rd. Gymea Bay 491 B9
NORTHWOOD
cl. Mona Vale 199 A2
la. Camperdwn...... 17 F7
pl. Dundas Vy...... 280 D8
rd. Lane Cove 314 F6
rd. Longueville..... 314 F6
rd. Northwood 314 F6
st. Camperdwn...... 17 F7
wy. Cherrybrook ... 219 E11
NORTON
av. Chipping Ntn .. 366 F13
av. Dover Ht......... 348 E8
av. Springwood.... 171 K16
ct. Berowra Ht 133 A7
la. Lane Cove W .. 284 G15
la. Kingsford, off Barker St......... 376 J16
pl. Glenmore Pk... 265 E10
pl. Minto............. 483 A1
rd. North Ryde..... 282 G13
st. Ashfield 372 F3
st. Croydon 372 D3
st. Glebe............... 12 D14
st. Kingsford 376 J16
st. Leichhardt.......... 9 J8
st. Lilyfield............. 9 J8
st. Surry Hills 20 B1
NORTONS BASIN
rd. Warragamba... 323 K12
NORVAL
pl. Illawong 459 G5
st. Auburn 339 C6
NORVEGIA
av. Tregear.......... 240 C4
NORVIC
pl. Seven Hills 275 D9
NORWEST
bvd. Baulkham Hl ... 216 G16
bvd. Bella Vista....... 246 B2

NORWICH
la. Rose Bay........348 B11
pl. Cherrybrook...219 A13
rd. Ingleburn.......453 B5
rd. Rose Bay........348 A11
NORWIN
pl. Stanhpe Gdn..215 G9
NORWOOD
av. Beecroft..........250 B12
av. Carlingford.....250 B12
av. Lindfield.........284 C3
la. Marrickville.......15 K16
pl. Baulkham Hl...246 K3
rd. Vineyard..........152 F13
st. Burwood..........341 H15
st. Sandringham..463 D4
NOTE
st. Hunters Hill....313 B6
NOTLEY
st. Mount Druitt...241 E12
NOTT
la. Longueville.....314 E8
pl. Mt Annan.......479 F14
NOTTING
la. Cottage Pt......135 F10
NOTTINGHAM
av. Castle Hill.......217 K10
cr. Chipping Ntn..366 F13
pl. Ryde...............312 B4
pl. Yowie Bay......492 B12
pwy. Chipping Ntn, off Nottingham Cr...366 H13
st. Old Tngabbie..277 E9
NOTTINGHILL
rd. Berala............339 F13
rd. Lidcombe........339 F13
rd. Regents Pk.....369 F1
NOTTLE
st. Ashfield..........373 A4
NOTTS
av. Bondi Beach...378 D5
NOUMEA
av. Bankstown.....399 E5
st. Lethbrdg Pk...240 K1
st. Shalvey..........210 K16
NOVA
pl. Mount Druitt...241 H12
pl. S Penrith........267 D4
NOVAR
st. St Johns Pk....364 H1
NOVARA
cr. Como.............460 H10
cr. Jannali...........460 H10
NOWILL
st. Condell Park...398 H6
st. Rydalmere......309 J5
NOWLAND
pl. Abbotsbury....333 B14
st. Seven Hills....246 B14
wy. Bradbury........511 J12
NOWRA
cl. Prestons.........423 B2
la. Campsie.........372 D12
pl. Gymea Bay.....491 C11
st. Campsie.........372 D12
st. Greystanes.....305 H2
st. Marayong.......244 B3
st. Merrylands.....308 D15
NOWRANIE
pl. Windsor Dn....151 A15
st. Summer Hill....373 D5
NOYANA
av. Grays Point....491 A15
NUGENT
pl. Prairiewood....334 E12
NULANG
rd. Forestville.......255 E8
st. Old Tngabbie..276 K8
NULGARRA
av. Gymea Bay.....491 E11
pl. Bradbury........511 E15
st. Frenchs Frst...256 D8
st. Northbridge....285 H16
NULLA
st. Vaucluse........348 C6
NULLABOR
pl. Yarrawarrah...489 G12
NULLABURRA
rd. Newport.........169 H10
rd.n, Caringbah.......493 B7
rd.s, Caringbah.......493 B7
NULLAGA
wy. Clarmnt Ms....268 H2
NULLA NULLA
st. Turramurra.....222 K13
NULLAWARRA
av. Concord.........341 G1
av. Concord W.....311 F13
NUMA
rd. North Ryde.....282 F13
st. Birchgrove......314 K16
NUMANTIA
rd. Engadine........518 G7
NUMBRUCK
cl. Cranebrook.....207 E7
NUNANA
pl. Frenchs Frst....255 H1
NUNATAK
la. Tregear...........240 E6
NUNDA
cl. Pennant Hills..220 B14
NUNDAH
pl. Woronora.......460 A15
st. Lane Cove W..284 E16
st. St Johns Pk....334 F16
NUNDLE
st. Smithfield.......335 F1
NUNGA
pl. Baulkham Hl...246 E10
pl. Marayong.......243 K6
NUNGEROO
av. Jamisontown..266 A3
NUNKERE
cr. Rouse Hill.......185 D6
NURLA
av. Little Bay........437 B10
NURRAGI
pl. Belrose...........225 G15
st. Villawood.......367 J5
NURRAN
rd. Vaucluse.........348 B2
NURSEL
pl. Tregear...........240 C4
NURSERY
pl. Belrose...........226 A10
st. Hornsby.........221 E2
NURSES
dr. Randwick.......377 A16
wk. The Rocks..........A K6
NUTMANS
la. Grose Wold....116 A11
rd. Grose Wold....116 B11
NUTMEG
cl. Casula...........424 A2
NUTT
rd. Londonderry...177 F8
NUTWOOD
la. Windsor Dn....151 A13
NUWARRA
rd. Chipping Ntn..396 F4
rd. Moorebank.....396 E12
NYALLA
pl. Castle Hill.......247 G3
NYAN
st. Chifley............437 B9
NYARA
rd. Mt Krng-gai....162 J12
NYARDO
pl. Jannali...........460 H10
NYARI
rd. Kenthurst........157 A3
wy. Narraweena....258 B3
NYDEGGAR
av. Glenwood.......215 D14
NYINYA
av. Gymea............491 G4
NYLETA
st. Doonside........243 D13
NYMAGEE
st. Glenwood.......215 E16
NYMBOIDA
av. Hoxton Park...392 J8
cr. Ruse...............512 D6
cr. Sylvania Wtr...462 D13
st. Greystanes.....306 A2
st. S Coogee........407 G6
NYNGAN
pl. Miranda..........462 D16
st. Hoxton Park...392 H7
st. Quakers Hill....244 A2
wy. Mcquarie Pk...282 E4
NYORA
av. Smithfield.......336 B8
st. Chester Hill.....368 C3
st. Killara............254 C10
NYORIE
pl. Frenchs Frst....256 B2
NYRANG
pl. Kirrawee........490 J5
rd. Allambie Ht.....257 F16
st. Lidcombe.......339 H4

O

OADBY
st. Chipping Ntn...396 G1
OAG
cr. Kingswood.....267 E2
OAK
dr. Georges Hall...367 F11
la. Potts Point.........4 K1
la. N St Marys, off Oak St.............240 A10
pl. Banksia...........403 F12
pl. Bradbury.........511 G13
pl. Mt Pritchard....364 D10
rd. Kirrawee.........490 K6
rd.n, Kirrawee.........460 K16
st. Ashfield..........372 K2
st. Clovelly...........377 K13
st. Greystanes......306 F9
st. Lugarno..........429 J16
st. Normanhurst..221 D12
st. N Narrabeen...199 A14
st. N St Marys......240 A10
st. N Sydney...........K A5
st. N Sydney............5 D7
st. Parramatta......308 H5
st. Prestons.........394 A14
st. Rosehill..........308 H5
st. Schofields.......183 K12
OAKBORNE
rd. Liverpool........395 B9
OAKDALE
av. Kogarah..........433 E6
pl. Baulkham Hl...246 J4
pl. Cartwright.......394 E5
OAKES
av. Eastwood........281 F6
pl. North Bondi....348 F15
rd. Carlingford......249 F9
rd. Old Tngabbie..277 A6
rd. W Pnnant Hl...249 F9
rd. Winston Hills..277 A6
st. Westmead......307 H2
OAKHAM
st. Sylvania..........461 J13
OAKHILL
cl. St Ives............224 F11
dr. Castle Hill.......218 J8
OAKLAND
av. Baulkham Hl...248 A13
la. Wrrngtn Dns, off Oakland Pde....237 K5
pde. Wrrngtn Dns...237 K5
OAKLANDS
av. Beecroft..........250 F9
av. Summer Hill...373 B3
OAKLEA
pl. Canley Ht........335 C15
wy. Castle Hill.......218 J6
OAKLEAF
st. Glenwood.......245 C1
OAKLEIGH
av. Banksia..........403 J13
av. Milperra..........397 F11
av. S Granville......338 E6
av. Thornleigh......220 J11
OAKLEY
rd. Long Point......454 B7
rd. Mcquarie Fd....454 B7
rd. North Bondi....348 D16
OAKMONT
av. Glenmore Pk...266 G9
wy. Rouse Hill.......185 C9
OAKRIDGE
pl. Kenthurst........156 H2
OAKS
av. Cremorne.......316 C7
av. Dee Why.........258 H6
rd. Mowbray Pk....561 B7
rd. Thirlmere........561 F16
rd. Thirlmere........561 B7
rd. Thirlmere........564 F1
st. Cronulla..........523 K2
st. Thirlmere........564 J3
st. Thirlmere........565 A3
OAKTREE
gr. Prospect.........274 H11
pl. Penshurst.......431 D1
OAKURA
st. Rockdale.........403 C14
OAKVILLE
rd. Oakville...........122 G15
rd. Willoughby.....285 F12
OAKWOOD
pl. Busby.............363 H16
pl. Hornsby Ht.....162 A8
rd. Toongabbie.....275 F14
st. Sutherland......490 C1
wy. Menai.............458 H10
OAKY
rd. Luddenham.....326 B7
OATES
av. Gladesville......312 J5
pl. Belrose...........226 B9
pl. Leumeah.........482 J11
rd. Mortdale.........430 J7
OATLANDS
cr. Oatlands.........279 A8
ct. Wattle Grove...426 B3
st. Wentwthvle.....276 G16
OATLEY
av. Oatley.............431 B14
av. Oatley.............431 C11
pde. Oatley.............431 B14
pl. Padstow Ht.....429 C6
rd. Paddington.......21 A3
st. Kingsgrove.....401 H6
OATLEY PARK
av. Oatley.............430 G12
OATS
pl. Rooty Hill........242 F13
OATWAY
pde. North Manly....258 C15
OBA
pl. Toongabbie.....275 E12
OBADIAH
pl. S Penrith.........266 H4
OBAN
cl. Windsor Dn....180 H3
pl. St Andrews.....481 K2
st. Schofields.......183 B16
OBELISK
av. Mosman.........317 K7
OBERON
cr. Gordon...........253 G9
cr. S Penrith.........267 C4
la. Randwick, off Oberon St........407 B2
rd. Ruse...............512 F6
st. Blakehurst.......462 C1
st. Coogee...........407 F3
st. Georges Hall...367 J10
st. Randwick........407 C2
O'BRIEN
la. Windsor...........121 C9
pde. Liverpool.........365 A14
pl. Barden Rdg.....488 G3
rd. Londonderry...148 C10
rd. Mt Annan........479 F14
st. Bondi Beach....378 A2
st. Chatswood......284 H8
st. Mount Druitt...241 E11
O'BRIENS
la. Darlinghurst........4 D9
rd. Hurstville........431 J6
rd. Maroota S.........64 G1
OCCUPATION
rd. Kyeemagh.......404 A14
OCEAN
av. Double Bay.......13 K11
av. Newport..........169 J9
gr. Collaroy..........229 B15
la. Manly.............288 F8
la. Mortdale.........431 B4
la. Pagewood.......405 K10
la. Bondi, off Bennett St........377 J4
la. Clovelly, off Warner Av.......378 B12
pl. Illawong..........459 H4
pl. Palm Beach.....139 K1
pl. Woodbine.......481 K9
rd. Manly.............288 F8
rd. Palm Beach.....109 K16
st. Bnksmeadw....405 K10
st. Beverley Pk.....433 C7
st. Bondi..............377 J5
st. Clovelly...........378 B13
st. Cronulla..........493 K8
st. Edgecliff............13 K12
st. Kogarah..........433 A6
st. Kogarah..........433 C7
st. Narrabeen.......229 A6
st. Pagewood.....405 K10
st. Penshurst.....431 C5
st. Woollahra........22 A1
st.n, Bondi............377 J4
OCEANA
st. Narraweena....258 C5
st.e, Dee Why.......258 D7
OCEAN GROVE
av. Cronulla.........493 K12
OCEANIA
cr. Newport.........169 K13
OCEAN VIEW
rd. Harbord.........258 H16
st. Woolooware...493 E11
wy. Belrose...........226 C10
OCEANVIEW
av. Dover Ht........348 F7
av. Vaucluse........348 F7
O'CONNELL
av. Killarney Ht....286 C1
av. Matraville.......407 A15
cl. Lurnea...........394 D14
st. Clarmnt Ms....268 C1
st. Greenwich.......314 K14
st. Kingswood......268 C1
st. Monterey........433 G6
st. Newtown...........17 J8
st. N Parramatta..278 B12
st. Parramatta.....308 A4
st. Smithfield.......335 H5
st. Sydney...............B B14
st. Sydney...............1 J15
st. Vineyard.........152 G11
O'CONNOR
la. Marrickville, off Llewellyn St......374 F10
la. Beaconsfield, off Queen St.........375 G11
st. Chippendale.....19 A2
st. Eastlakes........405 K5
st. Guildford........337 C1
st. Haberfield......343 D16
O'CONNORS
rd. Beacon Hill.....257 F7
OCTAGON
rd. Darling Point....13 J8
OCTAVIA
av. Rsemeadow...540 F3
st. Narrabeen......229 B2
st. Toongabbie....276 A8
O'DEA
av. Kyeemagh......404 D13
av. Waterloo........375 J9
av. Zetland..........375 J9
pl. N Richmond.....87 A12
rd. Mt Annan.......479 D16
ODELIA
cr. Plumpton.......241 G10
O'DELL
st. Vineyard.........153 A9
ODEON
pl. Heathcote.......518 G8
ODETTE
rd. Dural.............189 F12
ODNEY
pl. Castle Hill.......219 A10
O'DONNELL
av. Greenacre......369 H11
st. North Bondi...348 D16
st. North Bondi...348 F16
O'DOWD
cl. Edensor Pk.....333 H16
st. Waverley.........377 G7
O'FARRELL
la. Penrith...........236 K11
OFFENBACH
av. Emerton.........240 H5
OFFERTON
wy. Cranebrook....207 F13
OFT
pl. Blacktown......274 G9
OGDEN
cl. Abbotsbury....333 B14
cl. St Clair...........270 H13
la. Redfern............19 K9
la. St Clair, off Ogden Cl.........270 H13
rd. Oakville..........122 K12
OGILVIE
pl. Blackett..........241 C4
st. East Hills.......427 H2
OGILVY
rd. Clontarf..........287 H16
st.n, Peakhurst.......430 A3

st.s, Peakhurst......430 A6
OGMORE
ct. Bankstown......399 B4
O'GRADY
pl. Kellyville......216 D2
O'HAGON
st. Chester Hill......368 A3
O'HARA
st. Marrickville......373 K14
O'HARAS CREEK
rd. Middle Dural......158 B3
O'HARES
rd. Wedderburn......540 A9
rd. Wedderburn......541 E16
OHIO
pl. Erskine Park......271 A16
pl. Kearns......451 A15
pl. Quakers Hill......214 D9
OHLFSEN
rd. Minto......453 A15
O'KEEFE
cr. Eastwood......281 G6
rd. Annangrove......156 B11
O'KEEFES
la. Kogarah, off Kensington St......433 B5
pl. Horngsea Pk......392 C14
OKLAHOMA
av. Toongabbie......275 H12
OKRA
pl. Quakers Hill......243 E4
OLA
pl. Oakhurst......241 J3
OLBURY
pl. Airds......512 B13
OLD
la. Cremorne, off Waters La......316 D8
st. Tempe......404 B4
OLDAKER
st. Doonside......243 C5
OLD BARRENJOEY
rd. Avalon......170 A3
OLD BATHURST
rd. Blaxland......233 J7
rd. Emu Heights......235 A6
rd. Emu Plains......235 A6
OLD BEECROFT
rd. Cheltenham......251 A11
OLD BELLS LINE OF
rd. Kurrajong......55 H16
OLD BEROWRA
rd. Hornsby......191 G9
OLD BRIDGE
st. Windsor......121 D7
OLDBURY
ct. Wattle Grove......426 A2
pl. West Hoxton......392 B12
OLD BUSH
rd. Engadine......489 D14
OLD CANTERBURY
rd. Ashfield......373 A8
rd. Dulwich Hill......373 A8
rd. Lewisham......15 A10
rd. Summer Hill......373 A8
OLD CASTLE HILL
rd. Castle Hill......218 D14
OLD CHURCH
la. Prospect......275 B11
OLD EAST KURRAJONG
rd. E Kurrajong......60 C9
rd. Glossodia......60 C9
OLD FERRY
rd. Illawong......459 F4
OLDFIELD
ct. St Clair......269 K14
la. St Clair, off Oldfield Ct......269 K14
pl. Menai......458 G8
rd. Seven Hills......275 D3
st. Greystanes......305 G9
OLD FOREST
rd. Lugarno......429 K14
OLD FORT
rd. Mosman......317 K6
OLD GLENFIELD
rd. Casula......424 A4
rd. Glenfield......424 A4
OLD GLENHAVEN
rd. Glenhaven......187 J14
OLD GRAND
dr. Moore Park......20 J10
OLDHAM
av. Wrrngtn Cty......238 H4
cr. Dolls Point......433 E16
OLD HAWKESBURY
rd. McGraths Hl......122 A12
rd. Vineyard......152 C1
rd. Vineyard......152 E6
OLD HILL
lk. Homebush B......M C12
OLD HILL ROAD
lk. Homebush B......310 C16
OLD HUME
hwy. Camden......507 A5
OLD ILLAWARRA
rd. Barden Rdg......488 F2
rd. Barden Rdg......488 F4
rd. Holsworthy......426 E16
rd. Illawong......458 G8
rd. Illawong......459 A6
rd. Lucas Ht......487 G11
rd. Menai......458 G8
OLD JERUSALEM
rd. Oakdale......500 H10
OLD KENT
rd. Greenacre......369 J14
rd. Greenacre......370 D15
rd. Kentlyn......512 F5
rd. Mt Lewis......369 J14
rd. Ruse......512 F5
OLD KURRAJONG
rd. Casula......394 G14
rd. Richmond......118 C1
OLD LEUMEAH
rd. Leumeah......482 A13
OLD LIVERPOOL
rd. Lansvale......366 B10
OLD LLANDILO
rd. Llandilo......179 B16
OLD MENANGLE
rd. Campbelltwn......511 C7
OLD NORTHERN
rd. Baulkham Hl......247 H9
rd. Castle Hill......218 C15
rd. Dural......188 G16
rd. Dural......189 A14
rd. Glenhaven......218 E3
rd. Glenorie......128 B2
rd. Middle Dural......158 H1
OLD PEATS FERRY
rd. Cowan......104 C14
OLD PITT TOWN
rd. Box Hill......153 K4
rd. Nelson......154 F8
rd. Oakville......153 H2
rd. Pitt Town......92 K15
rd. Pitt Town......93 A15
OLD PITTWATER
rd. Brookvale......257 J10
OLD POST OFFICE
rd. Cattai......64 K14
OLD PRINCES
hwy. Engadine......518 G5
hwy. Sutherland......490 E3
OLD PROSPECT
rd. Greystanes......306 D5
rd. S Wntwthvle......306 D5
rd. S Wntwthvle......307 A4
OLD RACECOURSE
cl. Picton......561 E2
OLD RAZORBACK
rd. Cawdor......506 D16
OLD SACKVILLE
rd. Wilberforce......61 K16
OLD SAMUEL
st. Mona Vale......198 G1
OLDSMOBILE
pl. Ingleburn......453 K8
OLD SOUTH HEAD
rd. Bellevue Hill......377 F3
rd. Bondi......377 F3
rd. Bondi Beach......348 B16
rd. Bondi Jctn......377 F3
rd. Dover Ht......348 B16
rd. North Bondi......348 B16
rd. Rose Bay......348 B16
rd. Vaucluse......348 E5
rd. Watsons Bay......318 G15
rd. Woollahra......377 F3
OLD STOCK ROUTE
rd. Oakville......122 F15
rd. Pitt Town......93 F13
OLD SYDNEY
rd. Seaforth......287 C10
OLD TAREN POINT
rd. Taren Point......462 J11
OLD WALLGROVE
rd. Eastern Ck......302 B3
rd. Horsley Pk......301 G9
OLD WINDSOR
rd. Bella Vista......246 A1
rd. Glenwood......215 E3
rd. Kellyville......215 E3
rd. Kings Lngly......246 D8
rd. Old Tngabbie......277 B7
rd. Seven Hills......246 F14
rd. Stanhpe Gdn......215 E3
rd. Toongabbie......276 G2
rd. Winston Hills......246 F14
OLEA
pl. Mcquarie Fd......454 C4
OLEANDER
av. Baulkham Hl......246 K14
av. Lidcombe......339 F11
cr. Riverstone......182 K4
ct. Peakhurst......430 E1
la. N St Marys, off Oleander Rd......240 A12
pde. Caringbah......493 B10
rd. N St Marys......239 J10
rd. Wahroonga......222 B4
st. Greenacre......370 G9
st. Greystanes......306 A11
OLGA
cl. Bossley Park......334 C5
pl. Belrose......225 E14
pl. Cecil Hills......362 H7
pl. Leumeah......482 G12
st. Blacktown......243 K10
st. Chatswood......285 B9
st. Greystanes......306 G8
OLIN
cl. Cranebrook......207 B13
OLINDA
cr. Carlingford......279 D1
pl. St Ives......254 C1
OLIPHANT
st. Mt Pritchard......364 H11
OLIVE
cr. Peakhurst......430 E1
la. Neutral Bay......6 F1
la. Turramurra......222 H13
pl. Mcquarie Fd......454 G1
st. Artarmon......285 A16
st. Asquith......191 K12
st. Baulkham Hl......247 H11
st. Condell Park......398 J6
st. Fairfield......336 C16
st. Kingsgrove......402 B5
st. Liverpool......395 D6
st. Minto Ht......483 F8
st. Paddington......13 B15
st. Ryde......281 K10
st. Seven Hills......275 G3
st. Wentwthvle......276 J13
OLIVE LEE
st. Quakers Hill......213 J7
OLIVER
av. Rookwood......339 K12
la. Roseville, off Oliver Rd......284 G4
rd. Chatswd W......284 G11
rd. Roseville......284 G3
st. Bexley North......402 C10
st. Curl Curl......258 F16
st. Harbord......288 E2
st. Heathcote......518 D10
st. Mascot......405 D3
st. Queenscliff......288 E2
st. Riverstone......183 A6
wy. Mona Vale......199 A4
OLIVERI
cl. Edensor Pk......363 H1
cr. Green Valley......363 G10
pl. Schofields......213 K6
OLIVET
st. Glenbrook......233 K12
OLIVIA
cl. Rsemeadow......540 F6
la. Surry Hills......20 C5
OLIVIERI
pl. Ryde......282 C12
OLLIER
cr. Prospect......274 F12
OLLIVER
cr. St Clair......270 B9
OLOLA
av. Castle Hill......218 D16
av. Vaucluse......348 B3
O'LOUGHLIN
st. Surry Hills......19 H1
OLPHERT
av. Vaucluse......348 F3
OLSEN
st. Guildford......338 D9
OLSSON
cl. Hornsby Ht......161 J11
OLWEN
pl. Quakers Hill......214 C8
OLWYN
pl. Earlwood......403 G2
OLYMPIA
rd. Naremburn......315 D1
OLYMPIC
bvd. Homebush B......310 E15
bvd. Newington......M C9
ct. Bradbury......511 D8
ct. Carlingford......279 D2
dr. Lidcombe......339 H5
dr. Milsons Pt......1 K1
pde. Bankstown......399 D1
pde. Mt Riverview......204 C16
pl. Doonside......243 E7
OLYMPUS
dr. St Clair......269 G11
st. Winston Hills......276 K1
OMAGH
pl. Killarney Ht......256 B14
OMAHA
st. Belfield......371 E12
O'MALLEY
pl. Glenfield......424 E13
OMAR
cl. Illawong......459 F3
pl. Winston Hills......277 F2
st. Greenwich......314 J6
OMAROO
av. Doonside......243 B14
OMARU
av. Miranda......491 H2
cr. Bradbury......511 F16
st. Beverly Hills......400 H16
OMATI
st. Whalan......240 J8
OMDURMAN
st. Harbord......288 D1
O'MEALLY
st. Prairiewood......334 E11
O'MEARA
st. Carlton......432 K9
OMEGA
av. Lapstone......264 H5
cl. Prestons......392 K14
la. St Clair, off Omega Pl......270 E16
pl. Greenacre......370 A12
pl. St Clair......270 E16
OMEO
st. St Clair......269 K9
OMNIBUS
la. Ultimo......3 C13
rd. Kingsgrove......401 J8
ONA
cl. Bossley Park......333 K11
ONDIEKI
ct. Blacktown......273 H6
ONDINE
pl. Kareela......461 E10
ONEATA
la. Lakemba......401 A1
st. Lakemba......401 A2
O'NEIL
wk. Mosman......317 D7
O'NEILE
cr. Lurnea......394 D6
O'NEILL
la. Btn-le-Sds......433 H4
la. Lilyfield......10 E4
rd. Menai......458 F8
st. Btn-le-Sds......433 H5
st. Granville......308 E16
st. Guildford......337 F2
st. Guildford......337 F4
st. Lalor Park......245 G13
st. Lilyfield......10 E4
ONSLOW
av. Camden......507 B6
av. Elizabeth Bay......13 A3
la. Gordon......254 B5
la. Canterbury, off Onslow St......372 D15
pl. Elizabeth Bay......13 A3
pl. Leumeah......482 B14
pl. Rose Bay......348 E13
pl. Sylvania......462 A14
st. Canterbury......372 D15
st. Granville......308 H10
st. Rose Bay......348 C12
st. St Clair......269 K10
st. Seven Hills......275 K4
ONTARIO
av. Roseville......284 E4
av. St Clair......269 H15
cl. Illawong......459 D5
cl. Seven Hills......275 E6
ONUS
av. Richmond......118 F8
la. Lowlands......118 F2
ONYX
cl. Bossley Park......333 K8
pl. Eagle Vale......481 A7
rd. Artarmon......285 B14
OORANA
av. Phillip Bay......436 J12
OORIN
rd. Hornsby Ht......191 H4
OPAL
cl. S Penrith......267 B1
la. Northmead......278 A5
pl. Bossley Park......333 K8
pl. Cartwright......393 H6
pl. Eagle Vale......481 H7
pl. Greystanes......306 B2
pl. Gymea......461 F16
pl. Northmead......278 A5
pl. Padstow Ht......429 F8
pl. Rooty Hill......242 A12
OPALA
st. Belrose......225 J15
OPEL
pl. Ingleburn......453 J10
OPHELIA
pl. Oakhurst......241 K1
st. Rsemeadow......540 J6
OPHIR
gr. Mount Druitt......271 A4
pl. Illawong......459 E4
OPREY
cl. Minto......452 J14
OPUS
pl. Cranebrook......207 E16
ORALLO
av. Blacktown......244 F14
ORAMZI
rd. Girraween......275 K11
ORAN
pl. Fairfield W......335 E12
ORANA
av. Hornsby......191 J9
av. Kirrawee......490 J2
av. Penrith......237 D6
av. Pymble......253 F2
av. Seven Hills......275 C3
cr. Blakehurst......432 D16
cr. Peakhurst......430 D7
la. Merrylands......307 H14
pde. Homebush B......M B8
pl. Greenacre......369 J11
pl. Liverpool......394 J3
pl. Telopea......279 E8
rd. Kenthurst......156 F5
rd. Mona Vale......199 G2
st. North Ryde......282 F8
ORANGE
av. Clarmnt Ms......238 G16
gr. Castle Hill......218 C16
gr. Frenchs Frst......255 J2
la. Hurstville......432 C5
la. Randwick, off Clovelly Rd......377 C9
pl. Seven Hills......275 G7
st. Eastwood......281 F8
st. Greystanes......305 H5
st. Greystanes......305 J5
st. Hurstville......432 C3
ORANGE GROVE
rd. Cabramatta......365 B12
rd. Liverpool......365 B12
rd. Warwick Frm......365 B12
ORANGERY
pl. Bella Vista......246 G4
ORANGEVILLE
st. Marsden Pk......181 K11
ORARA
ct. Wattle Grove......395 J13
pl. Plumpton......242 C10
rd. Allambie Ht......257 J15
st. Chatswood......285 D6
st. Waitara......221 J3

ORATAVA
av. W Pnnant Hl 249 D7
ORBELL
st. Kingsgrove 401 G12
ORCAM
la. Rooty Hill 272 E5
ORCHARD
av. Winston Hills 277 G1
cr. Ashfield 372 J3
pl. Glenwood 215 E12
pl. Ingleburn 453 D8
rd. Bass Hill 368 A7
rd. Beecroft 250 B10
rd. Brookvale 258 B11
rd. Busby 363 G13
rd. Chatswood 284 J12
rd. Chatswood 284 J9
rd. Chester Hill 368 A4
rd. Colyton 270 A8
rd. Fairfield 336 F16
st. Balgowlah 287 K9
st. Baulkham Hl 247 K12
st. Croydon 342 E14
st. Epping 280 D2
st. Pennant Hills 221 A15
st. Pymble 223 D15
st. Thornleigh 221 A15
st. Warriewood 198 F9
st. West Ryde 281 F14
ORCHARDLEIGH
st. Old Guildfrd 337 C10
st. Yennora 337 C10
ORCHID
cl. Colyton 270 H6
ct. Quakers Hill 214 A10
pl. Mcquarie Fd 454 C5
pl. W Pnnant Hl 248 G8
rd. Old Guildfrd 337 E8
st. Loftus 489 K12
ORD
cl. Bossley Park 333 G5
cr. Sylvania Wtr 462 E14
pl. Leumeah 482 G11
ORDAK
av. Gymea Bay 491 D8
ORDE
pl. Prospect 274 H13
ORDER
pl. Redfern 19 E7
ORE
la. Erskine Park 300 G5
pl. Eagle Vale 481 G6
OREADES
wy. Bidwill 211 D16
O'REGAN
dr. Ryde 312 B3
OREGON
st. Blacktown 243 J14
O'REILLY
cl. Menai 458 F9
st. Parramatta 307 K5
wy. Rouse Hill 184 J8
ORELIA
wy. Minto 482 J6
ORFORD
pl. Illawong 459 B7
ORIANA
dr. Illawong 459 A6
ORIELTON
rd. Smeaton Gra 479 A8
st. Narellan 478 E8
ORIENT
av. Cronulla 524 A2
rd. Greendale 385 C9
rd. Padstow 429 E2
st. Gladesville 312 H5
ORIENTAL
st. Bexley 402 K13
ORINOCO
cl. Seven Hills 275 E8
st. Pymble 253 C5
ORIOLE
pl. Green Valley 363 D9
pl. Ingleburn 453 D9
st. Glenmore Pk 265 G12
st. Woronora Ht 489 D2
ORION
cl. Castle Hill 218 J9
pl. Leonay 234 J15
rd. Lane Cove W 283 F15
st. Bardwell Vy 403 A9
st. Engadine 488 D12
st. Rooty Hill 272 B2
O'RIORDAN
st. Alexandria 375 D16
st. Beaconsfield 375 D16
st. Mascot 405 B5
ORISON
st. Georges Hall 367 H13
ORISSA
la. Cammeray 316 A3
st. Campsie 371 K15
wy. Doonside 243 H16
ORLANDER
av. Glenmore Pk 266 H15
ORLANDO
av. Mosman 316 G11
cr. Seven Hills 275 E3
cr. Voyager Pt 427 D4
pl. Edensor Pk 333 E14
rd. Cromer 228 H14
ORLEANS
cct. Cecil Hills 362 E4
cr. Toongabbie 275 E12
ORLETON
la. Wrrngtn Cty, off Orleton Pl 238 D7
pl. Wrrngtn Cty 238 D7
ORLICK
st. Ambarvale 510 G16
ORMISTON
av. Gordon 253 F9
av. N Sydney 5 K8
av. West Hoxton 392 C11
ORMOND
gdn. Coogee 377 F16
st. Ashfield 373 B2
st. Bondi Beach 378 B4
st. Paddington 13 B16
ORMONDE
av. Epping 251 D16
cl. Glenmore Pk 266 F13
pde. Hurstville 432 A6
rd. E Lindfield 255 B14
rd. Roseville Ch 255 E15
ORMSBY
pl. Wetherill Pk 334 A2
ORNELLA
av. Glendenning 242 F4
ORO
pl. Glenfield 424 G14
ORONGA
av. Baulkham Hl 248 B8
ORONTES
la. Burwood 341 J16
O'ROURKE
cr. Eastlakes 405 J2
OROYA
pde. Roseville 285 A2
ORPHAN
st. Horsley Pk 332 E3
ORPHEUS
cl. Green Valley 363 B12
ORPINGTON
st. Ashfield 373 A2
st. Bexley 402 G12
st. Bexley North 402 G11
ORR
pl. Davidson 255 D3
st. Bondi 377 H2
st. Gladesville 312 H10
ORRS
la. Strathfield 341 G12
ORSINO
pl. Rsemeadow 540 G5
ORTH
st. Kingswood 237 F13
ORTON
la. Concord 311 K15
pl. Currans Hill 479 J12
st. Barden Rdg 488 G6
st. Kings Lngly 245 E4
ORTONA
pde. Como 460 J6
rd. Lindfield 284 D4
ORWELL
la. Potts Point 4 K5
st. Blacktown 274 E10
st. Potts Point 4 J5
OSBERT
pl. Acacia Gdn 214 H16
OSBORN
rd. Normanhurst 221 G12
OSBORNE
av. Dundas Vy 279 K9
av. Ryde 311 H6
la. Woollahra 22 B1
rd. Greenwich 314 G5
rd. Lane Cove 314 G5
rd. Manly 288 H12
rd. Marayong 244 A8
st. Chipping Ntn 396 F5
OSBURN
pl. St Helens Pk 541 B6
OSCAR
pl. Acacia Gdn 214 H14
st. Chatswood 285 A9
st. Greenwich 315 A8
OSGATHORPE
rd. Gladesville 312 G7
OSGOOD
av. Marrickville 373 E14
st. Guildford 338 A2
O'SHANNASSY
st. Mt Pritchard 364 F10
OSHEA
cl. Edensor Pk 363 F1
O'SHEAS
la. Surry Hills 4 C16
la. Surry Hills 20 C1
OSLO
st. Marsfield 281 J1
OSMOND
av. Warwck Frm 365 D14
gr. Hassall Gr 212 A15
OSMUND
la. Bondi Jctn 22 D5
OSPREY
av. Glenmore Pk 266 C13
av. Green Valley 363 D12
ct. Maroubra 407 D14
dr. Illawong 459 F6
pl. Clarmnt Ms 268 H4
OSROY
av. Earlwood 403 D3
OSSARY
st. Mascot 404 K1
OSTEND
st. Bankstown 399 A5
st. Lidcombe M K13
st. Lidcombe 340 C5
st. S Granville 338 F6
O'SULLIVAN
av. Maroubra 406 J11
la. Queens Park 22 E12
pl. Kellyville 216 D2
rd. Bellevue Hill 347 H11
rd. Leumeah 482 A15
rd. Rose Bay 347 H11
OSWALD
cl. Warrawee 222 E13
cr. Rsemeadow 540 J7
la. Darlinghurst 13 A10
la. Darling Point 13 F9
la. Campsie, off Redman St 372 C13
la. Canterbury, off Redman St 372 C13
st. Campsie 372 C13
st. Edgecliff 13 F9
st. Guildford 337 C6
st. Mosman 316 H10
st. Randwick 377 D14
OSWELL
st. Rockdale 403 A12
OSWIN
la. Rockdale 403 C13
OTAGO
cl. Glenorie 128 C1
pde. Miranda 492 A8
pl. Northmead 248 C15
st. Vineyard 152 H12
OTAKI
pl. St Ives Ch 223 J3
OTHELLO
av. Rsemeadow 540 H6
pl. St Clair 270 D15
st. Blakehurst 432 B15
OTTAWA
cl. Cranebrook 207 H10
st. Toongabbie 275 E12
OTTER
la. Erskine Park, off Otter Pl 301 A1
pl. Erskine Park 301 A1
OTTLEY
st. Quakers Hill 244 A3
OTTO
st. Merrylnds W 307 A16
OTTWAY
cl. St Ives 224 D9
OTWAY
cl. Wetherill Pk 334 J5
pl. Illawong 459 C5
OULTON
av. Concord W 311 C12
av. Rhodes 311 C12
st. Prospect 274 G10
OURIMBAH
rd. Mosman 316 H4
OUSE
cl. West Hoxton 392 C6
OUSLEY
pl. Milperra 397 E9
OUTLOOK
av. Emu Heights 235 A6
av. Mt Riverview 204 G15
OUTRAM
pl. Currans Hill 479 J14
st. Chippendale 19 D2
OVAL
la. Glenbrook 234 A15
la. Kingsford 376 J15
st. Old Tngabbie 276 K8
OVENS
cl. Hornsea Pk 392 F15
dr. Wrrngtn Cty 238 G6
pl. St Ives Ch 224 A3
OVER
pl. Shalvey 210 K15
OVERETT
av. Kemps Ck 359 G1
OVERTON
av. Chipping Ntn 366 F14
cl. Berowra 133 C16
rd. Comleroy 56 A5
OWEN
av. Baulkham Hl 247 G12
av. Kyeemagh 404 C13
la. Ultimo 12 K16
pl. Horngsea Pk 392 D16
pl. Illawong 459 D7
pl. S Windsor 150 F3
rd. Georges Hall 367 J15
st. E Lindfield 254 G15
st. Gladesville 312 H5
st. Glendenning 242 H8
st. Lindfield 254 G15
st. North Bondi 348 C14
st. N Willghby 285 E10
st. Punchbowl 400 C5
st. Thirlmere 562 D14
st. Ultimo 12 K16
st. Wentwthvle 277 B13
OWEN JONES
row. Menai 458 G15
OWENS
pl. Cranebrook 207 F10
OWEN STANLEY
av. Allambie Ht 257 E10
av. Beacon Hill 257 D9
rd. Glenfield 424 F13
st. Mt Annan 479 C11
OWL
cl. Green Valley 363 D11
pl. Ingleburn 453 D9
pl. St Clair 269 H11
OXFORD
av. Bankstown 399 B4
av. Castle Hill 217 K10
cl. Belrose 226 C13
la. Cambrdg Pk 237 H8
la. Mount Druitt 241 C15
la. Newtown 17 D10
pl. St Ives 224 A7
rd. Ingleburn 453 D6
rd. Strathfield 341 C13
sq. Darlinghurst 4 B11
sq. Surry Hills 4 B11
st. Belmore 371 D15
st. Berala 339 E10
st. Blacktown 244 J16
st. Bondi Jctn 22 E6
st. Burwood 341 H15
st. Cambrdg Pk 237 G7
st. Centnnial Pk 21 C1
st. Chipping Ntn 366 G16
st. Darlinghurst F G3
st. Darlinghurst 4 A10
st. Epping 251 B15
st. Gladesville 312 J7
st. Guildford 337 J2
st. Lidcombe 339 E10
st. Merrylands 307 E14
st. Mortdale 431 A8
st. Newtown 17 C10
st. Paddington 4 F13
st. Petersham 15 H13
st. Riverstone 182 K8
st. Rozelle 344 D8
st. St Marys 269 J6
st. Smithfield 335 J8
st. Surry Hills F G3
st. Surry Hills 4 A10
st. Sutherland 490 D2
st. Woollahra 21 K6
OXFORD FALLS
rd. Beacon Hill 257 C1
rd. Oxford Falls 257 C1
rd.w, Oxford Falls 226 H12
OXFORD ST
ml. Bondi Jctn 22 H6
OXLEY
av. Castle Hill 247 H4
av. Jannali 460 G11
av. Panania 428 E2
av. St Ives 224 E10
dr. Mt Colah 162 B10
gr. Tahmoor 566 A11
la. Centnnial Pk 21 A14
pl. Frenchs Frst 256 D1
rd. Ingleburn 423 A10
st. Camden 477 A15
st. Crows Nest 315 E5
st. Ermington 280 C16
st. Fairfield 336 B14
st. Glebe 11 K6
st. Lalor Park 245 C14
st. Matraville 437 C1
st. St Leonards 315 D7
OYAMA
av. Manly 288 F13
OYSTER BAY
rd. Como 460 K8
rd. Oyster Bay 461 A8
OZARK
pl. Cranebrook 207 D9
st. Seven Hills 275 B9
OZONE
pde. Dee Why 259 B9
st. Cronulla 494 A12
st. Harbord 258 C15

P

PAAVO NURMI
av. Newington L J12
av. Newington, off Bobby Pearce Av 310 C12
PACEY
av. North Ryde 282 K12
PACHA
pl. Shalvey 210 G14
PACIFIC
av. Penshurst 431 F6
av. Tamarama 378 B7
cr. Maianbar 523 B7
hwy. Artarmon 284 H15
hwy. Asquith 192 A9
hwy. Berowra 133 E14
hwy. Brooklyn 75 A13
hwy. Chatswood 284 H6
hwy. Chatswd W 284 H6
hwy. Cowan 104 D13
hwy. Crows Nest 5 D3
hwy. Gordon 253 J10
hwy. Greenwich 315 A5
hwy. Hornsby 221 G2
hwy. Killara 253 J10
hwy. Lane Cove 314 G1
hwy. Lane Cove W 284 H15
hwy. Lindfield 284 D1
hwy. Mooney 75 A13
hwy. Mt Colah 162 F16
hwy. Mt Krng-gai 162 F16
hwy. N Sydney K B2
hwy. N Sydney 315 G8
hwy. Osborne Pk 314 G1
hwy. Pymble 253 B1
hwy. Roseville 284 D1
hwy. St Leonards 315 A5
hwy. Turramurra 222 H13
hwy. Wahroonga 222 C8
hwy. Waitara 221 G2
hwy. Warrawee 222 C8
hwy. Waverton 5 D3
hwy. Wollstncraft 5 D3
la. Manly 288 G6
la. Penshurst 431 F6

la. *Crows Nest, off Clarke St* 315 F6
la. *St Clair, off Pacific Rd* 270 H15
pde. Dee Why 258 G6
pde. Manly 288 F6
pl. Palm Beach 140 B3
rd. Erskine Park 270 H15
rd. Palm Beach 139 J1
rd. Quakers Hill 213 F14
st. Blakehurst 462 C2
st. Bronte 378 A9
st. Caringbah 492 F9
st. Clovelly 377 J11
st. Greystanes 306 E7
st. Kingsgrove 401 K7
st. Manly 288 G5
st. Watsons Bay 318 E13
PACIFIC PALMS
cct. Hoxton Park 392 G6
PACKARD
av. Castle Hill 217 E16
cl. Ingleburn 453 G11
pl. Horngsea Pk 392 C13
PACKENHAM
pl. Mt Annan 509 F1
PACKSADDLE
st. Glenwood 215 F16
PADBURY
st. Chipping Ntn 396 G2
PADDINGTON
la. Paddington 21 G1
st. Paddington 21 F1
PADDISON
av. Gymea 491 G4
PADDOCK
cl. Casula 394 B16
PADDY MILLER
av. Currans Hill 479 H13
PADEMELON
av. St Helens Pk 541 F3
PADSTOW
pde. Padstow 399 E16
st. Rozelle 10 G1
PADUA
pl. Hebersham 241 G4
st. Prestons 393 E13
PADULLA
pl. Castle Cove 286 C5
PAGANINI
cr. Clarmnt Ms 268 G3
PAGE
av. Ashfield 342 J13
av. Illawong 459 D3
av. N Wahrnga 192 F14
cl. Minto 452 J14
ct. Carlingford 249 G15
la. Canterbury 402 C2
pl. Cabramtta W 364 H5
pl. Moorebank 396 D9
rd. East Ryde 283 C14
rd. North Ryde 283 C14
st. Canterbury 402 C2
st. Pagewood 405 K11
st. Wentwthvle 277 A12
PAGES
rd. St Marys 269 D3
PAGET
ct. Winmalee 173 G12
st. Richmond 118 H7
PAGODA
cr. Quakers Hill 214 B9
PAILS
pl. Shalvey 210 K12
PAINE
av. Moorebank 396 D11
pl. Bligh Park 150 J8
st. Kogarah 433 A4
st. Maroubra 406 H10
PAINS
pl. Currans Hill 479 H10
rd. Hunters Hill 313 C3
PAINTERS
pde. Dee Why 258 E7
PAINTS
la. Chippendale 18 H2
PAISLEY
cl. St Andrews 482 A2
pl. Carlingford 249 J16
rd. Burwood 342 B14
rd. Croydon 342 B14
rd. Croydon 372 E1
PALACE
la. Mortlake 312 A13
la. Petersham 15 J8
rd. Baulkham Hl 247 D8
st. Ashfield 372 G6
st. Petersham 15 H9
PALAMARA
pl. Chester Hill 337 H10
PALANA
cl. West Hoxton 392 F5
PALARA
pl. Dee Why 258 J1
PALAU
cr. Lethbrdg Pk 240 G1
PALAWAN
av. Kings Park 244 J2
PALENA
cr. St Clair 269 F15
la. *St Clair, off Rotarua Rd* 269 F14
PALERMO
pl. Allambie Ht 257 C9
PALFREY
pl. Emu Heights 235 C3
PALING
pl. Beacon Hill 257 K4
st. Cremorne 316 F7
st. Lilyfield 10 F11
st. Thornleigh 220 K14
PALINGS
la. Sydney C J1
PALISADE
cr. Bonnyrigg 364 D6
PALISANDER
pl. Castle Hill 218 G12
PALLAMANA
pde. Beverly Hills 401 B12
PALLISTER
st. Kings Lngly 246 B10
PALM
av. North Manly 288 D2
cl. Green Valley 362 J13
ct. Narellan Vale 479 A13
ct. Woodbine 481 J11
gr. Beverly Hills 400 K15
gr. Normanhurst 221 D13
pl. Bidwill 211 C14
rd. Newport 169 J11
st. Girraween 275 K12
st. St Ives 224 D5
tce. N Narrabeen 228 H3
PALM BEACH
rd. Palm Beach 109 J16
PALMER
av. Strathfield 371 A2
cl. Illawong 459 E2
cr. Bexley 403 A14
la. Darlinghurst 4 D10
la. *Parramatta, off Palmer St* 278 D16
pl. Blacktown 274 J3
pl. Emu Plains 235 C13
st. Artarmon 284 J14
st. Balmain 7 G10
st. Belmore 371 H16
st. Cammeray 315 J4
st. Campsie 371 H16
st. Darlinghurst 4 D12
st. Guildford W 336 K3
st. Ingleburn 453 C8
st. Parramatta 308 D1
st. Sefton 368 E6
st. S Coogee 407 J6
st. Windsor 121 F7
st. Woolmloo 4 E6
wy. Bonnyrigg 364 D5
PALMERSTON
av. Bronte 377 H7
av. Glebe 12 B11
av. Winston Hills 247 H15
pl. Seaforth 287 B11
rd. Fairfield W 335 D12
rd. Hornsby 192 B16
rd. Mount Druitt 241 A16
rd. Waitara 222 B2
st. Canley Ht 365 H3
st. Canley Vale 365 H3
st. Kogarah 433 C2
st. Vaucluse 318 F16
PALMETTO
cl. Stanhpe Gdn 215 E9
PALMGROVE
rd. Avalon 169 K3
PALMYRA
av. Lethbrdg Pk 240 F1
av. St Marys 210 B12
av. Shanes Park 209 G10
av. Willmot 210 B12
PALOMAR
pde. Harbord 288 E1
pde. Yagoona 369 C11
PALOMINO
cl. Eschol Park 481 B4
rd. Emu Heights 235 B4
PALONA
cr. Engadine 488 F15
st. Marayong 244 A4
PALYA
pl. Narraweena 258 E3
PAMBULA
av. Prestons 393 D16
av. Revesby 398 G16
cr. Woodpark 306 G14
pl. Forestville 255 J7
rd. Engadine 489 A12
PAMELA
av. Peakhurst 430 D10
cr. Bayview 168 J12
cr. Berala 339 B13
cr. Bowen Mtn 83 K12
la. *Leonay, off Pamela Pde* 235 B14
pde. Leonay 235 B14
pde. Leonay 235 C14
pde. Marayong 244 D6
pl. Concord 342 A3
pl. Girraween 276 A12
pl. Kenthurst 157 E9
st. North Ryde 282 H9
PAM GREEN
pl. Doonside 273 G1
PAMPAS
cl. Clarmnt Ms 238 H15
PAMSHAW
pl. Bidwill 211 C15
PAN
cr. Greystanes 306 E7
PANAMA
cl. Illawong 459 G5
PANANIA
av. Panania 398 A15
PANAVIEW
cr. North Rocks 279 C1
PANDALA
pl. Woolooware 493 C9
PANDANUS
ct. Stanhpe Gdn 215 D10
PANDORA
cr. Greystanes 306 E7
pl. Tahmoor 566 A12
st. Greenacre 370 D11
PANETH
st. Lucas Ht 487 H13
PANETTA
av. Liverpool 394 J8
PANGARI
cr. Dharruk 241 B5
rd. Glenorie 127 J3
PANGEE
st. Kingsgrove 402 A7
PANICUM
pl. Glenmore Pk 265 G12
PANIMA
pl. Newport 169 F14
PANK
pde. Blacktown 243 J12
PANKLE
st. S Penrith 266 H5
PANMURE
st. Rouse Hill 184 K9
PANORA
av. North Rocks 248 H16
PANORAMA
av. Cabramatta 365 C11
av. Leonay 264 K1
av. Woolooware 493 F9
cr. Freemns Rch 90 A3
cr. Frenchs Frst 256 E7
cr. Mt Riverview 234 C4
la. Seaforth 287 B11
pde. Blacktown 274 K3
pde. Panania 428 D1
pde. Seaforth 287 C10
rd. Kingsgrove 401 K5
rd. Lane Cove 314 H4
rd. Penrith 237 B6
st. Bargo 567 D6
st. Penshurst 431 E9
PANTHER
pl. Penrith 236 D12
PANTON
cl. Glenmore Pk 266 F9
PAPEETE
av. Lethbrdg Pk 240 G1
PAPER BARK
pl. Mcquarie Fd 454 E1
PAPERBARK
cct. Casula 423 J3
cl. Glenmore Pk 265 H10
cr. Kellyville 186 A16
cr. Kellyville 216 A1
pl. Alfords Point 429 B16
pl. Narellan Vale 478 J13
PAR
cl. Pymble 252 J7
la. Randwick 377 F10
PARADISE
av. Avalon 139 H12
av. Roseville 284 K5
cl. Cherrybrook 219 E13
cl. Plumpton 242 B10
pl. St Clair 269 H9
PARAGON
dr. North Rocks 249 B16
la. *Belmore, off Collins St* 371 E16
rd. Dural 189 C16
PARAKA
cl. Bangor 459 E14
pl. Bradbury 511 C15
PARAKEET
pl. W Pnnant Hl 248 E9
PARAMOUNT
cr. Kellyville 185 E8
PARANA
av. Revesby 428 G1
PARAPET
pl. Glenhaven 217 K6
st. Fairfield 336 D6
PARBURY
la. Dawes Point 1 G7
la. Ultimo 12 K12
PARDALOTE
pl. Glenmore Pk 265 H12
st. Ingleburn 453 F7
wy. W Pnnant Hl 249 D7
PARDEY
st. Kingsford 406 J6
PARE
av. Loftus 490 A11
PARER
av. Condell Park 398 C2
st. Kings Park 244 E1
st. Maroubra 406 G11
st. Melrose Pk 310 J2
st. Springwood 202 D12
PARINGA
pl. Bangor 459 F14
PARIS
av. Earlwood 403 A2
pl. Miranda 461 K15
pl. Toongabbie 276 C4
st. Balgowlah 287 G7
st. Carlton 432 G11
PARK
av. Ashfield 372 F5
av. Avalon 140 A15
av. Beecroft 250 F4
av. Bexley 403 A16
av. Blaxland 233 J6
av. Burwood 341 K12
av. Cammeray 316 B7
av. Chatswd W 284 E10
av. Concord 341 K9
av. Cremorne 316 B7
av. Denistone 281 C13
av. Drummoyne 344 A4
av. Glebe 11 H9
av. Gordon 253 H7
av. Hurstville Gr 431 F10
av. Kingswood 237 H12
av. Manly 288 F9
av. Mosman 316 H10
av. Neutral Bay 316 B8
av. Oatley 430 G11
av. Penshurst 431 E9
av. Punchbowl 370 F16
av. Randwick 377 D10
av. Roseville 285 A2
av. Springwood 201 K1
av. Tahmoor 566 C8
av. Waitara 221 K4
av. Westmead 277 H16
av. West Ryde 281 C13
cr. Pymble 253 D2
dr. Bondi Beach 378 E2
dr. Lilyfield 10 E1
la. Caringbah 492 H7
la. Erskineville 18 D14
la. Glebe 12 F12
la. Gordon 253 H7
la. Greenwich 315 B7
la. Newtown 18 A10
la. Sydenham 374 D15
la. Waitara 221 K3
la. Waterloo 19 F12
la. *Mosman, off Lower Almora St* 317 D6
la. *Clovelly, off Park St* 378 A12
pde. Bondi 377 H5
pde. Pagewood 406 F8
pde. Parramatta 307 J1
pl. Caringbah 492 H7
rd. Alexandria 18 J14
rd. Auburn 339 B8
rd. Baulkham Hl 248 B11
rd. Berala 339 A15
rd. Burwood 341 J13
rd. Cabramatta 365 J6
rd. Carlton 432 G9
rd. Cowan 104 B14
rd. Dundas 279 G13
rd. East Hills 427 G4
rd. Five Dock 343 A10
rd. Homebush 341 A7
rd. Homebsh W 340 K6
rd. Hunters Hill 313 C6
rd. Hurstville 431 K3
rd. Kenthurst 157 K6
rd. Kogarah Bay 432 J11
rd. Leppington 420 J12
rd. Liverpool 395 A2
rd. Luddenham 325 C13
rd. Maianbar 522 K9
rd. Marrickville 15 K16
rd. Marrickville 373 K9
rd. Marsden Pk 181 J13
rd. Naremburn 315 D2
rd. Panania 427 G4
rd. Regents Pk 339 A15
rd. Riverstone 181 J9
rd. Rydalmere 309 G3
rd. St Leonards 315 B7
rd. Sans Souci 433 D14
rd. Seven Hills 246 A16
rd. Springwood 202 D8
rd. Sydenham 374 D15
rd. Vineyard 152 A4
rd. Wallacia 325 C13
rd.s, Mulgrave 151 J5
row. Bradbury 511 E13
st. Arncliffe 403 E7
st. Bexley North 402 C12
st. Camden 507 A1
st. Campsie 372 B13
st. Carlton 432 K7
st. Clovelly 378 A12
st. Collaroy 229 A10
st. Croydon Pk 371 K9
st. Curl Curl 258 H13
st. Emu Plains 235 F9
st. Epping 280 F2
st. Erskineville 18 D13
st. Glenbrook 234 A16
st. Homebush B 310 H16
st. Ingleburn 453 C8
st. Kingsgrove 402 C12
st. Kogarah 433 A7
st. Merrylands 308 B16
st. Mona Vale 199 A2
st. Mortdale 431 D8
st. Mulgoa 325 C3
st. Narrabeen 229 A10
st. Newington M D6
st. Northmead 277 G10
st. Peakhurst 430 B4
st. Petersham 15 E6
st. Riverstone 182 J7
st. Rossmore 390 C5
st. Rozelle 344 D8
st. Sutherland 490 D4
st. Sydney C J12
st. Sydney 3 G6
st. Tahmoor 565 G9
st. Woronora 489 J1
PARKCREST
pl. Kenthurst 156 H2

PARKER
av. Earlwood 402 C5
av. West Pymble 252 F9
cl. Beecroft 250 F9
la. Haymarket E F10
la. Padstow 399 F16
rd. Kentlyn 513 D8
rd. Londonderry 149 E14
st. Canley Vale 335 J15
st. Fairfield 335 J15
st. Granville 308 J9
st. Guildford 337 D5
st. Haymarket E G10
st. Haymarket 3 F13
st. Kings Lngly 246 A10
st. Kingswood 237 D15
st. McMahons Pt 5 D15
st. Northbridge 286 B14
st. Rockdale 403 C14
PARKERS
la. Erskineville, off Victoria St 17 K16
PARKES
av. Werrington 239 A11
cr. Blackett 241 A1
dr. Centnnial Pk 21 G6
rd. Artarmon 315 A1
rd. Collaroy 228 J16
rd. Collaroy Plat 228 G12
rd. Cromer 228 J16
st. Ermington 310 D1
st. Guildford W 337 A2
st. Harris Park 308 D5
st. Heathcote 518 F10
st. Kirribilli 6 C16
st. Manly Vale 288 B4
st. Naremburn 315 H3
st. Parramatta 308 D5
st. Ryde 281 G15
st. Thornleigh 221 A13
st. West Ryde 281 G15
PARKHAM
la. Surry Hills 20 D5
pl. Surry Hills 20 D5
rd. Oatlands 279 C7
st. Chester Hill 337 H11
st. Surry Hills 20 C5
PARK HILL
rd. Minchinbury 271 B8
PARKHILL
av. Leumeah 482 E14
cr. Cherrybrook 220 A11
st. Croydon Pk 371 K6
PARKHOLME
cct. Campbelltwn 510 J10
PARKHURST
av. Panania 428 F4
PARKIN
rd. Colyton 270 C6
PARKINSON
av. S Turramrra 252 A4
gr. Minchinbury 272 C9
st. Kings Lngly 245 E6
PARKLAND
av. Mcquarie Fd 424 A16
av. Pendle Hill 276 D14
av. Punchbowl 400 D7
av. Rydalmere 279 H16
pl. Thornleigh 220 J10
rd. Carlingford 249 F16
rd. Mona Vale 198 J1
PARKLANDS
av. Heathcote 519 A10
av. Lane Cove W 284 D16
av. Leonay 265 A2
rd. Glenbrook 264 B3
rd. Mt Colah 192 C1
rd. North Ryde 282 E5
PARKLAWN
la. N St Marys, off Parklawn Pl 239 K11
pl. N St Marys 239 K11
PARKLEA
cl. Dural 190 A13
pde. Canley Ht 335 C15
pl. Carlingford 279 J2
PARKRIVER
cl. Mulgoa 323 C3
PARKSIDE
av. Miranda 491 K2
av. Wrrngtn Dns 238 C5
ct. Currans Hill 479 J10
dr. Kogarah Bay 432 H13
dr. Lalor Park 245 F12
dr. Sandringham 463 D3
dr. S Hurstville 432 C13
la. Chatswood 284 K11
la. Westmead 307 J2
pl. Mt Pritchard 364 H14
PARKTREE
pl. Narellan 478 H13
PARK VIEW
gr. Blakehurst 432 C16
PARKVIEW
av. Belfield 371 F11
av. Glenorie 128 C6
av. Picnic Point 428 F9
av. S Penrith 236 J16
dr. Homebush B M D4
dr. Homebush B 310 J16
la. Fairlight, off Parkview Rd 288 E9
la. Manly, off Parkview Rd 288 E9
pl. Westleigh 220 H8
rd. Abbotsford 343 C3
rd. Chiswick 343 C3
rd. Fairlight 288 E8
rd. Russell Lea 343 C3
st. Miranda 492 D7
PARKWOOD
cl. Castle Hill 218 K8
dr. Menai 459 A12
gr. Emu Heights 234 K3
gr. West Pymble 253 A13
pl. North Rocks 279 B2
PARLAND
cl. Illawong 459 D1
PARLIAMENT
rd. Mcquarie Fd 454 A2
tce. Bexley 402 J11
PARMA
cr. St Helens Pk 541 F3
pl. Carlingford 249 F14
PARMAL
av. Padstow 399 F16
PARNELL
av. Quakers Hill 214 D16
cl. Minto 483 A2
st. East Killara 254 J7
st. Strathfield 341 G12
PARNI
pl. Frenchs Frst 256 D7
PARNOO
av. Castle Cove 285 J4
PAROO
av. Sylvania Wtr 462 F14
ct. Wattle Grove 395 J13
pl. Hornsby Ht 191 H4
pl. Seven Hills 275 G8
pl. S Turramrra 252 B7
st. Greystanes 306 B5
st. Ruse 512 D6
PARR
av. N Curl Curl 258 H9
cl. Bossley Park 333 G9
pde. Beacon Hill 257 J3
pde. Faulconbdg 171 D14
pde. Narraweena 258 B3
pl. Marayong 243 H5
PARRAMATTA
rd. Annandale 16 C4
rd. Ashfield 343 A15
rd. Auburn 309 B13
rd. Burwood 341 H10
rd. Camperdwn 17 C3
rd. Canada Bay 342 E11
rd. Concord 341 H10
rd. Croydon 342 E11
rd. Five Dock 342 E11
rd. Forest Lodge 17 C3
rd. Glebe 18 D1
rd. Granville 308 G10
rd. Haberfield 373 C1
rd. Homebush 341 B8
rd. Homebsh W 339 J1
rd. Leichhardt 15 C6
rd. Lewisham 15 C6
rd. Lidcombe M G13
rd. Lidcombe 339 J1
rd. N Strathfield 341 B8
rd. Petersham 15 C6
rd. Silverwater 309 B13
rd. Stanmore 16 C4
rd. Strathfield 341 B8
rd. Summer Hill 15 C6
st. Cronulla 493 K15
PARRAWEEN
st. Cremorne 316 F8
PARRAWEENA
av. Baulkham Hl 248 B7
rd. Caringbah 462 J16
rd. Miranda 462 C16
PARRELLA
gr. Glendenning 242 F3
PARRISH
pl. Mt Colah 162 C15
PARRIWI
rd. Mosman 317 B2
PARROO
cl. St Clair 299 J2
PARROT
rd. Green Valley 363 F11
PARRY
av. Narwee 400 K12
cl. Bonnyrigg 364 B8
st. Pendle Hill 276 C14
st. Putney 312 B6
wy. Glenmore Pk 265 J6
PARSLEY
rd. Vaucluse 348 E2
PARSON
pl. Harringtn Pk 478 F6
PARSONAGE
rd. Castle Hill 247 F1
st. Ryde 311 G5
PARSONS
av. S Penrith 266 F2
av. Strathfield 341 E15
pl. Barden Rdg 488 H2
st. Ashcroft 364 D15
st. Rozelle 7 D16
PARTANNA
av. Matraville 436 G4
PARTHENIA
st. Caringbah 493 A16
st. Dolans Bay 492 K16
PARTRIDGE
av. Castle Hill 217 F13
av. Hinchinbrk 393 C1
av. Miranda 492 B6
av. Yennora 336 K10
PARUKALA
pl. N Narrabeen 199 B15
PARUNA
pl. Cromer 228 A15
PARYS
cl. Menai 458 K10
PASADENA
pl. St Clair 270 J12
st. Monterey 433 G10
PASCHA
pl. Kareela 461 F9
PASHLEY
st. Balmain 7 F10
PASKIN
st. Kingswood 237 H14
PASLEY
rd. Georges Hall 368 B15
PASSEFIELD
st. Liverpool 395 A7
PASSEY
av. Belmore 371 D13
PASSIONFRUIT
wy. Glenwood 215 E13
PASSY
av. Hunters Hill 313 K12
PASTUREGATE
av. Cmbrdg Gdn 237 J4
av. Wrrngtn Dns 237 J4
PATAK
rd. Ingleside 167 K16
PATANGA
rd. Frenchs Frst 257 A5
PATCHING
cl. Minto 482 K4
PAT DEVLIN
cl. Chipping Ntn 396 K5
PATE
av. East Ryde 313 B1
PATEN
st. Revesby 398 E14
PATENT
sq. Holroyd 308 A10
PATER
st. Bnksmeadw 406 A13
PATERNOSTER
row. Pyrmont 12 H4
PATERSON
av. Kingsgrove 401 K11
av. Lurnea 394 C13
cr. Fairfield W 335 B12
pl. Colyton 270 H8
rd. Springwood 172 F15
st. Camden S 507 B9
st. Campbelltwn 512 A6
st. Carlingford 250 B16
st. Matraville 436 J1
PATEY
st. Dee Why 258 H7
PATHERTON
pl. Narellan Vale 478 H15
PATIENCE
av. Yagoona 369 E8
PATON
pl. Balgowlah 288 A5
st. Kingsford 406 K4
st. Merrylnds W 306 H12
st. Merrylnds W 307 A12
st. Rookwood 340 B11
PATONGA
cl. Woodbine 481 J8
pl. Engadine 489 A11
st. Kingsgrove 401 G10
PATONS
la. Orchard Hills 299 A6
PATRICIA
av. Mt Pritchard 364 D12
ct. Castle Hill 248 B3
pl. Cherrybrook 220 A4
st. Belfield 371 B10
st. Blacktown 274 F10
st. Cecil Hills 362 H6
st. Chester Hill 368 B2
st. Colyton 270 F5
st. Marsfield 282 A7
st. Mays Hill 307 G6
st. Rydalmere 309 J3
PATRICK
av. Castle Hill 217 J12
pl. Berowra Ht 133 B5
pl. Currans Hill 479 G10
st. Avalon 139 K11
st. Beacon Hill 257 E8
st. Blacktown 274 F2
st. Campbelltwn 511 E4
st. Casula 424 F3
st. Greystanes 306 C8
st. Hurstville 431 H1
st. N Willghby 285 E8
st. Punchbowl 400 E8
PATRICK O'POSSUM
pl. Faulconbdg 171 G13
PATRINE
pl. Bella Vista 246 E6
PATRIOT
pl. Rouse Hill 185 D8
PATSY
pl. Kings Park 244 E2
PATTEN
av. Merrylands 307 J15
pl. Kings Lngly 245 D4
PATTERN
pl. Woodcroft 243 G7
PATTERSON
av. Kellyville 216 H7
av. West Pymble 252 H12
cl. Padstow 429 H5
la. Concord 341 J7
la. Surry Hills 4 D14
la. Avalon, off Central Rd 170 C1
rd. Heathcote 518 C16
rd. Lalor Park 245 D11
st. Concord 341 G8
st. Double Bay 14 D11
st. Ermington 310 B1
st. North Bondi 348 C15
st. Rydalmere 309 K1
st. Tahmoor 565 H10
PATTERSONS
la. Grose Vale 85 A8
PATTISON
av. Hornsby 221 H3
av. Waitara 221 H3
PATTON
la. Willoughby 285 D13
PATTYS
pl. Jamisontown 265 K1
PATU
pl. Cherrybrook 219 D12
PATYA
cl. Epping 250 J14
ct. Kellyville 186 F16
pl. N Richmond 87 D16
PAUL
av. St Ives 224 F14
cl. Camden 507 B2
cl. Cranebrook 207 C15
cl. Hornsby Ht 161 J13
cl. Mona Vale 199 E2
cr. Canley Ht 335 F16
cr. S Wntwthvle 306 H8
ct. Baulkham Hl 247 G15
la. Coogee 407 G2
la. Bondi Jctn, off Paul St 377 G4
pl. Carlingford 279 J2
st. Auburn 339 A3
st. Balmain East 8 G9
st. Blacktown 274 B1
st. Bondi Jctn 377 G4
st. Dundas 279 J14
st. Hunters Hill 313 B8
st. Milsons Pt 5 K16
st. North Ryde 282 G6
st. Panania 428 E5
st. Pitt Town 93 B5
st.n, Mcquarie Pk 282 F5
PAULA
st. Marayong 244 A9
PAULA PEARCE
pl. Bella Vista 246 E8
PAUL ELVSTROM
av. Newington M B14
av. Newington 310 B15
PAULINE
pl. Baulkham Hl 247 D3
PAULING
av. Coogee 377 E13
PAULL
st. Mount Druitt 271 C3
PAULWOOD
av. Winmalee 172 J11
PAVASOVIC
pl. Bonnyrigg Ht 363 D5
PAVER
pl. Woodcroft 243 F8
PAVESI
st. Guildford 336 F1
st. Guildford W 336 F1
st. Smithfield 336 F1
PAVEY
pl. Cranebrook 207 E12
PAVIA
rd. Como 460 H9
rd. Jannali 460 H9
PAVILION
dr. Little Bay 437 G14
st. Queenscliff 288 H3
PAVO
cl. Hinchinbrk 393 D4
PAVONIA
wy. Blacktown 274 F12
PAWLEY
st. Surry Hills 20 C5
PAWSON
pl. S Windsor 150 K2
PAXTON
av. Belmore 371 D13
cr. Cherrybrook 219 E16
la. Belmore, off Paxton Av 371 E13
pl. Castle Hill 217 G16
st. Frenchs Frst 257 A4
PAYNE
st. Oakhurst 211 J16
st. S Penrith 237 C16
PAYTEN
av. Roselands 400 F8
st. Kogarah Bay 432 H11
st. Menangle Pk 539 A6
st. Putney 312 A6
PAYTON
ct. Narellan Vale 509 A2
st. Canley Vale 366 B5
PEACE
av. Peakhurst 430 D7
av. Pymble 253 H1
av. St Clair 299 H1
PEACH
ct. Carlingford 249 G16
gdn. Glenwood 215 D13
PEACH TREE
la. Kirrawee 490 J2
rd. Mcquarie Pk 282 E3
PEACHTREE
av. Wentwthvle 277 B8

la. Penrith, off Peachtree Rd...236 E7
rd. Penrith...236 E7
wy. Menai...458 H10
PEACOCK
cl. Green Valley...363 F11
pde. Frenchs Frst...255 G1
st. Bardwell Pk...402 K7
st. Seaforth...287 A8
wy. Claymore...481 A11
wy. Currans Hill...479 G11
PEAK
st. Engadine...488 D12
st. Glenwood...215 G16
PEAKE
pde. Peakhurst...430 E3
PEAKER
la. Woollahra...21 K3
PEAL
pl. Warriewood...199 E14
PEAR
cl. Casula...424 C2
PEARCE
av. Peakhurst...430 E2
la. Hurlstone Pk, off Fernhill St...373 A10
pl. Emu Plains...235 E11
pl. Narellan Vale...508 F1
rd. Quakers Hill...213 J13
st. Baulkham Hl...247 K6
st. Double Bay...14 E7
st. Ermington...280 A16
st. Liverpool...395 A6
st. S Coogee...407 H5
wk. Rockdale...403 F15
PEARL
av. Belmore...371 E13
av. Chatswd W...284 G12
av. Epping...281 C4
cl. Erskine Park...270 H16
ct. Woodbine...481 K10
la. Newtown...374 H10
pl. Seven Hills...275 B7
st. Hurstville...431 H4
st. Newtown...374 H10
st. West Ryde...311 B1
PEARL BAY
av. Mosman...287 A15
PEARRA
wy. Clarmnt Ms...268 H1
PEARSON
av. Gordon...253 G6
cr. Harringtn Pk...478 G7
la. Gladesville...312 J10
pl. Baulkham Hl...247 B15
st. Balmain East...8 H9
st. Bligh Park...150 H5
st. Gladesville...312 J11
st. Kingswood...237 K14
st. S Wntwthvle...307 C6
PEAT
cl. Eagle Vale...481 D7
pl. Camden S...507 D12
st. Brooklyn...75 F12
PEBBLEWOOD
ct. W Pnnant Hl...248 K1
PEBBLY HILL
rd. Cattai...94 E8
rd. Maraylya...94 E11
PEBWORTH
pl. S Penrith...267 A8
PECAN
cl. Cherrybrook...220 A9
cl. St Clair...269 G16
PECK
la. Bardwell Pk...402 J6
PECKHAM
av. Chatswd W...284 G7
PECKS
rd. Kurrajong Ht...54 A6
rd. N Richmond...87 A12
PECOS
cl. St Clair...299 J2
pl. Seven Hills...275 D7
PEDDER
cl. Woodcroft...243 G10
ct. Wattle Grove...396 A14
st. Glenbrook...264 C5
PEDIT
pl. Cherrybrook...219 C12
PEDRICK
pl. Dundas Vy...280 B11
PEDVIN
pl. Annangrove...155 K9
PEEBLES
av. Kirrawee...461 A15
rd. Fiddletown...129 H1
st. Winston Hills...277 E4
PEEK
pl. Chester Hill...338 A14
PEEL
pde. Comleroy...56 A8
pl. Sylvania Wtr...462 F12
pl. Winston Hills...277 J2
rd. Baulkham Hl...246 G8
st. Belmore...371 C15
st. Belmore...371 C16
st. Canley Ht...365 E4
st. Dover Ht...348 F9
st. Glenbrook...233 J16
st. Granville...308 A10
st. Kirribilli...2 D1
st. Lakemba...371 C15
st. Quakers Hill...214 D11
st. Ruse...512 D8
PEELER
pl. Milperra...397 D10
PEERLESS
cl. Ingleburn...453 G11
PEFFER
st. Panania...428 C1
PEGAR
pl. Marayong...243 H5
PEGASUS
av. Hinchinbrk...393 D5
la. Erskine Park, off Weaver St...301 A3
st. Erskine Park...301 A2
PEGGOTTY
av. Ambarvale...511 A15
PEGGY
st. Mays Hill...307 G6
PEGLER
av. S Granville...338 E5
la. S Granville...338 E4
wy. Ambarvale...511 A16
PEITA
cr. Mona Vale...198 J2
PEKE
pl. Rooty Hill...272 D5
PELARGONIUM
cr. Mcquarie Fd...454 G6
PELICAN
la. St Clair, off Swamphen St...271 A13
pl. Hinchinbrk...393 C1
pl. Woronora Ht...489 D5
rd. Schofields...213 E3
st. Erskine Park...271 A13
st. Gladesville...312 K6
st. Surry Hills...F H6
st. Surry Hills...4 B11
PELLATT
pl. Emu Plains...235 F9
PELLEAS
st. Blacktown...275 A9
PELLION
st. Blaxland...233 E9
PELLISIER
pl. Putney...312 A9
rd. Putney...312 B9
PELLITT
la. Dural...188 G11
PELMAN
av. Belmore...371 E14
av. Greenacre...370 F14
PELORUS
av. Voyager Pt...427 D5
PELSART
av. Penrith...237 D2
av. Willmot...210 D12
PEMBERTON
la. Parramatta...308 J1
st. Botany...405 H15
st. Parramatta...308 J2
st. Strathfield...340 H14
PEMBREW
cr. Earlwood...403 C3
PEMBROKE
av. Earlwood...402 F3
av. Summer Hill...373 B3
av. Turramurra...252 F5
pl. Belrose...226 A13
rd. Leumeah...482 B14
rd. Marsfield...251 G15
rd. Minto...452 H16
st. Ashfield...373 A2
st. Blacktown...273 J5
st. Bronte...377 K10
st. Cambrdg Pk...237 F8
st. Epping...251 C15
st. Epping...251 E15
st. Surry Hills...19 G4
st. Sylvania...462 C9
PEMBURY
av. North Rocks...249 B15
cl. Denham Ct...422 C9
rd. Minto...482 B6
PEMELL
la. Newtown...17 C14
st. Newtown...17 C15
PENDANT
av. Blacktown...274 J8
PENDERGAST
av. Minto...482 J7
PENDERLEA
dr. W Pnnant Hl...248 K6
PENDEY
st. Northbridge...285 G16
st. Willoughby...285 G16
PENDLE
wy. Pendle Hill...306 D1
PENDLEBURY
pl. Abbotsbury...333 D11
PENDLEY
cr. Quakers Hill...214 C12
PENDOCK
la. Cranebrook, off Pendock Rd...207 F14
rd. Cranebrook...207 E14
PENDRILL
st. Glebe...11 H7
PENELOPE
cr. Arndell Park...273 D9
la. Cranebrook, off Milligan Rd...207 C13
pl. Cranebrook...207 C13
PENELOPE LUCAS
la. Rosehill...308 J8
PENFOLD
pl. Edensor Pk...333 E15
pl. Sydney...D A1
st. Eastern Ck...272 E7
PENGILLY
st. Riverview...314 A5
PENGUIN
pde. Hinchinbrk...393 C1
pl. Tregear...240 B4
pl. Woronora Ht...489 C6
PENINSULA
rd. Valley Ht...202 F4
PENINSULAR
rd. Grays Point...491 E15
PENKIVIL
st. Bondi...377 J4
st. Willoughby...285 D13
PENMON
cl. Menai...458 H9
PENN
cr. Quakers Hill...213 G15
PENNA
pl. Bonnyrigg Ht...363 C4
PENNANT
av. Denistone...281 G11
av. Gordon...253 G10
pde. Carlingford...250 C13
pde. Epping...280 C1
st. Castle Hill...218 B14
st. N Parramatta...278 J15
st. Parramatta...278 J15
wy. Castle Hill...218 C13
PENNANT HILLS
rd. Beecroft...249 J9
rd. Carlingford...279 A7
rd. Normanhurst...221 A13
rd. N Parramatta...278 D13
rd. Oatlands...279 A7
rd. Pennant Hills...220 H16
rd. Thornleigh...221 A13
rd. Wahroonga...221 A13
rd. W Pnnant Hl...249 J7
PENNICOOK
la. Pennant Hills, off Hillcrest Rd...220 G16
PENNINGTON
av. Georges Hall...367 K14
PENNSYLVANIA
rd. Riverwood...400 A13
PENNY
la. Thirlmere...565 B3
pl. Arndell Park...274 B11
PENNYBRIGHT
pl. Kellyville...216 C2
PENNYS
la. Potts Point...4 J8
PENOLA
ct. Baulkham Hl...247 A2
PENPRASE
la. Miranda...491 K3
st. Riverstone...182 D11
PENRHYN
av. Beecroft...249 K7
av. Pymble...253 C6
pl. Castle Hill...217 K7
rd. Bnksmeadw...435 K4
PENRITH
av. Collaroy Plat...228 D13
pl. St Ives...224 F4
st. Jamisontown...236 D16
PENROSE
av. Belmore...401 G5
av. Cherrybrook...219 J10
av. East Hills...428 A5
cl. Prestons...392 K14
cr. S Penrith...237 A15
pl. Frenchs Frst...256 G9
pl. Menai...458 H6
st. Lane Cove...313 G3
st. Lane Cove W...313 G3
st. Minto...483 A2
PENRUDDOCK
st. S Windsor...150 K2
PENSACOLA
pl. Casula...395 A11
PENSAX
la. Cranebrook, off Pensax Rd...207 G14
rd. Cranebrook...207 F14
PENSHURST
av. Neutral Bay...6 H8
av. Penshurst...431 G6
la. Penshurst...431 E5
rd. Narwee...400 J13
rd. Roselands...400 J13
st. Beverly Hills...401 A15
st. Chatswood...285 C5
st. N Willghby...285 D9
st. Penshurst...431 C1
st. Roseville...285 C5
st. Willoughby...285 D9
PENTECOST
av. Pymble...223 G13
av. St Ives...223 C12
av. Turramurra...223 C12
st. Hinchinbrk...392 K2
PENTLAND
av. Roselands...400 G6
st. Quakers Hill...213 K14
PENTLANDS
dr. Winmalee...173 E11
PENZA
pl. Quakers Hill...214 C10
PEONY
pl. Quakers Hill...243 F3
PEPLER
rd. Cabramtta W...365 B7
PEPLOW
pl. Doonside...273 E3
PEPPER
la. Clovelly, off Thorpe St...377 K14
PEPPERCORN
av. Mt Hunter...505 B8
av. Narellan...478 G14
dr. Frenchs Frst...256 H1
pl. Cranebrook...207 B8
pl. Glenwood...245 H2
pl. Horngsea Pk...392 F13
pl. Kirrawee...460 K16
PEPPERIDGE
av. Oakhurst...242 D1
PEPPERINA
pl. Carlingford...249 H11
PEPPERMINT
cl. Prestons...394 C14
cr. Kingswood...267 G1
cr. Mcquarie Fd...454 G3
gr. Engadine...518 D2
gr. Panania...428 E5
PEPPERMINT GUM
pl. Westleigh...220 F7
PEPPERTREE
dr. Erskine Park...270 G15
gr. Quakers Hill...214 C14
la. St Clair, off Swallow Dr...270 K16
PEPPIN
cl. St Clair...270 B13
cr. Airds...512 D9
la. St Clair, off Peppin Cl...270 B13
pl. Elderslie...507 H1
PERA
pl. Fairfield W...335 C9
PERABO
cl. Bossley Park...333 F9
PERAK
st. Mona Vale...199 E2
PERCEVAL
cl. Abbotsbury...333 A11
PERCHERON
st. Blairmount...480 K14
PERCIVAL
av. Appin...568 F9
la.e, Stanmore...16 G5
la.w, Stanmore...16 F5
rd. Caringbah...492 J16
rd. Smithfield...336 C1
rd. Stanmore...16 F5
st. Bexley...432 H3
st. Carlton...432 H3
st. Clarendon...120 B4
st. Lilyfield...10 G9
st. Maroubra...406 J7
st. Penshurst...431 E3
PERCY
st. Auburn...339 G2
st. Bankstown...399 F3
st. Fairfield Ht...335 H10
st. Gladesville...312 J7
st. Greystanes...306 D9
st. Haberfield...373 E1
st. Ingleburn...453 D10
st. Marayong...244 C10
st. Rozelle...10 J1
PEREGRINE
cl. Green Valley...363 E11
PERENTIE
rd. Belrose...226 D13
PERFECTION
av. Kellyville...215 C2
av. Stanhpe Gdn...215 C8
PERI
cl. Woodcroft...243 J11
ct. Wattle Grove...395 K15
PERIDOT
cl. Eagle Vale...481 E5
PERIGEE
cl. Doonside...243 F14
PERIMETER
rd. Mascot...404 J11
rd. Mascot...404 C12
rd. Mascot...404 E4
PERINA
cl. Bangor...459 E14
cl. Casula...424 C3
PERISHER
st. Horngsea Pk...392 C15
PERKINS
dr. Kellyville...215 J5
pl. Bonnyrigg Ht...363 E8
st. Bligh Park...150 K7
st. Denistone W...280 K12
st. Rooty Hill...272 B1
wy. Maroubra...407 C12
PERMANENT
av. Earlwood...372 H15
PERMIAN
dr. Cartwright...394 D4
PERON
pl. Willmot...210 D14
PERONNE
av. Clontarf...287 E11
cl. Milperra...397 D12
pde. Allambie Ht...257 J16
wy. Matraville...407 A15
PEROUSE
rd. Randwick...377 B15
PERRETT
st. Rozelle...7 D14
PERREY
st. Collaroy Plat...228 H13
PERRI
la. Haberfield...343 C15
PERRIN
av. Plumpton...241 H6
PERRITT
pl. S Penrith...236 K15

PERRUMBA
pl. Bradbury........511 G16
PERRY
av. Springwood....201 G2
cr. Engadine........518 F4
ct. Harringtn Pk...478 E5
la. Campsie.........372 B15
la. Lilyfield...............9 G6
la. Lilyfield...............9 J7
la. Paddington.......13 B16
rd. Arcadia............129 J8
st. Bossley Park..334 B5
st. Campsie.........372 B15
st. Dundas Vy......280 C9
st. Kings Lngly....245 H8
st. Lilyfield...............9 H6
st. Lilyfield...............9 K6
st. Marrickville.......16 G16
st. Marrickville.....374 D9
st. Matraville.......436 F2
st. North Rocks...248 F15
st. Surry Hills........19 H5
st. Wentwthvle....307 A1
wy. Auburn...........338 K2
PERRYMAN
pl. Cronulla.........494 A11
PERRYS
av. Bexley............432 F3
PERSEUS
cct. Kellyville.........186 G16
PERSHORE
la. Cranebrook, off
Pendock Rd....207 G13
rd. Cranebrook....207 G13
PERSIC
st. Belfield...........371 C10
PERSIMMON
wy. Glenwood.......215 E14
PERTAKA
pl. Narraweena....258 B1
PERTARINGA
wy. Glenorie.........128 A6
PERTH
av. Campbelltwn..512 C4
av. E Lindfield......254 K14
cl. West Hoxton..392 D6
st. Kirrawee.........461 A14
st. Oxley Park......270 E1
st. Riverstone......152 F15
st. Vineyard.........152 F15
PERU
pl. Illawong.........459 K3
PESSOTTO
pl. Wakeley.........334 F14
PETER
av. Camden...........507 B6
cl. Hornsby Ht.....161 J12
cr. Greenacre.........370 B7
ct. Jamisontown..266 A2
pde. Old Tngabbie..277 B6
pl. Bligh Park.......150 K8
pl. Gymea Bay.....491 F9
st. Baulkham Hl...247 E11
st. Blacktown.......244 J14
st. Glossodia.........59 F10
PETERLEE
pl. Hebersham.....241 E7
rd. Canley Ht........365 B3
PETER MEADOWS
rd. Kentlyn...........483 A15
rd. Leumeah........482 J14
PETER PAN
av. Wallacia.........324 K14
gln. St Clair...........270 D11
la. St Clair, off
Peter Pan Gln..270 D11
PETERS
pl. Maroubra.......407 E14
pl. Ruse..............512 H8
PETERS CORNER
Randwick.......377 A12
PETERSEN
cr. Tregear...........240 C4
PETERSHAM
la. Petersham........16 A5
rd. Marrickville.....373 K13
st. Bonnyrigg Ht..363 C7
st. Petersham........16 A5
PETERSON
pl. North Rocks...248 K14
PETER WILSON
st. Glenwood.......245 J1
PETITE
la. Springwood....201 K3
PETITH
la. Hurstville.......401 H16
PETRARCH
av. Vaucluse.........348 E5
PETREL
pl. Hinchinbrk......393 C1
pl. Tregear...........240 B4
pl. Woronora Ht...489 E4
PETRIE
cl. Bidwill............211 D15
pl. Georges Hall...368 C15
PETRINA
cr. Baulkham Hl...248 B13
PETRIZZI
pl. Baulkham Hl...247 E8
PETTIT
av. Lakemba.........371 A13
PETTY
av. Yagoona.........368 K11
PETUNIA
av. Bankstown......399 G3
pl. Mcquarie Fd...454 E4
st. Marayong.......244 A6
PEUGEOT
dr. Ingleburn........453 J9
PEVENSEY
st. Canley Vale.....365 J4
PHAR LAP
cl. Casula............394 E16
la. St Clair, off
Phar Lap Pl......270 E12
pl. St Clair...........270 E11
PHARLAP
st. Bossley Park...333 J8
PHEASANT
st. Canterbury......402 E2
PHEASANTS
rd. Wedderburn...540 D9
PHELPS
cr. Bradbury........511 E7
la. Surry Hills........20 D3
st. Canley Vale.....365 K4
st. Surry Hills........20 C3
PHILBY
pl. Bonnyrigg.......363 H8
PHILIP
la. West Pymble..252 J10
ml. West Pymble..252 J10
pl. Carlingford.....249 F13
pl. Cherrybrook...220 B4
rd. Leppington.....420 D7
rd. Mona Vale......169 G16
st. Blacktown.......244 B11
st. Bondi.............377 K5
st. Strathfield.......341 H11
st. Woolooware...493 J9
PHILIPPA
cl. Cecil Hills.......362 E2
PHILLIP
av. Cabramatta.....365 F9
av. Seaforth.........287 B7
cr. Btn-le-Sds......403 K15
la. Newtown.........17 C12
la. Penshurst.......431 B3
la. Sydney...............B F13
la. St Marys, off
Champness Cr..239 K15
la. Parramatta, off
Phillip St.........308 C2
pky. Eastern Ck......272 H4
pky. Rooty Hill.......272 F1
pl. McGraths Hl...121 J12
rd. Putney............311 K6
rd. Ryde...............311 K6
rd. St Ives Ch.......194 B16
st. Balmain..............7 F8
st. Birchgrove..........7 F8
st. Blakehurst......432 C15
st. Campbelltwn...511 J6
st. Glebe...............12 E12
st. Guildford W....336 J4
st. Kingswood.....237 F11
st. Liverpool........394 H2
st. Newtown.........17 B12
st. Oatlands.........278 K10
st. Oyster Bay......461 B8
st. Panania.........428 B5
st. Parramatta......308 C2
st. Petersham.......16 C4
st. Redfern............19 C10
st. Riverwood......400 C15
st. Roselands......401 C5
st. St Marys.........239 H14
st. Seven Hills.....245 E16
st. S Coogee........407 G6
st. Stanmore..........16 C4
st. Sydney...............B E15
st. Sydney...............D D4
st. Sydney...............1 K16
st. Sydney...............3 K2
st. Waterloo...........19 C10
PHILLIPA
ct. Kellyville.........217 C1
ct. Kellyville.........217 D1
pl. Bargo.............567 B5
PHILLIPS
av. Canterbury......372 D13
av. Regents Pk......339 C16
la. Marrickville.....373 F15
la. Neutral Bay.........6 C6
rd. Kogarah..........433 D10
st. Alexandria.........18 J13
st. Auburn...........339 A4
st. Cabarita..........342 E2
st. Neutral Bay.........6 D7
st. Rookwood......340 C12
PHILLIPSON
la. Springwood....172 A15
PHILO
cl. Rsemeadow....540 E2
PHILOS
st. Minchinbury...272 B8
PHILPOTT
la. Marrickville, off
Philpott St.......374 D9
st. Marrickville.......16 H16
st. Marrickville.....374 D9
PHINEY
rd. Ingleburn........453 E1
PHIPPS
rd. Maraylya...........94 C10
st. Oatley............461 D1
PHLOX
cl. Lalor Park.......245 C10
PHOEBE
st. Balmain..............7 A7
PHOENIX
av. Ingleburn........453 A9
av. Kellyville.........215 J3
av. Rhodes...........311 D11
av. Stanhpe Gdn...215 A11
cl. Castle Hill.......218 K9
cr. Casula............395 A11
cr. Erskine Park....270 H15
la. St Clair, off
Phoenix Cr.......270 J15
pl. Illawong..........459 G3
pl. Narellan Vale...479 B14
st. Lane Cove.......314 E1
PHYLLIS
av. Picnic Point....428 G5
av. Thornleigh......221 B12
cr. Guildford........337 D3
la. N Curl Curl, off
Phyllis St.........259 C10
st. Minto.............482 G2
st. Mt Pritchard....364 G12
st. N Curl Curl......259 C10
PHYSICS
rd. Camperdwn......18 B4
PIAF
cl. Bonnyrigg Ht..363 C4
PIANOSA
pl. Glenwood.......245 K3
PIBRAC
av. Warrawee.......222 G10
PICASSO
cr. Old Tngabbie..276 K6
la. Emu Plains, off
Picasso Pl........236 A7
pl. Emu Plains.....236 A7
PICCADILLY
pl. Maroubra.........407 A9
st. Riverstone......183 A6
st. Riverstone......183 B8
PICCOLO
wy. Shalvey...........210 H14
PICHOLA
pl. Castle Hill.......218 E15
PICKEN
la. Blacktown.......244 F13
st. Silverwater..........L D16
st. Silverwater......309 K8
PICKERING
la. Woollahra.........22 B2
PICKERING PATH
Winmalee.......173 A14
PICKERSGILL
st. Kings Lngly.....245 H7
PICKETT
av. Minto.............453 A15
PICKFORD
av. Eastwood........281 F7
PICKWICK
wy. Ambarvale.......541 A1
PICKWORTH
av. Balgowlah.......287 G8
pl. Menai............458 J6
PICNIC
gln. Springwood....201 H6
gr. Ingleburn........454 A8
pl. Clarmnt Ms.....238 K16
PICNIC POINT
rd. Panania..........428 D5
rd. Picnic Point.....428 C8
PICOT
pl. Blackett..........241 C1
PICTON
av. Picton.............563 F5
rd. Picton............563 H11
st. Mascot............405 H6
st. Quakers Hill....244 A1
PICTOR
st. Erskine Park....300 K3
PIDCOCK
st. Camperdwn......17 D4
PIDDING
rd. Ryde..............312 G1
PIER
st. Haymarket..........E A4
st. Haymarket..........3 B10
st. Prospect.........274 H11
st. Sydney...............E A4
st. Sydney...............3 B10
PIERCE
pl. Bonnet Bay.....460 D10
st. Mount Druitt...241 F13
st. Newtown..........17 A10
st. Prairiewood....334 H7
PIERRE
cl. Mt Colah.........192 C3
PIERSON
la. Canterbury......372 G13
PIESLEY
st. Prairiewood....334 K9
PIGEON
cl. Hinchinbrk......393 C4
PIGGERY
la. Richmond.......118 K12
PIGGOTT
wy. Ingleburn........452 K10
PIGOTT
la. Marrickville.....373 E15
st. Dulwich Hill.....373 D8
PIKE
rd. Hornsby Ht.....191 F2
st. Rydalmere......309 E4
PIKES
la. Eastern Ck......272 J11
la. Newtown..........17 E11
PILBARA
pl. Grays Point.....491 A14
PILBARRA
pl. Cartwright.......394 A4
PILCHER
av. Castle Hill.......218 J12
st. Strathfield S....370 K7
PILCHERS
la. Burwood, off
Belmore St.......342 A15
PILDRA
av. St Ives............223 J14
pl. Frenchs Frst....256 E8
PILE
pl. N Sydney............6 A10
st. Dulwich Hill.....373 G9
st. Gladesville......312 G13
st. Marrickville.....373 H9
st.n, Bardwell Pk.....402 K8
st.s, Bardwell Vy.....403 A9
PILGRIM
av. Marrickville.....373 D14
av. Strathfield.......341 F11
PILLARS
pl. Matraville........436 J1
PILLIGA
cr. Bossley Park...333 G12
ct. Wattle Grove....426 C3
pl. Bangor...........459 E14
PIMA
cl. Greenfld Pk.....334 B16
PIMELEA
pl. Rooty Hill.......272 B3
PIMELIA
ct. Voyager Pt.....427 C5
st. Tahmoor........565 H8
PINANG
pl. Whalan..........240 K7
PINAROO
cr. Bradbury........511 C16
pl. Gymea Bay.....491 H8
pl. Lane Cove W..283 J14
PINCOMBE
cr. Harringtn Pk...478 F8
PINDARI
av. Camden.........506 K4
av. Carlingford.....279 F3
av. Castle Cove....285 H3
av. Loftus............490 B10
av. Mosman.........287 A16
av. St Ives...........254 A2
cr. S Wntwthvle...306 H7
dr. S Penrith........266 J7
pl. Bardwell Vy....403 C7
pl. Bayview.........168 K13
rd. Dover Ht........348 F14
rd. Peakhurst.......430 C9
st. Hornsby Ht.....191 G2
st. North Ryde......282 F8
st. Winmalee.......173 A9
PINDARUS
wy. Rsemeadow...540 H3
PINDOS
pl. Emu Heights..235 B5
PINDRIE
pl. Belrose...........225 H16
st. Miranda.........492 C9
PINDURO
pl. Cromer...........227 H13
PINE
av. Bradbury........511 C13
av. Brookvale.......258 C9
av. Earlwood........403 H2
av. Five Dock.......343 B7
av. Narraweena....258 C7
av. Russell Lea....343 B7
av. Wareemba......343 B7
cr. Bella Vista......246 E5
cr. Bidwill............211 G13
la. Chippendale.....18 H3
la. Manly.............288 G6
la. Newtown..........18 A11
la. Rydalmere.......309 H1
la. Bondi Jctn, off
Hollywood Av...377 F3
la. Engadine, off
Mianga Av........518 J2
pl. Chippendale.....18 J3
pl. Grose Vale........84 J13
pl. Narraweena....258 C7
pl. Riverstone......182 K4
rd. Auburn...........339 A6
rd. Casula...........423 J1
rd. Casula...........423 K1
rd. Casula...........424 D2
rd. Fairfield.........336 H7
rd. Yennora.........336 H7
sq. Leichhardt........16 B1
st. Cammeray......316 A3
st. Chippendale.....18 J3
st. Lugarno.........429 J15
st. Manly.............288 E6
st. Manly.............288 F6
st. Marrickville....373 F11
st. Newtown..........18 B10
st. Normanhurst..221 D13
st. North Ryde......282 F7
st. Randwick.......377 D9
st. Rozelle...............7 D14
st. Rydalmere......309 G1
st.e, Cammeray......316 B4
PINE CREEK
cct. St Clair..........299 H1
PINECREST
st. Winmalee.......173 E5
PINEDALE
pl. Kurrajong Ht....53 K4
PINEGROVE
tce. Minchinbury...272 D8
PINE HILL
av. Double Bay.......14 D12
PINEHURST
av. Glenmore Pk..266 G10
av. Rouse Hill......185 B9
PINELEIGH
rd. Lalor Park......245 K13

PINERA
cl. Hornsby ... 221 B2
PINERIDGE
cr. Silverdale ... 383 A11
cr. Silverdale ... 413 A4
PINES
av. Little Bay ... 437 G13
pde. Gymea ... 491 G7
PINETREE
av. Cranebrook ... 237 E1
dr. Carlingford ... 249 H13
PINE VALLEY
rd. Galston ... 160 D13
PINEVIEW
av. Manly Vale ... 287 H3
av. Roselands ... 400 G8
pl. Dural ... 219 B7
PINNACLE
st. Miranda ... 491 H4
st. Sadleir ... 394 B1
wy. Glenwood ... 215 G16
PINNER
cl. N Epping ... 251 G11
PIN OAK
gr. Menai ... 458 J15
pl. Narellan Vale ... 479 A12
PINOT
pl. Minchinbury ... 271 G7
st. Eschol Park ... 481 D2
PINTA
pl. Cromer ... 228 B15
PINTO
la. St Clair, off Pinto Pl ... 270 E12
pl. St Clair ... 270 E11
PINUS
av. Glenorie ... 128 F12
PIO
wy. Acacia Gdn ... 214 J16
PIONEER
av. Thornleigh ... 221 B11
dr. Menai ... 459 A12
gr. Wrrngtn Dns ... 238 C6
la. Wrrngtn Dns, off Pioneer Gr ... 238 D5
pl. Castle Hill ... 218 F13
rd. Cronulla ... 493 J16
st. Seven Hills ... 245 E15
st. Wentwthvle ... 276 H13
PIPER
cl. Kingswood ... 267 E3
cl. Milperra ... 397 C10
la. Annandale ... 11 A12
la. Kingswood, off Piper Cl ... 267 F2
pl. Minchinbury ... 271 H8
st. Annandale ... 10 J11
st. Lilyfield ... 10 D9
st. West Hoxton ... 392 C9
st.n, Annandale ... 11 B12
st.s, Annandale ... 11 A12
wy. Minto ... 482 K2
wy. Narellan ... 478 G13
PIPERITA
cl. Mt Colah ... 191 K3
pl. Winmalee ... 173 E8
PIPERS
la. Silverdale ... 384 A4
PIPET
pl. Hinchinbrk ... 393 C3
PIPINO
pl. Dee Why ... 258 H1
PIPIT
pl. Ingleburn ... 453 H8
PIPON
cl. Green Valley ... 362 K11
PIPPA
st. Seven Hills ... 246 A11
PIPPEN
pl. Rooty Hill ... 242 A12
st. Harringtn Pk ... 478 F6
PIPPITA
pl. Bangor ... 459 F14
st. Lidcombe ... 340 D6
PIPPITTA
st. Marayong ... 244 B2
PIQUET
pl. Toongabbie ... 276 D5
PIRA
pl. Forestville ... 255 F8
PIRIE
cl. Wakeley ... 334 J14
st. Liverpool ... 395 D5

PIRIWAL
cl. Bangor ... 459 D14
PIROL
pl. Dean Park ... 242 K1
PIRON
pl. Woronora Ht ... 489 C6
PIRRAMA
rd. Pyrmont ... 8 F16
PISA
pl. Plumpton ... 241 G8
PISCES
la. Erskine Park, off Pisces Pl ... 300 H1
pl. Erskine Park ... 300 H1
PITAPUNGA
cl. Woodcroft ... 243 G11
PITCAIRN
av. Lethbrdg Pk ... 210 F16
PITLOCHRY
rd. St Andrews ... 452 A15
PITMAN
av. Hornsby Ht ... 161 F15
PITT
la. N Richmond ... 87 F14
la. Rockdale ... 403 E15
la. Parramatta, off Steele St ... 307 K5
rd. N Curl Curl ... 258 G10
st. Badgerys Ck ... 358 G4
st. Balgowlah ... 287 J6
st. Canley Ht ... 335 G16
st. Concord ... 341 H7
st. Granville ... 307 K8
st. Haymarket ... E F13
st. Haymarket ... 3 F15
st. Holroyd ... 307 J12
st. Hunters Hill ... 313 E11
st. Kirribilli ... 6 A16
st. Loftus ... 490 C9
st. Manly Vale ... 287 J5
st. Mays Hill ... 307 K8
st. Merrylands ... 307 J12
st. Mortdale ... 431 B9
st. Parramatta ... 308 A4
st. Randwick ... 377 C14
st. Redfern ... 19 E10
st. Richmond ... 119 B5
st. Riverstone ... 182 J7
st. Rockdale ... 403 E15
st. Springwood ... 201 E4
st. Sydney ... C K16
st. Sydney ... 1 H16
st. Sydney ... 3 H6
st. Tahmoor ... 565 H13
st. Waterloo ... 19 E11
st. Waterloo ... 19 F15
st. Windsor ... 121 F7
PITTMAN STEPS
pl. Blair Athol ... 511 B4
PITT-OWEN
av. Arncliffe ... 403 F9
PITT TOWN
rd. Kenthurst ... 157 A13
rd. McGraths Hl ... 121 J12
rd. Maraylya ... 125 B2
rd. Pitt Town ... 122 F7
PITT TOWN BOTTOMS
rd. Pitt Town ... 92 A8
rd. Pitt Twn Bttms 122 A3
PITT TOWN DURAL
rd. Maraylya ... 94 A14
rd. Pitt Town ... 93 E12
PITT TOWN FERRY
rd. Wilberforce ... 92 D2
PITT VIEW
st. Scotland I ... 168 J2
PITTWATER
rd. Bayview ... 168 J10
rd. Brookvale ... 258 A12
rd. Church Point ... 168 F7
rd. Collaroy ... 229 A6
rd. Dee Why ... 258 F7
rd. East Ryde ... 283 B11
rd. Gladesville ... 312 J9
rd. Hunters Hill ... 313 A7
rd. Mcquarie Pk ... 283 A6
rd. Manly ... 288 G8
rd. Mona Vale ... 199 C6
rd. Narrabeen ... 229 A6
rd. North Manly ... 258 A13
rd. N Narrabeen ... 229 A2
rd. North Ryde ... 283 B11
rd. Queenscliff ... 288 D2
rd. Warriewood ... 199 A16

PITURI
pl. Alfords Point ... 429 A14
PIUS
la. Marsden Pk ... 211 J2
PIVETTA
st. Revesby ... 399 A14
PLAINS VIEW
cr. Mt Riverview ... 204 H14
PLANA
cr. Springwood ... 202 B2
PLANE
st. Prestons ... 393 J14
PLANE TREE
dr. Narellan Vale ... 479 A13
dr. Stanhpe Gdn ... 215 D10
PLANT
la. Mortlake, off Herbert St ... 312 B16
st. Balgowlah ... 287 E10
st. Carlton ... 432 H11
PLANTE
wk. Lalor Park ... 245 G12
PLANTHURST
rd. Carlton ... 432 F10
PLASSER
cr. N St Marys ... 240 A13
PLASSEY
rd. Mcquarie Pk ... 283 D7
PLASTO
st. Greenacre ... 370 F15
PLATEAU
cl. Hornsby Ht ... 161 H15
pde. Blaxland ... 233 C6
rd. Avalon ... 169 K4
rd. Bilgola ... 169 F6
rd. Collaroy Plat ... 228 J15
rd. Springwood ... 201 D1
PLATFORM
st. Lidcombe ... 340 A6
PLATO
pl. Wetherill Pk ... 335 A6
PLATTS
av. Belmore ... 401 H3
PLAYER
st. St Marys ... 269 D3
PLAYFAIR
rd. Mt Colah ... 192 D1
rd. N Curl Curl ... 258 H11
st. The Rocks ... A K2
PLAYFORD
rd. Padstow Ht ... 429 E8
PLEASANT
av. E Lindfield ... 255 A13
av. Erskineville ... 374 K9
ct. Carlingford ... 279 G5
pl. Leonay ... 234 K16
pl. Yarramundi ... 145 F8
st. Bossley Park ... 334 B10
wy. Blakehurst ... 462 B1
PLEASURE POINT
rd. Pleasure Pt ... 427 G9
PLIMSOLL
la. Belmore, off Plimsoll St ... 401 H1
st. Belmore ... 401 H1
st. McGraths Hl ... 122 A11
st. Sans Souci ... 462 J4
PLOUGH INN
rd. Leumeah ... 481 K13
PLOUGHMAN
cr. Wrrngtn Dns ... 238 A4
cr. Wrrngtn Dns ... 238 A5
rd. Currans Hill ... 479 K8
PLOVER
cl. St Clair ... 270 B14
gln. Bella Vista ... 246 F1
la. St Clair, off Plover Cl ... 270 B14
pl. Ingleburn ... 453 G10
st. Grays Point ... 491 F15
st. Newington ... L J16
st. Newington ... 310 D12
st. Plumpton ... 241 K9
PLOWMAN
rd. Minto ... 453 C15
st. North Bondi ... 348 D16
PLUKAVEC
cct. Prestons ... 393 C14
PLUM
cl. Casula ... 424 B2
gdn. Glenwood ... 215 D13
PLUME
cl. Mcquarie Fd ... 454 A3

PLUMER
rd. Rose Bay ... 347 G12
PLUMPTON
rd. Glendenning ... 242 C7
rd. Plumpton ... 242 C7
PLUMTREE
ct. W Pnnant Hl ... 248 K4
PLUNKETT
cr. Kingswood ... 267 F1
cr. Mount Druitt ... 241 G11
la. Drummoyne ... 343 H4
pl. Gladesville ... 312 K12
rd. Mosman ... 317 E8
st. Drummoyne ... 343 G5
st. Kirribilli ... 2 F2
st. Marsfield ... 281 K2
st. St Leonards ... 315 D5
st. Woolmloo ... 4 F4
PLYMOUTH
av. Chester Hill ... 338 C14
av. North Rocks ... 278 H3
cl. Wahroonga ... 222 G7
cr. Kings Lngly ... 246 C8
st. Enfield ... 371 G3
PLYMPTON
rd. Carlingford ... 250 C12
rd. Epping ... 250 C12
wy. Glenhaven ... 218 E5
POA
pl. Glenmore Pk ... 265 H12
POATE
la. Centnnial Pk ... 21 D5
pl. Davidson ... 225 B15
rd. Centnnial Pk ... 21 C6
rd. Moore Park ... 21 C6
POBJE
av. Birrong ... 368 K6
POBJOY
pl. Bnkstn Aprt ... 397 K1
POCKET
cl. Ambarvale ... 540 G1
POCKLEY
av. Roseville ... 284 F5
PODARGUS
pl. Ingleburn ... 453 G8
PODMORE
pl. Hillsdale ... 406 G14
POETS
gln. Wrrngtn Dns ... 238 E6
la. Wrrngtn Dns, off Poets Gln ... 238 E6
POGSON
dr. Cherrybrook ... 219 K9
POIDEVIN
la. Wilberforce ... 91 J1
POINCIANA
cl. Greystanes ... 306 E12
cl. Mt Colah ... 192 B2
row. Menai ... 458 J15
POINSETTIA
av. North Rocks ... 279 B1
POINT
la. Northwood ... 314 H9
rd. Mooney ... 75 D1
rd. Northwood ... 314 H9
rd. Lilyfield, off Central Av ... 344 A7
st. Lilyfield ... 10 B6
st. Pyrmont ... 8 F15
POINT PIPER
la. Paddington ... 21 H2
POKOLBIN
pl. Edensor Pk ... 363 E2
POLAR
st. Tregear ... 240 E7
POLARIS
pl. Rooty Hill ... 272 B2
POLDING
la. Drummoyne ... 343 H4
pl. Telopea ... 279 G10
rd. Lindfield ... 283 J2
st. Bossley Park ... 334 C6
st. Drummoyne ... 343 G4
st. Fairfield Ht ... 335 G8
st. Fairfield W ... 335 G8
st. Smithfield ... 335 G8
st. Wetherill Pk ... 334 C6
st.n, Fairfield ... 336 F9

POLE
la. Crows Nest, off Hume St ... 315 F6
la. St Leonards, off Oxley St ... 315 E6
POLITO
ct. Kellyville ... 217 A2
POLK
pl. Bonnet Bay ... 460 C10
POLLACK
st. Blacktown ... 274 B5
POLLARD
pl. Sutherland ... 490 G6
POLLOCK
st. Georges Hall ... 367 H12
POLLUX
cl. Erskine Park ... 301 A1
POLLY
pl. Plumpton ... 241 H10
POLO
av. Mona Vale ... 199 E3
cr. Girraween ... 276 A11
pl. Jamisontown ... 236 A16
pl. Prestons ... 392 J16
rd. Rossmore ... 419 H4
st. Kurnell ... 466 D7
st. Revesby ... 398 G15
POLONIA
av. Plumpton ... 242 D12
POLONIUS
st. Rsemeadow ... 540 J5
POLWARTH
pl. Bradbury ... 511 D13
st. Miller ... 393 F3
POLWORTH
cl. Elderslie ... 507 J2
POLYBLANK
pde. North Bondi ... 348 C14
pde. Rose Bay ... 348 C14
POLYGON
cr. Earlwood ... 372 K16
POMARA
gr. Narellan Vale ... 508 G2
POMEGRANATE
pl. Glenwood ... 215 F13
POMEROY
st. Homebush ... 341 C6
st. N Strathfield ... 341 C6
POMO
cl. Greenfld Pk ... 334 A16
POMONA
st. Greenacre ... 370 H12
st. Pennant Hills ... 220 K15
POMROY
av. Earlwood ... 373 B16
PONDAGE
lk. Homebush B ... M B11
lk. Homebush B ... 310 D15
PONDEROSA
pde. Warriewood ... 198 G5
pl. Lugarno ... 430 A12
PONDS
rd. Prospect ... 275 A15
rd. Wilberforce ... 62 A6
wy. Airds ... 511 J16
PONSFORD
av. Rouse Hill ... 184 K5
PONSONBY
pde. Seaforth ... 287 A10
PONTIAC
pl. Ingleburn ... 453 J7
PONTO
pl. Kings Lngly ... 245 J8
PONYARA
rd. Beverly Hills ... 401 C13
PONYTAIL
dr. Stanhpe Gdn ... 215 B10
POOL
la. Glenbrook ... 233 H15
pl. Fairfield W ... 335 C11
st. Maroubra ... 407 H7
POOLE
rd. Kellyville ... 216 B4
rd. West Hoxton ... 392 C12
st. Kingsgrove ... 402 B8
st. Longueville ... 314 E10
st. Wrrngtn Cty ... 238 J6
POOLEY
st. Ryde ... 282 G15
POOLMAN
st. Abbotsford ... 342 H1
POPE
pl. Campbelltwn ... 512 B2
pl. Fairfield W ... 334 K11

rd. Londonderry .. 147 G8
rd. Mount Druitt... 241 A15
st. Matraville 436 J5
st. Ryde 312 A1

POPIO
wy. Woodcroft...... 243 H11

POPLAR
av. Sans Souci..... 463 B2
cr. Bradbury........ 511 C13
ct. Castle Hill....... 218 E16
la. Narraweena.... 258 C7
pl. Kirrawee......... 490 K1
pl. Lugarno 429 J14
pl. Picton 561 B3
pl. Westleigh 220 G9
st. N St Marys 240 B11
st. Surry Hills .... F G5
st. Surry Hills 4 A11

POPONDETTA
pl. Glenfield 424 H12
rd. Bidwill 211 C16
rd. Blackett 211 C16
rd. Dharruk 241 A6
rd. Emerton 240 H8
rd. Whalan 240 H8

POPPERWELL
dr. Menai 458 H11

POPPLE
cl. Casula 394 C15

POPPLEWELL
pl. S Coogee........ 407 F7

POPPY
cl. Clarmnt Ms 238 J16
pl. Greystanes 306 A12
pl. Mcquarie Fd ... 454 B6

PORLOCK
wy. Canley Vale..... 366 E5

PORPOISE
cr. Bligh Park....... 150 H7
pl. Willmot 210 C13

PORRENDE
st. Narellan.......... 478 C6

PORST
pl. Guildford 338 B3

PORT
pl. Kings Lngly 245 D5
st. Tempe............ 404 C2

PORTADOWN
rd. Wentwthvle 277 D11

PORTAL
rd. Glenbrook, off Great Western Hwy................ 234 E15

PORTEOUS
st. Edensor Pk..... 363 H3

PORTER
av. Marrickville..... 373 H9
pl. Blackett 241 B3
rd. Engadine 489 A16
st. Bondi Jctn 377 F5
st. Minto 453 C14
st. Ryde 311 H5

PORT ERRINGHI
rd. Ebenezer 63 K1

PORTERS
la. St Ives............ 224 A13
rd. Kenthurst 158 A10

PORT HACKING
rd. Miranda.......... 492 C1
rd. Sylvania 462 B10
rd.s, Caringbah....... 492 H16
rd.s, Dolans Bay 522 H1
rd.s, Port Hacking .. 522 H1

PORTIA
cl. Rsemeadow ... 541 A4
rd. Toongabbie 275 K8

PORTICO
pde. Toongabbie 276 B5

PORTLAND
cl. Illawong 459 F6
cr. Maroubra 407 D14
st. Croydon Pk 371 G7
st. Dover Ht......... 348 F11
st. Enfield 371 G7
st. Waterloo 19 H12

PORT MACQUARIE
av. Hoxton Park ... 392 H9

PORTMADOC
dr. Menai............. 459 A10

PORTMAN
la. Zetland, off Merton St........ 375 H10
st. Zetland 375 H10

PORTSEA
pl. Castle Hill 217 J7

PORTSMOUTH
st. Cronulla.......... 493 J16

PORTVIEW
pl. Burraneer 523 E3
rd. Greenwich 315 B7

POST OFFICE
la. Kogarah.......... 433 B5
la. Merrylands 307 H13
la. Pymble 253 C2
la. Croydon, off Paisley Rd 372 D1
la. Mosman, off Upper Almora St........ 317 B7
la. Chatswood, off Victor St........... 284 J10
rd. Castlereagh...... 176 A4
rd. Ebenezer........... 63 C8
rd. Glenorie.......... 128 B8
st. Carlingford 279 H3
st. Pymble 253 C2

POTOROO
av. St Helens Pk ... 511 H16

POTTER
av. Earlwood 372 F16
cl. Wetherill Pk 303 H16
st. Old Tngabbie .. 276 J9
st. Quakers Hill 214 F12
st. Russell Lea 343 D7

POTTERY
cct. Woodcroft 243 E9
la. Richmond....... 119 A5

POTTINGER
st. Dawes Point 1 F8

POTTS
st. Beverly Hills... 401 E9
st. Homebush...... 340 K7
st. Kingsgrove 401 E9
st. Richmond...... 118 D9
st. Ryde.............. 312 E5

POULET
st. Matraville........ 406 J16

POULTER
av. Engadine 488 G13

POULTON
av. Beverley Pk.... 432 K10
pde. Frenchs Frst.... 257 A2

POULTRY
la. Richmond....... 118 H13

POUND
av. Frenchs Frst.... 255 F2
cl. Hamondvle 396 G16
la. Ashfield, off Frederick St 372 G1
rd. Hornsby 221 G2

POWDER WORKS
rd. Elanora Ht....... 198 D12
rd. Ingleside......... 197 J7
rd. N Narrabeen ... 198 H14

POWDRILL
rd. Prestons 394 B9

POWELL
cl. Edensor Pk..... 333 H15
cl. Liberty Gr 311 B11
la. Coogee, off Melody St........ 377 E16
pl. Cherrybrook 219 F13
rd. Rose Bay 347 G11
rt. Westleigh 220 G7
st. Blaxland 233 G12
st. Coogee........... 377 E16
st. Glenbrook....... 233 G12
st. Homebush...... 341 C8
st. Killara 253 K11
st. Neutral Bay 6 H6
st. Richmond....... 118 E6
st. Waterloo.......... 19 G16
st. Yagoona 369 E9

POWELLS
la. Brookvale 258 B11
la. Lowlands........... 88 F9
rd. Brookvale 258 B12

POWER
av. Alexandria 19 A15
cl. Eagle Vale....... 481 A10
pl. Kings Lngly 245 G6
pl. Menai 458 F12
st. Doonside 243 A9
st. Glendenning ... 242 G9
st. Plumpton 242 C8
st. Prairiewood 334 H7
st. St Marys 239 G10

POWERS
pl. Bass Hill 368 C13
rd. Seven Hills...... 276 E2

POWHATAN
st. Greenfld Pk..... 334 A13

POWIE
cl. Clarmnt Ms..... 268 J3

POWYS
av. Bardwell Pk..... 402 K6
cct. Castle Hill 217 C9
cl. S Penrith 267 C7

POZIERES
av. Matraville........ 407 A16
av. Milperra.......... 397 D11
pde. Allambie Ht 257 J14
st. Woolooware ... 493 J7

PRAHRAN
av. Davidson 255 D2
av. Frenchs Frst.... 255 G4
rd. Engadine 518 G8

PRAIRIE
gln. Clarmnt Ms..... 268 G1

PRAIRIE VALE
rd. Bankstown...... 369 H15
rd. Bossley Park 333 E12
rd. Mt Lewis......... 369 H15
rd. Prairiewood 334 B11

PRAIRIEVALE
rd. S Hurstville 432 B12

PRATIA
pl. Glenmore Pk... 265 G12

PRATO
ct. Glenwood 245 K5

PRATTEN
av. Ryde.............. 282 C16
la. Punchbowl 399 J5
st. Kemps Ck....... 360 H6

PREDDYS
rd. Bexley............ 402 E13
rd. Bexley North ... 402 E13

PRELI
pl. Quakers Hill 214 C11

PRELL
pl. Airds 512 B10

PREMIER
la. Darlinghurst........ 4 F8
la. Rooty Hill........ 272 C1
st. Canley Vale 366 D3
st. Gymea............ 491 E7
st. Gymea............ 491 F3
st. Kogarah.......... 433 C4
st. Marrickville 373 H16
st. Neutral Bay 6 D4
st. Toongabbie..... 276 C5

PRENTICE
la. Strathfield 371 A3
la. Willoughby 285 F15
st. Bnkstn Aprt..... 398 A1

PRENTIS
la. Ebenezer........... 63 F2

PRESCOT
pde. Milperra.......... 397 D12

PRESCOTT
av. Cromer........... 258 E3
av. Dee Why......... 258 E3
av. Narraweena 258 E3
cct. Quakers Hill 214 D13

PRESIDENT
av. Caringbah 492 D7
av. Gymea............ 491 B5
av. Kirrawee 491 B5
av. Kogarah.......... 433 D4
av. Miranda.......... 491 H6
av. Monterey 433 D4
av. Rockdale......... 433 D4
av. Sutherland 490 F4
rd. Kellyville 216 G6
st. Croydon Pk..... 371 K7

PRESLAND
av. Revesby.......... 398 F13

PRESTIGE
av. Bella Vista....... 246 E6
av. Roselands....... 401 C4

PRESTON
av. Bellevue Hill...... 14 G7
av. Double Bay 14 G7
av. Engadine 518 H3
av. Five Dock........ 342 J7
pl. Roseville......... 284 G1
rd. Old Tngabbie .. 276 J10
st. Jamisontown .. 236 D14
wy. Claymore 481 F10

PRESTWICK
tce. Glenmore Pk... 266 G8

PRETORIA
av. Mosman 317 F9
pde. Hornsby.......... 221 A1
rd. Seven Hills...... 275 H5
st. Lilyfield 10 D9

PRIAM
st. Chester Hill 338 C16

PRICE
av. Belmore 401 G5
la. Agnes Banks ... 117 B12
la. Bankstown...... 369 F12
la. Riverwood 400 B15
st. Merrylands...... 307 C13
st. Ryde.............. 282 A15
st. S Penrith......... 266 F5
st. Wetherill Pk 334 G6

PRICES
cct. Woronora 459 K16

PRIDDIS
av. Carlingford...... 279 D1

PRIDDLE
st. Warwck Frm ... 365 J16
st. Westmead....... 307 G1
wy. Bonnyrigg 364 B4

PRIEST
pl. Barden Rdg..... 458 K16

PRIESTLEY
cl. St Ives 224 B14

PRIMA
pl. Arndell Park 273 E7

PRIME
dr. Seven Hills...... 276 D1

PRIMROSE
av. Frenchs Frst.... 256 G6
av. Rosebery 375 H16
av. Rydalmere 309 K5
av. Ryde.............. 311 J2
av. Sandringham .. 463 E3
cct. Clarmnt Ms..... 268 G1
pl. Loftus 490 B7
pl. Windsor.......... 121 A8

PRIMULA
st. Lindfield.......... 283 J2

PRINCE
la. Mosman, off Macpherson St.. 316 G7
la. Randwick, off Prince St........ 376 K10
la. Mosman, off Union St 317 B11
rd. Killara 253 J15
st. Blacktown 244 H15
st. Canley Ht 365 G1
st. Canley Vale 365 G1
st. Cronulla 494 B10
st. Glenbrook 233 G15
st. Granville 308 F9
st. Mosman 316 H6
st. Mosman 316 H7
st. Newtown 374 G9
st. N Parramatta ... 278 D11
st. Oatlands 279 A12
st. Picnic Point..... 428 G7
st. Picton 563 F8
st. Randwick......... 376 K12
st. Rozelle............. 11 A1
st. Springwood 202 A1
st. Wrrngtn Cty 238 H9

PRINCE ALBERT
rd. Sydney............... D G6
rd. Sydney................ 4 A4
st. Mosman 317 B12

PRINCE ALFRED
pde. Newport.......... 169 C7

PRINCE CHARLES
pde. Kurnell 465 E7
rd. Belrose 226 C16
rd. Frenchs Frst.... 256 B4

PRINCE EDWARD
av. Earlwood 372 J16
av. Earlwood 373 A16
cir. Daceyville........ 406 F6
cir. Pagewood....... 406 F6
pde. Hunters Hill..... 314 C13
rd. Seaforth.......... 287 A5
st. Carlton........... 432 J8
st. Gladesville 313 A12
st. Malabar 437 D3

PRINCE EDWARD PARK
rd. Woronora 460 A16

PRINCE GEORGE
pde. Hunters Hill..... 314 C13

PRINCE HENRY
av. Little Bay......... 437 G14

PRINCE OF WALES
dr. Matraville 436 B13
dr. Phillip Bay 436 B13
dr. Port Botany 436 B13
dr. West Pymble.. 253 A11

PRINCES
av. Vaucluse 348 G2
hwy. Arncliffe 403 K5
hwy. Banksia 403 D14
hwy. Beverley Pk 433 A8
hwy. Blakehurst....... 432 E15
hwy. Carlton 432 H11
hwy. Carss Park...... 432 E15
hwy. Engadine........ 489 C16
hwy. Engadine........ 518 D15
hwy. Gymea 491 B3
hwy. Heathcote....... 518 D15
hwy. Kirrawee......... 490 J3
hwy. Kirrawee......... 491 B3
hwy. Kogarah 433 C6
hwy. Kogarah Bay ... 432 H11
hwy. Rockdale........ 403 D16
hwy. Rockdale........ 403 D14
hwy. St Peters 374 E16
hwy. Sutherland 490 C9
hwy. Sydenham....... 374 E16
hwy. Sylvania 461 F16
hwy. Tempe............ 374 E16
hwy. Waterfall 519 D11
hwy. Yarrawarrah ... 489 C16
la. Kogarah 433 B6
la. Newport......... 169 E11
pl. McMahons Pt...... 5 D13
prm. Seaforth 286 K11
rd. Schofields 183 B14
rd.e, Auburn........... 339 A14
rd.e, Regents Pk..... 339 A14
rd.w, Auburn........... 338 G14
st. Bexley 402 K10
st. Burwood 342 C12
st. Guildford W ... 336 J3
st. Hunters Hill 313 B5
st. McMahons Pt..... 5 D13
st. Marrickville 373 E15
st. Mortdale 431 D9
st. Newport......... 169 E11
st. Penshurst 431 F8
st. Putney 311 J6
st. Riverstone....... 153 A14
st. Ryde 312 A4
st. Turramurra 223 D11

PRINCESS
av. N Strathfield ... 341 F8
av. Rodd Point...... 343 E8
av. Rosebery 375 G13
la. N Strathfield, off Queens La........ 341 F8
st. Ashbury 372 G10
st. Btn-le-Sds 433 K2
st. Canterbury 372 G10
st. Hurlstone Pk .. 372 G10
st. Lidcombe 340 B6
st. Rose Bay........ 348 E10
st. Werrington 238 J10

PRINCESS MARY
st. Beacon Hill 257 K5
st. St Marys 269 F1

PRINCETON
av. Oatlands......... 279 B8

PRINCE WILLIAM
dr. Seven Hills 276 F3

PRINDLE
st. Oatlands......... 279 A10

PRING
st. Woolmloo 4 H4

PRINGLE
av. Bankstown 399 A4
av. Belrose........... 225 K13
av. Frenchs Frst ... 256 A2
la. Woollahra, off Kendall St 377 G2
pl. Woollahra, off Old South Head Rd.................. 377 G2
rd. Hebersham 241 G10
rd. Plumpton 241 G10

PRION
pl. Hinchinbrk 393 C2

PRIOR
av. Cremorne 6 K7
cl. Illawong 459 F4
rd. Prestons 394 A8
st. Winston Hills.. 246 G16

PRIORY
cl. Cherrybrook... 219 F14

cl. St Ives Ch 224 B2
ct. Baulkham Hl ... 247 A12
pde. Cmbrdg Gdn ... 237 J2
rd. Waverton 5 C5
PRISCILLA
pl. Baulkham Hl ... 247 D3
pl. Quakers Hill 213 J7
PRITCHARD
av. Hamondvle 396 E15
la. Annandale 10 K8
pl. Glenmore Pk ... 265 K9
pl. Peakhurst 430 F4
rd. Mcquarie Fd 453 K3
st. Annandale 10 K8
st. Auburn 339 B3
st. Marrickville 16 H16
st. Mt Pritchard ... 364 G8
st. Thornleigh 220 H13
st.e, Wentwthvle 277 A16
st.w, Wentwthvle 276 K16
PRIVATE
rd. Northwood 314 H8
rd. Sydney .... B K10
PRIVET
wy. Blacktown 274 E12
PRIYA COOPER
av. Newington .... L J16
av. Newington, off
Michael Jordan
Av 310 B15
PROBATE
st. Naremburn 315 G2
PROBERT
la. Camperdwn 17 C8
st. Camperdwn 17 D8
st. Newtown 17 D8
PROCTER
cl. Abbotsbury 333 A14
PROCTOR
av. Kingsgrove 402 A5
pde. Chester Hill 368 B3
pde. Sefton 368 E3
pl. Berowra 163 D2
wy. Claymore 481 D11
PROCYON
pl. Cranebrook 207 G5
PRODUCTION
av. Kogarah 433 D11
av. St Marys 239 D8
av. Warragamba ... 353 F10
la. Kogarah 433 E11
pl. Jamisontown .. 266 D1
rd. Taren Point 462 K14
PROGRESS
av. Eastwood 281 A8
la. Cranebrook, off
Pendock La 207 F14
rd. Eveleigh 18 E12
st. Tahmoor 566 A12
wy. Cranebrook 207 F14
PROSPECT
av. Cremorne 316 G6
cr. Canley Vale 366 D2
hwy. Prospect 275 A13
hwy. Seven Hills 275 G2
la. Carlton 432 K5
pl. Como 460 F4
rd. Canley Vale 366 D3
rd. Peakhurst 430 G2
rd. Summer Hill 373 A4
st. Blacktown 274 C4
st. Carlton 432 K5
st. Erskineville 17 K16
st. Greenwich 314 K14
st. Leichhardt 16 B1
st. Newtown 17 H9
st. Paddington 4 J15
st. Rosehill 308 G7
st. Surry Hills 20 D2
st. Waverley 377 G8
PROSPER
la. Rozelle 7 A15
st. Condell Park ... 398 F6
st. Rozelle 7 A15
PROSPERITY
pde. Warriewood 198 H6
PROSPERO
cl. Rsemeadow 540 K5
PROSS
ct. Ambarvale 540 G1
PROSSER
av. Padstow 429 F2
PROTEA
pl. Cherrybrook ... 219 E7

PROTEUS
pl. Kellyville 216 G3
PROTHERO
pl. Pagewood 406 D8
PROUT
pl. Quakers Hill 214 E11
st. Cabramatta 366 B9
wy. Claymore 481 A11
PROVIDENCE
dr. Bella Vista 246 F6
la. Darlinghurst .... F K7
pl. Darlinghurst .... F K7
rd. Ryde 312 D3
PROVINCE
st. Abbotsbury 333 A14
PROVINCIAL
rd. Lindfield 254 A16
st. Auburn 339 B5
PROVINS
la. Cranebrook, off
Milligan Rd 207 C14
wy. Cranebrook 207 C13
PROVOST
mw. Holsworthy 426 F3
PROYART
av. Milperra 397 G12
PRUNE
st. Wentwthvle 277 B8
PRUNELLA
pl. Faulconbdg 171 E15
PRUNUS
cl. Glenmore Pk ... 265 G11
PRYCE
ct. Kellyville 186 K16
pl. Rooty Hill 272 C6
PRYOR
st. Rydalmere 279 D15
st. Springwood 202 D3
PUEBLO
st. Greenfld Pk 333 K13
PUKARA
pl. Cromer 258 C1
PULBROOK
pde. Hornsby 192 A15
PULHAM
pl. Chipping Ntn ... 366 F14
PULLMAN
pl. Emu Plains 235 C7
PULPIT
la. Mosman 286 J16
PUNCH
la. Mosman 317 B5
pl. Glenbrook 264 E1
st. Artarmon 315 B1
st. Balmain 7 C5
st. Mosman 317 B5
PUNCHBOWL
rd. Belfield 371 B10
rd. Belmore 371 B11
rd. Lakemba 370 H15
rd. Minto 482 C4
rd. Punchbowl 400 C3
rd. Wiley Park 400 C3
PUNCTATA
ct. Voyager Pt 427 B5
PUNICEA
wy. Mcquarie Fd 454 H4
PUNKA
pl. Glenmore Pk ... 266 D7
PUNT
rd. Emu Plains 236 B7
rd. Gladesville 312 J13
rd. Pitt Town 92 G8
PURCELL
cr. Lalor Park 245 E13
rd. Londonderry 148 H12
st. Elderslie 477 F16
PURCHASE
rd. Cherrybrook 219 D9
st. Parramatta 308 G4
PURDIE
la. Pendle Hill 276 E14
PURDY
st. Minchinbury ... 271 C5
PURKIS
st. Camperdwn 17 E2
PURLEY
pl. Cronulla 493 K12
PURRI
av. Baulkham Hl ... 246 E10
PURSELL
av. Mosman 287 B16
PURSER
av. Castle Hill 217 K15

PURVES
st. Glebe 12 A14
PURVINES
rd. Yellow Rock 204 A3
PUSAN
pl. Belrose 226 A15
PUTARRI
av. St Ives 223 J14
PUTLAND
cl. Kirrawee 490 K8
pl. Vineyard 153 A8
st. Clarmnt Ms 269 A1
st. St Marys 269 E1
PUTNEY
pde. Putney 312 C10
PUTTY
rd. Wilberforce 91 J2
PYALLA
st. Northbridge 285 H16
PYE
av. Northmead 278 C6
rd. Acacia Gdn 214 F15
rd. Bringelly 386 K10
rd. Quakers Hill 214 A15
st. Westmead 307 G2
PYES
rd. Dural 219 F2
PYKETT
pl. Dural 219 A5
PYLARA
pl. Busby 363 H15
PYMBLE
av. Pymble 253 A5
av. Winmalee 173 F5
st. Dharruk 241 C7
PYRAMID
av. Padstow 399 C14
st. Emu Plains 235 B9
PYRAMUS
cct. Rsemeadow 540 H9
pl. St Clair 270 D16
PYREE
st. Bangor 459 D14
PYRENEES
wy. Kellyville 185 J13
PYRITE
pl. Eagle Vale 481 H5
PYRL
rd. Artarmon 285 B15
PYRMONT
st. Ashfield 372 J5
st. Pyrmont 12 G2
st. Sydney 3 A8
st. Ultimo 3 A8
PYRMONT BRIDGE
rd. Annandale 17 C3
rd. Camperdwn 17 C3
rd. Pyrmont 12 F7

Q

QANTAS
dr. Mascot 405 A4
QUAAMA
cl. Prestons 393 B16
QUADRANT
cl. Pymble 252 J4
la. Sadleir 364 B16
QUAIL
pl. Grays Point 491 F16
pl. Hinchinbrk 393 C2
pl. Ingleburn 453 D8
pl. Woronora Ht ... 489 C6
rd. Blacktown 274 B9
st. Coogee 377 H13
st. Cranebrook 207 C16
QUAKERS
rd. Marayong 243 G1
rd. Mosman 316 K1
rd. Mosman 317 A1
rd. Quakers Hill 243 G1
QUAKERS HILL
pky. Acacia Gdn 214 F14
pky. Quakers Hill 213 H12
pky. Quakers Hill 243 C3
QUALLEE
pl. Engadine 488 G16
QUAMBI
pl. Edgecliff 14 B13
QUAMBY
ct. Wattle Grove ... 425 J6
QUANDONG
av. Burwood 371 J2
pl. Concord W 341 G1

st. Concord W 341 F1
QUARRION
pl. Woronora Ht .. 489 D4
QUARRY
cl. Yagoona 369 B8
la. Dural 189 F14
la. Ultimo 12 J10
la. Glebe, off
Quarry St 12 B9
pl. Pymble 253 C5
rd. Bossley Park .. 333 F6
rd. Dundas Vy 280 A10
rd. Dural 189 C14
rd. Greystanes 275 F16
rd. Hornsby 191 E16
rd. Prospect 275 F16
rd. Ryde 281 K10
rd. The Oaks 501 K11
st. Glebe 12 B9
st. Naremburn 315 J3
st. Paddington 13 K16
st. Tempe 404 A3
st. Ultimo 12 H10
st. Woollahra 13 J16
QUARRY MASTER
dr. Pyrmont 12 D3
QUARTERS
pl. Currans Hill 480 A11
QUARTER SESSIONS
rd. Church Point .. 168 E7
rd. Glenfield 423 G9
rd. Westleigh 220 G10
QUARTZ
pl. Eagle Vale 481 G8
QUAY
st. Haymarket .... E B8
st. Haymarket 3 D13
QUEANBEYAN
av. Miranda 462 A15
QUEBEC
av. Killara 283 E1
rd. Chatswd W 283 J9
st. Toongabbie 275 F12
QUEEN
la. St Marys, off
Queen St 239 H15
rd. Paddington 21 E1
st. Arncliffe 403 G8
st. Ashfield 372 J10
st. Auburn 339 C2
st. Auburn 339 E4
st. Beaconsfield ... 375 F13
st. Botany 405 J12
st. Burwood 342 D13
st. Campbelltwn .. 511 E4
st. Canley Ht 365 G1
st. Canley Vale 365 G1
st. Chippendale 19 B3
st. Concord W 341 D1
st. Croydon 342 D13
st. Croydon Pk 371 F6
st. Glebe 12 G14
st. Granville 308 E12
st. Guildford W 336 H3
st. Hurlstone Pk .. 372 J10
st. Kurrajong Ht 54 B9
st. Marrickville 374 A14
st. Mosman 317 B10
st. Narellan 478 F10
st. Newtown 18 C8
st. N Strathfield ... 341 E6
st. Petersham 15 J5
st. Randwick 377 D15
st. Revesby 398 F14
st. Riverstone 182 D13
st. Rosebery 375 G14
st. St Marys 239 G16
st. Woollahra 21 G4
QUEEN ELIZABETH
dr. Bondi Beach ... 378 D3
QUEENS
av. Avalon 140 A13
av. Kogarah 433 B6
av. McMahons Pt 5 C13
av. Parramatta 308 E2
av. Rcuttrs Bay 13 C8
av. Vaucluse 348 B5
la. Mortdale 431 D7
la. N Strathfield, off
Princess Av 341 F8
la. Beaconsfield, off
William St 375 F13
pde. Newport 169 E12
pde.e, Newport 169 H12
pl. Balmain 7 K9

rd. Asquith 192 B8
rd. Btn-le-Sds 433 J3
rd. Canada Bay 342 E10
rd. Connells Pt 431 F16
rd. Five Dock 342 E10
rd. Hurstville 432 A4
rd. Westmead 277 H15
st. Sydney .... A K10
sq. Sydney 3 K3
QUEENSBOROUGH
rd. Croydon Pk 372 C7
QUEENSBURY
rd. Padstow Ht 429 H7
rd. Penshurst 431 A2
QUEENSCLIFF
dr. Woodbine 481 H10
rd. Queenscliff 288 E3
QUEENSHILL
dr. Luddenham 326 C7
QUEENS PARK
rd. Queens Park 22 E13
QUEENSWAY
Blacktown 274 H4
QUEEN VICTORIA
st. Bexley 402 J16
st. Drummoyne ... 344 A2
st. Kogarah 433 A2
QUENDA
pl. St Helens Pk ... 541 G1
QUENTIN
pl. Oatlands 279 B9
st. Bass Hill 368 B11
QUEST
av. Carramar 366 J4
av. Miranda 491 K8
QUIAMONG
st. Naremburn 315 F2
QUIBEREE
st. Miranda 462 B16
QUIG
pl. Narellan Vale .. 508 G1
QUIGG
la. Lakemba 401 C4
st. Lakemba 371 A16
st. Lakemba 401 B1
QUILP
pl. Ambarvale 510 K11
QUILPIE
st. North Manly ... 258 C13
QUINDALUP
pl. Bella Vista 246 H2
QUINE
la. Punchbowl 400 C3
QUINION
pl. Ambarvale 510 J16
QUINLAN
pde. Manly Vale 287 H2
QUINN
av. Seven Hills 245 H15
pl. Prairiewood 334 E11
st. Castlereagh 176 G9
st. S Wntwthvle ... 306 K4
QUINTANA
av. Baulkham Hl ... 246 J13
QUINTON
la. Manly, off
Birkley Rd 288 E7
rd. Manly 288 F8
QUIRK
rd. Balgowlah 288 A6
rd. Manly Vale 288 B4
st. Dee Why 258 G8
st. Rozelle 11 A1
QUIROS
av. Fairfield W 335 D9
QUIST
av. Lurnea 394 C9
pl. Greystanes 306 B10
pl. Menai 458 J6
pl. Shalvey 211 B14
QUOKKA
pl. St Helens Pk ... 541 D2
QUOTA
av. Chipping Ntn .. 396 A5
pl. Edensor Pk 333 J15

R

RABAT
cl. Cranebrook 207 G6
RABAUL
av. Whalan 240 J10
cl. Bossley Park ... 333 J6
rd. Bnkstn Aprt 367 D16

rd. Georges Hall 367 D16
rd. N Curl Curl 258 G10
wy. Matraville 407 B16

RABBETT
st. Frenchs Frst 256 E5

RABETT
cr. Horngsea Pk 392 F13

RABY
la. Randwick 377 F10
rd. Catherine Fd 450 E5
rd. Leppington 450 E5
rd. Raby 481 E1
rd. St Andrews 481 E1
rd. Varroville 450 G10

RACECOURSE
av. Menangle Pk 538 K7
av. Menangle Pk 539 A7
pl. Eastlakes 406 A2
pl. S Penrith 236 J14
rd. Clarendon 119 J14
rd. S Penrith 236 H16

RACEMOSA
cl. Kemps Ck 360 B9

RACHAEL
cl. Silverwater 310 A11

RACHEL
av. W Pnnant Hl 249 E8
cr. Mt Pritchard 364 G11
ct. Minto 482 K6
la. Belmore, off Dean Av 371 E15
st. Greystanes 305 J6

RACO
cl. Edensor Pk 333 J14

RADALJ
cl. Rooty Hill 271 K2

RADBURN
rd. Hebersham 241 E4

RADCLIFFE
st. Ingleburn 453 A11

RADFORD
av. Bondi Jctn 377 F5
pl. Castle Hill 218 C10
pl. Gordon 253 G7
pl. Oakhurst 242 B2

RADIATA
av. Baulkham Hl 247 F14

RADIO
av. Balgowlah Ht 287 H13

RADISSON
pl. Kellyville 185 E8

RADLEY
pl. Cherrybrook 219 E16
rd. Seven Hills 245 B16

RADNOR
pl. Campbelltwn 511 H9
pl. Smithfield 335 D1
pl. S Turramrra 252 C8
rd. Bargo 567 D4
rd. Galston 160 E5

RAE
av. Moorebank 396 D12
la. Randwick 377 C12
pl. Currans Hill 479 J11
pl. Woolmloo 4 H6
st. Randwick 377 C13
st. Seven Hills 245 D15

RAEBURN
av. Castlecrag 285 K11

RAEMOT
la. Baulkham Hl 247 J11

RAFFO
la. Harbord 258 E15

RAFTREE
st. Padstow Ht 429 J7

RAGLAN
av. Ingleburn 453 A9
la. Waterloo 19 F12
rd. Auburn 339 A13
rd. Miranda 491 H7
st. Darlington 18 F6
st. Drummoyne 313 J16
st. Malabar 437 E5
st. Manly 288 E8
st. Mosman 316 J13
st. Mosman 317 C8
st. Turramurra 223 D12
st. Waterloo 19 C11

RAHT
pl. Doonside 273 H3

RAIDELL
pl. N Epping 251 F10

RAIL
pl. Chipping Ntn 396 C6

RAILSIDE
av. Bargo 567 E4

RAILWAY
av. Eastwood 281 B6
av. Lavender Bay K E16
av. Seven Hills 276 A3
av. Stanmore 16 G9
av. Strathfield 341 H12
av. Wahroonga 222 D7
cr. Burwood 341 J13
cr. Jannali 460 G11
la. Newtown 17 G13
la. N Strathfield 341 E8
la. Sydenham 374 E15
la. Kogarah, off Railway Pde 433 B2
pde. Allawah 432 F7
pde. Annandale 10 K7
pde. Belmore 371 C16
pde. Blacktown 244 B14
pde. Blaxland 233 E2
pde. Burwood 341 J13
pde. Cabramatta 365 J10
pde. Cabramatta 365 K6
pde. Canley Vale 366 B3
pde. Carlton 432 F7
pde. Condell Park 398 G4
pde. Condell Park 398 E3
pde. Eastwood 281 B7
pde. Engadine 518 H7
pde. Erskineville 18 B14
pde. Eveleigh 18 B14
pde. Fairfield 336 D16
pde. Glenfield 424 A12
pde. Granville 308 D10
pde. Hornsby 191 H14
pde. Hurstville 432 B7
pde. Kogarah 433 A6
pde. Lakemba 400 J2
pde. Lidcombe 339 G6
pde. Mcquarie Fd 423 K14
pde. Mcquarie Fd 423 H16
pde. Marrickville 374 D14
pde. Mortdale 431 D7
pde. Penshurst 431 D7
pde. Springwood 202 C4
pde. Thornleigh 220 K13
pde. Warrimoo 203 D13
pde. Waverton 5 A8
pde. Westmead 277 G16
pde. Marrickville, off Edinburgh Rd 374 G11
pde.n, Kogarah 433 B3
pwy. Warwck Frm, off Station St 365 H15
rd. Como 460 J7
rd. Marayong 244 D4
rd. Meadowbnk 311 E3
rd. Quakers Hill 213 J13
rd. Sydenham 374 D15
rd.n, Mulgrave 151 H1
rd.s, Mulgrave 151 H1
rd.s, Vineyard 151 H1
row. Emu Plains 235 K7
sq. Haymarket 3 F15
st. Banksia 403 C15
st. Baulkham Hl 247 J11
st. Campbelltwn 511 E3
st. Carlton 433 A5
st. Chatswood 284 H9
st. Croydon 372 F1
st. Emu Plains 235 J6
st. Glebe 12 C10
st. Glenbrook 233 J14
st. Granville 308 A9
st. Hurlstone Pk 373 A13
st. Kogarah 433 A5
st. Lidcombe 339 J9
st. Liverpool 395 E4
st. Mount Druitt 241 H14
st. N Strathfield 341 E8
st. Old Guildfrd 337 A10
st. Parramatta 307 H7
st. Pennant Hills 250 G1
st. Petersham 15 K8
st. Rockdale 403 C15
st. Rookwood 340 A9
st. Rooty Hill 241 H14
st. Wentwthvle 277 B15
st. Werrington 239 A12
st. Yennora 337 A10
tce. Granville 308 A11
tce. Guildford 337 F5
tce. Lewisham 15 C9
tce. Merrylands 307 J16
tce. Petersham 373 G5
tce. Riverstone 182 J9
tce. Schofields 183 A12

RAILWAY VIEW
pde. Rooty Hill 242 B15

RAIMONDE
rd. Carlingford 280 E7
rd. Eastwood 280 E7

RAINBOW
cl. Glenmore Pk 265 H9
cr. Kingsgrove 402 C6
la. Randwick 407 A2
la. St Clair, off Dobell Cct 270 C14
pde. Peakhurst 430 C12
pl. Kareela 461 E11
pl. St Clair 270 C14
st. Coogee 407 F3
st. Kingsford 406 H2
st. Randwick 406 H2
st. Randwick 407 C3
st. S Coogee 407 F3
st. S Wntwthvle 307 D6
wy. Agnes Banks 117 E16

RAINE
av. Liverpool 394 H8
av. North Rocks 248 G11
pl. Barden Rdg 458 H16
rd. Padstow 399 A15
rd. Revesby 399 A15
st. Woollahra 377 G2

RAINFORD
st. Surry Hills 20 B3

RAIN RIDGE
rd. Kurrajong Ht 53 J7

RAJ
pl. Mount Druitt 241 H13

RAJOLA
pl. North Rocks 248 F13

RALEIGH
av. Caringbah 493 A3
cl. St Clair 270 J12
cr. St Ives Ch 224 A7
pl. Bonnyrigg Ht 363 A6
rd. Milperra 397 D12
st. Artarmon 284 J13
st. Blakehurst 462 E2
st. Cammeray 315 K5
st. Coogee 377 E13
st. Dover Ht 348 F13
st. Guildford 337 C3

RALFE
st. Tahmoor 565 K14

RALPH
pl. Mount Druitt 241 F15
st. Alexandria 375 F16
st. Cabramatta 366 D7
st. Westmead 307 G3

RALSTON
av. Belrose 225 H11
rd. Palm Beach 139 J1
rd. Palm Beach 139 K3
st. Lane Cove W 284 F15

RAMATA
pl. Wetherill Pk 334 A2

RAMBLER
pl. Ingleburn 453 K9

RAMEAU
wy. Clarmnt Ms 268 G4

RAMILLIES
wy. Kellyville 185 K15

RAMLEH
st. Hunters Hill 313 D5

RAMONA
st. Quakers Hill 213 J13

RAMOSUS
wy. Bidwill 211 F13

RAMSAY
av. West Pymble 252 F7
cl. Narellan Vale 479 C10
rd. Five Dock 342 K10
rd. Kemps Ck 359 E16
rd. Panania 428 D7
rd. Pennant Hills 220 F15
rd. Picnic Point 428 D7
rd. Rossmore 389 E8
st. Canley Vale 366 G3
st. Collaroy 229 A10
st. Haberfield 343 B13
st. Picton 563 G1
wy. Claymore 481 E12

RAMSEY
st. Kings Lngly 245 H7

RAMSGATE
av. Bondi Beach 378 E1
av. North Bondi 378 G3
rd. Beverley Pk 433 A13
rd. Kogarah Bay 433 A13
rd. Ramsgate 433 D13
rd. Ramsgate Bch 433 D13
rd. Sans Souci 433 A13
st. Botany 405 G12

RAMU
cl. Sylvania Wtr 462 D15
pl. Whalan 240 J10

RANCE
rd. Werrington 239 B13

RANCH
av. Glenbrook 264 B5

RANCOM
st. Botany 405 H15

RAND
av. Pymble 253 C5

RANDAL
cr. North Rocks 248 F14

RANDALL
av. Minto 453 B16
ct. Collaroy Plat 228 H15
st. Agnes Banks 117 D12
st. Marrickville 373 G13

RANDELL
av. Lilli Pilli 522 F2

RANDLE
la. Newtown 18 B11
la. Surry Hills E K16
la. Surry Hills 19 H1
st. Granville 308 B11
st. Newtown 18 B10
st. Surry Hills 19 G1

RANDOLPH
la. Wahroonga, off Billyard Av 222 H7
st. Campbelltwn 511 K5
st. Guildford 338 D7
st. Rosebery 405 J3
st. S Granville 338 D7
st. Wahroonga 222 H7

RANDWICK
cl. Casula 394 D15
st. Randwick 377 B11

RANELAGH
cr. Chatswood 285 C10

RANFURLEY
rd. Bellevue Hill 14 J16

RANGE
pl. Engadine 488 C14
rd. W Pnnant Hl 249 B9
st. Chatswd W 284 D9

RANGER
rd. Croydon 342 G14

RANGERS
av. Mosman 316 G9
la. Cremorne 6 H2
rd. Cremorne 6 J2
rd. St Helens Pk 541 H4
rd. Yagoona 368 G8

RANGERS RETREAT
rd. Frenchs Frst 256 F8

RANGIHOU
cr. Parramatta 308 G3

RANI
pl. Kareela 461 D9

RANIERI
pl. Hoxton Park 392 K8

RANKIN
pl. Doonside 273 F1

RANMORE
rd. St Marys 269 K4

RANNOCH
pl. Thornleigh 221 C12
st. St Andrews 451 K14

RANSLEY
st. Penrith 236 E12

RAPER
st. Newtown 17 H8
st. Surry Hills 20 C4

RAPHAEL
dr. Hornsby Ht 191 F3
pl. Old Tngabbie 277 A7
st. Greenfld Pk 364 B1
st. Lidcombe 339 K9

RAPLEYS
lp. Werombi 443 H3

RASCHKE
st. Cambrdg Pk 237 G10

RASP
cl. West Hoxton 392 B13

RASPA
pl. Quakers Hill 213 K10

RATA
pl. Sutherland 460 C16

RATCLIFFE
st. Ryde 312 D2

RATHANE
rd. Royal N P 521 J7

RATHMORE
cct. Glendenning 242 J3
ct. Kellyville 216 D2

RATHOWEN
pde. Killarney Ht 256 B14

RAU
pl. Bonnyrigg Ht 363 B5

RAUPACH
st. Dean Park 212 F16

RAUSCH
st. Toongabbie 276 G6

RAVEL
st. Seven Hills 246 D12

RAVEN
gr. Bidwill 211 D13
pl. Ingleburn 453 H6
pl. S Windsor 150 D3
st. Gladesville 312 G9

RAVENGLASS
pl. Cranebrook 207 F12

RAVENHILL
rd. Turramurra 252 E6
st. Kings Lngly 245 B4

RAVENNA
st. Strathfield 371 A1

RAVENSBOURNE
cct. Dural 219 B4

RAVENSWOOD
av. Gordon 253 J9
av. Randwick 377 E11
st. Canley Vale 366 G4

RAVENSWORTH
pl. Airds 512 B10

RAVENUE
la. Stanmore 16 H9

RAVINE
av. Blaxland 233 J6
cl. Cranebrook 207 B11

RAW
av. Bankstown 369 E14
sq. Strathfield 341 F12

RAWDON
pl. Airds 512 A15

RAWHITI
st. Roseville 284 F3

RAWSON
av. Bexley 432 G3
av. Drummoyne 343 J4
av. Loftus 490 C8
av. Penrith 236 H14
av. Queens Park 22 D11
av. Sutherland 490 C8
cr. Horngsea Pk 392 F15
cr. Pymble 223 D13
la. Haymarket E F11
la. Newtown 17 D15
la. Queens Park 22 D11
la. Sans Souci 433 B16
la. Mascot, off Rawson St 405 E3
la. Mosman, off Rawson St 317 C4
pde. Caringbah 493 A13
pl. Cromer 227 J14
pl. Haymarket E F11
pl. Haymarket 3 F14
rd. Berowra 133 C14
rd. Fairfield W 335 F11
rd. Greenacre 369 K9
rd. Guildford 337 K8
rd. Rose Bay 348 C8
rd. S Wntwthvle 306 J4
st. Auburn 309 B15
st. Croydon Pk 371 H7
st. Epping 251 A15
st. Haberfield 343 D14
st. Lidcombe 340 A7
st. Mascot 405 E3
st. Mosman 317 B4
st. Neutral Bay 6 A7
st. Newtown 17 E15
st. Rockdale 403 B16
st. Sans Souci 433 B16
st. Wiley Park 400 F4

RAWTON
av. Northmead 277 H8

RAY
av. Vaucluse 348 C5

la. Erskineville.......18 A13
pl. Kings Lngly....245 C5
pl. Minto.............453 B15
pl. Penrith...........237 C3
pl. Woodpark.......306 G14
rd. Epping............251 A13
st. Blakehurst......462 B4
st. Turramurra.....222 H13
st. Vaucluse.........348 G7
RAYBEN
st. Glendenning...242 H8
RAYFORD
cl. Bossley Park...333 J8
RAYM
rd. Kenthurst........187 C7
RAYMENT
av. Kingsgrove.....401 J14
RAYMOND
av. Campbelltwn...511 K5
av. Drummoyne...313 F16
av. Matraville........436 E2
av. Northmead.....277 J9
av. Roselands......400 J10
av. Warrawee.......222 H9
la. Springwood......201 K3
pl. Engadine........518 F5
pl. Epping............251 F15
rd. Bilgola............169 E8
rd. Kurrajong.........85 J5
rd. Neutral Bay.........6 E4
rd. Neutral Bay.........6 F6
rd. Springwood......201 K6
st. Bankstown......399 F1
st. Blacktown.......245 A7
st. Eastwood........281 G3
st. Freemns Rch....90 E2
st. Glenbrook.......264 A1
st. Granville........308 D7
st. Harris Park.....308 D7
st. Oatley............430 H14
st.e, Lidcombe.......339 H10
st.w, Lidcombe.......339 G10
RAYNER
av. Narraweena....258 D2
pl. Bonnyrigg.......364 A8
rd. Whale Beach...140 E9
st. Lilyfield.............10 A7
RAYNOR
av. Abbotsford.....342 K3
pl. Baulkham Hl...247 D6
st. Mount Druitt...241 C13
REA
st. Greenacre.......370 E9
REACH
cl. Abbotsbury.....333 B15
READ
la. Bronte...........377 J7
pl. Seven Hills......276 E1
pl. W Pnnant Hl...249 F7
st. Blakehurst......462 C1
st. Bronte...........377 J7
st. Eastwood........280 H11
wy. Claymore........481 B11
READFORD
pl. Ryde..............282 B13
READING
av. East Killara......254 F7
av. Kings Lngly....246 B9
rd. Btn-le-Sds......404 A16
st. Glenbrook.......233 G15
REAGHS FARM
rd. Minto.............482 E7
REALM
st. Arncliffe..........403 D7
REARDEN
av. Kings Lngly....245 K9
REARWIN
pl. Bnkstn Aprt....397 K1
REBECCA
ct. Rouse Hill.......184 K8
pde. Winston Hills..276 J3
pl. Cherrybrook...219 H4
pl. Ingleburn........453 D10
rd. Greenacre.......370 F4
st. Colyton...........270 D8
RECHELLE HAWKES
av. Newington.........L J16
av. Newington, off Newington Dr.. 310 A15
RECREATION
av. Penrith...........236 C8
av. Roseville.........284 J4
dr. Wollstncraft....315 D11
pl. Busby............363 H12
RECTORY
av. Ashfield..........342 K15
RED
pl. Westleigh........220 J8
REDAN
la. Mosman..........317 C7
st. Mosman..........317 C7
REDBANK
pl. Northmead......277 G9
pl. Picton............563 B14
rd. Killara............253 K16
rd. Kurrajong..........86 A7
rd. Northmead......277 G9
rd. Northmead......277 H11
rd. N Richmond......86 A7
REDBUSH
cl. Rouse Hill.......185 C8
gr. Menai.............458 K15
RED CEDAR
dr. Mt Colah.........162 E14
RED-CROWNED
ct. Winmalee........173 G6
REDDALL
st. Campbelltwn...511 G5
st. Manly.............288 J11
wy. Mcquarie Lk....423 G13
REDDAN
av. Penrith...........237 C13
REDDEN
dr. Kellyville.........216 D3
REDDINGTON
av. St Clair...........270 E12
REDDISH
cl. Lane Cove W, off Whitfield Av.....283 F12
REDDITCH
cr. Hebersham......241 E7
wy. Cranebrook.....207 G13
REDDY
la. Edgecliff............13 E10
st. Edgecliff............13 F10
REDFERN
gln. St Clair............270 D10
la. Redfern..............19 G8
pde. Dee Why.........258 F5
pl. Gymea............461 H16
pl. Pitt Town..........93 A12
rd. Minto.............482 F3
st. Blaxland..........234 B7
st. Granville..........338 F1
st. Ingleburn........453 E3
st. Redfern..............19 C8
st. Wetherill Pk....335 A1
REDFIELD
rd. East Killara......254 H7
RED GABLES
rd. Box Hill...........124 C14
REDGRAVE
pl. W Pnnant Hl...248 K9
rd. Normanhurst..221 H12
REDGROVE
av. Beecroft..........250 E10
RED GUM
cr. Bowen Mtn.......83 K7
REDGUM
av. Cronulla..........523 J3
av. Killara............254 D11
av. Pennant Hills...220 D13
cct. Glendenning....242 J5
cl. Kellyville.........186 A16
dr. Lugarno..........429 K9
dr. Padstow..........429 G2
pl. Frenchs Frst....256 B2
REDHEAP
rd. Faulconbdg.....172 A5
RED HOUSE
cr. McGraths Hl....121 J13
REDIN
pl. Connells Pt.....431 H14
REDLEAF
av. Wahroonga.....222 D8
cl. Galston...........159 F9
la. Wahroonga, off Redleaf Av.......222 D8
RED LION
st. Rozelle............344 E8
REDMAN
av. Illawong..........459 J7
la. Belmore..........371 E14
pde. Belmore..........371 F15
pl. W Pnnant Hl...248 K2
rd. Dee Why.........258 E6
st. Campsie..........372 B14
st. Canterbury......372 B14
st. Seaforth..........287 B8
REDMAYNE
rd. Horsley Pk......302 G13
REDMILL
cl. Cheltenham.....250 J10
REDMOND
av. Baulkham Hl....246 K15
st. Leichhardt........16 C3
REDMYRE
rd. Strathfield.......341 C14
rd. Strathfield.......341 G12
REDNAL
st. Mona Vale.......169 D14
REDSHAW
st. Ryde..............312 E1
REDSTONE
pl. St Clair...........299 H1
REDWOOD
av. Berowra..........133 C16
cl. Castle Hill........218 D8
pl. Clarmnt Ms.....238 G16
pl. Forestville........256 B7
pl. Mcquarie Fd....424 E15
pl. Padstow Ht......429 E7
rd. Engadine.........488 G15
st. Blacktown.......244 K7
REE
pl. Bidwill.............211 C16
pl. St Clair............299 K2
REED
la. Cremorne, off Florence La......316 F10
pl. Fairfield W......335 C9
pl. Shalvey...........211 B13
st. Cremorne........316 F11
st. Croydon..........342 D16
REEDE
st. Turrella...........403 D5
REEDY
rd. Cattai..............94 G6
rd. Horsley Pk......302 F10
rd. Maraylya..........94 G6
REEF
st. Bundeena........524 A11
st. Manly Vale......287 H5
st. Quakers Hill....213 G14
REELY
st. Pymble...........223 C12
REEN
rd. Prospect.........274 A16
REES
av. Belmore..........401 H4
cl. Eagle Vale.......480 K10
st. Mays Hill.........307 G6
REEVE
cr. Doonside........243 D9
pl. Barden Rdg.....488 G7
pl. Camden S.......507 A13
st. Waterloo..........19 E13
REEVES
av. Epping............251 D16
cr. Bonnyrigg.......364 C4
REFALO
pl. Quakers Hill....213 H7
REFRACTORY
ct. Holroyd, off Brickworks Dr...308 A10
REGAL
av. Kings Lngly.....245 D6
ct. North Rocks....278 J3
st. Regents Pk......338 J15
REGAN
cl. Jamisontown..266 B4
pl. Rooty Hill........272 A4
st. Hurstville.........401 G15
st. Rsemeadow....540 J5
REGATTA
av. Caringbah.......492 H16
pl. Leonay............265 A2
rd. Canada Bay.....342 E10
rd. Five Dock........342 E11
REGATTA
la. Leonay, off Regatta Pl........264 K2
REGENCY
ct. Oatlands.........279 A8
gr. Woodcroft........243 F8
REGENT
cr. Moorebank......396 A9
la. Kogarah..........433 D3
la. Newtown..........17 E12
la. Paddington......21 C3
la. Ryde..............311 J5
pl. Castle Hill........217 C8
pl. Illawong.........459 G3
pl. Redfern............19 B7
st. Berala............339 B16
st. Bexley............432 E1
st. Chippendale.......E B16
st. Chippendale.....19 C4
st. Dee Why........258 G4
st. Kogarah.........433 B3
st. Leichhardt..........9 E15
st. Paddington.......21 C4
st. Petersham........15 J11
st. Redfern............19 B9
st. Regents Pk.....339 B16
st. Riverstone......182 K10
st. Rozelle............10 G1
st. Ryde.............311 J6
st. Summer Hill...373 C5
REGENTVILLE
rd. Glenmore Pk..265 F5
rd. Jamisontown..236 C16
rd. Mulgoa...........265 B5
REGIMENTAL
sq. Sydney...............C G2
REGINA
av. Brookvale.......258 C9
st. Guildford W....306 K16
REGINALD
av. Belmore.........401 F2
pl. Merrylnds W..307 B15
st. Bexley...........402 J12
st. Chatswd W......284 E10
st. Mosman.........316 G10
st. Wareemba......342 K5
REGREME
rd. Picton...........561 B3
rd. Picton...........563 G1
REGULUS
la. Erskine Park, off Regulus St...... 300 H2
st. Erskine Park...300 F2
REIBA
cr. Revesby.........399 A10
REIBY
dr. Baulkham Hl...247 G5
la. Newtown..........17 D14
pl. Bradbury........511 H11
pl. McGraths Hl...122 A12
pl. Sydney...............B B8
rd. Hunters Hill....313 F9
st. Newtown..........17 D14
REID
av. Campsie.........402 A3
av. Castle Hill.......247 K5
av. Greenacre.......370 D7
av. Matraville.......436 K8
av. Narraweena....258 C6
av. N Curl Curl.....258 J10
av. Wentwthvle....277 C16
av. Woolmloo...........4 G6
cir. Winmalee.......173 D10
dr. Chatswd W.....283 K9
pl. Chipping Ntn..396 C6
pl. Illawong.........459 A7
rd. Winmalee.......173 C11
st. Ermington.......310 C1
st. Lindfield.........254 C15
st. Merrylands.....308 D16
st. Seaforth.........287 C9
st. Werrington......238 K9
REILLEYS
rd. Winston Hills..277 F6
REILLY
la. Sydenham......374 E15
st. Liverpool.......395 A9
st. Lurnea...........394 C8
REIMS
st. Russell Lea.....343 E5
REIN
rd. Greystanes.....306 G8
REINA
st. North Bondi....348 D15
REINDEER
la. Werrington, off Reindeer Pl.....238 G11
pl. Werrington.....238 F11
RELIANCE
av. Yagoona.........368 E16
cr. Willmot..........210 C13
pl. Illawong.........459 G5
wy. Airds.............511 J16
REMBRANDT
dr. Baulkham Hl...247 G10
dr. Middle Cove...285 K8
st. Carlingford.....280 A1
REMEMBRANCE
av. Warwck Frm...365 H15
dr. Bargo............567 D1
dr. Bargo............567 G9
dr. Yanderra.........567 E16
dwy. Camden S.......537 A3
dwy. Cawdor..........537 A3
dwy. Menangle.......537 A3
dwy. Picton...........561 D4
dwy. Picton...........563 F16
dwy. Picton...........563 K1
dwy. Tahmoor........565 G16
REMI
st. Bankstown......369 G12
REMLY
st. Roselands......401 B5
REMUERA
st. Willoughby.....285 H13
REMUS
pl. Winston Hills..276 K1
RENA
st. S Hurstville.....432 C10
RENARD
cl. Illawong.........460 B3
RENATA
pl. Hassall Gr.......211 J15
RENAULT
pl. Ingleburn........453 J9
RENE
pl. Cecil Hills.......362 E1
pl. Doonside........243 B9
st. East Ryde.......313 C2
RENEE
cl. Glenhaven......218 C3
RENFORD
cl. Menai.............458 F15
RENFREW
st. Guildford W....337 A5
st. St Andrews.....452 C12
RENMARK
pl. Engadine........518 H8
st. Engadine........518 H7
RENN
st. Kogarah Bay...432 H12
RENNELL
av. Green Valley...362 K8
st. Kings Park......244 H2
RENNIE
rd. Woodbine.......481 K12
st. Redfern............20 C8
st. Wetherill Pk....333 K5
RENNY
la. Paddington.......21 B1
st. Paddington.......21 B2
RENOIR
st. Old Tngabbie..276 K6
RENOWN
av. Miranda..........492 E2
av. Oatley............431 D10
av. Wiley Park......400 G3
rd. Baulkham Hl...248 C12
st. Canada Bay.....342 D9
RENSHAW
av. Auburn...........339 A10
st. Warwck Frm...365 E15
RENTON
av. Moorebank.....396 C12
RENTOUL
st. Glenfield.........424 H12
RENWAY
av. Lugarno..........429 H11
RENWICK
cl. Blaxland.........234 D8
la. Alexandria........18 F14
la. Leichhardt, off Norton St..........15 K4
st. Alexandria........18 F14
st. Drummoyne...343 K2
st. Leichhardt.........15 K1
st. Marrickville.....373 H15
st. Redfern............19 C9
REPON
pl. Belfield...........371 D8
REPPAN
av. Baulkham Hl...248 B11
RESERVE
av. Blaxland.........233 K7
la. Annandale........16 H2
la. Chatswd W......284 D8
la. Mona Vale......198 J1
la. Randwick.......407 B2
rd. Artarmon.......315 A2
rd. Casula...........394 H14
rd. Clarmnt Ms.....239 A16

rd. Freemns Rch....60 H13
rd. Kurnell.......466 E8
rd. St Leonards....315 A2
rd. St Leonards....315 C5
st. Abbotsford.....312 J16
st. Alexandria......375 F12
st. Annandale........16 G1
st. Beaconsfield...375 F12
st. Denistone.....281 E13
st. Hunters Hill....313 B10
st. Neutral Bay........6 E6
st. Penrith..........236 H11
st. Rydalmere......279 C15
st. Seaforth........287 A3
st. Smithfield.......335 H8
st. West Ryde......281 E13
RESERVOIR
av. Greenacre.......369 G10
la. Ryde.............281 J13
la. Surry Hills.........F J12
rd. Bargo............567 J11
rd. Blacktown......274 D9
rd. Mt Pritchard....364 F13
rd. Prospect.........274 C15
rd. Prospect.........275 B16
rd. Pymble...........253 B1
st. Little Bay........437 A12
st. Surry Hills.........F B10
st. Surry Hills..........3 J13
RESIDENTIAL
sq. Mt Annan.......479 E15
RESOLUTE
av. Gt Mckrl Bch..109 A14
RESOLUTION
av. Willmot..........210 G13
dr. Caringbah.......493 B3
RESOURCES
rd. Richmond......118 G12
RESTHAVEN
rd. Bankstown.....369 J15
rd. S Hurstville.....432 A12
RESTIO
ct. Voyager Pt.....427 B5
RESTON
av. Hebersham.....241 F4
gra. Bella Vista......246 G1
RESTORMEL
st. Woolooware...493 G6
RESTWELL
rd. Bossley Park..333 F9
rd. Bossley Park..333 J9
rd. Prairiewood....334 C8
st. Bankstown.....399 E3
RETFORD
wy. Hornsby Ht.....161 J14
RETIMO
cl. St Ives Ch.......224 A4
RETREAT
dr. Penrith...........236 E11
st. Alexandria........19 C16
REUBEN
st. Winston Hills..276 K3
REUSS
st. Birchgrove..........7 F4
st. Glebe...............12 A14
st. Leichhardt........15 G3
REVESBY
pl. Revesby.........398 J16
REVINGSTONE
st. Prairiewood....334 J7
REX
pl. Rooty Hill.......241 K14
rd. Georges Hall...367 E14
st. West Ryde......311 B1
REXHAM
pl. Chipping Ntn..366 F15
REXROTH
pl. Huntingwd.....273 E11
REYCROFT
av. Quakers Hill....213 F7
REYES
la. Merrylands, off Merrylands Rd...307 H13
REYNALDO
pl. Rsemeadow...540 J8
REYNELL
st. Eastern Ck......272 E7
REYNELLA
cl. Edensor Pk.....363 E1
REYNOLDS
av. Bankstown.....369 D15
av. Richmond......118 F8
av. Rozelle.............7 F13
cr. Beacon Hill.....257 E4
pl. Galston..........160 H9
rd. Londonderry...148 D3
st. Balmain.............7 C12
st. Cremorne.......316 F7
st. Old Tngabbie..276 J6
st. Pymble..........223 E14
st. Toongabbie....276 J6
RHINE
cl. Kearns...........481 B2
st. St Clair..........270 B10
RHODES
av. Guildford........337 H6
av. Naremburn.....315 G3
pl. Harringtn Pk...478 E1
pl. Kellyville.........216 F6
st. Hillsdale.........406 G16
st. West Ryde......311 F1
RHONDA
av. Frenchs Frst....256 D9
av. Narwee...........400 G11
cl. Wahroonga.....222 D10
pl. Concord.........342 B6
pl. Plumpton.......241 H6
st. Pendle Hill......306 D1
st. Revesby.........399 A15
RHONDDA
st. Smithfield.......335 F1
RHYL
st. Auburn..........338 H1
RHYS
pl. Edensor Pk.....363 H1
RIALTO
av. Cremorne Pt...316 G14
la. Manly............288 H10
pl. Heathcote.......518 F7
RIBBLE
rd. Bringelly.........357 G14
RIBBON GUM
cl. Alfords Point..459 C3
pl. Picton............561 B3
RICE
pl. Oxley Park......270 E2
pl. Shalvey...........211 C13
RICH
cl. Bligh Park.......150 A6
pl. Jamisontown..266 E3
st. Marrickville.....374 C10
RICHARD
av. Campbelltwn...512 A4
av. Earlwood........402 H5
cl. North Rocks...278 D1
cr. Bardwell Pk....402 H8
cr. Cecil Hills.......362 E3
la. Bardwell Pk....402 H8
rd. Emu Plains.....235 F7
rd. St Ives...........224 B13
rd. Scotland I.......168 G3
st. Colyton...........270 D7
st. Greenwich......314 J13
st. Panania.........428 F4
st. Richmond.......118 J6
RICHARD ARTHUR
wk. Mosman, off Ballantyne St...316 K9
RICHARD JOHNSON
cr. Ryde..............311 F3
sq. Sydney..............B B16
sq. Sydney..............1 J16
RICHARD PORTER
wy. Pymble..........253 B1
RICHARDS
av. Drummoyne...343 G5
av. Eastwood.......280 J8
av. Marrickville.....403 H1
av. Peakhurst.......430 B2
av. Riverstone......182 G6
av. Surry Hills........20 C2
cl. Berowra..........133 G10
la. Surry Hills........20 C2
pl. Concord.........342 B6
rd. Riverstone......181 K6
rd. Wakeley.........334 G12
st. Blaxland.........233 J10
RICHARDSON
av. Padstow Ht.....429 C6
av. Regents Pk.....339 C16
cr. Hebersham.....241 E2
pl. Bella Vista......246 H3
pl. Glenmore Pk...265 J6
pl. North Ryde.....283 E10
rd. Narellan.........478 E10
rd. Narellan Vale..478 F16
rd. Spring Farm...508 D6
st. Fairfield.........335 K14
st. Merrylands.....307 D9
st. Thirlmere.......562 C14
st.e, Lane Cove.......314 G5
st.w, Lane Cove.......314 E5
wk. Hillsdale.........406 H15
RICHARDSONS
cr. Marrickville.....403 K1
RICHLAND
st. Kingsgrove.....401 J8
RICHLANDS
pl. Prestons.........392 K12
RICHMOND
av. Ashfield.........342 J15
av. Auburn...........338 J8
av. Cremorne.......316 G5
av. Dee Why.........258 J5
av. Padstow Ht.....429 G6
av. St Ives...........224 E4
av. Sylvania Wtr...462 C10
av. Willoughby.....285 D16
cl. St Johns Pk....364 D3
cr. Campbelltwn...511 K7
cr. Cecil Hills........362 E7
cr. Cecil Hills........362 E7
cr. Hunters Hill.....313 B11
ct. Castle Hill.......219 A11
la. Cambrdg Pk, off Richmond Rd..237 F8
rd. Berkshire Pk...180 F1
rd. Blacktown.......244 C11
rd. Cambrdg Pk....237 F8
rd. Clarendon.......120 C9
rd. Colebee..........212 C10
rd. Dean Park.......242 F1
rd. Doonside.........243 G7
rd. Glendenning...242 F1
rd. Hassall Gr.......212 C10
rd. Homebsh W....340 F9
rd. Kingswood.....237 F8
rd. Marayong.......243 G7
rd. Marsden Pk....211 J2
rd. Penrith...........237 E6
rd. Plumpton........212 C10
rd. Quakers Hill....243 A3
rd. Rose Bay........348 B10
rd. Seaforth..........286 J12
rd. Windsor..........120 C9
rd. Windsor Dn....180 F1
rd. Woodcroft......243 G7
st. Banksia...........403 G14
st. Croydon..........342 F13
st. Denistone E....281 H10
st. Earlwood.........402 G2
st. Merrylands.....307 A8
st. Rockdale.........403 G14
st. S Wntwthvle...307 A8
RICHMOUNT
st. Cronulla..........493 J15
RICHTER
cr. Davidson........255 D3
RICKABY
st. Clarendon.......119 K13
st. S Windsor......150 C1
RICKARD
av. Bondi Beach...378 A3
av. Mosman.........317 A13
rd. Bankstown......369 E15
rd. Berowra.........133 D14
rd. Bossley Park...334 B9
rd. Chipping Ntn...397 D4
rd. Leppington.....421 B1
rd. N Narrabeen...228 G1
rd. Oyster Bay......461 E5
rd. Quakers Hill....213 K16
rd. S Hurstville.....431 K11
rd. Strathfield.......371 B3
rd. Warrimoo.......203 E12
st. Auburn...........339 A6
st. Balgowlah.......287 H8
st. Carlingford......280 B3
st. Concord.........342 A1
st. Denistone E....281 J12
st. Five Dock........343 C10
st. Guildford........337 J5
st. Merrylands.....307 H9
st. Punchbowl......400 D3
st. Ryde..............281 J12
st. Turrella..........403 C6
RICKARDS
rd. Agnes Banks...146 C11
rd. Castlereagh.....146 A13
rd. Castlereagh.....146 C11
RICKETTY
st. Mascot..........404 J1
RICKMAN
st. Kings Lngly.....245 E4
RIDDELL
cl. Glenmore Pk...265 K8
cr. Blackett..........241 B4
la. Bellevue Hill, off Riddell St.........377 H1
st. Bellevue Hill...347 G16
st. West Hoxton...392 C8
RIDDLES
la. Pymble...........253 H1
RIDER
pl. Minto.............453 B14
RIDGE
la. N Sydney...........5 F2
la. Surry Hills.........20 C7
pl. Richmond.......118 H7
pl. Surry Hills.........20 C7
rd. Arcadia...........129 H9
rd. Engadine.........488 D12
sq. Leppington......420 H10
st. Chester Hill.....368 A4
st. Epping............250 D14
st. Glenwood.......215 G16
st. Gordon...........253 D8
st. Merrylands......307 A11
st. N Sydney............5 E2
st. S Penrith.........266 G1
st. Surry Hills.........20 C6
RIDGECROP
dr. Castle Hill........217 F2
RIDGEHAVEN
pl. Baulkham Hl...216 G16
pl. Baulkham Hl...246 G1
pl. Bella Vista.......246 G1
rd. Silverdale........353 J14
RIDGELAND
av. Killara.............253 F12
RIDGEMONT
cl. Cherrybrook....219 D15
cl. W Pnnant Hl....248 K10
pl. Kings Park......244 G2
RIDGES
la. Lowlands.........88 B15
la. Richmond.........88 B15
RIDGETOP
dr. Glenmore Pk...266 B13
dr. Glenmore Pk...266 F15
pl. Dural...............219 F4
RIDGE VIEW
cl. Winmalee........173 D4
pl. Narellan..........478 C9
RIDGEVIEW
cr. Erskine Park....300 E2
pl. Oakhurst.........242 D3
wy. Cherrybrook....219 E11
RIDGEWAY
cr. Quakers Hill....213 H15
cr. Valley Ht.........203 A5
RIDGEWELL
st. Roselands.......401 A6
RIDGEWOOD
pl. Dural...............219 C5
RIDLEY
pl. Blacktown.......275 A6
RIESLING
pl. Eschol Park.....481 B3
RIFLE RANGE
rd. Bligh Park.......150 H6
rd. Northmead......278 B1
rd. S Windsor.......150 D3
RIGA
av. Greenacre.......370 A8
RIGEL
pl. Glendenning...242 F5
RIGELSFORD
st. Mt Annan........479 E16
RIGG
pl. Bonnyrigg.......364 B7
RIGNEY
av. Kingsford........406 K3
la. Kingsford, off Rigney Av........407 A3
la. Cranebrook, off Rigney Pl.........207 D10
pl. Cranebrook.....207 C9
pl. Harringtn Pk...478 F6
RIGNOLD
st. Doonside........243 C9
st. Seaforth..........286 K7
RIGO
pl. Glenfield.........424 D13
RIKARA
pl. Frenchs Frst....256 A2
RILEY
av. W Pnnant Hl....249 E8
la. Burwood........342 A11
pl. Quakers Hill....213 E16
rd. Leppington.....420 D14
st. Darlinghurst........F K4
st. Darlinghurst.......4 C10
st. N Sydney...........5 C7
st. Oatley............430 H11
st. Penrith...........236 H9
st. Surry Hills..........F H10
st. Surry Hills..........F G16
st. Surry Hills........19 K5
st. Surry Hills........20 A3
st. Woolmloo..........4 C7
RIMA
pl. Hassall Gr......211 K16
RIMFIRE
cl. Bossley Park..334 A8
RIMMINGTON
st. Artarmon........284 H16
RIMU
st. Cherrybrook...219 J6
RING
st. Belmore.........371 D14
st. Sefton............368 G1
RINGAROOMA
cct. West Hoxton..392 D6
RINGBARK
av. Kellyville.........216 A1
RINGROSE
av. Greystanes.....306 F6
RINGTAIL
cr. Bossley Park..333 H7
RIO
wk. Seven Hills.....275 J4
RIPLEY
gld. Bella Vista......246 F3
pl. Hassall Gr......212 A16
RIPON
rd. Moorebank.....425 B2
wy. Rosebery.......375 K15
RIPPLE
cl. Greenfld Pk....334 C13
st. Kareela..........461 E10
RIPPON
av. Dundas..........279 C15
RISBEY
pl. Bligh Park......150 J9
RISCA
pl. Quakers Hill....214 B9
RISDONI
wy. Mcquarie Fd...424 D16
RISORTA
av. St Ives..........254 E1
RITA
av. Faulconbdg.....171 K8
pl. Oakhurst........241 J5
st. Merrylands.....307 E6
st. Narwee..........400 H15
st. Thirlmere.......565 C3
RITCHARD
av. Coogee..........377 E12
RITCHIE
la. Mosman, off Upper Almora St.........317 B6
rd. Silverdale.......354 B13
rd. Yagoona.........369 A11
st. Rosehill..........308 G8
st. Sans Souci.....433 C15
RIVAL
pl. Shalvey..........210 H12
st. Kareela..........461 C11
RIVATTS
dr. Yarramundi....145 F6
RIVENDELL
cr. Wrrngtn Dns..237 J5
wy. Glenhaven......217 K4
RIVENOAK
av. Padstow.........429 E3
RIVER
av. Carramar........366 H2
av. Chatswd W.....283 J9
av. Villawood.......367 A1
cl. Freemns Rch....89 H5
la. Drummoyne....313 G16
la. Wollstncraft....315 E7
la. Chatswd W, off River Av..........283 J8
la. Emu Plains, off River Rd..........235 H12
rd. Elderslie........507 E3
rd. Emu Plains.....235 D16
rd. Ermington......310 A5
rd. Greenwich......314 G6

rd. Lane Cove 314 G6
rd. Leonay 235 D16
rd. Northwood 314 G6
rd. Oatley 431 B12
rd. Osborne Pk 314 G6
rd. Parramatta 278 A13
rd. St Leonards 315 D7
rd. Sutherland 460 C14
rd. Tahmoor 566 D7
rd. Tahmoor 566 D9
rd. Wollstncraft 315 D7
rd. Woronora 489 H1
rd. Yarramundi 115 K16
rd.w, Camellia 308 J4
rd.w, Lane Cove 314 B3
rd.w, Longueville 314 B3
rd.w, Parramatta 308 J4
rd.w, Riverview 314 B3
st. Birchgrove 7 E4
st. Blakehurst 462 C2
st. Earlwood 402 G2
st. Silverwater L E16
st. Silverwater 309 J9
st. Strathfield S 371 A4
RIVERDALE
av. Marrickville 373 K14
RIVERFORD
cl. Menangle 538 J16
RIVERGLEN
pl. Illawong 459 K6
RIVERGUM
wy. Rouse Hill 185 A6
RIVERHAVEN
pl. Oyster Bay 461 B6
RIVER HEIGHTS
rd. Pleasure Pt 427 J8
RIVERHILL
av. Forestville 255 J10
RIVERINA
av. Homebush B M D7
RIVERPARK
dr. Liverpool 395 E7
RIVERPLAINS
la. Mt Riverview 204 H14
RIVERS
st. Bellevue Hill 347 G16
RIVERSDALE
av. Connells Pt 431 G15
pl. Glen Alpine 510 B13
pl. Mt Annan 479 J15
RIVERSIDE
av. Picnic Point 427 K7
av. Ryde 311 H5
cr. Dulwich Hill 373 D13
cr. Marrickville 373 D14
dr. Airds 512 A11
dr. Lugarno 429 H14
dr. Mcquarie Pk 283 B2
dr. North Ryde 283 F9
dr. Sandringham 463 B6
dr. Sans Souci 463 B6
dr. Yarramundi 145 F10
rd. Chipping Ntn 397 A1
rd. Croydon Pk 371 K9
rd. Emu Heights 205 A15
rd. Lansvale 366 K8
rd. Royal N P 520 E5
RIVERSTONE
pde. Riverstone 182 G2
pde. Vineyard 152 E12
rd. Riverstone 183 A11
RIVERTOP
cl. Normanhurst 221 F12
RIVER VIEW
rd. Pleasure Pt 427 J7
RIVERVIEW
av. Connells Pt 431 K14
av. Dangar I 76 G8
av. Kyle Bay 431 K16
av. Woolooware 493 H8
cr. Mt Riverview 204 H14
pde. Leonay 264 K1
pde. North Manly 288 C2
pl. Oatlands 278 K8
rd. Avalon 139 H13
rd. Earlwood 373 C15
rd. Fairfield 336 F16
rd. Kentlyn 513 C2
rd. Oyster Bay 460 K6
rd. Padstow Ht 429 H5
rd. Pleasure Pt 427 H7
st. Chiswick 343 C1
st. Concord 342 C2
st. N Richmond 87 E14
st. Riverview 313 J5
st. West Ryde 281 B15
RIVETT
pl. Doonside 273 H1
rd. North Ryde 283 C10
RIVIERA
av. Avalon 139 J13
av. North Rocks 249 A15
pl. Glenmore Pk 266 E9
RIX
av. Hamondvle 396 D14
pl. Camden S 507 D13
RIXON
rd. Appin 568 F8
st. Bass Hill 368 B8
ROA
pl. Blacktown 274 J9
ROACH
av. Thornleigh 220 J10
st. Arncliffe 403 E10
st. Marrickville 373 H15
ROAD J
Kurnell 466 A10
ROAD L
Kurnell 466 A10
ROAD N
Kurnell 466 B12
ROAD 4
Kurnell 466 D12
ROAD 6
Kurnell 466 C12
ROAD 9
Kurnell 466 B11
ROAD 12
Kurnell 466 A10
ROAD 13
Kurnell 466 A10
ROATH
pl. Prospect 274 G12
ROB
pl. Vineyard 152 A3
ROBARDS
pl. Stanhpe Gdn 215 G10
ROBB
av. Bexley 432 K1
st. Revesby 398 G15
ROBBIE
cr. Carlingford 249 F16
ROBBINS
rd. Box Hill 154 F16
st. Fairfield W 335 C14
ROBBS
pl. Dundas Vy 279 K7
ROBECQ
av. Cheltenham 251 A7
ROBENS
cr. Catherine Fd 419 B6
ROBERT
av. North Manly 258 A13
av. Russell Lea 343 D7
la. Arncliffe 403 K7
la. Marrickville 373 H12
la. St Peters, off Mary St 374 G14
rd. Cherrybrook 219 C15
st. Artarmon 284 J15
st. Ashfield 372 J5
st. Ashfield 372 K5
st. Belmore 401 H4
st. Canterbury 372 F13
st. Gordon 253 J8
st. Granville 307 K9
st. Greenwich 314 J12
st. Harbord 258 E14
st. Kingsgrove 401 H4
st. Marrickville 373 H12
st. Marsden Pk 182 A12
st. N Richmond 87 B15
st. N Willghby 285 G11
st. Penrith 237 A8
st. Petersham 16 B6
st. Riverstone 182 A12
st. Rozelle 7 D16
st. Ryde 311 G3
st. Sans Souci 433 C15
st. Smithfield 336 A3
st. Telopea 279 D9
st. Telopea 279 E9
st. Willoughby 285 G11
ROBERTA
st. Greystanes 305 J8
ROBERTS
av. Mortdale 430 F7
av. Mt Pritchard 364 K12
av. Randwick 377 E11
av. Wahroonga 222 B6
cl. Liberty Gr 311 B11
la. Camperdwn 17 F7
la. Hurstville 432 D5
la. Lane Cove W, off Whitfield Av 283 F12
pde. Hawksbry Ht 174 H3
pl. McGraths Hl 121 K11
rd. Casula 424 H2
rd. Greenacre 370 F16
rd. Greenacre 370 F9
rd. Strathfield S 370 F9
rd. Werombi 443 A11
st. Cabarita 342 D1
st. Camperdwn 17 F7
st. Jannali 460 H13
st. Rose Bay 348 D10
st. St Peters 374 G14
st. Strathfield 341 H11
wy. Claymore 481 E10
ROBERTSON
av. Seven Hills 245 J15
cl. Holsworthy, off Chauvel Av 396 B13
cr. Mt Lewis 370 B16
la. Kirribilli 6 B16
la. Sutherland, off Adelong St 490 D2
pl. Bella Vista 246 G3
pl. Jamisontown 266 D1
pl. Watsons Bay 318 G14
rd. Bass Hill 368 C9
rd. Centnnial Pk 21 A13
rd. Chester Hill 368 C6
rd. Moore Park 21 A13
rd. Newport 169 H9
rd. N Curl Curl 259 B10
rd. Scotland I 168 G3
st. Campsie 372 B16
st. Greenwich 314 J10
st. Guildford 338 C9
st. Guildford 338 D4
st. Guildford W 337 A2
st. Kogarah 433 A4
st. Kurrajong 85 E4
st. Merrylands 338 D4
st. Narrabeen 229 A6
st. Parramatta 308 E2
st. Sutherland 490 D2
ROBERTSWOOD
av. Blaxland 234 B5
ROBEY
st. Maroubra 407 A10
st. Mascot 405 A5
st. Matraville 407 A10
ROBILLIARD
st. Mays Hill 307 H6
ROBIN
av. S Turramrra 252 D8
cr. S Hurstville 432 A10
pl. Caringbah 492 J9
pl. Glenmore Pk 265 J13
pl. Ingleburn 453 G8
pl. Roselands 400 H9
st. Carlingford 250 A15
st. Hinchinbrk 363 D16
ROBINA
st. Blacktown 274 H3
st. St Ives Ch 223 K2
ROBINIA
pl. Alfords Point 429 C14
ROBINSON
cl. Hornsby Ht 191 G3
cl. Lurnea 394 D14
dr. Centnnial Pk 22 B10
la. Woollahra 22 F4
la. Eastlakes, off Robinson St 405 K4
pl. Baulkham Hl 247 C12
pl. S Turramrra 252 A8
rd. Bringelly 388 F15
rd. Cranebrook 207 E11
st. Belfield 371 B9
st. Campbelltwn 510 J7
st. Chatswood 285 B9
st. Croydon 342 F15
st. Eastlakes 405 J4
st. E Lindfield 254 J12
st. Greenacre 370 E3
st. Minchinbury 271 F7
st. Monterey 433 H7
st. Riverstone 182 K10
st. Ryde 312 F2
st. Wiley Park 400 E2
st. Wiley Park 400 F4
st. Woolmloo 4 D7
st. Woolooware 493 J8
ROBIN VALE
pl. Baulkham Hl 247 G11
ROBSHAW
rd. Marayong 244 C4
ROBSON
cr. St Helens Pk 541 B2
rd. Kenthurst 187 A11
ROBVIC
av. Kangaroo Pt 461 H7
ROBYN
av. Belfield 371 E11
av. Frenchs Frst 256 K3
av. S Penrith 266 J2
cr. Mt Pritchard 364 H14
la. Panania 428 B1
pl. Northmead 277 H8
pl. Tahmoor 565 F10
rd. Winmalee 173 J6
st. Blacktown 243 K12
st. Peakhurst 430 C10
st. Revesby 398 K14
st. Woodpark 306 G16
ROBYNE
pl. W Pnnant Hl 249 D10
ROCCA
st. Ryde 281 K10
ROCCO
pl. Green Valley 362 J10
ROCHE
gr. Shalvey 211 C13
la. Northbridge 316 B1
pl. Merrylnds W 306 K11
ROCHER
av. Hunters Hill 313 C11
ROCHES
av. Bayview 169 B13
ROCHESTER
gr. Castle Hill 217 B10
st. Botany 405 F13
st. Camperdwn 17 H6
st. Strathfield 341 C11
ROCHFORD
st. Erskineville 17 J16
st. Erskineville 374 K9
st. St Clair 269 H9
wy. Cherrybrook 219 B15
ROCK
la. Balgowlah 288 A6
la. Glebe 11 G12
st. Yagoona 368 G10
ROCK BATH
rd. Palm Beach 140 B3
ROCKDALE
st. Banksia 403 D13
st. Rockdale 403 D13
ROCKDALE PLAZA
dr. Rockdale 433 C1
ROCK FARM
av. Dundas 279 E11
ROCKFORD
rd. Tahmoor 565 J14
ROCKLANDS
la. Wollstncraft 5 A1
rd. Crows Nest 5 A2
rd. Wollstncraft 5 A2
ROCKLEA
cr. Sylvania 461 F12
ROCKLEIGH
st. Croydon 342 E13
wy. Epping 251 C14
ROCKLEY
av. Baulkham Hl 247 A9
st. Bondi 378 A4
st. Castlecrag 286 C13
ROCKLILY
av. Westleigh 220 G8
ROCKTON
pl. Prestons 393 C15
ROCKWALL
cr. Potts Point 4 K3
la. Potts Point 4 K3
pl. Potts Point 4 K3
pl. W Pnnant Hl 249 B6
ROCK WALLABY
wy. Blaxland 233 D12
ROCKY
cl. East Killara 254 F6
ROCKY HALL
rd. Wilberforce 61 G2
ROCKY MAIN
dr. Holsworthy 426 K7
ROCKY POINT
rd. Beverley Pk 433 C8
rd. Kogarah 433 C8
rd. Ramsgate 433 C8
rd. Sans Souci 463 A3
ROD
st. Belmore 401 H3
RODBOROUGH
av. Crows Nest 315 J7
rd. Frenchs Frst 257 B6
RODD
la. Five Dock 343 A8
rd. Five Dock 343 A8
st. Birrong 368 H5
st. Sefton 368 E4
RODENS
la. Millers Point A A1
la. Millers Point 1 C9
RODEO
dr. Green Valley 362 K9
RODERIGO
cl. Rsemeadow 540 G5
RODGERS
av. Kingsgrove 402 A12
av. Panania 428 E3
st. Kingswood 237 F12
RODLEY
av. Penrith 236 F11
la. Penrith, off Rodley Av 236 G10
RODMAN
av. Maroubra 407 E15
RODNEY
av. Beecroft 250 B3
cr. Beverly Hills 401 B16
pl. Ingleburn 453 D11
pl. W Pnnant Hl 249 B8
st. Dover Ht 348 G11
st. East Ryde 283 B15
RODWELL
pl. Kellyville 216 E4
ROE
pl. Wetherill Pk 304 E15
st. North Bondi 348 C14
ROEBOURNE
st. Yarrawarrah 489 H13
ROEBUCK
cr. Willmot 210 E12
pl. Illawong 459 A6
rd. Werrington 238 E11
st. Cabramatta 366 D8
ROENTGEN
st. Lucas Ht 487 J12
ROFE
cr. Hornsby Ht 191 F7
pl. Grasmere 505 J1
st. Leichhardt 15 J2
ROGAL
pl. Mcquarie Pk 282 K1
ROGAN
cr. Wakeley 334 F13
ROGER
av. Castle Hill 248 C1
cr. Mt Riverview 234 D3
pl. Blacktown 275 C6
st. Brookvale 258 A11
ROGER BOWMAN
la. Chester Hill 337 G12
ROGERS
av. Haberfield 343 B16
av. Liverpool 365 A14
pl. Campbelltwn 511 J8
st. Kingsgrove 401 C8
st. Merrylands 307 J16
st. Roselands 401 C8
st. Wentwthvle 276 H16
wy. Mt Annan 479 D15
ROHAN
pl. N Richmond 87 A13
st. Naremburn 315 F3
ROHINI
st. Turramurra 222 H13
ROKEBY
rd. Abbotsford 342 K1
ROKER
st. Cronulla 494 A14
ROKEVA
st. Eastwood 281 F6
ROLAND
av. Liverpool 394 G5
av. Northmead 248 B15
av. Wahroonga 222 C15
la. Warrawee 222 C15
la. Wilberforce 61 D10

st. Bossley Park ... 334 B5
st. Greystanes ... 306 D11
st. Mulgoa ... 265 C3
ROLESTONE
av. Kingsgrove ... 401 H7
ROLF
la. St Peters ... 374 F14
ROLFE
st. Manly ... 288 F5
st. Rosebery ... 405 E2
ROLLA
wy. Kellyville ... 185 K14
ROMA
av. Blacktown ... 244 F14
av. Kensington ... 376 D13
av. Mt Pritchard ... 364 F11
av. Padstow Ht ... 429 E7
av. Wallacia ... 324 K14
ct. W Pnnant Hl ... 248 J8
la. Blacktown ... 244 F12
pl. Ingleburn ... 453 C10
pl. Sylvania ... 462 A12
rd. St Ives ... 224 F7
st. N Epping ... 251 E10
ROMAINE
av. Wrrngtn Cty ... 238 D8
ROMANA
sq. Prestons ... 393 F15
ROMANI
av. Hurstville ... 432 C2
av. Riverview ... 314 B7
pde. Matraville ... 437 B1
st. N Parramatta ... 278 F12
wy. Matraville ... 407 B16
ROMANO
cl. Edensor Pk ... 333 H15
ROME
pl. Shalvey ... 211 A14
st. Canterbury ... 372 F15
ROMEO
cr. Rsemeadow ... 540 H4
pl. Dural ... 219 A6
ROMFORD
rd. Epping ... 250 J12
rd. Frenchs Frst ... 256 K4
rd. Kings Park ... 244 K6
ROMILLY
pl. Ambarvale ... 540 D2
st. Riverwood ... 400 D15
ROMINA
rd. Winmalee ... 173 G10
ROMLEY
cr. Oakhurst ... 242 C1
ROMNEY
cr. Miller ... 393 H3
pl. Wakeley ... 334 K16
rd. St Ives Ch ... 224 A6
wy. Airds ... 512 A13
ROMSEY
st. Waitara ... 221 J4
ROMSLEY
rd. Jamisontown ... 266 C2
ROMULUS
st. Winston Hills ... 277 A1
RON
pl. Plumpton ... 241 H10
RONA
cl. Berowra Ht ... 132 K10
st. Peakhurst ... 430 D6
RONALD
av. Dundas ... 279 K14
av. Earlwood ... 372 H15
av. Greenwich ... 314 J4
av. Harbord ... 258 J16
av. Lane Cove ... 314 H3
av. Narraweena ... 258 A4
av. Ryde ... 281 K9
pl. Guildford ... 337 D1
st. Birchgrove ... 8 C4
st. Blacktown ... 243 K12
st. Campbelltwn ... 511 K3
st. Carramar ... 366 J2
st. Hornsby ... 221 F6
st. Padstow ... 399 B12
RON CLARKE
st. Newington ... L J16
st. Newington ... 310 B12
RONDELAY
dr. Castle Hill ... 247 H3
RON FILBEE
pl. Maroubra ... 407 H8
RON SCOTT
cct. Greenacre ... 370 F5
ROOKE
ct. Kellyville ... 186 H15
la. Hunters Hill ... 313 K11
st. Hunters Hill ... 314 A12
ROOKIN
pl. Minchinbury ... 271 J10
ROOKWOOD
rd. Bankstown ... 369 F10
rd. Potts Hill ... 369 F10
rd. Yagoona ... 369 F10
ROONY
av. Abbotsbury ... 333 A12
ROOSEVELT
av. Allambie Ht ... 257 D12
av. Riverwood ... 400 A12
av. Sefton ... 338 F15
la. Allambie Ht, off Roosevelt Av ... 257 D12
pl. Bonnet Bay ... 460 A10
ROOTS
av. Luddenham ... 356 G3
ROOTY HILL
rd.n, Oakhurst ... 242 B11
rd.n, Plumpton ... 242 B11
rd.n, Rooty Hill ... 242 B14
rd.s, Eastern Ck ... 272 F4
rd.s, Rooty Hill ... 272 D2
ROPE
st. Dundas Vy ... 280 B10
ROPER
av. S Coogee ... 407 G5
cr. Sylvania Wtr ... 462 E14
la. Hornsby ... 191 G13
pl. East Killara ... 254 H10
rd. Colyton ... 270 H5
ROPES CREEK
rd. Mount Druitt ... 271 A2
RORKE
st. Beecroft ... 250 B6
ROSA
cr. Castle Hill ... 218 D14
pl. West Hoxton ... 392 C8
st. Acacia Gdn ... 214 H14
st. Croydon ... 342 D16
st. Oatley ... 431 D12
ROSAKI
cl. Edensor Pk ... 333 E16
ROSALIE
av. Camden ... 507 A6
cr. Greenacre ... 370 C7
ROSALIND
cr. Campbelltwn ... 511 K4
rd. Marayong ... 244 B7
st. Cammeray ... 315 J6
st. Crows Nest ... 315 J6
st. Greystanes ... 305 J7
ROSAMOND
st. Hornsby ... 191 F11
ROSANNAH
wy. Cranebrook ... 207 E13
ROSCOE
st. Bondi Beach ... 378 B1
ROSCOMMON
cr. Killarney Ht ... 286 B2
rd. Arcadia ... 129 F14
ROSCREA
av. Randwick ... 377 D10
ROSE
av. Bexley ... 402 C16
av. Collaroy Plat ... 228 D9
av. Concord ... 341 K6
av. Connells Pt ... 431 F16
av. Mt Pritchard ... 364 D9
av. Neutral Bay ... 6 A2
cir. Winmalee ... 173 E9
cr. Glossodia ... 58 K9
cr. Mosman ... 316 H12
cr. N Parramatta ... 278 E10
cr. Regents Pk ... 369 A1
dr. Mt Annan ... 479 F16
la. Annandale ... 11 C10
la. Cmbrdg Gdn, off Rose Pl ... 237 G2
pl. Cmbrdg Gdn ... 237 G2
pl. Lalor Park ... 245 C12
st. Annandale ... 11 A9
st. Ashfield ... 372 H5
st. Auburn ... 309 D16
st. Baulkham Hl ... 247 G13
st. Birchgrove ... 7 G2
st. Botany ... 405 F10
st. Bronte ... 377 J9
st. Campbelltwn ... 481 G16
st. Chatswood ... 284 K7
st. Chippendale ... 18 H3
st. Cronulla ... 524 A3
st. Croydon Pk ... 371 K6
st. Darlington ... 18 E7
st. Epping ... 281 C2
st. Hurstville ... 432 B6
st. Liverpool ... 395 A8
st. Newtown ... 17 J9
st. Pendle Hill ... 306 F1
st. Petersham ... 15 K15
st. Punchbowl ... 400 A5
st. Sefton ... 368 G8
st. Smithfield ... 335 C7
st. Wilberforce ... 91 K6
st. Winmalee ... 173 D9
st. Yagoona ... 368 F10
tce. Paddington ... 4 F14
ROSEA
pl. Glenmore Pk ... 265 H12
ROSEANNE
av. Roselands ... 400 H10
ROSEBANK
av. Dural ... 188 G12
av. Epping ... 250 K14
av. Kingsgrove ... 401 E8
cr. Hurstville ... 431 J6
st. Darlinghurst ... 4 G9
st. Glebe ... 12 B12
st. Panania ... 398 D13
ROSE BAY
av. Bellevue Hill ... 347 E11
ROSEBERRY
pl. Balmain ... 7 H12
st. Balgowlah ... 287 K6
st. Balmain ... 7 C11
st. Manly Vale ... 287 K6
st. Merrylands ... 337 F1
st. Riverstone ... 153 C14
ROSEBERY
av. Rosebery ... 375 J15
la. Mosman, off Rosebery St ... 316 K4
rd. Guildford ... 337 H7
rd. Kellyville ... 217 B4
rd. Killara ... 254 D8
st. Heathcote ... 518 F12
st. Mosman ... 316 J5
st. Penshurst ... 431 B2
ROSEBRIDGE
av. Castle Cove ... 285 F3
ROSEBUD
la. Paddington ... 4 G15
ROSEBY
st. Drummoyne ... 344 B4
st. Leichhardt ... 15 H3
st. Marrickville ... 403 G1
ROSEDALE
av. Bankstown ... 369 G10
av. Fairlight ... 288 A9
av. Greenacre ... 369 G10
av. Penrith ... 237 C14
cr. Croydon Pk ... 371 K8
pl. W Pnnant Hl ... 248 K3
rd. Gordon ... 253 J6
rd. Pymble ... 223 K16
rd. St Ives ... 223 K16
st. Canley Ht ... 335 B15
st. Dulwich Hill ... 373 C7
ROSEGREEN
ct. Glendenning ... 242 H3
ROSEGUM
pl. Alfords Point ... 429 B15
pl. Silverdale ... 384 B2
st. Quakers Hill ... 213 K7
ROSEHILL
cl. Casula ... 394 D15
st. Parramatta ... 308 A7
st. Redfern ... 19 A8
ROSELAND
av. Roselands ... 400 J8
ROSELANDS
av. Frenchs Frst ... 255 H3
dr. Roselands ... 400 J8
ROSELEA
wy. Beecroft ... 249 J13
ROSELLA
cl. Blaxland ... 234 E5
gr. Bidwill ... 211 D13
la. Darlinghurst ... 4 D8
pl. Cranebrook ... 207 C15
rd. Prestons ... 423 A1
st. Dural ... 190 A7
st. Prestons ... 423 A1
wy. W Pnnant Hl ... 249 E7
ROSEMARY
cr. Glenmore Pk ... 265 G10
pl. Blacktown ... 244 K9
pl. Cherrybrook ... 219 F10
pl. Mcquarie Fd ... 454 D2
row. Menai ... 458 K14
ROSEMEAD
rd. Hornsby ... 221 B1
ROSEMEADOW
dr. Cabarita ... 342 F2
ROSEMEATH
av. Kingsgrove ... 402 A5
ROSEMONT
av. Emu Plains ... 235 H9
av. Mortdale ... 431 D7
av. Smithfield ... 335 H7
av. Woollahra ... 14 B15
pl. Gymea Bay ... 491 G13
st. Punchbowl ... 400 E3
st. Punchbowl ... 400 E4
ROSEMOUNT
av. Pennant Hills ... 220 G15
av. Summer Hill ... 373 B7
ROSEN
st. Epping ... 250 J14
ROSENEATH
pl. Baulkham Hl ... 247 G6
pl. Engadine ... 518 F6
ROSENTHAL
av. Lane Cove ... 314 D1
la. Valley Ht ... 203 B7
la. Lane Cove, off Rosenthal Av ... 314 D1
st. Doonside ... 273 E2
ROSE PAYTEN
dr. Leumeah ... 482 A11
dr. Minto ... 482 A11
ROSES RUN
Westleigh ... 220 G7
ROSETTA
av. Killara ... 254 E11
cl. Cranebrook ... 207 D11
la. Cranebrook, off Rosetta Cl ... 207 D11
la. Beverly Hills, off Rosetta St ... 401 A12
pl. N Richmond ... 87 G13
st. Beverly Hills ... 401 A12
st. Warwck Frm ... 366 D16
ROSEVALE
pl. Narellan ... 478 H12
ROSEVEAR
st. Stanmore ... 16 H8
ROSEVIEW
av. Roselands ... 400 H9
ROSEVILLE
av. Roseville ... 284 H4
la. Roseville, off Roseville Av ... 284 G4
tce. Glenmore Pk ... 266 G12
ROSEWALL
dr. Menai ... 458 G6
pl. Shalvey ... 210 J13
st. Greystanes ... 306 B10
st. N Willghby ... 285 E10
st. Willoughby ... 285 E10
ROSEWOOD
av. Carlingford ... 249 E16
dr. Greystanes ... 306 F11
dr. Mcquarie Fd ... 454 E1
dr. Prestons ... 393 J14
dr. Prestons ... 393 K14
pl. Cherrybrook ... 219 K13
row. Menai ... 458 K12
wy. Werrington ... 239 B11
ROSFORD
av. Petersham ... 15 G13
st. Smithfield ... 335 D1
ROSHERVILLE
rd. Mosman ... 317 D2
ROSIEVILLE
la. Balmain ... 7 A8
ROSINA
cr. Kings Lngly ... 245 G4
st. Fairfield ... 335 G13
st. Fairfield W ... 335 G13
ROSITANO
pl. Rooty Hill ... 271 H4
ROSLEEN
pl. Baulkham Hl ... 247 E10
ROSLYN
av. Btn-le-Sds ... 433 J5
av. Northmead ... 277 H9
av. Panania ... 428 E1
av. Roseville ... 284 F2
gdn. Elizabeth Bay ... 13 A8
gdn. Rcuttrs Bay ... 13 A8
la. Elizabeth Bay ... 13 A7
pl. Cherrybrook ... 219 C13
st. Ashbury ... 372 D8
st. Elizabeth Bay ... 13 A7
st. Lane Cove W ... 284 D15
st. Liverpool ... 394 J1
st. Potts Point ... 4 K7
st. Rcuttrs Bay ... 13 A7
ROSLYNDALE
av. Woollahra ... 14 D15
ROSS
av. Kingsgrove ... 401 G6
cr. Blaxland ... 233 D7
pl. Kellyville ... 185 F1
pl. Minto ... 452 K13
pl. N Wahrnga ... 222 K1
pl. St Marys ... 239 H14
pl. Wetherill Pk ... 303 H15
st. Bankstown ... 399 E3
st. Blacktown ... 274 J4
st. Brooklyn ... 75 H11
st. Camperdwn ... 17 C6
st. Chipping Ntn ... 396 C5
st. Dulwich Hill ... 373 A10
st. Epping ... 280 B1
st. Forest Lodge ... 11 H13
st. Gladesville ... 312 G10
st. Glenbrook ... 264 A1
st. Naremburn ... 315 E4
st. Newport ... 169 J10
st. N Curl Curl ... 258 J10
st. Parramatta ... 278 C16
st. Seaforth ... 287 C10
st. Seven Hills ... 275 K6
st. Waverton ... 315 D12
st. Windsor ... 121 D8
ROSSELL
pl. Glenfield ... 424 E13
ROSSER
la. Rozelle ... 7 E14
st. Balmain ... 7 E13
st. Rozelle ... 7 E13
wy. Ryde, off O'Regan Dr ... 312 C4
ROSSETTI
st. Wetherill Pk ... 334 H4
ROSSFORD
av. Jannali ... 460 J13
ROSSI
st. S Hurstville ... 432 B10
ROSSIAN
pl. Cherrybrook ... 219 H10
ROSSINI
dr. Hinchinbrk ... 393 A4
ROSSITER
av. Maroubra ... 407 F11
la. Maroubra, off Rossiter Av ... 407 F11
st. Granville ... 308 G15
st. Smithfield ... 335 K7
ROSSIVILLE
pl. Glen Alpine ... 510 F12
ROSSKELLY
la. Quakers Hill ... 243 B2
ROSSLYN
st. Bellevue Hill ... 347 G16
st. Berowra ... 133 E10
ROSSMORE
av. Punchbowl ... 400 C5
av.e, Rossmore ... 389 J14
av.w, Rossmore ... 389 C13
cr. Rossmore ... 419 E3
ROSSMOYNE
la. Ellis Lane ... 476 C8
ROSS PHILLIPS
la. Padstow, off Alice St ... 399 D15
ROSS SMITH
av. Mascot ... 405 B6
av. Meadowbnk ... 311 D3
pde. Gt Mckrl Bch ... 109 A14
pde. Lane Cove ... 313 K2
st. Kings Park ... 244 C1
st. Quakers Hill ... 244 C1
ROSTHERNE
av. Croydon ... 342 D12
ROSTREVOR
st. Cronulla ... 524 A2
ROSTROV
st. Penshurst ... 431 D4

ROTA
pl. Kings Park 244 K2
ROTARUA
rd. St Clair, off Rotarua Rd 269 F14
ROTARY
st. Liverpool 365 B15
ROTHBURY
pl. Cherrybrook 219 C13
st. Edensor Pk 333 F16
ROTHERWOOD
av. Asquith 192 A7
pl. Turramurra 222 H16
ROTHERY
st. Gordon 254 A4
ROTHESAY
av. Ryde 311 F5
st. Winston Hills 277 C3
ROTHSCHILD
av. Rosebery 375 H16
ROTHWELL
av. Concord W 341 C3
av. N Strathfield 341 C3
cct. Glenwood 215 G10
cr. Lane Cove 314 E3
la. Schofields 183 C15
rd. Turramurra 222 C15
rd. Warrawee 222 C15
st. Eastwood 280 K4
ROTORUA
pl. St Ives Ch 223 J2
rd. St Clair 269 F14
st. Lethbrdg Pk 240 E1
ROTTNEST
av. Hinchinbrk 362 J14
ROTUMA
st. Oakhurst 211 J16
ROUGHLEY
rd. Kenthurst 157 K5
ROUNCE
av. Forestville 256 A6
ROUND TABLE
cl. Mt Colah 162 E9
ROUSE
la. N Richmond 87 G7
pl. Illawong 459 H5
rd. Rouse Hill 184 F11
ROWALLAN
av. Castle Hill 217 K13
ROWAN
st. Mona Vale 199 B6
ROWANY
cl. Bonnyrigg 363 H9
ROWE
av. Lurnea 394 E7
cl. Wetherill Pk 334 F6
la. Bondi Jctn 22 G6
la. Eastwood 281 B8
la. Paddington 4 J14
la. Sydenham, off Park Rd 374 D15
pl. Baulkham Hl 247 E5
pl. Doonside 273 H3
pl. Greystanes 305 J9
st. Eastwood 280 H9
st. Eastwood 281 B8
st. Harbord 288 E2
st. Manly 288 F10
st. Roseville Ch 285 D1
st. S Hurstville 432 A12
st. Sydenham 374 D15
st. Sydney D A3
st. Woollahra 22 H5
ROWELL
st. Granville 308 G10
st. North Ryde 282 J10
st. Revesby Ht 428 K7
ROWENA
pl. Cherrybrook 219 C9
pl. Potts Point 4 H5
rd. Narraweena 258 D2
st. Greystanes 305 J7
ROWLAND
av. Bondi 378 C6
av. Kurmond 56 E16
st. Revesby 428 H3
ROWLEY
la. Camperdwn 17 B8
la. Eveleigh 18 F11
la. Eveleigh 375 C6
pl. Airds 511 J15
rd. Guildford 338 A7
rd. Russell Lea 343 C5
st. Btn-le-Sds 404 A15
st. Burwood 341 J11
st. Camperdwn 17 A9
st. Eveleigh 18 F12
st. Eveleigh 375 C6
st. Pendle Hill 276 E16
st. Seven Hills 245 F16
st. Smithfield 335 F4
ROWLEYS POINT
rd. Lansvale 366 J11
ROWLISON
pde. Cammeray 316 B3
ROWNTREE
st. Balmain 7 F7
st. Birchgrove 7 F7
st. Quakers Hill 213 G16
ROWOOD
rd. Prospect 275 B14
ROXANA
rd. Kurrajong 55 H15
ROXBOROUGH PARK
rd. Baulkham Hl 247 F6
rd. Castle Hill 247 F6
ROXBURGH
pl. Bella Vista 246 H3
ROXBY
gr. Quakers Hill 214 D8
pl. Hinchinbrk 362 J14
ROY
pl. Marayong 244 C8
st. Kingsgrove 401 J5
ROYAL
arc. Sydney 3 G5
av. Baulkham Hl 247 G8
av. Birrong 368 J3
av. Plumpton 242 C5
pl. Bardwell Pk 402 K8
pl. Blair Athol 511 A3
pl. Greystanes 306 H10
pl. St Clair 270 E10
row. Menai 459 A14
st. Chatswood 285 C7
st. Maroubra 406 J9
ROYALA
cl. Prestons 393 D16
ROYAL GEORGE
dr. Harringtn Pk 478 C3
ROYALIST
rd. Mosman 316 G11
ROYAL OAK
dr. Alfords Point 459 A3
pl. W Pnnant Hl 248 J4
ROYCE
av. Croydon 342 D12
st. Greystanes 306 C10
ROYCROFT
pl. Edensor Pk 363 C2
ROYENA
wy. Blacktown 274 E12
ROYLSTON
la. Paddington 13 F13
st. Fairfield W 335 D13
st. Paddington 13 F14
ROYSTON
cl. Pymble 223 D16
pde. Asquith 192 A10
pde. Mt Colah 192 A10
st. Darlinghurst 4 J9
ROY WATTS
rd. Glenfield 423 J7
RUBIDA
wy. Mcquarie Fd 424 D16
RUBIE
la. Malabar, off Nix Av 437 F7
RUBINA
st. Merrylnds W 307 B12
RUBY
ct. Kellyville 185 F7
pl. Seven Hills 275 D8
rd. Gymea 461 F16
st. Carramar 366 G1
st. Guildford 337 J2
st. Hurstville 431 G3
st. Marrickville 373 K15
st. Mosman 317 B12
st. Yagoona 368 G11
wy. Claymore 481 C12
RUCKLE
pl. Doonside 273 E5
RUDD
cl. Casula 424 G3
cl. Edensor Pk 363 F3
pde. Campsie 371 K14
pl. Blackett 241 C4
pl. Doonside 243 B8
rd. Leumeah 481 J16
st. East Ryde 283 A16
st. Narellan 478 F12
RUDDERS
la. Eastern Ck 273 B12
RUDELLE
cr. Yagoona 369 B9
RUDGE
pl. Ambarvale 511 A15
RUDHAM
pl. Chipping Ntn 366 H15
RUDOLF
rd. Seven Hills 275 F7
RUDYARD
st. Winston Hills 247 G16
RUFUS
av. Glenwood 215 E15
RUGBY
cr. Chipping Ntn 396 F1
pl. Sydney A K8
pwy. Chipping Ntn, off Rugby Cr 396 G1
rd. Marsfield 281 G2
st. Cambrdg Pk 238 B7
st. Wrrngtn Cty 238 B7
RULANA
st. Acacia Gdn 214 H16
RULE
st. Cambrdg Pk 237 H9
RULES
pl. Horngsea Pk 392 F16
RULWALLA
pl. Gymea 491 C7
RUM CORP
la. Windsor 120 J9
RUMKER
st. Picton 563 D10
st. Picton 563 D12
RUMSAY
la. Rozelle 7 F13
st. Rozelle 7 F14
RUMSEY
cr. Dundas Vy 279 K11
RUNCORN
av. Hebersham 241 E8
st. St Johns Pk 334 F16
RUNDLE
pl. Gladesville 312 K5
rd. Busby 363 F14
rd. Green Valley 363 F14
st. S Granville 338 F3
RUNIC
la. Maroubra 406 K7
RUNNYMEDE
wy. Carlingford 249 H11
RUNYON
av. Greystanes 306 G5
RUPARI
pl. Belrose 225 F15
RUPERT
st. Bass Hill 368 A11
st. Ingleburn 453 B10
st. Merrylnds W 307 B14
st. Mt Colah 192 A6
RUPERTSWOOD
av. Bellevue Hill 14 K9
rd. Rooty Hill 271 H5
RUSDEN
ml. Mt Riverview 234 C1
rd. Blaxland 234 A7
rd. Mt Riverview 234 A7
RUSE
pl. Campbelltwn 511 H9
pl. Illawong 459 E4
st. Harris Park 308 F5
st. North Ryde 282 C7
RUSH
pl. Quakers Hill 243 E4
st. Woollahra 21 H3
RUSHALL
st. Pymble 223 C14
RUSHES
pl. Minto 453 B14
RUSKIN
cl. Wetherill Pk 334 F6
RUSKIN ROWE
Avalon 169 H2
RUSSELL
av. Dolls Point 463 C1
av. Frenchs Frst 256 D4
av. Lindfield 284 E1
av. Sans Souci 463 C1
av. Valley Ht 202 H11
av. Wahroonga 221 J7
av. Winston Hills 277 J1
cl. Green Valley 363 B13
cr. Westleigh 220 H2
ct. Maroubra 407 E13
la. Allawah 432 D9
la. Lindfield 254 F16
la. Oakdale 500 C16
la. Sans Souci 463 C1
la. Strathfield 341 G14
rd. N Parramatta 279 A7
st. Blacktown 274 G4
st. Campbelltwn 511 J5
st. Clontarf 287 F11
st. Denistone E 281 F8
st. Emu Heights 235 C7
st. Emu Plains 235 B12
st. Granville 308 F11
st. Greenacre 370 E7
st. Lilyfield 10 E9
st. Mt Pritchard 364 H11
st. Northmead 248 B14
st. Oatley 431 D14
st. Riverwood 400 B10
st. Russell Lea 343 C6
st. Strathfield 341 G13
st. The Oaks 502 E10
st. Vaucluse 318 G16
st. Wollstncraft 315 C8
st. Woollahra 22 G3
RUSSELL MOCKRIDGE
av. Newington L K16
av. Newington 310 B11
RUSTIC
pl. Woodcroft 243 G7
RUTAR
pl. Abbotsbury 333 B10
RUTH
pl. Cherrybrook 219 J4
pl. Minto 482 G2
pl. Panania 398 D15
st. Canley Ht 365 A2
st. Marsfield 281 K5
st. Merrylnds W 307 C12
st. Naremburn 315 E1
st. Winston Hills 277 A4
RUTHERFORD
av. Burraneer 523 E4
av. Lucas Ht 487 G12
st. Blacktown 274 A3
RUTHERGLEN
av. Northmead 278 C1
av. Richmond 118 D8
dr. St Andrews 481 K2
pl. Minchinbury 271 J10
RUTHVEN
av. Milperra 397 D9
la. Bondi Jctn 22 D6
st. Bondi Jctn 22 D8
RUTLAND
av. Baulkham Hl 247 F4
av. Castlecrag 285 K11
pl. N Wahrnga 222 J2
st. Allawah 432 F8
st. Blacktown 274 J7
st. Surry Hills 19 G2
RUTLEDGE
cr. Quakers Hill 214 C8
st. Eastwood 280 H10
st. West Ryde 280 F10
RUZAC
st. Campbelltwn 511 J5
RYAN
av. Beverly Hills 401 B16
av. Cabramatta 365 D9
av. Hornsby Ht 191 G6
av. Maroubra 407 E8
av. Mosman 317 D6
cl. St Andrews 452 C14
cr. Riverstone 183 A6
la. Forest Lodge 11 E15
la. St Leonards 315 F5
la. Yagoona 369 D10
la. East Hills, off Park Rd 427 G5
pl. Beacon Hill 257 J9
pl. Emu Plains 235 B9
pl. Illawong 459 E4
pl. Mount Druitt 270 K2
rd. Padstow 399 F16
st. Bnkstn Aprt 367 J16
st. Dundas Vy 280 B11
st. Lilyfield 10 G4
st. St Marys 269 J2
st. Thirlmere 564 J4
st. Thirlmere 564 J6
RYDAL
av. Castle Hill 247 J5
pl. Collaroy Plat 228 E11
pl. Cranebrook 207 E11
st. Prospect 274 G12
RYDE
pl. St Johns Pk 364 G5
rd. Gladesville 312 J6
rd. Gordon 253 B14
rd. Hunters Hill 313 C8
rd. Pymble 253 B14
rd. West Pymble 253 B14
st. Epping 280 G1
RYDER
ct. Rouse Hill 184 K9
rd. Greenfld Pk 334 D14
st. Darlinghurst 4 C13
st. Glenwood 215 E13
RYDGE
la. Belmore, off Rydge St 371 G16
la. Belmore, off Rydge St 401 G1
st. Belmore 401 G1
RYE
av. Bexley 402 F14
RYEDALE
la. West Ryde, off Wattle St 281 F15
rd. Denistone 281 E13
rd. Eastwood 281 D9
rd. West Ryde 281 E13
RYELAND
cl. Elderslie 507 J3
pl. Airds 512 A12
st. Miller 393 F2
RYLAND
cl. Wakeley 334 K15
RYMILL
pl. Bundeena 523 K11
pl. Leumeah 482 J11
rd. Tregear 240 B4
RYNAN
av. Edmndsn Pk 422 G3
RYRIE
av. Cromer 228 D15
av. Forestville 255 F10
rd. Earlwood 402 C3
rd. N Parramatta 278 K6
st. Mosman 317 A2
st. North Ryde 282 H10
RYRIES
pde. Cremorne 316 G4

S

SABA
st. Fairfield W 335 G10
SABER
st. Woollahra 22 H5
SABINA
pl. St Ives 224 F8
st. Mosman 317 D3
SABRE
cr. Holsworthy 426 F3
pl. Raby 451 E16
SABRINA
gr. Plumpton 241 J8
SABUGAL
rd. Engadine 488 D13
SACKVILLE
rd. Ebenezer 63 A9
rd. Wilberforce 62 G16
st. Bardwell Vy 402 K10
st. Bexley 402 K10
st. Blacktown 245 A13
st. Canley Ht 365 H4
st. Canley Vale 365 H4
st. Fairfield 336 A15
st. Hurstville 401 G16
st. Ingleburn 453 A10
st. Lalor Park 245 A13
st. Maroubra 407 J10
SACOYA
av. Bella Vista 246 G6
SADDINGTON
st. St Marys 269 E2
st. S Turramrra 252 A8
SADDLE
row. Holsworthy 426 E4
SADDLEBACK
cl. Hinchinbrk 363 B16
SADDLER
wy. Glenmore Pk 266 H14

SADLEIR
av. Ashcroft 394 D1
av. Heckenberg 364 C14
av. Sadleir 394 D1
SADLIER
av. Milperra 397 D9
cr. Fairfield W 335 A10
cr. Petersham 15 G11
wk. *Mosman, off*
Awaba St 317 A4
SAFORD
st. Forestville 256 A5
SAGARS
rd. Kenthurst 188 A11
SAGE
av. Oyster Bay 461 C8
st. Mount Druitt 270 K3
st. St Ives 253 K2
SAGER
pl. East Ryde 282 K16
SAGGART FIELD
rd. Minto 482 C1
SAGGAS
st. Springwood 171 D16
SAIALA
rd. East Killara 254 G7
SAIDOR
rd. Whalan 241 A13
SAIL
pl. Illawong 459 B7
SAILORS BAY
rd. Northbridge 285 H15
SAINSBURY
st. St Marys 269 G1
ST AGNES
av. Rooty Hill 272 F6
ST AGNESS
wy. Blair Athol 511 C2
ST AIDANS
av. Oatlands 279 A11
av. Oatlands 279 A12
ST ALBANS
rd. Kingsgrove 401 H7
rd. Schofields 183 C14
st. Abbotsford 342 J1
ST ANDREWS
bvd. Casula 395 A11
dr. Glenmore Pk 266 F11
dr. Pymble 252 J4
gte. Elanora Ht 198 D12
pl. Cronulla 493 J11
rd. Leppington 420 J15
rd. Raby 451 G8
rd. St Andrews 451 K13
rd. Varroville 451 C3
st. Balmain 8 B9
st. Rydalmere 279 E14
wy. Rouse Hill 185 B8
ST ANN
st. Merrylands 307 F14
ST ANNE
pl. Blair Athol 510 K2
ST ANNES
cl. Belrose 226 B12
sq. Strathfield S 371 A5
st. Ryde 312 A3
ST ANTHONY
cl. Kings Park 244 E5
ST AUBINS
pl. Glen Alpine 510 F12
ST BARBARAS
av. Manly 289 A16
ST BARNABAS
st. Ultimo 12 J16
ST BARTHOLOMEWS
pl. Prospect 275 B15
ST CATHERINE
st. Mortdale 431 B6
ST CLAIR
av. St Clair 269 H9
st. Belmore 371 E14
ST DAVID
av. Dee Why 258 G5
ST DAVIDS
rd. Haberfield 343 C16
rd. Varroville 451 G3
ST ELMO
pde. Kingsgrove 401 H12
st. Mosman 317 C13
ST GEORGE
cr. Sandy Point 428 A14
ST GEORGES
cr. Cecil Hills 362 E7
cr. Drummoyne 344 A2
pde. Allawah 432 C7
pde. Earlwood 402 K4
pde. Hurstville 432 C7
rd. Bexley 402 D14
rd. Penshurst 431 D4
ST GILES
av. Greenwich 315 B8
ST HELENA
la. Eastlakes 405 K4
pde. Eastlakes 405 K5
ST HELENS
av. Mt Krng-gai 162 J14
cl. West Hoxton 392 D8
ST HELENS PARK
dr. St Helens Pk 541 B3
ST HILLIERS
rd. Auburn 339 G1
ST IVES
av. Hunters Hill 314 A12
ST JAMES
arc. Sydney 3 J3
av. Baulkham Hl 247 E7
av. Earlwood 402 J4
av. Glebe 11 K13
av. Menangle 538 G16
la. Glebe 12 A13
la. Turramurra 222 H12
pl. Narellan 478 H12
pl. Seven Hills 276 D1
rd. Bondi Jctn 22 C8
rd. Sydney D D6
rd. Sydney 3 K3
rd. Varroville 451 D4
rd. Vineyard 152 D10
ST JOHN
st. Balmain 8 B9
st. Lewisham 15 B7
st. Newtown 17 G16
ST JOHNS
av. Auburn 339 A12
av. Gordon 253 F9
cl. Brookvale 258 A8
la. *Gordon, off*
St Johns Av 253 H8
pl. Appin 568 F13
pl. Narellan 478 B10
rd. Auburn 339 A12
rd. Blaxland 233 F10
rd. Bradbury 511 C14
rd. Busby 363 K14
rd. Busby 363 K15
rd. Cabramatta 365 E4
rd. Cabramatta W 365 A4
rd. Campbelltwn 511 H12
rd. Canley Ht 365 A4
rd. Forest Lodge 11 J16
rd. Glebe 11 J16
rd. Heckenberg 363 K14
rd. Heckenberg 363 K15
rd. Maraylya 95 C12
rd. Maraylya 95 D8
rd. St Johns Pk 364 H3
wk. Gordon 253 F9
ST JUDE
cr. Belmore 401 H3
rd. Varroville 451 G3
ST KILDA
la. *Woolmloo, off*
Bourke St 4 E6
st. Bexley North 402 C10
st. Kingsgrove 402 C10
st. St Johns Pk 364 F3
ST LAWRENCE
av. Kearns 451 A16
st. Greenwich 314 J13
ST LUKE
st. Randwick 377 D15
ST MALO
av. Hunters Hill 314 A14
ST MARKS
av. Castle Hill 217 K9
la. Randwick 377 C10
rd. Darling Point 13 J8
rd. Randwick 377 D13
ST MARTINS
cr. Blacktown 274 K5
ST MARYS
av. Bondi Jctn 377 G5
la. Camperdwn 17 C10
la. Newtown 17 C10
rd. Berkshire Pk 180 A13
rd. Sydney D H7
rd. Sydney 4 B4
st. Balmain East 8 H10
st. Camperdwn 17 C10
st. Newtown 17 C10
st. West Hoxton 392 D9
ST MATTHEWS
la. *Baulkham Hl, off*
Rose St 247 G13
ST MERVYNS
av. Point Piper 14 J4
ST MICHAELS
pl. Baulkham Hl 247 D4
pl. Vaucluse 348 B5
ST NEOT
av. Potts Point 4 K1
ST PAULS
cl. Burwood 341 K16
cr. Emu Plains 235 D9
cr. Liverpool 394 G5
la. Cobbitty 446 J11
pl. Chester Hill 337 H12
pl. Chippendale 19 C5
rd. N Balgowlah 287 C6
st. Randwick 377 B16
wy. Blacktown 274 B6
ST PETER
cl. Hinchinbrk 392 K2
ST PETERS
la. Darlinghurst 4 E8
la. Redfern 19 D10
st. Darlinghurst 4 E8
st. St Peters 374 H13
ST THOMAS
rd. Mulgoa 295 D11
st. Bronte 377 K11
st. Clovelly 377 K11
ST VINCENT
rd. Bexley 432 D1
ST VINCENTS
rd. Greenwich 314 K8
rd. Greenwich 315 A7
SAIPAN
av. Lethbrdg Pk 240 H1
SALADILLO
gr. Wallacia 325 A16
SALADINE
av. Punchbowl 399 H4
SALAMANDER
gr. Baulkham Hl 246 K2
pl. Mt Lewis 370 A15
pl. Raby 451 E12
st. St Clair 269 F15
SALAMAUA
cr. Holsworthy 426 D3
pl. Glenfield 424 G12
rd. Whalan 241 A13
SALECICH
pl. Bonnyrigg 364 E6
SALEM
cl. St Clair 269 G13
SALERNO
cl. Emu Heights 235 B5
la. *Emu Heights, off*
Salerno Cl 235 B4
pl. St Ives Ch 223 J5
st. Forestville 256 A6
SALERWONG
pl. Ryde 282 E12
SALES
av. Silverdale 353 J15
SALFORD
st. Ingleburn 453 E5
st. St Clair 270 G10
SALIGNA
wy. Mcquarie Fd 424 E16
SALIGNUS
pl. Narellan Vale 478 J14
SALINA
av. W Pnnant Hl 249 H7
SALISBURY
av. Bexley 402 H14
av. Glenfield 424 C11
av. Kemps Ck 360 E1
ct. West Hoxton 392 B11
la. Camperdwn 17 A7
la. Stanmore 17 A7
la. *Rosebery, off*
Queen St 375 G13
pl. Gymea Bay 491 C7
pl. Watsons Bay 318 F15
rd. Asquith 192 A12
rd. Bellevue Hill 347 G11
rd. Camperdwn 17 E7
rd. Camperdwn 17 G6
rd. Castle Hill 217 A13
rd. East Killara 254 H11
rd. Guildford 337 H7
rd. Hornsby 192 A12
rd. Kensington 376 D10
rd. Rose Bay 347 G11
rd. Stanmore 16 F9
rd. Willoughby 285 F15
sq. Seaforth 287 A10
st. Botany 405 G14
st. Canley Ht 365 F4
st. Concord 342 A8
st. Mount Druitt 241 B14
st. Penshurst 431 C3
st. Riverwood 400 F14
st. Silverwater 309 H13
st. S Hurstville 432 A9
st. Watsons Bay 318 F15
st. Waverley 377 G6
SALISBURY DOWNS
dr. W Pnnant Hl 249 A2
SALIX
pl. Engadine 488 H16
SALLAWAY
pl. W Pnnant Hl 249 B1
rd. Galston 159 B8
rd. Middle Dural 159 B8
SALLEE
gln. Kingswood 267 F2
la. *Kingswood, off*
Sallee Gln 267 F2
SALLY
pl. Glendenning 242 E4
pl. Kellyville 217 C2
SALMON
cl. Asquith 192 C8
rd. S Windsor 150 F2
SALT
rd. Church Point 168 F9
st. Concord 342 D4
SALTASH
st. Yagoona 368 F15
SALTBUSH
pl. Bossley Park 333 J9
SALTER
av. Minto 452 K14
cr. Denistone E 281 H9
ct. Harringtn Pk 478 E6
rd. Bossley Park 333 K9
st. Gladesville 313 A12
SALTERS
rd. Wilberforce 62 D12
SALT PAN
rd. Riverwood 429 J1
SALTPETRE
cl. Eagle Vale 481 H5
SALVANA
wy. Claymore 481 C11
SALVESTRO
pl. Bella Vista 246 G6
SALVIA
av. Bankstown 399 H2
cl. Cherrybrook 219 F10
SAMANTHA
cr. Glendenning 242 J4
pl. Smeaton Gra 479 E9
SAMANTHA RILEY
dr. Kellyville 215 H5
SAMARAI
pl. Beacon Hill 257 H4
rd. Whalan 241 A12
SAMES
cl. Mona Vale 198 K3
SAM JOHNSON
wy. Lane Cove W 283 G15
SAMMUT
cr. Chipping Ntn 396 D4
st. Smithfield 305 F14
SAMOA
av. Picnic Point 428 D8
pl. Lethbrdg Pk 240 H1
SAMORA
av. Cremorne 316 F4
SAMPSON
cr. Acacia Gdn 214 F16
cr. Quakers Hill 214 F16
pl. Rsemeadow 540 J4
SAMUEL
la. *Tempe, off*
Samuel St 374 C16
pl. Airds 512 B14
pl. Quakers Hill 214 A8
pl. St Clair 269 K11
st. Bligh Park 150 J8
st. Lidcombe 339 G8
st. Mona Vale 198 H3
st. Peakhurst 430 B5
st. Ryde 281 K15
st. Surry Hills F F10
st. Surry Hills 4 A13
st. Tempe 374 C16
st. Wiley Park 400 J3
SAMUEL FOSTER
dr. S Penrith 267 A4
SAMUEL MARSDEN
rd. Orchard Hills 269 A10
SAMUELS
av. Jannali 461 A9
SANANANDA
av. Allambie Ht 257 D11
rd. Holsworthy 396 D16
SANBROOK
la. Newtown 17 A10
SAN CRISTOBAL
dr. Green Valley 363 A8
SANCTUARY
av. Avalon 140 A15
cl. Cherrybrook 219 F14
dr. Windsor Dn 180 F1
pl. Chipping Ntn 366 K14
SANCTUARY PARK
dr. Plumpton 242 A9
SANCTUARY POINT
rd. W Pnnant Hl 248 F8
SAND
pl. Illawong 459 C3
SANDAKAN
cr. Lethbrdg Pk 210 H16
rd. Revesby Ht 428 J7
SANDAL
cr. Carramar 366 G2
SANDALWOOD
av. St Clair 270 G11
cl. Casula 423 K3
SANDBAR
pl. Port Hacking 522 K3
SANDEFORD
wy. Minto 482 K1
wy. Minto 483 A1
SANDELL
pl. Dean Park 242 K2
SANDERLING
st. Hinchinbrk 393 E1
SANDERS
cr. Kings Lngly 245 H6
la. Avalon 170 B2
pde. Concord 342 D4
rd. Baulkham Hl 247 B10
SANDERSON
st. Carramar 366 J1
st. Cronulla 494 C6
SANDFORD
rd. Turramurra 223 D10
SANDGATE
st. Botany 405 F14
SANDHURST
cr. Glenhaven 218 C4
SAN DIEGO
st. Clarmnt Ms 268 J2
SANDILANDS
rd. Bonnyrigg 364 E5
SANDLER
av. North Rocks 279 A2
SANDLEWOOD
cl. Rouse Hill 185 B8
SANDO
cr. Roselands 401 C7
SANDON
st. Seven Hills 275 J8
SANDOVER
ct. Wattle Grove 395 K13
SANDOWN
cl. Casula 394 D15
cl. St Johns Pk 364 F5
SANDPIPER
av. Hinchinbrk 363 D15
cr. Clarmnt Ms 268 H4
cr. Newington L H11
cr. Newington L J11
cr. Newington 310 D12
pl. Kenthurst 188 A1
pl. Woronora Ht 489 C6
tce. Plumpton 241 K10
SANDPLOVER
pl. Hinchinbrk 363 D15
SAND POINT
la. *Palm Beach, off*
Iluka Rd 139 H3
SANDRA
av. Panania 398 A15
cr. Roselands 401 A8

pl. Ingleburn 453 D11
pl. Miranda 491 J1
pl. Mount Druitt 241 D14
pl. Seaforth 286 K6
pl. S Penrith 267 A1
st. Ryde 312 D7
st. Woodpark 306 G16
SANDRIDGE
st. Bondi 378 C5
SANDRINGHAM
av. Cambrdg Pk 237 J10
dr. Carlingford 279 D5
dr. Cecil Hills 362 G4
st. Dolls Point 463 H1
st. St Johns Pk 364 D4
st. Sans Souci 433 C16
SANDS
st. Sydney C D14
SANDSTOCK
pl. Woodcroft 243 F7
SANDWELL
st. Surry Hills 20 D1
SANDY
gln. Wrrngtn Dns 238 B3
la. Thirlmere 561 G11
rd. Burraneer 493 E15
SANDY BAY
rd. Clontarf 287 E12
SANFORD
st. Glendenning 242 F3
SANGRADO
st. Seaforth 287 A10
SAN MARINO
dr. Prestons 393 E14
SAN MICHEL
cr. Ryde, off O'Regan Dr 312 B4
SAN MICHELLE
av. Baulkham Hl 247 G14
SANONI
av. Sandringham 463 E2
SAN REMO
av. Gymea 491 E2
pl. Dural 189 C5
pl. Guildford 337 D2
SAN STEFANO
pl. Ryde, off O'Regan Dr 312 B4
SANTA
pl. Bossley Park 334 C11
SANTA FE
pl. Dural 189 D6
SANTA MARINA
av. Waverley 377 F8
SANTANGELO
cl. Edensor Pk 363 G3
SANTA ROSA
av. Ryde 282 B11
SANTIAGO
pl. Seven Hills 275 H4
SANTLEY
cr. Kingswood 237 H13
SANTON
pl. Cranebrook 207 F12
SANTOS
pl. Toongabbie 275 F11
SAPIUM
wy. Mcquarie Fd 454 F3
SAPPHIRE
pl. Eagle Vale 481 C7
st. Greystanes 306 A1
SAPPHO
rd. Warwck Frm 365 K13
st. Canley Ht 365 B1
SARACEN
rd. Beecroft 250 E10
SARAH
cr. Baulkham Hl 247 F7
pl. Appin 568 F10
pl. Bossley Park 334 C9
pl. Cecil Hills 362 J4
pl. Illawong 459 D8
pl. Minchinbury 271 G8
st. Enmore 17 B16
st. Mascot 405 A5
wy. Minto 482 J3
SARAH DURACK
av. Homebush B 340 G4
av. Newington M H8
SARAH HOLLANDS
dr. Horngsea Pk 392 D14
SARAH JANE
av. Kellyville 185 K12
SARAHS
wk. Mosman 317 E13
SARAH WEST
pl. Mt Annan 509 G1
SARDAM
av. Cranebrook 206 H8
SARDAN
av. Fairfield 336 F8
SARDINIA
av. Glenwood 245 J3
pl. Birchgrove 7 G4
SARDONYX
av. Richmond 118 E9
SARDYGA
st. Plumpton 242 A7
SARGENTS
rd. Ebenezer 62 H7
rd. Minchinbury 271 B7
rd. Wilberforce 61 K11
SARIC
av. Georges Hall 368 C16
SARISSA
wy. Mcquarie Fd 454 H4
SARK
gr. Minto 482 F8
SARNER
rd. Greenwich 315 A7
SARNIA
cr. Killara 253 G11
SARRE
pl. Prospect 274 G12
SARSFIELD
cct. Bexley North 402 E9
st. Blacktown 244 K14
SARTOR
cr. Bossley Park 333 G11
SASSAFRAS
cl. Bradbury 511 G12
la. Cabramatta 365 H8
la. Vaucluse 318 E16
SASSAFRAS GULLY
rd. Springwood 201 G5
SATARA
av. Cabramtta W 365 B6
SATELBERG
st. Holsworthy 426 D4
SATINWOOD
cl. Alfords Point 429 B14
SATTERLEY
av. Turramurra 252 D4
SATURN
pl. Doonside 243 D15
SAUNDERS
av. Liverpool 365 B16
la. Pyrmont 12 E2
la. Quakers Hill 243 C2
la. Yagoona 368 K11
pl. Menai 458 H14
pl. Raby 451 D11
rd. Ermington 310 E4
rd. Oakville 122 G8
st. N Parramatta 278 E12
st. Pyrmont 12 E3
SAUNDERS BAY
rd. Caringbah 492 K12
SAURINE
st. Bankstown 368 H15
SAUTERNE
cr. Minchinbury 272 A8
SAUTERNES
pl. Eschol Park 481 D5
SAUVAGE
pl. Doonside 273 F5
SAUVIGNON
cl. Eschol Park 481 B4
SAVA
pl. Bonnyrigg 364 A10
SAVANNAH
la. St Clair, off Fantail Cr 271 A15
pl. Erskine Park 271 A15
SAVERY
cr. Blacktown 274 C8
pl. Fairfield W 335 C12
SAVIC
pl. Bonnyrigg Ht 363 C7
SAVOY
av. East Killara 254 H6
cr. Chester Hill 368 B3
ct. W Pnnant Hl 249 H9
SAWAO KATO
av. Newington L K16
av. Newington 310 A15
SAWELL
st. Bossley Park 333 G11
SAWMILL
ct. Castle Hill 248 E5
SAWTELL
cl. Hoxton Park 392 K9
SAWYER
cr. Lane Cove W, off Whitfield Av 283 F12
la. Artarmon 314 H2
SAXBY
st. Girraween 276 C14
wy. Blacktown 273 G5
SAXON
pl. Cecil Hills 362 E7
pl. Wentwthvle 277 C9
st. Belfield 371 D9
wy. Airds 512 A13
SAXONVALE
cr. Edensor Pk 333 E14
rd. Baulkham Hl 246 H3
rd. Bella Vista 246 H3
SAXONY
rd. Horsley Pk 332 G6
SAYERS
st. N Balgowlah 287 E4
SAYONARA
pl. Greenfld Pk 334 E14
SAYWELL
la. Btn-le-Sds 433 K2
rd. Mcquarie Fd 453 J1
rd. Mcquarie Fd 454 A2
st. Chatswood 284 K12
st. Marrickville 374 D12
SCADDAN
st. Quakers Hill 214 E9
SCAHILL
st. Campsie 372 B16
SCAIFE
st. Padstow 429 B4
SCALES
pde. Balgowlah Ht 287 H12
SCANLEN
wy. Ingleburn 452 K10
SCAPOLITE
pl. Eagle Vale 481 E7
SCARAB
st. Bnkstn Aprt 397 K1
SCARBOROUGH
cl. Lurnea 394 C12
cl. Narellan 478 E16
cl. W Pnnant Hl 249 A1
cr. North Bondi 378 G3
la. Kogarah 433 E8
pl. Beacon Hill 257 G2
st. Bundeena 523 J10
st. Monterey 433 G9
wy. Cherrybrook 219 A14
SCARCELLA
pl. Edensor Pk 333 J15
SCARFE
st. Fairfield W 335 F13
SCARSBOROUGH
cr. Bligh Park 150 C5
SCARUS
pl. Rsemeadow 540 F3
SCARVELL
av. McGraths Hl 121 J13
SCENIC
cct. Cranebrook 237 C1
cir. Blaxland 234 A5
cr. Mt Riverview 204 G15
cr. S Hurstville 432 A13
gr. Glenwood 246 A5
SCHAEFER
tce. Glenwood 215 K16
SCHERELL
pl. Shalvey 211 A14
st. Dharruk 241 B7
SCHEYVILLE
rd. Maraylya 124 B5
rd. Oakville 122 K8
rd. Scheyville 123 B8
SCHILLER
pl. Emerton 240 K6
SCHLEICHER
st. St Marys 269 D3
SCHOEFFEL
gr. Horngsea Pk 392 F13
SCHOFIELD
av. Earlwood 402 F4
av. Rockdale 433 D2
pde. Pennant Hills 220 D12
pl. Menai 458 J11
rd. Pitt Town 122 K3
rd. Scheyville 123 B5
st. Riverwood 400 A10
SCHOFIELDS
rd. Rouse Hill 185 A13
rd. Schofields 183 G16
SCHOFIELDS FARM
rd. Schofields 183 F13
SCHOOL
av. Villawood 337 G16
la. Five Dock 342 J10
la. Earlwood, off William St 402 H4
pde. Doonside 243 C13
pde. Marrickville 373 F13
pde. Padstow 429 C2
pde. Westmead 307 E4
rd. Galston 159 D8
st. Balmain East 8 G7
SCHOOL HOUSE
la. Glenbrook, off Mann St 233 K16
rd. Regentville 265 H4
SCHUBERT
pl. Bonnyrigg Ht 363 E5
wy. Clarmnt Ms 268 G4
SCHULTZ
st. Balmain 7 A9
st. St Marys 269 K4
SCHUMACK
st. North Ryde 282 J11
SCHWEBEL
la. Glenorie 127 G3
st. Marrickville 373 J14
SCIARRA
cr. Acacia Gdn 244 J1
SCIENCE
rd. Camperdwn 18 B2
rd. Richmond 118 G12
SCINTILLA
gr. Doonside 243 H15
SCIPIO
st. Yagoona 368 D15
SCOBIE
pl. Mt Annan 479 B13
st. Doonside 273 F1
SCONE
pl. Doonside 243 A11
SCORPIUS
pl. Cranebrook 207 F5
SCOT
st. Bargo 567 C3
SCOTCHEY
st. Prairiewood 334 F12
SCOTLAND
rd. Ingleburn 423 B12
SCOTNEY
pl. Collaroy Plat 228 K13
pl. Quakers Hill 213 H10
SCOTT
cl. Rossmore 389 F4
cr. Roseville 285 D4
ct. Cherrybrook 249 F1
la. Kogarah 433 D7
la. Maroubra 407 F13
pl. Baulkham Hl 247 D5
pl. Kirrawee 460 J16
pl. St Ives 224 G8
rd. Colyton 270 H8
st. Bankstown 400 A3
st. Belfield 371 D9
st. Bronte 377 J11
st. Campbelltwn 512 B3
st. Croydon 342 G12
st. Fairfield E 337 F12
st. Five Dock 342 H9
st. Kogarah 433 D7
st. Liverpool 395 E4
st. Maroubra 407 F13
st. Marsfield 282 C5
st. Mortdale 430 K6
st. Narellan 478 H12
st. Punchbowl 399 J3
st. Pyrmont 12 F1
st. Springwood 202 A5
st. Toongabbie 276 E11
st. Willoughby 285 E16
SCOTTS DALE
cct. West Hoxton 392 D5
SCOTTS-DALE
cct. West Hoxton 392 E5
SCOTTSDALE
st. Stanhpe Gdn 215 B12
SCOTTS FARM
rd. Grose Wold 115 E9
SCOULLER
la. Marrickville 374 E9
st. Marrickville 374 E9
SCOUT
pl. Sydney B E8
SCOUTS
la. Paddington 21 F1
SCRIBBLY
pl. Mcquarie Fd 454 F4
SCRIBBLY GUM
cl. Hornsby Ht 161 K9
ct. Voyager Pt 427 B4
pl. Alfords Point 459 B3
SCRIBBLYGUM
cct. Rouse Hill 184 K7
SCRIVENER
la. Springwood 202 E3
st. Warwck Frm 395 J3
SCRIVIN
st. Leumeah 482 A16
SCROGGIES
rd. Thirlmere 561 A12
SCRUBWREN
pl. Glenmore Pk 265 J12
SCULLIN
pl. N Wahrnga 192 G14
pl. Penrith 237 C6
SCULLY
pl. Mt Annan 479 F15
SCYLLA
rd. Oyster Bay 461 A6
SEA
st. Hunters Hill 313 H10
SEABEACH
av. Mona Vale 199 F4
SEABORG
av. Lucas Ht 487 J12
SEABROOK
av. Grays Point 491 B11
av. Russell Lea 343 E7
cr. Doonside 273 G3
SEAEAGLE
cr. Green Valley 363 C11
SEAFORTH
av. Oatley 430 J10
av. Woolooware 493 F11
cr. Seaforth 287 A10
st. Bexley 402 K16
SEAL
pl. Tregear 240 C3
SEALE
cl. Beecroft 250 G5
cr. Leumeah 512 A1
la. Darlinghurst F J2
st. Burwood 371 J2
st. Darlinghurst F J2
st. Leichhardt 15 F3
wy. Oakhurst 242 D3
SEALY
st. Mt Lewis 369 K16
SEAMAN
av. Villawood 337 C16
st. Greenwich 314 J9
SEAMANS
pl. Horngsea Pk 392 D14
SEAMER
st. Forest Lodge 12 B16
SEARL
rd. Cronulla 493 H11
st. Petersham 15 G9
SEARLE
av. Randwick 377 E11
st. Canterbury 372 G11
st. Ryde 312 F6
SEARS
pl. Prairiewood 334 K8
SEASIDE
pde. S Coogee 407 J7
SEA SPRAY
ct. Chipping Ntn 366 K15
SEATON
av. Wahroonga 222 A10
cr. Cranebrook 207 G13
SEATTLE
cl. St Clair 270 J11
SEAVIEW
av. Harbord 258 J14
av. Newport 169 H10
pde. Collaroy 229 D15
st. Ashfield 372 J7
st. Balgowlah 287 G10
st. Clovelly 377 G11

st. Cronulla 493 K9
st. Dulwich Hill....373 F9
st. Mt Krng-gai....163 B10
st. Summer Hill...373 A7
st. Waverley........377 H7
SEBASTIAN
av. Rsemeadow....540 F6
dr. Dural..............219 A2
SEBASTOPOL
rd. Emu Heights...235 A1
st. Enmore............16 G14
SECANT
st. Liverpool........395 D1
SECOND
av. Berala.............339 E15
av. Blacktown.......244 H14
av. Campsie..........371 G10
av. Canley Vale.....366 B3
av. Condell Park....398 D4
av. Eastwood........281 C9
av. Epping............280 G3
av. Five Dock........343 A9
av. Gymea Bay......491 D10
av. Jannali............460 J11
av. Kingswood.......237 H14
av. Lane Cove.......314 G4
av. Lindfield..........254 F13
av. Llandilo...........208 K9
av. Loftus.............490 A5
av. Mcquarie Fd....454 A1
av. Mcquarie Pk....283 C7
av. Maroubra.........407 G9
av. Narrabeen.......228 G9
av. North Ryde......282 H13
av. Seven Hills......275 H2
av. Toongabbie.....276 F8
av. West Hoxton...362 D16
av. West Hoxton...392 C6
av. Willoughby......285 H11
rd. Berkshire Pk...180 B2
st. Ashbury..........372 G9
st. Granville.........308 G13
st. Parramatta......279 A15
st. Warragamba...353 G6
wk. Chester Hill.....337 J13
SEDDON
pl. Campbelltwn...511 K3
st. Bankstown......399 F6
SEDDON HILL
rd. Harbord...........258 J16
SEDGEMAN
av. Menai.............458 G7
SEDGER
rd. Kenthurst........187 G4
SEDGMAN
cr. Shalvey...........210 J14
st. Greystanes......306 A10
SEDGWICK
st. Leumeah.........482 A16
st. Leumeah.........512 B1
st. Smeaton Gra...479 E10
SEE
la. Kingsford.........406 E1
st. Kingsford.........406 E1
st. Meadowbnk.....311 F3
SEEANA
pl. Belrose............225 K10
SEEBREES
st. Manly Vale......287 J3
SEELAND
pl. Padstow Ht......429 B6
SEFTON
rd. Thornleigh.......221 A9
SEGEFIELD
pl. Casula............395 B12
SEGENHOE
pl. Richmond.......118 C5
st. Arncliffe...........403 G11
SEGERS
av. Padstow..........399 D16
SEIDEL
av. Picnic Point....428 G7
pl. Abbotsbury.....333 C13
SEINE
pl. Kearns............451 C16
pl. Miranda...........461 K15
SELBORNE
st. Burwood.........342 C12
SELBY
av. Dee Why.........258 E6
pl. Blacktown.......274 D5
pl. Minto..............482 K10
pl. St Johns Pk.....364 G3
SELDON
st. Quakers Hill....213 F7
SELEMS
pde. Revesby.........398 H15
SELF
pl. Shalvey...........211 B13
SELINA
pl. Cherrybrook....219 D7
SELKIRK
av. Cecil Park.......331 E12
pl. Bligh Park.......150 B7
pl. Camden S.......507 B12
pl. St Andrews......452 B13
st. Winston Hills..277 D4
SELLERS
la. Greenacre.......370 D12
SELLWOOD
st. Btn-le-Sds......434 A1
SELMA
pl. Oakhurst.........242 A2
SELMON
st. Sans Souci......433 D14
SELMS
pl. Minto..............452 J16
SELWA
pl. Kareela...........461 C12
SELWAY
av. Moorebank.....396 D10
SELWYN
av. Cmbrdg Gdn...237 G2
cl. Pennant Hills..220 D14
pl. Cartwright......393 K6
pl. Fairfield W......335 E10
pl. Quakers Hill....243 J3
st. Artarmon........285 B13
st. Paddington.......20 F1
st. Pymble...........223 B15
st. Wollstncraft.....315 D9
SEMAAN
st. Werrington.....238 H10
SEMANA
pl. Winmalee.......173 G12
st. Whalan...........241 B13
SEMILLON
cr. Eschol Park....481 D2
SEMPLE
st. Ryde..............282 C15
SENIOR
st. Canley Vale.....366 C3
SENNAR
la. Erskine Park, off
Sennar Rd.......271 A16
rd. Erskine Park...271 A16
SENTA
rd. Londonderry...177 J12
SENTINEL
av. Kellyville.........216 H3
cl. Horngsea Pk...392 F16
SENTRY
dr. Parklea...........215 A13
dr. Stanhpe Gdn...215 A10
SEPIK
pl. Kearns............451 C16
st. Holsworthy.....426 G7
SEPPELT
pl. Edensor Pk.....333 D15
st. Eastern Ck......272 F8
SEPTIMUS
av. Punchbowl......399 K7
st. Chatswood......285 B9
st. Erskineville......17 K13
SEQUOIA
cl. West Pymble..252 H11
gr. Menai, off
Fern Cct W......458 J14
SERA
st. Lane Cove......314 C2
SERAM
pl. Kings Park......244 D2
SERCIAL
pl. Eschol Park....481 C3
SERGEANT LARKIN
cr. Daceyville.......406 G3
SERGEANTS
la. St Leonards, off
Chandos St......315 D5
SERI
pl. Bossley Park...333 K10
SERINA
av. Castle Hill.......248 C3
SERMELFI
dr. Glenorie..........127 K1
SERPENTINE
cr. N Balgowlah...287 E7
la. Bowen Mtn.......84 D11
pde. Vaucluse.........348 E4
pl. Eagle Vale.......481 B7
rd. Hunters Hill.....314 C12
rd. Kirrawee.........491 A9
st. Bossley Park...333 G5
st. Merrylnds W...306 J11
SERVICE
av. Ashfield..........372 K9
la. Five Dock........343 A8
SESTO
pl. Bossley Park...333 G8
SETA
cl. St Clair...........299 H2
SETON
rd. Moorebank.....395 K8
SETTLERS
bvd. Liberty Gr.......311 C14
cl. Castle Hill.......218 F11
cr. Bligh Park.......150 H7
gld. Wrrngtn Dns...238 B4
wy. Westleigh.......220 G7
SEVEN HILLS
rd. Baulkham Hl...247 A11
rd. Bella Vista.......246 E9
rd. Seven Hills......246 A14
rd.s, Seven Hills......275 D6
wy. Baulkham Hl...246 F9
SEVENOAKS
cr. Bass Hill.........367 G7
pl. Jannali............461 A13
SEVENTEENTH
av. Austral............361 F16
av.e, West Hoxton...391 K1
SEVENTH
av. Austral............391 A12
av. Berala............339 D14
av. Campsie.........371 H11
av. Jannali............460 K12
av. Llandilo..........207 J4
av. Loftus............490 A7
av. Seven Hills......275 K3
st. Granville.........308 G15
st. Mascot...........405 A7
st. Warragamba...353 G4
SEVEN WAYS
Bondi Beach...348 C16
North Bondi....348 C16
SEVERN
pl. Kearns............450 K16
rd. Bringelly.........387 G3
rd. Woronora........489 H1
st. Maroubra........407 H11
st. St Marys.........239 G6
SEVILLE
pl. Glenwood........215 F12
pl. Kenthurst........157 J11
st. Fairfield E........337 A13
st. Lane Cove.......314 B3
st. N Parramatta..278 B10
SEWELL
av. Padstow Ht.....429 E7
av. Seven Hills......246 A13
st. Ryde..............311 H1
SEXTANS
pl. Cranebrook.....207 H6
SEXTON
av. Castle Hill.......217 G13
SEYMOUR
cl. Wahroonga.....221 H16
la. Marrickville, off
Frampton Av....374 A13
pde. Belfield...........371 C10
pl. Bossley Park...333 E11
pl. Paddington.......20 F1
st. Croydon Pk.....372 B6
st. Drummoyne.....343 J1
st. Dundas Vy......280 A7
st. Hurstville Gr....431 G11
wy. Kellyville.........216 K3
SEYTON
pl. Rsemeadow....540 C3
SHAARON
ct. Banksia...........403 F12
la. Banksia, off
Shaaron Ct.......403 F12
SHACKEL
av. Brookvale.......258 C8
av. Clovelly...........378 A13
av. Concord..........341 J6
av. Gladesville......312 G12
av. Kingsgrove.....401 K5
av. Old Guildfrd....337 E7
rd. Bangor............459 D14
SHACKLETON
av. Birrong...........368 J5
av. Tregear...........240 F4
SHADDOCK
av. Pymble...........253 B10
av. Villawood........367 F2
SHADE
pl. Lugarno..........429 K9
SHADFORTH
pl. Paddington.........4 K16
st. Mosman.........316 J11
st. Paddington.........4 K15
st. Wiley Park.......400 G1
SHADLOW
cr. St Clair...........269 H10
SHADWELL
cr. Kings Lngly.....246 A7
SHAFT
st. Silverwater..........L E16
st. Silverwater......309 K9
st. Silverwater......309 K10
SHAFTESBURY
rd. Burwood.........342 B15
st. Carlton............432 H7
SHAFTSBURY
rd. Denistone W...281 A10
rd. Eastwood........280 K7
rd. West Ryde......281 A11
SHAKESPEARE
dr. St Clair............270 C15
dr. Winmalee........173 J8
pl. Sydney................B G15
st. Campbelltwn...512 A3
st. Campsie..........372 A11
st. Wetherill Pk....334 G5
SHALOM
cl. Old Guildfrd....337 F8
SHAMROCK
cl. Winmalee........173 D10
ct. St Clair...........269 K10
pde. Killarney Ht.....286 D1
pl. Glendenning...242 H3
st. Smithfield.......335 F2
SHAND
cl. Illawong..........459 G4
cr. Turramurra.....252 G2
SHANDLIN
pl. S Penrith.........267 A7
SHANE
pl. Bella Vista.......246 E5
pl. Kurrajong Ht.....53 K6
st. Colyton...........270 E4
SHANE GOULD
av. Homebush B.....M G9
SHANE PARK
rd. Shanes Park....209 H9
SHANKE
cr. Kings Lngly.....245 C3
SHANNON
av. Killarney Ht.....256 C15
av. Merrylands......307 E10
gln. St Clair...........270 A12
la. St Clair, off
Menzies Cct.....270 A13
pl. Kearns............481 A2
rd. Bringelly.........387 J1
rd. Mt Colah.........162 B16
st. Greenacre.......370 F7
st. Lalor Park.......245 G9
st. St Ives............224 E11
SHANUK
st. Frenchs Frst....255 G1
SHARAN
pl. Forestville.......255 G8
SHARI
av. Picnic Point.....428 G5
av. Picnic Point.....428 G6
SHARK
av. Vaucluse.........348 B5
rd. Kurnell...........495 B1
SHARLAND
av. Chatswd W.....284 F14
pl. Smithfield.......335 C3
SHARMAN
cl. Harringtn Pk...478 H8
SHARN
st. Kurnell...........466 E8
SHARON
cl. Bossley Park...333 J11
cl. Hornsby..........192 A16
pl. Engadine.........488 E15
pl. N Richmond......86 K15
pl. Rooty Hill........271 J6
st. Holsworthy.....426 D12
SHARP
cl. Castle Hill.......218 A9
st. Belmore.........401 G1
st. Matraville.......406 K15
SHARPE
pl. Camden S......507 B15
SHARROCK
av. Glenwood.......215 J13
SHARWEN
pl. Blaxland.........234 B5
SHAUGHNESSY
st. Oakhurst.......242 C4
SHAULA
cr. Erskine Park...300 H2
la. Erskine Park, off
Shaula Cr.........300 H2
SHAUN
dr. Glenwood.......215 J15
SHAW
av. Earlwood........402 E6
av. Kingsford.......376 C16
cl. Barden Rdg.....488 G1
la. Sefton............368 F2
pl. Fairfield W......335 D13
pl. Prospect.........274 G12
pl. Rooty Hill.......242 A12
rd. Ingleburn.......452 K7
st. Beverly Hills....401 B15
st. Bexley North..402 A10
st. Cambrdg Pk....238 B11
st. East Ryde.......283 A14
st. Kingsgrove.....402 A10
st. Kogarah.........433 C8
st. North Bondi....348 B14
st. Petersham.......15 J14
SHAWNEE
st. Greenfld Pk....334 A13
SHAWS
pl. Yarramundi....145 B7
SHAYNE
ct. Oakdale..........500 D13
SHEAFFE
pl. Davidson........225 A16
SHEAHAN
av. Guildford........338 D7
pwy. Warwck Frm, off
Sheahan St......365 H15
st. Warwck Frm....365 H15
SHEARER
la. Padstow.........399 C15
la. St Clair, off
Shearer St.......270 F12
pl. Elderslie.........477 H16
st. St Clair...........270 F12
SHEARING
pl. Bonnyrigg......364 C5
SHEARS
wy. Minto.............482 J5
SHEARWATER
av. Woronora Ht..489 D4
cr. Yarramundi....145 E6
dr. Glenmore Pk..266 A13
rd. Hinchinbrk.....393 E2
SHEAS
st. Mascot...........405 A4
SHEATHER
av. St Ives...........254 D1
pl. Campbelltwn..511 H8
SHEATHERS
la. Camden.........506 E2
la. Cawdor..........506 E2
la. Grasmere.......506 E2
SHEBA
cr. S Penrith........267 C1
SHEDWORTH
st. Marayong.......244 B5
SHEEHAN
st. Eastwood.......281 H7
st. Wentwthvle....276 H14
SHEEHY
st. Glebe..............12 A7
SHEENS
la. Penrith...........205 F16
SHEFFIELD
st. Auburn...........339 A1
st. Kingsgrove.....401 J9
st. Merrylands.....307 G11
SHEILA
pl. Kellyville.........216 F6
SHELBY
rd. St Ives Ch.......223 K5

SHELDON
pl. Bellevue Hill 14 J8
SHELL
rd. Burraneer 493 E15
SHELLBANK
av. Mosman 316 H2
pde. Cremorne 316 G3
SHELLCOTE
rd. Greenacre 370 C6
SHELLCOVE
rd. Neutral Bay 6 H5
SHELLEY
cr. Blacktown 273 G6
pl. Wetherill Pk 334 K6
rd. N Turramrra 223 E8
rd. Wallacia 324 J13
st. Campbelltwn 512 B3
st. Campsie 372 A10
st. Enfield 371 H3
st. Winston Hills 277 F2
SHELLEYS
la. Thirlmere 561 G15
la. Marrickville, off Llewellyn St 374 F10
SHELLY
cr. Kellyville 185 J16
SHELSLEY
pl. S Penrith 267 A7
SHELTON
av. Winmalee 173 E6
la. Richmond 119 A5
SHENSTONE
rd. Riverwood 429 J1
SHENTON
av. Bankstown 399 B4
SHE-OAK
gr. Narellan Vale 478 J14
SHEOAK
cl. Cherrybrook 219 G11
pl. Alfords Point 459 A2
pl. Bossley Park 333 G8
pl. Colyton 270 J6
pl. Glenmore Pk 265 H11
SHEPHARD
st. Marayong 244 D7
SHEPHERD
av. Padstow Ht 429 G7
la. Ashfield 372 G5
la. Baulkham Hl 248 A7
la. Chippendale 18 J2
la. Darlington 18 J5
pde. Bardwell Vy 403 B8
rd. Artarmon 285 A13
st. Ashfield 372 G5
st. Chippendale 18 J3
st. Colyton 270 E8
st. Darlington 18 H6
st. Kurnell 466 B9
st. Lalor Park 245 D10
st. Liverpool 395 D8
st. Maroubra 406 K8
st. Marrickville 374 B10
st. Ryde 311 H2
st. St Marys 269 K7
SHEPHERDS
dr. Cherrybrook 219 E10
rd. Freemns Rch 60 B15
rd. Freemns Rch 90 B2
SHEPPARD
la. Emu Plains, off Sheppard Rd 235 J9
rd. Emu Plains 235 H11
rd. Narraweena 258 D4
SHER
pl. Prospect 275 A11
SHERACK
pl. Minto 453 A14
SHERARS
av. Strathfield 341 H16
SHERBORNE
pl. Glendenning 242 G2
SHERBROOK
rd. Asquith 192 A12
rd. Hornsby 221 K1
SHERBROOKE
av. Double Bay 14 F7
rd. West Ryde 311 D2
st. Darlinghurst 4 D11
st. Rooty Hill 242 A16
SHEREDAN
rd. Castlereagh 176 D11
SHERIDAN
cl. Milperra 398 A7
pl. Manly 288 F7
st. Granville 308 F16
wy. Mt Annan 479 E16
SHERIFF
st. Ashcroft 394 D1
SHERLOCK
av. Panania 428 A1
SHERMAN
st. Greenacre 370 B5
SHERRIDON
cr. Quakers Hill 214 C16
SHERRINGHAM
la. Cranebrook, off Sherringham Rd 207 E13
la. Cranebrook, off Sherringham Rd 207 F13
rd. Cranebrook 207 D12
SHERRITT
pl. Prairiewood 334 H8
SHERRY
pl. Minchinbury 271 G7
st. Mona Vale 199 B5
SHERWIN
av. Castle Hill 217 K14
st. Henley 313 B15
wy. Minto 482 J6
SHERWOOD
av. Springwood 201 F2
av. Yowie Bay 492 B11
cct. Penrith 237 D10
cl. Pennant Hills 250 E2
cr. Narraweena 258 C2
ct. Carlingford 249 E13
la. Penrith, off Sherwood Cct 237 D10
pl. North Ryde 282 J14
pl. St Ives 254 A2
rd. Merrylnds W 306 K14
st. Kensington 376 C12
st. Kurrajong 85 D3
st. Old Tngabbie 277 D9
st. Revesby 398 G13
SHETLAND
rd. Blairmount 481 A13
SHIEL
pl. St Andrews 452 B13
SHIELDS
la. Pennant Hills 220 H15
rd. Colyton 270 F7
st. Marayong 244 C3
SHIELS
ct. Glenmore Pk 265 E10
SHIERS
av. Mascot 404 J6
SHINFIELD
av. St Ives 223 J13
SHINNICK
dr. Oakhurst 241 H4
SHIPHAM
st. Concord 342 A3
SHIPLEY
av. N Strathfield 341 F6
SHIPROCK
rd. Port Hacking 523 A3
SHIPTON
pl. Dean Park 242 F1
SHIPWAY
st. Marsfield 251 J14
SHIPWRIGHT
pl. Oyster Bay 461 A6
SHIRAZ
cl. Edensor Pk 363 E1
pl. Eschol Park 481 D2
pl. Minchinbury 271 K7
SHIRLEY
av. Roselands 400 J10
cl. Narraweena 258 E3
cr. Matraville 436 J4
la. Wollstncraft 315 D9
la. Campsie, off Canterbury Rd 372 A16
la. Matraville, off Jordons La 436 J3
rd. Crows Nest 315 E8
rd. Miranda 462 G16
rd. Roseville 284 C7
rd. Wollstncraft 315 B11
rd. Wollstncraft 315 E8
st. Alexandria 375 F15
st. Bexley 432 G1
st. Blacktown 245 A15
st. Carlingford 279 K3
st. Epping 250 D16
st. Padstow 429 A1
st. Rosehill 309 B9
SHIRLEY STRICKLAND
av. Homebush B M J6
av. Homebush B 340 H4
SHIRLOW
st. Marrickville 374 D13
SHOAL
pl. Illawong 459 C5
SHOALHAVEN
rd. Sylvania Wtr 462 C11
st. Homebush B M C6
st. Ruse 512 D6
st. Wakeley 334 K12
SHOEMAKER
pl. Bonnyrigg 364 C6
SHOEMARK
pl. Narellan 478 F15
SHOPLANDS
rd. Annangrove 155 F4
SHORE
br. Avalon 139 H10
cl. Illawong 459 C3
st. Warwck Frm 366 A16
SHOREHAM
cr. Chipping Ntn 366 G15
SHORLAND
av. Jannali 460 K13
SHORT
av. Bundeena 523 G9
la. Woollahra, off Fletcher St 377 G2
la. Rose Bay, off Hamilton St 348 C11
la. Neutral Bay, off Military Rd 316 B8
la. Emu Plains, off Short St 235 E9
la. S Hurstville, off Short St 432 B11
pl. Surry Hills 4 D15
rd. Riverwood 400 A16
st. Auburn 309 B13
st. Balmain 7 F7
st. Banksia 403 F12
st. Bankstown 399 G8
st. Birchgrove 7 F7
st. Blaxland 233 G8
st. Brookvale 258 B13
st. Campbelltwn 511 E3
st. Canterbury 372 D16
st. Carlton 432 H5
st. Chatswood 285 D5
st. Croydon 342 F11
st. Double Bay 14 C9
st. Drummoyne 343 F3
st. Dulwich Hill 373 E7
st. Emu Plains 235 E9
st. Enfield 371 H4
st. Enmore 16 J16
st. Enmore 374 F9
st. Forest Lodge 17 J1
st. Gladesville 313 A5
st. Heathcote 518 E13
st. Hunters Hill 313 D10
st. Hurlstone Pk 373 A11
st. Kogarah 433 C6
st. Leichhardt 9 K15
st. Lidcombe 339 J6
st. Lindfield 254 F16
st. Liverpool 395 C5
st. Manly 288 H9
st. Mosman 316 K6
st. North Manly 258 B13
st. N St Marys 239 J8
st. N Sydney 5 D8
st. Oatley 430 H11
st. Oyster Bay 461 B9
st. Paddington 4 F16
st. Parramatta 278 F15
st. Randwick 377 B14
st. Redfern 19 D6
st. Rooty Hill 242 C15
st. Rosehill 308 J8
st. St Peters 374 J12
st. S Hurstville 432 B11
st. Springwood 201 G4
st. Summer Hill 373 B4
st. Surry Hills 4 D14
st. Tahmoor 565 G12
st. Thornleigh 221 A15
st. Waterloo 19 F16
st. Watsons Bay 318 F13
st. Waverley 377 F7
st. Wentwthvle 277 B15
st. Woolooware 493 E8
st.e, Homebush 341 C7
st.w, Homebush 341 B8
SHORTER
av. Beverly Hills 400 G10
av. Narwee 400 G10
la. Darlinghurst 4 E10
la. Narwee 400 H10
la. Roselands 400 H10
SHORTLAND
av. Lurnea 394 B12
av. Strathfield 341 A12
cl. N Richmond 87 F15
pl. Doonside 273 E2
pl. Ruse 512 H5
st. Canley Vale 366 E4
st. Lidcombe 339 J6
st. Telopea 279 G10
st. Wrrngtn Cty 238 G8
SHOULTS
la. Padstow 399 E16
SHOWFREIGHT
wy. Berala 339 D14
SHOWGROUND
rd. Castle Hill 217 J13
rd. Homebush B M D8
rd. Homebush B 340 G1
SHRIKE
gln. Erskine Park 270 K11
pl. Ingleburn 453 H6
SHROPSHIRE
cl. Wakeley 334 K16
st. Miller 393 G3
SHUTE
wy. Casula 424 E3
SHUTTLEWORTH
av. Raby 451 F13
SIANDRA
av. Fairfield 336 D5
av. Shalvey 210 H14
dr. Kareela 461 B11
SIBBICK
st. Chiswick 343 C6
st. Russell Lea 343 C6
SIBELIUS
cl. Seven Hills 246 E12
SIBLEY
cl. Abbotsbury 333 C11
SICILIA
st. Prestons 393 F14
SICKLES
dr. Grasmere 475 J15
SIDDELEY
pl. Raby 451 F16
SIDDINS
av. Pagewood 406 F7
SIDNEY
cl. Quakers Hill 213 K7
pl. Casula 424 E3
SIDON
pl. Mt Pritchard 364 H15
SIDWELL
av. Shalvey 210 J14
SIEBEL
st. Blacktown 243 K11
SIEMENS
cr. Emerton 240 J3
SIENA
cl. Prestons 393 D13
SIENNA
gr. Woodcroft 243 F6
SIERRA
pl. Baulkham Hl 246 F14
pl. Seven Hills 275 B10
rd. Engadine 488 C12
SIGLINGEN
st. Emerton 240 J7
SIKES
pl. Ambarvale 510 H12
SILAS
wy. Ambarvale 511 A16
SILDOR
ct. Kenthurst 188 A1
SILEX
rd. Mosman 317 C12
SILICA
cr. Eagle Vale 481 B8
rd. Bargo 567 E15
rd. Yanderra 567 E15
SILKS
la. N Richmond 87 A1
rd. Kurmond 56 K16
SILKWOOD
gr. Quakers Hill 214 D14
SILKY
cl. Bossley Park 333 E8
SILKY OAK
pl. Castle Hill 248 E4
SILKY-OAK
gr. Elderslie 507 F2
SILKYOAK
gr. Greenacre 370 G6
pl. Glenwood 245 H1
SILLOT
pl. Narellan Vale 508 H1
SILLWOOD
pl. West Hoxton 392 A12
SILVA
rd. Springwood 202 A2
st. Tamarama 378 B6
SILVER
cr. Westleigh 220 G3
la. St Peters 374 H14
la. Marrickville, off Calvert St 373 K13
st. Marrickville 374 A12
st. Randwick 376 K13
st. St Peters 374 G13
st. Silverwater L D16
st. Silverwater 309 K9
SILVER BEACH
rd. Kurnell 466 A8
SILVERBURN
av. Richmond 118 A6
SILVERDALE
rd. Silverdale 353 F16
rd. The Oaks 502 G7
rd. Wallacia 324 A15
rd. Warragamba 324 A15
rd. Warragamba 353 K10
rd. Warragamba 354 A1
SILVEREYE
cl. Glenmore Pk 265 H13
ct. Woronora Ht 489 C3
pl. Hinchinbrk 363 F15
SILVERFERN
cr. W Pnnant Hl 248 K2
SILVERLEAF
row. Menai 458 J15
SILVER MIST
cr. Castle Hill, off Barker Dr 218 J13
SILVERTON
st. Glenwood 215 F16
SILVERTOP
cl. Glenwood 245 H1
cl. Westleigh 220 F7
SILVERWATER
cr. Lansvale 366 E10
cr. Miranda 462 B16
rd. Auburn 309 H16
rd. Dundas 280 A15
rd. Ermington 280 A15
rd. Rydalmere 309 K10
rd. Silverwater L D15
rd. Silverwater 309 K10
SILVERWOOD
av. Luddenham 356 A6
rd. Brownlow Hl 475 E11
SILVIA
st. Hornsby 191 G13
SIMBLIST
rd. Port Botany 436 B11
SIMEON
pl. Liberty Gr 311 B11
rd. Orchard Hills 267 D8
st. Clovelly 377 G10
SIMEON PEARCE
dr. Randwick, off Easy St 377 A16
SIMLA
rd. Denistone 281 B12
st. Lidcombe 340 B4
SIMMAT
av. Condell Park 398 F6
SIMMONDS
la. Avalon 170 B2
pl. W Pnnant Hl 249 A6
st. Kings Lngly 246 A9
SIMMONS
rd. Kingsgrove 401 J13
st. Balmain East 8 F7
st. Enmore 17 C14
st. Enmore 17 C16
st. Newtown 17 C14
st. Revesby 398 J15
st. Warwck Frm 365 F13
SIMMS
rd. Glendenning 242 D2
rd. Oakhurst 242 D2

SIMON
av. Bonnyrigg 364 A8
cl. Illawong 459 D7
pl. Hornsby Ht 191 E8
st. Winston Hills 246 G15
wk. Pagewood 406 A11
SIMONE
cr. Casula 394 G14
cr. Strathfield 341 A11
pl. Peakhurst 430 C4
SIMPSON
av. Baulkham Hl 247 C13
av. Burwood 342 B13
av. Casula 394 G13
cl. Narrabeen 228 G8
la. Lidcombe 339 F9
pl. Kings Lngly 245 D4
pl. Leumeah 482 H11
rd. Bonnyrigg Ht 363 E5
rd. Bundeena 523 G9
st. Artarmon 315 A1
st. Auburn 339 F1
st. Bondi 377 K2
st. Bondi Beach 377 K2
st. Dundas Vy 279 J10
st. Greystanes 306 B9
st. Mosman 317 A13
st. Northmead 278 A1
st. Ryde 311 J4
SIMPSON HILL
rd. Mount Druitt 270 J3
SIMS
gr. Maroubra 407 D13
la. Maroubra 407 D13
pl. St Johns Pk 364 J2
st. Darlinghurst 4 F14
SINAI
av. Milperra 397 H10
SINCLAIR
av. Blacktown 274 K4
av. Thornleigh 220 K11
rd. Ashcroft 394 E1
st. Wollstncraft 5 B1
SINDEL
cl. Bonnyrigg 363 K7
st. West Ryde 280 J13
SINDONE
pl. Caringbah 492 J3
SINFIELD
st. Ermington 280 B15
SINGER
pl. Ingleburn 453 J8
SINGH
la. Chester Hill 368 C2
SINGLE
la. S Penrith, off Single Rd 267 B4
rd. S Penrith 267 A4
SINGLE RIDGE
rd. The Slopes 56 E8
SINGLES RIDGE
rd. Winmalee 173 A12
rd. Yellow Rock 203 G1
SINGLETON
av. East Hills 428 A3
av. Wrrngtn Cty 238 E5
pl. Kirrawee 491 B7
rd. Wilberforce 91 J3
st. Earlwood 402 F5
st. Horngsea Pk 392 D14
SINNOTT
st. Villawood 336 K16
SIOBHAN
pl. Mona Vale 198 J2
SIOUX
cl. Greenfld Pk 334 A15
SIOVI
rd. Londonderry 177 J12
SIR BERTRAM STEVENS
dr. Royal N P 520 E7
SIR HENRYS
pde. Faulconbdg 201 A1
pde. Springwood 201 A1
SIRIUS
av. Mosman 316 K12
cct. Narellan 478 E15
pde. Beacon Hill 257 G3
pl. Berkshire Pk 179 H14
pl. Engadine 488 D12
pl. Kellyville 215 H3
pl. Riverwood 400 C13
rd. Bligh Park 150 D5
rd. Lane Cove W 283 F16
rd. Voyager Pt 427 D4
rd. Voyager Pt 427 C6
st. Cremorne Pt 316 F13
st. Dundas Vy 280 C8
st. Fairfield W 335 B10
st. Ruse 512 H4
SIRIUS COVE
rd. Mosman 317 A12
SIR JOHN JAMISON
cct. Glenmore Pk 265 D9
SIR JOHN YOUNG
cr. Sydney 4 D5
cr. Woolmloo 4 D5
SIR JOSEPH BANKS
dr. Kurnell 465 J12
st. Bankstown 369 G14
st. Botany 405 G15
SIROIS
st. Toongabbie 276 J5
SIR REGINALD ANSETT
dr. Mascot 405 A7
SIR THOMAS MITCHELL
dr. Davidson 255 B1
rd. Bondi Beach 378 B3
rd. Chester Hill 367 K3
rd. Villawood 367 K3
SISKIN
st. Quakers Hill 214 E11
SISTERS
cr. Drummoyne 343 K4
la. Edgecliff 14 A13
SITAR
pl. Plumpton 241 H9
SITELLA
pl. Ingleburn 453 D9
SITTELLA
pl. Glenmore Pk 265 J12
SIWA
st. Holsworthy 426 F7
SIWARD
pl. Rsemeadow 540 D4
SIXTEENTH
av. Austral 391 F2
av.e, West Hoxton 391 K2
SIXTH
av. Austral 391 A14
av. Berala 339 D15
av. Campsie 371 K10
av. Condell Park 398 E5
av. Denistone 281 D11
av. Jannali 460 K9
av. Llandilo 208 C3
av. Loftus 489 K7
av. Seven Hills 275 J3
av. West Hoxton 391 F14
rd. Berkshire Pk 179 H6
st. Granville 308 G15
st. Mascot 404 K7
st. Warragamba 353 G5
SIXTH MILE
la. Roseville 284 G4
SKAIN
pl. Horngsea Pk 392 C13
SKARRATT
av. Glenbrook 233 J13
st,n, Silverwater 309 E12
st,s, Auburn 309 D14
SKATE
st. Cranebrook 207 A10
SKELTON
st. Leichhardt 16 C1
SKENE
pl. Belrose 225 K9
SKENES
av. Eastwood 280 G6
SKERRETT
la. Doonside 243 C13
SKILLCORN
av. Jannali 460 G9
SKINNER
av. Riverwood 400 F10
pde. Roseville 284 J1
SKINNERS
av. Dolls Point 463 H1
SKIPTON
la. Prestons 393 H15
SKONE
st. Condell Park 398 J6
SKYE
cl. Merrylnds W 306 K13
ct. Kellyville 216 K1
pl. Engadine 488 J12
pl. Prospect 274 G10
pl. St Andrews 481 K2
pl. Winston Hills 277 B3
SKYFARMER
pl. Raby 481 F2
SKYHAWK
av. Raby 481 F1
SKYLARK
cct. Bella Vista 246 F1
cr. Erskine Park 270 H14
SKYLINE
pl. Frenchs Frst 256 J5
st. Greenacre 370 H13
SKYROS
la. Emu Heights, off Skyros Pl 235 B4
pl. Emu Heights 235 B5
SLADDEN
rd. Engadine 489 B15
SLADE
av. Castle Hill 218 J13
av. Lindfield 254 F14
la. Bardwell Pk 402 H7
pl. Prospect 274 G12
rd. Bardwell Pk 402 F8
rd. Bexley North 402 F8
rd. Ingleside 196 G11
st. Narellan 478 H9
st. Naremburn 315 G3
st. Rozelle 7 A12
SLADES
rd. Couridjah 564 E10
SLAPP
st. Merrylands 307 E8
SLATER
rd. Ingleburn 452 J8
SLATTERY
pl. Eastlakes 406 B2
wy. Eastlakes 406 C3
SLAVIN
st. S Penrith 267 D6
SLEIGH
pl. Wetherill Pk 303 H15
SLENDER
av. Smithfield 335 J8
SLESSOR
pl. Blackett 241 C3
pl. Heathcote 518 D14
rd. Casula 424 F5
SLIGAR
av. Hamondvle 396 E16
SLIGO
cl. Killarney Ht 255 J14
SLIM
pl. Cabramatta 365 D11
pl. Wentwthvle 277 A12
SLIP
st. Sydney C C3
st. Sydney 3 D2
SLOANE
cr. Allambie Ht 287 J1
cr. Manly Vale 287 J1
la. Marrickville 374 D13
st. Haberfield 373 D3
st. Marrickville 374 D13
st. Newtown 17 D15
st. Summer Hill 373 D3
SLOOP
st. Seven Hills 275 B5
SLOPER
av. Richmond 118 F8
SLOPES
rd. Comleroy 56 F7
rd. Kurmond 57 A12
rd. N Richmond 87 C6
rd. The Slopes 56 F7
SLOUGH
av. Silverwater 309 K11
SLUMAN
st. Denistone W 281 A11
SMAIL
la. Ultimo 12 J15
st. Ultimo 12 J15
SMALL
cr. Glenmore Pk 265 F7
la. Petersham 15 G11
la. Woollahra, off Fletcher St 377 F2
rd. Illawong 459 D4
st. Marayong 244 D4
st. Northbridge 285 F16
st. Ryde 311 J4
st. Willoughby 285 F16
st. Woollahra 377 F2
SMALLS
pl. Kellyville 185 H7
rd. Arcadia 129 J16
rd. Brownlow Hl 475 G15
rd. Grasmere 475 G15
rd. Ryde 282 B11
SMALLWOOD
av. Homebush 341 A8
rd. Glenorie 96 E3
rd. McGraths Hl 121 K13
SMART
av. Camden S 507 B15
cl. Minto 482 K4
st. Fairfield 336 E10
st. Fairfield Ht 336 B9
SMARTS
cr. Burraneer 493 F14
SMEATON GRANGE
rd. Smeaton Gra 479 A8
SMEE
av. Roselands 400 F8
SMEETON
rd. Londonderry 177 A9
SMERDON
pl. Kenthurst 126 G15
SMIDMORE
st. Marrickville 374 F11
SMIKE
pl. Ambarvale 510 H16
SMITH
av. Allambie Ht 257 J14
av. Hurlstone Pk 373 A14
av. Richmond 118 E10
cr. Liverpool 394 J5
gr. Shalvey 211 C13
la. Newtown 17 F14
la. Five Dock, off Ramsay Rd 342 K11
pl. Mt Annan 509 D1
rd. Artarmon 285 B14
rd. Castlereagh 175 G6
rd. Oakville 122 J14
st. Annandale 10 J11
st. Balmain 7 E13
st. Bexley 402 J13
st. Chatswood 285 E5
st. Eastgardens 406 F13
st. Emu Plains 235 J6
st. Epping 251 C16
st. Granville 308 D10
st. Hillsdale 406 F13
st. Kentlyn 513 B6
st. Kingsford 406 K6
st. Kingswood 267 E1
st. Lindfield 254 E15
st. Manly 288 G6
st. Marrickville 374 D10
st. Parramatta 308 D4
st. Pendle Hill 306 E1
st. Regents Pk 369 E2
st. Rozelle 7 E13
st. Ryde 282 B16
st. St Marys 269 D3
st. S Penrith 237 A16
st. Summer Hill 373 B4
st. Surry Hills F F11
st. Surry Hills 4 A14
st. Taren Point 462 J12
st. Tempe 404 C2
st. Wentwthvle 306 E1
st. Woollahra 21 H4
st. Yagoona 368 E10
SMITHERS
st. Chippendale 19 A2
SMITHFIELD
av. Coogee 377 G15
rd. Edensor Pk 363 J4
rd. Fairfield W 335 A9
rd. Greenfld Pk 334 C15
rd. Prairiewood 335 A9
rd. Smithfield 335 F7
rd. Wakeley 334 C15
SMITHS
av. Cabramatta 365 C10
av. Hurstville 401 J15
la. Freemns Rch 90 J3
la. Glenorie 127 E14
la. Erskineville, off Victoria St 374 K9
SMITHYS
pl. Richmond 118 F12
SMOOTHY
pl. Arndell Park 273 H10
SMYTHE
st. Merrylands 307 K13
SMYTHES
st. Concord 342 A3
SNAILHAM
cr. S Windsor 150 J1
SNAKE GULLEY
cl. Narrabeen 228 E8
SNAPE
st. Kingsford 406 H6
st. Maroubra 406 H6
SNAPPER
cl. Green Valley 362 K12
SNAPPERMAN
la. Palm Beach, off Iluka Rd 139 J3
SNELL
pl. West Hoxton 392 B12
SNIPE
cl. Hinchinbrk 363 E15
pl. Ingleburn 453 H7
wy. Mt Annan 479 B15
SNOWBIRD
la. Erskine Park, off Snowbird Pl 300 K1
la. Erskine Park, off Snowbird Pl 301 A1
pl. Erskine Park 301 A1
SNOWDEN
av. Sylvania 461 K10
cl. Cecil Hills 362 F3
pl. St Ives Ch 224 C1
st. Jamisontown 266 B1
SNOWDON
av. Carlingford 279 B4
cr. Smithfield 335 D1
SNOWDRIFT
ct. St Clair 270 D13
SNOW GUM
pl. Alfords Point 429 C12
SNOWSILL
av. Revesby 399 B9
SNOWY
cl. St Clair 269 H15
pl. Heckenberg 364 A12
pl. Sylvania Wtr 462 D10
st. Seven Hills 275 E10
SNOWY BAKER
av. Newington M B15
av. Newington 310 A15
SNUG
pl. West Hoxton 392 E8
SNUGGLEPOT
dr. Faulconbdg 171 D15
SOBRAON
rd. Marsfield 282 A4
SODBURY
st. Chipping Ntn 396 F2
SOFA
st. Marayong 244 B6
SOFALA
av. Riverview 314 A4
st. Riverwood 400 B11
SOL
pl. Rooty Hill 272 A2
SOLANDER
av. West Hoxton 392 B13
cl. Turramurra 252 D4
dr. St Clair 269 F13
la. Daceyville, off Cook Av 406 F3
pl. Mt Annan 509 G3
rd. Daceyville 406 F3
rd. Kings Lngly 245 K9
st. Kurnell 466 A9
st. Matraville 436 G1
st. Monterey 433 H6
st. Ruse 512 H3
SOLAR
av. Baulkham Hl 246 F9
SOLARIS
dr. Doonside 243 H16
SOLDIERS
av. Harbord 258 D16
pl. Woodbine 481 K10
rd. Jannali 460 F9
SOLENT
cct. Baulkham Hl 216 F14
cct. Baulkham Hl 216 F16
SOLERO
pl. Eschol Park 481 B4
SOLING
cr. Cranebrook 207 A9
SOLITAIRE
ct. Stanhpe Gdn 215 B10
SOLITARY
pl. Ruse 512 H7

SQUIRE
pl. Castle Hill 217 G6
st. Ryde 311 G2
SQUIRES
rd. Springwood 202 E10
STABLE SQUARE
pl. Richmond 118 F12
STABLE VIEW
pl. Narellan 478 B9
STACEY
rd. Castlereagh 176 F12
st. Bankstown 369 G10
st. Cronulla 523 J3
st. Fairfield W 335 G11
st. Greenacre 369 G10
st.s, Bankstown 399 G5
st.s, Punchbowl 399 G5
STACK
st. Balmain East 8 E8
st. Narrabeen 228 G8
STADDON
cl. St Ives 224 C6
STAFF
av. Glenwood 215 D14
STAFFORD
la. Paddington 13 C15
la. Stanmore 16 K9
pl. N Turramrra 223 G4
rd. Artarmon 285 A12
st. Cabramatta 365 C11
st. Double Bay 14 E7
st. Kingswood 237 E14
st. Minto 482 F2
st. Paddington 13 C15
st. Penrith 237 A13
st. S Granville 338 E8
st. Stanmore 16 K9
wy. Kellyville 216 A1
STAGG
pl. Ambarvale 510 F16
STAHLS
rd. Oakville 153 A2
STAINSBY
av. Kings Lngly 246 A9
cl. Turramurra 252 A2
STALEY
ct. W Pnnant Hl 249 C1
STALLION
gln. Glenwood 245 J4
STALWART
st. Prairiewood 334 J7
STAMFORD
av. Cabarita 342 D1
av. Ermington 280 D12
STAN
st. N Willghby 285 G10
STANBROOK
st. Fairfield Ht 335 K9
STANBURY
pl. Quakers Hill 214 A12
st. Gladesville 312 F8
STANDARD
wy. Minto 482 H7
STANDISH
av. Oakhurst 241 H3
STANFORD
cct. Rouse Hill 185 D4
wy. Airds 511 H15
STANHOPE
pky. Parklea 215 B8
pky. Stanhpe Gdn 215 B8
rd. Killara 254 A14
row. Bella Vista 246 G3
st. Auburn 338 J3
STANIER
cl. Cherrybrook 219 K7
STANLEA
pde. Wiley Park 400 G2
STANLEY
av. Kurrajong Ht 54 B12
av. Mosman 317 C5
av. W Pnnant Hl 249 G5
cl. St Ives 224 A12
la. Darlinghurst D K16
la. Darlinghurst 4 C8
la. Ermington 310 B2
la. Queens Park 22 H11
la. St Ives 224 A12
la. Stanmore 16 B9
la. Kogarah, off Regent St 433 C3
la. Arncliffe, off Stanley St 403 F9
pl. Illawong 459 H5
rd. Epping 251 E15
rd. Hunters Hill 313 H11
rd. Ingleburn 453 B7
rd. Lidcombe 339 F7
st. Arncliffe 403 F9
st. Bankstown 399 F2
st. Blacktown 274 G7
st. Burwood 341 J15
st. Campsie 372 A15
st. Chatswood 285 C11
st. Concord 342 A8
st. Croydon Pk 371 J7
st. Darlinghurst D G16
st. Darlinghurst 4 B8
st. Fairfield Ht 335 H12
st. Kogarah 433 C2
st. Leichhardt 10 B15
st. Marrickville 373 J11
st. Merrylands 307 C10
st. Mona Vale 199 G3
st. Newport 169 K12
st. Peakhurst 430 F4
st. Putney 312 B9
st. Queens Park 22 G11
st. Randwick 377 B10
st. Redfern 20 C9
st. St Ives 224 A12
st. St Marys 269 H5
st. Shanes Park 209 K1
st. Silverwater 309 J13
st. Stanmore 16 B9
st. Tempe 404 B2
st. Woollahra 22 E3
STANMORE
la. Stanmore 16 G8
rd. Enmore 16 B12
rd. Petersham 16 B12
rd. Stanmore 16 B12
STANNARDS
pl. N Sydney 6 D13
STANNIX PARK
rd. Ebenezer 62 D3
rd. Wilberforce 61 F4
STANNUM
cl. Hinchinbrk 392 H5
STANSBURY
st. Emu Plains 235 E11
STANSELL
av. Jannali 460 J10
st. Gladesville 312 J8
STANTON
dr. W Pnnant Hl 249 C9
la. Mosman, off Spit Rd 317 B3
pl. Emu Plains 236 B6
rd. Haberfield 373 D1
rd. Mosman 317 B3
rd. Mosman 317 E3
rd. Seven Hills 246 B15
st. Liverpool 394 H3
STANWAY
av. Springwood 201 E4
STANWELL
cr. Ashcroft 394 E2
STAPLES
pl. Glenmore Pk 265 F8
st. Kingsgrove 402 B10
STAPLETON
av. Sutherland 490 F2
la. St Marys, off Stapleton Pde 239 J16
pde. St Marys 269 J1
pl. Pymble 223 G16
st. Pendle Hill 276 E14
st. Wentwthvle 276 E14
STAPLEY
st. Kingswood 237 E16
STAPYLTON
st. Winmalee 173 D5
STAR
cr. Pennant Hills 220 B15
cr. W Pnnant Hl 220 B15
ct. Cmbrdg Gdn 237 F4
la. Rooty Hill 272 B2
st. Eastwood 281 H6
st. Picton 563 C9
STARFIGHTER
av. Raby 481 F1
STARK
st. Coogee 377 D16
STARKEY
dr. Bnkstn Aprt 397 F5
st. Forestville 256 A13
st. Hurlstone Pk 373 B13
st. Killarney Ht 256 A14
STARLEAF
wy. Mcquarie Fd 454 H3
STARLIGHT
pl. Kellyville 186 B16
pl. Richmond 118 D5
pl. St Clair 270 C13
STARLING
st. Green Valley 363 F12
st. Lilyfield 10 G10
st. Rozelle 7 C15
STARR
av. Padstow 429 E5
cl. Camden 507 A9
pl. Blacktown 274 A5
STARTOP
pl. Ambarvale 510 J14
STATHAM
av. Faulconbdg 171 C16
av. North Rocks 278 K2
st. Belfield 371 G11
STATION
av. Concord W 341 C1
la. Hurstville 432 E7
la. Narwee 400 J13
la. Newtown 17 E14
la. Penrith 236 G11
la. Wahroonga, off Coonabarra Rd 222 D7
la. Penshurst, off The Strand 431 F6
pl. Eveleigh 18 E12
rd. Auburn 309 F16
rd. Belmore 371 C16
rd. Menangle Pk 539 A5
rd. Seven Hills 245 K15
rd. Toongabbie 276 A2
st. Arncliffe 403 E9
st. Ashfield 372 J2
st. Blaxland 233 F7
st. Camden 477 B15
st. Concord 341 G6
st. Couridjah 564 E15
st. Dundas 279 D14
st. Engadine 518 J2
st. Fairfield 335 K10
st. Fairfield Ht 335 K10
st. Glenbrook 263 K2
st. Guildford 337 G6
st. Homebush 341 D9
st. Hornsby 221 G1
st. Kogarah 433 B4
st. Marrickville 373 J14
st. Menangle 538 H16
st. Mortdale 431 A7
st. Naremburn 315 C1
st. Newtown 17 D12
st. Newtown 17 F15
st. Penrith 236 H10
st. Petersham 15 E6
st. Picton 563 G8
st. Pymble 253 E2
st. Regents Pk 368 K1
st. Rooty Hill 242 D16
st. St Marys 239 H14
st. Schofields 183 C15
st. S Wntwthvle 307 A3
st. Thirlmere 564 H9
st. Thirlmere 565 A6
st. Thornleigh 221 A14
st. Warwck Frm 365 H14
st. Wentwthvle 307 A3
st. West Ryde 281 C16
st. Springwood, off Jerseywold Av 201 J3
st.e, Harris Park 308 D4
st.e, Parramatta 308 D4
st.e, Tempe 404 B3
st.s, Emu Plains 235 K7
st.w, Harris Park 308 D7
st.w, Tempe 404 A3
STAUNER
pl. Quakers Hill 213 H13
STEAD
cl. Edensor Pk 363 H2
pl. Casula 424 F5
STEAMER
pl. Currans Hill 480 A12
STEDHAM
gr. Oakhurst 241 J4
STEEL
la. Surry Hills 19 K3
st. Blacktown 244 H10
st. S Granville 338 E7
st. Surry Hills 19 K3
STEELE
av. Revesby Ht 428 K8
pl. Bligh Park 150 F5
pl. Bonnyrigg 364 A6
st. Mays Hill 307 K6
st. Parramatta 307 K6
STEEPLE
wy. Narellan 478 B10
STEERFORTH
wy. Ambarvale 510 K16
wy. Ambarvale 511 A16
STEFAN
la. Doonside 243 C12
STEFANIE
pl. Bonnyrigg 364 A11
STEFIE
pl. Kings Lngly 245 G8
STEIN
pl. Cecil Hills 362 K5
pl. Glenmore Pk 265 F8
STEINTON
st. Manly 288 H8
STELLA
cl. East Killara 254 E6
dr. Green Valley 362 K9
pl. Blacktown 274 F8
st. Collaroy Plat 228 J12
st. Fairfield Ht 335 H12
STENHOUSE
dr. Mt Annan 509 F2
STENNETT
rd. Ingleburn 452 E9
STEPHANIE
la. Belmore 371 G16
la. Belmore 401 G1
pl. Bella Vista 246 F5
pl. N Turramrra 223 G5
st. Padstow 399 E15
STEPHANO
pl. Rsemeadow 540 C3
STEPHEN
av. Matraville 436 G9
av. Ryde 281 K11
cl. Castle Hill 218 F16
la. Paddington 13 C12
la. Randwick 377 B10
pl. Roselands 401 B9
rd. Botany 405 K12
rd. Engadine 518 G6
st. Balmain 8 A10
st. Beacon Hill 257 E7
st. Blacktown 245 A10
st. Bondi 377 J5
st. Chatswood 285 C12
st. Hornsby 191 J13
st. Newtown 17 K9
st. N Richmond 87 B14
st. Paddington 13 B13
st. Penshurst 431 A2
st. Randwick 377 B10
st. Woolmloo 4 G5
STEPHENS
la. Padstow 399 E16
STEPHENSON
pl. Currans Hill 479 J14
st. Birrong 368 J4
st. Leumeah 512 D1
st. Roselands 400 J6
st. Winston Hills 277 E5
STERLAND
av. North Manly 258 A14
STERLING
rd. Minchinbury 271 C6
STERLINI
pl. Blacktown 274 D10
STERN
pl. Roselands 400 K7
STEVEN
pl. Vineyard 152 A2
STEVENAGE
rd. Canley Ht 365 B3
rd. Hebersham 241 E5
STEVENS
av. Miranda 491 K1
cr. Smithfield 336 C5
la. Marrickville, off Philpott St 374 D9
rd. Glenorie 128 G2
rd. Ingleburn 422 J11
st. East Hills 428 A2
st. Ermington 310 C1
st. Panania 428 A2
st. Pennant Hills 220 G14
STEVENSON
st. Lane Cove 314 F6
st. S Penrith 266 K1
st. S Penrith 267 A1
st. Wetherill Pk 334 G4
STEVEYS FOREST
rd. Oakdale 499 H7
STEWARD
st. Lilyfield 9 K7
STEWART
av. Blacktown 244 E12
av. Curl Curl 258 H12
av. Hamondvle 396 F15
av. Hornsby 191 E11
av. Mcquarie Pk 283 B7
av. Matraville 406 J16
av. Peakhurst 430 B3
cl. Cheltenham 251 A11
dr. Castle Hill 248 C2
la. Bankstown 399 E1
la. Sydenham, off Park Rd 374 E16
pl. Balmain 7 E10
pl. Glenmore Pk 265 J7
pl. Paddington 21 D4
pl. Strathfield 341 E12
pwy. Hamondvle, off Stewart Av 396 G16
st. Arncliffe 403 D9
st. Artarmon 285 A13
st. Balmain 7 E11
st. Campbelltwn 511 G7
st. Eastwood 280 K10
st. Ermington 280 C11
st. Glebe 11 J7
st. Harringtn Pk 478 G8
st. North Bondi 348 D14
st. Paddington 21 B2
st. Paddington 21 D3
st. Parramatta 308 F2
st. Randwick 407 C1
st. S Windsor 150 H3
STEWARTS
la. Wilberforce 61 D10
STILES
av. Padstow 399 B9
st. Croydon Pk 371 H6
STILL
cl. Arcadia 129 J10
STILLER
pl. Greenacre 369 J12
STILT
av. Cranebrook 207 H10
cl. Hinchinbrk 363 D16
STILTON
la. Picton 563 C16
STIMPSON
cr. Grasmere 505 J3
STIMSON
st. Guildford 337 D3
st. Smithfield 336 A6
STINGRAY
cl. Raby 451 C13
st. Cranebrook 207 B10
STINSON
cr. Bnkstn Aprt 367 J16
la. Marrickville, off Warren Rd 373 J15
pl. Forestville 256 A7
STIPA
pl. Mt Annan 509 D3
STIRGESS
av. Curl Curl 258 G12
STIRLING
av. Kirrawee 461 A15
av. North Rocks 248 J16
ct. Castle Hill 219 A11
la. Chatswood 285 D8
la. Glebe 12 G13
pl. Belrose 225 K12
pl. Glenfield 424 E10
st. Cambrdg Pk 237 K9
st. Cecil Hills 362 E7
st. Glebe 12 G13
st. Redfern 19 D6
STOCK
av. Kingswood 237 H15
pl. Winston Hills 276 H1
STOCKADE
la. Emu Plains, off Stockade St 235 D10
pl. Woodcroft 243 E8
st. Emu Plains 235 D10

STOCKALLS
pl. Minto 452 K16
STOCKDALE
cr. Abbotsbury 333 C12
rd. Orchard Hills 298 C11
STOCK FARM
av. Bella Vista 246 F2
STOCKHOLM
av. Hassall Gr 211 H13
STOCKMAN
pl. Wrrngtn Dns 238 D5
rd. Currans Hill 479 K9
STOCKTON
av. Moorebank 396 C7
STOCKWOOD
st. S Penrith 266 G4
STODDART
pl. Dee Why 258 F3
rd. Prospect 275 A13
st. Roselands 400 K6
STOKE
av. Marrickville 373 H9
cr. S Penrith 266 G5
STOKES
av. Alexandria 375 E9
av. Asquith 192 B11
pl. Lindfield 254 B16
pwy. Springwood 201 H1
rd. Tahmoor 565 D15
st. Lane Cove W 284 F15
STOKOE
st. Warwck Frm 365 F14
STOLLE
cl. Menai 458 J7
st. Shalvey 210 K14
STONE
pde. Davidson 225 C14
pl. Wrrngtn Dns 238 C3
st. Earlwood 402 G2
st. Glendenning 242 F2
st. Lidcombe 339 E10
st. Meadowbnk 311 F2
tce. Kurrajong Hl 54 E13
STONE BRIDGE
dr. Glenbrook 234 B12
STONEBRIDGE
pl. Gymea Bay 491 C7
STONECROP
rd. N Turramrra 193 E15
STONEHAVEN
pde. Cabramatta 365 D11
pl. Castle Hill 218 A7
rd. Mt Colah 162 D14
STONELEA
ct. Dural 188 G13
STONE PINE
wy. Bella Vista 246 G4
STONEQUARRY
pl. Picton 563 F9
STONES
rd. Ebenezer 63 K1
STONEX
la. Turramurra 222 H14
STONEY CREEK
rd. Beverly Hills 401 C16
rd. Bexley 402 A14
rd. Kingsgrove 401 C16
rd. Narwee 430 J2
STONNY BATTER
rd. Minto 482 E7
STONY CREEK
rd. Shanes Park 209 K9
STOREY
av. West Hoxton 391 G13
st. Maroubra 406 J7
st. Ryde 311 J5
STORNOWAY
av. St Andrews 451 J15
STORY
pl. Quakers Hill 213 H15
STOTT
cl. Bonnyrigg 363 G8
STOTTS
av. Bardwell Pk 402 G8
STOULTON
wy. Cranebrook 207 G13
STOUT
rd. Mount Druitt 241 A15
STOW
cl. Edensor Pk 363 K2
pl. Illawong 459 G3
STOWE
ct. Wattle Grove 426 A5

STRABANE
av. Killarney Ht 256 C15
STRACHAN
ct. Kellyville 217 A2
la. Kingsford, off Houston Rd 406 F1
st. Kingsford 406 F1
STRADBROKE
av. Green Valley 363 A13
STRAITS
av. Guildford 338 E10
STRAND
arc. Sydney 3 G3
la. Penshurst 431 F6
STRANG
pl. Bligh Park 150 F6
pwy. Castle Hill 218 E14
STRANRAER
dr. St Andrews 481 K3
STRAPPER
cl. Casula 394 F16
STRASSMANN
cr. Lucas Ht 487 G12
STRATFORD
av. Denistone 281 E12
cl. Asquith 192 E10
dr. Belrose 225 K10
pl. St Ives 254 A3
rd. North Rocks 278 J2
rd. Tahmoor 565 H16
st. Cammeray 316 C4
STRATH
pl. Kenthurst 157 F5
STRATHALBYN
dr. Oatlands 278 H11
STRATHALLEN
av. Northbridge 315 K1
STRATHAM
pl. Belrose 225 K12
STRATHCARRON
av. Castle Hill 218 B7
STRATHDARR
st. Miller 393 F1
STRATHDON
cr. Blaxland 233 F12
la. Emu Heights, off Strathdon Rd 205 B15
rd. Emu Heights 205 A15
STRATHEDEN
av. Kellyville 185 J14
STRATHFIELD
av. Strathfield 341 F14
cl. St Johns Pk 364 G5
sq. Strathfield 341 G12
STRATHFILLAN
wy. Kellyville 186 K16
STRATHLORA
st. Strathfield 341 A16
STRATHMORE
la. Glebe 11 K7
pde. Chatswood 284 K6
pl. Glen Alpine 510 F13
STRATHWOOD
ct. Pymble 253 G2
STRATTON
cr. Milperra 397 D11
STRAUSS
cl. Bonnyrigg Ht 363 F5
pl. Seven Hills 246 E12
rd. St Clair 300 A2
STRAWBERRY
rd. Casula 424 E1
wy. Glenwood 215 F12
STREAM
st. Darlinghurst D K15
STREATFIELD
rd. Bellevue Hill 347 E16
STREBER
pl. Hornsby 191 D12
STREETON
av. Mt Pritchard 364 J12
pl. Plumpton 242 C8
STRETHAM
av. Picnic Point 428 G6
STRETTON
la. Illawong 460 A7
wy. Claymore 481 F11
STRIATA
wy. Mcquarie Fd 454 G4
STRICKLAND
av. Cromer 227 H13
av. Lindfield 284 E2
av. Maroubra 407 C15
cr. Ashcroft 364 D15
la. Lindfield, off Strickland Av 284 E3
la. St Clair, off Strickland Pl 270 G16
pl. Edensor Pk 363 C2
pl. Erskine Park 270 F16
pl. Wentwthvle 276 K14
rd. Guildford 338 C9
st. Bass Hill 368 B8
st. Heathcote 518 G11
st. Rose Bay 348 D11
STRICTA
pl. Oxford Falls 226 G16
STRINGER
pl. Oatlands 279 E12
rd. Kellyville 185 G2
STRINGYBARK
av. Cranebrook 237 E1
cl. Westleigh 220 F7
pl. Alfords Point 429 C12
pl. Bradbury 511 E10
pl. Castle Hill 248 G3
STROKER
st. Canley Ht 365 C1
STROMBOLI
pl. Bilgola 169 F3
STROMEFERRY
cr. St Andrews 481 J5
STROMLO
pl. Ruse 512 F4
st. Bossley Park 334 D9
STRONE
av. Wahroonga 221 K13
STRONG
pl. Richmond 119 A4
STROUD
pl. Belrose 226 B12
st. North Ryde 282 G13
st. Warwck Frm 365 K16
wy. Bonnyrigg 364 D5
STROUTHION
ct. Green Valley 363 F14
STRUAN
st. Tahmoor 566 A9
STRUEN MARIE
st. Kareela 461 C10
STRUTHERS
st. Cronulla 524 A1
STRZELECKI
cl. Wakeley 334 G15
STRZLECKI
dr. Horngsea Pk 392 E13
STUART
av. Normanhurst 221 D11
av. Springwood 201 H3
cl. Illawong 460 G1
cr. Blakehurst 462 B4
cr. Drummoyne 343 H1
la. Blakehurst 432 D15
la. Wahroonga, off Illoura Av 222 E7
pl. Tahmoor 565 F9
rd. Dharruk 241 B5
st. Blakehurst 432 C16
st. Burwood 342 C11
st. Canley Vale 366 A2
st. Collaroy 229 A9
st. Concord W 341 D2
st. Granville 308 E16
st. Jamisontown 236 C15
st. Kogarah 433 A5
st. Longueville 314 C9
st. Manly 288 G12
st. Newport 169 F12
st. Padstow 399 F12
st. Ryde 282 E13
st. Wahroonga 222 D6
wk. Mosman, off Bloxsome La 316 G9
STUART MOULD
cr. Lalor Park 245 D10
STUBBS
pl. Bonnyrigg 364 C6
pl. Ingleburn 453 C12
st. Auburn 309 E14
st. Beverley Pk 432 K10
st. Silverwater 309 E14
STUCKEY
pl. Narellan Vale 478 G15
STUDDY
cl. Bligh Park 150 D5
STUDENTS
la. Mt Riverview 204 D16

STUDLEY
ct. Narellan 478 B10
st. Carramar 366 J3
st. Londonderry 148 B14
STUKA
cl. Raby 451 D12
STURDEE
la. Lovett Bay 168 B2
pde. Dee Why 258 G7
st. North Ryde 282 K10
st. Wentwthvle 306 H1
STURGESS
pl. Eagle Vale 481 A9
STURT
av. Georges Hall 368 A15
la. Kingsford 406 J3
pl. Camden S 507 A12
pl. Castle Hill 218 D9
pl. Mt Colah 162 C11
pl. St Ives 224 A11
pl. Windsor Dn 151 B15
rd. Ingleburn 423 A9
rd. Woolooware 493 G7
st. Campbelltwn 511 G6
st. Darlinghurst 4 E14
st. Frenchs Frst 256 C1
st. Kingsford 406 G3
st. Lalor Park 245 D13
st. Smithfield 336 E2
st. Telopea 279 G10
STUTT
pl. S Windsor 150 G2
st. Kings Park 244 D2
STUTZ
pl. Ingleburn 453 G13
STYLES
cr. Minto 482 G6
pl. Merrylands 307 F14
st. Leichhardt 10 D16
STYPANDRA
pl. Springwood 201 K2
SUAKIN
dr. Mosman 317 F10
st. Pymble 253 D6
SUBIACO
pl. Carlingford 280 D4
SUBWAY
la. Homebush 341 C9
rd. Banksia 403 D11
rd. Rockdale 403 C16
SUCCESS
av. Kellyville 216 H1
st. Greenfld Pk 334 D13
SUDBURY
st. Belmore 371 E14
SUE
pl. Mt Colah 162 G13
SUEZ CANAL
The Rocks A K4
SUFFOLK
av. Collaroy 229 A15
cl. St Ives 224 D9
la. Paddington 13 D15
pl. Colyton 270 E5
pl. Elderslie 507 J1
pl. Tahmoor 566 E8
st. Blacktown 244 C13
st. Ingleburn 453 B7
st. Miller 393 G2
st. Paddington 13 D15
st. Windsor 121 C9
SUGAR HOUSE
rd. Canterbury, off Hutton St 372 H14
SUGARLOAF
cr. Castlecrag 285 K10
rd. Ingleside 198 C4
SUGARWOOD
gr. Greenacre 370 F6
SULLIVAN
av. Lurnea 394 C7
st. Blacktown 273 K5
st. Fairfield W 335 A12
SULLY
st. Randwick 407 D1
SULMAN
pl. Doonside 273 F3
pl. Menangle 538 G16
rd. Cabramtta W 365 B5
SULTANA
gr. Glenwood 215 D15
SULU
wy. Glenfield 424 E11

SUMBRAY
av. Kemps Ck 359 J3
SUMMER
rd. Faulconbdg 171 B13
SUMMERCROP
pl. Wrrngtn Dns 237 K4
SUMMERFIELD
av. Quakers Hill 214 B15
av. Quakers Hill 214 E15
cct. Cmbrdg Gdn 237 H2
SUMMERHAZE
pl. Hornsby Ht 161 H15
SUMMER HILL
la. St Clair, off Summer Hill Pl 270 C10
pl. St Clair 270 C10
st. Lewisham 15 A11
SUMMERS
av. Hornsby 191 F13
pl. Bradbury 511 J12
st. Dundas Vy 279 K11
SUMMERSTONE
wy. Ambarvale 510 J16
SUMMERVILLE
cr. N Willghby 285 E9
SUMMERWOOD
wy. Beecroft 250 J7
SUMMIT
av. Dee Why 259 B9
cl. Glenwood 215 G16
cl. Marsfield 281 J4
gln. Cranebrook 207 B11
la. Cranebrook, off Summit Gln 207 B11
pl. Baulkham Hl 246 F11
pl. Strathfield 341 C16
st. Earlwood 402 E5
st. Mt Riverview 204 G14
SUMNER
st. Hassall Gr 212 B15
st. Sutherland 460 F15
SUNART
pl. St Andrews 481 J5
SUNBEAM
av. Burwood 371 J2
av. Croydon 342 H13
av. Kogarah 433 D10
la. Campsie 401 K2
pl. Ingleburn 453 K7
SUNBIRD
cl. Hinchinbrk 393 B4
tce. Glenmore Pk 266 A12
SUNBLEST
cr. Mount Druitt 240 K15
SUNBURY
st. Sutherland 460 D15
SUNCREST
av. Newport 169 G15
pl. Doonside 243 H15
SUNCROFT
av. Georges Hall 368 D15
SUNDA
av. Whalan 241 B13
SUNDALE
pl. Chester Hill 368 C2
SUNDERLAND
av. Rose Bay, off New South Head Rd 347 K10
cr. Bligh Park 150 J6
dr. Raby 451 F15
SUNFLOWER
dr. Clarmnt Ms 268 H1
SUNHAVEN
st. Beecroft 250 A11
SUNHILL
pl. North Ryde 282 F7
SUNLAND
cr. Mt Riverview 204 G16
SUNLEA
av. Mortdale 430 J5
cr. Belfield 371 C8
pl. Allambie Ht 257 B8
SUNNDAL
cl. St Clair 269 H15
SUNNING
pl. Summer Hill 373 C3
SUNNINGDALE
dr. Glenmore Pk 266 F10
SUNNY
cr. Punchbowl 399 J6
pl. St Johns Pk 334 E15

SUNNYDALE
pl. Narellan, off Links Wy 478 B10
SUNNYHOLT
rd. Acacia Gdn 215 A16
rd. Blacktown 244 J15
rd. Glenwood 215 A16
rd. Kings Lngly 244 K8
rd. Kings Park 244 K8
rd. Parklea 215 A16
rd. Stanhpe Gdn 215 D12
SUNNYMEADE
cl. Asquith 192 C10
rd. Berkshire Pk 179 E9
SUNNY RIDGE
rd. Winmalee 172 K12
SUNNYRIDGE
pl. Bayview 168 J11
rd. Arcadia 129 E8
SUNNYSIDE
av. Caringbah 492 J6
av. Lilyfield 10 G3
cr. Castlecrag 285 K11
cr. N Richmond 87 E15
dr. Ellis Lane 476 D5
pl. Blakehurst 462 C2
st. Gladesville 312 K11
SUNNYVALE
rd. Middle Dural 158 K10
SUNRAY
cr. St Clair 270 D14
SUNRIDGE
pl. W Pnnant Hl 248 K3
SUNRISE
pl. Horngsea Pk 392 C14
pl. Kellyville 216 H3
rd. Palm Beach 109 J16
SUNSET
av. Bankstown 399 B5
av. Cabramtta W 365 C5
av. Cronulla 523 J2
av. Elderslie 507 F2
av. Hornsby Ht 161 G12
av. Lurnea 394 C7
av. S Penrith 266 F1
bvd. Winmalee 173 E5
la. Seaforth 286 K11
pl. Earlwood 402 H5
pl. Frenchs Frst 256 K4
pl. North Rocks 278 G3
SUNSHINE
av. Penrith 237 A7
pde. Peakhurst 430 C11
st. Manly Vale 287 J3
SUNTER
wy. Castle Hill 217 K6
SUNTOP
pl. Glenmore Pk 266 H14
SUN VALLEY
pl. Carlingford 279 F2
rd. Valley Ht 203 A6
SUNVILLE
ct. Blacktown 274 B8
SUPERBA
av. Cronulla 494 C6
la. Mosman, off Superba Pde 317 C6
pde. Mosman 317 C6
SUPERIOR
av. Seven Hills 275 F7
SUPPLY
av. Beacon Hill 257 G2
av. Lurnea 394 C12
cl. Narellan 478 E16
ct. Kellyville 216 H1
pl. Bligh Park 150 E4
rd. Lilyfield 10 A2
st. Dundas Vy 280 B7
st. Ruse 512 H3
SURADA
av. Riverview 314 B7
SURF
la. Cronulla 493 K12
rd. Cronulla 493 K12
rd. N Curl Curl 259 A11
rd. Palm Beach 140 B7
rd. Whale Beach 140 B7
SURFERS
pde. Harbord 258 E16
SURFSIDE
av. Avalon 170 C2
av. Clovelly 377 K12
SURFVIEW
rd. Mona Vale 199 G4
SURGEONS
ct. The Rocks A K5
SURPRISE
cr. Bligh Park 150 C7
SURREY
av. Castle Hill 217 K9
av. Collaroy 258 K1
av. Georges Hall 368 B15
la. Darlinghurst 4 J9
la. Waterloo 19 F11
pl. Kareela 461 B13
rd. Turramurra 223 D9
st. Blacktown 274 G6
st. Darlinghurst 4 H10
st. Epping 251 B13
st. Guildford 337 G3
st. Marrickville 374 A9
st. Minto 452 G16
st. Stanmore 16 G9
st. Waterloo 19 F11
SURVEY
pl. St Ives 224 B16
SURVEYOR
av. Heathcote 518 D13
SURVEYOR ABBOT
dr. Glenbrook 234 C11
SURVEYORS CREEK
rd. Glenmore Pk 266 E9
SUSAN
av. Padstow Ht 429 D6
ct. Glenwood, off Shaun Dr 215 K16
la. Annandale 11 B16
la. Clovelly, off Fern St 377 G12
pde. Castle Hill 217 K16
pl. Eastwood 281 G6
pl. Gymea Bay 491 F9
pl. Minto 482 G3
st. Annandale 17 B2
st. Auburn 339 D5
st. Camperdwn 17 J6
st. Newtown 17 J7
st. S Wntwthvle 306 H8
SUSANNE
la. Cambrdg Pk, off Susanne Pl 238 C7
pl. Cambrdg Pk 238 C7
SUSAN O'NEILL
av. Newington M A13
av. Newington 310 B14
SUSELLA
cr. N Richmond 87 A12
SUSSEX
la. Sydney A C15
pl. Narellan 478 H12
pl. Seven Hills 275 E5
rd. St Ives 254 A2
st. Cabramatta 365 G10
st. Epping 251 C12
st. Haymarket E E2
st. Haymarket 3 E7
st. Minto 482 E1
st. Sydney A B13
st. Sydney E E2
st. Sydney 1 D15
SUSSMAN
av. Bass Hill 368 C13
cr. Smithfield 336 C5
SUTCLIFFE
pl. Barden Rdg 488 G4
st. Kingsgrove 401 H12
SUTHERLAND
av. Kings Lngly 245 D6
av. Paddington 13 F14
av. Ryde 311 H3
av. Wahroonga 222 F8
cr. Darling Point 14 B4
la. Merrylands 307 J13
la. Sutherland 490 D2
la. Cremorne, off Ben Boyd La 316 D7
la. Chippendale, off O'Connor St 19 A2
rd. Beecroft 250 F5
rd. Chatswd W 284 G12
rd. Cheltenham 251 A9
rd. Jannali 460 F14
rd. Londonderry 148 J16
rd. N Parramatta 278 E11
st. Canley Ht 365 B3
st. Cremorne 316 C7
st. Granville 308 H12
st. Lane Cove 314 B1
st. Mascot 405 F6
st. Paddington 13 F14
st. Rosebery 405 F6
st. St Peters 374 F14
st. Sutherland 490 D3
st. Yagoona 369 D8
SUTTIE
rd. Bellevue Hill 14 H16
rd. Double Bay 22 G1
rd. Woollahra 22 G1
SUTTON
av. Earlwood 402 K5
grn. W Pnnant Hl 249 C4
la. Darlinghurst, off Bourke St 4 E9
la. Balmain, off Sutton St 7 F11
pl. Minto 453 C15
pl. St Ives 224 B16
rd. Ashcroft 364 D16
rd. Cambrdg Pk 238 B8
st. Balmain 7 F10
st. Blacktown 274 H4
st. Five Dock 343 A9
st. Hornsby 191 F9
SUTTOR
av. Ryde 311 J4
pl. Baulkham Hl 247 E4
rd. N Parramatta 278 K6
st. Alexandria 18 F15
st. Silverwater 309 G12
st. Woolmloo 4 C7
SUVA
cr. Greenacre 369 K14
pl. Lethbrdg Pk 240 G1
SUWARROW
st. Fairlight 288 D7
SUZANNE
cl. Berowra Ht 133 A6
rd. Mona Vale 198 H2
st. Seven Hills 275 J6
SVENSDEN
pl. Ingleburn 453 B12
SVERGE
st. Mosman 316 K12
SWAFFHAM
rd. Minto 482 A6
SWAGER
pl. Canley Ht 335 E16
SWAGMAN
la. Wrrngtn Dns, off Swagman Pl 238 D4
pl. Wrrngtn Dns 238 D4
SWAIN
st. Moorebank 395 H9
st. Sydenham 374 D14
SWALES
pl. Colyton 270 J9
SWALLOW
dr. Erskine Park 270 G16
dr. Erskine Park 270 J14
la. Ebenezer 63 G2
la. St Clair, off Swallow Dr 270 J14
pl. Hinchinbrk 363 D15
pl. Ingleburn 453 G9
st. Jamisontown 236 B16
SWALLOW ROCK
dr. Grays Point 491 C15
SWAMP
rd. Tempe 404 D3
SWAMPHEN
la. St Clair, off Swamphen St 271 A14
st. Erskine Park 271 A13
SWAN
av. Strathfield 341 G10
cct. Green Valley 363 C14
ct. Harringtn Pk 478 D4
la. Granville 308 H12
pl. Ingleburn 453 D9
pl. Jamisontown 266 D4
pl. Lalor Park 245 J11
pl. Pennant Hills 220 D16
rd. Edensor Pk 333 G16
st. Gladesville 312 K5
st. Lilli Pilli 522 E3
st. Revesby 398 H15
st. Rydalmere 279 F16
st. Woolooware 493 G9
SWANE
st. Ermington 310 F2
SWANLEY
st. Mt Pritchard 364 C11
SWANN
pl. Kellyville 215 F4
SWANNELL
av. Chiswick 343 D2
SWANNS
la. Allawah 432 G9
SWANSEA
ct. Glenwood 215 J14
pl. West Hoxton 392 E5
SWANSON
la. Erskineville 18 C15
st. Erskineville 18 B14
st. Eveleigh 18 A14
wy. Claymore 481 B11
SWANSTON
st. St Marys 269 H2
SWEENEY
av. Plumpton 241 G10
SWEETHAVEN
rd. Bossley Park 333 J10
rd. Edensor Pk 333 J13
rd. Greenfld Pk 333 J13
st. Bankstown 399 E1
SWEETWATER
gr. Orchard Hills 268 H12
SWETE
st. Lidcombe 339 K8
SWETTENHAM
rd. Minto 482 B3
SWIFT
gln. Erskine Park 270 K11
pl. Hinchinbrk 393 C3
pl. Ingleburn 453 F6
pl. Wetherill Pk 334 K6
st. Guildford 337 F5
SWINBORNE
cr. Wetherill Pk 335 A4
SWINBOURNE
st. Bnksmeadw 405 J13
st. Botany 405 J13
SWINDON
cl. Turramurra 222 J16
pl. Chipping Ntn 366 E16
SWINSON
rd. Blacktown 274 G3
SWIVELLER
cl. Ambarvale 540 F1
SWORDFISH
av. Raby 481 G2
SWORDS
pl. Mount Druitt 271 A1
SYBIL
la. Btn-le-Sds 433 H4
st. Beverley Pk 432 K10
st. Eastwood 280 G8
st. Guildford W 306 J16
st. Newport 169 H7
SYCAMORE
av. Casula 394 F14
cr. Quakers Hill 243 D3
gr. Menai 458 J13
st. N St Marys 240 B9
SYD EINFELD
dr. Bondi Jctn 22 E5
dr. Woollahra 22 E5
SYDENHAM
la. Marrickville, off Shirlow St 374 D13
rd. Brookvale 258 B11
rd. Marrickville 373 K9
SYDNEY
arc. Sydney 3 G3
gte. Waterloo 19 K15
la. Erskineville 18 B14
la. Marrickville 374 B14
pl. Ruse 512 G1
pl. Woolmloo 4 H5
rd. Balgowlah 287 F9
rd. E Lindfield 254 J14
rd. Fairlight 288 B8
rd. Hornsby Ht 191 E4
rd. Manly 288 B8
rd. Seaforth 287 D10
rd. Warriewood 199 E13
rd. Warwck Frm 365 D16
st. Artarmon 285 C14
st. Blacktown 245 A15
st. Chatswood 285 C12
st. Concord 341 H8
st. Erskineville 18 C14
st. Marrickville 374 C13
st. N Willghby 285 C12
st. Panania 398 B15
st. Randwick 377 A11
st. Riverstone 182 H4
st. St Marys 270 B2
st. Willoughby 285 C14
SYDNEY HARBOUR TUNNEL
Milsons Pt 2 A4
Sydney B H1
Sydney 2 A4
SYDNEY JOSEPH
dr. Seven Hills 246 B13
SYDNEY LUKER
rd. Cabramtta W 365 C6
SYDNEY-NEWCASTLE
fwy. Asquith 192 D16
fwy. Berowra 163 A9
fwy. Brooklyn 75 A13
fwy. Cowan 104 E13
fwy. Krngai Ch NP 192 D16
fwy. Mooney 75 A13
fwy. Mt Colah 162 F16
fwy. Mt Krng-gai 162 F16
fwy. N Wahrnga 222 B6
fwy. Wahroonga 222 B6
SYDNEY PARK
rd. Alexandria 375 A11
rd. Erskineville 374 K11
SYDNEY STEEL
rd. Marrickville 374 E12
SYKES
pl. Colyton 270 E4
pl. Mount Druitt 271 A1
SYLVA
av. Miranda 491 J4
SYLVAN
av. E Lindfield 255 B12
gr. Glenhaven 187 K16
gr. Picnic Point 428 C12
pl. Leonay 264 K2
st. Galston 159 E10
st. Sylvania 461 J10
SYLVANIA
av. Springwood 201 G3
av. Thornleigh 221 C10
rd.n, Miranda 491 H4
rd.n, Sylvania 461 H16
rd.s, Gymea Bay 491 G8
rd.s, Miranda 491 G7
SYLVAN RIDGE
dr. Illawong 459 C1
SYLVANUS
st. Greenacre 370 H11
SYLVESTER
av. Roselands 400 J8
SYLVIA
av. Carlingford 249 F12
pl. Frenchs Frst 256 F4
pl. Greystanes 305 H8
st. Blacktown 273 H1
st. Chatswd W 284 D10
st. Rydalmere 309 K5
SYLVIA CHASE
sq. Sydney 4 C5
sq. Woolmloo 4 C5
SYM
av. Burwood 341 K15
la. Burwood, off Livingstone St 341 K15
SYMONDS
av. Parramatta 278 J15
rd. Colebee 213 A16
rd. Dean Park 242 K2
rd. Londonderry 148 F7
SYMONS
st. Fairfield 336 D16
SYNCARPIA
wy. Winmalee 173 E8
SYRUS
pl. Quakers Hill 213 H8
SYSTRUM
st. Ultimo 3 B12

T

TABALI
st. Whalan 241 A11
TABALUM
rd. Balgowlah Ht 287 J16
TABARD
pl. Illawong 459 D5
TABELL
cl. Hornsby Ht 191 F8
TABER
pl. Bradbury 511 G11
st. Menangle Pk 539 A3
TABERS
rd. Orangeville 473 E10

TABITHA
pl. Plumpton 241 H6
TABLETOP
cct. Horngsea Pk ... 392 C15
TABOOBA
st. Wentwthvle 277 A9
TABOR
st. Glenbrook 233 K14
TABORA
st. Forestville 255 K13
TABOURIE
st. Leumeah 482 F15
TABRETT
st. Banksia 403 E12
TADMORE
rd. Cranebrook 206 K1
TAFFS
av. Lugarno 430 A10
TAFT
pl. Bonnet Bay 460 F11
TAGGARTS
la. Darlinghurst 4 C13
TAGU
pl. Kings Park 244 K3
TAGUDI
pl. Bangor 459 E12
TAGULA
pl. Glenfield 424 H10
TAHITI
av. Lethbrdg Pk 240 H2
pl. Kings Lngly 245 C6
TAHLEE
cl. Castle Hill 218 J8
cr. Leumeah 482 A15
st. Burwood 342 B16
TAHMOOR
rd. Tahmoor 566 A10
TAHOE
pl. Erskine Park ... 271 A15
TAILBY
st. Campbelltwn ... 510 H7
TAIN
pl. Schofields 183 B16
TAIO
pl. Kings Lngly 245 E8
TAIRORA
st. Whalan 241 A10
TAIT
la. Russell Lea 343 E5
st. Russell Lea 343 E5
st. Smithfield 336 A1
TAIWAN
pl. Sylvania 462 A12
TAIYUL
rd. N Narrabeen ... 198 H14
TALARA
av. Glenmore Pk ... 266 A8
rd.n, Gymea 491 D3
rd.s, Gymea 491 D6
TALASEA
st. Whalan 241 A11
TALAVERA
rd. Mcquarie Pk ... 282 F1
rd. Marsfield 252 C13
TALBINGO
pl. Heckenberg 364 D13
pl. Ruse 512 H6
pl. Woodcroft 243 H9
TALBOT
cl. Menai 458 E15
ct. Wattle Grove ... 395 K16
pl. Ingleburn 453 G13
pl. Woolmloo 4 F7
rd. Guildford 337 H4
rd. Yagoona 368 K8
st. Riverwood 400 D16
st. St Peters 374 E16
TALBRAGAR
st. Ruse 512 D7
TALC
pl. Eagle Vale 481 B7
TALEEBAN
rd. Riverview 314 B5
TALFOURD
la. Glebe 12 B12
st. Glebe 12 C12
TALGAI
av. Wahroonga 251 H1
TALGARA
pl. Beacon Hill 257 J8
TALIA
cl. Kingswood 267 J3

TALINGA
av. Georges Hall ... 368 A15
pl. Cherrybrook 219 B12
pl. Lilli Pilli 522 G2
st. Carlingford 280 B3
TALISMAN
av. Castle Hill 247 H3
TALKOOK
pl. Baulkham Hl ... 246 K6
TALLAGANDRA
dr. Quakers Hill 243 D3
TALLARA
pl. Busby 363 J15
pl. Terrey Hills 196 F5
TALLAROOK
cl. Mona Vale 199 D1
pl. Bangor 459 F12
TALLAWALLA
st. Beverly Hills 401 C12
TALLAWARRA
av. Padstow 429 G2
pl. Narrabeen 229 A5
rd. Leumeah 482 A15
TALLAWONG
av. Blacktown 273 H4
rd. Rouse Hill 184 A9
TALLAWUNG
pl. Kenthurst 156 E11
TALLGUMS
av. W Pnnant Hl ... 249 J2
TALLINN
gr. Rooty Hill 271 K5
TALLONG
pl. Caringbah 492 F13
pl. Turramurra 223 D11
st. Prestons 393 B13
TALLOW
pl. Glenwood 245 J2
pl. S Coogee 407 E5
TALLOWOOD
av. Casula 394 F14
cr. Bossley Park ... 333 E8
gdn. Blaxland 234 B8
gr. Kellyville 186 A16
pl. Cranebrook 207 B8
wy. Frenchs Frst 256 F1
TALLOW WOOD
cl. Wilberforce 93 F4
TALLOW-WOOD
av. Narellan Vale ... 479 A13
TALLOWWOOD
av. Cherrybrook 219 F11
av. Lugarno 429 K9
cl. Alfords Point ... 429 C15
cr. Bradbury 511 F12
TALL SHIPS
av. W Pnnant Hl ... 249 A1
TALL TIMBERS
rd. Winmalee 173 E12
TALL TREES
av. Castle Hill, off Barker Dr 218 J13
TALLWOOD
av. Eastwood 281 K8
dr. North Rocks 278 G3
pl. St Clair 270 D9
TALMIRO
st. Whalan 241 A11
TALOFA
pl. Castle Hill 218 C8
TALOMA
av. Lurnea 394 E6
la. S Penrith 237 A16
st. Picnic Point 428 G6
st. S Penrith 237 A15
TALOOMBI
st. Cronulla 493 H16
TALPA
cl. Thornleigh 221 A5
TALUS
st. Naremburn 315 D3
TALWONG
st. Hornsby Ht 161 K11
TAMAR
ct. Glenhaven 218 D5
pl. Fairfield W 335 B10
pl. N Wahrnga 223 A1
st. Marrickville 373 F13
st. Sutherland 490 C1
TAMARA
cl. Oakdale 500 D12
pl. Kellyville 186 C16
rd. Faulconbdg 171 E13

TAMARAMA
st. Tamarama 378 A6
TAMARAMA MARINE
dr. Tamarama 378 B7
TAMARIND
pl. Alfords Point ... 429 B16
TAMARISK
cr. Cherrybrook 219 H6
TAMARIX
cr. Banksia 403 G12
st. Greystanes 305 E11
TAMARO
av. Whalan 241 A10
TAMBA
pl. Port Hacking ... 522 H2
TAMBAROORA
cr. Marayong 243 H6
pl. W Pnnant Hl 248 G7
TAMBOON
av. Turramurra 252 F2
TAMBOURA
av. Baulkham Hl 247 B14
TAMBOURINE BAY
rd. Lane Cove 314 C3
rd. Riverview 314 A6
TAMBOY
av. Carlingford 279 C1
TAMBU
st. St Ives 224 F10
TAMINA
pl. S Penrith 267 C6
TAMINGA
rd. Green Valley 363 H10
st. Bayview 168 H11
TAMMAR
pl. St Helens Pk 541 F3
TAMPLIN
rd. Guildford 337 B5
TAMWORTH
cr. Hoxton Park 392 G6
pl. Allambie Ht 257 D13
pl. Engadine 488 G13
TANA
pl. Kings Park 244 H2
TANAMI
cl. Belrose 225 J12
cl. Wakeley, off Mallacoota St ... 334 J12
pl. Bow Bowing 452 C15
TANBARK
cct. Wrrngtn Dns ... 238 C4
pl. Dural 219 B7
TANCRED
av. Kyeemagh 404 C13
TANDARA
av. Bradbury 511 C16
TANDERAGEE
st. Wentwthvle 277 D10
TANDERRA
av. Carlingford 279 J2
pl. Curl Curl 258 J14
st. Colyton 270 F6
st. Wahroonga 222 C10
TANGALOA
cr. Lethbrdg Pk 240 J2
TANGARA
st. Eveleigh 18 H11
TANGARRA
st. Croydon Pk 371 F6
st.e, Croydon Pk 371 H6
TANGERINE
st. Fairfield E 337 A14
TANGLEWOOD
cl. Glenmore Pk ... 266 F10
pl. W Pnnant Hl 248 H5
wy. Hornsby Ht 161 H15
TANGO
av. Dee Why 258 F8
TANIA
av. S Penrith 267 C3
cl. Hornsby Ht 161 K8
st. Greystanes 305 H5
TANJA
cl. Prestons 393 D16
TANK STREAM
wy. Sydney .... B A12
TANNER
av. Allawah 432 G9
av. Carlton 432 G9
la. Carlton 432 G8
pl. Minchinbury 271 H7
TANNERS
wy. Kellyville 216 J1

TANTALLON
av. Arncliffe 403 G10
la. Arncliffe 403 G11
rd. Lane Cove W .. 284 A15
TANTANGARA
pl. Woodcroft 243 E11
st. Heckenberg 363 K14
TANTANI
av. Green Valley ... 363 G11
TANYA
pl. Tahmoor 566 A13
TAO
cl. St Clair 269 H15
TAPI
gln. St Clair 300 A3
TAPIOLA
av. Hebersham 241 E4
TAPLAN
st. Como 460 F7
TAPLEY
wy. Ambarvale 511 B15
TAPLIN
pl. Camden S 506 K15
TAPP
pl. Bidwill 211 B15
TAPPEINER
ct. Baulkham Hl ... 217 A16
TARA
cl. Yennora 336 K11
pl. Lugarno 430 A13
rd. Blacktown 273 J1
st. Kangaroo Pt ... 461 H7
st. Merrylands 308 D15
st. Sylvania 461 H7
st. Woollahra 21 K1
TARAGO
pl. E Lindfield 255 B11
pl. Prestons 392 J15
TARAKAN
cr. Northbridge 285 J14
pl. Narraweena 257 K4
rd. Moorebank 425 A4
st. Holsworthy 396 D16
TARALGA
st. Old Guildfrd 337 G9
st. Prestons 392 H14
TARANA
cl. Casula 394 C16
cr. Baulkham Hl ... 246 J9
cr. Dharruk 241 B7
TARANAKI
av. Lethbrdg Pk ... 240 H2
pl. Northmead 248 B16
TARANTO
rd. Marsfield 252 B13
TARAWA
rd. Lethbrdg Pk ... 240 H3
TARBAN
st. Gladesville 313 B11
TARBERT
pl. St Andrews 481 J3
TARCOOLA
pl. Ellis Lane 476 C6
pl. Engadine 488 D13
TAREE
av. N Balgowlah ... 287 B5
cr. Greystanes 305 J5
pl. Dharruk 241 B8
pl. Hoxton Park ... 392 J9
TARELLA
pl. Cammeray, off Amherst St 315 J5
TAREN
rd.s, Caringbah 492 E11
TAREN POINT
rd. Caringbah 492 G5
rd. Taren Point 462 H15
TARGO
rd. Beverley Pk 433 B13
rd. Girraween 276 B16
rd. Toongabbie 276 C8
TARI
wy. Glenfield 424 E11
TARINGA
st. Ashfield 342 J15
TARINGHA
st. Blaxland 233 D6
TARLINGTON
pde. Bonnyrigg 364 A5
pl. Prospect 275 C15
pl. Smithfield 305 D12
TARO
pl. Quakers Hill 243 F4
st. Blakehurst 462 D1

TARONGA
pde. Caringbah 492 K5
pl. Mona Vale 199 D3
st. Blacktown 274 E8
st. Como 460 F6
st. Hurstville 401 K15
wy. Faulconbdg 171 A13
TAROO
pl. Forestville 255 G11
TAROOK
av. S Turramrra 252 A5
TAROONA
st. St Marys 239 G14
TARPAN
pl. Emu Heights ... 235 B2
TARPEIAN
wy. Sydney .... B H5
TARPLEE
av. Hamondvle 396 F15
TARRA
cr. Dee Why 258 J2
TARRABUNDI
dr. Glenmore Pk ... 266 C7
TARRAGON
av. Richmond 118 C7
TARRAGUNDI
rd. Epping 250 J12
TARRANT
av. Bellevue Hill 14 G10
cl. Picton 563 F12
pl. Doonside 243 E16
TARRANTS
av. Eastwood 280 J9
TARRILLI
pl. Kellyville 216 E4
st. Beverly Hills 401 B12
TARRO
av. Revesby 428 G1
cl. Hornsby 191 H7
TARUN
pl. Dharruk 241 B6
TARWIN
av. Glenwood 215 H12
TASKER
av. Campsie 402 A3
av. Peakhurst 430 A4
TASMA
pl. Airds 512 C11
TASMAN
av. Lethbrdg Pk 240 H2
cr. Killara 254 C10
ct. Castle Hill 218 D10
la. Bundeena 524 B11
pde. Fairfield W 335 C11
pl. Mcquarie Pk ... 282 J1
pl. S Windsor 150 E3
rd. Avalon 140 D16
rd. Mulgoa 325 G4
st. Bondi 377 K6
st. Cambrdg Pk ... 237 H6
st. Dee Why 259 A9
st. Hinchinbrk 363 B15
st. Kurnell 465 G9
st. Phillip Bay 436 J12
TATE
cr. Horngsea Pk ... 392 F16
pl. Lugarno 429 J16
st. Panania 428 C4
TATES
la. Kurrajong 85 B5
TATHIRA
cr. Merrylnds W ... 306 J11
TATHRA
av. Prestons 393 D16
ct. Dural 219 B3
pl. Bow Bowing ... 452 D12
pl. Castle Hill 218 D16
pl. Forestville 255 G8
pl. Gymea Bay 491 C8
TATIARA
cr. N Narrabeen ... 198 G14
TATLER
pl. Woronora Ht ... 489 B4
TATTERSALL
pl. Emu Plains 235 D14
rd. Kings Park 244 H6
TATTLER
pl. Hinchinbrk 363 E16
TAUBMAN
dr. Horngsea Pk ... 392 E14
TAUNTON
la. Pymble, off Taunton St 253 D2
rd. Hurstville 432 A1

st. Blakehurst...... 432 D12
st. Pymble.......... 253 D2
TAUPO
rd. Glenorie 128 C1
TAURUS
pl. Gilead............ 540 F8
st. Erskine Park ... 300 K2
TAVISTOCK
rd. Homebsh W ... 340 F10
rd. Kemps Ck....... 360 B7
rd. S Hurstville..... 432 A12
st. Auburn.......... 338 J4
st. Croydon Pk 371 G7
st. Drummoyne ... 343 H2
TAWA
st. Ashfield......... 342 J15
TAWARRI
cr. Kyle Bay 431 J16
TAWMII
pl. Castle Hill 218 H9
TAWNY
cl. Glenwood....... 215 E15
TAWORRI
st. Doonside........ 243 C15
TAY
la. Kensington..... 376 E9
pl. St Andrews..... 481 K6
pl. Winston Hills .. 277 E4
pl. Woronora....... 489 G2
st. Kensington....... 20 K16
TAYLEE
pl. Rouse Hill....... 185 D6
TAYLER
rd. Valley Ht......... 202 E4
TAYLOR
av. Banksia 403 E12
av. Melrose Pk..... 310 H1
av. Turramurra...... 252 E3
cl. Miranda......... 492 B5
ct. Springwood.... 202 D11
la. Artarmon........ 315 A2
la. Glebe............... 12 B9
la. N Strathfield, off Carrington St... 341 G8
pl. Ermington....... 280 A14
pl. Kings Lngly 245 H8
pl. Pennant Hills .. 220 F12
pl. Theresa Park .. 445 A11
rd. Badgerys Ck ... 328 E16
rd. Cranebrook 177 D15
sq. Darlinghurst 4 D13
st. Annandale 17 C1
st. Condell Park ... 398 H3
st. Darlinghurst 4 E14
st. Fairfield 336 E16
st. Five Dock 342 D10
st. Glebe............... 12 B8
st. Gordon........... 254 A6
st. Greystanes 305 K10
st. Kogarah 433 A4
st. Lakemba 371 B16
st. Lakemba 401 C1
st. Lidcombe 339 J9
st. Maroubra 406 H11
st. N Curl Curl 259 B10
st. Paddington....... 21 H1
st. Queens Park... 377 F7
st. Waterloo 20 C16
st. W Pnnant Hl ... 248 K5
wy. Claymore........ 481 B10
TAYLORS
dr. Lane Cove W .. 283 F13
la. Lane Cove W .. 284 F16
rd. Dural 189 G3
rd. Silverdale 353 G16
TAYLORS POINT
rd. Clareville 169 D2
TAYNISH
av. Camden S 507 B14
TAYWOOD
av. Winston Hills .. 277 G4
st. Woolooware ... 493 F8
TEAGAN
pl. Blacktown 274 B6
TEA GARDENS
av. Kirrawee 491 C1
TEAGUE
st. Girraween....... 276 A10
st. Toongabbie 276 A10
TEAK
cl. Bossley Park .. 333 F8
pl. Cherrybrook 219 H7
pl. Miranda 462 C16
st. St Clair 269 G10
wy. Prestons......... 393 K14
TEAKLE
st. Summer Hill ... 373 B5
TEAL
pl. Blacktown....... 273 K7
pl. Hinchinbrk...... 363 C15
pl. Ingleburn........ 453 H9
pl. Woronora Ht... 489 C4
TEALE
pl. Parramatta...... 278 G15
TEA TREE
cr. Mcquarie Fd ... 424 F16
gln. Jamisontown .. 266 A3
pl. Bossley Park... 333 H9
pl. Kellyville......... 216 A1
pl. Kirrawee......... 460 K15
wy. Colyton.......... 270 H7
TEA-TREE
pl. Mt Annan........ 509 E5
TEAWA
cr. Glenwood....... 215 G14
TEBBUTT
st. Leichhardt 15 C5
st. Windsor 121 A9
TECHNOLOGY
dr. Appin 568 D15
TECOMA
dr. Glenorie.......... 128 C2
st. Heathcote 518 K12
TEDDICK
pl. Cherrybrook ... 219 G6
TEDDLES
rt. Moorebank 396 F13
TEDMAN
pde. Sylvania.......... 461 H12
TEDWIN
av. Kensington 376 C14
st. Mt Pritchard ... 364 C11
TEELE
rd. Harringtn Pk ... 478 F2
TEEMER
st. Tennyson 312 E9
TEESWATER
pl. Airds 512 A13
TEGGS
la. Chippendale...... 19 B3
TEKLA
st. W Pnnant Hl ... 249 K2
TEKOPA
rd. Glenorie.......... 128 C3
TELAK
cl. N Willghby...... 285 H7
TELEGRAPH
rd. Eastern Ck 272 J5
rd. Pymble........... 253 C1
TELFER
pl. Westmead 307 H4
rd. Castle Hill 218 G14
wy. Castle Hill 218 G15
TELFORD
la. Willoughby 285 J11
pl. N St Marys 239 J11
pl. Prairiewood 335 B8
st. Leumeah 512 C1
TELL
cl. Abbotsbury..... 333 B16
TELLICHERRY
cct. Kellyville 185 J13
TELOPEA
av. Caringbah....... 492 F12
av. Homebsh W ... 340 G6
av. Strathfield....... 371 D4
cl. Glenmore Pk... 265 J9
la. Redfern 20 A9
pl. Mcquarie Fd ... 454 G3
st. Collaroy Plat ... 228 G12
st. Mt Colah 192 D3
st. Punchbowl 370 D16
st. Redfern 19 K9
st. Telopea 279 G9
st. Wollstncraft.... 315 B10
TELOPIA
st. Mt Annan........ 509 B2
TELOWIE
ct. Dural 219 C4
TEME
pl. Jamisontown .. 266 A3
TEMI
pl. Marayong 243 G6
TEMORA
rd. Glenhaven 187 G16
st. Prestons 393 E14
TEMPE
st. Earlwood 403 H3
st. Greenacre 370 D11
TEMPI
pl. Dharruk 241 C7
TEMPLAR
st. Blacktown 274 K7
TEMPLE
la. Stanmore.......... 16 E8
st. Stanmore.......... 16 C8
TEMPLEMAN
cr. Hillsdale.......... 406 G13
TEMPLETON
cr. Baulkham Hl ... 247 E5
cr. Moorebank 396 C9
rd. Elderslie.......... 507 H1
wy. Airds............... 512 C13
TENBY
st. Blacktown 274 H9
TENCH
av. Jamisontown .. 235 G14
pl. Glenmore Pk ... 265 F5
wy. West Hoxton ... 392 A11
TENELLA
st. Canley Ht 335 A16
TENGAH
cr. Mona Vale 199 E2
TENILBA
rd. Northbridge 285 J14
TENISON
av. Cmbrdg Gdn ... 237 H5
ct. Baulkham Hl ... 247 B2
TENNANT
pl. Blackett........... 241 A3
pl. Edensor Pk 363 J3
pl. Illawong.......... 459 C7
rd. Werrington 239 B15
st. Casula 424 F3
TENNENT
pde. Dulwich Hill 373 A14
pde. Hurlstone Pk ... 373 A14
TENNESSEE
pl. Riverwood 400 A13
TENNIS COURT
la. Mosman, off Countess St..... 316 J4
TENNYSON
av. Turramurra 222 K8
dr. Cherrybrook.... 219 D9
pde. Guildford W 306 K15
pl. Sylvania.......... 462 C14
rd. Breakfast Pt 312 A13
rd. Concord.......... 312 B16
rd. Cromer 258 E1
rd. E Kurrajong....... 59 A2
rd. Gladesville 312 F8
rd. Greenacre 370 B7
rd. Mortlake 312 A13
rd. Ryde.............. 312 F8
rd. Tennyson.......... 87 H1
rd. Tennyson......... 312 E11
st. Campsie 372 A10
st. Dulwich Hill 373 C13
st. Enfield 371 H3
st. Granville 309 B11
st. Parramatta 308 J1
st. Wetherill Pk 334 J7
st. Winston Hills .. 277 G1
TENT
st. Kingswood 267 E1
TENTERDEN
rd. Botany 405 G11
TENTERFIELD
av. Hinchinbrk...... 392 J5
st. N Strathfield.... 341 E5
TENTH
av. Austral........... 391 B9
av. Loftus 490 B9
av. Oyster Bay 461 B11
rd. Berkshire Pk ... 180 C11
st. Warragamba ... 353 F5
TEOFILO STEVENSON
av. Newington .... L K16
av. Newington, off Heidelberg Av .. 310 B14
TEPKO
rd. Terrey Hills 196 C6
TERALBA
rd. Btn-le-Sds 433 J4
rd. Leumeah 482 A15
TERAMA
st. Bilgola 169 F8
TERANGLE
cl. Prestons 393 A13
TERAWEYNA
cl. Woodcroft 243 G11
TERESA
pl. Cromer 228 A16
st. Birrong 369 B5
TERGUR
cr. Caringbah 492 F3
TERMEIL
st. Prestons 392 K16
TERMINAL
ct. Bnkstn Aprt..... 397 J2
pl. Merrylands...... 307 J12
TERMINUS
la. Petersham, off Terminus St....... 15 K9
rd. Seven Hills...... 275 G1
rd. Seven Hills...... 275 H1
st. Castle Hill........ 218 C15
st. Liverpool......... 395 D5
st. Petersham 15 J9
TERN
pl. Erskine Park.... 300 F1
pl. Hinchinbrk 393 C2
pl. Tregear 240 C4
pl. Woronora Ht ... 489 B3
pl. Yarramundi 145 C3
TERNEN
st. Balmain East 8 E9
TERONE
pl. Bossley Park ... 333 G8
TERPENTINE
pl. Yagoona 369 C9
TERRA
ct. Glenmore Pk ... 266 E7
st. Thornleigh 221 C10
TERRACE
av. Sylvania 461 K10
dr. Cranebrook 207 F15
la. Dulwich Hill..... 373 C11
rd. Dulwich Hill..... 373 C11
rd. Freemns Rch..... 89 A5
rd. Killara 253 C16
rd. N Richmond...... 87 F12
TERRACOTTA
cl. Woodcroft....... 243 E9
TERRAL
pl. Kings Lngly..... 246 A8
TERRANORA
pl. Bangor............ 459 F10
wy. Woodcroft....... 243 G11
TERRA NOVA
pl. Tregear 240 D6
TERRELL
av. Wahroonga 221 K16
TERRENE
st. Regents Pk 369 B1
TERRIE
pl. Kellyville.......... 216 G4
TERRIGAL
av. Turramurra 222 K15
pl. Engadine......... 489 B13
pl. Woodbine 481 K8
rd. Terrey Hills 196 C7
st. Marayong 243 H5
TERROL
cr. Mona Vale....... 199 F4
TERRY
av. Seven Hills...... 245 B15
la. Arncliffe 403 G11
rd. Box Hill 154 B15
rd. Denistone 281 F11
rd. Dulwich Hill..... 373 C8
rd. Eastwood 280 G8
rd. Rouse Hill 184 H10
rd. Theresa Park... 444 K9
rd. West Ryde 281 F13
st. Arncliffe 403 G11
st. Balmain 344 E6
st. Blakehurst....... 432 A14
st. Connells Pt 431 G16
st. Greenacre 370 F4
st. Greystanes 306 C9
st. Kyle Bay.......... 431 G16
st. Rozelle............ 344 D6
st. Surry Hills.......... F A16
st. Tempe 374 D16
TERRYBROOK
rd. Llandilo.......... 208 A7
TERRYMONT
rd. Warrimoo 203 C12
TESSA
st. Chatswd W 284 G8
TETBURY
cl. Cambrdg Pk.... 238 C9
TEUMA
pl. Glendenning ... 242 F5
TEVIOT
av. Abbotsford 312 K15
pl. St Andrews 452 A15
st. Richmond 118 H7
TEWINGA
rd. Birrong........... 369 A4
TEWKESBURY
av. Darlinghurst 4 G10
st. Chipping Ntn .. 396 F3
THACKER
cl. Gymea 491 G5
st. Gymea 491 G4
THACKERAY
cl. Wetherill Pk.... 335 A6
st. Camellia 309 G5
st. Winston Hills .. 277 E1
THALIA
st. Hassall Gr 211 K14
THALLON
st. Carlingford 279 J3
THAMES
pl. Kearns 481 B2
pl. Seven Hills 275 D7
rd. Bringelly......... 388 C11
st. Balmain.............. 7 J8
st. Merrylnds W .. 306 H11
st. Woronora....... 460 B15
THANE
cl. Rsemeadow ... 540 D3
st. Pendle Hill...... 276 H12
st. Wentwthvle 276 H13
THARAWAL
rd. Thirlmere 564 G8
THARKINNA
cl. Cranebrook 207 J10
THEA
pl. Rooty Hill 272 B5
THEA DARE
dr. Castle Hill 219 A13
THE APPIAN
wy. Avalon............ 139 H14
wy. Bankstown 369 F16
wy. Mt Vernon 331 D5
wy. S Hurstville 432 A12
THE ARCADE
Arncliffe 403 G8
THE AVENUE
Annandale 16 K3
Ashfield.......... 372 G2
Balmain East 8 D8
Bankstown 368 H12
Bundeena 524 A9
Canley Vale 366 B1
Collaroy 229 A12
Condell Park... 368 G16
Eastwood 281 A8
Gladesville...... 312 H6
Glenmore Pk .. 265 F6
Granville......... 308 D14
Heathcote 518 J9
Hunters Hill 313 F10
Hurlstone Pk .. 372 K10
Hurstville 432 A3
Kingsgrove..... 402 A11
Leichhardt 16 D1
Linley Point 313 F8
Mount Druitt .. 271 B1
Newport 169 F14
N Sydney 6 B10
Petersham 15 G8
Randwick 377 B12
Riverstone 182 D10
Rose Bay........ 348 C13
Valley Ht......... 202 D4
Voyager Pt 427 C6
Waitara 221 H4
Warrimoo 203 B13
Yagoona 368 H12
THE BARBETTE
Castlecrag 286 C13
THE BARBICAN
Castlecrag 286 C12
THE BARRICADE
Castlecrag 286 D12
THE BARTIZAN
Castlecrag 286 C11
THE BASTION
Castlecrag 286 B12
Hornsby......... 221 B4
THE BATTLEMENT
Castlecrag 286 B12
THE BOOMERANG
Freemns Rch.... 90 B5

THE BOULEVARD
Harringtn Pk...478 E2
THE BOULEVARDE
Btn-le-Sds...433 K3
Cammeray...316 A3
Canley Vale...335 J15
Caringbah...492 B1
Cheltenham...250 K9
Dulwich Hill...15 A14
Epping...280 J2
Fairfield...335 J15
Fairfield Ht...335 J10
Fairfield W...335 J15
Gymea...491 F1
Kirrawee...460 G15
Kirrawee...461 A16
Lakemba...400 K1
Lewisham...15 A14
Lidcombe...339 G11
Lilyfield...10 D5
Malabar...437 E5
Miranda...492 B1
Newport...169 J11
Petersham...15 A14
Punchbowl...400 E4
Sans Souci...462 K3
Smithfield...335 J10
Strathfield...341 F16
Sutherland...460 G15
Warrimoo...203 C14
Wiley Park...400 E4
Yagoona...369 E11
THE BROADWAY
Enfield...371 E3
Penrith...236 H11
Strathfield...371 E3
Strathfield S...371 E3
Wahroonga...221 H16
THE BULWARK
Castlecrag...286 C12
THE CARRIAGEWAY
Glenmore Pk...265 E10
North Rocks...278 D6
THE CASCADES
Mt Annan...479 C14
Oatlands...278 K8
Oatlands...279 A8
THE CAUSEWAY
Beverley Pk...433 A13
Maroubra...407 G10
Strathfield S...371 D6
THE CENTRE
Forestville...256 A10
THE CHASE
Orchard Hills...267 E14
Valley Ht...202 G4
rd. Turramurra...223 A9
THE CIRCLE
Bilgola...169 J3
Jannali...461 A10
Narraweena...258 C6
Oatlands...279 A8
THE CITADEL
Castlecrag...286 C11
THE CLEARWATER
Mt Annan...479 B14
THE CLOISTERS
Cherrybrook...219 E15
St Ives...224 E8
THE CLOSE
Hunters Hill...313 G11
Strathfield...340 J12
THE COAL
rd. Bickley Vale...506 E8
rd. Camden...506 E8
rd. Camden S...506 E8
rd. Cawdor...506 E8
rd. Grasmere...506 E8
THE COMENARRA
pky. S Turramrra...251 K2
pky. Thornleigh...221 B13
pky. Turramurra...252 D5
pky. Wahroonga...221 B13
pky. West Pymble...252 D5
THE CORSO
Manly...288 G10
Maroubra...407 J9
THE COTTELL
wy. Baulkham Hl...247 G9
THE CREEL
Lansvale...366 E10
THE CRESCENT
Annandale...11 B5
Auburn...339 B1
Avalon...170 B3
Beecroft...250 G8
Berala...339 D11
Chatswd W...284 F9
Cheltenham...250 G8
Dee Why...258 J7
Fairfield...336 F13
Forest Lodge...11 C8
Homebush...341 A9
Homebsh W...340 G9
Hurstville Gr...431 F12
Kingsgrove...401 F11
Linley Point...313 G8
Manly...288 D10
Marayong...244 C5
Mosman...317 A6
Narrabeen...228 F7
N Narrabeen...198 J15
Pennant Hills...250 H1
Penrith...237 A9
Rozelle...11 B4
Russell Lea...343 D7
Toongabbie...275 F11
Vaucluse...348 E1
Woronora...489 G3
Yagoona...369 A12
THE CRESENT
North Ryde...282 H12
THE CREST
Frenchs Frst...256 D1
Hornsby Ht...161 E14
Killara...254 E11
THE CROFT
wy. W Pnnant Hl...249 H6
THE DRIFTWAY
Agnes Banks...117 F13
Londonderry...149 B3
S Windsor...149 B3
THE DRIVE
Concord W...311 E16
Harbord...258 K16
North Ryde...282 G11
THE ENTRANCE
Earlwood...402 F1
THE ESPLANADE
Ashfield...372 H2
Botany...405 E15
Cronulla...524 A4
Drummoyne...343 G1
Drummoyne...343 E3
Frenchs Frst...256 C1
Guildford...337 E4
Mosman...317 D4
Narrabeen...228 H7
S Hurstville...432 B12
Sylvania...461 E12
Thornleigh...220 K13
THE FAIRWAY
Chatswd W...283 K9
Elanora Ht...198 D14
THE FRESHWATER
Mt Annan...479 B16
THE GLADE
Belrose...226 D16
Galston...159 F10
Kirkham...477 G4
Wahroonga...222 B9
W Pnnant Hl...249 C4
wk. Wahroonga...222 C9
THE GLEN
Beecroft...250 B4
cr. Springwood...201 J4
rd. Bardwell Vy...403 A8
THE GRAND
pde. Btn-le-Sds...404 B16
pde. Btn-le-Sds...433 J9
pde. Monterey...433 J9
pde. Ramsgate Bch.433 G16
pde. Sans Souci...433 G16
pde. Sutherland...490 B1
pde. Sutherland...490 D1
THE GRANDSTAND
St Clair...270 A15
THE GRANGE
Cherrybrook...219 E14
Kirkham...477 F5
THE GREENWAY
Duffys Frst...195 C1
Elanora Ht...198 D13
THE GROVE
Belrose...226 D16
Fairfield...336 A15
Mosman...317 C4
Padstow Ht...429 H8
Penrith...237 B6
Roseville...284 G3
Woollahra...22 C3
Oatlands, off Hunterford Cr...279 A8
wy. Normanhurst...221 H10
THE GULLY
rd. Berowra...133 F13
THE HAVEN
Orchard Hills...267 G14
THE HERMITAGE
W Pnnant Hl...248 G6
THE HIGH
rd. Blaxland...234 A8
THE HIGH TOR
Castlecrag...286 F11
THE HIGHWATER
Mt Annan...479 D14
THE HILLS
cr. Seven Hills...275 E2
THE HORSLEY
dr. Carramar...366 K1
dr. Fairfield...336 G11
dr. Horsley Pk...302 H16
dr. Smithfield...336 B5
dr. Villawood...367 A1
dr. Wetherill Pk...334 A5
THE KINGSWAY
Roseville Ch...255 E15
St Marys...239 B15
Wentwthvle...277 A16
Werrington...239 B15
THE KNOLL
Avalon...169 K2
Blakehurst...462 B2
Galston...159 G10
Lansvale...366 F10
Miranda...461 J14
THE KRAAL
dr. Blair Athol...511 A4
THE LAKES
dr. Glenmore Pk...266 A8
THE LAMBETH
wk. Bundeena...524 A8
THE LEE
Middle Cove...285 K10
THELLA
st. Strathfield S...370 J3
THELMA
av. Panania...398 D13
st. Greystanes...305 H7
st. Lurnea...394 G6
st. Marsfield...281 H2
THE MAIN
av. Mcquarie Pk...283 C6
THE MALL
Bankstown...369 F16
S Hurstville...432 B11
Turramurra...223 D9
Warrimoo...203 C15
Wiley Park...400 G6
THE McKELL
av. Waterfall...519 E13
THE MEADOWS
Kirkham...477 F6
THE MEADOWS FIRE
trl. Royal N P...521 C5
THE MEWS
Kirkham...477 G6
THE NINE WAYS
Kingsford...406 H2
THE NOOK
West Ryde...281 F16
THE NORTHERN
rd. Bringelly...388 B8
rd. Cobbitty...448 B6
rd. Cranebrook...207 G16
rd. Glenmore Pk...266 J16
rd. Harringtn Pk...448 A10
rd. Llandilo...207 H7
rd. Londonderry...149 D15
rd. Luddenham...356 G2
rd. Mulgoa...296 D14
rd. Narellan...478 B2
rd. Oran Park...448 A10
rd. Orchard Hills...267 A9
rd. S Penrith...267 A9
THEO
st. Liverpool...365 B15
THE OAKS FIRE
trl. Blue Mtn N P...263 B15
THEODORE
st. Balmain...7 D9
THE OLD OAKS
rd. Brownlow Hl...505 H6
rd. Grasmere...505 H6
THE OUTLOOK
Bilgola...169 H5
Harringtn Pk...477 F4
Hornsby Ht...191 D4
Kirkham...477 F4
THE OUTPOST
Castlecrag...286 A14
Northbridge...286 A14
THE PALISADE
Castlecrag...286 A13
THE PARADE
Drummoyne...343 E4
Dulwich Hill...373 C12
Enfield...371 H3
Russell Lea...343 E4
Telopea...279 H9
THE PARAPET
Castlecrag...286 A12
THE PARKWAY
Bradbury...511 D14
Bradbury...511 D8
Kellyville...185 H13
THE PINNACLE
Bilgola...169 J3
THE PLATEAU
Lansvale...366 F9
THE PLAZA
Rose Bay...348 D13
THE POINT
S Wntwthvle...306 H7
rd. Woolwich...314 F12
THE PONDS
Mt Annan...479 B15
Mt Annan...479 C15
THE PORTICO
Toongabbie...276 C7
THE POSTERN
Castlecrag...285 K12
THE PROMENADE
Cheltenham...250 J9
Old Guildfrd...337 D9
Sans Souci...433 A16
Sylvania...461 G10
Yennora...337 D9
THE QUARTERDECK
Middle Cove...286 A7
Mt Annan...479 B15
THE RAMPART
Castlecrag...286 A13
Hornsby...221 C3
THE RAPIDS
Mt Annan...479 C15
THE REDOUBT
Castlecrag...286 B13
THERESA
st. Blacktown...274 E5
st. Greystanes...306 F6
st. Smithfield...336 B8
THERESA VIEW
dr. Theresa Park...444 A5
THERESE
cct. Baulkham Hl...247 C3
THE RETREAT
Bringelly...388 G5
THE RIDGE
Frenchs Frst...256 D1
Lansvale...366 D10
THE RIVER
rd. Picnic Point...428 J7
rd. Revesby...428 J5
rd. Revesby Ht...428 J7
THE RIVULET
Mt Annan...509 C1
THE ROAD
Penrith...237 B7
THE ROCKS
sq. The Rocks...A K2
THERRY
rd. Ambarvale...511 A10
rd. Campbelltwn...510 K10
st. Avalon...139 K13
st. Bligh Park...150 K7
st. Drummoyne...343 H5
st.e, Strathfield S...371 B5
st.w, Strathfield S...371 A5
THE SANCTUARY
dr. Leonay...264 J1
THE SCARP
Castlecrag...286 D11
THE SERPENTINE
Bilgola...170 A6
Kensington...376 C10
THESEUS
cct. Rsemeadow...540 J10
THE SEVEN WAYS
Rockdale...403 C16
THESIGER
rd. Bonnyrigg...363 J7
THE SPRINGS
Mt Annan...479 B16
Mt Annan...509 B1
THE STABLES
la. Darlinghurst...F H2
THE STONE COTTAGE
pl. Blair Athol...511 A2
THE STRAIGHT
rd. Mulgoa...325 B2
THE STRAND
Croydon...372 E1
Dee Why...259 A7
Gladesville...313 A4
Mortdale...431 A6
Penshurst...431 F6
Rockdale...403 E16
Whale Beach...140 C7
THE TAR
Mosman, off Wolseley Rd...317 D9
THE TERRACE
Abbotsford...312 J15
Birchgrove...7 G3
Warrimoo...203 B12
Windsor...121 A9
Windsor...121 C7
Oatlands, off Governors Wy...279 A8
THE TOR
wk. Castlecrag...286 F10
THE TRONGATE
Granville...308 F16
S Granville...338 F2
THE UPPER SANCTUARY
dr. Leonay...234 J16
THE VALE
Belrose...225 K13
THE VALLEY
rd. Valley Ht...202 G5
THE VILLAGE
pl. Dural...188 J13
THEW
pde. Cromer...228 F14
THE WALK
Clontarf...287 G12
Earlwood...403 B5
THE WATER
la. Box Hill...184 G1
la. Rouse Hill...184 G1
THE WATERMARK
Mt Annan...479 B15
THE WATERS
Mt Annan...479 C15
THE W E MIDDLETON MEMORIAL
dr. Couridjah...564 B16
THE WHITE WATER
Mt Annan...479 C16
THE WOODS
cct. Menai...458 J14
THIELE
rd. Kenthurst...156 J12
THIRD
av. Berala...339 E15
av. Blacktown...244 F14
av. Campsie...371 H10
av. Canley Vale...366 B4
av. Condell Park...398 D5
av. Eastwood...281 C9
av. Epping...280 E3
av. Gymea Bay...491 D11
av. Jannali...460 J10
av. Lane Cove...314 G5
av. Lindfield...254 F13
av. Llandilo...208 E8
av. Loftus...490 A6
av. Mcquarie Fd...454 A2
av. North Ryde...282 H13
av. N Willghby...285 H11
av. Seven Hills...275 H3
av. Willoughby...285 H11
rd. Berkshire Pk...180 A3
st. Ashbury...372 G8
st. Granville...308 G14
st. Parramatta...279 A16
st. Warragamba...353 F7
THIRLMERE
av. Northmead...278 D5

pl. Leumeah 482 F12
wy. Picton 562 C16
wy. Picton 563 B11
wy. Tahmoor 565 C9
wy. Thirlmere 562 C16
wy. Thirlmere 565 B8
wy. Thirlmere 565 C3
THIRROUL
cct. Prestons 393 C13
THIRTEENTH
av. Austral 391 B5
st. Warragamba 353 F5
THIRTIETH
av. West Hoxton 391 F14
THIRTYFIRST
av. West Hoxton 391 F14
THIRTYSECOND
av. West Hoxton 391 G7
THIRTYTHIRD
av. West Hoxton 391 G9
THISBE
pl. Rsemeadow 540 H9
THISTLE
cct. Green Valley 363 A8
st. Ryde 311 H3
wy. Blacktown 274 E12
THOAR
pl. Clarmnt Ms 268 J3
THOM
av. West Hoxton 391 J6
THOMAS
av. Hamondvle 396 H16
av. Lurnea 394 C10
av. Roseville 284 D5
la. Darlington 18 K5
la. Haymarket E C10
la. Crows Nest, off Huntingdon St 315 H6
la. St Marys, off Thomas St 269 J6
pl. Bligh Park 150 F6
rd. Freemns Rch 60 J10
rd. Galston 159 C6
rd. Londonderry 178 A9
st. Ashfield 372 E1
st. Birchgrove 7 E5
st. Campbelltwn 511 J2
st. Chatswood 284 H10
st. Coogee 407 E2
st. Croydon 372 E1
st. Darlington 18 J5
st. Fairfield 336 C13
st. Granville 308 E15
st. Haymarket E B11
st. Haymarket 3 D14
st. Hornsby 221 J2
st. Hurstville 401 E16
st. Kingsgrove 401 K6
st. Lewisham 15 C8
st. McMahons Pt 5 C12
st. Merrylands 307 J9
st. Merrylands 308 E15
st. Newtown 17 G13
st. North Manly 258 C13
st. Northmead 277 J7
st. Parramatta 308 F1
st. Picnic Point 428 G8
st. St Marys 269 H6
st. Seven Hills 246 B11
st. Strathfield 371 E2
st. Ultimo 3 A15
st. Woolooware 493 J10
wy. Currans Hill 479 H10
THOMAS BELL
av. Wrrngtn Cty 238 H6
THOMAS CLARKE
st. Westmead 307 H3
THOMAS FRANCIS
wy. Rouse Hill 184 K8
THOMAS HOLT
dr. Mcquarie Pk 282 J6
THOMAS KELLY
cr. Lalor Park 245 G12
THOMAS LAYCOCK
pl. Bringelly 388 J9
THOMAS MITCHELL
dr. Barden Rdg 488 F7
THOMAS NELSON
pl. Glenbrook 234 B11
THOMAS ROSE
dr. Rsemeadow 540 K3
THOMAS TELFORD
pl. Glenbrook 234 B11
THOMAS WILKINSON
av. Dural 219 A5
THOMOND
st. Hurstville 401 G16
THOMPSON
av. Illawong 459 J3
av. Maroubra 407 E15
av. Moorebank 396 B8
av. Richmond 118 D6
av. St Marys 240 A15
cl. W Pnnant Hl 250 B1
cr. Glenwood 215 E12
dr. Terrey Hills 196 C11
la. Belmore 401 F2
la. Bondi Jctn 22 C9
la. East Hills 427 G5
la. Five Dock 342 K10
pl. Baulkham Hl 247 D7
pl. Camden S 507 A15
pl. Darlinghurst 4 E10
pl. Minto 482 H8
sq. Windsor 121 D7
st. Arncliffe 403 H5
st. Bundeena 523 H9
st. Drummoyne 343 G3
st. Earlwood 372 H16
st. Gladesville 312 K4
st. Marrickville 374 B11
st. Mosman 317 B12
st. Scotland I 168 G3
st. Scotland I 168 G4
st. Tamarama 378 B7
st. Turrella 403 G5
st. Wetherill Pk 334 G4
THOMPSONS
la. Yagoona 369 B12
rd. Bringelly 387 H8
THOMSON
av. Artarmon 285 A16
av. Beverly Hills 430 J1
av. Lucas Ht 487 J11
av. Springwood 172 C12
la. Darlinghurst 4 E10
st. Darlinghurst 4 E11
THOR
pl. Hebersham 241 G4
THORA
st. Greystanes 305 H6
THORBY
av. Leichhardt 10 E16
THORLEY
st. S Windsor 150 A6
THORN
pl. Mt Pritchard 364 D9
pl. North Rocks 248 F14
st. Hunters Hill 313 E5
st. Liverpool 395 A8
st. Pennant Hills 220 E12
st. Revesby 398 J13
st. Ryde 311 G3
wy. Penrith 237 D2
THORNBILL
cr. Glenmore Pk 265 J13
wy. W Pnnant Hl 249 D8
wy. Yarramundi 145 C6
THORNBURY
pl. Bella Vista 246 H3
pl. Minto 483 A2
THORNCRAFT
pde. Campsie 371 J16
THORNCROFT
pl. Bargo 567 B3
THORNE
av. Pendle Hill 276 G14
st. Edgecliff 13 K14
st. Ingleburn 453 B12
THORNEY
rd. Fairfield W 335 B13
THORNFLAT
rd. Cranebrook 207 F12
THORNHILL
cr. Wrrngtn Dns 238 B6
pl. Cherrybrook 219 C14
THORNLEIGH
av. Concord 341 G8
st. Thornleigh 221 A14
THORNLEY
la. Drummoyne, off Roseby St 344 B4
rd. Prospect 305 A1
st. Drummoyne 344 A4
st. Leichhardt 15 J2
st. Marrickville 403 G1
THORNTON
av. Bass Hill 368 C13
av. Carlingford 279 E2
av. Glenmore Pk 266 E14
pl. Kangaroo Pt 461 H7
st. Canada Bay 342 D9
st. Darling Point 13 J2
st. Fairlight 288 D8
st. Rozelle 7 A10
THORP
rd. Woronora 489 J3
THORPE
av. Cherrybrook 219 J11
av. Liberty Gr 311 B11
rd. Kingsgrove 401 J14
st. Clovelly 377 K13
st. Colyton 270 G7
THORSBY
pl. Emu Plains 235 E9
THOW
pl. Currans Hill 479 G12
THREDBO
st. Heckenberg 364 C13
THRELFALL
st. Eastwood 281 G5
THRELKELD
dr. Cattai 94 A5
THRIFT
cl. W Pnnant Hl 249 A7
st. Colyton 270 B7
THROSBY
dr. Narellan Vale 508 G1
st. Casula 394 C16
st. Fairfield Ht 335 H11
wy. Ambarvale 511 B12
THRUPP
st. Neutral Bay 6 F8
THUDDUNGRA
rd. Duffys Frst 194 K4
THUNDERBOLT
dr. Raby 451 C13
THURBON
av. Peakhurst 430 H1
THURLGONA
rd. Engadine 488 F13
THURLOW
la. Redfern 20 C9
st. Redfern 20 C9
st. Riverwood 400 C15
THURN
pl. Elderslie 507 F4
THURNBY
la. Newtown 17 C13
st. Chipping Ntn 396 G1
THUROONG
pl. Cranebrook 207 D5
THURSDAY
pl. Green Valley 362 K8
THURSO
pl. St Andrews 452 A12
THURSTON
st. Penrith 237 B8
THURWOOD
av. Jamisontown 266 D2
THYME
st. Quakers Hill 243 F5
THYRA
rd. Palm Beach 140 A6
TIA
pl. Hoxton Park 392 J10
pl. Ruse 512 D9
TIANIE
pl. Rouse Hill 185 D7
TIARA
pl. Granville 307 K8
TIARRI
av. Terrey Hills 196 B7
TIBBETT
pl. Kellyville 216 E5
TIBER
pl. Heathcote 518 E7
pl. Kearns 451 B16
st. Seven Hills 275 D8
TIBOOBURRA
rd. Hoxton Park 392 G7
st. Engadine 489 B12
TICH
pl. Doonside 243 C5
TICHBORNE
dr. Quakers Hill 213 J14
TICKLE
dr. Tahmoor 565 G5
TICKNER
st. Castlereagh 146 B14
TIDESWELL
st. Ashfield 373 C2
TIDSWELL
st. Mount Druitt 271 E2
st. St Marys 270 A3
TIERNAN
av. North Rocks 248 J14
TIERNEY
av. Eastgardens 406 G13
rd. Kurmond 56 H15
rd. The Slopes 56 H15
TIFFANY
pl. Rooty Hill 271 K2
TIFFIN
pl. Harringtn Pk 478 E1
TIGG
pl. Ambarvale 511 A10
TIGRIS
st. Kearns 450 K16
TILBA
av. Balmain 7 A6
pl. Woodpark 306 G14
pl. Yarrawarrah 489 F14
rd. Mulgoa 295 H15
st. Berala 339 D11
TILDEN
st. Plumpton 242 C11
TILEY
la. Cammeray, off Tiley St 316 B4
st. Cammeray 316 B4
TILFORD
st. Zetland 375 J10
TILLEARD
dr. Winston Hills 277 C3
TILLETT
pde. Lansdowne 367 C5
TILLEY
st. Dundas Vy 279 J10
TILLFORD
gr. Rooty Hill 272 C6
rd. Kenthurst 187 F6
rd. Royal N P 522 D9
TILLOCK
st. Haberfield 9 B10
st. Pennant Hills 220 G13
st. Thornleigh 220 H13
TILPA
pl. Hoxton Park 392 F7
TIMARU
gr. S Penrith 266 J7
pl. Kirrawee 491 B8
rd. Terrey Hills 196 E4
st. Glenorie 128 B2
st. Turramurra 222 K16
TIMBARA
ct. Wattle Grove 395 K12
TIMBARAM
wy. Woodcroft 243 E10
TIMBARRA
pl. Sutherland 460 C16
rd. St Ives Ch 194 A15
rd. Westleigh 220 G10
TIMBER
gr. Glenhaven 217 K5
gr. Wrrngtn Dns 238 D4
la. Wrrngtn Dns, off Timber Gr 238 D4
TIMBERLEA
cl. Bradbury 511 E14
TIMBERLINE
av. W Pnnant Hl 249 F6
av. W Pnnant Hl 249 G7
TIMBERTOP
av. Carlingford 249 H11
wy. Beecroft 250 J5
TIMBILLICA
pl. Prestons 393 C15
TIMBRELL
dr. Five Dock 343 D10
TIMESWEEP
dr. St Clair 270 C13
TIMGALEN
av. S Penrith 237 A16
TIMMS
cl. Edensor Pk 363 F4
st. Hebersham 241 E2
TIMMS HILL
rd. Kurrajong 85 F2
TIMOR
cl. Kirrawee 490 K8
pl. Kings Park 244 F1
TIMOTHY
av. Castle Hill 248 E1
cl. Cherrybrook 219 D7
la. Belmore 401 G3
pl. Edensor Pk 363 G2
rd. Londonderry 178 B8
st. Hurstville 431 J3
TIMOTHY LACEY
la. The Oaks 502 F9
TIMS
cr. Guildford W 336 H1
TIM WHIFFLER
pl. Richmond 118 A6
TINA
av. Lethbrdg Pk 210 G15
TINAKILL
av. Engadine 488 K11
TINAM
av. Whalan 240 K11
TINANA
pl. Bidwill 211 F16
st. Haberfield 343 B16
TINARRA
cr. Erskine Park 300 C2
cr. Erskine Park 300 D2
TINCOMBE
st. Canterbury 372 G13
TINDAL
wy. Mt Annan 479 H16
TINDALE
la. Woollahra 377 F2
rd. Artarmon 284 K14
st. Penrith 236 J11
TINDALL
av. Liverpool 395 F1
st. Campbelltwn 511 A6
TINDELL
st. Bligh Park 150 H5
TINGARA
av. Vaucluse 348 B4
la. Cabarita 342 E1
TINGCOMBE
pl. Camden 507 B2
TINGHA
av. S Penrith 266 E6
cl. Hinchinbrk 392 G4
st. Chatswood 284 K11
st. Engadine 488 F12
TINGIRA
pl. Forestville 255 K12
TINTAGEL
pl. Glenhaven 217 J6
pl. Turramurra 222 G15
TINTERN
av. Carlingford 279 E9
av. Telopea 279 E9
rd. Ashfield 373 A5
TINTO
pl. Acacia Gdn 244 K1
TIPANI
pl. Erskine Park 300 E2
TIPPER
av. Bronte 378 A10
TIPPERARY
av. Killarney Ht 256 D14
TIPPET
pl. Quakers Hill 214 C8
TIPPING
pl. Ambarvale 510 H15
TIPTREE
av. Strathfield 341 E16
TIPTREES
av. Carlingford 279 H5
la. Carlingford 279 J5
TIRAGE
pl. Minchinbury 272 B10
TIRANNA
pl. Oyster Bay 461 C4
TIREE
av. Hunters Hill 314 B13
TIRRABEENA
pl. Bangor 459 E12
TIRTO
st. Barden Rdg 488 F8
TISANE
av. Frenchs Frst 256 G2
TISHER
pl. Ambarvale 511 A14
TITANIA
la. Randwick, off Lion St 407 B2
la. Randwick, off Rainbow La 407 A1
la. Cranebrook, off Titania Pl 207 E10
pl. Cranebrook 207 F10

pl. Rsemeadow....540 J10
st. Randwick.......407 B2

TI TREE
cr. Berowra..........163 C1
pl. Wilberforce.......62 G12

TITUS
pl. Acacia Gdn.....244 K1

TIVERTON
wy. Airds.............512 E9

TIVOLI
av. Rose Bay........348 B7
ct. Wattle Grove...426 C3
esp. Como............460 J6
pl. Doonside........243 B9
st. Mosman..........317 C3
st. Paddington.......21 F3

TIVY
pl. Marayong.......243 H6

TIZZANA
rd. Ebenezer...........63 E6

TOBERMORY
av. St Andrews.....481 J2

TOBIAS
pl. Kings Lngly....245 A4

TOBIN
pl. Marayong.......243 H6

TOBRUK
av. Allambie Ht.....257 F11
av. Balmain..............7 E12
av. Belmore..........371 F16
av. Carlingford.....250 A13
av. Cremorne.......316 F4
av. Engadine........488 J16
av. Liverpool........394 J4
av. St Ives Ch.......223 J4
pl. Bossley Park...334 A6
rd. Narellan Vale...479 A11
st. North Ryde.....282 K11
st. N St Marys.....239 J10

TOBY
cr. Panania..........398 A13
mw. Bella Vista.......246 G3
pl. Kings Lngly....246 B10

TOBYS
bvd. Mt Pritchard...364 G13

TOCAL
ct. Wattle Grove...426 A1

TOD
pl. Minchinbury...271 G9

TODD
cir. Old Tngabbie..277 B6
cr. Peakhurst.......400 H16
ct. Wattle Grove...395 H12
la. St Clair, off Banks Dr.........269 K13
pl. Bossley Park...333 J6
pl. Cherrybrook...219 J11
pl. Illawong.........459 J5
pl. Leumeah........482 G11
pl. Mt Annan........509 F1
row. St Clair..........269 J12
st. Kingsgrove.....402 A12
st. Merrylnds W...307 A12

TODMAN
av. Kensington.....376 B9
av. Kensington.....376 D12
av. West Pymble..252 H9
la. St Clair, off Todman Pl.......270 E12
pl. St Clair..........270 E11
pl. Strathfield.......341 B14
rd. Warwck Frm...365 J14

TOELLE
st. Rozelle...........344 C7

TOGGERAI
st. Appin.............568 F13

TOGIL
st. Canley Vale.....366 E2

TOKANUE
pl. St Ives Ch.......223 J3

TOKARA
st. Allambie Ht.....257 G15

TOKAY
ct. Edensor Pk.....363 D1
pl. Eschol Park....481 E2

TOLEDO
pl. Baulkham Hl...246 J13

TOLL
st. N Parramatta..278 A10

TOLLAND
st. Prestons.........393 B15

TOLLEY
pl. Edensor Pk.....333 F14

TOLLGATE
cr. Windsor..........121 C9

TOLL HOUSE
wy. Windsor..........121 C9

TOLMER
st. Bossley Park...334 C5

TOLOL
av. Miranda..........491 H2

TOM
st. Ermington.......310 F3
st. Sylvania..........462 A8
wy. Casula............424 H2

TOMAGO
ct. Wattle Grove...425 K3

TOMAH
pl. Bossley Park...334 B10
pl. Ruse...............512 G5
pl. Sylvania..........461 K8
pl. Westleigh........220 G9
st. Carlingford......280 C4
st. Kurrajong Ht.....54 B7
st. St Ives Ch.......224 B1

TOMINTOUL
wy. Glenhaven.......218 A6

TOMKI
st. Carramar........366 J1

TOMKINS
st. Bexley North...402 E11

TOMPSON
rd. Panania...........428 E3
rd. Revesby..........428 E3

TOM SCANLON
cl. Kellyville.........216 E1

TONBRIDGE
st. Ramsgate.......433 F14
st. Sans Souci.....433 F14

TONGA
cl. Greenacre.......370 C14
cl. St Clair............270 B16
cr. Smithfield.......336 B6
pl. Lethbrdg Pk....240 H2

TONGARIRO
tce. Bidwill.............211 F15

TONGARRA
cl. Bangor............459 G10
pl. Westleigh........220 F6

TONI
cr. Ryde...............282 D15
pl. Baulkham Hl...247 F9

TONITTO
av. Peakhurst.......430 E5

TONKIES
pl. Menai.............459 A11

TONKIN
cr. Schofields.......213 H6
st. Cronulla..........493 K13

TONY
cr. Padstow.........399 B16
pl. Glendenning...242 F1
st. Collaroy..........229 A10

TOOCOOYA
la. Hunters Hill.....313 J12
rd. Hunters Hill.....313 J12

TOOGOOD
la. Erskineville.......17 J14

TOOHEY
av. Westmead.......307 D2
cr. Bexley.............402 D15
rd. Wetherill Pk....333 H4

TOOHEYS
la. Lidcombe.......339 H8

TOOLANG
rd. St Ives............223 J6

TOOLE
st. Doonside........243 E5

TOOLONG
st. Horngsea Pk...392 E15
st. Horngsea Pk...392 D15

TOOMA
pl. Heckenberg....364 A15

TOOMEVARA
st. Kogarah..........433 D7

TOOMEY
cr. Quakers Hill....213 J7

TOOMUNG
cct. Clarmnt Ms.....268 G2

TOONA
pl. Bossley Park...333 H8

TOONGABBIE
rd. Girraween.......275 H14
rd. Toongabbie.....275 H15
rd. Toongabbie.....276 B9

TOONGARAH
rd. Roseville.........284 D6

rd. Waverton...........5 C6

TOORADIN
pl. W Pnnant Hl....250 A2

TOORAH
rd. Londonderry...149 H9

TOORAK
av. Beverly Hills....401 A15
av. Taren Point.....462 J13
cl. St Johns Pk.....364 E4
cr. Emu Plains......234 K9
ct. Cherrybrook.....219 D10
pl. Avalon.............140 B12

TOORONGA
rd. Terrey Hills......195 F5
tce. Beverly Hills....401 C14

TOOTH
la. Camperdwn.....17 E6

TOOTHILL
la. Lewisham, off Old Canterbury Rd...................15 B10
st. Lewisham........15 A11

TOOTHS
pl. Camperdwn.....17 E7

TOPAROA
cl. Casula............394 F16

TOPAZ
cr. Seven Hills......275 B7
pl. Bankstown......399 E6
pl. Bossley Park...334 A7
pl. Eagle Vale.......481 B7

TOPE
pl. Ambarvale.......510 J15

TOPEKA
gln. St Clair...........270 H13
la. St Clair, off Topeka Gln.......270 H13

TOPHAM
rd. Smeaton Gra...479 B6

TOPIN
pl. Moorebank......396 C12

TOPLICA
pl. Canloy Ht........365 D4

TOPNOT
av. Hinchinbrk......393 C4

TOPPER
pl. Campbelltwn...510 J10

TOPPING
st. Panania...........398 A16

TOR
rd. Dee Why.........258 F3

TORA
pl. Dharruk...........241 A6
pl. Forestville.......255 K12

TORBERT
av. Quakers Hill....214 F10

TORCH
st. Voyager Pt......427 C4

TORICELLI
av. Whalan...........241 A11

TORKINGTON
rd. Londonderry...147 D7

TORNADO
cr. Cranebrook.....207 B10
la. Cranebrook, off Tornado Cr.......207 B10
pl. Raby..............451 E16

TORNAROS
av. Penrith............237 A13

TOROKINA
av. St Ives............224 C15

TORONTO
av. Cromer...........227 J12
pde. Jannali...........460 F16
pde. Sutherland......490 F1

TORQUAY
tce. Glenmore Pk...266 G14

TORQUIL
av. Carlingford......250 A15

TORRANCE
cr. Quakers Hill....214 C12

TORRENS
ct. Wattle Grove...396 A14
pl. Cherrybrook....219 F12
pl. Cromer...........228 C16
pl. Kearns............481 A2
st. Blakehurst.......432 F16
st. Canley Ht........365 E3
st. Canley Vale.....365 E3
st. Matraville.......437 B3
st. Merrylnds W...306 K13
st. Punchbowl......400 B8
st. St Ives............254 F1

TORRES
cl. Emu Plains.....234 K11
cr. Whalan...........241 A10
cr. Whalan...........241 A11
pl. Kings Lngly....245 D3
pl. St Ives...........224 A8
st. Kurnell...........465 H8

TORRINGTON
av. Sefton............368 G3
dr. Marsfield........281 H3
rd. Maroubra.......407 H9
rd. Strathfield.......341 F14

TORRS
st. Baulkham Hl...247 J14

TORTON
pl. Penrith...........236 J13

TORULOSA
pl. Winmalee.......173 F8

TORUMBA
av. Bayview..........168 E11
cl. Bangor...........459 E11

TORVER
pl. Collaroy Plat...228 D10

TORWOOD
pl. St Johns Pk.....334 E16
st. Sans Souci.....433 B14
st. Warrimoo.......203 A10

TOSCANA
st. Prestons.........393 E13

TOSCANO
ct. Erskine Park...300 F2

TOSH
la. Zetland, off Dunning Av.....375 H11

TOSICH
pl. Bonnyrigg Ht..363 F5

TOTALA
pl. Elanora Ht......198 F12

TOTEM
la. Balgowlah......287 J8

TOTTENHAM
pl. Blakehurst.......462 F2
st. Granville.........308 D8
st. N Balgowlah...287 F5

TOUCAN
cr. Plumpton.......241 H7

TOULOUSE
st. Cecil Hills.......362 C4

TOURMALINE
st. Eagle Vale.......481 F8
st. Narrabeen......229 B1

TOURNAY
st. Peakhurst.......430 H2

TOUT
rd. Bidwill............211 F12
rd. Marsden Pk....211 F12

TOWARRI
pl. Belrose...........226 C16

TOWER
ct. Castle Hill.......217 B9
pl. Berowra.........133 E12
rd. Bnkstn Aprt....397 E5
res. Castlecrag, off Edinburgh Rd..286 C11
st. Coogee...........377 K13
st. Glenwood.......215 C15
st. Manly.............288 F9
st. Panania..........428 A2
st. Revesby.........428 E2
st. Vaucluse........348 G5

TOWERS
pl. Arncliffe..........403 E9
st. Arncliffe..........403 E9
st. Cabramatta.....365 C9

TOWN
st. Richmond......118 E7

TOWNER
av. Milperra.........397 D10
gdn. Pagewood......406 F7
st. Galston..........160 H6

TOWN HALL
la. Auburn, off Queen St.........339 D3

TOWNS
pl. Millers Point.......1 D8
rd. Vaucluse........348 C7
st. Gladesville......312 G8

TOWNSEND
av. Frenchs Frst...255 H4
rd. N Richmond.....86 J14
st. Condell Park...398 E3
st. Guildford........337 J3

TOWNSON
av. Leumeah........482 F11

av. Minto.............482 G8
rd. Marsden Pk....212 D9
rd. Schofields......212 D9
st. Blakehurst......462 D2

TOWNSVILLE
rd. Wakeley.........334 K14

TOWNVIEW
rd. Mt Pritchard...364 J9

TOWRADGI
pl. Bangor...........459 G10
st. Narraweena....257 K3

TOWRA POINT
rd. Kurnell...........463 K12

TOWRI
cl. St Ives...........224 C15
pl. Marsfield........251 H16

TOWSON
la. Bexley............402 C16

TOXANA
st. Richmond.......118 J4

TOXTETH
la. Glebe...............11 H11
rd. Glebe...............11 G11

TOYER
av. Sans Souci.....463 B3
st. Tempe............374 B16

TRABB
pl. Ambarvale......510 J16

TRACEY
av. Carlingford.....249 F13
cl. Normanhurst..221 H7
la. Chippendale......18 H3
pl. Orchard Hills..268 E8
st. Revesby.........398 D11

TRACY
st. Rooty Hill.......242 A15

TRADE
la. Newtown..........17 B10
st. Newtown..........17 B10

TRADEWINDS
pl. Kareela...........461 E10

TRAFALGAR
av. Lindfield.........284 F1
av. Roseville.........284 F1
la. Annandale........11 B14
la. Concord, off Trafalgar Pde...341 K4
pde. Concord..........341 J4
pl. Marsfield.........252 A13
pl. Northmead.......278 C6
rd. Emu Heights...235 A2
st. Annandale........16 K3
st. Belmore..........401 F4
st. Btn-le-Sds.......433 K3
st. Bronte............378 A10
st. Crows Nest.....315 J6
st. Engadine........488 J14
st. Enmore............17 A11
st. Glenfield.........424 E10
st. Peakhurst........430 C2
st. Petersham........15 H10
st. Riverstone......182 F13
st. Stanmore.........16 C10

TRAHLEE
rd. Bellevue Hill......14 H9
rd. Londonderry...148 D10

TRAIL
cl. Mt Annan........479 J16

TRAINER
av. Casula...........394 F16

TRALEE
av. Killarney Ht.....256 A16

TRAM
la. Randwick, off Church St........376 K12

TRAMINER
gr. Orchard Hills..268 G14
pl. Eschol Park...481 E3
pl. Minchinbury...272 B8

TRAMORE
pl. Killarney Ht.....256 B16

TRAMWAY
arc. Rockdale, off Frederick St.... 403 B15
arc. Rockdale, off Princess Hwy..403 C15
av. Camellia.........308 J4
av. Parramatta......308 J4
dr. Currans Hill....479 J12
la. Randwick.......377 A10
la. Rosebery........405 F1
la. Concord, off Frederick St.....342 B2
st. Denistone W...280 J13

st. Rosebery 405 F1
st. Tempe 404 A2
st. West Ryde 280 J13
TRANMERE
st. Drummoyne 343 J3
TRANQUILITY
ct. Bella Vista 246 F6
TRANSVAAL
av. Double Bay 14 D9
TRAPPERS
wy. Avalon 139 H10
TRAVERS
rd. Curl Curl 258 J13
TRAVIS
pl. Menai 458 K6
TRAWALLA
st. Hebersham 241 E9
TRAYNOR
av. Kogarah 433 E6
TREACY
st. Hurstville 432 B6
TREADGOLD
st. Leichhardt 15 D4
st. Milperra 397 F10
TREATT
av. Padstow 429 A1
TREATTS
rd. Lindfield 254 B15
TREBARTHA
st. Bass Hill 368 C9
TREBBIANO
pl. Eschol Park 481 B4
TREBLE
cl. Hamondvle 396 D13
TREBOR
rd. Pennant Hills 250 F1
TREBORTH
pl. Menai 459 B9
TREELANDS
av. Ingleburn 453 C8
cl. Galston 160 J4
TREES
wy. Rooty Hill 271 K6
TREE TOPS
av. S Penrith 267 A1
pl. Valley Ht 202 E6
TREETOPS
rd. Cherrybrook 219 A13
TREEVIEW
pl. Epping 251 A12
pl. North Rocks 248 K15
TREGENNA
cl. St Ives 224 E11
TREHARNE
cl. Marsfield 282 B4
TRELAWNEY
st. Croydon Pk 371 H9
st. Eastwood 280 K11
st. Eastwood 281 A9
st. Thornleigh 221 C11
st. Woollahra 14 A15
TRELOAR
av. Mortdale 430 J5
cr. Chester Hill 338 A13
pl. Edensor Pk 363 C2
pl. Menai 458 D12
TREMA
pl. Mt Annan 509 D3
TREMAIN
av. Kellyville 216 E4
TREMERE
st. Concord 342 D6
TREMLOW
cr. Ambarvale 511 B11
TRENT
pl. Ambarvale 511 B14
pl. Hassall Gr 211 J14
pl. N Richmond 87 C12
rd. North Rocks 278 F1
st. S Penrith 266 J4
TRENTBRIDGE
rd. Belrose 225 J12
TRENTHAM PARK
ct. Wattle Grove 425 K5
TRENTINO
rd. Turramurra 222 K7
TRENTON
rd. Guildford 337 D5
TRENTWOOD
pk. Avalon 139 J16
TRESALAM
st. Mt Pritchard 364 H15
TRESCO
st. St Marys 239 G7
TRESIDDER
av. Kingsford 406 C1
TRESS
st. Blacktown 274 K5
TRESSIDER
av. Haberfield 9 A16
av. Haberfield 343 E16
TREUER
la. Yagoona, off The Crescent 369 A12
pde. Yagoona 368 F14
TREVALGAN
pl. St Ives 224 F5
TREVALSA
pl. Burraneer 523 D3
TREVANION
st. Five Dock 343 A8
TREVANNA
st. Busby 363 H13
TREVELLYAN
st. Cronulla 523 J1
TREVELYAN
st. Botany 405 J13
TREVENA
la. Enfield 371 J3
TREVENAR
st. Ashbury 372 F7
TREVES
st. Merrylands 307 G12
TREVILYAN
av. Rosebery 375 K16
TREVITHICK
st. Riverstone 182 J10
TREVITT
rd. North Ryde 282 D6
TREVLYN
wy. Acacia Gdn 244 K1
TREVONE
st. Padstow 399 G16
TREVOR
pl. Castle Hill 217 G15
rd. Newport 169 H12
st. Lilyfield 10 D6
TREVORS
la. Cherrybrook 220 A3
TREVOR TOMS
dr. Acacia Gdn 214 K16
TREWILGA
av. Earlwood 372 J16
TREZISE
pl. Quakers Hill 213 K16
TRIABUNNA
av. West Hoxton 392 E5
TRIAL
pl. Illawong 459 D5
TRIANGLE
la. Lowlands 88 C16
la. Richmond 88 C16
TRICKETT
rd. Woolooware 493 G11
TRIDA
pl. Emu Plains 235 G11
TRIDENT
cl. Raby 481 H1
TRIESTE
cl. Prestons 393 D13
TRIGALANA
pl. Frenchs Frst 256 E1
TRIGG
av. Carlingford 279 J1
TRIGGS
st. St Marys 239 E2
TRIGON
rd. Abbotsbury 362 G1
TRILLER
pl. Ingleburn 453 F10
st. Green Valley 363 D10
TRINA
cr. Canterbury 402 E1
pl. Hassall Gr 211 K16
TRINDER
av. Kingswood 237 F15
TRINERVIS
wy. Mcquarie Fd 454 H4
TRINEURA
ct. Wattle Grove 396 B15
TRINITY
av. Dawes Point A G2
av. Dawes Point 1 F9
dr. Cmbrdg Gdn 237 G2
la. Cmbrdg Gdn, off Trinity Dr 237 G5
pl. Cherrybrook 219 F14
pl. Kings Lngly 245 H5
TRIPOD
st. Concord 342 C5
TRIPOLI
av. Carlingford 249 K14
pl. Eagle Vale 481 H4
rd. Fairfield W 335 F13
TRIPP
pwy. Warwick Frm, off Tripp St 365 E14
st. Warwick Frm 365 E14
TRIS
pl. Kings Lngly 246 B9
TRISH
pl. Castle Hill 248 F3
TRISTAN
cl. Oakhurst 242 D2
ct. Castle Hill 217 G4
TRISTANIA
ct. Baulkham Hl 247 C15
gr. Greenacre 370 F5
gr. Menai 459 A14
pl. West Pymble 252 G11
st. Mt Annan 509 C3
wy. Beecroft 250 F3
wy. Winmalee 173 F7
TRISTRAM
rd. Beacon Hill 257 F5
st. Ermington 310 B4
TRITEN
av. Greenfld Pk 334 D15
TRITON
pl. S Penrith 267 C4
TRITTONS
la. Lakemba 370 H15
TRIUMPH
pl. Ingleburn 453 G11
TRIVET
st. Horsley Pk 303 G13
TRIVETTS
la. Balmain 7 H8
TROBRIAND
cr. Glenfield 424 H11
TROON
ct. Glenmore Pk 266 E11
pl. Pymble 252 J4
pl. St Andrews 481 K5
TROOPERS
mw. Holsworthy 426 F4
TROPIC-BIRD
cr. Hinchinbrk 393 C3
TROTT
st. Parramatta 278 C15
TROTWOOD
av. Ambarvale 510 H15
TROUT
pl. St Clair 269 H16
TROUTON
st. Balmain 7 K6
TROUVE
st. Lane Cove 314 B3
TROY
la. Campsie 401 K2
pl. Winston Hills 277 D1
rd. Heathcote 518 F7
st. Campsie 401 K1
st. Emu Plains 235 D13
TRUDY
pl. Hassall Gr 211 J14
TRUEMAN
pl. North Rocks 278 J3
TRUK
pl. Kings Park 244 J3
TRUMAN
av. Bonnet Bay 460 C8
av. Cromer 227 J13
av. Riverwood 400 B14
pl. Bonnet Bay 460 C8
rd. Horsley Pk 331 H4
st. Hurstville 431 K9
st. S Hurstville 431 K9
TRUMBLE
av. Ermington 310 C3
TRUMFIELD
la. Mosman 316 H13
TRUMPER
pl. Menai 458 F9
st. Ermington 310 E2
wy. Rouse Hill 184 J6
TRURAN
cl. Hornsby 221 E4
TRURO
pde. Padstow 429 G1
pl. Kenthurst 188 A12
TRUSCOTT
av. Matraville 407 C16
la. Panania 427 K1
pl. Bidwill 211 C15
pl. East Killara 254 G9
st. North Ryde 282 J10
st. Panania 427 K1
TRYAL
pl. Willmot 210 C11
TRYON
av. Wollstncraft 315 C12
la. Lindfield 254 E16
la. Chatswood, off Orchard Rd 284 J12
pl. Lindfield, off Pacific Hwy 284 D1
rd. E Lindfield 254 G15
rd. Lindfield 254 E16
st. Chatswood 284 J12
TSAR
cl. Cecil Hills 362 J5
TUAM
pl. Killarney Ht 255 H11
st. Concord 342 D6
TUART
pl. Narellan Vale 478 J15
TUCABIA
av. Georges Hall 367 H10
st. S Coogee 407 G7
TUCANA
st. Erskine Park 300 G2
TUCKER
la. Bass Hill, off Tucker St 368 D11
pl. Edensor Pk 363 G2
rd. Casula 424 D4
st. Bass Hill 368 D11
st. N Sydney 5 G1
st. Ryde 312 A1
st. Wiley Park 400 H4
TUCKS
rd. Seven Hills 276 E2
rd. Toongabbie 276 F6
TUCKWELL
pl. Mcquarie Pk 283 A2
rd. Castle Hill 217 G10
TUCSON
gr. Stanhpe Gdn 215 B11
TUDAR
rd. Bonnet Bay 460 D10
rd. Sutherland 460 D10
TUDOR
av. Blacktown 275 A6
av. Cherrybrook 219 K9
cl. Belrose 226 C12
cr. Cecil Hills 362 E7
pl. Carlingford 279 B5
pl. Glenfield 424 C11
pl. St Ives Ch 224 B6
pl. Surry Hills 20 B3
st. Belmore 401 J1
st. Campsie 401 J1
st. Surry Hills 20 A3
TUFFY
av. Sans Souci 463 B6
TUGA
pl. Glenmore Pk 266 A11
TUGGERAH
cl. St Clair 300 C1
pl. Woodcroft 243 H11
st. Leumeah 482 E14
TUGLOW
pl. Leumeah 482 C14
TUGRA
cl. Glenmore Pk 266 C10
TUKARA
rd. S Penrith 267 A6
TUKIDALE
cl. Elderslie 507 J2
TULA
pl. Tregear 240 F6
TULICH
av. Dee Why 258 H2
av. Prestons 393 A15
TULIP
cl. Alfords Point 459 A2
gr. Fairfield W 335 B9
pl. Quakers Hill 243 D3
pl. St Clair 269 G10
st. Chatswood 284 J8
st. Greystanes 306 A12
st. North Ryde 282 C8
TULIPWOOD
dr. Colyton 270 H7
TULLAMORE
av. Killarney Ht 256 A14
TULLIMBAR
rd. Cronulla 494 A8
st. Croydon Pk 371 F7
TULLOCH
av. Rhodes 311 D11
cl. Casula 394 G15
la. St Clair, off Tulloch Pl 270 D11
pl. Baulkham Hl 246 J3
pl. Edensor Pk 333 E15
pl. St Clair 270 E11
st. Blacktown 243 K10
TULLOH
st. Willoughby 285 F15
TULLOONA
st. Mount Druitt 241 C12
TULLY
av. Liverpool 394 H10
pl. Quakers Hill 214 D14
TULONG
av. Oatlands 279 B13
pl. Kirrawee 491 A9
TULSA
ct. Quakers Hill 214 F11
TULUKERA
pl. Bangor 459 G10
TUMBARUMBA
cr. Heckenberg 364 C13
TUMBRIDGE
cr. Cambrdg Pk 238 C8
TUMBURRA
st. Ingleside 197 D6
TUMMUL
pl. St Andrews 452 B15
TUMUT
cl. Bankstown 399 B5
la. St Clair, off Tumut Pl 269 J15
pl. Bossley Park 333 J5
pl. Heckenberg 363 K15
pl. St Clair 269 J16
pl. Seven Hills 275 E10
pl. Sylvania Wtr 462 D11
st. Ruse 512 G8
TUNA
pl. St Clair 269 H16
TUNBRIDGE
pl. Cherrybrook 219 H5
pl. Jannali 461 A13
st. Busby 363 G14
st. Mascot 405 E4
TUNCOEE
rd. Villawood 367 A4
TUNCURRY
st. Bossley Park 333 E12
TUNGARRA
rd. Girraween 276 B10
TUNGOO
pl. St Helens Pk 511 J16
TUNIS
pl. Quakers Hill 214 C9
TUNKS
av. Cammeray 316 A3
pl. Barden Rdg 488 G3
rd. Dural 190 C4
st. Northbridge 286 B16
st. Ryde 282 B14
st. Waverton 315 D11
TUNLEY
pl. Kings Lngly 245 B3
TUNNACK
cl. West Hoxton 392 E7
TUNNEL
pl. Horsley Pk 333 B9
TUNSTALL
av. Kensington 376 C16
av. Kingsford 376 C16
TUNUNDA
pl. Eschol Park 481 A3
TUOHY
la. Marrickville 373 K13
TUPELO
gr. Menai 458 J12
TUPIA
pl. Kings Lngly 245 H6
st. Botany 405 G16
TUPPEL
wy. Airds 512 C12

TUPPER
st. Enmore 16 H15
TURBO
rd. Kings Park 244 F5
TURELLA
cl. Belrose 225 K14
st. Glenbrook 264 D2
TURF
pl. Quakers Hill 214 G16
TURI
cl. Bangor 459 F12
TURIMETTA
av. Leumeah 482 B16
st. Mona Vale 199 B6
TURLINJAH
cl. Prestons 393 A13
TURNBERRY
cr. Glenmore Pk 266 F11
wy. Rouse Hill 185 B8
TURNBULL
av. Kemps Ck 359 J5
av. Wilberforce 92 C1
st. Winmalee 173 J6
TURNER
av. Baulkham Hl 247 D13
av. Concord 342 A1
av. Haberfield 9 A11
av. Haberfield 343 E13
av. Ryde 312 C2
cl. Bligh Park 150 G5
la. Punchbowl 400 B4
la. Woolmloo 4 D6
pl. Casula 424 D4
rd. Berowra Ht 133 A7
rd. Currans Hill 479 D3
rd. Smeaton Gra 479 D3
st. Balmain 7 D7
st. Blacktown 244 K8
st. Bronte 378 A7
st. Colyton 270 J8
st. Dee Why 258 H1
st. Ermington 310 D2
st. Guildford 337 E6
st. Punchbowl 400 D5
st. Redfern 19 C8
st. Riverwood 399 K16
st. Ryde 311 K2
st. Thirlmere 565 C3
TURON
av. Baulkham Hl 247 B8
av. Kingsgrove 401 J11
pl. Ruse 512 C9
TUROSS
av. Five Dock 343 C7
av. Sylvania Wtr 462 F12
cl. Prestons 393 D16
pl. Leumeah 482 G14
st. Seven Hills 275 E10
TURPENTINE
av. Peakhurst 430 E4
cl. Alfords Point 429 C16
TURQUOISE
cr. Bossley Park 333 K7
pl. Eagle Vale 481 A7
TURRA
st. S Turramrra 252 C5
TURRAMURRA
av. Turramurra 222 J13
TURRELLA
rd. Yarrawarrah 489 E13
st. Turrella 403 E5
TURRET
pl. Castle Hill 217 F4
pl. Glenmore Pk 266 D6
TURRIELL BAY
rd. Caringbah 492 G16
rd. Lilli Pilli 492 F16
TURRIELL POINT
rd. Port Hacking 522 H2
TURTLE
cct. Green Valley 363 B9
la. Erskineville 17 K16
la. Newtown 17 D10
rd. Caringbah 492 D11
TURTON
av. Belmore 401 J5
la. Belmore, off Turton Av 401 J5
pl. Castle Hill 217 H15
TURUGA
pl. Bangor 459 F11
st. Turramurra 223 A14
TURUNEN
av. Warragamba 353 H12
TURVEY
rd. Blacktown 274 F3
st. Padstow 399 A10
st. Revesby 398 K10
TUSCAN
av. Kellyville 186 H15
av. Kellyville 186 H16
pl. Beacon Hill 257 G7
pl. Casula 395 A13
wy. Cherrybrook 220 A5
wy. Glenwood 245 K4
TUSCANY
gr. S Penrith 267 B6
TUSCULUM
ct. Wattle Grove 425 J5
la. Potts Point 4 J4
rd. Valley Ht 202 D5
st. Potts Point 4 K4
TUSMORE
st. Punchbowl 400 A9
TUTOR
cl. Winmalee 173 G7
TUTT
cr. Chiswick 343 D2
TUTUS
st. Balgowlah Ht 288 A12
TWAIN
st. Winston Hills 277 E1
TWEED
ct. Wattle Grove 395 K13
pl. Ruse 512 C9
pl. St Clair 270 E10
pl. Sylvania Wtr 462 D10
TWEEDMOUTH
av. Rosebery 405 G1
TWELFTH
av. Austral 391 B6
av. Rossmore 390 B5
av. West Hoxton 392 C8
st. Warragamba 353 F4
TWENTIETH
av. Hoxton Park 393 A7
st. Warragamba 353 E8
TWENTYEIGHTH
av. Austral 391 J1
TWENTYFIFTH
av. West Hoxton 391 H16
TWENTY FIRST
st. Warragamba 353 D7
TWENTYFOURTH
av. West Hoxton 391 H14
TWENTYNINTH
av. Austral 391 G9
TWENTY SECOND
st. Warragamba 353 C8
TWENTYSECOND
av. West Hoxton 391 K5
TWENTYSEVENTH
av. West Hoxton 391 J1
TWENTYSIXTH
av. West Hoxton 391 H16
TWENTY THIRD
st. Warragamba 353 B7
TWENTYTHIRD
av. West Hoxton 391 H8
TWICKENHAM
av. Cambrdg Pk 238 B7
cl. Normanhurst 221 D9
TWIN
rd. North Ryde 282 E11
TWINGLETON
av. Ambarvale 510 H16
TWYFORD
av. Earlwood 403 A3
TWYNAM
pl. Horngsea Pk 392 F15
rd. Davidson 255 C1
TYAGARAH
pl. Cromer 228 A15
st. Ryde 312 E7
TYALGUM
av. Panania 428 G2
TYALLA
av. Frenchs Frst 256 D8
cl. Casula 394 G14
TYARAN
pl. Bangor 459 E12
TYCANNAH
pl. Bangor 459 H9
rd. Northbridge 286 F14
TYGH
st. Lapstone 264 G5
TYLER
cr. Abbotsford 343 A3
pl. Bonnet Bay 460 D10
st. Campbelltwn 511 H2
TYLERS
rd. Bargo 567 A10
rd. Bargo 567 E9
TYNE
cl. Baulkham Hl 246 J5
cr. N Richmond 87 A13
ct. St Clair 299 K1
pl. Prospect 274 G13
TYNESIDE
av. N Willghby 285 G7
TYPHOON
pl. Raby 451 E16
TYRELL
cr. Fairfield W 335 G9
st. Gladesville 312 G9
TYRINGHAM
cl. Hoxton Park 392 J8
TYRONE
av. Forestville 256 B11
pl. Blacktown 275 A8
TYRRELL
st. Rockdale 403 A13
TYRWHITT
st. Maroubra 407 F14
TYSON
pl. Emu Plains 235 D14
pl. North Rocks 278 J3
rd. Bringelly 387 G11

U

UDALL
av. Five Dock 342 J8
UHRIG
rd. Homebush B 340 D2
rd. Newington M F11
UHRS
la. Rhodes 311 E7
UKI
av. Picnic Point 428 G5
ULA
cr. Baulkham Hl 247 K11
ULANDI
pl. Northmead 277 J4
ULINGA
pl. Engadine 488 G14
ULLADULLA
dr. Prestons 393 B14
pl. Kareela 461 B13
ULLATHORNE
st. Drummoyne 343 H5
ULM
av. S Turramrra 251 K6
pl. Doonside 273 F4
rd. Orchard Hills 268 C6
st. Ermington 280 A14
st. Lane Cove W 283 J13
st. Maroubra 406 G11
ULMARRA
av. Camden S 507 B10
pl. E Lindfield 255 D11
ULOLO
av. Hornsby Ht 191 D1
ULONGA
av. Greenwich 314 K5
pl. Toongabbie 276 E9
ULOOLA
pl. Gymea Bay 491 E11
ULPHA
pl. Cranebrook 207 E12
ULRIC
la. Northbridge 316 B2
ULSTER
st. Cecil Hills 362 E6
st. Paddington 21 E4
st. Peakhurst 430 A7
ULTIMO
rd. Haymarket E A11
rd. Haymarket E E9
rd. Haymarket 3 C14
rd. Ultimo E A11
rd. Ultimo 3 C14
st. Caringbah 492 G10
ULUNDRI
dr. Castle Hill 218 A9
ULVERSTONE
st. Fairfield 336 F14
UMBRIA
st. Prestons 393 E15
UMINA
pl. Woodbine 481 J10
UNA
la. Campsie, off Una St 372 B15
pl. Toongabbie 276 G10
st. Campsie 372 C15
st. Harris Park 308 F5
st. Wentwthvle 306 H2
st. Redfern, off Regent Pl 19 B7
UNARA
la. Campsie 372 A14
st. Campsie 372 A15
UNCLE WATTLEBERRY
cr. Faulconbdg 171 F11
UNDERCLIFF
rd. Harbord 288 G2
st. Neutral Bay 6 E5
UNDERCLIFFE
la. Earlwood 403 G3
rd. Earlwood 403 F2
st. Dee Why 259 A8
UNDERDALE
la. Meadowbnk, off Railway Rd 311 E4
UNDERWOOD
av. Botany 405 E11
la. Paddington 21 E1
la. Sydney A J10
la. Sydney 1 G13
pl. Barden Rdg 488 H4
rd. Homebush M J2
rd. Homebush 341 A4
rd. Prairiewood 334 K8
rd. St Clair 270 E9
st. Minto 482 G7
st. Paddington 13 B16
st. Paddington 21 D1
st. Sydney A K10
UNDINE
st. Maroubra 407 K9
st. Russell Lea 343 F6
UNDULA
pl. Belrose 225 J13
UNGARRA
st. Rydalmere 279 J14
UNICOMBE
cr. Oakhurst 242 A2
UNION
ct. Bella Vista 246 B1
la. Carlton 432 K5
la. Dulwich Hill 373 C9
la. Newtown 17 J15
la. Paddington 13 D16
la. Penrith 236 G10
la. Pyrmont 12 K4
la. Windsor 121 C8
la. Erskineville, off Union St 374 K9
la. Fairlight, off William St 288 D8
rd. Auburn 339 A5
rd. Penrith 236 F10
st. Arncliffe 403 F8
st. Balmain East 8 F9
st. Dulwich Hill 373 C9
st. Eastwood 280 G7
st. Erskineville 17 J16
st. Erskineville 374 J9
st. Granville 308 B10
st. Kogarah 432 K4
st. Lidcombe 340 A8
st. McMahons Pt 5 B10
st. Mosman 317 B11
st. Newtown 17 J16
st. N Sydney 5 B10
st. Paddington 13 D16
st. Parramatta 308 E3
st. Pyrmont 12 H3
st. Riverstone 152 J12
st. Riverwood 399 K14
st. Tempe 404 B1
st. Toongabbie 276 B5
st. Vineyard 152 J12
st. Waterloo 19 F11
st. Waverton 5 B10
st. West Ryde 311 D2
UNITED
la. Parramatta 308 C3
UNIVERSAL
av. Georges Hall 367 G12
la. Eastlakes, off Universal St 405 K3
st. Eastlakes 405 J3
st. Mortdale 431 A7
UNIVERSITY
pl. Camperdwn 18 E2
rd. Miranda 491 J4
UNSTED
cr. Hillsdale 406 G14
UNSWORTH
st. Abbotsbury 333 A16
UNWIN
la. Earlwood, off Unwin St 403 H3
rd. Cabramtta W 365 B7
rd. Wahroonga 221 H7
rd. Waitara 221 H7
st. Bexley 402 C16
st. Canterbury 372 G12
st. Earlwood 403 H3
st. Rosehill 309 A8
UNWINS
la. Hunters Hill 313 B5
UNWINS BRIDGE
rd. St Peters 374 E14
rd. Sydenham 374 E14
rd. Tempe 374 B16
UPFIELD
la. Catherine Fd 449 D5
st. Edensor Pk 363 H2
UPPER
rd. Forest Lodge 11 E14
UPPER ALMORA
st. Mosman 317 B7
UPPER AVENUE
rd. Mosman 316 J11
UPPER BEACH
st. Balgowlah 287 G10
UPPER CLIFF
av. Northbridge 316 A1
rd. Northwood 314 H7
UPPER CLIFFORD
av. Fairlight 288 B9
UPPER CLONTARF
st. Seaforth 287 A3
UPPER FAIRFAX
rd. Mosman 317 B2
UPPER FORT
st. Millers Point A E5
st. Millers Point 1 E11
UPPER GILBERT
st. Manly 288 F9
UPPER GREYCLIFF
st. Queenscliff, off Greycliff St 288 H3
UPPER MINIMBAH
rd. Northbridge 286 E14
UPPER PITT
st. Kirribilli 2 C1
st. Kirribilli 6 B16
UPPER SERPENTINE
rd. Greenwich 314 J13
UPPER SPIT
rd. Mosman 287 B16
UPPER WASHINGTON
dr. Bonnet Bay 460 B9
dr. Bonnet Bay 460 D10
UPPER WILSONS
rd. Bardwell Vy 403 B9
UPTON
pl. Bonnyrigg 364 A5
st. S Penrith 236 K16
UPWARD
st. Leichhardt 15 C5
UPWEY
cl. Mt Krng-gai 162 H7
pl. St Johns Pk 364 E2
st. Prospect 274 G10
URALBA
av. Caringbah 492 F10
pl. N Wahrnga 192 E16
pl. Oatlands 279 B14
URALLA
av. Padstow 429 D3
pl. S Coogee 407 E4
rd. Dural 189 D4
rd. E Kurrajong 56 H4
st. Hebersham 241 E9
URAMBI
pl. Engadine 488 G14
URANA
pl. Leumeah 482 F15
rd. Yarrawarrah 489 D12
st. Villawood 367 D2
URANUS
rd. Padstow 429 A1
rd. Revesby 428 K1

URARA
rd. Avalon 140 E14
URBANE
st. Leonay 235 D15
URDALA
pl. Sutherland 490 C1
UREN
pl. Bligh Park 150 E6
pl. Merrylands 308 A16
st. S Penrith 237 C16
URIAH
pl. Ambarvale 510 H14
URQUHART
st. Riverwood 400 D15
URSULA
pl. Cecil Hills 362 E2
st. Winston Hills 276 G1
URUNGA
cl. Hoxton Park 392 K9
pde. Miranda 492 B4
pde. Punchbowl 400 D3
pde. Wiley Park 400 D3
pl. Bossley Park 333 F10
st. N Balgowlah 287 B4
USHER
cl. Abbotsbury 333 A13
cr. Sefton 368 E5
UTAH
pl. Erskine Park 270 K15
pl. Toongabbie 275 H12
UTE
pl. Bossley Park 333 K10
UTHER
av. Bradbury 511 G12
st. Surry Hills 19 K1
UTINGU
pl. Bayview 168 K15
UTYANA
pl. Frenchs Frst 256 G11
UTZON
ct. St Clair 270 A10
rd. Cabramtta W 365 B5

V

VAIRYS
cr. Merrylands 337 J1
VALDA
av. Arncliffe 403 J8
pl. Baulkham Hl 247 C2
pl. Ingleburn 453 D10
pl. Marsfield 281 K5
st. Bexley 402 G12
st. Blacktown 274 F6
st. Merrylnds W 306 H13
st. W Pnnant Hl 249 H1
VALDER
av. Richmond 118 C8
VALE
av. Dee Why 258 F4
cct. Narellan Vale 478 K10
cct. Narellan Vale 479 A10
ct. Canley Vale 366 A4
la. Peakhurst 430 B10
rd. Thornleigh 221 A4
st. Cabramatta 366 C7
st. Cammeray 315 J4
st. Canley Vale 366 C7
st. Clovelly 377 H11
st. Gordon 253 E7
st. Woodpark 306 F15
VALEDICTION
rd. Kings Park 244 J5
VALENCIA
cr. Toongabbie 275 F11
st. Dural 188 J12
st. Greenacre 370 E10
VALENTIA
av. Lugarno 429 H11
st. Woolwich 314 G12
VALENTINE
av. Parramatta 308 D5
cl. Winston Hills 277 C2
pl. Rsemeadow 540 G6
st. Blacktown 274 F6
st. Haymarket E D12
st. Haymarket 3 E14
st. Horngsea Pk 392 E16
st. Yagoona 368 F11
VALERIA
st. Toongabbie 276 B6
VALERIE
av. Baulkham Hl 246 F12
av. Chatswd W 284 A9
st. Mt Pritchard 364 G12
st. Pendle Hill 306 E1
VALES
la. Auburn 339 D2
VALETTA
ct. Blacktown 274 G6
VALEWOOD
cr. Marsfield 281 K4
VALINDA
cr. Campbelltwn 512 A5
VALLANCE
st. St Marys 239 F5
VALLEN
pl. Quakers Hill 214 D13
VALLEY
cl. Bayview 168 J12
gln. W Pnnant Hl 249 A5
la. Lindfield 254 F16
rd. Balgowlah Ht 287 J12
rd. Campbelltwn 512 A6
rd. Eastwood 280 G5
rd. Epping 280 G5
rd. Forestville 255 G11
rd. Hornsby 221 A1
rd. Lindfield 254 F16
rd. Padstow Ht 429 F8
rd. Springwood 201 G5
rd. Valley Ht 202 D4
st. Balmain 7 G10
wy. Glossodia 59 A5
wy. Gymea Bay 491 G9
wy. Tennyson 59 A5
VALLEYFIELD
ct. Wattle Grove 395 K15
VALLEY PARK
cr. N Turramrra 223 E5
VALLEY VIEW
cl. Roseville 284 B6
cr. Engadine 489 A14
cr. N Epping 251 C10
dr. Narellan 478 B9
rd. Frenchs Frst 257 A3
VALLEYVIEW
cr. Greenwich 314 J6
cr. Wrrngtn Dns 237 K5
pl. Kellyville 186 K15
VALLINGBY
av. Hebersham 241 E4
VALMA
pl. Colyton 270 G4
VALMAY
av. Picnic Point 428 E9
VALPARAISO
av. Toongabbie 275 F12
VALS
ct. St Ives 224 B15
VALVE HOUSE
rd. Warragamba 353 C5
VAL WHEELER
dr. Kurrajong Ht 53 F3
VAN BENTUM
pl. Blacktown 273 H6
VAN BUREN
cct. Bonnet Bay 460 D9
VANCE
st. Dean Park 212 H16
VANCOUVER
av. Toongabbie 275 E12
pl. Fairfield W 335 C10
VAN DIEMAN
cr. Fairfield W 335 C10
pl. Caringbah 492 F7
rd. St Clair 299 J3
VAN DIEMEN
av. Willmot 210 B11
VAN DYKE
pl. Punchbowl 400 D4
VANE
st. Cranebrook 206 J2
VANESSA
av. Baulkham Hl 247 D9
ct. Glenwood 215 J15
pl. Mcquarie Fd 424 F15
st. Beverly Hills 401 E13
st. Kingsgrove 401 E13
VANGELI
st. Arndell Park 273 H9
VAN HEE
st. Concord 342 A1
VANIMO
pl. Eastwood 281 D4
VANNAN
la. Padstow 399 C14
VANNON
cct. Currans Hill 479 J9
VANNY
pl. Maroubra 407 F9
VANSTON
pde. Sandringham 463 E4
VANTAGE
cr. Kellyville 216 H2
la. Peakhurst 430 C10
pl. Thornleigh 221 A4
VARDEN
wy. Ambarvale 541 A1
VARDYS
rd. Blacktown 245 A6
rd. Kings Lngly 245 A6
rd. Kings Park 244 E5
rd. Lalor Park 245 F8
VARGA
pl. Hassall Gr 212 C15
VARIAN
st. Mount Druitt 241 C15
VARIDEL
av. Belfield 371 F10
VARNA
st. Clovelly 377 G10
st. Mt Colah 192 A4
VARNDELL
pl. Dundas Vy 280 D9
VARUNA
pl. Doonside 243 E16
VASEY
cl. St Ives Ch 224 B2
VASSALLO
pl. Glendenning 242 E3
VASTA
av. Moorebank 396 E13
VAUCLUSE
rd. Vaucluse 348 A3
VAUDAN
st. Kogarah Bay 433 A13
VAUGHAN
av. Pennant Hills 220 E14
av. Revesby 398 J14
pl. Glenorie 128 E15
pl. Redfern 20 D8
st. Auburn 339 C8
st. Blakehurst 432 D16
st. Lidcombe 339 C8
VAUTIN
rd. Marsden Pk 211 J7
VAUXHALL
st. Ingleburn 453 G12
VEAL
gr. Plumpton 242 B11
VEALE
wy. Bella Vista 246 H4
VEGA
cr. Bnkstn Aprt 367 J16
pl. Hinchinbrk 393 D5
st. Revesby 428 J5
VELA
pl. Erskine Park 301 A2
VELLA
cr. Blacktown 273 K6
VENESS
cct. Narellan Vale 478 J16
VENETIA
st. Kangaroo Pt 461 J10
st. Sylvania 461 J10
VENETIAN
rd. N Narrabeen 228 J1
VENETTA
rd. Glenorie 128 A14
VENEZIA
st. Prestons 393 E14
VENICE
pl. Guildford W 336 J3
VENN
av. Lalor Park 245 B11
VENO
st. Heathcote 518 G11
VENTURA
av. Miranda 492 C3
av. Narwee 400 G13
pl. Hornsby Ht 161 J15
pl. Warriewood 199 C8
rd. Northmead 248 B16
VENTURE
cr. Yagoona 369 B10
VENUS
cl. Cranebrook 207 G6
pl. Kings Lngly 245 C6
pl. Lansvale 366 H8
rd. Lane Cove W 283 F15
st. Gladesville 312 K8
VERA
av. Earlwood 373 C16
ct. Cabramatta 365 G11
la. Earlwood 373 C15
pl. Padstow Ht 429 C6
st. Baulkham Hl 247 K11
st. Eastwood 281 J8
st. Seven Hills 245 C16
VERBENA
av. Bankstown 399 G3
av. Casula 394 G12
av. Lurnea 394 G12
pl. Caringbah 493 A12
VERBRUGGHEN
pl. Mt Pritchard 364 K10
VERDELHO
wy. Orchard Hills 268 F13
VERDI
gln. St Clair 300 A3
la. St Clair, off Verdi Gln 300 A3
VERDUN
pl. Engadine 489 A13
st. Bexley 432 J2
VERGE
pl. Doonside 273 F2
pl. West Hoxton 392 D11
VERITY
pl. Oakhurst 242 C1
VERLETTA
av. Castle Hill 217 J15
VERLEY
dr. Homebush 341 A6
VERLIE
st. Merrylands 307 D6
st. S Wntwthvle 307 D6
VERMONT
cr. Riverwood 400 B12
ct. Seven Hills 275 C6
st. Sutherland 460 E16
VERN
la. Chatswd W 284 G7
VERNEY
dr. W Pnnant Hl 220 A16
VERNON
av. Eastlakes 406 A6
av. Gymea Bay 491 F10
cl. Rsemeadow 540 H8
cl. W Pnnant Hl 220 B15
la. Eastlakes 405 K6
la. Woollahra 22 F4
st. Balmain East 8 G9
st. Bondi Jctn 22 F6
st. Cammeray 316 C3
st. Greystanes 306 B8
st. Hunters Hill 314 B12
st. Lewisham 15 D14
st. Marayong 244 D10
st. Punchbowl 399 J8
st. S Turramrra 252 A8
st. Strathfield 341 E14
st. Woollahra 22 G6
wy. Cranebrook 207 C14
VERON
rd. Bexley 402 H11
rd. Schofields 213 A2
st. Fairfield E 336 K12
st. Wentwthvle 307 B1
VERONA
av. Mt Pritchard 364 G11
st. Auburn 339 D1
st. N Narrabeen 228 K2
st. Paddington 4 G15
st. Strathfield 371 A3
VERONA RANGE
Como 460 J5
VERONICA
cr. Seven Hills 245 K11
pl. Cherrybrook 219 F10
pl. Glenmore Pk 265 H10
pl. Greystanes 305 F11
pl. Loftus 490 A7
pl. Narellan Vale 479 B15
st. Chester Hill 368 C2
VERRELL
st. Wetherill Pk 335 B1
VERRILLS
gr. Oakhurst 241 H4
VESCEY
st. Waterloo 19 F11
VESPER
st. Mona Vale 199 A3
wy. Doonside 243 G15
VESPERMAN
rd. Glenorie 126 H3
VESTA
st. Sutherland 460 F16
VESUVIUS
st. Seven Hills 275 B8
VETERANS
pde. Collaroy Plat 228 G11
pde. Narrabeen 228 G11
VEZEY
pl. Blacktown 274 B5
VIALOUX
av. Paddington 13 C12
VIALS
la. Paddington 21 E2
VIA MARE
Cronulla 524 A1
VIANNEY
cr. Toongabbie 276 E5
VIBURNUM
rd. Loftus 489 H11
VICAR
st. Coogee 377 G16
VICAR PARK
la. Luddenham 356 F11
VICARS
av. North Bondi 348 F16
pl. Wetherill Pk 334 B3
VICKERS
av. Mascot 404 K7
pl. Raby 451 D15
VICKERY
av. Carlingford 279 J1
av. Rose Bay 347 K10
rd. Greendale 355 A14
rd. Wallacia 355 A14
VICKY
av. Castle Hill 217 G9
pl. Glendenning 242 E1
VICLIFFE
av. Campsie 402 A1
VIC RENALSON
cl. Newington L K16
cl. Newington, off Ron Clarke St 310 B12
VICTA
pl. Thirlmere 564 K2
VICTOR
av. Kemps Ck 359 G11
av. Panania 428 F5
av. Picnic Point 428 E8
cl. Baulkham Hl 247 C12
pl. Illawong 459 G4
pl. Raby 451 F15
rd. Brookvale 258 D9
rd. Dee Why 258 D7
rd. Narraweena 258 D7
st. Chatswood 284 J10
st. Greystanes 306 B8
st. Kogarah 433 C2
wy. Bonnyrigg 364 D5
VICTORIA
av. Castle Hill 217 C12
av. Chatswood 284 H10
av. Chatswood 284 K9
av. Concord W 341 C1
av. Mortdale 431 C7
av. N Willghby 285 D8
av. Penshurst 431 C7
av. West Pymble 252 H12
av. Woollahra 21 H4
cr. Auburn 338 J4
cs. N Sydney 5 G8
la. Malabar 437 D3
la. Marrickville 374 B13
la. Ryde 311 J5
la. Werrington 239 A12
la. Beaconsfield, off Beaconsfield St 375 F13
la. Rydalmere, off John St 309 J2
la. Waverley, off Victoria St 377 F7
pde. Manly 288 H10
pl. Drummoyne 313 F15
pl. McMahons Pt 5 D11
pl. Paddington 21 D1
pl. Richmond 117 K6
rd. Bellevue Hill 14 J6
rd. Castle Hill 217 A7
rd. Drummoyne 343 J1
rd. Dundas 279 A16
rd. Ermington 309 K2
rd. Gladesville 312 H6

rd. Glebe 11 G9
rd. Henley 313 B13
rd. Huntleys Pt 313 B13
rd. Kellyville 217 A7
rd. Mcquarie Fd 423 K15
rd. Marrickville 374 D10
rd. Marrickville 374 A14
rd. Minto 452 F15
rd. Parramatta 278 D16
rd. Pennant Hills 249 H2
rd. Punchbowl 400 B5
rd. Punchbowl 400 B9
rd. Rooty Hill 241 K14
rd. Rozelle 7 A16
rd. Rydalmere 309 C1
rd. Ryde 311 G1
rd. Thirlmere 565 A2
rd. Wedderburn 540 C14
rd. W Pnnant Hl 249 G2
rd. West Ryde 281 A15
sq. Ashfield 373 A6
st. Ashfield 372 K9
st. Beaconsfield 375 G13
st. Botany 405 K12
st. Cambrdg Pk 237 J11
st. Darlinghurst 4 F13
st. Dulwich Hill 373 E7
st. Epping 281 A1
st. Erskineville 17 K16
st. Granville 308 E9
st. Greenwich 314 K13
st. Jannali 460 G13
st. Kingswood 237 J11
st. Kogarah 433 C3
st. Lewisham 15 A11
st. Lewisham 373 E7
st. Lilyfield 10 F3
st. McMahons Pt 5 C12
st. Malabar 437 E3
st. Merrylands 307 G9
st. Mount Druitt 270 J1
st. Newtown 17 H9
st. Paddington 21 D2
st. Picton 563 G8
st. Potts Point 4 H7
st. Queens Park 22 K14
st. Queens Park 377 F7
st. Randwick 377 B13
st. Redfern 19 J7
st. Revesby 398 J14
st. Riverstone 152 F16
st. Riverstone 153 A13
st. Roseville 284 J5
st. St Peters 374 J14
st. Smithfield 335 G3
st. Strathfield 341 C15
st. Turrella 403 E6
st. Warrimoo 203 B13
st. Watsons Bay 318 E12
st. Waverley 377 F7
st. Werrington 238 D12
st. Wetherill Pk 333 J1
st. Wetherill Pk 334 F1
st.e, Burwood 342 A13
st.e, Lidcombe 339 H11
st.w, Burwood 341 K13
st.w, Lidcombe 339 G10
wy. Kogarah 433 A3

VICTORY
av. Belfield 371 D8
av. Camden 507 A3
la. Camperdwn 17 D3
pl. Concord 341 J4
rd. Oatley 430 K16
st. Asquith 192 B10
st. Belmore 401 F3
st. Clovelly 378 A14
st. Dover Ht 348 E11
st. Engadine 488 K14
st. Fairfield E 336 K12
st. Rose Bay 348 E11
st. S Penrith 236 J15

VIDAL
st. Wetherill Pk 334 D5

VIDILINI
la. Northmead 277 H9

VIDLER
pl. Mt Annan 479 F15

VIENNA
st. Seven Hills 275 C5

VIEW
la. Chatswd W 284 G9
rd. Ingleside 198 B3
st. Annandale 11 A14
st. Arncliffe 403 F10
st. Blaxland 233 F7
st. Cabramatta 365 C11
st. Camden 477 B16
st. Chatswd W 284 G9
st. Concord 342 C4
st. Cowan 104 B14
st. Cremorne 316 C6
st. Earlwood 402 K4
st. Forestville 256 C10
st. Gymea 491 G5
st. Hurstville Gr 431 G11
st. Linley Point 313 G7
st. Marrickville 373 G15
st. Miranda 491 G5
st. Peakhurst 430 B12
st. Picton 563 F7
st. Queens Park 22 K13
st. Sefton 368 E4
st. Telopea 279 G8
st. Tempe 404 A4
st. W Pnnant Hl 249 B5
st. Woollahra 22 H3
st. Woolwich 314 G12

VIEW PARK
st. Prospect 275 B10

VIGNES
st. Ermington 280 B15

VIKING
st. Campsie 402 A1

VILLA
pl. Wentwthvle 277 B11

VILLAGE
cr. Penrith 237 C10
wy. Wattle Grove 426 B1

VILLAGE GREEN
pde. St Ives 223 K12

VILLAGE HIGH
rd. Vaucluse 348 F1

VILLAGE LOWER
rd. Vaucluse 348 E3

VILLAWOOD
pl. Villawood 367 C1
rd. Villawood 367 C1

VILLERS BRETT
Engadine 489 A13

VILLIERS
av. Mortdale 431 B4
la. Rockdale 403 C13
pl. Cromer 228 H14
pl. Oxley Park 240 E16
rd. Cecil Park 332 F10
rd. Padstow Ht 429 F7
st. Kensington 376 E12
st. Merrylands 307 C16
st. Parramatta 278 C16
st. Rockdale 403 A11

VIMIERA
rd. Eastwood 281 C5
rd. Marsfield 251 H16

VIMY
cl. Mt Colah 162 E12
la. Earlwood 403 A1
st. Bankstown 399 E3
st. Earlwood 403 A1

VINCENNES
av. Tregear 240 D3

VINCENT
av. Emu Plains 235 J9
av. Liverpool 365 A15
av. Mulgoa 325 C3
cr. Canley Vale 366 F1
pl. Davidson 225 B14
rd. Cranebrook 206 J3
rd. Kurrajong 85 G2
st. Balmain 8 A11
st. Baulkham Hl 247 H14
st. Blacktown 274 C3
st. Canterbury 372 H11
st. Marrickville 374 C13
st. Merrylands 307 D8
st. Mount Druitt 271 C2
st. St Marys 269 D3

VINCENTIA
st. Marsfield 281 K3

VINCENTS
av. Arncliffe 403 F11

VINCENZ
la. Mosman, off Awaba St 316 K4

VINE
gr. Darlington 18 J4
la. Condell Park 398 G3
la. Darlington 18 K4
st. Ashfield 342 G15
st. Darlington 18 J4
st. Fairfield 336 G14
st. Hurstville 432 C3
st. Redfern 19 A5
st.e, Schofields 182 E16
st.w, Marsden Pk 211 K1

VINEGAR HILL
rd. Kellyville 185 B16
rd. Kellyville 215 C1

VINES
av. Forestville 256 A6
ct. Minto 482 K5
dr. Richmond 118 E11

VINEY
st. N St Marys 239 J9

VINEYARD
av. Smithfield 336 B5
rd. Mulgoa 296 C16
st. Mona Vale 199 A5
st. Rydalmere 279 D15

VINEYS
la. Dural 189 C12
rd. Dural 189 C12

VINTAGE
pl. Minchinbury 272 A8

VIOLA
pl. Glenmore Pk 265 H8
pl. Greystanes 305 J12
pl. Heathcote 518 K9
pl. Lalor Park 245 C10
pl. Rsemeadow 540 F6
st. Punchbowl 399 K6
wy. Mt Annan 509 F3

VIOLET
av. Forestville 256 A11
av. Liverpool 365 A15
cl. Wilberforce 92 A5
ct. Quakers Hill 214 A10
pl. Greystanes 306 G5
st. Balgowlah 287 F9
st. Bronte 377 J9
st. Chatswood 284 J7
st. Croydon Pk 371 K5
st. Miranda 461 J16
st. Revesby 398 E10
st. Roselands 400 G8
st. Surry Hills 20 C4
swy. Liverpool, off Violet Av 365 A15

VIRET
st. Hunters Hill 314 A11

VIRGIL
av. Chester Hill 338 A16
av. Sefton 368 E1
la. Bronte 377 K9
st. Greystanes 306 D7

VIRGINIA
av. Bardwell Vy 403 A9
av. Baulkham Hl 247 B9
pl. Forestville 256 A7
pl. Riverwood 400 B13
pl. W Pnnant Hl 249 B11
st. Blacktown 244 A11
st. Guildford W 306 J15
st. Kensington 376 B12
st. Rosehill 308 G7

VIRGINIUS
st. Padstow 429 B4

VIRGO
pl. Erskine Park 300 G2

VIRIA
ct. Glenhaven 218 C3

VIRTUE
st. Condell Park 398 H5

VISCOUNT
cl. Raby 451 F13
pl. Warwck Frm 365 C13

VISCOUNT VAMPIRE
pl. Richmond, off Davis St 120 B5

VISION VALLEY
rd. Arcadia 130 A13

VISTA
av. Balgowlah Ht 287 H15
av. Bayview 169 A14
av. Peakhurst 430 C11
cl. Hornsby 191 H9
cl. Kings Park 244 G2
cr. Chester Hill 338 C13
la. Bellevue Hill 347 J14
la. Greenwich, off Edwin St 315 A10
la. Penrith, off Vista St 236 F10
pde. Mt Riverview 204 J13
pl. Kurrajong Ht 53 K4
pl. Narellan 478 C10
st. Caringbah 492 G8
st. Greenwich 315 A10
st. Mosman 316 K7
st. Oatlands 278 J9
st. Penrith 236 F10
st. Pymble 223 H16
st. Sans Souci 462 J3

VISTA HEIGHTS
rd. Miranda 461 K16

VITTORIA SMITH
av. Castle Hill 218 J14

VIVALDI
cr. Clarmnt Ms 268 G4
pl. Kellyville 216 C1

VIVIAN
cr. Berala 339 E11
st. Bellevue Hill 347 G15
st. Bexley 432 G1
st. Manly 288 J12
st. Scotland I 168 G4

VIVIEN
pl. Castle Hill 218 C12

VIVIENNE
av. Lakemba 371 A13
st. Kingsgrove 401 J12
st. Woodpark 306 G15

VIVYAN
cl. Denistone 281 H12

VLADIMIR KUTS
av. Newington L K16

VLADIMUR KUTS
av. Newington 310 B13

VLATKO
dr. West Hoxton 392 C11

VOGAN
st. Mt Riverview 234 E3

VOLANS
la. Erskine Park, off Volans Pl 300 J1
pl. Erskine Park 300 J2

VOLLERS
la. Freemns Rch 90 K1

VOLMER
rd. Scheyville 123 E1
st. Oatlands 279 C7

VOLTA
pl. Winston Hills 277 B5

VOLTAIRE
rd. Winston Hills 277 F2

VOLUNTEER
rd. Kenthurst 188 A4

VONN
av. Smithfield 335 B3

VONNE
pl. Condell Park 398 H8

VON NIDA
pl. Menai 458 J5

VORE
st. Silverwater 309 H13

VOYSEY
cl. Quakers Hill 213 D15

VUKAS
pl. Bonnyrigg Ht 363 C7

VUKO
pl. Warriewood 199 C11

VULCAN
pl. Raby 451 H15
st. Guildford 337 C3
wy. Currans Hill 479 G10

W

WABASH
av. Cromer 228 A13

WABBA
st. Marayong 243 J6

WACKETT
st. Bnkstn Aprt 398 B2
st. Maroubra 406 H11

WADDELL
cr. Hornsby Ht 161 J9

WADDS
av. Cabramatta 366 D8

WADE
cl. Illawong 459 J5
la. Gordon 253 H7
la. Ryde 311 J6
pl. Kings Lngly 246 B9
pl. Surry Hills F F13
rd. Leumeah 481 J13
rd. N Parramatta 278 K6
st. Campsie 401 K1
st. Maroubra 407 A13
st. Ryde 311 J6
st. Telopea 279 G10
st. Toongabbie 276 E5

WADSLEY
cr. Connells Pt 431 H16

WAGGA WAGGA
st. Prestons 393 B15

WAGNER
pl. Cranebrook 207 G9
pl. Seven Hills 246 D12

WAGSTAFF
st. Edensor Pk 363 D2

WAGTAIL
cr. Ingleburn 453 E9
pl. Erskine Park 270 K13

WAHROONGA
av. Wahroonga 222 G5
pl. W Pnnant Hl 248 G6
rd. Winmalee 173 F4

WAIKANDA
cr. Whalan 240 H9

WAIMEA
av. Woollahra 22 B3
rd. Lindfield 284 E2
st. Burwood 342 B14
st. N Balgowlah 287 D4

WAINE
la. Cabarita 312 E16
st. Cabarita 342 E1
st. Harbord 288 D1
st. Surry Hills F H6
st. Surry Hills 4 B11

WAINES
cr. Rockdale 403 D14

WAINWRIGHT
av. Padstow 429 G5
la. Kingswood 237 G12
rd. Mount Druitt 241 A14
rd. Whalan 241 A14
st. Guildford 337 D1

WAIPORI
st. St Ives Ch 223 J3

WAIROA
av. Bondi Beach 378 E2
av. North Bondi 378 E2
la. Canterbury 372 D12
st. Campsie 372 D12
st. Canterbury 372 D12

WAITAKI
st. Lethbrdg Pk 240 F1

WAITANGI
pl. Glenorie 128 C2

WAITARA
av. Waitara 221 K3
pde. Hurstville Gr 431 H10
pl. Dharruk 241 D8

WAITE
av. Balmain 8 B10

WAITOVU
st. Mosman 317 D5

WAIWERA
av. North Manly 258 C16
st. Lavender Bay K B16
st. Lavender Bay 5 E13

WAKE
pl. Kings Park 244 J3

WAKEFIELD
st. North Manly 258 B16

WAKEFORD
pl. Blaxland 233 F12
rd. Strathfield 371 E1

WAKEHURST
pky. Belrose 227 E6
pky. Elanora Ht 228 B3
pky. Frenchs Frst 256 H6
pky. N Narrabeen 228 B3
pky. Oxford Falls 227 B15
pky. Seaforth 286 J3

WAKELIN
av. Mt Pritchard 364 J11
wy. Claymore 481 D12

WAKELY
av. Quakers Hill 214 D7
pl. Forestville 256 A5

WAKOOKA
av. Elanora Ht 198 C16

WALANA
cr. Warriewood 198 F3

WALAR
cr. East Killara 254 K6

WALBURGA
cl. Bradbury 511 J10

WALCHA
ct. Mt Krng-gai 162 G3
la. S Penrith, off Walcha Pl 266 H6
pl. S Penrith 266 G6
wy. Hoxton Park 392 G5
WALDEN
rd. N Parramatta 278 F10
WALDER
rd. Hamondvle 396 E15
WALDO
cr. Peakhurst 430 C3
WALDON
rd. Belrose 225 K5
WALDRON
la. Sandringham, off Norwood St 463 D4
pl. Cambrdg Pk 238 A6
rd. Chester Hill 368 A1
rd. Sefton 368 E2
st. Sandringham 463 D5
WALENORE
av. Kingsford 406 H5
av. Newtown 374 H9
WALER
pl. Blairmount 481 A13
WALES
cl. Illawong 459 E5
la. Greenacre 370 G14
pl. Kings Lngly 245 B3
st. Greenacre 370 G15
WALGETT
cl. Hinchinbrk 392 H4
WALKER
av. Edgecliff 13 F11
av. Gymea 491 F7
av. Haberfield 343 A14
av. Mascot 405 E4
av. Narrabeen 228 J8
av. Peakhurst 430 H3
av. St Ives 224 E6
cl. Silverdale 353 H15
la. Lavender Bay K G13
la. Lavender Bay 5 H11
la. Paddington 4 K15
pde. Riverstone 181 K10
pl. Church Point 168 C9
pl. N Epping 251 F9
pl. Wetherill Pk 334 A1
rd. Port Hacking 522 J2
st. Belmore 371 C12
st. Canada Bay 342 D10
st. Clovelly 378 A13
st. Five Dock 342 D10
st. Lavender Bay K F14
st. Lavender Bay 5 G11
st. Merrylands 307 G16
st. N Sydney K G10
st. N Sydney 5 H9
st. Putney 312 C8
st. Quakers Hill 213 G7
st. Redfern 19 H10
st. Rhodes 311 D9
st. S Windsor 120 J16
st. Springwood 202 H1
st. Turrella 403 F5
st. Waterloo 19 H12
st. Werrington 239 A13
wy. Minto 482 H5
WALKERS
cr. Emu Plains 234 K10
dr. Lane Cove W 283 F12
la. St Clair 300 A1
WALKOM
av. Forestville 256 B9
WALL
av. Asquith 192 A7
av. Panania 398 C13
pl. Bonnyrigg 364 C5
WALLABA
pl. Greystanes 305 H10
WALLABY
cl. Blacktown 273 J5
cl. Bossley Park 333 F7
gr. Winmalee 173 K5
WALLACE
av. Hunters Hill 313 A8
av. Hurlstone Pk 373 A11
cl. Hornsby Ht 161 J10
la. Balmain 8 C10
la. Hurlstone Pk 372 K11
la. Kingsford, off Wallace St 406 J2
pde. Lindfield 254 B16
pl. Mt Pritchard 364 J9
rd. Vineyard 152 C7
st. Ashfield 373 A2
st. Balmain 8 C10
st. Bexley 432 G3
st. Blacktown 244 J15
st. Burwood 342 C16
st. Concord 342 B6
st. Eastwood 280 H8
st. Granville 308 C10
st. Greenwich 314 J13
st. Kingsford 406 H2
st. Marrickville 373 F16
st. Sefton 368 G5
st. Waverley 377 G10
st. Willoughby 285 D12
WALLAGA
av. Leumeah 482 G16
wy. Woodcroft 243 G10
WALLALONG
cr. West Pymble 252 G11
WALLAMI
st. Caringbah 492 G16
WALLAN
av. Glenmore Pk 266 B6
WALLANGRA
rd. Dover Ht 348 E13
WALLARINGA
av. Neutral Bay 6 G10
cl. Mt Colah 162 B15
WALLAROO
cl. Killara 253 K11
WALLAROY
cr. Woollahra 14 D13
rd. Woollahra 14 E14
rd. Woollahra 22 D2
st. Concord W 311 D14
WALLAWA
av. Engadine 488 H15
WALLCLIFFE
ct. Wattle Grove 425 H6
WALLENDBEEN
av. Port Hacking 523 A2
pl. Bardwell Vy 403 C7
WALLGROVE
rd. Cecil Park 332 E13
rd. Eastern Ck 302 G2
rd. Horsley Pk 302 H15
WALLINA
av. Belrose 225 H14
WALLINGA
pl. Airds 512 A14
WALLINGTON
rd. Mosman 317 D2
WALLIS
av. Matraville 436 K8
av. Strathfield 371 B3
cr. Cecil Hills 362 J6
gln. Cranebrook 207 E9
la. Woollahra 22 D4
pde. North Bondi 378 F1
pl. St Ives 224 B15
pl. Willmot 210 B11
st. Leumeah 482 G14
st. Maianbar 522 K9
st. Woollahra 21 J5
st. Woollahra 22 C4
WALL PARK
av. Blacktown 275 C2
av. Seven Hills 275 C2
WALLUMATTA
rd. Newport 169 D8
rd.n, Caringbah 493 B8
rd.s, Caringbah 493 B8
WALMAN
av. Lurnea 394 B10
WALMER
st. Ramsgate 433 E14
st. Sans Souci 433 E14
WALMSLEY
cl. Prairiewood 334 K9
WALNUT
gr. Cherrybrook 219 H7
st. Greystanes 306 E5
WALPA
pl. Quakers Hill 213 G7
WALPOLE
cl. Wetherill Pk 334 J3
pl. Wahroonga 222 D11
st. Granville 307 K10
st. Holroyd 307 K10
st. Merrylands 307 F9
WALRUS
pl. Raby 451 D15
WALSH
av. Castle Hill 248 E2
av. Croydon Pk 371 F8
av. Glebe 11 J12
av. Maroubra 406 H11
cl. Edensor Pk 333 H13
cl. Illawong 459 E7
la. Greenacre 369 J10
pl. Kingswood 267 F1
st. Eastwood 281 H7
st. N Narrabeen 199 B13
WALSHE
gr. Bidwill 211 B15
WALTER
cl. Bligh Park 150 D5
pl. Greystanes 306 E12
pl. Northmead 278 D4
rd. Ingleside 198 C2
st. Balmain 7 C8
st. Bondi Jctn 22 G9
st. Croydon 372 E1
st. Granville 308 D11
st. Kingswood 237 K12
st. Leichhardt 9 B16
st. Mortdale 431 A5
st. Paddington 21 B2
st. Roselands 401 B5
st. Sans Souci 433 E15
st. Wetherill Pk 334 H1
st. Willoughby 285 E16
WALTERS
av. Glenbrook 234 E16
rd. Arndell Park 274 A10
rd. Berala 339 D14
rd. Blacktown 274 B4
st. Arncliffe 403 E8
st. Auburn 339 A2
wy. Castle Hill, off Kerle Cr 218 J14
WALTHAM
st. Artarmon 315 A2
st. Coogee 407 G1
wy. Glenwood 215 C13
WALTHER
av. Bass Hill 367 E7
WALTON
cl. Pymble 253 F5
cr. Abbotsford 342 K1
la. Abbotsford 312 K15
la. Picton 563 F3
pl. Emu Plains 235 B12
pl. Minchinbury 271 F6
st. Blakehurst 432 C14
WALUMETTA
dr. Wollstncraft 315 D10
WALWORTH
av. Newport 169 H13
ct. Newport 169 H12
rd. Horsley Pk 302 E11
WALZ
la. Rockdale, off Walz St 403 C15
st. Rockdale 403 C15
WAMBIRI
pl. Cromer 227 K14
WAMBOOL
pl. Brooklyn 76 C11
st. Turramurra 222 J16
WAMINDA
av. Campbelltwn 511 J8
WANAARING
tce. Glenwood 215 E16
WANAKA
pl. Belrose 226 A16
pl. Glenorie 128 C3
WANARI
rd. Terrey Hills 196 E7
WANAWONG
dr. Thornleigh 220 J12
rd. Avalon 139 K12
WANDA
cr. Berowra Ht 133 C7
pl. Woodbine 481 D15
st. Merrylnds W 307 B14
st. Strathfield S 371 E7
WANDANA
av. Baulkham Hl 247 C4
WANDARRA
cr. Bradbury 511 D15
WANDARRI
rd. Kenthurst 157 E10
WANDEARAH
av. Avalon 139 J12
WANDEEN
av. Beecroft 250 F5
pl. St Ives Ch 223 K3
rd. Clareville 169 D2
WANDELLA
av. Hunters Hill 313 F12
av. Northmead 278 C2
av. Roseville 284 K4
pl. Glen Alpine 510 E14
rd. Allambie Ht 257 G16
rd.n, Miranda 491 K4
rd.s, Miranda 491 K5
WANDOBAH
st. Engadine 489 E8
WANDOO
av. Ryde 311 K4
gln. Kingswood 237 H16
pl. Bradbury 511 E10
WANDSWORTH
st. Parramatta 308 G1
WANGAL
pl. Five Dock 342 K12
WANGALLA
rd. Riverview 314 C5
WANGANELLA
cl. Mt Colah 162 B15
rd. St Ives Ch 223 K3
st. Balgowlah 287 G10
st. Balgowlah 287 G8
st. Miller 393 F4
wy. Airds 512 E10
WANGANUI
rd. Kirrawee 491 B8
WANGARA
st. Doonside 243 B15
st. Mona Vale 199 A3
WANGAROA
cr. Lethbrdg Pk 240 E1
WANGEE
rd. Greenacre 370 E12
rd. Lakemba 370 K14
WANGI
av. Cronulla 523 J4
WANGOOLA
wy. Minto 482 K3
WANILL
pl. Berowra 133 E10
WANINGA
rd. Hornsby Ht 161 J8
WANJINA
pl. North Rocks 278 H2
WANNITI
rd. Belrose 225 H14
WANNYL
rd. Kirrawee 490 J5
WANSEY
rd. Randwick 376 J14
WANSTEAD
av. Earlwood 403 G2
WANT
st. Caringbah 492 K14
st. Mosman 317 B9
st. Rosebery 405 H2
WARABIN
st. Waterfall 519 D12
WARAGAL
av. Rozelle 344 E6
WARANA
rd. Cecil Park 331 E14
WARANDOO
st. Gordon 254 C6
st. Hornsby 221 G6
WARATAH
av. Casula 394 J11
av. Randwick 377 A14
cr. Mcquarie Fd 453 G1
ct. Narellan Vale 478 K12
la. Canterbury 372 C14
la. Sutherland 490 E4
pde. Narraweena 258 B6
pl. Glenorie 127 K10
rd. Berowra 133 D14
rd. Botany 405 H16
rd. Engadine 518 E3
rd. Ingleside 197 H6
rd. Ingleside 198 A6
rd. Kentlyn 483 C13
rd. Palm Beach 109 J14
rd. Turramurra 252 E3
rd. Warrimoo 202 K11
st. Arncliffe 403 D10
st. Balgowlah 288 A8
st. Bexley 432 D2
st. Blakehurst 432 B15
st. Bowen Mtn 83 K13
st. Burwood Ht 372 A6
st. Canterbury 372 D14
st. Chatswood 284 J6
st. Cronulla 493 K14
st. Croydon Pk 372 A6
st. Eastwood 281 H8
st. Ermington 310 H3
st. Granville 308 B10
st. Haberfield 9 A10
st. Haberfield 343 D12
st. Harbord 258 F14
st. Kirrawee 490 G1
st. Kyle Bay 432 B15
st. Leichhardt 10 B14
st. Mona Vale 199 A2
st. North Bondi 348 F15
st. N Strathfield 341 E6
st. Oatley 431 A12
st. Oatley 431 A14
st. Old Guildfrd 337 E9
st. Punchbowl 400 C2
st. Rooty Hill 272 E4
st. Rcuttrs Bay 13 C8
st. St Marys 239 F14
st. Stanhpe Gdn 215 D10
st. Sutherland 490 G1
WARBLER
av. Ingleburn 453 F10
cl. Hinchinbrk 363 E15
la. St Clair, off Warbler St 271 A12
st. Erskine Park 270 K14
WARBRICK
st. Concord 342 A5
WARBROON
ct. Bella Vista 246 H2
WARBURTON
cr. Wrrngtn Cty 238 E4
la. Earlwood 402 D4
pde. Earlwood 402 E3
st. Chifley 437 A5
st. Condell Park 398 F1
st. Gymea 491 E3
st. Marrickville 373 J14
WARBY
st. Campbelltwn 511 G2
WARCOO
av. Gymea Bay 491 G12
WARD
av. Canterbury 372 D14
av. Darlinghurst 4 K9
av. Elizabeth Bay 13 A7
av. Potts Point 4 K9
cl. Prairiewood 334 J7
cr. Oyster Bay 461 F5
la. Concord 342 D6
pl. Dural 188 H13
pl. Hinchinbrk 362 J16
pl. Northmead 277 H8
st. Bass Hill 368 E9
st. Concord 342 D6
st. Eastwood 280 J6
st. Epping 250 G16
st. Kurnell 465 F8
st. N Sydney K F3
st. N Sydney 5 G6
st. Pymble 253 A7
st. Willoughby 285 E12
st. Yagoona 368 E9
wy. Minto 482 K1
WARDANG
rd. Hinchinbrk 362 J16
WARDELL
dr. Barden Rdg 488 H2
dr. S Penrith 267 C4
la. Blaxland 233 E10
la. Dulwich Hill, off Keith St 373 E12
pl. Agnes Banks 117 C12
rd. Dulwich Hill 15 E16
rd. Dulwich Hill 373 G9
rd. Earlwood 403 A3
rd. Lewisham 373 G9
rd. Marrickville 373 D13
rd. Petersham 373 G9
st. Arncliffe 403 G10
wy. Minto 482 J6
WARDIA
st. Glenwood 245 E1
WARDINGTON
ri. Bella Vista 246 H2
WARDLE
cl. Currans Hill 479 F12

WARDROP
st. Greenwich 315 A9
WARE
st. Fairfield 336 E12
st. Fairfield Ht 336 B10
WAREEMBA
av. Thornleigh 221 A4
pl. Lilli Pilli 492 F16
st. Wareemba 343 A5
WAREHAM
cr. Frenchs Frst 256 D3
WAREJEE
st. Kingsgrove 402 A8
WAREKILA
cl. Berowra Ht 133 D8
rd. Beacon Hill 257 H8
WARESLEY
la. Cranebrook, off Waresley Wy 207 G14
wy. Cranebrook 207 F14
WARFIELD
pl. Cecil Hills 362 J9
WARGON
cr. Glenmore Pk 266 A10
WARHAM
la. Marrickville 374 A11
WARI
av. Glenmore Pk 266 D10
WARIALDA
st. Kogarah 433 A3
st. Merrylnds W 307 B13
wy. Hinchinbrk 392 H5
WARILDA
av. Engadine 489 B10
la. Beverly Hills 401 C13
st. Villawood 367 F4
WARILI
rd. Frenchs Frst 255 K2
WARILLA
pl. Riverview 314 A6
WARIN
pl. Glenmore Pk 266 B12
WARING
av. Caringbah 492 D15
cr. Plumpton 242 C11
st. Marsfield 282 B2
WARINGA
cr. Glenmore Pk 266 A6
WARK
av. Pagewood 406 G6
WARKS HILL
rd. Kurrajong Ht 53 J3
WARLENCOURT
av. Milperra 397 F12
WARMAN
st. Dundas Vy 280 C11
st. Pendle Hill 276 C14
WARNDON
la. Cranebrook, off Warndon Rd 207 E13
rd. Cranebrook 207 E13
WARNE
cr. Beverly Hills 400 K11
pl. Marrickville 373 G16
st. Pennant Hills 220 G15
WARNER
av. Clovelly 378 A12
av. S Turramrra 252 A5
pl. Greystanes 306 D12
st. Gladesville 312 E6
WARNERS
av. Bondi Beach 378 D1
av. North Bondi 348 B16
av. Willoughby 285 J12
WARNING
pl. Ruse 512 F7
WARNOCK
rd. Agnes Banks 117 C11
st. Guildford W 336 H3
WAROOGA
av. Baulkham Hl 246 E10
WAROON
rd. Cromer 228 C15
WARRA
st. Wentwthvle 276 K13
WARRABA
rd. N Narrabeen 198 H13
st. Como 460 F7
st. Hurstville 402 A15
WARRABINA
av. St Ives 224 C9
WARRABRI
pl. West Pymble 252 H11
WARRADALE
rd. Warragamba 353 F9
WARRAGAL
rd. Turramurra 222 J16
WARRAGAMBA
cr. Bossley Park 333 H5
cr. Jamisontown 266 A3
cr. Leumeah 482 G13
WARRAH
pl. Greystanes 305 G10
rd. Miranda 492 A9
rd. Yowie Bay 492 A9
st. Chatswood 285 C5
WARRAMUNGA
st. St Marys 239 H16
WARRAN
pl. Castle Hill 218 B12
WARRANA
st. Botany 405 J13
WARRANE
pl. Castle Cove 285 E3
rd. Chatswood 285 G7
rd. N Willghby 285 G7
rd. Roseville Ch 285 D1
WARRANGARREE
dr. Woronora Ht 489 C3
WARRANGI
st. Turramurra 223 A15
WARRAROON
rd. Riverview 314 D5
WARRAROONG
st. Beverly Hills 401 C13
WARRATTA
pl. Oatlands 279 B13
WARRAWEE
av. Castle Cove 285 K5
av. Warrawee 222 F9
pl. Beverly Hills 401 C13
WARRAWIDGEE
rd. Chester Hill 337 F13
WARRAWONG
st. Eastwood 280 H11
st. Glenmore Pk 266 H16
WARREGO
av. Sylvania Wtr 462 D12
ct. Wattle Grove 395 K12
pl. East Killara 254 E9
pl. Greystanes 306 B4
rd. Berowra Ht 133 D8
st. N St Marys 239 J10
WARRELL
ct. Rooty Hill 272 B4
WARREN
av. Bankstown 399 F7
av. Bankstown 399 G7
av. Grays Point 491 A15
av. Kogarah 433 E5
la. Marrickville, off Church St 373 H14
pde. Punchbowl 400 E5
pl. Wakeley 334 H12
pl. Warragamba 353 J9
rd. Bellevue Hill 14 J15
rd. Marrickville 373 G14
rd. Smithfield 336 B2
rd. Woodpark 306 E16
rd. Woodpark 306 F16
st. Quakers Hill 244 B2
st. Ryde 282 B10
swy. Liverpool 395 E3
WARREN BALL
av. Newtown 18 A9
WARRENTON
la. St Clair, off Warrenton St 270 J11
st. St Clair 270 J11
WARRI
cl. Narraweena 258 A6
WARRICK
la. Blacktown 244 H15
WARRIEWOOD
rd. Warriewood 199 A8
st. Woodbine 481 G11
WARRIGAL
dr. Westleigh 220 H5
gln. Wrrngtn Dns 238 E5
la. Canterbury, off Warrigal St 372 D13
rd. Frenchs Frst 256 G2
st. Blacktown 244 A10
st. Canterbury 372 D13
st. Jannali 460 G9
WARRIGO
st. Sadleir 364 B15
WARRIMOO
av. St Ives 223 G9
av. St Ives Ch 223 K4
dr. Quakers Hill 243 J1
WARRINA
av. Baulkham Hl 246 K6
av. Parramatta 278 A13
pl. Glendenning 242 G5
pl. Greystanes 305 H10
pl. Londonderry 148 B11
rd. Bradbury 511 C16
rd. Caringbah 492 G12
st. Berowra Ht 133 D9
WARRING
av. Emu Plains 235 H10
WARRINGA
rd. Cammeray 316 A6
st. Bass Hill 368 E14
st. Yagoona 368 E14
WARRINGAH
fwy. Cammeray 315 G4
fwy. Crows Nest 315 G4
fwy. Naremburn 315 G4
fwy. N Sydney K K6
fwy. N Sydney 5 J6
la. Mosman 317 C3
rd. Beacon Hill 257 B5
rd. Dee Why 258 A6
rd. Forestville 255 F16
rd. Frenchs Frst 256 C8
rd. Mosman 317 C3
rd. Narraweena 258 A6
st. N Balgowlah 287 D3
WARRINGTON
av. Caringbah 493 A6
av. East Killara 254 F7
av. Epping 281 A2
WARRIOR
pl. St Marys 239 F9
WARROWA
av. West Pymble 252 J7
WARRUGA
cr. Berowra Ht 133 C8
pl. N Narrabeen 198 H13
pl. Riverview 313 J6
WARRUMBUNGLE
pl. Bow Bowing 452 D12
st. Fairfield W 335 E11
WARRUNG
rd. St Helens Pk 541 E2
WARSAW
st. N Strathfield 341 C5
WARSOP
st. Kurnell 464 C16
WARUDA
av. Kirribilli 2 D2
pl. Tarban 313 D12
st. Bankstown 368 E14
st. Kirribilli 2 C2
st. Yagoona 368 E14
WARUMBUI
av. Baulkham Hl 246 H8
av. Miranda 492 A1
WARUMBUL
rd. Royal N P 520 K10
WARUNG
av. Frenchs Frst 255 F2
st. Georges Hall 368 D15
st. McMahons Pt 5 E16
st. Yagoona 368 D15
WARWICK
av. Cabramatta 365 C10
av. Cammeray 316 B5
cl. Berowra 133 E9
cl. Blaxland 234 A9
cr. Canterbury 402 E1
la. Hurstville 401 F16
la. Stanmore 16 H9
pde. Castle Hill 217 J15
pl. Wahroonga 221 K15
rd. Dundas Vy 280 A6
rd. Merrylands 307 F12
st. Hurstville 401 E16
st. Killara 253 H11
st. Minto 482 F1
st. North Ryde 283 B11
st. Penrith 236 J13
st. Punchbowl 399 J5
st. St Marys 269 F3
st. Stanmore 16 H9
st. Sylvania 461 K13
st. Warwck Frm 365 J15
WARWILLA
av. Wahroonga 222 C6
wk. Wahroonga, off Warwilla Av 222 D7
WARWILLAH
rd. Russell Lea 343 C5
WASCOE
st. Glenbrook 233 H14
WASDALE
st. Collaroy Plat 228 E12
WASHINGTON
av. Cromer 228 A13
av. Riverwood 400 B13
dr. Bonnet Bay 460 A10
dr. Bonnet Bay 460 E11
pl. Castle Hill 247 E1
st. Bexley 432 K2
st. Bexley 433 A1
wy. Cecil Park 332 A12
WASSALL
la. Alexandria 18 J13
WASSELL
st. Chifley 437 A4
st. Dundas 279 K12
st. Matraville 437 A4
WATCH HOUSE
rd. Prospect 304 K1
WATER
la. Carlton 432 K5
la. Mosman 317 A12
la. Emu Plains, off Water St 235 D10
st. Annandale 17 B2
st. Auburn 339 D7
st. Bardwell Pk 402 K6
st. Belfield 371 C8
st. Birchgrove 7 E4
st. Blakehurst 432 E16
st. Cabramtta W 365 A8
st. Caringbah 493 B13
st. Emu Plains 235 C10
st. Hornsby 191 J15
st. Lidcombe 339 D7
st. Sans Souci 462 K5
st. Strathfield S 371 C7
st. Wahroonga 222 F6
st. Wallacia 324 J11
st. Wentwthvle 277 B15
st. Werrington 238 K15
st. Werrington 239 A15
WATERFALL
av. Forestville 256 A13
cr. Cranebrook 207 B12
pl. Duffys Frst 195 C7
rd. Heathcote 518 F10
rd. Oatley 430 H10
rd. Oatley 430 J11
WATERFORD
pl. Killarney Ht 255 J14
WATERFRONT
dr. Lilyfield, off Military Dr 10 A1
wy. Harringtn Pk 478 D5
WATERGUM
cl. Rouse Hill 185 C8
cr. Silverdale 384 A2
pl. Alfords Point 459 C1
wy. Greenacre 370 F5
WATERHOUSE
av. St Ives 254 D1
dr. Silverdale 353 K10
pl. Airds 511 J14
pl. Camden S 507 C10
st. Abbotsbury 333 C12
WATER LILY
tce. Bidwill 211 E14
WATERLOO
av. Castle Hill 217 K11
pl. Glenfield 424 E9
rd. Greenacre 370 C15
rd. Mcquarie Pk 251 J13
rd. Mcquarie Pk 282 F2
rd. Mcquarie Pk 283 A6
rd. Marsfield 251 J13
rd. Mt Lewis 370 C15
rd. N Epping 251 G11
st. Narrabeen 229 B4
st. Rozelle 344 D8
st. Surry Hills F F16
st. Surry Hills 19 K2
WATER RESERVE
rd. N Balgowlah 287 F5
WATERS
la. Cremorne 316 E8
la. Lowlands 88 E9
la. Neutral Bay 316 E8
rd. Cremorne 6 J1
rd. Cremorne 316 E8
rd. Glenbrook 264 B2
rd. Naremburn 315 E2
rd. Naremburn 315 D3
rd. Neutral Bay 6 J1
WATERSIDE
av. Maroubra 407 J8
cr. Carramar 366 H4
cr. Earlwood 372 J15
gr. Woodcroft 243 G9
pde. Peakhurst 430 D11
WATERSLEIGH
la. Cremorne, off Illiliwa St 316 E7
WATERTON
av. Matraville 436 J2
WATERVIEW
av. Caringbah 492 E12
cr. Blaxland 233 H12
st. Balmain 8 A9
st. Carlton 432 F11
st. Five Dock 342 K10
st. Mona Vale 199 E1
st. Oyster Bay 461 C7
st. Putney 311 J6
st. Ryde 311 J6
st. Seaforth 286 K3
WATERWORTH
dr. Mt Annan 479 A15
dr. Narellan Vale 478 G16
dr. Narellan Vale 508 F1
WATFORD
cl. N Epping 251 G9
WATKIN
av. Earlwood 403 A3
la. Newtown 17 K10
la. Concord, off Watkin St 312 A16
st. Bexley 403 A16
st. Concord 342 A1
st. Hurlstone Pk 372 J11
st. Newtown 17 K10
st. Rockdale 403 A16
WATKINS
cr. Currans Hill 479 H13
rd. Avalon 140 F14
rd. Baulkham Hl 247 E15
st. Bondi 377 H3
WATKIN WOMBAT
wy. Faulconbdg 171 H12
WATKISS
st. Glenwood 215 H16
WATLING
av. West Hoxton 392 A14
wy. Claymore 481 B11
WATSFORD
rd. Campbelltwn 511 F2
WATSON
av. Ashbury 372 E6
av. Hornsby 191 F12
av. N Wahrnga 192 F16
dr. Penrith 237 C7
la. Balmain 7 H9
la. Narwee, off Arrow Rd 400 F15
pl. Doonside 243 B5
pl. Minto 453 A13
pl. Northmead 278 C4
rd. Lapstone 264 F2
rd. Millers Point A E3
rd. Millers Point 1 E10
rd. Mt Annan 479 G14
rd. Padstow 399 D14
st. Bondi 377 K5
st. Ermington 310 D1
st. Glenbrook 264 A4
st. Hamondvle 396 E14
st. Neutral Bay 6 E1
st. Paddington 21 E3
st. Pennant Hills 220 D14
st. Putney 311 J7
st. Rosehill 308 H8
WATSONIA
st. Emu Plains 235 H8
WATT
av. Ryde 282 B16
pde. Lansdowne 367 C6
pl. Emu Plains 235 E9
st. Leumeah 512 C1
st. Rooty Hill 272 B2

WATTING
st. Abbotsbury ... 333 B11
WATTLE
av. Carramar ... 366 H2
av. Fairlight ... 288 C7
av. Mcquarie Fd ... 453 K4
av. N St Marys ... 239 K11
av. Villawood ... 367 A1
cr. Glossodia ... 59 C5
cr. Pyrmont ... 12 G7
la. N St Marys ... 239 K11
la. Ultimo ... 12 K13
la. West Ryde ... 281 G15
la. Asquith, off Amor St ... 191 K10
la. Hurlstone Pk, off New Canterbury Rd ... 372 K10
pl. Carlingford ... 249 F15
pl. Rooty Hill ... 272 D3
pl. Turramurra ... 252 D2
pl. Ultimo ... 3 A16
pl. Ultimo ... 12 K16
rd. Brookvale ... 258 C12
rd. Casula ... 423 H2
rd. Ingleside ... 197 K8
rd. Jannali ... 460 H14
rd. Jannali ... 460 J9
rd. North Manly ... 258 C12
rd. Ruse ... 512 E8
rd. Sutherland ... 460 H15
st. Asquith ... 191 K10
st. Bankstown ... 369 J16
st. Bargo ... 567 G4
st. Blacktown ... 243 J14
st. Bowen Mtn ... 84 A10
st. Enfield ... 371 G5
st. Greystanes ... 306 E4
st. Haberfield ... 343 A13
st. Killara ... 254 B10
st. Peakhurst ... 430 H4
st. Punchbowl ... 370 B16
st. Rydalmere ... 309 G1
st. Springwood ... 202 E8
st. Ultimo ... 3 A15
st. Ultimo ... 12 G9
st. West Ryde ... 281 F14
WATTLEBIRD
cr. Glenmore Pk ... 266 A14
WATTLE CREEK
dr. Theresa Park ... 445 A10
WATTLE GREEN
pl. Narellan Vale ... 478 J13
WATTLE GROVE
dr. Wattle Grove ... 396 A16
WATTON
rd. Carlingford ... 249 F12
st. Quakers Hill ... 214 F16
WATTS
gr. Blacktown ... 273 H5
pl. Cherrybrook ... 220 A11
pl. Prairiewood ... 335 B8
pl. West Hoxton ... 392 C10
rd. Kemps Ck ... 359 G13
rd. Ryde ... 281 K9
st. Canada Bay ... 342 E9
st. North Rocks ... 249 A16
WAU
pl. Glenfield ... 424 J10
pl. Holsworthy ... 426 C3
pl. Whalan ... 240 K8
WAUCHOPE
rd. Hoxton Park ... 392 H10
WAUGH
av. N Parramatta ... 278 G13
cr. Blacktown ... 273 H3
WAUGOOLA
la. Gordon ... 254 B5
st. Gordon ... 254 A5
WAUHOPE
cr. S Coogee ... 407 F4
WAVEHILL
av. Windsor Dn ... 180 J1
WAVELL
av. Carlingford ... 250 A15
pde. Earlwood ... 403 D4
WAVERLEY
cr. Bondi Jctn ... 377 F3
la. Belmore, off Plimsoll St ... 401 H1
st. Belmore ... 401 H1
st. Bondi Jctn ... 22 K7
st. Bondi Jctn ... 377 F4
st. Fairfield W ... 335 D8
st. Randwick ... 377 B11

WAVERLY
pl. Illawong ... 459 K5
WAVERTON
av. Waverton ... 5 B6
la. Waverton ... 5 B6
WAY
cl. Carlingford ... 250 B13
st. Kingsgrove ... 402 B11
st. Tempe ... 374 B16
WAYCOTT
av. Kingsgrove ... 402 B13
WAYELLA
st. West Ryde ... 280 J12
WAYFIELD
rd. Dural ... 218 F2
rd. Glenhaven ... 218 F2
WAYGARA
av. Green Valley ... 363 H11
WAYGROVE
av. Earlwood ... 402 F3
WAYLAND
av. Lidcombe ... 339 H13
WAYMAN
pl. Merrylands ... 307 G13
WAYNE
av. Lugarno ... 430 A11
cr. Condell Park ... 398 F5
cr. Greystanes ... 306 F13
st. Dean Park ... 242 J2
WAYS
tce. Pyrmont ... 8 G16
WAZIR
st. Bardwell Vy ... 403 C8
WEALTHEASY
st. Riverstone ... 182 B9
WEARDEN
rd. Belrose ... 226 C15
rd. Frenchs Frst ... 226 C15
rd. Frenchs Frst ... 256 J1
rd. Frenchs Frst ... 257 A1
WEARNE
av. Pennant Hills ... 220 E14
rd. Bonnyrigg ... 363 K10
st. Canterbury ... 402 C1
WEATHERBY
av. Cambrdg Pk ... 238 A10
WEAVER
la. Erskine Park, off Weaver St ... 301 B2
pl. Minchinbury ... 271 G7
pl. Woronora Ht ... 489 C5
st. Erskine Park ... 300 K2
st. Erskine Park ... 301 A1
st. Ryde ... 312 F6
WEBB
av. Hornsby ... 221 F2
av. Liberty Gr ... 311 B11
cl. Edensor Pk ... 333 H16
cl. Illawong ... 459 J5
pl. Blackett ... 241 D1
pl. Bligh Park ... 150 J7
pl. W Pnnant Hl ... 249 G3
st. Croydon ... 342 D15
st. McMahons Pt ... 5 C12
st. Merrylands ... 307 E7
st. N Parramatta ... 278 H15
st. Parramatta ... 278 H15
st. Riverwood ... 399 J16
st. Werrington ... 238 K12
tce. Westleigh ... 220 G7
WEBBER
pl. Kings Lngly ... 245 A2
pl. Prairiewood ... 335 A8
st. Greenacre ... 370 G11
st. Sylvania ... 461 K12
WEBBS
av. Ashfield ... 372 J1
av. Auburn ... 338 J5
la. Burwood ... 342 A11
st. Ashfield ... 342 H16
WEBER
cr. Emerton ... 240 H6
WEBSTER
av. Peakhurst ... 430 B6
rd. Lurnea ... 394 E10
st. Milperra ... 397 D16
st. Pendle Hill ... 276 B16
st. Picton ... 563 G7
WEDDELL
av. Tregear ... 240 E4
WEDDERBURN
rd. St Helens Pk ... 541 F4
rd. Wedderburn ... 540 B9
rd. Wedderburn ... 541 F11

WEDDIN
pl. Ruse ... 512 F7
WEDDLE
av. Abbotsford ... 343 B3
av. Chiswick ... 343 B3
WEDGE
pl. Lurnea ... 394 C7
WEDGEWOOD
cr. Beacon Hill ... 257 G8
rd. The Oaks ... 502 J1
WEDMORE
la. Emu Heights, off Wedmore Rd ... 235 A5
rd. Emu Heights ... 235 A5
wy. Canley Vale ... 366 D5
WEEDON
av. Paddington ... 13 A16
rd. Artarmon ... 285 A14
WEEKES
av. Rookwood ... 340 B12
la. Newtown ... 17 F11
rd. Clontarf ... 287 H15
WEEKS
pl. Narellan Vale ... 508 J1
WEELSBY PARK
dr. Cawdor ... 505 E16
WEEMALA
av. Doonside ... 243 B14
av. Kirrawee ... 490 J2
av. Riverwood ... 399 K16
cr. Bradbury ... 511 H14
rd. Duffys Frst ... 195 A3
rd. Northbridge ... 286 F16
rd. Pennant Hills ... 220 F16
rd. Terrey Hills ... 195 A3
st. Chester Hill ... 338 B16
st. Northmead ... 277 K3
WEEM FARM
rd. Grose Vale ... 84 G16
WEENA
rd. Kurrajong Hl ... 55 A15
WEENAMANA
pl. Padstow ... 429 G2
WEENEY
st. Beverley Pk ... 433 C11
st. Kurnell ... 464 C16
WEERONA
pl. Caringbah ... 492 D14
WEEROONA
av. Elanora Ht ... 228 F1
av. Woollahra ... 22 D1
pl. Dundas ... 279 H15
pl. Rouse Hill ... 185 C5
rd. Edensor Pk ... 363 G1
rd. Lidcombe ... 369 H2
rd. Rookwood ... 340 E16
rd. Rookwood ... 340 F14
rd. Strathfield ... 340 F14
WEETA
st. Picton ... 561 D3
WEETALIBAH
rd. Northbridge ... 286 E15
WEETAWA
rd. Northbridge ... 286 D15
WEETAWAA
rd. Bilgola ... 169 J3
WEE WAA
cl. Hoxton Park ... 392 J7
WEGG
pl. Ambarvale ... 511 A14
WEHLOW
st. Mount Druitt ... 271 D1
WEIGAND
av. Bankstown ... 369 C15
WEIL
av. Croydon Pk ... 371 H8
WEIPA
cl. Green Valley ... 363 J11
WEIR
cr. Lurnea ... 394 F10
pl. Kings Lngly ... 246 A10
rd. Warragamba ... 353 F8
WEISEL
pl. Willmot ... 210 D12
WEJA
cl. Prestons ... 422 J1
WELBY
st. Eastwood ... 281 E8
tce. Acacia Gdn ... 214 G14
WELCH
av. Greenacre ... 370 A10
pl. Minto ... 452 K15
st. North Manly ... 258 B14

WELCOME
st. Wakeley ... 334 H13
WELD
pl. Prestons ... 393 G8
WELDER
rd. Seven Hills ... 246 F15
WELDON
la. Woollahra ... 21 K2
st. Burwood ... 372 A2
WELFARE
av. Beverly Hills ... 400 K12
av. Narwee ... 400 K12
st. Homebsh W ... 340 J6
WELHAM
st. Beecroft ... 250 E8
WELL
st. Ryde ... 311 G5
WELLAND
cl. Jamisontown ... 236 B15
WELLARD
pl. Bonnyrigg ... 364 A7
WELLBANK
st. Concord ... 341 J5
st. N Strathfield ... 341 E6
WELLE
cl. St Clair ... 299 H1
WELLER
pl. Rydalmere ... 279 F16
WELLERS
rd. Bargo ... 567 B1
WELLESLEY
cr. Kings Park ... 244 K3
pl. Green Valley ... 363 A10
rd. Pymble ... 253 E3
st. Pitt Town ... 92 J15
st. Summer Hill ... 373 D5
WELLGATE
av. Kellyville ... 185 F9
WELLING
dr. Mt Annan ... 479 F13
dr. Narellan Vale ... 508 F1
pl. Mt Pritchard ... 364 C10
WELLINGTON
av. Ingleburn ... 453 A8
la. Lavender Bay ... 5 E13
la. McMahons Pt ... 5 E13
la. Waterloo ... 19 G12
la. E Lindfield, off Wellington Rd ... 255 A12
pl. Bondi ... 377 J4
rd. Auburn ... 338 G8
rd. Auburn ... 339 C9
rd. Birrong ... 368 J3
rd. Chester Hill ... 368 B2
rd. Earlwood ... 403 B3
rd. E Lindfield ... 255 A12
rd. Hurstville ... 432 A1
rd. Ryde ... 312 H2
rd. Sefton ... 368 E2
rd. S Granville ... 338 G8
st. Bondi ... 377 K3
st. Bondi Beach ... 378 A2
st. Chippendale ... 19 C2
st. Croydon ... 342 E13
st. Mascot ... 405 F4
st. Narrabeen ... 229 A3
st. Riverstone ... 153 A16
st. Riverstone ... 182 H3
st. Rosebery ... 405 F4
st. Rozelle ... 344 E7
st. Sans Souci ... 462 J4
st. Wakeley ... 334 H13
st. Waterloo ... 19 C13
st. Woollahra ... 22 B1
WELLMAN
rd. Forestville ... 256 B6
WELLS
av. Tempe ... 404 A1
ct. Baulkham Hl ... 247 E5
st. Annandale ... 11 A16
st. Balmain ... 8 A8
st. Chifley ... 437 B5
st. Jamisontown ... 266 C5
st. Newtown ... 374 G11
st. Pitt Town ... 92 J9
st. Redfern ... 19 C7
st. S Granville ... 338 F2
st. Thornleigh ... 220 H13
WELLUMBA
st. Horngsea Pk ... 392 D15
st. Horngsea Pk ... 392 E15
WELLWOOD
av. Moorebank ... 396 B11

WELSFORD
st. Merrylands ... 307 C8
WELSH
pl. Narellan Vale ... 479 A16
WELSTED
st. S Windsor ... 150 H3
WELWYN
rd. Canley Ht ... 365 A3
rd. Hebersham ... 241 E8
WEMBLEY
av. Cambrdg Pk ... 238 B7
WEMBURY
rd. St Ives ... 224 C6
WEMYSS
la. Surry Hills ... F E5
st. Enmore ... 16 F16
st. Marrickville ... 16 F16
WENBAN
la. Mosman, off Dugald Rd ... 317 D9
pl. Wetherill Pk ... 304 F14
WENDEN
av. Kellyville ... 215 H6
av. West Hoxton ... 392 A7
st. Fairfield ... 335 K14
WENDLEBURY
rd. Chipping Ntn ... 396 G3
WENDOUREE
st. Busby ... 363 G14
WENDOVER
st. Doonside ... 243 B10
WENDRON
cl. St Ives ... 224 G9
WENDY
av. Georges Hall ... 367 F10
av. Normanhurst ... 221 F11
cl. Cabramatta ... 365 E9
pl. Glenwood ... 215 D13
pl. Toongabbie ... 276 G8
WENKE
cr. Yagoona ... 368 H10
WENONA
la. N Sydney ... 5 J5
WENTON
av. Liberty Gr ... 311 B11
WENTWORTH
av. Bnksmeadw ... 406 A8
av. Blakehurst ... 432 B15
av. Eastgardens ... 406 A8
av. East Killara ... 254 F8
av. Eastlakes ... 405 E7
av. Glenfield ... 424 C11
av. Hillsdale ... 406 A8
av. Mascot ... 405 E7
av. North Rocks ... 278 F3
av. Pagewood ... 406 A8
av. Pendle Hill ... 276 G14
av. Surry Hills ... F C7
av. Surry Hills ... 3 J12
av. Sydney ... F C7
av. Sydney ... 3 J12
av. Toongabbie ... 276 D9
av. Waitara ... 222 A2
av. Wentwthvle ... 276 G14
av. Wentwthvle ... 277 B16
dr. Camden S ... 507 A13
dr. Liberty Gr ... 311 C13
pde. Yennora ... 337 B10
pl. Belrose ... 226 C16
pl. Point Piper ... 14 K1
pl. Point Piper ... 347 E8
rd. Burwood ... 341 H16
rd. Eastwood ... 280 J9
rd. Ingleburn ... 423 B9
rd. Orchard Hills ... 266 K12
rd. Orchard Hills ... 267 A12
rd. Strathfield ... 371 H1
rd. Vaucluse ... 348 B3
rd. Vaucluse ... 348 C3
rd.n, Homebush ... 341 A5
rd.s, Homebush ... 341 A6
st. Auburn ... 309 C16
st. Bardwell Vy ... 403 C7
st. Birrong ... 368 J4
st. Caringbah ... 492 J14
st. Croydon Pk ... 372 A7
st. Dolans Bay ... 492 J14
st. Dover Ht ... 348 G15
st. Ermington ... 310 C1
st. Glebe ... 12 F12
st. Granville ... 308 K11
st. Greenacre ... 370 H7
st. Greenacre ... 370 J12
st. Manly ... 288 H10
st. Paddington ... 21 F3

st. Parramatta 308 D5
st. Petersham 15 F8
st. Point Piper 14 K2
st. Point Piper 347 E8
st. Randwick 22 C16
st. Randwick 377 A11
st. Tempe 404 B3
WENTWORTH PARK
rd. Glebe 12 E9
WEONGA
rd. Dover Ht 348 F10
WERAMBIE
st. Woolwich 314 H11
WERINGA
av. Cammeray 316 B4
WERNA
pl. Hornsby 221 F4
WERNICKE
cl. Prairiewood 335 A9
WEROMBI
rd. Brownlow Hl 475 G9
rd. Ellis Lane 476 B11
rd. Grasmere 506 C1
rd. Orangeville 444 A10
rd. Theresa Park 445 A12
rd. Werombi 443 D2
WEROMBIE
rd. Mt Colah 192 B4
WERONA
av. Abbotsford 342 J3
av. Clarmnt Ms 268 J1
av. Gordon 253 H7
av. Killara 253 H7
av. Padstow 429 G3
av. Punchbowl 400 E8
pl. Dharruk 241 D8
rd. Riverview 314 C6
st. Pennant Hills 220 H15
WERRIBEE PARK
pl. Glen Alpine 510 A15
WERRINGTON
rd. Werrington 239 B9
WESCOE
pl. Cranebrook 207 F11
WESLEY
pl. Cherrybrook 220 A5
pl. Greystanes 306 D12
pl. Horngsea Pk 392 C13
st. Elanora Ht 198 D11
st. Greenacre 370 F3
st. Oatlands 279 C8
st. Telopea 279 C8
WESSEL
cl. Hinchinbrk 363 A15
WESSEX
la. Wentwthvle 277 C9
pl. Raby 451 H12
WESSON
rd. W Pnnant Hl 249 G1
WEST
av. Darlinghurst 4 J12
cir. Blaxland 233 J6
cl. Illawong 459 B7
cr. Hurstville Gr 431 F10
ct. Carlingford 279 G5
dr. Bexley North 402 C10
esp. Manly 288 F10
la. Carlton 432 J5
la. Darlinghurst 4 H12
la. Randwick 407 B2
la. St Marys 239 G15
lk. Eveleigh 18 H12
pde. Chatswd W 284 F8
pde. Couridjah 564 D16
pde. Denistone 281 D12
pde. Eastwood 281 B8
pde. Riverstone 182 J9
pde. Roseville 284 F8
pde. Thirlmere 564 G12
pde. West Ryde 281 E15
pl. Camden S 506 K14
prm. Manly 288 G10
st. Auburn 338 J6
st. Balgowlah 287 H10
st. Balgowlah 287 H8
st. Blacktown 274 H4
st. Blakehurst 432 E11
st. Brookvale 258 D9
st. Cammeray 315 H6
st. Canley Vale 366 B4
st. Carlton 432 E11
st. Crows Nest 315 H6
st. Croydon 342 J12
st. Darlinghurst 4 H12
st. Darlinghurst 4 G14
st. Five Dock 342 K9
st. Glenbrook 233 G14
st. Guildford 337 J5
st. Hurstville 432 B7
st. Kingswood 237 G16
st. Lewisham 15 E10
st. Lurnea 394 C9
st. Naremburn 315 J3
st. N Sydney 5 E3
st. Paddington 4 G14
st. Parramatta 279 A16
st. Petersham 15 D7
st. Petersham 15 E10
st. Pymble 253 D6
st. S Hurstville 432 B7
st. Strathfield 371 B1
st. Waterloo 19 E13
tce. Bankstown 399 F1
WESTACOTT
la. Canley Vale, off Railway Pde 366 A3
WESTALL
cl. Abbotsbury 333 C12
WESTBANK
av. Emu Plains 235 H11
WEST BOTANY
st. Arncliffe 403 H11
st. Kogarah 433 F4
st. Rockdale 403 G16
WESTBOURNE
av. Thirlmere 565 B3
la. Petersham 16 B7
la. Stanmore 16 B7
rd. Lindfield 284 D4
st. Artarmon 315 A5
st. Bexley 432 E3
st. Carlton 432 J9
st. Drummoyne 343 H1
st. Petersham 16 B7
st. St Leonards 315 A5
st. Stanmore 16 B7
WESTBROOK
av. Wahroonga 223 A5
rd. Bickley Vale 505 F13
rd. Cawdor 505 F13
rd. Mt Hunter 504 K8
st. Beverly Hills 401 F13
WESTBURY
rd. Grose Vale 84 H10
st. Chipping Ntn 396 E3
WESTCHESTER
av. Casula 395 A12
WESTCOMBE
pl. Rooty Hill 272 B2
WESTCOTT
pl. Oakhurst 241 J1
st. Eastlakes 405 J5
WEST CRESCENT
st. McMahons Pt 5 D15
WESTELLA
av. Roselands 401 B7
WEST END
la. Ultimo 12 H15
WESTERLY
wy. Glenmore Pk 266 G13
WESTERN
av. Blaxland 234 A5
av. Camperdwn 18 B5
av. North Manly 258 C16
cr. Blacktown 274 D5
cr. Gladesville 312 G10
cr. Gladesville 312 H8
cr. Westleigh 220 H1
mwy. Auburn 309 C12
mwy. Blacktown 273 C14
mwy. Clarmnt Ms 269 B7
mwy. Eastern Ck 272 C11
mwy. Emu Plains 235 A12
mwy. Glenbrook 234 H15
mwy. Granville 308 C8
mwy. Greystanes 306 E3
mwy. Harris Park 308 C8
mwy. Homebush 341 A7
mwy. Homebush B 340 A1
mwy. Homebsh W 340 A1
mwy. Huntingwd 273 C14
mwy. Jamisontown 265 G1
mwy. Lapstone 234 H15
mwy. Leonay 234 H15
mwy. Lidcombe 340 A1
mwy. Mays Hill 307 B4
mwy. Merrylands 307 B4
mwy. Minchinbury 271 C10
mwy. N Strathfield 341 A7
mwy. Orchard Hills 267 D8
mwy. Parramatta 308 C8
mwy. Prospect 275 B16
mwy. St Clair 270 A8
mwy. Silverwater 309 C12
mwy. S Penrith 266 D6
mwy. S Wntwthvle 307 B4
rd. Castle Hill 218 H13
rd. Kemps Ck 359 K13
wy. Chatswd W 284 G10
WESTERN DISTRIBUTOR
Pyrmont 12 E5
Sydney A C16
Sydney 1 D16
WESTFIELD
dr. Eastgardens 406 F11
pl. Blacktown, off Rushcombe Rd 244 G16
st. Earlwood 402 E3
WESTHALL
wy. Claymore 481 B10
WEST HEAD
rd. Krngai Ch NP 167 E13
rd. Terrey Hills 196 G4
WEST HILL
pl. Green Valley 362 J11
st. McGraths Hl 121 K11
WESTLAKE
pl. Balgowlah 287 G7
WESTLAND
cl. Raby 451 G13
WESTLEIGH
dr. Westleigh 220 D6
la. Neutral Bay 6 F4
st. Neutral Bay 6 F5
WEST MARKET
st. Richmond 118 F5
WESTMEATH
av. Killarney Ht 286 D1
WESTMINSTER
av. Carlingford 279 D5
av. Dee Why 258 H4
dr. Castle Hill 219 A12
rd. Gladesville 312 J6
st. Bexley 402 J11
st. Rooty Hill 242 A16
st. Schofields 183 C13
wy. Rsemeadow 540 J2
WESTMONT
dr. S Penrith 267 B1
WESTMOOR
gr. Wrrngtn Dns 238 A5
WESTMORE
dr. W Pnnant Hl 249 C11
WESTMORELAND
av. Collaroy 259 A1
la. Glebe 12 B14
rd. Leumeah 482 F9
rd. Minto 482 F9
st. Glebe 12 B15
WESTON
av. Narwee 400 H11
la. Rooty Hill 242 C16
pl. West Hoxton 392 A10
rd. Hurstville 431 K1
st. Balmain East 8 H9
st. Dulwich Hill 373 D7
st. Fairfield 336 G13
st. Harris Park 308 F6
st. Panania 428 C1
st. Revesby 428 E1
st. Rosehill 308 F6
WESTRINGIA
pl. Gymea Bay 491 J10
pl. Mcquarie Fd 454 D3
WESTVILLE
pl. Westmead 307 E2
WESTWARD
av. Shalvey 210 J12
st. Kareela 461 C11
WEST WILCHARD
rd. Castlereagh 176 A7
WESTWOOD
av. Belmore 401 H2
pl. Theresa Park 445 B8
st. Bossley Park 334 D10
st. Pennant Hills 220 G13
st. Prairiewood 334 D10
wy. Bella Vista 246 D2
WETHERILL
cr. Bligh Park 150 B5
st. Croydon 372 E2
st. Croydon 372 E3
st. Leichhardt 10 A16
st. Narrabeen 229 A9
st. Smithfield 335 A6
st. Wetherill Pk 335 A6
st.n, Silverwater 309 J15
st.s, Lidcombe 309 J16
WETSTONE
wy. Dural 219 C6
WEWAK
pl. Allambie Ht 257 F13
pl. Bossley Park 333 K5
rd. Holsworthy 396 C16
WEXFORD
pl. Killarney Ht 255 K13
WEYLAND
st. Punchbowl 399 J7
WEYMOUTH
av. Auburn 338 J9
WEYNTON
la. Annandale 11 A7
mw. Bella Vista 246 G5
st. Annandale 11 B8
WHADDON
av. Dee Why 258 E6
WHALAN
pl. Gymea 491 G1
pl. Whalan 240 K10
WHALANS
rd. Greystanes 305 G8
WHALE
pl. Woodbine 481 K9
WHALE BEACH
rd. Avalon 140 D12
rd. Palm Beach 140 B2
rd. Whale Beach 140 B7
WHALING
rd. N Sydney 5 K9
WHARF
rd. Birchgrove 7 K2
rd. Ermington 280 H15
rd. Gladesville 312 H13
rd. Kogarah Bay 432 J14
rd. Lansvale 367 A10
rd. Lilyfield 10 B4
rd. Longueville 314 B9
rd. Melrose Pk 280 H15
rd. Vaucluse 318 F16
rd. Cremorne Pt, off Cremorne Rd 316 G15
st. Brooklyn 75 F11
st. Marrickville 403 E1
WHARF HOUSE STEPS
The Rocks B B1
WHATELEY
la. Newtown 17 H11
st. Newtown 17 J11
WHATMORE
la. Waverton, off Bay Rd 315 E12
st. Waverton 315 D12
WHEAT
pl. Horngsea Pk 392 E15
rd. Sydney C A11
rd. Sydney C B2
WHEATLEIGH
st. Crows Nest 315 G4
st. Naremburn 315 G4
WHEATLEY
pl. Harringtn Pk 478 G7
rd. Hawksbry Ht 174 E7
rd. Yarrawarrah 489 E15
st. St Johns Pk 364 J2
WHEEDON
st. Glenwood 215 H14
WHEELER
av. Camden S 507 C16
av. Lurnea 394 C10
la. N Sydney K A6
la. Surry Hills, off Brumby St 19 H3
pde. Dee Why 258 K8
pl. Minto 453 B16
st. Carlton 432 K8
st. Lalor Park 245 C13
st. Narrabeen 228 F9
WHEENEY
rd. Kurrajong 84 J5
WHEENY
st. Maroota S 65 B6
WHELAN
av. Chipping Ntn 396 A5
av. Rookwood 340 E14
la. Paddington 21 G3
WHELLER
st. Bossley Park 334 D8
WHERRITT
cl. Picton 563 F10
WHIBLEY
av. Glenwood 215 J13
WHIDDON
cl. Denham Ct 422 C8
WHIMBREL
av. Hinchinbrk 393 D1
pl. Woronora Ht 489 E4
wy. Glenmore Pk 266 A13
WHIPBIRD
av. Ingleburn 453 G9
la. St Clair, off Whipbird Pl 270 J14
pl. Castle Hill 219 B10
pl. Erskine Park 270 J14
pl. Green Valley 363 E9
WHISSON
cl. Abbotsbury 333 D12
WHISTLER
av. Ingleburn 453 F10
cr. Erskine Park 270 K14
la. St Clair, off Whistler Cr 271 A14
st. Green Valley 363 E9
st. Manly 288 G9
WHITAKER
rd. Rossmore 389 F7
st. Old Guildfrd 337 C9
st. Yennora 337 C9
WHITBAR
wy. Cherrybrook 219 B12
WHITBECK
la. Cranebrook, off Whitbeck Pl 207 G11
pl. Cranebrook 207 F11
WHITBREAD
pl. North Rocks 278 C7
WHITBY
rd. Kings Lngly 245 F7
WHITCROFT
pl. Oxley Park 270 D2
pl. Thornleigh 220 K10
WHITE
av. Bankstown 399 C4
av. Maroubra 407 D15
la. Paddington 13 C15
pde. St Marys 270 A3
pl. Bossley Park 334 C5
pl. Castle Hill 217 J13
pl. Rooty Hill 272 D3
pl. S Windsor 120 K16
rd. Pagewood 406 G6
st. Artarmon 284 H16
st. Artarmon 284 J16
st. Balgowlah 287 G9
st. Balmain 7 A6
st. Brookvale 257 K12
st. Jannali 460 H12
st. Lilyfield 10 G12
st. Randwick 377 A9
st. Strathfield 341 J11
wy. Casula 424 F3
WHITE CEDAR
dr. Castle Hill 217 F16
WHITECHAPEL
cl. Ambarvale 510 K16
WHITE CLIFFS
av. Hoxton Park 392 F8
WHITE CROSS
rd. Winmalee 173 E4
WHITEFRIARS
wy. Winston Hills 276 H1
WHITEGATES
av. Peakhurst 430 C8
rd. Londonderry 178 B4
WHITE GUM
pl. Greystanes 306 C4
pl. Kellyville 185 H8
WHITEHALL
rd. Kenthurst 187 A5
WHITEHAVEN
av. Quakers Hill 213 H9
pl. Castle Hill 217 H16
rd. Northmead 277 H6
st. St Ives 224 F7
WHITEHEAD
ct. Glendenning 242 F8
WHITEHORSE
st. Newtown 17 F15
WHITELEY
cl. Casula 424 C4
WHITEMAN
av. Bella Vista 246 H2

la. Ellis Lane 476 C11
WHITEMORE
av. Georges Hall 367 H11
WHITES
av. Caringbah 492 G15
la. Darlinghurst 4 G11
rd. Glenorie 128 C8
rd. Shanes Park 209 F5
WHITES CREEK
la. Annandale 16 E3
WHITESIDE
st. North Ryde 282 E5
WHITES RIDGE
rd. Annangrove 156 B14
WHITEWOOD
pl. Caringbah 492 K10
WHITFIELD
av. Ashbury 372 F7
av. Beverly Hills 400 K16
av. Lane Cove W 283 F12
pde. Hurstville Gr 431 H12
pl. Picton 563 E6
WHITFORD
rd. Green Valley 363 E12
rd. Hinchinbrk 393 C5
WHITING
st. Artarmon 314 J2
st. Leichhardt 9 E12
st. Regents Pk 369 E1
WHITING BEACH
rd. Mosman 317 A13
WHITLAM
av. Edensor Pk 333 H13
WHITLAM SQUARE
Darlinghurst 4 A9
Surry Hills 4 A9
Sydney F F3
WHITLEY
pl. Abbotsbury 332 K14
WHITLING
av. Castle Hill 217 K15
WHITMONT
cr. St Ives Ch 224 B1
WHITMORE
rd. Maraylya 94 A12
WHITNEY
row. Mona Vale 198 H2
st. East Killara 254 K8
st. Mona Vale 198 H2
WHITSUNDAY
cct. Green Valley 362 J11
WHITTAKER
st. Mortlake 312 A13
WHITTALL
st. Russell Lea 343 E7
WHITTELL
st. Surry Hills 20 C4
WHITTIER
st. Quakers Hill 213 G16
WHITTLE
av. Balgowlah 287 E10
av. Milperra 397 F9
WHITTON
pl. Bligh Park 150 H5
pl. Doonside 273 E3
rd. Chatswd W 284 G11
st. Heathcote 518 F12
WHITWORTH
pl. Raby 451 F16
st. Westmead 307 F5
WHORLONG
st. St Helens Pk 541 A7
WHYALLA
cl. Wakeley 334 J13
pl. Prestons 393 H8
WIAK
rd. Jannali 460 H10
WIANAMATTA
dr. Cartwright 394 A5
WIBLIN
st. Silverwater 309 J12
WICK
pl. St Andrews 481 K5
WICKFIELD
cct. Ambarvale 511 A12
WICKHAM
la. Avalon 170 B2
st. Arncliffe 403 H9
WICKLOW
pl. Killarney Ht 255 K14
pl. Rouse Hill 185 B6
st. Bidwill 211 C16
WICKS
av. Marrickville 373 E14
la. Kogarah, off South St 433 B4
rd. Mcquarie Pk 282 F11
rd. North Ryde 282 F11
WIDE BAY
cct. Bidwill 211 F14
WIDEMERE
rd. Wetherill Pk 304 K14
WIDEVIEW
rd. Berowra Ht 133 C7
WIDGIEWA
rd. Northbridge 286 D14
WIGAN
rd. Dee Why 258 E3
WIGENS
av. Como 460 D5
WIGGAN
pl. Cranebrook 207 C10
WIGGINS
av. Beverly Hills 430 K1
pl. Concord 342 B1
st. Botany 405 J15
WIGGS
rd. Punchbowl 399 J9
rd. Riverwood 399 J9
WIGHT
st. Bnksmeadw 406 D12
WIGMORE
gr. Glendenning 242 G4
WIGNELL
pl. Mt Annan 479 G16
WIGRAM
la.e, Glebe 11 H13
la.w, Forest Lodge 11 E15
rd. Annandale 11 D15
rd. Faulconbdg 201 A2
rd. Forest Lodge 11 D15
rd. Glebe 11 D15
rd. Hinchinbrk 392 K2
st. Harris Park 308 E8
WILBAR
av. Cronulla 493 J11
WILBERFORCE
av. Rose Bay 348 B11
rd. Revesby 398 K14
rd. Revesby 399 A15
rd. Wilberforce 91 J7
st. Ashcroft 394 F2
WILBOW
pl. Bligh Park 150 H7
WILBUNG
rd. Illawong 459 F5
WILBUR
la. Greenacre 370 K13
st. Greenacre 370 E12
WILBY
st. Chipping Ntn 396 F1
WILCANNIA
wy. Hoxton Park 392 F8
wy. Mcquarie Pk 282 D3
WILCO
av. Cabramtta W 365 A7
WILCOCK
st. Carramar 366 H1
st. Regents Pk 338 K16
WILCOX
la. Marrickville, off Black St 374 F10
WILD
la. Maroubra 406 G9
st. Maroubra 406 G9
st. Picton 563 E12
WILDARA
av. W Pnnant Hl 249 G9
WILDE
av. Killarney Ht 256 B16
av. Parramatta 308 E1
pl. Wrrngtn Cty 238 J5
st. Carramar 366 J3
WILDEN
cl. Jamisontown 236 B14
WILDFLOWER
pl. Dural 219 B7
pl. Kellyville 216 G3
WILDING
st. Edensor Pk 363 G2
st. Marsfield 282 B5
WILDMAN
av. Liverpool 365 A14
WILD ORANGE
pl. Mcquarie Fd 424 F16
WILDTHORN
av. Dural 188 F1
WILDWOOD
wy. Dural 219 D6
WILES
pl. Cambrdg Pk 238 A10
WILEY
av. Greenacre 370 F16
ct. Wrrngtn Cty 238 E8
la. Wiley Park 400 G2
pl. Guildford W 336 G1
st. Chippendale 18 K3
st. Waverley 377 G7
WILFIELD
av. Vaucluse 348 F7
WILFORD
la. Newtown 17 D13
st. Newtown 17 D13
WILFRED
av. Campsie 371 K13
av. Chatswd W 284 D10
la. Campsie 371 J13
pl. Jamisontown 266 A2
st. Lidcombe 339 D8
WILFRID
st. Mcquarie Fd 424 A15
WILGA
av. Dulwich Hill 373 E12
cl. Casula 394 G14
la. Concord W 341 E1
pl. Hornsby 191 D12
pl. Mcquarie Fd 454 E4
pl. Marsfield 281 K5
rd. Caringbah 492 F12
st. Blacktown 273 H4
st. Bondi 378 C5
st. Burwood 342 A13
st. Concord W 341 F1
st. Elanora Ht 197 K11
st. Fairfield 336 E15
st. Ingleside 197 K11
st. N St Marys 240 B12
st. Punchbowl 399 K4
st. Regents Pk 369 C1
st. W Pnnant Hl 249 K1
WILIMA
pl. Frenchs Frst 256 F7
WILKES
av. Artarmon 284 K15
av. Matraville 437 B2
av. Moorebank 396 D11
cr. Tregear 240 E9
WILKIE
cr. Doonside 243 C8
WILKINS
pl. Leumeah 482 J11
st. Bankstown 368 J15
st. Turrella 403 C6
st. Yagoona 368 J15
WILKINSON
av. Kings Lngly 245 B3
cr. Ingleburn 452 H10
la. Marrickville 374 C14
la. Telopea 279 F8
pl. Cranebrook 207 H10
pl. Hornsby 192 A14
rd. Bexley North 402 G10
st. Elderslie 477 F15
WILKSCH
la. Naremburn 315 E2
WILL
cl. Glendenning, off Vicky Pl 242 E1
WILLABURRA
rd. Woolooware 493 D13
WILLAN
dr. Cartwright 394 B4
WILLANDRA
pde. Heathcote 518 F10
rd. Beacon Hill 257 H4
rd. Cromer 258 A1
rd. Narraweena 257 H4
st. Lane Cove W 283 J14
st. Miller 393 F3
st. Ryde 311 J3
wy. Airds 512 E10
WILLARA
av. Merrylands 307 E9
WILLARONG
rd. Caringbah 492 H5
rd. Mt Colah 191 K6
rd.s, Caringbah 492 G10
WILLAROO
av. Kellyville 216 F3
av. Woronora Ht 489 B4
WILLARRA
la. Point Piper, off Wunulla Rd 347 G7
WILLAWA
av. Penrith 237 D7
la. Penrith, off Kareela Av 237 E6
st. Balgowlah Ht 287 J15
WILLEE
st. Strathfield 371 G2
WILLEROO
av. Rooty Hill 272 E4
dr. Windsor Dn 151 A16
dr. Windsor Dn 180 J3
st. Lakemba 401 A4
WILLETT
pl. Ambarvale 510 G15
st. Yagoona 368 F12
WILLFOX
st. Condell Park 398 H7
WILLIAM
av. Camden 507 A3
cl. Liberty Gr 311 B11
dr. Rookwood 340 A10
la. Alexandria 375 F13
la. Earlwood 402 D4
la. Redfern 19 A9
la. Woolmloo 4 F7
la. Ryde, off William St 312 A3
pl. North Rocks 278 F4
pwy. Caringbah 492 D15
rd. Riverwood 399 K15
st. Alexandria 375 F13
st. Annandale 11 D10
st. Ashfield 372 K6
st. Avalon 140 A14
st. Balmain East 8 H10
st. Bankstown 368 K15
st. Beaconsfield 375 F13
st. Blacktown 244 B14
st. Botany 405 H11
st. Brooklyn 76 D11
st. Brookvale 258 A13
st. Cambrdg Pk 238 B8
st. Chatswood 284 J6
st. Concord 342 B1
st. Darlinghurst D H13
st. Double Bay 14 B7
st. Earlwood 402 G4
st. Epping 281 A1
st. Ermington 280 F14
st. Fairfield 336 E13
st. Fairlight 288 D8
st. Five Dock 342 F11
st. Granville 307 K10
st. Granville 308 A12
st. Henley 313 B14
st. Hornsby 221 D1
st. Kingsgrove 401 J5
st. Leichhardt 9 E11
st. Lewisham 15 B9
st. Lidcombe 339 G9
st. Lurnea 394 G7
st. Marrickville 16 B14
st. Merrylands 308 A12
st. North Manly 258 A13
st. Northmead 278 B3
st. N Parramatta 278 D11
st. N Richmond 87 D12
st. N Sydney K B12
st. N Sydney 5 E10
st. Paddington 21 D1
st. Randwick 376 J10
st. Redfern 19 E7
st. Richmond 118 K6
st. Riverstone 152 K14
st. Riverstone 183 A1
st. Rockdale 403 H14
st. Rose Bay 348 C13
st. Roseville 284 J6
st. Ryde 312 A2
st. St Marys 269 J4
st. Schofields 182 H15
st. Seven Hills 275 H3
st. S Hurstville 431 K10
st. Strathfield S 371 C6
st. Tempe 404 C1
st. The Oaks 502 E11
st. Turramurra 222 H13
st. Werrington 238 D10
st. Wilberforce 91 J3
st. Woolmloo D H13
st. Woolmloo 4 B7
st. Yagoona 368 K15
st.e, Roseville 285 B5
st.s, Condell Park 398 J3
WILLIAM CAMPBELL
av. Harringtn Pk 478 D5
av. Harringtn Pk 478 F7
WILLIAM COX
dr. Richmond 118 A6
WILLIAM DOWLE
pl. Grasmere 475 K13
WILLIAM EDWARD
st. Longueville 314 C9
WILLIAM FAHY
pl. Camden S 507 B9
WILLIAM HENRY
st. Ultimo 3 A11
st. Ultimo 12 H12
WILLIAM HOWE
pl. Narellan Vale 508 F2
WILLIAM HOWELL
dr. Glenmore Pk 265 K9
WILLIAM MAHONEY
dr. Prestons 393 K14
WILLIAM MANNIX
av. Currans Hill 479 H9
WILLIAMS
av. Richmond 119 K5
cl. Hoxton Park 392 K6
la. Paddington 4 F16
pde. Campsie 371 J12
pde. Dulwich Hill 373 C9
rd. North Rocks 248 E14
WILLIAMSON
av. Seven Hills 245 J15
cr. Warwck Frm 365 E13
rd. Ingleburn 423 C16
WILLIAMTOWN
ct. Glenhaven 218 E6
WILLINGTON
st. Turrella 403 D6
WILLIS
av. Guildford 338 C7
av. Pennant Hills 220 H15
av. St Ives 224 E9
la. Kingsford 406 H2
pl. Winston Hills 277 F1
rd. Castle Cove 286 D7
st. Arncliffe 403 H6
st. Kensington 376 H16
st. Kingsford 406 H2
st. Lansvale 366 K7
st. Oakdale 500 D11
st. Rooty Hill 272 A6
WILLISON
rd. Carlton 432 G3
WILLMOT
av. Toongabbie 276 F7
st. Bossley Park 334 C10
WILLMOTT
av. Winston Hills 277 H2
pl. Glenmore Pk 265 E9
WILLOCK
av. Miranda 492 A3
WILLORING
cr. Jamisontown 236 B15
la. Jamisontown, off Willoring Cr 236 B14
WILLOUGHBY
cct. Grasmere 475 K14
la. Crows Nest, off Falcon St 315 F6
rd. Crows Nest 315 F6
rd. Naremburn 315 F1
rd. Naremburn 315 F6
rd. St Leonards 315 F6
rd. Willoughby 285 E15
rd. Willoughby 315 F1
st. Colyton 270 G8
st. Epping 280 D2
st. Guildford 338 C6
st. Kirribilli 6 A14
st. Milsons Pt 6 A14
wy. Rsemeadow 540 J2
WILLOW
cl. East Killara 254 G7
cl. Epping 250 D15
cl. Lansvale 366 K9
cr. Ryde 281 K13
ct. Bradbury 511 G11
dr. Baulkham Hl 248 B11
gr. Plumpton 242 A9
la. Earlwood 402 G1
pl. Bass Hill 368 C11
pl. Kirrawee 490 J5
rd. N St Marys 239 K10

st. Casula 423 K2
st. Greystanes 306 E4
st. Lugarno..........429 J16
wy. Forestville.......256 A13
wy. Leonay 265 B2

WILLOW BROOK
pl. Tennyson 58 G5

WILLOWBROOK
pl. Castle Hill 218 H8
pl. Sylvania..........462 B11

WILLOWDENE
av. Luddenham 356 C5

WILLOW GLEN
rd. Kurrajong 85 A4

WILLOWGUM
cr. Cranebrook.....207 D7

WILLOWIE
cl. Hornsby Ht.....191 E1
rd. Castle Cove.....286 A5

WILLOWLEAF
cl. Glenwood 245 D1
pl. W Pnnant Hl ...248 H5

WILLOW TREE
av. Emu Plains 235 K8
cr. Belrose...........226 B14

WILLOWTREE
st. Normanhurst..221 E12

WILLS
av. Castle Hill 218 C16
av. Chifley 437 A6
av. Waverley 377 G10
cr. Daceyville 406 F4
gln. St Clair 270 E11
pl. Camden S.......507 A11
pl. Guildford 337 J4
rd. Long Point......454 E7
rd. Mcquarie Fd....454 E7
rd. Woolooware ...493 G10
rd. Woolooware ...493 G9
st. Lalor Park.......245 B12

WILLUNGA
av. Earlwood 402 D6
cr. Forestville.......255 G10
pl W Pnnant Hl ...249 A1
rd. Berowra..........133 G11

WILLYAMA
av. Fairlight 288 A9
la. Fairlight 288 A9
st. Dharruk 241 C7

WILMA
pl. Hassall Gr.......211 K14

WILMAR
av. Berala 339 D15

WILMETTE
pl. Mona Vale 199 D2

WILMOT
st. Sydney ....C H16
st. Sydney 3 G8

WILONA
av. Greenwich 315 B8
av. Lavender Bay......K D13
av. Lavender Bay......5 F11

WILSHIRE
av. Carlingford 249 D12
av. Cronulla...........523 J1
rd. Agnes Banks...147 B2
rd. Londonderry...147 G3
st. Surry Hills 20 B5

WILSON
av. Belmore..........401 E3
av. Ingleside.........197 K10
av. Regents Pk.....339 C16
av. Winston Hills..247 H16
cr. Narellan..........478 C11
gr. Thirlmere........565 C5
la. Belmore..........401 E3
la. Darlington 18 E9
la. Jamisontown..235 K13
la. Longueville.....314 E9
la. Newtown 18 B10
la. Padstow Ht.....429 F6
pde. Heathcote 518 G13
pl. Bonnet Bay 460 A9
pl. Ruse...............512 F6
pl. St Marys..........269 D4
rd. Acacia Gdn 214 F15
rd. Bonnyrigg Ht ..363 C9
rd. Green Valley ...363 C9
rd. Hinchinbrk......393 B4
rd. Pennant Hills ..250 D1
rd. Quakers Hill ...214 F15
st. Botany............405 J15
st. Cammeray......316 A4
st. Chatswood 284 H8
st. Darlington 18 E9
st. Eveleigh 18 E9
st. Harbord 258 E16
st. Kogarah 433 D8
st. Maroubra........407 K9
st. Narwee 400 F15
st. Newtown 17 G12
st. Newtown 17 H11
st. North Ryde 282 D7
st. Panania...........398 B16
st. St Marys 269 D4
st. Strathfield 340 J16
st. Woolmloo...........4 F4
wy. Blaxland..........233 E4
wy. Blaxland..........233 H7

WILSONS
rd. Arncliffe 403 B9

WILTON
cl. Castle Hill........217 K16
cl. Gordon 253 G4
pl. Georges Hall ...367 G9
rd. Appin 568 C16
rd. Doonside 243 B9
st. Narellan 478 F12
st. Surry Hills.........19 J5
wy. Bonnyrigg 363 K5

WILTONA
pl. Girraween 275 K10

WILTSHIRE
cl. Liberty Gr 311 B11
ct. Cherrybrook, off Glamorgan Wy.. 219 E9
pl. Turramurra 222 J8
rd. The Slopes.......56 K6
st. Miller 393 H3
st. Minto..............482 E3

WIMBLEDON
av. N Narrabeen....228 J3
ct. Wattle Grove...426 B5

WIMBOW
pl. S Windsor.......150 E3

WINANI
cl. Belrose 225 J13

WINBOURNE
pl. Airds..............511 K15
rd. Brookvale........258 B10
rd. Mulgoa 295 C16
st. West Ryde 280 F11
st. West Ryde 280 G13
st.e, West Ryde 280 G11

WINBURN
av. Kingsford.........376 D15

WINBURNDALE
rd. Wakeley..........334 F14

WINCHCOMBE
av. Haberfield 343 C15
pl. Castle Hill........218 E13

WINCHESTER
av. Lindfield..........283 J5
la. Clovelly, off Winchester Rd. 377 J11
rd. Clovelly...........377 J12
st. Carlton............432 J7

WINCHMORE
st. Merrylands 307 G16

WINDAM
pl. Westleigh........220 D8

WINDARRA
cr. Wahroonga.....221 K7
pl. Castle Hill........217 D6
pl. Cromer 258 B1
st. Narwee 400 H12

WINDEMERE
av. Woodcroft 243 F10

WINDERMERE
av. Cambrdg Pk....237 J10
av. Miranda..........492 C3
av. Northmead......278 B3
cr. Panania...........398 D14
pl. Collaroy Plat ...228 D10
rd. Epping 250 J12

WINDERS
la. Revesby..........398 H15

WINDEYER
av. Gladesville 313 A10
rd. N Parramatta...279 A6
st. Thirlmere 565 C2
st. Woolmloo...........4 H5

WINDHOVER
ct. Bella Vista 246 E6

WINDLE
av. Hoxton Park....392 J7
pl. Menai 458 E15

WINDMILL
cl. Seven Hills......275 C6
pl. Wrrngtn Dns ...237 K3
st. Dawes Point.......A C1
st. Dawes Point....... 1 E9
st. Millers Point.......A B1
st. Millers Point.......A C1
st. Millers Point....... 1 D9

WINDMILL STEPS
Millers Point.......A C1

WINDORRA
av. Glenmore Pk ...266 G13

WINDRUSH
av. Belrose 225 J11
cct. St Clair............269 J15
la. St Clair, off Windrush Cct...269 K14

WINDSOR
av. Carlingford 279 B6
av. Croydon Pk.....371 J8
ct. Castle Hill........219 A11
dr. Mcquarie Pk....282 D2
la. Paddington 13 F15
la. Dulwich Hill, off Weston St.......373 E6
pde. N Narrabeen....228 K2
pl. Bargo..............567 C4
pl. St Ives Ch 223 J5
rd. Baulkham Hl....247 G10
rd. Box Hill 184 C1
rd. Castle Hill........247 E1
rd. Cecil Hills 362 K3
rd. Cronulla 493 J16
rd. Dulwich Hill.....373 C8
rd. Kellyville..........215 E1
rd. Kellyville..........217 A14
rd. McGraths Hl....121 G10
rd. Merrylands......307 G12
rd. Northmead 277 K7
rd. Padstow..........429 D2
rd. Richmond 119 E7
rd. Riverstone.......184 C1
rd. Rouse Hill 184 C1
rd. Vineyard..........152 A1
rd. Willoughby......285 J13
rd. Windsor 121 G10
st. Mcquarie Fd 423 K16
st. Matraville 436 K1
st. Paddington 13 F16
st. Paddington 21 G1
st. Richmond 118 J5
wy. West Pymble...253 A12

WINDWARD
av. Mosman 317 F9

WINES
st. Emu Plains......235 G9

WINESHOP
rd. Oakdale...........500 J12

WINFORD
dr. Mulgrave.........121 K15

WINGADAL
pl. Point Piper....... 14 H1

WINGADEE
pl. Windsor Dn.....150 F16
st. Lane Cove W...284 B16

WINGARA
gr. Belrose 225 H15
st. Chester Hill 338 A15

WINGARIE
pl. Berowra Ht......133 C7

WINGATE
av. Eastwood 281 A6
pl. Guildford W 336 H1
rd. Mulgrave.........121 J14

WINGELLO
rd. Miranda 492 B1
st. Guildford.........337 F6

WINGHAM
rd. Hoxton Park....392 H10

WINGROVE
av. Epping 250 G12

WINIFRED
av. Caringbah 492 F6
av. Epping 281 E3
cr. Blacktown 245 A16
st. Condell Park....398 H5

WINIFRED FALLS FIRE
trl. Royal N P.......521 A11

WINJEEL
av. Richmond 119 K3

WINKIN
av. Gymea Bay......491 E11

WINKURRA
st. Kensington.....376 B10

WINNA
pl. Glenmore Pk ...266 B7

WINNALEAH
st. West Hoxton .. 392 C7

WINNALL
pl. Ashcroft 364 E14

WINNICOOPA
rd. Blaxland 233 F4

WINNIE
st. Cremorne....... 316 E7

WINNIFRED
rd. McGraths Hl... 121 K10

WINNIPEG
st. Seven Hills..... 275 G6

WINNOW DOWN
la. Cobbitty 446 A16

WINNUNGA
rd. Dural............. 158 D10
rd. Lilli Pilli 522 G3
rd. Middle Dural... 158 D10

WINPARA
cl. Tahmoor 565 H8

WINSFORD
av. Hebersham..... 241 E5

WINSLEA
av. Frenchs Frst ... 257 B4

WINSLOW
av. Castle Hill....... 217 C6
av. Stanhpe Gdn .. 215 D11
la. Milsons Pt......... 6 B13
st. Milsons Pt......... 6 A13

WINSOME
av. N Balgowlah ... 287 E6
av. Plumpton 241 J9

WINSPEAR
av. Bankstown 369 C16

WINSTANLEY
pl. Mt Pritchard ... 364 K9

WINSTON
av. Bass Hill......... 368 C6
av. Cammeray...... 316 D4
av. Earlwood........ 372 G15
av. Guildford W.... 336 H1
cl. Badgerys Ck... 358 D3
ct. Baulkham Hl ... 248 A8
pl. Narellan Vale .. 479 B11
pl. Sylvania 462 A10
st. Asquith 192 A11
st. Marsfield 282 B5
st. Penrith 236 H14

WINTAROO
cr. St Helens Pk ... 541 G1

WINTEN
dr. Glendenning ... 242 G3
dr. Glendenning ... 242 H5

WINTER
av. Neutral Bay......... 6 A3
pl. Oatley............ 431 B14
rd. Springwood ... 203 B2
st. Telopea 279 F11

WINTERCORN
row. Wrrngtn Dns .. 237 J4

WINTERGREEN
pl. W Pnnant Hl ... 248 J3

WINTHINGTON
pky. Denistone....... 281 C11

WINTON
av. Edensor Pk..... 333 J14
av. Northmead 248 C15
cl. Wedderburn 540 E12
st. Appin 568 G9
st. Warrawee....... 222 G12

WIRANDA
ct. Windsor Dn.... 151 A14

WIRE
la. Camden S 507 A16
la. Cawdor 506 E14
la. Freemns Rch 88 K5
la. N Richmond..... 88 K5

WIREGA
av. Kingsgrove..... 401 G7

WIRILDA
wy. Blacktown 274 E11

WIRRA
cl. Edensor Pk...... 333 F16
cl. St Ives........... 224 D16
pl. Glenorie 128 C4

WIRRABARA
rd. Dural............. 188 H11

WIRRALEE
st. S Wntwthvle ... 306 K7

WIRRALIE
av. Baulkham Hl... 247 A7

WIRRAWAY
pl. Doonside........ 273 F4
st. Raby 451 D13

WIRREANDA
cl. Warrawee....... 222 E13
rd. Ingleside....... 197 B8
rd.n, Ingleside......... 197 C6

WIRRILDA
wy. Forestville 256 A12

WIRRINA
pl. N Narrabeen ... 198 H13

WIRRINDA
rd. Mt Krng-gai 162 H6

WIRRINGULLA
av. Elvina Bay....... 168 C3

WIRRUNA
st. Blacktown....... 244 A10

WIRUNA
cr. Narwee.......... 400 K14
cr. Newport 169 G14

WISBEACH
la. Balmain 7 B11
st. Balmain 7 A10

WISDOM
la. Darlinghurst 4 E8
rd. Greenwich 314 K5
st. Annandale 10 J12
st. Connells Pt 431 H15
st. Currans Hill 479 J12
st. Guildford W.... 336 K3
st. S Coogee 407 J5
wy. Connells Pt..... 431 H15

WISE
st. Maroubra 407 A11
st. Rozelle 7 A12

WISEMAN
rd. Castle Hill 247 G1

WISEMANS FERRY
rd. Cattai 64 F16
rd. Maroota S......... 65 C5

WISHART
rd. Kemps Ck....... 359 E15
st. Eastwood 281 F7

WISTARIA
pl. Baulkham Hl... 247 F15
pl. Blacktown....... 245 A9
st. Dolans Bay 492 J16

WISTERIA
cl. Glenmore Pk... 265 G10
cr. Cherrybrook ... 219 K6
cr. Stanhpe Gdn... 215 C11

WISTON
gdn. Double Bay 14 B6

WITCOM
st. Cranebrook..... 207 C11

WITHAM
pl. Chipping Ntn .. 366 H14

WITHECOMBE
st. Rozelle, off Belmore St 344 E8

WITHERS
la. Kurrajong Ht..... 54 B7
la. Surry Hills 20 A2
pl. Abbotsbury..... 333 B11
pl. Surry Hills 20 B2
rd. Kellyville 185 K11
rd. Rouse Hill....... 184 J4
st. Arncliffe......... 403 D11
st. Chiswick......... 343 D1
wy. Claymore........ 481 D12

WITHNELL
cr. St Helens Pk... 541 B9

WITHYBROOK
pl. Sylvania.......... 462 A12

WITLEY
cl. St Marys......... 269 K7

WITNEY
st. Prospect......... 274 G9

WITONGA
cr. Baulkham Hl... 248 C10

WITT
cl. Edensor Pk...... 333 J12

WITTAMA
dr. Glenmore Pk... 266 C7

WITTENOOM
pl. Yarrawarrah.... 489 H13

WOBURN
pl. Glenmore Pk... 266 F10

WOBURN ABBEY
ct. Wattle Grove... 425 K5

WODROW
pl. Rooty Hill 241 K13

WOIDS
av. Allawah.......... 432 D7
av. Carlton 432 D7
av. Hurstville........ 432 D7

WOKARI
st. Engadine........489 C10
WOLARA
av. Glenmore Pk..266 D8
WOLAROI
cr. Revesby.........399 B10
cr. Tamarama......378 B7
WOLBAH
pl. Cromer..........228 A11
WOLDHUIS
st. Quakers Hill....214 E15
WOLF
cl. St Clair..........269 H15
WOLFE
rd. East Ryde.......283 B14
WOLGER
la. Mosman.........316 J8
rd. Mosman.........316 K8
rd. Ryde..............282 A14
st. Como.............460 F8
WOLI
pl. Malabar..........437 F8
WOLLABI
cr. Glenmore Pk..266 A11
WOLLATON
gr. Oakhurst........241 H2
WOLLEMI
ct. Wattle Grove..426 B3
pl. Dural.............219 A4
pl. Kurrajong Ht.....53 E3
WOLLI
av. Earlwood........402 D8
av. Earlwood........402 E7
pl. Greenacre.......370 F9
st. Kingsgrove.....402 B10
WOLLI CREEK
rd. Arncliffe..........403 A10
rd. Banksia..........403 A10
WOLLOMBI
rd. Bilgola............169 J5
rd. Northbridge.....286 F16
WOLLOMOMBI
wy. Hoxton Park...392 H6
WOLLONDILLY
pl. Sylvania Wtr...462 G14
WOLLONGBAR
av. Panania..........428 F2
WOLLONGONG
rd. Arncliffe..........403 B10
WOLLSTONECRAFT
av. Avalon............140 B15
WOLLUN
st. Como.............460 G8
WOLLYBUTT
rd. Engadine........488 H12
WOLSELEY
cr. Point Piper.....347 E7
pl. Ingleburn.......453 H12
rd. Coogee..........407 H3
rd. Lindfield.........254 B15
rd. McGraths Hl...122 C11
rd. Mosman.........317 D9
rd. Oakville..........122 C11
rd. Point Piper.......14 J1
rd. S Coogee........407 H4
st. Bexley............433 A3
st. Drummoyne...313 J16
st. Fairfield..........335 K15
st. Fairfield..........336 B15
st. Guildford.........338 D4
st. Haberfield.......342 K13
st. Jamisontown..265 K2
st. Merrylands.....338 D3
st. Rooty Hill.......242 A13
WOLSLEY
av. Riverstone......183 B12
WOLSTEN
av. Turramurra.....223 A10
WOLSTENHOLME
av. Greendale.......385 H6
av. Gymea...........491 F2
WOLUMBA
st. Chester Hill.....338 B13
WOLVERTON
av. Chipping Ntn..366 E15
pl. Bringelly.........388 H8
pwy. Chipping Ntn, off Wolverton Av..366 E14
WOMBERRA
pl. S Penrith........266 H3
WOMBEYAN
ct. Wattle Grove..395 H12
pl. Leumeah........482 D14
st. Forestville.......255 K7
WOMBIDGEE
av. St Clair...........269 H8
WOMBOYNE
av. Kellyville.........216 F3
WOMERAH
av. Darlinghurst.......4 J11
la. Darlinghurst.......4 K10
st. Turramurra.....222 K15
WOMRA
cr. Glenmore Pk...266 A11
la. Glenmore Pk, off Womra Cr.......266 B10
WONAWONG
st. Belimbla Pk....501 F14
WONDABAH
pl. Carlingford.....249 H13
WONDAKIAH
dr. Waverton........315 D11
WONDERLAND
av. Tamarama......378 B6
WONGA
la. Canterbury......372 C12
pl. Ingleburn........453 F7
rd. Cremorne.......316 E4
rd. Lalor Park.......245 J11
rd. Lurnea............394 C9
rd. Miranda...........491 K9
rd. Mt Colah.........192 D2
rd. Picton.............563 F15
rd. Yowie Bay.......491 K9
st. Canterbury......372 D13
st. N Balgowlah....287 C4
st. Strathfield.......371 G1
WONGAJONG
cl. Castle Hill.......218 F10
WONGALA
av. Elanora Ht.......198 C16
cr. Beecroft..........250 F5
cr. Pennant Hills..250 F2
WONGALARA
pl. Woodcroft......243 H12
WONGALEE
av. Wahroonga.....251 H1
WONGAWILLI
st. Couridjah........564 G16
WONGA WONGA
st. Turramurra.....222 K12
WONIORA
av. Wahroonga.....222 D6
rd. Blakehurst......432 C9
rd. Hurstville........431 J5
rd. S Hurstville.....432 C9
WONNAI
pl. Clarmnt Ms.....268 G1
WONOONA
pde.e,Oatley..........431 C11
pde.w,Oatley..........431 A11
WOOD
cl. Green Valley...362 J8
ct. Mt Annan........479 G14
la. Cronulla..........493 K15
la. Randwick.......377 C12
pl. Emu Plains.....235 F13
st. Ashfield..........372 J2
st. Bexley............432 G2
st. Chatswd W.....284 D9
st. Eastwood.......281 F3
st. Fairfield..........336 C8
st. Forest Lodge.....11 F15
st. Lane Cove W..313 G2
st. Manly.............288 H12
st. Picton.............563 E13
st. Randwick.......377 C12
st. Richmond.......119 K3
st. Tempe............404 C2
st. Thornleigh......221 A14
st. Waverton........315 E13
WOODBERRY
rd. Winston Hills..277 B3
WOODBINE
av. Normanhurst..221 G7
cr. Ryde..............282 C15
st. N Balgowlah....287 D4
st. Yagoona.........369 C10
WOODBRIDGE
rd. Menangle.......538 B16
WOODBROOK
rd. Casula...........395 B11
WOODBURN
av. Panania..........428 D1
ct. Glenbrook.......234 B15
pl. Glenhaven......187 H15
rd. Berala............339 D12
rd. Kurrajong.........85 E2
rd. Lidcombe.......339 E10
st. Redfern............19 B5
WOODBURY
rd. St Ives...........224 C8
st. Marrickville.....373 H11
st. North Rocks...248 H16
WOODCHESTER
cl. Castle Hill.......217 H8
WOODCLIFF
pde. Lugarno.........430 B14
WOODCOCK
pl. Lane Cove W..283 F16
WOODCOURT
rd. Berowra Ht.....133 B6
st. Ambarvale......540 F2
st. Marrickville.....373 G11
WOODCREST
av. Ingleburn........453 G9
pl. Cherrybrook....219 J14
WOODCROFT
dr. Woodcroft......243 F8
WOODD
rd. Denham Ct......452 G2
WOODFIELD
av. Bundeena.......523 F10
bvd. Caringbah.......492 K2
pl. Castle Hill.......248 H2
pl. Lalor Park.......245 E12
WOODFORD
cl. Jamisontown..266 C5
cr. Heathcote.......519 A12
la. Lindfield.........284 C1
rd. Rockdale.........403 C12
st. Longueville.....314 F7
st. Northwood.....314 F7
WOODFULL
ct. Rouse Hill.......185 A8
WOODGATE
cr. Cranebrook.....207 E12
WOODGLEN
pl. Cherrybrook....219 C8
WOODGROVE
av. Castle Hill.......219 B11
av. Cherrybrook....219 B11
WOODHILL
st. Castle Hill.......248 B2
WOODHOUSE
dr. Ambarvale......511 A12
WOODI
cl. Glenmore Pk...266 B9
WOODLAKE
ct. Wattle Grove...395 K16
WOODLAND
av. Oxley Park......270 E2
cr. Narellan..........478 J9
rd. Annangrove....186 B1
rd. Bradbury.........541 C1
rd. Chester Hill.....337 K12
rd. St Helens Pk...541 C1
st. Coogee...........377 G13
st. Marrickville.....374 B10
st. Riverstone......153 C14
st.n, Balgowlah.......287 J8
st.s, Balgowlah.......287 H11
st.s, Balgowlah Ht..287 H13
WOODLANDS
av. Blakehurst......462 C4
av. Bossley Park...333 K11
av. Lugarno.........430 A16
av. Narwee..........400 K11
av. Pymble..........253 G2
dr. Glenmore Pk...265 J12
la. Glenmore Pk, off Woodlands Dr..265 J13
rd. Ashbury.........372 G6
rd. E Lindfield.......254 J16
rd. Forestville.......255 J9
rd. Liverpool........364 K16
rd. Taren Point.....462 J12
rd. Wilberforce........62 F11
st. Winston Hills..248 A15
WOODLARK
pl. Castle Hill.......219 B11
pl. Glenfield.........424 F14
st. Rozelle.............10 H1
WOODLAWN
av. Earlwood........402 E7
dr. Toongabbie.....276 D5
WOODLEAF
cl. W Pnnant Hl...249 B1
WOODLEY
cr. Glendenning...242 E4
st. St Peters.........374 K14
WOODMAN
pl. Abbotsbury.....333 B16
WOODPARK
rd. Guildford W....306 E14
rd. Smithfield.......305 G13
rd. Smithfield.......306 E14
rd. Woodpark.......306 E14
WOOD RIDGE
pl. Baulkham Hl...247 B10
WOODRIDGE
av. N Epping.........251 H9
WOODRIFF
st. Penrith............236 G13
st.n, Penrith............236 J10
WOODRUSH
ct. Dural..............219 C6
WOODS
av. Cabramatta.....365 D9
av. Woollahra.........22 C4
cl. Huntingwd......273 K12
la. Darlinghurst........4 D9
pde. Earlwood........373 B15
pde. Fairlight...........288 D10
rd. Birrong...........368 H6
rd. Sefton.............368 H6
rd. S Windsor........150 E1
rd. Yagoona.........368 G8
st. N Epping.........251 G8
st. Riverstone......183 B7
WOODSIDE
av. Blacktown.......243 J15
av. Hurlstone Pk...373 A10
av. Lindfield.........254 D15
av. West Hoxton...392 D9
av. West Hoxton...392 B9
av.e, Burwood.........341 J15
av.w, Strathfield.......341 G15
gln. Cranebrook.....207 B6
gr. Forestville.......256 B8
WOODS RESERVE
rd. Grose Wold.....115 A11
WOODSTOCK
av. Dharruk..........241 A7
av. Glendenning...242 B12
av. Hebersham.....241 E11
av. Mount Druitt...241 E11
av. Plumpton........241 E11
av. Rooty Hill........242 B12
av. Whalan...........241 A7
la. Bondi Jctn, off Paul St.............377 G3
rd. Carlingford......249 H15
st. Bondi Jctn......377 G3
st. Botany............405 G13
st. Guildford.........337 J3
st. St Johns Pk....364 F4
WOODVALE
av. N Epping.........251 G12
cl. Plumpton.........241 K11
cl. St Ives.............254 B2
pl. Castle Hill........218 D11
WOODVIEW
la. Oxley Park, off Woodview Rd..270 F2
rd. Oxley Park.......270 F2
WOODVILLE
av. Wahroonga.....222 E8
la. Hurstville, off Barratt St.........432 A5
rd. Chester Hill.....337 E15
rd. Fairfield E.......337 E15
rd. Granville.........308 A15
rd. Guildford.........337 K6
rd. Merrylands......308 A15
rd. Old Guildfrd....337 E15
rd. Villawood........367 C3
st. Glenbrook.......233 J16
st. Hurstville........432 A5
WOODWARD
av. Caringbah.......492 K11
av. Strathfield.......341 E14
cr. Miller.............393 J2
pl. St Ives............254 F1
rd. Hunters Hill.....313 H11
st. Cromer...........227 J12
st. Ermington.......280 B16
tce. Bella Vista.......246 G3
WOODY
av. Morning Bay...138 E16
WOOL
pl. Miller.............393 F4
WOOLCOTT
av. Wahroonga.....221 K6
st. Earlwood........372 G16
st. Newport..........169 G11
st. Waverton...........5 A9
st. Waverton.......315 E12
WOOLEY
la. Marrickville....373 H14
WOOLGEN PARK
rd. Leppington.....420 G13
WOOLGOOLGA
av. Hoxton Park...392 J9
st. N Balgowlah...287 B4
WOOLISIA
pl. Baulkham Hl...247 G15
WOOLLEY
ct. Agnes Banks..117 F16
la. Glebe...............11 K13
st. Glebe...............12 A13
WOOLLSIA
ct. Voyager Pt.....427 C6
WOOLLYBUTT
pl. Mcquarie Fd...454 E2
WOOLMERS
ct. Wattle Grove..425 H5
pl. Glen Alpine.....510 D14
WOOLNOUGH
pl. Cartwright......394 B5
WOOLOOWARE
rd.n, Woolooware...493 F8
rd.s, Burraneer.......493 E16
rd.s, Woolooware...493 E12
WOOLPACK
st. Elderslie.........477 G16
WOOLRYCH
cr. Davidson........255 C1
WOOLSHED
pl. Currans Hill....480 A10
WOOLWASH
rd. Airds.............512 A15
WOOLWICH
rd. Hunters Hill....313 K12
WOOLWONGA
pl. Bow Bowing...452 D14
WOOLYBUTT
pl. Mt Riverview..204 E15
WOOMBA
cl. Hornsby Ht.....161 H12
WOOMBYE
cl. Berowra Ht.....132 K6
WOOMERA
rd. Little Bay........437 A10
WOOMERA PATH
Winmalee.......173 B9
WOONAH
st. Little Bay........437 B10
st. Miranda.........492 C6
WOONGARA
wy. Glenhaven......218 D3
WOONGARRA
av. Chipping Ntn..396 B5
WOONONA
av. Wahroonga....222 C6
av.n, Wahroonga....222 C4
av.s, Wahroonga....222 C7
rd. Northbridge....286 B16
WOORAIL
av. Kingsgrove....402 C7
WOORAK
cr. Miranda.........491 J1
rd. Palm Beach....139 H2
WOORANG
st. Eastwood.......281 J7
st. Milperra.........398 C7
WOORARRA
av. Elanora Ht......228 D1
av. N Narrabeen...228 G1
WOOTTEN
rd. Ingleburn.......422 H13
st. Colyton..........270 B5
WORBOYS
pl. N St Marys.....239 H9
WORCESTER
pl. Turramurra....222 J8
rd. Cambrdg Pk...237 K11
rd. Rouse Hill......184 E6
st. Collaroy.........229 B14
WORDIE
pl. Padstow........399 E10
WORDOO
st. St Marys........239 H9
WORDSWORTH
av. Concord.........341 J7
av. Leumeah.......512 C2
pl. Sylvania.........462 B14
st. Wetherill Pk....334 K5
WORKMAN
pl. Leonay.........235 D15

WORKS
pl. Greenacre 370 H8
pl. Milperra 397 K8
WORLAND
st. Yagoona 368 K11
WORONORA
av. Leumeah 482 B15
cr. Como 460 E5
cr. Como 460 E6
pde. Oatley 431 A12
pl. St Clair 270 B16
rd. Engadine 518 E1
WORROBIL
st. N Balgowlah 287 D6
WORSLEY
st. East Hills 427 H2
WORTH
la. Blaxland 233 E9
st. Chullora 369 K5
st. Penrith 236 F10
WORTHING
av. Castle Hill 218 A14
pl. Cherrybrook 219 K11
WORTLEY
av. Belmore 371 E16
st. Balmain 7 F12
WOYLIE
pl. St Helens Pk 541 H1
WRAY
st. Fairfield Ht 336 A10
WRAYSBURY
pl. Oakhurst 241 H4
WREN
ct. Castle Hill 219 B9
ct. Woronora Ht 489 D6
pl. Clarmnt Ms 268 J4
pl. Greystanes 306 D3
pl. Lugarno 429 H13
pl. Thirlmere 565 C5
pl. Woolooware 493 E13
st. Condell Park 398 E1
tce. Plumpton 242 A9
WRENCH
pl. Kenthurst 157 H11
st. Cambrdg Pk 238 A10
WRENTMORE
st. Fairfield 336 C12
WRIDE
st. Maroubra 407 F10
WRIGHT
cl. Georges Hall 367 F14
cl. Heathcote 518 D15
la. Surry Hills F B11
pl. Bligh Park 150 H7
pl. Narellan Vale 479 A16
st. Blacktown 244 A9
st. Croydon 342 E15
st. Fairfield W 335 B12
st. Glenbrook 263 K3
st. Hurstville 432 B3
st. Merrylands 307 C9
st. Merrylands 308 C16
st. Sydenham, off Gleeson Av 374 D15
WRIGHTLAND
pl. Arndell Park 273 D7
WRIGHTS
av. Berala 339 B14
av. Marrickville 373 G14
rd. Castle Hill 217 A7
rd. Drummoyne 343 J1
rd. Kellyville 216 G8
WROXHAM
st. Prestons 393 C16
WUDGONG
st. Mosman 316 K6
wk. Mosman, off Cowles Rd 316 K6
WULUMAY
cl. Rozelle 344 D6
WULWORRA
av. Cremorne Pt 316 G15
WUNDA
rd. Concord W 311 D16
rd. Mosman 316 K8
WUNULLA
rd. Point Piper 14 K3
rd. Point Piper 347 F9
rd. Rose Bay 347 F9
WURLEY
av. Kingsford 406 E2
WURUMA
pl. Warriewood 199 A7
WYADRA
av. Harbord 258 F14
av. North Manly 258 C14
WYAGDON
st. Neutral Bay 6 A1
WYALONG
cl. Wakeley 334 G15
st. Burwood 342 B15
st. Panania 398 D15
st. Willoughby 285 D15
WYANBAH
rd. Cronulla 493 K9
WYANDOTTE
pl. Seven Hills 275 F6
WYANG
gln. Cranebrook 207 A6
pl. Engadine 489 B11
WYANGA
la. Beverly Hills, off Tooronga Tce 401 C13
rd. Elanora Ht 198 F14
WYANGALA
cct. Woodcroft 243 J10
cr. Leumeah 482 E14
cr. Leumeah 482 G10
pl. Miranda 491 H7
WYANNA
gr. Yennora 337 A8
st. Berowra Ht 132 J11
WYARAMA
st. Allambie Ht 257 D8
WYARGINE
st. Mosman 317 D4
WYATT
av. Belrose 225 H10
av. Burwood 372 A1
av. Earlwood 402 C6
av. Padstow 429 D5
av. Regents Pk 369 C1
cl. Wetherill Pk 335 A7
la. Burwood 371 K1
pde. Narwee 400 J13
pl. Doonside 243 C6
pl. Greystanes 306 E13
pl. Leumeah 482 D16
WYATTVILLE
dr. West Hoxton 392 C11
dr. West Hoxton 392 B12
WYBALENA
pl. Jannali 460 G9
rd. Hunters Hill 314 A13
WYBORN
la. Merrylands 306 K10
WYBURN
av. Carlingford 249 G16
WYCH
av. Lurnea 394 D7
WYCHBURY
av. Croydon 342 E11
la. Croydon 342 E11
WYCHWOOD
pl. Castle Hill 217 J9
WYCOMBE
av. Btn-le-Sds 433 J5
av. Monterey 433 J5
la. Neutral Bay 6 F9
rd. Neutral Bay 6 G9
st. Birrong 368 G10
st. Doonside 243 B10
st. Epping 250 G12
st. Yagoona 368 G10
WYE
cl. St Clair 299 H2
st. Blacktown 274 H9
WYEE
pl. Greystanes 305 H10
pl. Malabar 437 E8
st. Kogarah Bay 432 J13
WYEENA
cl. N Wahrnga 222 K2
WYENA
rd. Pendle Hill 276 C16
WYHARBOROUGH
pl. Canley Ht 335 B16
pl. Canley Ht 365 B1
WYLAH
pl. Woronora Ht 489 E2
WYLDE
cr. Abbotsbury 333 C16
st. Potts Point 2 K15
st. Potts Point 4 K1
st. Telopea 279 F9
WYLDS
rd. Arcadia 129 A15
rd. Glenorie 128 J14
WYLDWOOD
cr. Baulkham Hl 247 J6
WYLEENA
pl. Punchbowl 399 K6
WYLIE
st. Kirrawee 490 J1
WYLIES
la. Coogee 407 F1
WYLLIE
pl. Cherrybrook 219 F6
WYLMAR
av. Burraneer 493 F14
WYMAH
cr. Berowra Ht 132 H8
WYMARKS
la. Ebenezer 63 B2
WYMSTON
la. Wareemba, off Hill St 342 K6
pde. Abbotsford 342 J4
pde. Five Dock 342 J4
pde. Five Dock 342 J7
pde. Wareemba 342 J4
WYNDARRA
pl. Northwood 314 G7
WYNDHAM
av. Leumeah 482 F10
la. Alexandria 19 B13
pl. Baulkham Hl 247 C8
st. Alexandria 19 A11
WYNDORA
av. Harbord 258 D15
WYNGATE
cr. Forestville 256 B10
WYNN
cl. Edensor Pk 333 F16
st. Eschol Park 481 C6
WYNNE
av. Burwood 341 K14
WYNNSTAY
av. Enfield 371 G4
WYNWARD
pl. Barden Rdg 488 G2
WYNYARD
av. Bass Hill 367 K8
av. Rossmore 389 D9
la. Sydney A H16
st. Guildford 338 A4
st. Sydney C G1
st. Sydney 3 G1
WYOMEE
av. West Pymble 252 H8
WYOMING
av. Oatlands 278 J9
av. Valley Ht 202 G5
pl. Riverwood 400 A12
rd. Dural 188 E1
WYONG
rd. Cremorne 316 H3
rd. Duffys Frst 194 H6
rd. Mosman 316 H3
st. Canley Ht 365 E4
st. Oatley 431 B16
WYPERFELD
pl. Bow Bowing 452 C16
WYRALLA
av. Epping 280 G2
rd. Miranda 491 H6
WYREEMA
av. Padstow 399 A16
st. Merrylands 307 A11
WYUNA
av. Harbord 258 E15
cr. Padstow 429 G2
pl. Oatlands 279 D13
rd. Point Piper 347 E8
rd. West Pymble 253 B15
st. Beverley Pk 432 J10
WYVERN
av. Chatswd W 284 G7
av. Roseville 284 G7
st. Epping 250 J15

X

XENIA
av. Carlton 432 E5

Y

YABSLEY
av. Ashbury 372 F6
av. Marrickville 373 K11
YACHT
la. Lane Cove 314 F2
YACHTSMAN
dr. Chipping Ntn 366 J15
YACHTSMANS PARADISE
Newport 169 F16
YACHTVIEW
av. Newport 169 D9
YAGOONA
cl. Bangor 459 F13
la. Yagoona 369 A12
YAKIMA
av. Bossley Park 333 K10
YALA
rd. Bangor 459 E13
YALANGA
pl. Riverview 314 B5
YALDING
av. Carlingford 249 C16
av. North Rocks 249 C16
YALE
cl. North Rocks 249 A13
pl. Blacktown 274 K6
st. Epping 250 H15
YALGAR
rd. Kirrawee 461 A16
YALKIN
rd. Oakhurst 242 D2
YALLAH
st. Belimbla Pk 501 D12
YALLAMBEE
ct. Baulkham Hl 246 G8
pl. Terrey Hills 196 D7
rd. Berowra 133 A16
rd. Riverview 314 C5
YALLAMBI
st. Picton 561 D3
YALLARA
st. St Helens Pk 541 G2
YALLAROI
pde. Dangar I 76 J6
rd. Narraweena 258 B2
YALLEROI
av. West Pymble 252 K9
YALLOCK
pl. Prospect 274 E15
YALLUM
ct. Wattle Grove 425 H5
YALLUMBA
cl. Forestville 255 K8
YALTA
st. Sadleir 364 C15
YALUMBA
pl. Edensor Pk 363 E1
YALUNGA
pl. St Ives 224 B15
YALWAL
ct. Prestons 392 H13
YAMBA
cl. Marsfield 281 J4
la. Blacktown 274 J1
pl. Bossley Park 333 G10
pl. S Coogee 407 F4
rd. Bellevue Hill 14 H12
rd. Como 460 G7
st. N Balgowlah 287 C5
YAMMA
st. Sefton 368 G1
YAMPI
pl. Cartwright 394 A5
st. Leumeah 482 F10
YANAGANG
st. Waterfall 519 C13
YANAGIN
pl. W Pnnant Hl 249 A1
YANCANNIA
tce. Glenwood 215 E16
YANCHEP
pl. Yarrawarrah 489 G13
YANCO
av. Jamisontown 236 A15
cl. Frenchs Frst 255 K4
gln. Glenwood 215 F15
st. Merrylands 306 J10
YANDA
pl. Greystanes 306 A5
YANDARLO
st. Croydon Pk 371 H8
YANDERRA
av. Bangor 459 E13
cl. Hamondvle 396 H14
gr. Cherrybrook 219 J11
rd. Bargo 567 B15
rd. Duffys Frst 195 D1
rd. Yanderra 567 B15
st. Condell Park 398 D5
YANDIAH
pl. Castle Hill 218 C9
YANDINA
av. Winmalee 172 J11
YANGALLA
st. Marsfield 281 H1
YANGOORA
cl. Bangor 459 F13
rd. Belmore 371 A14
rd. Lakemba 370 K14
YANGTZE
pl. Kearns 481 A1
YANILLA
av. Wahroonga 251 G2
YANINA
pl. Bangor 459 E13
pl. Frenchs Frst 256 A1
YANKO
av. Bronte 377 J9
cl. Woronora 459 K16
rd. West Pymble 252 H10
rd. West Pymble 253 A13
YANNINA
av. Hornsby Ht 191 H5
YANTARA
pl. Woodcroft 243 J8
YARA
cl. Bangor 459 G14
YARAAN
av. Epping 281 A3
YARABAH
av. Gordon 253 H9
YARALLA
cr. Thornleigh 221 B8
la. Newtown 18 A10
pl. Baulkham Hl 246 K6
pl. Engadine 489 C11
rd. Putney 311 J8
st. Concord 341 E2
st. Concord W 341 E2
st. Newtown 18 A9
YARALLAH
pl. Beverly Hills 401 C13
YARBON
st. Wentwthvle 276 K13
YARDLEY
av. Narwee 400 F14
av. Riverwood 400 F14
av. Waitara 221 J5
YARENBOOL
wy. Bangor, off Yangoora Cl 459 F13
YARGO
rd. Winston Hills 277 A2
YARINGA
rd. Castle Hill 218 A8
YARMOUTH
pl. Smeaton Gra 479 B9
YARPOLE
av. W Pnnant Hl 218 K16
YARRA
cl. Kearns 481 B1
pl. Glenmore Pk 266 A12
pl. Prestons 392 K15
pl. St Johns Pk 364 F4
rd. Phillip Bay 436 J11
st. N St Marys 239 J9
YARRABEE
av. Bangor 459 F13
pl. Bilgola 169 E4
pl. Colyton 270 G8
rd. Northmead 277 J3
YARRABIN
cr. Berowra 133 C13
rd. Kenthurst 187 F8
st. Belrose 225 J15
YARRABUNG
av. Thornleigh 221 A8
rd. St Ives 224 C16
rd. St Ives 224 D14
YARRABURN
av. W Pnnant Hl 249 A2
YARRA BURRA
st. Gymea Bay 491 C11
YARRAGA
pl. Miranda 492 C9
YARRALUMLA
av. St Ives Ch 194 A16
dr. Carlingford 279 A4
YARRAM
st. Lidcombe 339 H5

YARRAMAN
av. Frenchs Frst 256 F9
cl. Quakers Hill 213 K8
rd. Grose Wold 116 C8
YARRAMUNDI
dr. Dean Park 212 G16
la. Agnes Banks 117 C6
la. Richmond 117 C6
rd. Richmond 118 F11
YARRAN
cl. Mona Vale 169 D16
ct. Wattle Grove 426 B1
pl. Mcquarie Fd 454 D3
rd. Oatley 431 A16
st. Punchbowl 400 A4
st. Pymble 253 C8
YARRANABBE
rd. Darling Point 13 J1
rd. Darling Point 13 J4
YARRANDALE
st. Stanhpe Gdn 215 D8
YARRANDI
pl. Northwood 314 F7
YARRANGOBILLY
st. Heckenberg 363 K11
YARRARA
la. Pymble 252 J8
la. West Pymble 252 J8
rd. Pennant Hills 220 H15
rd. Pymble 253 A7
rd. Terrey Hills 195 J14
rd. Thornleigh 220 H15
rd. West Pymble 252 J10
YARRA VISTA
ct. Yarrawarrah 489 G14
YARRAWA
st. Prestons 393 B9
YARRAWIN
wy. Airds 512 D10
YARRAWONGA
cl. Pymble 253 H3
st. S Windsor 120 E16
YARREN
av. Btn-le-Sds 403 K16
YARRENNAN
av. West Pymble 253 A10
YARROWEE
rd. Strathfield 370 K1
YARRUNGA
st. Prestons 393 A10
YARWOOD
la. Woollahra, off Fletcher St 377 G2
rd. Bligh Park 150 H5
st. Marsfield 281 K1
YASMAR
av. Haberfield 343 C15
YASS
cl. Bossley Park 333 E11
cl. Frenchs Frst 255 K4
pl. Prestons 392 K16
pl. Quakers Hill 244 B2
YATALA
rd. Mt Krng-gai 162 J6
YATAMA
st. Seaforth 287 C7
YATAY
cl. Plumpton 242 D5
YATE
av. Mt Riverview 204 E14
cl. Kingswood 267 J1
pl. Mcquarie Fd 454 E3
pl. Marayong 243 J6
pl. Narellan Vale 478 K15
YATES
av. Dundas Vy 280 A9
cr. Padstow 429 F4
rd. Bangor 459 H13
YATHONG
rd.n, Caringbah 493 A7
rd.s, Caringbah 493 A10
YATTENDEN
cr. Baulkham Hl 247 H12
YAWL
pl. Seven Hills 275 B5
YAWUNG
av. Baulkham Hl 246 H8
st. Dundas 279 G13
YEATS
av. Killarney Ht 256 D16
st. Wetherill Pk 334 K4
YEELANNA
pl. Kingswood 267 G2
YEEND
st. Birchgrove 8 A4
st. Merrylands 307 G9
YELL
pl. St Andrews 481 J5
YELLAMBIE
st. Yowie Bay 492 A13
YELLOW
pl. Clarmnt Ms 238 G15
YELLOW GUM
cl. Glenmore Pk 265 F11
YELLOWGUM
av. Rouse Hill 185 A6
gr. Glenwood 215 H16
YELLOW ROCK
rd. Yellow Rock 204 G2
YELVERTON
st. Sydenham 374 E15
YENA
st. Kurnell 466 C9
YENDA
av. Queens Park 22 J13
YENGO
ct. Holsworthy 426 E5
YENNA
pl. Glenmore Pk 266 B7
YENNORA
av. Yennora 337 A9
st. Campbelltwn 511 K6
YEO
av. Ashfield 372 K7
la. Bexley 402 H13
la. Neutral Bay 6 F1
pl. Menai 459 A12
st. Cremorne 6 D1
st. Neutral Bay 6 D1
st. Yagoona 368 J9
YEOMANS
rd. N Richmond 86 H7
YERAMBA
av. Caringbah 493 A15
cr. Berowra 133 C14
pl. Rydalmere 279 E15
st. Turramurra 252 D3
YERAN
st. Sylvania 462 C9
YERANDA
pl. Kenthurst 187 K8
YEREVAN
pl. Belrose 226 A12
YERONA
st. Prestons 423 B1
YERONG
pl. Castle Hill 218 B8
st. Ryde 311 H3
YERONGA
cl. St Johns Pk 364 F1
YERRAWAR
pl. Springwood 201 H4
YERRICK
rd. Lakemba 371 A13
rd. Lakemba 371 A14
YERRIEBAH
pl. Castle Hill 218 A8
YERRINBOOL
cl. Prestons 392 K12
YERROULBIN
st. Birchgrove 314 K16
YERTON
av. Hunters Hill 313 J12
YETHOLME
av. Baulkham Hl 246 K9
YETHONGA
av. Lane Cove W 313 J1
YEW
pl. Casula 424 A2
pl. Quakers Hill 214 E13
YILKI
cl. Cranebrook 207 E8
YILLOWRA
st. Auburn 309 C15
YIMBALA
st. Rydalmere 279 J15
YINDELA
st. Davidson 255 F3
YINDI
pl. Doonside 243 G14
YINNELL
pl. Castle Hill 218 C8
YIRAK
la. Como 460 G4
YIREMBA
pl. Forestville 255 F10
YIRGELLA
av. East Killara 254 G10
YIRRA
rd. Mt Colah 192 A5
YODALLA
av. Emu Plains 235 G11
la. Emu Plains, off Yodalla Av 235 G11
YONDELL
av. Springwood 201 G9
YOOGALI
st. Merrylands 306 J10
tce. Blaxland 234 D7
YOORAMI
rd. Beverly Hills 401 D12
YOORANA
pl. Castle Hill 219 A8
YORK
av. Five Dock 342 J11
cl. Yowie Bay 492 B12
cr. Petersham 16 A9
la. Glebe 11 J13
la. Queens Park 22 C10
la. Sydney A F15
pl. Bondi Jctn 22 C7
pl. Kensington 376 C11
pl. Rozelle 344 E6
rd. Bondi Jctn 22 C8
rd. Ingleburn 453 A4
rd. Jamisontown 236 F16
rd. Kellyville 216 G2
rd. Queens Park 22 C10
rd. Riverstone 182 D10
rd. S Penrith 266 E4
st. Beecroft 250 D6
st. Belmore 401 D2
st. Berala 339 B13
st. Casula 424 A3
st. Condell Park 398 K1
st. Emu Plains 235 K9
st. Epping 251 E12
st. Fairfield 336 D14
st. Gladesville 312 G11
st. Glebe 11 J14
st. Glenbrook 234 B14
st. Kingsgrove 401 K9
st. Marrickville 374 C9
st. Merrylands 307 H15
st. Oatlands 279 B9
st. Rockdale 403 E14
st. Sydney A F12
st. Sydney 1 F15
st. Tahmoor 565 J13
tce. Bilgola 169 G8
YORKSHIRE
cl. Catherine Fd 449 G1
st. Rosehill 309 B9
YORKTOWN
pde. Maroubra 407 C12
YORLIN
pl. Rouse Hill 185 C5
YORREL
cl. Alfords Point 429 A15
YOSEFA
av. Warrawee 222 F11
YOUL
pl. Bligh Park 150 E5
YOUNG
cr. Frenchs Frst 256 B3
la. Annandale 16 G3
la. Cremorne 316 D8
la. Neutral Bay 316 D8
la. Redfern 19 K7
la. Redfern 19 K9
pde. Eastwood 281 C9
pl. Eagle Vale 481 A10
pl. S Hurstville 431 K11
rd. Carlingford 279 K1
st. Annandale 16 F4
st. Balmain 7 B7
st. Chatswood 284 J12
st. Colyton 270 J8
st. Cremorne 316 D6
st. Cremorne 316 D8
st. Croydon 342 E15
st. Kings Lngly 245 E8
st. Mt Krng-gai 163 C11
st. Mt Pritchard 364 E9
st. Neutral Bay 6 G1
st. Neutral Bay 316 D8
st. N Strathfield 341 G9
st. Paddington 13 A16
st. Parramatta 307 J8
st. Penshurst 431 C1
st. Randwick 406 K1
st. Redfern 19 J10
st. Sydney B D12
st. Sydney 1 K14
st. Sylvania 461 H10
st. Tempe 404 B3
st. Vaucluse 348 F5
st. Wahroonga 222 H9
st. Warrawee 222 H9
st. Waterloo 19 H15
st. N Strathfield, off Parramatta Rd 341 F9
YOUNGER
av. Earlwood 372 K15
YOUTH
la. Burwood, off Deane St 342 A14
YOWAN
cl. Bangor 459 G13
YOWIE
av. Caringbah 492 F12
YPRES
rd. Moorebank 395 E12
YUGILBAR
av. Villawood 367 D3
YUKKA
rd. Regents Pk 369 D3
YUKON
cl. Kearns 481 A2
pl. Quakers Hill 214 C9
YULAN
rd. Narellan Vale 479 A13
YULE
pl. Glenfield 424 G9
st. Dulwich Hill 15 B16
YULONG
av. Terrey Hills 196 E7
YULUMA
cl. Bangor 459 F13
YULUNGA
pl. Bradbury 511 C14
YUMA
pl. Bossley Park 333 K12
YUNGA
rd. Glenmore Pk 266 C9
YUNGABURRA
st. Villawood 367 E5
YUNGANA
pl. Bangor 459 F13
YUROKA
st. Glenmore Pk 266 D8
YURONG
la. Darlinghurst D K14
la. Darlinghurst 4 C7
pky. Woolmloo D J12
pky. Woolmloo 4 C6
st. Darlinghurst D J16
st. Darlinghurst F J2
st. Darlinghurst 4 B10
st. Woolmloo D J12
YURREEL
cl. Bangor 459 H13
YURUGA
av. Caringbah 492 H12
av. Doonside 243 B15
pl. Allambie Ht 257 D13
pl. Lindfield 283 J3
rd. Kenthurst 188 D12
st. Beverly Hills 400 G16
YURUNGA
st. Telopea 279 E8
YVES
pl. Minchinbury 272 B10
YVETTE
st. Baulkham Hl 247 K12
YVONNE
av. Hawksbry Ht 174 H2
cl. Cobbitty 448 A13
cr. Bass Hill 367 G8
cr. Georges Hall 367 G8
pl. Castle Hill 248 C2
pl. N Richmond 87 B14
st. Cabramtta W 364 H6
st. Greystanes 306 G4
st. Seven Hills 246 A11

Z

ZADRO
av. Bossley Park 333 H8
ZAHEL
la. Mosman 316 H4
ZAHRA
pl. Quakers Hill 214 D13
ZAMBESI
rd. Seven Hills 275 F9
ZAMBEZI
pl. Kearns 450 K16
ZAMIA
st. Redfern 19 K10
ZAMMIT
av. Quakers Hill 213 K10
ZANCO
rd. Marsfield 282 A2
ZANE
cl. Bella Vista 246 E6
ZANITH
wy. Kellyville 186 K15
ZAPPIA
pl. Edensor Pk 363 J1
ZARA
cl. Cecil Hills 362 H7
rd. Willoughby 285 D13
ZARITA
av. Waverley 377 F6
ZARLEE
st. Fairfield W 335 F13
ZEALANDER
st. Sandringham 463 D5
ZEBRA
pl. Quakers Hill 214 B7
ZELA
st. Mortdale 430 J7
ZELDA
av. Wahroonga 222 K3
ZELENY
rd. Minchinbury 271 A6
ZENITH
cl. Wakeley 334 K16
ct. Glenwood 245 G1
ZEOLITE
pl. Eagle Vale 481 D9
ZEPPELIN
st. Raby 451 E13
ZERAFA
pl. Quakers Hill 214 A11
ZERMATT
av. Seven Hills 275 D11
ZETA
cl. Oakdale 500 D10
rd. Lane Cove 314 E4
ZEYA
cl. St Clair 269 H16
ZIERIA
pl. Belrose 225 G15
ZIG ZAG
la. Crows Nest, off Albany St 315 F6
ZILLAH
st. Guildford 338 C4
st. Merrylands 338 C4
ZINNIA
wy. Blacktown 274 E11
ZIONS
av. Malabar 437 F6
ZIRCON
pl. Bossley Park 334 A8
pl. Eagle Vale 481 F5
ZODIAC
pl. Erskine Park 270 K15
ZOE
cl. Yennora 336 K11
pl. Mount Druitt 241 G15
ZOELLER
st. Concord 342 C5
ZOLA
av. Ryde 282 B9
ZOLYOMI
la. Blacktown, off First Av 244 J15
ZONNEBEKE
cr. Milperra 397 H11
ZORIC
cl. Prestons 423 B1
ZOUCH
rd. Denham Ct 422 F9
ZULFI
pl. Cherrybrook 219 B14
ZULLO
ct. Castle Hill 217 B11
ZUNI
cl. Bossley Park 333 K11
ZUTTION
av. Beverly Hills 401 A12
la. Tempe, off Union St 404 B2

INFORMATION INDEX

AIRPORTS / AIRFIELDS

BAYS, BEACHES, ETC

Spring Creek 504 A15
Spring Gully Creek 222 D4
Springwood Creek 171 K14
Station Beach 109 J13
Steel Point 347 J1
Still Creek
  Berrilee 130 H16
  Menai 459 B7
Stokes Point 139 G8
Stonequarry Creek 563 G5
Stony Creek 253 J5
Store Beach 288 H15
Strangers Creek
  Kellyville 215 H2
  Ryde 282 J16
Stringybark Creek 283 G14
Subiaco Creek 309 D1
Sugarloaf Bay 286 F8
Sugarloaf Creek 286 A11
Sugarloaf Point 286 G9
Sutherland Point 466 D4
Swaines Creek 284 A11
Swallow Rock Reach 64 A6
Sydney Cove B D3
Tabbigai Gap 466 H15
Tabers Creek 473 A16
Tamarama Bay 378 C8
Tambourine Bay 314 B8
Tarban Creek 313 E12
Taren Point 462 J8
Taylors Bay 317 D14
Taylors Point 169 C1
Tedbury Creek 220 D11
Temptation Creek 490 H15
Terrys Creek 281 E3
The Basin
  Kentlyn 484 E11
  Ku-Ring-Gai Chase National Pk 138 G4
  Royal National Park 523 A12
The Big Gully 444 B12
The Cobblers 524 E15
The Gap 318 G14
The Long Swamp 125 K4
The Merries Reef 495 G7
The Old Mans Hat 318 K4
The Ponds Creek 279 H13
The Spit 287 C13
The Woolwash 132 E6
Thompsons Bay 460 E3
Thompsons Creek 388 A13
Three Brothers Rocks 313 B15
Thurns Weir 507 G10
Tom Uglys Point 462 F5
Toongabbie Creek 246 C16
Towlers Bay 138 G13
Towra Beach 464 E4
Towra Point 464 D4
Towra Spit Beach 464 A6
Trailers Lake 517 E11
Tree Fern Gully Creek 194 F14
Tuckawa Rill 519 F10
Tucker Creek 513 K16
Tunks Creek 190 G7
Tunnel Gully 264 G1
Turimetta Beach 199 F14
Turimetta Head 199 H12
Uhrs Point 311 G7
Vaucluse Bay 318 C16
Vaucluse Point 318 B15
Village Point 318 D15
Vineyard Creek 309 B2
Voodoo Point 496 A7
Vulcan Lake 375 A12
Waddells Gully 190 F1
Waitara Creek 191 A16
Walker Point 107 J3
Wallaby Gully 517 A7
Walls Gully 191 J3
Wallumatta Bay 313 C14
Walsh Bay 1 C6
Wanda Beach 494 E7
Wants Beach 520 F4
Wants Point 522 A1
Waratah Gully 133 H15
Warragamba Dam 353 B5
Warragamba River 353 D3
Warren Lake 375 A13
Warriewood Beach 199 E10
Washaway Beach 317 K1
Waterfall Gully 195 A9
Watsons Bay 318 D14
Wattle Creek 445 B10
Wearne Bay 460 A2
Wedding Cake Island 408 A2
Weeney Bay 464 D12
Wentworth Point 311 C5
Werrington Creek 238 C10
Werrington Lake 238 D9
West Head 109 F9
Whale Beach 140 C7
Wheeler Creek 227 H14
Wheeny Lagoon 65 B8
White Bay 7 K14
White Horse Point 344 E2
Whites Creek 10 H13
Whiting Beach 316 K15
Wilberforce Reach 91 J14
Wildlife Island 366 K9
Wildlife Lagoon 93 K1
Willarong Point 492 C16
Williams Creek 427 A4
Willoughby Bay 316 E4
Willow Pond 22 A14
Windsor Reach 121 G5
Winson Bay 163 K5
Wirreanda Creek 197 B6
Wolli Creek 401 G11
Wonga Creek 66 K11
Woodford Bay 314 F9
Woods Creek 115 A8
Woody Point 138 H14
Woollahra Point 347 G7
Woolloomooloo Bay 2 H15
Woolooware Bay 463 F14
Woronora River 460 A16
Wrights Point 313 J14
Wudyong Point 6 G15
Wyargine Point 317 F2
Yacht Bay 314 C11
Yaralla Bay 311 G13
Yarra Bay 436 F10
Yarramundi Lagoon 117 A13
Yarra Point 436 G12
Yatala Creek 134 C5
Yena Gap 466 J10
Yennahilli Point 522 J7
Yeoland Point 286 G4
Yeomans Bay 136 B6
Yeramba Lagoon 428 E11
York Reach 92 C7
Yowie Bay 492 C14
Yowie Point 492 A15
Yurulbin Point 315 A16

CARAVAN, TOURIST & MOBILE HOME PARKS

BASS HILL
Bass Hill Tourist Park
713 Hume Hwy 368 A9
BEROWRA
La Mancha Cara-Park
9 Pacific Hwy 163 C3
BUNDEENA
Bonnie Vale Camping Ground
Bundeena Dr 523 D9
Bundeena
Scarborough St 523 J10
CANLEY VALE
Lansdowne
61 Hume Hwy 366 H5
CARINGBAH
Cronulla Carapark
cnr Kingsway & Gannons Rd S 493 C9
CASTLE HILL
Carrington Rd 217 E11
DURAL
Dural Village Park
269 New Line Rd 189 A15
EBENEZER
Hawkesbury Waters Leisure Park
Port Erringhi Rd 64 A1
Kallawatta Park
Coromandel Rd 63 J6
ELDERSLIE
Poplars Park
Macarthur Rd 477 E16
EMU PLAINS
Nepean River
MacKellar St 236 B6
FAIRFIELD WEST
320 Polding St 335 C7
HEATHCOTE
Heathcote Tourist Park
Princes Hwy 518 F13
INGLEBURN
Denham Court
22 Campbelltown Rd 422 F14
KURNELL
Silver Beach Resort
288 Prince Charles Pde 465 F8
LEPPINGTON
Casa Paloma
105 Camden Valley Wy 421 G5
Four Lanterns
1481 Camden Valley Wy 421 E6
MACQUARIE PARK
Lane Cove River Caravan Park
Plassey Rd 283 E7
MARSDEN PARK
Town & Country
25 Hollinsworth Rd 211 G10
MIRANDA
Harts
215 Port Hacking Rd 462 C16
NORTH NARRABEEN
Lakeside
Lake Park Rd 199 C15
OAKDALE
Burragorang Rd 500 F11
PARKLEA
Merlton Mobile Vill
512 Sunnyholt Rd 215 A12
Parklea Garden Vill
30 Majestic Dr 215 C10
PITT TOWN
Percy Place
Hall St 93 B5
PITT TOWN BOTTOMS
Powers Ski Gardens
Pitt Town Bottoms Rd 92 B7
ROCKDALE
Sheralee
88 Bryant St 403 J15
ROUSE HILL
OK Caravan Corral
51 Terry Rd 184 J12
SANS SOUCI
Grand Pines Tourist Park The
289 The Grand Pde 433 G14
TERREY HILLS
319 Mona Vale Rd 196 A12
VINEYARD
A-Vina
217 Commercial Rd 153 A7
WALLACIA
cnr Silverdale Rd & Alwyn Av 324 H12
WILBERFORCE
Windsor Riverside
Putty Rd 91 J7
WORONORA
1 Menai Rd 460 A13

CLUBS

18 FOOT SAILING
76 McDougall St
Milsons Point 6 C13
ABRUZZI SPORTS
Elizabeth St
Wetherill Park 334 D3
AMERICAN
131 Macquarie St
Sydney B F12
API KELLYVILLE COUNTRY
Mungerie Rd
Kellyville 185 G13
ARNCLIFFE RSL
Wollongong Rd 403 E8
ARNCLIFFE SCOTS SPORTS & SOCIAL
29 Burrows St 403 G8
ASHFIELD CATHOLIC
7 Charlotte St 372 J2
ASHFIELD RSL
374 Liverpool Rd 372 F3
ASQUITH RUGBY LEAGUE
11 Alexandria Pde
Waitara 221 K3
AUBURN-LIDCOMBE BUSINESS
cnr Silverwater Rd & Clyde St 309 K8
AUBURN RSL
33 Northumberland Rd 339 E1
AUSTRALASIAN PIONEERS
61 York St
Sydney C F2
AUSTRALIAN
165 Macquarie St
Sydney B F16
AUSTRALIAN JOCKEY
Alison Rd
Randwick 376 F9
AUSTRALIAN OPERA FRIENDS
480 Elizabeth St
Surry Hills 19 H4
AUSTRIAN
20 Grattan Cr
Frenchs Forest 256 F10
AVALON BEACH RSL
1 Bowling Green La
Avalon 170 A1
BALGOWLAH RSL MEMORIAL
547 Sydney Rd
Seaforth 287 E9
BALMAIN LEAGUES
138 Victoria Rd
Rozelle 344 E7
BALMAIN ROZELLE RSL
440 Darling St
Balmain 7 B8
BANKSTOWN CATHOLIC
7 Cross St 399 G1
BANKSTOWN DISTRICT SPORTS
8 Greenfield Pde 399 E1
BANKSTOWN RSL
Kitchener Pde 369 D15
BANKSTOWN TROTTING RECREATIONAL
178 Eldridge Rd 398 F7
BASS HILL RSL
330 Hector St 368 C9
BAULKHAM HILLS SPORTING
6 Renown Rd 248 C12
BELFIELD RSL
cnr Persic & Bazentin Sts 371 C11
BELMORE RSL
427 Burwood Rd 371 F16
BERALA-CARRAMAR TENNIS & RECREATION
181 Chisholm Rd
Auburn 338 J7
BEROWRA RSL & CITIZENS
997 Pacific Hwy 133 F13
BEXLEY RSL
24 Stoney Creek Rd 402 J14
BLACKTOWN CITY SOCCER
106 Prospect Hwy
Seven Hills 245 K15
BLACKTOWN CITY RUGBY LEAGUE & FOOTBALL CLUB
122 Rooty Hill Rd N
Rooty Hill 242 B14
BLACKTOWN RSL
Second Av 244 G14
BLACKTOWN WORKERS
Campbell St 274 G1
BLACKTOWN WORKERS CLUB SPORTS
Reservoir Rd 274 C10
BONDI DIGGERS
Campbell Pde
Bondi Beach 378 E2
BONDI ICEBERGS
Notts Av
Bondi Beach 378 D5
BONDI JUNCTION-WAVERLEY RSL
Gray St
Bondi Junction 22 J8
BOTANY BAY YACHT
Endeavour St
Sans Souci 462 J2
BOTANY RSL
1421 Botany Rd 405 E11
BOWLERS CLUB OF NSW
95 York St
Sydney C G7
BRIGHTON-LE-SANDS AMATEUR FISHING
Bestic St
Kyeemagh 403 K14
BRIGHTON-LE-SANDS RSL
351 Bay St 433 K3
BRITISH EX-SERVICES
44 Market St
Sydney C G8
BRONTE RSL
113 Macpherson St
Waverley 377 K10
BUNDEENA RSL
71 Loftus St 523 K9
BURWOOD RSL
36 Shaftesbury Rd 342 B15
CABRA VALE EX-ACTIVE SERVICEMENS
1 Bartley St
Canley Vale 365 K4
CAMPBELLTOWN CATHOLIC
20 Camden Rd 511 C6
CAMPBELLTOWN RSL
6 Lithgow St 511 F5
CAMPBELLTOWN TENNIS
4 Leumeah Rd
Leumeah 482 B12
CAMPSIE RSL
25 Anglo Rd 371 K13
CANLEY HEIGHTS RSL
26 Humphries Rd
Wakeley 334 K16
CANTERBURY-BANKSTOWN LEAGUES
26 Bridge Rd
Belmore 371 E16
CANTERBURY-HURLSTONE PARK RSL
20 Canterbury Rd
Hurlstone Park 372 K11
CARINGBAH RSL
cnr Mackay St & Banksia Rd 492 K7
CASTELLORIZIAN
448 Anzac Pde
Kingsford 406 G1
CASTLE HILL RSL
Castle St 217 K12

CASTLE PINES COUNTRY
Spurway Dr
Baulkham Hills 216 J13

CATHOLIC
199 Castlereagh St
Sydney C B13

CHATSWOOD RSL
1 Thomas St 284 H10

CHESTER HILL-CARRAMAR RSL
cnr Proctor Pde &
Chester Hill Rd 368 B2

CITY OF SYDNEY RSL
565 George St
Sydney E G2

CITY TATTERSALLS
198 Pitt St
Sydney D A9

CLOVELLY RSL & AIR FORCE
Clovelly Rd 377 G12

COMBINED SERVICES RSL
5 Barrack St
Sydney C F3

COMMERCIAL TRAVELLERS ASSOC
MLC Centre,
Martin Pl
Sydney D B4

CONCORD RSL
Nirranda St 311 H16

CONNELLS POINT SAILING
Kyle Pde 431 J16

COOGEE LEGION
266a Coogee Bay Rd 377 G16

COOGEE RANDWICK RETURNED SERVICEMENS
Carr St
Coogee 407 E1

CORONATION
36 Burwood Rd
Burwood 342 A12

CROATIAN (JADRAN HAJDUK)
130 Edensor Rd
Bonnyrigg 364 C3

CRONULLA RSL
Gerrale St 494 A13

CROWS NEST
31 Hayberry St 315 G8

CRUISING YACHT
New Beach Rd
Darling Point 13 G7

CUMBERLAND CATHOLIC
Civic Av
Pendle Hill 276 E13

CYPRUS COMMUNITY CENTRE OF NSW
Stanmore Rd
Enmore 16 J14

CYPRUS HELLENE
150 Elizabeth St
Sydney F B4

DEEPWATER MOTOR BOAT
Webster St
Milperra 397 C16

DEE WHY RSL
932 Pittwater Rd 258 H4

DOBROYD AQUATIC
Rodd Park
Rodd Point 343 G8

DOUBLE BAY SAILING
79 Bay St 14 C6

DRUMMOYNE ROWING
Henley Marine Dr 344 A5

DRUMMOYNE RSL
162 Victoria Rd 343 K2

DRUMMOYNE SAILING
2 St Georges Cr 344 B3

DUNDAS VALLEY RUGBY UNION FOOTBALL
35 Quarry Rd 280 A10

EARLWOOD-BARDWELL PARK RSL
Hartill-Law Av 402 J6

EARLWOOD EX-SERVICEMENS
32 Fricourt Av 402 J2

EASTERN SUBURBS LEAGUES
93 Spring St
Bondi Junction 22 H7

EASTERN SUBURBS LEGION
213 Bronte Rd
Waverley 377 F8

ENFIELD RSL
236 Liverpool Rd 371 H2

ENGADINE RSL
1029 Old Princes Hwy 518 J1

EPPING RSL
Rawson St 251 A16

FAIRFIELD RSL
12 Dale St 336 G13

FIVE DOCK RSL
66 Great North Rd 342 K11

FOGOLAR FURLAN
Wharf Rd
Lansvale 367 A10

FORESTVILLE RSL
Melwood Av 255 J10

GALLIPOLI MEMORIAL
12 Loftus St
Sydney B C10

GEORGES RIVER SAILING
Sanoni Av
Sandringham 463 G2

GERMAN CONCORDIA
231 Stanmore Rd
Stanmore 16 E11

GLADESVILLE BOWLING & SPORTS
cnr Ryde Rd &
Halcyon St 312 K6

GLADESVILLE RSL
Linsley St 312 J10

GLENORIE RSL
Post Office Rd 128 B4

GOVERNMENT TRANSPORT SOCIAL
19 Regent St
Chippendale 19 D1

GRANVILLE RSL
Memorial Dr 308 G12

GRAPHIC ARTS
22 Regent St
Chippendale E B16

GREEK COMMUNITY
206 Lakemba St
Lakemba 400 K1

GREEK MACEDONIAN CLUB ALEXANDER THE GREAT
160 Livingstone Rd
Marrickville 373 J11

GROSVENOR
40 Flinders St
Darlinghurst 4 E14

GUILDFORD RUGBY LEAGUE
Tamplin Rd 337 B4

HAKOAH
61 Hall St
Bondi Beach 378 C2

HARBORD DIGGERS MEMORIAL
Evans St 288 K1

HAWKESBURY SPORTING
Beaumont Av
North Richmond 87 G13

HILLS DISTRICT MEMORIAL
21-25 Arcadia Rd
Galston 159 C10

HORNSBY RSL
4 High St 221 G1

HUBERTUS COUNTRY
Adams Rd
Luddenham 327 G16

HUBERTUS LIVERPOOL RIFLE
cnr Badgerys Creek
Rd & Elizabeth Dr
Badgerys Creek 328 H15

HUNTERS HILL RSL
cnr Ady &
Alexandra Sts 313 K11

HURSTVILLE RSL
1 Ormonde Pde 432 A6

HURSTVILLE UNITED SPORTS
311a Forest Rd 431 H5

INGLEBURN RSL
cnr Chester Rd &
Warbler Av 453 F10

JOHN EDMONDSON VC MEMORIAL
185 George St
Liverpool 395 E3

JOURNALISTS
36 Chalmers St
Surry Hills 19 G1

KENSINGTON WAR MEMORIAL
2 Goodwood St 376 F11

KIEV SPORTS
32 Broomfield Dt
Cabramatta 366 A5

KINGSGROVE RSL
The Avenue 401 K11

KIRRIBILLI EX-SERVICE
11 Harbour View Cr
Milsons Point 5 J13

KOGARAH BAY SAILING
Princes Hwy
Blakehurst 462 G2

KOGARAH RSL
254 Railway Pde 432 K6

KURING-GAI MOTOR YACHT
1 Cottage Point Rd
Cottage Point 135 G9

KURNELL COMMUNITY SPORTS & RECREATION
Captain Cook Dr 466 A10

KYEEMAGH RSL
Tancred Av 404 B12

LAKEMBA RETURNED SOLDIERS
60 Quigg St 401 B2

LEICHHARDT-LILYFIELD SOLDIERS SAILORS AIRMENS
38 Short St 10 A15

LEICHHARDT ROWING
Glover St
Lilyfield 9 H1

LEMNOS
44 Albert St
Belmore 371 F14

LE MONTAGE
38 Frazer St
Lilyfield 9 G5

LIDCOMBE CATHOLIC WORKMENS
24 John St 339 H8

LIDCOMBE RSL
Joseph St 339 J9

LIVERPOOL CATHOLIC
Hoxton Park Rd
Cartwright 393 G7

MALABAR RSL
Ireton St 437 E4

MANDARIN
396 Pitt St
Haymarket E K5

MANLY FISHING & SPORTING ASSOCIATION
270 Pittwater Rd 288 F5

MANLY-WARRINGAH MASTER BUILDERS
18 Fisher Rd
Dee Why 258 F6

MANLY WARRINGAH RUGBY LEAGUE
563 Pittwater Rd
Brookvale 258 D9

MARCONI
Marconi Rd
Bossley Park 333 H10

MAROUBRA RSL
Haig St 407 B11

MAROUBRA SEALS
212 Marine Pde 407 G12

MARRICKVILLE RSL
359 Illawarra Rd 373 J14

MASCOT RSL
1271 Botany Rd 405 E6

MATRAVILLE RSL
Norfolk Pde 436 J2

MERRYLANDS RSL
14 Military Rd 307 H13

MIDDLE HARBOUR YACHT
Spit Rd
Mosman 287 D14

MIRANDA RSL
615 Kingsway 491 K3

MOONEY MOONEY WORKERS SPORTS & RECREATION
Kowan Rd 75 D3

MORTDALE RSL
Macquarie Pl 431 B8

MOSMAN RETURNED SERVICEMENS
719 Military Rd 317 B6

MT PRITCHARD & DISTRICT COMMUNITY (MOUNTIES)
101 Meadows Rd 364 E8

NEPEAN ROWING
Bruce Neale Dr
Penrith 236 D7

NEWTOWN RSL
52 Enmore Rd 17 D13

NINEVEH CLUB
673 Smithfield Rd
Edensor Park 364 A2

NORTH BONDI RSL
120 Ramsgate Av 378 G3

NORTHBRIDGE SAILING
Clive Park 286 G13

NORTH RYDE RSL
cnr Magdala &
Pittwater Rds 283 C13

NORTH SYDNEY
88 Berry St K J3

NORTH SYDNEY ANZAC
cnr Miller &
Ernest Sts
Cammeray 315 J7

NORTH SYDNEY LEAGUES
12 Abbott St
Cammeray 315 J4

NSW CRICKETERS
11 Barrack St
Sydney C G3

NSW GUN
Booralie Rd
Duffys Forest 195 B2

NSW LEAGUES
165 Phillip St
Sydney D D4

NSW MASONIC
169 Castlereagh St
Sydney D A11

NSW SPORTS
10 Hunter St
Sydney A J14

OAKDALE WORKERS
Burragorang Rd 499 K12

OATLEY RSL
23 Letitia St 431 C13

PADDINGTON-WOOLLAHRA RSL
226 Oxford St 13 A16

PADSTOW RSL
Howard Rd 399 D16

PALM BEACH RSL
1087 Barrenjoey Rd 139 H2

PANANIA EAST HILLS RSL
28 Childs St
Panania 427 H1

PANTHERS-YOUR WORLD OF ENTERTAINMENT
Mulgoa Rd
Penrith 236 D12

PARRAMATTA LEAGUES
15 O'Connell St 278 B15

PARRAMATTA MASONIC
163 George St 308 G4

PARRAMATTA RETURNED EX-SERVICEMENS
Macquarie St 308 A3

PENRITH RSL
cnr Castlereagh &
Lethbridge Sts 236 J11

PENSHURST RSL
58a Penshurst St 431 E4

PETERSHAM RSL
7a Regent St 15 J10

PITT TOWN DISTRICT SPORTS
30 Old Pitt Town Rd 123 D2

PITTWATER AQUATIC
Esplanade
Mona Vale 169 C14

PITTWATER RSL
cnr Mona Vale Rd &
Foley St
Mona Vale 198 J4

PORT HACKING OPEN SAILING
224 Attunga Rd
Yowie Bay 492 C13

PUNCHBOWL & DISTRICT RETURNED EX-SERVICEMENS
1 Broadway 400 D4

QUEENS
cnr Elizabeth &
Markets Sts
Sydney D C8

RAMSGATE RSL
Chuter Av 433 F14

RANDWICK LABOR
135 Alison Rd 376 K13

RANDWICK RUGBY
104 Brook St
Coogee 377 F16

REDFERN RSL
Redfern St 19 B8

REVESBY HEIGHTS EX-SERVICEMENS
Donovan St 428 K6

REVESBY WORKERS
26 Brett St 398 H16

RIVERSTONE SCHOFIELDS RSL
Market St
Riverstone 182 J7

RIVERWOOD LEGION
32 Littleton St 400 C16

ROCKDALE RSL
Bay St 403 E16

ROOTY HILL RSL
cnr Sherbrooke Rd
& Railway St 241 J16

ROSE BAY RSL
New South Head Rd 347 K10

ROSEVILLE RETURNED SERVICEMENS MEMORIAL
64 Pacific Hwy..........284 G5
ROYAL AUTOMOBILE
89 Macquarie St
Sydney ....B G8
ROYAL MOTOR YACHT
Broken Bay
46 Prince Alfred Pde
Newport...................169 A8
New South Wales
21 Wunulla Rd
Point Piper...............347 F8
Port Hacking
228 Woolooware Rd
Burraneer..................493 F16
ROYAL PRINCE ALFRED YACHT
Mitala St
Newport...................169 B10
ROYAL SYDNEY YACHT SQUADRON
Peel St
Kirribilli........................6 F16
RUGBY
Rugby Pl
Sydney ....A K8
RUSSIAN CLUB THE
7 Albert Rd
Strathfield.................341 G11
RYDE DISTRICT EX-SERVICEMENS
724 Victoria Rd.........311 K3
RYDE EASTWOOD LEAGUES
117 Ryedale Rd
West Ryde 281 F14
ST GEORGE BUDAPEST SOCCER
84 Victoria Av
Mortdale...................431 D6
ST GEORGE LEAGUES
124 Princes Hwy
Beverley Park............433 A9
ST GEORGE MASONIC
86 Roberts Av
Mortdale...................430 G7
ST GEORGE MOTOR BOAT
2 Wellington St
Sans Souci 462 H4
ST GEORGE ROWING
1 Levey St
Arncliffe....................404 A6
ST GEORGE SAILING
Riverside Dr
Sans Souci 463 B7
ST MARYS DISTRICT BAND
411 Great Western Hwy..........................239 G16
ST MARYS RSL EX SERVICEMENS
Mamre Rd.................269 F5
ST MARYS RUGBY LEAGUE
Boronia Rd 239 J7
SERBIAN CENTRE
Simpson Rd
Bonnyrigg Heights....363 E4
SEVEN HILLS-TOONGABBIE RSL
Best Rd.....................275 H3
SHARKS INTERNATIONAL
Captain Cook Dr
Woolooware 493 E5
SILKS
202 Pitt St
Sydney ....D B11
SLOVENIAN
2 Elizabeth Dr
Wetherill Park...........334 E3
SMITHFIELD RSL
Smithfield Rd............335 J5
SOUTHERN DISTRICT RUGBY
233 Belgrave Esp
Sylvania Waters 462 D15
SOUTHERN SPORTS & RECREATIONAL
Old Princes Hwy
Sutherland 490 D5
SOUTH HURSTVILLE RSL
72 Connells Point Rd...432 B11
SOUTH SYDNEY BUSINESSMENS
182 Coward St
Mascot..................... 405 D2
SOUTH SYDNEY JUNIOR RUGBY LEAGUE
558a Anzac Pde
Kingsford 406 H3
SOUTH SYDNEY LEAGUES
263 Chalmers St
Redfern 19 F7
SPANISH
88 Liverpool St
Sydney .... E G2
SPRINGWOOD & DISTRICT COMMUNITY
Lawson Rd................ 202 D2
SUTHERLAND DISTRICT TRADE UNION
57 Manchester Rd
Gymea...................... 491 F3
SUTHERLAND UNITED SERVICES
7 East Pde................ 490 D4
SYDNEY
9 Rowe St ....D A4
SYDNEY AMATEUR SAILING
Karoola Rd
Cremorne Point........ 316 G13
SYDNEY AUSTRALIAN FOOTBALL
Driver Av
Moore Park 20 K3
SYDNEY FLYING SQUADRON
18 Foot Sailing Club,
76 McDougall St
Milsons Point................ 6 C13
SYDNEY LABOUR
464 Bourke St
Surry Hills.................. 20 D2
SYDNEY OLYMPIC SPORTING
64 Tennent Pde
Hurlstone Park 373 B14
SYDNEY PISTOL
Cape Banks
La Perouse............... 437 F16
TATTERSALLS
181 Elizabeth St
Sydney.........................D B10
TEACHERS
73 Bathurst St
Sydney.........................C E14
THE COVE SPORTS
325a Eastern Valley Wy
Middle Cove 285 F5
THE NEUTRAL BAY
Barry St........................ 6 F5
TRASANDINOS SPORTING
418 Gardeners Rd
Rosebery.................. 405 F1
UNION
24 Bent St
Sydney.........................B E14
UNIVERSITY & SCHOOLS
60 Phillip St
Sydney.........................B F12
UPPER HAWKESBURY POWER BOAT
George St
Windsor 121 G5
URUGUAYAN
31 Whitford Rd
Hinchinbrook...........393 C3
UTS HABERFIELD ROWING
Dobroyd Pde
Haberfield....................9 C4
VAUCLUSE AMATEUR 12 FOOT SAILING
Wharf Rd..................318 E15
VAUCLUSE YACHT
Marine Pde
Watsons Bay 318 E14
WENTWORTHVILLE LEAGUES
Smith St 306 H2
WENTWORTHVILLE MEMORIAL RSL
Dunmore St..............276 K16
WESTERN SUBURBS AUSTRALIAN FOOTBALL
40 Hampton St
Croydon Park............372 A8
WESTERN SUBURBS LEAGUES
115 Liverpool Rd
Ashfield 372 K3
Leumeah Rd
Leumeah 482 B13
WESTERN SUBURBS SOCCER
4 William St
Five Dock.................342 G9
WEST PENNANT HILLS SPORTS
103 New Line Rd
Cherrybrook 219 G15
WILLOUGHBY LEGION EX-SERVICES
26 Crabbes Av..........285 E9
WINDSOR LEAGUES
Rifle Range Rd
Bligh Park.................150 D4
WINDSOR RSL
Argyle St
South Windsor 120 K13
WINTERGARDEN PLAZA
1 O'Connell St
Sydney ....B B13
WOOLLAHRA SAILING
Vickery Av
Rose Bay..................347 K10
WORONORA RIVER RSL & CITIZENS
Prince Edward Park Rd
Woronora 489 J2
YARRA BAY SAILING
Yarra Rd
Phillip Bay 436 H11
YMCA (HEAD OFFICE)
154 Elizabeth St
Sydney ....F C5
YWCA (HEADQUARTERS)
5 Wentworth Av
Sydney ....F E3

COACH TERMINALS

Parramatta................308 D4
Sydney.........................E H12

GOLF COURSES & DRIVING RANGES

Antill Park.................561 H3
Ashlar.......................244 E10
Asquith......................192 C7
Auburn 338 H9
Avalon 170 B3
Avondale...................252 H5
Balgowlah 287 F7
Bankstown.................397 F7
Bardwell Valley 402 H9
Barnwell Park 342 F9
Barton Park
Driving Range.........403 K11
Bayview 198 J1
Beverley Park.............433 A10
Bexley Municipal........402 B15
Bondi.........................378 H1
Bonnie Doon 406 E10
Botany 435 J2
Cabramatta................365 A10
Camden 478 C12
Camden Lakeside.......450 E7
Camden Valley
Golf Resort 449 J13
Cammeray.................316 B6
Campbelltown 510 E11
Canterbury 401 D9
Capitol Hill
Golf Resort.............331 A7
Captain Cook 462 C16
Carnarvon 339 G14
Castlecove Country 285 H4
Castle Hill Country.......216 G11
Casula Powerhouse.....395 B13
Chatswood.................284 A12
Colonial......................239 C10
Commercial Rd
Reserve..................185 E10
Concord.....................341 H2
Cromer 228 B9
Cronulla 493 J6
Cronulla
Driving Range.........494 C3
Cullen Dan
Driving Range.........437 C13
Cumberland Country.....306 A6
Cumberland Grove
Country Club...........365 A13
Dunheved..................239 A5
Dural Golf
Driving Range.........189 B15
Eastlake 405 J8
Elanora Country 198 A13
Fairfield City Council....334 G8
Fox Hills 275 G14
Glenmore 265 C12
Golf Academy.............181 D13
Golf On Mars
Driving Range.........283 F16
Golf Paradise
Driving Range.........195 J13
Gordon 253 E11
Grose River 116 A12
Hawkesbury Waters......63 K1
Hudson Park 340 G12
Hurstville....................430 F9
Jasper Reserve 188 A8
Kareela......................461 E13
Kellyville Country 185 C11
Killara 253 F14
Kogarah 404 A9
Lane Cove Country......314 F3
Leonay.......................235 A15
Liverpool....................367 A11
Long Reef 259 D1
Longshot
Driving Range.........215 E3
Macquarie Links 423 H14
Macquarie University
Driving Range.........252 A16
Manly 288 B6
Marrickville.................403 D1
Massey Park...............342 C3
Milperra Sports Centre
Driving Range..........397 C9
Monash Country 197 H9
Mona Vale..................199 D5
Moore Park 20 E12
Mt Steele
Driving Range...........20 F10
Muirfield 248 G13
Narrabeen
Driving Range.........199 C12
New Brighton 396 G12
New South Wales 437 C16
Northbridge................286 D16
North Ryde.................282 E11
North Turramurra 193 F16
Oatlands................... 279 C10
Palm Beach.............. 109 J13
Parramatta................ 307 J2
Pennant Hills............. 250 A8
Penrith 266 H10
Pymble..................... 223 H12
RAAF Kingswood 296 G7
Randwick 437 G6
Rays Airport
Driving Range 398 A6
Richmond................. 118 K7
Riverlands 397 B11
Riverside Oaks 64 F5
Riverwood 397 D2
Roseville.................. 285 B1
Royal Australian
Engineers.............. 425 C5
Royal Sydney............ 348 A13
Rum Corps Barracks.....120 G8
Ryde-Parramatta 280 J15
St Marys
Driving Range 239 J6
St Michaels.............. 437 D13
Sefton 368 F6
Sharks Golf
Driving Range 333 B1
Springwood.............. 172 E13
Strathfield 370 F1
Terrey Hills Country.... 195 D1
The Australian 376 B13
The Baulkham Hills
Day Night
Driving Range 246 G14
The Coast 437 F9
The Lakes 405 H7
Tree Valley............... 423 F4
University
Driving Range 510 F6
Wakehurst................ 287 B1
Wallacia................... 325 B12
Warringah 257 K14
Windsor Country........ 120 G10
Woodville 338 A9
Woollahra................. 347 J12
Woolooware 493 D7

HOSPITALS

ALLOWAH CHILDRENS PRIVATE
8 Perry St
Dundas Valley.......... 280 E8
ALWYN REHABILITATION
1 Emu St
Strathfield................341 G16
ASHBURN HOUSE
30 Ashburn Pl
Gladesville 312 H12
AUBURN HOSPITAL & COMMUNITY HEALTH SERVICES
Norval St 339 D7
BALMAIN
29 Booth St..................7 H10
BANKSTOWN-LIDCOMBE
Eldridge Rd
Bankstown................398 K7
BANKSTOWN PRIVATE
74 Chiswick Rd
Greenacre.................370 A10
BELLEVUE
1a Edward St
Bondi.........................378 B5
BEXLEY
34 Harrow Rd...........403 A14
BIGGE STREET
40 Bigge St
Liverpool 395 F1
BLACKTOWN
Blacktown Rd 274 K2
BRADLEYS HEAD
66 Bradleys Head Rd
Mosman....................317 C11
BRAESIDE
Prairie Vale Rd
Prairiewood 334 F8

BUENA VISTA
132 Victoria Rd
Bellevue Hill.............347 H16

CALVARY
91 Rocky Point Rd
Beverley Park...........433 C10

CAMDEN
Menangle Rd...........507 A3

CAMPBELLTOWN
Therry Rds..............511 A9

CANTERBURY
Canterbury Rd
Campsie..................401 J1

CARRINGTON CENTENNIAL
90 Werombi Rd
Grasmere................476 C15

CASTLECRAG PRIVATE
150 Edinburgh Rd....286 B12

CHARLES WENTWORTH PRIVATE
21 Lytton St
Wentworthville.........307 B1

CONCORD REPATRIATION GENERAL
Hospital Rd
Concord West..........311 G12

CUMBERLAND
1 Hainsworth St
Westmead...............278 A12

DALCROSS PRIVATE
28 Stanhope Rd
Killara......................254 B13

DALWOOD CHILDRENS HOME
21 Dalwood Av
Seaforth..................286 K8

DAME EADITH WALKER DIALYSIS TRAINING CENTRE
Nullawarra Av
Concord West..........311 J13

DELMAR PRIVATE
58 Quirk St
Dee Why...................258 H8

EASTERN SUBURBS SRVS FOR DEVELOPMENTALLY DISABLED
York St
Queens Park...............22 D13

EVESHAM CLINIC
3 Harrison St
Cremorne....................6 H3

FAIRFIELD
cnr Polding St & Prairie Vale Rd
Prairiewood.............334 G8

GLADESVILLE MACQUARIE
Wicks Rd
North Ryde..............282 G12

GOVERNOR PHILLIP SPECIAL
Glebe Pl
Penrith.....................237 C9

GREENWICH
97 River Rd.............314 K7

HAWKESBURY DISTRICT
Day St
Windsor..................121 H10

HIRONDELLE
10 Wyvern Av
Chatswood West......284 H7

HMAS PENGUIN
Naval Depot
Mosman...................317 G7

HOLROYD PRIVATE
123 Chetwynd Rd
Guildford.................337 D1

HORNSBY & KU-RING-GAI COMMUNITY HEALTH SERVICES
Palmerston Rd.........192 B16

HUNTERS HILL PRIVATE
9 Mount St...............313 G11

HURSTVILLE COMMUNITY CO-OPERATIVE PRIVATE
37 Gloucester Rd......431 H4

JEAN COLVIN PRIVATE
9 Loftus Rd
Darling Point..............13 H7

KAREENA PRIVATE
86 Kareena Rd N
Miranda....................492 F4

KARITANE MOTHERCRAFT
171 Avoca St
Randwick.................377 B14

KENSINGTON PRIVATE
17 Alison Rd............376 F9

KING GEORGE V MEMORIAL
Missenden Rd
Camperdown.............17 J5

KOGARAH
18 Garden St...........433 B7

KURRAJONG COMMUNITY
Old Bells Line of Road
Kurrajong....................85 D2

LADY DAVIDSON REHABILITATION
Bobbin Head Rd
Turramurra...............193 F11

LANGTON CENTRE
cnr Dowling & Nobbs Sts
Surry Hills...................20 E5

LIVERPOOL
cnr Goulburn & Elizabeth Sts............395 G2

LIVERPOOL PRIVATE
55 Speed St.............395 D7

LONGUEVILLE PRIVATE
47 Kenneth St...........314 E7

LOTTIE STEWART
40 Stewart St
Ermington................280 D11

LYNTON PRIVATE
40 Fullers Rd
Chatswood West.......284 F10

MACARTHUR PRIVATE
92 Dumaresq St
Campbelltown...........511 F6

MANDALAY
2 Addison Rd
Manly.......................288 F14

MANDALAY PRIVATE
2 Addison Rd
Manly.......................288 F14

MANLY DISTRICT HOSPITAL & COMMUNITY HEALTH SERVICES
Darley Rd.................288 K13

MANLY WATERS PRIVATE
17 Cove Av
Manly.......................288 G13

MATER MISERICORDIAE PRIVATE
Rocklands Rd
Crows Nest....................5 B2

METROPOLITAN REHABILITATION
275 Addison Rd
Petersham..................15 K14

MINCHINBURY COMMUNITY
cnr Great Western Hwy & Rupertswood Rd
Mount Druitt............271 H5

MONA VALE HOSPITAL & COMMUNITY HEALTH SERVICES
Coronation St...........199 D7

MOSMAN PRIVATE
1 Ellamatta Av..........317 C10

MOUNT DRUITT
Railway St................241 H14

MT WILGA PRIVATE
2 Manor Rd
Hornsby...................191 E12

NEPEAN DISTRICT
Parker St
Penrith.....................237 E12

NEPEAN PRIVATE
Jamison Rd
Penrith.....................237 E12

NERINGAH
12 Neringah Av S
Wahroonga...............222 C7

NORTHCOTT CENTRE
2 Gross St
Parramatta...............278 B15

NORTH SHORE
Westbourne St
St Leonards.............315 B4

NORTHSIDE CLINIC PRIVATE
2 Greenwich Rd
Greenwich................315 A6

NSW PRIVATE HOSPITAL
Victoria St
Ashfield....................372 K5

PACIFIC
171 Bay St
Brighton-Le-Sands...433 G2

PARRAMATTA HEALTH SERVICE
Marsden St................308 B2

PEAT ISLAND
Mooney Mooney........75 A3

PENINSULAR PRIVATE
12 McDonald St
Harbord....................258 D15

POPLARS PRIVATE
66 Norfolk Rd
Epping......................251 D12

PRESIDENT PRIVATE
cnr President Av & Hotham Rd
Kirrawee...................491 B5

PRINCE HENRY THE
Anzac Pde
Little Bay.................437 C11

PRINCE OF WALES PRIVATE THE
Barker St
Randwick.................377 A16

PRINCE OF WALES THE
Avoca St
Randwick.................377 A15

PRIO 1 EMERGENCY
Masonic Hospital, cnr Victoria & Robert Sts
Ashfield....................372 K5

QUEEN VICTORIA MEMORIAL
Thirlmere Wy
Picton.......................562 G12

RACHEL FORSTER
150 Pitt St
Redfern.......................19 D9

ROMA PRIVATE
9 William St
Randwick.................376 J10

ROSE BAY
84 Newcastle St.......348 B12

ROYAL ALEXANDRA CHILDRENS (NEW CHILDRENS)
Hawkesbury Rd
Westmead.................277 J13

ROYAL FAR WEST CHILDRENS HOME
18 Wentworth St
Manly.......................288 H10

ROYAL HOSPITAL FOR WOMEN
Barker St
Randwick.................377 A16

ROYAL NORTH SHORE
Reserve Rd
St Leonards.............315 C5

ROYAL PRINCE ALFRED
Missenden Rd
Camperdown.............17 K5

ROYAL REHABILITATION CENTRE, SYDNEY
Coorabel
227 Morrison Rd
Ryde........................312 B6
Moorong
600 Victoria Rd
Ryde........................312 C4
Weemala
259 Morrison Rd
Ryde........................312 A5

ROYAL SOUTH SYDNEY COMMUNITY HEALTH COMPLEX
Joynton Av
Zetland....................375 J11

ROZELLE
cnr Church & Glover Sts
Lilyfield........................9 K2

RYDE HOSPITAL & COMMUNITY HEALTH SERVICES
Denistone Rd
Denistone................281 E10

SACRED HEART HOSPICE
279 Victoria St
Darlinghurst................4 F13

ST CATHERINES VILLA
162 Balaclava Rd
Marsfield.................281 K2

ST DAVIDS PRIVATE
7 Rowe St
Eastwood.................281 C8

ST EDMUNDS PRIVATE
13 Clanalpine St
Eastwood.................281 A9

ST GEORGE
Gray St
Kogarah...................433 B5

ST GEORGE PRIVATE & MEDICAL CENTRE
South St
Kogarah...................433 C5

ST JOHN OF GOD
North Richmond
135 Grose Vale Rd....116 J3

ST JOHN OF GOD PRIVATE
Burwood
13 Grantham St........341 J11

ST JOSEPHS
Normanby Rd
Auburn....................339 B2

ST LUKES PRIVATE
18 Roslyn St
Potts Point.................13 A7

ST MARGARETS
435 Bourke St
Darlinghurst................4 C15

ST VINCENTS
406 Victoria St
Darlinghurst................4 G12

ST VINCENTS CARITAS CENTRE
299 Forbes St
Darlinghurst................4 E11

SCOTTISH THE
2 Cooper St
Paddington.................13 A13

SOUTH PACIFIC PRIVATE
18 Beach St
Curl Curl..................258 J16

SPRINGWOOD
4 Huntley Grange Rd...172 A15

STRATHFIELD
3 Everton Rd............341 H12

SUTHERLAND HOSPITAL & COMMUNITY HEALTH SERVICES
cnr Kingsway & Kareena Rd N
Caringbah................492 F4

SYDNEY
Macquarie St................D G3

SYDNEY ADVENTIST PRIVATE
185 Fox Valley Rd
Wahroonga...............221 G14

SYDNEY CHILDRENS
High St
Randwick.................377 A15

SYDNEY EYE
Macquarie St................D G4

SYDNEY HOME NURSING SERVICE
36 Boyce St
Glebe.........................11 J11

SYDNEY UROLOGY & SURGERY CENTRE
5 Croydon St
Petersham..................16 A7

THE EASTERN SUBURBS PRIVATE
8 Chapel St
Randwick.................377 C12

THE HILLS PRIVATE
499 Windsor Rd
Baulkham Hills.........247 E4

TRESILLIAN
Petersham
cnr Addison Rd & Shaw St...................15 J14
Willoughby
Second Av................285 H12

UNITED DENTAL
2 Chalmers St
Surry Hills....................E K16

UNITED GARDENS
11a Moonbie St
Summer Hill.............373 C5

WANDENE PRIVATE
7 Blake St
Kogarah...................432 K6

WAR MEMORIAL
Birrell St
Waverley..................377 F6

WESLEY
84 Arthur St
Ashfield....................372 E5

WESTMEAD
cnr Darcy & Hawkesbury Rds......277 G14

WESTSIDE PRIVATE
55 Burwood Rd
Concord...................342 B9

WOLPER JEWISH PRIVATE
8 Trelawney St
Woollahra..................14 C15

HOTELS & MOTELS

ARNCLIFFE
Sydney Airport
Hilton.......................404 A7

ARTARMON
Artarmon Motor Inn...284 H15
Greenwich Inn Hotel...315 A5
Linwood Lodge Motel......................314 H3
Twin Towers Motor Inn................314 J3

ASHFIELD
Ashfields Philip Lodge Motel............373 B1
Metro Motor Inn.......373 B2
Philip Lodge Motel...372 K4

BANKSTOWN
International Pacific Hotel........................369 F13
Travelodge...............399 E1

BASS HILL
Banksia Motel 367 J7
Bass Hill Toursit Park & Motel 368 A9
Gardenia Motor Inn 368 B10
Rydges Bankstown 368 B9
BLACKTOWN
Travelodge 274 C10
BLAKEHURST
Country Comfort 432 E13
BONDI BEACH
Alice Motel 378 B6
Bondi Road Hotel 378 C2
City Beach Motel 378 C2
Grand All Suite Hotel 378 D2
Swiss Grand Hotel 378 D2
BRIGHTON-LE-SANDS
Novotel Brighton Beach 434 A2
BROOKVALE
Travelodge Manly Warringah 258 D9
CAMBRIDGE PARK
Overlander Hotel Motel 237 F5
CAMDEN
Camden Country Club 507 A16
Camden Valley Golf Resort 449 K12
CAMPBELLTOWN
Colonial Motor Inn 511 H1
Maclin Lodge Motel 511 H1
Motel Formula One 481 J12
CAMPERDOWN
Apia Hotel 17 G2
Travelodge 17 G3
Centra 17 G3
CASTLE HILL
Hills Lodge Boutique Hotel 217 A14
CASULA
Fountainebleau Inn 395 A12
Hunts Motel 424 A3
Jolly Knight Motel 394 H16
CHIPPENDALE
Mercure Hotel Sydney E C16
Metro Motor Inn 19 A3
COLYTON
Colyton Hotel/Motel 270 H4
COOGEE
Coogee Bay Boutique Hotel 407 G1
Coogee Bay Hotel 377 G16
Coogee Sands Motor Inn 377 H15
Holiday Inn Coogee Beach 407 G1
CREMORNE POINT
Cremorne Point Manor 316 G15
CRONULLA
Hotel Cronulla 494 A11
Rydges Cronulla Beach 494 A11
CROWS NEST
Sovereign Armada Inn 315 G8
DARLINGHURST
All Seasons On Crown 4 C13
Camelot Inn Motel 4 H10
Holiday Inn Park Suites F H3
Hotel Capital 4 H7
Hyde Park Plaza Hotel F G2
DAWES POINT
Pier One Parkroyal 1 H5
DOUBLE BAY
Metro Motor Inn 13 K11
Ritz-Carlton Hotel 14 C8
Sir Stamford Hotel 14 C9
EDGECLIFF
Bayside The 13 F9
Metro Motor Inn 13 K11
ELIZABETH BAY
Chateau Sydney Hotel 13 A2
De Vere Hotel 13 A4
Gazebo Hotel 13 A6
Madisons Central City Hotel 13 A7
Manhattan Hotel 13 B5
Roslyn Gardens Motor Inn 13 A7
Sebel of Sydney 13 B6
ENFIELD
Burwood Motel 371 K2
ENGADINE
Engadine Motor Inn 518 H7
ERMINGTON
Ermington Hotel/Motel 310 A2
FRENCHS FOREST
Parkway Hotel Motel 256 K5
GLADESVILLE
Gladesville Motel 312 J11
Sydney Huntley Inn 312 J11
GLEBE
A Line Hotel 12 H6
Haven Inn Sydney 12 B10
Rooftop Motel 12 B12
University Motor Inn Broadway 12 D16
GLENDENNING
Plumpton Motor Inn 242 K3
GREENACRE
Hotel 10 369 K8
Palms Motel The 370 B6
GREENWICH
Twin Tower Motor Inn 314 K4
GREYSTANES
Greystanes Inn Hotel/Motel 306 D10
GUILDFORD
Golf View Hotel/Motel 337 K8
GUILDFORD WEST
Sheridan Hotel/Motel 336 G3
HABERFIELD
Metro Motor Inn 343 B16
Palm Court Motor Inn 373 E3
HAYMARKET
Aarons Hotel E C10
All Seasons Darling Harbour Hotel Sydney E B4
Carlton Crest Hotel Sydney E B12
Country Comfort Sydney Central E D13
Furama Hotel Darling Harbour E C5
Goldspear Hotel E G7
Pacific International Inn Sydney E E10
Royal Garden International Sydney E H7
Sydney Central YHA E F11
HOMEBUSH
Novotel Hotel Ibis 340 G1
JAMISONTOWN
Grey Gums Hotel Motel 266 A1
KENSINGTON
Glensynd Motor Inn 376 F9
KILLARA
Killara Inn 254 A15
KINGSFORD
Barker Lodge Motor Inn 376 G16
KURMOND
Bellbird Motel 56 A16
LANE COVE
Country Comfort 314 G1
LANSVALE
Lansdowne Motor Inn 366 F7
LIDCOMBE
Liberty Plains Motor Inn 339 H6
Lidcombe Motor Inn 339 J9
MACQUARIE PARK
Travelodge Macquarie North Ryde 252 D15
MANLY
Manly Pacific Parkroyal 288 H8
Manly Seaview Motel 288 G5
Radisson Kestrel on Manly Beach 288 J10
MAROUBRA
Sands Hotel/Motel 407 E14
Tradewinds Hotel 407 B10
MASCOT
Hotel Ibis Sydney Airport 405 B4
Parkroyal Sydney Airport 405 B3
Sheraton Sydney Airport Hotel 405 B5
MILLERS POINT
Observatory Hotel A C6
Stamford On Kent A C10
MILSONS POINT
Duxton Hotel North Sydney 5 K14
Kirribilli Hotel 6 A14
MIRANDA
Metro Motor Inn 492 B4
MOORE PARK
Sydney Park Lodge Hotel 20 D9
MT KURING-GAI
Mt Kuring-Gai Motel 162 H13
NARELLAN
Angel Motel 478 F9
NEWPORT
Newport Mirage 169 D12
NORTH SYDNEY
Centra North Sydney K F12
North Sydney Harbourview Hotel K G12
Rydges North Sydney 5 H4
PADDINGTON
Sullivans Hotel 4 G15
PARRAMATTA
Courtyard by Marriott 308 D5
Gazebo Hotel 308 D1
Pacific International Hotel 308 D5
Parramatta City Motel 308 B5
Parramatta Parkroyal 308 C2
Ramada Hotel 308 D5
Travelodge 308 J5
PENNANT HILLS
Chifley on City View 250 F1
Country Comfort Inn 250 F1
PENRITH
Panthers Resort 236 D12
Penrith Hotel/Motel 237 A10
Penrith Vally Inn 236 D8
POTTS POINT
Astoria Hotel 4 K6
Barclay Hotel 4 J8
Chateau Sydney Hotel 13 A2
Cresent on Bayswater 4 J8
Hampton Court 4 J8
Holiday Inn 4 H7
Kingsview Motel 4 K6
Landmark Parkroyal Hotel 4 K4
Millennium Hotel 4 H8
Parkroyal Plaza 4 H6
Rex Hotel 4 K5
Top of The Town Hotel 4 H9
PYRMONT
Astor Goldsborough Apartment Hotel 12 K7
Ibis Hotel Darling Harbour 12 K5
Novotel Darling Harbour 12 K6
Star City Casino 12 H2
RANDWICK
Gemini Hotel 377 A13
REDFERN
Central Railway Motel 19 G6
RICHMOND
Colonial Motel 118 F4
Hawkesbury Conference Centre & Motel 118 F4
ROOTY HILL
Country Comfort 241 A16
ROSE BAY
Cranbrook International 347 F10
ROSEHILL
All Seasons Hotel 308 J7
Mercure Hotel Parramatta 308 J4
Rydges Parramatta 308 J7
RUSHCUTTERS BAY
Rushcutters Harbourside Sydney 13 C9
RYDE
Metro Motor Inn 311 G2
ST CLAIR
The Blue Cattle Dog Tavern 269 G9
ST LEONARDS
Mercure St Leonards Sydney Hotel 315 A5
SANS SOUCI
Sans Souci Motor Inn 433 C15
SPRINGWOOD
Pioneer Way Motel 201 D2
STRATHFIELD
Spanish Inn Motor Lodge 371 C4
STRATHFIELD SOUTH
Town & Country Motel 371 E4
SUMMER HILL
Marco Polo Motor Inn 373 E3
SURRY HILLS
Cambridge Park Inn International F J9
City Crown Lodge International 4 C14
Furama Central Hotel F C12
Oxford Koala Hotel & Apartments F H6
SUTHERLAND
Sutherland Inn Motel 490 G5
SYDNEY
All Seasons Premier Menzies Hotel A H15
Avillion Hotel Sydney E J3
Blacket Hotel C H4
Castlereagh Inn D B11
Grace Hotel C F5
Hotel Ibis World Square E K5
Hotel Inter-Continental B F10
Hotel Nikko C C6
Hotel No. 2 A J13
Hyde Park Inn F B1
Le Meridien Sydney A G13
Merchant Court Hotel C J8
Merchant Court Hotel C K8
Park Regis Hotel D A12
Parkroyal at Darling Harbour C C13
Pentura on Pitt C K15
Raddison Hotel E E1
Radisson Plaza Hotel B A14
Renaissance Sydney B B10
Sheraton on the Park D B9
Southern Cross F B6
Southern Cross on Harbour E D4
Sydney Hilton C J10
Sydney Marriott F G1
Sydney Vista Hotel A F14
The Ritz-Carlton B F8
Travelodge D D4
Travelodge Sydney Central F D5
Wentworth The B D14
Westin C K3
Y on the Park Hotel F F3
SYLVANIA
Abcot Motor Inn 461 G15
PARRAMATTA
The Parramatta 308 B3
THE ROCKS
ANA Hotel A G7
Harbour Rocks Hotel A K4
Observatory Hotel A C6
Old Sydney Parkroyal B A2
Park Hyatt 1 H7
Quay West A K6
The Stafford A J4
ULTIMO
Mercure Hotel E C16
Unilodge Sydney Motel 12 J16
WAHROONGA
Wahroonga Spainsh 222 A6
WARWICK FARM
El Toro Motor Inn 365 D15
Sunnybrook Hotel 366 B10
WENTWORTHVILLE
Motel Formula One 306 J3
WERRINGTON
Colonial Hotel Motel 238 H11
WESTMEAD
Wesley Lodge Motel 277 H15
WEST RYDE
Ryde Motor Inn 280 J15
WINDSOR
The Windsor Terrace 121 E7
Windsor Motel 121 E7
WINSTON HILLS
Winston Hotel/Motel 277 A1
WOOLLAHRA
Hughenden Hotel 21 G4
WOOLLOOMOOLOO
Sydney Boulevard Hotel 4 D7
Woolloomooloo Bay 4 F3
WOOLOOWARE
Cronulla Motor Inn 493 H10

LIBRARIES

Arncliffe 403 G8
Artarmon 284 K15
Ashfield 372 H3
Auburn 339 E3
Avalon 170 B1
Balmain 7 D8
Bankstown 369 F16
Baulkham Hills 247 J11
Beecroft Childrens 250 E5
Belrose 225 H16
Berowra 133 F12
Bexley 402 J14
Bexley North 402 D9
Blaxland 233 G8
Bondi 377 J4
Bondi Toy 378 E2
Bonnyrigg 364 A4
Botany 405 F11
Brighton-Le-Sands 433 K2
Brookvale Toy 258 B9
Bundeena 524 A11
Burwood 342 A14
Cabramatta 365 K6
Camden 477 A15
Campbelltown 511 F3
Campsie 371 K14
Caringbah 492 J8
Carlingford 279 J4
Castlecrag 285 K13
Castle Hill 218 C15
Casula 394 E15
Chatswood 284 K9
Chester Hill 368 B2
City Of Sydney C F12
Concord 342 A4
Concord West 341 F3
Cronulla 493 K12
Cubby House Toy 258 G7
Dee Why 258 G5
Double Bay 14 H5
Drummoyne 343 H2
Dulwich Hill 373 F9
Dundas Valley 279 G10
Dural 188 G12
Earlwood 402 H4
Eastwood 281 A7
Emu Plains 235 E10
Enfield 371 H2

Engadine 518 J2
Epping 251 C16
Ermington 310 A3
Fairfield 336 E12
Five Dock 342 K10
Forestville 256 A10
Galston 159 F11
Gladesville 312 J8
Glebe 12 A11
Glenquarie 424 C15
Gordon 253 H7
Granville 308 E11
Greenacre 370 C12
Green Valley 363 C13
Greenwich 315 A8
Greystanes 306 B10
Guildford 337 G4
Haberfield 343 D15
Haymarket E F8
H J Daley 511 B6
Holroyd Toy 337 F4
Homebush 341 C10
Hornsby 221 H1
Hurstville 431 K5
Ingleburn 453 D6
Jessie Street Womens 10 C4
Kogarah 433 B4
Lakemba 400 K1
Lalor Park 245 F12
Lane Cove 314 D2
Leichhardt 15 J1
Lidcombe 339 H8
Lindfield 284 D1
Liverpool 395 F2
Manly 288 H9
Maroubra 407 A8
Marrickville 373 J12
Mascot 405 D5
Matraville 437 D3
Max Webber 244 G16
Menai 458 K11
Merrylands 307 H13
Miller 393 K2
Minto 482 H2
Miranda 491 K4
Mona Vale 199 C4
Moorebank 396 E8
Mortdale 431 A3
Mosman 317 A6
Mount Druitt 241 E15
Narellan 478 G11
Naremburn 315 G2
Newtown 17 J10
Noahs Ark Toy 284 J15
Northbridge 286 C16
North Ryde 282 G9
Oatley 431 C13
Paddington 21 A1
Padstow 399 D15
Pagewood 406 E11
Panania 428 B2
Parramatta 308 C3
Pennant Hills 220 G16
Penrith 236 F9
Potts Point 13 A5
Randwick 377 B14
Regents Park 369 A1
Richmond 118 G4
Riverstone 182 J7
Riverwood 400 B14
Rockdale 403 D14
Ryde 312 A1
St Clair 270 D12
St Ives 223 J12
St Marys 269 G1
St Peters 374 D14
Sans Souci 463 E1
Seaforth 287 D9
Smithfield 335 J6
South Hurstville 432 B11
South Penrith 266 J3
Springwood 202 A3
Stanmore 16 F9
Stanton 5 G3
State Library of NSW B G16
Strathfield 371 C4
Surry Hills 20 B2
Sutherland 490 F2
Sylvania 462 B9
Terrey Hills 196 E7
Toongabbie 277 B9
Turramurra 222 H13
Warragamba 353 F8
Waterloo 19 G14
Watsons Bay 318 A14
Waverley 22 F8
Wentworthville 277 B16
West Ryde 281 D14
Wetherill Park 334 D8
Windsor 121 A10
Woollahra Childrens 21 K2

MOTOR REGISTRIES

BANKSTOWN
Shop 4a, Bankstown Square Shopping Centre 369 G15
BEVERLY HILLS
cnr Cambridge St & Stoney Creek Rd 401 C16
BLACKTOWN
85 Flushcombe Rd 274 G1
BONDI JUNCTION
88 Ebley St 22 J8
BOTANY
5 Lord St 405 F10
BURWOOD
Shops 1 & 2, 25 Belmore St 341 K15
CAMDEN
167 Argyle St 477 A16
CAMPBELLTOWN
Tindall St & Menangle Rd 511 A6
CAMPSIE
Shop 43, Campsie Centre 372 A14
CASTLE HILL
18 Anella Av 217 D12
CHATSWOOD
313 Victoria Av 285 B9
ENGADINE
Shop 3, 101 Caldarra Av 518 J2
FAIRFIELD
32 Harris St 336 E13
FAIRFIELD HEIGHTS
Shop 4, 144 Polding St 335 K8
FIVE DOCK
cnr Ramsay Rd & Henley Marine Dr 343 A12
FRENCHS FOREST
Shop 12, Forest Way Shopping Centre 256 D5
GLADESVILLE
230 Victoria Rd 312 J9
GREENACRE
Chullora
95 Hume Hwy 370 D5
HORNSBY
324 Pacific Hwy 191 G14
HURSTVILLE
8 Woodville St 432 A5
INGLEBURN
Shop 9, Centennial House, cnr Oxford & Ingleburn Rds 453 C6
JAMISONTOWN
Penrith South
81 York Rd 266 E1
KOGARAH
60a Gray St 433 C7
LIDCOMBE
cnr Swete & Mills Sts 339 K7
LIVERPOOL
357 Hume Hwy 395 A7
MACQUARIE PARK
North Ryde
Shop 2, Macquarie Centre 282 F1
MANLY
239 Pittwater Rd 288 F5
MAROUBRA
Maroubra Junction
930 Anzac Pde 407 A9
MARRICKVILLE
Shop 9, Marrickville Metro Shopping Centre 374 F10
MERRYLANDS
12 McFarlane St 307 H12
MIRANDA
Shop 5, Kiora Mall 492 A4
MOUNT DRUITT
23 Luxford Rd 241 F14
NORTH SYDNEY
154 Pacific Hwy K B3
PARRAMATTA
cnr Macquarie & Charles Sts 308 E3
REVESBY
Shop 13-15, Revesby Plaza 398 J16
RICHMOND
173 Windsor St 118 H4
ROSEBERY
52 Rothschild Av 375 H14
RYDE
cnr Blaxland & North Rds 281 K13
ST CLAIR
Shop 20, St Clair Shopping Centre 270 C12
SILVERWATER
1 River St 309 K9
SPRINGWOOD
Shop 1, Raymond Mall 201 K4
SURRY HILLS
City South
260 Elizabeth St F B12
SYDNEY
City
161 Clarence St C E3
THORNLEIGH
1 Central Av 221 A13
WARRIEWOOD
Shop 4, Warriewood Square Shopping Centre 199 A12
WETHERILL PARK
248 Victoria St 335 B2

PARKS, RESERVES, OVALS, ETC

36th Battalion Park
Leichhardt 10 C14
Abbotsford Cove Foreshore Park
Abbotsford 343 A1
Abbott Park
Chester Hill 367 K1
Abel Reserve
Revesby 398 H16
Acacia Park
Dundas Valley 279 K9
Eastwood 281 J8
Ace Reserve
Fairfield 336 G8
Acron Oval
St Ives 224 G11
Adams Park
Canley Vale 365 K3
Adam St Ground
Curl Curl 258 K12
Ador Reserve
Rockdale 403 G16
Adventure Park
Ryde 282 A14
A E Watson Reserve
Bexley 402 J16
Agnes Banks Nature Reserve 146 E8
Airey Park
Homebush 340 J10
Airport Reserve
Bankstown Airport 397 F6
Aitken Reserve
Queenscliff 288 F3
Akuna Av Oval
Bangor 459 G14
Alamein Park
Liverpool 394 K3
Albert Brown Park
Ermington 280 E11
Albert Park
Earlwood 403 A4
Alcheringa Reserve
Miranda 491 J8
Alderson Park
Merrylands 307 C7
Alexandria Park 19 A14
Alfred Henry Whaling Memorial Reserve
Baulkham Hills 247 G5
Algie Park
Haberfield 343 C14
Algona Reserve
Bilgola 169 F7
Alice Park
Bankstown 369 C13
Alison Playground
Dulwich Hill 373 C11
Allambie Heights Oval 257 C11
Allambie Rd Reserve
Edensor Park 333 G14
Allan Border Oval
Mosman 317 A7
Allan Small Park
East Killara 254 J6
Allder Park
Sefton 368 E4
Allenby Park
Allambie Heights 257 E9
Allen Robertson Reserve
Kings Langley 245 A5
Allison Park
Chiswick 343 B2
Allman Park
Ashfield 373 A4
Allsopp Oval
Cambridge Park 237 H7
Allum Park
Greenacre 370 E11
Alma Reserve
Padstow 429 G5
Alpha Park
Blacktown 244 F16
Alpha Rd Park
Greystanes 305 F12
Alroy Park
Plumpton 242 B6
Alston Reserve
Macquarie Park 282 K1
Amalfi Park
Lurnea 394 F9
Amaroo Reserve
Georges Hall 367 F13
Ambrose Hallen Park
Toongabbie 276 F9
Amour Park
Revesby 398 F15
Amundsen Reserve
Leumeah 482 J10
Amway Park
Castle Hill 217 E14
Amy St Playground
Marrickville 374 A9
Anana Reserve
Elanora Heights 198 E16
Anderson Park
Neutral Bay 6 B9
Rydalmere 309 K1
Anembo Reserve
Duffys Forest 194 J8
Angle Park
Chipping Norton 366 E12
Angophora Reserve
Avalon 169 G2
Bilgola 169 G2
Angus Park
Rooty Hill 272 C2
Annangrove Park 186 E3
Ann Cashman Reserve
Balmain 7 C10
Annie Prior Reserve
Glenhaven 187 G16
Annie Wyatt Park
Palm Beach 140 B3
Ann Thorn Park
Ryde 311 G3
Ansell Park (Private)
Clarendon 120 F8
Anzac Creek Park
Wattle Grove 395 K13
Anzac Oval
Engadine 488 F15
Anzac Park
Cammeray 315 K7
West Ryde 281 F15
A P Austin Field
Arncliffe 403 K11
Apex Community Park
Ingleburn 453 J6
Apex Park
Bradbury 511 D8
Liverpool 395 C2
Mona Vale 199 F4
Riverview 314 B4
Applegum Reserve
Glenmore Park 265 G7
Aquatic Park
Longueville 314 D11
Aquilina Reserve
Rooty Hill 242 H16
Ararat Reserve
Frenchs Forest 256 G10
Arcadia Park 130 A10
Arcadia St Park
Merrylands West 307 A12
Ardill Park
Warrimoo 203 C13
Argyle Bailey Memorial Park
Ebenezer 63 H9
Argyle Place Park
Millers Point A D2
A R Hurst Reserve
Sylvania 461 F10
Arlington Recreation Ground
Dulwich Hill 373 C9
Armitage Reserve
Chiswick 313 D16
Arncliffe Park 403 E7
Arnett Park
Guildford 337 B1
Arrowsmith Park
Hurstville 431 H5
Arrunga Gardens
Wentworthville 277 C12
Artarmon Oval 285 C16
Artarmon Park 315 B1
Artarmon Reserve 285 B16
Arthur Byrne Reserve
Maroubra 407 G13
Arthur Launchy Reserve
Bass Hill 367 G7
Arthur McElhone Reserve
Elizabeth Bay 13 B3
Arthur Park
Kings Cross 13 A9
Punchbowl 399 H5
Arthur Walker Reserve
Concord West 311 H16
Ashcroft Reserve
Georges Hall 367 E14
Ashfield Park 373 B1
Ashford Reserve
Milperra 397 G6
Ashley Brown Park
Lalor Park 245 J13
Ash Paddock
Centennial Park 376 G9
Ashton Park
Mosman 317 C15
Asquith Park 192 A7
A S Tanner Reserve
Monterey 433 G7
Astrolabe Park
Pagewood 406 D4
Atchison Reserve
Macquarie Fields 424 A14
Athol Barnes Reserve
South Granville 338 G7
Atkinson Reserve
Gladesville 312 K5
Atlas Reserve
Narellan Vale 508 H2
Attunga Reserve
Bilgola 169 K6
Newport 169 K6
Auburn Botanic Gardens 338 H6
Auburn Community Picnic Area 338 G7

Bronte Park 378 A8
Brooklyn Park 75 J11
Brookvale Park 258 B9
Brownlee Reserve
  Birchgrove 8 B3
Browns Field
  Wahroonga 222 A15
Browns Forest
  St Ives 223 H15
Browns Rd Reserve
  The Oaks 502 G9
Browns Reserve
  Croydon Park 371 H9
Bruce Reserve
  Panania 428 E4
Brunswick Park
  Liberty Grove 311 C14
Brush Farm Park
  Eastwood 280 F9
Brushwood Dr
  Reserve
  Rouse Hill 185 B7
Bryce Oval
  St Ives 254 F1
Buchanan Oval
  Newington College
  Stanmore 16 E14
Buckle Reserve
  Menai 458 E10
Buckley Park
  Winston Hills 276 J1
Buffalo Creek Reserve
  Hunters Hill 313 C3
Bugler Playground
  Enmore 17 B11
Bullock Reserve
  Chester Hill 337 J12
Bunbury Curran Park
  Glenfield 424 C14
  Macquarie Fields 424 D15
Bundara Reserve
  North Ryde 283 B9
Bundeena Oval 523 H10
Bundeena Reserve
  Woodbine 481 F13
Bundock Park
  Clovelly 378 A13
Bungan Head Reserve
  Newport 170 A13
Burgessiana Reserve
  Faulconbridge 171 A14
Burnie Park
  Clovelly 377 J12
Burns Bay Reserve
  Riverview 313 J5
Burraneer Park
  Woolooware 493 C12
Burrows Park
  Clovelly 378 B13
  Ryde 312 D2
Burwood Park 341 K12
Butler Park
  South Penrith 237 B15
Buttenshaw Park
  Springwood 201 D2
Buttercup Reserve
  Mount Annan 509 E4
Byrne Reserve
  St Andrews 451 J16
Byron Park
  Ryde 282 D12
Cabarita Park 312 F15
Caber Park
  Winston Hills 277 E4
Cabravale Park
  Cabramatta 365 K5
Caddies Creek Park
  Kellyville 185 E7
Caffyn Park
  Dover Heights 348 E11
Cahill Park
  Arncliffe 403 K6
Calangara Park
  Carlingford 279 G7
Caldew Reserve
  Macquarie Park 252 J16
Caley Park
  Macquarie Fields 454 F2
Calga Reserve
  Waverley 378 B10
Calgaroo
  Native Garden
  West Pennant Hills 249 F2
Calga St Reserve
  Roseville Chase 285 F1
Cambridge Park 237 H7
Camden Apex Park 506 K2
Camden Rugby Park
  Camden South 506 H14
Camden Showground 476 K16
Camdenville Park
  St Peters 374 H11
Cameron Park
  Holsworthy 426 C2
  Turramurra 222 J13
  Wattle Grove 426 C2
Campbell Hill
  Pioneer Reserve
  Guildford 338 C11
Campbell Oval
  Canterbury 372 G10
Campbell Park
  Chatswood West 284 F13
  Chiswick 343 C3
  West Pennant Hills 219 K16
Campbell Reserve
  Blacktown 244 C12
Campbelltown
  Showground 511 G3
Camperdown
  Memorial
  Rest Park 17 F9
Camperdown Park 17 D5
Canally Reserve
  Airds 512 F9
Canal Rd Park
  Greystanes 306 E13
Canberra Rd Reserve
  Sylvania 462 C10
Cann Park
  La Perouse 436 K14
Canterbury Park 372 G10
Captain Cook Oval
  Woolooware 493 D6
Captain Cook Reserve
  Blacktown 274 J2
Carara Reserve
  West Ryde 281 H14
C A Redmond Field
  Rockdale 403 J16
Careel Bay Ovals
  Palm Beach 140 B10
Careel Headland
  Reserve
  Avalon 140 G12
Carina Bay Reserve
  Como 460 K6
Caringbah Oval 492 H8
Carlingford
  Memorial Park 280 A4
Carmen Park
  Cherrybrook 219 H3
Carpenter Cr Reserve
  Warriewood 199 D11
Carrawood Park
  Carramar 366 J4
Carrington Park
  Wahroonga 222 E2
Carroll Park
  Casula 395 A14
Carrs Bush
  Galston 159 H4
Carss Bush Park
  Carss Park 432 G15
Carters Island
  Nature Reserve
  Kurnell 463 J9
Carysfield Park
  Bass Hill 368 B10
Casement Reserve
  Castlecrag 286 B13
Castle Cove Park 285 G3
Castle Glen Reserve
  Castle Hill 217 H5
Castle Haven Reserve
  Castlecrag 286 C12
Castle Hill Apex Park 218 G7
Castle Hill Heritage
  Park 218 F8
Castle Hill
  Lions Park 217 J6
Castle Hill Park 218 D14
Castle Hill
  Showground 217 E11
Castlereagh
  Nature Reserve
  Berkshire Park 178 F10
Castle Rock Reserve
  Clontarf 287 H16
Castlewood
  Village Green
  Castle Hill 248 H1
Casuarina Park
  Winston Hills 277 B3
Casuarina Rd Oval
  Alfords Point 429 B13
Casuarina Reserve
  Forestville 255 K11
Catherine Field
  Reserve 449 F3
Catherine Park
  Scotland Island 168 H2
Cattai Farm
  Picnic Ground 93 J1
Cattai National Park 95 B4
  Cattai 64 A13
Cattle Duffers Flat
  Picnic Point 428 E13
Cavanagh Reserve
  Lalor Park 245 C11
Cawarra Reserve
  Eastern Creek 272 F7
C D Hensley Field
  Hillsdale 406 E12
Centenary Park
  Campbelltown 511 J5
  Croydon 342 F13
Centennial Parklands
  Centennial Park 21 H10
Central Gardens
  Merrylands West 306 H11
Central Park
  Concord 341 H5
  Longueville 314 E6
  Maroubra 407 C8
Central Tree Reserve
  Glenmore Park 266 A10
C F Williams
  Reserve
  Lugarno 429 H12
Chadwick Reserve
  Lidcombe 339 H6
Chain of Ponds
  Reserve
  Ebenezer 62 E6
  Strathfield 371 A2
Chambers Park
  Chiswick 343 E1
Chaplin Oval
  Lane Cove West 283 G16
Chapman Gardens
  Kingswood 237 J13
Charles Herbert
  Reserve
  Northmead 277 J5
Charles Moore
  Reserve
  Mount Annan 509 F4
Charles Park
  Smithfield 335 C6
Charlotte Breen
  Memorial Park
  Kurnell 464 E15
Chatswood Park 284 J11
Chattan Park
  North Narrabeen 228 K3
Chauvel Park
  Chipping Norton 396 C3
Cheltenham Oval 250 G11
Cherrybrook Park
  Cabramatta 366 D11
Cherrywood Reserve
  Wahroonga 223 B4
Childs Park
  Chipping Norton 366 H13
Childs Reserve
  Glenfield 424 G12
Chilworth
  Recreation Reserve
  Beecroft 250 D8
Chisholm Park
  Canley Heights 364 J3
Chiswick Park
  Woollahra 22 A1
Choma Park
  Bossley Park 334 C9
Chopin Park
  Plumpton 242 A11
Christie Park
  Macquarie Park 252 E15
Christison Park
  Vaucluse 348 H3
Church Grounds
  Centennial Park 376 J9
Churchill Reserve
  Narellan Vale 479 A10
  Padstow Heights 429 D8
Church Point Reserve 168 F6
Cintra Park
  Concord 342 D9
Civic Park
  Auburn 339 D7
  Pendle Hill 276 D13
Clareville Beach
  Reserve
  Clareville 169 D1
Clareville Reserve
  Sandringham 463 D4
Clarke Reserve
  Padstow 429 F1
  Vaucluse 348 G4
Clarkes Point Reserve
  Woolwich 314 F14
Clark Oval
  Kearns 451 B15
Clark Park
  Milsons Point K G15
Claude Cameron
  Grove
  Wahroonga 223 A4
Claydon Reserve
  Kogarah Bay 433 B13
Claymore Park 481 B13
Clementson Park
  Bondi Junction 22 F8
Clemton Park
  Kingsgrove 401 G7
Cleopatra Reserve
  Ambarvale 540 F2
Cliff Reserve
  North Wahroonga 222 J1
Clifton Gardens
  Reserve
  Mosman 317 D12
Clinchs Pond Reserve
  Moorebank 395 H8
Clissold Reserve
  Emu Heights 234 K3
Clive Park
  Northbridge 286 G14
Clontarf Reserve 287 E14
Clyde Park
  Moorebank 396 E13
Clyne Reserve
  Millers Point 1 C8
Cobbitty Walk
  Cobbitty 446 H15
Cockayne Reserve
  Castle Hill 217 F14
Col Barratt Reserve
  Narellan 478 A10
Colbee Park
  Oakville 122 C14
Coleman Park
  Bankstown Airport 367 D16
  Berala 339 G12
Cole Park
  Moorebank 396 F7
Collimore Park
  Liverpool 395 B2
Collyer Playground
  Newtown 374 H10
Colonial Reserve
  Bligh Park 150 F6
Colquhoun Park
  South Granville 338 E2
Col Sutton Park
  Baulkham Hills 246 G12
Colvin Park
  Denistone East 281 J9
Comenarra
  Playing Field
  Turramurra 252 D5
Commercial Rd
  Reserve
  Kellyville 185 E10
Commercial Rd
  (Netball) Reserve
  Kellyville 185 G9
Community Hall Park
  Mt Riverview 204 D16
Community Park
  Pyrmont 8 H16
Como
  Pleasure Grounds 460 J4
Concord Oval 342 C10
Condor Cr Reserve
  Connells Point 432 A13
Connells Point
  Reserve 431 G16
Coogee Oval 377 G16
Cooinoo Reserve
  Enfield 371 F5
Cooke Park
  Belfield 371 B8
Cook Park
  Cabramatta West 364 G7
  Kyeemagh 404 C14
  St Marys 269 E3
  Sandringham 463 E5
  Sans Souci 433 G16
  Sans Souci 463 B6
  Sydney D H12
Cook Reserve
  Ruse 512 G2
Cooks Paddock
  Paddington 21 D1
Coolaroo Park
  Lane Cove West 284 D13
Cooleena Reserve
  Elanora Heights 198 F13
Coolibah Reserve
  Bardwell Valley 403 B7
Coolong Reserve
  Castle Hill 217 G16
Coonong Creek
  Bushland
  Gymea Bay 491 F9
Cooper Park
  Bellevue Hill 377 F1
  Woollahra 377 F1
Cooper St Reserve
  Engadine 518 H5
Copercornia Reserve
  Glenwood 215 C14
Copperfield Reserve
  Ambarvale 510 H13
Coralie Reserve
  Wareemba 343 A5
Coral Sea Park
  Maroubra 407 C12
Corbin Reserve
  Quakers Hill 214 D15
Corea Oval
  Miranda 461 K14
Coronation Park
  Minto 482 F3
Coronation View Point
  Greenwich 314 H3
Corroboree Park
  Wilberforce 91 J8
Corryton Park
  Wattle Grove 425 J2
Corteille Reserve
  Castlecrag 286 A12
Costa Park
  Busby 393 H1
Cowan Park
  Chipping Norton 396 G5
  Cowan 104 B12
Cowells La Reserve
  Ermington 280 E15
Cox Park
  Carlingford 279 K5
Craig St Reserve
  Punchbowl 399 J9
Craik Park
  Austral 391 B7
Crammond Park
  Stanmore 16 D10
Cranebrook Park 206 H9
Crane Rd Reserve
  Castle Hill 248 G1
Cremorne Reserve
  Cremorne Point 316 H16
Crest Park
  Georges Hall 368 A12
Crestwood Reserve
  Baulkham Hills 246 J6
Crete Reserve
  Rosebery 375 J16
Cripple Creek Reserve
  Blaxland 234 A2
  Mt Riverview 234 A2
Croatia Park
  Werrington 239 A15

Croft Playground, Marrickville 373 D14
Croker Park, Five Dock 342 K12
Cromer Park 228 F16
Cromwell Park, Malabar 437 E2
Cronulla Park 494 A13
Crookston Reserve, Camden South 506 K14
Croot Park, Hurstville 432 B2
Crosslands Reserve, Hornsby Heights 132 A16
Crown of Newport Reserve, Newport 169 G6
Croydon Park 372 C9
Cudal Reserve, Ryde 312 C6
Cumberland State Forest, Dural 219 B1
Cumberland State Forest, West Pennant Hills 249 F3
Cunninghams Reach Park, Linley Point 313 F7
Curagul Field, North Turramurra 193 E15
Curraghbeena Park, Mosman 316 J13
Currans Hill Park 479 H10
Curry Reserve, Elderslie 477 G15
Curtis Oval, Dundas Valley 280 B10
Cut Hill Reserve, Cobbitty 446 D9
C V Kelly Park, Girraween 276 A10
Cynthea Reserve, Palm Beach 140 A4
Cyprus Community Centre of NSW Stanmore Rd, Enmore 16 J14
Daisy St Park, Greystanes 305 H7
Dalton Reserve, Condell Park 398 E1
Dangar Oval, Rose Bay 347 K11
Daniel St Park, Greystanes 306 D7
Dan Mahoney Reserve, Dundas 278 H13
Dan Parklet, Lansvale 366 E8
Darcy Smith Oval, Emu Plains 235 F11
Dardabong Falls Reserve, Terrey Hills 195 J11
Dark Gully Park, Palm Beach 140 A6
Darks Common, Lapstone 264 E4
Darley St Playground, Newtown 374 G11
Darling Mills State Forest, West Pennant Hills 249 A12
Darling St Park, Greystanes 306 A3
Darnley Oval, Gordon 254 C6
Darook Park, Cronulla 523 H4
Darri Reserve, Gladesville 312 H10
Daruk Park, Casula 394 E15
Darvall Park, Denistone 281 B12
Davey Sq Reserve, Strathfield 341 B12
David Frater Reserve, Parramatta 308 D1
David Scott Reserve, Epping 280 G2
David Thomas Reserve, Manly Vale 287 J1

Davies Park, Springwood 201 C7
Davies Reserve, Padstow 429 G1
Davis Park, Claymore 481 C10
Dawes Point Park 1 H6
Dawes Point Reserve, The Rocks 1 J7
Day St Reserve, Drummoyne 344 B3
Deakin Park, Silverwater 309 H14
Dearin Park, Newport 169 E12
Deborah Wicks Walkway, Blacktown 273 K1
Deep Creek Reserve, Elanora Heights 228 C2
Deepwater Park, Milperra 397 D15
Deerbush Park, Prairiewood 334 F11
Deer Park, Royal National Park 521 J2
Deerubbin Park, Dangar Island 76 G8
Deerubbun Park, Cornwallis 120 K7
Deerubbun Reserve, Mooney Mooney 75 C4
Dee Why Park 258 J2
Dee Why West Recreation Reserve 227 F9
Degotardi Park, St Ives 254 B3
De Lardes Reserve, Illawong 459 J2
Dence Park, Epping 251 E16
Denistone Park 281 F11
Des Creagh Reserve, Avalon 140 D16
Deverall Park, Condell Park 398 D6
Devon Park, Cambridge Park 237 K9
D Hamilton Reserve, Eastwood 280 J7
Diamond Bay Reserve, Vaucluse 348 F6
Dickson Park, Bondi 377 K3
Digger Black Reserve, Ingleburn 453 F12
Dillon St Reserve, Paddington 13 B12
Dimeny Park, Claymore 481 C12
Dingley Dell, St Ives 224 D13
Discovery Park, Kings Langley 245 D4
Dixon Park, Rosehill 309 C6
Dobell Rd Reserve, Engadine 489 A15
Dog Kennel Reserve, Huntingwood 273 J11
Dolphin Park, Avalon 140 C9
Dominey Reserve, Bexley 432 H2
Don Moon Memorial Park, Camden 507 A4
Don Moore Reserve, North Rocks 248 J14
Donnans Reserve, Bexley 402 J13
Donnelly Park, Connells Point 431 J16
Donovan Park, Eastwood 281 K8
Don Stewart Park, Epping 280 D4
Doris Fitton Park, North Sydney K J5
Doris Sergeant Park, Old Toongabbie 276 J11
Dorothy Park, Bankstown 399 J2

Douglas Smith Memorial Park, Glenbrook 263 K2
Dover Heights Reserve 348 G8
Dover Park, Blakehurst 462 G2
Downes Park, Wallacia 324 K14
Doyle Gardens, Hurstville 401 E16
Doyle Ground, North Parramatta 278 H6
Doyle Ground, Parramatta 278 G15
Dr Charles McKay Reserve, Mount Druitt 271 H2
Dr H J Foley Rest Park, Glebe 12 B13
Drummoyne Park 343 G2
Drysdale Reserve, Elderslie 507 H3
Dudley Page Reserve, Dover Heights 348 F10
Duff Reserve, Point Piper 347 E7
Dukes Oval, Emu Plains 235 F10
Dumaresq Reserve, Rose Bay 348 B8
Dunbar Park, Avalon 170 B1
Dunbar Park, Marsfield 282 A3
Dunbar St Reserve, Silverdale 353 H16
Dunbier Park, Liverpool 395 C7
Duncan Park, Epping 280 J1
Duncan Park, Seven Hills 275 G5
Dundas Park, Dundas Valley 280 A10
Dunholm Reserve, Macquarie Park 252 H16
Dunningham Park, Cronulla 494 A11
Dunningham Reserve, Coogee 377 J15
Dunrossil Reserve, Carlingford 250 B15
Dural Park 189 H16
Duri Reserve, Malabar 437 G8
Durrant Oval, Warwick Farm 365 G12
Dwyer Oval, Warwick Farm 365 E13
Eagle Creek Reserve, Eschol Park 481 B5
Eagle Farm Reserve, Eagle Vale 481 F6
Eagleview Reserve, Minto 483 B4
Earl Reserve, Beacon Hill 257 G7
Earlwood Park 402 G3
East Gordon Park, Gordon 254 C5
East Hills Park 427 F6
Eastlakes Reserve 405 K3
East Lindfield Park 255 C11
Easton Park, Rozelle 405 K2
Eastwood Park 281 A7
Ebenezer Park 63 D5
Eccles Reserve, Belfield 371 D12
Echo Point Park, Roseville Chase 285 H1
Edenborough Park, Lindfield 284 A4
Edgecombe Park, Moorebank 396 C7
Edinburgh Rd Reserve, Castlecrag 286 D10
Edna Hunt Sanctuary, Epping 281 B4
Edna Reserve, Ingleburn 453 C11
Edward Bennett Oval, Cherrybrook 219 G15
Edwards Park, Concord 342 A4

Edwin Wheeler Oval, Sadleir 394 B3
Eggleton Park, Campbelltown 510 H9
E G Waterhouse National Camellia Gardens, Caringbah 492 E7
El Alamein Park, Rosebery 376 H16
Elder Reserve, Mount Annan 509 F1
Eldridge Reserve, Condell Park 398 J6
Elizabeth Chaffey Reserve, Castle Hill 217 D7
Elizabeth Macarthur Park, Telopea 279 F9
Elizabeth Macarthur Reserve, Camden South 507 C10
Elizabeth Park, Narellan Vale 478 J16
Elizabeth Park, Northbridge 286 G16
Elizabeth Park, Scotland Island 169 H3
Elkington Park, Balmain 7 B6
Ellerman Park, Dural 188 G11
Ellis Park, Miller 363 G16
Ellis Reserve, Ellis Lane 476 H1
Elms Reserve, Woollahra 22 B3
Elouera Reserve, Macquarie Park 282 E2
Eloura Nature Reserve, Liverpool 394 D3
Else Mitchell Park, Springwood 202 B1
E L S Hall Park, Marsfield 282 C6
Elvina Park, Elvina Bay 168 B3
Elyard Reserve, Narellan 478 G10
Embarkation Park, Potts Point 4 J2
Embrasure Reserve, Castlecrag 286 B12
Emerson St Reserve, Wetherill Park 334 J4
Emily McCarthy Park, South Coogee 407 G4
Empress Reserve, Hurstville 432 C8
Emu Park, Emu Plains 235 F10
Endeavour Park, Kings Langley 245 F5
Engadine Park 488 F15
Engesta Reserve, Camden 506 K6
Enmore Park, Marrickville 374 E9
Epping Oval 251 D11
Epworth Park, Elanora Heights 198 E12
Eric Green Reserve, Newport 170 A7
Eric Mobbs Park, Carlingford 280 A4
Eric Primrose Reserve, Rydalmere 309 K6
Eric Wood Reserve, Kenthurst 158 B16
Ernie Smith Recreation Area, Moorebank 396 B9
Erskineville Oval 18 E16
Erskineville Park 18 D15
Eskdale Reserve, Mount Annan 479 E12
E S Marks Memorial Field, Moore Park 20 J16
Esperance Reserve, Wakeley 334 K12
Esplanade Park, Fairlight 288 A10

Ethel Pyers Reserve, Greenacre 370 G12
Ettiesdale Reserve, Spring Farm 507 H6
Eugenie Byrne Park, Warragamba 353 G13
Eureka Cr Reserve, Sadleir 394 B3
Euston Park, Hurlstone Park 372 K12
Evatt Park, Bexley 432 D1
Everett Park, Liverpool 394 J8
Everley Park, Sefton 338 F12
Eve St Wetlands, Arncliffe 403 J11
Ewen Park, Hurlstone Park 372 K14
Ewenton Park, Balmain 8 D10
Excelsior Reserve, Baulkham Hills 248 B12
Excelsior Reserve, Baulkham Hills 248 D8
Excelsior Reserve, Castle Hill 248 D8
Excelsior Reserve, Northmead 248 D14
Excelsior Reserve, North Rocks 248 D14
Excelsior Reserve, West Pennant Hills 248 D8
Explosive Reserve, Castle Cove 286 F5
Fagan Park, Galston 159 G6
Fairfield Heights Park 336 A10
Fairfield Oval 336 G14
Fairfield Park 336 G15
Fairfield Rd Park, Yennora 336 F6
Fairfield Showground, Prairiewood 334 G10
Faulkland Cr Reserve, Kings Park 244 H2
Fay St Ground, North Curl Curl 258 F11
Fearnley Park, Beecroft 250 B6
Federal Park, Annandale 11 D8
Ferdinand St Reserve, Hunters Hill 313 J9
Ferndale Park, Chatswood West 284 D12
Fern Rd Reserve, Hunters Hill 314 A14
Fiddens Wharf Oval, Lindfield 283 E4
Fieldhouse Park, Ambarvale 511 A13
Field of Mars Wildlife Refuge, Ryde 312 K1
Field Park, Chipping Norton 396 G6
Fifth Av Reserve, Macquarie Fields 454 F5
Findlay Park, Mt Pritchard 364 E13
Fingleton Reserve, Bondi Junction 377 F3
First Fleet Park, The Rocks B A6
Firth Park, Ashcroft 394 F2
Fitzgerald Park, Homebush 341 C11
Fitzpatrick Park, Kensington 376 C15
Fitzpatrick Park, Picnic Point 428 C13
Fitzroy Gardens, Potts Point 4 K6
Fiveash Reserve, St Helens Park 541 A7
Five Dock Park 343 B9
Flagstaff Reserve, Rosemeadow 540 G8
Flat Rock Gully Reserve, Naremburn 315 H2
Fleming Playground, Newtown 17 E11
Flinders Field, Macquarie Fields 454 F1
Flinders Reserve, Camden South 506 K11

Flinders Slopes
Lansdowne 367 C10
Flockhart Park
Croydon Park 371 J9
Flood Reserve
Revesby 399 A9
Flora & Fauna Reserve
Hawkesbury Heights 174 H5
Flora & Richie
Roberts Reserve
Curl Curl 259 A12
Florence Cotton Park
Hornsby 221 C2
Florence Park
Newport 169 D7
Flynn Reserve
St Helens Park 541 F1
Flynns Reserve
Bexley 402 C16
Foley Reserve
Georges Hall 367 J14
Fontenoy Park
Macquarie Park 282 J1
Forbes Creek Reserve
Engadine 488 J11
Ford Park
Strathfield South 371 D7
Foreshore Reserve
Greenwich 314 K11
Forest Park
Epping 281 C1
Forest Redgum
Reserve
Glenmore Park 265 F6
Forestville Park 256 E9
Forestville
War Memorial
Playing Fields 255 J11
Formica Park
Busby 363 J15
Forrester Park
Epping 281 D4
Forrester Reserve
Kingsgrove 401 J9
Forshaw Field
Sylvania Waters 462 D15
Forsyth Park
Neutral Bay 6 B3
Foveaux Park
Parramatta 308 J1
Fowler Rd Park
Merrylands West 307 B16
Foxglove Oval
Mt Colah 162 F13
France Petanque Club
North Narrabeen 228 H3
Francis Park
Blacktown 244 E14
Francis Playground
Sydenham 374 E14
Francis St Park
Enmore 17 A16
Frappell Reserve
Narwee 400 G13
Fraser Park
Marrickville 374 C14
North Wahroonga 222 H1
Freame Park
Mays Hill 307 G6
Freda Park
Hammondville 396 B12
Fred Caterson Reserve
Castle Hill 217 E8
Fred Hollows Reserve
Randwick 377 D12
Fred Hutley Reserve
Naremburn 315 H4
Fred Spurway Reserve
Eastwood 280 F5
Fred Vassel Fields
Kings Langley 245 C6
Freeman Oval
Warwick Farm 365 F12
Freemans Reach Park 90 G3
Frenchs Forest
Showground 226 A16
Freres Crossing
Reserve
Kentlyn 483 G16
Freshwater Park
Strathfield 340 H16
Freshwater Reserve
Harbord 288 J2

Freya St Reserve
Kareela 461 D9
Friars Field
Pymble 223 F15
F Robertson Park
Dundas 279 C13
Frog Hollow
Centennial Park 21 E11
Frost Reserve
Narellan 478 G14
Frys Reserve
Kogarah 433 B2
F S Garside Park
Granville 308 H10
Fuchs Reserve
Elderslie 507 J1
Fullers Park
Chatswood West 284 A8
Fullers Rd Reserve
Chatswood West 284 E10
Fullwood Reserve
Claymore 481 F10
Eagle Vale 481 F10
Furber Park
Berowra Waters 132 E3
Gabo Park
Sadleir 394 A1
Gaden Park
Woollahra 22 D3
Gaiarine Gardens
Pagewood 405 J10
Galaringi Reserve
Carlingford 280 A5
Gallard Reserve
Greystanes 306 G7
Galston Park 159 D14
Gandangara Park
Casula 394 E16
Gannan Park
Ryde 282 F14
Gannons Park
Peakhurst 430 B8
Gap Park
Watsons Bay 318 H15
Gardenia Pde Park
Greystanes 306 B13
Gardiner Park
Banksia 403 C11
Gard Park
Ashcroft 364 F16
Garigal National Park
Belrose 226 D2
Davidson 224 H11
East Killara 254 J9
Forestville 256 E12
Frenchs Forest 255 G6
Ingleside 196 E14
Killarney Heights 255 H13
St Ives 224 K6
Seaforth 286 H1
Terrey Hills 196 E14
Garnet Jackson
Reserve
Botany 405 K12
Gayline Reserve
Mount Annan 479 C13
Gazzard Park
Yagoona 369 A11
George Caley Reserve
Mount Annan 509 G2
George Christie
Playing Field
Wahroonga 251 F3
George Harley
Reserve
Eastwood 280 K4
George Kendall
Riverside Park
Ermington 310 D5
Georges Heights Oval
Mosman 317 F10
Georges River
National Park
Alfords Point 429 A12
Illawong 459 D1
Lugarno 429 F15
Padstow Heights 429 C9
Picnic Point 428 F10
Georges River
Nature Reserve 454 A9
Airds 512 G9
Glenfield 424 J12
Kentlyn 484 A9

Georges River
Parkway Reserve
Airds 512 B14
Georges River
Softball Complex
Panania 397 F15
George W I Brown
Reserve
Quakers Hill 213 G12
Gibbs Park
Sadleir 364 C16
Gifford Park
Penshurst 431 C1
Gilbert Barry Reserve
Marrickville 373 F11
Gilchrist Oval
Campbelltown 511 A6
Gilgandra Reserve
North Bondi 348 C15
Gillespie Field
Warrawee 222 G9
Gilles Reserve
Beacon Hill 257 J5
Gillman Reserve
Yagoona 368 F12
Ginger Meggs Park
Hornsby 191 A16
Gipps Park
Smithfield 335 C5
Gipps Rd Oval
Greystanes 305 D14
Giriwa Picnic Ground
Oatley 430 H10
Girrahween Park
Earlwood 402 K5
Girraween Park
Toongabbie 276 A9
Glades Bay Park
Gladesville 312 G11
Gladesville Reserve
Henley 313 C13
Gladstone Park
Balmain 7 J10
Glenbrook
Native Plant
Reserve 234 B15
Glenbrook Oval 234 A15
Glenbrook Park 234 B16
Glendenning Reserve 242 H3
Glenfield Park 424 D11
Glenlee Reserve
Narellan Vale 508 F1
Glenmore Park
Jamisontown 266 F7
Glenorie Park 128 B3
Glenrock Reserve
Picton 563 G12
Glenroy Park
Claymore 481 C13
Glossodia Park
Freemans Reach 60 C13
Goanna Park
Greystanes 305 D14
Goddard Park
Concord 341 K9
Golden Grove Park
Kings Langley 245 B4
Golden Jubilee Field
North Wahroonga 223 B1
Gollan Park
Doonside 243 C14
South Coogee 407 G6
Goodacre Reserve
Fairfield West 335 B14
Gooden Reserve
Baulkham Hills 247 B16
Goodsells Field
Alexandria 375 B11
Gordon Park 254 A6
Gore Creek Reserve
Northwood 314 H7
Gore Hill Park
St Leonards 315 B5
Goroka Park
Beacon Hill 257 D8
Gosling Park
Greenacre 369 K10
Gough Whitlam Park
Earlwood 403 H2
Governor Phillip Park
Palm Beach 109 K14
Windsor 121 F6
Gowlland Reserve
Panania 398 D13

Gow Park
Mulgoa 205 F15
Graf Park
Yagoona 369 D10
Grange Avenue
Reserve
Schofields 212 F2
Granny Smith
Memorial Park
Eastwood 281 J6
Grantham Reserve
Seven Hills 275 E8
Grant Park
Enfield 371 H4
Grant Reserve
Coogee 407 H2
Granville Park
Merrylands 308 A14
Grasmere Reserve
Cremorne 316 E6
Gravestone Park
Rouse Hill 185 C8
Grays Point Oval 491 A14
Greenacre Heights
Reserve
Greenacre 369 J14
Green Ban Park
Erskineville 17 J13
Greendale Reserve
Greenwich 315 B9
Greenlees Park
Concord 342 A5
Green Park
Cammeray 316 B5
Darlinghurst 4 G12
Green Point Reserve
Oyster Bay 460 K5
Watsons Bay 318 D13
Greenup Park
Castle Hill 248 D1
Greenway
Kellyville 215 J1
Greenway Park
Cherrybrook 219 G8
Greenway Reserve
Camden South 507 B9
Revesby 398 E11
Greenwich Park 314 J14
Greenwich Pt Reserve
Greenwich 314 H13
Greenwood Park
North Ryde 282 D7
Greygums Oval
Cranebrook 207 B15
Griffith Park
Collaroy 229 D16
Longueville 314 F10
Griffiths Reserve
Camden South 507 B16
Grotto Pt Reserve
Balgowlah Heights 317 J2
Grove Park
Hurstville Grove 431 H9
Guildford Park 337 H2
Guilfoyle Park
Regents Park 369 B1
Gundungarra Reserve
Mount Annan 509 D2
Gundungurra Park
Belimbla Park 501 D14
Gundungurra Reserve
Narellan Vale 508 G2
Gunnamatta Park
Cronulla 493 J14
Gwandalan Reserve
North Ryde 283 C13
Gwarra Reserve
Forestville 255 H8
Gwawley Park
Sylvania Waters 462 H14
Gwendale Park
Eastwood 281 D5
Gymea Baths Reserve
Gymea Bay 491 G11
Gymea Bay Oval 491 D9
Hagan Reserve
Airds 511 K16
Haigh Park
Moorebank 395 J4
Halliday Park
Five Dock 342 J7
Hallstrom Park
Willoughby 285 F16

Ham Common
Bicentenary Park
Richmond 119 D7
Hamilton Park
Turramurra 252 E1
Hammond Park
Ashfield 342 H14
Hammondville Park 426 G2
Hampshire Reserve
Wakeley 334 J16
Hanna Laycock
Reserve
Bexley North 402 C13
Hanna Park
North Richmond 87 H14
Hannibal Macarthur
Park
Rydalmere 309 G2
Harbord Park 258 F14
Harbour View Park
Woollahra 22 G3
Harcourt Reserve
Campsie 371 H11
Haredale Reserve
Ambarvale 540 D2
Hargrave Park
Warwick Farm 365 F14
Harley Park
Mt Riverview 204 G14
Harnett Park
Mosman 316 G12
Harold Bull Reserve
Lakemba 402 D3
Harold Corr Oval
Cambridge Park 238 C10
Harold Fraser Reserve
Kogarah Bay 432 G12
Harold Moon Reserve
Auburn 338 J2
Harold Noakes
Reserve
The Oaks 502 G13
Harold Read Park
Girraween 275 K15
Harold Reid Reserve
Middle Cove 286 B8
Harold Reserve
Scotland Island 168 H5
Harold West Reserve
Carlingford 279 K1
Harrington Green
Elderslie 477 H14
Harrington Park 478 D5
Harris Creek Oval
Hammondville 426 J4
Harris Reserve
Harris Park 308 E7
Harry Dennison Park
Rooty Hill 242 C14
Harry Gapes Reserve
Merrylands 338 D2
Harry Lawler Park
Penrith 237 C11
Hartley Oval
Canley Vale 366 D4
Hart Park
Warwick Farm 365 H16
Harvey Brown Reserve
Blair Athol 511 A3
Harvey Dixon Reserve
Peakhurst 429 J4
Harvey Park
Marayong 243 K5
Hassell Park
St Ives 224 E6
Hastings Park
Castle Hill 218 K5
Haviland Park
Warragamba 353 D6
Hawken St Playground
Newtown 37 G10
Hawkesbury Park
North Richmond 87 E16
Hawkesbury Reserve
Sylvania Waters 462 G11
Hawkesbury
Showground
Richmond 119 H10
Hawthorne Canal
Reserve
Leichhardt 9 B13
Hayes Reserve
Ryde 311 H5

Hayter Reserve
  Camden South 506 H14
Hazlett Oval
  Macquarie Fields 454 A6
H C Press Park
  Castle Cove 286 F6
H D Robb Reserve
  Castle Cove 285 K3
Headen Park
  Thornleigh 220 K11
Heathcote
  National Park 517 J7
Heathcote Oval 518 G13
Heather King Park
  Cabramatta 366 D7
Heber Park
  Hebersham 241 G5
Heffron Park
  Maroubra 406 J13
Helen St Reserve
  Lane Cove West 284 G15
Helles Park
  Moorebank 395 D9
Henley Park
  Concord 341 J6
  Enfield 371 H5
Henningham
  Playground
  Greenwich 314 K7
Henri Dunant Reserve
  Ryde 282 C12
Henry Lawson Park
  Abbotsford 342 H2
Henson Park
  Marrickville 374 A10
Henty Park
  Yagoona 368 G9
Herald Square B A8
Herbert Crabtree
  Reserve
  Bass Hill 268 D9
Herbert Rumsey
  Reserve
  Dundas Valley 279 J7
Hercules St Reserve
  Dulwich Hill 373 D12
Heritage Dr Reserve
  Illawong 459 E3
Hermitage
  Foreshore Reserve
  Rose Bay 348 A6
Heron Park
  Chipping Norton 367 A14
Hewitt Park
  Bilgola 169 K4
Hews Reserve
  Belrose 226 A13
Heydon Park
  Hunters Hill 313 C11
  Rosemeadow 540 H6
Heynes Reserve
  Earlwood 372 G15
Hickeys Park
  Penrith 236 K4
Hickson Rd Reserve
  The Rocks 1 J6
Highfield Park
  Claymore 481 C11
Highlands Ridge
  Greenway
  Rouse Hill 185 D5
High St Reserve
  Mascot 405 C4
Hilder Reserve
  Elderslie 477 H15
Hillcrest Park
  Moorebank 396 C10
Hillier Oval
  Liverpool 395 B5
Hillside Park
  Glenbrook 234 E16
Hilltop Park
  Castle Hill 218 G7
Hind Park
  Chipping Norton 397 D6
Hinkler Park
  North Manly 288 F3
Hinsby Park
  Annandale 11 B12
Hitchcock Park
  Avalon 140 C12
H J Mahony
  Memorial Reserve
  Marrickville 403 E2
Hodgson Park
  Longueville 314 C8
Hogan Park
  Annandale 11 D13
Hogben Park
  Kogarah 433 C1
Holland Reserve
  Kenthurst 187 G11
Hollier Reserve
  Emu Plains 235 E13
Hollis Park
  Newtown 18 B10
Holloway Park
  Greenwich 315 A11
Holman Park
  Hornsby 191 K16
Holroyd Apex Park
  Greystanes 306 E11
Holt Park
  North Ryde 282 F6
Homelands Reserve
  Telopea 279 G7
Homepride Park
  Warwick Farm 365 D16
Homestead Park
  Chipping Norton 366 G12
Hopeville Park
  Hornsby 191 D8
Hopman St Park
  Greystanes 306 B10
Hordern Park
  Palm Beach 140 A2
Horlyck Reserve
  South Granville 338 H2
Hornsby Park 191 D15
Horsley Park 302 E15
Horton Reserve
  Burwood 372 A1
Hoskins Park
  Dulwich Hill 373 D8
Hospital Farm Reserve
  Northmead 277 J12
Howell Oval
  Penrith 236 E13
Howe Park
  Windsor 121 A7
Howley Park
  Drummoyne 313 F15
Howson Oval
  Turramurra 252 A1
Hoxton Park Reserve 393 B5
Hudson Park Oval
  Strathfield 340 G11
Hugh Bamford
  Reserve
  North Bondi 348 G16
Hughes Park
  Earlwood 402 E2
Hugh St Reserve
  Belmore 371 B12
Hume Oval
  Picton 563 F1
Hume Park
  Silverwater 309 H14
Hunter Park
  Bondi Beach 378 D5
Huntington Reserve
  Emu Plains 235 E14
Hunt Park
  Lakemba 401 D3
Hunt Reserve
  Mt Colah 162 F15
Hurley Park
  Campbelltown 511 G7
Hurstville Oval 431 K3
H V Evatt Park
  Lugarno 429 J13
Hyacinth Reserve
  Macquarie Fields 454 E5
Hycraft Park
  Five Dock 342 G9
Hyde Park
  Sydney D E10
Hyland Rd Park
  Greystanes 305 B12
Hyndes Park
  West Lindfield 283 J6
Ibbotson St Reserve
  Tahmoor 565 G10
Icely Park
  Richmond 119 D4
Ida Kennedy Park
  Green Valley 363 B12
Ilberry Park
  Neutral Bay 6 F5
Illawarra Reserve
  Leumeah 482 F14
Illoura Park
  Earlwood 402 F7
Illoura Reserve
  Balmain East 8 J9
Iluka Park
  Palm Beach 139 H3
Ingleside Park 198 D8
Innisfail Reserve
  Wakeley 334 K13
International
  Peace Park
  Seven Hills 275 D1
Inveresk Park
  Strathfield 341 A12
Ireland Park
  Liverpool 394 G3
Irelands Bridge
  Reserve
  Lansvale 366 B11
Irene Park
  Eastwood 281 G4
Iron Bark Reserve
  Colyton 270 J6
Ismay Reserve
  Homebush 341 D7
Ivanhoe Park
  Manly 288 F9
Ivanhoe Reserve
  Marsfield 251 J13
Jacka Park
  Harbord 258 G16
Jackett Reserve
  Burwood 341 H16
Jack Ferguson
  Recreation Area
  Greystanes 305 D13
Jack Nash Reserve
  Currans Hill 479 G11
Jackson Park
  Croydon Park 371 F7
  Faulconbridge 201 A1
  Woodbine 481 J7
Jacksons Rd Reserve
  North Narrabeen 199 B12
Jack Vanny
  Memorial Park
  Maroubra 407 K11
James Hoskin Reserve
  Eastwood 280 E6
James Meehan Park
  Macquarie Fields 454 C2
James Meehan
  Reserve
  Dee Why 259 A5
James Morgan
  Reserve
  Cromer 258 E1
James Park
  Hornsby 192 C15
  Lurnea 394 F7
James Ruse Park
  Ruse 512 G6
James Watkinson
  Reserve
  Pyrmont 10 G16
Jamieson Park
  Avalon 140 B14
  Casula 394 K15
  Narrabeen 228 E6
Jamison Park
  South Penrith 236 G14
Jannali Oval 460 F14
Jannali Reserve
  Bonnet Bay 460 C12
Jardine Park
  Casula 394 H14
Jarvie Park
  Marrickville 373 K11
Jasper Reserve
  Kenthurst 188 A8
Jegorow Reserve
  Haberfield 342 K12
Jelba Reserve
  Bangor 459 J11
Jellicoe Park
  Pagewood 406 F8
Jemina Jenkins Park
  Kearns 481 B2
Jenkins Park
  Penrith 237 D10
Jenola Park
  Woolooware 493 C8
Jensen Park
  Regents Park 368 J1
Jerome Dowling
  Reserve
  Eastlakes 406 A3
Jessie Stewart
  Reserve
  Concord 342 A5
Jessie Street Gardens
  Sydney B C9
J F Laxton Reserve
  Dulwich Hill 373 C9
J G McCartney
  Playground
  Ashfield 342 H15
Jim Crowgey Reserve
  Rydalmere 279 D15
Jim Ring Reserve
  Birrong 368 J3
Jindabyne Reserve
  Frenchs Forest 256 F2
J J Melbourne Hills
  Memorial Reserve
  Terrey Hills 196 D10
Joe Broad
  Memorial Park
  Mt Pritchard 364 K12
Joe McAleer Park
  Glendenning 242 J5
John Curtin Reserve
  Mascot 405 B5
  Winston Hills 277 H4
John Dwyer Park
  Caringbah 493 B9
John Fisher Park
  Wingala 258 G11
John Irving Park
  Harris Park 308 H8
John Knowles Park
  Merrylands West 306 G12
John Miller Park
  Ryde 282 G16
John Mountford
  Reserve
  Narwee 400 K11
John Paton Reserve
  Summer Hill 373 B4
John Peat Reserve
  Camden 507 C3
John Rider Reserve
  Minto 482 J10
John Roche Park
  Northbridge 316 C1
John Shore Park
  Maroubra 407 G12
Johnson Oval
  Newington College
  Stanmore 16 E13
Johnson Park
  Dulwich Hill 373 C8
Johnstone Reserve
  Revesby 398 G14
Johnston Park
  Canley Vale 366 C3
John Wearn Reserve
  Carlingford 249 E16
John Whitton
  Memorial Place
  Glenbrook 234 J10
Jones Park
  Parramatta 307 H6
Jones St Reserve
  Ryde 282 E15
Joseph Banks
  Native Plants
  Garden
  Kirrawee 461 E14
Josephine Park
  Moorebank 396 D12
Joseph Knox Park
  Pendle Hill 276 G11
Joshua Moore Park
  Sadleir 394 C3
J Peters Field
  Ruse 512 E5
Jubilee Park
  Bardwell Valley 402 K9
  Glebe 11 F7
  Mortdale 431 B9
  Parramatta 308 D5
Judges Park
  Penrith 236 H11
Jupp Reserve
  Eastwood 281 D4
J V McMahon
  Reserve
  Forest Lodge 11 D13
Kananga Reserve
  Kingswood 237 E8
Kanbyugal Reserve
  Woodbine 481 F14
Kangaroo Point
  Reserve 461 J4
Kanimbla Reserve
  Bilgola 169 J7
Kareela Oval
  Kirrawee 461 E16
Kareela Reserve
  Doonside 243 A15
Kareela Reserve West
  Doonside 242 K15
Kareena Park
  Caringbah 492 E8
Karuah Oval
  Turramurra 222 J11
Katandra
  Bushland Sanctuary
  Mona Vale 198 E1
Kathleen Reserve
  North Ryde 282 G9
Kayess Park
  Minto 452 H13
Keene Park
  Toongabbie 276 C9
Keep Reserve
  Castlecrag 286 A13
Keirle Park
  Manly 288 E4
Keith McKinnon Park
  Ermington 280 A15
Keith Smith Park
  Croydon 372 C3
Keith Willis Reserve
  Winston Hills 277 F2
Kelly Playground
  Newtown 18 A9
Kellys Bush
  Woolwich 314 D14
Kellyville Park 216 E9
Kelso Park
  Moorebank 396 A7
  Panania 397 H16
Kempt Field
  Hurstville 432 D6
Kendall St Reserve
  Sans Souci 463 A4
Kendrick Park
  Tempe 404 A4
Kenley Park
  Normanhurst 221 E9
Kennedy Park
  Bayview 168 D7
Kennett Park
  Glenfield 424 B13
Kensington Park 376 E16
Kenthurst Park 158 A5
Kentlyn Reserve 513 B6
Kent Oval
  North Turramurra 223 E9
Kentucky Reserve
  Bankstown Airport 397 D3
Kerry Park
  Blacktown 243 K16
Kessell Square
  Strathfield 340 J12
Kesterton Park
  North Sydney 6 E13
Kevin Wheatley
  Memorial Reserve
  Airds 512 B11
Kiah Reserve
  Clareville 169 D3
Kia Reserve
  Campbelltown 511 A2
Kibo Reserve
  Regents Park 339 D16
Killara Park 254 E9
Killara Reserve
  Panania 398 A14
Killarney Heights Oval 256 A15
Kilpack Park
  Carlingford 280 B1
Kimberley Park
  Rooty Hill 242 A14
Kinch Reserve
  Condell Park 398 C5

Mannix Park
Heckenberg ... 364 C14
Manns Point Park
Greenwich ... 315 A14
Manuka Reserve
Bass Hill ... 368 A10
Maraylya Park ... 124 G4
Marayong Oval ... 244 B7
Marconi Oval
Bossley Park ... 333 H9
Marden Reserve
Georges Hall ... 367 G12
Marella Avenue
Reserve
Kellyville ... 216 J2
Marine Park
Avalon ... 170 D3
Bilgola ... 170 D3
Marion Reserve
Yagoona ... 368 F15
Marjorie Park
Eastwood ... 281 J8
Marks Park
Tamarama ... 378 D6
Marrickville Park ... 373 J9
Marr Playground
Petersham ... 16 A12
Petersham ... 373 K6
Marsden Park
Campbelltown ... 511 B7
Marsfield Park ... 251 K15
Martin Knight Reserve
Kellyville ... 216 F3
Martin Reserve
North Ryde ... 283 B13
Martins Park
Springwood ... 202 C13
Marton Park
Kurnell ... 466 A9
Mary Howe Reserve
Narellan Vale ... 508 H2
Mary MacKillop Park
St Marys ... 269 F2
Mary O'Brien Reserve
Zetland ... 375 J10
Mary Wade Reserve
Woodbine ... 481 G11
Mascot
Memorial Park ... 405 D3
Mascot Oval ... 405 C3
Mascot Park ... 405 C3
Maserati Reserve
Ingleburn ... 453 G11
Masonic School Oval
Baulkham Hills ... 247 E13
Mason Park
Homebush ... 341 B4
South Windsor ... 120 G13
Mater Gardens
Crows Nest ... 5 C1
Matheson Park
Kurrajong ... 55 H15
Matraville Park
Maroubra ... 406 J15
Matthews Park
Greenacre ... 370 G8
Matt Hogan Reserve
Newtown ... 374 H9
Maundrell Park
Petersham ... 374 A6
Maurice Hughes
Reserve
Castle Hill ... 218 B12
Mawson Park
Campbelltown ... 511 F4
Max Ruddock Reserve
Winston Hills ... 277 B1
Maxwell Reserve
Bankstown ... 368 J15
May Cowpe Reserve
Rooty Hill ... 271 J4
Mays Hill Reserve ... 307 J5
Maze Park
West Ryde ... 280 J14
Meadowbank
Memorial Park ... 311 D5
Meadowbank Park ... 311 A3
Meere Park
Lurnea ... 394 C13
Melaleuca Reserve
Narellan Vale ... 478 J14
Melody Gardens
Seven Hills ... 246 D12
Melrose Park
Quakers Hill ... 243 G2
Melville Reserve
Homebush ... 340 H11
Memorial Oval
Ingleburn ... 453 C3
Memorial Park
Bankstown ... 399 E2
Kurrajong ... 85 E2
Matraville ... 407 B15
Merrylands ... 307 G12
Memorial
Playing Fields
Brighton-Le-Sands ... 433 H4
Memory Park
Mosman ... 316 K9
Memory Reserve
Sydenham ... 374 D15
Menai Park ... 458 J12
Menangle River
Reserve
Menangle Park ... 538 J11
Mercer St Reserve
Castle Hill ... 218 D15
Mereil Reserve
Campbelltown ... 511 K3
Merino Reserve
Airds ... 511 K16
Elderslie ... 507 G2
Merrett Playground
Waverton ... 315 E13
Merrylands Park ... 307 D11
Metcalfe Park
Moorebank ... 396 D9
Metella Reserve
Toongabbie ... 275 E13
Meyer Reserve
Oatley ... 430 J13
Michael Simpson
Reserve
Baulkham Hills ... 246 K11
Middle Creek Reserve
Narrabeen ... 228 A6
Middle Head Oval
Mosman ... 317 J6
Middleton Park
Yagoona ... 368 F10
Midgee Reserve
Marsfield ... 251 J13
Midlothian Reserve
St Andrews ... 452 B12
Mihkelson Reserve
Quakers Hill ... 214 B10
Miklouho-Maclay Park
Birchgrove ... 7 J2
Mildura Reserve
Campsie ... 372 B9
Mileham St
Netball Complex
South Windsor ... 120 G16
Milkmaids Reserve
North Turramurra ... 223 F7
Millennium Parklands
Homebush Bay ... 310 F8
Miller Park ... 393 G5
Miller Reserve
Ermington ... 310 E2
Millers Reserve
Manly Vale ... 287 K1
Mill Park
Liverpool ... 395 D9
Mills Park
Asquith ... 192 D11
Mill St Reserve
Riverstone ... 182 H6
Millwood Park
Lindfield ... 284 E3
Milperra Reserve ... 397 J10
Milray Reserve
Wollstonecraft ... 315 B10
Milson Park
Milsons Point ... 6 B13
Wentworthville ... 277 D13
Milton Park
Macquarie Fields ... 453 G3
Mimosa Rd Oval
Turramurra ... 252 F4
Minchinbury Reserve ... 271 J7
Minga Reserve
Ryde ... 282 F15
Minkara Reserve
Bayview ... 168 F12
Minnamurra Av
Reserve
Pymble ... 253 C8
Mirambeena
Regional Park
Lansdowne ... 367 A6
Miranda Park ... 491 J2
Mitchell Cr Oval
Turramurra ... 222 C16
Mitchell Park
Cattai ... 95 B6
Mitchell Reserve
Blacktown ... 275 A5
M J Bennett
Reserve
Westmead ... 307 E2
M Kenzie Field
Kingsford ... 407 B5
Mobbs La Reserve
Epping ... 280 F4
Model Farms Reserve
Northmead ... 277 J2
Model Farms
Siding Reserve
Northmead ... 278 A3
Moffatt Park
Lalor Park ... 245 J10
Molly Moore Park
Chipping Norton ... 396 G4
Mona Park
Auburn ... 338 J2
Monarch Field
Reserve
Macquarie Fields ... 453 K5
Monash Park
Gladesville ... 312 J6
Monash Reserve
East Hills ... 427 H5
Mona Vale
Headland Reserve ... 199 H3
Moncur Reserve
Woollahra ... 21 J2
Monfarville Reserve
St Marys ... 269 G6
Monro Park
Cronulla ... 493 K13
Montague Gardens
Stanmore ... 16 G11
Monteith Reserve
Baulkham Hills ... 247 D6
Montgomery Reserve
Padstow ... 428 K1
Montrose Reserve
Abbotsford ... 343 A1
Montview Park/oval
Hornsby Heights ... 161 E16
Monty Bennett Oval
Wentworthville ... 306 H3
Moolanda Av Reserve
West Pennant Hills ... 249 B9
Moore Park
Beverley Park ... 433 A9
Busby ... 363 J14
Eastwood ... 281 D5
Merrylands ... 307 E15
Moore Park ... 20 F4
Moore Reserve
Oatley ... 431 F11
Moorfield Hills
Reserve
Dural ... 219 A2
Morella Park
Palm Beach ... 140 B5
Morgan Park
Miller ... 393 G4
Morgan Power
Reserve
Kings Langley ... 245 B5
Mornington Reserve
Hunters Hill ... 314 B12
Morreau Reserve
Rooty Hill ... 272 G4
Morrison Bay Park
Putney ... 312 C8
Mort Bay Park
Birchgrove ... 7 K5
Mortlock Reserve
Cammeray ... 316 C3
Morton Park
Lewisham ... 15 C14
Morts Reserve
Woolwich ... 314 E14
Mount Annan
Botanic Garden ... 509 G7
Mountbatten Park
West Pymble ... 253 B14
Mount Druitt Park
Bonnyrigg ... 270 K3
Mount Druitt
Town Centre
Reserve ... 241 G15
Mt Kuring-gai Oval ... 162 J14
Mt Lewis Park ... 370 A16
Mt Pritchard Oval ... 364 E7
Mt Royal Reserve
Strathfield ... 341 A14
Mt Sion Park
Glenbrook ... 234 A11
Mt Wilberforce
Lookout Reserve
West Pennant Hills ... 249 J4
Mowbray Park
Lane Cove West ... 283 J12
Moxham Park
Northmead ... 277 J4
Mubo Park
Holsworthy ... 426 D3
Mulgoa Nature
Reserve
Glenmore Park ... 265 D8
Mulgoa Park ... 295 C15
Muller Reserve
Hillsdale ... 406 G13
Mundurama Reserve
Ambarvale ... 540 E2
Munn St Reserve
Millers Point ... A A2
Munro Park
Lurnea ... 394 E11
Northbridge ... 315 J1
Muogamarra
Nature Reserve
Cowan ... 75 A10
Murragan Reserve
Hinchinbrook ... 363 D15
Murray Farm Reserve
Carlingford ... 249 E12
Muston Park
Chatswood ... 285 D6
Mutch Park
Pagewood ... 406 D9
Nagle Park
Maroubra ... 406 J10
Nanbaree Reserve
Balgowlah Heights ... 287 J12
Nareen Reserve
North Narrabeen ... 198 J16
Narellan Park ... 478 B7
Naremburn Park ... 315 D3
Narnia Park
Alfords Point ... 459 A2
Narroy Park
North Narrabeen ... 198 H16
Natural Gas Square
Moore Park ... 21 B7
Navua Reserve
Grose Wold ... 116 F10
Navy Oval
Kingsford ... 407 E5
Neal Park
Hornsby ... 191 K16
Neat Reserve
Campsie ... 371 H14
Nemesia St Park
Greystanes ... 305 K12
Neptune Park
Revesby ... 428 K5
Nerang Park
Ryde ... 282 G14
Ness Park
Marrickville ... 373 G12
Neville Reserve
Bass Hill ... 368 D12
Newington Old Boys
Oval
Stanmore ... 16 F13
Newington Reserve
Silverwater ... 310 A10
Newington Road
Playground
Enmore ... 16 G15
Newland Reserve
Milperra ... 397 E10
Newlands La Reserve
Wollstonecraft ... 314 E10
Newlands Park
St Leonards ... 315 C7
Newport Heights
Reserve
Bilgola ... 169 E5
Newport Park ... 169 H11
Nichols Reserve
Lane Cove ... 314 A1
Nield Park
Rodd Point ... 343 E8
Nielsen Park
Vaucluse ... 348 A1
Nineveh Soccer Field
Edensor Park ... 364 A2
Nolan Oval
Rydalmere ... 279 K15
Nolan Reserve
North Manly ... 258 B16
Noorumba Reserve
Gilead ... 540 F10
Norfolk Reserve
Greenacre ... 370 E6
Norford Park
Sefton ... 338 G14
Norman Griffiths Oval
West Pymble ... 253 A11
Normanhurst Park ... 221 E7
Norman Park
Auburn ... 339 B9
Norman Peek Park
Penrith ... 237 B8
North Arm Reserve
Castle Cove ... 285 J6
Northbridge Park ... 286 D16
North Caringbah Oval
Caringbah ... 492 J4
Northcote Park
Greenacre ... 370 D9
North Epping Oval ... 251 J9
Northern Oval
Macquarie Park ... 252 D11
Northern Winter Field
Macquarie Park ... 252 E12
North Harbour
Reserve
Balgowlah ... 287 K10
Northmead Reserve ... 278 B4
North Narrabeen
Reserve
Warriewood ... 199 C12
North Parramatta
Reserve
Oatlands ... 279 A8
North Pymble Park
Pymble ... 223 D14
North Richmond Park ... 87 G12
North Rocks Park
Carlingford ... 249 E15
North Ryde Park ... 283 B12
North Sydney Oval ... 5 H2
North Turramurra
Oval ... 223 E4
Norton Russell
Reserve
Newtown ... 17 B11
Nott Oval
Narellan ... 478 F11
Nugent Park
Chester Hill ... 368 B2
Nundah Reserve
North Ryde ... 283 C12
Nunook Reserve
Marsfield ... 281 H3
Nurragingy Reserve
Doonside ... 242 J11
Nurra Reserve
Ambarvale ... 510 K14
Oakes Reserve
Old Toongabbie ... 277 A4
Oakleigh Park
Thornleigh ... 220 G11
Oak Park
Cronulla ... 524 A3
Oakville Reserve ... 122 G15
Oatley Heights Park
Mortdale ... 430 G10
Oatley Park ... 430 F11
Oatley
Pleasure Grounds ... 431 D14
Oatley Point Reserve
Oatley ... 461 D1
Oatley Reserve
Paddington ... 21 A2
O'Brien Park
Condell Park ... 398 J2

Riley Park
Airds 512 C11
Ringrose Park
Wentworthville 306 H2
Riverglade Reserve
Gladesville 313 B12
Riverine Park
Arncliffe 403 K10
River Rd Reserve
Emu Plains 236 A9
Revesby Heights 428 J9
River Reserve
Elderslie 507 D3
Riverstone Park 182 H9
Riverwood Park 399 J14
Rizal Park
Rooty Hill 241 J12
Rosemeadow 540 H3
R M Campbell
Reserve
Bankstown 366 G14
Roberta St Park
Greystanes 305 J6
Robertson Park
Watsons Bay 318 G14
Roberts Park
Greenacre 370 D14
Roberts Reserve
Five Dock 343 D8
Robertswood Park
Blaxland 234 C5
Robin Pl Reserve
Caringbah 492 K10
Robinson Park
Jamisontown 266 C3
Robin Thomas
Reserve
Parramatta 308 F4
Robson Park
Haberfield 9 A5
Rockdale Park 403 G15
Rock Farm Reserve
Dundas 279 E12
Rodd Park
Rodd Point 9 C1
Rodney Reserve
Dover Heights 348 G11
Rofe Park
Hornsby Heights 191 G7
Turramurra 252 G3
Roger Sheeran Oval
Macquarie Park 252 D12
Romney Park
Miller 393 J4
Ron Dine Reserve
Camden South 506 J11
Ron Gosling Reserve
Bardwell Park 403 A6
Ron Hill Park
Toongabbie 267 E7
Ron Routley Oval
Concord 311 J15
Rooty Hill
Central Park 272 D2
Rose Bay Park 347 F9
Rosedale Park
Warwick Farm 365 K16
Rosedale Reserve
Croydon Park 372 A9
Roselea Park
Beecroft 249 J12
Rosemeadow
Reserve 541 A2
Rose Park
Sefton 368 G6
Rosevale Reserve
Narellan 478 J12
Roseville Chase Oval 255 D15
Roseville Park 254 H16
Rosewood Oval
Waitara 221 H5
Rosford St Reserve
Smithfield 305 D16
Rosherville Reserve
Mosman 317 C2
Rosslyn Blay Park
Parramatta 278 E16
Rossmore Grange Park
Bringelly 389 D6
Rossmore Park 389 F15
Ross Reserve
Bangor 459 E14

Rotary Park
Condell Park 398 C2
Eastwood 281 G5
Kenthurst 158 B15
Ramsgate 433 F13
Riverwood 400 C11
Warwick Farm 365 G16
Rothwell Park
Concord 342 A6
Rouse Hill
Regional Park
Riverstone 184 B3
Rouse Hill 184 B3
Rowland Park
Daceyville 406 G5
Rowland Reserve
Bayview 169 C14
Rowley Park
Lansvale 367 A10
Roxborough Park
Rose Garden
Castle Hill 247 H4
Royal Botanic Gardens
Sydney B K12
Royal National Park 519 F3
Rozelle Common
Rozelle 10 H2
RSL Memorial Park
Picton 563 G2
Rubie Reserve
Malabar 437 G7
Ruddock Park
Westleigh 220 G8
Rudd Park
Belfield 371 F10
Ruse Park
Bankstown 399 F4
Rushcutters Bay Park
Darling Point 13 D8
Rushcutters Bay 13 D8
Russell Park
Drummoyne 343 E3
Rutherford Reserve
Burraneer 523 D5
R Whack Allen Field
Ingleburn 453 B4
Ryan Park
Chester Hill 337 J12
Ryan Playground
Enmore 16 G13
Rydalmere Park 309 F2
Ryde Park 312 B2
Sadleir Park 394 D1
Saggart Reserve
St Andrews 481 K2
Saiala Oval
East Killara 254 J7
Sailors Bay Park
Castlecrag 286 D13
St Andrews Oval
University of Sydney 18 A6
St Andrews Park 452 B16
St Crispens Green
Killara 283 D2
St Helens Park 541 B4
St Helens Park
Playing Fields
St Helens Park 541 C7
St Ives Showground 224 J1
St Ives Village Green 223 K12
St James Park
Glebe 11 K13
St Johns Oval
University
of Sydney 17 J3
St Johns Park
St Johns Park 364 C2
St Leonards Park
North Sydney 5 J1
St Lukes Park
Concord 342 C9
St Matthews
Farm Reserve
Cromer 228 D14
St Pauls Cobbitty
Reserve
Cobbitty 446 G15
St Pauls Oval
University
of Sydney 18 C5
St Peters Park
North Sydney K C12

St Pius X College
Playing Fields
Oxford Falls 227 A16
St Thomas
Rest Park
Crows Nest 315 H6
Salamaua Park
Holsworthy 426 D3
Sales Park
Luddenham 356 G3
Salmon Playground
Newtown 17 F15
Salton Reserve
Drummoyne 344 B3
Salt Pan Reserve
Padstow 399 H13
Samuel King Park
North Turramurra 223 D4
Samuel Marsden
Reserve
Orchard Hills 269 B8
Samuel Park
Vaucluse 348 E4
Sanananda Park
Holsworthy 396 D16
Sando Reserve
Croydon Park 371 J9
Sandringham Gardens
Sydney D F11
Sandstone Ridge
Centennial Park 21 K8
Sangrado Reserve
Seaforth 286 K10
Sans Souci Park 462 K6
Santa Rosa Park
Ryde 282 B10
Sassafra Park
Springwood 171 G16
Sassafras Gully
Reserve
Springwood 201 J8
Satelberg Park
Holsworthy 426 E4
Saunders Park
St Clair 270 A14
Sawmillers Reserve
McMahons Point 5 B14
Scarborough Park
Monterey 433 E10
Scattergood Reserve
St Helens Park 541 J1
SCEGS War Memorial
Playing Fields
Northbridge 285 H14
Schell Park
Liverpool 365 A15
Scheyville
National Park 123 E2
Schofields Park 183 D14
Scott Park
Sans Souci 463 C5
Scott Reserve
Roselands 400 E7
Scriven Reserve
Leumeah 482 A16
Scylla Bay Reserve
Como 460 J4
Seaforth Oval 286 J3
Seaforth Park
Bexley 403 A16
Searle Park
Telopea 279 G8
Seddon Park
Glenfield 424 B12
Sedgwick Reserve
Currans Hill 479 G11
Selkirk Park
Killara 254 A13
Sensory Garden
Lilyfield 9 F2
Septimus Reserve
Camden 507 A7
Settlers Park
Ryde 311 H6
Seven Little
Australians Park
Lindfield 254 G13
Seville Reserve
North Rocks 278 H3
Seymour Shaw Park
Miranda 492 A2
Shanes Park Reserve 209 F5
Shannon Reserve
Surry Hills 20 B2

Shark Park
Woolooware 493 E5
Shaw Park
Cambridge Park 238 B10
Sheas Field
Alexandria 374 K12
Sheldon Forest
Pymble 222 K16
Shell Park
Greenwich 314 K12
Shelly Beach Park
Manly 289 B10
Shelly Park
Cronulla 494 A16
Shepherd St Park
Colyton 270 C8
Sherwin Park
Canley Vale 366 E1
Sherwood Reserve
Quakers Hill 213 K12
Shields Playground
Leichhardt 9 C13
Shiprock
Aquatic Reserve
Port Hacking 523 B3
Shipwrights Bay
Reserve
Blakehurst 462 D4
Shortland Brush
Lansdowne 367 A5
Sickles Creek Reserve
Grasmere 475 J13
Sidney Smith Park
Westmead 307 G3
Sid Sharpe Oval
Oakdale 499 K13
Sid Teale
Memorial Grove
North Parramatta 278 G14
Sierra Pl Reserve
Baulkham Hills 246 G14
Signal Hill Reserve
Vaucluse 318 J16
Silverwater Park 309 K7
Simmons Point
Reserve
Balmain East 8 G6
Simmos Beach
Recreation Reserve
Macquarie Fields 454 J5
Simpson Hill Road
Reserve
Mount Druitt 270 K3
Simpson Park
St Peters 374 H12
Simpson Reserve
Canterbury 372 F14
Sir David Martin
Reserve
South Turramurra 252 B6
Sirius Cct Reserve
Narellan 478 F15
Sirius Cove Reserve
Mosman 316 K12
Sir Joseph Banks
Park
Botany 405 D13
Sir Robert Menzies
Park
Wahroonga 221 J16
Sir Thomas Mitchell
Reserve
Dundas Valley 280 B8
S J Harrison
Reserve
Earlwood 402 G6
Skarratt Park
Lapstone 234 H14
Skenes Reserve
Eastwood 280 H6
Skid Row Playground
Alexandria 375 A11
Skillinger Park
Busby 363 J16
Slade Rd Reserve
Bardwell Park 402 H7
Smalls Reserve
Grasmere 475 H16
Smart Av Reserve
Camden South 507 B16
Smithfield Park 336 B5
Smith Park
Castlereagh 176 A5
East Hills 427 J3
Richmond 118 E2

Smith Reserve
Kingsgrove 401 J11
Smiths Creek Reserve
Campbelltown 512 E1
Leumeah 512 E1
Ruse 512 E1
Smoothey Park
Wollstonecraft 315 B9
Smyths Field
Alexandria 375 A12
Snape Park
Maroubra 406 J7
Snapperman Beach
Reserve
Palm Beach 139 H1
Snowy Park
Heckenberg 364 A14
Snowy Reserve
Seven Hills 275 E10
Solander
Playing Fields
Woolooware 493 D5
Soldiers
Memorial Park
East Killara 254 G12
Somerset Park
Marsfield 251 H13
Somerville Park
Eastwood 281 C4
Sophia Doyle Reserve
Baulkham Hills 247 A10
Soudan St Playground
Paddington 13 H14
South Creek Park
St Marys 239 E13
South Down Reserve
Elderslie 507 H2
Southlands Oval
South Penrith 266 J4
South Park
Chipping Norton 366 D14
South Sydney
Rotary Park
Eveleigh 18 D13
Spain Reserve
Castle Hill 218 D9
Spencer St Reserve
Berala 339 C15
Springfield Gardens
Potts Point 4 J5
Springfield Park
Old Guildford 337 E8
Spring Reserve
Spring Farm 508 A6
Spring St Reserve
Dural 188 K13
Stafford Walk
Earlwood 403 C1
Stanhope Reserve
Stanhope Gardens 215 E8
Stanmore Reserve 16 F9
Stan Moses Reserve
Sans Souci 463 D5
Stan Thomson
Reserve
St Andrews 452 B13
Stanwell Oval
Ashcroft 394 F3
Stapleton Park
Avalon 139 K14
Starr Reserve
Camden 506 J8
Startop Reserve
Ambarvale 510 J14
Steel Park
Marrickville South 403 F1
Stevens Reserve
Bankstown 399 G2
Oatley 430 J11
Stewart Park
Marsfield 251 J16
Stewart St Reserve
Parramatta 308 F2
Steyne Park
Double Bay 14 C6
Stockdale Cr Reserve
Abbotsbury 333 C13
Stockmans Drift
Mount Annan 479 J15
Stoney Range Reserve
Camden South 507 D16
Stony Range
Flora Reserve
Dee Why 258 F8

Storey Park
Hornsby 191 H10
Stotts Reserve
Bexley North 402 G8
Strathfield Park 371 C1
Strathfield Square 341 G12
Stringybark Creek
Reserve
Lane Cove West 284 E15
Stromeferry Reserve
St Andrews 481 J4
Stromlo Reserve
Ruse 215 F4
Strong Park
Lansvale 366 K11
Stuart Park
Blakehurst 432 D16
Stuart St Reserve
Padstow 399 G13
Sturt Reserve
Georges Hall 367 K15
Telopea 279 H11
Styles St Playground
Leichhardt 10 F16
Summerhayes Park
Winmalee 173 C8
Summit Reserve
Mt Riverview 204 H15
Sunderland Park
Raby 451 F15
Sun Valley Reserve
Valley Heights 202 K6
Surf Reserve
North Curl Curl 259 A11
Surrey Reserve
Georges Hall 368 B15
Surveyors Creek
Public Reserve
Glenmore Park 266 E10
Sutherland Ovals 490 C1
Sutton Reserve
Earlwood 372 H14
Swain Gardens
Lindfield 254 E13
Swallow Rock Reserve
Grays Point 491 D16
Swan Reserve
Rosehill 308 H5
Sydney Field
Holsworthy 426 D6
Sydney Harbour
National Park
Balgowlah Heights 288 B13
Clontarf 317 H1
Goat Island 8 J3
Manly 289 B13
Mosman 317 H9
Vaucluse 347 J2
Watsons Bay 318 F13
Clarke Island 347 B7
Rodd Island 343 J7
Shark Island 347 H5
Sydney Park
St Peters 374 K12
Sydney University
Park
Brownlow Hill 475 F2
Sylvania Heights
Reserve
Sylvania 461 H14
Syme Park
Moorebank 396 D10
Symonds Reserve
Ingleburn 453 J9
Tahmoor Park 566 C7
Tait St Park
Smithfield 336 B1
Talavera Reserve
Marsfield 252 B13
Talinga Park
Carlingford 280 B4
Tallawang Rd Reserve
Forestville 255 D8
Tallawong Oval
Blacktown 273 H2
Taloma Park
South Penrith 237 A15
Talus Reserve
St Leonards 315 D3
Tamarama Park 378 B6
Tambourine Bay
Reserve
Riverview 314 A7

Tamplin Fields
Richmond 118 D8
Tandarra Reserve
Shalvey 210 J13
Tania Park
Balgowlah Heights 287 K15
Tantallon Oval
Lane Cove West 284 A15
Taplin Park
Drummoyne 343 G1
Tarakan Reserve
Rosebery 376 H16
Tarlington Reserve
Bonnyrigg 364 C3
Tasker Park
Canterbury 372 E13
Taunton Reserve
Blakehurst 432 D12
Ted Burge
Sportsground
Merrylands 307 A8
Ted Horwood Reserve
Baulkham Hills 248 C11
Tempe
Recreation Reserve 404 B5
Tench Reserve
Jamisontown 235 G14
Penrith 235 G14
Regentville 265 D1
Tennyson Park
Lane Cove 314 A3
Tennyson 312 D10
Terone Park
Bossley Park 334 B8
Terrace Park
Freemans Reach 89 E6
Terrey Hills
Playing Fields 196 E6
Terrigal Reserve
Terrey Hills 196 C7
Terry Lamb Reserve
Belmore 371 G16
The Breakaway Ovals
Freemans Reach 91 E14
The Charles
McLaughlin
Recreation Reserve
Baulkham Hills 246 K3
The Clive Evatt
Reserve
Turramurra 222 K6
The Dalrymple-Hay
Nature Reserve
St Ives 223 H15
The Domain
Sydney D K2
The Eric Mobbs
Recreation Reserve
Castle Hill 248 D6
The Esplanade
Cronulla 494 B15
The Glade Reserve
Wahroonga 222 C9
The Glen
Bushland Reserve
Bonnet Bay 460 E9
The Green
Blakehurst 432 A15
The Harry Noble
Reserve
Erskineville 18 D15
The Joseph Bugler
Playing Field
Waverton 315 E13
The Kingsway
Playing Fields
Werrington 239 C13
The Knoll
Northbridge 286 F14
The Lakes
Cherrybrook 219 J9
The Lilian Fraser
Garden
Pennant Hills 220 E15
Thella-Kenway
Reserve
Bankstown 368 H16
The Lookout
Turramurra 222 J14
The Rampart
Hornsby 221 C5
The Reg Bartley
Oval
Rushcutters Bay 13 C7

The Spit Reserve
Mosman 287 C14
The Village Green
Beecroft 250 F7
Kensington 376 G15
The Walter Read
Reserve
Paddington 21 B1
The William Cowan
Oval
St Ives 223 J11
Thew Reserve
Strathfield 371 A2
The Zig Zag
Balmain East 8 F7
Third Settlement
Reserve
Winston Hills 277 B5
Thirlmere Lakes
National Park 564 A8
Thirlmere
Memorial Park 565 A3
Thomas Acres
Reserve
Ambarvale 540 H1
Thomas Atkins Walk
Macquarie Fields 454 A5
Thomas Bourke
Reserve
Blairmount 481 B13
Thomas Clarkson
Reserve
Eagle Vale 481 C7
Thomas Extrem
Reserve
Baulkham Hills 247 B11
Thomas Hogan
Reserve
Bondi 377 K2
Thomas Moore Park
Chipping Norton 396 B4
Thomas Park
Blaxland 233 J6
Thomas Thompson
Park
Cherrybrook 219 J14
Thomas Wemyss
Park
Ermington 280 C14
Thomas Williams
Reserve
North Parramatta 278 E12
Thompsons Bay
Reserve
Illawong 460 D2
Thomson Park
Artarmon 284 K16
Thorley Park
Smithfield 335 K6
Thornleigh Park 221 C15
Thornleigh Reserve
Narellan Vale 479 B13
Thornton Park
Balmain East 8 H8
Thornton Playground
Bellevue Hill 347 H14
Thornton Reserve
Bass Hill 368 C12
Thorpe Park
Hurstville 401 H15
Padstow Heights 429 H8
Throsby Reserve
Ambarvale 511 A12
Thurina Park
Villawood 367 H5
Tillman Park
Tempe 374 C15
Timbergetters Reserve
Winston Hills 277 D1
Timbrell Park
Five Dock 343 D11
Tindal Reserve
Mount Annan 479 G16
Tindarra Reserve
North Ryde 282 C7
Tingira Reserve
Rose Bay 348 A10
Titalka Park
Moorebank 395 D13
Tobin Park
Telopea 279 F7
Tobruk Reserve
Narellan Vale 479 B11

Toby Reserve
Panania 398 B12
Todd Park
Blakehurst 432 E15
Tom Hunter Park
Faulconbridge 171 G15
Tom Kenny Reserve
Marrickville 373 E13
Tom Uren Park
Guildford West 336 G2
Tonbridge St Reserve
Ramsgate 433 F12
Tonkin Park
Cronulla 493 J12
Toolang Playing Field
St Ives Chase 223 K6
Topin Park
Moorebank 396 C11
Torry Burn Reserve
Baulkham Hills 247 D9
Towards Park
Macquarie Fields 454 E5
Tower Reserve
Castlecrag 286 C11
Townson Oval
Minto 482 H5
Towra Point
Aquatic Reserve
Kurnell 464 D3
Towra Point
Nature Reserve
Kurnell 464 D8
Tracey Reserve
Revesby 398 D11
Trafalgar Park
Newport 169 F12
Trafalgar Reserve
Marsfield 252 A14
Treelands Walk
Ingleburn 453 E9
Tregear Reserve 240 D7
Trenerry Reserve
Coogee 407 J3
Trewartha Park
Lurnea 394 C10
Trim Place
Gladesville 312 J10
Troubador Park
Kings Langley 246 D9
Truman Reserve
Cromer 227 J12
Trumper Oval
Paddington 13 G12
Trumper Park
Paddington 13 G13
Trumper Park
Playground
Paddington 13 G12
Tucker Reserve
Bass Hill 368 D12
Tuckwell Park
Macquarie Park 283 A2
Tumbalong Park
Sydney E A1
Tunks Park
Cammeray 316 A2
Tunnel Gully
Lapstone 264 F1
Turnbull Reserve
Box Hill 154 B16
Turramurra
Memorial Park 222 K10
Turramurra Oval 222 J11
Turrella Reserve
Earlwood 403 C4
Turrett Reserve
Castlecrag 286 A13
Turrumburra Park
Lane Cove West 284 A16
Turruwul Park
Rosebery 375 H16
Twin Creeks Reserve
Turramurra 222 B16
Wahroonga 222 B16
Twin Gums Reserve
Lalor Park 245 H11
Two Turners Reserve
Lindfield 284 C3
Tyagarah Park
Ryde 312 D6
Tynan Park
Ermington 280 C12
Tyrell Park
Ryde 282 H16

Uhrs Pt Reserve
Rhodes 311 F6
Ulmarra Park
North Ryde 283 H11
Ulundri Dr Reserve
Castle Hill 218 B9
University
Basin Reserve
Campbelltown 510 H6
University of Sydney
Ovals 18 A4
Upjohn Park
Rydalmere 279 K14
Upper Point Park
Pyrmont 8 F14
Utz Reserve
Drummoyne 313 H15
Vale Brook Reserve
Eschol Park 481 C3
Valentine Park
Glenwood 245 K2
Vale of Ah Reserve
Milperra 397 B7
Vale Reserve
Narellan Vale 478 K10
Valerie Park
Eastwood 281 C9
Valley View Reserve
Narellan 478 B8
Varna Park
Waverley 377 G10
Vasta Park
Moorebank 396 E13
Vaucluse Park 348 C3
Vesta Reserve
Milperra 397 E12
Victor Brazier Park
Guildford 338 B7
Victoria Park
Camperdown 18 F3
Minto 452 G15
Picton 563 G6
Queens Park 22 K14
St Marys 269 F1
Victoria St Park
Wetherill Park 335 A2
Victoria Wharf
Reserve
Watsons Bay 318 E13
Victory Reserve
Engadine 488 K14
Village Green
Bella Vista 246 F3
Liberty Grove 311 C14
West Pymble 252 J11
Villiers Reserve
Padstow Heights 429 G6
Vineyard Creek
Reserve
Dundas 279 E10
Vineyard Park 152 B3
Virginius Reserve
Padstow 429 A2
Voyager Park
Voyager Point 427 C4
Wabash Reserve
Cromer 228 D13
Wahroonga Park 222 D6
Waitara Park 221 K3
Wallis Reserve
Strathfield 371 B1
Wall Reserve
Panania 398 C12
Wallumatta
Nature Reserve
North Ryde 282 K14
Walpole St Park
Holroyd 307 K10
Walsh Av Reserve
Croydon Park 371 F8
Walshaw Park
Bass Hill 368 D8
Walsh Park
Eastwood 281 E6
Walter Gors Park
Dee Why 258 J5
Waminda Reserve
Campbelltown 512 C4
Leumeah 512 C4
Wanda Reserve
Cronulla 494 D6
Wandoo Reserve
Ryde 311 K3

Wangal Centenary
Bushland Reserve
Mortlake 311 K11
Wanstead Reserve
Earlwood 403 G1
Waratah Park
Duffys Forest 194 G4
Sutherland 490 D6
Ward Park
Surry Hills 20 A4
Warimoo Oval 203 H11
War Memorial
Pitt Town 92 H15
War Memorial Park
Leichhardt 10 E11
Warmul Oval
Greystanes 305 D15
Warners Park
Castlecrag 285 K13
Warragamba Park
Mulgoa 323 J10
Warraroon Reserve
Longueville 314 D5
Warrawong Reserve
Eastwood 280 J11
Warren Park
Marrickville South 403 H1
Warren Try Reserve
Merrylands 307 F15
Warrimoo Oval
St Ives Chase 224 A3
Warrina St Oval
Berowra 133 D9
Warringa Park
Neutral Bay 6 A7
Warwick Farm
Recreation Reserve ... 365 H12
Wascoe Park
Glenbrook 233 G14
Waterfall Oval 519 E13
Waterloo Park
Marsfield 252 A14
Waterloo 19 F14
Waterworth Park
Earlwood 403 J3
Waterworth Reserve
Narellan Vale 479 B14
Wattawa Reserve
Condell Park 398 G1
Wattlebird
Bushland Reserve
Caringbah 493 A13
Wattle Grove Park 396 A16
Watt Park
McMahons Point .... K D16
Watts Park
Ryde 281 K8
Waverley Park
Bondi Junction 377 H4
Waverton Park 315 E13
Weaver Park
Mosman 316 F9
Webbs Av
Playing Fields
Auburn 338 H5
Weekley Park
Stanmore 16 G7
Weil Park
Woolwich 314 D13
Weir Reserve
Penrith 236 D6
Weldon Park
Curl Curl 258 G12
Wellings Reserve
Balgowlah 287 K11
Wentworth Park
Ultimo 12 F9
Wentworth Reserve
Homebush 341 A6
Werrell Reserve
Abbotsford 312 K15
Werrington Creek Park
Cambridge Park 238 C10
West Epping Park 250 F15
Western Sydney
Regional Park
Horsley Park 332 J5
Westland
Memorial Park
Ingleburn 453 G4
Westminster Park
Gladesville 312 J5
Wetherill Park 334 J2
Whalan Reserve 240 F10

Wheat Park
Sadleir 364 B16
Wheeler Park
Lalor Park 245 D13
Narrabeen 228 K7
Whelan Reserve
Paddington 21 F5
Whiddon Reserve
Croydon Park 371 G9
Whitely Reserve
Stanmore 16 J7
Whitemore Reserve
Georges Hall 367 G11
Whiteoak Reserve
Brighton-Le-Sands 403 J14
White Oval
Kings School
North Parramatta 278 K7
Whites Creek
Valley Park
Annandale 10 J8
Leichhardt 10 J8
Whitlam Park
Busby 363 J12
Whitton Park
Glenbrook 233 K15
W H Wagener Oval
Ashbury 372 F6
Wicks Park
Marrickville 374 C12
Widemere Reserve
Greystanes 305 H12
Wiggins Park
Springwood 201 H10
Wilberforce Park 91 B1
Wild Flower Sanctuary
Warragamba 353 E7
Wildlife Sanctuary
North Rocks 279 A4
Wiley Park 400 J5
Wilga Park
Macquarie Park 282 E3
Wilkes Park
Moorebank 396 D11
William Howe Reserve
Narellan Vale 508 K3
William Joyce Reserve
Baulkham Hills 246 G11
William Lawson Park
Prospect 274 J10
William Lewis Park
Wahroonga 222 B12
Williams Park
Chipping Norton 396 E5
North Bondi 378 H2
Williams Reserve
Dundas 279 F14
Willis Park
Castle Cove 285 G5
Oakdale 500 E13
Willow Park
Lansvale 367 A9
Willow Tree Park
Neutral Bay 6 A6
Wills Ground
Earlwood 373 C14
Wills Playground
Kensington 376 D11
Willunga Reserve
Hurstville Grove 431 H12
Wilson Cr Reserve
Narellan 478 C11
Wilson Oval
St Marys 269 F4
Wilson Park
Llandilo 208 G5
Silverwater 310 A7
Wilton Reserve
Narellan 478 E11
Wiltshire Park
Palm Beach 139 K2
Windsor Downs
Nature Reserve 150 E11
Wingala Reserve
North Curl Curl 258 J8
Winji Jimmi Park
Mona Vale 169 D13
Winjoy Reserve
Dundas 279 C14
Winnal Reserve
Green Valley 363 D13
Winsor Park
Greenacre 369 J9

Wise Reserve
Riverwood 400 F11
Withers Rd Reserve
Kellyville 185 C9
Wollemi
National Park
Kurrajong Heights 53 H1
Wolseley St Reserve
South Granville 338 D4
Wonga Rd Reserve
Yowie Bay 492 B10
Woodbury Reserve
Glossodia 59 A7
Woodlands Park
Wilberforce 62 G14
Wood Park
Bankstown 369 G11
Ingleburn 453 E9
Woodriff Gardens.
Penrith 236 E8
Woodside Park
Hinchinbrook 362 J15
Woods St Reserve
North Epping 251 G7
Wood St Reserve
Epping 281 E3
Woodville Park
Hurstville 432 C5
Woodville Reserve
Villawood 367 D5
Woodward Park
Liverpool 395 A6
Woolcott Park
Newport 169 G11
Woollahra Oval
Rose Bay 347 K13
Woollahra
Playing Fields
Rose Bay 347 K12
Woolooware Oval 493 F10
Woolway Park
Meadowbank 311 D2
Woomera Reserve
Little Bay 437 A10
Woorarra Lookout
Reserve
Elanora Heights 228 D1
Worrell Park
Ruse 512 E5
Wright Reserve
Quakers Hill 214 A16
Writtle Park
Randwick 376 K14
Wrixton Park
Kirribilli 6 C14
W V Scott
Memorial Park
Austral 391 D16
Wyangala Reserve
Leumeah 482 G13
Wyatt Park
Lidcombe 339 G5
Wyatt Reserve
Belrose 225 K9
Wylde Park
Greenfield Park 334 A13
Wynyard Park
Sydney .... A G15
Yamble Reserve
Ryde 282 B12
Yarra Bay
Bicentennial Park
Phillip Bay 436 H10
Yarranabbe Park
Darling Point 13 H3
Yarran St Reserve
Pymble 253 B8
Yarra
Recreation Reserve
Phillip Bay 436 J10
Yarrawarrah Reserve 489 F14
Yatama Park
Campsie 402 A4
Yattenden Park
Baulkham Hills 247 J13
Yellow Rock Reserve 175 A14
Yeo Park
Ashfield 373 A8
Yeramba St Reserve
Turramurra 252 D3
Yinnell Reserve
North Ryde 283 C11
York Park
Berala 339 C12

York St Park
Tahmoor 565 K9
Young Place Reserve
South Hurstville 432 A11
Yulong Oval
Moorebank 395 E12
Yulong Playing Fields
Moorebank 395 F12
Yurrah Reserve
Macquarie Park 282 J2
Yurulbin Park
Birchgrove 315 A16

PLACES OF INTEREST

Addington Museum
(Sunday Afternoons)
813 Victoria Rd
Ryde 311 H2
Admiralty House
Kirribilli Av
Kirribilli 2 E4
Ahimsa Sanctuary
Day Rd
Cheltenham 251 B7
Animal Quarantine
Station
Eastern Creek 272 F10
Animal Welfare League
Herley Av
Rossmore 390 E3
ANSTO
New Illawarra Rd
Lucas Heights 487 H13
Anzac War Memorial
Hyde Park .... F E1
Archibald Fountain
Hyde Park .... D E8
Argyle Art Centre
The Rocks .... A J3
Arms of Australia
Inn (Museum)
cnr Gardenia Av &
Great Western Hwy
Emu Plains 235 H8
Art Gallery of NSW
The Domain 4 D2
Auburn
Botanic Gardens
cnr Chisholm &
Chiswick Rds 338 H6
Audley
Royal National Park 520 C7
Australiana Park
Camden Valley Wy
Catherine Field 450 A11
Australian Motor
Vehicle Museum
Harris St
Ultimo 12 J7
Australian Museum
College St .... D H14
Australian National
Maritime Museum
Darling Harbour 12 K3
Australian
Technology Park
Eveleigh 18 J11
Australian
Wildlife Park
Wallgrove Rd
Eastern Creek 272 C14
Australias First
Observatory
Parramatta 307 K2
Australia Square
cnr Bond &
Pitt Sts .... A J14
Austral Watergardens
Pacific Hwy
Cowan 104 H8
Aviation Museum
Harrington Park 478 G8
Bahai Temple
Ingleside 197 G8
Balmain Watch House
Darling St 8 B9

Bankstown
Aviation Museum
cnr Henry
Lawson Dr &
Milperra Rd
Bankstown 397 F5
Bare Island
La Perouse 436 H16
Barrenjoey Lighthouse
Palm Beach 110 B9
Bethlehem Monastery
Narellan Rd
Campbelltown 510 J2
Bicentennial Park
Homebush 311 A15
Blacktown City
Bicentennial
Museum
Blacktown 182 K7
Blue Gum Farm
Maxwell Av
Milperra 397 E14
Blue Pool
Glenbrook 263 K4
Springwood 202 B16
Bobbin Head
Ku-Ring-Gai Chase
National Pk 163 H12
Bondi Pavilion
Bondi Beach 378 E3
Botanical Gardens
Regreme Rd
Picton 563 F1
Braemar House
Springwood 202 A3
Bushrangers Cave
Silverdale 384 D12
Bus & Truck
Museum
Gannon St
Tempe 404 B2
Butterfly Farm
Wilberforce Rd
Wilberforce 91 J7
Cable
Water Ski Park
Panther Pl
Penrith 236 C13
Cadmans Cottage
110 George St .... B A3
Camden Park
Homestead
Camden South 508 B16
Cammeray
Suspension Bridge 315 K2
Campbelltown City
Bicentennial
Art Gallery
Art Gallery Rd 511 C7
Campbelltown
Steam Museum
Gilead 509 H16
Canterbury
Sugar Works
Sugar House Rd 372 G14
Captain Cooks
Landing Place
Kurnell 466 C5
Carss Cottage
Carss Park 432 H16
Casula Powerhouse
Arts Centre
1 Casula Rd
Casula 395 A15
Cenotaph
Martin Place .... C J2
Centennial Parklands
Centennial Park 21 H10
Central Gardens
Merrylands West 306 H11
Central Railway Station .... E H13
Chinatown
Dixon St .... E D4
Chinese Gardens
Darling Harbour .... E B3
Circular Quay .... B D6
Clarinda Falls 201 A5
Commodore Heights 109 A7
Convention Centre
Darling Harbour 3 A6
Cook Obelisk
Kurnell 466 D6
Cooks Landing Place
Museum 466 E6

INFORMATION

Crusader Union Centre Crusader Rd Galston 160 G14
CSIRO Research Station Badgerys Creek 328 F8
Cumberland State Forest West Pennant Hills 249 F3
Customs House Alfred St B D9
Darling Harbour C A16
Darlinghurst Court & Old Gaol Oxford St 4 E13
Dee Why Lagoon Wildlife Refuge 258 K3
Dobroyd Head Scenic Area Balgowlah Heights 288 B14
Dr H J Foley Memorial Glebe 12 B13
Dunmore House Dunmore St Pendle Hill 276 F15
Edgar Gornall Wildflower Gardens Edgecliff Bvd Narrabeen 228 K8
E G Waterhouse National Camellia Gardens President Av Caringbah 492 E7
El Alamein Fountain Kings Cross 4 K6
El Caballo Blanco Camden Valley Wy Catherine Field 450 B11
Elizabeth Bay House 7 Onslow Av 13 A3
Elizabeth Farmhouse Alice St Rosehill 308 H6
Elizabeth Macarthur Agricultural Institute Menangle 537 H9
Endeavour Light La Perouse 438 A14
Eryldene House & Garden 17 McIntosh St Gordon 253 K9
Exchange Centre 20 Bond St A K13
Experimental Farm Cottage Ruse St Harris Park 308 G5
Fairfield City Farm Abbotsbury 332 J13
Fairfield Regional Heritage Centre 632 The Horsley Dr Smithfield 336 A5
Farm Cove Sydney 2 E11
Featherdale Wildlife Park 217 Kildare Rd Doonside 243 H14
Federation Pavilion Centennial Park 22 A9
Fish Markets Gipps St Pyrmont 12 F6
Fitzroy Bridge Windsor 121 E8
Fleurs Radio Observatory Field Station Kemps Creek 329 K15
Fort Denison (Pinchgut) Sydney Harbour 2 J6
Fragrance Garden Sydney D J12
Galston Gorge 160 J16
Gardens of Many Nations Fagan Park Galston 159 F6
Garrison Church Argyle Place A F2
General Post Office (GPO) Martin Place C K3
Gilroy House Manly 288 J14
Gladesville Bridge 313 G14
Gledswood Homestead Camden Valley Wy Catherine Field 450 D9
Government House Sydney Cove B J4
Governors Bathhouse Parramatta 307 K2
Governors Dairy Parramatta 277 K15
Green Point Astronomical Observatory Oyster Bay 460 K5
Greycliffe House Vaucluse 343 A2
Hall of Champions State Sports Centre Homebush Bay 340 H4
Hambledon Cottage Hassall St Harris Park 308 G5
Harbour Ferry Wharves B D5
Harrington Park Homestead 478 H2
Hawkebury Heritage Farm Buttsworth La Wilberforce 91 K6
Hawkesbury River Railway Bridge 76 E5
Hills Centre Carrington Rd Castle Hill 217 F12
Hornby Lighthouse Watsons Bay 318 F9
Horseworld Stadium Maraylya 125 B14
Hurstville Historical Museum 319 Forest Rd 431 H5
Hyde Park Sydney D E10
Hyde Park Barracks Macquarie St D G6
Information Centre Great Western Hwy Glenbrook 234 B16
Ingleburn Military Camp 423 C12
Jackeroo Ranch Kenthurst 125 F10
Jackson Falls 235 F2
James Beres Bridge Silverdale 384 C3
Japanese Gardens cnr Chisholm & Chiswick Sts Auburn 338 J6
Jellybean Pool 263 K8
Jewish War Memorial & Museum cnr Darlinghurst Rd & Burton St Darlinghurst 4 G11
Joan Sutherland Performing Arts Centre Henry St Penrith 236 F9
John Tebbutts Observatory Palmer St Windsor 121 G8
Kalkari Visitors Centre Ku-Ring-Gai Chase National Pk 163 F16
Kidseum cnr Pitt & Walpole Sts Holroyd 307 K10
Kings Cross 4 H7
Kirinari Box Rd Sylvania 461 F13
Kirkham Stables Homestead 477 F7
Kirribilli House 2 F3
Knapsack Viaduct 234 G13
Koala Park Pennant Hills 249 H2
Ku-ring-gai Wildflower Garden St Ives 194 F16
Lancer Barracks Parramatta 308 D4
Lansdowne Bridge 366 K4
La Perouse Monument 436 J14
La Perouse Museum Anzac Pde 436 J14
Lapstone Hill 234 H9
Lapstone Zig Zag 234 G15
Lavender Bay Gallery Walker St North Sydney K G13
Law Courts D E5
Lennox Bridge Lapstone 234 E11
Lime Kiln Bay Bushland Sanctuary Oatley 430 G10
Linnwood Museum Byron Rd Guildford 337 C5
Liverpool Regional Museum cnr Hume Hwy & Congressional St 395 B8
Long Bay Correctional Centre Anzac Pde Malabar 437 C6
Luna Park Harbourside Functions Milsons Point 5 J16
Macarthur Bridge 507 D6
Macarthurs Homestead Elizabeth Macarthur Av Camden South 507 E13
Macquarie House Ferguson La Grasmere 476 F15
Macquarie Lighthouse Vaucluse 348 H2
Macquarie Place B B11
Magdala Falls 202 B16
Magic Kingdom Hollywood Dr Lansvale 367 B8
Mamre Homestead Tea Rooms Mamre Rd St Clair 269 E10
Manly Amusement Pier 288 G11
Manly Art Gallery & Museum 288 F10
Manly Dam 287 F2
Manly Oceanworld 288 F11
Man O'War Jetty 2 D9
Martin Plaza Martin Place C K2
Mary MacKillop Place (Museum) 7 Mount St North Sydney K B8
MLC Centre Martin Place D B4
Model Park (Open Last Sunday Each Month) Luddenham Rd Luddenham 327 H11
Model Steam Trains Darvall Park West Ryde 281 D14
Monorail C K9
Mount Annan Botanic Garden 509 G7
Mount Portal 264 F7
Mrs Macquaries Chair 2 J10
Museum Camden Aerodrome Cobbitty 476 J11
Museum of Applied Arts & Sciences Harris St Ultimo 3 B14
Museum of Contemporary Art Maritime Services Building, George St B A5
Museum of Fire Castlereagh Rd Penrith 236 G8
Museum of Sydney 37 Phillip St B E11
National Artillery Museum North Fort Rd Manly 290 C13
National Maritime Museum Shipyard Balls Head Dr Waverton 315 D15
National Park Office Glenbrook 264 A6
National Parks & Wildlife Service 110 George St The Rocks B A3
National Trust of Australia Observatory Hill Millers Point A D7
Native Gardens Picnic Point 428 C12
Norman Lindsey Home & Gallery 14 Norman Lindsey Cr Faulconbridge 171 G11
North Head Manly 290 D16
North Head Scenic Area Manly 290 B15
Notre Dame Mulgoa Rd Mulgoa 294 H4
NRMA Museum 137 Clarence St C E2
NSWFB Technical Services Amarina Av Greenacre 370 G8
NSW Govt Archives Claremont Meadows O'Connell St 268 F3
The Rocks Globe St A K5
Nutcote The Home of May Gibbs Wallaringa Av Neutral Bay 6 G10
Observatory Flagstaff Hill Millers Point A D4
Old Government House Parramatta 308 A2
Old Post Office Community Art Centre Great Western Hwy St Marys 269 H1
Old Quarantine Station (Organised Tours) Manly 318 H1
Overseas Passenger Terminal Darling Harbour C A3
Over The Road 70 Mulhollands Rd Mowbray Park 562 D2
Oxford Square East Sydney F J5
Parliament House Macquarie St D G2
Parramatta Museum Church St 308 D1
Peats Ferry Bridge 75 D7
Pier One Hickson Rd Millers Point 1 G6
Pitt Street Mall Sydney C K6
Pool of Reflection Hyde Park Sydney D E15
Port Operations & Communication Centre 1 B8
Powerhouse Museum Mary Ann St Ultimo 3 B11
Prospect Reservoir 304 B5
Queens Square Sydney D E5
Queen Victoria Building Sydney C H9
Railway Square E E13
Richmond Bridge 87 H15
Rose Lindsey Cottage Faulconbridge 171 H12
Rouse Hill Estate Guntawong Rd 184 F6
Royal Agricultural Society Showground Homebush Bay 310 F15
Royal Blind Society of NSW Enfield 371 J5
Royal Botanic Gardens B K12
RSPCA Animals Shelter Rookwood Rd Chullora 369 G4
St Andrews Cathedral George St C G14
St Andrews Home for Boys St Andrews Rd Leppington 450 H1
St Benedicts Monastery 121 Arcadia Rd Arcadia 129 H12
St Johns Church Menangle Rd Camden 507 B1
St Marys Cathedral St Marys Rd D H9
St Michaels Cave Avalon 140 F15
St Stephens Church Macquarie St D F2
Sandringham Gardens D F11
Scots Church Jamison St A F13
Shadforth Bridge Silverdale 384 G1
S H Ervin Gallery National Trust Centre, Observatory Hill Millers Point A D8
Shrine of Remembrance Hyde Park D D15
Silvicultural Demonstration Area Berkshire Park 178 H10
Sir Joseph Banks Memorial Kurnell 466 D5
Solander Monument Kurnell 466 E5
South Head Signal Station Vaucluse 348 H1
Sphinx War Memorial Ku-Ring-Gai Chase National Pk 193 H9
Star City Casino Pyrmont St Pyrmont 12 H2
State Library of NSW Macquarie St B G16
State Sports Centre Australia Av Homebush Bay 340 H4

Stony Range
Flora Reserve
Dee Why 258 F8
Strand Arcade .... C J6
Strickland House
Vaucluse 348 A3
Supreme Court
King St .... D E5
Sutherland
Entertainment Centre
30 Eton St N 490 F2
Sydney Aquarium
Darling Harbour .... C A6
Sydney Cove .... B E3
Sydney
Exhibition Centre 3 A8
Sydney
Harbour Bridge 1 H3
Sydney Mint Museum
Macquarie St .... D F5
Sydney Opera House
Bennelong Point .... B J1
Sydney Square .... C G13
Sydney Tower
Centrepoint .... D A7
Sydney Town Hall
George St .... C G12
Sydney
Tropical Centre
Royal
Botanic Gardens .... B K14
Sydney Wool Centre
Yennora 336 K6
Taronga
Zoological Park
Mosman 317 A14
Teen Ranch
Holiday Camp
Cobbitty Rd
Cobbitty 446 J15
The Domain .... D K2
The Gap
Watsons Bay 318 G14
The Rocks .... B A4
The Sydney Art Gallery
cnr Quarry &
Harris Sts
Ultimo 12 K9
Thirlmere
Railway Museum
Barbour Rd 565 A5
Tipperary Falls
Hunters Hill 313 E6
Tramway Museum
(open Sun, Wed &
Pub Hols)
Pitt St
Loftus 490 C9
Tudor Gatehouse The
Parramatta 308 B2
University of Sydney 18 A3
Vaucluse House
Wentworth Rd 348 C3
Victoria Barracks
Oxford St
Paddington 4 H16
Vision Valley
Recreation Centre
Vision Valley Rd
Arcadia 130 C13
Waratah Park
Namba Rd
Terrey Hills 194 G4
Warragamba Dam 353 B5
Wascoe Siding
Miniature Railway 233 H10
Watsons Bay
Naval Depot &
Memorial Chapel 318 F11
Watsons Bay School
Historical Site
Old South
Head Rd 318 G15
Willandra
Historical Home
Ryde 311 J3
Windsor Bridge 121 C7
Wollondilly
Heritage Centre
43 Edward St
The Oaks 502 G13
Wonderland Sydney
Wallgrove Rd
Eastern Creek 272 D14
World War One
Monument
Werombi Rd
Theresa Park 445 C13
World War Two
Monument
Aerodrome Rd
Cobbitty 476 K9
Yarra Bay House
La Perouse 436 H12
YMCA Yarramundi
Youth Camp 116 B14

SHOPPING COMPLEXES - MAJOR

Ashfield
Shopping Mall 372 H3
Auburn Home
Mega Mart 309 B13
Bankstown Square 369 G15
Bass Hill Plaza 367 K9
Bayside Plaza 433 K2
Birkenhead Point 344 B4
Bonnyrigg Plaza 364 A3
Bridgepoint 317 A5
Broadway 12 G15
Burwood Plaza 341 K14
Campbelltown Mall 511 D5
Campsie Centre 372 A14
Carlingford Court 280 A1
Castle Towers 218 C14
Casula Mall 394 F15
Centrepoint .... D A7
Chatswood Chase 284 K9
Cherrybrook Village 219 G9
Chifley Plaza .... B E15
Christies
Homemaker Centre
Bankstown 217 C14
Castle Hill 399 C7
Clocktower Square .... A J3
Cosmopolitan 14 C9
Cronulla Plaza 493 K11
Doncaster 376 E13
Eagle Vale
Marketplace 481 F5
Eastgate 22 H7
Eastlakes 406 A3
Eastwood Centre 281 B8
Edgecliff 13 H11
Fairfield Forum 336 E11
Forestway 256 D5
Glasshouse .... D A5
Glenquarie 424 C16
Glenrose 225 J16
Gordon Centre 253 G7
Greenfield
Shopping Village 334 A13
Greenway 308 C3
Harbourside 3 A5
Homebase 275 B13
Hunter Connection .... A K16
Hurstville
Super Centre 432 A6
Illawong Village 459 J4
Ingleburn Fair 453 D5
Kien Hay Centre .... E E7
Kingsgate 4 H8
Leichhardt
Market Place 15 D2
Lemon Grove 284 J9
Lennox 235 E10
Luxford Court 241 G15
Macarthur Square 510 J8
Macquarie 282 F1
Market City .... E C8
Marrickville Metro 374 F10
Menai Marketplace 458 J11
Mid City Centre .... C K6
Miller 393 J2
Minchinbury
Hometown 271 D5
Minto Mall 482 H4
MLC Centre .... D B4
Narellan Town Centre 478 G10
Neeta City 336 F11
Nepean Square 236 G12
Neutral Bay Village 6 J1
North Sydney
Shoppingworld .... K F6
Norwest Marketown 216 G15
Paddys Markets
Haymarket .... E C8
Paddys Markets
Flemington 340 J7
Parklea Markets 215 F11
Parkway Plaza 221 A13
Penrith Plaza 236 G9
Piccadilly .... D A9
Plumpton Marketplace 241 K5
Quakers Court 243 J3
Queen Victoria
Building .... C H9
Richmond
Marketplace 118 H6
Riverwood Plaza 400 B16
Rockdale Plaza 433 E1
Roselands 400 H8
Royal Randwick 377 B14
St Ives Village 223 K12
Skygarden .... D A6
Southgate 462 B9
Southpoint 406 H14
South Terrace Plaza 399 G1
Station Street Plaza 239 H14
Stockland City .... D A6
Stockland Mall
Baulkham Hills 247 H10
Maroubra 407 A9
Merrylands 307 H12
Wetherill Park 334 E7
Strathfield Plaza 341 F12
Supa Centa 20 D16
Surry Hills
Shopping Village 20 A7
Sussex Arcade .... E F6
Sydney Markets 340 J7
Sylvania Waters 462 F13
The Hills 275 F2
The Interchange 284 H10
The Valley Plaza 363 C13
Top Ryde
Shopping Square 312 A1
Triple CEE 243 G6
Village 239 F15
Warriewood Square 199 A12
Warringah Mall 257 J12
Westfield
Bondi Junction 22 K6
Burwood 342 A13
Chatswood 284 K10
Eastgardens 406 F11
Hornsby 221 H1
Hurstville 432 B6
Liverpool 395 D2
Miranda 491 K4
Mount Druitt 241 D14
Northgate 221 H1
North Rocks 249 B14
Parramatta 308 B4
Westpac Plaza .... A H13
Westpoint 244 F16
Winston Hills Mall 246 K16
Wintergarden Plaza .... B B13

SPORTING VENUES

Ahtletic Centre
Homebush Bay 340 F2
Alexandria
Basketball Stadium 375 E11
Ambarvale
Sports Complex 510 K12
Andrews Rd
Baseball Complex
Penrith 237 C1
Anzac Rifle Range
Malabar 437 G2
Arlington Oval
Dulwich Hill 373 C9
Australian
Tennis Academy
Frenchs Forest 257 C2
Bankstown
Basketball Stadium
Condell Park 398 C4
Bankstown City
Sports Complex 399 A5
Bankstown
Football Centre 399 F5
Bankstown Oval 399 D3
Baulkham Hills
Sportsground 247 J12
Bellingara
Netball Courts
Miranda 461 K15
Belmore Sportsground 371 G16
Blacktown
Equestrian Centre
Marsden Park 212 B5
Botany Athletic Centre
Hillsdale 406 E12
Broken Bay Sports &
Recreation Centre 107 E1
Brookvale Oval 258 B9
Cabramatta
Sportsground 365 G12
Calabria
Community Club
Prairiewood 334 D8
Campbelltown
Sportsground
Minto 482 B13
Camperdown
Velodrome 17 B6
Canterbury Velodrome
Earlwood 403 J3
Caringbah Oval 492 C8
Centennial Parklands
Equestrain Centre
Moore Park 21 B10
Chatswood Oval 284 J11
Chatswood
War Memorial
Athletic Field
Lane Cove West 283 F11
Chopin Park
Plumpton 242 A11
Clive Rogers
Equestrian Ground
Warriewood 199 C13
Concord Oval 342 C10
Coogee Oval 377 G16
Cromer Park 228 F16
Dangar-Cranbrook
Sportsground
Rose Bay 347 K12
David Phillips
Sports Field
Daceyville 406 E5
Drummoyne Oval 343 G2
Dudley Chesham
Sportsground
The Oaks 502 C13
Eastern Creek
Raceway 273 B16
E G Whitlam
Leisure Centre
Liverpool 395 A5
Endeavour
Sports Reserve
Fairfield 335 G15
Eschol Park
Sports Complex 481 D4
Fairfield Showground
Prairiewood 334 G10
Forshaw Field
Sylvania Waters 462 D15
Gabbie Stadium
Seven Hills 245 J14
Gipps Rd
Sporting Complex
Greystanes 305 A13
Greystanes
Sportsground 305 J10
Guildford West
Sportsground 336 F4
Harold Laybutt
Sporting Complex
Arndell Park 274 C11
Hawkesbury
Indoor Stadium
South Windsor 150 H1
Hills
Basketball Stadium
Castle Hill 217 E10
Hockey Centre
Homebush Bay 340 G4
Holroyd Sportsground 308 D9
Hordern Pavilion
Moore Park 20 K9
Howell Oval
Penrith 236 E13
Hurstville Oval 431 K3
Jacqui Osmond
Softball Centre
Warwick Farm 365 J12
Jim Campbell
Sportsfield
Macquarie Park 252 C12
King Tomislav Park
Edensor Park 333 E15
Kogarah Jubilee Oval
Carlton 433 A8
Lambert Park
Leichhardt 15 B1
Leichhardt Oval 9 H3
L H Waud
Sportsground 311 C3
Lidcombe Velodrome 339 G5
Little Bay
Sports Field 437 C9
McKay Sportground 21 C14
Makepeace
Athletic Field 336 H14
Marcellin
Sports Fields 407 A12
Marconi Oval
Bossley Park 333 H9
Mark Leece
Sporting Complex
St Clair 270 C10
Melita Stadium
South Granville 338 G11
Merrylands Park 307 D11
Merrylands
Velodrome 307 D11
National Equestrian
Sports Centre
Menangle Park 509 B13
Nepean
Rugby Union Oval
Penrith 237 B2
Nepean Short Circuit
Speedway
Castlereagh 146 D10
Nineveh
Soccer Field
Edensor Park 364 A2
North Sydney Oval 5 H2
NSW Academy
of Sport
Narrabeen 227 G7
NSW Catholic
Lawn Tennis Assn
Haberfield 9 A13
NSW Lawn Tennis
Assn Courts
(White City)
Paddington 13 E12
NSW Netball Assn
Lidcombe 339 F5
Old Kings Oval
Parramatta 278 A16
Oran Park Motorsport 448 F11
Oriole Stadium
Auburn 338 H3
Parramatta City
Raceway 309 A10
Parramatta Granville
Sportsground 309 A9
Parramatta Stadium 278 A16
Penrith City Archers
Werrington 239 C11
Penrith Park 236 E12
Penrith Sports Stadium
Cambridge Park 238 C10
Petersham Oval 15 E7
Pittwater Rugby Park
Warriewood 199 C12
Pratten Park
Ashfield 372 H5
Princess Anne
Equestrian Area
St Ives 194 J16
Raby Sports Complex 451 C14
RAS Showground
Homebush Bay 310 F15
Redfern Oval 19 F9
Reg Bartley Oval The
Rushcutters Bay 13 C7
Richmond
Ex-Servicemans
Sporting Complex 118 J3

Rockdale Womens
Sports Fields 403 H15

Roper Rd
Soccer Field
Colyton 270 H5

Ross Gwilliam
Sportsfield
Macquarie Park 252 D12

St George
Soccer Stadium
Banksia 403 K12

St Josephs College
Sportsground 313 B7

Serbian Centre
Bonnyrigg Heights 363 E4

Seymour Shaw Park
Miranda 492 A2

Shark Park
Woolooware 493 E5

Soldiers Hockey Field 460 F12

Somerville Park
Eastwood 281 C4

Stadium Australia
Homebush Bay 340 E1

State Sports Centre
Homebush Bay 340 H4

Sydney Aquatic Centre
Homebush Bay 340 G2

Sydney Athletic Field
Moore Park 20 J1

Sydney Cricket Ground
Moore Park 20 K6

Sydney
Football Stadium
Moore Park 21 A4

Sydney International
Aquatic Centre
Homebush Bay 340 G2

Sydney International
Athletic Centre
Homebush Bay 340 F2

Sydney International
Regatta Centre
Castlereagh 205 J13

Sydney University
Ovals 18 A4

Tahmoor Regional
Sporting Centre 565 D10

Tahmoor
Sportsground 565 D10

Tennis Centre
Homebush Bay 340 J4

T G Millner
Sportsground
Marsfield 281 H1

Thirlmere
Sportsground 565 A3

Trumper Oval
Paddington 13 G12

University of NSW
Oval
Kensington 376 G15

Warragamba
Sportsground 353 F9

Warwick Farm
Polo Field 366 C14

Waverley Oval 377 H5

Weigall Sportsground 13 D10

Wests Athletics Club
Lidcombe 339 F4

Womens
Athletic Field
Chifley 437 A8

Woodlands
Baseball Complex
St Helens Park 541 G2

TENPIN BOWLING

Balgowlah 287 J8

Bankstown 399 F1

Blacktown 244 H14

Blaxland 233 G3

Campbelltown 510 J8

Campbelltown 511 H1

Castle Hill
(Wondabowl)
Castle Hill 217 A14

Chester Hill 368 C1

Enfield 371 B4

Fairfield 336 E14

Hornsby 191 H15

Lessing Park
Hornsby 191 K13

Liverpool 395 C5

Mount Druitt 241 F15

Parramatta 308 D6

Penrith 236 G12

Randwick Bowl 377 A14

Rosebery 405 E1

Ryde 312 A1

Sylvania 462 B9

Windsor 150 H1

TERTIARY & OTHER INSTITUTIONS

ACTORS COLLEGE OF THEATRE AND TELEVISION
505 Pitt St
Sydney E F12

APM TRAINING INSTITUTE
33 Chandos St
St Leonards 315 D5

AQUINAS ACADEMY
152 Gloucester St
Sydney A G10

ASSOCIATED BUSINESS COLLEGE
91 York St
Sydney C D6

ASSOCIATED BUSINESS COLLEGE
3/3 Waverley St
Bondi Junction 377 F4
2 Crofts Av
Hurstville 432 A5

AUSTRALIAN CATHOLIC UNIVERSITY
Castle Hill Campus
521 Old Northern Rd 218 H9
MacKillop Campus
40 Edward St
North Sydney 5 D7
Main Campus
(Mt St Mary)
179 Albert Rd
Strathfield 341 A13

AUSTRALIAN COLLEGE OF APPLIED PSYCHOLOGY
414 Elizabeth St
Surry Hills 19 H2

AUSTRALIAN COLLEGE OF NATURAL THERAPIES
57 Foveaux St
Surry Hills F D16

AUSTRALIAN FILM, TELEVISION & RADIO SCHOOL
cnr Epping &
Balaclava Rds
Macquarie Park 282 A1

AUSTRALIAN INSTITUTE OF POLICE
Management
Collins Beach Rd
Manly 288 J15

AUSTRALIAN INTERNATIONAL CONSERVATORIUM OF MUSIC
31 Allen St
Parramatta 308 E7

AUSTRALIAN PACIFIC COLLEGE
ADC Building,
189 Kent St
Sydney A C11

BLACKTOWN COMMUNTIY COLLEGE
cnr Kildare Rd &
Lancaster St 244 B16

CANISIUS
102 Mona Vale Rd
Pymble 233 G15

CATHOLIC THEOLOGICAL
Albert Rd
Strathfield 341 C12

CHURCH OF CHRIST THEOLOGICAL COLLEGE
216 Pennant Hills Rd
Oatlands 279 C6

COLUMBAN MISSION INSTITUTE
420 Bobbin Head Rd
North Turramurra 193 F13

DEAF EDUCATION NETWORK
11 The Boulevarde
Strathfield 341 G12

EMMAUS BIBLE COLLEGE
25 Ray Rd
Epping 251 A14

HILLS DISTRICT COMMUNITY COLLEGE
129 Showground Rd
Castle Hill 217 G12

HORNSBY KU-RING-GAI COMMUNITY COLLEGE
45 Hunter St
Hornsby 191 H16

INTERNATIONAL COLLEGE OF TOURISM & HOTEL MANAGEMENT
151 Darley St
Manly 288 K12

KVB INSTITUTE OF TECHNOLOGY
99 Mount St
North Sydney K F8

MACQUARIE COMMUNITY COLLEGE
263b Marsden Rd
Carlingford 280 B4

MACQUARIE UNIVERSITY
Balaclava Rd
Macquarie Park 282 B1

MARTIN COLLEGE
169 Macquarie St
Parramatta 308 D3

SYDNEY PARK LODGE HOTEL
Moore Park 20 D9

MORLING COLLEGE (BAPTIST)
120 Herring Rd
Macquarie Park 282 D3

MOSMAN EVENING COLLEGE
Gladstone Av
Mosman 317 B8

NATURE CARE COLLEGE OF NATUROPATHIC AND TRADITIONAL MEDICINE
79 Lithgow St
St Leonards 315 D7

NORTHERN SYDNEY INSTITUTE OF TAFE
Bradfield Campus
192 Pacific Hwy
Crows Nest 5 C1
Brookvale Campus
154 Old Pittwater Rd 257 J13
Crows Nest Campus
Rodborough Av 315 H7
Hornsby Campus
205 Pacific Hwy 191 F15
Meadowbank
Campus
cnr See St &
Constitution Rd 311 E2
North Sydney
Campus
213 Pacific Hwy
Artarmon 315 A4
Ryde Campus
250 Blaxland Rd 281 J15
Seaforth Campus
cnr Sydney &
Frenchs Forest Rds 287 D9

NSW BUSINESS COLLEGE
Wembley House,
841 George St
Broadway E C14

OPEN TRAINING & EDUCATION NETWORK EXTERNAL STUDIES
Redfern
199 Regent St 19 B10
Strathfield
Wentworth Rd 341 H12

PATRICIAN BROTHERS TRAINING COLLEGE
134 Eastern Rd
Wahroonga 222 J6

CENTRAL RAILWAY MOTEL
Redfern 19 G6

REGENT COLLEGE
55 Regent St
Chippendale 19 D2

ST ANDREWS THEOLOGICAL
242 Cleveland St
Surry Hills 19 G5

ST GEORGE & SUTHERLAND COMMUNITY
Sutherland Rd
Jannali 460 F13

ST IVES INTENSIVE ENGLISH CENTRE
Warrimoo Av 224 B2

ST PATRICKS BUSINESS
cnr Devonshire &
Riley Sts
Surry Hills 20 A3

ST PAULS SEMINARY
1 Roma Av
Kensington 376 D14

SEMINARY OF THE GOOD SHEPHERD
50 Abbotsford Rd
Homebush 341 B10

SOUTHERN SYDNEY INSTITUTE OF TAFE
Bankstown Campus
500 Chapel Rd 369 E13
Gymea Campus
cnr Kingsway &
Hotham Rd 491 D2
Lidcombe Campus
East St 339 J14
Loftus Campus
Rawson Av 490 C8
Padstow College
Raine Rd 399 B13
St George Campus
cnr Princes Hwy &
President Av
Kogarah 433 D5

SOUTH WESTERN SYDNEY INSTITUTE OF TAFE
Campbelltown
Campus
Narellan Rd 510 J5
Granville College
136 William St 308 C12
Liverpool Campus
College St 395 G3
Macquarie Fields
Campus
Victoria Rd 424 C15
Miller Campus
cnr Hoxton Park &
Banks Rds 393 F5
Wetherill Park
Campus
The Horsley Dr 334 K3

SYDNEY BAPTIST BIBLE COLLEGE
214 Pennant Hills Rd
Oatlands 279 C7

SYDNEY COMMUNITY COLLEGE
cnr Victoria Rd &
Gordon St
Rozelle 11 B1

SYDNEY INSTITUTE OF TECHNOLOGY
Broadway Campus
George St E C14
Design Centre
110 Edgeware Rd
Enmore 374 F9
East Sydney
Campus
Forbes St
Darlinghurst 4 F12
Eora Centre
333 Abercrombie St 18 G7
Petersham Campus
27 Crystal St 16 B6
Petersham West
Campus
West St
Petersham 15 F10
Randwick Campus
cnr Darley Rd &
King St 376 H10
Ultimo Campus
Mary Ann St 3 B14

SYDNEY INSTITUTE OF TRADITIONAL CHINESE MEDICINE
92 Norton St
Leichhardt 15 K2

THE AUSTRALIAN ACADEMY
28 Margaret St
Sydney A E14

THE COLLEGE OF SOMATIC STUDIES
20 Hudson Av
Castle Hill 217 A12

THE WHITEHOUSE SCHOOL
53 Liverpool St
Sydney E F2

UNITED THEOLOGICAL
16 Masons Dr
North Parramatta 278 H8

UNIVERSITY OF NSW
College of Fine Arts
Selwyn St
Paddington 4 G16
Coogee Campus
Battery St
Clovelly 377 J13
Little Bay Campus
Prince Henry
Hospital 437 C11
Main Campus
High St
Kensington 376 H15
Randwick Campus
King St 376 J10
St George Campus
cnr Hurstville Rd &
Oatley Av
Oatley 431 C10

UNIVERSITY OF SYDNEY
Conservatorium of
Music
Conservatorium Rd B J11
Cumberland College
Campus
East St
Lidcombe 339 K15

Cumberland College of Health Sciences East St Lidcombe ... 339 K15
Faculty of Dentistry 2 Chalmers St Surry Hills ... E K16
Faculty of Dentistry cnr Darcy & Hawkesbury Rds Westmead ... 277 G14
Faculty of Nursing 88 Mallett St Camperdown ... 17 E4
Faculty of Nursing Reserve Rd St Leonards ... 315 C5
Graduate School of Management & Public Policy 144 Burren St Newtown ... 18 A11
Law School 173 Phillip St Sydney ... D E5
Main Campus Parramatta Rd Camperdown ... 18 B3
Sydney College of The Arts 44 Smith St Balmain ... 7 E13
Sydney College of The Arts 266 Glebe Point Rd Glebe ... 12 H7
Sydney College of The Arts Balmain Rd Lilyfield ... 10 D1

UNIVERSITY OF TECHNOLOGY, SYDNEY
Blackfriars Campus cnr Buckland & Blackfriars Sts Chippendale ... 18 K1
Kuring-gai Campus Eton Rd Lindfield ... 283 K6
Main Campus 1 Broadway Ultimo ... E A15
Markets Campus Quay St Haymarket ... E A8
St Leonards Campus cnr Pacific Hwy & Westbourne St ... 315 A5

UNIVERSITY OF WESTERN SYDNEY
Hawkesbury Bourke St Richmond ... 117 H12
Hawkesbury Blacktown Campus, Eastern Rd Schofields ... 213 E12
Macarthur Bankstown Campus, Bullecourt Av Milperra ... 397 J10
Macarthur Centre Campbelltown Campus, Goldsmith Av ... 510 D6
Nepean Second St Kingswood ... 238 B15
Nepean Great Western Hwy Werrington ... 238 F13
Nepean (North) Hawkesbury Rd Westmead ... 277 F15
Nepean, Parramatta Campus cnr Victoria Rd & James Ruse Dr ... 309 A1
Nepean (South) Hawkesbury Rd Westmead ... 277 F15

WESLEY INSTITUTE FOR MINISTRY-THE ARTS
Mary St Drummoyne ... 343 G5

WESTERN SYDNEY INSTITUTE OF TAFE
Baulkham Hills Campus cnr Old Northern Rd & Edward St ... 247 H6
Blacktown Campus cnr Main St & Newton Rd ... 274 J1
Mount Druitt Campus cnr Mount St & North Pde ... 241 G16
Nirimba Campus Eastern Rd Schofields ... 213 C11
Penrith Campus 117 Henry St ... 236 J9
Richmond Campus Ceremonial Dr ... 118 J10
Werrington Campus cnr Great Western Hwy & O'Connell St Kingswood ... 238 D15

WIVENHOE VOCATION
229 Macquarie Grove Rd Cobbitty ... 477 A2

THEATRES, CINEMAS & DRIVE-IN THEATRES

AVALON
Avalon Cinema Centre 39 Old Barrenjoey Rd ... 170 B3

BANKSTOWN
Hoyts Bankstown cnr Jacobs St & The Mall ... 369 F15

BASS HILL
Greater Union Drive-in Johnston Rd ... 367 J8

BELROSE
Glen Street Theatre Glen St ... 225 J16

BEVERLY HILLS
Beverly Hills Cinemas 449 King Georges Rd ... 401 C15

BLACKTOWN
Greater Union Twin Drive-in Cricketers Arms Rd ... 274 F15
Hoyts Cinema Westpoint Shopping Centre ... 244 F15

BONDI JUNCTION
Bondi Plaza Cinema 500 Oxford St ... 22 J6

BROOKVALE
Hoyts Warringah Mall cnr Pittwater Rd & Condamine St ... 257 J12

CAMPBELLTOWN
Greater Union Cinema Macarthur Square, Kellicar Rd ... 510 J8

CASTLE HILL
Greater Union Cinema Castle Towers ... 218 C14
Hills Centre Carrington Rd ... 217 F12
Pavilion Theatre Castle Hill Showground, Carrington Rd ... 217 E11

CHATSWOOD
Hoyts Cinema cnr Albert & Victor Sts ... 284 J10

COLLAROY
Collaroy Cinema 1097 Pittwater Rd ... 229 B13

CREMORNE
Hayden Orpheum Picture Palace 380 Military Rd ... 316 G7

CRONULLA
Arts Theatre Surf Rd ... 493 K12
Cronulla Cinema 2 Cronulla St ... 493 K13

DARLING HARBOUR
Imax Theatre ... C A13

DARLINGHURST
Govinders 112 Darlinghurst Rd ... 4 H9

DARLINGTON
Seymour Theatre Centre Downstairs, Everest, York, Nimrod cnr Cleveland St & City Rd ... 18 G4

DAWES POINT
Australian Theatre for Young People 4 Hickson Rd ... 1 F7
Wharf Theatres 1 & 2 4 Hickson Rd ... 1 F6

DOUBLE BAY
Village Cinema 377 New South Head Rd ... 14 D10

ENMORE
Enmore Theatre 130 Enmore Rd ... 17 C14

FAIRFIELD
Fairfield Twin Cinema cnr Station & Cunninghame Sts ... 336 E11

GLEBE
Footbridge Theatre Sydney University, Parramatta Rd ... 18 C1
Hoyts Broadway Shopping Centre ... 345 E16
Valhalla Cinema 166 Glebe Point Rd ... 12 A12

GLENBROOK
Glenbrook Theatre Great Western Hwy ... 234 A16

HAYMARKET
Capitol Theatre Campbell St ... E H7
Chinatown Cinema 27 Goulburn St ... E F4
Her Majestys Theatre 107 Quay St ... E C13
Hoover Cinema 27 Goulburn St ... E F4
Sydney Entertainment Centre Harbour St ... E B5

HOMEBUSH BAY
Sydney Superdome Edwin Flack Av ... 310 E16

HORNSBY
Hornsby Cinema 155 Pacific Hwy ... 191 G16

HURSTVILLE
Greater Union Cinema Westfield Shopping Centre ... 432 B5

KENSINGTON
Figtree Theatre High St ... 376 G14
NIDA Theatre Anzac Pde ... 376 F14
Parade Theatre 215 Anzac Pde ... 376 F14

KILLARA
Marian Street Theatre 2 Marian St ... 254 A13

KINGS CROSS
Stables Theatre 10 Nimrod St ... 4 H10

KOGARAH
Mecca Movie City 28 Station St ... 433 B3

LEICHHARDT
The Palace Norton Street ... 16 A3

LIVERPOOL
Greater Union Westfield Shoppingtown Elizabeth Dr ... 395 E2

MACQUARIE PARK
Greater Union Cinema Macquarie Centre ... 282 F1
Lighthouse Theatre Macquarie University, Waterloo Rd ... 252 C15

MANLY
Manly Twin Cinemas 43 East Esp ... 288 G10

MILSONS POINT
Ensemble Theatre 78 McDougall St ... 6 C13

MIRANDA
Greater Union Cinema Westfield Shoppingtown, Kingsway ... 491 K4

MOORE PARK
Cinema Paris Fox Studios Bent St ... 21 A9
Hordern Pavilion Driver Av ... 20 K9
Hoyts at Fox Studios Bent St ... 21 C9

MOSMAN
Greater Union Cinema cnr Clifford St & Spit Rd ... 3 H5

MOUNT DRUITT
Hoyts Cinema Westfield, Carlisle Av ... 241 D16

NEWTOWN
Dendy Cinema 261 King St ... 17 H11
New Theatre 542 King St ... 374 J9
New Theatre 542 King St ... 374 J9

NORTH SYDNEY
Walker Cinema The 121 Walker St ... K G7

PADDINGTON
Academy Twin Cinema 3a Oxford St ... 4 F14
Chauvel Cinemas cnr Oxford & Oatley Sts ... 21 A1
Verona cnr Oxford & Verona Sts ... 4 G14

PAGEWOOD
Hoyts Cinema Westfield Eastgardens Shopping Centre ... 406 E11

PARRAMATTA
Parramatta Riverside Theatres cnr Church & Market Sts ... 308 C1
Roxy Village Cinema 65 George St ... 308 D3
Village Cinema Westfield Shoppingtown ... 308 C4

PENRITH
Hoyts Cinema Lawson St ... 236 K10
Hoyts Penrith Plaza Riley St ... 236 G9

PRAIRIEWOOD
Hoyts Cinema Stockland Town Centre ... 334 E7

PYRMONT
Lyric Theatre Star City ... 12 H2

RANDWICK
Ritz Theatre 43 St Pauls St ... 377 C16

RICHMOND
Regent Theatre 149 Windsor St ... 118 H4

ROCKDALE
Guild Theatre cnr Railway & Waltz Sts ... 403 C15

ROSEVILLE
Roseville Theatre 112 Pacific Hwy ... 284 G4

SURRY HILLS
Belvoir Street Theatre 25 Belvoir St ... 19 G4
The Kirk 422 Cleveland St ... 20 A6
Tom Mann Theatre 136 Chalmers St ... 19 G3

SYDNEY
Australia Cinema The 59 Goulburn St ... E K5
Conservatorium of Music Conservatorium Rd ... B J11
Dendy Cinema 19 Martin Pl ... D A2
Dendy Cinema 624 George St ... E H1
Genesian Theatre Company 420 Kent St ... C F10
Greater Union Cinemas 232 Pitt St ... D A10
Greater Union Cinemas 525 George St ... C C16
Harbour City Cinema 6 Harbour St ... E D2
Hoyts Centre 505 George St ... C C16
State Theatre 49 Market St ... C J8
Sydney Opera House Bennelong Point ... B J1
Theatre Royal MLC Centre, King St ... D A4
Village Cinema City 545 George St ... E G1
Westpac Plaza 60 Margaret St ... A H13

THE ROCKS
Clocktower Square 35 Harrington St ... A J3

WINERIES

Winery	Map	Ref
Camden Estate	507	G6
Cobbitty	475	H2
Gledswood	450	D9
John Tebbutts	121	G8
Kirkham Estate	477	D15
Richmond Estate	57	C10
Vicarys	357	A10

PUBLISHING DATES

1st Edition	1967
2nd Edition	1968
3rd Edition	1975
4th Edition	1977
5th Edition	1978
6th Edition	1985
7th Edition	1989
8th Edition	1990
9th Edition	1991
10th Edition	1992
11th Edition	1993
12th Edition	1994
13th Edition	1995
14th Edition	1996
15th Edition	1998
16th Edition	1999
17th Edition	2000
18th Edition	2001

MAP A

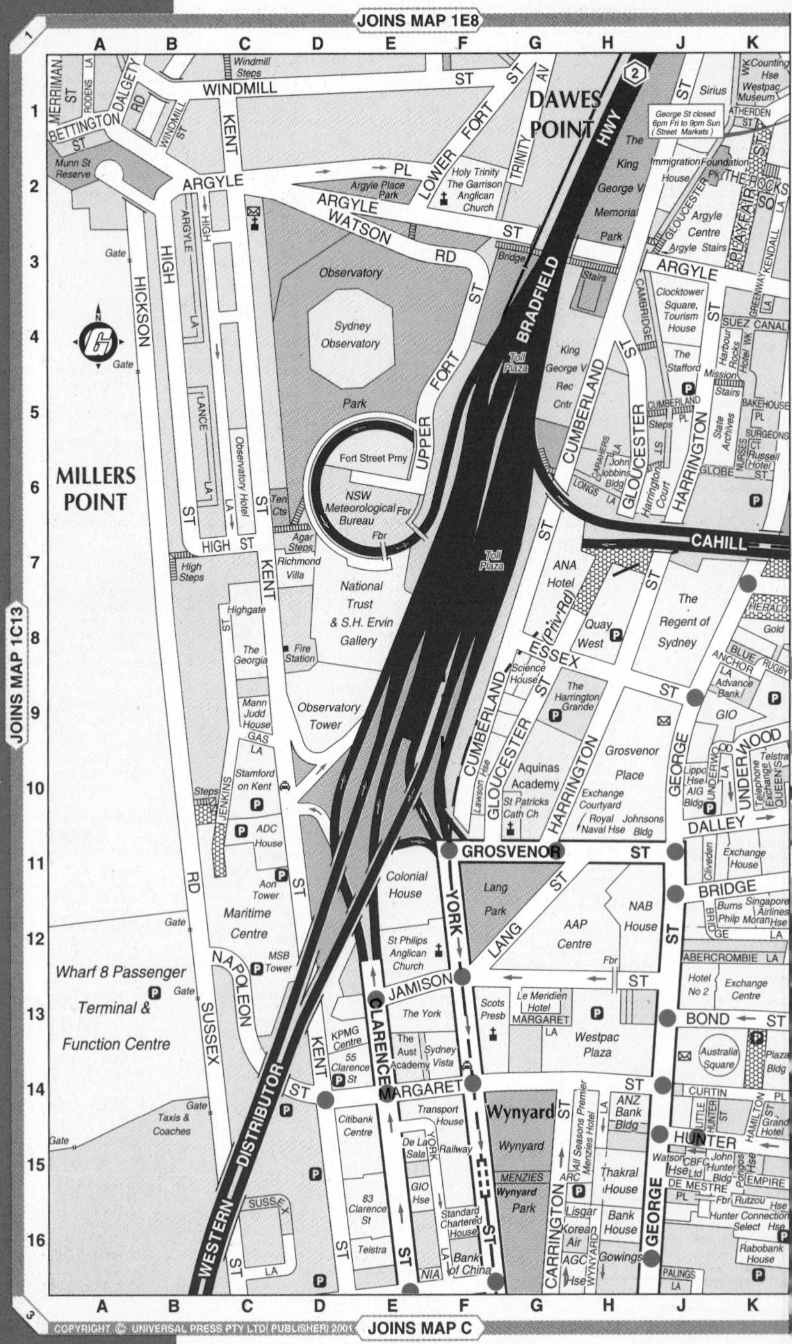

JOINS MAP 1E8
A B C D E F G H J K
1 2 3 4 5 6 7 8 9 10 11 12 13 14 15 16
JOINS MAP 1C13
MILLERS POINT
DAWES POINT
WINDMILL ST
Windmill Steps
MERRIMAN ST
RODENS LA
DALGETY RD
BETTINGTON ST
Munn St Reserve
ARGYLE PL
ARGYLE ST
Argyle Place Park
LOWER FORT ST
TRINITY AV
Holy Trinity The Garrison Anglican Church
WATSON RD
Observatory
Sydney Observatory
Park
UPPER FORT ST
Fort Street Pmy
NSW Meteorological Bureau
Agar Steps
Richmond Villa
National Trust & S.H. Ervin Gallery
Observatory Tower
Fire Station
HICKSON RD
HIGH ST
KENT ST
LANCE LA
Observatory Hotel
High Steps
Highgate
The Georgia
Mann Judd House
GAS LA
Stamford on Kent
JENKINS ST
Steps
ADC House
Aon Tower
Maritime Centre
MSB Tower
NAPOLEON ST
SUSSEX ST
Wharf 8 Passenger Terminal & Function Centre
Taxis & Coaches
Gate
WESTERN DISTRIBUTOR
BRADFIELD HWY
Toll Plaza
The King George V Memorial Park
King George V Rec Cntr
CUMBERLAND ST
GLOUCESTER ST
CAMBRIDGE ST
HARRINGTON ST
Clocktower Square, Tourism House
The Stafford
State Archives
Argyle Centre
Argyle Stairs
THE ROCKS SQ
PLAYFAIR ST
KENDALL LA
GREENWAY LA
SUEZ CANAL
Harbour Rocks Hotel
Mission Stairs
BAKEHOUSE PL
SURGEONS CT
NURSES WK
Russell (Hotel)
GLOBE ST
John Jobbins Bldg
Harrington Court
LONGS LA
CARAHERS LA
Immigration House
Foundation Pk
Sirius
Counting Hse
Westpac Museum
ATHERDEN ST
George St closed 6pm Fri to 9pm Sun (Street Markets)
CAHILL
ANA Hotel
Quay West
The Regent of Sydney
ESSEX ST
(Priv Rd)
Science House
The Harrington Grande
Grosvenor Place
Aquinas Academy
Lawson Hse
St Patricks Cath Ch
Exchange Courtyard
Royal Naval Hse
Johnsons Bldg
HERALD
Gold
BLUE
ANCHOR LA
RUGBY
Advance Bank
GIO
UNDERWOOD ST
Telstra
Telephone Exchange
Lippo Hse
AIG Bldg
DALLEY ST
GROSVENOR ST
Colonial House
Lang Park
LANG ST
AAP Centre
NAB House
YORK ST
St Philips Anglican Church
JAMISON ST
Scots Presb
Le Meridien Hotel
MARGARET LA
Westpac Plaza
Cliveden
Exchange House
BRIDGE ST
Burns Philp
Singapore Airlines Hse
Moran Hse
BRIDGE LA
ABERCROMBIE LA
Hotel No 2
Exchange Centre
BOND ST
Australia Square
Plaza Bldg
CURTIN PL
The York
The Aust Academy
Sydney Vista
KPMG Centre
55 Clarence St
CLARENCE ST
MARGARET ST
Citibank Centre
Transport House
De La Sala
Railway
GIO Hse
83 Clarence St
Telstra
Standard Chartered House
Bank of China
NIA
Wynyard
Wynyard Park
MENZIES
CARRINGTON ST
All Seasons Premier Menzies Hotel
ARC
Lisgar
Korean Air
AGC Hse
WYNYARD LA
ANZ Bank Bldg
Thakral House
Bank House
Gowings
GEORGE ST
LITTLE HUNTER ST
HAMILTON ST
Grand Hotel
HUNTER ST
Watson Hse
CBFC Ltd
John Hunter Bldg
Pongos Hse
EMPIRE
DE MESTRE PL
Rutzou Hse
Hunter Connection
Select Hse
Rabobank House
PALINGS LA
SUSSEX ST
Fbr
JOINS MAP C
COPYRIGHT © UNIVERSAL PRESS PTY LTD (PUBLISHER) 2001

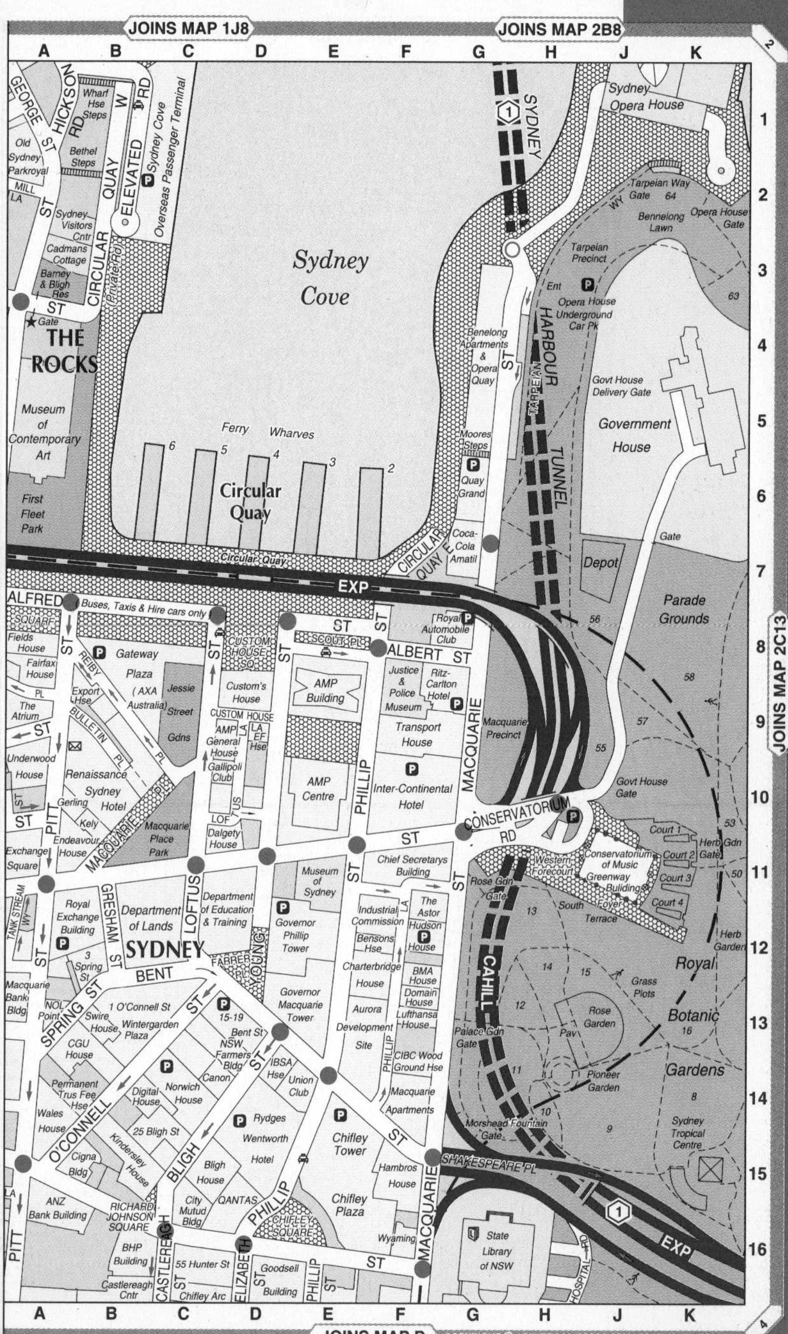
JOINS MAP 1J8
JOINS MAP 2B8
JOINS MAP 2C13
JOINS MAP D
Sydney Cove
Circular Quay
Ferry Wharves
THE ROCKS
SYDNEY
Sydney Opera House
Government House
Royal Botanic Gardens
Museum of Contemporary Art
First Fleet Park
Sydney Cove Overseas Passenger Terminal
Cadmans Cottage
Sydney Visitors Cntr
Old Sydney Parkroyal
Customs House
AMP Building
AMP Centre
Justice & Police Museum
Transport House
Inter-Continental Hotel
Museum of Sydney
Macquarie Place Park
Chifley Tower
Chifley Plaza
Chifley Square
Richard Johnson Square
State Library of NSW
Conservatorium of Music Greenway Building
Opera House Underground Car Pk
Parade Grounds
Depot
Rose Garden
Pioneer Garden
Sydney Tropical Centre
Tarpeian Precinct
Bennelong Lawn
Macquarie Precinct
Sydney Harbour Tunnel
Cahill Exp
Circular Quay Exp
COPYRIGHT © UNIVERSAL PRESS PTY LTD (PUBLISHER) 2001

MAP C

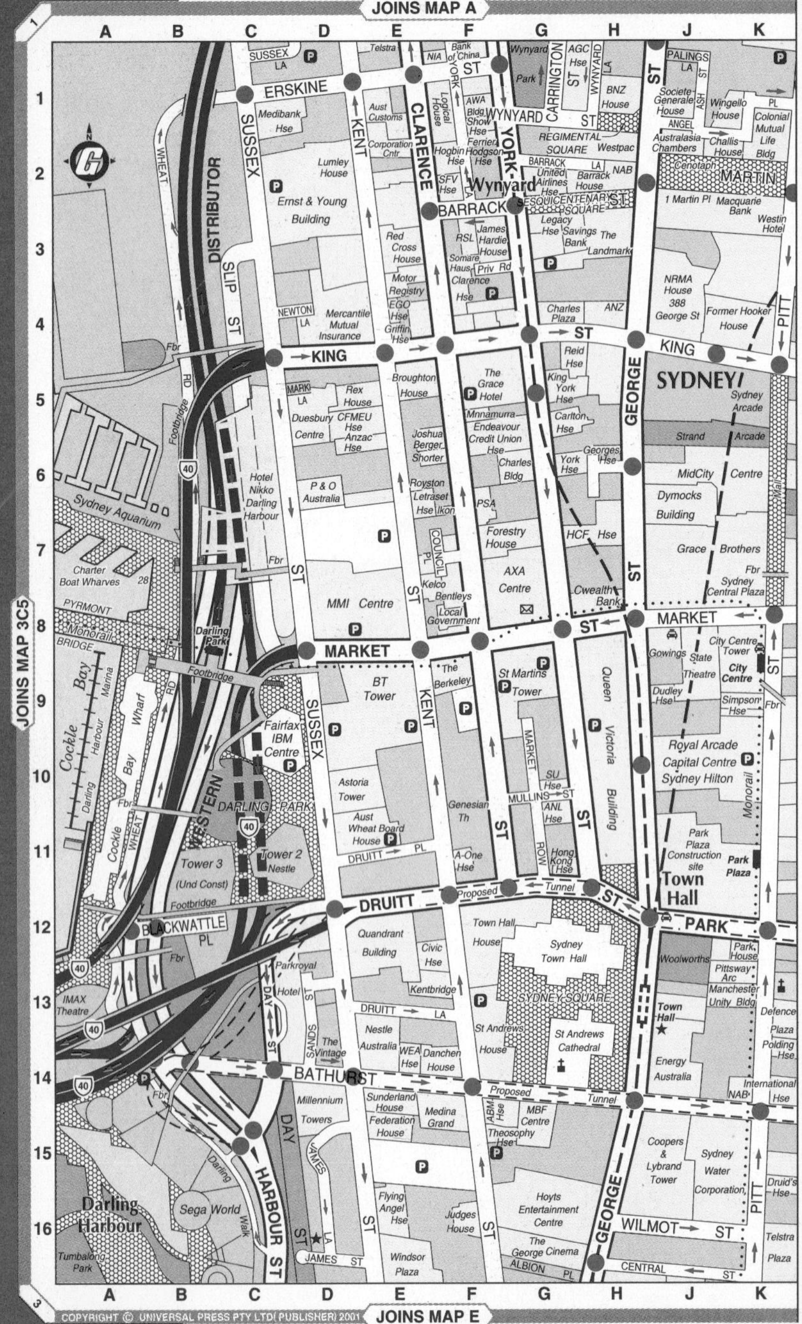
JOINS MAP A
JOINS MAP E
JOINS MAP 3C5
A B C D E F G H J K
1 2 3 4 5 6 7 8 9 10 11 12 13 14 15 16
SUSSEX LA
ERSKINE
Telstra
NIA
Bank of China
ST
Wynyard Park
CARRINGTON ST
AGC Hse
WYNYARD LA
ST
PALINGS LA
ST
Medibank Hse
KENT
Aust Customs
CLARENCE
Logical House
YORK
AWA Bldg
Show Hse
WYNYARD ST
BNZ House
Societe Generale House
ASH ST
Wingello House
PL
Colonial Mutual Life Bldg
WHEAT
DISTRIBUTOR
SUSSEX
Lumley House
Corporation Cntr
Hogbin Hse
Ferrier Hodgson Hse
REGIMENTAL SQUARE
Westpac
ANGEL
Australasia Chambers
Challis House
BARRACK LA
United Airlines Hse
Barrack House
NAB
Cenotaph
MARTIN
Ernst & Young Building
SFV Hse
Wynyard
SESQUICENTENARY SQUARE
1 Martin Pl
Macquarie Bank
BARRACK ST
Westin Hotel
SLIP ST
Red Cross House
RSL
James Hardie House
Legacy Hse
Savings Bank
The Landmark
Somare Haus
Priv Rd
Clarence Hse
Motor Registry
EGO Hse
Griffin Hse
NRMA House 388 George St
NEWTON LA
Mercantile Mutual Insurance
Charles Plaza
ANZ
Former Hooker House
PITT
Fbr
ST
KING
KING
RD
Broughton House
The Grace Hotel
Reid Hse
GEORGE
SYDNEY
MARK LA
Rex House
King York Hse
Sydney Arcade
Footbridge
Duesbury Centre
CFMEU Hse
Anzac Hse
Joshua Berger Shorter
Mnnamurra Endeavour Credit Union Hse
Carlton Hse
Strand Arcade
Georges Hse
York Hse
Charles Bldg
MidCity Centre
Hotel Nikko Darling Harbour
P & O Australia
Royston Letraset Hse
Ikon
PSA
Dymocks Building
Mall
Sydney Aquarium
Forestry House
HCF Hse
COUNCIL PL
Grace Brothers
Charter Boat Wharves
28
Fbr
ST
AXA Centre
ST
Kelco
Bentleys
Fbr
Sydney Central Plaza
PYRMONT
MMI Centre
ST
Cwealth Bank
Monorail
BRIDGE
Darling Park
Local Government
ST
MARKET
MARKET
Gowings
State Theatre
City Centre Tower
City Centre
ST
The Berkeley
St Martins Tower
Queen Victoria Building
Cockle Bay Marina
Footbridge
BT Tower
KENT
Dudley Hse
Simpson Hse
Fbr
Harbour
Wharf
RD
Fairfax IBM Centre
SUSSEX
MARKET ROW
Royal Arcade
Capital Centre
Sydney Hilton
Monorail
Darling
Bay
Astoria Tower
SU Hse
MULLINS ST
Fbr
WESTERN
DARLING PARK
Aust Wheat Board House
Genesian Th
ANL Hse
ST
Park Plaza Construction site
Cockle
WHEAT
Tower 2 Nestle
Tower 3 (Und Const)
DRUITT PL
A-One Hse
ST
Hong Kong Hse
Park Plaza
Town Hall
Footbridge
Proposed
Tunnel
ST
DRUITT
BLACKWATTLE PL
Quandrant Building
Civic Hse
Town Hall House
Sydney Town Hall
PARK
Woolworths
Park House
Fbr
Parkroyal Hotel
Pittsway Arc
Kentbridge
Manchester Unity Bldg
IMAX Theatre
DAY ST
SANDS ST
DRUITT LA
SYDNEY SQUARE
Town Hall
Defence Plaza
Nestle Australia
The Vintage
WEA Hse
Danchen House
St Andrews House
St Andrews Cathedral
Polding Hse
Energy Australia
BATHURST
Proposed
Tunnel
International Hse
NAB
Millennium Towers
Sunderland House
Federation House
Medina Grand
ABM Hse
MBF Centre
Theosophy Hse
Fbr
DAY
JAMES
Coopers & Lybrand Tower
Sydney Water Corporation
Darling
HARBOUR
Druid's Hse
Darling Harbour
Sega World
Walk
ST
Flying Angel Hse
ST
Judges House
ST
Hoyts Entertainment Centre
GEORGE
PITT
WILMOT ST
ST
LA
Telstra Plaza
Tumbalong Park
JAMES ST
Windsor Plaza
The George Cinema
ALBION PL
CENTRAL ST
COPYRIGHT © UNIVERSAL PRESS PTY LTD (PUBLISHER) 2001

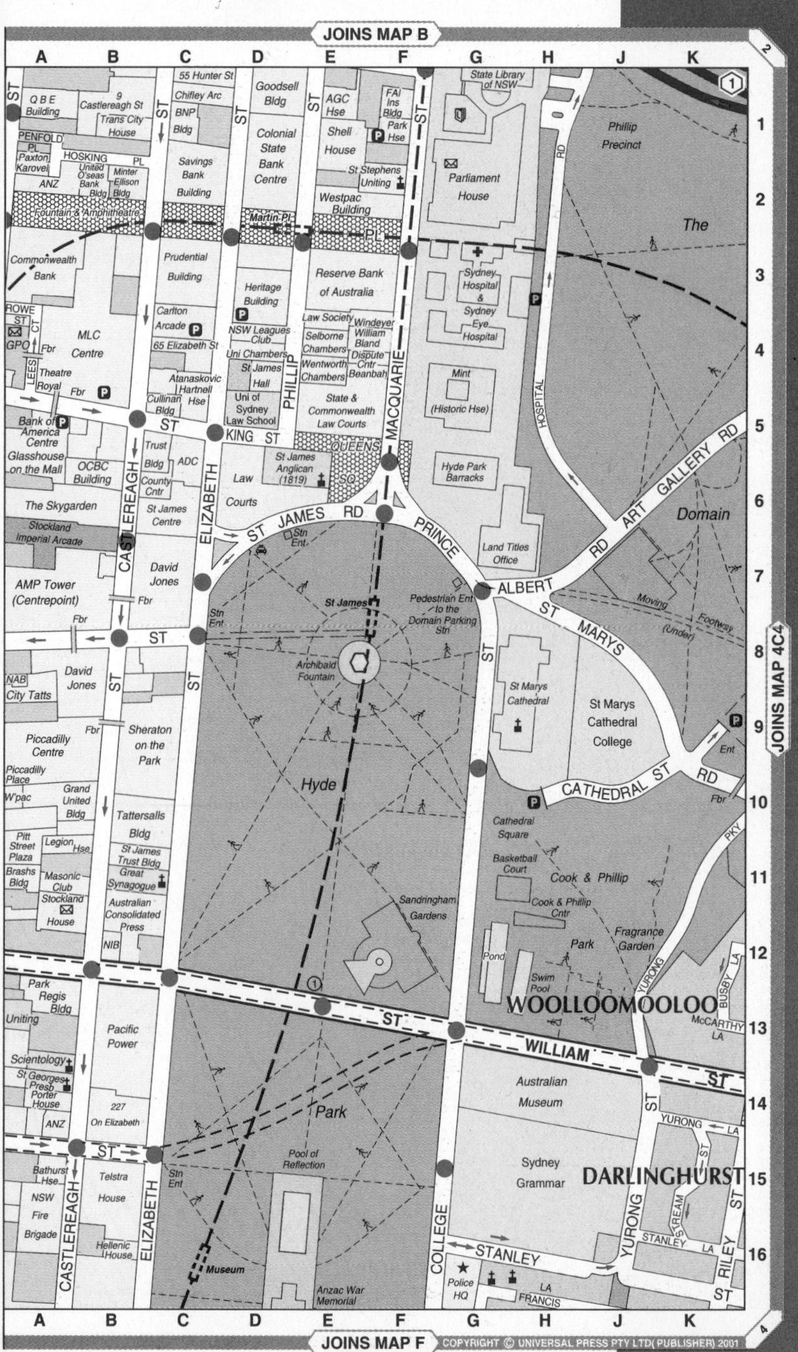
JOINS MAP B
JOINS MAP F
JOINS MAP 4C4
Hyde Park
The Domain
WOOLLOOMOOLOO
DARLINGHURST
Parliament House
Sydney Hospital & Sydney Eye Hospital
St Marys Cathedral
Australian Museum
Sydney Grammar
MACQUARIE ST
ELIZABETH ST
CASTLEREAGH ST
COLLEGE ST
WILLIAM ST
KING ST
PRINCE ALBERT RD
ST MARYS RD
ART GALLERY RD
ST JAMES RD
CATHEDRAL ST
STANLEY ST
YURONG ST
COPYRIGHT © UNIVERSAL PRESS PTY LTD(PUBLISHER) 2001

MAP E

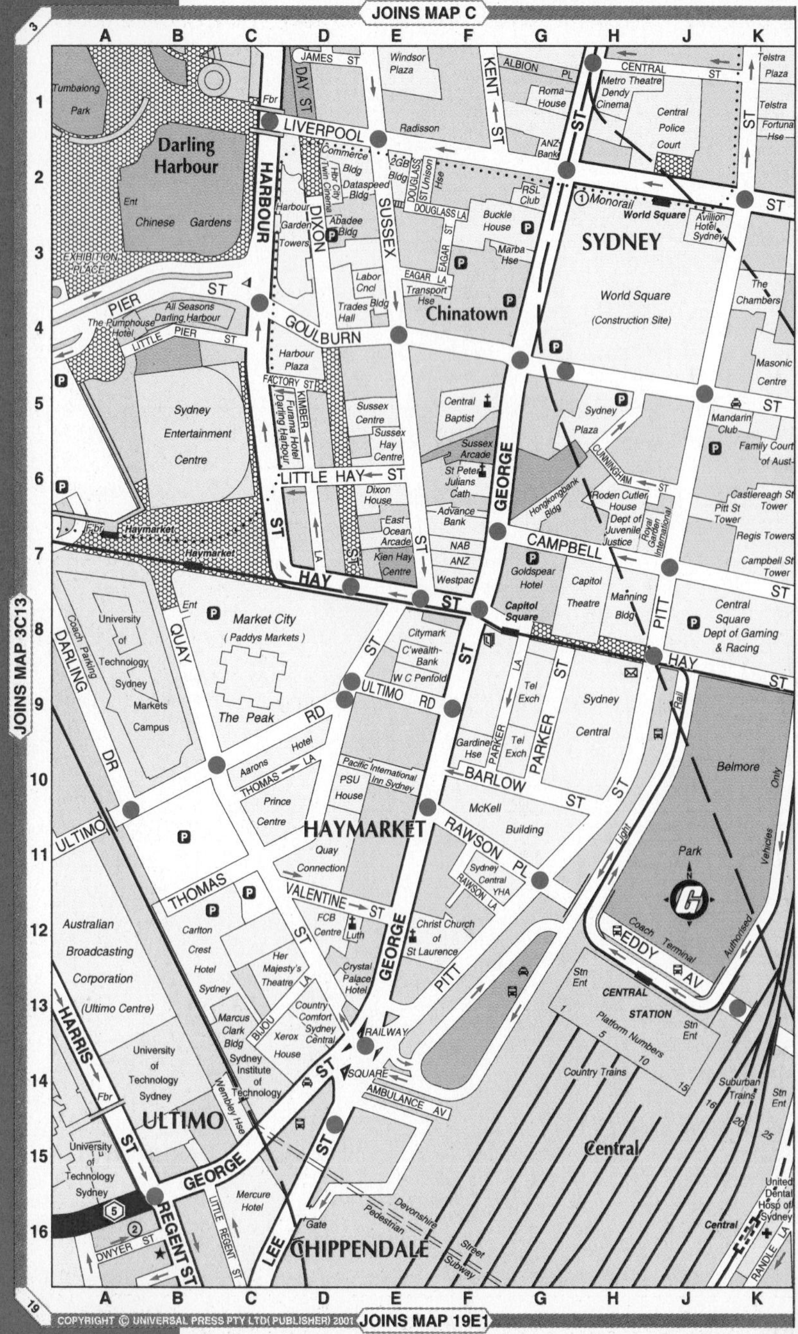

JOINS MAP C
JOINS MAP 3C13
JOINS MAP 19E1
Darling Harbour
Chinese Gardens
Tumbalong Park
EXHIBITION PLACE
Sydney Entertainment Centre
Market City (Paddys Markets)
The Peak
University of Technology Sydney Markets Campus
Chinatown
SYDNEY
World Square (Construction Site)
HAYMARKET
ULTIMO
CHIPPENDALE
Central
CENTRAL STATION
Belmore Park
Australian Broadcasting Corporation (Ultimo Centre)
Capitol Square
Sydney Central
LIVERPOOL
HARBOUR ST
GOULBURN
HAY ST
GEORGE ST
PITT ST
SUSSEX ST
DIXON
KENT ST
CAMPBELL
ULTIMO RD
BARLOW ST
RAWSON PL
THOMAS
QUAY ST
DARLING DR
HARRIS ST
REGENT ST
LEE ST
RAILWAY SQUARE
EDDY AV

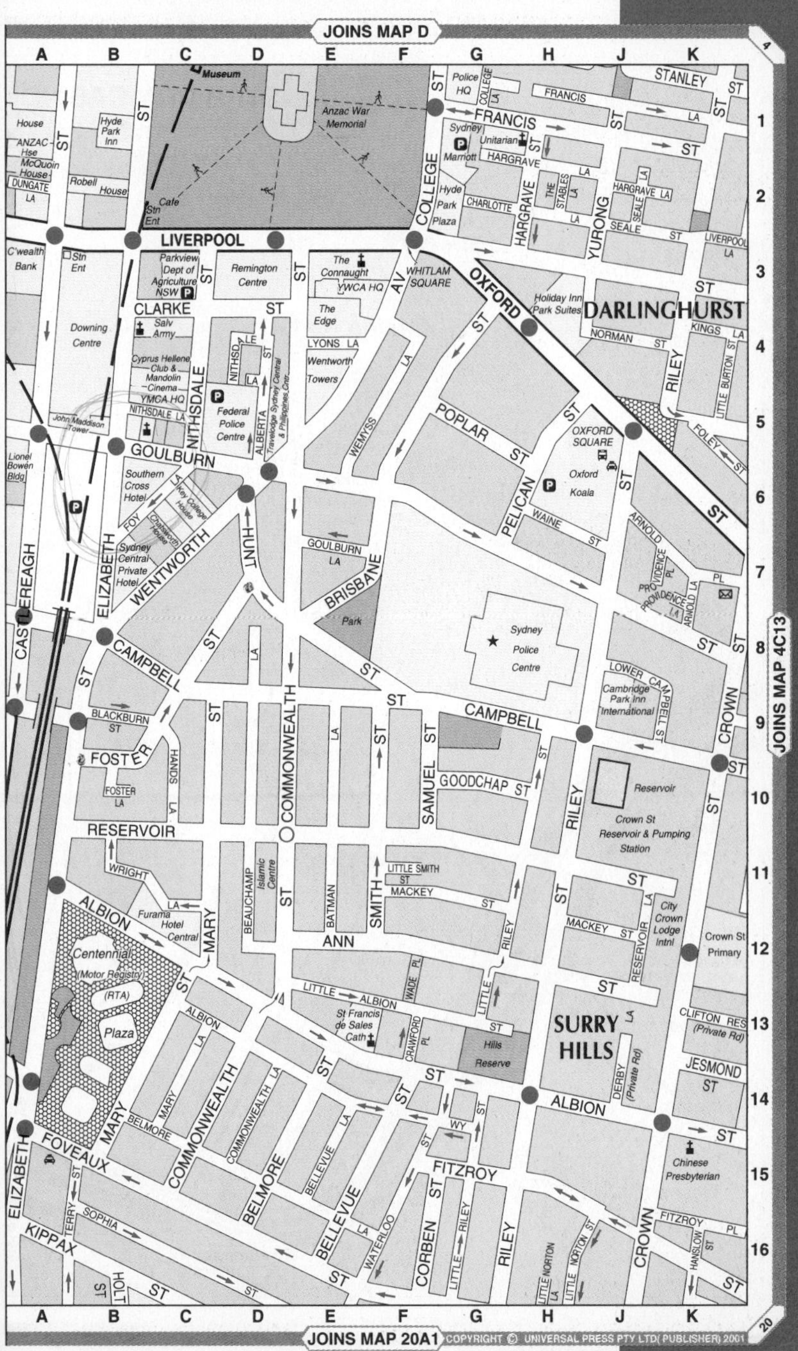
JOINS MAP D
JOINS MAP 4C13
JOINS MAP 20A1
DARLINGHURST
SURRY HILLS
LIVERPOOL
OXFORD ST
COLLEGE ST
ELIZABETH ST
CASTLEREAGH ST
GOULBURN
WENTWORTH
CAMPBELL ST
COMMONWEALTH ST
RILEY ST
CROWN ST
ALBION
FOVEAUX
FITZROY
RESERVOIR
Museum
Anzac War Memorial
Police HQ
Sydney Marriott
Downing Centre
Remington Centre
The Connaught
Federal Police Centre
Sydney Police Centre
Oxford Square
Crown St Reservoir & Pumping Station
Centennial (Motor Registry) (RTA) Plaza
St Francis de Sales Cath
Hills Reserve
Chinese Presbyterian
Crown St Primary
Wentworth Towers
WHITLAM SQUARE
Holiday Inn Park Suites
Cambridge Park Inn International

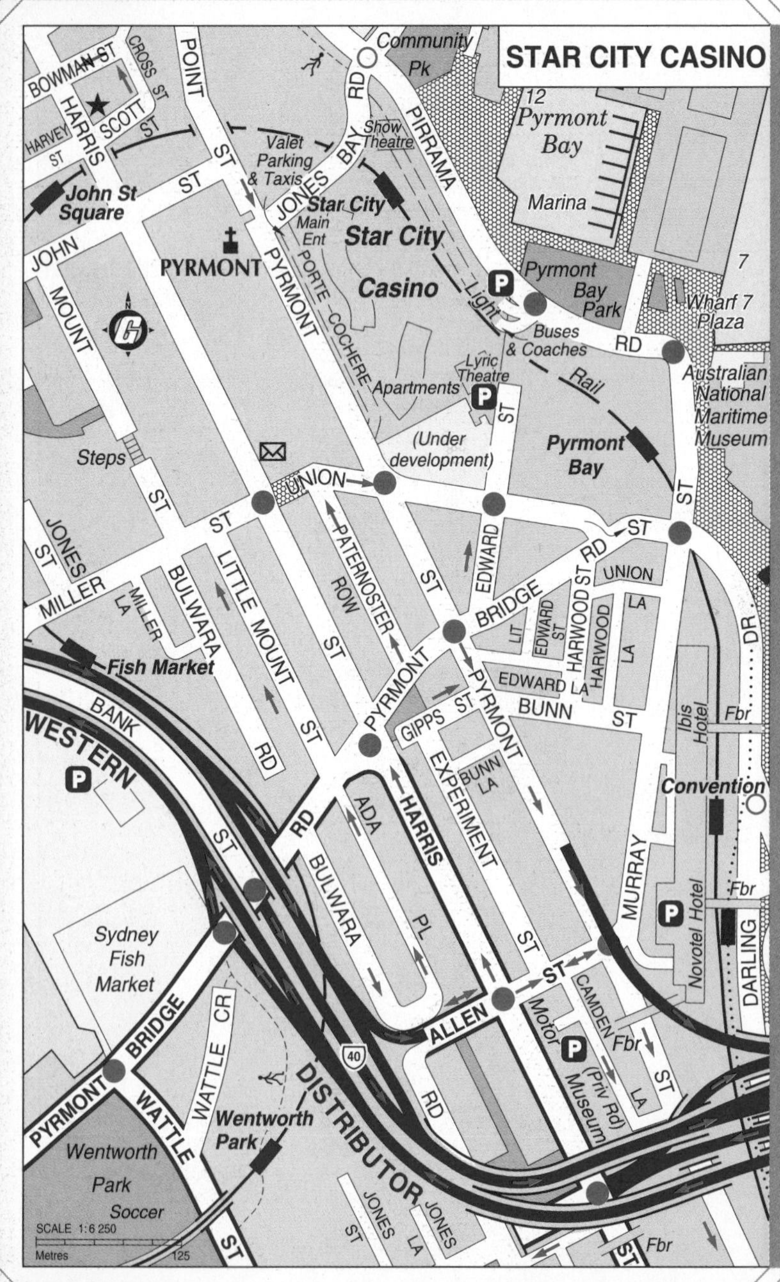
STAR CITY CASINO
Community Pk
Pyrmont Bay
Marina
Star City
Star City Casino
Show Theatre
Valet Parking & Taxis
Main Ent
Porte Cochere
PYRMONT
John St Square
Pyrmont Bay Park
Wharf 7 Plaza
Buses & Coaches
Light Rail
Lyric Theatre
Apartments
(Under development)
Australian National Maritime Museum
Pyrmont Bay
Steps
Fish Market
Sydney Fish Market
Wentworth Park
Wentworth Park Soccer
Convention
Ibis Hotel
Novotel Hotel
Motor Museum
Fbr
WESTERN DISTRIBUTOR
SCALE 1:6 250
Metres
125

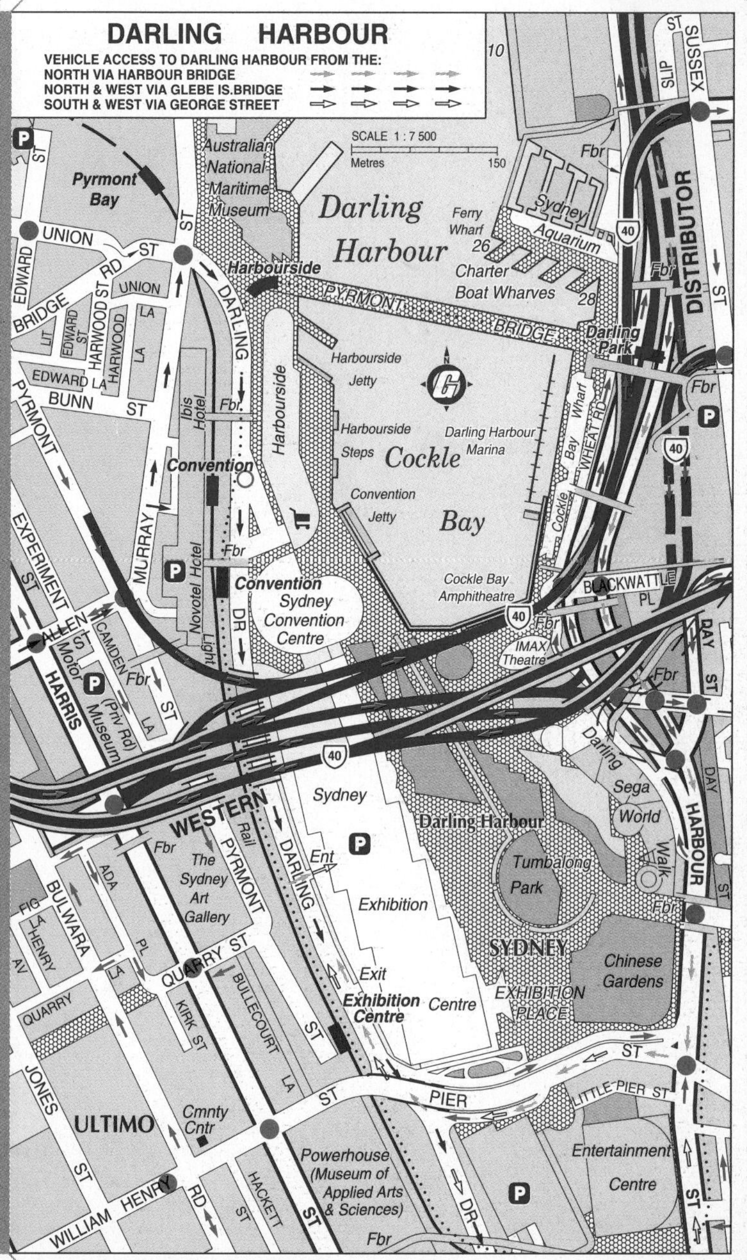
DARLING HARBOUR
VEHICLE ACCESS TO DARLING HARBOUR FROM THE:
NORTH VIA HARBOUR BRIDGE
NORTH & WEST VIA GLEBE IS.BRIDGE
SOUTH & WEST VIA GEORGE STREET
SCALE 1 : 7 500
Metres
150
Darling Harbour
Cockle Bay
Australian National Maritime Museum
Harbourside
Pyrmont Bay
Ferry Wharf
Charter Boat Wharves
Sydney Aquarium
Darling Park
Harbourside Jetty
Harbourside Steps
Darling Harbour Marina
Convention Jetty
Cockle Bay Amphitheatre
Cockle Bay Wharf
IMAX Theatre
Convention
Sydney Convention Centre
Ibis Hotel
Novotel Hotel
Motor Museum (Priv Rd)
Sydney Exhibition Centre
Darling Harbour
Tumbalong Park
Sega World
Darling Walk
Chinese Gardens
SYDNEY EXHIBITION PLACE
Exhibition Centre
Entertainment Centre
Powerhouse (Museum of Applied Arts & Sciences)
The Sydney Art Gallery
ULTIMO
Cmnty Cntr
PYRMONT BRIDGE
WESTERN DISTRIBUTOR
UNION ST
EDWARD ST
BRIDGE RD
PYRMONT ST
HARWOOD ST
BUNN ST
EDWARD LA
MURRAY ST
DARLING DR
EXPERIMENT ST
ALLEN ST
CAMDEN ST
HARRIS ST
WHEAT RD
BLACKWATTLE PL
DAY ST
SUSSEX ST
SLIP ST
HARBOUR ST
ADA PL
BULWARA RD
FIG LA
HENRY AV
QUARRY ST
KIRK ST
BULLECOURT LA
PIER ST
LITTLE PIER ST
JONES ST
WILLIAM HENRY ST
HACKETT ST
Light Rail
Fbr
Ent
Exit
40
COPYRIGHT © UNIVERSAL PRESS PTY LTD (PUBLISHER) 2001

MAP J

SCALE 1 : 20 800

Metres 200 400 600

CITY PARKING STATIONS

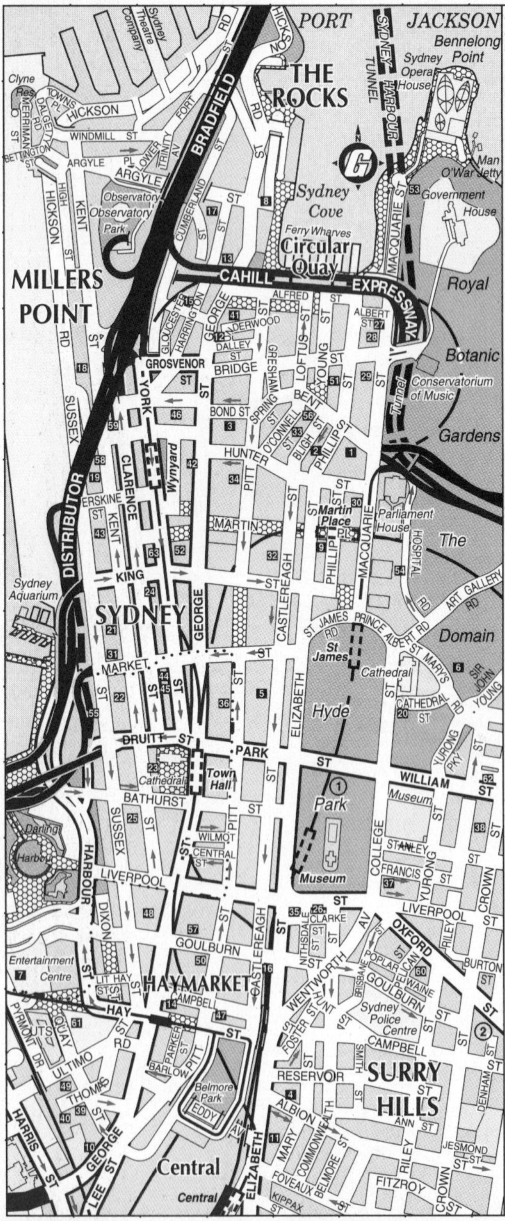

Location	Grid	No.
Albert St – 93 Macquarie St, Ritz-Carlton Hotel	F5	27
Albion St – Furama Hotel, 28 Albion St	E15	4
Argyle St – Circular Quay West	D3	8
Bent St – Chifley Tower, 27 Bent St	F6	1
Bijou La – 815 George St, Xerox House	B16	10
Bligh St – Rydges Wentworth Hotel	E6	2
Bond St – Australia Square	D6	3
Campbell St – Capitol	C14	14
Castlereagh St – Piccadilly, 133 Castlereagh St	D10	5
Cathedral St – Cathedral St Car Park	G10	20
Clarence St –		
Grace Hotel	C8	24
190 Clarence St, St Martins Tower	C9	44
Clarke St – 157 Liverpool St, Parkview	E13	35
Cunningham St – CKC Centre	C13	50
Dalley St – 2 Dalley St, AIG Building	D5	12
Darling Dr – Entertainment Centre	A13	7
Elizabeth St – 60 Elizabeth St, Heritage Building	E8	9
Francis St – Marriott Hotel	F12	37
George St –		
155 George St	D4	13
589 George St	C13	48
Goulburn St –		
cnr Castlereagh St	D13	16
30 Goulburn St, World Square	C13	57
Harrington St –		
Clocktower Square, 57 Harrington St	D3	17
Quay West, 111 Harrington St	C4	15
Hay St – 138 Hay St	D14	47
Hospital Rd – Sydney Hospital	F8	54
Jamison St – Le Meridien, 21 Jamison St	C6	46
Kent St –		
Cinema Centre, 521 Kent St	B11	25
cnr Napoleon St, 261 Kent St	B7	58
189 Kent St, ADC House	B5	18
196 Kent St	B6	59
279 Kent St	B7	19
321 Kent St & 86 Sussex St	B7	43
383 Kent St & 168 Sussex St	B9	21
427 Kent St, BT Tower	B10	22
464 Kent St, St Andrews House	C11	23
King St – MLC Centre, 106A King St	E8	32
Macquarie St –		
Opera House (Underground)	G3	53
131 Macquarie St, Hudson House	F5	29
187 Macquarie St, Park House	F7	30
Mary St – 300 Elizabeth St, Centennial Plaza	E15	11
Nithsdale St & Clarke St –		
175 Liverpool St, Remington Centre	E12	26
O'Connell St –		
O'Connell House	E6	56
6 O'Connell St, Norwich House	E6	33
Pelican St – Oxford Square	G13	60
Phillip St – 117 Macquarie St, Intercontinental Hotel	F5	28
Pitt St –		
Capital Centre, 255 Pitt St	D10	36
109 Pitt St, Hunter Connection	D7	34
Quay St –		
Market City	B14	61
89 Quay St	A15	49
Riley St – 70 Riley St	H11	38
St Marys Rd – The Domain	G9	6
Sussex St –		
Darling Park, 231 Sussex St	B10	55
MMI Centre, 182 Sussex St	B9	31
Suttor St – Terrace Tower	H11	62
Thomas St –		
Carlton Crest, 169 Thomas St	A15	40
cnr Quay St, Her Majesty's Theatre	B15	39
Underwood St – The Atrium, 3 Underwood St	D5	41
Wynyard La – All Seasons Premier Menzies Hotel	C7	42
York St –		
Queen Victoria Building, 111 York St	C9	45
22 York St, The Landmark	C8	52
York St – 71 York St, Company Director House	C8	63
Young St – 44 Young St, Governor Phillip Tower	E5	51

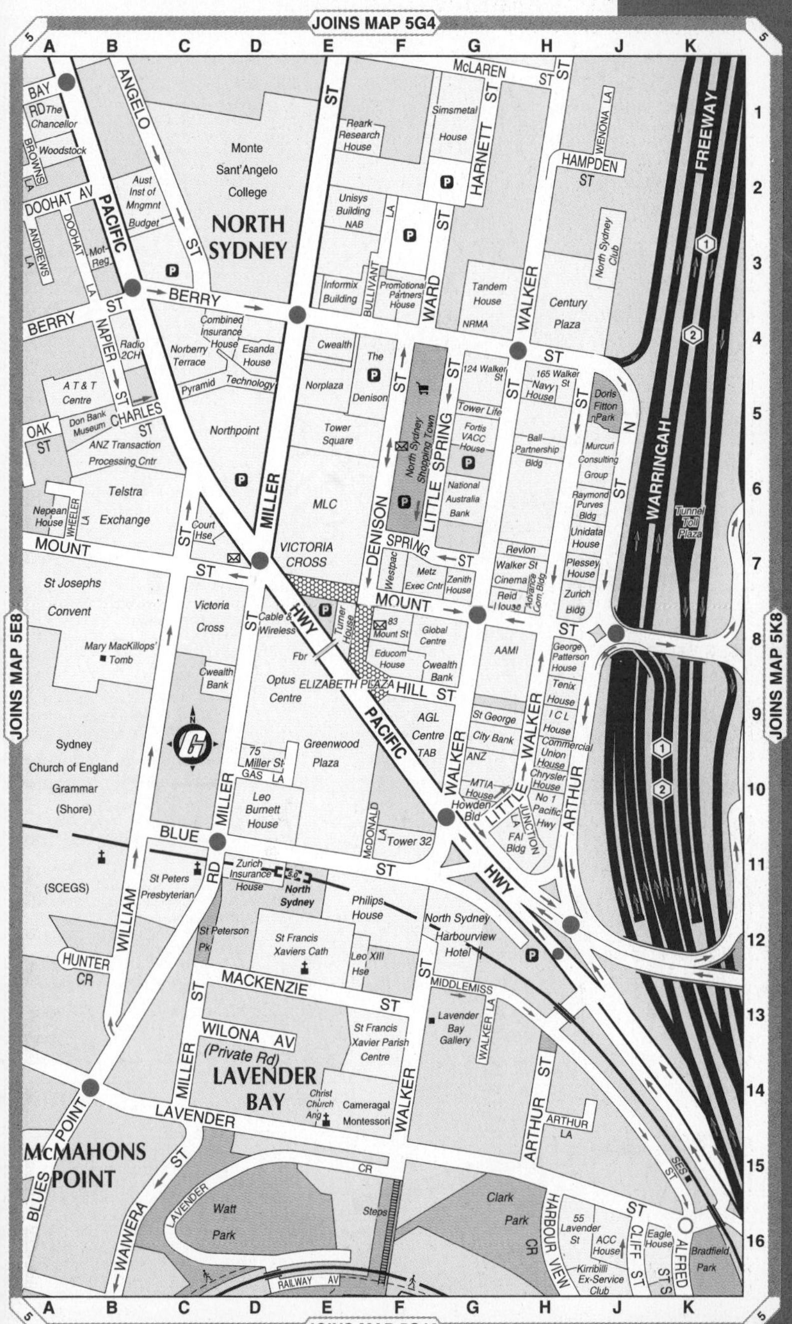
JOINS MAP 5G4
JOINS MAP 5E8
JOINS MAP 5K8
JOINS MAP 5G13
A B C D E F G H J K
1 2 3 4 5 6 7 8 9 10 11 12 13 14 15 16
NORTH SYDNEY
Monte Sant'Angelo College
BAY RD
The Chancellor
Woodstock
BROWNS LA
DOOHAT AV
DOOHAT LA
ANDREWS LA
PACIFIC
ANGELO ST
Aust Inst of Mngmnt
Budget
Mot Reg
BERRY ST
NAPIER ST
Radio 2CH
Combined Insurance House
Norberry Terrace
Esanda House
Pyramid
Technology
A T & T Centre
Don Bank Museum
CHARLES ST
OAK ST
ANZ Transaction Processing Cntr
Northpoint
Telstra Exchange
Nepean House
WHEELER LA
Court Hse
MOUNT ST
MILLER ST
St Josephs Convent
Mary MacKillops' Tomb
Victoria Cross
Cwealth Bank
Sydney Church of England Grammar (Shore)
(SCEGS)
McLAREN ST
Reark Research House
Simsmetal House
HARNETT ST
Unisys Building NAB
LA
WARD ST
Informix Building
BULLIVANT LA
Promotional Partners House
Tandem House
NRMA
WALKER ST
Century Plaza
HAMPDEN ST
WENONA LA
North Sydney Club
FREEWAY
Cwealth
The Denison
Norplaza
Tower Square
MLC
DENISON ST
North Sydney Shopping Town
LITTLE SPRING ST
124 Walker St
Tower Life
Fortis VACC House
National Australia Bank
165 Walker St
Navy House
Doris Fitton Park
Ball Partnership Bldg
Murcuri Consulting Group
Raymond Purves Bldg
Unidata House
Plessey House
Zurich Bldg
WARRINGAH
Tunnel Toll Plaza
VICTORIA CROSS
SPRING ST
Westpac
Metz Exec Cntr
Zenith House
Revlon
Walker St Cinema
Reid House
Advance Com Bldg
Cable & Wireless
Turner House
Fbr
83 Mount St
Global Centre
Educom House
Cwealth Bank
AAMI
George Patterson House
Tenix House
ICL House
Commercial Union House
Chrysler House
No 1 Pacific Hwy
Optus Centre
ELIZABETH PLAZA
HILL ST
AGL Centre
TAB
St George City Bank
ANZ
MTIA House
Howden Bld
LITTLE WALKER ST
JUNCTION LA
FAI Bldg
ARTHUR ST
HWY
75 Miller St
GAS LA
Greenwood Plaza
Leo Burnett House
McDONALD LA
Tower 32
BLUE ST
MILLER RD
Zurich Insurance House
North Sydney
St Peters Presbyterian
Philips House
North Sydney Harbourview Hotel
WILLIAM ST
HUNTER CR
St Peterson Pk
St Francis Xaviers Cath
Leo XIII Hse
MACKENZIE ST
MIDDLEMISS ST
Lavender Bay Gallery
WALKER LA
WILONA AV
(Private Rd)
LAVENDER BAY
St Francis Xavier Parish Centre
Christ Church Ang
Cameragal Montessori
WALKER ST
ARTHUR LA
POINT
LAVENDER ST
McMAHONS POINT
BLUES
WAIWERA ST
LAVENDER CR
Watt Park
Steps
Clark Park
HARBOUR VIEW CR
55 Lavender St
ACC House
Kirribilli Ex-Service Club
CLIFF ST
Eagle House
ALFRED ST S
SES
Bradfield Park
RAILWAY AV

MAP L

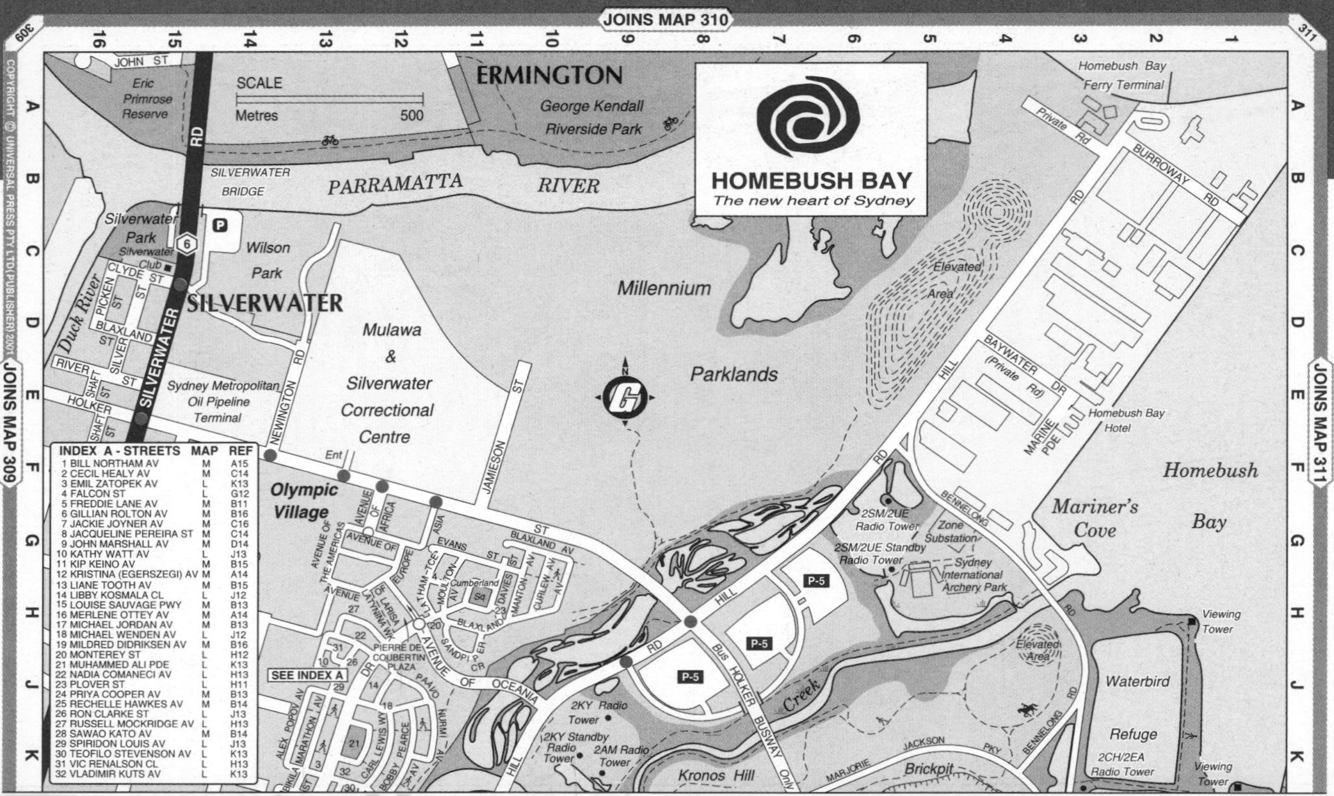

INDEX A - STREETS	MAP	REF
1 BILL NORTHAM AV	M	A15
2 CECIL HEALY AV	M	C14
3 EMIL ZATOPEK AV	L	K13
4 FALCON ST	L	G12
5 FREDDIE LANE AV	M	B11
6 GILLIAN ROLTON AV	M	B16
7 JACKIE JOYNER AV	M	C16
8 JACQUELINE PEREIRA ST	M	C14
9 JOHN MARSHALL AV	M	D14
10 KATHY WATT AV	L	J13
11 KIP KEINO AV	M	B15
12 KRISTINA (EGERSZEGI) AV	M	A14
13 LIANE TOOTH AV	M	B15
14 LIBBY KOSMALA CL	L	J12
15 LOUISE SAUVAGE PWY	M	B13
16 MERLENE OTTEY AV	M	A14
17 MICHAEL JORDAN AV	M	B13
18 MICHAEL WENDEN AV	L	J12
19 MILDRED DIDRIKSEN AV	M	B16
20 MONTEREY ST	L	H12
21 MUHAMMED ALI PDE	L	K13
22 NADIA COMANECI AV	L	H13
23 PLOVER ST	L	H11
24 PRIYA COOPER AV	M	B13
25 RECHELLE HAWKES AV	M	B14
26 RON CLARKE ST	L	J13
27 RUSSELL MOCKRIDGE AV	L	H13
28 SAWAO KATO AV	M	B14
29 SPIRIDON LOUIS AV	L	J13
30 TEOFILO STEVENSON AV	L	K13
31 VIC RENALSON CL	L	H13
32 VLADIMIR KUTS AV	L	K13

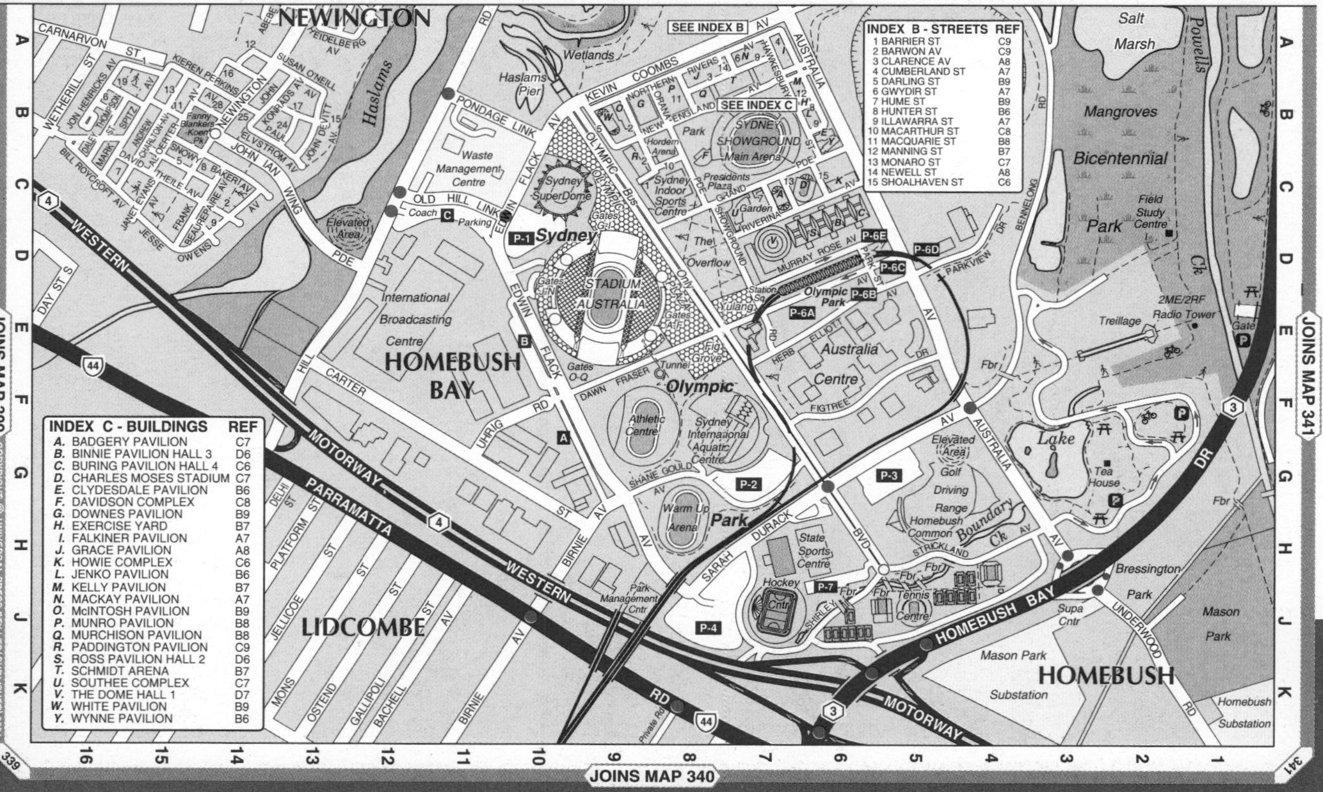
JOINS MAP 341
JOINS MAP 340
JOINS MAP 309
341
339
A B C D E F G H J K
1 2 3 4 5 6 7 8 9 10 11 12 13 14 15 16
INDEX B - STREETS REF
1 BARRIER ST C9
2 BARWON AV C9
3 CLARENCE AV A8
4 CUMBERLAND ST A7
5 DARLING ST B9
6 GWYDIR ST A7
7 HUME ST B9
8 HUNTER ST B6
9 ILLAWARRA ST A7
10 MACARTHUR ST C8
11 MACQUARIE ST B8
12 MANNING ST B7
13 MONARO ST C7
14 NEWELL ST A8
15 SHOALHAVEN ST C6
INDEX C - BUILDINGS REF
A. BADGERY PAVILION C7
B. BINNIE PAVILION HALL 3 D6
C. BURING PAVILION HALL 4 C6
D. CHARLES MOSES STADIUM C7
E. CLYDESDALE PAVILION B6
F. DAVIDSON COMPLEX C8
G. DOWNES PAVILION B9
H. EXERCISE YARD B7
I. FALKINER PAVILION A7
J. GRACE PAVILION A8
K. HOWIE COMPLEX C6
L. JENKO PAVILION B6
M. KELLY PAVILION B7
N. MACKAY PAVILION A7
O. McINTOSH PAVILION B9
P. MUNRO PAVILION B8
Q. MURCHISON PAVILION B8
R. PADDINGTON PAVILION C9
S. ROSS PAVILION HALL 2 D6
T. SCHMIDT ARENA B7
U. SOUTHEE COMPLEX C7
V. THE DOME HALL 1 D7
W. WHITE PAVILION B9
Y. WYNNE PAVILION B6
SEE INDEX B
SEE INDEX C
NEWINGTON
Wetlands
Haslams Pier
Haslams
Salt Marsh
Powells Ck
Mangroves
Bicentennial Park
Field Study Centre
2ME/2RF Radio Tower
Treillage
Gate
Lake
Tea House
Bressington Park
Mason Park
Supa Cntr
Mason Park Substation
HOMEBUSH
Homebush Substation
UNDERWOOD RD
HOMEBUSH BAY DR
MOTORWAY
BENNELONG DR
PARKVIEW
AUSTRALIA AV
Elevated Area
Golf Driving Range
Homebush Common
Boundary Ck
STRICKLAND AV
Tennis Centre
State Sports Centre
Hockey Cntr
SHIRLEY
DURACK
SARAH
BVD
Olympic Park
Australia Centre
HERB ELLIOTT AV
FIGTREE DR
Olympic Park Station Sq
Yulang
MURRAY ROSE AV
PARK ST
SYDNEY SHOWGROUND
Main Arena
Presidents Plaza
Garden
RIVERINA
GRAND PDE
SHOWGROUND RD
The Overflow
Sydney Indoor Sports Centre
Hordern Arena
Park
KEVIN COOMBS AV
NORTHERN
ORANA
NEW ENGLAND
RIVERS
HAWKESBURY
Sydney International Aquatic Centre
Warm Up Arena
Athletic Centre
SHANE GOULD AV
Fig Grove
Tunnel
Olympic
Sydney
STADIUM AUSTRALIA
Sydney SuperDome
OLYMPIC BLVD
Bus Only
PLAZA
DAWN FRASER
Gates
Park Management Cntr
BIRNIE AV
EDWIN FLACK AV
UHRIG RD
PONDAGE LINK
Waste Management Centre
OLD HILL LINK
Coach Parking
HOMEBUSH BAY
International Broadcasting Centre
Elevated Area
HILL RD
CARTER
MOTORWAY
PARRAMATTA RD
WESTERN
LIDCOMBE
BACHELL AV
GALLIPOLI ST
OSTEND ST
JELLICOE ST
MONS
PLATFORM ST
DELHI ST
JOHN IAN WING PDE
JOHN DEVITT AV
SUSAN O'NEILL
HEIDELBERG AV
ABEBE
KONRADS AV
PAUL
JOHN NEWINGTON
ELVSTROM AV
KIEREN PERKINS
BAKER AV
BEAUREPAIRE AV
FRANK
OWENS
JANET EVANS AV
JESSE
SNOWY
THEILE AV
DAVID
MARK
ANDREW
SPITZ
DALEY THOMPSON
Fanny Blankers Koen Pk
BILL ROYCROFT AV
JON HENRICKS AV
WETHERILL ST
CARNARVON ST
DAY ST S
P-1 P-2 P-3 P-4 P-6A P-6B P-6C P-6D P-6E P-7
Private Rd

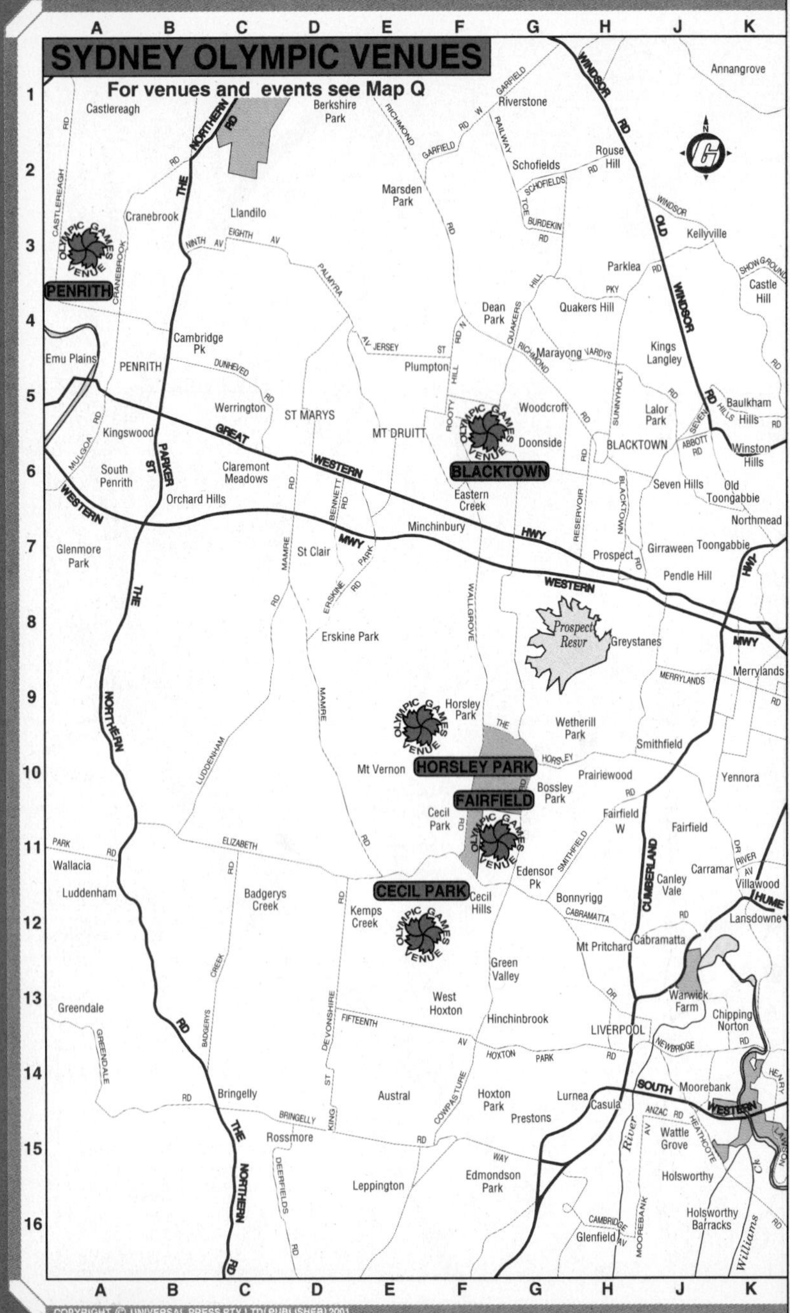
SYDNEY OLYMPIC VENUES
For venues and events see Map Q
A B C D E F G H J K
1 2 3 4 5 6 7 8 9 10 11 12 13 14 15 16
PENRITH
BLACKTOWN
HORSLEY PARK
FAIRFIELD
CECIL PARK
OLYMPIC GAMES VENUE
Castlereagh
Berkshire Park
Riverstone
Annangrove
Rouse Hill
Schofields
Marsden Park
Cranebrook
Llandilo
Kellyville
Parklea
Castle Hill
Dean Park
Quakers Hill
Cambridge Pk
Emu Plains
PENRITH
Plumpton
Marayong
Kings Langley
Werrington
ST MARYS
MT DRUITT
Woodcroft
Lalor Park
Baulkham Hills
Kingswood
Doonside
BLACKTOWN
Winston Hills
South Penrith
Claremont Meadows
Seven Hills
Old Toongabbie
Orchard Hills
Eastern Creek
Northmead
Minchinbury
Glenmore Park
St Clair
Prospect
Girraween
Toongabbie
Pendle Hill
Erskine Park
Prospect Resvr
Greystanes
Merrylands
Horsley Park
Wetherill Park
Smithfield
Mt Vernon
Prairiewood
Yennora
Bossley Park
Cecil Park
Fairfield W
Fairfield
Wallacia
Carramar
Villawood
Luddenham
Badgerys Creek
Kemps Creek
Edensor Pk
Canley Vale
Cecil Hills
Bonnyrigg
Lansdowne
Mt Pritchard
Cabramatta
Green Valley
Warwick Farm
Greendale
West Hoxton
Hinchinbrook
LIVERPOOL
Chipping Norton
Bringelly
Austral
Hoxton Park
Lurnea
Casula
Moorebank
Prestons
Wattle Grove
Rossmore
Leppington
Edmondson Park
Holsworthy
Holsworthy Barracks
Glenfield
THE NORTHERN RD
GREAT WESTERN HWY
WESTERN MWY
PARKER ST
WINDSOR RD
OLD WINDSOR RD
CUMBERLAND HWY
HUME HWY
SOUTH WESTERN
River
Williams Ck

MAP P

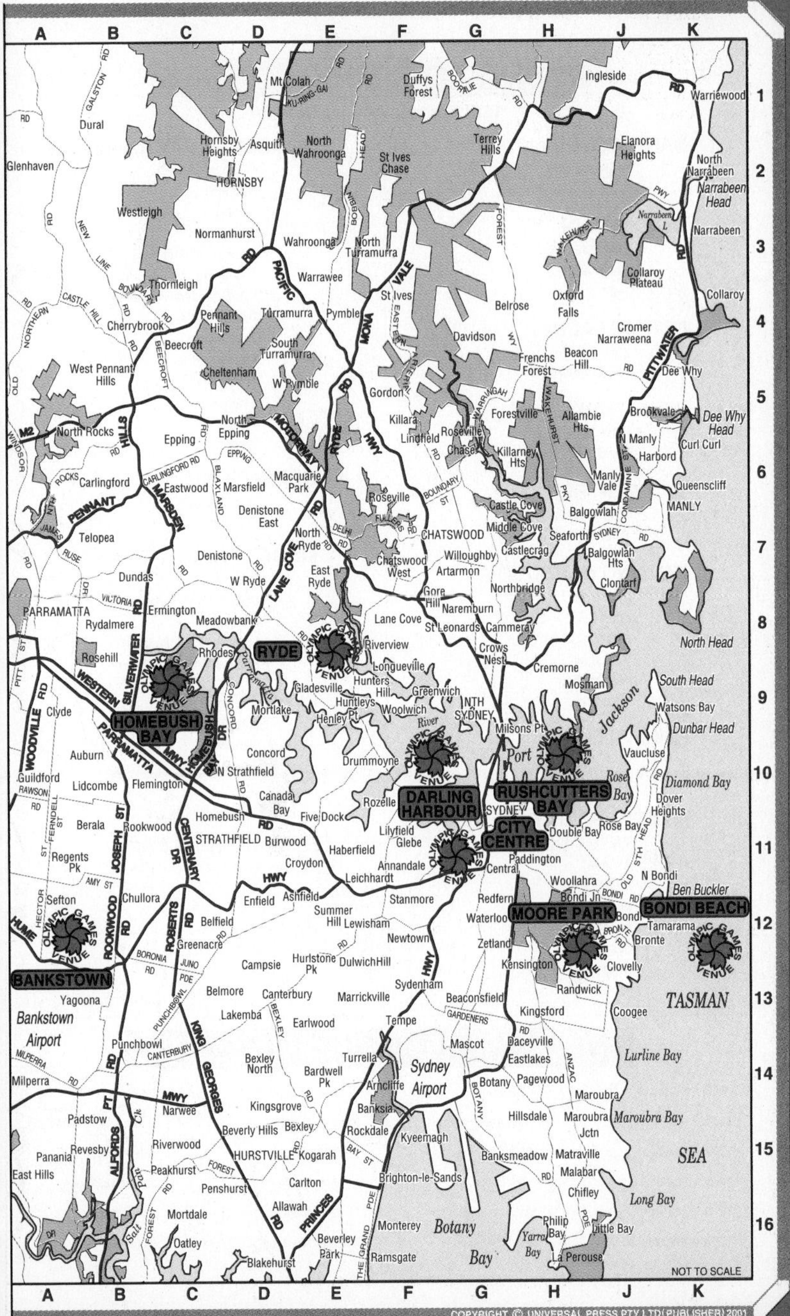
A B C D E F G H J K
1 2 3 4 5 6 7 8 9 10 11 12 13 14 15 16
Mt Colah
Duffys Forest
Ingleside
Warriewood
Dural
Hornsby Heights
Asquith
North Wahroonga
St Ives Chase
Terrey Hills
Elanora Heights
Glenhaven
HORNSBY
North Narrabeen
Narrabeen Head
Westleigh
Narrabeen
Normanhurst
Wahroonga
North Turramurra
Thornleigh
Warrawee
Collaroy Plateau
Collaroy
St Ives
Belrose
Oxford Falls
Pennant Hills
Turramurra
Pymble
Cherrybrook
Beecroft
South Turramurra
Davidson
Cromer
Narraweena
West Pennant Hills
Cheltenham
W Pymble
Frenchs Forest
Beacon Hill
Dee Why
Gordon
Forestville
Allambie Hts
Brookvale
Dee Why Head
North Rocks
North Epping
Killara
Roseville Chase
Epping
Lindfield
Killarney Hts
N Manly
Curl Curl
Harbord
Carlingford
Eastwood
Marsfield
Macquarie Park
Manly Vale
Queenscliff
Denistone East
Roseville
Castle Cove
MANLY
Telopea
North Ryde
Middle Cove
Balgowlah
Seaforth
CHATSWOOD
Chatswood West
Willoughby
Castlecrag
Balgowlah Hts
Denistone
Artarmon
Dundas
W Ryde
East Ryde
Clontarf
Northbridge
Gore Hill
PARRAMATTA
Ermington
Naremburn
Rydalmere
Meadowbank
Lane Cove
St Leonards
Cammeray
North Head
Rhodes
RYDE
Riverview
Rosehill
Crows Nest
Cremorne
Longueville
Mosman
South Head
Gladesville
Hunters Hill
Greenwich
Clyde
HOMEBUSH BAY
Mortlake
Huntleys Pt
Henley
Woolwich
NTH SYDNEY
Watsons Bay
Jackson
Dunbar Head
Milsons Pt
Port
Auburn
Concord
Vaucluse
Drummoyne
Guildford
N Strathfield
Lidcombe
Flemington
Rose Bay
Diamond Bay
Canada Bay
Rozelle
DARLING HARBOUR
RUSHCUTTERS BAY
Dover Heights
Homebush
SYDNEY
Berala
Rookwood
Five Dock
CITY CENTRE
Double Bay
Rose Bay
STRATHFIELD
Burwood
Lilyfield
Glebe
Haberfield
Regents Pk
Paddington
Croydon
Annandale
Central
N Bondi
Leichhardt
Woollahra
Sefton
Chullora
Enfield
Ashfield
Stanmore
Redfern
Bondi Jn
Ben Buckler
BONDI BEACH
Summer Hill
Lewisham
Waterloo
MOORE PARK
Bondi
Tamarama
Belfield
Bronte
Greenacre
Newtown
Zetland
Campsie
Hurlstone Pk
Dulwich Hill
Kensington
Clovelly
BANKSTOWN
Sydenham
Randwick
Belmore
Canterbury
Marrickville
Yagoona
Beaconsfield
TASMAN
Lakemba
Kingsford
Coogee
Bankstown Airport
Earlwood
Tempe
Mascot
Punchbowl
Daceyville
Lurline Bay
Turrella
Eastlakes
Bexley North
Sydney Airport
Bardwell Pk
Botany
Pagewood
Milperra
Arncliffe
Maroubra
Narwee
Kingsgrove
Banksia
Maroubra Bay
Padstow
Hillsdale
Maroubra Jctn
Beverly Hills
Bexley
Rockdale
Kyeemagh
Revesby
Riverwood
Panania
HURSTVILLE
Kogarah
Banksmeadow
Matraville
SEA
Peakhurst
East Hills
Malabar
Carlton
Brighton-le-Sands
Penshurst
Chifley
Allawah
Long Bay
Mortdale
Monterey
Botany Bay
Philip Bay
Little Bay
Oatley
Beverley Park
Yarra Bay
Blakehurst
Ramsgate
La Perouse
NOT TO SCALE
OLYMPIC GAMES VENUE

SYDNEY OLYMPIC VENUES

15th September - 1st October

BANKSTOWN
MAP 368 B12
Cycling - Velodrome

BLACKTOWN
MAP 242 J16
Baseball 2
Softball

BONDI BEACH
MAP 378 E4
Beach Volleyball

CECIL PARK
MAP 361 E3
Shooting

CITY CENTRE
MAP C K3
Triathlon

DARLING HARBOUR
MAP 3 B8
Boxing
Judo
Volleyball
Weightlifting
Wrestling

FAIRFIELD
MAP 332 J13
Cycling - Mountain Bike

HOMEBUSH BAY
MAP 340 H2
Archery
Athletics
Badminton
Baseball
Basketball
Diving
Football

HOMEBUSH BAY (continued)
Gymnastics
Handball
Hockey
Marathon
Modern Pentathlon
Swimming
Synchronised Swimming
Table Tennis
Taekwondo
Tennis
Trampolining
Volleyball
Water Polo
Walk

HORSLEY PARK
MAP 333 B2
Equestrian

MOORE PARK
MAP 20 J7
Cycling Road Race and Time Trials
Fencing
Football (Preliminaries)
Football (Womens Final)

PENRITH
MAP 206 A14
Canoeing
Kayaking
Rowing
Slalom Canoe

RUSHCUTTERS BAY
MAP 13 F4
Sailing

RYDE
MAP 312 F5
Water Polo

THE GAMES OF THE OLYMPIAD

1896 Athens	1924 Paris	1956 Melbourne	1980 Moscow
1900 Paris	1928 Amsterdam	1960 Rome	1984 Los Angeles
1904 St Louis	1932 Los Angeles	1964 Tokyo	1988 Seoul
1908 London	1936 Berlin	1968 Mexico City	1992 Barcelona
1912 Stockholm	1948 London	1972 Munich	1996 Atlanta
1920 Antwerp	1952 Helsinki	1976 Montreal	2000 Sydney

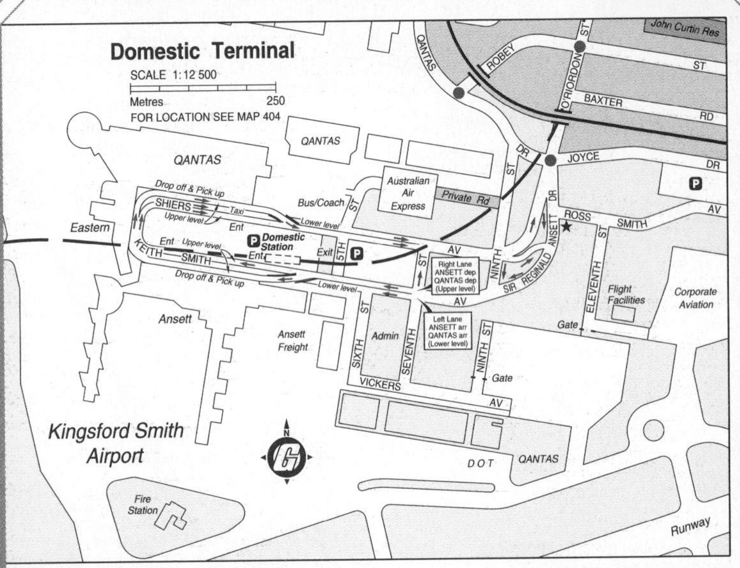

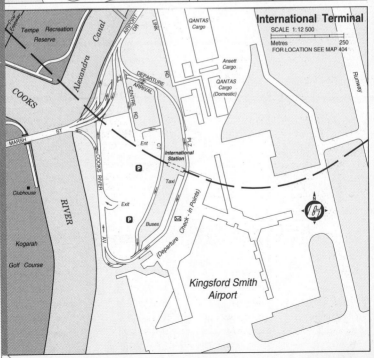

International Terminal

SCALE 1:12 500
Metres 250
FOR LOCATION SEE MAP 404

Prop Freeway
Tempe Recreation Reserve
Alexandra Canal
COOKS RIVER
MARSH ST
AIRPORT DR
LINK RD
DEPARTURE
ARRIVAL
CENTRE RD
QANTAS Cargo
Ansett Cargo
QANTAS Cargo (Domestic)
Runway
Ent
CT
PLZ
International Station
COOKS RIVER AV
Taxi
Exit
Buses
(Departure Check - in Points)
Clubhouse
Kogarah Golf Course
Kingsford Smith Airport

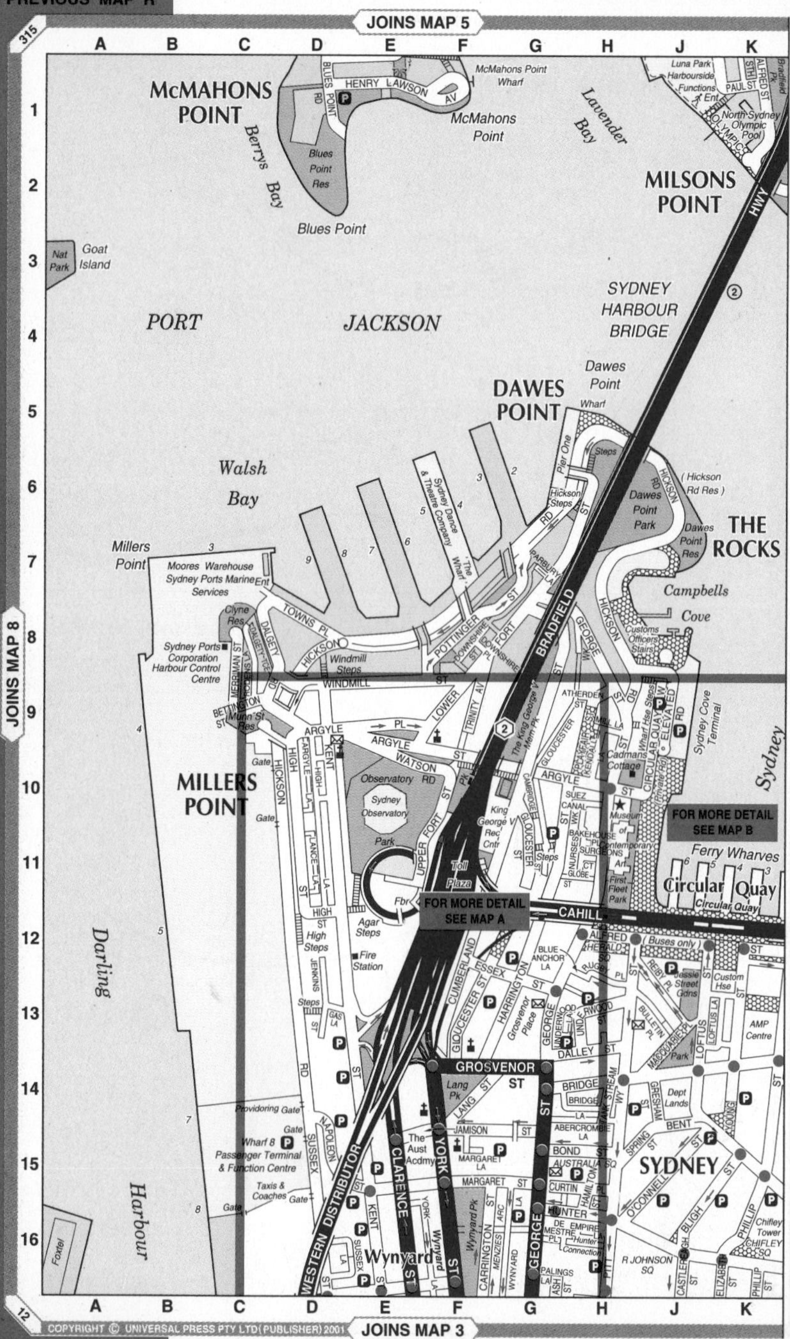

JOINS MAP 5
JOINS MAP 8
JOINS MAP 3
315
12
A B C D E F G H J K
1 2 3 4 5 6 7 8 9 10 11 12 13 14 15 16
McMAHONS POINT
Berrys Bay
Blues Point Res
Blues Point
HENRY LAWSON AV
BLUES POINT RD
McMahons Point Wharf
McMahons Point
Lavender Bay
Luna Park Harbourside Functions Ent
North Sydney Olympic Pool
OLYMPIC
PAUL ST
ALFRED ST
Bradfield Pk
MILSONS POINT
HWY
Nat Park
Goat Island
PORT
JACKSON
SYDNEY HARBOUR BRIDGE
Dawes Point
Wharf
DAWES POINT
Walsh Bay
Pier One
Sydney Dance & Theatre Company
'The Wharf'
Hickson Steps
Steps
Dawes Point Park
(Hickson Rd Res)
Dawes Point Res
THE ROCKS
Millers Point
Moores Warehouse
Sydney Ports Marine Services
Ent
Campbells Cove
Customs Officers Stairs
TOWNS PL
HICKSON RD
Windmill Steps
POTTINGER
DOWNSHIRE ST
FORT ST
PARBURY LA
BRADFIELD
GEORGE ST
Clyne Res
DALGETY RD
Sydney Ports Corporation Harbour Control Centre
MERRIMAN ST
WINDMILL ST
BETTINGTON ST
Munn St Res
LOWER
TRINITY AV
ATHERDEN ST
MILL LA
ARGYLE
ARGYLE PL
WATSON RD
KENT
The King George V Mem Pk
PLAYFAIR ST
KENDALL LA
Wharf Hse Steps
CIRCULAR QUAY W
ELEVATED
Cadmans Cottage
Sydney Cove Terminal
Sydney
MILLERS POINT
Gate
HICKSON
HIGH
Observatory RD
Sydney Observatory
Park
UPPER FORT ST
King George V Rec Cntr
GLOUCESTER ST
CAMBRIDGE
SUEZ CANAL
Museum of Contemporary Art
FOR MORE DETAIL SEE MAP B
Ferry Wharves
Circular Quay
Toll Plaza
Fbr
FOR MORE DETAIL SEE MAP A
CAHILL
First Fleet Park
BAKEHOUSE PL
NURSES WK
SURGEONS CT
GLOBE
Steps
Agar Steps
High Steps
Fire Station
JENKINS
GAS LA
Darling
Harbour
CUMBERLAND
ESSEX
HARRINGTON
Grosvenor Place
BLUE ANCHOR LA
ALFRED
HERALD SQ
RUGBY PL
(Buses only)
REIBY PL
Jessie Street Gdns
Custom Hse
LOFTUS LA
AMP Centre
BULLETIN PL
MACQUARIE PL
Park
DALLEY ST
UNDERWOOD ST
GROSVENOR ST
Lang Pk
LANG ST
BRIDGE ST
TANK STREAM WY
GRESHAM
Dept Lands
YOUNG
Providoring Gate
Gate
Wharf 8 Passenger Terminal & Function Centre
Taxis & Coaches
NAPOLEON
SUSSEX
WESTERN DISTRIBUTOR
CLARENCE ST
YORK ST
The Aust Acdmy
JAMISON ST
MARGARET LA
MARGARET ST
ABERCROMBIE LA
BOND ST
AUSTRALIA SQ
CURTIN
HUNTER ST
DE MESTRE PL
EMPIRE LA
Hunter Connection
HAMILTON
SPRING ST
BENT ST
SYDNEY
O'CONNELL ST
BLIGH ST
PHILLIP ST
Chifley Tower
CHIFLEY SQ
Foxtel
KENT ST
Wynyard
Wynyard Pk
CARRINGTON ST
MENZIES
WYNYARD
GEORGE ST
PALINGS LA
ASH ST
PITT ST
R JOHNSON SQ
CASTLEREAGH ST
ELIZABETH ST

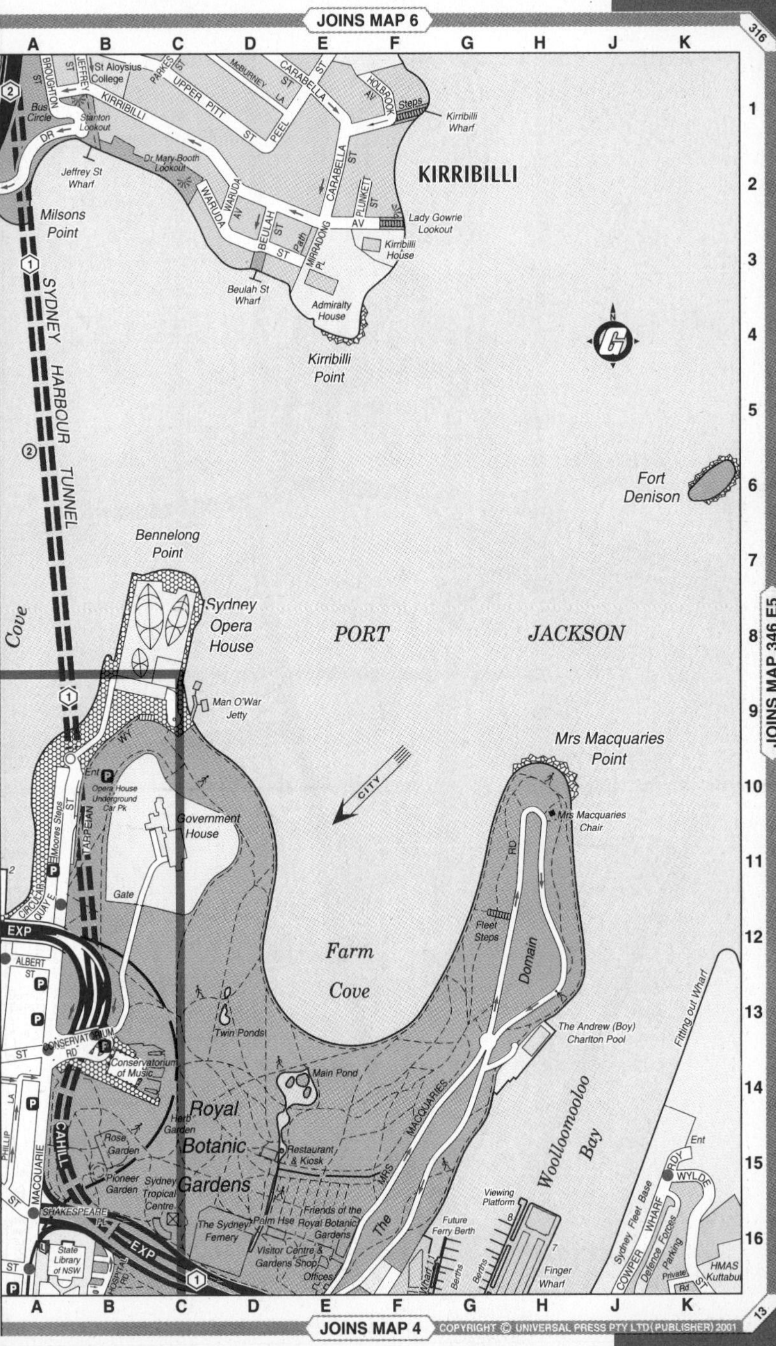
JOINS MAP 6
KIRRIBILLI
Kirribilli Wharf
Lady Gowrie Lookout
Kirribilli House
Admiralty House
Kirribilli Point
Beulah St Wharf
Jeffrey St Wharf
Milsons Point
St Aloysius College
Stanton Lookout
Dr Mary Booth Lookout
Bus Circle
SYDNEY HARBOUR TUNNEL
Fort Denison
Bennelong Point
Sydney Opera House
PORT
JACKSON
Cove
Man O'War Jetty
Mrs Macquaries Point
Mrs Macquaries Chair
CITY
Opera House Underground Car Pk
Government House
Gate
Farm Cove
Fleet Steps
Domain
The Andrew (Boy) Charlton Pool
Woolloomooloo Bay
Fitting out Wharf
Twin Ponds
Main Pond
Royal Botanic Gardens
Herb Garden
Rose Garden
Pioneer Garden
Sydney Tropical Centre
Conservatorium of Music
Restaurant & Kiosk
Palm Hse
The Sydney Fernery
Friends of the Royal Botanic Gardens
Visitor Centre & Gardens Shop
Offices
Viewing Platform
Future Ferry Berth
Finger Wharf
Sydney Fleet Base
Defence Forces Parking
HMAS Kuttabul
State Library of NSW
JOINS MAP 346 E5
JOINS MAP 4

MAP 3

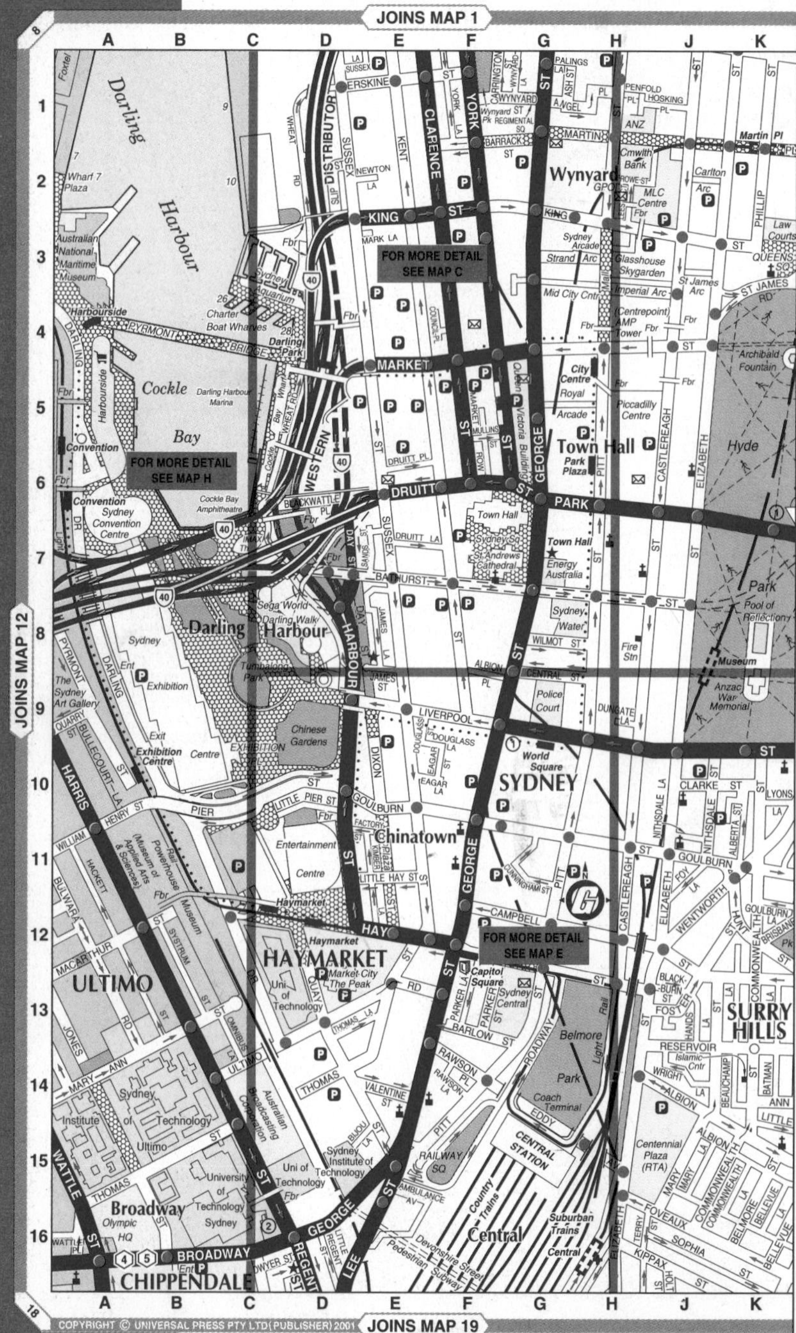
JOINS MAP 1
JOINS MAP 12
JOINS MAP 19
FOR MORE DETAIL SEE MAP C
FOR MORE DETAIL SEE MAP H
FOR MORE DETAIL SEE MAP E
Darling Harbour
Cockle Bay
Darling Harbour
Wynyard
Town Hall
SYDNEY
Chinatown
HAYMARKET
ULTIMO
SURRY HILLS
CHIPPENDALE
Broadway
Central
Hyde Park
CENTRAL STATION
Belmore Park
World Square
Australian National Maritime Museum
Sydney Convention Centre
Sydney Aquarium
Chinese Gardens
Entertainment Centre
Powerhouse Museum (Museum of Applied Arts & Sciences)
Sydney Exhibition Centre
Queen Victoria Building
St Andrews Cathedral
Sydney Institute of Technology
University of Technology Sydney
Australian Broadcasting Corporation
Centennial Plaza (RTA)
Anzac War Memorial
Archibald Fountain
Pool of Reflection
Museum

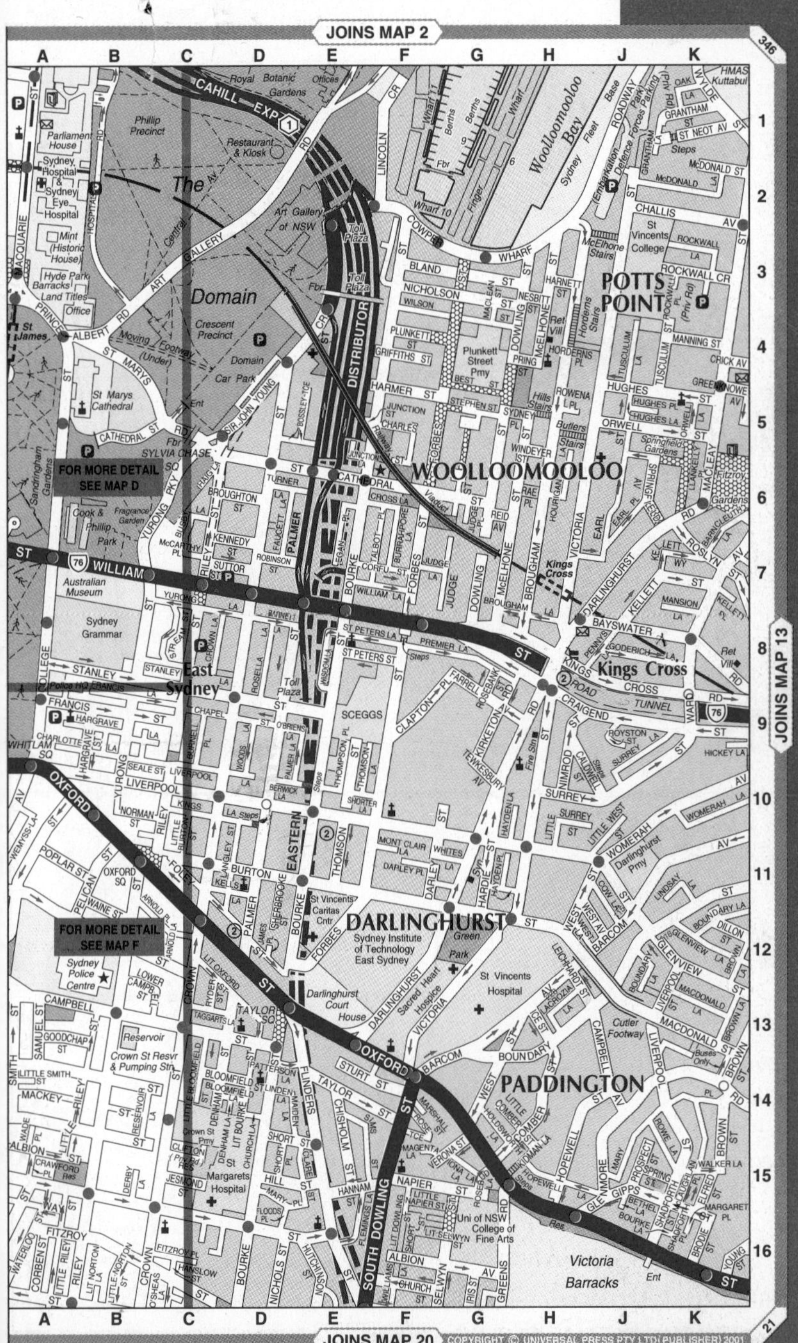
JOINS MAP 2
A B C D E F G H J K
346
Royal Botanic Gardens
CAHILL EXP
Phillip Precinct
Parliament House
Sydney Hospital & Sydney Eye Hospital
Mint (Historic House)
Hyde Park Barracks
Land Titles Office
St James
Restaurant & Kiosk
The Domain
Art Gallery of NSW
Crescent Precinct
Domain Car Park
St Marys Cathedral
FOR MORE DETAIL SEE MAP D
Cook & Phillip Park
Australian Museum
Sydney Grammar
East Sydney
Woolloomooloo Bay
Wharf 10
Sydney Fleet Base
POTTS POINT
St Vincents College
Plunkett Street Pmy
WOOLLOOMOOLOO
DISTRIBUTOR
Toll Plaza
Kings Cross
WILLIAM ST
SCEGGS
Fitzroy Gardens
JOINS MAP 13
FOR MORE DETAIL SEE MAP F
Sydney Police Centre
DARLINGHURST
St Vincents Caritas Cntr
Sydney Institute of Technology East Sydney
Green Park
St Vincents Hospital
Darlinghurst Court House
Sacred Heart Hospice
Darlinghurst Pmy
Cutler Footway
PADDINGTON
Reservoir
Crown St Resvr & Pumping Stn
Crown St Pmy
St Margarets Hospital
Uni of NSW College of Fine Arts
Victoria Barracks
OXFORD ST
SOUTH DOWLING ST
1 2 3 4 5 6 7 8 9 10 11 12 13 14 15 16
JOINS MAP 20
21

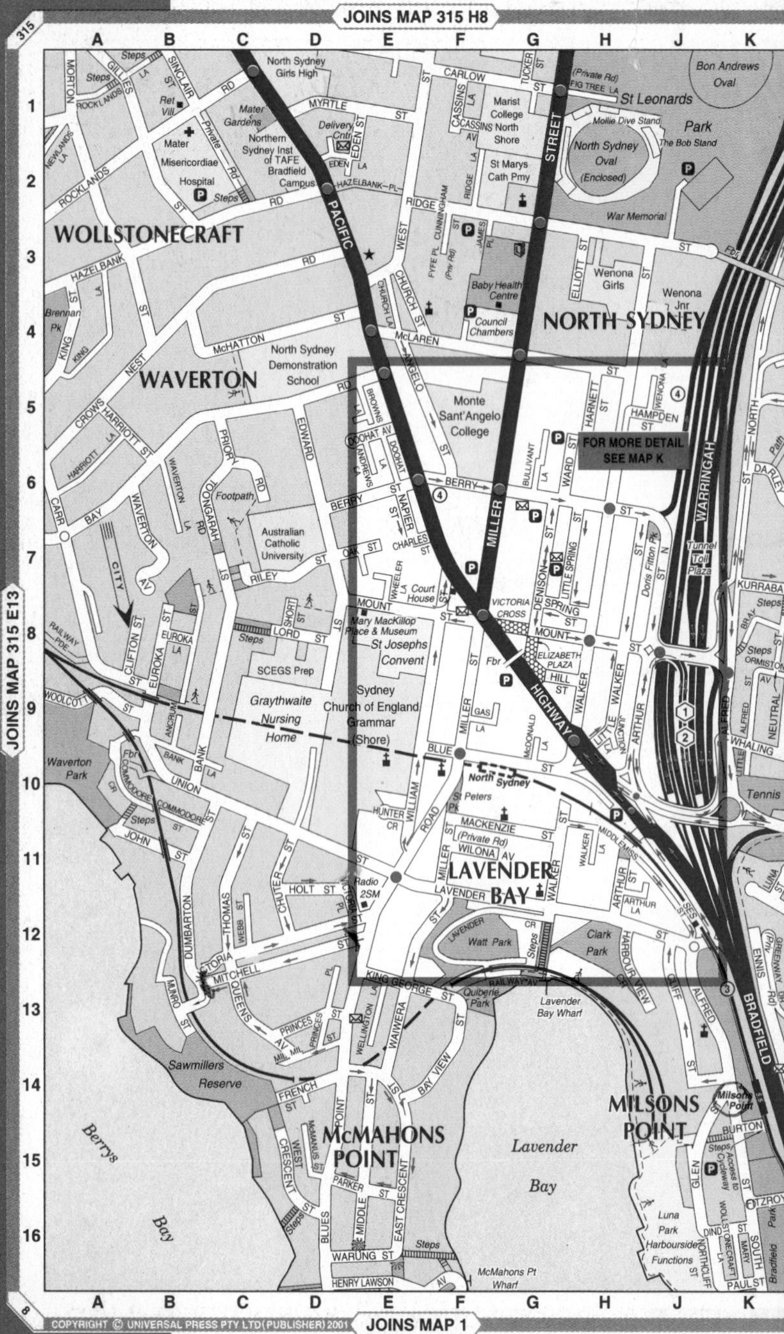
JOINS MAP 315 H8
JOINS MAP 315 E13
JOINS MAP 1
315
8
A B C D E F G H J K
1 2 3 4 5 6 7 8 9 10 11 12 13 14 15 16
WOLLSTONECRAFT
WAVERTON
NORTH SYDNEY
LAVENDER BAY
McMAHONS POINT
MILSONS POINT
North Sydney Girls High
Mater Gardens
Northern Sydney Inst of TAFE Bradfield Campus
Mater Misericordiae Hospital
Delivery Cntr
Marist College North Shore
St Marys Cath Pmy
St Leonards Park
North Sydney Oval (Enclosed)
Mollie Dive Stand
The Bob Stand
Bon Andrews Oval
War Memorial
Wenona Girls
Wenona Jnr
Baby Health Centre
Council Chambers
North Sydney Demonstration School
Monte Sant'Angelo College
FOR MORE DETAIL SEE MAP K
Australian Catholic University
Court House
Mary MacKillop Place & Museum
St Josephs Convent
SCEGS Prep
Graythwaite Nursing Home
Sydney Church of England Grammar (Shore)
VICTORIA CROSS
ELIZABETH PLAZA
Doris Fitton Pk
Tunnel Toll Plaza
Waverton Park
Brennan Pk
North Sydney
St Peters Pk
Radio 2SM
Watt Park
Clark Park
Quiberie Park
Lavender Bay Wharf
Sawmillers Reserve
Berrys Bay
Lavender Bay
Luna Park Harbourside Functions
McMahons Pt Wharf
Milsons Point
Access to Cycleway
Tennis
PACIFIC HIGHWAY
MILLER STREET
WARRINGAH
BRADFIELD
CITY
Footpath
Steps
COPYRIGHT © UNIVERSAL PRESS PTY LTD (PUBLISHER) 2001

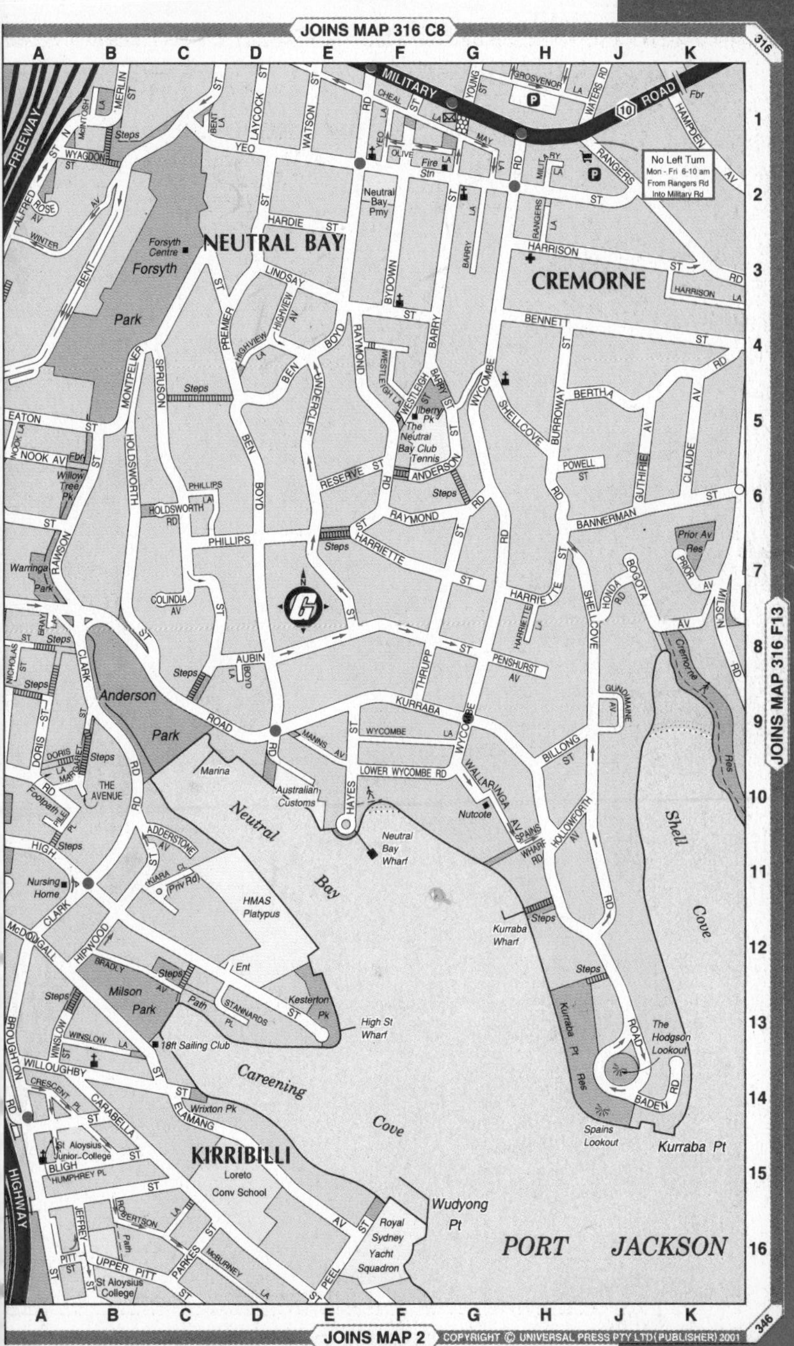
JOINS MAP 316 C8
JOINS MAP 316 F13
JOINS MAP 2
NEUTRAL BAY
CREMORNE
KIRRIBILLI
PORT JACKSON
Neutral Bay
Careening Cove
Shell Cove
MILITARY ROAD
No Left Turn
Mon - Fri 6-10 am
From Rangers Rd
Into Military Rd
Forsyth Park
Anderson Park
Milson Park
HMAS Platypus
Kurraba Pt
Wudyong Pt
Royal Sydney Yacht Squadron
Loreto Conv School
St Aloysius Junior College
St Aloysius College
The Hodgson Lookout
Spains Lookout
Neutral Bay Wharf
Kurraba Wharf
High St Wharf
18ft Sailing Club
Nutcote
Australian Customs
Marina
Kesterton Pk
Wrixton Pk
Ilbery Pk
The Neutral Bay Club Tennis
Forsyth Centre
Neutral Bay Pmy
Fire Stn
Willow Tree Pk
Warringa Park
Prior Av Res
Nursing Home
Kurraba Pt Res
COPYRIGHT © UNIVERSAL PRESS PTY LTD (PUBLISHER) 2001

JOINS MAP 314 H16

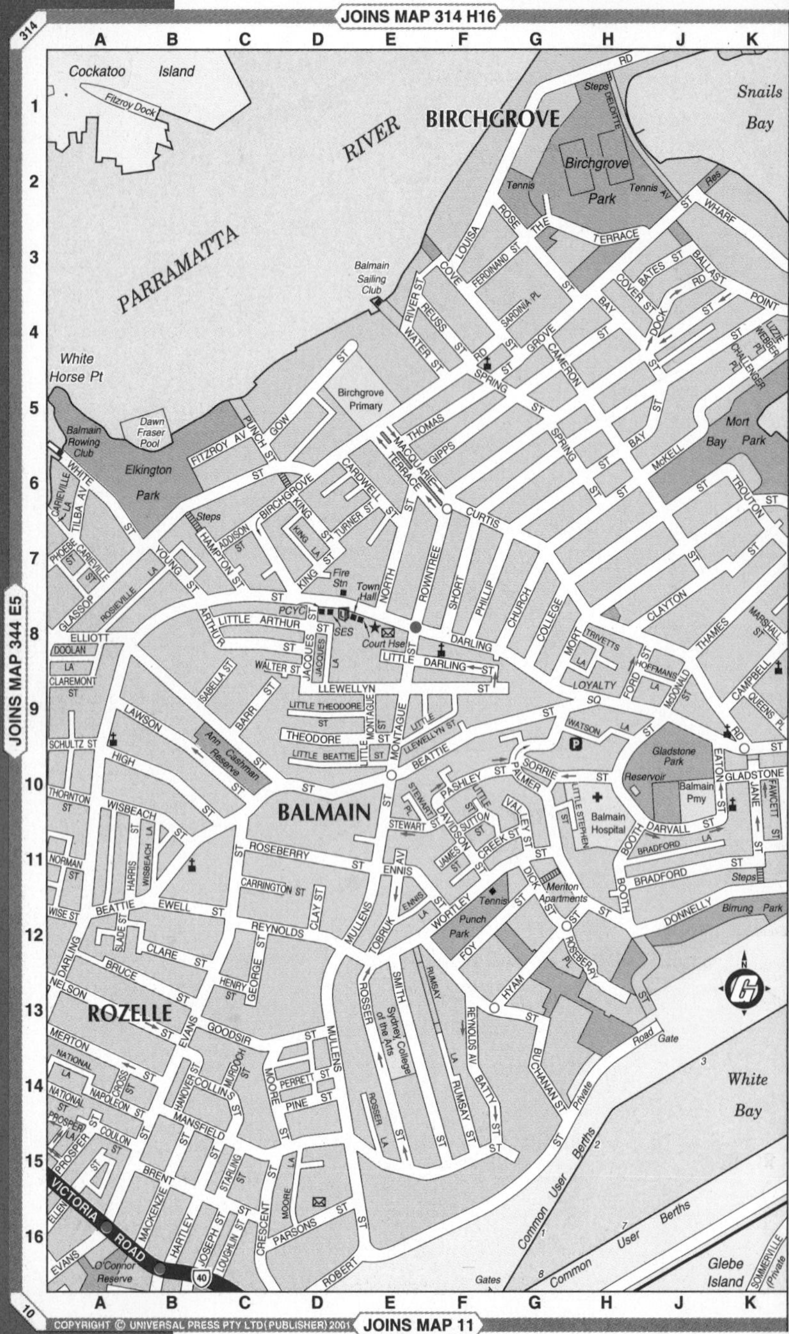

JOINS MAP 344 E5

JOINS MAP 11

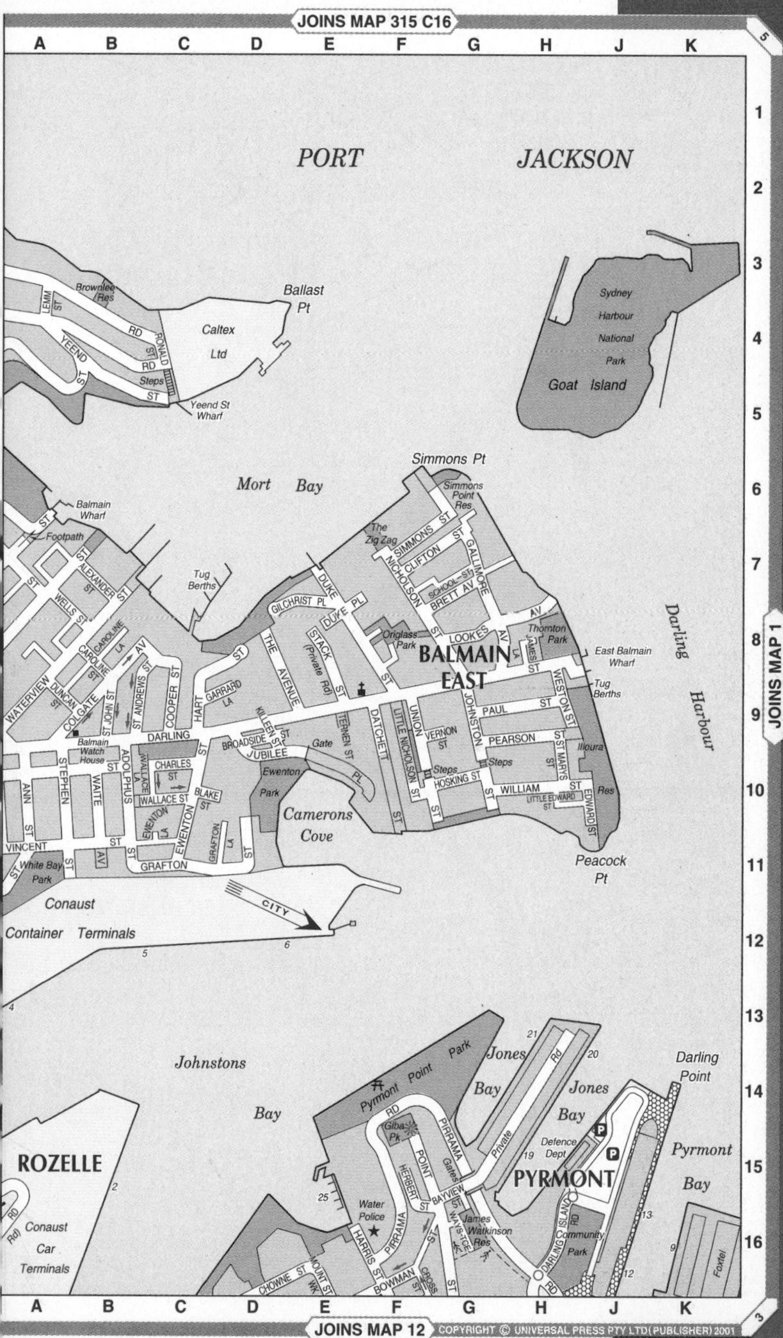
JOINS MAP 315 C16
A B C D E F G H J K
1 2 3 4 5 6 7 8 9 10 11 12 13 14 15 16
PORT JACKSON
Sydney Harbour National Park
Goat Island
Ballast Pt
Caltex Ltd
Brownlee Res
LEMM ST
YEEND ST
RONALD ST
RD
Steps
Yeend St Wharf
Simmons Pt
Simmons Point Res
Mort Bay
Balmain Wharf
Footpath
Tug Berths
The Zig Zag
SIMMONS ST
CLIFTON ST
GALLIMORE AV
NICHOLSON ST
SCHOOL ST
BRETT AV
LOOKES AV
GILCHRIST PL
DUKE PL
DUKE ST
Origlass Park
Thornton Park
JAMES LA
STACK ST (Private Rd)
THE AVENUE
BALMAIN EAST
East Balmain Wharf
Tug Berths
Darling Harbour
JOINS MAP 1
ALEXANDER ST
WELLS ST
CAROLINE LA
CAROLINE ST
WATERVIEW ST
DUNCAN ST
COLGATE AV
ST JOHN ST
ST ANDREWS ST
COOPER ST
HART ST
GARRARD LA
DARLING ST
KILLEEN ST
BROADSIDE ST
JUBILEE PL
Gate
TERNEN ST
DATCHETT ST
LITTLE NICHOLSON ST
UNION ST
VERNON ST
JOHNSTON ST
PAUL ST
WESTON ST
PEARSON ST
ST MARYS ST
Illoura Res
Steps
HOSKING ST
WILLIAM ST
LITTLE EDWARD ST
EDWARD ST
Balmain Watch House
ANN ST
STEPHEN ST
WAITE AV
ADOLPHUS ST
WALLACE LA
CHARLES ST
WALLACE ST
BLAKE ST
EWENTON LA
EWENTON ST
GRAFTON LA
GRAFTON ST
Ewenton Park
Camerons Cove
Peacock Pt
VINCENT ST
White Bay Park
Conaust Container Terminals
CITY
Johnstons Bay
ROZELLE
Conaust Car Terminals
Pyrmont Point Park
Jones Bay
Private Rd
Darling Point
Gilba Pk
PIRRAMA RD
POINT ST
HERBERT ST
BAYVIEW ST
Gates
Water Police
HARRIS ST
CHOWNE ST
MOUNT ST WK
BOWMAN ST
CROSS ST
James Watkinson Res
Defence Dept
PYRMONT
DARLING ISLAND RD
Community Park
Pyrmont Bay
Foxtel
JOINS MAP 12

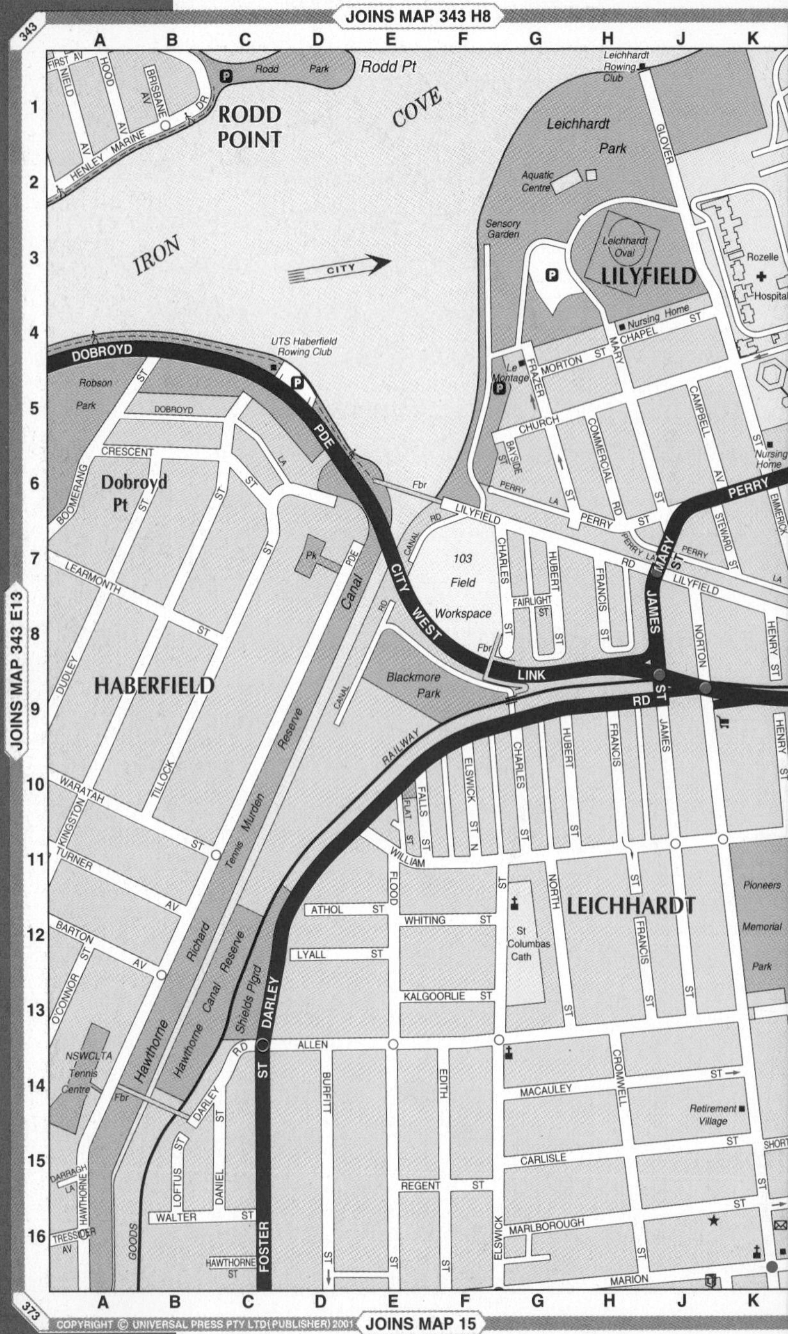
JOINS MAP 343 H8
JOINS MAP 343 E13
JOINS MAP 15
RODD POINT
Rodd Pt
Rodd Park
COVE
IRON
CITY
Leichhardt Rowing Club
Leichhardt Park
Aquatic Centre
Sensory Garden
Leichhardt Oval
LILYFIELD
Rozelle Hospital
Nursing Home
UTS Haberfield Rowing Club
Robson Park
Le Montage
Dobroyd Pt
103 Field Workspace
Blackmore Park
HABERFIELD
Tennis
Murden Reserve
Canal
Richard
Hawthorne Canal Reserve
Shields Plgrd
NSWCLTA Tennis Centre
LEICHHARDT
St Columbas Cath
Pioneers Memorial Park
Retirement Village
CITY WEST LINK
DOBROYD PDE
LILYFIELD RD
PERRY ST
MARY ST
JAMES ST
PARRAMATTA RD
DARLEY RD
FOSTER ST
WILLIAM ST
ALLEN ST
MACAULEY ST
CARLISLE ST
MARLBOROUGH ST
MARION ST
RAILWAY
GOODS
Fbr

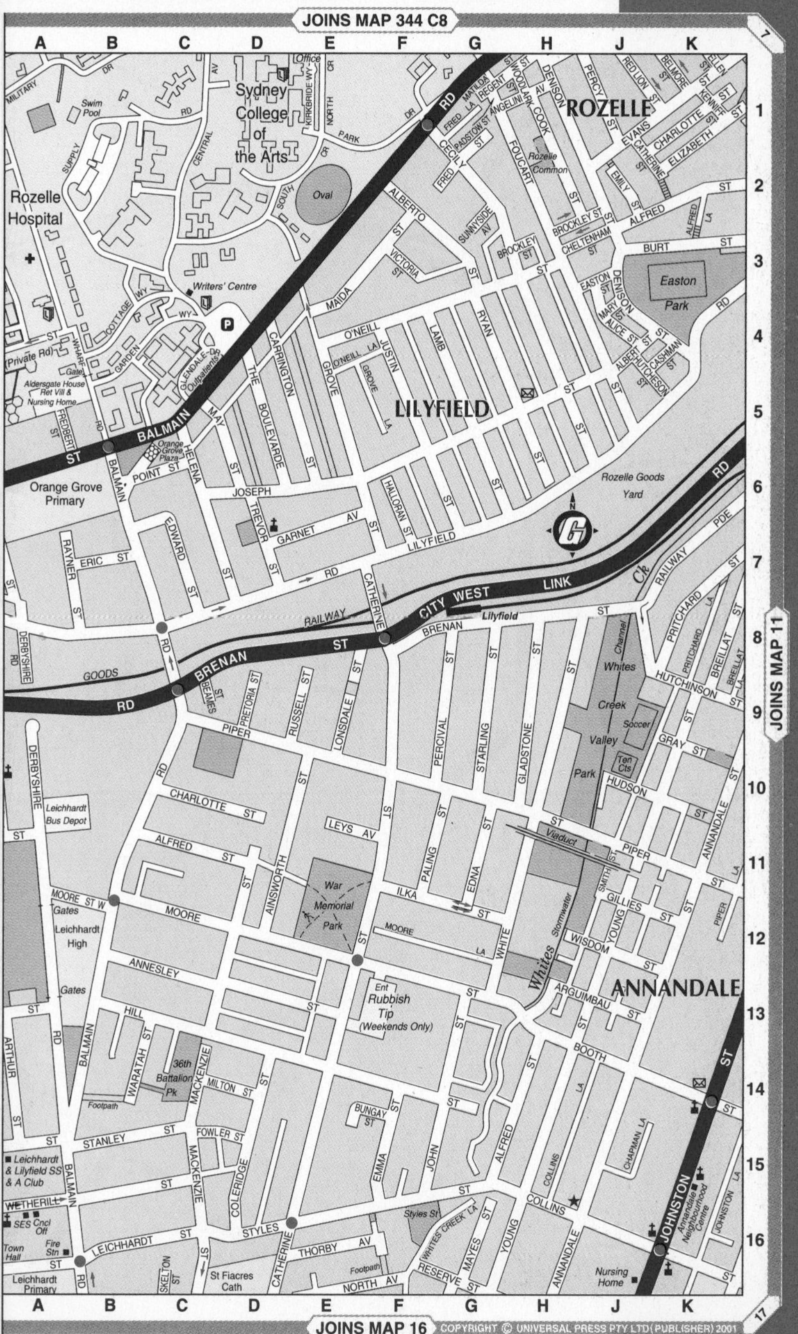
JOINS MAP 344 C8
JOINS MAP 11
JOINS MAP 16
7
17
A B C D E F G H J K
1 2 3 4 5 6 7 8 9 10 11 12 13 14 15 16
ROZELLE
LILYFIELD
ANNANDALE
Sydney College of the Arts
Office
Oval
Rozelle Hospital
Swim Pool
Writers' Centre
Outpatients
Aldersgate House Ret Vill & Nursing Home
(Private Rd)
Gate
Orange Grove Plaza
Orange Grove Primary
Rozelle Common
Easton Park
Rozelle Goods Yard
Lilyfield
Whites Creek Valley Park
Channel
Soccer
Ten Cts
Viaduct
Stormwater
Whites
Leichhardt Bus Depot
Leichhardt High
Gates
War Memorial Park
Ent
Rubbish Tip (Weekends Only)
36th Battalion Pk
Footpath
Leichhardt & Lilyfield SS & A Club
SES
Cncl Off
Town Hall
Fire Stn
Leichhardt Primary
St Fiacres Cath
Styles St
Nursing Home
Annandale Neighbourhood Centre
VICTORIA RD
BALMAIN RD
BALMAIN ST
CITY WEST LINK
BRENAN ST
RAILWAY PDE
GOODS RD
JOHNSTON ST
MILITARY DR
SUPPLY
CENTRAL AV
KIRKBRIDE WY
NORTH CR
SOUTH CR
PARK DR
COTTAGE WY
GARDEN
GLENDALE DR
WHARF RD
FREDBERT ST
MAY ST
HELENA ST
POINT ST
THE BOULEVARDE
CARRINGTON ST
GROVE ST
GROVE LA
JUSTIN ST
O'NEILL ST
O'NEILL LA
MAIDA ST
ALBERTO ST
VICTORIA ST
LAMB ST
RYAN ST
CECILY ST
FRED ST
FRED LA
MATILDA ST
REGENT ST
PADSTOW ST
ANGELINE ST
WOODLARK ST
COOK ST
FOUCART ST
DENISON ST
PERCY ST
RED LION ST
BELMORE ST
ELLEN ST
KENNIFF ST
EVANS ST
CHARLOTTE ST
CATHERINE ST
ELIZABETH ST
EMILY ST
ALFRED ST
ALFRED LA
BURT ST
BROCKLEY ST
CHELTENHAM ST
SUNNYSIDE AV
EASTON ST
MARY ST
ALICE ST
ALBERT ST
HUTCHESON ST
CASHMAN ST
JOSEPH ST
TREVOR ST
GARNET AV
HALLORAN ST
LILYFIELD RD
EDWARD ST
RAYNER ST
ERIC ST
DERBYSHIRE RD
BEAMES ST
PRETORIA ST
RUSSELL ST
LONSDALE ST
PIPER ST
PERCIVAL ST
STARLING ST
GLADSTONE ST
PRITCHARD ST
PRITCHARD LA
BREILLAT ST
HUTCHINSON ST
GRAY ST
HUDSON ST
ANNANDALE ST
CHARLOTTE ST
ALFRED ST
LEYS AV
AINSWORTH ST
PALING ST
EDNA ST
ILKA ST
MOORE ST W
MOORE ST
MOORE LA
WHITE ST
SMITH ST
GILLIES ST
YOUNG ST
WISDOM ST
PIPER LA
ANNESLEY ST
ARGUIMBAU ST
HILL ST
WARATAH ST
MACKENZIE ST
MILTON ST
BOOTH ST
ARTHUR ST
STANLEY ST
FOWLER ST
BUNGAY ST
EMMA ST
JOHN ST
ALFRED ST
COLLINS ST
COLLINS LA
CHAPMAN LA
WETHERILL ST
COLERIDGE ST
STYLES ST
LEICHHARDT ST
CATHERINE ST
THORBY AV
WHITES CREEK LA
MAYES ST
YOUNG ST
ANNANDALE ST
RESERVE ST
NORTH AV
SKELTON ST
JOHNSTON LA
Ck
N

MAP 11

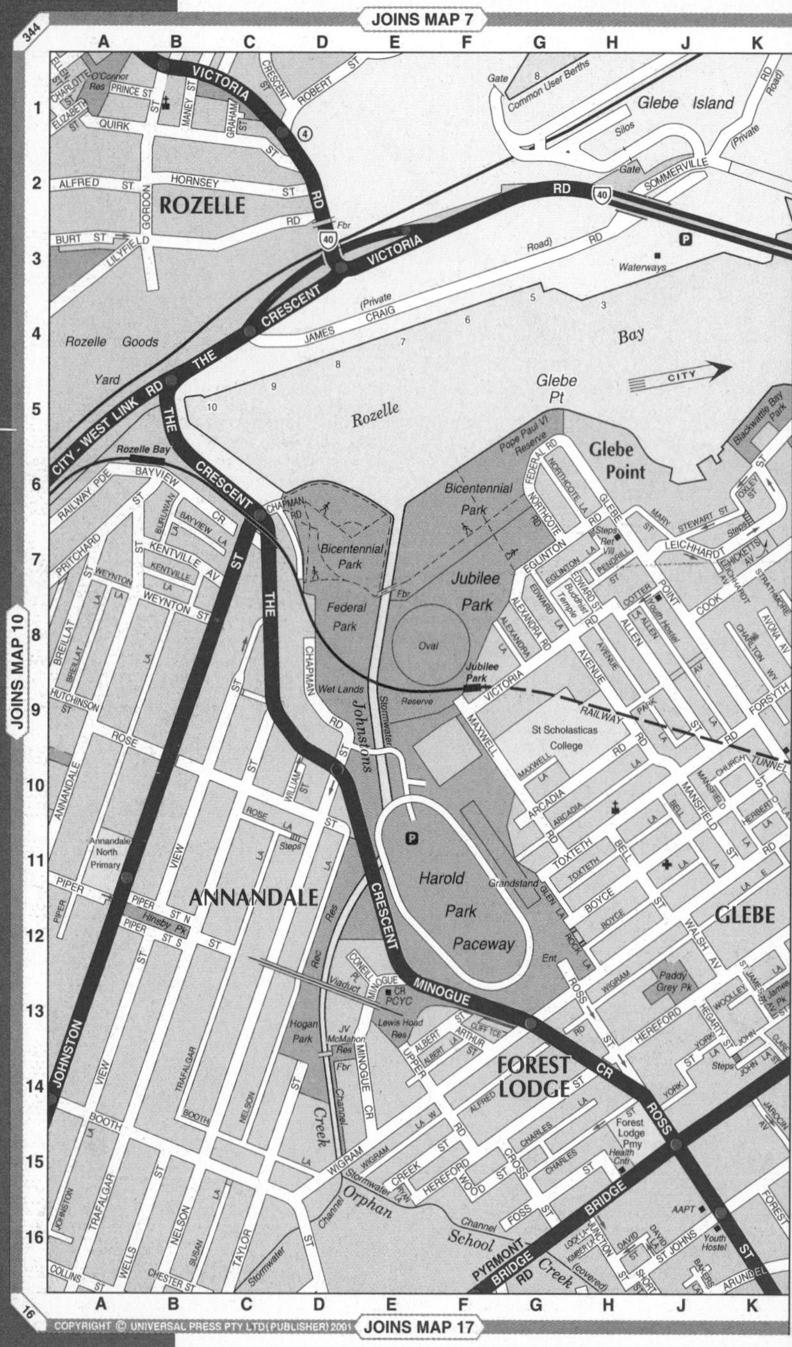

JOINS MAP 7
JOINS MAP 10
JOINS MAP 17
344
16
A B C D E F G H J K
ROZELLE
ANNANDALE
GLEBE
FOREST LODGE
Glebe Point
Glebe Island
Rozelle Bay
Glebe Pt
Rozelle Goods Yard
Bicentennial Park
Jubilee Park
Federal Park
Harold Park Paceway
St Scholasticas College
Wet Lands Reserve
Johnstons Creek
Orphan School Creek
Hogan Park
Paddy Grey Pk
Pope Paul VI Reserve
Blackwattle Bay Park
Annandale North Primary
Hinsby Pk
Forest Lodge Pmy Health Cntr
Youth Hostel
Waterways
Silos
Common User Berths
Oval
Grandstand
VICTORIA RD
THE CRESCENT
CITY - WEST LINK RD
JOHNSTON ST
MINOGUE CR
ROSS ST
PYRMONT BRIDGE RD
GLEBE POINT RD
JAMES CRAIG (Private Road) RD
WIGRAM RD
CITY

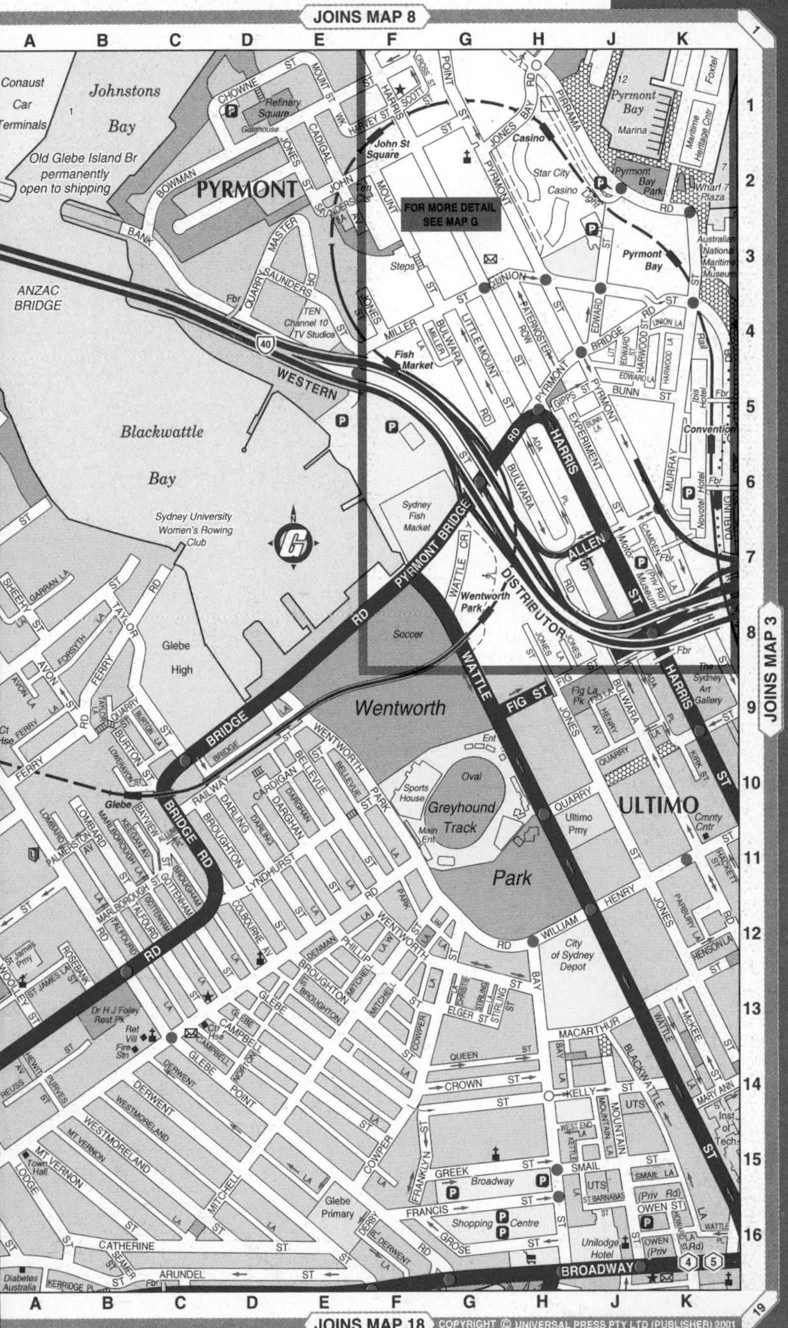
JOINS MAP 8
JOINS MAP 3
JOINS MAP 18
PYRMONT
ULTIMO
Johnstons Bay
Blackwattle Bay
Pyrmont Bay
Conaust Car Terminals
Old Glebe Island Br permanently open to shipping
ANZAC BRIDGE
Refinery Square
John St Square
FOR MORE DETAIL SEE MAP G
Star City Casino
Pyrmont Bay Park
Wharf 7 Plaza
Australian National Maritime Museum
Maritime Heritage Cntr
Pyrmont Bay Marina
TEN Channel 10 TV Studios
Fish Market
Sydney Fish Market
Sydney University Women's Rowing Club
Wentworth Park
Soccer
Glebe High
Greyhound Track
Sports House
Ultimo Pmy
Cmnty Cntr
City of Sydney Depot
UTS
Inst of Tech
Broadway Shopping Centre
Unilodge Hotel
Novotel Hotel
Ibis Hotel
Convention
Motor Museum
The Sydney Art Gallery
Glebe Primary
Dr H J Foley Rest Pk
Diabetes Australia
St James Pmy
Town Hall
WESTERN DISTRIBUTOR
PYRMONT BRIDGE RD
WATTLE ST
HARRIS ST
BROADWAY
GLEBE POINT RD
BRIDGE RD

MAP 13

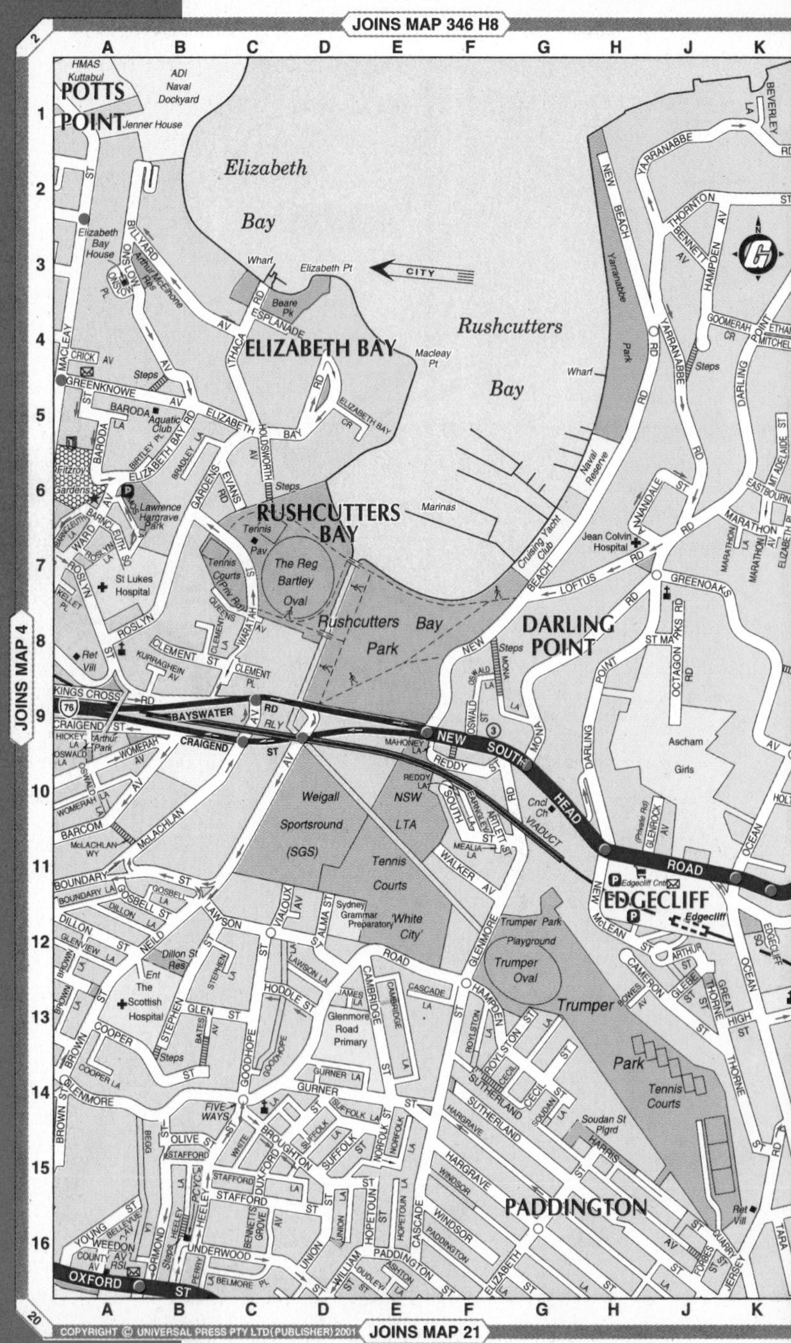
JOINS MAP 346 H8
JOINS MAP 4
JOINS MAP 21
POTTS POINT
ELIZABETH BAY
RUSHCUTTERS BAY
DARLING POINT
EDGECLIFF
PADDINGTON
Elizabeth Bay
Rushcutters Bay
Rushcutters Bay Park
The Reg Bartley Oval
Weigall Sportsground (SGS)
NSW LTA Tennis Courts
Sydney Grammar Preparatory
'White City'
Trumper Park
Trumper Oval
Ascham Girls
St Lukes Hospital
The Scottish Hospital
Jean Colvin Hospital
Glenmore Road Primary
Cruising Yacht Club
Naval Reserve
Yarranabbe Park
ADI Naval Dockyard
HMAS Kuttabul
Elizabeth Bay House
Fitzroy Gardens
Lawrence Hargrave Park
Beare Pk
Arthur Park
Marinas
CITY
NEW SOUTH HEAD ROAD
OXFORD ST
BAYSWATER RD
KINGS CROSS RD
CRAIGEND ST
McLACHLAN AV
BOUNDARY ST
GLENMORE RD
GLENMORE
HAMPDEN ST
NEW BEACH RD
DARLING POINT RD
OCEAN ST
LOFTUS RD
GREENOAKS AV
ELIZABETH BAY RD
MACLEAY ST
GREENKNOWE AV
WARATAH ST
CLEMENT ST
ROSLYN ST
FIVE WAYS
GURNER ST
UNDERWOOD ST
CASCADE ST
SUTHERLAND ST
HARGRAVE ST
WINDSOR ST
ELIZABETH ST
QUARRY ST
JERSEY RD
HIGH ST
THORNE ST
MARATHON RD
YARRANABBE RD
Edgecliff

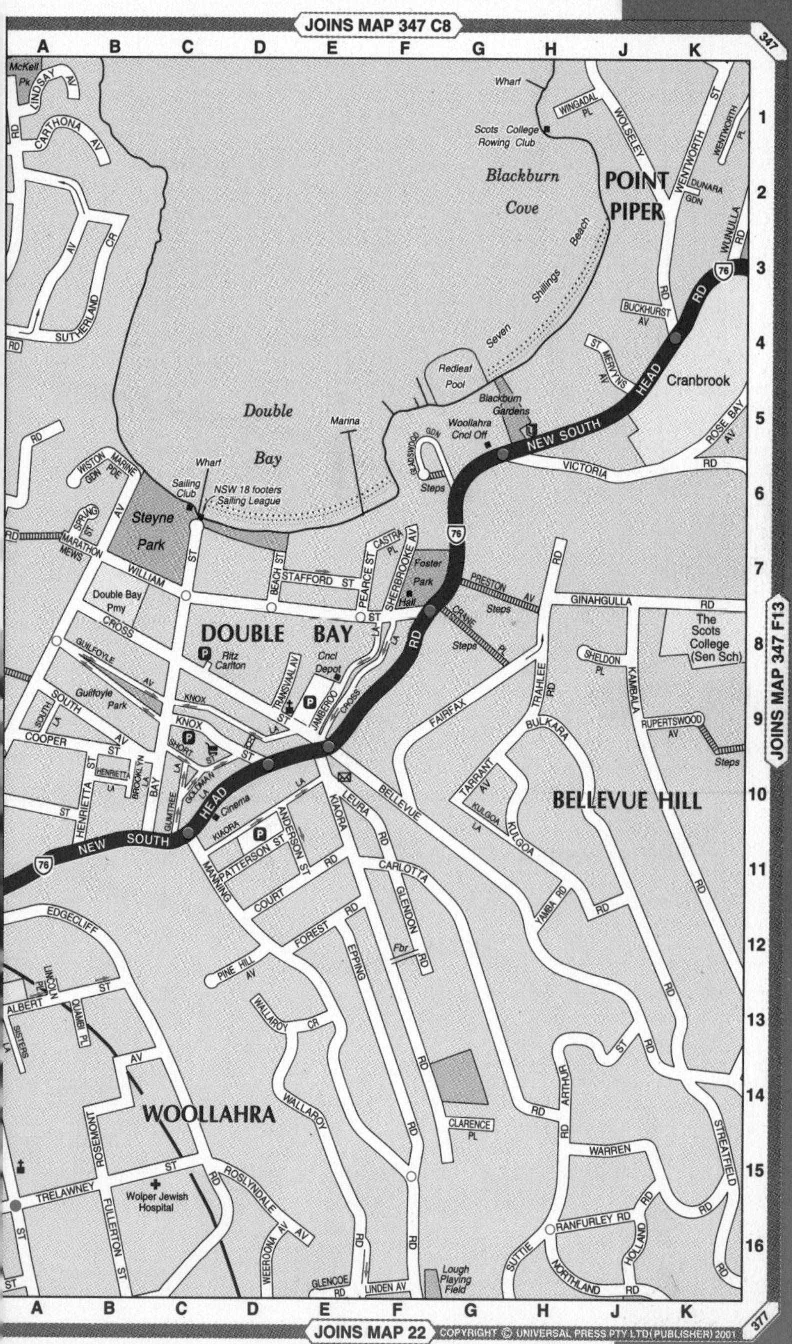
JOINS MAP 347 C8
JOINS MAP 347 F13
JOINS MAP 22
Blackburn Cove
POINT PIPER
Double Bay
DOUBLE BAY
BELLEVUE HILL
WOOLLAHRA
Cranbrook
Scots College Rowing Club
Seven Shillings Beach
Redleaf Pool
Blackburn Gardens
Woollahra Cncl Off
Marina
Wharf
Sailing Club
NSW 18 footers Sailing League
Steyne Park
Foster Park
Hall
Double Bay Pmy
Ritz Carlton
Cncl Depot
Guilfoyle Park
Cinema
The Scots College (Sen Sch)
Wolper Jewish Hospital
Lough Playing Field
Steps
NEW SOUTH HEAD RD
VICTORIA RD
BELLEVUE RD
EDGECLIFF RD
COPYRIGHT © UNIVERSAL PRESS PTY LTD (PUBLISHER) 2001

MAP 15

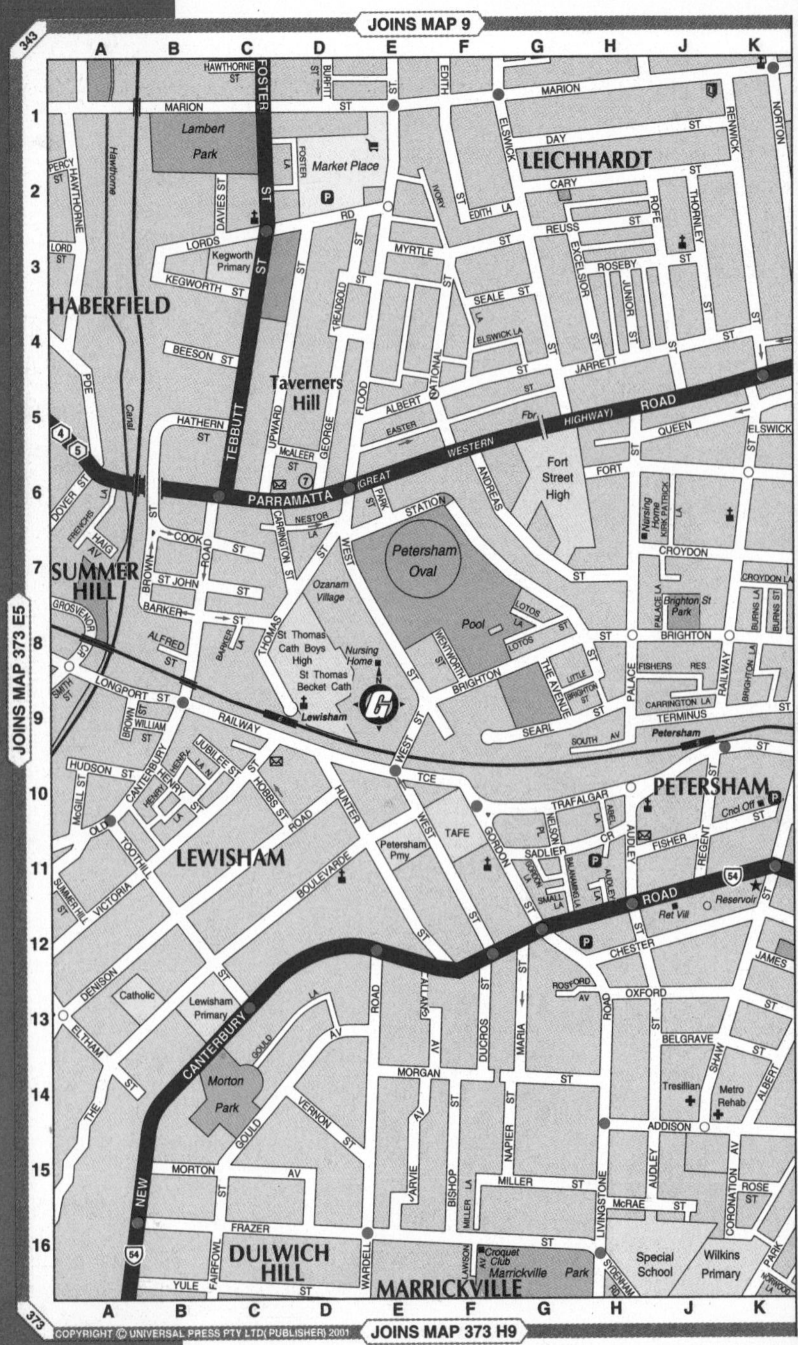

JOINS MAP 9
343
A B C D E F G H J K
1 2 3 4 5 6 7 8 9 10 11 12 13 14 15 16
JOINS MAP 373 E5
HAWTHORNE ST
FOSTER ST
BURFITT ST
EDITH ST
MARION ST
Lambert Park
Market Place
LEICHHARDT
DAY ST
ELSWICK ST
RENWICK ST
NORTON ST
PERCY ST
HAWTHORNE
Hawthorne Canal
DAVIES ST
CARY ST
ROFE ST
THORNLEY ST
IVORY
EDITH LA
REUSS ST
LORDS RD
MYRTLE ST
Kegworth Primary
KEGWORTH ST
LORD ST
EXCELSIOR ST
ROSEBY ST
JUNIOR ST
SEALE ST
ELSWICK LA
HABERFIELD
TREADGOLD ST
BEESON ST
JARRETT ST
NATIONAL ST
Taverners Hill
ALBERT ST
FLOOD ST
PDE
EASTER
UPWARD ST
GEORGE ST
HATHERN ST
TEBBUTT ST
McALEER ST
PARRAMATTA (GREAT WESTERN HIGHWAY) ROAD
Fbr
QUEEN ST
ELSWICK ST
FORT ST
Fort Street High
DOVER ST
FRENCHS LA
HAIG AV
PARK ST
STATION ST
ANDREAS ST
Nursing Home
KIRK PATRICK LA
COOK ST
ROAD
NESTOR LA
CARRINGTON ST
WEST ST
Petersham Oval
CROYDON ST
CROYDON LA
SUMMER HILL
BROWN
ST JOHN ST
BARKER ST
Ozanam Village
PALACE LA
Brighton St Park
BURNS LA
BURNS ST
GROSVENOR CR
ALFRED ST
BARKER LA
THOMAS ST
St Thomas Cath Boys High
Nursing Home
St Thomas Becket Cath
Pool
LOTOS LA
LOTOS ST
WENTWORTH ST
BRIGHTON ST
THE AVENUE
LITTLE
BRIGHTON ST
FISHERS RES
RAILWAY ST
BRIGHTON LA
SMITH ST
LONGPORT ST
WILLIAM ST
Lewisham
CARRINGTON LA
TERMINUS ST
SEARL ST
SOUTH AV
Petersham
HUDSON ST
CANTERBURY
HENRY ST
HENRY LA
JUBILEE ST
RAILWAY TCE
HOBBS ST
McGILL ST
PETERSHAM
TRAFALGAR ST
ABEL
NELSON PL
Cncl Off
OLD
TOOTHILL
LEWISHAM
HUNTER ST
ROAD
WEST ST
TAFE
GORDON ST
Petersham Pmy
SADLIER CR
AUDLEY ST
FISHER ST
REGENT ST
BOULEVARDE
GORDON LA
BALMAIN LA
SMALL LA
SUMMER HILL ST
VICTORIA
54
ROAD
Reservoir
Ret Vill
CHESTER ST
JAMES ST
DENISON ST
ROSFORD AV
OXFORD ST
Catholic
Lewisham Primary
CALLAN ST
ROAD
DUCROS AV
MARIA ST
ROAD
ELTHAM ST
CANTERBURY
GOULD
BELGRAVE ST
SHAW
Morton Park
MORGAN ST
Tresillian
Metro Rehab
ALBERT
THE
VERNON ST
JARVIE AV
BISHOP ST
NAPIER ST
ADDISON
NEW
MORTON AV
GOULD
MILLER ST
LIVINGSTONE
AUDLEY
CORONATION AV
ROSE ST
McRAE ST
MILLER LA
FRAZER ST
Croquet Club
Marrickville Park
Special School
Wilkins Primary
DULWICH HILL
FAIRFOWL
WARDELL
LAWSON AV
SYDENHAM RD
NORWOOD
PARK
YULE ST
MARRICKVILLE
373
COPYRIGHT © UNIVERSAL PRESS PTY LTD (PUBLISHER) 2001
JOINS MAP 373 H9

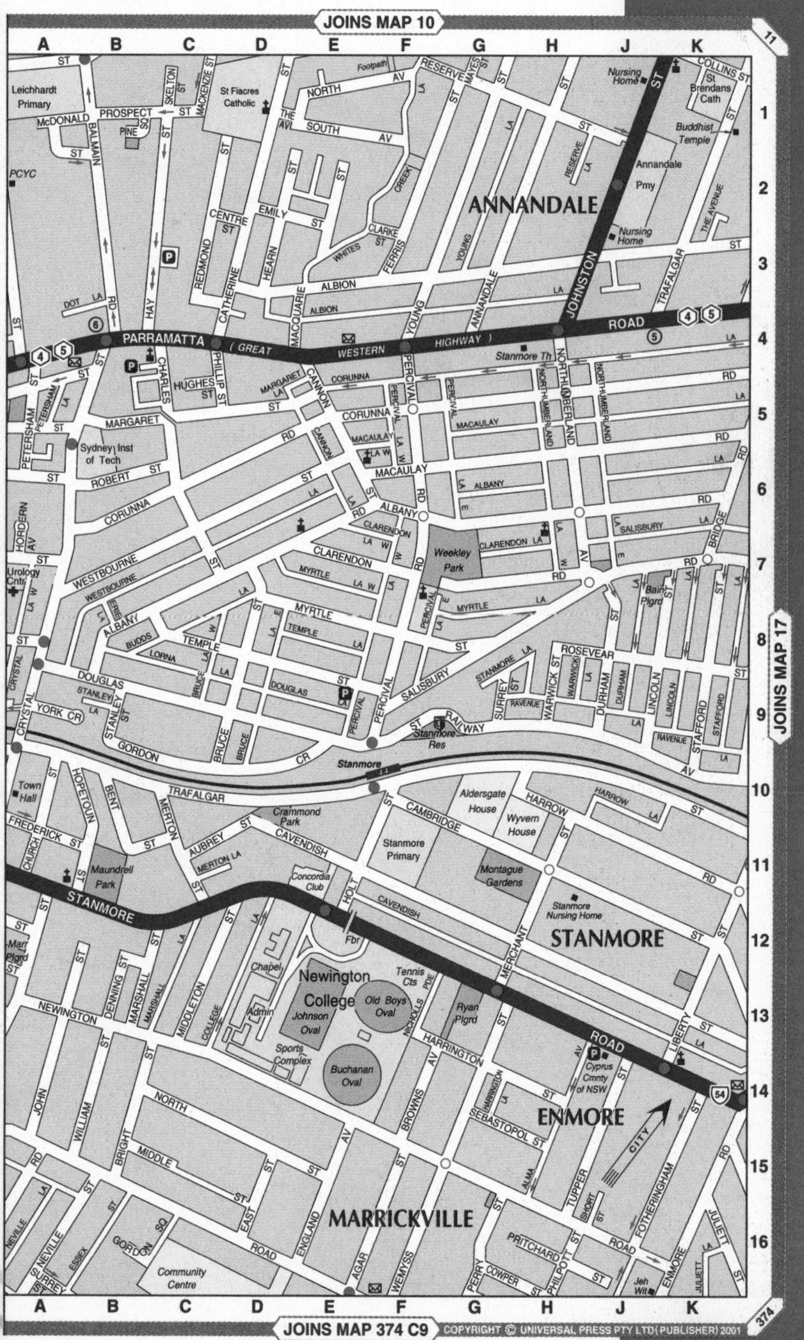
JOINS MAP 10
ANNANDALE
STANMORE
ENMORE
MARRICKVILLE
PARRAMATTA (GREAT WESTERN HIGHWAY) ROAD
STANMORE ROAD
JOINS MAP 17
Leichhardt Primary
St Fiacres Catholic
St Brendans Cath
Buddhist Temple
Annandale Pmy
Nursing Home
PCYC
Sydney Inst of Tech
Stanmore Th
Weekley Park
Urology Cntr
Bain Plgrd
Stanmore Res
Stanmore
Town Hall
Crammond Park
Aldersgate House
Wyvern House
Stanmore Primary
Montague Gardens
Maundrell Park
Concordia Club
Stanmore Nursing Home
Newington College
Chapel
Admin
Johnson Oval
Old Boys Oval
Tennis Cts
Ryan Plgrd
Sports Complex
Buchanan Oval
Cyprus Cmnty of NSW
CITY
Community Centre
Jeh Wit
JOINS MAP 374 C9

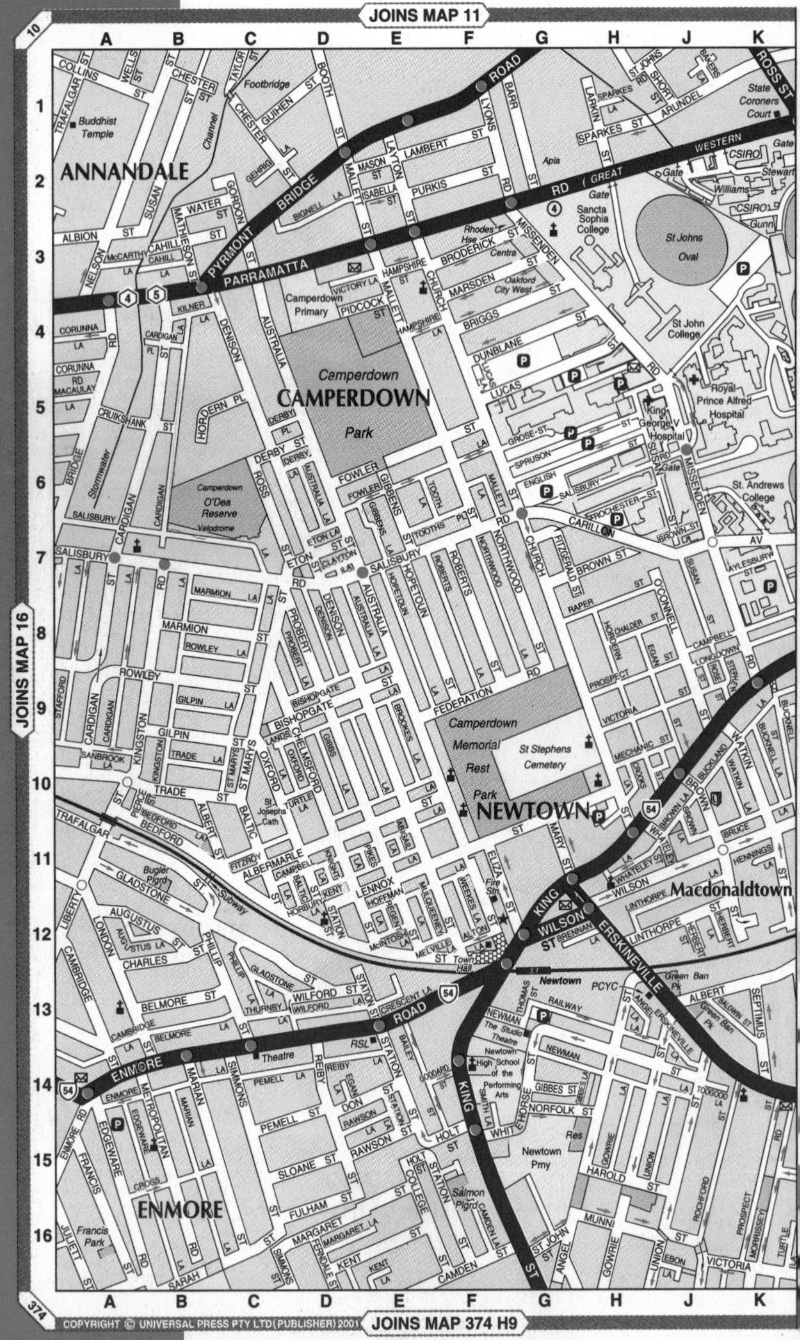
JOINS MAP 11
JOINS MAP 16
JOINS MAP 374 H9
ANNANDALE
CAMPERDOWN
NEWTOWN
ENMORE
Macdonaldtown
Camperdown Park
Camperdown O'Dea Reserve
Camperdown Memorial Rest Park
St Stephens Cemetery
St Johns Oval
Royal Prince Alfred Hospital
King George V Hospital
St John College
St. Andrews College
Sancta Sophia College
Buddhist Temple
State Coroners Court
Camperdown Primary
Newtown Pmy
Newtown High School of the Performing Arts
Francis Park
Salmon Plgrd
Bugler Plgrd
Green Ban Pk
PARRAMATTA RD
PYRMONT BRIDGE RD
ENMORE ROAD
KING ST
MISSENDEN RD
CITY RD
ERSKINEVILLE RD
WILSON ST
STATION ST
CHURCH ST
AUSTRALIA ST
DENISON ST
SALISBURY RD
CAMDEN ST
Newtown
Footbridge
Channel
Stormwater
Subway
Apia
Gate
Fire Stn
Town Hall
Theatre
RSL
PCYC
Res
CSIRO
The Studio Theatre
St Josephs Cath

JOINS MAP 12

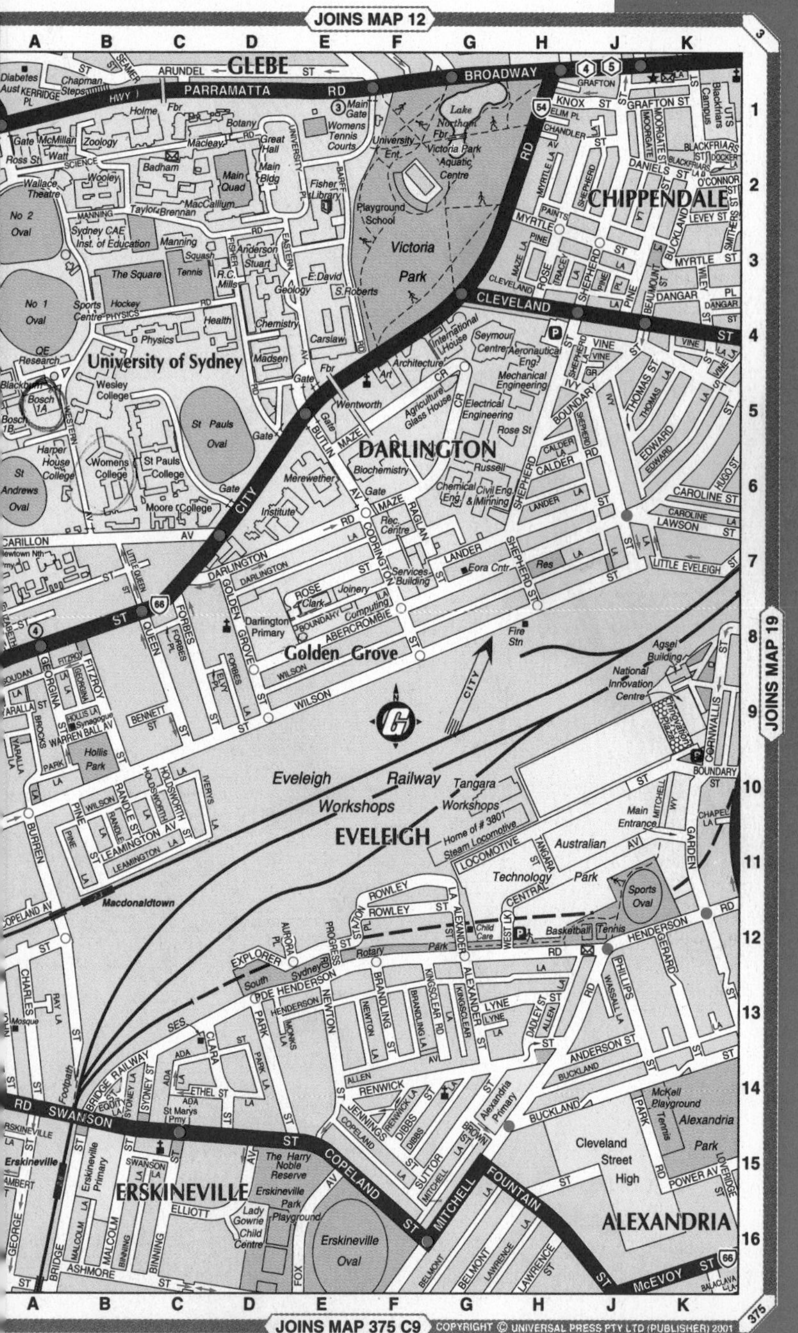

JOINS MAP 375 C9

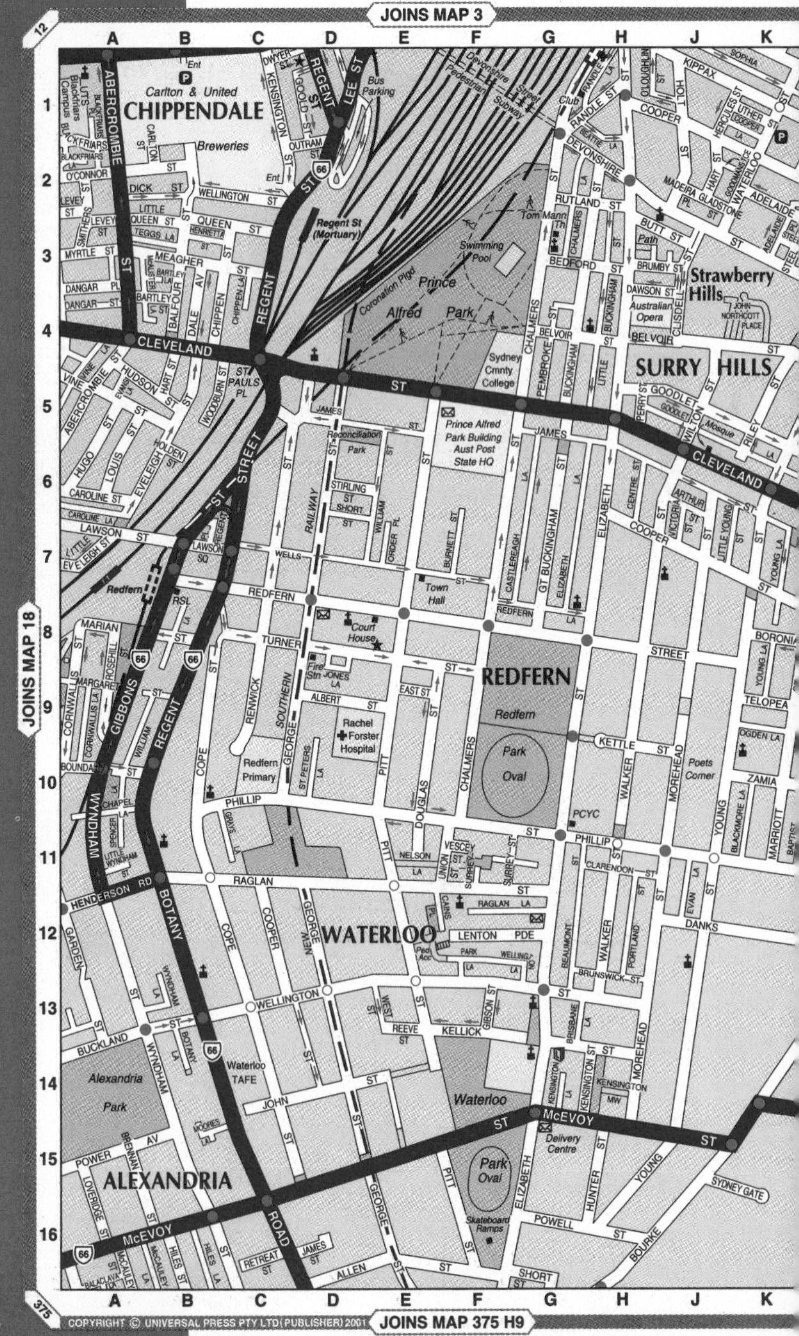
JOINS MAP 3
JOINS MAP 18
JOINS MAP 375 H9
12
375
A B C D E F G H J K
1 2 3 4 5 6 7 8 9 10 11 12 13 14 15 16
CHIPPENDALE
Carlton & United Breweries
UTS Blackfriars Campus
Regent St (Mortuary)
Bus Parking
Devonshire Street Pedestrian Subway
Club
Tom Mann Th
Swimming Pool
Coronation Plgd
Prince Alfred Park
Strawberry Hills
Australian Opera
SURRY HILLS
Sydney Cmnty College
Prince Alfred Park Building Aust Post State HQ
Reconciliation Park
Mosque
Redfern
RSL
Town Hall
Court House
Fire Stn
REDFERN
Redfern Park
Park Oval
Rachel Forster Hospital
Redfern Primary
PCYC
Poets Corner
WATERLOO
Ped Acc
Waterloo TAFE
Alexandria Park
ALEXANDRIA
Waterloo
Delivery Centre
Park Oval
Skateboard Ramps
ABERCROMBIE ST
REGENT ST
CLEVELAND ST
LEE ST
CHALMERS ST
ELIZABETH ST
BOTANY RD
McEVOY ST
RAGLAN ST
PHILLIP ST
REDFERN ST
WELLINGTON ST
GEORGE ST
BOURKE ST
SYDNEY GATE

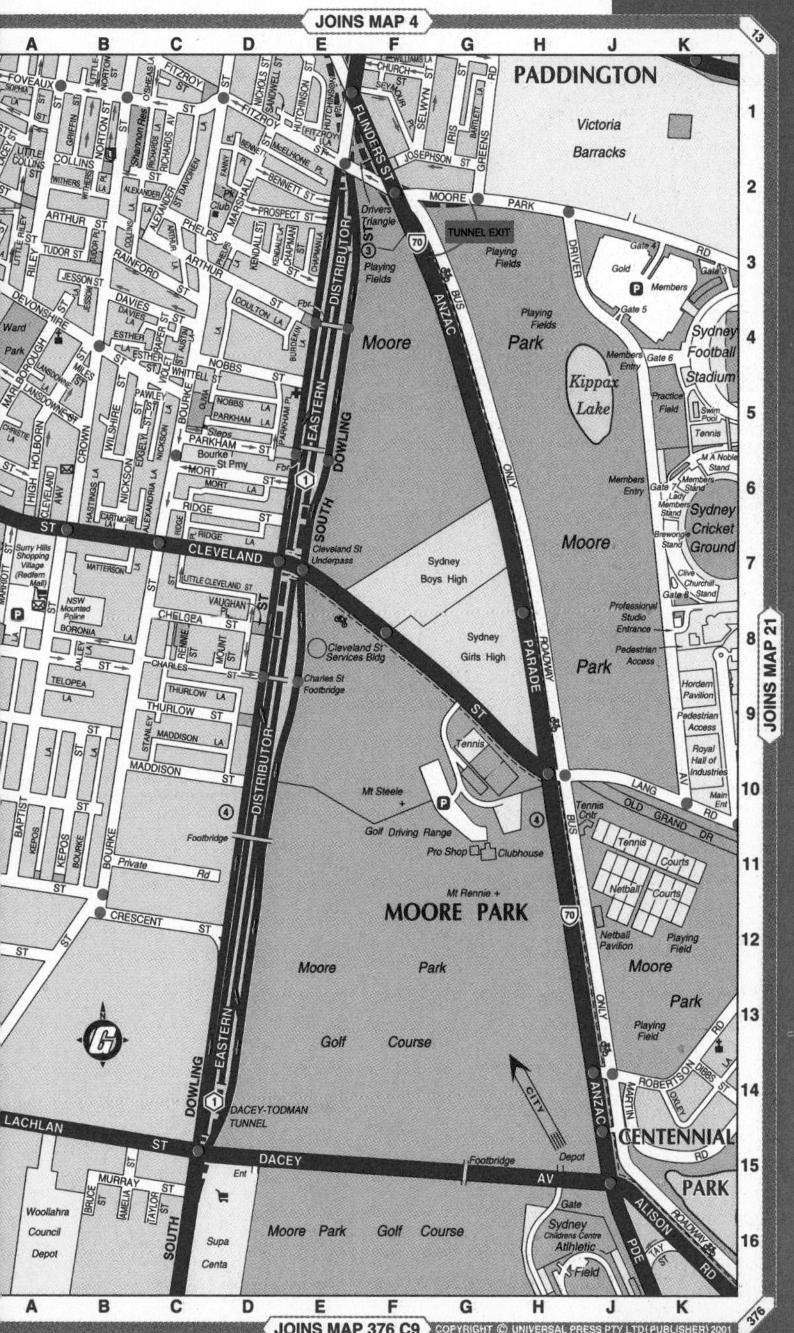
JOINS MAP 4
PADDINGTON
Victoria
Barracks
MOORE
PARK
FLINDERS ST
DISTRIBUTOR
EASTERN
DOWLING
SOUTH
ANZAC
PARADE
TUNNEL EXIT
Drivers Triangle
Playing Fields
Moore
Park
Kippax Lake
Sydney Football Stadium
Sydney Cricket Ground
Members Entry
Practice Field
Swim Pool
Tennis
M A Noble Stand
Lady Members Stand
Brewongle Stand
Clive Churchill Stand
Professional Studio Entrance
Pedestrian Access
Hordern Pavilion
Royal Hall of Industries
CLEVELAND
ST
Cleveland St Underpass
Sydney Boys High
Sydney Girls High
Cleveland St Services Bldg
Charles St Footbridge
Tennis
Mt Steele
Golf Driving Range
Pro Shop
Clubhouse
Mt Rennie
MOORE PARK
Moore Park Golf Course
LANG
RD
OLD GRAND DR
Tennis Cntr
Tennis Courts
Netball Courts
Netball Pavilion
Playing Field
ROBERTSON RD
CENTENNIAL
PARK
DACEY-TODMAN TUNNEL
LACHLAN
DACEY AV
Footbridge
Depot
Gate
Sydney Childrens Centre Athletic Field
ALISON RD
Woollahra Council Depot
Supa Centa
Ent
CRESCENT ST
BOURKE
Private Rd
MADDISON ST
THURLOW ST
TELOPEA
BORONIA
NSW Mounted Police
Surry Hills Shopping Village (Redfern Mall)
Ward Park
DEVONSHIRE
FOVEAUX
COLLINS
ARTHUR
RAINFORD
FITZROY
MOORE PARK
JOSEPHSON
JOINS MAP 21
JOINS MAP 376 C9
CITY

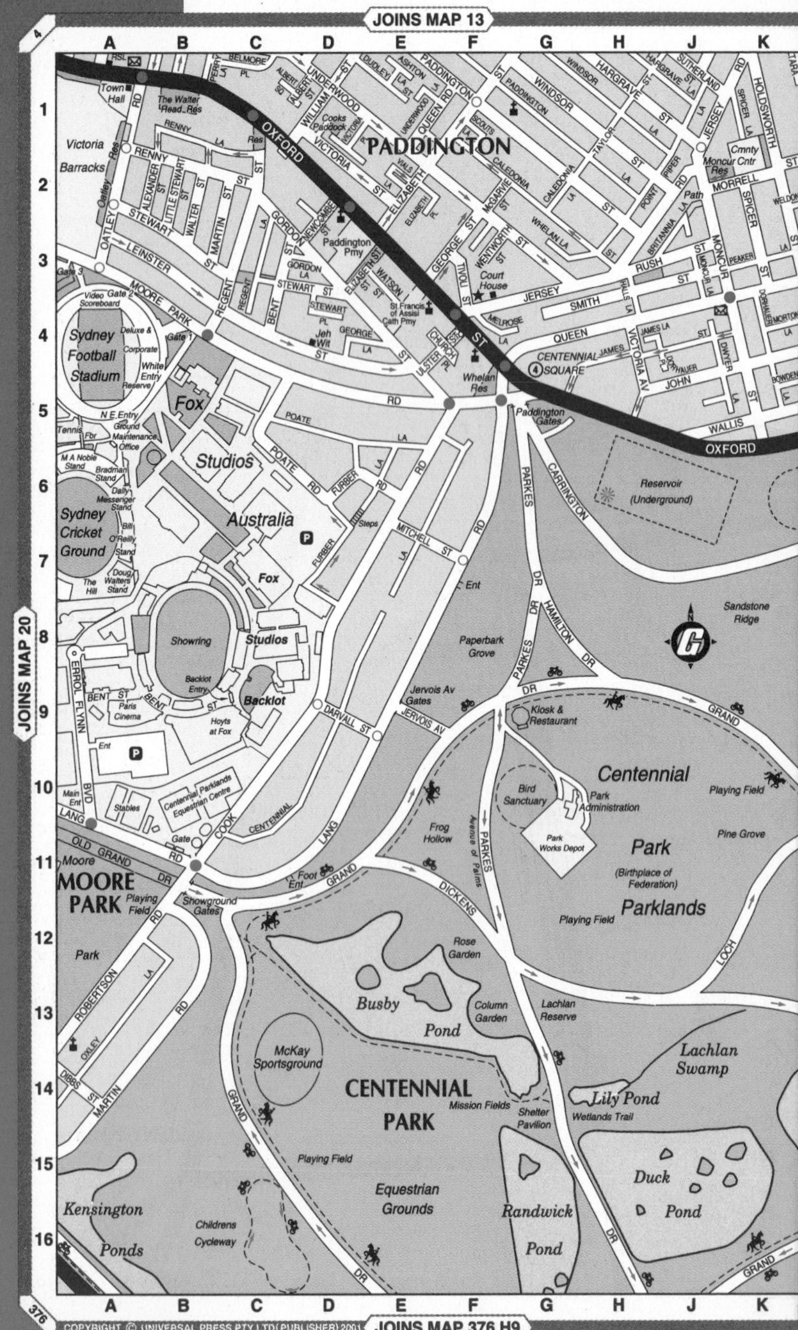
JOINS MAP 13
JOINS MAP 20
JOINS MAP 376 H9
A B C D E F G H J K
1 2 3 4 5 6 7 8 9 10 11 12 13 14 15 16
PADDINGTON
OXFORD ST
Town Hall
The Walter Read. Res
Victoria Barracks
Cooks Paddock
Paddington Pmy
St Francis of Assisi Cath Pmy
Court House
Whelan Res
Cmnty Moncur Cntr Res
CENTENNIAL SQUARE
Paddington Gates
Reservoir (Underground)
Sydney Football Stadium
Sydney Cricket Ground
Fox Studios Australia
Showring
Backlot
Hoyts at Fox
Paris Cinema
Centennial Parklands Equestrian Centre
Stables
Showground Gates
MOORE PARK
Playing Field
Paperbark Grove
Jervois Av Gates
Kiosk & Restaurant
Bird Sanctuary
Park Administration
Park Works Depot
Centennial Park (Birthplace of Federation) Parklands
Playing Field
Pine Grove
Sandstone Ridge
Frog Hollow
Avenue of Palms
Rose Garden
Busby Pond
Column Garden
Lachlan Reserve
Lachlan Swamp
Lily Pond
Wetlands Trail
McKay Sportsground
CENTENNIAL PARK
Mission Fields
Shelter Pavilion
Playing Field
Equestrian Grounds
Randwick Pond
Duck Pond
Kensington Ponds
Childrens Cycleway
Moore Park
GRAND DR
PARKES DR
DICKENS DR
LOCH
CARRINGTON DR
HAMILTON DR
COOK RD
LANG RD
MOORE PARK RD
OATLEY RD
ROBERTSON RD
ERROL FLYNN BVD
DARVALL ST
MITCHELL ST
JERVOIS AV
POATE RD

JOINS MAP 14

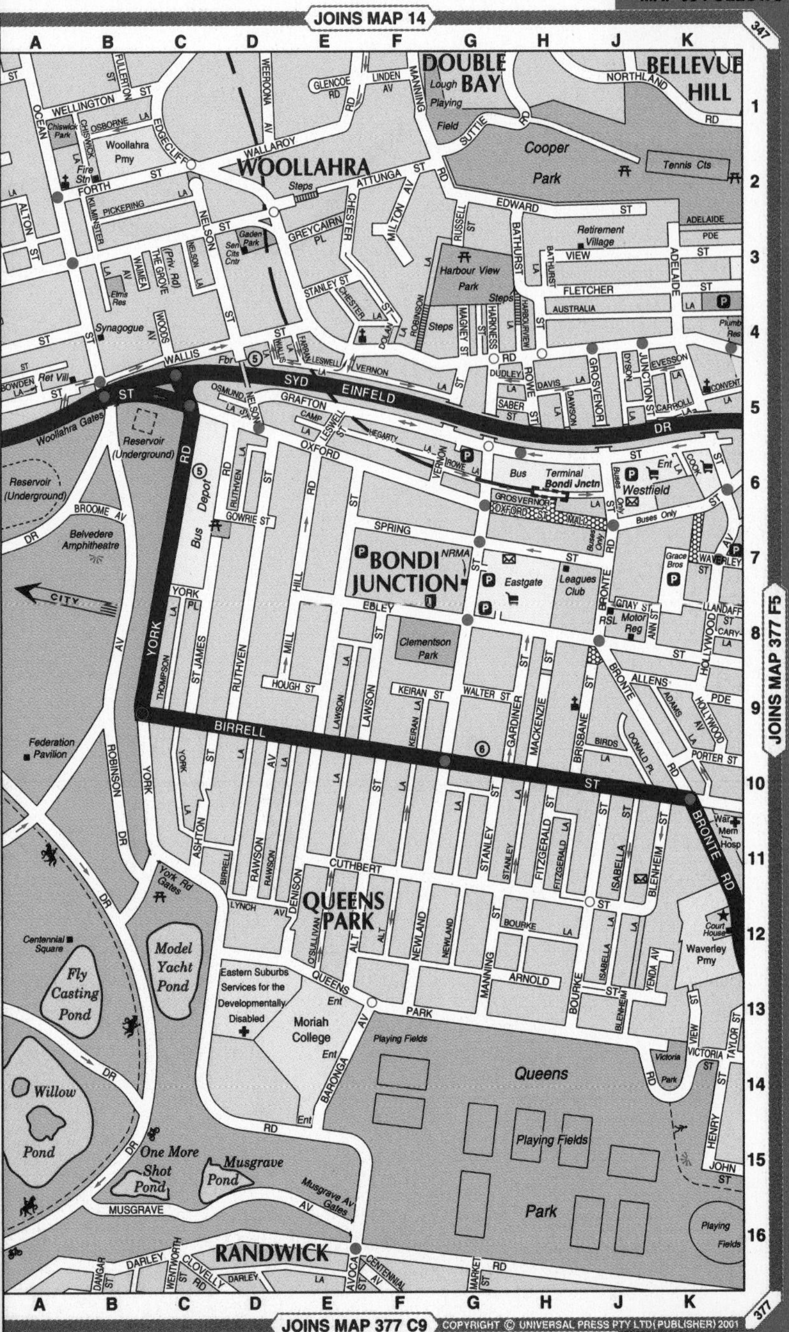

JOINS MAP 377 F5

JOINS MAP 377 C9

LIMIT OF MAPS

JOINS MAP 83

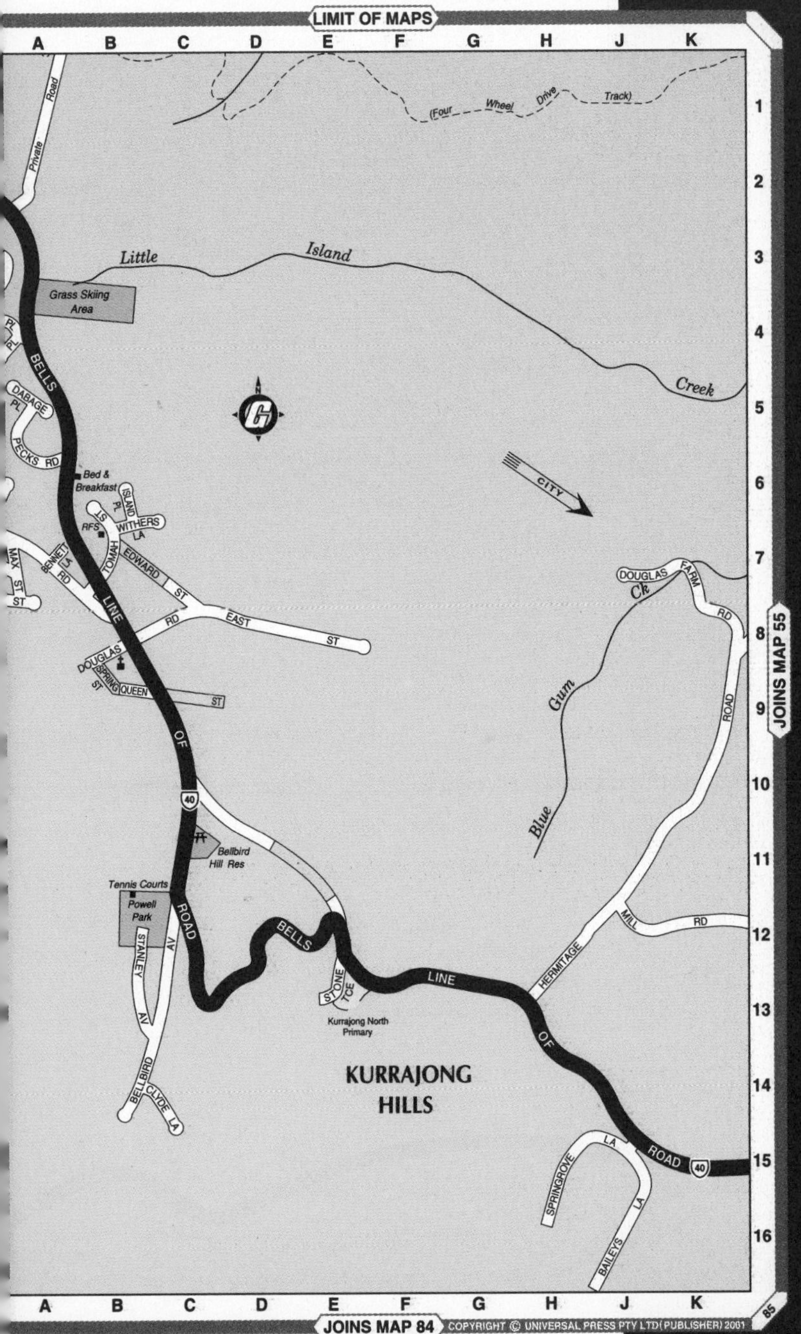
LIMIT OF MAPS
A B C D E F G H J K
1 2 3 4 5 6 7 8 9 10 11 12 13 14 15 16
Private Road
(Four Wheel Drive Track)
Little Island Creek
Grass Skiing Area
BELLS LINE OF ROAD
DABAGE PL
PECKS RD
Bed & Breakfast
ISLAND PL
TOMAH ST
WITHERS LA
RFS
MAX ST
BENNET LA
RD
EDWARD ST
EAST ST
RD
DOUGLAS
SPRING ST
QUEEN ST
CITY
DOUGLAS FARM RD
Blue Gum Ck
40
Bellbird Hill Res
Tennis Courts
Powell Park
STANLEY AV
AV
BELLBIRD
CLYDE LA
STONE ST
TCE
Kurrajong North Primary
KURRAJONG HILLS
HERMITAGE
MILL RD
SPRINGROVE LA
BAILEYS LA
ROAD
JOINS MAP 55
JOINS MAP 84

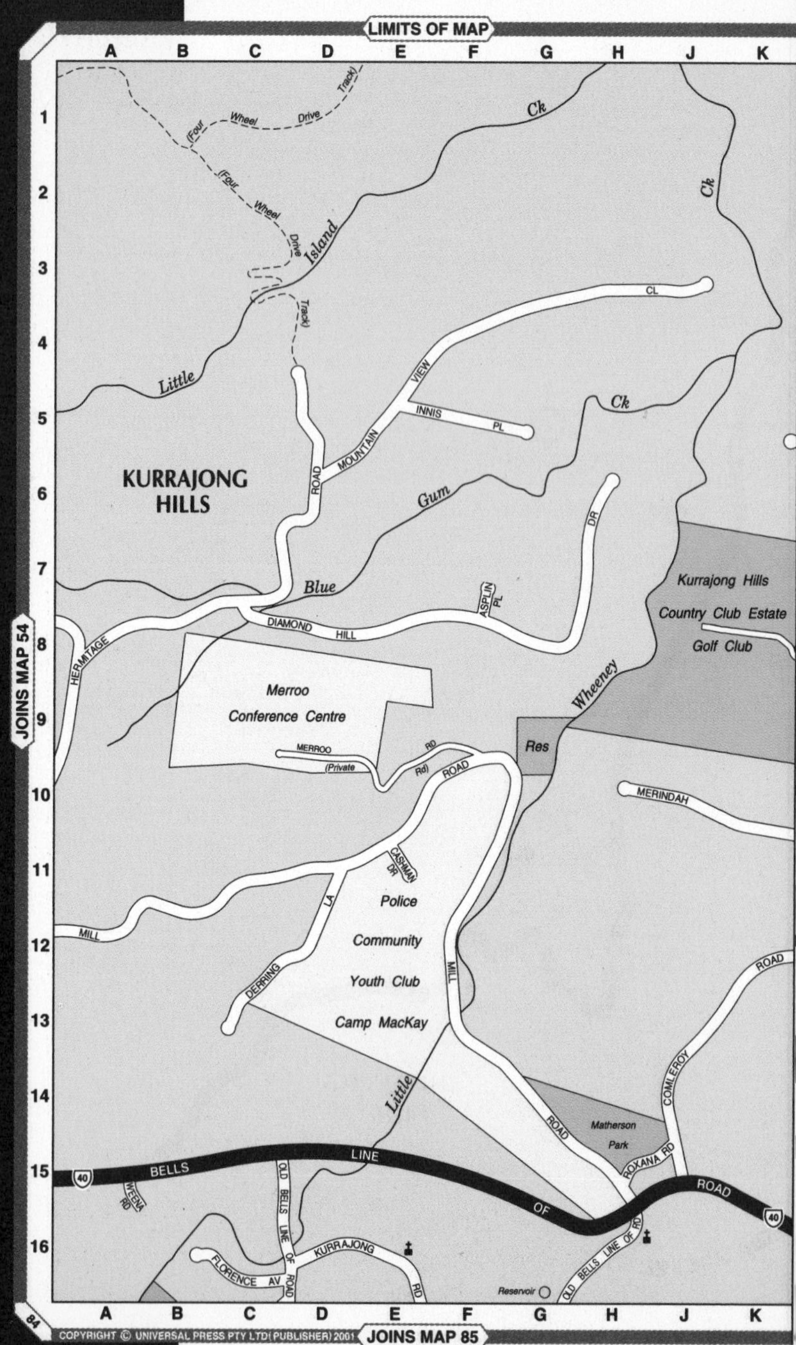
LIMITS OF MAP
A B C D E F G H J K
1 2 3 4 5 6 7 8 9 10 11 12 13 14 15 16
JOINS MAP 54
KURRAJONG HILLS
(Four Wheel Drive Track)
Little Island Ck
Ck
MOUNTAIN VIEW CL
INNIS PL
ROAD
Gum
Ck
DR
Blue
ASPLIN PL
DIAMOND HILL
HERMITAGE
Kurrajong Hills Country Club Estate Golf Club
Merroo Conference Centre
Wheeney
MERROO (Private Rd)
RD
ROAD
Res
MERINDAH
CASHMAN DR
LA
Police Community Youth Club Camp MacKay
MILL
MILL
DERRING
ROAD
Little
COMLEROY
ROAD
Matherson Park
ROXANA RD
BELLS LINE OF ROAD
40
WEENA RD
OLD BELLS LINE OF ROAD
KURRAJONG RD
FLORENCE AV
Reservoir
OLD BELLS LINE OF RD
JOINS MAP 85

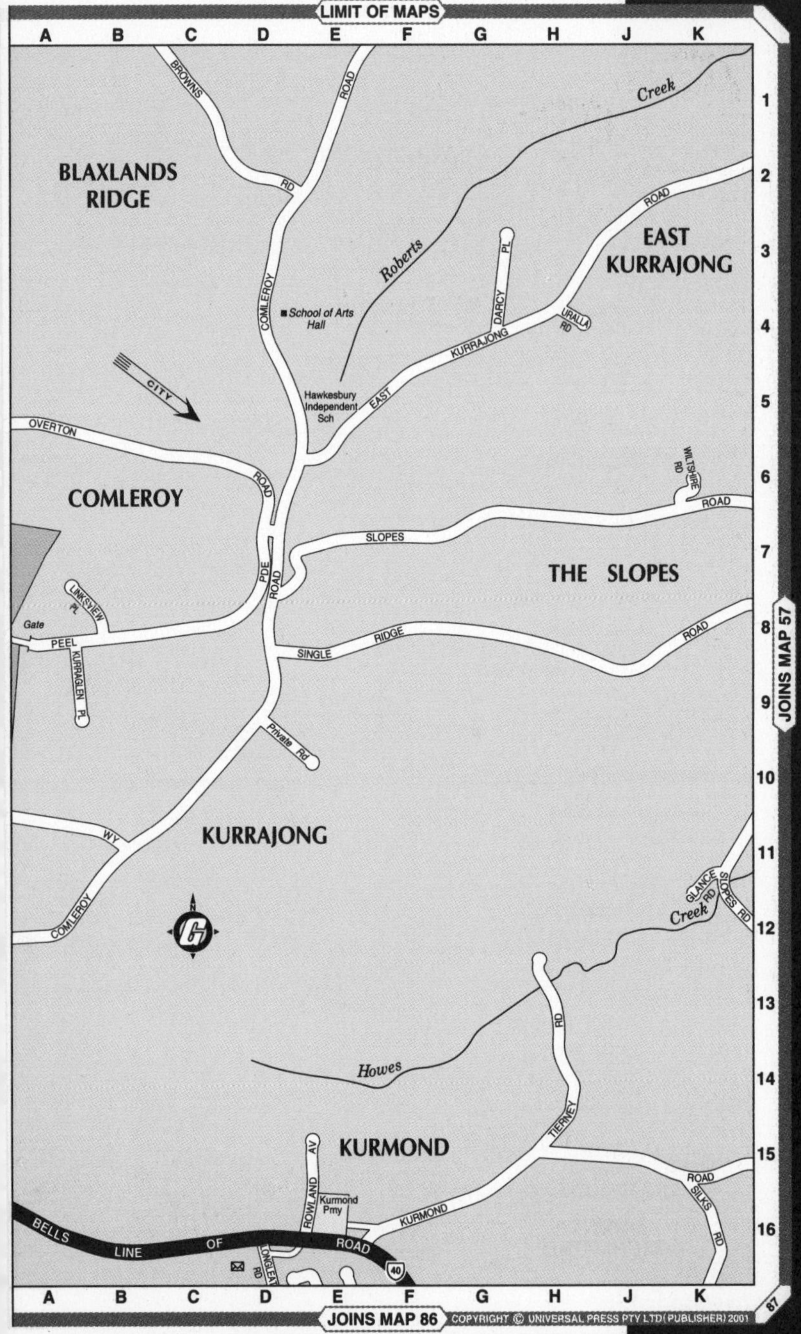
LIMIT OF MAPS
A B C D E F G H J K
1 2 3 4 5 6 7 8 9 10 11 12 13 14 15 16
BLAXLANDS RIDGE
EAST KURRAJONG
COMLEROY
THE SLOPES
KURRAJONG
KURMOND
BROWNS RD
ROAD
COMLEROY RD
Creek
Roberts
School of Arts Hall
Hawkesbury Independent Sch
EAST KURRAJONG ROAD
DARCY PL
URALLA RD
CITY
OVERTON ROAD
WILTSHIRE RD
ROAD
SLOPES
PDE
ROAD
LINKSVIEW PL
Gate
PEEL
KURRAGLEN PL
SINGLE RIDGE ROAD
Private Rd
WY
COMLEROY
GLANCE RD
SLOPES RD
Creek
RD
Howes
TIERNEY
ROWLAND AV
Kurmond Pmy
KURMOND
ROAD
SILKS RD
BELLS LINE OF ROAD
LONGLEAT RD
40
JOINS MAP 57
JOINS MAP 86
87

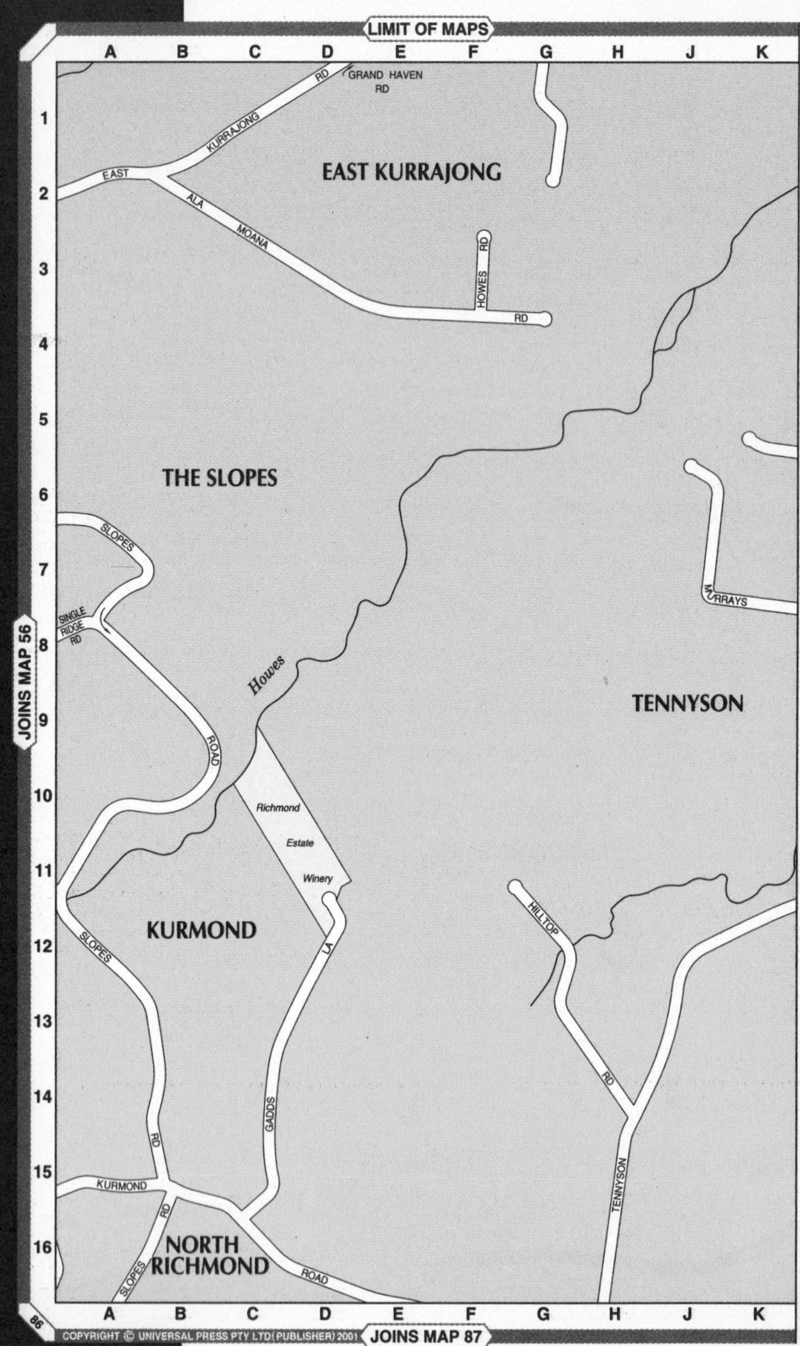
LIMIT OF MAPS
A B C D E F G H J K
1 2 3 4 5 6 7 8 9 10 11 12 13 14 15 16
JOINS MAP 56
GRAND HAVEN RD
EAST KURRAJONG RD
EAST KURRAJONG
ALA MOANA
HOWES RD
RD
THE SLOPES
SLOPES
SINGLE RIDGE RD
ROAD
Howes
TENNYSON
MURRAYS
Richmond
Estate
Winery
KURMOND
SLOPES
LA
HILLTOP
RD
GADDS
RD
TENNYSON
KURMOND
RD
NORTH RICHMOND
SLOPES
ROAD
86
JOINS MAP 87

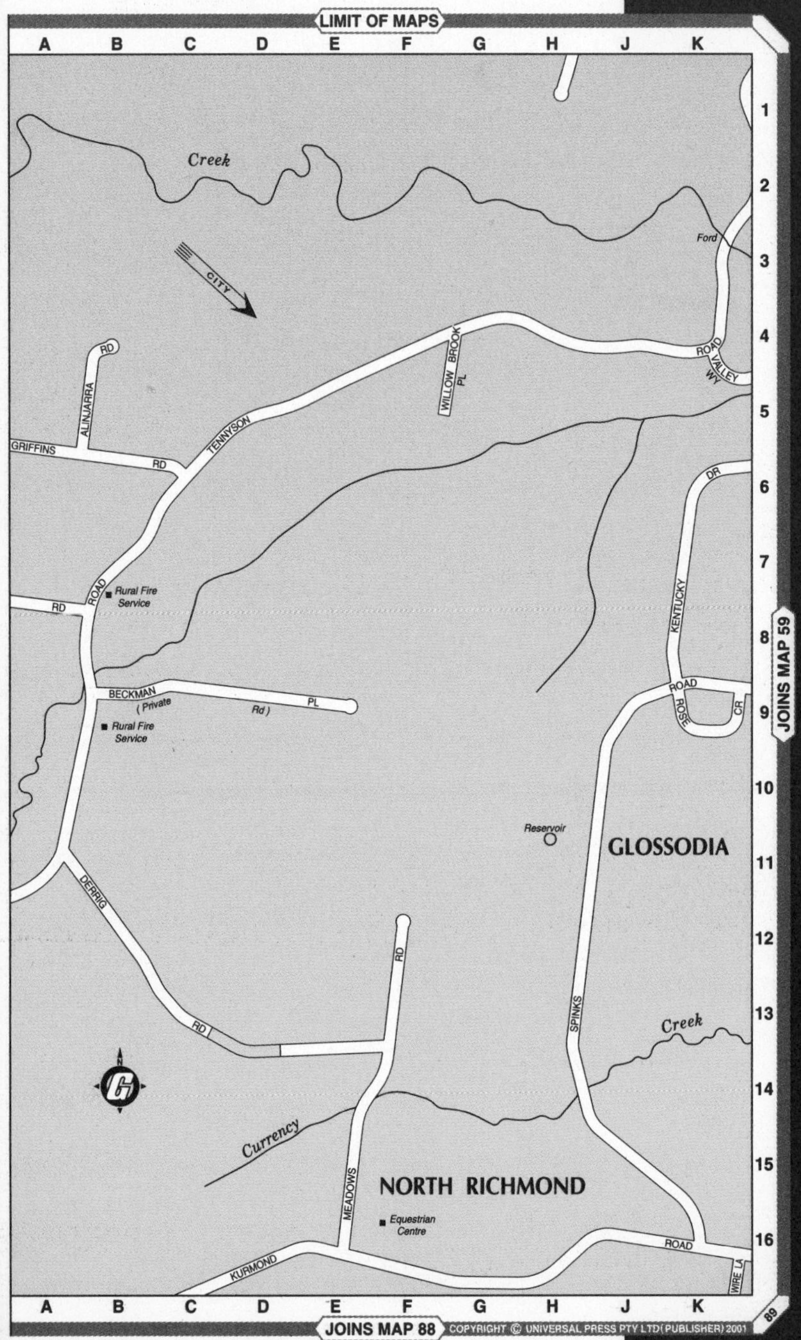
LIMIT OF MAPS
A B C D E F G H J K
1 2 3 4 5 6 7 8 9 10 11 12 13 14 15 16
Creek
CITY
Ford
ALINJARRA RD
GRIFFINS RD
TENNYSON ROAD
WILLOW BROOK PL
ROAD
VALLEY WY
DR
KENTUCKY
ROAD
ROSE CR
JOINS MAP 59
RD
Rural Fire Service
BECKMAN PL
(Private Rd)
Rural Fire Service
Reservoir
GLOSSODIA
DERRIG RD
RD
SPINKS
Creek
Currency
MEADOWS
NORTH RICHMOND
Equestrian Centre
KURMOND ROAD
WIRE LA
89
JOINS MAP 88

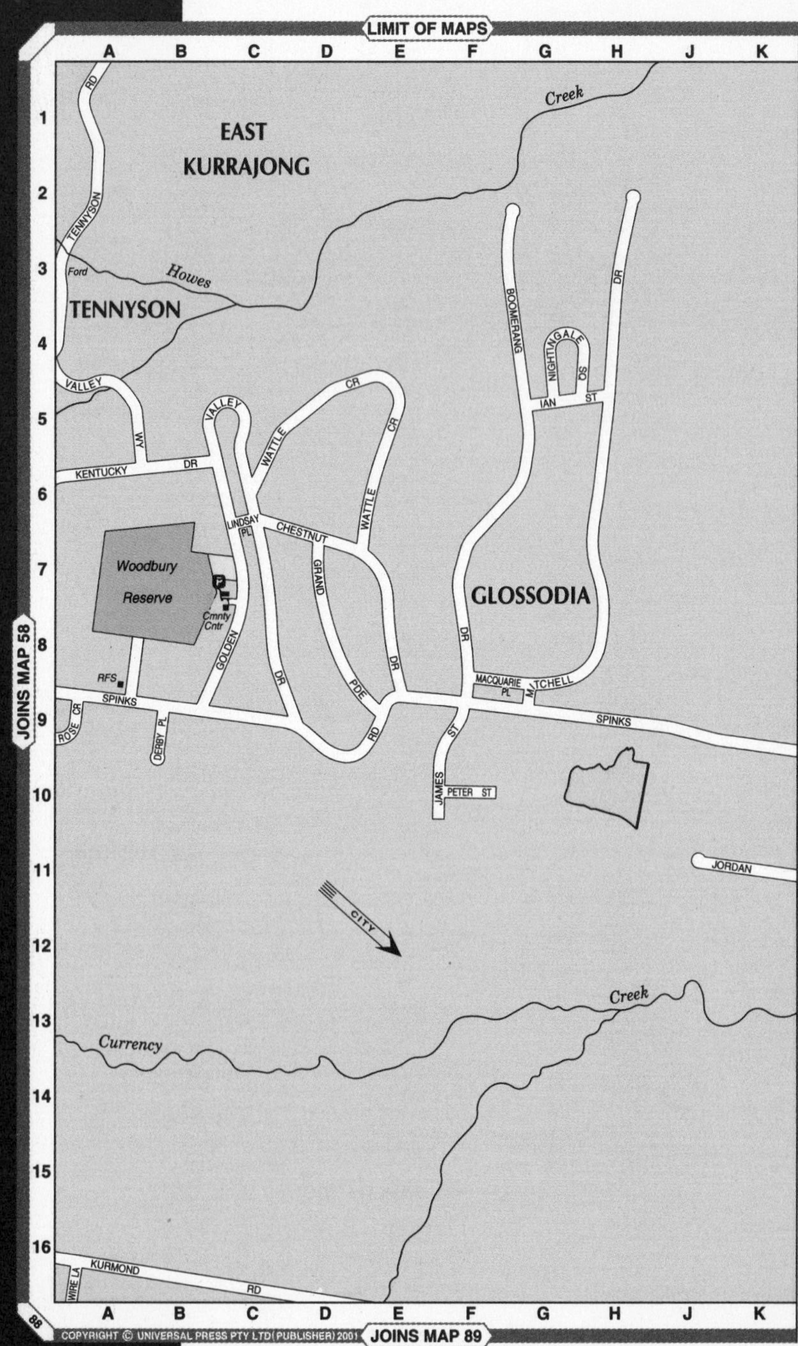
LIMIT OF MAPS
A B C D E F G H J K
1 2 3 4 5 6 7 8 9 10 11 12 13 14 15 16
EAST
KURRAJONG
TENNYSON
GLOSSODIA
Creek
Howes
Ford
TENNYSON
RD
VALLEY
WY
KENTUCKY
DR
VALLEY
WATTLE
CR
CR
WATTLE
LINDSAY
PL
CHESTNUT
GRAND
PDE
DR
DR
GOLDEN
Woodbury
Reserve
Cmnty
Cntr
RFS
SPINKS
ROSE
CR
DERBY PL
RD
BOOMERANG
DR
NIGHTINGALE
SQ
IAN
ST
DR
MACQUARIE
PL
MITCHELL
SPINKS
JAMES
ST
PETER ST
JORDAN
CITY
Creek
Currency
KURMOND
RD
WIRE LA
JOINS MAP 58
88

JOINS MAP 89

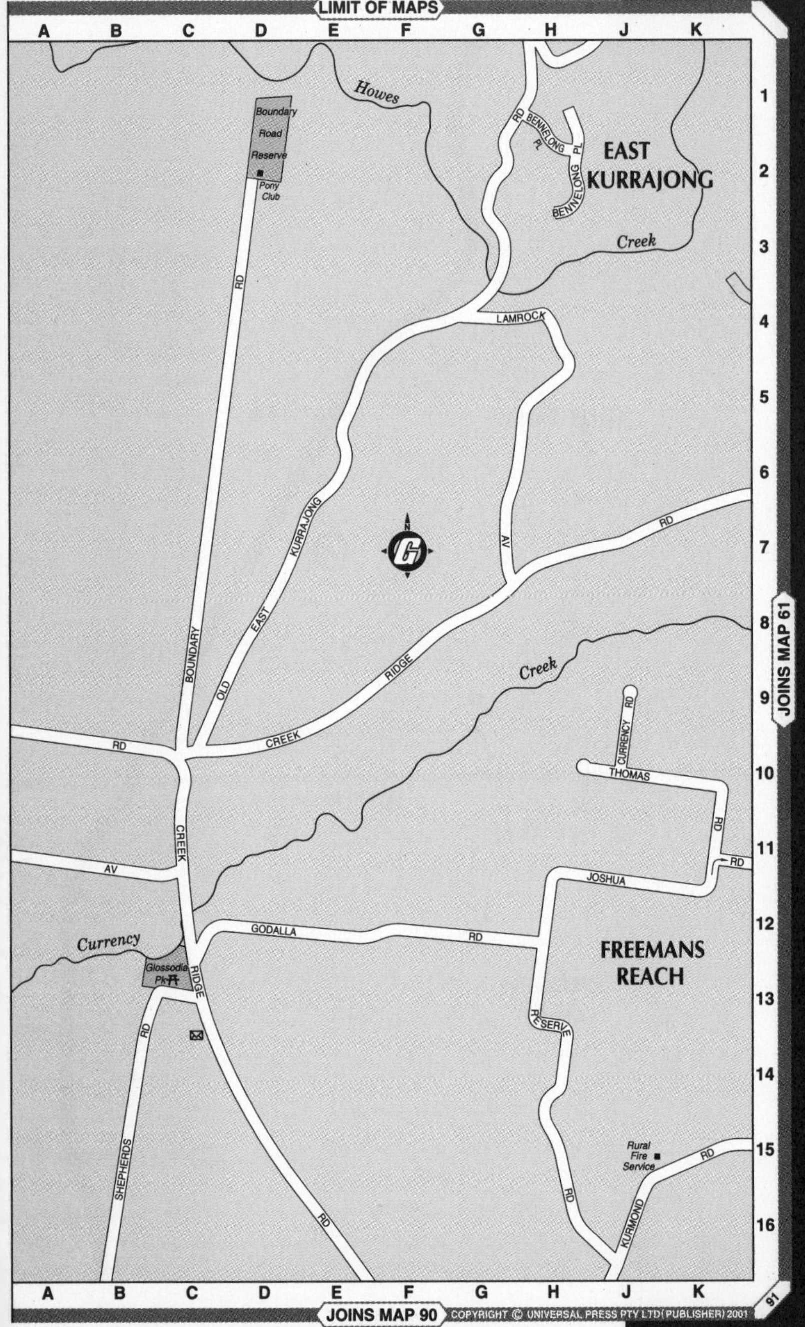
LIMIT OF MAPS
A
B
C
D
E
F
G
H
J
K
1
2
3
4
5
6
7
8
9
10
11
12
13
14
15
16
Howes
Creek
Boundary
Road
Reserve
Pony
Club
EAST
KURRAJONG
BENNELONG
PL
RD
LAMROCK
AV
OLD
EAST
KURRAJONG
RD
BOUNDARY
RD
CREEK
RIDGE
RD
Creek
JOINS MAP 61
CURRENCY
RD
THOMAS
RD
RD
JOSHUA
AV
CREEK
GODALLA
RD
Currency
Glossodia
Pk
RIDGE
FREEMANS
REACH
RESERVE
RD
SHEPHERDS
RD
Rural
Fire
Service
KURMOND
RD
JOINS MAP 90

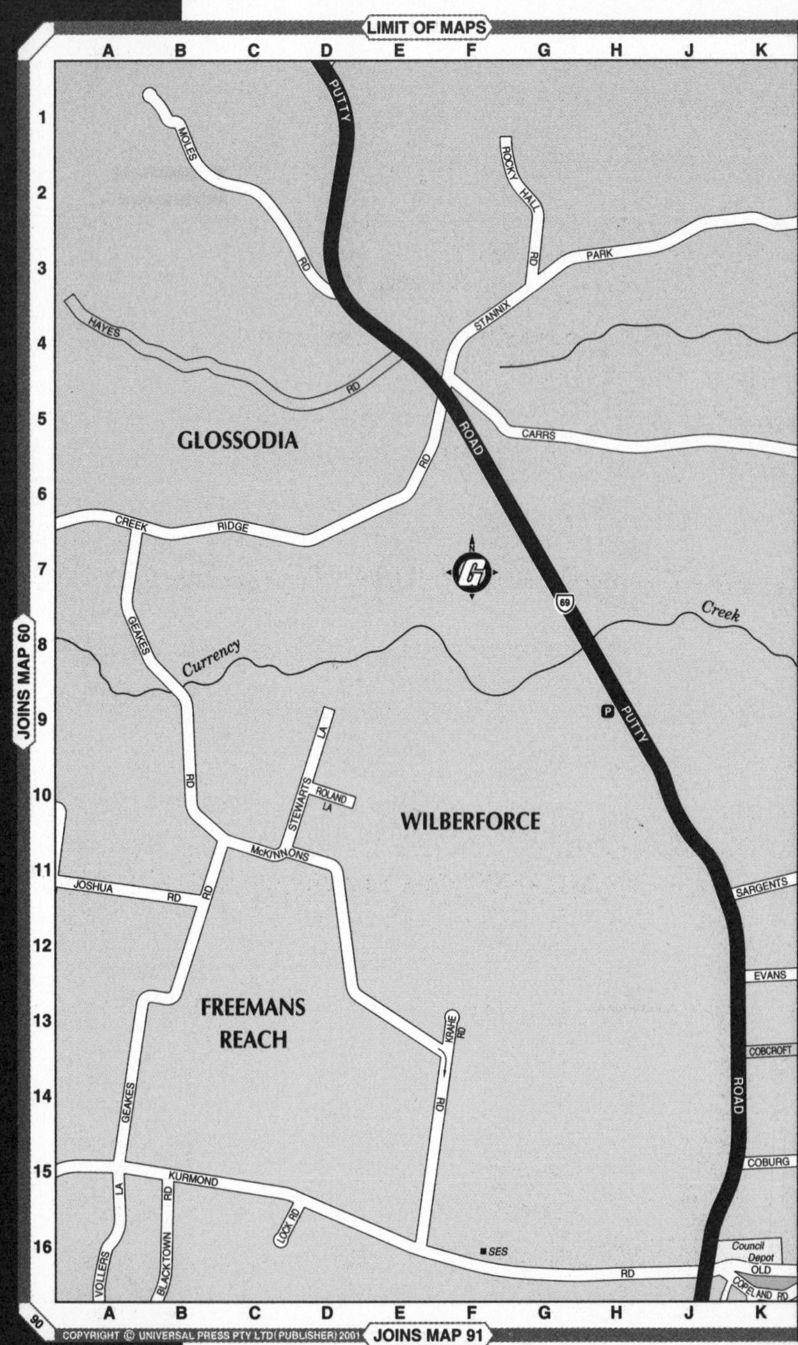
LIMIT OF MAPS
A B C D E F G H J K
1 2 3 4 5 6 7 8 9 10 11 12 13 14 15 16
PUTTY ROAD
MOLES RD
ROCKY HALL RD
PARK
STANNIX
HAYES RD
CARRS
GLOSSODIA
RD
CREEK RIDGE
69
Creek
GEAKES RD
Currency
PUTTY
STEWARTS LA
ROLAND LA
WILBERFORCE
McKINNONS
JOSHUA RD
SARGENTS
EVANS
FREEMANS REACH
KRAHE RD
RD
COBCROFT
ROAD
GEAKES
COBURG
KURMOND
LA
RD
LOCK RD
SES
Council Depot
OLD
COPELAND RD
RD
VOLLERS
BLACKTOWN
JOINS MAP 60
JOINS MAP 91
90

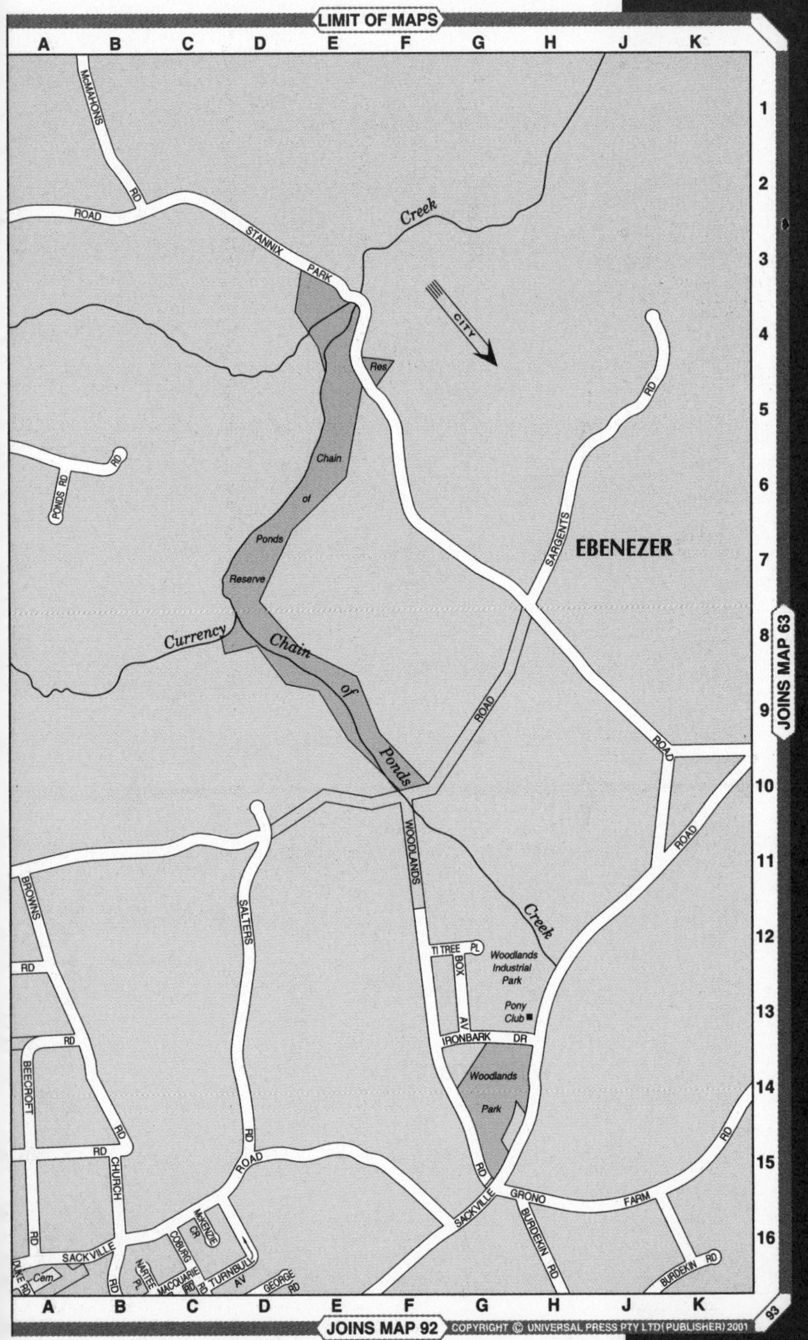
LIMIT OF MAPS
A B C D E F G H J K
1 2 3 4 5 6 7 8 9 10 11 12 13 14 15 16
McMAHONS RD
ROAD
STANNIX PARK
Creek
CITY
Res
RD
PONDS RD
RD
Chain of Ponds Reserve
SARGENTS
EBENEZER
Currency
Chain of Ponds
ROAD
ROAD
JOINS MAP 63
ROAD
WOODLANDS
BROWNS
SALTERS
Creek
RD
TI TREE PL
BOX AV
Woodlands Industrial Park
Pony Club
IRONBARK DR
RD
BEECROFT
Woodlands Park
RD
RD
RD
CHURCH
ROAD
RD
RD
SACKVILLE
GRONO
FARM
BURDEKIN RD
McKENZIE CR
COBURG RD
RD
SACKVILLE
DUKE RD
Cem
RD
NARTEE PL
MACQUARIE RD
TURNBULL AV
GEORGE RD
BURDEKIN RD
A B C D E F G H J K
JOINS MAP 92
93

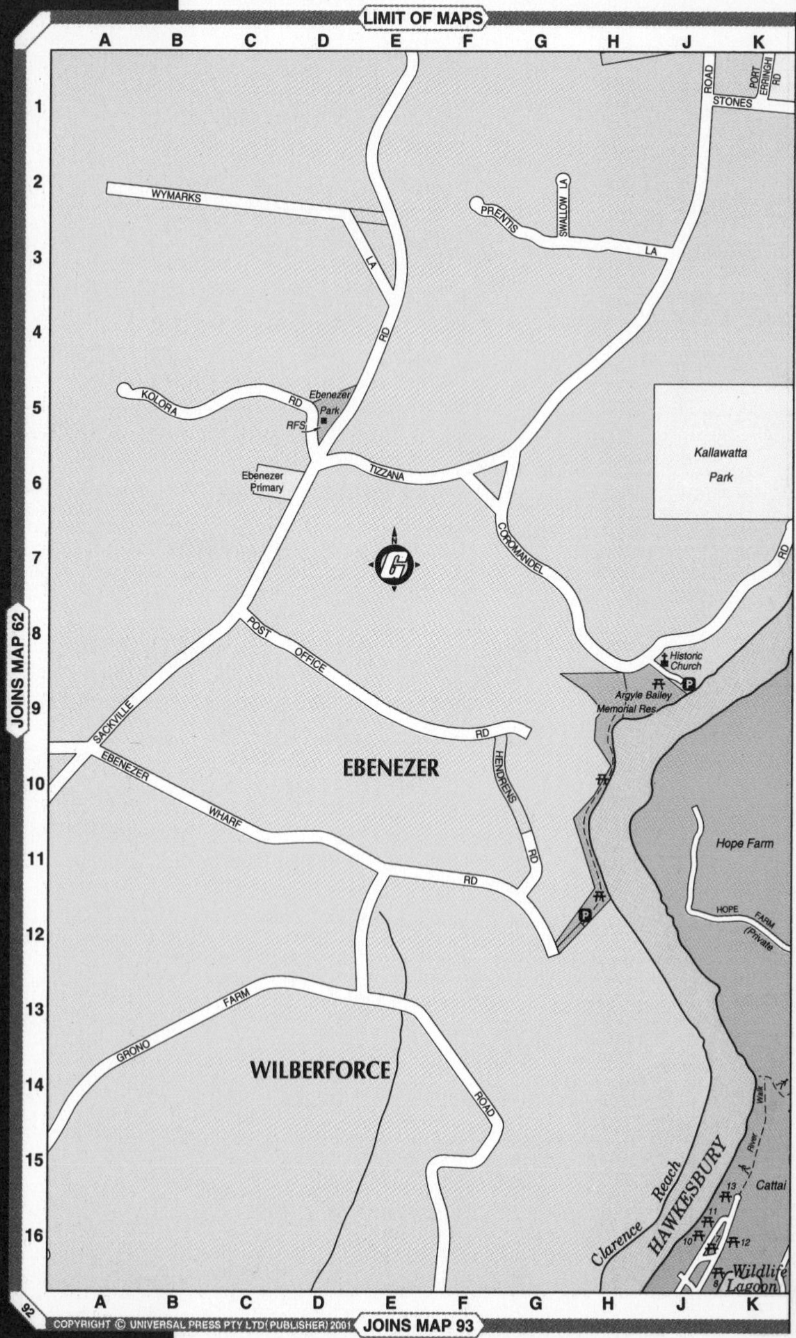
LIMIT OF MAPS
A
B
C
D
E
F
G
H
J
K
1
2
3
4
5
6
7
8
9
10
11
12
13
14
15
16
ROAD
STONES
PORT ERRINGHI RD
WYMARKS
LA
RD
SWALLOW LA
PRENTIS
LA
KOLORA
RD
Ebenezer Park
RFS
Ebenezer Primary
TIZZANA
Kallawatta Park
CORONMANDEL
RD
POST
OFFICE
RD
SACKVILLE
EBENEZER
WHARF
RD
HENDRENS
RD
Historic Church
Argyle Bailey Memorial Res.
EBENEZER
Hope Farm
HOPE FARM
(Private
GRONO
FARM
WILBERFORCE
ROAD
Clarence Reach
HAWKESBURY
River
Walk
Cattai
Wildlife Lagoon
JOINS MAP 62
JOINS MAP 93
92

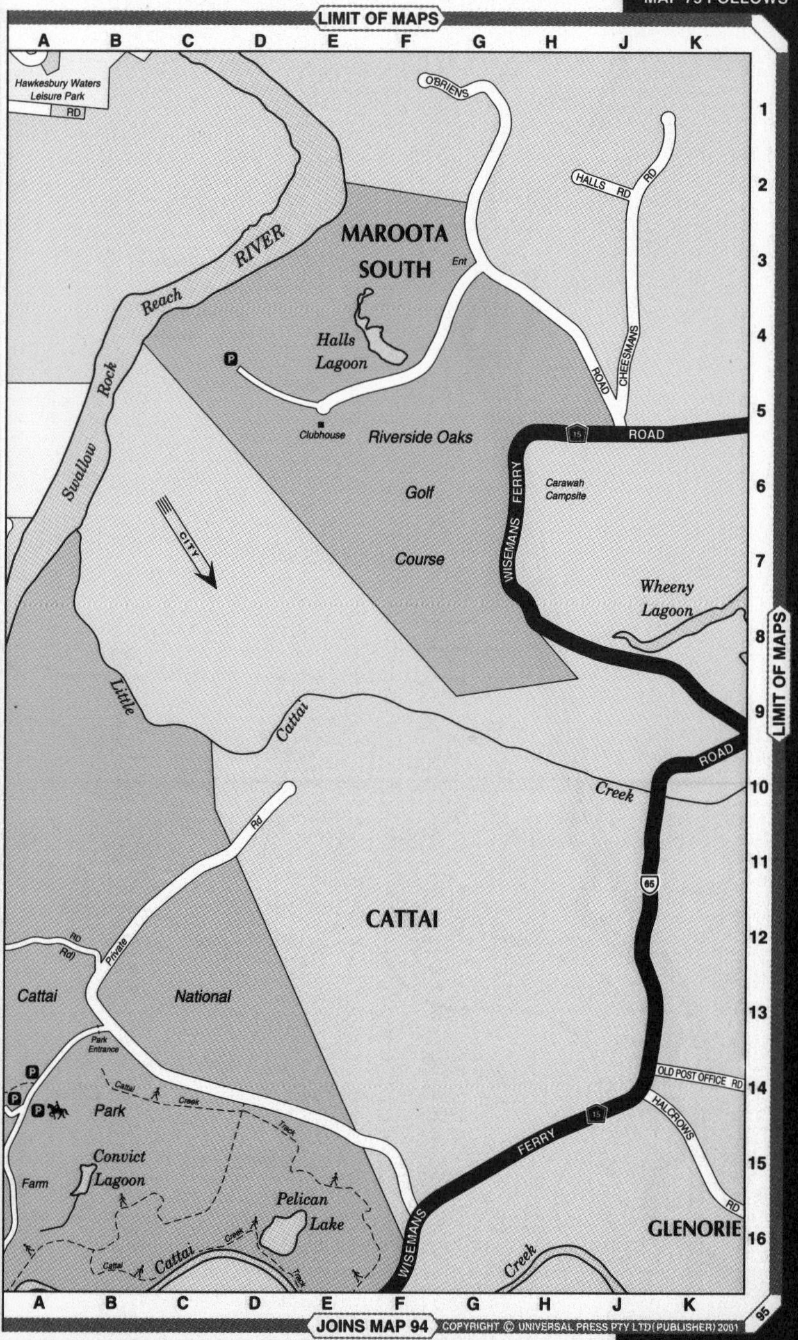
LIMIT OF MAPS
A B C D E F G H J K
1 2 3 4 5 6 7 8 9 10 11 12 13 14 15 16
Hawkesbury Waters Leisure Park
RD
O'BRIENS
HALLS RD
RD
MAROOTA SOUTH
Ent
RIVER
Reach
Rock
Swallow
Halls Lagoon
Clubhouse
Riverside Oaks
Golf
Course
CITY
CHEESMANS
ROAD
ROAD
15
WISEMANS FERRY
Carawah Campsite
Wheeny Lagoon
LIMIT OF MAPS
Little
Cattai
Creek
ROAD
Rd
65
CATTAI
RD
Rd)
Private
Cattai
National
Park Entrance
Cattai
Creek
Park
Track
Convict Lagoon
Farm
Pelican Lake
Creek
Cattai
Cattai
Track
OLD POST OFFICE RD
HALCROWS
RD
15
FERRY
WISEMANS
GLENORIE
Creek
A B C D E F G H J K

MAP 75
PREVIOUS MAP 64

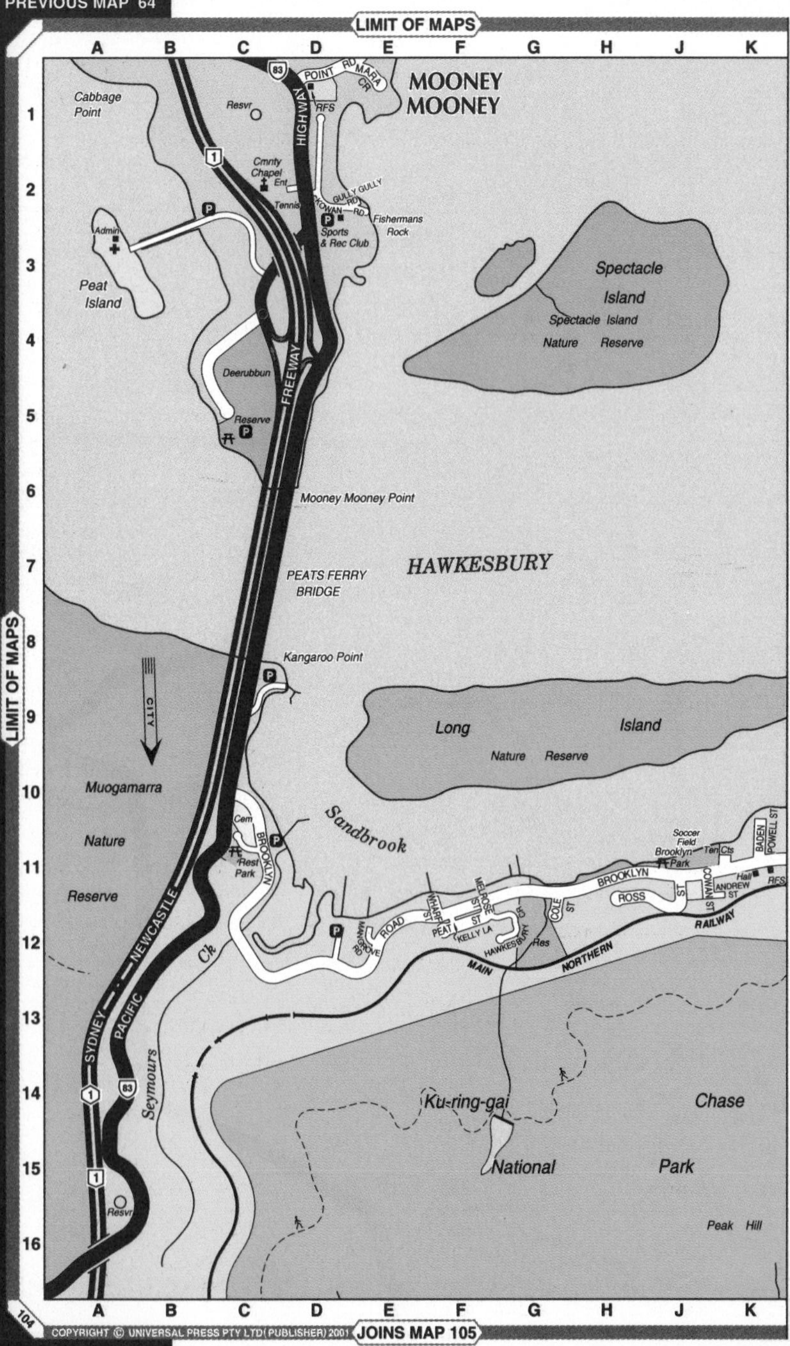

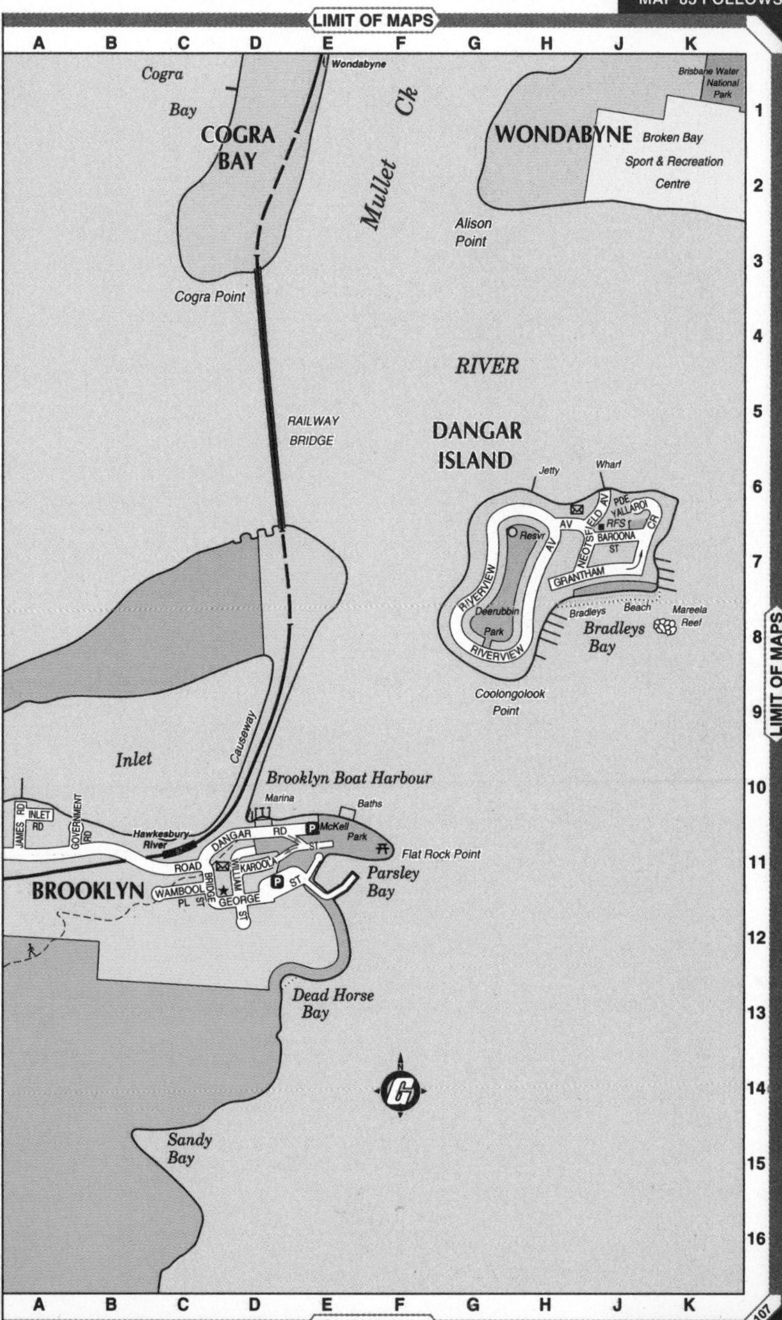
LIMIT OF MAPS
A B C D E F G H J K
Wondabyne
Cogra
Bay
COGRA
BAY
Mullet Ck
Brisbane Water
National
Park
WONDABYNE
Broken Bay
Sport & Recreation
Centre
Alison
Point
Cogra Point
RIVER
RAILWAY
BRIDGE
DANGAR
ISLAND
Jetty
Wharf
PDE
YALLAROI
RFS
BAROONA
ST
CR
NEOTSFIELD AV
AV
Resvr
GRANTHAM
RIVERVIEW
Deerubbin
Park
Bradleys
Beach
Mareela
Reef
Bradleys
Bay
Coolongolook
Point
LIMIT OF MAPS
Inlet
Causeway
Brooklyn Boat Harbour
Marina
Baths
JAMES
RD
INLET
RD
GOVERNMENT
RD
Hawkesbury
River
DANGAR
RD
McKell
Park
ST
Flat Rock Point
ROAD
KAROOLA
WILLIAM
BRIDGE
ST
Parsley
Bay
BROOKLYN
WAMBOOL
PL
GEORGE
ST
Dead Horse
Bay
Sandy
Bay
1 2 3 4 5 6 7 8 9 10 11 12 13 14 15 16

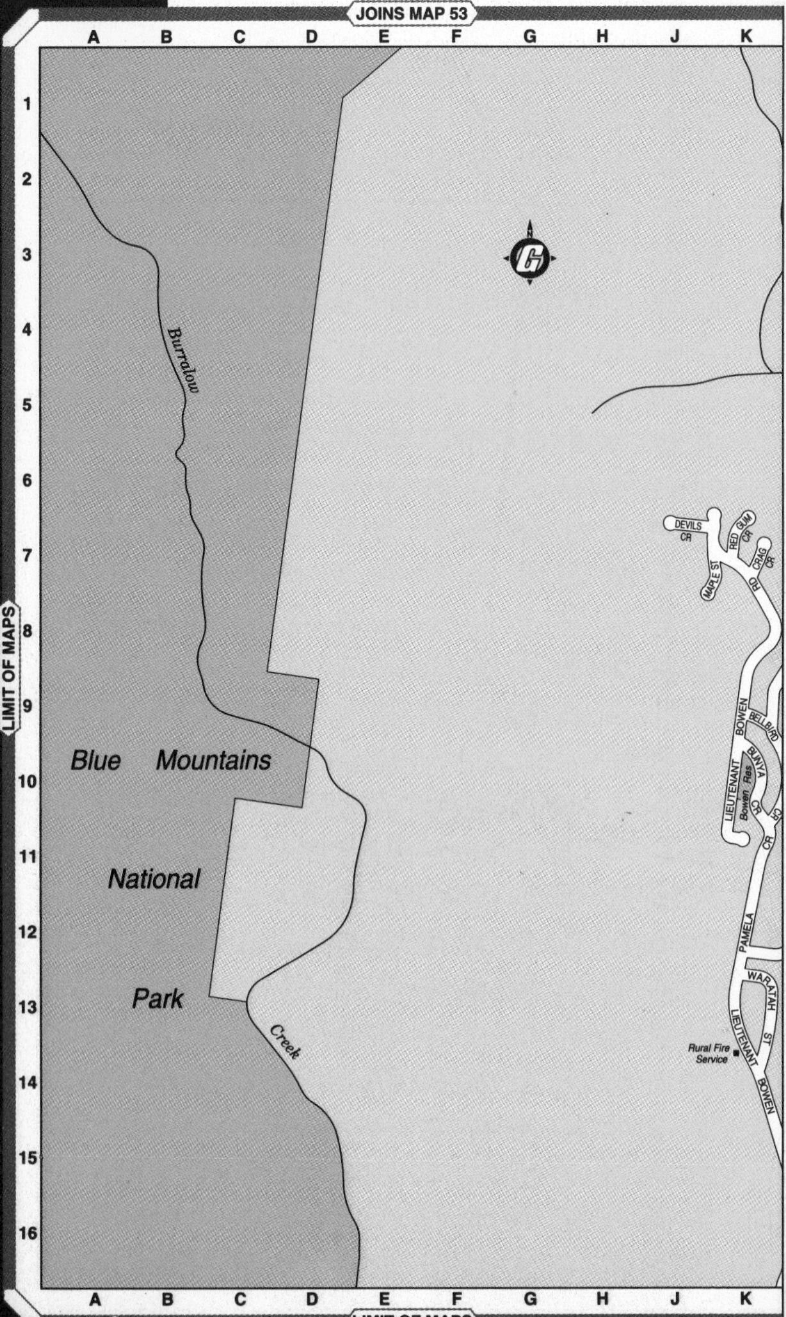

JOINS MAP 53

A B C D E F G H J K

1 2 3 4 5 6 7 8 9 10 11 12 13 14 15 16

Burralow Creek

Blue Mountains National Park

DEVILS CR
RED GUM CR
CRAG CR
MAPLE ST
RD
BOWEN
BELLBIRD
BUNYA
LIEUTENANT
Bowen Res
CR
CR
CR
PAMELA
WARATAH ST
LIEUTENANT BOWEN
Rural Fire Service

A B C D E F G H J K

LIMIT OF MAPS

LIMIT OF MAPS

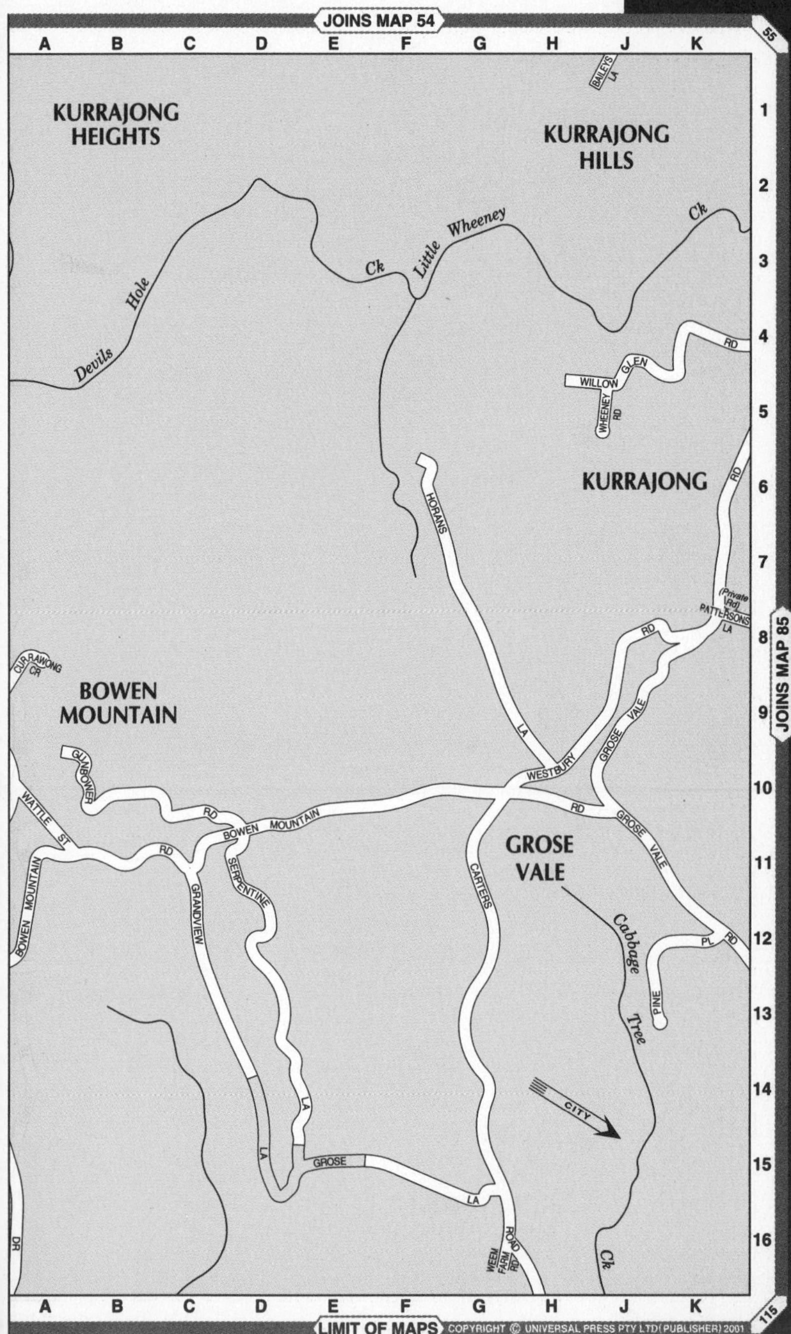
JOINS MAP 54
A B C D E F G H J K
1 2 3 4 5 6 7 8 9 10 11 12 13 14 15 16
55
KURRAJONG HEIGHTS
KURRAJONG HILLS
KURRAJONG
BOWEN MOUNTAIN
GROSE VALE
BAILEYS LA
Devils Hole
Ck
Little Wheeney
Ck
RD
WILLOW GLEN
WHEENEY RD
HORANS LA
RD
(Private Rd)
PATTERSONS LA
RD
GROSE VALE
WESTBURY
RD
GROSE VALE RD
CURRAWONG CR
GUNBOWER
RD
WATTLE ST
BOWEN MOUNTAIN
RD
BOWEN MOUNTAIN
SERPENTINE
GRANDVIEW
CARTERS
Cabbage Tree Ck
PINE PL
CITY
LA
LA
GROSE
LA
ROAD
WEEM FARM RD
DR
JOINS MAP 85
115
LIMIT OF MAPS

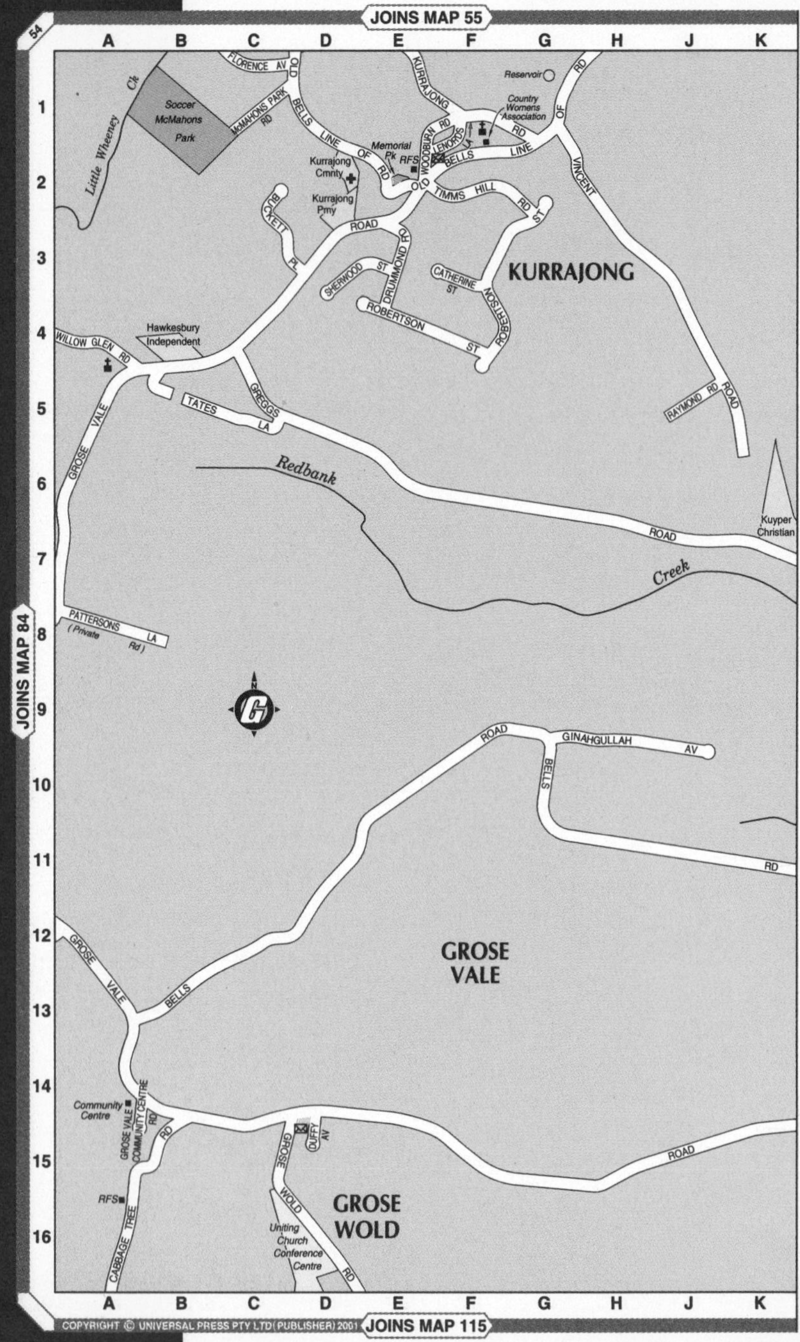

JOINS MAP 115

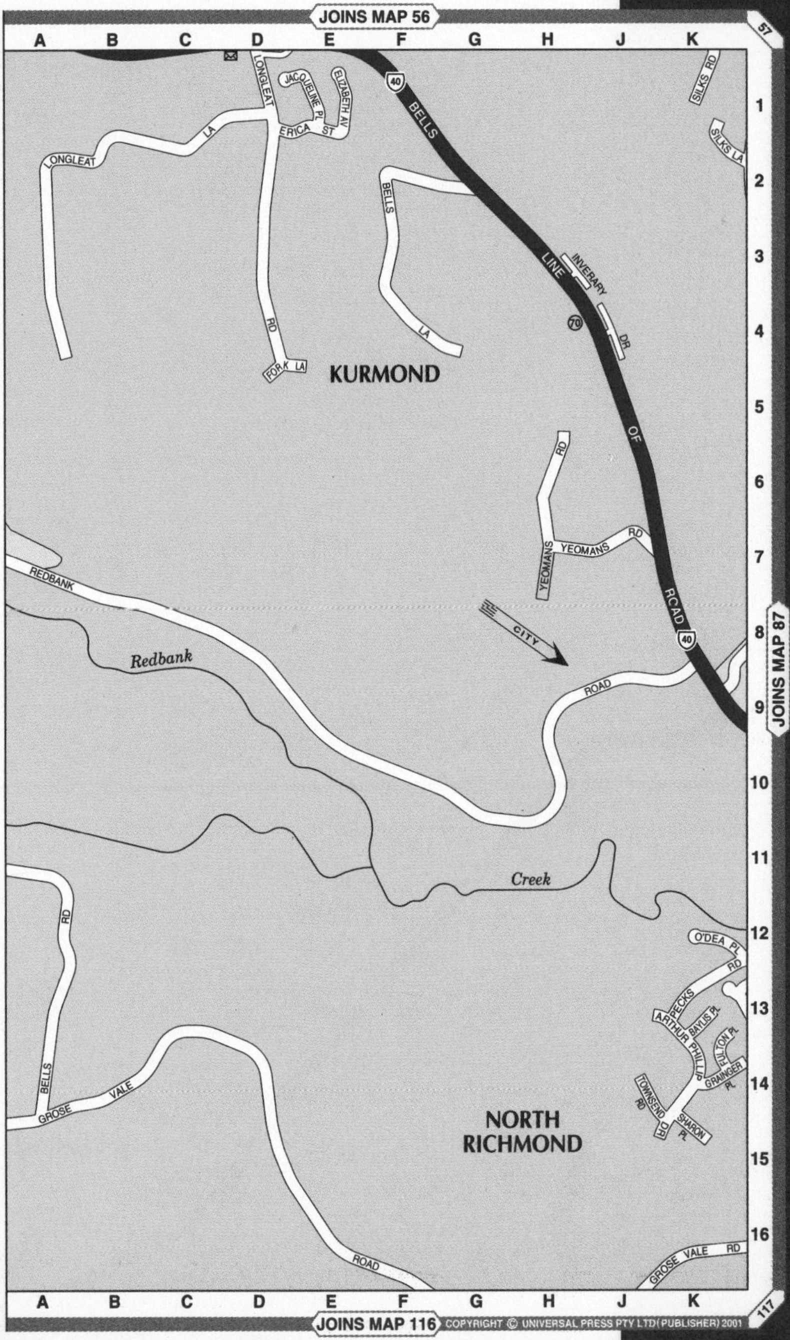
JOINS MAP 56
57
A
B
C
D
E
F
G
H
J
K
1
2
3
4
5
6
7
8
9
10
11
12
13
14
15
16
LONGLEAT
LA
JACQUELINE PL
ELIZABETH AV
ERICA ST
LONGLEAT
RD
FORK LA
40
BELLS
LINE
OF
ROAD
BELLS
LA
INVERARY
DR
70
SILKS RD
SILKS LA
KURMOND
RD
YEOMANS
YEOMANS
RD
REDBANK
Redbank
CITY
ROAD
40
Creek
JOINS MAP 87
RD
BELLS
GROSE
VALE
ROAD
NORTH RICHMOND
O'DEA PL
RD
PECKS
ARTHUR PHILLIP
BAYLIS PL
FULTON PL
GRAINGER PL
TOWNSEND RD
DR
SHARON PL
GROSE VALE RD
117
JOINS MAP 116

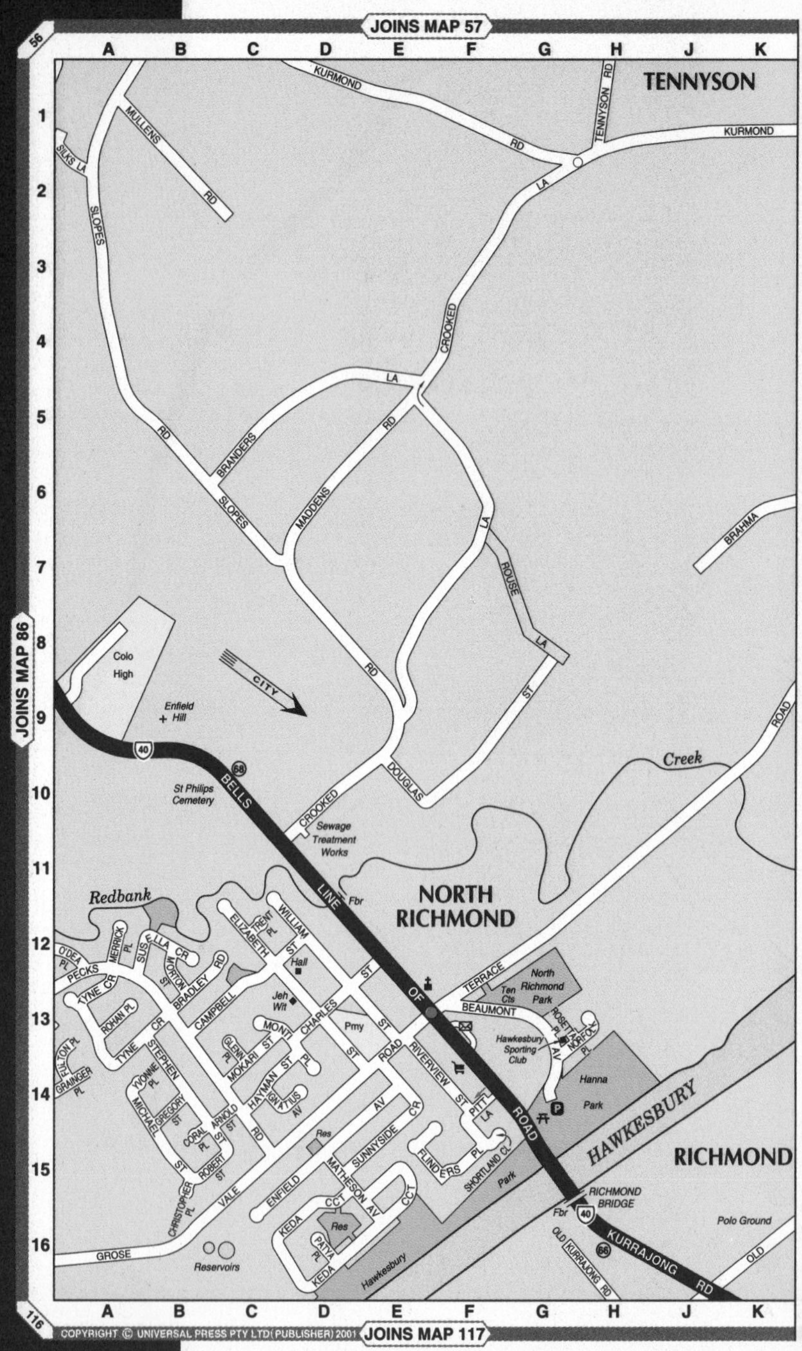
JOINS MAP 57
JOINS MAP 86
JOINS MAP 117
TENNYSON
NORTH RICHMOND
RICHMOND
KURMOND RD
TENNYSON RD
MULLENS RD
SILKS LA
SLOPES RD
CROOKED LA
BRANDERS LA
MADDENS RD
CROOKED RD
ROUSE LA
DOUGLAS ST
BRAHMA RD
Creek
Colo High
Enfield Hill
CITY
St Philips Cemetery
BELLS LINE OF ROAD
Sewage Treatment Works
Fbr
Redbank
TERRACE
North Richmond Park
Ten Cts
BEAUMONT
Hawkesbury Sporting Club
Hanna Park
HAWKESBURY
RICHMOND BRIDGE
KURRAJONG RD
OLD KURRAJONG RD
Polo Ground
Park
Hawkesbury
Reservoirs
GROSE VALE RD
Hall
Jeh Wit
Pmy
Res
O'DEA PL
PECKS
MERRICK PL
SUSELLA CR
MORTON ST
BRADLEY RD
TYNE CR
ROHAN PL
FULTON PL
GRAINGER PL
STEPHEN ST
YVONNE PL
MICHAEL ST
GREGORY ST
CORAL PL
ARNOLD ST
ROBERT ST
CHRISTOPHER PL
CAMPBELL ST
ELIZABETH ST
TRENT PL
WILLIAM ST
CHARLES ST
MONTI PL
GLENN PL
MOKARI ST
HAYMAN ST
IGNATIUS AV
RIVERVIEW ST
PITT LA
SHORTLAND CL
FLINDERS PL
SUNNYSIDE CR
ENFIELD AV
MATHESON AV
KEDA CCT
PATYA PL
ROSETTA PL
NORFOLK PL
AV
56
116
COPYRIGHT © UNIVERSAL PRESS PTY LTD (PUBLISHER) 2001

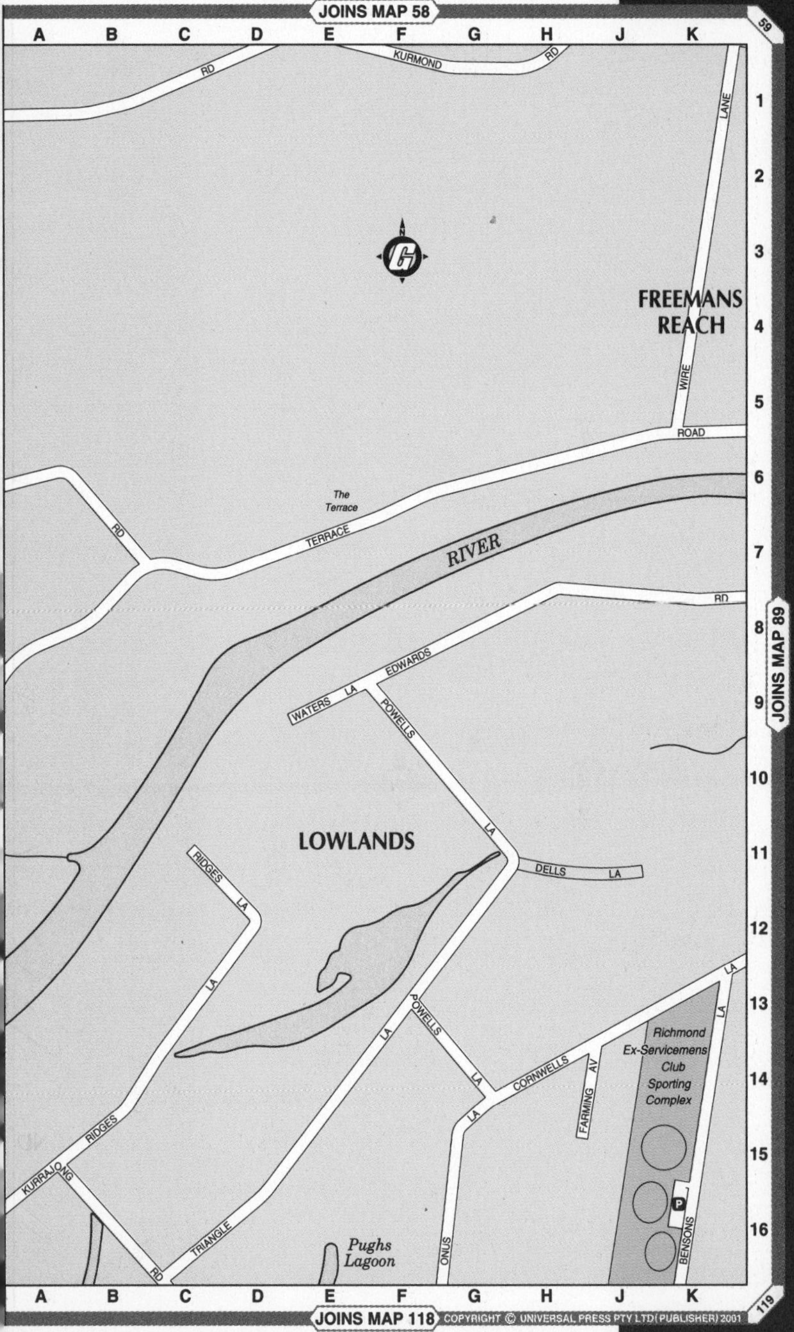
JOINS MAP 58
A B C D E F G H J K
59
KURMOND
RD
RD
LANE
FREEMANS
REACH
WIRE
ROAD
The
Terrace
TERRACE
RD
RIVER
RD
EDWARDS
WATERS LA
POWELLS
JOINS MAP 89
LA
DELLS LA
LOWLANDS
RIDGES
LA
LA
LA
POWELLS
LA
LA
CORNWELLS
LA
FARMING AV
LA
Richmond
Ex-Servicemens
Club
Sporting
Complex
P
RIDGES
KURRAJONG
TRIANGLE
RD
ONUS
BENSONS
Pughs
Lagoon
1 2 3 4 5 6 7 8 9 10 11 12 13 14 15 16
A B C D E F G H J K
JOINS MAP 118
119

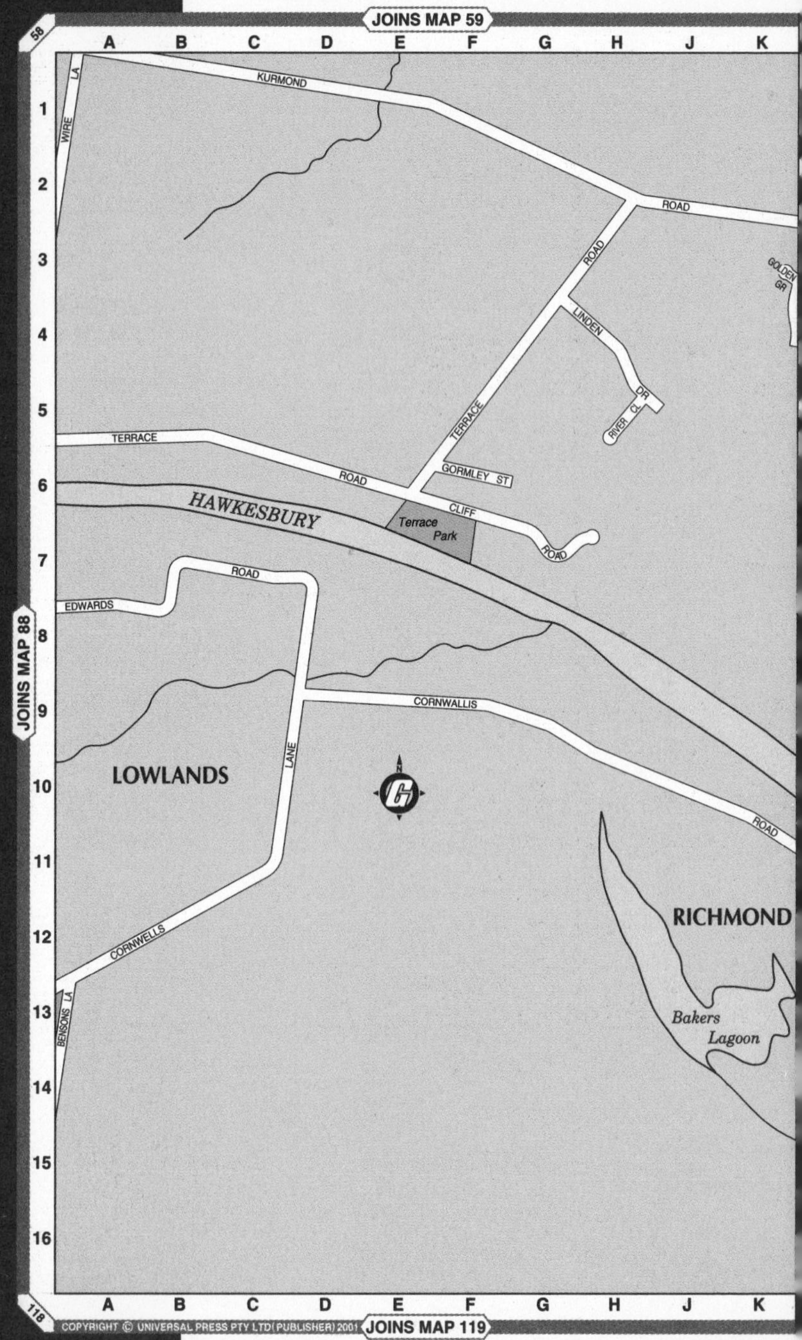
JOINS MAP 59
58
A
B
C
D
E
F
G
H
J
K
1
2
3
4
5
6
7
8
9
10
11
12
13
14
15
16
WIRE LA
KURMOND
ROAD
ROAD
GOLDEN GR
LINDEN
DR
RIVER CL
TERRACE
TERRACE
ROAD
GORMLEY ST
CLIFF
ROAD
HAWKESBURY
Terrace Park
ROAD
EDWARDS
CORNWALLIS
ROAD
LANE
LOWLANDS
RICHMOND
Bakers Lagoon
CORNWELLS
BENSONS LA
JOINS MAP 88
118
JOINS MAP 119

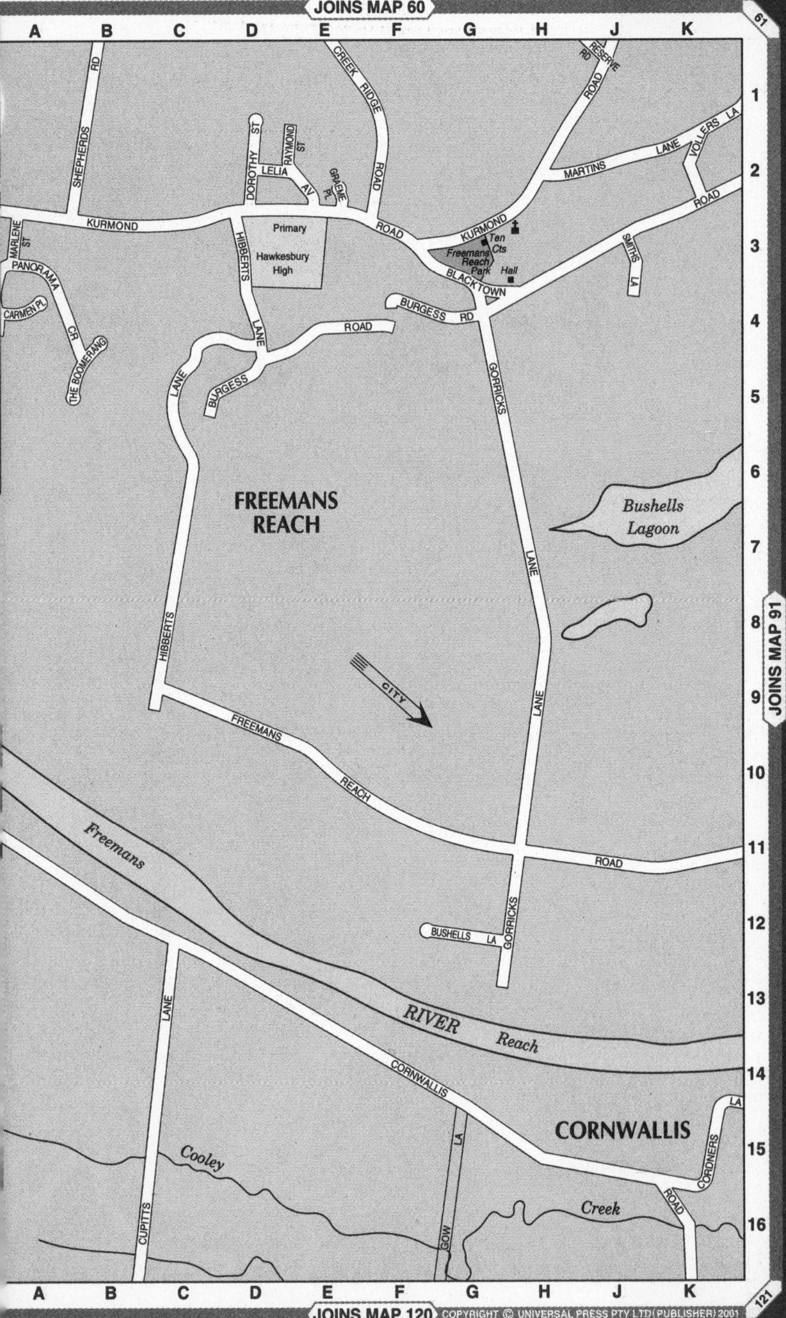
JOINS MAP 60
61
A B C D E F G H J K
1 2 3 4 5 6 7 8 9 10 11 12 13 14 15 16
SHEPHERDS RD
CREEK RIDGE ROAD
RESERVE RD
ROAD
DOROTHY ST
RAYMOND ST
LELIA AV
GRAEME PL
MARTINS LANE
VOLLERS LA
ROAD
KURMOND ROAD
KURMOND
Primary
Hawkesbury High
Ten Cts
Freemans Reach Park
Hall
MARLENE ST
PANORAMA CR
CARMEN PL
THE BOOMERANG
HIBBERTS LANE
BLACKTOWN
SMITHS LA
BURGESS RD
ROAD
BURGESS
LANE
GORRICKS LANE
FREEMANS REACH
Bushells Lagoon
HIBBERTS
CITY
FREEMANS REACH ROAD
JOINS MAP 91
Freemans
BUSHELLS LA
GORRICKS
RIVER
Reach
CUPITTS LANE
CORNWALLIS
GOW LA
CORNWALLIS
CORDNERS LA
ROAD
Cooley
Creek
121
JOINS MAP 120

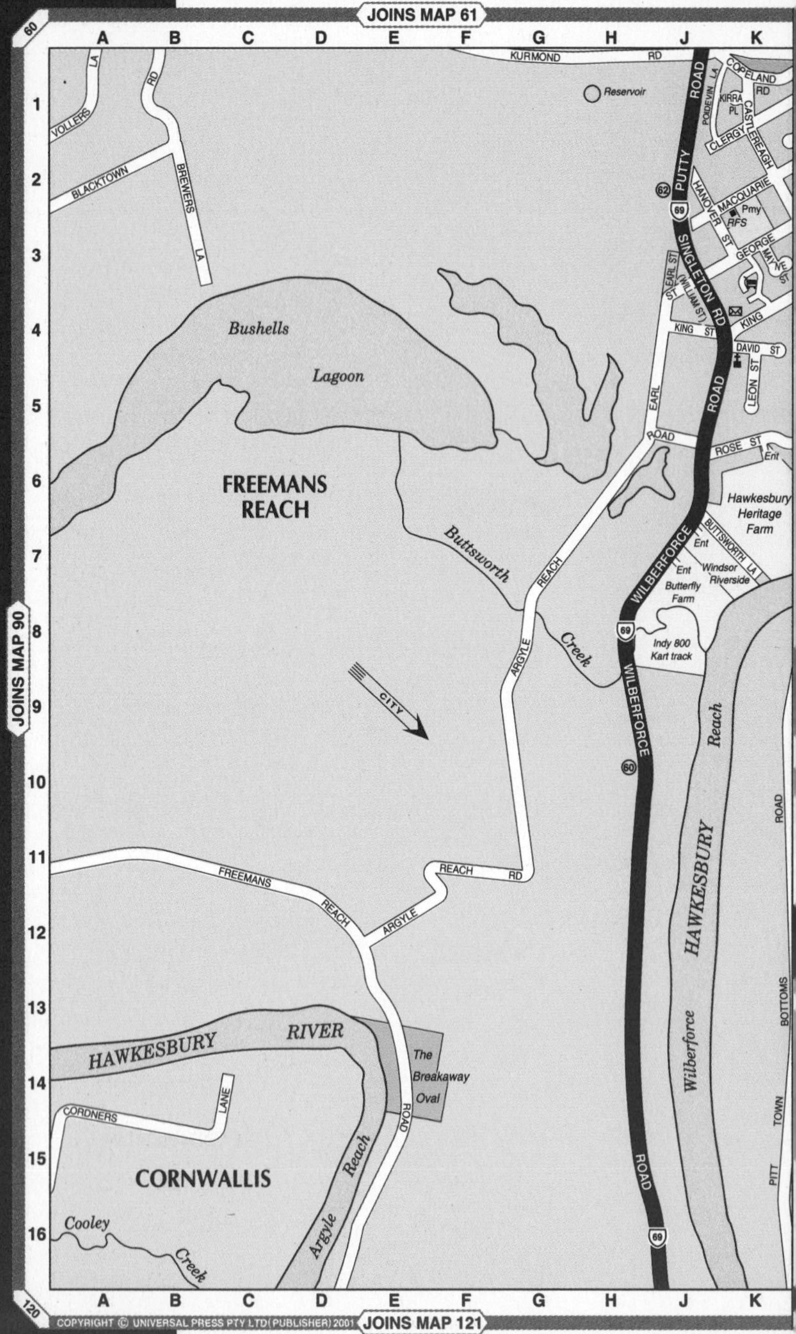
JOINS MAP 61
60
A B C D E F G H J K
1 2 3 4 5 6 7 8 9 10 11 12 13 14 15 16
JOINS MAP 90
VOLLERS LA
BREWERS RD
BLACKTOWN RD
BREWERS LA
KURMOND RD
Reservoir
PUTTY ROAD
COPELAND RD
POIDEVIN LA
KIRRA PL
CASTLEREAGH
CLERGY
HANOVER ST
MACQUARIE
Pmy
RFS
GEORGE
MAYNE ST
EARL ST
(WILLIAM ST)
SINGLETON RD
KING ST
KING
DAVID ST
LEON ST
EARL ROAD
ROAD
ROSE ST
Ent
Hawkesbury Heritage Farm
BUTTSWORTH LA
Ent
Windsor Riverside
Ent
Butterfly Farm
Indy 800 Kart track
WILBERFORCE
WILBERFORCE
62
69
60
Bushells
Lagoon
FREEMANS REACH
Buttsworth
Creek
REACH
ARGYLE
CITY
Reach
HAWKESBURY
Wilberforce
ROAD
BOTTOMS
TOWN
PITT
FREEMANS
REACH
ARGYLE
REACH RD
HAWKESBURY
RIVER
The Breakaway Oval
ROAD
CORDNERS
LANE
CORNWALLIS
Reach
Argyle
Cooley
Creek
ROAD
120
JOINS MAP 121

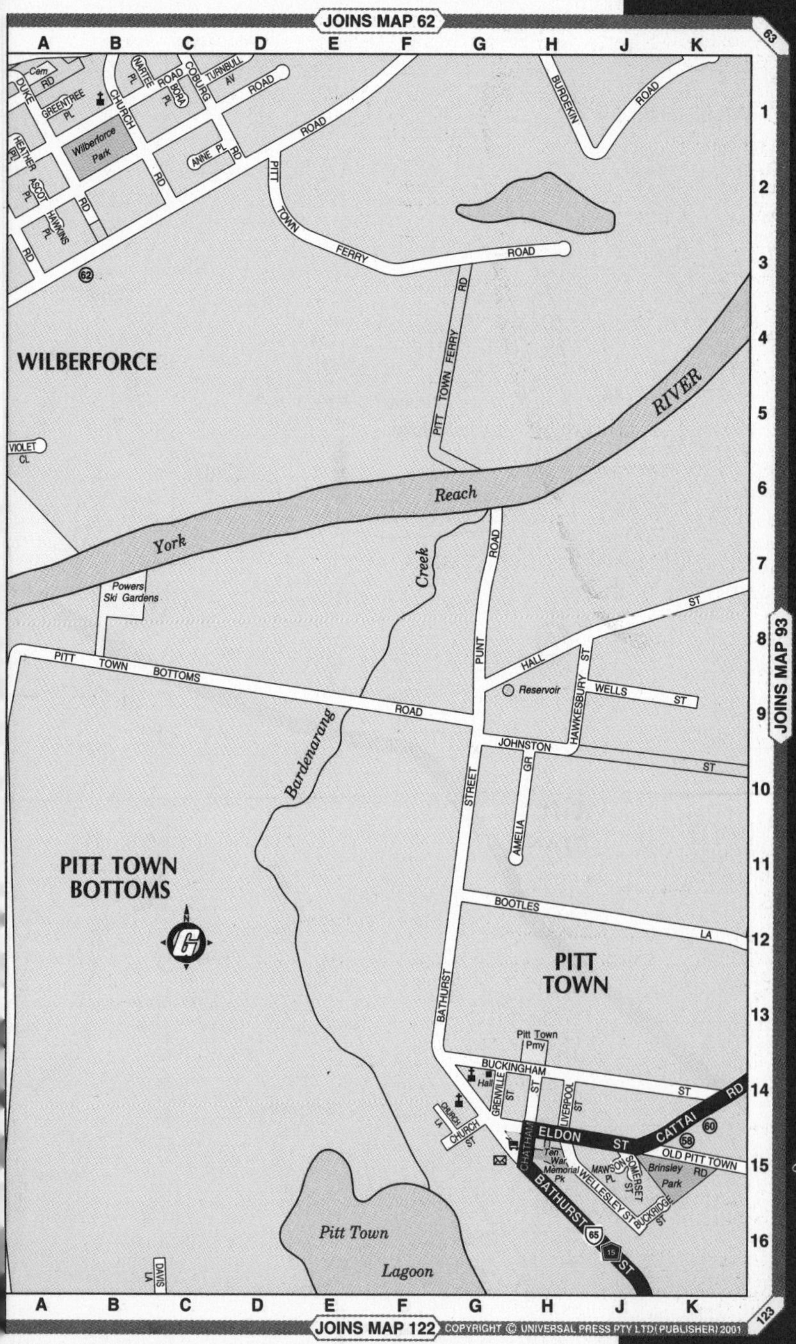

JOINS MAP 62
JOINS MAP 93
JOINS MAP 122
WILBERFORCE
PITT TOWN BOTTOMS
PITT TOWN
York
Reach
RIVER
Creek
Bardenarang
Pitt Town
Lagoon
Wilberforce Park
Powers Ski Gardens
Reservoir
Pitt Town Pmy
Hall
Ten War Memorial Pk
Brinsley Park
PITT TOWN FERRY ROAD
PITT TOWN FERRY RD
PITT TOWN BOTTOMS ROAD
PUNT ROAD
STREET
BATHURST
BATHURST ST
HALL ST
WELLS ST
HAWKESBURY ST
JOHNSTON ST
AMELIA GR
BOOTLES LA
BUCKINGHAM ST
GRENVILLE ST
LIVERPOOL ST
ELDON ST
CATTAI RD
OLD PITT TOWN RD
CHATHAM
MAWSON PL
SOMERSET ST
WELLESLEY ST
BUCKRIDGE ST
CHURCH ST
CHURCH LA
BURDEKIN ROAD
CHURCH ROAD
COBURG ROAD
TURNBULL AV
NARTEE PL
BORA PL
GREENTREE PL
DUKE RD
Cem
HEATHER PL
ASCOT PL
HAWKINS PL
ANNE PL
VIOLET CL
DAVIS LA
RD
A B C D E F G H J K
1 2 3 4 5 6 7 8 9 10 11 12 13 14 15 16
62
63
123
65
15
58
60
N

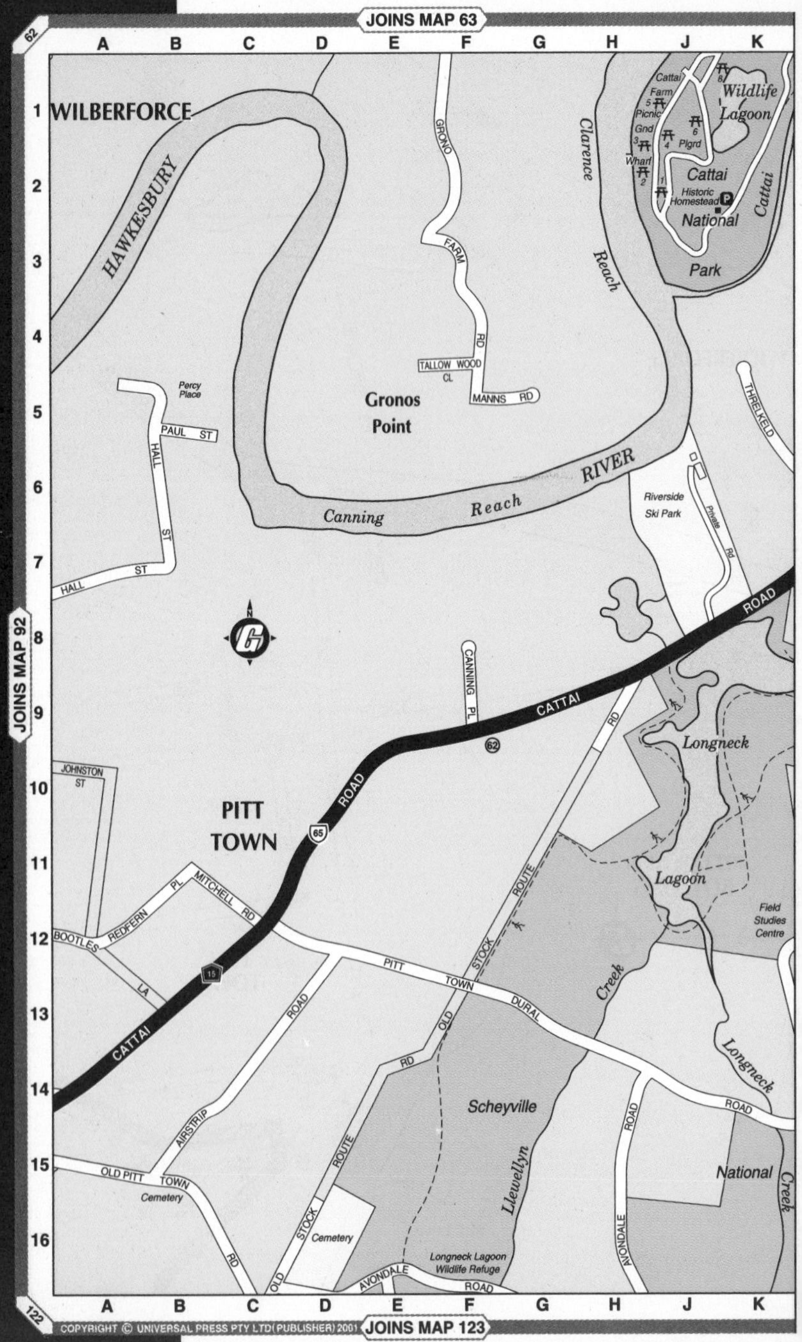
JOINS MAP 63
JOINS MAP 92
JOINS MAP 123
62
122
A B C D E F G H J K
1 2 3 4 5 6 7 8 9 10 11 12 13 14 15 16
WILBERFORCE
HAWKESBURY
RIVER
Canning
Reach
Clarence
Reach
Gronos
Point
GRONO
FARM
RD
TALLOW WOOD
CL
MANNS RD
Percy
Place
PAUL ST
HALL
ST
HALL ST
Cattai
Farm
Picnic
Gnd
Wharf
Plgrd
Wildlife
Lagoon
Cattai
Historic
Homestead
National
Park
Cattai
THRELKELD
Riverside
Ski Park
Private
Rd
CATTAI
ROAD
CANNING
PL
62
65
Longneck
Lagoon
Creek
Field
Studies
Centre
JOHNSTON
ST
PITT
TOWN
MITCHELL
RD
REDFERN
PL
BOOTLES
LA
15
PITT
TOWN
DURAL
ROAD
OLD
STOCK
ROUTE
RD
Longneck
Creek
AIRSTRIP
OLD PITT
TOWN
Cemetery
RD
Scheyville
Llewellyn
National
Creek
AVONDALE
ROAD
Cemetery
Longneck Lagoon
Wildlife Refuge
AVONDALE
ROAD

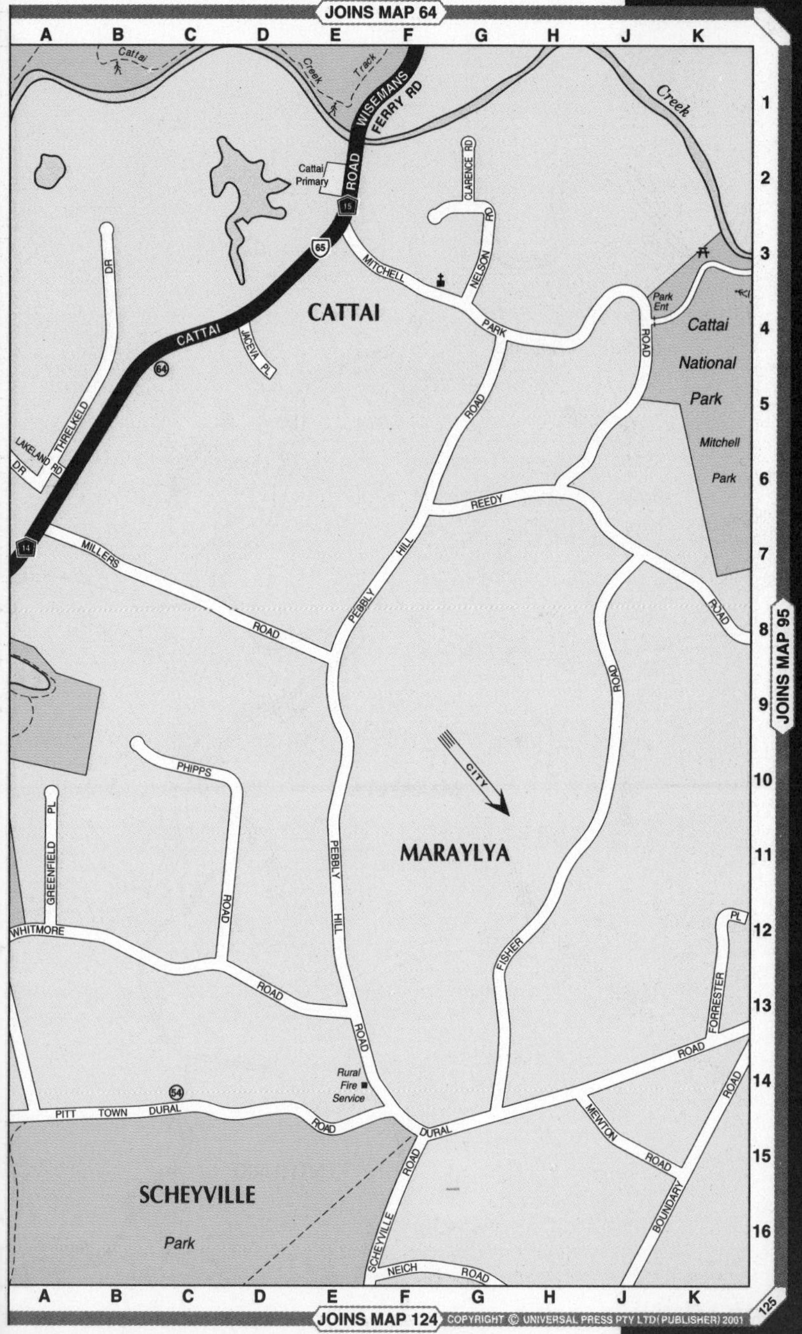
JOINS MAP 64
A B C D E F G H J K
1 2 3 4 5 6 7 8 9 10 11 12 13 14 15 16
Cattai
Cattai Creek Track
Creek
WISEMANS FERRY RD
ROAD
Cattai Primary
CLARENCE RD
NELSON RD
MITCHELL
PARK
CATTAI
CATTAI
JACEVA PL
THRELKELD DR
LAKELAND DR
RD
Park Ent
ROAD
Cattai National Park
Mitchell Park
REEDY
ROAD
HILL
PEBBLY
MILLERS ROAD
ROAD
ROAD
JOINS MAP 95
CITY
PHIPPS ROAD
GREENFIELD PL
MARAYLYA
PEBBLY HILL ROAD
FISHER
WHITMORE ROAD
FORRESTER PL
ROAD
ROAD
Rural Fire Service
PITT TOWN DURAL ROAD
DURAL
MEWTON ROAD
BOUNDARY
SCHEYVILLE ROAD
SCHEYVILLE
Park
NEICH ROAD
JOINS MAP 124

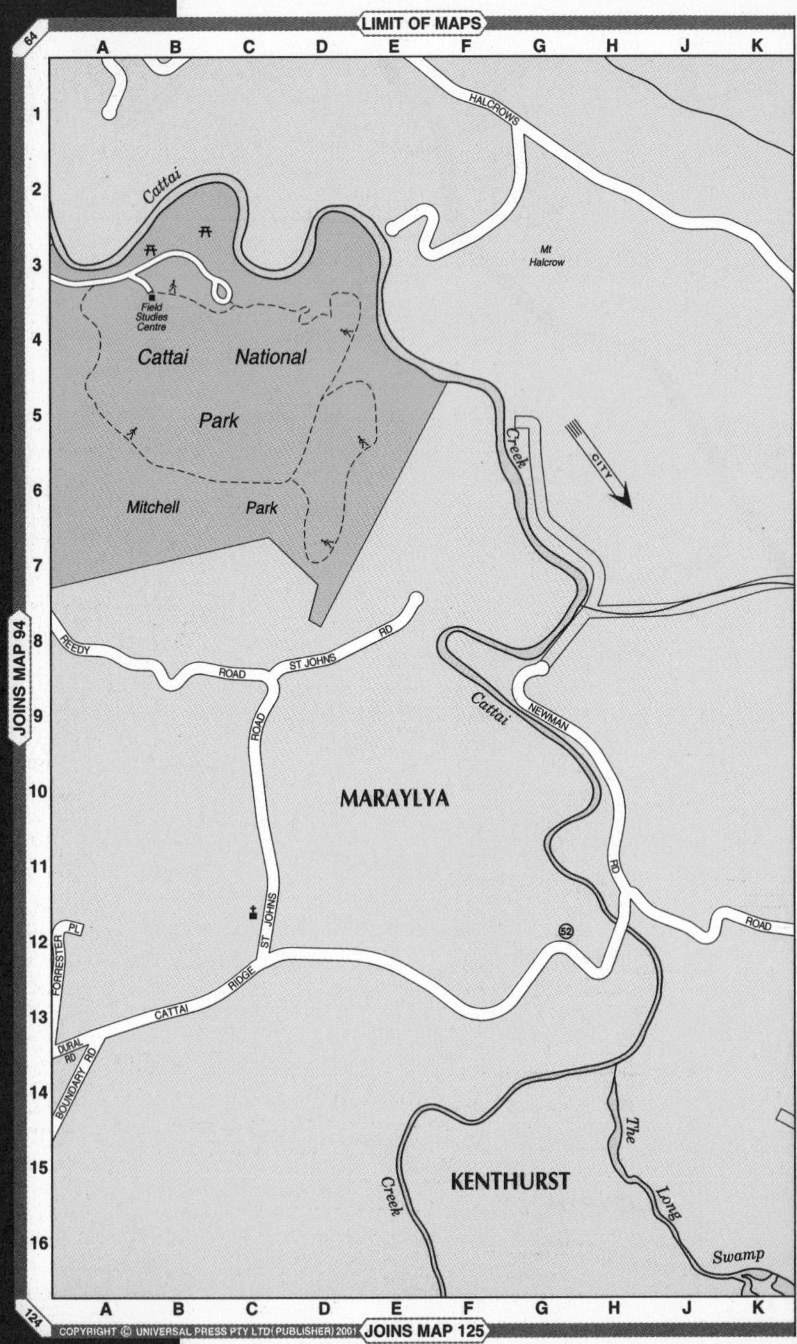
LIMIT OF MAPS
64
A B C D E F G H J K
1 2 3 4 5 6 7 8 9 10 11 12 13 14 15 16
HALCROWS
Cattai
Mt
Halcrow
Field
Studies
Centre
Cattai National
Park
Mitchell Park
Creek
CITY
REEDY
ROAD
ST JOHNS
RD
ROAD
Cattai
NEWMAN
MARAYLYA
RD
ROAD
52
PL
FORRESTER
ST JOHNS
RIDGE
CATTAI
DURAL
RD
BOUNDARY RD
The
Long
Swamp
Creek
KENTHURST
JOINS MAP 94
124
JOINS MAP 125

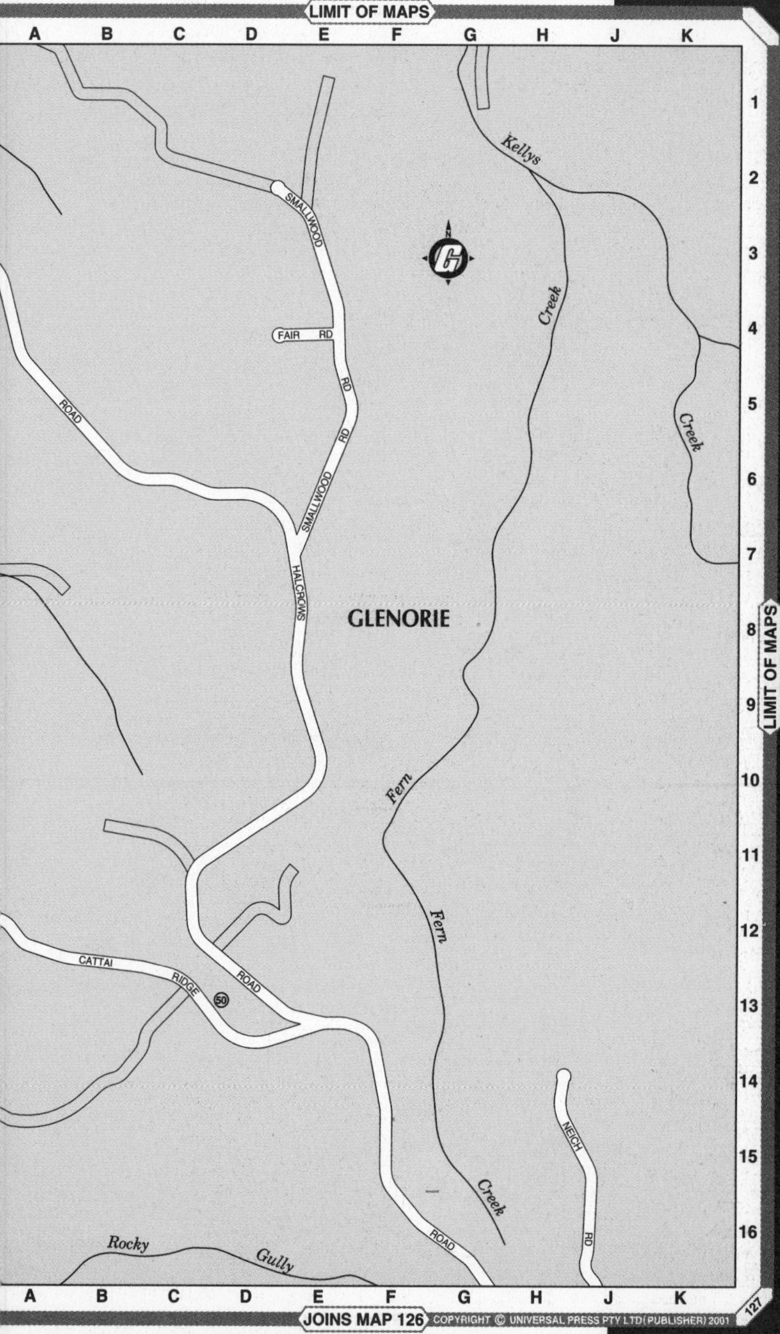
LIMIT OF MAPS
A B C D E F G H J K
1 2 3 4 5 6 7 8 9 10 11 12 13 14 15 16
SMALLWOOD RD
FAIR RD
ROAD
HALCROWS
GLENORIE
Kellys
Creek
Creek
Fern
Fern
Creek
CATTAI RIDGE ROAD
50
NEICH RD
ROAD
Rocky Gully
LIMIT OF MAPS

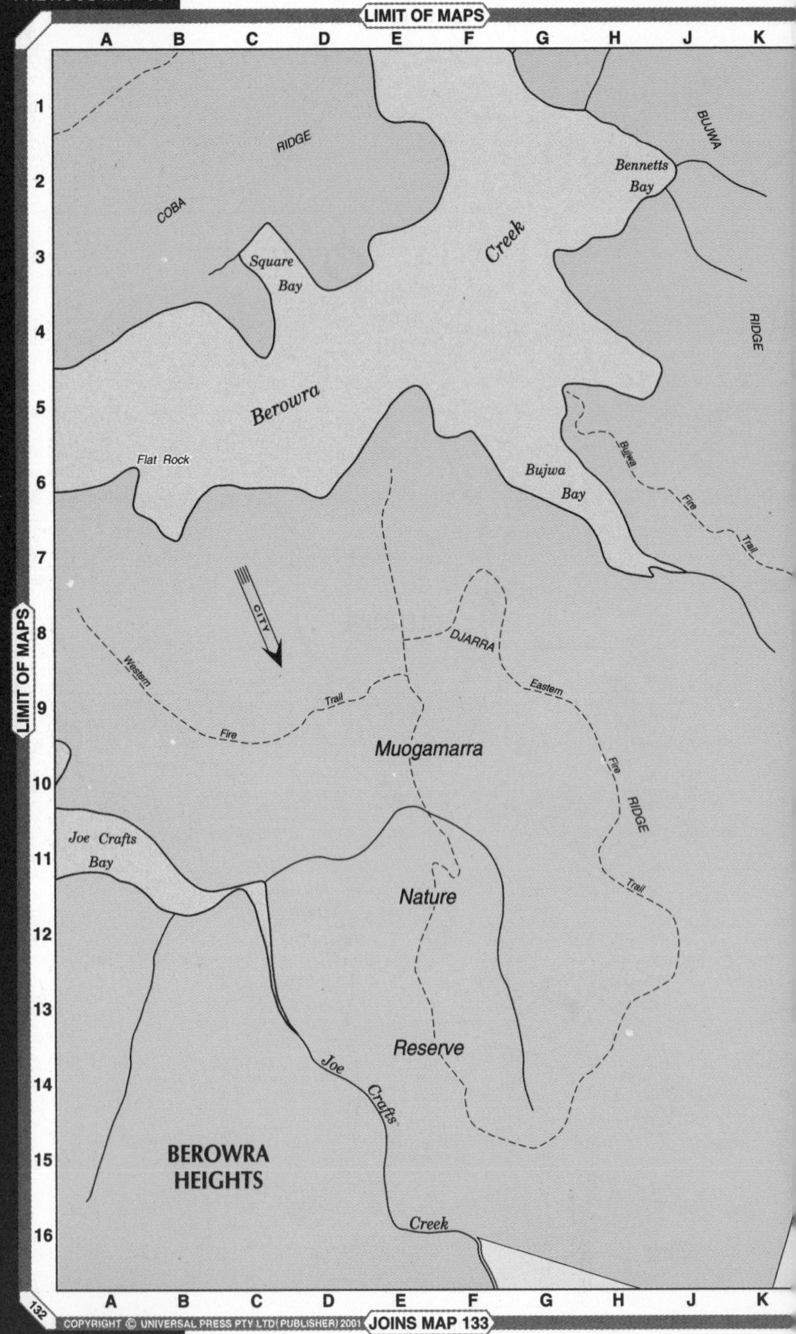
LIMIT OF MAPS
A B C D E F G H J K
1 2 3 4 5 6 7 8 9 10 11 12 13 14 15 16
COBA
RIDGE
Square
Bay
Creek
Bennetts
Bay
BUJWA
RIDGE
Berowra
Flat Rock
Bujwa
Bay
Bujwa
Fire
Trail
CITY
DJARRA
Western
Fire
Trail
Eastern
Fire
RIDGE
Trail
Muogamarra
Joe Crafts
Bay
Nature
Reserve
Joe
Crafts
BEROWRA
HEIGHTS
Creek
LIMIT OF MAPS

LIMIT OF MAPS

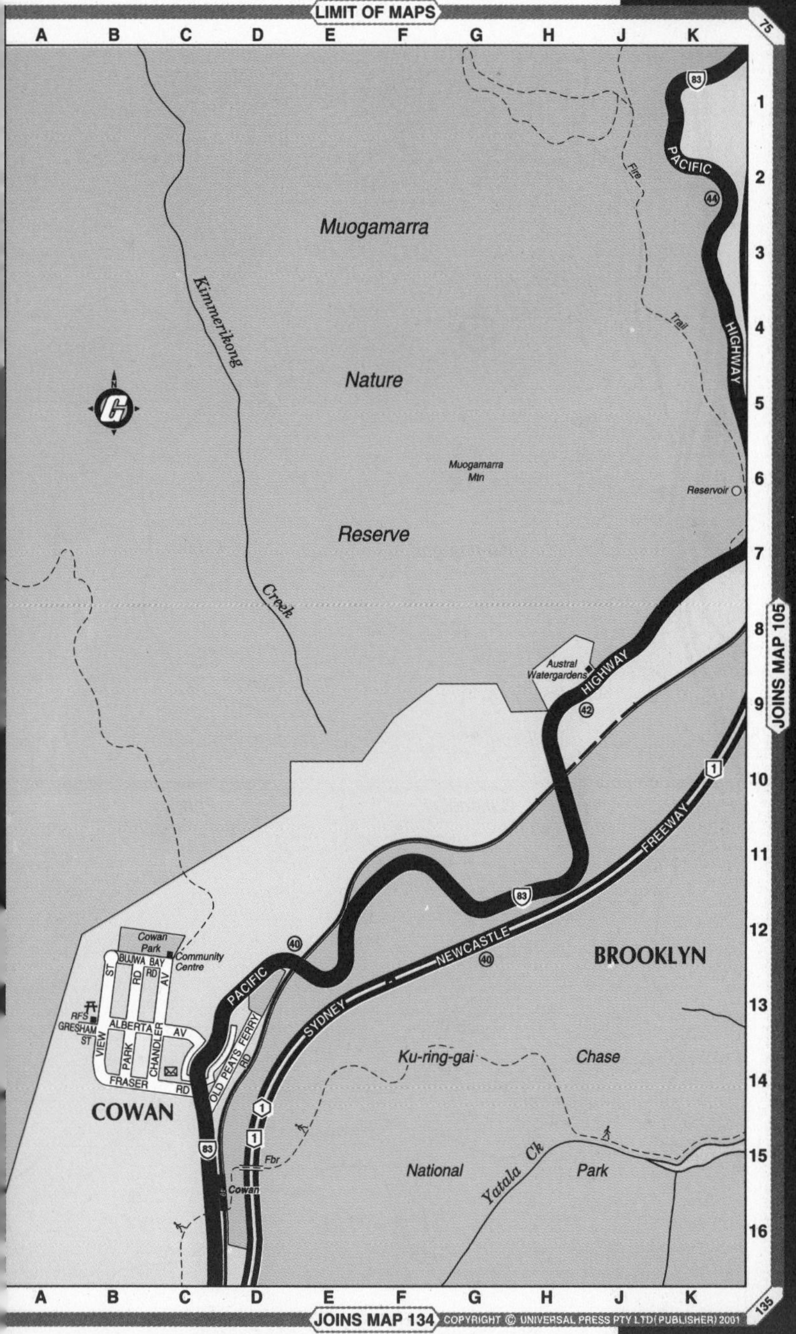

JOINS MAP 134

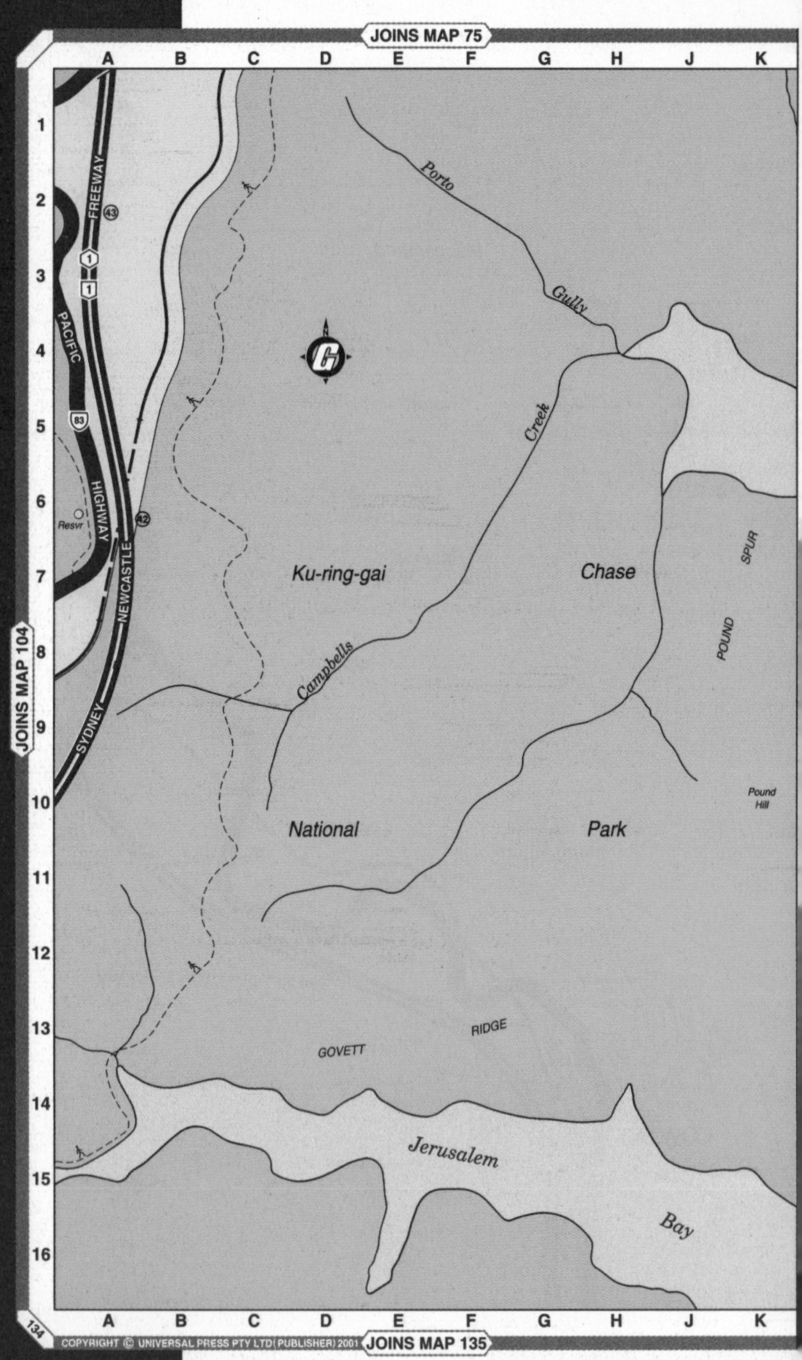
JOINS MAP 75
A B C D E F G H J K
1 2 3 4 5 6 7 8 9 10 11 12 13 14 15 16
FREEWAY
PACIFIC
HIGHWAY
SYDNEY
NEWCASTLE
43
1
83
42
Resvr
Porto
Gully
Creek
Campbells
Ku-ring-gai
Chase
National
Park
SPUR
POUND
Pound
Hill
GOVETT
RIDGE
Jerusalem
Bay
JOINS MAP 104
JOINS MAP 135

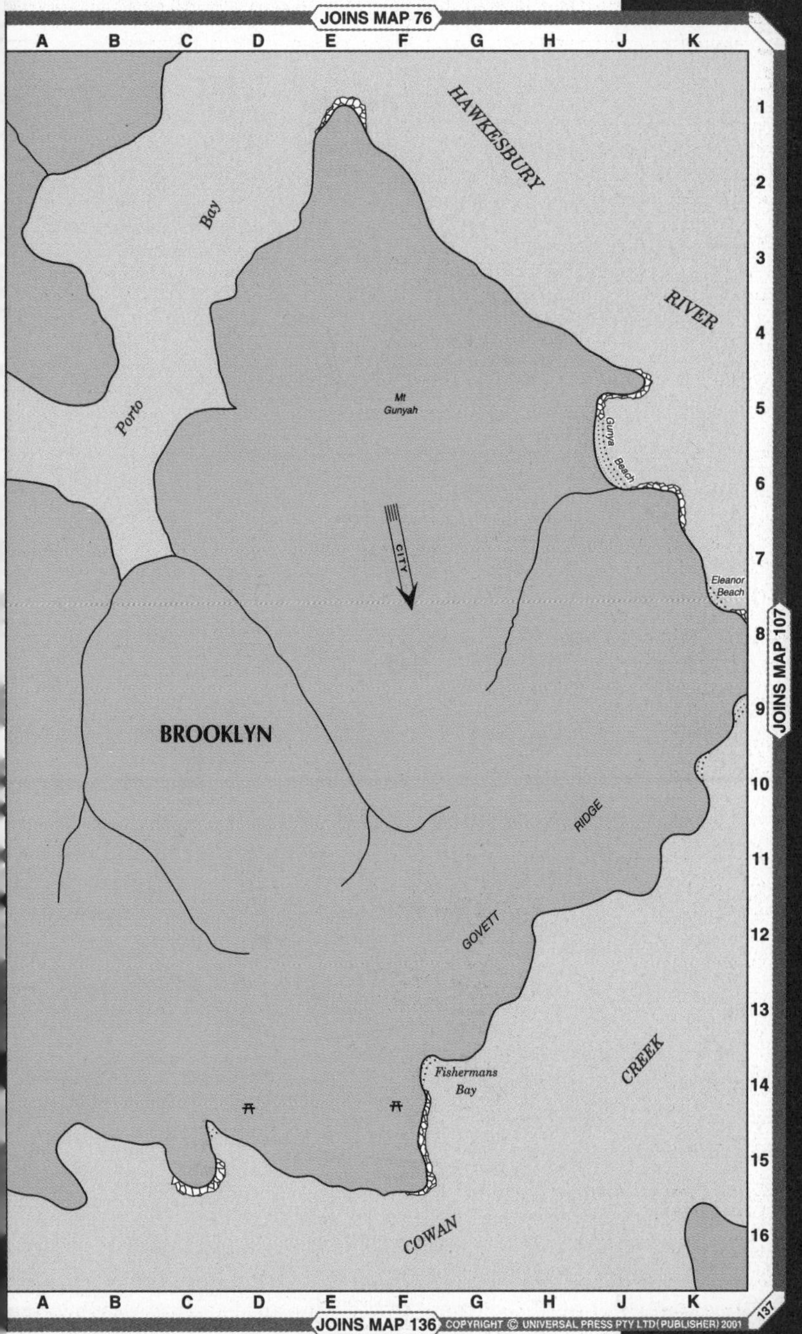
JOINS MAP 76
A B C D E F G H J K
1 2 3 4 5 6 7 8 9 10 11 12 13 14 15 16
HAWKESBURY
RIVER
Porto
Bay
Mt
Gunyah
Gunya Beach
CITY
Eleanor Beach
JOINS MAP 107
BROOKLYN
RIDGE
GOVETT
CREEK
Fishermans Bay
COWAN
JOINS MAP 136

MAP 107

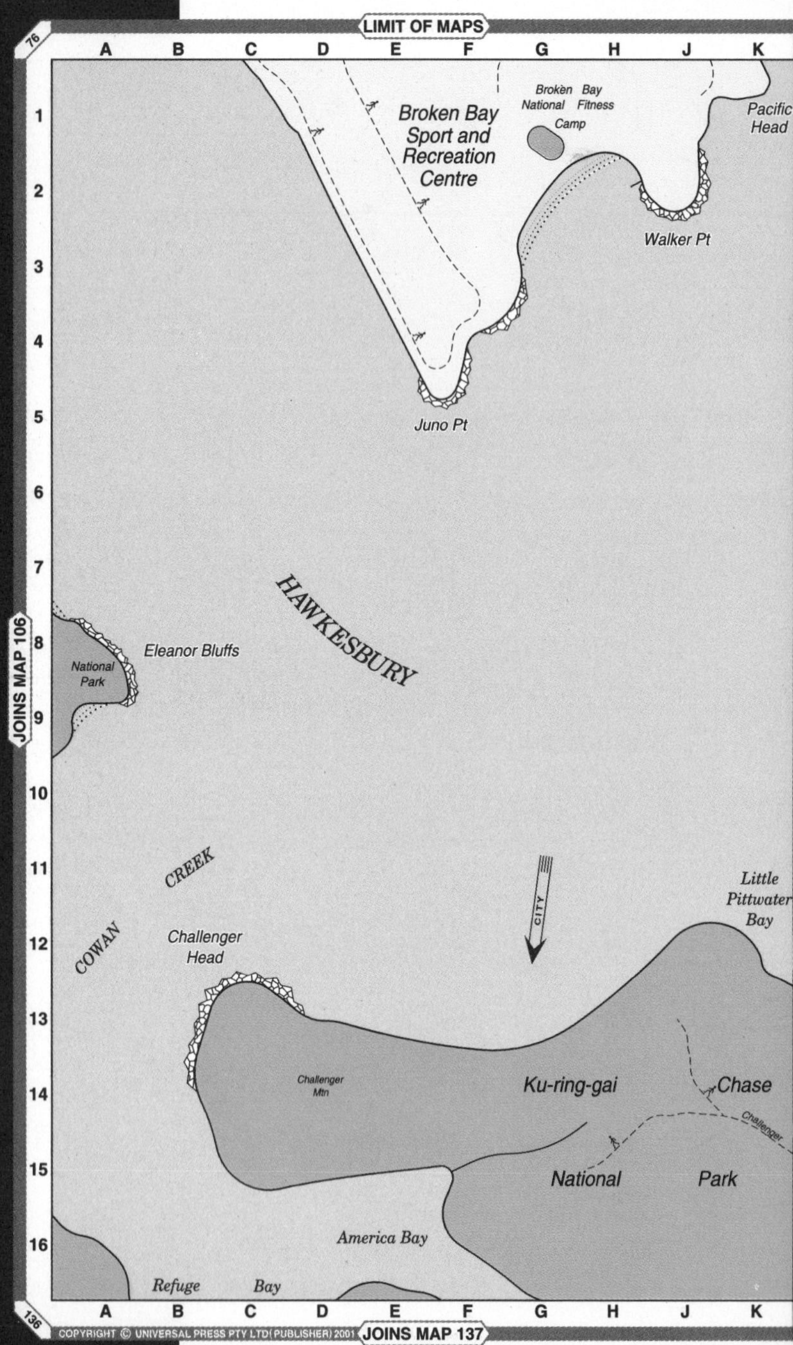

LIMIT OF MAPS
76
A B C D E F G H J K
1 2 3 4 5 6 7 8 9 10 11 12 13 14 15 16
Broken Bay Sport and Recreation Centre
Broken Bay National Fitness Camp
Pacific Head
Walker Pt
Juno Pt
HAWKESBURY
Eleanor Bluffs
National Park
JOINS MAP 106
CREEK
COWAN
Challenger Head
CITY
Little Pittwater Bay
Challenger Mtn
Ku-ring-gai Chase National Park
Challenger
America Bay
Refuge Bay
136
JOINS MAP 137

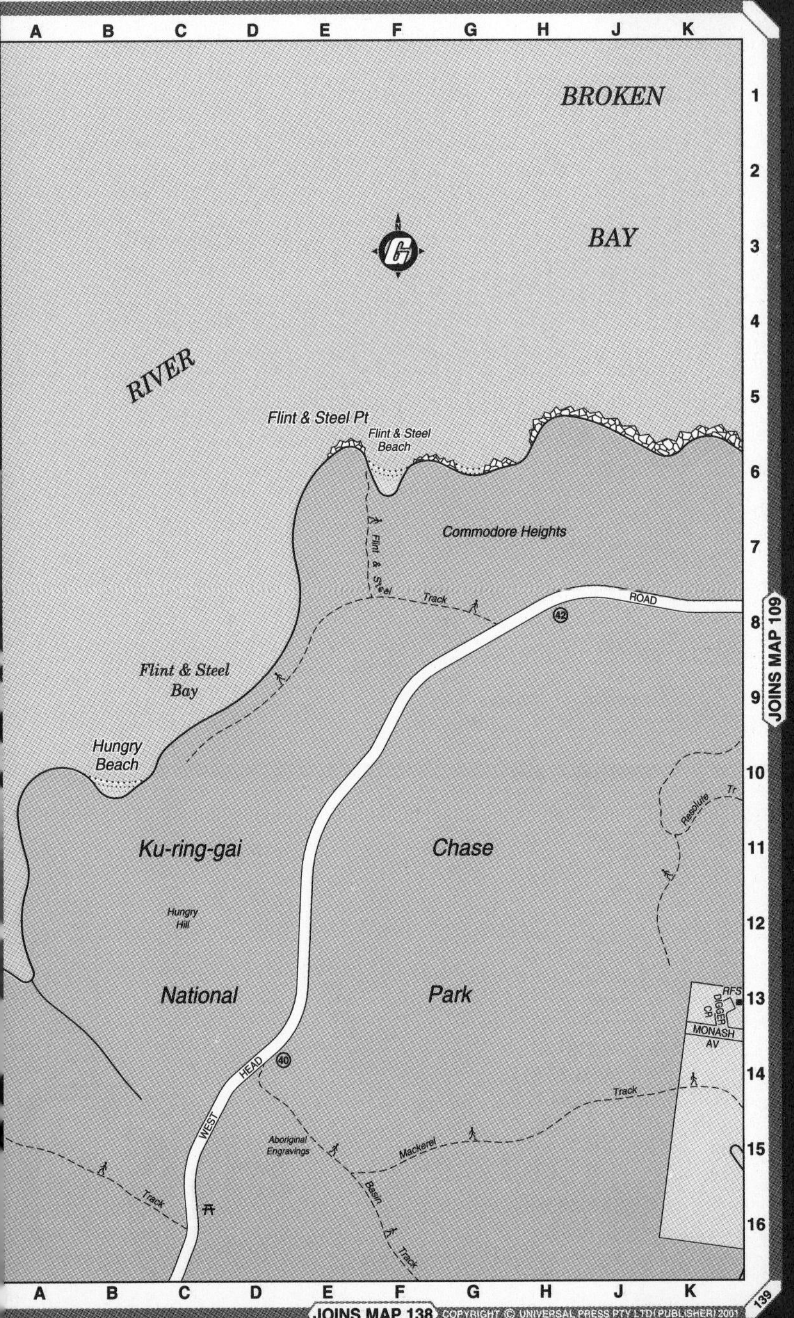
A B C D E F G H J K
1 2 3 4 5 6 7 8 9 10 11 12 13 14 15 16
BROKEN
BAY
RIVER
Flint & Steel Pt
Flint & Steel Beach
Commodore Heights
Flint & Steel Track
ROAD
42
Flint & Steel Bay
Hungry Beach
Ku-ring-gai
Chase
Hungry Hill
National
Park
Resolute Tr
RFS
DIGGER CR
MONASH AV
WEST HEAD
40
Track
Aboriginal Engravings
Mackerel
Basin
Track
Track
JOINS MAP 109
139

JOINS MAP 138

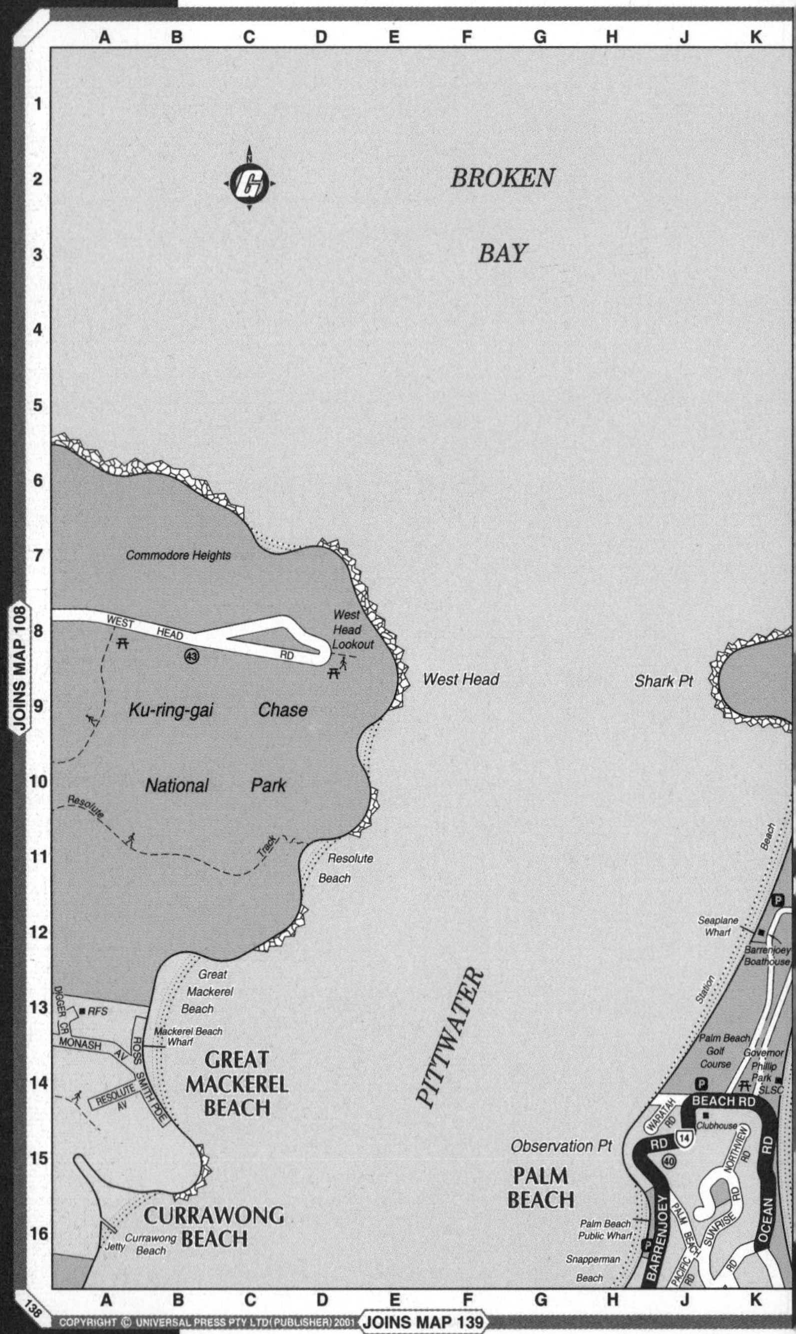

JOINS MAP 139

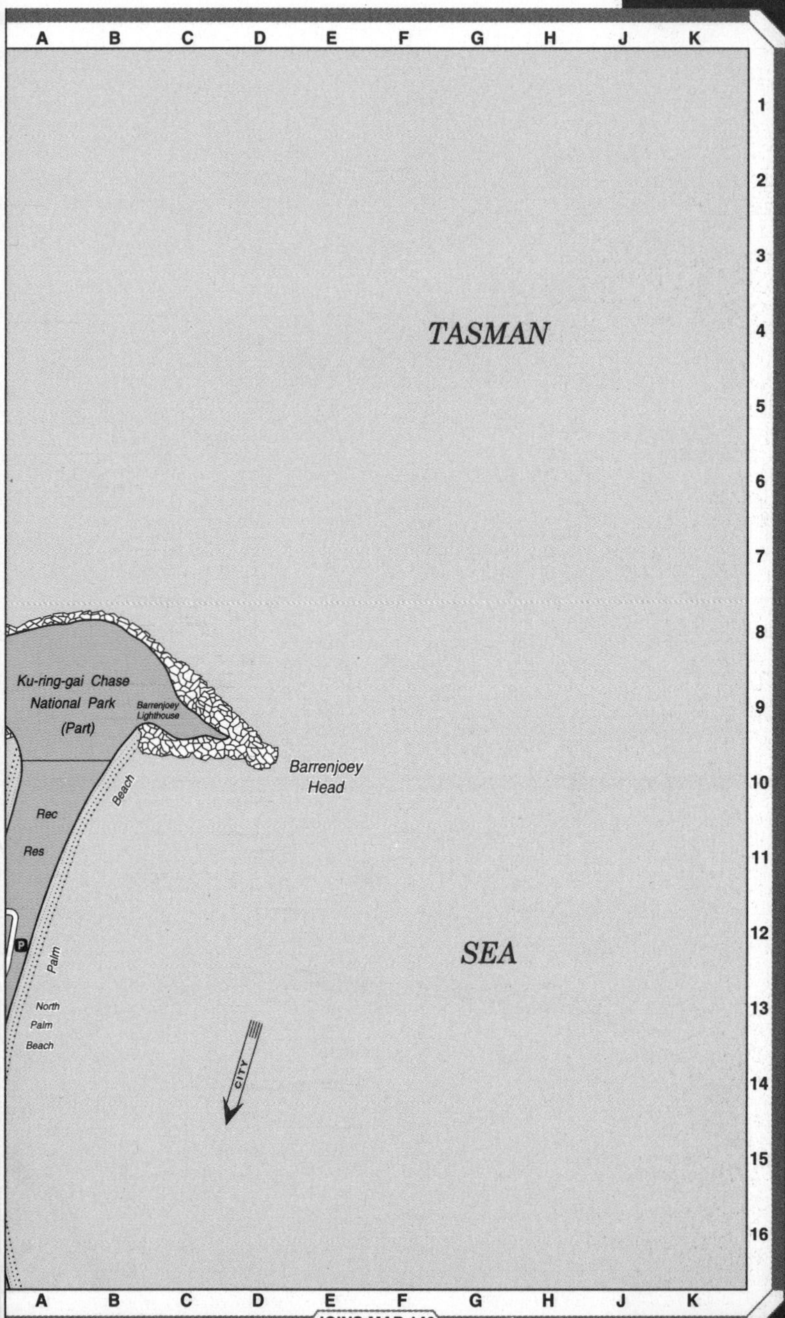

JOINS MAP 140

JOINS MAP 85

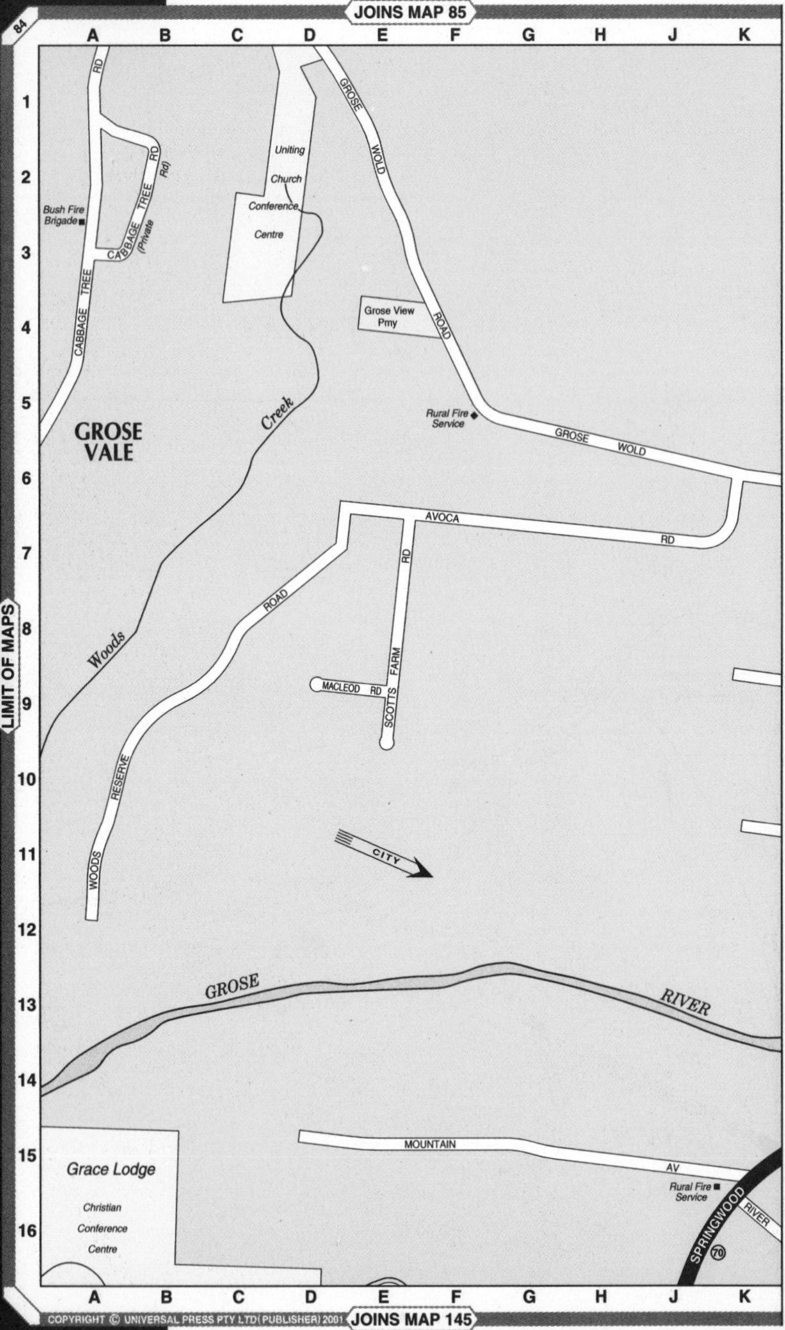

84

A B C D E F G H J K

1 2 3 4 5 6 7 8 9 10 11 12 13 14 15 16

LIMIT OF MAPS

GROSE VALE

CABBAGE TREE RD
CABBAGE TREE RD
(Private Rd)
Bush Fire Brigade
Uniting Church Conference Centre
GROSE WOLD ROAD
Grose View Pmy
Rural Fire Service
GROSE WOLD
AVOCA RD
Woods Creek
ROAD
SCOTTS FARM RD
MACLEOD RD
WOODS RESERVE
CITY
GROSE RIVER
MOUNTAIN AV
Grace Lodge
Christian Conference Centre
Rural Fire Service
SPRINGWOOD
RIVER
70

A B C D E F G H J K

JOINS MAP 145

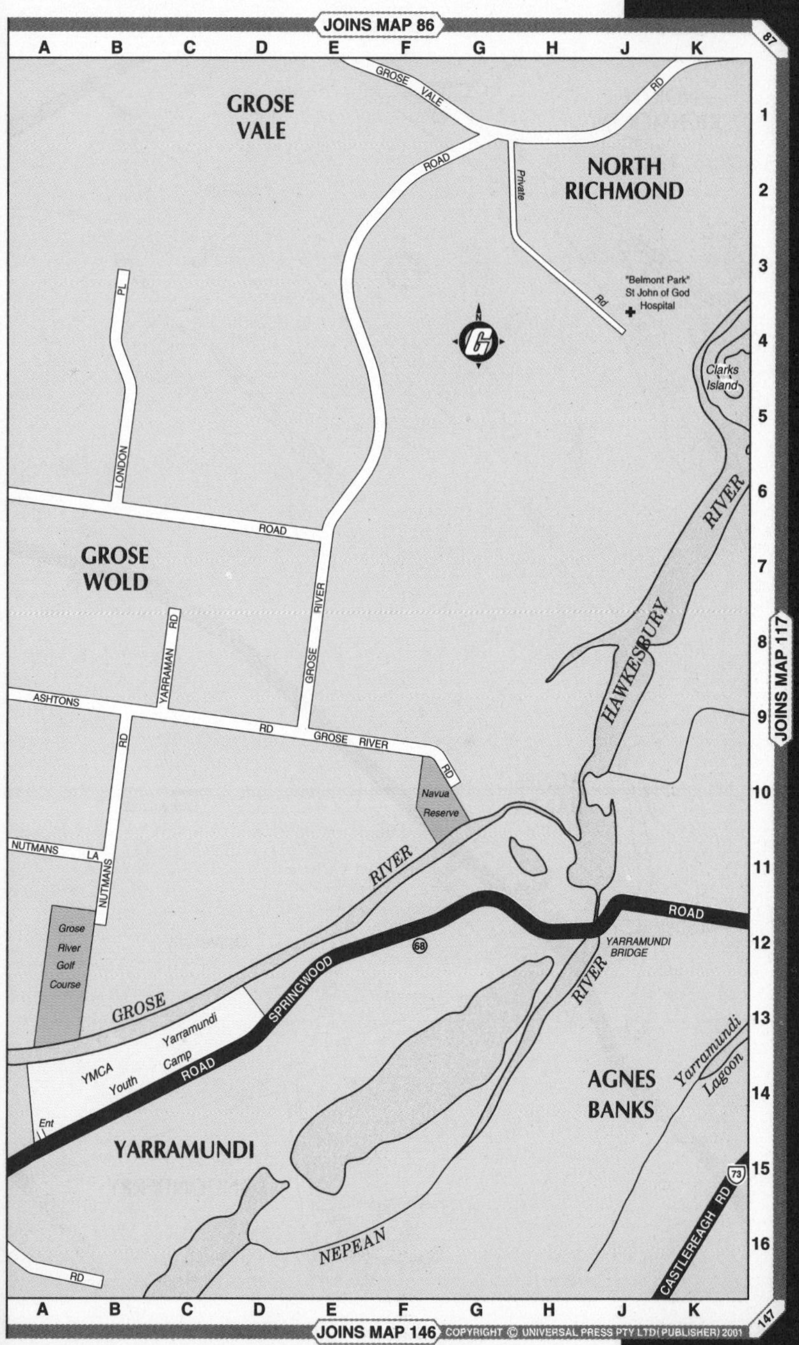
JOINS MAP 86
87
A B C D E F G H J K
1 2 3 4 5 6 7 8 9 10 11 12 13 14 15 16
GROSE VALE
GROSE VALE ROAD
RD
NORTH RICHMOND
Private Rd
"Belmont Park" St John of God Hospital
Clarks Island
LONDON PL
ROAD
GROSE WOLD
GROSE RIVER
YARRAMAN RD
ASHTONS RD
RD
GROSE RIVER RD
HAWKESBURY RIVER
JOINS MAP 117
Navua Reserve
NUTMANS LA
NUTMANS
RIVER
ROAD
Grose River Golf Course
68
YARRAMUNDI BRIDGE
GROSE
SPRINGWOOD ROAD
Yarramundi YMCA Youth Camp
RIVER
AGNES BANKS
Yarramundi Lagoon
Ent
YARRAMUNDI
73
CASTLEREAGH RD
NEPEAN
RD
JOINS MAP 146
147

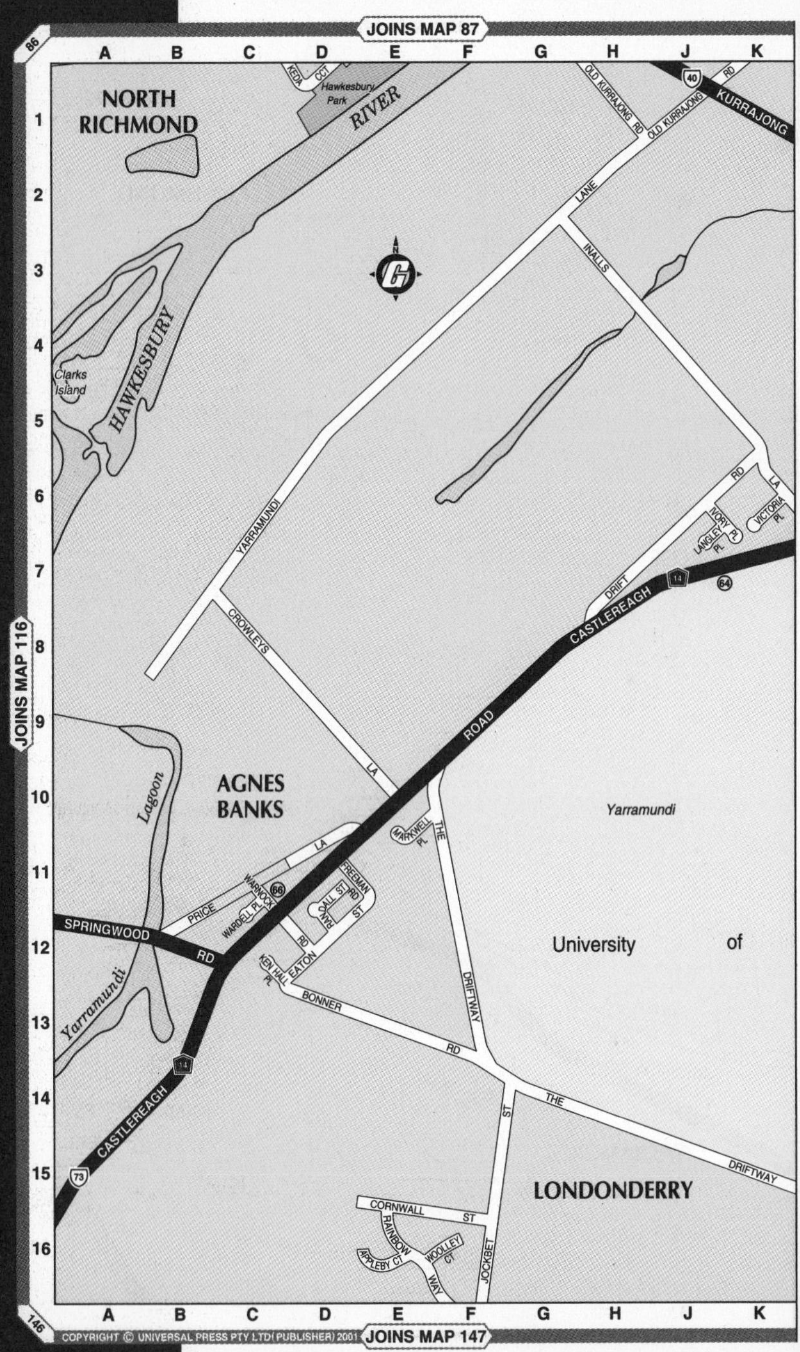
JOINS MAP 87
86
A B C D E F G H J K
NORTH RICHMOND
KEDA CCT
Hawkesbury Park
RIVER
OLD KURRAJONG RD
OLD KURRAJONG RD
40
KURRAJONG
LANE
INALLS
HAWKESBURY
Clarks Island
YARRAMUNDI
RD
LA
IVORY PL
VICTORIA PL
LANGLEY PL
DRIFT
CASTLEREAGH
14
64
CROWLEYS
ROAD
LA
JOINS MAP 116
Lagoon
AGNES BANKS
Yarramundi
MARKWELL PL
THE
LA
FREEMAN RD
WARNOCK
66
PRICE
WARDELL PL
CALL ST
RAN
ST
SPRINGWOOD RD
RD
EATON
KEN HALL PL
University of
Yarramundi
BONNER RD
DRIFTWAY
14
CASTLEREAGH
THE DRIFTWAY
ST
73
LONDONDERRY
CORNWALL ST
RAINBOW WAY
APPLEBY CT
WOOLLEY CT
JOCKBET
1 2 3 4 5 6 7 8 9 10 11 12 13 14 15 16
146
JOINS MAP 147

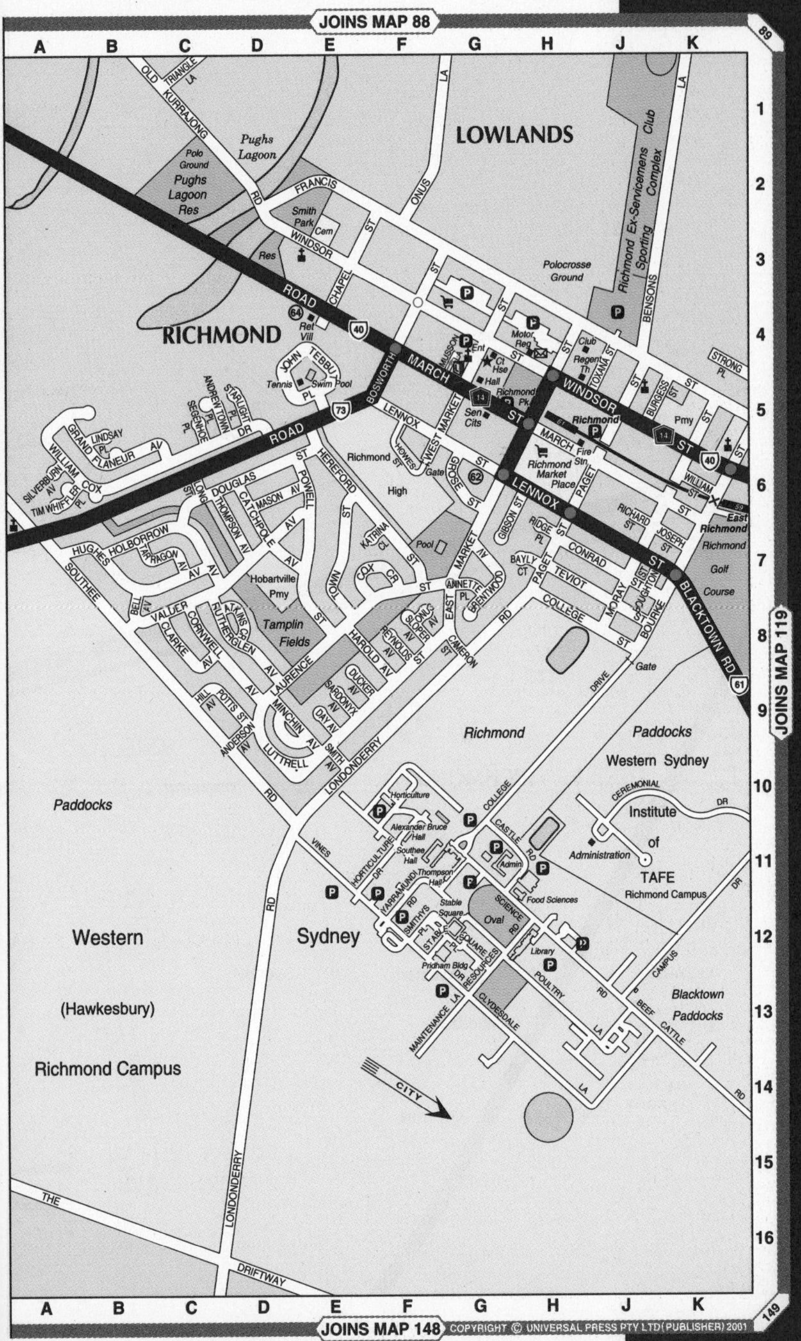
JOINS MAP 88
JOINS MAP 119
JOINS MAP 148
LOWLANDS
RICHMOND
Pughs Lagoon
Pughs Lagoon Res
Richmond Ex-Servicemens Club Sporting Complex
Polocrosse Ground
Richmond High
Hobartville Pmy
Tamplin Fields
Richmond Golf Course
Richmond Paddocks
Western Sydney Institute of TAFE Richmond Campus
Blacktown Paddocks
Western Sydney (Hawkesbury) Richmond Campus
Paddocks
WINDSOR ROAD
MARCH ST
WINDSOR ST
LENNOX ST
BLACKTOWN RD
LONDONDERRY RD
COLLEGE DRIVE
THE DRIFTWAY
CITY

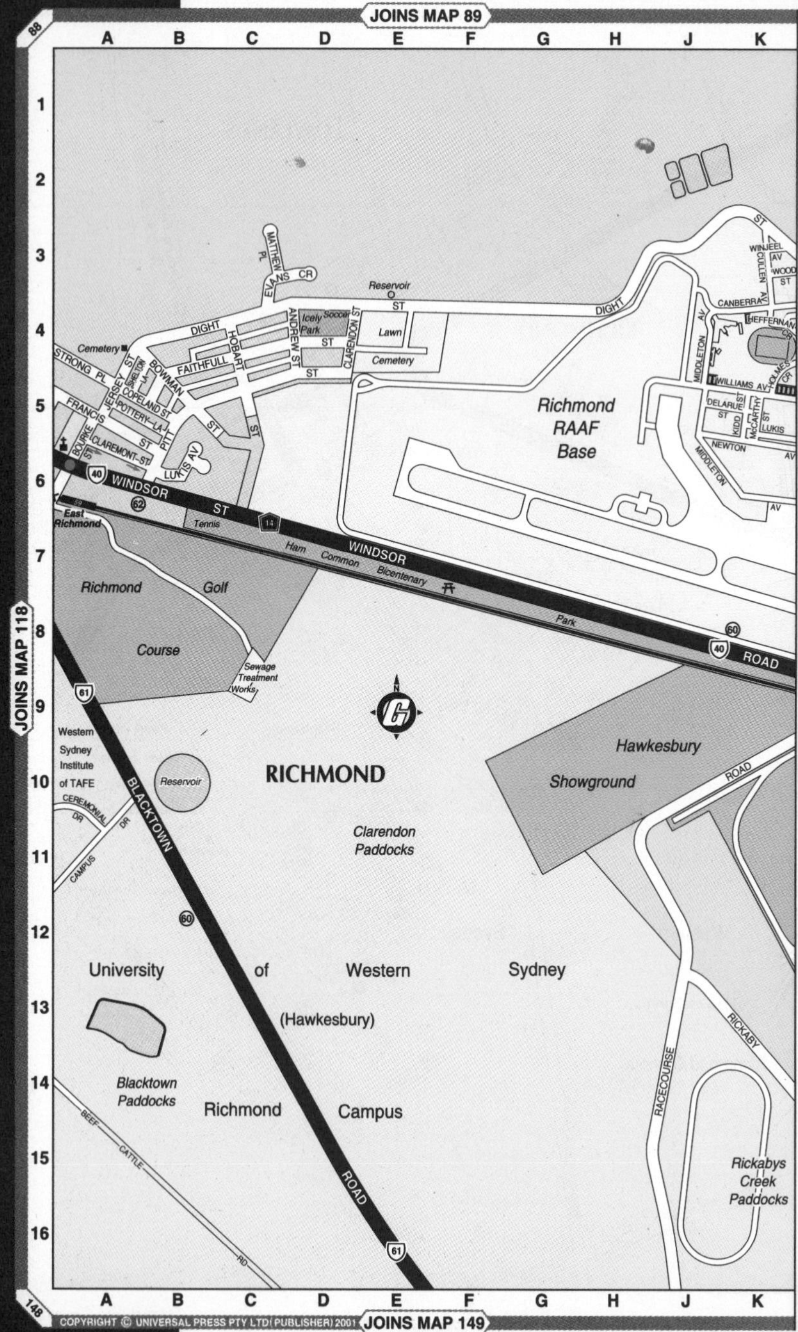
JOINS MAP 89
JOINS MAP 118
JOINS MAP 149
Richmond RAAF Base
Richmond Golf Course
Sewage Treatment Works
RICHMOND
Hawkesbury Showground
Clarendon Paddocks
Western Sydney Institute of TAFE
Reservoir
University of Western Sydney (Hawkesbury) Richmond Campus
Blacktown Paddocks
Rickabys Creek Paddocks
Ham Common Bicentenary Park
East Richmond
Tennis
Icely Park
Soccer
Lawn
Cemetery
WINDSOR ST
WINDSOR ROAD
BLACKTOWN ROAD
RACECOURSE
RICKABY
ROAD
DIGHT ST
BEEF CATTLE RD
CEREMONIAL DR
CAMPUS DR
MATTHEW PL
EVANS CR
HOBART ST
ANDREW ST
CLARENDON ST
FAITHFULL ST
BOWMAN ST
STRONG PL
FRANCIS ST
BOURKE ST
JERSEY ST
COPELAND ST
POTTERY LA
CLAREMONT ST
PITT ST
LUKIS AV
MIDDLETON AV
WILLIAMS AV
DELARUE ST
KIDD ST
McCARTHY ST
NEWTON AV
CANBERRA AV
HEFFERNAN CR
HOLMES CR
WINJEEL AV
CULLEN AV
WOOD ST

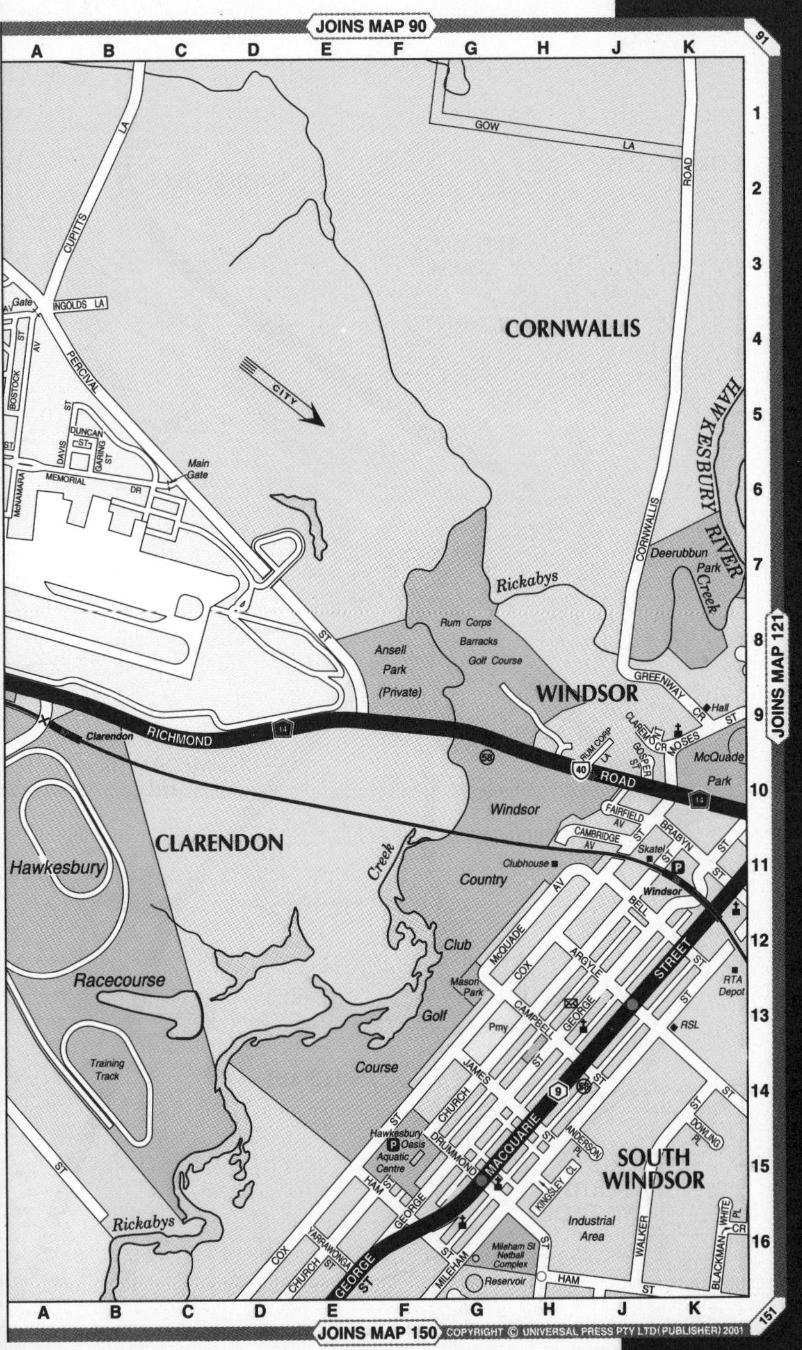
JOINS MAP 90
JOINS MAP 121
JOINS MAP 150
91
151
CORNWALLIS
WINDSOR
CLARENDON
SOUTH WINDSOR
HAWKESBURY RIVER
CITY
GOW LA
ROAD
CUPITTS LA
INGOLDS LA
PERCIVAL
BOSTOCK ST
DUNCAN
DAVIS
GARING ST
McNAMARA
MEMORIAL DR
Main Gate
Gate
Rickabys
Rickabys Creek
Deerubbun Park
Creek
CORNWALLIS
Rum Corps Barracks Golf Course
Ansell Park (Private)
GREENWAY CR
Hall
CLAREMONT CR
MOSES ST
GOSPER ST
RUM CORP LA
McQuade Park
RICHMOND ROAD
Clarendon
Windsor
FAIRFIELD AV
CAMBRIDGE AV
BRABYN ST
Skate
Clubhouse
Windsor Country Club Golf Course
Hawkesbury Racecourse
Training Track
Mason Park
McQUADE AV
COX
ARGYLE
BELL
GEORGE STREET
CAMPBELL
Pmy
RTA Depot
RSL
JAMES
CHURCH
DRUMMOND
MACQUARIE
ANDERSON PL
KINGSLEY CL
DOWLING PL
Hawkesbury Oasis Aquatic Centre
HAM ST
GEORGE
Industrial Area
WALKER
WHITE PL
BLACKMAN CR
YARRAWONGA
MILEHAM
Mileham St Netball Complex
Reservoir
HAM ST
GEORGE ST

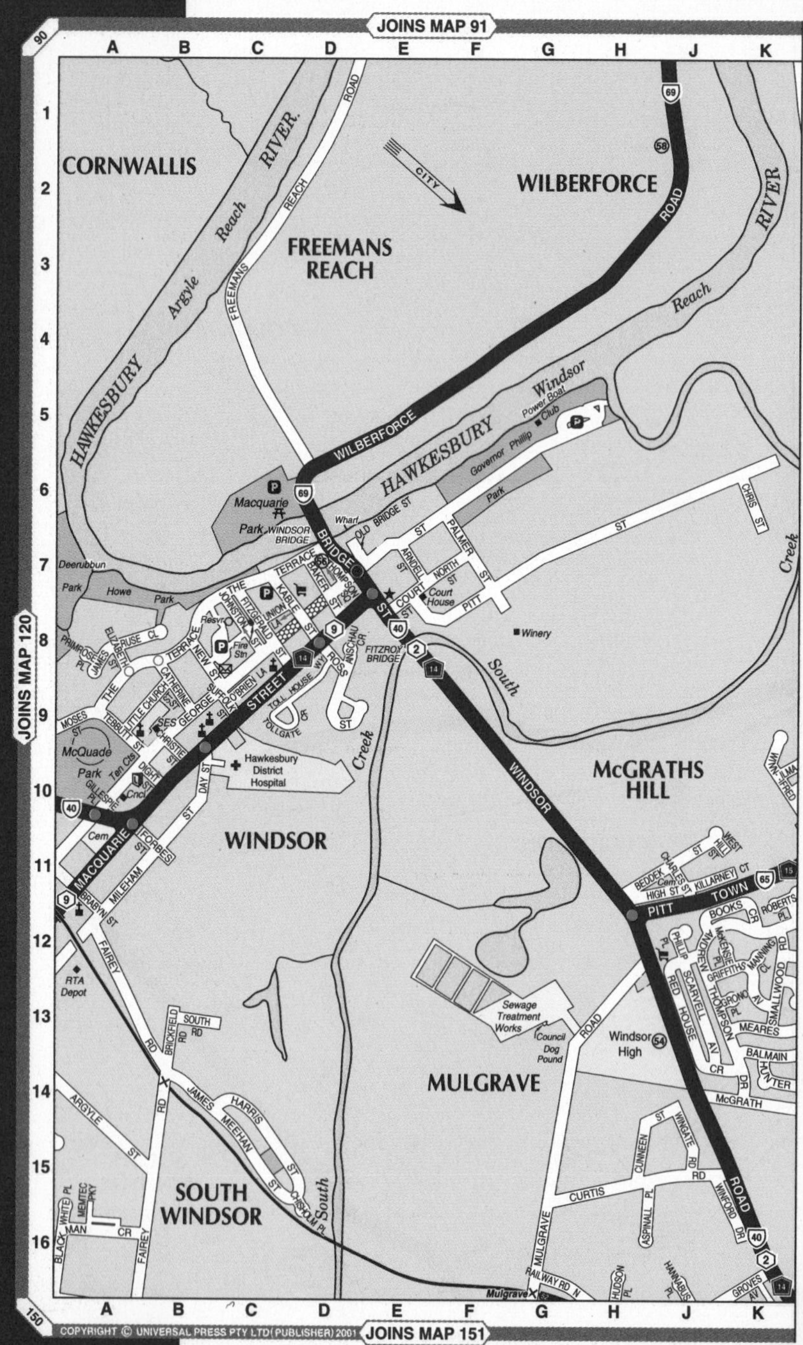
JOINS MAP 91
JOINS MAP 120
JOINS MAP 151
CORNWALLIS
WILBERFORCE
FREEMANS REACH
McGRATHS HILL
WINDSOR
MULGRAVE
SOUTH WINDSOR
HAWKESBURY
RIVER
Argyle
Reach
Windsor
Power Boat Club
Governor Phillip Park
Macquarie Park
WINDSOR BRIDGE
Wharf
Deerubbun Park
Howe Park
McQuade Park
Hawkesbury District Hospital
Court House
Winery
FITZROY BRIDGE
South Creek
Sewage Treatment Works
Council Dog Pound
Windsor High
RTA Depot
Mulgrave
WILBERFORCE ROAD
FREEMANS REACH ROAD
WINDSOR ROAD
GEORGE ST
MACQUARIE ST
BRIDGE ST
PITT TOWN RD
CITY

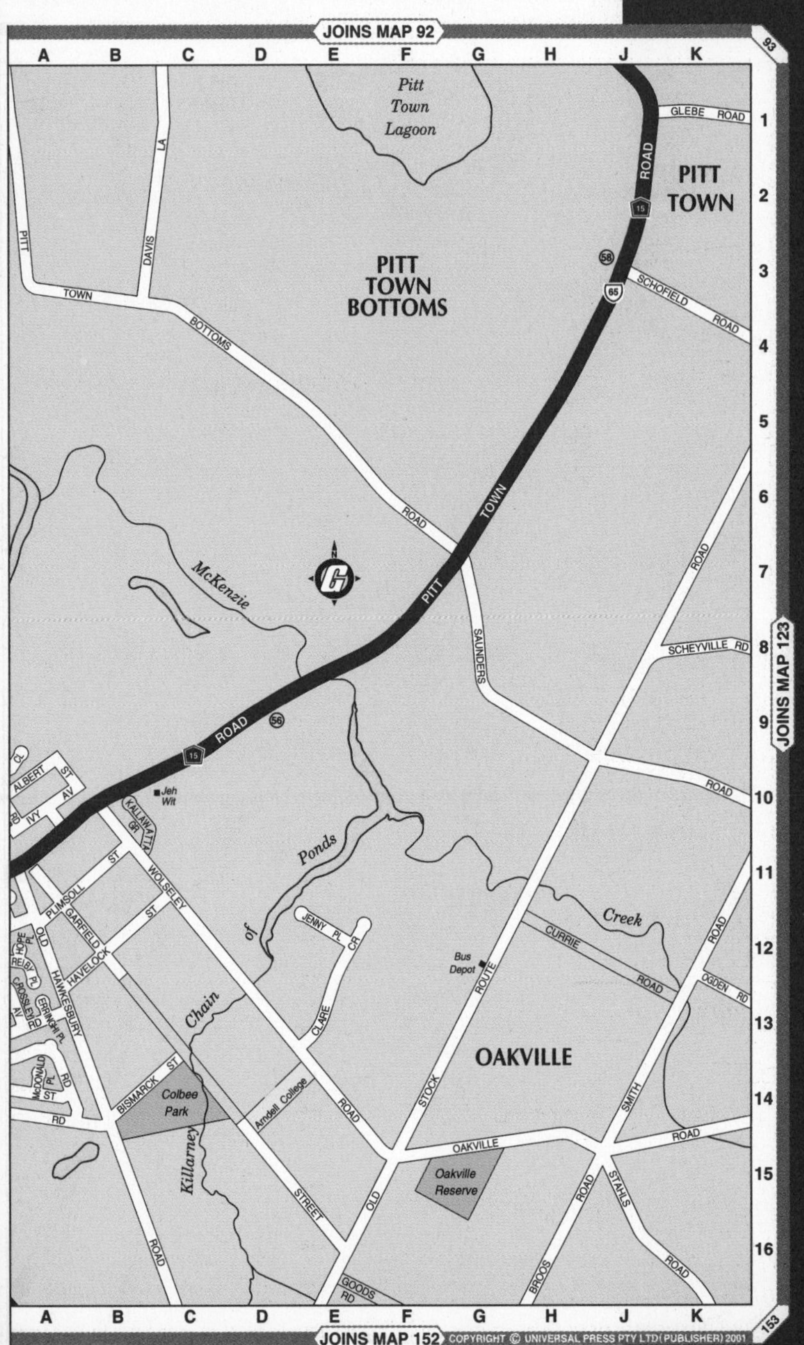
JOINS MAP 92
A B C D E F G H J K
1 2 3 4 5 6 7 8 9 10 11 12 13 14 15 16
93
Pitt Town Lagoon
GLEBE ROAD
PITT TOWN
PITT TOWN BOTTOMS
PITT
DAVIS LA
TOWN
BOTTOMS
SCHOFIELD ROAD
ROAD
PITT TOWN ROAD
McKenzie
SAUNDERS
SCHEYVILLE RD
ROAD
JOINS MAP 123
Jeh Wit
ALBERT ST
CL
AV
IVY
KALLAWATTA GR
Ponds
Chain of
PLIMSOLL ST
WOLSELEY
GARFIELD
ST
HAVELOCK
JENNY PL
CR
CLARE
HOPE PL
OLD
REIBY PL
CROSSLEY AV
RD
ERRINGHI PL
HAWKESBURY
McDONALD PL
RD
ST
RD
BISMARCK ST
Colbee Park
Killarney
Arndell College
ROAD
STREET
ROAD
Creek
CURRIE ROAD
OGDEN RD
ROAD
Bus Depot
ROUTE
STOCK
OLD
OAKVILLE
SMITH
OAKVILLE ROAD
Oakville Reserve
ROAD
BROOS
STAHLS ROAD
GOODS RD
153

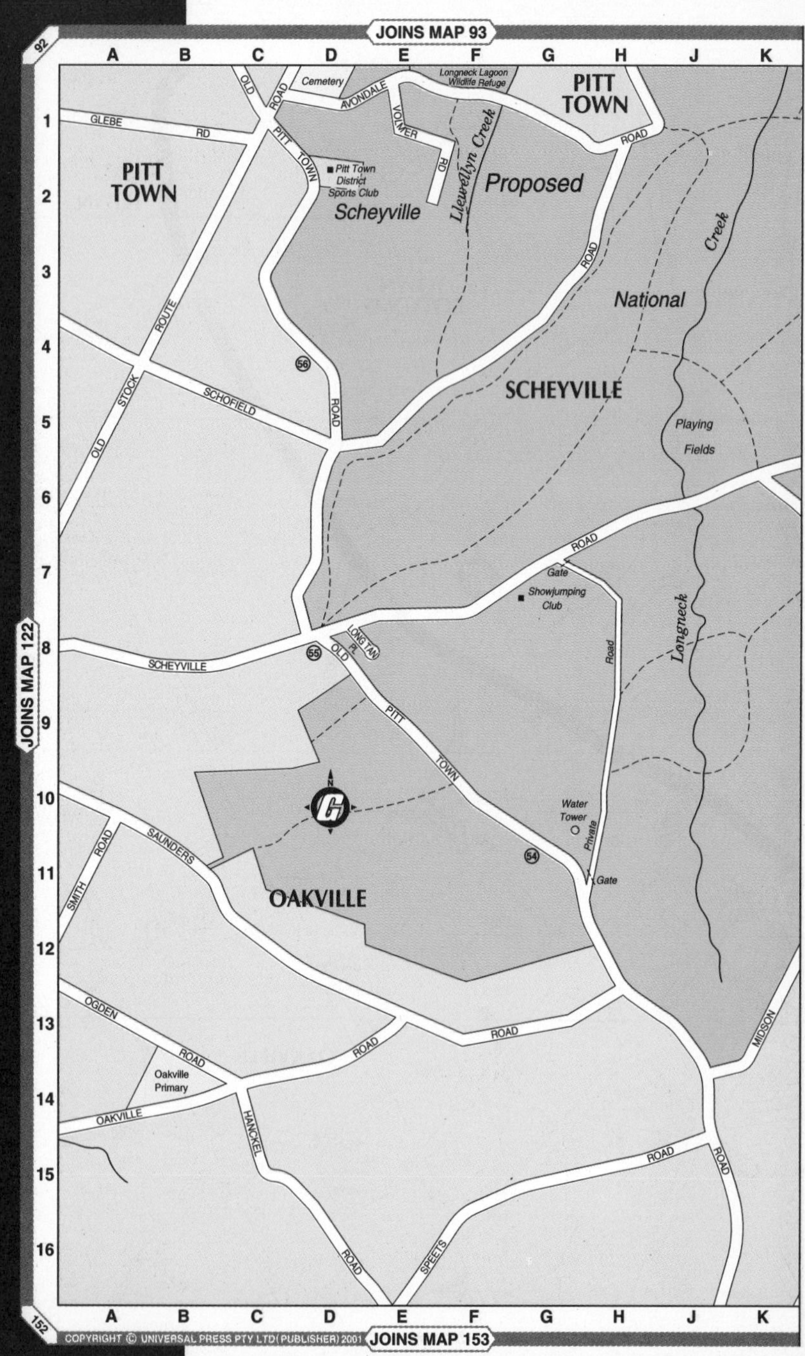
JOINS MAP 93
92
A B C D E F G H J K
1 2 3 4 5 6 7 8 9 10 11 12 13 14 15 16
Cemetery
Longneck Lagoon
Wildlife Refuge
PITT TOWN
OLD ROAD
AVONDALE
VOLMER RD
Lleurellyn Creek
GLEBE RD
ROAD
PITT TOWN
Pitt Town District Sports Club
PITT TOWN
Proposed
Scheyville
ROAD
Creek
ROUTE
National
56
ROAD
OLD STOCK
SCHOFIELD
SCHEYVILLE
Playing Fields
ROAD
Gate
Showjumping Club
LONG TAN PL
55
OLD
SCHEYVILLE
Road
Longneck
PITT
TOWN
Water Tower
SAUNDERS
ROAD
SMITH
54
Private
Gate
OAKVILLE
OGDEN
ROAD
ROAD
ROAD
MIDSON
Oakville Primary
OAKVILLE
HANCKEL
ROAD
ROAD
ROAD
SPEETS
A B C D E F G H J K
152
JOINS MAP 122
JOINS MAP 153

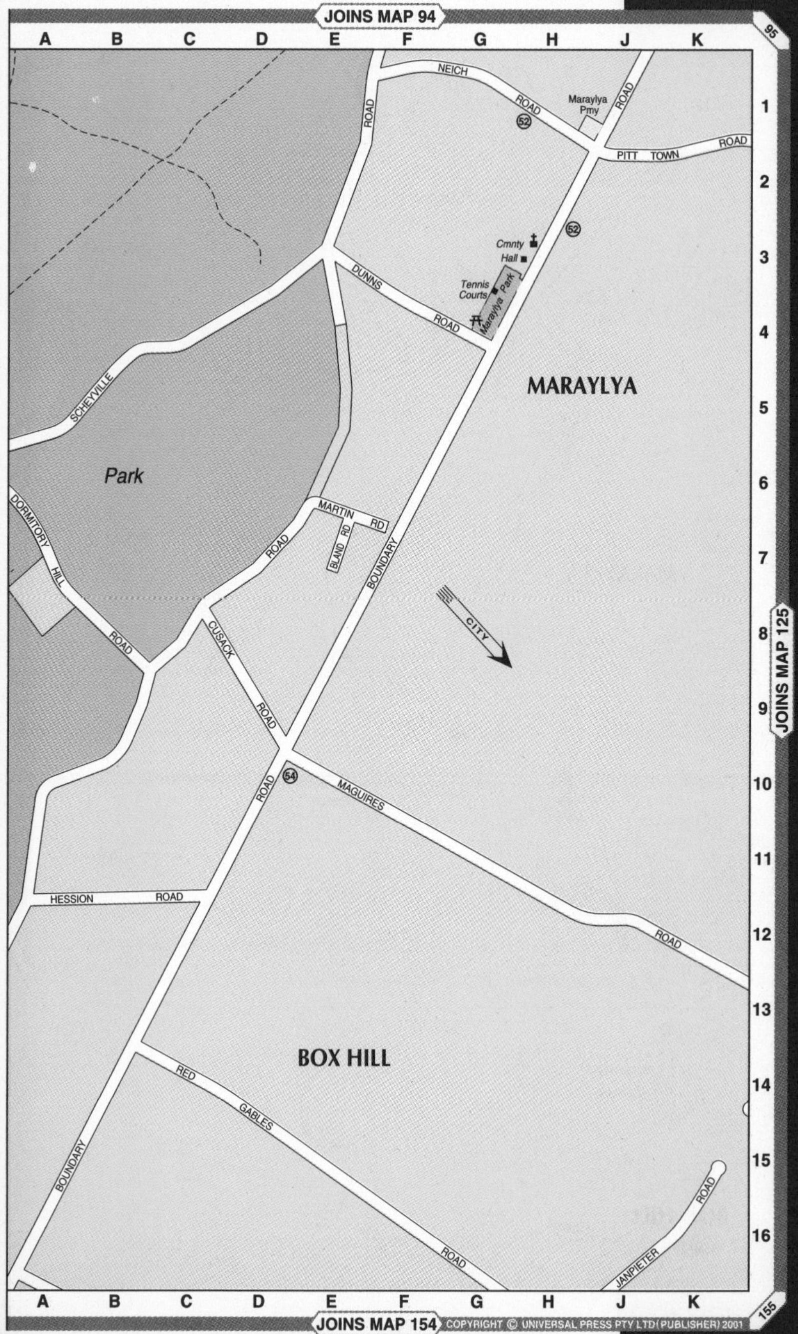
JOINS MAP 94
95
A
B
C
D
E
F
G
H
J
K
1
2
3
4
5
6
7
8
9
10
11
12
13
14
15
16
NEICH
ROAD
ROAD
Maraylya
Pmy
ROAD
52
PITT
TOWN
ROAD
52
Cmnty
Hall
Tennis
Courts
Maraylya Park
DUNNS
ROAD
MARAYLYA
SCHEYVILLE
Park
DORMITORY
HILL
ROAD
MARTIN
RD
BLAND RD
ROAD
BOUNDARY
CITY
JOINS MAP 125
CUSACK
ROAD
54
ROAD
MAGUIRES
ROAD
HESSION
ROAD
BOX HILL
RED
GABLES
ROAD
BOUNDARY
ROAD
JANPIETER
155
JOINS MAP 154

JOINS MAP 95

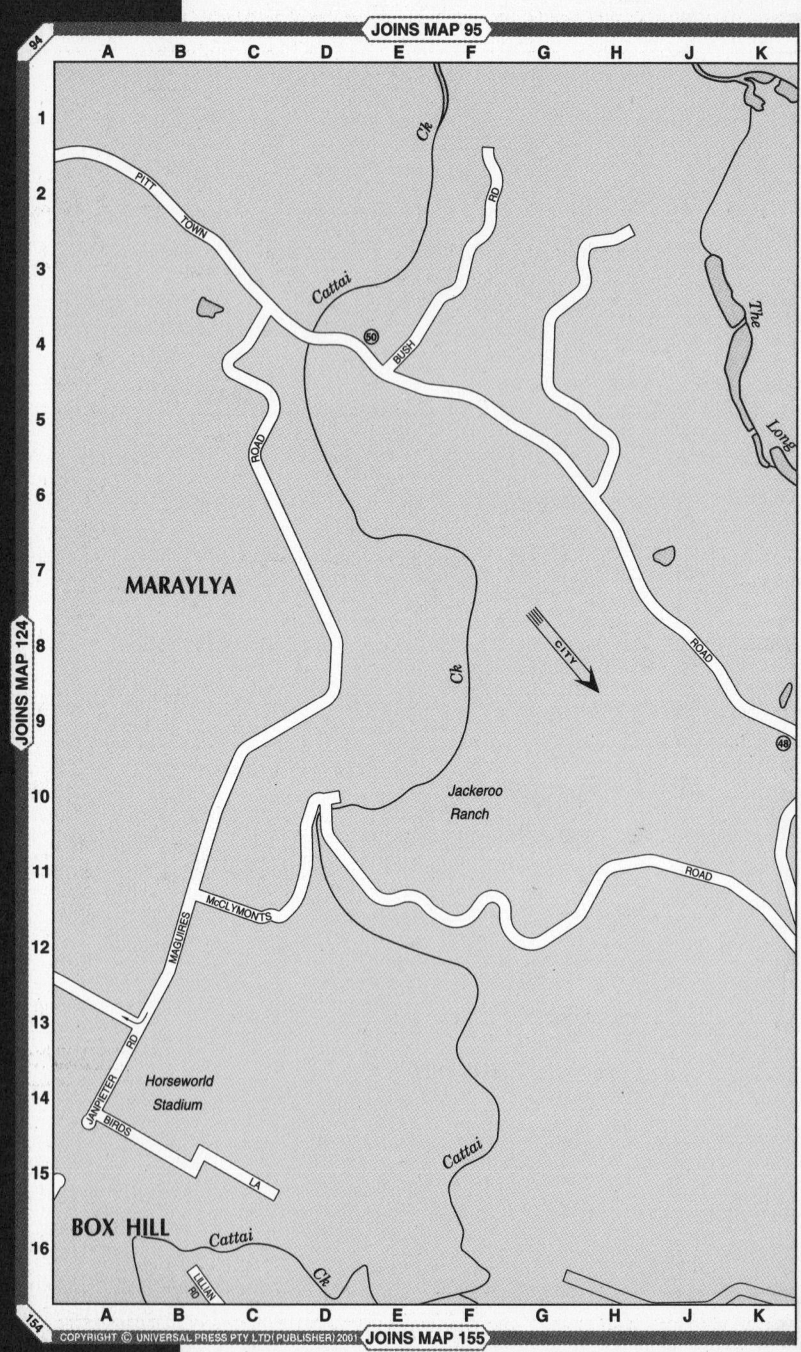

JOINS MAP 124

JOINS MAP 155

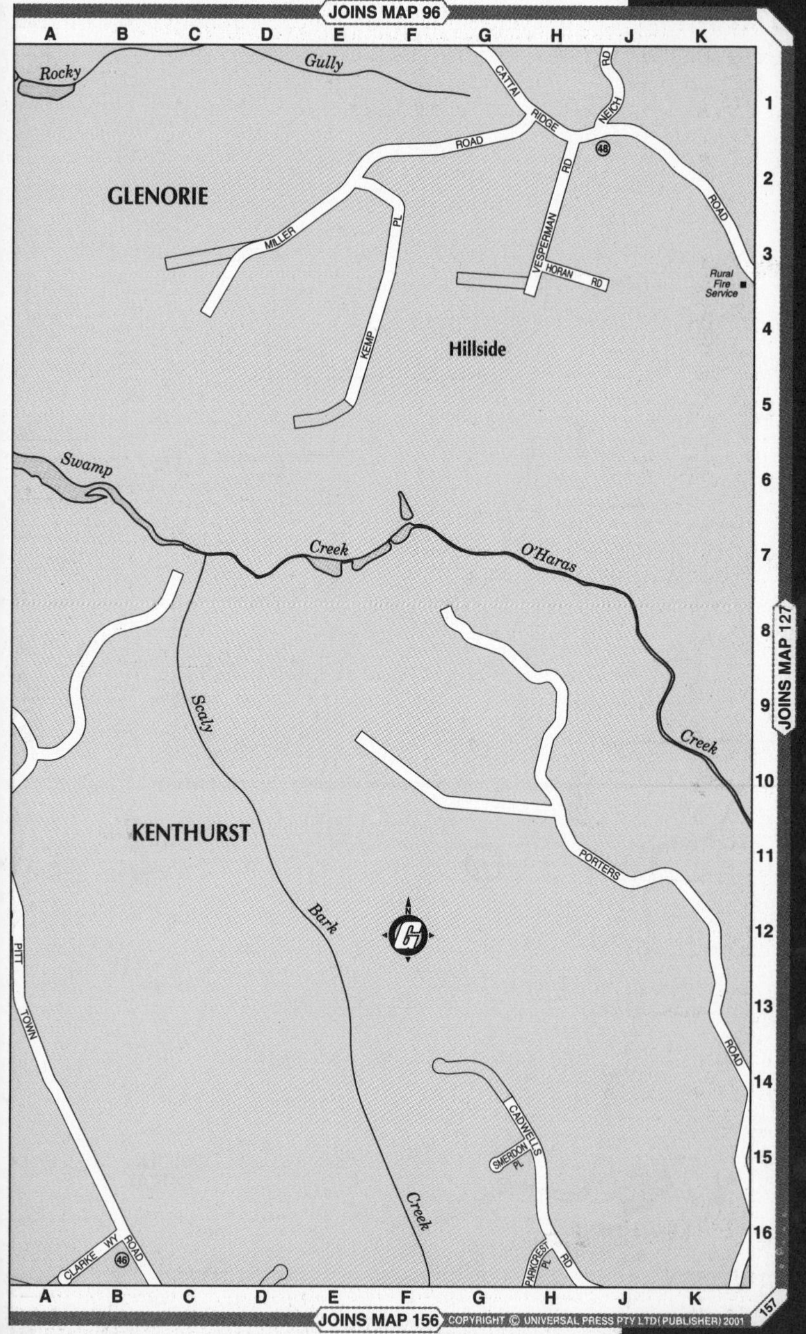
JOINS MAP 96
A
B
C
D
E
F
G
H
J
K
Rocky
Gully
CATTAI
RIDGE
ROAD
RD
NEICH
48
ROAD
GLENORIE
MILLER
PL
KEMP
RD
VESPERMAN
HORAN
RD
Rural
Fire
Service
Hillside
Swamp
Creek
O'Haras
Creek
JOINS MAP 127
Scaly
KENTHURST
PORTERS
Bark
ROAD
PITT
TOWN
CADWELLS
SMERDON
PL
Creek
CLARKE
WY
ROAD
46
PARKCREST
PL
RD
1
2
3
4
5
6
7
8
9
10
11
12
13
14
15
16
JOINS MAP 156

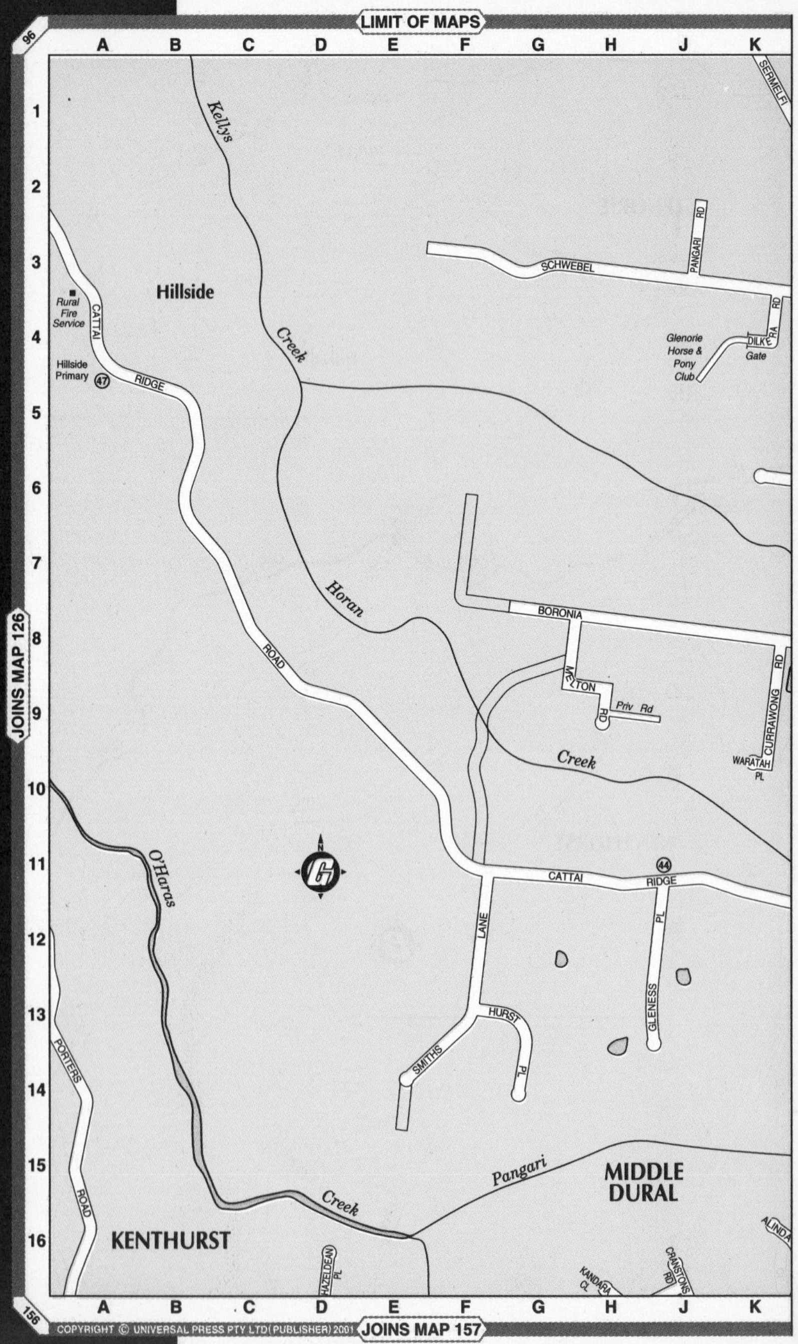
LIMIT OF MAPS
96
A
B
C
D
E
F
G
H
J
K
1
2
3
4
5
6
7
8
9
10
11
12
13
14
15
16
SERMELFI
Kellys
Creek
Horan
Creek
Hillside
Rural
Fire
Service
CATTAI
RIDGE
ROAD
Hillside
Primary
47
PANGARI
RD
SCHWEBEL
RD
DILKE
RA
Gate
Glenorie
Horse &
Pony
Club
BORONIA
MELTON
RD
Priv Rd
CURRAWONG
RD
WARATAH
PL
JOINS MAP 126
O'Haras
CATTAI
RIDGE
44
LANE
PL
GLENESS
HURST
PL
SMITHS
PORTERS
ROAD
Pangari
Creek
MIDDLE
DURAL
KENTHURST
HAZELDEAN
PL
KANDARA
CL
CRANSTONS
RD
ALINDA
156
JOINS MAP 157

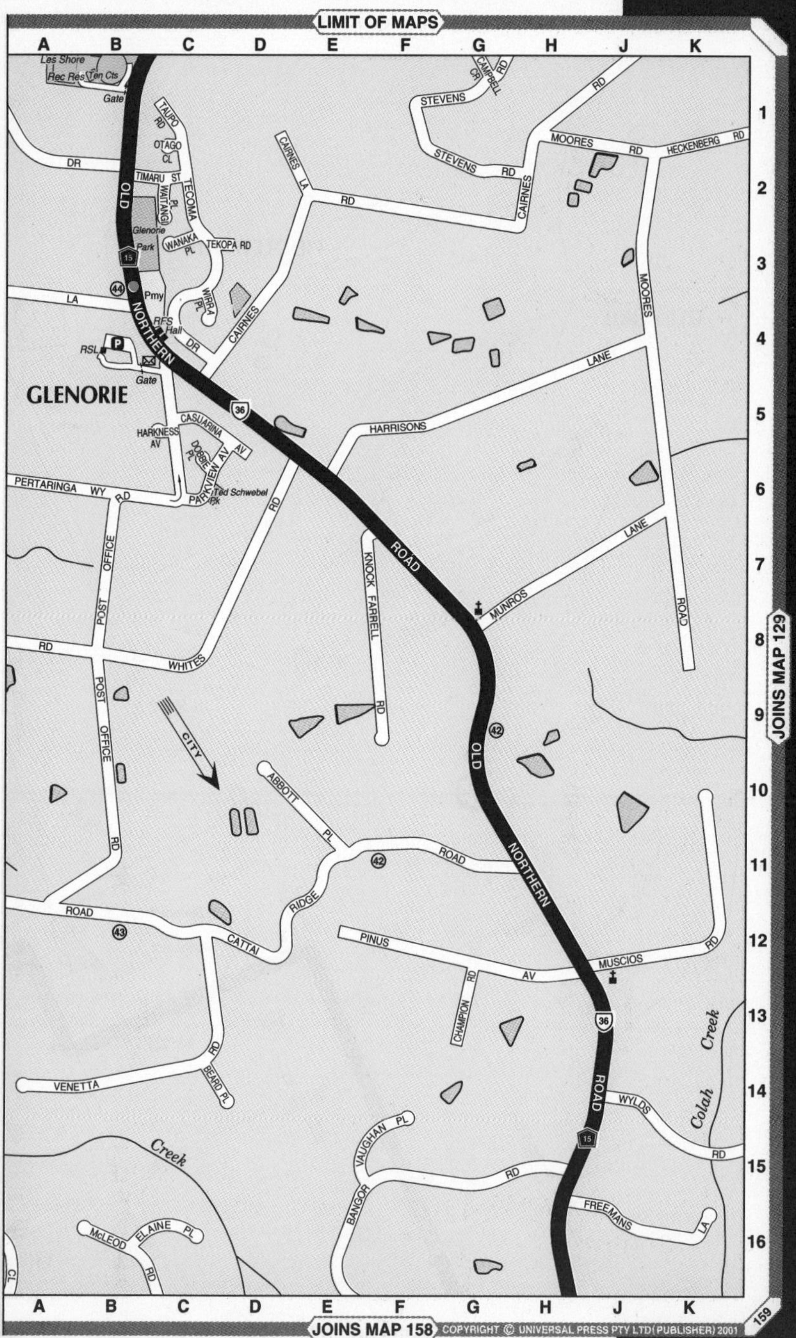
LIMIT OF MAPS
A B C D E F G H J K
1 2 3 4 5 6 7 8 9 10 11 12 13 14 15 16
GLENORIE
Les Shore
Rec Res
Ten Cts
Gate
TAUPO RD
OTAGO CL
DR
TIMARU ST
WAITANGI PL
TECOMA
OLD
Glenorie Park
WANAKA PL
TEKOPA RD
WIRRA PL
LA
Pmy
NORTHERN
RFS Hall
DR
CAIRNES
RSL
P
Gate
CASUARINA AV
HARKNESS AV
DOBBIE PL
PARKVIEW AV
PERTARINGA WY
RD
PARK
Ted Schwebel Pk
RD
POST OFFICE
RD
WHITES
POST OFFICE RD
CITY
ABBOTT PL
ROAD
RIDGE
CATTAI
ROAD
BEARD PL
RD
VENETTA
Creek
McLEOD
ELAINE PL
RD
CL
STEVENS
CAMPBELL CR
RD
STEVENS RD
CAIRNES LA
RD
CAIRNES
MOORES RD
HECKENBERG RD
MOORES
LANE
HARRISONS
KNOCK FARRELL RD
ROAD
MUNROS LANE
ROAD
OLD NORTHERN ROAD
PINUS AV
CHAMPION RD
MUSCIOS RD
WYLDS RD
Colah Creek
VAUGHAN PL
BANGOR
RD
FREEMANS LA
15 36 44 42 43
JOINS MAP 129

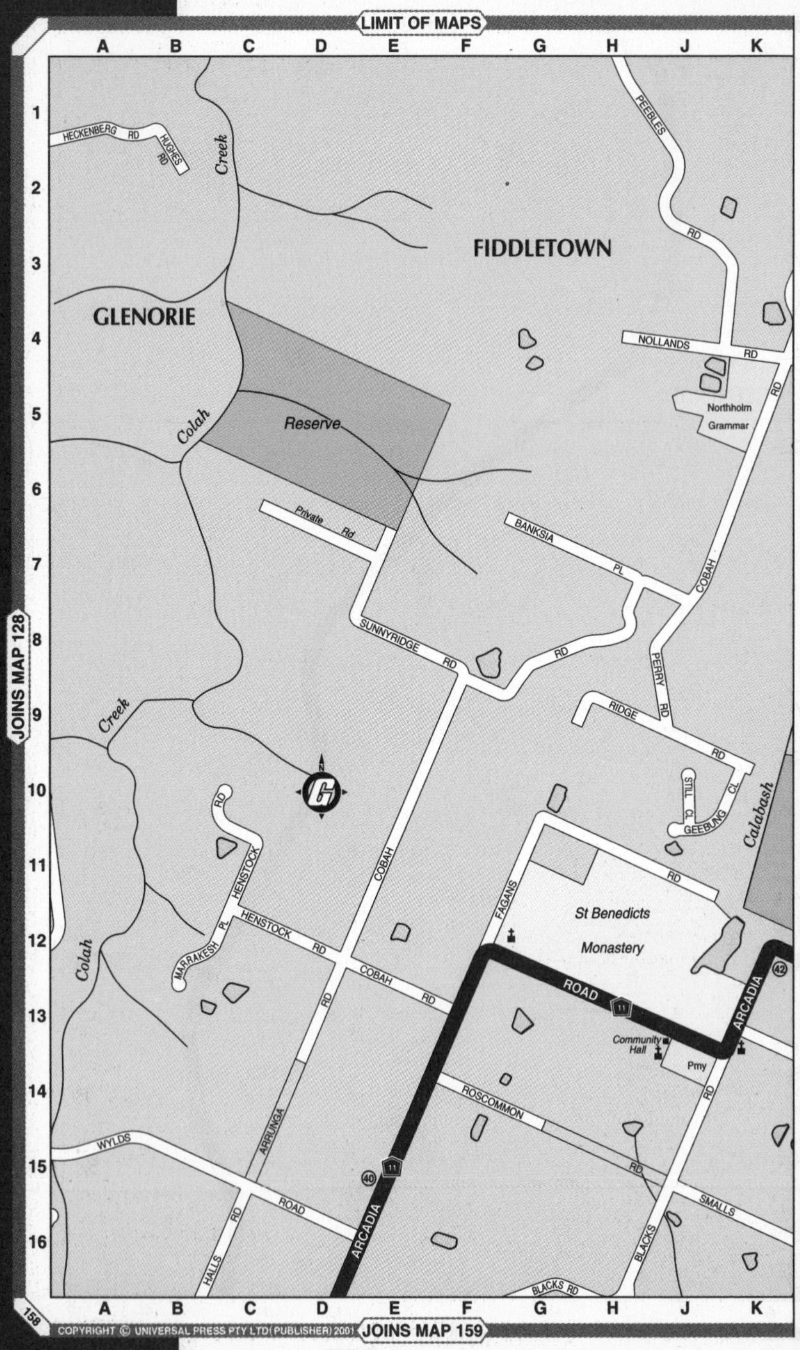
LIMIT OF MAPS
A B C D E F G H J K
1 2 3 4 5 6 7 8 9 10 11 12 13 14 15 16
JOINS MAP 128
FIDDLETOWN
GLENORIE
HECKENBERG RD
HUGHES RD
Colah Creek
PEEBLES RD
NOLLANDS RD
Northholm Grammar
Reserve
Private Rd
BANKSIA PL
COBAH RD
SUNNYRIDGE RD
PERRY RD
RIDGE RD
STILL CL
GEEBUNG CL
Calabash
HENSTOCK RD
MARRAKESH PL
HENSTOCK RD
COBAH RD
FAGANS RD
St Benedicts
Monastery
ROAD
ARCADIA
Community Hall
Pmy
ROSCOMMON RD
SMALLS
ARRUNGA
WYLDS ROAD
HALLS RD
BLACKS RD
BLACKS RD
40
42
11
JOINS MAP 159
158

LIMIT OF MAPS

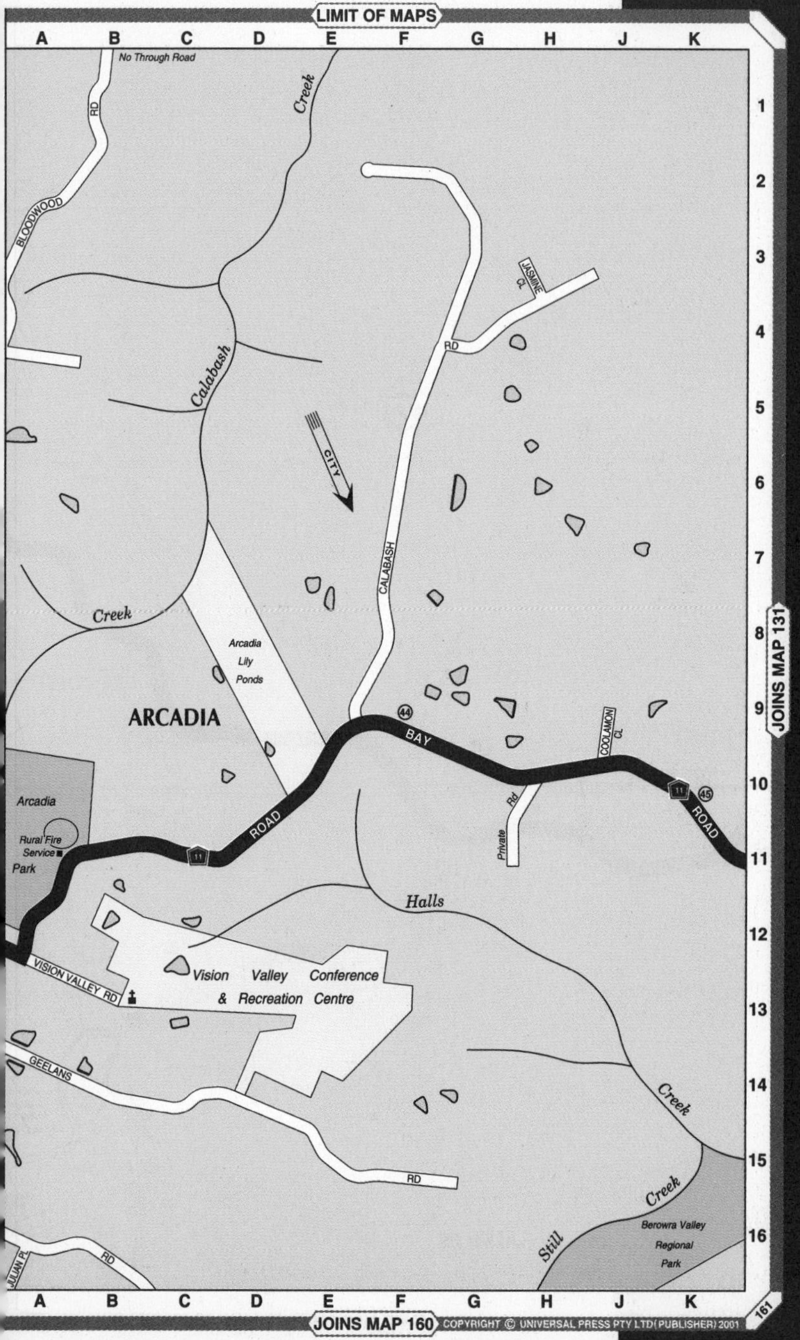

JOINS MAP 131

JOINS MAP 160

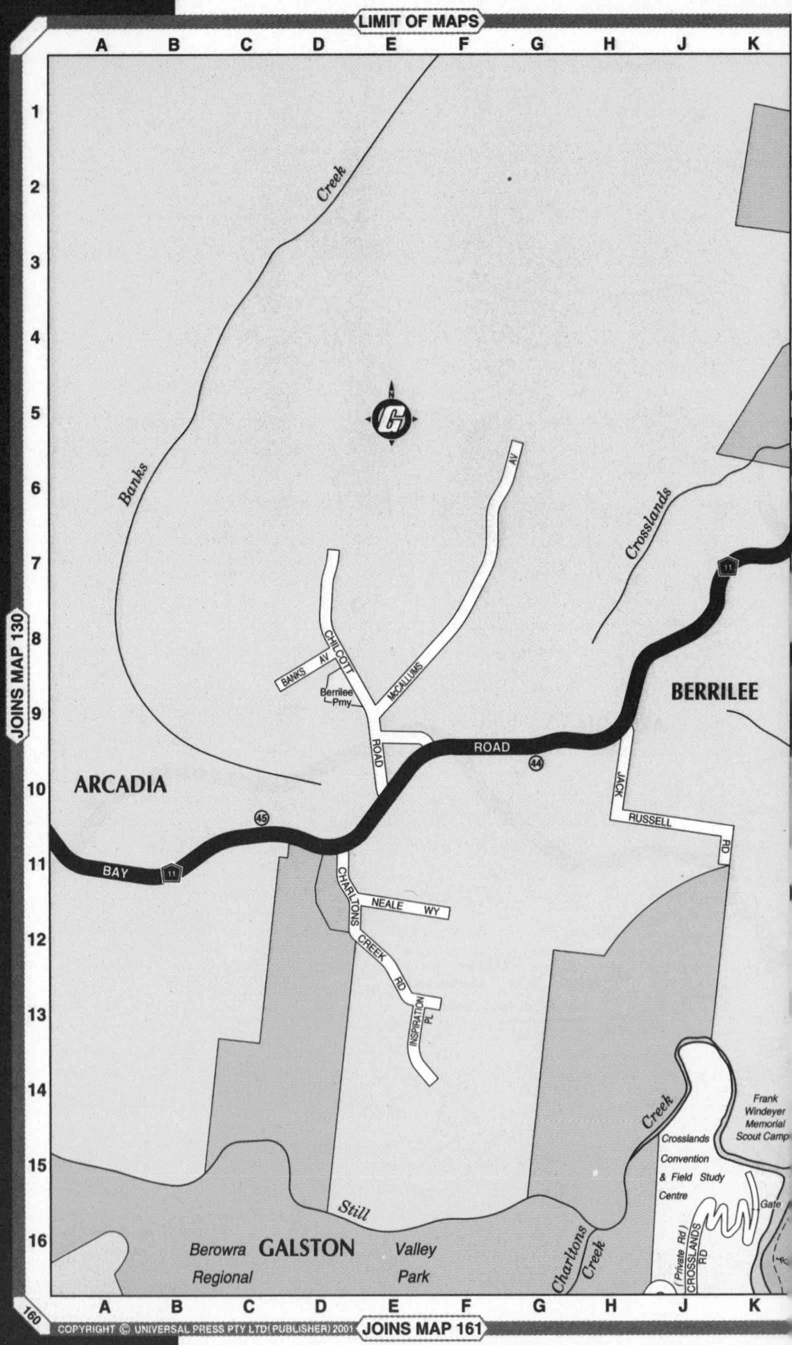

JOINS MAP 161

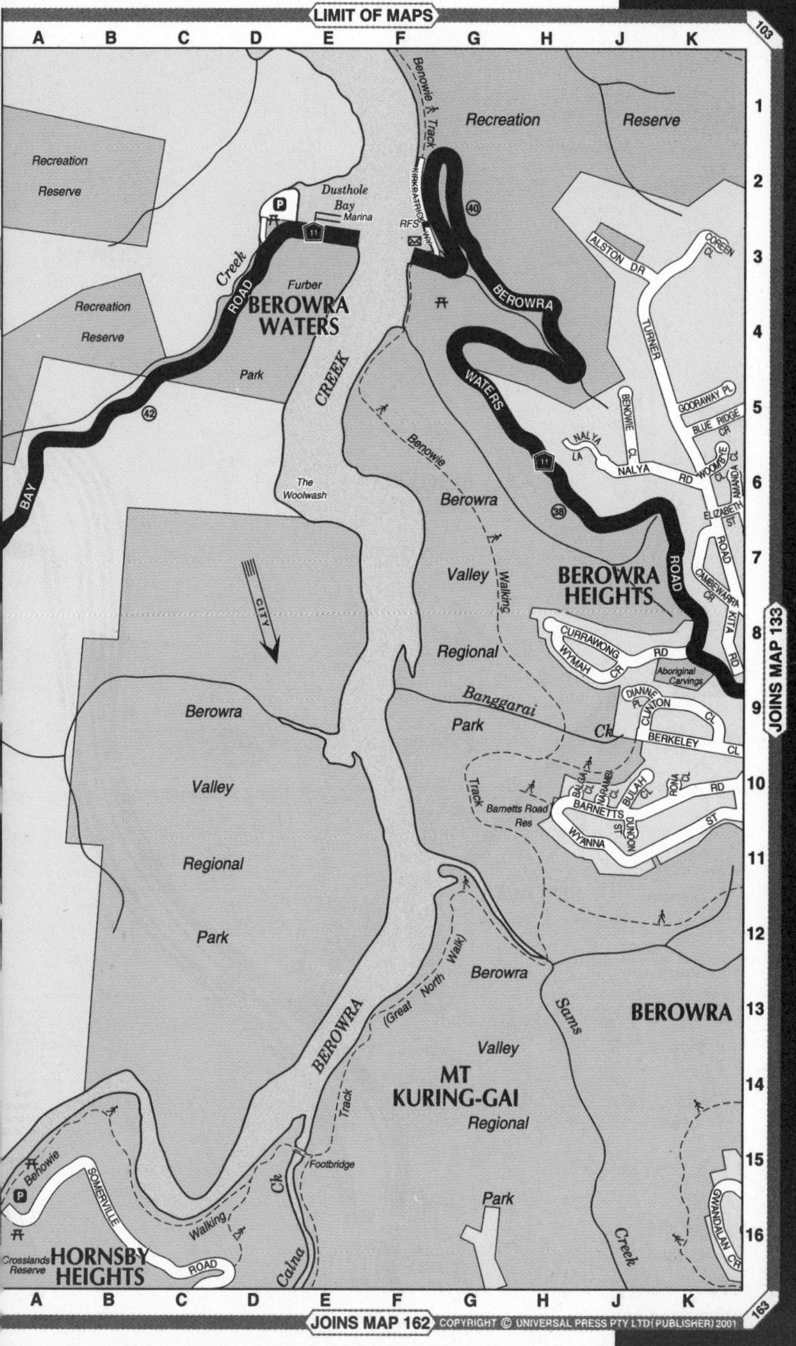
LIMIT OF MAPS
103
A B C D E F G H J K
1 2 3 4 5 6 7 8 9 10 11 12 13 14 15 16
Recreation Reserve
Dusthole Bay
Marina
RFS
KIRKPATRICK
Benowie Track
Creek
ROAD
Furber
BEROWRA WATERS
Park
CREEK
BEROWRA
WATERS
ALSTON DR
COREEN CL
TURNER
GOORAWAY PL
BLUE RIDGE CR
BENOWIE CL
NALYA LA
NALYA RD
WOOMBYE
AMANDA CL
ELIZABETH ST
ROAD
The Woolwash
Benowie
Berowra Valley Regional Park
Walking
BEROWRA HEIGHTS
CAMBEWARRA CR
KITA RD
CITY
CURRAWONG RD
WYMAH CR
Aboriginal Carvings
Banggarai Ck
DIANNE PL
CLINTON CL
BERKELEY CL
BALGA CL
NARAMBI CL
BULAH CL
RONA CL
RD
BARNETTS ST
Barnetts Road Res
DUNOON ST
WYANNA
Track
(Great North Walk)
Sams Creek
BEROWRA
MT KURING-GAI
Berowra Valley Regional Park
Footbridge
Calna Ck
Benowie
SOMERVILLE ROAD
Walking
Crosslands Reserve
HORNSBY HEIGHTS
BAY
JOINS MAP 133
JOINS MAP 162
163

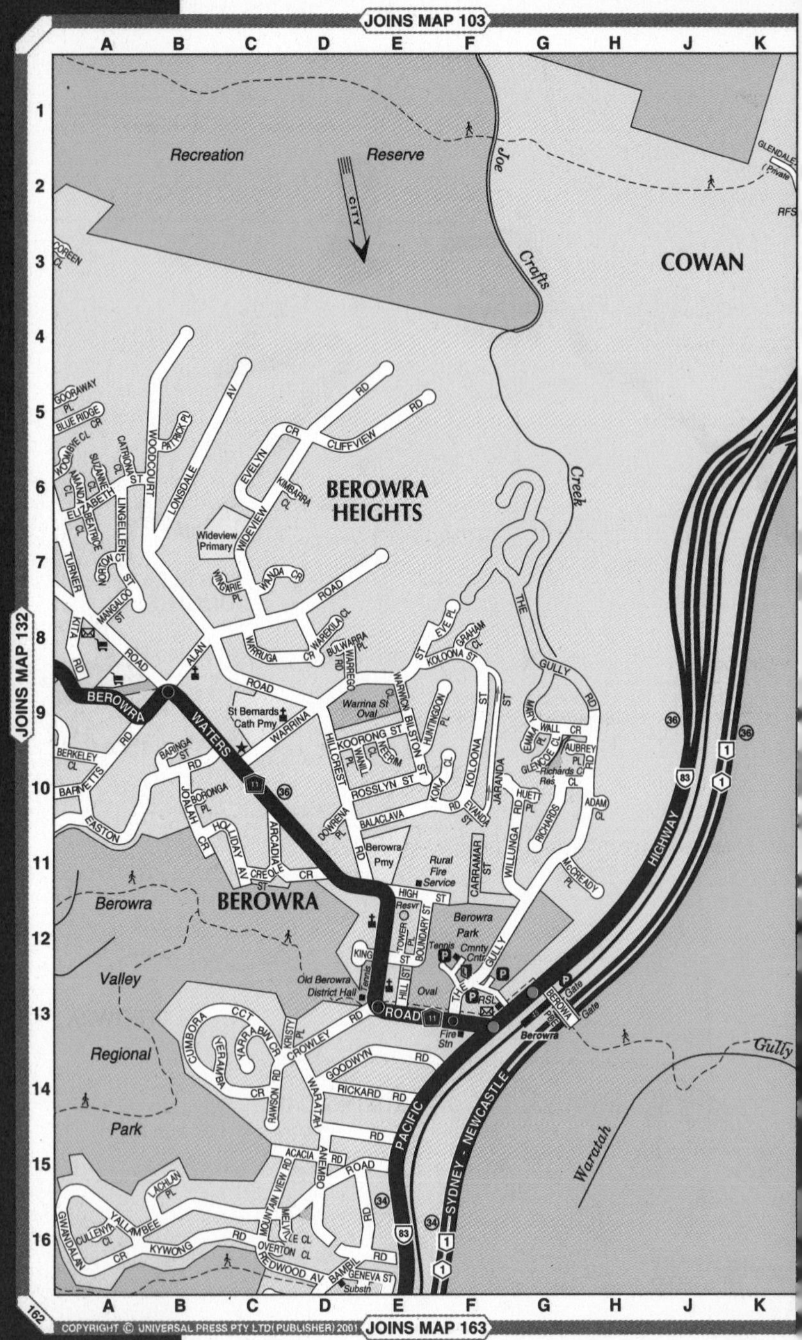
JOINS MAP 103
JOINS MAP 132
JOINS MAP 163
Recreation
Reserve
CITY
Joe
Crafts
Creek
COWAN
GLENDALE
Private
RFS
BEROWRA
HEIGHTS
Wideview
Primary
Warrina St
Oval
St Bernards
Cath Pmy
BEROWRA
Berowra
Valley
Regional
Park
Berowra
Pmy
Rural
Fire
Service
Berowra
Park
Tennis
Cmnty
Cntr
Oval
RSL
Old Berowra
District Hall
Fire
Stn
Berowra
Gully
Waratah
Richards Cl
Res
PACIFIC
HIGHWAY
SYDNEY - NEWCASTLE
WATERS
ROAD
WARRINA
COREEN CL
GOORAWAY PL
BLUE RIDGE CR
WOOMBYE CL
SUZANNE CL
CATRIONA CL
AMANDA CL
ELIZABETH
BEATRICE CL
LINGELLEN ST
WOODCOURT
PATRICK PL
LONSDALE
AV
EVELYN
CR
CLIFFVIEW
RD
KIMBARRA CL
WIDEVIEW
TURNER
NORTON CT
MANGALOO ST
KITA RD
WINGARIE PL
WANDA CR
WAREKILA CL
WARRUGA CR
BULWARRA PL
WARREGO RD
ALAN
EVE PL
GRAHAM CL
KOLOONA ST
THE GULLY RD
MARY PL
EMMA PL
WALL CR
GLENCOE CL
AUBREY PL
HUETT PL
ADAM CL
RICHARDS
MCCREADY PL
WARWICK CL
BILSTON ST
HUNTINGDON PL
KOORONG ST
WANILL PL
LE CL
NEERIM
HILLCREST
ROSSLYN ST
KONA CL
KOLOONA
EVANDA ST
JARANDA
WILLUNGA RD
CARRAMAR ST
DOWRENA PL
BALACLAVA RD
BARINGA ST
BERKELEY CL
BARNETTS RD
EASTON
JOALAH
BORONGA PL
HOLLIDAY AV
CREOLE ST
ARCADIA
HIGH ST
Resvr
TOWER PL
BOUNDARY ST
KING
HILL ST
CUMBORA
CCT
YERAMBA
YARRABIN CR
KRISTY PL
CROWLEY RD
GOODWYN RD
RICKARD RD
WARATAH
RAWSON RD
ACACIA RD
ANEMBO
MOUNTAIN VIEW RD
MELVYLE CL
OVERTON CL
REDWOOD AV
BAMBIL
GENEVA ST
Substn
LACHLAN PL
YALLAMBEE
GWANDALAN
CULLENYA CL
KYWONG RD
CR
BEROWRA
Gate
11
36
83
1
34
A B C D E F G H J K
1 2 3 4 5 6 7 8 9 10 11 12 13 14 15 16
162

JOINS MAP 104

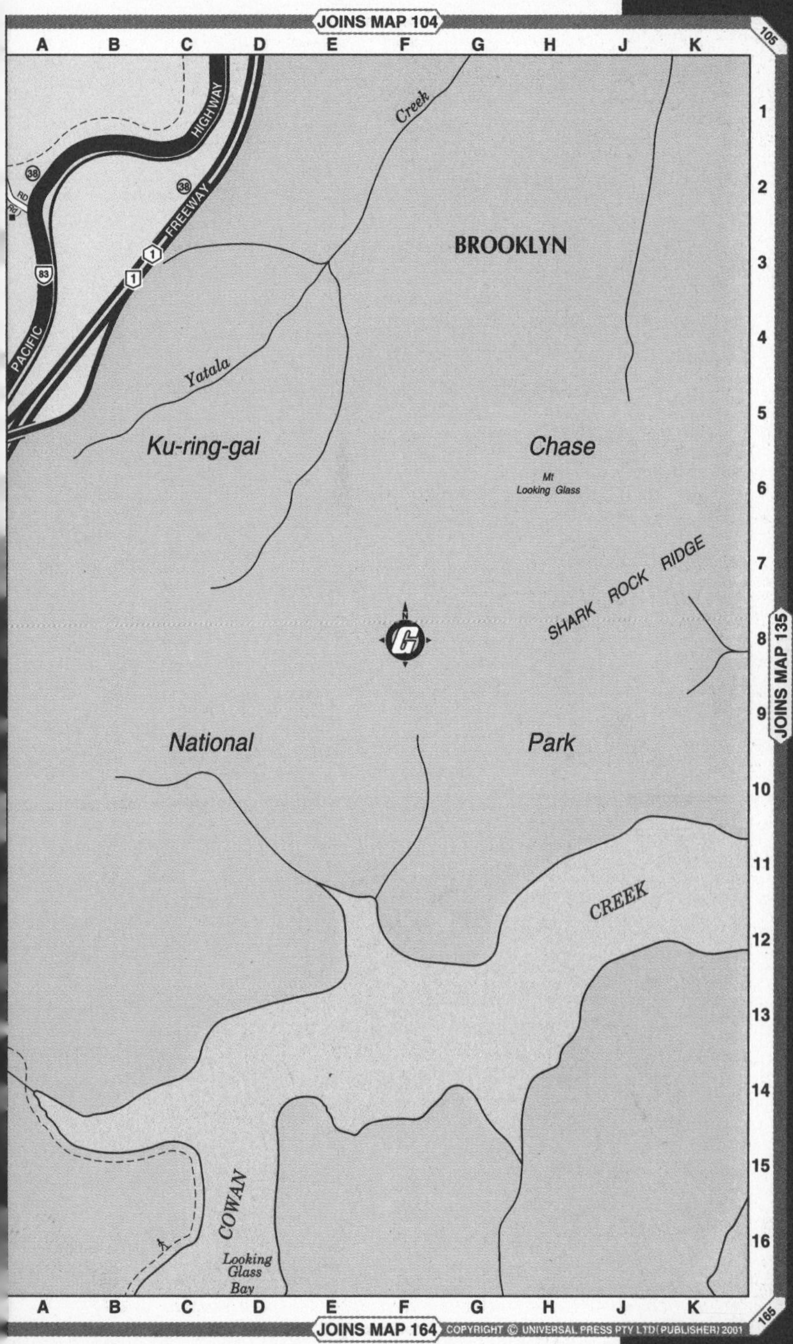

JOINS MAP 135

JOINS MAP 164

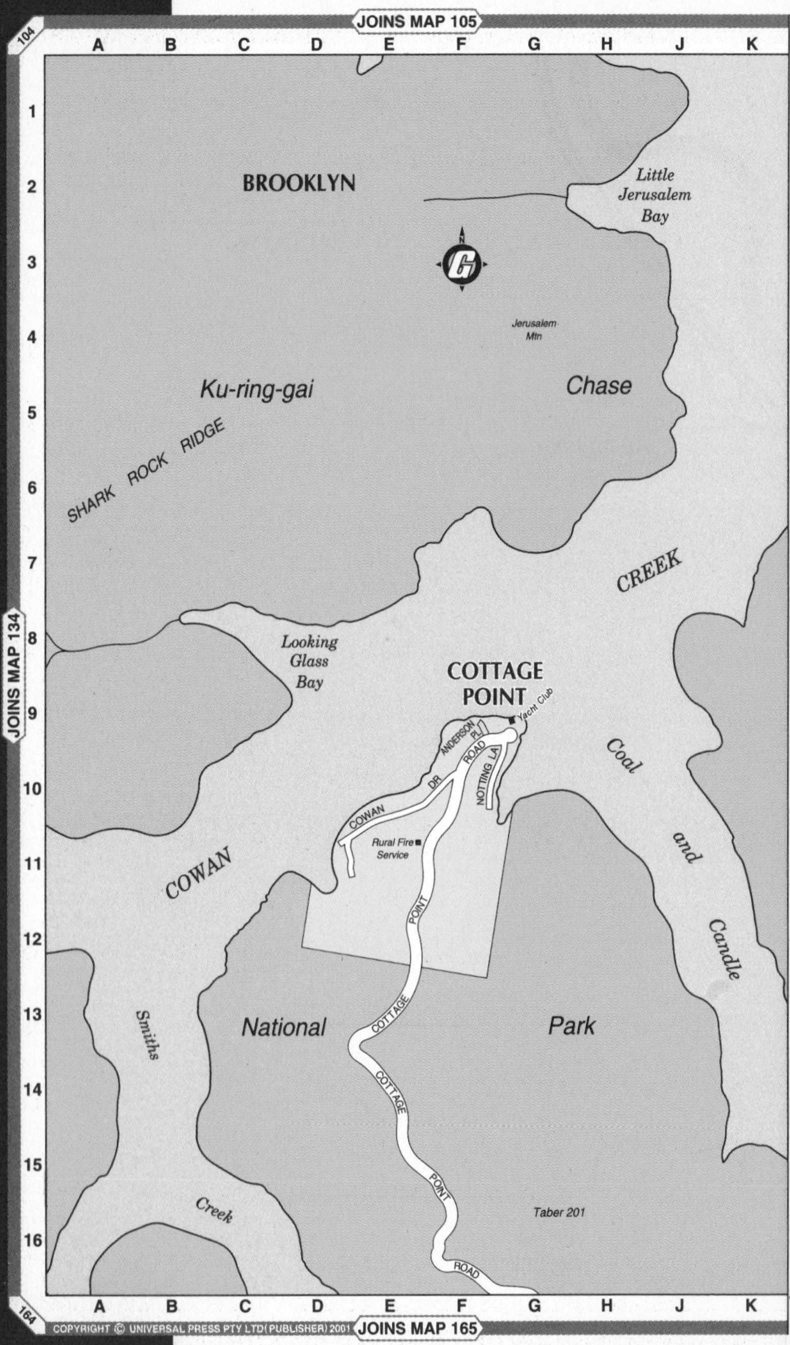
JOINS MAP 105
104
A B C D E F G H J K
1
2
3
4
5
6
7
8
9
10
11
12
13
14
15
16
BROOKLYN
Little Jerusalem Bay
Jerusalem Mtn
Ku-ring-gai
Chase
SHARK ROCK RIDGE
CREEK
Looking Glass Bay
COTTAGE POINT
Yacht Club
ANDERSON PL
ROAD
NOTTING LA
COWAN DR
Rural Fire Service
COWAN
Coal and Candle
POINT
COTTAGE
National
Park
Smiths Creek
COTTAGE POINT ROAD
Taber 201
JOINS MAP 134
164
JOINS MAP 165

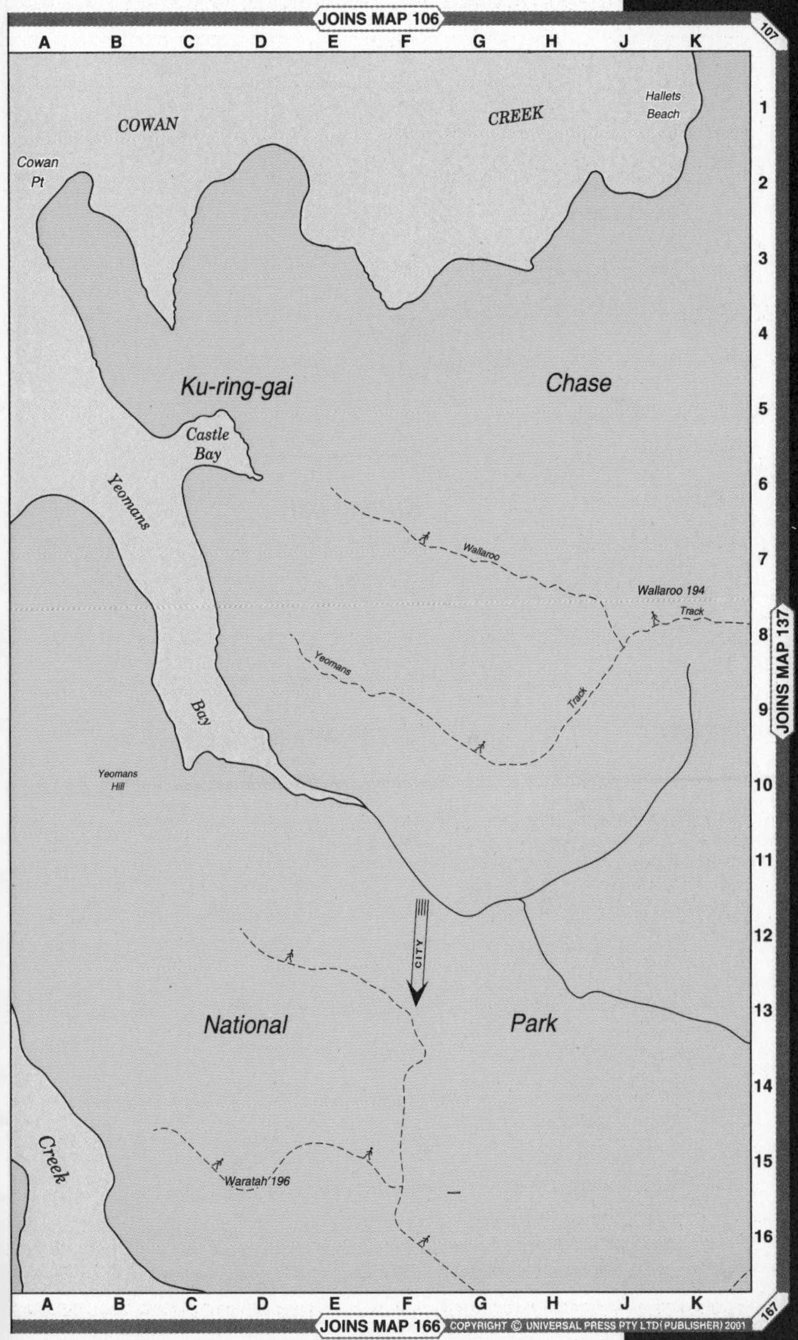
JOINS MAP 106
107
A B C D E F G H J K
1 2 3 4 5 6 7 8 9 10 11 12 13 14 15 16
COWAN
CREEK
Hallets
Beach
Cowan
Pt
Ku-ring-gai
Chase
Castle
Bay
Yeomans
Wallaroo
Wallaroo 194
Track
Yeomans
Track
JOINS MAP 137
Bay
Yeomans
Hill
CITY
National
Park
Creek
Waratah 196
JOINS MAP 166
167

MAP 137

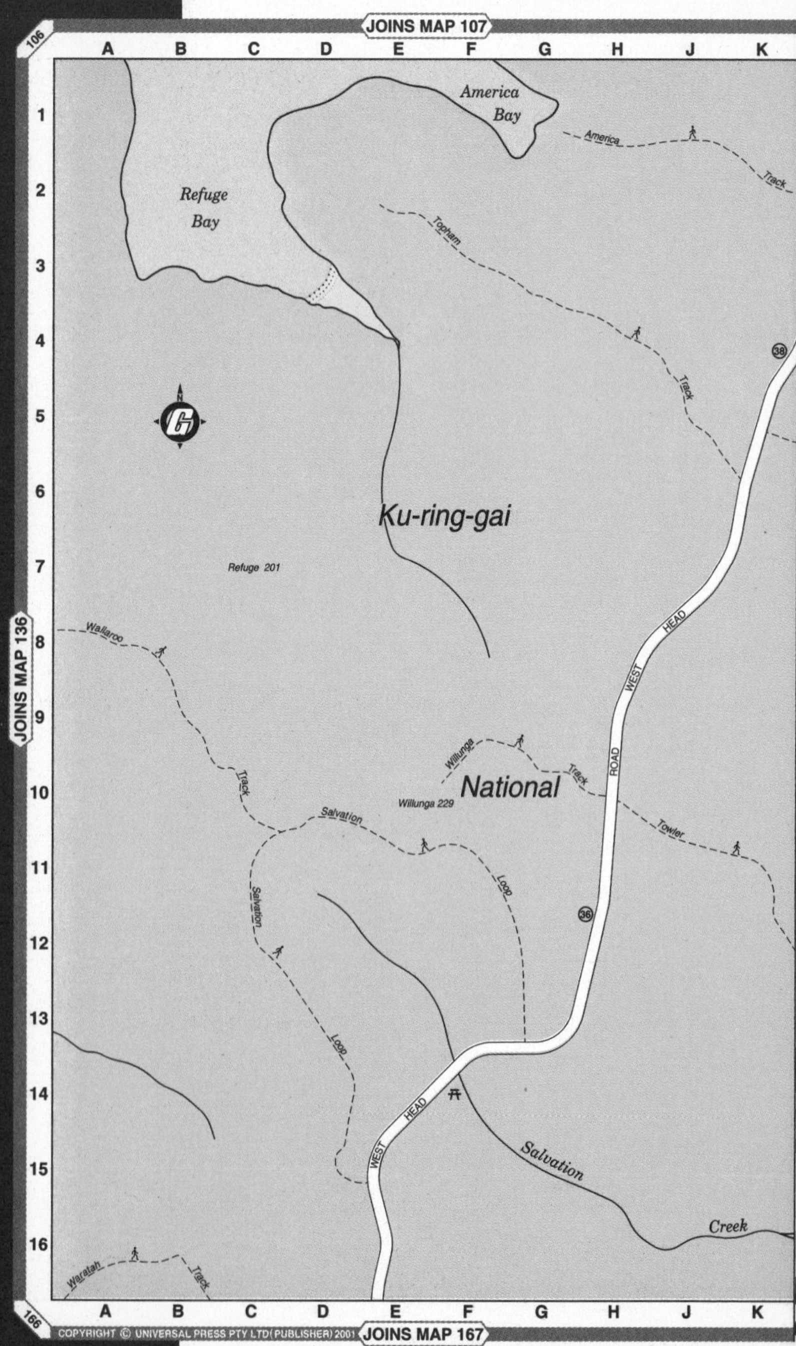

JOINS MAP 107
106
A
B
C
D
E
F
G
H
J
K
1
2
3
4
5
6
7
8
9
10
11
12
13
14
15
16
America
Bay
America
Track
Refuge
Bay
Topham
Track
38
Ku-ring-gai
Refuge 201
Wallaroo
Track
HEAD
WEST
ROAD
Willunga
Track
National
Willunga 229
Salvation
Towler
Loop
Salvation
36
Loop
HEAD
WEST
Salvation
Creek
Waratah
Track
JOINS MAP 136
166
JOINS MAP 167

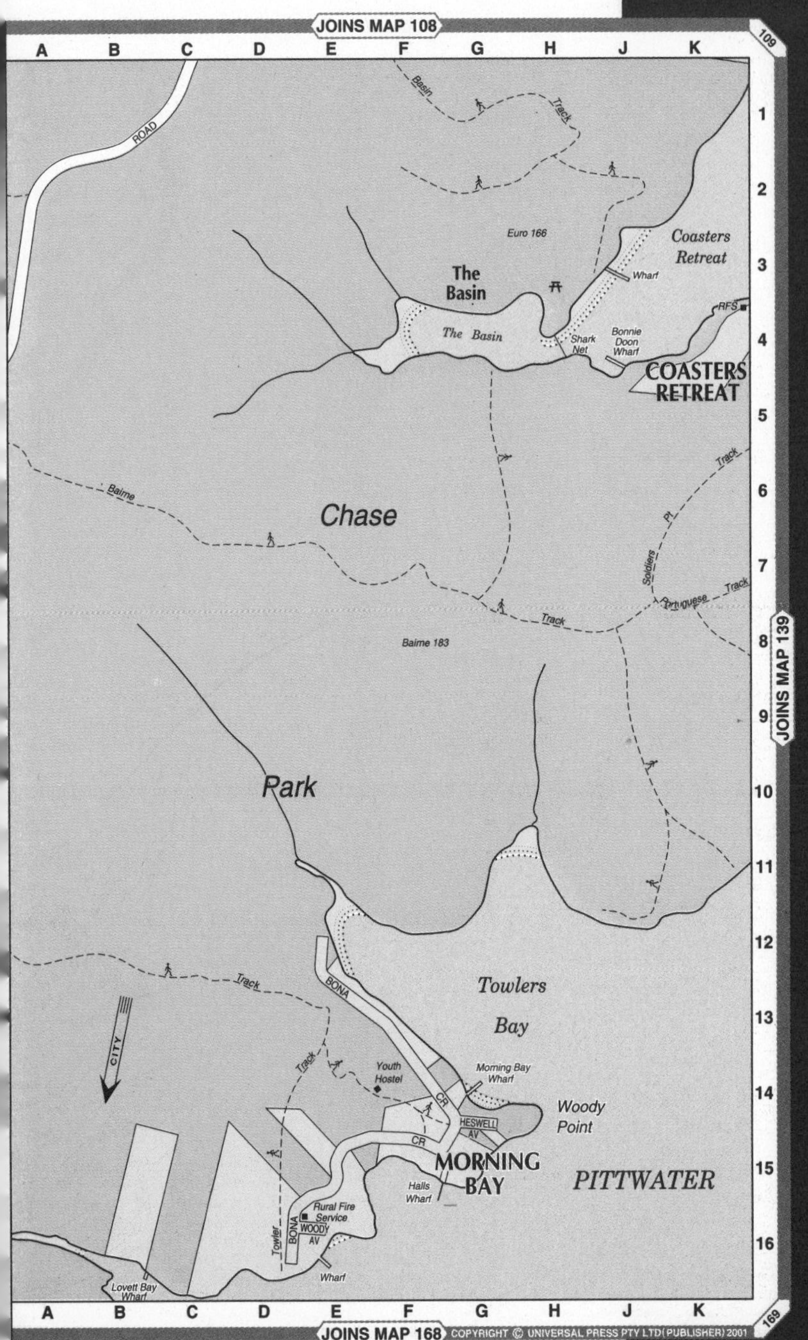
JOINS MAP 108
109
A B C D E F G H J K
1 2 3 4 5 6 7 8 9 10 11 12 13 14 15 16
ROAD
Basin
Track
Euro 166
Coasters
Retreat
The
Basin
Wharf
RFS
The Basin
Shark
Net
Bonnie
Doon
Wharf
COASTERS
RETREAT
Track
Baime
Chase
Pt
Soldiers
Portuguese
Track
Track
Baime 183
JOINS MAP 139
Park
Towlers
Bay
Track
BONA
CITY
Track
Youth
Hostel
Morning Bay
Wharf
Woody
Point
CR
HESWELL
AV
CR
MORNING
BAY
PITTWATER
Halls
Wharf
Rural Fire
Service
BONA
WOODY
AV
Towler
Wharf
Lovett Bay
Wharf
169

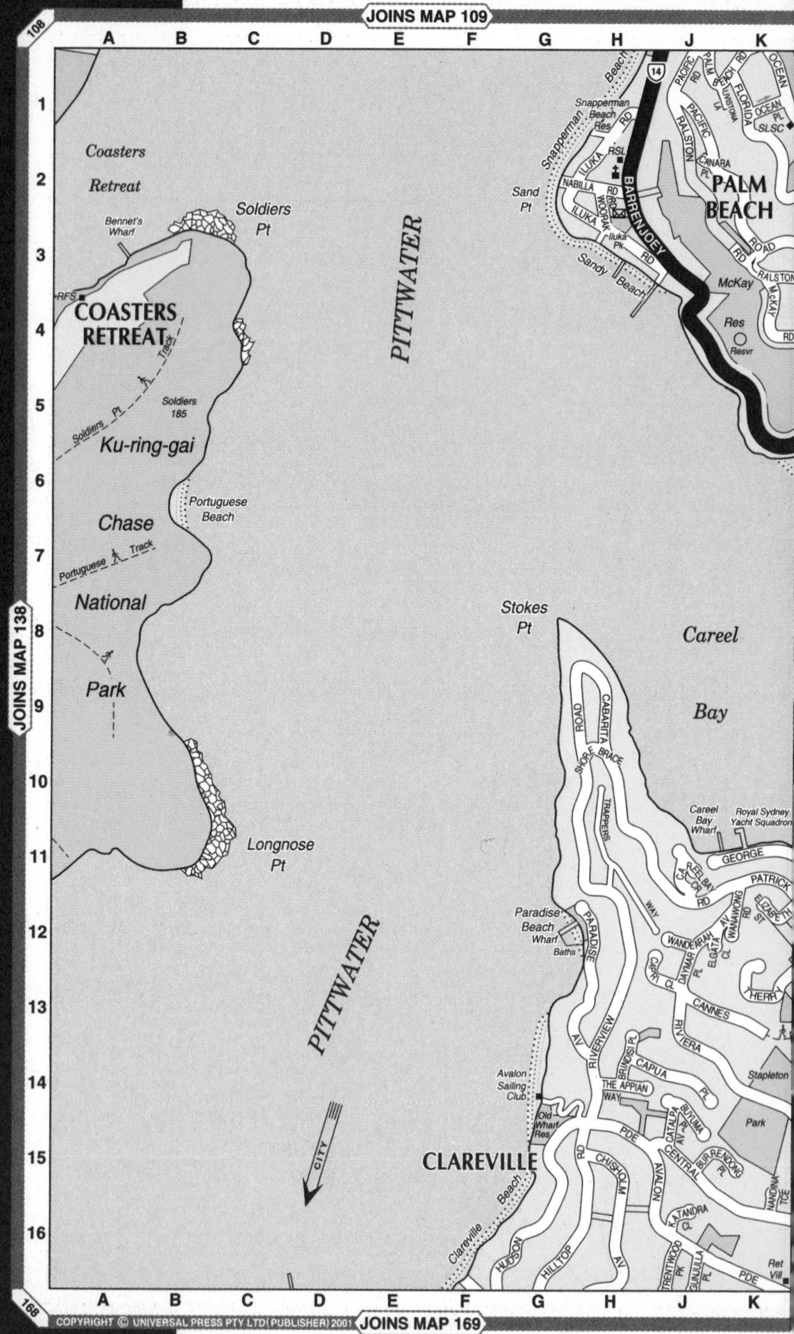
JOINS MAP 109
108
A B C D E F G H J K
1 2 3 4 5 6 7 8 9 10 11 12 13 14 15 16
Coasters
Retreat
Bennet's Wharf
Soldiers Pt
RFS
COASTERS RETREAT
Track
Soldiers Pt
Soldiers 185
Ku-ring-gai
Portuguese Beach
Chase
Portuguese Track
National
Park
PITTWATER
Longnose Pt
PITTWATER
CITY
Beach
Snapperman Beach Res
Snapperman
ILUKA
RD
RSL
NABILLA
WOORAK
Sand Pt
BARRENJOEY
Iluka Pk
Sandy Beach
PACIFIC
PALM BEACH
FLORIDA
OCEAN
SLSC
RALSTON
CANARA PL
PALM BEACH
ROAD
McKay
Res
Resvr
MCKAY
Stokes Pt
Careel
Bay
CABARITA
ROAD
SHORE BRACE
TRAPPERS
Careel Bay Wharf
Royal Sydney Yacht Squadron
GEORGE
PATRICK
Paradise Beach Wharf
Baths
PARADISE
WAY
WANDEARAH
DAYMAR PL
ELGATA AV
WANAWONG RD
CAPRI CL
CANNES
RIVIERA
RIVERVIEW
AV
BRINDISI PL
CAPUA
Stapleton
Avalon Sailing Club
Old Wharf Res
THE APPIAN WAY
CATALPA AV
BUYUMA PL
PDE
CENTRAL
BURRENDONG PL
Park
CLAREVILLE
Clareville Beach
RD
CHISHOLM
AVALON
KATANDRA CL
NANDINA TCE
HUDSON
HILLTOP
AV
TRENTWOOD PK
GUNJULLA PL
Ret Vill
JOINS MAP 138
168

JOINS MAP 110

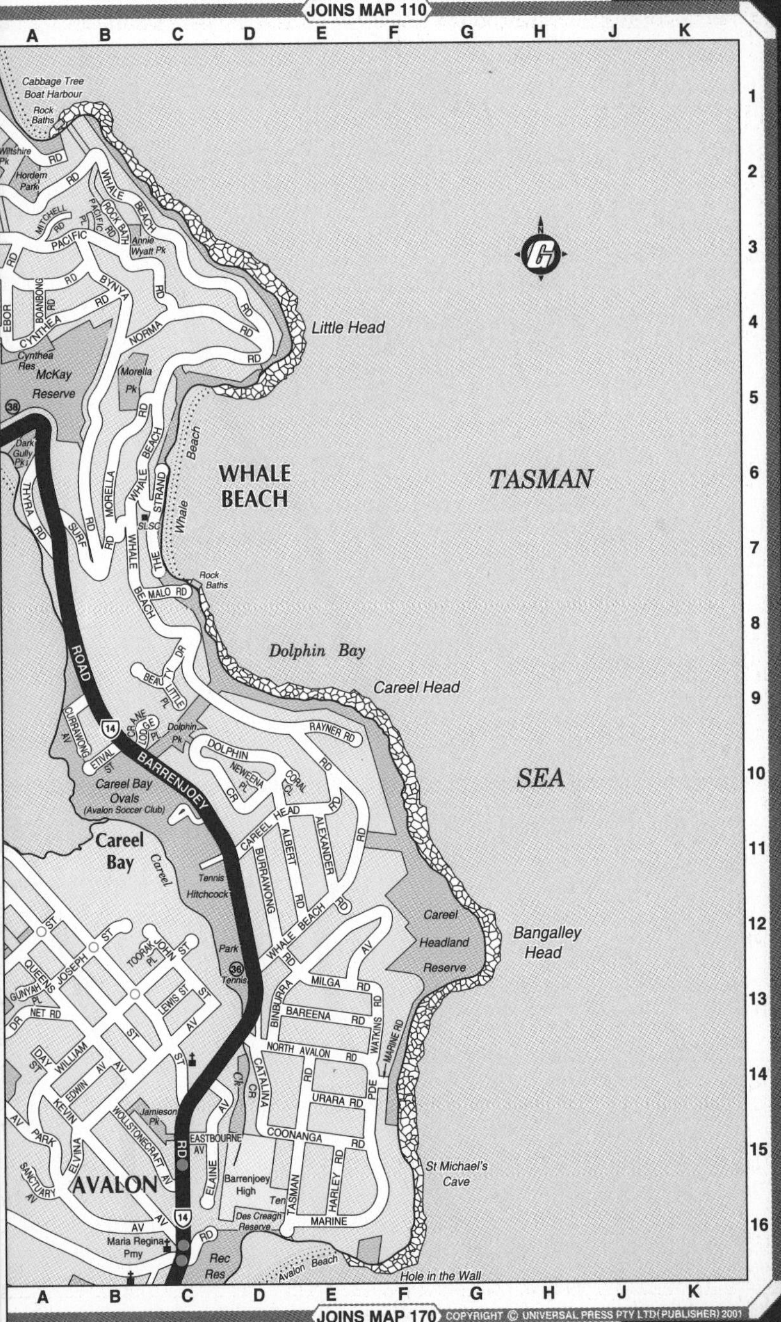

JOINS MAP 170

JOINS MAP 115

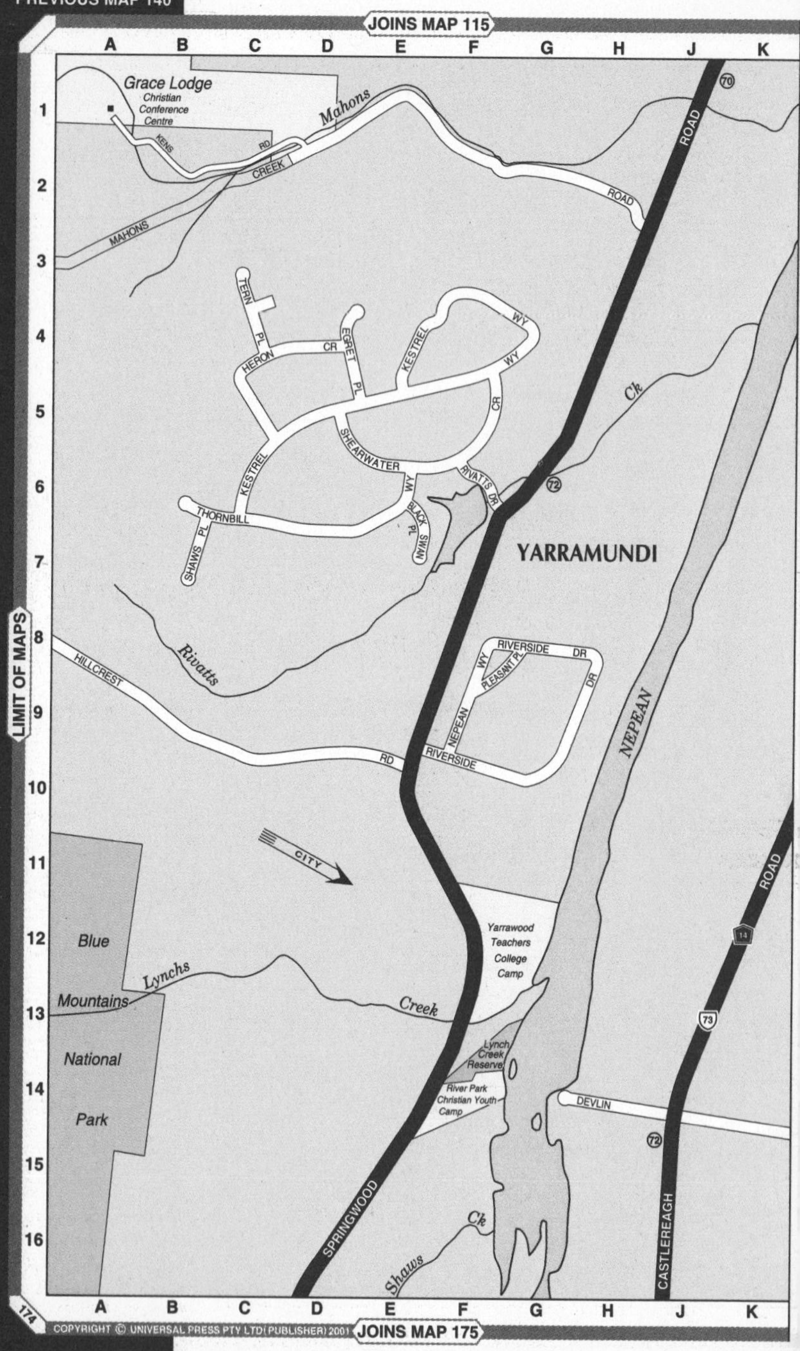

JOINS MAP 175

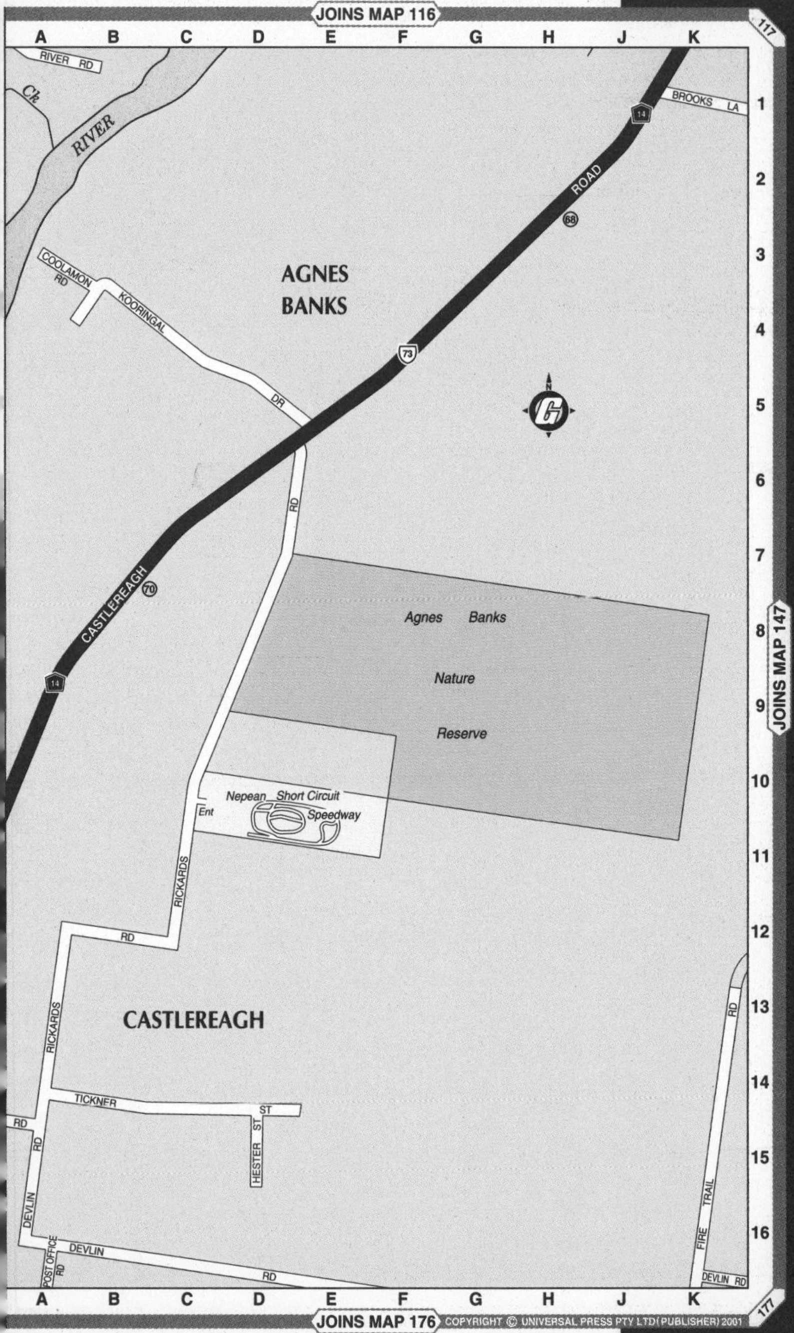
JOINS MAP 116
A
B
C
D
E
F
G
H
J
K
117
RIVER RD
Ck
RIVER
BROOKS LA
14
ROAD
68
COOLAMON RD
KOORINGAL
DR
AGNES
BANKS
73
RD
CASTLEREAGH
70
14
Agnes Banks
Nature
Reserve
Nepean Short Circuit
Speedway
Ent
RICKARDS
RD
CASTLEREAGH
RICKARDS
TICKNER
ST
HESTER ST
RD
RD
DEVLIN
DEVLIN
POST OFFICE RD
RD
RD
FIRE TRAIL
DEVLIN RD
JOINS MAP 147
1
2
3
4
5
6
7
8
9
10
11
12
13
14
15
16
177
JOINS MAP 176

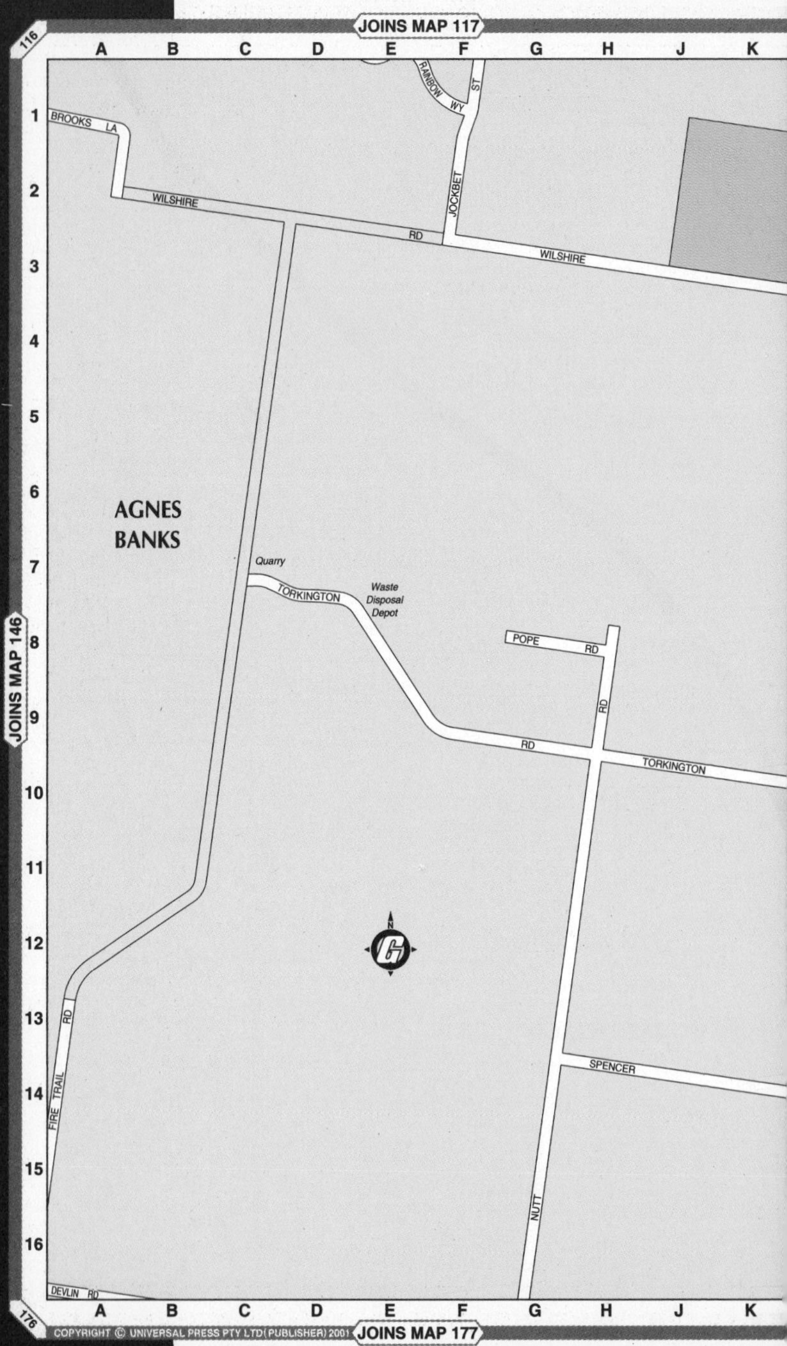
JOINS MAP 117
116
A B C D E F G H J K
1 2 3 4 5 6 7 8 9 10 11 12 13 14 15 16
BROOKS LA
WILSHIRE RD
RAINBOW WY
JOCKBET ST
WILSHIRE
AGNES
BANKS
Quarry
TORKINGTON RD
Waste
Disposal
Depot
POPE RD
RD
TORKINGTON
SPENCER
NUTT
FIRE TRAIL RD
DEVLIN RD
JOINS MAP 146
176
JOINS MAP 177

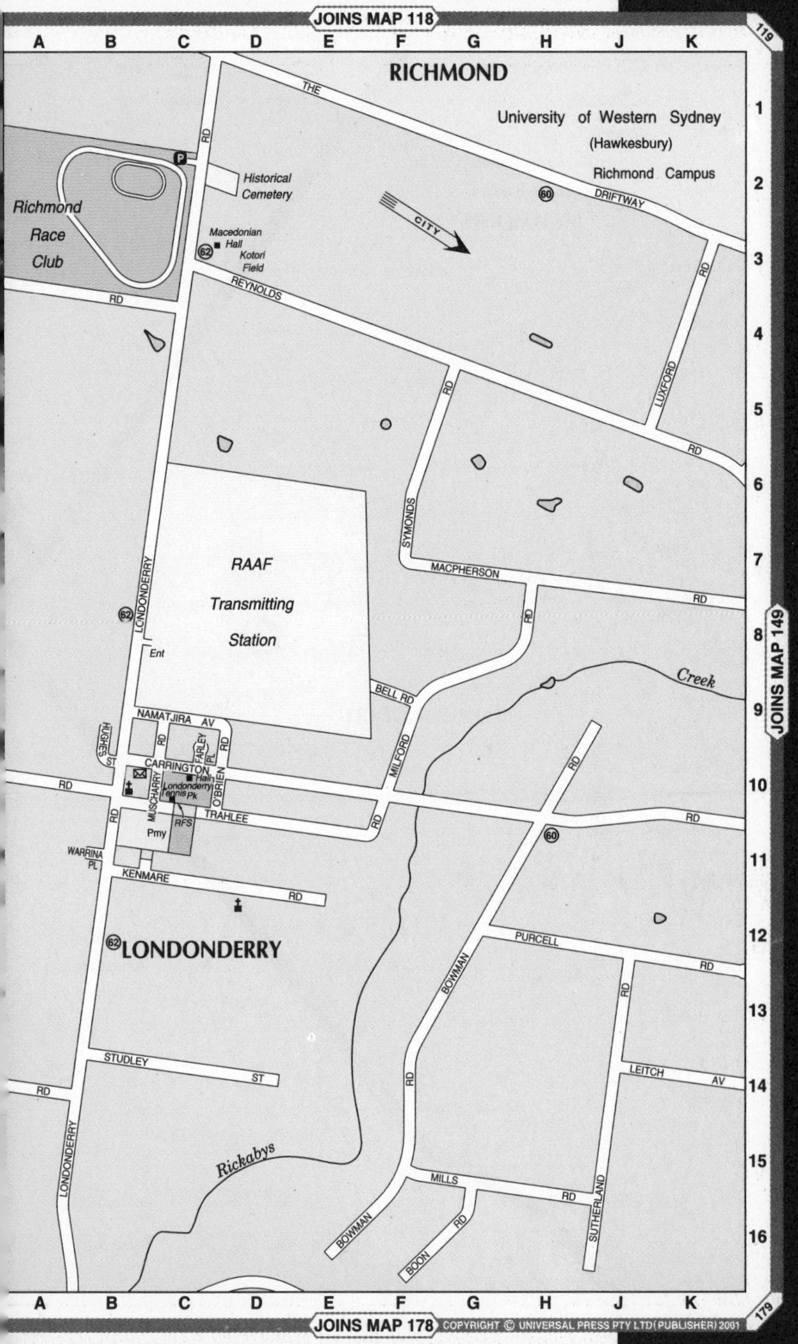
JOINS MAP 118
119
A B C D E F G H J K
RICHMOND
University of Western Sydney
(Hawkesbury)
Richmond Campus
Richmond
Race
Club
Historical
Cemetery
Macedonian
Hall
Kotori
Field
CITY
THE
DRIFTWAY
REYNOLDS
RD
LUXFORD
SYMONDS
MACPHERSON
RAAF
Transmitting
Station
Ent
LONDONDERRY
BELL RD
Creek
NAMATJIRA AV
HUGHES ST
FARLEY PL
CARRINGTON
Hall
Londonderry
Tennis Pk
O'BRIEN
MUSCHARRY
TRAHLEE
RFS
Pmy
WARRINA PL
KENMARE
MILFORD
PURCELL
BOWMAN
LONDONDERRY
LEITCH AV
STUDLEY ST
Rickabys
MILLS
BOON
SUTHERLAND
1 2 3 4 5 6 7 8 9 10 11 12 13 14 15 16
JOINS MAP 149
179
JOINS MAP 178

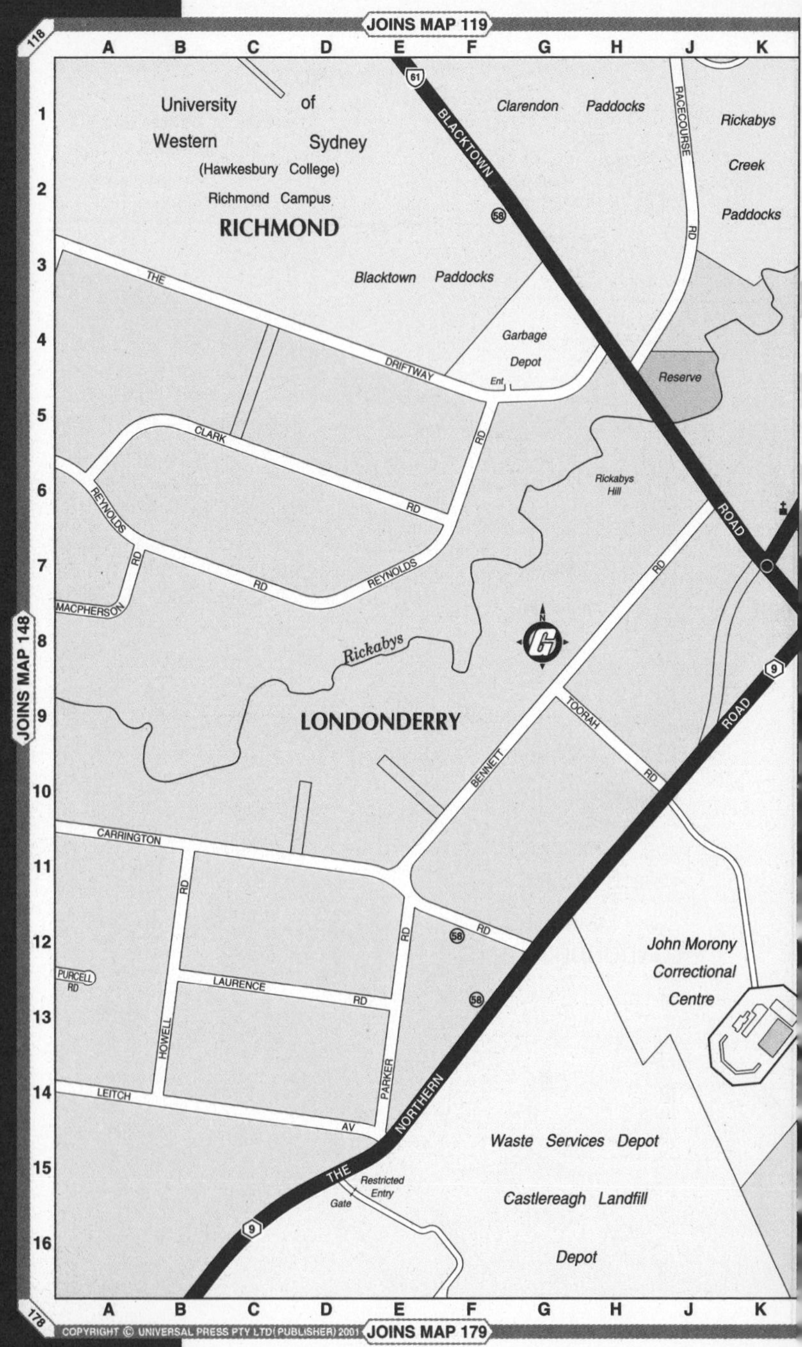
JOINS MAP 119
118
A B C D E F G H J K
1 2 3 4 5 6 7 8 9 10 11 12 13 14 15 16
University of Western Sydney
(Hawkesbury College)
Richmond Campus
RICHMOND
61
BLACKTOWN
Clarendon Paddocks
RACECOURSE RD
Rickabys Creek Paddocks
58
THE DRIFTWAY
Blacktown Paddocks
Garbage Depot
Ent
Reserve
CLARK RD
RD
Rickabys Hill
ROAD
REYNOLDS RD
REYNOLDS
RD
MACPHERSON
Rickabys
LONDONDERRY
BENNETT RD
TOORAH RD
9
ROAD
CARRINGTON
RD
RD
RD
PURCELL RD
LAURENCE RD
John Morony Correctional Centre
HOWELL
PARKER
LEITCH AV
THE NORTHERN
Restricted Entry
Gate
Waste Services Depot
Castlereagh Landfill
Depot
JOINS MAP 148
178
JOINS MAP 179

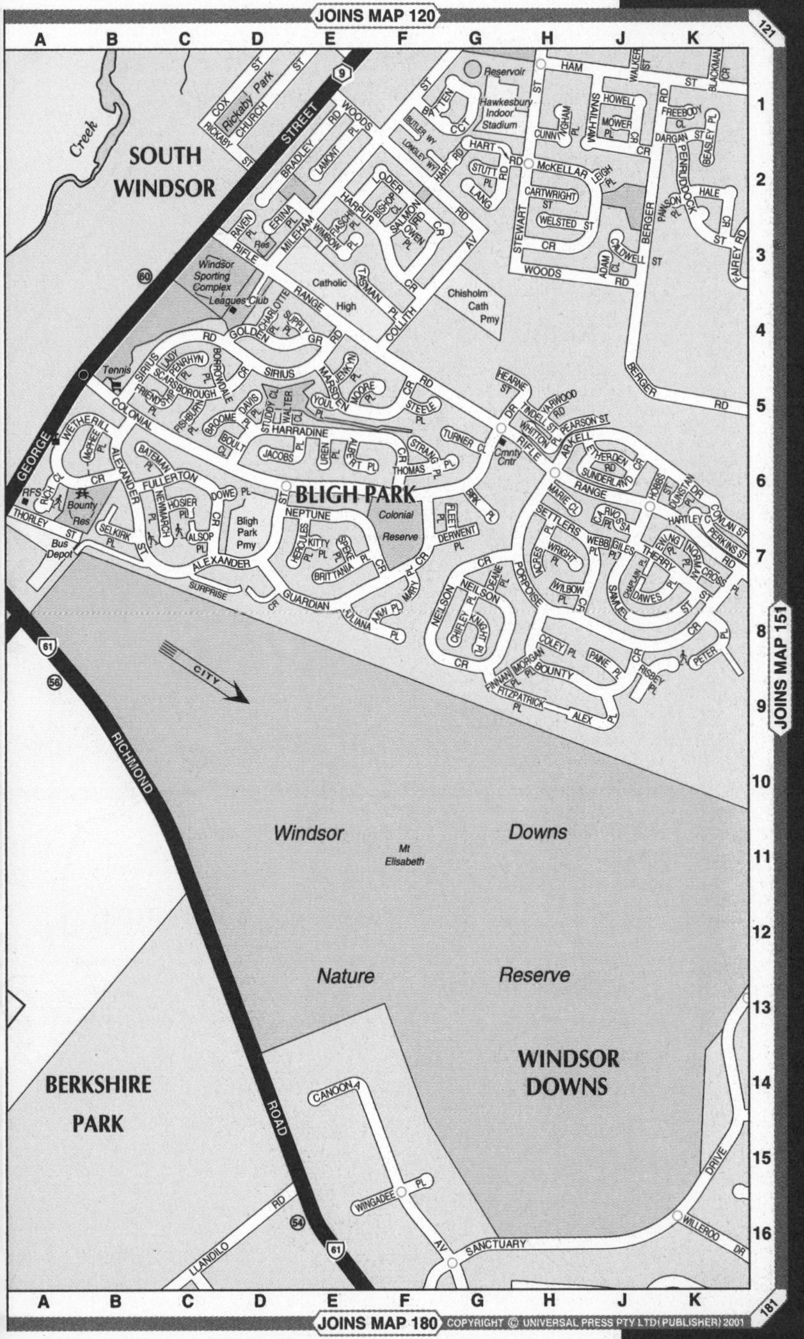
JOINS MAP 120
JOINS MAP 151
JOINS MAP 180
121
181
A B C D E F G H J K
1 2 3 4 5 6 7 8 9 10 11 12 13 14 15 16
SOUTH WINDSOR
BLIGH PARK
WINDSOR DOWNS
BERKSHIRE PARK
Windsor Downs Nature Reserve
Mt Elisabeth
Creek
GEORGE STREET
RICHMOND ROAD
CITY
Reservoir
Hawkesbury Indoor Stadium
Windsor Sporting Complex
Leagues Club
Catholic High
Chisholm Cath Pmy
Bligh Park Pmy
Colonial Reserve
Cmnty Cntr
Tennis
RFS
Bounty Res
Bus Depot
Res
RICKABY
COX ST
Rickaby Park
CHURCH ST
WOODS RD
BRADLEY
LAMONT PL
BUTLER WY
LONGLEY WY
BATTEN CCT
HART RD
STUTT PL
LANG
HAM
STEWART ST
CUNNINGHAM
SNAILHAM
HOWELL
MOWER PL
McKELLAR
LEIGH PL
CARTWRIGHT
WELSTED ST
CR
WOODS
ADAM CL
CALDWELL ST
BERGER RD
WALKER ST
FREEBODY CL
DARGAN ST
PENRUDDOCK
BEASLEY PL
PAWSON PL
HALE CR
BLACKMAN CR
FAIREY RD
RAVEN PL
ERINA PL
MILEHAM
WIMBOW
FIASCHI
HARPUR
LODER
BISHOP CL
SALMON
OWEN PL
RD
AV
RIFLE RANGE
TASMAN PL
COLLITH
CHARLOTTE
SUPPLY
GOLDEN GR
SIRIUS
LADY PENRHYN
BORROWDALE
SCARSBOROUGH
FRIENDSHIP
FISHBURN
MARSDEN
JENKYN
MOORE PL
YOUL PL
STUDDY CL
WALTER CL
DAVIS
BROOME
BOULT CL
HARRADINE
JACOBS
UREN
ALBERT PL
STEELE
HEARNE ST
TINDELL ST
YARWOOD RD
WHITTON
PEARSON ST
ARKELL
ETHERDEN RD
SUNDERLAND CR
TURNER CL
STRANG PL
THOMAS
COLONIAL
WETHERILL
McPHEE
ALEXANDER
RICH CL
FULLERTON
BATEMAN
HOSIER
NEWMARCH
DOWE PL
ALSOP
THORLEY ST
SELKIRK PL
NEPTUNE
HERCULES
KITTY
SPEKE
BRITTANIA
FLEET
DERWENT PL
BIRK
MARIE CL
SETTLERS
RANGE
HOBBS
DUNSTAN DR
HARTLEY
CONLAN ST
PERKINS ST
NORMAN
CROSS
WEBB PL
GILES PL
THERRY
WRIGHT PL
ACRES
PORPOISE
WILBOW
CHAPLAIN
DAWES
SAMUEL
DEANE
NEILSON
CHIFLEY
KNIGHT
COLEY PL
PAINE PL
MORGAN PL
FINNAN PL
BOUNTY
FITZPATRICK PL
ALEX
RISBEY PL
PETER
SURPRISE CR
GUARDIAN
JULIANA
MARY
CANOONA
WINGADEE PL
LLANDILO RD
SANCTUARY
WILLEROO DR
DRIVE
9
60
61
56
54

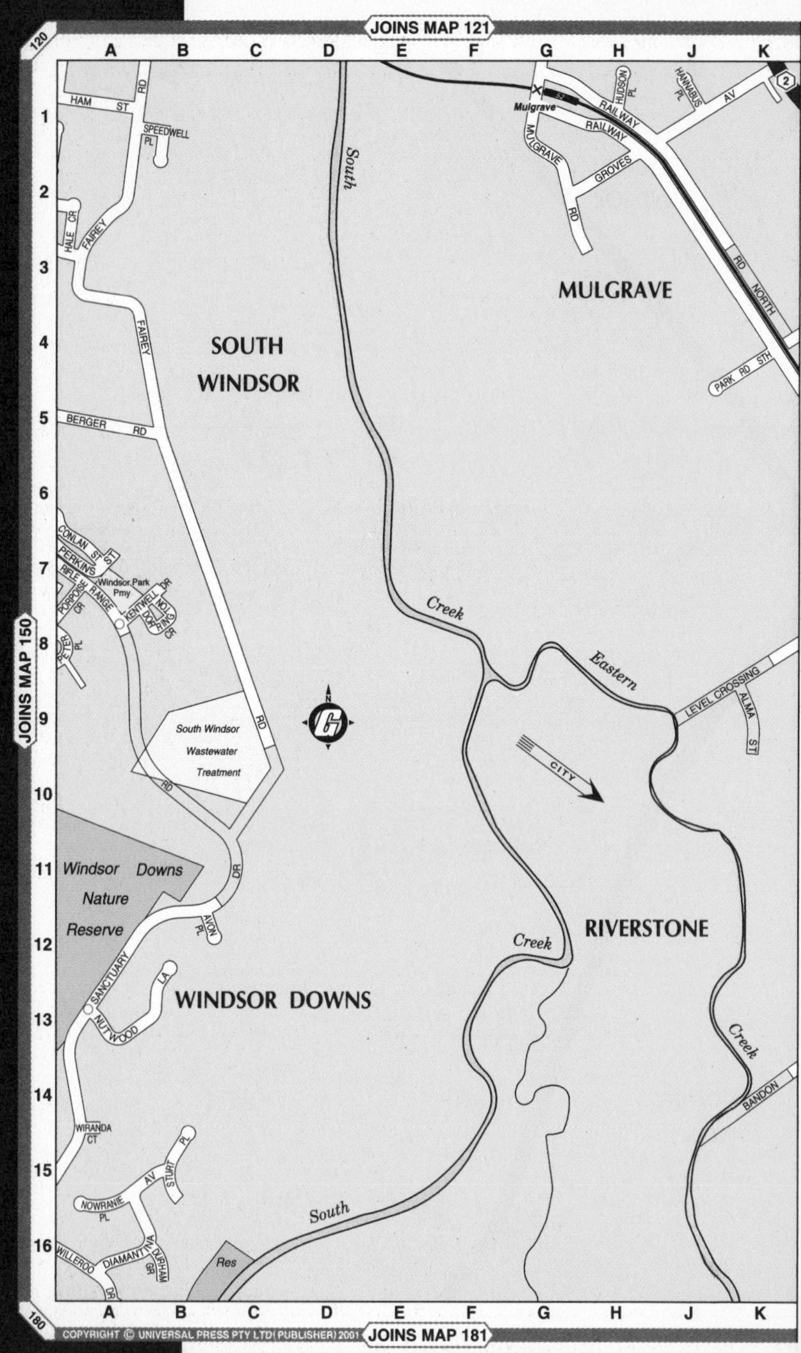
JOINS MAP 121
120
A B C D E F G H J K
1 2 3 4 5 6 7 8 9 10 11 12 13 14 15 16
HAM ST
RD
SPEEDWELL PL
HALE CR
FAIREY
Mulgrave
HUDSON PL
HANNABUS PL
AV
RAILWAY
RAILWAY
MULGRAVE
GROVES
RD
2
South
MULGRAVE
RD
NORTH
SOUTH WINDSOR
FAIREY
PARK RD STH
BERGER RD
CONLAN ST
PERKINS ST
RIFLE RANGE
Windsor Park Pmy
KENTWELL DR
NOLTING CR
DORRING
PORPOISE CR
PETER PL
Creek
Eastern
LEVEL CROSSING
ALMA ST
South Windsor Wastewater Treatment
RD
CITY
RD
DR
Windsor Downs Nature Reserve
AVON PL
RIVERSTONE
Creek
SANCTUARY
LA
WINDSOR DOWNS
NUTWOOD
Creek
BANDON
WIRANDA CT
STURT PL
AV
NOWRANIE PL
South
WILLEROO
DIAMANTINA GR
DURHAM
DR
Res
JOINS MAP 150
180
JOINS MAP 181

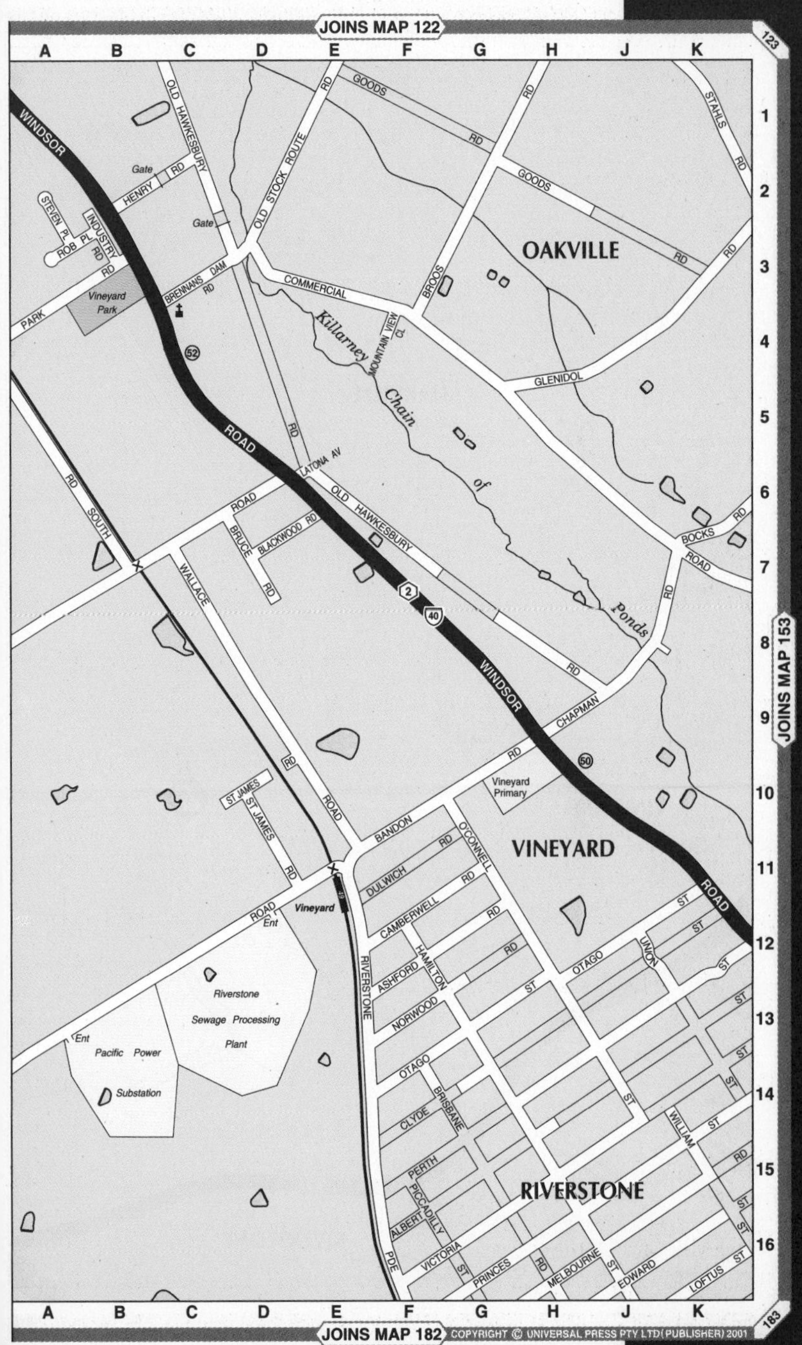
JOINS MAP 122
JOINS MAP 153
JOINS MAP 182
OAKVILLE
VINEYARD
RIVERSTONE
WINDSOR ROAD
OLD HAWKESBURY RD
OLD STOCK ROUTE RD
GOODS RD
STAHLS RD
HENRY RD
Gate
STEVEN PL
ROB PL
INDUSTRY RD
PARK RD
Vineyard Park
BRENNANS DAM RD
COMMERCIAL RD
BROOS RD
MOUNTAIN VIEW CL
Killarney Chain of Ponds
GLENIDOL RD
SOUTH RD
LATONA AV
ROAD
BRUCE RD
BLACKWOOD RD
WALLACE RD
BOCKS RD
CHAPMAN RD
Vineyard Primary
ST JAMES RD
BANDON RD
O'CONNELL ST
DULWICH RD
CAMBERWELL RD
Vineyard
Ent
Riverstone Sewage Processing Plant
Pacific Power Substation
RIVERSTONE PDE
ASHFORD
HAMILTON
NORWOOD
OTAGO ST
UNION ST
BRISBANE
CLYDE
PERTH
PICCADILLY
ALBERT
VICTORIA
PRINCES
MELBOURNE ST
EDWARD
WILLIAM ST
LOFTUS ST
COPYRIGHT © UNIVERSAL PRESS PTY LTD (PUBLISHER) 2001

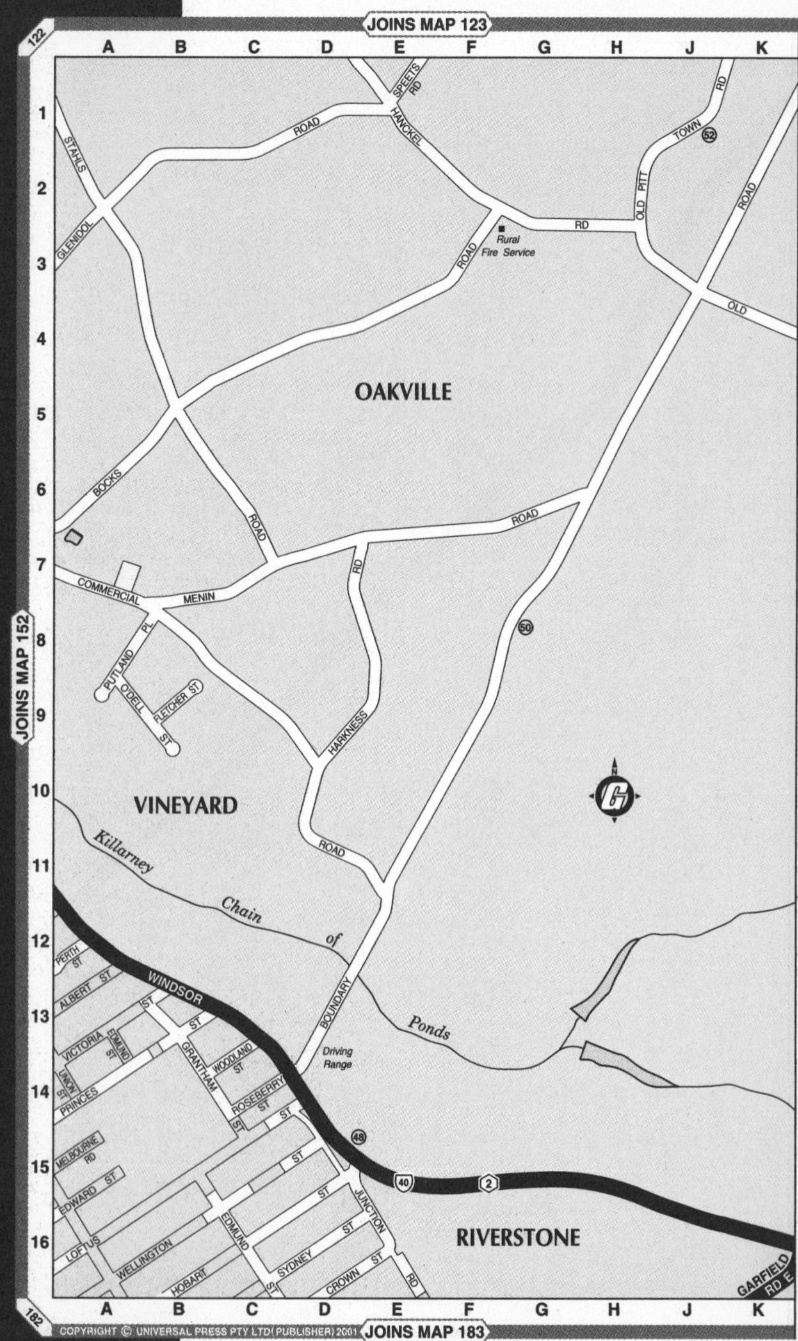
JOINS MAP 123
JOINS MAP 152
JOINS MAP 183
122
182
OAKVILLE
VINEYARD
RIVERSTONE
Rural Fire Service
Killarney Chain of Ponds
Driving Range
SPEETS RD
HANCKEL ROAD
OLD PITT TOWN RD
RD
ROAD
OLD
STAHLS
GLENIDOL
BOCKS
ROAD
RD
COMMERCIAL
MENIN
PUTLAND PL
O'DELL ST
FLETCHER ST
HARKNESS ROAD
BOUNDARY
WINDSOR
PERTH ST
ALBERT ST
VICTORIA
EDMUND ST
UNION ST
PRINCES
GRANTHAM ST
WOODLAND ST
ROSEBERRY ST
MELBOURNE RD
EDWARD ST
LOFTUS
WELLINGTON
HOBART
EDMUND
SYDNEY
CROWN ST
JUNCTION RD
GARFIELD RD E
52
50
48
40
2

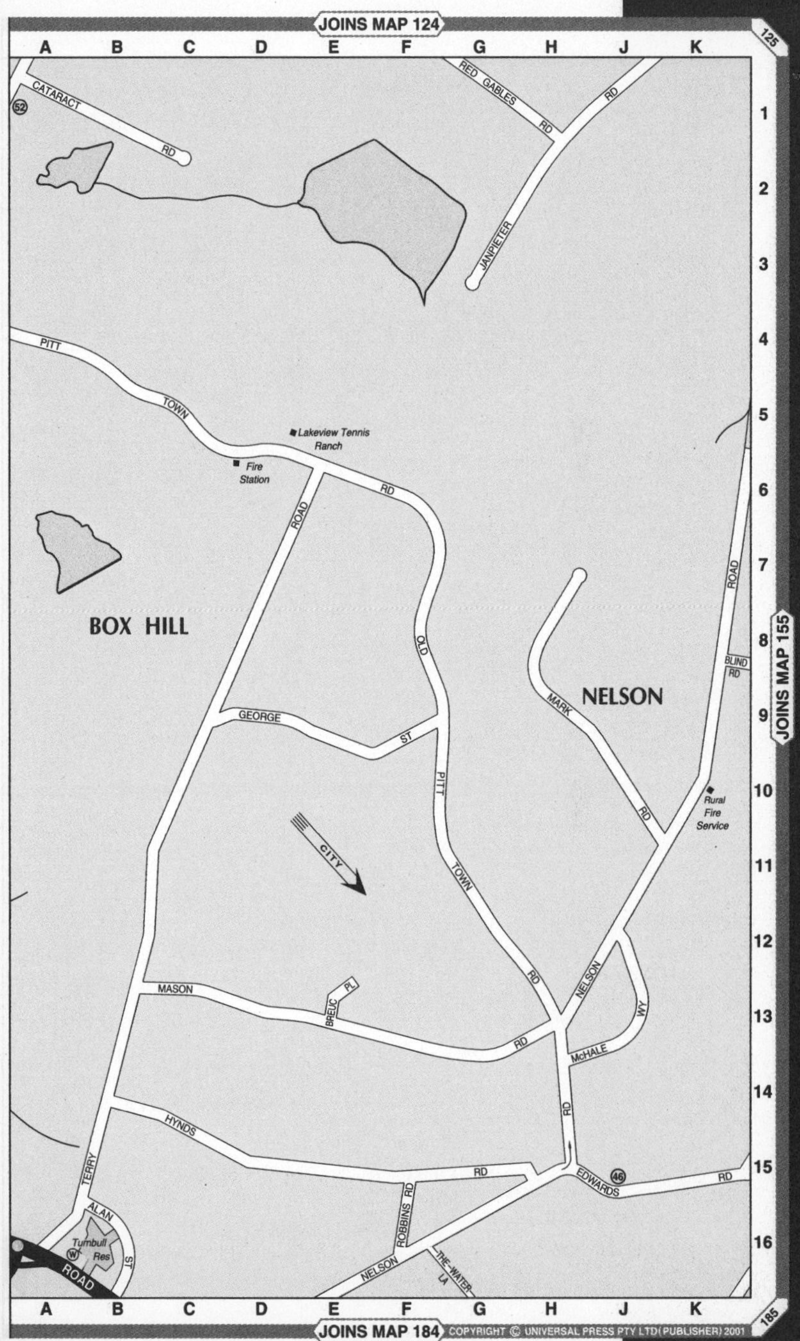
JOINS MAP 124
125
A B C D E F G H J K
1 2 3 4 5 6 7 8 9 10 11 12 13 14 15 16
CATARACT RD
52
RED GABLES RD
JANPIETER RD
PITT TOWN RD
Lakeview Tennis Ranch
Fire Station
ROAD
BOX HILL
OLD PITT TOWN RD
GEORGE ST
CITY
NELSON
MARK RD
ROAD
BLIND RD
Rural Fire Service
JOINS MAP 155
NELSON RD
WY
McHALE
MASON RD
BREUC PL
HYNDS RD
EDWARDS RD
46
TERRY
ALAN ST
Turnbull Res
ROAD
ROBBINS RD
NELSON
THE WATER LA
JOINS MAP 184
185

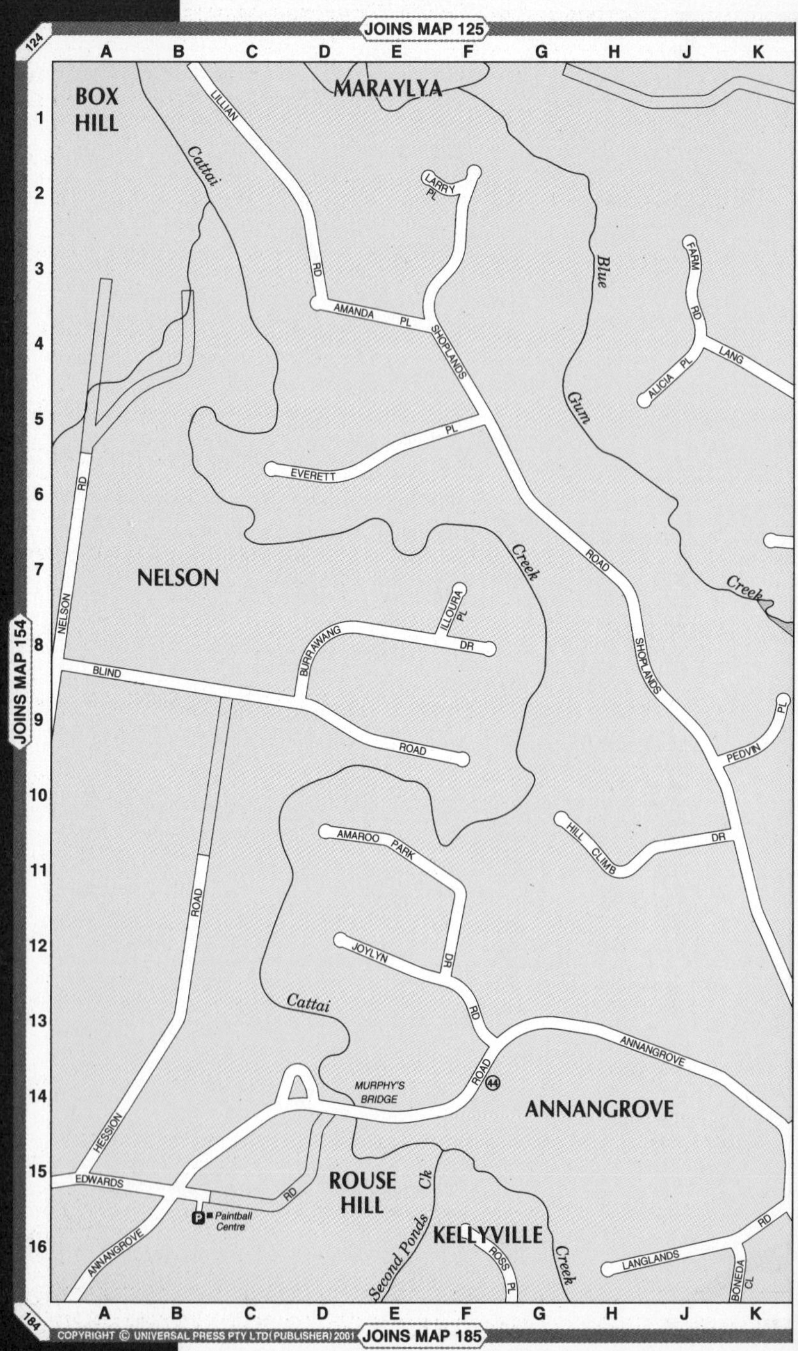
JOINS MAP 125
JOINS MAP 154
JOINS MAP 185
124
184
A B C D E F G H J K
1 2 3 4 5 6 7 8 9 10 11 12 13 14 15 16
BOX HILL
MARAYLYA
NELSON
ANNANGROVE
ROUSE HILL
KELLYVILLE
LILLIAN RD
AMANDA PL
LARRY PL
SHOPLANDS ROAD
EVERETT PL
NELSON RD
BLIND ROAD
BURRAWANG DR
ILLOURA PL
FARM RD
ALICIA PL
LANG
PEDVIN PL
HILL CLIMB DR
AMAROO PARK DR
JOYLYN RD
ANNANGROVE ROAD
HESSION ROAD
EDWARDS RD
LANGLANDS RD
BONEDA CL
ROSS PL
MURPHY'S BRIDGE
Paintball Centre
44
Cattai
Creek
Blue Gum Creek
Second Ponds Ck
Creek

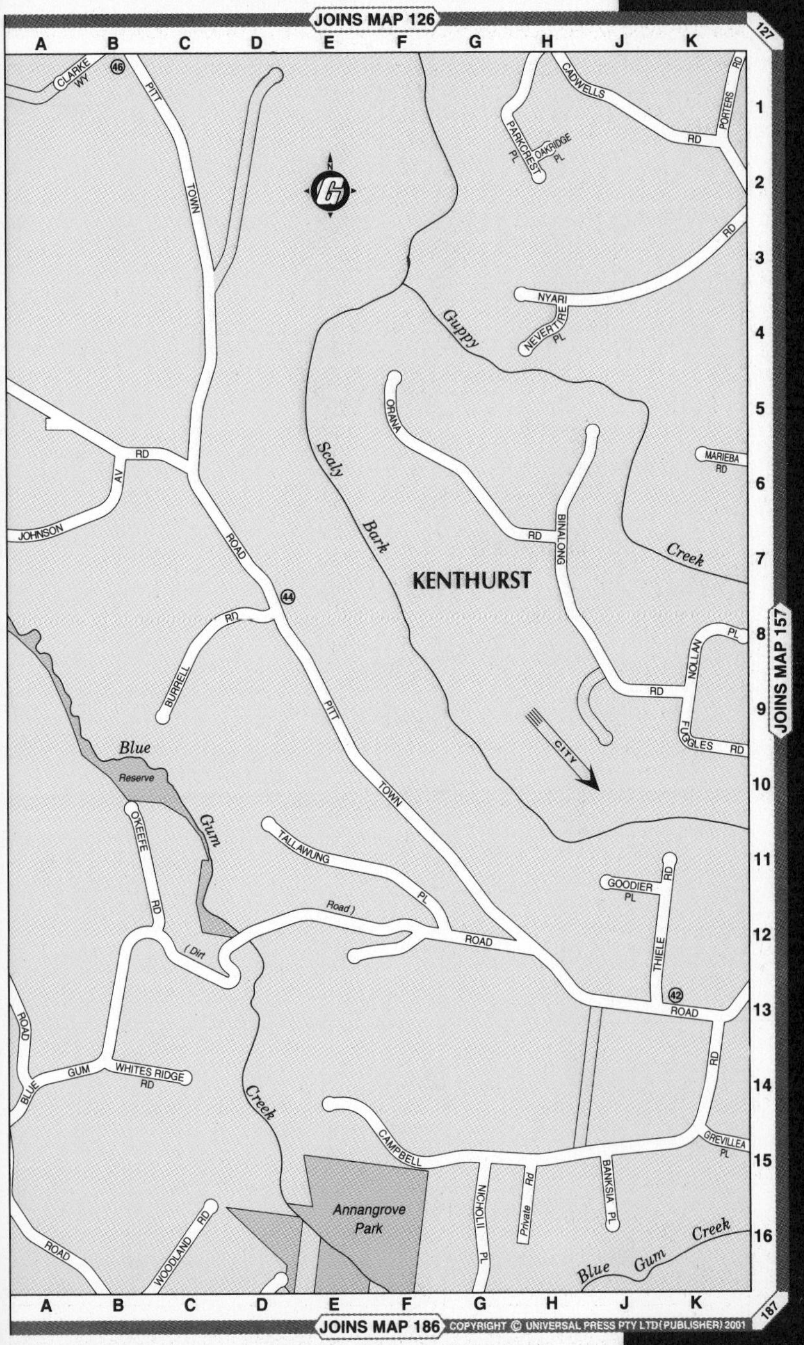
JOINS MAP 126
127
A B C D E F G H J K
1 2 3 4 5 6 7 8 9 10 11 12 13 14 15 16
CLARKE WY
PITT
TOWN
ROAD
PITT
TOWN
ROAD
CADWELLS RD
PORTERS RD
PARKCREST PL
OAKRIDGE PL
RD
NYARI
NEVERTYRE PL
Guppy
Scaly Bark
ORANA RD
BINALONG RD
Creek
MARIEBA RD
RD
AV
JOHNSON
KENTHURST
BURRELL RD
NOLLAN PL
FUGGLES RD
RD
CITY
Blue Reserve Gum
OKEEFE RD
TALLAWUNG PL
Road)
(Dirt
ROAD
GOODIER PL
THIELE RD
ROAD
RD
ROAD
BLUE GUM
WHITES RIDGE RD
Creek
CAMPBELL
GREVILLEA PL
NICHOLII PL
Private Rd
BANKSIA PL
Annangrove Park
WOODLAND RD
ROAD
Blue Gum Creek
JOINS MAP 157
A B C D E F G H J K
187

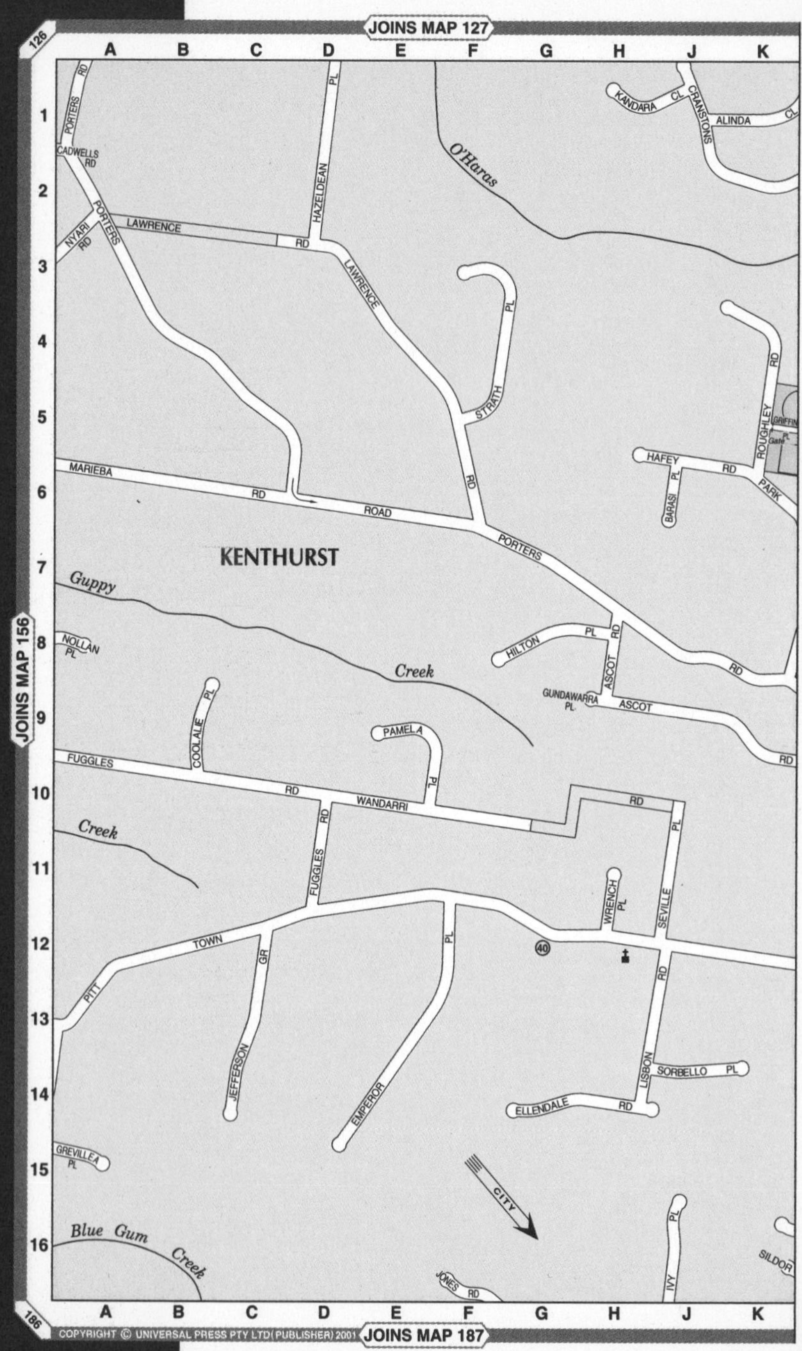
JOINS MAP 127
JOINS MAP 156
JOINS MAP 187
126
186
KENTHURST
PORTERS RD
CADWELLS RD
NYARI RD
LAWRENCE RD
HAZELDEAN PL
O'Haras
KANDARA CL
CRANSTONS
ALINDA CL
STRATH PL
ROUGHLEY RD
GRIFFIN PL
Gate
HAFEY RD
BARASI PL
PARK
MARIEBA RD
ROAD
PORTERS RD
Guppy Creek
NOLLAN PL
HILTON PL
ASCOT RD
GUNDAWARRA PL
ASCOT RD
COOLALIE PL
PAMELA PL
FUGGLES RD
WANDARRI RD
FUGGLES RD
Creek
WRENCH PL
SEVILLE PL
TOWN
PITT
GR
JEFFERSON
PL
EMPEROR
40
RD
LISBON
SORBELLO PL
ELLENDALE RD
GREVILLEA PL
CITY
Blue Gum Creek
JONES RD
IVY PL
SILDOR

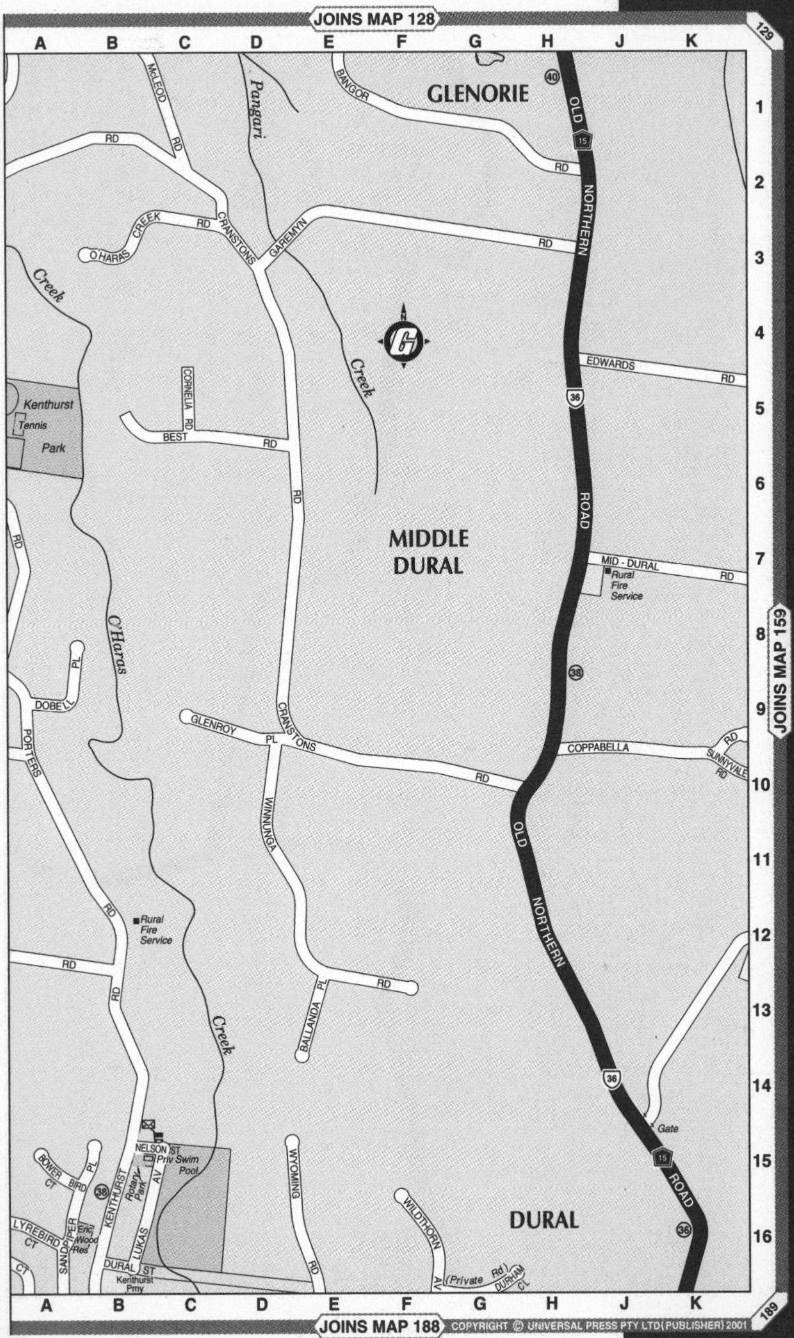
JOINS MAP 128
JOINS MAP 159
JOINS MAP 188
129
189
GLENORIE
MIDDLE DURAL
DURAL
OLD NORTHERN ROAD
BANGOR RD
McLEOD RD
Pangari Creek
CRANSTONS RD
GAREMYN RD
O'HARAS CREEK RD
Creek
EDWARDS RD
CORNELIA RD
BEST RD
Kenthurst Tennis Park
MID - DURAL RD
Rural Fire Service
O'Haras Creek
DOBELL PL
PORTERS RD
GLENROY PL
COPPABELLA RD
SUNNYVALE RD
WINNUNGA RD
BALLANDA PL
Gate
NELSON ST
Priv Swim Pool
Rotary Park
BOWER BIRD CT
KENTHURST RD
LUKAS AV
Eric Wood Res
LYREBIRD CT
SANDPIPER
DURAL ST
Kenthurst Pmy
WYOMING RD
WILDTHORN AV
(Private Rd)
DURHAM CL

JOINS MAP 129

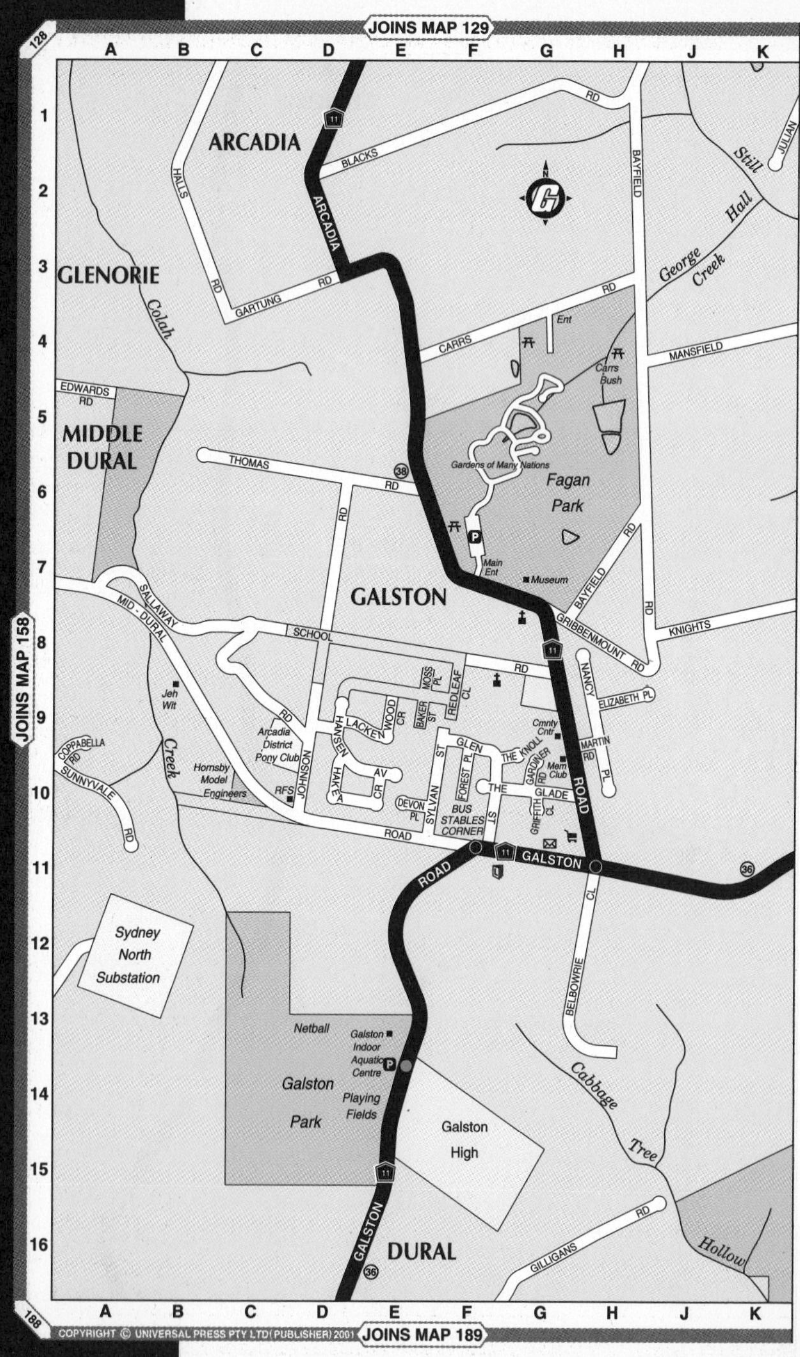

JOINS MAP 189

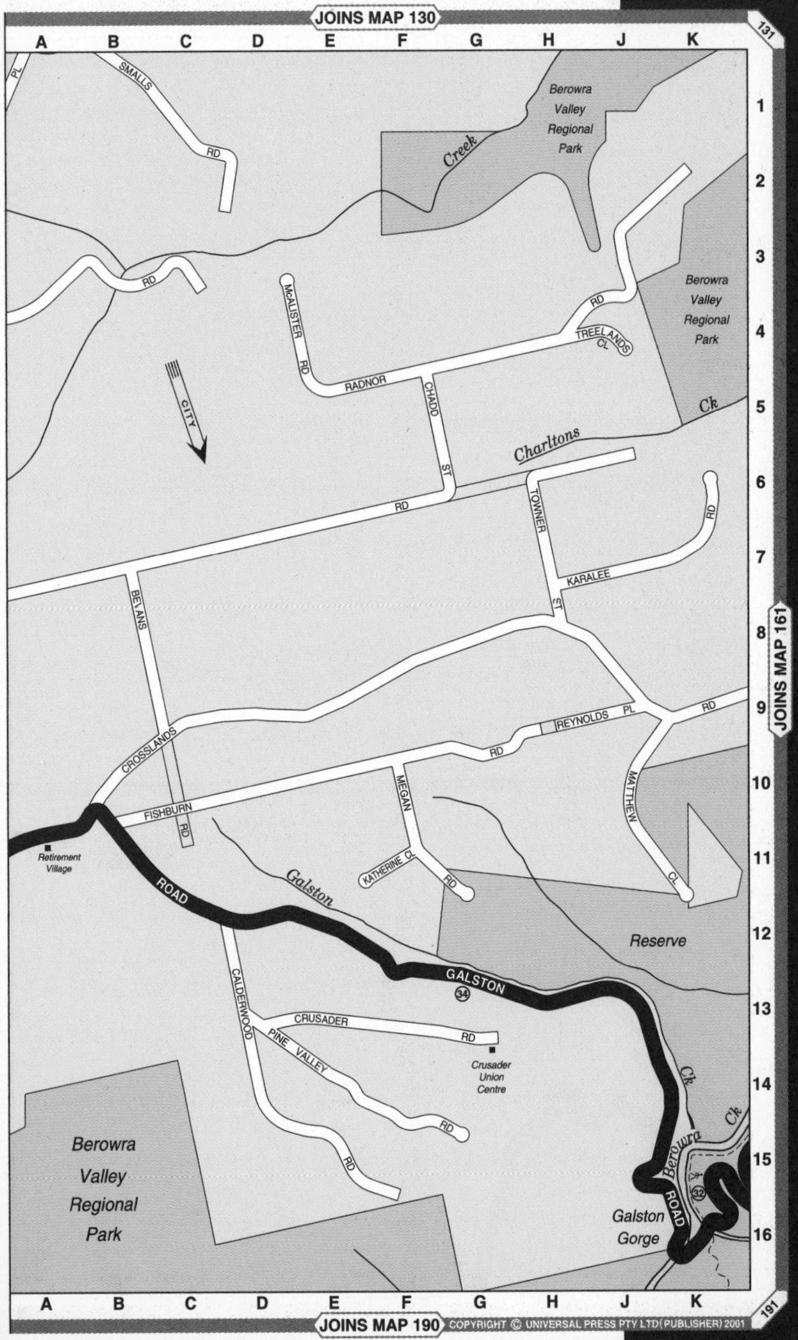
JOINS MAP 130
131
A
B
C
D
E
F
G
H
J
K
1
2
3
4
5
6
7
8
9
10
11
12
13
14
15
16
PL
SMALLS
RD
Berowra
Valley
Regional
Park
Creek
RD
McALISTER
RD
RADNOR
CHADD
ST
RD
TREELANDS
CL
Berowra
Valley
Regional
Park
Ck
CITY
Charltons
RD
TOWNIER
ST
RD
KARALEE
BELANS
JOINS MAP 161
CROSSLANDS
REYNOLDS
PL
RD
RD
MEGAN
MATTHEW
FISHBURN
RD
Retirement
Village
KATHERINE CL
RD
CL
Galston
ROAD
Reserve
GALSTON
34
CALDERWOOD
CRUSADER
RD
PINE
VALLEY
Crusader
Union
Centre
Ck
Ck
RD
Berowra
Valley
Regional
Park
RD
Berowra
ROAD
32
Galston
Gorge
A
B
C
D
E
F
G
H
J
K
JOINS MAP 190
191

MAP 161

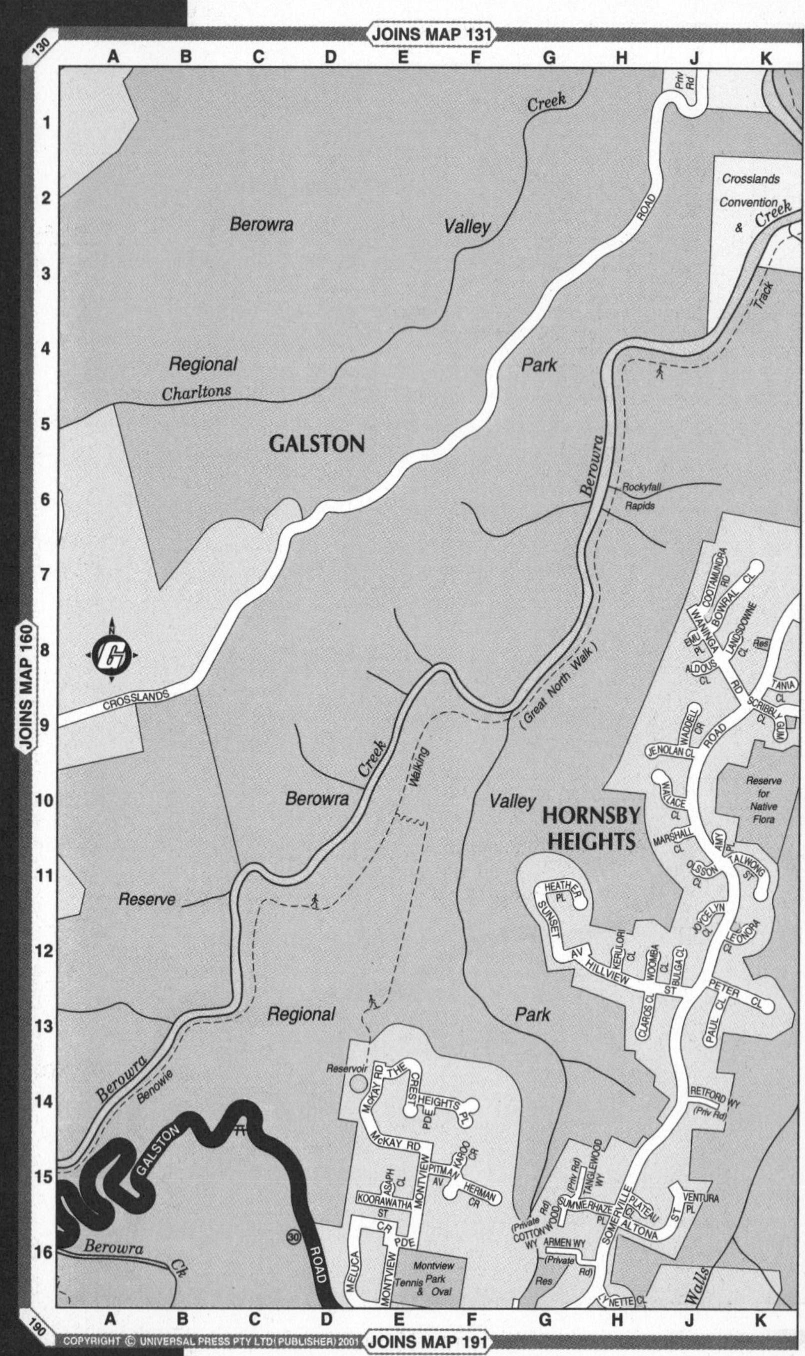

JOINS MAP 131
JOINS MAP 160
JOINS MAP 191
130
190
GALSTON
HORNSBY HEIGHTS
Berowra Valley Regional Park
Berowra Valley Regional Park
Charltons
Creek
Berowra Creek
Crosslands Convention
Rockyfall Rapids
Great North Walk
Walking
Track
Reserve for Native Flora
CROSSLANDS ROAD
GALSTON ROAD
Montview Park Tennis & Oval
Reservoir
Berowra Ck
Benowie
Walls
Res

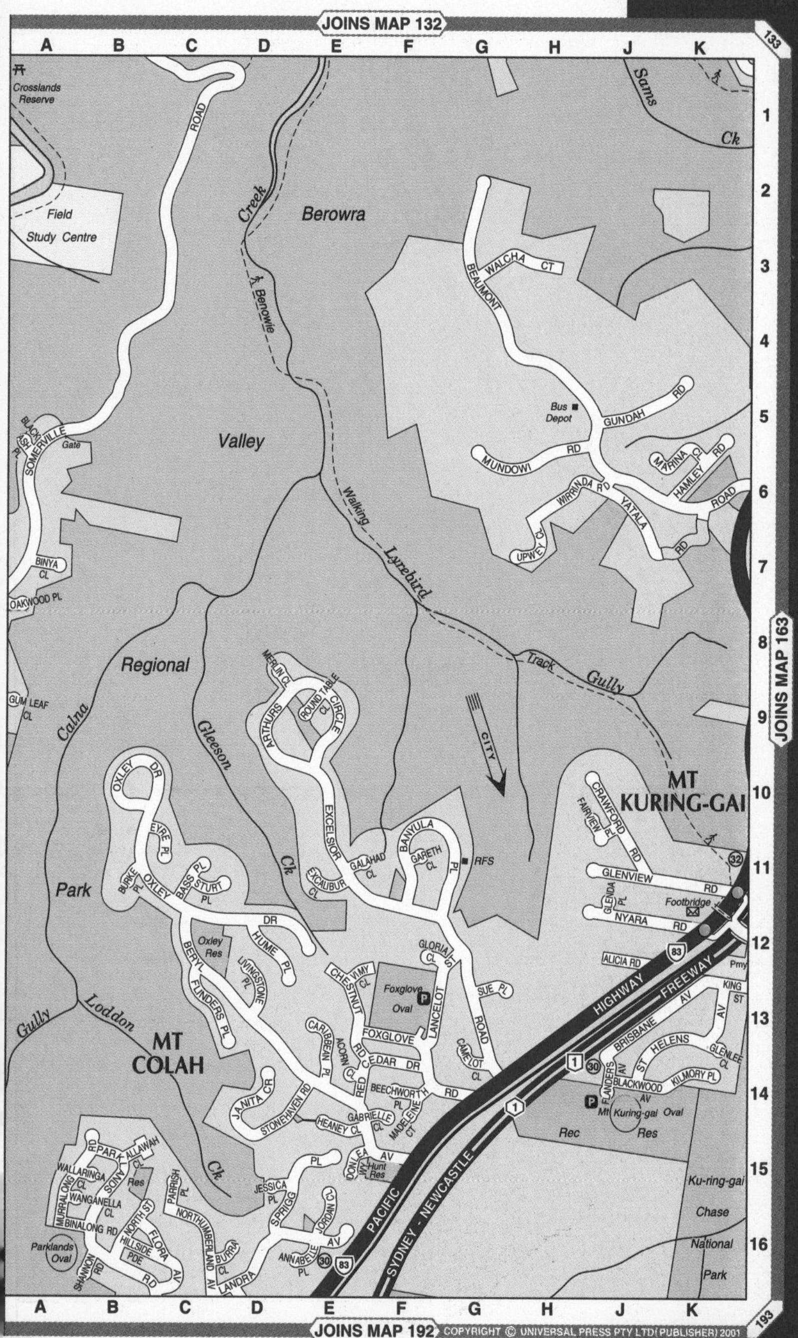
JOINS MAP 132
JOINS MAP 163
JOINS MAP 192
Berowra
Valley
Regional
Park
Field Study Centre
Crosslands Reserve
MT KURING-GAI
MT COLAH
Ku-ring-gai Chase National Park
Foxglove Oval
Oxley Res
Mt Kuring-gai Oval
Rec Res
Parklands Oval
Bus Depot
RFS
Footbridge
PACIFIC HIGHWAY
SYDNEY - NEWCASTLE FREEWAY
Lyrebird Gully
Calna Gully
Gleeson Ck
Loddon Gully
Sams Ck
Berowra Creek
Benowie Walking Track
CITY

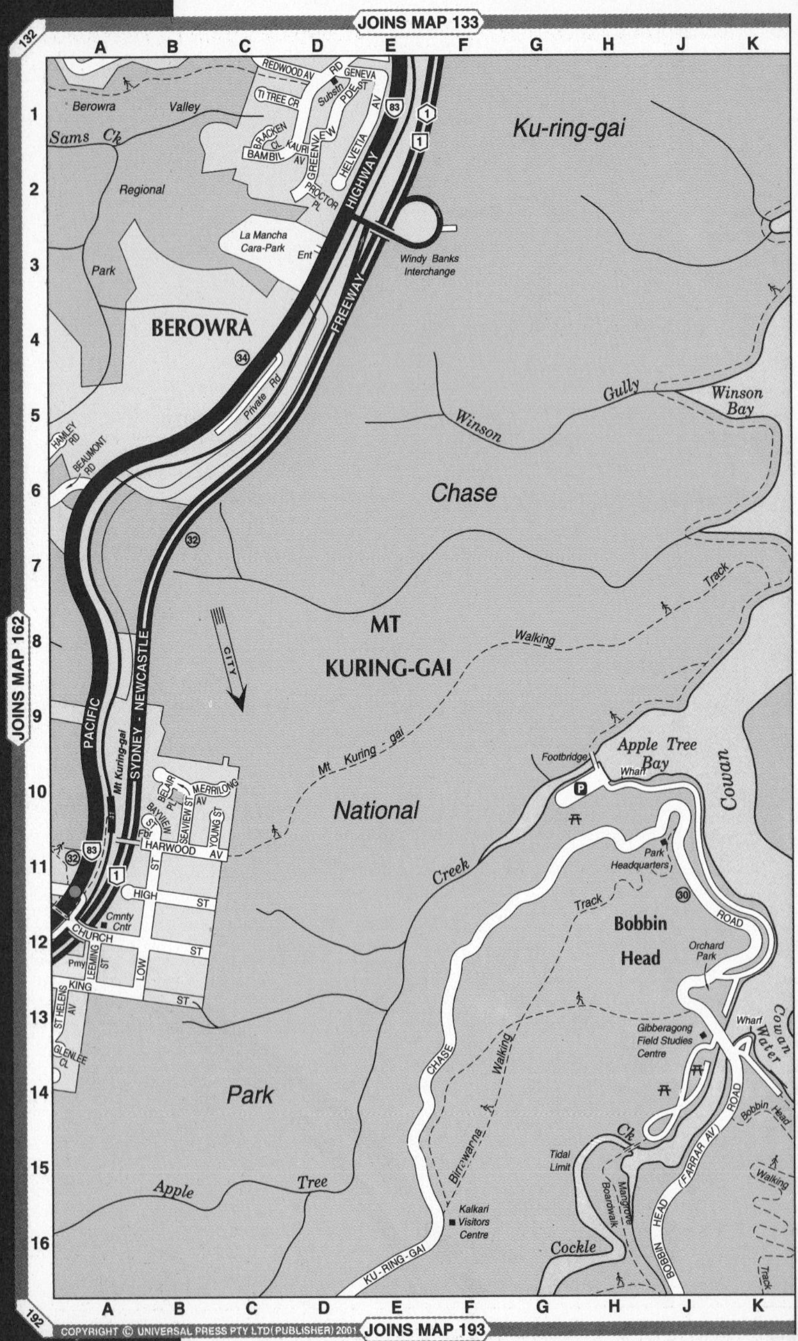
JOINS MAP 133
JOINS MAP 162
JOINS MAP 193
132
192
A B C D E F G H J K
1 2 3 4 5 6 7 8 9 10 11 12 13 14 15 16
Ku-ring-gai
Chase
National
Park
MT KURING-GAI
BEROWRA
Berowra Valley Regional Park
Sams Ck
REDWOOD AV
GENEVA
RD
TI TREE CR
Substn
PDE ST
BRACKEN CL
KAURI
GREENVIEW
BAMBIL AV
HELVETIA AV
PROCTOR PL
HIGHWAY
La Mancha Cara-Park
Ent
Windy Banks Interchange
FREEWAY
Private Rd
HAMLEY RD
BEAUMONT RD
PACIFIC
SYDNEY - NEWCASTLE
CITY
Mt Kuring-gai
BELAIR PL
MERRILONG AV
BAYVIEW ST
SEAVIEW ST
YOUNG ST
Fbr
HARWOOD AV
HIGH ST
Cmnty Cntr
CHURCH ST
Pmy
LEEMING ST
LOW
KING ST
ST HELENS AV
GLENLEE CL
Winson Gully
Winson Bay
Walking Track
Mt Kuring-gai
Footbridge
Apple Tree Bay
Wharf
Cowan
Creek
Park Headquarters
Track
Bobbin Head
ROAD
Orchard Park
Wharf
Cowan Water
Gibberagong Field Studies Centre
CHASE
Walking
Birrawarna
KU-RING-GAI
Kalkari Visitors Centre
Ck
Tidal Limit
Boardwalk
Mangrove
Cockle
BOBBIN HEAD
(FARRAR AV)
ROAD
Bobbin Head
Walking
Track
Apple
Tree
83
1
34
32
30

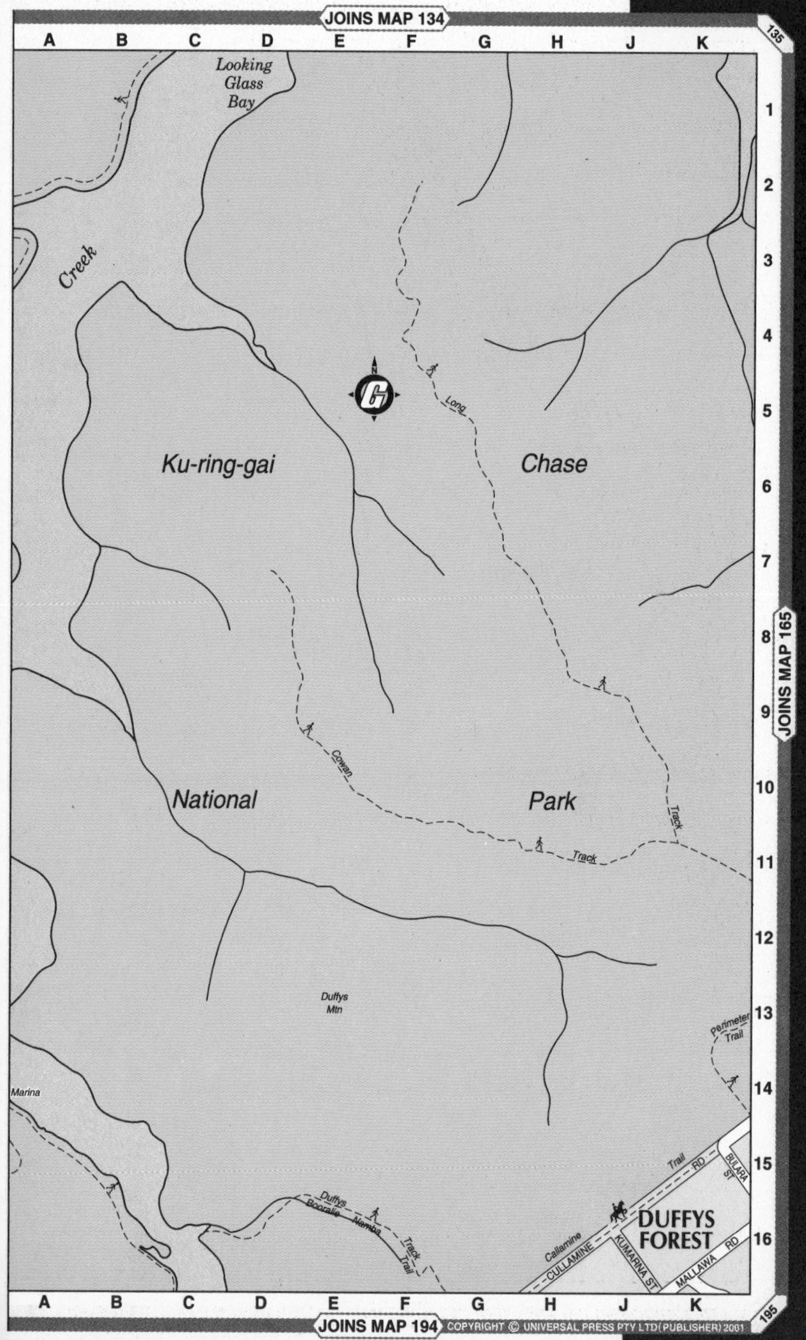
JOINS MAP 134
135
A
B
C
D
E
F
G
H
J
K
Looking Glass Bay
Creek
Ku-ring-gai
Chase
Long
National
Park
Cowan
Track
Track
Duffys Mtn
Perimeter Trail
Marina
Duffys
Booralie
Namba
Track
Trail
Trail
RD
BULARA ST
DUFFYS FOREST
Callamine
CULLAMINE
KUMARNA ST
MALLAWA
RD
1
2
3
4
5
6
7
8
9
10
11
12
13
14
15
16
JOINS MAP 165
JOINS MAP 194
195

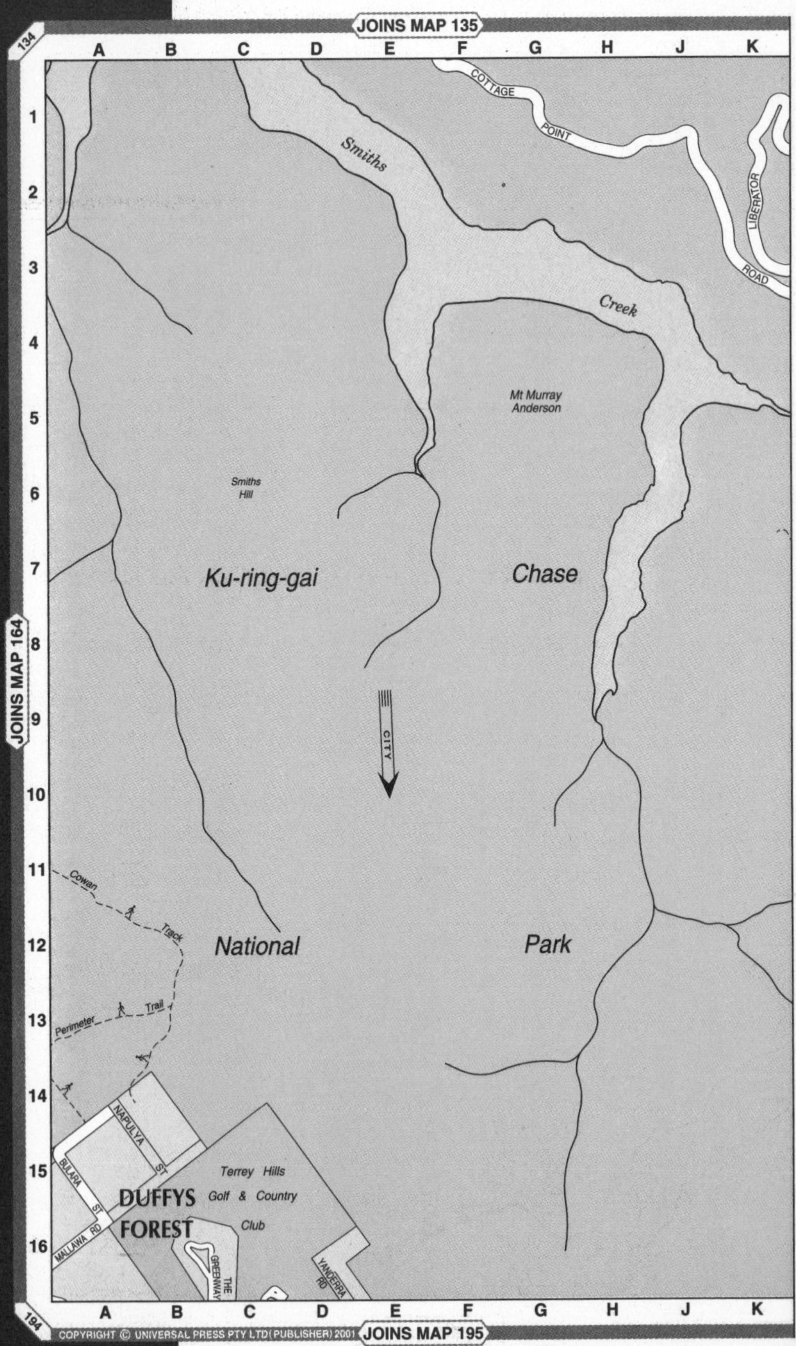
JOINS MAP 135
134
A B C D E F G H J K
1 2 3 4 5 6 7 8 9 10 11 12 13 14 15 16
COTTAGE
POINT
ROAD
LIBERATOR
Smiths
Creek
Mt Murray
Anderson
Smiths
Hill
Ku-ring-gai
Chase
National
Park
CITY
Cowan
Track
Perimeter
Trail
NAPULYA
ST
BULARA
ST
MALLAWA RD
DUFFYS
FOREST
Terrey Hills
Golf & Country
Club
THE
GREENWAY
YANDERRA
RD
JOINS MAP 164
194
JOINS MAP 195

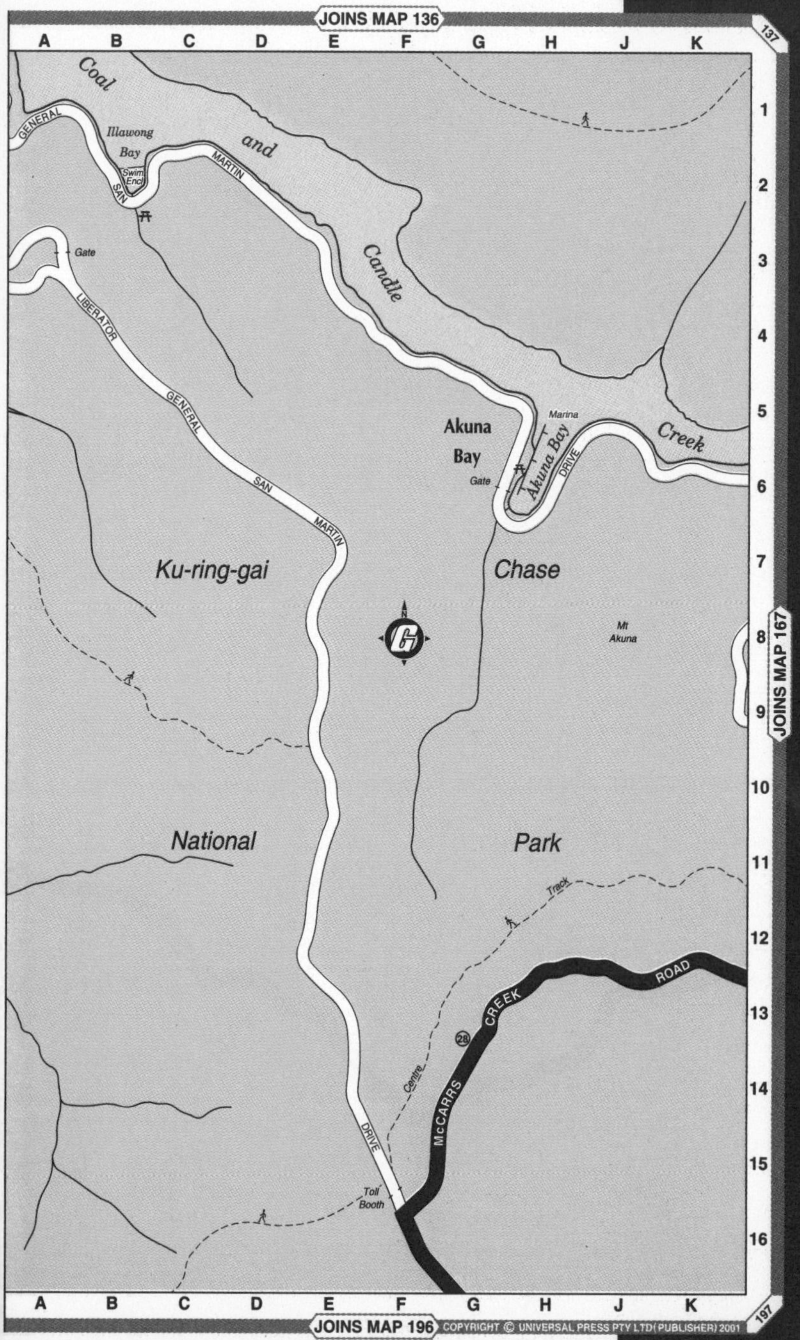
JOINS MAP 136
A B C D E F G H J K
137
Coal
and
Candle
Creek
Illawong Bay
Swim Encl
GENERAL SAN MARTIN
Gate
LIBERATOR GENERAL SAN MARTIN
Akuna Bay
Marina
Akuna Bay
DRIVE
Gate
Ku-ring-gai
Chase
National
Park
Mt Akuna
JOINS MAP 167
Track
Centre
Toll Booth
DRIVE
McCARRS CREEK ROAD
28
1 2 3 4 5 6 7 8 9 10 11 12 13 14 15 16
A B C D E F G H J K
JOINS MAP 196
197

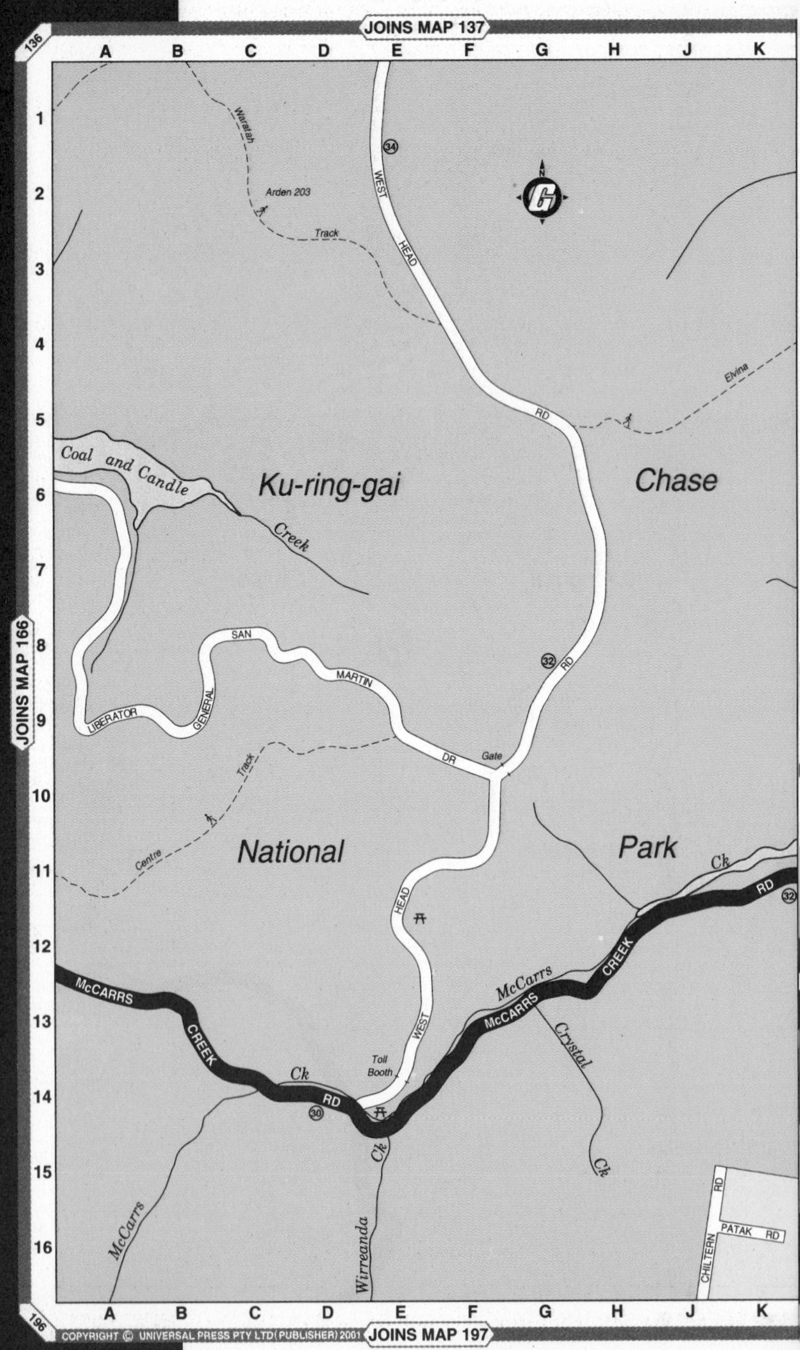
JOINS MAP 137
136
A
B
C
D
E
F
G
H
J
K
1
2
3
4
5
6
7
8
9
10
11
12
13
14
15
16
Waratah
Arden 203
Track
34
WEST
HEAD
RD
Elvina
Coal and Candle
Creek
Ku-ring-gai
Chase
JOINS MAP 166
SAN
MARTIN
GENERAL
LIBERATOR
DR
Gate
32
RD
Track
Centre
National
Park
Ck
RD
32
HEAD
McCARRS
CREEK
RD
McCarrs
McCARRS
CREEK
Crystal
WEST
Toll
Booth
Ck
RD
30
Ck
Ck
McCarrs
Wirreanda
RD
PATAK
RD
CHILTERN
196
JOINS MAP 197

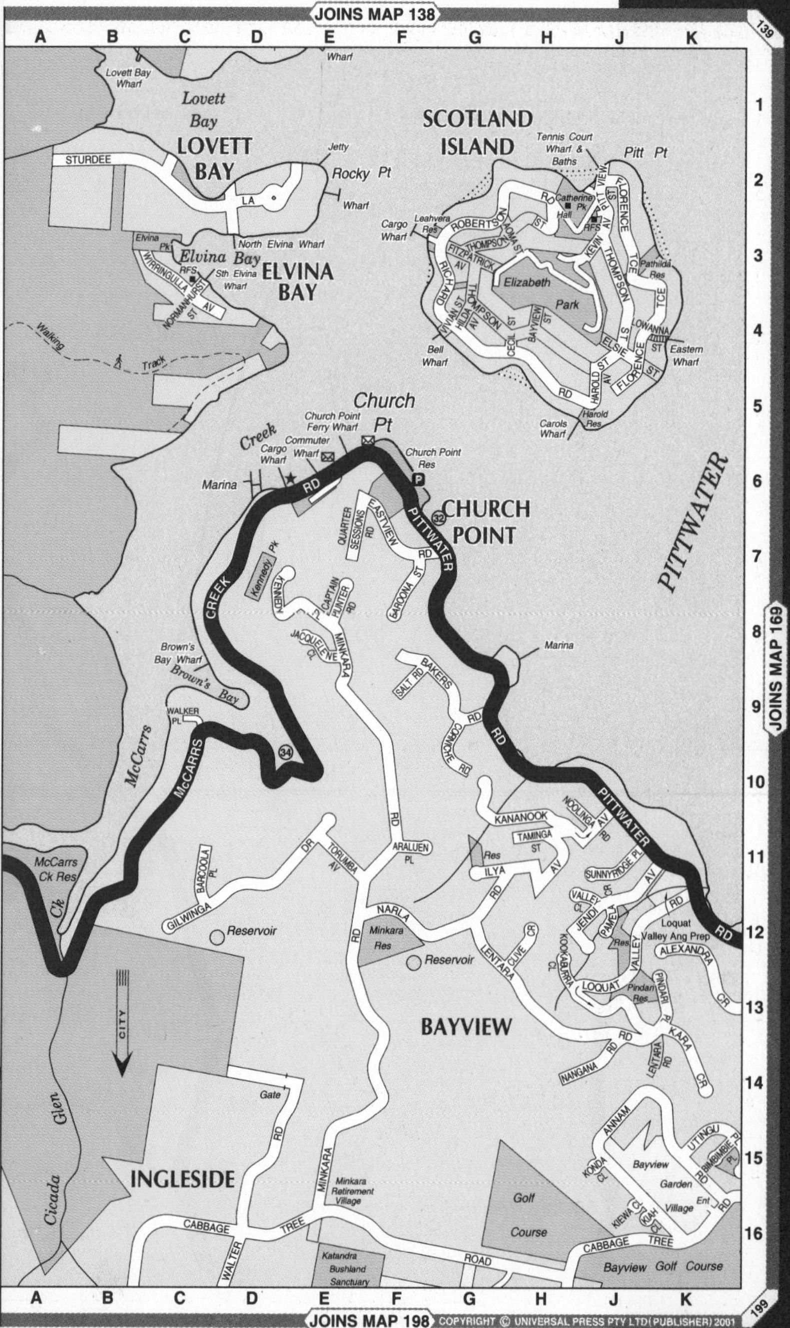
JOINS MAP 138
JOINS MAP 169
JOINS MAP 198
139
199
A B C D E F G H J K
1 2 3 4 5 6 7 8 9 10 11 12 13 14 15 16
Lovett Bay Wharf
Lovett Bay
LOVETT BAY
STURDEE
LA
Jetty
Rocky Pt
Wharf
North Elvina Wharf
Elvina Pk
Elvina Bay
ELVINA BAY
WIRRINGULLA
RFS
Sth Elvina Wharf
NORMANHURST
AV
ST
Walking Track
SCOTLAND ISLAND
Tennis Court Wharf & Baths
Pitt Pt
Cargo Wharf
Leahvera Res
ROBERTSON
THOMPSON
FITZPATRICK
RICHARD
Catherine Pk
Hall
RFS
PITT VIEW
FLORENCE
KEVIN
THOMPSON
TCE
Pathilda Res
Elizabeth Park
VIVIAN ST
HILDA
JOHN
CECIL ST
BAYVIEW ST
LOWANNA
ELSIE
Eastern Wharf
Bell Wharf
HAROLD ST
RD
Harold Res
Carols Wharf
Church Pt
Church Point Ferry Wharf
Creek
Cargo Wharf
Commuter Wharf
Church Point Res
Marina
RD
CHURCH POINT
QUARTER SESSIONS RD
EASTVIEW
PITTWATER
RD
GAROONA ST
Kennedy Pk
KENNEDY
CAPTAIN HUNTER RD
JACQUELENE CL
MINKARA
CREEK
PITTWATER
Marina
BAKERS
SALT RD
RD
CORNICHE RD
Brown's Bay Wharf
Brown's Bay
WALKER PL
McCarrs
McCARRS
RD
KANANOOK
NOOLINGA AV
TAMINGA ST
Res
ILYA
AV
RD
ARALUEN PL
TORUMBA AV
DR
BARCOOLA PL
GILWINGA
Reservoir
McCarrs Ck Res
Ck
NARLA
Minkara Res
Reservoir
LENTARA
OLIVE CR
SUNNYRIDGE PL
VALLEY CL
JENDI CR
PAMELA
Res
Loquat Valley Ang Prep
ALEXANDRA CR
KOOKABURRA CL
LOQUAT
VALLEY
Pindari Res
PINDARI PL
KARA CR
BAYVIEW
NANGANA RD
LENTARA RD
CITY
Gate
RD
Glen
Cicada
INGLESIDE
MINKARA
Minkara Retirement Village
ANNAM
KONDA CL
Bayview Garden Village
UTINGU PL
BIMBIMBIE PL
KIEWA CL
KUAH CL
Ent
Golf Course
CABBAGE TREE
WALTER
ROAD
CABBAGE TREE
Bayview Golf Course
Katandra Bushland Sanctuary
PITTWATER

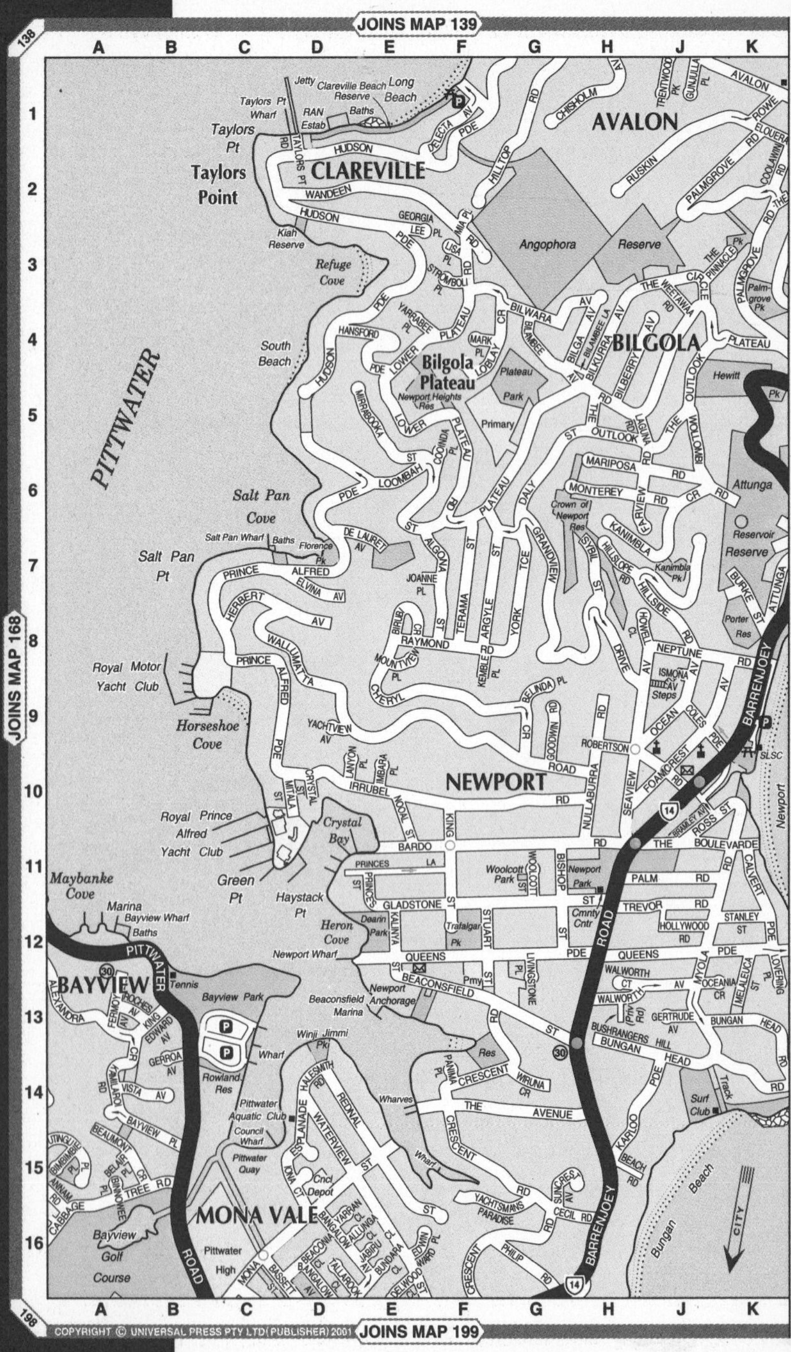
JOINS MAP 139
138
A B C D E F G H J K
1 2 3 4 5 6 7 8 9 10 11 12 13 14 15 16
JOINS MAP 168
PITTWATER
Taylors Point
Taylors Pt
Taylors Pt Wharf
Jetty
Clareville Beach Reserve
Long Beach
RAN Estab
Baths
CLAREVILLE
AVALON
BILGOLA
Bilgola Plateau
Newport Heights Res
Angophora
Reserve
Plateau Park
Primary
Kiah Reserve
Refuge Cove
South Beach
Salt Pan Cove
Salt Pan Wharf
Baths
Florence Pk
Salt Pan Pt
Royal Motor Yacht Club
Horseshoe Cove
Royal Prince Alfred Yacht Club
Green Pt
Crystal Bay
Haystack Pt
Heron Cove
Maybanke Cove
Marina
Bayview Wharf
Baths
Newport Wharf
NEWPORT
Crown of Newport Res
Attunga Reservoir Reserve
Kanimbla Pk
Porter Res
Hewitt Pk
Palmgrove Pk
Ismona Av Steps
SLSC
Woolcott Park
Newport Park
Cmnty Cntr
Dearin Park
Trafalgar Pk
Pmy
Newport Anchorage
Beaconsfield Marina
Res
BAYVIEW
Tennis
Bayview Park
Rowland Res
Winji Jimmi Pk
Wharf
Pittwater Aquatic Club
Council Wharf
Pittwater Quay
Cncl Depot
Wharves
Wharf
MONA VALE
Pittwater High
Bayview Golf Course
Surf Club
Bungan Beach
CITY
Newport
HUDSON PDE
TAYLORS PT RD
WANDEEN RD
DELECTA AV
HILLTOP RD
CHISHOLM RD
RUSKIN
PALMGROVE RD
AVALON PDE
ROWE
GEORGIA LEE PL
MIA PL
LISA PL
STROMBOLI PL
YARRABEE PL
HANSFORD
LOWER PLATEAU RD
BILWARA AV
BILAMBEE LA
BILGA AV
BILKURRA AV
BILBERRY AV
THE OUTLOOK
THE WEETAWAA
THE CIRCLE
PLATEAU RD
MIRRABOOKA
LOOMBAH ST
COOINDA PL
MARIPOSA RD
MONTEREY CR
FAIRVIEW RD
KANIMBLA
HILLSLOPE RD
HILLSIDE RD
GRANDVIEW
DALY ST
ALGONA ST
DE LAURET AV
PRINCE ALFRED PDE
ELVINA AV
HERBERT AV
WALLUMATTA
JOANNE PL
TERAMA ST
ARGYLE ST
YORK TCE
KEMBLE PL
RAYMOND RD
MOUNTVIEW PL
CHERYL CR
BELINDA PL
GOODWIN RD
ROBERTSON RD
NEPTUNE RD
OCEAN AV
COLES
YACHTVIEW AV
IRRUBEL RD
NULLABURRA RD
SEAVIEW
FOAMCREST
BARRENJOEY RD
KING ST
BARDO RD
THE BOULEVARDE
PRINCES LA
PALM RD
GLADSTONE ST
TREVOR RD
HOLLYWOOD RD
STANLEY ST
QUEENS PDE
BEACONSFIELD ST
LIVINGSTONE
WALWORTH AV
GERTRUDE AV
BUNGAN HEAD RD
BUSHRANGERS HILL
PANIMA PL
CRESCENT
WIRUNA CR
THE AVENUE
KARLOO PDE
BEACH RD
SUNCREST AV
CECIL RD
YACHTSMANS PARADISE
PHILIP RD
ALEXANDRA CR
GERROA AV
VISTA AV
BAYVIEW PL
BEAUMONT
TREE RD
CABBAGE
HALESMITH RD
WATERVIEW ST
REDNAL
ESPLANADE
BASSETT
BARRENJOEY
ROAD
PITTWATER ROAD
30
14
198
JOINS MAP 199

JOINS MAP 140

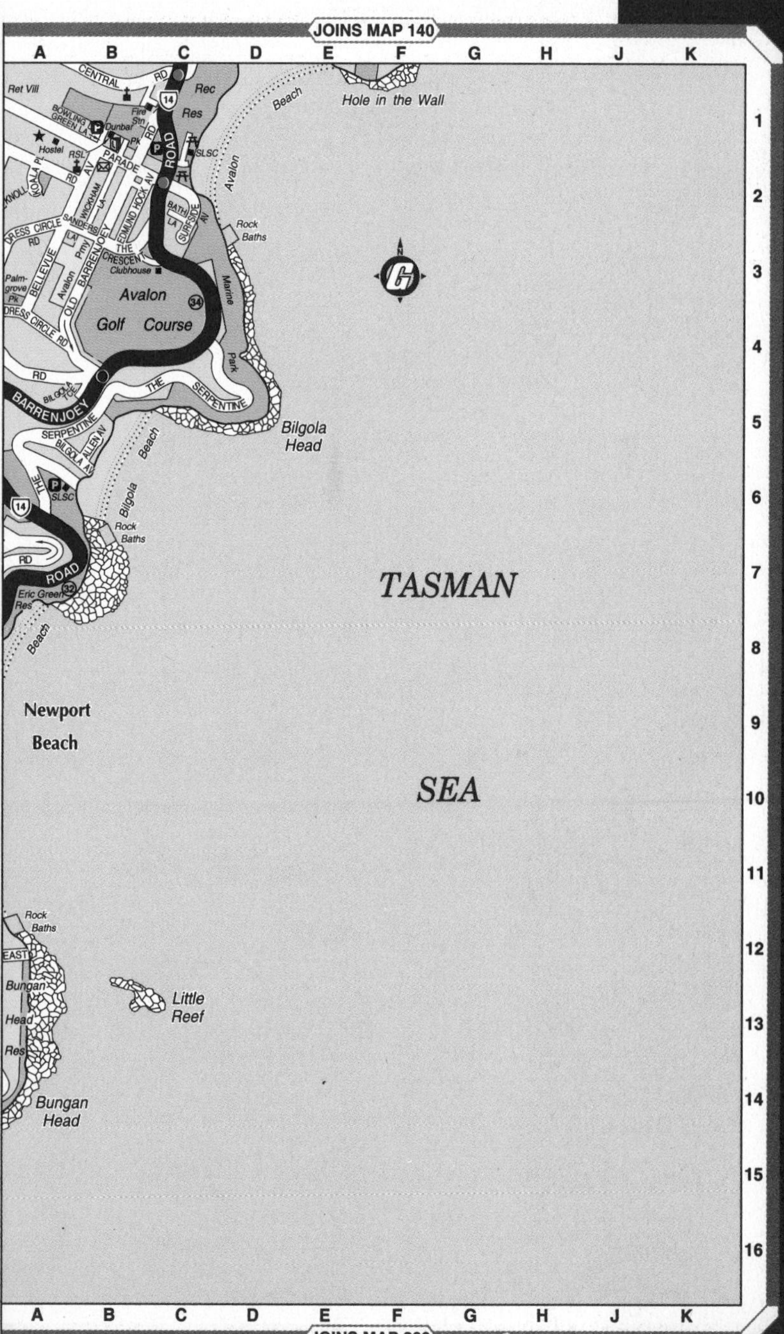

JOINS MAP 200

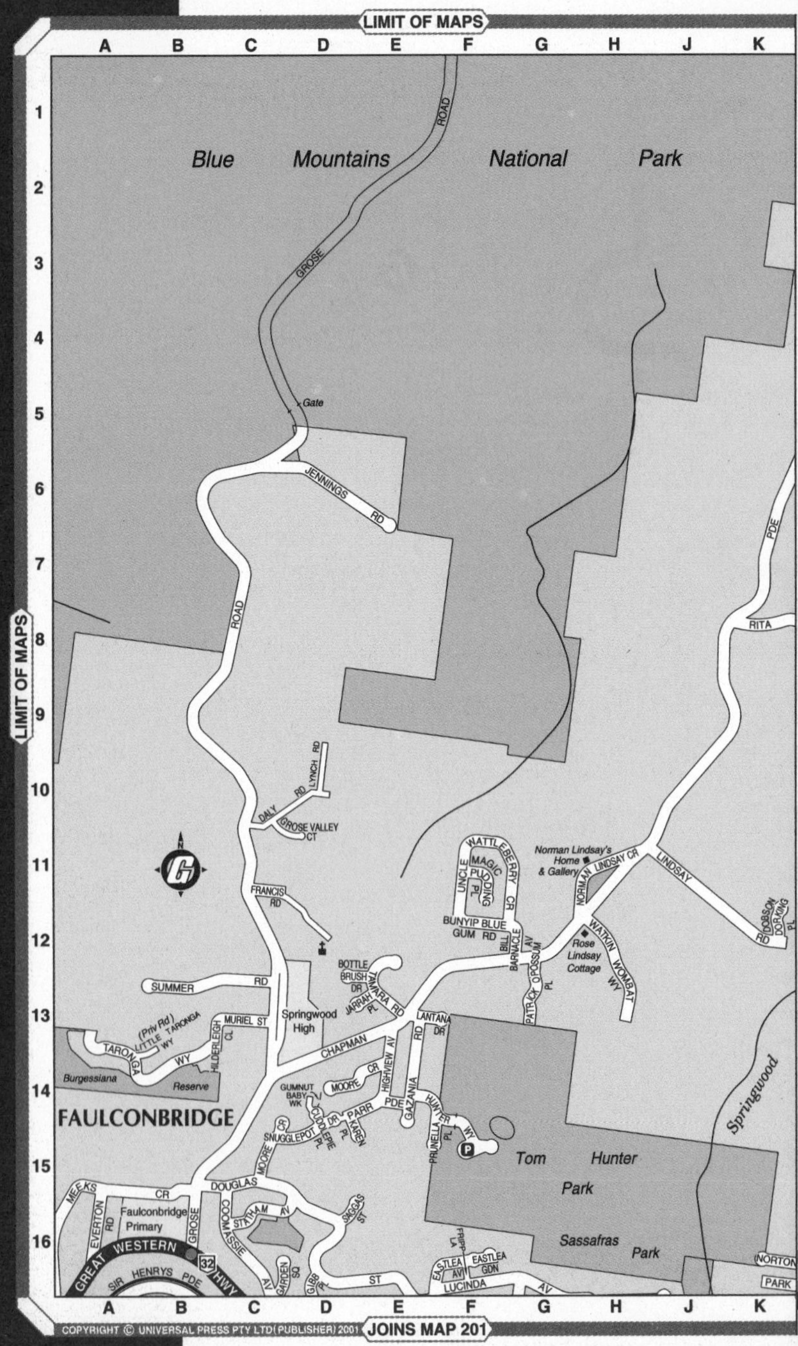

JOINS MAP 201

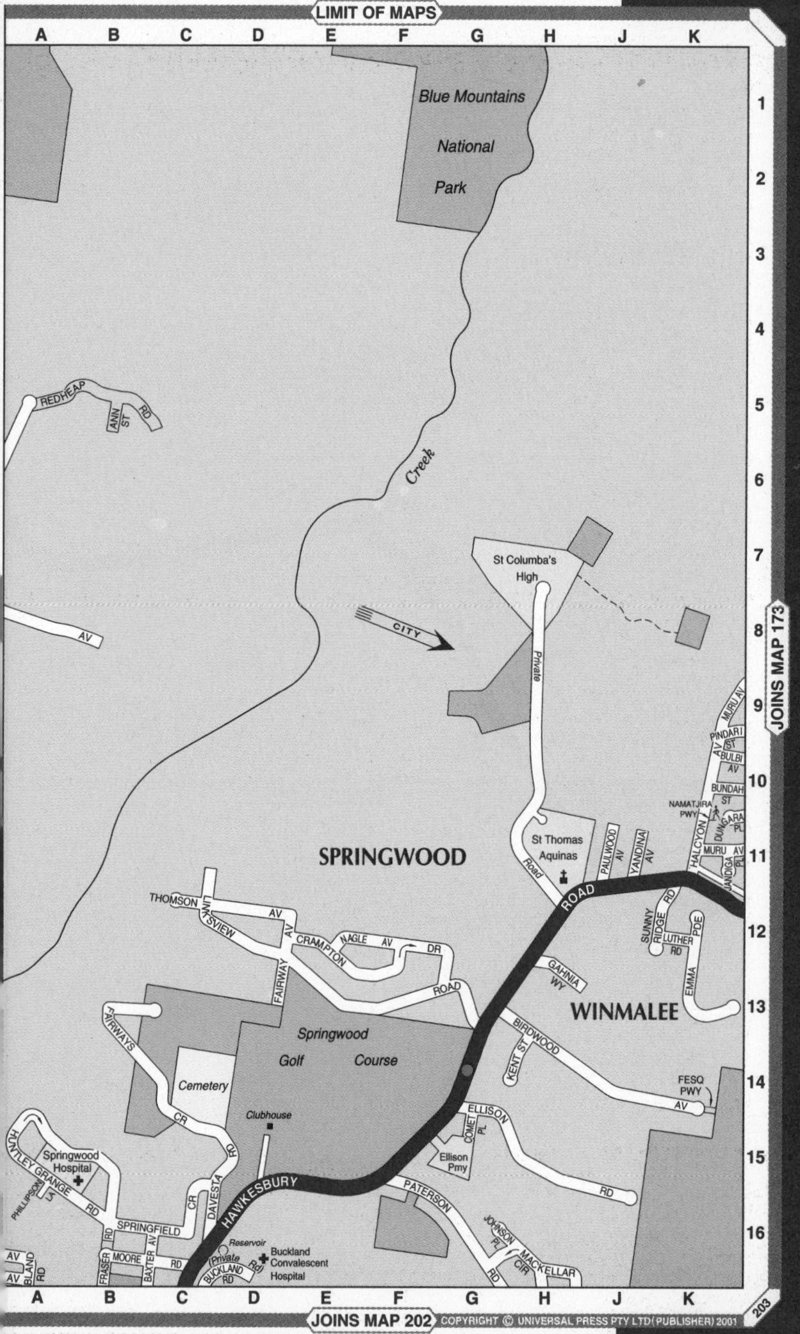

JOINS MAP 202

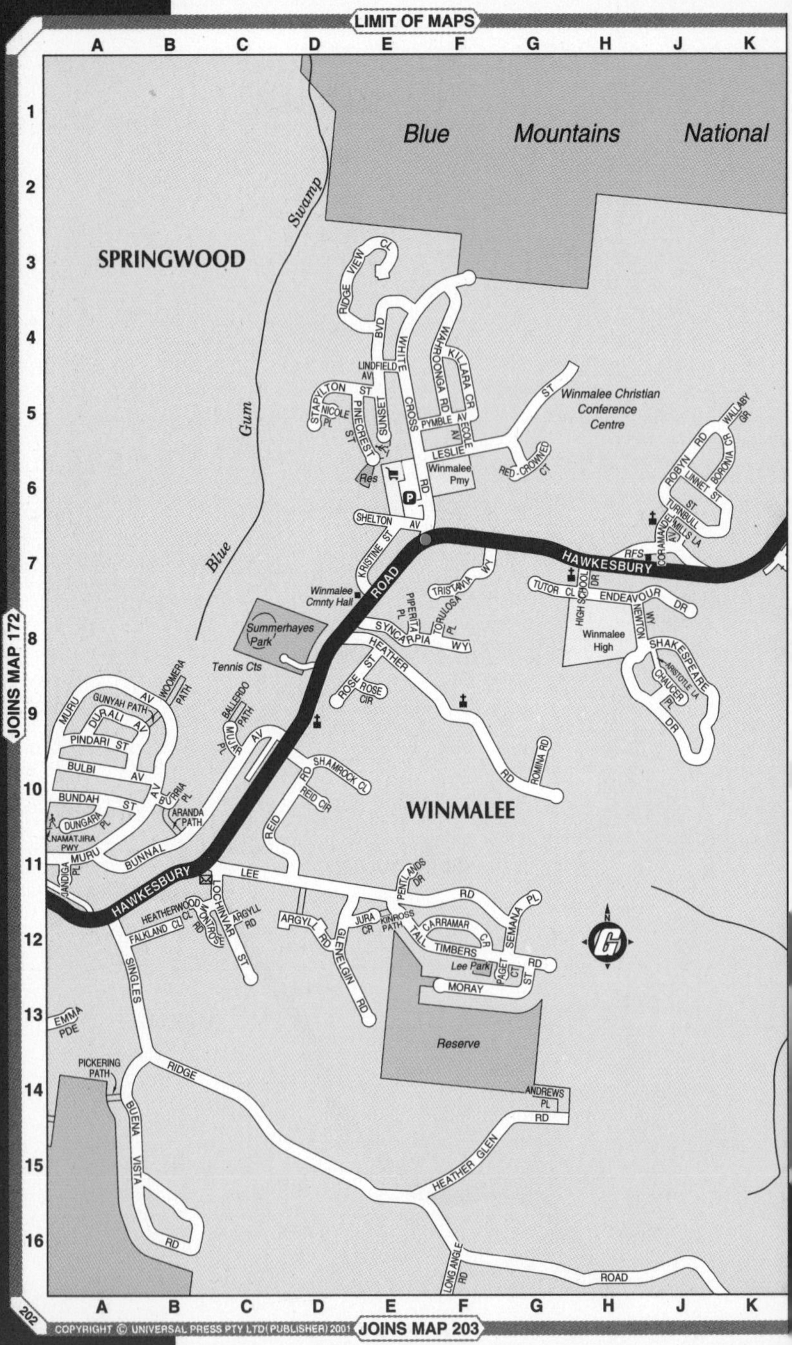
LIMIT OF MAPS
JOINS MAP 172
JOINS MAP 203
202
Blue Mountains National
SPRINGWOOD
WINMALEE
Blue Gum Swamp
Winmalee Christian Conference Centre
Winmalee Pmy
Winmalee Cmnty Hall
Summerhayes Park
Tennis Cts
Winmalee High
Lee Park
Reserve
Res
RFS
HAWKESBURY ROAD
RIDGE VIEW CL
LINDFIELD AV
WHITE CROSS RD
WAHROONGA RD
KILLARA CR
PYMBLE AV
ECOLE AV
LESLIE ST
RED-CROWNED CT
STAPYLTON ST
NICOLE PL
PINECREST ST
SUNSET
SHELTON AV
KRISTINE ST
TRISTANIA WY
PIPERITA PL
TORULOSA PL
SYNCARPIA WY
HEATHER RD
ROSE ST
ROSE CIR
ROMINA RD
SHAMROCK CL
REID CIR
REID RD
ROBYN RD
WALLABY GR
BORONIA CR
LINNET ST
TURNBULL ST
MILLS LA
CORAMANDEL AV
TUTOR CL
HIGH SCHOOL DR
ENDEAVOUR DR
NEWTON WY
SHAKESPEARE DR
ARISTOTLE LA
CHAUCER PL
MURU AV
WOOMERA PATH
GUNYAH PATH
DURALI AV
PINDARI ST
BULBI AV
BUNDAH ST
BURRIA PL
ARANDA PATH
DUNGARA PL
NAMATJIRA PWY
MURU
BUNNAL AV
JANDIGA PL
BALLERDO PATH
MUJAR PL
LEE RD
PENTLANDS DR
SEMANA PL
HEATHERWOOD CL
MONTROSE RD
LOCHINVAR ST
ARGYLL RD
FALKLAND CL
ARGYLL RD
GLENELGIN RD
JURA CR
KINROSS PATH
TALL TIMBERS RD
CARRAMAR CR
PAGET CT
MORAY ST
SINGLES RIDGE
EMMA PDE
PICKERING PATH
BUENA VISTA RD
ANDREWS PL
HEATHER GLEN RD
LONG ANGLE RD
ROAD

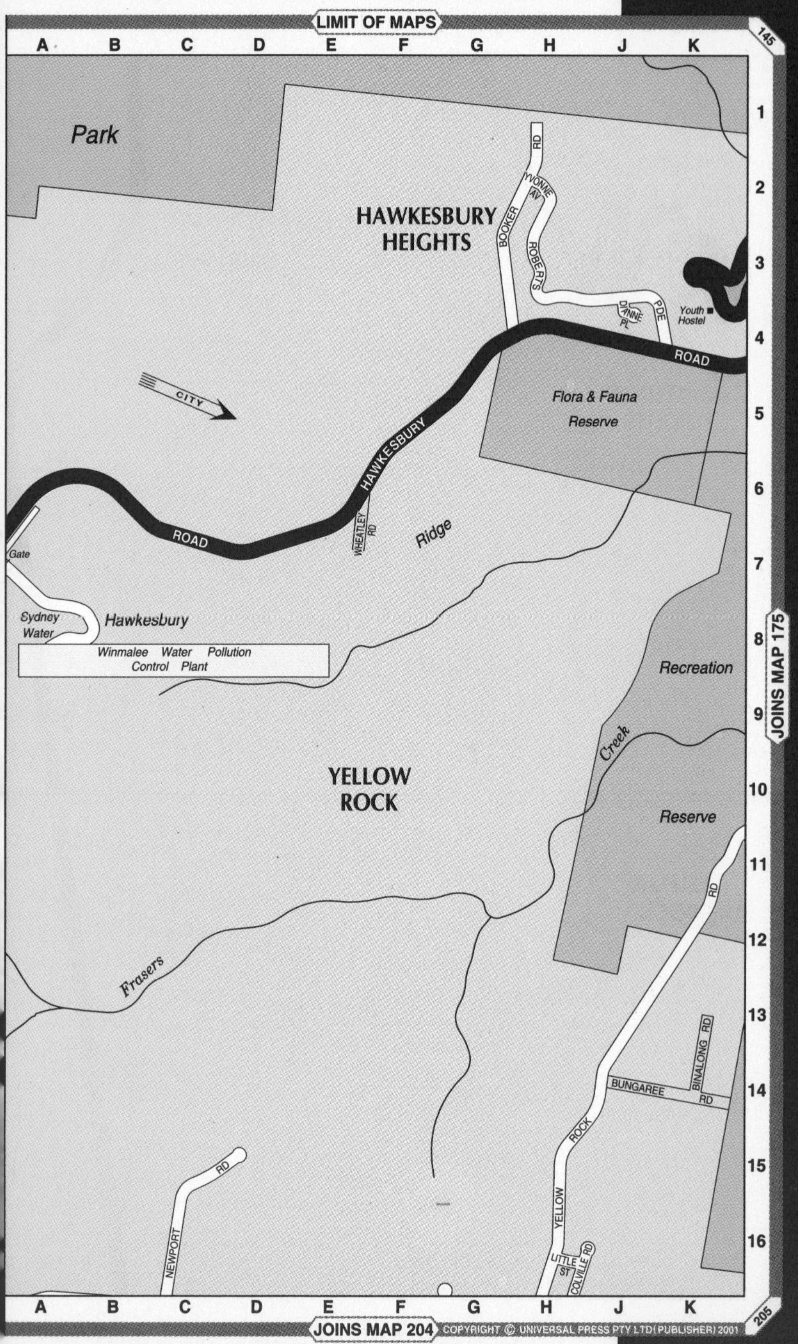

JOINS MAP 204

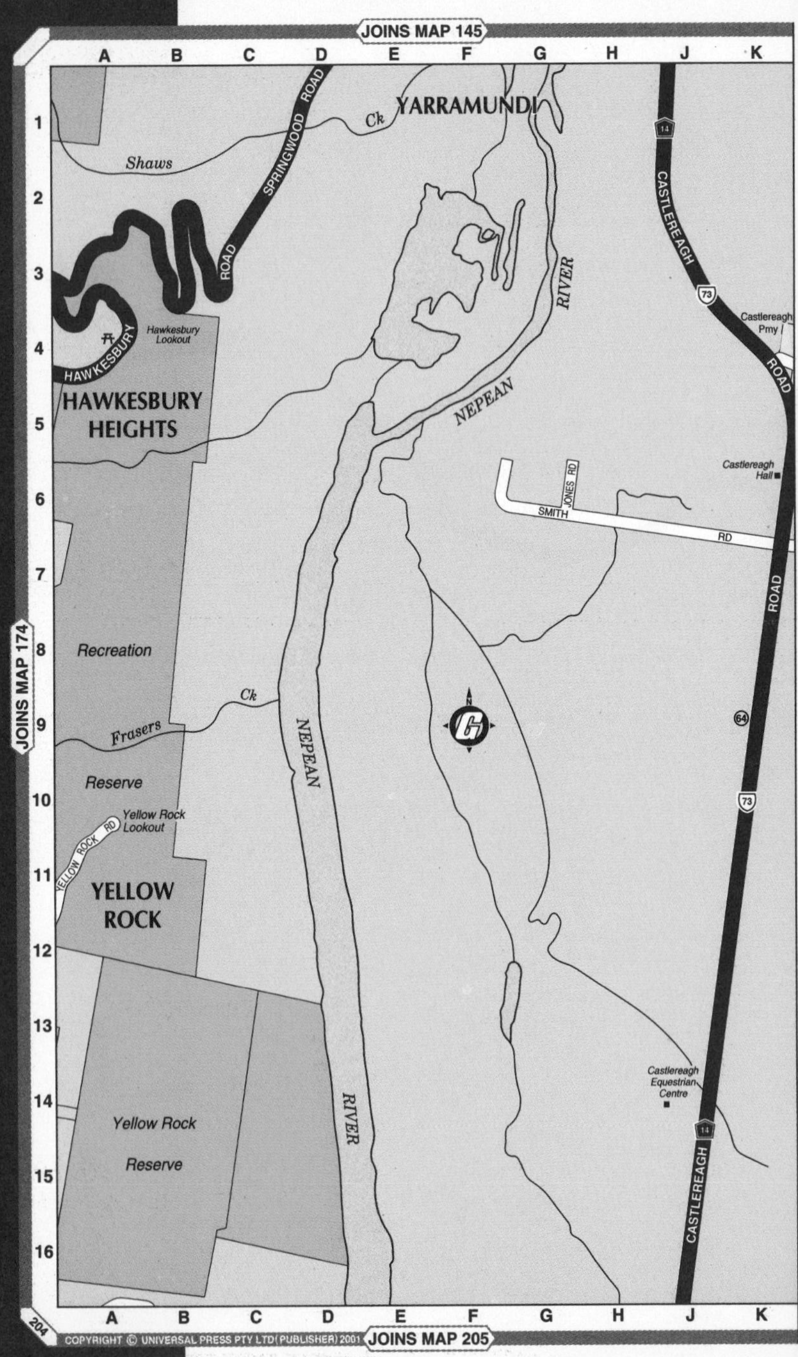
JOINS MAP 145
A B C D E F G H J K
1 2 3 4 5 6 7 8 9 10 11 12 13 14 15 16
YARRAMUNDI
Shaws
Ck
SPRINGWOOD ROAD
ROAD
HAWKESBURY
Hawkesbury Lookout
HAWKESBURY HEIGHTS
NEPEAN
RIVER
CASTLEREAGH
ROAD
Castlereagh Pmy
Castlereagh Hall
JONES RD
SMITH
RD
JOINS MAP 174
Recreation
Frasers
Ck
Reserve
Yellow Rock Lookout
YELLOW ROCK RD
YELLOW ROCK
Yellow Rock
Reserve
NEPEAN
RIVER
Castlereagh Equestrian Centre
CASTLEREAGH
14
73
64
JOINS MAP 205
204

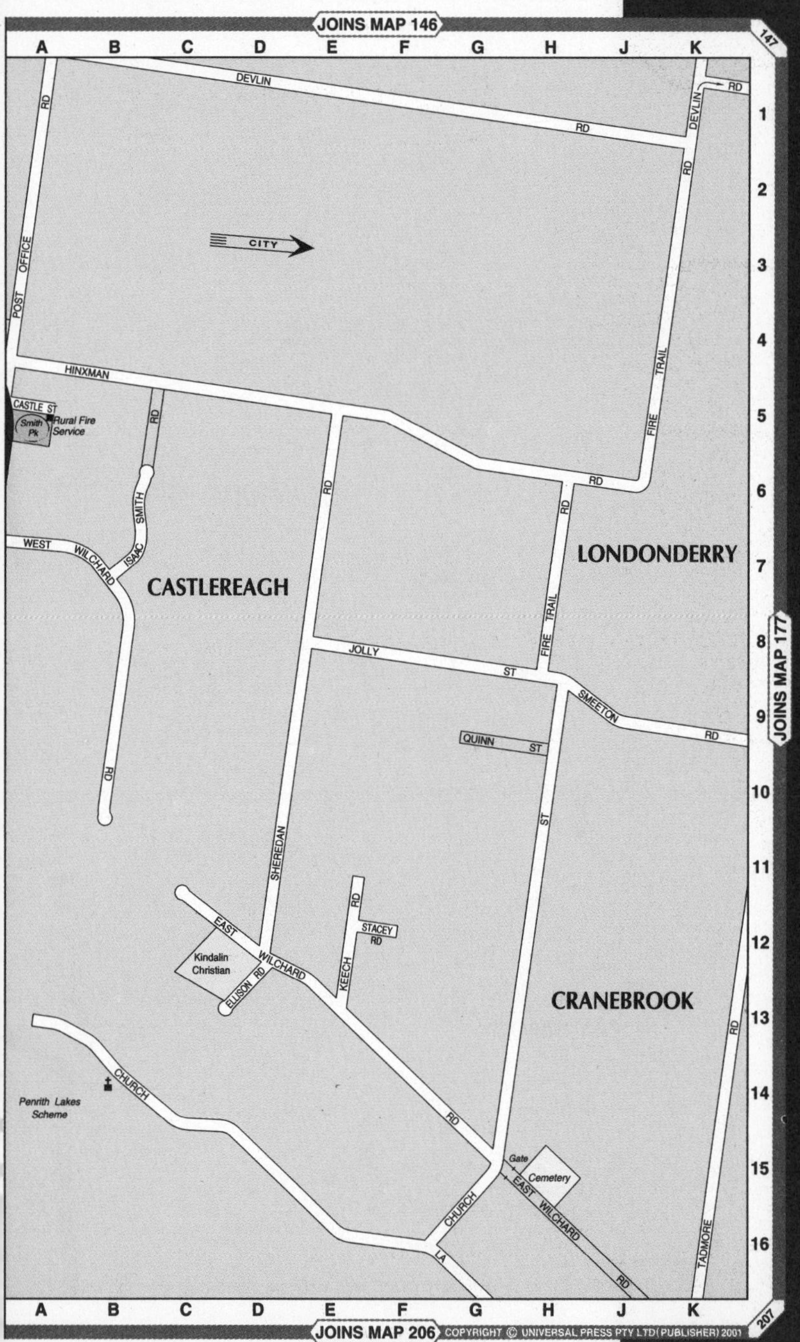
JOINS MAP 146
147
A B C D E F G H J K
1 2 3 4 5 6 7 8 9 10 11 12 13 14 15 16
DEVLIN RD
DEVLIN RD
RD
POST OFFICE RD
CITY
HINXMAN RD
FIRE TRAIL
CASTLE ST
Smith Pk
Rural Fire Service
ISAAC SMITH RD
WEST WILCHARD RD
CASTLEREAGH
LONDONDERRY
SHEREDAN RD
FIRE TRAIL RD
JOLLY ST
SMEETON RD
QUINN ST
ST
EAST WILCHARD RD
Kindalin Christian
ELLISON RD
KEECH RD
STACEY RD
CRANEBROOK
Penrith Lakes Scheme
CHURCH LA
Gate
Cemetery
EAST WILCHARD RD
TADMORE RD
JOINS MAP 177
JOINS MAP 206
207

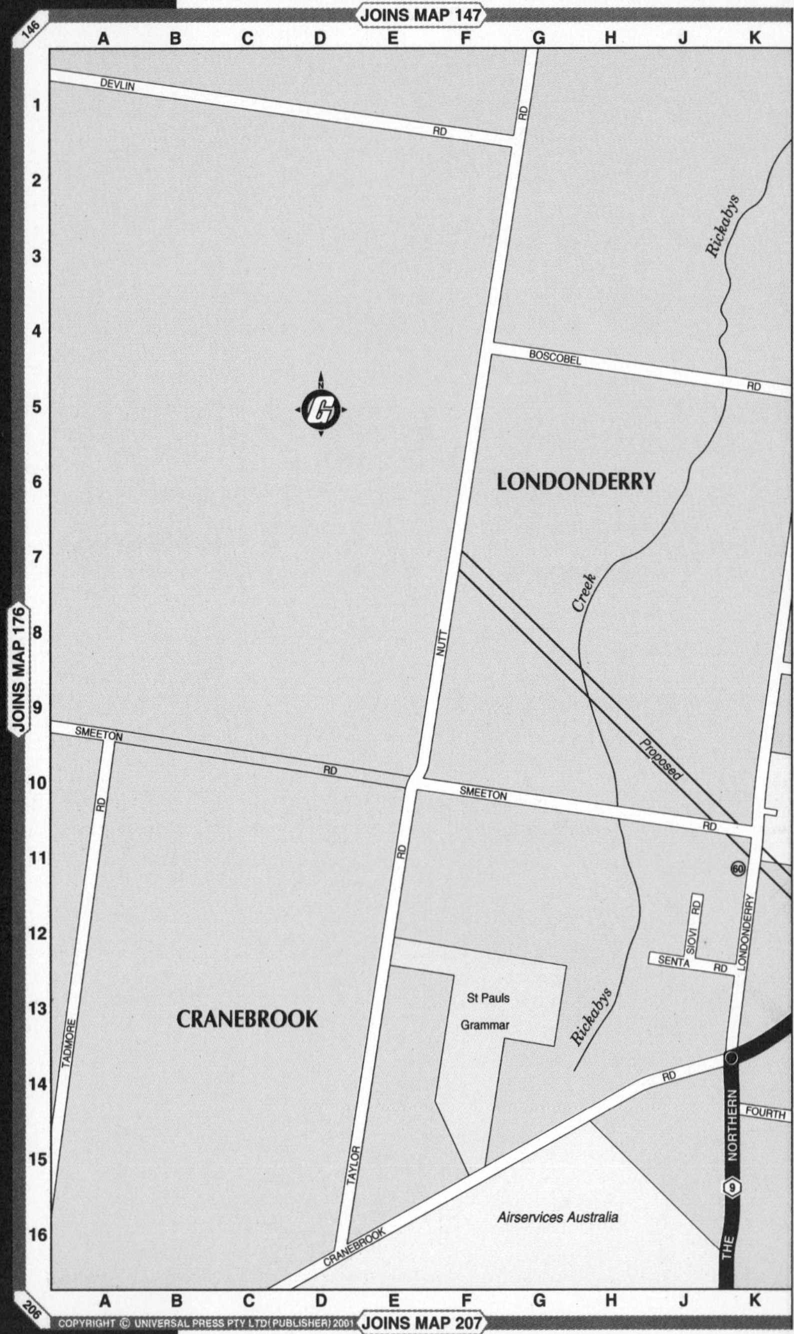
JOINS MAP 147
146
A
B
C
D
E
F
G
H
J
K
1
2
3
4
5
6
7
8
9
10
11
12
13
14
15
16
JOINS MAP 176
DEVLIN
RD
RD
Rickabys
BOSCOBEL
RD
LONDONDERRY
Creek
NUTT
Proposed
SMEETON
RD
RD
SMEETON
RD
RD
RD
60
SIOVI
RD
LONDONDERRY
SENTA
RD
St Pauls
Grammar
Rickabys
CRANEBROOK
TADMORE
RD
RD
FOURTH
NORTHERN
9
TAYLOR
Airservices Australia
CRANEBROOK
THE
206
JOINS MAP 207

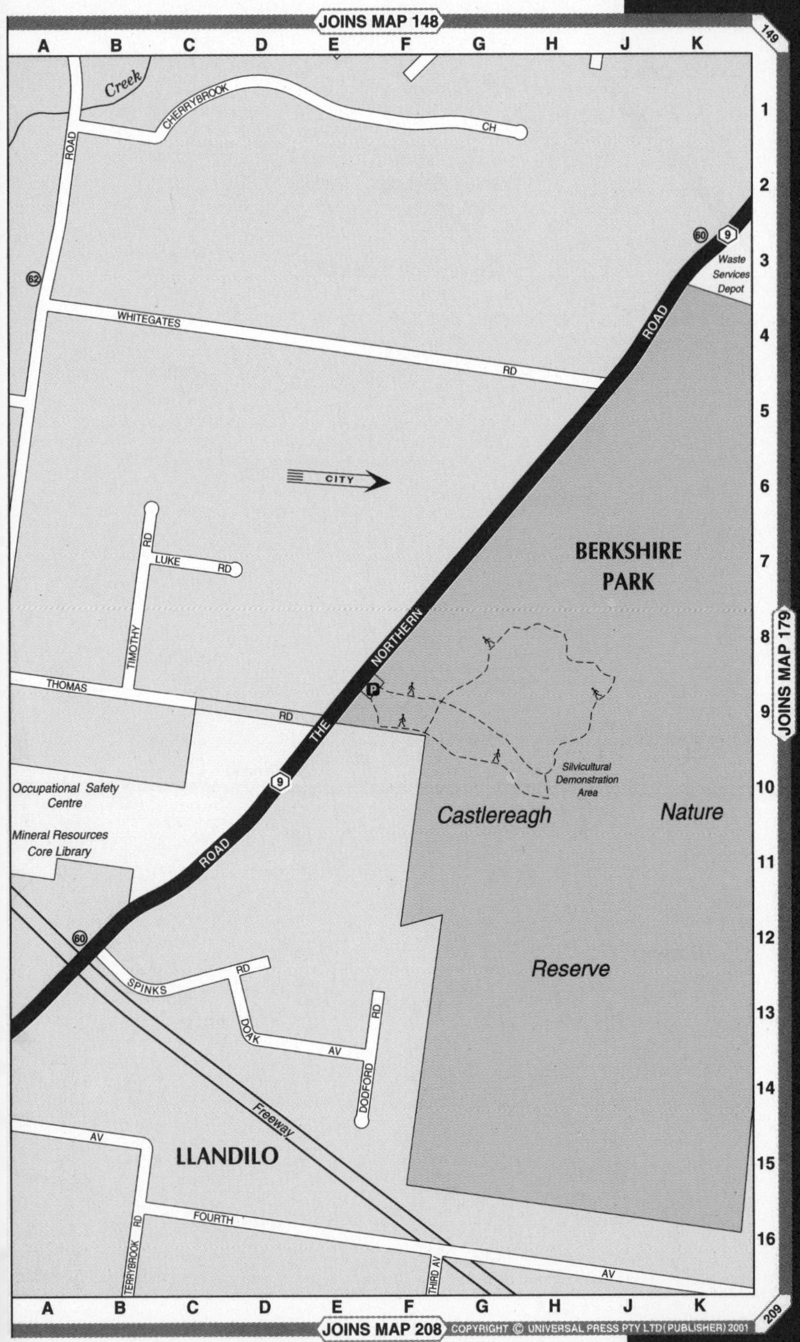
JOINS MAP 148
149
A B C D E F G H J K
1 2 3 4 5 6 7 8 9 10 11 12 13 14 15 16
Creek
CHERRYBROOK
CH
ROAD
62
WHITEGATES
RD
60
9
Waste
Services
Depot
ROAD
CITY
BERKSHIRE
PARK
RD
LUKE
RD
TIMOTHY
THE
NORTHERN
THOMAS
RD
Silvicultural
Demonstration
Area
Occupational Safety
Centre
Mineral Resources
Core Library
Castlereagh
Nature
Reserve
ROAD
60
SPINKS
RD
DOAK
AV
RD
DODFORD
Freeway
AV
LLANDILO
FOURTH
RD
TERRYBROOK
THIRD AV
AV
JOINS MAP 179
JOINS MAP 208
209

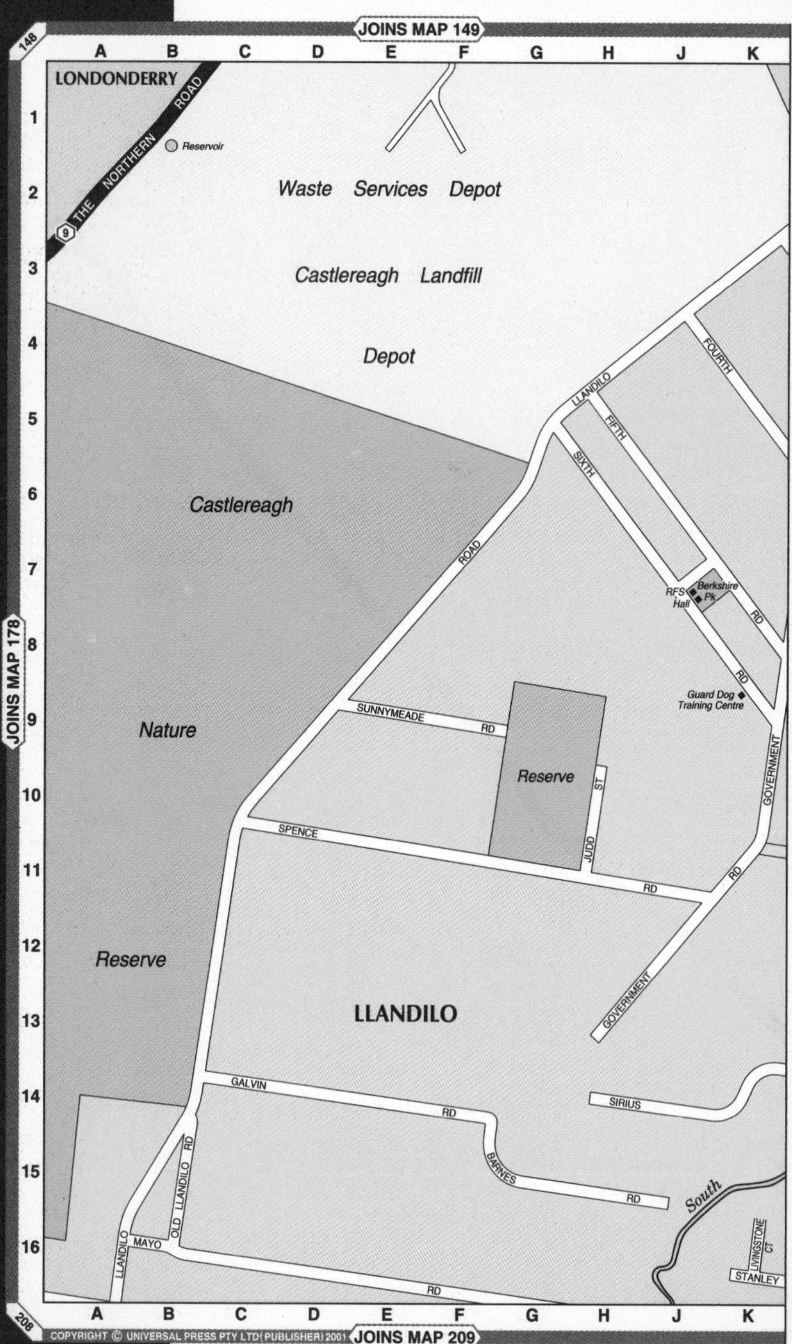
JOINS MAP 149
148
A B C D E F G H J K
1 2 3 4 5 6 7 8 9 10 11 12 13 14 15 16
LONDONDERRY
THE NORTHERN ROAD
9
Reservoir
Waste Services Depot
Castlereagh Landfill
Depot
Castlereagh
Nature
Reserve
LLANDILO ROAD
FOURTH
FIFTH
SIXTH
RD
RFS Hall
Berkshire Pk
Guard Dog Training Centre
SUNNYMEADE RD
Reserve
JUDD ST
SPENCE RD
GOVERNMENT RD
GOVERNMENT
LLANDILO
GALVIN RD
SIRIUS
BARNES RD
OLD LLANDILO RD
MAYO RD
LLANDILO
South
LIVINGSTONE CT
STANLEY
JOINS MAP 178
208

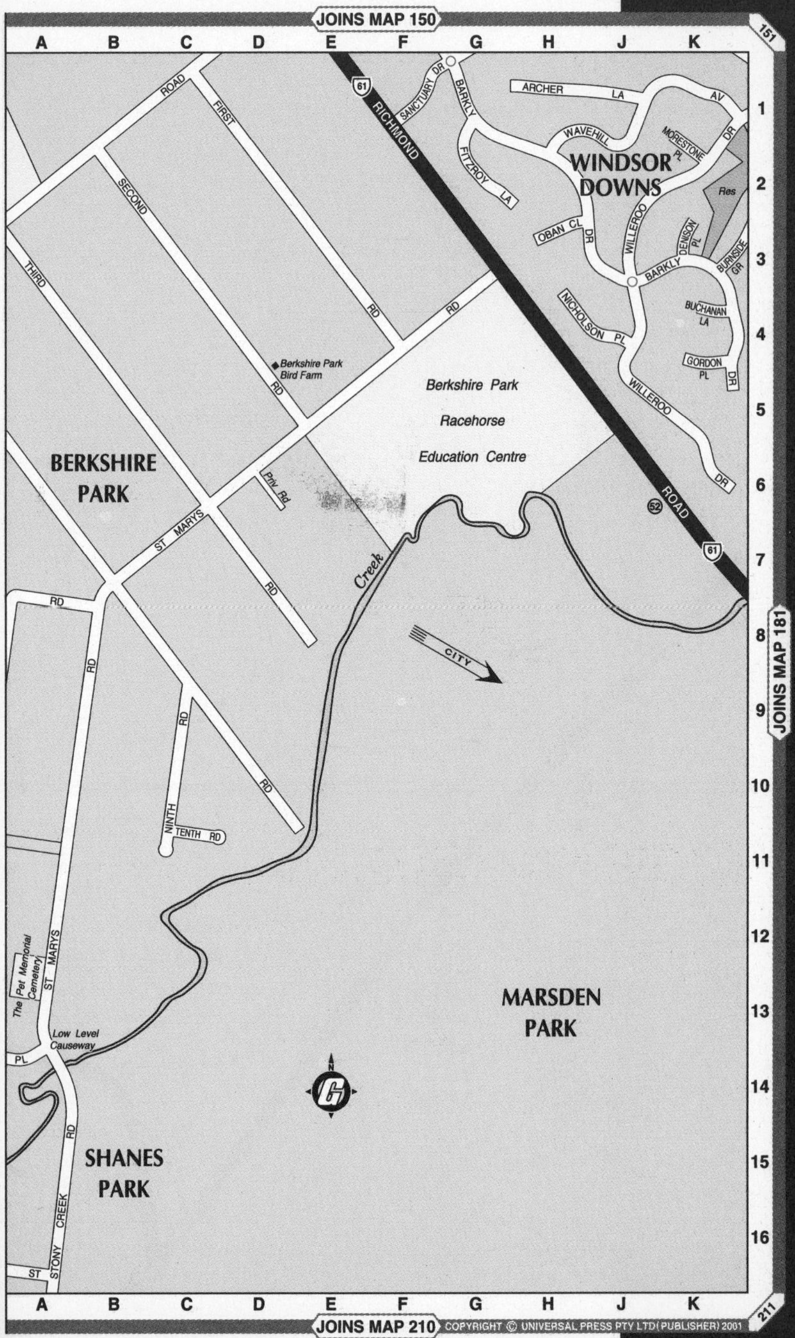
JOINS MAP 150
151
A B C D E F G H J K
1 2 3 4 5 6 7 8 9 10 11 12 13 14 15 16
ROAD
FIRST
SECOND
THIRD
RD
RICHMOND
61
SANCTUARY DR
BARKLY
ARCHER LA
AV
WAVEHILL
MORESTONE PL
DR
WINDSOR
DOWNS
FITZROY LA
Res
OBAN CL
DR
WILLEROO
DENISON PL
BARKLY
BURNSIDE GR
NICHOLSON PL
BUCHANAN LA
GORDON PL
DR
WILLEROO
DR
Berkshire Park Bird Farm
Berkshire Park
Racehorse
Education Centre
BERKSHIRE
PARK
Priv Rd
ST MARYS
ROAD
52
61
Creek
CITY
JOINS MAP 181
RD
RD
RD
NINTH
TENTH RD
The Pet Memorial Cemetery
ST MARYS
Low Level Causeway
PL
MARSDEN
PARK
SHANES
PARK
STONY CREEK RD
ST
JOINS MAP 210
211

MAP 181

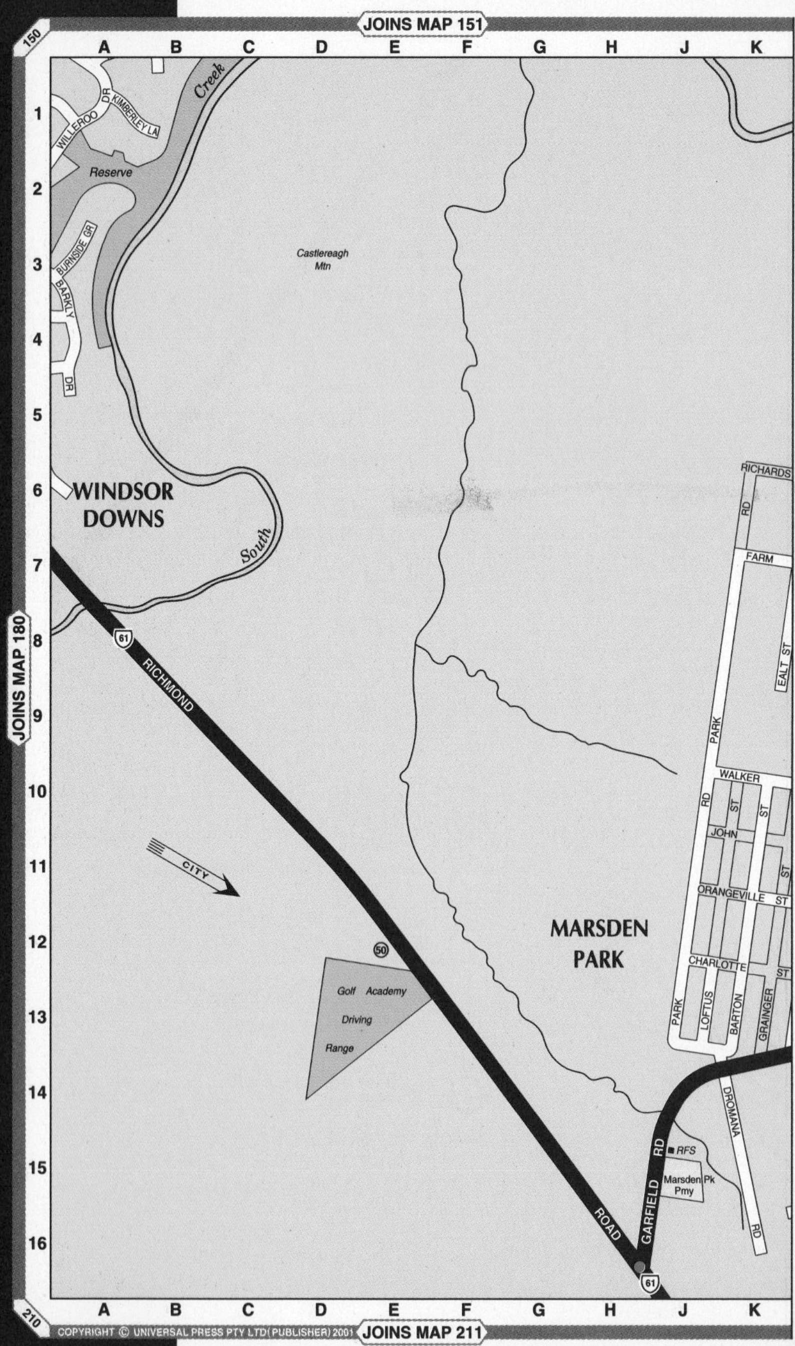
JOINS MAP 151
JOINS MAP 180
JOINS MAP 211
150
210
A B C D E F G H J K
1 2 3 4 5 6 7 8 9 10 11 12 13 14 15 16
WILLEROO
DR
KIMBERLEY LA
Reserve
Creek
BURNSIDE GR
BARKLY
DR
Castlereagh Mtn
WINDSOR DOWNS
South
61
RICHMOND
ROAD
CITY
50
Golf Academy
Driving
Range
MARSDEN PARK
RICHARDS
RD
FARM
EALT ST
PARK
WALKER
RD
ST
ST
JOHN
ST
ORANGEVILLE ST
CHARLOTTE
ST
PARK
LOFTUS
BARTON
GRAINGER
DROMANA
RD
GARFIELD
RD
RFS
Marsden Pk Pmy

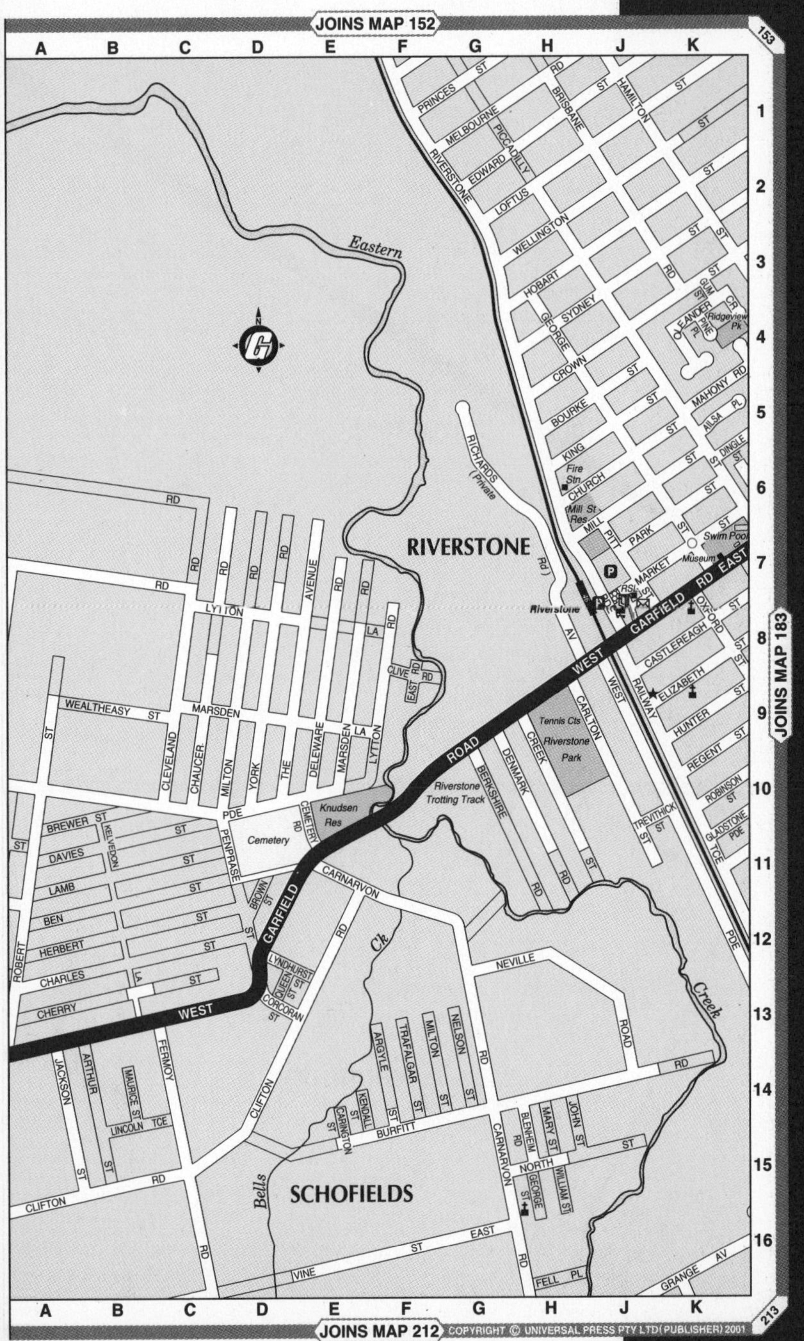
JOINS MAP 152
JOINS MAP 183
JOINS MAP 212
153
213
RIVERSTONE
SCHOFIELDS
Eastern
Creek
Bells
Ck
Riverstone
Knudsen Res
Cemetery
Riverstone Trotting Track
Tennis Cts
Riverstone Park
Fire Stn
Mill St Res
Swim Pool
Museum
RSL
Ridgeview Pk
GARFIELD RD EAST
WEST GARFIELD ROAD
RICHARDS (Private Rd)
PRINCES ST
MELBOURNE
PICCADILLY
EDWARD
LOFTUS
WELLINGTON
HOBART
SYDNEY
GEORGE
CROWN
BOURKE
KING
CHURCH
MILL
PITT
PARK
MARKET
BRISBANE
HAMILTON
OLEANDER
GUM ST
PINE PL
MAHONY RD
AILSA PL
DINGLE
OXFORD
CASTLEREAGH
ELIZABETH
HUNTER
REGENT
ROBINSON ST
GLADSTONE PDE
TCE
RAILWAY
CARLTON
WEST
TREVITHICK ST
DENMARK
CREEK
BERKSHIRE
LYTTON
AVENUE
CLIVE
EAST RD
WEALTHEASY ST
MARSDEN
MARSDEN LA
CLEVELAND
CHAUCER
MILTON
YORK
THE
DELEWARE
PDE
CEMETERY RD
PENPRASE
BREWER ST
KELVEDON
DAVIES
LAMB
BEN
HERBERT
CHARLES
CHERRY
ROBERT
BROWN ST
LYNDHURST ST
QUEEN ST
CORCORAN ST
CARNARVON
CLIFTON
FERMOY
JACKSON ST
ARTHUR ST
MAURICE ST
LINCOLN TCE
ARGYLE
TRAFALGAR ST
NELSON ST
KENDALL
CARRINGTON
BURFITT
NEVILLE
BLENHEIM RD
MARY ST
JOHN ST
NORTH
WILLIAM ST
GEORGE ST
VINE
EAST ST
FELL PL
GRANGE AV
CLIFTON RD

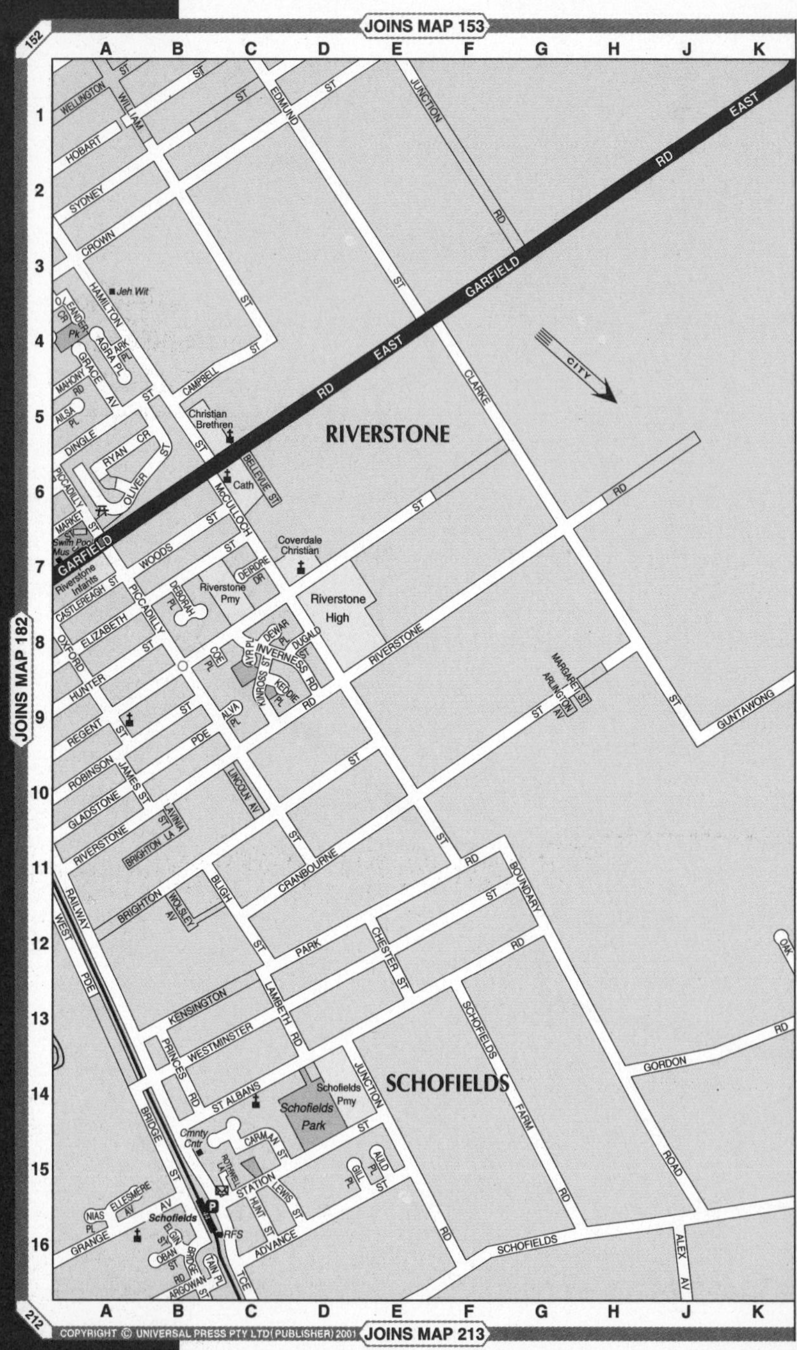
JOINS MAP 153
JOINS MAP 182
JOINS MAP 213
152
212
RIVERSTONE
SCHOFIELDS
GARFIELD RD EAST
CITY
Riverstone High
Riverstone Pmy
Riverstone Infants
Coverdale Christian
Christian Brethren
Cath
Schofields Pmy
Schofields Park
Cmnty Cntr
Schofields
RFS
RIVERSTONE PDE
RIVERSTONE RD
CLARKE ST
JUNCTION RD
EDMUND ST
McCULLOCH ST
PICCADILLY
WINDSOR ST
BOUNDARY RD
SCHOFIELDS FARM RD
SCHOFIELDS RD
GUNTAWONG RD
GORDON RD
ALEX AV
RAILWAY TCE
WEST PDE
BRIDGE ST
STATION ST
ADVANCE ST
ST ALBANS RD
CARMAN ST
LEWIS ST
HUNT ST
GILL PL
AULD ST
PRINCES RD
LAMBETH RD
CHESTER ST
PARK ST
KENSINGTON
WESTMINSTER
BLIGH ST
CRANBOURNE ST
BRIGHTON
WOLSLEY AV
LINCOLN AV
LAVINIA ST
BRIGHTON LA
GLADSTONE
ROBINSON
JAMES ST
REGENT ST
HUNTER ST
OXFORD
ELIZABETH
CASTLEREAGH ST
WOODS
DEBORAH PL
DEIRDRE DR
COE PL
AYR PL
DEWAR PL
DUGALD ST
INVERNESS RD
KINROSS ST
KEDDIE PL
ALVA PL
MARGARET ST
ARLINGTON AV
BELLEVUE ST
OLIVER ST
RYAN CR
DINGLE
AILSA PL
MAHONY RD
GRACE AV
AGRA PL
ARK PL
LEANDER CR
HAMILTON
CAMPBELL
CROWN
SYDNEY
HOBART
WELLINGTON
WILLIAM
MARKET ST
Swim Pool
Mus
Jeh Wit
Pk
ELLESMERE AV
NIAS PL
GRANGE AV
ELGIN ST
OBAN ST
ARGOWAN RD
TAIN PL
OAK
ROTHWELL LA

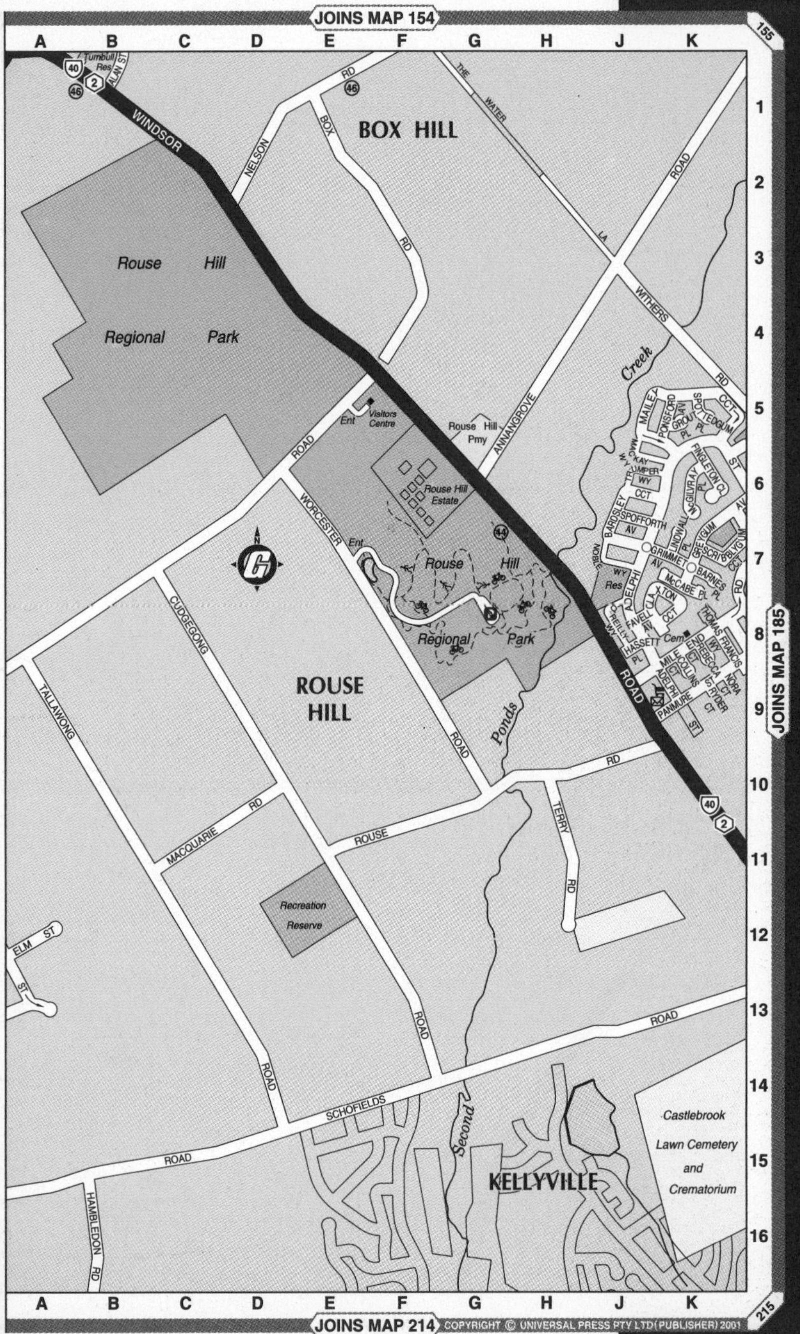
JOINS MAP 154
JOINS MAP 185
JOINS MAP 214
155
215
A B C D E F G H J K
1 2 3 4 5 6 7 8 9 10 11 12 13 14 15 16
BOX HILL
ROUSE HILL
KELLYVILLE
Rouse Hill Regional Park
WINDSOR ROAD
NELSON ROAD
BOX RD
THE WATER LA
WITHERS RD
ROAD
ANNANGROVE
Creek
Visitors Centre
Ent
Rouse Hill Pmy
Rouse Hill Estate
WORCESTER ROAD
Rouse Hill Regional Park
CUDGEGONG ROAD
TALLAWONG
MACQUARIE RD
ROUSE RD
TERRY RD
Ponds
Second
Recreation Reserve
ELM ST
SCHOFIELDS ROAD
HAMBLEDON RD
Castlebrook Lawn Cemetery and Crematorium
MAILEY
PONSFORD
GROUT
SPOTTEDGUM CCT
FINGLETON CL
McGILVRAY PL
BARDSLEY
SPOFFORTH AV
GRIMMETT AV
BARNES PL
McCABE PL
ADELPHI
FAVELL AV
HASSETT PL
THOMAS FRANCIS
REBECCA
COLLINS CT
RYDER CT
PANMURE ST
NOBLE
Res
Cem
Turnbull Res
ALAN ST
40 2 46 44

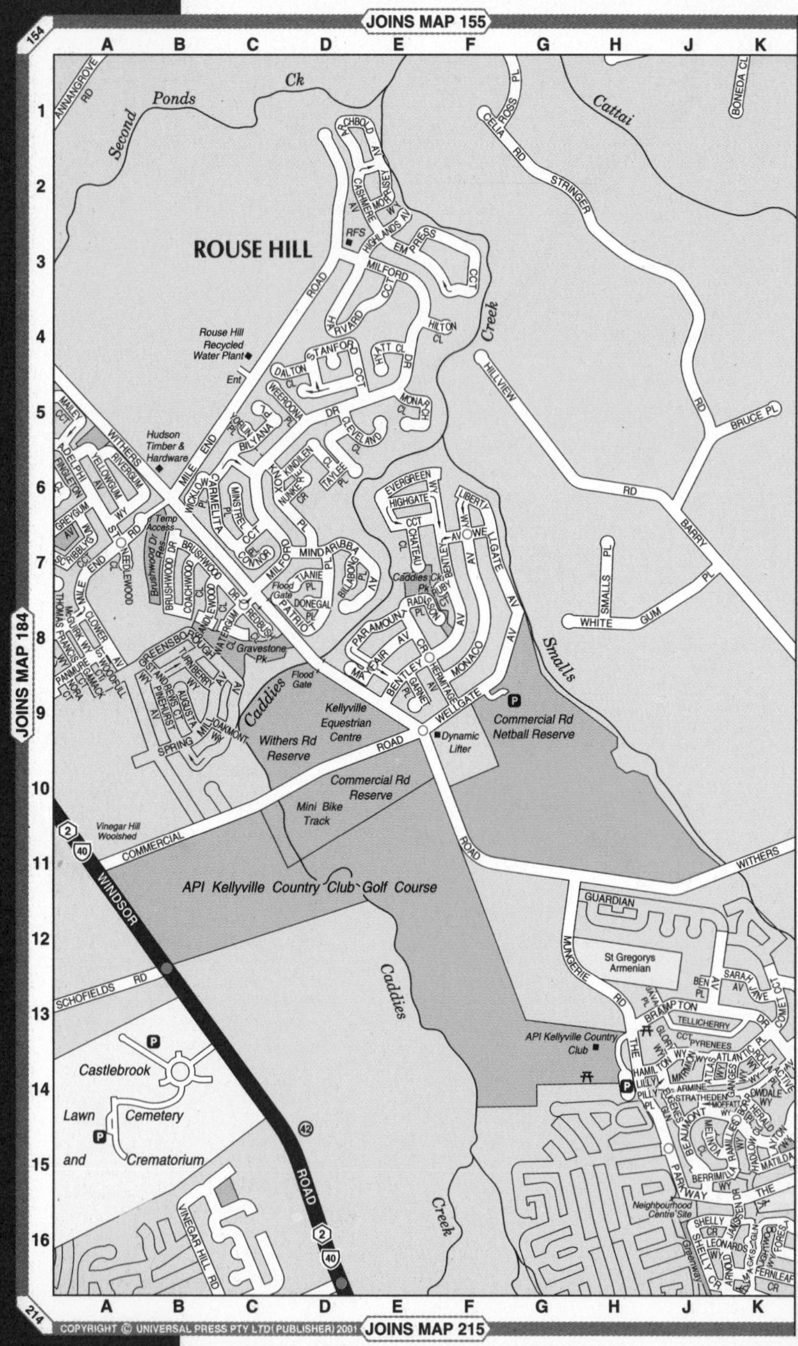
JOINS MAP 155
JOINS MAP 184
JOINS MAP 215
154
214
ROUSE HILL
Second Ponds Ck
Cattai Creek
Caddies Creek
Smalls Creek
Rouse Hill Recycled Water Plant
Hudson Timber & Hardware
RFS
Temp Access
Brushwood Dr Res
Gravestone Pk
Flood Gate
Caddies Ck Pk
Kellyville Equestrian Centre
Withers Rd Reserve
Commercial Rd Netball Reserve
Dynamic Lifter
Commercial Rd Reserve
Mini Bike Track
Vinegar Hill Woolshed
API Kellyville Country Club Golf Course
St Gregorys Armenian
API Kellyville Country Club
Castlebrook Lawn Cemetery and Crematorium
Neighbourhood Centre Site
Greenway
WINDSOR ROAD
COMMERCIAL ROAD
WITHERS RD
MILE END RD
STRINGER RD
BARRY RD
HILLVIEW
SCHOFIELDS RD
VINEGAR HILL RD
MUNGERIE RD
THE PARKWAY
ANNANGROVE RD

JOINS MAP 156

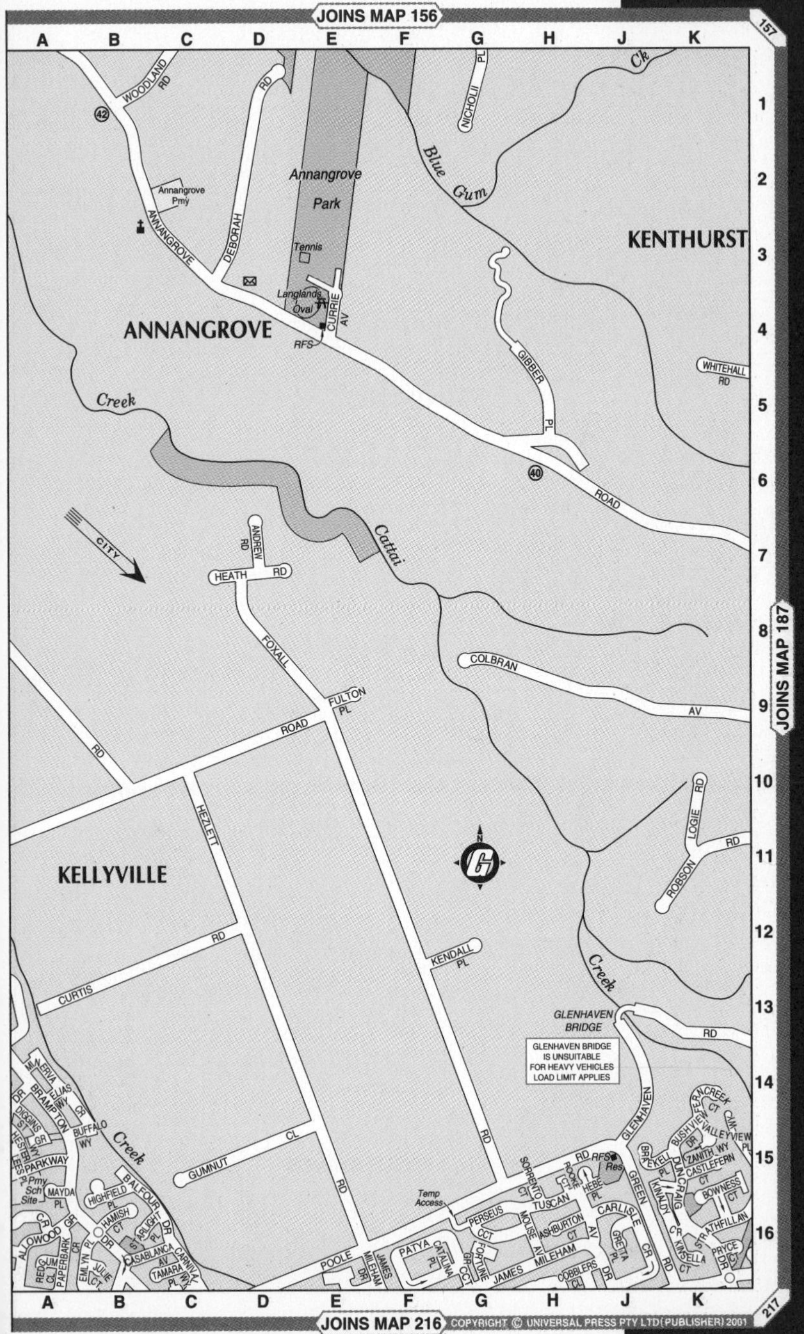

JOINS MAP 187

JOINS MAP 216

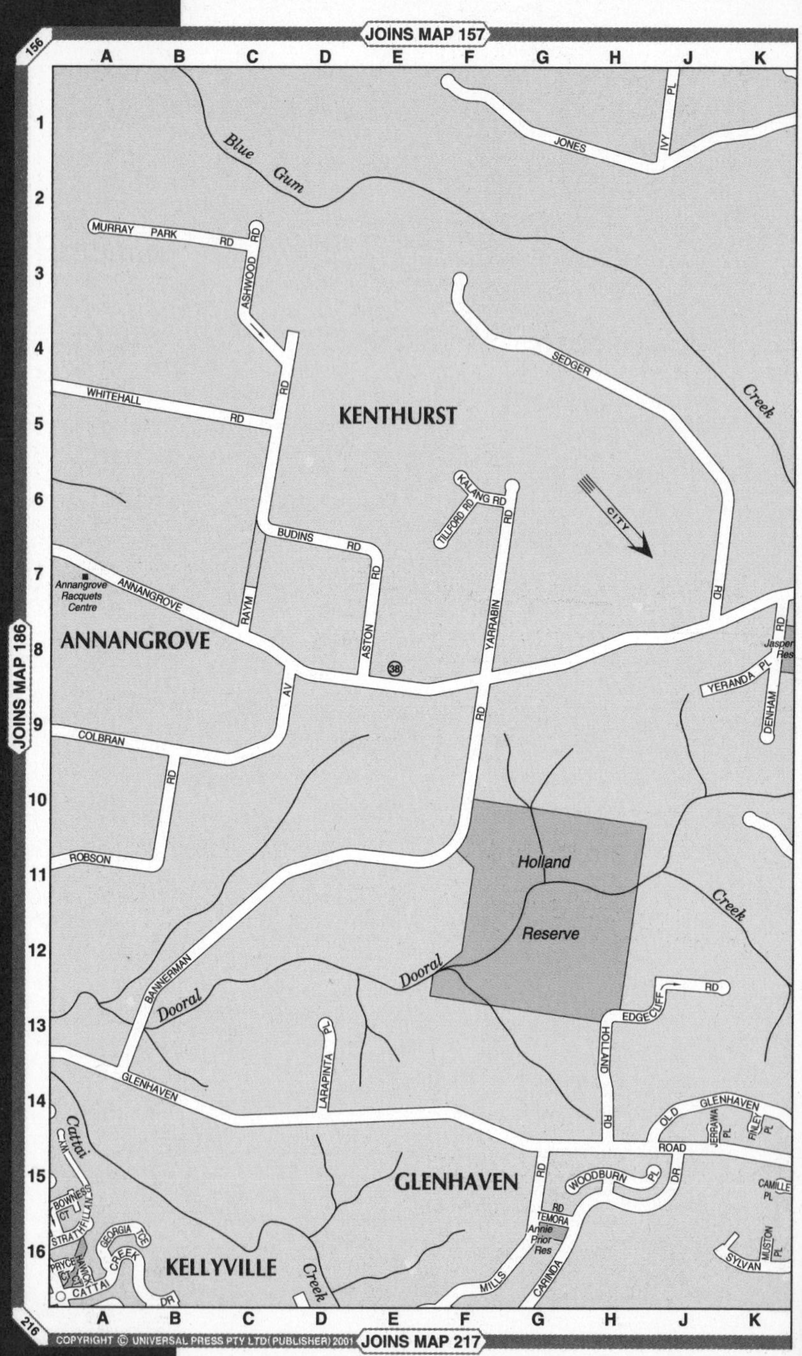
JOINS MAP 157
JOINS MAP 186
JOINS MAP 217
156
216
A B C D E F G H J K
1 2 3 4 5 6 7 8 9 10 11 12 13 14 15 16
KENTHURST
ANNANGROVE
GLENHAVEN
KELLYVILLE
Blue Gum
Creek
Dooral
Dooral
Creek
Cattai
Creek
Holland
Reserve
Annangrove Racquets Centre
Jasper Res
Annie Prior Res
JONES
IVY PL
MURRAY PARK RD
ASHWOOD RD
WHITEHALL RD
SEDGER RD
KALANG RD
TILLFORD RD
CITY
BUDINS RD
ASTON RD
RAYM
ANNANGROVE AV
YARRABIN RD
38
YERANDA PL
DENHAM
COLBRAN RD
ROBSON
BANNERMAN
EDGECLIFF RD
HOLLAND RD
LARAPINTA PL
GLENHAVEN
OLD GLENHAVEN ROAD
JERRAWA PL
FINLEY PL
WOODBURN PL
DR
RD
TEMORA RD
CAMILLE PL
MUSTON PL
SYLVAN
MILLS
CARINDA
BOWNESS CT
FILLAN
STRATH
GEORGIA TCE
PRYCE CT
HAMICK CT
CREEK
CATTAI
DR
WK

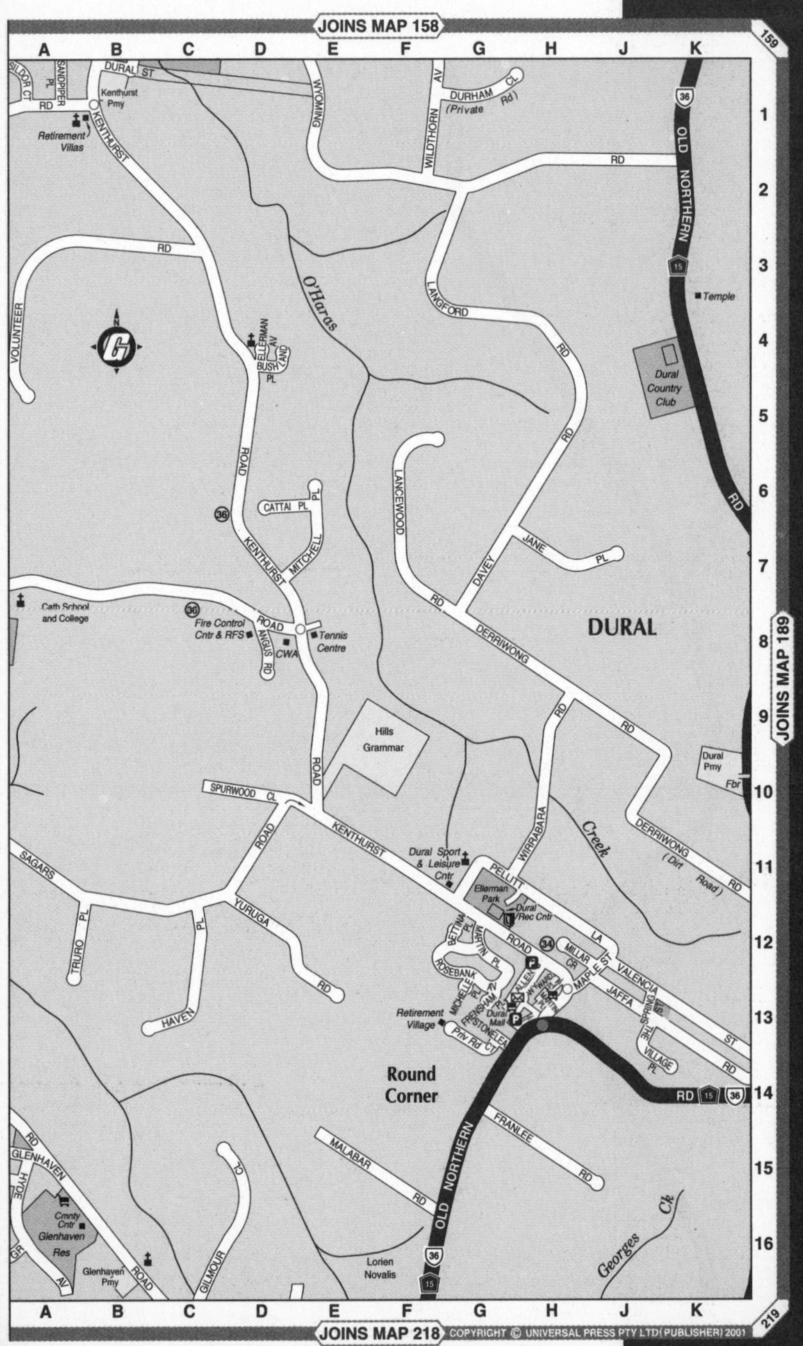
JOINS MAP 158
159
A B C D E F G H J K
1 2 3 4 5 6 7 8 9 10 11 12 13 14 15 16
DURAL ST
SANDPIPER PL
RD
Kenthurst Pmy
Retirement Villas
KENTHURST
WYOMING
WILDTHORN AV
DURHAM CL
(Private Rd)
RD
OLD NORTHERN
RD
VOLUNTEER
O'Haras
LANGFORD RD
RD
ELLERMAN AV
BUSHLAND PL
Temple
Dural Country Club
ROAD
LANCEWOOD
RD
CATTAI PL
PL
MITCHELL
KENTHURST
JANE PL
DAVEY
RD
Cath School and College
ROAD
Fire Control Cntr & RFS
ANGUS RD
CWA
Tennis Centre
DERRIWONG
DURAL
JOINS MAP 189
RD
RD
Hills Grammar
ROAD
SPURWOOD CL
Dural Pmy
Fbr
WIRRABARA
Creek
DERRIWONG (Dirt Road)
RD
KENTHURST
ROAD
SAGARS
Dural Sport & Leisure Cntr
PELLITT
Ellerman Park
Dural Rec Cntr
TRURO PL
PL
YURUGA
RD
BETTINA PL
MARTIN PL
ROAD
LA
MILLAR CR
MAPLE ST
VALENCIA
JAFFA
ROSEBANK
MICHELLE PL
FRENSHAM PL
AV
ALLEN
Dural Mall
STONELEA
Retirement Village
Priv Rd CT
HAVEN
THE SPRING ST
VILLAGE PL
ST
RD
Round Corner
RD
FRANLEE
RD
MALABAR
RD
OLD NORTHERN
GLENHAVEN RD
HYDE AV
Cmnty Cntr
Glenhaven Res
CL
GILMOUR
ROAD
Glenhaven Pmy
Lorien Novalis
Georges Ck
JOINS MAP 218
219

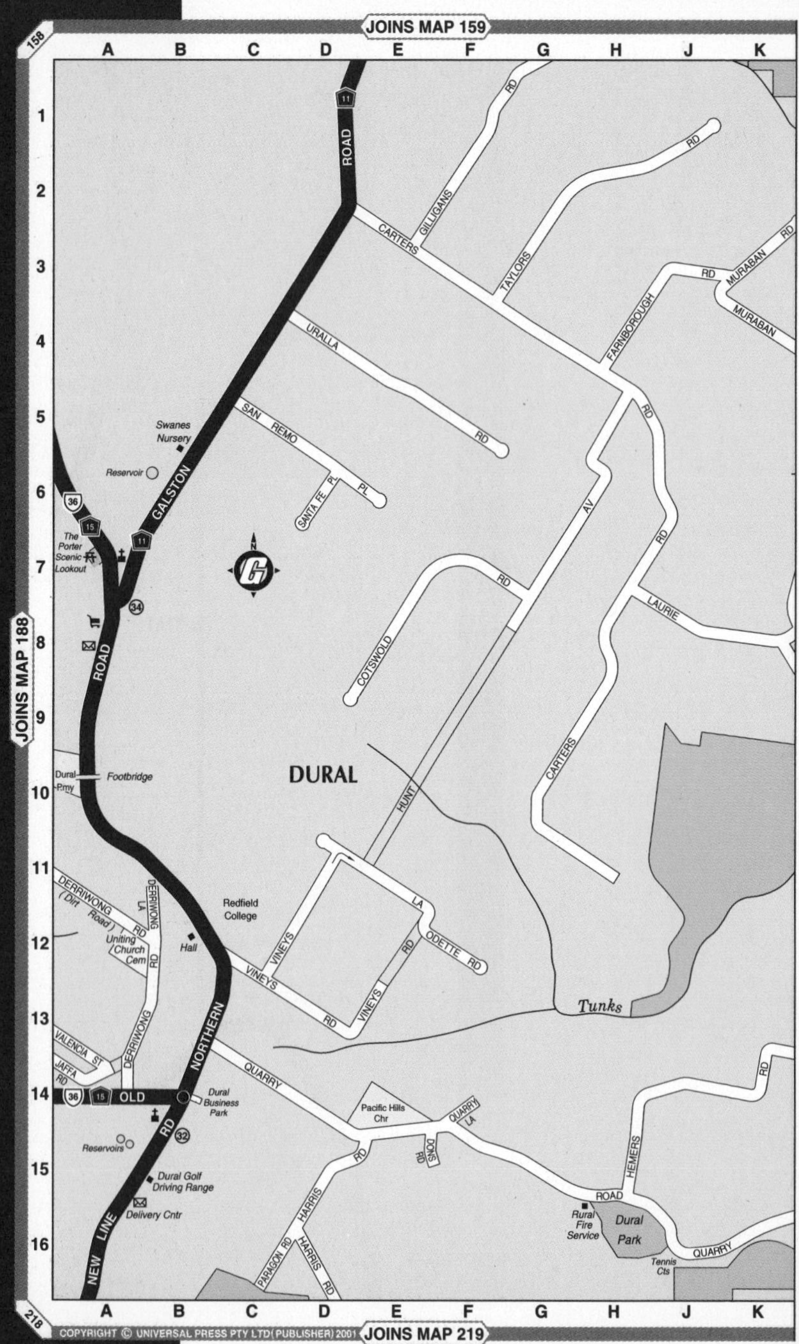

JOINS MAP 219

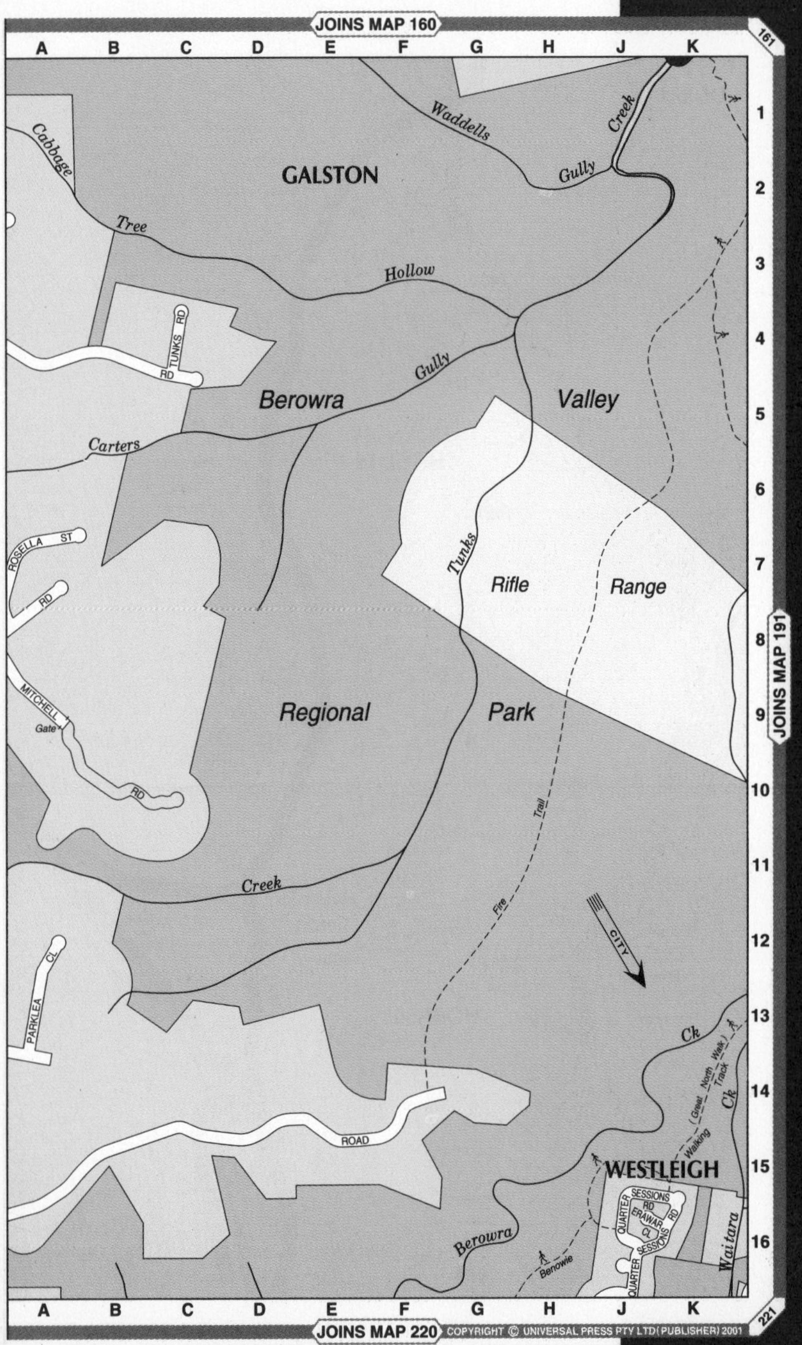

JOINS MAP 160
161
A B C D E F G H J K
1 2 3 4 5 6 7 8 9 10 11 12 13 14 15 16
GALSTON
Waddells
Gully
Creek
Cabbage
Tree
Hollow
TUNKS RD
RD
Gully
Berowra
Valley
Carters
ROSELLA ST
RD
Tunks
Rifle
Range
JOINS MAP 191
MITCHELL
Gate
RD
Regional
Park
Trail
Creek
Fire
CITY
PARKLEA
CL
Ck
Great North Walk
Track
Walking
Ck
ROAD
WESTLEIGH
QUARTER SESSIONS RD
ERAWAR CL
SESSIONS RD
Berowra
Benowie
QUARTER
Waitara
JOINS MAP 220
221

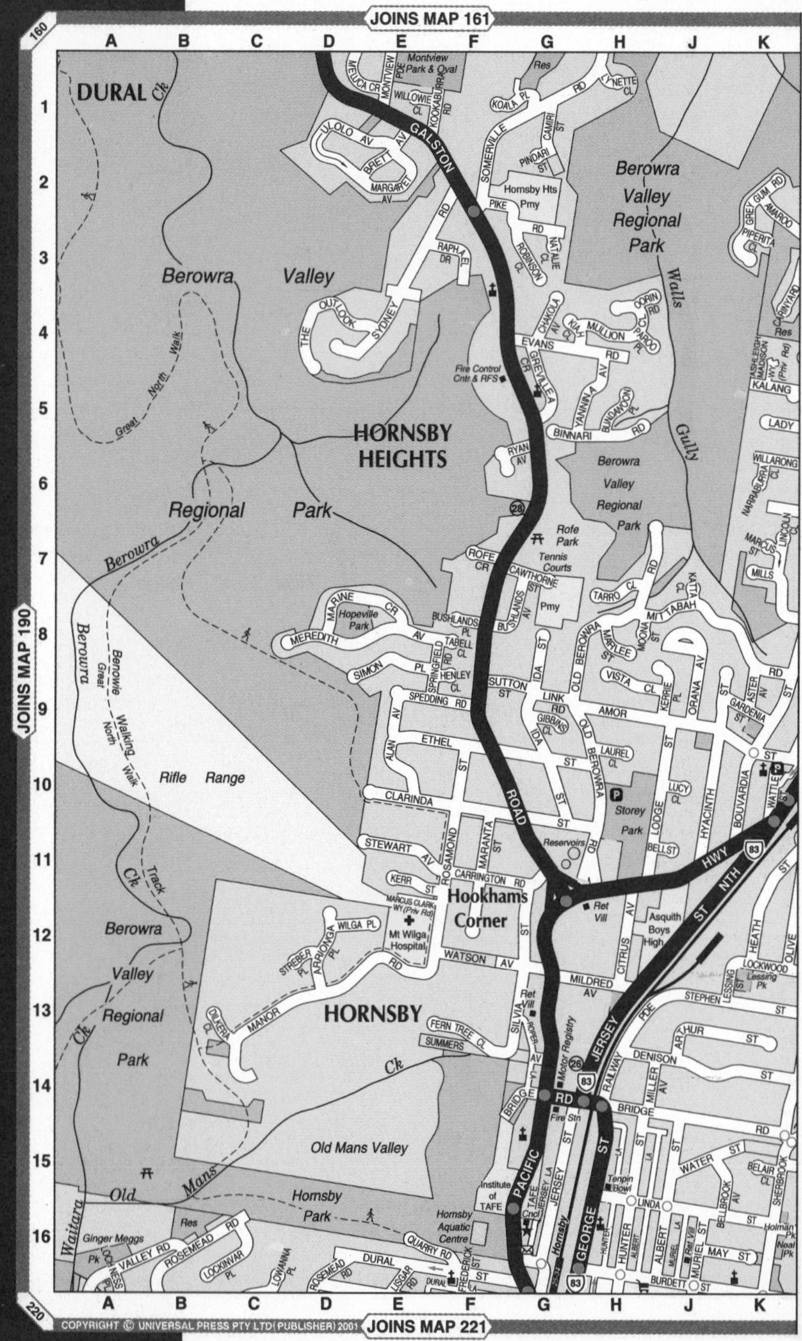
JOINS MAP 161
JOINS MAP 190
JOINS MAP 221
160
220
A B C D E F G H J K
1 2 3 4 5 6 7 8 9 10 11 12 13 14 15 16
DURAL Ck
Berowra Valley Regional Park
HORNSBY HEIGHTS
Great North Walk
Berowra Ck
Berowie Great North Walking Track
Rifle Range
Berowra Valley Regional Park
Old Mans Valley
Old Mans Ck
Waitara Ck
Hornsby Park
Ginger Meggs Pk
Res
Montview Park & Oval
GALSTON RD
SOMERVILLE RD
Hornsby Hts Pmy
Walls Gully
Fire Control Cntr & RFS
Rofe Park
Tennis Courts
Pmy
Hopeville Park
Hookhams Corner
Mt Wilga Hospital
MARCUS CLARK WY (Priv Rd)
Storey Park
Reservoirs
Ret Vill
Asquith Boys High
Lessing Pk
HORNSBY
Motor Registry
Fire Stn
Institute of TAFE
TAFE Cnd
Hornsby Aquatic Centre
Tenpin Bowl
Holman Pk
Neal Pk
PACIFIC HWY
ROAD
GEORGE ST
JERSEY RD
BRIDGE RD
PEATS FERRY RD
83
26
28
MELUCA CR
MONTVIEW PDE
WILLOWIE CL
KOOKABURRA RD
KOALA PL
LYNETTE CL
CAMIRI ST
PINDARI ST
ULOLO AV
BRETT AV
MARGARET AV
PIKE RD
ROBINSON CL
NATALIE CL
RAPHAEL DR
SYDNEY RD
THE OUTLOOK
CHAKOLA AV
KIAH CL
MULLION CL
OORIN RD
PAROO PL
EVANS RD
GREVILLEA CR
YANNINA AV
BUNDANOON RD
BINNARI RD
RYAN AV
GREY GUM RD
AMAROO
PIPERITA CL
CARINYA RD
ASHLEIGH WY
MADISON WY (Priv Rd)
KALANG
LADY
WILLARONG CL
NARRABURRA CL
LINCOLN CL
MARCUS ST
MILLS
ROFE CR
CAWTHORNE ST
BUSHLANDS AV
TARRO CL
KATTA CL
MITTABAH RD
MARINE CR
MEREDITH AV
BUSHLANDS PL
TABELL CL
SPRINGFIELD RD
HENLEY CL
SIMON PL
SUTTON ST
IDA ST
OLD BEROWRA RD
MARLEE ST
MOONA
VISTA CL
KERRIE PL
ORANA AV
ASTER AV
GARDENIA ST
SPEDDING RD
LINK RD
GIBBINS CL
AMOR ST
ALAN AV
ETHEL ST
LAUREL CL
LODGE
LUCY CL
HYACINTH
BOUVARDIA
WATTLE ST
CLARINDA ST
STEWART AV
ROSAMOND ST
MARANTA ST
BELL ST
CARRINGTON RD
KERR ST
WILGA PL
ARRIONGA PL
STREBER PL
WATSON AV
CITRUS AV
MILDRED AV
HEATH
OLIVE
LOCKWOOD
LESSING ST
STEPHEN ST
MANOR RD
DILKERA CL
FERN TREE CL
SUMMERS
SILVIA ST
ROPER AV
PDE
RAILWAY ST
ARTHUR ST
DENISON ST
MILLER AV
WATER ST
BELAIR CL
SHERBROOK
BELLBROOK AV
HUNTER ST
ALBERT ST
MURIEL ST
LINDA
MAY ST
BURDETT ST
JERSEY LA
VALLEY RD
ROSEMEAD RD
LOCKINVAR PL
LOWANNA PL
DURAL ST
LISGAR RD
QUARRY RD
FREDERICK ST
LOCHNESS PL
COPYRIGHT © UNIVERSAL PRESS PTY LTD (PUBLISHER) 2001

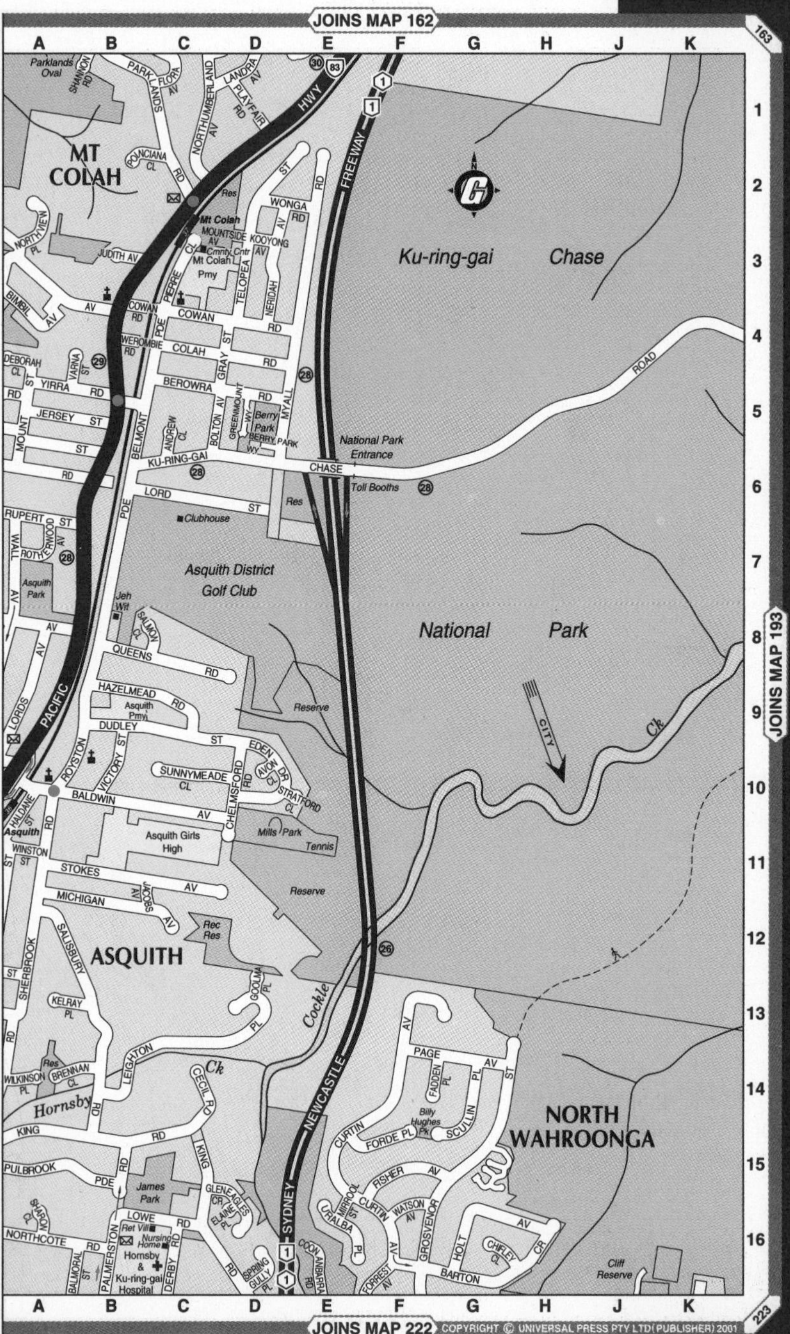
JOINS MAP 162
JOINS MAP 193
JOINS MAP 222
163
223
MT COLAH
ASQUITH
NORTH WAHROONGA
Ku-ring-gai Chase National Park
Asquith District Golf Club
National Park Entrance
Toll Booths
Asquith Girls High
PACIFIC HWY
FREEWAY
SYDNEY NEWCASTLE
KU-RING-GAI CHASE ROAD
Cockle Ck
Hornsby Ck
Hornsby & Ku-ring-gai Hospital
Cliff Reserve
James Park
Mills Park
Berry Park
Asquith Park
Parklands Oval
Reserve
Clubhouse

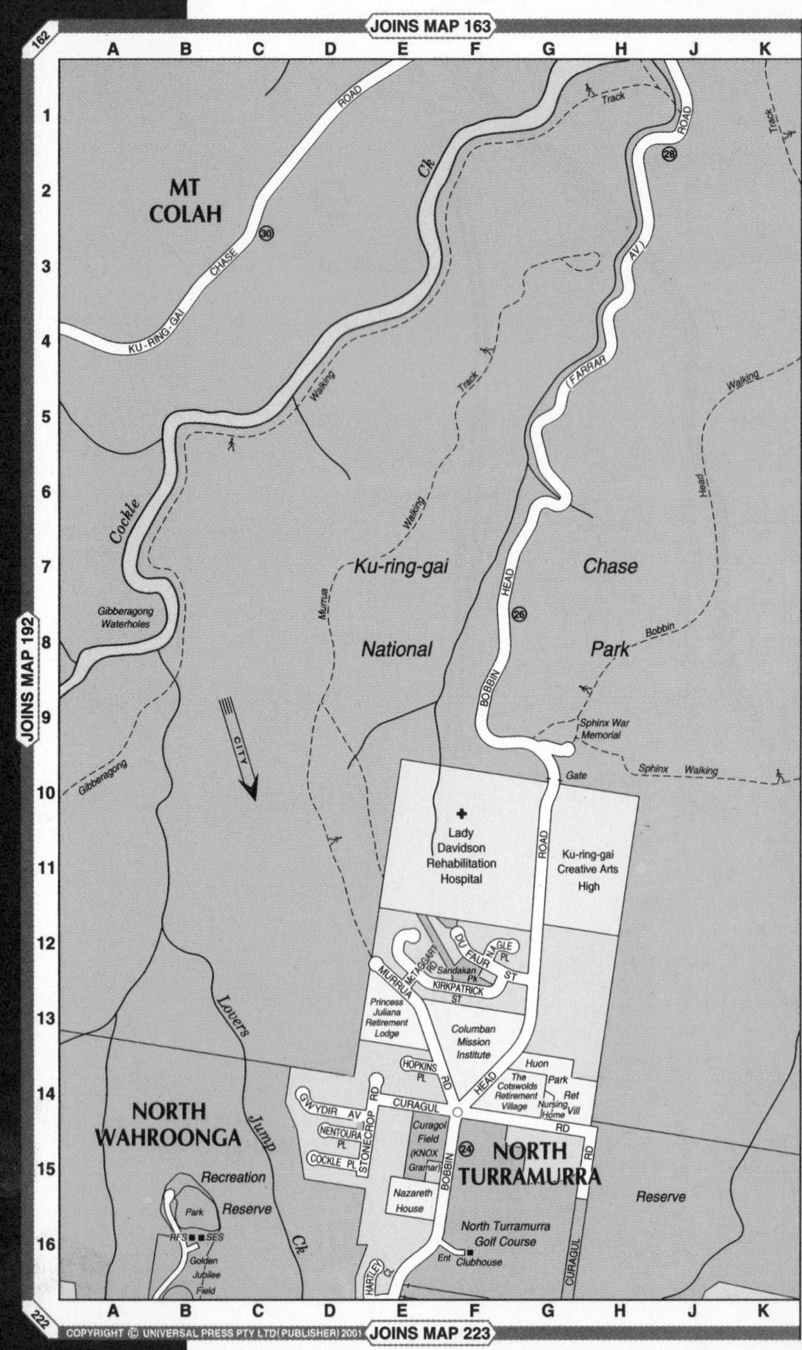
JOINS MAP 163
162
A B C D E F G H J K
1 2 3 4 5 6 7 8 9 10 11 12 13 14 15 16
JOINS MAP 192
MT COLAH
KU-RING-GAI CHASE ROAD
30
Ck
Track
ROAD
28
FARRAR AV
Walking
Track
Cockle
Walking
Ku-ring-gai
Chase
Gibberagong Waterholes
Murrua
National
Park
HEAD
26
Bobbin
BOBBIN
Head
Walking
CITY
Sphinx War Memorial
Gibberagong
Gate
Sphinx Walking
Lady Davidson Rehabilitation Hospital
ROAD
Ku-ring-gai Creative Arts High
DU FAUR
NAGLE PL
McTAGGART RD
Sandakan Pk
ST
MURRUA
KIRKPATRICK ST
Princess Juliana Retirement Lodge
Columban Mission Institute
Lovers
HOPKINS PL
RD
HEAD
Huon Park
The Cotswolds Retirement Village
Nursing Home
Ret Vill
NORTH WAHROONGA
GWYDIR AV
CURAGUL
RD
NENTOURA PL
COCKLE PL
STONECROP RD
Curagol Field (KNOX Grammar)
24
NORTH TURRAMURRA
RD
Jump
Recreation Reserve
Park
Nazareth House
BOBBIN
Reserve
RFS SES
Ck
North Turramurra Golf Course
Golden Jubilee Field
HARTLEY Cl
Ent
Clubhouse
CURAGUL
222
JOINS MAP 223

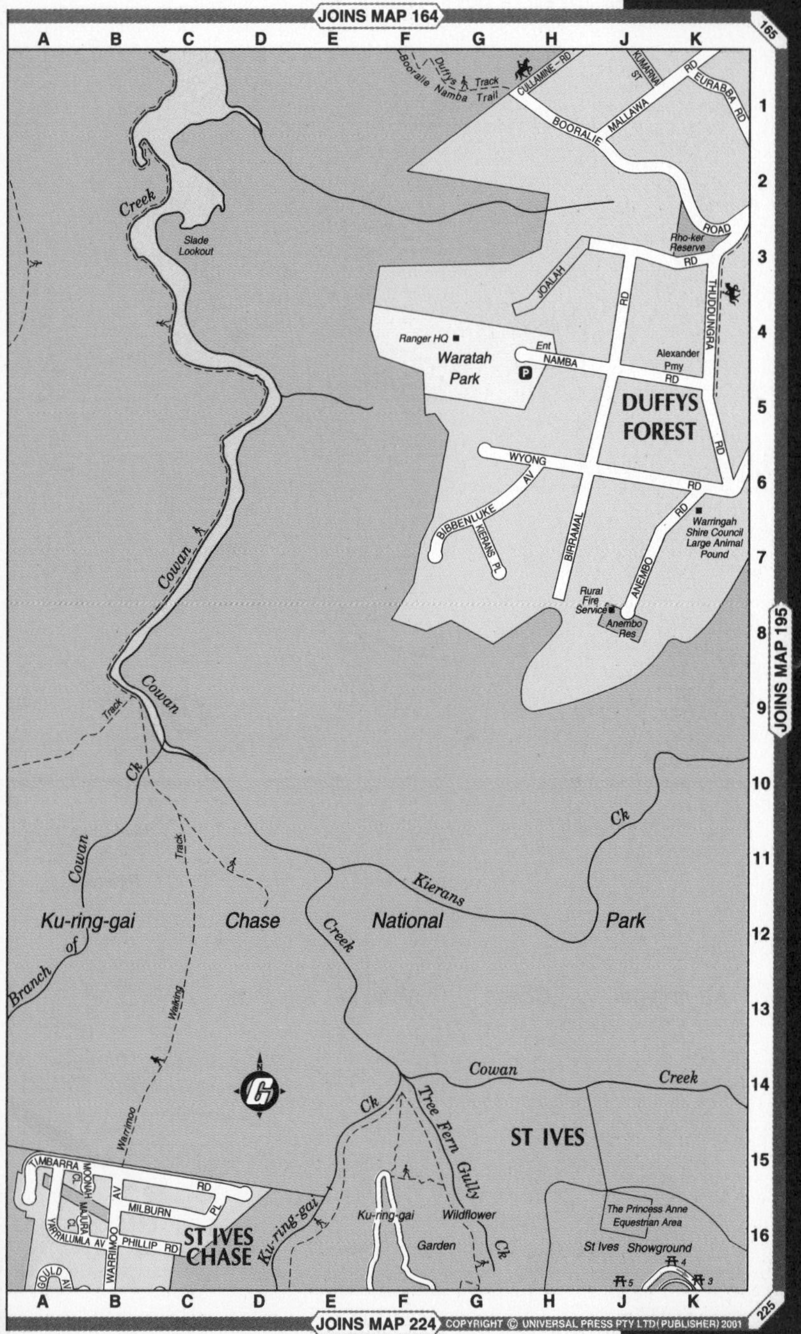
JOINS MAP 164
165
A B C D E F G H J K
1 2 3 4 5 6 7 8 9 10 11 12 13 14 15 16
Booralie Namba Trail
Duffys Track
CULLAMINE RD
KUMARNA ST
RD
EURABBA RD
MALLAWA
BOORALIE
ROAD
Rho-ker Reserve
RD
JOALAH
RD
THUDDUNGRA
Creek
Slade Lookout
Ranger HQ
Waratah Park
Ent
NAMBA
RD
Alexander Pmy
DUFFYS FOREST
WYONG
AV
RD
RD
BIBBENLUKE
KIERANS PL
BIRRAMAL
Warringah Shire Council Large Animal Pound
ANEMBO
Rural Fire Service
Anembo Res
Cowan
Cowan
Track
Ck
JOINS MAP 195
Cowan
Track
Ck
Kierans
Ku-ring-gai
Chase
National
Park
Creek
of
Branch
Walking
Cowan
Creek
Ck
Tree Fern Gully
Warrimoo
ST IVES
TIMBARRA
MOONAH CL
MAJURA CL
AV
RD
MILBURN
PL
YARRALUMLA AV
WARRIMOO
PHILLIP RD
ST IVES CHASE
GOULD AV
Ku-ring-gai
Ku-ring-gai
Wildflower
Garden
Ck
The Princess Anne Equestrian Area
St Ives Showground
5
4
3
JOINS MAP 224
225

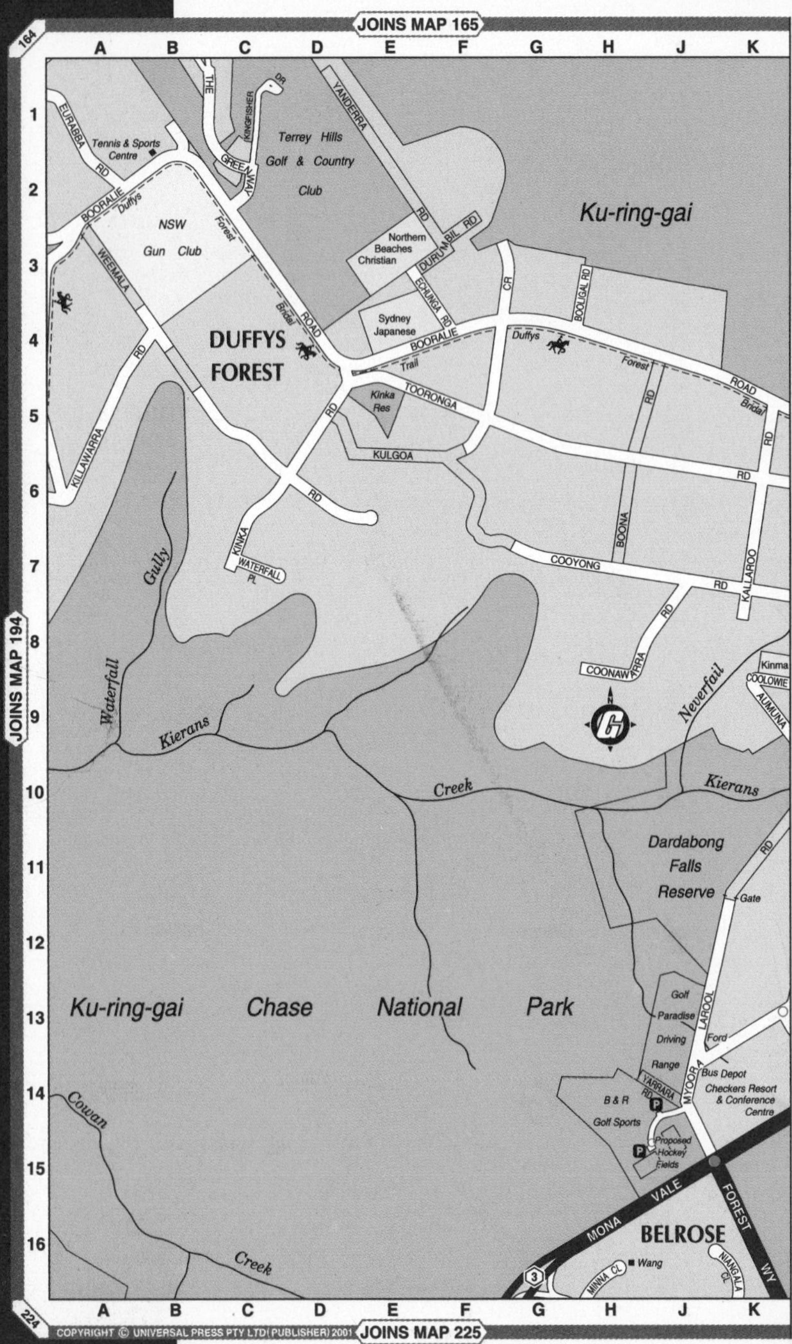
JOINS MAP 165
JOINS MAP 194
JOINS MAP 225
164
224
Tennis & Sports Centre
Terrey Hills Golf & Country Club
NSW Gun Club
Northern Beaches Christian
Sydney Japanese
Ku-ring-gai
DUFFYS FOREST
Kinka Res
Duffys Forest Bridal Trail
BOORALIE ROAD
TOORONGA RD
KULGOA
COOYONG RD
KINKA RD
WATERFALL PL
COONAWARRA RD
KALLAROO RD
BOONA RD
BOOLIGAL RD
YANDERRA RD
DURUMBIL RD
ECHUNGA RD
WEEMALA RD
KILLAWARRA
EURABBA RD
KINGFISHER
GREENWAY
Waterfall Gully
Kierans Creek
Neverfail
Kinma
COOLOWIE
AUMUNA
Dardabong Falls Reserve
Gate
Ku-ring-gai Chase National Park
Golf Paradise Driving Range
Ford
Bus Depot
Checkers Resort & Conference Centre
B & R Golf Sports
Proposed Hockey Fields
YARRARA RD
MYOORA
LAROOL
MONA VALE
FOREST WY
BELROSE
Wang
MINNA CL
NIANGALA CL
Cowan Creek
3

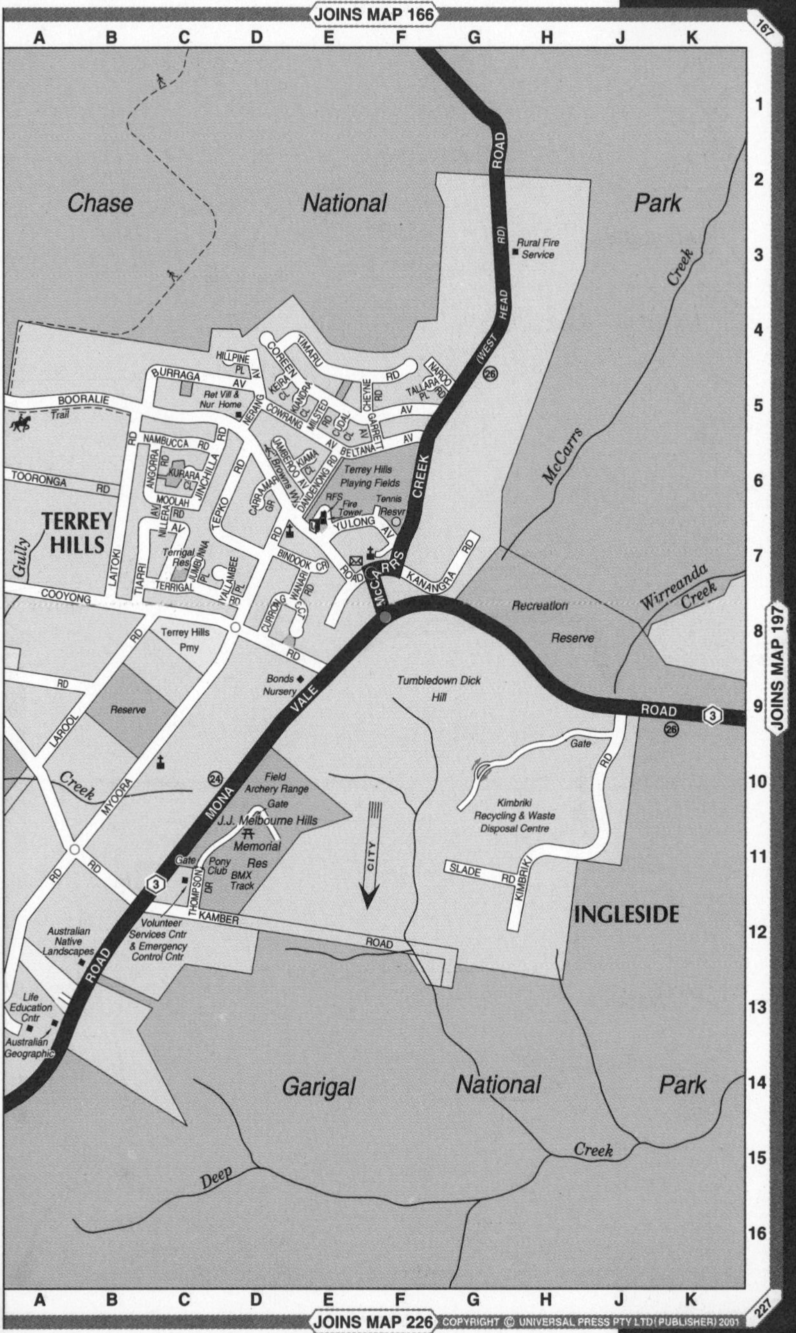
JOINS MAP 166
JOINS MAP 197
JOINS MAP 226
Chase National Park
Garigal National Park
TERREY HILLS
INGLESIDE
MONA VALE ROAD
McCARRS CREEK ROAD
(WEST HEAD RD)
Rural Fire Service
Terrey Hills Playing Fields
RFS Fire Tower
Tennis
Resvr
Recreation Reserve
Tumbledown Dick Hill
Bonds Nursery
Terrey Hills Pmy
Reserve
Field Archery Range
Gate
J.J. Melbourne Hills Memorial Res
Pony Club
BMX Track
Volunteer Services Cntr & Emergency Control Cntr
Australian Native Landscapes
Life Education Cntr
Australian Geographic
Kimbriki Recycling & Waste Disposal Centre
Ret Vill & Nur Home
Terrigal Res
BOORALIE Trail
TOORONGA RD
COOYONG RD
BURRAGA AV
HILLPINE PL
NAMBUCCA RD
KURARA CL
MOOLAH RD
ANGORRA RD
JINCHILLA RD
TEPKO RD
NILLERA AV
JUMBUNNA PL
YALLAMBEE PL
TERRIGAL RD
TIARRI
LAITOKI RD
BINDOOK CR
CURRONG
WANARI RD
CARRAMAR GR
JAMBEROO AV
Browns Wy
KIAMA CL
DANDENONG RD
BELTANA AV
YULONG AV
KANANGRA RD
COWRANG AV
NERANG
KEIRA CL
KIANDRA CL
MILSTED RD
CUDAL CL
GARRETT AV
CHEYNE RD
TALLARA PL
NAROO RD
TIMARU RD
COREEN
LAROOL
MYOORA RD
THOMPSON DR
KAMBER ROAD
SLADE RD
KIMBRIKI RD
McCarrs Creek
Wirreanda Creek
Deep Creek
Gully
CITY

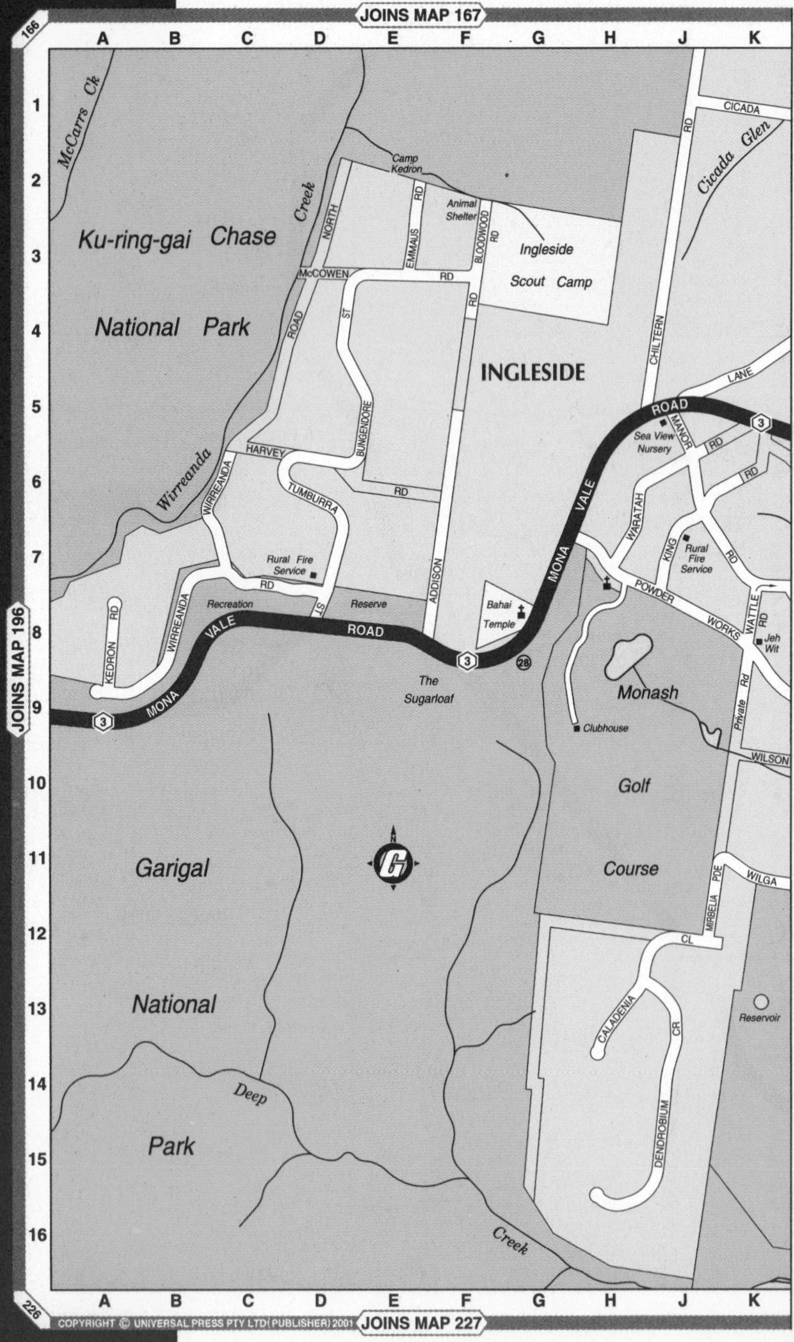
JOINS MAP 167
JOINS MAP 196
JOINS MAP 227
166
226
A B C D E F G H J K
1 2 3 4 5 6 7 8 9 10 11 12 13 14 15 16
McCarrs Ck
Ku-ring-gai Chase
National Park
Creek
Camp Kedron
Animal Shelter
NORTH
EMMAUS RD
BLOODWOOD RD
Ingleside
Scout Camp
McCOWEN RD
ROAD
ST
BUNGENDORE
INGLESIDE
CHILTERN RD
CICADA
Cicada Glen
LANE
ROAD
MANOR
Sea View Nursery
RD
VALE
MONA
HARVEY
Wirreanda
WIRREANDA
TUMBURRA
RD
RD
WARATAH
KING
Rural Fire Service
Rural Fire Service
ADDISON
POWDER
WORKS
WATTLE RD
Jeh Wit
Recreation
Reserve
RD
ST
Bahai Temple
28
KEDRON RD
WIRREANDA
VALE
ROAD
MONA
The Sugarloaf
Monash
Private Rd
Clubhouse
WILSON
Golf
Course
WILGA
MIRBELIA PDE
CL
Garigal
National
Park
CALADENIA
CR
Reservoir
DENDROBIUM
Deep
Creek

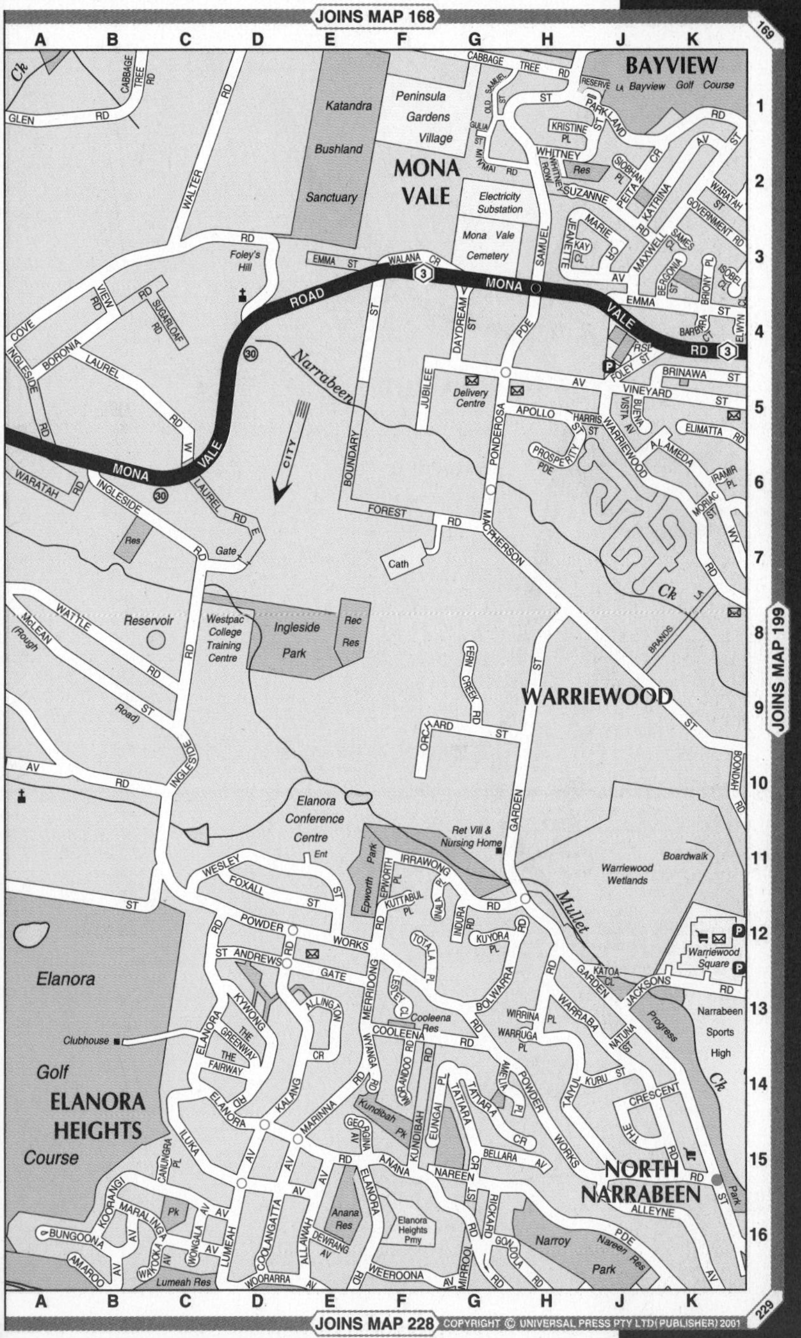
JOINS MAP 168
JOINS MAP 199
JOINS MAP 228
BAYVIEW
MONA VALE
WARRIEWOOD
ELANORA HEIGHTS
NORTH NARRABEEN
Katandra Bushland Sanctuary
Peninsula Gardens Village
Electricity Substation
Mona Vale Cemetery
Bayview Golf Course
Foley's Hill
Delivery Centre
Cath
Reservoir
Westpac College Training Centre
Ingleside Park
Rec Res
Elanora Conference Centre
Ret Vill & Nursing Home
Warriewood Wetlands
Boardwalk
Warriewood Square
Narrabeen Sports High
Elanora Golf Course
Clubhouse
Kundibah Pk
Anana Res
Elanora Heights Pmy
Narroy Park
Nareen Res
Lumeah Res
Cooleena Res
Epworth Park
MONA VALE ROAD
Narrabeen
Mullet
Progress
CITY
COPYRIGHT © UNIVERSAL PRESS PTY LTD (PUBLISHER) 2001

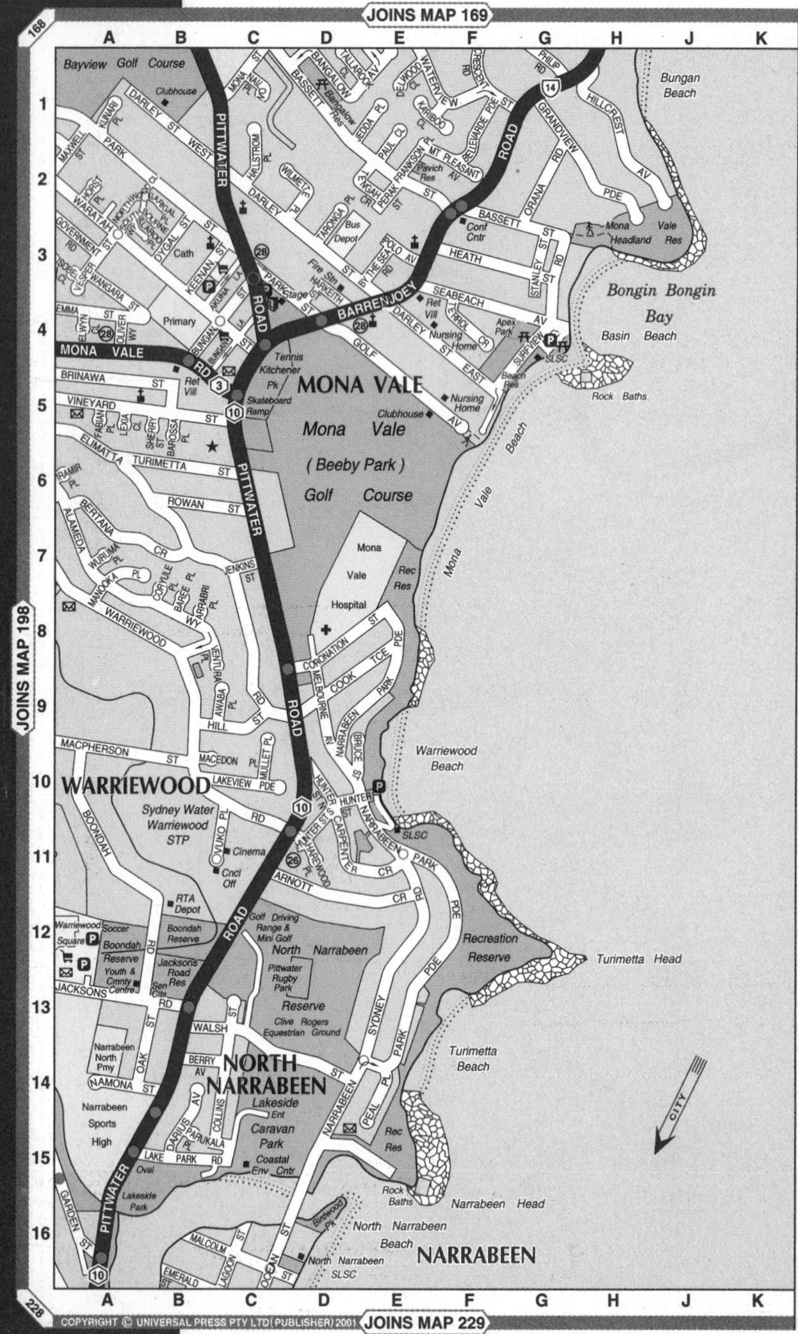
JOINS MAP 169
JOINS MAP 198
JOINS MAP 229
168
228
A
B
C
D
E
F
G
H
J
K
1
2
3
4
5
6
7
8
9
10
11
12
13
14
15
16
MONA VALE
WARRIEWOOD
NORTH NARRABEEN
NARRABEEN
Bayview Golf Course
Clubhouse
Mona Vale (Beeby Park) Golf Course
Mona Vale Hospital
Rec Res
Tennis
Kitchener Pk
Skateboard Ramp
Bungan Beach
Mona Headland
Vale Res
Bongin Bongin Bay
Basin Beach
Rock Baths
Mona Vale Beach
Warriewood Beach
Sydney Water Warriewood STP
Cinema
Cncl Off
RTA Depot
Boondah Reserve
Warriewood Square
Soccer
Boondah Reserve
Youth & Cmnty Centre
Jacksons Road Res
Sen Cits
Golf Driving Range & Mini Golf
North Narrabeen
Pittwater Rugby Park
Reserve
Clive Rogers Equestrian Ground
Recreation Reserve
Turimetta Head
Turimetta Beach
Narrabeen North Pmy
Narrabeen Sports High
Lakeside Caravan Park
Coastal Env Cntr
Oval
Lakeside Park
Rock Baths
Narrabeen Head
North Narrabeen Beach
North Narrabeen SLSC
Birdwood Pk
SLSC
Nursing Home
Ret Vill
Apex Park
Beach Res
Conf Cntr
Bus Depot
Fire Stn
Stage
Cath
Primary
Pavich Res
Bangalow Res
CITY
PITTWATER ROAD
BARRENJOEY ROAD
MONA VALE RD
GOLF AV
DARLEY ST
BASSETT ST
HEATH ST
SEABEACH AV
SURFVIEW RD
GRANDVIEW PDE
HILLCREST AV
WARRIEWOOD RD
MACPHERSON ST
JACKSONS RD
NARRABEEN PARK PDE
OCEAN ST
LAKE PARK RD

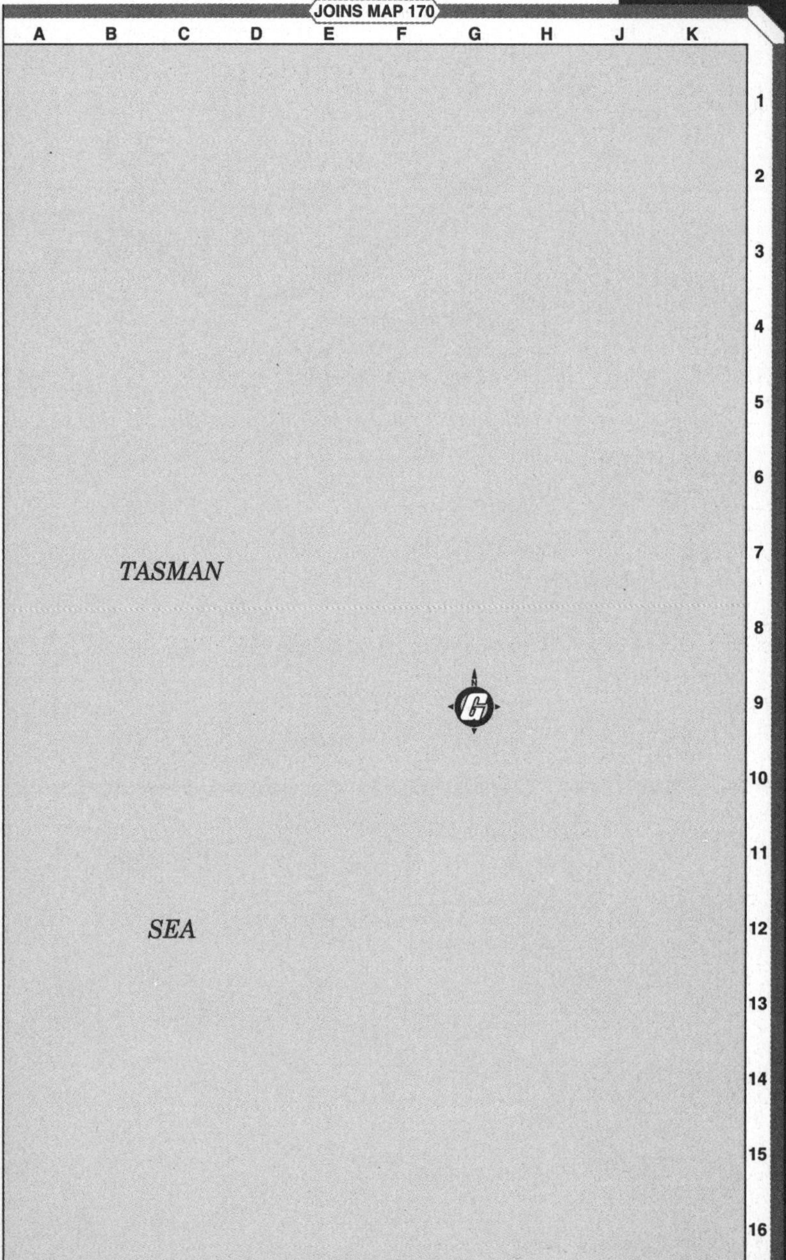

JOINS MAP 170

A B C D E F G H J K

1 2 3 4 5 6 7 8 9 10 11 12 13 14 15 16

TASMAN

SEA

A B C D E F G H J K

JOINS MAP 230

JOINS MAP 171

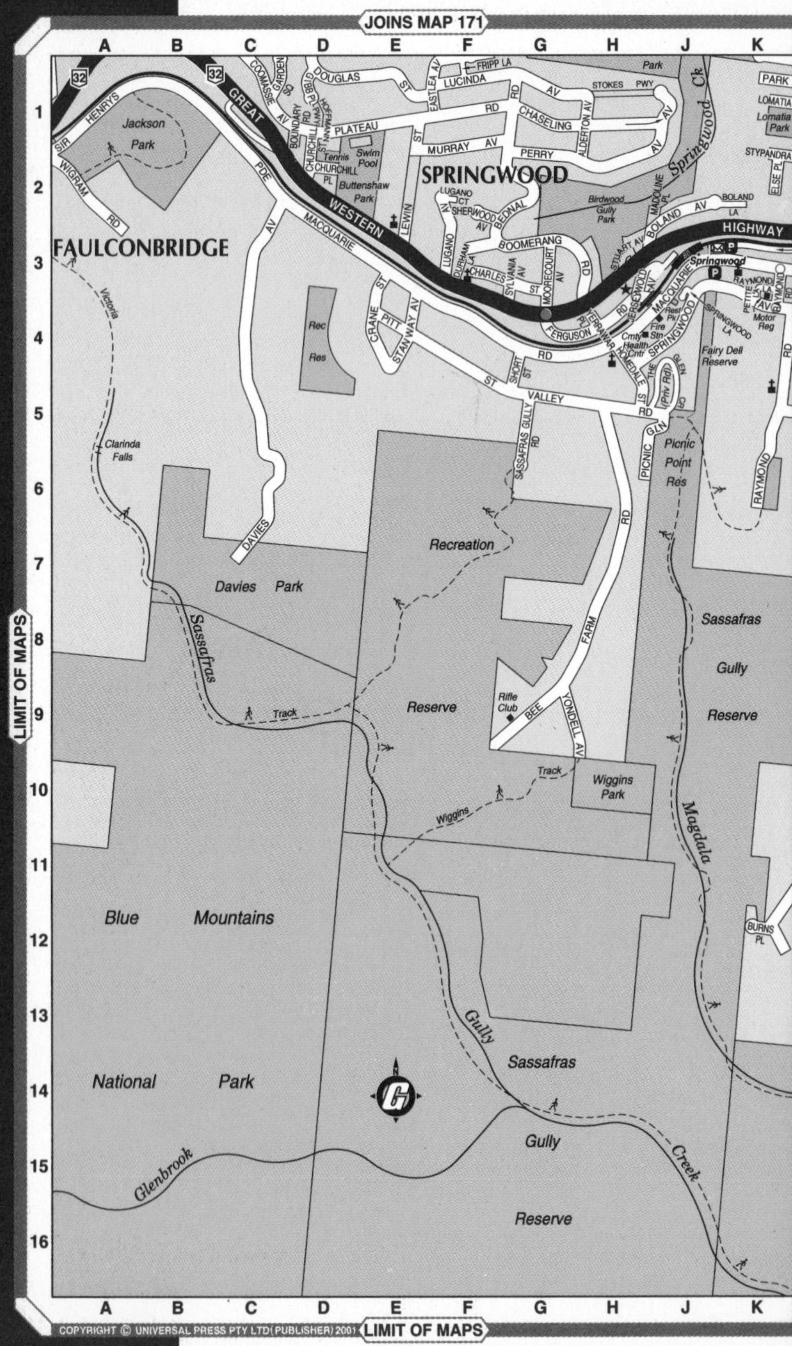

LIMIT OF MAPS

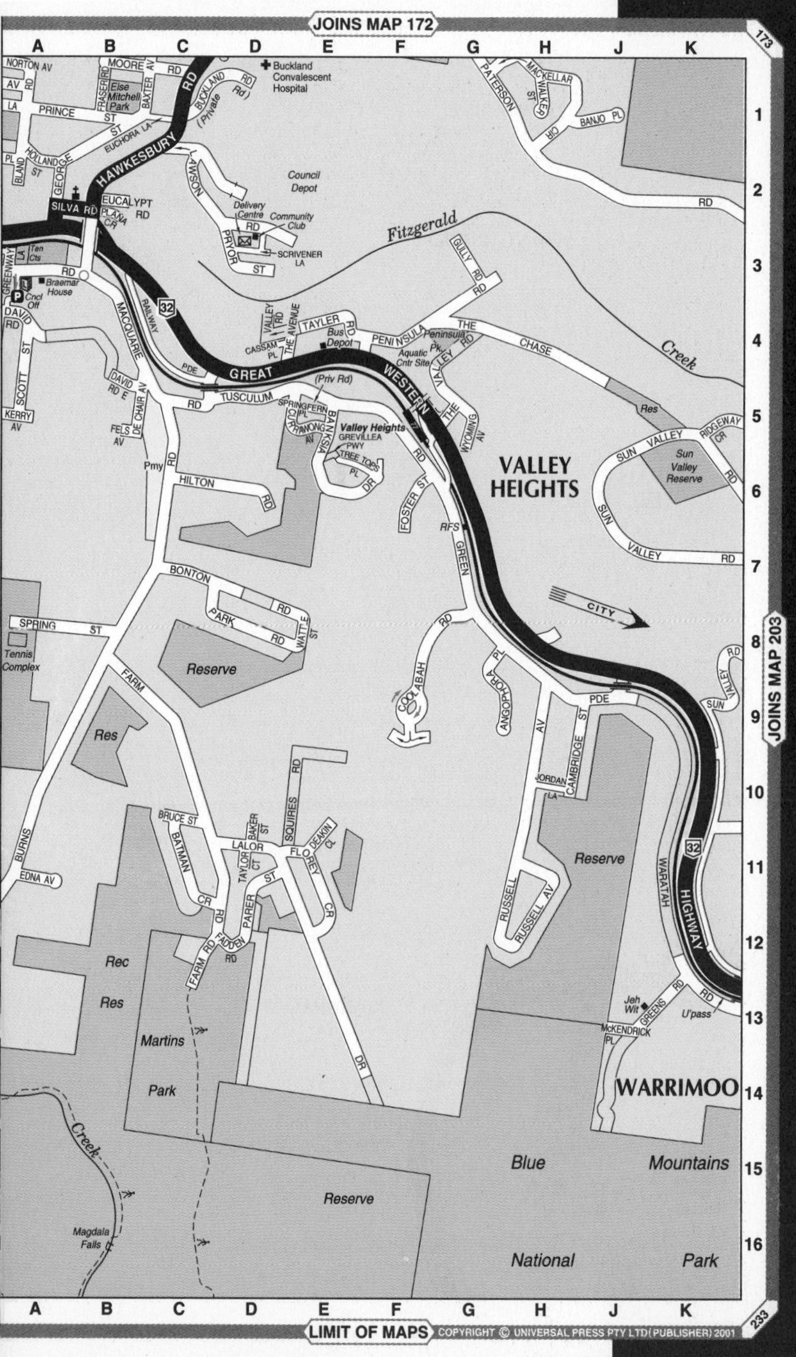
JOINS MAP 172
173
VALLEY HEIGHTS
WARRIMOO
Buckland Convalescent Hospital
Council Depot
Fitzgerald
Creek
HAWKESBURY RD
GREAT WESTERN
HIGHWAY
Valley Heights
Sun Valley Reserve
Reserve
Res
Rec Res
Martins Park
Blue Mountains National Park
Magdala Falls
CITY
JOINS MAP 203
LIMIT OF MAPS
233

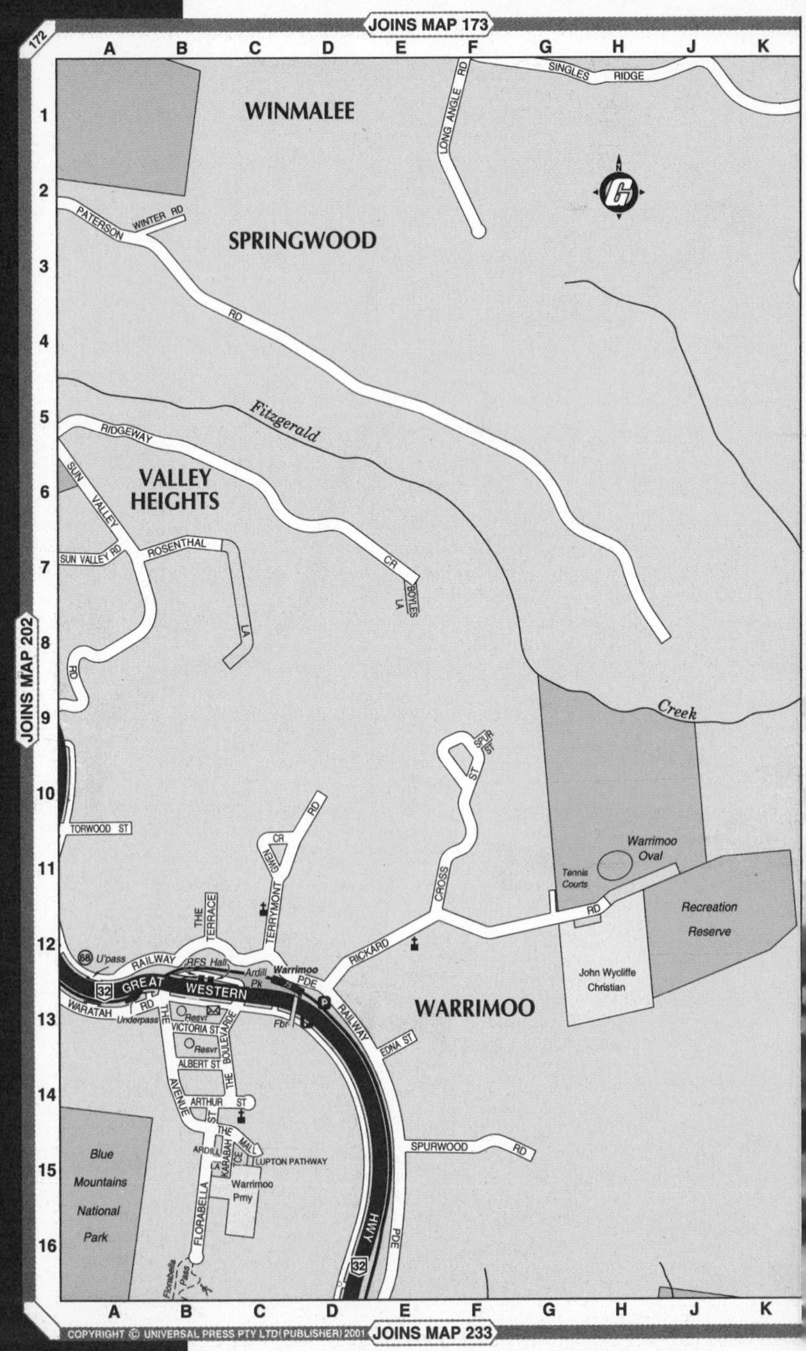
JOINS MAP 173
172
A B C D E F G H J K
1 2 3 4 5 6 7 8 9 10 11 12 13 14 15 16
WINMALEE
SPRINGWOOD
VALLEY HEIGHTS
WARRIMOO
SINGLES RIDGE
LONG ANGLE RD
PATERSON RD
WINTER RD
RIDGEWAY CR
Fitzgerald
Creek
SUN VALLEY RD
ROSENTHAL LA
BOYLES LA
SPUR ST
CROSS ST
RICKARD RD
TERRYMONT RD
GWEN CR
THE TERRACE
TORWOOD ST
U'pass
RAILWAY PDE
RFS Hall
Ardill Pk
Warrimoo
GREAT WESTERN HWY
32
WARATAH RD
Underpass
Resvr
VICTORIA ST
ALBERT ST
THE BOULEVARDE
THE AVENUE
ARTHUR ST
THE MALL
ARDILL LA
KARABAH TCE
LUPTON PATHWAY
Warrimoo Pmy
FLORABELLA ST
Florabella Pass
EDNA ST
SPURWOOD RD
Fbr
Warrimoo Oval
Tennis Courts
Recreation Reserve
John Wycliffe Christian
Blue Mountains National Park
JOINS MAP 202
JOINS MAP 233

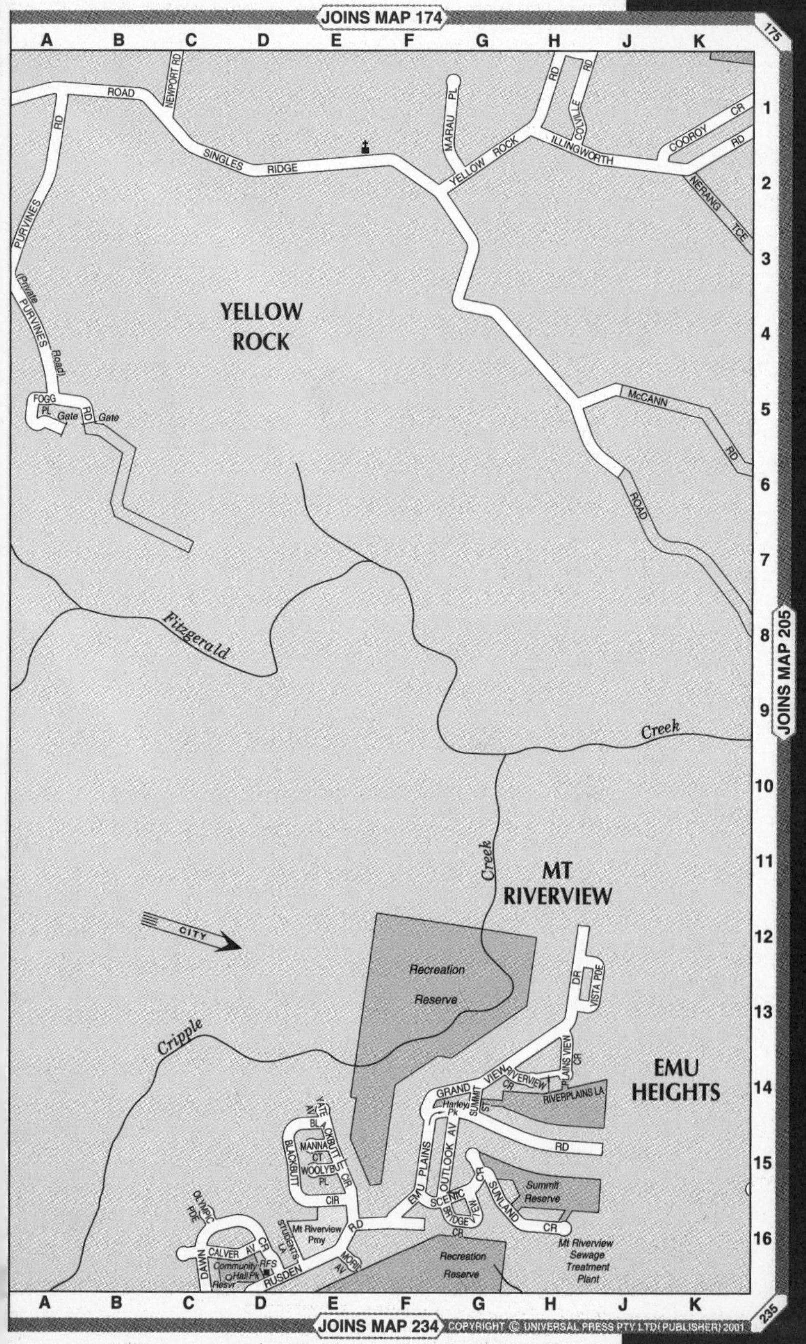
JOINS MAP 174
A B C D E F G H J K
1 2 3 4 5 6 7 8 9 10 11 12 13 14 15 16
175
YELLOW ROCK
SINGLES RIDGE ROAD
NEWPORT RD
PURVINES RD
(Private PURVINES Road)
FOGG PL
Gate
RD
Gate
MARAU PL
YELLOW ROCK
ILLINGWORTH
COLVILLE RD
RD
COOROY CR
RD
NERANG TCE
McCANN RD
ROAD
Fitzgerald
Creek
Creek
JOINS MAP 205
CITY
MT RIVERVIEW
Recreation Reserve
Cripple
VISTA PDE
DR
GRAND VIEW
RIVERVIEW CR
PLAINS VIEW CR
RIVERPLAINS LA
SUMMIT ST
Harley Pk
EMU HEIGHTS
RD
OUTLOOK AV
EMU PLAINS
SCENIC CR
BRIDGEVIEW CR
SUNLAND CR
Summit Reserve
Mt Riverview Sewage Treatment Plant
YATE AV
BLACKBUTT CIR
BLACKBUTT
MANNA CT
WOOLYBUTT PL
CIR
Mt Riverview Pmy
STUDENTS LA
OLYMPIC PDE
DAWN
CALVER AV
CR
Community Hall Pk
RFS
Resvr
RUSDEN RD
MORIC AV
Recreation Reserve
JOINS MAP 234
235

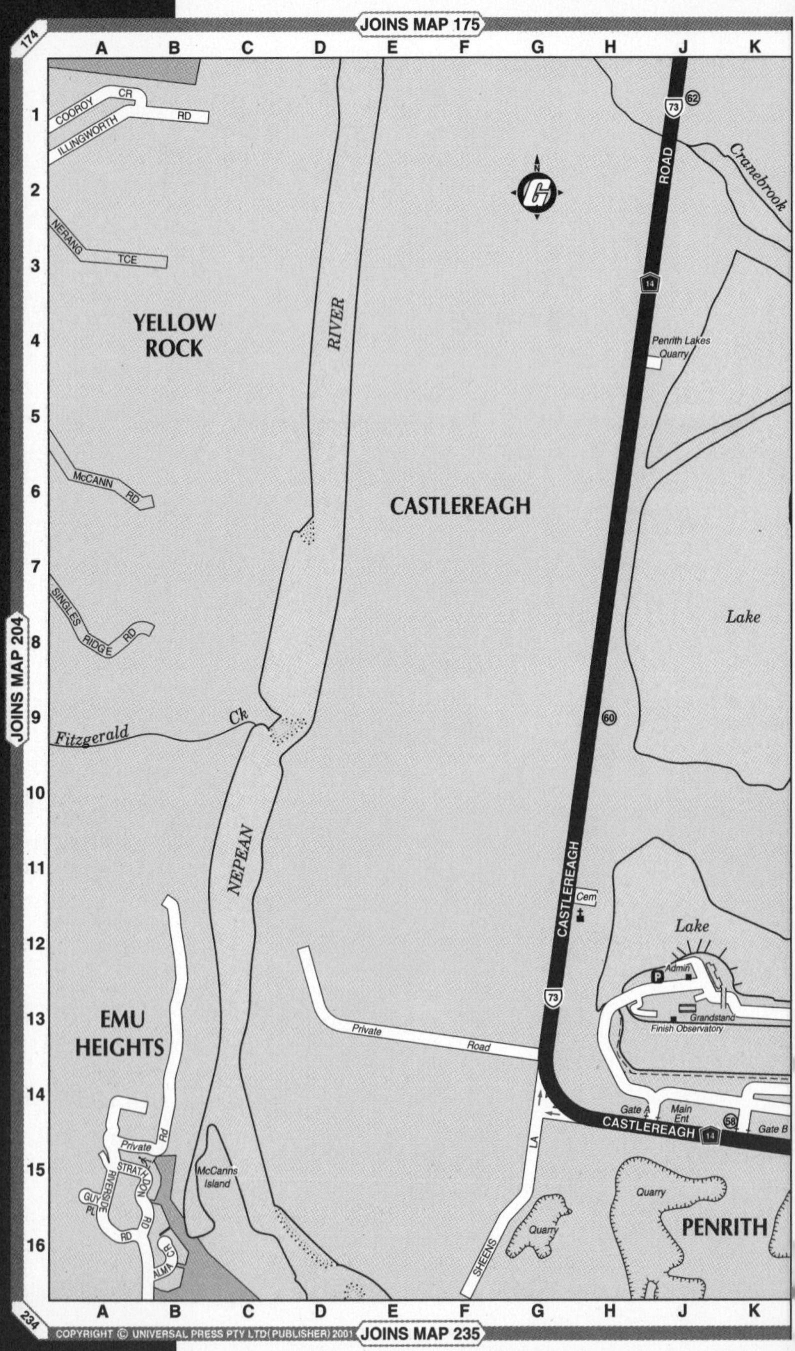
JOINS MAP 175
174
A B C D E F G H J K
1 2 3 4 5 6 7 8 9 10 11 12 13 14 15 16
COOROY CR
ILLINGWORTH RD
NERANG TCE
YELLOW ROCK
McCANN RD
SINGLES RIDGE RD
Fitzgerald Ck
RIVER
NEPEAN
CASTLEREAGH
Cranebrook
ROAD
73
62
14
Penrith Lakes Quarry
Lake
60
CASTLEREAGH
Cem
Lake
Admin
Grandstand
Finish Observatory
Private Road
Gate A
Main Ent
58
Gate B
CASTLEREAGH
EMU HEIGHTS
Private Rd
STRATHDON RD
RIVERSIDE RD
GUY PL
ALMA CR
McCanns Island
SHEENS LA
Quarry
Quarry
PENRITH
JOINS MAP 204
234
JOINS MAP 235

JOINS MAP 176

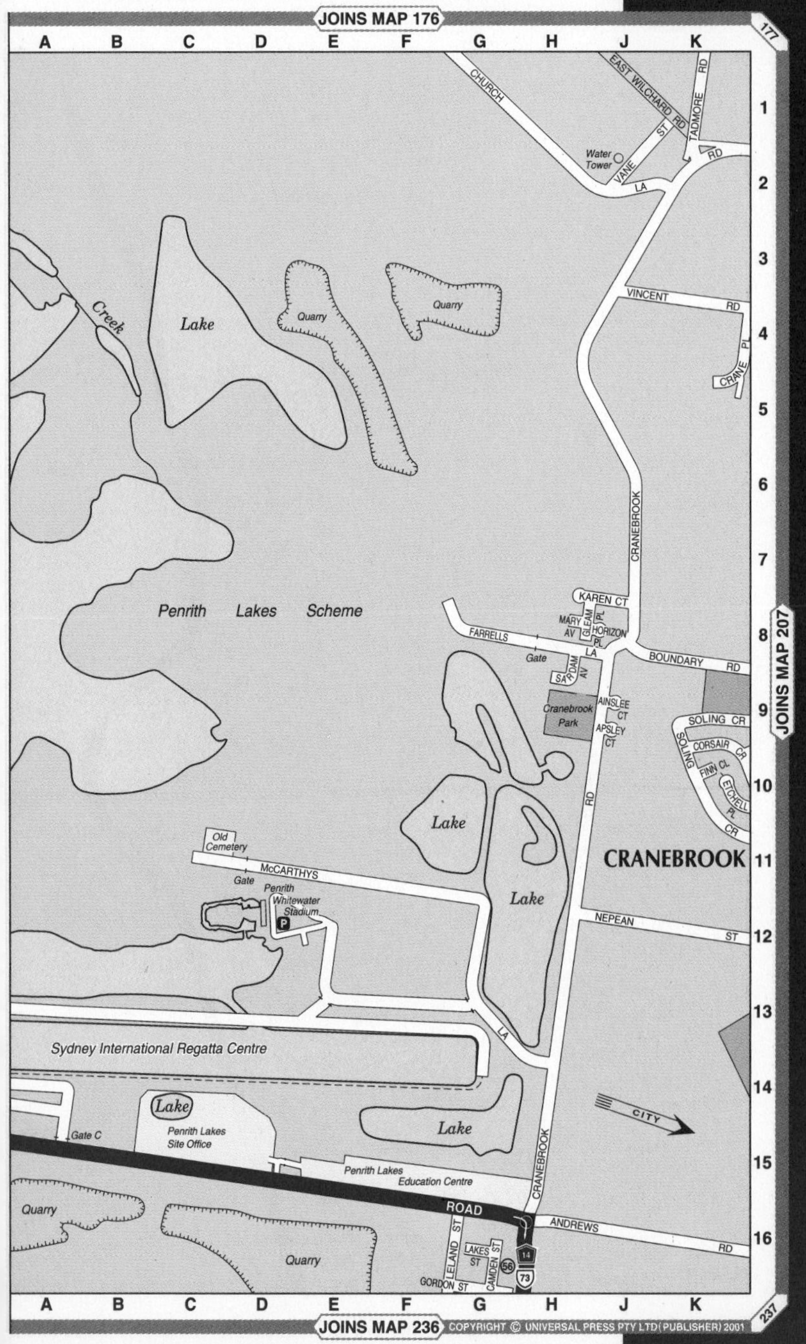

JOINS MAP 207

JOINS MAP 236

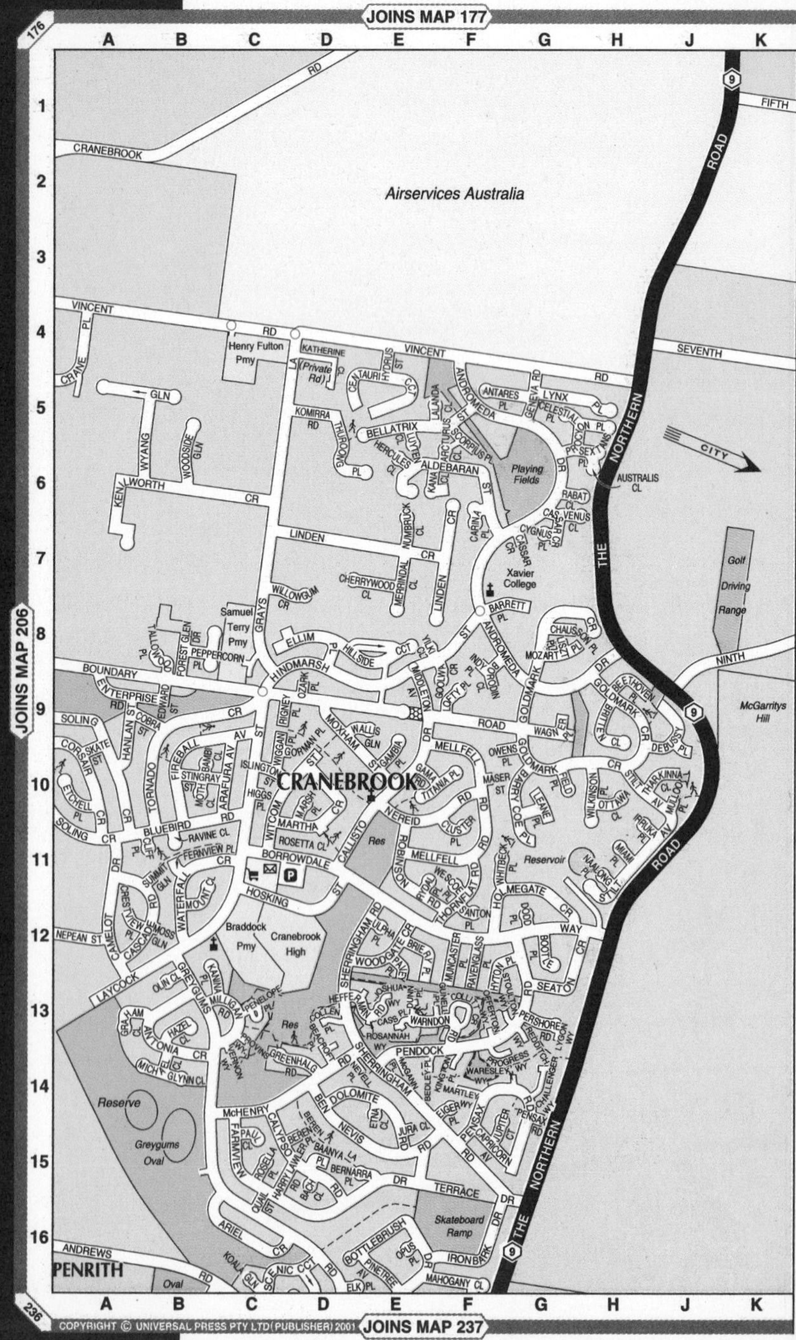
JOINS MAP 177
176
A B C D E F G H J K
1 2 3 4 5 6 7 8 9 10 11 12 13 14 15 16
JOINS MAP 206
RD
FIFTH
CRANEBROOK
Airservices Australia
ROAD
VINCENT
RD
Henry Fulton Pmy
KATHERINE
(Private Rd)
HYDRUS
VINCENT
SEVENTH
RD
CRANE
PL
GLN
KOMIRRA RD
CENTAURI
CCT
ANDROMEDA
ANTARES PL
LYNX
CELESTIAL
GENEVA RD
WYANG
WOODSIDE GLN
BELLATRIX
LUYTEN
ARCTURUS
SCORPIUS PL
HERCULES CL
THURGONG PL
ALDEBARAN
KANA CL
Playing Fields
NORTHERN
SEXTANS
CITY
AUSTRALIS CL
KENILWORTH
CR
RABAT
CASSIOPEIA
VENUS CL
CYGNUS PL
LINDEN
NUMBRUCK CL
CARINA PL
CASSAR CR
CR
THE
Golf Driving Range
CHERRYWOOD CL
MERRINDAL CL
LINDEN
Xavier College
WILLOWGUM CR
BARRETT PL
Samuel Terry Pmy
GRAYS
TALLOWOOD PL
FOREST GLEN DR
PEPPERCORN PL
ELLIM
HILLSIDE
CCT
YILKI CL
ANDROMEDA
INDY CL
BORODIN
MOZART
CHAUSSON PL
LISZT PL
GOLDMARK
NINTH
BOUNDARY
HINDMARSH
MIDDLETON AV
GOOLWA CR
LOFTY PL
BEETHOVEN PL
McGarritys Hill
ENTERPRISE RD
EDWARD ST
SOLING
HANLAN ST
COBRA ST
CR
RIGNEY
OZARK
MOXHAM
WALLIS GLN
ROAD
WAGNER PL
BRITTEN CL
DEBUSSY PL
CORSAIR
SKATE ST
TORNADO
FIREBALL
BAMBI
AV
ST
GORMAN PL
MELLFELL
OWENS PL
GOLDMARK
ETCHELL PL
STINGRAY CL
MOTH CL
ARAFURA AV
ISLINGTON
WIGGAN
GAMBIA
GAMA
TITANIA PL
MASER ST
BARRY COE PL
CR
WILKINSON PL
THARKINNA
CRANEBROOK
HIGGS PL
WITCOM
MARSH PL
CR
RD
OTTAWA CL
STILT
MULLOO
CL
SOLING
CR
BLUEBIRD
RAVINE CL
RD
MARTHA
ROSETTA CL
CALLISTO
NEREID
CLUSTER PL
LEANE
FIELD
IRRUKA AV
CLIFF PL
FERNVIEW PL
BORROWDALE
Res
ROBINSON
MELLFELL
WHITBECK PL
Reservoir
MIAMI PL
NAALONG PL
STILT
DR
SUMMIT GLN
WATERFALL
MOUNT CL
CR
HOSKING
ST
WESCOE
RYDAL PL
THORNFLAT RD
SANTON PL
HOLMEGATE
DODD PL
CR
ROAD
CRESTVIEW PL
CASCADE
MOSS GLN
Braddock Pmy
Cranebrook High
SHERRINGHAM
ULPHA PL
WOODGATE
BRIERY PL
MUNCASTER
RAVENGLASS
HYTON PL
STOULTON
BOOTLE PL
WAY
CR
NEPEAN ST
CAMELOT
LAYCOCK
OLIN CL
GREYGUMS
KANINA PL
MILLIGAN RD
PENELOPE
HEFFERMAN
JOSHUA
DUNN
COLLU
OFFERTON
SEATON
PERSHORE
REDDITCH
LYGON
GRAHAM CL
HAZEL CL
ANTONIA
CR
Res
COLLEN
BEACROFT
ROSANNAH WY
CASS PL
WARNDON
PENDOCK
PROGRESS WY
WARESLEY WY
CHALLENGER
MICHAEL GLYNN CL
PROVINS WY
VERNON WY
GREENHALGH RD
RD
NEVELL
SHERRINGHAM
McGANN
BEDLEY PL
KINGTON PL
MARTLEY
EIGER PL
PENSAX
JUPITER CT
CAPRICORN AV
Reserve
McHENRY
CALYPSO
BEREN PL
BEN
DOLOMITE
NEVIS
ETNA CL
JURA CL
RD
Greygums Oval
FARMVIEW
PAUL CL
ROSELLA PL
HARRY LAWLER RD
BAANYA LA
BERNARRA PL
BACH CL
RD
DR
TERRACE
DR
QUAIL ST
Skateboard Ramp
ARIEL
CR
BOTTLEBRUSH
OPUS PL
IRONBARK
ANDREWS
PENRITH
KOALA
SCENIC CCT
ELK PL
PINETREE AV
MAHOGANY CL
Oval
GLN
RD
9
236
JOINS MAP 237

JOINS MAP 178

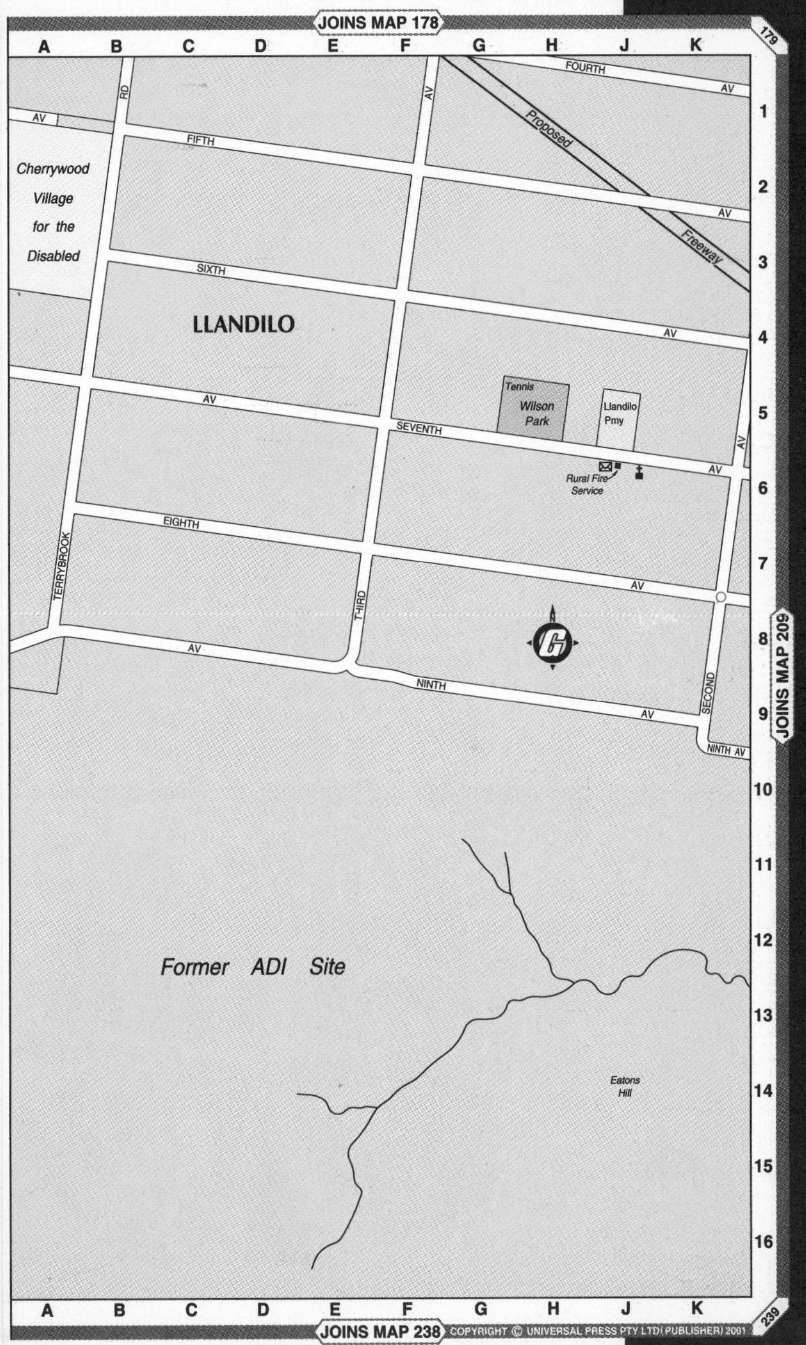

JOINS MAP 209

JOINS MAP 238

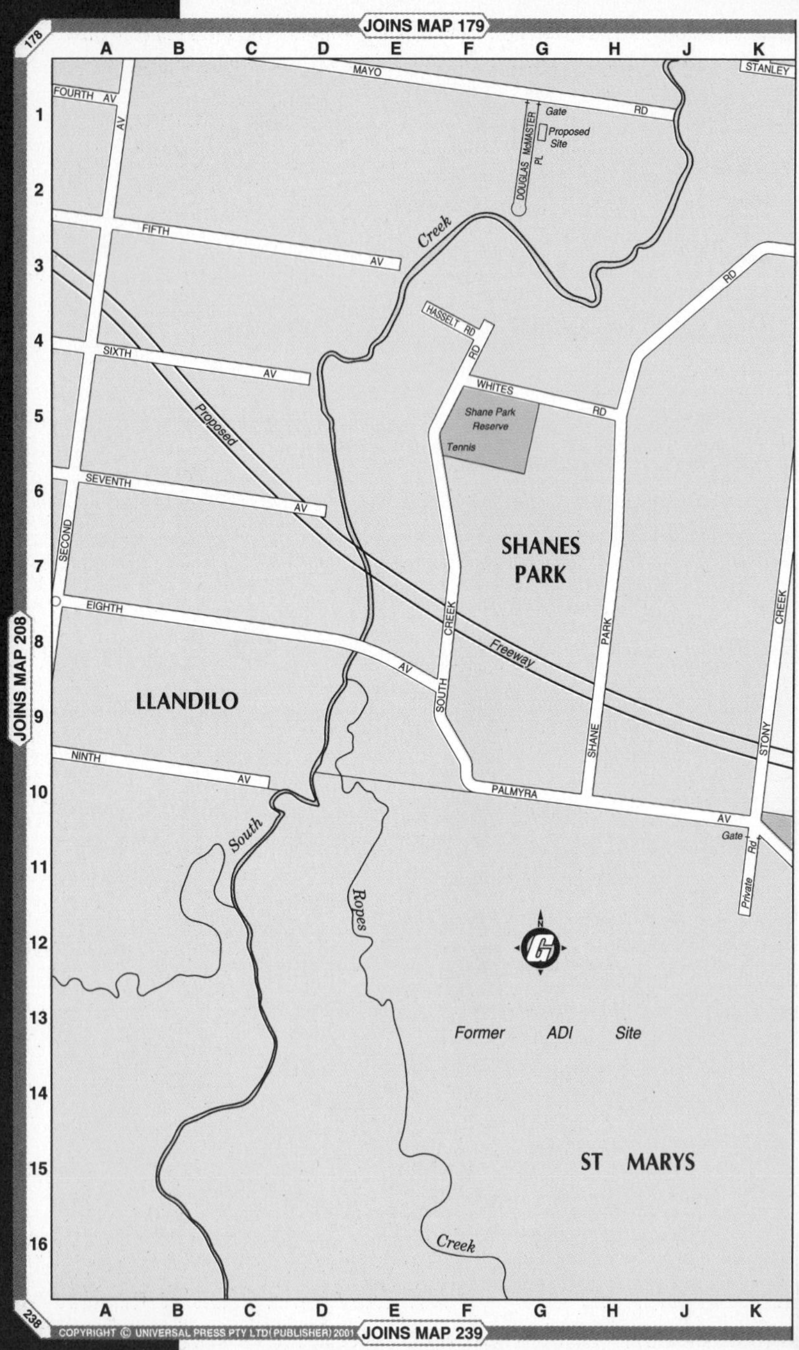
JOINS MAP 179
178
A B C D E F G H J K
1 2 3 4 5 6 7 8 9 10 11 12 13 14 15 16
MAYO RD
STANLEY
FOURTH AV
AV
Gate
Proposed Site
DOUGLAS McMASTER PL
FIFTH AV
Creek
RD
HASSELT RD
RD
SIXTH AV
Proposed
WHITES RD
Shane Park Reserve
Tennis
SEVENTH AV
SECOND
SHANES PARK
EIGHTH AV
SOUTH CREEK
Freeway
SHANE PARK
STONY CREEK
JOINS MAP 208
LLANDILO
NINTH AV
PALMYRA AV
Gate
Private Rd
South
Ropes
Former ADI Site
ST MARYS
Creek
238
JOINS MAP 239

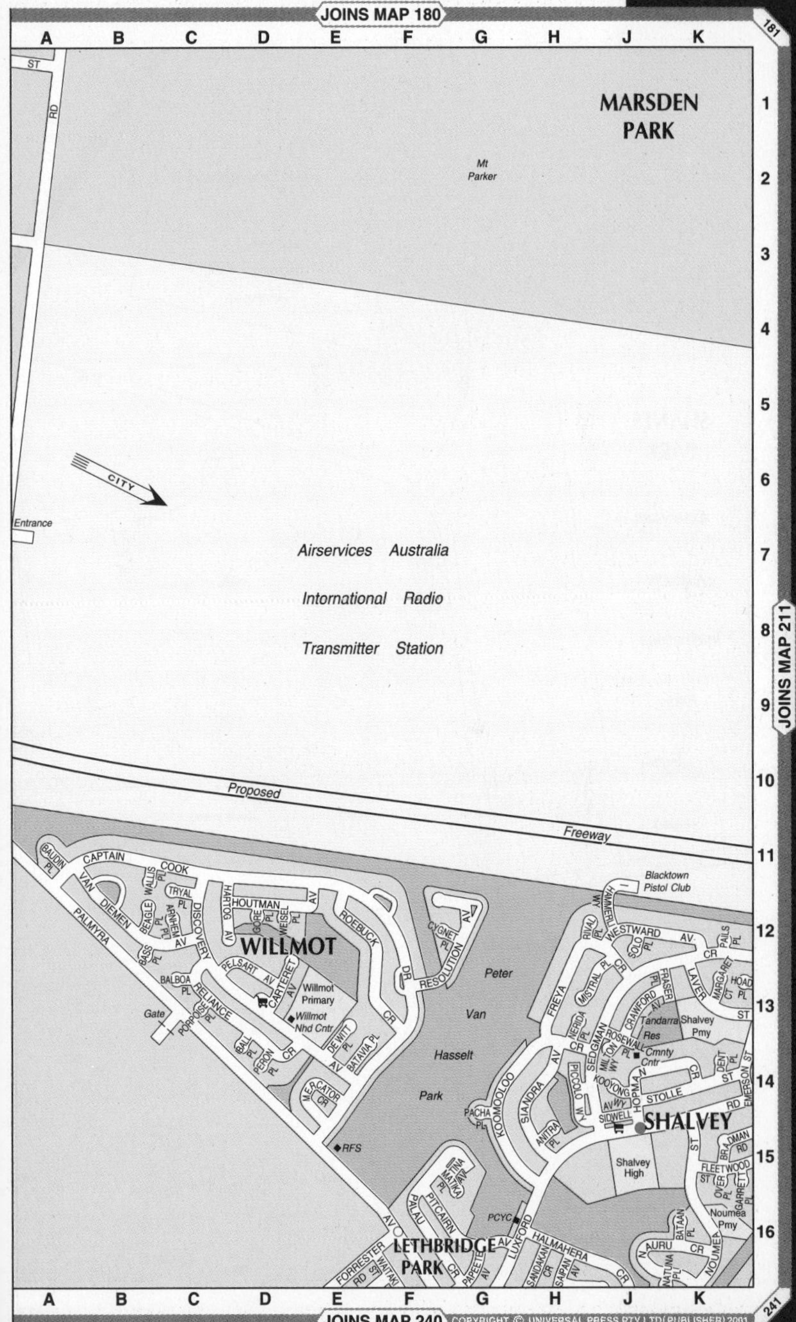
JOINS MAP 180
A B C D E F G H J K
181
MARSDEN PARK
Mt Parker
CITY
Entrance
Airservices Australia
International Radio
Transmitter Station
JOINS MAP 211
Proposed
Freeway
Blacktown Pistol Club
WILLMOT
Willmot Primary
Willmot Nhd Cntr
Peter Van Hasselt Park
RFS
PCYC
LETHBRIDGE PARK
SHALVEY
Tandarra Res
Shalvey Pmy
Cmnty Cntr
Shalvey High
Noumea Pmy
Gate
CAPTAIN COOK
PALMYRA
VAN DIEMEN
DISCOVERY
HOUTMAN
RESOLUTION
ROEBUCK
WESTWARD AV
STOLLE
HALMAHERA
LUXFORD
1 2 3 4 5 6 7 8 9 10 11 12 13 14 15 16
241

JOINS MAP 181

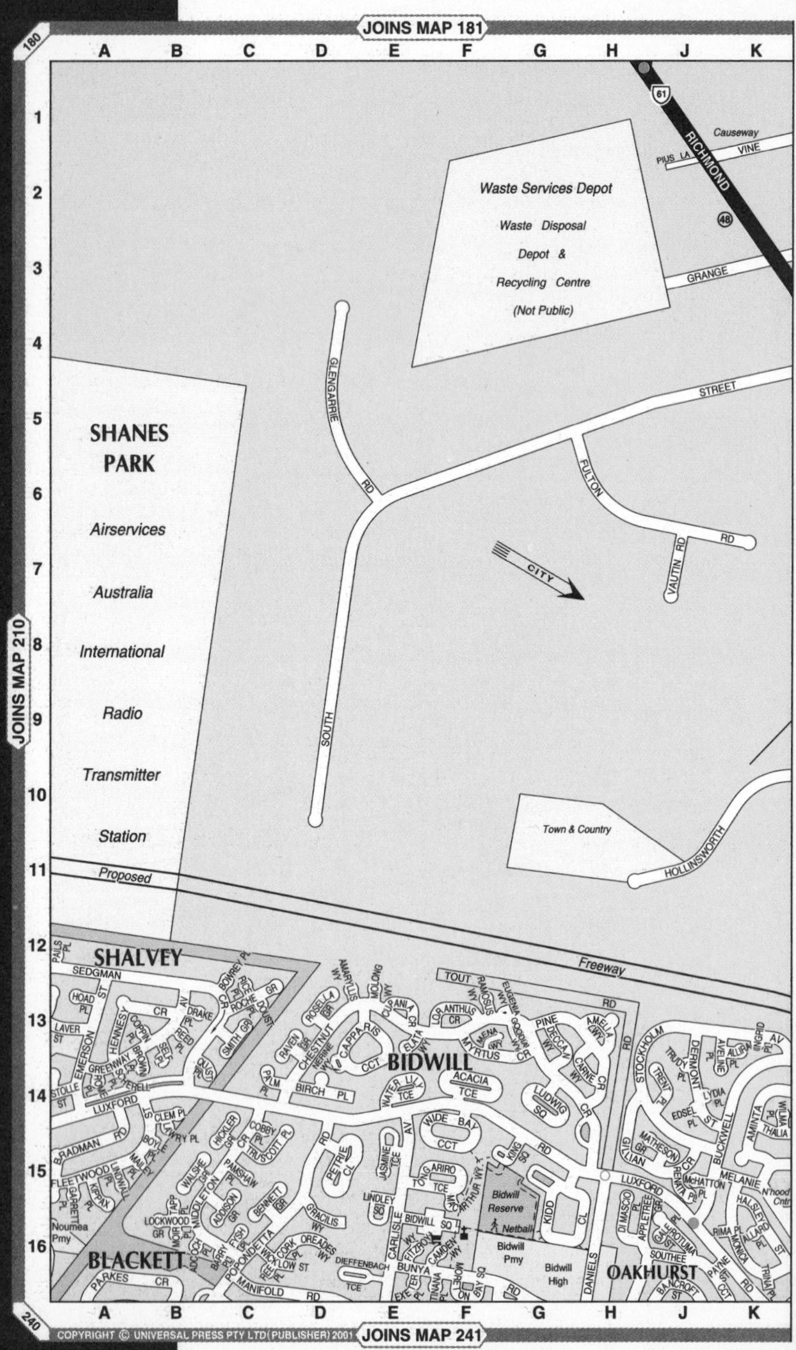

JOINS MAP 210

JOINS MAP 241

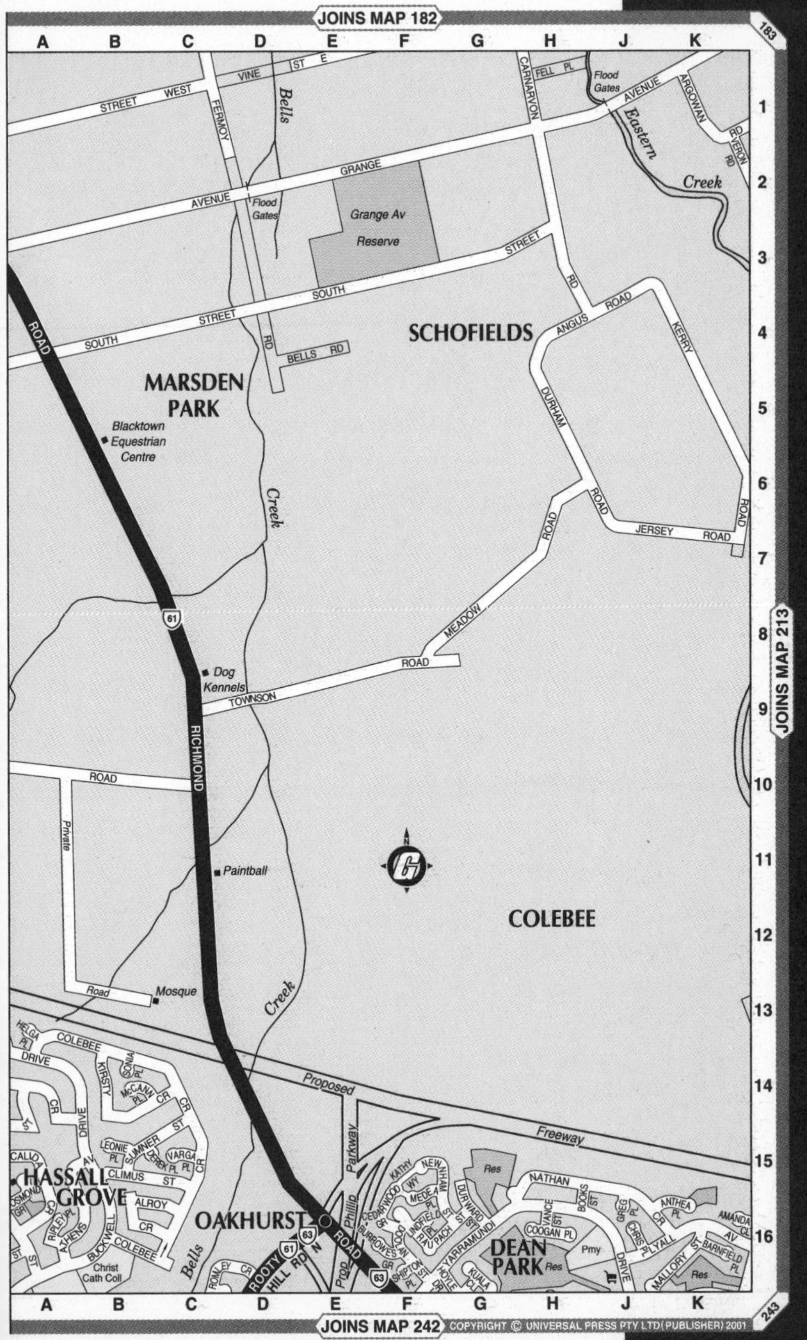
JOINS MAP 182
JOINS MAP 213
JOINS MAP 242
SCHOFIELDS
MARSDEN PARK
COLEBEE
HASSALL GROVE
OAKHURST
DEAN PARK
Grange Av Reserve
Blacktown Equestrian Centre
Dog Kennels
Paintball
Mosque
Flood Gates
Bells Creek
Eastern Creek
RICHMOND ROAD
SOUTH STREET
GRANGE AVENUE
WEST STREET
VINE ST
TOWNSON ROAD
MEADOW ROAD
DURHAM ROAD
ANGUS ROAD
KERRY ROAD
JERSEY ROAD
CARNARVON RD
BELLS RD
Proposed Freeway
Parkway
Private Road
COLEBEE DRIVE
ROOTY HILL RD N
NATHAN ST
Christ Cath Coll
Pmy
Res

JOINS MAP 183

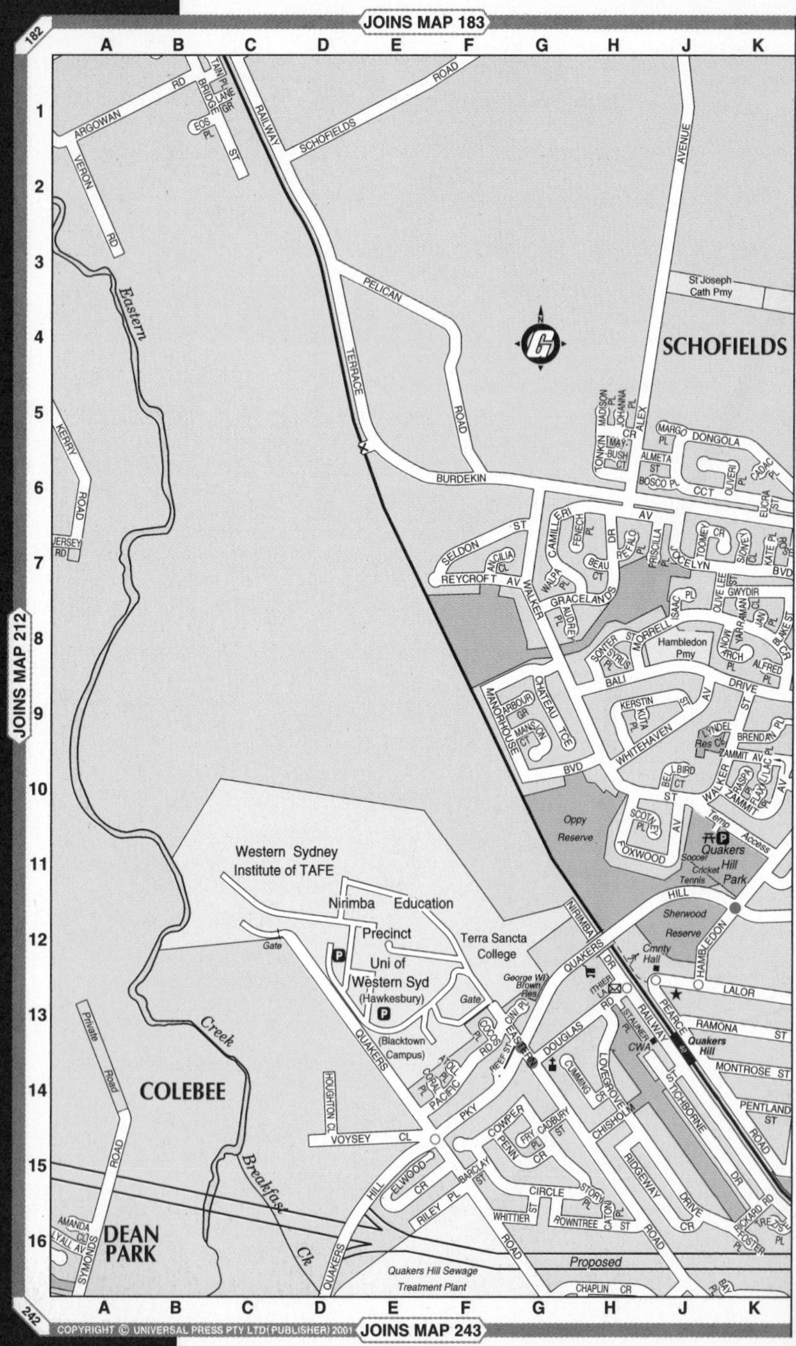

JOINS MAP 212

JOINS MAP 243

JOINS MAP 184

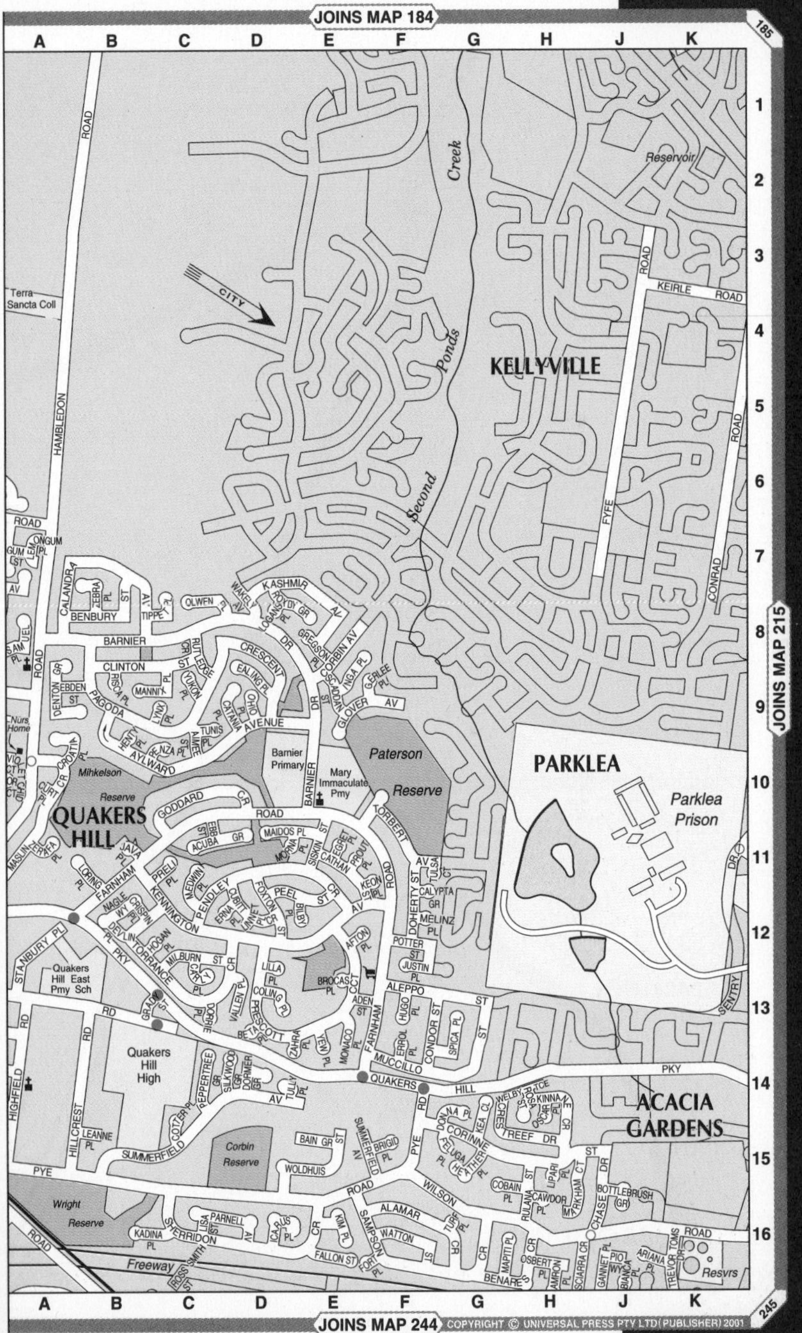

JOINS MAP 215
185
245
JOINS MAP 244

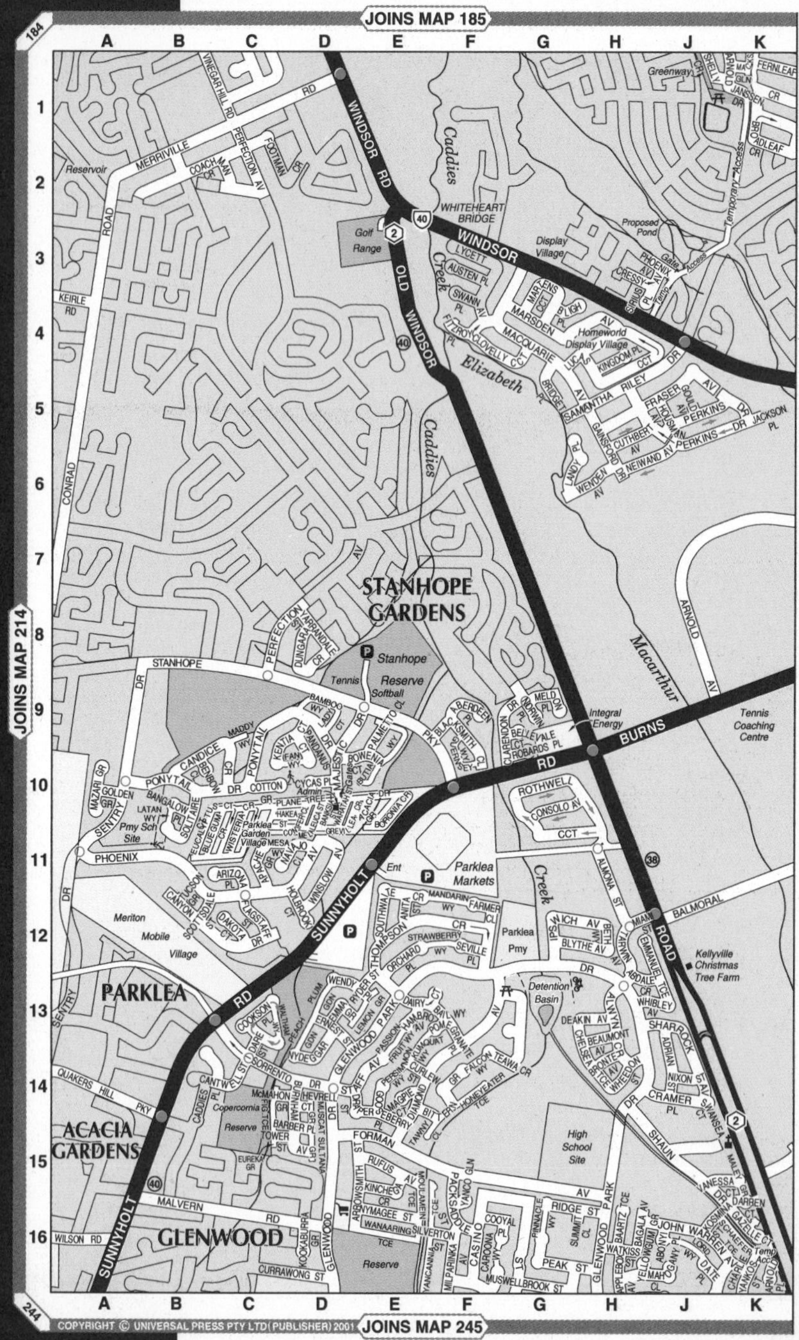
JOINS MAP 185
JOINS MAP 214
JOINS MAP 245
184
244
STANHOPE GARDENS
PARKLEA
ACACIA GARDENS
GLENWOOD
WINDSOR RD
OLD WINDSOR RD
SUNNYHOLT RD
BURNS RD
Caddies Creek
Elizabeth Macarthur Creek
Golf Range
WHITEHEART BRIDGE
Display Village
Homeworld Display Village
Proposed Pond
Stanhope Reserve
Tennis
Softball
Integral Energy
Tennis Coaching Centre
Parklea Markets
Parklea Pmy
Detention Basin
Kellyville Christmas Tree Farm
High School Site
Meriton Mobile Village
Pmy Sch Site
Parklea Garden Village
Copercornia Reserve
Reservoir
Reserve

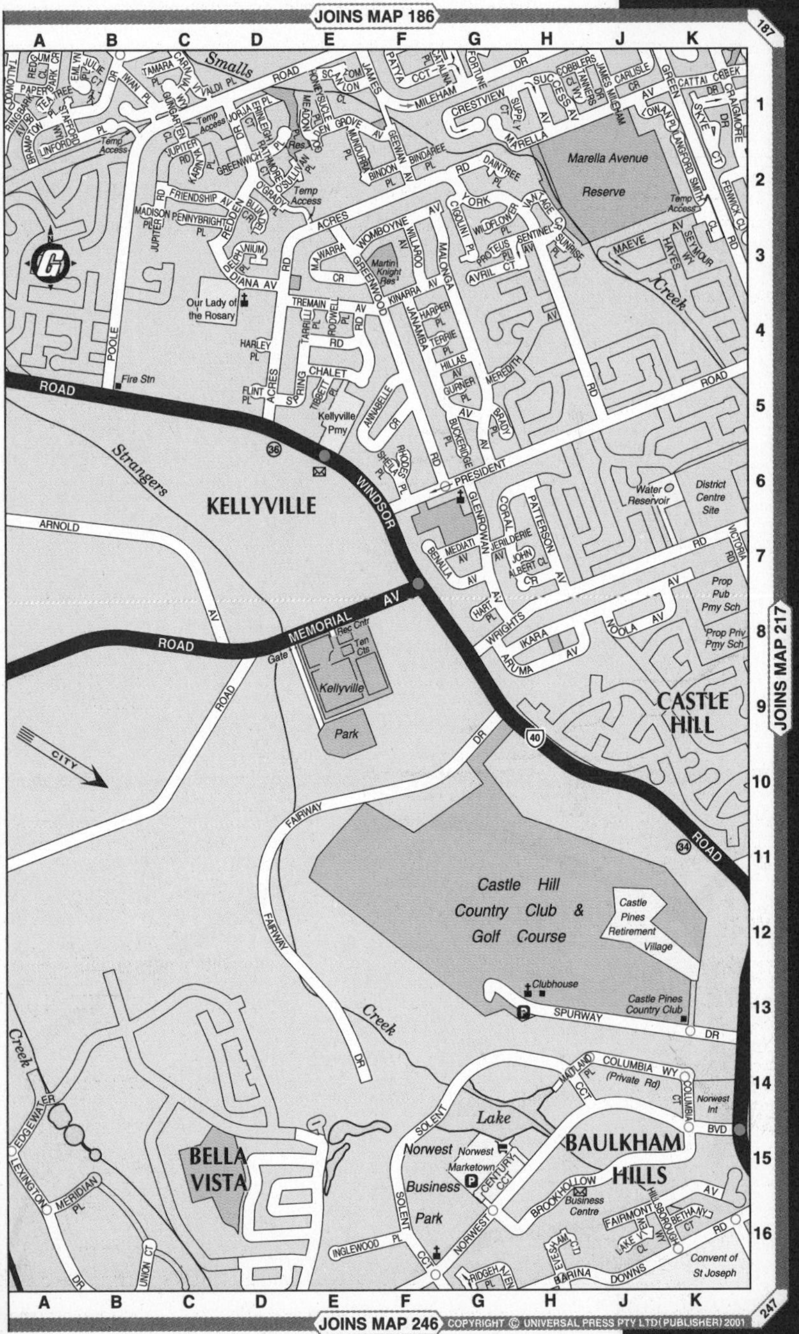
JOINS MAP 186
JOINS MAP 217
JOINS MAP 246
KELLYVILLE
CASTLE HILL
BAULKHAM HILLS
BELLA VISTA
Marella Avenue Reserve
Castle Hill Country Club & Golf Course
Castle Pines Retirement Village
Kellyville Park
Norwest Business Park
Our Lady of the Rosary
Water Reservoir
District Centre Site
WINDSOR ROAD
MEMORIAL AV
Strangers Creek
Smalls Creek
Lake
CITY

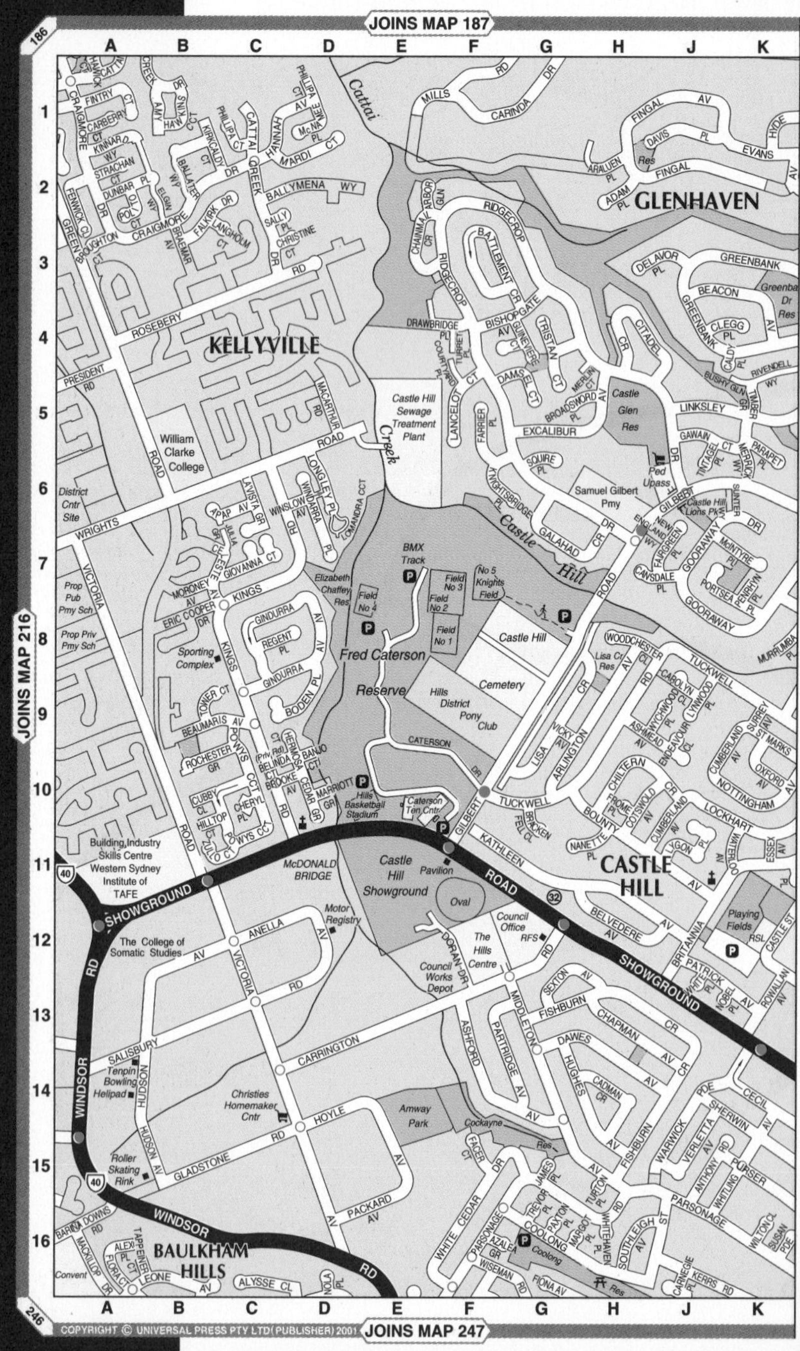
JOINS MAP 187
186
A B C D E F G H J K
1 2 3 4 5 6 7 8 9 10 11 12 13 14 15 16
GLENHAVEN
KELLYVILLE
CASTLE HILL
BAULKHAM HILLS
Castle Hill Sewage Treatment Plant
William Clarke College
District Cntr Site
Prop Pub Pmy Sch
Prop Priv Pmy Sch
Sporting Complex
Elizabeth Chaffey Res
BMX Track
Field No 4
Field No 3
Field No 2
Field No 1
No 5 Knights Field
Fred Caterson Reserve
Castle Hill Cemetery
Hills District Pony Club
Hills Basketball Stadium
Caterson Ten Cntr
Castle Glen Res
Samuel Gilbert Pmy
Ped Upass
Castle Hill Lions Pk
Lisa Cr Res
Greenbank Dr Res
Building Industry Skills Centre Western Sydney Institute of TAFE
McDONALD BRIDGE
Motor Registry
Castle Hill Showground
Pavilion
Oval
Council Office
RFS
The Hills Centre
Council Works Depot
Playing Fields
RSL
The College of Somatic Studies
Tenpin Bowling
Helipad
Christies Homemaker Cntr
Amway Park
Cockayne Res
Roller Skating Rink
Coolong Res
Convent
SHOWGROUND ROAD
WINDSOR RD
OLD WINDSOR RD
GILBERT RD
VICTORIA RD
CARRINGTON RD
GLADSTONE RD
WRIGHTS RD
ROSEBERY RD
CASTLE HILL RD
40
32
JOINS MAP 216
246
COPYRIGHT © UNIVERSAL PRESS PTY LTD (PUBLISHER) 2001
JOINS MAP 247

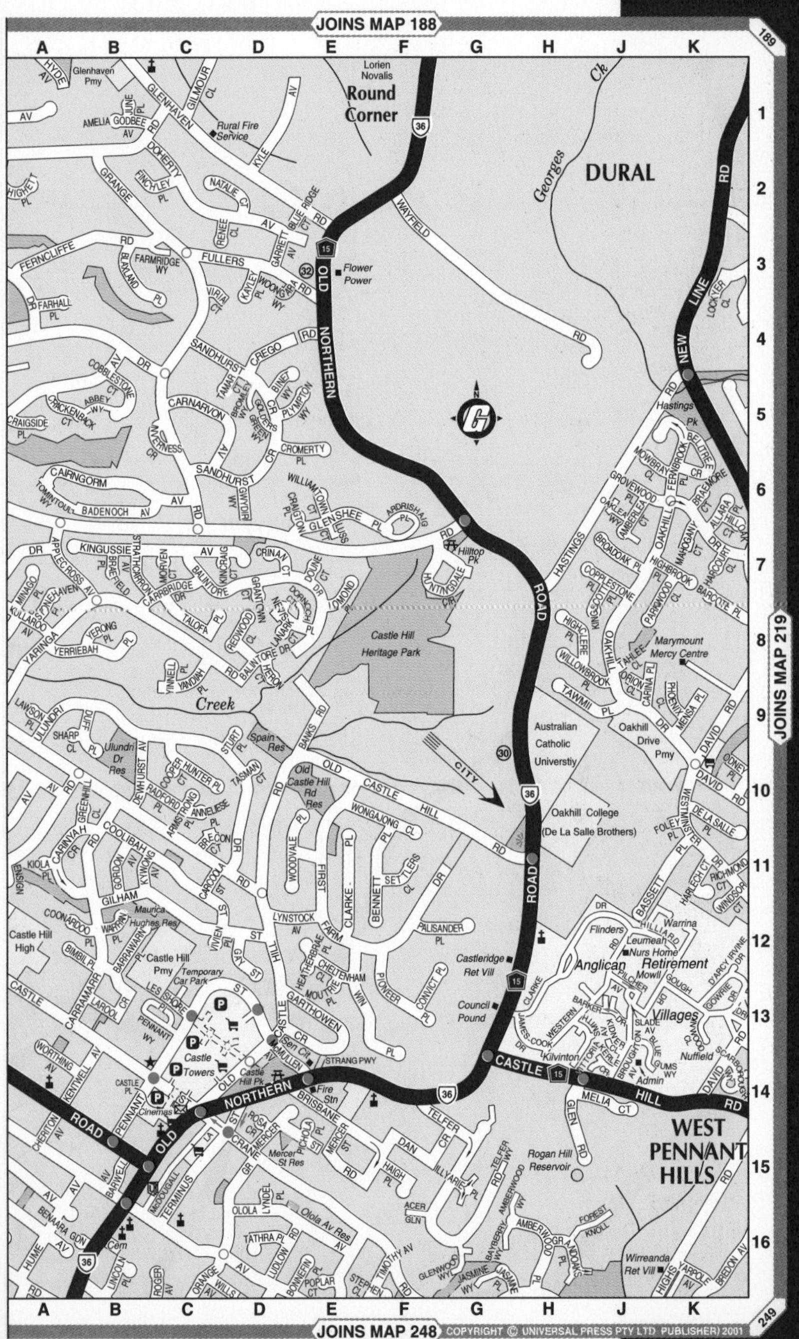
JOINS MAP 188
JOINS MAP 219
JOINS MAP 248
189
249
A B C D E F G H J K
1 2 3 4 5 6 7 8 9 10 11 12 13 14 15 16
Round Corner
DURAL
WEST PENNANT HILLS
Lorien Novalis
Glenhaven Pmy
Rural Fire Service
Flower Power
Georges Ck
Hastings Pk
Hilltop Pk
Castle Hill Heritage Park
Creek
Spain Res
Old Castle Hill Rd Res
Ulundri Dr Res
Marymount Mercy Centre
Australian Catholic Universtiy
Oakhill Drive Pmy
Oakhill College (De La Salle Brothers)
Castleridge Ret Vill
Council Pound
Anglican Retirement Villages
Flinders
Leumeah
Nurs Home
Mowll
Kilvinton
Admin
Nuffield
Warrina
Castle Hill High
Maurica Hughes Res
Castle Hill Pmy
Temporary Car Park
Castle Towers
Castle Hill Pk
Sen Cit
Cinemas
Fire Stn
Mercer St Res
Rogan Hill Reservoir
Olola Av Res
Cem
Wirreanda Ret Vill
CITY
OLD NORTHERN ROAD
CASTLE HILL RD
NEW LINE RD
OLD CASTLE HILL RD
HASTINGS RD
WAYFIELD RD
GLENHAVEN RD
SANDHURST DR
FULLERS RD
FERNCLIFFE RD
KINGUSSIE AV
GLENSHEE PL
OAKHILL DR
DAVID RD
BANKS RD
HILL ST
BRISBANE RD
36
15
32
30

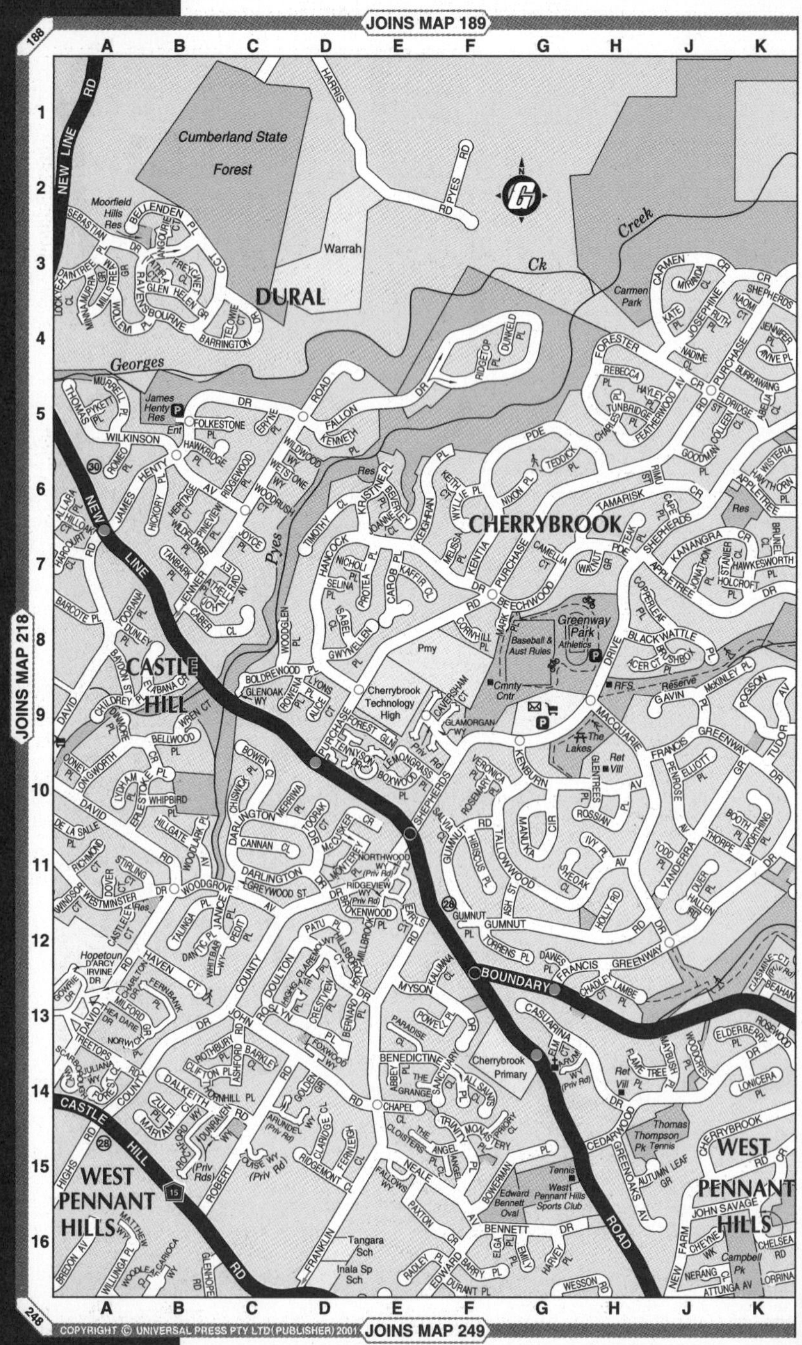
JOINS MAP 189
JOINS MAP 218
JOINS MAP 249
188
248
A B C D E F G H J K
1 2 3 4 5 6 7 8 9 10 11 12 13 14 15 16
Cumberland State Forest
DURAL
CHERRYBROOK
CASTLE HILL
WEST PENNANT HILLS
WEST PENNANT HILLS
Warrah
Moorfield Hills Res
James Henty Res
Carmen Park
Georges
Creek
Ck
Pyes
NEW LINE RD
CASTLE HILL RD
BOUNDARY ROAD
SHEPHERDS DR
PURCHASE RD
COUNTY DR
FRANCIS GREENWAY DR
MACQUARIE DRIVE
JOHN RD
Cherrybrook Technology High
Cherrybrook Primary
Greenway Park
Baseball & Aust Rules
Athletics
Cmnty Cntr
The Lakes
Ret Vill
RFS
Reserve
Thomas Thompson Pk
Tennis
Edward Bennett Oval
West Pennant Hills Sports Club
Tangara Sch
Inala Sp Sch
Hopetoun
Campbell Pk
Pmy
Res

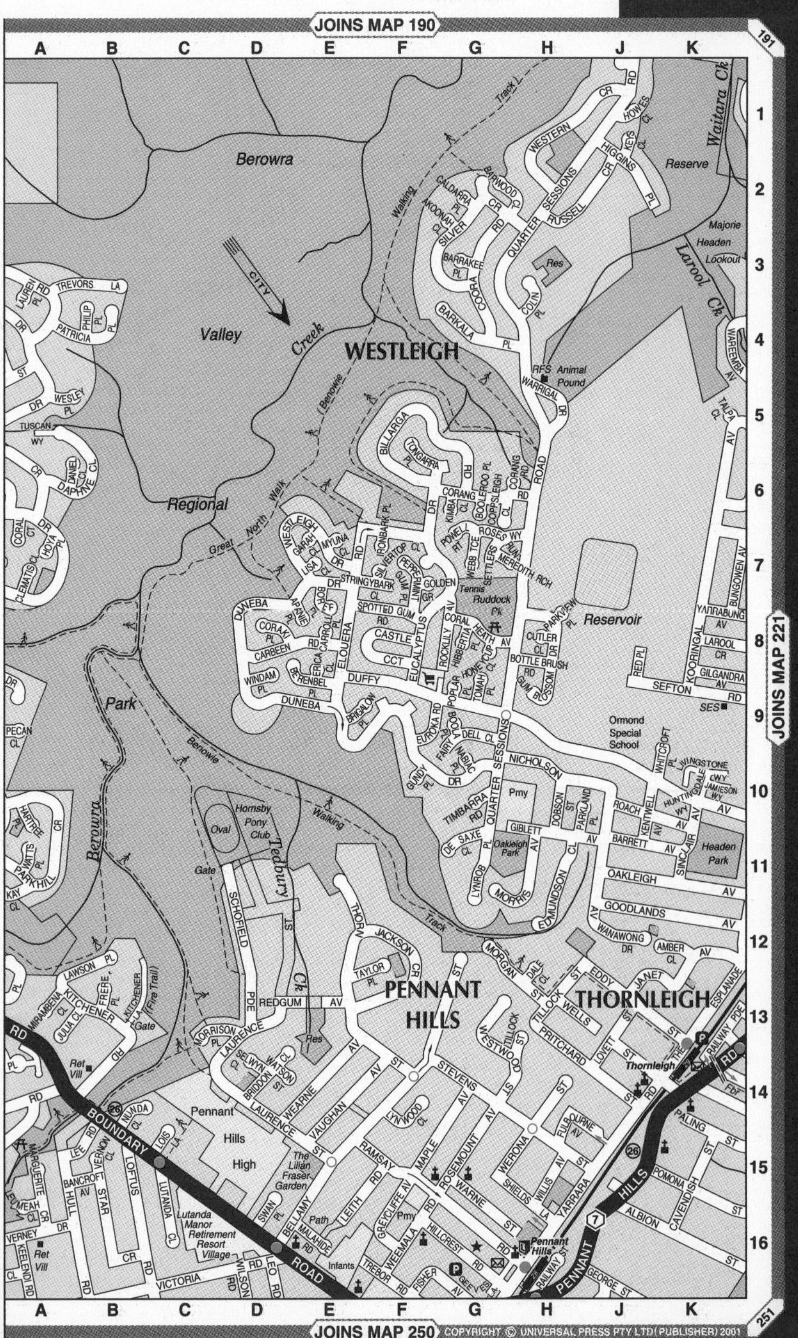
JOINS MAP 190
191
A B C D E F G H J K
1 2 3 4 5 6 7 8 9 10 11 12 13 14 15 16
JOINS MAP 221
JOINS MAP 250
251
COPYRIGHT © UNIVERSAL PRESS PTY LTD (PUBLISHER) 2001
WESTLEIGH
PENNANT HILLS
THORNLEIGH
Berowra
Valley
Regional
Park
Creek
CITY
Great North Walk
Walking Track
Benowie
Berowra
Tedbury Ck
Waitara Ck
Larool Ck
Reserve
Majorie Headen Lookout
Res
RFS
Animal Pound
Tennis
Ruddock Pk
Reservoir
Ormond Special School
SES
Hornsby Pony Club
Oval
Gate
Pmy
Oakleigh Park
Headen Park
Pennant Hills High
The Lilian Fraser Garden
Lutanda Manor Retirement Resort Village
Ret Vill
Infants
Path
Thornleigh
Pennant Hills
Fire Trail
WESTERN CR
HOWES CL
KEYS CL
HIGGINS PL
RUSSELL CR
SESSIONS
QUARTER SESSIONS RD
BARWOOD CL
CALDARRA PL
AKOONAH CL
SILVER RD
BARRAKEE PL
COORA CR
BARKALA PL
COLIN PL
WARRIGAL DR
WAREEMBA AV
TALPA CL
BILLARGA RD
TONGARRA PL
CORANG RD
BOOLEROO PL
COPPSLEIGH CL
KIMBA CL
POWELL PT
WEBB TCE
ROSES WY
SETTLERS
MEREDITH RCH
PARKVIEW PL
WESTLEIGH DR
GARAH
MYUNA CL
LISA
IRONBARK PL
SILVERTOP
PEPPERMINT GUM PL
GOLDEN GR
STRINGYBARK CL
SPOTTED GUM RD
CASTLE CCT
EUCALYPTUS AV
CORAL HEATH AV
ROCKLILY
HIBBERTIA
HONEYCUP CL
TOMAH PL
POPLAR
CUTLER DR
BOTTLE BRUSH RD
GUM BLOSSOM
DUNEBA DR
CORAKI PL
CARBEEN RD
APANIE PL
BORONIA
ELOUERA
ERICA
CARROLL CT
BERENBEL PL
WINDAM PL
DUFFY AV
BRIGALOW PL
EUROKA RD
FAIRY BOWER
DELL CL
NABIAC PL
GUNDY PL
NICHOLSON AV
TIMBARRA RD
DE SAXE CL
GIBLETT AV
DOBSON ST
PARKLAND PL
LYNROB PL
MORRIS
EDMUNDSON CL
YARRABUNG AV
LAROOL CR
GILGANDRA AV
KOORINGAL AV
BUNGOWEN AV
RED PL
SEFTON RD
WHITCROFT PL
LIVINGSTONE CWY
JAMIESON WY
HUNTINGDALE AV
ROACH ST
KENTWELL AV
BARRETT AV
SINCLAIR AV
OAKLEIGH AV
GOODLANDS AV
WANAWONG DR
AMBER CL
TREVORS LA
LAUREN RD
PHILIP PL
PATRICIA DR
WESLEY PL
TUSCAN WY
DANIEL CL
DAPHNE CL
CORAL CT
HOYA DR
CLEMATIS CL
PECAN CL
HARTREE CR
WATTS PL
PARKHILL
KAY CL
LAWSON PL
KITCHENER RD
FRERE PL
MIRAMBENA
JULIA CL
SCHOFIELD PDE
REDGUM AV
MORRISON PL
LAURENCE ST
SELWYN CL
WATSON ST
BRIDDON CL
THORN
JACKSON CR
TAYLOR PL
MORGAN ST
DALE CL
TILLOCK ST
EDDY
JANET
ESPLANADE
WELLS
PRITCHARD
LOVETT ST
WESTWOOD ST
STEVENS ST
WEARNE AV
VAUGHAN AV
LYNWOOD CL
FULBOURNE AV
WERONA AV
ROSEMOUNT AV
MAPLE AV
RAMSAY RD
SHIELDS LA
WILLIS
YARRARA RD
WARNE ST
GREYCLIFFE AV
LEITH
WEEMALA
HILLCREST RD
FISHER AV
TREBOR RD
BELLAMY ST
SWAN PL
MALAHIDE RD
GEORGE ST
RAILWAY ST
RAILWAY PDE
PENNANT HILLS RD
BOUNDARY ROAD
PALING ST
POMONA ST
CAVENDISH ST
ALBION ST
NUNDA CL
LOIS LA
LUTANDA CL
LOFTUS
STAR
VERNON CL
LEE RD
BANCROFT AV
HULL
MARGUERITE CR
LEUMEAH CL
VERNEY DR
KEELEND RD
VICTORIA RD
WILSON RD
LEO RD
GEE LA

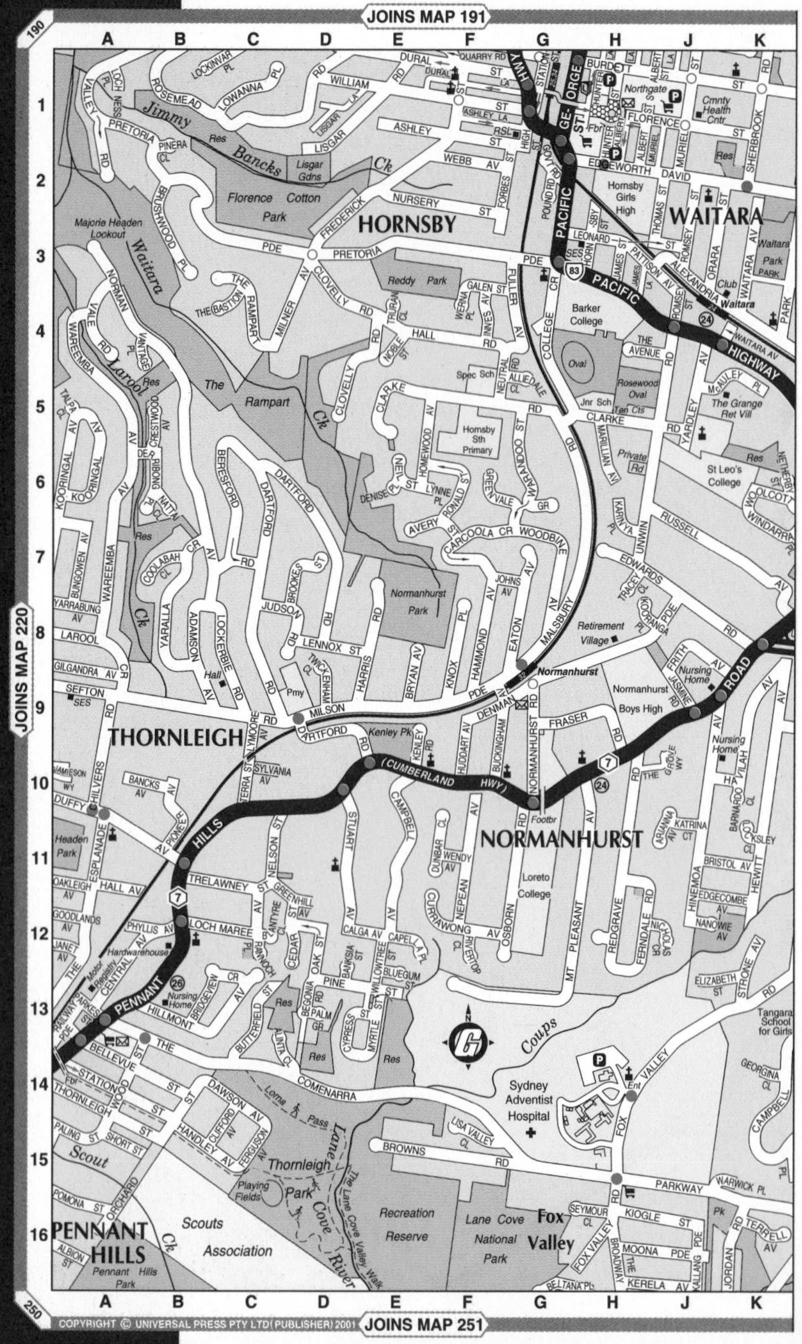
JOINS MAP 191
JOINS MAP 220
JOINS MAP 251
190
250
HORNSBY
WAITARA
THORNLEIGH
NORMANHURST
PENNANT HILLS
Fox Valley
Florence Cotton Park
Reddy Park
Normanhurst Park
Barker College
Hornsby Girls High
Normanhurst Boys High
Loreto College
Sydney Adventist Hospital
St Leo's College
Tangara School for Girls
Thornleigh Park
Recreation Reserve
Lane Cove National Park
Scouts Association
Pennant Hills Park
Majorie Headen Lookout
Hornsby Sth Primary
Retirement Village
PACIFIC HIGHWAY
CUMBERLAND HWY
PENNANT HILLS ROAD
PRETORIA PDE
COMENARRA PKWY
The Lane Cove Valley Walk
Lane Cove River
COPYRIGHT © UNIVERSAL PRESS PTY LTD (PUBLISHER) 2001

JOINS MAP 192

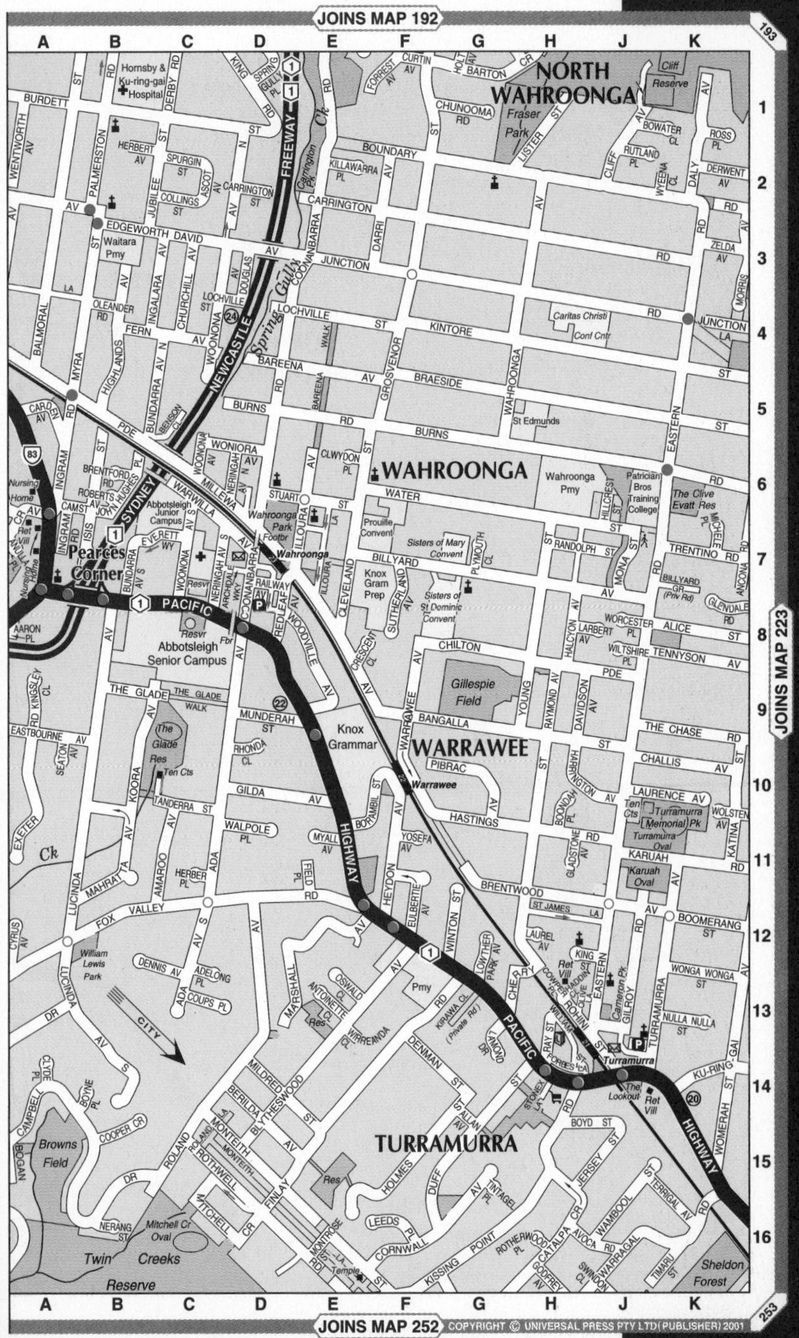

JOINS MAP 223

JOINS MAP 252

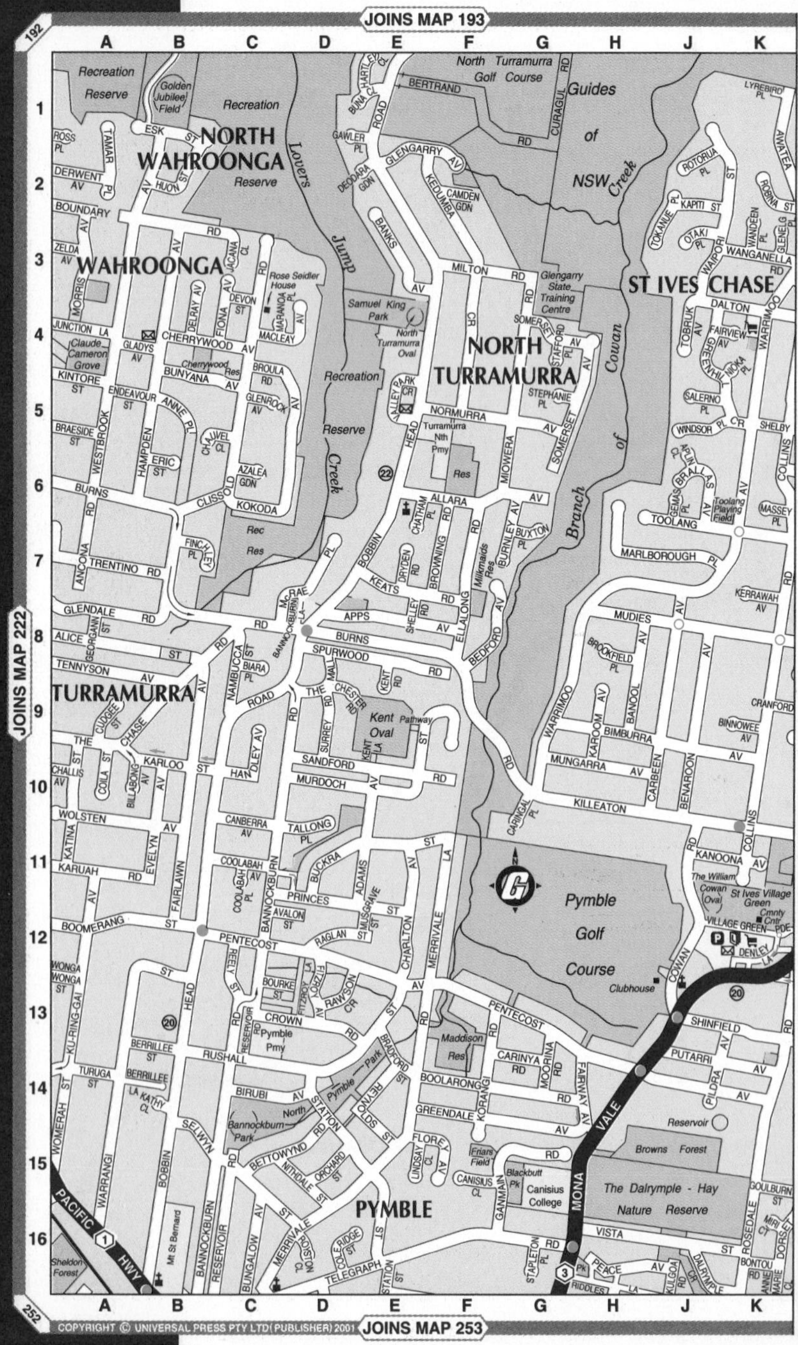
JOINS MAP 193
JOINS MAP 222
JOINS MAP 253
192
252
A
B
C
D
E
F
G
H
J
K
1
2
3
4
5
6
7
8
9
10
11
12
13
14
15
16
NORTH WAHROONGA
WAHROONGA
NORTH TURRAMURRA
ST IVES CHASE
TURRAMURRA
PYMBLE
Recreation Reserve
Golden Jubilee Field
Recreation Reserve
North Turramurra Golf Course
Guides of NSW
Lovers Jump Creek
Cowan Creek
Branch of Cowan Creek
Rose Seidler House
Samuel King Park
North Turramurra Oval
Recreation Reserve
Glengarry State Training Centre
Claude Cameron Grove
Cherrywood Res
Turramurra Nth Pmy
Res
Rec Res
Milkmaids Res
Toolang Playing Field
Kent Oval
Pathway
Pymble Golf Course
Clubhouse
The William Cowan Oval
St Ives Village Green
Cmnty Cntr
Maddison Res
Pymble Pmy
Pymble Park
Bannockburn Park
Friars Field
Blackbutt Pk
Canisius College
Reservoir
Browns Forest
The Dalrymple - Hay Nature Reserve
Mt St Bernard
Sheldon Forest
PACIFIC HWY
ESK ST
TAMAR
ROSS PL
DERWENT AV
HUON ST
BOUNDARY AV
ZELDA AV
JACANA CL
MORRIS
DELRAY AV
FIONA AV
DEVON ST
MARANOA PL
MACLEAY
JUNCTION LA
CHERRYWOOD AV
GLADYS AV
BUNYANA AV
BROULA RD
KINTORE ST
ENDEAVOUR ST
ANNE PL
GLENROCK AV
BRAESIDE ST
WESTBROOK AV
HAMPDEN AV
CHAJUVEL CL
ERIC ST
AZALEA GDN
CLISSOLD RD
BURNS RD
KOKODA
FINCHLEY PL
ANCONA
TRENTINO RD
GLENDALE RD
ALICE ST
GEORGANN
TENNYSON AV
NAMBUCCA
BIARA PL
CUDGEE ST
THE CHASE
KARLOO ST
CHALLIS AV
COILA ST
BILLABONG AV
WOLSTEN AV
KATINA
KARUAH RD
EVELYN
FAIRLAWN AV
HANDLEY AV
CANBERRA AV
COOLABAH AV
COOLABAH PL
BOOMERANG ST
WONGA WONGA ST
KU-RING-GAI
HEAD ST
BERRILLEE ST
TURUGA ST
KATHY CL
WOMERAH
WARRANGI
BOBBIN
SELWYN
BANNOCKBURN
RESERVOIR
BUNGALOW AV
BUNA CL
HARTLEY CL
ROAD
GAWLER PL
DEODARA GDN
GLENGARRY AV
BANKS AV
KEDUMBA
CAMDEN GDN
BERTRAND RD
CURAGUL RD
MILTON RD
CR
SOMERSET
STAFFORD PL
VALLEY PARK CR
NORMURRA AV
STEPHANIE PL
MIOWERA
ALLARA AV
CHATHAM PL
BROWNING RD
BURNLEY AV
BUXTON PL
DRYDEN RD
BOBBIN HEAD RD
KEATS RD
SHELLEY RD
ELLALONG
BEDFORD AV
APPS AV
McRAE LA
BANNOCKBURN LA
BURNS
SPURWOOD RD
KENT RD
THE MALL
THE CHESTER RD
SURREY RD
SANDFORD
MURDOCH AV
TALLONG PL
BUCKRA
ADAMS
MUSGRAVE ST
PRINCES ST
AVALON ST
RAGLAN ST
PENTECOST AV
CHARLTON
MERRIVALE LA
REELY ST
BOURKE ST
FITZROY LA
RAWSON CR
CROWN RD
RUSHALL
BIRUBI AV
STATION ST
BRADFORD ST
REYNOLDS AV
BETTOWYND RD
NITHDALE ST
ORCHARD ST
MERRIVALE RD
ROSTON CL
COLERIDGE ST
TELEGRAPH
LYREBIRD PL
AWATEA
ROTORUA PL
ROBINA ST
TOKANUE PL
KAPITI ST
OTAKI PL
WAIPORI
WANDEEN PL
GLENELG PL
WANGANELLA RD
DALTON RD
TOBRUK AV
FAIRVIEW AV
GREENHILL
NOKA PL
WARRIMOO
SALERNO PL
WINDSOR PL
SHELBY
COLLINS
BRALLAS AV
APPIN CL
GEMAS
TOOLANG
MASSEY PL
MARLBOROUGH PL
KERRAWAH AV
MUDIES AV
BROOKFIELD PL
BANOOL AV
KAROOM AV
BIMBURRA
CRANFORD
BINNOWEE AV
MUNGARRA AV
CARBEEN
BENAROON
KILLEATON
CARINGAL PL
KANOONA AV
VILLAGE GREEN PDE
DENLEY LA
COWAN
SHINFIELD AV
PUTARRI AV
PILDRA AV
CARINYA RD
MOORINA RD
FAIRWAY AV
BOOLARONG
KORANGI
GREENDALE AV
FLOREY AV
LINDSAY CL
CANISIUS CL
GANMAIN
MONA VALE
VISTA ST
STAPLETON PL
PEACE AV
RIDDLES LA
KULGOA
DALRYMPLE
BONTOU RD
ANNE MARIE
DORSET
MIRI CT
GOULBURN ST
ROSEDALE
1
3
20
22
COPYRIGHT © UNIVERSAL PRESS PTY LTD (PUBLISHER) 2001

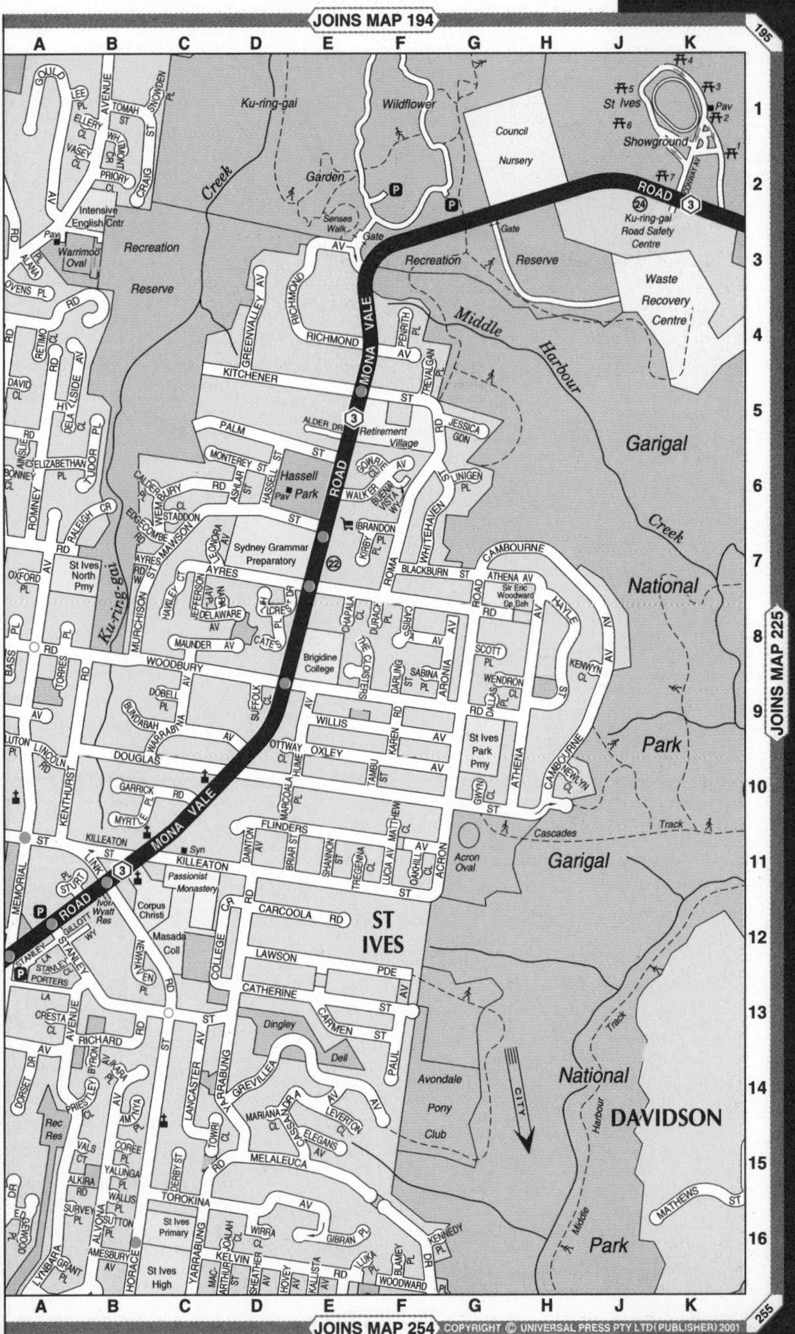
JOINS MAP 194
JOINS MAP 225
JOINS MAP 254
Ku-ring-gai
Wildflower
Garden
Council
Nursery
St Ives
Showground
Ku-ring-gai
Road Safety
Centre
Waste
Recovery
Centre
Recreation
Reserve
Middle
Harbour
Creek
Garigal
National
Park
MONA VALE ROAD
Sydney Grammar
Preparatory
Hassell
Park
Retirement
Village
Brigidine
College
St Ives
North
Pmy
St Ives
Park
Pmy
Acron
Oval
Passionist
Monastery
Corpus
Christi
Masada
Coll
ST
IVES
Dingley
Dell
Avondale
Pony
Club
DAVIDSON
St Ives
Primary
St Ives
High
Intensive
English Cntr
Warrimoo
Oval
Rec
Res
Cascades
Track

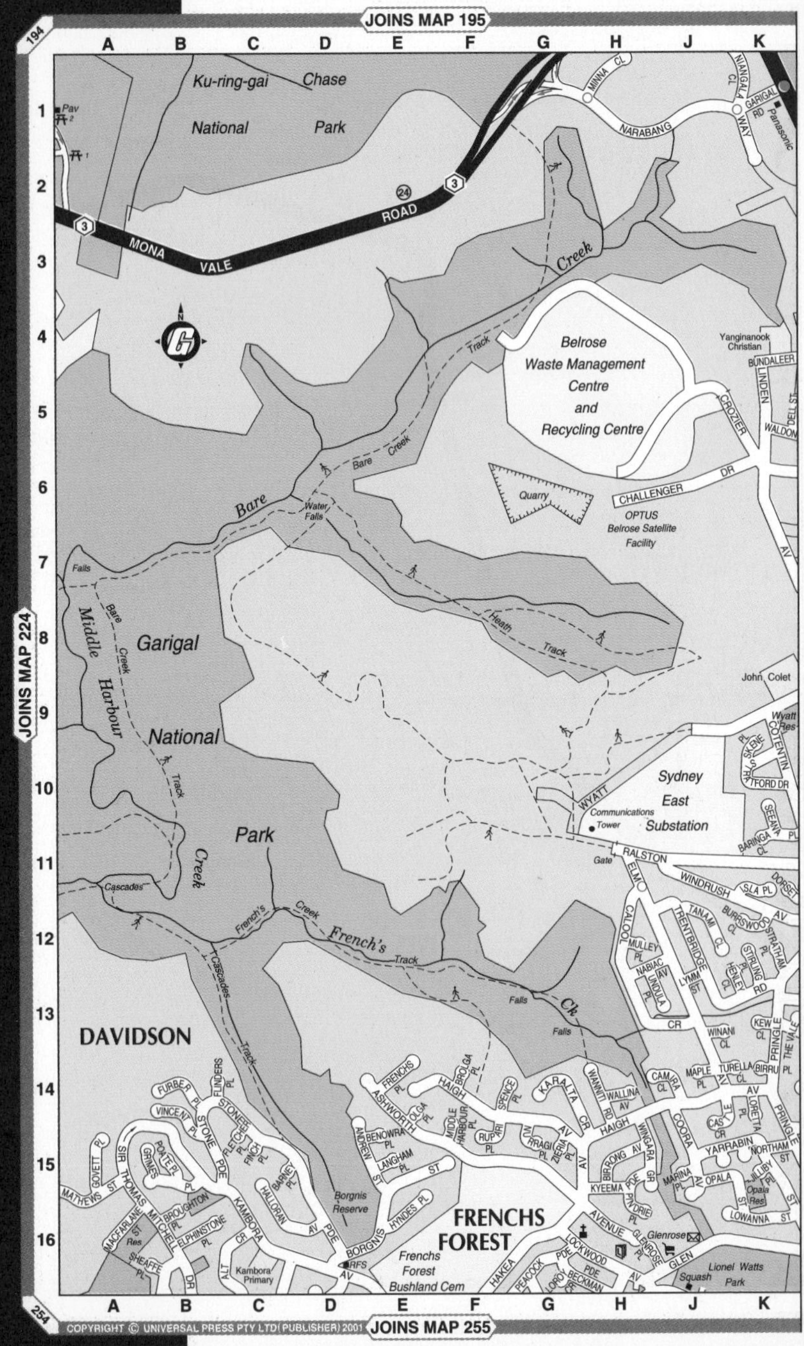
JOINS MAP 195
JOINS MAP 224
JOINS MAP 255
194
254
Ku-ring-gai Chase National Park
MONA VALE ROAD
Garigal National Park
Middle Harbour Creek
Bare Creek
French's Creek
French's Ck
Heath Track
Cascades Track
Belrose Waste Management Centre and Recycling Centre
Quarry
OPTUS Belrose Satellite Facility
CHALLENGER DR
NARABANG WAY
MINNA CL
NIANGALA CL
GARIGAL RD
Panasonic
CROZIER
Yanginanook Christian
BUNDALEER
LINDEN
WALDON
DELL ST
John Colet
Wyatt Res
WYATT
Sydney East Substation
Communications Tower
Gate
RALSTON
WINDRUSH
DORSET
COTENTIN
SKENE PL
STRATFORD DR
SEEANA PL
BARINGA CL
DAVIDSON
FRENCHS FOREST
Frenchs Forest Bushland Cem
Borgnis Reserve
Kambora Primary
RFS
Lionel Watts Park
Squash
Glenrose
Opala Res
Falls
Water Falls
Cascades
Track
FURBER PL
FLINDERS PL
VINCENT PL
STONE PDE
STONER
FLETCHER PL
FINCH PL
POATE PL
GRIMES PL
GOVETT PL
MATHEWS ST
SIR THOMAS MITCHELL DR
BROUGHTON PL
ELPHINSTONE PL
MACFARLANE ST
SHEAFFE PL
KAMBORA AV
HALLORAN
BARNEY PL
ALT CR
BORGNIS AV
HYNDES PL
LANGHAM PL
BENOWRA PL
ANDREW ST
ASHWORTH AV
FRENCHS PL
OLGA PL
HAIGH AV
BROLGA PL
MIDDLE HARBOUR PL
SPENCE PL
RUPARI PL
KARALTA CR
MURRAGI PL
ZIERIA PL
WANNITI RD
WALLINA AV
BIRRONG AV
WINGARA GR
KYEEMA PDE
PINDARI PL
AVENUE
GLENROSE PL
GLEN
HAKEA AV
PEACOCK
LOROY CR
LOCKWOOD PDE
BECKMAN PDE
CAMIRA CL
COORA RD
MARINA PL
OPALA ST
JILLIBY PL
LOWANNA ST
YARRABIN
NORTHAM
CASTLE CR
LORETTA AV
PRINGLE AV
MAPLE PL
TURELLA CL
BIRRU PL
THE VALE
KEW CL
WINANI CL
CR
LYMM ST
HENLEY CL
STIRLING PL
STRATHAM PL
BURSWOOD CL
TANAMI CL
TRENTBRIDGE RD
MULLEY PL
NABIAC AV
UNDULA PL
CALOOL
ELM
SLA PL

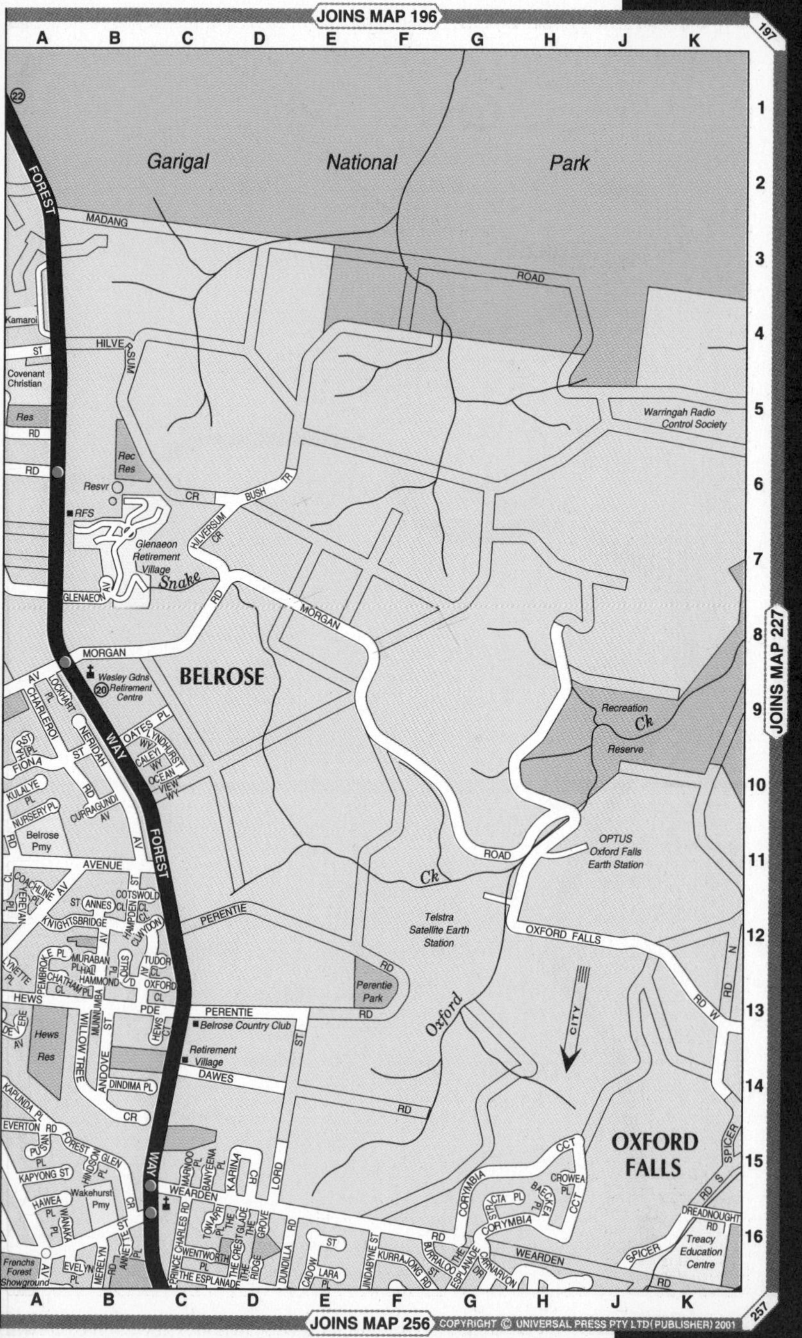
JOINS MAP 196
197
A B C D E F G H J K
1 2 3 4 5 6 7 8 9 10 11 12 13 14 15 16
Garigal National Park
FOREST WAY
MADANG
ROAD
Kamaroi
HILVERSUM
ST
Covenant Christian
Res
RD
Rec Res
Resvr
RFS
CR
BUSH TR
HILVERSUM CR
Glenaeon Retirement Village
Snake
GLENAEON AV
MORGAN RD
MORGAN
Wesley Gdns Retirement Centre
BELROSE
Warringah Radio Control Society
Recreation Reserve
Ck
JOINS MAP 227
OATES PL
LYNDHURST WY
CALEYI WY
OCEAN VIEW WY
LOCKHART PL
CHARLEROI AV
NERIDAH ST
HARST PL
FIONA
KULALYE PL
NURSERY PL
CURRAGUNDI AV
CURRAGUNDI RD
Belrose Pmy
AVENUE
COACHLINE
YEREVAN
ST ANNES CL
COTSWOLD CL
HAMPDEN CL
KNIGHTSBRIDGE
CLWYDON
PEMBROKE PL
MURABAN PL
HAL PL
HAMMOND
CHATHAM PL
TUDOR AV
STROUD
OXFORD CL
LYNETTE PL
HEWS
PDE
DEVERE AV
Hews Res
WILLOW TREE
MUNNUMBA
HEWS CT
ANDOVE ST
DINDIMA PL
CR
KAPUNDA PL
EVERTON RD
PUSAN PL
FOREST GLEN
HINDSON PL
KAPYONG ST
HAWEA PL
WANAKA PL
Wakehurst Pmy
ANNETTE PL
EVELYN PL
MERELYN RD
Frenchs Forest Showground
OPTUS Oxford Falls Earth Station
ROAD
Ck
PERENTIE
Telstra Satellite Earth Station
OXFORD FALLS
Perentie Park
PERENTIE RD
Belrose Country Club
Retirement Village
ST
DAWES
RD
Oxford
CITY
RD W
RD N
OXFORD FALLS
SPICER
RD S
WEARDEN
MARNOO PL
BANYEENA PL
KARINA CR
LORD
PRINCE CHARLES RD
TOWARRI PL
THE CRESTGLADE
THE GROVE
THE RIDGE
WENTWORTH PL
THE ESPLANADE
DUNDILLA RD
CADOW ST
LARA PL
JINDABYNE ST
KURRAJONG RD
BURRALOO ST
THE ESPLANADE
CARNARVON DR
CORYMBIA
CORYMBIA CCT
ACACIA PL
BAECKEA PL
CROWEA PL
DREADNOUGHT RD
WEARDEN RD
Treacy Education Centre
SPICER RD
JOINS MAP 256
257

JOINS MAP 197

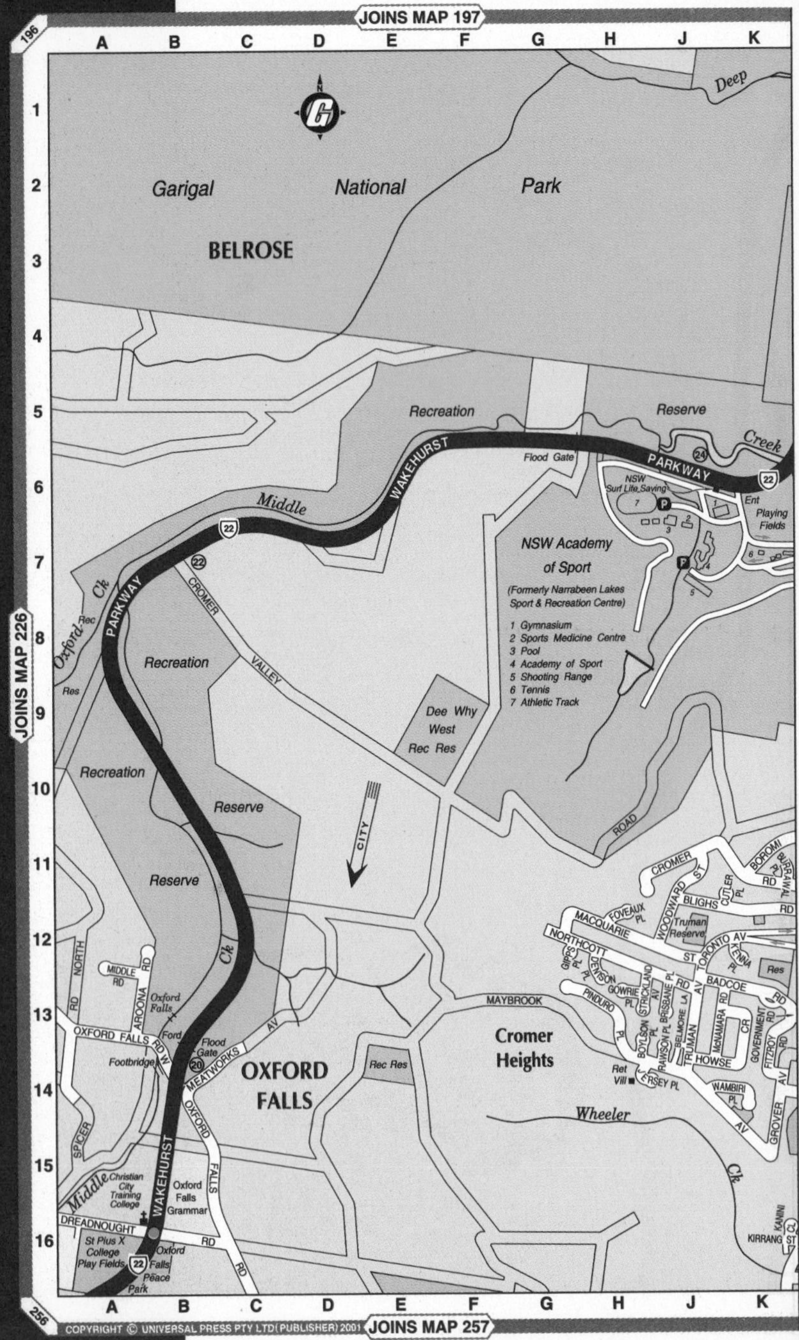

JOINS MAP 226

JOINS MAP 257

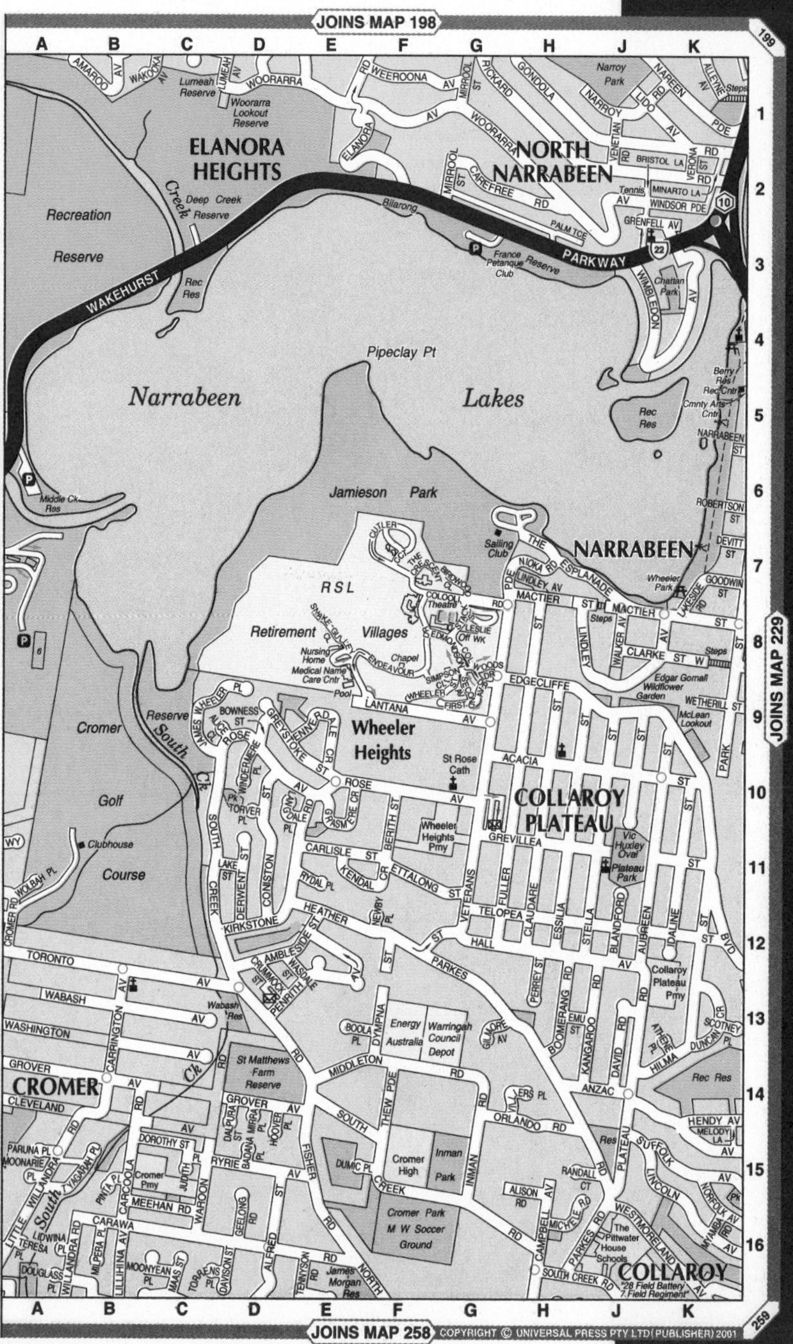
JOINS MAP 198
JOINS MAP 229
JOINS MAP 258
199
259
ELANORA HEIGHTS
NORTH NARRABEEN
NARRABEEN
Wheeler Heights
COLLAROY PLATEAU
CROMER
COLLAROY
Narrabeen Lakes
Pipeclay Pt
Jamieson Park
RSL Retirement Villages
Recreation Reserve
Cromer Golf Course
WAKEHURST PARKWAY
Deep Creek Reserve
Woorarra Lookout Reserve
Lumeah Reserve
France Petanque Club Reserve
Narroy Park
Chattan Park
Sailing Club
Wheeler Park
Edgar Gornall Wildflower Garden
McLean Lookout
St Rose Cath
Wheeler Heights Pmy
Vic Huxley Oval
Plateau Park
Collaroy Plateau Pmy
Energy Australia
Warringah Council Depot
St Matthews Farm Reserve
Cromer High
Inman Park
Cromer Park M W Soccer Ground
James Morgan Res
Cromer Pmy
The Pittwater House Schools
"28 Field Battery 7 Field Regiment"
Berry Res
Rec Cntr
Cmnty Arts Cntr
Rec Res
Wabash Res
Clubhouse
Nursing Home
Medical Name Care Cntr
Chapel
Pool
Colool Theatre

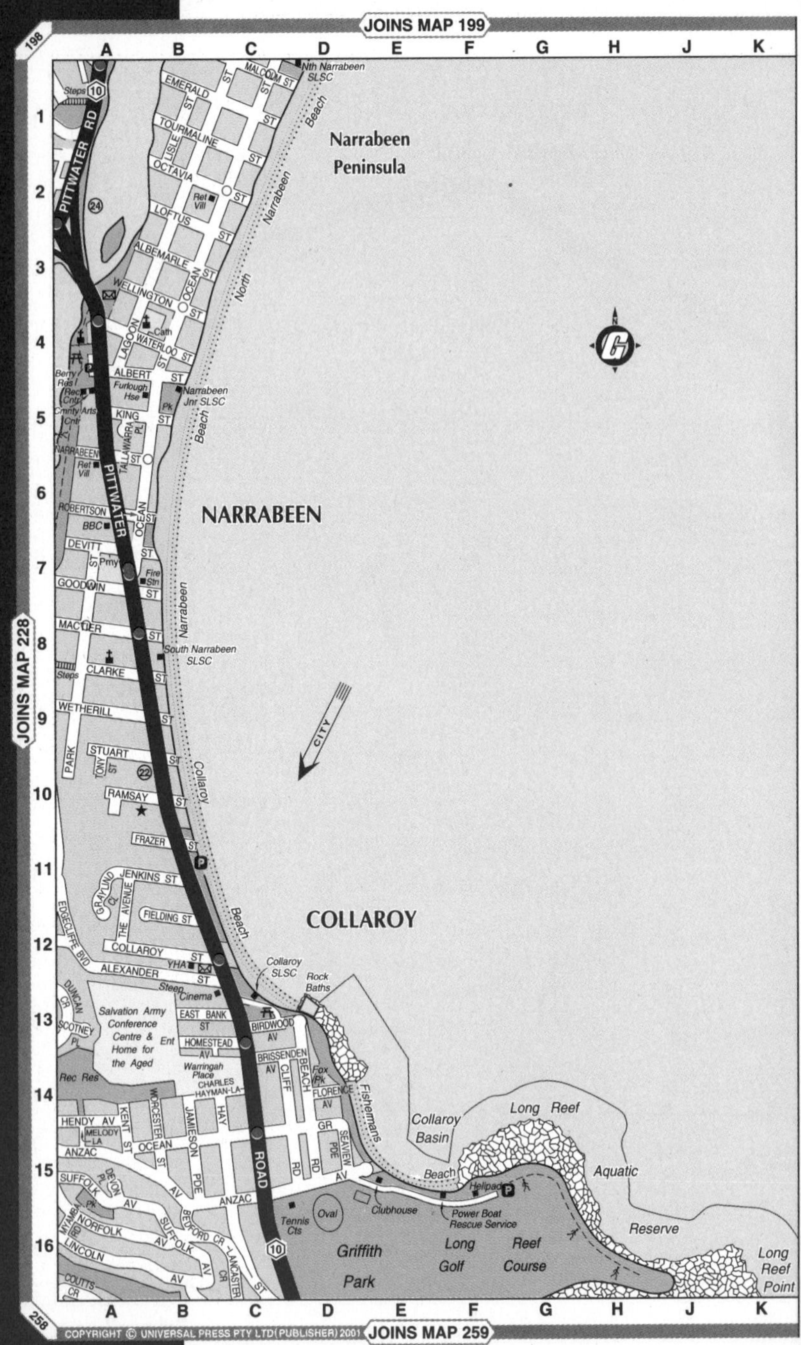
JOINS MAP 199
JOINS MAP 228
JOINS MAP 259
198
258
Narrabeen
Peninsula
NARRABEEN
COLLAROY
Nth Narrabeen
SLSC
Narrabeen Jnr SLSC
South Narrabeen
SLSC
Collaroy
SLSC
Rock
Baths
North Narrabeen Beach
Narrabeen Beach
Collaroy Beach
Fishermans Beach
Collaroy
Basin
Long Reef
Aquatic
Reserve
Long
Reef
Point
Griffith
Park
Long Reef Golf Course
Clubhouse
Power Boat
Rescue Service
Helipad
Oval
Tennis
Cts
Salvation Army
Conference
Centre &
Home for
the Aged
Ent
Rec Res
Warringah
Place
PITTWATER RD
PITTWATER ROAD
EMERALD ST
MALCOLM ST
TOURMALINE ST
LISLE ST
OCTAVIA ST
LOFTUS ST
ALBEMARLE ST
WELLINGTON ST
OCEAN ST
LAGOON ST
WATERLOO ST
ALBERT ST
KING ST
TALLAWARRA PL
NARRABEEN ST
ROBERTSON
DEVITT ST
GOODWIN ST
MACTIER ST
CLARKE ST
WETHERILL ST
PARK
STUART ST
TONY ST
RAMSAY ST
FRAZER ST
JENKINS ST
GRAYLUND CL
THE AVENUE
FIELDING ST
EDGECLIFFE BVD
COLLAROY ST
ALEXANDER ST
DUNCAN CR
SCOTNEY PL
EAST BANK ST
HOMESTEAD AV
BIRDWOOD AV
BRISSENDEN AV
CLIFF RD
BEACH RD
FLORENCE AV
CHARLES HAYMAN LA
WORCESTER ST
JAMIESON PDE
HAY
HENDY AV
KENT ST
MELODY LA
OCEAN GR
SEAVIEW PDE
ANZAC AV
ANZAC PDE
SUFFOLK AV
DEVON PL
NORFOLK AV
MYAMBA RD
LINCOLN AV
BEDFORD CR
LANCASTER CR
COUTTS CR
Steps
Ret Vill
Cath
Berry Res
Rec Cntr
Cmnty Arts Cntr
Furlough Hse
Pk
BBC
Pmy
Fire Stn
YHA
Steps
Cinema
Fox Pk
CITY
10
24
22
A B C D E F G H J K
1 2 3 4 5 6 7 8 9 10 11 12 13 14 15 16

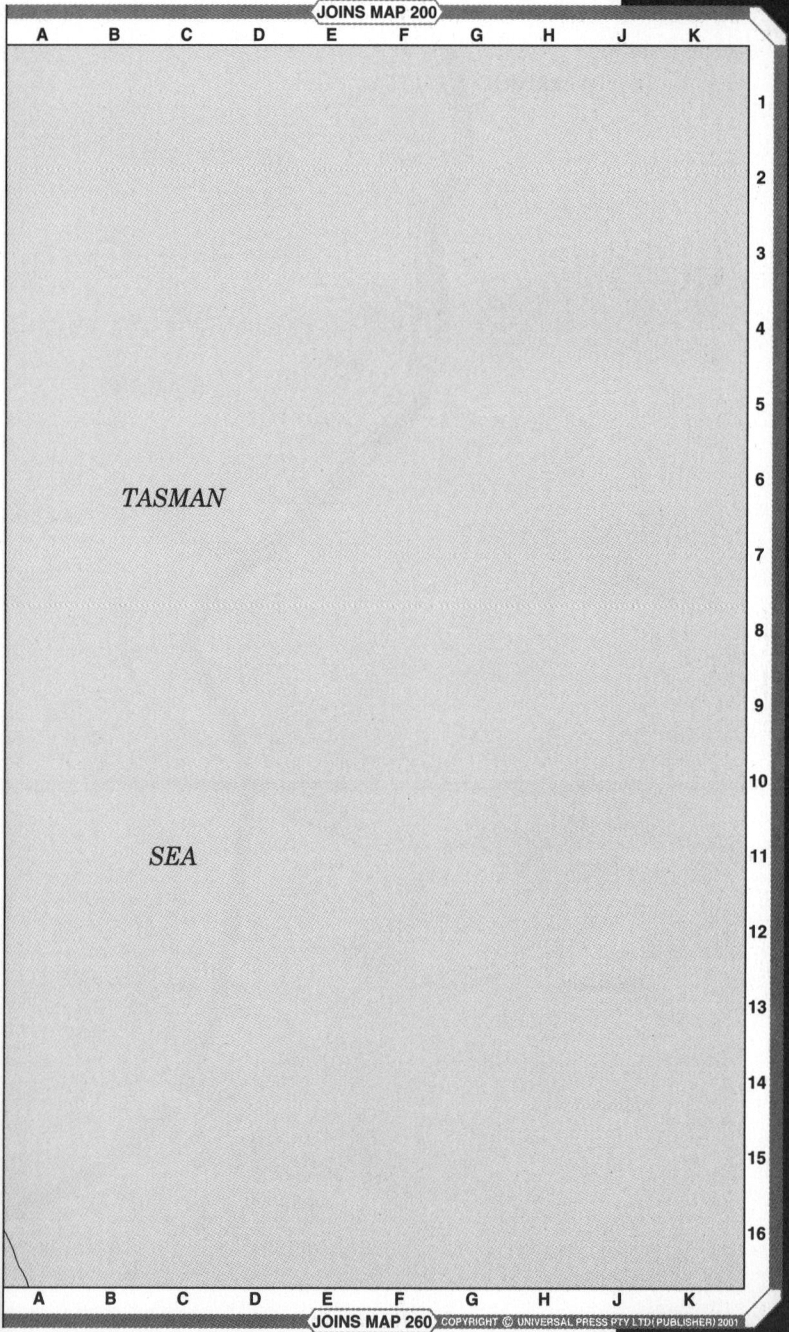

JOINS MAP 200

A B C D E F G H J K

1 2 3 4 5 6 7 8 9 10 11 12 13 14 15 16

TASMAN

SEA

A B C D E F G H J K

JOINS MAP 260

JOINS MAP 203

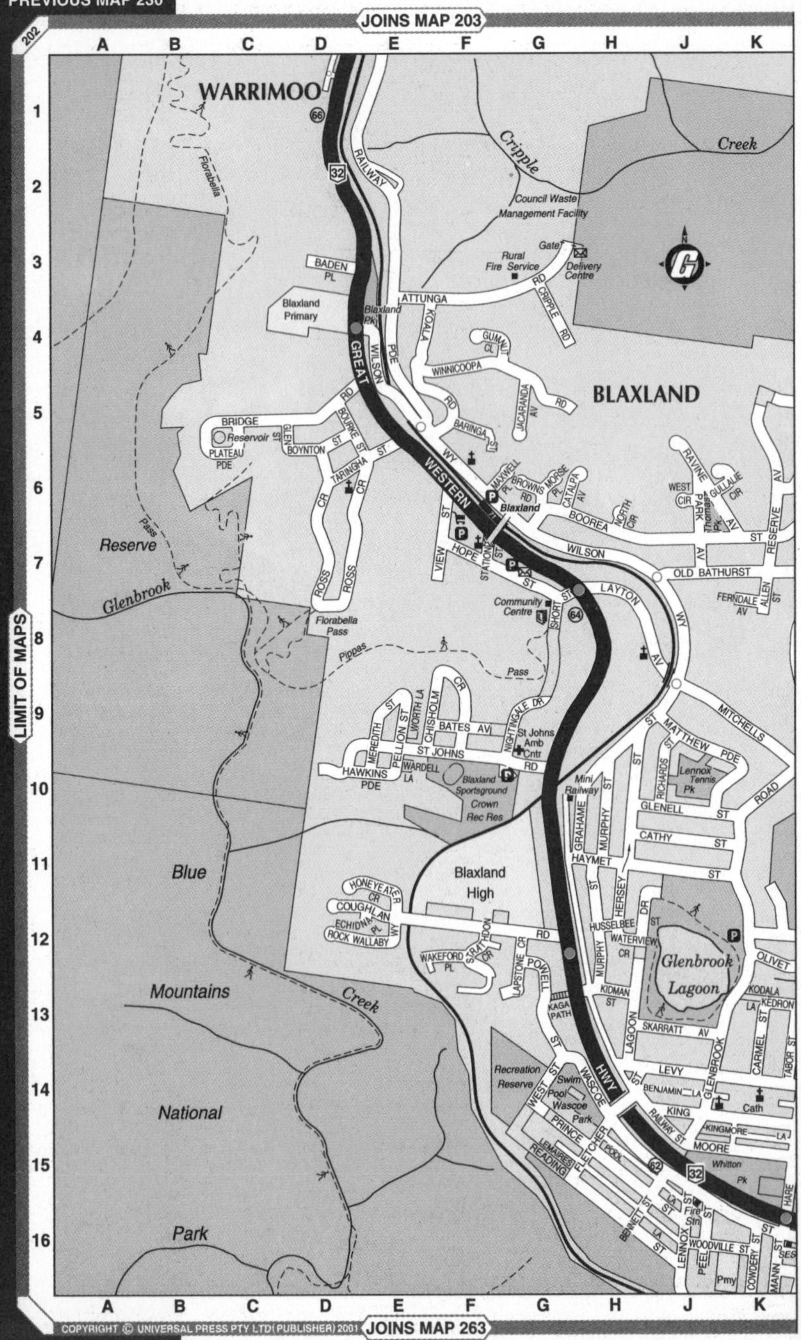

JOINS MAP 263

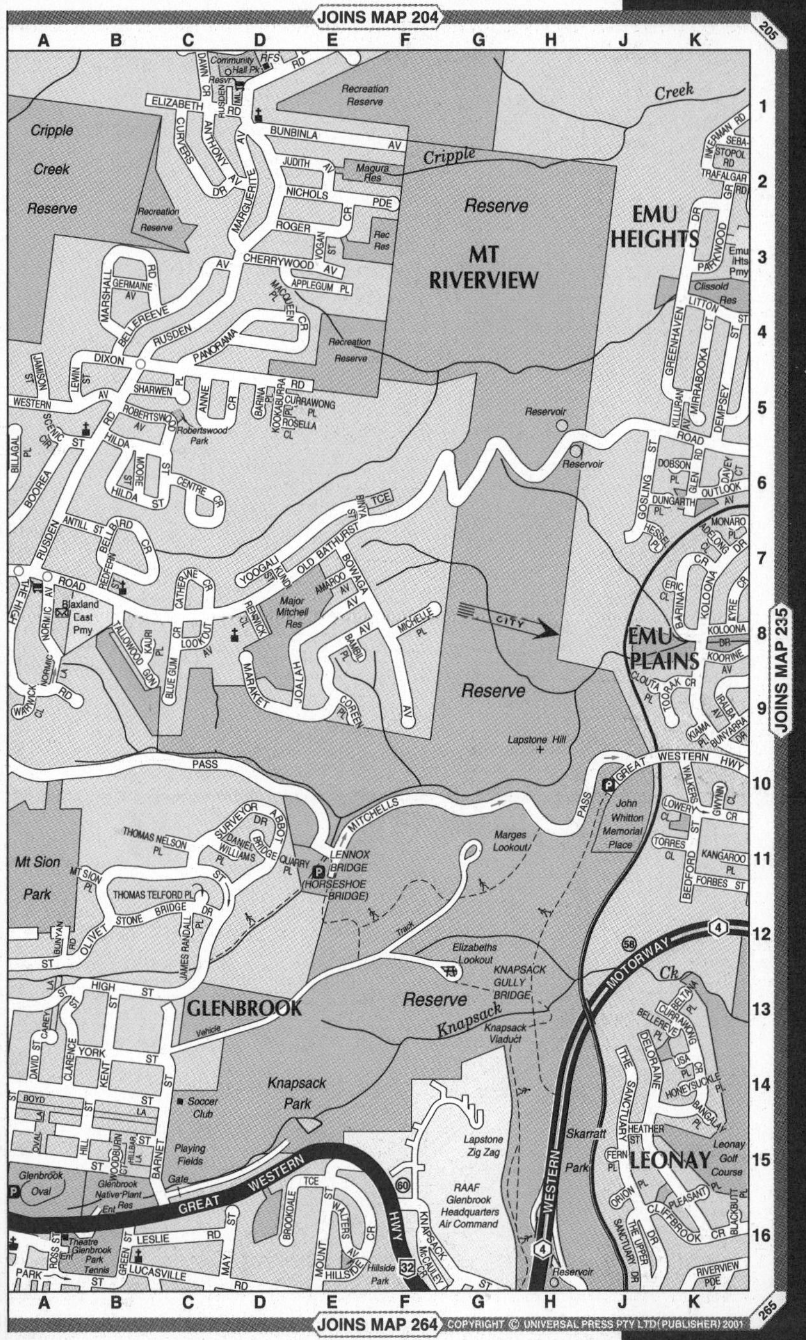
JOINS MAP 204
205
JOINS MAP 235
JOINS MAP 264
265
Cripple Creek Reserve
Recreation Reserve
Reserve
MT RIVERVIEW
EMU HEIGHTS
EMU PLAINS
Cripple
Creek
Magura Res
Rec Res
Recreation Reserve
Robertswood Park
Blaxland East Pmy
Major Mitchell Res
Reservoir
Lapstone Hill
Reserve
John Whitton Memorial Place
Marges Lookout
LENNOX BRIDGE (HORSESHOE BRIDGE)
Mt Sion Park
Elizabeths Lookout
KNAPSACK GULLY BRIDGE
Knapsack Viaduct
Knapsack
GLENBROOK
Reserve
Knapsack Park
Soccer Club
Playing Fields
Lapstone Zig Zag
RAAF Glenbrook Headquarters Air Command
Skarratt Park
LEONAY
Leonay Golf Course
Glenbrook Oval
Glenbrook Native Plant Res
Theatre Glenbrook Park Tennis
Hillside Park
Community Hall Pk
RFS
CITY
GREAT WESTERN HWY
MOTORWAY
WESTERN
OLD BATHURST RD
MITCHELLS PASS
Emu Hts Pmy
Clissold Res
Track
Vehicle
Gate
Ent

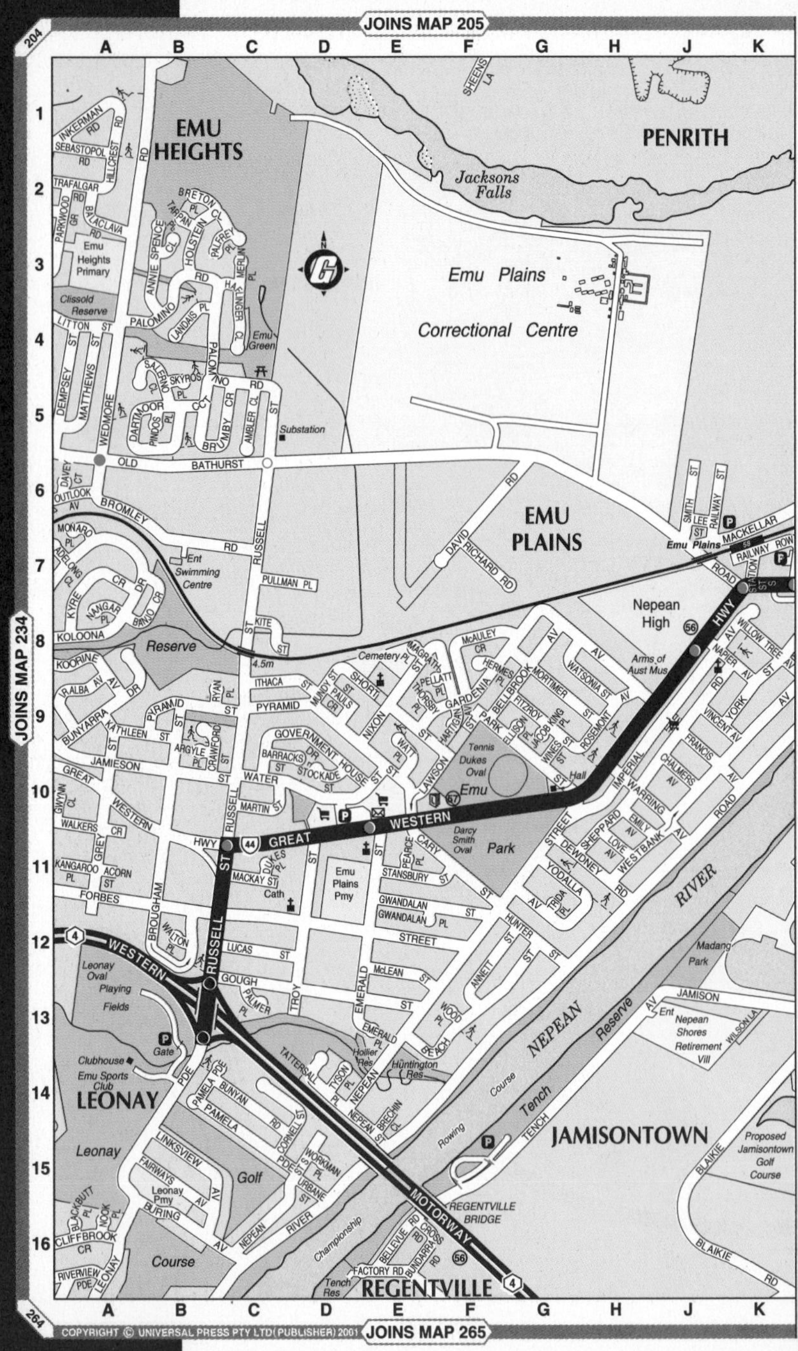
JOINS MAP 205
JOINS MAP 234
JOINS MAP 265
204
264
EMU HEIGHTS
PENRITH
Jacksons Falls
Emu Plains Correctional Centre
EMU PLAINS
LEONAY
JAMISONTOWN
REGENTVILLE
NEPEAN RIVER
Emu Heights Primary
Clissold Reserve
Emu Green
Substation
Ent Swimming Centre
Reserve
Nepean High
Arms of Aust Mus
Tennis Dukes Oval
Emu
Darcy Smith Oval
Park
Emu Plains Pmy
Cath
Hall
Madang Park
Ent Nepean Shores Retirement Vill
Proposed Jamisontown Golf Course
Leonay Oval Playing Fields
Clubhouse
Emu Sports Club
Gate
Leonay Golf Course
Leonay Pmy
Championship
Rowing Course
Tench Reserve
REGENTVILLE BRIDGE
Hollier Res
Huntington Res
Tench Res
Emu Plains
OLD BATHURST RD
GREAT WESTERN HWY
WESTERN MOTORWAY
RUSSELL ST
MACKELLAR
RAILWAY ROW
COPYRIGHT © UNIVERSAL PRESS PTY LTD (PUBLISHER) 2001

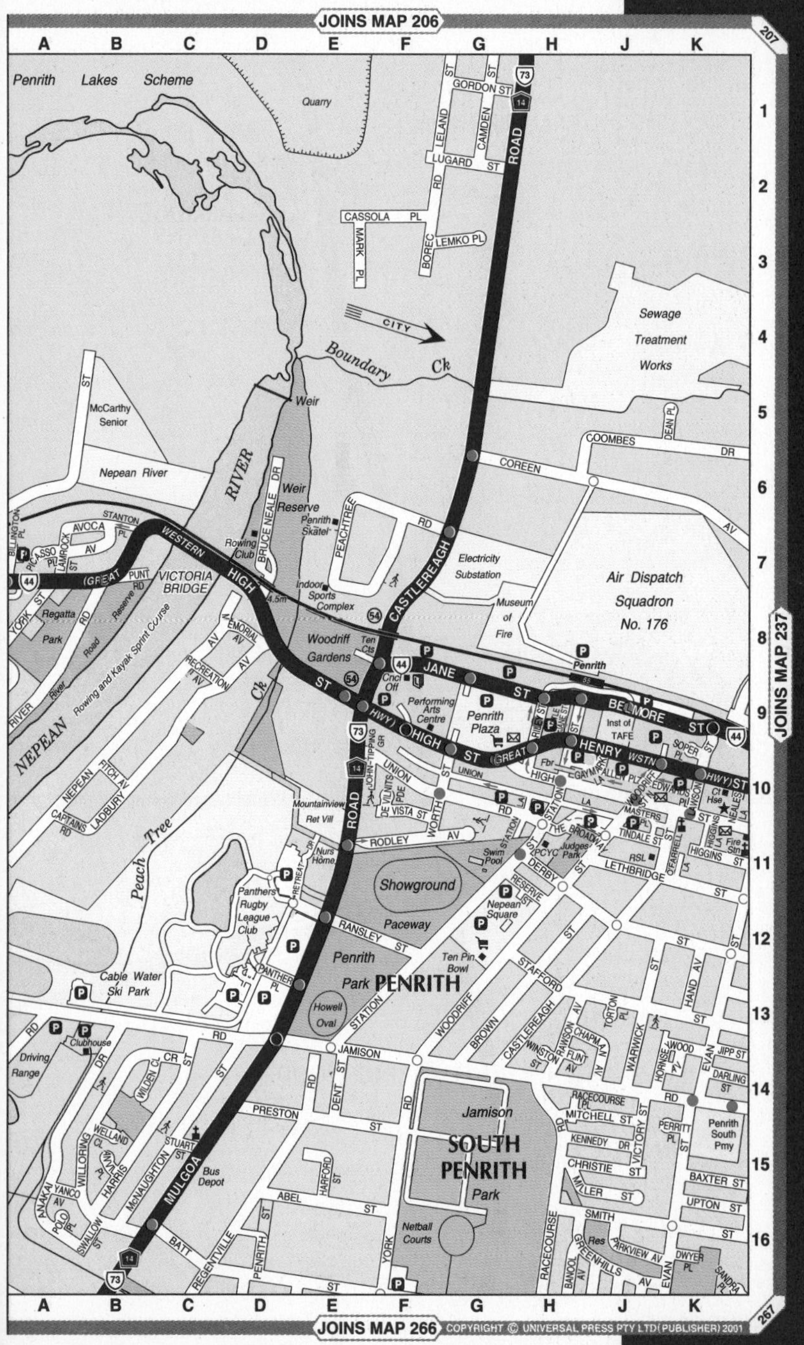

JOINS MAP 206
JOINS MAP 237
JOINS MAP 266
207
267
Penrith Lakes Scheme
Quarry
Sewage Treatment Works
Boundary Ck
CITY
Weir
McCarthy Senior
Nepean River
RIVER
Weir Reserve
Penrith Skatel
Rowing Club
Indoor Sports Complex
Electricity Substation
Museum of Fire
Air Dispatch Squadron No. 176
VICTORIA BRIDGE
Regatta Park
Woodriff Gardens
Ten Cts
Cncl Off
Performing Arts Centre
Penrith Plaza
Penrith
Inst of TAFE
NEPEAN
Nepean Rowing and Kayak Sprint Course
Mountainview Ret Vill
Nurs Home
Swim Pool
PCYC
Judges Park
RSL
Fire Stn
Ct Hse
Showground
Paceway
Panthers Rugby League Club
Nepean Square
Ten Pin Bowl
Penrith Park
PENRITH
Howell Oval
Cable Water Ski Park
Peach Tree Ck
Clubhouse
Driving Range
Bus Depot
Jamison
SOUTH PENRITH
Park
Netball Courts
Res
Penrith South Pmy
CASTLEREAGH ROAD
GREAT WESTERN HWY
HIGH ST
JANE ST
BELMORE ST
HENRY ST
MULGOA ROAD
JAMISON RD
COREEN AV
COOMBES DR

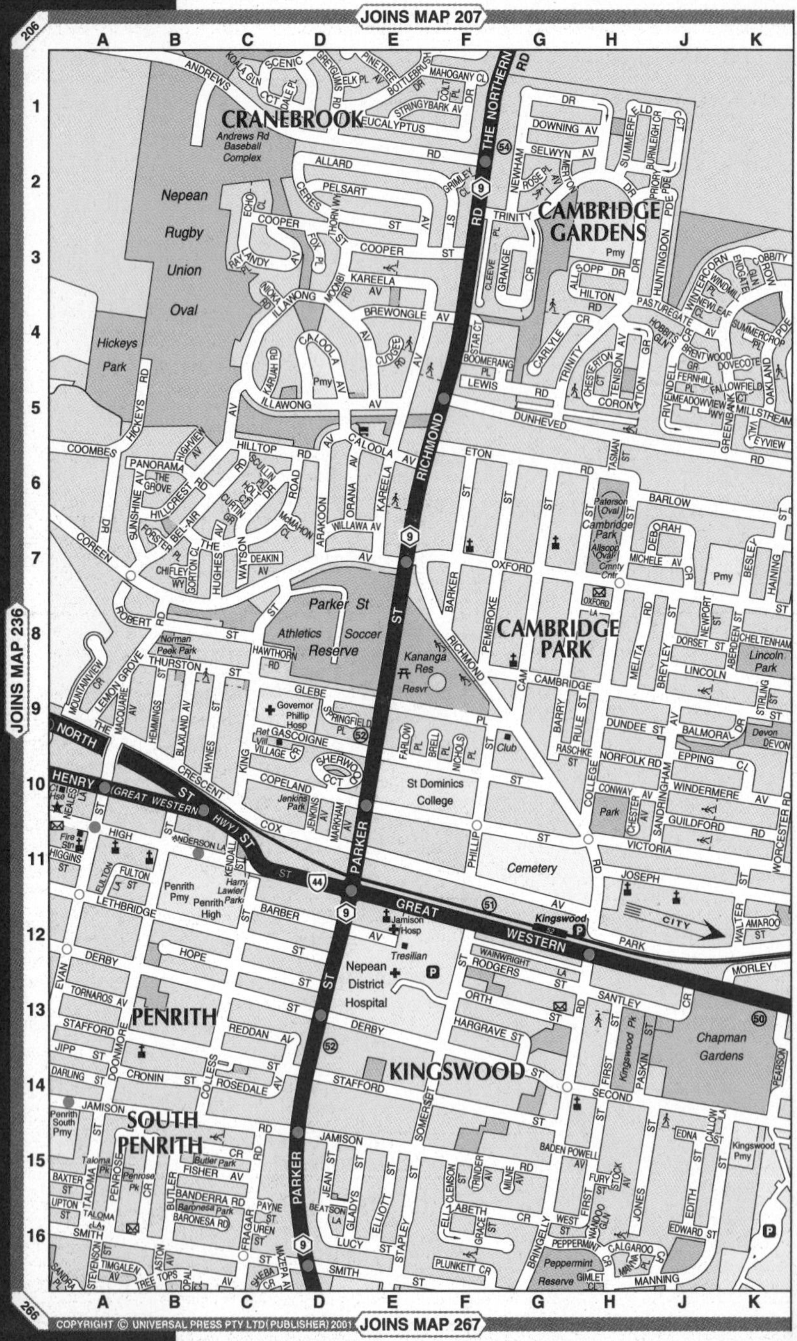
JOINS MAP 207
JOINS MAP 236
JOINS MAP 267
206
266
A
B
C
D
E
F
G
H
J
K
1
2
3
4
5
6
7
8
9
10
11
12
13
14
15
16
CRANEBROOK
Andrews Rd Baseball Complex
Nepean Rugby Union Oval
Hickeys Park
CAMBRIDGE GARDENS
CAMBRIDGE PARK
Parker St Athletics Soccer Reserve
Kananga Res
Resvr
Governor Phillip Hosp
Ret Vill
St Dominics College
Cemetery
Paterson Oval
Cambridge Park
Allsopp Oval
Cmnty Cntr
Lincoln Park
Norman Peek Park
Jenkins Park
Penrith Pmy
Penrith High
Harry Lawler Park
Jamison Hosp
Tresilian
Nepean District Hospital
PENRITH
KINGSWOOD
SOUTH PENRITH
Penrith South Pmy
Taloma Pk
Penrose Pk
Butler Park
Baronesa Park
Kingswood Pk
Chapman Gardens
Kingswood Pmy
Peppermint Reserve
Kingswood
CITY
Fire Stn
Ct Hse
Club
Park
Pmy
THE NORTHERN RD
RICHMOND RD
PARKER ST
GREAT WESTERN HWY
HENRY ST
NORTH
GREAT WESTERN
ANDREWS RD
CAMBRIDGE
JAMISON
SMITH
COPYRIGHT © UNIVERSAL PRESS PTY LTD (PUBLISHER) 2001

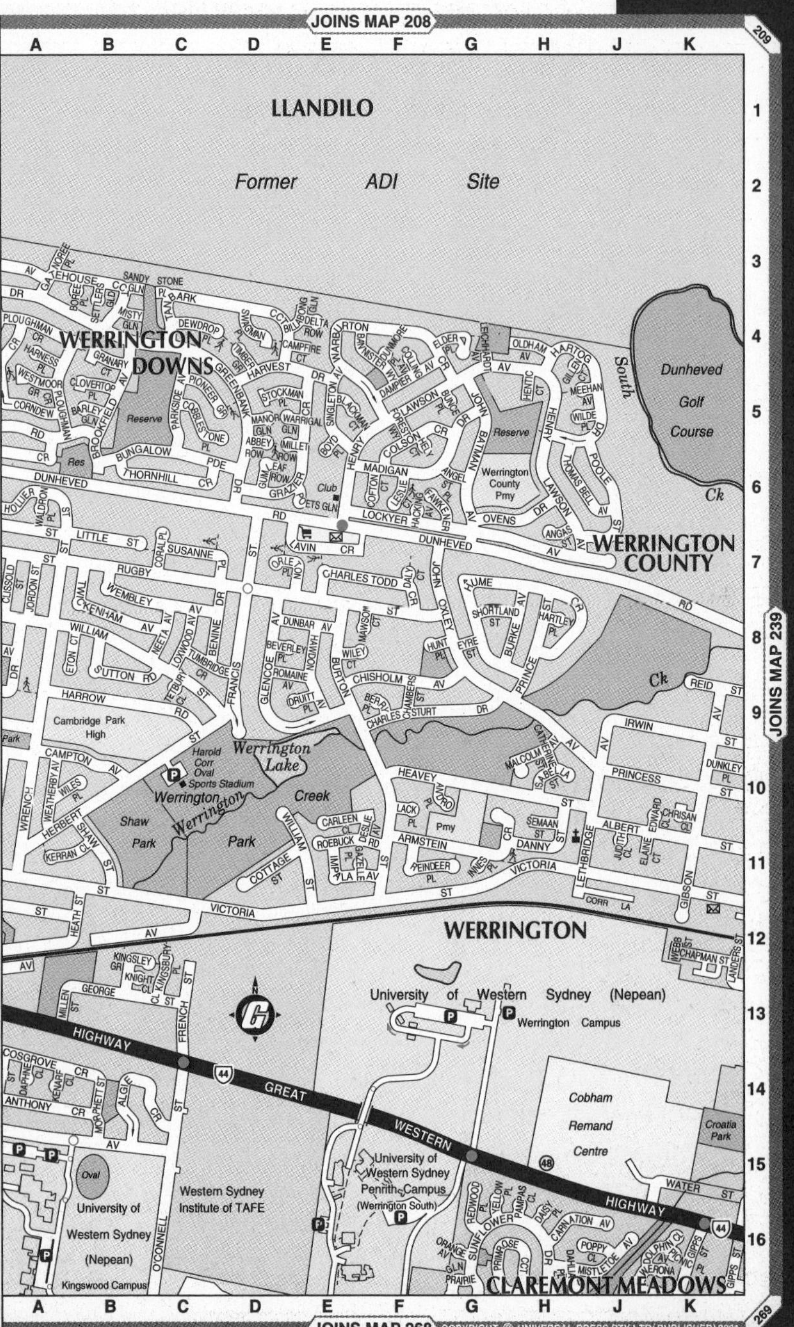
JOINS MAP 208
LLANDILO
Former ADI Site
WERRINGTON DOWNS
WERRINGTON COUNTY
WERRINGTON
CLAREMONT MEADOWS
Dunheved Golf Course
Werrington Lake
Werrington Park
Shaw Park
University of Western Sydney (Nepean)
Werrington Campus
Cobham Remand Centre
Western Sydney Institute of TAFE
University of Western Sydney Penrith Campus (Werrington South)
University of Western Sydney (Nepean) Kingswood Campus
Cambridge Park High
GREAT WESTERN HIGHWAY
JOINS MAP 239
JOINS MAP 268

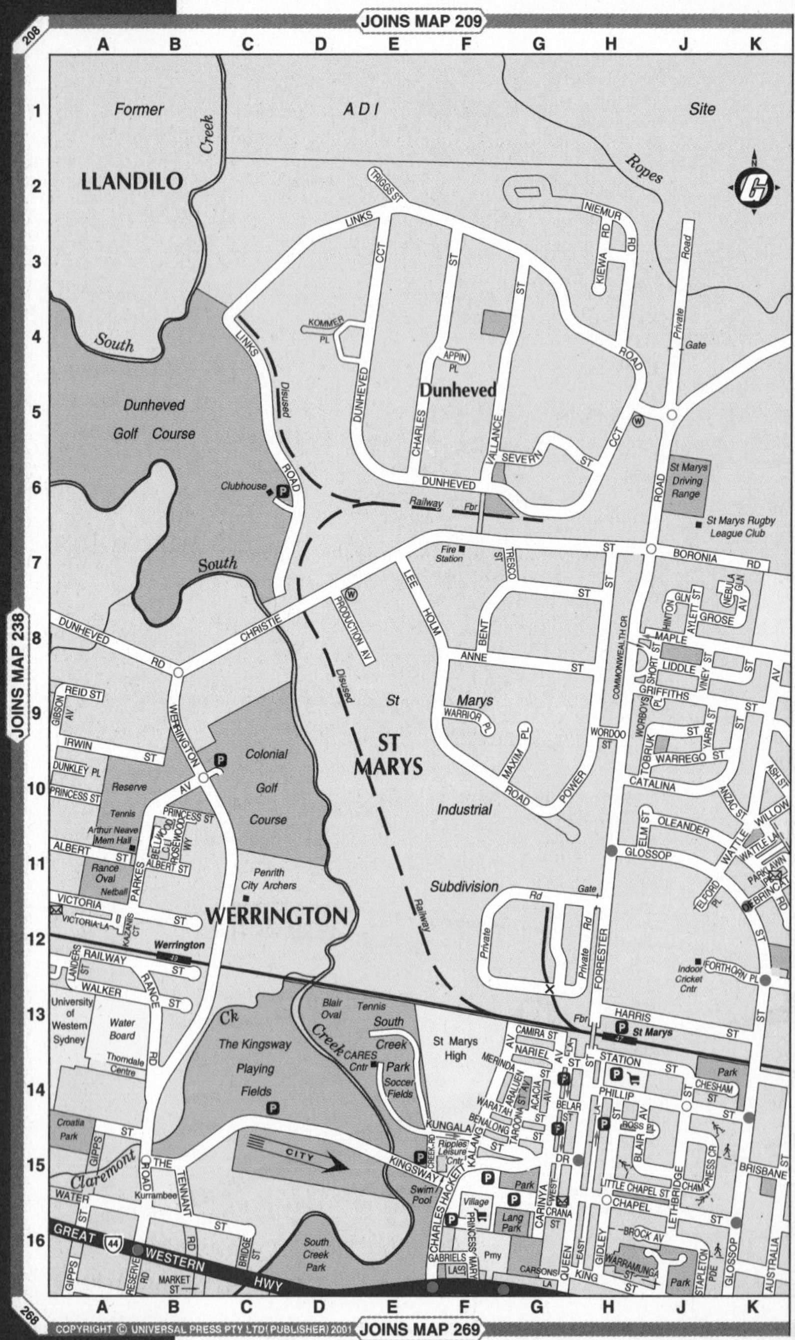
JOINS MAP 209
JOINS MAP 238
JOINS MAP 269
208
268
A B C D E F G H J K
1 2 3 4 5 6 7 8 9 10 11 12 13 14 15 16
Former ADI Site
LLANDILO
Dunheved
ST MARYS
WERRINGTON
Dunheved Golf Course
Colonial Golf Course
St Marys Industrial Subdivision
The Kingsway Playing Fields
South Creek Park
St Marys Driving Range
St Marys Rugby League Club
St Marys High
University of Western Sydney
Water Board
Thomdale Centre
Rance Oval
Netball
Reserve
Tennis
Arthur Neave Mem Hall
Penrith City Archers
Clubhouse
Fire Station
Indoor Cricket Cntr
Blair Oval
CARES Cntr
Ripples Leisure Cntr
Swim Pool
Village
Lang Park
Pmy
Croatia Park
Kurrambee
South Creek Park
Werrington
St Marys
LINKS CCT
LINKS ROAD
TRIGGS ST
DUNHEVED CCT
CHARLES ST
VALLANCE ST
NIEMUR RD
KIEWA RD
KOMMER PL
APPIN PL
SEVERN ST
DUNHEVED RD
CHRISTIE ST
BORONIA RD
PRODUCTION AV
LEE HOLM RD
TRESCO ST
BENT ST
ANNE ST
WARRIOR PL
MAXIM PL
POWER ST
COMMONWEALTH CR
WORDOO ST
FORRESTER RD
HARRIS ST
STATION ST
PHILLIP ST
CHAPEL ST
KING ST
QUEEN ST
GLOSSOP ST
GREAT WESTERN HWY
KINGSWAY
WERRINGTON RD
RAILWAY ST
WALKER ST
VICTORIA ST
ALBERT ST
PRINCESS ST
IRWIN ST
REID ST
GIBSON AV
DUNKLEY PL
PARKES AV
TENNANT RD
BRIDGE ST
MARKET ST
BRISBANE ST
AUSTRALIA ST
MAPLE
LIDDLE
GRIFFITHS
CATALINA
OLEANDER
WATTLE
WILLOW
TELFORD PL
FORTHORN PL
DEBRINCAT
CHESHAM ST
KUNGALA
BELAR AV
NARIEL ST
CAMIRA ST
MERINDA
WARATAH
BENALONG
TAROONA ST
CARINYA AV
CRANA ST
CHARLES HACKETT DR
PRINCESS MARY ST
GABRIELS LA
CARSONS LA
GIDLEY ST
LETHBRIDGE ST
BLAIR AV
ROSS PL
BROCK AV
WARRAMUNGA ST
STAPLETON PDE
LITTLE CHAPEL ST
South Creek
Ropes Creek
Claremont Creek
Disused Railway
Private Road
Gate
CITY
COPYRIGHT © UNIVERSAL PRESS PTY LTD (PUBLISHER) 2001

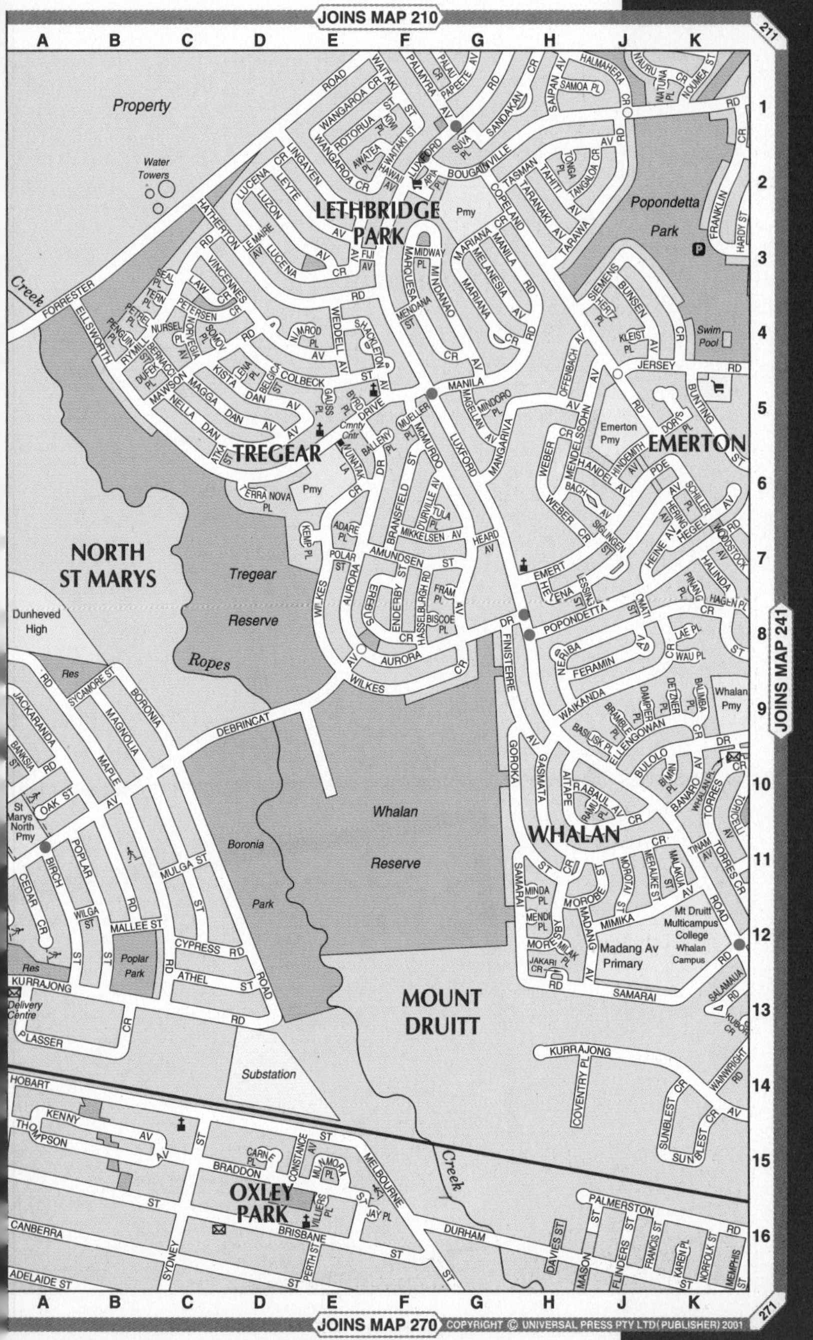
JOINS MAP 210
211
A B C D E F G H J K
1 2 3 4 5 6 7 8 9 10 11 12 13 14 15 16
LETHBRIDGE PARK
TREGEAR
EMERTON
NORTH ST MARYS
WHALAN
MOUNT DRUITT
OXLEY PARK
Property
Water Towers
Creek
Popondetta Park
Swim Pool
Pmy
Emerton Pmy
Cmnty Cntr
Tregear Reserve
Ropes
Dunheved High
Res
St Marys North Pmy
Whalan Reserve
Boronia Park
Poplar Park
Whalan Pmy
Mt Druitt Multicampus College Whalan Campus
Madang Av Primary
Delivery Centre
Substation
FORRESTER RD
WAITAKI ST
PALMYRA AV
PALAU CR
PAPEETE AV
SANDAKAN CR
SAIPAN AV
HALMAHERA CR
NAURU CR
NATUNA PL
NOUMEA ST
SAMOA PL
WANGAROA CR
ROTORUA ST
KIWI PL
AWATEA PL
HAWAII AV
LUXFORD RD
APIA PL
SUVA PL
BOUGAINVILLE RD
TASMAN AV
TONGA PL
TAHITI AV
TANGALOA CR
TARANAKI AV
TARAWA AV
LINGAYEN AV
LUCENA CR
LEYTE AV
LUZON AV
LE MAIRE AV
FIJI AV
HATHERTON RD
MIDWAY PL
MARQUESA CR
MINDANAO AV
MENDANA ST
MARIANA CR
MELANESIA AV
MANILA RD
COPELAND RD
FRANKLIN ST
HARDY ST
SIEMENS CR
HERTZ PL
BUNSEN AV
KLEIST PL
JERSEY RD
BUNTING ST
DORYS PL
OFFENBACH AV
MENDELSSOHN AV
WEBER CR
HANDEL AV
HINDEMITH AV
BACH PL
SCHILLER PL
HERING PL
HEGEL AV
HEINE AV
SIGLINGEN ST
WOODSTOCK AV
HALINDA ST
PINANG PL
HAGEN PL
OMATI ST
EMERT
HEENA
LESSING
POPONDETTA DR
VINCENNES CR
SEAL PL
TERN PL
PETREL PL
PENGUIN PL
RYMILL PL
ELLSWORTH RD
LAW CR
PETERSEN CR
NURSEL PL
NORVEGIA AV
SOMOV PL
NIMROD PL
WEDDELL AV
SHACKLETON AV
BERNACCI
DUFEK PL
MAWSON RD
KISTA DAN AV
LENA PL
BELGICA ST
COLBECK ST
MAGGA DAN AV
NELLA DAN AV
GAUSS PL
BYRD PL
DRIVE
MUELLER PL
McMURDO ST
BALLENY PL
NUNATAK LA
ATKA ST
TERRA NOVA PL
MINDORO PL
MAGELLAN AV
MANGARIVA AV
BRANSFIELD ST
DURVILLE AV
TULA PL
MIKKELSEN AV
HEARD AV
ADARE PL
KEMP PL
POLAR ST
AMUNDSEN ST
AURORA AV
EREBUS
ENDERBY ST
HASSELBURGH RD
FRAM PL
BISCOE PL
WILKES CR
FINISTERRE AV
NERIBA
FERAMIN
LAE PL
WAU PL
WAIKANDA CR
DAMPIER ST
DETZNER PL
BALIMBA PL
BRAMBLE PL
BASILISK PL
ELLENGOWAN CR
BULOLO DR
BIMIN PL
BANARO AV
WHALAN PL
TORRES CR
TORICELLI AV
GOROKA ST
GASMATA
AITAPE
RABAUL AV
RAMU PL
SAMARAI RD
MINDA PL
MENDI PL
MORESBY
MOROBE ST
MADANG AV
MOROTAI ST
MERAUKE ST
MALAKUA ST
MIMIKA AV
MILAK PL
JAKARI CR
TINAM AV
SALAMAUA RD
KUBOR CR
WAINWRIGHT RD
KURRAJONG AV
COVENTRY PL
SUNBLEST CR
DEBRINCAT AV
SYCAMORE ST
BORONIA RD
MAGNOLIA
MAPLE
JACKARANDA
BANKSIA ST
OAK ST
BIRCH
POPLAR
CEDAR CR
WILGA ST
MALLEE ST
MULGA ST
CYPRESS RD
ATHEL ST
KURRAJONG RD
PLASSER CR
HOBART
KENNY AV
THOMPSON AV
BRADDON ST
CARNE PL
CONSTANCE AV
MUNMORA PL
MELBOURNE ST
VILLIERS PL
JAY PL
CANBERRA ST
BRISBANE ST
PERTH ST
SYDNEY ST
ADELAIDE ST
DURHAM ST
PALMERSTON RD
DAVIES ST
MASON ST
FLINDERS ST
FRANCIS ST
KAREN PL
NORFOLK ST
MEMPHIS ST
JOINS MAP 241
JOINS MAP 270
271

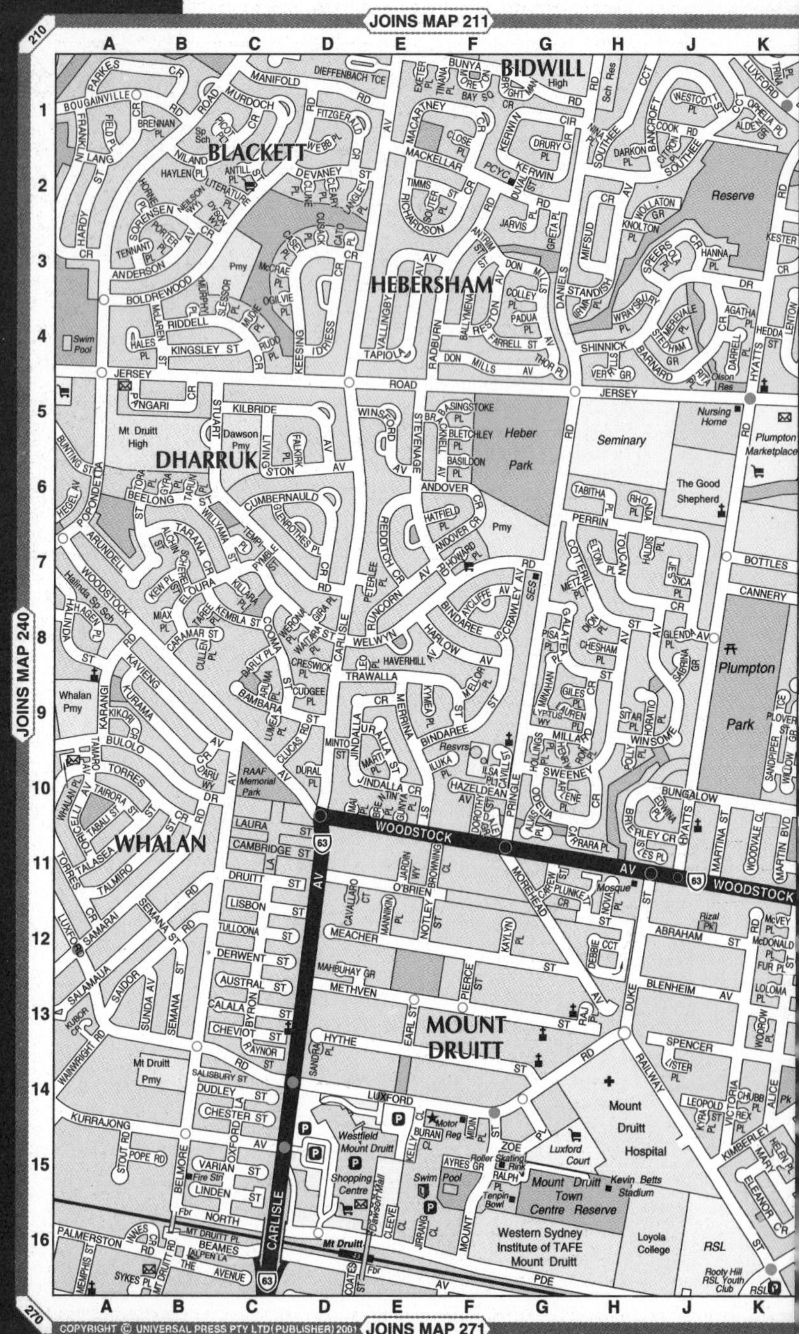
JOINS MAP 211
JOINS MAP 240
JOINS MAP 271
210
270
A B C D E F G H J K
1 2 3 4 5 6 7 8 9 10 11 12 13 14 15 16
BLACKETT
BIDWILL
HEBERSHAM
DHARRUK
WHALAN
MOUNT DRUITT
JERSEY RD
WOODSTOCK AV
CARLISLE AV
Heber Park
Seminary
Plumpton Park
Plumpton Marketplace
The Good Shepherd
Nursing Home
Mt Druitt High
Dawson Pmy
Whalan Pmy
Mt Druitt Pmy
RAAF Memorial Park
Westfield Mount Druitt Shopping Centre
Luxford Court
Mount Druitt Hospital
Mount Druitt Town Centre Reserve
Kevin Betts Stadium
Western Sydney Institute of TAFE Mount Druitt
Loyola College
RSL
Rooty Hill RSL Youth Club
Swim Pool
Mt Druitt
COPYRIGHT © UNIVERSAL PRESS PTY LTD (PUBLISHER) 2001

JOINS MAP 212

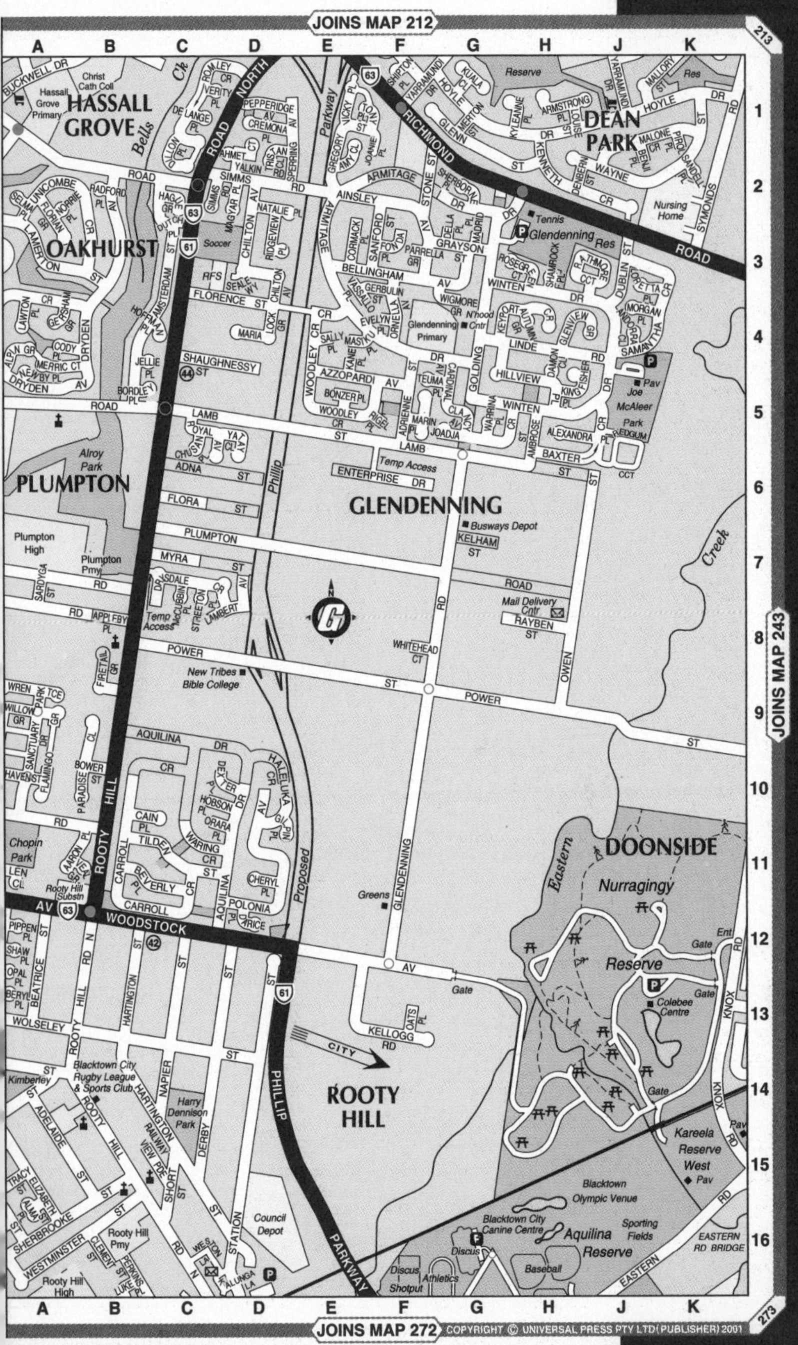

JOINS MAP 243

JOINS MAP 272

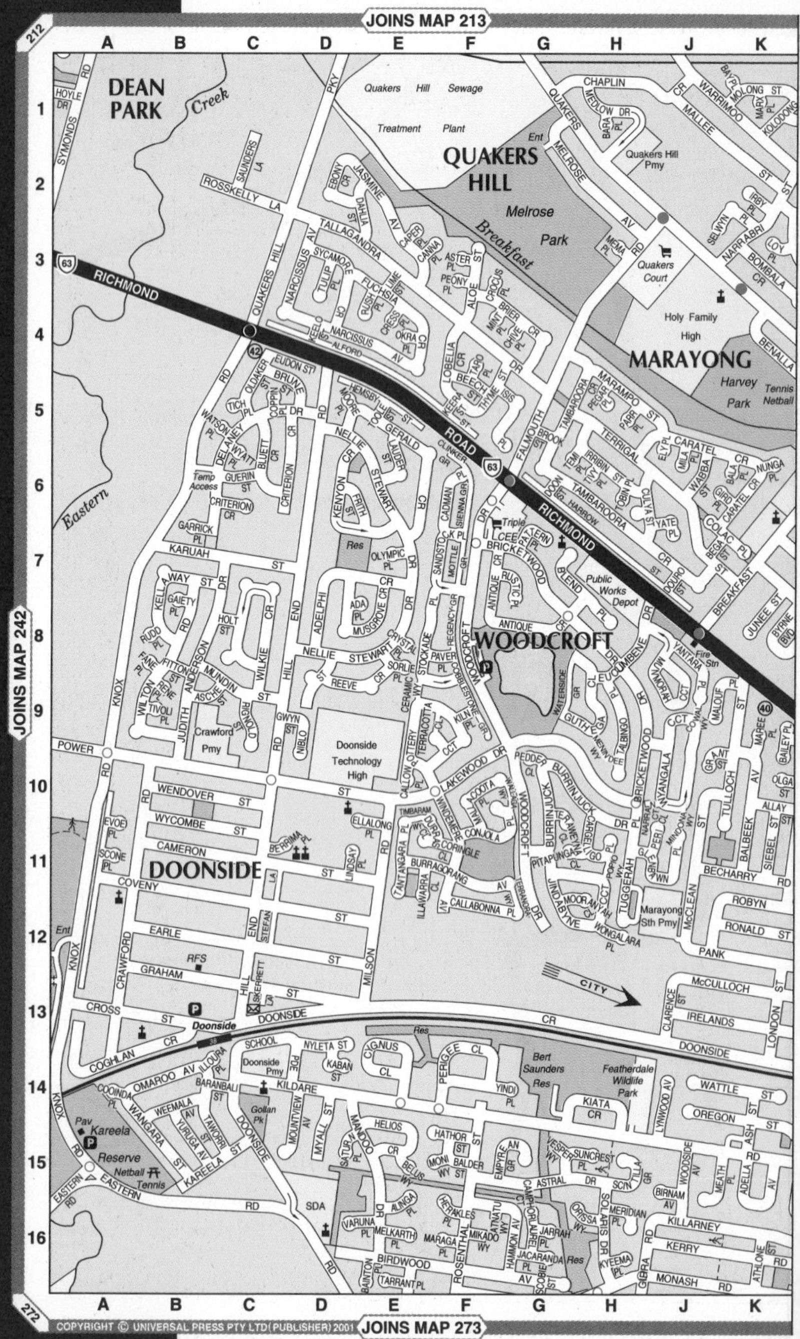
JOINS MAP 213
JOINS MAP 242
JOINS MAP 273
212
272
DEAN PARK
QUAKERS HILL
MARAYONG
WOODCROFT
DOONSIDE
Quakers Hill Sewage Treatment Plant
Melrose Park
Quakers Hill Pmy
Quakers Court
Holy Family High
Harvey Park
Tennis Netball
Public Works Depot
Fire Stn
Crawford Pmy
Doonside Technology High
Marayong Sth Pmy
Doonside Pmy
Bert Saunders Res
Featherdale Wildlife Park
Kareela Reserve
Gollan Pk
RICHMOND ROAD
CITY

JOINS MAP 214

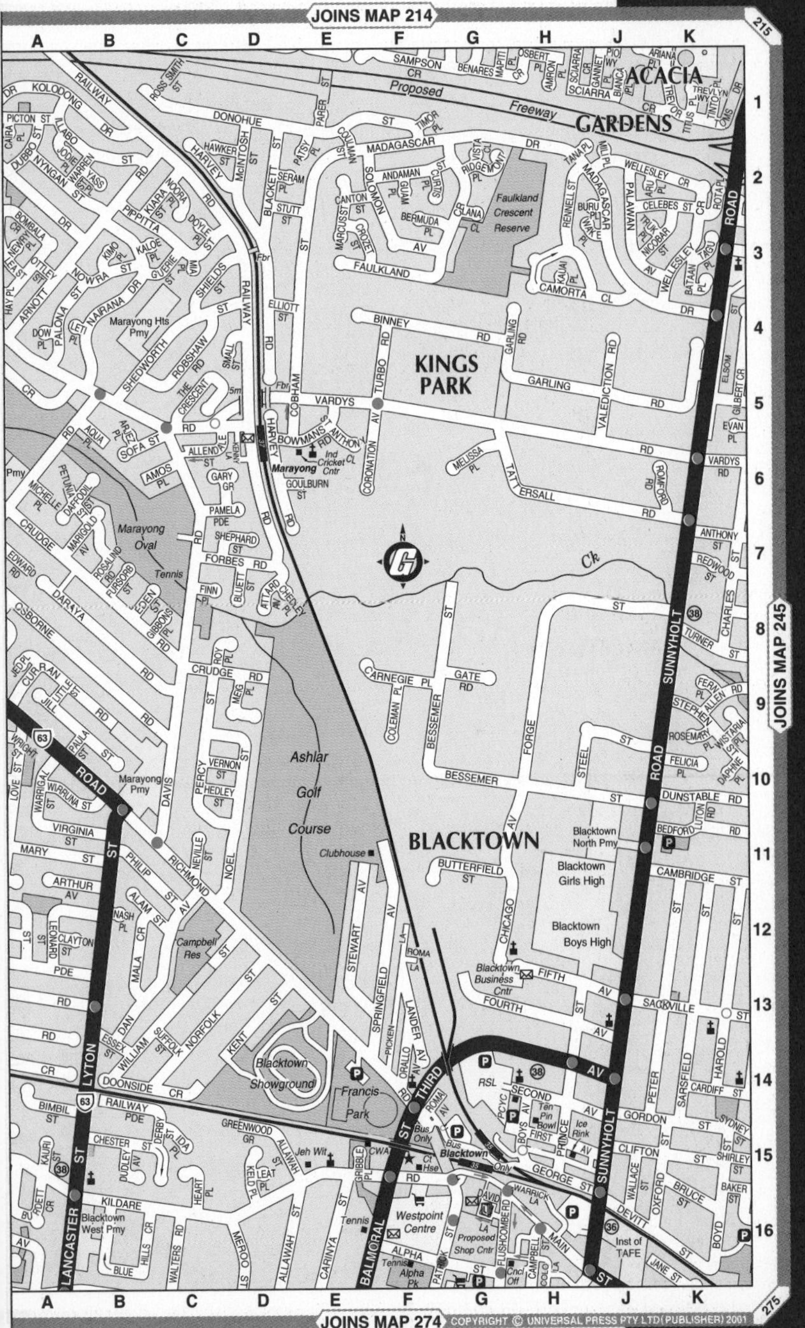

JOINS MAP 245

JOINS MAP 274

MAP 245

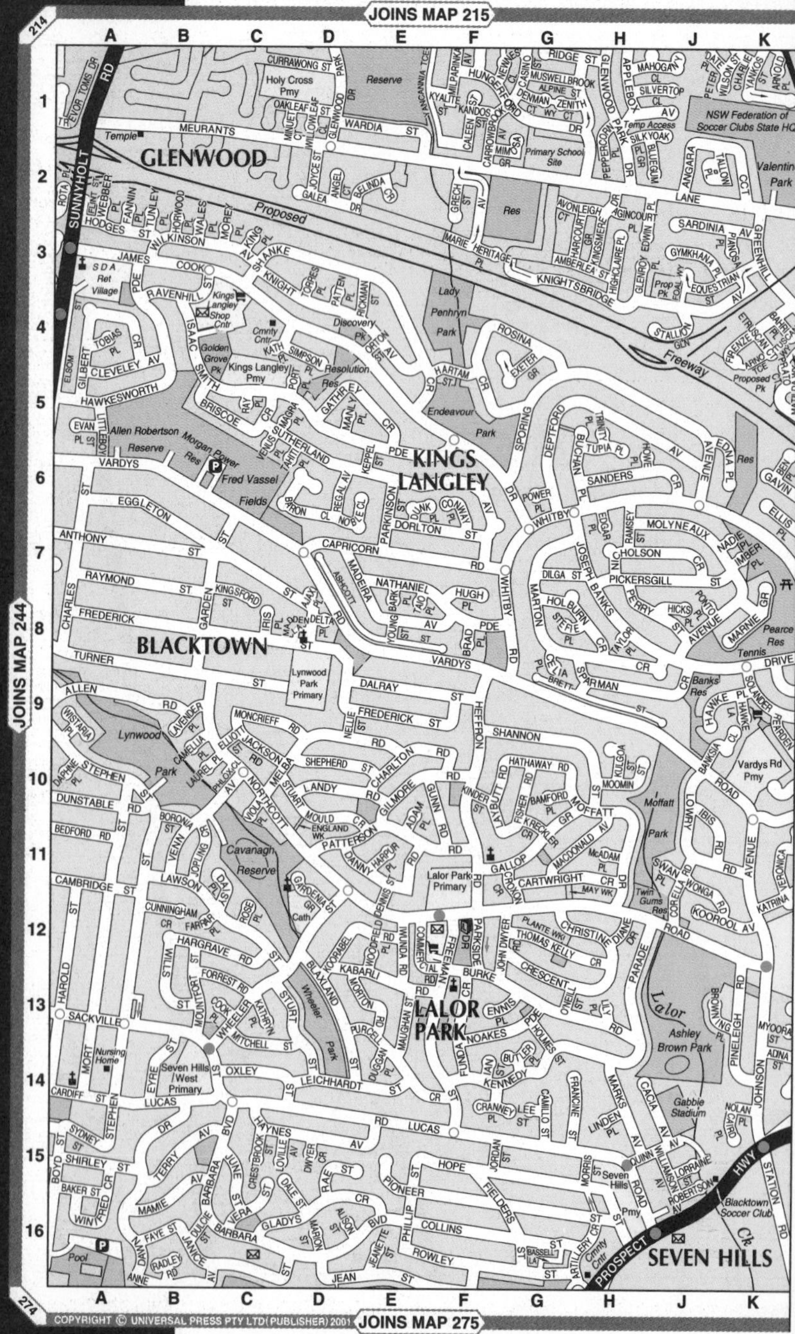

JOINS MAP 215
JOINS MAP 244
JOINS MAP 275
214
274
A B C D E F G H J K
1 2 3 4 5 6 7 8 9 10 11 12 13 14 15 16
GLENWOOD
KINGS LANGLEY
BLACKTOWN
LALOR PARK
SEVEN HILLS
Proposed
Freeway
SUNNYHOLT RD
MEURANTS
WARDIA ST
Temple
Holy Cross Pmy
Reserve
Res
NSW Federation of Soccer Clubs State HQ
Valentine Park
Primary School Site
Temp Access
Lady Penhryn Park
Endeavour Park
Discovery Pk
Resolution Res
Kings Langley Shop Cntr
Kings Langley Pmy
Cmnty Cntr
Golden Grove Pk
S D A Ret Village
Allen Robertson Reserve
Morgan Power Res
Fred Vassel Fields
HAWKESWORTH
VARDYS
EGGLETON
ANTHONY ST
RAYMOND ST
FREDERICK
TURNER
ALLEN
CAPRICORN RD
Lynwood Park Primary
Lynwood Park
DALRAY
SHANNON
Pearce Res
Tennis
Banks Res
Vardys Rd Pmy
Moffatt Park
Twin Gums Res
Cavanagh Reserve
Cath
Lalor Park Primary
Wheeler Park
Lalor
Ashley Brown Park
Gabbie Stadium
Nursing Home
Seven Hills West Primary
Seven Hills Pmy
Cmnty Cntr
Blacktown Soccer Club
Pool
PROSPECT HWY
LUCAS RD
LEICHHARDT ST
OXLEY
SACKVILLE
CAMBRIDGE ST
DUNSTABLE RD
BEDFORD RD
COPYRIGHT © UNIVERSAL PRESS PTY LTD (PUBLISHER) 2001

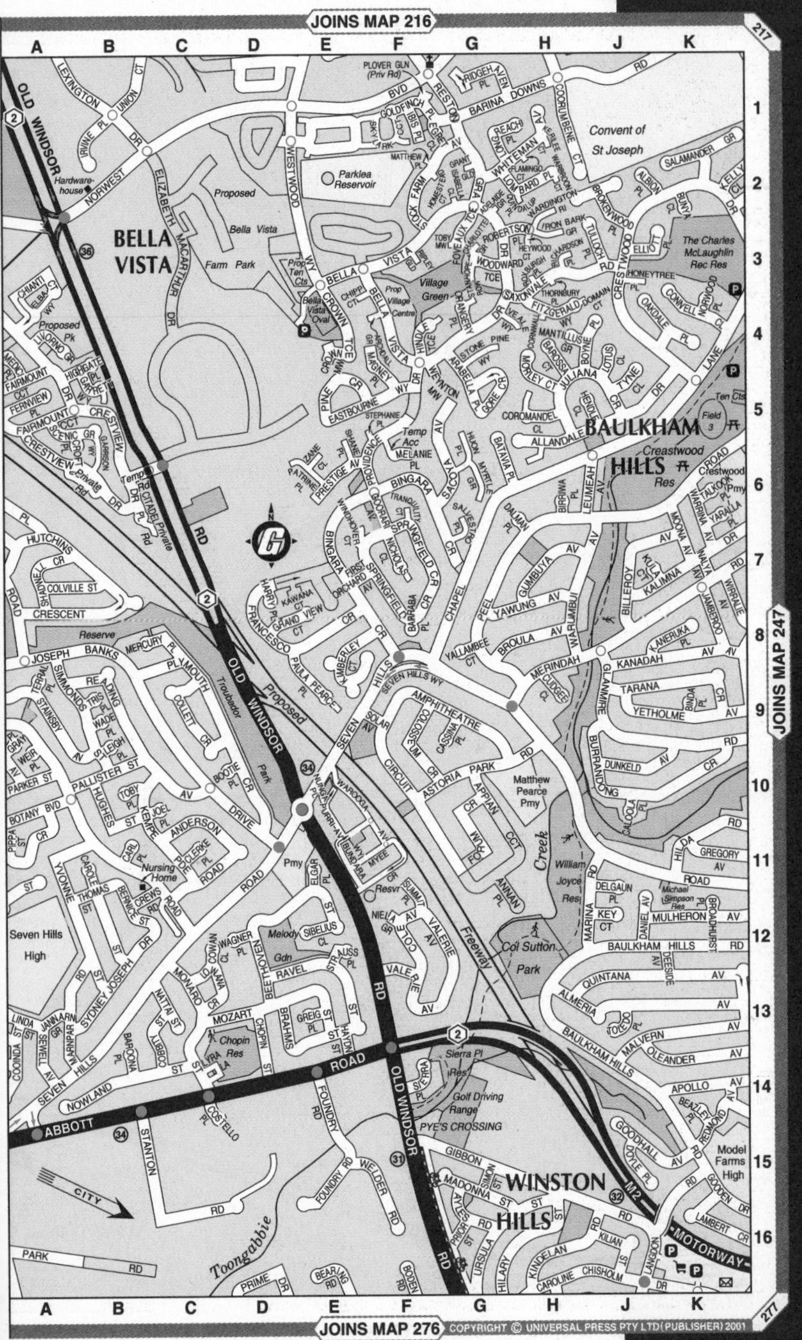
JOINS MAP 216
JOINS MAP 247
JOINS MAP 276
217
277
A B C D E F G H J K
1 2 3 4 5 6 7 8 9 10 11 12 13 14 15 16
BELLA VISTA
BAULKHAM HILLS
WINSTON HILLS
OLD WINDSOR RD
NORWEST BVD
Hardware-house
Proposed Bella Vista Farm Park
Parklea Reservoir
Convent of St Joseph
The Charles McLaughlin Rec Res
Bella Vista Oval
Village Green
Prop Village Centre
Prop Ten Cts
Proposed Pk
Creastwood Res
Crestwood Pmy
Field 3
Ten Cts
Temp Acc
Troubador Park
Proposed Freeway
Reserve
Matthew Pearce Pmy
William Joyce Res
Creek
Col Sutton Park
Michael Simpson Res
Nursing Home
Seven Hills High
Melody Gdn
Chopin Res
Resvr
Pmy
Sierra Pl Res
Golf Driving Range
PYE'S CROSSING
Model Farms High
SEVEN HILLS RD
ABBOTT ROAD
MOTORWAY
M2
Toongabbie
CITY
BAULKHAM HILLS RD
BARINA DOWNS RD
CRESTWOOD DR
CHAPEL LANE
SEVEN HILLS WY
ASTORIA PARK RD
FOUNDRY RD
STANTON RD
PARK RD
WELDER RD

MAP 247

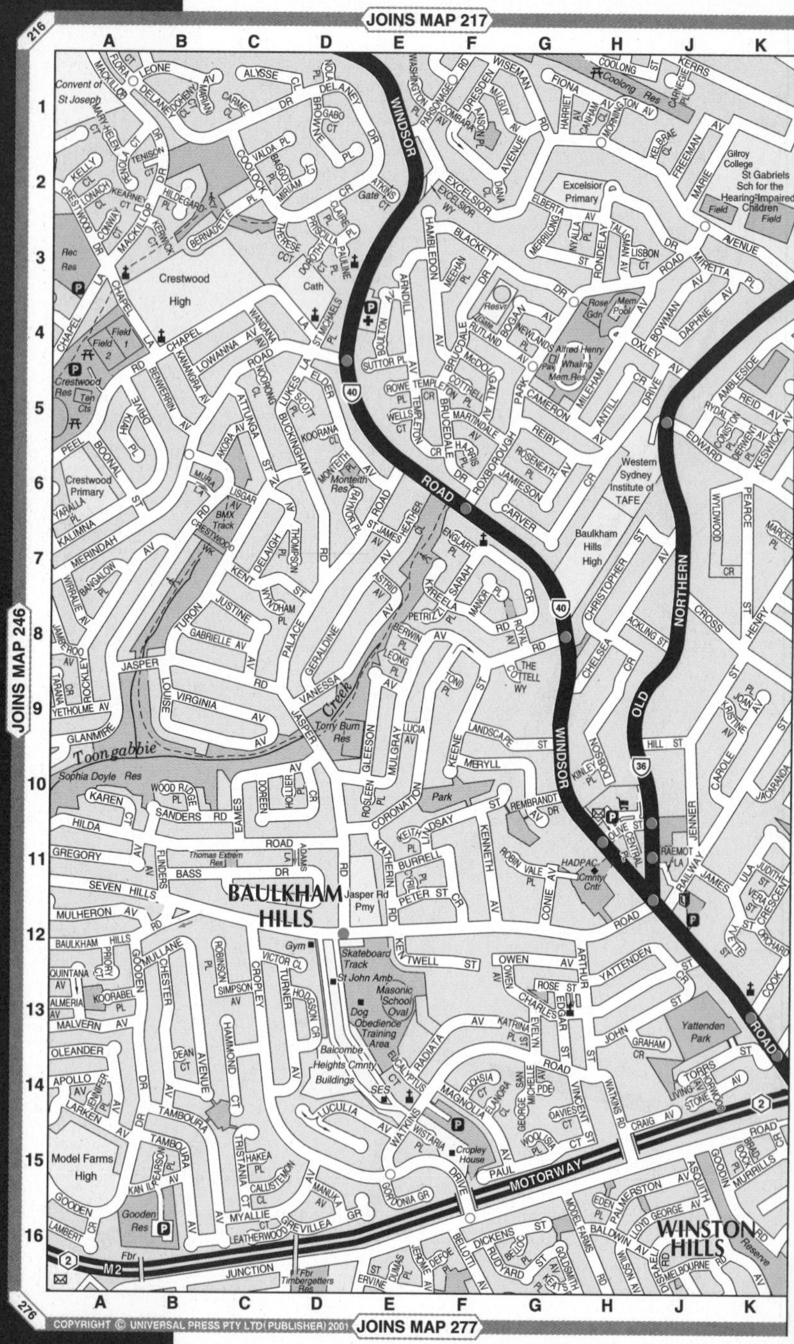

JOINS MAP 217
JOINS MAP 246
JOINS MAP 277
216
276
A B C D E F G H J K
1 2 3 4 5 6 7 8 9 10 11 12 13 14 15 16
BAULKHAM HILLS
WINSTON HILLS
WINDSOR ROAD
OLD NORTHERN ROAD
MOTORWAY
M2
Convent of St Joseph
Crestwood High
Cath
Crestwood Res
Ten Cts
Crestwood Primary
Rec Res
Field 1
Field 2
BMX Track
Monteith Res
Torry Burn Res
Toongabbie Creek
Sophia Doyle Res
Thomas Extrem Res
Jasper Rd Pmy
Gym
Skateboard Track
St John Amb
Masonic School Oval
Dog Obedience Training Area
Balcombe Heights Cmnty Buildings
SES
Cropley House
Model Farms High
Gooden Res
Timbergetters Res
Excelsior Primary
Gilroy College
St Gabriels Sch for the Hearing-Impaired Children
Field
Alfred Henry Whaling Mem.Res.
Rose Gdn
Mem Pool
Resvr
Western Sydney Institute of TAFE
Baulkham Hills High
Park
HADPAC
Cmnty Cntr
Yattenden Park
Coolong Res
Reserve
COPYRIGHT © UNIVERSAL PRESS PTY LTD (PUBLISHER) 2001

JOINS MAP 218

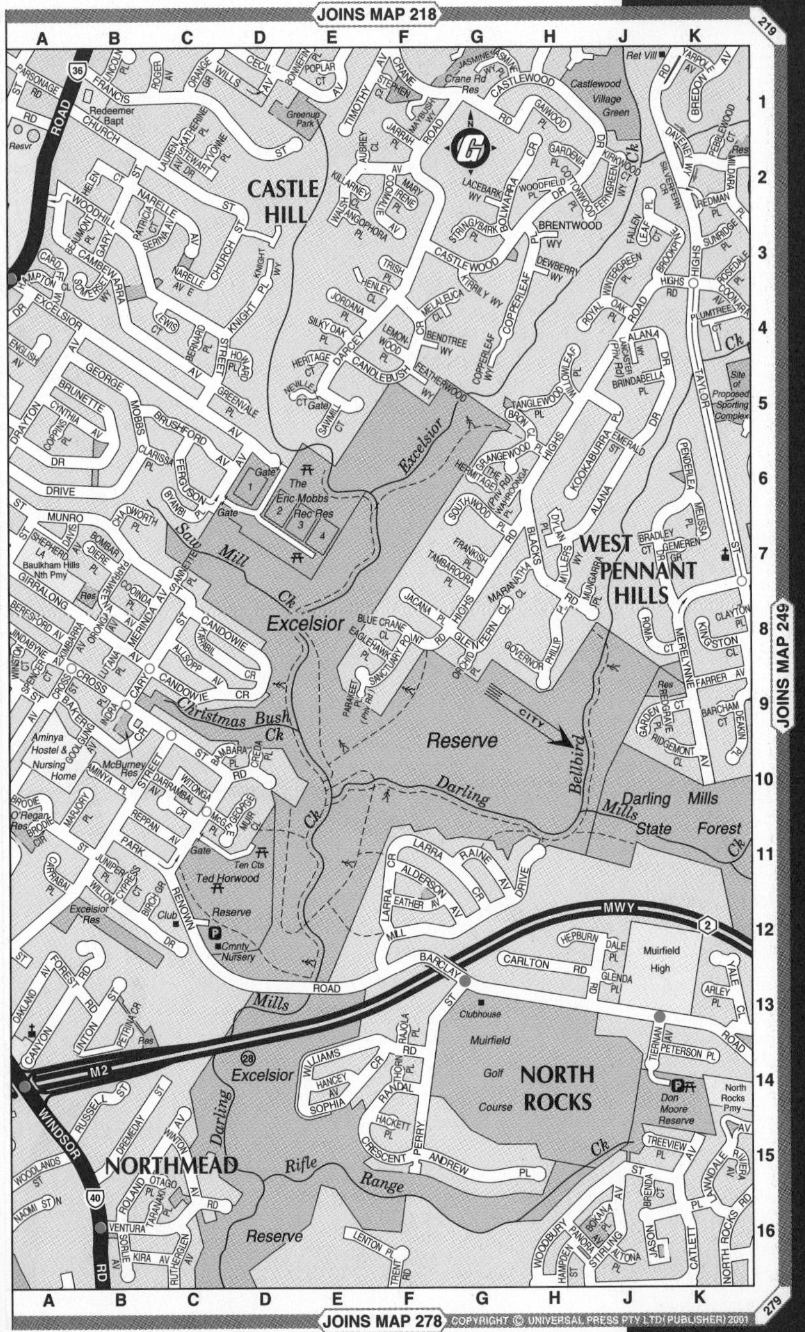

JOINS MAP 249

JOINS MAP 278

279

MAP 249

JOINS MAP 219

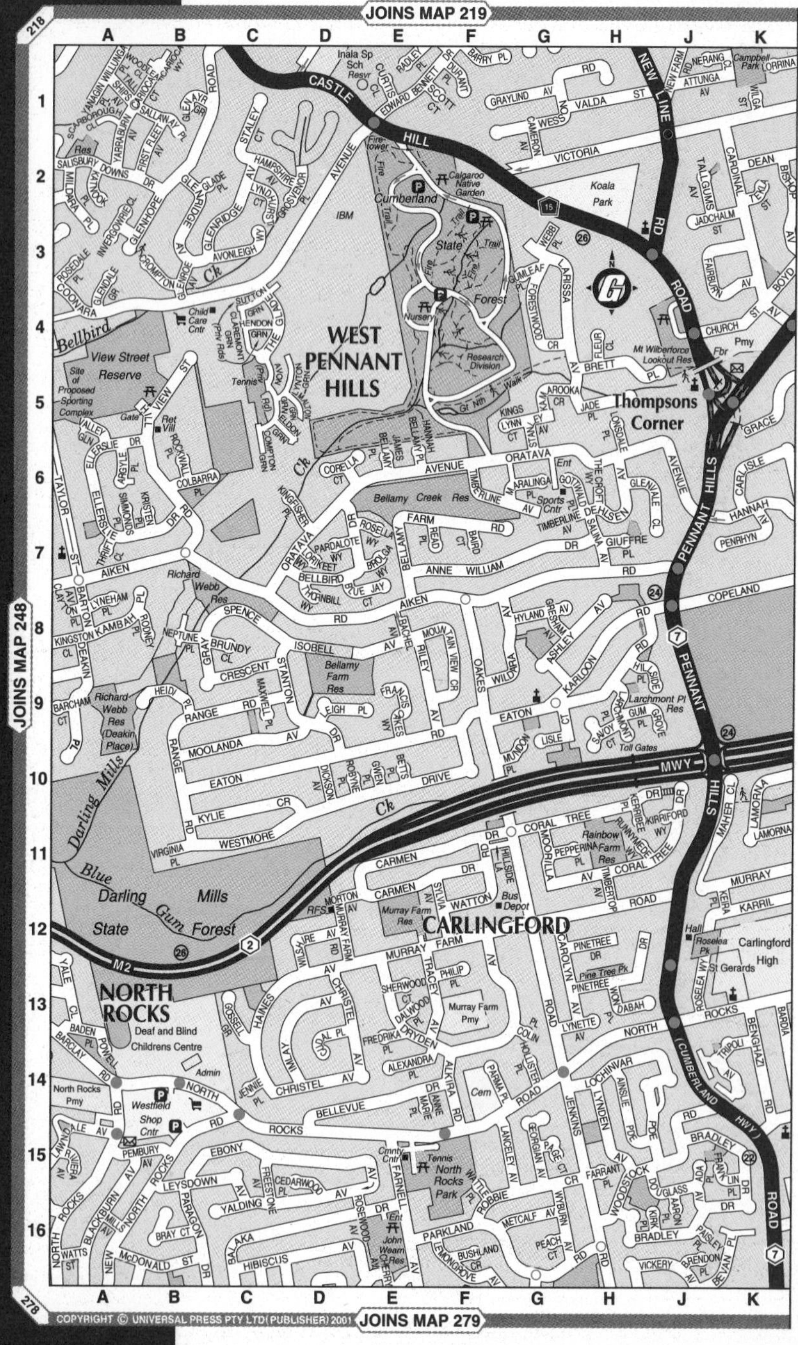

JOINS MAP 248

JOINS MAP 279

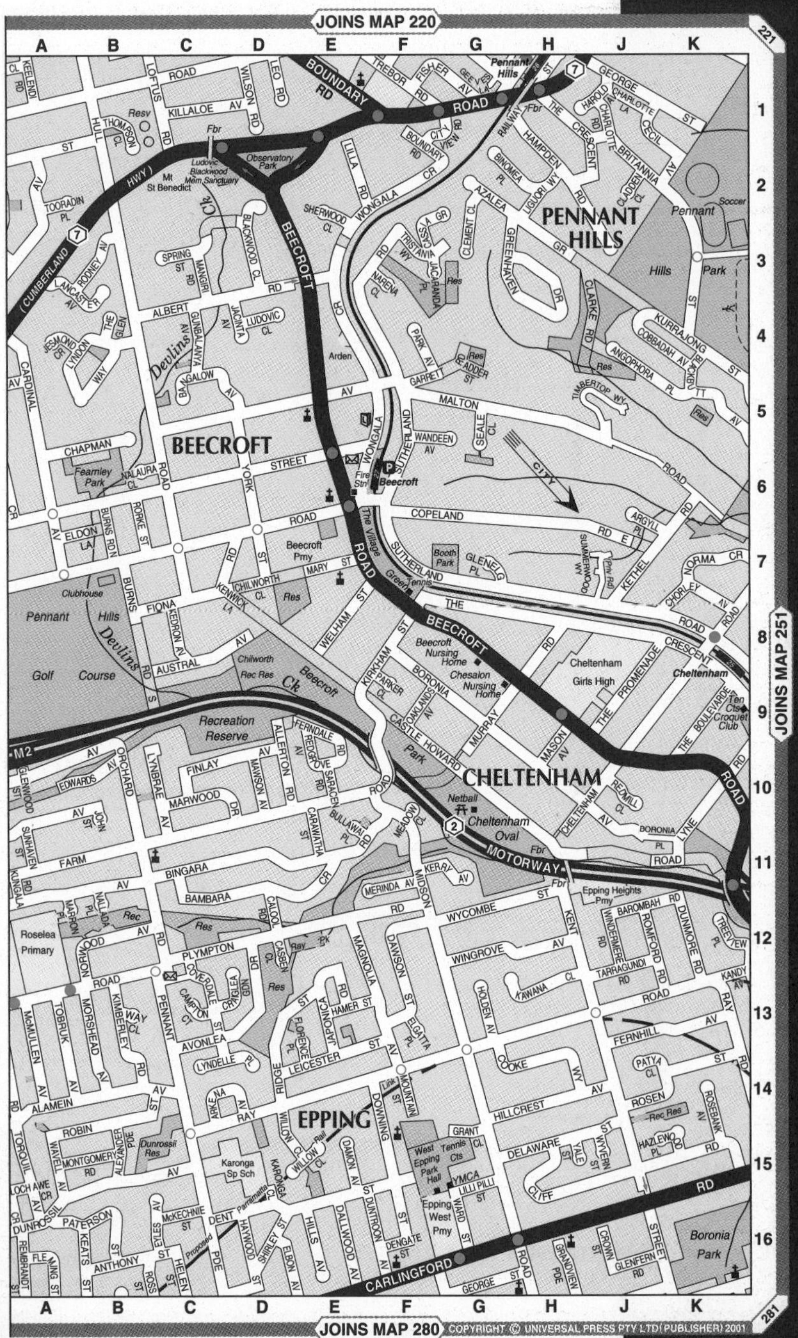
JOINS MAP 220
221
JOINS MAP 251
JOINS MAP 280
281
A B C D E F G H J K
1 2 3 4 5 6 7 8 9 10 11 12 13 14 15 16
PENNANT HILLS
BEECROFT
CHELTENHAM
EPPING
BOUNDARY RD
ROAD
CUMBERLAND HWY
BEECROFT ROAD
Observatory Park
Ludovic Blackwood Mem Sanctuary
Mt St Benedict
Resv
Fbr
KILLALOE AV
LOFTUS RD
WILSON RD
LEO RD
TREBOR RD
FISHER AV
GEORGE ST
HAROLD
CHARLOTTE
CECIL
BRITANNIA AV
CLADDEN CL
THE CRESCENT
HAMPDEN RD
BINOMEA PL
LIGUORI WY
RAILWAY
CITY VIEW RD
BOUNDARY RD
LILLA RD
WONGALA CR
SHERWOOD CL
AZALEA GR
CLEMENT CL
GREENHAVEN DR
TRISTANIA WY
CASSIA GR
JACARANDA PL
NARENA CL
Res
Pennant Hills Park
Soccer
KURRAJONG ST
COBBADAH AV
ANGOPHORA PL
BLACKBUTT
TIMBERTOP WY
CLARKE RD
THOMPSON CL
HULL RD
TOORADIN PL
SPRING ST
MANGIRI RD
BLACKWOOD CL
LANCASTER AV
RODNEY AV
THE GLEN
JESMOND CR
LYNDON WAY
ALBERT RD
GUNBALANYA AV
JACINTA AV
LUDOVIC CL
Devlins Ck
BANGALOW AV
Arden
PARK AV
GARRETT RD
ADDER ST
MALTON RD
WANDEEN AV
SEALE CL
SUTHERLAND RD
CITY
CARDINAL AV
CHAPMAN AV
Fearnley Park
NALAURA CL
YORK ST
STREET
Fire Stn
Beecroft
COPELAND RD
ARGYLL PL
ELDON LA
BURNS RD
RORKE ST
Beecroft Pmy
MARY ST
CHILWORTH CL
The Village Green
Booth Park
GLENELG PL
SUMMERWOOD WY
KETHEL RD
NORMA CR
CHORLEY AV
Tennis
Clubhouse
Pennant Hills Golf Course
FIONA
KEDRON AV
KENWICK LA
WELHAM ST
THE CRESCENT
Cheltenham
Beecroft Nursing Home
Chesalon Nursing Home
Cheltenham Girls High
THE PROMENADE
THE BOULEVARDE
Ten Cts
Croquet Club
AUSTRAL AV
Chilworth Rec Res
Beecroft Ck
KIRKHAM ST
PARKER CL
BORONIA AV
OAKLANDS AV
CASTLE HOWARD RD
MURRAY RD
MASON AV
Recreation Reserve
M2
GLENWOOD
EDWARDS
ORCHARD
LYNBRAE AV
FINLAY
MAWSON AV
ALLERTON RD
FERNDALE RD
REDGROVE AV
SARACEN RD
MARWOOD DR
CARAWATHA ST
BULLAWAI PL
Park
Netball
Cheltenham Oval
MEADOW CL
REDMILL CL
CHELTENHAM AV
BORONIA PL
LYNE
ROAD
MOTORWAY
2
7
SUNHAVEN
FARM
BINGARA
BAMBARA
CALOOL
KERAY AV
MERINDA AV
MIDSON RD
Epping Heights Pmy
KENT
WINDERMERE
BAROMBAH RD
ROMFORD RD
DUNMORE RD
TREEVIEW PL
NALLADA PL
MARRON
Rec
Res
Roselea Primary
NORWOOD
PLYMPTON
WYCOMBE
WINGROVE AV
TARRAGUNDI RD
KANDY AV
RAY
ROAD
MAGNOLIA
DAWSON ST
CASSEN CL
COVERDALE
CRAGLEA
CAMPTON CT
TOBRUK
MORSHEAD
KIMBERLEY RD
PENNANT
McMULLEN
HAMER ST
JAPONICA
FLORENCE PL
ELGATA PL
HOLDEN AV
KAWANA CL
FERNHILL
AVONLEA
LYNDELLE PL
LEICESTER ST
RIDGE
COOKE WY
PATYA CL
ALAMEIN
ARKENA AV
MOUNTAIN
DOWNING
HILLCREST AV
ROSEN ST
ROSEBANK AV
Rec Res
ROBIN
WAVELL
MONTGOMERY RD
ALEXANDER PDE
Dunrossil Res
Karonga Sp Sch
WILLOW CL
DAMON AV
GRANT CL
West Epping Park Hall
Tennis Cts
YMCA
DELAWARE
YALE
WYVERN
HAZLEWOOD PL
CLIFF
LOCH AWE CR
TORQUIL
DUNROSSIL
PATERSON
McKECHNIE ST
DENT
Parramatta Rail
Proposed
HAYWOOD
SHIRLEY ST
ELBON AV
HILLS AV
DALLWOOD AV
DUNTROON
LILLI PILLI
Epping West Pmy
WARD ST
DENGATE ST
CARLINGFORD RD
GRANDVIEW PDE
CROWN
GLENFERN RD
STREET
Boronia Park
REMBRANDT
FLEMING ST
KEATS
ANTHONY
ROSS ST
HELEN ST
GEORGE ST

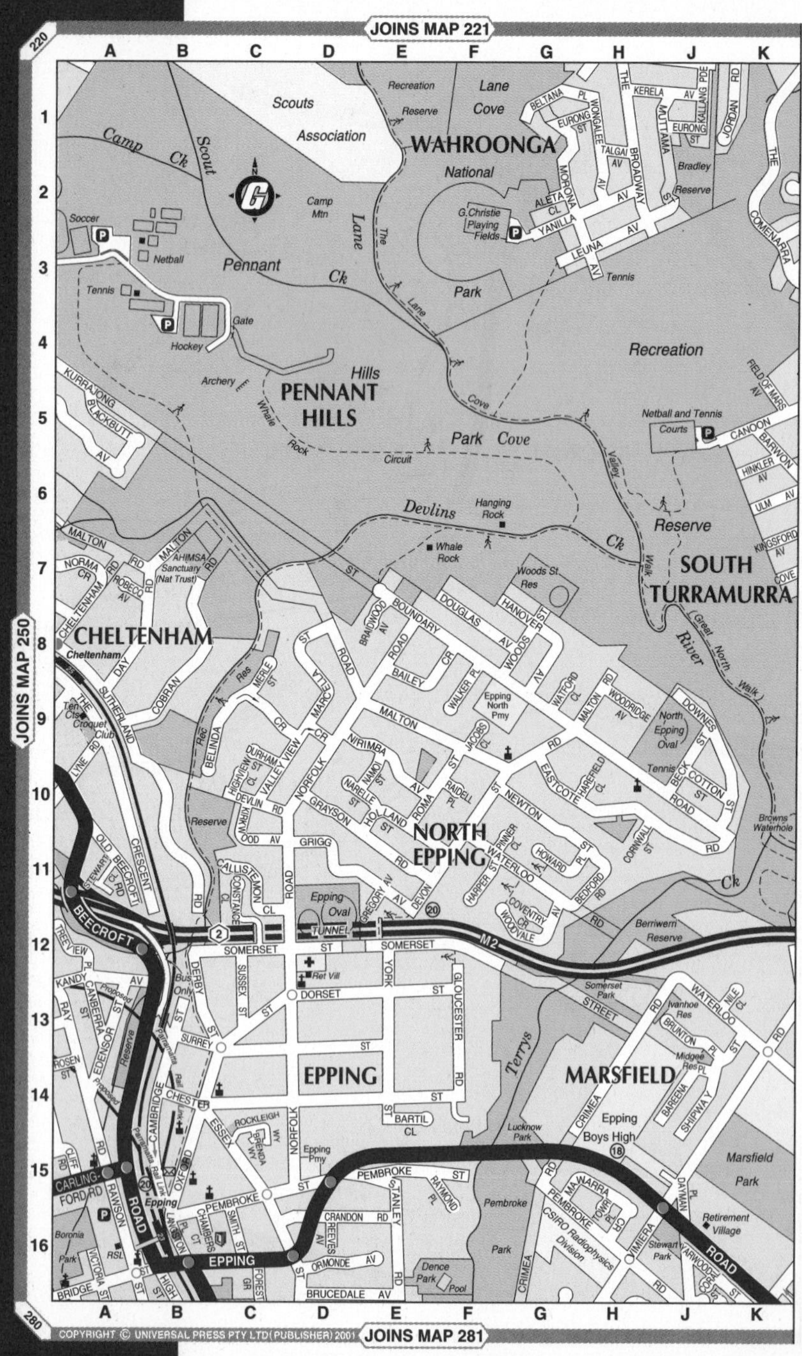
JOINS MAP 221
JOINS MAP 250
JOINS MAP 281
220
280
A B C D E F G H J K
1 2 3 4 5 6 7 8 9 10 11 12 13 14 15 16
WAHROONGA
National
Park
Lane
Cove
Scouts
Association
Camp Ck
Scout
Pennant
Ck
Soccer
Netball
Tennis
Hockey
Gate
Archery
Camp
Mtn
Recreation
Reserve
G.Christie
Playing
Fields
PENNANT
HILLS
Hills
Whale
Rock
Circuit
Park Cove
Devlins
Ck
Hanging
Rock
Whale
Rock
Recreation
Netball and Tennis
Courts
Valley
Walk
Reserve
SOUTH
TURRAMURRA
Great North Walk
River
Bradley
Reserve
Tennis
CHELTENHAM
Cheltenham
Croquet
Club
AHIMSA
Sanctuary
(Nat Trust)
Woods St
Res
Epping
North
Pmy
North
Epping
Oval
NORTH
EPPING
Browns
Waterhole
Reserve
Epping
Oval
TUNNEL
M2
Berriwerri
Reserve
Somerset
Park
Terrys
Ivanhoe
Res
Midgee
Res
EPPING
MARSFIELD
Epping
Boys High
Marsfield
Park
Lucknow
Park
Pembroke
Park
CSIRO Radiophysics
Division
Retirement
Village
Stewart
Park
Dence
Park
Pool
Epping
Pmy
Ret Vill
Bus
Only
Proposed
Parramatta
Rail
Link
Epping
RSL
Boronia
Park
BOUNDARY
MALTON RD
EPPING RD
BEECROFT RD
CARLINGFORD RD
SOMERSET ST
DORSET ST
CHESTER ST
PEMBROKE ST
WATERLOO RD
EPPING RD
ESSEX ST
NORFOLK RD
VALLEY VIEW CR
CHELTENHAM RD

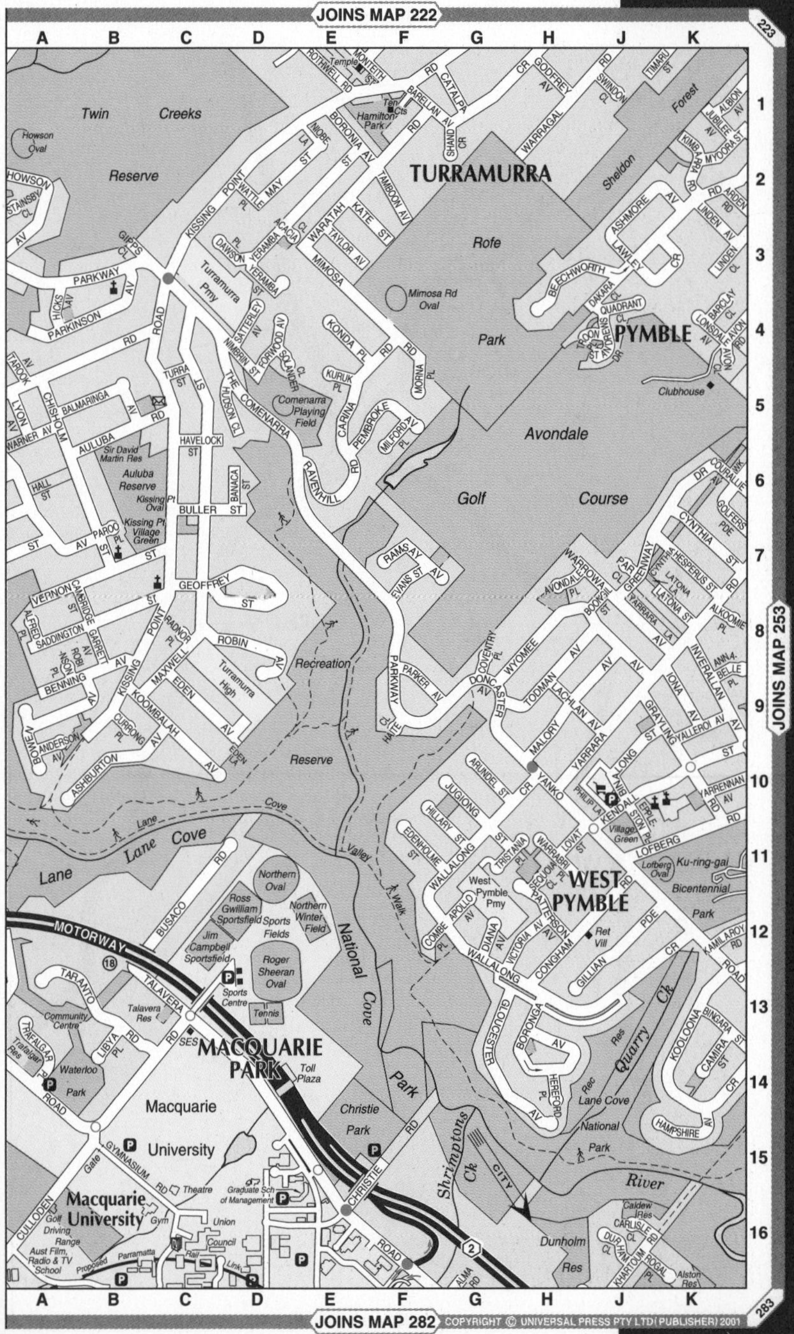
JOINS MAP 222
JOINS MAP 253
JOINS MAP 282
223
283
TURRAMURRA
PYMBLE
WEST PYMBLE
MACQUARIE PARK
Twin Creeks Reserve
Rofe Park
Avondale Golf Course
Sheldon Forest
Lane Cove National Park
Macquarie University
Turramurra Pmy
Turramurra High
Recreation Reserve
Comenarra Playing Field
Mimosa Rd Oval
Northern Oval
Roger Sheeran Oval
Christie Park
Waterloo Park
Ku-ring-gai Bicentennial Park
Lofberg Oval
Dunholm Res
Shrimptons Ck
Quarry Ck
Lane Cove River
MOTORWAY

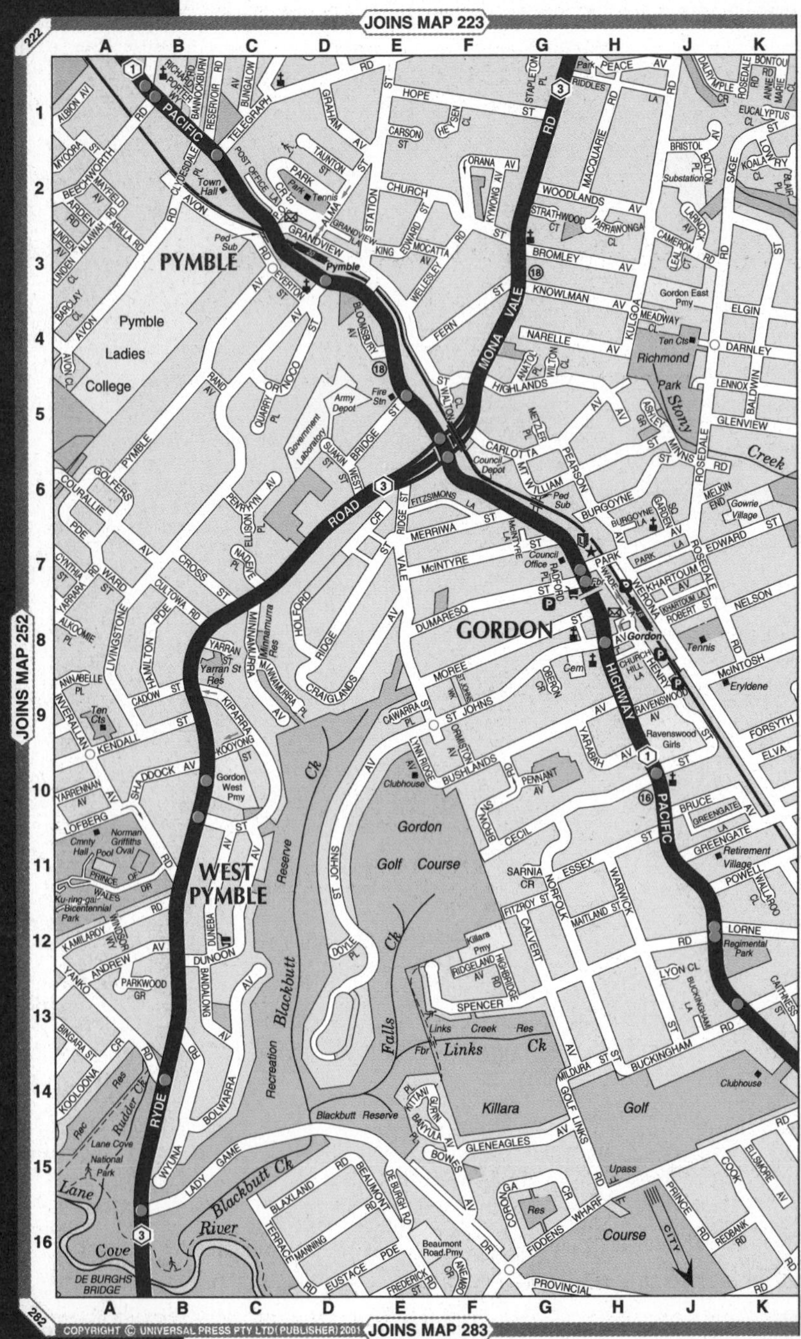
JOINS MAP 223
JOINS MAP 252
JOINS MAP 283
222
282
A B C D E F G H J K
1 2 3 4 5 6 7 8 9 10 11 12 13 14 15 16
PYMBLE
GORDON
WEST PYMBLE
Pymble Ladies College
PACIFIC HIGHWAY
MONA VALE RD
RYDE ROAD
Town Hall
Ped Sub
Pymble
Park
Tennis
Army Depot
Fire Stn
Government Laboratory
Council Depot
Council Office
Gordon
Tennis
Eryldene
Richmond Park
Ten Cts
Gordon East Pmy
Gowrie Village
Stony Creek
Ravenswood Girls
Retirement Village
Regimental Park
Gordon West Pmy
Yarran St Res
Cmnty Hall
Pool
Norman Griffiths Oval
Ku-ring-gai Bicentennial Park
Gordon Golf Course
Clubhouse
Killara Pmy
Killara Golf Course
Links Creek Res
Links Ck
Falls Ck
Blackbutt Reserve
Blackbutt Recreation Reserve
Blackbutt Ck
Lane Cove National Park
Rudder Ck
Lane Cove River
DE BURGHS BRIDGE
Beaumont Road Pmy
Res
Upass
CITY
Cem
Substation
HOPE ST
CHURCH
STATION ST
GRANDVIEW
TELEGRAPH
BROMLEY AV
KNOWLMAN AV
NARELLE AV
HIGHLANDS
FERN AV
WOODLANDS AV
ELGIN
DARNLEY
LENNOX
GLENVIEW
EDWARD ST
NELSON
McINTOSH
FORSYTH
ELVA
BRUCE AV
GREENGATE RD
POWELL
LORNE
BUCKINGHAM RD
GLENEAGLES AV
PROVINCIAL RD
FIDDENS WHARF RD
MERRIWA ST
McINTYRE ST
DUMARESQ ST
MOREE ST
ST JOHNS AV
BUSHLANDS AV
CECIL ST
ESSEX
KENDALL ST
SHADDOCK AV
LOFBERG
CADOW ST
KOOYONG
KIPARRA
LADY GAME DR
BLAXLAND RD
BEAUMONT ST
COPYRIGHT © UNIVERSAL PRESS PTY LTD (PUBLISHER) 2001

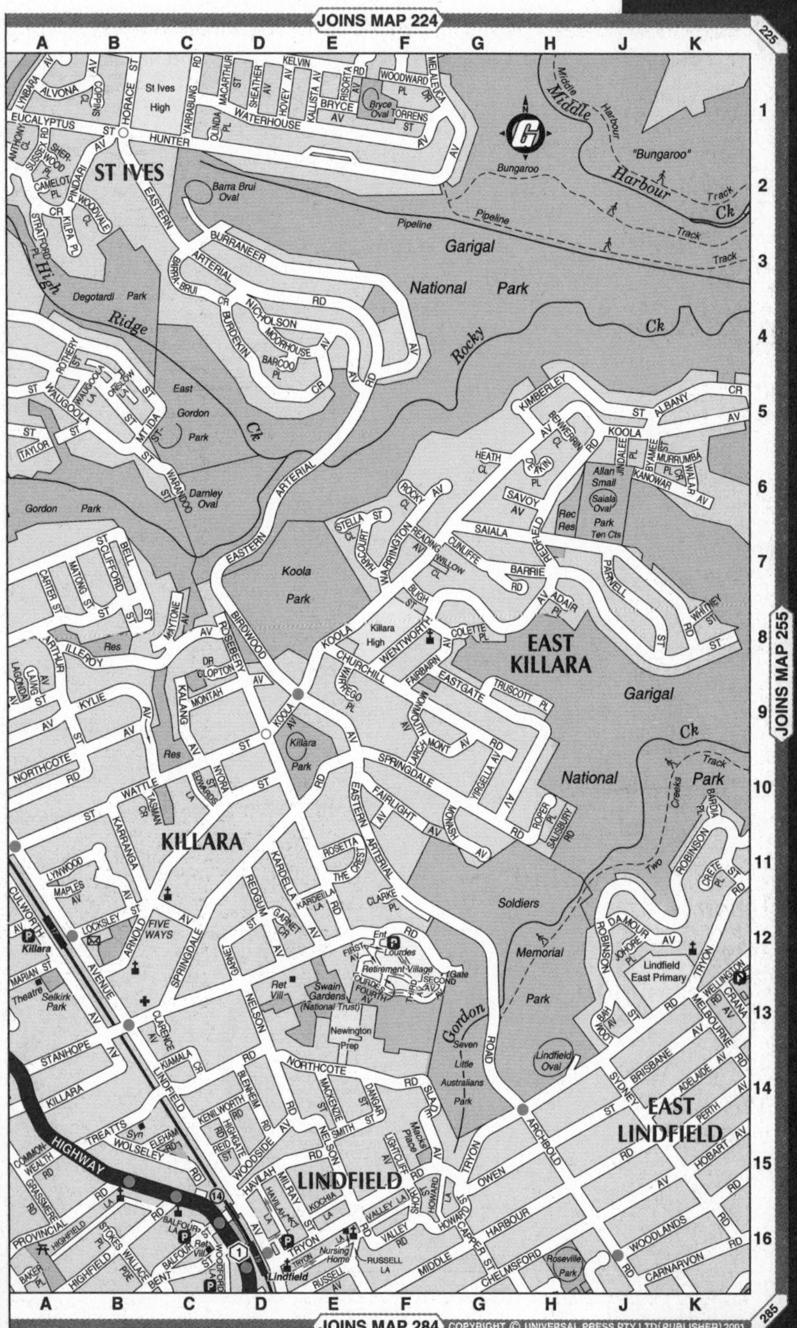
JOINS MAP 224
JOINS MAP 255
JOINS MAP 284
225
285
ST IVES
EAST KILLARA
KILLARA
EAST LINDFIELD
LINDFIELD
Garigal National Park
Middle Harbour
"Bungaroo"
Bungaroo
Track
Pipeline
Rocky Ck
High Ridge
Degotardi Park
East Gordon Park
Gordon Park
Darnley Oval
Barra Brui Oval
St Ives High
Bryce Oval
Koola Park
Killara High
Killara Park
Soldiers Memorial Park
Lindfield Oval
Roseville Park
Allan Small Park
Saiala Oval
Lindfield East Primary
Swain Gardens (National Trust)
Newington Prep
Seven Little Australians Park
Selkirk Park
Macks Place
Nursing Home
Retirement Village
FIVE WAYS
EASTERN ARTERIAL RD
PACIFIC HIGHWAY
COPYRIGHT © UNIVERSAL PRESS PTY LTD (PUBLISHER) 2001

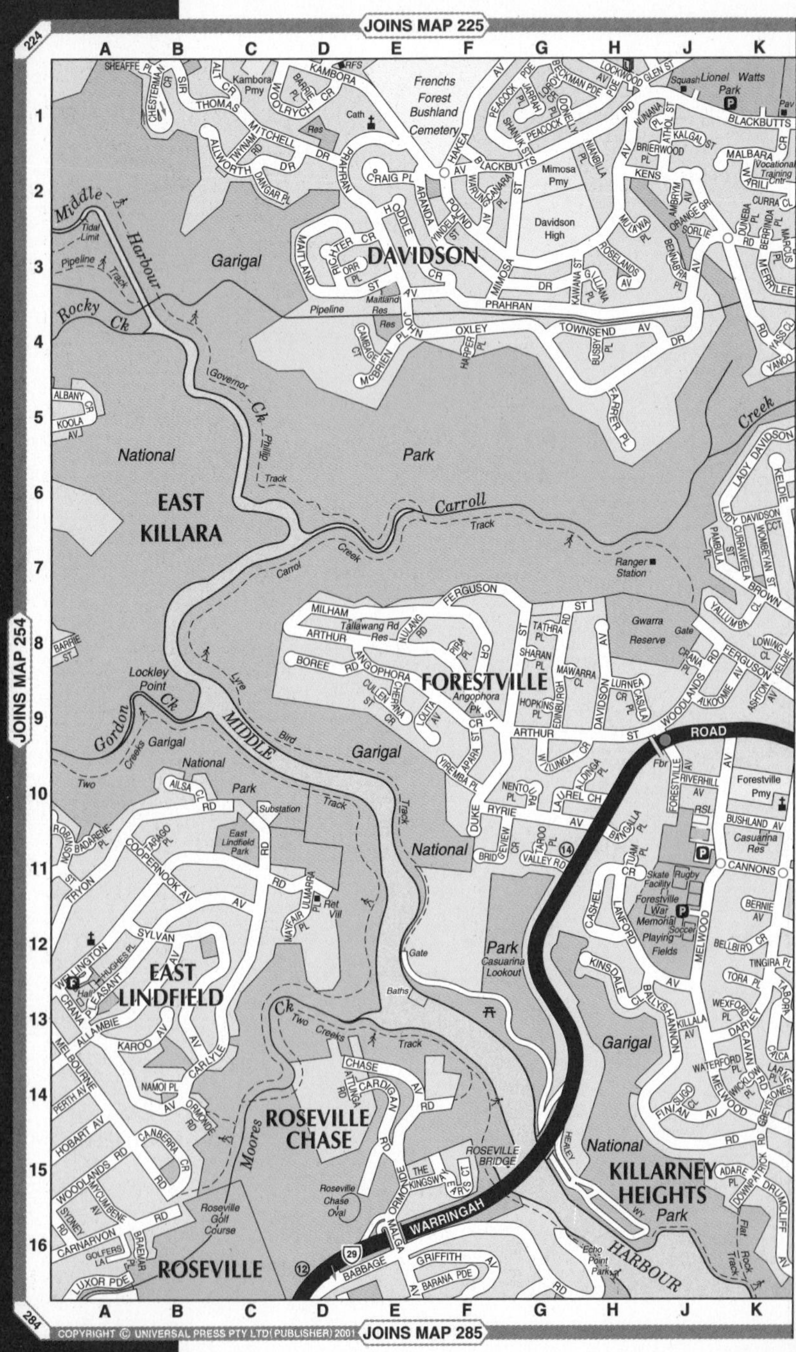
JOINS MAP 225
JOINS MAP 254
JOINS MAP 285
224
284
DAVIDSON
EAST KILLARA
FORESTVILLE
EAST LINDFIELD
ROSEVILLE CHASE
KILLARNEY HEIGHTS
ROSEVILLE
Garigal National Park
Frenchs Forest Bushland Cemetery
Lionel Watts Park
Davidson High
Mimosa Pmy
Gwarra Reserve
Ranger Station
Lockley Point
Forestville War Memorial Playing Fields
Casuarina Lookout
Roseville Golf Course
Roseville Chase Oval
ROSEVILLE BRIDGE
Echo Point Park
MIDDLE HARBOUR
WARRINGAH ROAD
Carroll Creek
Middle Harbour Ck
Rocky Ck
Gordon Ck
Moores Ck
Two Creeks Track
Governor Phillip Track
Lyre Bird Track
Flat Rock Track
Pipeline Track
Tidal Limit

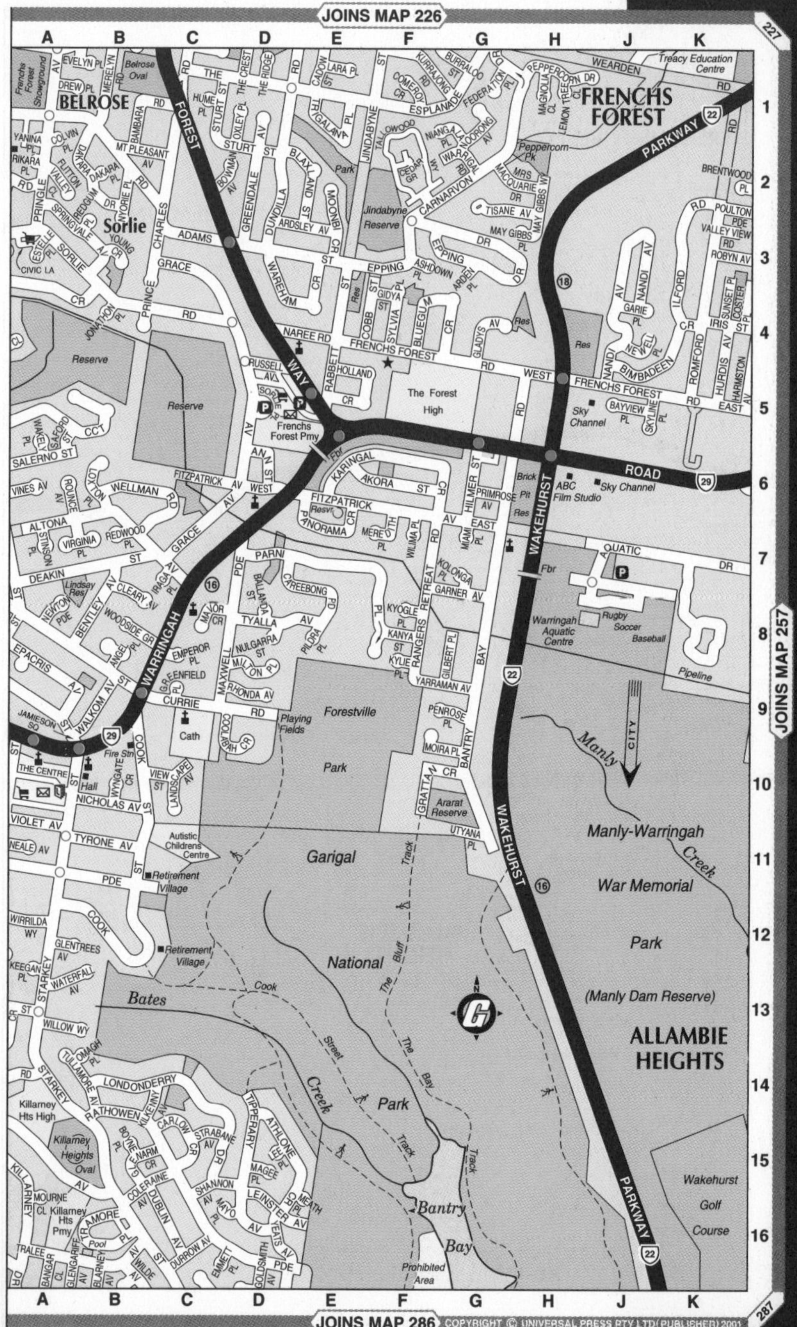
JOINS MAP 226
JOINS MAP 257
JOINS MAP 286
227
287
BELROSE
Sorlie
FRENCHS FOREST
ALLAMBIE HEIGHTS
FOREST WAY
WARRINGAH ROAD
WAKEHURST PARKWAY
FRENCHS FOREST RD WEST
FRENCHS FOREST RD EAST
The Forest High
Frenchs Forest Pmy
Jindabyne Reserve
Reserve
Forestville Park
Playing Fields
Garigal National Park
Manly-Warringah War Memorial Park
(Manly Dam Reserve)
Manly Creek
Bates Creek
Bantry Bay
Prohibited Area
Warringah Aquatic Centre
Rugby
Soccer
Baseball
Wakehurst Golf Course
ABC Film Studio
Sky Channel
Killarney Hts High
Killarney Heights Oval
Killarney Hts Pmy
Ararat Reserve
Autistic Childrens Centre
Retirement Village
Treacy Education Centre
Peppercorn Pk
Frenchs Forest Showground
Belrose Oval
CITY
COPYRIGHT © UNIVERSAL PRESS PTY LTD (PUBLISHER) 2001

JOINS MAP 227

226

JOINS MAP 256

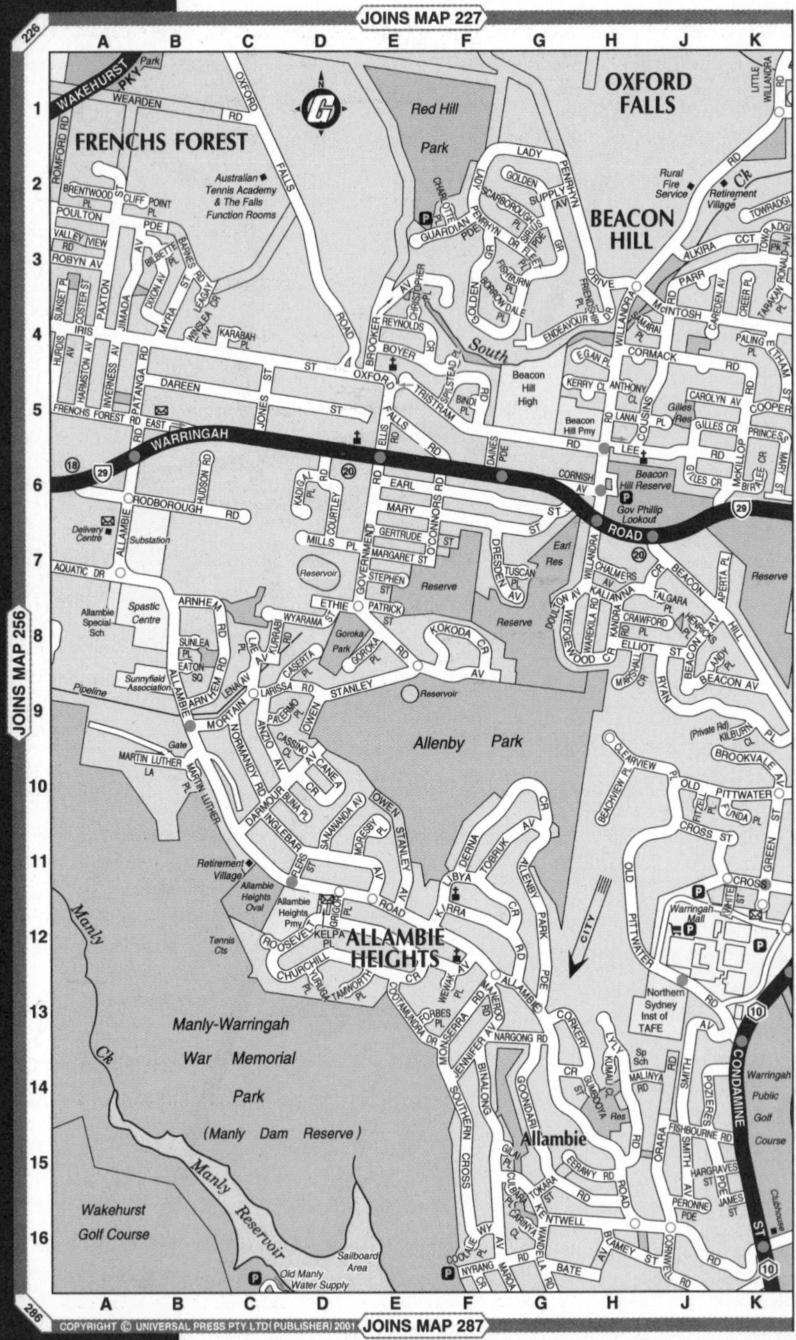

JOINS MAP 287

286

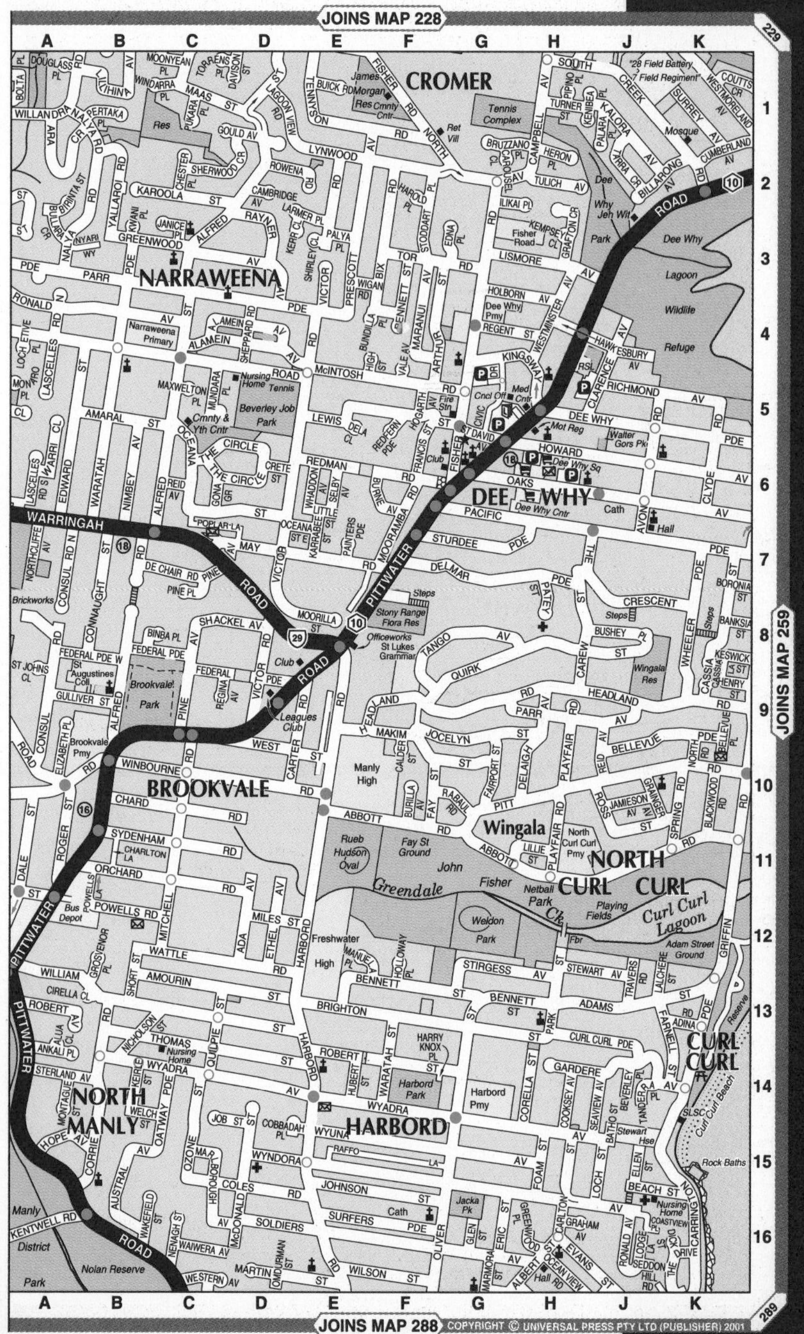
JOINS MAP 228
229
A B C D E F G H J K
1 2 3 4 5 6 7 8 9 10 11 12 13 14 15 16
CROMER
NARRAWEENA
DEE WHY
BROOKVALE
Wingala
NORTH CURL CURL
CURL CURL
NORTH MANLY
HARBORD
Dee Why Lagoon Wildlife Refuge
Curl Curl Lagoon
Greendale Ck
John Fisher Park
Weldon Park
Brookvale Park
Beverley Job Park
Harbord Park
Jacka Pk
Manly District Park
Nolan Reserve
Stony Range Flora Res
Wingala Res
Rueb Hudson Oval
Fay St Ground
Adam Street Ground
Netball Park
Playing Fields
Tennis Complex
Narraweena Primary
Manly High
Freshwater High
Harbord Pmy
North Curl Curl Pmy
Brookvale Pmy
Dee Why Pmy
St Augustines Coll
St Lukes Grammar
Leagues Club
Dee Why Cntr
Dee Why Sq
Cncl Off
Med Cntr
Fire Stn
RSL
Mot Reg
Walter Gors Pk
Cmnty & Yth Cntr
Nursing Home
Bus Depot
Brickworks
Officeworks
Rock Baths
SLSC
Curl Curl Beach
Stewart Hse
"28 Field Battery 7 Field Regiment"
Mosque
Ret Vill
James Morgan Res
Cmnty Cntr
Fisher Road
Cath
Hall
Steps
Reserve
WARRINGAH ROAD
PITTWATER ROAD
10
18
29
16
JOINS MAP 259
JOINS MAP 288
289
COPYRIGHT © UNIVERSAL PRESS PTY LTD (PUBLISHER) 2001

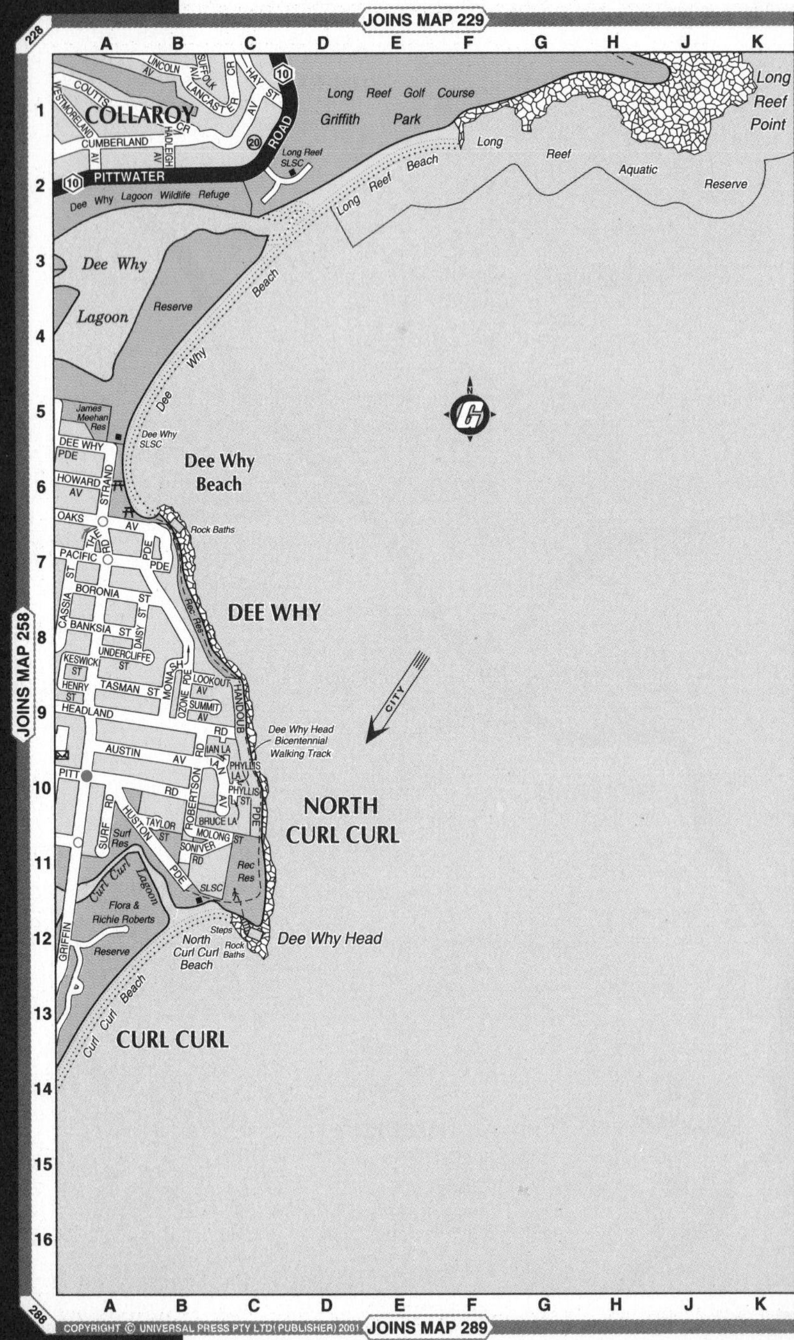
JOINS MAP 229
JOINS MAP 258
JOINS MAP 289
228
288
COLLAROY
Long Reef Golf Course
Griffith Park
Long Reef Point
Long Reef Aquatic Reserve
Long Reef SLSC
Long Reef Beach
PITTWATER ROAD
Dee Why Lagoon Wildlife Refuge
Dee Why Lagoon
Reserve
Dee Why Beach
James Meehan Res
Dee Why SLSC
Rock Baths
DEE WHY
Dee Why Head Bicentennial Walking Track
NORTH CURL CURL
CITY
Curl Curl Lagoon
Flora & Richie Roberts Reserve
North Curl Curl Beach
Steps
Rock Baths
Dee Why Head
Curl Curl Beach
CURL CURL
Rec Res
Surf Res
SLSC

JOINS MAP 230

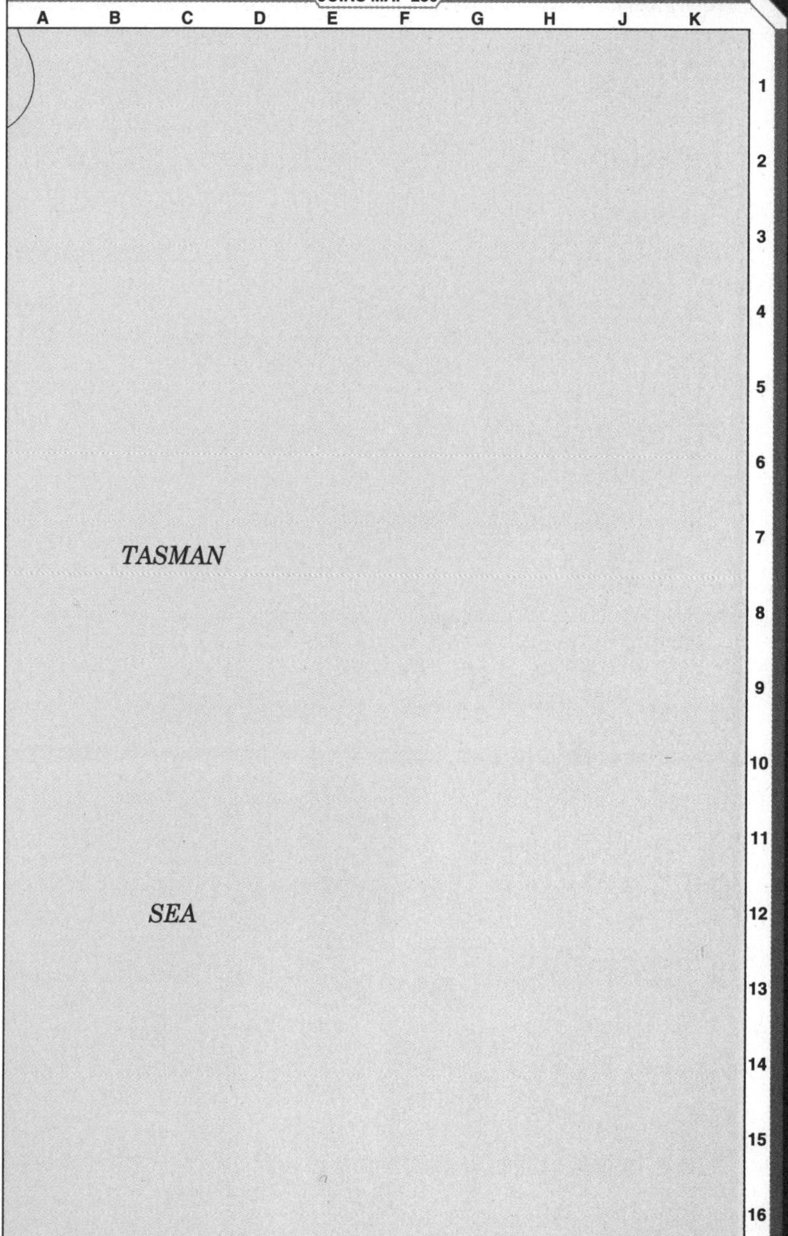

A B C D E F G H J K

1 2 3 4 5 6 7 8 9 10 11 12 13 14 15 16

TASMAN

SEA

A B C D E F G H J K

JOINS MAP 290

JOINS MAP 233

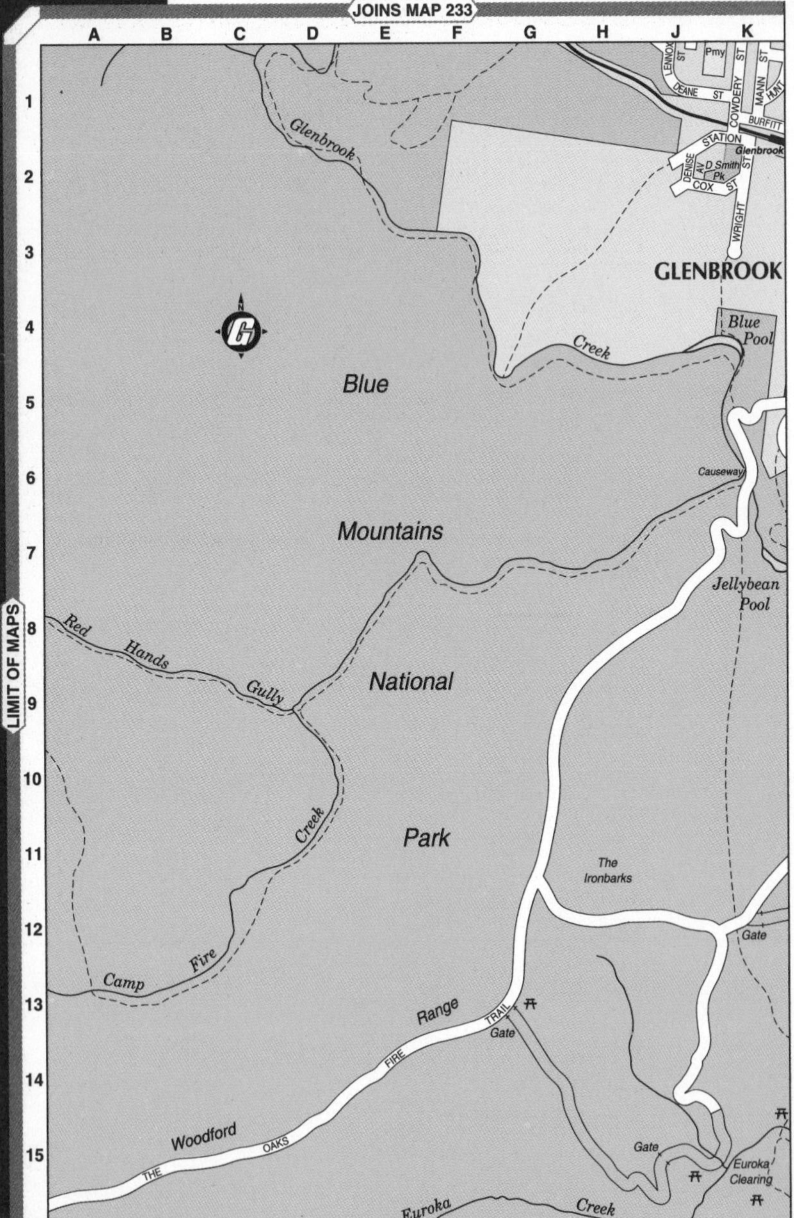

A B C D E F G H J K

1 2 3 4 5 6 7 8 9 10 11 12 13 14 15 16

GLENBROOK

Blue Mountains National Park

Glenbrook Creek
Blue Pool
Causeway
Jellybean Pool
LENNOX ST
Pmy
DEANE ST
COWDERY ST
MANN ST
HUNT
BURFITT
STATION
Glenbrook
DENISE AV
D Smith Pk
COX ST
WRIGHT ST
Red Hands Gully
Camp Fire Creek
The Ironbarks
Gate
Woodford Range
THE OAKS FIRE TRAIL
Euroka Creek
Euroka Clearing

LIMIT OF MAPS

LIMIT OF MAPS

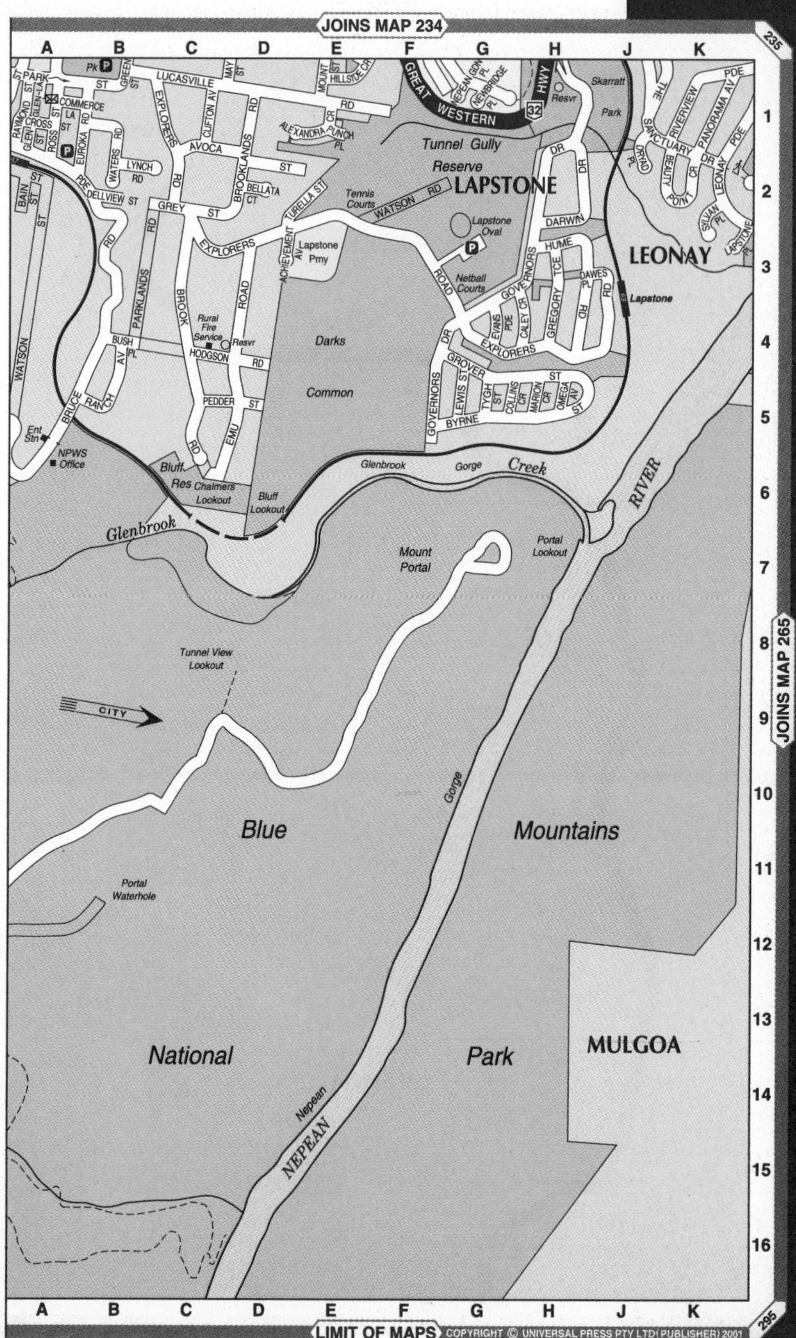
JOINS MAP 234
JOINS MAP 265
LIMIT OF MAPS
LAPSTONE
LEONAY
MULGOA
Blue Mountains National Park
Tunnel Gully Reserve
Darks Common
Glenbrook Gorge Creek
NEPEAN RIVER
Mount Portal
Portal Lookout
Tunnel View Lookout
Portal Waterhole
Bluff Res
Chalmers Lookout
Bluff Lookout
Lapstone Oval
Lapstone Pmy
Netball Courts
Tennis Courts
Skarratt Park
Rural Fire Service
NPWS Office
GREAT WESTERN HWY
CITY

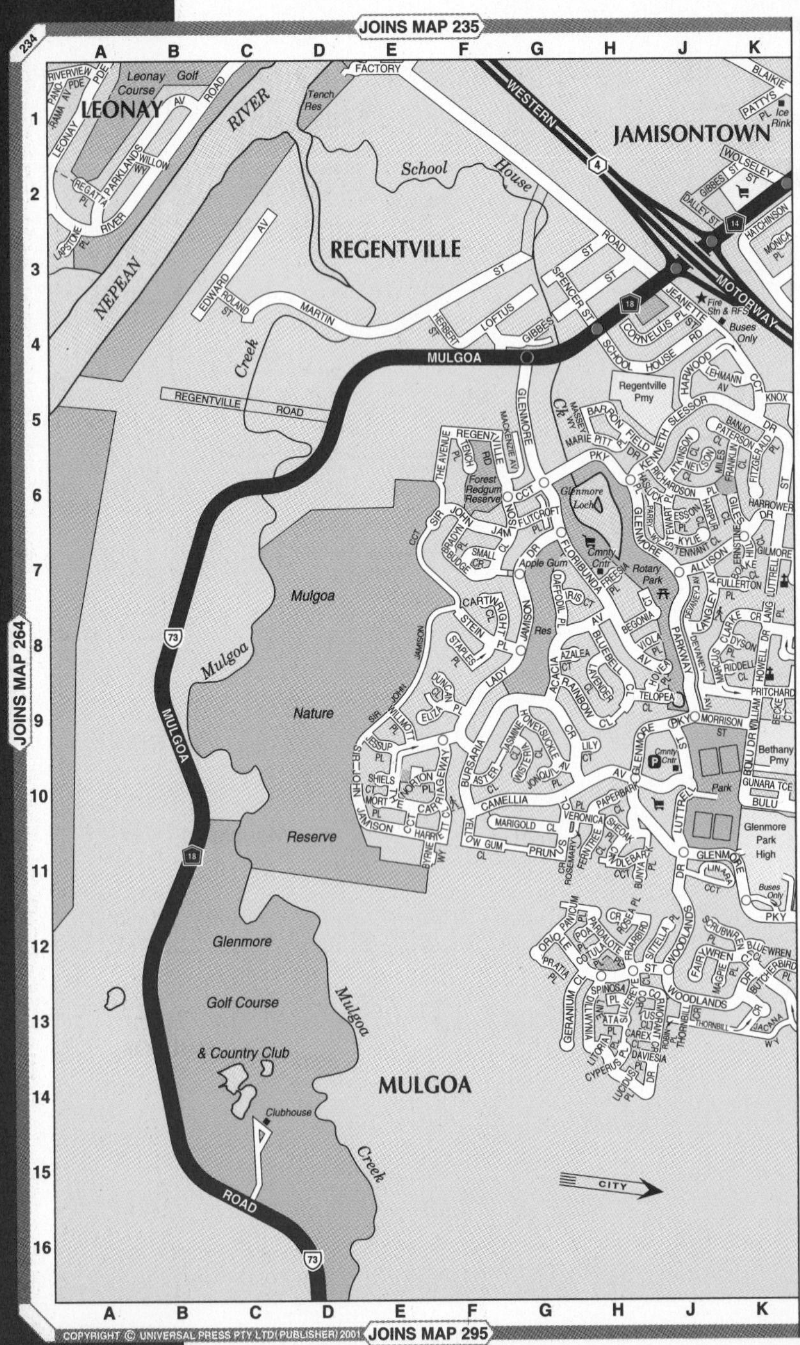
JOINS MAP 235
JOINS MAP 264
JOINS MAP 295
234
264
LEONAY
JAMISONTOWN
REGENTVILLE
MULGOA
Leonay Golf Course
NEPEAN RIVER
School House
Creek
WESTERN MOTORWAY
MULGOA ROAD
REGENTVILLE ROAD
Mulgoa Nature Reserve
Glenmore Golf Course & Country Club
Clubhouse
Mulgoa Creek
Tench Res
Forest Redgum Reserve
Glenmore Loch
Rotary Park
Regentville Pmy
Bethany Pmy
Glenmore Park High
Park
Res
Cmnty Cntr
Fire Stn & RFS
Buses Only
Ice Rink
CITY
COPYRIGHT © UNIVERSAL PRESS PTY LTD (PUBLISHER) 2001

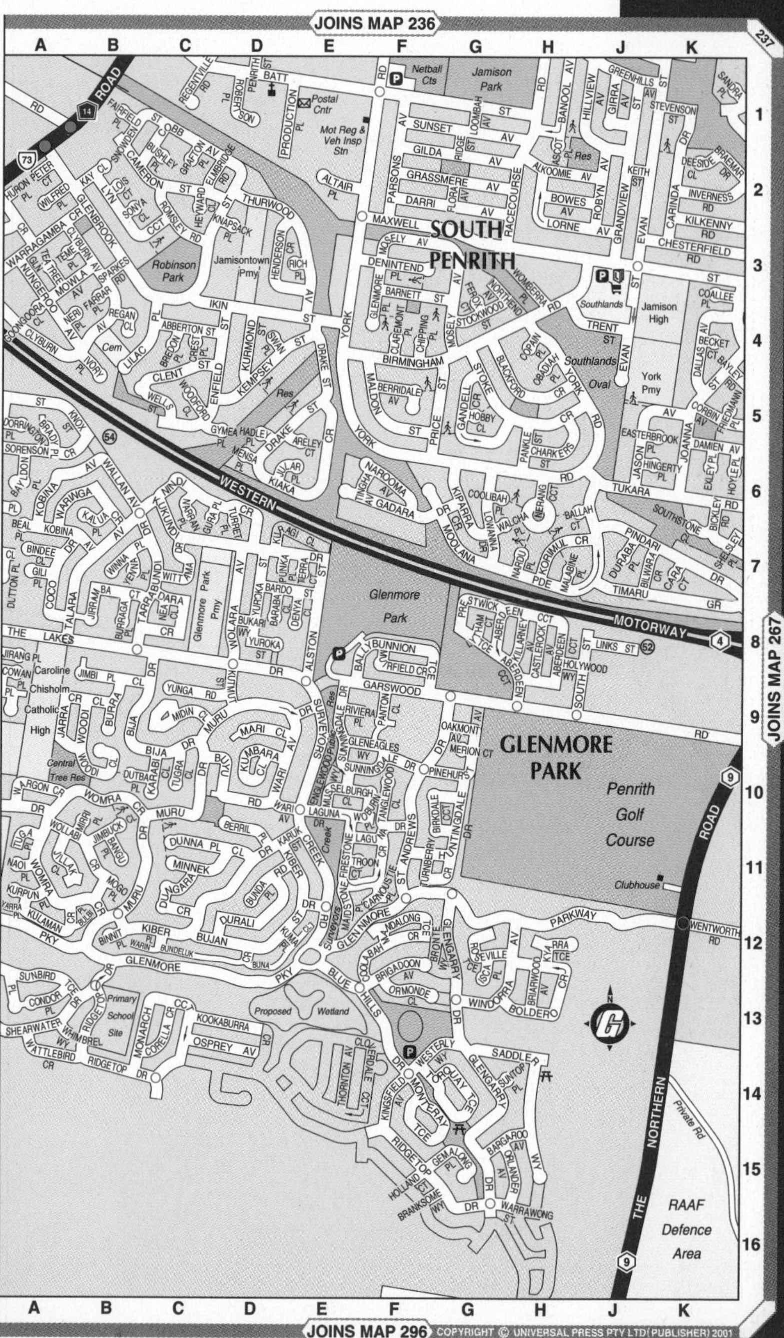
JOINS MAP 236
A B C D E F G H J K
1 2 3 4 5 6 7 8 9 10 11 12 13 14 15 16
237
SOUTH PENRITH
GLENMORE PARK
Netball Cts
Jamison Park
Postal Cntr
Mot Reg & Veh Insp Stn
Robinson Park
Jamisontown Pmy
Southlands
Jamison High
Southlands Oval
York Pmy
Cem
Res
Glenmore Park
Glenmore Park Pmy
Caroline Chisholm Catholic High
Central Tree Res
Penrith Golf Course
Clubhouse
Proposed Wetland
Primary School Site
RAAF Defence Area
Private Rd
ROAD
WESTERN
MOTORWAY
THE NORTHERN ROAD
WENTWORTH RD
PARKWAY
GLENMORE PKY
MAXWELL ST
YORK RD
BIRMINGHAM AV
SUNSET AV
GILDA AV
GRASSMERE AV
DARRI AV
BOWES AV
LORNE AV
CHESTERFIELD RD
KILKENNY RD
INVERNESS RD
TRENT ST
TUKARA RD
TIMARU GR
SOUTHSTONE CL
PINDARI DR
IKIN ST
THURWOOD AV
PRODUCTION PL
PARSONS AV
RACECOURSE RD
EVAN ST
GRANDVIEW ST
SURVEYORS CREEK RD
ALSTON ST
WOLARA AV
THE LAKES DR
GARSWOOD RD
SOUTH ST
BLUE HILLS DR
GLENGARRY DR
RIDGETOP DR
KOOKABURRA CR
OSPREY AV
WINDORRA AV
BOLDER CR
SADDLER CR
WESTERLY WY
MONTERAY TCE
WARRAWONG ST
BRANKSOME WY
CLOVERDALE CCT
THORNTON AV
KINGSFIELD AV
MURU DR
BIJA DR
KIBER DR
BUJAN ST
DURALI CR
MINNEK CL
DUNNA PL
WOMRA CR
KURPUN PL
KULAMAN PKY
SUNBIRD TCE
CONDOR PL
SHEARWATER WY
WHIMBREL WY
WATTLEBIRD CR
MONARCH CR
CORELLA CR
73
14
54
4
52
9
JOINS MAP 267
JOINS MAP 296
COPYRIGHT © UNIVERSAL PRESS PTY LTD (PUBLISHER) 2001

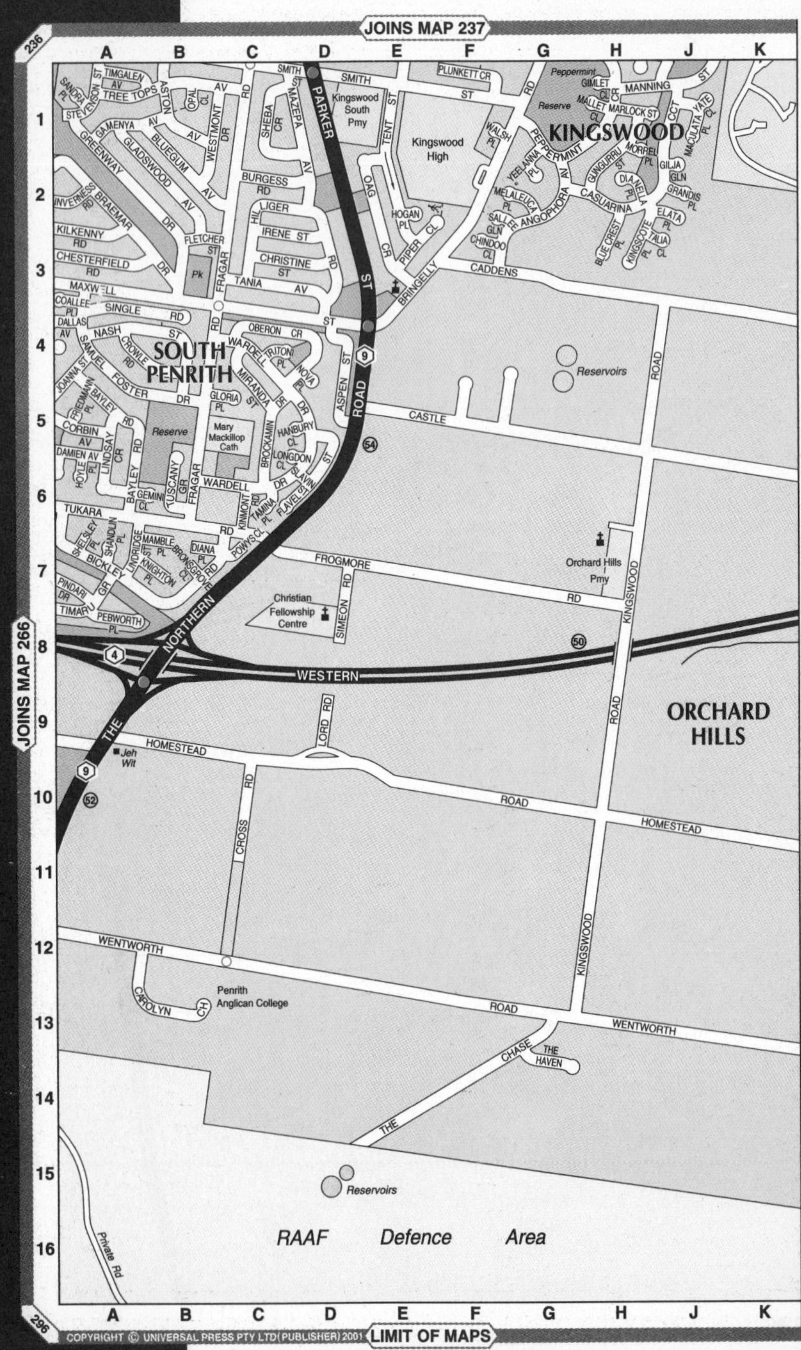

JOINS MAP 237
JOINS MAP 266
LIMIT OF MAPS
236
296
KINGSWOOD
SOUTH PENRITH
ORCHARD HILLS
RAAF Defence Area
Kingswood South Pmy
Kingswood High
Peppermint Reserve
Reserve
Pk
Mary Mackillop Cath
Reservoirs
Orchard Hills Pmy
Christian Fellowship Centre
Jeh Wit
Penrith Anglican College
PARKER ST
NORTHERN ROAD
THE NORTHERN
WESTERN
HOMESTEAD ROAD
WENTWORTH ROAD
KINGSWOOD ROAD
CADDENS
CASTLE
FROGMORE RD
CROSS RD
LORD RD
SIMEON RD
THE CHASE
THE HAVEN
CAROLYN CH
BRINGELLY
Private Rd

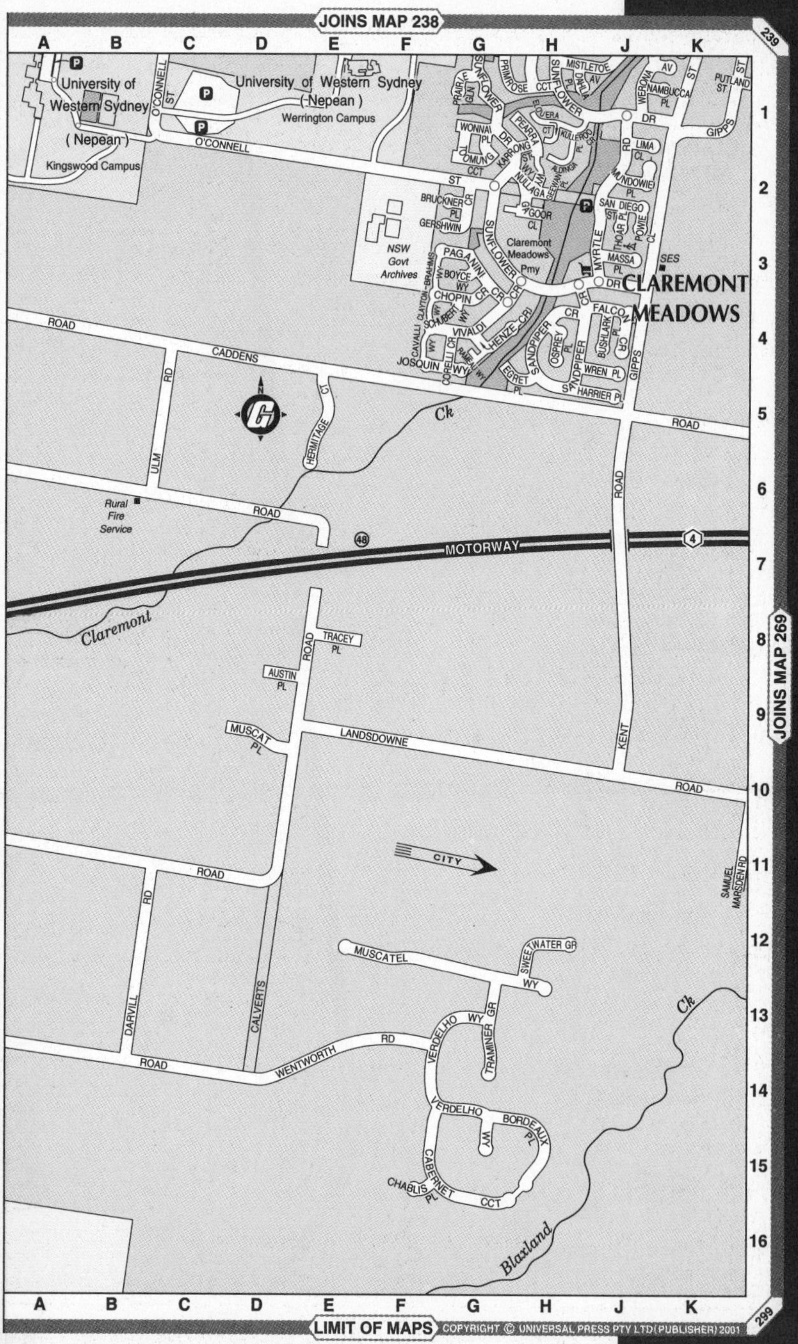
JOINS MAP 238
239
JOINS MAP 269
LIMIT OF MAPS
299
University of Western Sydney (Nepean)
Kingswood Campus
University of Western Sydney (Nepean)
Werrington Campus
O'CONNELL ST
NSW Govt Archives
Claremont Meadows Pmy
CLAREMONT MEADOWS
SES
CADDENS ROAD
ULM RD
HERMITAGE CT
Rural Fire Service
MOTORWAY
Claremont Ck
TRACEY PL
AUSTIN PL
MUSCAT PL
LANDSDOWNE ROAD
KENT ROAD
GIPPS ST
PUTLAND ST
SAMUEL MARSDEN RD
CITY
DARVILL RD
CALVERTS ROAD
WENTWORTH RD
MUSCATEL WY
SWEETWATER GR
TRAMINER GR
VERDELHO WY
BORDEAUX PL
CABERNET CCT
CHABLIS PL
Blaxland Ck
SUNFLOWER DR
PAGANINI CR
CHOPIN CR
VIVALDI
HENZE CR
SANDPIPER CR
MYRTLE DR
FALCON CR
WREN PL
HARRIER PL
EGRET PL
OSPREY PL
BUSHLARK PL
JOSQUIN WY
CORELLI CR
BRUCKNER PL
GERSHWIN
BOYCE WY
SCHUBERT WY
MISTLETOE AV
PRIMROSE CCT
WEROWA AV
NAMBUCCA PL
LIMA CL
MUNDOWIE PL
SAN DIEGO ST
THOAR PL
POWIE CL
MASSA PL
GOOR CL
WONNAI PL
KARRONG
PEARRA
KULLEROO
ALDINGA
GEEWAN
NULLAGA
COPYRIGHT © UNIVERSAL PRESS PTY LTD (PUBLISHER) 2001

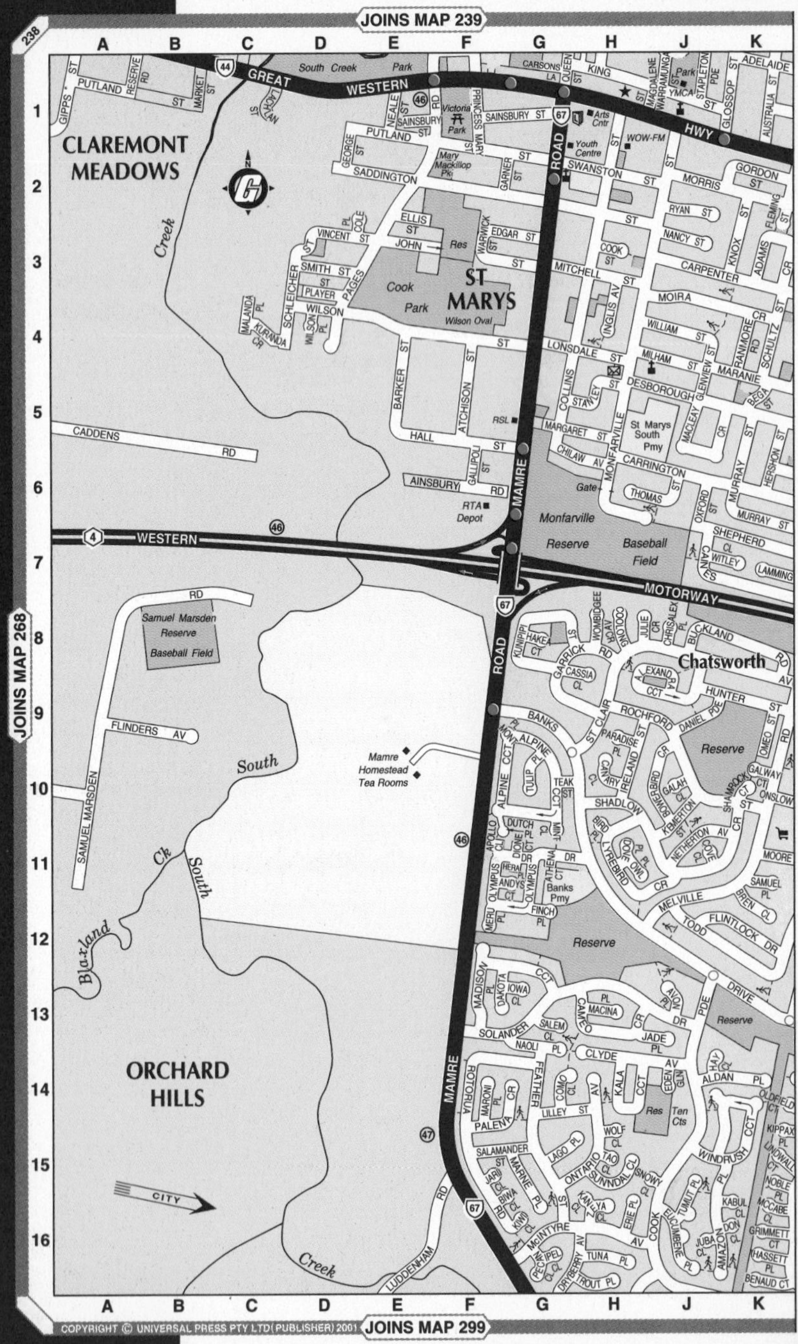
JOINS MAP 239
JOINS MAP 268
JOINS MAP 299
238
CLAREMONT MEADOWS
ST MARYS
Chatsworth
ORCHARD HILLS
GREAT WESTERN HWY
WESTERN MOTORWAY
MAMRE ROAD
CADDENS RD
Cook Park
Wilson Oval
Monfarville Reserve
Baseball Field
Samuel Marsden Reserve Baseball Field
Mamre Homestead Tea Rooms
St Marys South Pmy
Banks Pmy
South Creek
Blaxland Ck
CITY

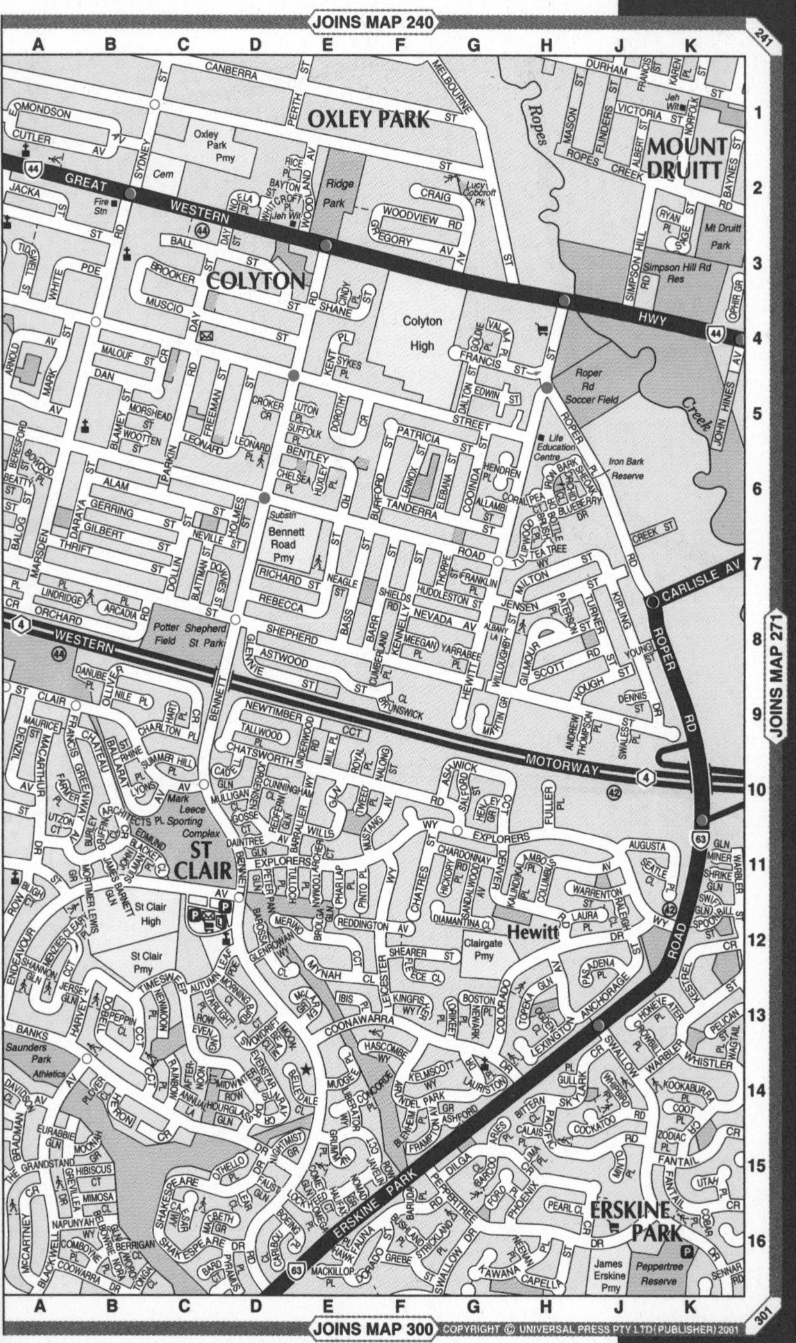
JOINS MAP 240
JOINS MAP 271
JOINS MAP 300
241
301
OXLEY PARK
COLYTON
MOUNT DRUITT
ST CLAIR
Hewitt
ERSKINE PARK
GREAT WESTERN HWY
WESTERN MOTORWAY
ROPER RD
ERSKINE PARK ROAD
CARLISLE AV
Colyton High
St Clair High
Bennett Road Pmy
Oxley Park Pmy
St Clair Pmy
Clairgate Pmy
James Erskine Pmy
Mark Leece Sporting Complex
Roper Rd Soccer Field
Iron Bark Reserve
Potter Field
Shepherd St Park
Saunders Park Athletics
Peppertree Reserve
Mt Druitt Park
Simpson Hill Rd Res
Ridge Park
Lucy Cobcroft Pk
Ropes Creek

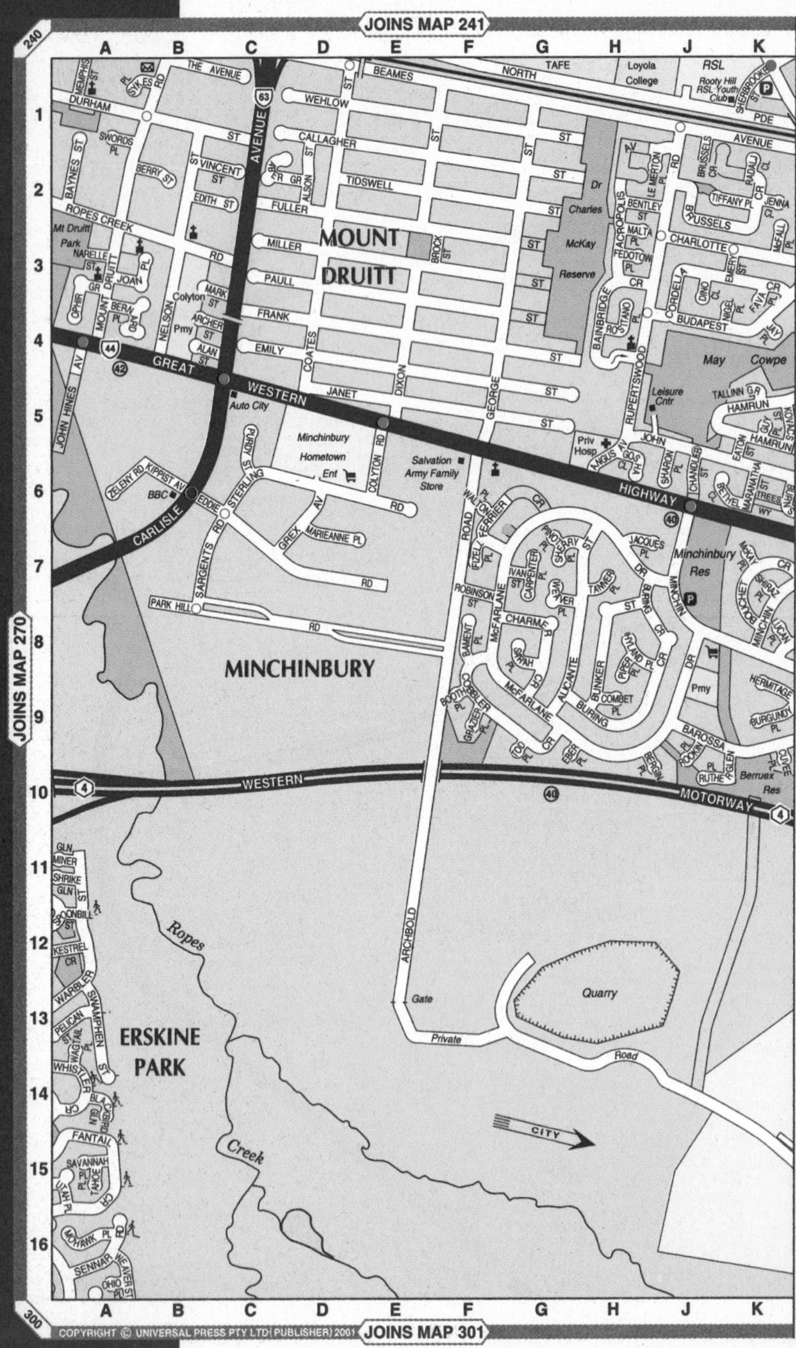
JOINS MAP 241
JOINS MAP 270
JOINS MAP 301
240
300
MOUNT DRUITT
MINCHINBURY
ERSKINE PARK
GREAT WESTERN HIGHWAY
WESTERN MOTORWAY
CARLISLE AVENUE
NORTH PDE
ROPES CREEK RD
Ropes Creek
Mt Druitt Park
Dr Charles McKay Reserve
May Cowpe
Minchinbury Res
Minchinbury Hometown Ent
Salvation Army Family Store
Auto City
BBC
Leisure Cntr
Priv Hosp
Loyola College
RSL
Rooty Hill RSL Youth Club
TAFE
Berruex Res
Quarry
Gate
Private Road
ARCHBOLD RD
CITY

JOINS MAP 242

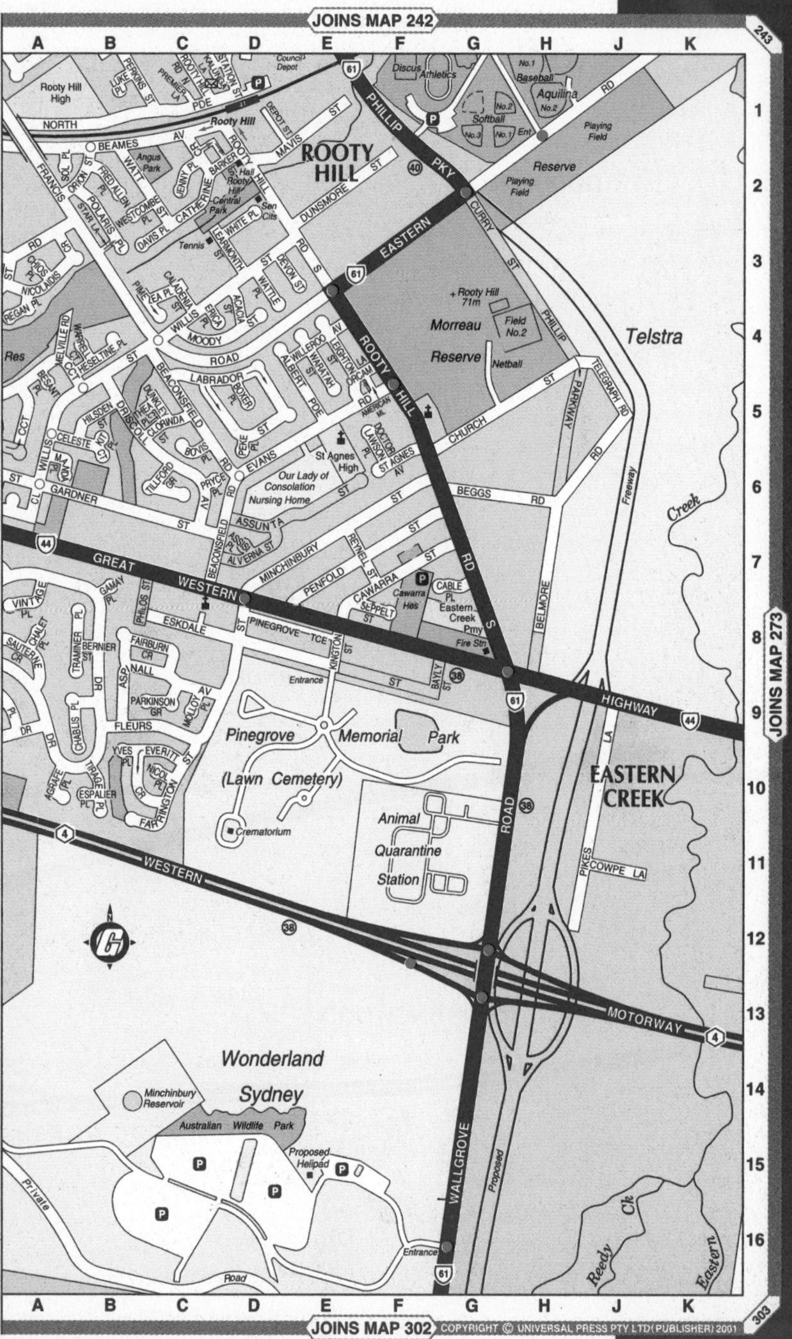

JOINS MAP 273

JOINS MAP 302

MAP 273

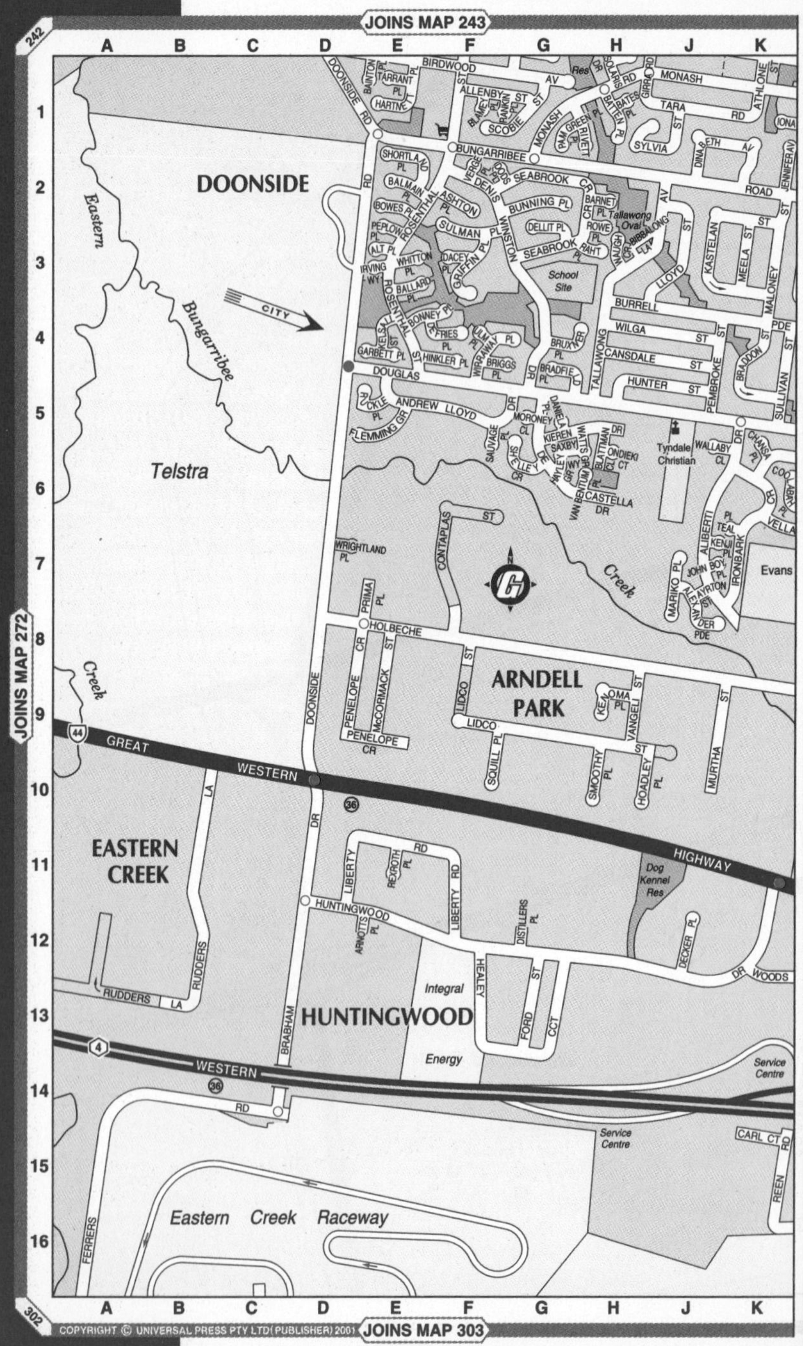
JOINS MAP 243
JOINS MAP 272
JOINS MAP 303
242
302
A B C D E F G H J K
1 2 3 4 5 6 7 8 9 10 11 12 13 14 15 16
DOONSIDE
ARNDELL PARK
EASTERN CREEK
HUNTINGWOOD
Telstra
Eastern Creek Raceway
Eastern Creek
Bungarribee Creek
CITY
GREAT WESTERN HIGHWAY
WESTERN
44
4
36
DOONSIDE RD
DOONSIDE DR
BIRDWOOD AV
MONASH RD
BUNGARRIBEE RD
ALLENBY ST
SCOBIE PL
SEABROOK CR
BUNNING PL
DELLIT PL
WINSTON
ROSENTHAL ST
SULMAN PL
ASHTON
GRIFFIN PL
DACEY PL
WHITTON PL
BALLARD PL
BONNEY PL
DE FRIES PL
HINKLER PL
BRIGGS PL
WIRRAWAY PL
ULM PL
GARBETT PL
KELSALL ST
IRVING WY
ALT PL
PEPLOW PL
BOWES PL
BALMAIN PL
SHORTLAND PL
VERGE
DENIS
DOUGLAS RD
ANDREW LLOYD DR
FLEMMING GR
RUCKLE PL
MORONEY CL
DANIELA PL
KIEREN
SAXBY
SHELLEY CR
SAUVAGE PL
WATTS GR
HAYLEY
VAN BENTUM PL
BLATTMAN PL
ONDIEKI CT
CASTELLA DR
BRUXNER PL
BRADFIELD
School Site
Tallawong Oval
TALLAWONG AV
BARNET PL
ROWE PL
RAHT
WAUGH
BIBBALONG LA
LLOYD
BURRELL
WILGA ST
CANSDALE ST
HUNTER ST
PEMBROKE
KASTELAN ST
MEELA ST
MALONEY PDE
BRADDON
SULLIVAN
TARA RD
SYLVIA
DINAH BETH AV
ATHLONE ST
JENNIFER AV
IONA
RES
SOLARIS
BATTEN PL
BATES PL
GIRRARD
RIVETT
PAM GREEN PL
Tyndale Christian
WALLABY CL
CHANSA PL
COOLABAH CR
VELLA
ALIBERTI
TEAL PL
KENJI PL
IRONBARK
JOHN BOY PL
AYRTON ST
ALEXANDER PDE
MARIKO PL
Evans
Creek
CONTAPLAS ST
WRIGHTLAND PL
PRIMA PL
HOLBECHE RD
PENELOPE CR
McCORMACK ST
LIDCO ST
SQUILL PL
KEA
OMA PL
VANGELI ST
SMOOTHY PL
HOADLEY PL
MURTHA ST
Dog Kennel Res
LIBERTY RD
REXROTH PL
HUNTINGWOOD DR
ARNOTTS PL
DISTILLERS PL
HEALEY
FORD ST
CCT
Integral Energy
DECKER PL
WOODS
BRABHAM DR
RUDDERS LA
FERRERS
RD
Service Centre
CARL CT
REEN RD

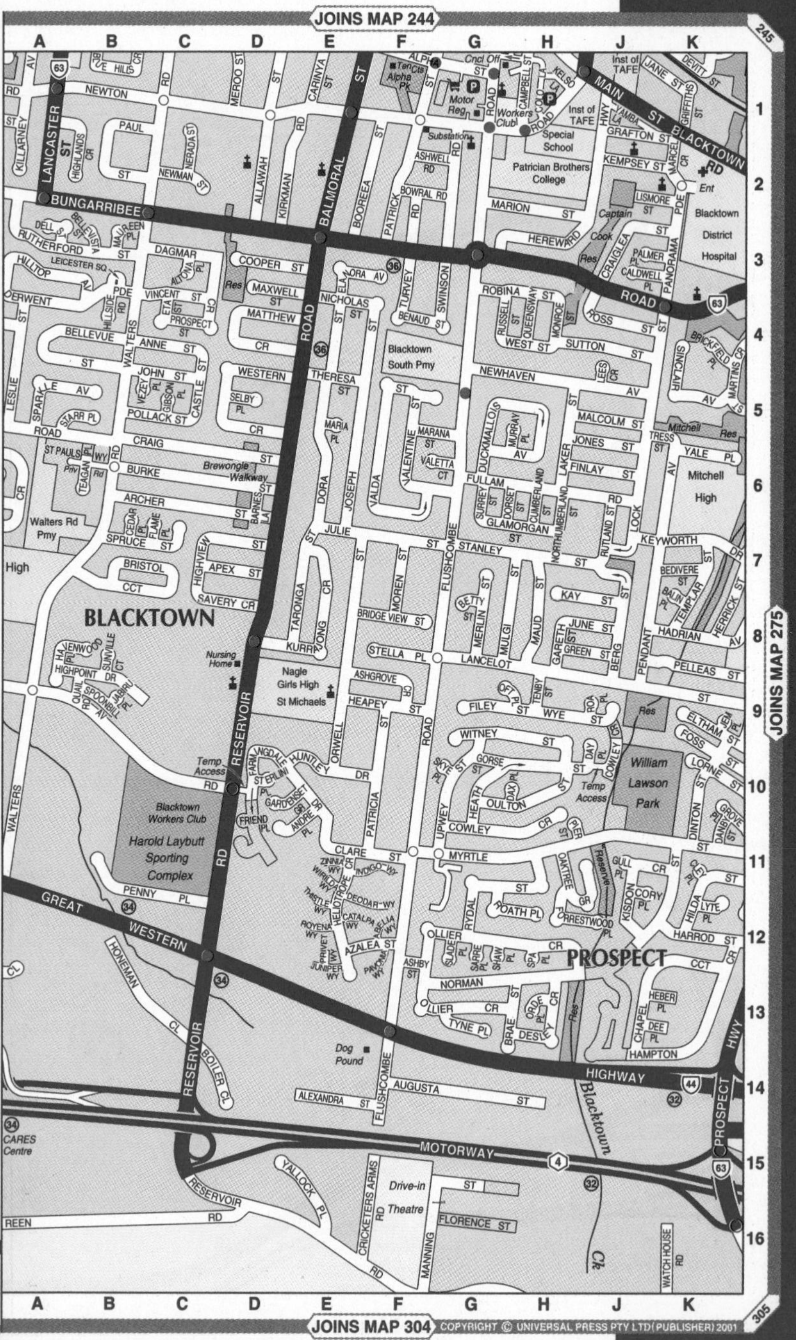
JOINS MAP 244
JOINS MAP 275
JOINS MAP 304
BLACKTOWN
PROSPECT
MAIN ST BLACKTOWN RD
BUNGARRIBEE ROAD
BALMORAL ST
ROAD
RESERVOIR RD
GREAT WESTERN HIGHWAY
MOTORWAY
PROSPECT HWY
Blacktown District Hospital
Patrician Brothers College
Special School
Workers Club
Blacktown South Pmy
Mitchell High
Walters Rd Pmy
Nagle Girls High
St Michaels
Blacktown Workers Club
Harold Laybutt Sporting Complex
William Lawson Park
Dog Pound
Drive-in Theatre
CARES Centre
Blacktown Ck

MAP 275

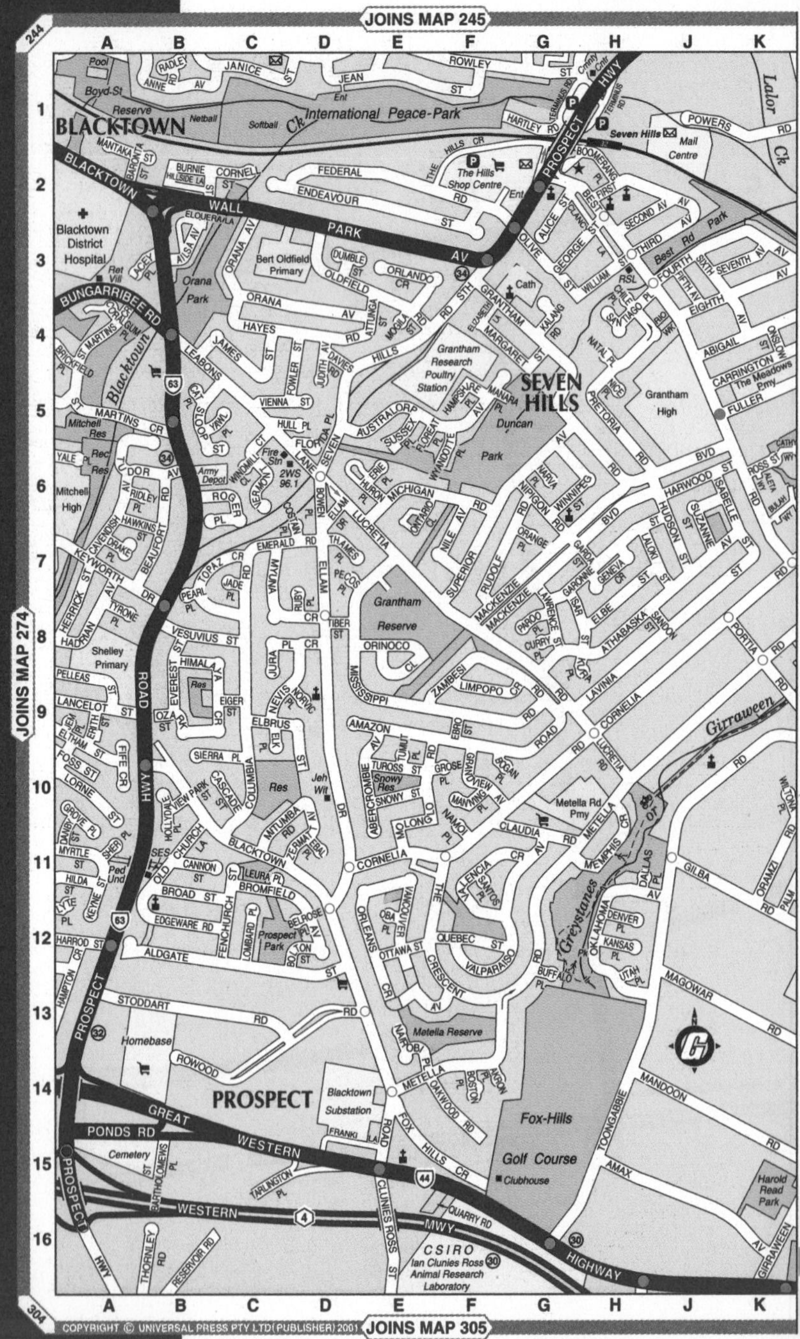
JOINS MAP 245
JOINS MAP 274
JOINS MAP 305
244
304
BLACKTOWN
SEVEN HILLS
PROSPECT
International Peace-Park
Blacktown District Hospital
Orana Park
Bert Oldfield Primary
The Hills Shop Centre
Seven Hills Mail Centre
Grantham Research Poultry Station
Duncan Park
Grantham High
Mitchell High
Shelley Primary
Grantham Reserve
Prospect Park
Metella Rd Pmy
Metella Reserve
Homebase
Blacktown Substation
Cemetery
Fox-Hills Golf Course
Clubhouse
CSIRO
Ian Clunies Ross Animal Research Laboratory
Harold Read Park
The Meadows Pmy
Greystanes
Girraween
Lalor Ck
BLACKTOWN RD
WALL PARK AV
PROSPECT HWY
GREAT WESTERN HIGHWAY
WESTERN MWY
BUNGARRIBEE RD
SEVEN HILLS RD STH
LUCRETIA RD
CORNELIA RD
BLACKTOWN RD
OLD CHURCH LA
STODDART RD
PONDS RD
CLUNIES ROSS ST
REWOOD
ALDGATE ST
MAGOWAR RD
MANDOON RD
TOONGABBIE RD
AMAX AV
POWERS RD
FULLER
HARWOOD ST
PORTIA RD
LAVINIA ST
QUARRY RD
THORNLEY RD
RESERVOIR RD

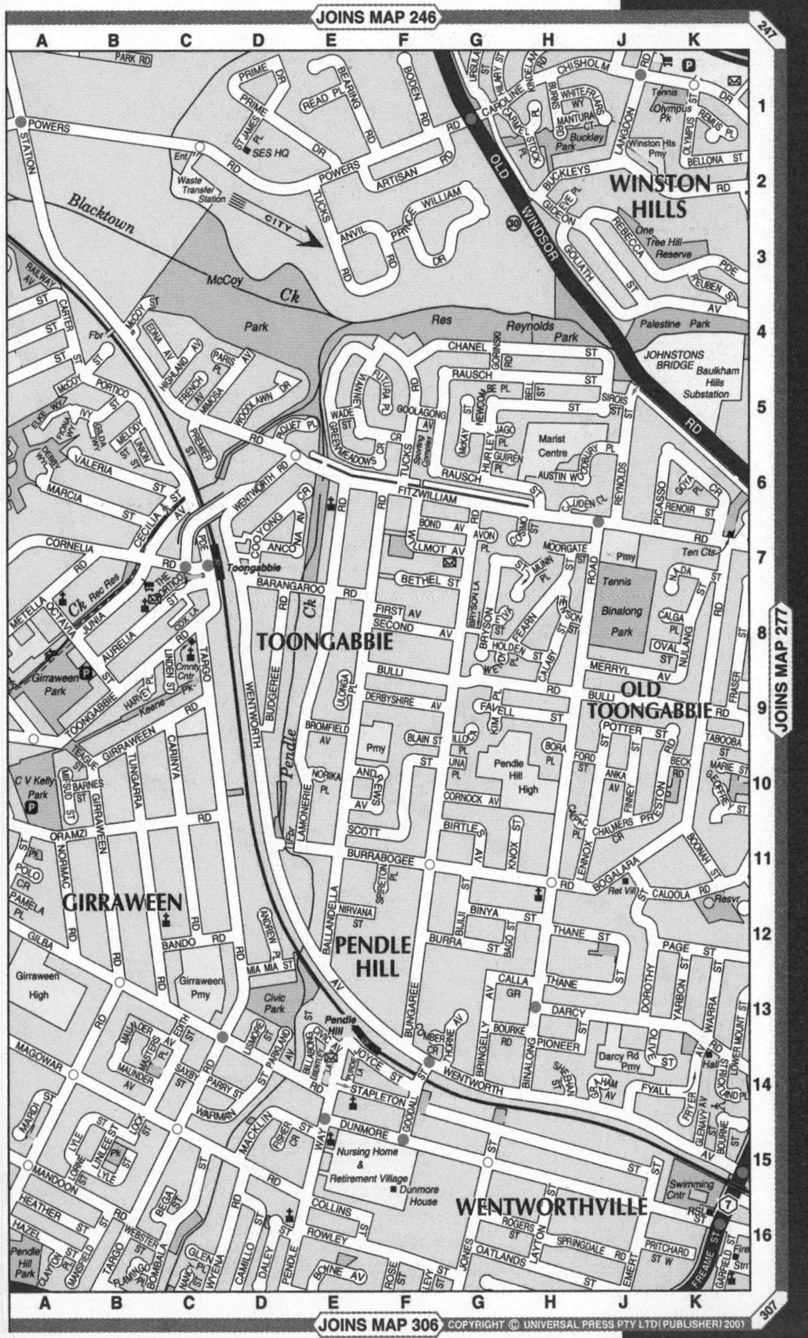
JOINS MAP 246
JOINS MAP 277
JOINS MAP 306
247
307
A B C D E F G H J K
1 2 3 4 5 6 7 8 9 10 11 12 13 14 15 16
WINSTON HILLS
TOONGABBIE
OLD TOONGABBIE
GIRRAWEEN
PENDLE HILL
WENTWORTHVILLE
OLD WINDSOR RD
POWERS RD
STATION
PARK RD
PRIME DR
PRIME PL
ST JAMES PL
SES HQ
BEARING RD
READ PL
BODEN RD
ARTISAN
TUCKS RD
ANVIL
PRINCE WILLIAM DR
Waste Transfer Station
Ent
CITY
Blacktown
McCoy Ck
Park
Res
Reynolds Park
Palestine Park
JOHNSTONS BRIDGE
Baulkham Hills Substation
One Tree Hill Reserve
URSULA ST
HILARY ST
CAROLINE
KINDELAN
CHISHOLM
WHITEFRIARS WY
MANTURA CT
Buckley Park
BUCKLEYS RD
CARMEL
STOCK PL
BURNS RD
LANGDON RD
Tennis
Olympus Pk
OLYMPUS
REMUS PL
BELLONA ST
Winston Hts Pmy
GIDEON
EVE PL
GOLIATH
REBECCA ST
REUBEN ST
PDE
AV
RAILWAY AV
CARTER ST
McCOY ST
EDNA AV
HIGHLAND AV
PARIS PL
FRENCH AV
MIMOSA
WOODLAWN DR
PORTICO
Fbr
ELKE WY
IVY
FIONA WY
GILDA WY
MELODY ST
UNION ST
DEBBY WY
VALERIA ST
MARCIA ST
CECILIA ST
CORNELIA RD
PREMIER ST
PIQUET PL
WENTWORTH RD
CHANEL ST
GORINSKI RD
RAUSCH ST
VIANNEY
FUTURA PL
WADE ST
GOOLAGONG AV
GREENMEADOWS CR
Sporting Complex
BE PL
BELL ST
NEWCOMB
McKAY ST
JAGO PL
HURLEY
GUIREN PL
Marist Centre
AUSTIN WOODBURY PL
SIROIS ST
REYNOLDS
PICASSO
GOYA PL
RENOIR ST
CLUDEN CL
FITZWILLIAM
BOND AV
AVON PL
COSIMO ST
WILLMOT AV
MOORGATE ST
COOYONG CR
ANCONA AV
PDE
Toongabbie
THE PORTICO
Rec Res
Ck
METELLA
OCTAVIA
JUNIA
AURELIA
COX LA
BARANGAROO RD
BETHEL ST
FIRST AV
SECOND AV
BRYSON LA
MUNN PL
FEARN
HOLDEN ST
JAYSON ST
Pmy
Tennis
Binalong Park
Ten Cts
NADA
CALGA PL
OVAL ST
NULANG
MERRYL AV
Girraween Park
TOONGABBIE
HARVEY PL
LINDEN ST
Cmnty Cntr
Pk
TARGO
Keene
BUDGEREE
WENTWORTH
ULONGA PL
BULLI RD
DERBYSHIRE AV
FAVELL ST
KIM PL
CALABY
POTTER ST
FRASER
TABOOBA ST
MARIE ST
GEOFFREY ST
BECK RD
Pendle
BROMFIELD AV
BLAIN ST
ILLOCA PL
UNA PL
Pendle Hill High
BORA PL
FORD ST
ANKA AV
FINNEY
PRESTON
CHALMERS CR
NORIKA PL
ANDREWS AV
CORNOCK AV
BIRTLE AV
KNOX ST
CAPPAC PL
LENNOX
SCOTT
BURRABOGEE RD
BOGALARA
Ret Vill
CALOOLA RD
Resvr
BOONAH ST
TEAGUE
GIRRAWEEN
TUNGARRA
CARINYA
C V Kelly Park
MIFSUD ST
BARNES ST
ORAMZI RD
NORMAC
POLO CR
PAMELA PL
LAMONERIE
SPIRETON PL
BALLANDELLA
NIRVANA ST
BINYA ST
BURRA ST
BIJIJI
BAGO
THANE ST
PAGE ST
GILBA RD
BANDO RD
Girraween High
Girraween Pmy
ANDREW PL
MIA MIA ST
Civic Park
CALLA GR
DARCY
BUNGAREE
BRINGELLY AV
DOROTHY
YARBON ST
WARRA
LOWER MOUNT ST
MAGOWAR
MAUNDER AV
MASTERS PL
EDITH ST
SAXBY ST
PARRY ST
USMORE ST
PARKLAND
BILLABONG ST
CIVIC LA
Pendle Hill
JOYCE ST
PURDIE LA
COMBER CR
THORNE AV
BOURKE RD
PIONEER
BINALONG
SHEEHAN ST
GRAHAM AV
Darcy Rd Pmy
OLIVE ST
FYALL
FRYER
GLENAVY AV
STRICKLAND PL
Hall
WENTWORTH AV
STAPLETON
WARMAN
MACKLIN
FISHER CR
DUNMORE
WAY
GOODALL
Nursing Home & Retirement Village
Dunmore House
BOURNE ST
Swimming Cntr
RSL
MARDI ST
LYLE
LINLEE ST
LORNE
LOCK ST
Pk
MANDOON
HEATHER ST
HAZEL
BEGA ST
WEBSTER
COLLINS
ROWLEY
ROGERS ST
SPRINGDALE RD
PRITCHARD ST W
FREAME ST
Fire Stn
GARFIELD ST
Pendle Hill Park
CLAYTON
MANSFIELD
TARGO
FLAMINGO PL
BOMBALA
GLEN ST
NANCY PL
WYENA
CAMILLO
DALEY
PENDLE
BOYNE AV
ROSE ST
LEVY ST
JONES
OATLANDS
LAYTON
EMERT
30
7

JOINS MAP 247

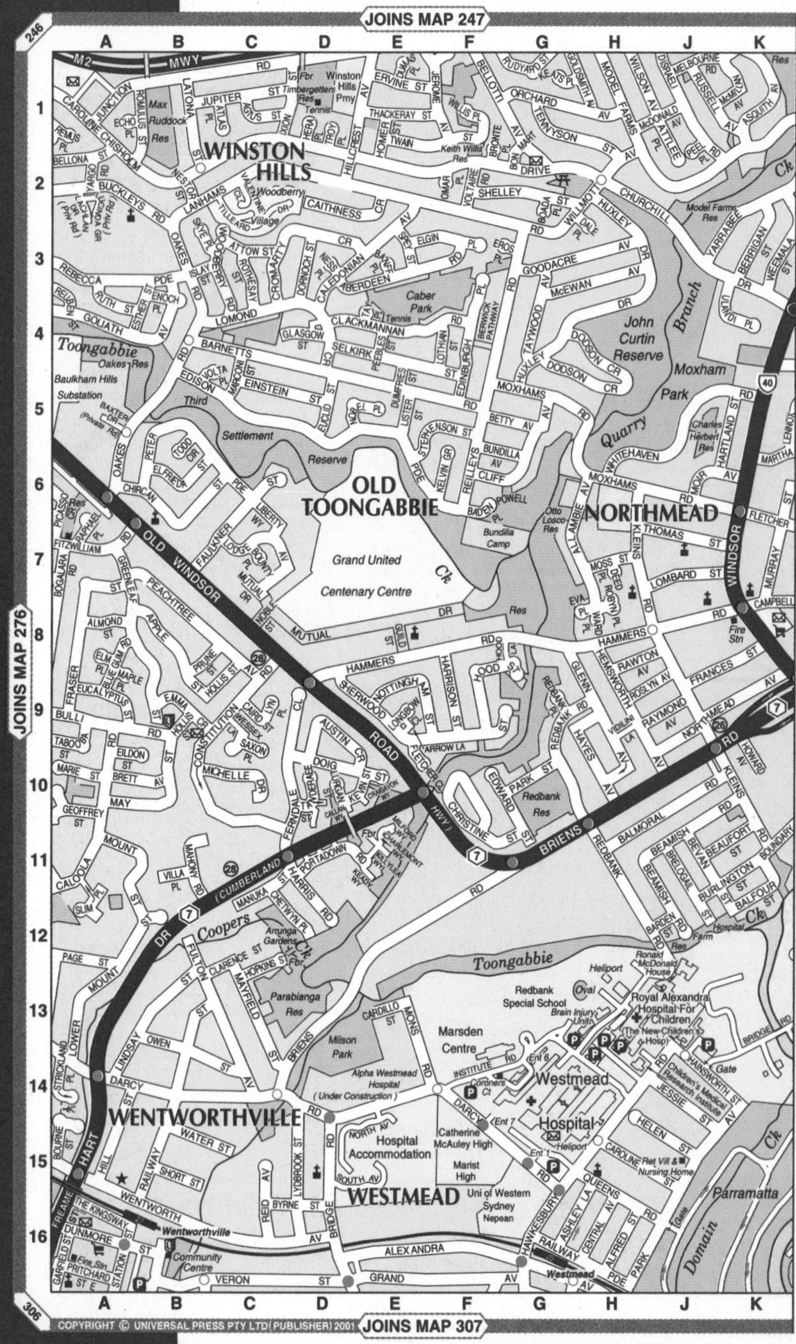

JOINS MAP 276

JOINS MAP 307

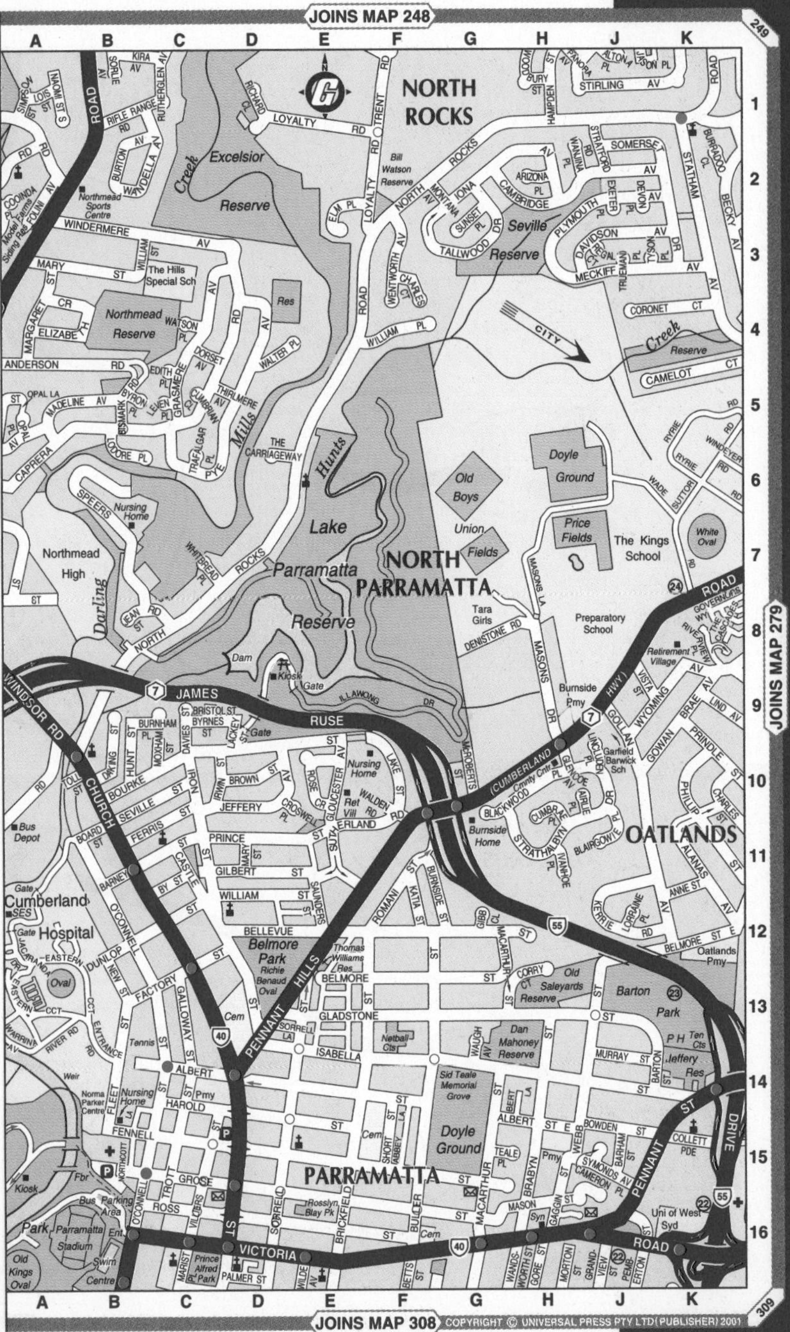

JOINS MAP 248
JOINS MAP 279
JOINS MAP 308
NORTH ROCKS
NORTH PARRAMATTA
OATLANDS
PARRAMATTA
Excelsior Reserve
Seville Reserve
Northmead Reserve
Lake Parramatta Reserve
Old Boys Union Fields
Doyle Ground
Price Fields
The Kings School
Preparatory School
Cumberland Hospital
Belmore Park
Barton Park
Old Saleyards Reserve
Dan Mahoney Reserve
Parramatta Stadium
Old Kings Oval
Northmead High
JAMES RUSE DR
CUMBERLAND HWY
PENNANT HILLS RD
CHURCH ST
WINDSOR RD
VICTORIA RD
NORTH ROCKS RD

MAP 279

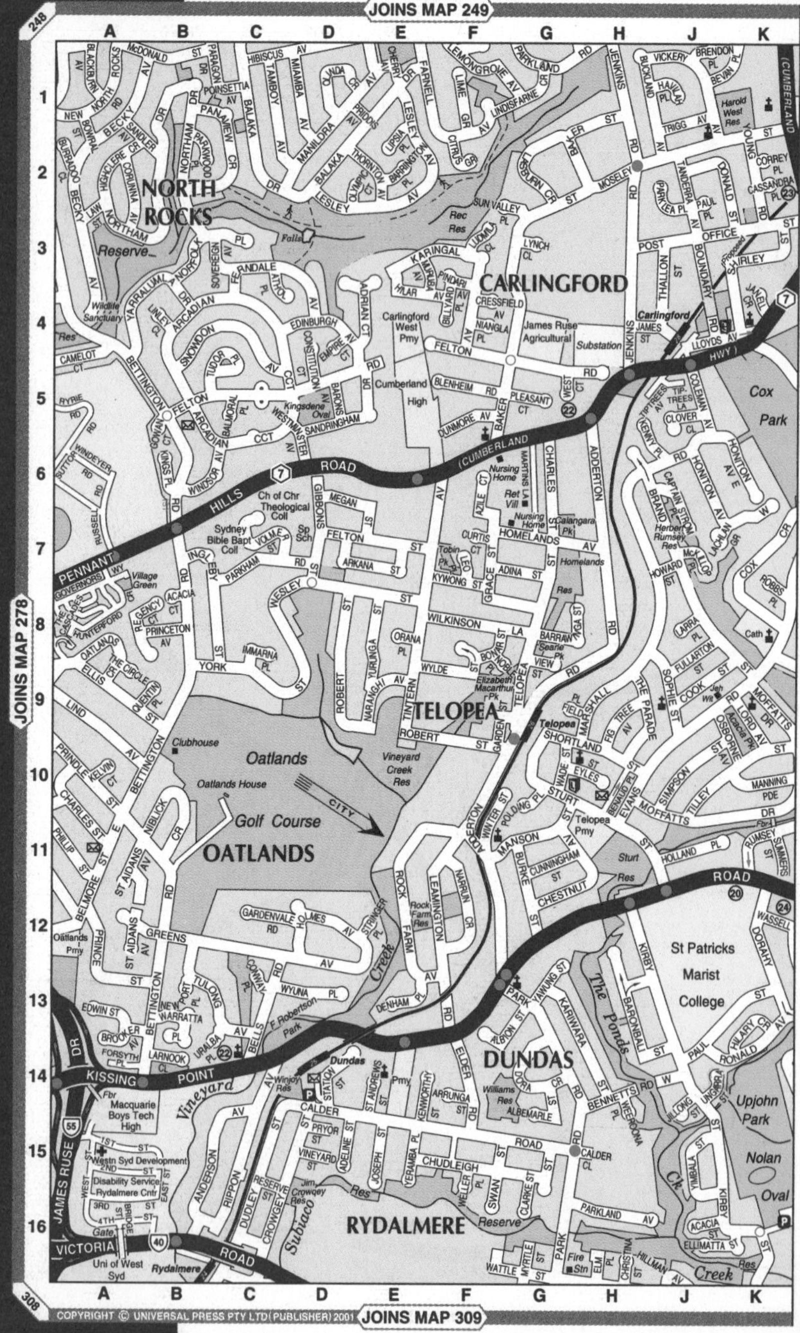

JOINS MAP 249
JOINS MAP 278
JOINS MAP 309
248
308
A B C D E F G H J K
1 2 3 4 5 6 7 8 9 10 11 12 13 14 15 16
NORTH ROCKS
CARLINGFORD
TELOPEA
OATLANDS
DUNDAS
RYDALMERE
Reserve
Wildlife Sanctuary
Rec Res
Falls
Carlingford West Pmy
James Ruse Agricultural
Substation
Carlingford
Cumberland High
Kingsdene Oval
Nursing Home
Ret Vill
Calangara Pk
Homelands Res
Harold West Res
Cox Park
Herbert Rumsey Res
Ch of Chr Theological Coll
Sydney Bible Bapt Coll
Sp Sch
Village Green
Tobin Pk
Searle Pk
Elizabeth Macarthur Pk
Telopea
Clubhouse
Oatlands House
Oatlands Golf Course
CITY
Vineyard Creek Res
Rock Farm Res
Telopea Pmy
Sturt Res
St Patricks Marist College
Upjohn Park
Nolan Oval
Oatlands Pmy
F. Robertson Park
Creek
Dundas
Winjoy Res
Williams Res
The Ponds
Macquarie Boys Tech High
Westn Syd Development
Disability Service
Rydalmere Cntr
Jim Crowgey Res
Subiaco
Vineyard
Fire Stn
Uni of West Syd
Rydalmere
Cath
Acacia Pk
PENNANT HILLS ROAD
CUMBERLAND HWY
KISSING POINT ROAD
VICTORIA ROAD
JAMES RUSE DR
CALDER ROAD
7
22
20
23
24
40
55
COPYRIGHT © UNIVERSAL PRESS PTY LTD (PUBLISHER) 2001

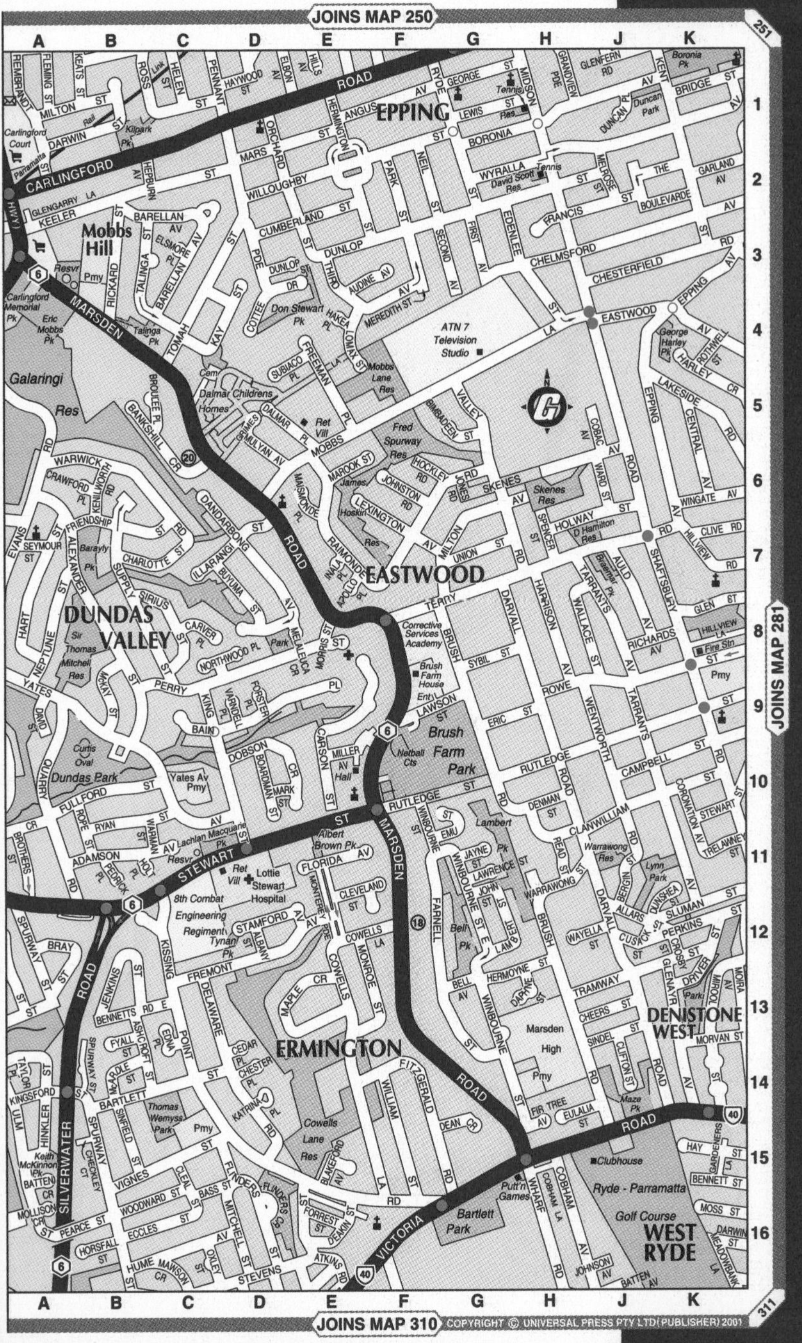

JOINS MAP 250
JOINS MAP 281
JOINS MAP 310
EPPING
EASTWOOD
DUNDAS VALLEY
ERMINGTON
DENISTONE WEST
WEST RYDE
Mobbs Hill
CARLINGFORD RD
MARSDEN RD
VICTORIA RD
STEWART ST
SILVERWATER RD
ATN 7 Television Studio
Brush Farm Park
Ryde - Parramatta Golf Course
Marsden High
Corrective Services Academy
Lottie Stewart Hospital
Galaringi Res
Dundas Park
Bartlett Park
COPYRIGHT © UNIVERSAL PRESS PTY LTD (PUBLISHER) 2001

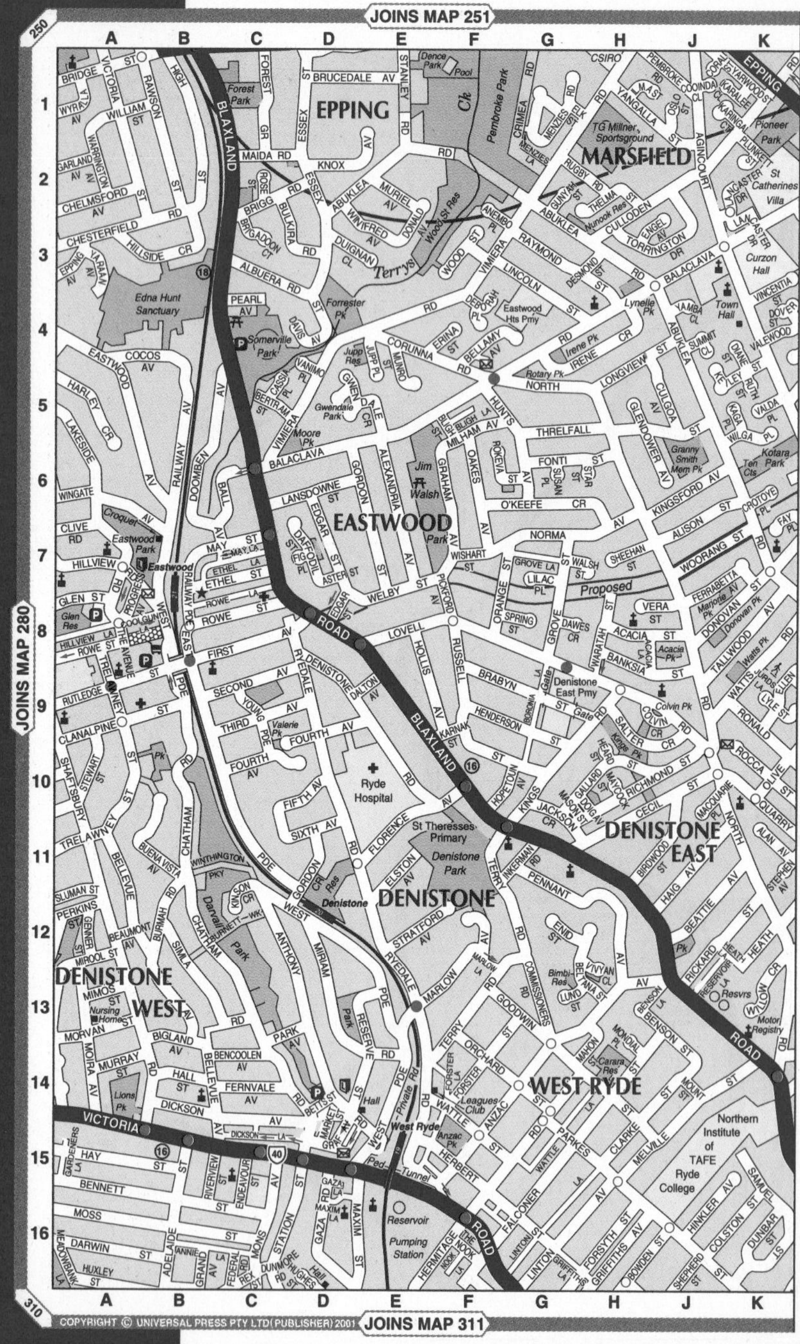
JOINS MAP 251
JOINS MAP 280
JOINS MAP 311
250
310
A B C D E F G H J K
1 2 3 4 5 6 7 8 9 10 11 12 13 14 15 16
EPPING
MARSFIELD
EASTWOOD
DENISTONE
DENISTONE EAST
DENISTONE WEST
WEST RYDE
BLAXLAND
BLAXLAND RD
VICTORIA RD
EPPING RD
Forest Park
Dence Park
Pool
Pembroke Park
TG Millner Sportsground
Pioneer Park
St Catherines Villa
Curzon Hall
Town Hall
Edna Hunt Sanctuary
Somerville Park
Forrester Pk
Jupp Res
Gwendale Park
Moore Pk
Eastwood Hts Pmy
Irene Pk
Rotary Pk
Lynelle Pk
Wood St Res
Nunook Res
Terrys Ck
Jim Walsh Park
Granny Smith Mem Pk
Kotara Park
Ten Cts
Croquet
Eastwood Park
Eastwood
Glen Res
Proposed
Marjorie Pk
Donovan Pk
Acacia Pk
Watts Pk
Denistone East Pmy
Gate
Colvin Pk
Kings Pk
Valerie Pk
Ryde Hospital
St Theresses Primary
Denistone Park
Denistone
Res
Darvall Park
Winthington Pky
Bimbi Res
Resvrs
Motor Registry
Nursing Home
Lions Pk
Carara Res
Leagues Club
Anzac Pk
West Ryde
Hall
Reservoir
Pumping Station
Private Rd
Ped Tunnel
Northern Institute of TAFE Ryde College
COPYRIGHT © UNIVERSAL PRESS PTY LTD (PUBLISHER) 2001

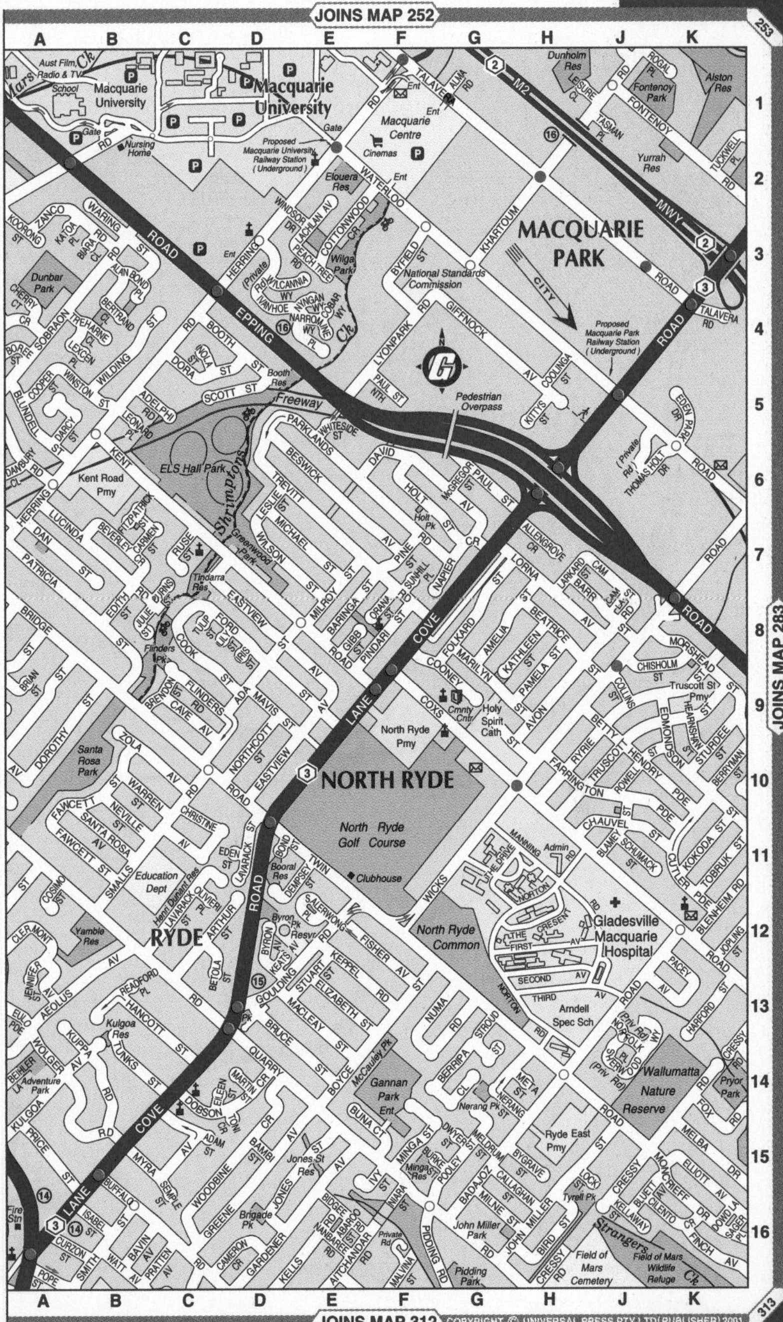
JOINS MAP 252
JOINS MAP 283
JOINS MAP 312
253
313
Macquarie University
Aust Film, Radio & TV School
Macquarie Centre
Cinemas
Proposed Macquarie University Railway Station (Underground)
MACQUARIE PARK
Proposed Macquarie Park Railway Station (Underground)
National Standards Commission
Pedestrian Overpass
Freeway
EPPING ROAD
TALAVERA RD
WATERLOO RD
M2 MWY
Dunholm Res
Fontenoy Park
Alston Res
Yurrah Res
Elouera Res
Wilga Park
Dunbar Park
ELS Hall Park
Shrimptons Ck
Kent Road Pmy
Greenwood Park
Tindarra Res
Flinders Pk
Booth Res
Holt Pk
Santa Rosa Park
Education Dept
Henri Dunant Res
RYDE
Yamble Res
NORTH RYDE
North Ryde Pmy
Holy Spirit Cath
Cmnty Cntr
North Ryde Golf Course
Clubhouse
North Ryde Common
Gladesville Macquarie Hospital
Arndell Spec Sch
Booral Res
Byron Pk
Resvr
Truscott St Pmy
Kulgoa Res
Adventure Park
Gannan Park
McCauley Pk
Jones St Res
Brigade Pk
Minga Res
Nerang Pk
Ryde East Pmy
Wallumatta Nature Reserve
Pryor Park
John Miller Park
Tyrell Pk
Field of Mars Cemetery
Field of Mars Wildlife Refuge
Strangers Ck
Pidding Park
Fire Stn
LANE COVE ROAD
BLENHEIM RD
COPYRIGHT © UNIVERSAL PRESS PTY LTD (PUBLISHER) 2001

MAP 283

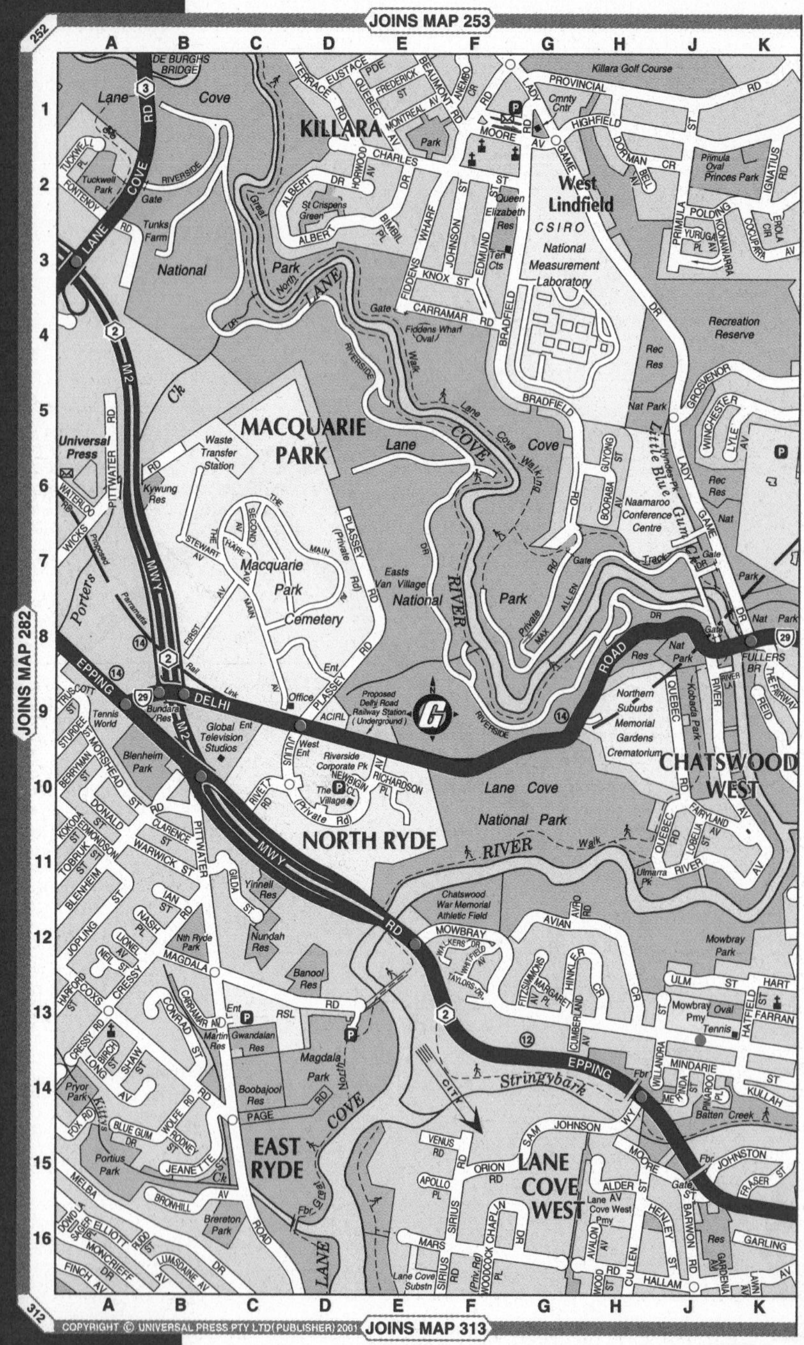

JOINS MAP 253
JOINS MAP 282
JOINS MAP 313
252
312
A B C D E F G H J K
1 2 3 4 5 6 7 8 9 10 11 12 13 14 15 16
DE BURGHS BRIDGE
Lane Cove
KILLARA
West Lindfield
Killara Golf Course
PROVINCIAL RD
Cmnty Cntr
HIGHFIELD
MOORE AV
CHARLES ST
St Crispens Green
Tuckwell Park
Tunks Farm
National Park
Queen Elizabeth Res
Ten Cts
CSIRO
National Measurement Laboratory
KNOX ST
CARRAMAR RD
Fiddens Wharf Oval
Primula Oval
Princes Park
Recreation Reserve
Rec Res
Nat Park
Little Blue Gum Ck
Universal Press
Waste Transfer Station
Kywung Res
MACQUARIE PARK
Macquarie Park Cemetery
Lane Cove Walk
Lane Cove National Park
Easts Van Village
LANE COVE RIVER
Naamaroo Conference Centre
Porters
EPPING RD
DELHI RD
Global Television Studios
Proposed Delhi Road Railway Station (Underground)
Riverside Corporate Pk
The Village
Tennis World
Bundara Res
Blenheim Park
Northern Suburbs Memorial Gardens Crematorium
CHATSWOOD WEST
FULLERS BR
NORTH RYDE
Yinnell Res
Nundah Res
Nth Ryde Park
Banool Res
Chatswood War Memorial Athletic Field
Mowbray Park
Mowbray Pmy
Ulmarra Pk
RSL
Martin Res
Gwandalan Res
Magdala Park
Boobajool Res
Pryor Park
Portius Park
Brereton Park
EAST RYDE
Stringybark
Batten Creek
LANE COVE WEST
Lane Cove West Pmy
Lane Cove Substn
COPYRIGHT © UNIVERSAL PRESS PTY LTD (PUBLISHER) 2001

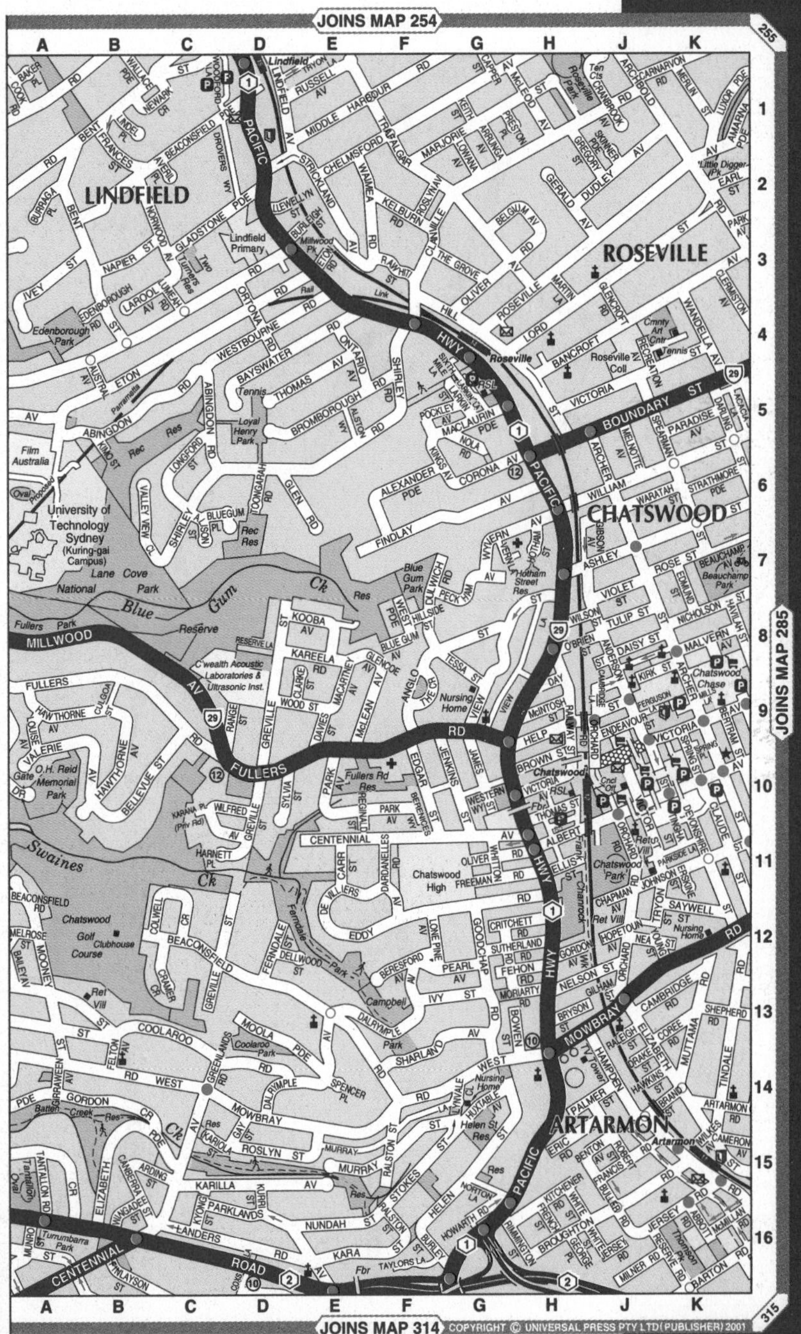
JOINS MAP 254
255
JOINS MAP 285
JOINS MAP 314
315
A B C D E F G H J K
1 2 3 4 5 6 7 8 9 10 11 12 13 14 15 16
LINDFIELD
ROSEVILLE
CHATSWOOD
ARTARMON
Lindfield
Roseville
Chatswood
Artarmon
PACIFIC HWY
BOUNDARY ST
MILLWOOD AV
FULLERS RD
CENTENNIAL ROAD
MOWBRAY RD
Lindfield Primary
Edenborough Park
Film Australia
University of Technology Sydney (Kuring-gai Campus)
Lane Cove National Park
Blue Gum Reserve
Loyal Henry Park
C'wealth Acoustic Laboratories & Ultrasonic Inst.
O.H. Reid Memorial Park
Chatswood Golf Course
Chatswood High
Chatswood Park
Chatswood Chase
Roseville Coll
Cmnty Art Cntr
Roseville Park
Blue Gum Park
Hotham Street Res
Fullers Rd Res
Coolaroo Park
Dalrymple Park
Campbell Park
Ferndale Park
Thomson Pk
Turrumbarra Park
Tantallon Oval
Swaines Ck
Blue Gum Ck
Batten Creek Res
Nursing Home
Ret Vill
COPYRIGHT © UNIVERSAL PRESS PTY LTD (PUBLISHER) 2001

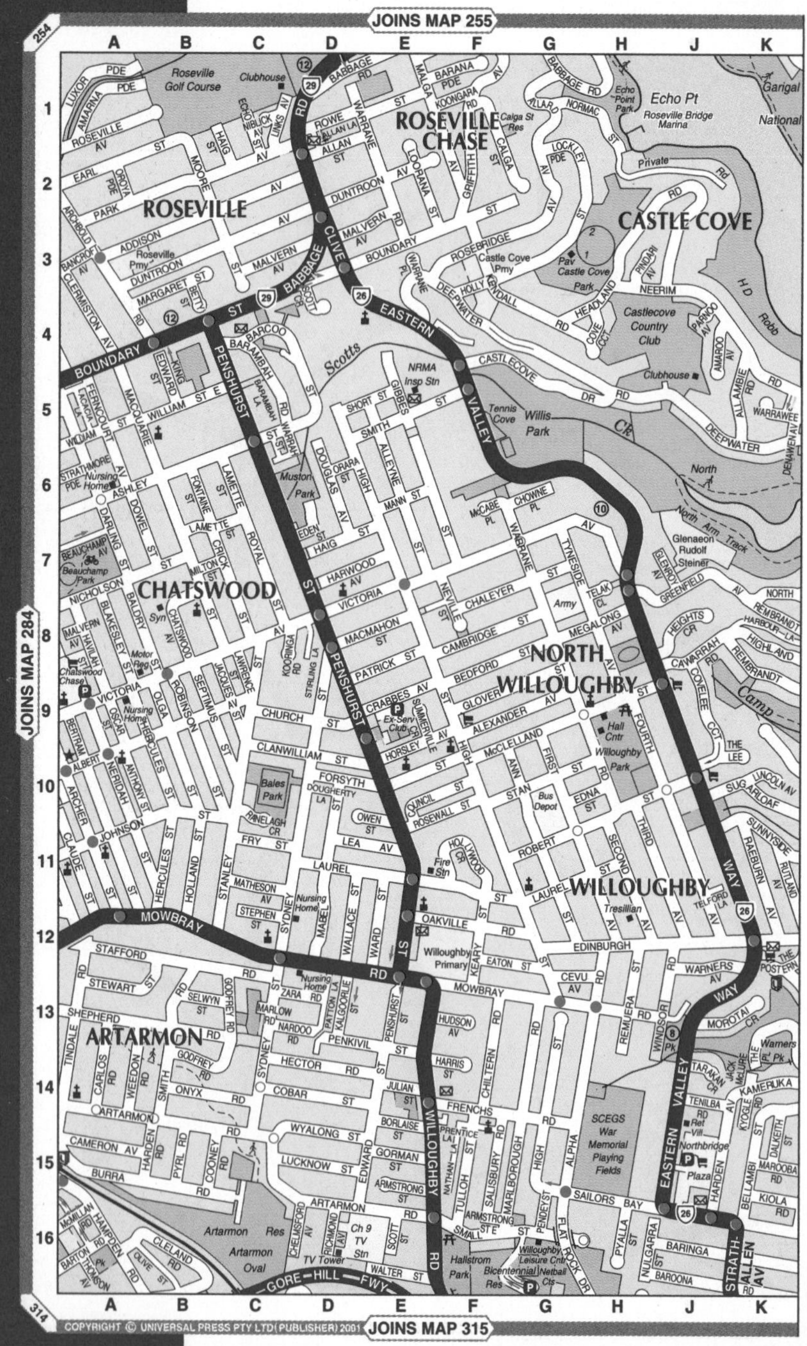
JOINS MAP 255
254
JOINS MAP 284
314
JOINS MAP 315
ROSEVILLE
ROSEVILLE CHASE
CASTLE COVE
CHATSWOOD
NORTH WILLOUGHBY
WILLOUGHBY
ARTARMON
Roseville Golf Course
Clubhouse
Echo Point Park
Echo Pt
Roseville Bridge Marina
Garigal National
Calga St Res
Private
Castle Cove Pmy
Pav
Castle Cove Park
Castlecove Country Club
Clubhouse
Roseville Pmy
Scotts
NRMA Insp Stn
Tennis Cove
Willis Park
Ck
North
North Arm Track
Glenaeon Rudolf Steiner
Muston Park
Beauchamp Park
Nursing Home
Syn
Motor Reg
Chatswood Chase
Army
Camp
Ex-Serv Club
Hall Cntr
Willoughby Park
Bales Park
Bus Depot
Fire Stn
Tresillian
Willoughby Primary
Warners Pk
Ret Vill
Northbridge Plaza
SCEGS War Memorial Playing Fields
Artarmon Res
Artarmon Oval
Ch 9 TV Stn
TV Tower
Hallstrom Park
Willoughby Leisure Cntr
Bicentennial Res
Netball Cts
BOUNDARY ST
BABBAGE RD
PENSHURST ST
EASTERN VALLEY WAY
MOWBRAY RD
WILLOUGHBY RD
GORE HILL FWY
STRATH-ALLEN AV
SAILORS BAY RD
HD Robb
A B C D E F G H J K
1 2 3 4 5 6 7 8 9 10 11 12 13 14 15 16

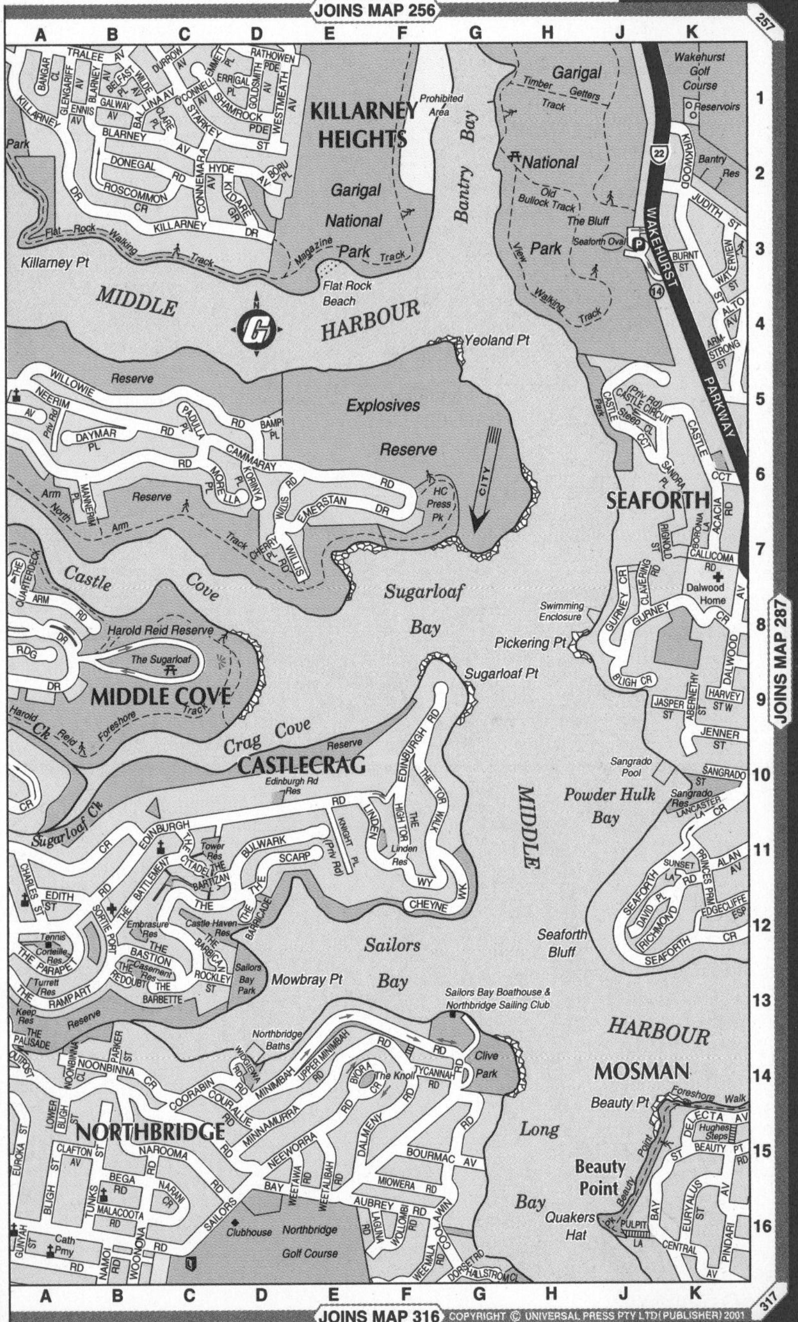

JOINS MAP 256
257
JOINS MAP 287
JOINS MAP 316
317
KILLARNEY HEIGHTS
Garigal National Park
Killarney Pt
Flat Rock Walking Track
Magazine Track
Flat Rock Beach
MIDDLE HARBOUR
Prohibited Area
Bantry Bay
Garigal National Park
Timber Getters Track
Old Bullock Track
The Bluff
Seaforth Oval
View Walking Track
Wakehurst Golf Course
Reservoirs
Bantry Res
WAKEHURST PARKWAY
Yeoland Pt
Explosives Reserve
HC Press Pk
CITY
Willowie Reserve
North Arm Reserve
North Arm Track
Castle Cove
Sugarloaf Bay
Harold Reid Reserve
The Sugarloaf
MIDDLE COVE
Harold Reid Foreshore Track
Crag Cove Reserve
CASTLECRAG
Edinburgh Rd Res
Sugarloaf Pt
Pickering Pt
Swimming Enclosure
SEAFORTH
Dalwood Home
Sangrado Pool
Powder Hulk Bay
Sangrado Res
MIDDLE
Seaforth Bluff
Sailors Bay
Mowbray Pt
Sailors Bay Park
Sailors Bay Boathouse & Northbridge Sailing Club
Northbridge Baths
Clive Park
The Knoll
HARBOUR
MOSMAN
Beauty Pt
Foreshore Walk
Hughes Steps
Long Bay
Beauty Point
Quakers Hat
NORTHBRIDGE
Clubhouse
Northbridge Golf Course
Tower Res
Linden Res
Embrasure Res
Castle Haven Res
Corteille Res
Casement Res
Turrett Res
Keep Res
Reserve
COPYRIGHT © UNIVERSAL PRESS PTY LTD (PUBLISHER) 2001

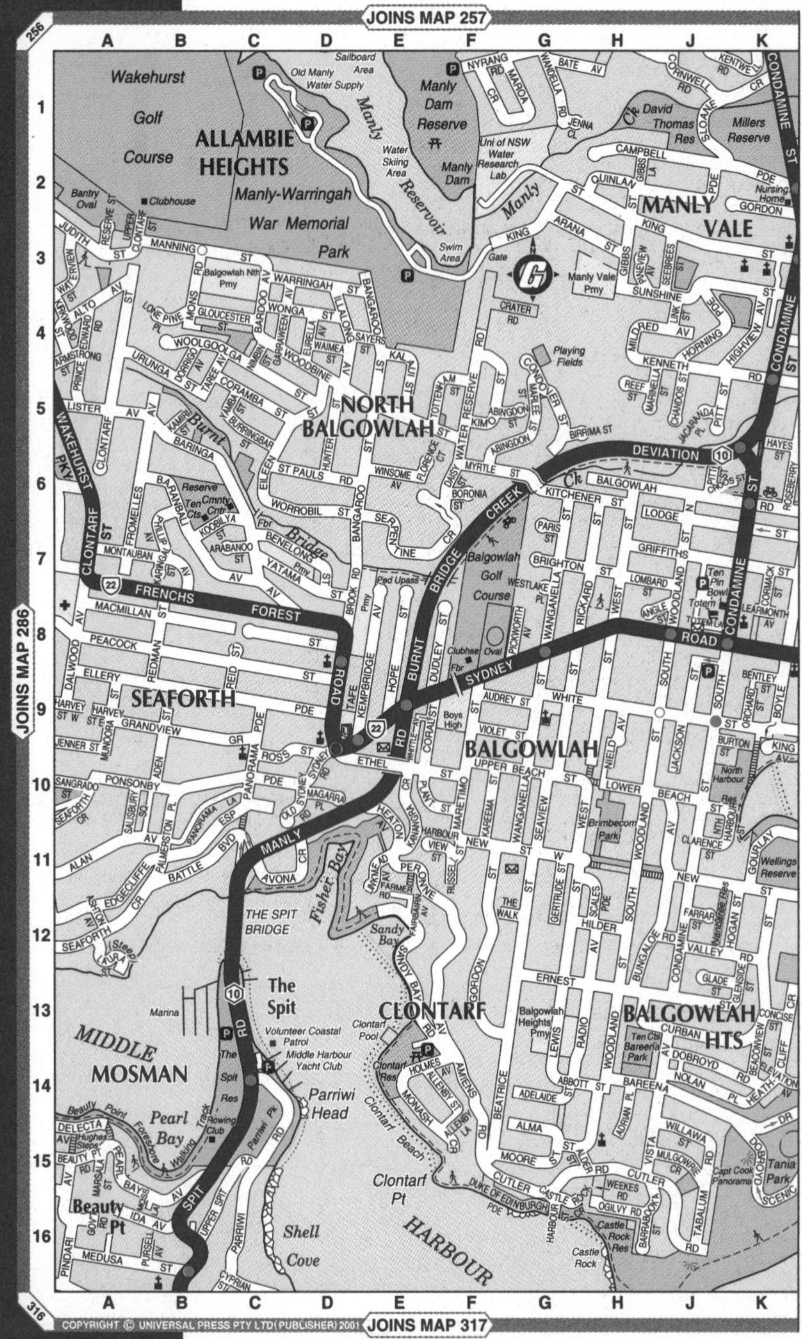
JOINS MAP 257
JOINS MAP 286
JOINS MAP 317
256
316
A B C D E F G H J K
1 2 3 4 5 6 7 8 9 10 11 12 13 14 15 16
Wakehurst Golf Course
ALLAMBIE HEIGHTS
Manly-Warringah War Memorial Park
Bantry Oval
Clubhouse
Old Manly Water Supply
Sailboard Area
Manly Reservoir
Water Skiing Area
Manly Dam Reserve
Manly Dam
Swim Area
Gate
Uni of NSW Water Research Lab
David Thomas Res
Millers Reserve
MANLY VALE
Nursing Home
Manly Vale Pmy
Balgowlah Nth Pmy
Playing Fields
NORTH BALGOWLAH
Burnt Bridge Ck
Reserve
Ten Cts
Cmnty Cntr
Fbr
Pmy
DEVIATION
Ten Pin Bowl
Totem
Balgowlah Golf Course
Clubhse
Oval
Ped Upass
FRENCHS FOREST ROAD
SYDNEY ROAD
SEAFORTH
BALGOWLAH
Boys High
North Harbour Res
Brimbecom Park
Wellings Reserve
MANLY RD
THE SPIT BRIDGE
Fisher Bay
Sandy Bay
The Spit
Marina
Volunteer Coastal Patrol
Middle Harbour Yacht Club
The Spit Res
Rowing Club
MIDDLE HARBOUR
MOSMAN
Pearl Bay
Beauty Pt
Parriwi Head
Shell Cove
CLONTARF
Clontarf Pool
Clontarf Res
Clontarf Beach
Clontarf Pt
HARBOUR
Balgowlah Heights Pmy
BALGOWLAH HTS
Ten Cts Bareena Park
Capt Cook Panorama
Tania Park
Castle Rock Res
Castle Rock
Forestore Walking Track
Hughes Steps

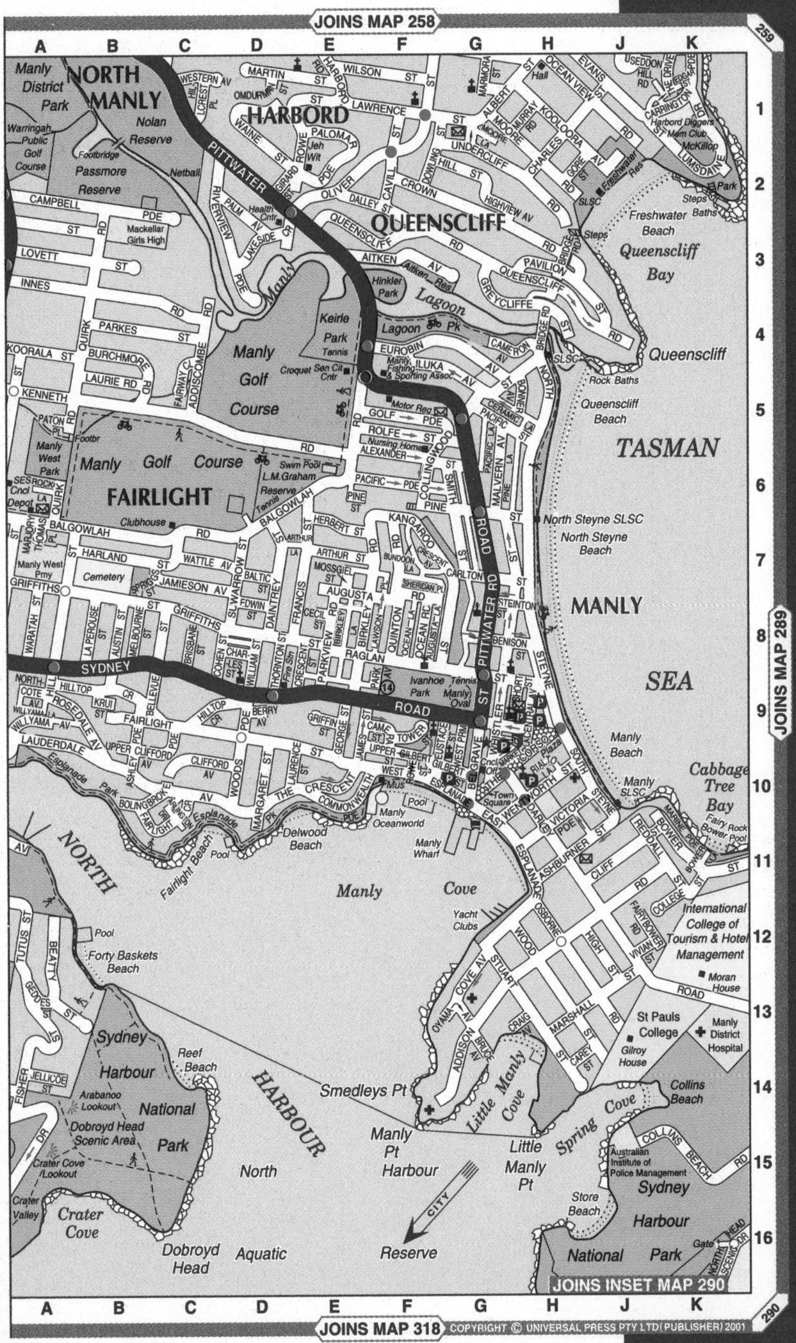
JOINS MAP 258
JOINS MAP 289
JOINS MAP 318
JOINS INSET MAP 290
259
290
NORTH MANLY
HARBORD
QUEENSCLIFF
FAIRLIGHT
MANLY
TASMAN
SEA
Manly District Park
Warringah Public Golf Course
Nolan Reserve
Passmore Reserve
Footbridge
Netball
Mackellar Girls High
Manly Golf Course
Keirle Park
Hinkler Park
Manly Lagoon
Lagoon Pk
Aitken Res
Croquet
Sen Cit Cntr
Manly Fishing & Sporting Assoc
Motor Reg
Nursing Home
Manly West Park
SES Cncl Depot
Swim Pool
L.M.Graham Reserve
Tennis
Clubhouse
Cemetery
Manly West Pmy
Fire Stn
Ivanhoe Park
Tennis
Manly Oval
Town Square
Cncl Offices
Mus
Pool
Manly Oceanworld
Manly Wharf
Delwood Beach
Fairlight Beach
Manly Cove
Yacht Clubs
Freshwater Beach
Queenscliff Bay
Queenscliff
Rock Baths
Queenscliff Beach
North Steyne SLSC
North Steyne Beach
Manly Beach
Manly SLSC
Cabbage Tree Bay
Fairy Bower Rock Pool
Harbord Diggers Mem Club
McKillop Park
Steps
Baths
Freshwater Res
SLSC
Hall
Health Cntr
Jeh Wit
International College of Tourism & Hotel Management
Moran House
St Pauls College
Gilroy House
Manly District Hospital
Collins Beach
Australian Institute of Police Management
Sydney Harbour National Park
Store Beach
Gate
Little Manly Cove
Little Manly Pt
Spring Cove
Smedleys Pt
Manly Pt Harbour
North Harbour Aquatic Reserve
CITY
Reef Beach
Forty Baskets Beach
Pool
Arabanoo Lookout
Dobroyd Head Scenic Area
Crater Cove Lookout
Crater Valley
Crater Cove
Dobroyd Head
PITTWATER RD
SYDNEY ROAD
BALGOWLAH RD
CAMPBELL PDE
LOVETT ST
INNES RD
PARKES ST
KOORALA ST
BURCHMORE RD
LAURIE RD
KENNETH RD
HARLAND ST
WATTLE AV
JAMIESON AV
GRIFFITHS ST
RAGLAN ST
AUGUSTA RD
FAIRLIGHT ST
LAUDERDALE AV
CLIFFORD AV
THE CRESCENT
WEST ESPLANADE
EAST ESPLANADE
WENTWORTH ST
CORSO
NORTH STEYNE
SOUTH STEYNE
ASHBURNER ST
CLIFF ST
DARLEY RD
VICTORIA PDE
MARSHALL ST
STUART ST
CARLTON ST
WILSON ST
LAWRENCE ST
MARTIN ST
OLIVER ST
CROWN RD
DALLEY ST
QUEENSCLIFF RD
AITKEN AV
EUROBIN AV
ILUKA AV
GOLF PDE
ROLFE ST
ALEXANDER ST
PACIFIC PDE
PINE ST
KANGAROO ST
HERBERT ST
ARTHUR ST
BELGRAVE ST
A B C D E F G H J K
1 2 3 4 5 6 7 8 9 10 11 12 13 14 15 16
COPYRIGHT © UNIVERSAL PRESS PTY LTD (PUBLISHER) 2001

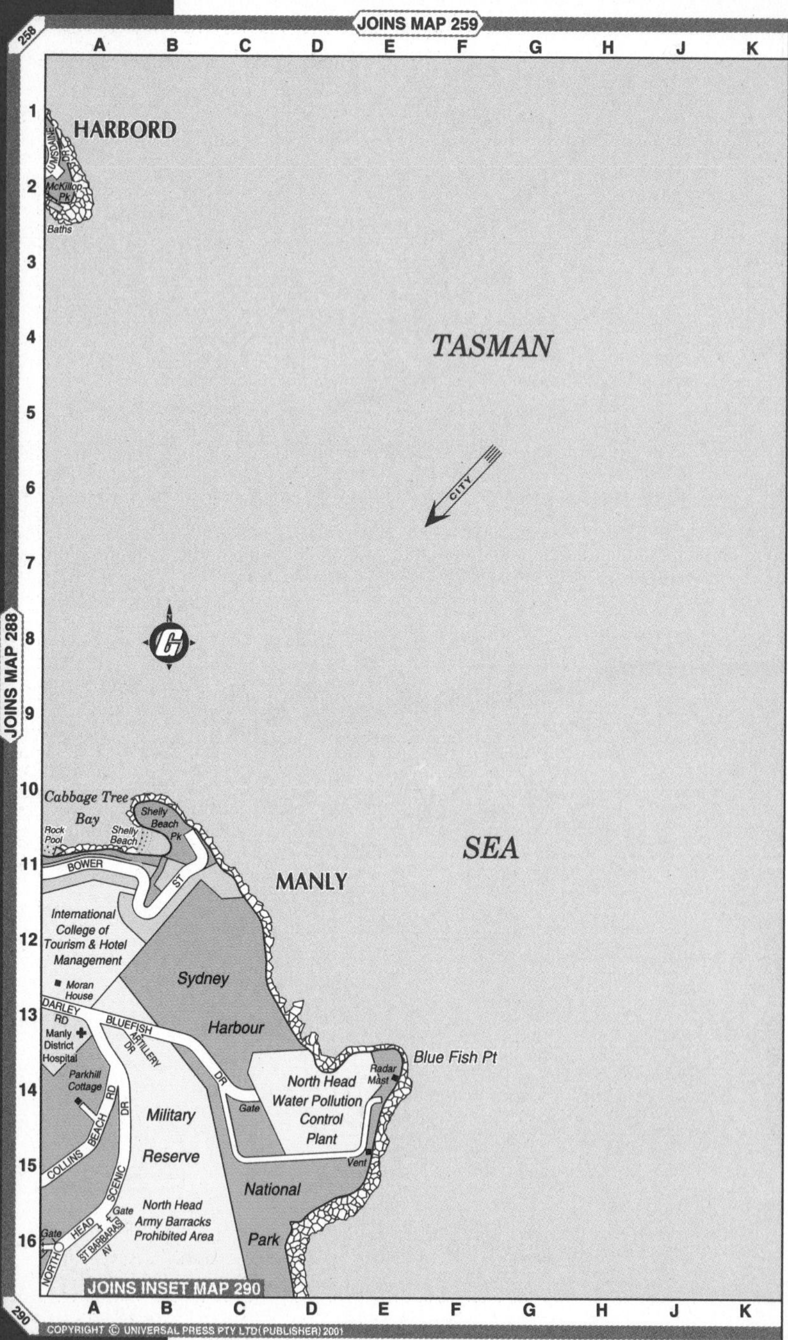

JOINS MAP 259
258
A B C D E F G H J K
1 2 3 4 5 6 7 8 9 10 11 12 13 14 15 16
HARBORD
LUNSDAINE
DR
McKillop Pk
Baths
TASMAN
SEA
CITY
N
JOINS MAP 288
Cabbage Tree Bay
Rock Pool
Shelly Beach
Shelly Beach Pk
BOWER
ST
MANLY
International College of Tourism & Hotel Management
Moran House
DARLEY RD
BLUEFISH
Manly District Hospital
ARTILLERY DR
Sydney Harbour
DR
Blue Fish Pt
Radar Mast
North Head Water Pollution Control Plant
Gate
Vent
Parkhill Cottage
BEACH RD
DR
Military Reserve
COLLINS
SCENIC
National Park
North Head Army Barracks Prohibited Area
Gate
Gate
HEAD
NORTH
ST BARBARAS AV
Park
JOINS INSET MAP 290
290

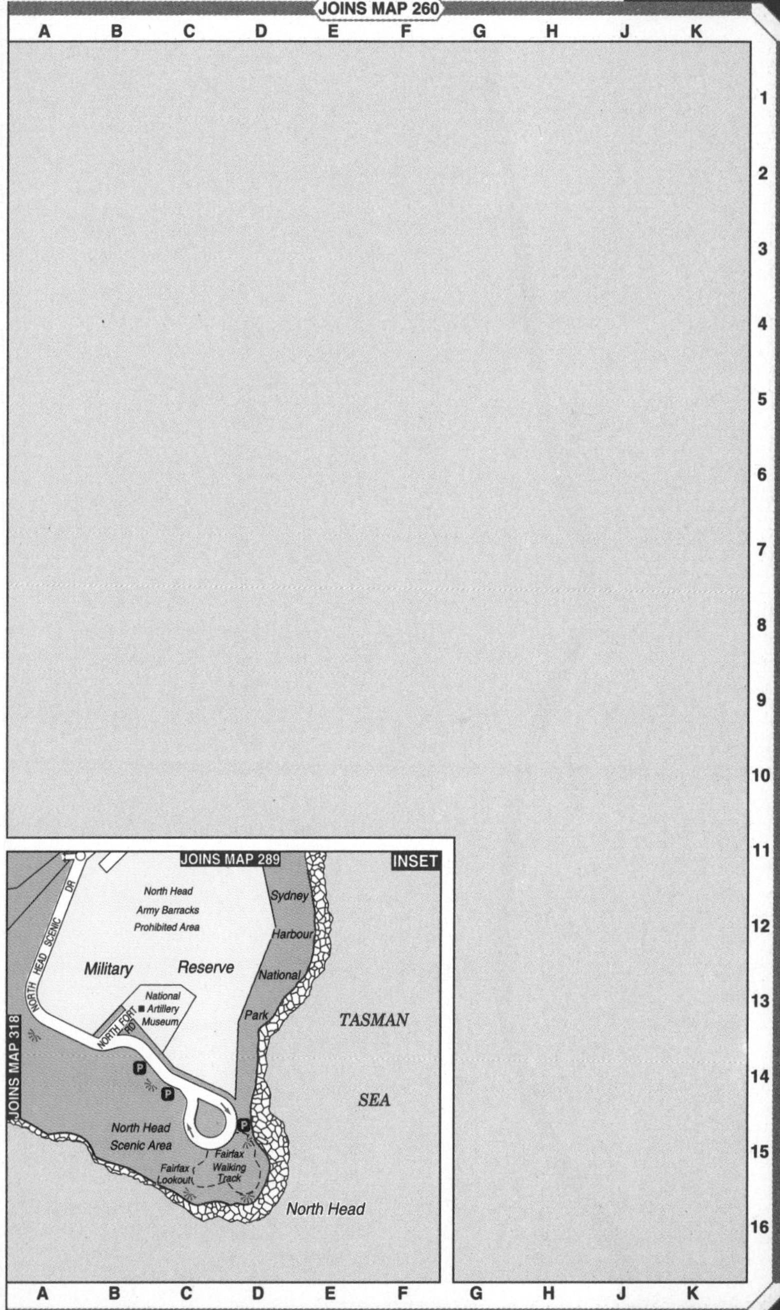
JOINS MAP 260
A B C D E F G H J K
1 2 3 4 5 6 7 8 9 10 11 12 13 14 15 16
JOINS MAP 289
INSET
North Head
Army Barracks
Prohibited Area
Military
Reserve
Sydney
Harbour
National
Park
NORTH HEAD SCENIC DR
National
Artillery
Museum
NORTH FORT RD
JOINS MAP 318
TASMAN
SEA
North Head
Scenic Area
Fairfax
Lookout
Fairfax
Walking
Track
North Head

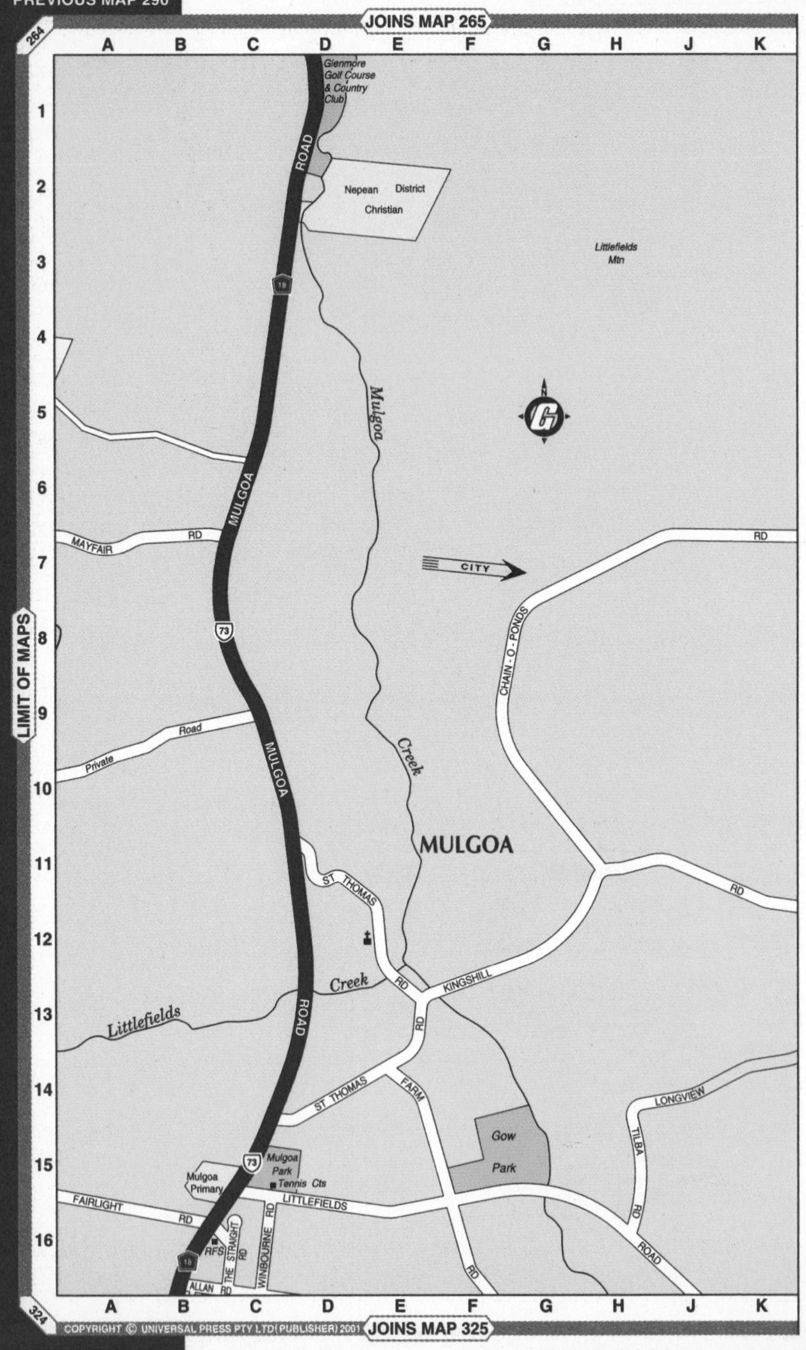
JOINS MAP 265
264
A B C D E F G H J K
1 2 3 4 5 6 7 8 9 10 11 12 13 14 15 16
LIMIT OF MAPS
Glenmore Golf Course & Country Club
ROAD
Nepean District Christian
Littlefields Mtn
Mulgoa
MULGOA
MAYFAIR RD
CITY
RD
CHAIN - O - PONDS
Private Road
MULGOA
Creek
MULGOA
ST THOMAS
RD
Creek
RD
KINGSHILL
Littlefields
ROAD
RD
ST THOMAS
FARM
LONGVIEW
TILBA
Gow Park
Mulgoa Park
Tennis Cts
Mulgoa Primary
FAIRLIGHT RD
LITTLEFIELDS
RD
WINBOURNE
THE STRAIGHT RD
RFS
ALLAN RD
RD
ROAD
73
19
324
JOINS MAP 325

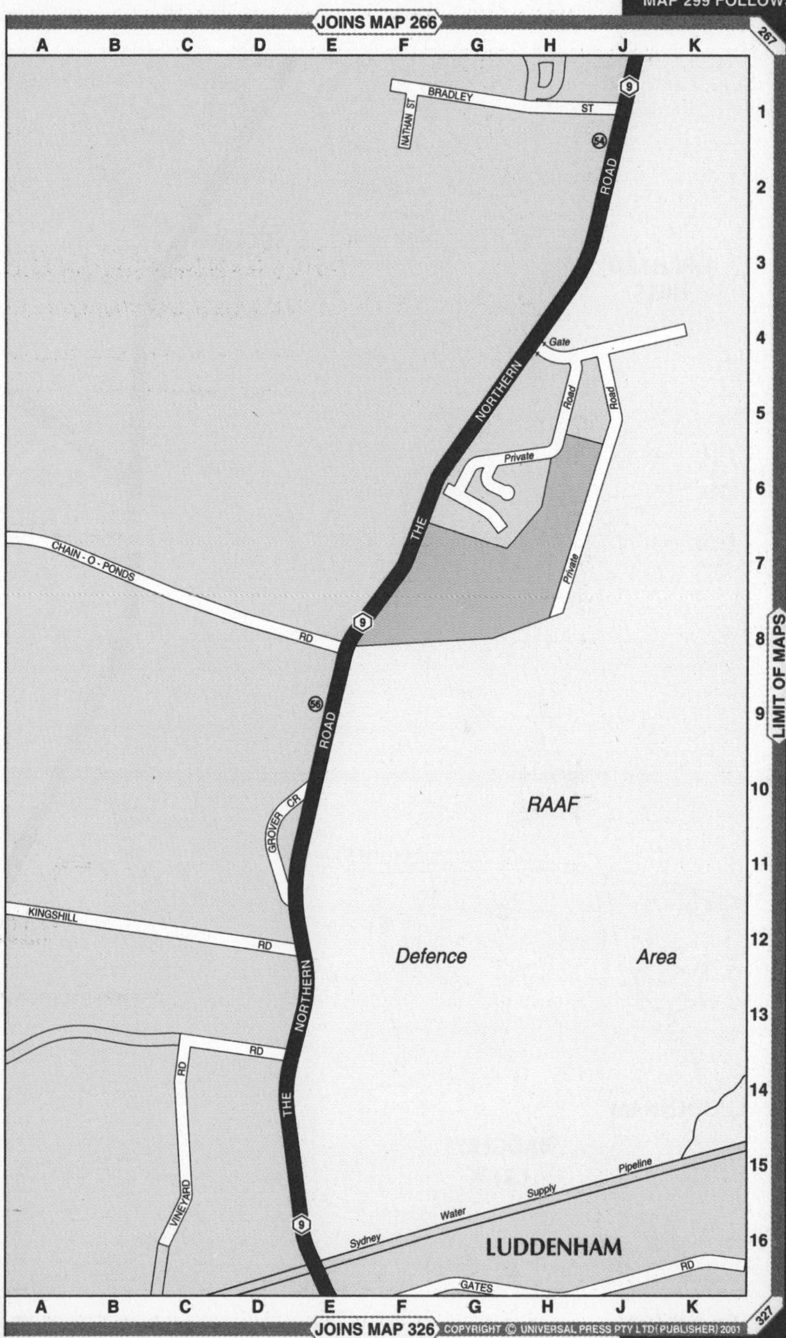
JOINS MAP 266
267
A B C D E F G H J K
1 2 3 4 5 6 7 8 9 10 11 12 13 14 15 16
BRADLEY ST
NATHAN ST
THE NORTHERN ROAD
9
54
56
Gate
Private Road
Road
Private
CHAIN - O - PONDS RD
GROVER CR
KINGSHILL RD
RD
RD
VINEYARD RD
RAAF
Defence Area
LIMIT OF MAPS
Sydney Water Supply Pipeline
LUDDENHAM
GATES RD
JOINS MAP 326
327

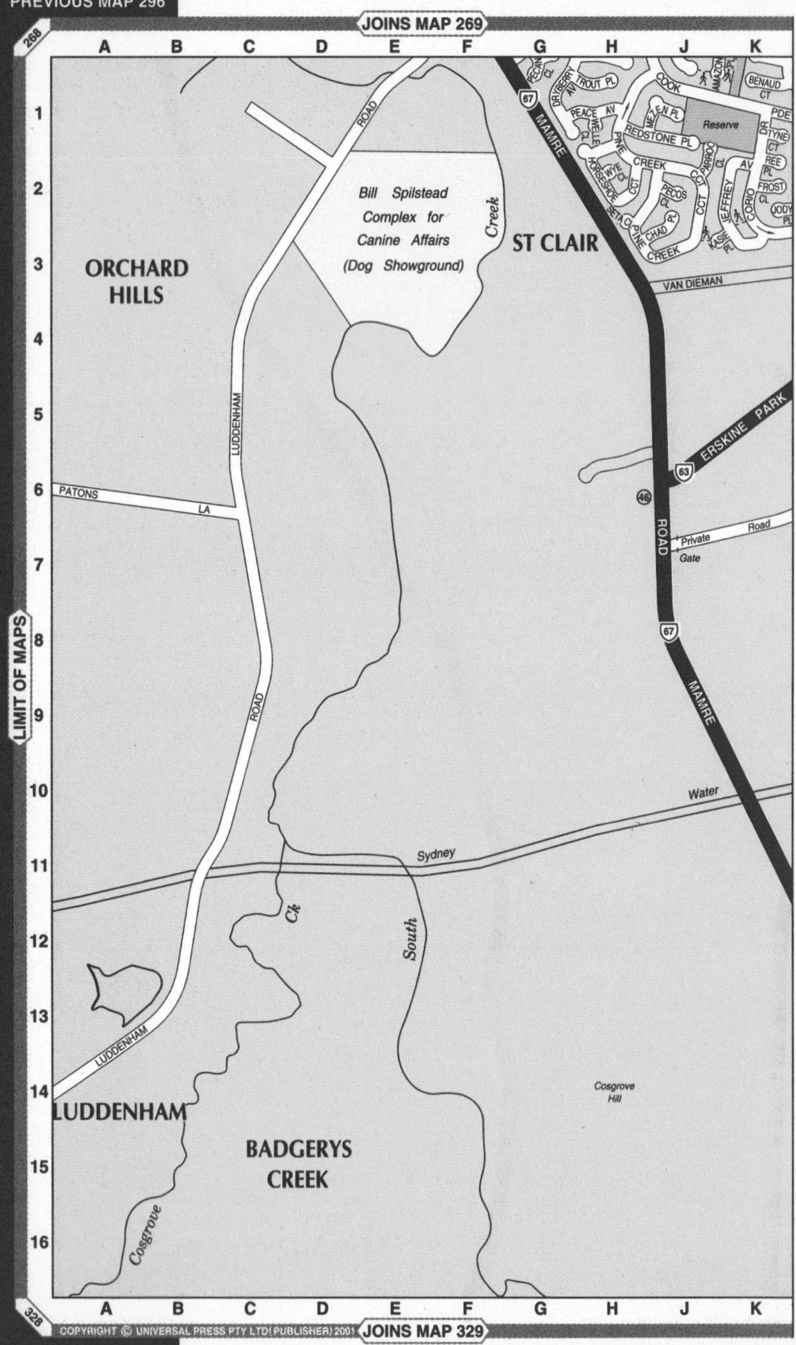
JOINS MAP 269
268
LIMIT OF MAPS
ORCHARD
HILLS
ST CLAIR
Bill Spilstead
Complex for
Canine Affairs
(Dog Showground)
Creek
LUDDENHAM
ROAD
PATONS
LA
MAMRE
ROAD
VAN DIEMAN
ERSKINE PARK
Private
Road
Gate
Water
Sydney
Ck
South
Cosgrove
Hill
LUDDENHAM
BADGERYS
CREEK
Cosgrove
COOK
TROUT PL
DRYBERRY
AV
PEACE
WELLEY
CL
REDSTONE PL
Reserve
PINE
CREEK
HORSESHOE
WYE
CCT
PARROO
CL
PECOS
CL
JEFFREY
AV
CORIO
CL
CHAD
PL
KASIE
PL
BENAUD
CT
PDE
TYNE
CT
REE
PL
FROST
CL
JODY
PL
328
JOINS MAP 329

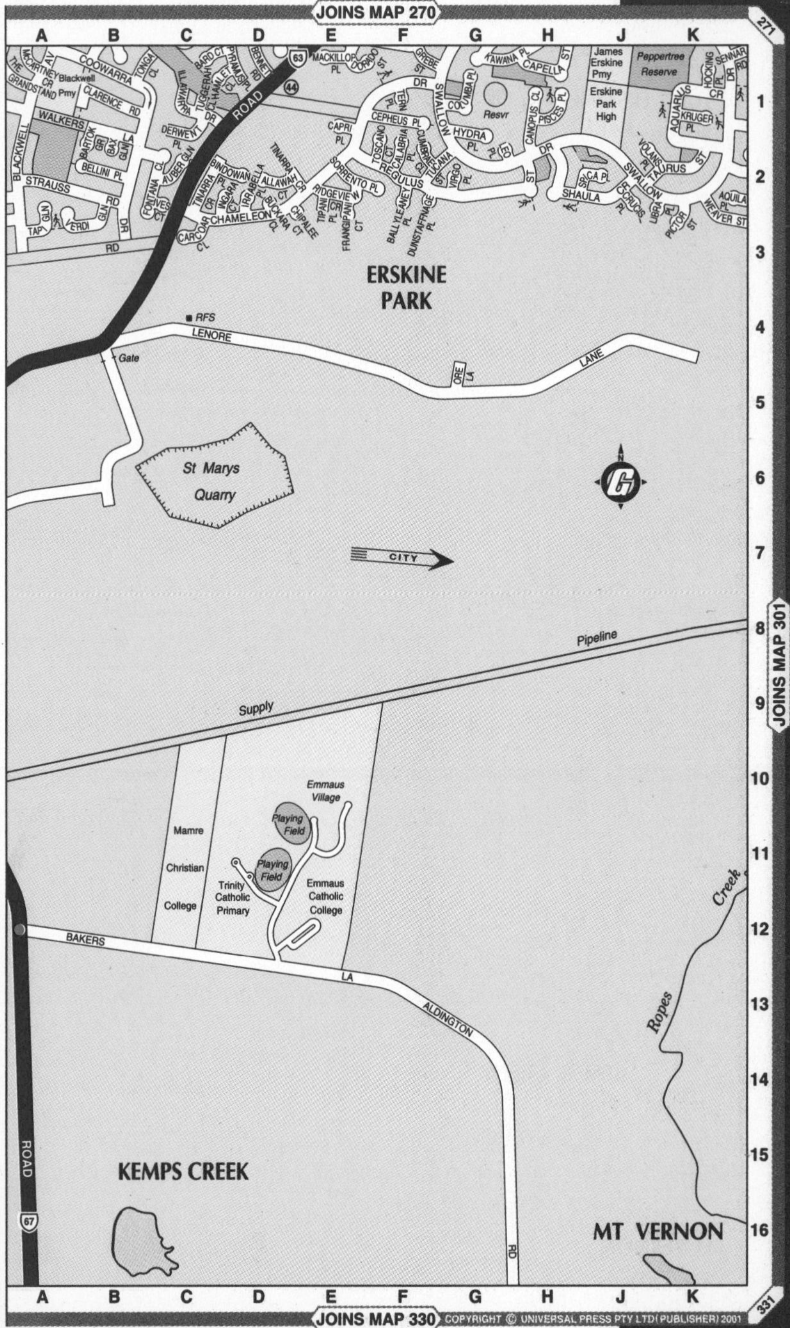

JOINS MAP 270
JOINS MAP 301
JOINS MAP 330
271
331
ERSKINE PARK
KEMPS CREEK
MT VERNON
St Marys Quarry
LENORE LANE
ORE LA
RFS
Gate
CITY
Supply Pipeline
Mamre Christian College
Trinity Catholic Primary
Emmaus Village
Emmaus Catholic College
Playing Field
Playing Field
BAKERS LA
ALDINGTON RD
ROAD
Ropes Creek
James Erskine Pmy
Erskine Park High
Peppertree Reserve
Resvr
Blackwell Pmy
COOWARRA
CLARENCE RD
WALKERS
BLACKWELL
STRAUSS RD
VERDI
TAP
CHAMELEON
CARCOAR CL
ERSKINE PARK RD
SWALLOW DR
REGULUS ST
SHAULA
HYDRA PL
CEPHEUS PL
SORRENTO PL
RIDGEVIEW
TAURUS ST
WEAVER ST
AQUILA PL
KRUGER PL
CAPELLA ST
KAWANA PL
MACKILLOP PL
DORADO ST
GREBE ST

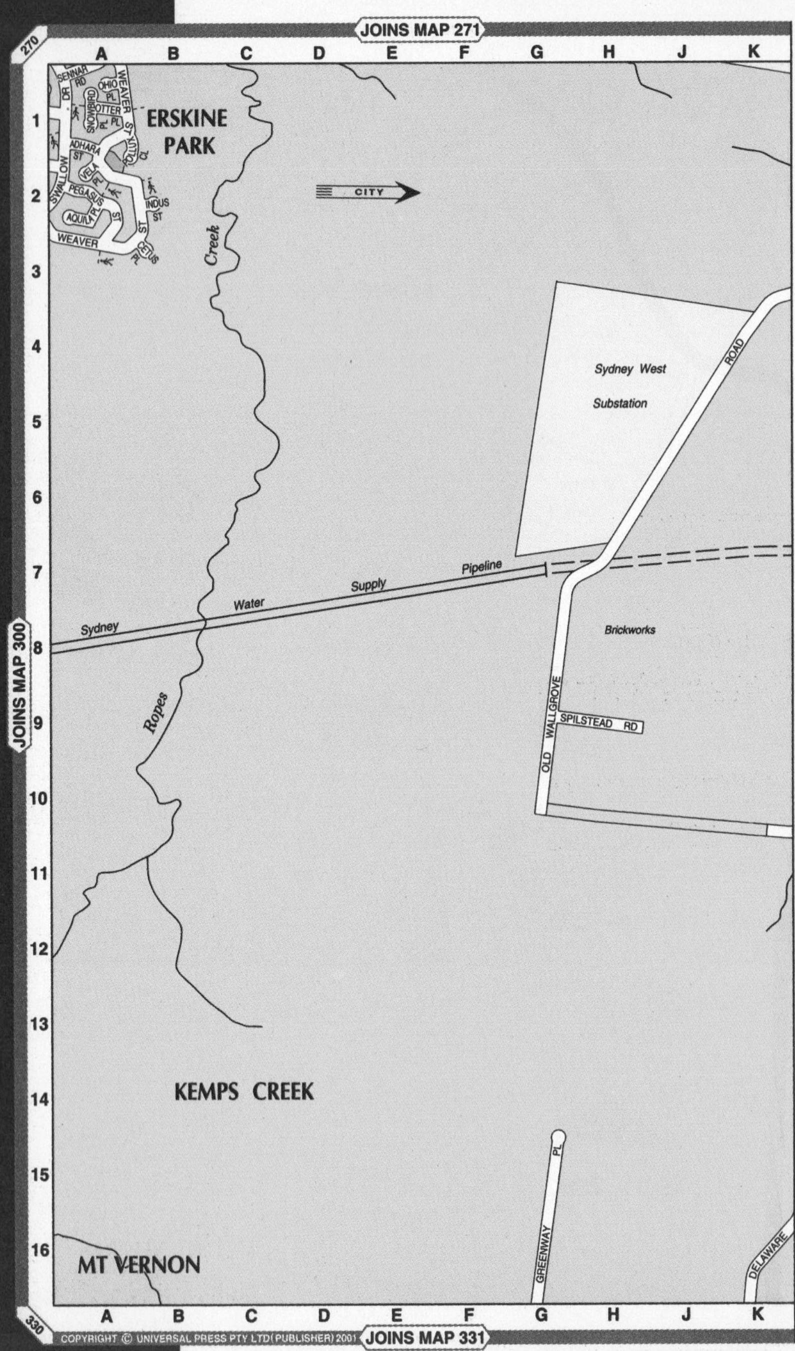

JOINS MAP 271
270
A B C D E F G H J K
1 2 3 4 5 6 7 8 9 10 11 12 13 14 15 16
ERSKINE PARK
SENNAR RD
OHIO PL
WEAVER ST
SNOWBIRD
OTTER PL
ADHARA ST
VELA PL
SWALLOW DR
PEGASUS ST
AQUILA PL
INDUS ST
WEAVER
CETUS PL
CITY
Creek
Ropes
Sydney Water Supply Pipeline
Sydney West Substation
ROAD
Brickworks
OLD WALLGROVE
SPILSTEAD RD
KEMPS CREEK
GREENWAY PL
DELAWARE
MT VERNON
JOINS MAP 300
330
JOINS MAP 331

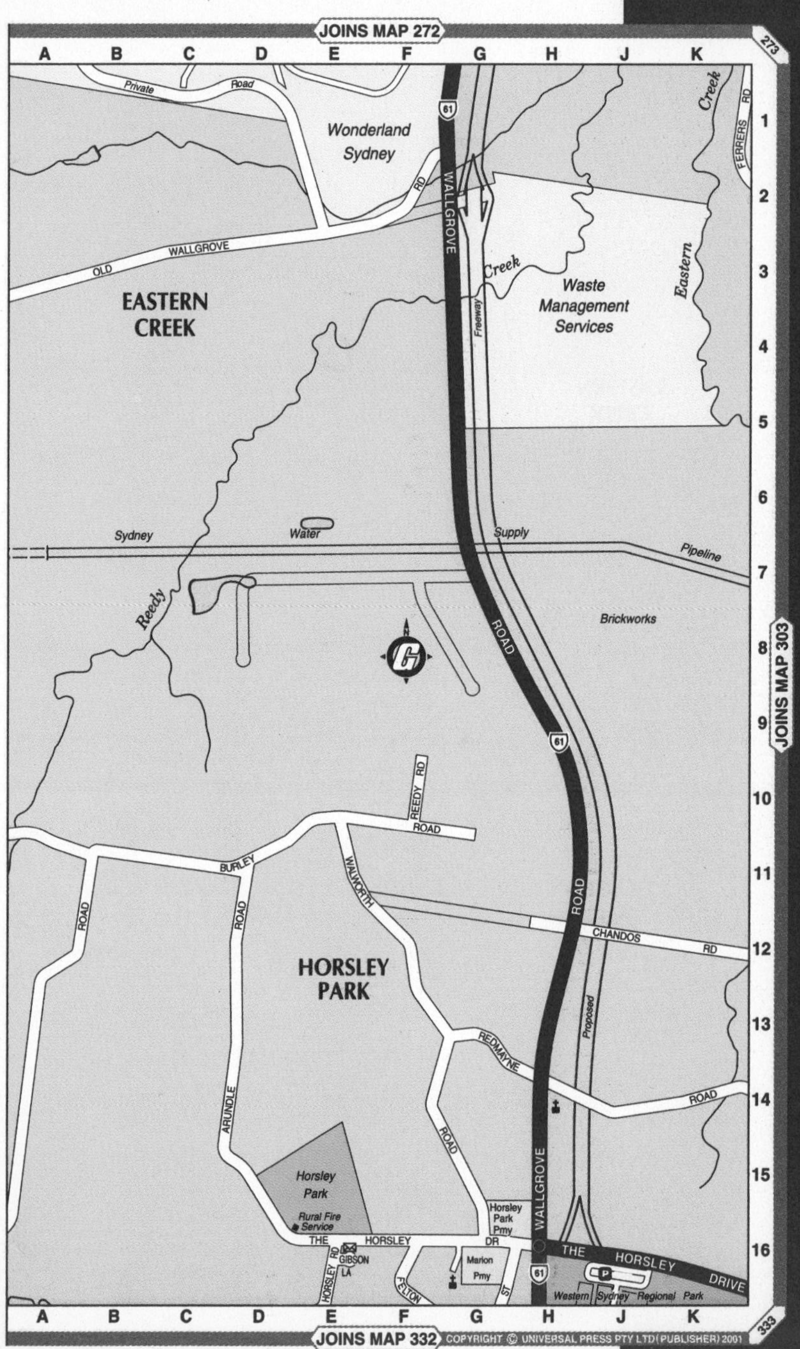

JOINS MAP 272
273
A B C D E F G H J K
1 2 3 4 5 6 7 8 9 10 11 12 13 14 15 16
Private Road
Wonderland Sydney
RD
WALLGROVE
61
FERRERS RD
Creek
OLD WALLGROVE
EASTERN CREEK
Creek
Freeway
Waste Management Services
Eastern
Sydney
Water
Supply
Pipeline
Reedy
Brickworks
ROAD
JOINS MAP 303
REEDY RD
ROAD
BURLEY
ROAD
ROAD
WALWORTH
ROAD
CHANDOS
RD
HORSLEY PARK
Proposed
REDMAYNE
ROAD
ARUNDLE
ROAD
Horsley Park
Rural Fire Service
WALLGROVE
Horsley Park Pmy
THE HORSLEY DR
GIBSON LA
HORSLEY RD
FELTON
Marion Pmy
ST
THE HORSLEY DRIVE
Western Sydney Regional Park
A B C D E F G H J K
JOINS MAP 332
333

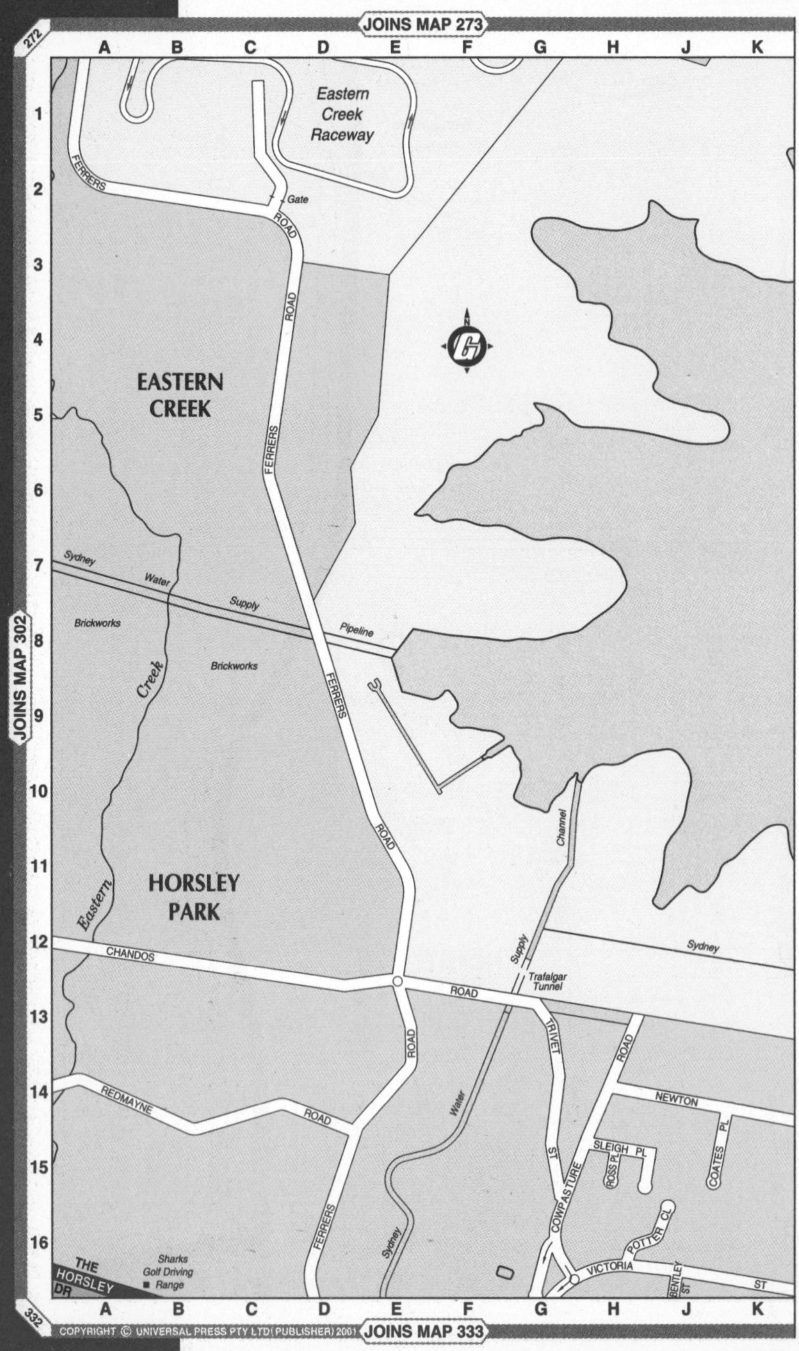
JOINS MAP 273
272
A B C D E F G H J K
1 2 3 4 5 6 7 8 9 10 11 12 13 14 15 16
Eastern
Creek
Raceway
FERRERS
Gate
ROAD
EASTERN
CREEK
Sydney
Water
Supply
Pipeline
Brickworks
Brickworks
Creek
Eastern
Channel
HORSLEY
PARK
CHANDOS
ROAD
Supply
Trafalgar
Tunnel
Sydney
TRIVET
ST
NEWTON
SLEIGH PL
ROSS PL
COATES PL
REDMAYNE
Water
COWPASTURE
POTTER CL
VICTORIA
BENTLEY ST
Sydney
Sharks
Golf Driving
Range
THE
HORSLEY
DR
JOINS MAP 302
332
JOINS MAP 333

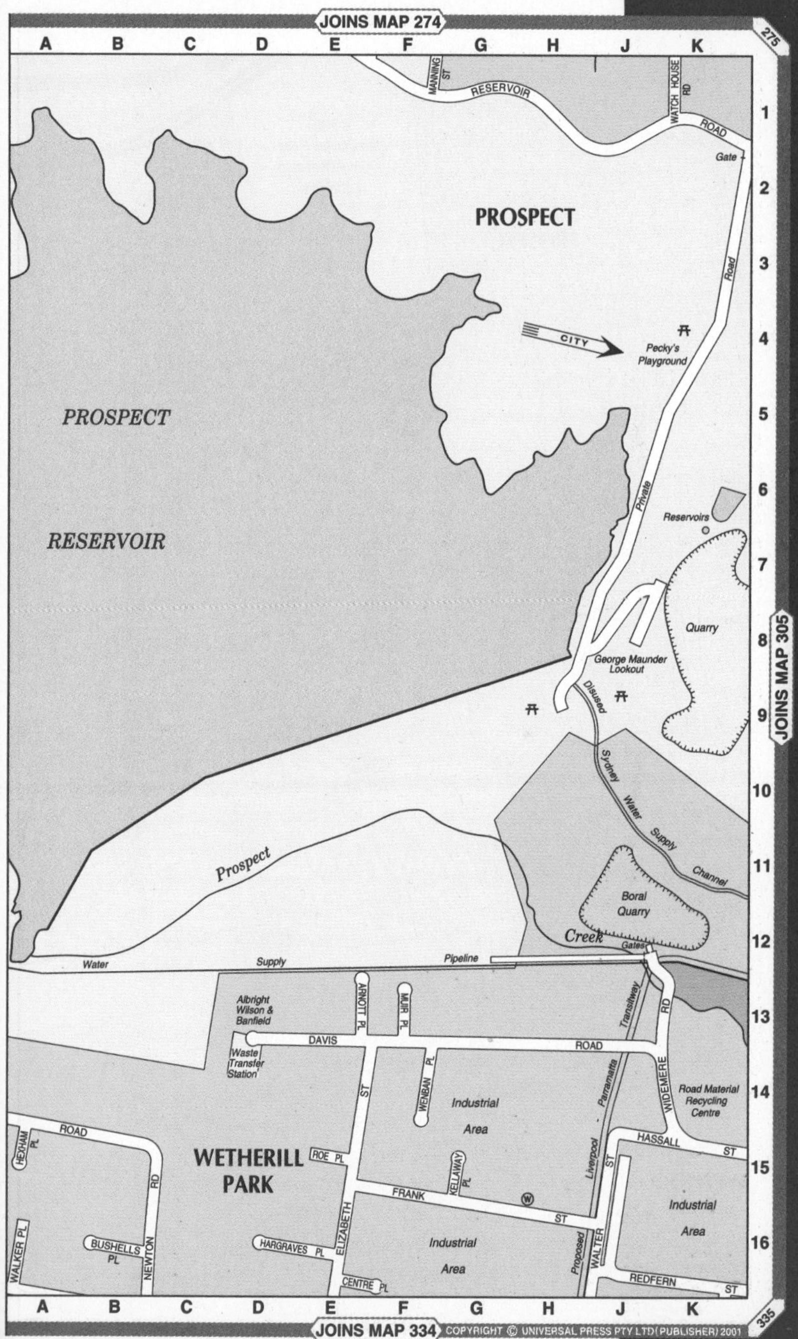
JOINS MAP 274
275
A
B
C
D
E
F
G
H
J
K
MANNING ST
RESERVOIR
WATCH HOUSE RD
ROAD
Gate
PROSPECT
Road
CITY
Pecky's Playground
PROSPECT
RESERVOIR
Private
Reservoirs
Quarry
George Maunder Lookout
Disused
Sydney
Water
Supply
Channel
JOINS MAP 305
Prospect
Boral Quarry
Creek
Gates
Water
Supply
Pipeline
Albright Wilson & Banfield
Waste Transfer Station
ARNOTT PL
MUIR PL
DAVIS
ROAD
Transitway
RD
WIDEMERE
Parramatta
Road Material Recycling Centre
ST
WENBAN PL
Industrial Area
HEXHAM PL
ROAD
WETHERILL PARK
ROE PL
KELLAWAY PL
HASSALL
ST
RD
FRANK
ST
Liverpool
ST
Industrial Area
WALKER PL
BUSHELLS PL
NEWTON
HARGRAVES PL
ELIZABETH
Industrial Area
Proposed
WALTER
REDFERN
ST
CENTRE PL
1
2
3
4
5
6
7
8
9
10
11
12
13
14
15
16
JOINS MAP 334
335

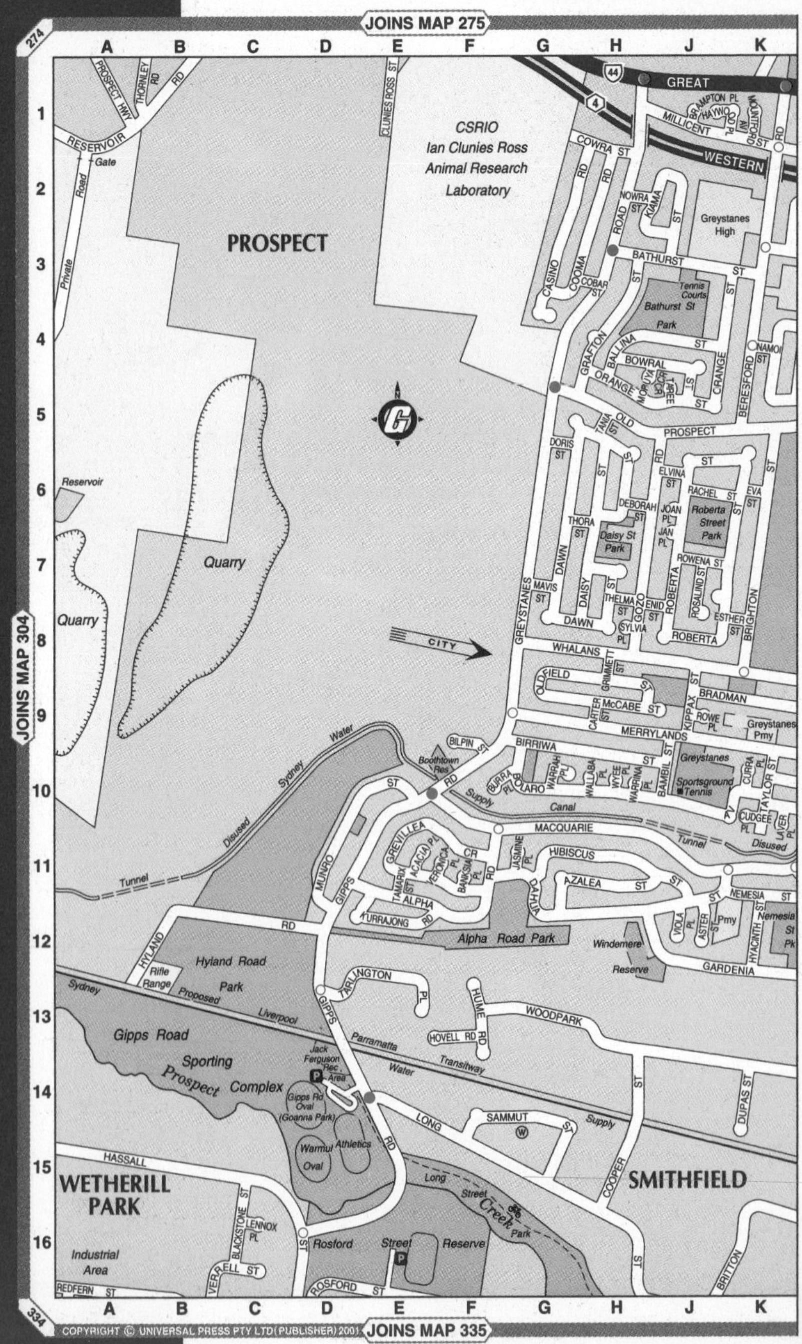
JOINS MAP 275
JOINS MAP 304
JOINS MAP 335
274
334
PROSPECT
CSRIO
Ian Clunies Ross
Animal Research
Laboratory
Quarry
Quarry
Reservoir
CITY
SMITHFIELD
WETHERILL PARK
Industrial Area
GREAT WESTERN
Greystanes High
Bathurst St Park
Tennis Courts
Daisy St Park
Roberta Street Park
Greystanes Sportsground
Tennis
Greystanes Pmy
Alpha Road Park
Windemere Reserve
Nemesia St Pk
Pmy
Hyland Road Park
Rifle Range
Gipps Road Sporting Complex
Prospect
Jack Ferguson Rec. Area
Gipps Rd Oval (Goanna Park)
Warmul Oval
Athletics
Rosford Street Reserve
Long Street Creek Park
Sydney Water
Disused Tunnel
Supply Canal
Proposed Liverpool Parramatta Transitway
Boothtown Res
GREYSTANES RD
PROSPECT HWY
RESERVOIR
Private Road
Gate
CLUNIES ROSS ST
HYLAND RD
GIPPS RD
LONG ST
MACQUARIE
HIBISCUS
WOODPARK
SAMMUT ST
COOPER ST
HASSALL
BLACKSTONE ST
LENNOX PL
VERRELL ST
REDFERN ST
ROSFORD ST
BRITTON
DUPAS ST
HUME RD
HOVELL RD
TARLINGTON PL
MUNRO
GREVILLEA
ACACIA PL
VERONICA PL
BANKSIA PL
TAMARIX
ALPHA
KURRAJONG RD
JASMINE PL
DAHLIA
AZALEA ST
NEMESIA ST
VIOLA PL
ASTER PL
HYACINTH ST
GARDENIA
WHALANS
OLDFIELD
GRIMMETT ST
McCABE ST
CARTER ST
KIPPAX ST
BRADMAN
ROWE PL
MERRYLANDS
BIRRIWA
BURRA PL
BOLARO
WARRAH PL
WALLABA PL
WYEE PL
WARRINA PL
BAMBIL ST
CURRA PL
TAYLOR ST
CUDGEE PL
LAVER PL
BILPIN ST
DAWN
DAISY
MAVIS ST
THORA ST
THELMA ST
SYLVIA PL
GOZO
ENID ST
ROBERTA
ROSALIND ST
ESTHER ST
BRIGHTON
ROWENA ST
JOAN PL
JAN PL
DEBORAH ST
ELVINA ST
RACHEL ST
EVA ST
DORIS ST
TANIA ST
OLD PROSPECT
ORANGE
GRAFTON
BALLINA
BOWRAL
MOPOIVA
ANCKOR
TAREE
ORANGE
BERESFORD
NAMOI ST
CASINO
COOMA
COBAR ST
BATHURST ST
NOWRA ST
KIAMA
COWRA ST
MILLICENT
BRAMPTON PL
HAYWOOD PL
MOUNTFORD AV
THORNLEY RD

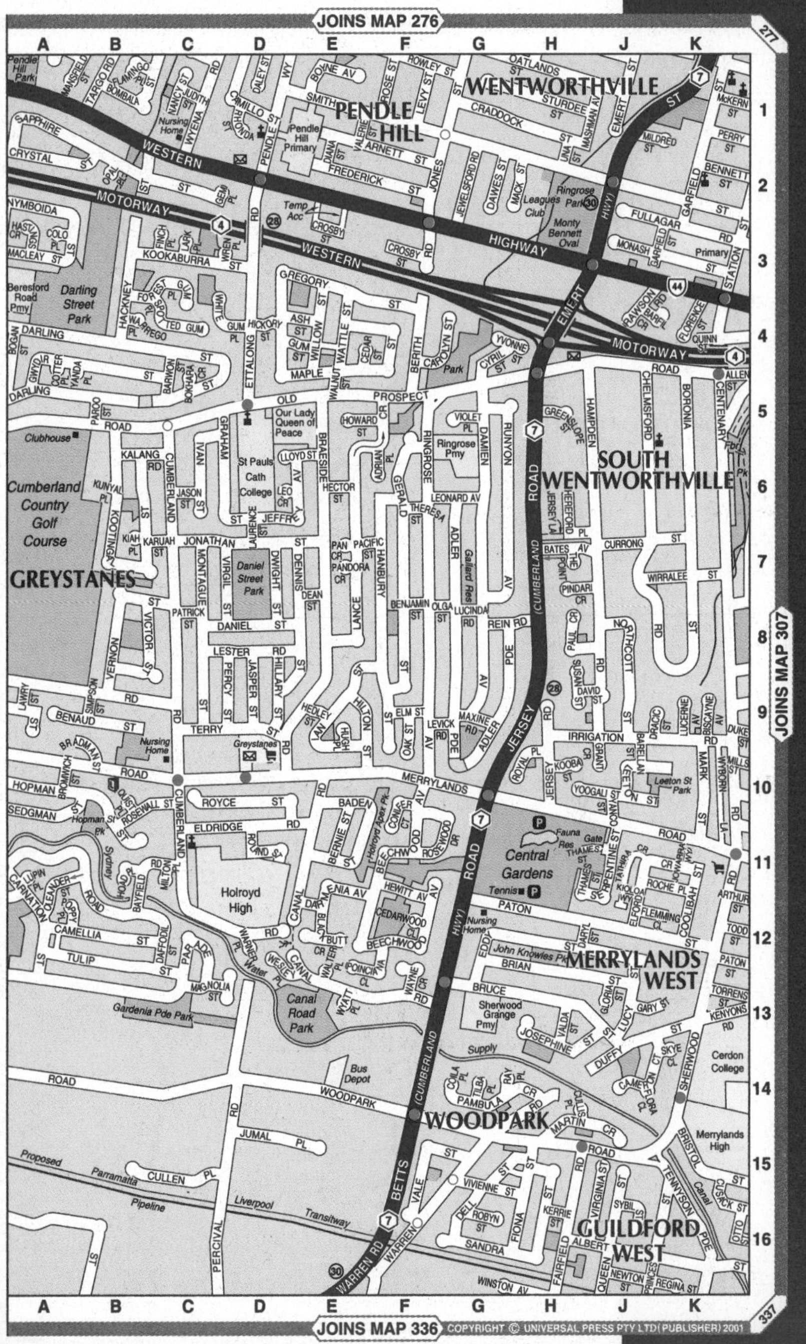
JOINS MAP 276
JOINS MAP 307
JOINS MAP 336
277
337
A B C D E F G H J K
1 2 3 4 5 6 7 8 9 10 11 12 13 14 15 16
WENTWORTHVILLE
PENDLE HILL
SOUTH WENTWORTHVILLE
GREYSTANES
MERRYLANDS WEST
WOODPARK
GUILDFORD WEST
WESTERN MOTORWAY
WESTERN HIGHWAY
CUMBERLAND HWY
OLD PROSPECT ROAD
MERRYLANDS ROAD
WOODPARK ROAD
JERSEY ROAD
BETTS RD
WARREN RD
CUMBERLAND RD
Pendle Hill Park
Pendle Hill Primary
Nursing Home
Temp Acc
Leagues Club
Ringrose Park
Monty Bennett Oval
Primary
Beresford Road Pmy
Darling Street Park
Park
Clubhouse
Cumberland Country Golf Course
Our Lady Queen of Peace
St Pauls Cath College
Ringrose Pmy
Daniel Street Park
Gallard Res
Greystanes
Leeton St Park
Hopman St Pk
Holroyd High
Holroyd Apex Pk
Central Gardens
Fauna Res
Tennis
Nursing Home
John Knowles Pk
Sherwood Grange Pmy
Gardenia Pde Park
Canal Road Park
Bus Depot
Cerdon College
Merrylands High
Proposed Parramatta Pipeline
Liverpool Transitway
Sydney Water
Supply
Canal
FREDERICK ST
CRADDOCK ST
OATLANDS ST
STURDEE ST
KOOKABURRA ST
DARLING ST
GREGORY ST
MAPLE ST
KALANG RD
JONATHAN ST
DANIEL ST
TERRY RD
HOPMAN ST
SEDGMAN ST
ROYCE ST
ELDRIDGE RD
CAMELLIA ST
TULIP ST
PATON ST
BRIAN ST
BRUCE ST
JOSEPHINE ST
IRRIGATION RD
CURRONG ST
NORTHCOTT RD
BENNETT ST
FULLAGAR RD
MONASH RD
JUMAL PL
CULLEN PL
VIVIENNE ST
SANDRA ST
WINSTON AV

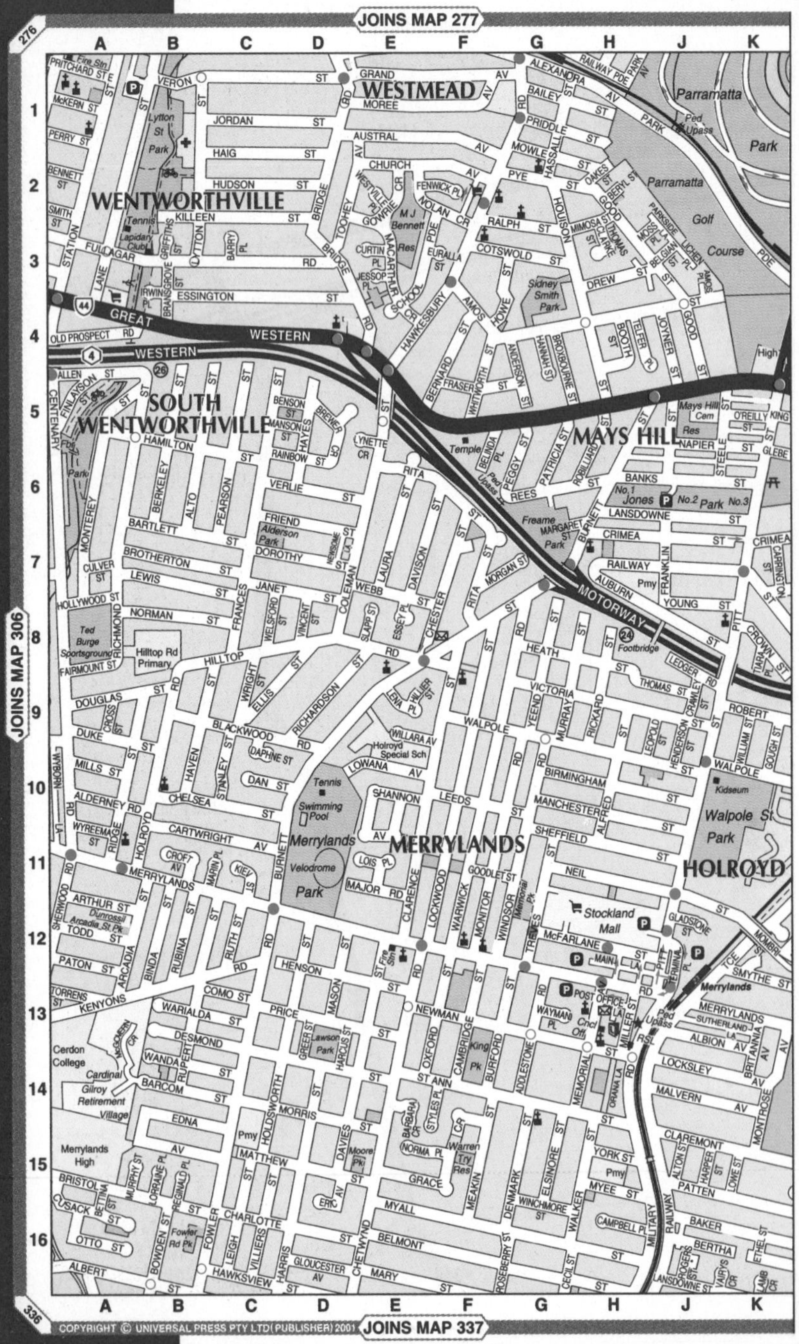

JOINS MAP 277
JOINS MAP 306
JOINS MAP 337
276
336
A B C D E F G H J K
1 2 3 4 5 6 7 8 9 10 11 12 13 14 15 16
WESTMEAD
WENTWORTHVILLE
SOUTH WENTWORTHVILLE
MAYS HILL
MERRYLANDS
HOLROYD
Parramatta Park
Parramatta Golf Course
Lytton St Park
Tennis
Lapidary Club
Sidney Smith Park
M J Bennett Res
Mays Hill Cem
Res
Temple
Jones Park No.1 No.2 No.3
Freame Park
Alderson Park
Ted Burge Sportsground
Hilltop Rd Primary
Holroyd Special Sch
Merrylands Velodrome Park
Tennis
Swimming Pool
Kidseum
Walpole St Park
Stockland Mall
Post Office
Cncl Off
Merrylands
RSL
Ped Upass
Footbridge
Dunrossil Arcadia St Pk
Cerdon College
Cardinal Gilroy Retirement Village
Merrylands High
Lawson Park
King Pk
Warren Try Res
Moore Pk
Fowler Rd Pk
Memorial Pk
Pmy
Fire Stn
GREAT WESTERN
WESTERN
MOTORWAY
44
4
26
24
GRAND AV
ALEXANDRA AV
RAILWAY PDE
PARK AV
BAILEY ST
MOREE
JORDAN ST
HAIG ST
HUDSON ST
AUSTRAL AV
CHURCH
PRIDDLE ST
MOWLE ST
HASSALL
PYE ST
OAKES
BERYL ST
KILLEEN ST
FULLAGAR RD
ESSINGTON ST
OLD PROSPECT RD
COTSWOLD ST
RALPH ST
DREW ST
HAMILTON ST
RAINBOW ST
VERLIE ST
BARTLETT ST
BROTHERTON ST
LEWIS ST
NORMAN ST
HILLTOP RD
DOUGLAS ST
DUKE ST
MILLS ST
ALDERNEY RD
CHELSEA ST
CARTWRIGHT AV
MERRYLANDS RD
ARTHUR ST
TODD ST
PATON ST
KENYONS RD
WARIALDA ST
DESMOND ST
WANDA
BARCOM
EDNA
BRISTOL
CUSACK
OTTO ST
ALBERT
HAWKSVIEW ST
GLOUCESTER AV
MARY ST
BELMONT ST
MYALL
CHARLOTTE ST
GRACE
MATTHEW
MORRIS
HENSON ST
PRICE
NEWMAN
ST ANN
WINCHMORE ST
MYEE ST
YORK ST
CLAREMONT
PATTEN
MALVERN AV
LOCKSLEY
ALBION AV
MERRYLANDS
SUTHERLAND
SMYTHE ST
McFARLANE
NEIL
SHEFFIELD
MANCHESTER
BIRMINGHAM
WALPOLE ST
VICTORIA
HEATH
THOMAS ST
ROBERT
LEDGER RD
CROWN ST
YOUNG ST
RAILWAY
AUBURN
CRIMEA ST
LANSDOWNE ST
BANKS
REES
NAPIER
O'REILLY ST
KING
GLEBE
BURNETT
RITA ST
WEBB ST
JANET
DOROTHY
FRIEND
BENSON
MANSON
LYNETTE CR
BLACKWOOD RD
LOWANA AV
SHANNON
LEEDS
MAJOR RD
LOIS PL
CROFT AV
KIEV ST
DAN ST
DAPHNE ST
WILLARA AV
HILLIER ST
LENA PL
GOODLET ST
RICHARDSON
CHESTER
LAURA
DAVISON
COLEMAN
FRANCES
BERKELEY
ALTO
PEARSON
MONTEREY
CENTENARY
FINLAYSON
RICHMOND
HOLROYD
RIDGE
WYREEMA ST
WYBORN LA
SHERWOOD RD
ARCADIA
BINDA
RUBINA
RUTH ST
BURNETT
CLARENCE
LOCKWOOD
WARWICK
MONITOR
WINDSOR
TREVES
ADDLESTONE
OXFORD
CAMBRIDGE
BURFORD
MEAKIN
DENMARK
ELSINORE
WALKER
MILITARY
HOLDSWORTH
DAVIES
HARRIS
VILLIERS
LEIGH
FOWLER
BOWDEN ST
MEMORIAL
MILLER ST
TERMINAL PL
GLADSTONE ST
MOMBRI
TCE
BRITANNIA
MONTROSE
ALTON ST
HARPER ST
LOWE ST
BAKER
BERTHA
ETHEL ST
LAMB
ROGERS
LANSDOWNE ST
CAMPBELL PL
ROSEBERRY ST
CECIL ST
CHETWYND
WELSFORD
VINCENT
SLAPP ST
ESSEY PL
HAWKESBURY
BERNARD
FRASER
WHITWORTH
BELINDA PL
PEGGY
PATRICIA ST
ROBILLIARD
ANDERSON
HANNAH ST
BROXBOURNE ST
BOOTH
TELFER
JOYNER
GOOD
HOUISON
MIMOSA ST
CLARKE
THOMAS
BELGIAN
LICHEN
AMOS
HOWE
MACARTHUR
SCHOOL
TOOHEY
BRIDGE
EURALLA
NOLAN CR
GOWRIE
CURTIN PL
JESSOP PL
FENWICK PL
WESTVILLE PL
LYTTON
GRIFFITHS
BARRY PL
STATION
LANE
IRWIN PL
BRANSGROVE
PRITCHARD ST
McKERN ST
PERRY ST
BENNETT ST
SMITH ST
VERON
ALLEN ST
CULVER ST
HOLLYWOOD ST
FAIRMOUNT ST
CROSS ST
MILLS ST
TORRENS ST
COMO ST
GREER ST
HARCUS ST
STYLES PL
BARBARA CR
NORMA PL
ERIC AV
YEEND
MURRAY
RICKARD
LEOPOLD
HENDERSON
CRAWLEY
WILLIAM ST
GOUGH
STEELE
FRANKLIN
PITT
CARRINGTON
TARA PL
MORGAN ST
MARGARET ST
SUTHERLAND LA
ORANA LA
WAYMAN PL
MAIN
HIGH

JOINS MAP 278

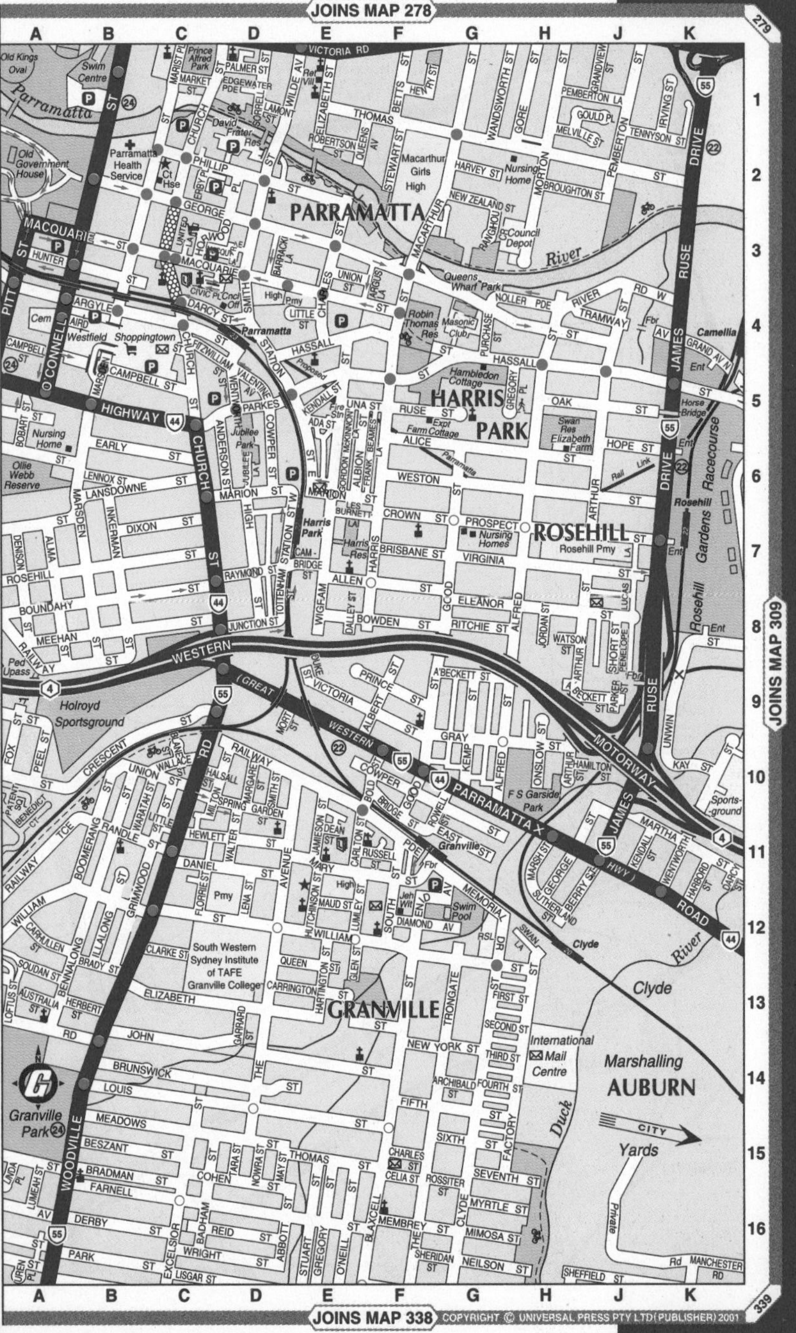

JOINS MAP 309

JOINS MAP 338

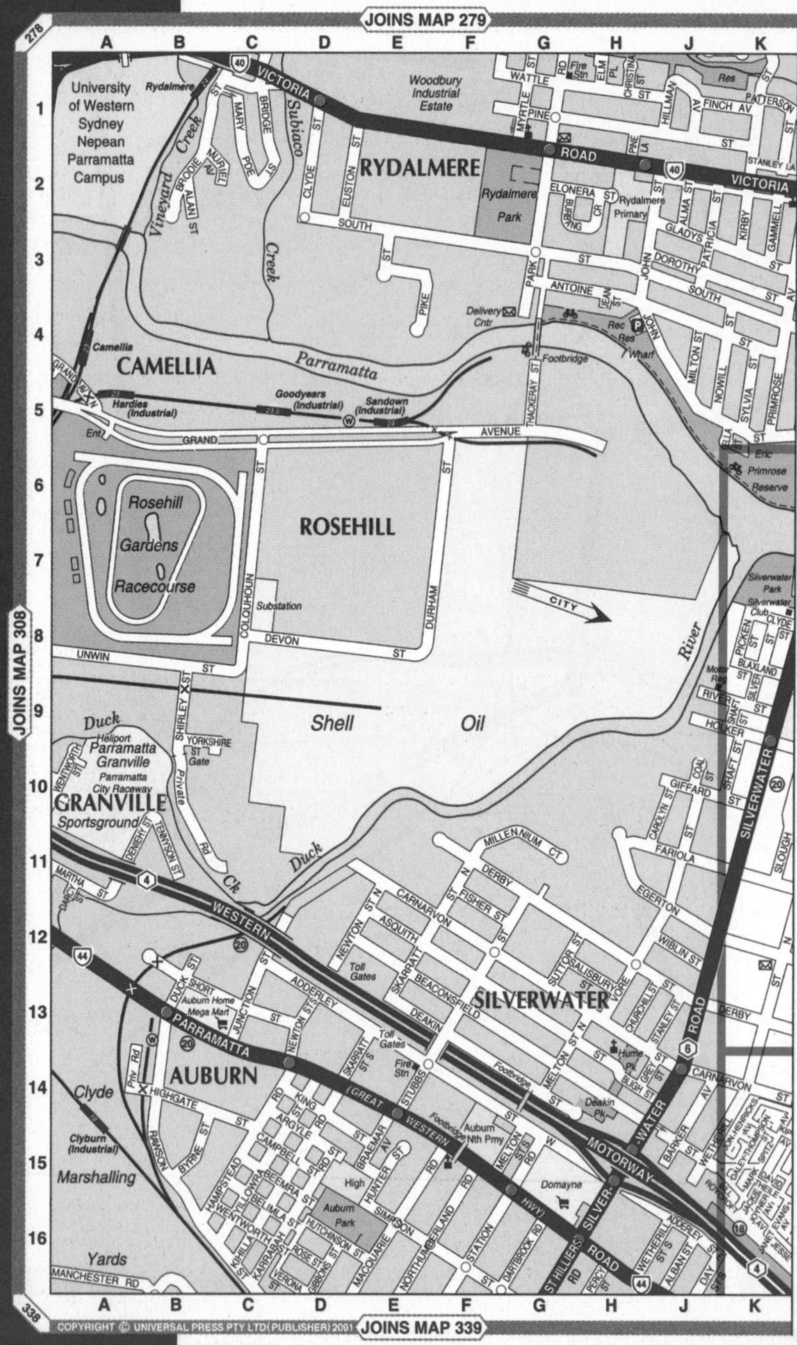
JOINS MAP 279
University of Western Sydney Nepean Parramatta Campus
Woodbury Industrial Estate
RYDALMERE
Rydalmere Park
Rydalmere Primary
CAMELLIA
Hardies (Industrial)
Goodyears (Industrial)
Sandown (Industrial)
Eric Primrose Reserve
Rosehill Gardens Racecourse
ROSEHILL
Substation
Shell Oil
Parramatta River
Duck Ck
Parramatta Granville City Raceway
GRANVILLE
Sportsground
Silverwater Park
Silverwater Club
SILVERWATER
AUBURN
Auburn Home Mega Mart
Auburn Park
Auburn Nth Pmy
Domayne
Clyburn (Industrial)
Marshalling Yards
VICTORIA ROAD
GRAND AVENUE
WESTERN MOTORWAY
PARRAMATTA ROAD
SILVERWATER ROAD
JOINS MAP 308
JOINS MAP 339

JOINS MAP 280

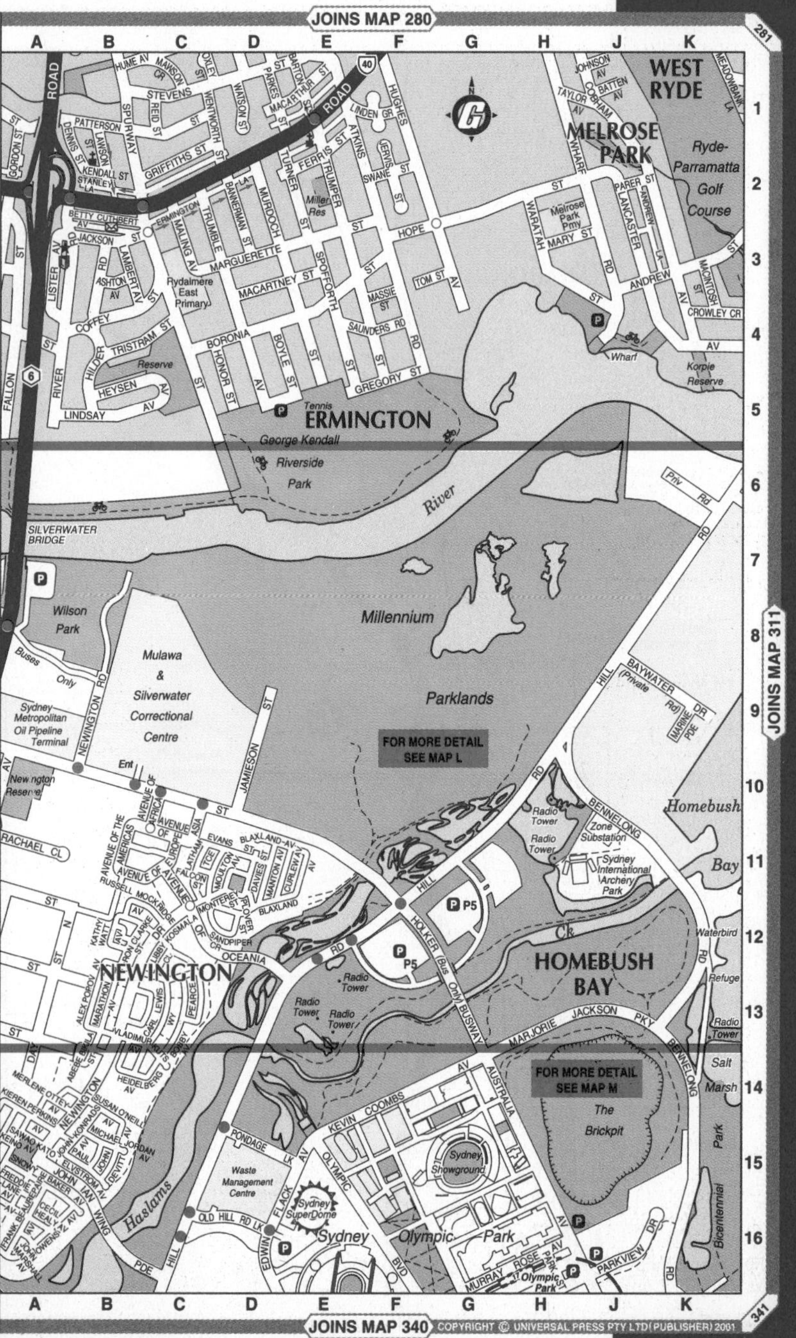

JOINS MAP 311

JOINS MAP 340

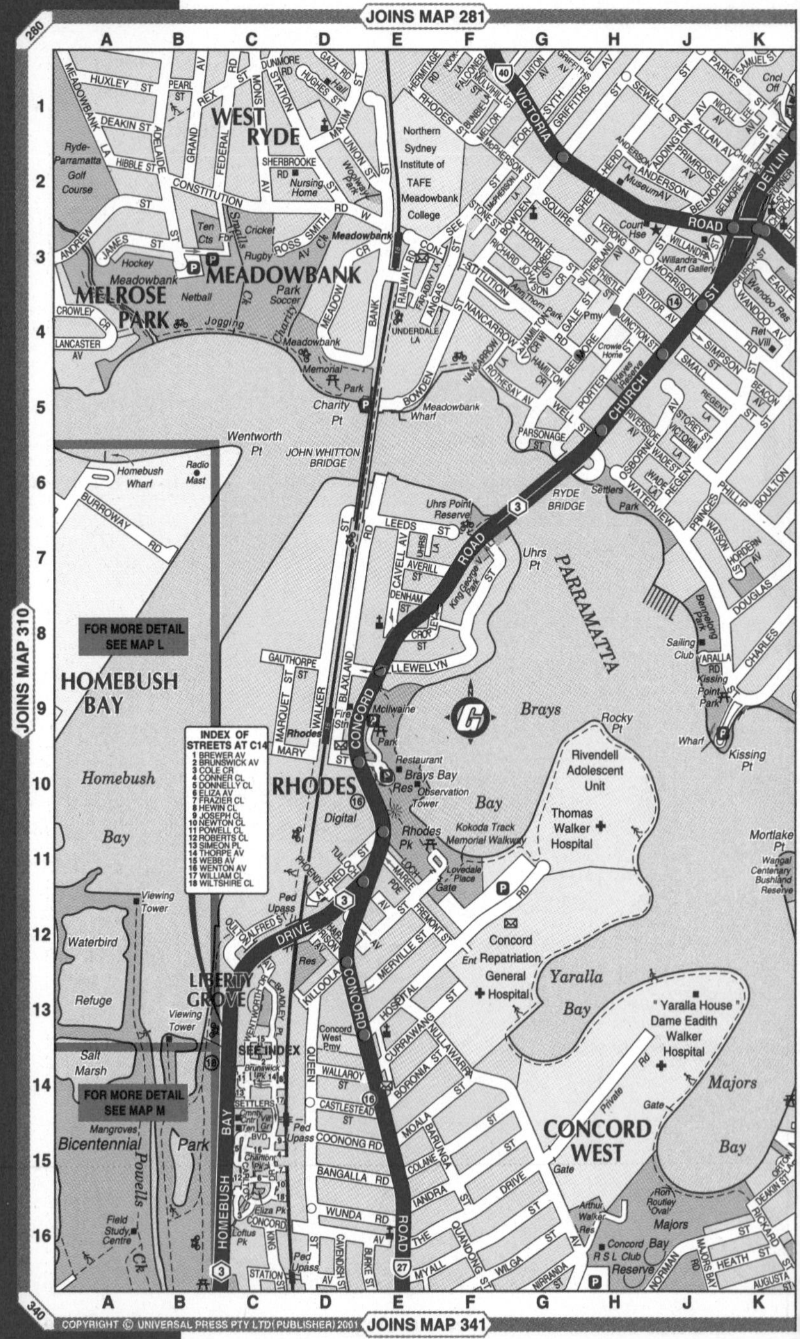
JOINS MAP 281
JOINS MAP 310
JOINS MAP 341
280
340
WEST RYDE
MEADOWBANK
MELROSE PARK
RHODES
HOMEBUSH BAY
LIBERTY GROVE
CONCORD WEST
PARRAMATTA
Brays
Bay
Homebush
Bay
Yaralla
Bay
Majors
Bay
Northern Sydney Institute of TAFE Meadowbank College
Ryde-Parramatta Golf Course
JOHN WHITTON BRIDGE
RYDE BRIDGE
Wentworth Pt
Charity Pt
Uhrs Pt
Rocky Pt
Kissing Pt
Mortlake Pt
Rivendell Adolescent Unit
Thomas Walker Hospital
Concord Repatriation General Hospital
"Yaralla House" Dame Eadith Walker Hospital
Concord R S L Club
Waterbird Refuge
Salt Marsh
Bicentennial Park
Kokoda Track Memorial Walkway
Brays Bay Res
Observation Tower
Settlers Park
Bennelong Park
Sailing Club
Wangal Centenary Bushland Reserve
Homebush Wharf
Meadowbank Wharf
Radio Mast
FOR MORE DETAIL SEE MAP L
FOR MORE DETAIL SEE MAP M
SEE INDEX
VICTORIA ROAD
DEVLIN ST
CHURCH ST
CONCORD ROAD
HOMEBUSH BAY DRIVE
CONSTITUTION RD
INDEX OF STREETS AT C14
1 BREWER AV
2 BRUNSWICK AV
3 COLE CR
4 CONNER CL
5 DONNELLY CL
6 ELIZA AV
7 FRAZIER CL
8 HEWIN CL
9 JOSEPH CL
10 NEWTON CL
11 POWELL CL
12 ROBERTS CL
13 SIMEON PL
14 THORPE AV
15 WEBB AV
16 WENTON AV
17 WILLIAM CL
18 WILTSHIRE CL

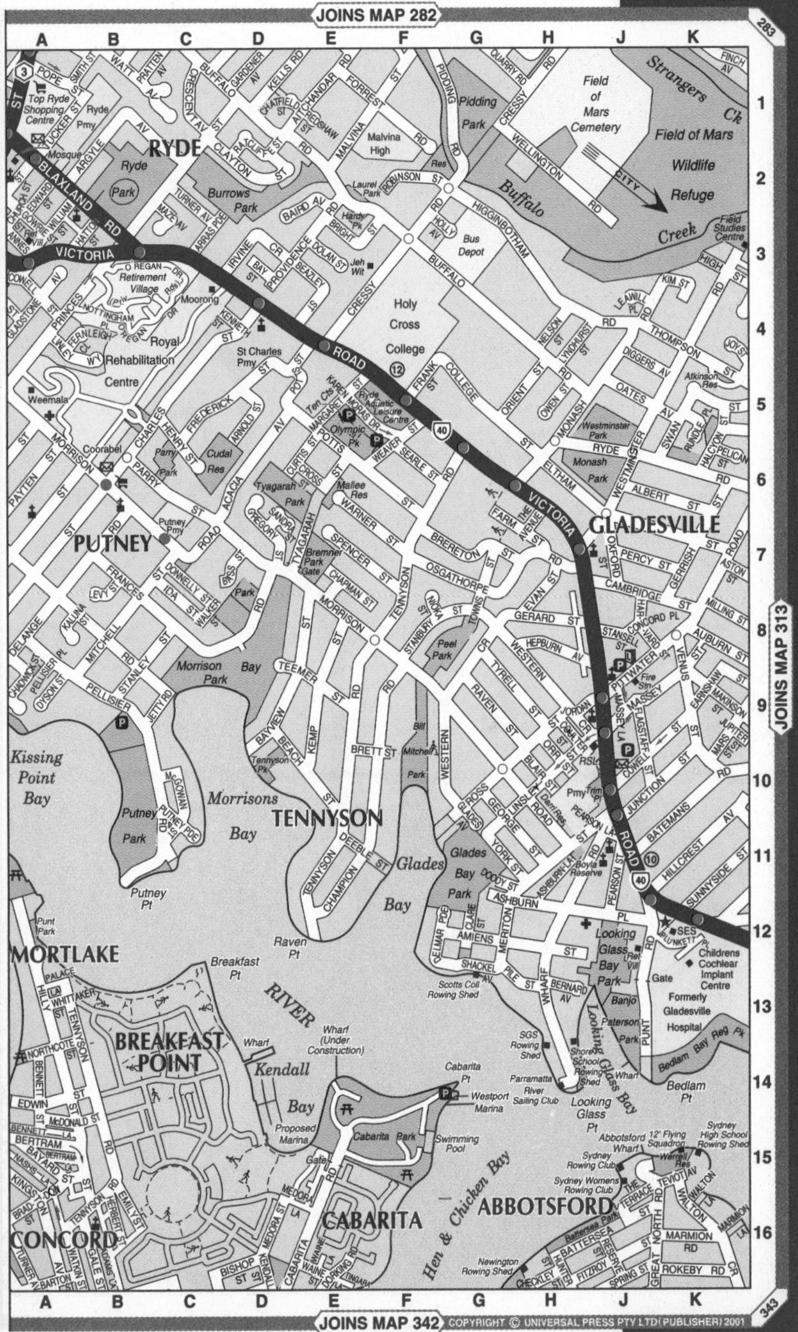
JOINS MAP 282
JOINS MAP 313
JOINS MAP 342
283
343
A B C D E F G H J K
1 2 3 4 5 6 7 8 9 10 11 12 13 14 15 16
RYDE
PUTNEY
GLADESVILLE
TENNYSON
MORTLAKE
BREAKFAST POINT
CABARITA
ABBOTSFORD
CONCORD
Top Ryde Shopping Centre
Ryde Park
Burrows Park
Pidding Park
Malvina High
Field of Mars Cemetery
Field of Mars Wildlife Refuge
Strangers Ck
Buffalo Creek
Field Studies Centre
Bus Depot
Holy Cross College
Retirement Village
Royal Rehabilitation Centre
Weemala
Coorabel
Cudal Res
Tyagarah Park
Mallee Res
Bremner Park
Ryde Aquatic Leisure Centre
Olympic Pk
Westminster Park
Monash Park
Peel Park
Morrison Bay Park
Kissing Point Bay
Putney Park
Putney Pt
Morrisons Bay
Tennyson Pk
Bill Mitchell Park
Glades Bay
Glades Bay Park
Looking Glass Bay Park
Banjo Paterson Park
Childrens Cochlear Implant Centre
Formerly Gladesville Hospital
Bedlam Bay Reg Pk
Bedlam Pt
Looking Glass Bay
Looking Glass Pt
Raven Pt
Breakfast Pt
PARRAMATTA RIVER
Kendall Bay
Proposed Marina
Cabarita Pt
Cabarita Park
Westport Marina
Swimming Pool
Parramatta River Sailing Club
Hen & Chicken Bay
Abbotsford Wharf
Sydney Rowing Club
Sydney Womens Rowing Club
12' Flying Squadron
Sydney High School Rowing Shed
Newington Rowing Shed
Scotts Coll Rowing Shed
SGS Rowing Shed
Shore School Rowing Shed
Wharf (Under Construction)
VICTORIA RD
BLAXLAND RD
COPYRIGHT © UNIVERSAL PRESS PTY LTD (PUBLISHER) 2001

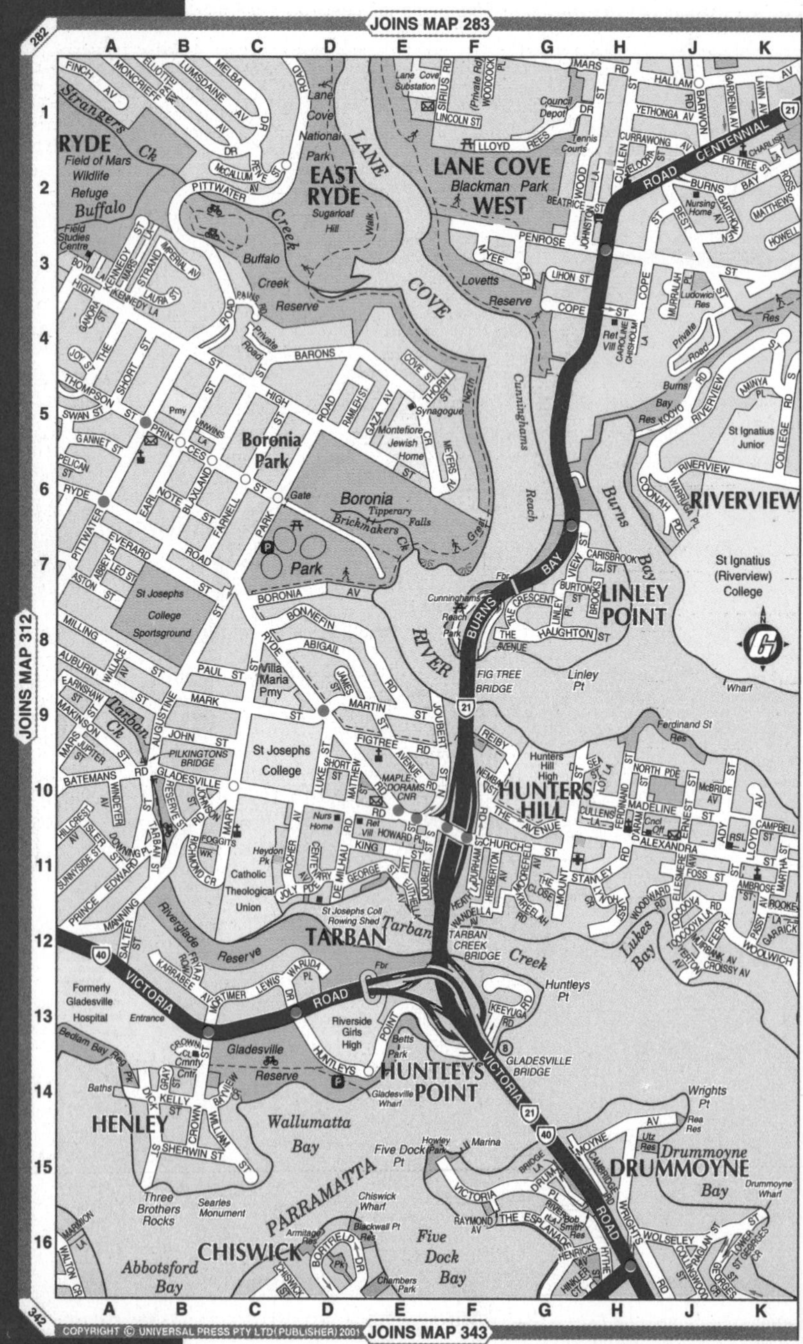
JOINS MAP 283
282
A B C D E F G H J K
1 2 3 4 5 6 7 8 9 10 11 12 13 14 15 16
JOINS MAP 312
RYDE
Field of Mars
Wildlife
Refuge
Buffalo
Strangers Ck
Field Studies Centre
EAST RYDE
Sugarloaf Hill
Lane Cove National Park
LANE COVE
LANE COVE WEST
Blackman Park
Lane Cove Substation
Council Depot
Tennis Courts
Buffalo Creek Reserve
Lovetts Reserve
Walk
COVE
Boronia Park
Boronia Park
Tipperary Falls
Brickmakers Ck
Great North Walk
Cunninghams Reach
Cunninghams Reach Park
Synagogue
Montefiore Jewish Home
St Josephs College Sportsground
Villa Maria Pmy
St Josephs College
Pmy
Burns Bay
Burns Bay Res
Ret Vill
Nursing Home
Ludowici Res
Res
St Ignatius Junior
RIVERVIEW
St Ignatius (Riverview) College
LINLEY POINT
Linley Pt
FIG TREE BRIDGE
Wharf
RIVER
Ferdinand St Res
Hunters Hill High
HUNTERS HILL
MAPLE DORAMS CNR
PILKINGTONS BRIDGE
Tarban Ck
Nurs Home
Ret Vill
Cncl Off
RSL
Heydon Pk
Catholic Theological Union
St Josephs Coll Rowing Shed
TARBAN
Tarban Creek
TARBAN CREEK BRIDGE
Lukes Bay
Riverglade Reserve
Formerly Gladesville Hospital
Entrance
Bedlam Bay Reg Pk
Riverside Girls High
Huntleys Pt
Betts Park
GLADESVILLE BRIDGE
Gladesville Reserve
HUNTLEYS POINT
Gladesville Wharf
Cmnty Cntr
Baths
HENLEY
Wallumatta Bay
Five Dock Pt
Howley Park
Marina
Wrights Pt
Rea Res
Utz Res
Drummoyne Res
DRUMMOYNE
Drummoyne Bay
Drummoyne Wharf
Three Brothers Rocks
Searles Monument
PARRAMATTA
Chiswick Wharf
Armitage Res
Blackwall Pt Res
Bob Smith Res
Five Dock Bay
CHISWICK
Abbotsford Bay
Chambers Park
Pk
VICTORIA ROAD
BURNS BAY ROAD
CENTENNIAL ROAD
21
40
8
FINCH AV
MONCRIEFF
ELLIOTT AV
LUMSDAINE AV
MELBA DR
PITTWATER RD
McCALLUM AV
RENE ST
HIGH ST
BARONS CR
PRINCES ST
BLAXLAND RD
FARNELL ST
PARK RD
RYDE RD
EARL ST
NOTE ST
THOMPSON ST
SWAN ST
GANNET ST
PELICAN ST
SHORT ST
JOY ST
GANORA ST
KENNEDY ST
KENNEDY LA
BOYD LA
MARS ST
STRAND
IMPERIAL AV
LAURA ST
EVERARD ST
ROAD
ABBEY ST
LEO ST
ASTON ST
MILLING ST
AUBURN ST
WALLACE AV
PAUL ST
MARK ST
EARNSHAW ST
MAKINSON ST
JOHN ST
AUGUSTINE ST
BATEMANS RD
GLADESVILLE RD
BORONIA AV
BONNEFIN RD
ABIGAIL ST
JAMES ST
MARTIN ST
JOUBERT ST
FIGTREE AVENUE
LUKE ST
MATTHEW ST
HOWARD PL
KING ST
GEORGE ST
JOLY PDE
CENTENARY AV
ROCHER AV
DE MILHAU RD
PITT ST
EUTHELLA AV
RAMLEH ST
GAZA AV
COVE ST
THORN ST
MEYERS AV
MARS RD
HALLAM AV
YETHONGA AV
CURRAWONG AV
BARWON RD
GARDENIA AV
LAWN AV
LLOYD REES DR
LINCOLN ST
SIRIUS RD
WOODCOCK PL
PENROSE ST
BEATRICE ST
JOHNSTON ST
WOOD ST
CULLEN ST
MYEE CR
LIHON ST
COPE ST
CAROLINE CHISHOLM LA
FIG TREE ST
BURNS BAY RD
GARTHOWEN AV
MATTHEWS AV
HOWELL AV
ROSS ST
CHARLISH LA
BEST ST
MURRALAH AV
RIVERVIEW RD
AMINYA PL
COLLEGE RD
COONAH PDE
WARRUGA PL
KOOYO
CARISBROOK ST
BURTONS ST
BROOKS ST
VIEW ST
LINLEY PL
THE CRESCENT
HAUGHTON ST
THE AVENUE
REIBY RD
NEMBA ST
THE AVENUE
NORTH PDE
MADELINE ST
CULLENS LA
FERDINAND ST
D'ARAM ST
ERNEST ST
McBRIDE AV
CAMPBELL ST
ALEXANDRA ST
CHURCH ST
DURHAM ST
HERBERTON AV
MOOREFIELD AV
THE CLOSE
MOUNT ST
STANLEY ST
LLOYD AV
MARTHA ST
FOSS ST
AMBROSE ST
BOOKER
GARRICK
WOOLWICH RD
WOODWARD RD
ELLESMERE AV
TOOCOOYA RD
FERRY ST
MUIRBANK AV
CROISSY AV
PASSY AV
HEATH
WANDELLA AV
KAREELAH
KEEYUGA RD
WINDEYER AV
HILLCREST AV
ISLER ST
DOWNING ST
SUNNYSIDE ST
EDWARD ST
PRINCE ST
MANNING ST
SALTER ST
KARRABEE AV
FRIAR ROW
MORTIMER
LEWIS DR
WARUDA PL
RESERVE ST
TARBAN ST
JOHNSON RD
RICHMOND CR
FOGGITS WK
MARY ST
CROWN ST
GRAY
DICK
KELLY
WILLIAM
BAYVIEW
SHERWIN ST
HUNTLEYS PT RD
MOYNE
CAMBRIDGE ST
WRIGHTS RD
DRUMMOYNE AV
BRIDGE LA
RIVER LA
VICTORIA PL
RAYMOND AV
THE ESPLANADE
HENRICKS AV
HINKLER CT
HYTHE
WOLSELEY
COLLINGWOOD ST
RAGLAN ST
ST GEORGES CR
LOWER ST GEORGES
MARMION LA
WALTON CR
BORTFIELD DR
CHISWICK ST
342
A B C D E F G H J K
COPYRIGHT © UNIVERSAL PRESS PTY LTD (PUBLISHER) 2001
JOINS MAP 343

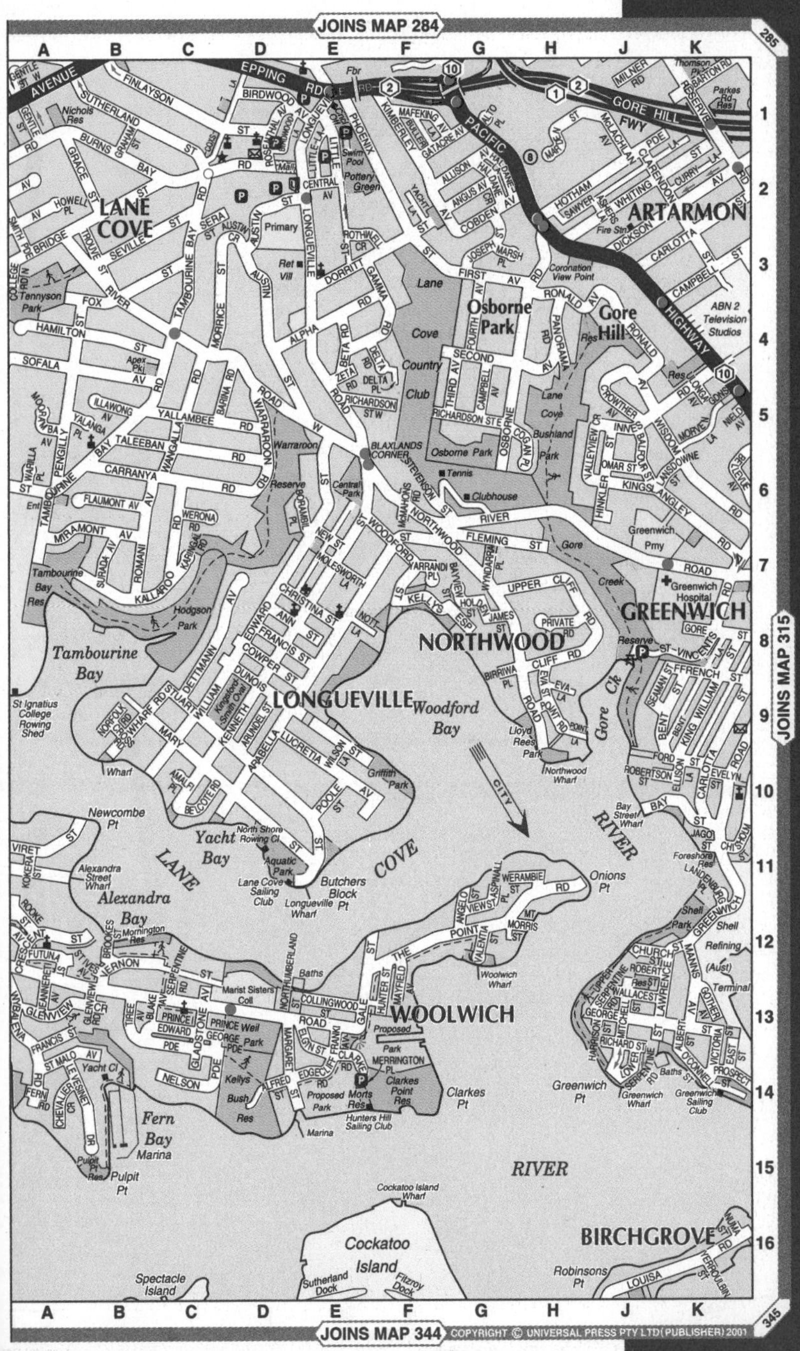

JOINS MAP 284
JOINS MAP 315
JOINS MAP 344
285
345
A B C D E F G H J K
1 2 3 4 5 6 7 8 9 10 11 12 13 14 15 16
LANE COVE
ARTARMON
Osborne Park
Gore Hill
GREENWICH
NORTHWOOD
LONGUEVILLE
WOOLWICH
BIRCHGROVE
EPPING RD
AVENUE
GORE HILL FWY
PACIFIC HIGHWAY
RIVER RD
LONGUEVILLE RD
Lane Cove Country Club
Lane Cove Bushland Park
Tennyson Park
Nichols Res
Warraroon Reserve
Hodgson Park
Tambourine Bay Res
Tambourine Bay
St Ignatius College Rowing Shed
BLAXLANDS CORNER
Central Park
Coronation View Point
ABN 2 Television Studios
Greenwich Pmy
Greenwich Hospital
Gore Creek
Gore Ck
Woodford Bay
CITY
Lloyd Rees Park
Northwood Wharf
Griffith Park
Kingsford-Smith Oval
Newcombe Pt
Yacht Bay
North Shore Rowing Cl
Aquatic Park
Lane Cove Sailing Club
Longueville Wharf
Butchers Block Pt
LANE COVE RIVER
Alexandra Street Wharf
Alexandra Bay
Mornington Res
Marist Sisters Coll
Baths
Onions Pt
Bay Street Wharf
Foreshore Res
Shell Park
Shell Refining (Aust) Terminal
Woolwich Wharf
Proposed Park
Kellys Bush Res
Clarkes Point Res
Clarkes Pt
Morts Res
Hunters Hill Sailing Club
Marina
Yacht Cl
Fern Bay Marina
Pulpit Pt Res
Pulpit Pt
Greenwich Pt
Greenwich Wharf
Greenwich Sailing Club
RIVER
Cockatoo Island Wharf
Cockatoo Island
Sutherland Dock
Fitzroy Dock
Spectacle Island
Robinsons Pt
COPYRIGHT © UNIVERSAL PRESS PTY LTD (PUBLISHER) 2001

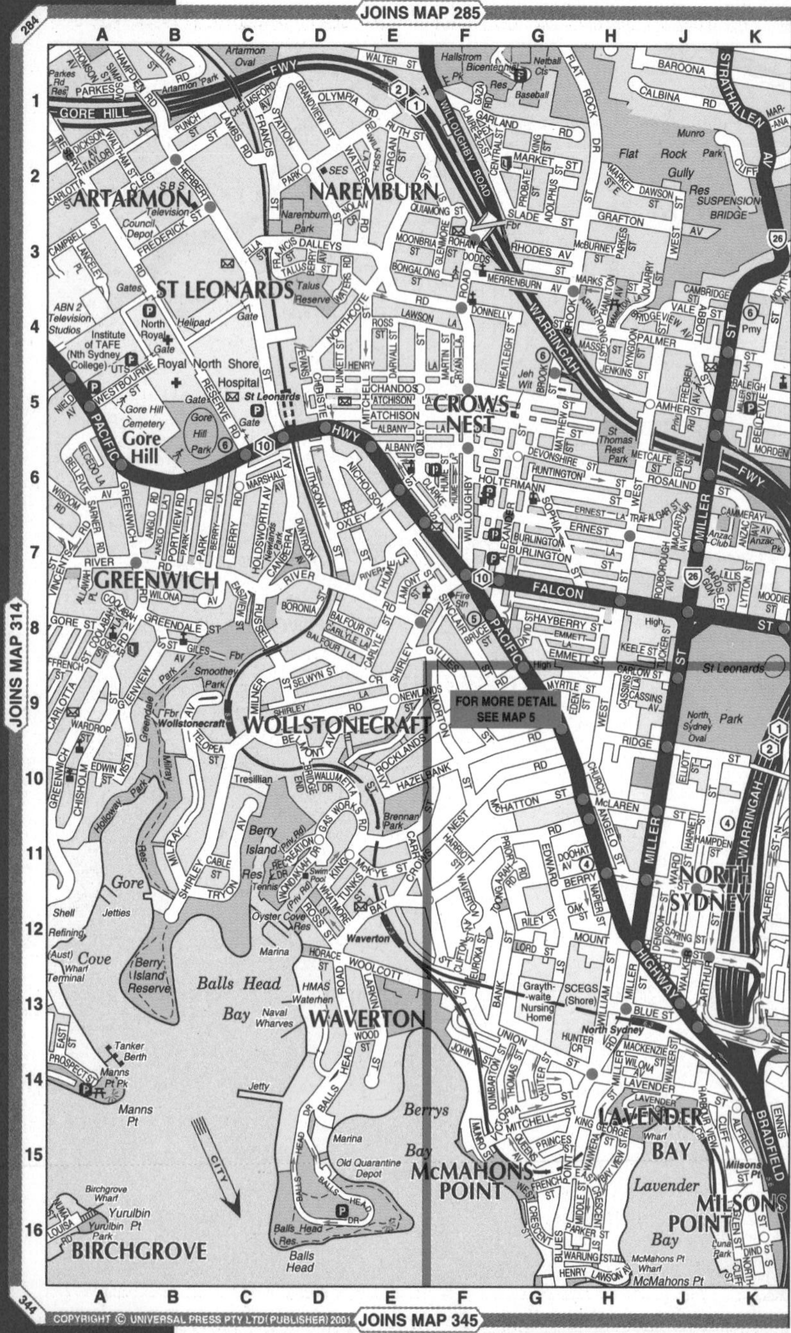

JOINS MAP 285
JOINS MAP 314
JOINS MAP 345
284
344
A B C D E F G H J K
1 2 3 4 5 6 7 8 9 10 11 12 13 14 15 16
ARTARMON
NAREMBURN
ST LEONARDS
CROWS NEST
Gore Hill
GREENWICH
WOLLSTONECRAFT
NORTH SYDNEY
WAVERTON
McMAHONS POINT
LAVENDER BAY
MILSONS POINT
BIRCHGROVE
Royal North Shore Hospital
Institute of TAFE (Nth Sydney College)
ABN 2 Television Studios
Gore Hill Cemetery
Gore Hill Park
Naremburn Park
Talus Reserve
Smoothey Park
Berry Island Reserve
Balls Head Bay
Balls Head
Balls Head Res
Gore Cove
Berrys Bay
Lavender Bay
Flat Rock Gully
Munro Park
St Thomas Rest Park
North Sydney Oval
Brennan Park
HMAS Waterhen
Naval Wharves
Old Quarantine Depot
Manns Pt
Yurulbin Pt
Birchgrove Wharf
Tanker Berth
Shell Refining (Aust) Wharf Terminal
SCEGS (Shore)
Graythwaite Nursing Home
Oyster Cove Res
Marina
Jetty
CITY
Artarmon Oval
Hallstrom Bicentennial
Netball Cts
Baseball
SUSPENSION BRIDGE
GORE HILL FWY
PACIFIC HWY
WARRINGAH FWY
WILLOUGHBY ROAD
MILLER ST
FALCON ST
BRADFIELD
St Leonards
Wollstonecraft
Waverton
North Sydney
Milsons Pt
McMahons Pt Wharf
FOR MORE DETAIL SEE MAP 5

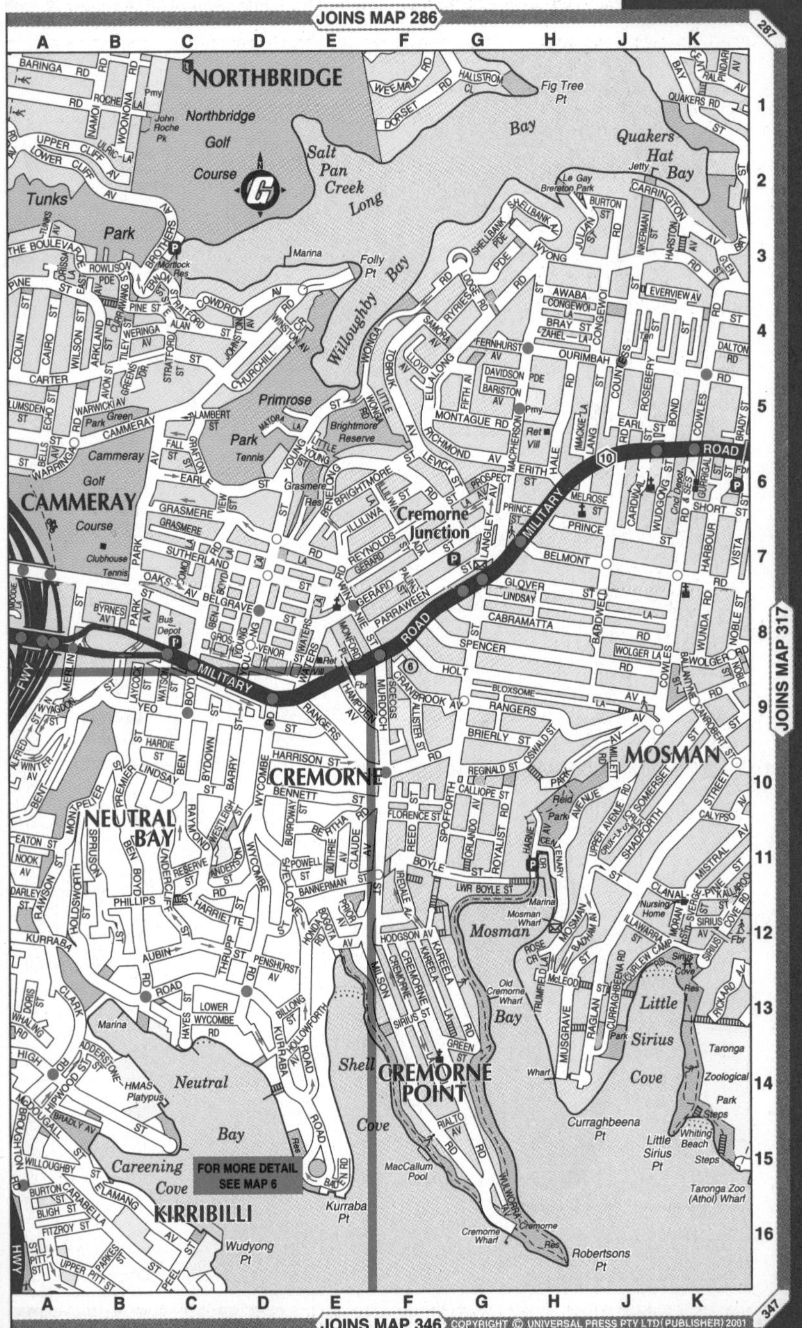

JOINS MAP 286
JOINS MAP 317
JOINS MAP 346
287
347
A B C D E F G H J K
1 2 3 4 5 6 7 8 9 10 11 12 13 14 15 16
NORTHBRIDGE
Northbridge Golf Course
John Roche Pk
Salt Pan Creek
Long Bay
Fig Tree Pt
Quakers Hat Bay
Jetty
Le Gay Brereton Park
Tunks Park
Mortlock Res
Marina
Folly Pt
Willoughby Bay
Primrose Park
Tennis
Brightmore Reserve
Grasmere Res
Cammeray Golf Course
CAMMERAY
Clubhouse
Tennis
Cremorne Junction
Ret Vill
Bus Depot
MILITARY ROAD
CREMORNE
NEUTRAL BAY
MOSMAN
Reid Park
Mosman Wharf
Mosman Bay
Old Cremorne Wharf
Little Sirius Cove
Nursing Home
Sirius Cove
Taronga Zoological Park
Steps
Whiting Beach
Little Sirius Pt
Curraghbeena Pt
Wharf
Taronga Zoo (Athol) Wharf
CREMORNE POINT
Shell Cove
MacCallum Pool
Cremorne Wharf
Cremorne Res
Robertsons Pt
Neutral Bay
HMAS Platypus
Careening Cove
KIRRIBILLI
Wudyong Pt
Kurraba Pt
FOR MORE DETAIL SEE MAP 6
BARINGA RD
ROCHE LA
NAMOI RD
WOONONA RD
ULRIC LA
UPPER CLIFF AV
LOWER CLIFF AV
BROTHERS AV
THE BOULEVARDE
ROWLISON PDE
PINE ST
CURRAWANG ST
WERINGA AV
COWDROY AV
ALAN AV
STRATFORD ST
JOHNSTON AV
WINSTON AV
CHURCHILL CR
COLIN ST
CAIRO ST
WILSON ST
ARKLAND ST
CARTER ST
LUMSDEN ST
ECHO ST
WARWICK AV
CAMMERAY RD
WARRINGA RD
BELLS AV
LAMBERT ST
FALL ST
GRAFTON ST
EARLE ST
GRASMERE RD
VIEW ST
SUTHERLAND ST
PARK AV
OAKS AV
BELGRAVE ST
BYRNES AV
YOUNG ST
VENOR ST
WATERS RD
MONTFORD ST
WINNIE ST
GERARD ST
PARRAWEEN ST
REYNOLDS ST
ILLILIWA ST
BRIGHTMORE ST
BENELONG RD
WONGA RD
TOBRUK AV
SAMORA AV
RYRIES PDE
LODGE RD
SHELLBANK AV
SHELLBANK PDE
WYONG RD
AWABA ST
CONGEWOI RD
BRAY ST
ZAHEL LA
FERNHURST AV
DAVIDSON PDE
BARISTON AV
FIFTH AV
MONTAGUE RD
OURIMBAH RD
RICHMOND AV
LEVICK ST
MACPHERSON ST
PROSPECT AV
ERITH ST
HALE RD
LANGLEY AV
MILITARY ROAD
MELROSE ST
PRINCE ST
BELMONT RD
GLOVER ST
LINDSAY LA
CABRAMATTA RD
SPENCER RD
HOLT AV
CRANBROOK AV
BLOXSOME LA
RANGERS AV
BRIERLY ST
REGINALD ST
OSWALD ST
CALLIOPE ST
FLORENCE ST
SPOFFORTH ST
ORLANDO AV
ROYALIST RD
BOYLE ST
LWR BOYLE ST
HARNETT AV
CENTENARY DR
PARK AVENUE
MILLETT RD
UPPER AVENUE RD
SOMERSET ST
SHADFORTH ST
MISTRAL AV
CALYPSO AV
CLANALPINE ST
KALLAROO RD
MORAN ST
SIRIUS AV
ILLAWARRA ST
CURLEW CAMP RD
CURRAGHBEENA RD
RAGLAN ST
MUSGRAVE ST
McLEOD ST
BADHAM AV
ROSE CR
TRUMFIELD LA
RICKARD AV
BURTON ST
JULIAN ST
INKERMAN ST
HARSTON AV
CARRINGTON AV
GLEN ST
EVERVIEW AV
CARDINAL ST
WUDGONG ST
GURRIGAL ST
SHORT ST
HARBOUR ST
VISTA ST
ROSEBERY ST
BOND ST
COWLES RD
EARL ST
DALTON RD
BRADY ST
WUNDA RD
NOBLE ST
WOLGER RD
WOLGER LA
BALANTYNE ST
CARROBERT ST
QUAKERS RD
MERLIN ST
LAYCOCK ST
WATSON ST
BOYD ST
YEO ST
HARDIE ST
LINDSAY ST
BYDOWN ST
BARRY ST
WYCOMBE RD
HARRISON ST
BENNETT ST
MURDOCH ST
HAMPDEN AV
SCECGS
ALLISTER ST
REED ST
IREDALE AV
HODGSON AV
CREMORNE RD
KAREELA RD
SIRIUS ST
GREEN ST
MILSON RD
RIALTO AV
BERTHA RD
GUTHRIE AV
CLAUDE AV
POWELL ST
BANNERMAN ST
PRIOR AV
BOGOTA AV
HONDA RD
SHELL COVE RD
BURROWAY ST
RAYMOND RD
WESTLEIGH ST
ANDERSON ST
RESERVE ST
UNDERCLIFF ST
HARRIETTE ST
PHILLIPS ST
BEN BOYD RD
SPRUSON ST
HOLDSWORTH ST
MONTPELIER ST
PREMIER ST
WINTER AV
ALFRED ST
WYAGDON ST
EATON ST
NOOK AV
DARLEY ST
RAWSON ST
KURRABA RD
AUBIN ST
THRUPP ST
PENSHURST AV
LOWER WYCOMBE RD
HAYES ST
BILLONG ST
HOLLOWFORTH AV
CLARK RD
DORIS ST
WHALING RD
HIGH ST
ADDERSTONE AV
HIPWOOD ST
McDOUGALL ST
BRADLY AV
BROUGHTON ST
WILLOUGHBY ST
BURTON ST
CARABELLA ST
ELAMANG AV
BLIGH ST
FITZROY ST
PITT ST
UPPER PITT ST
PARKES ST
PEEL ST
BADEN RD
FWY
HWY
COPYRIGHT © UNIVERSAL PRESS PTY LTD (PUBLISHER) 2001

MAP 317

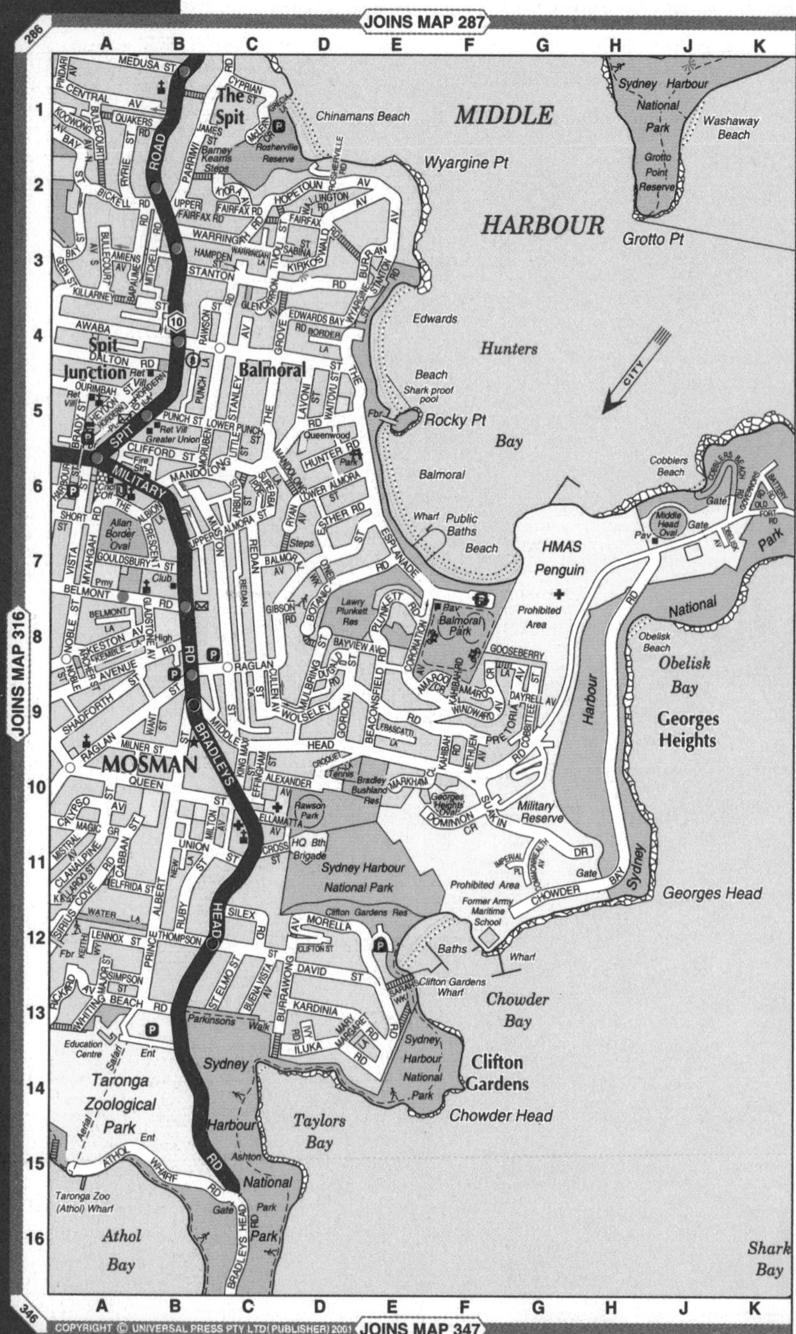
JOINS MAP 287
JOINS MAP 316
JOINS MAP 347
286
346
A
B
C
D
E
F
G
H
J
K
1
2
3
4
5
6
7
8
9
10
11
12
13
14
15
16
MIDDLE
HARBOUR
The Spit
Chinamans Beach
Rosherville Reserve
Barney Kearns Steps
Wyargine Pt
Sydney Harbour National Park
Washaway Beach
Grotto Point Reserve
Grotto Pt
Spit Junction
Balmoral
Edwards
Hunters
Beach
Shark proof pool
Rocky Pt
Bay
Balmoral
CITY
Public Baths
Beach
Wharf
Fbr
HMAS Penguin
Prohibited Area
Cobblers Beach
Middle Head Oval
Gate
Pav
National
Park
Obelisk Beach
Obelisk Bay
Georges Heights
Harbour
Sydney
Georges Head
Balmoral Park
Lawry Plunkett Res
Allan Border Oval
MOSMAN
Bradley Bushland Res
Georges Heights Oval
Military Reserve
Rawson Park
HQ Bth Brigade
Sydney Harbour National Park
Prohibited Area
Former Army Maritime School
Clifton Gardens Res
Baths
Wharf
Clifton Gardens Wharf
Chowder Bay
Sydney Harbour National Park
Clifton Gardens
Chowder Head
Taylors Bay
Parkinsons Walk
Ashton
Education Centre
Safari
Ent
Taronga Zoological Park
Aerial
Taronga Zoo (Athol) Wharf
Gate
Athol Bay
Shark Bay
SPIT RD
MILITARY RD
BRADLEYS HEAD RD
ESPLANADE
MIDDLE HEAD RD
CHOWDER BAY RD
MEDUSA ST
CENTRAL AV
QUAKERS
HOPETOUN AV
WARRINGAH RD
STANTON RD
EDWARDS BAY RD
PUNCH ST
CLIFFORD ST
RAGLAN ST
BELMONT RD
HEAD RD
QUEEN
ALEXANDER
UNION
WATER
THOMPSON
BEACH RD
ATHOL WHARF RD
DAVID ST
KARDINIA
ILUKA
MORELLA
DOMINION CR
SUAKIN
GOOSEBERRY
AMAROO
WINDWARD
PRETORIA
COBBITTEE
BEACONSFIELD
GORDON
WOLSELEY
MULBRING
BAYVIEW AV
PLUNKETT RD
CORONATION AV
KAHIBAH RD
BOTANIC RD
GIBSON RD
LOWER ALMORA ST
ESTHER RD
HUNTER RD
MANDOLONG
BURRAWONG
BUENA VISTA
ST ELMO ST
SILEX RD
CLIFTON ST
SARAHS WK
MILNER ST
RAGLAN
SHADFORTH
AVENUE
KEMBLE
NOBLE
VISTA
MYAHGAH RD
GOULDSBURY
SHORT
HARBOUR
BRADY
OURIMBAH
DALTON RD
AWABA
KILLARNEY
AMIENS
BULLECOURT
BICKELL RD
RYRIE ST
PINDARI AV
KOOWONG AV
BAY ST
GEN ST
MITCHELL
BAPAUME
PARRIWI RD
CYPRIAN
McLEAN CR
ROSHERVILLE RD
KIORA AV
FAIRFAX RD
WALLINGTON RD
BURRAN AV
WYARGINE ST
GLENCARRON AV
GROVE
STANLEY AV
RAWSON
LAVONI
WAITOVU ST
REDAN
MUSTON
ARBUTUS
UPPER ALMORA ST
BALMORAL AV
CULLEN AV
KING MAX
EFFINGHAM
ELLAMATTA AV
CROSS ST
MILTON AV
NEW
RUBY
ALBERT
PRINCE
LENNOX ST
SIMPSON ST
WHITING
RICKARD
CALYPSO AV
MISTRAL AV
CLANALPINE
ELFRIDA ST
CABBAN ST
SIRIUS COVE
MAGIC GR
WANT
PUNCH LA
HORDERN LA
CROQUET
MARKHAM CL
METHUEN
DAYRELL AV
IMPERIAL
COMMONWEALTH AV
FORT RD
BATTERY
GOVERNORS
OBELISK AV
COBBLERS BEACH
10

JOINS MAP 288

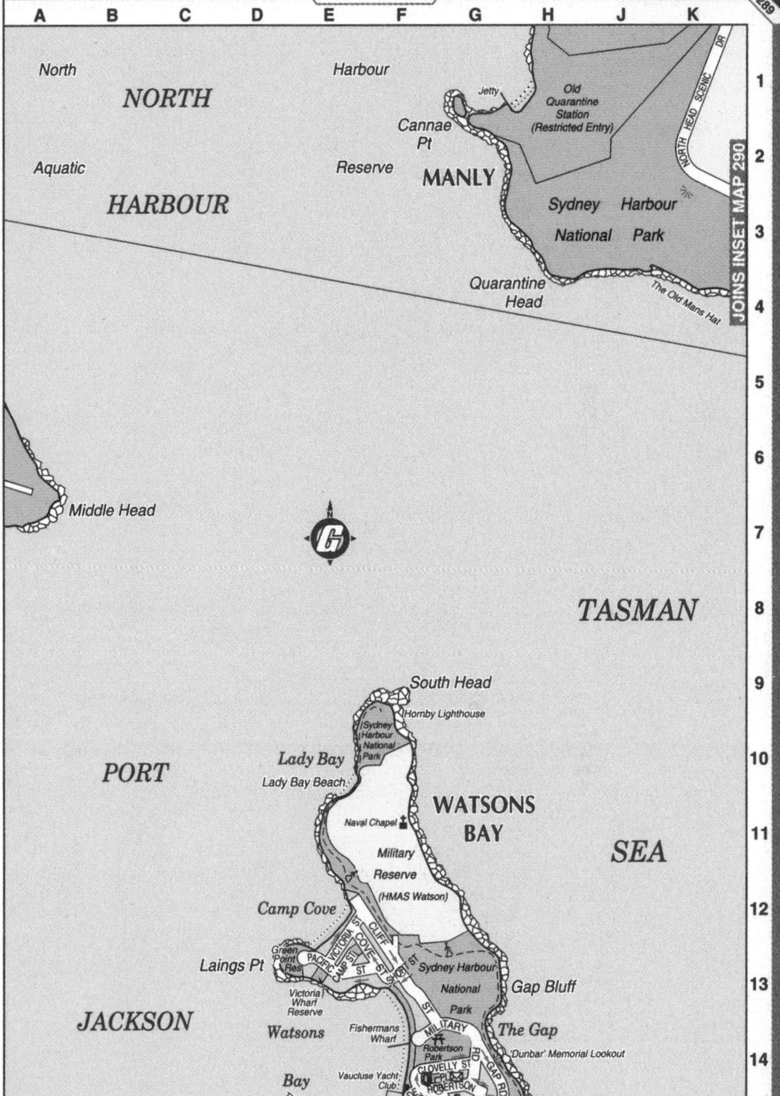

JOINS INSET MAP 290

289

JOINS MAP 348

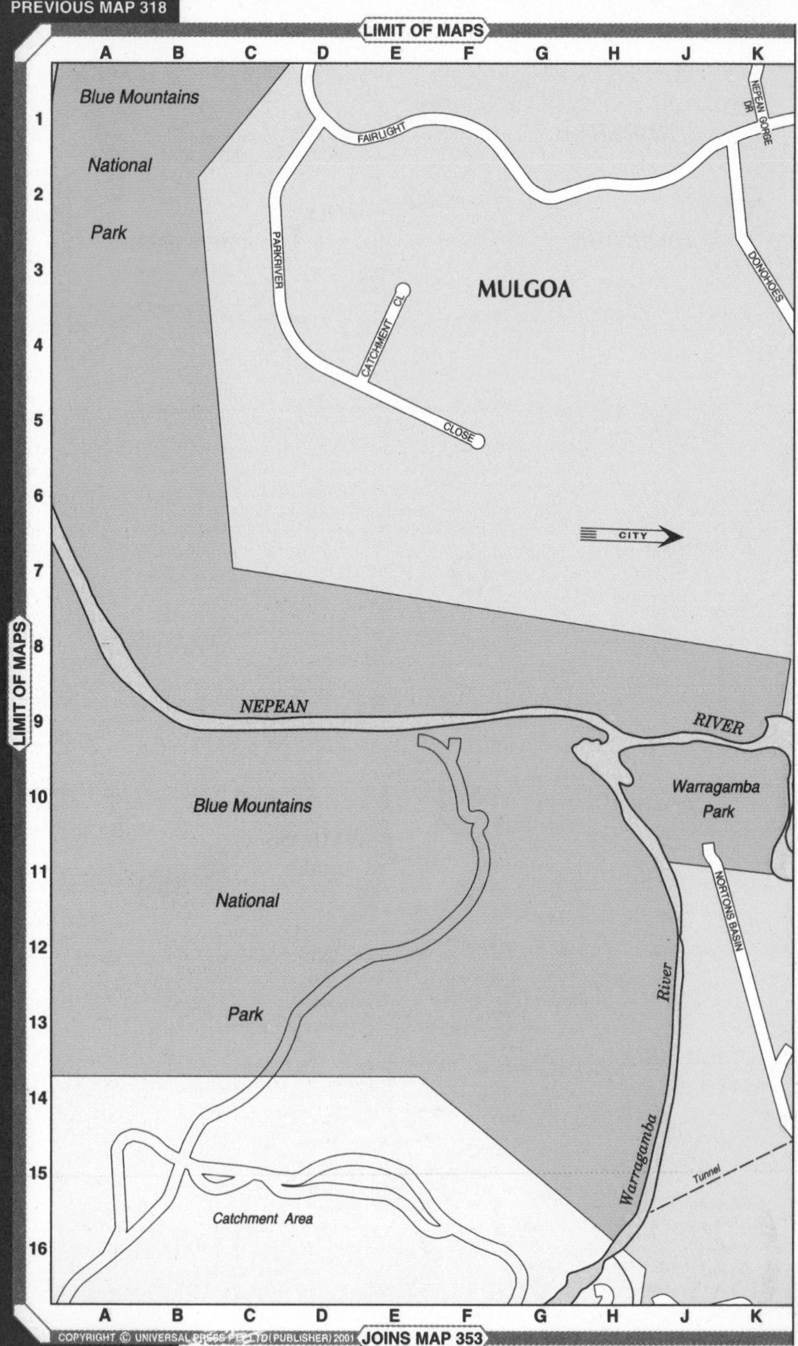
LIMIT OF MAPS
A B C D E F G H J K
1 2 3 4 5 6 7 8 9 10 11 12 13 14 15 16
Blue Mountains
National
Park
FAIRLIGHT
NEPEAN GORGE DR
PARKRIVER
DONOHOES
MULGOA
CATCHMENT CL
CLOSE
CITY
LIMIT OF MAPS
NEPEAN
RIVER
Warragamba
Park
Blue Mountains
National
Park
NORTONS BASIN
River
Warragamba
Tunnel
Catchment Area

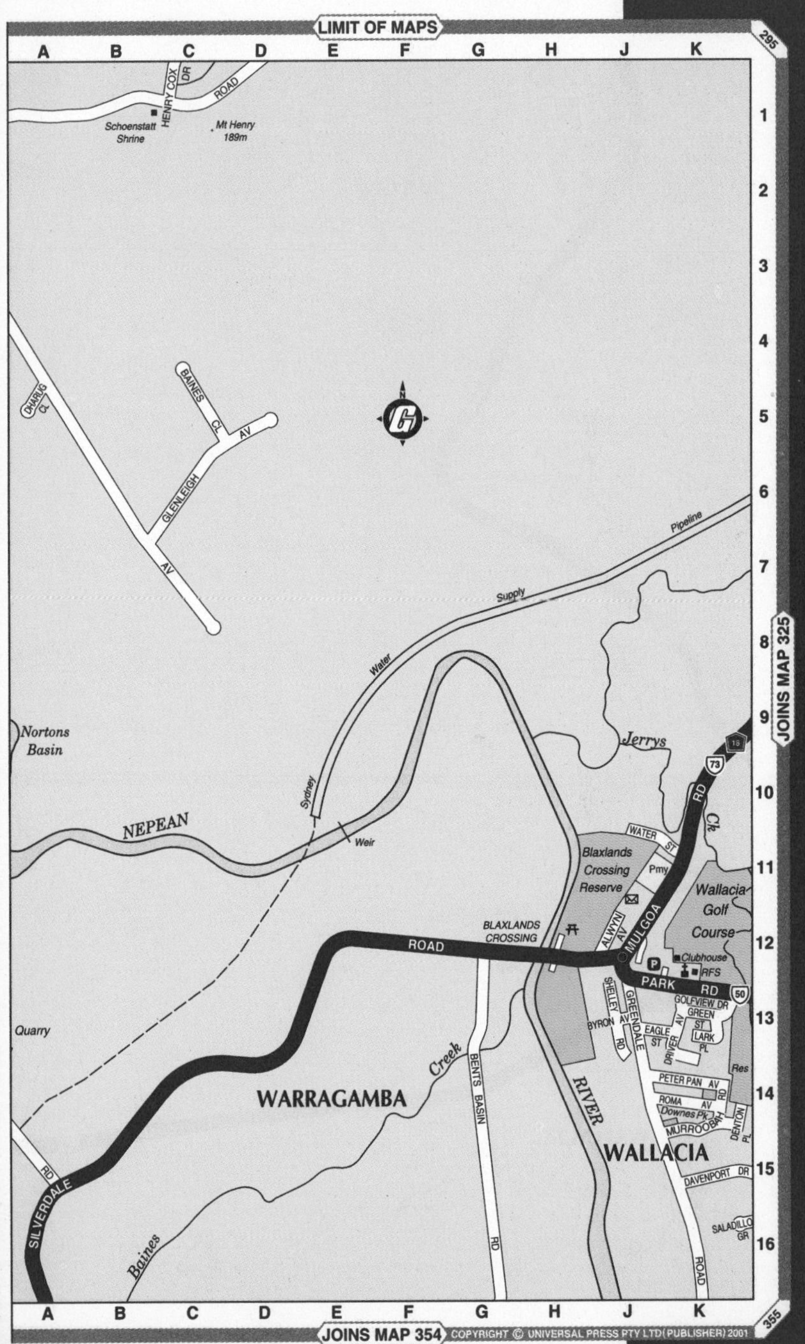
LIMIT OF MAPS
295
A B C D E F G H J K
1 2 3 4 5 6 7 8 9 10 11 12 13 14 15 16
HENRY COX DR
ROAD
Schoenstatt Shrine
Mt Henry 189m
DHARUG CL
BAINES CL
AV
GLENLEIGH
AV
Pipeline
Supply
Water
Sydney
Nortons Basin
NEPEAN
Weir
Jerrys
Ck
RD
73
15
WATER ST
Blaxlands Crossing Reserve
Pmy
Wallacia Golf Course
ALWYN AV
MULGOA
BLAXLANDS CROSSING
ROAD
Clubhouse
RFS
PARK RD
50
SHELLEY AV
GREENDALE
GOLFVIEW DR
GREEN ST
LARK PL
BYRON AV
RD
EAGLE ST
DRIVER AV
Res
Quarry
Creek
BENTS BASIN
PETER PAN AV
RD
ROMA AV
Downes Pk
MURROOBAH
DENTON PL
WARRAGAMBA
RIVER
WALLACIA
DAVENPORT DR
RD
SILVERDALE
SALADILLO GR
Baines
RD
ROAD
JOINS MAP 325
JOINS MAP 354
355

MAP 325

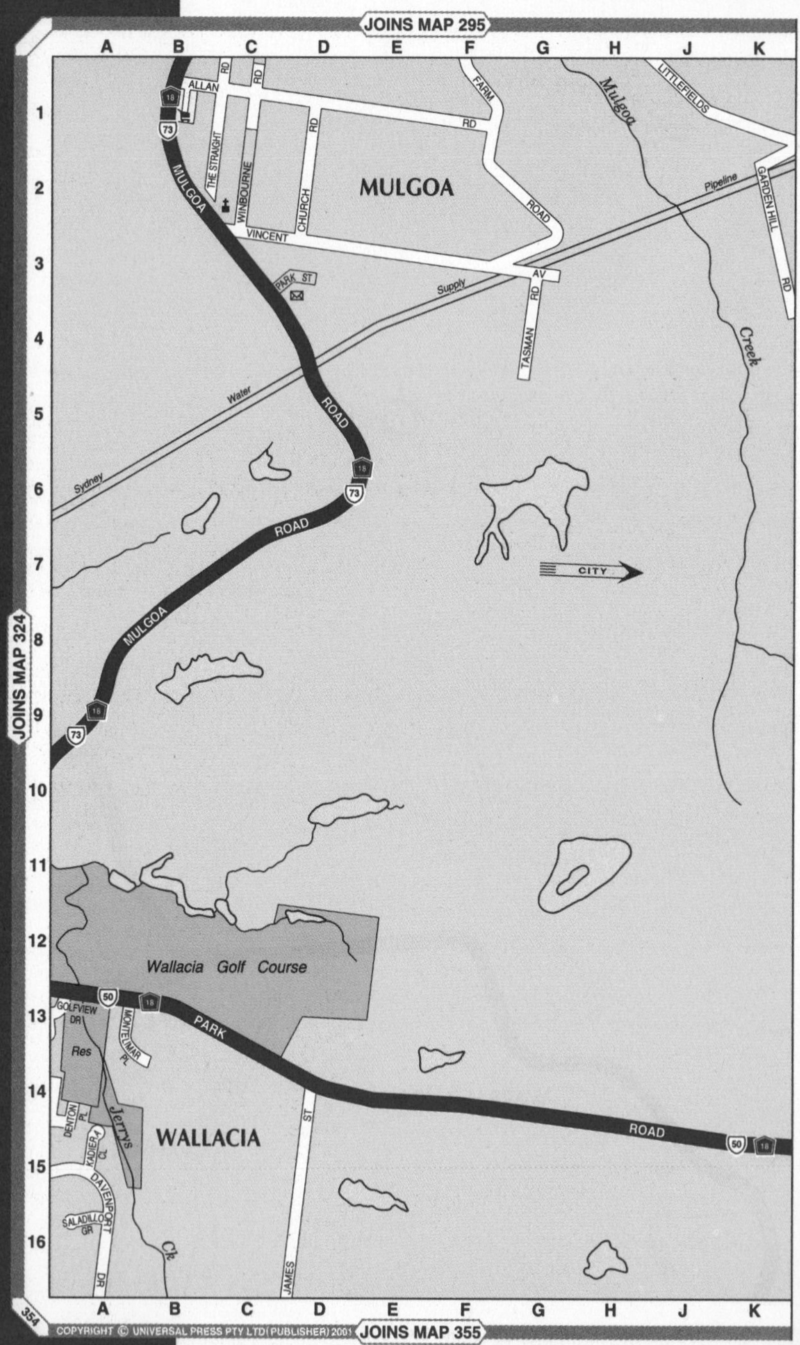
JOINS MAP 295
JOINS MAP 324
JOINS MAP 355
MULGOA
WALLACIA
Wallacia Golf Course
MULGOA ROAD
ALLAN
RD
THE STRAIGHT
WINBOURNE
CHURCH RD
FARM RD
ROAD
VINCENT
AV
PARK ST
TASMAN RD
Sydney Water Supply Pipeline
Mulgoa Creek
LITTLEFIELDS
GARDEN HILL RD
CITY
PARK ROAD
GOLFVIEW DR
MONTELIMAR PL
Res
DENTON PL
KADIERA CL
Jerrys Ck
DAVENPORT DR
SALADILLO GR
JAMES ST
354
COPYRIGHT © UNIVERSAL PRESS PTY LTD (PUBLISHER) 2001

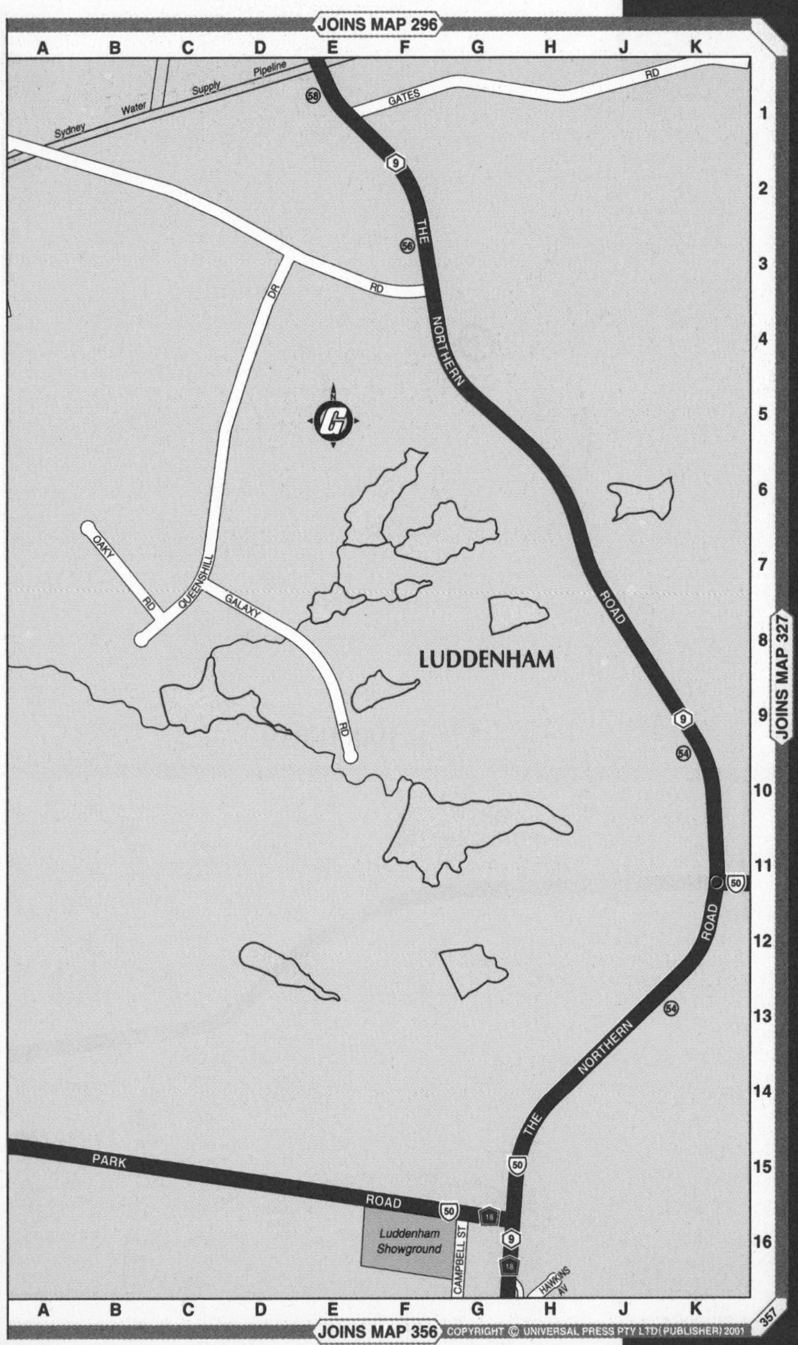
JOINS MAP 296
A B C D E F G H J K
1 2 3 4 5 6 7 8 9 10 11 12 13 14 15 16
Sydney Water Supply Pipeline
GATES RD
THE NORTHERN ROAD
RD
DR
QUEENSHILL
OAKY RD
GALAXY RD
LUDDENHAM
PARK ROAD
Luddenham Showground
CAMPBELL ST
HAWKINS AV
JOINS MAP 327
JOINS MAP 356
357

MAP 327

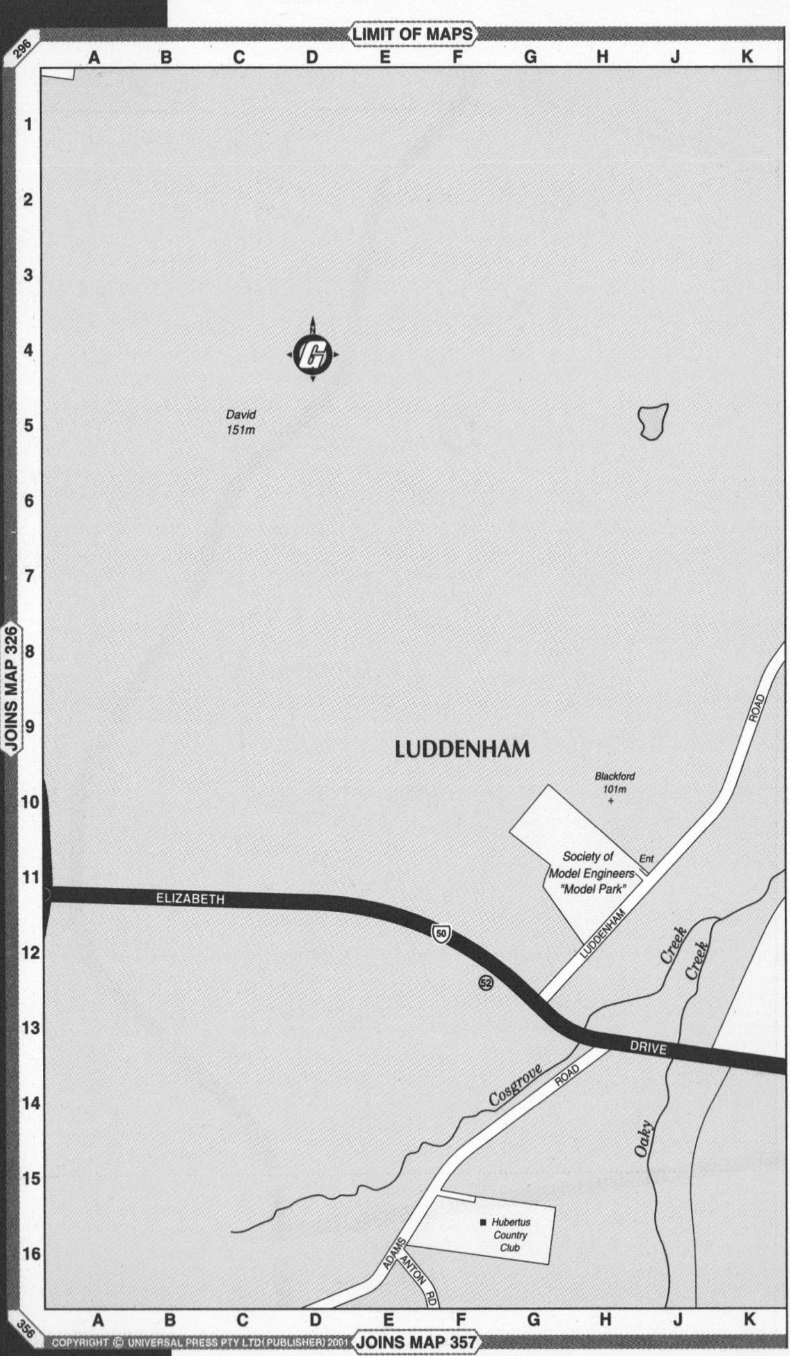

LIMIT OF MAPS
296
A B C D E F G H J K
1 2 3 4 5 6 7 8 9 10 11 12 13 14 15 16
JOINS MAP 326
David
151m
LUDDENHAM
Blackford
101m
Society of
Model Engineers
"Model Park"
Ent
ROAD
LUDDENHAM
ELIZABETH
50
52
DRIVE
Creek
Creek
Cosgrove
ROAD
Oaky
Hubertus
Country
Club
ADAMS
ANTON
RD
356
JOINS MAP 357

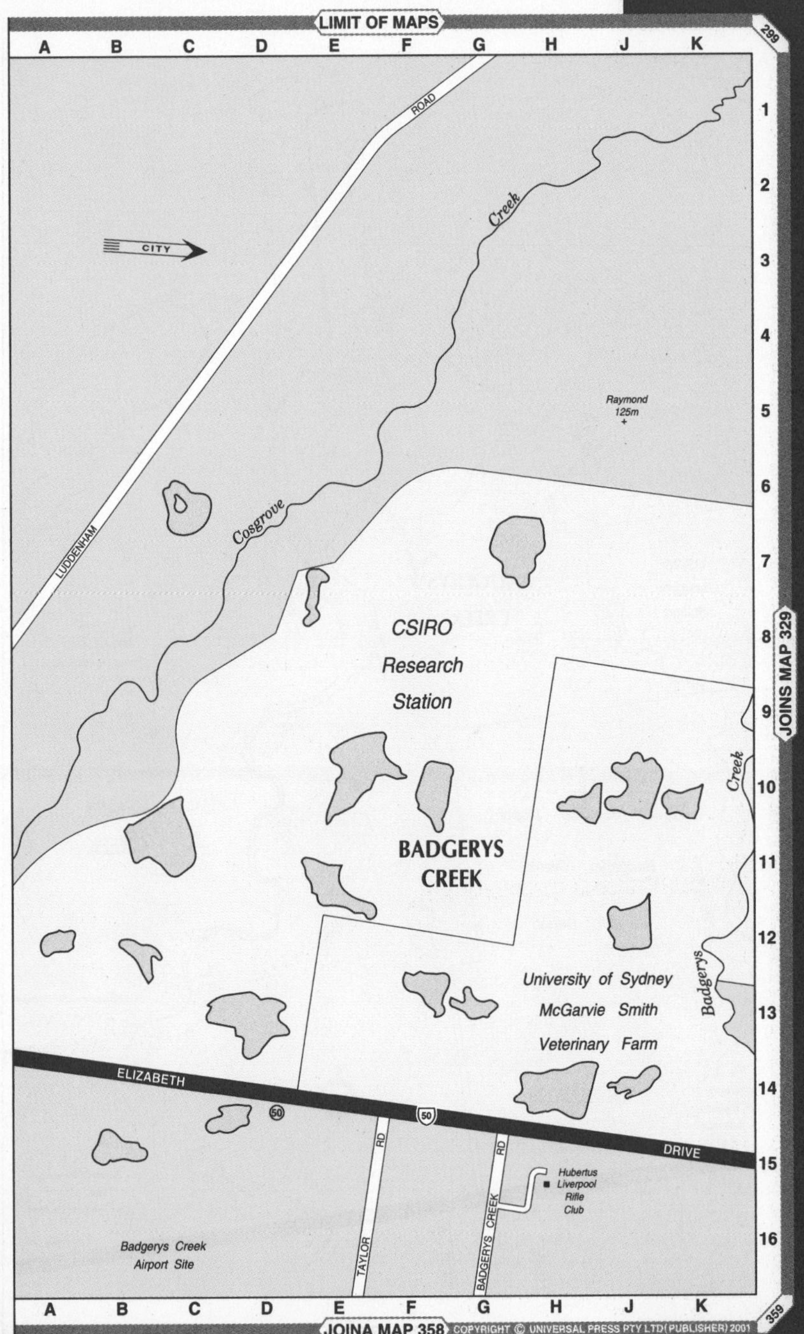
LIMIT OF MAPS
299
A B C D E F G H J K
1 2 3 4 5 6 7 8 9 10 11 12 13 14 15 16
ROAD
LUDDENHAM
CITY
Creek
Cosgrove
Raymond
125m
CSIRO
Research
Station
BADGERYS
CREEK
Creek
Badgerys
University of Sydney
McGarvie Smith
Veterinary Farm
ELIZABETH
50
DRIVE
TAYLOR RD
BADGERYS CREEK RD
Hubertus
Liverpool
Rifle
Club
Badgerys Creek
Airport Site
JOINS MAP 329
JOINA MAP 358
359

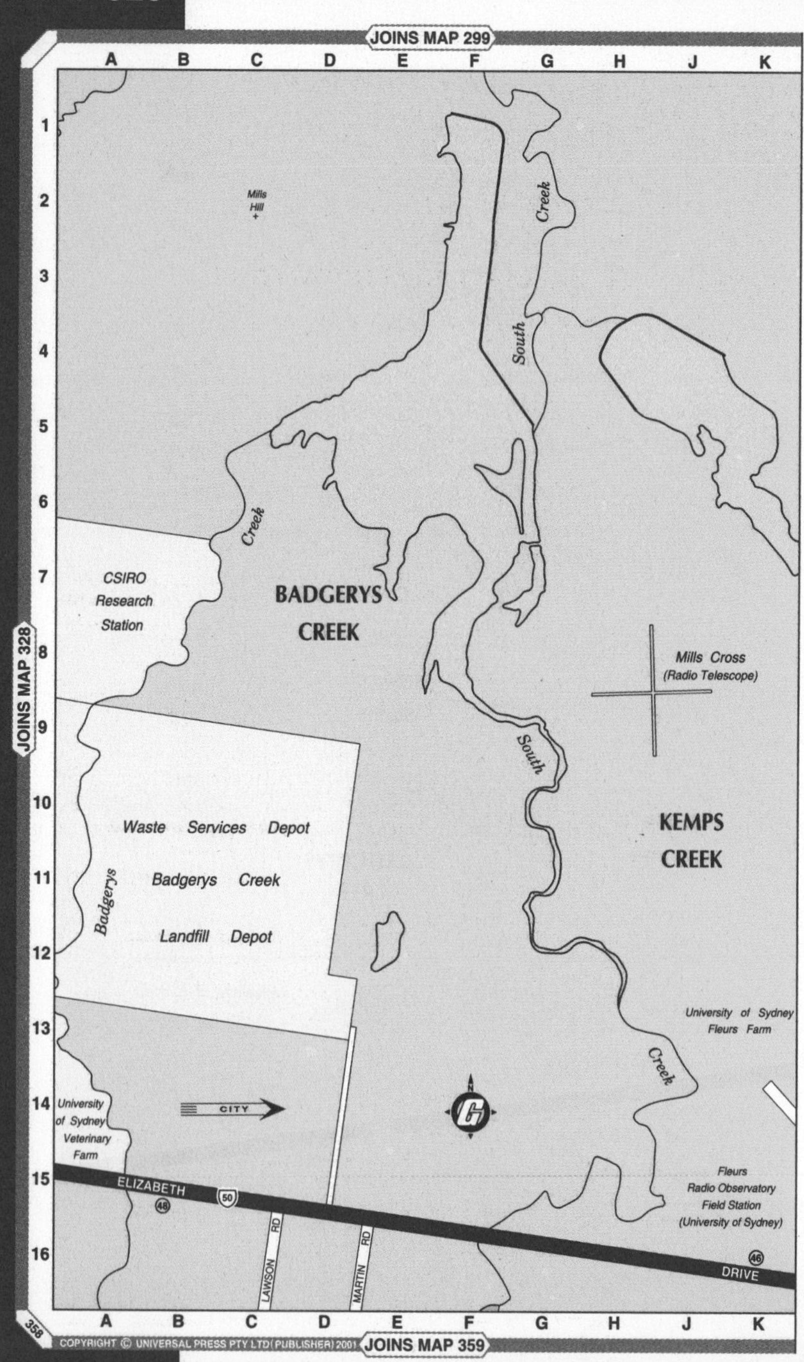
JOINS MAP 299
A B C D E F G H J K
1 2 3 4 5 6 7 8 9 10 11 12 13 14 15 16
Mills Hill
South Creek
Creek
CSIRO Research Station
BADGERYS CREEK
Mills Cross (Radio Telescope)
JOINS MAP 328
South
Waste Services Depot
Badgerys Creek
Landfill Depot
Badgerys
KEMPS CREEK
University of Sydney Fleurs Farm
Creek
University of Sydney Veterinary Farm
CITY
ELIZABETH
48
50
Fleurs Radio Observatory Field Station (University of Sydney)
LAWSON RD
MARTIN RD
46
DRIVE
358
JOINS MAP 359

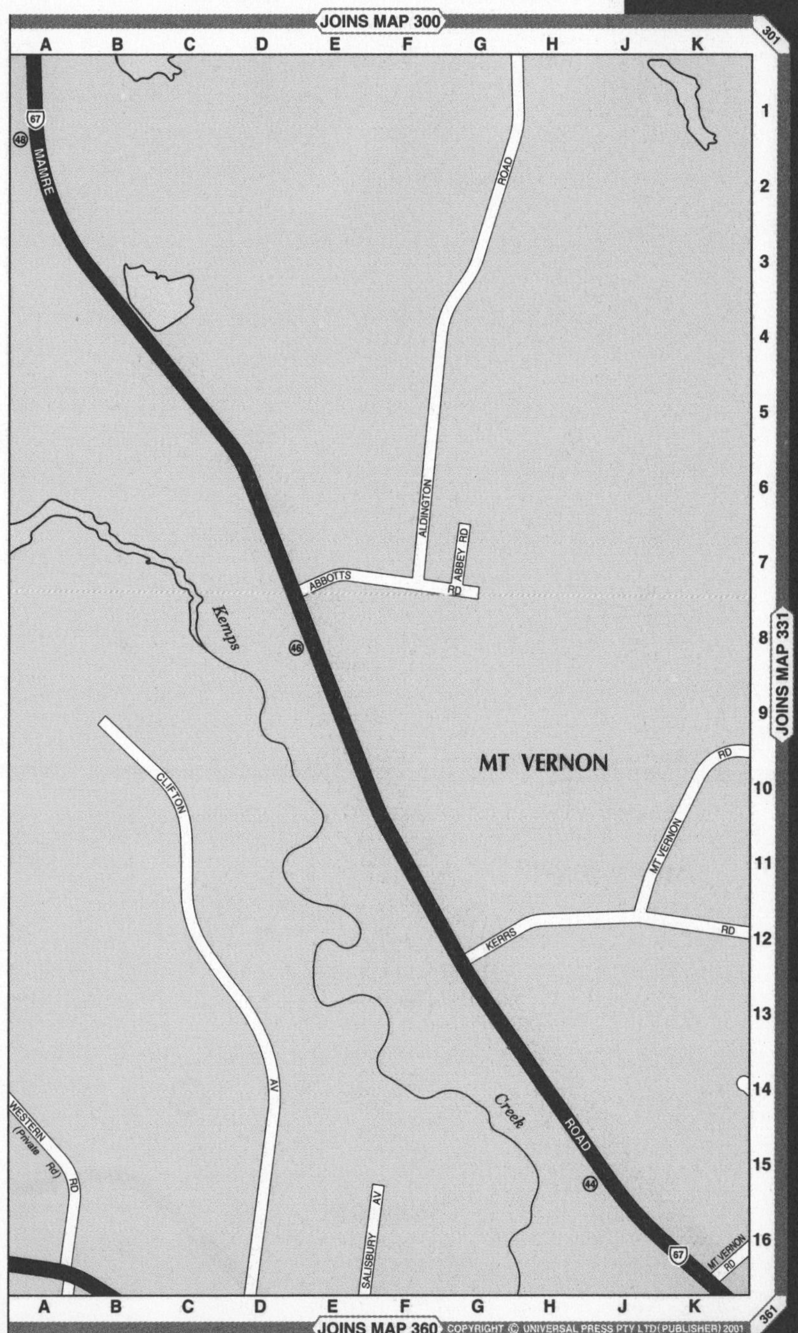
JOINS MAP 300
301
A
B
C
D
E
F
G
H
J
K
1
2
3
4
5
6
7
8
9
10
11
12
13
14
15
16
67
48
MAMRE
ROAD
ALDINGTON
ABBEY RD
ABBOTTS
RD
Kemps
46
JOINS MAP 331
MT VERNON
RD
MT VERNON
CLIFTON
KERRS
RD
AV
Creek
ROAD
44
WESTERN
(Private
Rd)
RD
SALISBURY
AV
67
MT VERNON
RD
JOINS MAP 360
361

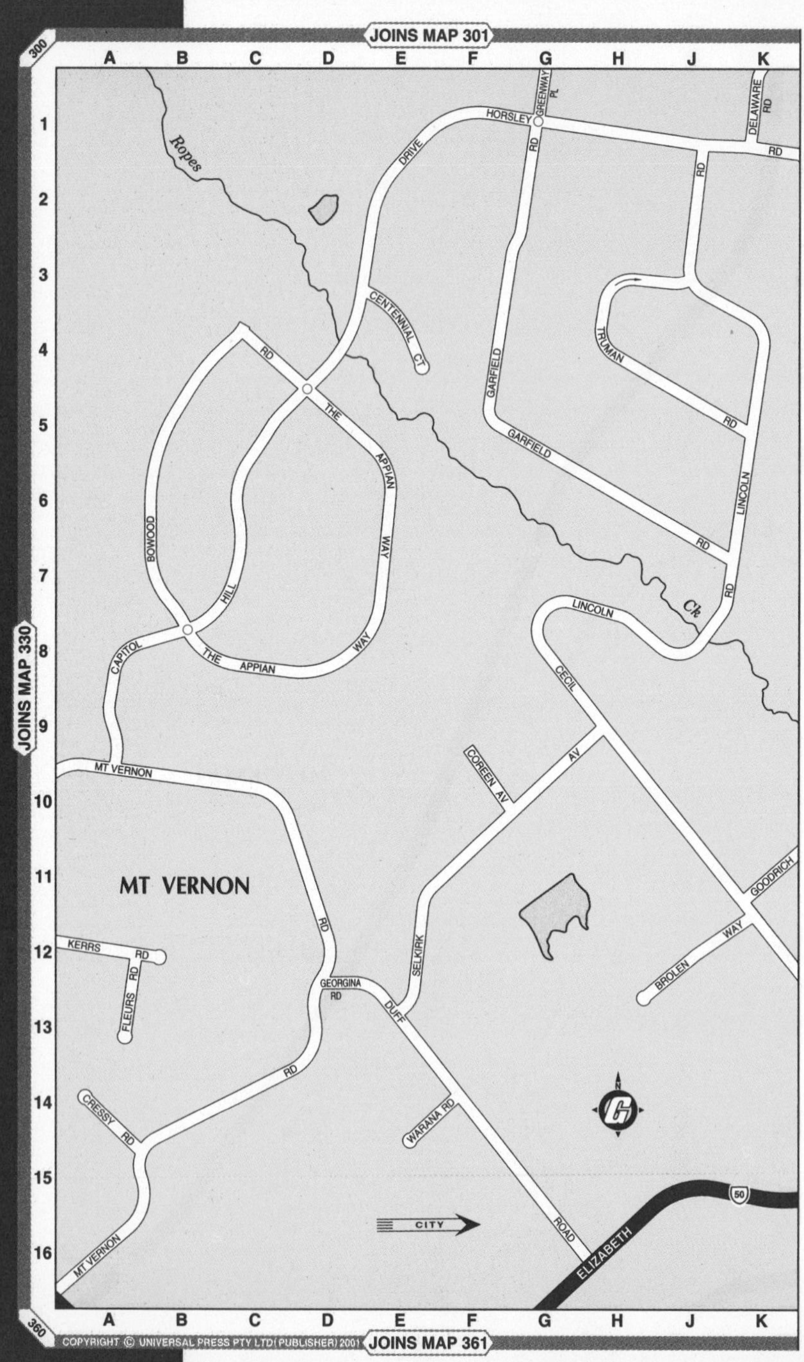
JOINS MAP 301
300
A B C D E F G H J K
1 2 3 4 5 6 7 8 9 10 11 12 13 14 15 16
JOINS MAP 330
Ropes
Ck
HORSLEY
GREENWAY PL
DRIVE
RD
DELAWARE RD
RD
RD
CENTENNIAL CT
TRUMAN
GARFIELD
GARFIELD
RD
RD
LINCOLN
RD
THE
APPIAN
WAY
BOWOOD
HILL
RD
CAPITOL
THE APPIAN
WAY
LINCOLN
CECIL
AV
COREEN AV
MT VERNON
MT VERNON
KERRS RD
FLEURS RD
RD
GEORGINA RD
SELKIRK
DUFF
GOODRICH
WAY
BROLEN
CRESSY RD
RD
WARANA RD
ROAD
CITY
ELIZABETH
50
MT VERNON
360

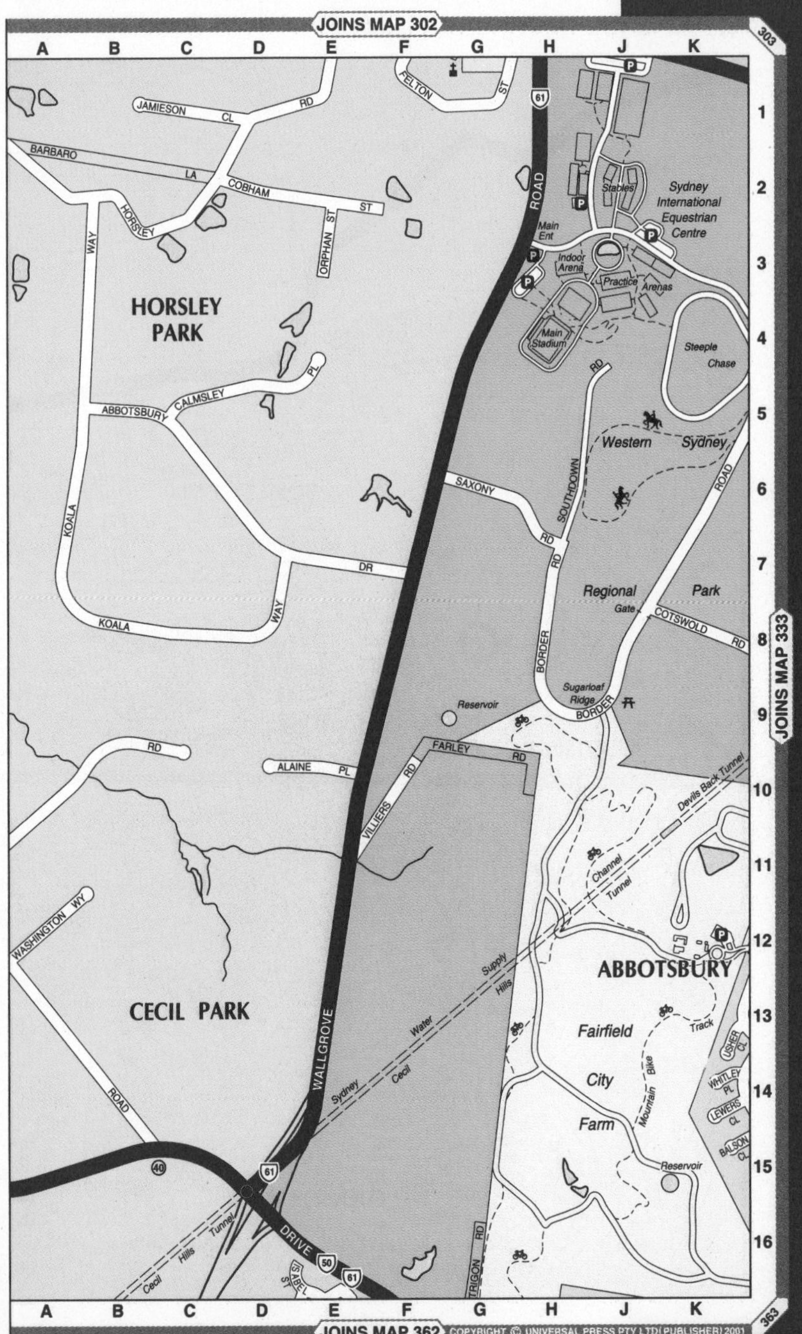
JOINS MAP 302
303
A B C D E F G H J K
1 2 3 4 5 6 7 8 9 10 11 12 13 14 15 16
JAMIESON CL RD
BARBARO LA
COBHAM ST
HORSLEY
ORPHAN ST
FELTON ST
61
ROAD
WAY
HORSLEY PARK
ABBOTSBURY
CALMSLEY PL
SAXONY RD
DR
KOALA WAY
KOALA
Stables
Sydney International Equestrian Centre
Main Ent
Indoor Arena
Practice Arenas
Main Stadium
Steeple Chase
Western Sydney Regional Park
SOUTHDOWN RD
RD
BORDER
Gate
COTSWOLD RD
Sugarloaf Ridge
BORDER
Reservoir
FARLEY RD
RD
ALAINE PL
VILLIERS RD
Devils Back Tunnel
Channel Tunnel
WASHINGTON WY
ABBOTSBURY
CECIL PARK
Sydney Water Supply Hills Cecil
WALLGROVE
Fairfield City Farm
Mountain Bike Track
USHER CL
WHITLEY PL
LEWERS CL
BALSON CL
Reservoir
ROAD
40
61
DRIVE
50
61
Cecil Hills Tunnel
ISABEL ST
TRIGON RD
JOINS MAP 333
A B C D E F G H J K
JOINS MAP 362
363

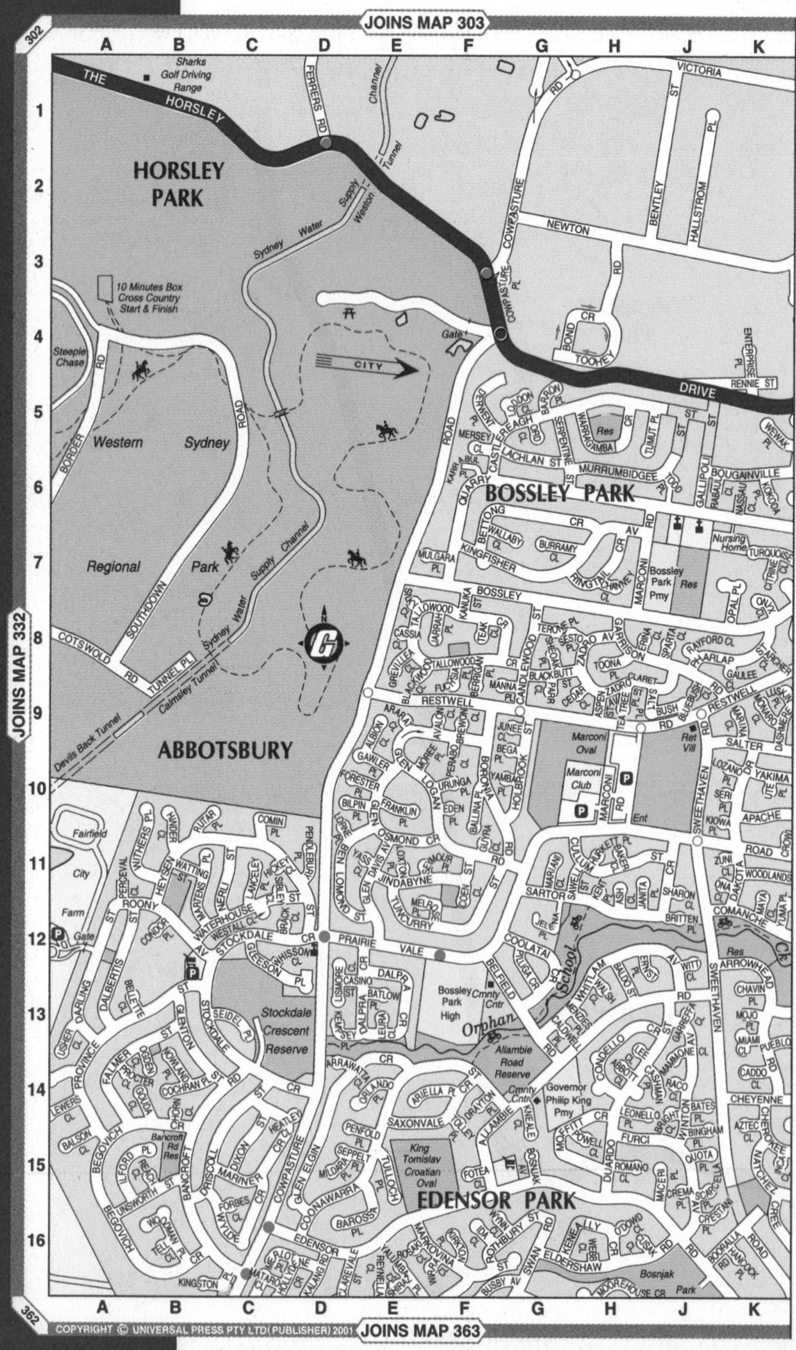
JOINS MAP 303
302
A B C D E F G H J K
1 2 3 4 5 6 7 8 9 10 11 12 13 14 15 16
JOINS MAP 332
HORSLEY PARK
BOSSLEY PARK
ABBOTSBURY
EDENSOR PARK
THE HORSLEY DRIVE
Sharks Golf Driving Range
Sydney Water Supply Channel
Weston
Tunnel
10 Minutes Box Cross Country Start & Finish
Steeple Chase
Western Sydney Regional Park
CITY
Gate
SOUTHDOWN ROAD
COTSWOLD RD
TUNNEL PL
Calmsley Tunnel
Devils Back Tunnel
BORDER
FERRERS RD
VICTORIA
COWPASTURE RD
COWPASTURE PL
NEWTON
BENTLEY
HALLSTROM
BOND CR
TOOHEY
ENTERPRISE
RENNIE ST
WEWAK PL
MERSEY CL
LOCHLAN ST
MURRUMBIDGEE
GALLIPOLI
BOUGAINVILLE
RABAUL CL
NASSAU CL
KOKODA
Nursing Home
TURQUOISE
Res
BETTONG
WALLABY CL
BURRAMY CL
KINGFISHER
RINGTAIL
MULGARA PL
MARCONI
Bossley Park Pmy
BOSSLEY
RESTWELL
CANDLEWOOD
ZADRO AV
GARRISON
RAYFORD CL
Marconi Oval
Marconi Club
Ret Vill
SALTER
SWEETHAVEN
YAKIMA
APACHE
ROAD
Ent
ALBION
GLEN LOGAN
OSMOND CR
JINDABYNE
TUNCURRY
PRAIRIE VALE
STOCKDALE CR
SARTOR
BRITTEN PL
COMANCHE
ARROWHEAD
School
Orphan
CR
Bossley Park High
Cmnty Cntr
Allambie Road Reserve
Governor Philip King Pmy
Stockdale Crescent Reserve
Fairfield City Farm
CHEYENNE
CHEROKEE
NATCHEL
PROVINCE
DARLING
BEGOVICH
BANCROFT
Bancroft Rd Res
DRISCOLL
DIXON
MARINER
COWPASTURE
GLEN ELGIN
COONAWARRA
SAXONVALE
King Tomislav Croatian Oval
EDENSOR
ROTHBURY ST
SWAN
ELDERSHAW
Bosnjak Park
MOOREHOUSE CR
KINGSTON
BUSBY AV
BOORALLA
HANCOCK PL
A B C D E F G H J K
362
JOINS MAP 363

JOINS MAP 304

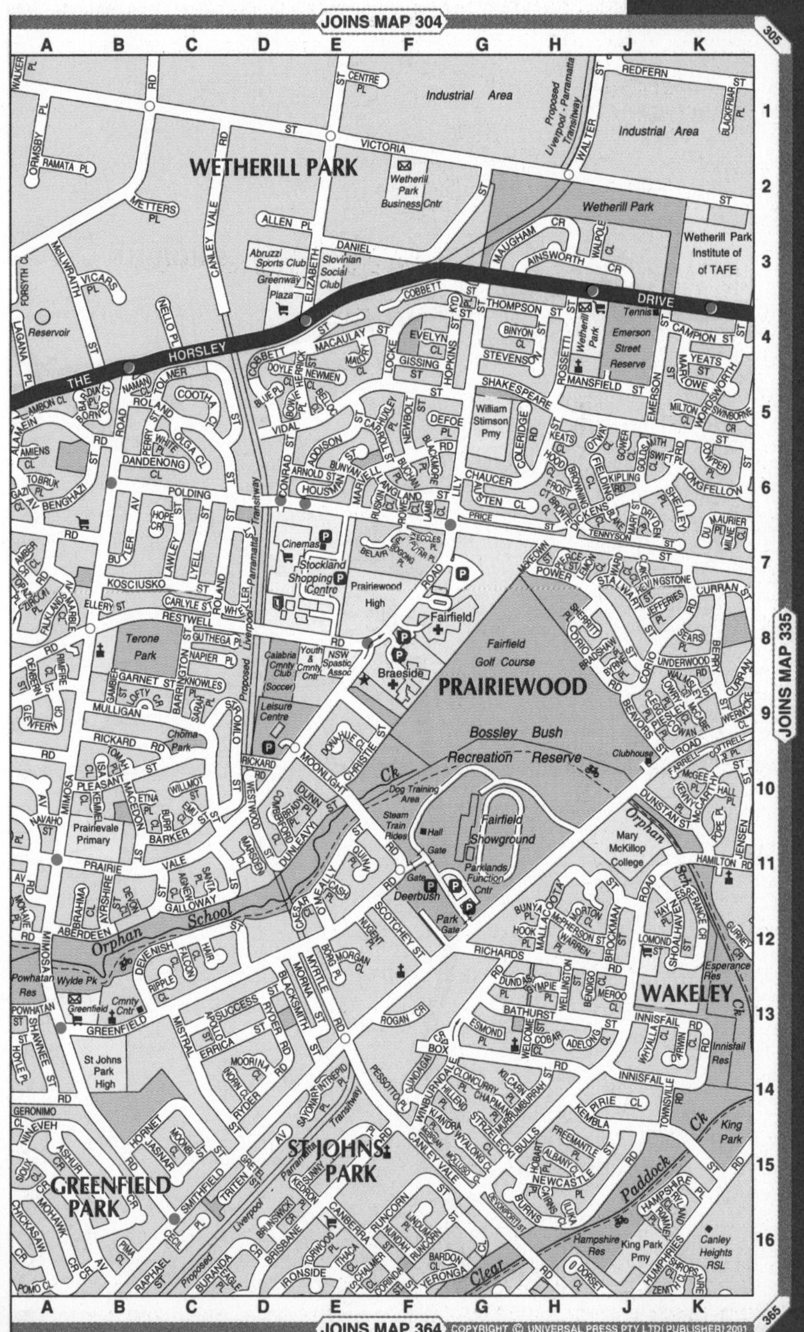

JOINS MAP 335

JOINS MAP 364

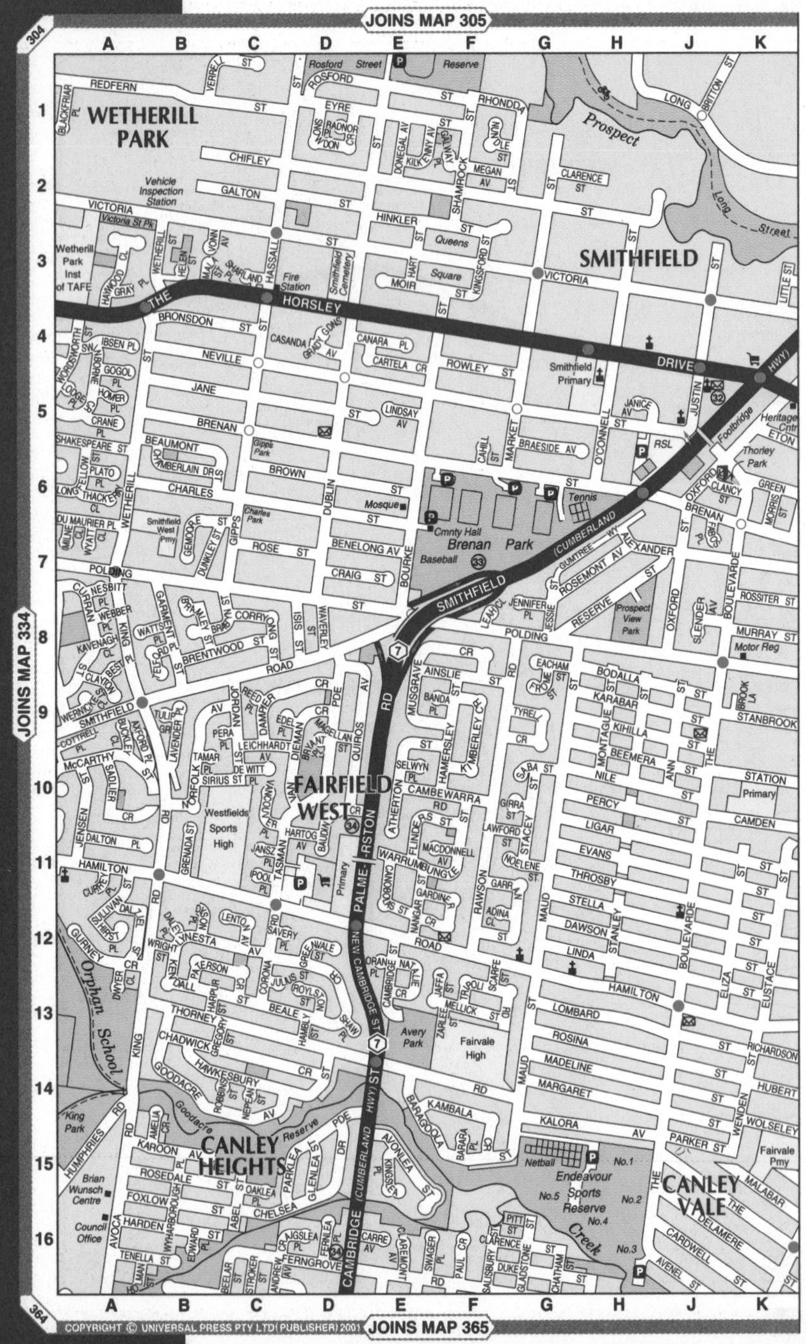
JOINS MAP 305
JOINS MAP 334
JOINS MAP 365
304
364
A B C D E F G H J K
1 2 3 4 5 6 7 8 9 10 11 12 13 14 15 16
WETHERILL PARK
SMITHFIELD
FAIRFIELD WEST
CANLEY HEIGHTS
CANLEY VALE
Prospect
Long Street
Orphan School
Goodacre Reserve
Creek
THE HORSLEY DRIVE
CUMBERLAND HWY
SMITHFIELD RD
CAMBRIDGE ST
NEW CAMBRIDGE ST
PALMERSTON RD
REDFERN ST
VICTORIA ST
CHIFLEY ST
GALTON ST
HINKLER ST
BRONSDON ST
NEVILLE ST
JANE ST
BRENAN ST
BROWN ST
CHARLES ST
ROSE ST
POLDING ST
HAMILTON RD
WETHERILL ST
DUBLIN ST
BOURKE ST
MARKET ST
O'CONNELL ST
OXFORD ST
BOULEVARDE
Vehicle Inspection Station
Wetherill Park Inst of TAFE
Fire Station
Smithfield Cemetery
Queens Square
Smithfield Primary
RSL
Heritage Cntr
Thorley Park
Gipps Park
Charles Park
Smithfield West Pmy
Mosque
Cmnty Hall
Brenan Park
Baseball
Tennis
Prospect View Park
Motor Reg
Westfields Sports High
Primary
Avery Park
Fairvale High
King Park
Brian Wunsch Centre
Council Office
Netball
Endeavour Sports Reserve
No.1 No.2 No.3 No.4 No.5
Fairvale Pmy
COPYRIGHT © UNIVERSAL PRESS PTY LTD (PUBLISHER) 2001

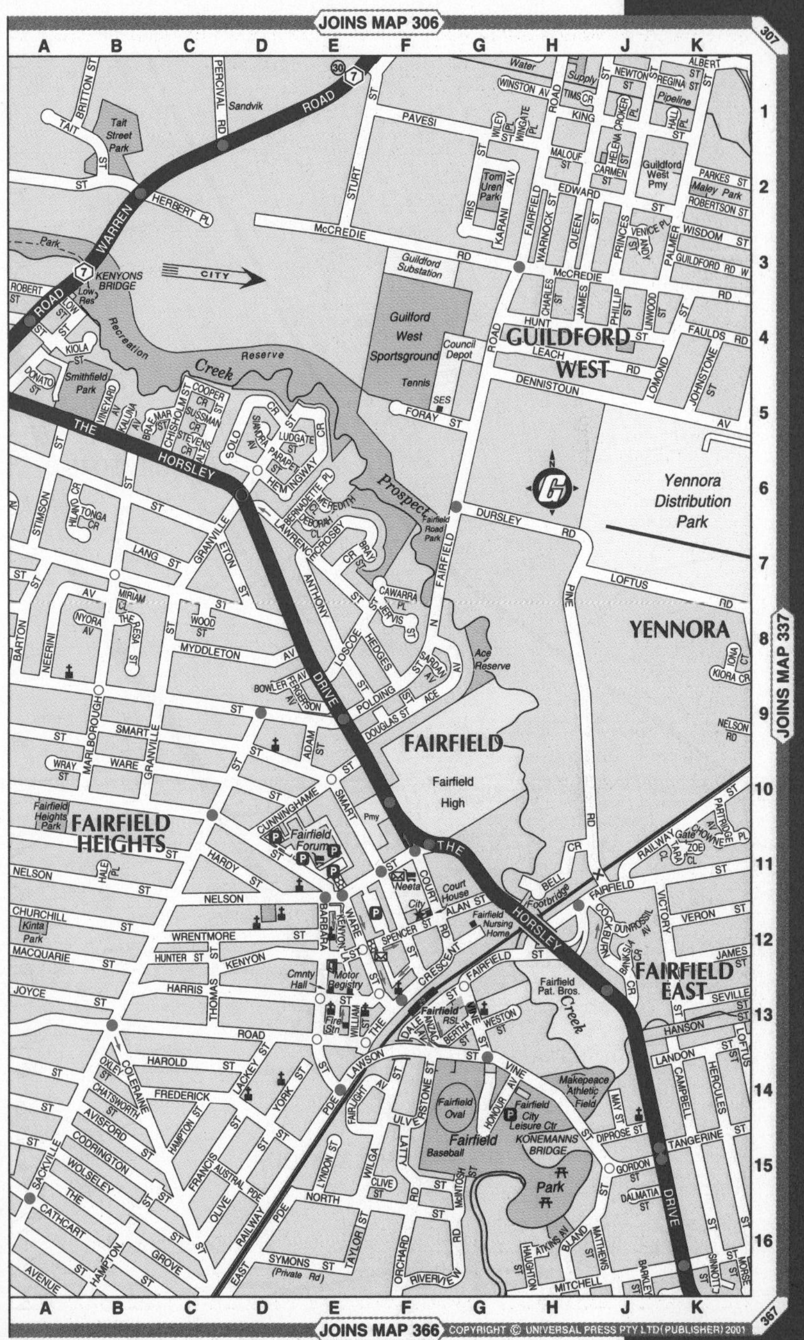
JOINS MAP 306
JOINS MAP 337
JOINS MAP 366
307
367
A B C D E F G H J K
1 2 3 4 5 6 7 8 9 10 11 12 13 14 15 16
GUILDFORD WEST
YENNORA
FAIRFIELD
FAIRFIELD HEIGHTS
FAIRFIELD EAST
Yennora Distribution Park
Guilford West Sportsground
Guildford Substation
Council Depot
Tennis
SES
Guildford West Pmy
Tom Uren Park
Maley Park
Tait Street Park
Smithfield Park
Fairfield Road Park
Ace Reserve
Fairfield High
Fairfield Heights Park
Kinta Park
Fairfield Forum
Court House
Fairfield Nursing Home
Cmnty Hall
Motor Registry
Fire Stn
Fairfield RSL
Fairfield Pat. Bros.
Makepeace Athletic Field
Fairfield Oval
Fairfield City Leisure Ctr
Fairfield Baseball
KONEMANNS BRIDGE
Park
KENYONS BRIDGE
Low Res
Prospect Creek
Recreation Reserve
Sandvik
Water Supply
Pipeline
Footbridge
CITY
WARREN ROAD
THE HORSLEY DRIVE
McCREDIE RD
FAIRFIELD RD
PINE RD
DURSLEY RD
LOFTUS RD
DENNISTOUN AV
FORAY ST
HUNT ST
LEACH RD
FAULDS RD
NELSON ST
CHURCHILL ST
MACQUARIE ST
JOYCE ST
SMART ST
WARE ST
POLDING ST
RAILWAY PDE
EAST PDE
LAWSON ST
VINE ST
DIPROSE ST
GORDON ST
HANSON ST
LANDON ST
TANGERINE ST
MITCHELL ST
SYMONS ST (Private Rd)
RIVERVIEW RD
HAROLD ST
FREDERICK ST
THE CATHCART ST
AVENUE ST
GROVE ST
SACKVILLE ST
NORTH ST
COPYRIGHT © UNIVERSAL PRESS PTY LTD (PUBLISHER) 2001

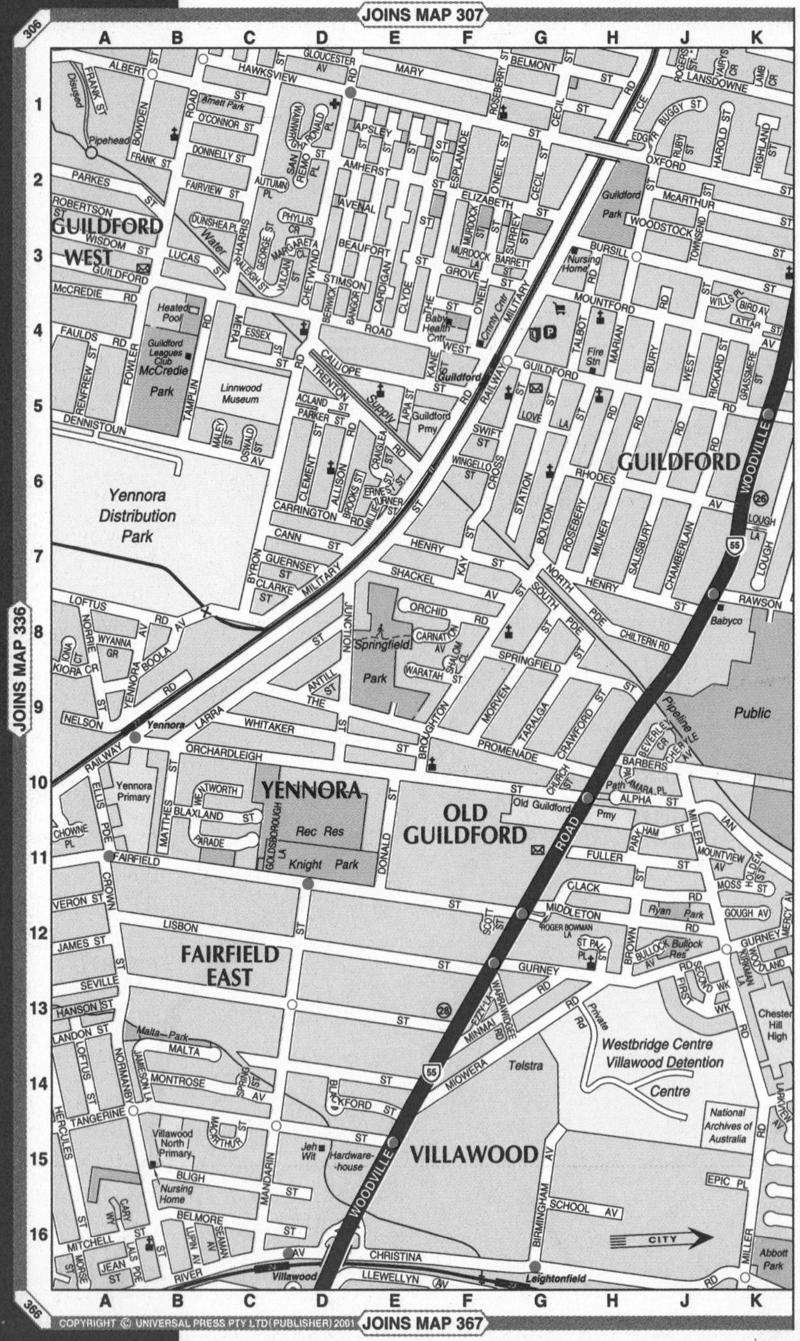
JOINS MAP 307
306
A B C D E F G H J K
JOINS MAP 336
GUILDFORD WEST
GUILDFORD
YENNORA
OLD GUILDFORD
FAIRFIELD EAST
VILLAWOOD
Yennora Distribution Park
McCredie Park
Linnwood Museum
Springfield Park
Rec Res
Knight Park
Guildford Park
Westbridge Centre Villawood Detention Centre
National Archives of Australia
Chester Hill High
Abbott Park
Public
Telstra
CITY
366
JOINS MAP 367

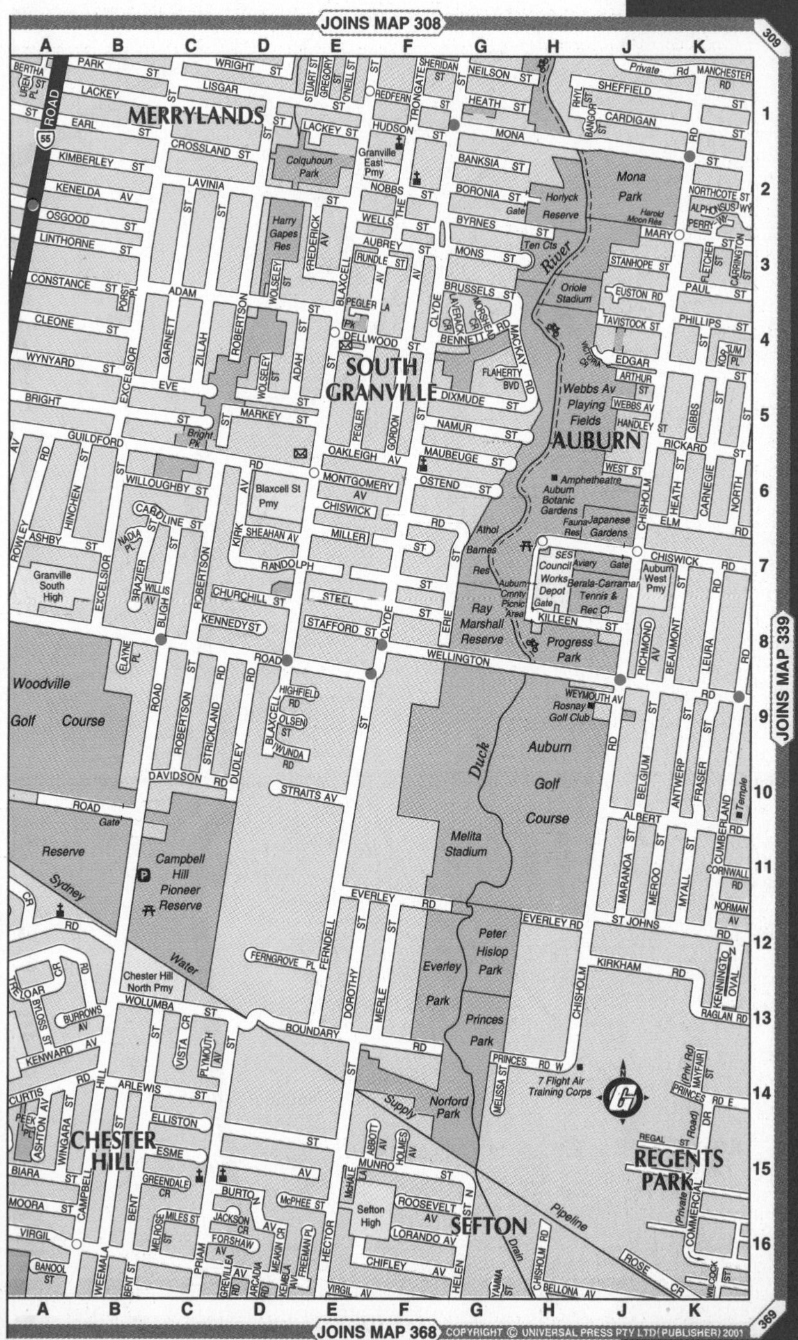
JOINS MAP 308
JOINS MAP 339
JOINS MAP 368
309
369
MERRYLANDS
SOUTH GRANVILLE
AUBURN
CHESTER HILL
SEFTON
REGENTS PARK
Colquhoun Park
Harry Gapes Res
Granville East Pmy
Horlyck Reserve
Mona Park
Oriole Stadium
Webbs Av Playing Fields
Auburn Botanic Gardens
Japanese Gardens
Athol Barnes Res
Ray Marshall Reserve
Progress Park
Auburn West Pmy
Blaxcell St Pmy
Granville South High
Woodville Golf Course
Rosnay Golf Club
Auburn Golf Course
Melita Stadium
Campbell Hill Pioneer Reserve
Chester Hill North Pmy
Peter Hislop Park
Everley Park
Princes Park
Norford Park
Sefton High
7 Flight Air Training Corps
Duck River
Sydney Water Supply Pipeline
WELLINGTON RD
GUILDFORD RD
WOODVILLE ROAD
EVERLEY RD
BOUNDARY RD
CHISHOLM RD

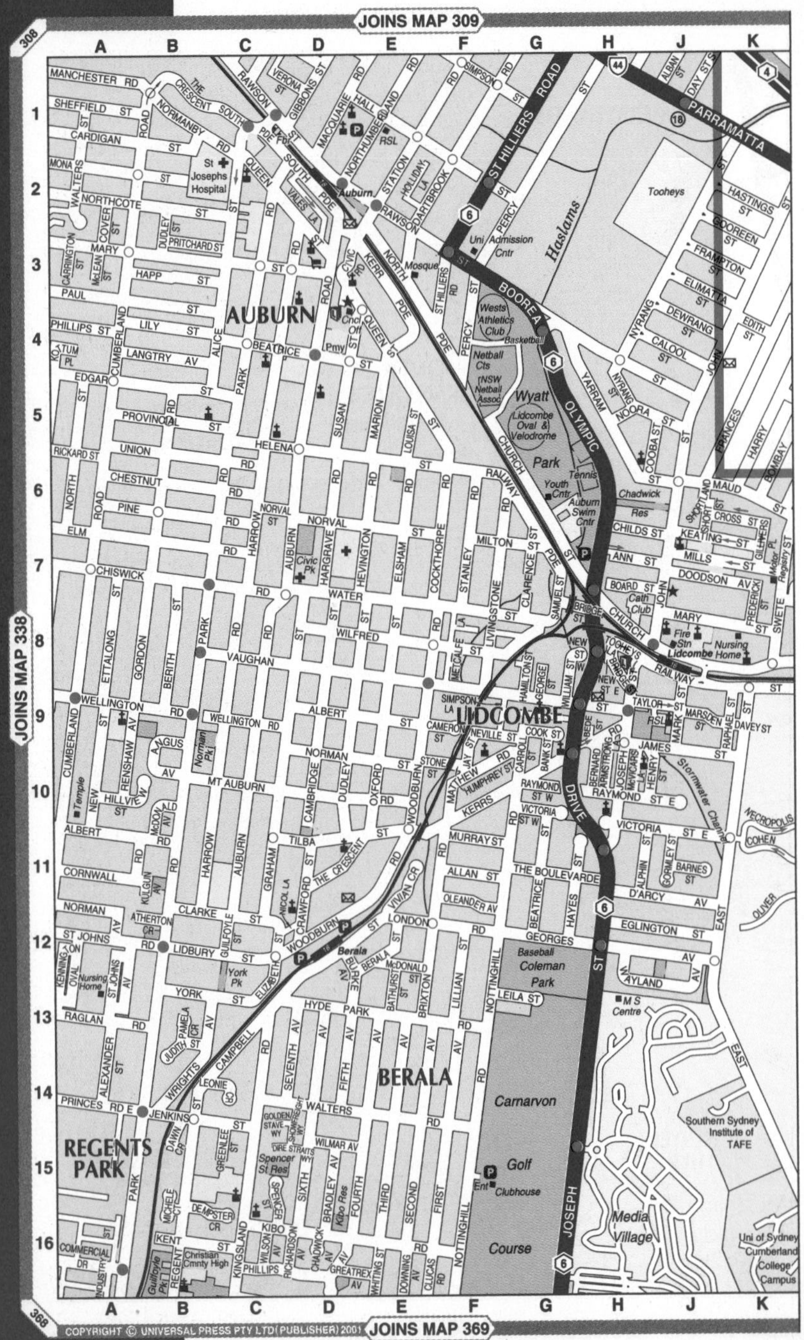
JOINS MAP 309
JOINS MAP 338
JOINS MAP 369
308
368
A B C D E F G H J K
1 2 3 4 5 6 7 8 9 10 11 12 13 14 15 16
AUBURN
LIDCOMBE
BERALA
REGENTS PARK
MANCHESTER RD
SHEFFIELD ST
CARDIGAN ST
NORTHCOTE ST
MARY ST
HAPP ST
PAUL ST
PHILLIPS ST
LILY ST
LANGTRY AV
EDGAR ST
PROVINCIAL ST
RICKARD ST
UNION ST
CHESTNUT RD
PINE RD
ELM
CHISWICK ST
WELLINGTON RD
ALBERT RD
CORNWALL RD
NORMAN AV
ST JOHNS RD
RAGLAN RD
PRINCES RD E
COMMERCIAL DR
THE CRESCENT
RAWSON ST
QUEEN ST
SOUTH PDE
NORTH PDE
PARRAMATTA RD
ST HILLIERS ROAD
BOOREA ST
OLYMPIC DRIVE
JOSEPH ST
CHURCH ST
RAILWAY ST
St Josephs Hospital
Auburn
Uni Admission Cntr
Mosque
Haslams
Tooheys
Wests Athletics Club
Netball Cts
NSW Netball Assoc
Wyatt Park
Lidcombe Oval & Velodrome
Youth Cntr
Auburn Swim Cntr
Chadwick Res
Cath Club
Fire Stn
Lidcombe
Nursing Home
Civic Pk
Norman Pk
Temple
York Pk
Berala
Coleman Park
Baseball
M S Centre
Carnarvon Golf Course
Clubhouse
Ent
Spencer St Res
Kibo Res
Christian Cmnty High
Guilfoyle Pk
Media Village
Southern Sydney Institute of TAFE
Uni of Sydney Cumberland College Campus
Stormwater Channel
NECROPOLIS
COHEN
OLIVER
EAST

JOINS MAP 310

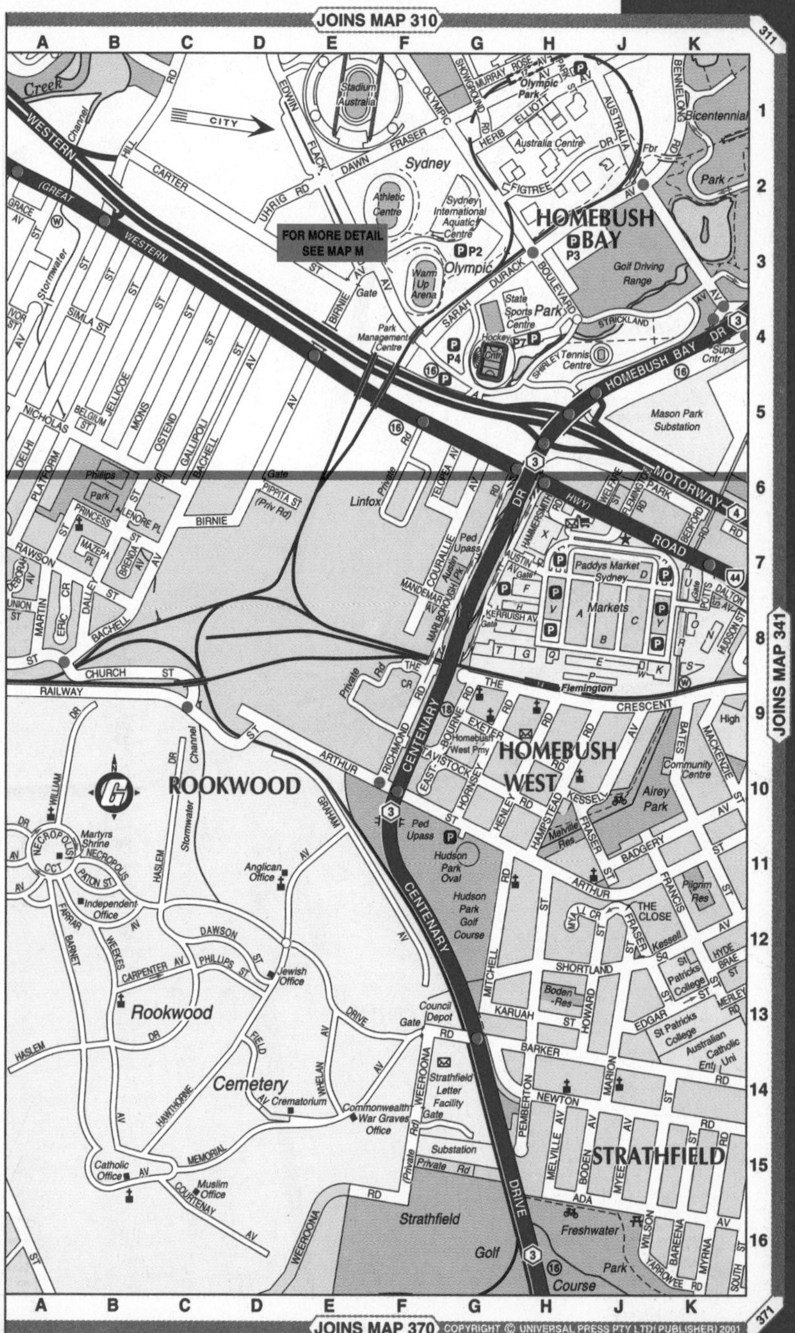

JOINS MAP 341

JOINS MAP 370

JOINS MAP 311

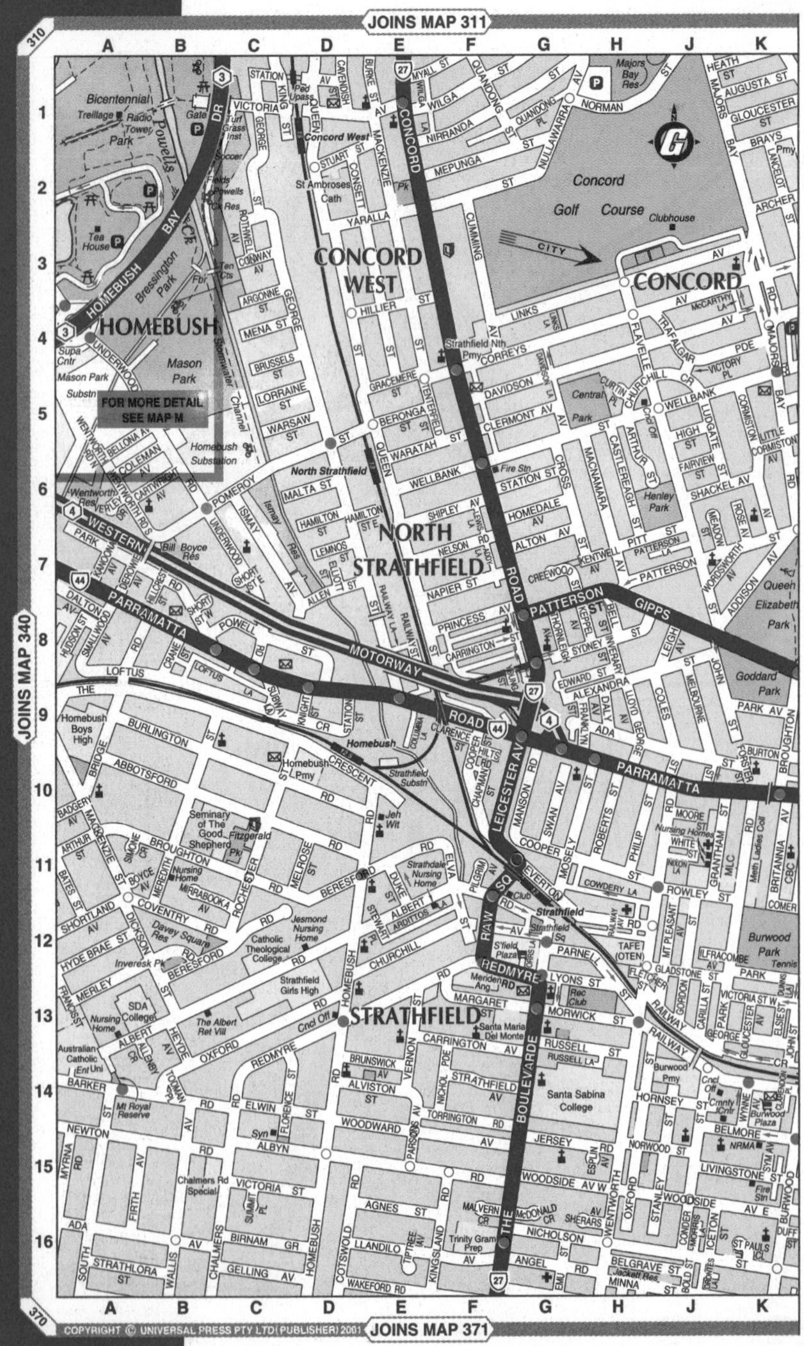

JOINS MAP 371

JOINS MAP 312

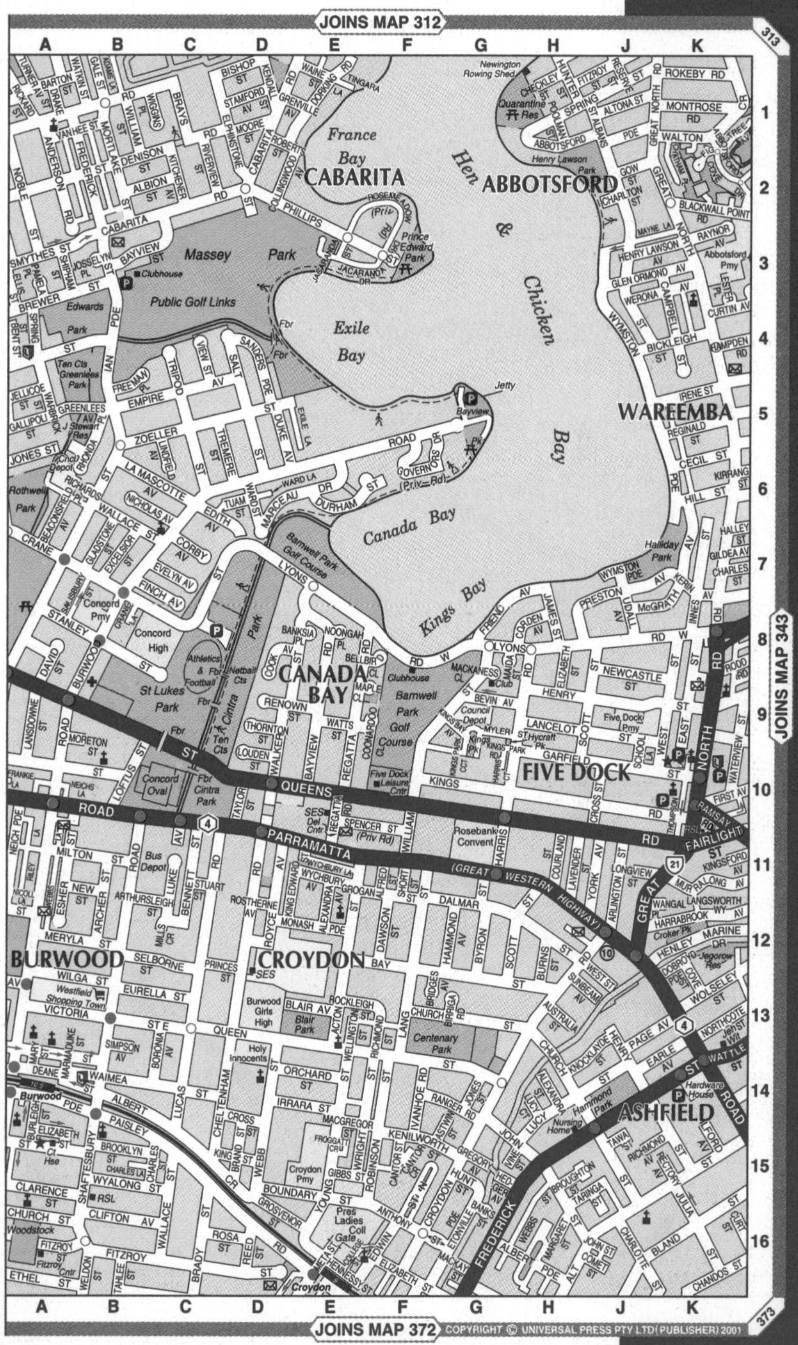

JOINS MAP 343

JOINS MAP 372

JOINS MAP 313

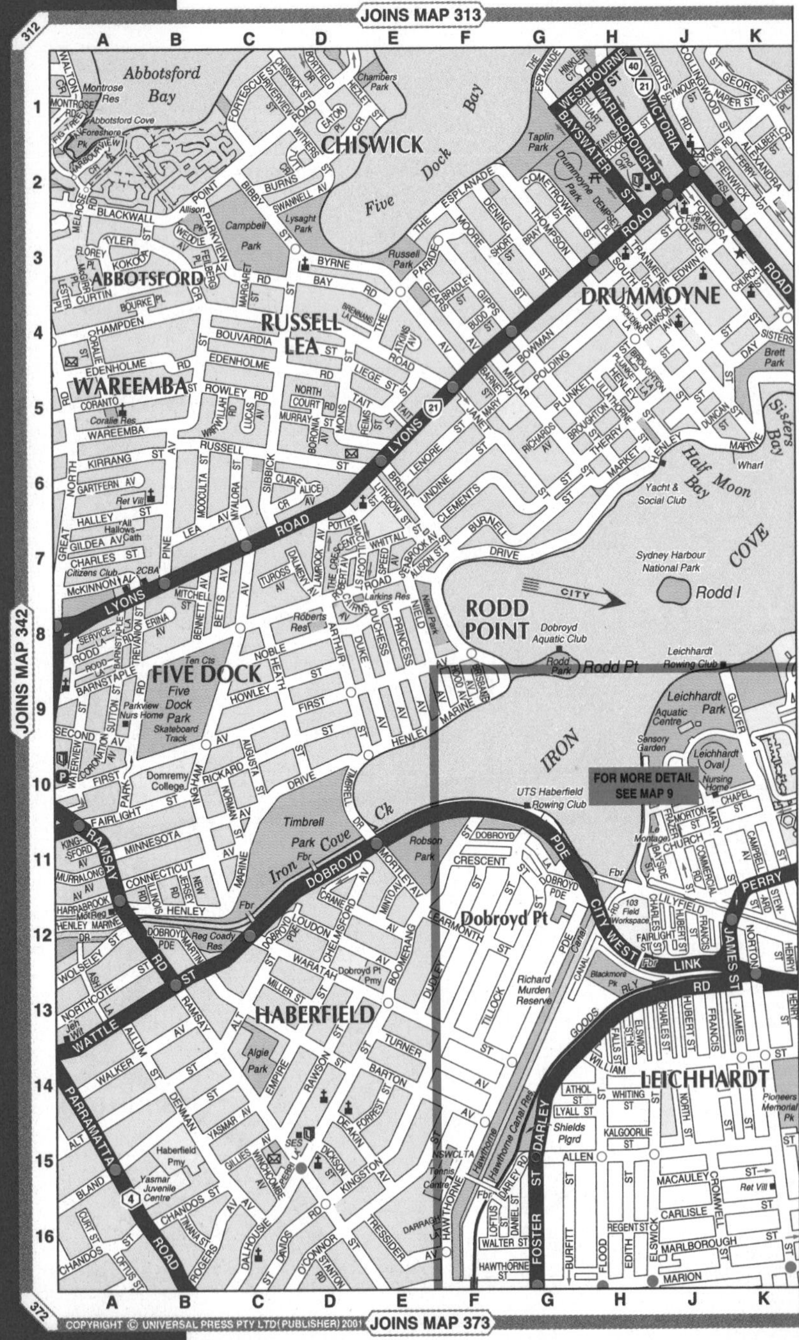

JOINS MAP 342

JOINS MAP 373

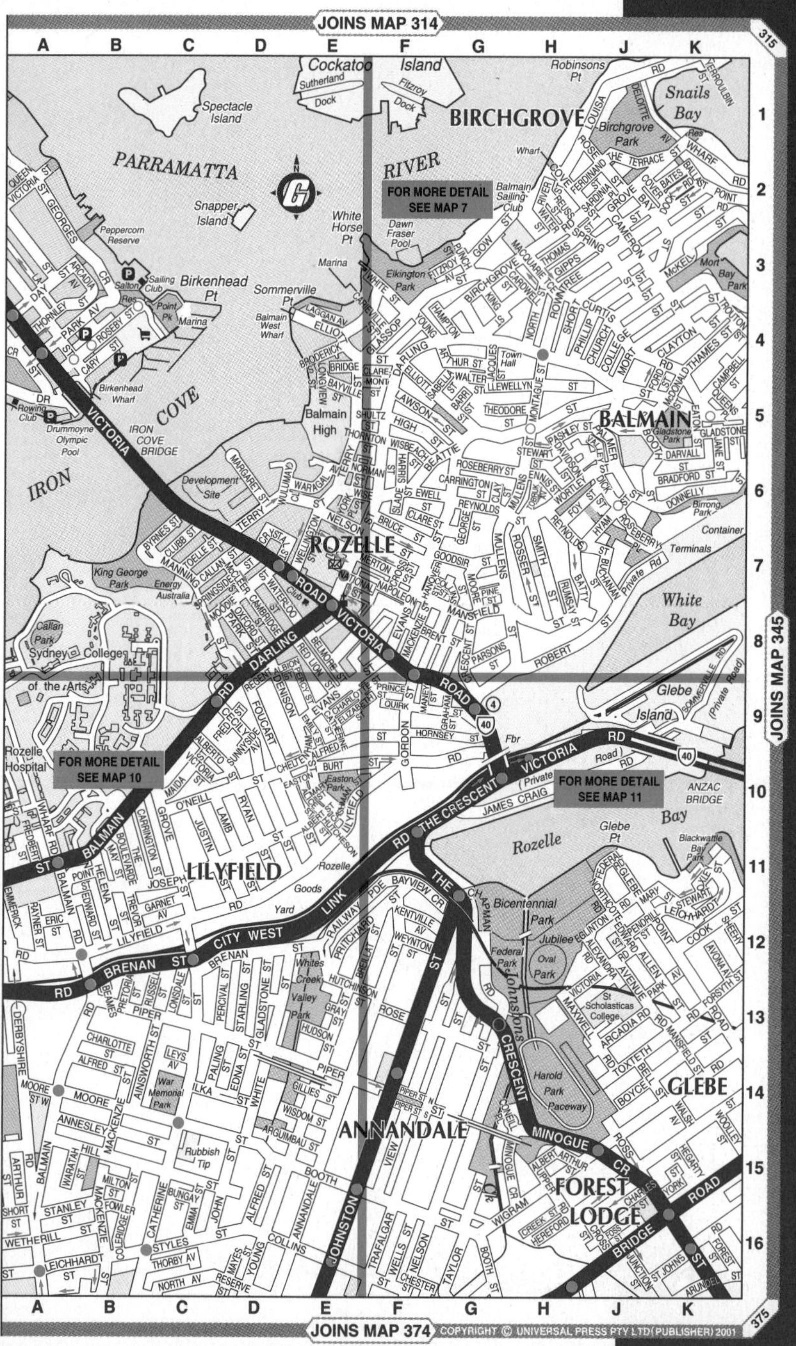
JOINS MAP 314
315
A B C D E F G H J K
1 2 3 4 5 6 7 8 9 10 11 12 13 14 15 16
Cockatoo Island
Sutherland Dock
Fitzroy Dock
Robinsons Pt
Snails Bay
Spectacle Island
BIRCHGROVE
Birchgrove Park
PARRAMATTA
RIVER
FOR MORE DETAIL SEE MAP 7
Snapper Island
Peppercorn Reserve
White Horse Pt
Balmain Sailing Club
Dawn Fraser Pool
Marina
Elkington Park
Mort Bay Park
Salton Res
Sailing Club
Birkenhead Pt
Point Pk
Marina
Sommerville Pt
Balmain West Wharf
Birkenhead Wharf
Town Hall
Rowing Club
Drummoyne Olympic Pool
IRON COVE
IRON COVE BRIDGE
Balmain High
BALMAIN
Gladstone Park
Development Site
Birrong Park
Container Terminals
ROZELLE
King George Park
Energy Australia
White Bay
Callan Park
Sydney College of the Arts
Glebe Island
Rozelle Hospital
FOR MORE DETAIL SEE MAP 10
FOR MORE DETAIL SEE MAP 11
ANZAC BRIDGE
Easton Park
Rozelle Bay
Glebe Pt
Blackwattle Bay Park
LILYFIELD
Rozelle Goods Yard
Bicentennial Park
Jubilee Oval Park
Federal Park
Whites Creek Valley Park
St Scholasticas College
War Memorial Park
Harold Park Paceway
GLEBE
Rubbish Tip
ANNANDALE
FOREST LODGE
VICTORIA RD
DARLING ST
CITY WEST LINK
THE CRESCENT
BRENAN ST
JOHNSTON ST
MINOGUE CR
BRIDGE ROAD
ROSS ST
JOINS MAP 345
JOINS MAP 374
375

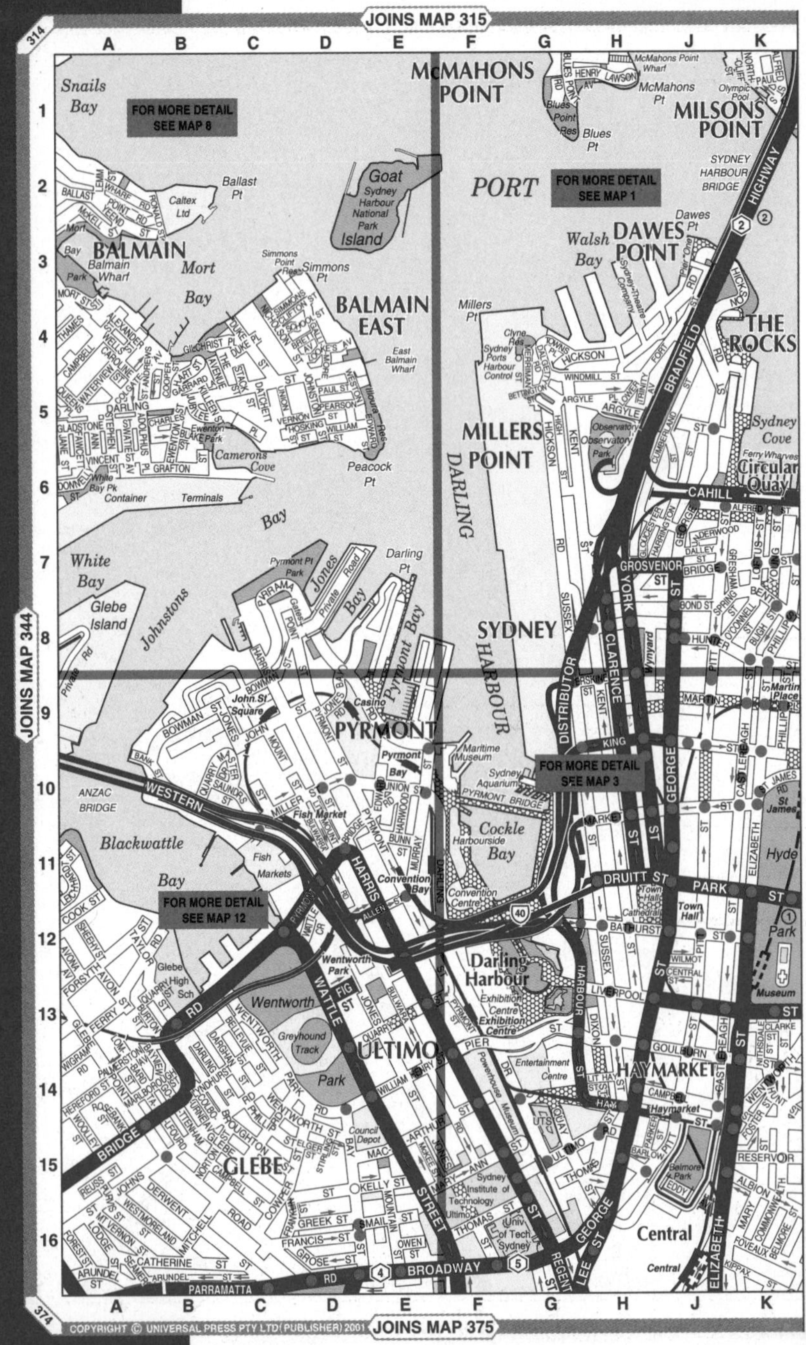
JOINS MAP 315
314
A B C D E F G H J K
1 2 3 4 5 6 7 8 9 10 11 12 13 14 15 16
Snails Bay
FOR MORE DETAIL SEE MAP 8
McMAHONS POINT
McMahons Point Wharf
McMahons Pt
Blues Point Res
Blues Pt
MILSONS POINT
SYDNEY HARBOUR BRIDGE
Ballast Pt
Caltex Ltd
Goat
Sydney Harbour National Park
Island
PORT
FOR MORE DETAIL SEE MAP 1
Dawes Pt
DAWES POINT
Walsh Bay
Sydney Theatre Company
BALMAIN
Balmain Wharf
Mort Bay
Simmons Point Res
Simmons Pt
BALMAIN EAST
East Balmain Wharf
Millers Pt
Clyne Res
Sydney Ports Harbour Control
THE ROCKS
HICKSON
WINDMILL ST
ARGYLE
Observatory Park
Sydney Cove
Ferry Wharves
Circular Quay
MILLERS POINT
DARLING
Peacock Pt
Camerons Cove
Container Terminals
Bay
CAHILL
White Bay
Glebe Island
Johnstons
Pymont Pt Park
Jones Bay
Darling Pt
Pyrmont Bay
SYDNEY
HARBOUR
John St Square
Casino
PYRMONT
Maritime Museum
Sydney Aquarium
PYRMONT BRIDGE
FOR MORE DETAIL SEE MAP 3
ANZAC BRIDGE
WESTERN
Fish Market
Blackwattle Bay
Cockle Bay
Harbourside
Fish Markets
Convention Bay
Convention Centre
FOR MORE DETAIL SEE MAP 12
Wentworth Park
Darling Harbour
Exhibition Centre
Greyhound Track
ULTIMO
Entertainment Centre
Powerhouse Museum
HAYMARKET
Haymarket
Town Hall
Hyde Park
Museum
GLEBE
Sydney Institute of Technology
Univ of Tech Sydney
UTS
Belmore Park
Central
BROADWAY
PARRAMATTA
GEORGE ST
ELIZABETH
BRADFIELD HIGHWAY
374
COPYRIGHT © UNIVERSAL PRESS PTY LTD (PUBLISHER) 2001
JOINS MAP 375
JOINS MAP 344

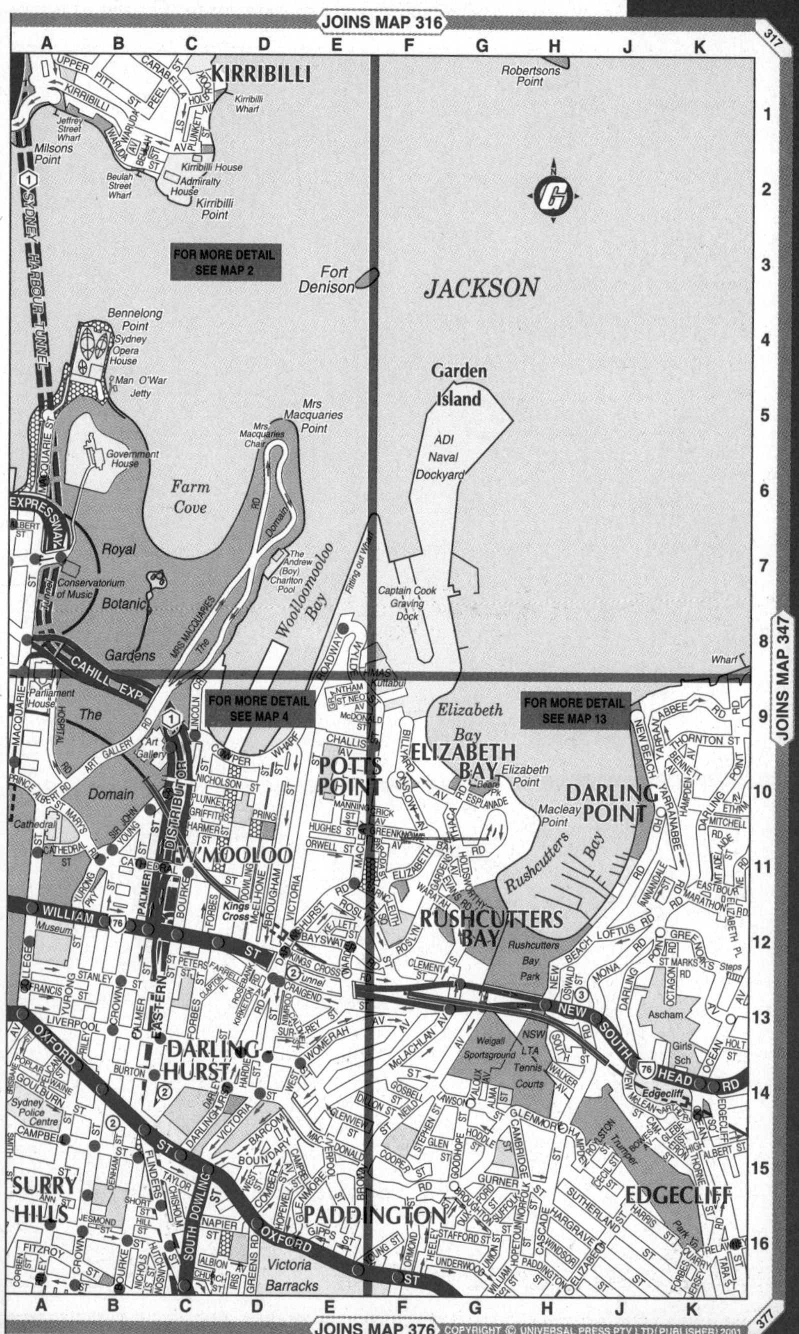
JOINS MAP 316
KIRRIBILLI
Milsons Point
Kirribilli House
Admiralty House
Kirribilli Point
Robertsons Point
FOR MORE DETAIL SEE MAP 2
Fort Denison
JACKSON
Bennelong Point
Sydney Opera House
Man O'War Jetty
Garden Island
ADI Naval Dockyard
Mrs Macquaries Point
Mrs Macquaries Chair
Government House
Farm Cove
Royal Botanic Gardens
Conservatorium of Music
Woolloomooloo Bay
The Andrew (Boy) Charlton Pool
Captain Cook Graving Dock
HMAS Kuttabul
FOR MORE DETAIL SEE MAP 4
FOR MORE DETAIL SEE MAP 13
Elizabeth Bay
POTTS POINT
ELIZABETH BAY
Elizabeth Point
DARLING POINT
Macleay Point
Rushcutters Bay
W'MOOLOO
The Domain
Art Gallery
Parliament House
Cathedral
Museum
Kings Cross
RUSHCUTTERS BAY
Rushcutters Bay Park
Ascham
Girls Sch
Edgecliff
DARLING-HURST
Weigall Sportsground
NSW LTA Tennis Courts
Sydney Police Centre
SURRY HILLS
PADDINGTON
Victoria Barracks
EDGECLIFF
Trumper Park
JOINS MAP 347
JOINS MAP 376

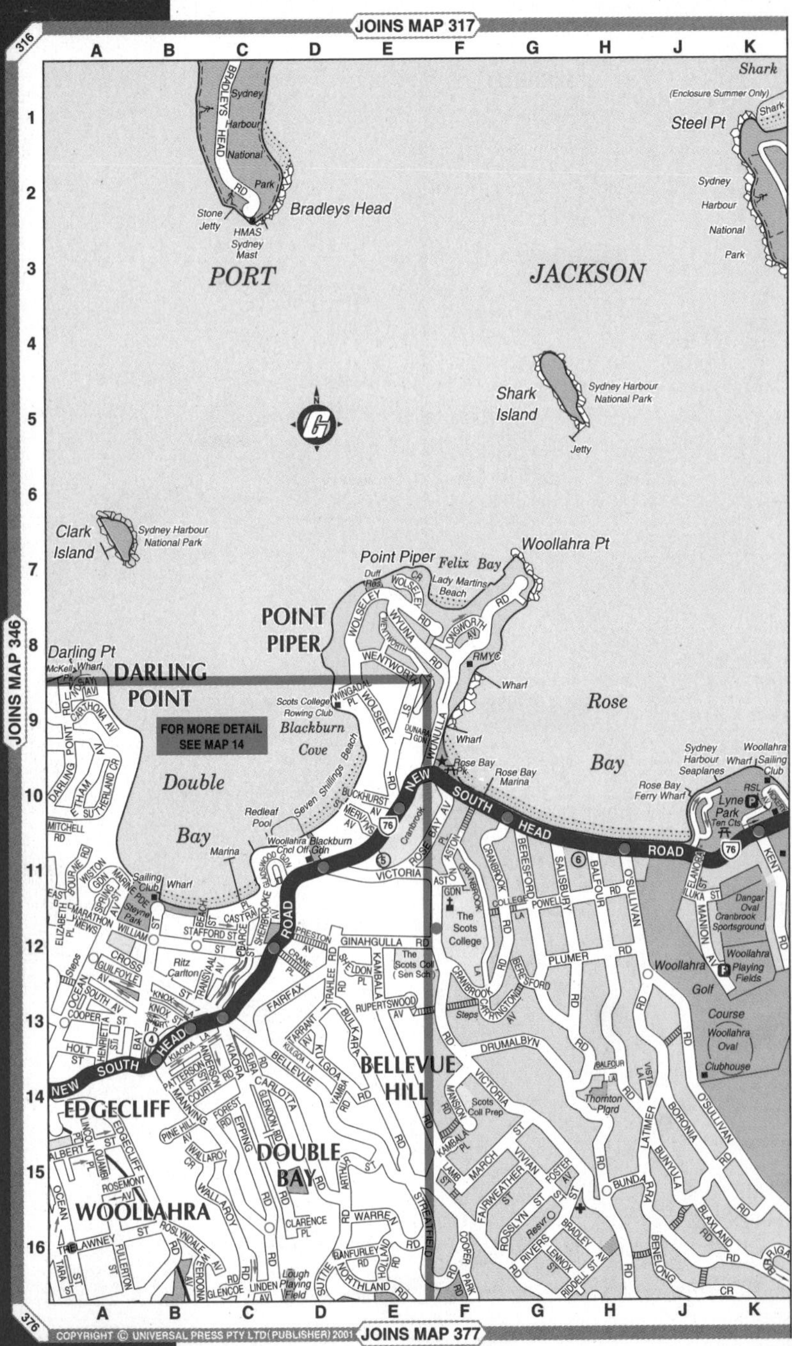
JOINS MAP 317
JOINS MAP 346
JOINS MAP 377
316
376
A B C D E F G H J K
1 2 3 4 5 6 7 8 9 10 11 12 13 14 15 16
PORT
JACKSON
Bradleys Head
BRADLEYS HEAD RD
Sydney Harbour National Park
Stone Jetty
HMAS Sydney Mast
Shark
(Enclosure Summer Only)
Steel Pt
Shark Island
Jetty
Clark Island
Woollahra Pt
Point Piper
Felix Bay
Lady Martins Beach
POINT PIPER
RMYC
Wharf
Rose Bay
Rose Bay Marina
Sydney Harbour Seaplanes
Woollahra Sailing Club
Rose Bay Ferry Wharf
Lyne Park
Ten Cts
Darling Pt
McKell Wharf
DARLING POINT
FOR MORE DETAIL SEE MAP 14
Scots College Rowing Club
Blackburn Cove
Seven Shillings Beach
Double Bay
Redleaf Pool
Woollahra Cncl Off
Blackburn Gdn
Marina
Sailing Club
Wharf
Steyne Park
NEW SOUTH HEAD ROAD
VICTORIA RD
Cranbrook
The Scots College
The Scots Coll (Sen Sch)
Ritz Carlton
Dangar Oval
Cranbrook Sportsground
Woollahra Playing Fields
Woollahra Golf Course
Woollahra Oval
Clubhouse
Thornton Plgrd
Scots Coll Prep
BELLEVUE HILL
EDGECLIFF
DOUBLE BAY
WOOLLAHRA
Lough Playing Field
Steps
Resvr
WOLSELEY RD
WYUNA RD
WENTWORTH RD
LONGWORTH AV
WUNULLA RD
ROSE BAY AV
ASTON GDNS
BERESFORD RD
SALISBURY RD
BALFOUR RD
O'SULLIVAN RD
KENT RD
ELANORA ST
LUKA ST
MANION AV
POWELL RD
COLLEGE LA
PLUMER RD
GINAHGULLA RD
KAMBALA RD
RUPERTSWOOD AV
DRUMALBYN RD
CARRINGTON AV
CRANBROOK RD
LATIMER RD
BORONIA RD
BUNYULA RD
BLAXLAND RD
BENELONG CR
BUNDARRA RD
FAIRWEATHER ST
VIVIAN ST
FOSTER AV
ROSSLYN ST
RIVERS ST
LENNOX ST
BRADLEY AV
RIDDELL ST
MARCH ST
LAMB ST
MANSION RD
COOPER PARK RD
STREATFIELD RD
BELLEVUE RD
CARLOTTA RD
KIAORA RD
FAIRFAX RD
TRAHLEE RD
BULKARA RD
KULGOA RD
YAMBA RD
WARREN RD
BANFURLEY RD
NORTHLAND RD
HOLLAND RD
SUTTIE RD
LINDEN AV
GLENCOE RD
WALLAROY RD
FOREST RD
EPPING RD
GLENDON RD
PINE HILL AV
MANNING RD
PATTERSON ST
ANDERSON ST
COURT RD
EDGECLIFF RD
ALBERT ST
OCEAN ST
ROSEMONT AV
QUAMBI PL
TRELAWNEY ST
FULLERTON ST
ROSLYNDALE AV
EEROONA AV
TARA ST
HOLT ST
COOPER ST
HENRIETTA ST
GUILFOYLE AV
CROSS ST
KNOX ST
TRANSVAAL AV
STAFFORD ST
CASTRA PL
BEACH ST
WILLIAM ST
MARATHON RD
ELIZABETH PL
SPRING ST
WISTON GDNS
MITCHELL RD
DARLING POINT RD
ETHAM AV
SUTHERLAND CR
CARTHONA AV
LINDSAY AV
MARINE PDE
PRESTON AV
CRANE AV
SHELDON PL
BUCKHURST AV
MERVYN AV
WINGADAL PL
DUNARA GDN
CLARENCE PL
ARTHUR ST

JOINS MAP 318

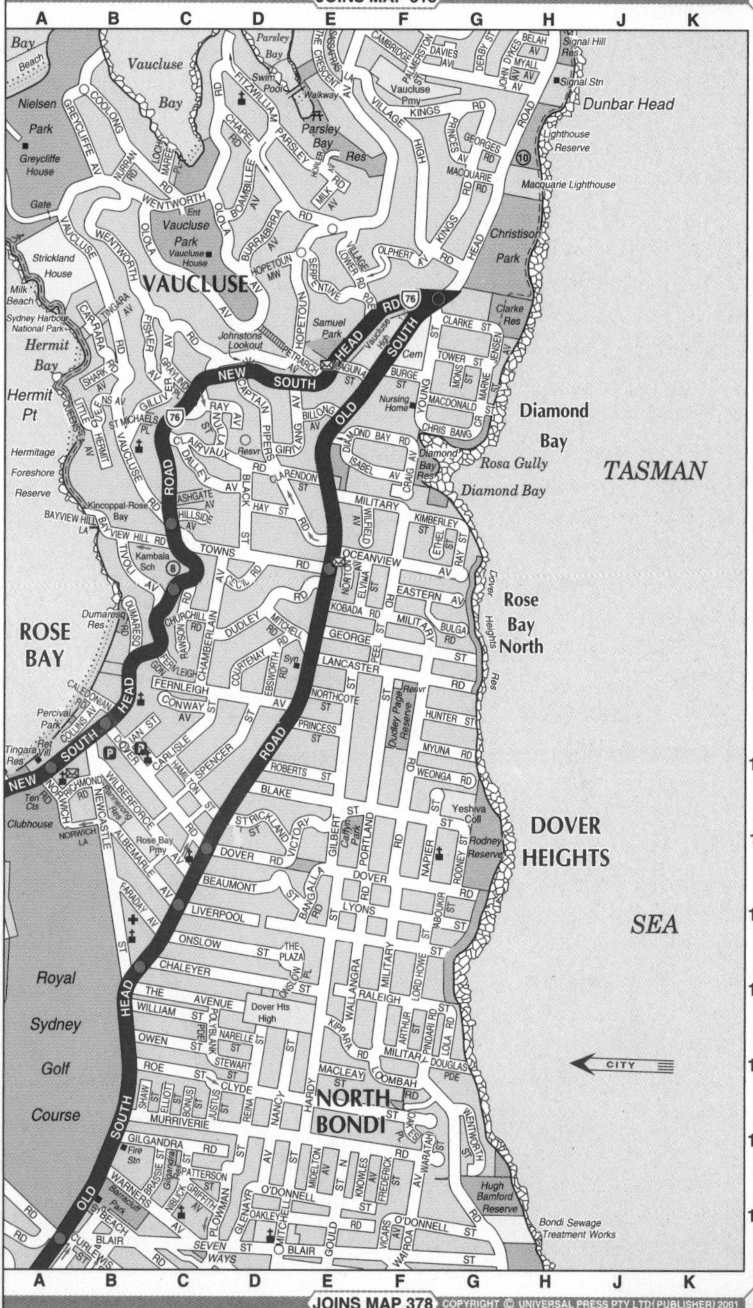

VAUCLUSE

ROSE BAY

DOVER HEIGHTS

NORTH BONDI

Rose Bay North

Diamond Bay

TASMAN SEA

JOINS MAP 378

JOINS MAP 323

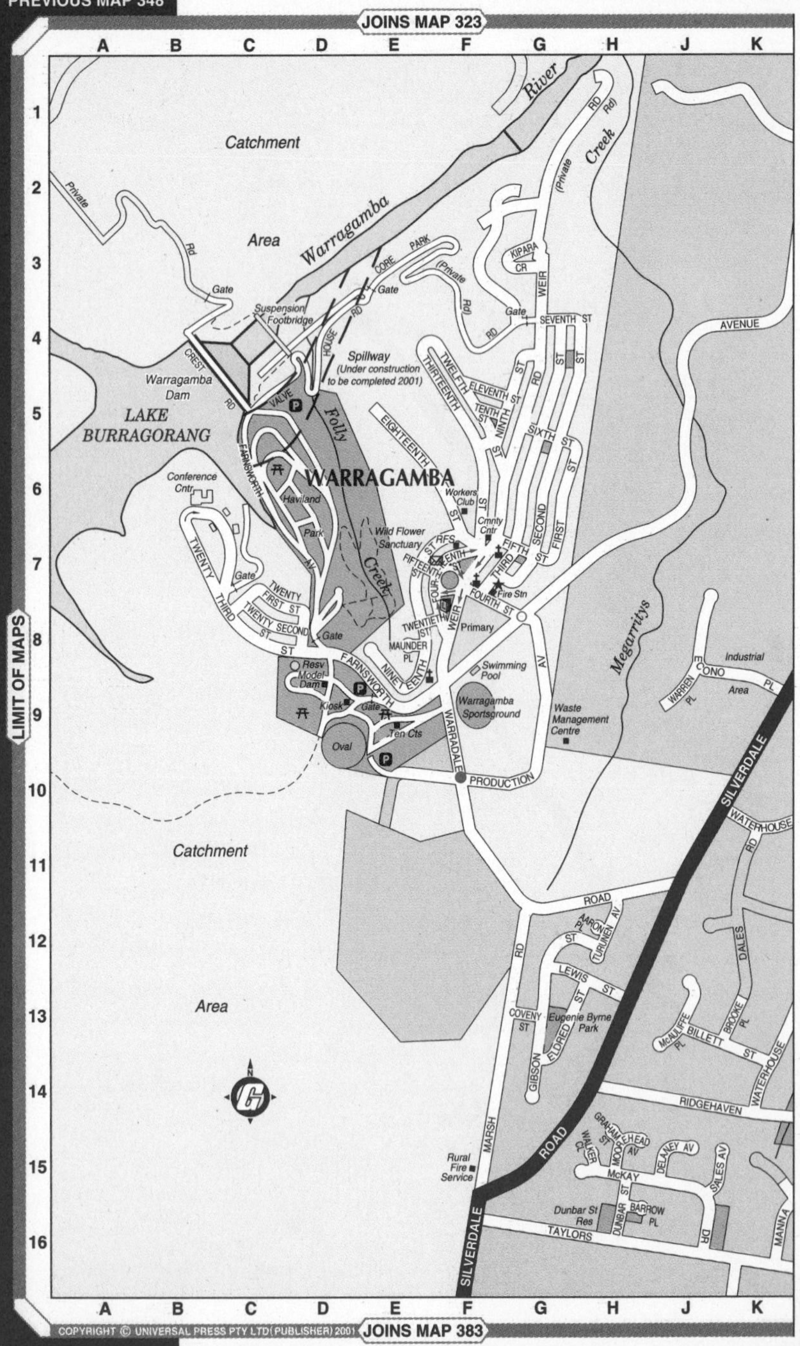

JOINS MAP 383

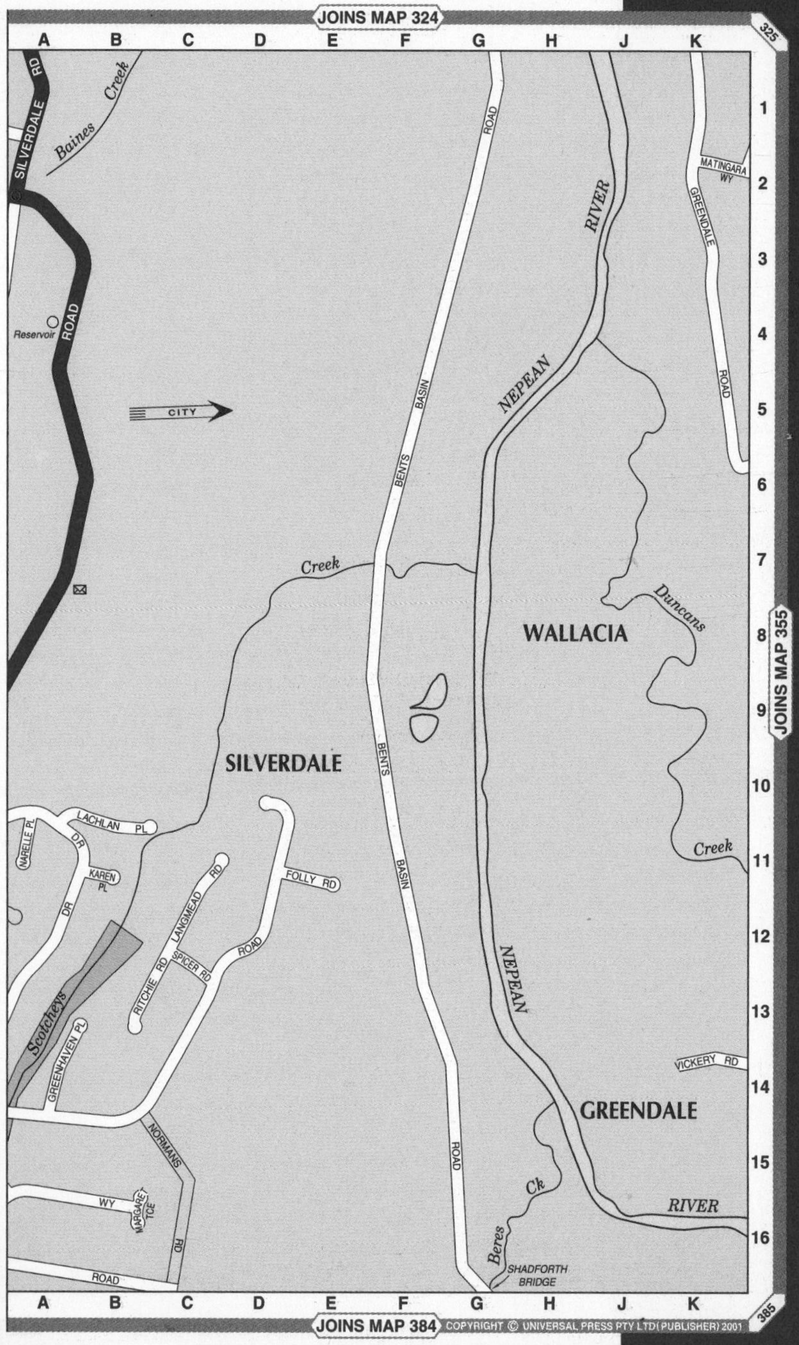
JOINS MAP 324
JOINS MAP 355
JOINS MAP 384
325
385
A B C D E F G H J K
1 2 3 4 5 6 7 8 9 10 11 12 13 14 15 16
SILVERDALE RD
Baines Creek
ROAD
Reservoir
CITY
BENTS BASIN ROAD
NEPEAN RIVER
MATINGARA WY
GREENDALE ROAD
Creek
Duncans
WALLACIA
SILVERDALE
LACHLAN PL
NARELLE PL
DR
KAREN PL
FOLLY RD
LANGMEAD RD
SPICER RD
RITCHIE RD
ROAD
Scotcheys
GREENHAVEN PL
NORMANS RD
WY
MARGARET TCE
ROAD
Creek
VICKERY RD
GREENDALE
Ck
Beres
SHADFORTH BRIDGE
RIVER
NEPEAN

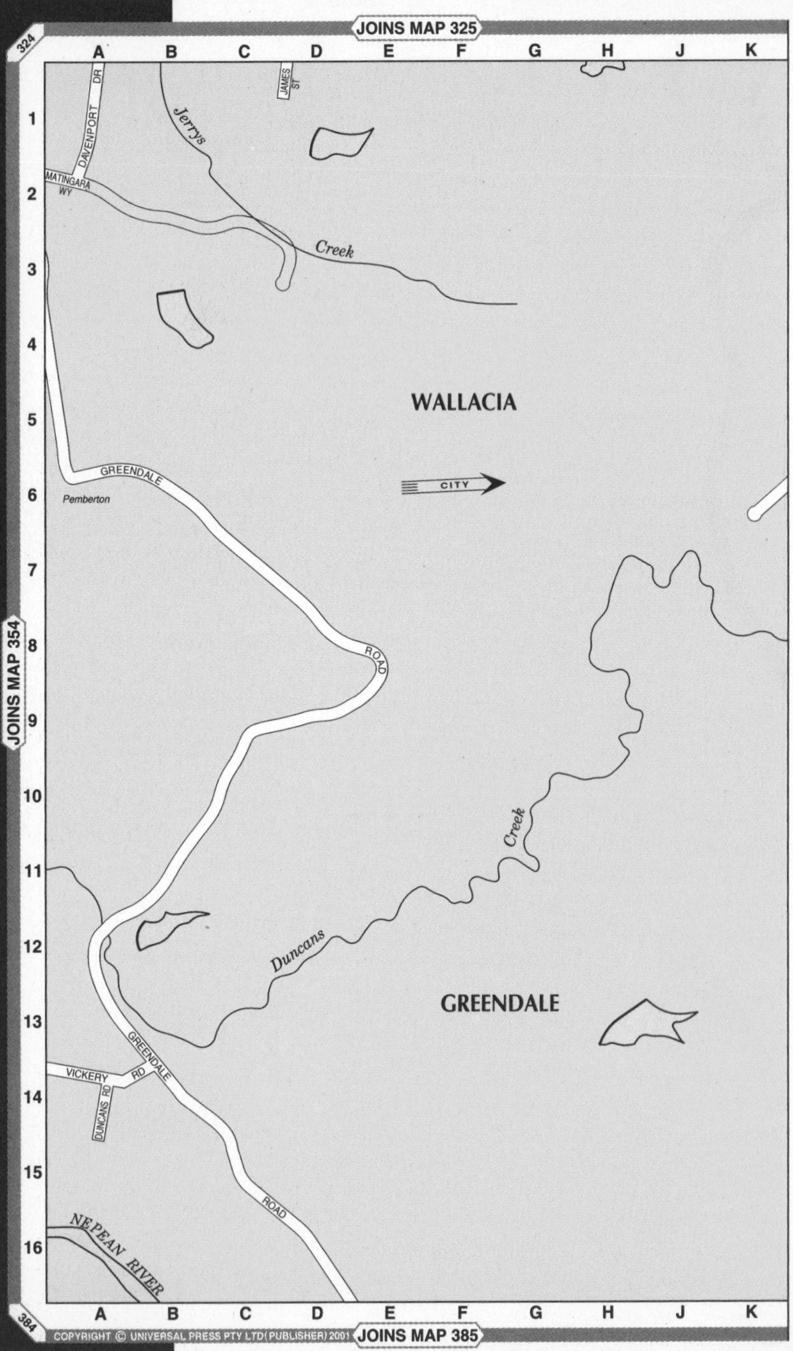
JOINS MAP 325
324
A
B
C
D
E
F
G
H
J
K
1
2
3
4
5
6
7
8
9
10
11
12
13
14
15
16
DAVENPORT DR
JAMES ST
Jerrys
MATINGARA WY
Creek
WALLACIA
GREENDALE
CITY
Pemberton
ROAD
JOINS MAP 354
Creek
Duncans
GREENDALE
GREENDALE
VICKERY RD
DUNCANS RD
ROAD
NEPEAN RIVER
384
JOINS MAP 385

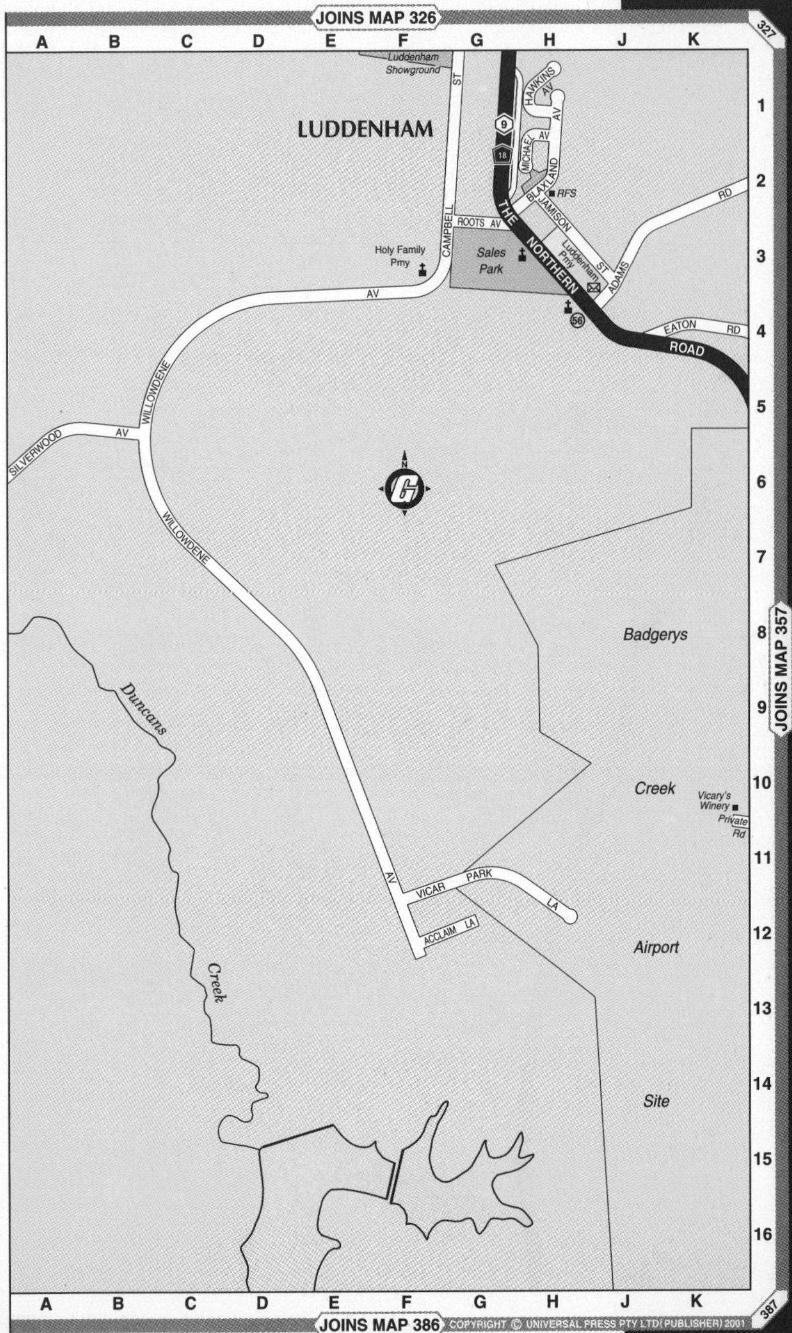
JOINS MAP 326
327
A
B
C
D
E
F
G
H
J
K
Luddenham Showground
LUDDENHAM
CAMPBELL ST
HAWKINS AV
MICHAEL AV
BLAXLAND AV
RFS
JAMISON ST
RD
ROOTS AV
THE NORTHERN ROAD
Holy Family Pmy
Sales Park
Luddenham Pmy
ADAMS
AV
EATON RD
ROAD
WILLOWDENE
SILVERWOOD AV
WILLOWDENE
Badgerys
Duncans
Creek
Vicary's Winery
Private Rd
AV
VICAR PARK LA
ACCLAIM LA
Airport
Creek
Site
1
2
3
4
5
6
7
8
9
10
11
12
13
14
15
16
JOINS MAP 357
A
B
C
D
E
F
G
H
J
K
387
JOINS MAP 386

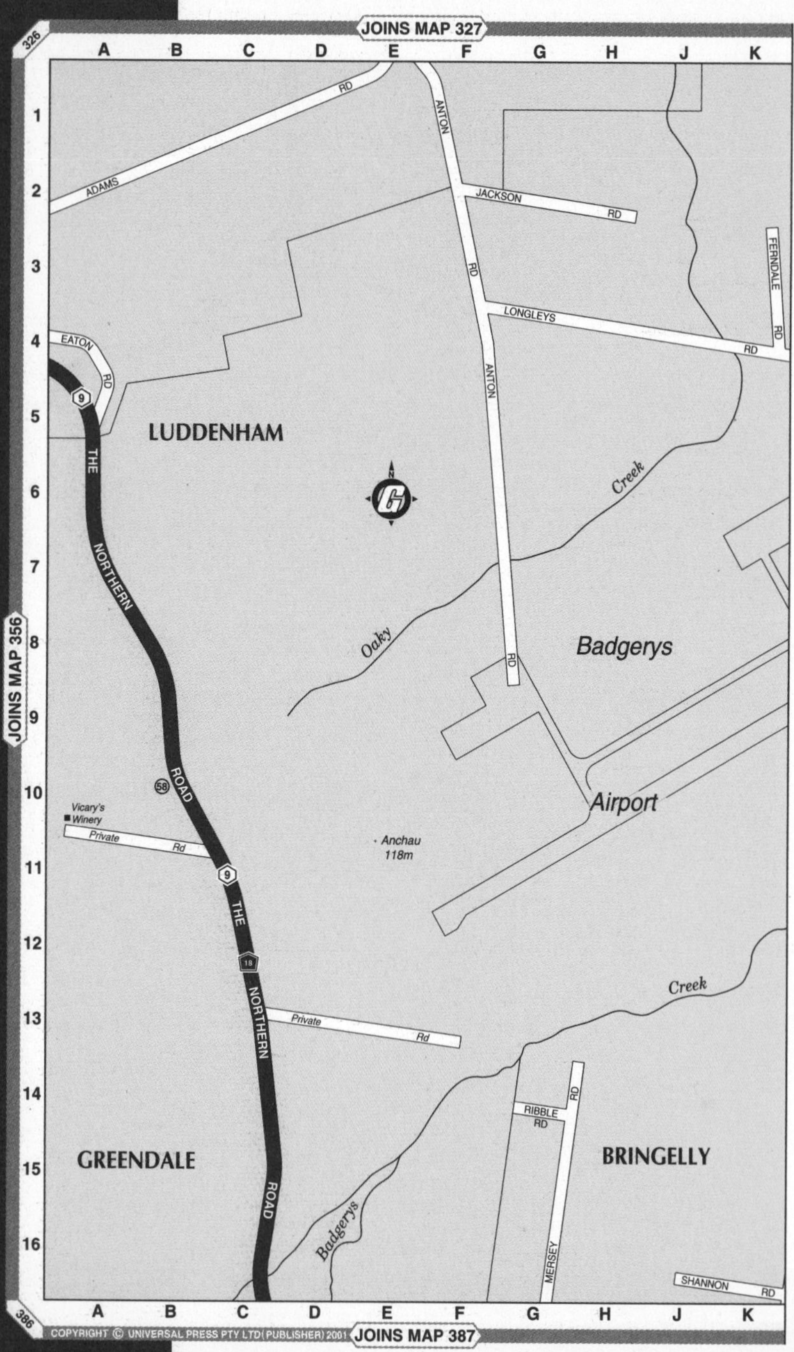
JOINS MAP 327
326
A B C D E F G H J K
1 2 3 4 5 6 7 8 9 10 11 12 13 14 15 16
ADAMS RD
ANTON RD
JACKSON RD
FERNDALE RD
LONGLEYS RD
EATON RD
9
LUDDENHAM
THE NORTHERN ROAD
Creek
Oaky
Badgerys
Airport
JOINS MAP 356
58
Vicary's Winery
Private Rd
Anchau 118m
18
Private Rd
Creek
RIBBLE RD
MERSEY RD
GREENDALE
BRINGELLY
Badgerys
SHANNON RD
386
JOINS MAP 387

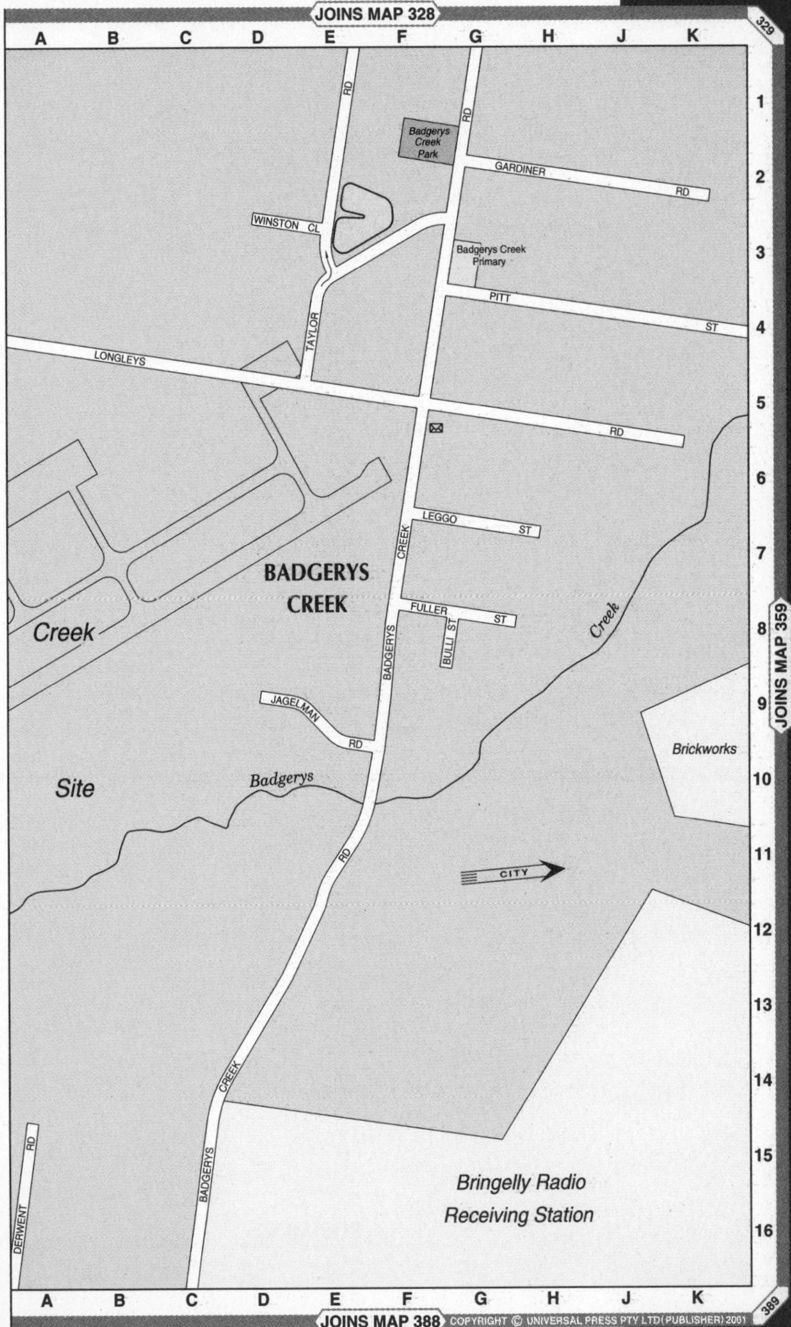
JOINS MAP 328
329
A B C D E F G H J K
1 2 3 4 5 6 7 8 9 10 11 12 13 14 15 16
Badgerys Creek Park
GARDINER RD
WINSTON CL
Badgerys Creek Primary
PITT ST
TAYLOR RD
LONGLEYS RD
LEGGO ST
BADGERYS CREEK
FULLER ST
BULLI ST
Creek
JAGELMAN RD
Site
Badgerys
Creek
Brickworks
CITY
BADGERYS CREEK RD
DERWENT RD
Bringelly Radio Receiving Station
JOINS MAP 359
JOINS MAP 388
389

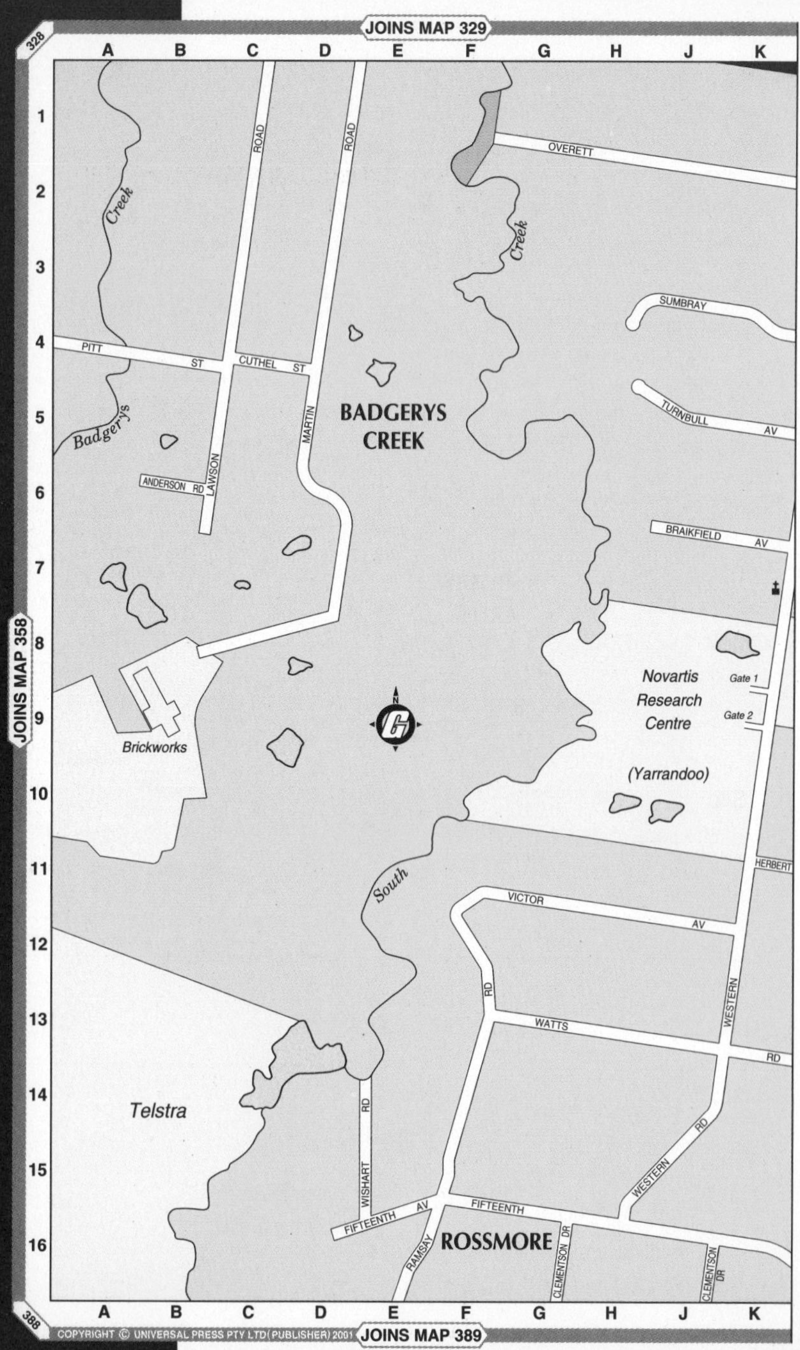
JOINS MAP 329
328
A B C D E F G H J K
1 2 3 4 5 6 7 8 9 10 11 12 13 14 15 16
OVERETT
ROAD
ROAD
Creek
Creek
SUMBRAY
PITT ST
CUTHEL ST
TURNBULL AV
MARTIN
BADGERYS CREEK
Badgerys
ANDERSON RD
LAWSON
BRAIKFIELD AV
Novartis Research Centre
Gate 1
Gate 2
(Yarrandoo)
Brickworks
JOINS MAP 358
HERBERT
South
VICTOR AV
RD
WATTS RD
WESTERN
Telstra
RD
WISHART
WESTERN RD
FIFTEENTH AV
FIFTEENTH
RAMSAY
ROSSMORE
CLEMENTSON DR
CLEMENTSON DR
388
JOINS MAP 389

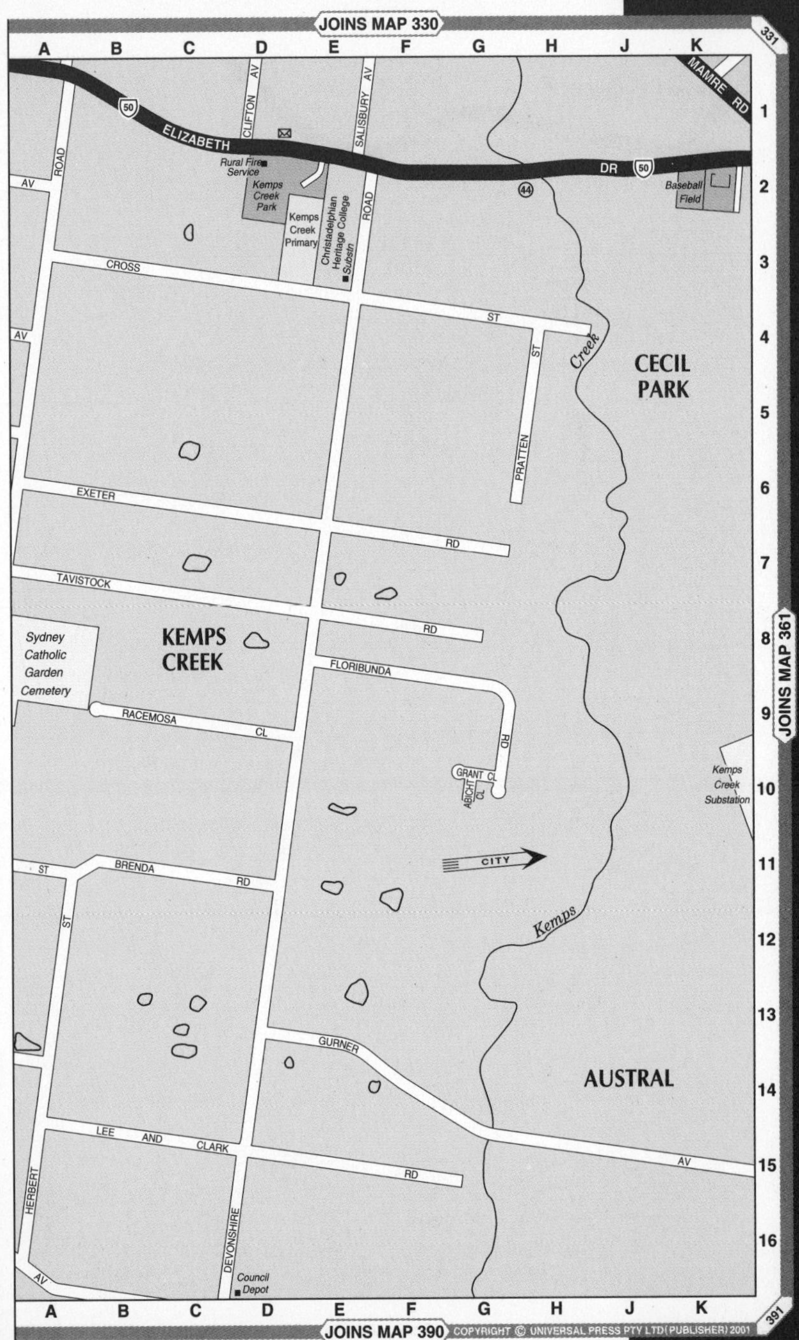
JOINS MAP 330
331
A
B
C
D
E
F
G
H
J
K
MAMRE RD
50
ELIZABETH
DR
50
CLIFTON AV
SALISBURY AV
ROAD
ROAD
AV
Rural Fire Service
Kemps Creek Park
Kemps Creek Primary
Christadelphian Heritage College
Substn
44
Baseball Field
CROSS
ST
PRATTEN ST
Creek
CECIL PARK
AV
EXETER
RD
TAVISTOCK
RD
Sydney Catholic Garden Cemetery
KEMPS CREEK
FLORIBUNDA
RD
RACEMOSA
CL
GRANT CL
ABICHT CL
Kemps Creek Substation
JOINS MAP 361
CITY
ST
BRENDA
RD
ST
Kemps
GURNER
AUSTRAL
LEE AND CLARK
RD
AV
HERBERT
DEVONSHIRE
AV
Council Depot
1
2
3
4
5
6
7
8
9
10
11
12
13
14
15
16
JOINS MAP 390
391

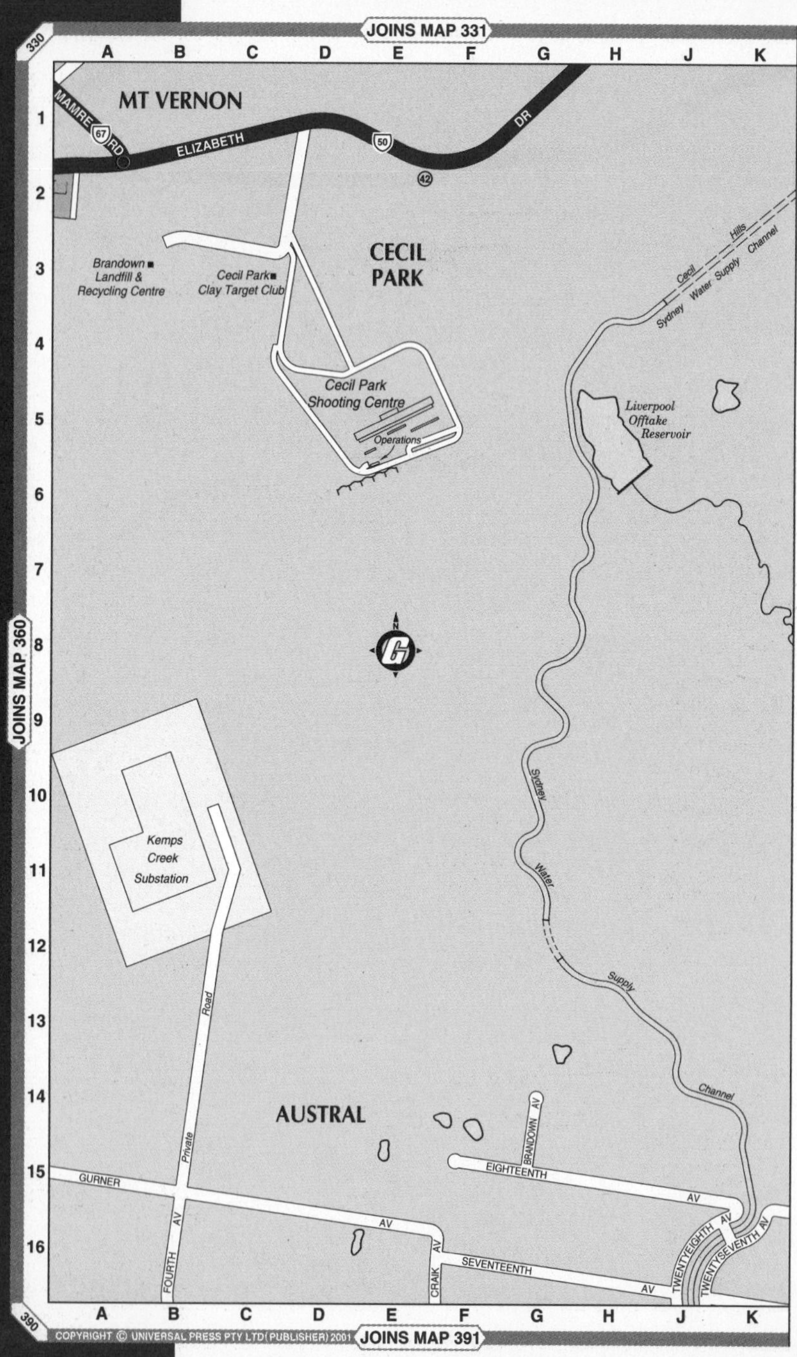
JOINS MAP 331
330
A
B
C
D
E
F
G
H
J
K
MT VERNON
MAMRE
RD
67
ELIZABETH
50
DR
42
Brandown
Landfill &
Recycling Centre
Cecil Park
Clay Target Club
CECIL
PARK
Cecil
Hills
Sydney Water Supply Channel
Cecil Park
Shooting Centre
Operations
Liverpool
Offtake
Reservoir
JOINS MAP 360
Kemps
Creek
Substation
Sydney
Water
Supply
Channel
Private
Road
AUSTRAL
BRANDOWN AV
EIGHTEENTH
AV
GURNER
AV
FOURTH
AV
CRAIK
AV
SEVENTEENTH
AV
TWENTYEIGHTH AV
TWENTYSEVENTH AV
390
JOINS MAP 391

JOINS MAP 332

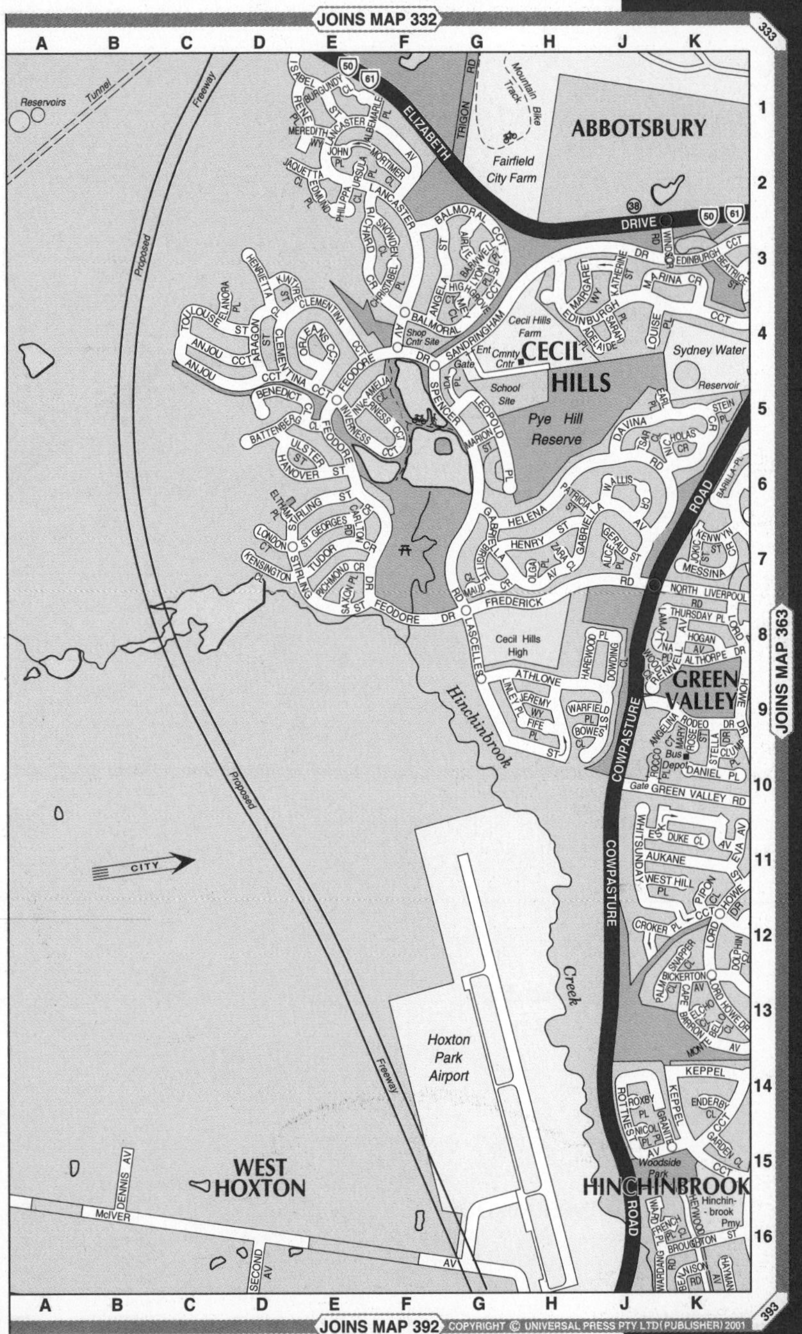

JOINS MAP 392

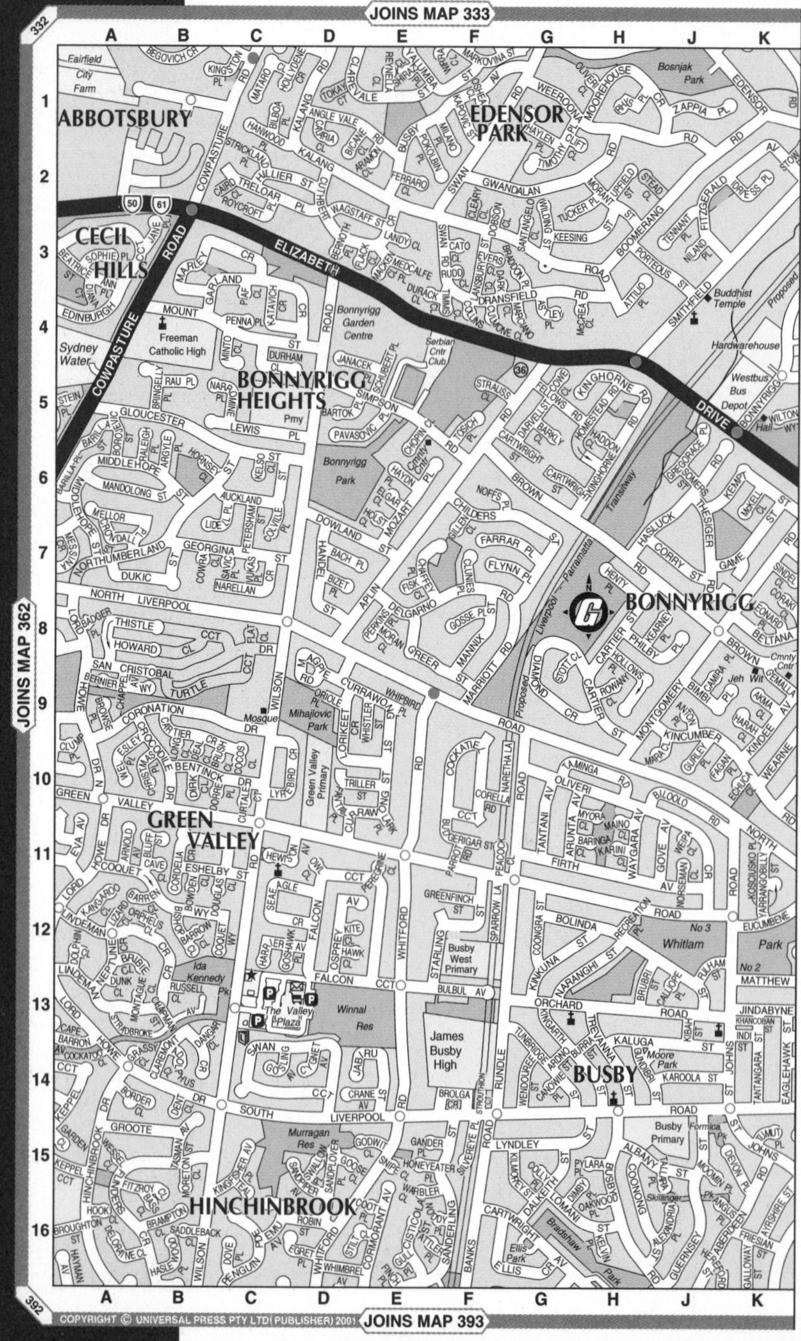

JOINS MAP 333
332
JOINS MAP 362
392
JOINS MAP 393
ABBOTSBURY
EDENSOR PARK
CECIL HILLS
BONNYRIGG HEIGHTS
BONNYRIGG
GREEN VALLEY
BUSBY
HINCHINBROOK
ELIZABETH
DRIVE
COWPASTURE
ROAD
NORTH LIVERPOOL
ROAD
SOUTH
LIVERPOOL
ROAD
Fairfield City Farm
Sydney Water
Freeman Catholic High
Bonnyrigg Garden Centre
Serbian Cntr Club
Bonnyrigg Park
Buddhist Temple
Hardwarehouse
Westbus Bus Depot
Wilton Hall
Mosque
Mihajlovic Park
Green Valley Primary
Ida Kennedy Pk
The Valley Plaza
Winnal Res
James Busby High
Busby West Primary
No 3 Whitlam Park No 2
Moore Park
Busby Primary
Formica Pk
Skillinger Pk
Murragan Res
Ellis Park
Bradshaw Park
Bosnjak Park
Transitway
Liverpool - Parramatta

JOINS MAP 334

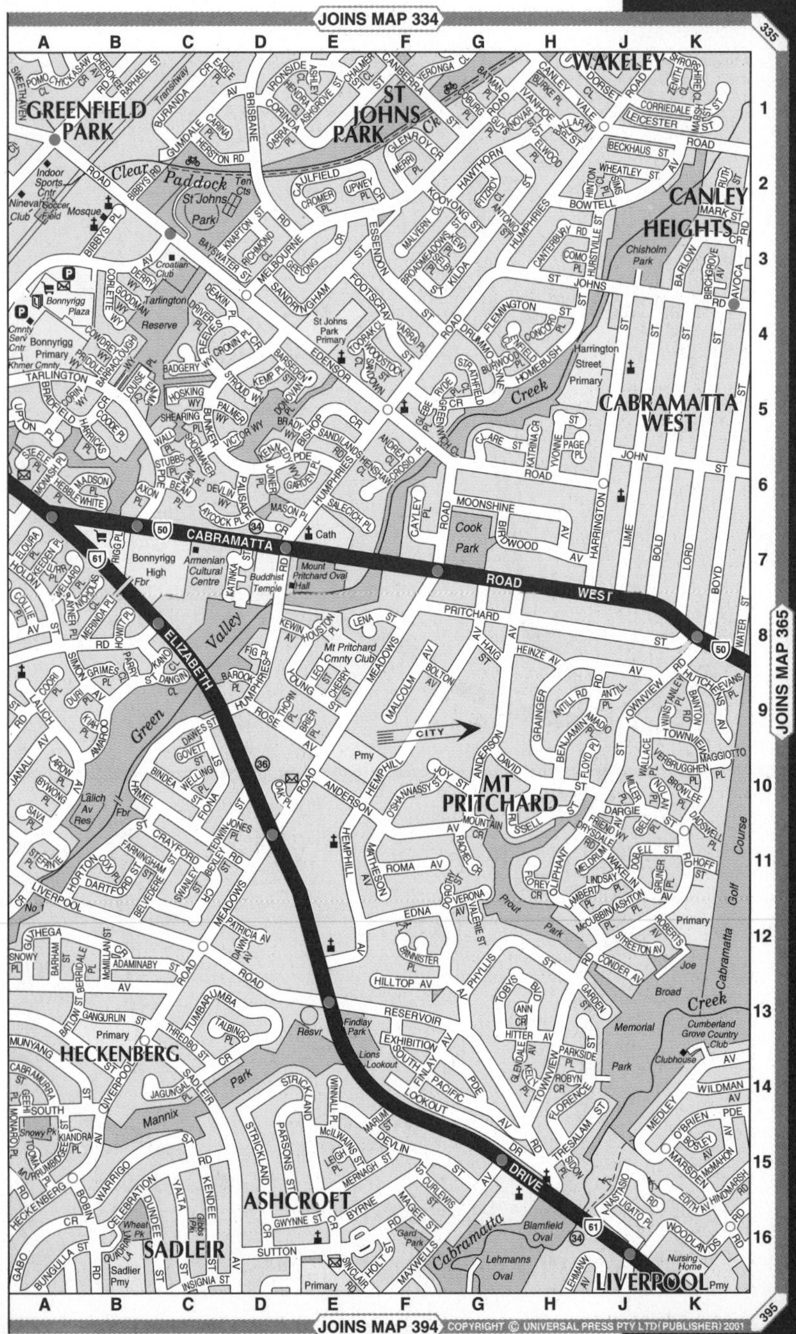

JOINS MAP 394

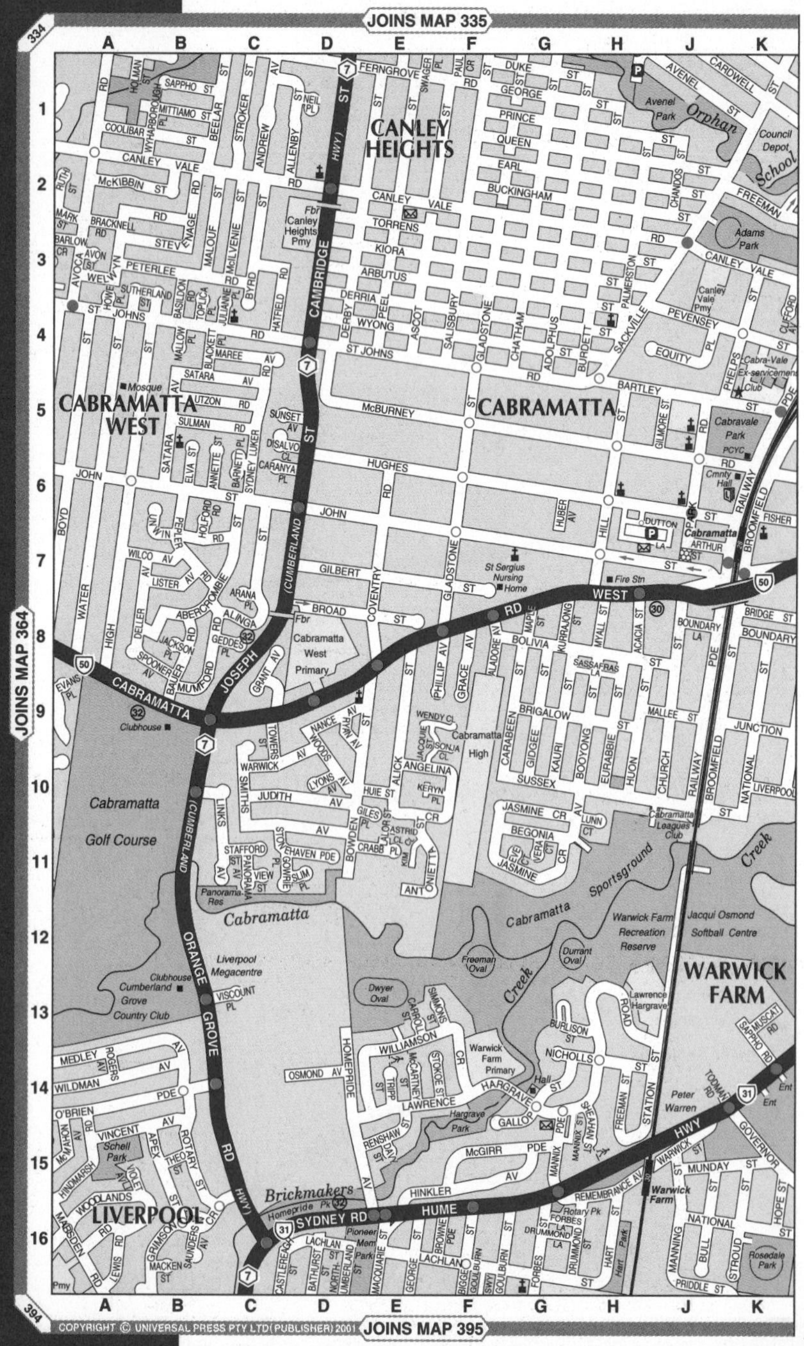
JOINS MAP 335
JOINS MAP 364
JOINS MAP 395
334
394
A B C D E F G H J K
1 2 3 4 5 6 7 8 9 10 11 12 13 14 15 16
CANLEY HEIGHTS
CABRAMATTA WEST
CABRAMATTA
WARWICK FARM
LIVERPOOL
Canley Heights Pmy
Canley Vale Pmy
Cabramatta West Primary
Cabramatta High
Warwick Farm Primary
Avenel Park
Adams Park
Council Depot
Cabravale Park
Cabra-Vale Ex-servicemens Club
Cabramatta Leagues Club
St Sergius Nursing Home
Cabramatta Golf Course
Cumberland Grove Country Club
Liverpool Megacentre
Panorama Res
Cabramatta Sportsground
Warwick Farm Recreation Reserve
Jacqui Osmond Softball Centre
Freeman Oval
Durrant Oval
Dwyer Oval
Lawrence Hargrave
Hargrave Park
Peter Warren
Schell Park
Rosedale Park
Pioneer Mem Park
Rotary Pk
Homepride Pk
Hart Park
Cabramatta Creek
Orphan School Creek
Brickmakers Creek
CAMBRIDGE ST
CUMBERLAND HWY
JOSEPH ST
ORANGE GROVE RD
CABRAMATTA RD WEST
HUME HWY
SYDNEY RD
CANLEY VALE RD
JOHN ST
HUGHES ST
McBURNEY RD
ST JOHNS RD
GILBERT ST
BROAD ST
RAILWAY PDE
STATION ST
COPYRIGHT © UNIVERSAL PRESS PTY LTD (PUBLISHER) 2001

JOINS MAP 336

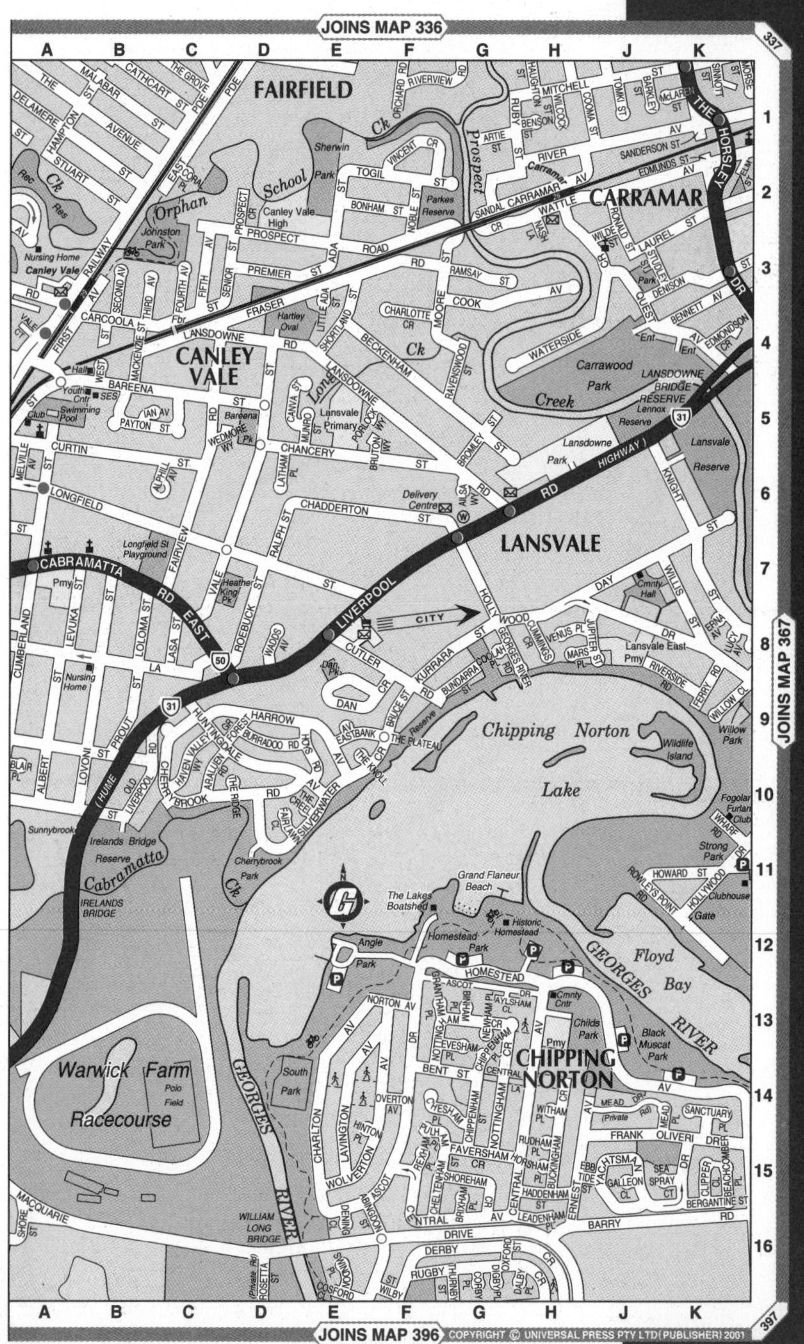

JOINS MAP 396

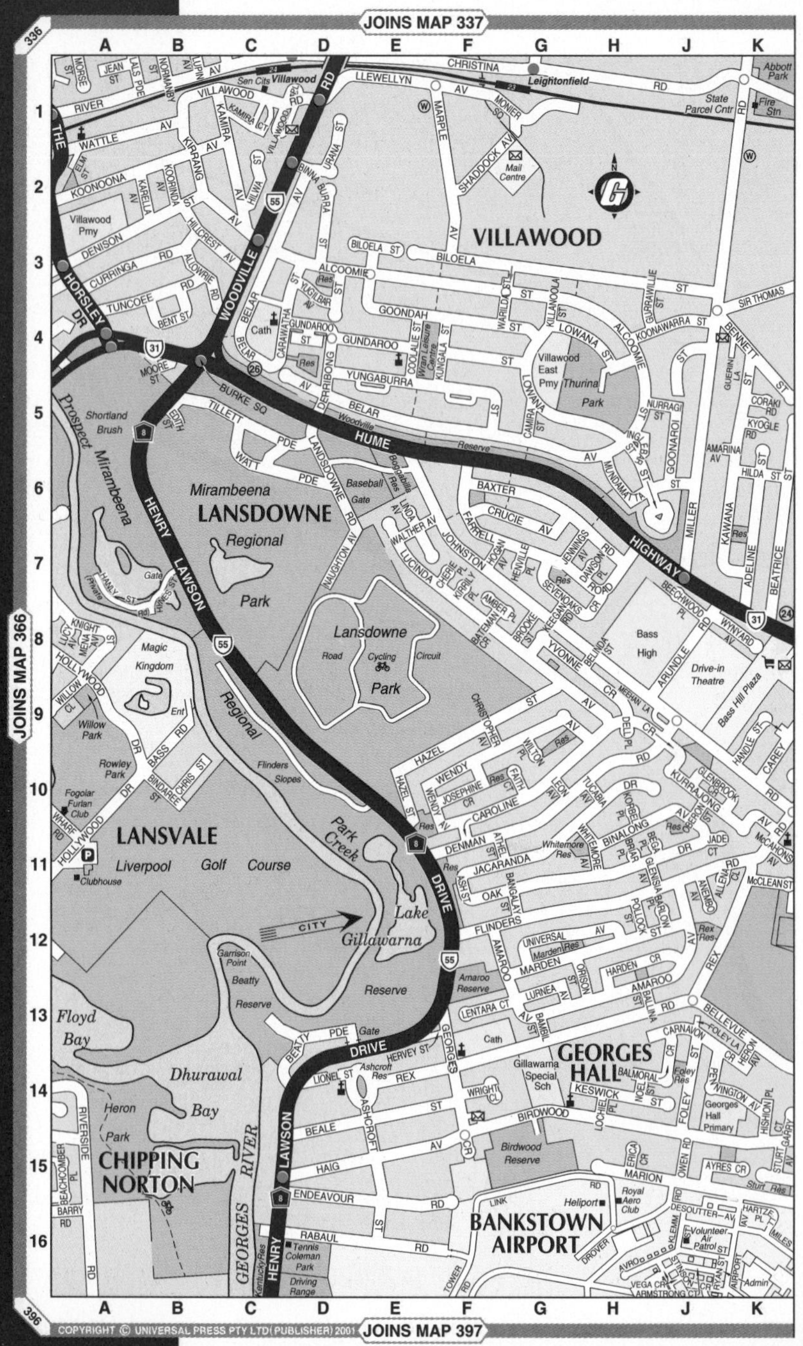
JOINS MAP 337
336
JOINS MAP 366
396
JOINS MAP 397
VILLAWOOD
LANSDOWNE
LANSVALE
GEORGES HALL
CHIPPING NORTON
BANKSTOWN AIRPORT
Mirambeena Regional Park
Lansdowne Road Cycling Circuit Park
Liverpool Golf Course
Lake Gillawarna
Beatty Reserve
Floyd Bay
Dhurawal Bay
Heron Park
Magic Kingdom
Willow Park
Rowley Park
Villawood Pmy
Villawood East Pmy
Bass High
Drive-in Theatre
Bass Hill Plaza
Georges Hall Primary
Gillawarna Special Sch
Birdwood Reserve
Amaroo Reserve
Royal Aero Club
Heliport
HUME HIGHWAY
HENRY LAWSON DRIVE
WOODVILLE RD
HORSLEY DR
GEORGES RIVER
Leightonfield
State Parcel Cntr
Mail Centre
Wran Leisure Centre
Tennis Coleman Park
Driving Range
Flinders Slopes
Fogolar Furlan Club
Clubhouse
Shortland Brush
Prospect
Abbott Park
Fire Stn
CITY

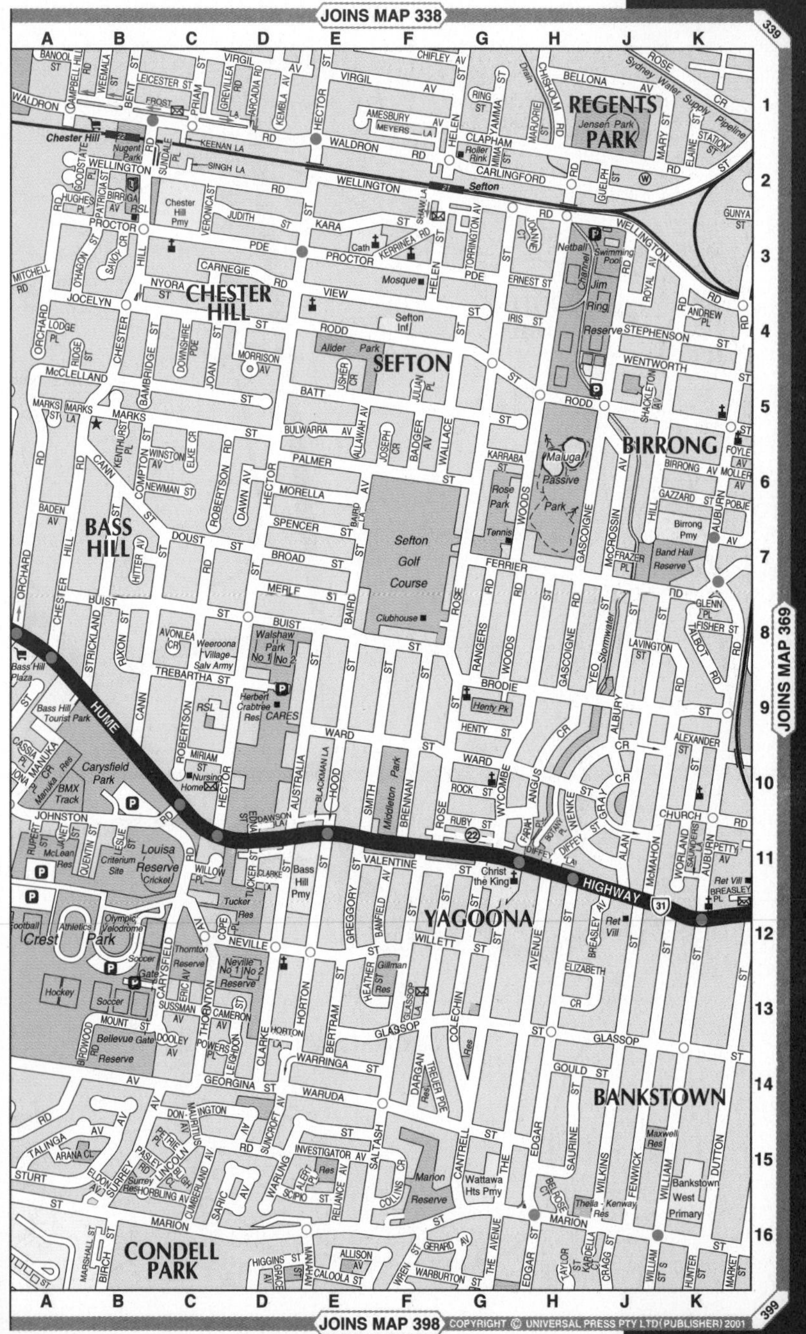
JOINS MAP 338
JOINS MAP 369
JOINS MAP 398
339
399
REGENTS PARK
CHESTER HILL
SEFTON
BIRRONG
BASS HILL
YAGOONA
BANKSTOWN
CONDELL PARK
Sefton Golf Course
Jim Ring Reserve
Maluga Passive Park
Louisa Reserve
Crest Park
Bellevue Reserve
Carysfield Park
Marion Reserve
HUME HIGHWAY
Chester Hill
Sefton

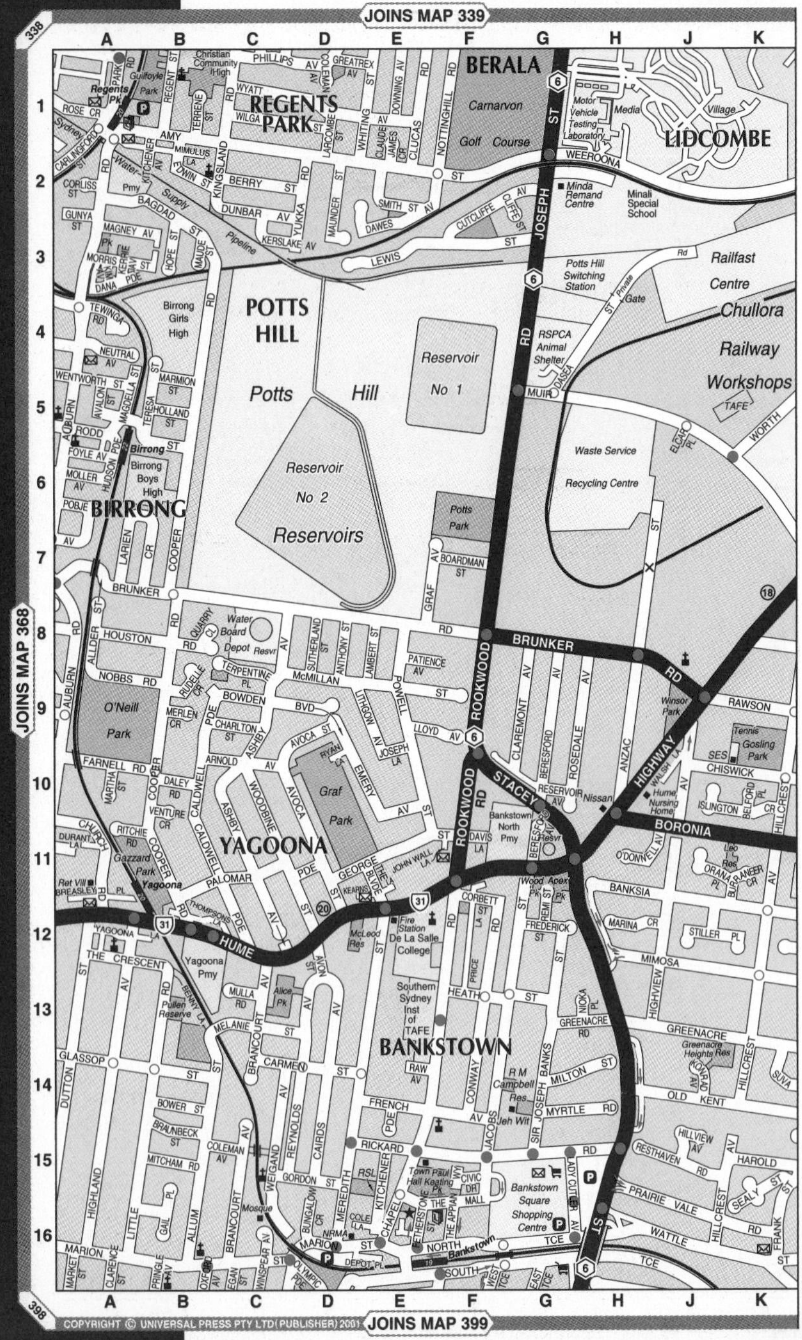
JOINS MAP 339
JOINS MAP 368
JOINS MAP 399
338
398
A B C D E F G H J K
1 2 3 4 5 6 7 8 9 10 11 12 13 14 15 16
BERALA
REGENTS PARK
LIDCOMBE
POTTS HILL
BIRRONG
YAGOONA
BANKSTOWN
Chullora Railway Workshops
Railfast Centre
Carnarvon Golf Course
Christian Community High
Regents Pk
Guilfoyle Park
Motor Vehicle Testing Laboratory
Media
Village
Minda Remand Centre
Minali Special School
Potts Hill Switching Station
RSPCA Animal Shelter
Birrong Girls High
Birrong Boys High
Birrong
Potts Hill
Reservoir No 1
Reservoir No 2
Reservoirs
Waste Service Recycling Centre
TAFE
Potts Park
Water Board Depot
Resvr
O'Neill Park
Graf Park
Gazzard Park
Yagoona
Ret Vill
Winsor Park
Tennis
Gosling Park
SES
Hume Nursing Home
Nissan
Bankstown North Pmy
Wood Pk
Apex Pk
Fire Station
De La Salle College
McLeod Res
Yagoona Pmy
Alice Pk
Pullen Reserve
Southern Sydney Inst of TAFE
R M Campbell Res
Jeh Wit
Leo Res
Greenacre Heights Res
RSL
Town Hall
Paul Keating Pk
Mosque
Bankstown Square Shopping Centre
Bankstown
PHILLIPS AV
GREATREX AV
COLEMAN
WYATT
WILGA
ROSE CR
Sydney
CARLINGFORD
AMY
MIMULUS LA
EDWIN ST
KINGSLAND
BERRY ST
DUNBAR AV
KERSLAKE AV
YUKKA
MAUNDER
LARCOMBE
WHITING AV
CLAUDE
JAMES CR
DOWNING AV
CLUCAS
NOTTINGHILL RD
WEEROONA
SMITH ST
DAWES
CUTCLIFFE AV
CLIFFE ST
LEWIS
JOSEPH ST
CORLISS ST
GUNYA ST
Water Supply Pipeline
BAGDAD
MAGNEY AV
MORRIS
DANA PDE
HOPE ST
MAUDE ST
TEWINGA RD
NEUTRAL AV
WENTWORTH ST
MARMION ST
HOLLAND ST
AVALON
MAGDALLA
TERESA
AUBURN RD
RODD
FOYLE AV
MOLLER AV
POBJE AV
HUDSON PDE
LARIEN CR
COOPER RD
BRUNKER RD
BOARDMAN ST
GRAF AV
MUIR
DIASEA
Private Rd
Gate
ELCAR PL
WORTH
HOUSTON RD
ALLDER ST
QUARRY CL
TERPENTINE PL
NOBBS RD
RUDELLE CR
BOWDEN ST
MERLEN CR
CHARLTON ST
ASHBY
McMILLAN
SUTHERLAND AV
ANTHONY ST
LAMBERT ST
PATIENCE AV
POWELL ST
LITHGOW AV
JOSEPH LA
LLOYD AV
AVOCA ST
RYAN LA
EMERY AV
BVD
ROOKWOOD RD
CLAREMONT AV
BERESFORD AV
ROSEDALE AV
ANZAC ST
HIGHWAY
RAWSON
WALSH LA
CHISWICK
FARNELL RD
MARTHA ST
DALEY RD
VENTURE CR
CALDWELL
ARNOLD AV
WOODBINE
STACEY
RESERVOIR AV
BORONIA
HILLCREST
ISLINGTON CR
BELFORD PL
CHURCH
RITCHIE RD
DURANT LA
DAVIS LA
JOHN WALL LA
GEORGE
THE BLVDE
O'DONNELL AV
ORANA PL
BURRANEER CR
PALOMAR PDE
BEASLEY PL
THOMPSONS LA
KEARNS
CORBETT PL
REMI ST
FREDERICK ST
BANKSIA
MARINA CR
STILLER PL
MIMOSA
HUME
YAGOONA LA
THE CRESCENT
MULLA RD
AVON
PRICE LA
HEATH ST
NIOKA PL
GREENACRE RD
GREENACRE
HIGHVIEW
BENNY LA
MELANIE
BRANCOURT AV
CARMEN
GLASSOP ST
DUTTON
RAW AV
CONWAY
MILTON ST
KONRAD
SUVA
OLD KENT RD
SIR JOSEPH BANKS ST
MYRTLE RD
FRENCH AV
BOWER ST
BRAUNBECK ST
MITCHAM RD
COLEMAN AV
WEIGAND
REYNOLDS
CAIRDS
JACOBS
RICKARD RD
HILLVIEW AV
RESTHAVEN RD
HAROLD
GORDON ST
MEREDITH
KITCHENER
WY
CIVIC DR
MALL
PRAIRIE VALE RD
SEALY ST
HIGHLAND
LITTLE
GAIL PL
ALLUM
BUNGALOW CR
COLE LA
CHAPEL
FETHERSTONE ST
THE APPIAN
LADY CUTLER AV
WATTLE
FRANK
MARION ST
NRMA
NORTH TCE
Bankstown
DEPOT PL
SOUTH TCE
WEST TCE
EAST TCE
MARKET ST
CLARENCE ST
PRINGLE AV
OXFORD AV
EGAN ST
WINSPEAR AV
OLYMPIC PDE
6
18
20
31
COPYRIGHT © UNIVERSAL PRESS PTY LTD (PUBLISHER) 2001

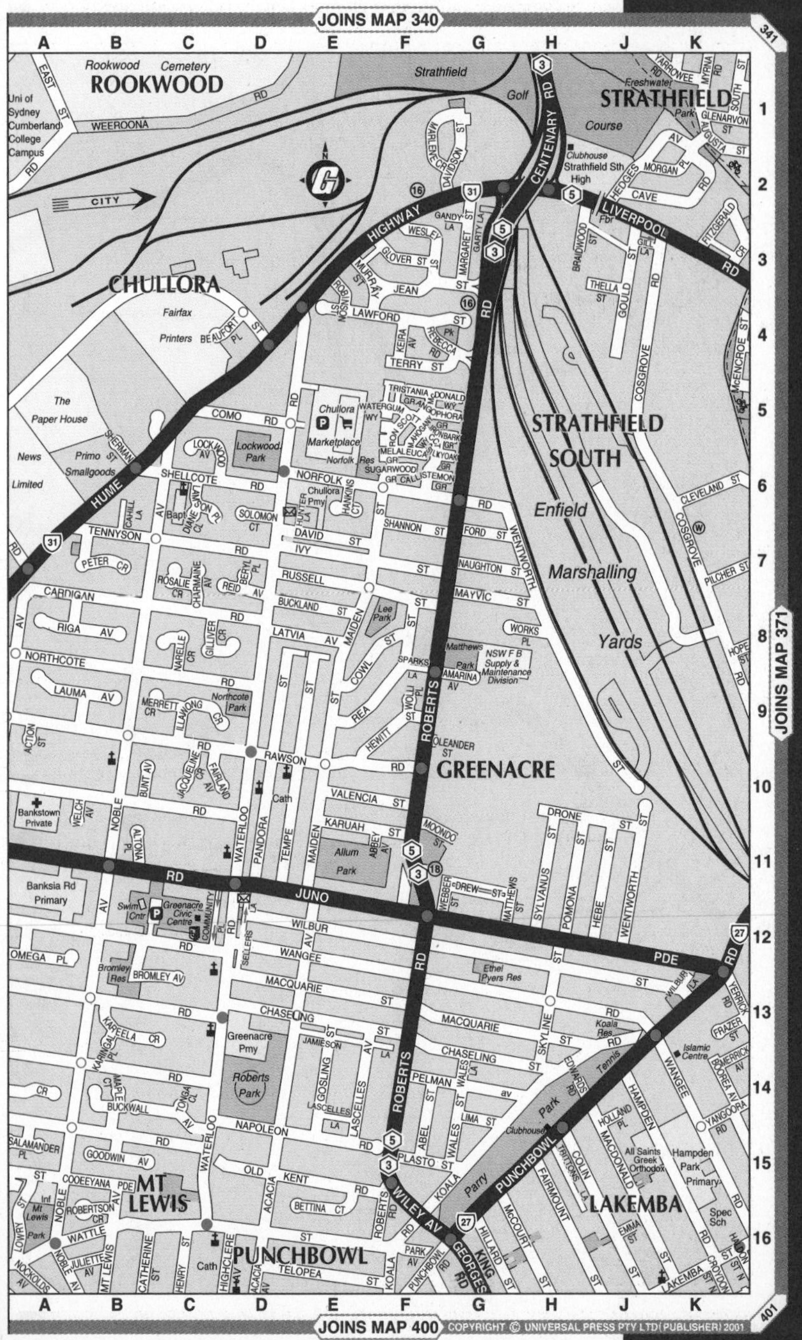
JOINS MAP 340
JOINS MAP 371
JOINS MAP 400
ROOKWOOD
Rookwood Cemetery
Uni of Sydney Cumberland College Campus
CHULLORA
Fairfax Printers
The Paper House
News Limited
Primo Smallgoods
Chullora Marketplace
STRATHFIELD
Strathfield Golf Course
Freshwater Park
Clubhouse
Strathfield Sth High
STRATHFIELD SOUTH
Enfield Marshalling Yards
NSW F B Supply & Maintenance Division
GREENACRE
Lockwood Park
Northcote Park
Lee Park
Matthews Park
Allum Park
Bankstown Private
Banksia Rd Primary
Greenacre Civic Centre
Bromley Res
Ethel Pyers Res
Koala Res
Greenacre Pmy
Roberts Park
Islamic Centre
Parry Park
Tennis
MT LEWIS
Mt Lewis Park
PUNCHBOWL
LAKEMBA
All Saints Greek Orthodox
Hampden Park Primary
Spec Sch
HUME HIGHWAY
LIVERPOOL RD
CENTENARY RD
ROBERTS RD
JUNO PDE
PUNCHBOWL RD
WILEY AV
KING GEORGES RD
WATERLOO RD

MAP 371

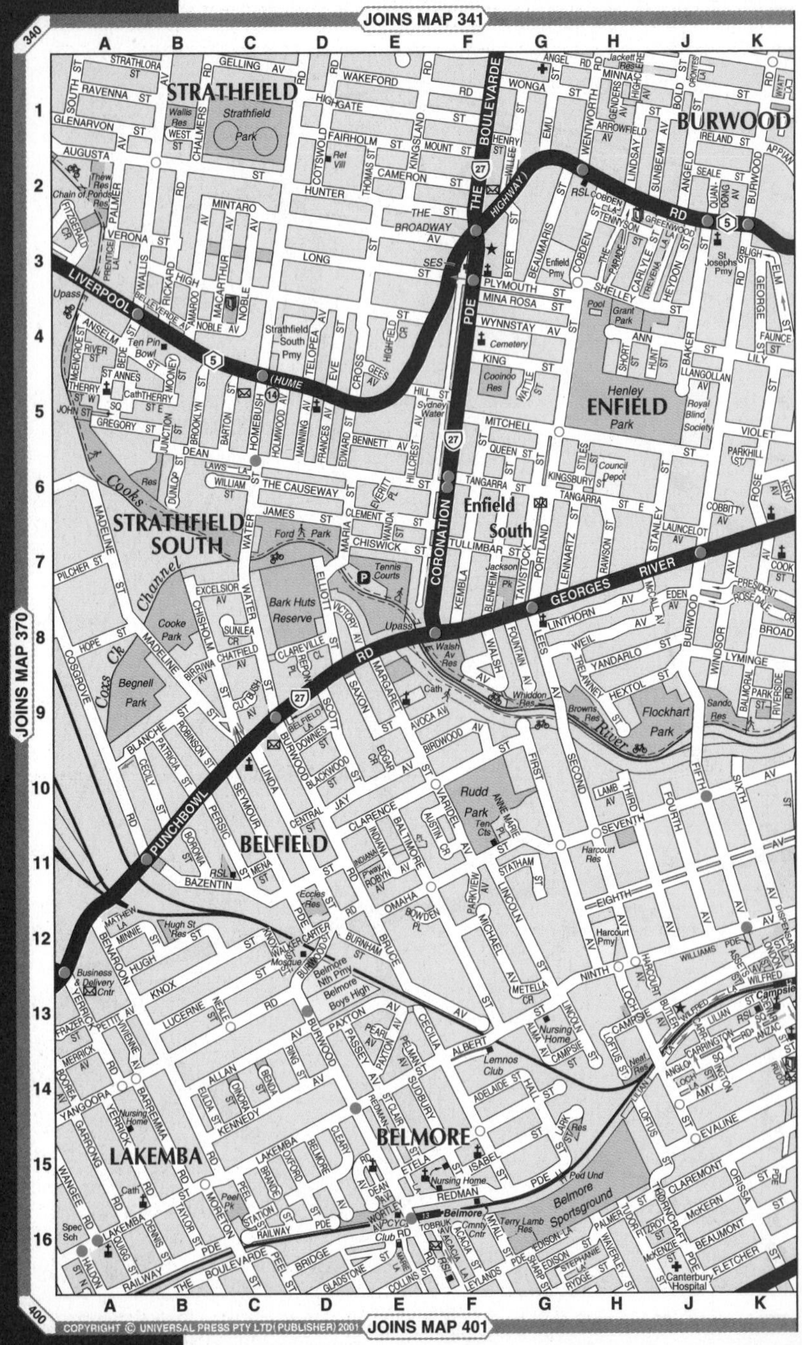

JOINS MAP 341
340
A B C D E F G H J K
1 2 3 4 5 6 7 8 9 10 11 12 13 14 15 16
JOINS MAP 370
STRATHFIELD
Strathfield Park
BURWOOD
ENFIELD
Henley ENFIELD Park
Enfield South
STRATHFIELD SOUTH
BELFIELD
BELMORE
LAKEMBA
Campsie
LIVERPOOL
(HUME HIGHWAY)
THE BOULEVARDE
CORONATION PDE
GEORGES RIVER RD
PUNCHBOWL RD
BURWOOD RD
Cooks River
Cooke Park
Begnell Park
Bark Huts Reserve
Ford Park
Flockhart Park
Rudd Park
Belmore Sportsground
Cemetery
Royal Blind Society
Belmore Boys High
Canterbury Hospital
400
JOINS MAP 401

JOINS MAP 342

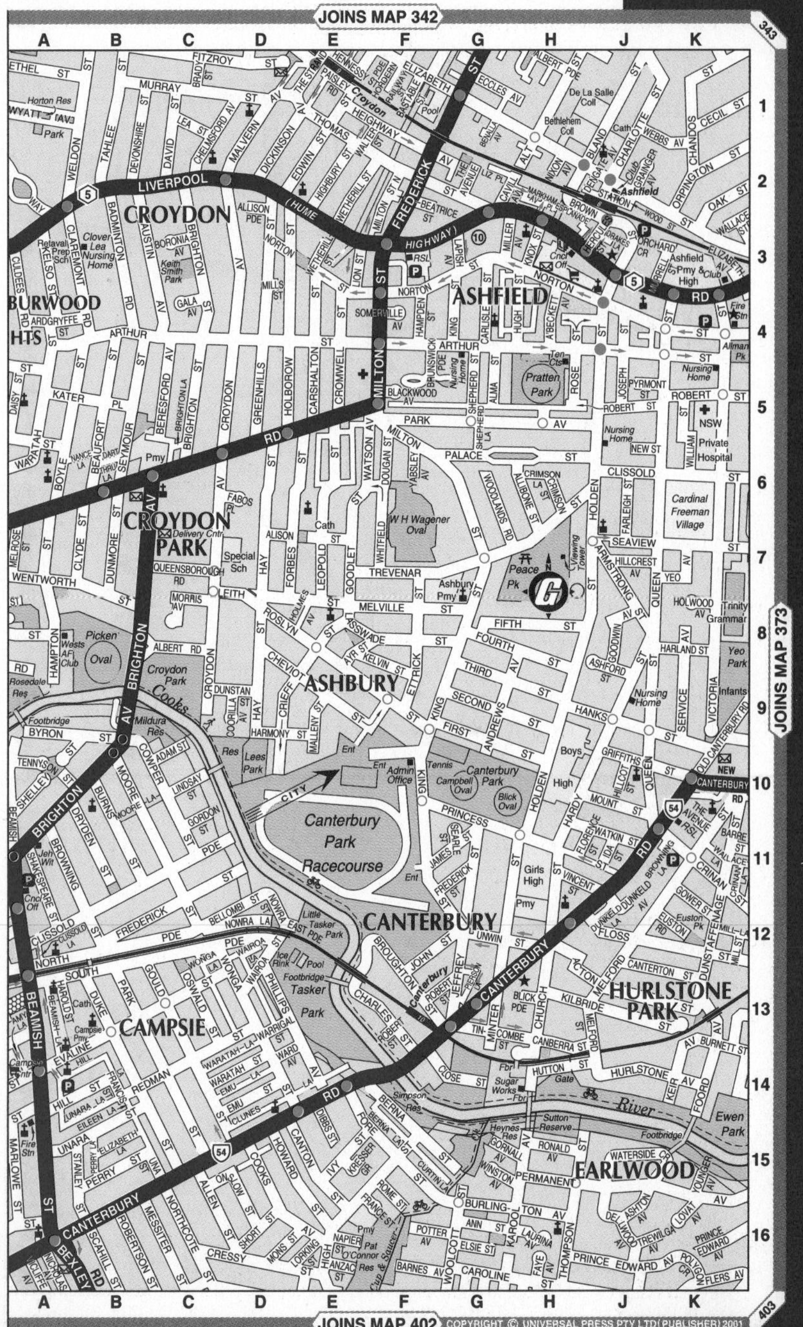

JOINS MAP 373

JOINS MAP 402

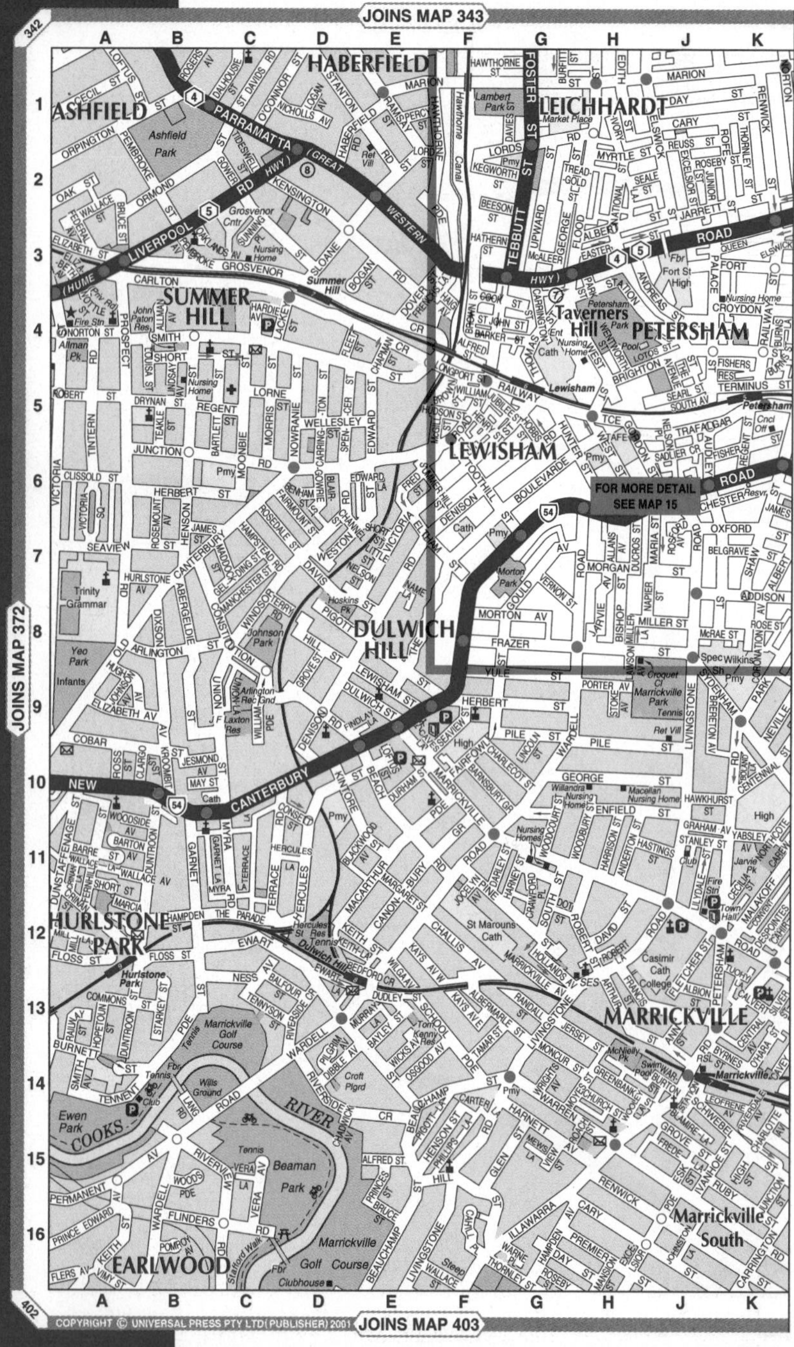
JOINS MAP 343
JOINS MAP 372
JOINS MAP 403
342
402
A B C D E F G H J K
1 2 3 4 5 6 7 8 9 10 11 12 13 14 15 16
HABERFIELD
ASHFIELD
LEICHHARDT
SUMMER HILL
Taverners Hill
PETERSHAM
LEWISHAM
DULWICH HILL
HURLSTONE PARK
MARRICKVILLE
Marrickville South
EARLWOOD
PARRAMATTA RD
(GREAT WESTERN HWY)
LIVERPOOL RD
(HUME HWY)
NEW CANTERBURY RD
FOR MORE DETAIL SEE MAP 15
Ashfield Park
Grosvenor Cntr
Summer Hill
Lambert Park
Hawthorne Canal
Market Place
Fort St High
Petersham Park
Lewisham
Petersham
Morton Park
Trinity Grammar
Yeo Park Infants
Johnson Park
Hoskins Pk
Arlington Rec Gnd
J F Laxton Res
Marrickville Park
St Marouns Cath
Casimir Cath College
Hurlstone Park
Dulwich Hill
Marrickville
Marrickville Golf Course
Wills Ground
Ewen Park
COOKS RIVER
Beaman Park
Croft Plgrd
Tom Kenny Res
McNielly Pk
Jarvie Pk
Town Hall
Clubhouse
Stafford Walk
COPYRIGHT © UNIVERSAL PRESS PTY LTD (PUBLISHER) 2001

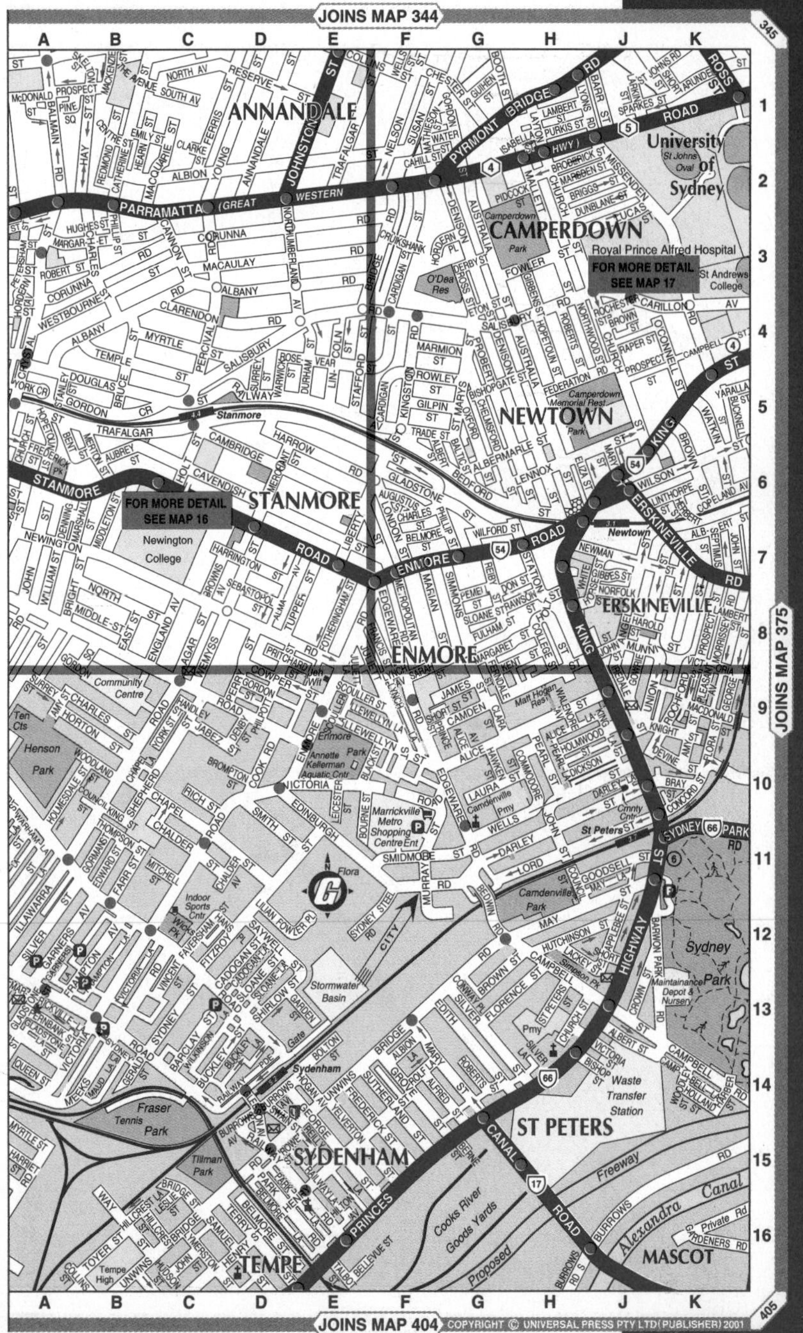
JOINS MAP 344
345
JOINS MAP 375
JOINS MAP 404
405
ANNANDALE
CAMPERDOWN
NEWTOWN
STANMORE
ENMORE
ERSKINEVILLE
SYDENHAM
ST PETERS
TEMPE
MASCOT
University of Sydney
St Johns Oval
Royal Prince Alfred Hospital
St Andrews College
FOR MORE DETAIL SEE MAP 17
FOR MORE DETAIL SEE MAP 16
Newington College
Camperdown Park
Camperdown Memorial Rest Park
O'Dea Res
Stanmore
Newtown
St Peters
Sydenham
PARRAMATTA (GREAT WESTERN HWY)
PYRMONT BRIDGE RD
ROSS ST
STANMORE ROAD
ENMORE ROAD
KING ST
ERSKINEVILLE RD
PRINCES HIGHWAY
CANAL ROAD
SYDNEY PARK RD
Henson Park
Community Centre
Enmore Park
Annette Kellerman Aquatic Cntr
Marrickville Metro Shopping Centre
Camdenville Pmy
Camdenville Park
Matt Hogan Res
Sydney Park
Maintainance Depot & Nursery
Stormwater Basin
Indoor Sports Cntr
Wicks Pk
Fraser Tennis Park
Tillman Park
Waste Transfer Station
Cooks River Goods Yards
Proposed Freeway
Alexandra Canal
Tempe High
CITY

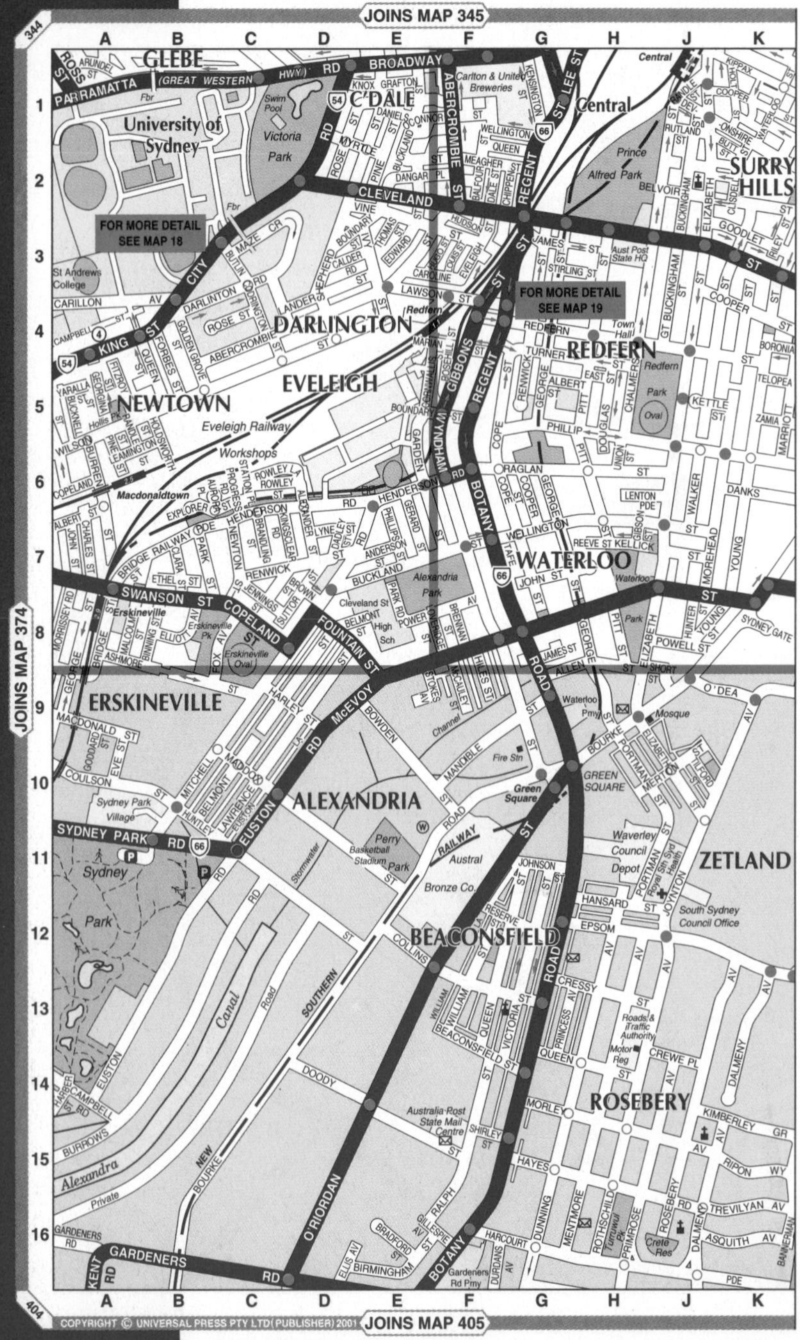
JOINS MAP 345
JOINS MAP 374
JOINS MAP 405
344
404
A B C D E F G H J K
1 2 3 4 5 6 7 8 9 10 11 12 13 14 15 16
GLEBE
C'DALE
Central
SURRY HILLS
DARLINGTON
EVELEIGH
REDFERN
NEWTOWN
WATERLOO
ERSKINEVILLE
ALEXANDRIA
ZETLAND
BEACONSFIELD
ROSEBERY
University of Sydney
Victoria Park
Swim Pool
Prince Alfred Park
Carlton & United Breweries
St Andrews College
FOR MORE DETAIL SEE MAP 18
FOR MORE DETAIL SEE MAP 19
Aust Post State HQ
Town Hall
Redfern Park Oval
Eveleigh Railway Workshops
Macdonaldtown
Erskineville
Erskineville Pk
Erskineville Oval
Alexandria Park
Cleveland St High Sch
Waterloo Park
Waterloo Pmy
Mosque
Fire Stn
Green Square
GREEN SQUARE
Sydney Park Village
Sydney Park
Perry Basketball Stadium Park
Austral Bronze Co.
Waverley Council Depot
Royal Sth Syd Health
South Sydney Council Office
Roads & Traffic Authority Motor Reg
Australia Post State Mail Centre
Turruwul Pk
Crete Res
Gardeners Rd Pmy
Alexandra Canal
PARRAMATTA RD
(GREAT WESTERN HWY)
BROADWAY
CITY RD
CLEVELAND ST
ABERCROMBIE ST
REGENT ST
KING ST
GIBBONS ST
WYNDHAM ST
BOTANY RD
SWANSON ST
COPELAND ST
FOUNTAIN ST
McEVOY ST
EUSTON RD
SYDNEY PARK RD
O'RIORDAN ST
GARDENERS RD
BOURKE RD
SOUTHERN CROSS DR
O'DEA AV
DALMENY AV
COPYRIGHT © UNIVERSAL PRESS PTY LTD (PUBLISHER) 2001

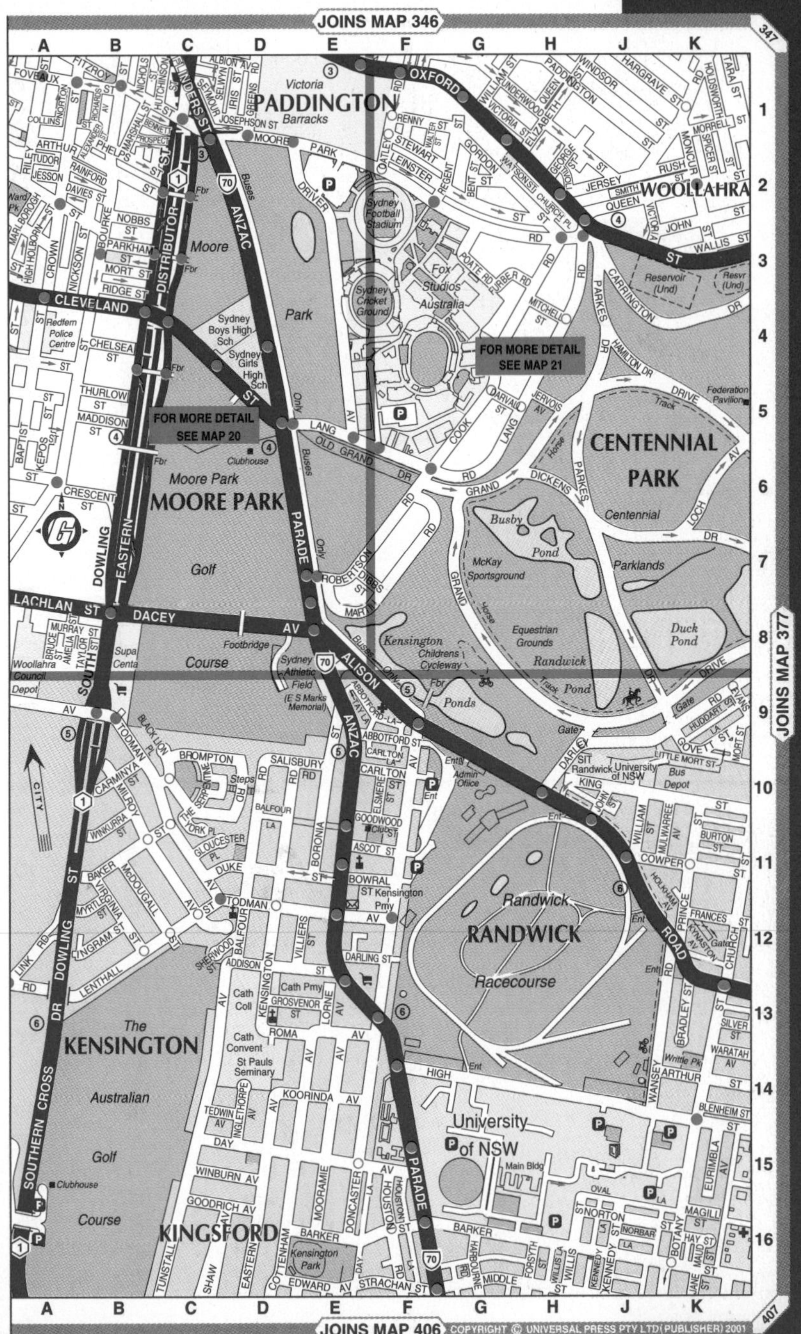
JOINS MAP 346
JOINS MAP 377
JOINS MAP 406
PADDINGTON
WOOLLAHRA
MOORE PARK
CENTENNIAL PARK
RANDWICK
KENSINGTON
KINGSFORD
Victoria Barracks
Sydney Football Stadium
Sydney Cricket Ground
Fox Studios Australia
Moore Park
Sydney Boys High Sch
Sydney Girls High Sch
FOR MORE DETAIL SEE MAP 20
FOR MORE DETAIL SEE MAP 21
Moore Park Golf Course
Centennial Parklands
Busby Pond
McKay Sportsground
Equestrian Grounds
Kensington Childrens Cycleway
Kensington Ponds
Duck Pond
Randwick Pond
Sydney Athletic Field (E S Marks Memorial)
Randwick Racecourse
University of NSW
The Australian Golf Course
Kensington Park
Redfern Police Centre
Woollahra Council Depot
Federation Pavilion
Reservoir (Und)
Resvr (Und)
OXFORD ST
CLEVELAND ST
ANZAC PARADE
ALISON ROAD
SOUTHERN CROSS DR
DOWLING ST
EASTERN DISTRIBUTOR
LACHLAN ST
DACEY AV
HIGH ST
BARKER ST

MAP 377

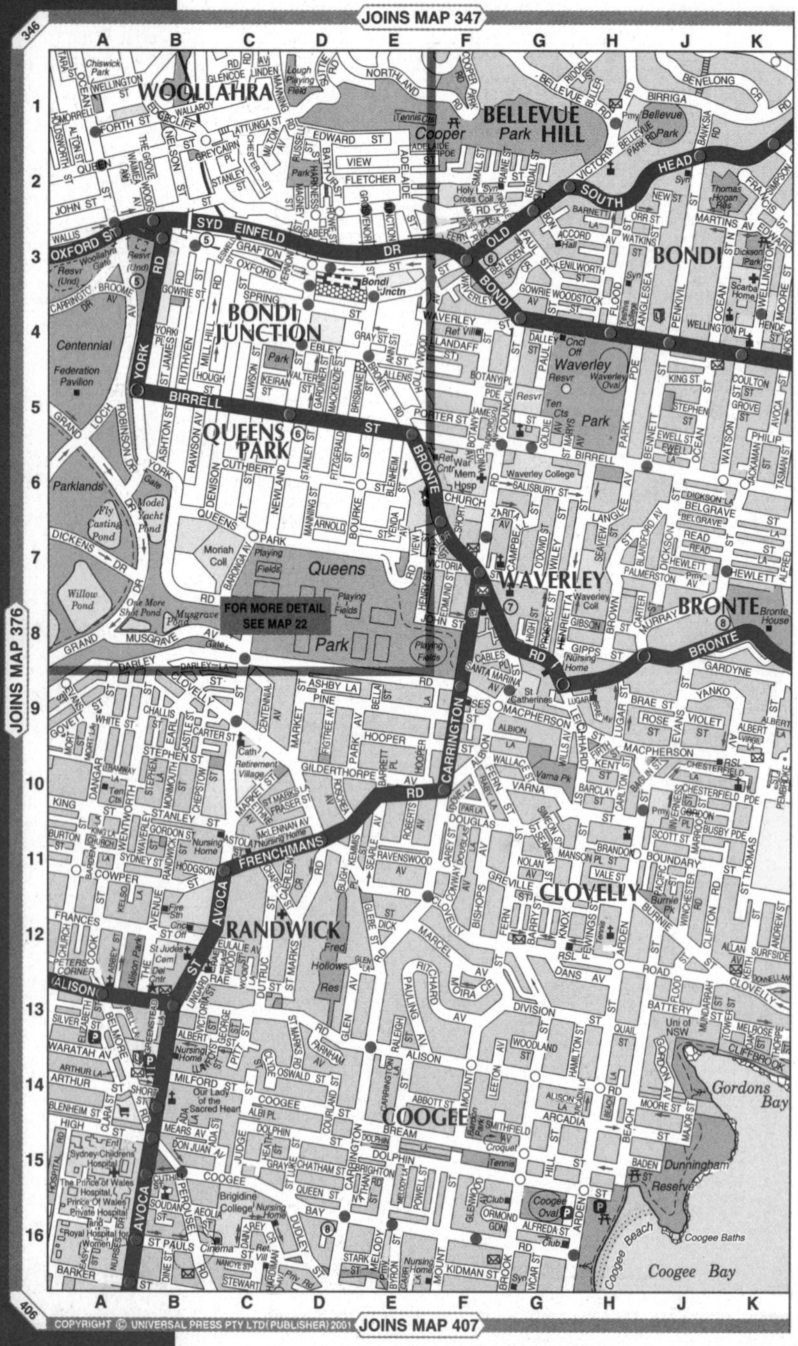

JOINS MAP 347
JOINS MAP 376
JOINS MAP 407
346
406
WOOLLAHRA
BELLEVUE HILL
Bellevue Park
BONDI
BONDI JUNCTION
QUEENS PARK
WAVERLEY
BRONTE
CLOVELLY
RANDWICK
COOGEE
Centennial
Federation Pavilion
Parklands
Fly Casting Pond
Model Yacht Pond
Willow Pond
One More Shot Pond
Musgrave Pond
Queens Park
Moriah Coll
Waverley Park
Waverley Oval
Waverley College
Waverley Coll
Bronte House
Uni of NSW
Gordons Bay
Dunningham Reserve
Coogee Beach
Coogee Baths
Coogee Bay
Coogee Oval
Brigidine College
Sydney Childrens Hospital
The Prince of Wales Hospital
Prince Of Wales Private Hospital
Royal Hospital for Women
Fred Hollows Res
FOR MORE DETAIL SEE MAP 22
OXFORD ST
SYD EINFELD DR
OLD SOUTH HEAD RD
BONDI RD
BIRRELL ST
BRONTE RD
CARRINGTON RD
FRENCHMANS RD
AVOCA ST
YORK RD
ALISON RD
COPYRIGHT © UNIVERSAL PRESS PTY LTD (PUBLISHER) 2001

JOINS MAP 348

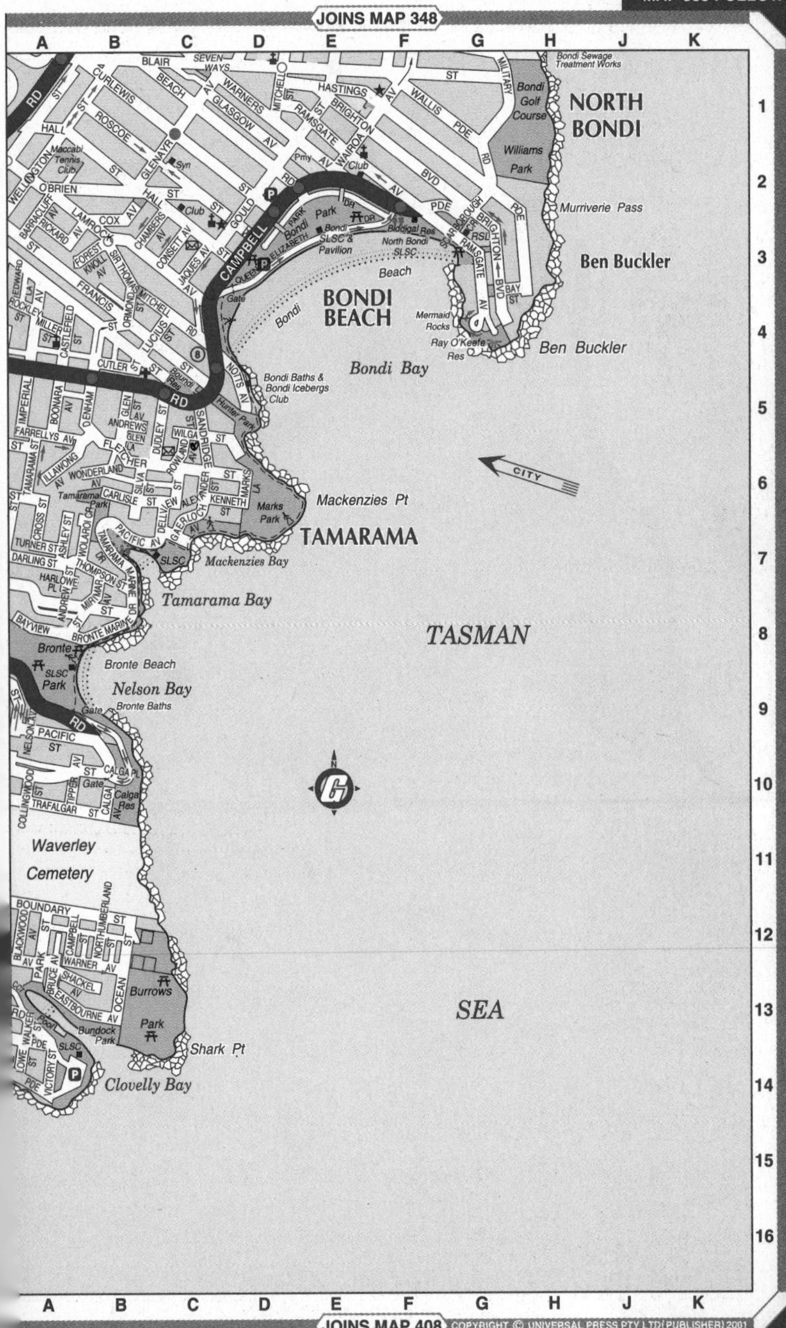

JOINS MAP 408

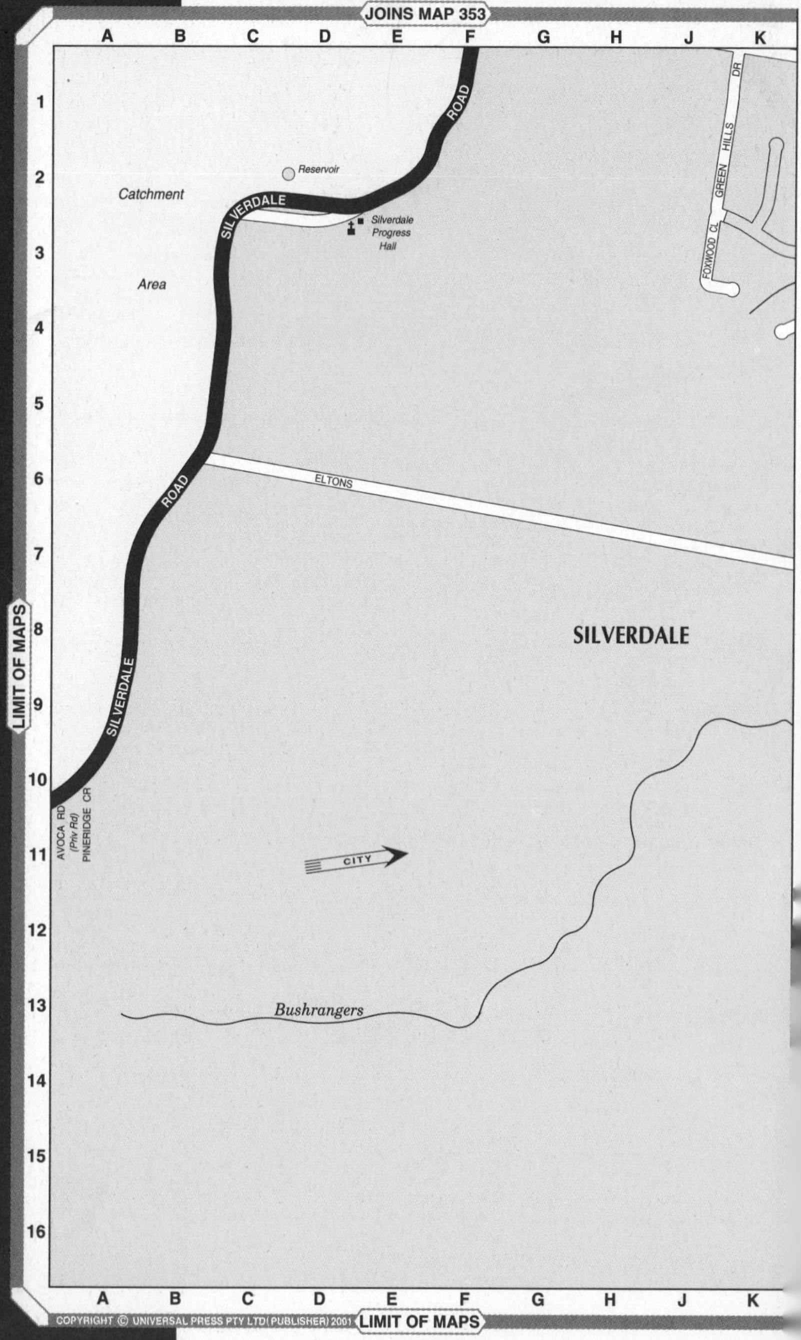
JOINS MAP 353
A B C D E F G H J K
1 2 3 4 5 6 7 8 9 10 11 12 13 14 15 16
Reservoir
Catchment
Area
SILVERDALE
ROAD
Silverdale
Progress
Hall
DR
GREEN
HILLS
FOXWOOD CL
ELTONS
LIMIT OF MAPS
SILVERDALE
SILVERDALE
AVOCA RD
(Priv Rd)
PINERIDGE CR
CITY
Bushrangers
LIMIT OF MAPS

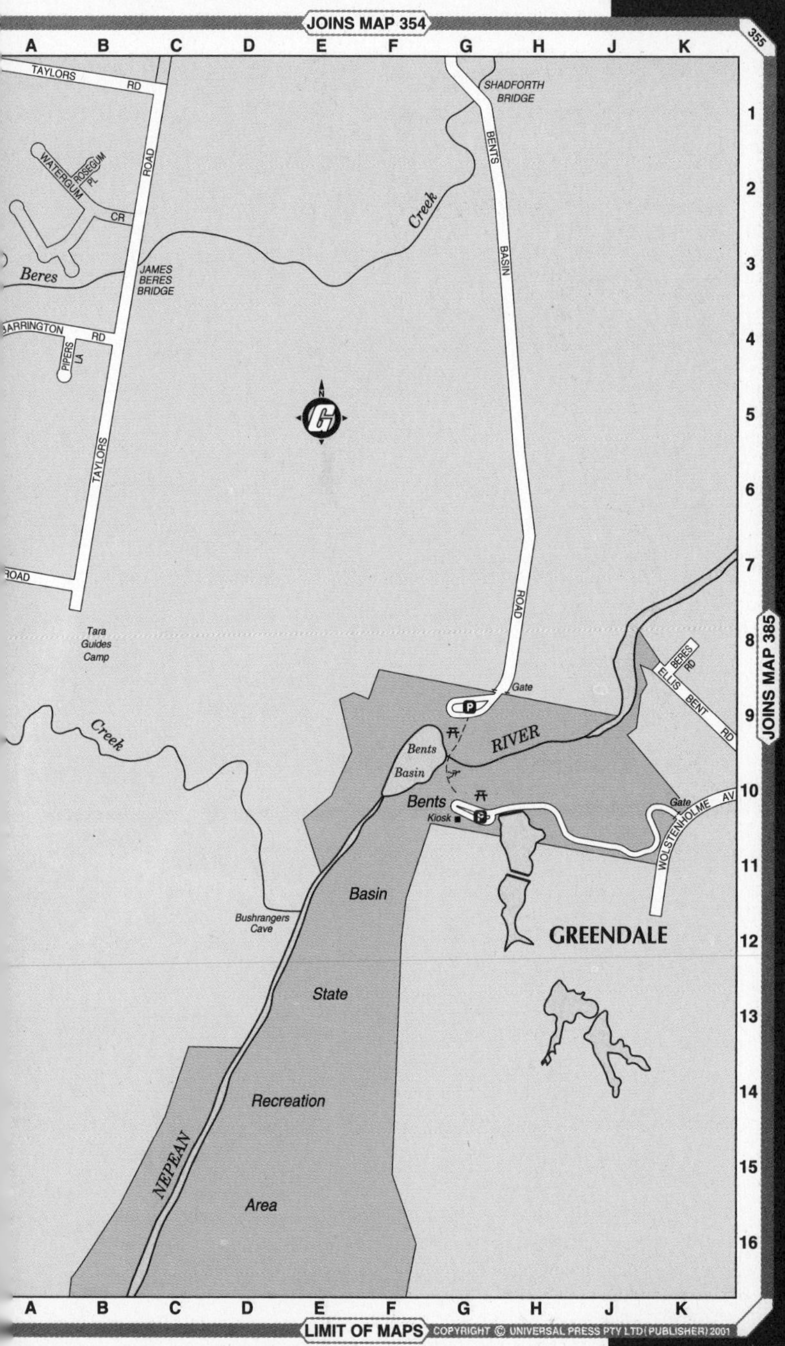
JOINS MAP 354
355
A
B
C
D
E
F
G
H
J
K
1
2
3
4
5
6
7
8
9
10
11
12
13
14
15
16
TAYLORS RD
SHADFORTH BRIDGE
BENTS BASIN ROAD
WATERGUM CR
ROSEGUM PL
ROAD
TAYLORS
Creek
Beres
JAMES BERES BRIDGE
BARRINGTON RD
PIPERS LA
ROAD
Tara Guides Camp
Creek
Gate
BERES RD
ELLIS BENT RD
RIVER
Bents Basin
Bents
Kiosk
Gate
WOLSTENHOLME AV
Basin
Bushrangers Cave
GREENDALE
State
Recreation
NEPEAN
Area
JOINS MAP 385
LIMIT OF MAPS

MAP 385

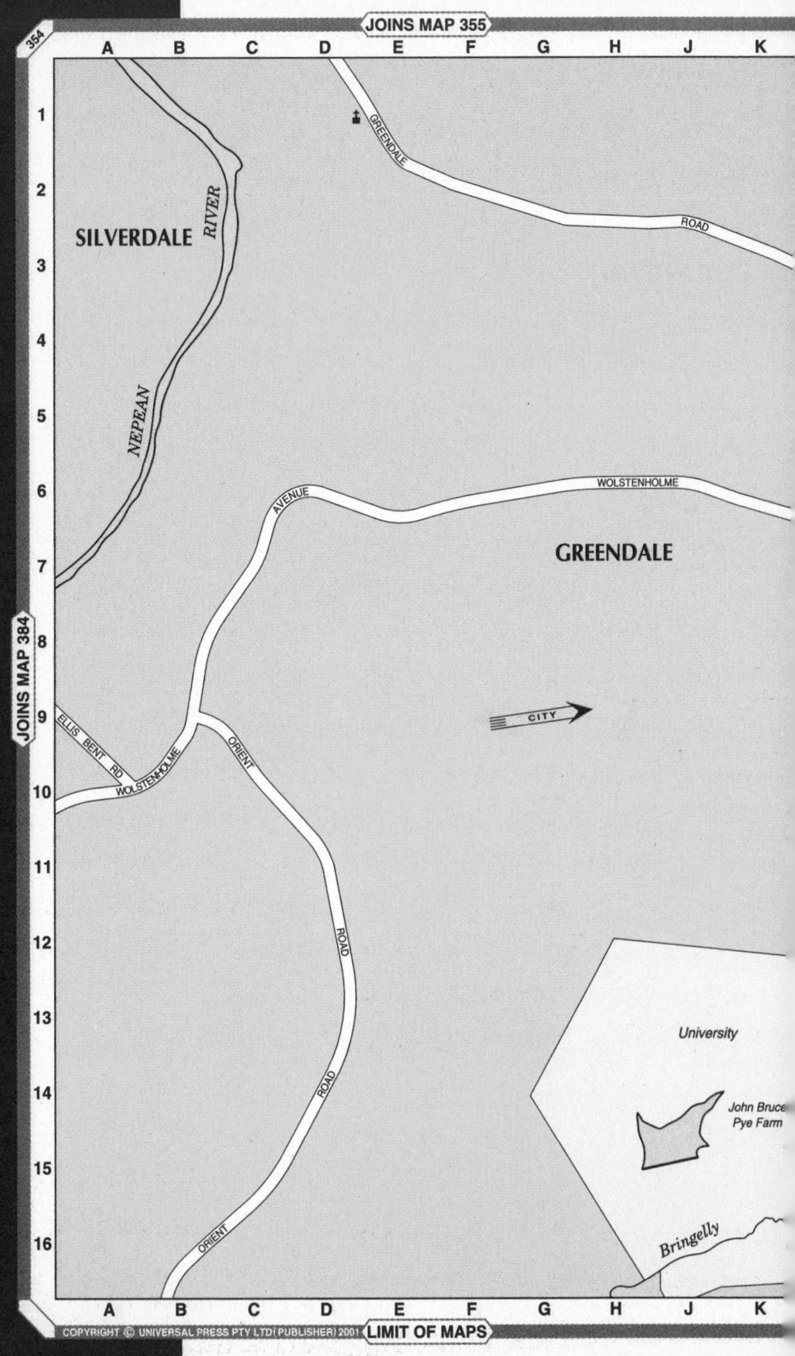
JOINS MAP 355
354
A B C D E F G H J K
1 2 3 4 5 6 7 8 9 10 11 12 13 14 15 16
JOINS MAP 384
SILVERDALE
NEPEAN
RIVER
GREENDALE
ROAD
WOLSTENHOLME
AVENUE
GREENDALE
ELLIS BENT RD
WOLSTENHOLME
ORIENT
ROAD
ROAD
ORIENT
CITY
University
John Bruce
Pye Farm
Bringelly
LIMIT OF MAPS

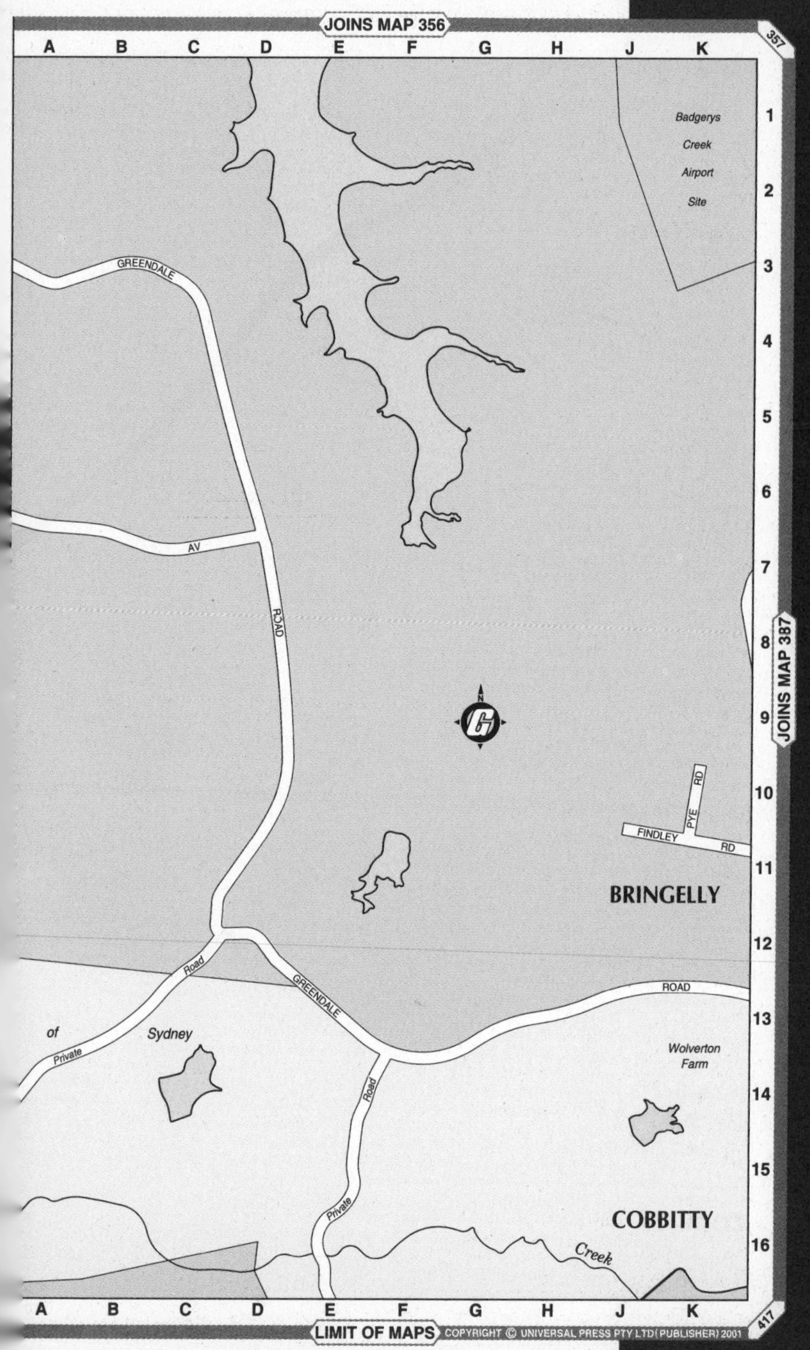
JOINS MAP 356
357
A
B
C
D
E
F
G
H
J
K
1
2
3
4
5
6
7
8
9
10
11
12
13
14
15
16
Badgerys
Creek
Airport
Site
GREENDALE
AV
ROAD
JOINS MAP 387
PYE
RD
FINDLEY
RD
BRINGELLY
Road
GREENDALE
ROAD
of
Private
Sydney
Road
Wolverton
Farm
Private
COBBITTY
Creek
LIMIT OF MAPS
417

JOINS MAP 357

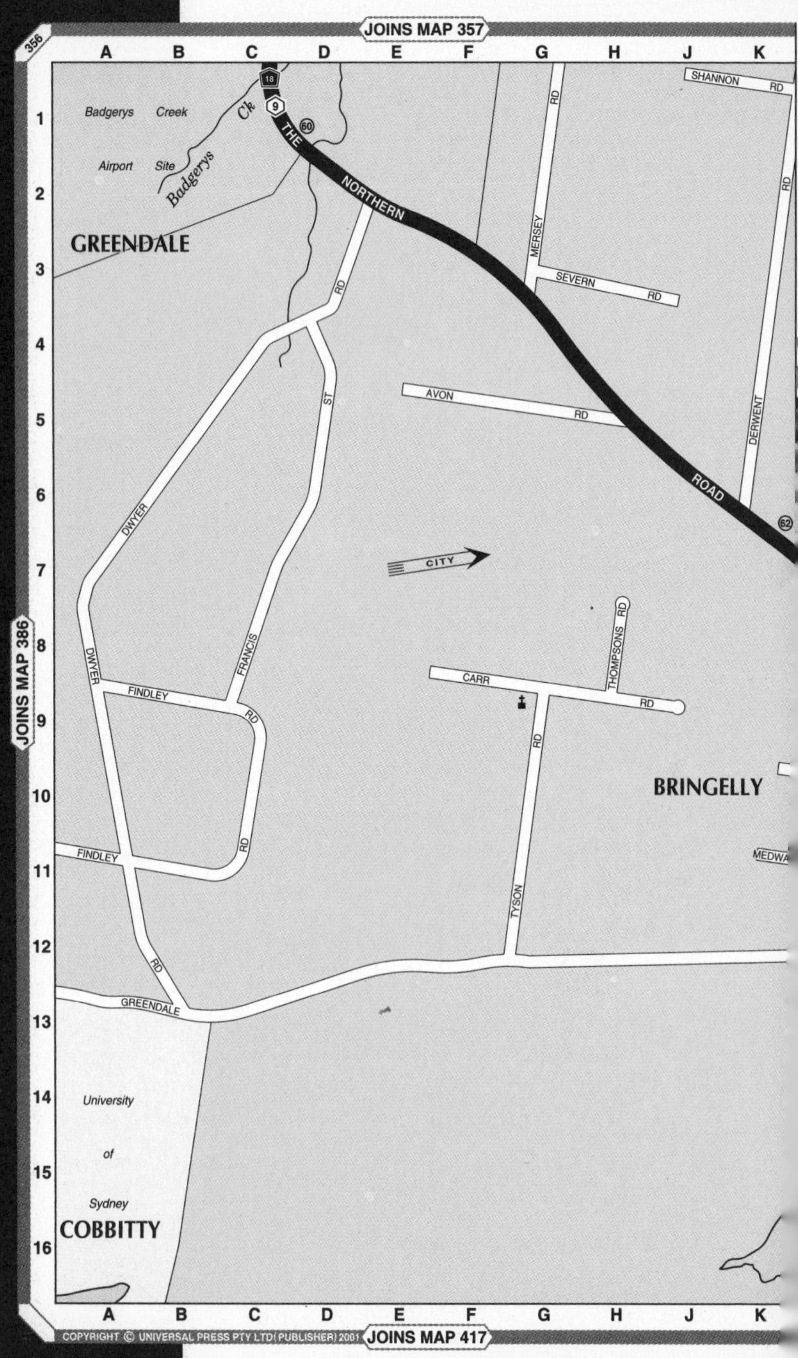

JOINS MAP 386

JOINS MAP 417

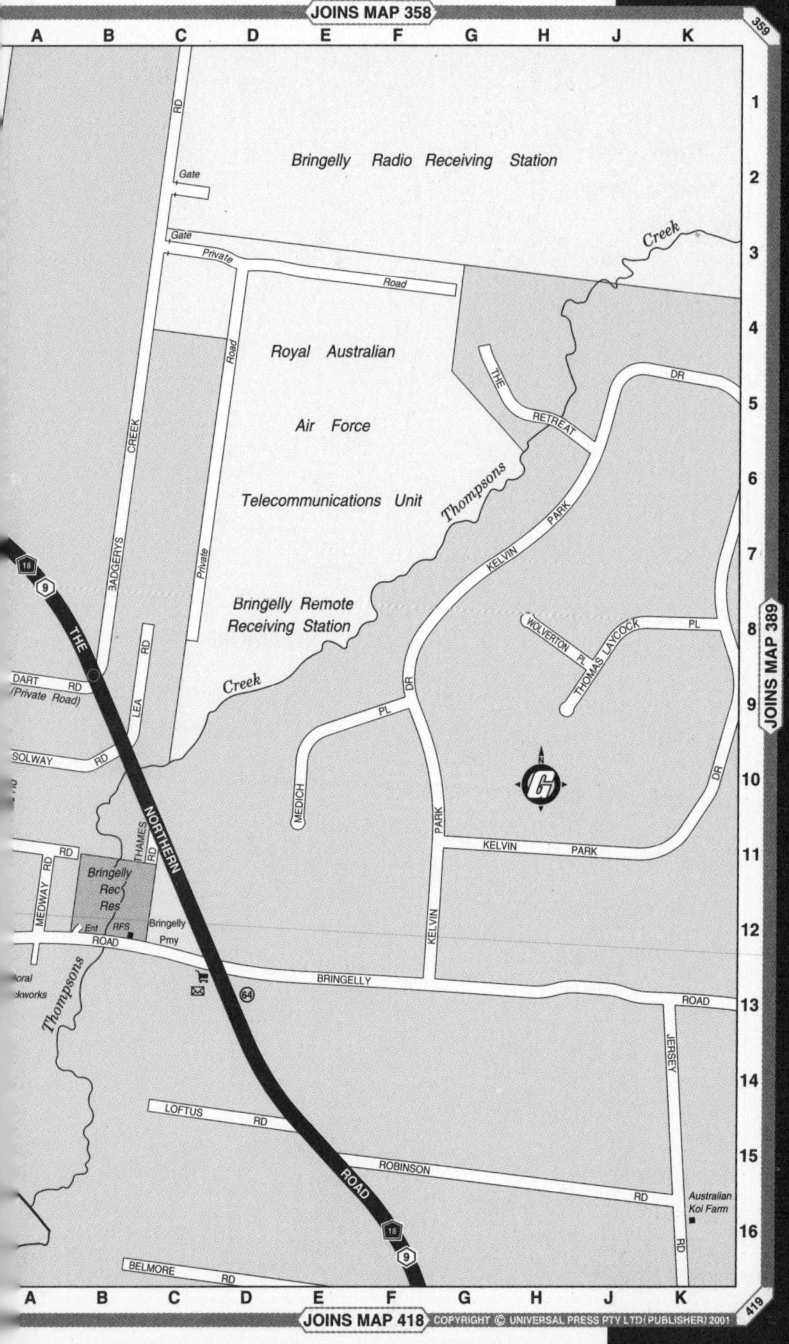
JOINS MAP 358
359
A B C D E F G H J K
1 2 3 4 5 6 7 8 9 10 11 12 13 14 15 16
Bringelly Radio Receiving Station
Gate
Gate
Private Road
Creek
Royal Australian
Air Force
Telecommunications Unit
Bringelly Remote
Receiving Station
Private Road
BADGERYS CREEK RD
THE RETREAT
KELVIN PARK DR
Thompsons
Creek
WOLVERTON PL
THOMAS LAYCOCK PL
DART RD
(Private Road)
LEA RD
SOLWAY RD
MEDICH PL
KELVIN PARK
KELVIN
THE NORTHERN ROAD
THAMES RD
MEDWAY RD
RD
Bringelly
Rec
Res
Ent
RFS
Bringelly
Pmy
ROAD
BRINGELLY ROAD
Boral
Brickworks
Thompsons
64
18
9
JERSEY RD
LOFTUS RD
ROBINSON RD
Australian
Koi Farm
BELMORE RD
JOINS MAP 389
JOINS MAP 418
419

MAP 389

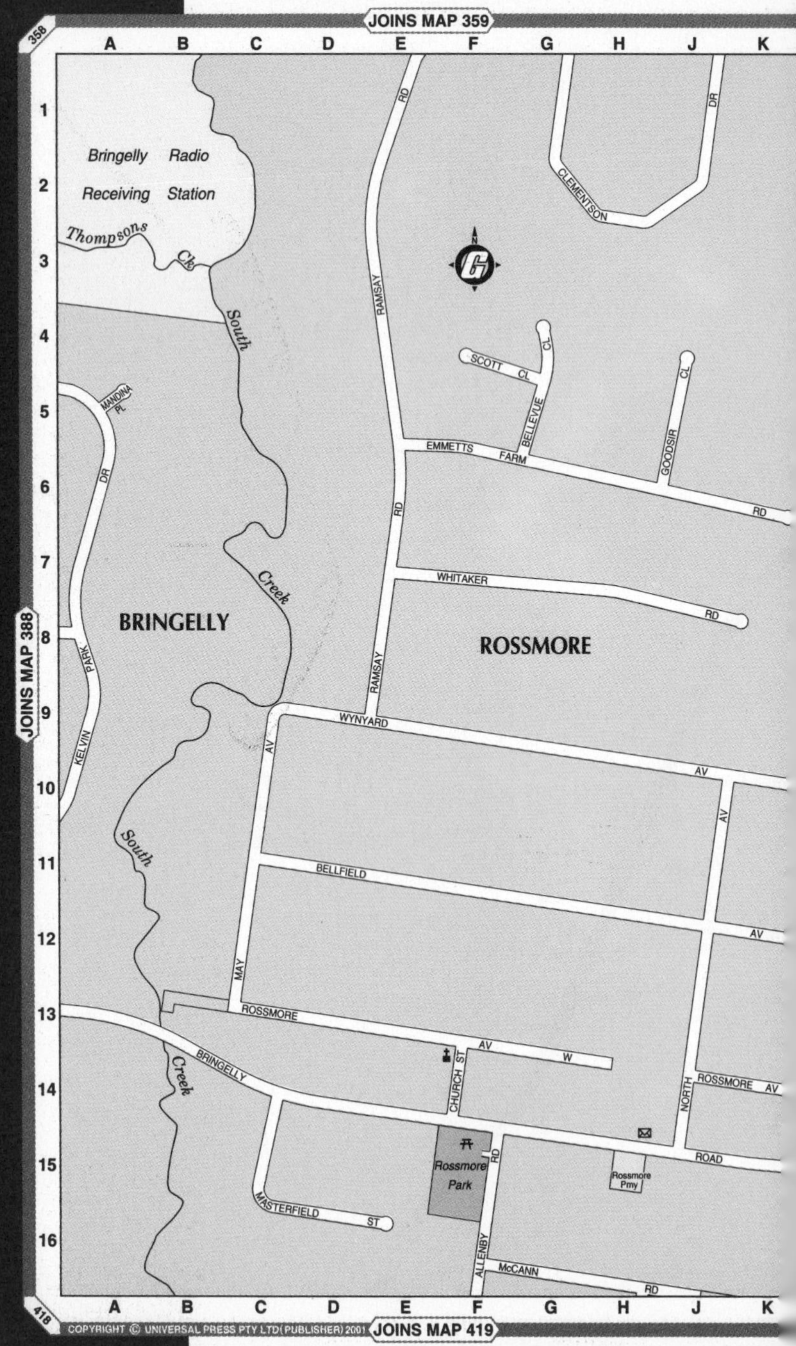

JOINS MAP 359
358
A B C D E F G H J K
1 2 3 4 5 6 7 8 9 10 11 12 13 14 15 16
Bringelly Radio Receiving Station
Thompsons Ck
South Creek
RAMSAY RD
CLEMENTSON DR
SCOTT CL
BELLEVUE CL
GOODSIR CL
MANDINA PL
KELVIN PARK DR
EMMETTS FARM RD
WHITAKER RD
BRINGELLY
ROSSMORE
WYNYARD AV
BELLFIELD AV
MAY AV
ROSSMORE AV W
ROSSMORE AV
NORTH
CHURCH ST
BRINGELLY ROAD
Rossmore Park
ALLENBY RD
Rossmore Pmy
MASTERFIELD ST
McCANN RD
JOINS MAP 388
418
JOINS MAP 419

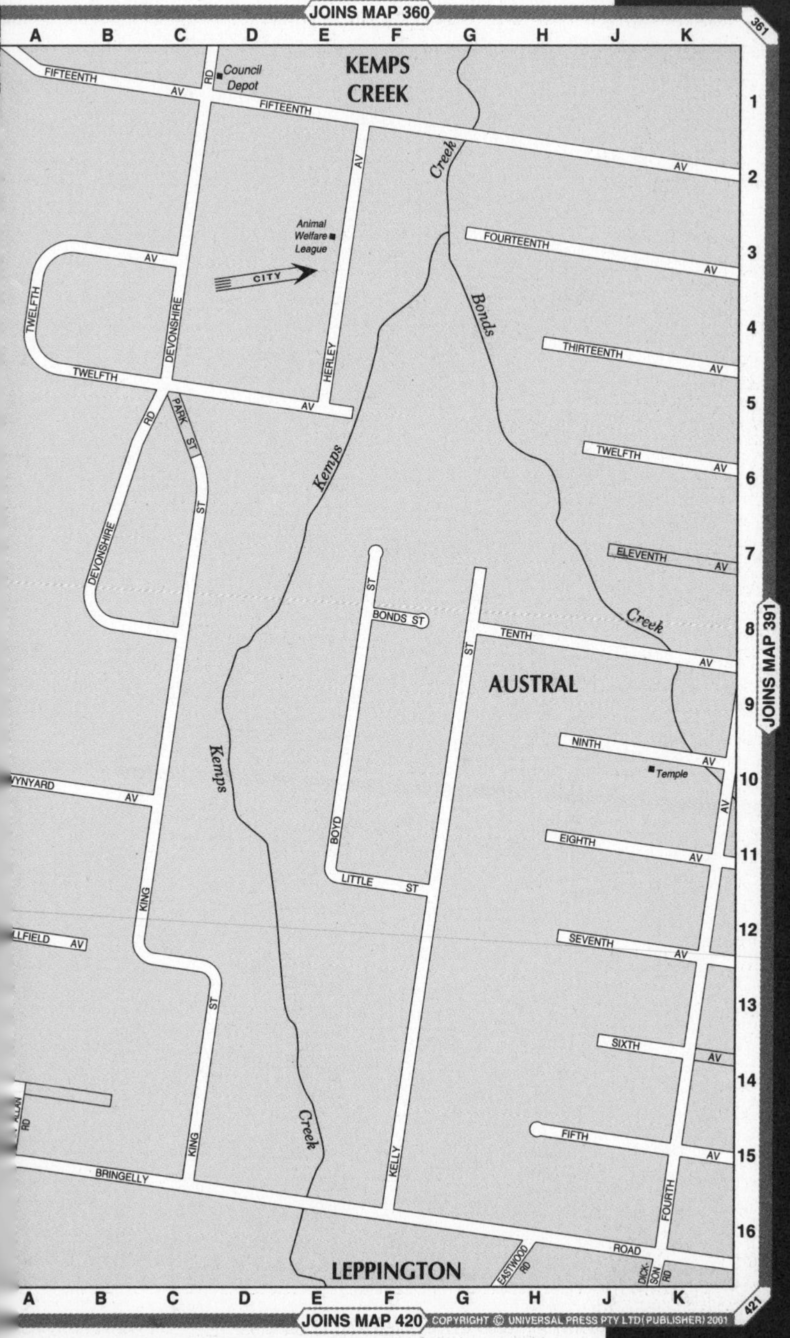
JOINS MAP 360
361
A B C D E F G H J K
KEMPS CREEK
Council Depot
FIFTEENTH AV
RD
FIFTEENTH AV
Creek
AV
Animal Welfare League
FOURTEENTH AV
AV
CITY
TWELFTH
DEVONSHIRE
HERLEY
Bonds
THIRTEENTH AV
TWELFTH AV
PARK ST
RD
TWELFTH AV
Kemps
ST
ELEVENTH AV
DEVONSHIRE
ST
BONDS ST
Creek
TENTH AV
ST
AUSTRAL
Kemps
NINTH AV
Temple
WYNYARD AV
AV
BOYD
EIGHTH AV
LITTLE ST
KING
LLFIELD AV
SEVENTH AV
ST
SIXTH AV
ALLAN RD
Creek
FIFTH AV
KING
KELLY
BRINGELLY
FOURTH
ROAD
LEPPINGTON
EASTWOOD RD
DICKSON RD
1 2 3 4 5 6 7 8 9 10 11 12 13 14 15 16
JOINS MAP 391
A B C D E F G H J K
JOINS MAP 420
421

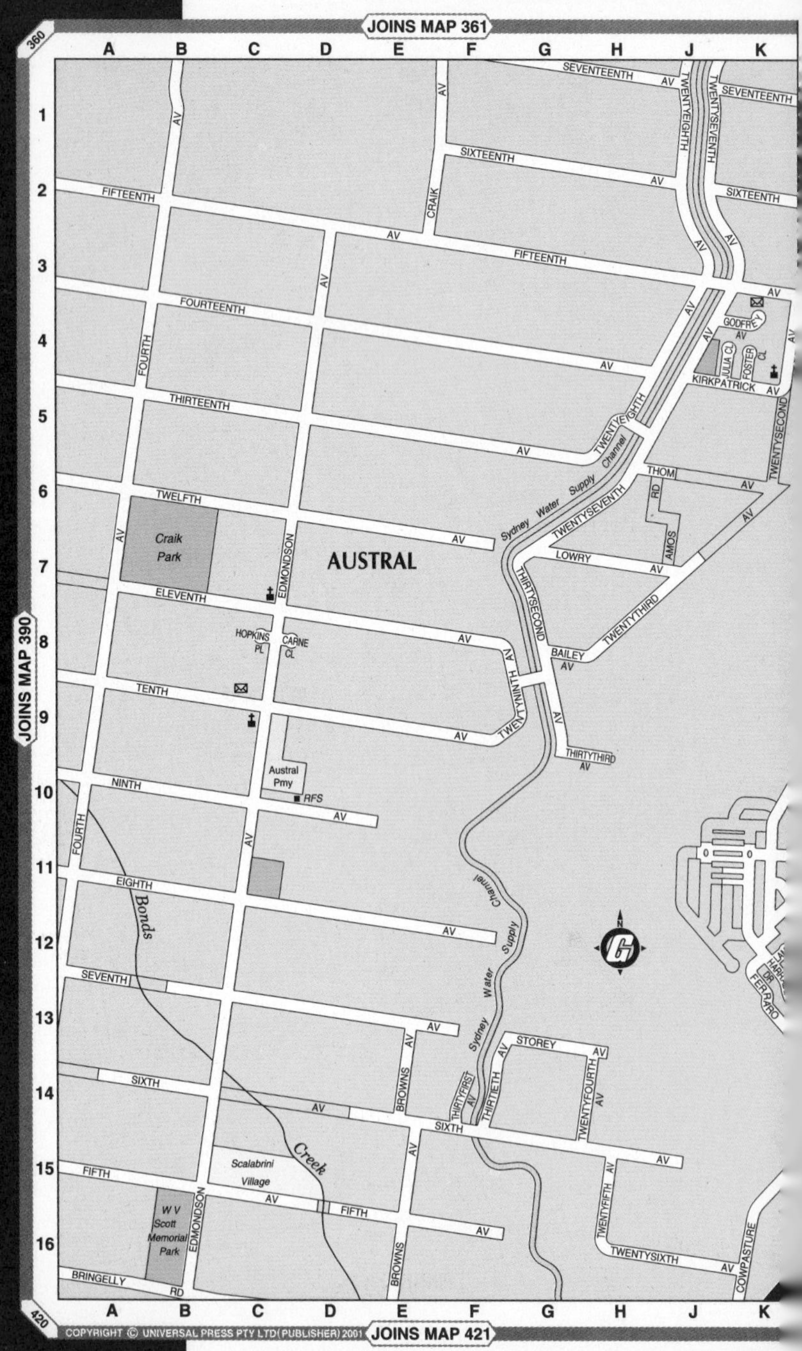
JOINS MAP 361
JOINS MAP 390
JOINS MAP 421
AUSTRAL
SEVENTEENTH AV
SIXTEENTH AV
FIFTEENTH AV
FOURTEENTH AV
THIRTEENTH AV
TWELFTH AV
ELEVENTH AV
TENTH AV
NINTH AV
EIGHTH AV
SEVENTH AV
SIXTH AV
FIFTH AV
BRINGELLY RD
FOURTH AV
CRAIK AV
EDMONDSON AV
BROWNS AV
TWENTYEIGHTH AV
TWENTYSEVENTH AV
TWENTYSECOND AV
THIRTYSECOND AV
TWENTYNINTH AV
THIRTYTHIRD AV
TWENTYTHIRD AV
BAILEY AV
LOWRY AV
AMOS RD
THOM RD
GODFREY AV
JULIA CL
FOSTER CL
KIRKPATRICK AV
HOPKINS PL
CARNE CL
STOREY AV
THIRTYFIRST AV
THIRTIETH AV
TWENTYFOURTH AV
TWENTYFIFTH AV
TWENTYSIXTH AV
COWPASTURE
FERRARO
Craik Park
Austral Pmy
RFS
Scalabrini Village
W V Scott Memorial Park
Bonds Creek
Sydney Water Supply Channel

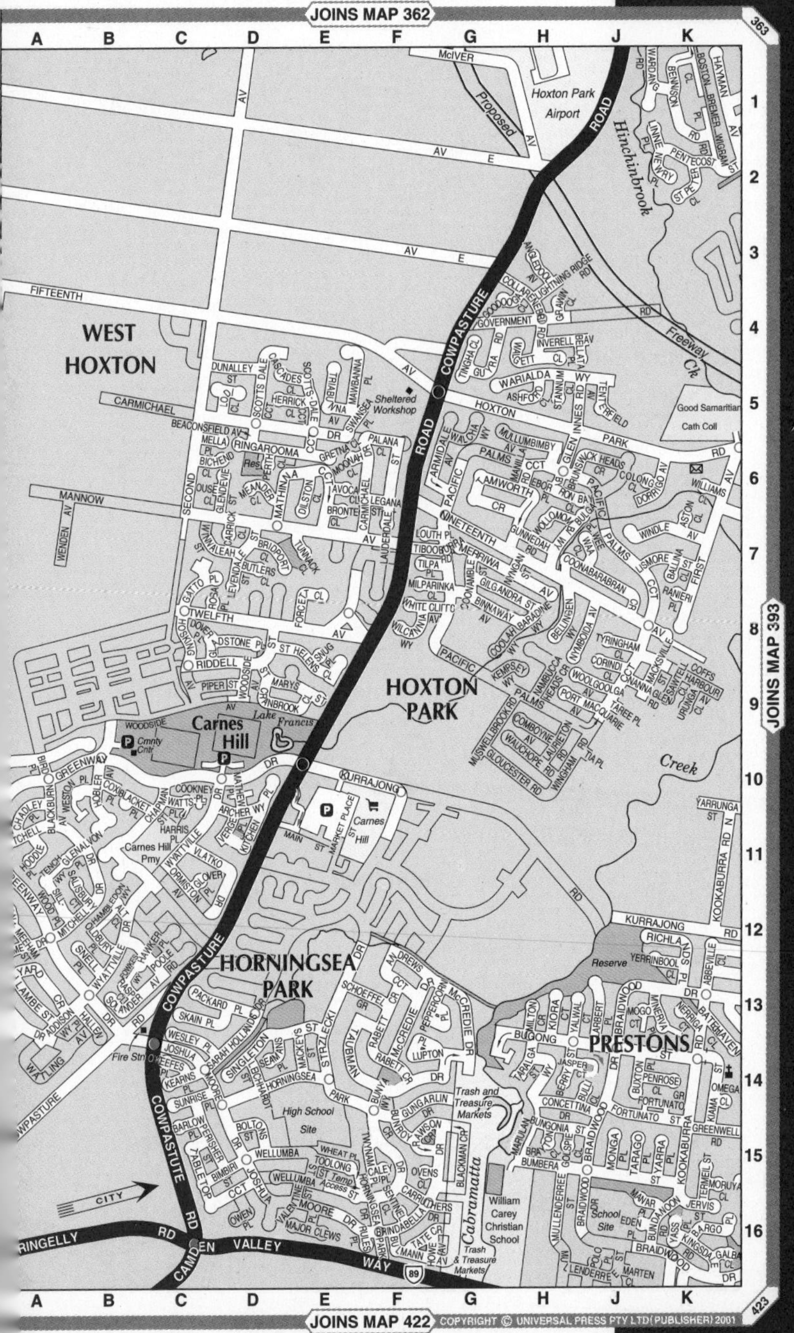
JOINS MAP 362
JOINS MAP 393
JOINS MAP 422
WEST HOXTON
HOXTON PARK
HORNINGSEA PARK
PRESTONS
Carnes Hill
Hoxton Park Airport
Good Samaritan Cath Coll
Sheltered Workshop
High School Site
William Carey Christian School
Trash and Treasure Markets
Hinchinbrook
Cabramatta
Creek
Reserve
COWPASTURE ROAD
CAMDEN VALLEY WAY
Carnes Hill Pmy
Fire Stn
Cmnty Cntr
Lake Francis
School Site
CITY

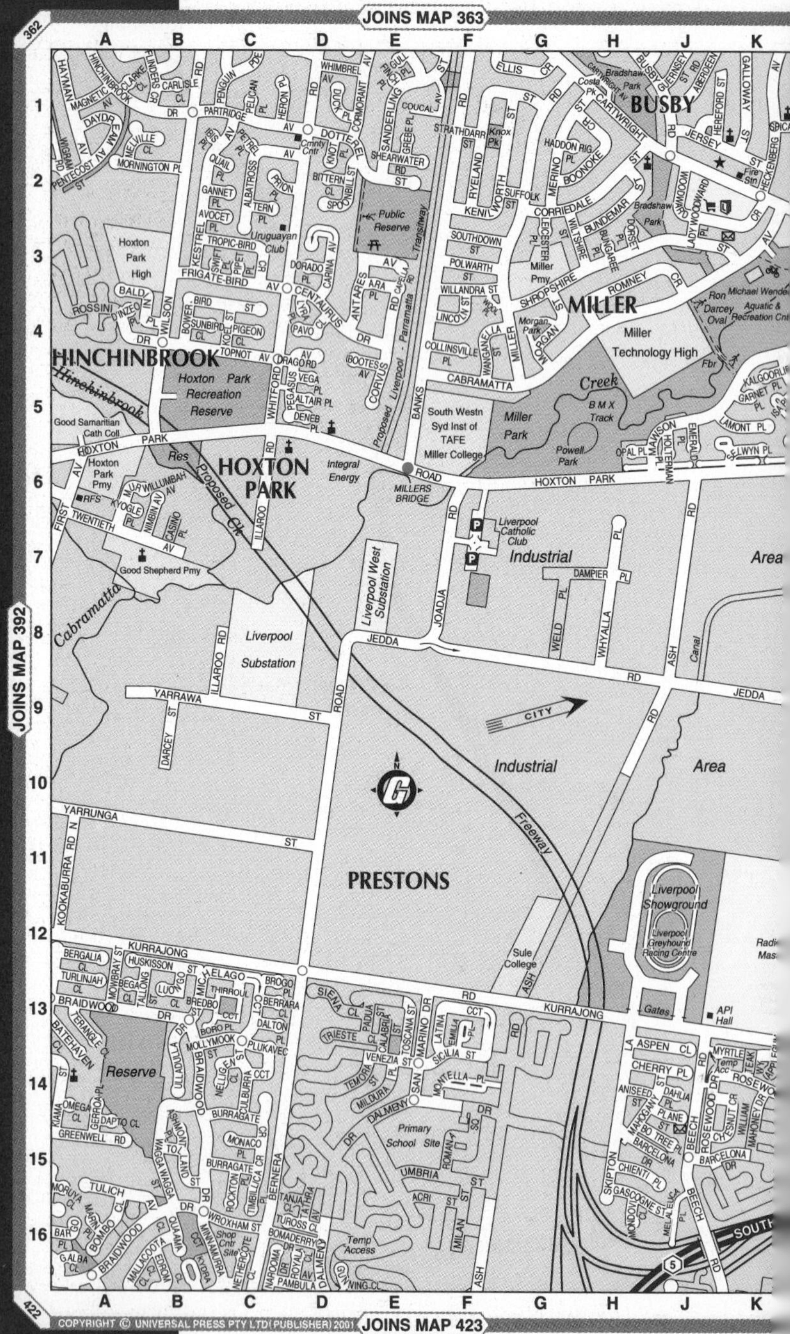
JOINS MAP 363
JOINS MAP 392
JOINS MAP 423
362
422
A B C D E F G H J K
1 2 3 4 5 6 7 8 9 10 11 12 13 14 15 16
HINCHINBROOK
HOXTON PARK
BUSBY
MILLER
PRESTONS
Hoxton Park High
Hoxton Park Recreation Reserve
Good Samaritan Cath Coll
Hoxton Park Pmy
RFS
Good Shepherd Pmy
Uruguayan Club
Cmnty Cntr
Public Reserve
Integral Energy
MILLERS BRIDGE
South Westn Syd Inst of TAFE Miller College
Miller Park
BMX Track
Powell Park
Knox Pk
Bradshaw Park
Miller Pmy
Morgan Park
Miller Technology High
Ron Darcey Oval
Michael Wenden Aquatic & Recreation Cnt
Liverpool Catholic Club
Industrial Area
Liverpool West Substation
Liverpool Substation
CITY
Freeway
Liverpool Showground
Liverpool Greyhound Racing Centre
Gates
API Hall
Sule College
Reserve
Primary School Site
Temp Access
Shop Cntr Site
Proposed Liverpool - Parramatta Transitway
Cabramatta Creek
Hinchinbrook Ck
Proposed Res
HOXTON PARK ROAD
CABRAMATTA RD
BANKS RD
JEDDA RD
JOADJA RD
ASH RD
YARRAWA ST
YARRUNGA ST
KURRAJONG RD
KOOKABURRA RD N
ILLAROO RD
WHITFORD RD
BRAIDWOOD DR
DALMENY DR
SOUTH

JOINS MAP 364
JOINS MAP 395
JOINS MAP 424
365
425
A
B
C
D
E
F
G
H
J
K
1
2
3
4
5
6
7
8
9
10
11
12
13
14
15
16
SADLEIR
ASHCROFT
LIVERPOOL
CARTWRIGHT
LURNEA
CASULA
Sadleir Pmy
Ashcroft Pmy
Ashcroft High
Lehmanns Oval
Landa Park
Creek
Cemetery
Nursing Home
Marsden Rd Pmy
Edwin Wheeler Oval
Eureka Cr Res
Landa Park
Joshua Moore Pk
Stanwell Oval
Ireland Park
Eloura Nature Res
Cabramatta
Tennis
McGirr Park
Cath Pmy
Gabo Pk
Sadleir Pk
Firth Pk
Alamein Pk
Cartwright Pmy
Prestons Mail Delivery Centre
Beswick Park
Mainsbridge Special
Liverpool West Pmy
Skating Rink
Civic Centre
Cncl Off.
Pearce Pk
Paciullo Park
Lion Pk
James Pk
SES
Council Depot
Everett Park
Canal
Res
Lurnea Pmy
Tennis
Phillips Park
Hall
St Francis Xaviers Cath
McCarthy Pk
Amalfi Park
Brickmakers
Fbr
Trewartha Pk
Kankama Village
Munro Pk
Cmnty Cntr
Lurnea High
Jeh Wit
Meere Park
National Broadcasting Station
Casula Pmy
Jardine Park
Prestons Pmy
Daruk Park
Casula Mall
Cmnty Cntr
Ben Prior Pk
Bollywood
Carroll Park
Jamieson Park
Casula
Steps
Resvr
Casula High
Gandangara Park
Glenfield Ck
ELIZABETH DR
HOXTON PARK ROAD
MEMORIAL AV
MOTORWAY
WESTERN
HUME HIGHWAY
CAMDEN VALLEY WAY
CABRAMATTA AV
DE MEYRICK AV
KURRAJONG RD
OLD KURRAJONG RD
CASULA RD
BOUNDARY
REILLY ST
COPYRIGHT © UNIVERSAL PRESS PTY LTD (PUBLISHER) 2001

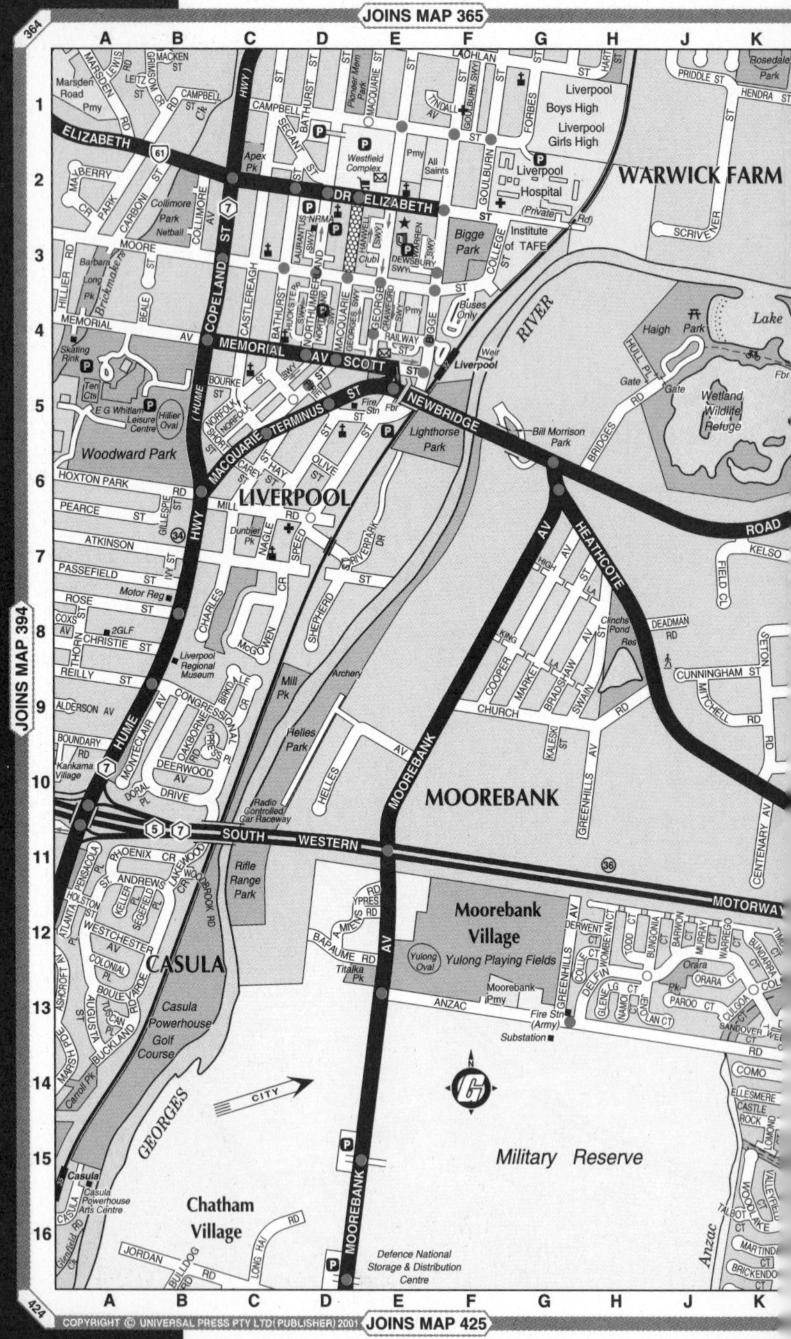

JOINS MAP 425

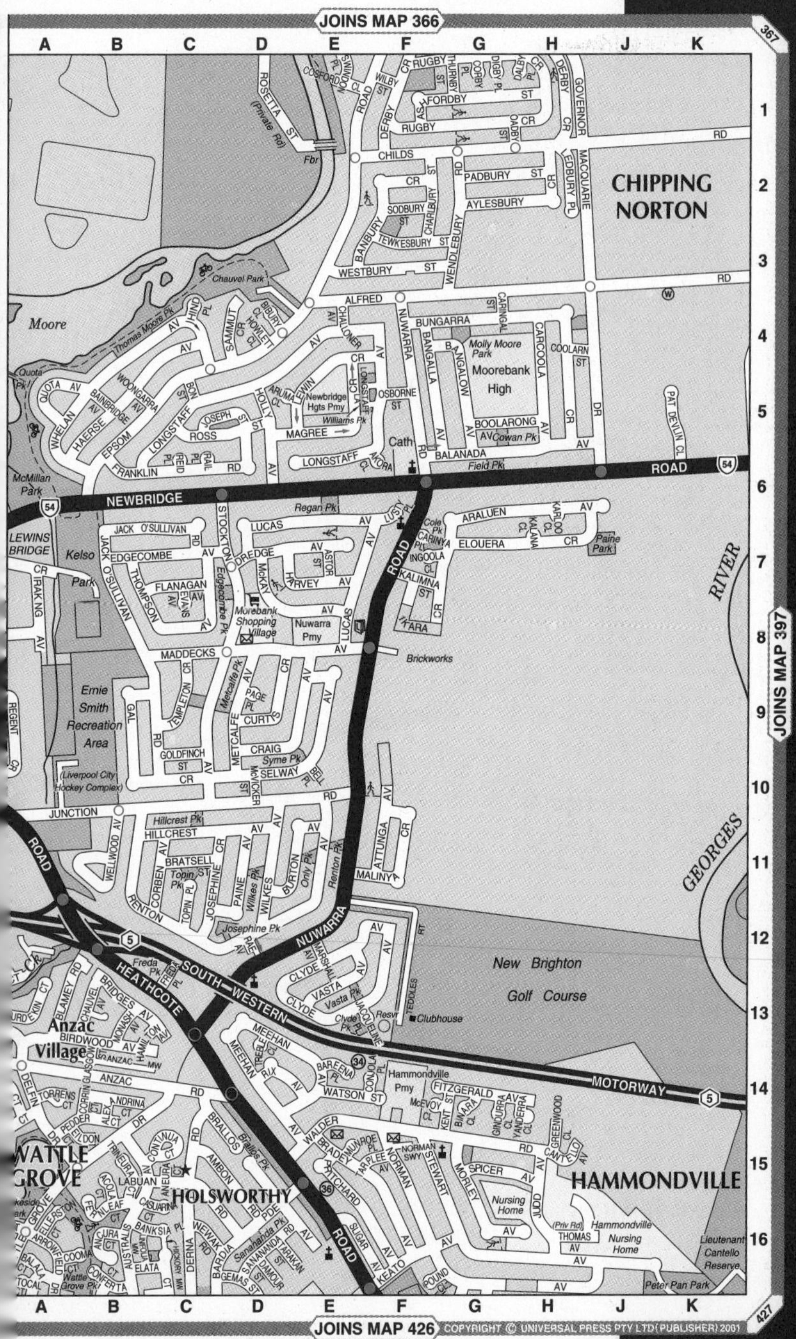
JOINS MAP 366
JOINS MAP 397
JOINS MAP 426
CHIPPING NORTON
HAMMONDVILLE
HOLSWORTHY
WATTLE GROVE
Anzac Village
Moore
NEWBRIDGE
ROAD
HEATHCOTE
SOUTH WESTERN
MOTORWAY
NUWARRA
GEORGES
RIVER
New Brighton Golf Course
Moorebank High
Ernie Smith Recreation Area
Kelso Park
Brickworks
Chauvel Park
McMillan Park
LEWINS BRIDGE
Molly Moore Park
Clubhouse
Hammondville Nursing Home
Lieutenant Cantello Reserve
Peter Pan Park

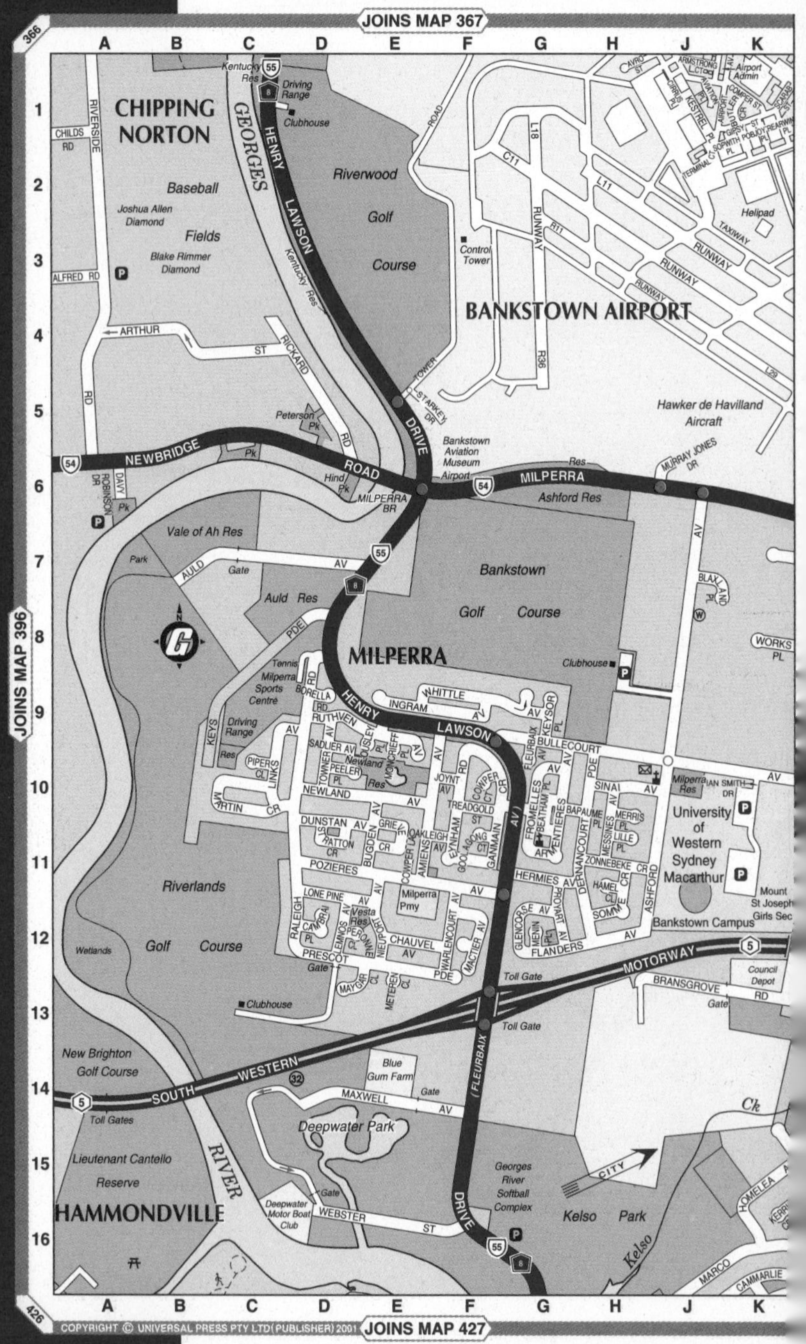
JOINS MAP 367
JOINS MAP 396
JOINS MAP 427
366
426
CHIPPING NORTON
BANKSTOWN AIRPORT
MILPERRA
HAMMONDVILLE
Baseball Fields
Joshua Allen Diamond
Blake Rimmer Diamond
Riverwood Golf Course
Bankstown Golf Course
Riverlands Golf Course
New Brighton Golf Course
Lieutenant Cantello Reserve
Deepwater Park
Kelso Park
Georges River Softball Complex
University of Western Sydney Macarthur
Bankstown Campus
Hawker de Havilland Aircraft
Bankstown Aviation Museum
Control Tower
Helipad
Airport Admin
Ashford Res
Vale of Ah Res
Auld Res
Milperra Sports Centre
Driving Range
Milperra Pmy
Blue Gum Farm
Deepwater Motor Boat Club
Council Depot
Mount St Joseph Girls Sec
Clubhouse
Toll Gate
Toll Gates
Wetlands
HENRY LAWSON DRIVE
NEWBRIDGE ROAD
MILPERRA ROAD
SOUTH WESTERN MOTORWAY
GEORGES RIVER
(FLEURBAIX AV)
BRANSGROVE RD
MAXWELL AV
WEBSTER ST
RIVERSIDE RD
ARTHUR ST
RICKARD RD
AULD AV
ASHFORD AV
CITY
COPYRIGHT © UNIVERSAL PRESS PTY LTD (PUBLISHER) 2001

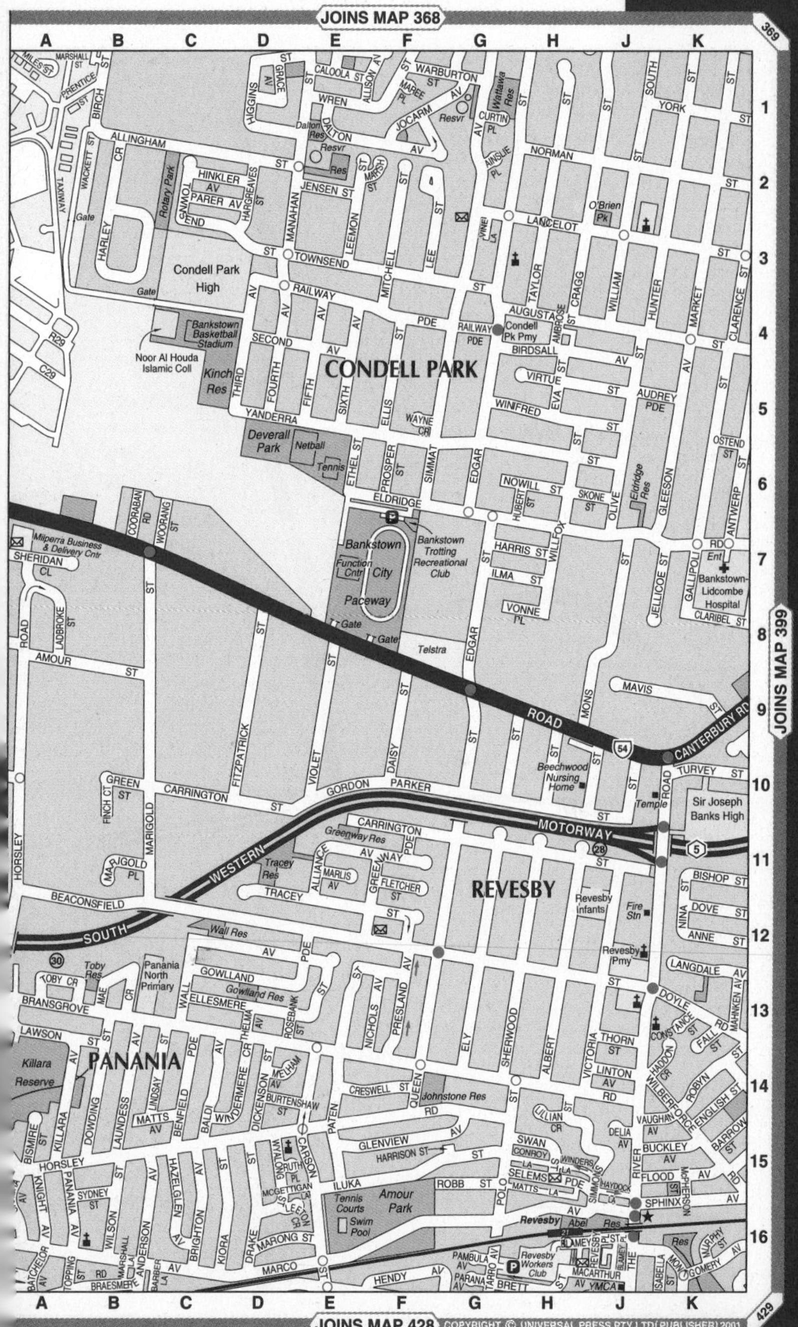
JOINS MAP 368
JOINS MAP 399
JOINS MAP 428
369
429
CONDELL PARK
REVESBY
PANANIA
Condell Park High
Bankstown Basketball Stadium
Noor Al Houda Islamic Coll
Kinch Res
Deverall Park
Netball
Tennis
Bankstown City Paceway
Function Cntr
Bankstown Trotting Recreational Club
Telstra
Milperra Business & Delivery Cntr
Bankstown-Lidcombe Hospital
Sir Joseph Banks High
Beechwood Nursing Home
Temple
Revesby Infants
Fire Stn
Revesby Pmy
Condell Pk Pmy
Panania North Primary
Killara Reserve
Johnstone Res
Amour Park
Tennis Courts
Swim Pool
Revesby Workers Club
YMCA
Rotary Park
Wattawa Res
Dalton Res
O'Brien Pk
Eldridge Res
Greenway Res
Tracey Res
Wall Res
Toby Res
Gowlland Res
CANTERBURY RD
WESTERN MOTORWAY
SOUTH
ROAD
ALLINGHAM
RAILWAY
RAILWAY PDE
CONDELL PARK
CARRINGTON
BEACONSFIELD
HORSLEY
GORDON PARKER
TOWNSEND
YANDERRA
ELDRIDGE
NORMAN
LANCELOT
AUGUSTA
BIRDSALL
WINIFRED
HARRIS ST
AMOUR ST
MAVIS
TURVEY ST
BISHOP ST
DOVE ST
ANNE ST
LANGDALE AV
DOYLE RD
THORN ST
LINTON AV
CRESWELL ST
QUEEN RD
GLENVIEW
HARRISON ST
ILUKA
ROBB ST
SWAN
SELEMS PDE
MATTS LA
MARCO
HENDY AV
BRETT
MACARTHUR AV
VAUGHAN AV
BUCKLEY AV
FLOOD AV
SPHINX
COPYRIGHT © UNIVERSAL PRESS PTY LTD (PUBLISHER) 2001

MAP 399

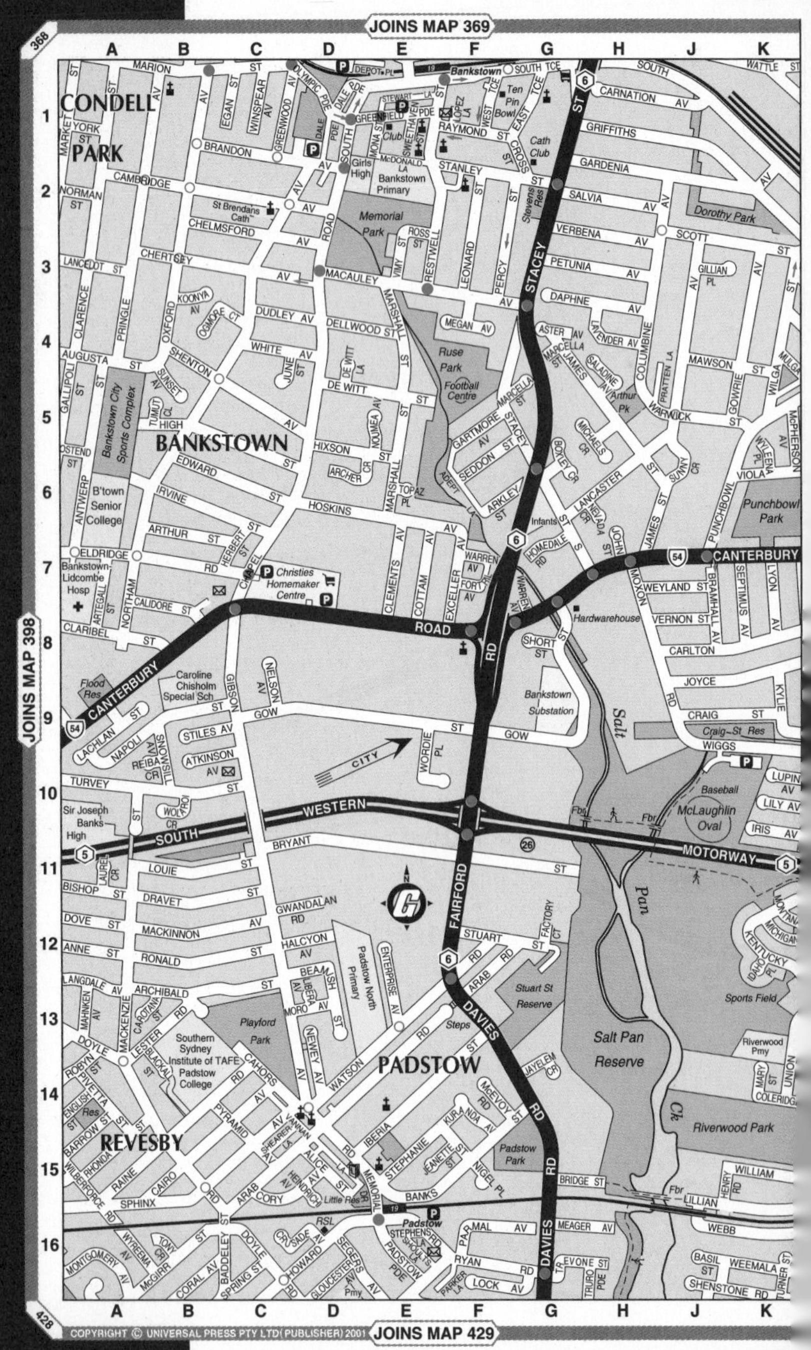

JOINS MAP 369
JOINS MAP 398
JOINS MAP 429
368
428
A B C D E F G H J K
1 2 3 4 5 6 7 8 9 10 11 12 13 14 15 16
CONDELL PARK
BANKSTOWN
PADSTOW
REVESBY
MARION ST
YORK
MARKET ST
NORMAN ST
BRANDON
CAMBRIDGE
CHELMSFORD
CHERTSEY
LANCELOT ST
EGAN ST
WINSPEAR AV
GREENWOOD AV
OLYMPIC PDE
DALE PDE
SOUTH TCE
DEPOT PL
STEWART LA
GREENFIELD PDE
MONA ST
SWEETHAVEN RD
McDONALD LA
RAYMOND ST
STANLEY ST
LOPEZ LA
WEST TCE
EAST TCE
CROSS ST
Bankstown
Ten Pin Bowl
Cath Club
Club
Girls High
Bankstown Primary
St Brendans Cath
Memorial Park
ROSS ST
VIMY ST
RESTWELL ST
LEONARD ST
PERCY AV
MACAULEY
Stevens Res
STACEY ST
CARNATION AV
GRIFFITHS
GARDENIA
SALVIA AV
VERBENA AV
SCOTT
PETUNIA AV
DAPHNE AV
ASTER AV
MARCELLA
JAMES
LAVENDER AV
SALADINE AV
COLUMBINE
PRATTEN LA
GILLIAN PL
MAWSON
GOWRIE ST
WILGA
MULGA
Dorothy Park
WATTLE ST
SOUTH
Arthur Pk
WARWICK
MICHAELS CR
BOXLEY CR
LANCASTER
NEVADA ST
JOHN ST
JAMES ST
SUNNY CR
PUNCHBOWL
WYLEENA PL
McPHERSON
VIOLA
Punchbowl Park
CLARENCE ST
PRINGLE AV
OXFORD AV
KOONYA AV
OGMORE CT
DUDLEY AV
DELLWOOD ST
MARSHALL ST
MEGAN AV
Ruse Park
Football Centre
AUGUSTA
GALLIPOLI ST
SHENTON AV
SUNSET AV
TUMUT CL
WHITE AV
JUNE ST
DE WITT LA
DE WITT
NOUMEA AV
HIGH
Bankstown City Sports Complex
HIXSON
ARCHER CR
TOPAZ PL
ADEPT LA
GARTMORE AV
SEDDON ST
ARKLEY ST
OSTEND ST
EDWARD
IRVINE
HOSKINS
B'town Senior College
ANTWERP
ARTHUR ST
HERBERT ST
CHAPEL
CLEMENTS AV
COTTAM AV
EXCELLER AV
WARREN AV
FORT AV
Infants
HOMEDALE RD
MOXON
WEYLAND ST
BRAMHALL AV
SEPTIMUS AV
LYON AV
VERNON ST
Hardwarehouse
CANTERBURY
ELDRIDGE
Bankstown-Lidcombe Hosp
ARTEGALL ST
NORTHAM
CALIDORE ST
Christies Homemaker Centre
ROAD
CLARIBEL ST
SHORT ST
CARLTON
JOYCE
KYLIE
CRAIG ST
Craig St Res
WIGGS
Flood Res
Caroline Chisholm Special Sch
GIBSON
NELSON AV
Bankstown Substation
Salt
LACHLAN
NAPOLI ST
SNOWSILL
REIBA CR
STILES AV
ATKINSON AV
GOW
WORDIE PL
CITY
LUPIN AV
LILY AV
IRIS AV
Baseball
McLaughlin Oval
TURVEY
Sir Joseph Banks High
WOLAROI CR
WESTERN
SOUTH
MOTORWAY
Fbr
BRYANT
LAUREL CR
LOUIE
BISHOP ST
DRAVET
DOVE ST
MACKINNON
ANNE ST
RONALD
LANGDALE AV
ARCHIBALD
GWANDALAN RD
HALCYON AV
FAIRFORD RD
Pan
MONTANA
MICHIGAN
KENTUCKY
IDAHO PL
Sports Field
STUART ST
FACTORY CT
Padstow North Primary
ENTERPRISE AV
BEAMISH ST
LIBERA AV
MORO AV
NEWEY AV
Playford Park
ARAB RD
Stuart St Reserve
DAVIES RD
Steps
Salt Pan Reserve
Riverwood Pmy
MAHNKEN AV
MACKENZIE
CAROTANA ST
LESTER RD
Southern Sydney Institute of TAFE Padstow College
CAHORS RD
WATSON
JAYELEM CR
MARY ST
UNION
COLERIDGE
DOYLE
ROBYN ST
PIVETTA
ENGLISH
Res
BLACKALL ST
PYRAMID
VANNAN
SHEARER
McGEVOY RD
Ck
Riverwood Park
BARROW ST
RHONDA
WILBERFORCE RD
RAINE
CAIRO
SPHINX
IBERIA
STEPHANIE
KURA
NOA
JEANETTE ST
NIGEL PL
Padstow Park
ALICE
HEINDRICH
MEMORIAL DR
CORY
Little Res
BANKS
BRIDGE ST
WILLIAM
HENRY RD
LILLIAN
RSL
Padstow
CRUSADE
STEPHENS RD
SHORTS LA
PARMAL AV
MEAGER AV
WEBB
WYREEMA AV
TONY CR
BADDELEY ST
DOYLE
MONTGOMERY AV
McGIRR
CORAL AV
SPRING ST
HOWARD
SEGERS AV
GLOUCESTER
PADSTOW PDE
RYAN
PARKER LA
LOCK AV
EVONE ST
TRURO PDE
BASIL ST
WEEMALA
SHENSTONE RD
TURNER ST
Pmy

JOINS MAP 370
JOINS MAP 401
JOINS MAP 430
371
431
PUNCHBOWL
WILEY PARK
LAKEMBA
ROSELANDS
RIVERWOOD
NARWEE
BEVERLY HILLS
PEAKHURST
KING GEORGES ROAD
CANTERBURY ROAD
SOUTH WESTERN MOTORWAY
Punchbowl
Wiley Park
Lakemba
Narwee
Riverwood
Punchbowl Boys High
Punchbowl Primary
Wiley Pk Girls High
Wiley Pk Pmy
Lakemba Pmy
Roselands
Bennett Park
Rotary Park
Lance Hutchinson Oval
Bland Oval
Hannans Rd Pmy
Narwee Pmy
Narwee Boys High
Bev Hills Nth Pmy
John Mountford Res
Richard Podmore Res
Wise Res
Scott Res
Spicers Paper Ltd
Retirement Village
Nursing Home
Legion Club
Sen Cits
Rasdall Park
Progress Pk
Greek Cmnty Club
Ten Cts
Cmnty Cntr
Sen Cits Cntr

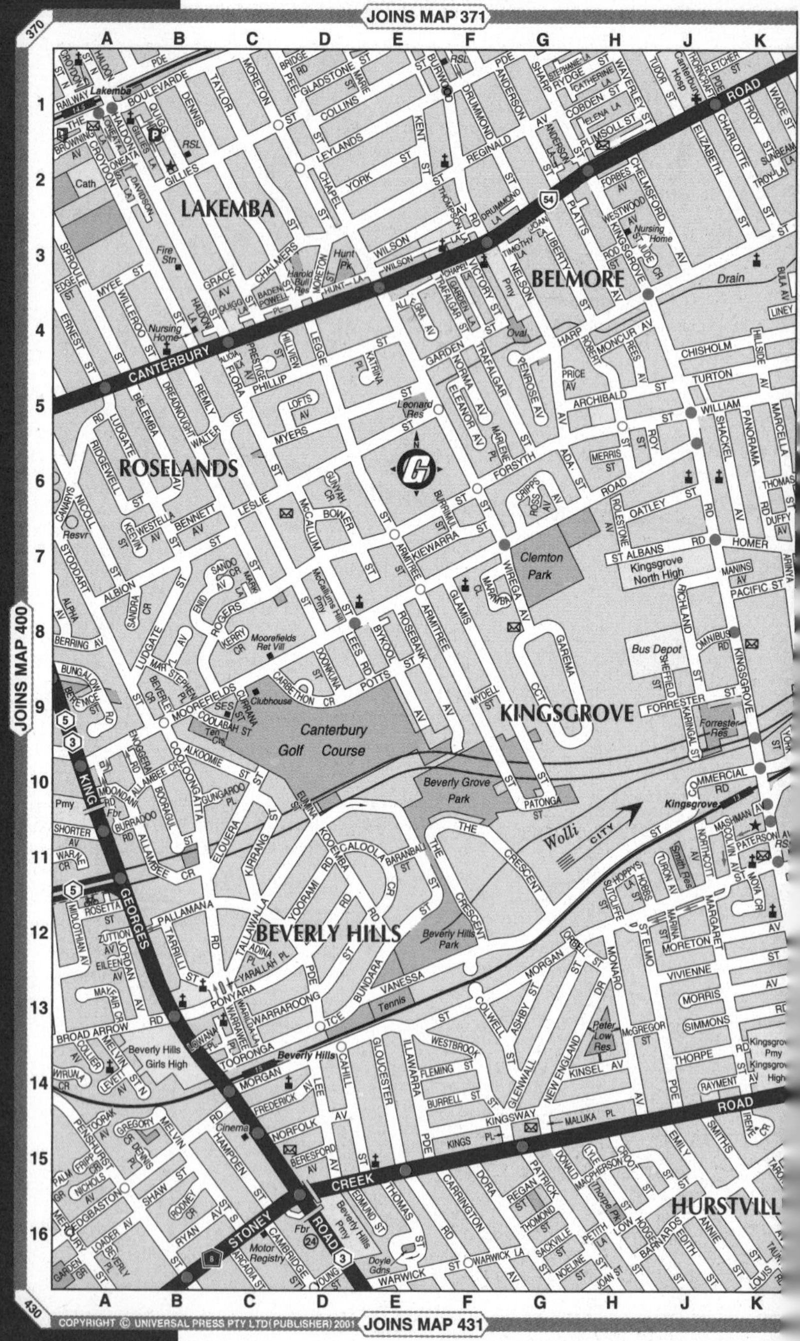
JOINS MAP 371
JOINS MAP 400
JOINS MAP 431
370
430
LAKEMBA
BELMORE
ROSELANDS
KINGSGROVE
BEVERLY HILLS
HURSTVILL
CANTERBURY
ROAD
KING GEORGES ROAD
STONEY CREEK ROAD
Canterbury Golf Course
Clemton Park
Kingsgrove North High
Bus Depot
Beverly Grove Park
Beverly Hills Park
Beverly Hills Girls High
Wolli
CITY
Kingsgrove
Lakemba
Beverly Hills
Moorefields Ret Vill
Leonard Res
Harold Bull Res
Hunt Pk
Forrester Res
Peter Low Res
Smith Res
Thorpe Pk
Doyle Gdns
Motor Registry
Cinema
Clubhouse
Fire Stn
Nursing Home
Drain
Oval
Tennis
Resvr
Cath
Pmy
Fbr
RSL
SES
Ten Cts
McCallums Hill Pmy
Beverly Hills Pmy
Kingsgrove Pmy
Kingsgrove High

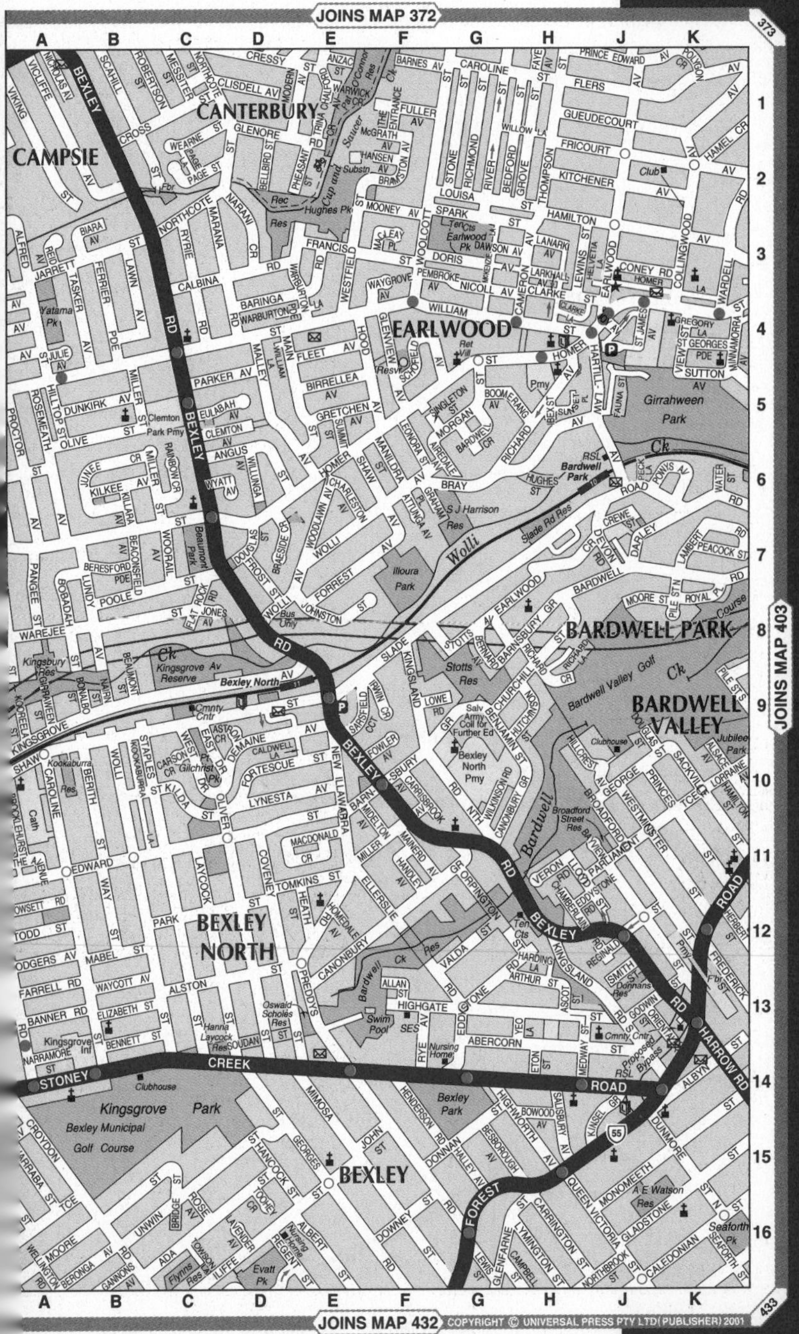
JOINS MAP 372
JOINS MAP 403
JOINS MAP 432
373
433
CANTERBURY
CAMPSIE
EARLWOOD
BARDWELL PARK
BARDWELL VALLEY
BEXLEY NORTH
BEXLEY
Kingsgrove Park
Bexley Municipal Golf Course
Girrahween Park
Illoura Park
Bexley Park
Bardwell Valley Golf Course
Kingsgrove Av Reserve
Beaumont Park
Yatama Pk
Hughes Pk
Earlwood Pk
S J Harrison Res
Stotts Res
Jubilee Park
Evatt Pk
Seaforth Pk
A E Watson Res
BEXLEY RD
STONEY CREEK ROAD
FOREST RD
HARROW RD
Bexley North
Bardwell Park
Cup and Saucer Ck
Wolli Ck
Bardwell Ck

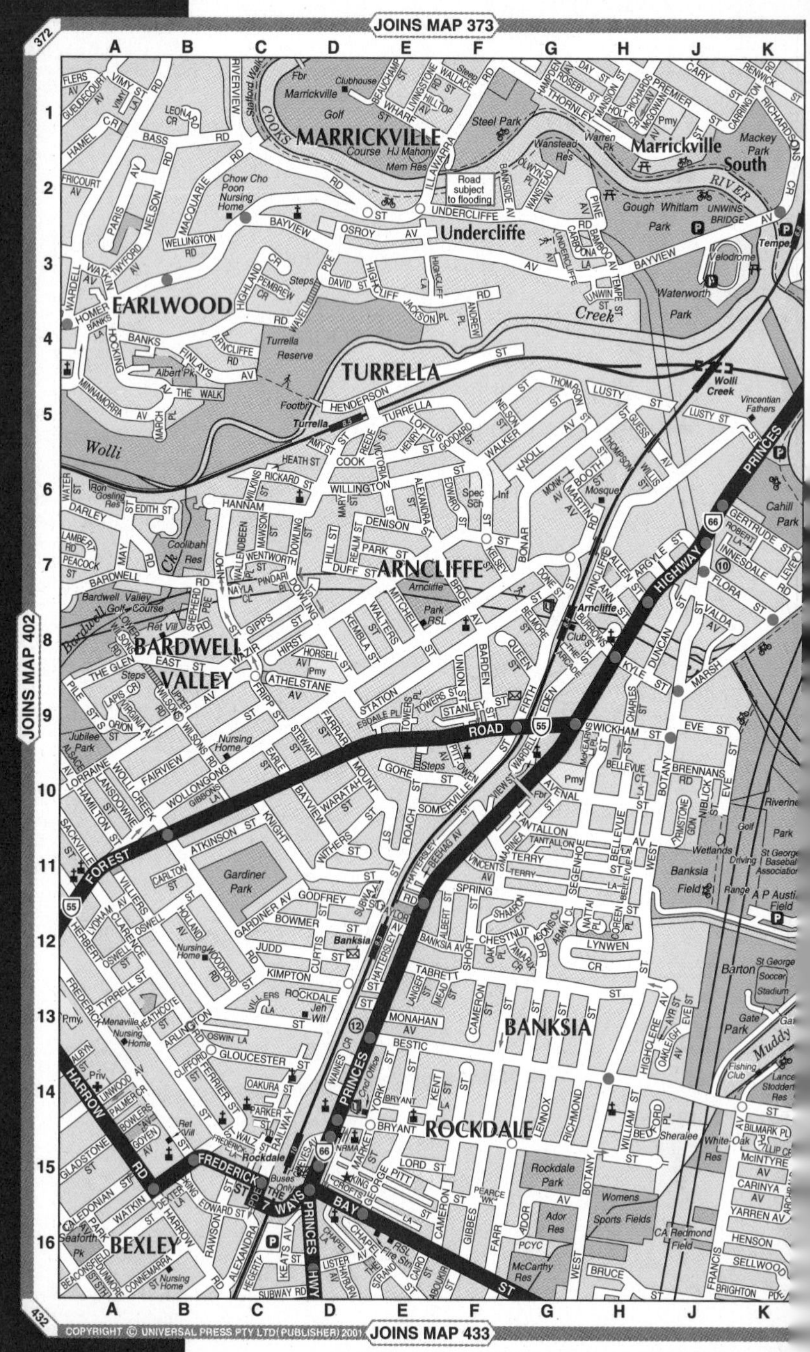
JOINS MAP 373
JOINS MAP 402
JOINS MAP 433
372
432
MARRICKVILLE
Marrickville South
Undercliffe
EARLWOOD
TURRELLA
ARNCLIFFE
BARDWELL VALLEY
BANKSIA
ROCKDALE
BEXLEY
Marrickville Golf Course
Steel Park
Gough Whitlam Park
Waterworth Park
Turrella Reserve
Cahill Park
Gardiner Park
Rockdale Park
Banksia Field
Bardwell Valley Golf Course
Jubilee Park
Wolli Creek
Cooks River
Road subject to flooding
FOREST RD
PRINCES HWY
WOLLONGONG RD
BAY ST
FREDERICK ST
HARROW RD
7 WAYS
Turrella
Arncliffe
Banksia
Rockdale
Tempe
Wolli Creek
Barton Park
St George Soccer Stadium
Riverine Park
Womens Sports Fields
McCarthy Res
Ador Res
CA Redmond Field
White Oak Res
Lance Stoddert Res

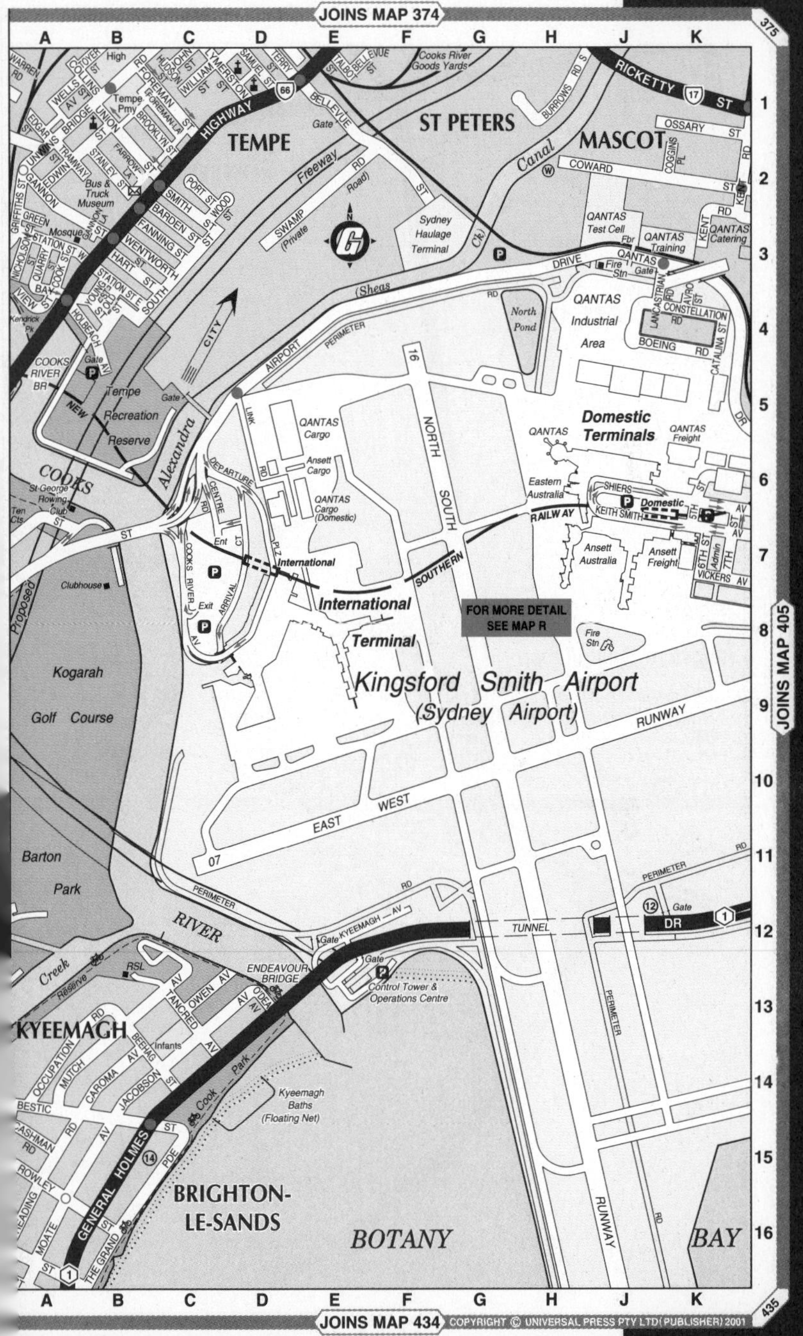
JOINS MAP 374
375
JOINS MAP 405
JOINS MAP 434
435
TEMPE
ST PETERS
MASCOT
Domestic Terminals
International Terminal
Kingsford Smith Airport
(Sydney Airport)
FOR MORE DETAIL SEE MAP R
Kogarah Golf Course
Barton Park
Tempe Recreation Reserve
KYEEMAGH
BRIGHTON-LE-SANDS
BOTANY BAY
COOKS RIVER
Sydney Haulage Terminal
QANTAS Industrial Area
Control Tower & Operations Centre
Kyeemagh Baths (Floating Net)
ENDEAVOUR BRIDGE
Bus & Truck Museum
Cooks River Goods Yards
North Pond
RICKETTY ST
GENERAL HOLMES DR
TUNNEL
RUNWAY
EAST WEST
SOUTHERN RAILWAY

JOINS MAP 375

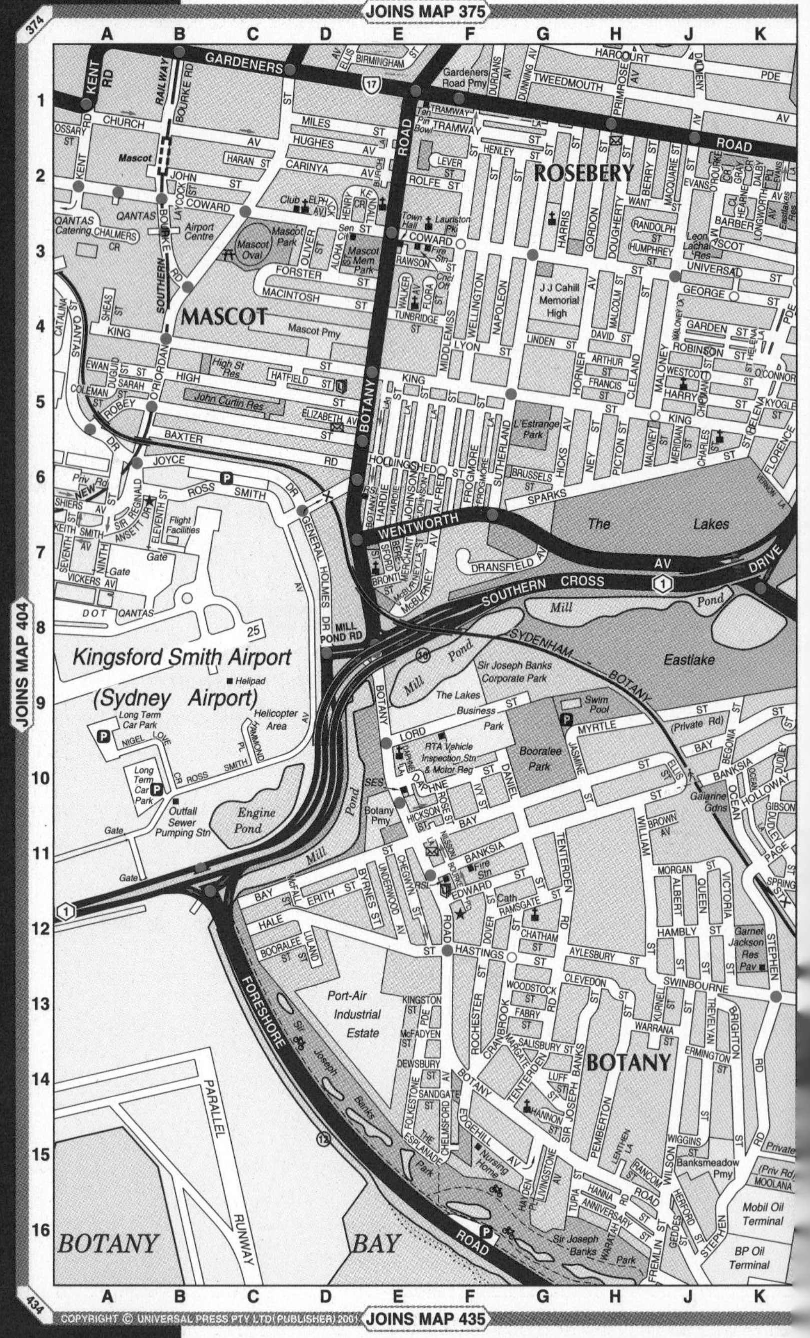

JOINS MAP 404

JOINS MAP 435

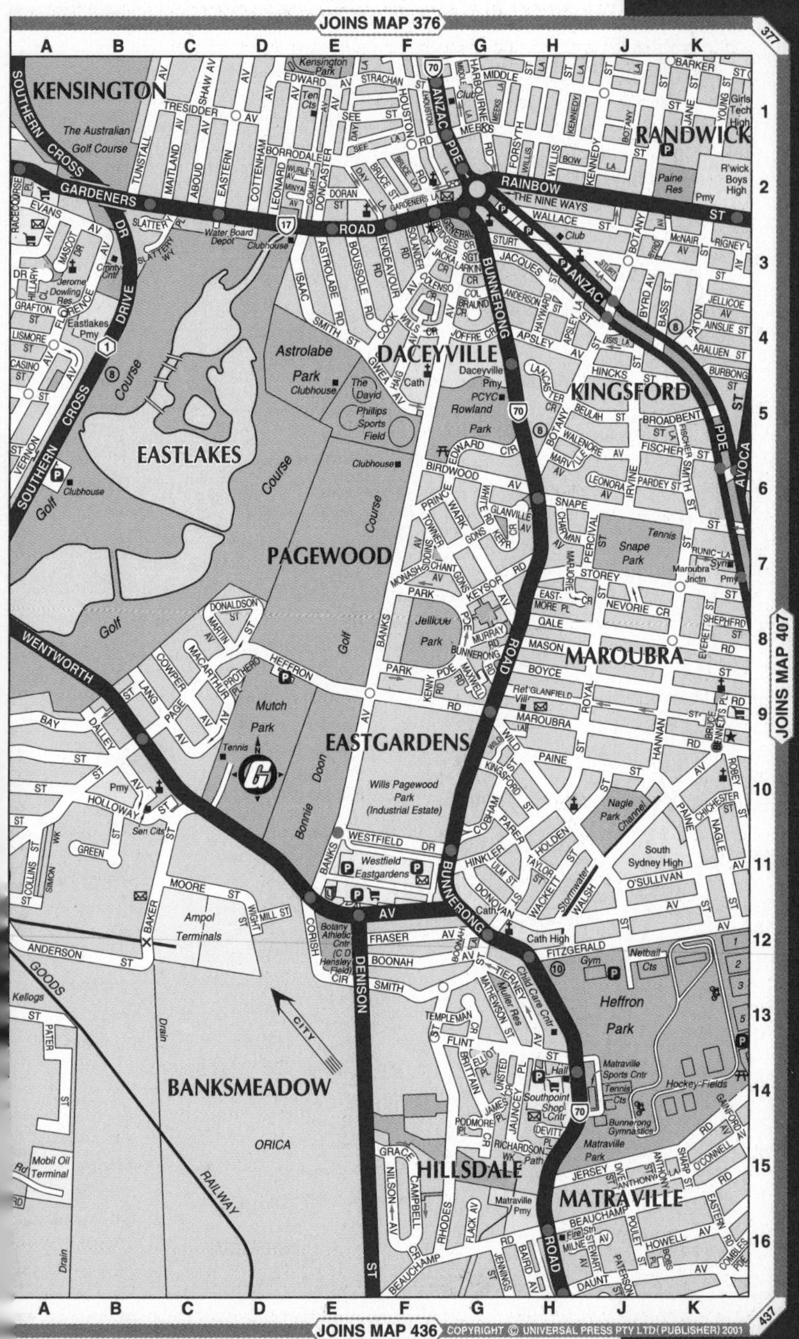
JOINS MAP 376
JOINS MAP 407
JOINS MAP 436
377
437
KENSINGTON
RANDWICK
EASTLAKES
DACEYVILLE
KINGSFORD
PAGEWOOD
MAROUBRA
EASTGARDENS
BANKSMEADOW
HILLSDALE
MATRAVILLE
The Australian Golf Course
Astrolabe Park
Mutch Park
Snape Park
Jellicoe Park
Heffron Park
Wills Pagewood Park (Industrial Estate)
Westfield Eastgardens
Ampol Terminals
ORICA
Mobil Oil Terminal
South Sydney High
Nagle Park
Rowland Park
The David Phillips Sports Field
Southern Cross Drive
Gardeners Road
Rainbow St
Anzac Pde
Bunnerong Road
Wentworth Av
Denison St
Botany St
Goods Railway

JOINS MAP 377

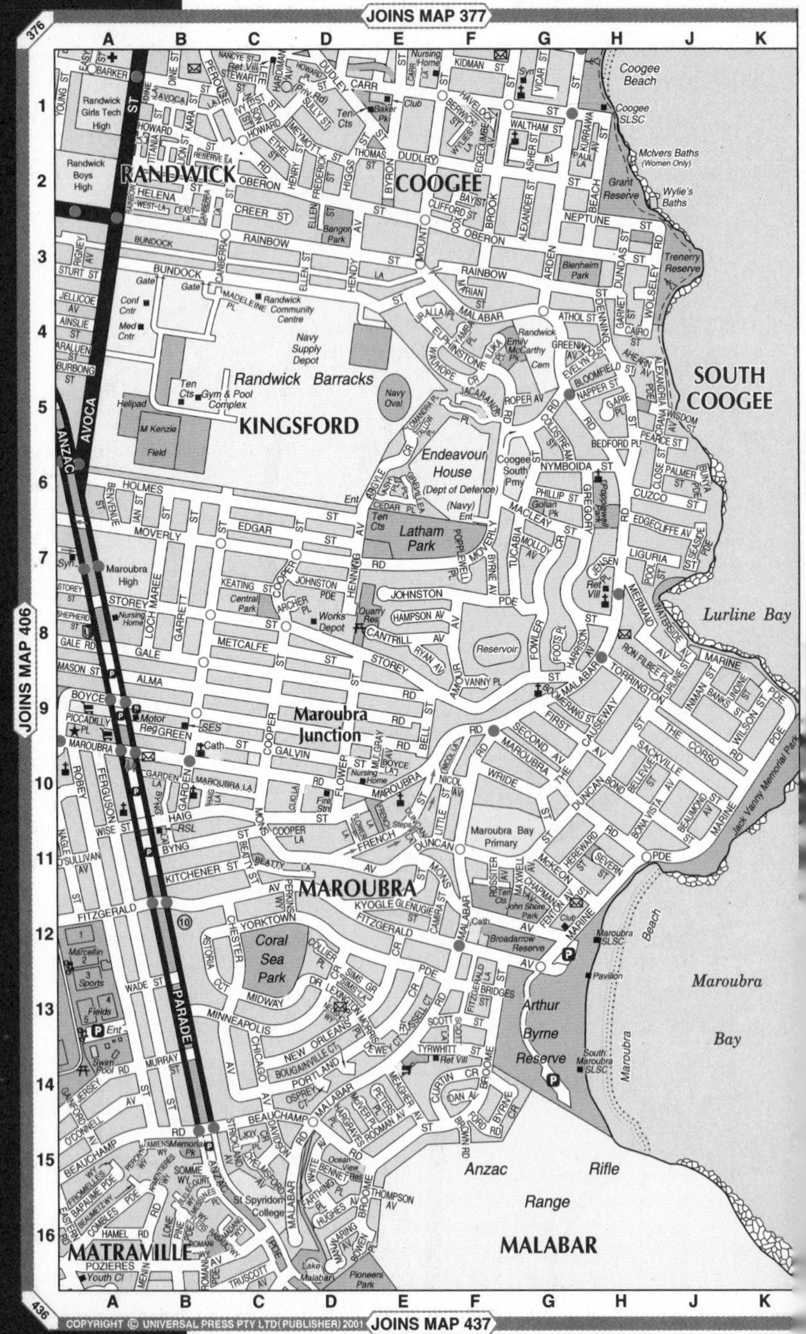

JOINS MAP 437

JOINS MAP 406

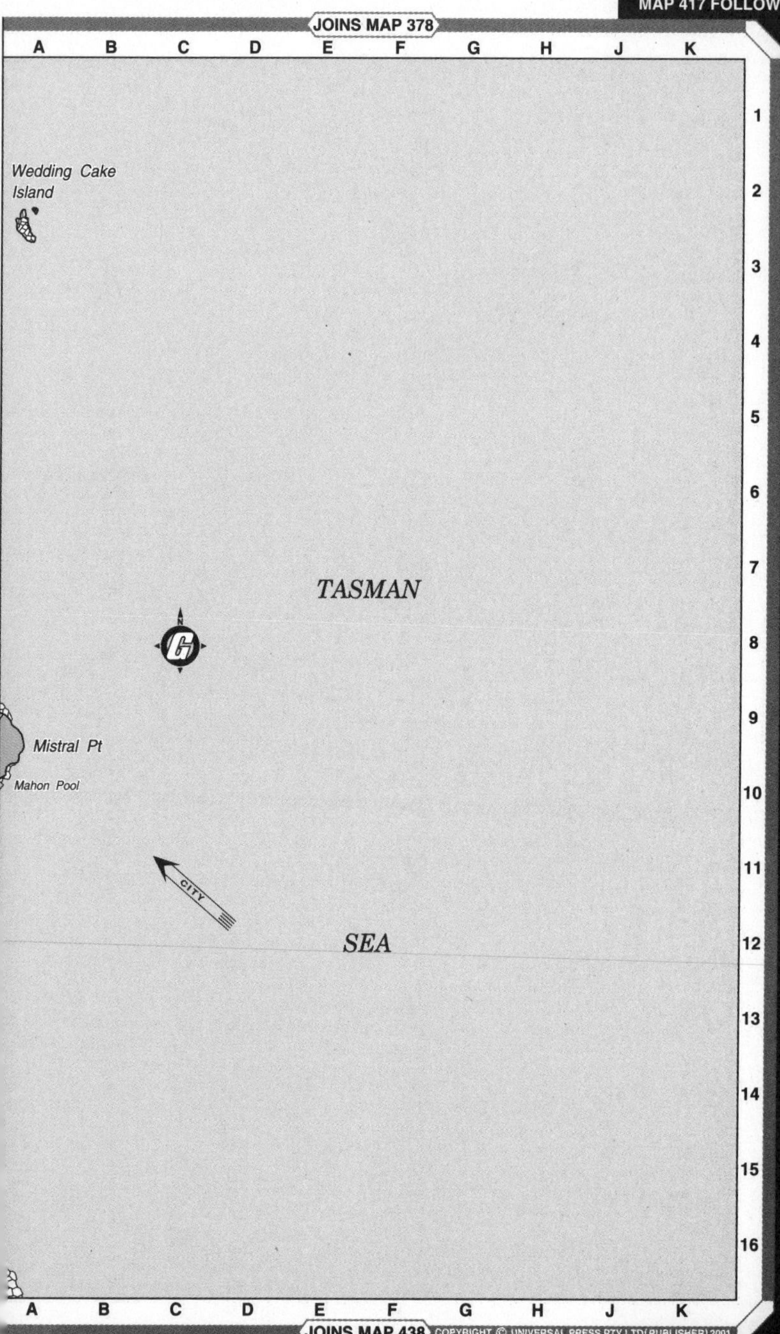
JOINS MAP 378
A B C D E F G H J K
1 2 3 4 5 6 7 8 9 10 11 12 13 14 15 16
Wedding Cake Island
TASMAN
SEA
Mistral Pt
Mahon Pool
CITY
JOINS MAP 438

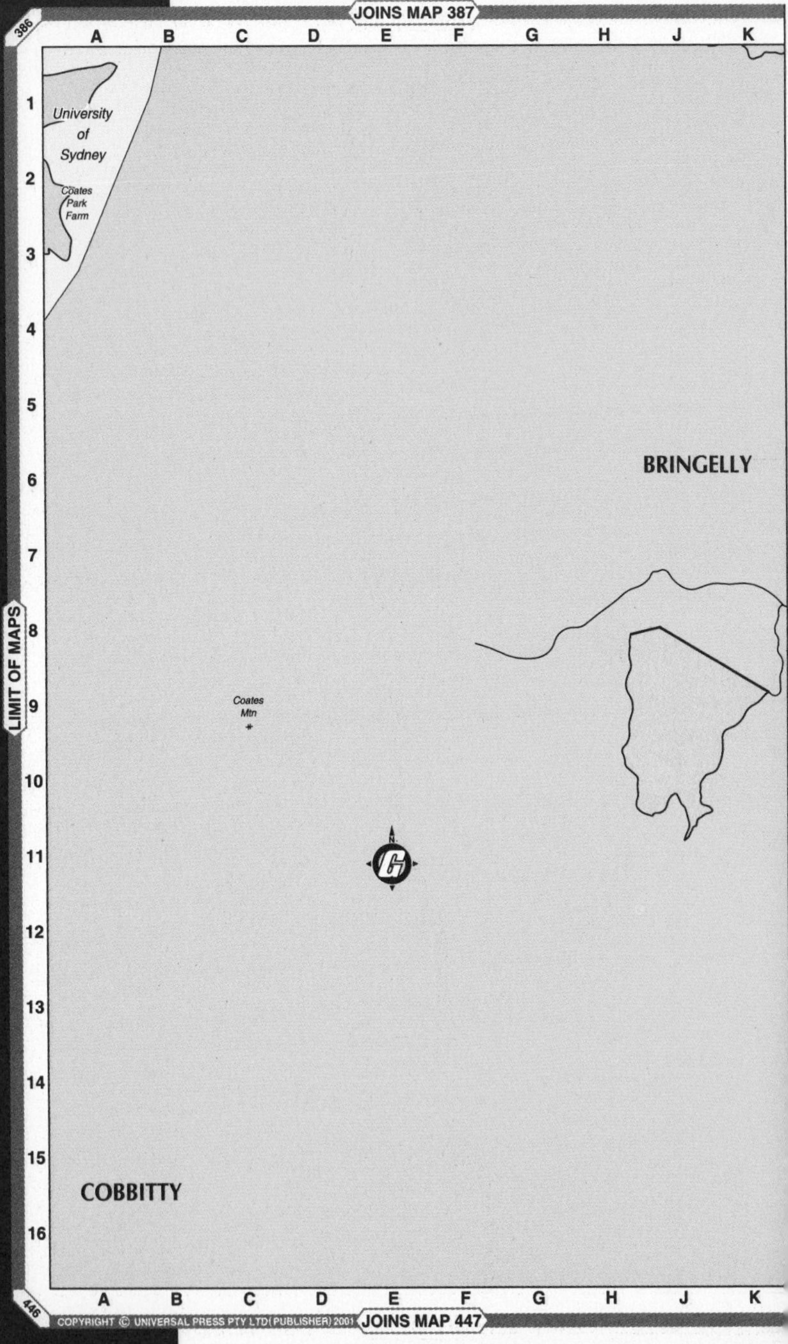

MAP 417
PREVIOUS MAP 408

JOINS MAP 387

JOINS MAP 447

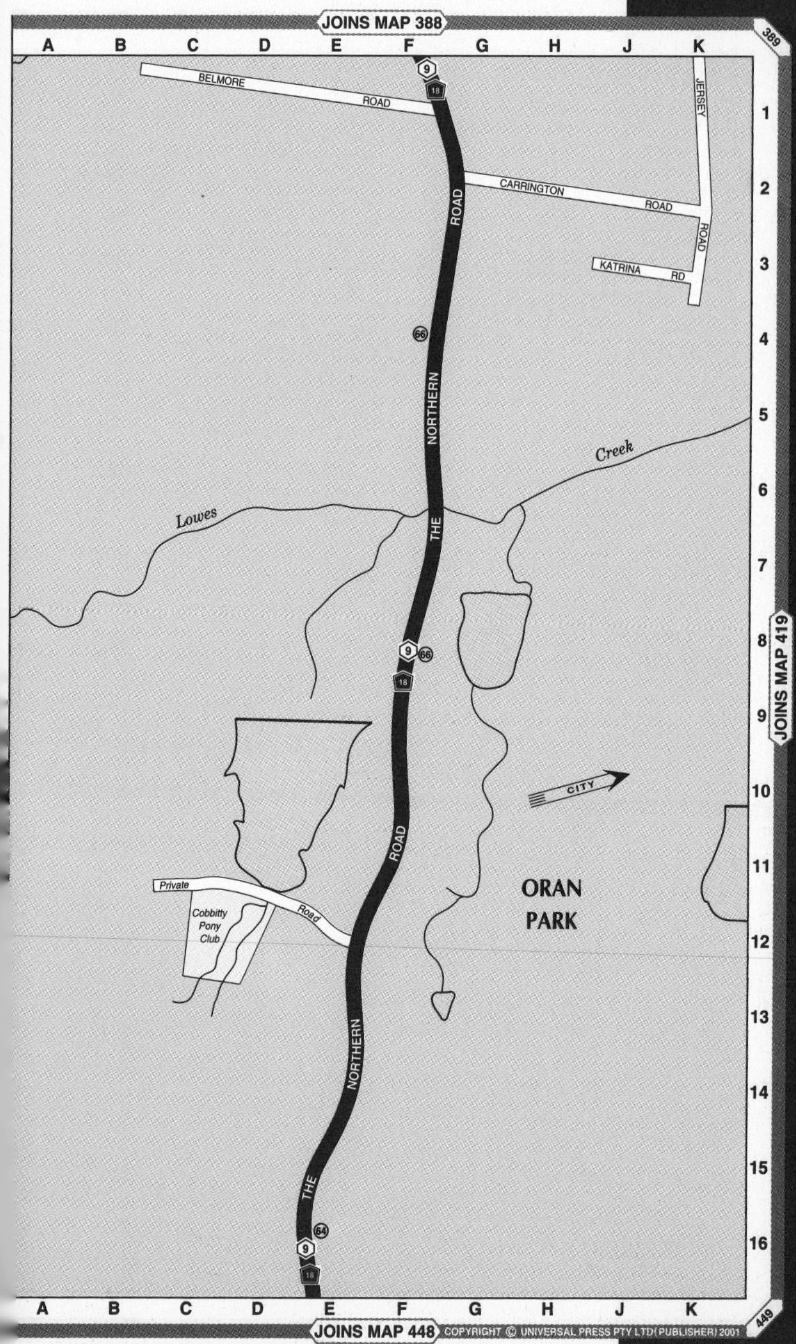
JOINS MAP 388
389
A B C D E F G H J K
BELMORE ROAD
JERSEY ROAD
CARRINGTON ROAD
KATRINA RD
THE NORTHERN ROAD
Lowes Creek
Private Road
Cobbitty Pony Club
CITY
ORAN PARK
1 2 3 4 5 6 7 8 9 10 11 12 13 14 15 16
JOINS MAP 419
JOINS MAP 448
449

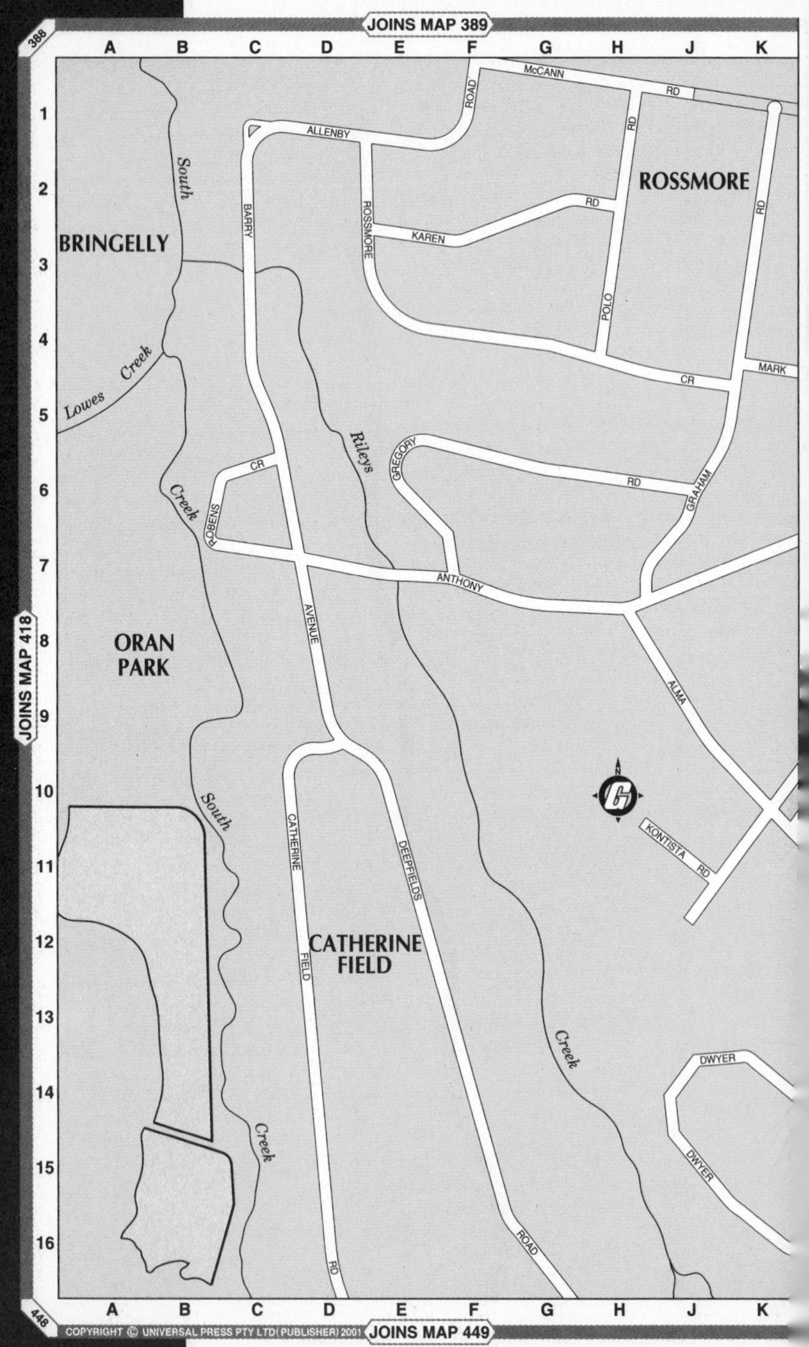

JOINS MAP 449

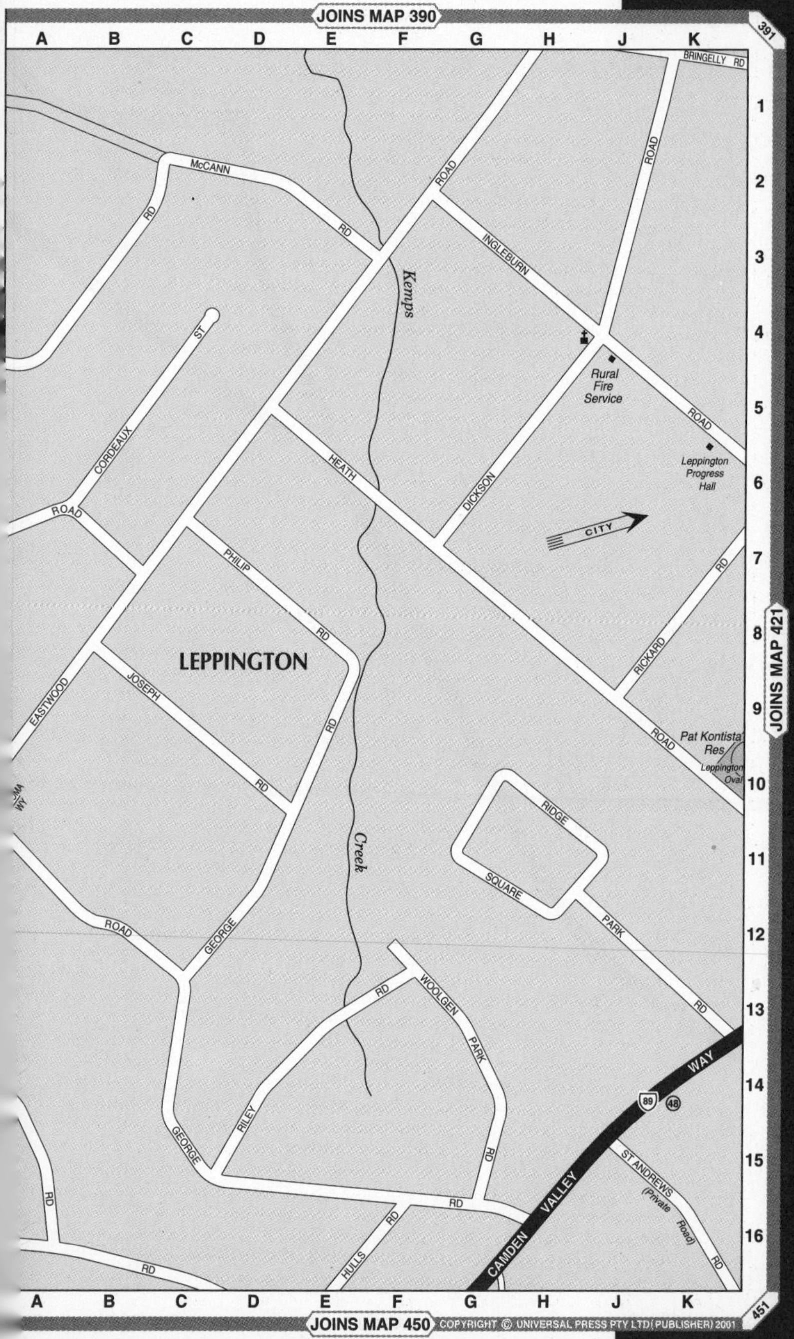
JOINS MAP 390
A
B
C
D
E
F
G
H
J
K
391
BRINGELLY RD
1
2
3
4
5
6
7
8
9
10
11
12
13
14
15
16
McCANN
RD
RD
ROAD
ROAD
Kemps
INGLEBURN
ST
Rural
Fire
Service
ROAD
CORDEAUX
HEATH
Leppington
Progress
Hall
ROAD
DICKSON
CITY
PHILIP
RD
RD
JOINS MAP 421
LEPPINGTON
RD
EASTWOOD
JOSEPH
RICKARD
ROAD
Pat Kontista
Res
Leppington
Oval
RD
RD
RIDGE
Creek
SQUARE
ROAD
GEORGE
PARK
RD
RD
WOOLGEN
PARK
WAY
89
48
RILEY
GEORGE
RD
ST ANDREWS
(Private
Road)
VALLEY
RD
RD
RD
CAMDEN
RD
HULLS
RD
A
B
C
D
E
F
G
H
J
K
JOINS MAP 450
451

JOINS MAP 391

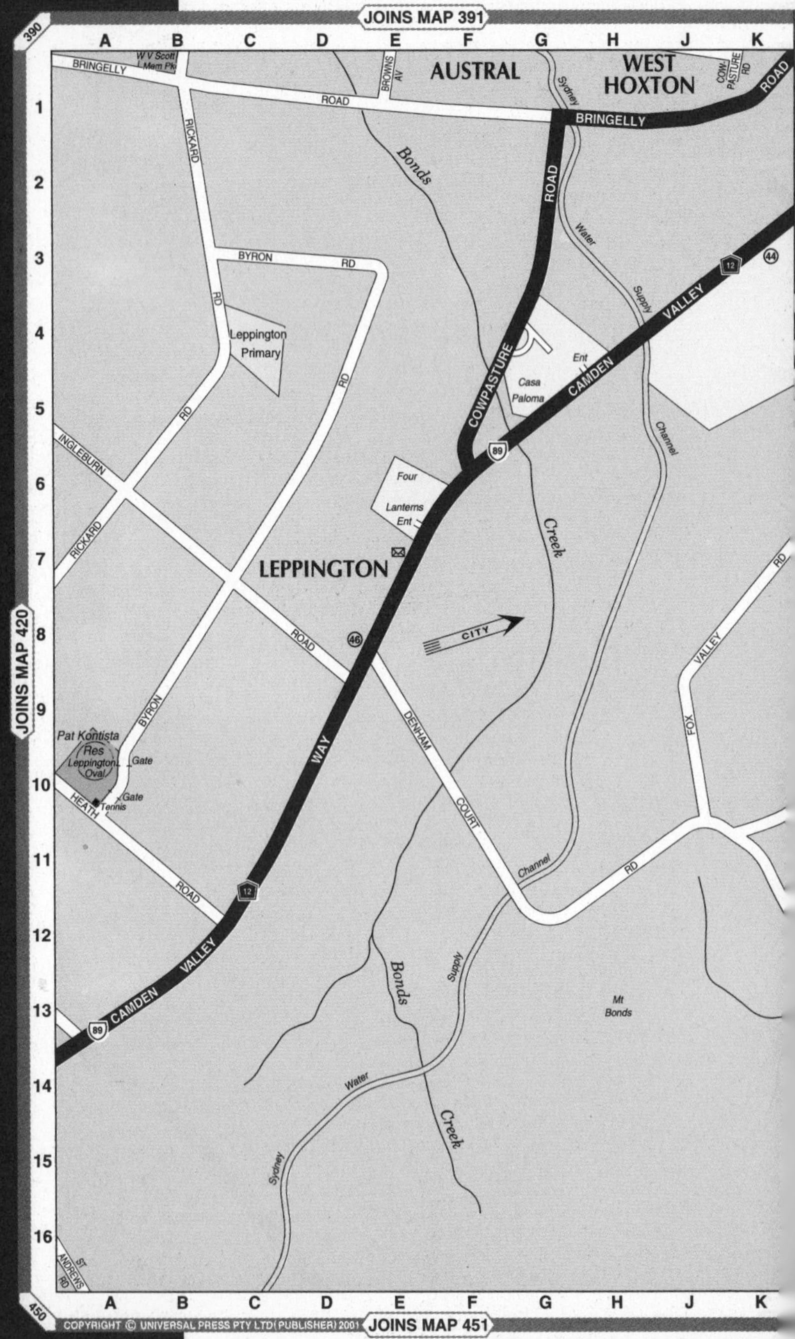

JOINS MAP 451

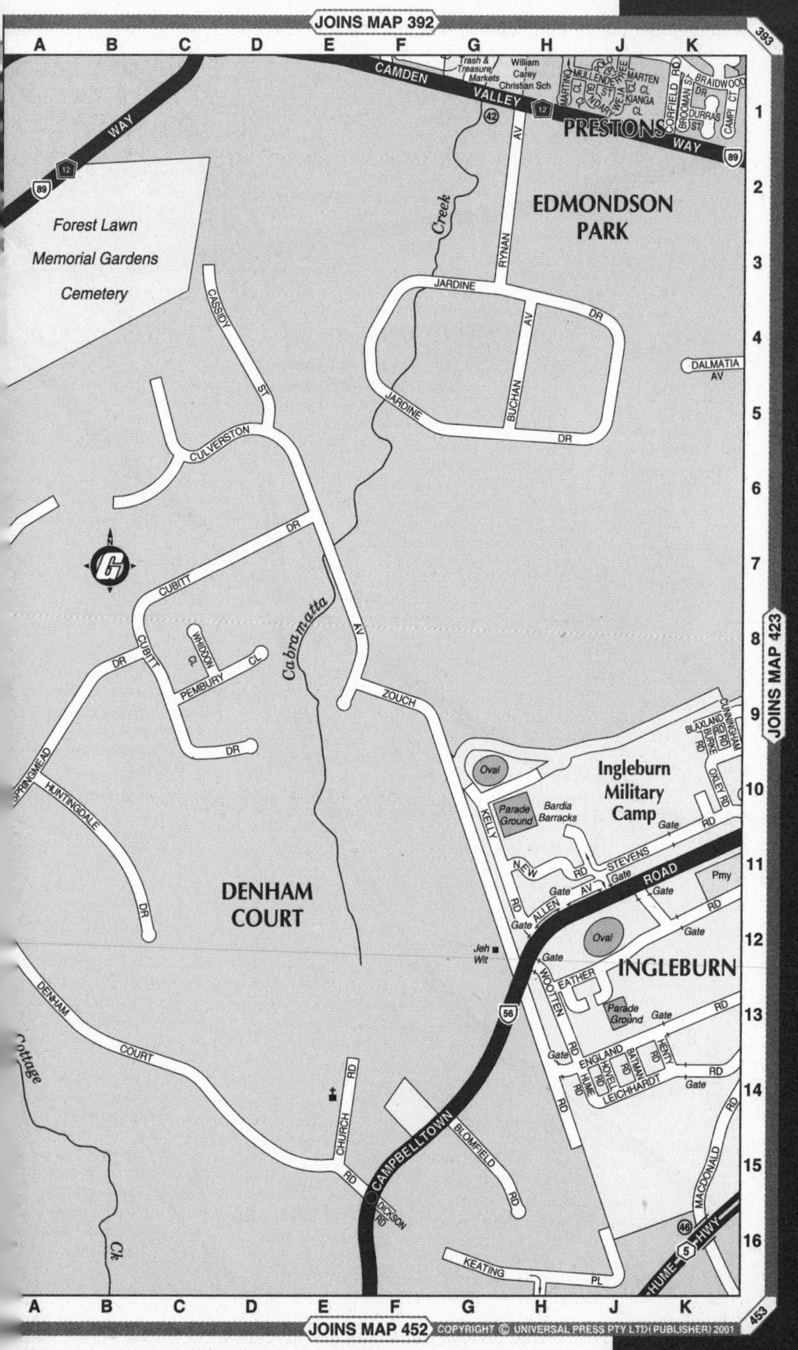
JOINS MAP 392
JOINS MAP 423
JOINS MAP 452
393
453
CAMDEN VALLEY WAY
Trash & Treasure Markets
William Carey Christian Sch
PRESTONS
EDMONDSON PARK
Forest Lawn Memorial Gardens Cemetery
Creek
RYNAN AV
JARDINE DR
BUCHAN AV
DALMATIA AV
CASSIDY ST
CULVERSTON
CUBITT DR
WHIDDON CL
PEMBURY CL
DR
Cabramatta
AV
ZOUCH
SPRINGMEAD
HUNTINGDALE DR
DENHAM COURT
Ingleburn Military Camp
Oval
Parade Ground
Bardia Barracks
KELLY
NEW RD
STEVENS RD
ALLEN AV
ROAD
Gate
Pmy
RD
BLAXLAND RD
BURKE RD
CUNNINGHAM
OXLEY RD
INGLEBURN
Jeh Wit
WOOTTEN RD
EATHER
ENGLAND
HOVELL RD
BATMAN RD
HENTY RD
HUME RD
LEICHHARDT
DENHAM COURT RD
Cottage
Ck
CHURCH RD
CAMPBELLTOWN RD
DICKSON RD
BLOMFIELD RD
KEATING PL
MACDONALD RD
HUME HWY
A B C D E F G H J K
1 2 3 4 5 6 7 8 9 10 11 12 13 14 15 16

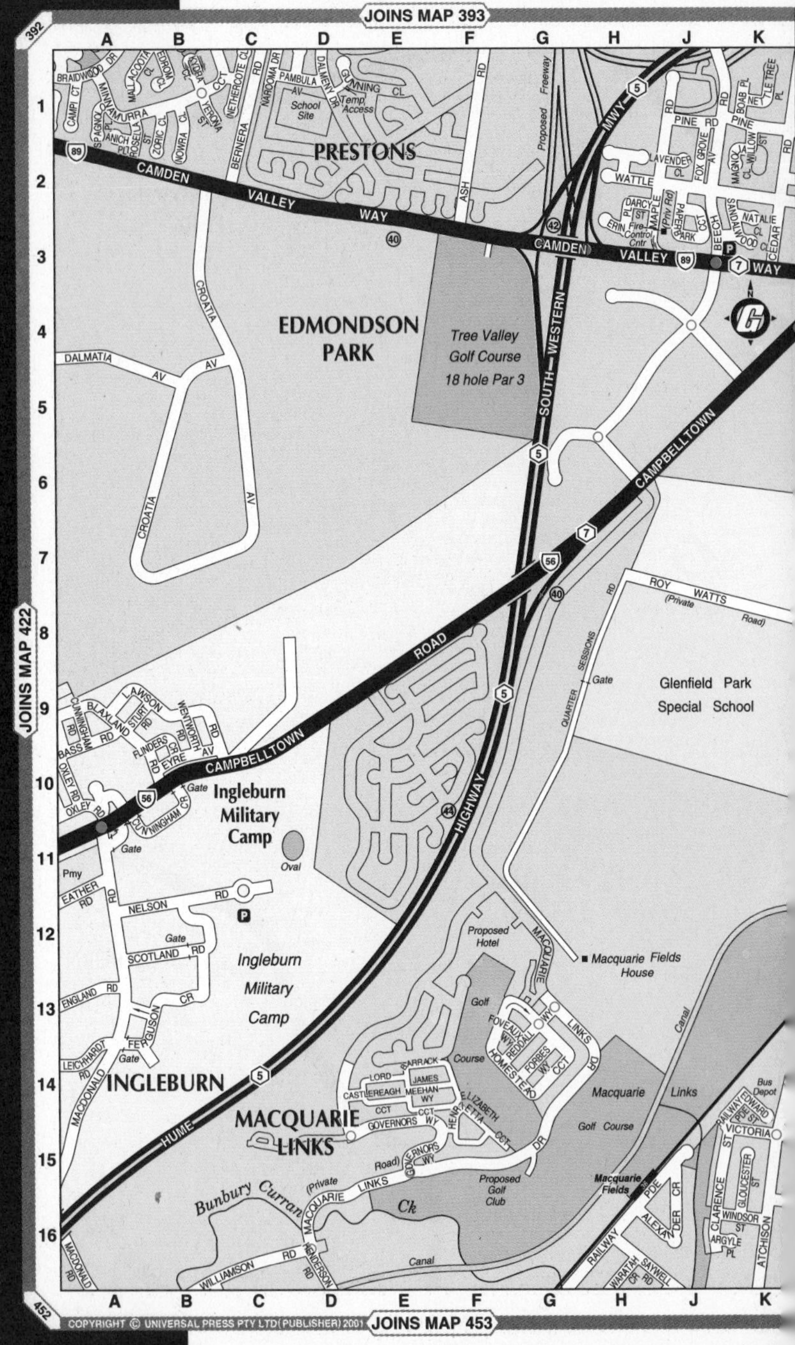
JOINS MAP 393
392
JOINS MAP 422
JOINS MAP 453
452
PRESTONS
EDMONDSON PARK
INGLEBURN
MACQUARIE LINKS
CAMDEN VALLEY WAY
CAMPBELLTOWN ROAD
HUME HIGHWAY
SOUTH WESTERN MWY
Proposed Freeway
Tree Valley Golf Course 18 hole Par 3
Ingleburn Military Camp
Oval
Glenfield Park Special School
ROY WATTS (Private Road)
QUARTER SESSIONS RD
Macquarie Fields House
Macquarie Links Golf Course
Proposed Hotel
Proposed Golf Club
Golf Course
Bunbury Curran Ck
Canal
Macquarie Fields
Bus Depot
School Site
Temp Access
Fire Control Cntr
CROATIA AV
DALMATIA AV
NELSON RD
SCOTLAND RD
ENGLAND RD
EATHER RD
LEICHHARDT RD
MACDONALD RD
FERGUSON CR
CUNNINGHAM CR
OXLEY RD
BASS RD
BLAXLAND RD
LAWSON AV
STURT RD
WENTWORTH RD
FLINDERS RD
EYRE CR
WILLIAMSON RD
HENDERSON RD
MACQUARIE LINKS (Private Road)
GOVERNORS WY
LORD CCT
CASTLEREAGH CCT
BARRACK
JAMES
MEEHAN WY
HENRIETTA
ELIZABETH CCT
FOVEAUX WY
REDDALL
HOMESTEAD
FORBES WY
LINKS DR
MACQUARIE
RAILWAY
WARATAH CR
SAYWELL RD
ALEXANDER CR
PDE
CLARENCE ST
GLOUCESTER ST
WINDSOR ST
ARGYLE PL
ATCHISON
VICTORIA
RAILWAY PDE
EDWARD ST
BRAIDWOOD DR
CAMPI CT
SPAGNOLO PL
MINNAMURRA
JANICH PL
ROSELLA ST
ZORIC CL
MALACOOTA CL
EDROM CL
NOWRA CL
KYORA
YERONA ST
NETHERCOTE CL
BERNERA RD
NAROOMA DR
PAMBULA AV
DALMENY DR
GUNNING CL
ASH RD
PINE RD
LAVENDER CL
WATTLE
FOX GROVE AV
MAGNOLIA CL
WILLOW ST
BOAB PL
NETTLE TREE PL
DARCY PL
MAPLE ST
(Priv Rd)
ERIN
PAPERBARK CCT
BEECH
SANDALWOOD CL
NATALIE CL
CEDAR
Gate
Pmy
CCT
Private

JOINS MAP 394

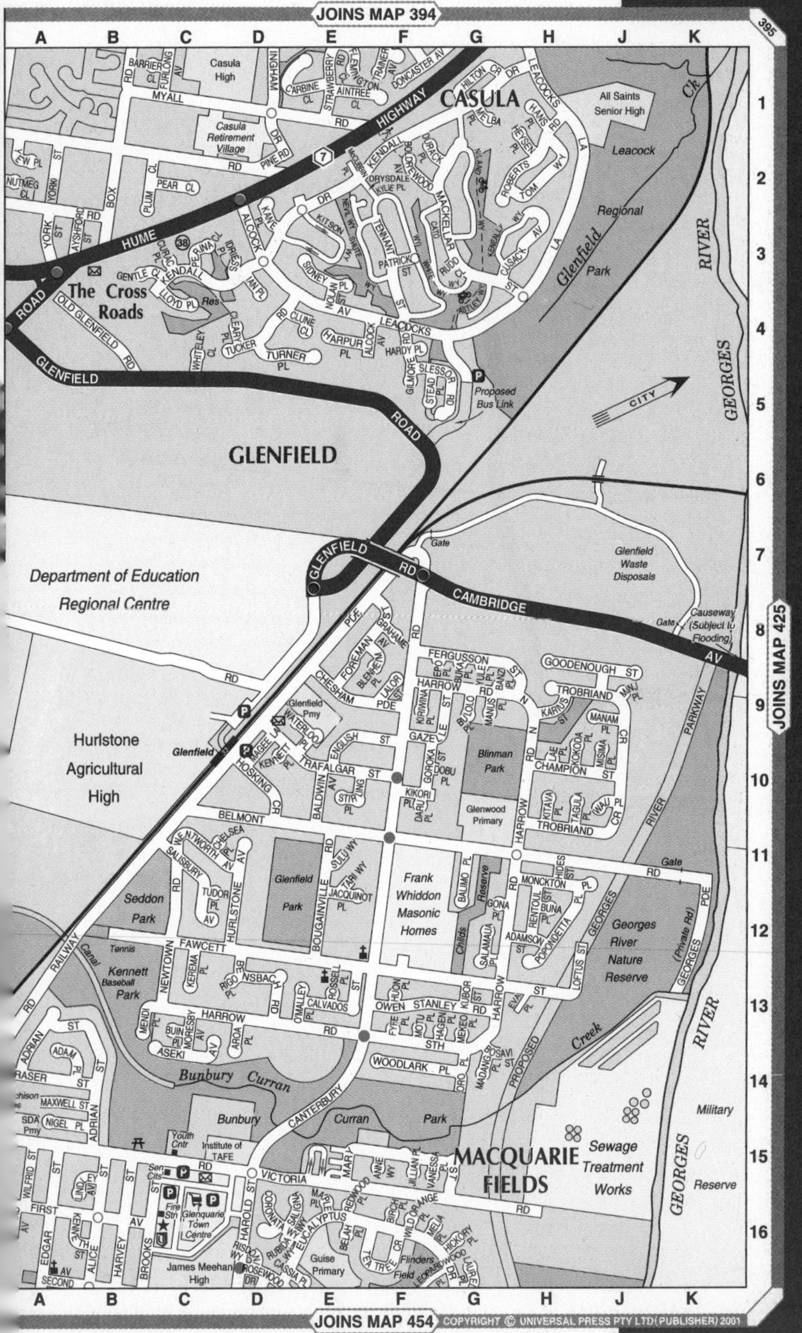

JOINS MAP 425

JOINS MAP 454

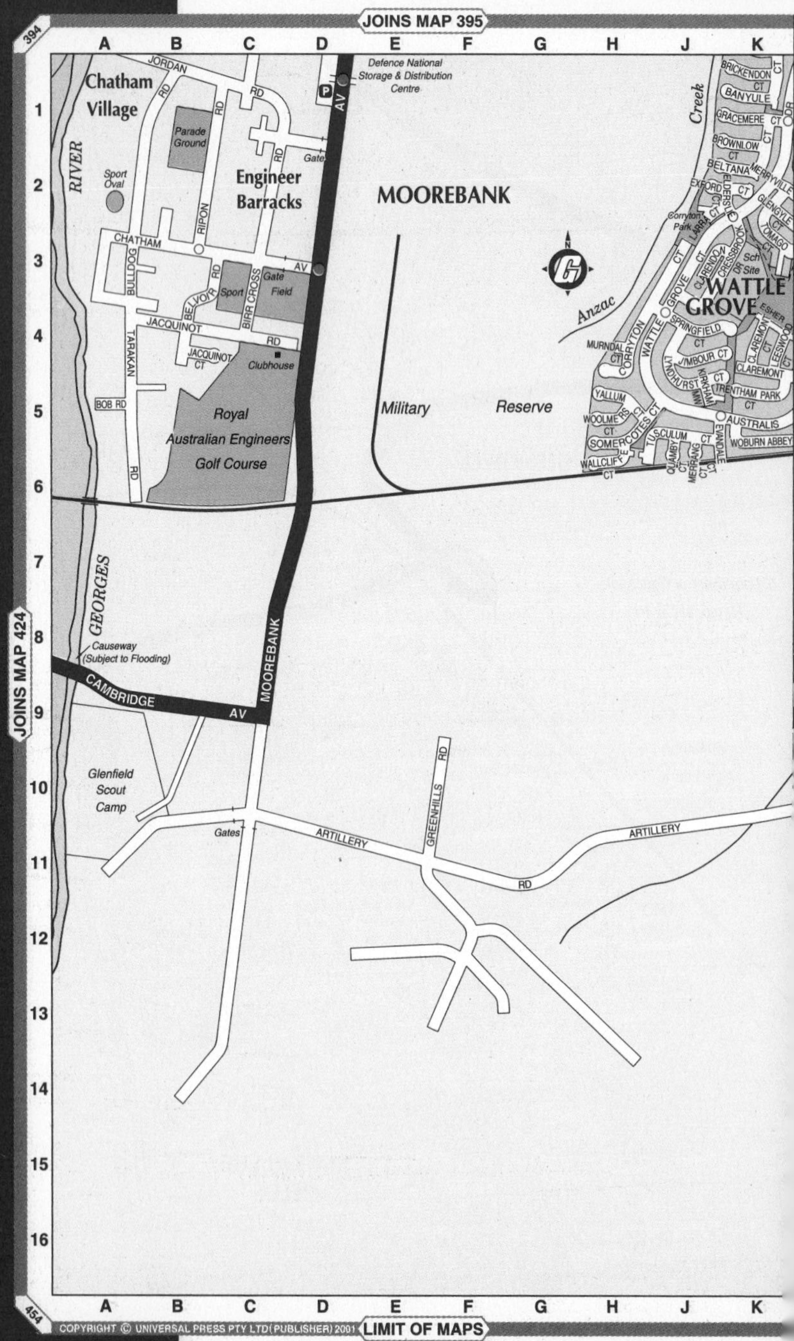

JOINS MAP 395
394
JOINS MAP 424
454
LIMIT OF MAPS
Chatham Village
Engineer Barracks
MOOREBANK
WATTLE GROVE
Defence National Storage & Distribution Centre
Parade Ground
Sport Oval
RIVER
GEORGES
Royal Australian Engineers Golf Course
Clubhouse
Military
Reserve
Anzac
Creek
Corryton Park
Sch Site
Causeway (Subject to Flooding)
Glenfield Scout Camp
Gates
Gate
Sport
Field
JORDAN RD
CHATHAM
BULLDOG
TARAKAN RD
JACQUINOT RD
JACQUINOT CT
BOB RD
RIPON RD
BELVOIR
BIRR CROSS
MOOREBANK AV
CAMBRIDGE AV
ARTILLERY RD
GREENHILLS RD
BRICKENDON CT
BANYULE CT
GRACEMERE CT
BROWNLOW CT
BELTANA
MERRYVILLE
EXFORD
ELDERSLIE
LARRA CT
GLENGYLE
TOMAGO
CLARENDON CT
CRESSBROOK DR
WATTLE GROVE
SPRINGFIELD CT
ESHER
CLAREMONT CT
LESSWOOD
MURNDAL CT
CORRYTON
JIMBOUR CT
LYNDHURST
KIRKHAM
TRENTHAM PARK CT
YALLUM
WOOLMERS CT
SOMERCOTES CT
AUSTRALIS
TUSCULUM
QUAMBY CT
MERRANG CT
EVANDALE CT
WOBURN ABBEY
WALLCLIFFE CT

JOINS MAP 396

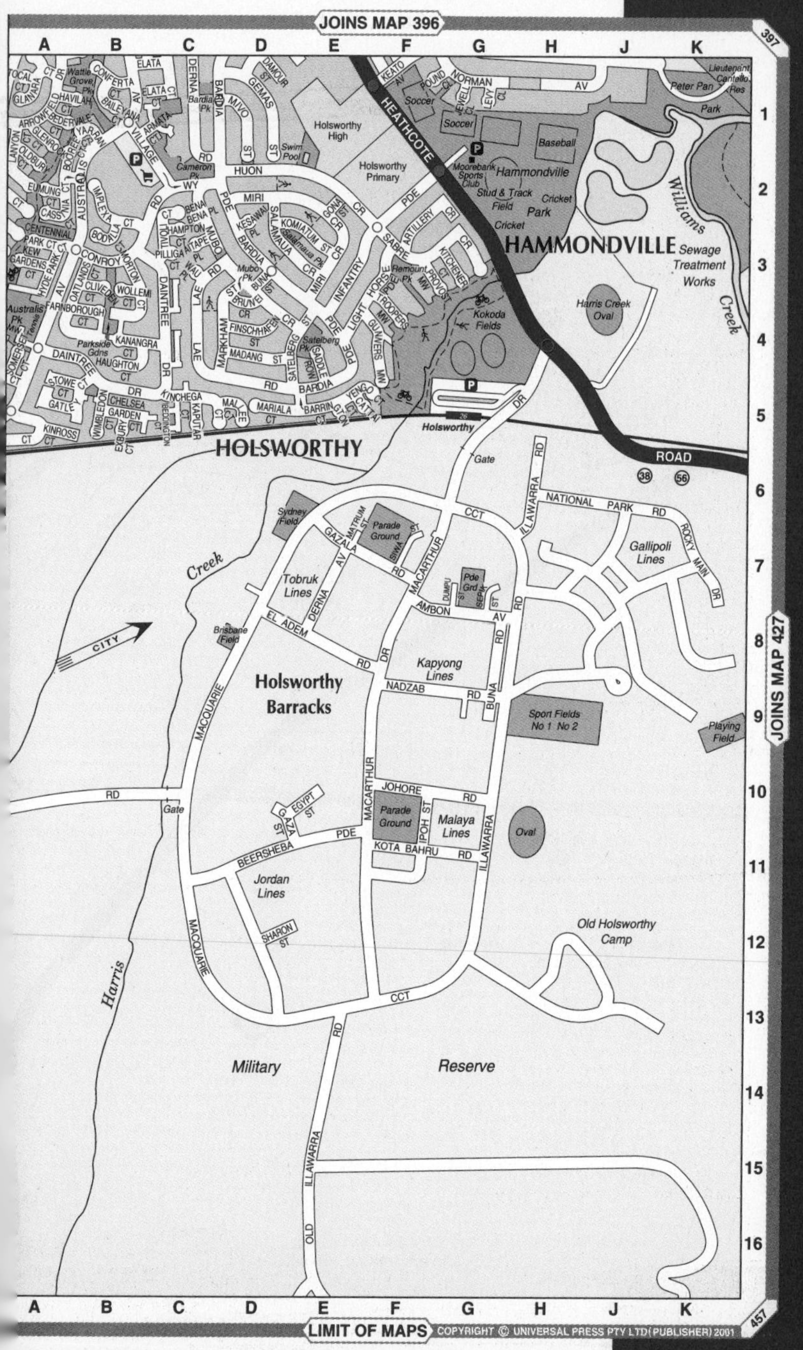

JOINS MAP 427

LIMIT OF MAPS

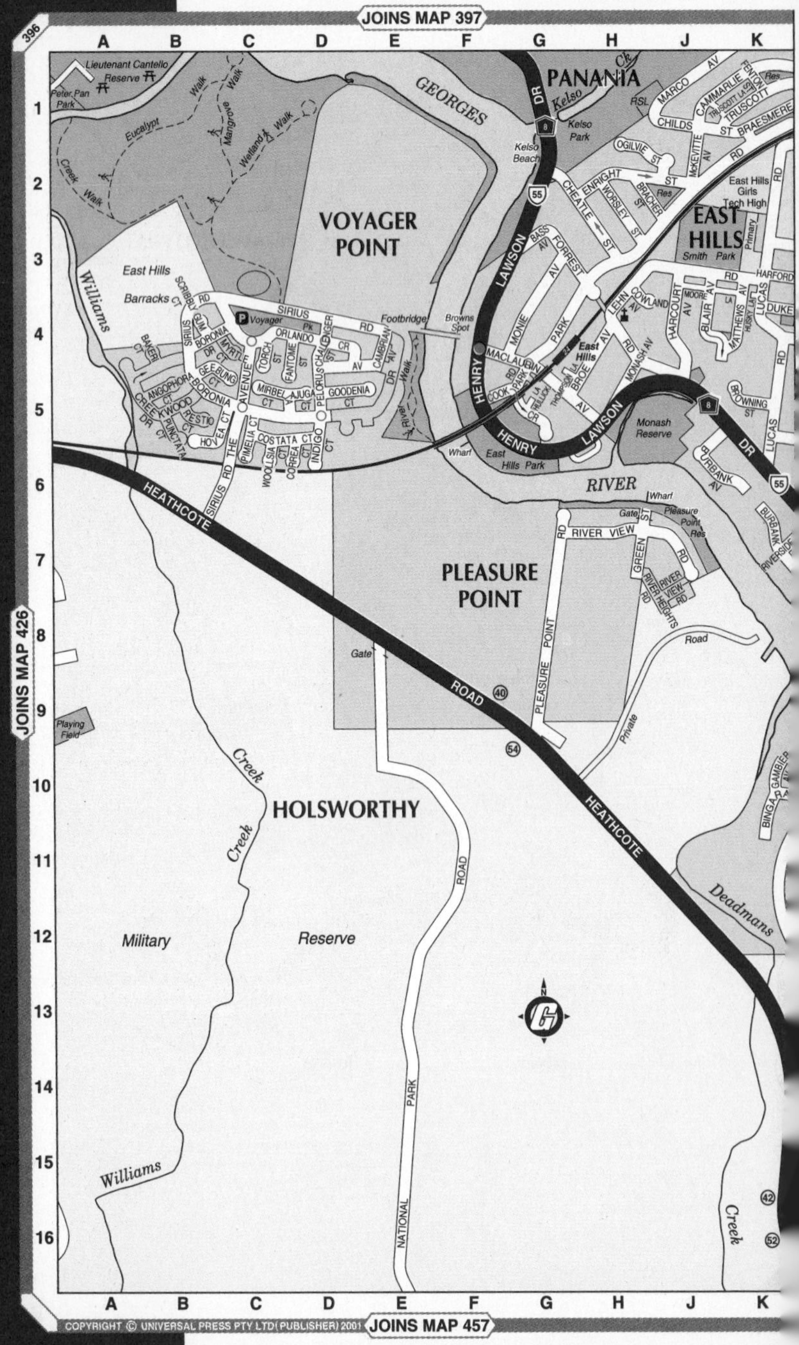
JOINS MAP 397
JOINS MAP 426
JOINS MAP 457
396
VOYAGER POINT
PANANIA
EAST HILLS
PLEASURE POINT
HOLSWORTHY
Military
Reserve
GEORGES
RIVER
HEATHCOTE
ROAD
HENRY LAWSON DR
NATIONAL PARK ROAD
PLEASURE POINT RD
RIVER VIEW RD
Lieutenant Cantello Reserve
Peter Pan Park
Eucalypt Walk
Mangrove Walk
Wetland Walk
Creek Walk
East Hills Barracks
Williams Creek
Deadmans Creek
Kelso Park
Kelso Beach
Monash Reserve
East Hills Park
Smith Park
East Hills Girls Tech High
Footbridge
Browns Spot
Wharf
Playing Field
Private Road
SIRIUS RD
Voyager Pk
THE AVENUE
BORONIA RD
ORLANDO
CHALLENGER AV
CAMBRIAN AV
GOODENIA CT
INDIGO CT
COSTATA CT
CHEATLE ST
FORREST RD
MONIE AV
PARK RD
MACLAURIN
BROE AV
MONASH AV
HARCOURT AV
BLAIR AV
MATTHEWS AV
LUCAS RD
HARFORD
BRAESMERE RD
CHILDS ST
MARCO AV
OGILVIE ST
ENRIGHT ST
WORSLEY ST
BRACHER
BURBANK AV
BROWNING ST
RIVERSIDE
BINGA
COPYRIGHT © UNIVERSAL PRESS PTY LTD (PUBLISHER) 2001

JOINS MAP 398

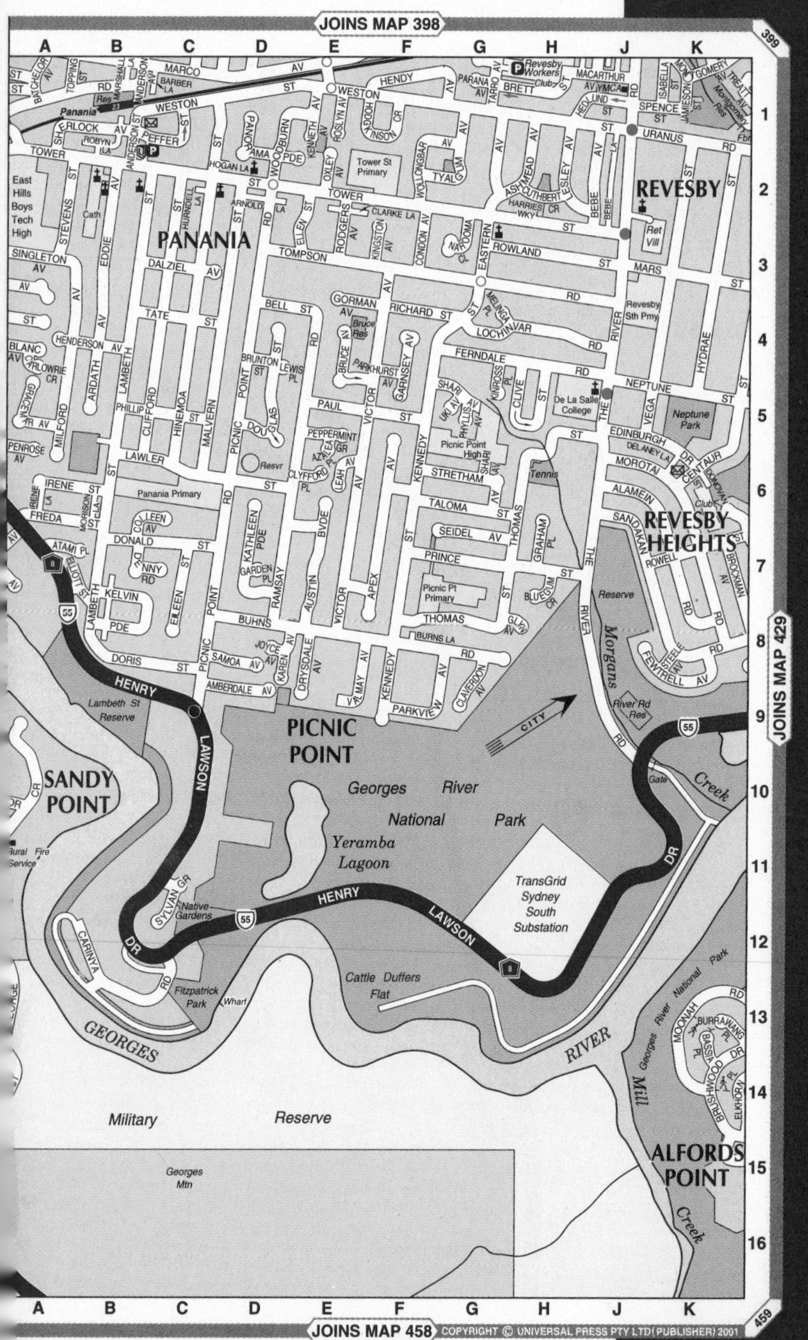

JOINS MAP 429

JOINS MAP 458

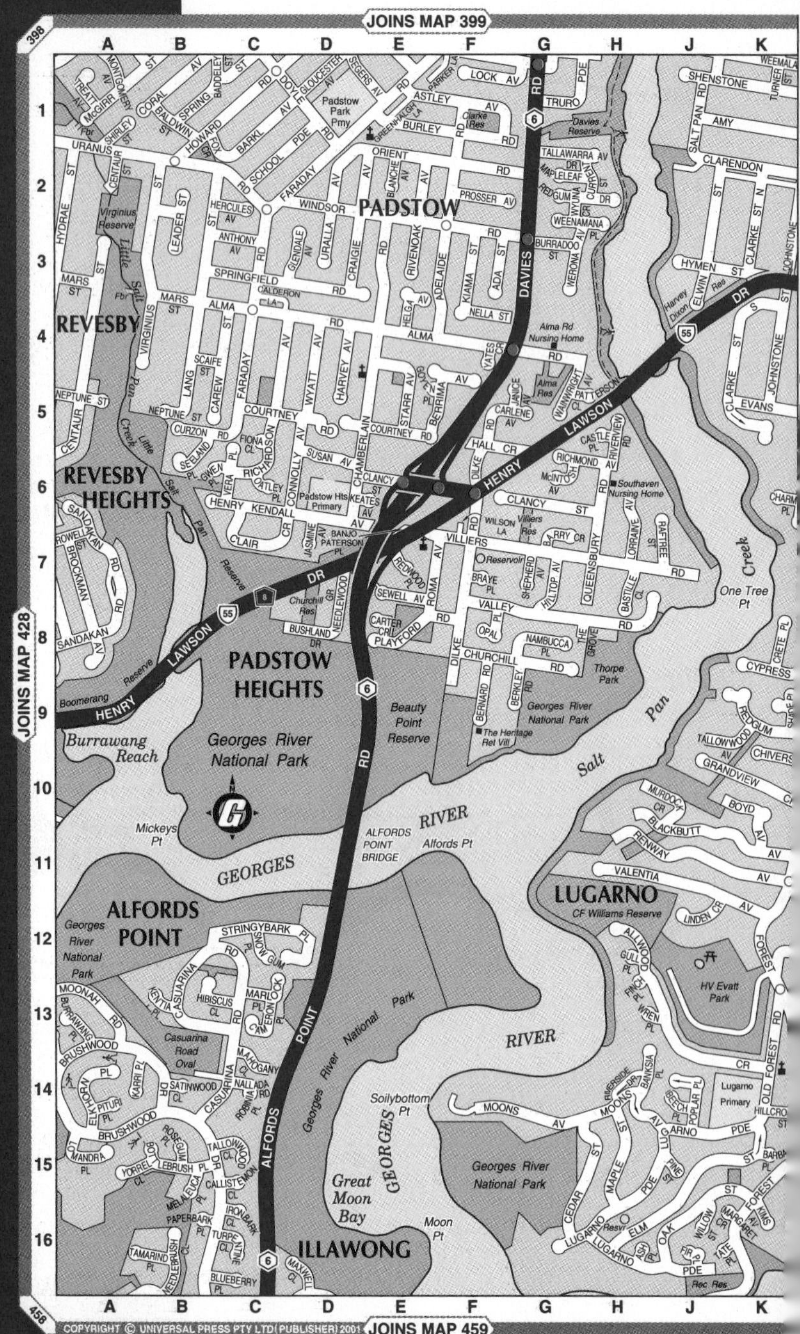
JOINS MAP 399
JOINS MAP 428
JOINS MAP 459
398
458
A B C D E F G H J K
1 2 3 4 5 6 7 8 9 10 11 12 13 14 15 16
PADSTOW
REVESBY
REVESBY HEIGHTS
PADSTOW HEIGHTS
ALFORDS POINT
LUGARNO
ILLAWONG
Padstow Park Pmy
Virginius Reserve
Little Salt Pan Creek
Davies Reserve
Clarke Res
Alma Rd Nursing Home
Alma Res
Southaven Nursing Home
Villiers Res
Padstow Hts Primary
BANJO PATERSON PL
Churchill Res
Thorpe Park
Beauty Point Reserve
Georges River National Park
The Heritage Ret Vill
Salt Pan Creek
One Tree Pt
Harvey Dixon Res
Boomerang Reserve
Burrawang Reach
Mickeys Pt
GEORGES RIVER
ALFORDS POINT BRIDGE
Alfords Pt
CF Williams Reserve
HV Evatt Park
Lugarno Primary
Casuarina Road Oval
Soilybottom Pt
Great Moon Bay
Moon Pt
Rec Res
DAVIES RD
HENRY LAWSON DR
ALFORDS POINT RD
FORREST RD
6
55
8

JOINS MAP 400

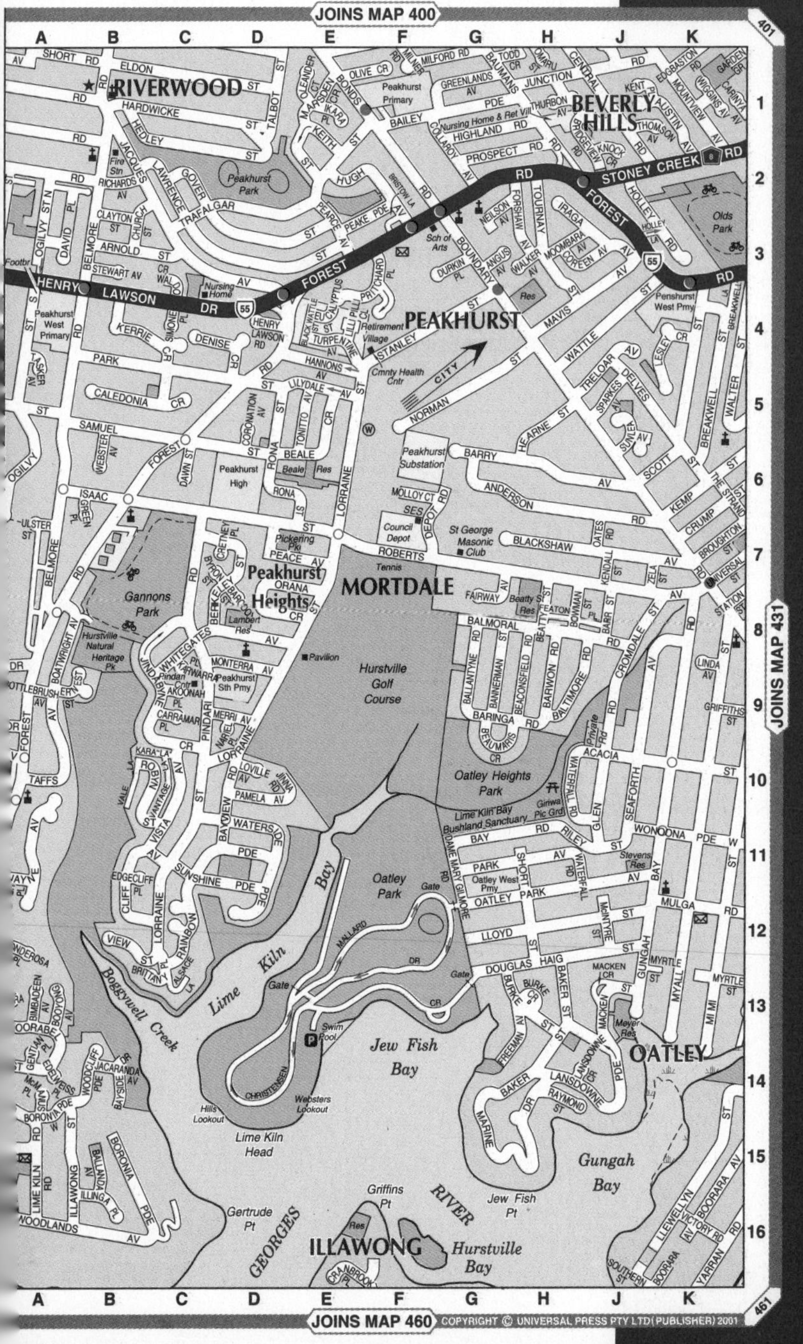

JOINS MAP 460

MAP 431

JOINS MAP 401

JOINS MAP 461

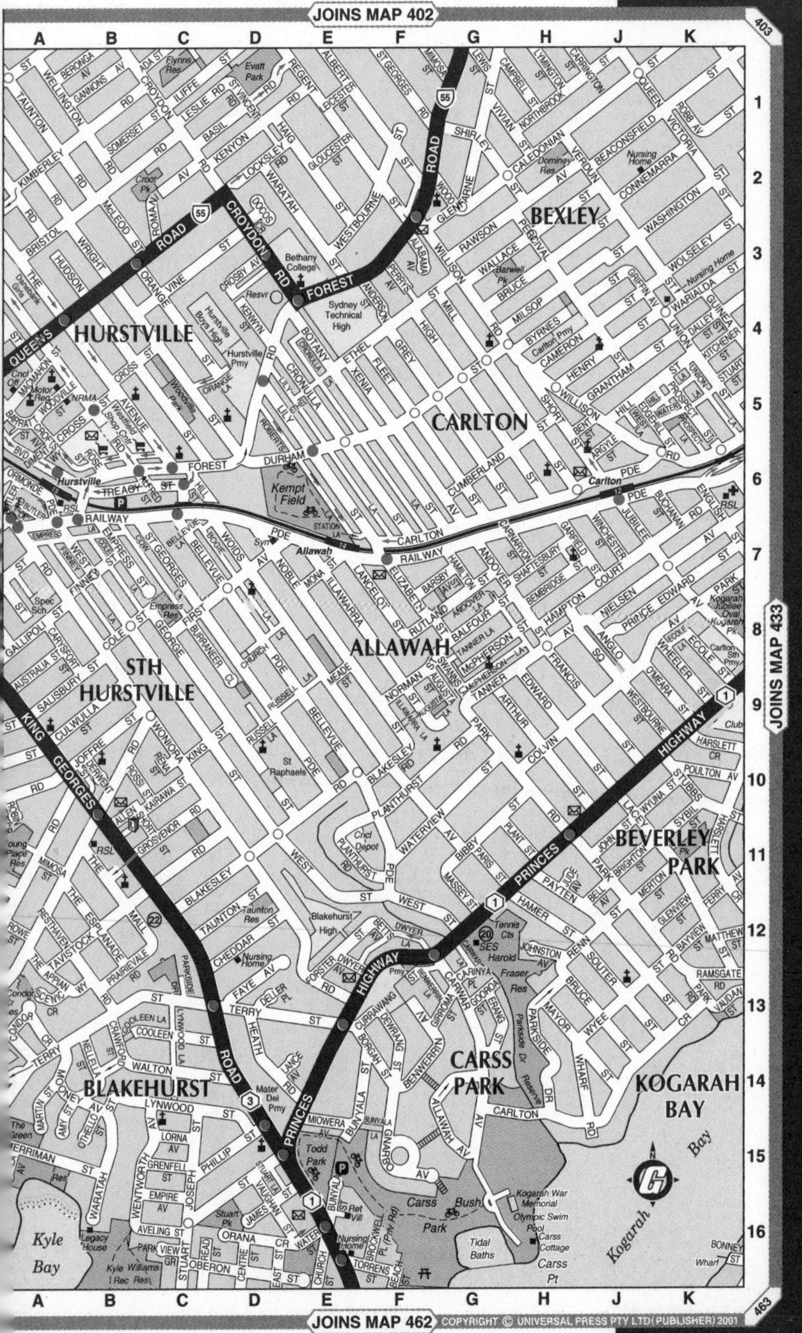

JOINS MAP 402
JOINS MAP 433
JOINS MAP 462
403
463
A B C D E F G H J K
1 2 3 4 5 6 7 8 9 10 11 12 13 14 15 16
HURSTVILLE
BEXLEY
CARLTON
ALLAWAH
STH HURSTVILLE
BEVERLEY PARK
CARSS PARK
BLAKEHURST
KOGARAH BAY
Kyle Bay
Kogarah Bay
QUEENS ROAD
CROYDON RD
FOREST RD
KING GEORGES ROAD
PRINCES HIGHWAY
Bethany College
Sydney Technical High
Hurstville Boys High
Hurstville Pmy
Kempt Field
Evatt Park
Woodville Park
Empress Res
Barwell Pk
Carlton Pmy
Dominey Res
Nursing Home
Hurstville
Allawah
Carlton
St Raphaels
Cncl Depot
Blakehurst High
Taunton Res
Tennis Cts
SES
Harold Fraser Res
Parkside Dr Reserve
Mater Dei Pmy
Todd Park
Carss Bush Park
Kogarah War Memorial Olympic Swim Pool
Carss Cottage
Carss Pt
Tidal Baths
Stuart Pk
Ret Vill
Legacy House
Kyle Williams Rec Res
Kogarah Jubilee Oval
Carlton Sth Pmy
RSL
Spec Sch
Young Place Res
The Danebank Girls
Motor Reg
NRMA
Westfield Shop Cntr
Cncl Off

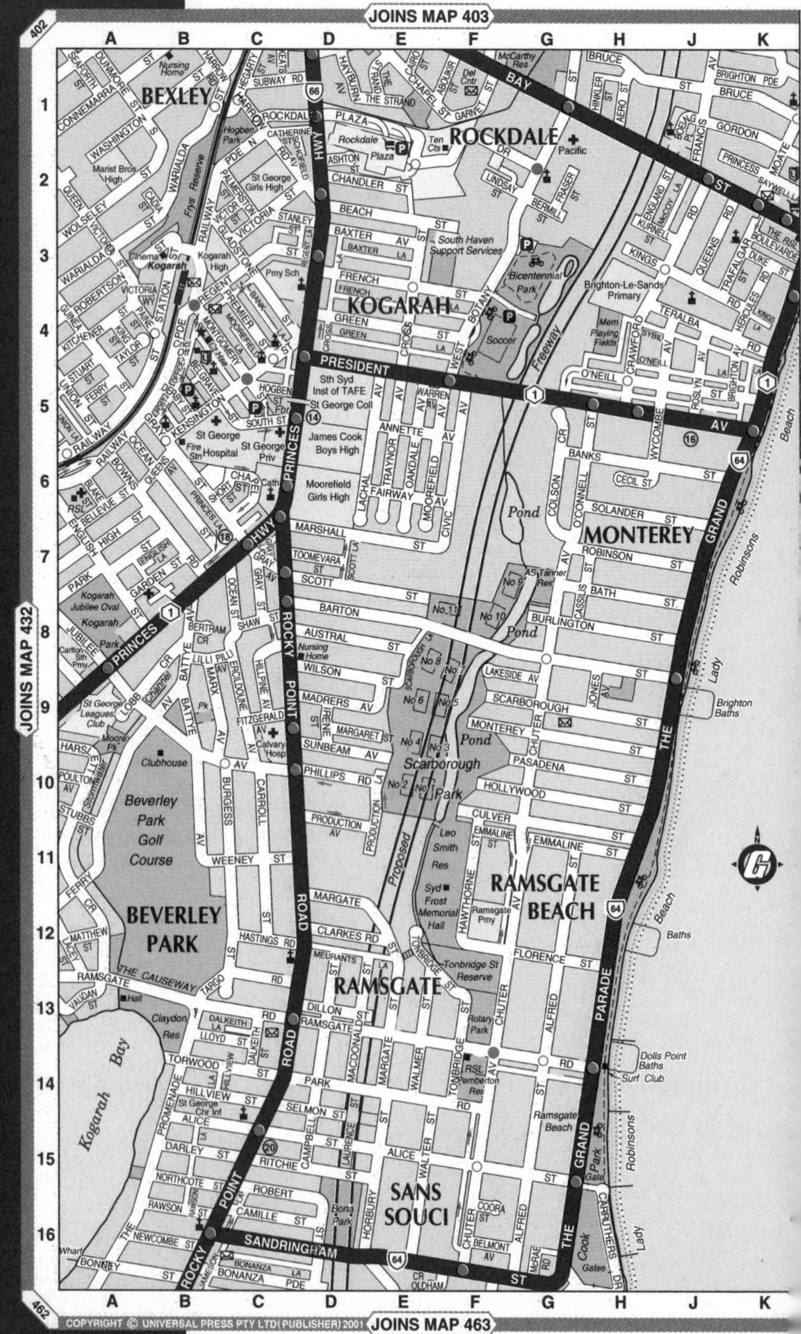
JOINS MAP 403
JOINS MAP 432
JOINS MAP 463
402
462
A B C D E F G H J K
1 2 3 4 5 6 7 8 9 10 11 12 13 14 15 16
BEXLEY
ROCKDALE
KOGARAH
MONTEREY
RAMSGATE BEACH
RAMSGATE
BEVERLEY PARK
SANS SOUCI
Beverley Park Golf Course
Kogarah Bay
Scarborough Park
Bicentennial Park
Frys Reserve
Hogben Park
Kogarah Jubilee Oval
St George Leagues Club
Claydon Res
Leo Smith Res
Tonbridge St Reserve
Rotary Park
Cook Park
Bona Park
Brighton Baths
Dolls Point Baths
Surf Club
Rockdale Plaza
St George Hospital
St George Girls High
Kogarah High
James Cook Boys High
Moorefield Girls High
Sth Syd Inst of TAFE
St George Coll
South Haven Support Services
Brighton-Le-Sands Primary
Calvary Hosp
Ramsgate Pmy
Syd Frost Memorial Hall
Marist Bros High
PRINCES HWY
ROCKY POINT ROAD
PRESIDENT AV
BAY ST
THE GRAND PARADE
SANDRINGHAM ST
Freeway
Proposed
Pond
Lady Robinsons Beach
COPYRIGHT © UNIVERSAL PRESS PTY LTD (PUBLISHER) 2001

JOINS MAP 404

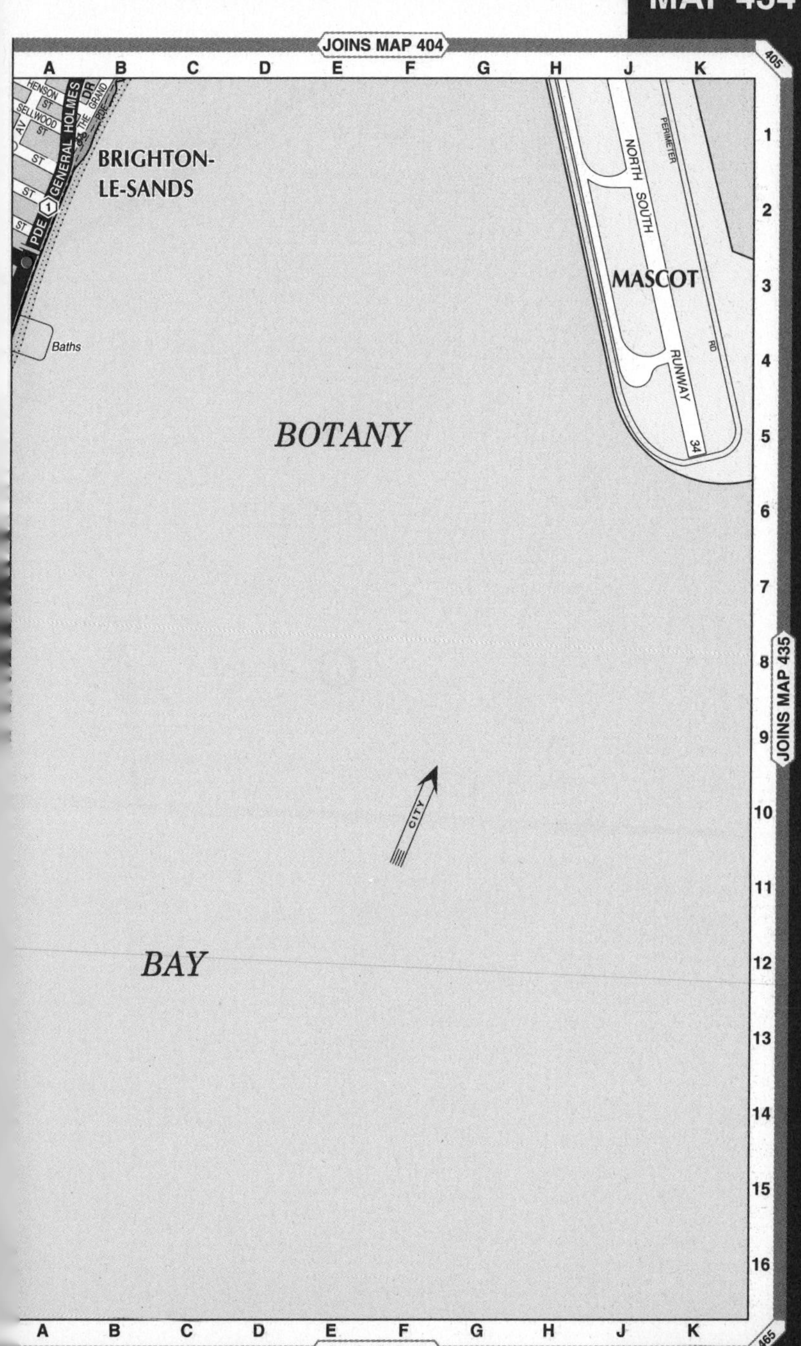

JOINS MAP 464

MAP 435

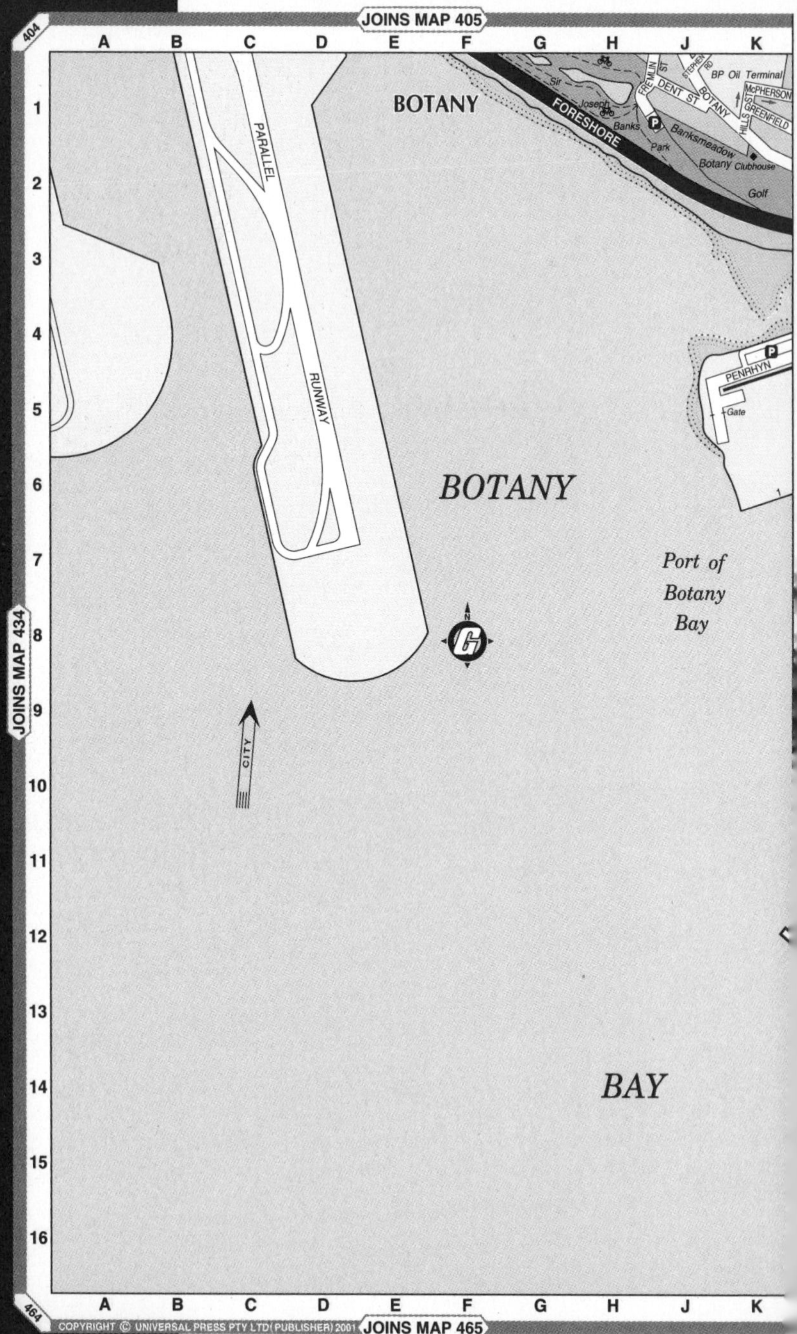

JOINS MAP 405
404
A
B
C
D
E
F
G
H
J
K
1
2
3
4
5
6
7
8
9
10
11
12
13
14
15
16
BOTANY
PARALLEL
RUNWAY
FORESHORE
Sir
Joseph
Banks
Park
Banksmeadow
Botany Clubhouse
Golf
FREMLIN ST
DENT ST
STEPHEN RD
BOTANY
BP Oil Terminal
McPHERSON
HILLS ST
GREENFIELD
PENRHYN
Gate
BOTANY
Port of
Botany
Bay
N
CITY
BAY
JOINS MAP 434
464
JOINS MAP 465

JOINS MAP 406

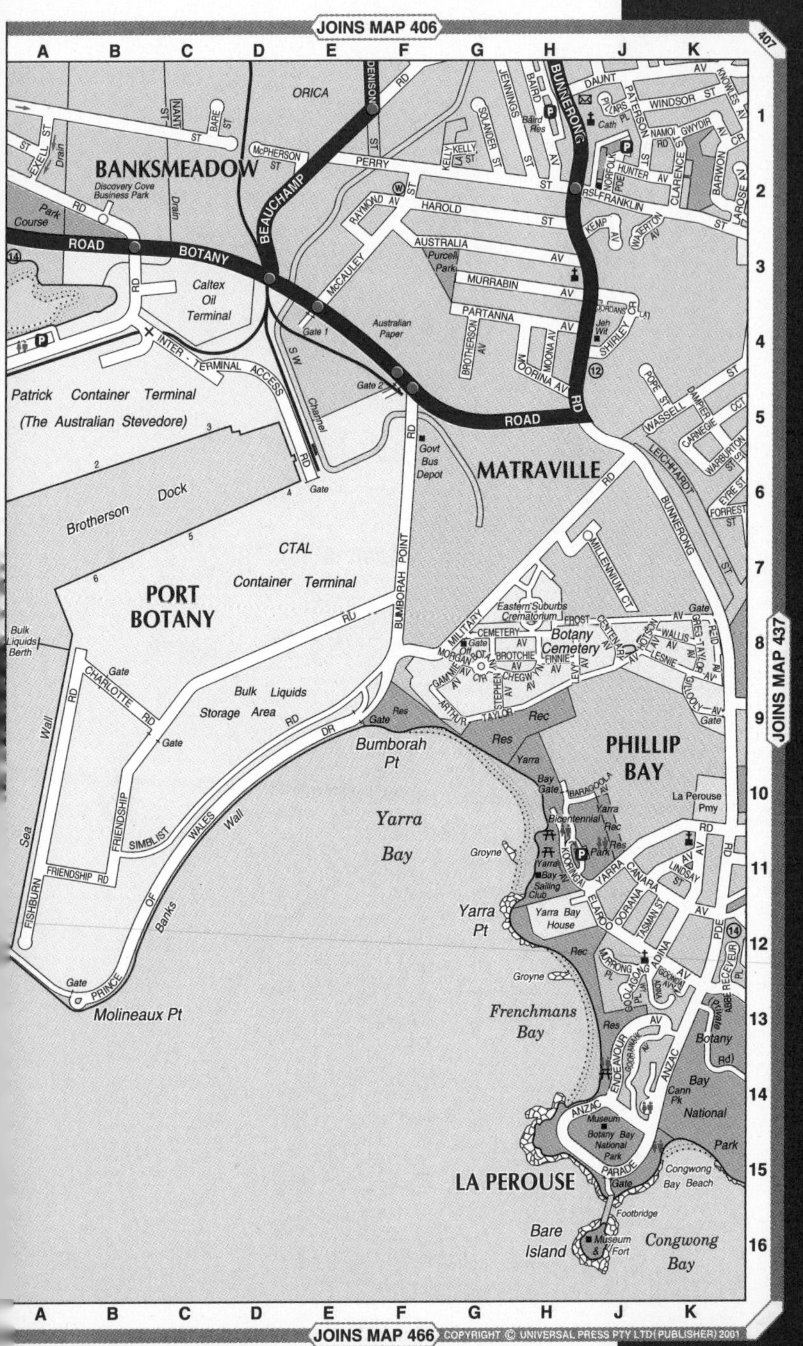

JOINS MAP 466

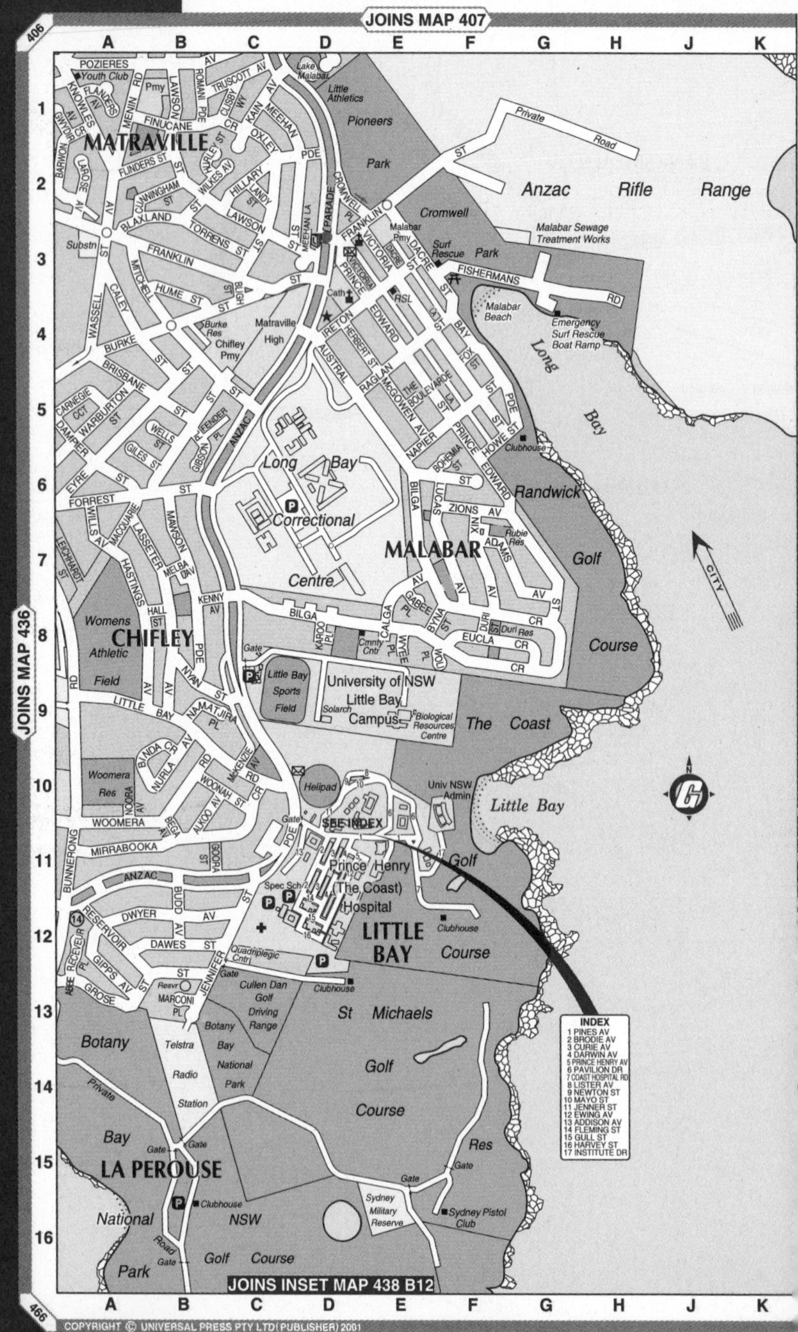
JOINS MAP 407
JOINS MAP 436
JOINS INSET MAP 438 B12
406
466
A B C D E F G H J K
1 2 3 4 5 6 7 8 9 10 11 12 13 14 15 16
MATRAVILLE
MALABAR
CHIFLEY
LITTLE BAY
LA PEROUSE
Lake Malabar
Little Athletics
Pioneers Park
Private Road
Anzac Rifle Range
Cromwell Park
Malabar Sewage Treatment Works
Surf Rescue
Malabar Beach
Emergency Surf Rescue Boat Ramp
Long Bay
Clubhouse
Randwick Golf Course
CITY
Long Bay Correctional Centre
Matraville High
Chifley Pmy
Burke Res
Womens Athletic Field
Little Bay Sports Field
University of NSW Little Bay Campus
Solarch
Biological Resources Centre
The Coast
Helipad
SEE INDEX
Univ NSW Admin
Little Bay
Prince Henry (The Coast) Hospital
Spec Sch
Quadriplegic Cntr
Golf Course
Woomera Res
Reservoir
Marconi Pl
Cullen Dan Golf Driving Range
Botany Bay National Park
Telstra Radio Station
St Michaels Golf Course
Res
Sydney Military Reserve
Sydney Pistol Club
NSW Golf Course
Botany Bay National Park
Gate
Pozieres
Youth Club
Substn
Cath
RSL
Rubie Res
Cmnty Cntr
INDEX
1 PINES AV
2 BRODIE AV
3 CURIE AV
4 DARWIN AV
5 PRINCE HENRY AV
6 PAVILION DR
7 COAST HOSPITAL RD
8 LISTER AV
9 NEWTON ST
10 MAYO ST
11 JENNER ST
12 EWING AV
13 ADDISON AV
14 FLEMING ST
15 GULL ST
16 HARVEY ST
17 INSTITUTE DR

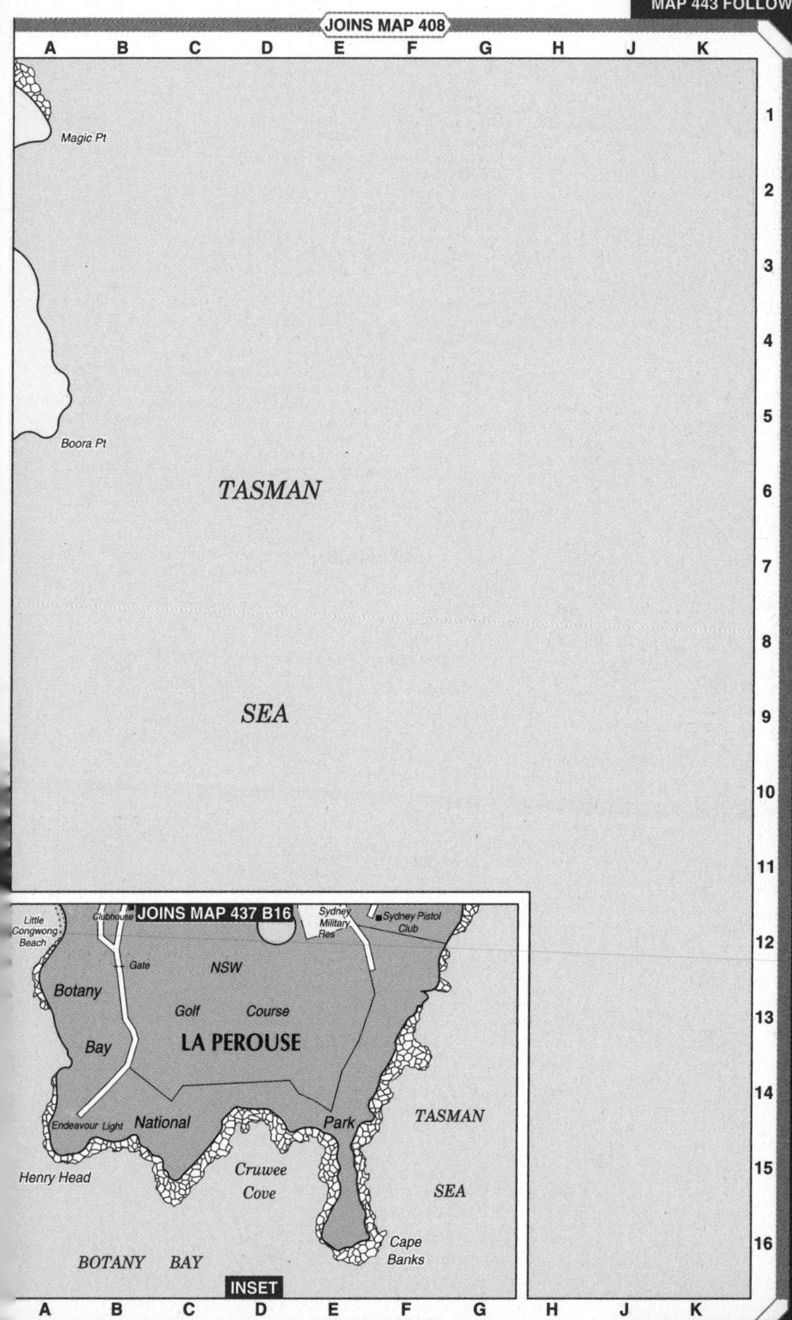
JOINS MAP 408
A B C D E F G H J K
1 2 3 4 5 6 7 8 9 10 11 12 13 14 15 16
Magic Pt
Boora Pt
TASMAN
SEA
Little Congwong Beach
Clubhouse
JOINS MAP 437 B16
Sydney Military Res
Sydney Pistol Club
Gate
NSW
Botany
Golf
Course
Bay
LA PEROUSE
Endeavour Light
National
Park
TASMAN
Henry Head
Cruwee Cove
SEA
Cape Banks
BOTANY BAY
INSET

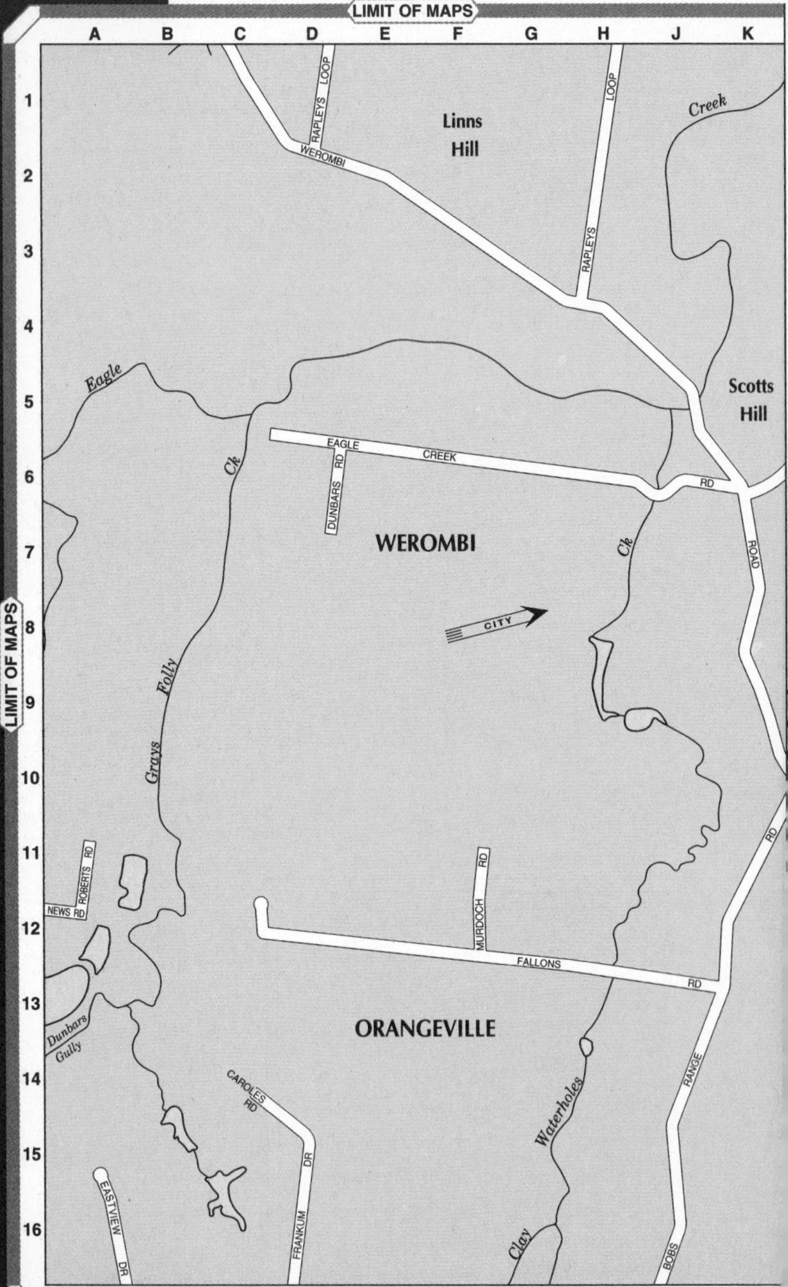

MAP 443
PREVIOUS MAP 438

LIMIT OF MAPS

LIMIT OF MAPS

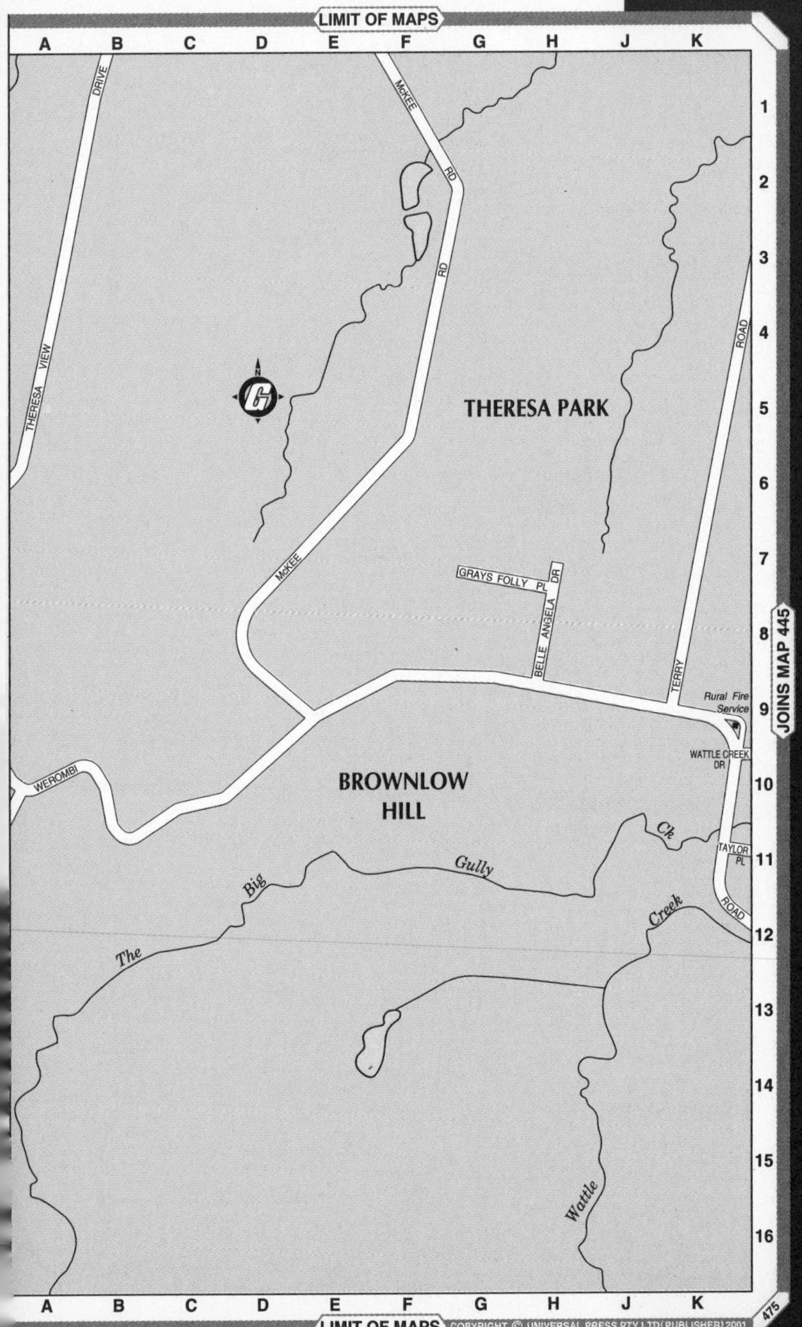
LIMIT OF MAPS
A B C D E F G H J K
1 2 3 4 5 6 7 8 9 10 11 12 13 14 15 16
THERESA VIEW DRIVE
McKEE RD
THERESA PARK
GRAYS FOLLY PL
BELLE ANGELA DR
TERRY ROAD
Rural Fire Service
WATTLE CREEK DR
WEROMBI
BROWNLOW HILL
TAYLOR PL
ROAD
Ck
The Big Gully
Creek
Wattle
JOINS MAP 445
LIMIT OF MAPS

LIMIT OF MAPS

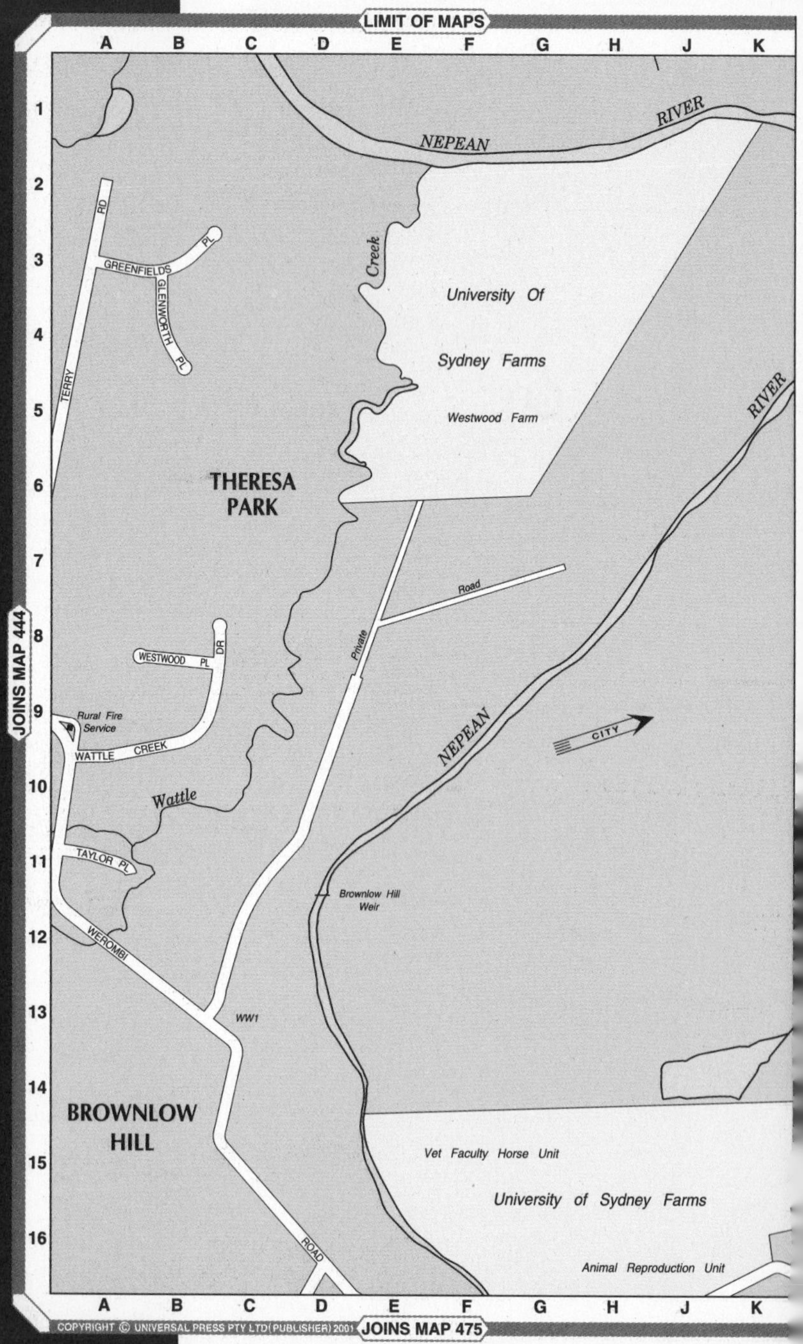

JOINS MAP 444

JOINS MAP 475

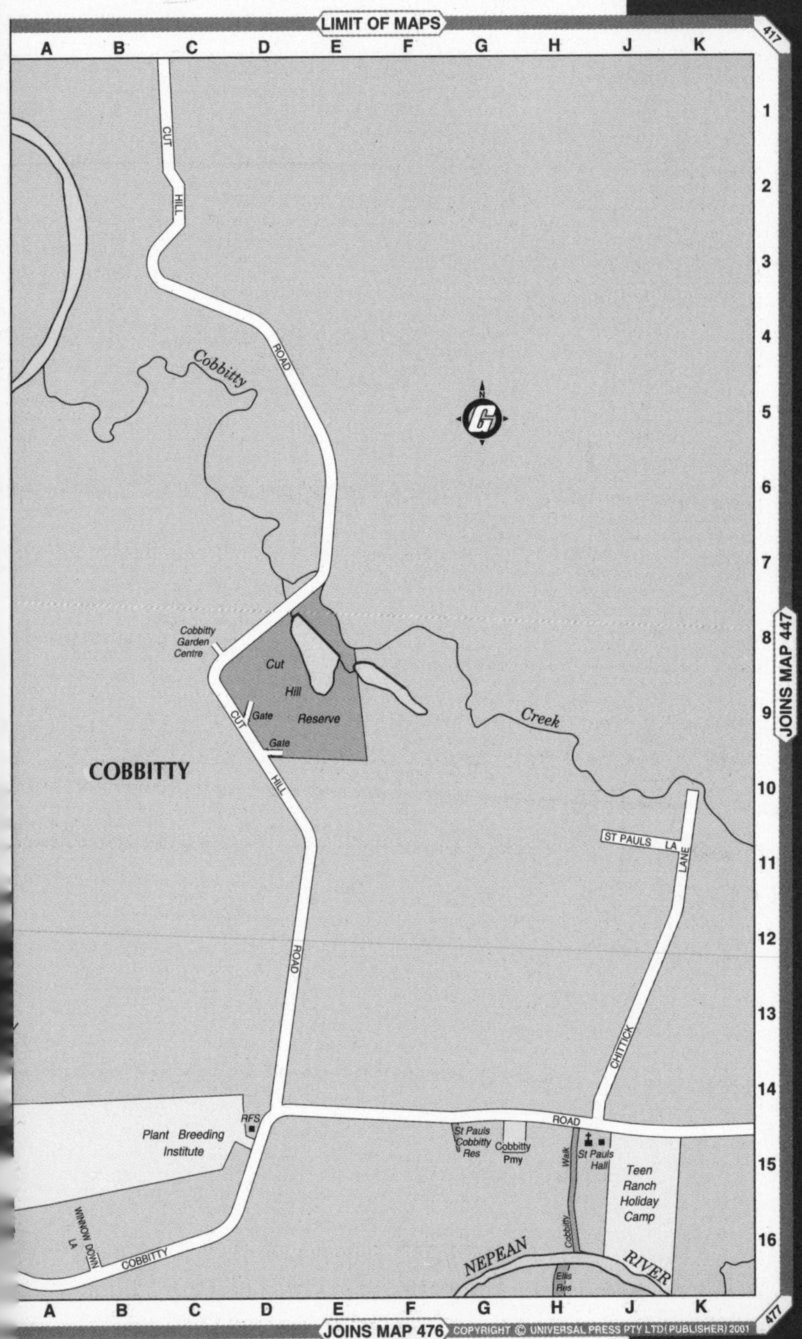

LIMIT OF MAPS
417
A B C D E F G H J K
1 2 3 4 5 6 7 8 9 10 11 12 13 14 15 16
CUT HILL
ROAD
Cobbitty
Creek
Cobbitty Garden Centre
Cut Hill Reserve
Gate
Gate
CUT HILL ROAD
COBBITTY
JOINS MAP 447
ST PAULS LA
LANE
CHITTICK
ROAD
RFS
Plant Breeding Institute
St Pauls Cobbitty Res
Cobbitty Pmy
Walk
St Pauls Hall
Teen Ranch Holiday Camp
Cobbitty
WINNOW DOWN LA
COBBITTY
NEPEAN RIVER
Ellis Res
477
JOINS MAP 476

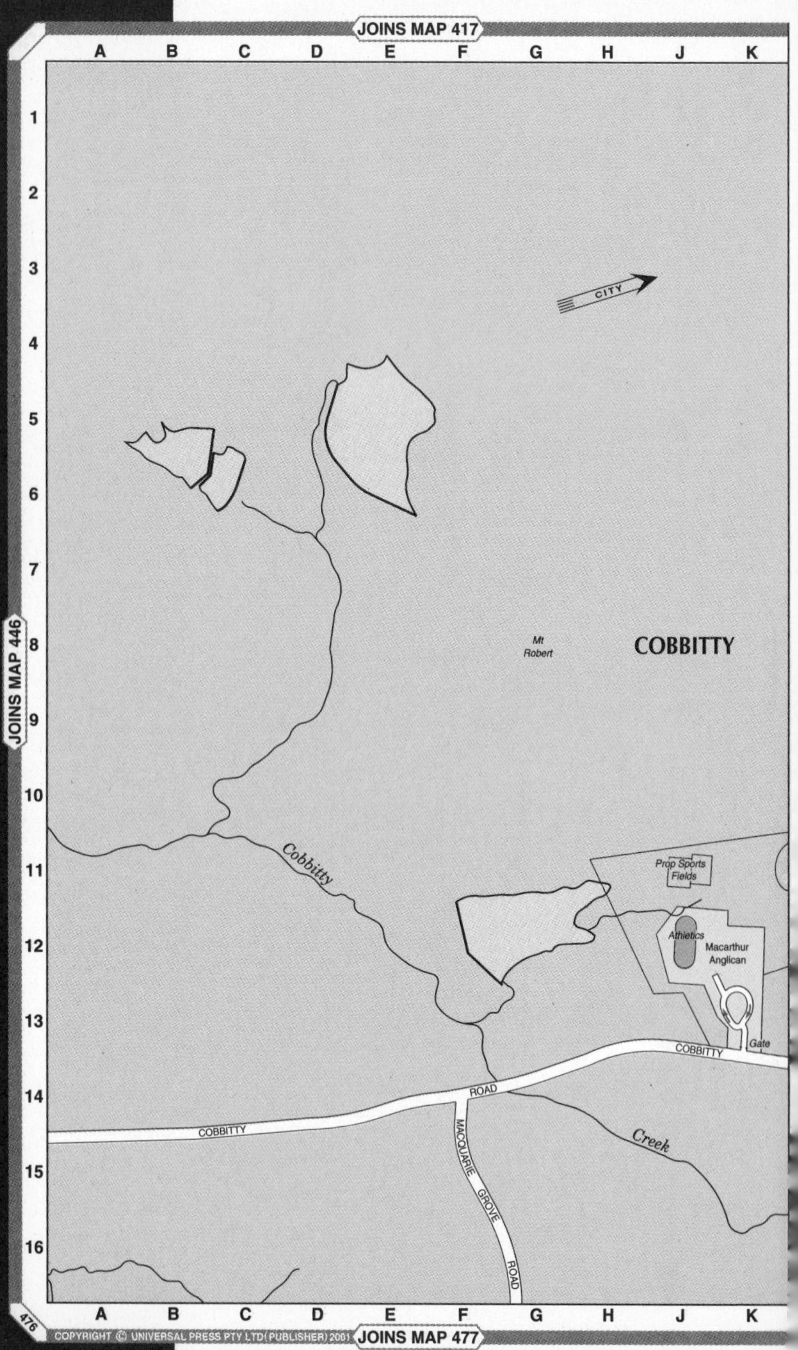
JOINS MAP 417
A B C D E F G H J K
1 2 3 4 5 6 7 8 9 10 11 12 13 14 15 16
CITY
Mt
Robert
COBBITTY
JOINS MAP 446
Cobbitty
Prop Sports
Fields
Athletics
Macarthur
Anglican
Gate
COBBITTY
ROAD
COBBITTY
MACQUARIE
GROVE
ROAD
Creek
JOINS MAP 477

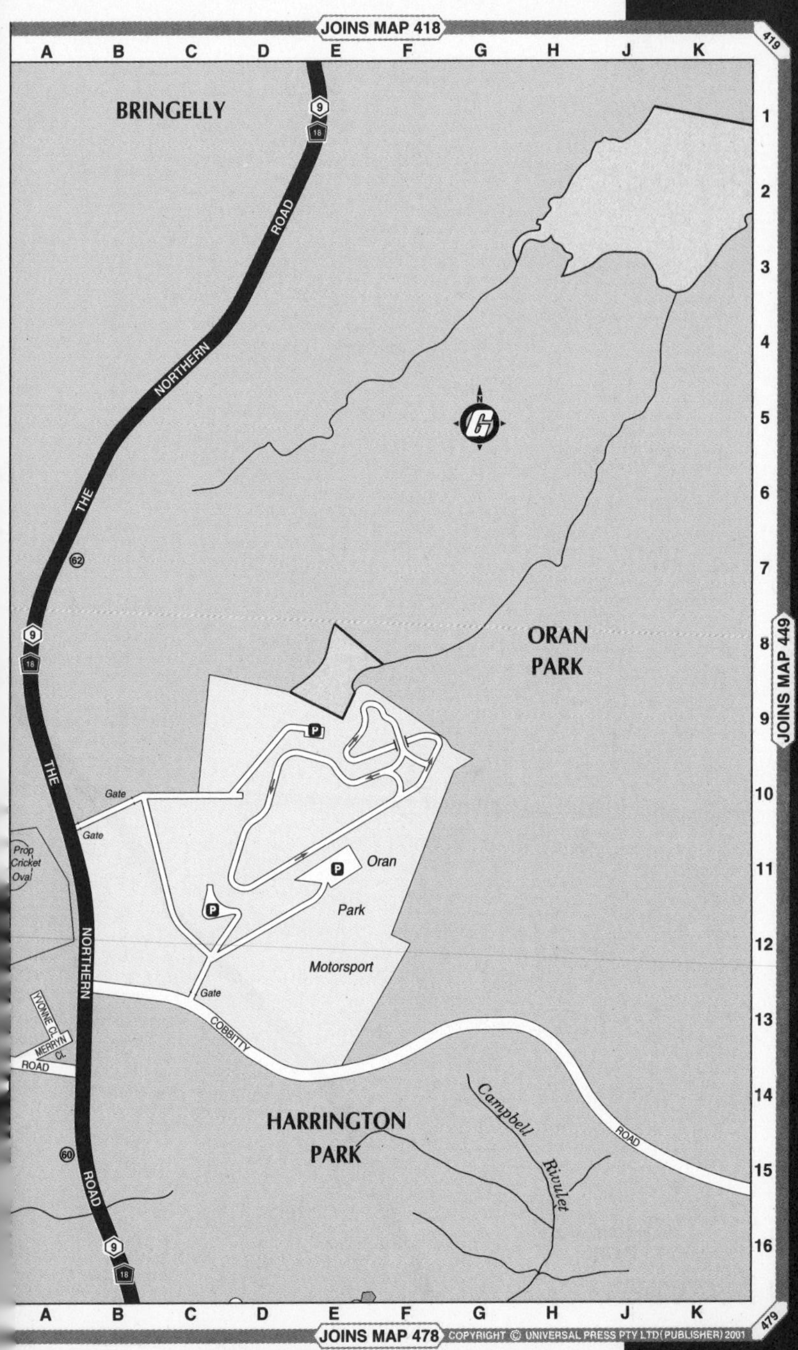
JOINS MAP 418
A B C D E F G H J K
419
1 2 3 4 5 6 7 8 9 10 11 12 13 14 15 16
BRINGELLY
THE NORTHERN ROAD
9
18
62
ORAN
PARK
JOINS MAP 449
Gate
Gate
Prop Cricket Oval
Oran
Park
Motorsport
Gate
YVONNE CL
MERRYN CL
ROAD
COBBITTY
ROAD
HARRINGTON
PARK
Campbell
Rivulet
60
479
JOINS MAP 478

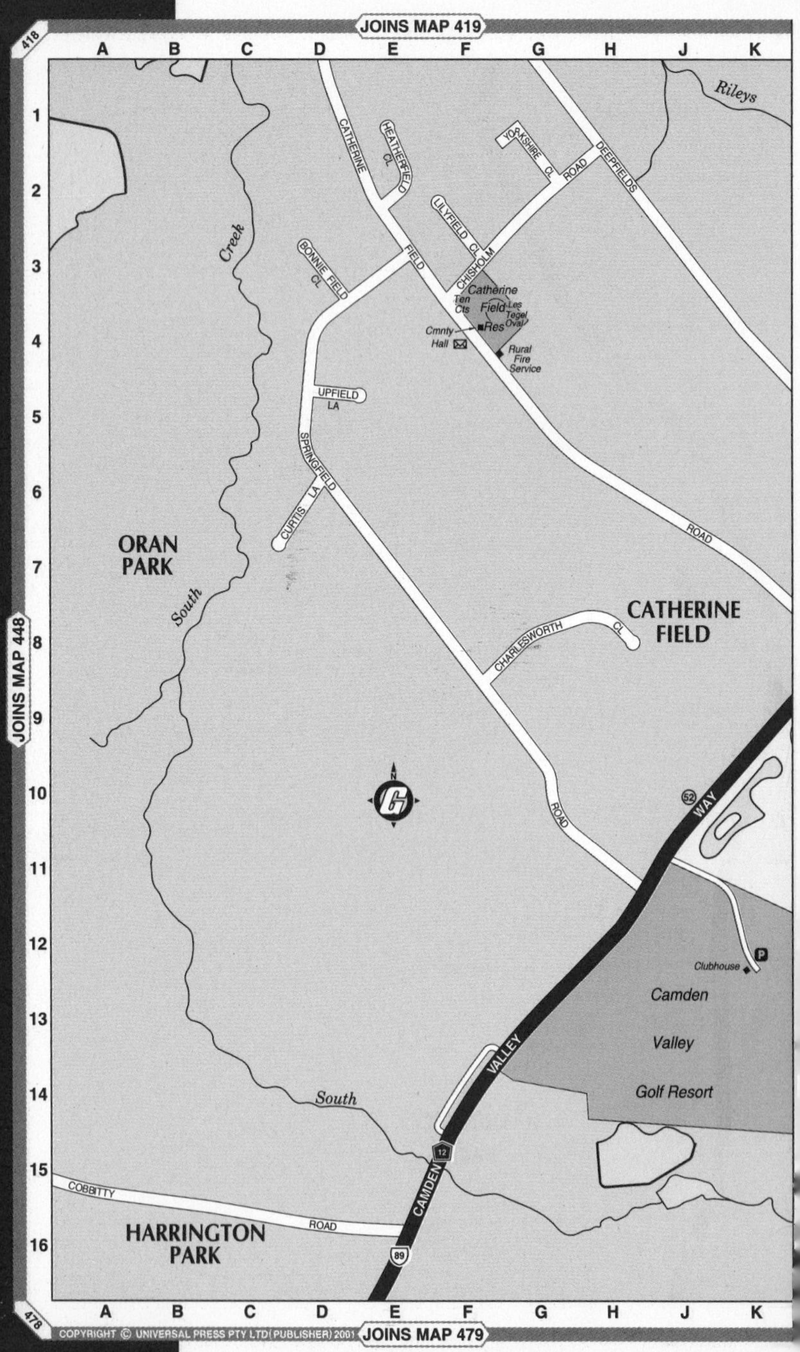
JOINS MAP 419
418
A B C D E F G H J K
1 2 3 4 5 6 7 8 9 10 11 12 13 14 15 16
JOINS MAP 448
Rileys
Creek
South
South
ORAN
PARK
CATHERINE
FIELD
HARRINGTON
PARK
CATHERINE
FIELD
ROAD
HEATHERFIELD
CL
YORKSHIRE
CL
ROAD
DEEPFIELDS
LILYFIELD
CL
CHISHOLM
BONNIE FIELD
CL
Catherine
Field
Res
Ten
Cts
Les
Tegel
Oval
Cmnty
Hall
Rural
Fire
Service
UPFIELD
LA
SPRINGFIELD
CURTIS
LA
ROAD
CHARLESWORTH
CL
ROAD
52
WAY
VALLEY
CAMDEN
12
89
Clubhouse
Camden
Valley
Golf Resort
COBBITTY
ROAD
478
JOINS MAP 479

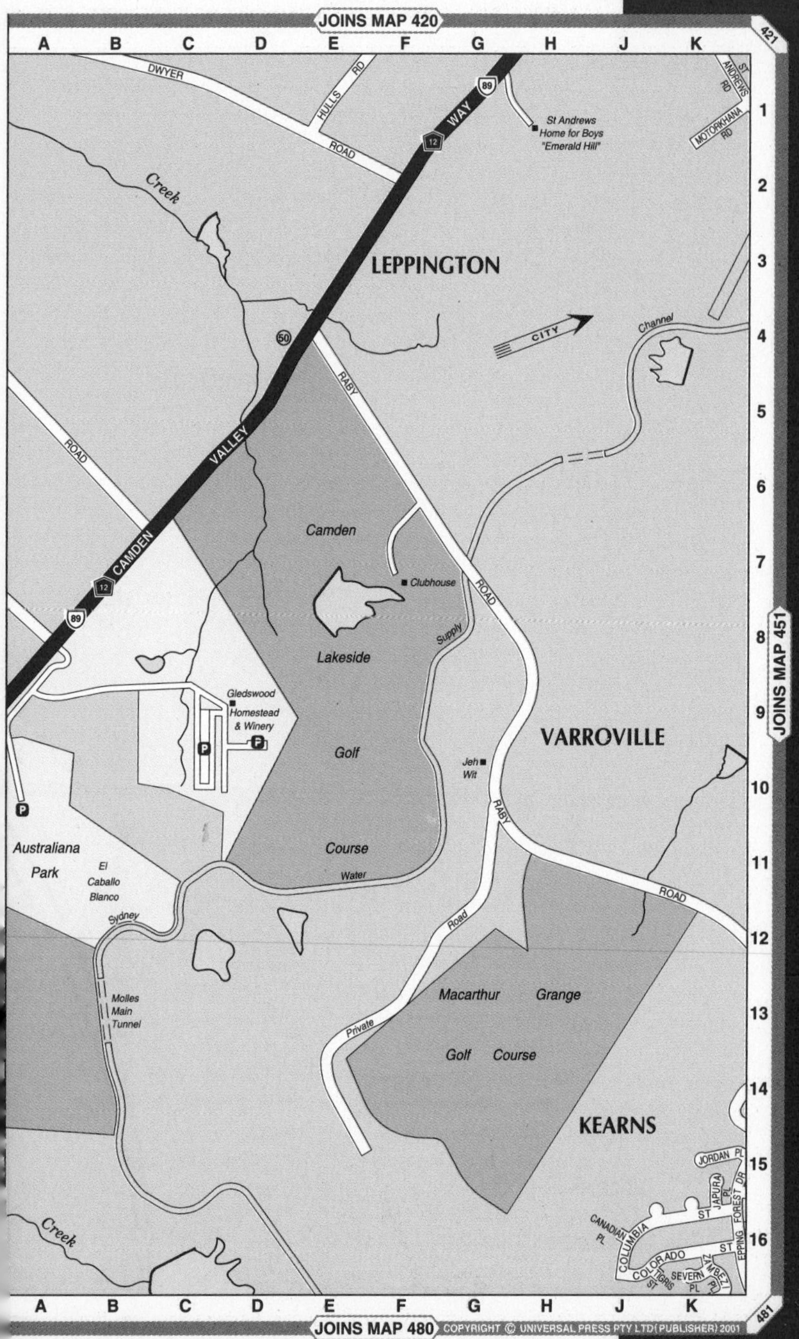

JOINS MAP 480

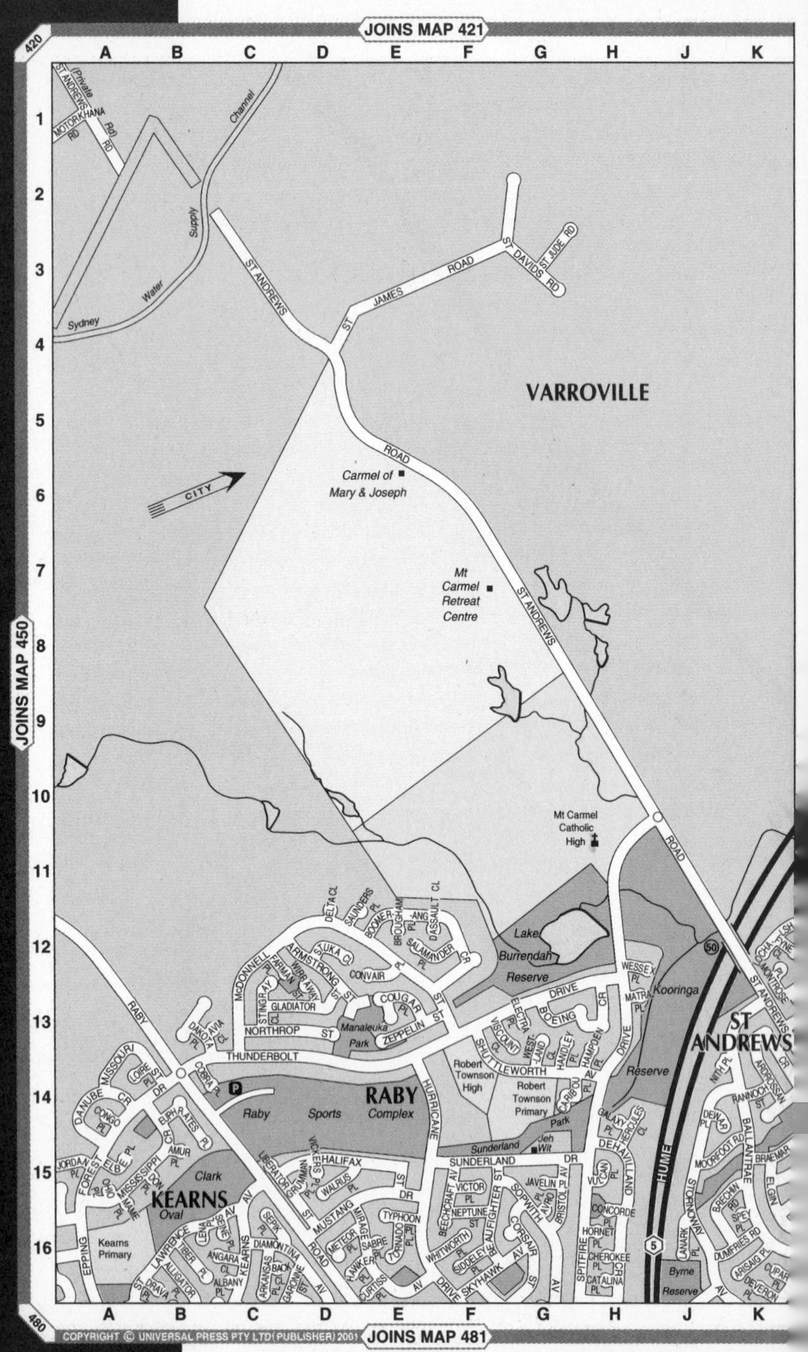
JOINS MAP 421
JOINS MAP 450
JOINS MAP 481
420
480
A B C D E F G H J K
1 2 3 4 5 6 7 8 9 10 11 12 13 14 15 16
VARROVILLE
RABY
KEARNS
ST ANDREWS
ST ANDREWS (Private Rd)
MOTORKHANA RD
Sydney Water Supply Channel
ST ANDREWS ROAD
ST JAMES ROAD
ST DAVIDS RD
ST JUDE RD
CITY
Carmel of Mary & Joseph
Mt Carmel Retreat Centre
Mt Carmel Catholic High
Lake Burrendah Reserve
Kooringa Reserve
Manaleuka Park
Raby Sports Complex
Robert Townson High
Robert Townson Primary
Sunderland Park
Jeh Wit
Clark Oval
Kearns Primary
Byrne Reserve
HUME
RABY ROAD
THUNDERBOLT DR
HURRICANE DRIVE
SUNDERLAND DR
DEHAVILLAND DRIVE
MISSOURI ST
LOIRE PL
DANUBE CR
CONGO PL
EUPHRATES PL
AMUR PL
ELBE PL
JORDAN PL
FOREST ST
OHIO PL
MISSISSIPPI CR
DON PL
MARNE PL
EPPING
LAWRENCE ST
TIBER PL
ALLIGATOR PL
DRAVA PL
LENA PL
SEINE PL
ANGARA CL
ALBANY PL
KEARNS AV
SEPIK PL
DIAMONTINA AV
ARKANSAS PL
BACK CL
GARONNE ST
DAKOTA PL
AVIA CL
COBRA PL
McDONNELL
FARMAN
STINGRAY CL
GLADIATOR
NORTHROP ST
ARMSTRONG ST
WIRRAWAY ST
STUKA CL
CONVAIR
DELTA CL
SAUNDERS PL
BOOMER PL
BROUGHAM
ANG
DASSAULT CL
SALAMANDER PL
COUGAR PL
ZEPPELIN ST
LIBERATOR
GRUMMAN ST
VICKERS
HALIFAX
WALRUS PL
MUSTANG AV
METEOR PL
MIRAGE
SABRE PL
HAWKER PL
CURTISS PL
TYPHOON
TORNADO PL
BEECHCRAFT AV
VICTOR PL
NEPTUNE ST
WHITWORTH DRIVE
SIDDELEY PL
BEAUFIGHTER ST
SKYHAWK AV
SOPWITH AV
AVRO PL
CORSAIR ST
JAVELIN PL
BRISTOL AV
VISCOUNT CL
ELECTRA PL
BOEING
WESTLAND CL
HANDLEY PL
HAMPDEN CR
SHUTTLEWORTH AV
CARIBOU PL
WESSEX PL
MATRA PL
GALAXY PL
HERCULES CL
VULCAN PL
CONCORDE PL
HORNET PL
CHEROKEE PL
CATALINA PL
SPITFIRE AV
LANARK PL
STORNOWAY
NITH PL
ARDROSSAN CR
RANNOCH ST
DEWAR PL
BALLANTRAE
MOORFOOT RD
BRECHIN RD
SPEY PL
DUMFRIES RD
ARISAIG PL
CUPAR PL
DEVERON
ELGIN
BRAEMAR
MONTROSE
50
5
COPYRIGHT © UNIVERSAL PRESS PTY LTD (PUBLISHER) 2001

JOINS MAP 422

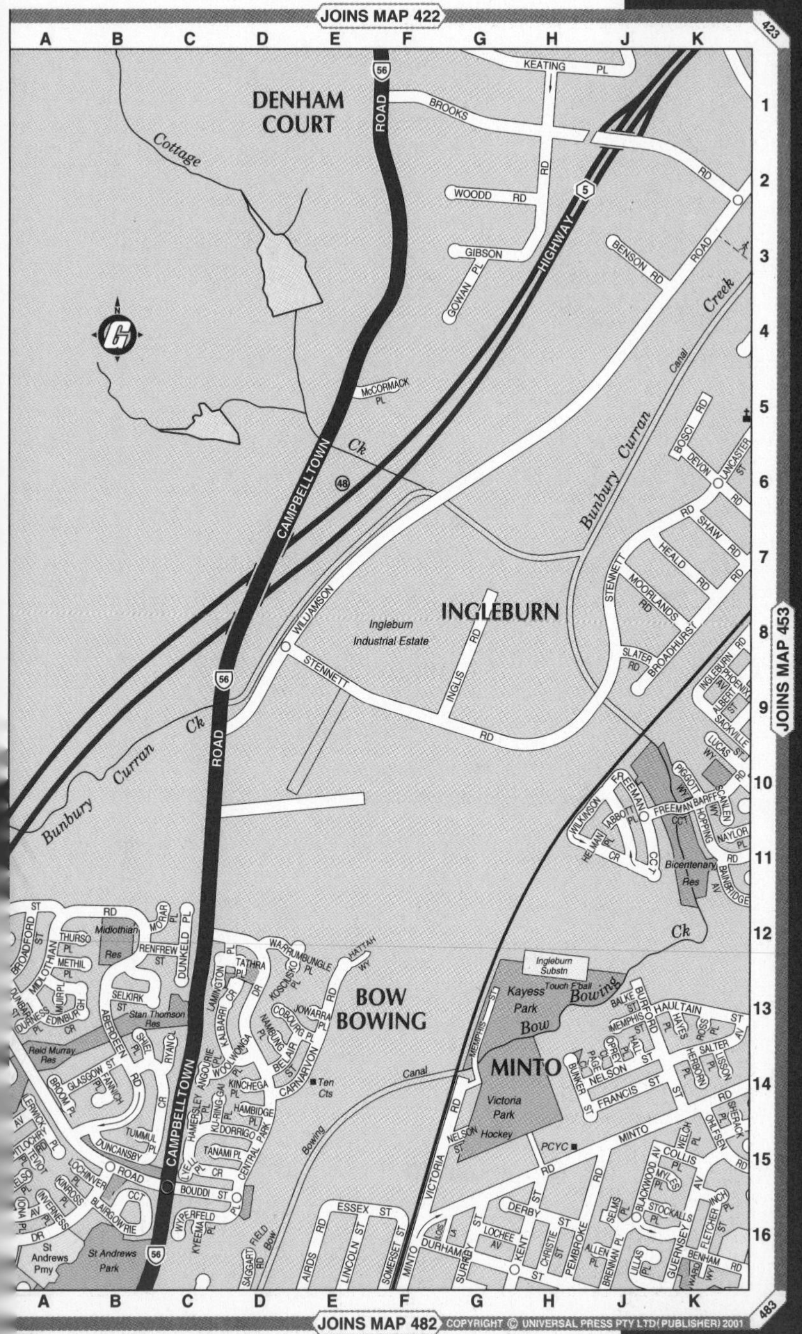

JOINS MAP 453

JOINS MAP 482

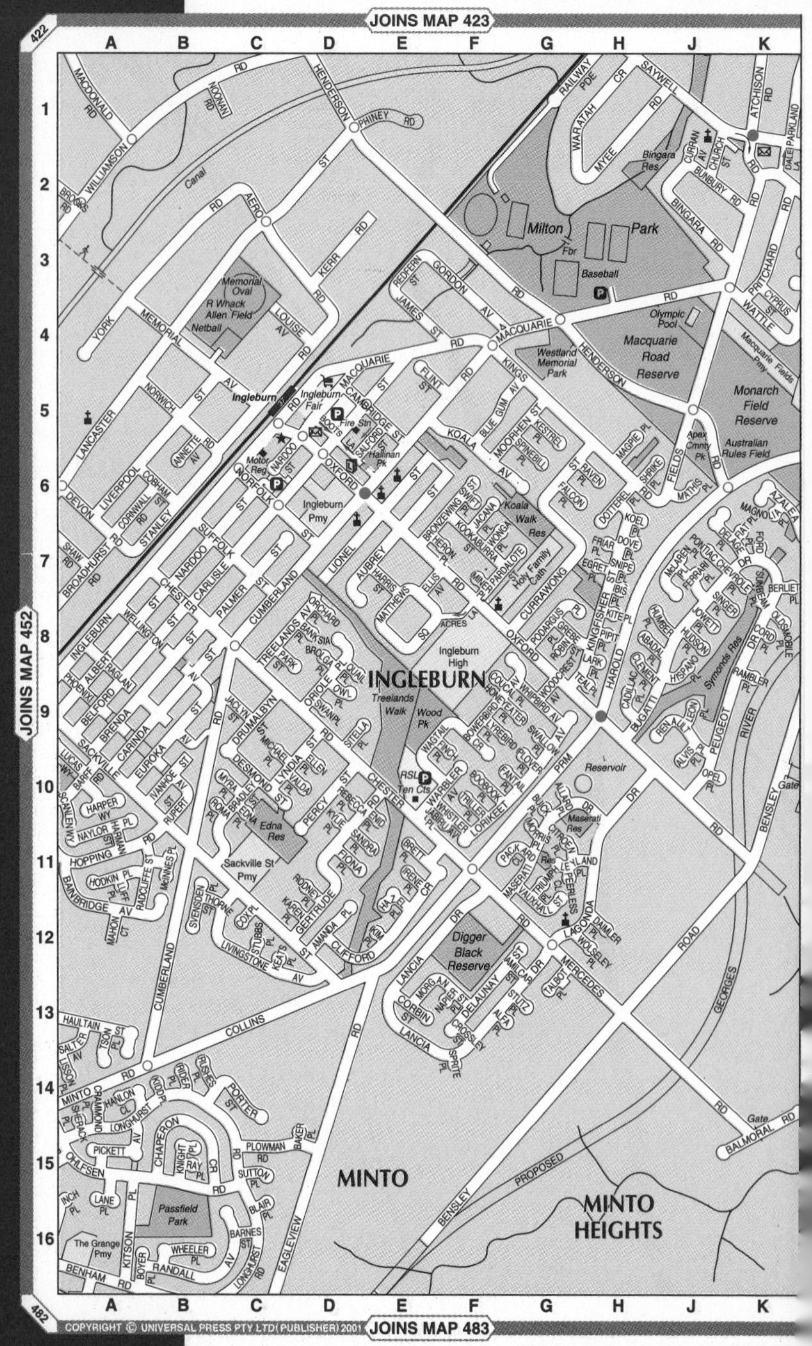
JOINS MAP 423
JOINS MAP 452
JOINS MAP 483
422
482
INGLEBURN
MINTO
MINTO HEIGHTS
Milton Park
Macquarie Road Reserve
Monarch Field Reserve
Digger Black Reserve
Passfield Park
Ingleburn High
Ingleburn Pmy
Sackville St Pmy
The Grange Pmy
Treelands Walk
Wood Pk
Koala Walk Res
Westland Memorial Park
Memorial Oval
R Whack Allen Field
Symonds Res
Edna Res
Reservoir
Olympic Pool
Baseball
Australian Rules Field
Apex Cmnty Pk
Hallinan Pk
Ingleburn Fair
Holy Family Cath
Bingara Res
Maserati Res
RSL
Ten Cts
Canal
Ingleburn

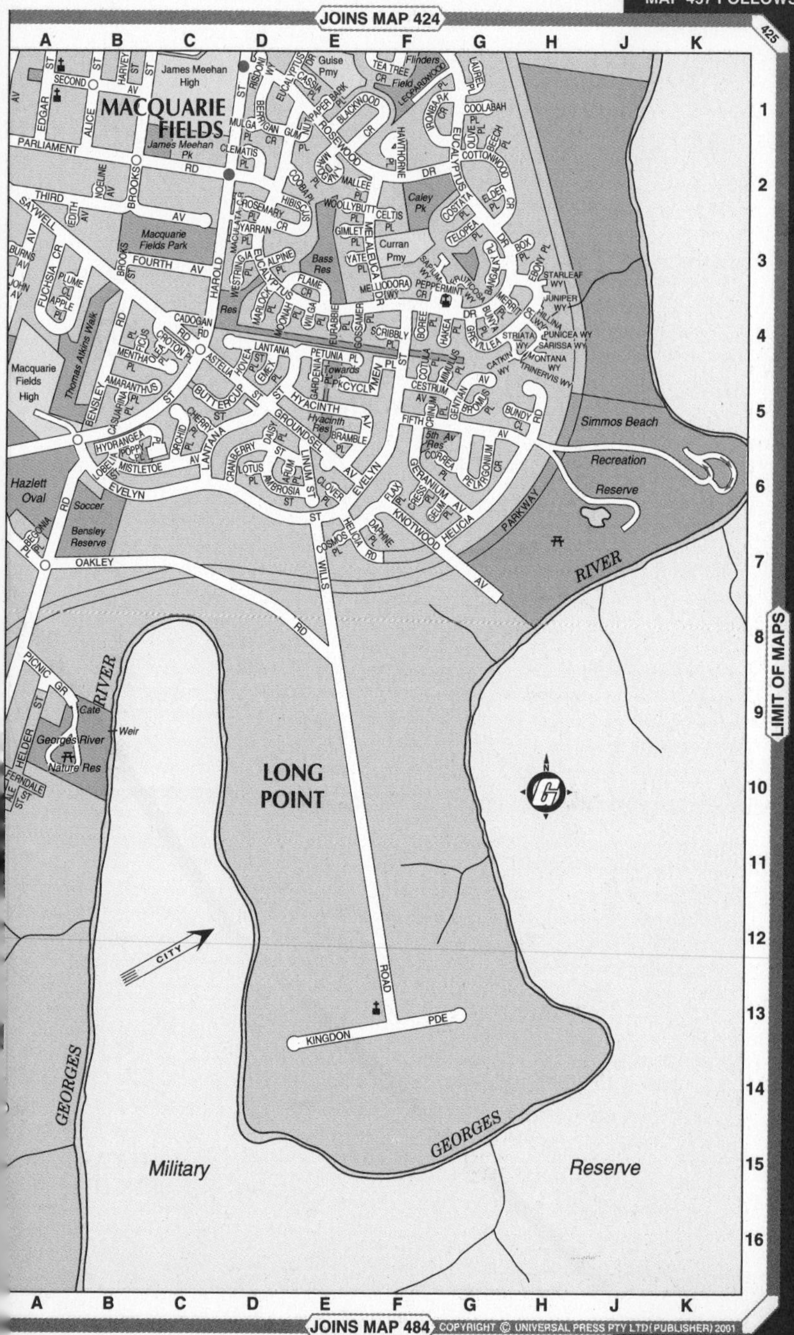
JOINS MAP 424
425
MACQUARIE FIELDS
James Meehan High
James Meehan Pk
Macquarie Fields Park
Macquarie Fields High
Thomas Atkins Walk
Guise Pmy
Flinders Field
Caley Pk
Curran Pmy
Bass Res
Towards Pk
Hyacinth Res
5th Av Res
Hazlett Oval
Soccer
Bensley Reserve
Simmos Beach
Recreation Reserve
PARKWAY
RIVER
OAKLEY
WILLS RD
Cate
Weir
Georges River Nature Res
LONG POINT
CITY
KINGDON PDE
GEORGES
Military
Reserve
LIMIT OF MAPS
JOINS MAP 484

JOINS MAP 427

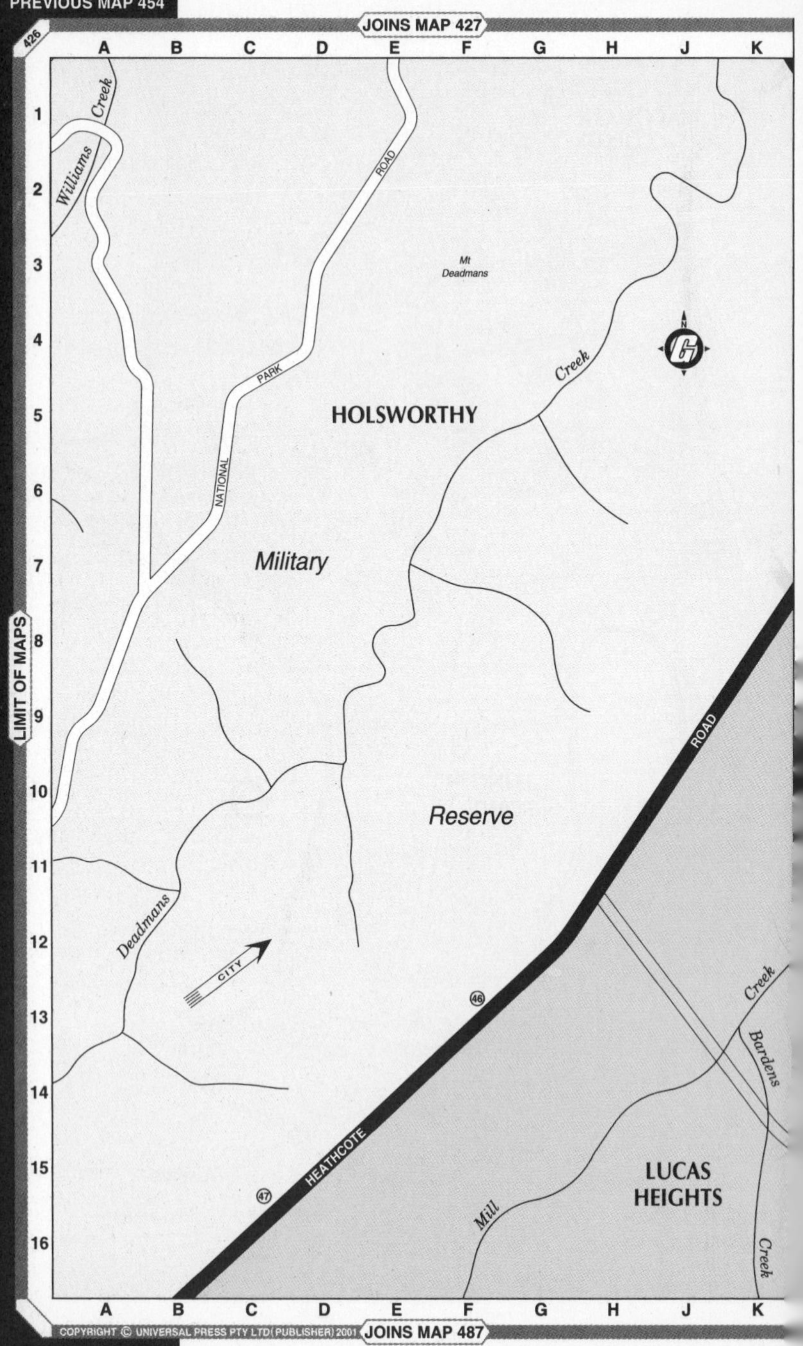

JOINS MAP 487

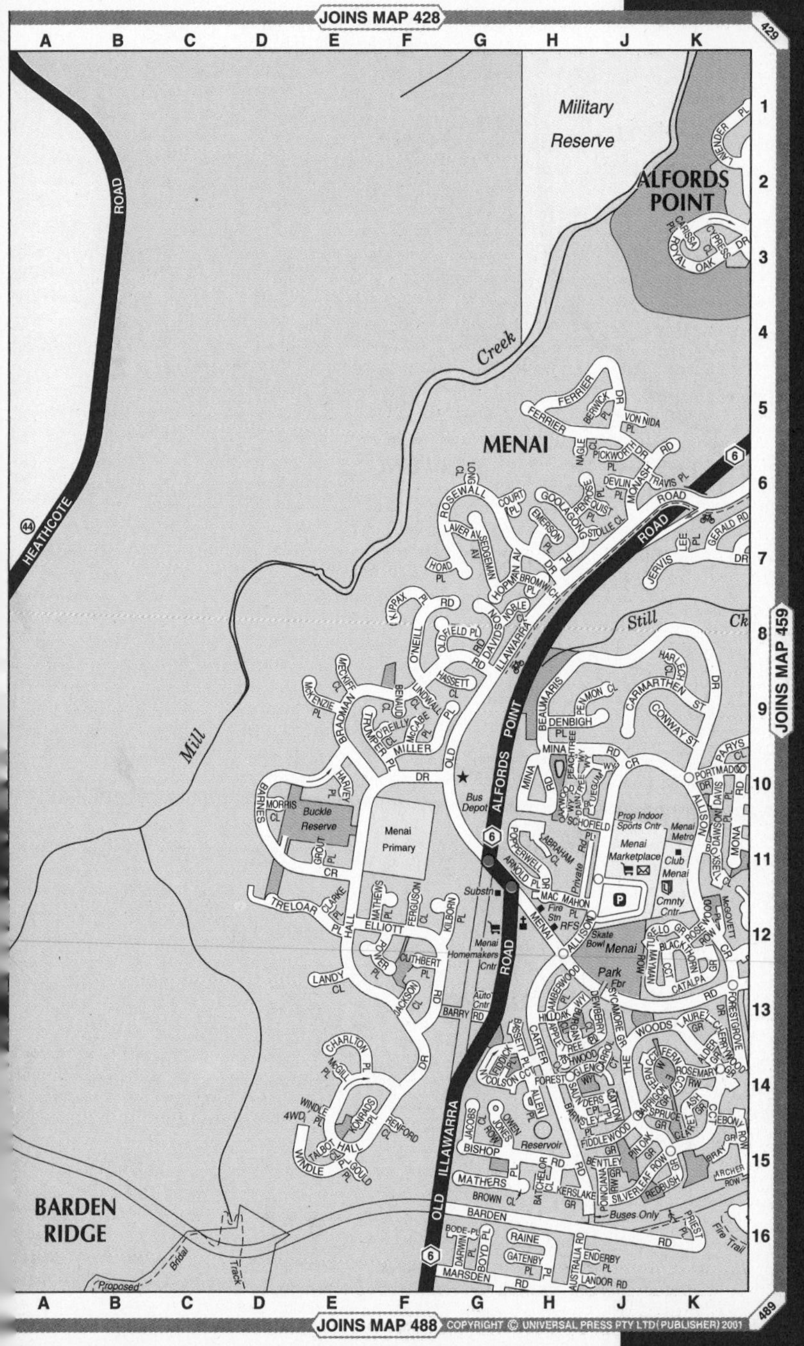
JOINS MAP 428
JOINS MAP 459
JOINS MAP 488
Military Reserve
ALFORDS POINT
MENAI
BARDEN RIDGE
HEATHCOTE ROAD
Mill Creek
Still Ck
ALFORDS POINT ROAD
OLD ILLAWARRA ROAD
Buckle Reserve
Menai Primary
Bus Depot
Menai Homemakers Cntr
Menai Marketplace
Club Menai
Cmnty Cntr
Menai Park
Prop Indoor Sports Cntr
Menai Metro
Reservoir
Buses Only
Fire Trail
Bridal Track
Proposed
BARDEN RD
MARSDEN RD
DR

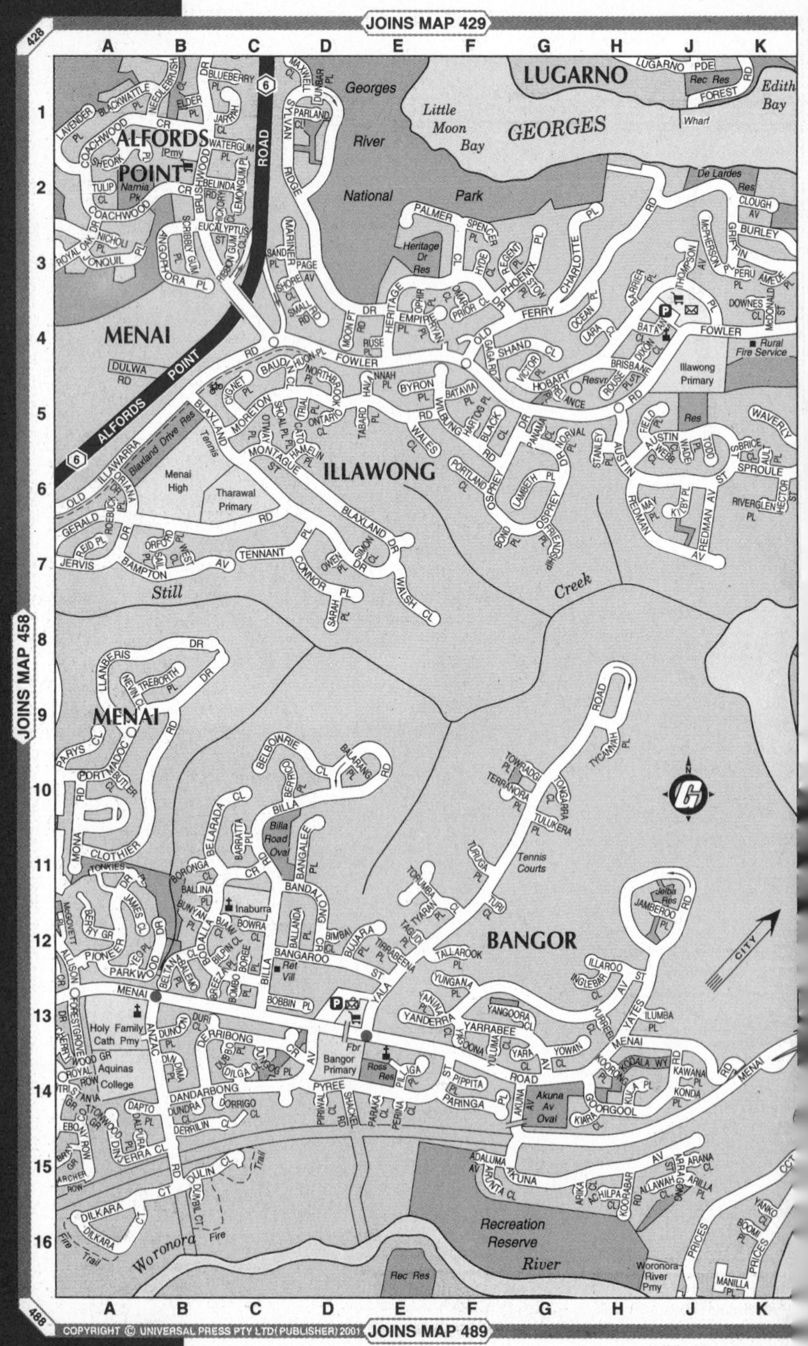
JOINS MAP 429
JOINS MAP 458
JOINS MAP 489
428
488
A B C D E F G H J K
1 2 3 4 5 6 7 8 9 10 11 12 13 14 15 16
LUGARNO
GEORGES
Georges River National Park
Little Moon Bay
Edith Bay
ALFORDS POINT
MENAI
ILLAWONG
BANGOR
ALFORDS POINT RD
FOWLER RD
BLAXLAND DR
MENAI RD
Still Creek
Woronora River
Recreation Reserve
Heritage Dr Res
Menai High
Tharawal Primary
Illawong Primary
Rural Fire Service
Billa Road Oval
Holy Family Cath Pmy
Aquinas College
Bangor Primary
Akuna Av Oval
Woronora River Pmy
Tennis Courts
Jelba Res
CITY

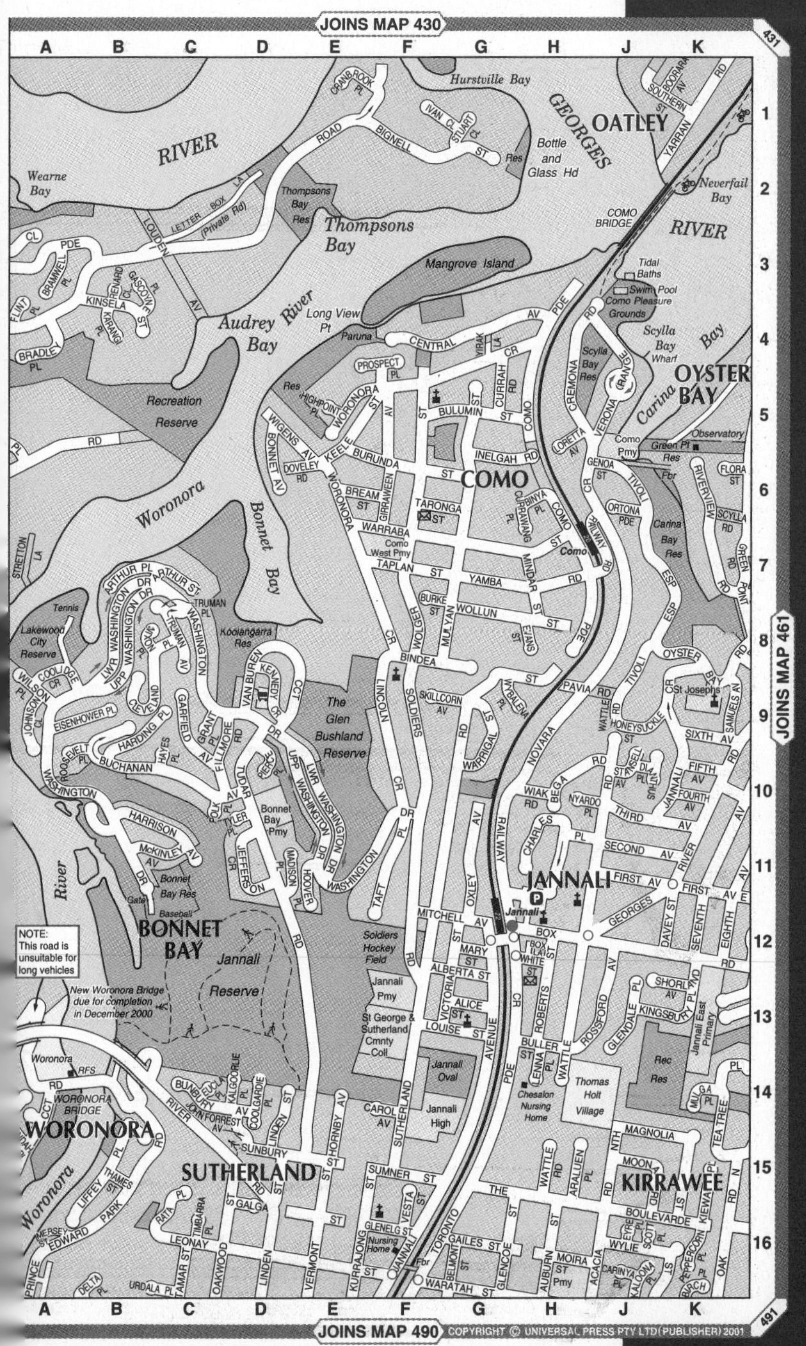
JOINS MAP 430
JOINS MAP 461
JOINS MAP 490
431
491
A B C D E F G H J K
1 2 3 4 5 6 7 8 9 10 11 12 13 14 15 16
GEORGES
RIVER
OATLEY
Hurstville Bay
Bottle and Glass Hd
Neverfail Bay
COMO BRIDGE
Wearne Bay
Thompsons Bay Res
Thompsons Bay
Mangrove Island
Tidal Baths
Swim Pool
Como Pleasure Grounds
Scylla Bay
Scylla Bay Wharf
Scylla Bay Res
Audrey Bay
Long View Pt
Paruna
Recreation Reserve
Carina Bay
OYSTER BAY
Observatory
Green Pt Res
Como Pmy
Carina Bay Res
COMO
Como West Pmy
Woronora
Bonnet Bay
Koolangarra Res
Tennis
Lakewood City Reserve
The Glen Bushland Reserve
St Josephs
Bonnet Bay Pmy
Bonnet Bay Res
Gate
Baseball
BONNET BAY
Jannali Reserve
River
NOTE: This road is unsuitable for long vehicles
New Woronora Bridge due for completion in December 2000
JANNALI
Soldiers Hockey Field
Jannali Pmy
St George & Sutherland Cmnty Coll
Jannali Oval
Jannali High
Chesalon Nursing Home
Thomas Holt Village
Rec Res
Jannali East Primary
WORONORA
WORONORA BRIDGE
RFS
SUTHERLAND
KIRRAWEE
Nursing Home
Moira St Pmy
Woronora
COPYRIGHT © UNIVERSAL PRESS PTY LTD (PUBLISHER) 2001

JOINS MAP 431

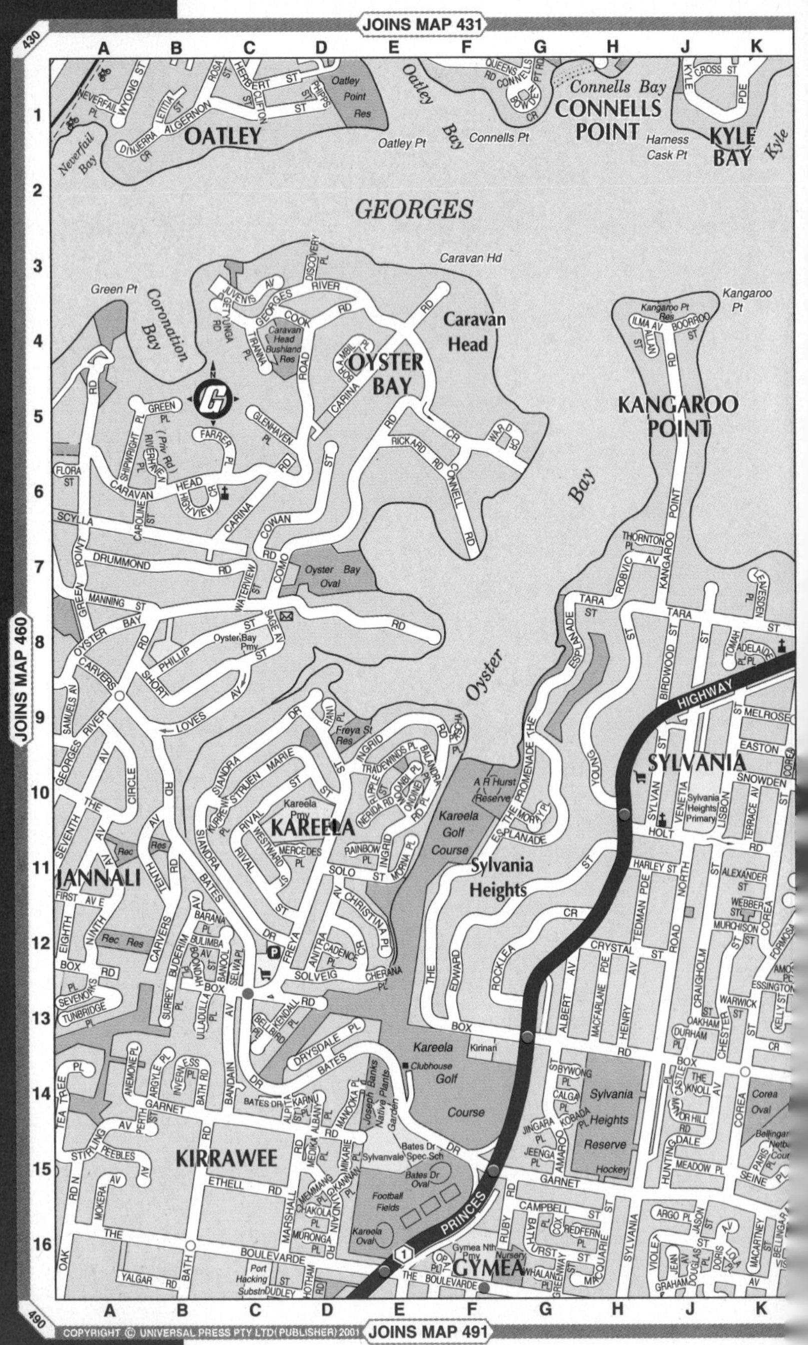

JOINS MAP 460

JOINS MAP 491

JOINS MAP 432

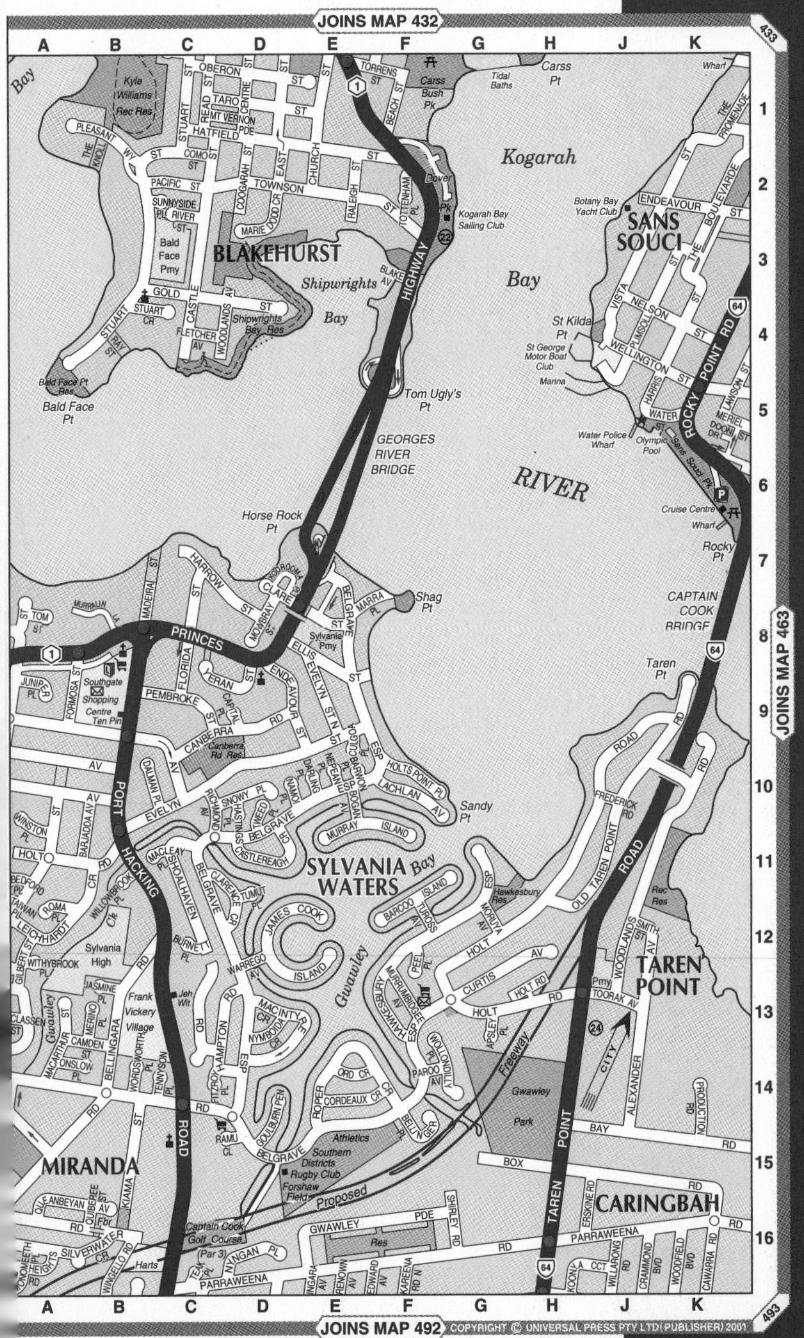

JOINS MAP 463

JOINS MAP 492

JOINS MAP 433

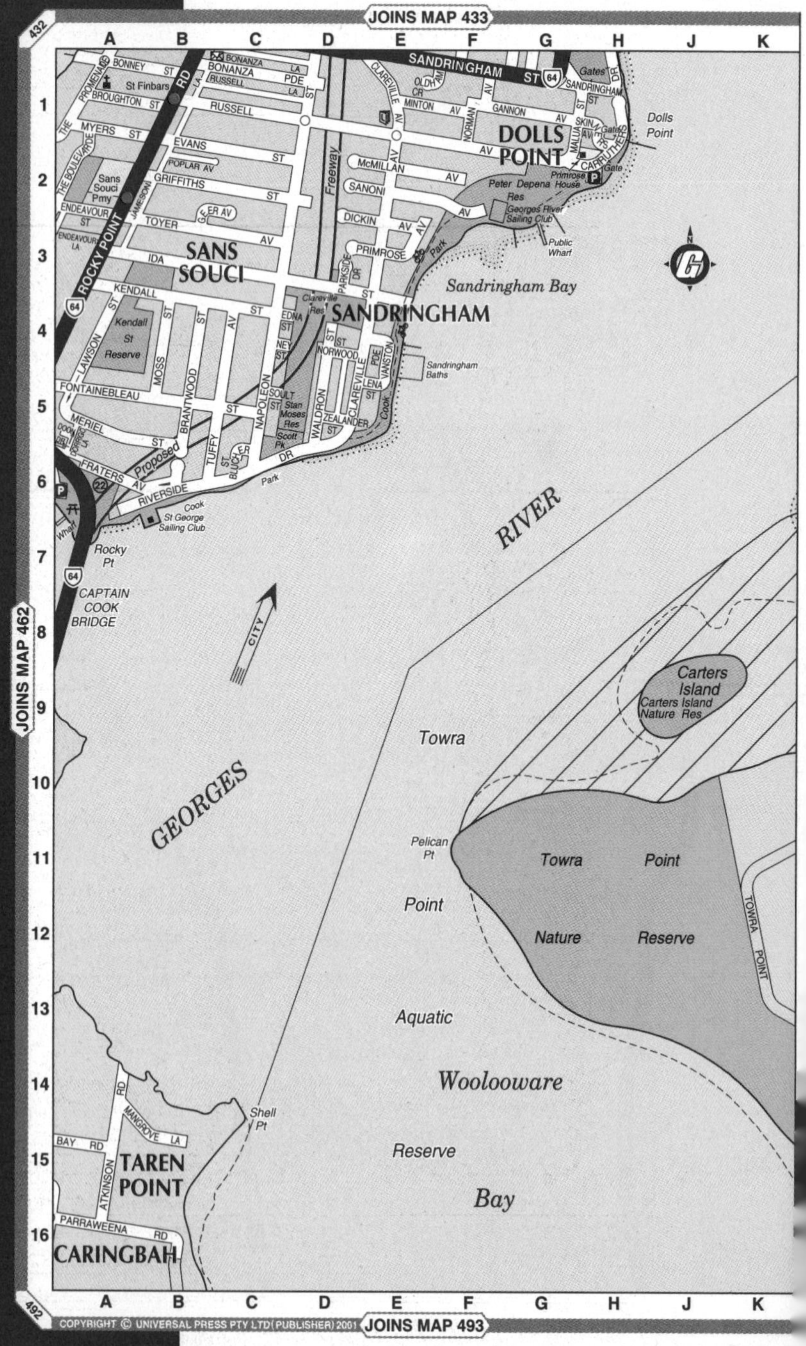

JOINS MAP 462

JOINS MAP 493

JOINS MAP 434

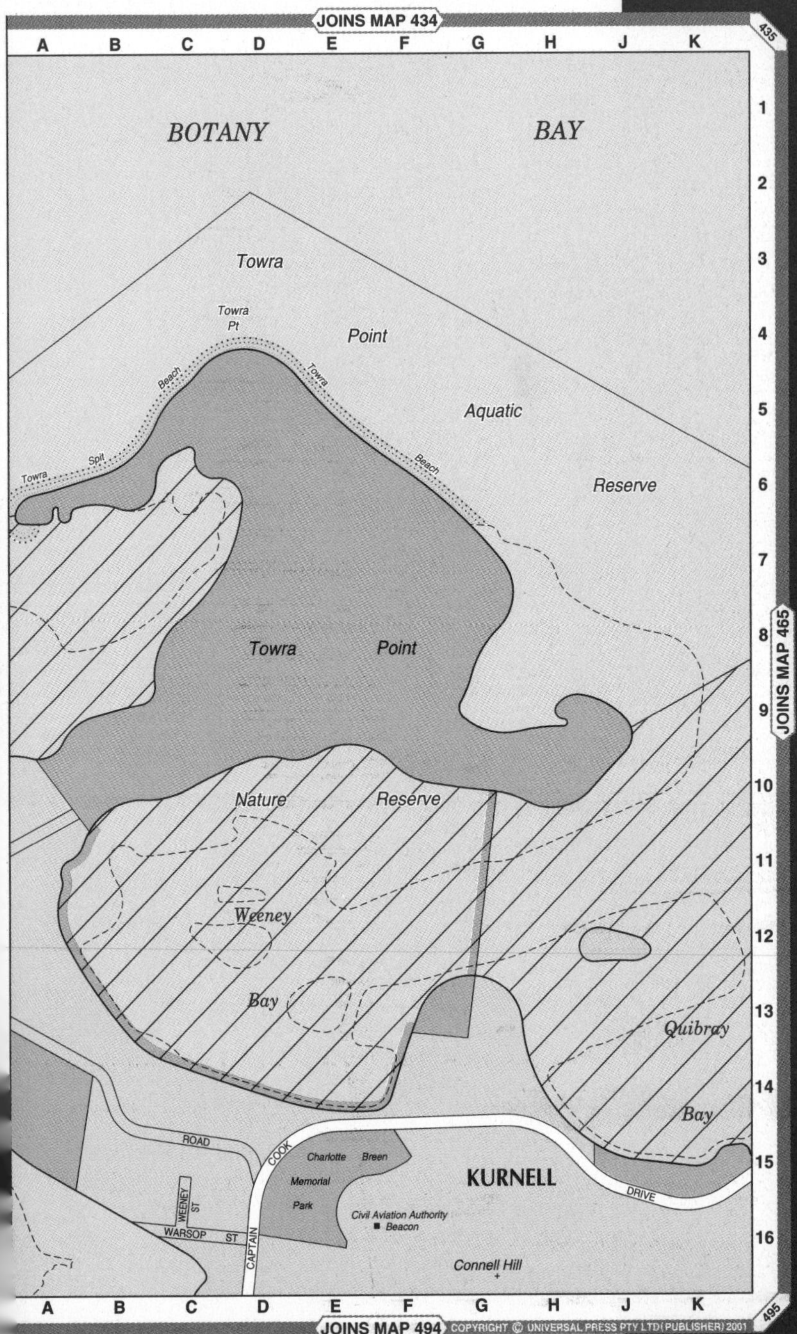

JOINS MAP 465

JOINS MAP 494

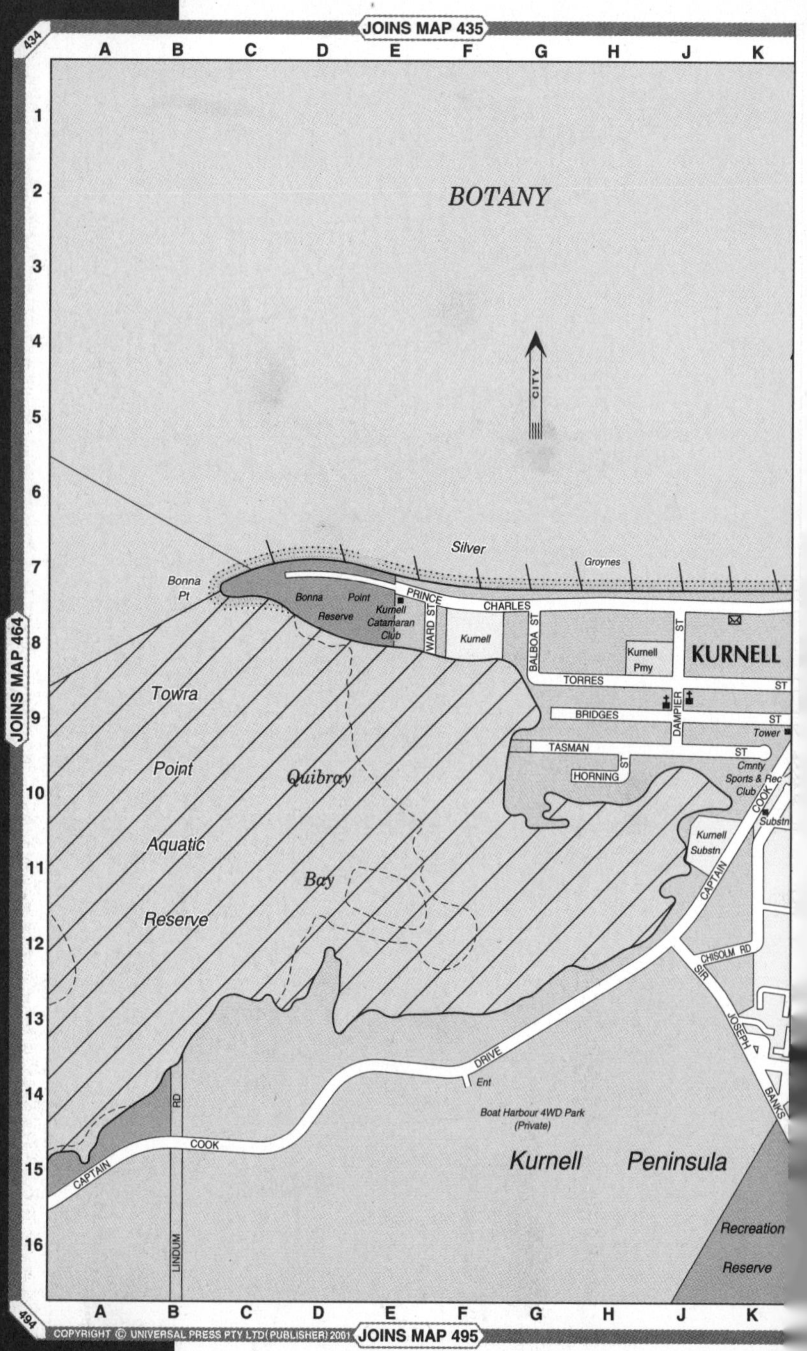
JOINS MAP 435
434
A B C D E F G H J K
1 2 3 4 5 6 7 8 9 10 11 12 13 14 15 16
JOINS MAP 464
BOTANY
CITY
Silver
Groynes
Bonna
Pt
Bonna Point Reserve
Kurnell Catamaran Club
PRINCE CHARLES
WARD ST
Kurnell
BALBOA ST
ST
KURNELL
Kurnell Pmy
TORRES ST
BRIDGES ST
DAMPIER
TASMAN ST
Tower
HORNING ST
Cmnty Sports & Rec Club
COOK
Substn
Kurnell Substn
CAPTAIN
CHISOLM RD
SIR JOSEPH BANKS
Towra Point Aquatic Reserve
Quibray Bay
DRIVE
Ent
Boat Harbour 4WD Park (Private)
Kurnell Peninsula
Recreation Reserve
RD
LINDUM
COOK
CAPTAIN
494
A B C D E F G H J K
JOINS MAP 495

JOINS MAP 436

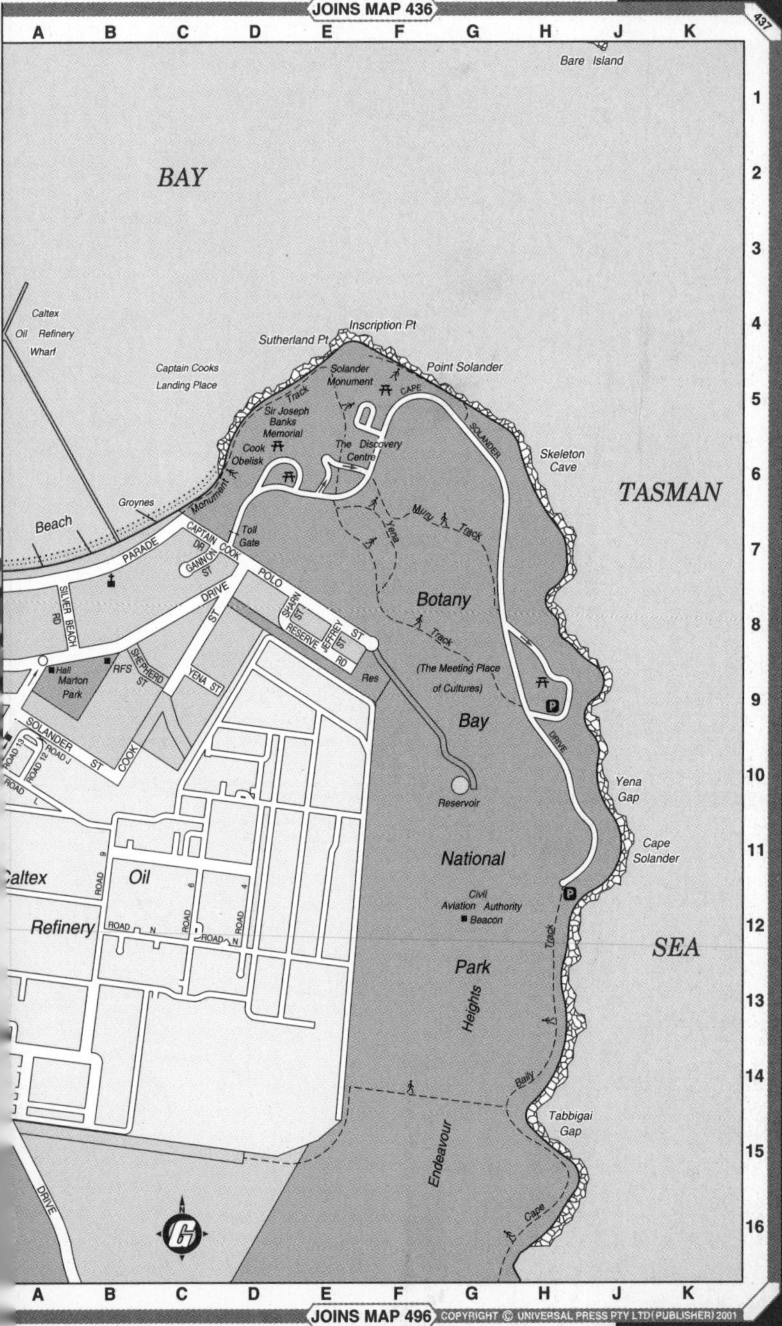

A B C D E F G H J K

1 2 3 4 5 6 7 8 9 10 11 12 13 14 15 16

BAY

TASMAN SEA

Bare Island
Caltex Oil Refinery Wharf
Inscription Pt
Sutherland Pt
Point Solander
Captain Cooks Landing Place
Solander Monument
Sir Joseph Banks Memorial
Cook Obelisk
The Discovery Centre
Skeleton Cave
Groynes
Beach
Monument Track
Toll Gate
CAPE SOLANDER DRIVE
Muru Track
Yena Track
CAPTAIN COOK DR
GANNON ST
PARADE
POLO ST
SHARK ST
JEFFREY ST
RESERVE RD
DRIVE
SILVER BEACH RD
ST
Botany Track (The Meeting Place of Cultures)
Botany Bay National Park
Res
Hall
Marton Park
RFS
SHEPHERD ST
YENA ST
SOLANDER ST
COOK
ROAD 13
ROAD 12
ROAD J
ROAD L
Reservoir
Yena Gap
Cape Solander
Caltex Oil Refinery
ROAD 9
ROAD 6
ROAD 4
ROAD N
Civil Aviation Authority Beacon
Heights
Track
Baily
Tabbigai Gap
Endeavour
Cape
DRIVE

A B C D E F G H J K

JOINS MAP 496

437

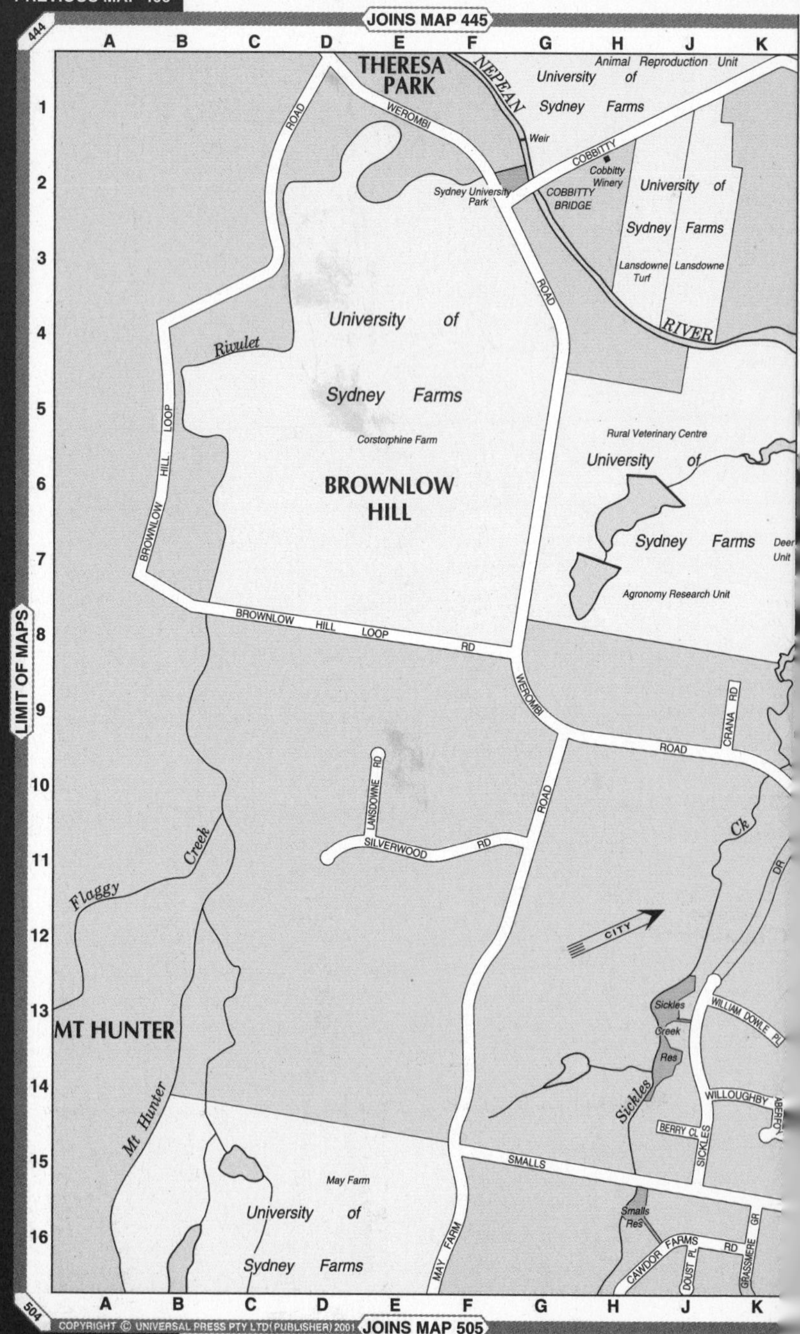
JOINS MAP 445
444
A B C D E F G H J K
1 2 3 4 5 6 7 8 9 10 11 12 13 14 15 16
LIMIT OF MAPS
THERESA PARK
NEPEAN
Animal Reproduction Unit
University of Sydney Farms
WEROMBI
ROAD
Weir
COBBITTY
Cobbitty Winery
Sydney University Park
COBBITTY BRIDGE
University of Sydney Farms
Lansdowne Turf
Lansdowne
RIVER
University of Sydney Farms
Rivulet
Corstorphine Farm
BROWNLOW HILL
BROWNLOW HILL LOOP
Rural Veterinary Centre
University of Sydney Farms
Deer Unit
Agronomy Research Unit
BROWNLOW HILL LOOP RD
WEROMBI ROAD
CRANA RD
LANSDOWNE RD
SILVERWOOD RD
Ck
DR
Flaggy Creek
CITY
MT HUNTER
Sickles Creek Res
WILLIAM DOWLE PL
WILLOUGHBY
ABERFOYL
Mt Hunter
Sickles
BERRY CL
SICKLES
SMALLS
May Farm
University of Sydney Farms
MAY FARM
Smalls Res
CAWDOR FARMS RD
DOUST PL
GRASSMERE GR
A B C D E F G H J K
504
JOINS MAP 505

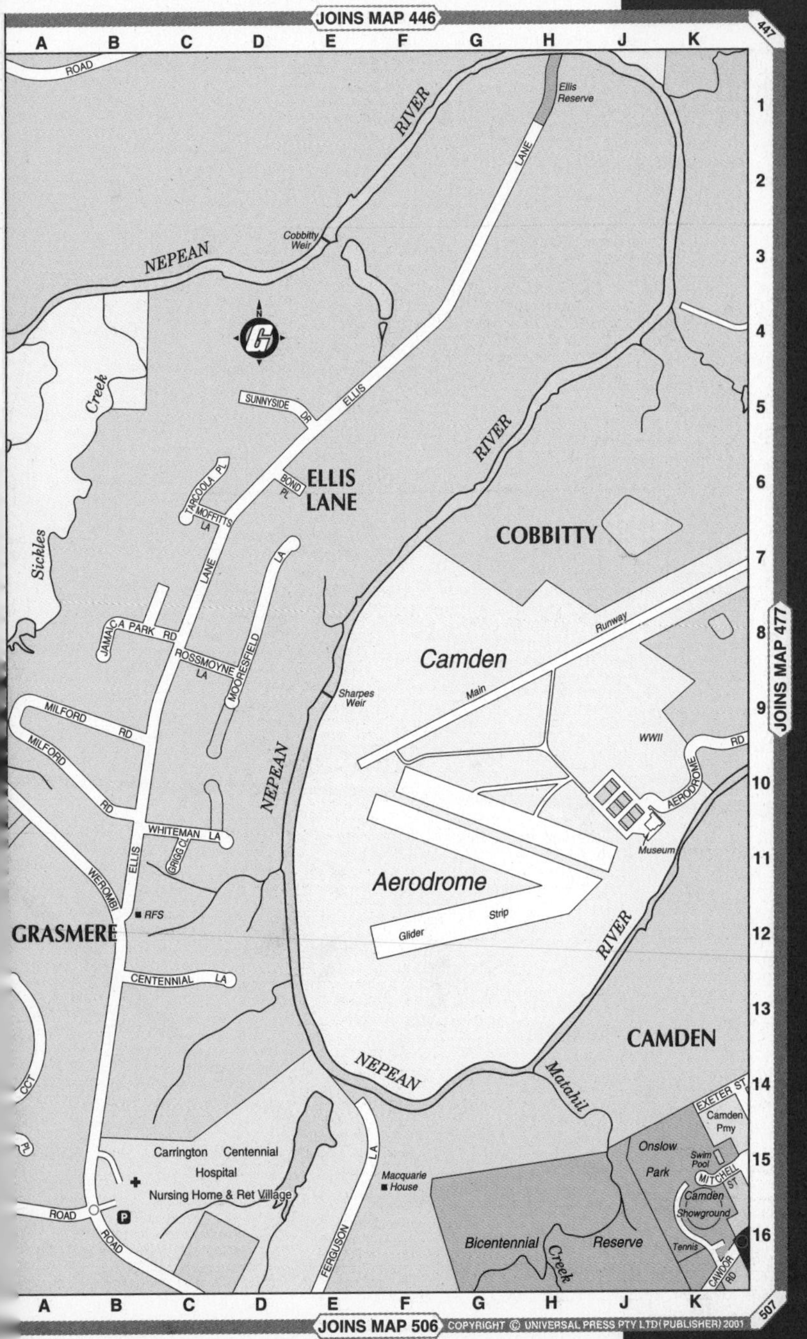
JOINS MAP 446
447
A
B
C
D
E
F
G
H
J
K
1
2
3
4
5
6
7
8
9
10
11
12
13
14
15
16
ROAD
Ellis
Reserve
RIVER
LANE
Cobbitty
Weir
NEPEAN
Creek
SUNNYSIDE
DR
ELLIS
RIVER
ELLIS
LANE
BOND
PL
TARCOOLA PL
MOFFITTS
LA
COBBITTY
Sickles
LA
LANE
Runway
JAMAICA PARK RD
ROSSMOYNE
LA
MOORESFIELD
Camden
Sharpes
Weir
Main
JOINS MAP 477
MILFORD
RD
MILFORD
RD
WWII
RD
NEPEAN
AERODROME
WHITEMAN LA
GRIGG CL
Museum
ELLIS
WEROMBI
Aerodrome
RFS
Strip
Glider
GRASMERE
RIVER
CENTENNIAL LA
CAMDEN
CCT
NEPEAN
Matahil
EXETER ST
Camden
Pmy
Onslow
Park
Swim
Pool
MITCHELL
ST
PL
Carrington Centennial
Hospital
Nursing Home & Ret Village
LA
Macquarie
House
Camden
Showground
ROAD
ROAD
FERGUSON
Bicentennial
Creek
Reserve
Tennis
CAWDOR
RD
507
JOINS MAP 506

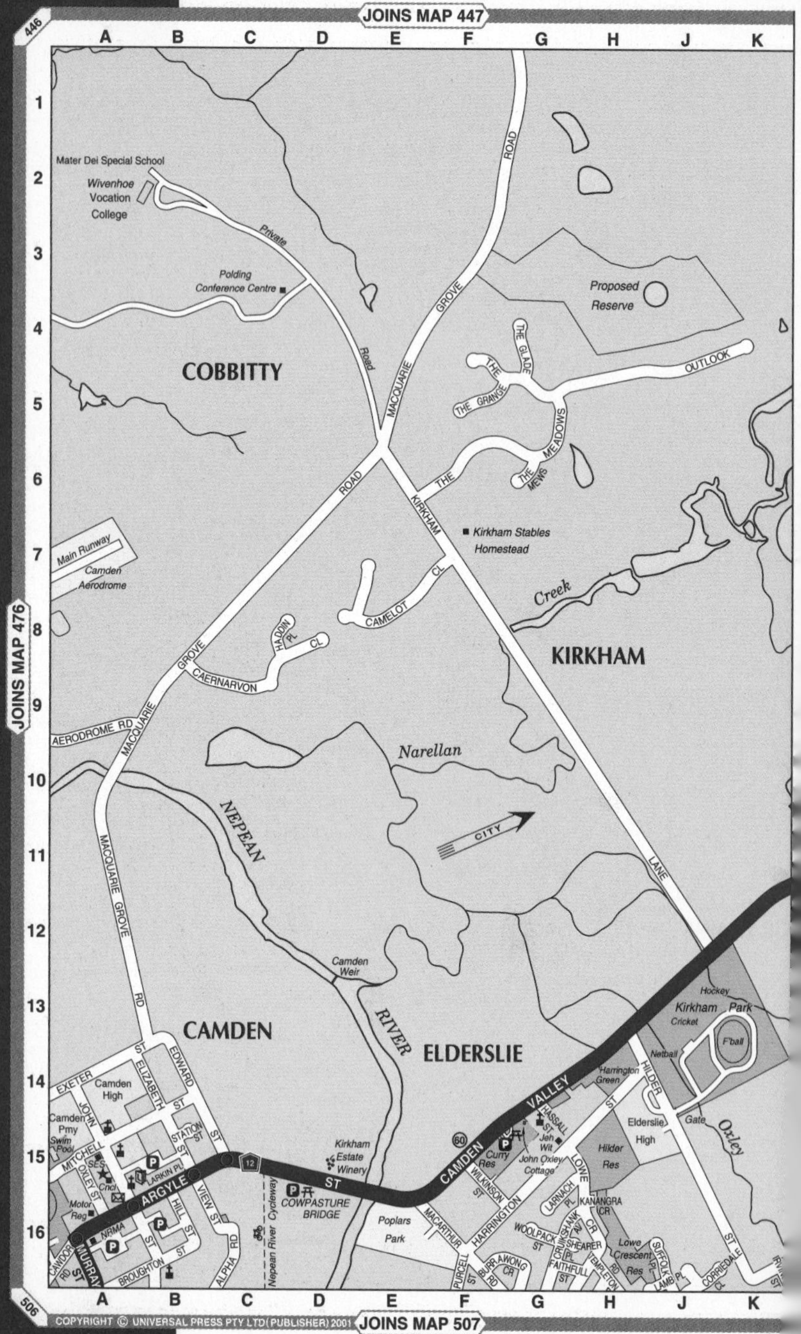
JOINS MAP 447
JOINS MAP 476
JOINS MAP 507
446
506
COBBITTY
KIRKHAM
CAMDEN
ELDERSLIE
Mater Dei Special School
Wivenhoe Vocation College
Private Road
Polding Conference Centre
MACQUARIE GROVE ROAD
Proposed Reserve
THE GLADE
THE GRANGE
OUTLOOK
THE MEADOWS
THE MEWS
KIRKHAM LANE
Kirkham Stables Homestead
Main Runway
Camden Aerodrome
CAMELOT CL
HADDIN PL
CAERNARVON CL
Creek
AERODROME RD
MACQUARIE GROVE RD
Narellan
NEPEAN RIVER
CITY
Camden Weir
Hockey
Kirkham Park
Cricket
F'ball
Netball
Harrington Green
HILDER ST
Gate
Oxley
Elderslie High
Hilder Res
CAMDEN VALLEY
HASSALL ST
Jeh Wit
John Oxley Cottage
Curry Res
WILKINSON ST
HARRINGTON
LOWE
LARNACH PL
KANANGRA CR
WOOLPACK ST
CRUIKSHANK AV
SHEARER PL
FAITHFULL ST
TEMPLETON RD
Lowe Crescent Res
SUFFOLK PL
LAMB PL
CORRIEDALE CL
BURRAWONG CR
PURCELL ST
MACARTHUR RD
Poplars Park
Kirkham Estate Winery
ARGYLE ST
COWPASTURE BRIDGE
Nepean River Cycleway
ALPHA RD
VIEW ST
HILL ST
BROUGHTON ST
NRMA
Motor Reg
Cncl
SES
LARKIN PL
STATION ST
OXLEY ST
MITCHELL
Camden Pmy
Swim Pool
JOHN
EXETER
Camden High
ELIZABETH ST
EDWARD
CAWDOR RD
MURRAY ST

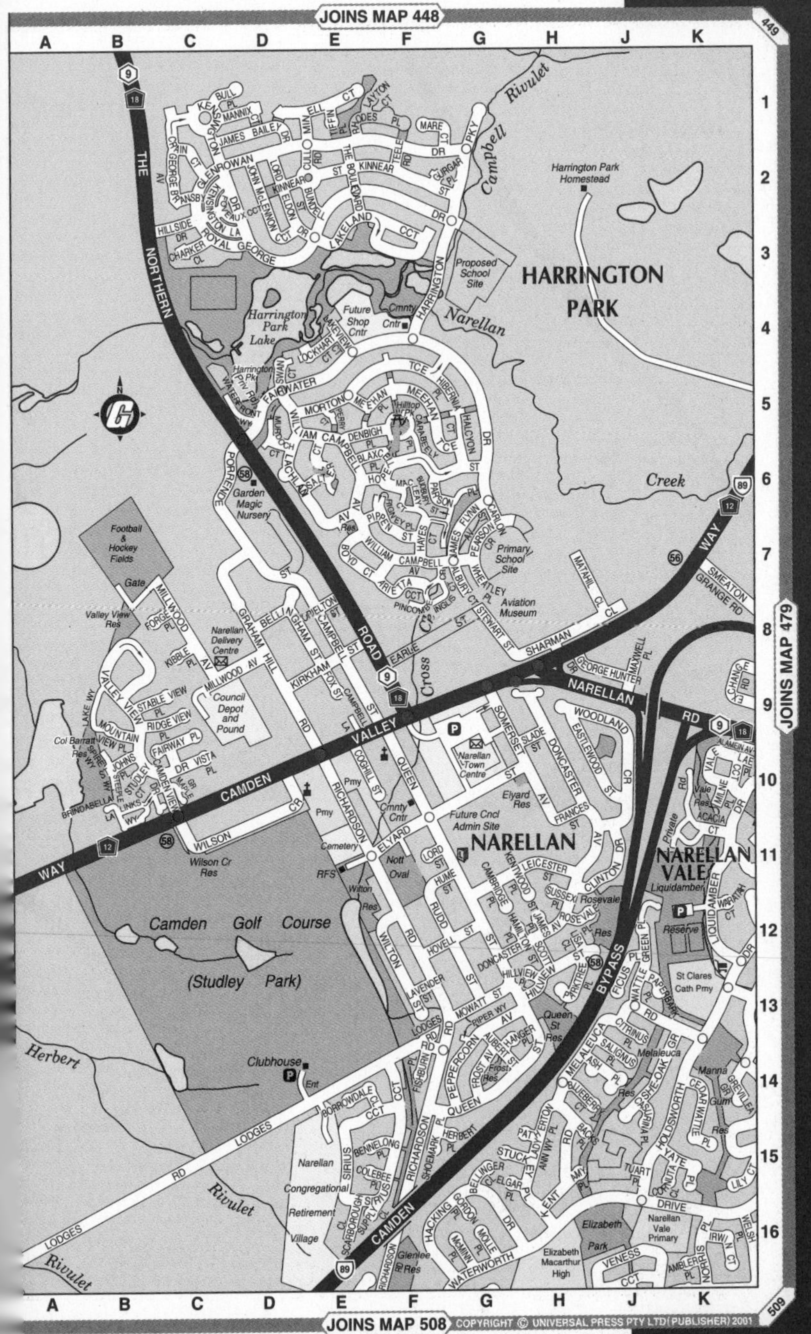
JOINS MAP 448
JOINS MAP 479
JOINS MAP 508
449
509
HARRINGTON PARK
NARELLAN
NARELLAN VALE
Harrington Park Homestead
Proposed School Site
Harrington Park Lake
Future Shop Cntr
Cmnty Cntr
Campbell Rivulet
Narellan Creek
Cross Creek
THE NORTHERN ROAD
CAMDEN VALLEY WAY
NARELLAN RD
CAMDEN BYPASS
LODGES RD
Garden Magic Nursery
Football & Hockey Fields
Valley View Res
Narellan Delivery Centre
Council Depot and Pound
Col Barratt Res
Wilson Cr Res
Camden Golf Course
(Studley Park)
Clubhouse
Herbert Rivulet
Narellan Town Centre
Elyard Res
Future Cncl Admin Site
Cemetery
RFS
Nott Oval
Witton Res
Primary School Site
Aviation Museum
Queen St Res
St Clares Cath Pmy
Liquidamber Reserve
Narellan Congregational Retirement Village
Glenlee Res
Elizabeth Park
Elizabeth Macarthur High
Narellan Vale Primary
Manna Gum Res
Rosevale Res
Vale Res
Melaleuca Res
COPYRIGHT © UNIVERSAL PRESS PTY LTD (PUBLISHER) 2001

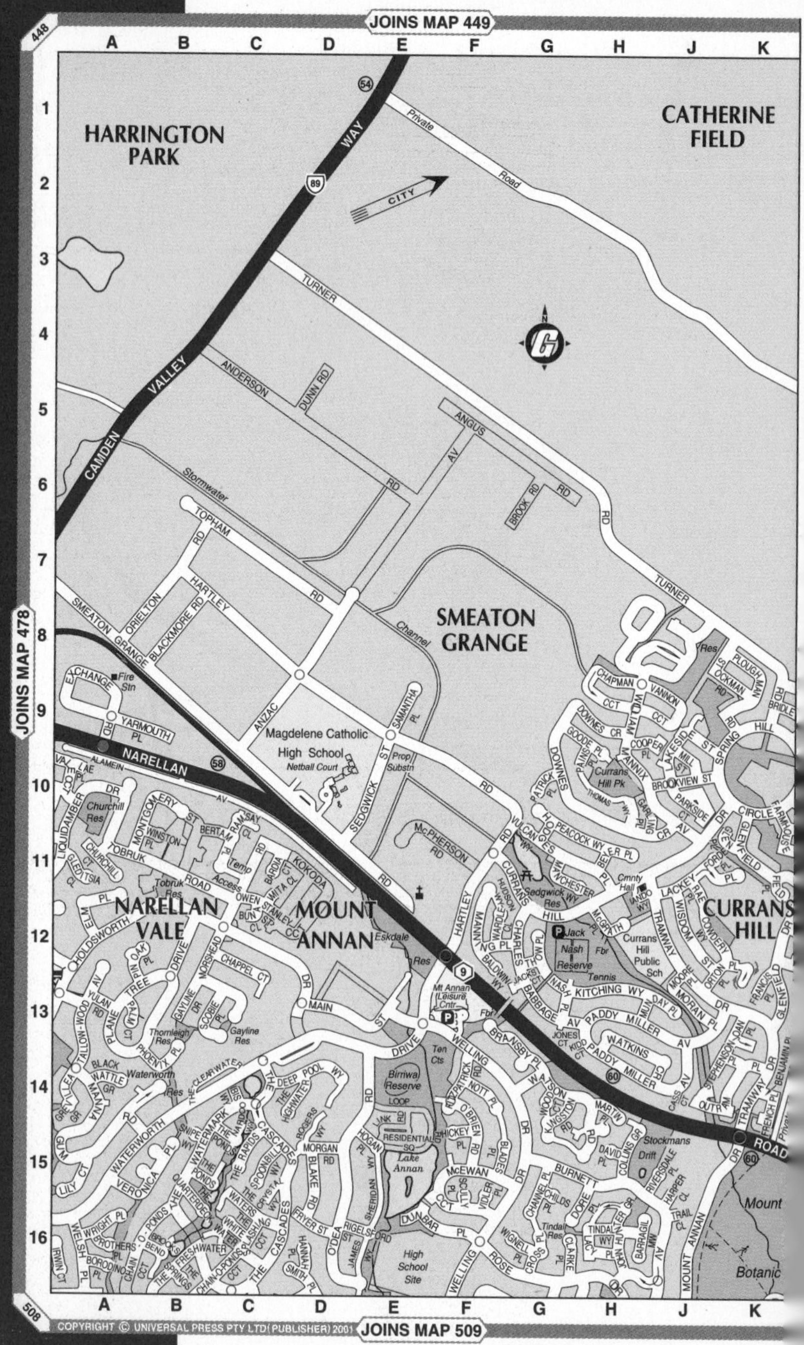
JOINS MAP 449
JOINS MAP 478
JOINS MAP 509
448
508
HARRINGTON PARK
CATHERINE FIELD
SMEATON GRANGE
NARELLAN VALE
MOUNT ANNAN
CURRANS HILL
CAMDEN VALLEY WAY
Private Road
CITY
TURNER RD
ANDERSON RD
DUNN RD
ANGUS AV
BROOK RD
Stormwater Channel
TOPHAM RD
HARTLEY RD
ORIELTON RD
BLACKMORE RD
SMEATON GRANGE RD
ANZAC
SAMANTHA PL
SEDGWICK ST
Prop Substn
McPHERSON RD
Magdelene Catholic High School
Netball Court
EXCHANGE
Fire Stn
YARMOUTH PL
NARELLAN RD
ALAMEIN AV
Churchill Res
MONTGOMERY ST
WINSTON PL
TOBRUK ROAD
Tobruk Res
CHURCHILL
LIQUIDAMBER
GLEDITSIA CL
BERTAM PL
RAMSAY CL
Temp Access
BARDIA CT
KOKODA
MITA CL
OWEN STANLEY CC
BUN ST
HOLDSWORTH
ELM
DRIVE
MORSHEAD
CHAPPEL CT
Eskdale Res
MAIN ST
DRIVE
Mt Annan Leisure Cntr
Fbr
HARTLEY
Thornleigh Res
Gayline Res
GAYLINE DR
SCOBIE PL
PHOENIX PL
PLANE TREE
PALM CT
PIN OAK PL
YULAN RD
TALLOW-WOOD
BLACK WATTLE GR
Waterworth Res
THE CLEARWATER
THE DEEP POOL WY
THE HIGHWATER
THE CASCADES
WATERWORTH
VERONICA
LILY CT
GUM
GREVILLEA GR
MANNA
WELSH PL
WRIGHT PL
BROTHERS BEND
BORODINO
IRWIN CT
CHAIN-O-PONDS
THE FRESHWATER
THE SPRINGS
BROOKS
THE WATERMARK
THE PONDS
THE RAPIDS
THE SPOONBILL WY
THE CRYSTAL WY
ROGERS WY
MORGAN RD
BLAKE RD
FRYER ST
HANNAH PL
SMITH PL
O'DEA
JAMES
RIGELSFORD
SHERIDAN WY
HOGAN PL
Birriwa Reserve
LOOP
LINK RD
RESIDENTIAL SQ
Lake Annan
Ten Cts
WELLING
FITZPATRICK RD
NOTT PL
O'BRIEN RD
HICKEY PL
McEWAN
SCULLY PL
VIDLER PL
BLADES
DUNBAR PL
CCT
High School Site
ROSE
WELLING
BRANSBY PL
WATSON
WOODS CL
KINGSTON RD
MARTIN RD
DAVID PL
COLLINS GR
Stockmans Drift
BURNETT
CHANNEL PL
CHILDS PL
DORE PL
Tindall Res
CLARKE
WIGNELL PL
CROSS PL
TINDAL WY
LACY PL
HUNTER GR
BARRAGIL
RIVERSDALE PL
HARPER CL
TRAIL CL
MOUNT ANNAN
Mount Annan Botanic
ROAD
VULCAN WY
HODGES PL
CURRANS
HUDSON WY
MANNING PL
WARDLE CL
CHARLES
Sedgwick Res
MANCHESTER WY
HILL
Jack Nash Reserve
Tennis
Fbr
McGRATH PL
Currans Hill Public Sch
THOW PL
BALDWIN WY
JACKSON
BABBAGE
NASH
KITCHING WY
PADDY MILLER AV
PADDY MILLER CR
JONES CT
KIDD CT
WATKINS CR
DAY PL
MUN PL
CASS AV
MORAN PL
MOORE PL
TRAMWAY
WISDOM
LACKEY
RAE PL
COWDERY WY
ORTON
FORDE PL
GLENFIELD
FARMHOUSE
CIRCLE
STEPHENSON
OUTRAM
FRENCH PL
BENJAMIN PL
FRANCIS PL
Cmnty Hall
IANDO WY
PEACOCK WY
BEER PL
PATRICK PL
DOWNES
DOWNES CR
GOODE PL
PAINS PL
Currans Hill Pk
THOMAS WY
GARLING PL
CR
AV
BROOKVIEW ST
PARKSIDE CT
LAKESIDE
MILL ST
COOPER PL
MANNIX
WILLIAM
CHAPMAN CCT
VANNON CCT
Res
COCKMAN RD
PLOUGHMAN
BRIDLE
SPRING HILL
RD
COPYRIGHT © UNIVERSAL PRESS PTY LTD (PUBLISHER) 2001

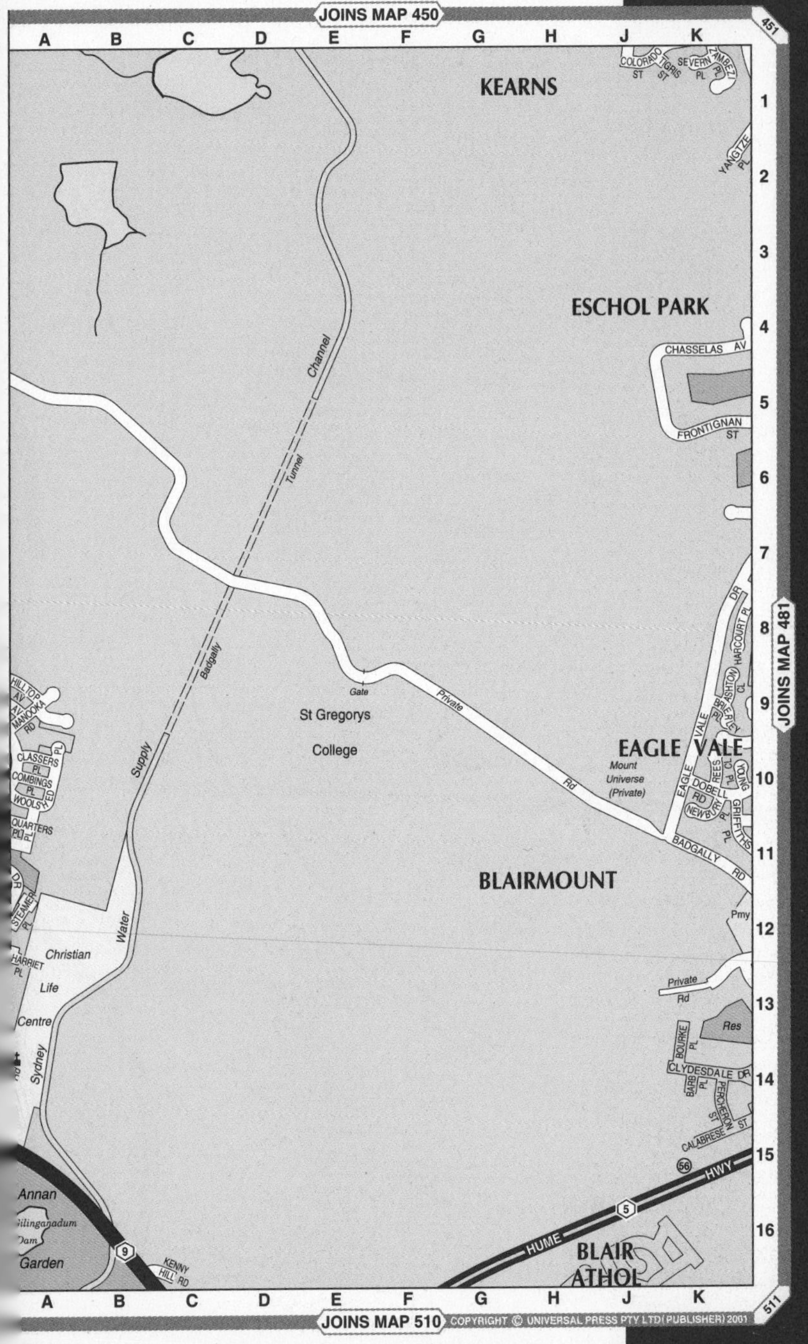

JOINS MAP 450
JOINS MAP 481
JOINS MAP 510
451
511
KEARNS
ESCHOL PARK
EAGLE VALE
BLAIRMOUNT
BLAIR ATHOL
St Gregorys College
Mount Universe (Private)
Christian Life Centre
Annan Gilinganadum Dam Garden
Supply Badgally Tunnel Channel
Water Supply
Sydney
Private Rd
Gate
Pmy
Res
HUME HWY
COLORADO ST
TIGRIS ST
SEVERN PL
ZAMBEZI PL
YANGTZE PL
CHASSELAS AV
FRONTIGNAN ST
BADGALLY RD
EAGLE VALE DR
HARCOURT PL
ASHTON CL
BRIERLEY
DOBELL RD
NEWBURY PL
GRIFFITHS PL
REES
YOUNG
BOURKE PL
CLYDESDALE DR
BARB PL
PERCHERON ST
CALABRESE ST
HILLTOP AV
MANOOKA RD
CLASSERS PL
COMBINGS PL
WOOLSHED
QUARTERS PL
STEAMER PL
HARRIET PL
KENNY HILL RD

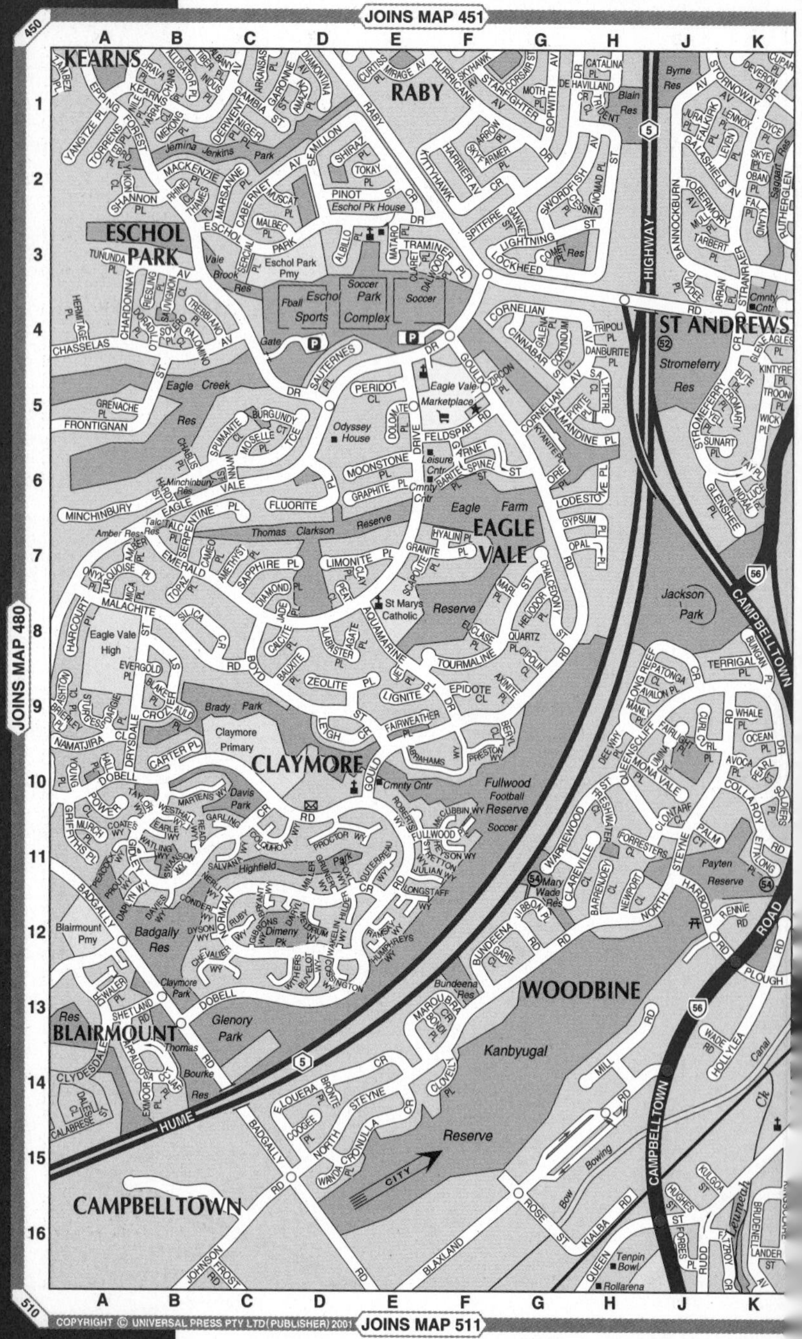
JOINS MAP 451
JOINS MAP 480
JOINS MAP 511
450
510
A B C D E F G H J K
1 2 3 4 5 6 7 8 9 10 11 12 13 14 15 16
KEARNS
RABY
ESCHOL PARK
ST ANDREWS
EAGLE VALE
CLAYMORE
WOODBINE
BLAIRMOUNT
CAMPBELLTOWN
Jemima Jenkins Park
Eschol Pk House
Eschol Park Pmy
Vale Brook Res
Fball Eschol Sports
Soccer Park Complex
Soccer
Eagle Creek Res
Odyssey House
Eagle Vale Marketplace
Leisure Cntr
Cmnty Cntr
Eagle Farm Reserve
Thomas Clarkson Reserve
Minchinbury Res
Amber Res
Talc Res
St Marys Catholic
Reserve
Eagle Vale High
Brady Park
Claymore Primary
Cmnty Cntr
Davis Park
Highfield Park
Dimeny Pk
Fullwood Football Reserve
Soccer
Mary Wade Res
Blairmount Pmy
Badgally Res
Claymore Park
Glenory Park
Thomas Bourke Res
Bundeena Res
Kanbyugal Reserve
Byme Res
Blain Res
Stromeferry Res
Jackson Park
Payten Reserve
Tenpin Bowl
Rollarena
HUME HIGHWAY
CAMPBELLTOWN ROAD
CITY
Bow Bowing
Canal
Ck
Leumeah

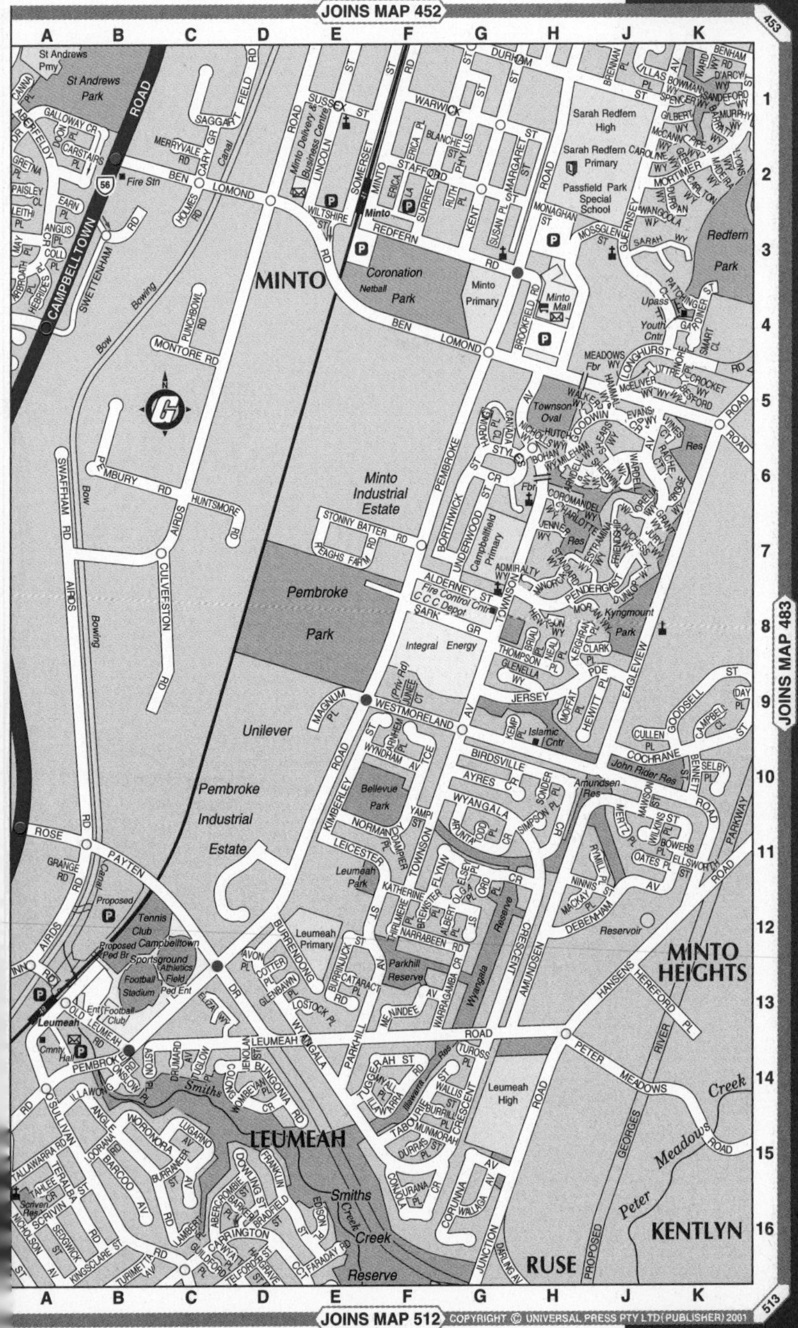
JOINS MAP 452
JOINS MAP 483
JOINS MAP 512
453
513
MINTO
MINTO HEIGHTS
LEUMEAH
KENTLYN
RUSE
St Andrews Park
St Andrews Pmy
Sarah Redfern High
Sarah Redfern Primary
Passfield Park Special School
Redfern Park
Coronation Park
Minto Primary
Minto Mall
Minto Industrial Estate
Pembroke Park
Unilever
Pembroke Industrial Estate
Integral Energy
Townson Oval
Campbellfield Primary
Kyngmount Park
Islamic Cntr
John Rider Res
Bellevue Park
Leumeah Park
Leumeah Primary
Parkhill Reserve
Wyangala Reserve
Reservoir
Leumeah High
Tennis Club
Campbelltown Sportsground
Football Stadium
Athletics Field
Smiths Creek
Smiths Creek Reserve
Peter Meadows Creek
Fire Stn
Fire Control Cntr
C C C Depot
Minto Delivery & Business Centre
Youth Cntr
Upass
CAMPBELLTOWN ROAD
BEN LOMOND RD
PEMBROKE RD
WESTMORELAND AV
LEUMEAH RD
PETER MEADOWS RD
GEORGES RIVER PARKWAY
AIRDS RD
PAYTEN AV
ROSE
Bow Bowing Canal
Minto
Leumeah
56

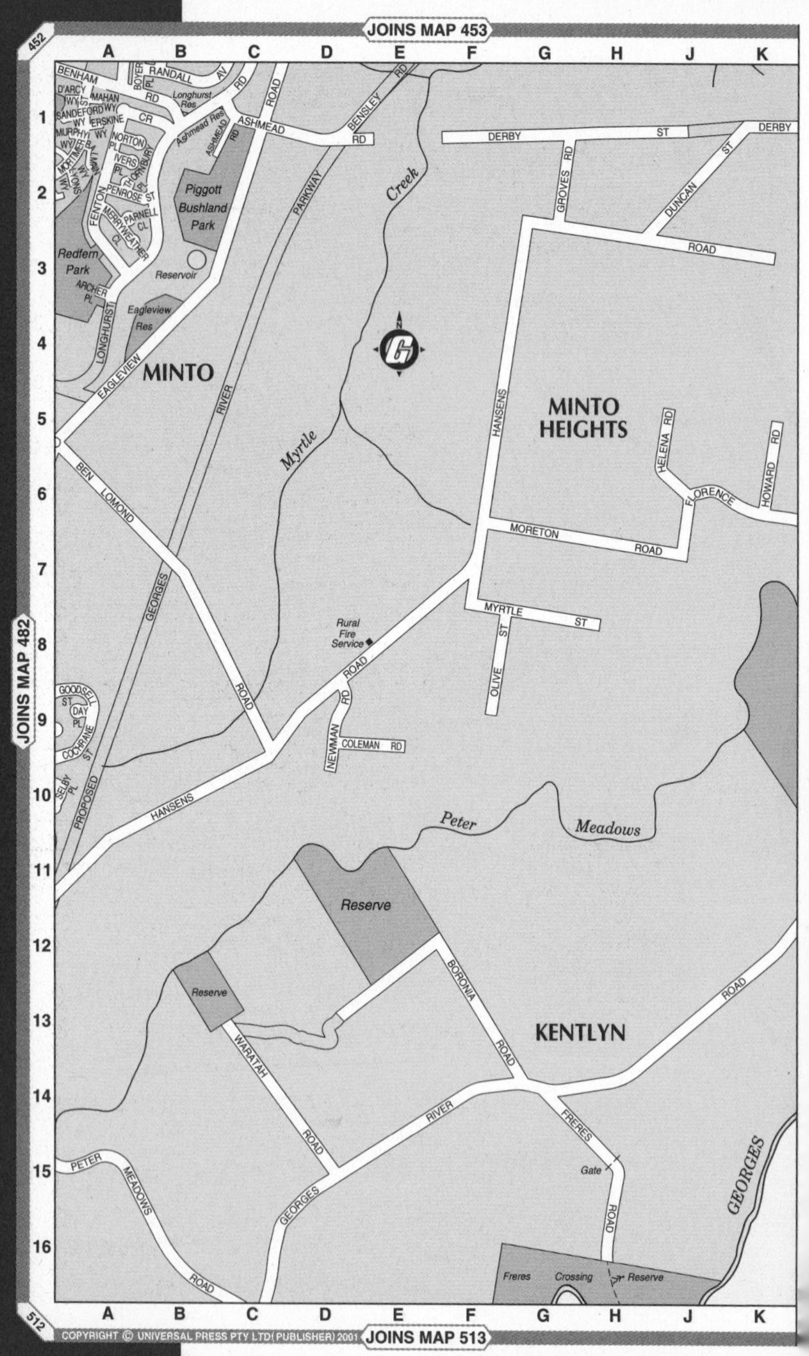
JOINS MAP 453
JOINS MAP 482
JOINS MAP 513
452
512
A B C D E F G H J K
1 2 3 4 5 6 7 8 9 10 11 12 13 14 15 16
MINTO
MINTO HEIGHTS
KENTLYN
Piggott Bushland Park
Redfern Park
Reservoir
Eagleview Res
Longhurst Res
Ashmead Res
Reserve
Freres Crossing Reserve
Rural Fire Service
Gate
Myrtle Creek
Peter Meadows
GEORGES
BENHAM
RANDALL AV
BOYER PL
D'ARCY WY
MAHAN WY
SANDEFORD WY
ERSKINE CR
MURPHY WY
MORTIMER
NORTON PL
IVERS PL
THORNBURY
PENROSE ST
FENTON
MERRYWEATHER CL
PARNELL CL
ARCHER PL
LONGHURST RD
ASHMEAD RD
BENSLEY RD
PARKWAY
RIVER ROAD
EAGLEVIEW RD
BEN LOMOND ROAD
GEORGES RIVER ROAD
DERBY ST
DERBY
GROVES RD
DUNCAN ST
ROAD
HANSENS ROAD
HELENA RD
FLORENCE
HOWARD RD
MORETON ROAD
MYRTLE ST
OLIVE ST
NEWMAN RD
COLEMAN RD
GOODSELL ST
DAY PL
COCHRANE ST
SELBY PL
PROPOSED
HANSENS
BORONIA ROAD
WARATAH ROAD
FRERES ROAD
PETER MEADOWS ROAD

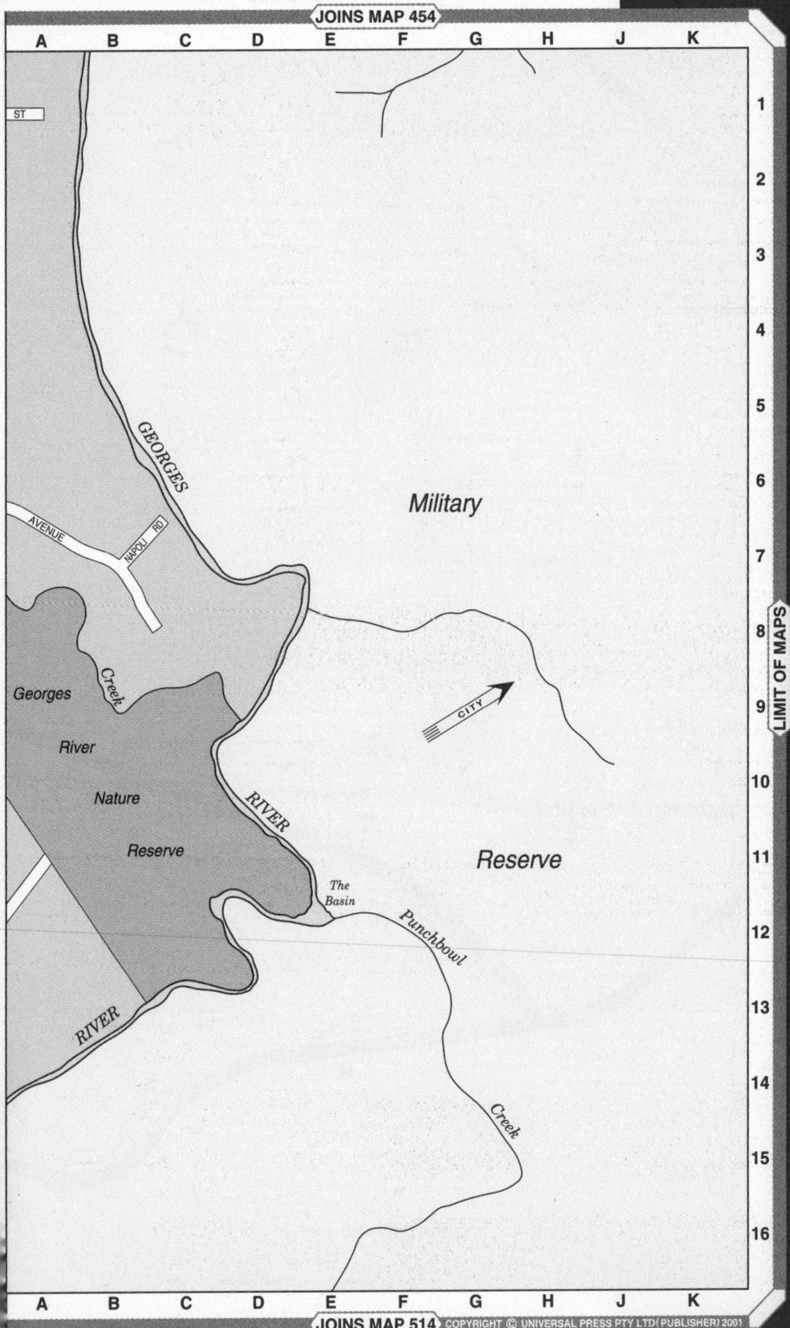
JOINS MAP 454
A B C D E F G H J K
1 2 3 4 5 6 7 8 9 10 11 12 13 14 15 16
ST
GEORGES
AVENUE
NAPOLI RD
Military
Creek
Georges
River
Nature
Reserve
CITY
RIVER
Reserve
The
Basin
Punchbowl
RIVER
Creek
LIMIT OF MAPS
JOINS MAP 514

JOINS MAP 457

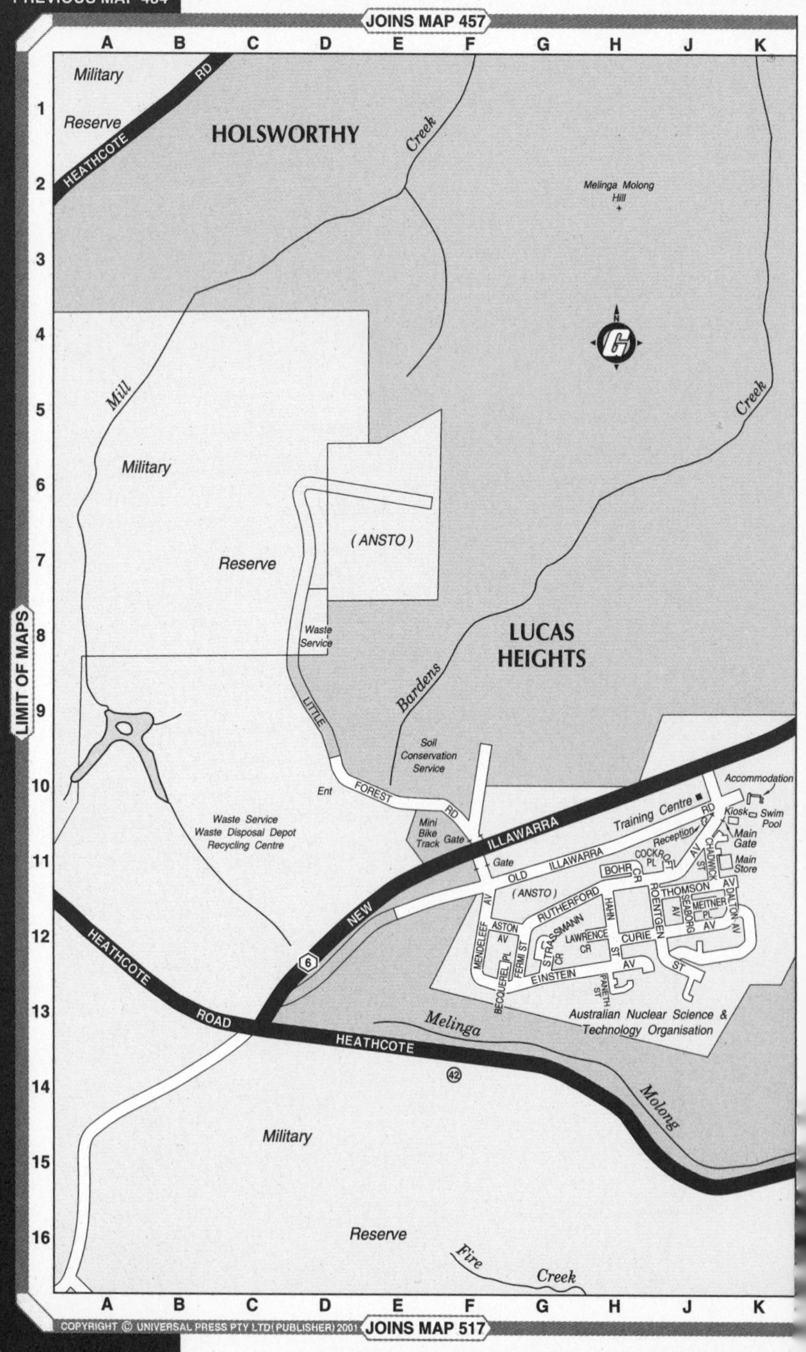

JOINS MAP 517

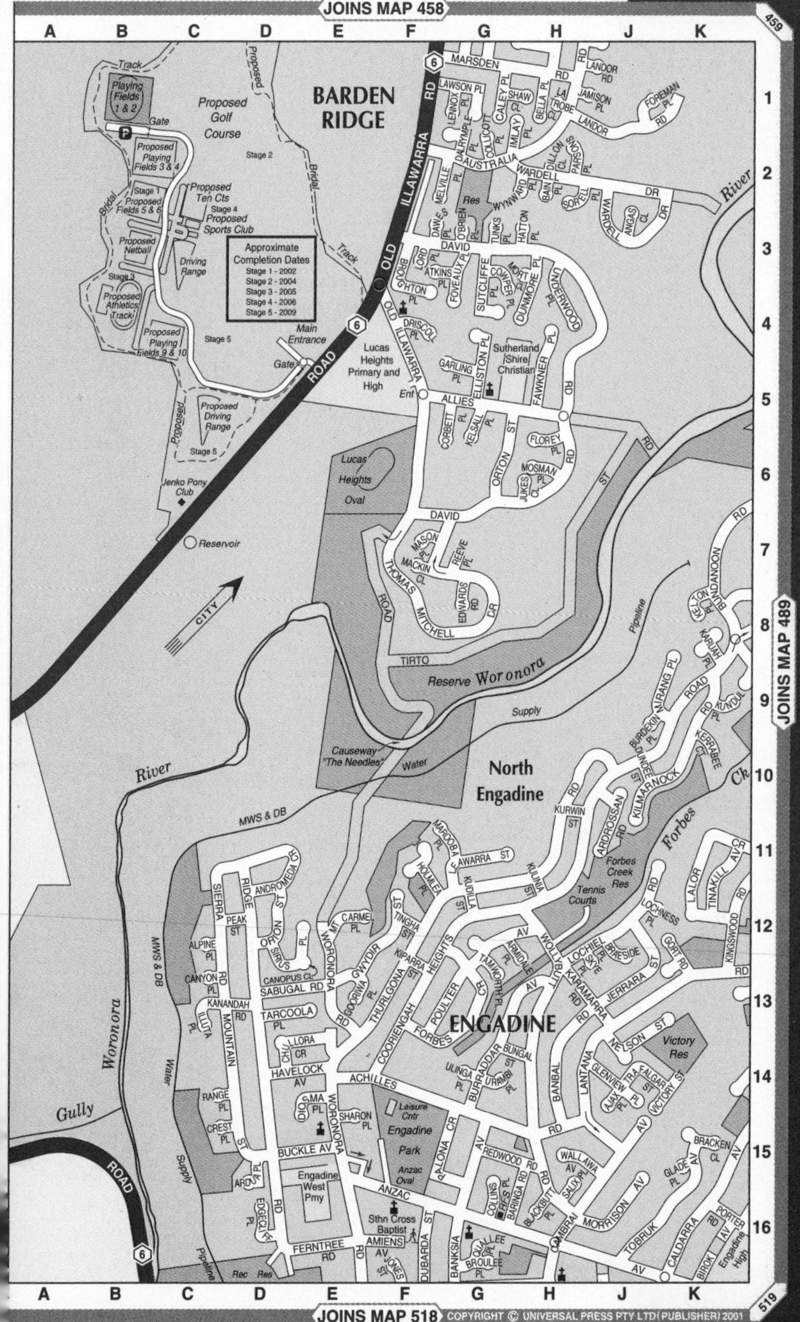
JOINS MAP 458
JOINS MAP 489
JOINS MAP 518
459
519
A B C D E F G H J K
1 2 3 4 5 6 7 8 9 10 11 12 13 14 15 16
BARDEN RIDGE
North Engadine
ENGADINE
Proposed Golf Course
Playing Fields 1 & 2
Proposed Playing Fields 3 & 4
Proposed Playing Fields 5 & 6
Proposed Ten Cts
Proposed Sports Club
Proposed Netball
Driving Range
Proposed Athletics Track
Proposed Playing Fields 9 & 10
Proposed Driving Range
Approximate Completion Dates
Stage 1 - 2002
Stage 2 - 2004
Stage 3 - 2005
Stage 4 - 2006
Stage 5 - 2009
Main Entrance
Gate
Lucas Heights Primary and High
Lucas Heights Oval
Sutherland Shire Christian
Jenko Pony Club
Reservoir
CITY
OLD ILLAWARRA RD
ROAD
Reserve Woronora
Causeway "The Needles"
Supply Water
MWS & DB
River
Woronora River
Gully
Forbes Creek Res
Tennis Courts
Victory Res
Leisure Cntr
Engadine Park
Anzac Oval
Engadine West Pmy
Sthn Cross Baptist
Engadine High
Rec Res

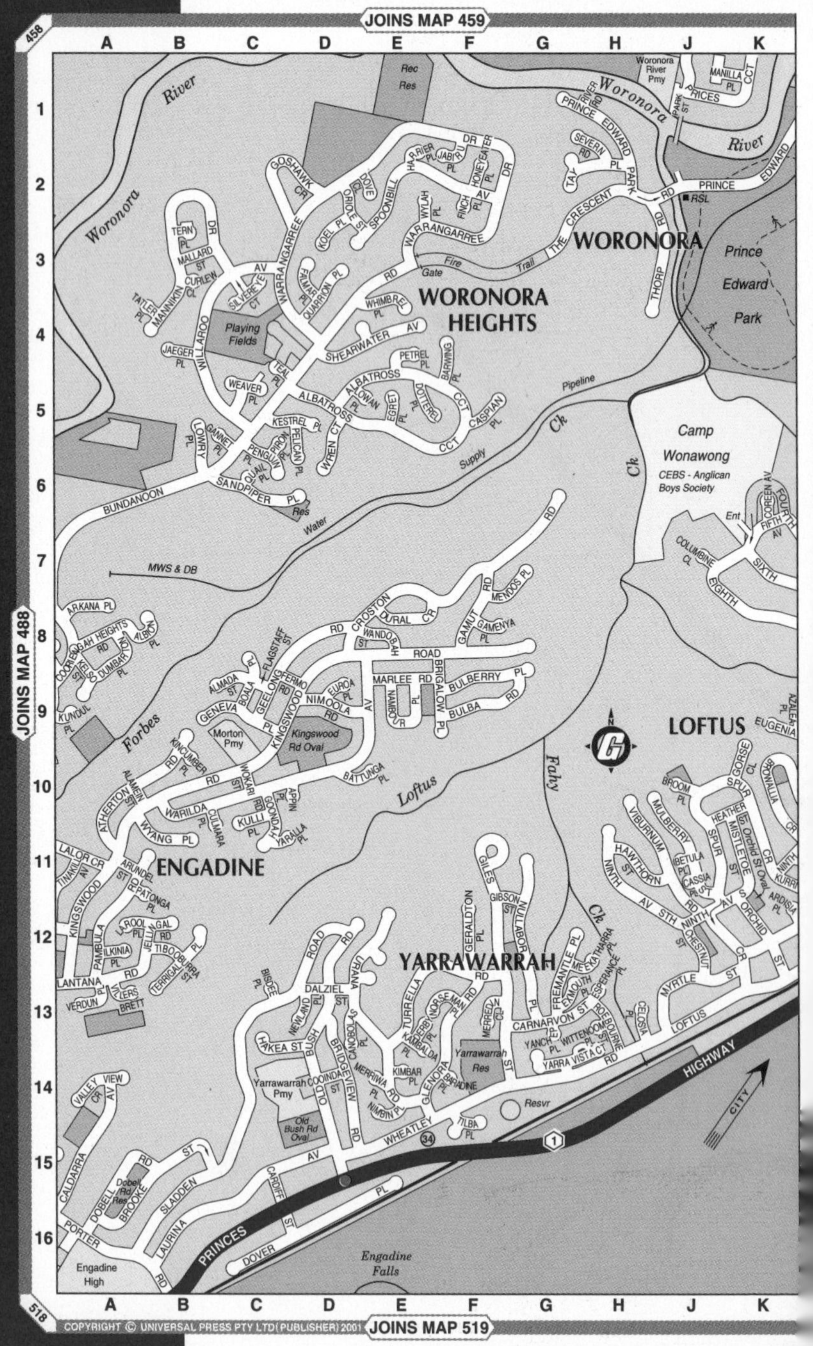

JOINS MAP 459
JOINS MAP 488
JOINS MAP 519
458
518
A B C D E F G H J K
1 2 3 4 5 6 7 8 9 10 11 12 13 14 15 16
WORONORA
WORONORA HEIGHTS
ENGADINE
YARRAWARRAH
LOFTUS
Woronora River
Woronora River Pmy
Prince Edward Park
RSL
Rec Res
Playing Fields
Camp Wonawong
CEBS - Anglican Boys Society
Morton Pmy
Kingswood Rd Oval
Yarrawarrah Pmy
Old Bush Rd Oval
Yarrawarrah Res
Dobell Rd Res
Engadine High
Engadine Falls
Resvr
MWS & DB
Supply Water
Pipeline
Fire Trail
Gate
Forbes Ck
Loftus Ck
Fahy Ck
PRINCE EDWARD PARK RD
PRINCE EDWARD RD
PRINCES HIGHWAY
CITY
THE CRESCENT
WARRANGARREE DR
WARRANGARREE RD
BUNDANOON RD
WILLAROO AV
SHEARWATER AV
ALBATROSS AV
CROSTON RD
KINGSWOOD RD
ROAD
LOFTUS AV
WHEATLEY AV
BUSH ST
BRIDGEVIEW RD
CARNARVON ST
YARRA VISTA CT
MYRTLE ST
NINTH AV
ORCHID ST
MISTLETOE ST
GORSE CL
BROOM PL
SPUR
HEATHER ST
VIBURNUM
MULBERRY
HAWTHORN ST
CASSIA ST
BETULA PL
CHESTNUT
COLUMBINE CL
EIGHTH
SIXTH
FIFTH AV
FOURTH
COREEN AV
EUGENIA
AZALEA PL
ARDISIA PL
DOVER
CARDIFF ST
SLADDEN ST
LAURINA
BROOKE
DOBELL
PORTER
CALDARRA
VALLEY VIEW CR
VERDUN
BRETT
LANTANA
TIBOOBURRA ST
TERRIGAL
PAMBULA
KINGSWOOD
ATHERTON ST
ALAMEIN
WARILDA
WYANG PL
KULLI PL
GOONDAH RD
YARALLA
APPIN
BATTUNGA PL
NIMOOLA RD
GENEVA
GEELONG RD
FERMO
EUROA PL
ALMADA ST
FLAGSTAFF ST
WANDOBAH ST
MARLEE RD
NAMBOUR
BRIGALOW PL
BULBERRY PL
BULBA RD
GAMUT RD
GAMENYA PL
MENDOS PL
DURAL CR
KINCUMBER PL
WOKARI ST
CULMARA
ARKANA PL
ALBION
GIBSON ST
GILES
GERALDTON PL
NULLABOR PL
FREMANTLE PL
EXMOUTH
ESPERANCE
ROEBOURNE
WITTENOOM
CELOSIA
KATHARRA PL
YANCHEP
MERREDIN CL
TURRELLA
NORSEMAN
KAMBALDA
KIMBAR PL
GLENORA
BARADINE
MERRIWA
NIMBIN PL
TILBA PL
URANA
DALZIEL ST
NEWLAND
HAKEA ST
BISDEE PL
CANOBOLAS
COOINDA ST
OLD
GOSHAWK CR
DOVE
ORIOLE ST
KOEL PL
SPOONBILL
HARRIER PL
JABIRU PL
HONEYEATER PL
FINCH AV
WYLAH PL
FALMAR
QUARRION PL
WHIMBREL PL
PETREL PL
BARWING PL
ALOWAN PL
EGRET PL
DOTTEREL
CASPIAN PL
WREN CT
KESTREL PL
PELICAN PL
PIRON
PENGUIN
QUAIL PL
SANDPIPER PL
GANNET PL
LOWRY PL
WEAVER PL
TEAL
JAEGER PL
TERN PL
MALLARD ST
CURLEW CL
MANNIKIN
TATLER PL
SILVEREYE CT
SEVERN RD
TAY
THORP RD
RIVER RD
PRICES
MANILLA PL
CCT
PARK ST
Res
Ent
34
1

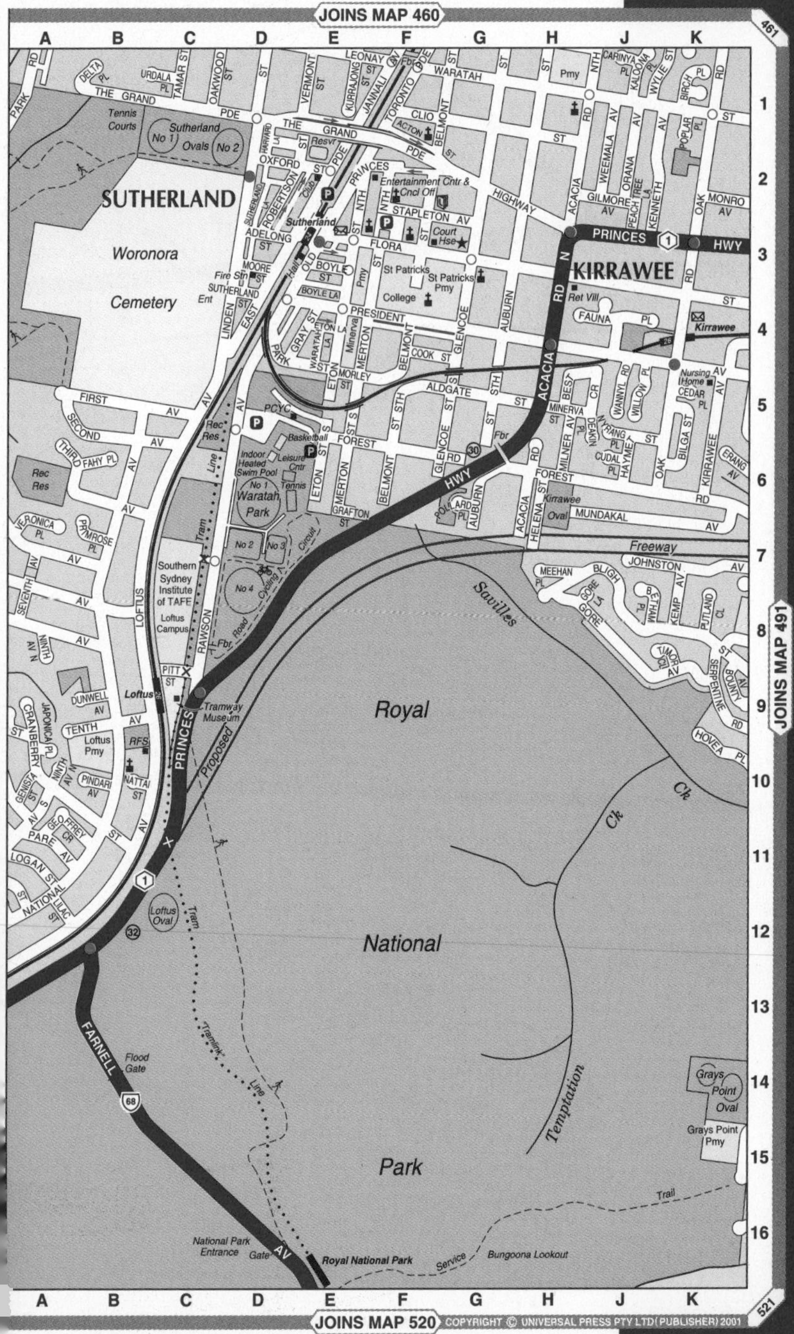

JOINS MAP 460
JOINS MAP 491
JOINS MAP 520
SUTHERLAND
KIRRAWEE
Woronora
Cemetery
Sutherland Ovals
Royal
National
Park
Southern Sydney Institute of TAFE
Loftus Campus
Tramway Museum
Waratah Park
St Patricks College
Entertainment Cntr & Cncl Off
Kirrawee Oval
Loftus Oval
Grays Point Oval
Grays Point Pmy
National Park Entrance
Royal National Park
Bungoona Lookout
Freeway
PRINCES HWY
FARNELL AV
Temptation
Savilles

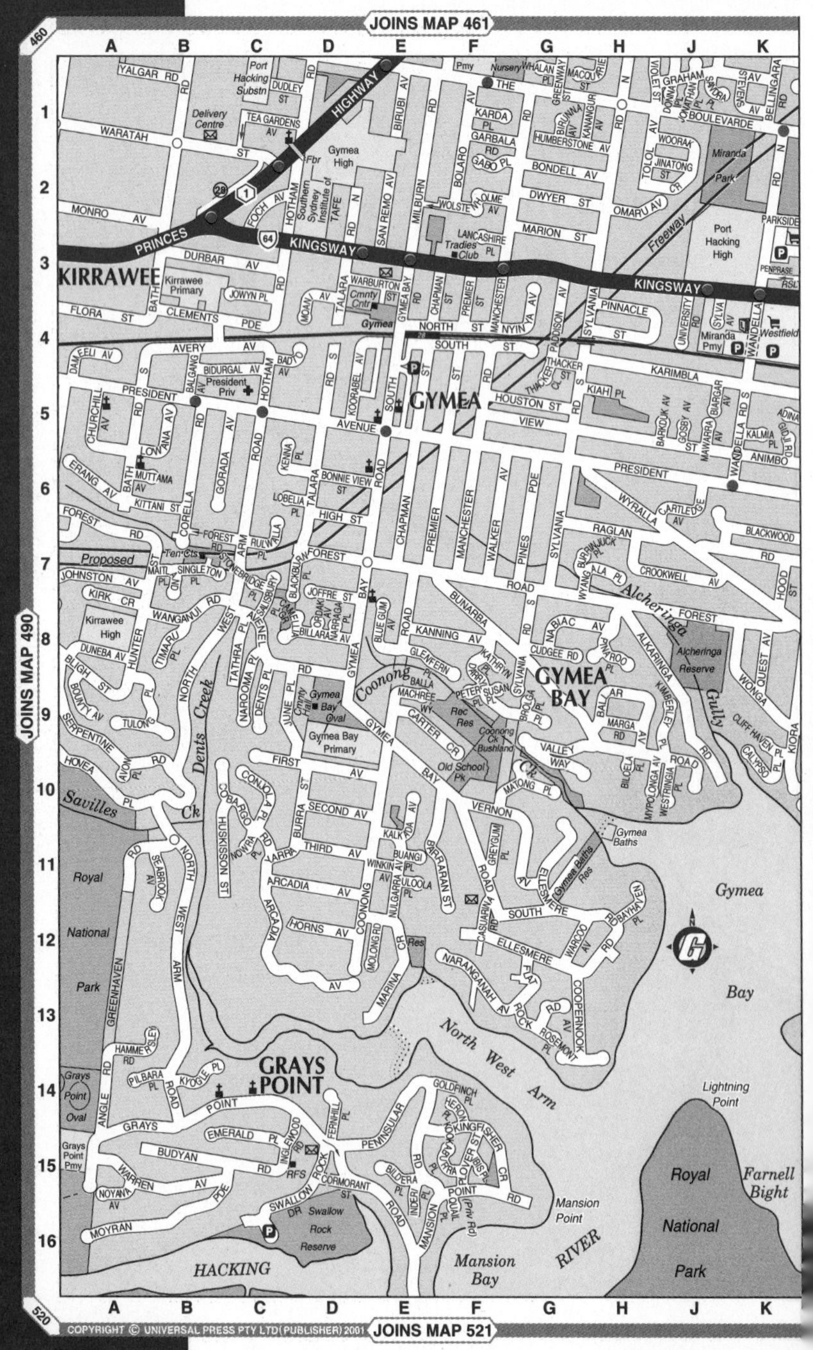
JOINS MAP 461
JOINS MAP 490
JOINS MAP 521
460
520
A B C D E F G H J K
1 2 3 4 5 6 7 8 9 10 11 12 13 14 15 16
KIRRAWEE
GYMEA
GYMEA BAY
GRAYS POINT
PRINCES HIGHWAY
KINGSWAY
Freeway
Port Hacking Substn
Delivery Centre
Gymea High
Southern Sydney Institute of TAFE
Tradies' Club
Kirrawee Primary
Cmnty Cntr
President Priv
Kirrawee High
Gymea Bay Oval
Gymea Bay Primary
Rec Res
Coonong Ck Bushland
Old School Pk
Miranda Park
Port Hacking High
Miranda Pmy
Westfield
Alcheringa Reserve
Alcheringa Gully
Gymea Baths
Gymea Baths Res
Gymea Bay
Savilles Ck
Dents Creek
Coonong Ck
Royal National Park
Grays Point Oval
Grays Point Pmy
Swallow Rock Reserve
North West Arm
Lightning Point
Farnell Bight
Mansion Point
Mansion Bay
HACKING RIVER
YALGAR RD
WARATAH ST
MONRO AV
DURBAR AV
FLORA ST
CLEMENTS PDE
AVERY AV
PRESIDENT AV
FOREST RD
JOHNSTON AV
KIRK CR
WANGANUI RD
HUNTER
NORTH WEST ARM RD
HOTHAM RD
GYMEA BAY RD
KINGSWAY
NORTH ST
SOUTH ST
HOUSTON ST
VIEW ST
RAGLAN RD
CROOKWELL AV
BUNARBA RD
KANNING AV
GLENFERN PL
VALLEY WAY
VERNON
FIRST AV
SECOND AV
THIRD AV
ARCADIA AV
HORNS AV
ELLESMERE RD
SOUTH
NARANGANAH AV
ROCK FLAT
ROSEMONT PL
COOPERNOOK AV
GREENHAVEN
GRAYS POINT RD
EMERALD PL
BUDYAN RD
WARREN AV
MOYRAN
PENINSULAR RD
KINGFISHER CR
POINT RD
CORMORANT
SWALLOW DR
BOULEVARDE
KARIMBLA
WYRALLA
PRESIDENT
FOREST
ANIMBO
BLACKWOOD
WONGA
CLIFF HAVEN PL
KIORA
COPYRIGHT © UNIVERSAL PRESS PTY LTD (PUBLISHER) 2001

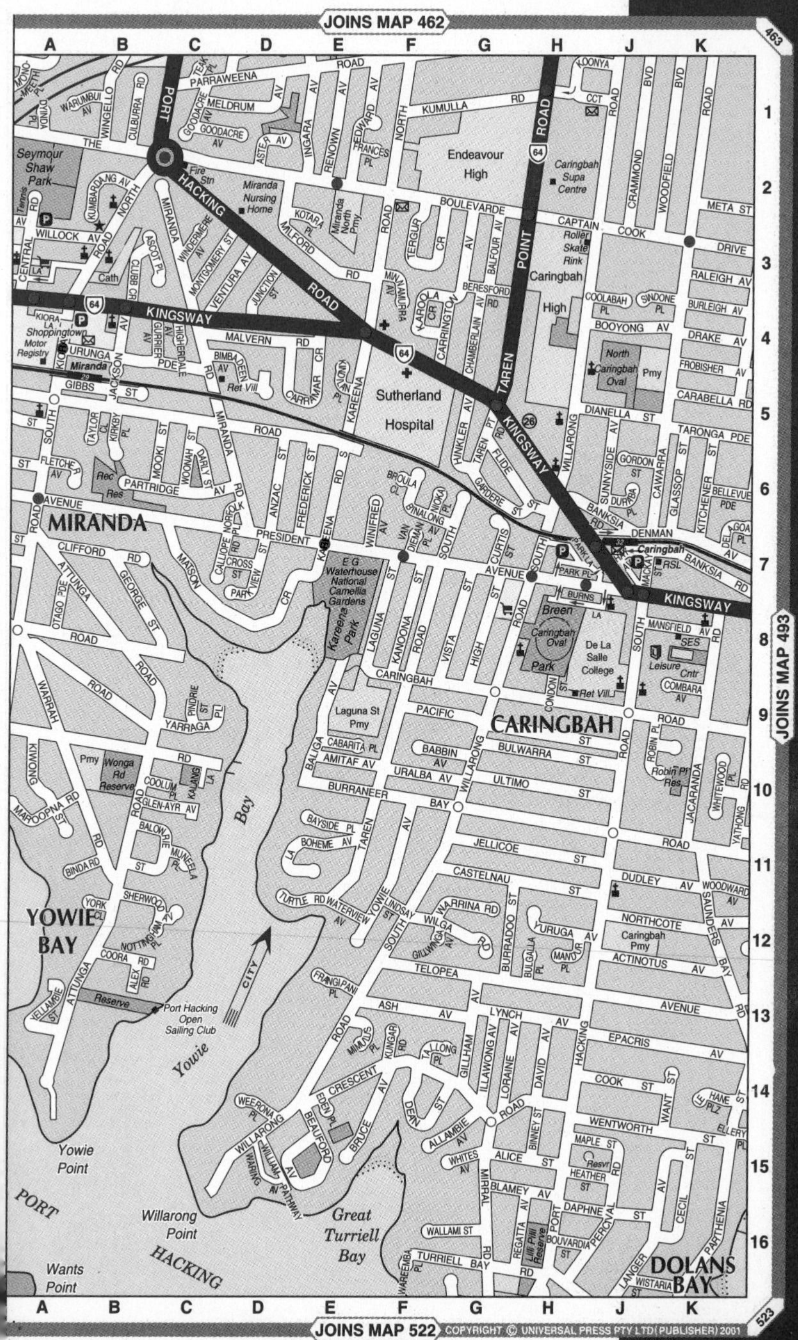

JOINS MAP 462
JOINS MAP 493
JOINS MAP 522
MIRANDA
CARINGBAH
YOWIE BAY
DOLANS BAY
Sutherland Hospital
Endeavour High
Caringbah High
E G Waterhouse National Camellia Gardens
Kareena Park
De La Salle College
Yowie Bay
Port Hacking
Great Turriell Bay
Yowie Point
Willarong Point
Wants Point
Port Hacking Open Sailing Club
Seymour Shaw Park
KINGSWAY
PORT HACKING ROAD
TAREN POINT ROAD

JOINS MAP 463

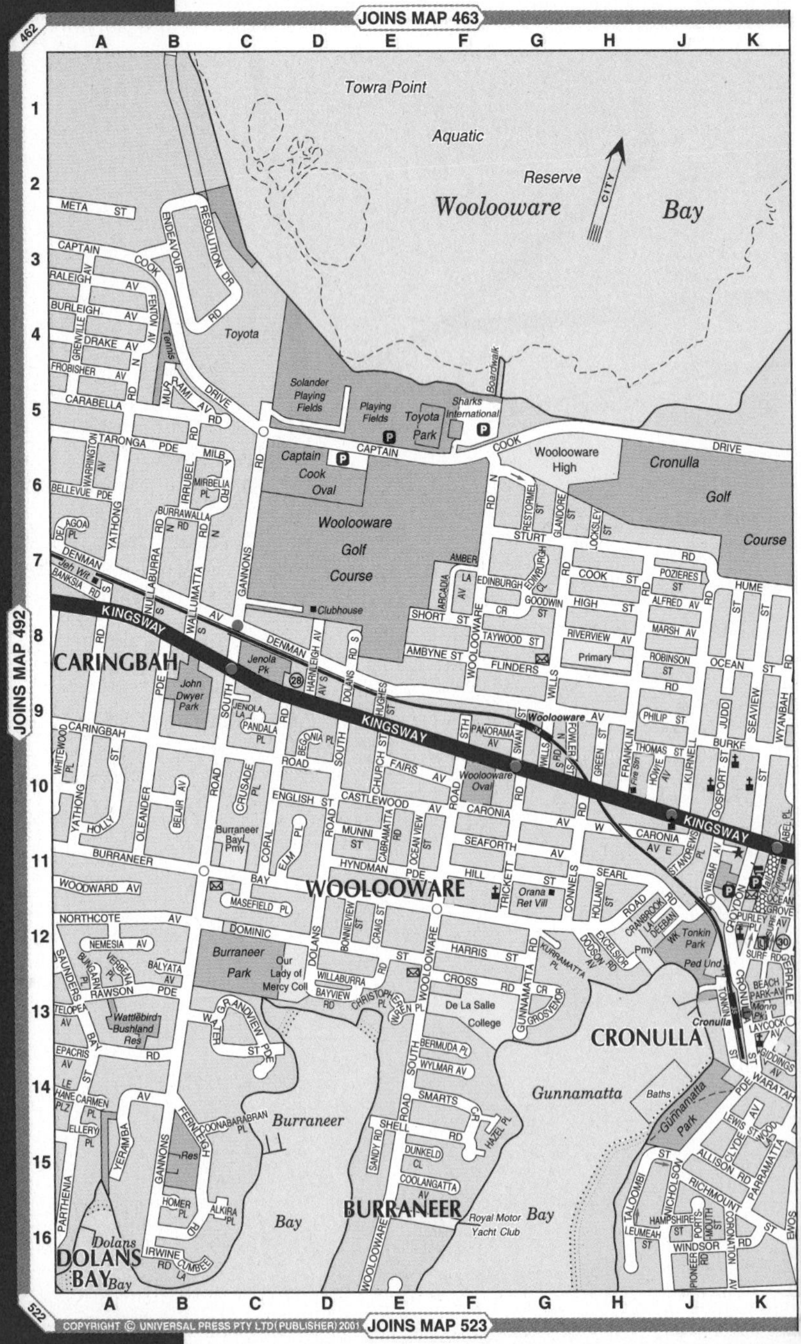

JOINS MAP 492

JOINS MAP 523

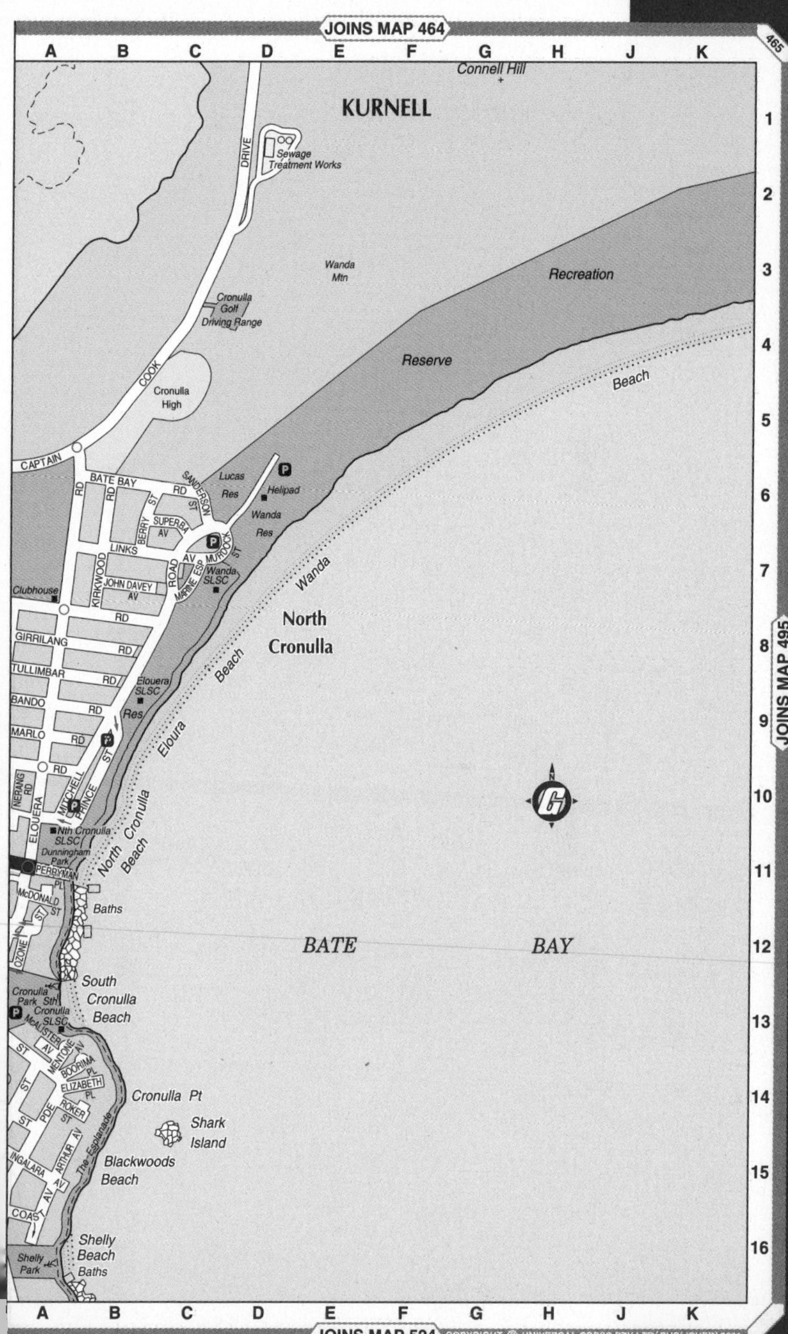
JOINS MAP 464
465
A B C D E F G H J K
Connell Hill
KURNELL
DRIVE
Sewage
Treatment Works
Wanda
Mtn
Recreation
Cronulla
Golf
Driving Range
Reserve
COOK
Cronulla
High
Beach
CAPTAIN
BATE BAY
RD
SANDERSON
ST
Lucas
Res
Helipad
Wanda
Res
BERRY ST
SUPERBA AV
LINKS
KIRKWOOD
MURDOCK ST
MARINE ESP
ROAD
AV
Wanda
SLSC
Wanda
Clubhouse
JOHN DAVEY AV
North
Cronulla
GIRRILANG RD
TULLIMBAR RD
Beach
Elouera
SLSC
BANDO RD
Res
MARLO RD
Eloura
NERANG RD
MITCHELL
PRINCE ST
ELOUERA
North Cronulla Beach
Nth Cronulla SLSC
Dunningham Park
PERRYMAN PL
McDONALD ST
Baths
OZONE
BATE
BAY
South
Cronulla
Beach
Cronulla Park Sth
Cronulla SLSC
McALISTER AV
MENTONE AV
BOORIMA PL
ELIZABETH PL
ROKER ST
Cronulla Pt
Shark
Island
PDE
ST
ARTHUR AV
The Esplanade
Blackwoods
Beach
INGALARA AV
COAST
Shelly
Beach
Baths
Shelly
Park
1 2 3 4 5 6 7 8 9 10 11 12 13 14 15 16
JOINS MAP 495
A B C D E F G H J K
JOINS MAP 524

MAP 495

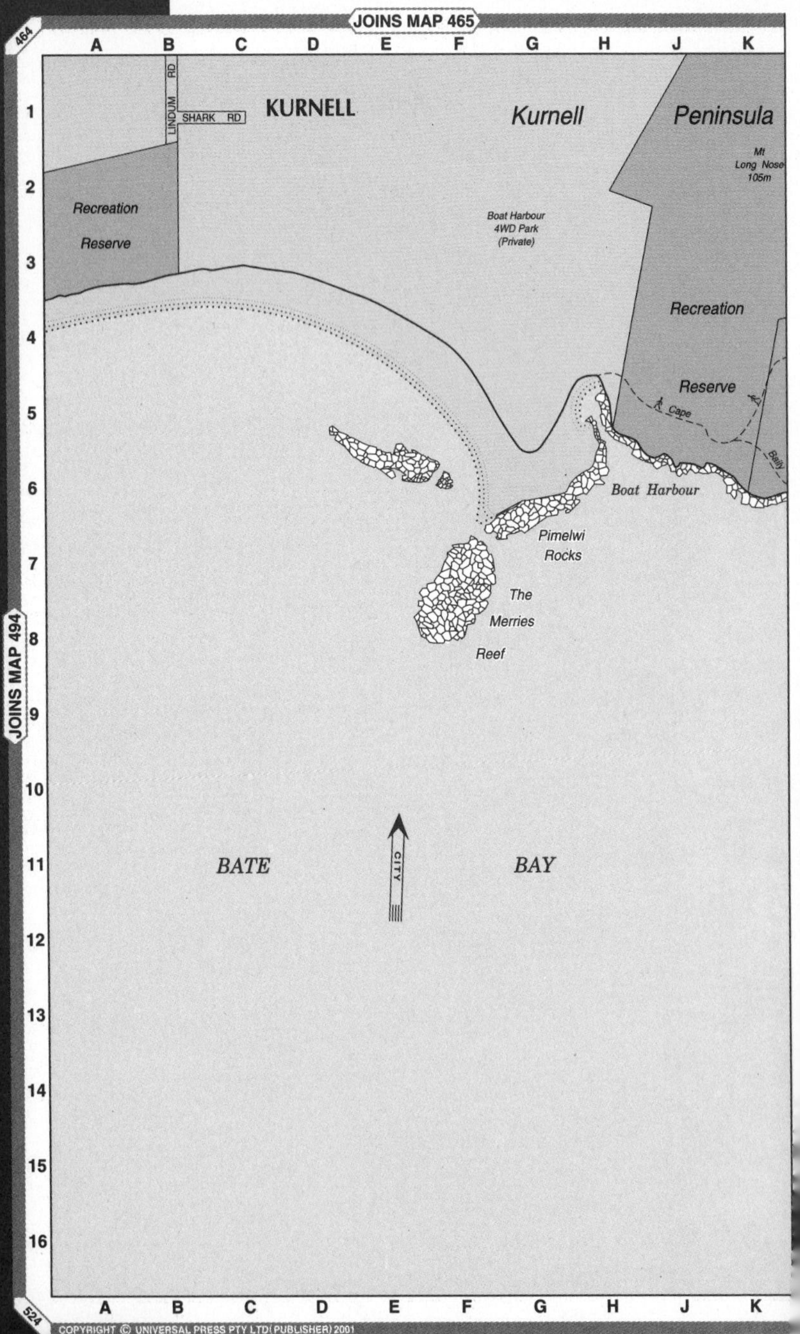

JOINS MAP 465
464
A
B
C
D
E
F
G
H
J
K
1
2
3
4
5
6
7
8
9
10
11
12
13
14
15
16
LINDUM RD
SHARK RD
KURNELL
Kurnell
Peninsula
Mt
Long Nose
105m
Recreation
Reserve
Boat Harbour
4WD Park
(Private)
Recreation
Reserve
Cape
Baily
Boat Harbour
Pimelwi
Rocks
The
Merries
Reef
JOINS MAP 494
BATE
CITY
BAY
524

JOINS MAP 466

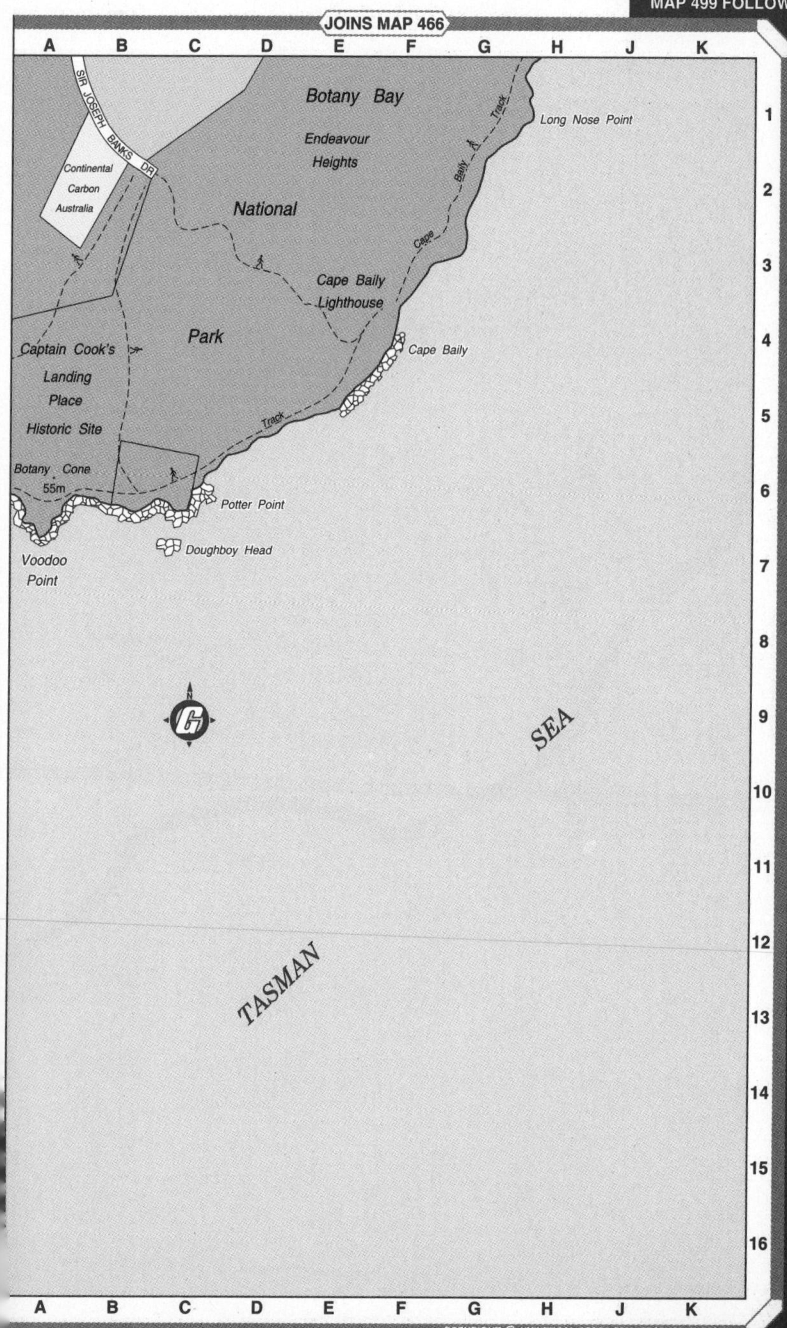

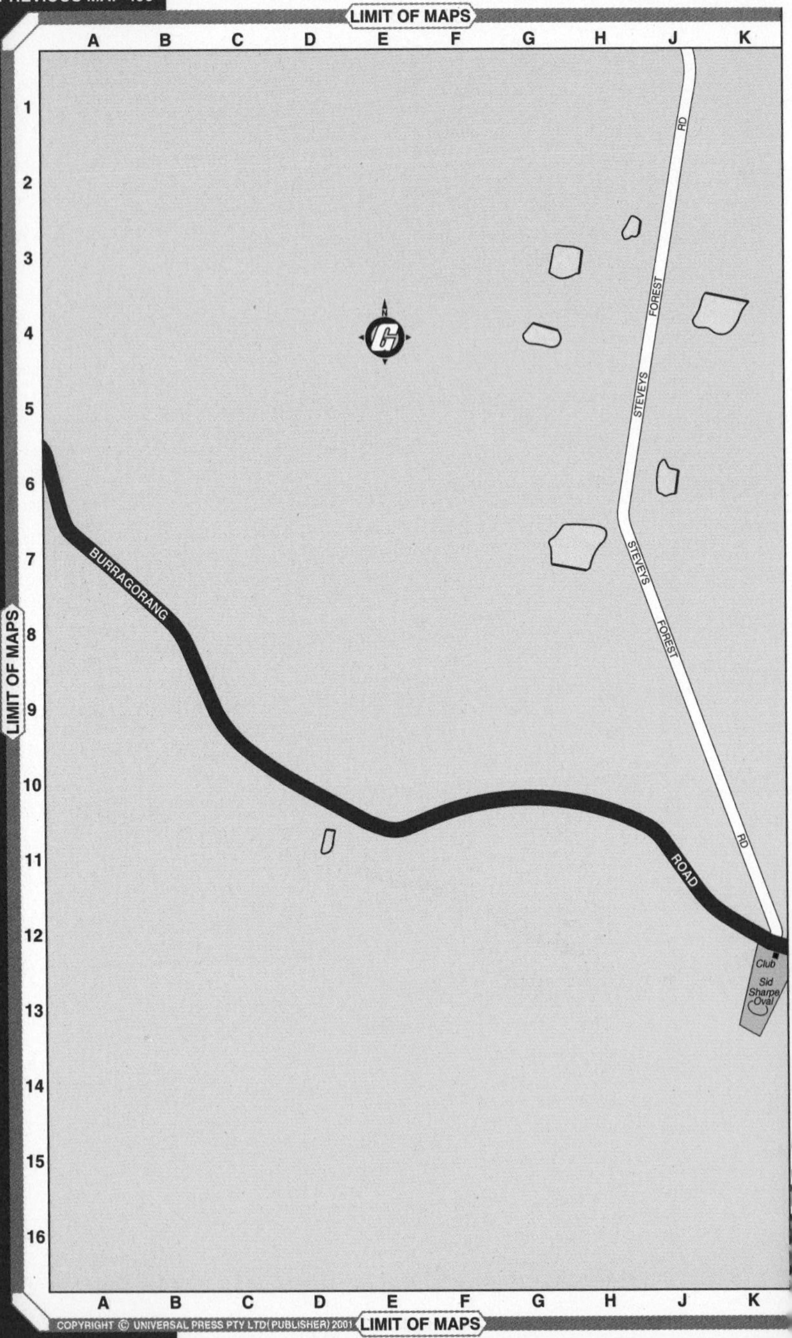
LIMIT OF MAPS
A B C D E F G H J K
1 2 3 4 5 6 7 8 9 10 11 12 13 14 15 16
LIMIT OF MAPS
STEVEYS FOREST RD
STEVEYS FOREST RD
BURRAGORANG ROAD
Club
Sid Sharpe Oval
LIMIT OF MAPS

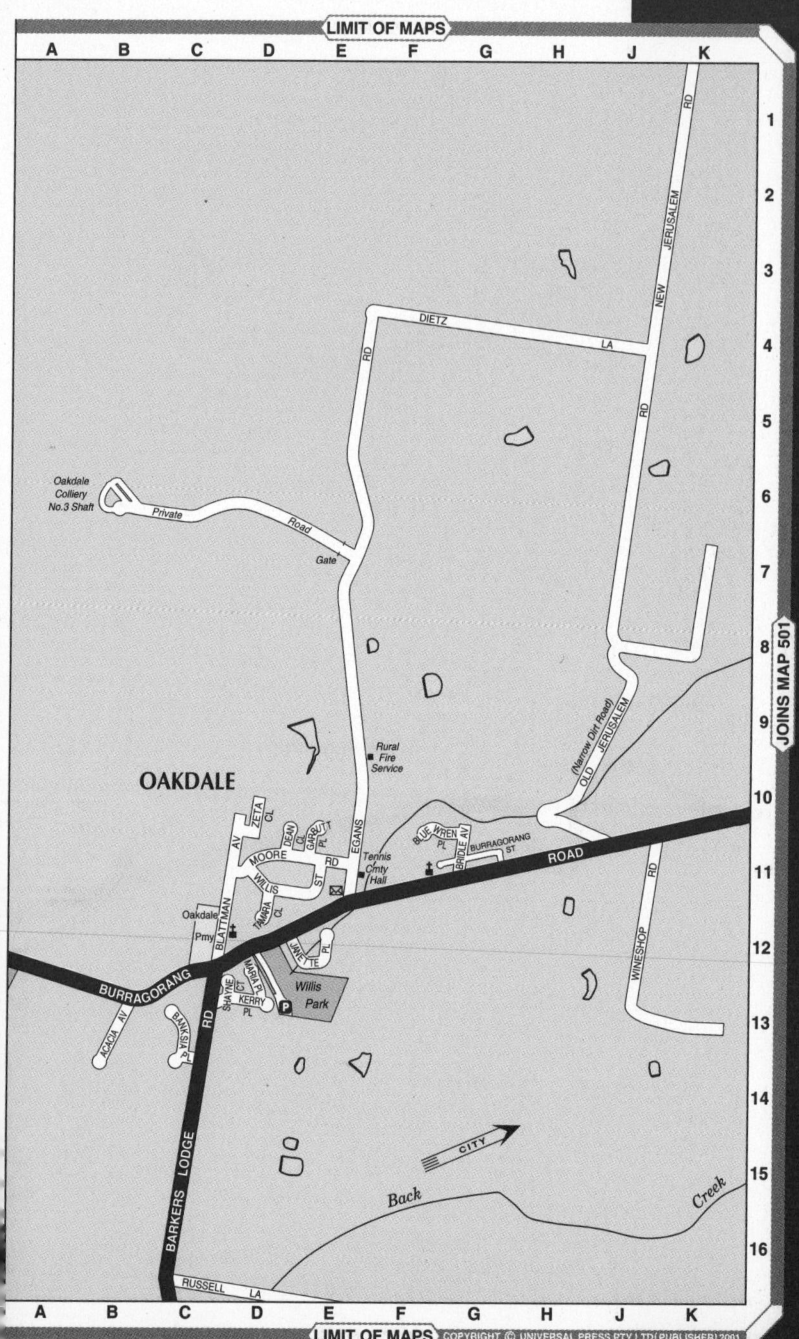
LIMIT OF MAPS
A B C D E F G H J K
1 2 3 4 5 6 7 8 9 10 11 12 13 14 15 16
JOINS MAP 501
OAKDALE
Oakdale Colliery No.3 Shaft
Private Road
Gate
DIETZ LA
NEW JERUSALEM RD
EGANS RD
Rural Fire Service
Tennis Cmty Hall
(Narrow Dirt Road)
OLD JERUSALEM RD
BURRAGORANG ROAD
BLUE WREN PL
BRIDLE AV
BURRAGORANG ST
WINESHOP RD
ZETA CL
DEAN CL
GARBUTT PL
MOORE RD
WILLIS ST
TAMARA CL
BLATTMAN AV
Oakdale Pmy
JANETTE PL
MARIA PL
SHAYNE CT
KERRY PL
Willis Park
BURRAGORANG RD
ACACIA AV
BANKSIA PL
BARKERS LODGE RD
CITY
Back Creek
RUSSELL LA
LIMIT OF MAPS

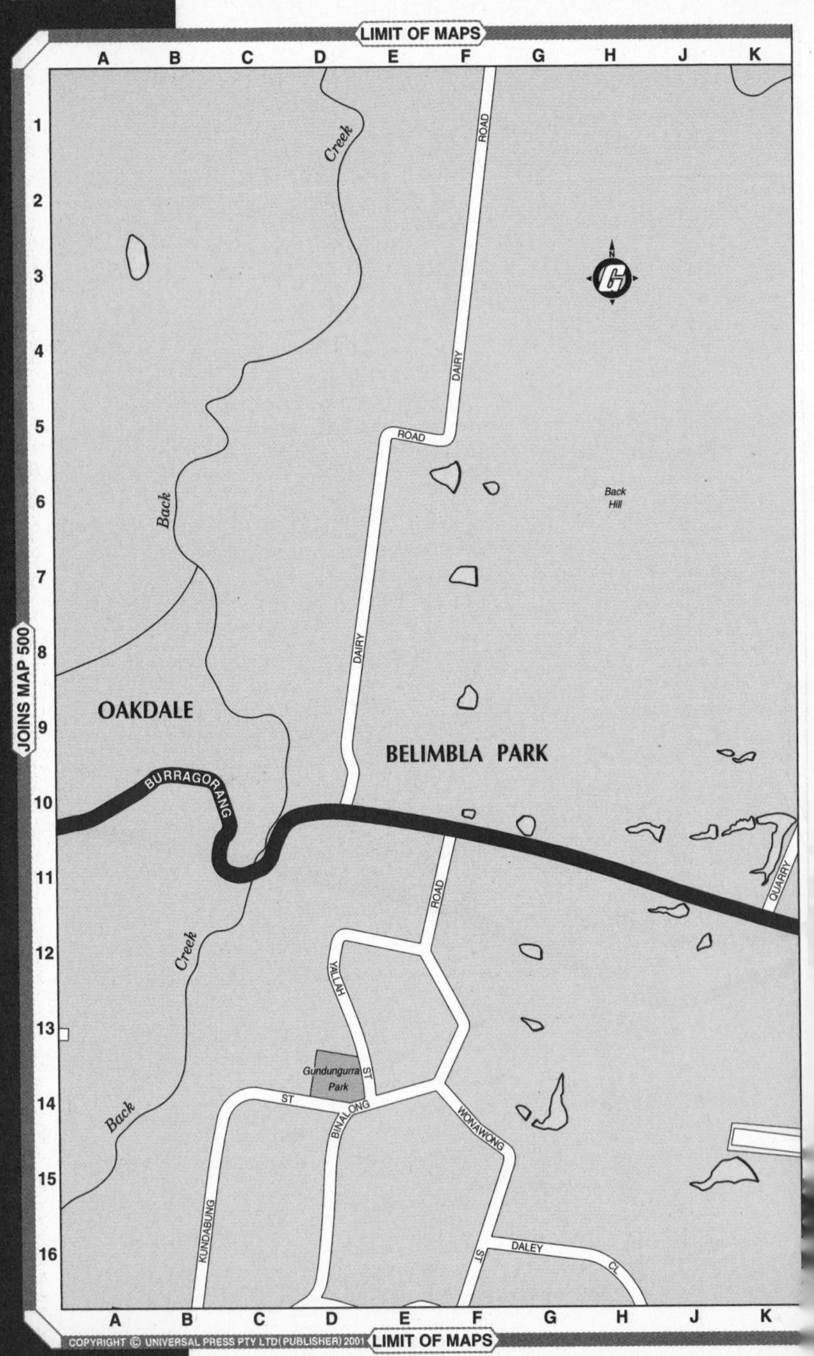
LIMIT OF MAPS
A B C D E F G H J K
1 2 3 4 5 6 7 8 9 10 11 12 13 14 15 16
JOINS MAP 500
Creek
DAIRY
ROAD
ROAD
Back
Back
Hill
DAIRY
OAKDALE
BELIMBLA PARK
BURRAGORANG
ROAD
QUARRY
Creek
YALLAH
Gundungurra
Park
ST
ST
BINALONG
WONAWONG
Back
KUNDABUNG
ST
DALEY
CL
LIMIT OF MAPS

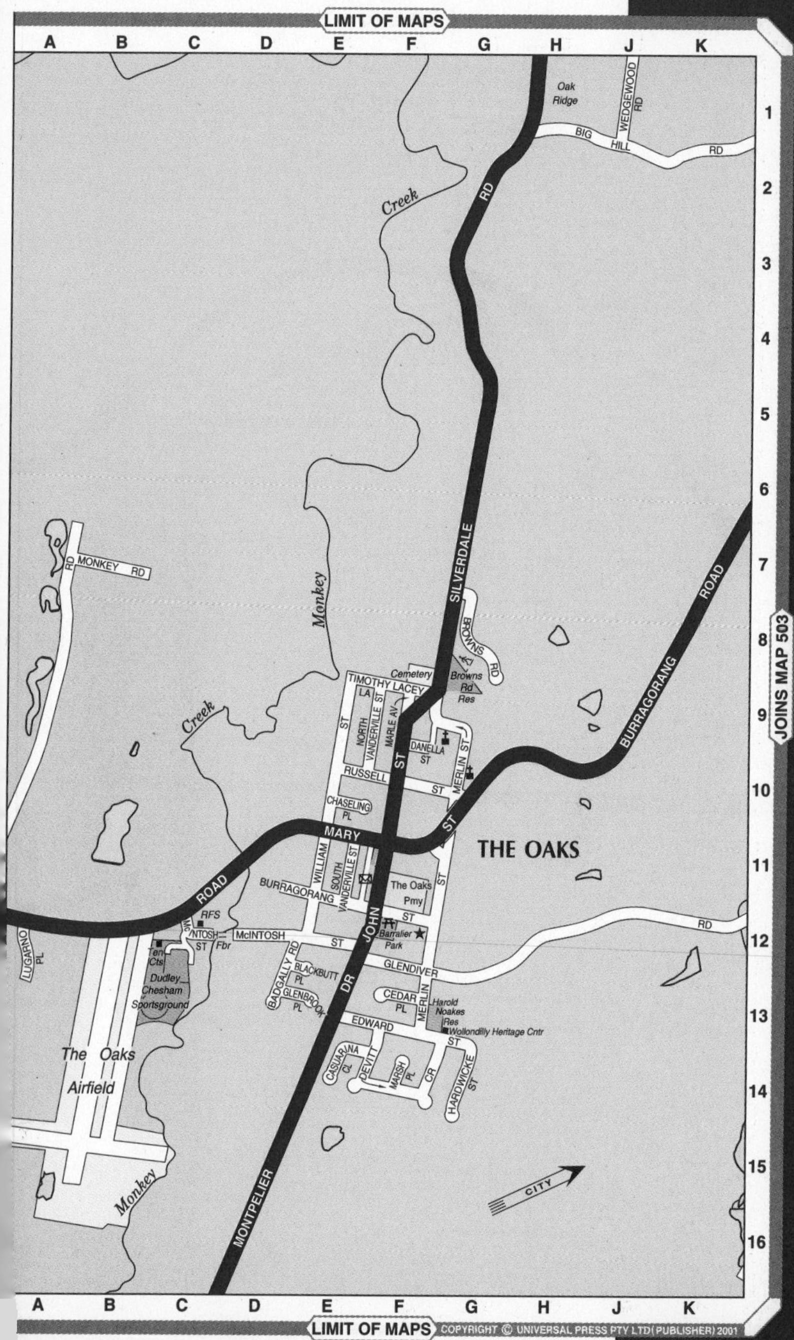
LIMIT OF MAPS
A B C D E F G H J K
1 2 3 4 5 6 7 8 9 10 11 12 13 14 15 16
Oak Ridge
WEDGEWOOD RD
BIG HILL RD
Creek
RD
SILVERDALE
Monkey
MONKEY RD
RD
BROWNS RD
Cemetery
Browns Rd Res
TIMOTHY LACEY
LA
ST
NORTH VANDERVILLE ST
MARLE AV
DANELLA ST
MERLIN ST
RUSSELL ST
CHASELING PL
Creek
ROAD
BURRAGORANG
MARY ST
JOINS MAP 503
THE OAKS
WILLIAM
SOUTH VANDERVILLE ST
The Oaks Pmy
BURRAGORANG
RFS
McINTOSH ST
Fbr
McINTOSH
ST
JOHN
Barralier Park
RD
GLENDIVER
LUGARNO PL
Ten Cts
Dudley Chesham Sportsground
BADGALLY RD
BLACKBUTT PL
GLENBROOK PL
DR
CEDAR PL
MERLIN
Harold Noakes Res
Wollondilly Heritage Cntr
EDWARD ST
CASUARINA CL
DEVITT
MARSH PL
CR
HARDWICKE ST
The Oaks Airfield
Monkey
MONTPELIER
CITY
A B C D E F G H J K
LIMIT OF MAPS

MAP 503

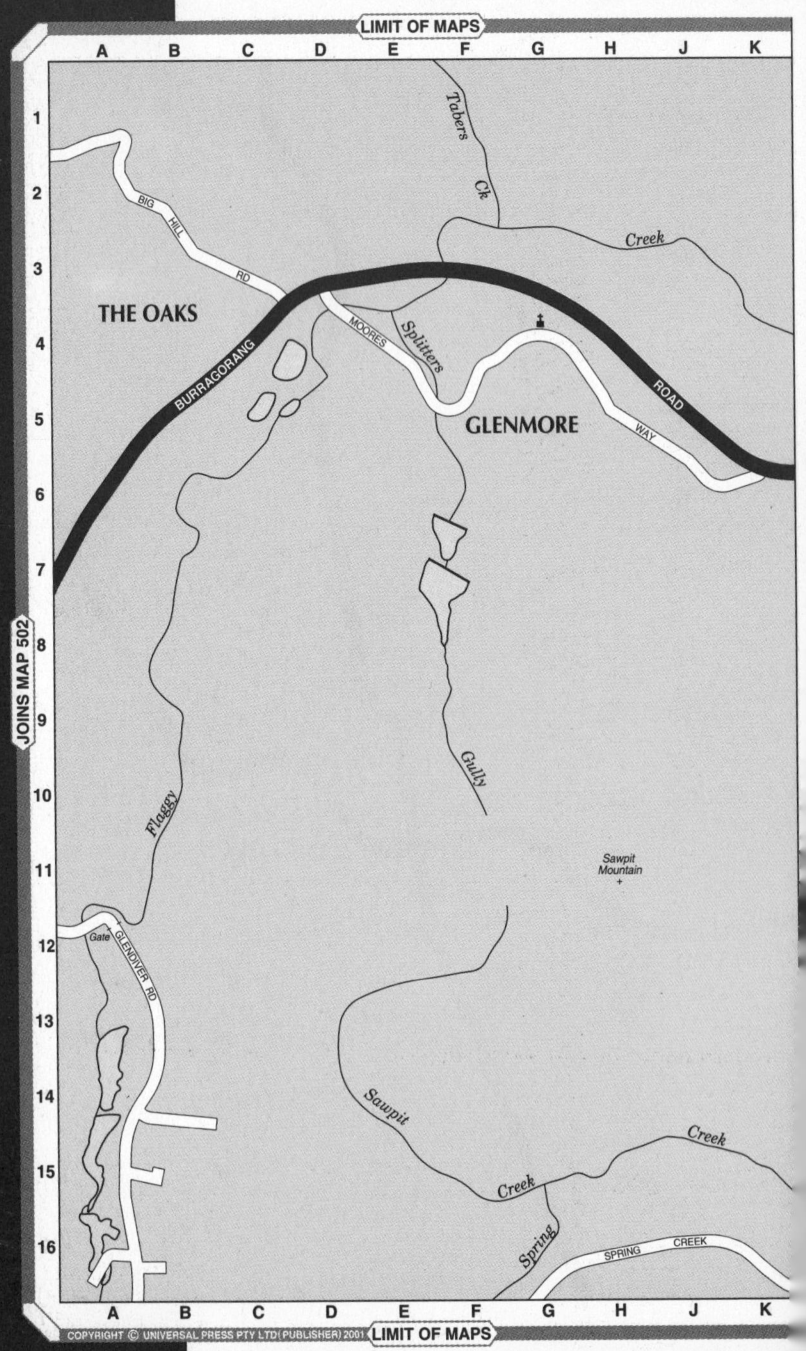

LIMIT OF MAPS
A
B
C
D
E
F
G
H
J
K
1
2
3
4
5
6
7
8
9
10
11
12
13
14
15
16
JOINS MAP 502
Tabers
Ck
Creek
BIG
HILL
RD
THE OAKS
BURRAGORANG
ROAD
MOORES
WAY
Splitters
GLENMORE
Gully
Flaggy
Sawpit
Mountain
Gate
GLENDIVER RD
Sawpit
Creek
Creek
Spring
SPRING
CREEK
COPYRIGHT © UNIVERSAL PRESS PTY LTD (PUBLISHER) 2001
LIMIT OF MAPS

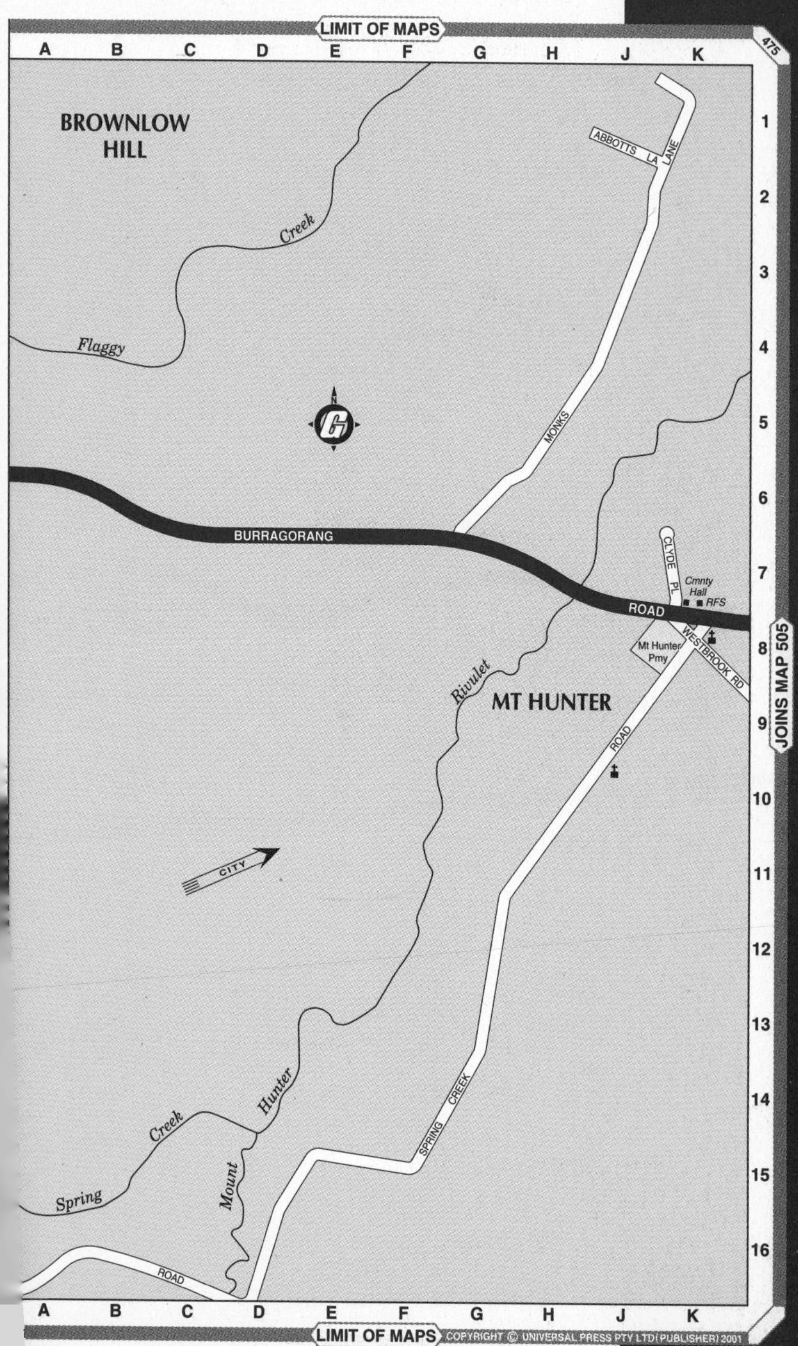
LIMIT OF MAPS
475
A
B
C
D
E
F
G
H
J
K
1
2
3
4
5
6
7
8
9
10
11
12
13
14
15
16
BROWNLOW
HILL
Flaggy
Creek
ABBOTTS LA
LANE
MONKS
BURRAGORANG
ROAD
CLYDE PL
Cmnty
Hall
RFS
Mt Hunter
Pmy
WESTBROOK RD
Rivulet
MT HUNTER
ROAD
JOINS MAP 505
CITY
Spring
Creek
Mount
Hunter
SPRING CREEK
ROAD
LIMIT OF MAPS

MAP 505

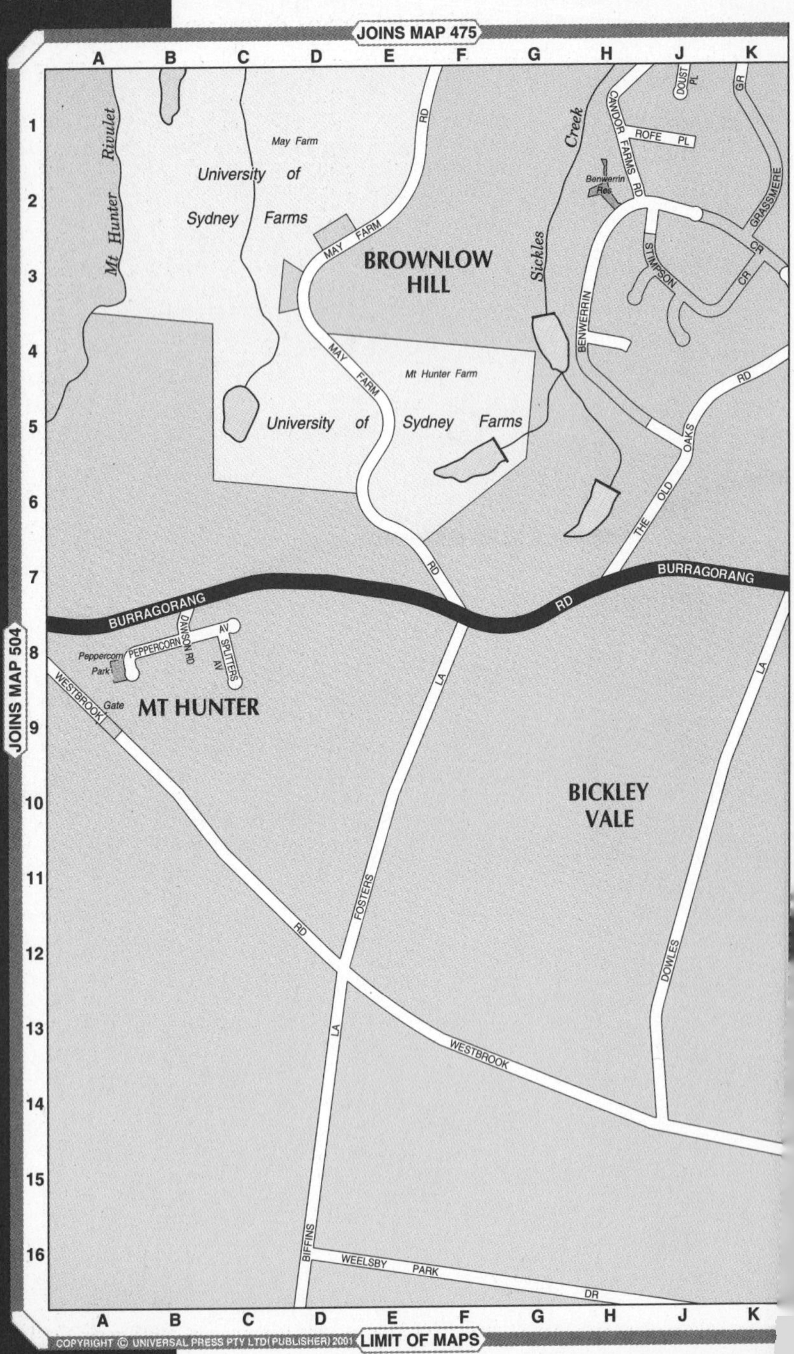

JOINS MAP 475
JOINS MAP 504
LIMIT OF MAPS
A B C D E F G H J K
1 2 3 4 5 6 7 8 9 10 11 12 13 14 15 16
BROWNLOW HILL
MT HUNTER
BICKLEY VALE
University of Sydney Farms
May Farm
Mt Hunter Farm
Mt Hunter Rivulet
Sickles Creek
Benwerrin Res
Peppercorn Park
Gate
MAY FARM RD
BURRAGORANG RD
THE OLD OAKS RD
CAWDOR FARMS RD
ROFE PL
DOUST PL
GRASSMERE GR
GRASSMERE CR
STIMPSON CR
BENWERRIN
PEPPERCORN AV
DAWSON RD
SPLITTERS AV
WESTBROOK RD
FOSTERS LA
DOWLES LA
BIFFINS LA
WEELSBY PARK DR

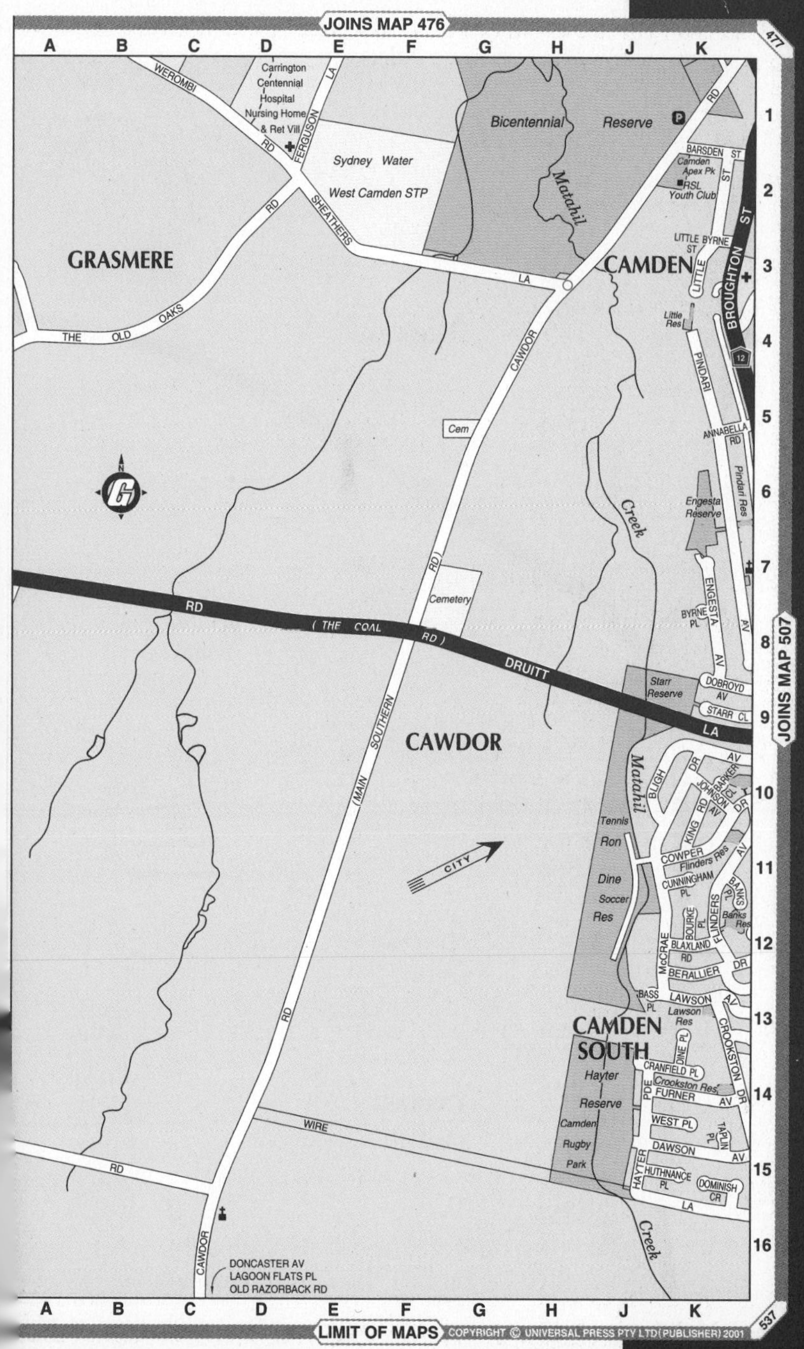
JOINS MAP 476
477
A B C D E F G H J K
1 2 3 4 5 6 7 8 9 10 11 12 13 14 15 16
WEROMBI RD
Carrington Centennial Hospital Nursing Home & Ret Vill
FERGUSON LA
Sydney Water West Camden STP
Bicentennial Reserve
BARSDEN ST
Camden Apex Pk
RSL Youth Club
SHEATHERS LA
GRASMERE
CAMDEN
LITTLE BYRNE ST
LITTLE ST
BROUGHTON ST
Little Res
THE OLD OAKS RD
Matahil
PINDARI
CAWDOR
Cem
ANNABELLA RD
Pindari Res
Engesta Reserve
Creek
(MAIN SOUTHERN RD)
Cemetery
RD (THE COAL RD) DRUITT LA
ENGESTA AV
BYRNE PL
Starr Reserve
DOBROYD AV
STARR CL
JOINS MAP 507
CAWDOR
Matahil
BLIGH DR
AV
BARKER CL
JOHNSON DR
KING RD
AV
Tennis
Ron Dine Soccer Res
COWPER
Flinders Res
AV
CUNNINGHAM PL
BANKS PL
Banks Res
CITY
BOURKE PL
FLINDERS
McCRAE
BLAXLAND RD
BERALLIER DR
BASS PL
LAWSON AV
Lawson Res
CAMDEN SOUTH
DINE PL
CROOKSTON DR
CRANFIELD PL
Crookston Res
PDE
FURNER AV
Hayter Reserve
Camden Rugby Park
WEST PL
TAPLIN PL
WIRE
DAWSON AV
RD
HAYTER
HUTHNANCE PL
DOMINISH CR
LA
Creek
CAWDOR
DONCASTER AV
LAGOON FLATS PL
OLD RAZORBACK RD
A B C D E F G H J K
LIMIT OF MAPS
537

JOINS MAP 477

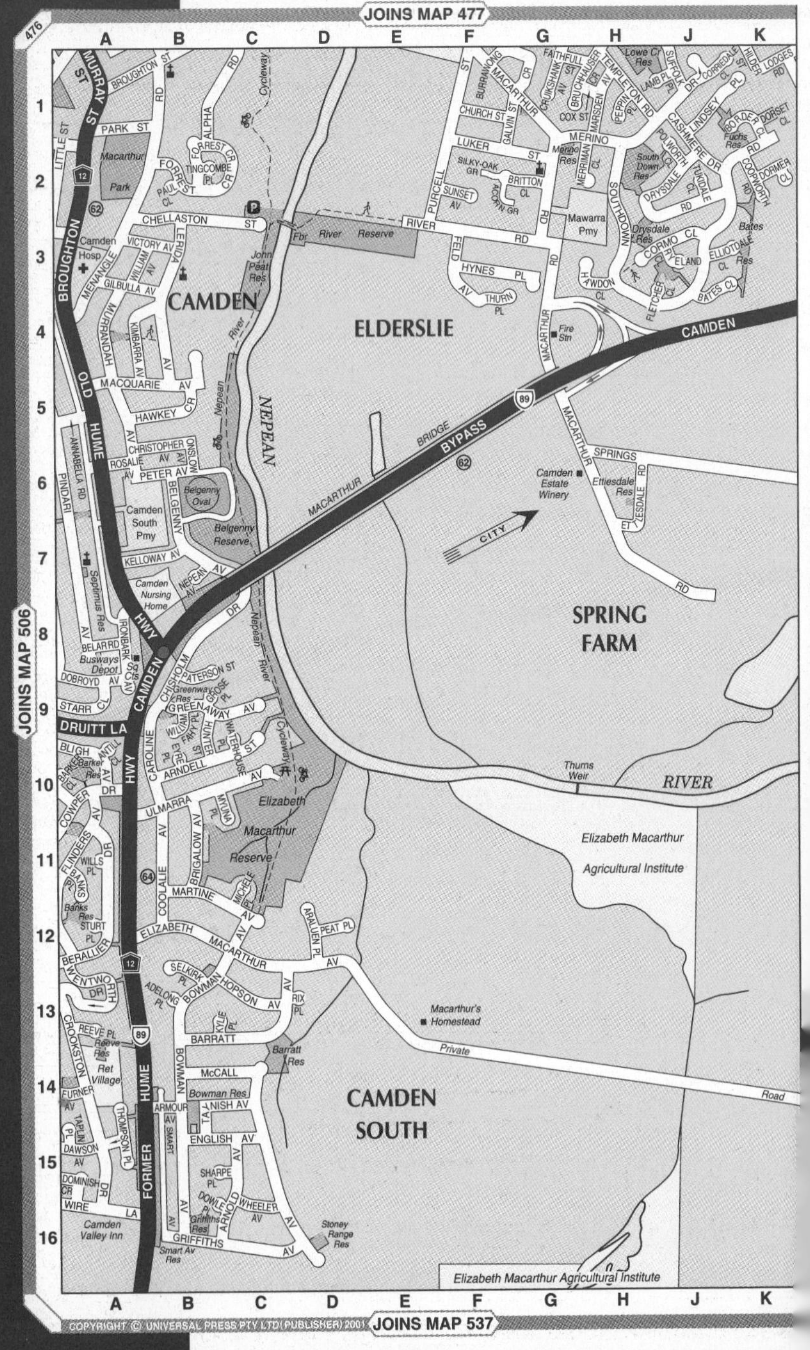

JOINS MAP 506

JOINS MAP 537

JOINS MAP 478

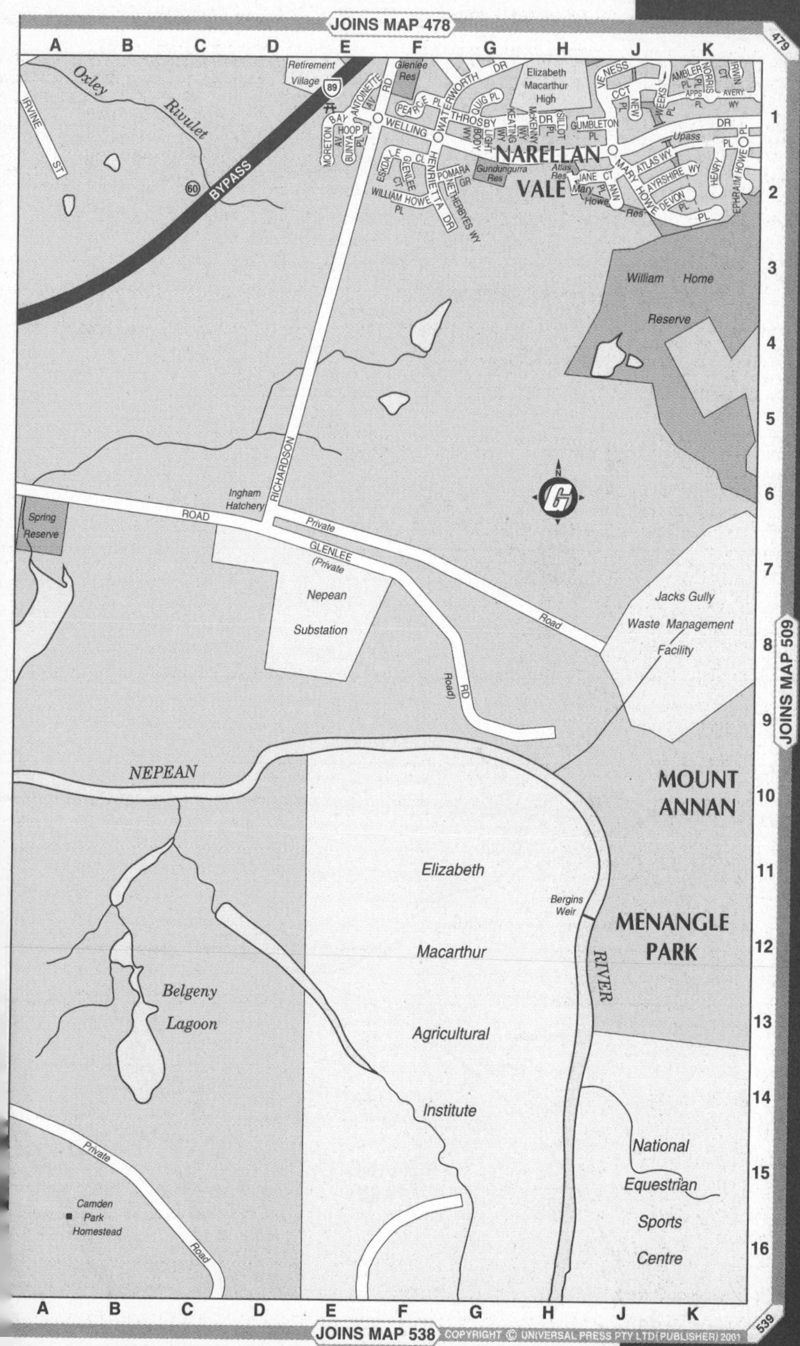

JOINS MAP 509

JOINS MAP 538

JOINS MAP 479

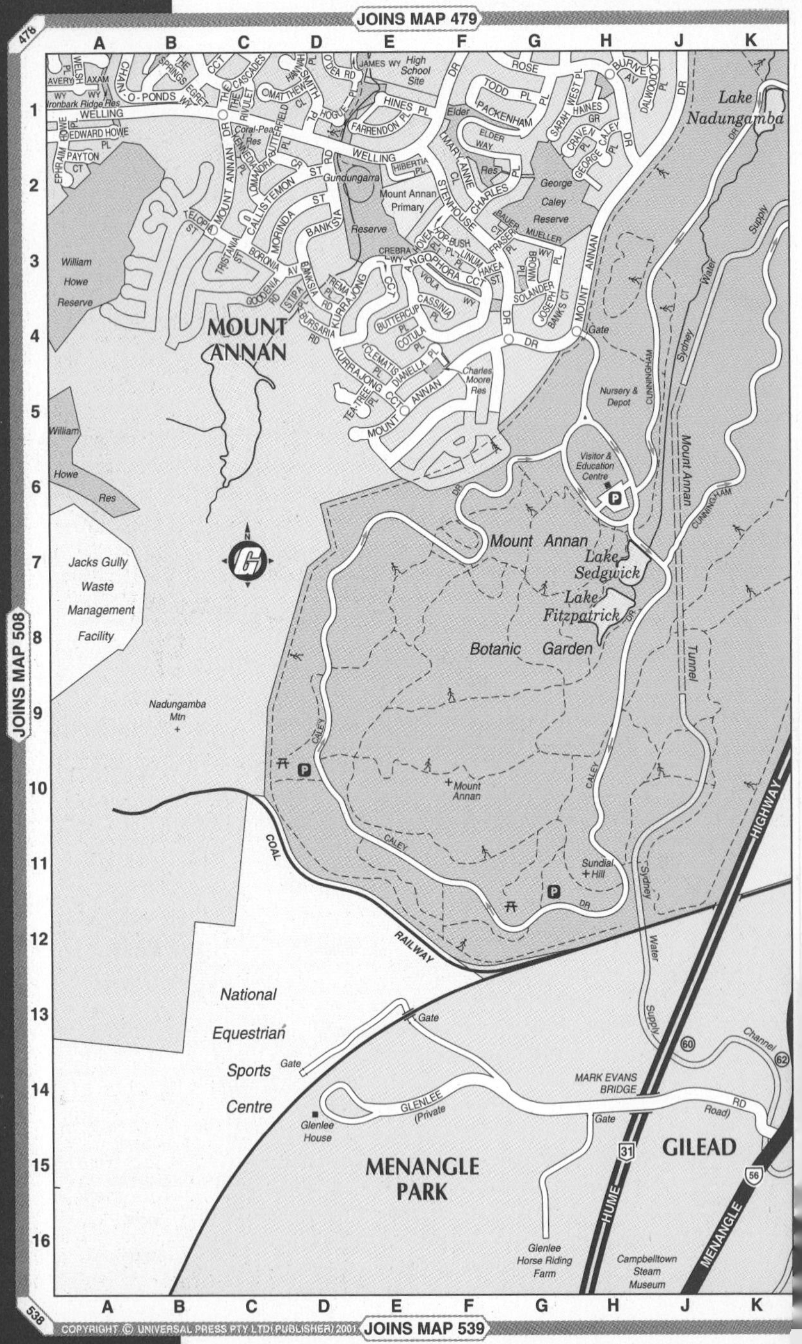

JOINS MAP 508

JOINS MAP 539

JOINS MAP 480

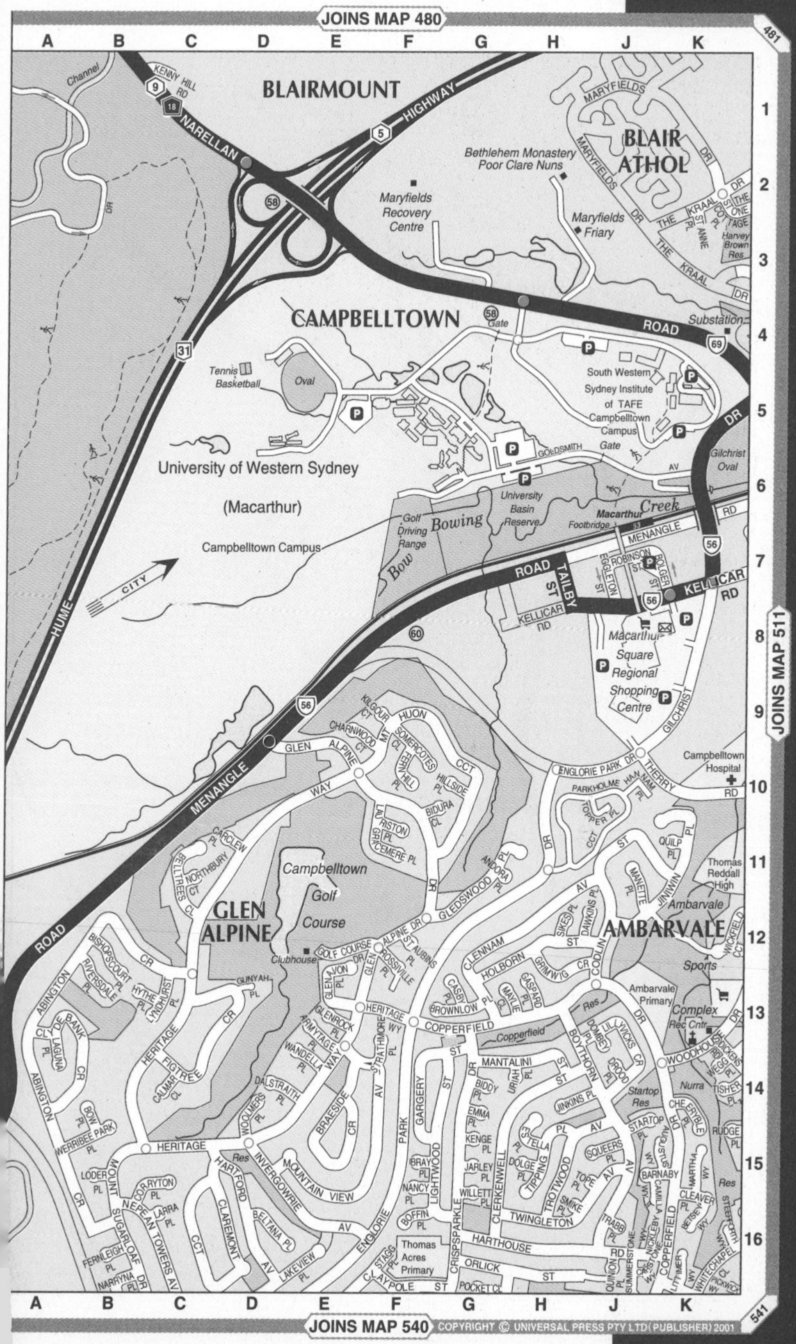

JOINS MAP 511

JOINS MAP 540

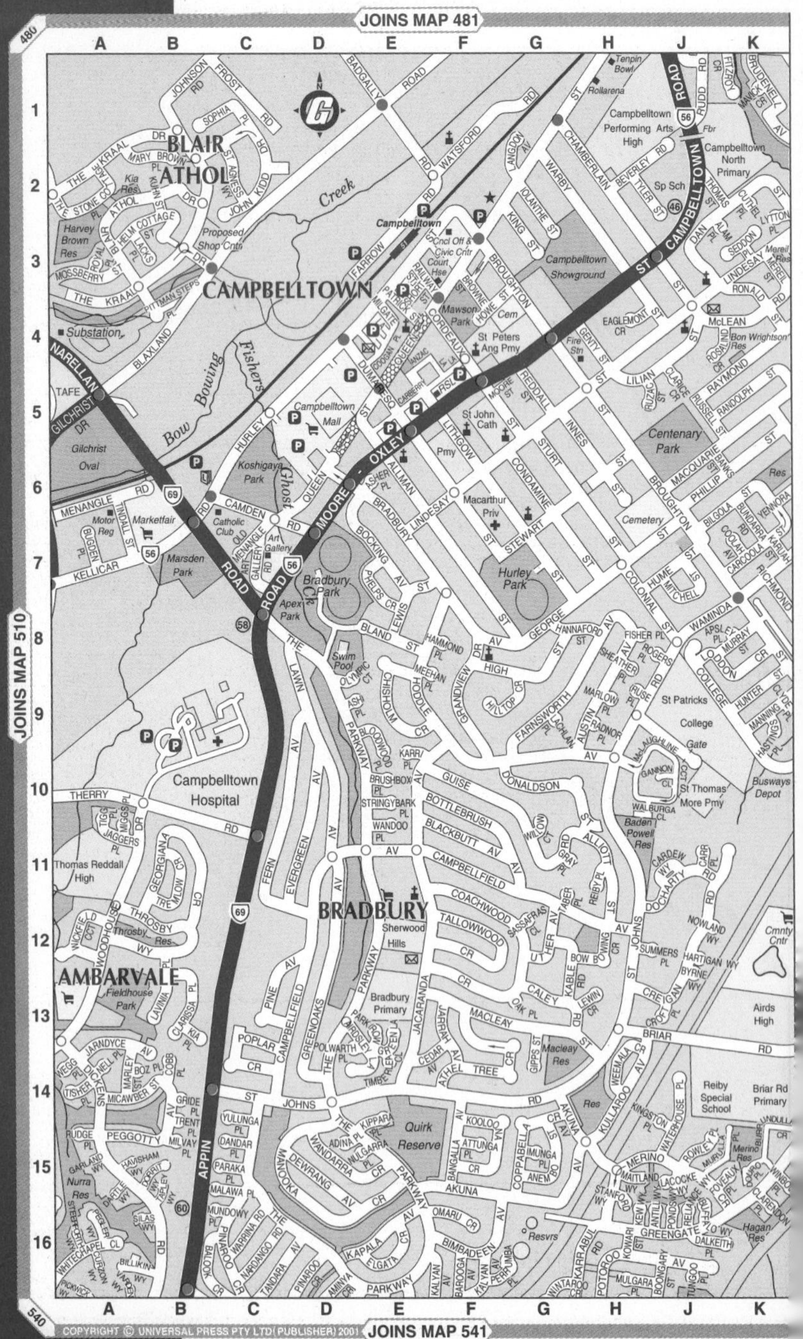
JOINS MAP 481
JOINS MAP 510
JOINS MAP 541
480
540
A B C D E F G H J K
1 2 3 4 5 6 7 8 9 10 11 12 13 14 15 16
BLAIR ATHOL
CAMPBELLTOWN
BRADBURY
AMBARVALE
Campbelltown
Campbelltown Performing Arts High
Campbelltown North Primary
Campbelltown Showground
Campbelltown Mall
Campbelltown Hospital
Cncl Off & Civic Cntr
Court Hse
Proposed Shop Cntr
Tenpin Bowl
Rollarena
Sp Sch
Substation
TAFE
Gilchrist Oval
Harvey Brown Res
Kia Res
Koshigaya Park
Catholic Club
Art Gallery
Marketfair
Motor Reg
Marsden Park
Bradbury Park
Apex Park
Swim Pool
Mawson Park
Cem
St Peters Ang Pmy
Fire Stn
McLEAN
Bon Wrightson Res
Centenary Park
St John Cath
Pmy
Macarthur Priv
Cemetery
Hurley Park
Res
Busways Depot
St Patricks College
Gate
St Thomas More Pmy
Baden Powell Res
Thomas Reddall High
Throsby Res
Fieldhouse Park
Sherwood Hills
Bradbury Primary
Macleay Res
Cmnty Cntr
Airds High
Reiby Special School
Briar Rd Primary
Quirk Reserve
Nurra Res
Merino Res
Hagan Res
Resvrs
Bow Bowing Creek
Fishers Ghost Ck
NARELLAN ROAD
APPIN ROAD
MOORE - OXLEY
CAMPBELLTOWN ROAD
QUEEN ST
CAMDEN RD
MENANGLE RD
KELLICAR RD
THERRY RD
BRIAR RD
JOHNS RD
THE PARKWAY
GILCHRIST DR
BADGALLY ROAD
WATSFORD RD
BROUGHTON ST
DUMARESQ ST
LINDESAY ST
BRADBURY AV
GEORGE ST
COLONIAL ST
HIGH ST
BLAND ST
DONALDSON ST
CAMPBELLFIELD AV
AKUNA AV
PEGGOTTY AV
MICAWBER ST
JARNDYCE AV
THROSBY WY
THE KRAAL
JOHNSON RD
FROST RD
JOHN KIDD DR
BLAXLAND RD
CHAMBERLAIN ST
WARBY ST
INNES ST
STURT ST
CONDAMINE ST
MACQUARIE AV
PHILLIP AV
WAMINDA AV
COLLEGE RD
GRANDVIEW DR
FARNSWORTH AV
EVERGREEN AV
FERN AV
CAMPBELLFIELD AV
GREENOAKS AV
PINE AV
POPLAR CR
JACARANDA AV
MACLEAY ST
KULLAROO AV
KINGSTON PL
WATERHOUSE PL
MERINO ST
GREENGATE RD

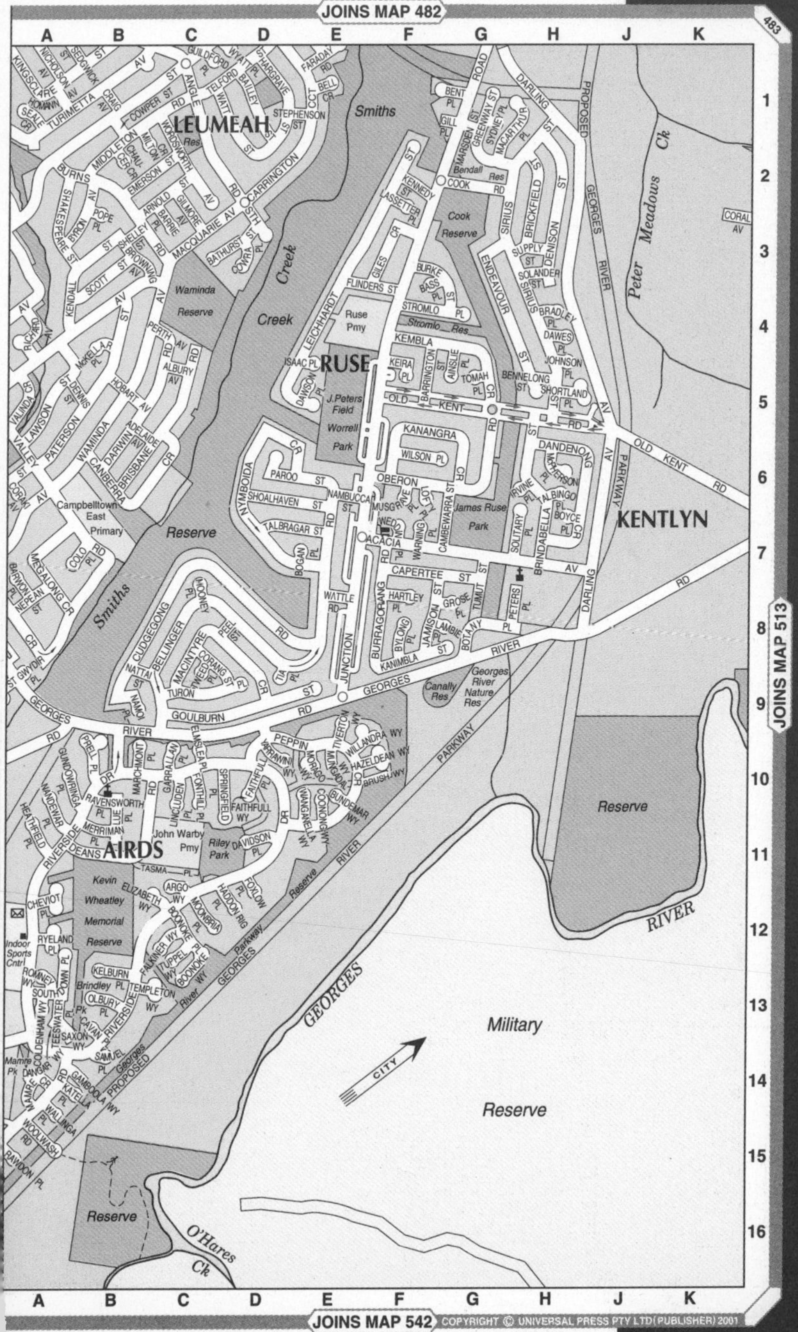
JOINS MAP 482
483
A B C D E F G H J K
1 2 3 4 5 6 7 8 9 10 11 12 13 14 15 16
LEUMEAH
RUSE
KENTLYN
AIRDS
Smiths Creek
Waminda Reserve
Ruse Pmy
J.Peters Field
Worrell Park
Cook Reserve
Bendall Res
Stromlo Res
James Ruse Park
Campbelltown East Primary
Reserve
Smiths
Canally Res
Georges River Nature Res
John Warby Pmy
Riley Park
Kevin Wheatley Memorial Reserve
Indoor Sports Cntr
Brindley Pk
Mamre Pk
Peter Meadows Ck
GEORGES RIVER
PROPOSED
GEORGES RIVER PARKWAY
OLD KENT RD
DARLING AV
Military Reserve
CITY
O'Hares Ck
JOINS MAP 513
JOINS MAP 542

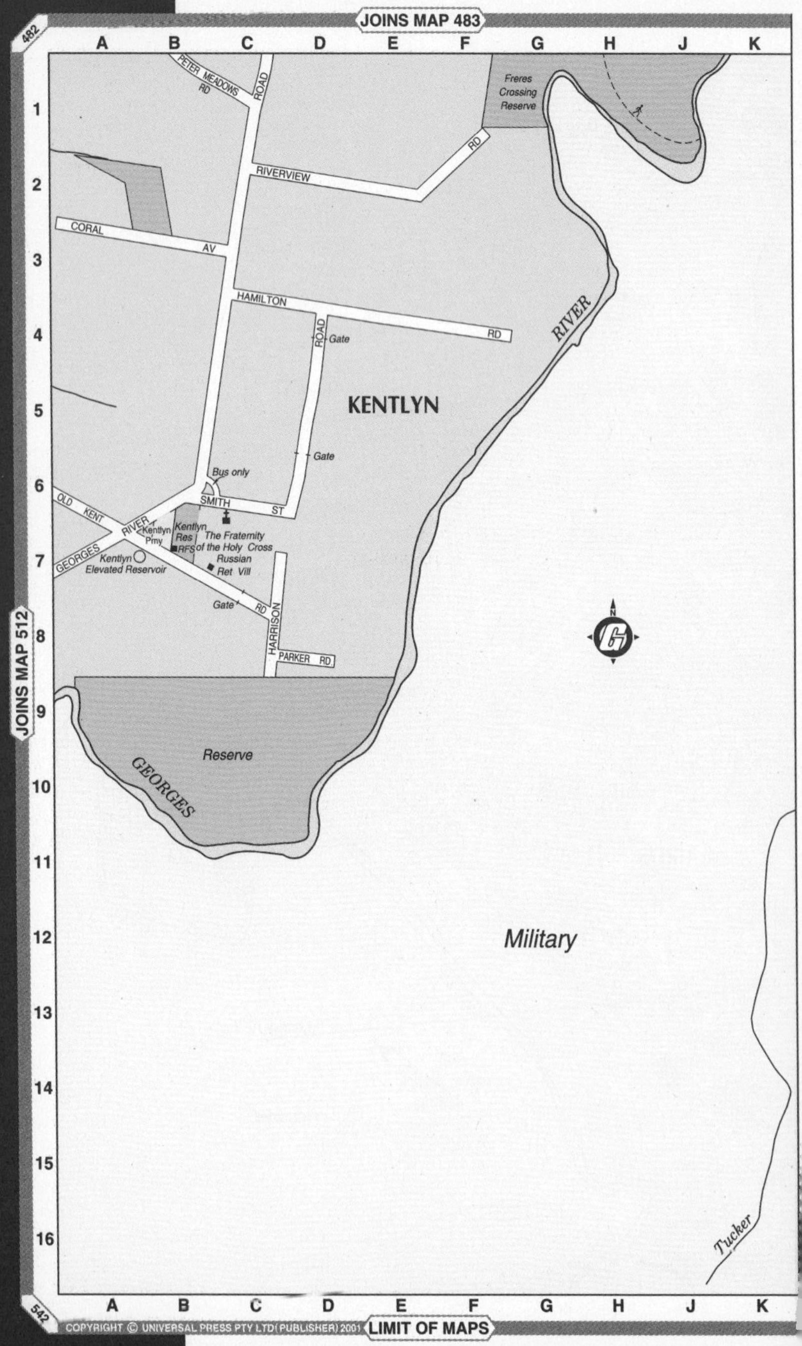
JOINS MAP 483
482
A
B
C
D
E
F
G
H
J
K
1
2
3
4
5
6
7
8
9
10
11
12
13
14
15
16
PETER MEADOWS RD
ROAD
Freres Crossing Reserve
RD
RIVERVIEW
CORAL AV
HAMILTON RD
ROAD
Gate
RIVER
KENTLYN
Gate
Bus only
SMITH ST
OLD KENT RIVER
GEORGES
Kentlyn Pmy
Kentlyn Res
RFS
The Fraternity of the Holy Cross
Russian Ret Vill
Kentlyn Elevated Reservoir
Gate
RD
HARRISON
PARKER RD
JOINS MAP 512
Reserve
GEORGES
Military
Tucker
542
LIMIT OF MAPS

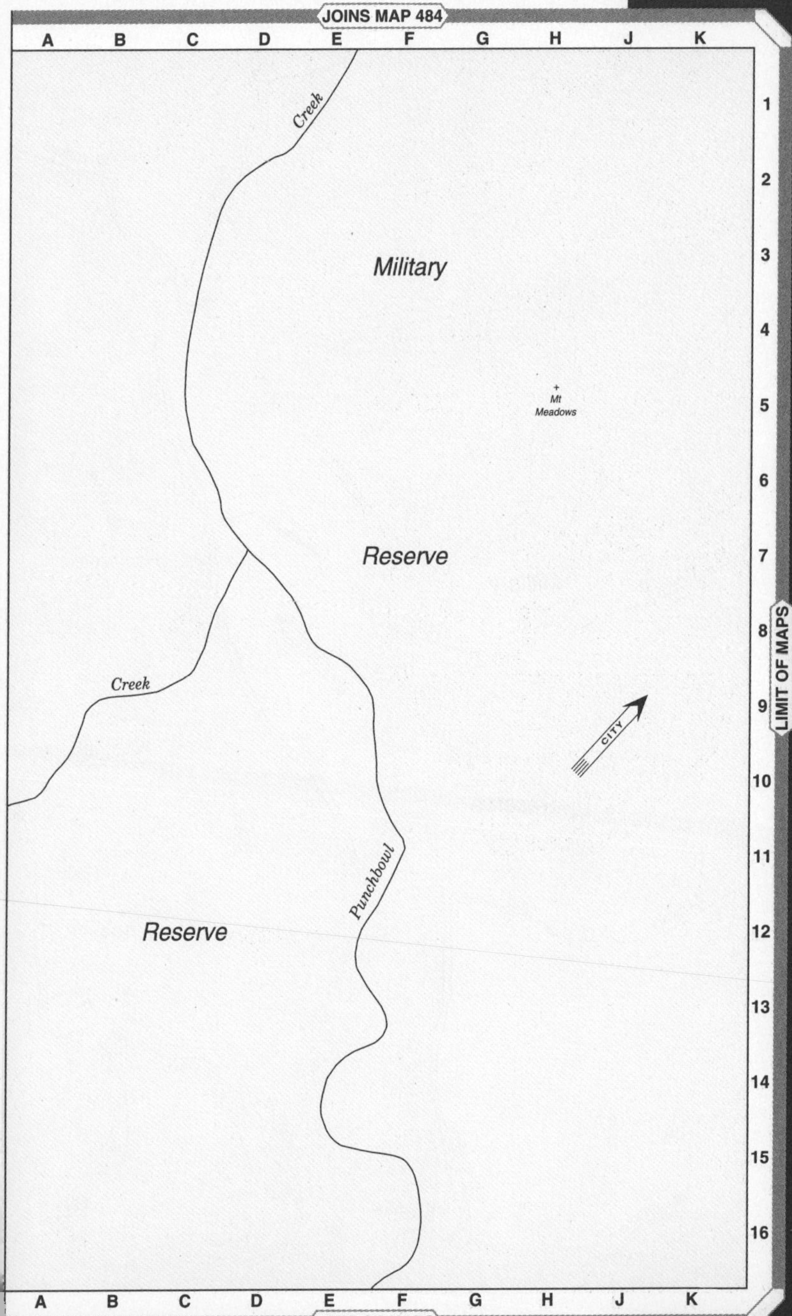
JOINS MAP 484
A
B
C
D
E
F
G
H
J
K
1
2
3
4
5
6
7
8
9
10
11
12
13
14
15
16
Creek
Military
Reserve
Mt
Meadows
Creek
CITY
Punchbowl
Reserve
LIMIT OF MAPS
LIMIT OF MAPS

JOINS MAP 487

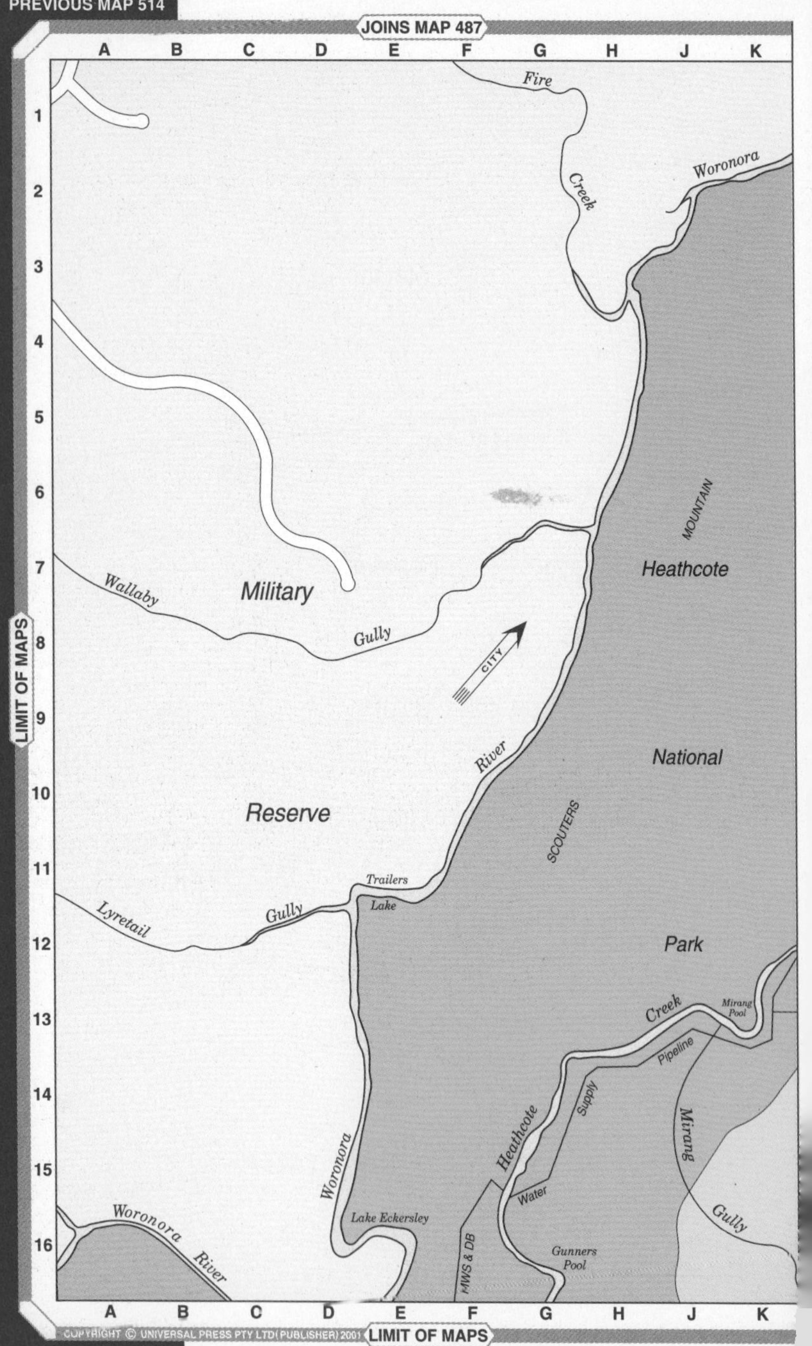

LIMIT OF MAPS

JOINS MAP 488

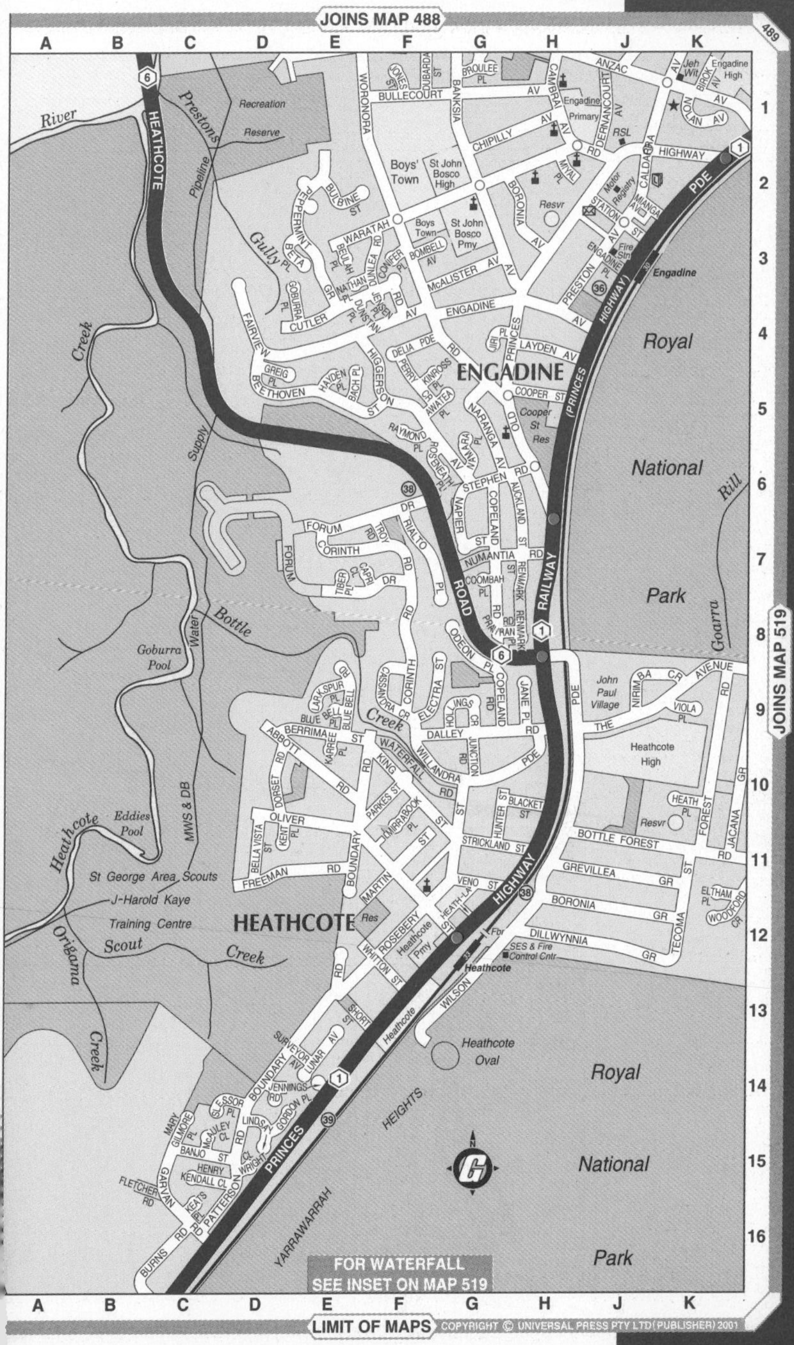

JOINS MAP 519

LIMIT OF MAPS

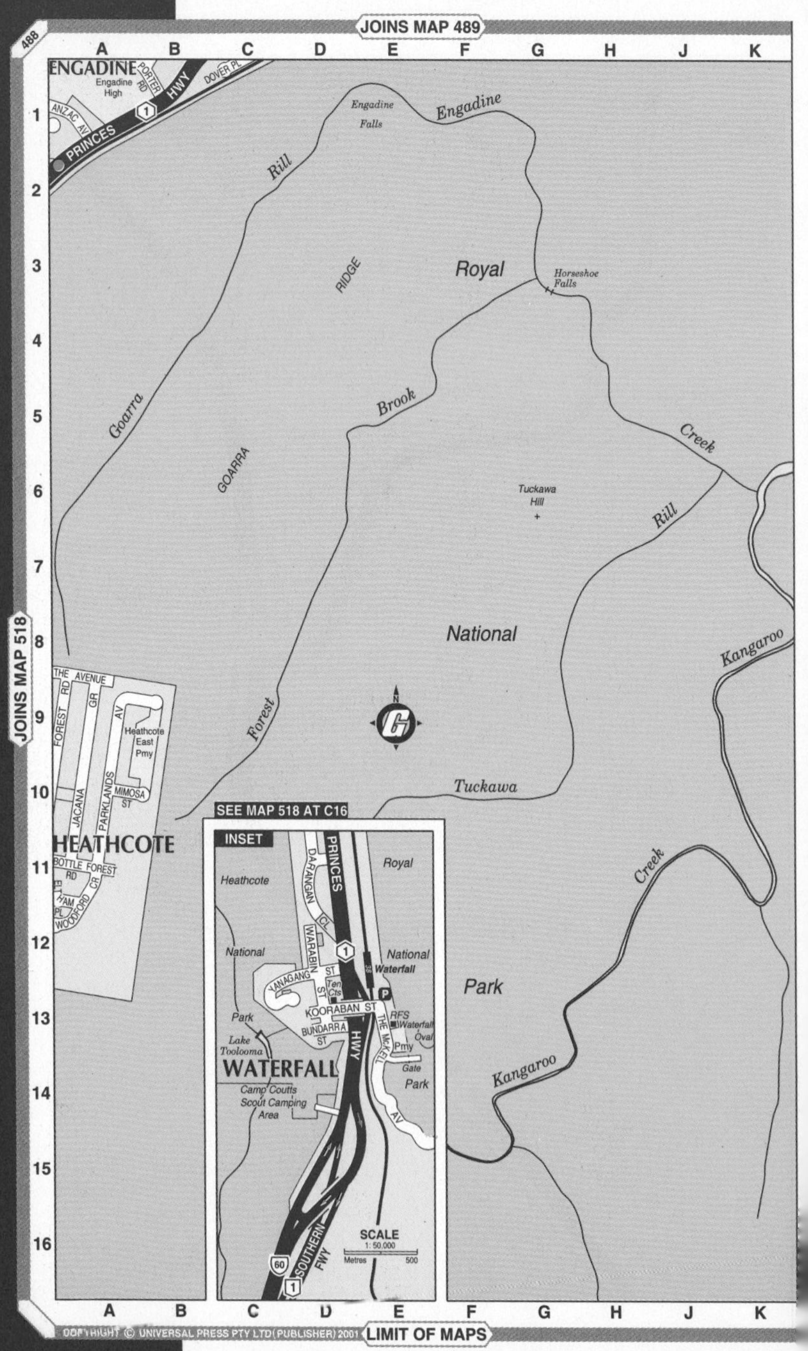
JOINS MAP 489
488
A B C D E F G H J K
1 2 3 4 5 6 7 8 9 10 11 12 13 14 15 16
ENGADINE
Engadine High
PORTER RD
DOVER PL
ANZAC AV
PRINCES HWY
Engadine Falls
Engadine
Rill
RIDGE
Royal
Horseshoe Falls
Brook
Goarra
GOARRA
Creek
Tuckawa Hill
Rill
National
Kangaroo
Forest
THE AVENUE
FOREST RD
GR
AV
Heathcote East Pmy
JACANA
PARKLANDS
MIMOSA ST
Tuckawa
HEATHCOTE
BOTTLE FOREST RD
ELTHAM PL
WOODFORD CR
Creek
Park
Kangaroo
SEE MAP 518 AT C16
INSET
PRINCES
DARANGAN CL
Royal
Heathcote
National
WARABIN ST
National
Waterfall
YANAGANG ST
Ten Cts
P
KOORABAN ST
RFS
Waterfall Oval
Park
BUNDARRA ST
HWY
THE McKELL AV
Pmy
Lake Toolooma
WATERFALL
Gate
Park
Camp Coutts Scout Camping Area
SOUTHERN FWY
SCALE 1: 50,000
Metres 500
JOINS MAP 518
LIMIT OF MAPS

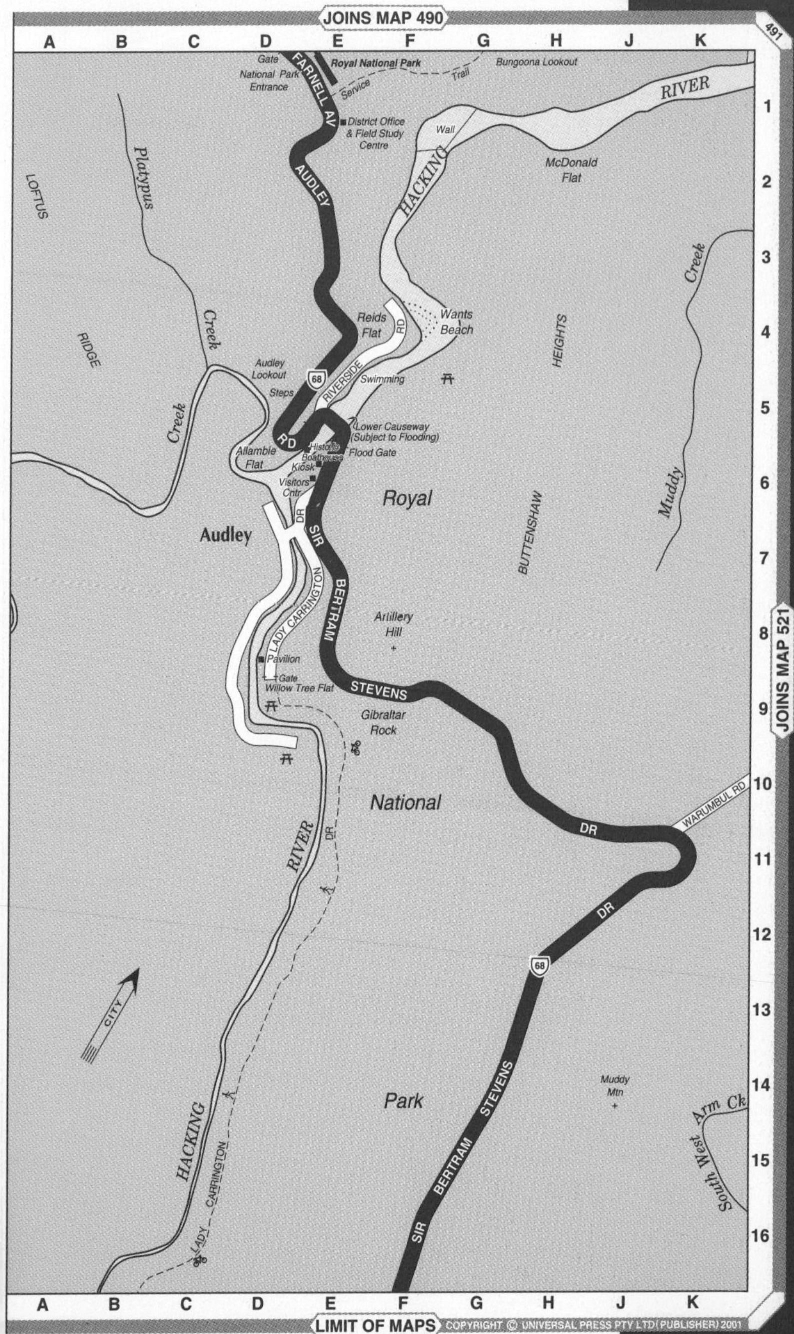
JOINS MAP 490
491
Royal National Park
Bungoona Lookout
Gate
National Park Entrance
FARNELL AV
Service
Trail
RIVER
District Office & Field Study Centre
Wall
McDonald Flat
AUDLEY
HACKING
Platypus
LOFTUS
Creek
Reids Flat
Wants Beach
RD
RIDGE
Creek
HEIGHTS
Audley Lookout
RIVERSIDE
68
Swimming
Steps
Creek
Lower Causeway (Subject to Flooding)
RD
Historic Boathouse
Flood Gate
Allambie Flat
Kiosk
Visitors Cntr
Royal
BUTTENSHAW
Muddy
DR
Audley
SIR
BERTRAM
LADY CARRINGTON
Artillery Hill
Pavilion
Gate
Willow Tree Flat
STEVENS
Gibraltar Rock
JOINS MAP 521
National
WARUMBUL RD
RIVER
DR
DR
DR
68
CITY
Muddy Mtn
Park
South West Arm Ck
HACKING
CARRINGTON
LADY
SIR
BERTRAM
STEVENS
LIMIT OF MAPS

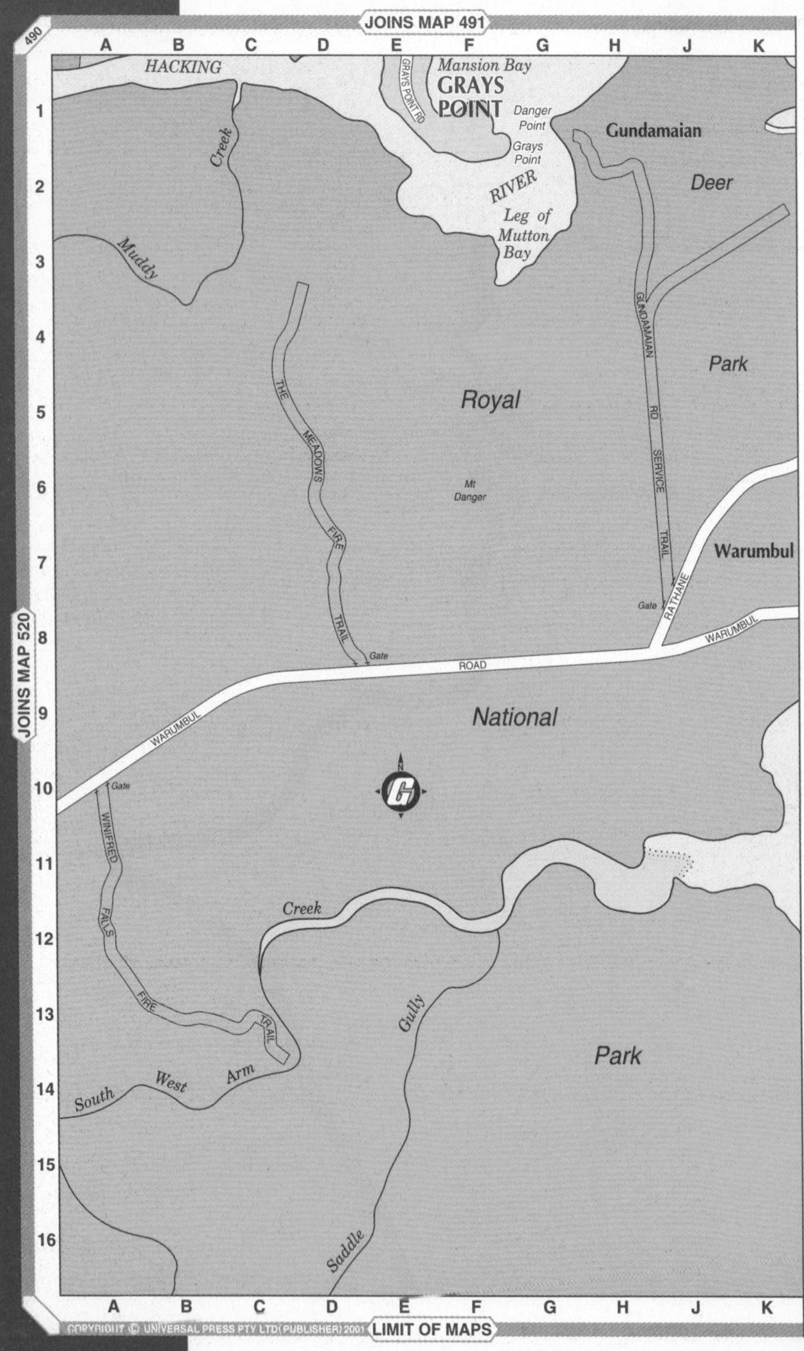
JOINS MAP 491
490
JOINS MAP 520
LIMIT OF MAPS
A B C D E F G H J K
1 2 3 4 5 6 7 8 9 10 11 12 13 14 15 16
HACKING
RIVER
Creek
Muddy
Mansion Bay
GRAYS POINT
GRAYS POINT RD
Danger Point
Grays Point
Leg of Mutton Bay
Gundamaian
Deer
Park
GUNDAMAIAN RD SERVICE TRAIL
Royal
Mt Danger
THE MEADOWS FIRE TRAIL
Warumbul
RATHANE
Gate
WARUMBUL
ROAD
National
WINIFRED FALLS FIRE TRAIL
Creek
Gully
Park
South West Arm
Saddle

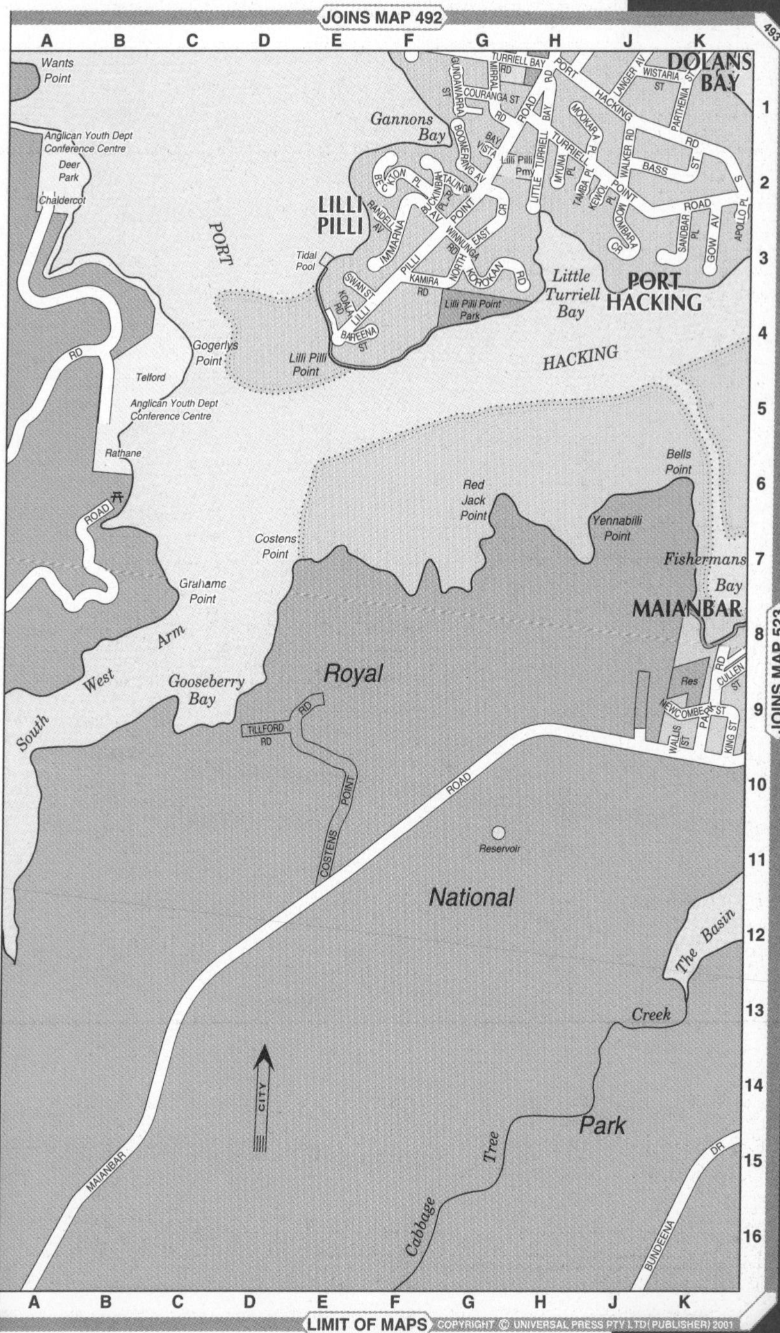

JOINS MAP 492
493
DOLANS BAY
Wants Point
Anglican Youth Dept Conference Centre
Deer Park
Chaldercot
Gannons Bay
LILLI PILLI
PORT
Tidal Pool
Lilli Pilli Pmy
Lilli Pilli Point Park
Little Turriell Bay
PORT HACKING
Gogerlys Point
Lilli Pilli Point
HACKING
Telford
Anglican Youth Dept Conference Centre
Rathane
Bells Point
Red Jack Point
Yennabilli Point
Costens Point
Fishermans Bay
Grahame Point
MAIANBAR
South West Arm
Gooseberry Bay
Royal
Res
JOINS MAP 523
Reservoir
National
The Basin
Creek
Park
Cabbage Tree
CITY
MAIANBAR
BUNDEENA DR
TILLFORD RD
COSTENS POINT RD
ROAD
LIMIT OF MAPS

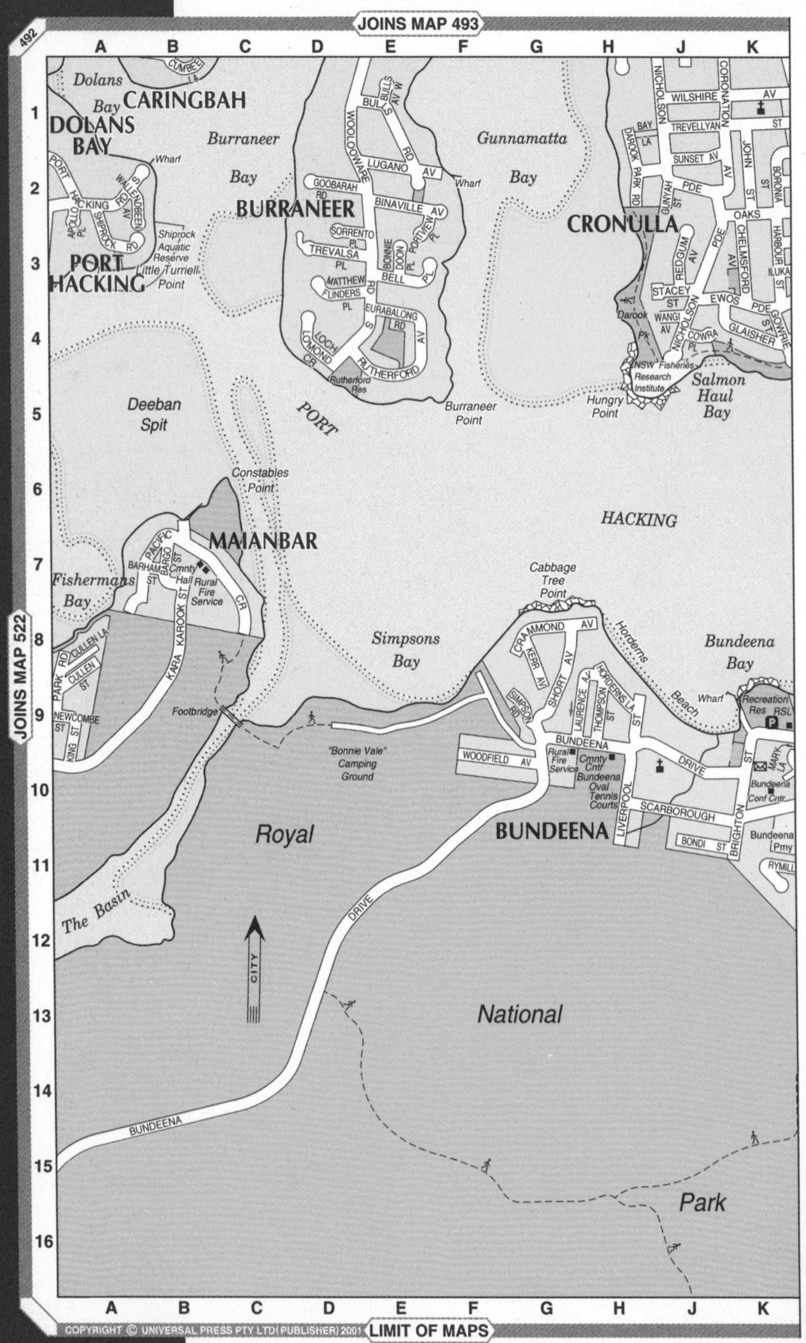
JOINS MAP 493
492
JOINS MAP 522
LIMIT OF MAPS
CARINGBAH
DOLANS BAY
Dolans Bay
PORT HACKING
BURRANEER
Burraneer Bay
Gunnamatta Bay
CRONULLA
Deeban Spit
PORT
HACKING
Constables Point
MAIANBAR
Fishermans Bay
Simpsons Bay
Cabbage Tree Point
Bundeena Bay
BUNDEENA
Royal
National
Park
The Basin
Burraneer Point
Hungry Point
Salmon Haul Bay
Shiprock Aquatic Reserve
Little Turriell Point
Darook Pk
NSW Fisheries Research Institute
"Bonnie Vale" Camping Ground
Footbridge
Cmnty Hall
Rural Fire Service
Cmnty Cntr
Bundeena Oval Tennis Courts
Recreation Res
RSL
Bundeena Conf Cntr
Bundeena Pmy
Rutherford Res
Wharf
Hordens Beach
CITY
BUNDEENA DRIVE

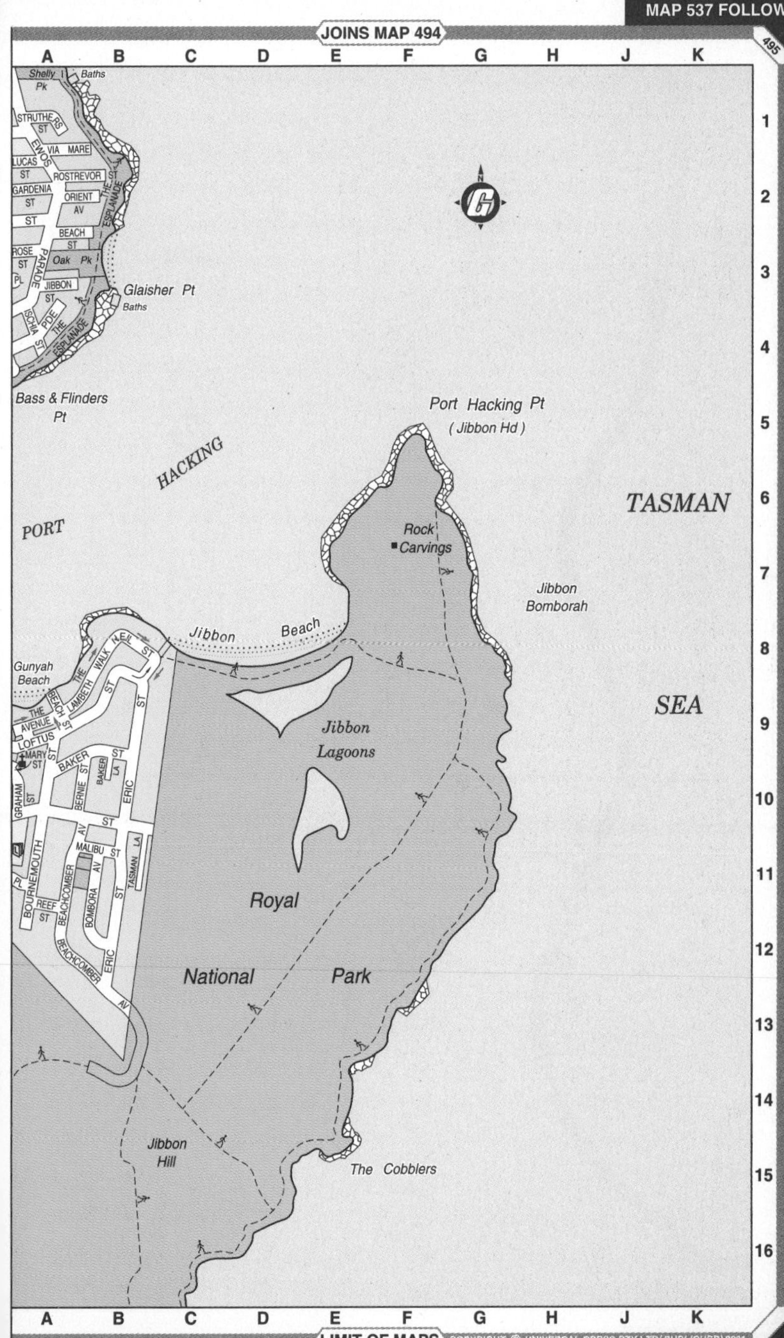
JOINS MAP 494
495
A B C D E F G H J K
1 2 3 4 5 6 7 8 9 10 11 12 13 14 15 16
Shelly Pk
Baths
STRUTHERS ST
EWOS
VIA MARE
LUCAS ST
ROSTREVOR ST
GARDENIA ST
ORIENT AV
ST
BEACH ST
THE ESPLANADE
ROSE ST
PARADE
Oak Pk
PL
JIBBON ST
ISCHIA ST
PDE
THE ESPLANADE
Glaisher Pt
Baths
Bass & Flinders Pt
PORT
HACKING
Port Hacking Pt
(Jibbon Hd)
TASMAN
Rock Carvings
Jibbon Bomborah
Jibbon Beach
Gunyah Beach
NEIL ST
THE WALK
LAMBETH ST
ST
BEACH ST
THE AVENUE
LOFTUS
MARY ST
ST
BAKER ST
BERNIE ST
BAKER LA
ERIC
GRAHAM ST
ST
AV
MALIBU ST
TASMAN LA
BOURNEMOUTH PL
BEACHCOMBER AV
BOMBORA AV
ST
REEF ST
BEACHCOMBER
ERIC AV
SEA
Jibbon Lagoons
Royal
National
Park
Jibbon Hill
The Cobblers
LIMIT OF MAPS

JOINS MAP 507
506

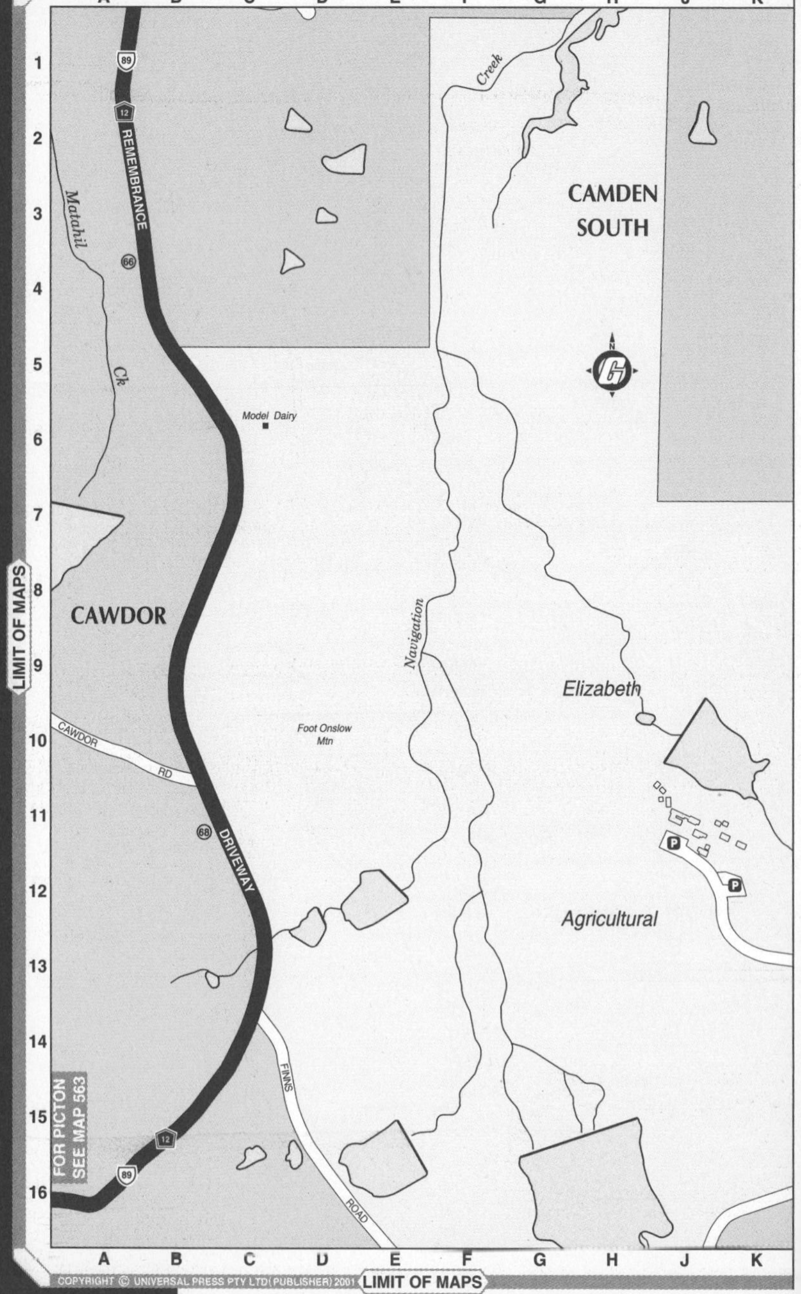

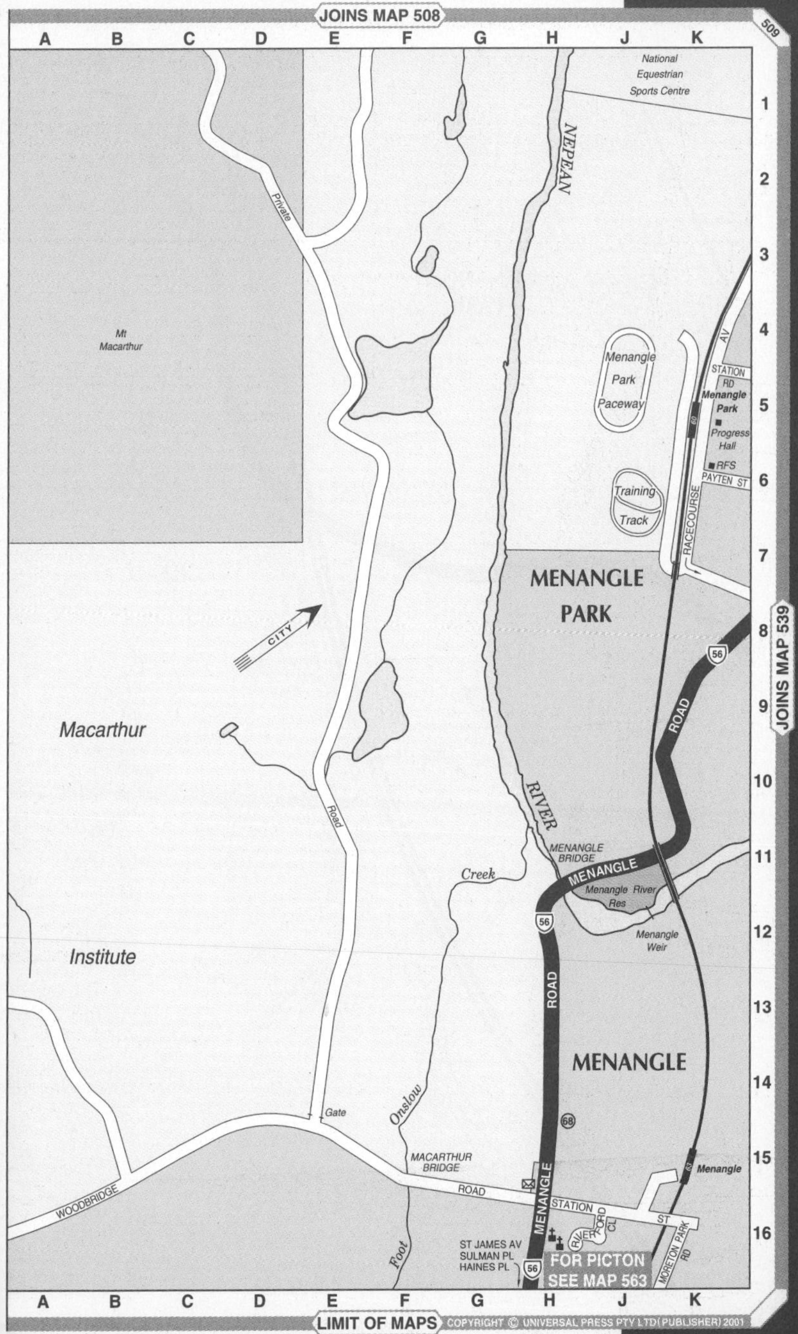
JOINS MAP 508
509
A B C D E F G H J K
1 2 3 4 5 6 7 8 9 10 11 12 13 14 15 16
National
Equestrian
Sports Centre
Mt
Macarthur
Private
NEPEAN
Menangle
Park
Paceway
AV
STATION
RD
Menangle
Park
Progress
Hall
RFS
PAYTEN ST
Training
Track
RACECOURSE
MENANGLE
PARK
CITY
JOINS MAP 539
ROAD
Macarthur
RIVER
Road
MENANGLE
BRIDGE
MENANGLE
Creek
Menangle River
Res
Menangle
Weir
Institute
ROAD
MENANGLE
Onslow
Gate
MACARTHUR
BRIDGE
Menangle
WOODBRIDGE
ROAD
MENANGLE
STATION
RIVERFORD
CL
ST
MORETON PARK
RD
ST JAMES AV
SULMAN PL
HAINES PL
Foot
FOR PICTON
SEE MAP 563
LIMIT OF MAPS

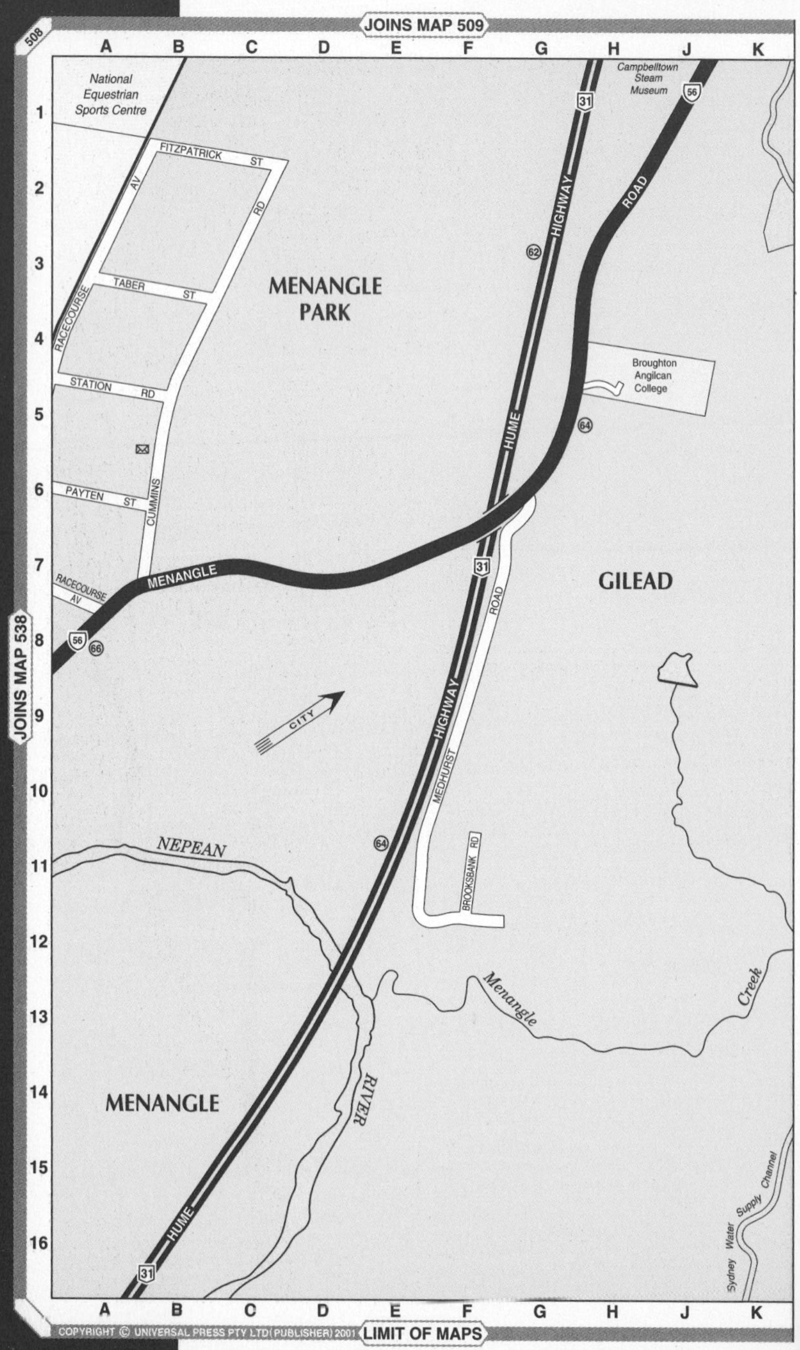
JOINS MAP 509
508
A
B
C
D
E
F
G
H
J
K
National
Equestrian
Sports Centre
Campbelltown
Steam
Museum
56
31
FITZPATRICK
ST
AV
RD
HIGHWAY
ROAD
62
TABER
ST
MENANGLE
PARK
RACECOURSE
STATION
RD
Broughton
Angilcan
College
HUME
64
PAYTEN
ST
CUMMINS
MENANGLE
GILEAD
RACECOURSE
AV
56
66
JOINS MAP 538
CITY
HIGHWAY
MEDHURST
NEPEAN
64
BROOKSBANK RD
Menangle
Creek
MENANGLE
RIVER
HUME
Sydney Water Supply Channel
1
2
3
4
5
6
7
8
9
10
11
12
13
14
15
16
LIMIT OF MAPS

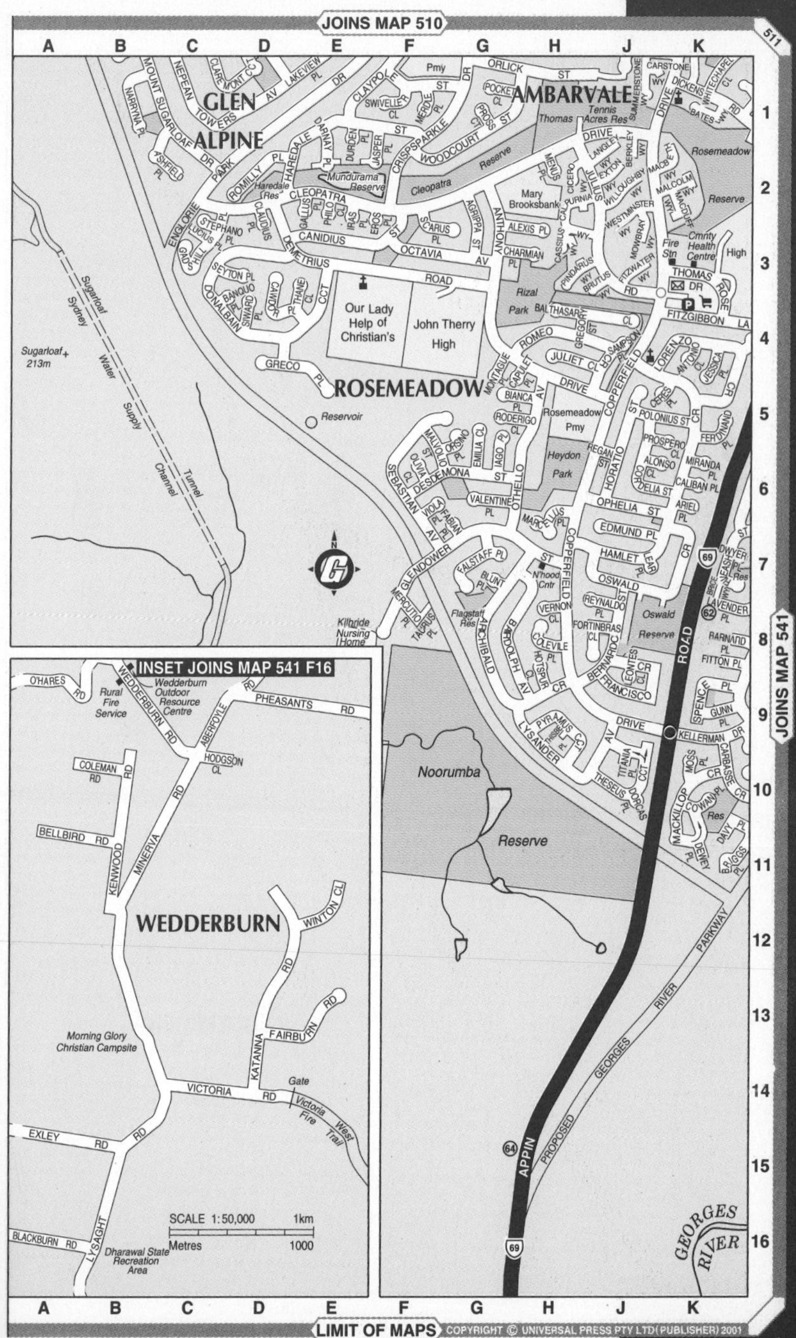
JOINS MAP 510
511
GLEN ALPINE
AMBARVALE
ROSEMEADOW
Our Lady Help of Christian's
John Therry High
Mundurama Reserve
Cleopatra Reserve
Thomas Acres Res
Rosemeadow Reserve
Mary Brooksbank
Rizal Park
Rosemeadow Pmy
Heydon Park
Oswald Reserve
Flagstaff Res
Kilbride Nursing Home
Sugarloaf 213m
Sugarloaf Sydney Water Supply Tunnel Channel
Reservoir
Noorumba Reserve
APPIN ROAD
PROPOSED GEORGES RIVER PARKWAY
GEORGES RIVER
JOINS MAP 541
INSET JOINS MAP 541 F16
WEDDERBURN
Rural Fire Service
Wedderburn Outdoor Resource Centre
Morning Glory Christian Campsite
Victoria West Fire Trail
Gate
Dharawal State Recreation Area
SCALE 1:50,000
1km
Metres
1000
LIMIT OF MAPS

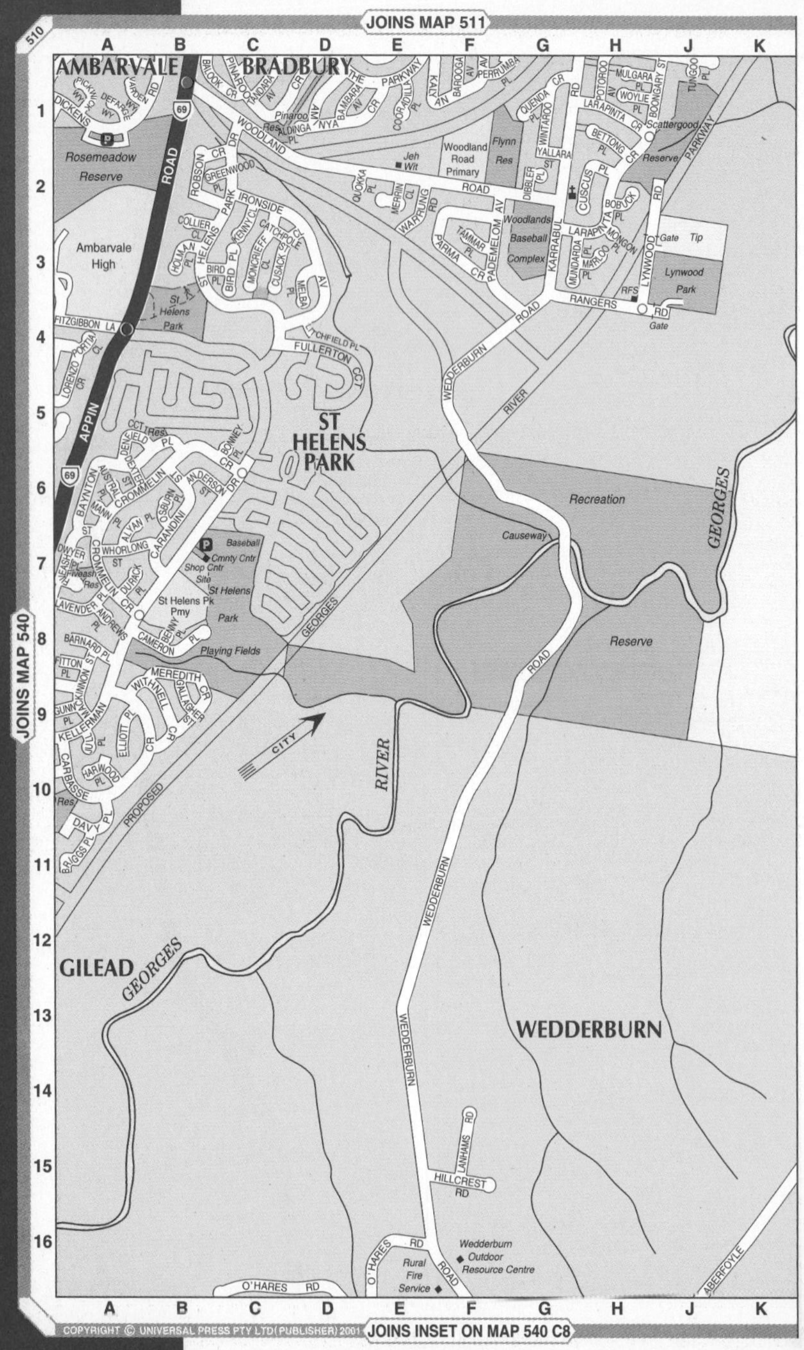
JOINS MAP 511
510
A B C D E F G H J K
1 2 3 4 5 6 7 8 9 10 11 12 13 14 15 16
AMBARVALE
BRADBURY
Rosemeadow Reserve
Ambarvale High
APPIN ROAD
69
FITZGIBBON LA
St Helens Park
ST HELENS PARK
Woodland Road Primary
Jeh Wit
Flynn Res
Woodlands Baseball Complex
Scattergood Reserve
PARKWAY
Gate Tip
Lynwood Park
RFS
RANGERS RD
Gate
WOODLAND ROAD
WEDDERBURN ROAD
RIVER
GEORGES RIVER
Recreation Reserve
Causeway
Baseball
Cmnty Cntr
Shop Cntr Site
St Helens Park
St Helens Pk Pmy
Playing Fields
Fiveash Res
CITY
PROPOSED
GEORGES
Res
GILEAD
WEDDERBURN
LANHAMS RD
HILLCREST RD
O'HARES RD
Rural Fire Service
Wedderburn Outdoor Resource Centre
ABERFOYLE
JOINS MAP 540
JOINS INSET ON MAP 540 C8

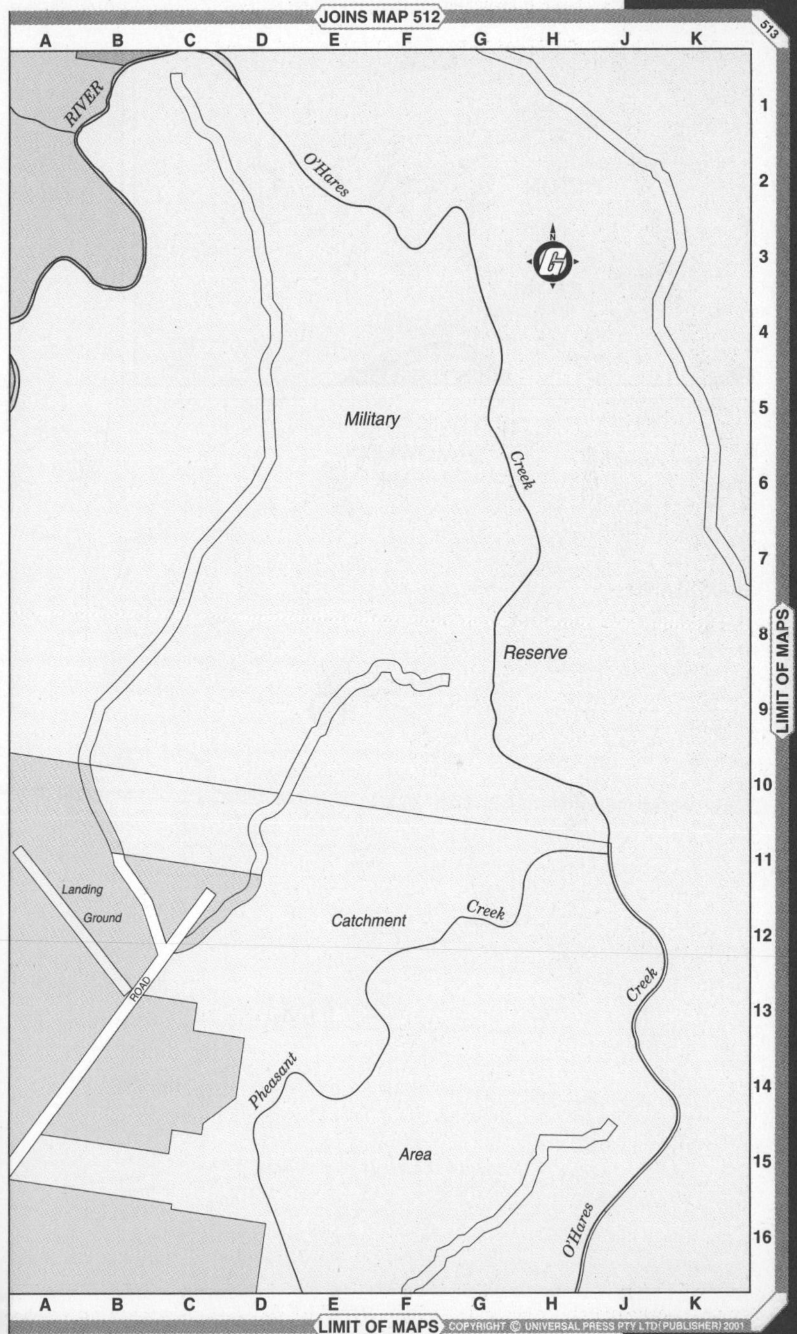
JOINS MAP 512
513
A B C D E F G H J K
1 2 3 4 5 6 7 8 9 10 11 12 13 14 15 16
RIVER
O'Hares
Military
Creek
Reserve
Landing
Ground
ROAD
Catchment
Creek
Creek
Pheasant
Area
O'Hares
LIMIT OF MAPS
LIMIT OF MAPS

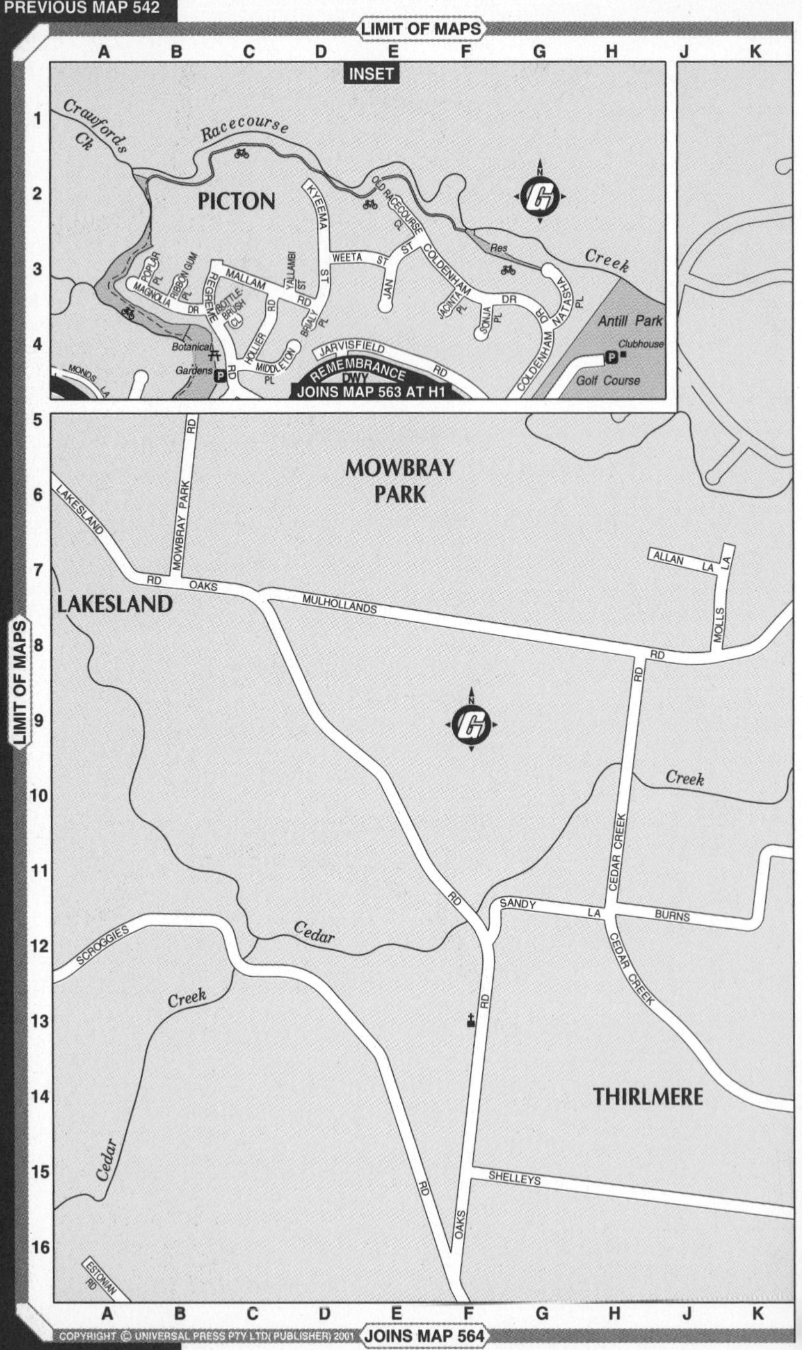

JOINS MAP 564

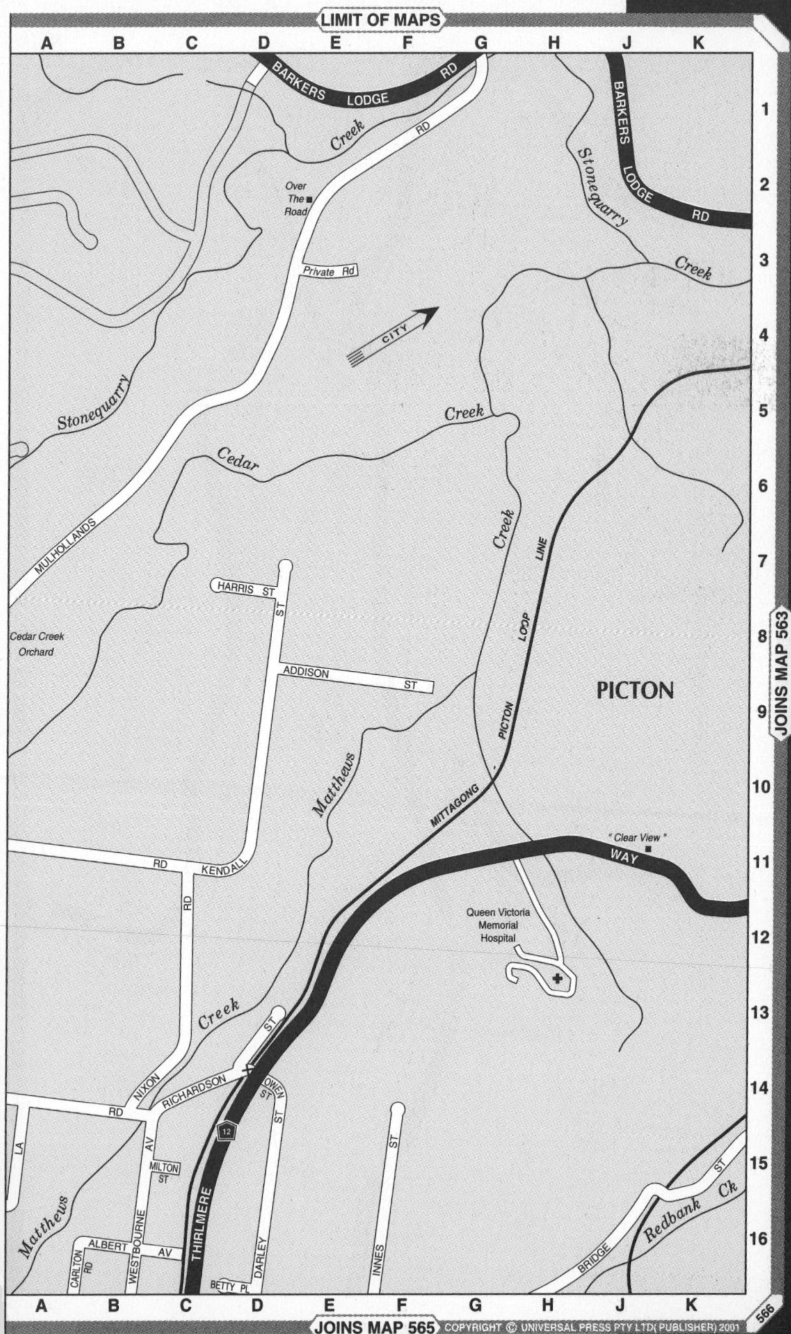
LIMIT OF MAPS
A B C D E F G H J K
1 2 3 4 5 6 7 8 9 10 11 12 13 14 15 16
BARKERS LODGE RD
Creek
RD
Over The Road
Stonequarry
Creek
Private Rd
CITY
Stonequarry
Creek
Cedar
MULHOLLANDS
Creek
LINE
LOOP
PICTON
HARRIS ST
ST
Cedar Creek Orchard
ADDISON ST
PICTON
JOINS MAP 563
Matthews
MITTAGONG
" Clear View "
WAY
RD KENDALL
RD
Queen Victoria Memorial Hospital
Creek
ST
NIXON
RICHARDSON
OWEN ST
ST
RD
12
LA
AV
MILTON ST
ST
ST
Redbank Ck
Matthews
THIRLMERE
WESTBOURNE
ALBERT AV
CARLTON RD
DARLEY
INNES
BRIDGE
BETTY PL
JOINS MAP 565
566

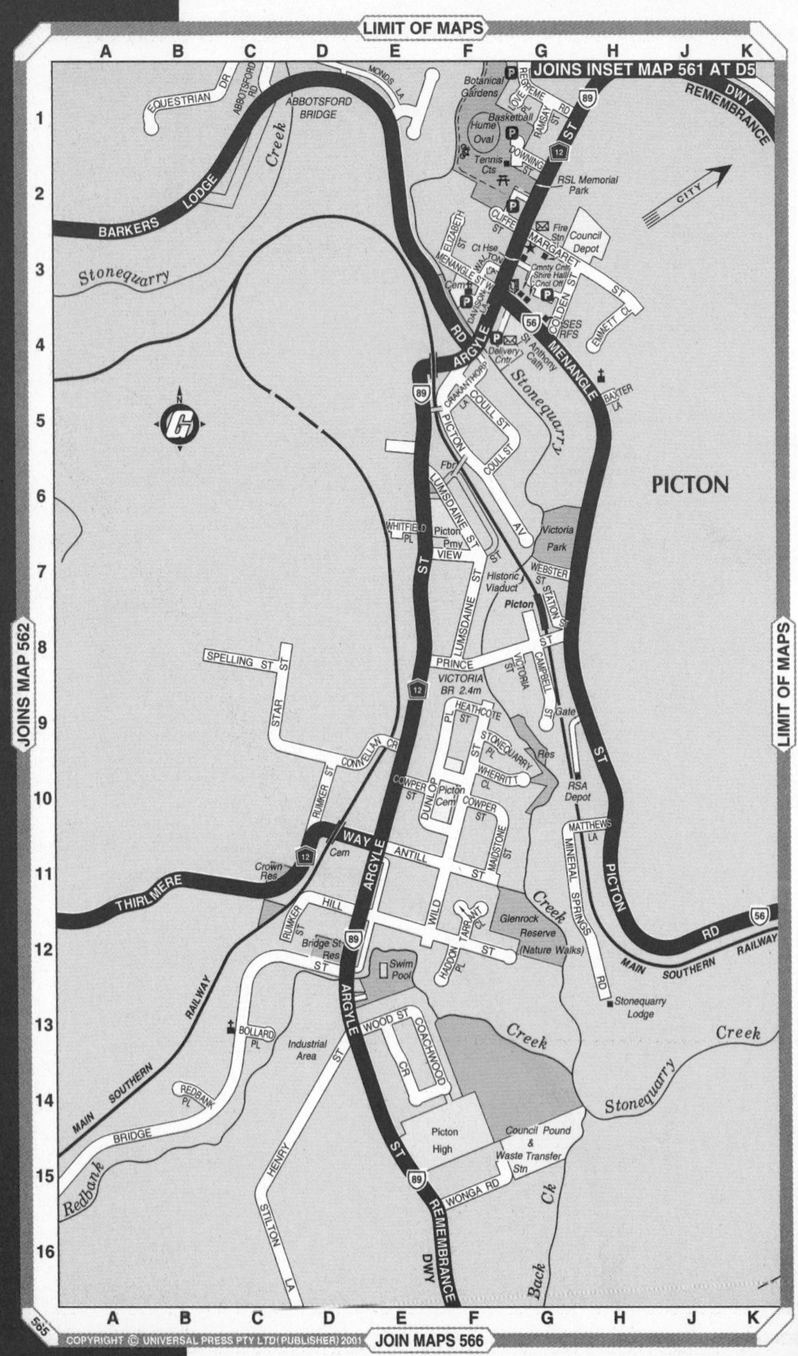
LIMIT OF MAPS
A B C D E F G H J K
1 2 3 4 5 6 7 8 9 10 11 12 13 14 15 16
JOINS INSET MAP 561 AT D5
JOINS MAP 562
LIMIT OF MAPS
JOIN MAPS 566
565
PICTON
EQUESTRIAN DR
ABBOTSFORD RD
ABBOTSFORD BRIDGE
MONDS LA
Botanical Gardens
Basketball
Hume Oval
Tennis Cts
REGREME RD
LOVE PL
RAMSAY ST
DOWNING ST
REMEMBRANCE DWY
RSL Memorial Park
CITY
BARKERS LODGE
Creek
Stonequarry
CLIFFE ST
ELIZABETH ST
Fire Stn
Council Depot
Ct Hse
MARGARET ST
WALTON LA
MENANGLE ST W
Cmnty Cntr
Shire Hall
Cncl Off
Cem
DAVISON LA
COLDEN ST
SES RFS
EMMETT CL
ARGYLE ST
RD
Delivery Cntr
St Anthony Cath
MENANGLE ST
BAXTER LA
CRAKANTHORP LA
COULL ST
PICTON AV
Fbr
LUMSDAINE ST
WHITFIELD PL
Picton Pmy
VIEW ST
Victoria Park
WEBSTER ST
STATION ST
Historic Viaduct
Picton
SPELLING ST
STAR ST
PRINCE ST
VICTORIA ST
CAMPBELL ST
VICTORIA BR 2.4m
HEATHCOTE ST
PL
Gate
STONEQUARRY PL
Res
WHERRITT CL
RSA Depot
CONVELLAN CR
RUMKER ST
COWPER ST
DUNLOP ST
Picton Cem
MAIDSTONE ST
MATTHEWS LA
WAY
ANTILL ST
Crown Res
THIRLMERE
MINERAL SPRINGS RD
PICTON RD
HILL ST
WILD ST
TARRANT CL
Glenrock Reserve (Nature Walks)
Bridge St Res
Swim Pool
HADDON PL
MAIN SOUTHERN RAILWAY
Stonequarry Lodge
BOLLARD PL
Industrial Area
WOOD ST
COACHWOOD CR
REDBANK PL
BRIDGE
Redbank
Picton High
Council Pound & Waste Transfer Stn
HENRY ST
WONGA RD
Ck
STILTON LA
Back Creek
12
56
89

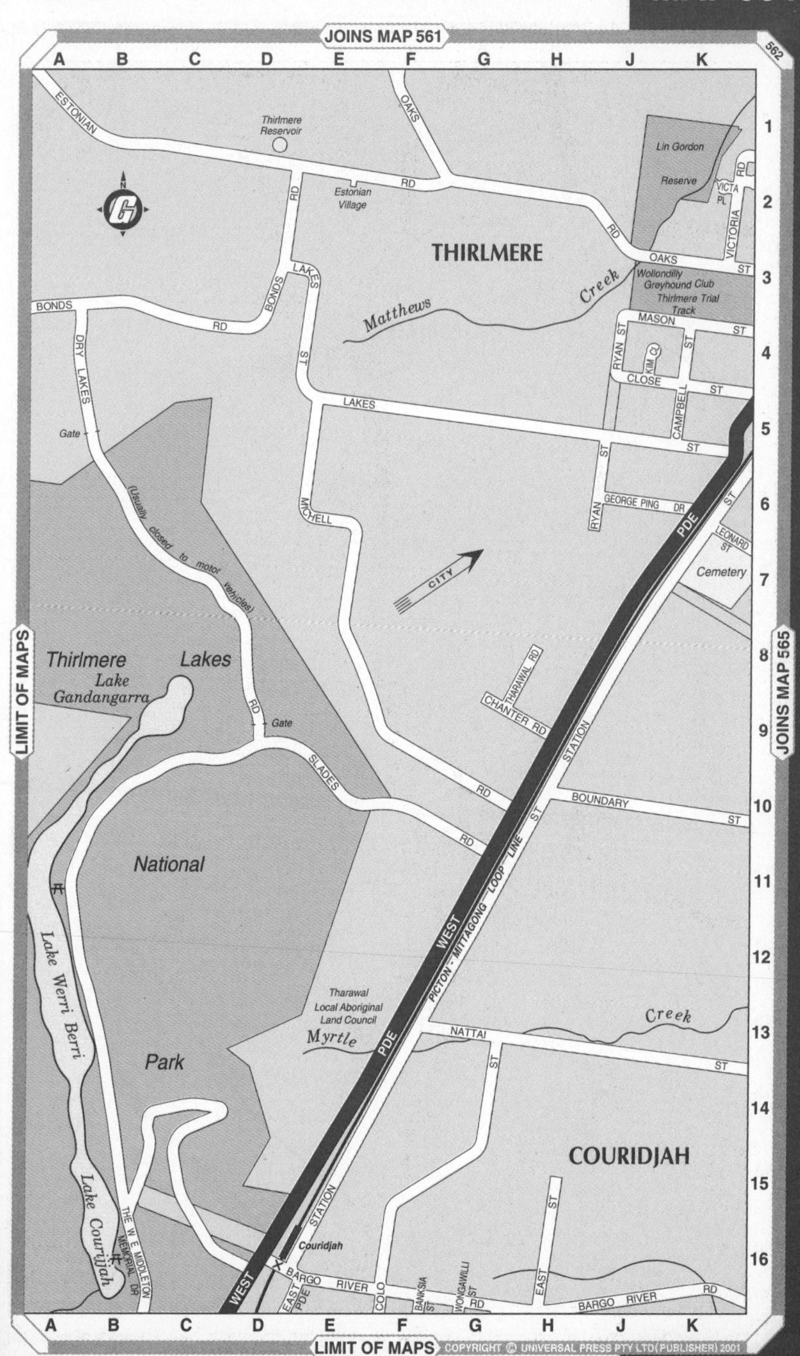
JOINS MAP 561
562
LIMIT OF MAPS
JOINS MAP 565
A B C D E F G H J K
1 2 3 4 5 6 7 8 9 10 11 12 13 14 15 16
THIRLMERE
COURIDJAH
Thirlmere Lakes
National Park
Thirlmere Reservoir
Estonian Village
Lin Gordon Reserve
Wollondilly Greyhound Club
Thirlmere Trial Track
Cemetery
Tharawal Local Aboriginal Land Council
Lake Gandangarra
Lake Werri Berri
Lake Couridjah
Matthews Creek
Myrtle Creek
ESTONIAN RD
OAKS RD
LAKES RD
BONDS RD
DRY LAKES RD
(Usually closed to motor vehicles)
Gate
MICHELL ST
LAKES ST
SLADES RD
VICTORIA RD
VICTA PL
MASON ST
RYAN ST
KIM CL
CLOSE ST
CAMPBELL ST
GEORGE PING DR
LEONARD ST
WEST PDE
STATION ST
PICTON - MITTAGONG LOOP LINE
THARAWAL RD
CHANTER RD
BOUNDARY ST
NATTAI ST
EAST ST
BARGO RIVER RD
EAST PDE
COLO
BANKSIA ST
WONGAWILLI ST
THE W E MIDDLETON MEMORIAL DR
Couridjah
CITY

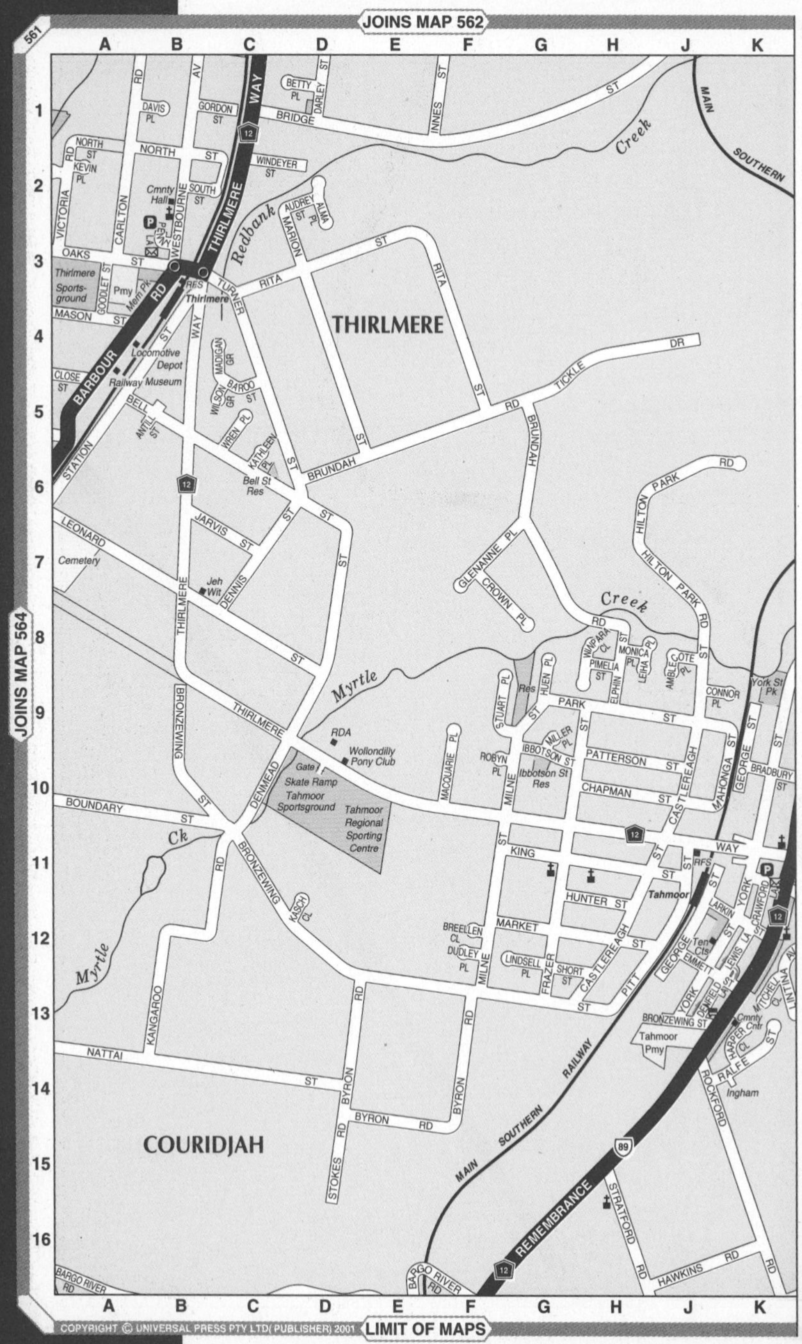
JOINS MAP 562
JOINS MAP 564
LIMIT OF MAPS
561
THIRLMERE
COURIDJAH
Thirlmere Sportsground
Locomotive Depot
Railway Museum
Cemetery
Bell St Res
Tahmoor Sportsground
Tahmoor Regional Sporting Centre
Wollondilly Pony Club
Skate Ramp
Tahmoor
Ingham
Redbank Creek
Myrtle Creek
THIRLMERE WAY
BARBOUR RD
MAIN SOUTHERN RAILWAY
REMEMBRANCE

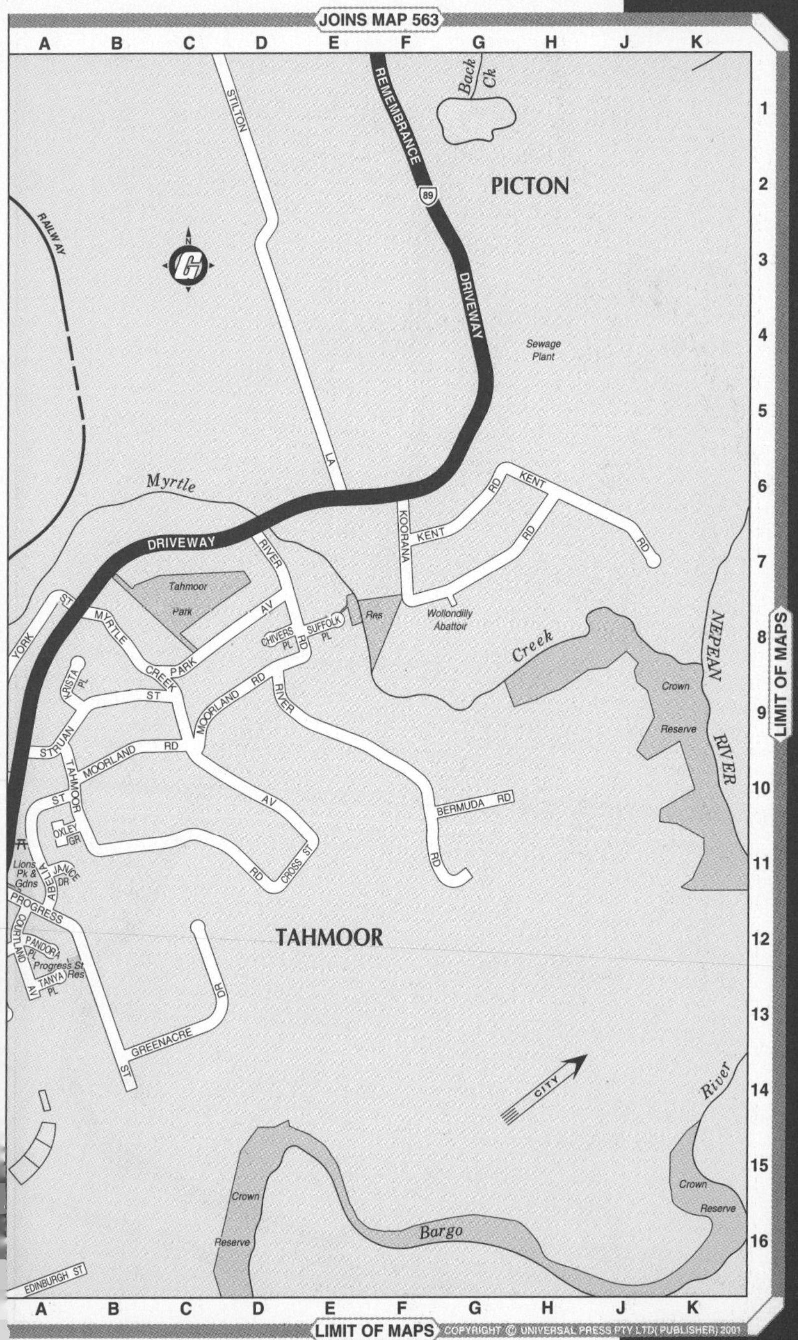

LIMIT OF MAPS

BARGO

SCALE 1:27 500
Metres 500 1000 1km

LIMIT OF MAPS

BARGO
YANDERRA
MAIN REMEMBRANCE DR
RAILSIDE AV
GREAT SOUTHERN RD
HAWTHORNE RD
IRONBARK RD
WATTLE ST
DYMOND RD
BARGO RD
GOVERNMENT RD
ANTHONY RD
WELLERS RD
HOGANS DR
FLORENCE CL
CLAREMONT
ELVY ST
NORMA CL
ASHBY AV
LLOYD CL
HORNE CL
SCOTT ST
HAMBRIDGE RD
THORNCROFT PL
JUSTINE CL
WINDSOR PL
PHILLIPA PL
LAURA CL
BIARA ST
CAMBALAN ST
RADNOR
MIMOSA ST
PANORAMA ST
KADER ST
DAISY LA
GWYNN HUGHES RD
NOONGAH PL
BERRICO
BINGARRA PL
NOORAL ST
Bargo Cmnty Park (Tahmoor Lions)
CWA
Child Care Centre
Bargo
Bargo Pmy
Berrico Plgrd
Tennis
Cmnty Hall
Skate Ramp
Bargo Sportsground & Bargo Paceway
AVON DAM RD
JOHNSTON RD
Inghams Breeding Farms & Hatchery
TYLERS RD
MARSHALL AV
Bargo Sports Club
RFS
Resvr
RESERVOIR RD
ARINA RD
BAYAN PL
RAILWAY
CARLISLE RD
CHANDOS RD
YANDERRA RD
SILICA
REMEMBRANCE
HUME HWY
MORTIMER ST
HARLEY ST
COBHAM ST
BERKELEY ST
CITY
Gate

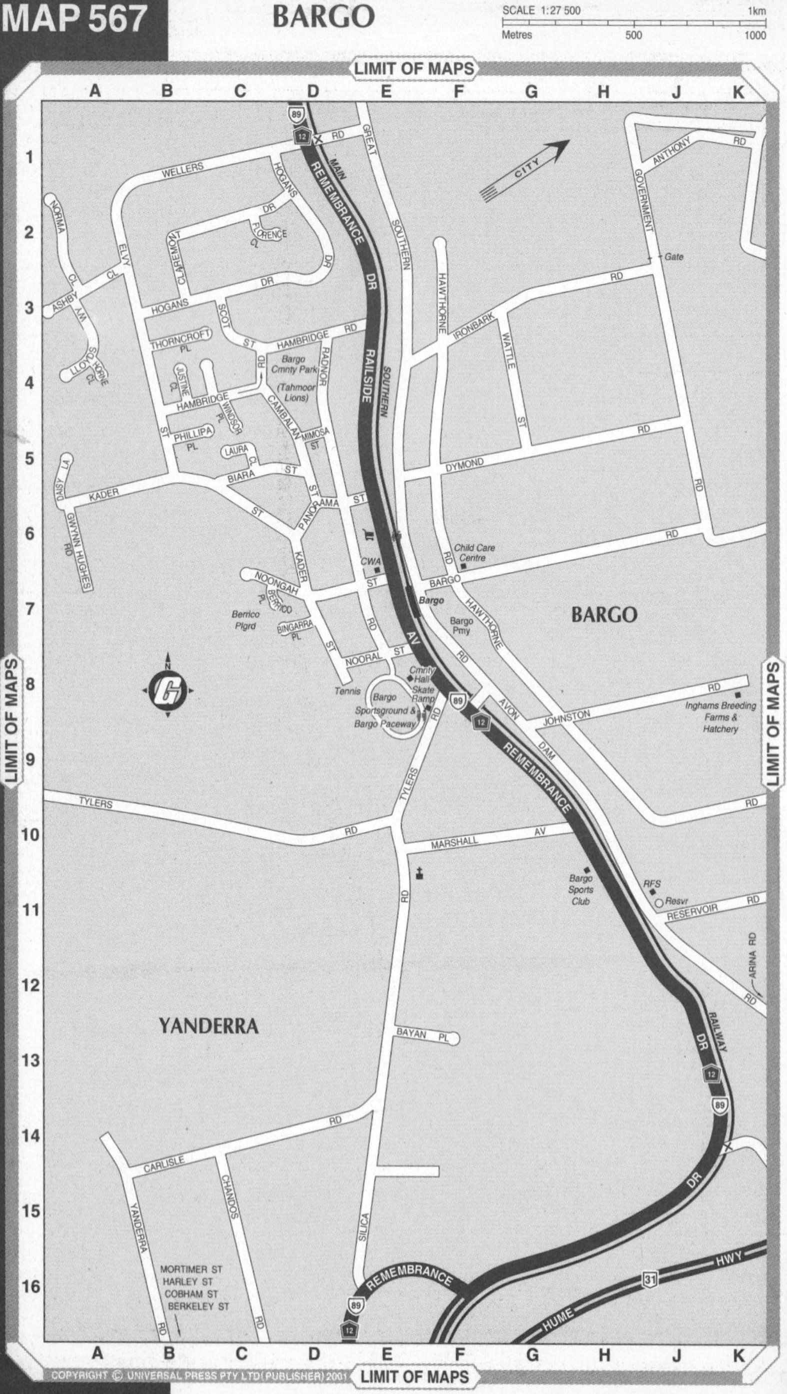

APPIN

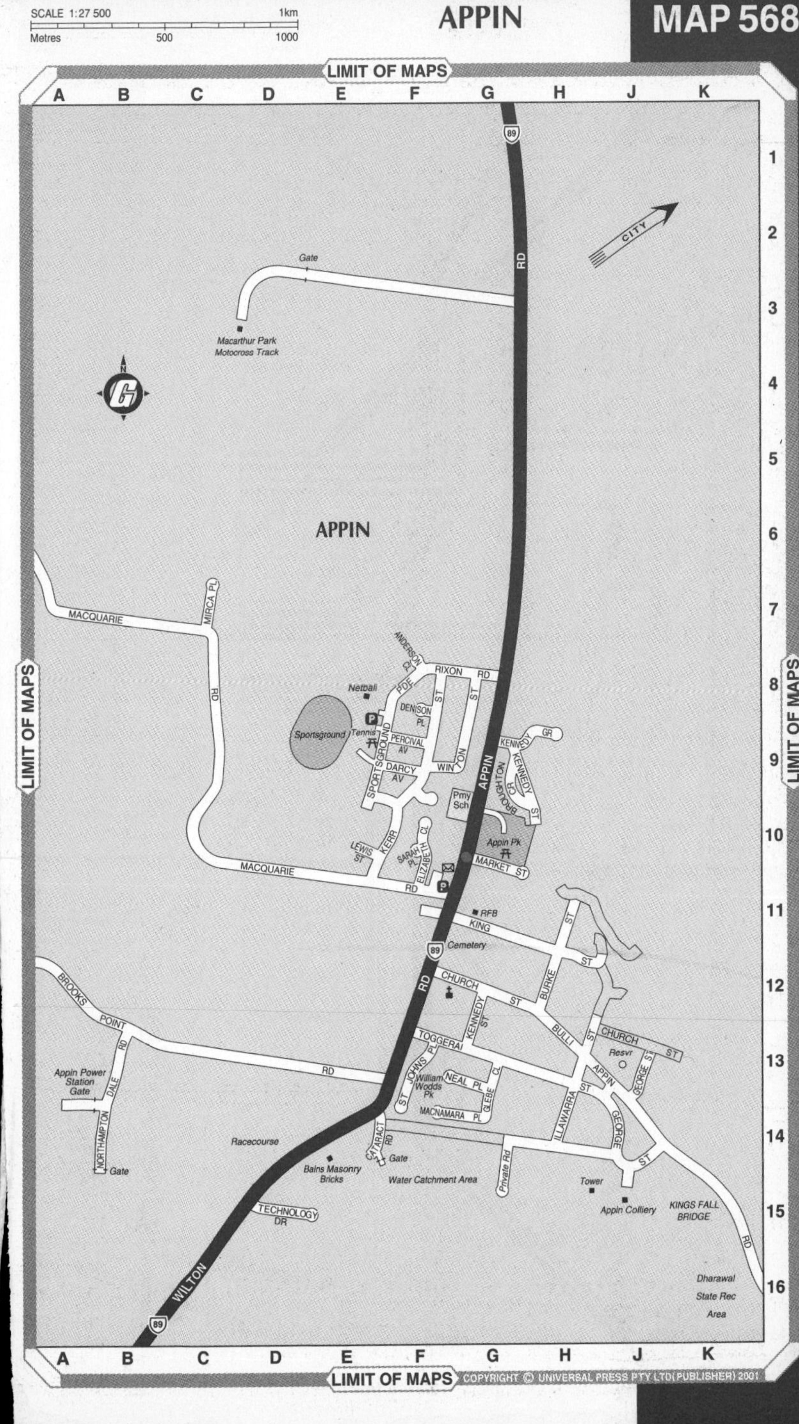
SCALE 1:27 500
1km
Metres
500
1000
LIMIT OF MAPS
APPIN
Gate
Macarthur Park Motocross Track
CITY
MACQUARIE
MIRCA PL
RD
ANDERSON CL
RIXON RD
PDE
Netball
DENISON PL
Sportsground
Tennis
SPORTSGROUND
PERCIVAL AV
DARCY AV
WINTON ST
KENNEDY GR
BROUGHTON CR
KENNEDY ST
Pmy Sch
Appin Pk
MARKET ST
LEWIS ST
KERR
SARAH PL
ELIZABETH CL
MACQUARIE RD
RFB
KING ST
Cemetery
BURKE ST
CHURCH ST
BROOKS POINT RD
DALE RD
Appin Power Station Gate
TOGGERAI
KENNEDY ST
BULLI ST
CHURCH ST
Resvr
GEORGE ST
APPIN
JOHNS PL
William Wodds Pk
NEAL PL
GLEBE CL
MACNAMARA PL
ILLAWARRA ST
GEORGE ST
NORTHAMPTON
Gate
Racecourse
CATARACT RD
Gate
Bains Masonry Bricks
Water Catchment Area
Private Rd
Tower
Appin Colliery
KINGS FALL BRIDGE
TECHNOLOGY DR
WILTON
Dharawal State Rec Area
LIMIT OF MAPS

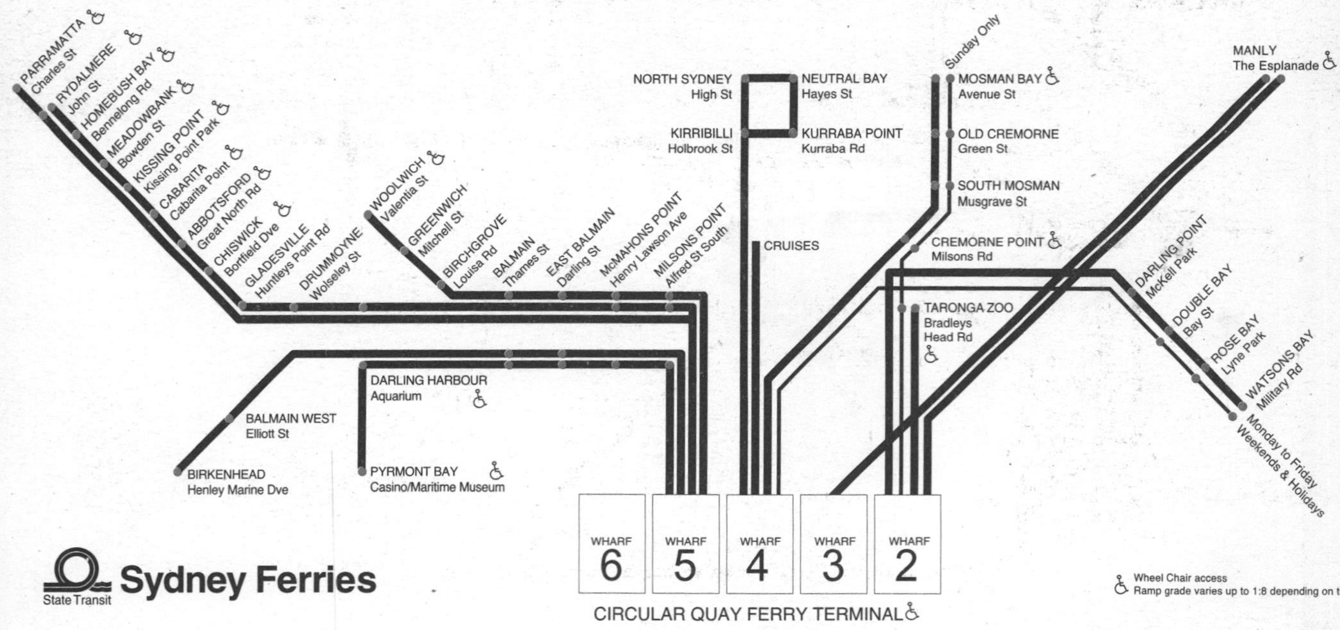

PARRAMATTA
Charles St
RYDALMERE
John St
HOMEBUSH BAY
Bennelong Rd
MEADOWBANK
Bowden St
KISSING POINT
Kissing Point Park
CABARITA
Cabarita Point
ABBOTSFORD
Great North Rd
CHISWICK
Bortfield Dve
GLADESVILLE
Huntleys Point Rd
DRUMMOYNE
Wolseley St
WOOLWICH
Valentia St
GREENWICH
Mitchell St
BIRCHGROVE
Louisa Rd
BALMAIN
Thames St
EAST BALMAIN
Darling St
McMAHONS POINT
Henry Lawson Ave
MILSONS POINT
Alfred St South
NORTH SYDNEY
High St
NEUTRAL BAY
Hayes St
KIRRIBILLI
Holbrook St
KURRABA POINT
Kurraba Rd
CRUISES
Sunday Only
MOSMAN BAY
Avenue St
OLD CREMORNE
Green St
SOUTH MOSMAN
Musgrave St
CREMORNE POINT
Milsons Rd
TARONGA ZOO
Bradleys
Head Rd
MANLY
The Esplanade
DARLING POINT
McKell Park
DOUBLE BAY
Bay St
ROSE BAY
Lyne Park
WATSONS BAY
Military Rd
Monday to Friday
Weekends & Holidays
BALMAIN WEST
Elliott St
BIRKENHEAD
Henley Marine Dve
DARLING HARBOUR
Aquarium
PYRMONT BAY
Casino/Maritime Museum
WHARF 6
WHARF 5
WHARF 4
WHARF 3
WHARF 2
CIRCULAR QUAY FERRY TERMINAL
Sydney Ferries
State Transit
Wheel Chair access
Ramp grade varies up to 1:8 depending on tide